HANDBOOK OF RESEARCH FOR EDUCATIONAL COMMUNICATIONS AND TECHNOLOGY

HANDBOOK OF RESEARCH FOR EDUCATIONAL COMMUNICATIONS AND TECHNOLOGY

A PROJECT OF THE ASSOCIATION FOR EDUCATIONAL COMMUNICATIONS AND TECHNOLOGY

EDITED BY
DAVID H. JONASSEN

Macmillan LIBRARY Reference USA
Simon & Schuster Macmillan
New York

Prentice Hall International
London   Mexico City   New Delhi   Singapore   Sydney   Toronto

Macmillan Library Reference USA
Simon & Schuster Macmillan
1633 Broadway
New York, NY 10019

Library of Congress Catalog Card Number: 96-21386

Printed in the United States of America

Printing number
1   2   3   4   5   6   7   8   9   10

Library of Congress Cataloging-in-Publication Data

Handbook of research for educational communications and technology/
    David H. Jonassen, editor.
        p.   cm.
    Includes bibliographical references and index.
    ISBN 0-02-864663-0 (alk. paper)
    1. Educational technology—Research—Handbooks, manuals, etc.
2. Communication in education—Research—Handbooks, manuals, etc.
3. Telecommunication in education—Research—Handbooks, manuals,
etc. 4. Instructional systems—Design—Research—Handbooks, manuals,
etc. I. Jonassen, David H., 1947–   .
    LB1028.3.H355   1996
    371.3'078'07—dc20   96-21386
                                                                           CIP

The paper used in this publication meets the minimum requirements of American National Standard for Information Sciences—Permanence of Paper for Printed Library Materials. ANSI Z39.48-1996.∞™

DEDICATION

To those who significantly advanced the discourse in this field, including Edgar Dale, W. W. Charters, Walt Wittich, Charles Hoban, Jim Finn, Arthur Lumsdaine, Wilbur Schramm, Ole Larsen, James Brown, Charles Schuller, Bob Gagné, Don Ely, Bob Heinich, Bob Glaser, and many others too numerous to mention.

CONTENTS

I

FOUNDATIONS FOR RESEARCH IN EDUCATIONAL COMMUNICATIONS AND TECHNOLOGY

John C. Belland, Ohio State University, Associate Editor

II

HARD TECHNOLOGIES: MEDIA-RELATED RESEARCH

Robert B. Kozma, Center for Technology in Learning, Associate Editor

III

SOFT TECHNOLOGIES: INSTRUCTIONAL AND INFORMATIONAL DESIGN RESEARCH

Robert D. Tennyson, University of Minnesota, Associate Editor

IV

INSTRUCTIONAL MESSAGE DESIGN RESEARCH

Francis M. Dwyer, Pennsylvania State University, Associate Editor

V

INSTRUCTIONAL STRATEGIES RESEARCH

Marcy P. Driscoll, Florida State University, Associate Editor

VI

ISSUES OF ORGANIZATION AND CHANGE IN EDUCATIONAL COMMUNICATIONS AND TECHNOLOGY

Donald P. Ely, Syracuse University, Associate Editor

VII

RESEARCH METHODOLOGIES IN EDUCATIONAL COMMUNICATIONS AND TECHNOLOGY

Rhonda Robinson, Northern Illinois University, Associate Editor

PREFACE

HISTORY

This handbook began in 1993 at the annual convention of the Association for Educational Communications and Technology, the professional association sponsor of the handbook. Lloyd Chilton, an editor for Scholastic and former editor for Macmillan Reference (publisher of the handbook series), had approached Stan Zenor about the prospects of producing a research handbook for our field. Stan deferred to the Research and Theory Division, which interviewed several people and selected me for the task of editing the book. Later that spring, at the annual Professors of Instructional Design and Technology conference on the shores of Lake Monroe in southern Indiana, a group of professors and students wrestled with the structure of the book for 2 days. After additional review by the associate editors and others, we agreed on a structure and set about imploring authors. Authors were selected for their reputation in the field and for their skills as researchers on the topics they were addressing. In some cases, we were not able to convince our first choices for chapter authors; however, for all chapters, we were fortunate to convince highly competent researchers and authors by late 1993.

For the next year and a half, authors presented detailed outlines for perusal by the editors and reviewers (listed in Acknowledgments), revised those outlines, wrote chapter drafts for the editors and reviewers, and again amended the drafts. The book was scheduled for completion early in 1996. The best-laid plans, however, went awry.

LIMITATIONS OF THE BOOK

Contemporaneity

The process for producing and publishing this book took longer than expected when Scholastic Inc. decided peremptorily in May 1995 that it wanted no more involvement with this project. Thankfully, Macmillan assumed responsibility for its publication, but the negotiations with two publishers, a professional association, and too many attorneys took more than 7 months. So the information in this handbook is already out of date. However, that is a phenomenon that has become a way of life in our field. The half-life of

new information has decreased a couple orders of magnitude (from decades to years to months and soon, no doubt, to weeks). While no book can be completely contemporary because of the print publication process, we made every attempt to make this one as contemporary as possible. During the transition of publishers and the resulting production hiatus, several authors took the opportunity to reflect once again on their work and to add the latest references and polish their manuscripts. Their efforts are greatly appreciated.

Comprehensiveness

Reviewing any field of research is a daunting task. Educational communications and technology is no exception. The thousands of studies that have been conducted and reported in various forms required amazing analysis and synthesis skills on the part of the authors. Deciding which studies to report, which to summarize, and which to ignore has challenged all of the authors in this book. The length, complexity, and detail of these chapters vary because of the quantity and quality of the research available. Chapter 11, on television research is, for instance, the longest (and one of the best written) in the book by far. Yet the authors cited only a fraction of the television research that has been reported. An exegesis of all of the research in our field would have required a book several times the length of this one. Not only would writing it have been a daunting task, reading would have been, as well. All of the chapters provide excellent overviews of their research domains and provide numerous avenues for continuing your research.

It will be easy to find omissions, important topics, or technologies that are not addressed in the book. Some were accidental, others intentional, and others necessary. For instance, we had intended to include chapters on film, programmed instruction, policy research in technology, and motivation and instructional design. These all represent important theoretical or technological foundations of our field, but we were unable to produce publishable chapters within the time restraints. Film and television were initially linked in Chapter 11. It became necessary, for reasons of sanity maintenance, to delete the film section. Within chapters, authors may have missed what you believe to be an important topic. Rest assured that we, the editors, coaxed as much out of the authors as they were able and willing to give. In any field, a definitive source is impossible, first because we are human and second because a field such as ours is changing so rapidly that a definitive source would remain definitive for only a matter of minutes.

FORMAT OF THE BOOK

You will notice that the headings in this handbook are numbered in a hierarchical manner. Opinions vary on the virtues of such a numbering system. Let me explain our reasoning. A handbook should be more than a static description of the state of the art. It should be a dynamic, working document that facilitates knowledge construction and problem solving for the readers. It should also reflect both the complexity and the interrelatedness of the field. To that end, many of the authors and I have worked to identify associations and relationships among the topics and methods described in this book. You will find references (e.g., "see 23.4.2"), distributed throughout the book. These references refer the reader to another section in the book about the same topic. We do not pretend that we have identified all or even a majority of the associations. Rather, we have provided a starting place. There are numerous inferences, implications, and associations that can yet be produced between all of the chapters. The more links that we can find as a profession, the more integrated our field becomes. The most usable document may have been a fully linked hypertext with typed links. However, I believe that the most meaningful links are the ones created by the user, so here is my own recommendation for studying this book: Create your own typed, hypertext links, and assemble them into some sort of link structure, either text based or computer mediated. Since we could not embed HTML code into this printed text (I believe that the handbook would be most useful in electronic form), we embedded references in the form of heading numbers.

USE OF THE BOOK

This is a handbook, not a novel. I would seriously doubt that many people will want to sit down and read it from cover to cover. Rather, it will be used to familiarize students and researchers with a domain of research in our field prior to beginning their own research. Or it may function as a handbook for selecting research topics or methodologies or for reflecting on proposed topics or hypotheses. The editors implored the authors to go beyond a review of research in a domain, evaluate prior research topics and methods, and suggest issues that need clarification. So, for the novice researcher in a domain, this book should provide some research direction as well as reflection. This handbook may also be used as a course text, probably not as a definitive text in a single course but rather as a reference source in some courses and a textbook in others. However you use this book, the reviewers, authors, editors, and I hope that it will help you to understand the issues better and formulate and execute better research, so that the next edition of this handbook may provide more answers and fewer questions. Best of luck!

DAVID JONASSEN, Editor

ACKNOWLEDGMENTS

So many people contributed to this effort.

The most important contributors were the authors, without whom there would be no handbook. Wedging chapters like these into overcommitted schedules required a strong commitment to the field and its propagation. These people are highlighted in the following section, "About the Authors."

Next, I want to acknowledge the contributions of the associate editors—John Belland, Marcy Driscoll, Frank Dwyer, Don Ely, Bob Kozma, Rhonda Robinson, and Bob Tennyson—who helped to shape this book and reviewed proposals, outlines, and chapter drafts. They also are highlighted in the next section, "About the Editors."

Producing a handbook as comprehensive as this one requires massive amounts of feedback, which were provided by a distinguished panel of expert reviewers, including Steve Alessi, Allen Avner, Dan Barron, Marge Cambre, Richard Carlson, John Cooper, David Crookall, Gayle Davidson, Chris Dede, Jack Dempsey, Walter Dick, Nick Eastmond, Elizabeth Ellsworth, Larry Frase, George Gropper, Bob Grover, Nick Hammond, Simon Hooper, Michael Huberman (special kudos from the author), Al Januszewski (two chapters), Jane Johnsen, Mable Kinzie, Randy Koetting, Raymond Kulhavy, David Lebow, John Leggett, Deborah Lieberman, Craig Locaitis, Jim Lockard, Richard Mayer, Barb McCombs, Bonnie Meyer, Keith Mielke, Bill Milheim, LaVerne Miller, Mike Moore, Gary Morrison, John Murphy, Randy Nichols, Charlie Reigeluth (two chapters), Susan Reilly, Bob Reiser, Steve Ross, Paul Saettler, David Salisbury, Gavriel Salomon, Peter Seidman, Pat Smith, Bill Taylor, Sigmund Tobias, Martin Tessmer (two chapters), Susan Tucker, John Wedman, Brent Wilson, Bill Winn, and Merlin Wittrock.

I would also like to acknowledge a number of people whom I cannot identify. At the 1993 Professors of Instructional Design and Technology conference at Bloomington, a number of faculty and students devoted a large portion of the conference to reviewing my proposals, brainstorming, and discussing the structure of the book. The Table of Contents was born there and refined later by the associate editors. My thanks to those people (only a few of whom I can recall—who said episodic memories were more resistant than semantic?) for their energy and wisdom.

A couple of people helped me sort through and mark up the mountains of manuscripts: Mauri Collins and Catlyn Gregory. Their contributions helped me to remain sane. A final check of the page proofs was provided by Karen Peters, a doctoral student in the Instructional Systems program, a future researcher, and the very first graduate student to read the *Handbook of Research for Educational Communications and Technology*.

My thanks and appreciation to all.

DAVID JONASSEN

ABOUT THE EDITORS

John C. Belland earned his B.A. in mathematics at Northwestern University, his M.S. in Ed. in curriculum and instruction at Northern Illinois University, and his Ph.D. in instructional systems technology at Syracuse. He served as an assistant professor at the University of North Carolina at Chapel Hill and then progressed through the faculty ranks in 25 years at the Ohio State University, serving as professor for the past decade, with joint appointments in the Department of Art Education and the Advanced Computing Center for the Arts and Design. He founded and directed the National Center on Educational Media and Materials for the Handicapped, served as program area coordinator for the Instructional Design and Technology Program, conducted research on how people learn from pictures and animations, edited the *Journal of Visual Literacy,* served on the editorial boards of the research section of Educational Technology and the Development section of Educational Technology Research & Development. He has received over $6 million of extramural funding for research and development projects. His publications include over 20 articles in refereed journals and the book *Paradigms Regained* (with Denis Hlynka).

Marcy P. Driscoll is professor of instructional systems and educational psychology at Florida State University. She is the author or coauthor of four textbooks in learning and instruction, including *Psychology of Learning for Instruction,* which won the 1995 Outstanding Book Award in Instructional Development from the Association of Educational Communications and Technology, and, with Robert M. Gagné, *Essentials of Learning for Instruction.* She has also published numerous articles in professional journals on learning, instructional theory, and educational semiotics. Professor Driscoll received her A.B. magna cum laude from Mt. Holyoke College and her M.S. and Ph.D. degrees in educational psychology from the University of Massachusetts at Amherst.

Francis M. Dwyer is professor of instructional systems in the College of Education at the Pennsylvania State University. He has served as president of the Association for Educational Communications and Technology and the International Visual Literacy Association. He has conducted more than 200 research studies related to visual learning, which have resulted in the publication of three texts directly related to the design and use of visualization in the instructional process. He received IVLA's Research Award for 25 years of sustained research contributions to the field of visual learning.

Donald P. Ely is professor emeritus, instructional design, development, and evaluation, Syracuse University. He has been an adjunct professor at the University of Twente in the Netherlands since 1980 and is currently a visiting professor in the Department of Educational Research at Florida State University. He served as program director for dissemination at the National Science Foundation (1992–93). His special interests are educational change, curriculum development in educational technology, the transfer of media and technology in developing nations, and the history and definition of the field of educational technology.

David H. Jonassen is professor and head of instructional systems at the Pennsylvania State University. Dr. Jonassen has previously taught at the University of Colorado, the University of North Carolina at Greensboro, Syracuse University, Temple University, and the University of Twente, and consulted with businesses, universities, and other institutions around the world. He has authored or edited 16 books and hundreds of articles, papers, and technical reports. His current research focuses on designing constructivist learning environments, cognitive tools for learning, knowledge representation methods, and individual differences and learning.

Robert B. Kozma is the director of the Center for Technology in Learning. For 20 years prior to assuming the directorship of CTL, Dr. Kozma was a professor at the School of Education and a research scientist at the Center for Research on Learning and Teaching at the University of Michigan. He directed or was coprincipal investigator of 19 projects accounting for over $6.5 million in revenue from federal agencies, foundations, and corporations. He directed the Program for Learning, Teaching, and Technology for the National Center for Research to Improve Postsecondary Teaching and Learning (NCRIPTAL), and he also founded and directed the EDUCOM/NCRIPTAL Higher Education Software Awards. His research has focused on media theory, the use of technology to improve teaching, the dissemination of educational innovations, and the development, use, and effectiveness of advanced computer-based tools, multimedia, and hypermedia software systems in the sciences and in English composition. He has authored or coauthored more than 40 academic works that include chapters, encyclopedia entries, books, and articles appearing in major academic journals. He has given more than 75 presentations and invited addresses at national and international conferences. And he has been the lead designer on several advanced multimedia and hypermedia educational software packages.

Rhonda S. Robinson is professor of instructional technology in the department of Leadership and Educational Policy Studies at Northern Illinois University in DeKalb, where she directs the master's degree and internship programs and teaches courses in research, design, development, and visual literacy. Rhonda has her Ph.D. in educational communications from the University of Wisconsin at Madison. She has been teaching at NIU for 16 years. Her research inter-

ests are in using interpretive and qualitative methods to look at technology applications in education and business. Her recent research includes a study on educational technology curriculum issues, an historical analysis of educational films, and an action research project involving the integration of technology into elementary school curricula.

Robert D. Tennyson is professor of educational psychology at the University of Minnesota and president of the Consortium of Courseware Engineering. He is editor of a professional journal, *Computers and Human Behavior,* as well as serving on editorial boards for four other journals. His research and publications include topics on problem solving and concept learning, intelligent systems, testing and measurement, instructional design, and advanced-learning technologies. Recently he has directed NATO-sponsored workshops and advanced-study institutes on automated instructional design and delivery. He has authored over 100 journal articles and has written numerous books and book chapters.

ABOUT THE AUTHORS

Brockenbrough S. Allen is professor of educational technology at San Diego State University, where he teaches advanced graduate courses on educational product design, multimedia, and the psychology of technology-based learning. He also advises corporations and government agencies on effective use of learning and performance technologies. Allen holds a bachelor's degree in ecology and an M.A. in education (emphasis in science education) from the University of California, Berkeley, and a Ph.D. in education from the University of Southern California, with specializations in instructional technology and communications. Allen's work as an instructional designer began in the late 1960s with his invention of a patented simulation game. Created in association with naturalist Robert Stebbins, "The Evolution Game" is still published in Europe and used widely in high school and college biology courses. Following a stint in New York as a consultant on high-technology office communications systems and multi-image production design, Allen worked for several years as a teacher-counselor and media producer before beginning doctoral work at the University of Southern California in 1979. There, he helped design early instructional authoring systems for interactive video, studied adoption patterns on ARPANET (forerunner of the Internet), and conducted research on metacognitive skills and computer-assisted instruction. In 1982, he joined the SDSU faculty and cofounded one of the first graduate programs for training multimedia designers. Allen writes widely on instructional design, is a consulting editor for several journals, including *Educational Technology Research & Development,* and lives near a mountain and a lake with his wife, Barbara.

Vanessa Allen-Brown is an assistant professor in the College of Education at the University of Cincinnati. She teaches both history and philosophy of education. Her research focuses on the life histories of African-American women educators. In particular, she is interested in understanding the role of schools, family, and the community in encouraging achievement in black women.

Jane H. Anderson (Ph.D., Ohio State, 1993) was picking flowers off a recently planted strawberry patch in her organic garden in the hills of Southern Oregon just before writing this biography. She believes picking these first flowers will enhance later fruit production. Dr. Anderson is not sure what this has to do with educational technology, but her former experience as an English teacher suggests that, if you think hard enough, you may find some connection.

Gary J. Anglin is associate professor of instructional systems design at the University of Kentucky. He received his Ed.D. in instructional systems technology from Indiana University. His research interests are in the area of visual learning. His most recent edited book is *Instructional Technology: Past, Present and Future* (2d ed.). He is an active member in the Association for Educational Communications and Technology, and is a consulting editor of the journal *Educational Technology Research and Development* and was on the editorial board of the journal. He has taught graduate courses in instructional design and development, and instructional computing.

Bela H. Banathy is a researcher, author, and educator. Until his retirement, he was senior research director at the Far West Laboratory for Research and Development, where he directed over 50 projects in the course of 2 decades. He is president of the International Systems Institute, a nonprofit research and educational agency, and professor emeritus of systems science at the Saybrook Graduate School. He is a past president of the International Society for the Systems Sciences and is now on the board of trustees of the society. He is president of the International Federation of Systems Research, an agency of 25 national systems organizations. He serves on the editorial board of several international journals. He authored several books, numerous chapters in books, and over 100 articles and research reports.

Louis H. Berry is associate professor in the Program in Instructional Design and Technology at the University of Pittsburgh He has researched and published in the area of instructional message design, particularly with regard to the effects of color and complexity in visual learning. This interest currently extends into the cognitive aspects of computer screen design in multimedia. Dr. Berry has been active in the Association for Educational Communications and Technology and is a past president of the Research and Theory Division of that organization.

Roberts A. Braden is a professor emeritus of instructional technology at California State University, Chico. He was twice a member of the board of directors of the Association for Educational Communications and Technology, and for 8 years has been the book review editor of that association's research journal *Educational Technology Research and Development.* He is also a consulting editor for the Development section of ETR&D and a contributing editor of *Educational Technology.* In addition to his numerous columns, articles, and other publications, he has edited a dozen books on visual literacy and is a past president of the International Visual Literacy Association. Roberts is a graduate of Fresno State, Radford University, and the University of Arkansas. His professional interests are systematic instructional design, instructional design models, formative evaluation, design of instructional visuals, and the research/theory literature of the field. He has written on all of those topics.

John K. Burton is a professor of instructional technology at Virginia Tech. He has been involved in research in the area of learning for over 20 years. For the last 10 years, his work has become increasingly focused on the use of computer technology in education and training. His most recent book, which he coedited with W. Michael Reed at West Virginia University and Liu Min at the University of Texas at Austin, is *Multimedia and Megachange.* He currently serves on the editorial boards of *Computers in the Schools,* the *Journal of Research and Development in Education,* and the *Journal of Research on Computing in Education.*

Rebecca P. Butler is an assistant professor of educational media and library science at Eastern Tennessee State University. Her expertise is in the area of historiography, including oral history. Her latest publication is "Gender Perceptions in Instructional Technology" in the *Journal of Visual Literacy.*

Peggy Cole is assistant coordinator of accountability and instructor of English at Arapahoe Community College in Colorado. She has published on topics in constructivist learning and elaboration theory. She is currently interested in strategies that use computers to assist teaching and learning composition.

Donald J. Cunningham is currently professor of education, cognitive science, and semiotic studies at Indiana University at Bloomington. He is also professor of the Department of Learning, Development, and Communication at the University of New England, Armidale, Australia (on leave). He is the founder of the Centre for Research into the Educational Application of Multimedia at the University of New England. He pursues an active program of research and development in computer-mediated instruction and is a frequent contributor to the development of semiotic/constructivist

theories of learning and instruction. During the 1990–91 academic year, he was Garfield Weston Visiting Professor at the University of Ulster at Coleraine, Northern Ireland, where he collaborated with the Language Development and Hypermedia Research Group. In his recent publications, Cunningham and his colleagues have described the development and testing of a variety of multimedia systems in primary, secondary, and higher education.

Suzanne K. Damarin is professor, College of Education, the Ohio State University.

Ann De Vaney is professor of curriculum and instruction and director of the graduate program in educational communications and technology at the University of Wisconsin at Madison. Her research incorporates literary models for the analysis of educational media texts. Her latest publication is an edited book, *Watching Channel One,* from SUNY Press.

Andrew Dillon is an associate professor of information science at Indiana University, Bloomington, Indiana. A human factors psychologist by background (M.A., Cork, 1987; Ph.D., Loughborough, 1991), he researches human-computer interaction (HCI) and cognitive ergonomics, with particular emphasis on the issue of usability. His current research focuses on the perception of shape and structure in information environments and the application of social and cognitive science to the design of usable interactive artifacts. He has authored widely in the area of HCI, most recently publishing *Designing Usable Electronic Text* (Taylor & Francis, 1994). He currently serves on the editorial boards of *International Journal of Human-Computer Studies, and Hypermedia.*

Marcy P. Driscoll is professor of instructional systems and educational psychology at Florida State University. She is the author or coauthor of four textbooks in learning and instruction, including *Psychology of Learning for Instruction,* which won the 1995 Outstanding Book Award in Instructional Development from the Association of Educational Communications and Technology, and, with Robert M. Gagné, *Essentials of Learning for Instruction.* She has also published numerous articles in professional journals on learning, instructional theory, and educational semiotics. Professor Driscoll received her A.B. magna cum laude from Mt. Holyoke College and her M.S. and Ph.D. degrees in educational psychology from the University of Massachusetts at Amherst.

Thomas M. Duffy is currently professor of education and cognitive science and director of the Corporate and Community Education Program at Indiana University at Bloomington. His work has focused on the implications of constructivist theory for the practice of instructional design and for the use of technology to support learning. His current work focuses on the design of problem-based learning environments from a constructivist perspective. This has included the design and development and evaluation of PBL environments. He has recently coauthored *Online Help: Design and Evaluation* and coedited *Constructivism and the Design of Instruction,* as well as *Designing Constructivist Learning Environments.*

Karen Fullerton is a doctoral candidate in the Program in Instructional Design and Technology at the University of Pittsburgh School of Education. She has been designing, writing, and producing award-winning media programs for over 15 years, specializing in educational videos and teleconferences for managers and health care workers. Her research interests include computer and television screen design. She currently teaches preservice teachers how to use computer applications and multimedia resources in the classroom. She has also taught courses in instructional technology, video production, and media management for Duquesne University and the University of Pittsburgh.

R. Scott Grabinger is associate professor and program leader of information and learning technologies in the Division of Technology and Special Services at the University of Colorado at Denver. In this position, he teaches classes in developing learning environments, telecommunications and computer-mediated communications, hypermedia authoring and applications, and message design and production. His research and publication interests include the educational applications of technology-supported learning environments, hypermedia, expert systems in education, and computer screen design.

Barbara L. Grabowski is associate professor of education in the Instructional Systems Program at the Pennsylvania State University. She had previously been an associate professor at Syracuse University and associate director of the Center for Instructional Development and Evaluation at the University of Maryland University College. While at Maryland, she developed many hours of computer-based instruction and designed an award-winning distance education program in nuclear science. Her current research interests are in the areas of generative learning, large-group college classroom learning, and using emerging technologies in generative ways.

Margaret E. Gredler is professor of educational psychology and research at the University of South Carolina. Her focus is the application of instructional design criteria to the design of games and simulations. In addition to numerous articles on games and simulations, she is the author of *Designing and Evaluating Games and Simulations: A Process Approach,* published by Kogan Page.

Charlotte Nirmalani Gunawardena is associate professor of distance education and instructional technology in the Training and Learning Technologies Program at the University of New Mexico. She teaches graduate courses in distance education, instructional design, adult learning, and cross-cultural teaching and learning. She is a reviewer for

The American Journal of Distance Education and is on the editorial board of the *International Journal of Educational Telecommunications.* In 1994, she was awarded a Regents Lectureship by the University of New Mexico for excellence in teaching, research, and service. She has published and made presentations at international and national conferences on topics related to distance education. Her current research examines learning styles, learner-centered learning, cognitive strategies, social presence, and collaborative learning in interactive distance learning systems.

Kathleen M. Hannafin is associate professor of education and director of educational design and development at the Medical College of Georgia. Her expertise and interests center around teaching and learning with emerging technologies. She has extensive experience in designing and developing innovative classroom models for science, mathematics, humanities, and social sciences curriculum.

Michael Hannafin is professor of instructional technology and eminent scholar of technology-enhanced learning at the University of Georgia, where he directs the Learning and Performance Support Laboratory. He has worked extensively in the theoretical and applied sides of both "traditional" computer-aided instruction and technology-supported learning environments that employ technology in seeking, manipulating, constructing, and connecting concepts and ideas. He has served as editor and guest editor, as well as served on the editorial boards of leading scholarly journals in technology and learning, including the *Journal of Computer-Based Instruction, Educational Technology Research and Development,* and *Journal of Educational Research.*

James Hartley is professor of applied psychology at the University of Keele, Staffordshire, U.K. He obtained his first degree in psychology in 1961 from the University of Sheffield, and his Ph.D. from the same institution some 3 years later on the topic of programmed instruction. His main research interests today are in written communication, with special reference to typography and layout, but he is also well known for his research into teaching and learning in the context of higher education. Professor Hartley is a prolific writer and has so far published 12 books and over 200 papers. He is a fellow of both the British Psychological Society and the American Psychological Association.

Denis Hlynka holds the rank of professor in the Department of Curriculum: Mathematics and Natural Sciences at the University of Manitoba, Winnipeg, Canada. He has published widely in the field of educational technology, including two books. The *Videotex/Teletext Handbook* (1985) was cowritten with Paul Hurly and Matthius Laucht; *Paradigms Regained: The Uses of Illuminative, Semiotic, and Post-modern Criticism as Modes of Inquiry in Educational Technology* (1991) was coedited with John Belland of Ohio State University. His papers deal with the intersection of technology and the humanities. A postmodern perspective permeates his thinking. Dr. Hlynka has served as consultant to the Ethiopian Nutrition Institute from 1983–85. He has presented papers in Australia, India, Ethiopia, the United States, and Canada and served a 3-year term as editor of the *Canadian Journal of Educational Communication.* In 1993–94, he was the acting director of the Centre for Ukranian Canadian Studies at the University of Manitoba.

Robert E. Holloway is an associate professor at the Center for Excellence in Education at Northern Arizona University. He has been on the faculty at Teachers College, Columbia University, New York, served as director for Project Advance, Center for Instructional Development, at Syracuse University, and as audiovisual coordinator in Guam, M.I. He has been professionally active on the National Forum on Information Literacy, and is past president of the Association for Educational Communications and Technology. His avocational service interest is as electronic coordinator in the Pacific Southwest District of the Unitarian-Universalist Association. His most recent publication, with Jason Ohler, is a chapter on distance education in the 1995 edition of *Instructional Technology: Past, Present, and Future.* His primary interest is in technological change and development.

Simon R. Hooper is an associate professor of education in the Instructional Systems and Technology Program at the University of Minnesota. His research applies learning theory to instructional design and examines how to use technology effectively in education. He has served as guest editor and on the editorial board of *Educational Technology Research and Development* and is a consulting editor for *Computers in Human Behavior.* His papers have been published in journals such as *Educational Technology Research and Development, Journal of Educational Research,* and *Educational Psychologist.*

Laura J. Horn is a doctoral student in instructional design and technology at the University of Pittsburgh. She has taught primary grades in both public and private schools and is concerned with the appropriate utilization of technology in the learning of young children. Currently, she is exploring aspects of the interaction between educational technologies and the commercial sector.

David W. Johnson is a professor of educational psychology at the University of Minnesota, where he holds the Emma M. Birkmaier Professorship in Educational Leadership. He is codirector of the Cooperative Learning Center. He received a master's and a doctoral degree from Columbia University. He is a past editor of the *American Educational Research Journal* and has published over 300 research articles and book chapters. He is the author of over 40 books and has received numerous national awards for his research and teaching. Currently listed in Marquis's *Who's Who in the World,* he is a leading authority in social interdependence, conflict resolution, the social psychology of education, organizational development and change, and experiential learning. For the past 30 years, he has served as

an organizational consultant to schools and businesses. He is a practicing psychotherapist.

Roger T. Johnson is a professor of curriculum and instruction, with an emphasis in science education, at the University of Minnesota. He holds an M.A. degree from Ball State University and an Ed.D. from the University of California in Berkeley. He is the codirector of the Cooperative Learning Center. He is the author of numerous books, research articles, and book chapters and has received a number of national and international awards for his research and teaching.

David H. Jonassen is professor of instructional systems at the Pennsylvania State University. He is widely published in the areas of constructivism, instructional design, hypertext and hypermedia learning environments, and computer-based learning, including *Computers in the Classroom: Mindtools for Critical Thinking.* His current research focuses broadly on knowledge representation and the design of learning environments, which include cognitive tools. He has taught previously at the University of Colorado, University of North Carolina, Temple University, Syracuse University, and the University of Twente in the Netherlands.

Stephen T. Kerr is professor of education in the College of Education at the University of Washington. He received his Ph.D. in education from the University of Washington. His research on educational technology has included studies of teachers' acceptance and use of technology in classroom settings, studies of roles and role changes in education as influenced by technology, the development of instructional design skills by practitioners, and way-finding in complex information systems. He has also examined how information technology has encouraged educational reform in the schools of Russia and the former Soviet Union. He edited the recent National Society for the Study of Education (NSSE) Yearbook on *Technology and the Future of Education.* He is currently studying models of technology and its effects on the popular imagination.

Asit S. Kini is a research associate in the College of Education at Texas A&M University, where he directs the Office of Computer and Network Support. His doctoral dissertation was in the area of human learning and development, with special emphasis on educational computing, instructional design, and visualization. In the past, he has served as a visiting assistant professor at the college. In his present role, he has been instrumental in the implementation of state-of-the-art technology at the college. His current research interests include design of networked interactive hypermedia documents and spatial and conceptual metaphors for data organization and storage.

Nancy Nelson Knupfer is associate professor of educational computing design and telecommunication at Kansas State University. Dr. Knupfer has been involved with education for approximately 25 years, first as a teacher of elementary, junior high, and high school, and now at the university level. A unique feature of Dr. Knupfer's experience was her involvement with starting a high school in a remote Alaskan village. She completed her doctorate at the University of Wisconsin at Madison and was a faculty member of Arizona State University prior to joining the faculty at Kansas State. Dr. Knupfer has been involved with the design, production, implementation, and evaluation of interactive, technology-based instructional materials for both local and distance education within industry, government, and education. She is involved with social and political issues concerning schooling and technology, visual literacy, alternative theories of instructional design, critical theory, and cognition. She has published numerous articles in professional journals and recently edited a book, *Computers in Education: Social, Political, and Historical Perspectives* (1993), Hampton Press, with Dr. Robert Muffoletto. Dr. Knupfer joined AECT in 1983, is an active member of several professional organizations, and is president of the International Visual Literacy Association. Today, her adventurous spirit and interest in multicultural issues is evident in her international research about educational uses of the Internet.

J. Randall Koetting is associate professor, Department of Curriculum and Instruction, University of Nevada, Reno. He received his Ph.D. in C&I from the University of Wisconsin at Madison, an M.A. in educational foundations from St. Louis University, and a B.A. in philosophy from LaSalette Major Seminary College. His areas of research and study include critical theory, curriculum theory, and pedagogy; the social foundations of education; issues that fall under the general heading of multicultural education; and the foundations of technology and education.

Kathy A. Krendl is presently professor of telecommunications and dean of the School of Continuing Studies at Indiana University. She received her Ph.D. in communication from the University of Michigan. Her research interests and publications have focused on the use of media in instructional sections. She has served as a visiting scholar at Children's Television Workshop and is currently working on research evaluating the effectiveness of distance learning programs.

W. Howard Levie (1933–89) was a professor of instructional systems design at Indiana University. He received his Ph.D. in mass communications from Indiana University. His research focus was in the area of instructional message design and visual learning. He has published numerous articles and, along with Malcolm Fleming, was coeditor of the book *Instructional Message Design*. He has written and directed numerous motion pictures and was head of the production department of the AV Center at Indiana University. He has taught graduate courses in research methodology and instructional design and development.

Susan G. Magliaro is associate professor of curriculum and instruction at Virginia Polytechnic Institute and State University. She teaches undergraduate and graduate courses

in educational psychology and graduate courses in instructional design and tests and measurements. Her two interrelated areas of research include change, instructional design, and program development. Among her projects are the development of a reflective and responsive model for teaching instructional design, and the design and implementation of a major curricular, instructional, and assessment change effort in a local school division.

Robin Mason is head of the Centre for Educational Technology at the Open University, where she carries out research and evaluation of new teaching technologies. She has authored several books on computer conferencing and other communication technologies, and has designed and taught on-line conferencing courses for teachers and trainers. She has worked on a range of European-funded projects involving telecommunications technologies, and has designed and organized several international conferences about these technologies.

Nancy Maushak is assistant professor of education at William Penn College in Oskaloosa, Iowa. She teaches undergraduate courses in elementary education and instructional technology and supervises education practicum experiences. Her current research focus is on distance education and the diffusion of innovations.

Marina Stock McIsaac is professor of educational media and computers at Arizona State University. She is on the editorial and research review boards of the *International Journal of Educational Telecommunications, The American Journal of Distance Education,* and *Educational Technology.* McIsaac's research focuses on the applications of technology to education, particularly distance learning in cross-cultural settings. She has published widely in the literature on distance learning. McIsaac is the recipient of two Fulbright Senior Scholar/Researcher awards to lecture and conduct research in Turkey at Anadolu University's Open Education Faculty, and has worked as a consultant with the National Institute for World Trade. McIsaac is past president of the Research and Theory Division and president-elect of the International Division of AECT. She has lectured widely in Europe, Australia, Asia, and the Middle East, and is an educational technology discipline evaluator for the United States Council for International Exchange of Scholars (CIES).

Cliff McKnight is reader in information studies at Loughborough University. A psychologist by background (B.Sc. 1973, Ph.D. 1976, Brunel University), he has an interest in human-computer interaction since working with the late Christopher Evans in 1971. His current research focuses on the impact of information technology on scholarly communication, particularly those issues relating to the development and use of digital libraries. He currently serves on the editorial board of the *International Journal of Human-Computer Studies, Hypermedia,* and the *Journal of Educational Multimedia and Hypermedia.*

Hilary McLellan is a partner with McLellan Wyatt Digital, a multimedia and virtual-reality development and consulting company. She received her Ph.D. in educational technology from the University of Wisconsin. Dr. McLellan's research and design interests include situated learning, interactive story design for electronic media, and social interactions in electronic learning environments. She is an internationally recognized expert concerning virtual reality, especially as it applies to education. In 1994, she received the International Visual Literacy Association Research Award for her work concerning virtual reality and education. Dr. McLellan served as an advisory editor for *Virtual Reality: An International Directory of Research Projects* and is a contributing editor of *Educational Technology* and *Virtual Reality Report*. In 1993 and 1994, she oversaw the selection of the annual Awards for the Advancement of the Virtual Reality Industry. Dr. McLellan is the author of over 75 publications concerning multimedia and virtual reality and has spoken at many conferences, workshops, and universities in the United States and Europe. She is the editor of the forthcoming book *Situated Learning Perspectives.*

G. F. McVey is a professor emeritus at Boston University, where during the period 1973–91, as a member of the Department in Educational Media and Technology in the School of Education, he taught graduate-level courses and engineering in display systems design and ergonomics in instructional systems design. He currently teaches part time in the same program and serves as research advisor on studies related to ergonomics and educational facilities planning and design. Since 1978, he has also served as president of McVey Associates, Inc. (d.b.a. MAI Consultants) of Newton, Massachusetts a firm specializing in ergonomics and AV facilities design and engineering, and serving educational, training, and conference organizations in the U.S. and overseas. To date, he has served as the principal planning and design specialist on more than 50 projects, ranging in size from a one-room training center for Allied Chemical in Richmond, to a $50-million information center for print and nonprint media for the National Center for Financial Information, Ministry of Finance, Riyadh, Saudi Arabia. All of his past and current projects are characterized by an emphasis on ergonomics and a strict application of research findings in their design. In 1993, one of his projects, the NYNEX Learning Center in Marlboro, was selected as one of the top-10 training centers in the U.S. by *Presentation Products Magazine*. In 1994, he received the Tradeline *Oracle of Architectural Design Award*. He received his M.Ed. in educational television production from Boston University and his Ph.D. degree from the University of Wisconsin at Madison, with a specialization in environmental design and human performance (ergonomics). He is an active member of numerous professional organizations and, for the past 3 years, has served on the national committee to revise the 1988 ANSI/HFES VDT Workstation Design Standard.

David M. (Mike) Moore is a professor of instructional technology at Virginia Polytechnic Institute and State University. He has been involved in research in the area of visual learning for almost 25 years. He has published more than 80 articles in professional journals primarily in the area of visual research. His most recent book, which he coedited with Francis Dwyer, is *Visual Literacy: A Spectrum of Visual Learning*. He is also a past president of the International Visual Literacy Association.

Gary R. Morrison is a professor of instructional design and technology at the University of Memphis, where he teaches graduate courses in instructional design and technology. He has written over 90 papers on instructional design and computer-based instruction, an instructional design textbook, and 10 textbook chapters. He has designed a variety of media materials, including television and radio programs that were broadcast nationally, and more recently he has designed a number of multimedia units for introductory chemistry. He is the associate editor of the research section of *Educational Technology Research and Development.*

Edna Holland Mory is assistant professor of instructional technology at the University of North Carolina at Wilmington, where she also serves as the director of the Donald K. Watson School of Education Instructional Technology Center. She received her Ph.D. in instructional systems from Florida State University in 1991. She was awarded the 1991 Dean & Sybil McClusky Research Award, the 1992 Educational Technology Research and Development Young Scholar Award, and the 1993 Robert M. Gagné Award for her research in the area of feedback in instruction. Her other research interests include technology in education, the use of interactive multimedia for learning, teacher planning, school restructuring, and student motivation. She is an active member of the Association for Educational Communications and Technology, the American Educational Research Association, and the Association for the Advancement of Computing in Education.

Robert Muffoletto is associate professor of education, University of Northern Iowa, Cedar Falls.

Robert J. Myers is a senior instructional designer at the NASA Classroom of the Future, Wheeling, West Virginia. Dr. Myers is currently a principal investigator on two major projects. The first is a grant from NASA Goddard Space Flight Center to develop earth science curricula featuring NASA's repository of remote-sensing databases. The second is a service-learning project to create opportunities for students with visual and hearing impairments to take part in simulated space missions. Dr. Myers has published widely on K-12 instructional technology infusions, hypermedia, and problem-based learning.

Wayne A. Nelson is associate professor of instructional technology and chair of the Department of Educational

Leadership at Southern Illinois University at Edwardsville. He is currently a member of the editorial review board for the *Journal of Educational Multimedia and Hypermedia,* the *Journal of Research on Computing in Education,* and the *Journal of Educational Computing Research.* He has conducted research and published in the areas of learning with hypermedia systems, interface design, intelligence tutoring systems, and the processes of instructional design. His current research is focused on the use of computer technology to support the development of reflective practice by teacher education students.

Randal G. Nichols is an associate professor of education at the University of Cincinnati, where his teaching and essays mainly reflect critical approaches to understanding education and educational technologies. He teaches technology, curriculum, and ethics courses. He suspects that overrationality and willfulness have gotten us into nearly irredeemable states of education, society, and ecology. His positive sustenance comes from fishing and the music of Alison Krauss.

Richard G. Otto is an independent research psychologist and consultant specializing in advanced applications of educational technology and multimedia publishing. He holds a bachelor's degree in mechanical engineering from Seattle University and a Ph.D. from Syracuse University in philosophy of natural sciences. From 1971 to 1980, Otto was associate professor at Metropolitan State College in Denver, Colorado, where he chaired the Department of Philosophy before taking a position as a researcher at the National University of Mexico. From 1984 to 1989, he served as director of the Mexican-American Cultural Institute in Guadalajara. Otto's research and development at SDSU has focused on visualization and scientific imagination, distance education, multimedia publishing, and the use of case-based learning in technical training. His recent design work has focused on the transformation of print-based Spanish language textbooks to CD-ROM-based multimedia.

Ok-choon Park is a senior research psychologist at the Advanced Training Methods Research Unit, the U.S. Army Research Institute (ARI). He is an editorial board member of several journals. He has also been serving as an advisor for the National Research Council Postdoctoral and Senior Research Associates Program and the Washington Metropolitan Area University Consortium Research Fellow program at ARI. After receiving his Ph.D. in instructional psychology and technology from the University of Minnesota in 1978, he worked as a faculty member at the State University of New York at Albany and as an instructional researcher and consultant at Control Data Corporation until he joined ARI in 1985. For the last few years, he has conducted research on the characteristics of mental models and applications of visual displays in media-based instruction.

Joseph Psotka is a research psychologist for the Research and Advanced Concepts Office at the Army Research Institute. He earned a Ph.D. degree in cognitive psychology from Yale University in 1975. He served as an advisory member of the General Officer Steering Committee on AI and Robotics. He has more than 30 published papers in refereed journals and numerous presentations at scientific conferences. In 1988, his edited volume on *Intelligent Tutoring Systems: Lessons Learned* was published. He edited a book on *Intelligent Instruction by Computer: Theory and Practice* with Marshall Farr in 1991. His research currently focuses on the application of cognitive science to learning and instruction, with a special emphasis on the use of virtual-reality technologies for immersive tutoring systems.

Tillman J. Ragan is a professor in the instructional psychology and technology program at the University of Oklahoma. He received his Ph.D. in instructional technology from Syracuse University in 1970. Ragan is author of five books, including *Instructional Design* with P. L. Smith, and numerous articles on instructional technology, and he has been a columnist for *Educational Technology* magazine. He has directed and contributed to research projects sponsored by IBM (technology effectiveness), the United States Air Force (cognitive styles), and the Army (training effectiveness). He has served on many committees and held the titles of president of Research and Theory Division and of the Division of Instructional Development of AECT, vice president of IVLA, and cochair of the Professors of Instructional Design Technology conference. His area of research and teaching is instructional technology, with specific interests in instructional design, learner characteristics, and applications of computer technology to instruction.

Thomas C. Reeves is professor of instructional technology at the University of Georgia, where he teaches program evaluation, instructional design, and research methods. In addition to numerous presentations and workshops in the United States, he has been an invited speaker in Australia, Brazil, Bulgaria, Finland, Peru, Russia, South Africa, Switzerland, Taiwan, and the Netherlands. His current research interests include evaluation of instructional technology for education and training, mental models and interactive multimedia user interface issues, electronic performance support systems, and instructional technology in developing countries.

Kim Reid is a graduate student in the Department of Telecommunications at Indiana University. She is interested in the interrelationship of communications and learning, and more specifically involved in children's informal learning from TV. In 1995, she was a graduate research associate at the Children's Television Workshop.

John Richardson is a research fellow at the HUSAT Research Institute at Loughborough University of Technology. As a psychologist, his primary research interest concerns the opportunities and problems surrounding the impact of digital technology on written communication. His previous work has looked at the transference of reading skills from the printed page to screen-based systems and at the limitations of hypertext presentations.

Rita C. Richey is professor and program coordinator of instructional technology at Wayne State University. She has conducted research and published in the areas of instructional design theory and trends and training design for adult learners. Her most recent book is a coauthored volume, *Instructional Technology: The Definition and Domains of the Field.* Currently, she is conducting developmental research with an emphasis on contextual analysis and studying the impact of training on organizational productivity. In addition, she is completing a book on the contributions of Robert M. Gagné and beginning a systematic exploration of the knowledge base of instructional design.

Lloyd P. Rieber is an associate professor of instructional technology at the University of Georgia. He is interested in visualization, cognitive psychology, and constructivistic orientations to instructional design. His research has focused on using computer animation in the design of interactive learning environments. His most relevant research is about the integration of computer-based microworlds, simulations, and games. He is a past president of the Association for the Development of Computer-Based Instructional Systems (ADCIS).

Warren B. Roby is director of the Language Learning Resource Center and assistant professor of foreign languages and literatures at Washington State University. He teaches French, Spanish, and pedagogy classes. He is also the coordinator of the university's Self-Instructional Language Program through which the study of Arabic and Hindi, with the assistance of a tutor, is organized. He has helped produce instructional videotapes and live teleconferences. Dr. Roby has coauthored several articles on the application of technology to foreign-language instruction. He also has published on the teaching of intercultural communication.

Alexander Joseph Romiszowski is currently research professor in instructional design, development, and evaluation at Syracuse University. He also works regularly overseas, holding the post of visiting professor/researcher at the "School of the Future" Research Institute at the University of Sao Paulo, Brazil, and currently conducting projects and consulting missions to educational and human resources development organizations in Indonesia, Venezuela, Singapore, and the Netherlands. He has published extensively on the topics of instructional design and development and the use of new media and technologies in education. Most of his research and development projects are concerned with aspects of the application of technology-based training and education solutions, in both conventional and distance education contexts. His recent research has focused on the use of hypermedia and computer-mediated communication environments, often in combination, for the conducting of small-group collaborative learning methods such as case study and discussion, on-line and at a distance. This research is part of a wider agenda that is concerned with cost-effective methods of distance education for the development of critical-thinking, problem-solving, and decision-making skills.

Steven M. Ross is professor of educational psychology and research and associate director of the Center for Research in Educational Policy at the University of Memphis. He teaches graduate courses in educational statistics, research, and adaptive instruction. He is the author of three textbooks and over 100 journal articles in the areas of educational technology, computer-based instruction, and at-risk learners. He is the editor of the research section of *Educational Technology Research and Development.*

Ernest Z. Rothkopf is Cleveland E. Dodge Professor of telecommunications and education at Columbia University's Teachers College. Prior to his present appointment, he served as head of the Learning and Instruction Research Department at AT&T Bell Laboratories. An experimental psychologist by training, he sees himself as trying to build bridges between the learning laboratory and teaching technology. He has written many articles on learning and instructional theory. His current research is focused on the interaction between analytic processes and episodic memory in problem solving. He has been awarded the Edward Lee Thorndike Medal for Psychological Contribution to Education by the American Psychological Association.

Wilhelmina C. Savenye is an associate professor of learning and instructional technology in the Division of Psychology in Education at Arizona State University. She has also served on the faculty at San Diego State University and at the University of Texas at Austin, and as an evaluation and instructional technology consultant with educational organizations, the military, corporations, botanical gardens, and museums. She serves as a reviewer for several educational technology research journals and recently served as chair of the special-interest group for instructional technology in AERA. Her research is in the areas of instructional design, design of interactive multimedia environments for learning, and use of both quantitative and qualitative methods for studying the use of interactive technologies in training and teaching.

Barbara Seels is associate professor and coordinator of the Program in Instructional Design and Technology at the University of Pittsburgh. She received her Ph.D. degree in mass communications from Ohio State University and her M.S. in instructional communications from Syracuse University. She has coauthored *Exercises in Instructional Design and Instructional Technology: The Definition and Domains of the Field,* and edited *Instructional Design Fundamentals: A Reconsideration.* Her research interests and publications are in the areas of instructional design, visual literacy, and theoretical development of the field of instructional technology.

Valerie J. Shute is a research psychologist at the Armstrong Laboratory, Brooks Air Force Base, Texas. As part of her basic research on individual differences in learning, she designs, develops, and evaluates intelligent tutoring systems, then uses these controlled ITS environments to systematically test for aptitude-treatment interactions. Her current research focuses on student modeling, cognitive diagnosis, and remediation, and has resulted in a broad and powerful new paradigm called SMART (Student Modeling Approach for Responsive Tutoring). Dr. Shute has written numerous journal articles and chapters on a range of topics, coedited a book on cognitive processes and automated instruction, and is on the editorial board of four journals.

Michael Simonson is professor of curriculum and instruction and associate director for research of the Research Institute for Studies in Education in the College of Education at Iowa State University, Ames, Iowa. Dr. Simonson teaches courses in instructional technology and has published over 50 research papers. He has been editor since 1977 of the *Proceedings of Research and Development Papers* presented at the annual conferences of the Association for Educational Communications and Technology, and has written five books and monographs on educational technology and educational computing. His research interests deal with the impact of instructional technology on attitude formation and change, distance education, and computer anxiety.

Patricia L. Smith is an associate professor in the instructional psychology and technology program at the University of Oklahoma. She received her Ph.D. in instructional systems from Florida State University in 1982. Smith is the author of two books, including *Instructional Design* with T. J. Ragan, and numerous journal articles on computer-based instruction and instructional design. She has directed and served on a variety of research projects, including a recent IBM-sponsored project on technology effectiveness. She has been on the board of directors of the Research and Theory Division and the Division of Instructional Development of AECT, as well as having served as president of the Research and Theory Division. Other positions include being cochair of the Professors of Instructional Design Technology conference in 1992 and president of the Instructional Technology Special Interest Group of AERA in 1993. Her area of research and teaching is instructional design, particularly the design of instructional strategies, the design of print-based instruction, and instructional feedback.

Daniel Snyder has recently completed his master's degree in educational technology at the University of Washington. His research interests include how various psychological theories inform and direct instructional decision making.

He has extensive experience in technology and training in the U.S. Navy. He currently teaches computing at a community college.

Robert L. Towers is an associate professor of technology at Eastern Kentucky University. He received his Ed.D. in instructional systems design from the University of Kentucky. Previously, he earned a bachelor's degree in electrical engineering from the University of Kentucky and a master's degree from Eastern Kentucky University, and worked as an engineering consultant. His most recent coauthored book is *Robotics Technology*. He has taught graduate and undergraduate courses in quality control, electronics, and automated manufacturing.

Steven D. Tripp is a professor in the Center for Language Research at the University of Aizu, in Aizu-Wakamatsu, Japan. He was previously at the University of Kansas and is on the editorial board of *Educational Technology, Research and Technology*. His current research interests focus on the applications of technology, especially computers, to language learning. He is working on various applications of the World Wide Web to the teaching of English for Special Purposes (ESP) in the field of computer science.

Dian Walster is an assistant professor of library media at the University of Colorado at Denver. She was the 1993 AASL/Highsmith research winner for a project developing alternative assessment for integrating content standards with information literacy skills. Her research areas are information access and attitudes toward information and information technologies. Recently, she published a book for practitioners, *Managing Time for School and Public Librarians.*

William H. Ware is a general research analyst for Michigan-based Consumers Power Company, where he directs the company's customer satisfaction research. He is currently a doctoral candidate in telecommunications at Indiana University and has lectured both there and at Florida State University in the areas of advertising and communication research. His research interests include analysis of television content, mass-communication processes and effects, and media imperialism.

Ron Warren (M.S., Colorado State University) is a graduate student in telecommunications at Indiana University. He has previously worked as a high school English teacher and as a lecturer in speech communication at Colorado State University. His principal research interest is media's role in socialization. His previous work has examined the use of instructional videos in high schools, violent television content, and research on children and media. He has also worked on distance education evaluation for a statewide network of Indiana colleges and universities.

Michael D. Williams is a lecturer in educational technology in the National Institute of Education, Nanyang Technological University in Singapore. He received his Ph.D. in instructional systems at the University of Minnesota, and has taught instructional design and computer-based instruction at San Diego State University, the University of Minnesota, and St. Thomas University. He has published several articles in the area of learner-control in relation to computer-based instructional designs. Current research interests focus on investigating the cross-cultural elements impacting the use and effectiveness of computer-based instructional technologies in schools.

Brent Wilson is associate professor of information and learning technologies at the University of Colorado at Denver. He has published widely on topics in instructional design theory, including constructivist learning environments, collaborative learning communities, and the Internet as a learning tool. Recently, he has become interested in how people choose to make use of learning resources and how technology can stimulate change within a learning setting.

William Winn is professor of educational technology in the College of Education, University of Washington. He holds a secondary appointment in educational psychology and is an affiliate faculty member in the Department of Technical Communication, College of Engineering. His research includes the study of how people learn from maps and diagrams and ways in which cognitive and constructivist theories of learning can be used as the basis for instructional design. He served as editor of *Educational Communication and Technology Journal* from 1983 to 1989.

Andrew R. J. Yeaman is an independent scholar and consultant located in Westminster, a suburb of Denver, Colorado. He is also president of the Industrial Training and Education Division of AECT. Previously, he worked as a media technician, as a school media specialist, and as an assistant professor. First educated in England, he gained an A.A. degree as a media technician from Bellevue Community College, and later received the Ph.D. in educational communication from the University of Washington. He has published over 50 scholarly reports, chapters, and articles on reading from computer displays, the ergonomics of human-computer interaction for students and trainees, utilizing cultural anthropology, interpreting computer anxiety as a myth produced by researchers, and applying poststructural thinking to instructional media design, analysis, and theory. Dr. Yeaman also edited the *Educational Technology* February 1994 special issue on social responsibility. The topic of his current research is the intersection of culture, thought, communication, and technology. He asks, "What is the connection between computers and civilization?

I

FOUNDATIONS FOR RESEARCH IN EDUCATIONAL COMMUNICATIONS AND TECHNOLOGY

John C. Belland, Ohio State University

Associate Editor

1. VOICES OF THE FOUNDERS: EARLY DISCOURSES IN EDUCATIONAL TECHNOLOGY

Ann De Vaney
UNIVERSITY OF WISCONSIN AT MADISON

Rebecca P. Butler
EASTERN TENNESSEE STATE UNIVERSITY

Discourses and their related disciplines and institutions are functions of power: They distribute the effects of power. They are power's relays throughout the modern social system (Bove, 1992).

. . . and when we got over to England, they didn't even know what the hell we were. They called us the audiovision boys. They thought that we had to do with hearing aids, improving of hearing and so on (Schuller, 1978).

1.1 INTRODUCTION

Educational technology is such a young and amorphous field that confusion about its objects of study, its audience, and the parameters of its operations is almost as common today as it was for Charles Schuller during World War II. Yet at the onset, only a few educators with a common goal to improve education through technology generated national interest in their cause, devised curricula, started graduate programs, and produced a spate of diverse texts while establishing new terrain in the academy. While academic audiovisual and educational technology programs started in the 1950s and proliferated in the 60s, the intellectual groundwork for this area emerged in the late 20s and peaked in the 40s with the capstone event of programmatic and extensive war research. Since texts produced during this time, 1932 to 1947, and oral accounts of this period form a solid base for the establishment of an academic field, we will consider these documents in our examination of the early history of educational technology.

Often, educational scholars, in and outside of educational technology, yearn for and pursue a monolithic academic project that would, once and for all, provide a unified definition of their enterprise and offer an objective account of their operations. While this is a futile exercise for social scientists who study human beings and their activity, it was and is a legitimate goal for academics working under the aegis of logical positivism. The fact that past and present educational technology scholars have failed in this monolithic effort is to the credit of the field. Heterogeneous texts produced during the period under consideration and later provide a rich account of objects of study, theories engaged, methods employed, and audiences included. The written and oral texts considered here disclose a set of common goals but are diverse projects whose structures are contingent on historically accepted concepts and values. They reflect prevailing notions of learning theory and pedagogy, research methods, economic, military, and political values, and other elements of the social milieu in which they were produced. The iterations of names, concepts, assumptions, and theories in these texts not only promoted ideas but actually created truisms in the field for the time in which they were written. The value of these texts cannot be measured by sophisticated standards of current research, nor by highly evolved notions of learning theory, but by how they achieved their common goals when they were written. From whatever perspective these authors spoke, we might ask how well they made their objects of study intelligible to specific audiences at specific moments in time. The rhetoric with which they spoke and the discourses that spoke through them energized an audience of scholars, educators, and students to participate in a new field, educational technology. By any measure they were successful.

It is with respect for the success of the founders of the field of educational technology that we attempt, from our specific moment in time, within our own community to describe the discourses of their early documents. Within this project we value the mutability and diversity of educational technology.

1.2 EARLY EDUCATIONAL TECHNOLOGY TEXTS

When people approach us today, they are often as confused about the title, *educational technology,* as they were about it's predecessor, *audiovisual instruction.* Educational technology is often mistakenly equated with computer education or instructional design, and for several years, in the 60s and 70s, definitions of the title and terms of the field proliferated. But definitions are historically contingent, and in a field constructed around ever-changing notions of technology, definitions as well as machines have obsolescence built into them.

Definitions, while helpful, can be limiting, and a description of the establishment, operation, and reception of a field may yield more understanding of its nature and scope than definitions. Imagine, for instance, what happens to many 60s and 70s definitions of educational technology concepts in light of virtual reality, or in light of all the new and startling research on the brain and the mind. What happens to definitions of interaction in virtual environments, and what happens to descriptions of learning from media in the new world of constructivist cognitivism? While not eschewing definitions, we will in this chapter try to examine the manner in which early discourses spawned the field of educational technology. When definitions are employed, we will attempt to place them in their historical context.

Within any discipline, the construction of knowledge and its subsequent cultural practice is always elusive. Yet, within each field there are specific early primary and secondary texts that have been authored and received over time. If carefully read, these texts can yield voluminous information about the formation of a field, such as who the founders were, which discourses influenced their communications, and to whom and with what authority they spoke. In psychiatry, for instance, one could analyze the primary texts of Freud, Jung, and Adler and the secondary texts of their disciples. In a field as young as educational technology, many early texts are available for analysis and may provide information about how specific discourses became inscribed in this area of scholarship.

This chapter will not be a traditional history of educational technology for several reasons. Paul Saettler (1968, 1990) has written an admirable history of the field, and that task need not be repeated. We are also limited by the strictures of one chapter. Since this is a handbook of research in educational technology, we have limited our investigation to a consideration of how knowledge in the academic field of educational technology was generated.

1.2.1 Purpose

In this chapter, we analyze early educational technology texts to ascertain the manner in which founders of the field constructed the base of knowledge that was to constitute educational technology. We explore their discourses to discover which ideas were included and which excluded from their writings; we examine how they spoke and with what authority; and we describe discourses they offered their readers. More specifically, in the early texts we locate repeated statements that describe concepts, theories, pedagogy, and values, and trace them to discourses outside the emerging field. We also attempt to describe the formation of discourses within the field. In tables of contents and indices, we explore the organization of information in the field by noting the hierarchy of topics and the inclusion or exclusion of subject matter. In prefaces and forewords, we investigate the intentions of the authors and note with what authority they speak. Additionally, we tell the stories of early women in the field.

1.2.2 Oral History

Edgar Dale, speaking with the authority of a renowned educational scholar, offers a description of some early (1930s) objects of study and intended audiences in the emerging audiovisual field.

> Well somewhere or another I got the concept there was a lot of rich knowledge available, and we ought to have some techniques for moving that rich knowledge into the minds and hearts of people. So I began—I didn't use the word then. I got the word (later) from Charters of—*communication.* And so there was this sharing of ideas and feelings in a *mood of mutuality.* Here's all this *information* the *librarians* want to share; the *teachers* want to share, but it isn't available; it isn't *packaged* right; it isn't *written* right; it isn't *pictured* right, and so on [italics ours] (Dale, 1977).

In this humanistic description of a nascent field, Dale suggests what would be studied—*communication, packaged information* with *pictures* and *text*—who would benefit—*librarians and teachers*—and most importantly identifies the professional esprit we found so common in the taped interviews. This rhetorical strand is woven through all the oral histories. We have reason to believe there was an authentic sharing of ideas and *mood of mutuality.*

> This mood is echoed in James Brown's statement: Many people were enthusiastically believing such things (that films would change education). It made a difference in their attitude toward education. There were a good many people who became convinced that this was a way of making education a good deal more effective than it had been (Brown, n.d.).

In describing what constituted the field, Kenneth Norberg addresses theoretical objects of study that came to be articulated and notes a discursive rift among scholars:

. . . I was interested in Jerry Torkelson's statement which he made a year or so ago, when he was still president of AECT, that the critical word in our association name is *communications,* and he went on to say that technology was secondary, in the sense that it implies a systematic approach to the solution of communication problems in an educational setting.

It seems to me that there are some unresolved conflicts —possibly—in the notion of what our field is. . . . I think there is a kind of theoretical rift between the communications people and the instructional development people who have been strongly influenced by learning psychologists, particularly behavioristic psychologists (Norberg, 1977).

Walter Wittich, in retrospect, speaks not of the objects of study but of the gatekeeping and mode of entry into the later field.

Well professionals are professionals. By that I mean that they have gone through a sequence of professional work which has been carefully designed to induct them into the strategies, into the philosophies, into the systems of the field, which is something that I—I say this unabashedly—I never had the advantage of. Because when I went looking for courses in the field, when I was working on my Ph.D. . . . and the education dean at the University of Wisconsin (John Guy Fowlkes) had to write a course so that we (Charles Schuller and Walter) would have something to take. This was way back in late 39 (Wittich, 1972).

And Elizabeth Golterman challenges the received wisdom about when the field started:

Many people, now that I'm retired, think of me as an audiovisual pioneer, but actually in 1930, when I became a member of the staff of the St. Louis School Audio Visual Center, I was joining the staff of an institution that had begun back in 1904, and had been reaching classrooms through weekly deliveries (of media software) since 1905. So that it had had 25 years of experience when I became part of it (Golterman, 1976).

1.2.3 Theory and Analytical Technique

Methods for reading these early written and oral texts are available to us. Poststructural reader theories provide an epistemology that frames this study (see 10.5), because according to these theories, truths are socially and linguistically constructed within and only within a discourse; they cannot be submitted to a transcendent authority for proof. Reader theories also supply us with a conceptual frame for a consideration of text, author, subjectivity, and discourse. What many of these theories fail to supply is an analytical technique, since they are, by and large, amethodological. In this study we have adopted a poststructural perspective to read historical texts and appropriated neorhetorical devices for our method of reading. Such methodological and theoretical pairings are gaining a foothold among scholars who analyze text (Rooney, 1989; Maillioux, 1989; Morrison, 1992). We will describe our adaptation of specific reader theory concepts and neorhetorical analysis for this study.

1.2.4 Readers, Texts, Discourses

While notions of text, author, subjectivity, and discourse are properly contested within poststructural literature, the presence of these concepts provides the paradigm with some cohesion. If one is to conduct rhetorical analysis within a poststructural frame, one must come to an understanding, however tentative or short lived, of these central concepts.

We consider our historical resources here to be physically bound texts that have been constructed with intent by authors; they contain socially encoded messages that may be variously interpreted by readers. Readers, however, must have linguistic access to the community that has encoded the message. We consider discourses, here, to be texts "writ large." They, too, have been constructed with intent by authors; they contain socially constructed messages that are variously interpreted by readers. While hard to define, discourses are invisible systems of thought (Bove, 1990) that operate at a linguistic level to produce and regulate knowledge. All communications are discourse specific, that is, they are rhetorically related to a system of thought that includes specific concepts, theories, assumptions, and values, while excluding others. Authors, by the virtue of the rhetoric they employ, are subjects of discourses; they produce only discourse-specific communication, and discourses speak through them. Authors offer potential readers invitations (Ellsworth, 1988) to believe in the discourses or systems of thought embodied in their texts.

1.2.4.1. Rhetoric. Rhetorical analysis, new or old, is concerned with the structure of a communication, such as a narration or an exposition. Even though the distinction between these two genres is blurred today in some scholarly circles, an analyst can locate significant rhetorical sites by examining traditional techniques for exposition in scholarly books and narrative in oral histories.

Our rhetorical techniques, then, include three approaches. To locate concepts, theories, assumptions, and values in expository texts and narrative texts, we examine the structure of the communication and question the text at specific organizational sites in the main sections or body of the texts. By examining the table of contents and indices of many old educational technology resources, we note the hierarchy of topics and the inclusion and exclusion of subject matter. In prefaces and forewords, we investigate the intention of the authors and note with what authority they speak. We group and relate our linguistic findings to the discourses from which they came. This is not a neat procedure, for as can be expected, there are many overlapping and conflated messages. Discourses are hard to pin down, but their operation can be seen. The specific rhetorical structure of one text acts like a vector that identifies the bodies of discourse from which it was drawn. We also explore the rhetoric of early women in the field.

1.2.4.2. Textual Sources. Representative historical (approximately early 1930s to early 1950s), educational technology texts were submitted to rhetorical analysis.

They include oral history audiotapes of the founders of the field, research reports, technical manuals, journal articles, textbooks, and books addressing theory, pedagogy, and application.

The value of articulating the linguistic presence of both dominant and subordinate discourses in these texts is to demonstrate a difficult process, to provide a partial example of the production, regulation, and institutionalizing of knowledge. Hopefully these analyses will partially explain how this happened and why similar discourses continue to shape the field of educational technology today.

1.3 OVERVIEW

1.3.1 Between Two Wars

Even though the modern field of educational technology emerged from training research of World War II, the objects of study, basic concepts, and intended audience had been circumscribed in the period between 1918 and 1941. While assessment of the efficacy of the Yale photoplays represents the first school research with students and film, earlier research on the value of health training films during World War I had been conducted. Between the wars, however, the area of audiovisual instruction for students was promoted by interested educators, librarians, school administrators, filmmakers, radio program designers, textbook producers, and other media enthusiasts throughout the country. We might say that early audiovisual practice was multivocal. Also, supporting the new audiovisual area was a substantial body of scholarly books and textbooks that were published in this period. The interest of educators in the field and researchers in the academy produced a flurry of additional books about classroom application of audiovisual instruction and building and district administration of audiovisual programs. We shall refer to all of these books as *texts*. Oral history audiotapes will also be called *texts*.

Audiovisual texts produced between the two wars were of several types. Late-20s and early-30s faculty research reports, published by university presses, were representative of prevailing scholarship of the decade. While seldom addressing the learning theory that informed their method and design, these texts reflected a heightened interest in connectionism and a growing reliance on statistical measurement, which was prevalent in the new departments of educational psychology. We speculate that these departments, many of which were established in the 20s, gained a foothold in the academy by imitating the practices of animal psychologists. We do not suggest that this was a self-serving move but one in which educational psychologists believed would bring rigor to an ill-formed field, education.

The applied audiovisual texts of the late 20s and early 30s reflect little research or learning theory. Rather, they were concerned with the operation of machines in public school classrooms, buildings, and districts. This direction was, of course, necessary, since most practitioners and potential practitioners were ignorant of the operation of these machines.

A different type of text, however, emerges in the late 30s and continues through the 40s. It is a text that attempts to ground audiovisual instruction in a learning theory and describe the manner in which theory suggests certain pedagogical practices. It is both theoretical and applied. The rhetoric of these texts engages the dominant educational discourse of the period, mid-30s to late 40s. It was a Deweyesque, child-centered, humanistic learning, and curricular theory. (That does not mean there was no behavioral subtext during this time. Learning theories, like discourses, are not pure, but conflated.) Atheoretical applied texts were still written during this period, but they proliferated in the area of audiovisual administration rather than pedagogy or instruction. Since this is a handbook of research, we have focused on the period from approximately the early 30s to the early 50s and on texts primarily, but not exclusively, produced in the academy. We have included chapters, but not whole texts devoted to administration of audiovisual programs. To understand the rhetoric of these texts, we provide some historical information about the context in which they were produced.

1.4 EDUCATIONAL TRENDS: LATE 20s AND EARLY 30s

When the National Academy of Visual Instruction (NAVI) merged with the Department of Visual Instruction (DVI) under the auspices of the National Education Association (NEA), the year was 1932, and the country was in the midst of a recession. Opposing national voices in the ongoing struggle for educational reform were surprised by the hybridized nature of local school reform. A bipolar debate for dominance of the U.S. curriculum had been mounted in the early years of the century and had reached a fevered pitch in the mid-20s. Kliebard (1987) characterizes these factions as social efficiency theorists and child study or developmental theorists. The manner in which these camps articulated their beliefs in curriculum theory and educational practice in the 1930s is important here, because their opposing discourses underpin the writings of audiovisual educators and researchers in the decade. Also, it is important to remember that the audiovisual movement was school based.

1.4.1 Social Efficiency

The powerful social efficiency movement, which borrowed ideas of social control and stability from Edward Ross and notions of efficiency from Frederick Winslow Taylor (Kliebard, 1987), spawned an interest in the compatible studies of behavioral psychology and mental measurement. "It was social efficiency that, for most people, held out the promise of social stability in the face of cries for massive social change" (Kliebard, 1987, 1989).

Early in the century, we hear John Franklin Bobbitt talking about the "scientific management" of education, the "elimination of inefficiency," the "platoon system," school superintendents as "educational engineers," and the school as a "plant" (Kliebard, 1987, pp. 97–99). While it was Taylor (1911) who actually introduced the business world to the twin gods of efficiency and effectiveness, it was Bobbitt and other early educational researchers and administrators such as Ellwood and Ayers (Kliebard, 1987, pp. 103–104) who graced the national educational discourse with that indelible metaphor of the school as a "factory."

1.4.2 Child Development

In opposition to the social efficiency movement, interest in child study or development grew in the early part of the century and had vocal proponents in the 1920s. Hall, Kilpatrick, Dewey, and others believed "that somewhere in the child lay the key to a revitalized curriculum" (Kliebard, 1987, p. 160). While generating varied child development theories, these scholars opposed the reformations suggested by the social efficiency movement. They felt that "education should be considered as life itself and not as a mere preparation for later living" (Kliebard, 1987, p. 162). (Although both movements claimed John Dewey, his experiential theories are more aligned with the child study group. He did, however, disagree with both groups on many points.) Like the social efficiency educators, child developmentalists believed that public school curriculum needed reform; students needed to participate in purposeful activity. To this end, Kilpatrick, diverging from his teacher Dewey, introduced the Project Method of education, which was to address, in an integrated manner, the problems of living. Child interests and their life activities were used as curriculum guides:

> By the 1930s, the Project Method movement had grown to such proportions that it outgrew its original identification with the project per se and came to be more grandly advertised as the activity curriculum or the experience curriculum (Kliebard, 1987, p. 168).

These utilitarian and pragmatic curricula were not the sole domain of elementary or secondary schools but were influential in determining experimental education at colleges such as Bennington, Sarah Lawrence, and a general college at the University of Minnesota (Brubacher & Rudy, 1968). We see the humanistic and pragmatic influence of this movement in the late 30s and 40s in the work of Dale and others.

1.4.3 Mental Measurement

At the same time, influential metaphors were being generated by another arm of the social efficiency movement: the mental measurement proponents. Thorndike's contribution of the mind as a machine with multitudinous, discrete, and nonconnected parts remains with us today. Indeed,

Thorndike, along with Goodard, Terman, Yerkes, and others, was responsible for the application of the IQ scale as a vehicle of social control, not just a diagnostic test (Kliebard, 1987).

Child development proponents were not the only educators who highlighted student needs. The social aspects of the efficiency movement also stressed education according to student needs; mental measurements allowed educators to ascertain those needs; and activity or job analysis became the means by which new curriculum was developed. W. W. Charters, who later figures prominently in the audiovisual movement, was one of the first educators to compile activity analyses for the tasks of such occupations as librarian and veterinarian (Kliebard, 1987). He transferred his model of task analysis to the curriculum for Stephens College in Missouri (Brubacher & Rudy, 1968).

Speaking of Charters and his early influence on curriculum theory and the emerging audiovisual field, Edgar Dale says:

> (Charters) had this whole idea of analysis of activities. . . . Now we'd call it, I suppose, behavioral analysis. . . . A very concrete approach to curricular processes (Dale, 1977).

But as Dale was learning Charters' activity analysis in the 30s and applying this curriculum technique to an articulation of Carleton Washburne's Winnetka plan, he was critiquing it:

> . . . And the individualized instruction involved analyzing a subject like arithmetic, loading the key steps, then preparing a set of almost textbook experience. So you would do a step at a time, take a test on it, take another test on it, and so on. And I thought it was very fruitful in terms of applying some of the Charters' approach. [There was] the old weakness of any kind of individualized instruction where you take it step by step, and you don't have the chance to tie the material together, to integrate it, and so on. That, that difficulty I thought of right along (Dale, 1977).

1.4.4 Learning Theory

One aspect of the curricular debate at this time influenced the research practices in our field, early and late. Aspects of early behaviorism need our attention (see 2.21.3). Educational psychology was dominated by Edward Thorndike in the early decades of this century (Guthrie & Powers, 1950; Hilgard, 1948; Kliebard, 1987), perhaps because he straddled the disciplines of psychology and education. Before the turn of the century, he had described his basic tenets of learning in *Animal Intelligence* (1898), and even though he applied his theory of connectionism to human beings in *The Psychology of Learning* (1913), it was not until the 30s that he elaborated his premises (Thorndike, 1935). Prior to that time, he applied his theory to education and mental measurements. Basically, he believed that the association between sense impressions (stimuli) and impulses to action (response) was the arena in which learning took place. His connectionism was an associative theory that peaked the interest of later (30s and 40s) psychologists concerned with the issues of learning and education. Guthrie, Skinner, and Hilgard, publishing in the 30s and beyond, and Hull in the 40s and beyond, each contributed their own behavioral theory to the scholarly and practical area of learning in the United States. Embracing the ideas of contiguity and association as a basis for learning, these men left an indelible mark on the rhetoric, discourses, and practices of the fields of educational psychology and educational technology. (For many decades educational technology research projects appeared to be simply imitations of educational psychology projects.)

Educational psychologists were not only influencing technology research but also publishing in the field. Hilgard, a popularizer and synthesizer of behavioral theory, contributed an important chapter in an influential audiovisual text, *New Teaching Aids for the American Classroom,* and is often cited in World War II research. Thorndike's name and, consequently, his brand of behaviorism, connectionism, appears in 30s audiovisual research reports. Hull's systematic behavioral theory appears in the 40s and 50s research of Neal Miller (1941, 1957). Another disciple of Hull whose work influenced educational technology scholarship was Albert Bandura, upon whose human modeling theory Gagne and Briggs (1965) based their Conditions of Learning.

A general definition of learning to which most of these behaviorists subscribed is offered by Hilgard:

> Learning is the process by which activity originates or is changed through training procedures (whether in the laboratory or in the natural environment) as distinguished from changes by factors not attributable to training (Hilgard, 1948, p. 4).

Neobehavioral theories, especially operant conditioning, provided a rigorous scaffolding for research in educational psychology from roughly the late 30s to the 70s and garnered for this field a reputation of serious scholarship in the academy. While educational technology was never accorded the same academic respect, most researchers in this field did imitate the learning theories and research methods practiced by educational psychologists. Educational psychologists gained the respect of arts and science colleagues by attempting to make the study of student learning as scientific as had the academic psychologists the study of animal learning. Although educational technology researchers adopted the behavioral posture of their colleagues, their reputations were tainted by their connection with audiovisual machines—not considered by many academics to be worthy of scholarship —before the advent of computers. If any one value was articulated in most academic discourses we examined, it was the valorization of words, especially words in print. (Such a value, in fact, may have led one leading researcher [Clark, 1986] to conduct a meta-analysis of educational technology research and conclude in 1986 that machines do not affect learning, and that media are dead when considered as variables in a learning experiment.)

The stature that educational technology scholars gained by adopting neobehavioral theories and practices was mitigated by other losses. If a discourse is a system of thought that produces knowledge, examination of the concepts included and excluded from the neobehavioral discourse will provide a partial understanding of the intellectual underpinning of educational technology. Within this discourse, the mind was considered a *tabula rasa* that could be modified by training. Key concepts of contiguity and association were borrowed intact from animal psychology and transferred to human beings. The paradigm excluded notions of culture, context, language production, internal action, and thinking (Becker, 1977). While current cognitive theories have gone a long way toward addressing some of these early exclusions, no one psychological theory of learning can account for learning that occurs because of one's membership in a group. When the research focus is on a unit of one, the brain and social and cultural factors elude scholarly efforts.

1.4.5 Behaviorism and Humanism

Educational practice and research in the United States ultimately fell under the sway of behaviorism and subsequent psychological theories of learning. Yet Western European curriculum and educational research emerged in a predominantly humanistic vein. National debates and their resolutions in the academy during the 30s and the 40s can partially account for this difference. During the 30s, U.S. philosophers began to adopt theories proposed by certain analytic European philosophers, particularly those logical positivists in the Vienna Circle and, secondarily, British analytic linguists. Quine, who had studied briefly with these philosophers in Vienna, paved the way for the migration of Carnap, Reichenbach, Hempel, Neurath, and Feigle to Ivy League universities where they remained to escape Naziism. In opposition to the European humanist philosophical traditions that these men believed accommodated fascism, they called themselves "scientists," not humanists (Borradori, 1994). Their project set the trajectory for U.S. philosophy for decades to come and contributed to the valorization of those academic disciplines based on positivism, i.e., science and mathematics. Even the pragmatists James and Dewey were convinced by some logical positivist arguments and incorporated them in their later works. And Quine's analytic work was strongly influenced by Skinner, a close Harvard colleague of his (Borradori, 1994). Ultimately the postwar culture in the U.S. academy was mainly positivist and in certain disciplines behaviorist, while the Western European academy remained predominantly humanist. While not the sole influence on curriculum development, this U.S. culture shaped educational practices and, finally, the development of the educational technology field.

Although scholarly audiovisual texts in the late 20s and early 30s were exclusively behavioral, applied books of that period were not. Also in the late 30s, scholarly audiovisual books began to reflect the child-centered notions of Dewey and others. For a brief time (approximately the late 30s and 40s), humanist, child-centered discourses were ascendant in departments of education, in curricular practices, and in the emergent audiovisual field. This was not the case in the 20s or early 30s, nor later when the AV field acquired the title of "educational technology." But membership in DVI in the 30s was eclectic (artists, commercial and educational filmmakers, librarians, school administrators, government officials, teachers, etc.), which suggests that the discourse that dominated the practice of audiovisual instruction during this period was multivocal. Many late 30s and 40s texts merged theory and pedagogy because of the pragmatic nature of the dominant Deweyesque discourse.

But the fact that child-centered theories dominated the audiovisual and general educational discourses from the mid-30s was a short aberration, both in U.S. curricular practice and audiovisual scholarship. Each of the neobehaviorists writing in the 20s and 30s contributed to educational technology scholarship in the 40s and 50s. And each theorist trained World War II researchers. This means that World War II film researchers, most often selected from educational psychology departments that had been established on university campuses approximately in the mid-20s, were steeped in a specific neobehavioral theory with its language, which included and excluded certain concepts. During World War II, they designed and executed experiments within a narrow psychological discourse, which was often well suited to the training taking place. The rigor we associate with the post–WW II period of educational technology research most likely came from the sophistication of measurements, and statistics for experimental and quasi-experimental designs, rather than from further articulation of behaviorism

1.5 EARLY AUDIO VISUAL SCHOLARSHIP

1.5.1 Connectionism and Mental Measurement

Scholarly audiovisual texts written in the early 30s display a convergence of the compatible discourses of social efficiency and Thorndike's brand of psychology and mental measurement. This convergence, which can be traced in educational psychology as well as educational technology, remains with us today. Of concern to AV scholars in the 30s was the effectiveness of film in teaching school subjects, the proper application of films in the classroom, and the intellectual and emotional impact of commercial films on students.

1.5.1.1. University Press. One way of ascertaining the status of a new area of study in the academy is to note if university presses, which print primarily scholarly material, publish books on the new area. Three books published by prestigious university presses in the early 30s were *The Educational Talking Picture* (Devereux, 1933), *The Sound Motion Picture* (Rulon, 1933), and *Motion Pictures in Edu-*

cation in the United States (Koon, 1934). These books begin to disclose what the founders of educational technology thought was knowledge important enough to be included in the field. The Devereux text (in the foreword, Robert Hutchins provides the text with an additional note of authority and a military connection when he refers to the author as "Colonel Devereux") and the Rulon textbook include reports of experiments with students and films. The language of the laboratory is employed, and strenuous efforts at objectivity are made. A list of the illustrations in the Devereux book and a list of the tables in the Rulon text will provide a picture of the depth of commitment to connectionism and mental measurements, even in the early 30s (see Fig. 1-1).

These lists indicate that the authors were following the lead of the few AV researchers who had preceded them in the 1920s. They were using experimental and control groups, and were controlling for some individual differences (students were not yet called *subjects*). They were measuring mean differences and were using standard IQ measures. In the light of today's more sophisticated statistics, the experiments were lacking. They did, for instance, measure the percent of mean difference and conclude that a film was X% better in teaching a subject than was standard teaching. But the base of a behavioral discourse complemented by specific mental measurements was there in its entirety. What was thought to be important were elements that could be isolated and controlled and, therefore, measured, i.e., intelligence and performance on immediate and delayed tests. Edgar Dale comments on the fact that the experimental model was de riguer even in the 20s.

> They employed Freeman, Frank Freeman of the University of Chicago and Ben Woods of Columbia University to make a study of audiovisual materials, films in this case. So they set up an experiment in the *usual fashion* (italics ours). They had control groups and experimental groups. They produced 20 films, 10 in general science and 10 in . . . general science and geography. . . . And plans were very care-

V.	Final Test Gains over Initial Test for Combined Cities
VI.	Final Test Gains on Picture-Unit Items for Combined Cities
VII.	Final Test Gains on Non-Picture Items for Combined Cities
VIII.	Final Test Gains over Initial Test for Groups of Below- and Above-Average Intelligence Levels
IX.	Recall Test Gains over Initial Test for Combined Cities
X.	Recall Test Gains on Picture-Unit Items
XI.	Recall Test Gains on Non-Picture Items

Figure 1-1. List of Illustrations, results of experimentation from *The Educational Talking Picture,* by F. Devereux, 1933, Cambridge: Harvard University Press, xiii.

1. Census Data by Occupations

2. Geographical Distribution of Students

3. Teaching Load

4. Group Balancing Data

5. Geographical Distribution of Balanced Groups

6. Teaching Load in Balanced Groups

7. Immediate Test-Group Results

8. Achievement Prediction Correlations

9. Immediate Group Comparisons

10. Immediate Percentage Comparisons

11. Immediate Percentage Comparison Standard Errors

12. Immediate Picture-Verbal Results

13. Immediate Text-Film Results

14. Immediate Rote-Education Results

15. Retention Group-Balancing Data

16. Retention Group Comparisons

17. Immediate-Retention Differences

18. Retention Percentage Comparisons

19. Retention Picture-Verbal Results

20. Retention Text-Film Results

21. Retention Rote-Education Results

Figure 1-2. List of Tables, from *The Sound Motion Picture,* by J. Rulon, 1933, Cambridge: Harvard University Press, xiii.

fully developed for the use of those materials. . . . Well, then they gave pretests and posttests. And speaking roughly, the youngsters having the films learned 15% more information than the ones that did not have it. Although it was a curious thing that happened. They let them (the schools) chose their own control groups. It turned out that the schools made the control groups typically brighter than the others. And this curious kind of reasoning (emerged), namely, because the control groups would not have the advantage of the film, so they ought to be just a little bit brighter and so on. Of course it's suspicious reasoning. That's what we're trying to test. . . . But they (the experimental groups) did better. And these (tests) would be simple information of what was in the film (Dale, 1977).

Early and late, the human factor confounded laboratory practices.

1.5.2 A Small Circle of Friends

Another way to discover the theoretical underpinnings of researchers is to note the resources included in their texts. In his bibliography, Rulon leans heavily on the audiovisual experiments of Freeman (1922, 1924) in the 20s, the behav-

iorism of Hull (1928), the experimental work of Knowleton and Tilton (1929), and McClusky (1924). (See Fig. 1-2.)

Other scholars often cited were J. J. Weber (who spanned the 20s and 30s), H. Wise (1939), L. Westfall (1937), V. Arnspiger (1937), and F. Consitt (Dale, p. 400). Weber's work compared silent film, slides, and diagrams as modes of instruction, while Westfall examined pupil interest and IQ in relation to film. Arnspiger, who later became director of educational research for Educational Research Pictures Incorporated (ERPI), explored retention of information after film screening and the type of information best suited to film, while Consitt wrote about grade-level differences for film learning and subject matter suited to film. Wise experimented with film for the teaching of history. Their research followed the lead of AV studies of the 20s and was built on a behavioral or connectionist base while employing mental measurements. The subject matter and rhetoric of their reports generally follow the topics and style of the texts reported above.

Like interlocking boards of directors, the names of a small group of AV experimental researchers from the late teens and 20s appear extensively in the literature of the 30s and even the 40s. They are Sumstine (1918), Lacy (1919), Weber (1922) and his pioneer study with 500 New York seventh-graders, Freeman (1924) and his large study at the University of Chicago, Knowlton and Tilton (1929) at Yale and their work with the Yale Chronicles of America, Freeman's joint project with Ben Wood at Columbia University (Wood & Freeman, 1929), and McClusky (1924) who became director of the Department of Visual Instruction of the National Education Association.

Media in the 20s and 30s classroom was certainly not restricted to sound films, however. James Brown tells us:

Well (we used) the famous Keystone 600 set for example in the social studies, which was a set of 600 3 1/4-by-4- inch black-and-white slides done by the Keystone Company in Meadville, Pennsylvania. [It] was one of the tools that we used. We had mostly silent films when I started, 16-mm silent films, that seems a long time ago. . . . They usually had captions in those days. Following the precepts of how you teach with a silent film—and I still think silent films have a great deal to offer in this regard—we would generally stop and start the film throughout; and stop and discuss or put it on hold for a still picture on the screen, even though it was a motion picture. . . . So you could do that and teach from the pictures (Brown, n.d.).

1.5.3 Film Usage in the 1930s

Research reports were not the only topics of scholarly audiovisual texts of the 1930s. Two (Koon & Devereux) of the three scholarly AV books (Koon, Devereux & Rulon) published by University Presses in the early 30s and cited above include discussions of subjects other than experiments. To introduce these topics, we include selections from their tables of contents.

1.5.4 Programs for Administration

The administration of audiovisual aids in schools and the utilization of these aids in classrooms was an important, almost dominant, aspect of general and some scholarly AV texts in the 30s. Whereas today, a university press or academic journal, such as *Educational Technology Research and Development,* would be reluctant to publish "how to" articles about technology, such was not the case in the early 30s. While all the scholarly texts we examined from that time did base their recommendations for film usage on experimentation, they also provided school-, district-, and statewide guidelines for administering AV programs; tips for screening films in the classroom; criteria for selection of films; and sometimes directions for local production of films. These topics were a vital aspect of a burgeoning field, since most educators had little or no knowledge of the application of films in the classroom. Because no rhetoric is neutral, language of administration and utilization of AV materials needs to be examined briefly.

Devereux elevates the pragmatic tasks of utilization and production by including them in a research agenda for the field in a chart (see Fig. 1-3).

Although Devereux's chart for film research appeared in 1933, it is similar to many later instructional development charts for either programmatic research in the field of design and development of curricular or training materials. A couple of decades later, systems theory appears in the educational technology literature. Springing from the human engineering field and the military, systems literature is replete with charts that partition and categorize concepts and tasks. Devereux had been a colonel in the Army and an executive for the American Telephone and Telegraph Company for many years (Saettler, 1990). When his book was published, he was vice president of Electrical Research Products Inc. (ERPI), a nontheatrical film production company that was a subsidiary of AT&T. Clearly, he had knowledge of administrative practices in the military and corporate sectors. This crossbreeding is not trivial when one attempts to understand the emergence of this technological field, and we will return to this point later. Briefly, we find no other educational field, or many early academic fields, so tied to machines and technology and, therefore, market economics.

I. A New Force in Education

II. Organizing Talking-Picture Materials

III. Translating Instructional Materials into Talking Films

IV. Standards of Excellence

V. Appraisal of the Educational Talking Picture

VI. Suggested Fields for Future Research in Educational Talking Pictures

VII. Utilizing the Educational Talking Picture on the Elementary- and the Secondary-School Levels

VIII. Administering a Local Program of Audio-Visual Instruction

IX. Use of Educational Talking Pictures on the College and University Level

X. Utilization of the Educational Talking Picture on the Adult Level

XI. School-Building Requirements for Audio-Visual Instruction

XII. Types of Equipment and Standards for their Selection

Figure 1-3. Tables of contents from *The Educational Talking Picture,* by F. Devereux, 1933, Cambridge: Harvard University Press, ix.

VII. The Technique of Making and Displaying Motion Pictures.
   A. The Production of Educational Films
   B. The Projection of Educational Films

VII. The Systematic Introduction of Motion Pictures in Teaching
   A. The Value of Visual Aids in Instruction
   B. The Extent of the Use of Motion Pictures in Teaching
   C. Reasons for Failure to Use More Motion Pictures in Schools
   D. More School Use of Films Probable
   E. Some Essentials in Introducing Films in Teaching

IX. Educational Problems of a General Nature Resulting from the Systematic Introduction of Motion Pictures in Teaching
   A. Methodology of the Use of Motion Pictures in Schools
   B. Comparison of the Effectiveness of Films and Other Didactic Auxiliaries
   C. Subjects in Which Films Could Be Used as an Auxiliary in Accordance with the Curricula
   D. Collaboration of Experts in the Production of Didactic Films
   E. Psychological Effects and Pedagogical Reform in Connection with the Film in Schools
   F. The Efficacy of the Intervention of the State in the Solution of the Systematic Introduction of Cinematography in Schools

X. General Conclusions
   A. The Theatrical Motion Picture Has Become a Powerful Force in National Life.
   B. Nontheatrical Uses of Motion Pictures are Varied.

Figure 1-4. Table of contents from *Motion Pictures in Education in the United States,* by C. Koon, 1934, Chicago: University of Chicago Press, xiv.

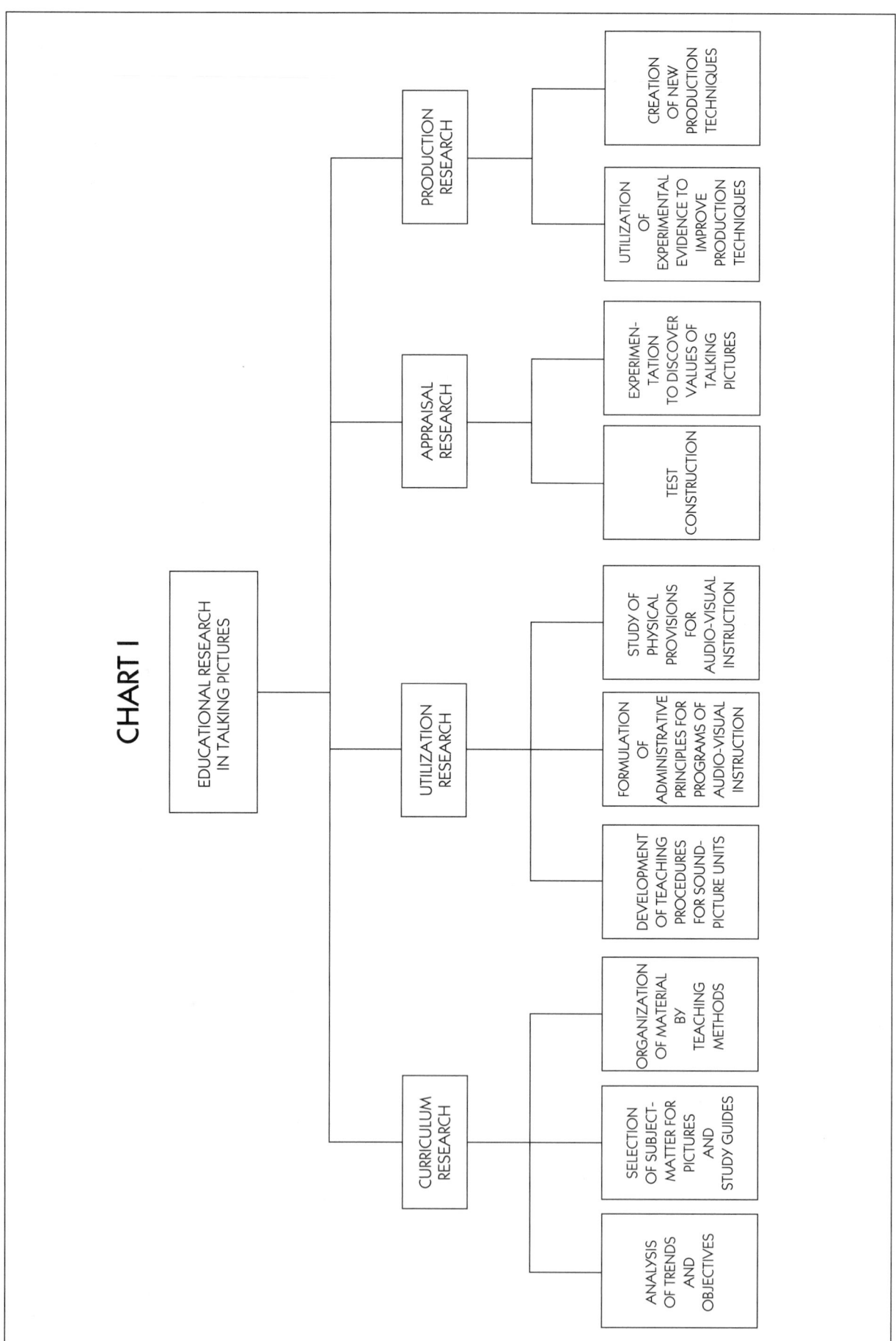

Figure 1-5.   Major research functions in developing the educational talking-picture program, Deuereux, 1933, p. 4.

1.5.5 Administration and Social Efficiency

When addressing administration of audiovisual programs, the authors of these texts (Koon & Devereux) invoke the vernacular of the social efficiency movement. In the first five pages of his text, Devereux (1934) uses some form of *effective* six times: "to increase the effectiveness of the process" (p. 1), "any effective use of the talking picture" (p. 2), "effective educational talking pictures," and "the working effectiveness of various elements of film" (p. 3), "depends upon effective utilization" (p. 5).

In a chapter entitled *The Systematic Introduction of Motion Pictures in Teaching*, Koon (1933) uses the following language ". . . a real need for improved methods of instruction, particularly the use of media which will furnish meaningful content to the school curriculum" (p. 57). Experiments, he claims, have shown that media "increases initial learning, *effects an economy of time* in learning, increases permanence of learning, aids in teaching *backward children* and motivates learning" (p. 57) [Italics ours.] (It should be noted that many authors writing in the 20s and 30s considered backward children to be a prime audience for audiovisual aids.) Koon was the senior specialist in radio and visual education, U.S. Department of the Interior, and was another researcher naturally concerned with the administrative aspects of these programs. Speaking with the authority of the federal government and as a representatives of corporate America, Koon and Devereux were invited to publish scholarship at university presses, although each author had collaborators who were university faculty. That their voices reflect the popular social efficiency movement of the day is not unusual. One of the lynchpins, however, of social efficiency is social control, and this effect surfaces obviously in Koon, and again in a more latent fashion in Devereux and Rulon when they use IQ and other tests to "isolate and control" differences.

Koon's (1933) subheadings in a chapter on problems with introduction of film in teaching are shown in Figure 1-6.

What is of interest here is another aspect of the language of social efficiency. Federal aid to education had not yet started in the 30s, but interest in some level of systematic governmental intervention was an issue for Koon.

1.5.6 Authors' Interests

Part of discourse analysis is the examination of author intention, and *prefaces and forwards* provide clues to reasons why writers have produced texts, disclose the authority with which they speak, and the manner in which they position their readers. Prefaces and forewords in Rulon (1933, pp. iix–xi), Devereux (1933, pp. v–vii) and Koon (1934, pp. v–xi) texts are rich sites for such examination. Some of the introductory comments of these books are written in a different style. The language of one (Rulon, 1933) remains terse, unelaborated, and scientific in style, but the other two display a different voice, one not heard in the body of the texts. The Koon (1934) foreword is some-

---

> A. Methodology of the Use of Motion Pictures in Schools
>
> B. Comparison of the Effectiveness of Films and Other Didactic Auxiliaries
>
> C. Subjects in Which Films Could Be Used as an Auxiliary in Accordance with the Curricula
>
> D. Collaboration of Experts in the Production of Didactic Films
>
> E. Psychological Effects and Pedagogical Reform in Connection with the Film in Schools
>
> F. The Efficacy of the Intervention of the State in the Solution of the Systematic Introduction of Cinematography

Figure 1-6. Chapter subheadings from *Motion Pictures in Education in the United States,* by C. Koon, 1934, Chicago: University of Chicago Press, xiv.

what literary, containing figures of speech such as "Let who will make my country's laws, so long as I may write her songs . . . " (p. v), and ". . . that is entertained and informed by this magical master teacher . . ." (p. v), ". . . but these are kaleidoscope times" (p.vi), and "As we approach the dawn of a new day in industrial life . . ." (p. vi). It is a rhetoric that runs counter to the unelaborated "scientific" language that academic researchers strove for then and now, but its voice breaks through the opening statements of these early texts and others in the 30s and 40s, despite the authors' attempts to control this voice, to be objective. However, the voice of objectivity, terse and scientific, efficient in its style, appears in these opening segments and is coexistent with an elaborated voice. In other AV texts of the 30s that are expositions or summaries and published by presses other than university presses, this conflated voice runs rampant in the discourses and uncovers some of the motives of the founders of the field. (As 1990s scholars in the field, we find it refreshing to hear this voice.)

1.5.6.1. Conflated Voice. Our thesis about the appearance of this conflated voice is that many discourses were conjoined in the turbulent 30s. Even though the early AV authors were highly influenced by the social efficiency movement in the schools and behavioral methods of research, they had been trained to write in public schools in the teens and 20s. Composition instruction, at that time, relied heavily on literary techniques. Whether students were writing narratives or expositions, they were taught to describe their plots or advance their arguments by employing figures of speech and by alluding to classical writings. Thirties AV writers had learned their expository rhetoric well, and their texts seek primarily to convince an audience of a point of view. They state their argument, provide proof, and summarize their points.

1.5.6.2. Technology as Progress. Methods of proof, however, do disclose a primary allegiance to social efficiency and behaviorism and adopt the language of those discourses. Nonetheless, persuasive techniques in an elaborated language seek to convince the reader of the goodness of technology for society and more specifically of the value of films in public classrooms. Indeed, the authors often become rhapsodic about this value.

Louis Forsdale's comment is typical of this stance:

> . . . one other thing that we also believed to be true was that if the moving image was indeed accessible to everybody— child, teacher, housewife, anybody—that it would then come closer to the role that the book has played (Forsdale, 1979).

If there is an underlying assumption that coalesces these early voices it is that *technology is progress*; technology is an ameliorative force in society. If some of the founders had private fears about the proliferation of technology, it rarely entered their public discourse. Within our texts, we found only one note of caution:

> We must be careful to avoid . . . one of the gravest dangers of the audiovisual field: the notion that the mere bringing of people physically and sensorially into contact with objects and materials always offers a communication of experience (Dale, 1977).

Floyde Brooker (1975) mentioned public concern, not about the cognitive nor moral effects of the films but about health:

> One of the great fears of the public at that time was that the children seeing motion pictures in a dark room would injure their eyes. . . . Eastman Kodak . . . they had tinted all their films a deep amber color, in order to prevent injury to the eyes. And all the people on the panels that were seeing the Teaching Film Custodian films had their eyes examined by a battery of ophthalmologists every week to make sure that their eyes were not being damaged by seeing so many motion pictures. And this was used throughout the educational journals of the time to give proof to the fact that seeing motion pictures was not injurious to the eyes of children (Brooker, 1975).

Although they were concerned with the appropriate projection of films in the classroom, and proper AV administration in schools and districts, those issues were primarily mechanistic. Founders' concerns about the criteria for selection of films mainly addressed the learning gains to be obtained from the screening of any one film. Where some of these authors did express concern about the proliferation of films and the effect on children, it was in relationship to students' exposure to Hollywood film. A modicum of that concern spilled over into the classroom; for example, see *Motion Pictures in Education: A Summary of the Literature: Source Book for Teachers and Administrators*, by Edgar Dale, Fannie W. Dunn, Charles F. Hoban, and Etta Schneider (1937). It is not unusual in the history of technology for discrete discourses about the social effects of mechanization to develop from the love-hate positions that people assume vis-à-vis machines (Benjamin, 1968; Nichols, 1981), but the cautious position is not present in the written or oral texts we examined. A general enthusiasm

for technology in the classroom permeated the public texts. It was one spoken value that partially unified the audiovisual project and probably accounts, in large measure, for the success in establishing the field.

1.6 TECHNOLOGY AND PSYCHOLOGY: EARLY AUDIOVISUAL SCHOLARSHIP

That the audiovisual scholars of the 20s and most of the 30s followed prevalent theoretical and methodological trends in educational psychology was a key step in the establishment of the field. The coin of the realm in the academy at this time was connectionism (*behaviorism* after Hull), mental measurements, and aspects of social efficiency. It was smart for these scholars to secure a berth for AV education by conducting psychological research. We are not suggesting that these were studied, deliberate moves on the part of AV scholars. Many of them were in and of the academy, and the culture of departments of education, especially in the 20s, was behavioral and experimental. We are also not suggesting that this culture did not gain academic status for departments of education, a status from which we still benefit. We do not contest the idea that before Thorndike, educational research in the United States was a helter-skelter affair.

We do suggest that connectionism, mental measurements, and social efficiency defined the dominant discourse in educational inquiry at a moment in time when the audiovisual field was emerging. We suggest that educational technology scholars have inherited a legacy, both fortunate and unfortunate. To start a field with the notion of the mind as a *tabula rasa* is unfortunate, because it is a concept ripe for imprinting and control. To trust that mental measurements are neutral and do not spring, originally, from a desire for control is naive. This issue was central for Thorndike and has been revisited recently by scholars such as Foucault (1977) and Curtis (1993), among others. Thorndike noted:

> The science of education can and will itself contribute abundantly to psychology. Not only do the laws derived by psychology from simple, specially arranged experiments help us to interpret and control mental action under the conditions of schoolroom life. Schoolroom life itself is a vast laboratory in which are made thousands of experiments of the utmost interest to "pure" psychology (Thorndike, 1910).

1.6.1 Residuals

Practically speaking, the fields of educational psychology and technology have suffered from the limits imposed by either behavioral or richer theories of the mind subsumed under cognitivism. Limitations imposed by the study of a unit of one, the brain, in a social setting have taken a toll on both fields. This toll can best be described by the inordinate focus of scholars from these fields, for practically 3 decades, on minuscule instructional problems. The psychological models available to us, and their concomitant statistics, demanded study of microaspects of learning and instruction. (Some of this may be partially redressed in educational psychology by the appearance of constructivism.) But what has the study of microaspects of learning contributed to the field of educational technology as a whole? When we compare experiments of the 20s with those of the 60s or 70s, we note similarities, a proliferation of nonconnected, nonprogrammatic microstudies. What is different about the later studies and concerned many graduate students was appropriate statistical application, not how to formulate more relevant research questions. How can we account for what educational technology has taught us through the years?

The current shift of power in the academy away from educational psychologists may be partially explained by their lack of ability to address macro-problems of learning, in this period of national dissatisfaction with the enterprise of public schooling.

1.6.2 General Audiovisual Texts

In addition to scholarly texts of the early 30s, many general audiovisual texts were published. Two texts were widely circulated. They are *Visual Instruction, Its Value and Its Needs* (McClusky, 1932) and *Motion Pictures in Education: A Summary of the Literature: Source Book for Teachers and Administrators* (Dale et al., 1937). F. Dean McClusky had been a student of Frank Freeman's at the University of Chicago, but carved a career for himself, not as a scholar but as an administrator. In fact, he became an authority within the AV economic realm who was devoted to the advance of machines in the classroom. In the 20s he had conducted the Freeman-Commonwealth Studies at the University of Chicago under the direction of Frank Freeman (Saettler, 1990) and written about the administration of AV programs and the preparation of teachers. His 1932 text is a summation of that work. Although he wrote articles and reports from the 20s until 1950, in keeping with the analysis here, we focus on his book *Visual Instruction, Its Value and Its Needs* (McClusky, 1932). Since his concerns were broad, his studies were surveys rather than experiments, and his style is not scientific. Structured survey research was in its infancy and was a method suited to claims for diffusion of innovation. He employs economic language such as *supply and demand, profit, service motive, commercial efforts, competition,* etc. (McClusky, 1932). In his book, he mixes economic arguments that were present in the oral vernacular of the early field but become central to general discussions in books such as McClusky's and administrative texts. McClusky has a delightful way of mixing professional esprit that we found so prevalent in the oral histories and sound administrative and economic advice about the field. (We looked forward to listening to Dr. McClusky's audiotape, but it was unclear.) This marketplace discourse, while not foreign to his audiovisual con-

temporaries, is prevalent in McClusky. His clear language and friendly authority were instrumental in starting the field.

Although not a textbook in the normal sense, *Motion Pictures in Education: A Summary of the Literature: Source Book for Teachers and Administrators* is written as a learning tool for researchers, teachers, and school administrators (the assumed students of visual instruction and educational motion pictures). It is a book consisting of six parts, each by a different author(s). Composed of annotated bibliographies of educational journal articles, books, and theses devoted to visual education from the mid-1920s through the mid-1930s, the text is arranged according to subject areas (administration of visual aids, teaching with visual aids—especially the motion picture, instructional materials selection, school film production, instructional films experimental research, and visual education teacher preparation). The authors summarize those materials they feel are most useful to their readers but do not evaluate these items. In addition, the authors assist their readers by adding editorial comments. Their hope is ". . . that this volume will acquaint the reader with the significant literature in the field, and will present information necessary to those who wish to be intelligent about the contribution of the motion picture to education" (Dale et al. 1937, p. 12).

1.7 NEW DISCURSIVE TERRAIN: A SUMMARY

In the 30s, multiple voices spoke for the nascent audiovisual field in the academy. A nexus of varied but complimentary discourses represented the new field of study. In this section, we have described some of these voices, and others have been uncovered in our extensive background reading. A story begins to emerge about the unique discursive terrain that was to become the academic field of educational technology. We will start to relate it here and unfold the rhetorical strands as they develop.

1.7.1 Machine Driven

No singular new or old discourse embodies the audiovisual field in the 1930s, although the appearance of this area is contingent on similar interests expressed in varied rhetoric. We have attempted to illustrate how similar values inherent in social efficiency, mental measurements, animal psychology, and educational psychology informed the scholarly audiovisual conversation. But educational technology was not educational psychology; they grew separately in the academy, and the convergence of similar discourses is not sufficient to describe the unique nature of educational technology. Despite efforts of some academics to deny it, this field is machine and market driven (see 37.1.4). A vision of the field arose with the invention of machines that could teach masses of citizens. This is undeniable when one examines the tables of contents of scholarly books from the

20s and 30s. It is an unescapable theme in the oral histories of the founders. We suggest that the frequent antitechnological values of the academy have tended to encourage educational technology scholars to deny their mechanistic origins and current status. (What better proof of this current status do we have than the issue of machines in public classrooms? Who influences decisions regarding educational technology in today's classrooms? We believe it is producers and distributors of hardware and software rather than educational technology professors.) This was the first educational field in the 30s to be based on the presence of hardware and one of very few, i.e., engineering, in the academy at large. Current academic research functions in numerous modern departments at the whim of technology. But for the 30s, the formation of a discursive space around machines, universities, and the enterprise of public education was unique. The terrain was historically related to industry not schooling.

1.7.2 Schools, Government, and Corporations

Early in this century, military and nonmilitary members of the federal government recognized the power of certain communication technologies to educate masses of citizens, young and old alike. Governmental alliance with audiovisual educators occurred well before official congressional aid was allotted to national public schools. The reason for this alliance, we believe, was the recognition by both academic and governmental officials of the power of radio and film to communicate mass messages. (In this chapter, we have mentioned some of the military and nonmilitary positions of early audiovisual scholars, but Saettler [1990] describes all of their positions.) This alliance was not a cabal as some critics would describe it. It was a convergence of interests and desires expressed in similar rhetoric. In the scholarly texts we have examined governmental and educational rhetoric converge loosely aligning the separate discourses and allowing educational language to take precedence.

Governmental interest in the outcome of audiovisual research, because of the presence of mass media, was not the only influence on the establishment of new discursive space in the academy. Private and corporate entrepreneurs were naturally interested in the market fallout from inventions of Edison and Marconi. A massive capital drive in the early part of the 20th century, around the production and distribution of machines, made the U.S. a leading world power. An offshoot of that venture was business investment in education, especially educational machines. As the field coalesced in the 20s and 30s, this tie with the marketplace became evident in the positions held by leading audiovisual scholars. (Again, we have mentioned some of them in this chapter, but Saettler [1990] gives a fuller account of the corporate contacts of AV scholars.) The language and values of the marketplace are evident in the earliest scholarly texts and continue throughout the period we have studied.

While this phenomenon may not be unusual in schools of education or public classrooms today, it was novel in the 1930s.

What is unique about the 1930s audiovisual studies in the academy is the discursive juncture of educational, governmental, and market interests. Again, we stress the manner in which this was formed. The language from two discourses outside of education was adopted by founders who held positions in and outside of education. And educational rhetoric was always ascendant. This new discursive terrain appears at least 2 1/2 decades before Eisenhower recommends a similar troika of government, education, and industry. (Because we have studied audiovisual texts over several decades, we note the continuance of this informal coalition.) As we continue, we will try to illustrate the manner in which the new and complex discursive plane was articulated in the later academic field, but first a few caveats.

As readers, you position yourselves within certain discourses; we believe it is impossible for you to do otherwise. You may value or repudiate the loose and informal alliance of business, government, and educational technology and its dependence on machines. We would like to stress that we believe the educational technology field originated and exists because of this juncture. In the academy, the founders could not have done otherwise: There was little initial support for machines, and had they not sought outside help we would have become a branch of educational psychology. We applaud the perspicacity of the founders in helping to establish this troika and, consequently, this field. There would have been no platform in the academy for views for or against educational machines unless the founders had forged this alliance. After all, they could have established a research and development arena in the corporate world and bypassed the niceties of academic freedom. And we, as authors, would not occupy the positions of privilege we have to recount history.

1.8 SHIFTING DISCOURSES

1.8.1 Edgar Dale

Edgar Dale, whose output spans the 30s to the 60s, was an influential leader and researcher, and his work is considered separately here, because it contains a specific learning discourse absent in the early experimental and administrative audiovisual literature. In fact, his turn away from experimentation and toward experience influenced most of the school-related audiovisual texts published in the 40s. Working as a researcher on the Payne Fund Studies, Dale published *How to Appreciate Motion Pictures* in 1933. His next publication was *Motion Pictures in Education* (1937). The language of his most influential text, *AudioVisual Methods in Teaching* (Dale, 1946), provides clues to his pragmatic discourse. In Dale's (1946) index, we note the appearance of entries that were unusual for the scholarly audiovisual arena. He includes an entry on chautauquas (p. 533) and one on direct experience (p. 534) that includes 51 pages of discussion on the topic. Unlike other AV researchers, he cites Dewey liberally (p. 534), includes Froebel (p. 536), William James (p. 537), and Johann Pestalozzi (p. 540), all humanistic educational theorists. In checking the references to these compatible authors in the body of the text, we found evidence that Dale incorporated their thinking to establish his theory of audiovisual education. Absent are entries on behaviorism, or mention of Thorndike, Hull, Guthrie, or Skinner; and the term *efficiency* is not evident in the book. What is evident is that Dale based his concepts of learning from media on humanistic and developmental theories, especially Dewey's pragmatic notion of experience and education. But Dale leans as well on educators who influenced Dewey, namely, Froebel and Pestalozzi. To distinguish his child-centered theory from behavioral theories of learning he reclaims the word *laboratory*. "You have seen the word *laboratory* widely discussed in books and articles on education. We talk of the community as a laboratory for learning" (Dale, 1946, p. 76). Dale accepts Dewey's working definition of the mind as "the power to understand things in terms of the use made of them" (Dale, 1946, p. 76). Laboratories, therefore, whether they are workrooms or field trips, allow students to pose their own questions, to explore, to see how things work, and to participate in direct experiential activity. For Dale, a learning theory was pragmatic, as it was for William James and John Dewey, and had to be based on experience.

The fact that child-centered theories enjoyed popularity in 1940s audiovisual texts is due, in large part, to Dale's influence. Note how a portion of his table of contents for *Audio-Visual Methods in Teaching* is drastically different from those we note from the early 30s (see Fig. 1-7).

Again, what tables of contents indicate is just what topics the founders deemed important enough to be included in the field, and their order indicates how they might wish the field to be organized. The topics Dale includes, which had been excluded from earlier audiovisual scholarly texts, are many aspects of experience, discussion of permanent learning, concept building, the new notion of a laboratory, dramatic participation, field trips, museums, etc.

Although Dale published from the 1930s until the 1960s, we have selected this text because it represents a theoretical summation point for him. Although he continued his inquiry into one pragmatic approach to education, his discourse was overshadowed after World War II by the reappearance of a behavioral rubric.

When Dale was asked why he did not do experimental research in which a scholar attempted to prove over and over that students learned from radio or film, he replied:

It always bothers me, because anybody knows that we learn from these things (media). There's no issue about that. . . . Well I suppose in any field, to be respectable you have to have a certain kind of research (Dale, 1977).

1.9 EDUCATIONAL TRENDS IN THE 40s

Scholarly texts about audiovisual aids in the schools were published primarily in the early 40s, between 1940 and 1942, and in the later 40s, in fact, mainly in 1949. Audiovisual scholars were caught up in the war effort and most were involved with military training. In the schools, however, curriculum was shifting. Arguments mounted in the 30s about the inadequacy of schools, and the necessity for drastic reform changed with the growing sense of patriotism that permeated U.S. institutions during World War II. Efforts to include students in the war drive became an official part of the U.S. curriculum and were operationalized in school-sponsored scrap-metal collections, bond drives, and encouragement for victory gardens. Oftentimes, reading groups were divided into platoons with sergeants and colonels as leaders. The language of WW II permeated formal and informal classroom activities (Tuttle, 1993).

1.9.1 Life Adjustment Curriculum

Curriculum design in the 40s was also altered. Kliebard (1990) points out that in times of worker shortages, consumer education must be stressed. Vocational education and courses such as physics and mathematics were restructured to place "greater stress on aeromechanics, aeronautics, auto mechanics, navigation, gunnery, and other aspects of modern warfare" (Smith, 1942). The original Smith article written for *Curriculum Journal* was "The War and the Educational Program." Leading educators were co-opting military rhetoric for classroom purposes. Vocational education was designed to stress preparation for manual labor as well as white-collar jobs, which it had encompassed to date, and the 40s became an era of adjusting the curriculum to more closely entail the life activities of U.S. citizens. Generally, this was known as the *life adjustment curriculum* (Kliebard, 1987). Its proponents built on the work of certain social efficiency proponents of the 30s who had generated long, detailed lists of job activities to be taught in the schools. (W. W. Charters was the most prominent among them.) But proponents were more directly influenced by the publication *What High Schools Ought to Teach* (Tyler, 1940). A functional, work-oriented curriculum was proposed in this 1940 report of the 8-year high school study directed by Ralph Tyler. Although Tyler eschewed the traditional curriculum and control of the secondary curriculum by college entry requirements, his recommendation for "life adjustment" study is informed by his theoretical assumptions. As early as 1931, he stated that it was crucial to define clearly the types of behavior that needed to be taught (Kliebard, 1987, p. 215). The recommendations of this report were couched in early Tyler rhetoric (Kliebard, 1987, p. 220), foreshadowing the Tyler rationale that shaped many years of curriculum and instructional practice. The formal response to this report occurred in 1945 when the Prosser resolution was passed in the U.S. Congress. It formalized the life adjustment curriculum and provided the

Figure 1-7.   Table of contents from *Audio-Visual Methods in Teaching*, by E. Dale, 1946, New York: The Dryden Press, xi–xiii.

first massive federal funding for public education. By the 1950s, the life adjustment curriculum was well entrenched in the schools (Becker, 1990). Edgar Dale remembers talking to Tyler about what part of his work was most important to him.

> Finally, about 6 months ago, I asked Ralph Tyler in terms of his career, what did he think stood out (as) the most fruitful, and so, he said "the 8-year study." And what the 8-year study did was loosen up the high school curriculum, make it easier for persons who had different curricula to get into college, and so on. . . . I think the most striking conclusion (of the 8-year study) was that the schools that had the most innovation had done the best in terms of school work. The greater the innovation, the greater the productivity of the school (Dale, 1977).

For a detailed description and assessment of the 8-year study, please see *The Struggle for the American Curriculum* (Kleibard, 1987).

1.9.2 Nonmilitary Audiovisual Scholarship of the 40s

Experimental research occurred under the auspices of the military in the 40s and deserves a separate examination, but scholarly texts of the decade were focused on application, not experimental studies. Although the social efficiency education proponents were gaining a foothold in public school curriculum through the emphases on vocational education and "job activities" lists, a humanistic educational discourse was ascendant. Classroom practices were complex, mixing child development, Deweyesque assumptions about learning with the "project method" from social efficiency proponents. Both camps wanted activities for the children, but for different ends and with different assumptions. Even though audiovisual writers concerned with schools were primarily influenced by the experiential child-centered camp, they mixed project and task analysis with their discussions. By and large, practical life experiences served as a basis for designing curriculum that would incorporate AV materials. The emphasis on vocational education, especially blue-collar jobs, gave the AV field an unexpected boost. Instead of following the Charters lead, however, and allowing curriculum developers to draw up lists of learning activities, most AV educators of the period went to teachers and students and attempted to decipher childhood experience and learning.

1.9.3 American Council on Education

Influential audiovisual texts from the American Council on Education (ACE) were published in the 40s, although research for the texts was conducted in the 30s. Both Paul Saettler and Floyde Brooker comment on their importance:

> Probably the most significant project in educational technology during the 1930s was the Motion Picture Project of

the ACE. This project generated insights and theories of instruction that led to instructional techniques that almost totally determined the pattern for the instructional programs of the U.S. Office of Education and the armed forces during World War II (Saettler, 1990, p. 230).

And Brooker agreed:

> Another final thing which I don't want to overlook, and which none of us anticipated, was that the Motion Picture Project of the American Council on Education became unwittingly a primary tool for the training of personnel for the tremendous advance of films in the war effort of the United States government (Brooker, 1975).

The Committee on Motion Pictures in Education, which was a branch of the ACE, conducted a 5-year study entitled *The Motion Picture Project*. The impetus for this enterprise came from opposite directions. Some American educators and governmental officials were interested in harnessing theatrical films for use in the classroom, while opponents to Hollywood were worried about the influence of cinema on the emotional lives of students. The Payne Fund Studies (1929–32) had created these discursive dichotomies, and the Motion Picture Project was partially undertaken to respond to Payne's study findings. Note Charters' rhetoric as he reports the Payne findings:

> The motion picture, as such, is a potent medium of education. . . . Emotions are measurably stirred as the scenes of a drama unfold, and this excitement may be recorded in deviations from the norm in sleep patterns, by visible gross evidences of bodily movement and by refined internal responses. They constitute patterns of conduct in daydreaming, phantasy [sic] and action. Second, for children the content of current pictures is not good. There is too much sex and crime and love for a balanced diet for children. Third, the motion picture situation is very complicated. It is one among many influences which mold the experience of children (Charters quoted in Saettler, 1990, p. 229).

This was strangely inflammatory language for Charters, who was (or became?) a proponent of the use of films in the classroom. We speculate that it helped crystallize positions around the benefits or danger of films in schools. A crystallized stance is obvious in one anecdote recounted by Floyde Brooker:

> When Dr. Hoban and I started out in the Motion Picture Project, we approached one of the prominent universities of the country in order to get the cooperation and assistance of their college of education. The dean of that college of education looked us square in the face. He said, "If a single professor on my faculty ever uses a motion picture in a class, he will be fired the very minute I discover it, because I will know that he is utterly incompetent.
> . . . And plenty of school superintendents would have supported it" (Brooker, 1975).

1.9.3.1. Motion Picture Project. But Charters wanted to harness the educational power of films. Perhaps the people or institutions that would harness the power would share that power themselves. In a report to the ACE encouraging them to initiate the Motion Picture Project, he notes:

> That this power (of film) may be utilized equally in raising the ideals and culture of a nation or debasing them is entirely clear. Attitudes toward races may be powerfully directed toward either a better understanding or increased hostility. Fact and error are indiscriminantly accepted by audiences.
>
> The United States should study authoritatively and in statesmanlike fashion the place of motion pictures in our culture, formulate the factors to be considered and work toward solutions in accordance with the temperament of our people (Charters quoted in Saettler, 1990, p. 232).

Charters did convince the ACE, and the Motion Picture Project went forward; it culminated in seven publications in the early 40s (Cochran, 1942; Noel, 1942; Bell et al., 1942; Brooker & Herrington, 1942; and staff of Tower Hill School, 1942). Two of the seven books list no authors: *The Other Americas through Films*, and *Records and Selected Educational Motion Pictures: A Descriptive Encyclopedia*. Two books are representative of the seven texts published by the Committee on Motion Pictures in Education, *Focus on Learning* (C. Hoban, Jr., 1942) and *Selected Educational Motion Pictures* (1942). The main thesis in these books is that films should be used in the classroom. Clearly all the authors, important audiovisual scholars, had entered the debate as proponents. Remember, their rhetoric had to oppose those voices who used the Payne studies and the Hays Act to condemn film. All of these founders, whether researchers or practitioners, had to overcome strong cultural objections to film. This rhetorical stance represented one way in which these early AV educators were unified. And perhaps this stance only represented their public voice.

1.9.3.2. Ace Texts. Many of the ACE texts spend long sections attempting to convince educators of the appropriateness of film for the classroom. To illustrate this point we include the tables of contents here (see Figs. 1-8 and 1-9).

The table of contents for the encyclopedia was most unusual for the 40s. This was the first scholarly text to list films exclusively, evaluate them, and offer classifications. The authors assume that films "have arrived" and are "good" for students.

In Hoban's contents, we see the word *movies* reflecting Hollywood influence (excerpts from Hollywood films were used in these studies) and suggestions for the place of movies in the school curriculum. We note that an authority, the teacher, will take a hand in controlling these powerful media, and judgment for selection will be passed. The polemic nature of audiovisual discourses has been present in scholarly texts before the ACE books, but not to this extent.

In the Foreword, we learn that the Hoban book was written for teachers and administrators:

> . . . the role of motion pictures in general education has been discussed from the viewpoint of the classroom teacher, so that general education may be improved through the effective use of motion pictures in the curriculum (Hoban 1942, p. v).

In this same Foreword, we learn how Hoban and other members of the Motion Picture Project negotiated the slippery moral path that surrounded cinema in the 30s:

> After the completion of the film catalog, it became apparent that, without any attempt to sort the good from the poor, a list of films available to schools might be more harmful than helpful. It was decided that available films should be evaluated and that these evaluations should be published in order to assist teachers in making proper selection and effective use of films in the curriculum. . . . When asking the question, "For what purpose, with whom and under what circumstances is this film good?" the Committee went directly to teachers and students for answers (Hoban, 1942, pp. v-vi).

Figure 1-8. Table of contents from *Selected Educational Motion Pictures: A Descriptive Encyclopedia*, 1942, Washington, DC, American Council on Education, ix.

Figure 1-9. Table of contents from *Focus on Learning*, by Charles F. Haban, Jr., 1942, Washington, DC, American Council on Education, xiii.

As we examine Hoban's rhetoric, we find it is consistent with his writings from the 30s; he has a foot in both camps. He wants *proper selection* and *effective use of films* in the classroom. In fact, he uses state-of-the-art statistical measures to ascertain the appropriateness of a specific film for the classroom. But for his evaluations, he went directly to teachers and students for answers. This action bespeaks the rhetoric of the child-centered, experimental discourse. And the task of effective use is preceded by his attempt to sort the *good* from the *poor* and to note films more *harmful* than *helpful*. Besides being child-centered, these last two phrases are drawn from the discourse that embodies notions of censorship for cinema. Hoban is faced with a moral dilemma. Obviously, there are films not suitable for children, but experimental research, on which he partially relied, did not have the power to address value statements; consequently the term *effective* in experimentation is used to denote that which produces measurable learning gains. For educators in the late 30s and early 40s, just as today, learning gains were only half the story. Hoban knew and stated that some films could be more *harmful* than *helpful*, that rhetoric comes from a moral discourse. Caught, as most of us are, between an attempt to assess the cognitive value of instructional materials and their socially responsible or irresponsible position, Hoban devised the following film-rating form. We include it because it is an important early film-rating form and typical of forms to come. Like many current forms, it represents a compromise that is still a compromise today. We note how this rating form foreshadows the later prescriptions for use, i.e., *educational purpose*, that became *objective*, *classroom procedure* that became *event of instruction*, and preparation that became *advance organizer*. Yet, Hoban went to teachers and students for their judgment, a humanistic move.

Finally, it is important to note that Hoban believed films were good at teaching concepts, critical thinking, and developing attitudes. World War II research indicated that films were good at teaching facts and adequate at developing attitudes. Subsequent research in educational technology did not approach the issue of critical thinking as a variable in film research, as did Hoban, Dale, and research members of the Payne Studies and the Motion Picture Project.

1.9.3.3. Anecdotal Information.

Floyd Brooker provides some specifics about the American Council on Education's Motion Picture Project.

> We had a prestigious advisory board on which such people like Mark May and Dr. W. W. Charters, one of the great men and one of the stimulators of the field. We set up a whole series of objectives: (1) Did the film have a role in the classroom as opposed to a role in the auditorium? (2) What did the teachers have to know in order to use a film effectively? (3) What body of films existed that were educationally effective and available? (4) What kinds of educational objectives could films serve?
>
> There were few films available for the K–3 level. . . . There were more films available in geography than there were in science, and more in science than there were in literature. We would be limited by the flexibility of the teach-

ers who volunteered, and no teacher was used if she was definitely opposed to the idea.

> Some of the side questions we considered were: Can students make motion pictures and can it be an educational process? Another one: If you see *Hamlet* performed in a motion picture, do you read the play? Another one: Does one [i.e., film] take the place or can it be considered as being educationally equal to the other [i.e., book]?
>
> We found that in the opinion of the teachers, the children of the third grade could get 80% or better of all of the concepts in the picture. What they couldn't get were the scientific names: larva, pupa and so forth. But they got 80% of all the meat of the film and they understood the life cycle of the butterfly as well as seniors in high school did. The seniors in high school could use all the technical terminology and, furthermore, they could write about it and spell it correctly. Now, another thing, we found that if we showed a silent motion picture on, let's say autumn, and the students write [sic] an essay on it, the teachers claimed that the students used more creative expression and a wider range of vocabulary than they did when given a verbal assignment (Brooker, 1975).

Brooker's rich description calls attention to new voices in the scholarly audiovisual terrain, that of teachers and students. For the first time, university researchers sought the opinion of students and teachers, believing that their evaluations were valid. And different research questions were being posed to students and teachers, questions such as: Can films teach addition and subtraction? What films can help children learn and are they good for them? We will return to a discussion of this later, but these humanistic interests were short-lived in the history of educational technology and psychology research.

1.9.3.4. Classroom Life.

As the audiovisual field was coalescing, educators encountered daily difficulties, not only with film selection but also with screening. A problem encountered in the 40s, as well as before and after, is recalled by Louis Forsdale. He and most of the founders were in positions where they had to "get their hands dirty" with machines on a daily basis. Participants of no other field of education were faced with such a dilemma. Evidence of the precarious nature of operation of audiovisual machines is rife in the oral histories.

Forsdale describes a film situation starting in the 20s and continuing well into the 60s that, while familiar to us today, would have discouraged many educators:

> . . . in the 20s they [schools] made the shift from 35-mm to 16-mm, but not many schools had 35-mm projectors when that first change was made. By the 60s large numbers of schools . . . had 16-mm projectors even though they weren't using them as much as we thought they could be used. They did have that commitment made . . . so it was natural for them to turn to 16-mm film. . . . Very few people were willing to make the shift to make 8-mm prints. . . . Standards for 8-mm projectors were very hard to come by, very hard, and I, for a while, chaired the standards committee for the 8-mm portion of the Society of Motion Picture and Television Engineers. The simple fact was that Fairchild had one projector that they began to bring out, which had a different

---

FILM RATING FORMS
Teacher Judgment of Usefulness of Educational Motion Picture

Title of film _____ Silent?_____ Sound?_____

Source of film _____ Grade in which used_____

Subject _____ Unit_____

Name of teacher_____ School _____ Date_____

   I.   What **educational purpose** did you expect to achieve in using this motion picture?

   II.   What were the **strong points** of this motion picture?

   III.   What were the **weak points** of this motion picture?

   IV.   From the standpoint of classroom procedure, where did you use this motion picture?

       1. _____ To introduce

       2. _____ To present material during a unit

       3. _____ To summarize

   V.   What, if anything, was done in preparation for using this motion picture

       1. _____ By the teacher?

       2. _____ By the students?

   VI.   What did the students do which indicated that your purposes were or were not fulfilled?

   VII.   In terms of what you were trying to achieve, what is your **general judgement** of this motion picture?

       1. _____ Excellent   4. _____ Poor

       2. _____ Good   5. _____ Usless

       3. _____ Fair

STUDENT JUDGEMENT OF EDUCATIONAL MOTION PICTURES

Name of student _____ Boy?_____ Girl?_____

Title of film _____ Silent?_____ Sound?_____

School _____ Grade?_____ Course?_____

Name of teacher_____ Date_____

   I.   What did you learn from this motion picture?

   II.   What were the strong points of this motion picture?

   III.   What were the weak points of this motion picture?

   IV.   What incidents, parts, or features of the picture did you like best?

   V.   What is your general judgment of this motion picture?

       1. _____ Excellent   4. _____ Poor

       2. _____ Good   5. _____ Usless

       3. _____ Fair

Figure 1-10. Film rating forms from *Focus on Learning,* by Charles F. Hoban, Jr., 1942, Washington, DC, American Council on Education, 171.

distance between sound and picture than did an MPO projector which was being brought out. . . . Technicolor at first brought out a silent projector and were headed all in the direction of silent, as they referred to them, single concept films. And only much later (Technicolor) brought out sound 8-mm equipment. And, in the midst of all this, there then came what was really a rather altering [?] development on the part of Eastman Kodak, namely, the development of Super 88 film which was incompatible with 8-mm film, because of the special size (Forsdale, 1979).

1.9.3.5. Encyclopedia. *The Encyclopedia* (1942) [*Selected Educational Motion Pictures: A Descriptive Encyclopedia*] is a compilation of 500 of the best educational films available before 1941. (It may have been a follow-up volume to the ACE project, led by Lorraine Noble, to catalog instructional films. The initial publication to emerge from this ACE project was a book with no author, the *Educational Film Catalog*, published by the H. W. Wilson Co., Saettler, 1990). In an unsigned introduction to the

1942 *Encyclopedia* we are told that the *Encyclopedia* is a "compendium, not of the 500 best films for general education, but of 500 films that have been reported as valuable when used for specific purposes" (*Encyclopedia*, 1942, p. 1). The claim is not made that objectives for the films will be listed, but clearly they are specified in the appraisals, although in terms of the film's properties, not in behavioral terms. The film descriptions are excellent detailed précis presented in terms of appraisals and contents. The introduction claims, "A complete, but concise, *objective* description of the content completes the information on each film" (*Encyclopedia*, 1942, p. 1) [italics are ours]. On the same page, the author refers to the specific objectives for the films. Again, the troublesome issue of evaluation arises. The appraisals presented for each film were evaluations, using the film-rating forms we presented in Figure 1-10. These were solicited from "teachers, and students in cooperating schools, school systems, colleges and universities. . . . About 5,500 teacher judgments and 12,000 student judgments were collected and used in this process" (Encyclopedia, 1942, p. 1). Thousands of films were evaluated in this manner and were further examined by preview panels assembled in Washington by the Motion Picture Project, and after that by the directors of the leading film libraries in the country. This was a complex process at best, which suggests that the project members did not fully trust the judgment of students and teachers. The amazing part of the project, however, is the fact that there were thousands of educational films, produced before 1941, to evaluate. These were sound films, and sound had only been introduced 11 years earlier (Saettler, 1990).

1.9.4 Additional 1940s Scholarship

A spate of scholarly books on audiovisual education appeared in the late 40s. Three representative texts, in fact, were published in 1949: *Audio-Visual Aids to Instruction* (McKown & Roberts, 1949), *Visual Aids* (Weaver & Bolinger, 1949), and *The Forty-Eighth Yearbook of the National Society for the Study of Education* [NSSE] (Brooker et al., 1949). The fact that the prestigious NSSE would devote a yearbook to audiovisual education was a recognition of the scholarly status of the field. By this time, Edgar Dale's *Audio-Visual Methods in Teaching*, first published in 1946, was in its seventh edition. The fact that Dryden Press had to publish seven editions of the Dale text within 3 years attests to the importance of Dale and his experiential approach in the AV world of the 40s. The authors of these three texts must have been highly influenced by Dale, because nowhere can we find a reference to behaviorism, or Thorndike, and very few social efficiency assumptions and language slip through their writings. There is a major difference, however, in the resources used to assemble these books, and this difference marks a critical point in the growth of the field (which was still identified with the adjective *audiovisual* at the time).

1.9.6 A Small Circle of Friends

AV researchers in the 20s and 30s based their learning theories primarily on Thorndike and other behaviorists, and we see them cited in 20s and 30s audiovisual texts. In these texts, we also see the mental measurement proponents cited. It has been shown that Dale took an opposing stance and called on Dewey, an opponent of behaviorism, to develop his learning theory. By the late 40s, however, many authors had stopped citing scholars outside the field and started relying only on the body of literature that had been generated by AV researchers in the 20s, 30s, and 40s. In the *NSSE Forty-Eighth Yearbook*, for instance, Dale, Finn, and Hoban cite early AV experimenters, Knowleton and Tilton, Rulon, Weber, Freeman, McClusky, and others. They also cite one another (Brooker, 1949). Writing other chapters in the same book, Larson cites Hoban, Dale, Brooker, and Herrington; Brown and VanderMeer cite themselves, Hoban, Carpenter, Dale, Meierhenry, and other AV writers. Similar citations exist in other chapters. These are not the exclusive realm of all citations. Many other business and administration texts are cited. What we would like to point out here, however, is that references to learning and curriculum theorists outside of the AV field have disappeared. This is both helpful to the field and harmful. Certainly, it indicates that finally there is a critical mass of AV scholars and a significant body of knowledge forming, and yet the theoretical stances and the epistemology of their discourses have gone underground. By citing Dale and earlier experimental researchers, these authors did not take the time to cite the primary sources of learning or curricular theory, as AV scholars of the 20s and 30s had done. Although their language discloses their theoretical foundations, underlying assumptions were undisclosed and unexamined. (This is also true of many texts in the early 50s, with the exception of the Wittich and Schuller book.)

1.9.6.1. Scholars of the 1940s. The table of contents in the Weaver and Bollinger, and the McKown and Roberts' texts, indicate that the scope of topics addressed has opened up, and we include a partial listing here (see Figs. 1-11 and 1-12).

What is different about these tables of contents and those of the 30s is the fact that experience replaces experimentation, and the view of media opens from a consideration of radio and film to include graphics, pictures, models, etc. A child's educational experience is carried outside the classroom to include trips and tours, and media play a large part in those excursions (McKown & Roberts, 1949). Weaver and Bollinger use a similar approach to categorize audiovisual knowledge and continue to offer administrative advice.

That the National Society for the Study of Education chose to publish a yearbook on audiovisual materials of instruction indicates that the scholarship of AV writers was finally garnering recognition from other education scholars. The book is noteworthy for several reasons. We are, of course, interested in the rhetoric of the specifically scholarly sections. (Several descriptive chapters of audiovisual departments in schools and school districts are also included.) We have already noted the manner in which scholars cite a small circle of friendly AV researchers, but several curriculum and learning discourses are present in the text as well. It is more multivocal than any AV text before that time.

In this yearbook, we note a conflated discourse growing up around Dale—almost every author quotes Dale; and Brown and VanderMeer use Dale's Cone of Experience. Dale's own voice is conflated as he mixes the humanistic and experiential aspects of the child development curricular and learning movement with the sequential and hierarchical structure of task analysis proponents such as Charters'. (He worked on the Winnetka Plan and for Charters in the Payne Fund Study). Dale's Cone of Experience stands as an example of this mixture. It is at once experiential and hierarchical in its listing of experiential events. And, while offering an intriguing and popular model, it was based on conflicting theoretical assumptions.

The research chapter by Dale, Hoban, and Finn does not lean on behaviorism, but touts early perception theory. And in this objective chapter, written in third-person singular, these authors shift to first person plural, to "we," when speaking about World War II and war research. It is an important reminder to us, almost half a century later, of the patriotism that permeated not only education but also society at large during what Turkle (1984) calls "The Good War." It is not a trivial point that this patriotism and close relationship with the military informed the design of instruction, educational media, and, as we see in this book, the rhetoric of the founding scholars of the field.

The full table of contents for the *Forty-Eighth NSSE Yearbook* is included here to illustrate the breadth and scope of the audiovisual field in 1949 (see Fig. 1-13).

In 1949, the official objects of study in the audiovisual field included teaching, learning, communications theory, and machines, with their application and administration. The audience was composed of teachers, librarians, and higher-education faculty interested in AV, government officials at the state and federal level, and people in the corporate sector. Its parameters of operation were primarily elementary and secondary school classrooms, libraries, and, secondarily university departments of education, and state and federal education agencies.

The book closes with a delightful first-person narrative by Walter Wittich of his experience in a small classroom. Film, in this classroom, transformed the learning experience not only for the students but for Walter and the teacher as well. Narratives are generally considered nonscholarly but are highly personal and can be persuasive. It is to the credit of NSSE that they allowed this touching story to be included at the end of a scholarly text. It is also indicative of the persuasive voice with which the founders spoke. For audiovisual education to be successful, for programs to be adopted and grants to be garnered, they had to be convincing. The rhetoric of persuasion existed side by side with that of scholarship.

Figure 1-11. Table of contents from *Visual Aids*, by G. Weaver and E. Bollinger, 1949, New York, Van Nostrand.

Figure 1-12. Table of contents from *Audiovisual Aids to Instruction*, by H. McKown and A. Roberts, 1949, New York, McGraw-Hill, ix–x.

Figure 1-13. Table of contents from the *Forty-Eighth Yearbook of the National Society for the Study of Education*, 1949, pp. vii–x.

1.9.7 Summary of Nonmilitary Audiovisual Scholarship in the 1940s

During a decade when Deweyesque ideas became entwined with social efficiency notions of curriculum in the schools and the country "went to war," audiovisual scholarship became closely allied with the classroom and students' practical life experiences. As we have shown, another conflated discourse was formed which primarily embodied a humanistic theory of learning, but incorporated some behavioral film research from the 20s and Charters' model of task analysis. The new discursive space was rich and multivocal, accommodating varying voices. The rhetoric had opened up from a narrow behavioral rubric to one that included recognition of the mind and consciousness in theories of learning. By the inclusion of concepts of experience and child development, social and cultural issues were perforce included in the scholarly inquiry of the period. Issues of ethics in the evaluation of "good or bad" films had to be broached. Research questions moved from a consideration of micro classroom issues to significant issues, and, most importantly, researchers consulted students and teachers to ascertain if something "worked," i.e., to find out if a film taught. (This humanistic technique is enjoying a return in schools of education today. Because U.S. citizens have sharply criticized the institution of public schools and schools of education, educators are reexamining their methods of inquiry; some are attempting to focus on larger learning issues.) This tendency to "go directly" to teacher and students would not be tolerated by experimental and quasi-experimental researchers.

That the opinions of teachers were valued in this decade is significant for many reasons. Such treatment recognized the professional nature of their work and certified them as experts. With the introduction of programmed instructional materials and behavioral objectives in the decades after the World War II, much of the art of teaching was replaced by prescriptions. Certainly, the curriculum became more standardized, but in Michael Apple's (1986) term, the teacher became "deskilled," much as craftspeople became deskilled by the introduction of machines to replace their work.

What emerges in the rhetoric of scholarly texts and oral histories of the 40s is a diverse field, tightly tied to classrooms, multivocal, and accepting of diverse concepts. In this climate, debates surely raged about what constituted the field, i.e., *communications, machines, films*; and about how to select films that would teach; about how to ascertain how films would teach; and about how to select wholesome films for children. It was probably an era of heated debate about these issues, but the issues were broad, the opinions varied, and the discourse open. What it did lack was rigor and agreement.

tional Technology. (Saettler recalls that W. W. Charters first used the term *educational technology,* and James Finn is often considered the first to write the term *instructional technology* [Saettler, 1990, p. 17n].) Generally speaking, communication researchers focused on those aspects of WWII research that impinged on the affect of audience groups. Even though Hoveland, Lumsdaine, and Sheffield conducted some research on training films, their main contribution was the extensive investigation of the *Why We Fight* film series and the attitudes of recruits. This work, in fact, became the basis for the first major scholarly work in the new communications field, *Experiments on Mass Communications* (Hoveland, Lumsdaine & Sheffield, 1949). Formal academic departments of educational technology did not coalesce at universities until the 60s, but informal work in audiovisual research had been conducted in colleges of education, such as Yale, Columbia, the University of Chicago, Indiana University, and the University of Wisconsin since the 20s (Hoban & Van Ormer, 1951). As we have seen, the discourses that informed academic audiovisual texts in the 30s included behaviorism, specifically connectionism; mental measurements, specifically early IQ work; social efficiency; and a mixture of persuasion, corporate economics, and governmental concerns. With Dale's work ascendant in the 40s, some of these discourses became subordinate for a short while. The nexus of discourses, however, from the late 20s and early 30s ran through the 30s, 40s, 50s, and 60s until university departments of educational technology were established. In fact, if this original amalgam had not existed, the field would not have been established.

If WWII research formed the basis for the modern field of educational technology, it is important to understand which theories of learning inform that work. What assumptions and concepts were important to the researchers, and what values impelled them to join the enterprise. Again, how this body of knowledge was established can be ascertained by examining the rhetoric of this research.

It is our theses that certain psychological strands of extant audiovisual discourses formed a basis for investigating film and other media in the Army and the Navy during this period, but that specific military discourses entered the field at this point in time and helped shape educational technology in the academy. Both psychological and military discourses are evident in the WWII research texts. Furthermore, we believe that the juncture of behaviorism (this time, operant conditioning, not connectionism) and military pedagogy was fortuitous (a marriage made in heaven), and together they formed a solid theoretical base for the field. The way knowledge was structured in operant conditioning and military pedagogy was quite similar.

1.10 MILITARY RESEARCH AND EDUCATIONAL TECHOLOGY

From the research on media during World War II, two new academic fields emerged, Communication Arts and Educa-

1.10.1 Military Training

Military pedagogy, which should more rightly be called *military training*, had existed for many years before WWII but was refined in the preparation of thousands of recruits during this conflict. It was training rather than education and had to accomplish very specific objectives in a short period of time. This training did not have time to be other than top-down in delivery. In addition to being hierarchical, it broke instruction down into small parts, often modularizing curriculum. It used demonstration, supplied opportunities for many trials or practice sessions, and was often self-paced. (Pressey's self-paced prewar teaching machine was ripe for induction into the military. With Skinner, Pressey expanded the capabilities of the machine to include simulations for pilots, but the innovation only built on former military practices of demonstration, trial and error, and self-paced, standardized instruction.) As had educational researchers in the 20s and early 30s, the Army and Navy made use of IQ tests as screening devices to place recruits in appropriate training units.

1.10.2 Training and Curriculum

There is ample evidence of the influence of military training on audiovisual and classroom practices. Books published after the war provide information on mass training. Military training had to be, of necessity, "quick, efficient, and standardized. . . . More learning in less time was perceived to be a necessity and became an immediate goal . . ." (U.S. Navy Department quoted in Miles & Spain, 1947, p. 4). We have already encountered notions that curriculum needs to be efficient and effective; but to those ideas, we now add goals of speed and standardization. It is important to point out that this approach was absolutely necessary to prepare recruits to fight:

> . . . the majority of men trained for military duty were not accustomed to serious study and prolonged mental concentration. This condition, plus the diversity of backgrounds, tended to encourage the development of instructional programs based on "learning by doing" and appeal to all the senses. Especially were these techniques of visualization thought applicable to trainees with less than average mental ability. The generally accepted thesis was that trainees would learn more in less time and retain more of what they did learn for a longer period of time through the use of visual aids. The following statement . . . is characteristic of a generally prevalent viewpoint in all military instruction: "To accelerate learning, as well as to graduate the lower-caliber student who reported in increasing numbers, instructors reduced difficult principles and operations to the simplest terms by visual, auditory, and other means" (Miles & Spain, 1947, pp. 4–5).

Several aspects of this passage are of interest, but the urgent overall message here is that the necessity to train quickly thousands of recruits with varied academic ability led to reducing instruction to its simplest terms. There was obviously no room for critical thinking in wartime training. Yet, at this specific moment in time, when behavioral educational psychologists were designing instruction and audiovisual specialists were producing training films, we believe that certain beliefs about instructions grew out of

these practices. In this curricular procedure, the audience had to be well understood, the objectives of instruction had to be precise and clear, and evaluation measures had to be concrete. It was as if education had to be reduced to instruction that further had to be reduced to training. The trouble with this reduction was that, after the war, a reductive training model was introduced to curriculum and textbook design and, ultimately, to teacher-training programs and classrooms. The constrained reductive model of *audience, task, and evaluation*, which served the Armed Forces so well, was transferred by the educators who designed it back into the public school arena. The training model was equated with instruction, and education for a time did not open up. The critique of behavioral objectives mounted in the mid-70s unseated the training model as the central trope of curriculum theory, but it is still part of the model that informs many instructional design techniques today.

About these training manuals, Walt Wittich says:

> Incidentally, the training guides (which I wrote) were based on the generalizations that I uncovered in writing my Ph.D. thesis . . . [They included training for] films on how to handle weapons, ah, also the Brooker films on how to weld bulkheads and how to weld steel plates together and that kind of how-to-do-it film. The whole objective, or the goal rather, was to give the instructor who was drafted into an instructional position, with which he was probably not too familiar, some tangible, direct guidance in how to introduce, how to involve the learner, and how to use intelligently, a 16-mm training film. . . . The guides were written for the instructors to be placed in the hands of the students, of the enlisted men, the draftees. But in many instances, it never got beyond the teacher, because the teacher then felt this was a good way to interpret the situation. I was so enthusiastic about the possibilities of increasing the usefulness of films through appropriate introduction techniques and preliminary techniques (Wittich, n.d.) [italics ours].

Here is fledgling rhetoric about what would later become *design elements*. Although certainly not the first, Wittich was writing about instructional design elements, but not identifying them as such in his dissertation of 1944.

1.10.2.1. Day-to-Day Military Training.   No matter what design or training models film educators used during the war, there were day-to-day problems about screening and reception. Louis Forsdale describes some hurdles:

> . . . there were some very interesting things that Jim [Finn] got involved with, and that I had the pleasure of helping him carry through. One of the interesting things was that the classrooms that were being used in Leavenworth were huge. I mean 800 students in a single room; that was the largest classroom probably, down to the smaller classrooms of, like, 200 in a single room. Those classrooms, by the way, were filled with people [whose] lowest rank [was] major. One of the things that Jim did was develop standards for the visibility of materials that could be seen by 800 people, by even the person in the last row (Forsdale, 1979).

This was training at its most basic. These educators, while following an efficient training model, often, did not have the luxury of time to create certain instructional films. Forsdale continues:

> We found that it would be terribly useful if we had raw footage, motion picture footage, on hand in Leavenworth, just raw footage, not cut into films at all. And one of my jobs every week was to go down to Kansas City, Missouri, which was about 30 miles away—45 revolver strapped around my waist, not having the slightest idea what I would do if push came to shove—accompanied by two MPs, and a plane came in every week (to Kansas City) with different footage of prime—was footage from all theaters. [I] brought it back and we had two men and they all but memorized what was in the footage. And then they would go to Colonel so and so, who was teaching about important bridges, new important bridges that the Germans were using, and he would say, "By the way, I've got 3 minutes of footage that came in last week. I wonder if we could incorporate that?" Whereupon the instructor took it upon himself [to say Yes]. It was very bad form to say No, because the general was always in favor of backing Jim up on these ventures (Forsdale, 1979).

For us, this anecdote provides a quick gloss on instructional design in wartime and the interplay of authority from both the military and audiovisual spheres.

Robert Frost says, "And reality broke in with all of its matter-of-factness." War was the reality of the 40s, and Floyde Brooker reminds us of the authenticity of Frost's observation:

> We had altogether 20 million men in the Armed Forces and all of them were trained with films. Some of the training was ridiculous. Well, I'll explain that. At one point in the war, they decided that there were too many motion pictures for all the soldiers to see. So the brass went down the list of films, and they selected 57 films that every soldier should see. So they sent out wires all over the country to all the forts and training places. The general out in charge of Fort Hayes in Columbus [said] "look at this list of films." He figured out that the biggest place he had on this post was the mess hall. So he had breakfast served at 5 o'clock. And by running them (the films) at 5-hour lots, all the men by midnight that night could see all 57 films. And they saw them one right after the other for 5 1/2 hours each sitting. But he was the most pleased commander you ever saw in the country, because he sent a telegram back to the War Department that night: "Order So and So Received. Order Executed." And we audiovisual people always said the word *executed*, that was really the word for it (Brooker, 1975).

1.10.2.2. Formalizing Training.   But the written war discourse formally entered curricular materials during and after the war. Miles and Spain help us understand the manner in which methods of training became inscribed in the Army and Navy and ultimately in public classroom texts:

> The most pervasive influence throughout the training program tending to extend the production and use of training aids was the fact of *military* [italics theirs] dominance and control of training. . . . Directives and "doctrine" in a military institution have the effectiveness of legal compulsion, in

practice if not in theory. If a decision, or even a suggestion, is made at the "top" to employ a particular device in teaching signaling, for example, this device will be used. Or if it is thought advisable for all trainees to see a particular film, then these trainees will see the film. A dramatic example of this thoroughgoing influence is the fact that most Army men in the continental United States saw the movie *Two Down and One to Go* within a few days after VE Day. . . . Training aids designed for particular instructional situations became virtually mandatory, and these inspections and visits tended to assure compliance with directives and recommendations (Miles & Spain, 1947, p. 8).

Far from being critical of military pedagogy, Miles and Spain were writing a descriptive book, *Audiovisual Aids in the Armed Services*, for the Commission on Implications of Armed Services Educational Programs. The transfer of this method of training was being explored for schools. This commission, authorized by the American Council on Education, published 12 books in 1947 and 1948 to explore the implications of military training for public education. Some titles were *Educational Lessons from Wartime Training* (Grace et al., 1947); *Area Studies in American Universities* (Fenton, 1947); *Improving Textbooks the Army and Navy Way* (Frauens, 1948); *Curriculum Implications of Armed Services Training* (Goodman, 1948); *Opinions on Gains for American Education from Wartime Armed Services Training* (Chambers, 1948). George Zook, president of the American Council of Education in the 40s said of this series:

> The Commission on Implications of Armed Services Educational Programs began work in July 1945. It undertakes to identify features of the wartime training and educational programs worthy of adaptation and experimentation in peacetime civilian education of any and all types of levels. It also undertakes to make available to the public well-considered answers to the questions: What should education in America gain from the experience of the vast wartime training efforts? What are the implications for education and the national culture and strength, now and in the future? (Miles & Spain, 1947, p. 97).

These texts are important here, in fact more important to public education than were the audiovisual set published by the American Council on Education and mentioned above. What they indicate is that general educators, not only AV educators, carried lessons about how to teach from the Army and Navy back to their civilian classrooms. Among them were teachers and administrators who were convinced of the efficacy of military training and, consequently, ripe for the upcoming "programming" of the curriculum by instructional designers and the fiat to teach by behavioral objectives.

To return a moment to the rhetoric of the quote from Miles and Spain, we note the introduction of words and concepts that had not been generally encountered in curriculum, nor in AV texts prior to WWII. There is *dominance* and *control*, *directives* and *doctrine*, *legal compulsion*; we had not often encountered the term *trainee* before this time. Also, notions of inspections and *compliance* are new.

Methods of teacher training in the Armed Services were explored for transfer to public classrooms. Teacher training, like behavioral protocol, was standardized in the military.

> Voice, diction, gestures and other personality traits were stressed as pertinent to the effectiveness of the teacher. . . . Supervisors also assisted instructors in developing other good teaching habits, for example, standing aside from blackboards or other graphic aids and using pointers (Miles & Spain, 1947, p. 10).

Although these were excellent teaching hints, there was an attempt to standardize the appearances of teaching, just as marching. The content to be taught was prewritten; strategies were ignored.

1.10.2.3. Designing Texts.

Methods of designing military manuals were gleaned for clues to the design of school-room texts. The pride of the Armed Forces, however, were the standardized manuals that they produced during the war years and released after the war. Many of them were self-instructional, stepwise texts "in modern magazine style containing all the basic information which students should acquire in primary training or in advanced training" (Miles & Spain, 1947, p. 11). Publicity men, professional editorial staffs, and commercial artists had been drafted into the Armed Forces to help design and produce these manuals:

> . . . the fact that such manuals were thought necessary and were accepted so wholeheartedly indicates that civilian textbooks perhaps could often be improved in format, size of print, and degree of visualization (Miles & Spain, 1947, p. 12).

Benefiting from these well-designed manuals, however, were the Army and Navy technical reports of audiovisual research. Most of them were presented in black textured covers with large gold lettering and official gold seals. The 8 1/2-by-11 report was designed in double columns with many different-sized headlines in both bold and plain text. Font size was varied in the heads, and there was plenty of white space in the text. Ample use was made of well-designed graphs and charts, and the text was easy to read. The magazine influence was evident in these reports and has remained so in at least part of the educational technology field today, namely, that of instructional design. To get a feeling for the structure of some of these training manuals, consult any one of a number of local production textbooks on the market today. They are good cookbooks and certainly supply the student in a production class with enough information to get started.

1.10.3 Content and Rhetoric of War Research

The research conducted in World War II consisted primarily of investigations into the training power of film, and the results are common knowledge today in many educational technology graduate programs. We learned that we use motion to teach motion tasks, that film was good for teaching facts, and adequate for teaching concepts, and that it had some effect on motivation and opinion. The reason educational technology researchers used these studies as a base for their work in the 50s and 60s was because they believed that the large number of participants used in the

studies supported the statistics employed to measure results. In a companion piece to Hoban and vanOrmer's 1950 well-designed, succinct, and terse *Instructional Film Research Report*, the Instructional Film Research Program, sponsored by the Army and Navy, prepared a 16-page booklet, *Practical Principles Governing the Production and Utilization of Sound Motion Pictures* (Hoban & vanOrmer, 1950) that summarizes the longer succinct version. The booklet again is handsomely designed in an 8 1/2-by-11 inch format with a professionally lettered buff cover with a brown binding. On the final page of the booklet the authors conclude:

> Four conclusions which apply to motion pictures in training, orientation, and information clearly emerge from the review of film research:
>
> 1. The educational effectiveness of films can be improved, but to do so steps must be taken all along the line from the origin of the film idea to the utilization of the film in instruction, and not simply at the production stage.
> 2. The effectiveness of films in instruction depends on the relationship of the film content to the audience and the context of their use, and not simply on the film itself.
> 3. Within the film, treatment of the content in terms of psychological and instructional principles governing audience reaction is of greatest importance. Film techniques involving special effects and elaborate musical scores are of minor importance.
> 4. Of all the devices of mass communication, motion pictures and their counterpart, television, are unquestionably the most powerful (Hoban & vanOrmer, 1950, p. 16).

Additional research, conducted during WWII, explored the effectiveness of other audiovisual modes of instruction as well as the appropriate environment for the presentation of instructional materials.

1.10.4 A Pre- and Postwar Voice

The difference in voice, namely, form of address, tone, and language use, may be compared in two similar pre- and postwar projects by the same author. In 1937, Charles Hoban, Jr., contributed "Part Three" and "Part Five" to *Motion Pictures in Education, A Summary of the Literature* (Dale et al., 1937). "Part Five" was a 54-page summary of "Experimental Research in Instructional Films" and recounted the film experiments conducted to date. In 1937, Hoban reports the findings of the Knowlton and Tilton studies in the following manner:

> Small, statistically reliable, differences in favor of the classroom groups, were obtained in six out of ten comparisons in immediate tests; in four of these six, a difference was still evident the following September (Hoban & vanOrmer, 1950, pp. 8–41).

The point of comparing the more general description with the precise, scientific version is not to cast aspersions on either. In fact, readers wishing to replicate Knowlton and Tilton will benefit from the second exposition. But it is important to note the evolution of this scientific language. With Knowleton and Tilton (1929), Freeman (1924), Rulon (1933), and Devereux (1933), practices of laboratory experimentation were introduced to the audiovisual field, and they applied these practices with state-of-the-art competency. These practices were refined, however, with the war research and, at that moment, permanently inscribed in the dominant discourse of the field. We do not suggest here that the child-centered theories of learning would have suited adult recruits in the Armed Forces, but the reverse did occur. The audiovisual discourse established in WWII training and research was applied to children in their classrooms. As we listen to Hoban's voice before and after the war, we can identify specific concepts that the more-sophisticated application of true experimental designs in the military contributed to the field.

In "Part Five" (Dale et al., 1937, pp. 307–61), Hoban rarely uses the word *experiment* but favors the phrases *experimental research* or *experimental study* or *experimental attack*. With the use of the adjective instead of the noun, Hoban implies these studies are not experiments but similar to experiments. In fact, he tips his hand on this topic when he notes, "In educational research, this law (holding one variable constant) is a principle to be approximated, not a condition readily obtained" (Dale et al., 1937, p. 315). The term *experiment* is used liberally in the *Army, Navy Report* (Hoban & vanOrme, 1950, 1-1–C-1) with no caveats; it has been sanctioned.

In writing a section of the 1937 text (Dale et al.), Hoban lists the "Criteria for Evaluation of Experimental Research in General." They are:

1. Significance of the problem
2. Selection of factors for study
3. Assumptions
4. Appropriateness of general procedure
5. Significance of raw measures
6. Representativeness of sampling
7. Adequacy of data
8. Analysis of data
9. Interpretation of observations and analytical findings (Dale et al., 1937, p. 312).

Yet, as Hoban (Hoban & vanOrmer, 1950. 1-1-C-1) evaluates research after WWII, his headings for reporting all studies are *Experimental Design, Findings, and Evaluation*. Some entire expositions under the "Evaluation" heading follow:

Evaluation. As we mentioned above, there seems to be a disagreement in the research findings on this problem. The collateral evidence is somewhat in favor of distributed showings. However, Ash's study involved a sufficient number of films and sufficient diversity of population to support the conclusion that, under instructional and physical conditions sometimes found in practice (where the instructor plans no immediate discussion of the film), 1-hour film sessions may be conducted without substantial loss in overall group learning. This conclusion applies to film sessions involving a subject divided into three or four major and self-contained sequences. Rate of development and content density probably also enter into the problem of long and short film sessions to influence the result (Hoban & vanOrmer, 1950, pp. 8–38).

Evaluation. This study lends support to the theory that relevant introductory remarks have an anticipational or motivational effect, as well as to the theory that learning results from the practice effect of repeating material in different symbolic forms (Hoban & vanOrmer, 1950, pp. 8–36).

A number of things occur in these quotes which clearly indicate the tacit formation of a professional discourse that will control entry into the field. It will constitute a style to be taught by professor to student. This rhetoric, complex with cumbersome sentence structure, yet with precise adjectives and nouns, is a laboratory style not seen to this extent in audiovisual discourse before this time. Was there a necessity for this voice? One might answer Yes when considering the culture of the academy, especially that of educational psychology departments. Founders were, after all, establishing academic turf. We speculate that writers hoped the "scientific" style would clarify the communication, or deliver a more accurate message. We note that it did reach for accuracy, yet in their haste for a professional style, Hoban and vanOrmer (and other authors) became sloppy epistomologists. They use the term *theory*, twice above, to designate a *thesis*. Hoban did not make such a mistake before the war, and the rich notion of *theory* becomes reduced to *thesis* or further reduced to *hypothesis*. In the Ash evaluation above, the phrases *rate of development* and *content density*, introduced for the first time at the end of this report, tend to obfuscate rather than clarify the evaluation. Their meanings are private.

1.10.5 Military Manuals in the Schools: Postwar Curriculum

In the late 40s and early 50s, Army and Navy training manuals such as *Photography, Vol. 1* and *Photography, Vol. 2* (Bureau of Naval Personnel, 1952) became quite popular in vocational and technical schools. This was, after all, the period of the life adjustment curriculum, and by 1949 more students were studying health, music, and art than any other fields. More than half the subjects in the public high school curriculum were in the fields of social studies, vocational education, home economics, and agriculture (Perkinson, 1968). There was a new emphasis on aviation in the curriculum which led to the founding of schools such as New York High School of Aviation Trades. Thousand of manuals were prepared by the Armed Services, either by their own personnel or by civilian subcontractors, sometimes at universities. The United States Armed Forces Institute at the University of Wisconsin-Madison was one such subcontractor (Kliebard, 1993). No author's name appears on these manuals, which were written in the formulaic stepwise fashion of military rhetoric. By 1952, the photography volumes were in their fourth printing, along with thousands of other training manuals. Although "how to" manuals existed in trade schools prior to WWII, it can be said that the military perfected this genre for vocational and technical education. Undoubtedly, these manuals influenced the structure of later instructional development texts. Although it was necessary during wartime to motivate men to fight, even a photography manual urged postwar students to arms:

> The camera is a weapon just as a battleship's big guns are weapons. . . . A vital reconnaissance or engagement picture may determine the plan or strategy that decides a battle. . . . You are the important man—the man who establishes the viewpoint of the camera, which means the viewpoint of the Navy (Bureau of Navy Personnel, 1952, Vols. 1, 3, p. 17).

Learning a topic for war or armament was a patriotic value that slipped into the public school curriculum in the 50s, not only in trade schools like Aviation Trades High School but also in the general teaching of mathematics and science. This value was reinforced by the passage of the National Defense Education Act (Becker, 1987). These training manuals were replete cookbook-like texts designed for self-study. Because of the premise, however, that recruits were not smart, the tone of these texts was often patronizing:

> "Now do you take off? Well not quite yet. But you're getting warmer. . . . Now use a bit of simple algebra. If that term frightens you, forget it. Just say that you will take a short cut to finding the amount of ground which the picture will cover" (Bureau of Naval Personnel, 1952, Vol. 2, pp. 172, 173).

On these pages of the photography volume and on many other pages, the author has employed what later became known as instructional design elements (Gagne & Allen). The unknown author uses questions to gain and/or maintain attention, and positive feedback is provided much as it is in programmed instruction.

The rhetoric of military training combined with that of operant conditioning entered the discursive audiovisual space during World War II and after. The mechanistic language of instructional materials distributed the effects of this combined discourse in classroom textbooks, programmed materials, and instructional media.

1.10.6 Postwar Scholarship

Research in the military and on university campuses became inextricably conflated after WWII and remains that way today. James Brown notes that "the universities then [during wartime] as now (1970s) were playing an important role in the whole armed forces program" (Brown, n.d.). Two representative military/university research studies to be published in the 50s were *Motion Pictures as a Medium of Instruction* (Fearing, 1950; see Fig. 1-14) and *Instructional Television Research Reports* (Twyford & Seitz,

1956). Both texts have some notable similarities; the studies are tightly controlled and true experiments, and the reports stress the statistical and experimental nature of this enterprise. This research appears to be more and more like that conducted in a psychology laboratory. The word *subject* indicating a study participant appears for the first time in our reading of audiovisual research. Fearing (1950), in fact, uses *subject* to indicate *participant* and elsewhere to indicate *topic to be studied*. Twyford and Seitz (1956) do not; for *topic to be studied* they use the word *lesson*. Neither text uses the word *audiovisual*; Fearing (1950) uses the words *film*, *motion picture*, and *medium*, but shies away from *audiovisual*, as do Twyford and Seitz (1956). They use the words *television*, *telecasts*, *moving pictures*, and *kinescopes*. These three authors were professionally located outside of colleges of education: Fearing in social science and Twyford and Seitz in psychology. We see a tendency here, and in other 50s texts, for some scholars to distance themselves from the prewar audiovisual research and to attach themselves to the "official," rigorous, and mechanistic research of the Armed Forces. Fearing, who finished his research in 1944, sounds, what we find, to be the last warning in this period about the borrowing of experimental design:

> There are important limitations in such a program. It is doubtful if complex relations between content and the individual exposed to it can be fully expressed within the limited and arbitrary confines of pencil and paper testing techniques. . . . Testing procedures may yield very useful information, but it is important to remember that the problem of the psychological impact of motion pictures is not solved by these devices alone (Fearing, 1950, pp. 102–03).

But after that caveat, he proceeds to ignore the limitations and interpret the results of his studies, as if they could measure the impact of films on viewers.

Twyford and Seitz, psychologists, do not discuss these limitations, and, gradually, we observe the erasure in the literature of the flaws of the experimental model. It becomes inscribed in the discourse as the appropriate model; it has been made official by military research. It may be said that the before-and-after design, using film as a stimulus, which was developed by Peterson and Thurstone (1933) for their part of the Payne Studies, grew into the true experimental design that still resides at the heart of educational technology research. The manner in which this model became inscribed is rhetorical and similar to the way the discourse on behavioral learning theory developed. Early in the century, when someone asked Watson how he would account for emotions within his stimulus-response model, he replied that emotions were distal variables that he and other behaviorists would address later, but, currently, he wished to study molar variables. Well, the distal variables fell out of the discourse and were never considered (or considered by a few as drives) when behaviorism dominated psychology (Becker, 1977).

The emphasis on experimentation can be seen in the contents of the Fearing (1950) book.

The Twyford and Seitz (1956) military technical report is bound in the same official-looking black-and-gold format as described before and makes good use of charts and diagrams. The variables studied tend to be similar to those employed in WWII film research, i.e., retention of learning, effectiveness, novelty, and screen size. It was strange that this particular set of instructional television findings were ignored by the initiators of instructional television in the 50s and 60s (Becker, 1987). These reports, which were sponsored by the Human Engineering Department of the U.S. Naval Training Device Center but conducted in the Psychology Department at Fordham University, have an early application of the flowchart in the audiovisual field.

Seitz was head of the Navy's Human Engineering Department, which may have appropriated concepts such as flow diagrams from the Navy's work on programmed machine language in the mid-40s (see Fig. 1-15). And the human engineering field was the area in which the systems concept was established (*Encyclopedia of Computers, Science and Technology*, Vol. 7, p. 429).

In both this and the Fearing text, we see an early use of the word *subject* to designate study participant, but here the word is never used to designate topic of study.

1.10.7 *See and Hear*

The audiovisual contingent returning from war duty organized an important journal, *See and Hear*. Although there had been journals in visual education before *See and Hear*, they had not been established by a group of educational technology founders. Walter Whittich recalls it's beginnings:

> I thought it would be a great idea now that the field was growing, and the war years were over—everybody was very enthusiastic—to gather up all this tremendous talent that had been developing in the training aids group. Such men as Noel and Bernardis and Jim Brown, oh, gosh, you know, that whole gang that came back from the war. I prevailed again upon my very good friend, John Guy [Fowlkes] to use his influence with a local businessman. . . . He ran Eau Claire Book and Stationary Company. And he had a printing press up there. . . . It was possible to gather together about 25 of these returned audiovisual buffs from the war (about 1946) and get them together and committed to the idea of starting a magazine that was a real forward-looking outreach and struck across the whole spread of education. Each would bring to it at least one article a year on his own innermost and most constructive thoughts. And this became *See and Hear* (Whittich, n.d.).

This journal represented an effort to get media formally adopted in the classroom. Audiences included not only teachers and librarians but school administrators and legislators as well. In the statement of purpose of Vol. 1, No. 1, the editors, Walter Wittich, C. J. Anderson, and John Guy Fowlkes say:

> We are well past the time when we should formulate plans for audiovisual education in terms of free materials. Audiovisual communication via good teaching equipment is here. It is here to stay as a working part of our classroom environment.
>
> We, therefore, have passed beyond the point of emergency appropriations, PTA gifts, service club sponsorship, scrap-paper drives, and other precarious policies of financing audiovisual education. Now that audiovisual materials must become an integral part of teaching techniques, more solid budget provision must be made. Only insofar as audiovisual materials enjoy a budgetary status comparable to that which other school equipment enjoys can the program of audiovisual learning approach full effectiveness.
>
> Isn't it, then, high time that we also examine the financial cost of a well-coordinated program of audiovisual education in our schools and make necessary budgetary provisions for it?

These are the purposes of *See and Hear* (Wittich, Anderson, Fawlkes, *See and Hear*, Vol. I, No. 1). These founders were attempting to move the audiovisual field from the periphery in classrooms to the center by establishing formal

I. INTRODUCTION
Use and limitations of psychological evaluation procedures
Other investigations
The present investigation
The tests
Groups tested

II. "THREE CADETS"
The film
Content analysis
Specific references
Thematic ambiguities
The subjects
Characteristics of group
Information on venereal disease
The tests
Attitude scales
Information test
Validity and reliability of information test
Administration of tests
Analysis of results of information test
Frequency distribution of test scores
Responses on individual test items
Individual items on which shift is slight
Responses as related to average for group
Items showing greatest change
Summary of results
Responses on attitude scales
Attitudes on which change is slight
Attitudes on which change is large
Summary of responses
Over-all evaluation of film by subjects

Figure 1-14. Table of contents from *Motion Pictures as a Medium of Instruction: An Experimental Analysis of the Effects of Two Films, 1950,* Berkeley, University of California Press, v–vi.

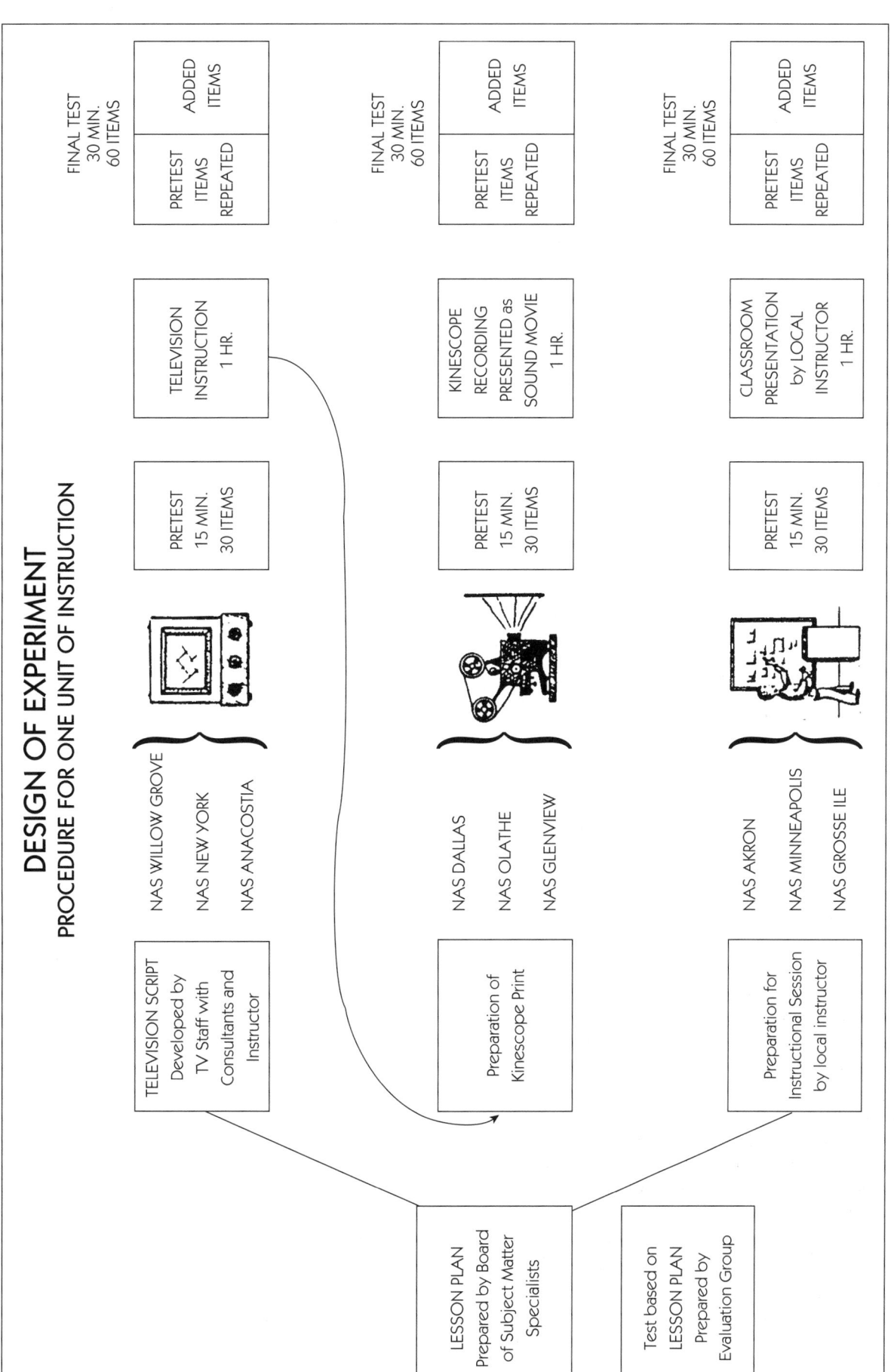

Figure 1-15. Flowchart, by Twyford and Seitz, 1956, p. 2.

links with funders, i.e., legislators private sector funders. Even at the classroom level, the area—to become professional—had to have alliances with government and business.

1.10.7.1. McClusky: While *See and Hear* was growing, there was a flurry of scholarly audiovisual activity. An AV pioneer, who had been writing since the 20s, published a helpful bibliography for the field in 1950, with a second edition in 1955 (McClusky, *The A-V Bibliography*, 1955). See Figure 1-16. The size and style of the book is similar to the military reports of media research released during and after WWII. An 8 1/2-by-11-inch format is covered in gray with maroon lettering; the book looks official. In the second edition, a condensed table of contents with graphics appears before the full table of contents.

The condensed table is similar to many tables in children's dictionarys and reference books of the time, and one used in some military training manuals. The full table of contents divides the field into the same categories as do the summary books and textbooks of the 30s and 40s. But even in the 1955 edition, McClusky—now at UCLA and, perhaps, with Frank Fearing who never uses the term *audiovisual*—still uses the term *audiovisual* and the initials A-V.

An interesting feature of this text and one that is important here, since we are exploring the formation of the academic field, is a listing of audiovisual doctoral dissertations completed in the late 40s and earlier. Two points are of interest here: the work of leaders and future chairs of Instructional Technology (IT) departments and the universities supporting AV research before the formation of IT departments. See Figure 1-17.

1.10.8 The Nebraska Study

In 1952, Wes Meierhenry published the final report on the "Nebraska Program of Educational Enrichment Through the Use of Motion Pictures" (Meierhenry, 1952). This had been a Carnegie-funded study and one of the first large, major educational media studies funded by private-sector money. It foreshadows the multimillion-dollar investment of the Ford Foundation just a few years later. (The Ford Foundation attempted to jump-start the diffusion of instructional television in public school classrooms.) The Nebraska statewide effort to introduce film in the public schools was based on the following premise:

> During and after World War II, reports from ex-servicemen and educators who served in the educational program of the Armed Forces showed that a wide variety of instructional materials, particularly motion pictures, had been found effective in the training of members of the Armed Forces. . . . The use of materials by the Armed Forces gave new impetus and direction to their general use (Meierhenry, 1952, p. 11).

In a chapter entitled, "Planning for Action," Meierhenry reviews several decades of experimentation with educational film, citing Wood and Freeman, and Knowleton and Tilton in the 20s; Rulon, Dale, and Arnspiger in the 30s; Carpenter, Whittich, Hoban, Jr., and Hovland, Lumsdaine and Scheffield in the 40s. Again, we see the 50s authors leaning on the substantial but limited (in number) work of a small circle of AV researchers. Gone again are any direct

I.	The Philosophy and Psychology of Teaching with Audio-Visual Materials
II.	Audio-Visual Teaching Materials and Their Use
III.	Elementary Schools
IV.	Secondary Schools
V.	Higher Education
VI.	Administration of Audio-Visual Instruction
VII.	Research on Value and Utilization of Audio-Visual Materials
VIII.	Miscellaneous

Figure 1-16. First table of contents from *The A-V Bibliography,* 1955, by F. McClusky, Dubuque, Iowa, Wm. C. Brown.

references to learning theories from the table of contents and the body of the text.

We conclude that tacit theoretical assumptions underpinning the Nebraska experiments are behavioral. Project members conducted state-of-the-art educational research in Nebraska public schools over a period of several years. Five of the book's chapters (V, VI, VII, VIII, and XIII) are based on doctoral dissertations conducted under the auspices of this project (see Fig. 1-18). Those aspects of students' learning from film are evident in the subheads of one of those chapters, "Motion Pictures Enrich Learning," based on Guy Scott's doctoral dissertation (Meierhenry, 1952, pp. 55–71). They are:

Experimental Design
Reliability of Film Tests
Statistical Procedure
Test Results for the First Experimental Period
Composite Test Results for Two Years
Tests Results for Retention
Summary of Test Results in the Science Area
Summary of Test Results in the Social Studies Area
Summary of Test Results in the Convocation Area
Summary of Tests Results on Retention
Conclusions

On the 16 pages of the chapter, there are 11 tables, almost one per page, and the chapter concludes with these paragraphs:

> In general, film groups and control groups learned about the same content as measured by standardized tests, and the film groups learned significantly more of the material presented by the films. It is possible to devote an amount of time at least equal to that used in this experiment for instruction by means of motion pictures and maintain a level of achievement equivalent to that where motion pictures are not used.
>
> A program of motion pictures can be used to supplement the subject-matter offering of the school and will result in

Weber, J. J. *Comparative Effectiveness of Some Visual Aids in Seventh Grade Instruction.* Columbia, Teachers College, 1921. Published by Educational Screen, 1922, pp. 131.

McClusky, F. D. *An Experimental Comparison of Different Methods of Visual Instruction.* Chicago, 1922. Condensed version, in Frank N. Freeman, ed., Visual Education, University of Chicago Press, 1924, pp. 83–166.

Arnspiger, V. C. *Measuring the Effectiveness of Sound Pictures as Teaching Aids.* Columbia, Teachers College, 1933. Teachers College Contributions to Education, No. 565.

Lewin, W. *Photoplay Appreciation in American High Schools.* New York, 1933, D. Appleton-Century, 1934, pp. 122.

Hoban, C. F. Jr. *A Critical Evaluation of the Experimental Literature on Instructional Films.* Duke, 1935. *Summarized in Motion Pictures in Education.* H. W. Wilson Co., 1937, pp. 307–66.

Ramseyer, L. L. *A Study of the Influence of Documentary Films on Social Attitudes.* Ohio, 1938.

Hall, C. C. *High School Science Students Preferences of Illustrated Materials.* Colorado State College of Education, 1940. Abstracted by David Goodman in *Educational Screen.* Vol. 20, Dec. 1941, pp. 434–35.

Brown, Kenneth William. *The Visual Arts in Secondary Education.* Ohio, 1942.

Cypher, Irene Fletcher. *The Development of the Diorama in the Museums of the United States.* New York, 1942. Abstracted by David Goodman in *Educational Screen,* Vol. 21, Sep. 1942, pp. 273–74.

Goodman, D. J. *Comparative Effectiveness of Pictorial Teaching Aids.* New York, 1942. Abstracted in *Educational Screen,* Vol. 21, Nov. 1942, pp. 358–59, 371.

Miles, John Robert. *An Evaluative Survey of Educational Recordings for Classroom Use.* Ohio, 1942.

Vandermeer, A. W. *The Economy of Time in Industrial Training: An Experimental Study of the Use of Sound Films in the Training of Engine Lathe Operators.* Chicago, 1943. *Summarized in Journal of Educational Psychology.*

Gibson, Ernest Dane. *Communication Sound-Slide Scripts,* New York, 1944.

Wittich, Walter Arno. *Sound Paths to Learning: A Comparison of Three Classroom Methods of Using Educational Sound Films.* Wisconsin, 1944. Condensed in, Wittich and Fowlkes, *Audio-Visual Paths to Learning,* Harper and Bros., 1946, pp. 135.

Miller, Mervyn Vincent. *The Development, Production, and Evaluation of a Vocational Guidance Film in Student Orientation on the College Level.* Stanford, 1945.

Witt, Paul W. F. *In-Service Education of Teachers in the Use of Audio-Visual Materials of Instruction.* Columbia, Teachers College, 1947.

De Kieffer, Robert E. *The Status of Teacher-Training in Audio-Visual Education in the Forty-Eight States.* Iowa, 1948.

Finn, James D. *A Study of Military Audio-Visual Programs, Particularly at the Command and General Staff School, With Some Implications for the Instructional Organization of Colleges.* Ohio, 1949. Abstract in, *The Audio-Visual Reader,* Wm. C. Brown, 1954, pp. 350–53.

Iverson, William. J. *A Definition of Teaching Competencies with Audio-Visual Materials.* Stanford, 1949.

Lumsdaine, A. A. *Ease of Learning with Pictorial and Verbal Symbols.* Stanford, 1949.

Allen, William H. *An Experimental Study of the Effectiveness of Commentary Variation in Educational Motion Pictures.* Los Angeles, California, 1951. Summarized in, *Journal of Applied Psychology,* Vol. 36, Jun. 1952, pp. 164–68.

De Bernardis, Amo. *A Study of Audio-Visual Education in Oregon Public Schools.* Oregon, 1951.

Guss, Carolyn. *A Study of Film Evaluation and Selection Practices in Twelve Universities and Colleges with Recommendations for Improvement.* Indiana, 1952.

Hyer, Anna L. *A Study of Possible Deterrents to the Use of Motion Pictures Within a School System Where Films and Faculties for Use Were Provided.* Indiana, 1952.

White, F. A. *An Evaluation of the Program of the University of Wisconsin School of Education for Giving Competency in the Use of Certain Selected Audio-Visual Methods.* Wisconsin, 1952.

Iverson, M. T. *A Historical and Structural Survey of Audio-Visual Techniques in Education, 1900–1950.* Iowa, 1953.

McTavish, C. L. *Effect of Repetitive Film Presentations on Learning.* Pennsylvania State, 1953.

Moldstad, John Alton. *A Study of the Relative Effects of Film Narration Listenability on the Learning of Factual Information and the Development of Incidental Vocabulary.* Indiana, 1953.

Saettler, L. P. *The Origin and Development of Audio-Visual Communication in Education in the United States.* Southern California, 1953.

Torkelson, G. M. *The Comparative Effectiveness of a Mockup, Cutaway, and Projected Charts in Teaching Nomenclature and Function of the 40mm Antiaircraft gun and the Mark 13 Type Torpedo.* Pennsylvania State, 1953.

Figure 1-17. University doctoral dissertations from *The A-V Bibilography,* 1955, by F. McClusky, Dubuque, Iowa, Wm. C. Brown, 190-97.

Figure 1-18. Table of contents from *Enriching the Curriculum Through Motion Pictures,* by W. Meierhenry, 1952, Lincoln, University of Nebraska Press.

significant achievement on a variety of topics. By this means, a school may increase the general educational development of the student body at relatively small cost in time and money.

There is no reason to believe that retention of material suffers as a result of the use of educational motion pictures. Rather, the evidence shows some overall gain in retention of information when films are used in instruction" (Meierhenry, 1952, p. 71).

The tacit assumption here is that variables can be isolated and controlled, and that careful measurement can locate cognitive gains in students. According to appropriate guidelines for the conduct of research at that time, there was no discussion of the students who were subjects in the studies. Even in the chapter "Motion Pictures Modify Beliefs," in which dissertator Jack Peterson quantifies student response (Meierhenry, 1952, pp. 88–134), there is no heading for students. The headings do include:

Administration of the Pretests
Administrations of the Post Test
Method of Scoring the Belief Scale

This action of ignoring the students does not reflect on the doctoral candidates in the project, or their major professors. They were, in fact, following rigorous methods for the conduct of scientific study, but the influence of the social efficiency movement and its concomitant learning and measurement theories are, by now, firmly inscribed in the dominant discourse running through educational technology, and it is, unfortunately, a narrow discourse. (There is not much use of the word *subject,* which is actually an interchangeable part, to indicate students here. Most often the authors use the terms, *experimental* or *control groups* and the word *student.*)

On the last page of the text, however, Meirehenry, for the first time, exposes his beliefs about media and learning:

Throughout the history of civilization there have been great teachers who have contributed much to the practice of teaching. Such men as Erasmus, Comenius, Pestalozzi, Rousseau, Froebel, and Dewey called attention to the sterility of many learning situations and urged the correction of these situations through the use of more concrete experiences. To provide concrete experiences out of which may develop meaningful concepts, generalizations, and principles is the main purpose for using audio-visual materials in education. When teachers understand more adequately than they do now, the essential elements for learning to take place in the complex human organism, when they understand more adequately the kinds of experiences necessary to produce desired changes in behavior, when they use more skillfully a variety of instruments and devices to discover whether the desired changes in behavior have taken place, at that time a happier, more satisfying, and more worthwhile educational experience will await the girls and boys in the schools of Nebraska. The Nebraska Program of Educational Enrichment Through the Use of Motion Pictures has helped to open the door to this new educational era (Meierhenry, 1952, p. 228).

This is an interesting statement, because the author cites a list of child-centered educators, in fact the very educators cited by many AV writers in the 40s. But, in the second paragraph, he switches back to the black-box theory of stimuli power to change behavior. It is as if his desire to help teachers and children breaks through the reductive epistemology that shackles the field at this moment in time.

1.10.9 Applied Texts in the 1950s

In the 50s, there was a new interest in the publication of audiovisual texts for the study of the field and the application of media in classrooms. Three of the texts had a wide distribution and are of interest to us here: *A-V Instruction, Materials and Methods, Audio-Visual Materials and Techniques,* and *Audio-Visual Materials: Their Nature and Use.* It is interesting to note that the field was officially still termed *audiovisual,* even though the war researchers were shying away from that title in their research publications. The paradox, however, was that most of these 50s education textbooks were authored by men who had participated, in or out of the services, in the writing of military training manuals. But for the first time, these books offered education professors and teachers in training a choice in selecting textbooks. Obviously, the market for these books in colleges of education existed, because major publishers, such as McGraw-Hill and Harper and Brothers joined the enterprise.

It is rare that we have an author of an important textbook talking about the manner in which the first edition was conceived and written, but Walter Wittich spoke frankly about *Audio-Visual Materials: Their Nature and Use*:

Well, the first edition was on the market in 1953, which was the culmination of 5 years of classroom tryout in the extension classes throughout Wisconsin, Northern Illinois, and the middle of Minnesota.

The book is the book because of the very wonderful working relationship that Charlie Schuller and I enjoyed in 1953 and still enjoy now.

[Charlie] came into the audiovisual department [University of Wisconsin] as my associate. . . . We began working very strenuously together on organizing extension classes in audiovisual throughout the state. In 1948, for example, we had 24 extension classes running simultaneously throughout the state of Wisconsin. There were six of us teaching those. One time we were using Edgar Dale and his very remarkable book. Due to a series of circumstances, we decided that we ought to try one of our own, so we began developing the materials" (Wittich, n.d.).

Schuller also talks about how the first edition of *Audio-Visual Materials; Their Nature and Use* came about:

It came about through accident, outside influence, and so on. John Guy Fowlkes had gotten a contract with Harper and Bros. by which he got a certain percentage out of generating needed books in the field—like a 1% royalty on all books produced, and he had a "Century in Education" series which was well conceived and well designed. Old John Guy came to us one day and said, "Well, you know I don't know of any real books in this field." He had heard of Edgar Dale's book and the impact it had. And he said, "Don't you think it would be a good idea if we put one up?" Neither Walt and I—although we had done some writing— were all that hot about writing a book, but the combination of our innate interest and John Guy's pushing created that first thing. And it was twice as much work as we had ever anticipated, maybe 3 or 4 times. And I doubt very much if we would have got into it, if not for that little accidental association. John Guy, of course, was both our major professors (Schuller, 1978).

Today, educational technology practitioners are often so focused on the details of academic life that the necessary political work on behalf of students and machines is accomplished by amateurs outside the field. That was not the case in the early years. Consider the work that I. Keith Tyler and the Institute for Education by Radio and Television (IERT) did to get public television channels reserved for education:

One thing that happened at the Institute [for Education by Radio and Television, IERT, at Ohio State] was that this became the place for the commissioners from the Federal Communications Commission to come out and get educated about the educational side of broadcasting. They saw commercial broadcasters all the time, but educators, in those days, didn't have money to have lawyers to appear before the commission. . . . And so those who really took

the public interest seriously used to come to the institute just to see what was being talked about and what was going on. . . . And if a new commissioner came on, they'd say, "Go out to Columbus and see what's going on." And so a new commissioner, a lawyer from the east side of New York who was very cause minded . . . Frieda Hennock, came out to the institute and was very impressed . . . and she said to herself "this is my cause." I am going to make this a cause (Tyler, 1977).

The FCC had put a freeze on the development of new television stations in 1948, until research about their positioning and operations could be assembled and presented to the commissioners. Originally, it was a 1-year freeze that was extended until 1952. Tyler and others mounted a case for the reserving of television stations for the exclusive use of education. It is an important moment, because it was the start of public television. His story is colorful:

. . . Let's see if we can . . . ask permission to come to the FCC while the freeze is on and insist, in their new allocation, that they reserve channels for education. So we had a meeting in the fall of 1950, and the NAEB (National Association for Educational Broadcasting) was represented, I . . . represented . . . the University [Ohio State] or the Institute [IERT], and the Office Of Education [was represented]. I would say there were about 12 of us, maybe 15. And the general idea . . . [was] we'd have to dig it out of our own universities or public school systems' pockets for the expenses.

. . . Frieda Hennock was there, the commissioner, and she said "This was a great cause, and we ought to do something about it" (Tyler, 1977).

Tyler relates that Hennock directed him to make a formal effort for the official FCC hearings on the allotment of channels in the fall of 1952. He chaired the effort, and Hennock recommended that his educational group be represented by an attorney:

And Frieda Hennock . . . said, "Why don't you go for General Telford Taylor?" And we said, "Who is he?" And she said that he was the chief prosecutor of the Nuremberg Trials for the Army. And before that he was the chief counsel for the Federal Communications Commission, and he really knows his way around, and he's with this very dedicated [to social causes] law firm on Wall Street (Tyler, 1977).

Taylor agreed, and they went about the business of assembling witnesses.

And so we had Democrats and Republicans; we had senators and representatives; we had AAUW; we had the PTA; we had labor; we had manufacturers (Tyler, 1977).

1.10.10 And They Were Successful

There remains a tendency today to say "Well, things are so complicated, we (educational technology scholars) could have little or no influence on the national scene." And the national scene, with the proliferation of computers in the classroom and the threat from the private sector of propri-etary schools, needs our input. In the 60s and 70s, many scholars were trained with monies from the National Defense Education Act, and there was an expectation that this funding would continue. Even though it did not, the field became entrenched in the academy, and there was less need for scholars to be political in the manner of the founders. As we nodded, we became shut out of national educational technology politics. One interpretation of this situation could be that only early innovators are politically effective. Another, although not separate, is that some aspects of national politics were anathema to the securing of tenure.

The rhetoric of the founders and those who follow indi-cate that the basis of this field will always be hardware, with its concomitant marketplace and governmental inter-ests. If we turn away from this, our voices will remain with-in the academy. We will be talking to ourselves. Whatever tempering influence we could have will be lost. Our founders presented us with a good model of action.

1.11 CONCLUSION

That which is valued by the cognoscenti and the practition-ers of a field is expressed in the rhetoric of their writing and speech. Such rhetoric inscribes those definitions, concepts, and theories that they value. That these important terms are based on values, and not on some constant nor objective reality, is uncovered in history, because one can see the manner in which they are always changing and always con-tingent on prevailing beliefs.

The progenitors of this field conducting ground-break-ing research in the 20s were naturally caught up in the refinement of educational studies by the introduction of connectionism and social efficiency principles. These two discourses permeated the social science literature of the decade—a decade of heavy immigration, a decade of expanding wealth. Methods for dealing with these social situations created by the 20s were being suggested by the prevalent discourses, particularly that of social efficiency. Film studies gained stature by joining the dominant dis-courses. Authority for film studies, and ultimately for the audiovisual field, however, became conflated with govern-mental and corporate offices.

That humanistic, Deweyesque discourses became ascen-dant in education, as well as in audiovisual education from the mid-30s, and was also culturally and historically contin-gent. The 30s was a period in which the common person was valorized and governmental agencies mistrusted (note Hollywood cinema and popular novels of the period). Social efficiency ideas, which were hierarchical and sought to control populations, became a subtext to humanism dur-ing this period. The experience and opinions of students and teachers entered the audiovisual discourse, and a multi-plicity of voices were heard.

The field of educational technology, however, as we know it today, garnered rhetorical currency and a berth in the academy with the discourses represented in World War II research, operant conditioning, and military training. That which is valued by scholars is always contingent on cultural norms, and these norms influence theory as well as practice in a field. One of the things that was valued in WWII was the preservation of democracy, and many pro-jects were conflated with that desire. Unfortunately, the methods for accomplishing that preservation at that moment in time were undemocratic, i.e., hierarchical and militaristic. Democratic desires had informed the enterprise of public education just prior to World War II (Apple, 1993). Perhaps audiovisual educators, imbued with democ-ratic values, noted the efficiency and effectiveness of mili-tary pedagogy operating particularly in the service of the preservation of democracy, and were convinced that educa-tion should proceed down the same road.

Nonetheless, a field was established in which many of us have careers. By any measure, the founders were successful. Walter Wittich is cognizant of this fact:

> I just want to say this, that any person who goes through a professional experience and is able to get something done, and is able to have people pay some attention to it, I think is very fortunate. And I consider myself extremely fortunate (Wittich, n.d.).

1.12 THE WOMEN'S STORIES

Within this chapter, we have focused on those people rec-ognized as most prominent historically in the field of edu-cational technology. However, another group of people worked with the field as well, also aspiring to bring educa-tional technology into the mainstream of the educational environment. These are the women of educational technol-ogy, and here are some of their stories. . . .

1.12.1 Introduction

Audiovisual education and ultimately educational technolo-gy was permanently inscribed in schools and training insti-tutions because of its presence in World War II. A small group of men did not allow the World War II years, that specific moment in time when there was a powerful conflu-ence of theory, pedagogy, and technology, to go unnoted.

Charles F. Hoban, Jr., James Finn, Walter A. Wittich, Charles F. Schuller, Kenneth Norberg, Edgar Dale, Lee Cochran, Amo DeBernardis, Frances Noel, John Guy Fowlkes, William Johnson, W. W. Charters, and Robert Gagne, these and other names represented the growth and development of educational technology preceding, during, and after World War II. In the eclectic Division of AudioVi-sual Instruction of the 30s that was peopled by teachers, artists, librarians, filmmakers, principals, and others, women's names were present in the rolls of leaders. The military adventure, however, was almost exclusively male, and audiovisual women were present only as helpmates. Gerda Lerner's insight applies to this era: "Women have been the one group in history longest excluded from political power, and they have, by and large, been excluded from military decision-making" (Lerner, 1979, p. 154). The position of women in the academic realms of educational technology after WWII was no different from the position of women in other educational fields, such as educational psychology. Historically, although women in audiovisual education played major roles, they were often overlooked and/or assigned minor ones. Therefore, we will inform you about some of these prominent women and answer this question: What contributions did women make to the development of the field of educational technology before, during, and after WWII?

1.12.2 Oral and Written Histories

In the 1950s and early 60s, the Archives Committee of the National Education Association, Department of Audio-Visual Instruction, sponsored a series of oral history interviews with audiovisual pioneers in the United States. Recorded on reel-to-reel audiotapes, the interviews follow similar formats. Although no prepared lists of questions have been found for these interviews, all conform to a similar style, taking the interviewee through his or her early days in the visual and/or audiovisual field and into the present 50s and early 60s. Questions asked include: "Didn't you dispute the very term *visual education?*" (Aughinbaugh, 1954); "Well now, just how far back does your interest in visual education go?" (McClusky, 1955); "How far back do you trace your interests in the motion picture?" (Milliken, 1954); and "As a former student of yours, I was always impressed with your ability to relate audiovisual materials to all levels of instruction. What factors or experiences have contributed to this ability?" (Wittich, 1959).

In all, seven interviews are available from this series: Rita Hocheimer, retired acting director of the Bureau of Visual Instruction of the Board of Education, City of New York (1955); B.A. Aughinbaugh, retired head of the Slide and Film Exchange of the Ohio State Education Department (1954); Ellsworth Dent, vice-president of Coronet Films (1961); F. Dean McClusky, professor of education and head of Audio-Visual Education and Extension, UCLA (1955); Bruce Mahan, retired dean of the State University of Iowa Extension Division (1961); Carl E. Milliken, head of Teaching Films Custodian Incorporated (1954); and Walter A. Wittich, professor of education at the University of Wisconsin-Madison (1959).

Additionally, in the mid- to late 1970s, the Educational Communications and Technology Foundation (ECT), which is part of the Association of Educational Communications and Technology (AECT), supported an oral history project. Young educational technologists interviewed and taped leaders from the early days of the formation of the field. An interview schedule was prepared to provide structure to the sessions, but both interviewers and interviewees strayed from the prepared list. The audiotapes consequently are quite rich. Some of the prepared questions were: What sorts of media/materials were predominant in the period prior to World War II? Who were some of the "big names" in the AV field at that time? What were some sources of professional information—textbooks, journals, etc.? Prepared questions concerned with World War II included: What was the name of your (military) position? Principal duties? Was military utilization of training films usually exemplary? Is it true that many of our current practices in film utilization were developed via military research and practice? Post–World War II questions included: Do you know of individuals who received their principal introduction to the media field in the military and later entered school or college AV work after the war? Who were some prominent names in ETV at that time?

The tapes of 1 woman and 12 men were available. Among those interviewed were Elizabeth Golterman, formerly of the St. Louis, Missouri, city school system (1976); Floyde Brooker, former director of the Division of Visual Aids for War Training of the U.S. Office of Education during the World War II years (1975); James W. Brown, San Jose State University (n.d.); Edgar Lee Dale, retired from Ohio State University (1977); C. Louis Forsdale, Teachers' College, Columbia University (1979); L. C. Larson, retired from Indiana University (1977); F. Dean McClusky, former school administrator and director of the Department of Visual Instruction (1980); Kenneth Norberg, retired professor of education at California State University in Sacramento, California (1977); Mendel Sherman, Indiana University (1976); Charles F. Schuller, retired director of the Instructional Media Center at Michigan State University (1978); Warren Stevens, Indiana University (1977); I. Keith Tyler, Ohio State University (1977); and Walt Wittich, professor emeritus at the University of Hawaii (n.d.).

The interviewees were immersed in the culture of their era: pre–World War II, the war years, and post–World War II, and were prominent, in the field of educational technology, over a wide time span, from approximately the 1930s through the 1960s. Social, political, and economic forces of these decades influenced the founders' attitudes, actions, and concerns about men and women and educational technology; women's equity in the workplace was not yet a focus of attention. In some cases, the comments of these founders reflected the position of women in the larger society; in other cases, they recognized and made space for the contributions of women to the formation of the field.

Additionally, we obtained information on early women in the field from a variety of reference books, educational technology textbooks, early audiovisual periodicals, DVI (Department of Visual Instruction, National Education Association) and DAVI (Department of Audio-Visual Instruction, National Education Association) publications, and other print sources.

1.12.3 Women in the Workplace During and After WWII

Although World War II did not revolutionize gender and race relations, it provided many more women, in industry and the military, with high-paid and skilled employment. While World War II was a "milestone" for American women in terms of career and employment, the 1950s found these same women fighting discrimination and sex segregation. Jobs they held during the war were often taken by men coming home. Housework was glamorized in magazines and finally television; women were ambivalent about losing their paid employment (Hewitt, 1990; Baxandall, 1976). The 50s, a period of apathy for many women, were also a time of general malaise in many parts of the U.S. educational community—until 1957. (Sputnik's launch in 1957 encouraged Americans across the nation to support improvement of the nation's education, especially in science, languages, counseling, and media services. Federal funds became available and audiovisual materials were introduced into the curriculum [Hopkins & Butler, 1991]). Women's ambivalence, as the "second sex," was captured during the following decade. The advent of the 1960s found many U.S. women in turmoil; an ideological shift highlighting their equity encouraged women to again work outside the home (Davies, 1974). Within educational technology, these decades were a period of growth for all involved in the profession. When viewed through women's eyes, these decades raise as many questions as they do answers.

1.12.4 Prominent Women: Oral Histories

1.12.3.1. Rita Hocheimer: A former president of the Department of Visual Instruction of the National Education Association and retired assistant director of visual instruction for the New York City Public Schools, Rita Hocheimer was one of the "old-timers" in the field of audiovisual instruction (Golterman, 1976; Lembo, 1970). Interviewed by Alfred E. Devereux, president of IBA House, Inc., Hocheimer states on the audiotape that she began teaching at Washington Irving High School in New York City in 1913. When World War I broke out, she went to France: "In those days, there was no USO. I asked for leave from the school system, which was granted. During the next few months, I lived with various units of the United States Army… we opened a lemonade stand. This was much appreciated by the men…" (Hocheimer, 1955). Hocheimer returned to the United States in 1918. Because of her work with slides and films, as well as her knowledge of French and German, she was assigned part-time to the New York City Schools' Bureau of Visual Instruction and part-time as a language teacher. Within a short period, she became a full-time employee of the Bureau and " . . . began going from school to school actually giving lessons in auditoriums on a weekly schedule" (Hocheimer, 1955). The films she used were commercial ones that she could obtain only by picking them up at 5 a.m. after theaters were through with them. Hocheimer continued in the Bureau of Visual Instruction in New York City, eventually becoming assistant director, a position she held for 25 years. For 20 of those years, she was also acting director. During this 25-year stint, she was active in a number of

audiovisual organizations including: the Academy of Visual Instruction, the New York Metropolitan Visual Instruction Association, and DAVI. People she worked closely with in the audiovisual field included: F. Dean McClusky, Grace Ramsey, and Irene Cypher. Hocheimer's expertise in the field of audiovisual materials was—in her own words—films, first silent and then also sound. Although retired from the New York City schools, Hocheimer was teaching a class in motion picture appreciation at New York University's New School at the time of her interview (Hocheimer, 1955).

1.12.3.2. Elizabeth Golterman: Elizabeth Golterman was one of two females, according to the AECT archives, interviewed during the ECT Oral History Project. She was also the only nonacademic in the group. (She and Professor L. C. Larson were the only two interviewees without Ph.D.s.) Involved in early audiovisual services for the St. Louis, Missouri, city school district, Golterman began in the St. Louis Audiovisual Center (a department specializing in audiovisual materials within the St. Louis school system) in 1930, and always viewed herself as a teacher first and an audiovisual person second. More than any other interviewees of the Oral History Project, Golterman named early women in the profession: Amelia Meissner, Alma Rogers, Lelia Trolinger, Camilla Best, Wanda Daniels, Margaret Devizia, Helen Rachford, Caroline Guss, Anna Hyer, Mickie Bloodworth, Emily Jones, Rita Hocheimer, Etta Schneider, and Bea Harding, among others. Her interviewer asked her how it felt to be a woman in a male-dominated profession:

> Interviewer: "Certainly as a young woman in education, and I hope my male chauvinism doesn't show too much by asking the question. How did you relate to the early administrators who were probably in the mainstream, at the upper level, male? And how do you anticipate the feminist movement for the future?"
>
> Golterman: "Well, I think . . . I certainly didn't feel we were part of any feminist movement back in the 30s when I began here. It is true that our staff had begun as a staff that was headed by a woman and staffed by women, and it continued this. I think largely, because we always had sought outstanding teachers of certain kinds. And the teachers in the St. Louis School System at that period were women teachers, except in the high schools. . . . my answer is that we tried to know our job. We cared a great deal for the teachers, and for the boys and girls, and I think that was the important thing, whether we were men or whether we were women. May I say, I am grateful and think that it is long overdue, to be recognizing some of the blocks that traditionally women have had in many fields. But fortunately, in St. Louis, I think that we had recognition, and we had good support as a department that was staffed by women. And there were some fine ones. I think that it was a privilege to have worked with Amelia Meissner; then the next generation of our associates that included teachers like Nelly Jenkinson, Dorothy Blackwell, Margery Fleming, Gertrude Hofstan, Harriet Bick. These were people that were tops. And I think that the department grew with them and through them" (Golterman, 1976).

Golterman's interviewer also asked her several other questions of interest to the subject of women in the profession:

Interviewer: "What are some names that you can recall from your experience—women nationally—that have made contributions to education, specifically media?"

Golterman: "Well, Cal, when you told me that the most recent AECT convention had had over 9,000 people, I thought back to the days when NEA Audiovisual Department was really held together by just a few loyal people, and when the first meeting I ever attended in St. Louis at the time of an NEA superintendents' meeting, mid-winter meeting, they met in our building. And I don't believe that there could have been more than 40 or 50 people there. In those early years, that I remember it, I think that it was held together by Lelia Trolinger from the University of Colorado; by Camilla Best, who was the New Orleans audiovisual head; by people like the elder Charles Hoban from the state of Pennsylvania; supported by a young Ohio State University man, Edgar Dale. . . .

" . . . Let me run down some of the women that I have had memories and associations with, certainly Miss Trolinger and Miss Best. Wanda Daniels up in Grosse Point, I think was one of the fine ones. Margaret Devizia in Los Angeles; Helen Rachford in Los Angeles County, who was killed in that tragic plane crash on her way to an audiovisual convention up in Minneapolis; Caroline Guss at the University of Indiana; at NEA, Anna Hyer and Mickie Bloodworth; Emily Jones at FWA; Rita Hocheimerr was one of the really old-timers. She headed up the services in New York, when first I came into this picture. Etta Schneider, and then the people here in our own area. Alma Rogers, certainly, and the members of our staff I think I've mentioned. . . . "

1.12.3.3. Margaret Devizia: " . . . now I appeared in the doorway and I didn't know anyone and it was kind of new to me and I felt a little bit shy about the whole thing, because it was mainly run by men and they were sitting around in the chairs in this room and draped over the furniture and having a smoke and a relaxing time and they looked up and one of them saw me in the door and he said to his friend, 'Get up off of that, that's the best chair in the room for God's sake. She's the representative from Los Angeles. She's got the biggest budget in the country' " (Devizia, 1979).

Interviewed in 1979 as part of the ECT Foundation Oral History Project, Margaret Devizia is probably best known as the first female audiovisual specialist in the military during World War II. Devizia began, in the 1930s, as an elementary school teacher in the Los Angeles City Schools, later becoming an audiovisual coordinator for the system. With the advent of World War II, she was approached by Francis Noel who had joined the Navy to direct an audiovisual services unit. Noel asked her to join this unit:

Devizia: " . . . the War came along and Francis Noel, who was in Santa Barbara, was invited by the Navy to come into the Navy to become an audiovisual . . . and I was invited by Francis to join that unit, and I was the only woman. There were 120 people, 120 men in the unit, and I was the only woman in the unit!"

Interviewer: "Where was the unit stationed?"

Devizia: "I went to Washington. Well, first of all, I went to Smith College for six weeks of training, and then I was sent to Washington for another six weeks of training . . . in the central unit there with Francis and the captain of training, and then I was allowed, which was almost unheard of, I was allowed to choose the place where I would work. Since they had only one woman, and some of them didn't know what in the world to do with her in a man's Navy and a man's world, really. I was asked . . . where I would like to go, so I was sent on a trip to a number of cities and was allowed to choose from that trip where I worked. So I decided to go to New York to work, because the captain of training in New York was very enthusiastic about having WAVEs, and that was not always true in the beginning when WAVEs were . . . first inducted into the Navy. So then I went to New York. . . . I had charge of the land schools in New Jersey and Connecticut and New York. . . . I was (the) audiovisuals materials officer. (In addition to the men's schools), I always had the women's training schools. We provided the (audiovisual) material" (Devizia, 1979).

After the war, Devizia returned to Los Angeles and the school audiovisual field. Eventually, she became head of the audiovisual section for the Los Angeles Public Schools and designed and operated a new citywide instructional materials center, which opened in 1962. Both before and after the Second World War, she was active in various audiovisual organizations at the state and national levels. (Elizabeth Golterman spoke of the fact that in early DAVI, she was the only woman until Margaret Devizia came into the picture [Golterman, 1976]). Devizia's strongest media interests were in the realms of educational film and television. "We had so much hope for television. We went into it with so much enthusiasm on the part of everyone as I said" (Devizia, 1979). At the end of her interview, Devizia's interviewer asked her to "… look into the future a little bit and predict some things or make some observations (about what in AV) we still have to look forward to" (Devizia, 1979). Devizia's reply was: "That'll be the day!" (Devizia, 1979).

1.12.4 Prominent Women: Written Histories

Even though little is recorded about women in educational technology, they played a significant role in the establishment of the field, particularly in the years surrounding World War II. Nine prominent women whose careers are recorded elsewhere are Amelia Meissner, Anna Verona Dorris, Etta Schneider, Fannie Dunn, Elizabeth (Betty) Noel, Helen Rachford, Frieda Hennock, Anna Hyer, and Carolyn Guss.

1.12.4.1. Amelia Meissner: Mentioned by Elizabeth Golterman as one of the people who most influenced her in educational technology, Amelia Meissner began the St. Louis School Audiovisual Center in 1904. At that time, it was called the "Educational Museum." The Educational Museum was a result of the Louisiana Purchase Exposition of 1904 (The World's Fair). St. Louis school superintendent, Dr. Soldan, appropriated $1,000.00—a large sum of money at that time—to purchase exhibits from the fair to be kept in St. Louis and used by teachers and students in the public schools. The subsequent large collection of realia was housed in one room and the corridors of one of the city schools, and Meissner, a former upper-grade teacher, was placed in charge of it. She was chosen by Soldan because of a shared hobby in photography (the two had first met on a train and later on a tour of Germany). In 1905, Meissner compiled the first printed catalog of visual materials. It was composed of object collections, sets of lantern slides and stereoscopic view sets. Golterman considers Meissner to be the first audiovisual pioneer in the United States (Golterman, 1976).

1.12.4.2. Anna Verona Dorris: Paul Saettler in *The Evolution of American Educational Technology* first mentions Dorris in a listing of early visual education bureaus in American city schools. He states that she was the director of visual instruction in Berkeley in 1922. Saettler later places her (also in 1922) at San Francisco State College, where she surveyed provisions made for teacher education across the nation in visual instruction. Dorris is also documented as having developed one of the earliest visual instruction course outlines and having written a book (published in 1928) entitled, *Visual Instruction in the Public Schools* (Saettler, 1990, pp. 137, 149, 153, 166). This text, along with an earlier book of Dorris's: *Visual Instruction: Course of Study for the Elementary Schools, Including the Kindergarten and First Six Grades* (1923), was documented and referenced by almost every other published visual or audiovisual textbook author through the 50s. Both are considered benchmarks in the field. In addition to this information, *Leaders in Education* (1941) places Dorris as president of the Department of Visual Instruction of the National Education Association (NEA) from 1927 to 1929.

1.12.4.3. Etta Schneider: We found very little biographical information on Etta Schneider (of Teachers College, Columbia University), other than the fact that she, along with Edgar Dale, Charles, F. Hoban, Jr., and Fannie Dunn (also of Teachers College), wrote the 1937 book, *Motion Pictures in Education: A Summary of the Literature: Source Book for Teachers and Administrators.* This text consists of nonevaluative summaries of articles and books written about educational films. According to its foreword, Schneider was involved in " . . . the bibliographical compilation, digesting and editing of a large amount of the material contained in this volume . . . " (Dale et al., 1937, 5). Schneider is mentioned by Golterman as one of the prominent women in the field (Golterman, 1976).

1.12.4.4. Fannie Dunn: Fannie Dunn was one of the coauthors of *Motion Pictures in Education: A Summary of the Literature: Source Book for Teachers and Administrators.* Along with Etta Schneider, she compiled and wrote three sections of the book: the administration of visual aids, teaching with the motion picture and other visual aids, and teacher preparation in visual education (Dale et al., 1937, pp. 7–8). Like Dorris's books, Motion Pictures in Educa-

tion was often referenced in educational technology books through the 50s.

1.12.4.5. Elizabeth Goudy (Betty) Noel: Another early woman pioneer in educational technology was Elizabeth Goudy (Betty) Noel. One of (Elizabeth) Noel's publications (coauthored with J. Paul Leonard), *Foundations for Teacher Education in Audio-Visual Instruction* (published in 1947), she describes as a " . . . guide for administrators and instructors in colleges and universities planning to include work in audiovisual education in their preservice and in-service teacher education program, and for administrators, supervisors, and directors of audiovisual departments in local school systems in planning in-service education programs" (Noel, 1947, p. iv). Here Noel refers to audiovisual education as

" . . . the carefully planned and integrated use of a wide range of teaching materials from the kindergarten through college . . . [which] includes the use of field trips or excursions, sound and silent motion pictures, television, objects, models, specimens, dioramas, slides, filmstrips, stereographs, study prints, posters, radio programs, recordings, maps, the bulletin board.

Instruction was improved by the use of these materials, she said, and by "life experiences which supplement and clarify the printed word" (Noel, 1947, p. 1). (This supports the life adjustment curriculum discussed previously in this chapter.) Although Noel's husband, Francis, is more well known in educational technology circles, this publication shows that Betty also influenced the field. As with other branches of education, educational technology textbooks were important for both college students and practitioners.

1.12.4.6. Helen Rachford: A former president of the Audiovisual Association of California and of the Film Council of America, Helen Rachford, was also active in DAVI and AECT (she was to assume the vice presidential office at the time of her death), and in several California educational and library organizations. Rachford, a contemporary of Margaret Devizia's (see above), was the Los Angeles County Schools director of the division of Audio-Visual Education. She was killed in a plane crash on her way to the 1958 AECT convention. The AECT Memorial Scholarship Fund, formerly the Helen Rachford Memorial Scholarship Fund, was established in her honor that same year.

1.12.4.7. Frieda Hennock: As first female member of the Federal Communications Commission (she was appointed by President Harry S. Truman in 1948), Frieda Hennock "… had a vision of a national educational television system and played a significant role in the movement toward educational television" (Saettler, 1990, p. 388). Although at first she knew little about broadcasting, Hennock learned rapidly, and was the only FCC commissioner in 1949 to protest the fact that no portion of the television spectrum had been set aside for education. Later, Hennock would be the one to suggest to I. Keith Tyler and Belmont Farley that they retain General Telford Taylor, chief prosecutor of the Nuremburg Trials, as lawyer in their quest to reserve television channels for education [see above] (Tyler, 1977). "She . . . became a kind of Joan of Arc, leading the campaign to reserve television channels for noncommercial educational use . . . [and] . . . she had a good relationship with [President] Harry Truman, which was helpful as well" (Robertson, 1993, pp. 61, 63).

1.12.4.3. Anna Hyer: Considered by Charles Schuller as "One of the great women in our business" (Schuller, 1978), Hyer is probably best noted as executive secretary of DAVI in the mid-50s. Before her tenure at DAVI (post–World War II), she served as assistant in administration at Indiana University under L. C. Larson. Later, she went to Syracuse, where she " . . . became involved in the international area" (Larson, 1977). When DAVI ceased being a part of the National Education Association (NEA), Hyer left DAVI and continued working for NEA. In 1977 she was awarded the AECT Distinguished Service Award in recognition of her contributions to the field (Larson, 1977).

1.12.4.9. Carolyn Guss: Carolyn Guss, according to various volumes of *Who's Who in American Education,* was (1960s) a professor of education at Indiana University in Bloomington, Indiana, where she taught administration of media and research. She was also active in the Audiovisual Department of NEA and various other audiovisual organizations, holding several administrative posts within these groups. In addition, she is one of the authors of the 1961 book *Guide to Newer Educational Media.*

1.13 CONCLUSION

A couple of decades after World War II, women in educational technology, as well as in other fields, rebelled against the "feminine mystique" and sought to gain equity in existing political, social, and economic structures in the United States. Although women in educational technology became more prominent, the placement of women in this field is still uneven today, as is the position of women in other areas of the academy, such as educational administration. The women mentioned above are just a few of the female contributors to the field of educational technology. There are others. Today, women continue working towards equal recognition, opportunity, and responsibility within educational technology.

REFERENCES

Apple, M.W. (1993). *Official knowledge: democratic education in a conservative age.* New York: Routledge.

— (1986). *Teachers and texts: a political economy of class and gender relations in education.* New York: Routledge & Kegan Paul.

Arnspiger, V.C. *In* E. Dale, F. W. Dunn, C. F. Hoban Jr. & E. Schneider (1937). *Motion pictures in education: a summary of the literature: source book for teachers and administrators,* 336. New York: Wilson.

Baxandall, R., Gordon, L. & Reverby, S. (1976). *America's working women.* New York: Vintage.

Becker, A. (1977). Alternate methodologies for instructional methods research. *Audiovisual Communication Review,* Summer, 181–94.

Becker, A. (1987). Instructional television and the talking Head. *Educational Technology,* Oct., 35-40.

Bell, R., Cain, L., Lamaroeaux, L., et al. (1942). Motion pictures in a modern curriculum, a report of the use of films in the Santa Barbara Schools. Washington, DC: American Council on Education.

Benjamin, W. (1968). *Illuminations.* New York: Harcourt, Brace.

Borradori, G. (1994). *The American philosopher.* Chicago, IL; University of Chicago Press.

Bove, P. (1992). *Mastering discourse.* Durham, NC: Duke University Press.

Brooker, F. (1975, Apr). Interview.

— & Herrington, E. (1942). Students make motion pictures, a report on film production in the Denver public schools. Washington, DC: American Council on Education.

Brown, J., Lewis, R. & Harcleroad, F. (1959). A-V instruction, materials and methods. New York: McGraw-Hill.

— (n.d.) Interview with Ron McBeth.

Brubacher, J. & Rudy, W. (1968). *Higher education in transition.* New York: Harper & Row.

Bureau of Naval Personnel (1947). *Photography,* Vol. 1. Washington, DC: United States Government Printing Office.

— (1947). *Photography,* Vol. 2. Washington, DC: United States Government Printing Office.

Cattell, J.M., Cattell, J. & Ross, E. E. (1941). *Leaders in education: a biographical directory.* New York: Science Press.

Chambers, M. (1948). Opinions on gains for American education from wartime armed services training. Washington, DC: American Council on Education.

Clark, R.E. & Salamon, G. (1986). Media in teaching. *In* M.C. Wittrock, ed. *The third handbook of research on teaching,* 468. Chicago, IL: Macmillan.

Cochran, B. (1942). *Films on war and American policy.* Washington, DC: American Council on Education.

Consitt, F. (1937). *In* E. Dale, F.W. Dunn, C.F. Hoban Jr. & E. Schneider (1937). *Motion pictures in education: a summary of the literature: source book for teachers and administrators,* 309. New York: Wilson.

Cook, R.C. & McDuff, M. (1968). *Who's who in American education.* Hattiesburg, MS: Who's Who in American Education.

Curtis, B. (1992). *True government by choice men?: inspection, education, and state formation in Canada west.* Toronto: University of Toronto Press.

Dale, E.L. (1977, Mar.). Interview with John C. Belland.

— (1946). *Audio-visual methods in teaching.* New York: Dryden.

— F.W. Dunn, C.F. Hoban Jr. & E. Schneider (1937). *Motion pictures in education: a summary of the literature: source book for teachers and administrators.* New York: Wilson.

Davies, M. (1974). *Woman's place is at the typewriter.* Cambridge, UK: Radical America.

DeVaney, A. (1990). Rules of evidence. *Journal of Thought 25* (172), 6–1.

Devereux, F. (1933). *The educational talking picture*. Chicago, IL : University of Chicago Press.

ECT Foundation. (1993). 1994 AECT Memorial Scholarships Information Paper. Washington, DC: ECT Foundation.

Fearing, F. (1950). *Motion pictures as a medium of instruction; an experimental analysis of the effects of two films*. Berkeley, CA : University of California Press.

Fenton, W.N. (1947). *Area studies in American universities*. Washington, DC: American Council on Education.

Forsdale, C.L. (1979, May). Interview with Bill Hugg.

Foucault, M. (1977). *Discipline and punish: the birth of the prison*. New York: Pantheon.

Frauens, M. (1948). *Improving textbooks the army and navy way*. Washington, DC: American Council on Education.

Freeman, F., ed. (1924). *Visual education: a comparative study of motion pictures and other methods of instruction*. Chicago, IL: University of Chicago Press.

Freeman, F.N., E.H. Reeder & J.A. Thomas (1924). An experiment to study the effectiveness of a motion picture film which consists largely of tables, maps, and charts as a means of teaching facts or giving abstract information. *In* F. Freeman et al. *Visual education: a comparative study of motion pictures and other methods of instruction*, 258–74. Chicago, IL: University of Chicago Press.

—(1922). Research versus propaganda in visual education. *Journal of Educational Psychology 13* (5), 257–66.

Gagne, R. & Briggs, L. (1965). *The conditions of learning*. New York: Rinehart & Winston.

Garce, A., et al. (1947). *Educational lessons from wartime training*. Washington, DC: American Council on Education.

Gluck, S.B. (1987). *Rosie the riveter revisited*. Boston, MA: Twayne.

Golterman, E. (1976, May). Interview with Calvin Owens.

Goodman, S. (1948). *Curriculum implications of armed services training*. Washington, DC: American Council on Education.

Guthrie, E.R. (1950). *The psychology of human conflict: the clash of motives within the individual*. New York: Smith.

Hewitt, N.A. (1990). *Women, families, and communities*. Glenview, IL : Scott, Foresman/Little, Brown Higher Education.

Hilgard, E.R. (1948). *Unconscious processes and man's rationality*. Urbana, IL.

Hoban, Jr., C. (1942). *Focus on learning*. Washington DC: American Council on Education, Committee on Motion Pictures in Education.

— & vanOrmer, E. (1951). Instructional film research 1918–1950 (Technical Report No. SDC 269-7-29). Port Washington, NY: Department of Commerce, Office of Technical Services, Special Devices Center.

Hopkins, D.M. & Butler, R.P. (1991). *The federal roles in support of school library media centers*. Chicago, IL: American Library Association.

Hoveland, C., Lumsdaine, A. & Sheffield. (1949). *Experiments on mass communication*. Princeton, NJ: Princeton University Press.

Hull, C. (1928). *Aptitude testing*. Yonkers on the Hudson, New York: World Book.

Kinder, J. (1950). *Audio-visual materials and techniques*. New York: American Book.

Kliebard, H.M. (1987). *The struggle for the American curriculum 1893–1958*. New York: Routledge.

Knowlton, D. & Tilton, J. (1929). *Motion pictures in history teaching*. New Haven, CT: Yale University Press.

Koon, C. (1934). Motion pictures in education in the United States, a report compiled for the International Congress of Educational and Instructional Cinematography. Chicago, IL: University of Chicago Press.

Lacy, J. (1919). The relative value of motion pictures as an educational agency. *Teachers College Record 20*, 452–65.

Larson, O. (1977). Interview with Bob Heinich.

Lerner, G. (1979). *The majority finds its past: placing women in history*. New York: Oxford University Press.

McClusky, F.D. (1924). Comparisons of different methods of visual instruction, and comparisons of six modes of presentation of the subject matter contained in a film on the iron and steel industry and one on lumbering in the north woods. *In* N. Freeman et al. *Visual Education*. Chicago, IL : University of Chicago Press.

— (1950). *The A-V bibliography*. Dubuque: Brown.

— (1955). *The A-V bibliography* (rev. ed.). Dubuque, IA: Brown.

— (1980). Interview with Bob Heinich.

— (1931). *Visual instruction: its value and need*. New York: Mancall.

McKown, H.C. & Roberts, A.B. (1949). *Audio-visual aids to instruction*. New York: McGraw-Hill.

Maillioux, S. (1989). *Rhetorical power*. Ithaca, NY: Cornell University Press.

Meierhenry, W.C. (1952). *Enriching the curriculum through motion pictures*. Lincoln, NE: University of Nebraska Press.

Mertz, N.T. & S.R. McNeely, (1990). *Getting to be a professor of educational administration: a study of how females "got" the job*. Boston, MA: American Educational Research Association.

Miles, J. R., & C.R. Spain, (1947). *Audio-visual aids in the armed services*. Washington, DC: American Council on Education.

Miller, N. & J. Dollard, (1941). *Social learning and imitation*. New Haven, CT: Yale University Press.

— et al. (1957). Graphic communication and the crisis in education. AVCR, 1-120.

Morrison, T. (1992). *Playing in the dark*. Cambridge, MA: Harvard University Press.

Motion Picture Project with the assistance of the Pan American Union (1942). *The other Americas through films and records*. Washington, DC: American Council on Education.

National Society for the Study of Education (1949). *The forty-eighth yearbook: part I: audio-visual materials of instruction*. Chicago, IL : University of Chicago Press.

(1960). *New teaching aids for the American classroom*. Palo Alto, CA: Stanford University, Institute for Communication Research.

Nichols, B. (1981). *Ideology and the image: social representation in the cinema and other media*. Bloomington, IN: Indiana University Press.

Noel, E.G. & Leonard, J.P. (1947). *Foundations for teacher education in audio-visual instruction*. Washington, DC: American Council On Education Studies.

Noel, F. (1942). Projecting motion pictures in the classroom. Washington, DC: American Council on Education.

Norberg, K. (1977, Apr.). Interview with Charles J. Vento.

Perkinson, H.J. (1968). *The imperfect panacea: American faith in education, 1865–1965.* New York: Random House.

Peterson, R. & Thurstone, L. (1933). *Motion pictures and the social attitudes of children.* New York: Macmillan.

Pounder, D. (1988). *Male/female salary disparity for professors of educational administration.* New Orleans, LA: American Educational Research Association.

Rooney, E. (1989). *Seductive reasoning.* Ithaca, NY: Cornell University Press.

Rulon, J. (1933). *The sound motion picture in science teaching. Cambridge,* MA: Harvard University Press.

Saettler, L.P. (1990). *The evolution of American educational technology.* Englewood, NJ: Libraries Unlimited,

Schuller, C.F. (1978, Feb.). Interview with Don Ely. *See and Hear 1,* (1).

— (1942). *Selected educational motion pictures: a descriptive encyclopedia.* Washington, DC: American Council on Education.

Sherman, M. (1976, Oct.). Interview with Michael Molenda.

Short, P.M., et al. (1989). *Women professors of educational administration: a profile and salient issues.* San Francisco, CA: American Educational Research Association.

Smith, B. (1942). *In* H.M. Kliebard (1987). *The struggle for the American curriculum 1893–1958,* 240. New York: Routledge.

— (1942). The War and the educational program. *Curriculum Journal* 13, 113–16.

Staff of the Tower Hill School (1942). *A school uses motion pictures.* Washington, DC: American Council on Education.

Stevens, W. (1977, Feb.). Interview with Michael Molenda.

Sumstine, D. (1918). A comparative study of visual instruction in the high school. *School and Society* 7, 235–38.

Symposium on the State of Research in Instructional Television and Tutorial Machines. (1959). *New teaching aids for the American classroom.* Stanford, CA: Institute for Communication Research, Stanford University.

Taylor, F.W. (1911). *The principles of scientific management.* New York: Harper & Brothers.

Thorndike. E. (1910). The contribution of psychology to education. *Journal of Educational Psychology 1* (1), 5–12.

Thurstone, L. & Peterson, R. (1933). *Motion pictures and the social attitudes of children.* New York: Macmillan.

Turkle, S. (1984). *The good war.*

Tuttle, W.M. (1993). *Daddy's gone to war: the Second World War in the lives of America's children.* New York: Oxford University Press.

Twyford, L. & C. Seitz (1956). *Instructional television research reports.* Port Washington, NY: U.S. Naval Training Device Center.

Tyler, K. (1977, Jun.). Interview with John Belland.

Vandermeer, A. (1954). Color and black and white in instructional films. *Audio-Visual Communication Review 2* (2), 121–34.

Weaver, G.G. & E.W. Bollinger (1949). *Visual aids: their construction and use.* New York: Van Nostrand.

Weber, J.J. (1922). *Comparative effectiveness of some visual aids in seventh grade instruction: the educational screen.*

— (1930). *Visual aids in education.* Valpariso, IN: Valparaiso University.

Westfall, L. (1937) E. Dale, F.W. Dunn, C.F. Hoban Jr. & E. Schneider (1937). *Motion pictures in education: a summary of the literature: source book for teachers and administrators,* 336. New York: Wilson.

Wise, H. (1939). *Motion pictures as an aid in teaching American history in the senior high school.* New Haven, CT : Yale University Press.

Wittich, W. (n.d.) Interview with Lillian Lum.

— & Schuller, C. (1953). *Audio-visual materials: their nature and use.* New York: Harper & Brothers.

Wood, B. & Freeman, F. (1929) *Motion pictures in the classroom.* Boston, MA : Houghton Mifflin.

2. BEHAVIORISM AND INSTRUCTIONAL TECHNOLOGY

John K. Burton   **David M. (Mike) Moore**   **Susan G. Magliaro**

VIRGINIA POLYTECHNIC INSTITUTE

In 1913, John Watson's *Psychology as the Behaviorist Views It* put forth the notion that psychology did not have to use terms such as *consciousness*, *mind*, or *images*. In a real sense, Watson's work became the opening round in a battle that the behaviorists dominated for nearly 60 years. During that period, behavioral psychology (and education) taught little about cognitive concerns, paradigms, etc. For a brief moment as cognitive psychology eclipsed behavioral theory (see 5.2.3), the commonalties between the two orientations were evident (see, e.g., Neisser, 1967, 1976). To the victors, however, go the spoils, and the rise of cognitive psychology has meant the omission, or in some cases misrepresentation, of behavioral precepts from current curricula. With that in mind, this chapter has three main goals. First, it is necessary to revisit some of the underlying assumptions of the two orientations and review some basic behavioral concepts. Second, we examine the research on instructional technology to illustrate the impact of behavioral psychology on the tools of our field. Finally, we conclude the chapter with an epilogue.

2.1 THE MIND/BODY PROBLEM

> The Western mind is European, the European mind is Greek; the Greek mind came to maturity in the city of Athens (Needham, 1978, p. 98).

The intellectual separation between mind and nature is traceable back to 650 BC and the very origins of philosophy itself. It certainly was a centerpiece of Platonic thought by the fourth century BC. Plato's student Aristotle ultimately separated mind from body (Needham, 1978). In modern times, it was René Descartes who reasserted the duality of mind and body and connected them at the pineal gland. The body was made of physical matter that occupied space; the mind was composed of "animal spirits," and its job was to think and control the body. The connection at the pineal gland made your body yours. While it would not be accurate to characterize current cognitivists as Cartesian dualists, it would be appropriate to characterize them as believers of what Churchland (1990) has called *popular dualism* (p. 91); that the "person" or mind is a "ghost in the machine." Current notions often place the "ghost" in a social group. It is this "ghost" (in whatever manifestation) that Watson objected to so strenuously. He saw thinking and hoping as things we *do* (Malone, 1990). He believed that when stimuli, biology, and responses are removed, the residual is not mind, it is nothing. As self-proclaimed mentalist William James (1904) wrote, " . . . but breath, which was ever the original 'spirit,' breath moving outwards, between the glottis and the nostrils, is, I am persuaded, the essence out of which philosophers have constructed the entity known to them as consciousness" (p. 478).

The view of mental activities as actions (e.g., "thinking is talking to ourself," Watson, 1919), as opposed to their being considered indications of the presence of a consciousness or mind as a separate entity, are central differences between the behavioral and cognitive orientations. According to Malone (1990), the goal of psychology from the behavioral perspective has been clear since Watson:

> We want to predict with reasonable certainty what people will do in specific situations. Given a stimulus, defined as an object of inner or outer experience, what response may be expected? A stimulus could be a blow to the knee or an architect's education; a response could be a knee jerk or the building of a bridge. Similarly, we want to know, given a response, what situation produced it. . . . In all such situations the discovery of the stimuli that call out one or another behavior should allow us to influence the occurrence of

We are deeply indebted to Dr. George Gropper and Dr. John "Coop" Cooper for their reviews of early versions of this manuscript. George was particularly helpful in reviewing the sections on methodological behaviorism, and Coop for his analysis of the sections on radical behaviorism and enormously useful suggestions. Thanks to Dr. David Jonassen for helping us reconcile their conflicting advice in the area that each did not prefer.

behaviors; prediction, which comes from such discoveries, allows control. What does the analysis of conscious experience give us? (p. 97).

Such notions caused Bertrand Russell to claim that Watson made "the greatest contribution to scientific psychology since Aristotle" (as cited in Malone, 1990, p. 96) while others called him the " . . . simpleton or archfiend . . . who denied the very existence of mind and consciousness (and) reduced us to the status of robots" (p. 96). Related to the issue of mind/body dualism are the emphases on structure versus function and/or evolution and/or selection.

2.1.1 Structuralism, Functionalism, and Evolution

> The battle cry of the cognitive revolution is "mind is back!" A great new science of mind is born. Behaviorism nearly destroyed our concern for it but behaviorism has been overthrown, and we can take up again where the philosophers and early psychologists left off (Skinner, 1989, p. 22).

Structuralism (see 5.3.1) also can be traced through the development of philosophy at least to Democritus's "heated psychic atoms" (Needham, 1978). Plato divided the soul/mind into three distinct components in three different locations: the impulsive/instinctive component in the abdomen and loins, the emotional/spiritual component in the heart, and the intellectual/reasoning component in the brain. In modern times, Wundt at Leipzig and Titchner (his student) at Cornell espoused structuralism as a way of investigating consciousness. Wundt proposed ideas, affect, and impulse, and Titchner proposed sensations, images, and affect as the primary elements of consciousness. Titchner eventually identified over 50,000 mental elements (Malone, 1990). Both relied heavily on the method of introspection (to be discussed later) for data. Cognitive notions such as schema, knowledge structures, duplex memory, etc., are structural explanations. There are no behavioral equivalents to structuralism because it is an aspect of mind/consciousness.

Functionalism, however, is a philosophy shared by both cognitive and behavioral theories. Functionalism is associated with John Dewey and William James who stressed the adaptive nature of activity (mental or behavioral) as opposed to structuralism's attempts to separate consciousness into elements. In fact, functionalism allows for an infinite number of physical and mind structures to serve the same functions. Functionalism has its roots in Darwin's *Origin of the Species* (1859) and Wittgenstein's *Philosophical Investigations* (Malcolm, 1954). The question, of course, is the focus of adaptation: mind or behavior. The behavioral view is, of course, that evolutionary forces and adaptations are no different for humans than for the first one-celled organisms; that organisms since the beginning of time have been vulnerable and, therefore, had to learn to discriminate and avoid those things that were harmful and discriminate and approach those things necessary to sustain themselves

(Goodson, 1973). This, of course, is the heart of the selectionist position long advocated by B. F. Skinner (1969, 1978, 1981, 1987a, 1987b, 1990).

The selectionist (Chiesa, 1992; Pennypacker, 1992, 1994; and Vargas, 1993) approach "emphasizes investigating changes in behavioral repertoires over time" (Johnson & Layng, 1992, p. 1475). Selectionism is related to evolutionary theory in that it views the complexity of behavior to be a function of selection contingencies found in nature (Donahoe, 1991; Donahoe & Palmer, 1989; Layng, 1991; Skinner, 1969, 1981, 1990). As Johnson and Layng (1992) point out, this "perspective is beginning to spread beyond the studies of behavior and evolution to the once structuralist-dominated field of computer science, as evidenced by the emergence of parallel distributed processing theory (McClelland & Rumelhart, 1986; Rumelhart & McClelland, 1986) and adaptive networks research" (Donahoe, 1991; Donahoe & Palmer, 1989, p. 1475).

2.1.2 Introspection and Constructivism

Constructivism (see 7.3.1, 12.3.1.1) the notion that meaning (reality) is made, is currently touted as a new way of looking at the world. In fact, there is nothing in any form of behaviorism that requires realism, naive or otherwise. The constructive nature of perception (see 16.2.1) has been accepted at least since von Helmholtz (1866) and his notion of "unconscious inference." Basically, von Helmholtz (see 26.2) believed that much of our experience depends on inferences drawn on the basis of a little stimulation and a lot of past experience. Most, if not all, current theories of perception rely on von Helmholtz's ideas as a base (Malone, 1990). The question is not whether perception is constructive but what to make of these constructions and where do they come from. Cognitive psychology draws heavily on introspection to "see" the "stuff" of construction.

In modern times, introspection was a methodological cornerstone of Wundt, Titchner, and the Gestaltist (see 5.1), Külpe (Malone, 1990). Introspection generally assumes a notion espoused by John Mill (1829) that thoughts are linear, that ideas follow each other one after another. Although it can (and has) been argued that ideas do not flow in straight lines, a much more serious problem confronts introspection on its face. Introspection relies on direct experience, that our "mind's eye" or inner observation reveals things as they are. We know, however, that our other senses do not operate that way.

> The red surface of an apple does not *look* like a matrix of molecules reflecting photons at a certain critical wavelength, but that is what it is. The sound of a flute does not *sound* like a sinusoidal compression wave train in the atmosphere, but that is what it is. The warmth of the summer air does not feel like the mean kinetic energy of millions of molecules, but that is what it is. If one's pains and hopes and beliefs do not *introspectively* seem like electrochemical states in a neural network, that may be only because our faculty of introspection, like our other senses,

is not sufficiently penetrating to reveal such hidden details. Which is just what we would expect anyway . . . unless we can somehow argue that the faculty of introspection is quite different from all other forms of observation (Churchland, 1990, p. 15).

Obviously, the problems with introspection become more problematic in retrospective paradigms, that is, when the learner/performer is asked to work from a behavior to a thought. This poses a problem on two counts: accuracy and causality. In terms of accuracy, James Angell stated his belief in his 1907 APA presidential address:

> No matter how much we may talk of the preservation of psychical dispositions, nor how many metaphors we may summon to characterize the storage of ideas in some hypo-thetical deposit chamber of memory, the obstinate fact remains that when we are not experiencing a sensation or an idea it is, strictly speaking, non-existent. . . . [W]e have no guarantee that our second edition is really a replica of the first; we have a good bit of presumptive evidence that from the content point of view the original never is and never can be literally duplicated (Herrnstein & Boring, 1965, p. 502).

The causality problem is perhaps more difficult to grasp at first, but, in general, behaviorists have less trouble with "heated" data (self-reports of mental activities at the moment of behaving) that reflect "doing in the head" and "doing in the world" at the same time than with going from behavior to descriptions of mental thought, ideas, or structures and then *saying* that the mental activity *caused* the behavior. In such cases of course, it is equally likely that the behavioral activities caused the mental activities.

A more current view of constructivism, social construc-tivism, focuses on the making of meaning through social interaction. In the words of Garrison (1994), meanings "are sociolinguistically constructed between two selves partici-pating in a shared understanding" (p. 11). This, in fact, is perfectly consistent with the position of behaviorists (see, for example, Skinner, 1974) as long as this does not also imply the substitution of a group of rather than an individ-ual "mind." Garrison, a Deweyian scholar, is, in fact, also a self-proclaimed behaviorist.

2.1.2.1. Behavioral and Cognitive Differences That Affect Instructional Design and Research.
In fact, behav-ioral and cognitive perspectives are not as far apart as it may appear (Slocum & Butterfield, 1994). Behaviorists have become more concerned with mental activities or "coverants," and cognitivists, although still interested in representations, are increasingly concerned with activities or behaviors in contexts, as well as the role of social feed-back. In a practical sense the differences are more a matter of emphases. Behaviorists like activities and dislike infer-ences (and inferential statistics; see, e.g., Michael, 1974), whereas cognitivists like representations and are willing to take bigger "leaps." Arguments such as: Cognitive psychol-ogy assumes more "active learners" (see 12.3.1.1) and behaviorists more "passive learners," or that behaviorism seeks to control behaviors while cognitivists seek to control

thoughts or "thought structures," make little sense and con-tribute little. Similarly, the idea that anyone, from any orientation, can design any activity that prohibits "con-struction" based on prior experience is false. Finally, although it is perhaps a central assumption in the early works of "methodological" behaviorists, logical positivism is not an essential or even widespread foundation for behaviorism any more than for cognitivists or construc-tivists. Behaviorists have always resisted inferential statis-tics, for example, in favor of description (e.g., Michael, 1974). Indeed, one of the criticisms of behavioral psycholo-gy is that it is too reliant on description (Malone, 1990).

2.2 THE BASICS OF BEHAVIORISM

Behaviorism in the United States may be traced to the work of E. B. Twitmyer (1902), a graduate student at the Uni-versity of Pennsylvania, and E. L. Thorndike (1898). Twit-myer's doctoral dissertation research on the knee-jerk (patellar) reflex involved alerting his participants with a bell that a hammer was about to strike their patellar tendon. As has been the case so many times in the history of the development of behavioral theory (see, for example, Skin-ner, 1956), something went wrong. Twitmyer sounded the bell, but the hammer did not trip. The participant, however, made a knee-jerk response in *anticipation* of the hammer drop. Twitmyer redesigned his experiment to study this phenomenon and presented his findings at the annual meet-ing of the American Psychological Association in 1904. His paper, however, was greeted with apathy, and it fell to Ivan Pavlov (1849–1936) to become the "Father of Classical Conditioning." Interestingly enough, Pavlov also began his line of research based on a casual or accidental observation. A Nobel Prize winner for his work in digestion, Pavlov noted that his subjects (dogs) seemed to begin salivating to the sights and sounds of feeding. He too altered the thrust of his research to investigate his serendipitous observations more thoroughly.

Operant or instrumental conditioning is usually associat-ed (particularly by educators) with B. F. Skinner. Yet, in 1898, E. L. Thorndike published a monograph on animal intelligence which made use of a "puzzle box" (a forerun-ner of what is often called a "Skinner Box") to investigate the effect of reward (e.g., food, escape) on the behavior of cats. Thorndike placed the cats in a box that could be opened by pressing a latch or pulling a string. Outside the box was a bowl of milk or fish. Not surprisingly, the cats tried anything and everything until they stumbled onto the correct response. Also, not surprisingly, the cats learned to get out of the box more and more rapidly. From these beginnings, the most thoroughly researched phenomenon in psychology evolves.

Behavioral theory is now entering its ninth decade. The pioneering work of such investigators as Mateer (1918), Watson and Rayner (1920), Cason (1922a, 1922b), and Liddell (1926) in classical conditioning, and Blodgett (1929), Hull (1943), Skinner (1938), and Hebb (1949) in operant conditioning has led to the development of the most powerful technology known to behavioral science. Behaviorism, however, is in a paradoxical place in American education today. In a very real sense, behavioral theory is the basis for innovations such as teaching machines, computer-assisted instruction, competency-based education (mastery learning), instructional design, minimal competency testing, "educational accountability," situated cognition, and even social constructivism, (see Chapter 7), yet behaviorism is no longer a "popular" orientation in education or instructional design. An exploration of behaviorism, its contributions to research and current practice in educational technology (despite its recent unpopularity), and its usefulness in the future are the concerns of this chapter.

2.2.1 BASIC ASSUMPTIONS AND CONCEPTS

Behavioral psychology has provided instructional technology with several basic assumptions, concepts, and principles. These components of behavioral theory are outlined in this section (albeit briefly) in order to ensure that the discussion of its applications can be clearly linked back to the relevant behavioral theoretical underpinnings. While some or much of the following discussion may be elementary for many, we believed it was crucial to lay the groundwork that illustrates the major role behavioral psychology has played and *continues* to play in the research and development of instructional technology applications.

Three major assumptions are directly relevant to instructional technology. These assumptions focus on the following: the role of the learner, the nature of learning, and the generality of the learning processes and instructional procedures.

2.2.1.1. The Role of the Learner. As mentioned earlier in this chapter, one of the most misinterpreted (misrepresented) assumptions of behavioral learning theory concerns the role of the learner. Quite often, the learner is characterized as a passive entity who merely reacts to environmental stimuli (cf. Anderson's receptive-accrual model, 1986). However, according to B. F. Skinner, knowledge is action (Schnaitter, 1987). Skinner (1968) stated that a learner "does not passively absorb knowledge from the world around him but must play an active role" (p. 5). He goes on to explain how learners learn by doing, experiencing, and engaging in trial and error. All three of these components work together and must be studied together to formulate any given instance of learning. It is only when these three components are describable that we can identify what has been learned, under what conditions the learning has taken place, and the consequences that support and maintain the learned behavior. The emphasis is on the active responding of the learner. The learner must be engaged in the behavior in order to learn and to validate that learning has occurred.

2.2.1.2. The Nature of Learning. Learning is frequently defined as a change in behavior due to experience. It is a function of building associations between the occasion on which the behavior occurs (stimulus events) and the

behavior itself (response events). These associations are centered in the experiences that produce learning, and differ to the extent to which they are *contiguous* and *contingent* (Chance, 1994). *Contiguity* refers to the close pairing of stimulus and response in time and/or space. *Contingency* refers to the dependency between the antecedent or behavioral event and either the response or consequence. Essential to the strengthening responses with these associations is the repeated continuous pairing of the stimulus with response and the pairing consequences (Skinner, 1968). It is the construction of functional relationships based on the contingencies of reinforcement under which the learning takes place. It is this functionality that is the essence of selection. Stimulus control develops as a result of continuous pairing with consequences (functions). In order to truly understand what has been learned, the entire relationship must be identified (Vargas, 1977). All components of this three-part contingency (i.e., functional relationship) must be observable and measurable to ensure the scientific verification that learning (i.e., a change of behavior) has occurred (Cooper, Heron & Heward, 1987).

Of particular importance to instructional technology is the need to focus on the individual in this learning process. Contingencies vary from person to person based on each individual's genetic and reinforcement histories and events present at the time of learning (Gagné, 1985). This requires designers and developers to ensure that instruction is aimed at aiding the learning of the individual (e.g., Gagné, Briggs & Wager, 1992). To accomplish this, a needs assessment (Burton & Merrill, 1991) or front-end analysis (Mager, 1984; Smith & Ragan, 1993) is conducted at the very beginning of the instructional design process. The focus of this activity is to articulate, among other things, learner characteristics; that is, the needs and capabilities of individual learners are assessed to ensure that the instruction being developed is appropriate and meaningful. The goals are then written in terms of what the learner will accomplish via this instructional event.

The material to be learned must be identified in order to understand clearly the requisite nature of learning. There is a natural order inherent in many content areas. Much of the information within these content areas is characterized in sequences; however, many form a network or a tree of related information (Skinner, 1968). Complex learning involves becoming competent in a given field by learning incremental behaviors that are ordered in these sequences, traditionally with very small steps, ranging from the simplest to more complex to the final goal. Two major considerations occur in complex learning. The first, as just mentioned, is the gradual elaboration of extremely complex patterns of behavior. The second involves the maintenance of the behavior in strength through the use of reinforcement contingent on successful achievement at each stage. Implicit in this entire endeavor to the observable nature of actual learning, public performance is crucial for the acknowledgment, verification (by self and/or others), and continued development of the present in similar behaviors.

2.2.1.3. The Generality of Learning Principles.
According to behavioral theory, all animals—including human beings—obey universal laws of behavior (Davey, 1981). All habits are formed from conditioned reflexes (Watson, 1924) or as a result of the experienced consequences of the organisms' behavior (Skinner, 1971). While Skinner (1969) does acknowledge species-specific behavior (e.g., adaptive mechanisms, differences in sensory equipment, effector systems, reactions to different reinforcers), he stands by the fact that the basic processes that promote or inhibit learning are universal of all organisms. Specifically, he states that the research does show an

> extraordinary uniformity over a wide range of reinforcement; the processes of extinction, discrimination, and generalization return remarkably similar and consistent results across species. For example, fixed-interval reinforcement schedules yield a predictable scalloped performance effect (low rates of responding at the beginning of the interval following reinforcement, high rates of responding at the end of the interval) whether the subjects are animals or humans" (Ferster & Skinner, 1957, p. 78).

Behavioral theory has contributed several important concepts and principles to the research and development of instructional technology. Three major types of behavior—respondent learning, operant learning, and observational learning—serve as the organizer for this section. Each of these models relies on building associations—the simplest unit that is learned—under the conditions of contiguity and repetition (Gagné, 1985). Each model also utilizes the processes of discrimination and generalization to describe the mechanisms humans use to adapt to situational and environmental stimuli (Chance, 1994). Discrimination is the act of responding differently to different stimuli, such as stopping at a red traffic light while driving through a green traffic light. Generalization is the act of responding in the same way to similar stimuli, specifically to those stimuli not present at time of training. For example, students generate classroom behavior rules based on previous experiences and expectations in classroom settings. Or, when one is using a new word-processing program, the individual attempts to apply what is already known about a word-processing environment to the new program. In essence, discrimination and generalization are inversely related, crucial processes that facilitate adaptation, and enable transfer to new environments.

2.2.1.3.1. Respondent Learning.   Involuntary actions, called *respondents*, are entrained using the classical conditioning techniques of Ivan Pavlov. In classical conditioning, an organism learns to respond to a stimulus that once prompted no response. The process begins with identification and articulation of an unconditional stimulus (US) that automatically elicits an emotional or physiological unconditional response (UR). No prior learning or conditioning is required to establish this natural connection (e.g., US = food; UR = salivation). In classical conditioning, a neutral stimulus is introduced, which initially prompts no response from the organism (e.g., a tone). The intent is to eventually have the tone (i.e., the conditioned stimulus or CS) elicit a

response that very closely approximates the original UR (i.e., will become the conditional response or CR). The behavior is entrained using the principles of contiguity and repetition (i.e., practice). In repeated trials, the US and CS are introduced at the same time or in close temporal proximity. Gradually the US is presented less frequently with the CS, being sure to retain the performance of the UR/CR. Ultimately, the CS elicits the CR without the aid of the US.

Classical conditioning is a very powerful tool for entraining basic physiological responses (e.g., increases in blood pressure, taste aversions, psychosomatic illness), and emotive responses (e.g., arousal, fear, anxiety, pleasure) since the learning is paired with reflexive, inborn associations. Classical conditioning is a major theoretical notion underlying advertising, propaganda, and related learning (see 7.4). Its importance in the formations of biases, stereotypes, etc., is of particular importance in the design of instructional materials and should always be considered in the design process.

The incidental learning of these responses is clearly a concern in instructional settings. Behaviors such as test anxiety and "school phobia" are maladaptive behaviors that are entrained without intent. From a proactive stance in instructional design, a context or environmental analysis is a key component of a needs assessment (Tessmer, 1990). Every feature of the physical (e.g., lighting, classroom arrangement) and support (e.g., administration) environment are examined to ascertain positive or problematic factors that might influence the learner's attitude and level of participation in the instructional events. Similarly, in designing software—video, audio, and so forth—careful attention is paid to the aesthetic features of the medium to ensure motivation and engagement. Respondent learning is a form of methodological behaviorism to be discussed later.

2.2.1.3.2. Operant Conditioning.   Operant conditioning is based on a single, simple principle: There is a functional and interconnected relationship between the stimuli that preceded a response (antecedents), the stimuli that follow a response (consequences), and the response (operant) itself. Acquisition of behavior is viewed as resulting from these three-term or three-component contingent relationships. While there are always contingencies in effect which are beyond the teacher's (or designer's) control, it is the role of the educator to control the environment so that the predominant contingent relationships are in line with the educational goal at hand.

2.2.1.3.2. Antecedents.   These are those objects or events in the environment that serve as cues. Cues set the stage or serve as signals for specific behaviors to take place. Antecedent cues determine and may include temporal cues (time), interpersonal cues (people), and covert or internal cues (inside the skin). Verbal and written directions, nonverbal hand signals and facial gestures, and highlighting with colors and boldfaced print are all examples of cues used by learners to discriminate the conditions for behaving in a way that returns a desired consequence. The behavior ultimately comes under stimulus control (i.e., controlled by the discriminative stimulus or cue) though the contiguous pairing in repeated trials, hence serving in a key functional role in this contingent relationship. Often the behavioral technologist seeks to increase or decrease antecedent (stimulus) control and must be cognizant of those cues to which generalized responding is desired or present. Antecedent control will increase with consequence pairing.

Unlike the involuntary actions entrained via classical conditioning, most behaviors of human beings are emitted or voluntarily enacted. People deliberately "operate" on their environment to produce desired consequences. Skinner termed these purposeful responses *operants*. Operants include both private (thoughts) and public (behavior) activities, but the basic measure in behavioral theory remains the observable measurable response. Operants range from simple to complex, verbal to nonverbal, fine to gross motor actions—the whole realm of what we as humans choose to do based on the consequences the behavior elicits.

While the first two components of operant conditioning (antecedents and operants) are relatively straightforward, the nature of *consequences* and interactions between consequences and behaviors is fairly complex. First, consequences may be classified as *contingent* and *noncontingent*. Contingent consequences are reliable and relatively consistent. A clear association between the operant and the consequences can be established. Noncontingent consequences, however, often produce accidental or superstitious conditioning. If perchance, a computer program has scant or no documentation, and the desired program features cannot be accessed via a predictable set of moves, the user would tend to press many keys, not really knowing what finally causes a successful screen change. This reduces the rate of learning, if indeed any learning occurs at all.

Another dimension focuses on whether or not the consequence is actually delivered. Consequences may be positive (something is presented following a response) or negative (something is taken away following a response). Note that positive and negative do not imply value (i.e., "good" or "bad"). Consequences can also be reinforcing, that is, tend to maintain or increase a behavior, or they may be punishing, that is, tend to decrease or suppress a behavior. Taken together, the possibilities then are positive reinforcement (presenting something to maintain or increase a behavior), positive punishment (presenting something to decrease a behavior), negative reinforcement (removing an aversive condition to increase a behavior), or negative punishment (taking away something to decrease a behavior). Another possibility obviously is that of no consequence following a behavior, which results in the disappearance or extinction of a previously reinforced behavior.

Examples of these types of consequences are readily found in the implementation of behavior modification. Behavior modification or applied behavior analysis is a widely used instructional technology that manipulates the use of these consequences to produce the desired behavior (Cooper, Heron & Heward, 1987). Positive reinforcers ranging from praise, to desired activities, to tangible rewards are delivered upon performance of a desired behavior. Positive punishments such as extra work, physical exertion, and demerits are imposed upon performance of an undesirable behavior. Negative reinforcement is used when aversive conditions such as a teacher's hard gaze or yelling are taken away when the appropriate behavior is performed (e.g., assignment completion). Negative punishment or response cost is used when a desirable stimulus such as free-time privileges are taken away when an inappropriate behavior is performed. When no consequence follows the behavior, such as ignoring an undesirable behavior, ensuring that no attention is given to the misdeed, the undesirable behavior often abates. But this typically is preceded by an upsurge in the frequency of responding until the learner realizes that the behavior will no longer receive the desired consequence. All in all, the use of each consequence requires consideration of whether one wants to increase or decrease a behavior, if it is to be done by taking away or giving some stimulus, and whether or not that stimulus is desirable or undesirable.

In addition to the type of consequence, the schedule for the delivery or timing of those consequences is a key dimension to operant learning. Often a distinction is made between simple and complex *schedules of reinforcement*. Simple schedules include continuous consequation and partial or intermittent consequation. When using a continuous schedule, reinforcement is delivered after each correct response. This procedure is important for the learning of new behaviors because the functional relationship between antecedent-response-consequence is clearly communicated to the learner through predictability of consequation.

When using intermittent schedules, the reinforcement is delivered after some but not all responses. There are two basic types of intermittent schedules: ratio and interval. A ratio schedule is based on the numbers of responses required for consequation (e.g., piecework, number of completed math problems). An interval schedule is based on the amount of time that passes between consequation (e.g., payday, weekly quizzes). Ratio and interval schedules may be either fixed (predictable) or variable (unpredictable). These procedures are used once the functional relationship is established, and the intent is to encourage persistence of responses. The schedule is gradually changed from continuous, to fixed, to variable (i.e., until it becomes very "lean"), in order for the learner to perform the behavior for an extended period of time without any reinforcement. A variation often imposed on these schedules is called *limited hold*, which refers to the consequence being available only for a certain period of time.

Complex schedules are comprised of the various features of simple schedules. Shaping requires the learner to perform successive approximations of the target behavior by changing the criterion behavior for reinforcement to become more and more like the final performance. A good example of shaping is the writing process, wherein drafts are constantly revised towards the final product. Chaining requires that two or more learned behaviors must be performed in a specific sequence for consequation. Each behavior sets up cues for subsequent responses to be performed (e.g., long division). In multiple schedules, two or more simple schedules are in effect for the same behavior, with each associated with a particular stimulus. Two or more schedules are available in a concurrent schedule procedure; however, there are no specific cues as to which schedule is in effect. Schedules may also be conjunctive (two or more behaviors that all must be performed for consequation to occur, but the behaviors may occur in any order), or tandem (two or more behaviors must be performed in a specific sequence without cues).

In all cases, the schedule or timing of the consequation is manipulated to fit the target response, using antecedents to signal the response, and appropriate consequences for the learner and the situation.

2.2.1.3.4. Observational Learning. By using the basic concepts and principles of operant learning, and the basic definition that learning is a change of behavior brought about by experience, organisms can be thought of as learning new behaviors by observing the behavior of others (Chance, 1994). This premise was originally tested by Thorndike (1989), with cats, chicks, and dogs, and later by Watson (1908), with monkeys, without success. In all cases, animals were situated in positions to observe and learn elementary problem-solving procedures (e.g., puzzle boxes) by watching successful same-species models perform the desired task. However, Warden and colleagues (1935, 1940) found that when animals were put in settings (e.g., cages) that were identical to the modeling animals, and the observers watched the models perform the behavior and receive the reinforcement, the observers did learn the target behavior, often responding correctly on the first trial (Chance, 1994).

Attention focused seriously on observational learning research with the work of Bandura and colleagues in the 1960s. In a series of studies with children and adults (with children as the observers and children and adults as the models), these researchers demonstrated that the reinforcement of a model's behavior was positively correlated with the observer's judgments that the behavior was appropriate to imitate. These studies formed the empirical basis for Bandura's Social Learning Theory (1977), which stated that people are not driven by either inner forces or environmental stimuli in isolation. His assertion was that behavior and complex learning must be "explained in terms of a continuous reciprocal interaction of personal and environmental determinants; . . . virtually all learning phenomena resulting from direct experience occurs on a vicarious basis by observing other people's behavior and its consequences for them" (pp. 11, 12).

The basic observational or vicarious learning experience consists of watching a live or filmed performance or listening to a description of the performance (i.e., symbolic modeling) of a model and the positive and/or negative consequences of that model's behavior. Four component processes govern observational learning (Bandura, 1977). First, *attentional processes* determine what is selectively observed and extracted: Valence, complexity, prevalence, and functional value influence the quality of the attention. Observer characteristics such as sensory capacities, arousal

level, perceptual set, and past reinforcement history mediate the stimuli. Second, the attended stimuli must be remembered or retained (i.e., *retentional processes*). Response patterns must be represented in memory in some organized, symbolic form. Humans primarily use imaginal and verbal codes for observed performances. These patterns must be practiced through overt or covert rehearsal to ensure retention. Third, the learner must engage in *motor reproduction processes* that require the organization of responses through their initiation, monitoring, and refinement on the basis of feedback. The behavior must be performed in order for cues to be learned and corrective adjustments made. The fourth component is *motivation*. Social learning theory recognizes that humans are more likely to adopt behavior that they value (functional) and reject behavior that they find punishing or unrewarding (not functional). Further, the evaluative judgments that humans make about the functionality of their own behavior mediate and regulate which observationally learned responses they will actually perform. Ultimately, people will enact self-satisfying behaviors and avoid distasteful or disdainful ones. Consequently, external reinforcement, vicarious reinforcement, and self-reinforcement are all processes that promote the learning and performance of observed behavior.

2.3 THE BEHAVIORAL ROOTS OF INSTRUCTIONAL TECHNOLOGY

2.3.1 Methodological Behaviorism

Stimulus-response (S-R) behaviorism, that is, behaviorism that emphasizes the antecedent as the *cause* of the behavior, is generally referred to as *methodological behaviorism* (see e.g., Day, 1983; Skinner, 1974). As such it is in line with much of experimental psychology; antecedents are the independent variables and the behaviors are the dependent variables. This transformational paradigm (Vargas, 1993) differs dramatically from the radical behaviorism of Skinner (e.g., 1945, 1974) which emphasizes the role of reinforcement of behaviors in the presence of certain antecedents, (see 7.3.3), in other words, the selectionist position. Most of the earlier work in instructional technology followed the methodological behaviorist tradition. In fact, from a radical behaviorist position, cognitive psychology is an extension of methodological behaviorism (Skinner, 1974). Although we have recast and reinterpreted where possible, the differences, particularly in the film and television research (see 11.5 to 11.7), are apparent. Nevertheless, the research is part of the research record in instructional technology and has been therefore necessary and, moreover, useful from an S-R perspective.

One of the distinctive aspects of the methodological behavioral approach is the demand for "experimental" data (manipulation) (see 11.2.4.1) to justify any interpretation of behavior as causal. Natural observation, personal experience, and judgment (see 40.2) fall short of the rules of evidence to support any psychological explanation

(Kendler, 1971). This formula means that a learner must make the "correct response when the appropriate stimulus occurs" and when the necessary conditions are present (Kendler, 1971):

> Usually there is no great problem in providing the appropriate stimulus, for audiovisual techniques have tremendous advantages over other educational procedures in their ability to present to the learner the stimuli in the most effective manner possible (p. 36).

In addition, Gropper (1963) suggests that visual materials should help students acquire, retain, and transfer responses, because visuals have the capacity to cue and reinforce specified responses.

A problem arises as to when to develop techniques (in which appropriate responses to specific stimuli can be practiced and reinforced). The developer of an instructional medium must know exactly what response is desired from the students, otherwise it is impossible to design and evaluate instruction. Once the response is specified, the problem becomes getting the student to make this appropriate response. This response must be practiced and the learner must be reinforced to make the correct response to this stimulus (Skinner, 1953b). Under the S-R paradigm, much of the research on the instructional media was based on the medium itself (i.e., the specific technology). The medium became the independent variable and media comparison studies became the norm until the middle 1970s (Smith & Smith, 1966). In terms of the methodological behavior model, much of the media (programmed instruction, film, television, etc.) functioned primarily within the stimulus component. From this position, Carpenter (1962) reasoned that any medium (e.g., film, television) "imprints" some of its own characteristics on the message itself. Therefore, the content and medium have more impact than the medium itself (see 11.3.3). The "way" the stimulus material (again, film, television, etc.) interacts with the learner instigates motivated responses. Carpenter (1962) developed several hypotheses based on his interpretations of the research on media and learning; these include the following possibilities:

1. The most effective learning will take place when there is similarity between the stimulus material (presented via a medium) and the criterion or learned performance.
2. Repetition of stimulus materials and the learning response is a major condition for most kinds of learning.
3. Stimulus materials that are accurate, correct, and subject to validation can increase the opportunity for learning to take place.
4. An important condition is the relationship between a behavior and its consequences. Learning will occur when the behavior is "reinforced" (Skinner, 1968). This reinforcement, by definition, should be immediately after the response.
5. Carefully sequenced combinations of knowledge and skills presented in logical and limited steps will be the most effective for most types of learning.
6. " . . . established principles of learning derived from studies where the learning situation involved from direct instruction by teachers are equally applicable in the use of instructional materials" (Carpenter, 1962, p. 305).

Practical aspects of these theoretical suggestions go back to the mid-1920s (see 1.5) with the development by Pressey of a self-scoring testing device. Pressey (1926, 1932) discussed the extension of this testing device into a self-instruction machine. Versions of these devices later (after World War II) evolved into several, reasonably sophisticated, teaching machines for the U.S. Air Force which were variations of an automatic self-checking technique. They included a punched card, a chemically treated card, a punchboard, and the Drum Tutor. The Drum Tutor used informational material with multiple-choice questions, but could not advance to the next question until the correct answer was chosen. All devices essentially allowed students to get immediate information concerning accuracy of response.

2.3.2 Teaching Machines

Peterson (1931) conducted early research on Pressey self-scoring testing devices. His experimental groups were given the chemically treated scoring cards used for self-checking while studying a reading assignment. The control group had no knowledge of their results. Peterson found the experimental groups had significantly higher scores than the group without knowledge of results. Little (1934), also using Pressey's automatic scoring device, had the experimental group as a test-machine group, the second group using his testing teaching machine as a drill machine, and the third group as a control group in a paired controlled experiment. Both experimental groups scored significantly higher mean scores than the control group. The drill-machine group scored higher than the test-machine group. After World War II, additional experiments using Pressey's devices were conducted. Angell and Troyer (1948) and Jones and Sawyer (1949) found that giving immediate feedback significantly enhanced learning in both citizenship and chemistry courses. Briggs (1947) and Jensen (1949) found that self-instruction by superior students using Pressey's punchboards enabled them to accelerate their course work. Pressey (1950) also reported efficacy of immediate feedback in English, Russian vocabulary, and psychology courses. Students given feedback via the punchboards received higher scores than those students who were not given immediate feedback. Stephens (1960), using Pressey's Drum Tutor, found that students using the device scored better than students who did not. This was true even though the students using the Drum Tutor lacked overall academic ability. Stephens "confirmed Pressey's findings that errors were eliminated more rapidly with meaningful material and found that students learned more efficiently when they could correct errors immediately" (Smith & Smith, 1966, p. 249). Severin (1960) compared the scores of students given the correct answers with no overt responses in a practice test with those of students using the punchboard practice test and found no significant differences. Apparently pointing out correct answers was enough, and an overt response was not required. Pressey (1950) concluded that the use of his punchboard created a single method of testing, scoring, informing students of their errors, and finding the correct solution all in one step (called *telescoping*). This telescoping procedure, in fact, allowed test taking to become a form of systematically directed self-instruction. His investigations indicated that when self-instructional tests were used at the college level, gains were substantial and helped improve understanding. However, Pressey (1960) indicated his devices may not have been sufficient to stand by themselves but were useful adjuncts to other teaching techniques.

Additional studies on similar self-instruction devices were conducted for military training research. Many of these studies used the automatic knowledge of accuracy devices such as the Tab Item and the Trainer-Tester (Smith & Smith, 1966). Glaser, Damrin, and Gardner (1954), and Cantor and Brown (1956), all found that scores for a troubleshooting task were higher for individuals using these devices than for those using a mock-up for training. Dowell (1955) confirmed this, but also found that even higher scores were obtained when learners used the Trainer-Tester and the actual equipment. Briggs (1958) further developed a device called the Subject-Matter Trainer that could be programmed into five teaching and testing modes. Irion and Briggs (1957) and Briggs (1958) found that prompting a student to give the correct response was more effective than just confirming correct responses.

Smith and Smith (1966) point out that while Pressey's devices were being developed and researched, they actually only attracted attention in somewhat limited circles. Popularity and attention were not generated until Skinner (1953a, b; 1954) used these types of machines. "The fact that teaching machines were developed in more than one context would not be particularly significant were it not true that the two sources represent different approaches to educational design . . . " (Smith & Smith, 1966, p. 245). Skinner developed his machines to test and develop his operant conditioning principles developed from animal research. Skinner's ideas attracted attention, and, as a result, the teaching machine and programmed instruction movement became a primary research emphasis during the 1960s. In fact, from 1960 to 1970 research on teaching machines and programming was the dominant type of media research in terms of numbers in the prestigious journal *AV Communication Review (AVCR)* (Torkelson, 1977). From 1960 to 1969, *AVCR* had a special section dedicated to teaching machines and programming concepts. Despite the fact of favorable research results from Pressey and his associates and the work done by the military, the technique was not popularized until Skinner (1954) recast self-instruction and self-testing. Skinner (1954) believed that any response could be reinforced. A desirable behavior could be taught by reinforcing a response that was close in time to this behavior. By reinforcing "successive" approximations, behavior will eventually approximate the desired pattern (Homme, 1957). Obviously, this reinforcement needed a great deal of supervision. Skinner believed that, in schools, reinforcement may happen hours, days, etc., after the initial event, and the effects would be greatly reduced. In addition, he felt that it was difficult to reinforce individually a response of an individual student in a large group. He also believed that schools used negative reinforcers—to punish, not necessarily as reinforcement (Skinner, 1954). To solve these problems, Skinner also turned to the teaching-machine concept. Skinner's (1958) machines in many respects were similar to Pressey's earlier teaching testing devices. Both employed immediate knowledge of results immediately after the response. The students were kept active by their participation, and both types of devices could be used in a self-instruction manner with students moving at their own rate. Differences in the types of responses in Pressey's and Skinner's machines should be noted. Skinner required students to "overtly" compose responses (e.g., writing words, terms, etc.). Pressey presented potential answers in a multiple-choice format, requiring students to "select" the correct answer. In addition, Skinner (1958) believed that answers could not be easy, but that steps would need to be small in order that there would be no chance for "wrong" responses. Skinner was uncomfortable with multiple-choice responses found in Pressey's devices because of the chance for mistakes (Homme, 1957; Porter, 1957; Skinner & Holland, 1960).

2.3.3 Films

The role and importance of military research (see 1.10, 11.2.3) during World War II and immediately afterward cannot be underestimated either in terms of amount or results. Research studies on learning, training materials, and instruments took on a vital role when it became necessary to train millions of individuals in skills useful for military purposes. People had to be selected and trained for complex and complicated machine systems (i.e., radio detection, submarine control, communication, etc.). As a result, most of the focus of the research by the military during and after the war was on the devices for training, assessment, and troubleshooting complex equipment and instruments. Much of the film research noted earlier stressed the stimulus, response, and reinforcement characteristics of the audiovisual device. "These [research studies] bear particularly on questions on the role of active response, size of demonstration and practice steps in procedural learning, and the use of prompts or response cues" (Lumsdaine & Glaser, 1960, p. 257). The major research programs during World War II were conducted on the use of films by the U.S. Army. These studies were conducted to study achievement of specific learning outcomes and the feasibility of utilizing film for psychological testings (Gibson, 1947; Hoban, 1946). After World War II, two major film research projects were sponsored by the United States Army and Navy at the Pennsylvania State University from 1947 to 1955 (Carpenter & Greenhill, 1955, 1958). A companion program on film research was sponsored by the United States Air Force from 1950 to 1957. The project at the Pennsylvania State University—the Instructional Film Research Program under the direction of C. R. Carpenter—was probably the "most extensive single program of experimentation dealing with instructional films ever conducted" (Saettler, 1968, p. 332). In 1954, this film research project was reorganized to include instructional films and instructional television because of the similarities of the two media. The Air Force Film Research Program (1950 to 1957) was conducted under the leadership of A. A. Lumsdaine (1961). The Air Force studies involved the manipulation of techniques for "eliciting and guiding overt responses during a course of instruction" (Saettler, 1968, p. 335). Both the Army and Air Force studies developed research that had major implications on the use and design of audiovisual materials (e.g., film). Although these studies developed a large body of knowledge, little use of the results was actually implemented in the production of instructional materials developed by the military. Kanner (1960) suggested that the reason for the lack of use of the results of these studies was because they created resentment among filmmakers, and much of the research was completed in isolation.

Much of the research on television was generated after 1950 and was conducted by the military because of television's potential for mass instruction. Some of the research replicated or tested concepts (variables) used in the earlier film research, but the bulk of the research compared television instruction to "conventional" instruction, and most results showed no significant differences between the two forms. Most of the studies were applied rather than using a theoretical framework, i.e., behavior principles (Kumata, 1961).

However, Gropper (1965a, b), Gropper and Lumsdaine (1961), and others used the television medium to test behavioral principles developed from the studies on programmed instruction. Klaus (1965) states that programming techniques tended to be either stimulus centered or response centered. Stimulus-centered techniques stressed meaning, structure, and organization of stimulus materials, while response-centered techniques dealt with the design of materials that ensure adequate response practice. For example, Gropper (1965, 1966) adopted and extended concepts developed in programmed instruction (particularly the response-centered model) to televised presentations. These studies dealt primarily with "techniques for bringing specific responses under the control of specific visual stimuli and . . . the use of visual stimuli processing such control within the framework of an instructional design" (1966, p. 41). Gropper, Lumsdaine, and Shipman (1961), Gropper and Lumsdaine (1961), and Gropper (1961a, b, c, d) all reported the value of pretesting and revising televised instruction and requiring students to make active responses. Gropper (1967) suggested that in television presentations it is desirable to

identify which behavioral principles and techniques that underlie programmed instruction are appropriate to television. Gropper and Lumsdaine (1961) reported that merely requiring students to respond actively to nonprogrammed stimulus materials (i.e., segments that are not well delineated or sequenced in systematic ways) did not lead to more effective learning (an early attempt at formative evaluation). However, Gropper (1967) reported that the success of using programmed instructional techniques with television depends on the effective design of the stimulus materials as well as on the design of the appropriate response practice.

Gropper (1963, 1965a, 1966, 1967) emphasized the importance of using visual materials to help students acquire, retain, and transfer responses based on the ability of such materials to cue and reinforce specified responses, and serve as examples. He further suggests that students should make explicit (active) responses to visual materials (e.g., television) for effective learning. Later, Gropper (1968) concluded that, in programmed televised materials, actual practice is superior to recognition practice in most cases and that the longer the delay in measuring retention, the more the active response was beneficial. The behavioral features that were original with programmed instruction and later used with television and film were attempts to minimize and later correct the defects in the effectiveness of instruction on the basis of what was known about the learning process (Klaus, 1966). The use of student responses were used in many studies (e.g., Gropper, 1963, 1966) as the basis for revisions of instructional design and content. In-depth reviews of the audiovisual research carried on by the military and civilian researchers are contained in the classic summaries of this primarily behaviorist approach of Hoban and Van Ormer (1950), May and Lumsdaine (1958), Cook (1960), Hoben (1960), Carpenter and Greenhill (1955, 1958), Schramm (1962), and Chu and Schramm (1968).

The following is a sample of some of the research results on the behavioral tenants of stimulus, response, and reinforcement gleaned from the World War II research and soon after, based on the study of audiovisual devices (particularly film).

2.3.3.1. Research on Stimuli.

Attempts to improve learning by manipulating the stimulus condition (see 11.3) can be divided into several categories. One category, that of the use of introductory materials to introduce content in film or audiovisual research has shown mixed results (Cook, 1960). Film studies by Wittich and Folkes (1946), Weiss and Fine (1955), and Wulff, Sheffield, and Kraeling (1954) reported that introductory materials presented prior to the showing of a film increased learning. But Lathrop (1949), Norford (1949), Peterman and Bouscaren (1954), and Jaspen (1948) found inconclusive or negative results by using introductory materials. Another category of stimuli, those that direct attention, uses the behavioral principle that learning is assisted by the association of the responses to stimuli (Cook, 1960). Film studies by Kimble and Wulff (1953), Lumsdaine and Sulzer (1951), Ryan and Hochberg

(1954), Gibson (1947), Roshal (1949), and McGuire (1953a) found that a version of the film that incorporated cues to guide the audience into making the correct responses produced increased learning. As might be expected, extraneous stimuli not focusing on relevant cues were not effective (Jaspen, 1950; Neu, 1950; Weiss, 1954). However, Miller and Levine (1952) and Miller, Levine, and Steinberger (1952a) reported the use of subtitles to associate content to be ineffective. Cook (1960) reported that many studies were conducted on the use of color, where it would provide an essential cue to understanding, with mixed results, and concluded it was impossible to say color facilitated learning results (i.e., Long, 1946; May & Lumsdaine, 1958). Note that the use of color in instruction is still a highly debated research issue.

2.3.3.2. Research on Response. Cook (1960) stated the general belief that unless the learner makes some form of response that is relevant to the learning task, no learning will occur. Responses (practice) in audiovisual presentations may range from overt oral, written, or motor responses to an implicit response (not overt). Cook (1960), in an extensive review of practice in audiovisual presentations, reported the effectiveness of students calling out answers to questions in an audiovisual presentation to be effective (i.e., Kanner & Sulzer, 1955; Kendler, Cook & Kendler, 1953; Kendler, Kendler & Cook, 1954; McGuire, 1954). Most studies that utilized overt written responses with training film and television were also found to be effective (i.e., Michael, 1951; Michael & Maccoby, 1954; Yale Motion Picture Research Project, 1947).

A variety of film studies on implicit practice found this type of practice to be effective (some as effective as overt practice) (i.e., Kanner & Sulzer, 1955; Kendler, Kendler & Cook, 1954; Michael, 1951; McGuire, 1954; Miller & Klier, 1953a, b). Cook (1960, p. 98) notes that the above-noted studies all reported that the effect of actual practice is "specific to the items practiced" and there appeared to be no carryover to other items. The role of feedback in film studies was positively supported (Gibson, 1947; Michael, 1951; Michael & Maccoby, 1954).

The use of practice, given the above results, appears to be an effective component of using audiovisual (film and television) materials. A series of studies were conducted to determine the amount of practice needed. Cook (1960) concludes that students will profit from a larger number of repetitions (practice). Film studies that used a larger number of examples or required viewing the film more than once found students fairing better than those with fewer examples or viewing opportunities (Brenner, Walter & Kurtz, 1949; Kendler, Cook & Kendler, 1953; Kimble & Wulff, 1954; Sulzer & Lumsdaine, 1952). A number of studies were conducted which tested when practice should occur. Was it better to practice concepts as a whole (massed) at the end of a film presentation or practice it immediately after it was demonstrated (distributed) during the film? Most studies reported that there was no difference in the time spacing of practice (e.g., McGuire, 1953b; Miller & Klier, 1953a, b, 1954;

Miller & Levine & Steinberger, 1952a, 1952b). Miller and Levine (1952), however, found results in favor of a massed practice at the end of the treatment period.

2.3.4 Programmed Instruction

Closely akin to and developed from Skinner's (1954) technology of teaching machine concepts were the teaching texts or programmed books (see 18.4.1). These programmed books essentially had the same characteristics as the machines: logical presentations of content, requirement of overt responses, and presentation of immediate knowledge of correctness (a correct answer would equal positive reinforcement (Porter, 1958, Smith & Smith, 1966). These programmed books were immediately popular for obvious reasons; they were easier to produce, portable, and did not require a complex, burdensome, costly device, i.e., a machine. As noted earlier during the decade of the 60s, research on *programmed instruction*, as the use of these types of books and machines became known, was immense (Campeau, 1974). Literally thousands of research studies were conducted. (See Campeau, 1974; Glaser, 1965; Lumsdaine & Glaser, 1960; Smith & Smith, 1966, among others for extensive summaries of research in this area.) The term *programming* is taken here to mean what Skinner called "the construction of carefully arranged sequences of contingencies leading to the terminal performances which are the object of education" (Skinner, 1953b, p. 169).

2.3.4.1. Linear Programming. Linear programming involves a series of learning frames presented in a set sequence. As in most of the educational research of the time, research on linear programmed instruction dealt with devices and/or machines and not on process or the learner. Most of the studies, therefore, generally compared programmed instruction to "conventional" or "traditional" instructional methods (see e.g., Teaching Machines and Programmed Instruction Department in *AV Communication Review,* 1962–1969). These types of studies were, of course, difficult to generalize from and often resulted in conflicting results (Holland, 1965). "The restrictions on interpretation of such a comparison arise from the lack of specificity of the instruction with which the instrument in question is paired" (Lumsdaine, 1962a or b, p. 251). Like other research of the time, many of the comparative studies had problems in design, poor criterion measures, scores prone to a ceiling effect, and ineffective and poor experimental procedures (Holland, 1965). Holland (1961), Lumsdaine (1965), and Rothkopf (1962) all suggested other ways of evaluating the success of programmed instruction. Glaser (1962) indicated that most programmed instruction was difficult to construct, was time consuming, and had few rules or procedures. Many comparative studies and reviews of comparative studies found no significance in the results of programmed instruction (e.g., Alexander, 1970; Barnes, 1970; Frase, 1970; Giese & Stockdale, 1966; McKeachie, 1967; Unwin, 1966; and Wilds & Zachert, 1966). However, Marsh and Pierce-Jones (1968), Hamilton and Heinkel (1967), and Daniel and Murdoch (1968) all reported positive and statistically significant findings in favor of programmed instruction. The examples noted above were based on gross comparisons. A large segment of the research on programmed instruction was devoted to "isolating or manipulating program or learner characteristics" (Campeau, 1974, p. 17). Specific areas of research on these characteristics included studies on repetition and dropout, e.g., Rothkopf (1960), Skinner and Holland (1960). Skinner and Holland (1960) suggested that various kinds of cueing techniques could be employed which would reduce the possibility of error but generally will cause the presentation to become linear in nature (Skinner, 1961; Smith, 1959). Karis, Kent, and Gilbert (1970) found that overt responding, such as writing a name in a (linear) programmed sequence, was significantly better for subjects who learned under covert response conditions. However, Valverde and Morgan (1970) concluded that eliminating redundancy in linear programs significantly increased achievement. Carr (1959) stated that merely confirming the correctness of a student's response, as in a linear program, is not enough. The learner must otherwise be motivated to perform (Smith & Smith, 1966). However, Coulson and Silberman (1960) and Evans, Glaser, and Homme (1962) found significant differences in favor of small (redundant) step programs over programs that had redundant and transitional materials removed. In the traditional linear program, after a learner has written his response (overt), the answer is confirmed by the presentation of the correct answer. Research on the confirmation (feedback) of results has shown conflicting results. Studies, for example, by Holland (1960), Hough and Revsin (1963), McDonald and Allen (1962), and Moore and Smith (1961, 1962) found no difference in mean scores due the added feedback. However, Meyer (1960), Kaess and Zeaman (1960), and Suppes and Ginsburg (1962) reported in their research the positive advantages for feedback on posttest scores. Homme and Glaser (1960) reported that when correct answers were omitted from linear programs, the learner felt it made no difference. Resnick (1963) felt that linear programs failed to make allowance for individual differences of the learners, and he was concerned about the "voice of authority" and the "right or wrong" nature of the material to be taught. Smith and Smith (1966) believed that a "linear program is deliberately limiting the media of communication, the experiences of the student, and thus the range of understanding that he achieves" (p. 293).

Holland (1965) summarized his extensive review of literature on general principles of programming and generally found that a contingent relationship between the answer and the content is important. A low error rate of responses received support, as did the idea that examples are necessary for comprehension. For long programs, overt responses are necessary. Results are equivocal concerning multiple-choice versus overt responses; however, many erroneous alternatives (e.g., multiple-choice foils) may interfere with later learning. Many of the studies concern-

ing the effects of the linear presentation of content introduced the "pall effect" (boredom) because of the many small steps and the characteristic of always being correct (Beck, 1959; Galanter, 1959; Rigney & Fry, 1961).

2.3.4.2. Intrinsic (Branching) Programming. Crowder (1961) used a similar approach to that developed by Pressey (1963), which suggested that a learner be exposed to a "substantial" and organized unit of instruction (e.g., a book chapter), and following this presentation a series of multiple-choice questions would be asked "to enhance the clarity and stability of cognitive structure by correcting misconceptions and deferring the instruction of new matter until there had been such clarification and education" (Pressey, 1963, p. 3). Crowder (1959, 1960) and his associates were not as concerned about error rate or the limited step-by-step process of linear programs. Crowder tried to reproduce, in a self-instructional program, the function of a private tutor; to present new information to the learner and have the learner use this information (to answer questions); then taking "appropriate" action based on learner's responses, such as going on to new information or going back and reviewing the older information if responses were incorrect. Crowder's intrinsic programming was designed to meet problems concerning complex problem solving but not necessarily based on a learning theory (Klaus, 1965). Crowder (1962) "assumes that the basic learning takes place during the exposure to the new material. The multiple-choice question is asked to find out whether the student has learned; it is not necessarily regarded as playing an active part in the primary learning process" (p. 3). Crowder (1961), however, felt that the intrinsic (also known as *branching*) programs were essentially "naturalistic" and kept students working at the "maximum practical" rate.

Several studies have compared, and found no difference between, the type of constructed responses (overt versus the multiple-choice response in verbal programs) (Evans, Homme & Glaser, 1962; Hough, 1962; Roe, Massey, Weltman & Leeds, 1960; Williams, 1963). Holland (1965) felt that these studies showed, however, that "the nature of the learning task determines the preferred response form. When the criterion performance includes a precise response . . . constructed responses seems to be the better form; whereas if mere recognition is desired the response form in the program is probably unimportant" (p. 104).

Although the advantages for the intrinsic (branching) program appears to be self-evident for learners with extreme individual differences, most studies found no advantages for the intrinsic programs over linear programs, but generally found time saving for students who used branching format (Beane, 1962; Campbell, 1961, 1962; Glaser, Reynolds & Harakas, 1962; Roe, Massey, Weltman & Leeds, 1962; Silberman, Melaragno, Coulson & Estavan, 1961).

2.3.5 Instructional Design

Behaviorism is prominent in the roots of the systems approach to the design of instruction. Many of the tenets, terminology, and concepts can be traced to behaviorial theories. Edward Thorndike in the early 1900s, for instance, had an interest in learning theory and testing. This interest greatly influenced the concept of instructional planning and the empirical approaches to the design of instruction. World War II researchers on training and training materials based much of their work on instructional principles derived from research on human behavior and theories of instruction and learning (Reiser, 1987). Heinich (1970) believed that concepts from the development of programmed learning influenced the development of the instructional design concept.

> By analyzing and breaking down content into specific behavioral objectives, devising the necessary steps to achieve the objectives, setting up procedures to try out and revise the steps, and by validating the program against attainment of the objectives, programmed instruction succeeded in creating a small but effective self-instructional system—a technology of instruction (Heinich, 1970, p. 123).

Task analysis, behavioral objectives, and criterion-referenced testing were brought together by Gagné (1962) and Silvern (1964). These individuals were among the first to use terms such as *systems development* and *instructional systems* to describe a connected and systematic framework for the instructional design principles currently used (Reiser, 1987).

Instructional design is generally considered to be a systematic process that uses tenants of learning theories to plan and present instruction or instructional sequences. The obvious purpose of instructional design is to promote learning. As early as 1900 Dewey called for a "linking science" that connected learning theory and instruction (1900). As the adoption of analytic and systematic techniques influenced programmed instruction and other "programmed" presentation modes, early instructional design also used learning principles from behavioral psychology. For example, discriminations, generalizations, associations, etc., were used to analyze content and job tasks. Teaching and training concepts such as shaping and fading were early attempts to match conditions and treatments, and all had behavioral roots (Gropper & Ross, 1987). Many of the current instructional design models use major components of methodological behaviorism such as specification of objectives (behavioral), concentration on behavioral changes in students, and the emphasis on the stimulus (environment) (Gilbert, 1962; Reigeluth, 1983). It is this association between the stimulus and the student response that characterizes the influence of behavioral theory on instructional design (Smith & Ragan, 1993). Many of the proponents of behavioral theory as a base for instructional design feel that there is an "inevitable conclusion that the quality of an educational system must be defined primarily in terms of change in student behaviors" (Tosti & Ball, 1969, p. 6). Instruction, thus, must be evaluated by its ability to change the behavior of the individual student. The influence of the behavioral theory on instructional design can be traced from writings by Dewey, Thorndike, and, of course, B. F. Skinner. In addition, during World War II, military trainers

(and psychologists) stated learning outcomes in terms of "performance" and found the need to identify specific "tasks" for a specific job (Gropper, 1983). Based on training in the military during the Second World War, a commitment to achieve practice and reinforcement became major components to the behaviorist-developed instructional design model (as well as other nonbehavioristic models). Gropper (1983) indicates that an instructional design model should identify a unit of behavior to be analyzed, the conditions that can produce a change, and the resulting nature of that change. The unit of analysis is the stimulus-response association. When the *appropriate* response is made and referenced after a (repeated) presentation of the stimulus, the response comes under the control of that stimulus.

> Whatever the nature of the stimulus, the response or the reinforcement, establishing stable stimulus control depends on the same two learning conditions: practice of an appropriate response in the presence of a stimulus that is to control it and delivery of reinforcement following its practice (Gropper, 1983, p. 106).

Gropper (1983) stated that this need for control over the response by the stimulus contained several components: practice (to develop stimulus construction) and suitability for teaching the skills.

Gagné, Briggs, and Wager (1988) have identified several learning principles that apply centrally to the behaviorial instructional design process. Among these are contiguity, repetition, and reinforcement in one form or another. Likewise, Gustafson and Tillman (1991) identify several major values that underline instructional design: (1) Goals and objectives of the instruction need to be identified and stated; (2) all instructional outcomes need to be measurable and meet standards of reliability and validity; (3) the instructional design concept centers on changes in behavior of the student (the learner).

Corey (1971) identified a model that would include the above components. These components include:

1. *Determination of objectives.* This includes a description of behaviors to be expected as a result of the instruction and a description of the stimulus to which these behaviors are considered to be appropriate responses.
2. *Analysis of instructional objectives.* This includes analyzing "behaviors under the learner's control" prior to the instruction sequence, behaviors that are to result from the instruction.
3. *Identifying the characteristics of the students.* This would be the behavior that is already under the control of the learner prior to the instructional sequence.
4. *Evidence of the achievement of instruction.* This would include tests or other measures that would demonstrate whether or not the behaviors the instruction "was designed to bring under his control actually were brought under his control" (p. 13).
5. *Constructing the instructional environment.* This involves developing an environment that will assist

the student to perform the desired behaviors as response to the designed stimuli or situation.

6. *Continuing instruction (feedback).* This involves reviewing if additional or revised instruction is needed to maintain the stimulus control over the learners' behavior.

Glaser (1965), also, described similar behavioral tenets of an instructional design system. He identified the following tasks to teach subject-matter knowledge. First, the behavior desired must be analyzed and standards of performance specified. The stimulus and desired response will determine what and how it is to be taught. Secondly, the characteristics of the students are identified prior to instruction. Thirdly, the student must be guided from one state of development to another using predetermined procedures and materials. Lastly, a provision for assessing the competence of the learner in relation to the predetermined performance criteria (objectives) must be developed.

Cook (1994) recently addressed the area of instructional effectiveness as it pertains to behavioral approaches to instruction. He noted that a number of behavioral instructional packages incorporate common underlying principles that promote teaching and student learning and examined a number of these packages concerning their inclusion of 12 components he considers critical to instructional effectiveness:

1. Task analysis and the specification of the objectives of the instructional system
2. Identification of the entering skills of the target population, and a placement system that addresses the individual differences among members of the target population
3. An instructional strategy in which a sequence of instructional steps reflects principles of behavior in the formation of discriminations, the construction of chains, the elaboration of these two elements into concepts and procedures, and their integration and formalization by means of appropriate verbal behavior such as rule statements
4. Requests and opportunities for active student responding at intervals appropriate to the sequence of steps in item 3
5. Supplementary prompts to support early responding
6. The transfer of the new skill to the full context of application (the facing of supporting prompts as the full context takes control, which may include the fading of verbal behavior that has acted as part of the supporting prompt system)
7. Provision of feedback on responses and cumulative progress reports, both at intervals appropriate to the learner and the stage in the program
8. The detection and correction of errors
9. A mastery requirement for each well-defined unit, including the attainment of fluency in the unit skills as measured by the speed at which they can be performed

10. Internalization of behavior that no longer needs to be performed publicly, which may include verbal behavior that remains needed but not in overt form
11. Sufficient self-pacing to accommodate individual differences in rates of achieving mastery
12. Modification of instructional programs on the basis of objective data on effectiveness with samples of individuals from the target population

2.3.6 Task Analysis and Behavioral Objectives

As we have discussed, one of the major components derived from behavioral theory in instructional design is the use of behavioral objectives. The methods associated with task analysis and programmed instruction stress the importance of the "identification and specification of observable behaviors to be performed by the learner" (Reiser, 1987, p. 23). Objectives have been used by educators as far back as the early 1900s. Although these objectives may have identified content that might be tested, usually they did not specify exact behaviors learners were to demonstrate based on exposure to the content (Reiser, 1987). Popularization and refinement of stating objectives in measurable or observable terms within an instructional design approach was credited by Reiser (1987) and Kibler, Cegala, Miles, and Barker (1974) to the efforts of Tyler (1934), Bloom, Engelhart, Furst, Hill & Krathwohl (1956), Mager (1962), Gagné (1965), Glaser (1962), and Popham and Baker (1970). Kibler and colleagues (1974) point out that there are many rational bases for using behavioral objectives, some of which are not based on learning theory, such as teacher accountability. They list, however, some of the tenets that are based on behavioral learning theories. These include (1) assisting in evaluating learners' performance, (2) designing and arranging sequences of instruction, (3) communicating requirements and expectations, and (4) providing and communicating levels of performance prior to instruction. In the Kibler et al. (1974) comprehensive review of the empirical bases for using objectives, they found only about 50 studies that dealt with the effectiveness of objectives. These researchers reported that results were inconsistent and provided little conclusive evidence of the effect of behavioral objectives on learning. They (1974) classified the research on objectives into four categories. These were:

1. *Effects of student knowledge of behavioral objectives on learning.* Of 33 studies, only 11 reported that student possession of objectives improved learning significantly (e.g., Doty, 1968; Lawrence, 1970; Olsen, 1972; Webb, 1971). The rest of the studies found no differences between student possession of objectives or not (e.g., Baker, 1969; Brown, 1970; Patton, 1972; Weinberg, 1970; Zimmerman, 1972).
2. *Effects of specific versus general objectives on learning.* Only two studies (Dalis, 1970; Janeczko, 1971) found that students receiving specific objectives performed higher than those receiving general objectives.

Other studies (e.g., Lovett, 1971; Stedman, 1970; Weinberg, 1970) found no significant differences between the form of objectives.

3. *Effects on student learning of teacher possession and use of objectives.* Five of eight students reviewed found no significant differences of teacher possession of objectives and those without (e.g., Baker, 1969; Crooks, 1971; Kalish, 1972). Three studies reported significant positive effects of teacher possession (McNeil, 1967; Piatt, 1969; Wittrock, 1962).

4. *Effects of student possession of behavioral objectives on efficiency (time).* Two of seven studies (Allen & McDonald, 1963; Mager & McCann, 1961) found that use of objectives reduced student time on learning. The rest found no differences concerning efficiency (e.g., Loh, 1972; Smith, 1970).

Kibler et al. (1974) found less than half of the research studies reviewed supported the use of objectives. However, they felt that many of the studies had methodological problems. These were: lack of standardization of operationalizing behavior objectives and unfamiliarity of the use of objectives by students, and few researchers provided teachers with training in the use of objectives. Although they reported no conclusive results in their reviews of behavioral objectives, Kibler et al. (1974) felt that there were still logical reasons (noted earlier) for their continued use.

2.4 CURRENT DESIGN AND DELIVERY MODELS

Three (radical) behavioral design/delivery models are worth examining in some detail: "personalized system of instruction," (PSI), "precision teaching," and "direct instruction." Each of these models has been in use for some 25 years and each shares some distinctively behavioral aspects. First and foremost, each model places the responsibility for success on the instruction/teacher as opposed to the learner. This places a high premium on validation and revision of materials. In fact, in all behavior models, instruction is always plastic—always in a formative stage. The major features are a task or logical analysis that is used to establish behavioral objectives and serve as the basis for precise assessment of learner entry behavior—lastly, the use of small groups, carefully planned or even scripted lessons, high learner response requirements coupled with equally high feedback, and, of course, data collection related to accuracy and speed. Each of these programs is consistent with all, or nearly all, of the principals from Cook (1994) listed previously.

2.4.1 Personalized System of Instruction

Following a discussion of B. F. Skinner's *Principles of the Analysis of Behavior* (Holland & Skinner, 1961), Fred Keller and his associates concluded that "traditional teaching methods were sadly out of date" (Keller & Sherman, 1974, p. 7). Keller suggested that if education were to improve, instructional design systems would need to be developed to improve and update methods of providing instructional information. Keller searched for a way in which instruction could follow a methodical pattern. The pattern should use previous success to reinforce the student to progress in a systematic manner toward a specified outcome. Keller and his associates developed such a system, called *personalized system of instruction* (PSI) or the Keller plan. This system, like programmed instruction, used tenets of behaviorism and mastery learning. PSI can be described as an interlocking system of instruction, consisting of sequentially, progressive tasks designed as highly individualized learning activities. In this design, students determine their own rate and amount of learning, as they progress through a series of instructional tasks. PSI has five defining characteristics: (a) use of proctors, (b) mastery learning, (c) self-pacing, (d) teacher as motivator, and (e) use of the written word. These characteristics determine decisions made within the design (Keller & Sherman, 1974).

PSI shares some of the same characteristics common to Bloom's "learning for mastery" (LFM) model (Siedentop, Mand & Taggart, 1986). Each task must be performed to a criterion established prior to the beginning of the course. On completion of each task, students have the option of moving to the next task or staying at that same task. Eventually the student must advance to the next task (Reiser, 1987).

Learning tasks are designed as highly individualized activities within the class. Students work at their own rate, largely independent from the teacher. The teacher usually provides motivation only through the use of cues and feedback on course content as students progress through the unit (Metzler, Eddleman, Treanor & Cregger, 1989).

Research on PSI in the classroom setting has been extensive (e.g., Callahan & Smith, 1990; Cregger & Metzler, 1992; Hymel, 1987; McLaughlin, 1991; and Zencias, Davis & Cuvo, 1990). Often it has been limited to comparisons with designs using conventional strategies. It has been demonstrated that PSI and similar mastery-based instruction can be extremely effective in producing significant gains in student achievement. Often PSI research focuses on comparisons to Bloom's LFM (Bloom, 1971). LFM and PSI share a few characteristics. Among these are the use of mastery learning, increased teacher freedom, and increased student skill practice time. In both systems, each task must be performed to a criterion determined prior to the beginning of the course (Metzler, Eddleman, Treanor & Cregger, 1989).

Reiser (1987) points to the similarity between LFM and PSI in the method of student progression through the separate systems. On completion of each task, the student is given the choice of advancing or continuing work within that unit. However, whereas PSI allows the student to continue working on the same task until mastery is reached, LFM recommends a "looping-back" to a previous lesson and proceeding forward from that point (Bloom, 1971).

This similarity between systems extends to PSI's use of providing information to the learners in small chunks, or tasks, with frequent assessment of these smaller learning units (Siedentop, Mand & Taggert, 1986). These chunks are built on simple tasks, to allow the learner success before advancing to more complex tasks. As in PSI, success LFM is developed through many opportunities for practice trials, with the instructor providing cues and feedback on the task being attempted. These cues and feedback are offered in the place of lectures and demonstrations. Though Bloom's LFM approach shares many similarities with Keller's design, PSI actually extends the concept of mastery to include attention to the individual student as he or she progresses through the sequence of learning tasks (Reiser, 1987).

Several studies have compared self-pacing approaches with reinforcement (positive or negative rewards) in a PSI setting. Keller (1968) has suggested that it was not necessary to provide any pacing contingencies. Others have used procedures that rewarded students for maintaining a pace (Cheney & Powers, 1971; Lloyd, 1971) or penalized students for failing to do so (Miller, Weaver & Semb, 1954; Reiser & Sullivan, 1977). Calhoun (1976), Semb, Conyers, Spencer, and Sanchez-Sosa (1975), Reiser (1980), and Morris, Surber, and Biyou (1978) report that learning was not effected by the type of pacing procedure. However, Allen, Grat, and Cheney (1974), Sheppard and MacDermont (1970), and Sutterer and Holloway (1975) reported that the "prompt completion of work is positively related to achievement in PSI courses" (Reiser, 1980, p. 200).

Reiser (1984), however, reported that student rates of progress are improved and learning is unhindered when pacing with penalties are used (e.g., Reiser & Sullivan, 1977; Robin & Graham, 1974). In most cases (except Robin & Graham, 1974; Fernald, Chiseri, Lawson, Scroggs & Riddell, 1975), student attitudes are as positive with a penalty approach as with a regular self-paced approach without penalty (e.g., Calhoun, 1976; Reiser, 1980; Reiser & Sullivan, 1977).

2.4.2 Precision Teaching

Precision teaching is the creation of O. R. Lindsley (Potts, Eshleman & Cooper, 1993). Building on his own early research with humans (e.g., Lindsley & Skinner, 1954; Lindsley, 1956, 1964, 1972, 1991a, 1991b), he proposed that rate, rather than percentage correct, might prove more sensitive to monitoring classroom learning. Rather than creating programs based on laboratory findings, Lindsley proposed that the measurement framework that had become the hallmark of the laboratories of Skinner and his associates be moved into the classroom. His goal was to put science in the hands of teachers and students (Binder & Watkins, 1990). In Lindsley's (1990a) words, he and his associates (e.g., Caldwell, 1966; Fink, 1968; Holzschuh & Dobbs, 1966) "did not set out to discover basic laws of behavior. Rather, we merely intended to monitor standard self-recorded performance frequencies in the classroom" (p. 7). The most conspicuous result of these efforts was the Standard Behavior Chart or Standard Celeration Chart, a six-cycle, semilogarithmic graph for charting behavior frequency against days. "By creating linear representations of learning (trends in performance) on the semilogarithmic chart, and quantifying them as multiplicative factors per week (e.g., correct responding $\times$ 2.0 per week, errors dividing by 1.5 per week), Lindsley defined the first simple measure of learning in the literature: *celeration*, either a multiplicative acceleration of behavior frequency or a dividing deceleration of behavior frequency per celeration period, e.g., per week" (Binder & Watkins, 1990, p. 78). Precision teachers distinguish between operational or descriptive definitions of an event, which require merely observation, versus functional definitions, which require manipulative (and continued) observation. Precision teachers apply the "dead man's test" to descriptions of behavior—i.e., "If a dead man can do it, then don't try to teach it" (Binder & Watkins, 1990)—to rule out objectives such as "sits quietly in chair" or "keeps eyes on paper." The emphasis of precision teaching has been on teaching teachers *and students* to count behaviors with an emphasis on counting and analyzing both correct and incorrect response, i.e., learning opportunities (White, 1986).

The precision teaching movement has resulted in some practical findings of potential use to education technologists. For example, precision teachers have consistently found that placement of students in more difficult tasks (which produce higher error rates) results in faster learning rates (see e.g., Johnson, 1971; Johnson & Layng, 1994; Neufeld & Lindsley, 1980). Precision teachers have also made fluency—accuracy plus speed of performance—a goal at each level of a student's progress. Fluency (or automaticity or "second nature" responding) has been shown to improve retention, transfer of training, and "endurance" or resistance to extinction (Binder, 1987, 1988; Binder, 1993; Binder, Haughton & VanEyk, 1990). (It is important to note that *fluency* is not merely a new word for "overlearning," or continuing to practice past mastery. Fluency involves speed, and, indeed, speed may be more important than accuracy, at least initially). Consistent with the findings that more difficult placement produces bigger gains are the findings of Bower and Orgel (1981) and Lindsley (1990b) that encouraging students to respond at very high rates from the beginning, even when error rates are high, can significantly increase learning rates. In addition, evidence suggests that celeration, a direct measure of learning, is not racially biased (Koening & Kunzelmann, 1981).

Large-scale implementations of Precision Teaching have found that improvements of two or more grade levels per year are common (e.g., West, Young & Spooner, 1990). "The improvements themselves are dramatic; but when cost/benefit is considered, they are staggering, since the time allocated to precision teach was relatively small and the materials used were quite inexpensive" (Binder & Watkins, 1990, pp. 82, 83).

2.4.3 Direct Instruction

Direct Instruction (DI) is a design and implementation model based on the work of Siegfried Engelmann (cf. Bereiter & Engelmann, 1966). DI is based on 25 years of research and development. According to Binder and Watkins (1990), over 50 commercially available programs are based on the DI model. Engelmann and Carnine (1982, 1991) state that designing instruction for cognitive learning requires three analyses: the analysis of behavior, the analysis of communications, and the analysis of knowledge systems.

The analysis of behavior is concerned with how the environment influences learner behavior (e.g., how to prompt and reinforce responses, how to correct errors, etc.). The analysis of communications seeks principles for the logical design of effective teaching sequences. These principles relate to ordering examples to maximize generalization (but minimize overgeneralization). The analysis of knowledge systems is concerned with the logical organization or classification of knowledge such that similar skills and concepts can be taught the same way, and instruction can proceed from simple to complex. Direct instruction uses scripted presentations not only to support quality control but also because most teachers lack training in design and are, therefore, not likely to select and sequence examples effectively without such explicit instructions (Binder & Watkins, 1990). Direct instruction also relies on small groups (10 to 15), unison responding (to get high response rates from *all* students) to fixed signals from the teacher, rapid pacing, and correction procedures for dealing with student errors (Carnine, Grossey & Silbert, 1994). Generalization and transfer are the result of six "shifts" that Becker and Carnine (1981) say should occur in any well-designed program: overtized to covertized problem solving, simplified contexts to complex contexts, prompts to no prompts, massed to distributed practice, immediate to delayed feedback, and teacher's roles to learner's role as a source of information.

Watkins (1988), in the Project Follow Through evaluation, compared over 20 different instructional models and found Direct Instruction to be the most effective of all programs on measures of basic skills achievement, cognitive skills, and self-concept. Direct Instruction with students has been shown to produce higher reading and math scores (Becker & Gerstein, 1982), more high school diplomas, less grade retention, and fewer dropouts than with students who did not participate (Gerstein, 1982; Gerstein & Carnine, 1983; Gerstein & Keating, 1983). Gerstein, Keating, and Becker (1988) found modest differences in Direct Instruction students 3, 6, and 9 years after the program, with one notable exception: reading. Reading showed a strong long-term benefit consistently across all sites.

2.4.3.1. The Morningside Model. The Morningside Model of Generative Instruction and Fluency (Johnson & Layng, 1992) puts together aspects of Precision Teaching, Direct Instruction, and Personalized System of Instruction with the Instructional Content Analysis of Markle and Tie-mann (Markle & Droege, 1980; Tiemann & Markle, 1990) and the guidelines provided by Markle (1964, 1969, 1991). The Morningside Model has apparently been used, to date, exclusively by the Morningside Academy in Seattle (since 1980) and Malcolm X College, Chicago (since 1991). The program offers instruction for both children and adults in virtually all skill areas. Johnson and Layng (1992) report impressive comparative gains "across the board." From the perspective of the Instructional Technologist, probably the most impressive statistic was the average gain per hour of instruction. Across all studies summarized, Johnson and Layng (1992) found that 20 to 25 hours of instruction per skill using Morningside Model instruction resulted in nearly a two-grade-level "payoff" as compared to the U.S. government standard of one grade level per 100 hours. Sixty hours of in-service was given to new teachers, and although design time/costs were not estimated, the potential cost-benefit of the model seem obvious.

2.5 EPILOGUE: RADICAL BEHAVIORISM

Thus, after 25 years of research, it is clear that behavioral design and delivery models "work." In fact, the large-scale implementations reviewed here were found to produce gains above two grade levels. Moreover, the models appear to be cost effective. Why are they no longer fashionable? Perhaps because what radical behaviorism is, and is not, is not well understood. The following section is our attempt to clarify some of the probable misconceptions.

Probably no psychologist in the modern era has been as misunderstood, misquoted, misjudged, and just plain maligned as B. F. Skinner and his form of Skinnerian, or radical, behaviorism. Much of this stems from the fact that many educational technology programs (or any educational program for that matter) do not teach, at least in any meaningful manner, behavioral theory and research. More recent notions such as cognitive psychology (see Chapter 5), constructivism (see Chapter 7), and social constructivism have become "featured" orientations. Potentially worse, recent students of educational technology have not been exposed to course work that emphasized history and systems, or theory building and theory analysis. In terms of the former problem, we will devote our conclusion to a brief synopsis of what radical behaviorism is and what it isn't. In terms of the latter, we will appeal to the simplest of the criteria for judging the adequacy and appropriateness of a theory: parsimony.

2.5.1 What Radical Behaviorism Does Not Believe

It is important to begin this discussion with what radical behaviorism rejects: structuralism (mind-body dualism), operationalism, and logical positivism.

That radical behaviorism rejects structuralism has been discussed earlier in the introduction of this article. Skinner (1938, 1945, 1953b, 1957, 1964, 1974) continually argued against the use of structures and mentalisms (see Chapters 5, 7, 14, and 29.2). His arguments are too numerous to deal with in this work, but let us consider what is arguably the most telling: copy theory. "The most important consideration is that this view presupposes three things: (a) a stimulus object in the external world, (b) a sensory registering of that object via some modality, and (c) the internal representation of that object as a sensation, perception, or image, different from (b) above (see Chapter 16). The first two are physical, and the third, presumably, something else (Moore, 1980, pp. 472–73).

In Skinner's (1964) words:

> The need for something beyond, and quite different from, copying is not widely understood. Suppose someone were to coat the occipital lobes of the brain with a special photographic emulsion which, when developed, yielded a reasonable copy of a current visual stimulus. In many quarters, this would be regarded as a triumph in the physiology of vision. Yet nothing could be more disastrous, for we should have to start all over again and ask how the organism sees a picture in its occipital cortex, and we should now have much less of the brain available from which to seek an answer. It adds nothing to an explanation of how an organism reacts to a stimulus to trace the pattern of the stimulus into the body. It is most convenient, for both organism and psychophysiologist, if the external world is never copied—if the world we know is simply the world around us. The same may be said of theories according to which the brain interprets signals sent to it and in some sense reconstructs external stimuli. If the real world is, indeed, scrambled in transmission but later reconstructed in the brain, we must then start all over again and explain how the organism sees the reconstruction (p. 87).

Quite simply, if we copy what we see, what do we "see" the copy with and what does this "mind's eye" do with its input? Create another copy? How do we, to borrow from our information-processing colleagues, exit this recursive process?

The related problem of mentalisms generally and their admission with the dialogue of psychology on largely historical grounds were also discussed often by Skinner. For example:

> Psychology, alone among the biological and social sciences, passed through a revolution comparable in many respects with that which was taking place at the same time in physics. This was, of course, behaviorism. The first step, like that in physics, was a reexamination of the observational bases of certain important concepts. . . . Most of the early behaviorists, as well as those of us just coming along who claimed some systematic continuity, had begun to see that psychology did not require the redefinition of subjective concepts. The reinterpretation of an established set of explanatory fictions was not the way to secure the tools then needed for a scientific description of behavior. Historical prestige was beside the point. There was no more reason to make a permanent place for "consciousness," "will," "felling," and so on, than for "phlogiston" or "vis anima." On the contrary, redefined concepts proved to be awkward

and inappropriate, and Watsonianism was, in fact, practically wrecked in the attempt to make them work.

Thus it came about while the behaviorists might have applied Bridgman's principle to representative terms from a mentalistic psychology (and were most competent to do so), they had lost all interest in the matter. They might as well have spent their time in showing what an 18th-century chemist was talking about when he said that the Metallic Substances consisted of a vitrifiable earth united with phlogiston. There was no doubt that such a statement could be analyzed operationally or translated into modern terms, or that subjective terms could be operationally defined. But such matters were of historical interest only. What was wanted was a fresh set of concepts derived from a direct analysis of newly emphasized data . . . (p. 292).

Operationalism is a term often associated with Skinnerian behaviorism, and, indeed, in a sense this association is correct; not however, in the historical sense of operationalism of Stevens (1939) or, in his attacks on behaviorism, by Spence (1948), or in the sense that it is assumed today: "how to deal scientifically with mental events" (Moore, 1981, p. 571). Stevens (1951) for example, states that "operationalism does not deny images, for example, but asks: What is the operational definition of the term "image"? (p. 231). As Moore (1980) explains, this "conventional approach entails virtually every aspect of the dualistic position" (p. 470). "In contrast, for the radical behaviorist, operationalism involves the functional analysis of the term in question, that is, an assessment of the discriminative stimuli that occasions the use of the term and the consequences that maintain it" (Moore, 1981, p. 59). In other words, radical behaviorism rejects the operationalism of methodology behaviorists but embraces the operationalism implicit in the three-part contingency of antecedents, behaviors, and consequences and would, in fact, apply it to the social dialogue of scientists themselves!

The final demon to deal with is the notion that radical behaviorism somehow relies on logical positivism (see 10.2.3). The rejection of this premise will be dealt with more thoroughly in the section to follow that deals with social influences, particularly social influences in science. Suffice it for now to point out that Skinner (1974) felt that methodological behaviorism and logical positivism "ignore consciousness, feelings, and states of mind," but radical behaviorism does not thus "behead the organism. . . . It was not designed to 'permit consciousness to atrophy.'" (p. 219). Day (1983) further describes the effect of Skinner's 1945 paper at the symposium on operationalism: "Skinner turns logical positivism upside down, while methodological behaviorism continues on its own, particular logical-positivist way" (p. 94).

2.5.2 What Radical Behaviorism Does Believe

Two issues that Skinnerian behaviorism is clear on, but not apparently well understood by critics, are the roles of private events and social cultural influences. The first problem, radical behaviorism's treatment of private events, relates to the confusion on the role of operationalism: "The position that psychology must be restricted to publicly observable, intersubjectivity, verifiable databases more appropriately characterizes what Skinner calls methodological behaviorism, an intellectual position regarding the admissibility of psychological data that is conspicuously linked to logical positivism and operationalism" (Moore, 1980, p. 459). Radical behaviorism holds as a central tenant that to rule out stimuli because they are not accessible to others not only represents inappropriate vestiges of operationalism and positivism; it also compromises the explanatory integrity of behaviorism itself (Skinner, 1953a, 1974). In fact, radical behavior does not only value private events; it says they are the same as public events, and herein lies the problem, perhaps. Radical behaviorism does not believe it is necessary to suppose that private events have any special properties simply because they are private (Skinner, 1953b). They are distinguished only by their limited accessibility but are assumed to be equally lawful as public events (Moore, 1980). In other words, the same analyses should be applied to private events as public ones. Obviously, some private or covert behavior involves the same musculature as the public or overt behavior in talking to oneself or "mental practice" of a motor event (Moore, 1980). Generally, we assume that private behavior began as a public event and then, for several reasons, became covert. Moore gives three examples of such reasons. The first is convenience: We learn to read publicly, but private behavior is faster. Another case is that we can engage in a behavior privately, and if the consequences are not suitable, reject it as a public behavior. A second reason is to avoid aversive consequences. We may sing a song over and over covertly but not sing it aloud because we fear social disapproval. Many of us, alone in our shower or in our car, with the negative consequences safely absent, may sing loudly indeed. A third reason is that the stimuli that ordinarily elicit an overt behavior are weak and deficient. Thus we become "unsure" of our response. We may think we see something but be unclear enough either to not say anything or to make a weak, low statement.

What the radical behaviorist does not believe is that private behaviors *cause* public behavior (see 23.6). Both are assumed to be attributable to common variables. The private event may have some discrimination stimulus control, but this is not the cause of the subsequent behavior. The cause is the contingencies of reinforcement that control both public and private behavior (Day, 1976). It is important, particularly in terms of current controversy, to point out that private events are in no way superior to public events, and in at least one respect important to our last argument, very much inferior: The verbal (social) community has trouble responding to these (Moore, 1980). This is because the reinforcing consequence "in most cases is social attention" (Moore, p. 461).

The influence of the social group, of culture, runs through all of Skinner's work (see, e.g., Skinner, 1945, 1953b, 1957, 1964, 1974). For this reason, much of this work focuses on language. As a first step (and to segue from private events), consider an example from Moore (1980). The example deals with pain, but feel free to substitute any private perception. Pain is clearly a case where the stimulus is available only to the individual who perceives it (as opposed to most events that have some external correlate). How do we learn to use the verbal response pain appropriately? One way is for the individual to report pain after some observable public event such as falling down, being struck, etc. The verbal community would support a statement of pain and perhaps suggest that sharp objects cause sharp pain, dull objects dull pain. The second case would involve a collateral, public response such as holding the area in pain. The final case would involve using the word *pain* in connection with some overt state of affairs such as a bent back or a stiff neck. It is important to note that if the individual reports pain too often *without* such overt signs, he or she runs the risk of being called a hypochondriac or malingerer (Moore, 1980). "Verbal behavior is a social phenomenon, and so in a sense all verbal behavior, including scientific verbal behavior, is a product of social-cultural influences" (Moore, 1984, p. 75). To examine the key role of social cultural influences, it is useful to use an example we are familiar with, science. As Moore (1984) points out, "Scientists typically live the first 25 years of their lives, and 12 to 16 hours per day thereafter, in the lay community" (p. 61). Through the process of social and cultural reinforcers, they become acculturated and as a result are exposed to popular preconceptions. Once the individual becomes a scientist, operations and contact with data cue behaviors, which lead to prediction and control. (See Fig. 2-1.) The two systems cannot operate separately. In fact, the behavior of the scientist may be understood as a product of the conjoint action of scientific and lay discriminative stimuli and scientific and lay reinforcer (Moore, 1984).

Figure 2-1.

Although it is dangerous to focus too hard on the "data" alone, Skinner (1974) also cautions against depending exclusively on the social/cultural stimuli and reinforcers for explanations, as is often the case with current approaches:

> Until fairly late in the 19th century, very little was known about the bodily processes in health or disease from which good medical practice could be derived, yet a person who was ill should have found it worthwhile to call in a physician. Physicians saw many ill people and were in the best possible position to acquire useful, if unanalyzed, skills in treating them. Some of them no doubt did so, but the history of medicine reveals a very different picture. Medical practices have varied from epoch to epoch, but they have often consisted of barbaric measures—bloodlettings, leechings, cuppings, poultices, emetics, and purgations—which more often than not must have been harmful. Such practices were not based on the skill and wisdom acquired from contact with illness; they were based on theories of what was going on inside the body of a person who was ill. . . .
>
> Medicine suffered, and in part just because the physician who talked about theories seemed to have a more profound knowledge of illness than one who merely displayed the common sense acquired from personal experience. The practices derived from theories no doubt also obscured many symptoms, which might have led to more effective skills. Theories flourished at the expense both of the patient and of progress toward the more scientific knowledge which was to emerge in modern medicine (Skinner, 1974, pp. x–xi.).

2.6 Conclusion

This brings us to the final points. First, what do current notions such as situated cognition and social constructive add to radical behaviorism? How well does each account for the other? Behaviorism is rich enough to account for both, is historically older, and has the advantage of parsimony; it is the simplest explanation of the observations. We do not believe that advocates of either could come up with a study that discriminates between their position as opposed to behaviorism *except* through the use of mentalistic explanations. Skinner's work was criticized often for being too descriptive, for not offering explanation. Yet it has been supplanted by a tradition that prides itself on qualitative, interpretive analysis. Do the structures and dualistic mentalisms add anything? We think not. Radical behaviorism provides a means both to describe events and to ascribe causality.

Anderson (1985) once noted that the problem in cognitive theory (although we could substitute all current theories in psychology) was that of nonidentifiability; they simply do not make different predictions that distinguish between them. Moreover, what passes as theory is a collection of minitheories and hypotheses without a unifying system. Skinner (1974) makes the point in his introduction to *About Behaviorism* that behaviorism is not the science of behaviorism; it is the philosophy of that science. As such it provides the best vehicle for educational technologists to describe and converse about human learning and behavior. Moreover, its assumptions that the responsibility for

teaching/instruction resides in the teacher or designer "makes sense" if we are to "sell our wares." In a sense, cognitive psychology and its offshoots are collapsing from the weight of the structures they postulate. Behaviorism "worked" even when it was often misunderstood and misapplied. The future for behaviorism may have been delayed (cf. Burton, 1981), but it is coming into fashion again as an orientation and firm foundation for research and practice.

REFERENCES

Alexander, J.E. (1970). *Vocabulary improvement methods, college level.* Knoxville, TN: Tennessee University.

Allen, D.W. & McDonald, F.J. (1963). *The effects of self-instruction on learning in programmed instruction.* Paper presented at the meeting of the American Educational Research Association, Chicago, IL.

Allen, G.J., Giat, L. & Cherney, R.J. (1974). Locus of control, test anxiety, and student performance in a personalized instruction course. *Journal of Educational Psychology 66,* 968–73.

Anderson, J.R. (1985). *Cognitive psychology and its implications,* 2d ed. New York: Freeman.

Anderson, L.M. (1986). Learners and learning. *In* M. Reynolds, ed. *Knowledge base for the beginning teacher,* 85–99. New York: AACTE.

Angell, G.W. & Troyer, M.E. (1948). A new self-scoring test device for improving instruction. *School and Society 67,* (84–85), 66–68.

Ausubel, D.P., Novak, J.D. & Hanesian, H. (1978). *Educational psychology: a cognitive view,* 2d ed. New York: Holt, Rinehart & Winston.

Baker, E.L. (1969). Effects on student achievement of behavioral and non-behavioral objectives. *The Journal of Experimental Education 37,* 5–8.

Bandura, A. (1977). *Social learning theory.* Englewood Cliffs, NJ: Prentice Hall.

Barnes, M.R. (1970). An experimental study of the use of programmed instruction in a university physical science laboratory. Paper presented at the annual meeting of the National Association for Research in Science Teaching, Minneapolis, MN.

Beane, D.G. (1962). A comparison of linear and branching techniques of programmed instruction in plane geometry. Technical Report No. 1. Urbana, IL: University of Illinois.

Beck, J. (1959). On some methods of programming. *In* E. Galanter, ed. *Automatic teaching: the state of the art,* 55–62. New York: Wiley.

Becker, W.C. & Carnine, D.W. (1981). Direct Instruction: a behavior theory model for comprehensive educational intervention with the disadvantaged. *In* S.W. Bijou & R. Ruiz, eds. *Behavior modification: contributions to education.* Hillsdale, NJ: Erlbaum.

— & Gersten, R. (1982). A follow-up of follow-through: meta-analysis of the later effects of the Direction Instruction Model. *American Educational Research Journal 19,* 75-93.

Bereiter, C. & Engelmann, S. (1966). *Teaching disadvantaged children in the preschool.* Englewood Cliffs, NJ: Prentice Hall.

Binder, C. (1987). *Fluency-building™ research background.* Nonantum, MA: Precision Teaching and Management Systems, Inc. (P.O. Box 169, Nonantum, MA 02195).

— (1988). Precision teaching: measuring and attaining academic achievement. *Youth Policy 10*(7), 12–15.

— (1993). Behavioral fluency: a new paradigm. *Educational Technology 33*(10), 8–14.

— Haughton, E. & VanEyk, D. (1990). Increasing endurance by building fluency: precision teaching attention span. *Teaching Exceptional Children 22*(3), 24–27.

— & Watkins, C.L. (1989). Promoting effective instructional methods: solutions to America's educational crisis. *Future Choices 1*(3), 33–39.

— & — (1990). Precision teaching and direct instruction: measurably superior instructional technology in schools. *Performance Improvement Quarterly 3*(4), 75–95.

Blodgett, R. (1929). The effect of the introduction of reward upon the maze performance of rats. *University of California Publications in Psychology 4*, 113–34.

Bloom, B. (1971). Master learning. *In* J.H. Block, ed. *Mastery learning: theory and practice*, 47–63. New York: Holt, Rinehart & Winston.

Bloom, B.S., Engelhart, N.D., Furst, E.J., Hill, W.H. & Krathwohl, D.R., eds. (1956). *Taxonomy of educational objectives—the classification of education goals, Handbook I: cognitive domain*. New York: McKay.

Borger, R. & Seaborne, A.E.M. (1982). *The psychology of learning*, 2d ed. New York: Penguin.

Bower, B. & Orgel, R. (1981). To err is divine. *Journal of Precision Teaching 2*(1), 3–12.

Brenner, H.R., Walter, J.S. & Kurtz, A.K. (1949). The effects of inserted questions and statements on film learning. Progress Report No. 10, State College, Pennsylvania: Pennsylvania State College, Instructional Film Research Program.

Briggs, L.J. (1947). Intensive classes for superior students. *Journal of Educational Psychology 38*, 207–215.

— (1958). Two self-instructional devices. *Psychological Reports 4*, 671–76.

— Gustafson, K.L. & Tillman, M.H. (1991). *Instructional design*. Englewood Cliffs, NJ: Educational Technology.

Brown, J.L. (1970). *The effects of revealing instructional objectives on the learning of political concepts and attitudes in two role-playing games*. Unpublished doctoral dissertation, University of California at Los Angeles.

Burton, J.K. (1981). Behavioral technology: foundation for the future. *Educational Technology XXI*(7), 21–28.

— & Merrill, P.F. (1991). Needs assessment: goals, needs, and priorities. *In* L.J. Briggs, K.L. Gustafson & M. Tillman, eds. *Instructional design: principles and applications*. Englewood Cliffs, NJ: Educational Technology.

Caldwell, T. (1966). *Comparison of classroom measures: percent, number, and rate* (Educational Research Technical Report). Kansas City: University of Kansas Medical Center.

Calhoun, J.F. (1976). The combination of elements in the personalized system of instruction. *Teaching Psychology 3*, 73–76.

Callahan, C. & Smith, R.M. (1990). Keller's personalized system of instruction in a junior high gifted program. *Roeper Review 13*, 39–44.

Campbell, V.N. (1961). *Adjusting self-instruction programs to individual differences: studies of cueing, responding and bypassing*. San Mateo, CA: American Institute for Research.

Campeau, P.L. (1974). Selective review of the results of research on the use of audiovisual media to teach adults. *AV Communication Review 22*(1), 5–40.

Cantor, J.H. & Brown, J.S. (1956). *An evaluation of the trainer-tester and punchboard tutor as electronics troubleshooting training aids*. (George Peabody College) Port Washington, NY: Special Devices Center, Office of Naval Research. Technical Report NTDC-1257-2-1.

Carnine, D., Grossen, B. & Silbert, J. (1994). Direct instruction to accelerate cognitive growth. *In* J. Block, T. Gluskey & S. Everson, eds. *Choosing research based school improvement innovations*. New York: Scholastic.

Carpenter, C.R. (1962). Boundaries of learning theories and mediators of learning. *AV Communication Review 10*(6), 295–306.

— & Greenhill, L.P. (1956). *Instructional film research reports*, Vol. 2. Technical Report 269-7-61, NAVEXOS P12543, Post Washington, NY: Special Devices Center.

— & — (1955). An investigation of closed-circuit television for teaching university courses, Report No. 1. University Park, PA: Pennsylvania State University.

— & — (1958). An investigation of closed-circuit television for teaching university courses, Report No. 2. University Park, PA: Pennsylvania State University.

Carr, W.J. (1959). Self-instructional devices: a review of current concepts. USAF Wright Air Dev. Cent. Tech. Report 59-503 [278, 286, 290].

Cason, H. (1922a). The conditioned pupillary reaction. *Journal of Experimental Psychology 5*, 108–46.

— (1922b). The conditioned eyelid reaction. *Journal of Experimental Psychology 5*, 153–96.

Chance, P. (1994). *Learning and behavior*. Pacific Grove, CA: Brooks/Cole.

Cheney, C.D. & Powers, R.B. (1971). A programmed approach to teaching in the social sciences. *Improving College and University Teaching 19*, 164–66.

Chiesa, M. (1992). Radical behaviorism and scientific frameworks: from mechanistic to relational accounts. *American Psychologist 47*, 1287–99.

Chu, G. & Schramm, W. (1968). *Learning from television*. Washington, DC: National Association of Educational Broadcasters.

Churchland, P.M. (1990). *Matter and consciousness*. Cambridge, MA: MIT Press.

Cook, D.A. (1994). The campaign for educational territories. Paper presented at the Annual meeting of the Association for Behavior Analysis, May, Atlanta, GA.

Cook, J.U. (1960). Research in audiovisual communication. *In* J. Ball & F.C. Byrnes, eds. *Research, principles, and practices in visual communication*, 91–106. Washington, DC: Department of Audiovisual Instruction, NEA.

Cooper, J.O., Heron, T.E. & Heward, W.L. (1987). *Applied behavior analysis*. Columbus, OH: Merrill.

Corey, S.M. (1971). Definition of instructional design. *In* M.D. Merrill, ed. *Instructional design: readings*. Englewood Cliffs, NJ: Prentice Hall.

Coulson, J.E. & H.F. Silberman (1960). Effects of three variables in a teaching machine. *Journal of Educational Psychology 51* 135–43.

Cregger, R. & Metzler, M. (1992). PSI for a college physical education basic instructional program. *Educational Technology 32*, 51–56.

Crooks, F.C. (1971). The differential effects of pre-prepared and teacher-prepared instructional objectives on the learning of educable mentally retarded children. Unpublished doctoral dissertation, University of Iowa.

Crowder, N.A. (1959). Automatic tutoring by means of intrinsic programming. *In* E. Galanter, ed. *Automatic teaching: the state of the art*, 109–16. New York: Wiley.

— (1960). Automatic tutoring by intrinsic programming. *In* A. Lumsdaine & R. Glaser, ed. *Teaching machines and programmed learning: a source book*, 286–98. Washington, DC: National Education Association.

— (1961). Characteristics of branching programs. The University of Kansas Conference on Programmed Learning (Edited by O.M. Haugh). Lawrence, KA: *University of Kansas Publications II*, (2), 22–27.

— (1962, Apr.). The rationale of intrinsic programming. *Programmed Instruction 1*, 3–6.

Dalis, G.T. (1970). Effect of precise objectives upon student achievement in health education. *Journal of Experimental Education 39*, 20–23.

Daniel, W.J. & P. Murdoch (1968). Effectiveness of learning from a programmed text compared with a conventional text covering the same material. *Journal of Educational Psychology 59*, 425–51.

Darwin, C. (1859). *On the origin of species by means of natural selection, or the preservation of the favored races in the struggle for life*. London: Murray.

Davey, G. (1981). *Animal learning & conditioning*. Baltimore: University Park.

Day, W.F. (1983). On the difference between radical and methodological behaviorism. *Behaviorism 11*(11), 89–102.

— (1976). Contemporary behaviorism and the concept of intention. *In* W.J. Arnold, ed. *Nebraska Symposium on Motivation*, 65–131 (1975). Lincoln, NE: University of Nebraska Press.

Dewey, J. (1957). *Human nature and conduct*. New York: Modern Library (original work published in 1922).

— (1900). Psychology and social practice. *The Psychological Review 7*, 105–24.

Donahoe, J.W. (1991). Selectionist approach to verbal behavior. Potential contributions of neuropsychology and computer simulation. *In* L.J. Hayes & P.N. Chase, eds. *Dialogues on verbal behavior,* 119–45. Reno, NV: Context.

— & Palmer, D.C. (1989). The interpretation of complex human behavior: some reactions to parallel distributed processing. J.L. McClelland, D.E. Rumelhart & the PDP Research Group, eds. *Journal of the Experimental Analysis of Behavior 51*, 399–416.

Doty, C.R. (1968). The effect of practice and prior knowledge of educational objectives on performance. Unpublished doctoral dissertation, Ohio State University.

Dowell, E.C. (1955). *An evaluation of trainer-testers*. Headquarters Technical Training Air Force, Keesler Air Force Base, MS. (Report No. 54-28.)

Englemann, S., Becker, W.C., Carnine, D. & Gersten, R. (1988). The direction instruction follow through model: design and outcomes. *Education and Treatment of Children 11*(4), 303–17.

— & Carnine, D. (1982). *Theory of instruction*. New York: Irvington.

— & — (1991). *Theory of instruction: principles and applications* (rev. ed.). Eugene, OR: ADI.

Evans, J.L., Glaser, R. & Homme, L.E. (1962). An investigation of "teaching machine" variables using learning programs in symbolic logic. *Journal of Educational Research 55*, 433–542.

— Homme, L.E. & Glaser, R. (1962, Jun.-Jul.). The Ruleg system for the construction of programmed verbal learning sequences. *Journal of Educational Research 55*, 513–18.

Fernald, P.S., Chiseri, M.J., Lawson, D.W., Scroggs, G.F. & Riddell, J.C. (1975). Systematic manipulation of student pacing, the perfection requirement, and contact with a teaching assistant in an introductory psychology course. *Teaching of Psychology 2*, 147–51.

Ferster, C.B. & Skinner, B.F. (1957). *Schedules of reinforcement*. New York: Appleton-Century-Crofts.

Fink, E.R. (1968). Performance and selection rates of emotionally disturbed and mentally retarded preschoolers on Montessori materials. Unpublished master's thesis, University of Kansas.

Frase, L.T. (1970). Boundary conditions for mathemagenic behaviors. *Review of Educational Research 40*, 337–47.

Gagné, R.M. (1962). Introduction. *In* R.M. Gagné, ed. *Psychological principles in system development*. New York: Holt, Rinehart & Winston.

— (1965). The analysis of instructional objectives for the design of instruction. *In* R. Glaser, ed. *Teaching machines and programmed learning, II*. Washington, DC: National Education Association of the US.

— ed. (1987). *Instructional technology foundations*. Hillsdale, NJ: Erlbaum.

— L.J. Briggs & W. W. Wager (1988). *Principles of instructional design,* 3d ed. New York: Holt, Rinehart & Winston.

—, — & — (1992). *Principles of instructional design*, 4th ed. New York: Harcourt, Brace.

Galanter, E. (1959). The ideal teacher. *In* E. Galanter, ed. *Automatic teaching: the state of the art*, 1–11. New York: Wiley.

Garrison, J.W. (1994). Realism, Deweyan pragmation, and educational research. *Educational Researcher 23*, (1), 5–14.

Gersten, R.M. (1982). High school follow-up of DI Follow Through. *Direct Instruction News 2*, 3.

— & Carnine, D.W. (1983). The later effects of Direction Instruction Follow Through. Paper presented at the annual meeting of the American Educational Research Association, Montreal, Canada.

— & Keating, T. (1983). DI Follow Through students show fewer dropouts, fewer retentions, and more high school graduates. *Direct Instruction News, 2*, 14–15.

—,— & Becker, W.C. (1988). The continued impact of the Direct Instruction Model: longitudinal studies of follow through students. *Education and Treatment of Children 11*(4), 318–27.

Gibson, J.J., ed. (1947). Motion picture testing and research. Report No. 7, Army Air Forces Aviation Psychology Program Research Reports, Washington, DC: Government Printing Office.

Giese, D.L. & Stockdale, W. (1966). Comparing an experimental and a conventional method of teaching linguistic skills. *The General College Studies 2*(3), 1–10.

Gilbert, T.F. (1962). Mathetics: the technology of education. *Journal of Mathetics*, 7–73.

Glaser, R. (1960). Principles and problems in the preparation of programmed learning sequences. Paper presented at the University of Texas Symposium on the Automation of Instruction, University of Texas, May 1960. [Also to be published as a report of a Cooperative Research Program Grant to the University of Pittsburgh under sponsorship of the U.S. Office of Education.]

— (1962). Psychology and instructional technology. *In* R. Glaser, ed. *Training research and education.* Pittsburgh, PA: University of Pittsburgh Press.

— ed. (1962). *Training research and education.* Pittsburgh, PA: University of Pittsburgh Press.

— (1965). Toward a behavioral science base for instructional design. *In* R. Glaser, ed. *Teaching machines and programmed learning, II: data and directions*, 771–809. Washington, DC: National Education Association.

— ed. (1965). *Teaching machines and programmed learning II.* Washington, DC: Association for Educational Communications and Technology.

— Damrin, D.E. & Gardner, F.M. (1954). The tab time: a technique for the measurement of proficiency in diagnostic problem-solving tasks. *Educational and Psychological Measurement 14*, 283–93.

— Reynolds, J.H. & Harakas, T. (1962). *An experimental comparison of a small-step single track program with a large-step multi-track (branching) program.* Pittsburgh, PA: Programmed Learning Laboratory, University of Pittsburgh.

Goodson, F.E. (1973). *The evolutionary foundations of psychology: a unified theory.* New York: Holt, Rinehart & Winston.

Gropper, G.L. (1963). Why is a picture worth a thousand words? *AV Communication Review 11*(4), 75–95.

— (1965a, Oct.). *Controlling student responses during visual presentations, report No. 2. Studies in televised instruction: the role of visuals in verbal learning, Study No. 1—an investigation of response control during visual presentations. Study No. 2—integrating visual and verbal presentations.* Pittsburgh, PA: American Institutes for Research.

— (1965b). A description of the REP style program and its rationale. Paper presented at NSPI Convention, Philadelphia, PA.

— (1966, Spring). Learning from visuals: some behavioral considerations. *AV Communication Review 14*: 37–69.

— (1967). Does "programmed" television need active responding? *AVCR 15*(1), 5–22.

— (1968). Programming visual presentations for procedural learning. *AVCR 16*(1), 33–55.

— (1983). A behavioral approach to instructional prescription. *In* C.M. Reigeluth, ed. *Instructional-design theories and models.* Hillsdale, NJ: Erlbaum.

— & Glasgow, Zita. (1966, Oct.). *Studies in televised instruction: an experimental evaluation of methods for improving "conventional" television lessons.* Pittsburgh, PA: American Institutes for Research.

—, A.A. Lumsdaine & V. Shipman (1961, Mar.). *Improvement of televised instruction based on student responses to achievement tests, Report No. 1. Studies in televised instruction: the use of student response to improve televised instruction.* Pittsburgh, PA: American Institutes for Research.

— & Ross, P.A. (1987). Instructional design. *In* R.L. Craig, ed. *Training and development handbook*, 3d ed. New York: McGraw-Hill.

Gustafson, K.L. & Tillman, M.H. (1991). Introduction. *In* L.J. Briggs, K.L. Gustafson & M.H. Tillman, eds. *Instructional design.* Englewood Cliffs, NJ: Educational Technology.

Hamilton, R.S. & Heinkel, O.A. (1967). *English A: an evaluation of programmed instruction.* San Diego, CA: San Diego City College.

Hebb, D.O. (1949). *Organization of behavior.* New York: Wiley.

Helmholtz, H.V. (1866). *Handbook of physiological optics* (J.P.C. Southhall, trans.). Rochester, NY: Optical Society of America.

Heinich, R. (1970). *Technology and the management of instruction* (Association for Educational Communication and Technology Monograph No. 4). Washington, DC: Association for Educational Communications and Technology.

Herrnstein, R.J. & Boring, E.G. (1973). *A source book in the history of psychology.* Cambridge, MA: Harvard University Press.

Hoban, C.F. (1946). *Movies that teach.* New York: Dryden.

— (1960). The usable residue of educational film research. *New teaching aids for the American classroom*, 95–115. Stanford University, CA: Institute for Communication Research.

— & Van Ormer, E.B. (1950). *Instructional film research 1918–1950.* Port Washington, NY: Special Devices Center, Office of Naval Research. Technical Report SDC 269-7-19.

Holland, J.G. (1960). Design and use of a teaching-machine program. Paper presented at the American Psychological Association, Chicago, IL.

Holland, J.G. (1961, Sep.). New directions in teaching-machine research. *Programmed learning and computer-based instruction. In* J.E. Coulson, ed., New York: Wiley.

Holland, J.G. (1965). Research on programmed variables. *In* R. Glaser, ed. *Teaching machines and programmed learning, II*, 66–117. Washington, DC: Association for Educational Communications and Technology.

Holland, J. & Skinner, B.V. (1961). *Analysis of behavior: a program of self-instruction.* New York: McGraw-Hill.

Holzschuh, R. & Dobbs, D. (1966). Rate correct vs. percentage correct. (Educational Research Technical Report). Kansas City, KS: University of Kansas Medical Center.

Homme, L.E. (1957). The rationale of teaching by Skinner's machines. *In* A.A. Lumsdaine & R. Glaser, eds. *Teaching machines and programmed learning: a source book*, Washington, DC: National Education Association.

Homme, L.E. & Glaser, R. (1960). Problems in programming verbal learning sequences. *In* A.A. Lumsdaine & R. Glaser, ed. *Teaching machines and programmed learning: a source book*, 486–96. Washington, DC: National Education Association.

Hough, J.B. (1962, Jun.-Jul.). An analysis of the efficiency and effectiveness of selected aspects of machine instruction. *Journal of Educational Research 55*, 467–71.

— & Revsin, B. (1963). Programmed instruction at the college level: a study of several factors influencing learning. *Phi Delta Kappan 44*, 286–91.

Hobland, C.I., Lumsdaine, A.A. & Sheffield, F.D. (1949). *Experiments on mass communication.* Princeton, NJ: Princeton University Press.

Hull, C.L. (1943). *Principles of behavior.* New York: Appleton-Century-Crofts.

Hymel, G. (1987, Apr.). A literature trend analysis in mastery learning. Paper presented at the Annual Meeting of the American Educational Research Association, Washington, DC.

Irion, A.L. & Briggs, L.J. (1957). *Learning task and mode of operation variables in use of the Subject Matter Trainer.* Lowry Air Force Base, CO: Air Force Personnel and Training Center, T.R. AFPTRC-TR-57-8.

James, W. (1890). *The principles of psychology.* New York: Holt, Rinehart & Winston.

— (1904). Does consciousness exist? *Journal of Philosophy 1*, 477–91.

Janeczko, R.J. (1971). The effect of instructional objectives and general objectives on student self-evaluation and psychomotor performance in power mechanics. Unpublished doctoral dissertation, University of Missouri-Columbia.

Jaspen, N. (1948). Especially designed motion pictures: I. assembly of the 40mm breechblock. Progress Report No. 9, State College, Pennsylvania: Pennsylvania State College, Instructional Film Research Program.

— (1950). Effects on training of experimental film variables, study II. Verbalization, "how it works," nomenclature audience participation and succinct treatment." Progress Report No., 14-15-16, State College, Pennsylvania: Pennsylvania State College, Instructional Film Research Program.

Jensen, B.T. (1949). An independent-study laboratory using self-scoring tests. *Journal of Educational Research 43*, 134–37.

Johnson, K.R. & Layng, T.V.J. (1992). Breaking the structuralist barrier; literacy and numeracy with fluency. *American Psychologist 47*(11), 1475–90.

— & — (1994). The Morningside model of generative instruction. *In* R. Gardner, D.M. Sainato, J.O. Cooper, T.E. Heron, W.L. Heward, J. Eshleman & T.A. Grossi, eds. *Behavior analysis in education: focus on measurably superior instruction,* 173–97. Pacific Grove, CA: Brooks/Cole.

Johnson, N.J. (1971). Acceleration of inner-city elementary school pupils' reading performance. Unpublished doctoral dissertation, University of Kansas, Lawrence, KS.

Jones, H.L. & Sawyer, M.O. (1949). A new evaluation instrument. *Journal of Educational Research 42*, 381–85.

Jordan, J.B. & Robbins, L.S. (1972). *Let's try doing something else kind of thing: behavioral principles and the exceptional child.* Arlington, VA: The Council for Exceptional Children.

Kaess, W. & Zeaman, D. (1960, Jul.). Positive and negative knowledge of results on a Pressey-type punchboard. *Journal of Experimental Psychology 60*, 12–17.

Kalish, D.M. (1972). The effects on achievement of using behavioral objectives with fifth grade students. Unpublished doctoral dissertation, Ohio State University.

Kanner, J.H. (1960). The development and role of teaching aids in the armed forces. *In New teaching aids for the American classroom.* Stanford, CA: The Institute for Communication Research.

— & Sulzer, R.L. (1955). *Overt and covert rehearsal of 50% versus 1005 of the material in filmed learning.* Chanute AFB, IL: TARL, AFPTRC.

Karis, C., Kent, A. & Gilbert, J.E. (1970). The interactive effect of responses per frame, response mode, and response confirmation on intraframe S-4 association strength. Final report. Boston, MA: Northeastern University.

Keller, F.S. (1968). Goodbye teacher . . . *Journal of Applied Behavior Analysis 1*, 79–89.

— & Sherman, J.G. (1974). *The Keller Plan handbook.* Menlow Park, CA: Benjamin.

Kendler, T.S., Cook, J.O. & Kendler, H.H. (1953). An investigation of the interacting effects of repetition and audience participation on learning from films. Paper presented at the annual meeting of the American Psychological Association, Cleveland, OH.

— Kendler, H.H. & Cook. J.O. (1954). Effect of opportunity and instructions to practice during a training film on initial recall and retention. Staff Research Memorandum, Chanute AFB, IL: USAF Training Aids Research Laboratory.

Kendler, H.H. (1971). Stimulus-response psychology and audiovisual education. *In* W.E. Murheny, ed. *Audiovisual Process in Education.* Washington, DC: Department of Audiovisual Instruction.

Kibler, R.J., Cegala, D.J., Miles, D.T. & Barker, L.L. (1974). *Objectives for instruction and evaluation.* Boston, MA: Allyn & Bacon.

Kimble, G.A. (1953). The effect of 'praise and reproof' on the value of training film instruction. Yale University. Unpublished manuscript.

Kimble, G.A. & Wulff, J.J. (1953). Response guidance as a factor in the value of audience participation in training film instruction. Memo Report No. 36, Human Factors Operations Research Laboratory.

— & — (1954). The teaching effectiveness of instruction in reading a scale as a function of the relative amounts of problem-solving practice and demonstration examples used in training. Staff Research Memorandum, USAF Training Aids Research Laboratory.

Klaus, D. (1965). An analysis of programming techniques. *In* R. Glaser (ed.). *Teaching machines and programmed learning, II.* Washington, DC: AECT.

Koenig, C.H. & Kunzelmann, H.P. (1981). *Classroom learning screening.* Columbus, OH: Merrill.

Kumata, H. (1961). History and progress of instructional television research in the U.S. Report presented at the International Seminar on Instructional Television. Lafayette, IN.

Lathrop, C.W., Jr. (1949). Contributions of film instructions to learning from instructional films. Progress Report No. 13, State College, Pennsylvania: Pennsylvania State College, Instructional Film Research Program.

Lawrence, R.M. (1970). The effects of three types of organizing devices on academic achievement. Unpublished doctoral dissertation, University of Maryland.

Layng, T.V.J. (1991). A selectionist approach to verbal behavior: Sources of variation. *In* L.J. Hayes & P.N. Chase, eds. *Dialogues on verbal behavior,* 146–50. Reno, NV: Context.

Liddell, H.S. (1926). A laboratory for the study of conditioned motor reflexes. *American Journal of Psychology 37*, 418–19.

Lindsley, O.R. (1956). Operant conditioning methods applied to research in chronic schizophrenia. *Psychiatric Research Reports 5*, 118–39.

— (1964). Direct measurement and prosthesis of retarded behavior. *Journal of Education 147,* 62-81.

— (1972). From Skinner to precision teaching. *In* J.B. Jordan & L.S. Robbins, eds. *Let's try doing something else kind of thing,* 1–12. Arlington, VA: Council on Exceptional Children.

— (1990a). Our aims, discoveries, failures, and problems. *Journal of Precision Teaching 7*(7), 7–17.

— (1990b). Precision Teaching: by children for teachers. *Teaching Exceptional Children* 22(3), 10–15.

— (1991a). Precision teaching's unique legacy from B.F. Skinner. *The Journal of Behavioral Education* 2, 253–66.

— (1991b). From technical jargon to plain English for application.. *The Journal of Applied Behavior Analysis* 24, 449–58.

— & Skinner, B.F. (1954). A method for the experimental analysis of the behavior of psychotic patients. *American Psychologist 9*, 419–20.

Little, J.K. (1934). Results of use of machines for testing and for drill upon learning in educational psychology. *Journal of Experimental Education 3*, 59–65.

Lloyd, K.E. (1971). Contingency management in university courses. *Educational Technology 11*(4), 18–23.

Loh, E.L. (1972). The effect of behavioral objectives on measures of learning and forgetting on high school algebra. Unpublished doctoral dissertation, University of Maryland.

Long, A.L. (1946). The influence of color on acquisition and retention as evidenced by the use of sound films. Unpublished doctoral dissertation, University of Colorado.

Lovett, H.T. (1971). The effects of various degrees of knowledge of instructional objectives and two levels of feedback from formative evaluation on student achievement. Unpublished doctoral dissertation, University of Georgia.

Lumsdaine, A.A., ed. (1961). *Student responses in programmed instruction*. Washington, DC: National Academy of Sciences, National Research Council.

— (1962a). Assessing the effectiveness of instructional programs. *In* R. Glaser, ed. *Teaching machines and programmed learning, II*, 267–320. Washington, DC: AECT.

— (1962b). Instruction materials and devices. *In* R. Glaser, ed. *Training research and education*. Pittsburgh, PA: University of Pittsburgh Press.

— & Sulzer, R.L. (1951). The influence of simple animation techniques on the value of a training film. Memo Report No. 24, Human Resources Research Laboratory.

— & Glaser, R., eds. (1960). *Teaching machines and programmed learning*. Washington, DC. Department of Audiovisual Instruction, NEA.

Mager, R.F. (1962). *Preparing instructional objectives*. San Francisco, CA: Fearon.

— (1984). *Goal analysis*, 2d ed. Belmont, CA: David S. Lake.

— & J. McCann (1961). *Learner-controlled instruction*. Palo Alto, CA: Varian.

Malcolm, N. (1954). Wittgenstein's philosophical investigation. *Philosophical Review* LXIII.

Malone, J.C. (1990). *Theories of learning: a historical approach*. Belmont, CA: Wadsworth.

Markle, S.M. (1964). *Good frames and bad: a grammar of frame writing*. New York: Wiley.

— (1967). Empirical testing of programs. *In* P.C. Lange, ed. *Programmed instruction: sixty-sixth yearbook of the National Society for the Study of Education: 2*, 104–38. Chicago, IL: University of Chicago Press.

— (1969). *Good frames and bad: a grammar of frame writing*, 2d ed. New York: Wiley.

— (1991). *Designs for instructional designers*. Champaign, IL: Stipes.

— & Droege, S.A. (1980). Solving the problem of problem solving domains. *NSPI Journal 19*, 30–33.

Marsh, L.A. & Pierce-Jones, J. (1968). Programmed instruction as an adjunct to a course in adolescent psychology. Paper presented at the annual meeting of the American Educational Research Association, Chicago, IL.

Mateer, F. (1918). *Child behavior: a critical and experimental study of young children by the method of conditioned reflexes*. Boston: Badger.

May, M.A. & Lumsdaine, A.A. (1958). *Learning from films*. New Haven, CT: Yale University Press.

McClelland, J.L. & Rumelhart, D.E. (1986). *Parallel distributed processing: explorations into the microstructure of cognition: Vol. 2. Psychological and biological models*. Cambridge, MA: Bradford Books/MIT Press.

McDonald, F.J. & Allen, D. (1962, Jun.-Jul.). An investigation of presentation response and correction factors in programmed instruction. *Journal of Educational Research 55*, 502–07.

McGuire, W.J. (1953a). Length of film as a factor influencing training effectiveness. Unpublished manuscript.

— (1953b). Serial position and proximity to reward as factors influencing teaching effectiveness of a training film. Unpublished manuscript.

— (1953c). Slow motion, added narration and distributed showings as factors influencing teaching effectiveness of a training film. Unpublished manuscript.

— (1954). The relative efficacy of overt and covert trainee participation with different speeds of instruction. Unpublished manuscript.

McKeachie, W.J. (1967). *New developments in teaching: new dimensions in higher education. No. 16*. Durham, NC: Duke University.

McNeil, J.D. (1967). Concomitants of using behavioral objectives in the assessment of teacher effectiveness. *Journal of Experimental Education 36*, 69–74.

McLaughlin, T.F. (1991). Use of a personalized system of instruction with and without a same-day retake contingency of spelling performance of behaviorally disordered children. *Behavioral Disorders 16*, 127–32.

Merrill, M.D. (1971). *Instructional design: readings*. Englewood Cliffs, NJ: Prentice Hall.

Metzler, M., Eddleman, K., Treanor, L. & Cregger, R. (1989, Feb.). Teaching tennis with an instructional system design. Paper presented at the annual meeting of the Eastern Educational Research Association, Savannah, GA.

Meyer, S.R. (1960). Report on the initial test of a junior high school vocabulary program. *In* A.A. Lumsdaine & R. Glaser, eds. *Teaching machines and programmed learning*, 229–46. Washington, DC: National Education Association.

Michael, D.N. (1951). Some factors influencing the effects of audience participation on learning from a factual film. Memo Report 13 A (rev.). Human Resources Research Laboratory.

Michael, D.N. & Maccoby, N. (1954). A further study of the use of 'audience participating' procedures in film instruction. Staff Research Memorandum, Chanute AFB, IL: AFPTRC, Project 504-028-0003.

Michael, J.L. (1974). Statistical inference for individual organism research: mixed blessings or curse. *Journal of Applied Behavior Analysis 7*, 647–53.

Mill, J. (1967). *Analysis of the phenomena of the human mind*, 2d ed. New York: Augustus Kelly Publishers (original work published 1829).

Miller, J. & Klier, S. (1953a). A further investigation of the effects of massed and spaced review techniques. Unpublished manuscript.

— & — (1953b). The effect on active rehearsal types of review of massed and spaced review techniques. Unpublished manuscript.

— & — (1954). The effect of interpolated quizzes on learning audio-visual material. Unpublished manuscript.

— & Levine, S. (1952b). A study of the effects of different types of review and of 'structuring' subtitles on the amount learned from a training film. Memo Report No. 17, Human Resources Research Laboratory.

—, — & Sternberger, J. (1952a). The effects of different kinds of review and of subtitling on learning from a training film (a replicative study). Unpublished manuscript.

—, — & — (1952). Extension to a new subject matter of the findings on the effects of different kinds of review on learning from a training film. Unpublished manuscript.

Miller, L.K., Weaver, F.H. & Semb, G. (1954). A procedure for maintaining student progress in a personalized university course. *Journal of Applied Behavior Analysis 7*, 87–91.

Moore, J. (1980). "On behaviorism and private events." *The Psychological Record 30*(4), 459–75.

— (1984). On behaviorism, knowledge, and causal explanation. *The Psychological Record 34*(1), 73-97.

— & Smith, W.I. (1961, December). Knowledge of results of self-teaching spelling. *Psychological Reports 9*, 717-26.

— & — (1962). A comparison of several types of "immediate reinforcement." *Programmed Learning*, 192–201. *In* W. Smith & J. Moore, eds. New York: Van Nostrand.

Morris, E. K., C. F. Surber & S. W. Biyou (1978). Self-pacing versus instructor-pacing: Achievement, evaluations, and retention. *Journal of Educational Psychology 70*, 224–30.

Needham, W.C. (1978). *Cerebral logic*. Springfield, IL: Charles C. Thomas.

Neisser, U. (1967). *Cognitive psychology*. New York: Appleton-Century-Crofts.

— (1976). *Cognition and reality*. San Francisco, CA: Freeman.

Neu, D.M. (1950). The effect of attention-gaining devices on film-mediated learning. Progress Report No. 14-15, 16, State College, Pennsylvania: Pennsylvania State College, Instructional Film Research Program.

Neufeld, K.A. & Lindsley, O.R. (1980). Charting to compare children's learning at four different reading performance levels. *Journal of Precision Teaching 1*(1), 9–17.

Norford, C.A. (1949). Contributions of film summaries to learning from instructional films. Progress Report No. 13, State College, Pennsylvania: Pennsylvania State College, Instructional Film Research Program.

Olsen, C.R. (1972). A comparative study of the effect of behavioral objectives on class performance and retention in physical science. Unpublished doctoral dissertation, University of Maryland.

Patton, C.T. (1972). The effect of student knowledge of behavioral objectives on achievement and attitudes in educational psychology. Unpublished doctoral dissertation, University of Northern Colorado.

Pennypacker, H.S. (1994). A selectionist view of the future of behavior analysis in education. *In* R. Gardner, D.M. Sainato, J.O. Cooper, T.E. Heron, W.L. Heward, J. Eshleman & T.A. Grossi, eds. *Behavior analysis in education: focus on measurably superior instruction*, 11–18. Pacific Grove, CA: Brooks/Cole.

Peterman, J.N. & Bouscaren, N. (1954). A study of introductory and summarizing sequences in training film instruction. Staff Research Memorandum, Chanute AFB, IL: Training Aids Research Laboratory.

Peterson, J.C. (1931). The value of guidance in reading for information. *Transactions of the Kansas Academy of Science 34*, 291–96.

Piatt, G.R. (1969). An investigation of the effect of the training of teachers in defining, writing, and implementing educational behavioral objectives on learner outcomes for students enrolled in a seventh grade mathematics program in the public schools. Unpublished doctoral dissertation, Lehigh University.

Popham, W.J. & Baker, E.L. (1970). *Establishing instructional goals*. Englewood Cliffs, NJ: Prentice Hall.

Porter, D. (1957). A critical review of a portion of the literature on teaching devices. *Harvard Educational Review 27*, 126–47.

— (1958). Teaching machines. *Harvard Graduate School of Education Association Bulletin 3*,1–15, 206–14.

Potts, L., Eshleman, J.W. & Cooper, J.O. (1993). Ogden R. Lindsley and the historical development of Precision Teaching. *The Behavioral Analyst 16*(2), 177–189.

Premack, D. (1965). Reinforcement theory. *In* D. Levin, ed. *Nebraska symposium on motivation*. Lincoln, NE: University of Nebraska Press.

Pressey, S.L. (1926). A simple apparatus which gives tests and scores—and teaches. *School and Society 23*, 35–41.

— (1932). A third and fourth contribution toward the coming "industrial revolution" in education. *School and Society 36*, 47–51.

— (1950). Development and appraisal of devices providing immediate automatic scoring of objective tests and concomitant self-instruction. *Journal of Psychology 29* (417–47) 69–88.

— (1960). Some perspectives and major problems regarding teaching machines. *In* A.A. Lumsdaine & R. Glaser, eds. *Teaching machines and programmed learning: a source book*, 497–505. Washington, DC: National Education Association.

— (1963). Teaching machine (and learning theory) crisis. *Journal of Applied Psychology 47*, 1–6.

Reigeluth, C.M. (1983). Instructional-design theories and models. Hillsdale, NJ: Erlbaum.

Reiser, R.A. (1980). The interaction between locus of control and three pacing procedures in a personalized system of instruction course. *Educational Communication and Technology Journal 28*, 194–202.

— (1984). Interaction between locus of control and three pacing procedures in a personalized system of instruction course. *ECTJ 28*(3), 194–202.

— (1987). Instructional technology: a history. *In* R.M. Gagné, ed. *Instructional technology: Foundations*. Hillsdale, NJ: Erlbaum.

— & Sullivan, H.J. (1977). Effects of self-pacing and instructor-pacing in a PSI course. *The Journal of Educational Research 71*, 8–12.

Resnick, L.B. (1963). Programmed instruction and the teaching of complex intellectual skills; problems and prospects. *Harvard Education Review 33*, 439–71.

Rigney, J.W. & Fry, E.B. (1961). Current teaching-machine programs and programming techniques. *Audio-Visual Communication Review 9*(3).

Robin, A. & Graham, M.Q. (1974). Academic responses and attitudes engendered by teacher versus student pacing in a personalized instruction course. *In* R.S. Ruskin & S.F. Bono, eds. *Personalized instruction in higher education: proceedings of the first national conference*. Washington, DC: Georgetown University, Center for Personalized Instruction.

Roe, A., Massey, M. Weltman, G. & Leeds, D. (1962, Jun.-Jul.). A comparison of branching methods for programmed learning. *Journal of Educational Research 55*, 407–16.

— et al.. (1960). Automated teaching methods using linear programs. No. 60-105. Los Angeles, CA: Automated Learning Research Project, University of California.

Roshal, S.M. (1949). Effects of learner representation in film-mediated perceptual-motor learning. Technical Report SDC 269-7-5, State College, Pennsylvania: Pennsylvania State College, Instructional Film Research Program.

Rothkopf, E.Z. (1960). Some research problems in the design of materials and devices for automated teaching. In A.A. Lumsdaine & R. Glaser, eds. Teaching machines and programmed learning: a source book, 318-328. Washington, DC: National Education Association.

— (1962). Criteria for the acceptance of self-instructional programs. Improving the efficiency and quality of learning. Washington, DC: American Council on Education.

Rumelhart, D.E. & McClelland, J.L. (1986). Parallel distributed processing: explorations into the microstructure of cognition: Vol. 1. Foundations. Cambridge, MA: Bradford Books/MIT Press.

Ryan, T.A. & Hochberg, C.B. (1954). Speed of perception as a function of mode of presentation. Unpublished manuscript, Cornell University.

Saettler, P. (1968). A history of instructional technology. New York: McGraw-Hill.

Schnaitter, R. (1987). Knowledge as action: the epistemology of radical behaviorism. In S. Modgil & C. Modgil, eds. B.F. Skinner: consensus and controversy. New York: Falmer.

Schramm, W. (1962). What we know about learning from instructional television. In L. Asheim et al., Educational television: the next ten years, 52–76. Stanford, CA: The Institute for Communication Research, Stanford University.

Semb, G., Conyers, D., Spencer, R. & Sanchez-Sosa, J.J. (1975). An experimental comparison of four pacing contingencies in a personalize instruction course. In J.M. Johnston, ed. Behavior research and technology in higher education. Springfield, IL: Thomas.

Severin, D.G. (1960). Appraisal of special tests and procedures used with self-scoring instructional testing devices. In A.A. Lumsdaine & R. Glaser, eds. Teaching machines and programmed learning: a source book. Washington, DC: National Education Association, 678–80. (Abstract.)

Sheppard, W.C. & MacDermot, H.G. (1970). Design and evaluation of a programmed course in introductory psychology. Journal of Applied Behavior Analysis 3, 5–11.

Siedentop, D., Mand, C. & Taggart, A. (1986). Physical education: teaching and curriculum strategies for grades 5-12. Palo Alto, CA: Mayfield.

Silberman, H.F., Melaragno, J.E., Coulson, J.E. & Estavan, D. (1961). Fixed sequence vs. branching auto-instructional methods. Journal of Educational Psychology 52, 166–72.

Silvern, L.C. (1964). Designing instructional systems. Los Angeles, CA: Education and Training Consultants.

Skinner, B.F. (1938). The behavior of organisms. New York: Appleton-Century-Crofts.

— (1945). The operational analysis of psychological terms. Psychological Review 52, 270–77, 291–94.

— (1953a). Science and human behavior. New York: Macmillan.

— (1953b). Some contributions of an experimental analysis of behavior to psychology as a whole. American Psychologist 8, 69–78.

— (1954). The science of learning and the art of teaching. Harvard Educational Review 24 (86–97), 99–113.

— (1956). A case history in the scientific method. American Psychologist 57, 221–233.

— (1957). Verbal behavior. Englewood Cliffs, NJ: Prentice Hall.

— (1958). Teaching machines. Science 128 (969–77), 137–58.

— (1961, Nov.). Teaching machines. Scientific American 205, 91–102.

— (1964). Behaviorism at fifty. In T.W. Wann, ed. Behaviorism and phenomenology. Chicago, IL: University of Chicago Press.

— (1968). The technology of teaching. Englewood Cliffs, NJ: Prentice Hall.

— (1969). Contingencies of reinforcement: a theoretical analysis. New York: Appleton-Century-Crofts.

— (1971). Beyond freedom and dignity. New York: Knopf.

— (1974). About behaviorism. New York: Knopf.

— (1978). Why I am not a cognitive psychologist. In B.F. Skinner, ed. Reflections on behaviorism and society, 97–112. Englewood Cliffs, NJ: Prentice Hall,.

— (1981). Selection by consequences. Science 213, 501–04.

— (1987a). The evolution of behavior. In B.F. Skinner, ed. Upon further reflection, 65-74. Englewood Cliffs, NJ: Prentice Hall.

— (1987b). The evolution of verbal behavior. In B.F. Skinner, ed. Upon further reflection, 75-92. Englewood Cliffs, NJ: Prentice Hall.

— (1987c). Cognitive science and behaviorism. In B.F. Skinner, ed. Upon further reflection, 93-111. Englewood Cliffs, NJ: Prentice Hall.

— (1989). Recent issues in the analysis of behavior. Columbus: OH. Merrill.

— (1990). Can psychology be a science of mind. American Psychologist 45, 1206–10.

— & Holland, J.G. (1960). The use of teaching machines in college instruction. In A.A. Lumsdaine & R. Glaser, eds. Teaching machines and programmed learning: a source book, 159–72. Washington, DC: National Education Association.

Smith, D.E.P. (1959). Speculations: characteristics of successful programs and programmers. In E. Galanter, ed. Automatic teaching: the state of the art, 91–102. New York: Wiley.

Smith, J.M. (1970). Relations among behavioral objectives, time of acquisition, and retention. Unpublished doctoral dissertation, University of Maryland.

Smith, K.U. & Smith, M.F. (1966). Cybernetic principles of learning and educational design. New York: Holt, Rinehart & Winston.

Smith, P.L. & Ragan, T.J. (1993). Instructional design. New York: Macmillan.

Spence, K.W. (1948). The postulates and methods of "Behaviorism." Psychological Review 55, 67–78.

Stedman, C.H. (1970). The effects of prior knowledge of behavioral objectives on cognitive learning outcomes using programmed materials in genetics. Unpublished doctoral dissertation, Indiana University.

Stephens, A.L. (1960). Certain special factors involved in the law of effect. In A.A. Lumsdaine & R. Glaser, eds. Teaching machines and programmed learning: a source book, 89-93. Washington, DC: National Education Association.

Stevens, S.S. (1939). Psychology and the science of science. Psychological Bulletin 37, 221–263.

— (1951). Methods, measurements, and psychophysics. In S.S. Stevens, ed. Handbook of experimental psychology, 1-49. New York: Wiley.

Sulzer, R.L. & Lumsdaine, A.A. (1952). The value of using multiple examples in training film instruction. Memo Report No. 25, Human Resources Research Laboratory.

Suppes, P. & Ginsberg, R. (1962, Apr.). Application of a stimulus sampling model to children's concept formation with and without overt correction response. *Journal of Experimental Psychology 63*, 330–36.

Sutterer, J.E. & Holloway, R.E. (1975). An analysis of student behavior in a self-paced introductory psychology course. *In* J.M. Johnson, ed. *Behavior research and technology in higher education*. Springfield, IL: Thomas.

Tessmer, M. (1990). Environmental analysis: a neglected stage of instructional design. *Educational Technology Research and Development 38*(1), 55–64.

Thorndike, E.L. (1913). The psychology of learning. *Educational psychology, Vol. 2*. New York: Teachers College Press.

— (1898). Animal intelligence: an experimental study of the associative processes in animals. *Psychological Review Monograph 2* (Suppl. 8).

Tiemann, P.W. & Markle, S.M. (1990). *Analyzing instructional content: a guide to instruction and evaluation*. Champaign, IL: Stipes.

Torkelson, G.M. (1977). AVCR-One quarter century. Evolution of theory and research. *AV Communication Review 25*(4), 317–358.

Tosti, D.T. & Ball, J.R. (1969). A behavioral approach to instructional design and media selection. *AV Communication Review 17*(1), 5–23.

Twitmeyer, E.B. (1902). A study of the knee-jerk. Unpublished doctoral dissertation, University of Pennsylvania.

Tyler, R.W. (1934). *Constructing achievement tests*. Columbus, OH: Ohio State University.

Unwin, D. (1966). An organizational explanation for certain retention and correlation factors in a comparison between two teaching methods. *Programmed Learning and Educational Technology 3*, 35–39.

Valverde, H. & Morgan, R.L. (1970). Influence on student achievement of redundancy in self-instructional materials. *Programmed Learning and Educational Technology 7*, 194–99.

Vargas, E.A. (1993). A science of our own making. *Behaviorology 1*, (1), 13–22.

Vargas, J.S. (1977). *Behavioral psychology for teachers*. New York: Harper & Row.

Warden, C.J., Fjeld, H.A. & Koch, A.M. (1940). Imitative behavior in cebus and rhesus monkeys. *Journal of Genetic Psychology 56*, 311–22.

Warden, C.J. & Jackson, T.A. (1935). Imitative behavior in the rhesus monkey. *Journal of Genetic Psychology 46*, 103–25.

Watkins, C.L. (1988). Project follow through: a story of the identification and neglect of effective instruction. *Youth Policy 10*(7), 7–11.

Watson, J.B. (1908). Imitation in monkeys. *Psychological Bulletin 5*, 169–78.

— (1913). Psychology as the behaviorist views it. *Psychological Review 20*, 158–77.

— (1919). *Psychology from the standpoint of a behaviorist*. Philadelphia, PA: Lippincott.

— (1924). Behaviorism. New York: Norton.

— & R. Rayner (1920). Conditioned emotional reactions. *Journal of Experimental Psychology 3*, 1–14.

Webb, A.B. (1971). Effects of the use of behavioral objectives and criterion evaluation on classroom progress of adolescents. Unpublished doctoral dissertation, University of Tennessee.

Weinberg, H. (1970). Effects of presenting varying specificity of course objectives to students on learning motor skills and associated cognitive material. Unpublished doctoral dissertation, Temple University.

Weiss, W. (1954). Effects on learning and performance of controlled environmental stimulation. Staff Research Memorandum, Chanute AFB, IL: Training Aids Research Laboratory.

— & Fine, B.J. (1955). Stimulus familiarization as a factor in ideational learning. Unpublished manuscript. Boston University.

West, R.P., Young, R. & Spooner, F. (1990). Precision teaching: an introduction. *Teaching Exceptional Children 22*(3), 4–9.

White, O.R. (1986). Precision teaching—precision learning. *Exceptional Children 25*, 522–34.

Wilds, P.L. & Zachert, V. (1966). Effectiveness of a programmed text in teaching gynecologic oncology to junior medical students, a source book on the development of programmed materials for use in a clinical discipline. Augusta, GA: Medical College of Georgia.

Williams, J.P. (1963, Oct.). A comparison of several response modes in a review program. *Journal of Educational Psychology 54*, 253–60.

Wittich, W.A. & Folkes, J.G. (1946). *Audio-visual paths to learning*. New York: Harper & Bros.

Wittrock, M.C. (1962). Set applied to student teachings. *Journal of Educational Psychology 53*, 175–80.

Wulff, J.J., Sheffield, F.W. & Kraeling, D.G. (1954). 'Familiarization' procedures used as adjuncts to assembly task training with a demonstration film. Staff Research Memorandum, Chanute AFB, IL: Training Aids Research Laboratory.

Yale Motion Picture Research Project (1947). Do 'motivation' and 'participation' questions increase learning? *Educational Screen 26*, 256–83.

Zencius, A.H., Davis, P.K. & Cuvo, A.J. (1990). A personalized system of instruction for teaching checking account skills to adults with mild disabilities. *Journal of Applied Behavior Analysis 23*, 245–52.

Zimmerman, C.L. (1972). An experimental study of the effects of learning and forgetting when students are informed of behavioral objectives before or after a unit of study. Unpublished doctoral dissertation, University of Maryland.

3. SYSTEMS INQUIRY AND ITS APPLICATION IN EDUCATION

Bela H. Banathy
INTERNATIONAL SYSTEMS INSTITUTE

3.1 PART 1: SYSTEMS INQUIRY

The first part of this chapter is a review of the evolution of the systems movement and a discussion of human systems inquiry.

3.1.1 A Definition of Systems Inquiry

Systems inquiry incorporates three interrelated domains of disciplined inquiry: systems theory, systems philosophy, and systems methodology. Bertalanffy (1968) notes that in contrast with the analytical, reductionist, and linear-causal paradigm of classical science, *systems philosophy* brings forth a reorientation of thought and world view, manifested by an expansionist, nonlinear dynamic, and synthetic mode of thinking. The scientific exploration of systems theories and the development of systems theories in the various sciences have brought forth a *general theory of systems*, a set of interrelated concepts and principles, applying to all systems. *Systems methodology* provides us with a set of models, strategies, methods, and tools that instrumentalize systems theory and philosophy in analysis, design, development, and management of complex systems.

3.1.1.1. Systems Theory. During the early 1950s, the basic concepts and principles of a general theory of systems were set forth by such pioneers of the systems movement as Ashby, Bertalanffy, Boulding, Fagen, Gerard, Rappoport, and Wienner. They came from a variety of disciplines and fields of study. They shared and articulated a common conviction: the unified nature of reality. They recognized a compelling need for a unified disciplined inquiry in understanding and dealing with increasing complexities, complexities that are beyond the competence of any single discipline. As a result, they developed a transdisciplinary perspective that emphasized the intrinsic order and interdependence of the world in all its manifestations. From their work emerged systems theory, the science of complexity. In defining systems theory, I review the key ideas of Bertalanffy and Boulding, who were two of the founders of the Society for the Advancement of General Systems Theory. Later, the name of the society was changed to the Society for General Systems Research, then the International Society for Systems research, and recently to the International Society for the Systems Sciences.

3.1.1.1.1. Bertalanffy (1956, pp. 1–10). He suggested that "modern science is characterized by its ever-increasing specialization, necessitated by the enormous amount of data, the complexity of techniques, and structures within every field. This, however, led to a breakdown of science as an integrated realm. "Scientists, operating in the various disciplines, are encapsulated in their private universe, and it is difficult to get word from one cocoon to the other." Against this background, he observes a remarkable development, namely, that "similar general viewpoints and conceptions have appeared in very different fields." Reviewing this development in those fields, Bertalanffy suggests that there exist models, principles, and laws that can be generalized across various systems, their components, and the relationships among them. "It seems legitimate to ask for a theory, not of systems of a more or less special kind, but of universal principles applying to systems in general."

The first consequence of this approach is the recognition of the existence of systems properties that are general and structural similarities or isomorphies in different fields:

> There are correspondences in the principles which govern the behavior of entities that are intrinsically widely different. These correspondences are due to the fact that they all can be considered, in certain aspects, "systems," that is, complexes of elements standing in interaction. [It seems] that a general

This paper is dedicated to the memory of my dear friend and colleague, Kenneth Boulding, one of the founders of the systems movement and the first president of the Society for General Systems Research.

theory of systems would be a useful tool providing, on the one hand, models that can be used in, and transferred to, different fields, and safeguarding, on the other hand, from vague analogies which often have marred the progress in these fields.

The second consequence of the idea of a general theory is to deal with organized complexity, which is a main problem of modern science.

Concepts like those of organization, wholeness, directiveness, teleology, control, self-regulation, differentiation, and the like are alien to conventional science. However, they pop up everywhere in the biological, behavioral, and social sciences and are, in fact, indispensable for dealing with living organisms or social groups. Thus, a basic problem posed to modern science is a general theory of organization. General Systems Theory is, in principle, capable of giving exact definitions for such concepts.

Thirdly, Bertalanffy suggested that it is important to say what a general theory of systems is not. It is not identical with the triviality of mathematics of some sort that can be applied to any sort of problems; instead "it poses special problems that are far from being trivial." It is not

a search for superficial analogies between physical, biological, and social systems. The isomorphy we have mentioned is a consequence of the fact that, in certain aspects, corresponding abstractions and conceptual models can be applied to different phenomena. It is only in view of these aspects that system laws apply.

Bertalanffy summarizes the aims of a general theory of systems as follows:

(a) There is a general tendency towards integration in the various sciences, natural and social. (b) Such integration seems to be centered in a general theory of systems. (c) Such theory may be an important means of aiming at exact theory in the nonphysical fields of science. (d) Developing unifying principles running "vertically" through the universe of the individual sciences, this theory brings us nearer to the goal of the unity of sciences. (e) This can lead to a much needed integration in scientific education.

Commenting later on education, Bertalanffy noted that education treats the various scientific disciplines as separate domains, where increasingly smaller subdomains become separate sciences, unconnected with the rest. In contrast, the educational demands of scientific generalists and developing transdisciplinary basic principles are precisely those that General Systems Theory (GST) tries to fill. In this sense, GST seems to make an important headway toward transdisciplinary synthesis and integrated education.

3.1.1.1.2. Boulding (1956, pp. 11–17). He underscored the need for a general theory as he suggested that in recent years increasing need has been felt for a body of theoretical constructs that will discuss the general relationships of the empirical world.

This is the quest of General Systems Theory (GST). It does not seek, of course, to establish a single, self-contained "general theory of practically everything" which will replace all the special theories of particular disciplines. Such a theory

would be almost without content, and all we can say about practically everything is almost nothing.

Somewhere between the specific that has no meaning and the general that has no content there must be, for each purpose and at each level of abstraction, an optimum degree of generality.

The objectives of GST, then, can be set out with varying degrees of ambitions and confidence. At a low level of ambition, but with a high degree of confidence, it aims to point out similarities in the theoretical constructions of different disciplines, where these exist, and to develop theoretical models having applicability to different fields of study. At a higher level of ambition, but perhaps with a lower level of confidence, it hopes to develop something like a "spectrum" of theories—a system of systems that may perform a "gestalt" in theoretical constructions. It is the main objective of GST, says Boulding, to develop "generalized ears" that overcome the "specialized deafness" of the specific disciplines, meaning that someone who ought to know something that someone else knows isn't able to find it out for lack of generalized ears. Developing a framework of a general theory will enable the specialist to catch relevant communications from others.

In the closing section of his paper, Boulding referred to the subtitle of his paper: GST as "the skeleton of science." It is a skeleton in the sense—he says—that:

It aims to provide a framework or structure of systems on which to hang the flesh and blood of particular disciplines and particular subject matters in an orderly and coherent corpus of knowledge. It is also, however, something of a skeleton in a cupboard—the cupboard in this case being the unwillingness of science to admit the tendency to shut the door on problems and subject matters which do not fit easily into simple mechanical schemes. Science, for all its success, still has a very long way to go. GST may at times be an embarrassment in pointing out how very far we still have to go, and in deflating excessive philosophical claims for overly simple systems. It also may be helpful, however, in pointing out to some extent where we have to go. The skeleton must come out of the cupboards before its dry bones can live.

The two papers introduced above set forth the "vision" of the systems movement. That vision still guides us today. At this point it seems to be appropriate to tell the story that marks the genesis of the systems movement. Kenneth Boulding told this story at the occasion when I was privileged to present to him the distinguished scholarship award of the Society of General Systems Research at our 1983 Annual Meeting. The year was 1954. At the Center for Behavioral Sciences, at Stanford University, four Center Fellows—Bertalanffy (biology), Boulding (economics), Gerard (psychology), and Rappoport (mathematics)—had a discussion in a meeting room. Another Center Fellow walked in and asked: "What's going on here?" Ken answered: "We are angered about the state of the human condition and ask: 'What can we—what can science—do about improving the human condition?'" "Oh!" their visitor said: "This is not my field. . . ." At that meeting the four scientists felt that in the statement of their visitor they heard the statement of the fragmented disciplines that have little concern for doing anything practical about the fate of humanity. So, they asked themselves, "What would happen if science would be redefined by crossing disciplinary boundaries and forge a general theory that would bring us together in the service of humanity?" Later they went to Berkeley, to the annual meeting of the American Association for the Advancement of Science, and established the Society for the Advancement of General Systems Theory. Throughout the years, many of us in the systems movement have continued to ask the question: How can systems science serve humanity?

3.1.1.2. Systems Philosophy. The next main branch of systems inquiry is systems philosophy. Systems philosophy is concerned with a systems view of the world and the elucidation of systems thinking as an approach to theoretical and real-world problems. Systems philosophy seeks to uncover the most general assumptions lying at the roots of any and all of systems inquiry. An articulation of these assumptions gives systems inquiry coherence and internal consistency. Systems philosophy (Laszlo, 1972) seeks to probe the basic texture and ultimate implications of systems inquiry. It "guides the imagination of the systems scientist and provides a general world view, the likes of which—in the history of science—has proven to be the most significant for asking the right question and perceiving the relevant state of affairs" (p. 10). The general scientific nature of systems inquiry implies its direct association with philosophy. This explains the philosophers' early and continuing interest in systems theory and the early and continuing interest of systems theorists and methodologists in the philosophical aspects of systems inquiry. In general, philosophical aspects are worked out in two directions. The first involves inquiry into the *What:* what things are, what a person or a society is, and what kind of world we live in. These questions pertain to what we call *ontology*. The second question is *How:* How do we know what we know; how do we know what kind of world we live in; how do we know what kind of persons we are? The exploration of these questions are the domain of epistemology. One might differentiate these two, but, as Bateson (1972) noted, ontology and epistemology cannot be separated. Our beliefs about what the world is will determine how we see it and act within it. And our ways of perceiving and acting will determine our beliefs about its nature. Blauberg, Sadovsky, and Yudin (1977) noted that the philosophical aspects of systems inquiry would give us an "unequivocal solution to all or most problems arising from a study of systems" (p. 94).

3.1.1.2.1. Ontology. The *ontological* task is the formation of a systems view of what is—in the broadest sense a systems view of the world. This can lead to a new orientation for scientific inquiry. As Baluberg (1977) noted, this orientation emerged into a holistic view of the world. Waddington (1977) presents a historical review of two great philosophical alternatives of the intellectual picture we have of the world. One view is that the world essentially consists of things. The other view is that the world consists of processes, and the things are only "stills" out of the moving picture. Systems philosophy developed as the main rival of the "thing view." It recognizes the primacy of organizing relationship processes between entities (of systems), from which emerge the novel properties of systems.

3.1.1.2.2. Epistemology. This philosophical aspect deals with general questions: How do we know whatever we know? How do we know what kind of world we live in and what kind of organisms we are? What sort of thing is the mind? Bateson (1972) notes that originating from systems theory, extraordinary advances have been made in answering these questions. The ancient question of whether the mind is immanent or transcendent can be answered in favor of immanence. Furthermore, any ongoing ensemble (system) that has the appropriate complexity of causal and energy relationships will: (a) show mutual characteristics, (b) compare and respond to differences, (c) process information, (d) be self-corrective, and (e) no part of an internally interactive system can exercise unilateral control over other parts of the system. "The mutual characteristics of a system are immanent not in some part, but in the system as a whole" (p. 316).

The epistomological aspects of systems philosophy address: (a) the principles of how systems inquiry is conducted; (b) the specific categorical apparatus of the inquiry, and that connected with it; and (c) the theoretical language of systems science. The most significant guiding principle of systems inquiry is that of giving prominence to synthesis, not only as the culminating activity of the inquiry (following analysis) but also as a point of departure. This approach to the "how do we know" contrasts with the epistemology of traditional science that is almost exclusively analytical.

3.1.1.3. Systems Methodology. Systems methodology—a vital part of systems inquiry—has two domains of inquiry: (1) the study of methods in systems investigations by which we generate knowledge about systems in general and (2) the identification and description of strategies, models, methods, and tools for the application of systems theory and systems thinking for working with complex systems. In the context of this second domain, systems methodology is a set of coherent and related methods and tools applicable to: (a) the analysis of systems and systems problems, problems concerned with the systemic/ relational aspects of complex systems; (b) the design, development, implementation, and evaluation of complex systems; and (c) the management of systems and the management of change in systems.

The task of those using systems methodology in a given context is threefold: (1) to identify, characterize, and classify the nature of the problem situation, i.e., (a), (b), or (c) above; (2) to identify and characterize the problem context and content in which the methodology is applied; (3) to identify and characterize the type of system in which the problem situation is embedded; and (4) to select specific strategies, methods, and tools that are appropriate to the nature of the problem situation, to the context/content, and to the type of systems in which the problem situation is located.

The brief discussion above highlights the difference between the methodology of systems inquiry and the methodology of scientific inquiry in the various disciplines.

The methodology of a discipline is clearly defined and is to be adhered to rigorously. It is the methodology that is the hallmark of a discipline. In systems inquiry, on the other hand, one selects methods and methodological tools or approaches that best fit the nature of the identified problem situation, and the context, the content, and the type of system that is the domain of the investigation. The methodology is to be selected from a wide range of systems methods that are available to us.

3.1.1.4. The Interaction of the Domains of Systems Inquiry. Systems philosophy, systems theory, and systems methodology come to life as they are used and applied in the functional context of systems. It is in the context of use that they are confirmed, changed, modified, and reconfirmed. Systems philosophy presents us with the underlying assumptions that provide the perspectives that guide us in defining and organizing the concepts and principles that constitute systems theory. Systems theory and systems philosophy then guide us in developing, selecting, and organizing approaches, methods, and tools into the scheme of systems methodology. Systems methodology then is used in the functional context of systems. But this process is not linear or forward-moving circular. It is recursive and multidirectional. One confirms or modifies the other. As theory is developed, it gets its confirmation from its underlying assumptions (philosophy), as well as from its application through methods in functional contexts. Methodology is confirmed or changed by testing its relevance to its theoretical/philosophical foundations and by its use. The functional context—the society in general and systems of all kinds in particular—is a primary source of placing demands on systems inquiry. It was, in fact, the emergence of complex systems that brought about the recognition of the need for new scientific thinking, new theory, and methodologies. It was this need that systems inquiry addressed and satisfied.

The dynamics of the recursive and multidirectional interaction of the four domains, described above, makes systems inquiry a living system. These dynamics are manifested in the interplay between confirmation and novelty. Novelty at times brings about adjustments and at other times it appears as discontinuities and major shifts. The process described here becomes transparent as the evolution of the systems movement is reviewed next.

3.1.2 The Evolution of the Systems Movement

Throughout the evolution of humanity there has been a constant yearning for understanding the wholeness of the human experience that manifests itself in the wholeness of the human being and the human society. Wholeness has been sought also in the disciplined inquiry of science as a way of searching for the unity of science and a unified theory of the universe. This search reaches back through the ages into the golden age of Greek philosophy and science in Plato's kybernetics, the art of steermanship, which is the origin of modern cybernetics: a domain of contemporary systems thinking. The search intensified during the Age of Enlightenment and the Age of Reason and Certainty, and it was manifested in the clockwork mechanistic world view. The search has continued in the current age of uncertainty (Heisenberg) and complexity, the science of relativity, (Einstein), quantum theory (Bohr & Shrodinger), and the theory of wholeness and the implicate order (Bohm).

In recent years, the major player in this search has been the systems movement. The genesis of the movement can be timed as the mid-50s (as discussed at the beginning of this chapter). But prior to that time, we can account for the emergence of the systems idea through the work of several philosophers and scientist.

3.1.2.1. The Pioneers. Some of the key notions of systems theory were articulated by the 18th-century German philosopher Hagel. He suggested that the whole is more than the sum of its parts, that the whole determines the nature of the parts, and the parts are dynamically interrelated and cannot be understood in isolation from the whole.

Most likely, the first person who used the term *general theory of systems* was the Hungarian philosopher and scientist Bela Zalai. Zalai, during the years 1913 to 1914, developed his theory in a collection of papers called *A Rendszerek Altalanos Elmelete*. The German translation was entitled *Allgemeine Theorie der Systeme* [General Theory of Systems]. The work was republished (Zalai, 1984) in Hungarian and was recently reviewed in English (Banathy & Banathy, 1989). In a three-volume treatise, *Tektologia*, Bogdanov (1921–1927), a Russian scientist, characterized *Tektologia* as a dynamic science of complex wholes, concerned with universal structural regularities, general types of systems, the general laws of their transformation, and the basic laws of organization. Bogdanov's work was published in English by Golerik (1980).

In the decades prior to and during World War II, the search intensified. The idea of a General Systems Theory was developed by Bertalanffy in the late 30s and was presented in various lectures. But his material remained unpublished until 1945 (*Zu einer allgemeinen Systemlehre*) followed by "An Outline of General Systems Theory" (1951). Without using the term GST, the same frame of thinking was used in various articles by Ashby during the years 1945 and 1947, published in his book *Design for a Brain*, in 1952.

3.1.2.2. Organized Developments. In contrast with the work of individual scientists, outlined above, since the 1940s we can account for several major developments that reflect the evolution of the systems movement, including "hard systems science," cybernetics, and the continuing evolution of a general theory of systems.

3.1.3 Hard-Systems Science

Under hard-systems science, we can account for two organized developments: operations research and systems engineering.

3.1.3.1. Operations Research. During the Second World War, it was again the "functional context" that challenged scientists. The complex problems of logistics and resource management in waging a war became the genesis of developing the earliest organized form of systems science: the quantitative analysis of rather closed systems. It was this orientation from which operations research and management science emerged during the 50s. This development directed systems science toward "hard" quantitative analysis. Operations research flourished during the 60s, but in the 70s, due to the changing nature of sociotechnical systems contexts, it went through a major shift toward a less quantitative orientation.

3.1.3.2. Systems Engineering. This is concerned with the design of closed man-machine systems and larger-scale sociotechnical systems. Systems engineering (SE) can be portrayed as a system of methods and tools, specific activities for problem solutions, and a set of relations between the tools and activities. The tools include language, mathematics, and graphics by which systems engineering communicates. The content of SE includes a variety of algorithms and concepts that enable various activities. The first major work in SE was published by A. D. Hall (1962). He presented a comprehensive, three-dimensional morphology for systems engineering. In a more recent work, Sage (1977) has changed the directions of SE.

> We use the word *system* to refer to the application of systems science and methodologies associated with the science of problem solving. We use the word *engineering* not only to mean the mastery and manipulation of physical data but also to imply social and behavioral consideration as inherent parts of the engineering design process (p. xi).

During the 60s and early 70s, practitioners of operations research and systems engineering attempted to transfer their approaches into the context of social systems. It led to disasters. It was this period when "social engineering" emerged as an approach to address societal problems. A recognition of failed attempts have led to changes in direction, best manifested by the quotation of Sage in the paragraph above.

3.1.4 Cybernetics

Cybernetics is concerned with the understanding of self-organization of human, artificial, and natural systems; the understanding of understanding; and its relation and relevance to other transdisciplinary approaches. Cybernetics, as part of the systems movement, evolved through two phases: first-order cybernetics, the cybernetics of the observed system, and second-order cybernetics, the cybernetics of the observing system.

3.1.4.1. First-Order Cybernetics. This early formulation of cybernetics inquiry was concerned with communication and control *in* the animal and the machine (Wiener, 1948). The emphasis on the *in* allowed focus on the process of self-organization and self-regulation, on circular causal feedback mechanisms, together with the systemic principles that underlie them. These principles underlay the

computer/cognitive sciences and are credited with being at the heart of neural network approaches in computing. The first-order view treated information as a quantity, as "bits" to be transmitted from one place to the other. It focused on "noise" that interfered with smooth transmission (Weatley, 1992). The content, the meaning, and the purpose of information was ignored (Gleick, 1987).

3.1.4.2. Second-Order Cybernetics. As a concept, this expression was coined by Foerster (1984), who describes this shift as follows: "We are now in the possession of the truism that a description (of the universe) implies one who describes (observes it). What we need now is a description of the 'describer' or, in other words, we need a theory of the observer" (p. 258). The general notion of second-order cybernetics is that "observing systems" awaken the notion of language, culture, and communication (Brier, 1992); and the context, the content, the meaning, and purpose of information becomes central. Second-order cybernetics, through the concept of self-reference, wants to explore the meaning of cognition and communication within the natural and social sciences, the humanities, and information science; and in such social practices as design, education, organization, art, management, and politics, etc. (p. 2).

3.1.5 The Continuing Evolution of Systems Inquiry

The first part of this chapter describes the emergence of the systems idea and its manifestation in the three branches of systems inquiry: systems theory, systems philosophy, and systems methodology. This section traces the evolution of systems inquiry. This evolutionary discussion will be continued later in a separate section by focusing on "human systems inquiry."

3.1.5.1. The Continuing Evolution of Systems Thinking. In a comprehensive report, commissioned by the Society of General Systems Research, Cavallo (1979) says that systems inquiry shattered the essential features of the traditional scientific paradigm characterized by analytic thinking, reductionism, and determinism. The systems paradigm articulates synthetic thinking, emergence, communication and control, expansionism, and teleology. The emergence of these core systems ideas was the consequence of a change of focus, away from entities that cannot be taken apart without loss of their essential characteristics, and hence can not be truly understood from analysis.

First, this change of focus gave rise to synthetic or systems thinking as complementary to analysis. In synthetic thinking an entity to be understood is conceptualized not as a whole to be taken apart but as a part of one or more larger wholes. The entity is explained in terms of its function, and its role in its larger context. Second, another major consequence of the new thinking is expansionism (an alternative to reductionism), which asserts that ultimate understanding is an ideal that can never be attained but can be continuously approached. Progress towards it depends on understanding ever-larger and more inclusive wholes. Third, the idea of nondeterministic causality, developed by Singer (1959), made it possible to develop the notion of objective teleology, a conceptual system in which such teleological concepts as free will, choice, function, and purpose could be operationally defined and incorporated into the domain of science.

3.1.5.2. A General Theory of Dynamic Systems. The theory was developed by Jantsch (1980). He argues that an emphasis on structure and dynamic equilibrium (steady-state flow), which characterized the earlier development of general systems theory, led to a profound understanding of how primarily technological structures may be stabilized and maintained by complex mechanisms that respond to negative feedback. (Negative feedback indicates deviation from established norms and calls for a reduction of such deviation.) In biological and social systems, however, negative feedback is complemented by positive feedback, which increases deviation by the development of new systems processes and forms. The new understanding that has emerged recognizes such phenomena as self-organization, self-reference, self-regulation, coherent behavior over time with structural change, individuality, symbiosis, and coevolution with the environment, and morphogenesis.

This new understanding of systems behavior, says Jantsch, emphasizes process in contrast to "solid" subsystems structures and components. The interplay of process in systems leads to evolution of structures. An emphasis is placed on "becoming," a decisive conceptual breakthrough brought about by Prigogine (1980). Prigogine's theoretical development and empirical conformation of the so-called *dissipative structures* and his discovery of a new ordering systems principle called *order through fluctuation* led to an explication of a "general theory of dynamic systems."

During the early 80s, a whole range of systems thinking–based methodologies emerged, based on what is called *soft-systems thinking*. These are all relevant to human and social systems and will be discussed under the heading of human systems inquiry. In this section, two additional developments are discussed: systems thinking based on "liberating systems theory" and "unbounded systems thinking."

3.1.5.3. Liberating Systems Theory (Flood, pp. 210–211, 1990). This theory is (1) in pursuit of freeing systems theory from certain tendencies and, in a more general sense, (2) tasking systems theory with liberation of the human condition. The first task is developed in three trends: (1) the liberation of systems theory generally from the natural tendency toward self-imposed insularity, (2) the liberation of systems concepts from objectivist and subjectivist delusions, and (3) the liberation of systems theory specifically in cases of internalized localized subjugations in discourse and by considering histories and progressions of systems thinking. The second task of the theory focuses on liberation and emancipation in response to domination and subjugation in work and social situations.

3.1.5.5. Unbounded Systems Thinking (Mitroff & Linstone, 1993). This development "is the basis for the 'new thinking' called for in the information age" (p. 91).

In unbounded systems thinking (UST), "everything interacts with everything."

All branches of inquiry depend fundamentally on one another. The widest possible array of disciplines, professions, and branches of knowledge—capturing distinctly different paradigms of thought—must be consciously brought to bear on our problems. In UST, the traditional hierarchical ordering of the sciences and the professions—as well as the pejorative bifurcation of the sciences into 'hard' vs. 'soft'—is replaced by a circular concept of relationship between them. The basis for choosing a particular way of modeling or representing a problem is not governed merely by considerations of conventional logic and rationality. It may also involve considerations of justice and fairness as perceived by various social groups and by consideration of personal ethics or morality as perceived by distinct persons" (p. 9).

3.1.5.6. Living Systems Theory. This theory was developed by Miller (1978) as a continuation and elaboration of the organismic orientation of Bertalanffy. The theory is a conceptual scheme for the description and analysis of concrete identifiable living systems. It describes seven levels of living systems, ranging from the lower levels of cell, organ, and organism, to higher levels of group, organizations, societies, and supranational systems.

The central thesis of living systems theory is that at each level a system is characterized by the same 20 critical subsystems whose processes are essential to life. A set of these subsystems processes information (input transducer, internal transducer, channel and net, decoder, associator, decider, memory, encoder, output transducer, and time). Another set processes matter and energy (ingestor, distributor, converter, producer, storage, extruder, motor, and supporter). Two subsystems (reproducer and boundary) process matter/energy and information.

Living system theory presents a common framework for analyzing structure and process and identifying the health and well-being of systems at various levels of complexity. A set of cross-level hypotheses was identified by Miller as a basis for conducting such analysis. During the 80s, Living systems theory has been applied by a method—called living systems process analysis—to the study of complex problem situations embedded in a diversity of fields and activities. [Living systems process analysis has been applied in educational contexts by Banathy and Mills (1988).]

3.1.6 Human Systems Inquiry

Human systems inquiry focuses systems theory, systems philosophy, and systems methodology and their applications on social or human systems. This section portrays human systems inquiry as follows: (1) present some of its basic characteristics, (2) describe the various types of human or social systems, (3) discuss the nature of problem situations and solutions in human systems inquiry, and (4) introduce the "soft-systems" approach and social systems design. The discussion of these issues will help us appreciate why human systems inquiry must be different from other modes of inquiry. Furthermore, inasmuch as education is a human system, such understanding and a review of approaches to human systems inquiry will lead to our discussion on systems inquiry in education.

3.1.6.1. The Characteristics of Human Systems. *Human Systems Are Different* is the title of the last book of the systems philosopher Geoffrey Vickers (1983). Discussing the characteristics of human systems, he provides a summary of their open nature as follows. (1) Open systems are nests of relations that are sustained through time. They are sustained by these relations and by the process of regulation. The limits within which they can be sustained are the conditions of their stability. (2) Open systems depend on and contribute to their environment. They are dependent on this interaction as well as on their internal interaction. These interactions/dependencies impose constraints on all their constituents. Human systems can mitigate but cannot remove these constraints, which tend to become more demanding and at times even contradictory as the scale of the organization increases. This might place a limit on the potential of the organization. (3) Open systems are wholes, but are also parts of larger systems, and their constituents may also be constituents of other systems.

Change in human systems is inevitable. Systems adapt to environmental changes, and in a changing environment this becomes a continuous process. At times, however, adaptation does not suffice, so the whole system might change. Through coevolution and cocreation, change between the systems and its environment is a mutual recursive phenomenon (Buckley, 1968; Jantch, 1976, 1980). Wheatley (1992), discussing stability, change, and renewal in self-organizing system, remarks that in the past, scientists focused on the overall structure of systems, leading them away from understanding the processes of change that makes a system viable over time. They were looking for stability. Regulatory (negative) feedback was a way to ensure the stability of systems, to preserve their current state. They overlooked the function of positive feedback that moves the system toward change and renewal.

Checkland (1981) presents a comprehensive characterization of what he calls *human activity systems* (HASs). HASs are very different from natural and engineered systems. Natural and engineered systems cannot be other than what they are.

> Human activity systems, on the other hand, are manifested through the perception of human beings who are free to attribute meanings to what they perceive. There will never be a single (testable) account of human activity systems, only a set of possible accounts, all valid according to particular *Weltanshaungen* (p. 14).

He further says, that HASs are structured sets of people who make up the system, coupled with a collection of such activities as processing information, making plans, performing, and monitoring performance.

According to Argyris and Schon (1979), a social group becomes an organization when members devise procedures for "Making decisions in the name of the collectivity, delegating to individuals the authority to act for the collectivity, and setting boundaries between the collectivity and the rest of the world" (p. 13). Ackoff and Emery (1972) characterize human systems as purposeful systems whose members are also purposeful individuals who intentionally and collectively formulate objectives. In human systems, "the state of the part can be determined only in reference to the state of the system. The effect of change in one part or another is mediated by changes in the state of the whole" (p. 218).

Ackoff (1981) suggests that human systems are purposeful systems that have purposeful parts and are parts of larger purposeful systems. This observation reveals three fundamental issues, namely, how to design and manage human systems so that they can effectively and efficiently serve (1) their own purposes, (2) the purposes of their purposeful parts and people in the system, and (3) the purposes of the larger system(s) of which they are part. These functions are called: (1) self-directiveness, (2) humanization, and (3) environmentalization, respectively.

Viewing human systems from an evolutionary perspective, Jantsch (1980) suggests that according to the dualistic paradigm, adaptation is a response to something that evolved outside of the systems. He notes, however, that with the emergence of the self-organizing paradigm, a scientifically founded nondualistic view became possible. This view is process oriented and establishes that evolution is an integral part of self-organization. True self-organization incorporates self-transcendence, the creative reaching out of a human system beyond its boundaries. Jantsch concludes that creation is the core of evolution, it is the joy of life, it is not just adaptation, not just securing survival. In the final analysis, says Laszlo (1987), social systems are value-guided systems. Insofar as they are independent of biological need-fulfillment and reproductive needs, cultures satisfy not body needs but values. All cultures respond to such suprabiological values. But in what form they do so depends on the specific kind of values people happen to have.

3.1.6.7. Types of Human Systems. Human activity systems (HASs), such as educational systems, are purposeful creations. People in these systems select, organize, and carry out activities in order to attain their purposes. Reviewing the research of Ackoff (1981), Jantsch (1976), Jackson and Keys (1984), and Southerland (1973), the author developed a comprehensive classification of HASs (1988) based on: (1) the degree to which they are open or closed, (2) their mechanistic vs. systemic nature, (3) their unitary vs. pluralistic position on defining their purpose, and (4) the degree and nature of their complexity (simple, detailed, dynamic). Based on these dimensions, we can differentiate five types of HASs: rigidly controlled, deterministic, purposive, heuristic, and purpose seeking.

3.1.6.2.1. Rigidly Controlled Systems. These systems are rather closed. Their structure is simple, consisting of few elements with limited interaction among them. They have a singleness of purpose and clearly defined goals, and act mechanically. Operational ways and means are prescribed.

There is little room for self-direction. They have a rigid structure and stable relationship among system components. Examples are assembly-line systems and man-machine systems.

3.1.6.3.2. Deterministic Systems.   These are still more closed than open. They have clearly assigned goals; thus, they are unitary. People in the system have a limited degree of freedom in selecting methods. Their complexity ranges from simple to detailed. Examples are bureaucracies, instructional systems, and national educational.

3.1.6.3.3. Purposive Systems.   These are still unitary but are more open than closed, and react to their environment in order to maintain their viability. Their purpose is established at the top, but people in the system have freedom to select operational means and methods. They have detailed to dynamic complexity. Examples are corporations, social service agencies, and our public education systems.

3.1.6.3.4. Heuristic Systems.   Such systems as R&D agencies and innovative business ventures formulate their own goals under broad policy guidelines; thus, they are somewhat pluralistic. They are open to changes and often initiate changes. Their complexity is dynamic, and their internal arrangements and operations are systemic. Examples of heuristic systems include innovative business ventures, educational R&D agencies, and alternative educational systems.

3.1.6.3.5. Purpose-Seeking Systems.   These systems are ideal seeking and are guided by their vision of the future. They are open and coevolve with their environment. They exhibit dynamic complexity and systemic behavior. They are pluralistic, as they constantly seek new purposes and search for new niches in their environments. Examples are (a) communities seeking to establish integration of their systems of learning and human development with social, human, and health service agencies, and their community and economic development programs, and (b) cutting-edge R&D agencies.

In working with human systems, the understanding of what type of system we are working with, or the determination of the type of systems we wish to design, is crucial in that it suggests the selection of the approach and the methods and tools that are appropriate to systems inquiry.

3.1.7 The Nature of Problem Situations and Solutions

Working with human systems, we are confronted with problem situations that comprise a system of problems rather than a collection of problems. Problems are embedded in uncertainty and require subjective interpretation. Churchman (1971) suggested that in working with human systems, subjectivity cannot be avoided. What really matters, he says, is that systems are unique, and the task is to account for their uniqueness; and this uniqueness has to be considered in their description and design. Our main tool in working with human systems is subjectivity: reflection on the sources of knowledge, social practice, community, and interest in and commitment to ideas, especially the moral idea, affectivity, and faith.

Working with human systems, we must recognize that they are unbounded. Factors assumed to be part of a problem are inseparably linked to many other factors. A technical problem in transportation, such as the building of a freeway, becomes a land-use problem, linked with economic, environmental, conservation, ethical, and political issues. Can we really draw a boundary? When we seek to improve a situation, particularly if it is a public one, we find ourselves facing not a problem but a cluster of problems, often called *problematique*. Peccei (1977), the founder of the Club of Rome, says that:

> Within the problematique, it is difficult to pinpoint individual problems and propose individual solutions. Each problem is related to every other problem; each apparent solution to a problem may aggravate or interfere with others; and none of these problems or their combination can be tackled using the linear or sequential methods of the past" (p. 61).

Ackoff suggests (1981) that a set of interdependent problems constitutes a system of problems, which he calls a *mess*. Like any system, the mess has properties that none of its parts has. These properties are lost when the system is taken apart. In addition, each part of a system has properties that are lost when it is considered separately. The solution to a mess depends on how its parts interact. In an earlier statement, Ackoff (1974) says that the era of "quest for certainty" has passed. We live an age of uncertainty in which systems are open, dynamic; in which problems live in a moving process. "Problems and solutions are in constant flux, hence problems do not stay solved. Solutions to problems become obsolete even if the problems to which they are addressed are not" (p. 31). Ulrich (1983) suggests that when working with human systems, we should reflect critically on problems. He asks: How can we produce solutions if the problems remain unquestioned? We should transcend problems as originally stated and should explore critically the problem itself with all of those who are affected by the problem. We must differentiate well-structured and well-defined problems in which the initial conditions, the goals, and the necessary operations can all be specified, from ill-defined or ill-structured problems, the kind in which initial conditions, the goals, and the allowable operations cannot be extrapolated from the problem. Discussing this issue, Rittel and Webber (1974) suggest that science and engineering are dealing with well-structured or tame problems. But this stance is not applicable to open social systems. Still, many social science professionals have mimicked the cognitive style of scientists and the operational style of engineers. But social problems are inherently wicked problems. Thus, every solution of a wicked problem is tentative and incomplete, and it changes as we move toward the solution. As the solution changes, as it is elaborated, so does our understanding of the problem. Considering this issue in the context of systems design, Rittel suggests that the "ill-behaved" nature of design problem situations frustrates all attempts to start out with an information and analysis phase, at the end of which a clear definition of the problem is rendered and objectives are defined that become the basis for synthesis, during which a "monastic" solution can be worked out. Systems design requires a continuous interaction between the initial phase that triggers design and the state when design is completed.

3.1.8 The Soft-Systems Approach and Systems Design

From the 70s on, it was generally realized that the nature of issues in human/social systems is "soft" in contrast with "hard" issues and problems in systems engineering and other quantitative focused systems inquiry.

> Hard-systems thinking and approaches were not usable in the context of human activity systems. "It is impossible to start the studies by naming 'the system' and defining its objectives, and without this naming/definition, hard systems thinking collapses" (Checkland, 1981; Checkland and Scholes, 1990).

Churchman in his various works (1968a, 1968b, 1971, 1979, 1981) has been the most articulate and most effective advocate of ethical systems theory and morality in human systems inquiry. Human systems inquiry, Churchman says, has to be value oriented, and it must be guided by the social imperative, which dictates that technological efficiency must be subordinated to social efficiency. He speaks for a science of values and the development of methods by which to verify ethical judgments. He took issue (Churchman, 1971) with the design approach where the focus is on various segments of the system. When the designer detects a problem in a part, he moves to modify it. This approach is based on the separability principle of incrementalism. He advocates "nonseperabilty" when the application of decision rules depends on the state of the whole system, and when a certain degree of instability of a part occurs, the designer can recognize this event and change the system so that the part becomes stable. "It can be seen that design, properly viewed, is an enormous liberation of the intellectual spirit, for it challenges this spirit to an unbounded speculation about possibilities" (p. 13). A liberated designer will look at present practice as a point of departure at best. Design is a thought process and a communication process. Successful design is one that enables someone to transfer thought into action or into another design.

Checkland (1981) and Checkland and Scholes (1990) developed a methodology based on soft-systems thinking for working with human activity systems. They consider the methodology as:

> a learning system which uses systems ideas to formulate basic mental acts of four kinds: perceiving, predicating, comparing, and deciding for action. The output of the methodology is very different from the output of systems engineering: It is learning which leads to decision to take certain actions, knowing that this will lead not to "the prob-

lem" being now "solved," but to a changed situation and new learning" (1981, p. 17).

The methodology defined here is a direct consequence of the concept, human activity system. We attribute meaning to all human activity. Our attributions are meaningful in terms of our particular image of the world, which, in general, we take for granted.

Systems design, in the context of social systems, is a future-creative disciplined inquiry. People engage in this inquiry to design a system that realizes their vision of the future, their own expectations, and the expectations of their environment. Systems design is a relatively new intellectual technology. It emerged only recently as a manifestation of open-system thinking and corresponding ethically based soft-systems approaches. This new intellectual technology emerged, just in time, as a disciplined inquiry that enables us to align our social systems with the new realities of the information/knowledge age (Banathy, 1991).

Early pioneers of social systems design include: Simon (1969), Jones (1970), Churchman (1968, 1971, 1978), Jantsch (1976, 1980), Warfield (1976), and Sage (1977). The watershed year of comprehensive statements on systems design was 1981, marked by the works of Ackoff, Checkland, and Nadler. Then came the work of Argyris (1982), Ulrich (1983), Cross (1984), Morgan (1986), Senge (1990), Warfield (1990), Nadler and Hibino (1990), Checkland and Scholes (1990), Banathy (1991), Hammer and Champy (1993), and Mitroff and Linstone (1993).

Prior to the emergence of social systems design, the improvement approach to systems change manifested traditional social planning (Banathy, 1991). This approach, still practiced today, reduces the problem to manageable pieces and seeks solutions to each. Users of this approach believe that solving the problem piece by piece ultimately will correct the larger issue it aims to remedy. But systems designers know that "getting rid of what is not wanted does not give you what is desired." In sharp contrast with traditional social planning, systems design—represented by the authors above—seeks to understand the problem situation as a system of interdependent and interacting problems, and seeks to create a design as a system of interdependent and interacting solution ideas. Systems designers envision the entity to be designed as a whole, as one that is designed from the synthesis of the interaction of its parts. Systems design requires both coordination and integration. We need to design all parts of the system interactively and simultaneously. This requires coordination, and designing for interdependency across all systems levels invites integration.

3.1.9 Reflections

In the first part of this chapter, systems inquiry was defined, and the evolution of the systems movement was reviewed. Then we focused on human systems inquiry, which is the conceptual foundation of the development of a systems view and systems applications in education. As we reflect on the ideas presented in this part, we realize how little of what was discussed here has any serious manifestation or application in education. Therefore, the second part of this chapter is devoted to the exploration of a systems view of education and its practical applications in working with systems of learning and human development.

3.2 PART TWO: THE SYSTEMS VIEW AND ITS APPLICATION IN EDUCATION

In the first section of this part of the chapter is a discussion of the systems view and its relevance to education. This is followed by a focus on the application of the intellectual technology of comprehensive systems design as an approach to the transformation of education.

3.2.1 A Systems View of Education

For any system of interest, a systems view enables us to explore and characterize the system of our interest, its environment, and its components and parts. We can acquire a systems view by integrating systems concepts and principles in our thinking and learning to use them in representing our world and our experiences with their use. A systems view empowers us to think of ourselves, the environments that surround us, and the groups and organizations in which we live in a new way: the systems way. This new way of thinking and experiencing enables us to understand and describe the following:

- Characteristics of the "embeddedness" of educational systems operating at several interconnected levels (e.g., institutional, administrative, instructional, learning experience levels)
- Relationships, interactions, and mutual interdependencies of systems operating at those levels
- Purposes, the goals, and the boundaries of educational systems
- Relationships, interactions, and information/matter/energy exchanges between our systems and their environments
- Dynamics of interactions, relationships, and patterns of connectedness among the components of systems
- Properties of wholeness and the characteristics that emerge at various systems levels as a result of systemic interaction and synthesis
- Systems processes, i.e., the behavior and change of systems and their environments over time.

The systems view generates insights into ways of knowing, thinking, and reasoning that enable us to pursue the kind of inquiry described above. Systemic educational renewal will become possible only if the educational community will develop a systems view of education, if it embraces the systems view, and if it applies the systems view in its approach to reform.

Systems inquiry and systems applications have been applied in the worlds of business and industry, in information technology, in the health services, in architecture and engineering, and in environmental issues. However, in education—except for a narrow application in instructional technology (discussed later)—systems inquiry is highly underconceptualized and underutilized, and it is often manifested in misdirected applications.

With very few exceptions, systems philosophy, systems theory, and systems methodology as subjects of study and applications are not yet on the agenda of our educational professional development programs. And, as a rule, capability in systems inquiry is not yet in the inventory of our educational research community. It is my firm belief that unless our educational communities and our educational professional organizations embrace systems inquiry, and unless our research agencies learn to pursue systems inquiry, the notions of "systemic" reform and "systemic approaches" to educational renewal will remain hollow and meaningless buzzwords.

The notion of systems inquiry enfolds large sets of concepts that constitute principles, common to all kinds of systems. Acquiring a "systems view of education" means that we learn to think about education as a system, we can understand and describe it as a system, we can put the systems view into practice and apply it in educational inquiry, and we can design education so that it will manifest systemic behavior. Once we individually and collectively develop a systems view, then—and only then—can we become "systemic" in our approach to educational reform, only then can we apply the systems view to the reconceptualization and redefinition of education as a system, and only then can we engage in the design of systems that will nurture learning and enable the full development of human potential.

During the past decade, we have applied systems thinking and the systems view in human and social systems. As a result we now have a range of systems models and methods that enable us to work creatively and successfully with education as a complex social system. We have organized these models and methods in four complementary domains of organizational inquiry (Banathy, 1988) as follows:

- The systems analysis and description of educational systems by the application of three systems models: the systems environment, functions/structure, and process/behavioral models
- Systems design, conducting comprehensive design inquiry with the use of design models, methods, and tools appropriate to education
- Implementation of the design by systems development and institutionalization
- Systems management and the management of change

Figure 3-1 depicts the relational arrangement of the four domains of organizational inquiry. In the center of the figure is the integrating cluster.

In the center, the core values, core ideas, and organizing perspectives constitute bases for both the development of the inquiry approach and the decisions we make in the course of the inquiry.

Of special interest to us in this chapter is the description and analysis of educational systems and comprehensive

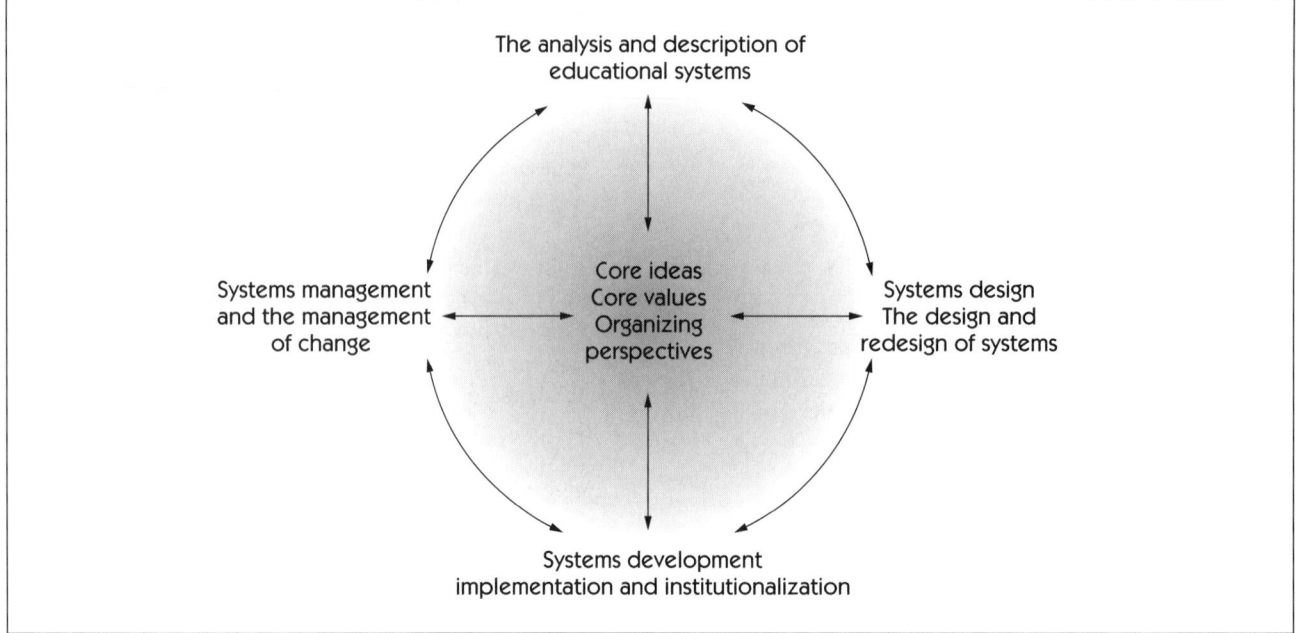

Figure 3-1.   A comprehensive system of educational inquiry.

systems design as a disciplined inquiry that offers potential for the development of truly systemic educational reform. In the rest of the chapter, we focus on these two aspects of systems inquiry.

3.2.2 Three Models That Portray Education as a System

Models are useful as a frame of reference to talk about the system the models represent. Because our purpose here is to understand and portray education as a system, it is important to create a common frame of reference for our discourse, to build systems models of education.

Models of social systems are built by the relational organization of the concepts and principles that represent the context, the content, and the process of social systems. I constructed three models (Banathy, 1992) that represent (a) systems-environment relationships, (b) the functions/structure of social systems, and (c) the processes and behavior of systems through time. These models are "lenses" that can be used to look at educational systems and understand, describe, and analyze them as open, dynamic, and complex social systems. These models are briefly described next.

3.2.2.1. Systems-Environment Model.   The use of the systems-environment model enables us to describe an educational system in the context of its community and the larger society. The concepts and principles that are pertinent to this model help us define systems-environment relationships, interactions, and mutual interdependencies. A set of inquiries, built into the model, guide the user to make an assessment of the environmental responsiveness of the system and, conversely, the adequacy of the responsiveness of the environment toward the system.

3.2.2.2. Functions/Structure Model.   The use of the functions/structure model focuses our attention on what the educational system *is* at a given moment of time. It projects a "still-picture" image of the system. It enables us to (a) describe the goals of the system (that elaborate the purposes that emerged from the systems-environment model), (b) identify the functions that have to be carried out to attain the goals, (c) select the components (of the system) that have the capability to carry out the functions, and (d) formulate the relational arrangements of the components that constitute the structure of the system. A set of inquiries are built into the model that guide the user to probe into the function/structure adequacy of the system.

3.2.2.3. Process/Behavioral Model.   The use of the process/behavioral model helps us to concentrate our inquiry on what the educational system *does* through time. It projects a "motion-picture" image of the system and guides us in understanding how the system behaves as a changing and living social system; how it (a) receives, screens, assesses, and processes input; (b) transforms input for use in the system; (c) engages in transformation operations by which to produce the expected output; (d) guides the transformation operations; (e) processes the output and assesses its adequacy; and (f) makes adjustment in the system if needed or imitates the redesign of the system if indicated. The model incorporates a set of inquiries that guides the user to evaluate the systems from a process perspective.

What is important for us to understand is that no single model can provide us with a true representation of an educational system. Only if we consider the three models jointly can we capture a comprehensive image of education as a social system.

3.2.3 Designing Social Systems

Systems design in the context of human activity systems is a future-creating disciplined inquiry. People engage in design in order to devise and implement a new system, based on their vision of what that system should be.

There is a growing awareness that most of our systems are out of sync with the new realities of the current era. Those who understand this and are willing to face these realities call for the rethinking and redesign of our systems. Once we understand the significance of these new realities and their implications for us individually and collectively, we will reaffirm that systems design is the only viable approach to working with and creating and recreating our systems in a changing world of new realities. These new realties and the societal and organizational characteristics of the current era call for the development of new thinking, new perspectives, new insight, and—based on these—the design of systems that will be in sync with those realities and emerged characteristics.

In times of accelerating and dynamic changes, when a new stage is unfolding in societal evolution, inquiry should not focus on the improvement of our existing systems. Such a focus limits perception to adjusting or modifying the old design in which our systems are still rooted. A design rooted in an outdated image is useless. We must break the old frame of thinking and reframe it. We should transcend the boundaries of our existing system, explore change and renewal from the larger vistas of our transforming society, envision a new image of our systems, create a new design based on the image, and transform our systems by implementing the new design.

3.2.3.1. Systems Design: A New Intellectual Technology. Systems design in the context of social systems is a relatively new intellectual technology. It emerged only recently as a manifestation of open-systems thinking and corresponding soft-systems approaches. This new intellectual technology emerged, just in time, as a disciplined inquiry that enables us to align our societal systems, most specifically our educational systems, with the "new realities" of the information/knowledge age.

3.2.4 When Should We Design?

Social systems are created for attaining purposes that are shared by those who are in the system. Activities in which people in the system are engaged are guided by those purposes. There are times when there is a discrepancy between what our system actually attains and what we designated as the desired outcome of the system. Once we sense such discrepancy, we realize that something has gone wrong, and we need to make some changes either in the activities or in the way we carry out activities. The focus is changes within the system. Changes within the system are accomplished by adjustment, modification, or improvement.

But there are times when we have evidence that changes within the system would not suffice. We might realize that our purposes are not viable anymore and we need to change them. We realize that we now need to change the whole system. We need a different system; we need to redesign our system; or we need to design a new system.

The changes described above are guided by self-regulation, accomplished, as noted earlier, by positive feedback that signals the need for changing the whole system. We are to formulate new purposes, introduce new functions, new components, and new arrangements of the components. It is by such self-organization that the system responds to positive feedback and learns to coevolve with its environment by transforming itself into a new state. The process by which this self-organization, coevolution, and transformation comes about is systems design.

3.2.5. Research Findings on the Nature of Design Activity

In Cross's compendium (1984), design researchers report their findings on the general nature of design. I briefly review their findings as follows.

3.2.5.1. Darke (1984). He has found that contemporary designers have rejected the earlier "systematic, objective, analysis-synthesis approach" to design and replaced it with what Hiller et al. (1972) called *conjecture-analysis*. The point of departure of this approach is not a detailed analysis of the situation but the formulation of a conjecture that Darke has termed *primary generator*. The primary generator is formed early in the design process as initiating concepts. (We later called this a system of core ideas: the first image of the system.) This primary generator helps designers make the creative leap between the problem formulation and a solution concept, as Cross noted (1982). Broad design requirements, in combination with the primary generator, help designers arrive at an initial conjecture that can be tested against specific requirements as an interactive process. Conjectures and requirements mutually shape each other. While earlier design approaches concentrated on design morphology as a sequence of boxes bearing preset labels, Darke (1982) finds that now designers fill the boxes with their own concepts and the sources of their concepts. An understanding of the subjectivity of designing reflects the diversity of human experience, which, in turn, should reflect the diversity in approaches to design.

3.2.5.2. Akin (1984). He challenges earlier assumptions about design. As Darke did, he also takes an issue with the analysis-synthesis-evaluation sequence in design. He says this approach was at the heart of almost all normative design methods of the past. He suggests that one of the unique aspects of designing is the constant generation of new task goals and the redefinition of task constraints. "Hence analysis is part of virtually all phases of design. Similarly, synthesis or solution development occurs as early as in the first stage" (p. 205). The rigid structuring of the design process into analysis-synthesis-evaluation and the tactics implied for these compartments are unrealistic. Solutions do not emerge from an analysis of all relevant aspects of the problem. Even a few cues in the design environment can be sufficient to evoke a recombined solution in the mind of the designers. Actually, this evoking is more the norm than a rational process of assembly of parts through synthesis. Many rational models of design violate the widely used criterion of designers, namely, to find a satisfying, rather than a scientifically optimized, solution. No fixed model is complex enough to represent the real-life complexities of the design process. That is why designers select approaches that produce a solution that satisfies an acceptable number of design criteria.

3.2.5.3. Lawson (1984). He conducted a controlled experiment between scientists and designers. He discovered that scientists used processes that focused on discovering the problem structure, while designers used strategies that focused on findings solutions. For the designers, the most successful and practical way to address design problem situations is not by analyzing them in depth but by quickly proposing solutions to them. This way, they discover more about the problem as well as what is an acceptable solution to it. On the other hand, scientists analyze the problem in order to discover its patterns and its rules before proposing a solution to it. Designers seek solutions by synthesis, scientists by analysis. Accordingly, designers evolve and develop methodologies that do not depend on the completion of analysis before synthesis begins.

3.2.5.4. Thomas and Carroll. Thomas and Carroll (1984) carried out a broad range of studies on design that indicated a wide range of similarities between the behavior of designers and their approaches to design, regardless of the particular subject of design. They said that they changed their original assumption that design is a form of problem solving to the opinion that design is "a way of looking at a problem." They considered design as a dialectic interactive process among the participants of the design activity. In this process, participants elaborate a goal statement into more explicit functional requirements, and then from these they elaborate the design solution.

In reviewing the four research findings, Cross (1982, pp. 172-73) arrives at two major conclusions. The first is an inevitable emphasis on the early generation of solutions so that a better understanding of the problem can be developed. Second is that the earlier systematic procedures tend to focus on an extensive phase of problem analysis, which seems an unrealistic approach to ill-defined problems.

In discussing systems design, the difference between systematic and systemic is a recurring issue. The term *systematic* was in vogue in the 50s and the 60s. During that period, a closed systems engineering thinking dominated the scene. The term implied regularity in a methodical procedure. In design, it means following the same steps, in a linear, one-directional causation mode; it means adhering to the same prescribed design method, regardless of the subject and the specific content and context of the design situation. Designers of the 70s and 80s have learned the confining and unproductive nature of the systematic approach. Once we understood the open-system, dynamic-

complexity, nonlinear, and mutually affecting nature of social systems, we developed a "systemic" approach that liberated us from the restrictive and prescriptive rigor of being systematic. Systemic relates to the dynamic interaction of parts from which the integrity of wholeness of the system emerges. Systemic also indicates uniqueness, which is the opposite of the sameness of systematic. Systemic recognizes the unique nature of each and every system. It calls for the use of methods that respect and are responsive to the uniqueness of the particular design situation, including the unique nature of the design environment.

3.2.6 Models for Building Social Systems

Until the 70s, design, as a disciplined inquiry, was primarily the domain of architecture and engineering. In social and sociotechnical systems, the nature of the inquiry was either systems analysis, operation research, or social engineering. These approaches reflected the kind of systematic, closed-systems, and hard-systems thinking discussed in the previous section. It was not until the 70s that we realized that the use of these approaches was not applicable; in fact they were counterproductive to working with social systems. We became aware that social systems are open systems; they have dynamic complexity; and they operate in turbulent and ever-changing environments. Based on this understanding, a new orientation emerged, based on "soft-systems" thinking. The insights gained from this orientation became the basis for the emergence of a new generation of designers and the development of new design models applicable to social systems. Earlier we listed systems researchers who made significant contributions to the development of approaches to the design of open social systems. Among them, three scholars—Ackoff, Checkland, and Nadler—were the ones who developed comprehensive process models of systems design. Their work did set the trend for continuing work in design research and social systems design.

3.2.6.1. Ackoff: A Model for the Design of Idealized Systems. The underlying conceptual base of Ackoff's design model (1981) is a systems view of the world. He explores how our concept of the world has changed in recent time from the machine age to the systems age. He defines and interprets the implications of the systems age and the systems view to systems design. He sets forth design strategies, followed by implementation planning. At the very center of his approach is what he calls *idealized design.*

Design commences with an understanding and assessment of what is now. Ackoff calls this process *formulating the mess.* The mess is a set of interdependent problems that emerges and is identifiable only in their interaction. Thus, the design that responds to this mess "should be more than an aggregation of independently obtained solutions to the parts of the mess. It should deal with messes as wholes, systemically" (1981, p. 52). This process includes systems analysis, a detailed study of potential obstructions to development, and the creation of projections and scenarios that explore the question: What would happen if things would not change?

Having gained a systemic insight into the current state of affairs, Ackoff proceeds to the idealized design. The selection of ideals lies at the very core of the process. As he says: "It takes place through idealized design of a system that does not yet exist, or the idealized design of one that does" (p. 105). The three properties of an idealized design are: (1) It should be technologically feasible, (2) operationally viable, and (3) capable of rapid learning and development. This model is not a utopian system but "the most effective ideal-seeking system of which designers can conceive" (p. 107). The process of creating the ideal includes selecting a mission, specifying desired properties of the design, and designing the system. Ackoff emphasizes that the vision of the ideal must be a shared image. It should be created by all who are in the system and those affected by the design. Such participative design is attained by the organization of interlinked design boards that integrate representation across the various levels of the organization.

Having created the model of the idealized system, designers engage in the design of the management system that can guide the system and can learn how to learn as a system. Its three key functions are: (1) identifying threats and opportunities, (2) identifying what to do and having it done, and (3) maintaining and improving performance. The next major function is organizational design, the creation of the organization that is "ready, willing, and able to modify itself when necessary in order to make progress towards its ideals" (p. 149). The final stage is implementation planning. It is carried out by selecting or creating the means by which the specified ends can be pursued, determining what resources will be required, planning for the acquisition of resources, and defining who is doing what, when, how, and where.

3.2.6.2. Checkland's Soft-Systems Model. Checkland in his work (1981, 1992) creates a solid base for his model for systems change by reviewing (a) science as human activity, (b) the emergence of systems science, and (c) the evolution of systems thinking. He differentiates between "hard-systems thinking," which is appropriate to work with, rather than closed, engineered type of systems and "soft-systems thinking," which is required in working with social systems. He says that he is "trying to make systems thinking a conscious, generally accessible way of looking at things, not the stock of trade of experts" (p. 162). Based on soft-systems thinking, he formulated a model for working with and changing social systems.

His seven-stage model generates a total system of change functions, leading to the creation of a future system. His conceptual model of the future system is similar in nature to Ackoff's idealized system. Using Checkland's approach, during the first stage we look at the problem situation of the system, which we find in its real-life setting as being "unstructured." At this stage, our focus is not on specific problems but the situation in which we perceive the problem. Given the perceived "unstructured situation," during stage 2 we develop a richest possible structured picture of the problem situation. These first two stages operate in the context of the real world.

The next two stages are developed in the conceptual realm of systems thinking. Stage 3 involves speculating about some systems that may offer relevant solutions to the problem situation and preparing concise "root definitions" of what these systems are (not what they do). During stage 4, the task is to develop abstract representations, models of the relevant systems, for which root definitions were formulated at stage 3. These representations are conceptual models of the relevant systems, comprised of verbs, denoting functions. This stage consists of two substages. First, we describe the conceptual model. Then, we check it against a theory-based, formal model of systems. Checkland adopted Churchman's model (1971) for this purpose.

During the last three stages, we move back to the realm of the real world. During stage 5, we compare the conceptual model with the structured problem situation we formulated during stage 2. This comparison enables us to identify, during stage 6, feasible and desirable changes in the real world. Stage 7 is devoted to taking action and introducing changes in the system.

3.2.6.3. Nadler's Planning and Design Approach. Nadler, an early proponent of designing for the ideal (1967), is the third systems scholar who developed a comprehensive model (Nadler, 1981) for the design of sociotechnical systems. During phase 1, his strategy calls for the development of a hierarchy of purpose statements, which are formulated so that each higher level describes the purpose of the next lower level. From this purpose hierarchy, the designers select the specific purpose level for which to create the system. The formulation of purpose is coupled with the identification of measures of effectiveness that indicate the successful achievement of the defined purpose. During this phase, designers explore alternative reasons and expectations that the design might accomplish.

During phase 2, "creativity is engaged as ideal solutions are generated for the selected purposes within the context of the purpose hierarchy," says Nadler (1981, p. 9). He introduced a large array of methods that remove conceptual blocks, nurture creativity, and widen the creation of alternative solutions ideas.

During phase 3, designers develop solution ideas into systems of alternative solutions. During this phase, designers play the believing game as they focus on how to make ideal solutions work, rather than on the reasons why they won't work. They try ideas out to see how they fit.

During phase 4, the solution is detailed. Designers build into the solution specific arrangements that might cope with potential exceptions and irregularities while protecting the desired qualities of solutions. As Nadler says: "Why discard the excellent solution that copes with 95% of the conditions because another 5% cannot directly fit into it?" (p. 11). As a result, design solutions are often flexible, multi-channeled, and pluralistic.

Phase 5 involves the implementation of the selected design solution. In the context of the purpose hierarchy, we set forth the ideal solution and plan for taking action necessary to install the solution. But we have to realize that the "most successful implemented solution is incomplete if it does not incorporate the seeds of its own improvement. An implemented solution should be treated as provisional" (p. 11). Therefore each system should have its own arrangements for continuing design and change.

In Nadler's recent book, coauthored by Hibino (1990), a set of principles are set forth that guide the work of designers. These principles can serve as guidelines that keep designers focused on seeking solutions rather than on being preoccupied by problems.

- The "uniqueness principle" suggests that whatever the apparent similarities, each problem is unique, and the design approach should respond to the unique contextual situation.
- The "purposes principle" calls for focusing on purposes and expectations rather than on problems. This focus helps us strip away nonessential aspects and prevents us from working on the wrong problem.
- The "ideal design principle" stimulates us to work back from the ideal target solution.
- The "systems principle" tells us that every design setting is part of a larger system. Understanding the systems matrix of embeddedness helps us to determine the multilevel complexities that we should incorporate into the solution model.
- The "limited information principle" points to the pitfall that too much knowing about the problem can prevent us from seeing some excellent alternative solutions.
- The "people design principle" underlines the necessity of involving in the design all those who are in the systems and who are affected by the design.
- The "betterment timeline principle" calls for the deliberate building into the design the capability and capacity for continuing betterment of the solution through time.

3.2.7 A Process Model of Social Systems Design

The three design models introduced above have been applied primarily in the corporate and business community. Their application in the public domain has been limited. Still, we can learn much from them as we seek to formulate an approach to the design of social and societal systems. In the concluding section of Part 2, we introduce a process model of social system design that has been inspired and informed by the work of Ackoff, Checkland, and Nadler, and is a generalized outline of our earlier work of designing educational systems (Banathy, 1991).

The process of design that leads us from an existing state to a desired future state is initiated by an expression of why we want to engage in design. We call this expression of

want the *genesis of design*. Once we decide that we want to design something other than what we now have, we must:

- Transcend the existing state or the existing system and leave it behind.
- Envision an image of the system that we wish to create.
- Design the system based on the image.
- Transform the system by developing and implementing the system based on the design.

Transcending, envisioning, designing, and transforming the system are the four major strategies of the design and development of social systems, which are briefly outlined below.

3.2.7.1. Transcending the Existing State. Whenever we have an indication that we should change the existing system or create a new system, we are confronted with the task of transcending the existing system or the existing state of affairs. We devised a framework that enables designers to accomplish this transcendence and create an option field, which they can use to draw alternative boundaries for their design inquiry and consider major solution alternatives. The framework is constructed of four dimensions: the focus of the inquiry, the scope of the inquiry, relationship with other systems, and the selection of system type. On each dimension, several options are identified that gradually extend the boundaries of the inquiry. The exploration of options leads designers to make a series of decisions that charts the design process toward the next strategy of systems design.

3.2.7.2. Envisioning: Creating the First Image. Systems design creates a description, a representation, a model of the future system. This creation is grounded in the designers' vision, ideas, and aspirations of what that future system should be. As the designers draw the boundaries of the design inquiry on the framework and make choices from among the options, they collectively form core ideas that they hold about the desired future. They articulate their shared vision and synthesize their core ideas into the first image of the system. This image becomes a magnet that pulls designers into designing the system that will bring the image to life.

3.2.7.3. Designing the New System Based on the Image. The image expresses an intent. One of the key issues in working with social systems is: How to bring intention and design together and create a system that transforms the image into reality? The image becomes the basis that initiates the strategy of transformation by design. The design solution emerges as designers: (1) formulate the mission and purposes of the future system, (2) define its specifications, (3) select the functions that have to be carried out to attain the mission and purposes, (4) organize these functions into a system, (5) design the system that will guide the functions and the organization that will carry out the functions, (6) define the environment that will have the resources to support the system, (7) describe the new system by using the three models we described earlier—the systems-environment model, the functions/structure model, and the process/behavioral model(Banathy, 1992)—and (8) prepare a development/implementation plan.

3.2.7.4. Transforming the System Based on the Design. The outcome of design is a description, a conceptual representation, or modeling of the new system. Based on the models, we can bring the design to life by developing the system based on the models that represent the design and then implementing and institutionalizing it (Banathy, 1986).

We elaborated the four strategies in the context of education in our earlier work (1991) as we described the processes of (1) transcending the existing system of education, (2) envisioning and defining the image of the desired future system, (3) designing the new system based on the image, and (4) transforming the existing system by developing/ implementing/institutionalizing the new system based on the design.

In this section, a major step has been taken toward the understanding of systems design by exploring some research findings about design, examining a set of comprehensive design models, and proposing a process model for the design of educational and other social systems. In the closing section, we present the disciplined inquiry of systems design as the new imperative in education and briefly highlight distinctions between instructional design and systems design.

3.2.8 Systems Design: The New Imperative in Education

Many of us share a realization that today's schools are far from being able to do justice to the education of future generations. There is a growing awareness that our current design of education is out of sync with the new realities of the information/knowledge era. Those who are willing to face these new realities understand that:

- Rather than improving education, we should *transcend* it.
- Rather than revising it, we should *revision* it.
- Rather then reforming, we should *transform* it by design.

We now call for a metamorphosis of education. It has become clear to many of us that educational inquiry should not focus on the improvement of existing systems. Staying within the existing boundaries of education constrains and delimits perception and locks us into prevailing practices. At best, improvement or restructuring of the existing system can attain some marginal adjustment of an educational design that is still rooted in the perceptions and practices of the 19th-century machine age.

But adjusting a design—rooted in an outdated image— creates far more problems than it solves. We have already found this out. The escalating rhetoric of educational reform has created high expectations, but the realities of improvement efforts have not delivered on those expectations. Improving what we have now does not lead to any

significant results, regardless of how much money and effort we invest in it.

> Two roads diverged in a woods—and I—I took the road less traveled by, and that has made all the difference" (Robert Frost).

Our educational communities—including our Educational Technology Community—have reached a juncture in our journey toward educational-renewal. We can continue to travel on the well-known road of our past and present practices with some attention paid to improving the road, so that we can travel faster. We can even restructure the schedules, the programs of—and the responsibilities for—the journey. None of these adjustments will make much difference. Or we can take the risk of choosing the less-traveled road so that we can make a difference in the education of this nation and in the development of our society.

But taking the less-traveled road, we must transcend our old ways of thinking and develop new ways. We must reframe our mindset from problem focus to solution focus. We must unload the baggage of our past practices, and must learn new ones.

The new thinking is systems thinking; the new mindset is a systems view of education; and the new practice is the application of systems design. These are the prerequisites of a purposeful and viable creation of new organizational capacities and individual and collective capabilities that enable us to empower our educational communities so that they can engage in the design and transformation of our educational systems by creating new systems of learning and human development.

3.2.9 Instructional Design Is Not Systems Design

Some of my friends in the educational technology community continue to ask me: Is there really a difference between the intellectual technology of instructional design and systems design? My answer continues to be a definite Yes. A review of this chapter should lead the reader to an understanding of the difference.

An understanding of the process of designing education as an open social system, reviewed here, and the comparison of this with the process of designing instructional or training systems, known well to the reader, will clearly show the difference between the two design inquiries. I discussed this difference at some length earlier (1987). Here I briefly highlight some of the differences:

> Education as social system is open to its environment, its community, and the larger society, and it constantly and dynamically interacts with its environment.
>
> An instructional system is a subsystem of an instructional program that delivers a segment of the curriculum. The curriculum is embedded in the educational system.
>
> An instructional system is three systems levels below education as a social system.
>
> We design an educational system in view of societal realities/expectations/aspirations and core ideas and values.

It is from these that an image of the future system emerges, based on which we then formulate the core definition, the mission, and purposes of the system.

We design an instructional system against clearly defined instructional objectives that are derived from the larger instructional program and—at the next higher level—from the curriculum.

An instructional system is a closed system. The technology of its design is an engineering (hard-system) technology. An educational system is open and is constantly coevolving with its environment. Its design applies soft-systems methods.

In designing an educational system we engage in the design activity those who are serving the system, those who are served by it, and those who are affected by it.

An instructional system is designed by the expert educational technologist who takes into account the characteristics of the user of the system.

A designed instructional system is often delivered by computer software and other mediation. An educational system is a human/social activity system that relies primarily on human/social interaction. Some of the interactions, e.g., planning or information storing, can be aided by the use of software.

3.2.10 The Challenge of the Educational Technology Community

We as members of the educational technology community face a four-pronged challenge: (1) We should transcend the constraints and limits of the means and methods of instructional technology. We should clearly understand the difference between the design of education as a social system and instructional design. (2) We should develop open-systems thinking, acquire a systems view, and develop competence in systems design. (3) We should create programs and resources that enable our larger educational community to develop systems thinking, a systems view, and competence in systems design. (4) We should assist our communities across the nation to engage in the design and development of their systems of learning and human development. Our societal challenge is to place ourself in the service of transforming education by design and help create just systems of learning and development for future generations.

Education creates the future, and there is no more important task and no more noble calling than participating in this creation.

REFERENCES

Ackoff, Russel L. (1981). *Creating the Corporate Future*. New York: Wiley.

— & Emery, F. E. (1972). *On purposeful systems*. Chicago, IL: Aldine-Atherton.

— (1974). *Redesigning the Future*. New York: Wiley.

— (1981). *Creating the Corporate Future*. New York: Wiley.

Akin, Omer (1984). An exploration of the design process, *In* N. Cross, ed. *Developments in design methodology*. New York: Wiley.

Argyris, Chris and Schon, Donald (1979). *Organizational learning*. Reading, MA: Addision Wesley.

— (1982). *Reasoning learning and action*. San Francisco, CA: Jossey-Bass.

Ashby, W. Ross (1952). *Design for a brain*. New York: Wiley.

Banathy, Bela H. (1986). A systems view of institutionalizing change in education, *In* S. Majumdar, ed. *1985-86 Yearbook of the National Association of Academies of Science*. Columbus, OH: Ohio Academy of Science.

— (1987) Instructional Systems Design, *In* R. Gagne, ed. *Instructional Technology Foundations*. Hillsdale, NJ: Erlbaum.

— (1988). Systems inquiry in education. *Systems Practice, No. 4*

— (1988). Matching design methods to system type. *Systems Research, No. 1*.

— & Banathy, Bela Antal (1989). A general theory of systems by Bela Zalai (book review). *Systems Practice 2(4)*.

— (1991). *Systems design of education*. Englewood Cliffs, NJ: Educational Technology.

— (1992). *A systems view of education*. Englewood Cliffs, NJ: Educational Technology.

Bateson, Gregory, (1972). *Steps to an ecology of mind*. New York: Random House.

Bertalanffy, Ludvig, von (1945). *Zu Einer Allgemeinen System Lehre. In* F. Blaetter, *Deutsche Philosophie 18* (3/4).

— (1951). General systems theory: a new approach to the unity of science. *Human Biology 23*.

— (1956) General systems theory, In *Vol. I. Yearbook*. Society for General Systems Research.

— (1968) *General systems theory*. New York: Braziller.

Blauberg, J.V., Sadovsky, V.N. & Yudin, E.G. (1977). *Systems theory: philosophical and methodological problems*. Moscow: Progress Publishers.

Bogdanov, A. (1921-27). Tektologia (a series of articles) *Proletarskaya Kultura*.

Boulding, Kenneth (1956). General systems theory-the skeleton of science, In *Vol I., Yearbook*. Society for General Systems Research.

Buckley, Walter (1968) *Modern systems research for the behavioral scientist*. Chicago, IL: Aldine.

Cavallo, Roger (1979). Systems research movement. *General Systems Bulletin IX,* (3).

Checkland, Peter (1981). *Systems thinking, systems practice*. New York: Wiley.

— & J. Scholes (1990). *Soft systems methodology*. New York: Wiley.

Churchman, C. West (1968a). *Challange to reason*. New York: McGraw-Hill.

— (1968b). *The systems approach*. New York: Delacorte.

— (1971). *The design of inquiring systems*. New York: Basic Books.

— (1979). *The systems approach and its enemies*. New York: Basic Books.

— (1981). *Thought and wisdom*. Salinas, CA: Intersystem.

Cross, Nigel (1984). *Developments in design methodology*. New York: Wiley.

Darke, Jane (1982). The primary generator and the design process, *In* N. Cross, ed. *Development in design methodology*. New York: Wiley.

Flood, Robert L. (1990). *Liberating systems theory*. New York: Plenum.

Foerster, Heinz von (1984). *Observing systems*. Salinas, CA: Intersystems.

Gleick, James (1987). *Chaos: making a new science*. New York: Viking.

Golerik, George, (1980). *Essays in tektology*. Salinas, CA: Intersystems.

Hall, Arthur (1962). *A methodology of systems engineering*, Princeton, NJ: Van Nostrand.

Hiller, W., Musgrove, J. & O'Sullivan, P. (1972). Knowledge and design. *In* W.J. Mitchell, ed. *Environmental design*. Berkeley, CA: University California Press.

Jackson, Michael & Keeys, Paul (1984) Towards a system of systems methodologies. *Journal of Operations Research* (35).

Jantsch, Erich (1976). *Design for evolution*. New York: Braziller.

— (1980). *The self-organizing universe*. Oxford: Pergamon.

Hammer, Michael & Champy, James (1993). *Reengineering the corporation*. New York: HarperCollins.

Jones, Christopher (1970). *Design methods*. New York: Wiley.

Laszlo, Ervin (1972). *The systems view of the world*. New York: Braziller.

— (1987). *Evolution: a grand synthesis*. Boston, MA: New Science Library.

Lawson, Bryan, R. Cognitive studies in architectural design, *In* N. Cross, ed. *Developments in design methodology*. New York: Wiley.

Miller, James (1978) Living Systems. New York: McGraw-Hill

Mitroff, Ian & Linstone, Harold (1993). *The unbounded mind*. New York: Oxford University Press.

Morgan, Gareth (1986). *Images of organization*. Beverly Hills, CA: Sage.

Nadler, Gerald (1976). *Work systems design: the ideals concept*. Homewood, IL: Irwin.

— (1981). *The planning and design approach*. New York: Wiley.

— & Hibino, Shozo (1990). *Breakthrough thinking*. Rocklin, CA: Prima.

Peccei, Aurel (1977). *The human quality*. Oxford, England: Pergamon.

Prigogine, Ilya & Stengers, Isabelle (1980). *La Nouvelle Alliance*. Paris: Gallimard. Published in English: (1984) *Order out of chaos*. New York: Bantam.

Rittel, Horst & Webber, Melvin (1973) Dilemmas in a general theory of planning. *Policy Sciences* (4).

Sage, Andrew (1977). *Methodology for large-scale systems*. New York: McGraw-Hill.

Sange, Peter (1990). *The fifth discipline*. New York: Doubleday

Simon, Herbert (1969). *The science of the artificial*. Cambridge, MA: MIT.

Singer, E.A. (1959). *Experience and reflection*. Philadelphia, PA: University Pennsylvania Press.

Southerland, J. (1973). *A general systems philosophy for the behavioral sciences*. New York: Braziller.

Thomas, John C. & Carroll, John M. (1984), The psychological study of design. *In* N. Cross, ed. *Developments on design methodology*. New York: Wiley.

Ulrich, Werner (1983). *Critical heuristics in social planning*. Bern, Switzerland: Haupt.

Waddington, Conrad (1977). *Evolution and consciousness*. Reading, MA: Addison-Wesley.

Warfield, John (1990). *A science of general design*. Salinas, CA: Intersystems.

Wheatley, Margaret (1992). *Leadership and the new science*. San Francisco, CA: Barrett-Koehler.

Vickers, Geoffrey (1983). *Human systems are different*. London, England: Harper & Row.

Wiener, N. (1948). *Cybernetics*. Cambridge, MA: MIT.

Zalai, Bela (1984). *General theory of systems*. Budapest, Hungary: Gondolat.

I. BIBLIOGRAPHY OF SYSTEMS-RELATED WRITINGS

The Design of Educational Systems

Banathy, Bela H. (1991). Systems design of education. Englewood Cliffs, NJ: Educational Technology.**

Banathy, Bela H. (1992). A systems view of education. Englewood Cliffs, NJ: Educational Technology. **

Banathy, B.H. & L, Jenks, (1991). The transformation of education by design. Far West Laboratory. **

Reigeluth, C., Banathy, B., Olson J., ed. (1993). Comprehensive systems design: a new educational technology. Stuttgart, Springer. **

---

* This mark means primary significance.

** This mark means primary and state of the art significance.

Articles (Representative Samples)

From *Systems Research:*

1. Social Systems Design

Vol. 2, #3: A.N. Christakis, The national forum on nonindustrial private forest lands.

Vol. 4, #1: A. Hatchel et al., Innovation as system intervention.

Vol. 4, #2 : J. Warfield & A. Christakis, Dimensionality; W. Churchman, Discoveries in an exploration into systems thinking.

Vol. 4, #4: J. Warfield, Thinking about systems.

Vol. 5, #1: B.H. Banathy, Matching design methods to systems type.

Vol. 5, #2: A.N. Christakis et al., Synthesis in a new age: a role for systems scientists in the age of design.

Vol. 5, #3: M.C. Jackson, Systems methods for organizational analysis and design.

Vol. 5, #3: R. Ackoff, A theory of practice in the social sciences.

Vol. 6, #4: B.H. Banathy, The design of evolutionary guidance systems.

Vol. 7, #3: F.F. Robb, Morhostasi and morphogenesis: context of design inquiry.

Vol. 7, #4: C. Smith, Self-organization in social systems: a paradigm of ethics.

Vol. 8, #2: T.F. Gougen, Family stories as mechanisms of evolutionary guidance.

From *Systems Practice:*

Vol. 1, #1: J. Oliga: Methodological foundations of systems methodologies, p. 3.

Vol. 1, #4: R. Mason, Exploration of opportunity costs; P. Checkland, Churchman's Anatomy of systems teleology; W. Ulrich, Churchman's Process of unfolding.

Vol. 2, #1: R. Flood, Six scenarios for the future of systems problem solving.

Vol. 2, #4: J. Vlcek, The practical use of systems approach in large-scale designing.

Vol. 3, #1: R. Flood & W. Ulrich, Critical systems thinking.

Vol. 3, #2: S. Beer, On suicidal rabbits: a relativity of systems.

Vol. 3, #3: M. Schwaninger, The viable system model.

Vol. 3, #5: R. Ackoff, The management of change and the changes it requires in management; P. Keys, Systems dynamics as a systems-based problem solving methodology.

Vol. 3, #6: I Tsivacou, An evolutionary design methodology.

Vol. 4, #2: M. Jackson, The origin and nature of critical systems thinking.

Vol. 4, #3: R. Flood & M. Jackson, Total systems intervention. 2. The systems design of education (very limited samples).

Vol. 9, #2: Banathy, B.H., New horizons through systems design, Educational Horizons.

Banathy, B.H. (Mar., May, Jul., Sep. 1991 and Jan. 1992), Columns on comprehensive systems design, Educational Technology.

Barth, R. (Oct. 1991) Restructuring schools, Phi Delta Kappan.

Branson, R. (Apr. 1990) Issues in the design of schooling, Educational Technology.

Reigeluth, C. (Vol. 10, #4) The search for meaningful reform: a third-wave educational system, *Journal of Instrument Development*.

Reigeluth, C. (Nov. 1991) Column: comprehensive systems design, Educational Technology.

Rowland, G. (Dec. 1991) Designing educational futures, Educational Technology, p. 4.

II. ELABORATION

Books: Design thinking—design action

Ackoff, R. (1974). *Redesigning the future:*. New York: Wiley.

— Ackoff, R., et al. (1984) *A guide to controlling your corporation's future*. New York: Wiley.

Alexander C. (1964). *Notes on the synthesis of form*. Cambridge, MA: Harvard University Press.

Banathy B., et al., (1979). *Design models and methodologies*. San Francisco, CA: Far West Laboratory.

Boulding, K. (1956). *The image*. Ann Arbor, MI: The University Michigan Press.

Checkland P. & Scholes, J. (1990). *Soft systems methodology in action*. New York: Wiley.

Emery, F. & Trist, E. (1973). *Towards a social ecology*. New York: Plenum.

Gasparski, W. (1984). *Understanding design*. Salinas, CA: Intersystems.

Harman, W. (1988). *Global mind change*. Indianapolis, IN: Knowledge Systems.

Harman, W. (1976). *An incomplete guide to the future*. San Francisco, CA: San Francisco Book Company.

Hausman, C. (1984). *A discourse on novelty and creation*. Albany, NY: SUNY Press.

Jantsch E. (1975). *Design for evolution*. New York: Braziller.

Jantsch E. (1980). *The self-organizing universe*. New York: Pergamon.

Jones C. (1980). *Design methods*. New York: Wiley.

Jones C. (1984). *Essays on design*. New York: Wiley.

Lawson, B. (1980). *How designers think*. Westfield, NJ: Eastview Editions, p. 5.

Lippit, G. (1973). *Visualizing change*. La Jolla, CA: University Associates.

Nadler, G. (1967). *Work systems design*. Ideals concept: Homewood, IL: Irwin.

Sage, A. (1977). *Methodology for large-scale systems*. New York: McGraw-Hill.

Senge, P. (1990). *The fifth discipline*. New York: Doubleday/Currency.

Simon, H. (1969). *The sciences of the artificial*. Cambridge, MA: MIT Press.

Ulrich, W. (1983). *Critical heuristics of social planning*. Bern, Switzerland: Haupt.

van Gigch J. (1974). *Applied systems theory*. New York: Harper & Row.

4. LEARNING BY ANY OTHER NAME: COMMUNICATION RESEARCH TRADITIONS IN LEARNING AND MEDIA

Kathy A. Krendl   William H. Ware   Kim A. Reid   Ron Warren

INDIANA UNIVERSITY

Students learn from any medium, in school or out, whether they intend to or not, whether it is intended or not that they should learn (as millions of parents will testify), providing that the content of the medium leads them to pay attention to it. Many teachers argue that learning from media is not the problem; it is hard to prevent a student from learning from media, and the real problem is to get him to learn what he is intended to learn. . . . Therefore, a teacher can feel a great deal of confidence that motivated students will learn from any medium if it is competently used and adapted to their needs. The existing evidence contributes to our confidence more in the media of instruction than in our ability to discriminate among them (Schramm, 1977, p. 267).

4.1 INTRODUCTION

The history of research on learning and media can be characterized as developing along two distinct paths, one that examines the role of media in out-of-school environments such as the home, and one that focuses on the role of media as teaching tools within the formal classroom setting (see, for review, Hornik, 1981; Krendl, 1989). Both of these research traditions trace their origins back to the same original models and theories that introduced the study of media and audiences. This chapter presents an overview of the evolution of theoretical models and research orientations that link these two traditions and that lay the foundation for future research on learning and media.

At the same time that research on learning and media has evolved and changed over time, so has the nature of the media systems examined. The media environment has changed significantly in recent years from the predominance of broadcast television as the delivery system of choice, characterized by its wide appeal to mass audiences, its one-way delivery, and its highly centralized distribution and production systems, to an environment characterized by an entirely different set of features.

First, this new environment offers an increasingly wide array of technologies and combinations of technologies (cable, videotape, DBS, computer, multimedia, etc.), rather than one dominant medium (see Chapter 12 and 24.6). Second, these technologies share characteristics that are in direct contrast to the earlier era of broadcast television. That is, these delivery systems are driven by their ability to serve small, specialized audiences—a narrow-cast orientation—as opposed to television's broadcast orientation. Third, they are designed to feature high levels of user control, flexibility, and interactivity, as well as decentralized production and distribution systems.

As the media environment has changed, the audience's relationship with media has changed. Audience members now expect systems that are responsive to their unique needs and interests. As consumer expectations have changed, inflexible, one-way systems featuring limited channel and content capabilities are increasingly threatened. Flexibility, user-friendliness, content diversity, and low cost appear to be characteristics that will drive the development of future media systems.

The dramatic changes in the dominant features that characterize emerging information and entertainment technologies and the blurring of the boundaries between what has traditionally been considered educational and what has traditionally been considered entertainment content suggest the need for reconsideration of the traditions, assumptions, and approaches used to study media and learning to date. Today, with the growth of "edutainment" products (products that combine elements of education and entertainment programming and are designed for use at home and at school), the traditional distinctions between research on learning in classrooms and on learning in out-of-school environments seem increasingly arbitrary and counterproductive. The following chapter is designed to provide a reconsideration of research on media and learning with an emphasis on the need for an integrated approach to the concepts, issues, and questions related to the field in future research.

In this chapter, we attempt to demonstrate the linkages between the two research traditions, beginning with early communication models. In the discussion of the research perspectives, we have focused on the definition of the approach, the basic components of the models, assumptions that have guided inquiry within the research orientations, and a discussion of representative research. Implicit in the models is an assumed structure to the communication process. The assumed structure has had profound implications for shaping research questions and influencing the direction and evolution of research within each particular research orientation.

4.2 RESEARCH BEGINNINGS

We trace the beginning of research on media and learning back to the 1930s and the Payne Fund studies, the first large-scale attempt to investigate the media's role in influencing people's beliefs and attitudes about society, other people, and themselves. These studies were designed to assess film content, identify audience size and composition, and examine effects resulting from exposure to the medium.

The Payne Fund studies explored many of the ideas later popularized by other writers in regard to the three types of learning that have become dominant in studies of media and learning: (1) knowledge acquisition or the reception and retention of specific information; (2) behavioral performance, defined as the imitation or repetition of actions performed by others in media portrayals; and (3) socialization or general knowledge, referring to attitudes about the world fostered by repeated exposure to mass media content.

Four studies that emerged from the Payne Fund research are of particular importance in regard to media and learning; each made fundamental arguments that would reappear in various forms and motivate later research. The first (Holaday & Stoddard, 1933) viewed learning from the knowledge acquisition perspective in an examination of both adults and children. After testing for the ability to retain film content accurately, the authors concluded that respondents acquired considerable general information from movie viewing, particularly in the areas of English,

history, and geography. These findings strongly suggested that movies could revolutionize the means by which traditional academic subjects could be taught in the classroom.

The Payne Fund studies also introduced the notion of learning from media as part of a socialization process. Researchers examined the ways in which attitudes among children could be changed by exposure to movies (Peterson & Thurstone, 1933). Topics addressed in the study included such issues as nationality, race, prohibition, war, and the punishment of criminals. The authors were particularly interested in the cumulative effects of films, that is, whether viewers of numerous movies were affected to a stronger degree than light viewers—a question that would inspire a multitude of studies on television's effects many years later. The results of the study concluded that "motion pictures have definite, lasting effects on the social attitudes of children" (Peterson & Thurstone, 1933, p. 66).

Taking the cumulative effects concept a step further, another study investigated the net effect of all film exposure on children's attitudes and behavior (Shuttleworth & May, 1933). Although the authors challenged Peterson's and Thurstone's conclusions regarding specific effects, they confirmed the general finding that movies reinforced existing behavior patterns and types of attitudes among those children who frequently attended movies. In other words, although the researchers accepted the notion that learning occurred while viewing movies, they recognized that learning from a mass medium could occur in different ways among different audiences, despite the uniform nature of the message.

A final example from the Payne Fund studies also dismissed the notions of powerful, aggregate film effects, arguing that a variety of mediating factors—situational, social background, and personality—should be taken into account when assessing learning from film (Cressey, 1934). Nevertheless, the study supported film's potential as an *informal* learning instrument, particularly in areas associated with social deviance:

> . . . when a child or youth goes to the movies he acquires from the experience much more than entertainment. General information concerning realms of life of which the individual does not have other knowledge, specific information and suggestions concerning fields of immediate personal interest, techniques of crime, methods of avoiding detection, and of escape from the law, as well as countless techniques for gaining special favors and for interesting the opposite sex in oneself are among the educational contributions of entertainment films" (Cressey, 1934, p. 506).

This study concluded by arguing that film's ability to educate was the result of the combination of important inherent qualities in the medium: wide variation in content, gripping narrative techniques, and appeal to "basic human motives and wishes." Compared to traditional classroom teaching, Cressey asserted, films offered an irresistible—and oppositional—new source of knowledge, especially for young people.

The Payne Fund studies represent one of the earliest and most important systematic investigations of the direct-effects model. This model was defined in simple, straightforward terms in the classic question: Who says what to whom with what effect? (Lasswell, 1948). However, though the direct, or magic-bullet, theory was the approach adopted in most of the Payne Fund studies, investigators like Shuttleworth, May, and Cressey proposed that more was at work when children viewed, read, or listened to mass media than direct-content effects. The Payne Fund studies explored the major concepts, research questions, and issues that would characterize studies of media and learning for the next 60 years. Unfortunately, later researchers opted for simpler models and explanations of learning outcomes resulting from media experiences.

Most subsequent research adopted the notion of a linear communication model based on Lasswell's 1948 question. According to this approach, the critical elements of communication thus were sender, message, receiver, and effect. The communication process began when a particular source with a specific intent initiated communication in order to achieve the desired effect. Research following this line of thinking adopted strong emphasis on the sender and the sender's intent in relation to the content of the message and its impact on the receiver.

A linear and sequential orientation to the study of communication outcomes became clear in early research and exerted strong influence on the evolution of subsequent research. The advantage of the model was that each of the elements of the model outlining the communication process could be focused on in relative isolation from the other components. Each communication had a clear beginning and end and followed the same sequence beginning with the sender's initiation of the message.

The disadvantage was that the model had severe limitations for adequately describing the components of the communication process, their interrelationships, and the role of other factors in influencing communication. Over time, researchers adopted more complex models that attempted to do so. The importance of a wide array of mediating factors gradually became clear. However, the basic linear structure, as well as the characterization of communication as a series of sequential steps, remained. The argument here proposes that future research on media and learning adopt a conceptualization of communication as an integrated process that cannot be broken out into sequential components in a linear fashion and that is more compatible with learning theory. Rather than conducting research that focuses on an individual component and its related factors, we have adopted a model that assumes the need for an integrated understanding of the dynamics and interrelationships among the components and factors.

If a metaphor for the previous model is the spotlight that focuses in on one or another component of the process, our model would adopt, instead, the metaphor of a light spectrum for understanding learning and media. The light spectrum is defined as "the series of colored bands diffracted through a prism or other diffracting medium and shading continuously from red . . . to violet . . . with invisible components at both ends" (*Webster's New World Dictionary*, 1966, p. 1400). Just as white light may be conceived as the presence of many different elements of light, visible or invisible, media experiences may be conceived as the presence of many different components and factors (internal and external). The mediating factors in the process of communication diffract, absorb, reflect, or filter what individuals take from their experiences. Communication passes through filters related to the production of the message, the symbol system and codes of the medium, the context in which the communication occurs, and the unique cognitive filters (beliefs, attitudes, experience, and so on) of individual learners. Thus, our understanding of mediated learning should account not only for different types of filtration mechanisms but should also realize the range of possibilities that arise from this process; that is, learning should be defined not as a narrow set of outcomes but rather as a diverse range of possibilities.

Since the introduction of electronic mass media in the 1920s and 1930s, the history of research on media and audiences may be understood as a series of inquiries adopting different emphases. Some research orientations focused on the technical aspects of media, others on the individual listener or viewer, and still others on an examination of media's role in shaping, reinforcing, or changing social relations. The theories and models that represent their major tenets can be loosely grouped under three philosophical perspectives: A technical perspective highlights the medium itself; a psychological perspective examines the ways in which individual viewers process messages from various sources; a social-cultural perspective examines how social relationships define media, determines how they are used, identifies audience expectations of media, and influences the way messages are interpreted. Each of these general perspectives will be discussed in terms of a definition of the orientation, an overview of the communication elements, an explanation of research assumptions, and a discussion of representative research traditions.

4.3 TECHNICAL PERSPECTIVE

4.3.1 Definition

The earliest models in the study of media and audiences were based on a conception of transmission. They developed in direct response to the advent of mass communication technologies that revolutionized the scale and speed of communication. The original intent was to assess the effects that the new and ubiquitous media systems had on their audience members and on society. From the beginning, research was highly influenced by mass media's potential to distribute singular messages from a central point in space to millions of individuals in a one-way flow of information.

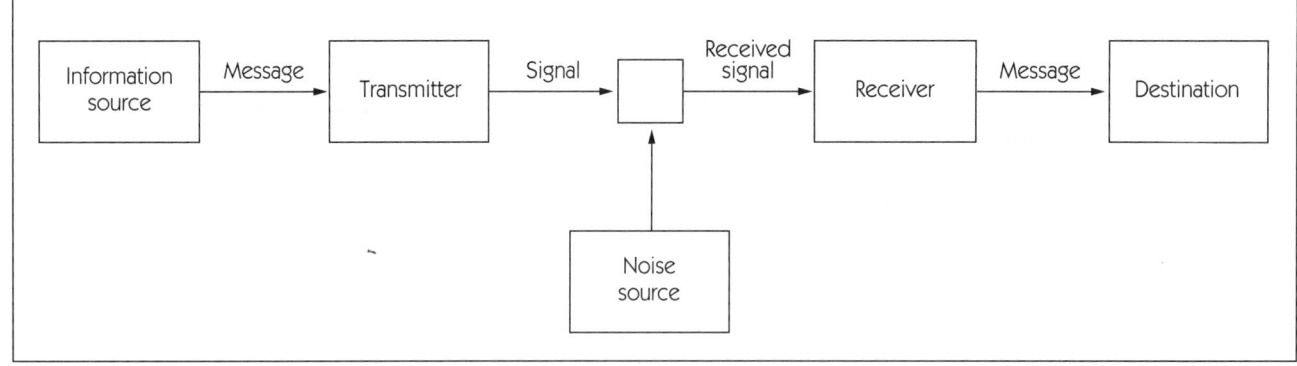

Figure 4-1.   Shannon and Weaver's "mathematical model" of a one-way, linear transmission of messages. (From Shannon & Weaver, *The Mathematical Theory of Communication,* Urbana, IL, University of Illinois Press, 1949, p. 98.) Copyright 1949 by the Board of Trustees of the University of Illinois. Used with permission of the University of Illinois Press.

The components of the models stemmed from Lasswell's (1948) question of "Who says what to whom with what effect?" Some of the earliest theoretical work in mass communication was done in conjunction with the development of electronic mass media and was grounded in information theory. This approach examined both the process of how information is transmitted from the sender to the receiver and the factors that influence the extent to which communication between individuals proceeds in a meaningful fashion. As telephone, radio, and television technologies advanced, researchers looked for scientific means of efficiently delivering messages from one person to another. In this case, *efficient* meant the degree that rational judgments are facilitated (Lasswell, 1948, p. 46). The person receiving the message should receive only the verbal or electronic signals intentionally sent by another person. These theories were based on 19th-century ideas about the transfer of energy (Trenholm, 1986). Such scientific theories held that research phenomena could be broken into component parts governed by universal laws that permitted prediction of future events. In short, the technical perspective on communication held that objects (for example, messages, their senders and receivers, etc.) follow laws of cause and effect.

One of the most popular examples of the technical perspective is the mathematical model of Shannon and Weaver (1949), developed during their work for Bell Laboratories (see Fig. 4-1).

The engineering focus of this work treated information as a mathematical constant, a fixed element of communication. Once a message source converted an intended meaning into electronic signals, this signal was fed by a sender through a channel to a receiver that converted the signal into comprehensible content for the destination of the message. Any interference in the literal transfer of the message (e.g., from electronic static, lack of knowledge about the communication system, or uncertainty on the part of either party) constituted noise that worked against the predictability of communication. If noise were kept at a minimum, the effect of a message on the destination could be predicted based on the source's intent. One important distinction in this model is the difference between information and meaning (Klapp, 1982). The former refers to bits of messages that reduce uncertainty between sources and destinations. The latter refers to making sense of information, or finding a comprehensible pattern among information bits.

4.3.2 Elements of Communication

The technical perspective, or transmission paradigm (Devito, 1986), sees communication as a linear process composed of several material objects: source, message, channel, noise, receiver, information, redundancy, entropy, and fidelity. Many of these concepts have remained fundamental concepts of communication theory since Shannon and Weaver's original work. Because of the emphasis on the transmission of the source's intended message, less attention was focused on outcomes or effects on the receiver. The greater the degree of similarity between the intention of the source and the outcome or effect at the receiver end, the more "successful" the communication was considered to be. If the intended effect did not occur, a breakdown in communication was assumed. Messages within information theory are bits of information that have any impact on uncertainty or the receiver's decision-making process. The concept of feedback was added later to account for messages the sender transmitted to gauge the success of each message. This notion was derived from learning theory, which provided for the teacher's "checks" on students' comprehension and learning (Heath & Bryant, 1992).

The channel in this perspective was linked to several other terms, including the signal, the channel's information capacity, and its rate of transmission. The technical capabilities of media were fundamental questions of information theory. The ability of senders and receivers to encode and decode mental intentions into/from various kinds of signals (verbal, print, or electronic) were paramount to successful communication. Each of these concepts emphasized the technical capabilities of media and the message source.

Two additional components critical within this perspective are *redundancy* and *entropy*. The former refers to the amount of information that must be repeated to overcome noise in the process and achieve the desired effect. Entropy, on the other hand, is a measure of randomness. It refers to the degree of choice one has in constructing messages. If a communication system is highly organized, the message source has little freedom in choosing the symbols that successfully communicate with others. Hence, the system would have low entropy and could require a great deal of redundancy to overcome noise. A careful balance between redundancy and entropy must be maintained in order to communicate successfully.

In the case of mass communication systems, the elements of the technical perspective have additional characteristics (McQuail, 1983). The sender, for instance, is often a professional communicator or organization, and messages are often standardized products requiring a great deal of work to produce, carrying with them an exchange value (for example, television air time that is sold as a product to advertisers). The relationship of sender and receiver is impersonal and noninteractive. A key feature here, of course, is that traditional notions of mass communication envision a single message source communicating to a vast audience with great immediacy. This audience is a heterogeneous, unorganized collection of individuals that share certain demographic or psychological characteristics with subgroups of their fellow audience members.

4.3.3 Assumptions and Research

The technical perspective of communication, including information theory and the mathematical model of Shannon and Weaver, adopts three major assumptions about communication (Trenholm, 1986). First, it assumes that the components of communication execute their functions in a linear, sequential fashion. Second, consequently, events occur as a series of causes and effects, actions and reactions. The source's message is transmitted to a receiver, who either displays or deviates from the intended effect of the source's original intent. Third, the whole of the communication process, from this engineering perspective, can be viewed as a sum of the components and their function. By understanding how each element receives and/or transmits a signal, the researcher may understand how communication works.

These assumptions have important consequences for the bulk of research conducted under a technical perspective (Fisher, 1978). First, and most importantly, it focuses attention on the channel of communication. Concepts such as the signal capacity of a given medium, the ability to reduce noise in message transmissions, and increased efficiency or fidelity of transmissions were important goals for researchers of new communication technologies. The use of multiple channels of communication (e.g., verbal and visual) also received a great deal of attention. These concepts, however, could be researched on more than a purely technological basis.

4.3.4 Discussion of Representative Research

4.3.4.1. Research on Radio.

Early studies focusing primarily on the communication channel emerged from research on the fledging medium, radio. The entrance of major corporations into radio advertising, beginning around 1928, inspired interest in how to best introduce products to listeners and to influence listeners' buying habits. J. B. Watson—generally regarded as the founder of behavioral science—was hired by a major advertising agency in the early 1930s to conduct studies on listener recall, recognition of product names, and willingness to buy advertised goods. Soon, numerous psychologists and sociologists (often sponsored by advertisers and networks) studied listeners' recall of radio content, as well as its influence on their behavior.

Another study of radio's role in reaching audience members emerged from the broadcast of the infamous 1938 "War of the Worlds," which inspired academic interest in how mass media could mobilize audiences who received and were affected by information (see, for example, Cantril, 1935). Concern with radio's ability to generate "serious" learning through educational programming and radio's threat to traditional learning from books became the focus of initial work (Lazarsfeld, 1940). This research analyzed learning from radio as knowledge acquisition and socialization. Researchers found that radio's potential to facilitate learning through instructional programs was thwarted by the fact that people at lower levels of educational achievement were least likely to listen to educational radio programs (or to read educational books). On the other hand, researchers found that listeners reported acquiring important forms of knowledge from entertainment programs such as quiz shows and soap operas—knowledge ranging from historical facts to lessons on how to be a successful wife (Herzog, 1948; Lazarsfeld, 1940).

4.3.4.2. Media Comparison Research.

Media comparison studies provide the best example of technical perspective research in the application of instructional technologies in classroom settings. These studies took Shannon and Weaver's model as the point of departure and focused primarily on the mode of delivery in a classroom setting. The primary assumption underlying this research orientation was that the instructional effectiveness of each medium was constant across all content and all students. Thus, the basic research design consisted of assigning subjects to treatment conditions in which the same instructional content was presented by different media. The most common comparisons were between new media and traditional (that is, lecture/discussion) classroom instruction. The "best" medium in these studies was the one that "caused" the highest posttest scores on comprehension and recall of content. Clark and Salomon (1985) have characterized this period as being preoccupied by "an intensive search for the 'one best medium.'" Schramm (1977) discussed this approach as a search for a "super-medium."

A series of meta-analyses (Cohen, Ebling & Kulik, 1981; Glass, 1976; Jamison, Suppes & Welles, 1974; Kulik,

Bangert & Williams, 1983; Kulik, Kulik & Cohen, 1979) suggested that students in treatments using media systems consistently scored slightly better on tests than did those in traditional classroom contexts. Modest positive gains in learning were noted with a variety of media and individual content areas (for example, math, science, foreign language). However, many individual studies have shown no significant differences between modes of delivery. No one medium emerged as consistently better or worse in delivering information to students.

In media comparison studies, measures of learning are typically pretest-posttest assessments of knowledge acquisition, comprehension, and retention; traditionally this research has focused on lower-order thinking skills. The media comparison perspective relies heavily on the application of behavioral teaching objectives (Mager, 1962), which stipulate the desired terminal behavior and the conditions under which it is to be performed. For example, "After being presented with verbal definitions of 10 new words, a child will be able to correctly identify at least 8 of those words and their correct definitions on a multiple-choice test." Thus the goal of media comparison studies is to show alternative means of committing information to long-term memory (as framed under cognitive learning theories) (Mayer, 1987).

Scholars have noted repeatedly the difficulties and limitations of this approach (see, for example, Clark, 1983; 1991; Krendl, 1989; Mielke, 1968; Schramm, 1977). The most serious criticisms focus on the inevitable confounding of instructional method and content in media comparison studies. Typically, the introduction of a new media system is accompanied by changes in curricular materials. For example, material taught through lecture may have to be redesigned for presentation over television, causing substantial changes in how the material is explained or elaborated on during the lesson. Thus, differences emerging from the treatment groups are likely attributable to differences in the curriculum rather than differences in the instructional effectiveness of the delivery systems.

Clark (1983, 1991) has also argued that the media comparison model fails to control for novelty effects linked to the new instructional mode. He proposed that the novelty of working with a computer, for example, will motivate some students to learn, aside from the medium's ability to teach. Positive learning effects attributed to the new media system might be more appropriately assigned to the novelty effect rather than the effectiveness of the delivery system. Media comparison studies are classic applications of Shannon and Weaver's technical model of communication. The delivery technology is seen as the primary variable in the learning process. The inherent differences between technologies are framed as the key to more or less effective instruction. Manipulations by the sender (in this case, the instructor) are measured in students' varying levels of information comprehension and retention.

As researchers began to expand such concepts to the abilities of humans to transmit, receive, and process mes-

sages, a second perspective of communication took hold that focused on psychological dimensions of the communication process.

4.4 PSYCHOLOGICAL PERSPECTIVE

4.4.1 Definition

Psychologically based communication theories share some fundamental characteristics (Trenholm, 1986). First, they represent a modification of technical theories in that messages are filtered primarily through individuals, not channels. Cognitive processes of handling information determine how a message is sent and received; the physical "signal" or channel is less important. Second, this view places more emphasis on the perceptions of senders and receivers. Communication takes place only when these parties perceive it. This perspective assumes that one person's outward behavior affects the cognitions or behavior of another. Such influences contribute to the messages and feedback of communicative events. Third, the goal of these behaviors is to arrive at a consistent meaning between sender and receiver, thereby reducing uncertainty in the meanings each carries for given objects and events.

The psychological perspective is the result of a synthesis of cognitive and behavioral psychology theories. In this tradition of research, three strategies are clear: (1) the adoption of attitude change as the most interesting dependent variable, (2) the modeling of communication (i.e., persuasion) as a special case of behavioral learning theory, and (3) the reliance on experimental social psychology for conceptual and methodological research strategies. The basic communication model proposed by Hovland and Janis (1959) conceived of the communication situation in terms of message content, source identity, type of channel, and setting operating through predispositional factors (situational elements that determine what audience members attend to and how) and internal mediating processes (attention, comprehension, and acceptance) in order to produce observable communication effects (changes in opinion, perception, affect, and action). The challenge of a message was to gain the receiver's interest, then produce the intended effect with understandable and memorable content. The receiver's interest, of course, could be affected by external qualities of the subject of communication or sender, as well as internal interests, beliefs, and cognitive processing capacities (Andersen, 1972). Thus, the model retained the linear notion of technical communication theories but adopted a strong emphasis on the effects component of the communication process.

Other theorists built on this model but emphasized the importance of the individual's abilities in understanding communication effects. The following models taken from Schramm (1954) demonstrate the inclusion of new components in the communication models being applied.

Schramm (1955), along with Osgood (1954; Osgood, Suci & Tannenbaum, 1958), conceived of each person as an entire communicative system with both sending and receiving abilities and, further, saw a more referential model of communication where the participants' experiences determined the meaning of symbols (including both verbal and nonverbal signals and gestures). Words had meaning only insofar as personal experience provided a context for interpretation. Thus, according to this view, for communication to occur, both sender and receiver must share similar experiences. Based on this model, Schramm argued that the effects of communication were limited by the cognitive capacities of senders/receivers and were not as direct as early technical theories of mass communication may have implied (see Fig. 4-2).

Theoretical orientations that adopted the psychological perspective were consistent with Newcomb's (1953) ABX model of social psychology, which held that communication is the way individuals orient to their environment and to one another. Persons develop attitudes toward objects consistent with other individuals who are perceived by them as socially attractive. This model is based on the concept of balance or consistency between one's belief and attitude systems with others who are important to the individual. Once the balance of this state is upset, all parties respond to the resulting dissonance by using communication to restore balance (Festinger, 1962).

Westley and MacLean (1957) contributed an important addition to this model by framing an event (e.g., a news event) as a starting point for communication designed to achieve this attitudinal balance among communicators. Their approach placed the mass media organization (e.g., newspapers) between the source and destination of messages. Assuming a gatekeeper function, the media funnel

information from infinite sources, encode messages, and transmit them to the destination. The model also formalized feedback loops in communication, recognizing that feedback to both the sources of messages and message distribution systems (media organizations) was an integral component of the process.

4.4.2 Elements of Communication

Most components of the communication process first laid out by technical theories are retained in the psychological perspective. Message sender and receivers are viewed as connected through feedback loops. Channels refer to material objects that produce or carry signals from one party to the next, but also include nonverbal gestures. Messages are seen in this perspective as "stimuli" that enact certain cognitive structures and recall past experiences on the part of all communicative participants. Noise in this perspective, then, highlights the internal interference that can result from unmatched experiences and perceptions among senders and receivers. The whole of the communication process is framed within individuals' cognitive processing abilities (Trenholm, 1986). The existence of individuals' mental constructs that shape information processing and interpretation represent the key contributions of psychological theories to communication.

The importance of beliefs, attitudes, and values of communicators (Andersen, 1972) becomes clear in the psychological perspective. These constructs are the result of prior experience, but also the motivation for further communication, thus acting as an influence over perception and behavior. They are, in Newcomb's (1953) and Festinger's (1962) terms, the measure of balance in social situations—the motivating force for communication. In addition, the role of attention, comprehension, and acceptance of information in the communication process is introduced in this perspective (Andersen, 1972). Because individuals seek to maintain cognitive balance, their attitudes and beliefs help them select information to which they will attend, how much of it they comprehend, and the ways in which they incorporate messages in their perception and experience. In short, psychological theories of communication hold that communicators selectively attend to and participate in those events that are consistent with their belief and value structures.

4.4.3 Assumptions and Research Focus

Psychological theories assume that human beings exist and process information independently. The reliance of psychological perspective research on S-R learning models focuses attention on cognitive processes, attitudes, beliefs, and so on. The psychological perspective also assumes that in using prior experience to shape cognitive constructs and attitudes, receivers are influenced by the messages they receive. Finally, according to this perspective, human beings are assumed to attend to incoming messages selec-

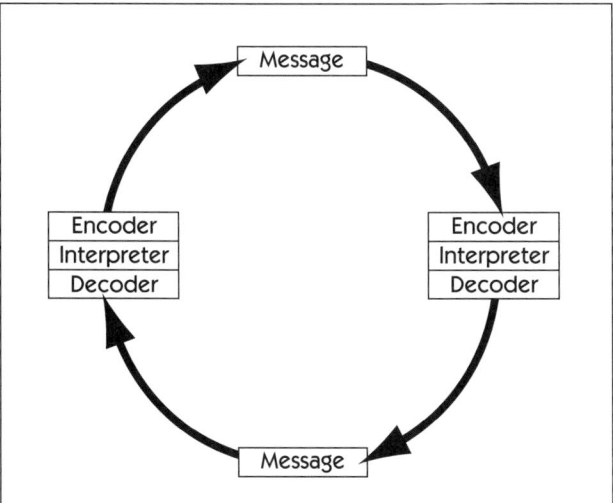

Figure 4-2. Osgood and Schramm's model of communication depicting both parties as fulfilling the same communicative functions. (From Schramm, *The Process and Effects of Mass Communication,* Urbana, IL, University of Illinois Press, 1954). Copyright 1965 by the Board of Trustees of the University of Illinois. Used with permission of the University of Illinois Press.

tively, and consciously choose future responses based on prior experience and anticipation of future events. This dimension of psychological perspectives, then, goes beyond traditional behaviorism in examining the influence of internal cognitive processing on communication.

Description and prediction of communication through each person's conceptual filters introduced research questions on the development, maintenance of, and changes in cognition and attitudes. Several new variables were introduced in experimental studies of communication, including person perception, attitudes, attention, comprehension, and a host of other psychological concepts (Trenholm, 1986). Indeed, later psychological theories (for example, the ABX model) introduced the notion that our perceptions of other people, especially our relational status with those people, is an important influence in the communication process.

4.4.4 Discussion of Representative Research

4.4.4.1. Persuasion Studies. One of the greatest and earliest influences in the development of the psychological perspective was a series of persuasion studies (Hovland & Janis, 1959; Hovland, Tanis & Kelley, 1953; Hovland, 1948). This programmatic research began in the American Soldier Studies, which used film as part of the indoctrination of new recruits during World War II. The *Why We Fight* series of film documentaries was designed to replace the traditional lecture-style orientation. A series of studies addressed the effectiveness of film as a vehicle for indoctrination (Hovland, Lumsdaine & Sheffield, 1949). Of interest to the researchers was the ability of the films to provide factual information about the war, to change attitudes of new recruits towards war, and to motivate the recruits to fight. Learning was addressed as persuasion in this instance, involving knowledge acquisition and attitude changes.

The researchers found that the films had significant impact on knowledge of factual material. They found that the soldiers' opinions or attitudes were also affected by the films to a lesser extent. Finally, they found no effect on the motivation of soldiers to fight. In addition, the researchers looked at links between personal factors, such as intellect and learning outcomes. Greater intellectual ability fostered more learning of factual information. However, intellectual ability had a much more complex relationship with opinion change, encompassing the concepts of learning ability, critical ability, and the ability to draw inferences.

The American Soldier Studies laid the foundation for future learning hierarchies of communication effects models such as the one suggested by McGuire (1973). McGuire looked at the process of persuasion (change in attitude or opinion) in conjunction with the factors of communications. In his model, persuasion is broken down into six states: presentation of the communication, attention to it, comprehension of the content, yielding to a new position, retention of that new position, and overt behavior based on the new position. These states are combined with the tradi-

tional elements of communication models to create a communication-persuasion matrix. The communication elements axis consists of source, message, channel, receiver, and destination, while the persuasion axis includes presentation, attention, comprehension, yielding, retention, and behavior (McGuire, 1973).

4.4.2. Research on Children and Television. Other examples of psychological research emerged from research on television and children. The first rigorous academic exploration of television's effects on children (Himmelweit, Oppenheim & Vince, 1959) set the stage for an examination of television's unintended effects on learning. Part of the study focused on the extent to which children's outlooks were colored by television: How were their attitudes affected? How were they socialized? Juxtaposing viewers and nonviewers, Himmelweit, Oppenheim, and Vince found that viewers were more ambitious than nonviewers and that girls who watched television were more concerned with issues such as adulthood and marriage than were those who were nonviewers.

At about the same time, Schramm, Lyle, and Parker (1961) initiated the first major exploration of television's effects on children in North America in a series of 11 studies on children from Canada and the United States. In particular, this research emphasized how children learn from television. Based on their research, Schramm, Lyle, and Parker developed the concept of "incidental learning":

> By this we mean that learning takes place when a viewer goes to television for entertainment and stores up certain items of information without seeking them (1961, p. 75).

In other words, the researchers found that learning took place whether or not programs were intended to be educational. The amount of incidental learning that occurred was linked to such qualities as children's age, television habits, and learning abilities.

4.4.4.3. Studies of Television and Aggression. The other major area of psychological perspective research on children and television focused on the study of violent television programming (see also 11.6.3.1 and 11.3.2). It seemed that if any type of content could be expected to demonstrate clear, direct effects on any particular segment of the audience, violent portrayals in children's programming ought to provide clear evidence of television's impact. The impetus for this research emerged from public outcries of educators and parents who argued that children were learning aggressive behaviors from television exposure. The theoretical model applied in this research was grounded in social learning theory. The early work in social learning theory involved children and imitative aggressive play after an exposure to filmed violence (Bandura, 1963). These studies were based in the highly controlled methodology of experimental psychology. The social learning model, which attempts to explain how children develop personality and learn behaviors by observing models in society, was extended to the study of mediated models of aggression. This approach examines learning as a broad-based variable that involves knowledge acquisition and behavioral performance.

In a series of experiments (Bandura, 1961; Bandura, Ross & Ross, 1963; Bandura, 1965), Bandura and his colleagues demonstrated that exposure to filmed aggression resulted in higher levels of imitative aggressive behavior. Such behaviors were conditioned not only on the role model to which the child was exposed but also on the physical setting and arousal of aggressive feelings in later situations. According to this approach, the message being sent, intentional or unintentional, is the notion of what constitutes appropriate behavior in society. The crux of the theory is that people learn how to behave from models viewed in society, live or mediated (Bandura, 1977). If the modeled behavior is seen as being desirable by the receiver, she or he may acquire that behavior. In addition, social learning research demonstrated that children were able to recall aggressive behavior up to 8 months after the initial exposure (Hicks, 1965). Bryant (1975) extended social learning theory beyond the realm of aggression to include the modeling of prosocial behavior. He concluded that children could also learn altruistic behaviors from mediated models.

Beyond the laboratory, researchers reported the results of a 10-year longitudinal study examining the relationship between television violence and aggressive behavior (Lefkowitz, Eron, Walder & Huesmann, 1972). This correlational study concluded that boys who reported viewing more violent content in the third grade displayed greater levels of aggression 10 years later. Finally, research indicated that children who had viewed violent films were more likely to tolerate violence (Drabman & Thomas, 1974, 1976, 1977). In response to the growing literature associating television and violence, NBC commissioned a panel study (Milavsky, Kessler, Stipp & Rubens, 1982) that revealed only small correlations between viewing televised violence and subsequent aggression, and no evidence at all indicating long-term effects.

4.4.4.4. Cultivation Research. Beginning in the late 1960s at the same time that initial research examined links between television exposure and aggressive behavior, research on the long-term socialization effects of television achieved prominence in the study of media and audiences. This approach, known as *cultivation research*, conceptualized learning as a generalized view of the world or perception of social reality as conveyed by the mass media. Concerned primarily with television as the foremost "storyteller" in modern society, researchers argued that television's power to influence world views was the result of two factors. First, television viewing was seen as ritualistic and habitual rather than selective (see 11.8.2). (That is, viewers chose to watch "television" in general rather than a specific program.) Second, the stories on television were all related in their content and in similar production processes.

Early cultivation research held that heavy television viewers would "learn" that the real world was more like that portrayed on television—particularly in regard to pervasive violence—than would light viewers (Gerbner, Gross,

Eleey, Jackson-Beeck, Jeffries-Fox & Signorielli, 1977; Gerbner, Gross, Jackson-Beeck, Jeffries-Fox & Signorielli, 1978; Gerbner, Gross, Morgan & Signorielli, 1980; Gerbner, Gross, Morgan & Signorielli, 1986; Gerbner, Gross, Signorielli, Morgan & Jackson-Beeck, 1979). Heavy viewers were expected to estimate the existence of higher levels of danger in the world and feel more alienated and distrustful than would light viewers. The scope of cultivation research was later broadened to include attitudes regarding race, sex roles, and various professions. Of crucial importance to cultivation theory, however, is the idea that such effects are more likely to take place in the absence of counter messages from the surrounding environment. Heavy viewers were thought to experience such effects because of the lack of other activities and interactions in their social lives. Without exposure to the real world, television served as the model.

Although cultivation has been a significant force in communication studies, its conclusions have been criticized repeatedly. Again, these criticisms focused on the role of contextual elements from the viewer's social environment. Doob and MacDonald (1979), for example, found that perceptions of personal danger were more influenced by one's area of residence than by television viewing. O'Keefe (1984), on the other hand, concluded that the amount of television exposure had no relationship with perceptions of crime, concern about victimization, and assessment of the criminal justice system. Such divergent conclusions are perhaps irreconcilable, but as new technologies develop, audiences become more fragmented, and program forms and themes become more diverse, such an approach seems increasingly irrelevant.

4.4.4.5. Agenda-Setting Research. Another example of psychological perspective research has focused on the study of news content and the process by which public learning about the world is influenced by mass-media news coverage. That is, to what extent does the content individuals read in the newspapers and watch on the television news affect their world view? This research tradition, referred to as *agenda setting*, was inspired by the writings of Walter Lippmann (1922), who proposed that the news media created the "pictures in our heads," providing a view of the world beyond people's limited day-to-day experiences. The basic hypothesis in such research is that there will be a positive relationship between media coverage of issues and what issues people regard as being important. In the 1960s, researchers extended the hypothesis by arguing that the media focus attention on specific issues, thereby suggesting what people should think, know, and have feelings about (Cohen, 1963; Lang & Lang, 1966).

In order to link mass media and public knowledge, a landmark study compared press coverage of the 1968 presidential campaign with the salience of campaign issues among a sample of undecided voters (McCombs & Shaw, 1972). Finding a significant positive correlation between voter knowledge and press coverage, the authors (Shaw & McCombs, 1977) concluded that the direction of influence was indeed from the press to the audience. That is, press coverage of events and issues was not preceded in time by audience interest in and demand for coverage of the topics.

Agenda-setting studies over the past 3 decades have employed both short-term and longitudinal designs to assess public awareness and concern about issues such as unemployment, energy, and inflation in relation to the amount and form of relevant news coverage (for example, Behr & Iyengar, 1985; Brosius & Kepplinger, 1990; Iyengar, Peters & Kinder, 1982). Recent research has attempted to broaden understanding of agenda setting by investigating both attitudinal and behavioral outcomes (e.g., Ghorpade, 1986; Roberts, 1992; Shaw & Martin, 1992).

Concern over possible mediating factors such as audience variations, issue abstractness, and interpersonal communication among audience members has fueled significant debate within the field concerning the strength of the agenda-setting effect on public learning. For example, some studies have suggested that agenda setting is strongly influenced by audience members' varying interests, the form of media employed, the tone of news stories toward issues, and the type of issue covered (Demers, Craff, Choi & Pessin, 1989; Protess, Leff, Brooks & Gordon, 1985; Yagade & Dozier, 1990). These theoretical problems face radical transformation, if not extinction, as audience members take an increasingly active role in setting their own media agendas through the use of video recordings, narrow-cast cable, and other new media technologies.

4.4.4.6. Media Attributes Research. The media attributes approach to the study of instructional media provides a good example of psychological research in in-school contexts (see 11.3, 16.3, 16.4, 26.4, 27.2, and 29.4). Rather than focusing on which mode of delivery resulted in the highest levels of learning as in the earlier media comparison studies, investigators turned to the more narrowly focused exploration of unique media characteristics and their connections to the development or enhancement of students' cognitive skills. Each medium was said to possess inherent codes or symbol systems that engaged specific cognitive abilities among users. In this research, the conceptualization of learning outcomes shifted away from consideration of the exclusively lower-order cognitive processes of the media comparison approach to include the learner's higher-order interpretive processes as well. For example, according to the media attributes perspective, a researcher might ask how students interpret use of a fade between scenes in a television show and its connection to the viewer's ability to draw inferences about the passage of time in a story.

Early media attributes studies (Salomon, 1974, 1979; Salomon & Cohen, 1977) concluded that mastery of certain skills was a requisite for satisfactory use of a medium. For instance, students had to be able to encode letters on a page as meaningful words in order to use a book. A series of laboratory and field experiments following this line of research reported that learning was mediated by the cognitive skills necessary for effective use of a particular medium.

In addition, scholars have analyzed the relationship between media attributes and the cultivation or development

of certain cognitive skills (see also 11.3). For television alone, studies have documented positive learning effects for the use of motion (Blake, 1977), screen placements (Hart, 1986; Zettl, 1973), split-screen displays (Salomon, 1979), and use of various camera angles and positions (Hoban & van Ormer, 1950). Researchers also explored cognitive skills linked to other media attributes, including the use of verbal previews, summaries, and repetition (Allen, 1973); amount of narration on audio/video recordings (Hoban & van Ormer, 1950; Travers, 1967); and the use of dramatization, background music, graphic aids, and special sound/visual effects (e.g., Beck, 1987; Dalton & Hannafin, 1986; Glynn & Britton, 1984; Morris, 1988; NIMH, 1982; Seidman, 1981).

The list of cognitive skills linked to such attributes included increases in attention, comprehension, and retention of information, as well as visualization of abstract ideas. Some intriguing results emerged from this research approach. For example, one study (Salomon, 1979) presented children with pictures of a particular scene, then asked them to choose an alternative view of the scene (e.g., from the back) from four pictures. The results demonstrated that frequent viewers of television were better at such perspective-taking skills.

Critics pointed out the potential weaknesses of this research. Some held that assertions about media's cognitive-cultivation capacities had yet to be proved (Johnston, 1987). One detailed review of the research (Clark, 1983) argued that media attributes research rests on three questionable expectations: (1) that attributes are an integral part of media, (2) that attributes provide for the cultivation of cognitive skills for learners who need them, and (3) that identified attributes would provide unique independent variables that specified causal relationships between media codes and the teaching of cognitive functions. A subsequent review found that no one attribute specific to any medium is necessary to learn any specific cognitive skill; other presentational forms may result in similar levels of skill development (Clark & Salomon, 1985). While some symbolic elements may permit the audience members to cultivate cognitive abilities, these elements are characteristic of several media, not unique attributes of any one medium (Clark, 1987).

4.5 SOCIAL-CULTURAL PERSPECTIVE

4.5.1 Definition

Even as psychologically oriented research was gaining attention and dominance in the field (i.e., during the 1940s and 1950s), theorists had begun to explore the influence of social relationships on communication. Whereas psychological theories saw messages filtered through individuals' cognitions, this perspective argues that communication occurs only through social interaction. One's definition of and experience with objects, events, other people, and even oneself, is determined through a network of interpersonal relationships. That is, the meanings we form are products of social "negotiation" with other people. These relationships determine both the symbols we use to communicate and the meanings of those symbols (Mead, 1934; Blumer, 1939, 1969). In essence, the symbols, objects, events, and self-images that make up our world are the creation of a shared meaning through social communication. This model clearly demonstrates the linkage between communication theory and social psychology. It explores the potential of media as a unifying force in society. This section will describe the contributions of research traditions that emphasize the social and cultural dimensions of the communication process. This model clearly demonstrated the linkage between communication theory and social psychology. It explored the potential of media as a unifying force in society. Rather than focusing on the filtering of messages solely through cognitive constructs, researchers were interested in the ways in which messages were mediated by interpersonal networks.

4.5.2 Elements of Communication

Social-cultural perspectives present a significant reframing of the communication process. Many of the elements presented by technical and psychological models are conceptualized in very different ways (Fisher, 1978; Swanson & Delia, 1976). Senders and receivers, for example, become "participants," or "interactants," stressing their mutually dependent roles as communicators. Each interactant's perception of self, others, and the situation, working within a framework of shared culture, knowledge, and language, is a major influence on communicative episodes. This reframing of senders and receivers takes Schramm (1955) and Osgood (1954) even further in the view of socially defined interaction.

Messages, in the social-cultural view, are products of negotiation: All participants must arrive at shared meaning for successful communication. Heath and Bryant (1992) state that the message, in this case, is the effect of the sender's behavior on the receiver. They cite Whorf (1956) and his colleague Sapir, who hypothesized that the rules of one's language system contain the society's culture, world view, and collective identity. This language, in turn, affects the way we perceive the world. In short, words define reality; reality does not give us objective meaning. This presents a problematic conception of feedback, because it is difficult to tell when feedback is truly a response to a message and not just another message in and of itself (Heath & Bryant, 1992).

The most compelling application of social-cultural perspectives to mass communication has been in the conceptualization of audience. McQuail (1983) points out that one meaning for "mass" audience has been an "aggregate in which individuality is lost" (*Oxford English Dictionary*, 1971). Blumer (1969), on the other hand, preferred to distinguish between the "mass" and smaller groups of "publics," "crowds," and "groups." Increasingly, media use occurs in these smaller aggregates of audience members,

each with a particular medium or content form that serves preexisting interests, goals, or values.

These groups form through "boundary properties" (such as demographic characteristics like political affiliation) and "internal structures" (such as belief or value systems) that arise through attention to particular media content and the possibility of interaction about that content (Ennis, 1961). Within such audience groups, three types of internal structures reveal the social character of audience experiences with media (McQuail, 1983). The first, social differentiation, refers to basic differences in audience members' interests, attention, and perceptions of various issues and topics.

A second internal structure is the extent of social interaction within the group. Four factors are included here. *Sociability* refers to the extent to which media use is primarily a social occasion and secondarily a communicative event between individuals (e.g., how much interaction is permitted while watching television in a group). Groups such as families often employ media for various *social purposes* (e.g., teaching children about values, avoiding arguments) as well (Lull, 1980). A third factor governing the extent of interaction is the degree of *social isolation* that may result from excessive media use (especially television). Finally, the presence of *para-social relationships* (e.g., a viewer's perceived relationship with a favorite TV or radio personality) may indicate the social interaction made possible between media users and easily recognized characters.

A third internal structure in the social character of audience experience with mass media is the control norms that a society holds for its mass media. This refers to the value systems and social norms that regulate media use, types of appropriate content for each medium, and audience expectations of media performance. For example, Americans may come to expect objective news reporting on television, but may not consider a graphic portrayal of murder appropriate for their evening newscast. The types of programming we expect to see may be identified with the medium itself.

4.5.3 Assumptions and Research Focus

The idea that communication is a product of social relationships is the most pervasive assumption of the social-cultural perspective. Several other assumptions guide this philosophical stance, however (Fisher, 1978). Establishment of self is believed primarily through symbolic communication with others. This means that until one acquires the cognitive or empathic ability to "take the role of the other," the self does not exist—nor does meaningful social activity. Such activity takes place only by assuming the role of others or the generalized other. This process of role taking is a collective sharing of selves; it cannot be centered in media structures. It is not an individual act but one clearly dependent on social interaction for its purpose and existence. The concepts of self, roles, and collective meaning creation, then, are the focus of a great deal of investigation within social-cultural communication theories.

4.5.4 Discussion of Representative Research

4.5.4.1. Two-Step Flow Research. A prime example of social-cultural research is the two-step flow model of mass communication (Katz & Lazarsfeld, 1955). A landmark study that examined voters in Erie County, Ohio, during the 1940 presidential election, focused on the content of political media messages and social interaction about the election. The study (Lazarsfeld, Berelson & Gaudet, 1948), was based on a 6-month panel survey of voting behaviors and decision making. The study sought to chart various influences on voting decisions, including the emerging medium of radio. Findings demonstrated only limited media impact. People who reported making an initial decision or changing their minds did so after speaking with others about the election. Often these "opinion leaders" received a great deal of information from mass media. The study reframed the one-way, direct-effects model of mass communication processes to account for this "two-step flow" in media influence. The first step reflects the role of opinion leaders in a community who seek out media content related to politics. In the second step, they filter and pass along political information to their social contacts. Media effects, then, were achieved by reaching opinion leaders, not mass audiences.

These findings were later elaborated in a subsequent panel study of women in Decatur, Illinois. Researchers examined the role of opinion leaders on more subtle, day-to-day issues (for example, fashions and household products) (Katz & Lazarsfeld, 1955). The hypothesis was that on less significant topics, the two-step flow would prove to be an even more dynamic and powerful process than with phenomena such as presidential elections. The findings confirmed this expectation, again noting the existence of a two-step flow of information.

Both of these studies demonstrated clearly that mediating factors intervened in the media effects process. They were among the first to identify social factors that intervened between message and audience response based on the earlier stimulus-response model. Within this theoretical framework, however, the flow of information is still linear and universal. In other words, the media message remains relatively intact. Opinion leaders, often only those wealthy enough to own radio or television and subscribe to magazines, were conduits of media messages.

4.5.4.2. Research on Social Context of Media Use. Another research tradition that falls under the general category of social-cultural research is the body of literature examining social contexts of media use such as on family and home media use (see also 11.5.4). A great deal of research has examined parent-child coviewing of media. According to one study (Desmond, Singer, Singer, Calum & Calimore, 1985), parental mediation in the media-child relationship takes three forms: (1) critical comments about programs or the medium in general, (2) interpretive comments that explain content or media to younger children, and (3) rule making/disciplinary intervention that forcibly regulates the child's viewing habits. Parental inter-pretation and rule making were framed as a major influence on children's viewing and comprehension of media content. One study (St. Peters, Fitch, Huston, Eakins & Wright, 1991) found that when such coviewing did take place, it was predicted more by the adult's personal viewing habits than the child's. In other words, children and parents coviewed more adult than children's programming. Further, parents' participation in regulating viewing declined as children grew older; and parental guidance or mediation with content was not related to coviewing. Dorr, Kovaric, and Doubleday (1989) echoed the finding that coviewing was largely a coincidence of viewing habits and preferences. They also found weak evidence for the positive consequences of such coviewing, but questioned the value of this concept as an indicator of parental mediation of content.

Such concerns were also discussed by Bryce and Leichter (1983) on a methodological level. They argued that quantitative measures of viewing habits and coviewing may not capture more routine or subtle processes of family viewing that mediate potential effects. They proposed using ethnographic methods (see 40.2) to study the unintentional and nonverbal behaviors that mediate television effects, as well as assessing those mediating behaviors that take place away from television. Jordan (1992) used ethnographic and depth interview techniques for just such a purpose. She concluded that family routines, use and definition of time, and the social roles of family members all played a part in the use of media. Children learned at least as much, if not more, from these daily routines than any formal efforts to regulate media use.

Corder-Bolz (1980) proposed that groups and institutions such as family, peers, school, and church should be considered as primary socializing agents that both provide social information (e.g., facts, ideas, and values) and respond to social communication about this information. McDonald (1986) pointed out that peer coviewing is more frequent and influential among young viewers. Media were defined by Corder-Bolz as the group of "secondary socializing agents" that can provide social information but cannot enforce their messages with child viewers. Media, then, can provide social facts, ideas, and values, but this information's influence is limited to the extent that the child's environment presents no competing messages or that the viewer uncritically adopts such views from media content. Thus, external factors limit the potential impact of content.

Desmond et al. (1985) studied the cognitive skills necessary to comprehend and interpret television content and the effects of family communication on these skills. In their sample of kindergarten and first-grade children, comprehension of and beliefs about the reality of television content were linked to parental mediation styles and general patterns of discipline. Children who watched low levels of TV, in environments that included family control of television, TV-related rules, and strong discipline, were better able to discern reality from fantasy in programming. Those who were raised with TV-specific rules, positive communication between child and mother, and a pattern of explanation of content from adults and older siblings were better able to gain knowledge from television content and about television techniques (e.g., camera zooms and slow motion). Further, this study found that family environmental variables influence the amount of television children viewed. Heavy viewers in this study grew up in homes where parents were heavy viewers and did not mediate viewing often. Family communication was considered the critical variable that determined a child's ability to comprehend televised material and develop the cognitive skills necessary to understand and interpret content.

The research on families and media use suggests that, especially in early childhood, family members are a prime influence on the images children form of media. The amount of and motivations for media use are part of the family's daily social routine (Bryce & Leichter, 1983). Further, other family members' responses to media content serve to shape the developing child's own responses (Corder-Bolz, 1980; Desmond et al., 1985). Such influences likely originate with both family and peers with older, school-aged children. As these children encounter media within classroom contexts, new images of mass media must compete with the definitions and expectations shaped by home media use.

4.5.4.3. Learner-Centered Studies.
In addition, a series of learner-centered studies has begun to emerge from research on instructional media applications. Many of these studies address contextual and social factors that influence the communication process. Thus, they are included in the discussion of social-cultural research. One important research tradition began with a strong psychological orientation exploring students' attitudes toward the individual media systems as determinants of the amount and kinds of learning experienced. Clark (1982, 1983) identified three fundamental dimensions of people's expectations about the media: preference, difficulty, and learning. Salomon used the notion of media expectations as the foundation of a series of studies (1981, 1983, 1984) based on the learner's preconceptions about a given media activity and the relationship of those expectations to learning outcomes. His conception of the model relied on predicted relationships among three constructs: the perceived demand characteristics of the activity, the individual's perceived self-efficacy for using a particular medium, and the amount of mental effort the individual invested in processing the presentation. Oltman (1983) elaborated on Salomon's model by suggesting that older students may be especially familiar with certain media characteristics or the meaning of certain media codes. This familiarity may increase their perceived self-efficacy with a medium and form attitudes about the medium's impact on their thinking about both the content and the medium. It is clear that this approach assumes an active processor who approaches media activities in an individualistic but relatively sophisticated manner.

However, an additional concept missing from Salomon's model is the notion of a kind of cultural identity or stereotype associated with individual media systems and its role in influencing learning outcomes. In his research he failed to disentangle individual and cultural perceptions of media experiences. Both contributed to the kinds of outcomes he examined. That is, individuals' expectations about media experiences are based, at least in part, on the cultural identity of a medium. For example, television in the U.S. is considered primarily an entertainment medium. Though Salomon did not address the significance of a medium's cultural identity in his model, later research attempted to disentangle media perceptions and expectations to include some understanding of the broad cultural identity of media systems. Thus, the model has been included in the discussion under the social-cultural perspective. Despite its original emphasis only on the learner and the psychological orientation of the model, subsequent studies evolved to embrace a stronger social-cultural approach.

According to Salomon's original model, the relationships among these three constructs—perceived demand characteristics, perceived self-efficacy, and amount of invested mental effort—would explain the amount of learning that would result from media exposure. For example, he compared students' learning from reading a book with learning from a televised presentation of the same content. Salomon found more learning from print media, which he attributed to the high perceived demand characteristics of book learning. Students confronted with high demands, he argued, would invest more effort in processing instructional content. Conversely, students would invest the least effort, he predicted, in media perceived to be the easiest to use, thus resulting in lower levels of learning.

In a test of this model, Salomon and Leigh (1984) concluded that students preferred the medium they found easiest to use; the easier it was to use, the more they felt they learned from it. However, measures of inference making suggested that these perceptions of enhanced learning from the "easy" medium were misleading. In fact, students learned more from the "hard" medium, the one in which they invested more mental effort. A series of studies extended Salomon's work to examine the effect of media predispositions and expectations on learning outcomes. Several studies used the same medium, television, to deliver the content but manipulated instructions to viewers about the purpose of viewing. The treatment groups were designed to yield one group with high investments and one with low investments of mental effort.

Though this research began as an extension of traditional research on learning in planned, instructional settings, it quickly evolved to include consideration of context as an independent variable related to learning outcomes. Krendl and Watkins (1983) demonstrated significant differences between treatment groups following instructions to students to view a program and compare it to other programs they watched at home (entertainment context), as opposed to viewing in order to compare it to other videos they saw in school (educational context). This study reported that students instructed to view the program for educational purposes responded to the content with a deeper level of understanding. That is, they recalled more story elements and included more analytical statements about the show's meaning or significance when asked to reconstruct the content than did students in the entertainment context.

Two other studies (Beentjes, 1989; Beentjes & van der Voort, 1991) attempted to replicate Salomon's work in another cultural context, the Netherlands. In these studies children were asked to indicate their levels of mental effort in relation to two media (television and books) and across content types within those media. The second study asked children either watching or reading a story to reproduce the content in writing. Beentjes concluded, "the invested mental effort and the perceived self-efficacy depend not only on the medium, but also on the type of television program or book involved" (1989, p. 55). Bordeaux and Lange (1991) supported these findings in a study of home television viewing. Children and parents were surveyed about the former's active cognitive processing of program content. The researchers concluded that the amount of mental effort invested varied as a function of viewer age and the type of program being viewed. These studies raise the possibility of profound cultural differences in response to various media and genres. Though few studies have examined the notion of cultural differences, clearly the learner-centered approach must investigate the existence and nature of cultural factors related to the understanding of media experiences and learning outcomes.

A longitudinal study emerging from the learner-centered studies (Krendl, 1986) asked students to compare media (print, computer, and television) activities on Clark's (1982, 1983) dimensions of preference, difficulty, and learning. That is, students were asked to compare the activities on the basis of which activity they would prefer, which they would find more difficult, and which they thought would result in more learning. Results suggested that students' judgments about media activities were directly related to the particular dimension to which they were responding. Media activities have multidimensional, complex sets of expectations associated with them. The findings suggest that simplistic, stereotypical characterizations of media experiences (for example, books are hard) are not very helpful in understanding audiences' responses to media.

These studies begin to merge the traditions of mass communication research on learning and studies of the learning process in formal instructional contexts. The focus on individuals' attitudes toward, and perceptions of, various media has begun to introduce a multidimensional understanding of learning in relation to media experiences. Multiple factors influence the learning process-mode of delivery, content, context of reception, as well as individual characteristics such as perceived self-efficacy and cognitive abilities.

One additional approach (Becker, 1985) points to the perspectives offered by poststructural reader theories that define the learner as a creator of meaning. The student interacts with media content and actively constructs meaning from texts, previous experience, and outside influences (e.g., family and peers) rather than passively receiving and remembering content. According to this approach, cultural and social factors are seen as active forces in the construction of meaning.

Abelman (1989) offered a similar perspective in his study of experiential learning, within the context of computer-mediated instruction. The emphasis in this research is on cooperative or collaborative learning; students are seen in partnership with teachers, each other, and delivery systems. The idea is that media can create "microworlds" where students can have some direct experience with new, sophisticated ideas (see 12.3.1.3). Abelman described a program called "Space Shuttle Commander" that teaches principles of motion through student-computer interaction in a simulated space environment. In effect, the student and the computer form a learning partnership.

Jonassen (1985) and Rowntree (1982) have pointed out that such perspectives force us to ask how the student controls learning rather than letting our concerns about the technology drive the research agenda. The concern with technology clearly describes early research on educational media, which took an ad hoc approach to measuring learning outcomes in relation to instructional treatments for each new advance in technology.

4.6 REVIEW OF ELEMENTS OF COMMUNICATION

The three philosophical perspectives discussed above have differing conceptualizations of successful communication. Technical theories of communication looked for improvements in the transmission of the intended message and achievement of the intended effect. The focus in such research remained on channels and symbol systems. Psychological perspectives examined the development of cognitive processing abilities in individual communicators and the influence of their respective attitudes, beliefs, values, and knowledge on communication outcomes. The focus has been on the effects or outcomes of media experiences. Social-cultural perspectives saw social influences as the crux of communication. Individuals exist as parts of social networks. These social networks collectively give meaning to all aspects of communication.

From these theoretical perspectives, we can review the concepts that are included in current models of communication. Each of the major elements is discussed here, with a brief list and description of the significant variables developed in each of theoretical perspectives described above.

Sender/receiver relationships have become so interrelated as to be indistinguishable in recent psychological and social-cultural theories of communication. Among the important variables here are the individual communicator's knowledge, attitudes, beliefs, values, goals, and interest. Also relevant are each communicator's group and social role memberships, as well as their perceptions of themselves and their relations with other people. These elements, combined with the communicative abilities of each sender/receiver, are but a short list of the elements behind the people engaging in communication.

Channels of communication, once confined to the technical realms of telephones, film, radio, and television, have been at once even more limited and expanded. Berlo (1960) confined signals to sensory channels, but in doing so opened the concept to intentional and unintentional communication through verbal and nonverbal, interpersonal, and mediated modes of interaction. Likewise, the forms of messages now include examinations of content, symbol systems, and the stylistic use of symbols. Ironically, through such theoretical developments, the clear distinction between channel and message is more ambiguous; that is, the medium is the message (McLuhan, 1964).

Perhaps the most significant theoretical development has been the explication of the communication context, or social situation. Andersen (1972) states that the setting of communicative events may be seen in two levels. The first is the general environment, including macro-level social attitudes and norms governing the form and content of communication, the number of communicators, the availability of given media channels, and the public or private nature of the setting (see also 7.3.5). The second is the communication-binding context, which refers to the very specific dimensions of a single communicative episode. This includes the exact time and place of the encounter, the social roles of the participants, the participants' perceptions of all the situational elements present during the encounter, and any complexities resulting from barriers in the symbol system or channel of communication (e.g., language barriers, technical difficulties in mass media). In short, context now refers to more than a time and place; it is the combination of these elements with the social status and relationships of all those seeking to communicate or share meaning (Heath & Bryant, 1992). Different kinds of contexts may overlap, such as viewing television programs in the small group setting of a family's living room. In such situations, rules of the communication-binding context are necessarily influenced by more than one set of general norms.

In the research orientations related to the three philosophical perspectives reviewed here, a transmission paradigm has clearly dominated communication models, particularly in the study of mass communication systems. The influence of the technical perspective, born of a concern for scientific efficiency and engineering quality, made examinations of human communication a problematic endeavor. Applications of mass media to learning environments have usually shared such concerns but have attempted to apply these theories to situations distinct from the traditional "one-to-many" situations associated with mass communication. The settings of broadcast media reception and classroom education share some elements. Both contain carefully prepared and distributed messages, both operate in a more public than private sphere, in both cases the message "source" (broadcaster or teacher) carries some degree of power (political or economic) over the "receivers."

4.7 AN INTEGRATED APPROACH TO LEARNING

While much of the previous research has studied learning from the media in formal and informal settings independently, some research has begun to examine learning as a phenomenon that cuts across both types of communication contexts. Educational programming for children has been purposefully designed to obscure this boundary, so that while they are being entertained, children will also be exposed to curriculum-based content. This area of research is a first step in the direction of a more integrated approach to learning from the media.

4.7.1 Edutainment Research

Research on edutainment or planned programming integrates studies of incidental and formal learning contexts. Examinations of such programming, involving the study of programming designed to combine entertainment and a planned curriculum, date back to early concerns over the positive effects of programs such as *Sesame Street*. Studies by Bogatz and Ball (1971) and Schramm, Lyle, and Parker (1961) showed that a great deal of incidental learning occurred in entertainment programming. More recently, Morris (1988) demonstrated positive learning gains related to the use of dramatic or entertaining elements within instructional programming.

Edutainment programs, designed to exploit the opportunity of incidental learning, package planned curricula within traditional entertainment formats (for example, the magazine show format of *3-2-1 Contact*, or the game show format of *Where in the World Is Carmen San Diego*). This hybrid, edutainment, thrives on the notion that a curriculum can ride, somewhat surreptitiously, on the crest of viewer engagement. Curriculum goals may be narrowly defined, but they are integrated into a much broader context; entertainment programming. Research on such programs has demonstrated that learning is occurring on many levels at one time.

The Children's Television Workshop (CTW), creators of *Sesame Street*, the original edutainment program for preschool kids, has been exploring this nexus of education and entertainment for the last 25 years. The educational goals of its programming often reflect a broad understanding of learning. The goal of *Sesame Street* was "to promote the intellectual and cultural growth of preschool children" (Cooney, 1968, as quoted in Cook et al., 1975, p. 7). This definition of learning encompasses lower-level knowledge acquisition, as well as higher-level cognitive processes.

A number of edutainment shows have emerged from CTW: *Sesame Street*, *3-2-1 Contact*, *Square One TV*, and *Ghostwriter*. Goals for these programs concern not only basic literacy and numeracy skills but also more broadly defined cultural goals. For example, for the program *3-2-1 Contact,* the workshop expressed three primary goals: "(1) to help children experience the joy of scientific exploration;

(2) to help children become familiar with various styles of scientific thinking; and (3) to help children, with a special appeal to girls and minorities, to recognize science and technology as open to their participation" (Children's Television Workshop, 1980). These stated goals address learning at levels of cognitive processes, affect and behavior; moreover, they express an ineluctable link between the three.

The exploratory studies for *3-2-1 Contact* discussed the importance of a broad conceptualization of learning, citing "a closer dynamic than is sometimes assumed between the motivational and educational effects . . . motivation and mastery should be seen as close companions in a common educational enterprise" (Chen, 1984, p. 7).

Another recent example is *Square One TV*. This show, aimed at an at-home audience of 8- to 12-year-old children, is designed to "promote positive attitudes toward, and enthusiasm for, mathematics . . . to encourage the use and application of problem-solving processes . . . and to present sound mathematical content in an interesting, accessible and meaningful way" (Hall, Esty & Fisch, 1990, p. 162). The definition of learning in effect at Children's Television Workshop is integrated in the sense that the stated goals of its programming recognize that cognitive and affective learning cannot be separated.

But our conceptualization of learning can be broader still. If cognitive and affective learning are contiguous gradations of color in the spectrum of learning outcomes, there is still the process of filtration to be understood. One child watching *Sesame Street* may come away with an understanding of near and far (courtesy of Grover). Another may come away with an understanding of cooperation.

4.8 CONCLUSION

Application of the metaphor of a spectrum to research on media and learning enriches the conceptualization of the learning process, including consideration of multiple factors, for example, different types of context and content, various delivery media, and a wide array of learner characteristics. This chapter has attempted to demonstrate through the reviewing of various research orientations and transitions the arguments for a more integrated approach to the study of media and learning.

Though much of the research to date remains focused on either formal classroom media applications or uses of media in at-home contexts, on one media system or another media system, on one type of content or another type of content, on one segment of the audience or another segment of the audience, research on new communication systems will gradually eliminate such distinctions. What ultimately shapes a learning experience is the series of filters that learning must pass through. Filtered by the inherent attributes of the medium, filtered by the social context and the culture in which learning occurs, and most certainly filtered by the perceptual framework and cognitive abilities of the learner, this experience can be broad or narrow, intentional or incidental, profound or superficial. Moreover, from one

learning opportunity, an infinite number of possible learning outcomes may emerge.

Therefore, assessing learning by any preconceived and narrowly defined set of outcomes is futile. Forecasting what will be learned given only attributes of a medium, the level of the learner's motivation, or the context in which the experience occurred will give rise to incomplete understanding of the learning possibilities. The argument presented here proposes that researchers consider multiple learning possibilities.

One illustration of the breadth of learning possibilities lies in *Ghostwriter*, a multimedia project of the Children's Television Workshop that strives to teach literacy but is valued for its strong social messages as well. The *Ghostwriter* project centers around a one-half hour television show (PBS), but also employs magazines, newspaper pages, teacher guides, and guides for after-school program directors. The result is that kids can experience *Ghostwriter* by watching television in the home; they can read the magazines or see the show in school; they can be involved in *Ghostwriter* activities in after-school settings also.

As part of the summative research of *Ghostwriter*, the Children's Television Workshop commissioned a study of the use of *Ghostwriter* in after-school and school settings in the hope that understanding how these materials were used would inform understanding of the possible learning outcomes. In this naturalistic study (EDC, 1993) the researchers indicated that use of *Ghostwriter* materials was deeply entangled with setting and with the individual goals of adult mediators of the experience. "Use in context is the most appropriate way to characterize [*Ghostwriter*] materials use, given that adults in these settings brought to *Ghostwriter* a deep understanding of the goals of their program needs and the needs of their children" (EDC, p. 117). A *Ghostwriter* experience, then, ends up being a rich experience defined not by the content of the materials, by a particular medium, by the agenda of an adult mediator, or by the child alone, but by all of these things at once.

In the history of research on media and learning is a history that has evolved from a conceptualization of learning as a relatively narrow set of predicted outcomes based on message content and sender intent to a broader definition of learning that recognizes multiple components and factors as contributing to a complex process. The former approach, in effect, examined the learning process backwards, missing the breadth of possibilities inherent in any learning experience. The new media environments—flexible, interactive, and decentralized—highlight something that has always been true, that learning by nature cannot be constrained, not by content, not by context, not by culture, not by medium. Learning occurs as a spectrum of possibilities, filtered by complex factors until it becomes, for each learner, a unique experience. Throughout the discussion of the various research traditions examined here, we have come to understand that learning is not an outcome but a process affected by many factors. The mandate for future research is to explore this process and the relationships among the factors.

REFERENCES

Abelman, R. (1989). From here to eternity: children's acquisitions of understanding of projective size of television. *Human Communication Research 15,* 463–81.

Allen, W.H. (1973). Research in education media. *In* J. Brown, ed. *Educational media yearbook, 1973.* New York: Bowker.

Andersen, K.E. (1972). *Introduction to communication theory and practice.* Menlo Park, CA: Cummings.

Bandura, A. (1965). Influence of model's reinforcement contingencies on the acquisition of imitative responses. *Journal of Personality and Social Psychology 1,* 589–95.

— (1977). *Social learning theory.* Englewood Cliffs, NJ: Prentice Hall.

—, Ross, D. & Ross, S. (1963). Imitation of film-mediated aggressive models. *Journal of Abnormal and Social Psychology 66,* 3–11.

—, — & — (1961). Transmission of aggression through imitation of aggressive models. *Journal of Abnormal and Social Psychology 63,* 575–82.

Beck, C.R. (1987). Pictorial cueing strategies for encoding and retrieving information. *International Journal of Instructional Media 14*(4), 332–45.

Becker, A. (1985). Reader theories, cognitive theories, and educational media research. Paper presented at the Annual Meeting of the Association for Educational Communications and Technology. (ERIC Document Reproduction Service No. ED 256 301.)

Beentjes, J.W.J. (1989). Learning from television and books: a Dutch replication study based on Salomon's model. *Educational Technology, Research, and Development 37*(2), 47–58.

— & T.H.A. van der Voort (1991). Children's written accounts of televised and printed stories. *Educational Technology, Research, and Development 39*(3), 15–26.

Behr, R.L. & Iyengar, S. (1985). Television news, real world cues, and changes in the public agenda. *Public Opinion Quarterly 49,* 38–57.

Berlo, D.K. (1977). *The process of communication.* New York: Holt, Rinehart & Winston.

Blake, T. (1977). Motion in instructional media: some subject-depth display mode interactions. *Perceptual and Motor Skills 44,* 975–85.

Blumer, H. (1939). The mass, public & public opinion. *In* A. M. Lee, ed. *New outlines of the principles of sociology.* New York: Barnes & Noble.

— (1969). *Symbolic interactionism: perspective and method.* Englewood Cliffs, NJ: Prentice Hall.

Bogatz, G.A. & Ball, S. (1971). *The second year of Sesame Street: a continuing evaluation, Vols. I and II.* Princeton, NJ: Education Testing Service.

Bordeaux, B.R. & Lange, G. (1991). Children's reported investment of mental effort when viewing television. *Communication Research 18,* 617–35.

Brosius, H. & Kepplinger, H.M. (1990). The agenda setting function of television news. *Communication Research 17,* 183–211.

Bryant, J.H. (1975). Children's cooperation and helping behavior. *In* E.M. Hethrington, ed. *Review of child development research, Vol. 5.* Chicago, IL: University of Chicago Press.

Bryant J.W. & Leichter H.J. (1983). The family and television: forms of mediation. *Journal of Family Issues 4,* 309–28.

Cantril, H. (1935). *The psychology of radio.* New York: Harper & Bros.

Chen, M. (1984). *A review of research on the educational potential of 3-2-1 Contact: a children's television series on science and technology.* New York: Children's Television Workshop.

Children's Television Workshop (1980). *3-2-1 Contact: a children's television series on science and technology: Proposal for season II.* New York: Author.

Clark, R.E. (1982). Individual behavior in different settings. *Viewpoints in Teaching and Learning 58*(3), 33–39.

— (1983). Reconsidering research on learning from media. *Review of Educational Research 53*(4), 445–59.

— (1987). Which technology for what purpose? The state of the argument about research on learning from media. Paper presented at the Annual Convention of the Association for Educational Communications and Technology. (ERIC Document Reproduction Service No. ED 285 520.)

— (1991). When researchers swim upstream: reflections on an unpopular argument about learning from media. *Education Technology 31*(2), 34–40.

— & Salmon, G. (1985). Media in teaching. *In* M. Wittrock, ed. *Handbook of Research on Teaching,* 3d ed., 464–78. New York: Macmillan.

Cohen, B. (1963). *The press, the public, and foreign policy.* Princeton, NJ: Princeton University Press.

Cohen, P.A., Eberling, B.J. & Kulik, J.A. (1981). A meta-analysis of outcome studies of visual-based instruction. *Educational Communication and Technology: A Journal of Theory, Research, and Development 29*(1), 26–36.

Cook, T.D., Appleton, H., Connor, R.F., Shaffer, A., Tamkin, G. & Weber. S.J. (1975). *Sesame Street revisited.* New York: Sage.

Corder-Bolz, C.R. (1980). Mediation: the role of significant others. *Journal of Communication 30*(2), 106–118.

Cressey, P. (1934). The motion picture as informal education. *Journal of Education Sociology 7,* 504–15.

Dalton, D.W. & Hannafin, M.J. (1986). The effects of video only, CAI only, and interactive video instructional systems on learner performance and attitude: an exploratory study. Paper presented at the Annual Convention of the Association for Educational Communications and Technology. (ERIC Document Reproduction Service No. ED 267 762.)

Demers, D.P., Craff, D., Choi, Y. & Pessin, B.M. (1989). Issue obtrusiveness and the agenda setting effects of national network news. *Communication Research 16,* 793–812.

Desmond, R.J., Singer, J.L., Singer, D.G., Calam, R. & Colimore, K. (1985). Family mediation patterns and television viewing: young children's use and grasp of the medium. *Human Communication Research 11,* 461–80.

Devito, J.A. (1986). *The communication handbook: a dictionary.* New York: Harper & Row.

Doob, A. & MacDonald, G. (1979). Television viewing and fear of victimization, is the relationship causal? *Journal of Personality and Social Psychology 37,* 170–79.

Dorr, A., Kovaric, P. & Doubleday, C. (1989). Parent-child coviewing of television. *Journal of Broadcasting and Electronic Media 33,* 35–51.

Drabman, R.S. & Thomas, M.H. (1974). Does media violence increase children's toleration of real-life aggression? *Developmental Psychology 10,* 418–21.

— & — (1976). Does watching violence on television cause apathy? *Pediatrics 57,* 329–31.

— & — (1977). Children's imitation of aggressive and prosocial behavior when viewing alone and in pairs. *Journal of Communication 27*(3), 199–205.

EDC (1993). *A naturalistic study of Ghostwriter use in after-school and school settings.* Newton, MA: Educational Developmental Center.

Ennis, P.H. (1961). The social structure of communication systems: a theoretical proposal. *Studies in Public Communication 3,* 120–44.

Festinger, L.A. (1962). *A theory of cognitive dissonance.* Stanford, CA: Stanford University.

Fisher, B.A. (1978). *Perspectives on human communication.* New York: Macmillan.

Gerbner, G., Gross, L., Eleey, M.F., Jackson-Beeck, M., Jeffries-Fox, S. & Signorielli, N. (1977). Violence profile no. 8: the highlights. *Journal of Communication 27*(2), 171–80.

—, —, —, —, — & — (1978). Cultural indicators: violence profile no. 9. *Journal of Communication 28*(3), 176–206.

—, —, Morgan, M. & Signorielli, N. (1980). The mainstreaming of America: violence profile no. 11. *Journal of Communication 30*(3), 10–28.

—, —, — & — (1986). Living with television: the dynamics of the cultivation process. *In* J. Bryant & D. Zillman, ed. *Perspectives on media effects,* 17–40. Hillsdale, NJ: Erlbaum.

—, —, Signorielli, N., Morgan, M. & Jackson-Beeck, M. (1979). The demonstration of power: violence profile no. 10. *Journal of Communications 29,* 177–96.

Ghorpade, S. (1986). Agenda setting: a test of advertising's neglected function. *Journal of Advertising Research 25,* 23–27.

Glass, G.V. (1976). Primary, secondary, and meta-analysis of research. *Educational Researcher 5,* 3–8.

Glynn, S. & Britton, B. (1984). Supporting readers' comprehension through effective text design. *Educational Technology 24,* 40–3.

Hall, E.R., Esty, E.T. & Fisch, S.M. (1990). Television and children's problem-solving behavior: a synopsis of an evaluation of the effect of Square One TV. *Journal of Mathematical Behavior 9,* 161–74.

Hart, R.A. (1986). The effects of fluid ability, visual ability, and visual placement within the screen on a simple concept task. Paper presented at the Annual Convention of the Association for Educational Communications and Technology. (ERIC Document Reproduction Service No. ED 267 774.)

Heath, R. & Bryant, J. (1992). *Human communication theory and research.* Hillsdale, NJ: Erlbaum.

Herzog, H. (1948). On borrowed experience: an analysis of listening to daytime sketches. *Studies in Philosophy and Social Science 9,* 65–95.

Hicks, D. (1965). Imitation and retention of film-mediated aggressive peer and adult models. *Journal of Personality and Social Psychology 2,* 97–100.

Himmelweit, H., Oppenheim, A.N. & Vince, P. (1959). *Television and the child: an empirical study of the effects of television on the young.* London: Oxford University Press.

Hoban, C.F. & van Ormer, E.B. (1950). *Instructional film research, 1918-1950.* Technical Report No SDC 269-7-19. Port Washington, NY: U.S. Naval Special Devices Center.

Hovland, P.W. & Stoddard, G.D. (1933). *Getting ideas from the movies.* New York: Macmillan.

Hornik, R. (1981). Out-of-school TV and schooling: hypotheses and methods. *Review of Educational Research 51,* 193–214.

Hovland, C.I. & Janis. I.L. (1959). *Personalityy and persuasibility.* New Haven, CT: Yale University Press.

— (1948). Psychology of the communication process. *In* W. Schramm, ed. *Communication in modern society* 58–65.

Urbana, IL: University of Illinois Press.

—, Janis, I.L. & Kelley, H.H. (1953). *Communication and persuasion.* New Haven, CT: Yale University Press.

—, Lumsdaine, A.A. & Sheffield, F.D. (1949). *Experiments on mass communication,* Vol. 3. Princeton, NJ: Princeton University Press.

Iyengar, E., Peters, M.D. & Kinder, D.R. (1982). Experimental demonstrations of the "not-so-minimal" consequences of television news programs. *American Political Science Review 76,* 848–58.

Jamison, D., Suppes, P. & Wells, S. (1974). The effectiveness of alternative instructional media: a survey. *Review of Education Research 44,* 1–68.

Johnston, J. (1987). *Electronic learning: from audiotape to videodisk.* Hillsdale, NJ: Erlbaum.

Jonassen, D.H. (1985). Learning strategies: a new education technology. *Programmed Learning and Educational Technology 22*(1), 26–34.

Jordan, A.B. (1992). Social class, temporal orientation, and mass media use within the family system. *Critical Studies in Mass Communication 9,* 374–86.

Katz, E. & Lazarfeld, P.F. (1955). *Personal influence: the part played by people in the flow of mass communication.* Glencoe, IL: Free Press.

Klapp, O.E. (1982). Meaning lag in the information-society. *Journal of Communication 32*(2), 55–66.

Krendl, K.A. (1986). Media influence on learning: examining the role of preconceptions. *Educational Communication and Technology Journal 34,* 223–34.

— (1989). Two roads converge: the synthesis of research on media influence on learning. *In* B. Derwin & M. Voigt, ed. *Progress in communication sciences,* Vol. 9, 105–22. Norwood, NY: Ablex.

— & Watkins, B. (1983). Understanding television: an exploratory inquiry into the reconstruction of narrative content. *Educational Communication and Technology Journal 31,* 201–12.

Kulik, J.A. Bangert, R. & Williams, G. (1983). Effects of computer-based teaching on secondary school students. *Journal of Educational Psychology 75,* 19–26.

—, Kulik, C.L.C. & Cohen. P.A. (1979). A meta-analysis of outcome studies of Keller's Personalized System of Instruction. *American Psychologist 38,* 307–18.

Lang, K. & Lang, G.E. (1966). The mass media and voting. *In* B. Berelson & M. Janowitz, ed. *Reader in public opinion and communication,* 2d ed., 217–235. New York: Free Press.

Lasswell H.D. (1948). The structure and function of communication society. *In* L. Bryson, ed. *The communication of ideas.* New York: Harper & Bros.

Lazarsfeld, P.F.. (1940). *Radio and the printed page: an introduction to the study of radio and its role in the communication of ideas.* New York: Duell, Sloan & Pearce.

—, Berelson, B. & Gaudet, H. (1944). *The people's choice.* New York: Free Press.

Lefkowitz, M.M., Eron, L.D., Walder, L.O. & Huesmann, L.R. (1972). Television violence and child aggression: a follow-up study. *In* G.A. Comstock & E.A. Rubinstein, ed. *Television and social behavior, Vol. III: Television and adolescent aggressiveness,* 35–135. Washington, DC: U.S. Government Printing Office.

Lippmann, W. (1922). *Public opinion.* New York: Free Press.

Lull, J. (1980). Social uses of television. *Human Communication Research 6*(3), 197–209.

Mager, R.F. (1962). *Preparing instructional objectives.* Palo Alto, CA: Fearon.

Mayer, R.E. (1987). *Educational psychology: a cognitive approach.* Boston, MA: Little, Brown.

McCombs, M.E. & Shaw, D.L. (1972). The agenda setting function of mass media. *Public Opinion Quarterly 36,* 176–87.

McDonald, D.G. (1986). Generational aspects of television coviewing. *Journal of Broadcasting and Electronic Media 30,* 75–85.

McGuire, W.J. (1973). Persuasion, resistance, and attitude change. *In* I.D.S. Pool, W. Schramm, F.W. Frey, N. Macoby & E.B. Parker, ed. *Handbook of communication,* 216–252. Chicago, IL: Rand McNally.

McLuhan, M. (1964). *Understanding media: the extensions of man.* New York: New American Library.

McQuail, D. (1983). *Mass communication theory: an introduction.* Beverly Hills, CA: Sage.

Mead, G.H. (1934). *Mind, self, and society.* Chicago, IL: University of Chicago Press.

Mielke, K.W. (1968). Asking the right ETV research questions. *Educational Broadcasting Review 2*(6), 54–61.

Milavsky, J.R., Kessler, R., Stipp, H. & Rubens, W.S. (1982). Television and aggression: results of a panel study. *In* D. Pearl, L. Bouthilet & J. Lazar, ed., *Television and behavior: ten years of scientific progress and implications for the eighties,* Vol. 2, 138–57. Washington, DC: U.S. Government Printing Office.

Morris, J.D. (1988). The use of television production techniques to facilitate the learning process: an experiment. *International Journal of Instructional Media 15*(3), 244–56.

National Institute of Mental Health (1982). *In* D. Pearl, L. Bouthilet & J. Lazar, ed. *Television and behavior: ten years of scientific progress and implications for the eighties,* Vol. 2, 138–157. Washington, DC: U.S. Government Printing Office.

Newcomb, T.M. (1953). An approach to the study of communicative acts. *Psychological Review 60,* 393–404.

Noble, G. (1975). *Children in front of the small screen.* Beverly Hills, CA: Sage.

O'Keefe, G.J. (1984). Public views on crime: television exposure and media credibility. *In* R.N. Bostrom, ed., *Communication yearbook, Vol. 8,* 514–35. Newbury Park, CA: Sage.

Oltman, P.K. (1983). *Cognitive assessment and the media.* College Board Report No. 83–1. New York: College Entrance Examination Board. (ERIC Document Reproduction Service No. ED 229 445.)

Osgood, C.E., ed. (1954). Psycholinguists: a survey of theory and research problems. *Journal of Abnormal and Social Psychology 49* (Oct.). Morton Prince Memorial Supplement.

—, Suci, G.J. & Tannenbaum, P.H. (1958). *The measurement of meaning.* Urbana, IL: University of Illinois Press.

Oxford English Dictionary, 2d ed. (1971). New York: Oxford University Press.

Peterson, R.C. & Thurstone, L.L. (1933). *Motion pictures and the social attitudes of children.* New York: Macmillan.

Protess, D.L., Leff, D.R., Brooks, S.C. & Gordon, M.T. (1985). Uncovering rape: the watchdog press and the limits of agenda setting. *Public Opinion Quarterly 49,* 19–37.

Roberts, M.S. (1992). Predicting voting behavior via the agenda-setting tradition. *Journalism Quarterly 69,* 878–92.

Rowntree, D. (1982). *Educational technology in curriculum development.* London: Harper & Row.

Salomom, G. (1974). Internalization of filmic schematic operations in interaction with learners' aptitudes. *Journal of Educational Psychology 66,* 499–511.

— (1979). *Interaction of media, cognition, and learning.* San Francisco, CA: Jossey-Bass.

— (1981). *Communication and education: social and psychological interactions.* Beverly Hills, CA: Sage.

— (1983). Television watching and mental effort: a social psychological view. *In* J. Bryand & D.R. Anderson, ed. *Children's understanding of television,* 181–98. New York: Academic.

— (1984). Television is "easy" and print is "tough": the different investment of mental effort in learning as a function of perceptions and attributions. *Journal of Educational Psychology 76,* 647–58.

— & Cohen, A.A. (1977). Television formats, mastery of mental-skills, and the acquisition knowledge. *Journal of Education Psychology 69,* 612–19.

— & Leigh, T. (1984). Predispositions about learning from print and television. *Journal of Communication 34*(2), 119–35.

Schramm, W. (1954). How communication works. *In* W. Schramm, ed. *The process and effects of mass communication.* Urbana, IL: University of Illinois Press.

— (1955). Information theory and mass communication. *Journalism Quarterly 32,* 131–46.

— (1977). *Big media, little media.* Beverly Hills, CA: Sage.

—, Lyle, J. & Parker E.B. (1961). *Television in the lives of our children.* Stanford, CA: Stanford University Press.

Seidman, S.A. (1981). On the contributions of music to media productions. *Educational Communication and Technology Journal 29* (Spring), 49–61.

Shannon, C. & Weaver, W. (1949). *The mathematical theory of communication.* Urbana, IL: University of Illinois Press.

Shaw, D.L. & Martin, S.E. (1992). The function of mass media agenda setting. *Journalism Quarterly 69,* 902–20.

— & McCombs, M.E., ed. (1977). *The emergence of American political issues: the agenda setting function of the press.* St. Paul, MN: West.

Shuttleworh, F.K. & May, M.A. (1933). *The social conduct and attitudes of movie fans.* New York: Macmillan.

St. Peters, M., Fitch, M., Huston, A.C., Wright, J.C. & Eakins. D.J. (1991). Television and families: what do young children watch with their parents? *Child Development 62,* 1409–23.

Swanson, D.L. & Delia, J.G. (1976). *Modules of speech: the nature of human communication.* Palo Alto, CA: Science Research Associates.

Travers. R.M.W. (1967). *Research and theory related to audiovisual information transmission.* Kalamazoo, MI: Western Michigan University Press.

Trenholm, S. (1986). *Human communication theory.* Englewood Cliffs, NJ: Prentice Hall.

Webster's new world dictionary of the American language. (1966). Cleveland, OH: World.

Westley, B.H. & MacLean, M. (1957). A conceptual model for communication research. *Journalism Quarterly 34,* 31–38.

Whorf, B. (1956). *In* J.B. Carroll, ed. *Language, thought, and reality; selected writings.* Cambridge, MA: Technical Press of the Massachusetts Institute of Technology.

Yagade, A. & Dozier, D. M. (1990). The media agenda-setting effect of concrete versus abstract issues. *Journalism Quarterly 67,* 3–10.

Zettl, H. (1973). *Sight, sound, motion: applied media aesthetics.* Belmont, CA: Wadsworth

5. COGNITIVE PERSPECTIVES IN PSYCHOLOGY

William Winn   Daniel Snyder

UNIVERSITY OF WASHINGTON

5.1 INTRODUCTION

The purpose of this chapter is to discuss some of the developments in cognitive psychology that have been influential in educational technology research. Since cognitive psychology is a broad, eclectic, and sometimes elusive discipline, this chapter is of necessity selective. Nonetheless, it provides discussion of the most important research in cognitive psychology that has a bearing on the theory and practice of educational technology.

Educational technology came of age as a discipline at a time when relevant psychological theory was based almost entirely on behavioral principles (see 2.2). This meant that the procedures and practice of educational technology evolved to accommodate behavioral accounts of learning and instruction (Winn, 1989). History teaches us that theories change more readily than practice. Therefore, when researchers started to develop cognitive theories that compensated for the inadequacy of behaviorism to explain many aspects of human activity, the technologies and practices by means of which psychological theory is applied changed much more slowly, and in some cases not at all. The practices recommended by some schools of thought in instructional design are still exclusively behavioral. This chapter is colored by the tension that exists between some aspects of traditional practice in educational technology and cognitive theory, a tension that arises from the difficulty of trying to reconcile one kind of theory with procedures for application developed for another kind.

The different rates of change in the theory and practice of educational technology mean that the true importance of research in cognitive psychology to our field must be examined in its historical context. For this reason, the chapter begins with a brief review of the antecedents of cognitive theory and of behaviorism against which it reacted. The historical development of cognitive psychology and cognitive science is addressed in a little more detail. The next two sections deal with two of the cornerstones of cognitive theory, mental representation, and mental processes. It will

become clear that these topics are not entirely dissociable one from the other. Nonetheless, we feel that this somewhat artificial distinction is a better compromise for the sake of clarity than the muddle that would surely ensue from trying to treat both at once. The final section speaks specifically to the relevance of cognitive psychology to the practice of educational technology, namely, instructional design. It examines ways in which cognitive theory has been brought to both the theory of instruction and the design procedures by means of which that theory is applied to practical tasks.

5.2 HISTORICAL OVERVIEW

Most readers will already know that cognitive theory came into its own as an extension of (some would say a replacement of) behavioral theory (see 2.2.1). However, many of the tenets of cognitive theory are not new and date back to the very beginnings of the autonomous discipline of psychology in the 19th century. We therefore begin with a brief discussion of introspection and of Gestalt theory before turning to the story of cognitive psychology's reaction to behaviorism.

5.2.1 Introspection

One of the major forces that helped psychology emerge as a distinct discipline at the end of the 19th century was the work of the German psychologist Wundt (Boring, 1950). Wundt made two significant contributions, one conceptual and the other methodological. First, he clarified the boundaries of the new discipline. Psychology was the study of the inner world, not the outer world, which was the domain of physics. And the study of the inner world was to be the study of thought, or mind, not of the physical body, which was the domain of physiology. At first glance, these two distinctions may strike us as somewhat naive. However, it is worth noting that a great deal of recent research in cognitive psychology has looked at the issue of how the physical world is mapped onto memory, and in some cases it is not always clear where the physical world ends and the mental world begins. Also, there is now a growing interest in neurophysiological explanations of perception and cognition. This interest is occurring at a time when philosophers and psychologists are questioning Cartesian dualism, which proposes that mind and body are separate and which has held sway in Western thought since the 17th century. The distinction between mind and brain is becoming blurred. Thus, today, physics and physiology are not necessarily cleanly separated from psychology.

Wundt's methodological contribution was the development of introspection as a means for studying the mind. Physics, and to a large extent physiology, deals with phenomena that are objectively present and therefore directly observable and measurable. Thought is both highly subjective and intangible. Therefore, Wundt proposed, the only access to it, if one was to study it directly, was for a person to examine his or her own thoughts. And the only way to do that was through introspection. Wundt developed a program of research that extended over many decades and attracted adherents from laboratories in many countries. Typically, his experimental tasks were simple: pressing buttons, watching displays. The data of greatest interest were the descriptions his subjects gave of what they were thinking about as they performed the tasks.

On the face of it, Wundt's approach was very sensible. You best learn about things by studying them directly. And the only direct route to thought is via a subject's description of his or her own thinking. The danger of introspection lies in the difficulty persons have thinking about their own thinking. Behaviorists would soon decry the lack of objectivity in the method. What is more, we have to ask whether the act of thinking about thinking interferes with and changes the thinking that one is interested in studying. Is there an "uncertainty principle" at work whereby the act of thinking about thought changes its very nature?

It is important to note that, in spite of criticism that led to its ultimate demise, introspection (the first psychology) was unashamedly cognitive. What is more, the same general access route to cognitive processes is used today in think-aloud protocols (Ericsson & Simon, 1984) obtained while subjects perform natural or experimental tasks. The method is respected, judged to be valid if properly applied, and essential to the study of thought and behavior in the real world or in simulations of it.

5.2.2 Gestalt Psychology

The word *Gestalt* is a German noun that

> has two meanings: besides the connotation of "shape" or "form" as a property of things, it has the meaning of a concrete individual and characteristic entity, existing as something detached and having a shape or form as one of its attributes. Following this tradition, in Gestalt theory, the word *Gestalt* means any segregated whole . . . (Hartmann, 1935).

Thus, Gestalt psychology is the study of how people see and understand the relation of the whole to the parts that make up that whole.

Wertheimer (1924) stated that Gestalt psychology was not trying to find the meaning of each individual part at the expense of the whole. He stated:

> Gestalt theory will not be satisfied with sham solutions suggested by a simple dichotomy of science and life. Instead, Gestalt theory is resolved to penetrate the problem itself by examining the fundamental assumptions of science. It has long seemed obvious—and is, in fact, the characteristic tone of European science—that "science" means breaking up complexes into their component elements. Isolate the elements, discover their laws, then reassemble them, and the problem is solved. All wholes are reduced to pieces and piecewise relations between pieces. The fundamental "formula" of Gestalt theory might be expressed this way: There are wholes, the behavior of which is not determined by that of their individual elements, but where the part-processes are themselves determined by the intrinsic nature of the whole. It is the hope of Gestalt theory to determine the nature of such wholes (Wertheimer, 1924).

Although the major features of this "new" psychology were developed by Wertheimer, his two protégés, Kohler and Koffka, were responsible for the wide dissemination of this school of thought. This spread was assisted by the rise in Germany of the Nazi party in 1933. Hitler expelled Wertheimer, Levin, von Hornbostel, Stern, Werner, and other Gestalt scholars, ensuring the spread of the concept. Koffka was appointed a research professor at Smith College, and Kohler would soon be at Harvard. Both had been giving lecture tours explaining the principles and concepts of this new school.

One of the best illustrations of the whole being different from the sum of the parts is provided by Ehrenfels in a musical example. If a melody is played on an instrument, it is recognizable. If the melody is played again, but this time in another key, it is still recognizable. However, if the same notes, in the same key, were played in a different sequence, the listener will not recognize any similarity between the first and the second melody. As an example, if the sequence of notes for the first melody was *e e f g g f e d c c d e e d d*, and the second melody played was *b b c d d c b a g g a b b a a*, the listener would recognize the melody immediately as being the same even though different notes are involved. But if the second sequence used the same notes but in a different order, *e e g g f f c c d d e e e d d*, the similarity would not be recognized unless, of course, the listener understood the precise way in which the melody has been transformed.

Based on this difficulty, and the ability of a person to recognize and even reproduce a melody in a key different from the original one,

> Ehrenfels concludes that the resemblance between spatial and tonal patterns rests upon something other than a similarity of their accompanying elements. The totals themselves, then, must be different entities than the sums of their parts.

In other words, the "*Gestaltqualität*" ("form quality") or whole has been reproduced: the elements or Parts have not" (Hartmann, 1935).

The central tenet of Gestalt theory—that our perception and understanding of objects and events in the world depends on the appearance and actions of whole objects, not of their individual parts—has had some influence on the evolution of research in educational technology. The key to that influence are the well-known Gestalt laws of perceptual organization, codified by Wertheimer (1938). These include the principles of "good figure," "figure-ground separation," and "continuity." These laws formed the basis for a considerable number of message design principles (see 26.2) (Fleming & Levie, 1978), in which Gestalt theory about how we perceive and organize information that we see is used in prescriptive recommendations about how to present information on the page, or screen. A similar approach to what we hear is taken by Hereford and Winn (1994).

More broadly, the influence of Gestalt theory is evident in much of what has been written about visual literacy (see 16.4). In this regard, Arnheim's book *Visual Thinking* (1969) is a key work. It was widely read and cited by scholars of visual literacy and proved influential in the development of that movement.

Finally, it is important to note the recent renewal of interest in Gestalt theory (Henle, 1987; Epstein, 1988). The Gestalt psychologists provided little empirical evidence for their laws of perceptual organization beyond everyday experience of their effects. Recently, perceptual psychologists (Pomerantz, 1986; Rock, 1986) have provided explanations for how perceptual organization works from the findings of controlled experiments. The effects of such stimulus features as symmetry on perceptual organization has been explained in terms of the "emergent properties" (Rock, 1986) of what we see in the world around us. We see a triangle as a triangle, not as three lines and three angles. Emergent properties, of course, are the same as the Gestaltist's "whole" that has features all its own that are, indeed, greater than the sum of the parts.

5.2.3 The Rise of Cognitive Psychology

Behavioral theory is described in detail elsewhere in this handbook (see 2.2). Suffice it to say that behaviorism embodies two of the key principles of positivism: that our knowledge of the world can only evolve from the observation of objective facts and phenomena; and that theory can only be built by applying this observation in experiments where only one or two factors are allowed to vary as a function of an experimenter's manipulation or control of other related factors. The first of these principles therefore banned from behavioral psychology unobservable mental states, images, insights, and Gestalts. The second principle banned research methods that involved the subjective techniques of introspection, phenomenology, and the drawing of inferences from observation rather than from objective measurement. Ryle's (1949) relegation of the concept of

"mind" to the status of "the ghost in the machine," both unbidden and unnecessary for a scientific account of human activity, captures the behaviorist ethos exceptionally well.

Behaviorism's reaction against the suspect subjectivity of introspection was necessary at the time if psychology were to become a scientific discipline. However, the imposition of the rigid standards of objectivism (see 7.3) and positivism excluded from accounts of human behavior many of those experiences with which we are extremely familiar. We all experience mental images, feelings, insight, and a whole host of other unobservable and unmeasurable phenomena. To deny their importance is to deny much of what it means to be human (Searle, 1992). Cognitive psychology has been somewhat cautious in acknowledging the ability or even the need to study such phenomena, often dismissing them as "folk psychology" (Bruner, 1990). Only recently, this time as a reaction against the inadequacies of cognitive rather than behavioral theory, do we find serious consideration of subjective experiences. (These are discussed in Bruner, 1991; Clancey, 1993; Edelman, 1992; Searle, 1992; and Varela, Thompson & Rosch, 1991, among others. They are also touched on elsewhere in this handbook.)

Cognitive psychology's reaction against the inability of behaviorism to account for much human activity arose mainly from a concern that the link between a stimulus and a response was not straightforward, that there were mechanisms that intervened to reduce the predictability of a response to a given stimulus, and that stimulus-response accounts of complex behavior unique to humans, like the acquisition and use of language, were extremely complex and contrived. (Chomsky's [1964] review of Skinner's [1957] S-R account of language acquisition is a classic example of this point of view and is still well worth reading.) Cognitive psychology therefore focuses on mental processes that operate on stimuli presented to the perceptual and cognitive systems, and which usually contribute significantly to whether or not a response is made, when it is made, and what it is. Whereas behaviorists claim that such processes cannot be studied because they are not directly observable and measurable, cognitive psychologists claim that they *must* be studied because they alone can explain how people think and act the way they do.

Let me give two examples of the transition from behavioral to cognitive theory. The first concerns memory, the second mental imagery.

Behavioral accounts of how we remember lists of items are usually associationist. Memory in such cases is accomplished by learning S-R associations among pairs of items in a set and is improved through practice (Gagné, 1965; Underwood, 1964). However, we now know that this is not the whole story and that mechanisms intervene between the stimulus and the response that affect how well we remember. The first of these is the collapsing of items to be remembered into a single "chunk." Chunking is imposed by the limits of short-term memory to roughly seven items (Miller, 1956). Without chunking, we would never be able to remember more than seven things at once. When we have to remember more than this limited number of items, we tend to learn them in groups that are manageable in short-term memory, and then to store each group as a single unit. At recall, we "unpack" (Anderson, 1983) each chunk and retrieve what is inside. Chunking is more effective if the items in each chunk have something in common, or form a spatial (McNamara 1986; McNamara, Hardy & Hirtle, 1989) or temporal (Winn, 1986) group.

A second mechanism that intervenes between a stimulus and response to promote memory for items is interactive mental imagery. When people are asked to remember pairs of items and recall is cued with one item of the pair, performance is improved if they form a mental image in which the two items appear to interact (Paivio, 1971, 1983; Bower, 1970). For example, it is easier for you to remember the pair *Whale Cigar* if you imagine a whale smoking a cigar. The use of interactive imagery to facilitate memory has been developed into a sophisticated instructional technique by Levin and his colleagues (Morrison & Levin, 1987; Peters & Levin, 1986). The considerable literature on the role of imagery in paired-associate and other kinds of learning is summarized by Paivio (1971, 1983; Clark & Paivio, 1991).

The importance of these memory mechanisms to the development of cognitive psychology is that, once understood, they make it very clear that a person's ability to remember items is improved if the items are meaningfully related to each other or to the person's existing knowledge. The key word here is *meaningful*. For now, we shall simply assert that what is meaningful to people is determined by what they can remember of what they have already learned. This implies a circular relationship among learning, meaning, and memory—that what we learn is affected by how meaningful it is, that meaning is determined by what we remember, and that memory is affected by what we learn. However, this circle is not a vicious one. The reciprocal relationship between learning and memory, between environment and knowledge, is the driving force behind established theories of cognitive development (Piaget, 1968) and of cognition generally (Neisser, 1976), as we shall see in our examination of schema theory. It is also worth noting that Ausubel's (1963) important book on meaningful verbal learning proposed that learning is most effective when memory structures appropriate to what is about to be learned are created or activated through advance organizers. More generally, then, cognitive psychology is concerned with meaning, or semantics, while behavioral psychology is not.

Mental imagery provides another interesting example of the differences between behavioral and cognitive psychology. Imagery was so far beyond the behaviorist pale that Mandler's article, which reintroduced the topic, was subtitled "The return of the ostracized." Images were, of course, central to Gestalt theory, as we have seen. But because they could not be observed, and because the only route to them was through introspection and self-report, they had no place in behavioral theory.

Yet we can all, to some degree, conjure up mental images. We can also deliberately manipulate them. Kosslyn, Ball, and Reiser (1978) trained their subjects to "zoom" in and out of images of familiar objects and found that the "distance" between the subject and the imagined object constrained the subject's ability to describe the object. To discover the number of claws on an imaged cat, for example, the subject had to move closer to it in the mind's eye.

This ability to manipulate images is useful in some kinds of learning. The method of "Loci" (Kosslyn, 1985; Yates, 1966), for example, requires a person to create a mental image of a familiar place in the mind's eye and to place in that location images of objects that are to be remembered. Recall consists of mentally walking through the place and describing the objects you find. The effectiveness of this technique, which was known to the orators of ancient Greece, has been demonstrated empirically (Cornoldi & De Beni, 1991; De Beni & Cornoldi, 1985).

Mental imagery will be discussed in more detail in the section on representation (5.3). For now, we will draw attention to two methodological issues that are raised by its study. First, some studies of imagery are symptomatic of a conservative color to some cognitive research. As Anderson (1978) has commented, any conclusions about the existence and nature of images can only be inferred from observable behavior. You can only really tell if the Loci method has worked if a person can name items in the set to be remembered. On this view, the behaviorists were right. Objectively observable behavior is all even cognitive researchers have to go on. This means that cognitive psychology has to study mental representation and processes indirectly and to draw conclusions about them by inference rather than from direct measurement. (This will doubtless change as techniques for directly observing brain functions during cognitive activity become available and reliable. See Farah, 1989.)

The second methodological issue is exemplified by Kosslyn's (1985) use of introspection and self-report by subjects to obtain his data on mental images. The scientific tradition that established the methodology of behavioral psychology considered subjective data to be biased, tainted, and therefore unreliable. This precept has carried over into the mainstream of cognitive research. Yet, in his invited address to the 1976 AERA conference, the sociologist Uri Bronfenbrenner (1976) expressed surprise, indeed dismay, that educational researchers do not ask subjects their opinions about the experimental tasks they carry out, nor about whether they performed the tasks as instructed or in some other way. Certainly, this stricture has eased in much of the educational research that has been conducted since 1976, and nonexperimental methodology, ranging from ethnography to participant observation to a variety of phenomenologically based approaches to inquiry is the norm for certain types of educational research (see, for example, the many articles that appeared in the mid-80s, among them Baker, 1984; Eisner, 1984; Howe, 1983; Phillips, 1983). Nonetheless, strict cognitive psychology still tends to adhere to experimental methodology, based on positivism, which makes research such as Kosslyn's on imagery somewhat suspect.

5.2.4 Cognitive Science

Inevitably, cognitive psychology has come face to face with the computer. This is not merely a result of the times in which the discipline has developed but also emerges from the intractability of many of the problems cognitive psychologists seek to solve. The necessity for cognitive researchers to build theory by inference rather than from direct measurement has always been problematic. And it seems that it will remain so until such time as the direct measurement of brain activity is possible on a large scale.

One way around this problem is to build theoretical models of cognitive activity, to write computer simulations that predict what behaviors are likely to occur if the model is an accurate instantiation of cognitive activity, and to compare the behavior predicted by the model—the output from the program—to the behavior observed in subjects. A good example of this approach is found in the work of David Marr (1982) on vision.

Marr began with the assumption that the mechanisms of human vision are too complex to understand at the neurological level. Instead, he set out to describe the functions that these mechanisms need to perform as what is seen by the eye as it moves from the retina to the visual cortex and is interpreted by the viewer. The functions Marr developed were mathematical models of such processes as edge detection, the perception of shapes at different scales and stereopsis (Marr & Nishihara, 1978). The observed electrical activity of certain types of cell in the visual system matched the activity predicted by the model almost exactly (Marr & Ullman, 1981).

Marr's work has had implications that go far beyond his important work on vision, and as such serves as a paradigmatic case of cognitive science. *Cognitive science* is not called that because of its close association with the computer but because it adopts the functional or computational approach to psychology that is so much in evidence in Marr's work. By "functional" (see Pylyshyn, 1984), we mean that it is concerned with the functions the cognitive system must perform, not with the devices through which cognitive processes are implemented. A commonly used analogy is that cognitive science is concerned with cognitive software, not hardware. By "computational" (Arbib & Hanson, 1987; Richards, 1988), we mean that the models of cognitive science take information that a learner encounters, perform logical or mathematical operations on it, and describe the outcomes of those operations. The computer is the tool that allows the functions to be tested, the computations to be performed.

The tendency in cognitive science to create theory around computational rather than biological mechanisms points to another characteristic of the discipline. Cognitive scientists conceive of cognitive theory at different levels of description. The level that comes closest to the brain mechanisms that create cognitive activity is obviously biological. However, as Marr presumed, this level is virtually inaccessible to cognitive researchers, consequently requiring the construction of more abstract functional models. The number, nature, and names of the levels of cognitive theory vary from theory to theory and from researcher to researcher. Anderson (1990, Chapter 1) provides a useful discussion of levels, including those of Chomsky (1965), Pylyshyn (1984), Rumelhart and McClelland (1986), and Newell (1982), in addition to Marr's and his own. In spite of their differences, each of these approaches to levels of cognitive theory implies that if we cannot explain cognition in terms of the mechanisms through which it is actually realized, we can explain it in terms of more abstract mechanisms that we can profitably explore. In other words, the different levels of cognitive theory are really different metaphors for the actual processes that take place in the brain.

The computer has assumed two additional roles in cognitive science beyond that of a tool for testing models. First, some have concluded that, because computer programs written to test cognitive theory accurately predict observable behavior that results from cognitive activity, cognitive activity must itself be computerlike (see 19.2.3.1). Cognitive scientists have proposed numerous theories of cognition that embody the information-processing principles and even the mechanisms of computer science (Boden, 1988; Johnson-Laird, 1988). Thus we find reference in the cognitive science literature to input and output, data structures, information processing, production systems, and so on. More significantly, we find descriptions of cognition in terms of the logical processing of symbols (Larkin & Simon, 1987; Salomon, 1979; Winn, 1982).

Second, cognitive science has provided both the theory and the impetus to create computer programs that "think" just as we do. Research in artificial intelligence blossomed during the 80s, and was particularly successful when it produced intelligent tutoring systems (see 19.3; Anderson & Reiser, 1985; Anderson, Boyle & Yost, 1985; Wenger, 1987) and expert systems (see 24.8; Forsyth, 1984). The former are characterized by the ability to understand and react to the progress a student makes working through a computer-based tutorial program. The latter are smart "consultants," usually to professionals whose jobs require them to make complicated decisions from large amounts of data.

Its successes notwithstanding, AI has shown up the weaknesses of many of the assumptions that underlie cognitive science, especially the assumption that cognition consists in the logical mental manipulation of symbols. Recently, scholars (Clancey, 1993; Dreyfus, 1979; Dreyfus & Dreyfus, 1986; Edelman, 1992; Searle, 1992) have been vigorous in their criticism of this and other assumptions of cognitive science, as well as of computational theory and, more basically, functionalism. The critics imply that cognitive scientists have lost sight of the metaphorical origins of the levels of cognitive theory and have assumed that the brain really does compute the answer to problems by symbol manipulation. Searle's comment sets the tone: "If you are tempted to functionalism, we believe you do not need refutation, you need help" (1992, p. 9). As we shall see in the last section of this chapter, cognitive science is at the point behavioral theory was in the early 60s—facing criticism from proponents of a new paradigm for psychology.

5.2.5 Section Summary

Although many of the ideas in this section will be developed in what follows, we think it is useful at this point to provide a short summary of the ideas presented so far. We have seen that cognitive psychology returned to center stage largely because stimulus-response theory did not adequately or efficiently account for many aspects of human behavior that we all observe from day to day. The research on memory and mental imagery that we briefly described indicated that psychological processes and prior knowledge intervene between the stimulus and the response, making the latter less predictable by behavioral theory. We have also seen that nonexperimental and nonobjective methodology is now deemed appropriate for certain types of research. However, it is possible to detect a degree of conservatism in mainstream cognitive psychology that still insists on the objectivity and quantifiability of data.

Cognitive science, emerging from the confluence of cognitive psychology and computer science, has developed its own set of assumptions, not least among which are computer models of cognition. These have served well, at different levels of abstraction, to guide cognitive research, leading to such applications as intelligent tutors and expert systems. However, the computational theory and functionalism that underlie these assumptions have been the source of considerable recent criticism and point perhaps to the closing of the current chapter in the history of psychology.

The implications of all of this for research and practice in educational technology will be dealt with in section 5.5. We would nonetheless like to anticipate three aspects of that discussion. First, educational technology research, and particularly mainstream instructional design practice, needs to catch up with cognitive theory. As we have suggested elsewhere (Winn, 1989), it is not sufficient simply to substitute cognitive objectives for behavioral objectives and to tweak our assessment techniques to gain access to knowledge schemata rather than just to observable behaviors. More fundamental changes are required.

Second, shifts in the technology itself away from rather prosaic and ponderous computer-assisted programmed instruction to highly interactive multimedia environments permit educational technologists to develop serious alternatives to didactic instruction. We can now use technology to do more than direct teaching. We can use it to help students construct meaning for themselves through experience in ways proposed by constructivist theory and practice described elsewhere in this handbook (see 7.4, 20.3, 20.4, 23.4, 24.6) and by Duffy and Jonassen (1992), Duffy, Jonassen, and Lowyck (1993), and others.

Third, the proposed alternatives to computer models of cognition—which explain first-person experience, nonsymbolic thinking and learning, and reflection-free cognition—

lay the conceptual foundation for educational developments of virtual realities (see Chapter 15; Winn, 1993). The full realization of these new concepts and technologies lies in the future. However, we need to get ahead of the game and prepare for when these eventualities become a reality.

5.3 MENTAL REPRESENTATION

The previous section showed the historical origins of the two major aspects of cognitive psychology that are addressed in this and the next section. These are mental representation and mental processes. Our example of representation was the mental image, and passing reference was made to memory structures and hierarchical chunks of information. We also talked generally about the input, processing, and output functions of the cognitive system, and paid particular attention to Marr's account of the processes of vision.

This section deals with cognitive theories of mental representation. How we store information in memory, represent it in our mind's eye, or manipulate it through the processes of reasoning has always seemed relevant to researchers in educational technology. Our field has sometimes supposed that the way in which we represent information mentally is a direct mapping of what we see and hear about us in the world (see Knowlton, 1966; Cassidy & Knowlton, 1983; Sless, 1981). Educational technolgists have paid a considerable amount of attention to how visual presentations of different levels of abstraction affect our ability to reason literally and analogically (Winn, 1982). Since the earliest days of our discipline (Dale, 1946), we have been intrigued by the idea that the degree of realism with which we present information to students determines how well they learn. More recently (Salomon, 1979), we have come to believe that our thinking uses various symbol systems as tools, enabling us both to learn and to develop skills in different symbolic modalities. How mental representation is affected by what a student encounters in the environment has become inextricably bound up with the part of our field we call *message design* (Fleming & Levie, 1993; Rieber, 1994; Chapter 7).

5.3.1 Schema Theory

The concept of "schema" is central to cognitive theories of representation. There are many descriptions of what schemata are. All descriptions concur that a schema has the following characteristics: (1) It is an organized structure that exists in memory and, in aggregate with all other schemata, contains the sum of our knowledge of the world (Paivio, 1974). (2) It exists at a higher level of generality, or abstraction, than our immediate experience with the world. (3) It consists of concepts that are linked together in propositions. (4) It is dynamic, amenable to change by general experience or through instruction. (5) It provides a context for interpreting new knowledge as well as a structure to hold it. Each of these features requires comment.

5.3.1.1. Schema as Memory Structure. The idea that memory is organized in structures goes back to the work of Bartlett (1932). In experiments designed to explore the nature of memory that required subjects to remember stories, Bartlett was struck by two things: First, recall, especially over time, was surprisingly inaccurate; second, the inaccuracies were systematic in that they betrayed the influence of certain common characteristics of stories and turns of event that might be predicted from common occurrences in the world. Unusual plots and story structures tended to be remembered as closer to "normal" than in fact they were. Bartlett concluded from this that human memory consisted of cognitive structures that were built over time as the result of our interaction with the world and that these structures colored our encoding and recall of subsequently encountered ideas. Since Bartlett's work, both the nature and function of schemata have been amplified and clarified experimentally. The next few paragraphs describe how.

5.3.1.2. Schema as Abstraction. A schema is a more abstract representation than a direct perceptual experience. When we look at a cat, we observe its color, the length of its fur, its size, its breed if that is discernible, and any unique features it might have, such as a torn ear or unusual eye color. However, the schema that we have constructed from experience to represent "cat" in our memory, and by means of which we are able to identify any cat, does not contain these details. Instead, our "cat" schema will tell us that it has eyes, four legs, raised ears, a particular shape, and habits. However, it leaves those features that vary among cats, like eye color and length of fur, unspecified. In the language of schema theory, these are "place-holders," "slots," or "variables" to be "instantiated" through recall or recognition (Norman & Rumelhart, 1975).

It is this abstraction, or generality, that makes schemata useful. If memory required that we encode every feature of every experience that we had, without stripping away variable details, recall would require us to match every experience against templates in order to identify objects and events, a suggestion that has long since been discredited for its unrealistic demands on memory capacity and cognitive processing resources (Pinker, 1985). On rare occasions, the generality of schemata may prevent us from identifying something. For example, we may misindentify a penguin because, superficially, it has few features of a bird. As we shall see below, learning requires the modification of schemata so that they can accurately accommodate unusual instances, like penguins, while still maintaining a level of specificity that makes them useful.

5.3.1.3. Schema as Network. Schemata have been conceived of and described in many ways. One of the most prevalent conceptions of schema has been as a network of concepts connected by links. Illustrative is Palmer's (1975) description of a schema to represent the concept "face." The schema consists of nodes and links that describe the relations between node pairs. The central node in the network is the head, which is roughly oval in shape. The other nodes, representing other features of a face such as eyes,

nose, and mouth, are described in terms of their relationship to the head. The right eye is connected to the head by three links specifying shape, size, and location. Thus, the eye is an oval, like the head, but turned through an angle of 90° relative to the head; it is roughly one-eighth the size of the head; it is located above and to the right of the head's center. In this schema, the relationships—size, shape, and orientation—are constant, and the nodes—eye, nose, mouth—are "placeholders" whose exact nature varies from case to case. Eye color, for example, is not specified in the face schema. But eyes are always above the nose. As in most cases, it is therefore the schema's structure, determined by the links, rather than characteristics of individual nodes that is encoded and against which new information is compared.

5.3.1.4. Schema as Dynamic Structure. A schema is not immutable. As we learn new information, either from instruction or from day-to-day interaction with the environment, our memory and understanding of our world will change. Schema theory proposes that our knowledge of the world is constantly interpreting new experience and adapting to it. These processes, which Piaget (1968) has called *assimilation* and *accommodation*, and which Thorndyke and Hayes-Roth (1979) have called *bottom-up* and *top-down* processing, interact dynamically in an attempt to achieve cognitive equilibrium without which the world would be a tangled blur of meaningless experiences. The process works like this: (1) When we encounter a new object, experience, or piece of information, we attempt to match its features and structure (nodes and links) to a schema in memory (bottom-up). On the basis of the success of this first attempt at matching, we construct a hypothesis about the identity of the object, experience, or information, on the basis of which we look for further evidence to confirm our identification (top-down). If further evidence confirms our hypothesis, we assimilate the experience to the schema. If it does not, we revise our hypothesis, thus accommodating to the experience.

Let us return to Palmer's (1975) "face" schema to illustrate. Palmer describes what happens when a person is shown a "face," whose head consists of a watermelon, whose eyes are apples, whose nose is a pear, and whose mouth is a banana. At first glance, on the basis of structural cues, one interprets the picture as a face. However, this hypothesis is not borne out when confirming evidence is sought and a "fruit" schema (or perhaps "fruitface" schema) is hypothesized. Admittedly, this example is a little unusual. However, it brings home the importance of structure in schemata and illustrates the fact that accommodation of a schema to new information is often achieved by reconciling discrepancies between global and local features.

Learning takes place as schemata change, as they accommodate to new information in the environment, and as new information is assimilated by them. Rumelhart and Norman (1981) discuss important differences in the extent to which these changes take place. Learning takes place by accretion, by schema tuning, or by schema creation.

In the case of accretion, the match between new information and schemata is so good that the new information is simply added to an existing schema with almost no accommodation of the schema at all. A hiker might learn to recognize a golden eagle simply by matching it to an already-familiar bald eagle schema, noting only the absence of the former's white head and tail.

Schema tuning results in more radical changes in a schema. A child raised in the inner city might have formed a "bird" schema on the basis of seeing only sparrows and pigeons. The features of this schema might be: a size of between 3 and 10 inches, flying by flapping wings, found around and on buildings. This child's first sighting of an eagle would probably be confusing, and might lead to a misidentification as an airplane, which is bigger than 10 inches long and does not flap its wings. Learning, perhaps through instruction, that this creature was indeed a bird would lead to changes in the "bird" schema, to include soaring as a means of getting around, large size, and mountain habitat.

Rumelhart and Norman describe schema creation as occurring by analogy. Stretching the bird example to the limits of credibility, imagine someone from a country that has no birds but lots of bats for whom a "bird" schema does not exist. The creation of a bird schema could take place by temporarily substituting the features birds have in common with bats and then specifically teaching the differences. The danger, of course, is that a significant residue of bat features could persist in the bird schema, in spite of careful instruction. Analogies can therefore be misleading (Spiro, Feltovich, Coulson & Anderson, 1989) if they are not used with extreme care.

5.3.1.5. Schema as Context. Not only does a schema serve as a repository of experiences. It provides a context that affects how we interpret new experiences and even directs our attention to particular sources of experience and information. From the time of Bartlett, schema theory has been developed largely from research in reading comprehension. And it is from this area of research that the strongest evidence comes for the decisive role of schemata in interpreting text.

The research design for these studies requires the activation of a well-developed schema to set a context, the presentation of a text that is often deliberately ambiguous, and a comprehension posttest. For example, Bransford and Johnson (1972) had subjects study a text that was so ambiguous as to be meaningless without the presence of an accompanying picture. Anderson, Reynolds, Schallert, and Goetz (1977) presented ambiguous stories to different groups of people. A story that could have been about weight lifting or a prison break was interpreted to be about weight lifting by students in a weight-lifting class, but in other ways by other students. Musicians interpreted a story that could have been about playing cards or playing music as if it were about music.

Neisser (1976) has argued that schemata not only determine interpretation but also affect people's anticipations of what they are going to find in the environment. Thus, in what Neisser calls a *perceptual cycle*, "anticipatory schemata" direct our exploration of the environment. Our exploration of the environment leads us to some sources of information rather than others. The information we find modifies our schemata, in ways we have already encountered, and the cycle repeats itself.

5.3.2 Schema Theory and Educational Technology

Schema theory has influenced educational technology in a variety of ways. For instance, the notion of activating a schema in order to provide a relevant context for learning finds a close parallel in Gagné, Briggs, and Wager's (1988) third instructional "event," "stimulating recall of prerequisite learning." Reigeluth's (Reigeluth & Stein, 1983) "elaboration theory" of instruction consists of, among other things, prescriptions for the progressive refinement of schemata. The notion of a "generality," which has persisted through the many stages of Merrill's instructional theory (Merrill, 1983, 1988; Merrill, Li & Jones, 1991), is close to a schema.

There are however three particular ways in which educational technology research has used schema theory (or at least some of the ideas it embodies, in common with other cognitive theories of representation). The first concerns the assumption, and attempts to support it, that schemata can be more effectively built and activated if the material that students encounter is somehow isomorphic to the putative structure of the schema. This line of research extends into the realm of cognitive theory's earlier attempts to propose and validate a theory of audiovisual (usually more visual than audio) education and concerns the role of pictorial and graphic illustration in instruction (Dale, 1946; Carpenter, 1953; Dwyer, 1972, 1978, 1987).

The second way in which educational technology has used schema theory has been to develop and apply techniques for students to use to impose structure on what they learn and thus make it more memorable. These techniques are referred to, collectively, by the term *information mapping*.

The third line of research consists of attempts to use schemata to represent information in a computer and thereby to enable the machine to interact with information in ways analogous to human assimilation and accommodation. This brings us to a consideration of the role of schemata, or "scripts" (Schank & Abelson, 1977) or "plans" (Minsky, 1975) in AI and "intelligent" instructional systems (see 19.2.3.1). The next sections examine these lines of research.

5.3.3 Schema-Message Isomorphism: Imaginal Encoding

There are two ways in which pictures and graphics can affect how information is encoded in schemata. Some research suggests that a picture is encoded directly as a mental image. This means that encoding leads to a schema that retains many of the properties of the message that the student saw, such as its spatial structure and the appearance of its features. Other research suggests that the picture or graphic imposes a structure on information first and that propositions about this structure rather than the structure itself are encoded. The schema therefore does not contain a mental image but information that allows an image to be created in the mind's eye when the schema becomes active. This and the next section examine these two possibilities.

Research into imaginal encoding is typically conducted within the framework of theories that propose two (at least) separate, though connected, memory systems (see 29.2.3). Paivio's (1983; Clark & Paivio, 1992) "dual coding" theory and Kulhavy's (Kulhavy, Lee & Caterino, 1985; Kulhavy, Stock & Caterino, 1994) "conjoint retention" theory are typical. Both theories assume that people can encode information as languagelike propositions or as picturelike mental images. This research has provided evidence that (1) pictures and graphics contain information that is not contained in text, and (2) that information shown in pictures and graphics is easier to recall because it is encoded in both memory systems, as propositions and as images, rather than just as propositions, which is the case when students read text. As an example, Schwartz and Kulhavy (1981) had subjects study a map while listening to a narrative describing the territory. Map subjects recalled more spatial information related to map features than nonmap subjects, while there was no difference between recall of the two groups on information not related to map features. In another study, Abel and Kulhavy (1989) found that subjects who saw maps of a territory recalled more details than subjects who read a corresponding text, suggesting that the map provided "second stratum cues" that made it easier to recall information.

5.3.4 Schema-Message Isomorphism: Structural Encoding

Evidence for the claim that graphics help students organize content by determining the structure of the schema in which it is encoded comes from studies that have examined the relationship between spatial presentations and cued or free recall. The assumption is that the spatial structure of the information on the page reflects the semantic structure of the information that gets encoded. For example, Winn (1980) used text with or without a block diagram to teach about a typical food web to high school subjects. Estimates of subjects' semantic structures representing the content were obtained from their free associations to words naming key concepts in the food web (e.g., *consumer herbivore*). It was found that the diagram significantly improved the closeness of the structure the students acquired to the structure of the content.

More recently, McNamara, Hardy, and Hirtle (1989) had subjects learn spatial layouts of common objects. Ordered trees, constructed from free-recall data, revealed hierarchical clusters of items that formed the basis for organizing the information in memory. A recognition test, in which targeted items were primed by items either within or outside the same cluster, produced response latencies that were faster for same-cluster items than for different-item clusters. The placement of an item in one cluster or another was determined, for the most part, by the spatial proximity of the items in the original layout.

In another study, McNamara (1986) had subjects study the layout of real objects placed in an area on the floor. The area was divided by low barriers into four quadrants of equal size. Primed recall produced response latencies suggesting that the physical boundaries imposed categories on the objects when they were encoded that overrode the effect of absolute spatial proximity. For example, recall reposes were slower to items physically close but separated by a boundary than two items further apart but within the same boundary. The results of studies like these have been the basis for recommendations about when and how to use pictures and graphics in instructional materials (Levin, Anglin & Carney, 1987; Winn, 1989b).

5.3.5 Schemata and Information Mapping

Strategies exploiting the structural isomorphism of graphics and knowledge schemata have also formed the basis for a variety of text- and information-mapping schemes aimed at improving comprehension (Armbruster & Anderson, 1982, 1984) and study skills (Dansereau et al., 1979; Holley & Dansereau, 1984). Research on the effectiveness of these strategies and its application is one of the best examples of how cognitive theory has come to be used by instructional designers.

The assumptions underlying all information-mapping strategies are that if information is well organized in memory, it will be better remembered and more easily associated with new information, and that students can be taught techniques exploiting the spatial organization of information on the page that make what they learn better organized in memory (see 24.7). We have already given examples of research that bears out the first of these assumptions. We turn now to research on the effectiveness of information-mapping techniques.

All information-mapping strategies (reviewed and summarized by Hughes, 1989) require students to learn ways to represent information, usually text, in spatially constructed diagrams. With these techniques, they construct diagrams that represent the concepts they are to learn as verbal labels often in boxes and that show interconcept relations as lines or arrows. The most obvious characteristic of these techniques is that students construct the information maps for themselves rather than studying diagrams created by someone else. In this way, the maps require students to process the information they contain in an effortful manner, while allowing a certain measure of idiosyncrasy in the ideas shown, both of which are attributes of effective learning strategies.

Some mapping techniques are radial, with the key concept in the center of the diagram and related concepts on arms reaching out from the center (Hughes, 1989). Other schemes are more hierarchical, with concepts placed on branches of a tree (Johnson, Pittelman & Heimlich, 1986).

Still others maintain the roughly linear format of sentences but use special symbols to encode interconcept relations, like equals signs or different kinds of boxes (Armbruster & Anderson, 1984). Some computer-based systems provide more flexibility by allowing "zooming" in or out on concepts to reveal subconcepts within them and by allowing users to introduce pictures and graphics from other sources (see 24.7; Fisher et al., 1990).

Regardless of format, information mapping has been shown to be effective. In some cases, information-mapping techniques have formed part of study skills curricula (Holley & Dansereau, 1984; Schewel, 1989). In other cases, the technique has been used to improve reading comprehension (Ruddell & Boyle, 1989) or for review at the end of a course (Fisher et al., 1990). Information mapping has been shown to be useful for helping students write about what they have read (Sinatra, Stahl-Gemake & Morgan, 1986) and works with disabled readers as well as with normal ones (Sinatra, Stahl-Gemake & Borg, 1986). Information mapping has proved to be a successful technique in all of these tasks and contexts, showing it to be remarkably robust.

Information mapping can, of course, be used by instructional designers (Jonassen, 1991, 1996; Jonassen, Bersner & Yacci, 1993). In this case, the technique is used not so much to improve comprehension as to help designers understand the relations among concepts in the material they are working with. Often, understanding such relations makes strategy selection more effective. For example, a radial outline based on the concept "zebra" (Hughes, 1989) shows, among other things, that a zebra is a member of the horse family and also that it lives in Africa on the open grasslands. From the layout of the radial map, it is clear that membership of the horse family is a different kind of interconcept relation than the relation with Africa and grasslands. The designer will therefore be likely to organize the instruction so that a zebra's location and habitat are taught together and not at the same time as the zebra's place in the mammalian taxonomy is taught. We will return to instructional designers' use of information mapping techniques in our discussion of cognitive objectives in section 5.5.

All of this seems to suggest that imagery-based and information-structuring strategies based on graphics have been extremely useful in practice. However, the whole idea of isomorphism between an information display outside the learner and the structure and content of a memory schema implies that information in the environment is mapped fairly directly into memory. As we have seen, this basic assumption of much of cognitive theory is currently being seriously challenged. The extent to which this challenge threatens the usefulness of using pictures and graphics in instruction remains to be seen.

5.3.6 Schemata and AI

Another way in which theories of representation have been used in educational technology is to suggest ways in which computer programs designed to "think" like people might represent information. Clearly, this application embodies the "computer models of mind" assumption that we looked at above (Boden, 1988).

The structural nature of schemata makes them particularly attractive to cognitive scientists working in the area of artificial intelligence. The reason for this is that they can be described using the same "language" that is used by computers and therefore provide a convenient link between human and artificial thought. The best examples are to be found in the work of Minsky (1975) and of Schank and his associates (Schank & Abelson, 1977). Here, schemata provide constraints on the meaning of information that the computer and the user share that make the interaction between them more manageable and useful. The constraints arise from only allowing what typically happens in a given situation to be considered. For example, certain actions and verbal exchanges commonly take place in a restaurant. You enter. Someone shows you to your table. Someone brings you a menu. After a while, the waiter comes back, and you order your meal. Your food is brought to you in a predictable sequence. You eat it in a predictable way. When you have finished, someone brings you the bill, which you pay. You leave. It is not likely (though not impossible, of course) that someone will bring you a basketball rather than the food you ordered. Usually, you will eat your food rather than sing to it. You use cash or a credit card to pay for your meal rather than offering a giraffe. In this way, the almost infinite number of things that can occur in the world are constrained to relatively few, which means that the machine has a better chance of figuring out what your words or actions mean.

Even so, schemata (or "scripts" as Schank [1984] calls them) cannot contend with every eventuality. This is because the assumptions about the world that are implicit in our schemata, and therefore often escape our awareness, have to be made explicit in scripts that are used in AI. Schank (1984) provides examples as he describes the difficulties encountered by TALE-SPIN, a program designed to write stories in the style of Aesop's fables.

> One day Joe Bear was hungry. He asked his friend Irving Bird where some honey was. Irving told him there was a beehive in the oak tree. Joe walked to the oak tree. He ate the beehive."

Here, the problem is that we know beehives contain honey, and while they are indeed a source of food, they are not themselves food but contain it. The program did not know this, nor could it infer it. A second example, with Schank's own analysis, makes a similar point:

> Henry Ant was thirsty. He walked over to the river bank where his good friend Bill Bird was sitting. Henry slipped and fell in the river. He was unable to call for help. He drowned.
>
> This was not the story that TALE-SPIN set out to tell. [. . .] Had TALE-SPIN found a way for Henry to call to Bill for help, this would have caused Bill to try to save him. But the program had a rule that said that being in water prevents speech. Bill was not asked a direct question, and there was no way for any character to just happen to notice something. Henry drowned because the program knew that that's

what happens when a character that can't swim is immersed in water (1984, p. 84).

The rules that the program followed, leading to the sad demise of Henry, are rules that normally apply. People do not usually talk when they're swimming. However, in this case, a second rule should have applied, as we who understand a calling-for-help-while-drowning schema are well aware of.

The more general issue that arises from these examples is that people have extensive knowledge of the world that goes beyond any single set of circumstances that might be defined in a script. And human intelligence rests on the judicious use of this general knowledge. Thus, on the rare occasion that we do encounter someone singing to their food in a restaurant, we have knowledge from beyond the immediate context that lets us conclude the person has had too much to drink, or is preparing to sing a role at the local opera and is therefore not really singing to her food at all, or belongs to a cult for whom praising the food about to be eaten in song is an accepted ritual. The problem for the AI designer is therefore how much of this general knowledge to allow the program to have? Too little, and the correct inferences cannot be made about what has happened when there are even small deviations from the norm. Too much, and the task of building a production system that embodies all the possible reasons for something to occur becomes impossibly complex.

It has been claimed that AI has failed (Dreyfus & Dreyfus, 1986) because "intelligent" machines do not have the breadth of knowledge that permits human reasoning. A current project called "Cyc" (Guha & Lenat, 1991; Lenat, Guha, Pittman, Pratt & Shepherd, 1990) has as its goal to imbue a machine with precisely the breadth of knowledge that humans have. Over a period of years, programmers will have worked away at encoding an impressive number of facts about the world. If this project is successful, it will be testimony to the usefulness of general knowledge of the world for problem solving and will confirm the severe limits of a "schema" or "script" approach to AI. It may also suggest that the schema metaphor is misleading. Maybe people do not organize their knowledge of the world in clearly delineated structures. A lot of thinking is "fuzzy," and the boundaries among schemata are permeable and indistinct.

5.3.7 Mental Models

Another way in which theories of representation have influenced research in educational technology is through psychological and human factors research on mental models. A mental model, like a schema, is a putative structure that contains knowledge of the world. For some, mental models and schemata are synonymous. However, there are two properties of mental models that make them somewhat different from schemata. Mayer (1992, p. 431) identifies these as (1) representations of objects in whatever the model describes and (2) descriptions of how changes in one

object effect changes in another. Roughly speaking, a mental model is broader in conception than a schema because it specifies causal actions among objects that take place within it. However, you will find any number of people who disagree with this distinction.

The term *envisionment* is often applied to the representation of both the objects and the causal relations in a mental model (DeKleer & Brown, 1981; Strittmatter & Seel, 1989). This term draws attention to the visual metaphors that often accompany discussion of mental models. When we use a mental model, we "see" a representation of it in our "mind's eye." This representation has spatial properties akin to those we notice with our biological eye. Some objects are "closer to" some than to others. And from seeing changes in our mind's eye in one object occurring simultaneously with changes in another, we infer causality between them. This is especially true when we consciously bring about a change in one object ourselves. For example, Sternberg and Weil (1980) gave subjects such problems to solve as: "If A is bigger than B and C is bigger than A, who is the smallest?" Subjects who changed the representation of the problem by placing the objects A, B, and C in a line from tallest to shortest were most successful in solving the problem, because envisioning it in this way allowed them simply to "see" the answer. Likewise, envisioning what happens in an electrical circuit that includes an electric bell (DeKleer & Brown, 1981) allows someone to come to understand how it works. In short, a mental model can be "run" like a film or computer program and watched in the mind's eye while it is running. You may have observed world-class skiers "running" their model of a slalom course, eyes closed, body leaning into each gate, before they make their run.

The greatest interest in mental models by educational technologists lies in ways of getting learners to create good ones. This implies, as in the case of schema creation, that instructional materials and events act with what learners already understand in order to construct a mental model that the student can use to develop understanding. Just how instruction affects mental models has been the subject of considerable research, summarized by Gentner and Stevens (1983), Mayer (1989a), and Rouse and Morris (1986), among others. At the end of his review, Mayer lists seven criteria that instructional materials should meet to induce mental models that are likely to improve understanding. (Mayer refers to the *materials*, typically illustrations and text, as "conceptual models" that describe in graphic form the objects and causal relations among them.) A good model is: Complete—it contains all the objects, states, and actions of the system; Concise—it contains just enough detail; Coherent—it makes "intuitive sense"; Concrete—it is presented at an appropriate level of familiarity; Conceptual—it is potentially meaningful; Correct—the objects and relations in it correspond to actual objects and events; and Considerate—it uses appropriate vocabulary and organization.

If these criteria are met, then instruction can lead to the

creation of models that help students understand systems and solve problems arising from the way the systems work. For example, Mayer (1989b) and Mayer and Gallini (1990) have demonstrated that materials, conforming to these criteria, in which graphics and text work together to illustrate both the objects and causal relations in systems (hydraulic drum brakes, bicycle pumps) were effective at promoting understanding. Subjects were able to answer questions requiring them to draw inferences from their mental models of the system using information they had not been explicitly taught. For instance, the answer (not explicitly taught) to the question "Why do brakes get hot?" can be found only in an understanding of the causal relations among the pieces of a brake system. A correct answer implies that an accurate mental model has been constructed.

A second area of research on mental models in which educational technologists are now engaging arises from a belief that interactive multimedia systems are effective tools for model building (Hueyching & Reeves, 1992; Kozma, Russell, Jones, Marx & Davis, 1993; Seel & Dörr, 1994). For the first time, we are able, with reasonable ease, to build instructional materials that are both interactive and that, through animation, can represent the changes of state and causal actions of physical systems. Kozma et al. describe a computer system that allows students to carry out simulated chemistry experiments. The graphic component of the system (which certainly meets Mayer's criteria for building a good model) presents information about changes of state and causality within a molecular system. It "corresponds to the molecular-level mental models that chemists have of such systems" (Kozma et al., 1993, p. 16). Analysis of constructed student responses and of think-aloud protocols have demonstrated the effectiveness of this system at helping students construct good mental models of chemical reactions. Byrne, Furness, and Winn (1995) describe a virtual environment in which students learn about atomic and molecular structure by building atoms from their subatomic components. The most successful treatment for building mental models was a highly interactive one.

5.3.8 Mental Representation and the Development of Expertise

The knowledge we represent as schemata or mental models changes as we work with it over time. It becomes much more readily accessible and useable, requiring less conscious effort to use it effectively. At the same time, its own structure becomes more robust, and it is increasingly internalized and automatized. The result is that its application becomes relatively straightforward and automatic, and frequently occurs without our conscious attention. When we drive home after work, we do not have to think hard about what to do or where we are going. It is important in the research that we shall examine below that this process of "knowledge compilation and translation" (Anderson, 1983) is a slow process. One of the biggest oversights in

our field has occurred when instructional designers have assumed that task analysis should describe the behavior of experts rather than novices, completely ignoring the fact that expertise develops in stages and that novices cannot simply "get there" in one jump.

Out of the behavioral tradition that continues to dominate a great deal of thinking in educational technology comes the assumption that it is possible for mastery to result from instruction. In mastery learning, the only instructional variable is the time required to learn something. Therefore, given enough time, anyone can learn anything. The evidence that this is the case is compelling (Bloom, 1984, 1987; Kulik, 1990a, b). However, "enough time" typically comes to mean the length of a unit, module, or semester, and "mastery" means mastery of performance, not of high-level skills such as problem solving.

There is a considerable body of opinion that expertise arises from a much longer exposure to content in a learning environment than that implied in the case of mastery learning. Labouvie-Vief (1990) has suggested that wisdom arises during adulthood from processes that represent a fourth "stage" of human development, beyond Piaget's traditional three. Achieving a high level of expertise in chess (Chase & Simon, 1973) or in the professions (Schon, 1983, 1987) takes many years of learning and applying what one has learned. This implies that learners move through stages on their way from novicehood to expertise, and that, as in the case of cognitive development (Piaget & Inhelder, 1969), each stage is a necessary prerequisite for the next and cannot be skipped. In this case, expertise does not arise directly from instruction. It may start with some instruction, but it develops fully only with maturity and experience on the job (Lave & Wenger, 1991).

An illustrative account of the stages a person goes through on the way to expertise is provided by Dreyfus and Dreyfus (1986). The stages are: novice, advanced beginner, competence, proficiency, and expertise. Dreyfus and Dreyfus's examples are exceptionally useful in clarifying the differences between stages. The following few paragraphs are therefore based on their narrative (1986, pp. 21–35).

Novices learn objective and unambiguous facts and rules about the area that they are beginning to study. These facts and rules are typically learned out of context. For example, beginning nurses learn how to take a patient's blood pressure and are taught rules about what to do if the reading is normal, high, or very high. However, they do not yet necessarily understand what blood pressure really indicates or why the actions specified in the rules are necessary or how they affect the patient's recovery. In a sense, the knowledge they acquire is "inert" (Cognition and Technology Group at Vanderbilt, 1990) in that, though it can be applied, it is applied blindly and without a context or rationale.

Advanced beginners continue to learn more objective facts and rules. However, with their increased practical experience, they also begin to develop a sense of the larger context in which their developing knowledge and skill operate. Within that context, they begin to associate the objective rules and facts they have learned with particular situations they encounter on the job. Their knowledge becomes "situational" or "contextualized." For example, student nurses begin to recognize patients' symptoms by means that cannot be expressed in objective, context-free rules. The way a particular patient's breathing sounds may be sufficient to indicate that a particular action is necessary. However, the sound itself cannot be described objectively, nor can recognizing it be learned anywhere except on the job.

As the student moves into competence and develops further sensitivity to information in the working environment, the number of context-free and situational facts and rules begins to overwhelm the student. The situation can be managed only when the student learns effective decision-making strategies. Student nurses at this stage often appear to be unable to make decisions. They are still keenly aware of the things they have been taught to look out for and the procedures to follow in the maternity ward. However, they are also now sensitive to situations in the ward that require them to change the rules and procedures. They begin to realize that the baby screaming its head off requires immediate attention even if to give that attention is not something set down in the rules. They are torn between doing what they have been taught to do and doing what they sense is more important at that moment. And often they dither, as Dreyfus and Dreyfus put it, ". . . like a mule between two bales of hay" (1986, p. 24).

Proficiency is characterized by quick, effective, and often unconscious decision making. Unlike the merely competent student, who has to think hard about what to do when the situation is at variance with objective rules and prescribed procedures, the proficient student easily grasps what is going on in any situation and acts, as it were, automatically to deal with whatever arises. The proficient nurse simply notices that a patient is psychologically ready for surgery, without consciously weighing the evidence.

With expertise comes the complete fusion of decision making and action. So completely is the expert immersed in the task, and so complete is the expert's mastery of the task and of the situations in which it is necessary to act, that ". . . When things are proceeding normally, experts don't solve problems and don't make decisions; they do what normally works" (Dreyfus & Dreyfus, 1986, pp. 30–31). Clearly, such a state of affairs can arise only after extensive experience on the job. With such experience comes the expert's ability to act quickly and correctly from information without needing to analyze it into components. Expert radiologists can perform accurate diagnoses from X rays by matching the pattern formed by light and dark areas on the film to patterns they have learned over the years to be symptomatic of particular conditions. They act on what they see as a whole and do not attend to each feature separately. Similarly, early research on expertise in chess (Chase & Simon, 1973) revealed that grand masters rely on the recognition of patterns of pieces on the chessboard to guide their play and engage in less in-depth analysis of situations than merely proficient players. Expert nurses sometimes sense that a patient's situation has become critical without there being

any objective evidence, and, although they cannot explain why, they are usually correct.

A number of things are immediately clear from his account of the development of expertise. The first is that any student must start by learning explicitly taught facts and rules even if the ultimate goal is to become an expert who apparently functions perfectly well without using them at all. Spiro et al. (1992) claim that learning by allowing students to construct knowledge only works for "advanced knowledge" that assumes the basics have already been mastered.

Second, though, is the observation that students begin to learn situational knowledge and skills as early as the "advanced beginner" stage. This means that the abilities that appear intuitive, even magical, in experts are already present in embryonic form at a relatively early stage in a student's development. The implication is that instruction should foster the development of situational, nonobjective knowledge and skill as early as possible in a student's education. This conclusion is corroborated by the study of situated learning (Brown, Collins & Duguid, 1989) and apprenticeships (Lave & Wenger, 1991) in which education is situated in real-world contexts from the start (see also 7.4.4, 20.3).

Third is the observation that as students becomes more expert, they are *less* able to rationalize and articulate the reasons for their understanding of a situation and for their solutions to problems. Instructional designers and knowledge engineers generally are acutely aware of the difficulty of deriving a systematic and objective description of knowledge and skills from an expert as they go about content or task analyses. Experts just do things that work and do not engage in specific or describable problem solving. This also means that assessment of what students learn as they acquire expertise becomes increasingly difficult and eventually impossible by traditional means, such as tests. Tacit knowledge (Polanyi, 1962) is extremely difficult to measure.

Finally, we can observe that what educational technologists spend most of their time doing—developing explicit and measurable instruction—is only relevant to the earliest step in the process of acquiring expertise. There are two implications of this. First, we have, until recently, ignored the potential of technology to help people learn anything except objective facts and rules. And these, in the scheme of things we have just described, though necessary, are intended to be quickly superseded by other kinds of knowledge and skills that allow us to work effectively in the world. We might conclude that instructional design, as traditionally conceived, has concentrated on creating nothing more than training wheels for learning and acting that are to be jettisoned for more important knowledge and skills as quickly as possible. The second implication is that by basing instruction on the knowledge and skills of experts, we have completely ignored the protracted development that has led up to that state. The student must go through a number of qualitatively different stages that come between novicehood and expertise, and can no more jump directly from stage 1 to stage 5 than a child can go from Piaget's preoperational stage of development to formal operations without passing through the intervening developmental steps. If we try to teach the skills of the expert directly to novices, we shall surely fail.

The Dreyfus and Dreyfus account is by no means the only description of how people become experts. Nor is it to any great extent given in terms of the underlying psychological processes that enable it to develop. In the next paragraphs, we look briefly at more specific accounts of how expertise is acquired, focusing on two cognitive processes: automaticity and knowledge organization.

5.3.8.1. Automaticity. From all accounts of expertise, it is clear that experts still do the things they learned to do as novices, but, more often than not, they do them without thinking about them. The automatization of cognitive and motor skills is a step along the way to expertise that occurs in just about every explanation of the process. By enabling experts to function without deliberate attention to what they are doing, automaticity frees up cognitive resources that the expert can then bring to bear on problems that arise from unexpected and hitherto unexperienced events, as well as allowing more attention to be paid to the more mundane though particular characteristics of the situation. This has been reported to be the case for such diverse skills as learning psychomotor skills (Romiszowski, 1993), developing skill as a teacher (Leinhart, 1987), typing (Larochelle, 1982), and the interpretation of X rays (Lesgold et al., 1988).

Automaticity occurs as a result of overlearning (Shiffrin & Schneider, 1977). Under the mastery learning model (Bloom, 1984), a student keeps practicing and receiving feedback, iteratively, until some predetermined criterion has been achieved. At that point, the student is taught and practices the next task. In the case of overlearning, the student continues to practice after attaining mastery, even if the achieved criterion is 100% performance. The more students practice using knowledge and skill beyond just mastery, the more fluid and automatic their skill will become. This is because practice leads to discrete pieces of knowledge and discrete steps in a skill becoming fused into larger pieces, or "chunks." Anderson (1983, 1986) speaks of this process as "knowledge compilation" in which declarative knowledge becomes procedural. Just as a computer compiles statements in a computer language into a code that will actually run, so, Anderson claims, the knowledge that we first acquire as explicit assertions of facts or rules is "compiled" by extended practice into knowledge and skill that will run on its own without our deliberately having to attend to them. Likewise, Landa (1983) describes the process whereby knowledge is transformed first into skill and then into ability through practice. At an early stage of learning something, we constantly have to refer to statements in order to be able to think and act. Fluency only comes when we no longer have to refer explicitly to what we know. Further practice will turn skills into abilities that are characterized by being our natural, intuitive manner of doing things.

5.3.8.2. Knowledge Organization. We mentioned briefly above that experts appear to solve problems by recognizing

and interpreting the patterns in bodies of information, not by breaking down the information into its constituent parts. If automaticity corresponds to the "cognitive process" side of expertise, then knowledge organization is the equivalent of "mental representation" of knowledge by experts.

There is considerable evidence that experts organize knowledge in qualitatively different ways from novices. It appears that the chunking of information that is characteristic of experts' knowledge leads them to consider patterns of information when they are required to solve problems rather than improving the way they search through what they know to find an answer. For example, chess masters are far less affected by time pressure than lesser players (Calderwood, Klein & Crandall, 1988). Requiring players to increase the number of moves they make in a minute will obviously reduce the amount of time they have to search through what they know about the relative success of potential moves. However, pattern recognition is a much more instantaneous process and will therefore not be as affected by increasing the number of moves per minute. Since masters were less affected than less-expert players by increasing the speed of a game of chess, it seems that they use pattern recognition rather than search as their main strategy.

Charness (1989) reported changes in a chess player's strategies over a period of 9 years. There was little change in the player's skill at searching through potential moves. However, there were noticeable changes in recall of board positions, evaluation of the state of the game, and chunking of information, all of which, Charness claims, are pattern-related rather than search-related skills. Moreover, Saariluoma (1990) reported, from protocol analysis, that strong chess players in fact engaged in *less* extensive search than intermediate players, concluding that what is searched is more important than how deeply the search is conducted.

It is important to note that some researchers (Patel & Groen, 1991) explicitly discount pattern recognition as the primary means by which some experts solve problems. Also, in a study of expert X-ray diagnosticians, Lesgold et al. (1988) propose that experts' knowledge schemata are developed through "deeper" generalization and discrimination than novices'. It is important to note that in cases where pattern recognition is not taken to be the key to expert performance, studies nonetheless supply evidence of qualitative differences in the nature and use of knowledge between experts and novices.

5.3.9 Summary

In this section we have seen that theories of mental representation have influenced research in educational technology in a number of ways. Schema theory, or something very much like it, is basic to just about all cognitive research on representation. And schema theory is centrally implicated in what we call *message design*. Establishing predictability and control over what appears in instructional materials and how the depicted information is represented has been high on the research agenda. So it has been of prime importance to discover (a) the nature of mental schemata and (b) how changing messages affects how schemata change or are created.

Mental representation is also the key to information-mapping techniques that have proved to help students understand and remember what they read. Here, however, the emphasis is on how the relations among objects and events are encoded and stored in memory and less on how the objects and events are shown. Also, these interconcept relations are often metaphorical. Within the graphical conventions of information maps—hierarchies, radial outlines, and so on—"above," "below," "close to," and "far from" use the metaphor of space to convey semantic, not spatial, structure (see Winn & Solomon, 1991, for research on these "metaphorical" conventions). Nonetheless, the supposition is that representing these relations in some kind of structure in memory improves comprehension and recall.

The construction of schemata as the basis for computer reasoning has not been entirely successful. This is largely because computers are literal minded and cannot draw on general knowledge of the world outside the scripts they are programmed to follow. The results of this, for storywriting at least, are often whimsical and humorous. However, some would claim that the broader implication is that AI is impossible to attain.

Mental model theory has a lot in common with schema theory. However, studies of comprehension and transfer of changes of state and causality in physical systems suggest that well-developed mental models can be "envisioned" and "run" as students seek answers to questions. The ability of multimedia computer systems to show the dynamic interactions of components suggests that this technology has the potential for helping students develop models that represent the world in accurate and accessible ways.

The way in which mental representation changes with the development of expertise has perhaps received less attention from educational technolgists than it should. This is partly because instructional prescriptions and instructional design procedures (particularly the techniques of task analysis) have not taken into account the stages a novice must go through on the way to expertise, each of which requires the development of qualitiatively different forms of knowledge. This is an area to which educational technologists could profitably devote more of their attention.

5.4 MENTAL PROCESSES

The second major body of research in cognitive science has sought to explain the mental processes that operate on the representations we construct of our knowledge of the world. Of course, it is not possible to separate our understanding, nor our discussion, of representations and processes. Indeed, the sections on mental models and expertise made this abundantly clear! However, a body of research exists that has tended to focus more on process than representation. It is to this that we now turn.

All of what follows in this section rests on the assumption that cognitive actions operate on mental representations. As the cognitive actions occur, mental representations change in some way. And changes in mental representations mean changes in our knowledge of the world, which we call *learning*. By and large, we can therefore think of three families of cognitive processes, each bringing about its own kind of change in mental representation, and therefore resulting in its own kind of learning. The distinctions, predictably, are not always clear. But the three kinds of mental processes have to do with (1) information processing, (2) symbol manipulation, and (3) knowledge construction. We shall examine each of these in turn.

5.4.1 Information-Processing Accounts of Cognition

As we have seen, one of the basic tenets of cognitive theory is that information that is present in an instructional stimulus is acted on by a variety of mediating variables before the student produces a response. Information-processing accounts of cognition describe stages that information moves through in the cognitive system and suggests processes that operate at each step. We therefore begin this section with a general account of information processing in human beings. This account sets the stage for our consideration of cognition as symbol manipulation and as knowledge construction.

Although the rise of information-processing accounts of cognition cannot be ascribed uniquely to the development of the computer, the early cognitive psychologists' descriptions of human thinking use distinctly computerlike terms. Like computers, people were supposed to take information from the environment into "buffers," to "process" it before "storing it in memory." Information-processing models describe the nature and function of putative "units" within the human perceptual and cognitive systems, and how they interact. They trace their origins to Atkinson and Shiffrin's (1968) model of memory, which was the first to suggest that memory consisted of a sensory register, a long-term and a short-term store. According to Atkinson and Shiffrin's account, information is registered by the senses and then placed into a short-term storage area. Here, unless it is worked with in a "rehearsal buffer," it decays after about 15 seconds. If information in the short-term store is rehearsed to any significant extent, it stands a chance of being placed into the long-term store, where it remains more or less permanently. With no more than minor changes, this model of human information processing has persisted in the instructional technology literature (R. Gagné, 1974; E. Gagné, 1985) and in recent ideas about long-term and short-term, or working, memory (Gagné & Glaser, 1987). The importance that every instructional designer gives to practice stems from the belief that rehearsal improves the chance of information passing into long-term memory.

A major problem that this approach to explaining human cognition pointed to was the relative inefficiency of human beings at information processing. This is to be a result of the limited capacity of working memory to roughly seven (Miller, 1956) or five (Simon, 1974) pieces of information at one time. (E. Gagné [1985, p. 13] makes an interesting comparison between a computer's and a person's capacity to process information. The computer wins handily. However, human capacity to be creative, to imagine, and to solve complex problems does not enter into the equation.) It therefore became necessary to modify the basic model to account for these observations. One modification arose from studies like those of Shiffrin and Schneider (1977) and Schneider and Shiffrin (1977). In a series of memory experiments, these researchers demonstrated that, with sufficient rehearsal, people automatize what they have learned so that what was originally a number of discrete items become one single "chunk" of information. With what is referred to as "overlearning," the limitations of working memory can be overcome. The notion of chunking information in order to make it possible for people to remember collections of more than five things has become quite prevalent in the information-processing literature (see Anderson, 1983). And rehearsal strategies intended to induce chunking became part of the standard repertoire of tools used by instructional designers.

Another problem with the basic information-processing account arose from research on memory for text in which it was demonstrated that people remembered the ideas of passages rather than the text itself (Bransford & Franks, 1971; Bransford & Johnson, 1972). This suggested that what was passed from working memory to long-term memory was not a direct representation of the information in short-term memory but a more abstract representation of its meaning. These abstract representations are, of course, schemata, which we discussed at some length earlier. Schema theory added a whole new dimension to ideas about information processing. So far, information-processing theory assumed that the driving force of cognition was the information that was registered by the sensory buffers—that cognition was data driven, or bottom-up. Schema theory proposed that information was, at least in part, top-down. This meant, according to Neisser (1976), that cognition is driven as much as by what we know as by the information we take in at a given moment. In other words, the contents of long-term memory play a large part in the processing of information that passes through working memory. For instructional designers, it became apparent that strategies were required that guided top-down processing by activating relevant schemata and aided retrieval by providing the correct context for recall. The "elaboration theory of instruction" (Reigeluth & Stein, 1983; Reigeluth & Curtis, 1987) achieves both of these ends (see 18.4.3). Presenting an epitome of the content at the beginning of instruction activates relevant schemata. Providing synthesizers at strategic points during instruction helps students remember, and integrate, what they have learned up to that point.

Bottom-up, information-processing approaches have recently regained ground in cognitive theory as the result of the recognition of the importance of preattentive perceptual processes (Marr, 1982; Arbib & Hanson, 1987; Boden,

1988; Treisman, 1988; Pomerantz, Pristach & Carlson, 1989). Our overview of cognitive science, mentioned before, described computational approaches to cognition. In this return to a bottom-up approach, however, we can see marked differences from the bottom-up, information-processing approaches of the 60s and 70s. Bottom-up processes are now clearly confined within the barrier of what Pylyshyn (1984) called *cognitive impenetrability*. These are processes over which we can have no attentive, conscious, effortful control. Nonetheless, they impose a considerable amount of organization on the information we receive from the world. In vision, for example, it is likely that all information about the organization of a scene, except for some depth cues, is determined preattentively (Marr, 1982). What is more, preattentive perceptual structure predisposes us to make particular interpretations of information, top-down (Owens, 1985a, 1985b; Duong, 1994). In other words, the way our perception processes information determines how our cognitive system will process it. Subliminal advertising works!

Although we still talk rather glibly about short-term and long-term memory and use rather loosely other terms that come from information-processing models of cognition, information-processing theories have matured considerably since they first appeared in the late 50s. The balance between bottom-up and top-down theories, achieved largely within the framework of computational theories of cognition, offers researchers a good conceptual framework within which to design and conduct studies. Equally, instructional designers who are serious about bringing cognitive theory into educational technology will find in this latest incarnation of information-processing theory an empirically valid and rationally tenable basis for making decisions about instructional strategies.

5.4.2 Cognition as Symbol Manipulation

How is information that is processed by the cognitive system represented by it? One very popular answer is "as symbols." This notion lies close to the heart of cognitive science and, as we saw in the very first section of this chapter, it is also the source of some of the most virulent attacks on cognitive theory (Clancey, 1993). The idea is that we think by mentally manipulating symbols that are representations, in our mind's eye, of referents in the real world. There is a direct mapping between objects and actions in the external world and the symbols we use internally to represent them. Our manipulation of these symbols places them into new relationships with each other, allowing new insights into objects and phenomena. Our ability to reverse the process by means of which the world was originally encoded as symbols therefore allows us to act on the real world in new and potentially more effective ways.

We need to consider both how well people can manipulate symbols mentally and what happens as a result. The clearest evidence for people's ability to manipulate symbols in their "mind's eye" comes from Kosslyn's (1985) studies of mental imagery. Kosslyn's basic research paradigm was to have his subjects create a mental image and then to instruct them directly to change it in some way, usually by "zooming" in and out on it. Evidence for the success of his subjects at doing this was found in their ability to answer questions about properties of the imaged objects that could only be inspected as a result of such manipulation.

The work of Shepard and his colleagues (Shepard & Cooper, 1982) represents another "classical" case of our ability to manipulate images in our mind's eye. The best known of Shepard's experimental methods is as follows. Subjects are shown two three-dimensional solid figures seen from different angles. The figures may be the same or different. The subjects are asked to judge whether the figures are the same or different. In order to make the judgment, it is necessary to rotate mentally one of the figures in three dimensions in an attempt to orient it to the same position as the target, so that a direct comparison may be made. Shepard consistently found that the time it took to make the judgment was almost perfectly correlated with the number of degrees through which the figure had to be rotated, suggesting that the subject was rotating it in real time in the mind's eye.

Finally, Salomon (1979) speaks more generally of "symbol systems" and of people's ability to internalize them and use them as "tools for thought." In an early experiment (Salomon, 1974), he had subjects study paintings in one of the following three conditions: (a) A film showed the entire picture, zoomed in on a detail, and zoomed out again, for a total of 80 times. (b) The film cut from the whole picture directly to the detail without the transitional zooming. (c) The film showed just the whole picture. In a posttest of cue attendance, in which subjects were asked to write down as many details as they could from a slide of another picture, low-ability subjects performed better if they were in the "zooming" group. High-ability subjects did better if they just saw the entire picture. Salomon concluded that zooming in and out on details, which is a symbolic element in the symbol system of film, television, and any form of motion picture, modeled for the low-ability subjects a strategy for cue attendance that they could execute for themselves cognitively. This was not necessary for the high-ability subjects. Indeed, there was evidence that modeling the zooming strategy reduced performance of high-ability subjects because it got in the way of mental processes that were activated without prompting. Bovy (1983) found results similar to Salomon's using "irising" rather than zooming. A similar interaction between ability and modeling was reported by Winn (1986) for serial and parallel pattern-recall tasks.

Salomon has continued to develop the notion of internalized symbol systems serving as cognitive tools. Educational technologists have been particularly interested in his research on how the symbolic systems of computers can "become cognitive," as he put it (Salomon, 1988). The internalization of the symbolic operations of computers led to the development of a word processor, called the "Writing Partner" (Salomon, Perkins & Globerson, 1991), that

helped students write. The results of a number of experiments showed that interacting with the computer led the users to internalize a number of its ways of processing, which led to improved metacognition relevant to the writing task. Most recently (Salomon, 1993), this idea has evolved even further, to encompass the notion of distributing cognition among students and machines (and, of course, other students).

This research has had two main influences on educational technology. The first, derived from work in imagery of the kind reported by Kosslyn and Shepard, provided an attractive theoretical basis for the development of instructional systems that incorporate large amounts of visual material (Winn, 1980, 1982). The promotion and study of visual literacy (Dondis, 1973; Sless, 1981) is one manifestation of this activity. A number of studies have shown that the use of visual instructional materials can be beneficial for some students studying some kinds of content. For example, Dwyer (1972, 1978) has conducted an extensive research program on the differential benefits of different kinds of visual materials, and has generally reported that realistic pictures are good for identification tasks, line drawings for teaching structure and function, and so on. Explanations for these different effects rest on the assumption that different ways of encoding material facilitate some cognitive processes rather than others—that some materials are more effectively manipulated in the mind's eye for given tasks than others.

The second influence of this research on educational technology has been in the study of the interaction between technology and cognitive systems. Salomon's research, which we just described, is of course an example of this. The work of Papert and his colleagues at MIT's Media Lab is another important example. Papert (1983) began by proposing that young children can learn the "powerful ideas" that underlie reasoning and problem solving by working (perhaps *playing* is the more appropriate term) in a microworld over which they have control. The archetype of such a microworld is the well-known LOGO environment (see 24.5.1.3) in which the student solves problems by instructing a "turtle" to perform certain tasks. Learning occurs when the children develop problem definition and debugging skills as they write programs for the turtle to follow. Working with LOGO, children develop fluency in problem solving as well as specific skills, like problem decomposition and the ability to modularize problem solutions. Like Salomon's (1988) subjects, the children who work with LOGO (and in other technology-based environments [Harel & Papert, 1991]) internalize a lot of the computer's ways of using information and develop skills in symbol manipulation that they use to solve problems.

There is, of course, a great deal of research into problem solving through symbol manipulation that is not concerned particularly with technology. The work of Simon and his colleagues is central to this research. (See Klahr & Kotovsky's [1989] edited volume that pays tribute to his work.) It is based largely on the notion that human reasoning operates by applying rules to encoded information that manipulate the information in such a way as to reveal solutions to problems. The information is encoded as a "production system" that operates by testing whether the conditions of rules are true or not, and following specific actions if they are (see also 24.8.1). A simple example: "If the sum of an addition of a column of digits is greater than 10, then write down the right-hand integer and carry 1 to add to the next column." The "if . . . then . . ." structure is a simple production system in which a mental action is carried out (add 1 to the next column) if a condition is true (the number is greater than 10).

An excellent illustration is to be found in Larkin and Simon's (1987) account of the superiority of diagrams over text for solving certain classes of problems. Here, they develop a production system model of pulley systems to explain how the number of pulleys attached to a block, and the way in which they are connected, affects the amount of weight that can be raised by a given force. The model is quite complex. It is based on the idea that people need to search through the information presented to them in order to identify the conditions of a rule (e.g., if a rope passes over two pulleys between its point of attachment 'and a load, its mechanical advantage is doubled) and then compute the results of applying the production rule in those given circumstances. The two steps, searching for the conditions of the production rule and computing the consequences of its application, draw on cognitive resources (memory and processing) to different degrees. Larkin and Simon's argument is that diagrams require less effort to search for the conditions and to perform the computation, which is why they are so often more successful than text for problem solving.

It is easier to explain the symbol manipulation required to search for information and use it to compute the answer to a question with a simpler example. Winn, Li, and Schill (1991) conducted an empirical test of some aspects of Larkin and Simon's account using family trees rather than pulley systems. Subjects examined either family trees or statements about who was related to whom. They were given questions to answer about kinship, such as, "Is Mary Jack's second cousin?" The dependent measure of most interest was the speed at which subjects were able to answer the questions. Arguing that the information presented in the text required more cognitive manipulation than that provided by the family trees, from which answers could be obtained by simple inspection, it was expected that subjects seeing diagrams would be able to answer kinship questions quicker than those who saw text. This turned out to be the case.

These results, along with analysis of strategies that subjects used to find answers to the questions, supported the following interpretation. The text condition provided simple factual statements about who was whose parent, such as "Jack is Mary's parent; Jack is Edward's parent; Mary is Penny's parent. . . ." To answer a question from

text, such as, "Is Amy Joseph's first cousin?", the subject has to read through the list until the first relevant piece of information was found, which in this case would be a statement about who Amy's parent was. That information had to be stored in memory, while the second piece of information, about Joseph's parents, was sought and remembered. For first cousins, it was necessary to repeat this search-and-store process twice more, to find who were the parents of Amy's and Joseph's parents, before all the conditions of the production could be satisfied. This required encoding and retrieval of at least four pieces of information, assuming the subject was 100% efficient. Next, the answer had to be computed from this information. Either the lineage of Amy and Joseph made them second cousins or it did not.

In the case of family trees, once the first person in the problem had been found, all that was necessary to do was to trace up and down the tree the required number of branches and read off the name at the end. Nothing had to be stored in memory, and no computations were required. This, of course, was only the case when kinship terms (*cousin, sibling*) and the conventions of family trees were known to subjects. When this was not the case, and subjects had to apply kinship rules explicitly, the advantage of the graphic was reduced. For example, in one experiment, some subjects worked with Chinese names and kinship terms defined for them in a rule. So the requirements of symbol manipulation to solve problems are removed when the conventions of the graphic representation are known. Interestingly, the most rapid responses were given by subjects, in the graphic condition, who were told no kinship rules at all. They simply used their knowledge that cousins are always on the same level of a family tree and did not examine parents at all.

This study, and Larkin and Simon's production system model that lay behind it, illustrate very well the symbol manipulation approach to theories of cognitive processing. In the case of both pulleys and families, subjects encode objects (pulleys, ropes, weights, people's names, and kinship) as symbols that they are required to store in memory and manipulate through comparisons, tracing relationships among them, and so on. When the symbols are represented as diagrams of pulley systems or family trees, relationships among them that are crucial to understanding the systems, and answering questions about them are made explicit by their relative placement on the page and by drawings of the links among them: ropes between pairs of pulleys, lines between names in the family tree. This makes the search for conditions of production rules much simpler and does not draw on memory at all. Computation consists of reading off the answer once all the conditions have been met. If, in addition, the graphic representation uses conventions with which the reader is familiar, search and computation can be short-circuited completely, making the task trivial by comparison.

Many other examples of symbol manipulation through production systems exist. In the area of mathematics education, the interested reader will wish to look at projects reported by Resnick (1976) and Greeno (1980) in which instruction makes it easier for students to encode and manipulate mathematical concepts and relations. Applications of Anderson's (1983) ACT* production system in intelligent computer-based tutors to teach geometry, algebra, and LISP are also illustrative (Anderson & Reiser, 1985; Anderson, Boyle & Yost, 1985).

For the educational technologist, the question arises of how to make symbol manipulation easier so that problems may be solved more rapidly and accurately. Larkin and Simon and Winn, Li, and Schill show that one way to do this is to show conceptual relationships by layout and links in a graphic. A related body of research concerns the relations between illustrations and text. (See summaries in Willows & Houghton, 1987; Houghton & Willows, 1987; Mandl & Levin, 1989; Schnotz & Kulhavy, 1994.) Central to this research is the idea that pictures and words can work together to help students understand information more effectively and efficiently. There is now considerable evidence that people encode information in one of two memory systems, a verbal system and an imaginal system. This "dual coding" (Paivio, 1983; Clark & Paivio, 1991) or "conjoint retention" (Kulhavy, Lee & Caterino, 1985) has two major advantages. The first is redundancy. Information that is hard to recall from one source is still available in the other. Second is the uniqueness of each coding system. As Levin, Anglin, and Carney (1987) have ably demonstrated, different types of illustration are particularly good at performing unique functions. Realistic pictures are good for identification, cutaways and line drawings for showing the structure or operation of things. Text is more appropriate for discursive and more abstract presentations.

Specific guidelines for instructional design have been drawn from this research, many presented in the summaries mentioned in the previous paragraph. Other useful sources are chapters by Mayer and by Winn in Fleming and Levie's (1993) volume on message design. The theoretical basis for these principles is by and large the facilitation of symbol manipulation in the mind's eye that comes from certain types of presentation.

However, as we saw at the beginning of this chapter, the basic assumption that we think by manipulating symbols that represent objects and events in the real world has been called into question (Clancey, 1993). There are a number of grounds for this criticism. The most compelling is that we do not carry around in our heads representations that are accurate "maps" of the world. Schemata, mental models, symbol systems, search, and computation are all metaphors that give a superficial appearance of validity because they predict behavior. However, the essential processes that underlie the metaphors are more amenable to genetic and biological than to psychological analysis. We are, after all, living systems that have evolved like other living systems. And our minds are embodied in our brains, which are organs just like any other. We shall leave the implications of this line of argument to those writing other chapters in this handbook. For now, we shall turn to a relatively uncon-

troversial and well-rooted corollary, that people construct knowledge for themselves rather than receiving it from someone else.

5.4.3 Cognition as Knowledge Construction

One result of the mental manipulation of symbols is that new concepts can be created. Our combining and recombining of mentally represented phenomena leads to the creation of new schemata that may or may not correspond to things in the real world. When this activity is accompanied by constant interaction with the environment in order to verify new hypotheses about the world, we can say that we are accommodating our knowledge to new experiences in the "classic" interactions described by Neisser (1976) and Piaget (1968), mentioned earlier. When we construct new knowledge without direct reference to the outside world, then we are perhaps at our most creative, conjuring from memories thoughts and expressions of it that are entirely novel.

When we looked at schema theory, we described Neisser's (1976) "perceptual cycle," which describes how what we know directs how we seek information; how we seek information determines what information we get; and how the information we receive affects what we know. This description of knowledge acquisition provides a good account of how top-down processes, driven by knowledge we already have, interact with bottom-up processes, driven by information in the environment, to enable us to assimilate new knowledge and accommodate what we already know to make it compatible.

What arises from this description, which we did not make explicit earlier, is that the perceptual cycle and thus the entire knowledge acquisition process is centered on the person not the environment. Some (Duffy & Jonassen, 1992; Cunningham, 1992a; and Chapters 7 and 23 in this handbook) extend this notion to mean that the schemata a person constructs do not correspond in any absolute or objective way to the environment. A person's understanding is therefore built from that person's adaptations to the environment entirely in terms of the experience and understanding that the person has already constructed. There is no process whereby representations of the world are directly "mapped" onto schemata. We do not carry representational images of the world in our mind's eye. Semiotic theory, which has recently made an appearance on the educational stage (Cunningham, 1992b; Driscoll, 1990; Driscoll & Lebow, 1992) goes one step further, claiming that we do not apprehend the world directly at all. Rather, we experience it through the signs we construct to represent it. Nonetheless, if students are given responsibility for constructing their own signs and knowledge of the world, semiotic theory can guide the development and implementation of learning activities as Winn, Hoffman, and Osberg (1995) have demonstrated.

A thorough discussion of these ideas takes place in Chapters 7 and 23 and so will therefore not be pursued here. What is of relevance in this discussion of cognitive processes, however, is the notion that people do construct understanding for themselves in ways that are often idiosyncratic and that often defy expression to someone else. We all "know the world" in ways that differ, sometimes quite sharply, from other people. This idiosyncracy of knowledge has led some (Merrill, 1992) to react severely against instructional theories that aim at fostering construction of knowledge that varies among individuals on the grounds that some knowledge and skills must be acquired and expressed in a uniform manner. Idiosyncratic understanding of brain surgery or how to fly a plane could lead to disaster! However, one can reasonably make the case that some knowledge can be, indeed is best, constructed by individuals for themselves without the imposition of a right answer or a correct set of actions to follow as a result.

The significance of knowledge construction for educational technology lies in its marking a shift away from didactic, content-specific instruction to building environments that make it easy for students to construct their understanding of knowledge domains. Zuccermaglio (1993) describes "filled" and "empty" technologies. The former are instructional systems, like CAI and intelligent tutors, that consist of shells plus content. For example, Anderson, Boyle, and Yost's (1985) algebra tutor consists of a variety of generic components, found in any intelligent tutorial, such as the capability of constructing a student model, of making inferences, and so on (see chapters in Polson & Richardson, 1988). In addition, it contains a knowledge base about algebra from which the other components draw. On the other hand, empty technologies are shells that provide teachers and students with the capability of interacting with content, exploring information, and creating output, but which do not contain a predetermined knowledge base. An example is the "Bubble Dialogue" project (McMahon & O'Neil, 1993), which consists of a HyperCard stack that permits students to construct dialogues. The program allows students to write both the overt speech and the covert thoughts of the characters whose roles they play. Yet what the students write about is not prescribed, and the tool has been used for many purposes ranging from teaching writing to developing understanding about social problems.

If cognition is understood to involve the construction of knowledge by students, it is therefore essential that they be given the freedom to do so. This means that, within Spiro et al.'s (1992) constraints of "advanced knowledge acquisition in ill-structured domains," instruction is less concerned with content, and sometimes only marginally so. Instead, educational technologists need to become more concerned with how students interact with the environments within which technology places them and with how objects and phenomena in those environments appear and behave. This requires educational technologists to read carefully in the area of human factors (for example, Ellis, 1993; Barfield & Furness, 1995) where a great deal of research exists on the cognitive consequences of human-machine interaction. It requires less emphasis on instructional design's traditional attention to task and content analysis. It requires alternative ways of thinking about (Winn, 1993b) and doing (Cunningham, 1992a) evaluation. In short, it is only through the cognitive activity that interaction with content engenders, not the content itself, that people can learn anything at all.

5.4.4 Summary

Information-processing models of cognition have had a great deal of influence on research and practice of educational technology. Instructional designers' day-to-day frames of reference for thinking about cognition, such as working memory and long-term memory, come directly from information-processing theory. The emphasis on rehearsal in many instructional strategies arises from the small capacity of working memory. Attempts to overcome for this problem have led designers to develop all manner of strategies to induce chunking. Information-processing theories of cognition continue to serve our field well.

Research into cognitive processes involved in symbol manipulation have been influential in the development of intelligent tutoring systems (Wenger, 1987), as well as in information-processing accounts of learning and instruction. The result has been that the conceptual bases for some (though not all) instructional theory and instructional design models have embodied a production system approach to instruction and instructional design (see Landa, 1983; Scandura, 1983; Merrill, 1992). To the extent that symbol manipulation accounts of cognition are being challenged, these approaches to instruction and instructional design are also challenged by association.

Accounts of learning through the construction of knowledge by students have been generally well accepted since the mid-70s and have served as the basis for a number of the assumptions educational technologists have made about how to teach. Attempts to set instructional design firmly on cognitive foundations (DiVesta & Rieber, 1987; Bonner, 1988; Tennyson & Rasch, 1988) reflect this orientation. We examine these in the next section.

5.5 COGNITIVE THEORY AND EDUCATIONAL TECHNOLOGY

Educational technology has for some time been influenced by developments in cognitive psychology. Up until now, we have focused mainly on research that has fallen outside the traditional bounds of our field. We have referred to sources in philosophy, psychology, computer science, and so on. In this section, we review the work of those who bear the title "educational technologist" who have been primarily responsible for bringing cognitive theory to our field. We are, again, of necessity selective, focusing on the applied side of our field, instructional design. We begin with some observations about what scholars consider design to be. We then examine the assumptions that underlay behavioral theory and practice at the time when instructional design became established as a discipline. We then argue that research in our field has helped the theory that designers use to make decisions about how to instruct keep up with developments in cognitive theory. However, design procedures have not evolved as they should have. We conclude with some implications about where design should go.

5.5.1 Theory, Practice, and Instructional Design

At the beginning of this chapter we noted that the discipline of educational technology hit its stride during the heyday of behaviorism. This historical fact was entirely fortuitous. Indeed, our field could have started equally well under the influence of Gestalt or of cognitive theory. However, the consequences of this coincidence have been profound and to some extent troublesome for our field. To explain why, we need to examine the nature of the relationship between theory and practice in our field. (Our argument is equally applicable to any discipline.)

The purpose of any applied field, such as educational technology, is to improve practice. The way in which theory guides that practice is through what Simon (1981) and Glaser (1976) call *design*. The purpose of design, seen this way, is to select the alternative from among several courses of action that will lead to the best results. Since these results may not be optimal, but the best one can expect given the state of our knowledge at any particular time, design works through a process Simon (1981) calls *satisficing*.

The degree of success of our activity as instructional designers relies on two things: first, the validity of our knowledge of effective instruction in a given subject domain and, second, the reliability of our procedures for applying that knowledge. Here is an example. We are given the task of writing a computer program that teaches the formation of regular English verbs in the past tense. To simplify matters, let us assume that we know the subject matter perfectly. As subject-matter specialists, we know a procedure for accomplishing the task: Add *ed* to the infinitive, and double the final consonant if it is immediately preceded by a vowel. Would our instructional strategy therefore be to do nothing more than show a sentence on the computer screen that says, "Add *ed* to the infinitive, and double the final consonant if it is immediately preceded by a vowel"? Probably not (though such a strategy might be all that is needed for students who already understand the meanings of *infinitive, vowel,* and *consonant*). If we know something about instruction, we will probably consider a number of other strategies as well. Maybe the students would need to see examples of correct and incorrect verb forms. Maybe they would need to practice forming the past tense of a number of verbs. Maybe they would need to know how well they were doing. Maybe they would need a mechanism that explained and corrected their errors. The act of designing our instructional computer program in fact requires us to choose from among these and other strategies

the ones that are most likely to "satisfice" the requirement of constructing the past tense of regular verbs.

Knowing subject matter and something about instruction are therefore not enough. We need to know how to choose among alternative instructional strategies. Reigleuth (1983) has pointed the way. He observes that the instructional theory that guides instructional designers' choices is made up of statements about relations among the conditions, methods, and outcomes of instruction. When we apply prescriptive theory, knowing instructional conditions and outcomes leads to the selection of an appropriate method. For example, an instructional prescription might consist of the statement, "To teach how to form the past tense of regular English verbs (outcome) to advanced students of English who are familiar with all relevant grammatical terms and concepts (conditions), present them with a written description of the procedure to follow (method)." All the designer needs to do is learn a large number of these prescriptions and all is well.

There are a number of difficulties with this example, however. First, instructional prescriptions rarely, if at all, consist of statements at the level of specificity as the previous one about English verbs. Any theory gains power by its generality. This means that instructional theory contains statements that have a more general applicability, such as "to teach a procedure to a student with a high level of entering knowledge, describe the procedure." Knowing only a prescription at this level of generality, the designer of the verb program needs to determine whether the outcome of instruction is indeed a procedure—it could be a concept, or a rule, or require problem solving—and whether or not the students have a high level of knowledge when they start the program.

A second difficulty arises if the designer is not a subject-matter specialist, which is often the case faced by designers. In our example, this means that the designer has to find out that "forming the past tense of English verbs" requires adding *ed* and doubling the consonant.

Finally, the prescription itself might not be valid. Any instructional prescription that is derived empirically, from an experiment or from observation and experience, is always a generalization from a limited set of cases. It could be that the present case is an exception to the general rule. The designer needs to establish whether or not this is so.

These three difficulties point to the requirement that instructional designers know how to perform analyses that lead to the level of specificity required by the instructional task. We all know what these are. Task analysis permits the instructional designer to identify exactly what the student must achieve in order to attain the instructional outcome. Learner analysis allows the designer to determine the most critical of the conditions under which instruction is to take place. And the classification of tasks, described by task analysis, as facts, concepts, rules, procedures, problem solving, and so on links the designer's particular case to more general prescriptive theory. Finally, if the particular case the designer is working on is an exception to the general prescription, the designer will have to experiment with a variety of potentially effective strategies in order to find the best one, in effect inventing a new instructional prescription along the way.

Even from this simple example, it is clear that, in order to be able to select the best instructional strategies, the instructional designer needs to know *both* instructional theory *and* how to do task and learner analysis, to classify learning outcomes into some theoretically sound taxonomy, and to reason about instruction in the absence of prescriptive principles. Our field, then, like any applied field, provides to its practitioners both theory and procedures through which to apply the theory. These procedures are predominantly, though not exclusively, analytical.

Embedded in any theory are sets of assumptions that are amenable to empirical verification. If the assumptions are shown to be false, then the theory must be modified or abandoned as a paradigm shift takes place (Kuhn, 1970). The effects of these basic assumptions are clearest in the physical sciences. For example, the assumption in modern physics that it is impossible for the speed of objects to exceed that of light is so basic that, if it were to be disproved, the entire edifice of physics would come tumbling down. What is equally important is that the procedures for applying theory rest on the same set of assumptions. The design of everything from cyclotrons to radio telescopes relies on the inviolability of the "light barrier."

It would seem reasonable, therefore, that both the theory and procedures of instruction should rest on the same set of assumptions and, further, that should the assumptions of instructional theory be shown to be invalid, the procedures of instructional design should be revised to accommodate the paradigm shift. In the next section, we show that this was the case when instructional design established itself within our field within the behavioral paradigm. However, we do not believe that this is the case today.

5.5.2 The Legacy of Behaviorism

The most fundamental principle of behavioral theory is that there is a predictable and reliable link between a stimulus and the response it produces in a student. Behavioral instructional theory therefore consists of prescriptions for what stimuli to employ if a particular response is intended (see 2.2.1.3). The instructional designer can be reasonably certain that with the right sets of instructional stimuli all manner of learning outcomes can be attained. Indeed, behavioral theories of instruction can be quite intricate (Gropper, 1983) and can account for the acquisition of quite complex behaviors. This means that a basic assumption of behavioral theories of instruction is that human behavior is predictable. The designer assumes that if an instructional strategy, made up of stimuli, has had a certain effect in the past, it will probably do so again.

The assumption that behavior is predictable also underlies the procedures that instructional designers originally developed to implement behavioral theories of instruction

(Andrews & Goodson, 1981; Gagné, Briggs & Wager 1988; Gagné & Dick, 1983). If behavior is predictable, then all the designer needs to do is to identify the subskills the student must master that, in aggregate, permit the intended behavior to be learned, and select the stimulus and strategy for its presentation that builds each subskill. In other words, task analysis, strategy selection, try-out, and revision also rest on the assumption that behavior is predictable. The procedural counterpart of behavioral instructional theory is therefore analytical and empirical, that is, reductionist. If behavior is predictable, then the designer can select the most effective instructional stimuli simply by following the procedures described in an instructional design model. Instructional failure is ascribed to the lack of sufficient information, which can be corrected by doing more analysis and formative testing.

5.5.3 Cognitive Theory and the Predictability of Behavior

The main theme of this chapter has been cognitive theory. We have argued that cognitive theory provides a much more complete account of human learning and behavior because it considers factors that mediate between the stimulus and the response, such as mental processes and the internal representations that they create. We have documented the ascendancy of cognitive theory and its replacement of behavioral theory as the dominant paradigm in educational psychology and technology. However, the change from behavioral to cognitive theories of learning and instruction has not been accompanied by a parallel change in the procedures of instructional design through which the theory is implemented.

You might well ask why a change in theory should be accompanied by a change in procedures for its application. The reason is that cognitive theory has essentially invalidated the basic assumption of behavioral theory, that behavior is predictable. Since the same assumption underlies the analytical, empirical, and reductionist technology of instructional design, the validity of instructional design procedures is inevitably called into question.

Cognitive theory's challenges to the predictability of behavior are numerous and have been described in detail elsewhere (Winn, 1987, 1990, 1993). The main points may be summarized as follows:

1. Instructional theory is incomplete. This point is trivial at first glance. However, it reminds us that there is not a prescription for every possible combination of instructional conditions, methods, and outcomes. In fact, instructional designers frequently have to select strategies without guidance from instructional theory. This means that there are often times when there are no prescriptions with which to predict student behavior.

2. Mediating cognitive variables differ in their nature and effect from individual to individual. There is a good chance that everyone's response to the same stimulus

will be different because everyone's experiences, in relation to which the stimulus will be processed, are different. The role of individual differences in learning and their relevance to the selection of instructional strategies has been a prominent theme in cognitive theory for 2 decades (Cronbach & Snow, 1977; Snow, 1992). Individual differences make it extremely difficult to predict learning outcomes for two reasons. First, to choose effective strategies for students, it would be necessary to know far more about the student than is easily discovered. The designer would need to know the student's aptitude for learning the given knowledge or skills, the student's prior knowledge, motivation, beliefs about the likelihood of success, learning style, level of anxiety, and stage of intellectual development. Such a prospect would prove daunting even to the most committed determinist! Second, for prescriptive theory, it would be necessary to construct an instructional prescription for every possible permutation of, say, high, low, and average levels on every factor that determines an individual difference. This obviously would render instructional theory too complex to be useful for the designer. In both the case of the individual student and of theory, the interactions among many factors make it impossible in practice to predict what the outcomes of instruction will be. One way around this problem has been to let students decide strategies for themselves. Learner control (Merrill, 1988; Tennyson & Park, 1987) is a feature of many effective computer-based instructional programs (see 33.1). However, this does not attenuate the damage to the assumption of predictability. If learners choose their course through a program, it is not possible to predict the outcome.

3. Some students know how they learn best and will not necessarily use the strategy the designer selected for them. Metacognition is another important theme in cognitive theory. It is generally considered to consist of two complementary processes (Brown, Campione & Day, 1981). The first is students' ability to monitor their own progress as they learn. The second is to change strategies if they realize they are not doing well. If students do not use the strategies that instructional theory suggests are optimal for them, then it becomes impossible to predict what their behavior will be. Instructional designers are now proposing that we develop ways to take instructional metacognition into account as we do instructional design (Lowyck & Elen, 1994).

4. People do not think rationally as instructional designers would like them to. Many years ago, Collins (1978) observed that people reason "plausibly." By this he meant that they make decisions and take actions on the basis of incomplete information, hunches, and intuition. Hunt (1982) has gone so far as to claim that

plausible reasoning is necessary for the evolution of thinking in our species. If we were creatures who made decisions only when all the information needed for a logical choice was available, we would never make any decisions at all and would not have developed the degree of intelligence that we have! Schon's (1983, 1987) study of decision making in the professions comes to a conclusion that is similar to Collins's. More recently, research in situated learning (Brown, Collins & Duguid, 1989; Lave & Wenger, 1991; Suchman, 1987) has demonstrated that most everyday cognition is not "planful" and is most likely to depend on what is afforded by the particular situation in which it takes place. The situated nature of cognition has led Streibel (1991) to claim that standard cognitive theory can never act as the foundational theory for instructional design. Be that as it may, if people do not reason logically, and if the way they reason depends on specific and usually unknowable contexts, their behavior is certainly unpredictable.

These and other arguments (see Csiko, 1989) are successful in their challenge to the assumption that behavior is predictable. The bulk of this chapter has described the factors that come between a stimulus and a student's response that make the latter unpredictable. Scholars working in our field have for the most part shifted to a cognitive orientation when it comes to theory. However, they have not shifted to a new position on the procedures of instructional design. Since these procedures are based, like behavioral theory, on the assumption that behavior is predictable, and since the assumption is no longer valid, the procedures whereby educational technologists apply their theory to practical problems are without foundation.

5.5.4 Cognitive Theory and Educational Technology

The evidence that educational technologists have accepted cognitive theory is prominent in the literature of our field (Gagné & Glaser, 1987; Richey, 1986; Spencer, 1988; Winn, 1989a). Of particular relevance to this discussion are those who have directly addressed the implications of cognitive theory for instructional design (Bonner, 1988; Champagne, Klopfer & Gunstone, 1982; DiVesta & Rieber, 1987; Schott, 1992; Tennyson & Rasch, 1988). Collectively, scholars in our field have described cognitive equivalents for all stages in instructional design procedures. Here are some examples.

Twenty years ago, Resnick (1976) described "cognitive task analysis" for mathematics. Unlike behavioral task analysis, which produces task hierarchies or sequences (Gagné, Briggs & Wager, 1988), cognitive analysis produces either descriptions of knowledge schemata that students are expected to construct, or descriptions of the steps information must go through as the student processes it, or both. Greeno's (1976, 1980) analysis of mathematical tasks illustrates the knowledge representation approach and corresponds in large part to instructional designers' use of information mapping that we discussed in section 5.3. Resnick's (1976) analysis of the way children perform subtraction exemplifies the information-processing approach.

Cognitive task analysis gives rise to cognitive objectives, counterparts to behavioral objectives. In Greeno's (1976) case, these appear as diagrammatic representations of schemata, not written statements of what students are expected to be able to do, to what criterion, and under what conditions (Mager, 1962).

The cognitive approach to learner analysis aims to provide descriptions of students' mental models (Bonner, 1988), not descriptions of their levels of performance prior to instruction. Indeed, the whole idea of "student model" that is so important in intelligent computer-based tutoring (Van Lehn, 1988) very often revolves around ways of capturing the ways students represent information in memory and how that information changes, not on their ability to perform tasks.

With an emphasis on knowledge schemata and the premise that learning takes place as schemata change, cognitively oriented instructional strategies are selected on the basis of their likely ability to modify schemata rather than to shape behavior. If schemata change, DiVesta and Rieber (1987) claim, students can come truly to understand what they are learning, not simply modify their behavior.

These examples show that educational technologists concerned with the application of theory to instruction have carefully thought through the implications of the shift to cognitive theory for instructional design. Yet in almost all instances, no one has questioned the procedures that we follow. We do cognitive task analysis, describe students' schemata and mental models, write cognitive objectives, and prescribe cognitive instructional strategies. But the fact that we do task and learner analysis, write objectives, and prescribe strategies has not changed. The performance of these procedures still assumes that behavior is predictable, a cognitive approach to instructional theory notwithstanding. Clearly something is amiss.

5.5.5 Can Instructional Design Remain an Independent Activity?

We are at the point where our acceptance of the assumptions of cognitive theory forces us to rethink the procedures we use to apply it through instructional design. The key to what is necessary lies in a second assumption that follows from the assumption of the predictability of behavior. That assumption is that the design of instruction is an activity that can proceed independent of the implementation of instruction. If behavior is predictable and if instructional theory contains valid prescriptions, then it should be possible to perform analysis, select strategies, try them out, and

revise them until a predetermined standard is reached, and then deliver the instructional package to those who will use it, with the safe expectation that it will work as intended. If, as we have demonstrated, that assumption is not tenable, we must also question the independence of design from the implementation of instruction (Winn, 1990).

There are a number of indications that educational technologists are thinking along these lines. All conform loosely with the idea that decision making about learning strategies must occur during instruction rather than ahead of time. In their details, these points of view range from the philosophical argument that thought and action cannot be separated, and therefore the conceptualization and doing of instruction must occur simultaneously (Nunan, 1983; Schon, 1987), to more practical considerations of how to construct learning environments that are adaptive, in real time, to student actions (Merrill, 1992). Another way of looking at this is to argue that, if learning is indeed situated in a context (for arguments on this issue, see McLellan, 1996), then instructional design must be situated in that context, too.

A key concept in this approach is the difference between learning environments and instructional programs. Other chapters in this volume address the matter of media research. Suffice it to say here that the most significant development in our field that occurred between Clark's (1983) argument that media do not make a difference to what and how students learn and Kozma's (1991) revision of this argument was the development of software that could create rich multimedia environments. Kozma (1994) makes the point that interactive and adaptive environments can be used by students to help them think, an idea that has a lot in common with Salomon's (1979) notion of media as "tools for thought." The kind of instructional program that drew much of Clark's (1985) disapproval was didactic—designed to do what teachers do when they teach towards a predefined goal. What interactive multimedia systems do is allow students a great deal of freedom to learn in their own way rather than in the way the designer prescribes. Zucchermaglio (1993) refers to them as "empty technologies" that, like shells, can be filled with anything the student or teacher wishes. By contrast, "full technologies" comprise programs whose content and strategy are predetermined, as is the case with computer-based instruction (see 12.2.3).

We believe that the implementation of cognitive principles in the procedures of educational techology requires a reintegration of the design and execution of instruction. This is best achieved when we develop stimulating learning environments whose function is not entirely prescribed but which can adapt in real time to student needs and proclivities. This does not necessarily require that the environments be "intelligent" (although at one time that seemed to be an attractive proposition [Winn, 1987]). It requires, rather, that the system be responsive to the student's intelligence in such a way that the best ways for the student to learn are determined, as it were, "on the fly."

5.5.6 The Three "Ages" of Scholarship in Educational Technology

We summarize the main points in this section by describing the three ages of educational technology. We call these the *age of instructional design*, the *age of message design*, and the *age of environment design*.

The age of instructional design is dominated by behavioral theories of learning and instruction and by procedures for applying theory to practice that are based ultimately on the assumption that behavior is predictable. The decisions instructional designers make are driven almost exclusively by the nature of the content students are to master. Thus, task analysis, which directs itself to an analysis of content, dominates the sources of information from which strategy selection is made. The most important criterion for the success of the techniques used during the age of instructional design is whether or not they produce instruction that is as successful as a teacher. Clark's (1983) criticism of research in our field is leveled at instructional systems that attempt to meet this criterion.

In the age of message design, the emphasis shifts from instructional content to instructional formats. We believe that this is the immediate result of the concern among cognitive theorists with the way information is represented in memory, schemata, and mental models. There is an assumption (doubtless incorrect; see Salomon, 1979) that the format selected to present information to students in some way determines the way in which the information is encoded in memory. A less-restrictive form of this assumption has, however, produced a great deal of useful research about the relationship between message forms and cognition. Fleming and Levie (1993) provide an excellent summary of this work.

The age of environment design is likewise based on cognitive theory. However, its emphasis is on providing information from which students can construct understanding for themselves through interaction that is more or less constrained, depending on students' needs and wishes. The key to success in this third, current, age is in the interaction between student and environment rather than in content or information format. A good example of this orientation in instructional design is Merrill's (1992) transaction theory, where the instructional designer's main focus in prescribing instruction is the kind of transaction (interaction) that occurs between the student and the instructional program. Another example is the design of learning environments based in the technologies of virtual reality (Winn, 1993). In virtual environments, the interaction with the environment is potentially so intuitive as to be entirely transparent to the user (Bricken, 1991). However, just what the participant in a virtual environment is empowered to do and particularly the way in which the environment reacts to participant actions (Winn & Bricken, 1992) requires the utmost care and attention from the instructional designer.

5.5.7 Section Summary

In this section we have reviewed a number of important issues concerning the importance of cognitive theory to what educational technologists actually do, namely, design instruction. This has led us to consider the relations between theory and the procedures employed to apply it in practical ways. We observed that when behaviorism was the dominant paradigm in our field, both the theory and the procedures for its application adhered to the same basic assumption, namely, that human behavior is predictable. We then noted that our field was effective in subscribing to the tenets of cognitive theory, but that the procedures for applying that theory remained unchanged and continued to subscribe to the by-now discredited assumption that behavior is predictable. We concluded by suggesting that cognitive theory requires of our design procedures that we create learning environments in which learning strategies are not entirely predetermined, which requires that the environments be highly adaptive to student actions. Recent technologies that permit the development of virtual environments offer the best possibility for realizing this kind of learning environment.

REFERENCES

Abel, R. & Kulhavy, R.W. (1989). Associating map features and related prose in memory. *Contemporary Educational Psychology 14*, 33–48.

Anderson, J.R. (1978). Arguments concerning representations for mental imagery. *Psychological Review 85*, 249–77.

— (1983). *The architecture of cognition*. Cambridge, MA.: Harvard University Press.

— (1986). Knowledge compilation: the general learning mechanism. *In* R. Michalski, J. Carbonell & T. Mitchell, eds. *Machine learning*, Vol. 2. Los Altos, CA: Kaufmann.

— (1990). *Adaptive character of thought*. Hillsdale, NJ: Erlbaum.

—, Boyle, C.F. & Yost, G. (1985). *The geometry tutor*. Pittsburgh, PA: Carnegie Mellon University, Advanced Computer Tutoring Project.

— & Reiser, B.J. (1985). The LISP tutor. *Byte 10* (4), 159–75.

Anderson, R.C., Reynolds, R.E., Schallert, D.L. & Goetz, E.T. (1977). Frameworks for comprehending discourse. *American Educational Research Journal 14*, 367–81.

Andrews, D.H. & Goodson, L.A. (1980). A comparative analysis of models of instructional design. *Journal of Instructional Development 3* (4), 2–16.

Arbib, M.A. & Hanson, A.R. (1987). Vision, brain and cooperative computation: an overview. *In* M.A. Arbib & A.R. Hanson, eds. *Vision, brain and cooperative computation*. Cambridge, MA: MIT Press.

Armbruster, B.B. & Anderson, T.H. (1982). *Idea mapping: the technique and its use in the classroom, or simulating the "ups" and "downs" of reading comprehension*. Urbana, IL University of Illinois Center for the Study of Reading. Reading Education Report #36.

— & Anderson, T.H. (1984). Mapping: representing informative text graphically. *In* C.D. Holley & D.F. Dansereau, eds. *Spatial learning strategies*. New York: Academic.

Arnheim, R. (1969). *Visual thinking*. Berkeley, CA: University of California Press.

Atkinson, R.L. & Shiffrin. R.M. (1968). Human memory: a proposed system and its control processes. *In* K.W. Spence & J.T. Spence, eds. *The psychology of learning and motivation: advances in research and theory*, Vol. 2. New York: Academic.

Ausubel, D.P. (1968). *The psychology of meaningful verbal learning*. New York: Grune & Stratton.

Baker, E.L. (1984). Can educational research informa educational practice? Yes! *Phi Delta Kappan 56*, 453–55.

Barfield, W. & Furness, T., eds., (1995). *Virtual environments and advanced interface design*. Oxford, England: Oxford University Press.

Bartlett, F.C. (1932). *Remembering: a study in experimental and social psychology*. London: Cambridge University Press.

Bloom, B.S. (1984). The 2 sigma problem: the search for methods of group instruction as effective as one-to-one tutoring. *Educational Researcher 13* (6), 4–16.

— (1987). A response to Slavin's mastery learning reconsidered. *Review of Educational Research 57*, 507–08.

Boden, M. (1988). *Computer models of mind*. New York: Cambridge University Press.

Bonner, J. (1988). Implications of cognitive theory for instructional design: revisited. *Educational Communication and Technology Journal 36*, 3–14.

Boring, E.G. (1950). *A history of experimental psychology*. New York: Appleton-Century-Crofts.

Bovy, R.C. (1983, Apr.). *Defining the psychologically active features of instructional treatments designed to facilitate cue attendance*. Presented at the meeting of the American Educational Research Association, Montreal, Canada.

Bower, G.H. (1970). Imagery as a relational organizer in associative learning. *Journal of Verbal Learning and Verbal Behavior 9*, 529–33.

Bransford, J.D. & Franks, J.J. (1971). The abstraction of linguistic ideas. *Cognitive Psychology 2*, 331–50.

— & Johnson, M.K. (1972). Contextual prerequisits for understanding: some investigations of comprehension and recall. *Journal of Verbal Learning and Verbal Behavior 11*, 717–26.

Bricken, M. (1991). Virtual worlds: no interface to design. *In* M. Benedikt, ed. *Cyberspace: first steps*. Cambridge, MA: MIT Press.

Bronfenbrenner, U. (1976). The experimental ecology of education. *Educational Researcher 5* (9), 5–15.

Brown, A.L., Campione, J.C. & Day, J.D. (1981). Learning to learn: on training students to learn from texts. *Educational Researcher 10* (2), 14–21.

Brown, J.S., Collins, A. & Duguid, P. (1989). Situated cognition and the culture of learning. *Educational Researcher 18* (1), 32–43.

Bruner, J. (1990). *Acts of meaning*. Cambridge, MA: Harvard University Press.

Byrne, C.M., Furness, T. & Winn, W.D. (1995, Apr.). *The use of virtual reality for teaching atomic/molecular structure*. Paper presented at the annual meeting of the American Educational Research Association, San Francisco, CA.

Calderwood, B., Klein, G.A. & Crandall, B.W. (1988). Time pressure, skill and move quality in chess. *American Journal of Psychology 101*, 481–93.

Carpenter, C.R. (1953). A theoretical orientation for instructional film research. *AV Communication Review 1*, 38–52.

Cassidy, M.F. & Knowlton, J.Q. (1983). Visual literacy: a failed metaphor? *Educational Communication and Technology Journal 31*, 67–90.

Champagne, A.B., Klopfer, L.E. & Gunstone, R.F. (1982). Cognitive research and the design of science instruction. *Educational Psychologist 17*, 31–51.

Charness, N. (1989). Expertise in chess and bridge. *In* D. Klahr & K. Kotovsky, eds. *Complex information processing: the impact of Herbert A. Simon*. Hillsdale, NJ: Erlbaum.

Chase, W.G. & Simon, H.A. (1973). The mind's eye in chess. *In* W.G. Chase, ed. *Visual information processing*. New York: Academic.

Chomsky, N. (1964). A review of Skinner's *Verbal Behavior*. *In* J.A. Fodor & J.J. Katz, eds. *The structure of language: readings in the philosophy of language*. Englewood Cliffs, NJ: Prentice Hall.

— (1965). *Aspects of the theory of syntax*. Cambridge, MA: MIT Press.

Clancey, W.J. (1993). Situated action: a neuropsychological interpretation: response to Vera and Simon. *Cognitive Science 17*, 87–116.

Clark, J.M. & Paivio, A. (1991). Dual coding theory and education. *Educational Psychology Review 3*, 149–210.

Clark, R.E. (1983). Reconsidering research on learning from media. *Review of Educational Research 53*, 445–60.

— (1985). Confounding in educational computing research. *Journal of Educational Computing Research 1*, 137–48.

Cognition and Technology Group at Vanderbilt (1990). Anchored instruction and its relationship to situated learning. *Educational Researcher 19* (3), 2–10.

Collins, A. (1978). *Studies in plausible reasoning: final report, Oct. 1976 to Feb. 1978. Vol. 1: Human plausible reasoning*. Cambridge MA: Bolt Beranek and Newman, BBN Report No. 3810.

Cornoldi, C. & De Beni, R. (1991). Memory for discourse: loci mnemonics and the oral presentation effect. *Applied Cognitive Psychology 5*, 511–18.

Cronbach, L.J. & Snow, R. (1977). *Aptitudes and instructional methods*. New York: Irvington.

Csiko, G.A. (1989). Unpredictability and indeterminism in human behavior: arguments and implications for educational research. *Educational Researcher 18* (3), 17–25.

Cunningham, D.J. (1992a). Assessing constructions and constructing assessments: a dialogue. *In* T. Duffy & D. Jonassen, eds. *Constructivism and the technology of instruction: a conversation*. Hillsdale, NJ: Erlbaum.

— (1992b). Beyond educational psychology: steps towards an educational semiotic. *Educational Psychology Review 4*(2), 165–94.

Dale, E. (1946). *Audio-visual methods in teaching*. New York: Dryden.

Dansereau, D.F., Collins, K.W., McDonald, B.A., Holley, C.D., Garland, J., Diekhoff, G. & Evans, S.H. (1979). Development and evaluation of a learning strategy program. *Journal of Educational Psychology 71*, 64–73.

De Beni, R. & Cornoldi, C. (1985). Effects of the mnemotechnique of loci in the memorization of concrete words. *Acta Psychologica 60*, 11–24.

De Kleer, J. & Brown, J.S. (1981). Mental models of physical mechanisms and their acquisition. *In* J.R. Anderson, ed. *Cognitive skills and their acquisition*. Hillsdale, NJ: Erlbaum.

DiVesta, F.J. & Rieber, L.P. (1987). Characteristics of cognitive instructional design: the next generation. *Educational Communication and Technology Journal 35*, 213–30.

Dondis, D.A. (1973). *A primer of visual literacy*. Cambridge, MA: MIT Press.

Dreyfus, H.L. (1972). *What computers can't do*. New York: Harper & Row.

Dreyfus, H.L. & Dreyfus, S.E. (1986). *Mind over machine*. New York: Free Press.

Driscoll, M. (1990, Aug.). Semiotics: an alternative model. *Educational Technology*, 33–35.

— & Lebow, D. (1992). Making it happen: possibilities and pitfalls of Cunningham's semiotic. *Educational Psychology Review 4*, 211–21.

Duffy, T.M. & Jonassen, D.H. (1992). Constructivism: new implications for instructional technology. *In* T. Duffy & D. Jonassen, eds. *Constructivism and the technology of instruction: a conversation*. Hillsdale, NJ: Erlbaum.

—, Lowyck, J. & Jonassen, D.H. (1983). *Designing environments for constructive learning*. New York: Springer.

Duong, L-V. (1994). *An investigation of characteristics of pre-attentive vision in processing visual displays*. Ph.D. dissertation, University of Washington, Seattle, WA.

Dwyer, F.M. (1972). *A guide for improving visualized instruction*. State College, PA: Learning Services.

— (1978). *Strategies for improving visual learning*. State College, PA: Learning Services.

— (1987). *Enhancing visualized instruction: recommendations for practitioners*. State College, PA: Learning Services.

Edelman, G.M. (1992). *Bright air, brilliant fire*. New York: Basic Books.

Eisner, E (1984). Can educational research inform educational practice? *Phi Delta Kappan 65*, 447–52.

Ellis, S.R., ed. (1993). *Pictorial combination in virtual and real environments*. London: Taylor & Francis.

Epstein, W. (1988). Has the time come to rehabilitate Gestalt psychology? *Psychological Research 50*, 2–6.

Ericsson, K.A. & Simon, H.A. (1984). *Protocol analysis: verbal reports as data*. Cambridge, MA: MIT Press.

Farah, M.J. (1989). Knowledge of text and pictures: a neuropsychological perspective. *In* H. Mandl & J.R. Levin, eds. *Knowledge acquisition from text and pictures*. North Holland: Elsevier.

Fisher, K.M., Faletti, J., Patterson, H., Thornton, R., Lipson, J. & Spring, C. (1990). Computer-based concept mapping. *Journal of Science Teaching 19*, 347–52.

Fleming, M.L. & , Levie, W.H. (1978). *Instructional message design: principles from the behavioral science*. Englewood Cliffs, NJ: Educational Technology.

Fleming, M.L., Levie, W.H., & Anglin, G., eds. (1993). *Instructional message design: principles from the behavioral and cognitive sciences*, 2d ed. Hillsdale, NJ: Educational Technology.

Gagné, E.D. (1985). *The cognitive psychology of school learning*. Boston, MA: Little, Brown.

Gagné, R.M. (1965). *The conditions of learning*. New York: Holt, Rinehart & Winston.

— (1974). *Essentials of learning for instruction*. New York: Holt, Rinehart & Winston.

—, Briggs, L.J. & Wager, W.W. (1988). *Principles of instructional design*, 3d ed. New York: Holt, Rinehart & Winston.

— & Dick, W. (1983). Instructional psychology. *Annual Review of Psychology 34*, 261–95.

— & Glaser, R. (1987). Foundations in learning research. *In* R.M. Gagné, ed. *Instructional technology: foundations*. Hillsdale, NJ: Erlbaum.

Gentner, D. & Stevens, A.L. (1983). *Mental models*. Hillsdale, NJ: Erlbaum.

Glaser, R. (1976). Components of a psychology of instruction: towards a science of design. *Review of Educational Research 46*, 1–24.

Greeno, J.G. (1976). Cognitive objectives of instruction: theory of knowledge for solving problems and answering questions. *In* D. Klahr, ed. *Cognition and instruction*. Hillsdale, NJ: Erlbaum.

— (1980). Some examples of cognitive task analysis with instructional implications. *In* R.E. Snow, P-A. Federico & W.E. Montague, eds. *Aptitude, learning and instruction*, Vol. 2. Hillsdale, NJ: Erlbaum.

Gropper, G.L. (1983). A behavioral approach to instructional prescription. *In* C.M. Reigeluth, ed. *Instructional design theories and models*. Hillsdale, NJ: Erlbaum.

Guha, R.V. & Lenat, D.B. (1991). Cyc: a mid-term report. *Applied Artificial Intelligence 5*, 45–86.

Harel, I. & Papert, S., eds. (1991). *Constructionism*. Norwood, NJ: Ablex.

Hartman, G.W. (1935). *Gestalt psychology: a survey of facts and principles*. New York: Ronald.

Henle, M. (1987). Koffka's *Principles* after fifty years. *Journal of the History of the Behavioral Sciences 23*, 14–21.

Hereford, J. & Winn, W.D. (1994). Non-speech sound in the human-computer interaction: a review and design guidelines. *Journal of Educational Computing Research 11*, 209–31.

Holley, C.D. & Dansereau, D.F., eds. (1984). *Spatial learning strategies*. New York: Academic

Houghton, H.A. & Willows, D.H., eds. (1987). *The psychology of illustration*. Vol. 2. New York: Springer.

Howe, K.R. (1985). Two dogmas of educational research. *Educational Researcher 14* (8), 10–18.

Hueyching, J.J. & Reeves, T.C. (1992). Mental models: a research focus for interactive learning systems. *Educational Technology Research and Development 40*, 39–53.

Hughes, R.E. (1989). *Radial outlining: an instructional tool for teaching information processing*. Ph.D. dissertation. Seattle, WA: University of Washington, College of Education.

Hunt, M. (1982). *The universe within*. Brighton: Harvester.

Johnson, D.D., Pittelman, S.D. & Heimlich, J.E. (1986). Semantic mapping. *Reading Teacher 39*, 778–83.

Johnson-Laird, P.N. (1988). *The computer and the mind*. Cambridge, MA: Harvard University Press.

Jonassen, D.H. (1991). Hypertext as instructional design. *Educational Technology, Research and Development 39*, 83–92.

— (1996). Computers in the classroom; mindtools for critical thinking. Columbus, OH: Prentice Hall.

—, Bressner, K & Yacci, M.A. (1993). Structural knowledge: techniques for assessing, conveying, and acquiring structural knowledge. Hillsdale, NJ: Erlbaum.

Klahr, D. & Kotovsky, K., eds. (1989) *Complex information processing: the impact of Herbert A. Simon*. Hillsdale, NJ: Erlbaum.

Knowlton, J.Q. (1966). On the definition of 'picture.' *AV Communication Review 14*, 157–83.

Kosslyn, S.M. (1985). *Image and mind*. Cambridge, MA: Harvard University Press.

—, Ball, T.M. & Reiser, B.J. (1978). Visual images preserve metric spatial information: evidence from studies of image scanning. *Journal of Experimental Psychology: Human Perception and Performance 4*, 47–60.

Kozma, R.B. (1991). Learning with media. *Review of Educational Research 61*, 179–211.

— (1994). *Will* media influence learning? Reframing the debate. *Educational Technology Research and Development 42*, 7–19.

—, Russell, J., Jones, T., Marz, N. & Davis, J. (1993, Sep.). *The use of multiple, linked representations to facilitate science understanding*. Paper presented at the fifth conference of the European Association for Research in Learning and Instruction, Aix-en-Provence, France.

Kuhn, T.S. (1970). *The structure of scientific revolutions*, 2d ed. Chicago, IL: University of Chicago Press.

Kulhavy, R.W., Lee, J.B. & Caterino, L.C. (1985). Conjoint retention of maps and related discourse. *Contemporary Educational Psychology 10*, 28–37.

—, Stock, W.A. & Caterino, L.C. (1994). Reference maps as a framework for remembering text. *In* W. Schnotz & R.W. Kulhavy, eds. *Comprehension of graphics*. North-Holland: Elsevier.

Kulik, C.L. (1990). Effectiveness of mastery learning programs: a meta-analysis. *Review of Educational Research 60*, 265–99.

Kulik, J.A. (1990). Is there better evidence on mastery learning? A reply to Slavin. *Review of Educational Research 60*, 303–07.

Labouvie-Vief, G. (1990). Wisdom as integrated thought: historical and development perspectives. *In* R.E. Sternberg, ed. *Wisdom: its nature, origins and development*. Cambridge, England: Cambridge University Press.

Landa, L. (1983). The algo-heuristic theory of instruction. *In* C.M. Reigeluth, ed. *Instructional design theories and models*. Hillsdale, NJ: Erlbaum.

Larkin, J.H. & Simon, H.A. (1987). Why a diagram is (sometimes) worth ten thousand words. *Cognitive Science 11*, 65–99.

Larochelle, S (1982). *Temporal aspects of typing. Dissertation Abstracts International 43*, 3-B, 900.

Lave, J. & Wenger, E. (1991). *Situated learning: legitimate peripheral participation*. Cambridge, MA: Cambridge University Press.

Lenat, D.B., Guha, R.V., Pittman, K., Pratt, D. & Shepherd, M. (1990). Cyc: towards programs with common sense. *Communications of ACM 33* (8), 30–49.

Leinhardt, G. (1987). Introduction and integration of classroom routines by expert teachers. *Curriculum Inquiry 7*, 135–76.

Lesgold, A., Robinson, H., Feltovich, P., Glaser, R., Klopfer, D. & Wang, Y. (1988). Expertise in a complex skill: diagnosing x-ray pictures. *In* M. Chi, R. Glaser & M.J. Farr, eds. *The nature of expertise*. Hillsdale, NJ: Erlbaum.

Levin, J.R., Anglin, G.J. & Carney, R.N. (1987). On empirically validating functions of pictures in prose. *In* D.H. Willows & H.A. Houghton, eds. *The psychology of illustration*. New York: Springer.

Lowyck, J. & Elen, J. (1994). *Students' instructional metacognition in learning environments (SIMILE)*. Unpublished paper. Leuven, Belgium: Centre for Instructional Psychology and Technology, Catholic University of Leuven.

Mager, R. (1962). *Preparing instructional objectives*, Palo Alto, CA: Fearon.

Mandl, H. & Levin, J.R., eds. (1989). *Knowledge acquisition from text and pictures*. North Holland: Elsevier.

Marr, D. (1982). *Vision*. New York: Freeman.

Marr, D. & Nishihara, H.K. (1978). Representation and recognition of the spatial organization of three-dimensional shapes. *Proceedings of the Royal Society of London 200*, 269–94.

— & Ullman, S. (1981). Directional selectivity and its use in early visual processing. *Proceedings of the Royal Society of London 211*, 151–80.

Mayer, R.E. (1989a). Models for understanding. *Review of Educational Research 59*, 43–64.

— (1989b). Systematic thinking fostered by illustrations of scientific text. *Journal of Educational Psychology 81*, 240–46.

— (1992). *Thinking, problem solving, cognition*, 2d ed. New York: Freeman.

—, & Gallini, J.K. (1990). When is an illustration worth ten thousand words? *Journal of Educational Psychology 82*, 715–26.

McLellan, H., ed. (1996). *Situated learning perspectives*. Englewood Cliffs, NJ: Educational Technology.

McNamara, T.P. (1986). Mental representations of spatial relations. *Cognitive Psychology 18*, 87–121.

McNamara, T.P, Hardy, J.K. & Hirtle, S.C. (1989). Subjective hierarchies in spatial memory. *Journal of Experimental Psychology: Learning, Memory and Cognition 15*, 211–27.

McMahon, H. & O'Neill, W. (1993). Computer-mediated zones of engagement in learning. *In* T.M. Duffy, J. Lowyck & D.H. Jonassen, eds. *Designing environments for constructive learning*. New York: Springer.

Merrill, M.D. (1983). Component display theory. *In* C.M. Reigeluth, ed. *Instructional design theories and models*. Hillsdale, NJ: Erlbaum.

— (1988). Applying component display theory to the design of courseware. *In* D. Jonassen, ed. *Instructional designs for microcomputer courseware*. Hillsdale, NJ: Erlbaum.

— (1992). Constructivism and instructional design. *In* T. Duffy & D. Jonassen, eds. *Constructivism and the technology of instruction: a conversation*. Hillsdale, NJ: Erlbaum.

—, Li, Z. & Jones, M.K. (1991). Instructional transaction theory: an introduction. *Educational Technology 30* (3), 7–12.

Miller, G.A. (1956). The magical number seven, plus or minus two: some limits on our capacity for processing information. *Psychological Review 63*, 81–97.

Minsky, M. (1975). A framework for representing knowledge. *In* P.H. Winston, ed. *The psychology of computer vision*, New York: McGraw-Hill.

Morrison, C.R. & Levin, J.R. (1987). Degree of mnemonic support and students' acquisition of science facts. *Educational Communication and Technology Journal 35*, 67–74.

Neisser, U. (1976). *Cognition and reality*. San Francisco, CA: Freeman.

Newell, A. (1982). The knowledge level. *Artificial Intelligence 18*, 87–127.

Norman, D.A. & Rumelhart, D.E. (1975). Memory and knowledge. *In* D.A. Norman & D.E. Rumelhart, eds. *Explorations in cognition*. San Francisco, CA: Freeman.

Nunan, T. (1983). *Countering educational design*. New York: Nichols.

Owen, L.A. (1985a). Dichoptic priming effects on ambiguous

picture processing. *British Journal of Psychology 76*, 437–47.

— (1985b). The effect of masked pictures on the interpretation of ambiguous pictures. *Current Psychological Research and Reviews 4*, 108–18.

Paivio, A. (1971). *Imagery and verbal processes*. New York: Holt, Rinehart & Winston.

Paivio, A. (1974). Language and knowledge of the world. *Educational Researcher 3* (9), 5–12.

— (1983). The empirical case for dual coding. *In* J.C. Yuille, ed. *Imagery, memory and cognition*. Hillsdale, NJ: Erlbaum.

Palmer, S.E. (1975). Visual perception and world knowledge. *In* D.A. Norman & D.E. Rumlehart, eds. *Explorations in cognition*. San Francisco, CA: Freeman.

Papert, S. (1983). *Mindstorms: children, computers and powerful ideas*. New York: Basic Books.

Patel, V.L. & Groen, G.J. (1991). The general and specific nature of medical expertise: a critical look. *In* K.A. Ericsson & J. Smith (1991). *Toward a general theory of expertise*. Cambridge, England: Cambridge University Press.

Peters, E.E. & Levin, J.R. (1986). Effects of a mnemonic strategy on good and poor readers' prose recall. *Reading Research Quarterly 21*, 179–92.

Phillips, D.C. (1983). After the wake: postpositivism in educational thought. *Educational Researcher 12* (5), 4–12.

Piaget, J. (1968). The role of the concept of equilibrium. *In* D. Elkind, ed. *Six psychological studies by Jean Piaget*. New York: Vintage.

— & Inhelder, B. (1969). *The psychology of the child*. New York: Basic Books.

Pinker, S. (1985). Visual cognition: an introduction. *In* S. Pinker, ed. *Visual cognition*. Cambridge, MA: MIT Press.

Polanyi, M. (1962). *Personal knowledge: towards a post-critical philosophy*. Chicago, IL: University of Chicago Press.

Polson, M.C. & Richardson, J.J. (1988). *Foundations of intelligent tutoring systems*. Hillsdale, NJ: Erlbaum.

Pomerantz, J.R. (1986). Visual form perception: an overview. *In* E.C. Schwab & H.C. Nussbaum, eds. *Pattern recognition by humans and machines; Vol. 2: visual perception*. New York: Academic.

— Pristach, E.A. & Carson, C.E. (1989). *Attention and object perception. In* B.E. Shepp & S. Ballesteros, eds. *Object perception: structure and process*, 53–90. Hillsdale, NJ: Erlbaum.

Pylyshyn Z. (1984). *Computation and cognition: toward a foundation for cognitive science*. Cambridge, MA: MIT Press.

Reigeluth, C.M (1983). Instructional design: what is it and why is it? *In* C.M. Reigeluth, ed. *Instructional design theories and models*. Hillsdale, NJ: Erlbaum.

— & Curtis, R.V. (1987). Learning situations and instructional models. *In* R.M. Gagne, ed. *Instructional technology: foundations*. Hillsdale NJ: Erlbaum.

— & Stein, F.S. (1983). The elaboration theory of instruction. *In* C.M. Reigeluth, ed. *Instructional design theories and models*. Hillsdale, NJ: Erlbaum.

Resnick, L.B. (1976). Task analysis in instructional design: some cases from mathematics. *In* D. Klahr, ed. *Cognition and instruction*. Hillsdale, NJ: Erlbaum.

Richards, W., ed. (1988) *Natural computation*. Cambridge, MA: MIT Press.

Richey, R. (1986). *The theoretical and conceptual bases of instructional design*. London: Kogan Page.

Rieber, L.P (1994). *Computers, graphics and learning*. Madison, WI: Brown & Benchmark.

Rock, I. (1986). The description and analysis of object and event perception. *In* K.R. Boff, L. Kaufman & J.P. Thomas, eds. *The handbook of perception and human performance, Vol. 2*, 33–1, 33–71.

Romiszowski, A.J. (1993). Psychomotor principles. *In* M.L. Fleming & W.H. Levie, eds. *Instructional message design: principles from the behavioral and cognitive sciences*, 2d ed. Hillsdale, NJ: Educational Technology.

Rouse, W.B. & Morris, N.M. (1986). On looking into the black box: prospects and limits in the search for mental models. *Psychological Bulletin 100*, 349–63.

Ruddell, R.B. & Boyle, O.F. (1989). A study of cognitive mapping as a means to improve summarization and comprehension of expository text. *Reading Research and Instruction 29*, 12–22.

Rumelhart, D.E. & McClelland, J.L.(1986). *Parallel distributed processing: explorations in the microstructure of cognition*. Cambridge MA: MIT Press.

— & Norman, D.A. (1981). Analogical processes in learning. *In* J.R. Anderson, ed. *Cognitive skills and their acquisition*. Hillsdale, NJ.: Erlbaum.

Ryle, G. (1949). *The concept of mind*. London: Hutchinson.

Saariluoma, P. (1990). Chess players' search for task-relevant cues: are chunks relevant? *In* D. Brogan, ed. *Visual search*. London: Taylor & Francis.

Salomon, G. (1974). Internalization of filmic schematic operations in interaction with learners' aptitudes. *Journal of Educational Psychology 66*, 499–511.

— (1979). *Interaction of media, cognition and learning*. San Francisco, CA: Jossey Bass.

— (1988). Artificial intelligence in reverse: computer tools that turn cognitive. *Journal of Educational Computing Research 4*, 123–40.

—, ed. (1993). *Distributed cognitions: psychological and educational considerations*. Cambridge, England: Cambridge University Press.

—, Perkins, D.N. & Globerson, T. (1991). Partners in cognition: extending human intelligence with intelligent technologies. *Educational Researcher 20*, 2–9.

Scandura, J.M. (1983). Instructional strategies based on the structural learning theory. *In* C.M. Reigeluth, ed. *Instructional design theories and models*. Hillsdale, NJ: Erlbaum.

Schank, R.C. (1984). *The cognitive computer*. Reading, MA: Addison-Wesley.

— & Abelson, R. (1977). *Scripts, plans, goals and understanding*. Hillsdale, NJ: Erlbaum.

Schewel, R. (1989). Semantic mapping: a study skills strategy. *Academic Therapy 24*, 439–47.

Schneider, W. & Shiffrin, R.M. (1977). Controlled and automatic human processing: I. detection, search and attention. *Psychological Review 84*, 1–66.

Schnotz, W. & Kulhavy, R.W., eds. (1994). *Comprehension of graphics*. North-Holland: Elsevier.

Schon, D.A. (1983). *The reflective practitioner*. New York: Basic Books.

— (1987). *Educating the reflective practitioner*. San Francisco, CA: Jossey-Bass.

Schott, F. (1992). The contributions of cognitive science and educational technology to the advancement of instructional design. *Educational Technology Research and Development 40*, 55–7.

Schwartz, N.H. & Kulhavy, R.W. (1981). Map features and the

recall of discourse. *Contemporary Educational Psychology* 6, 151–8.

Searle, J.R. (1992). *The rediscovery of the mind*. Cambridge, MA: MIT Press.

Seel, N.M. & Dörr, G. (1994). The supplantation of mental images through graphics: instructional effects on spatial visualization skills of adults. *In* W. Schnotz & R.W. Kulhavy, eds. *Comprehension of graphics*. North-Holland: Elsevier.

— & Strittmatter, P. (1989). Presentation of information by media and its effect on mental models. *In* H. Mandl & J.R. Levin, eds. *Knowledge acquisition from text and pictures*. North Holland: Elsevier.

Shepard, R.N. & Cooper, L.A. (1982). *Mental images and their transformation*. Cambridge, MA: MIT Press.

Shiffrin, R.M. & Schneider, W. (1977). Controlled and automatic information processing: II. perceptual learning, automatic attending, and a general theory. *Psychological Review 84*, 127–90.

Simon, H.A. (1974). How big is a chunk? *Science 183*, 482–8.

— (1981). *The sciences of the artificial*. Cambridge, MA: MIT Press.

Sinatra, R.C., Stahl-Gemake, J. & Borg, D.N. (1986, Oct.). Improving reading comprehension of disabled readers through semantic mapping. *The Reading Teacher,*, 22–9.

—, — & Morgan, N.W. (1986). Using semantic mapping after reading to organize and write discourse. *Journal of Reading 30* (1), 4–13.

Sless, D. (1981). *Learning and visual communication*. New York: Wiley.

Skinner, B.F. (1957). *Verbal behavior*. New York: Appleton-Century-Crofts.

Snow, R.E. (1992). Aptitude theory: yesterday, today and tomorrow. *Educational Psychologist 27*, 5–32.

Spencer, K. (1988). *The psychology of educational technology and instructional media*. London: Routledge.

Spiro, R.J., Feltovich, P.J., Coulson, R.L & Anderson, D.K. (1989). Multiple analogies for complex concepts: antidotes to analogy-induced misconception in advanced knowledge acquisition. *In* S. Vosniadou & A. Ortony, eds. *Similarity and analogical reasoning*. Cambridge, England: Cambridge University Press.

—, —, Jacobson, M.J. & Coulson, R.L. (1992). Cognitive flexibility, constructivisim, and hypertext: random access instruction for advanced knowledge acquisition in ill-structured domains. *In* T.M. Duffy & D.H. Jonassen, eds. *Constructivism and the technology of instruction*. Hillsdale, NJ: Erlbaum.

Sternberg, R.J. & Weil, E.M. (1980). An aptitude X strategy interaction in linear syllogistic reasoning. *Journal of Educational Psychology 72*, 226–39.

Streibel, M.J. (1991). Instructional plans and situated learning: the challenge of Suchman's theory of situated action for instructional designers and instructional systems. *In* G.J. Anglin, ed. *Instructional technology past, present and future*. Englewood, CO: Libraries Unlimited.

Suchman, L. (1987). *Plans and situated actions: the problem of human/machine communication*. New York: Cambridge University Press.

Suzuki, K. (1987, Feb.). *Schema theory: a basis for domain integration design*. Paper presented at the Annual Convention of the Association for Educational Communication and Technology, Atlanta, GA.

Tennyson, R.D. & Park, O.C. (1987). Artifical intelligence and computer-based learning. *In* R.M. Gagné, ed. *Instructional technology: foundations*. Hillsdale, NJ: Erlbaum.

— & Rasch, M. (1988). Linking cognitive learning theory to instructional prescriptions. *Instructional Science 17*, 369–85.

Thorndyke, P.W. & Hayes-Roth, B. (1979). The use of schemata in the acquisition and transfer of knowledge. *Cognitive Psychology 11*, 82–106.

Treisman, A. (1988). Features and objects: the fourteenth Bartlett Memorial Lecture. *Quarterly Journal of Experimental Psychology: Human Experimental Psychology*, 40A, 210–37.

Underwood, B.J. (1964). The representativeness of rote verbal learning. *In* A.W. Melton, ed. *Categories of human learning*. New York: Academic.

Van Lehn, K. (1988). Student modeling. *In* M.C. Polson & J.J. Richardson. *Foundations of intelligent tutoring systems*. Hillsdale, NJ: Erlbaum.

Varela, F.J., Thompson, E. & Rosch, E. (1991). *The embodied mind*. Cambridge, MA: MIT Press..

Wenger, E. (1987). *Artificial intelligence and tutoring systems*. Los Altos, CA: Kaufman.

Wertheimer, M. (1924/1955). Gestalt theory. *In* W.D. Ellis, ed. *A source book of Gestalt psychology*. New York: Humanities Press.

Wertheimer, M. (1938). *Laws of organization in perceptual forms in a source book for Gestalt psychology*. London: Routledge & Kegan Paul.

Willows, D.H. & Houghton, H.A., eds. (1987) *The psychology of illustration*, Vol. 1. New York: Springer.

Winn, W.D. (1980). The effect of block-word diagrams on the structuring of science concepts as a function of general ability. *Journal of Research in Science Teaching 17*, 201–11.

— (1980). Visual information processing: a pragmatic approach to the "imagery question." *Educational Communication and Technology Journal 28*, 120–33.

— (1982). Visualization in learning and instruction: a cognitive approach. *Educational Communication and Technology Journal 30*, 3–25.

— (1986). Knowledge of task, ability and strategy in processing letter patterns. *Perceptual and Motor Skills 63*, 726.

— (1987). Instructional design and intelligent systems: shifts in the designer's decision-making role. *Instructional Science 16*, 59–77.

— (1989a). Toward a rationale and theoretical basis for educational technology. *Educational Technology Research and Development 37*, 35–46.

— (1989b). The design and use of instructional graphics. *In* H. Mandl & J.R. Levin, eds. *Knowledge acquisition from text and pictures*. North Holland: Elsevier.

— (1990). Some implications of cognitive theory for instructional design. *Instructional Science 19*, 53–69.

— (1993a). *A conceptual basis for educational applications of virtual reality*. Human Interface Technology Laboratory Technical Report. Seattle, WA: Human Interface Technology Laboratory.

— (1993b). A constructivist critique of the assumptions of instructional design. *In* T.M. Duffy, J. Lowyck & D.H. Jonassen, eds. *Designing environments for constructive learning*. New York: Springer.

— & Bricken, W. (1992). Designing virtual worlds for use in mathematics education: the example of experiential algebra.

Educational Technology 32 (12), 12–19.

—, Li, T-Z. & Schill, D.E. (1991). Diagrams as aids to problem solving: their role in facilitating search and computation. *Educational Technology Research and Development 39*, 17–29.

— & Solomon, C. (1993). The effect of the spatial arrangement of simple diagrams on the interpretation of English and nonsense sentences. *Educational Technology Research and Development 41*, 29–41.

Yates, F.A. (1966). *The art of memory*. Chicago, IL: University of Chicago Press.

Zucchermaglio, C. (1993). Toward a cognitive ergonomics of educational technology. *In* T.M. Duffy, J. Lowyck & D.H. Jonassen, eds. *Designing environments for constructive learning*. New York: Springer.

6. TOWARD A SOCIOLOGY OF EDUCATIONAL TECHNOLOGY

Stephen T. Kerr
UNIVERSITY OF WASHINGTON

6.1 INTRODUCTION

Common images of technology, including educational technology, highlight its rational, ordered, and controlled aspects. These are the qualities that many observers see as its advantages, the qualities that encouraged the United States to construct ingenious railway systems in the last century, to develop a national network of telegraph and telephone communication, and later to blanket the nation with television signals. In the American mind, technology seems to be linked with notions of efficiency and progress; it is a distinguishing and preeminent value, a characteristic of the way Americans perceive the world in general, and the possible avenues for resolving social problems in particular (Boorstin, 1973; Segal, 1985).

Education is one of those arenas in which Americans have long assumed that technological solutions might bring increased efficiency, order, and productivity. Our current interest in computers and multimedia was preceded by a century of experimentation with precisely articulated techniques for organizing school practice, carefully specific approaches to the design of school buildings (down to the furniture they would contain), and an abiding enthusiasm for systematic methods of presenting textual and visual materials (Saettler, 1968; Godfrey, 1965).

There was a kind of mechanistic enthusiasm about many of these efforts. If we could just find the right approach, the thinking seemed to go, we could address the problems of schooling and improve education immensely. The world of the student, the classroom, the school, was, in this interpretation, a machine (perhaps a computer) needing only the right program to run smoothly.

But technology frequently has effects in areas other than those intended by its creators. Railroads were not merely a better way to move goods across the country; they also brought standard time and a leveling of regional and cultural differences. Telephones allowed workers in different locations to speak with each other, but they also changed the ways workplaces were organized and the image of what office work was. Television altered the political culture of the country in ways we still struggle to comprehend. Those who predicted the social effects that might flow from these new technologies typically either missed entirely or foresaw inaccurately what their impact might be.

Similarly with schools and education, the focus of researchers interested in educational technology has usually been on what is perceived to be the outcome of these approaches on what is thought of as their principal target: learning by pupils. Occasionally, other topics related to the way technology is perceived and used have been studied. Attitudes and opinions by teachers and principals about the use of computers are an example. Generally, however, there have been few attempts to define a "sociology of educational technology" (exceptions: Kerr & Taylor, 1985; Hlynka & Belland, 1991). In their 1992 review, Scott, Cole, and Engel also went beyond traditional images to focus on what they called a "cultural constructivist perspective." The task here, then, has these parts: to say what ought to be included under such a rubric, to review the relatively small number of works from within the field that touch on these issues, and the larger number of works from related fields or on related topics that may be productive in helping us think about a sociology of educational technology; and, finally, to consider future directions for work in this field.

6.1.1 What to Include?

To decide what we should consider under the suggested heading of a "sociology of educational technology," we need to think about two sets of issues: those that are important to sociologists, and those that are important to educators and to educational technologists. Sociology is concerned with many things, but if there is a primary assertion, it is that we cannot adequately explain social phenomena if we look only at individuals. Rather, we must examine how people interact in group settings, and how those settings shape and constrain individual action.

Defining what is central to educators (including educational technologists) is also difficult, but central is probably (to borrow a sociological term) cultural reproduction: the passing on to the next generation of values, skills, and knowledge that are judged to be critical, and the improvement of the general condition of society. Three aspects of this vision of education are important here: (1) direct relationships among educators, students, administrators, parents, community members, and others who define what education is to be ("what happens in schools and classrooms"); (2) attempts to deal with perceived social problems and inequities, and thus provide a better life for the next generation ("what happens after they finish"); and (3) efforts to reshape the educational system itself, so that it carries out its work in new ways and thus contributes to social improvement.

The questions about educational technology's social effects that will be considered here, then, are principally those relating (or potentially relating) to what sociologists call *collectivities*: groups of individuals (teachers, students, administrators, parents), organizations, and social movements.

6.1.1.1. Sociology of Organizations. If our primary interest is in how educational technology affects the ways that people work together in schools, then what key topics ought we to consider? Certainly a prime focus must be organizations, the ways that schools are structured so as to carry out their work. It is important to note that we can use the term *organization* to refer to more than the administration of schools or universities. It can also refer to the organization of classrooms, of interactions among students or among teachers, of the ways individuals seek to shape their work environment to accomplish particular ends, and so forth.

Organizational sociology is a well-established field, and there have been some studies on educational organizations. Subparts of this field include the functioning of schools as bureaucracies; the ways in which new organizational forms are born, live, and die; the expectations of actors within the school setting of themselves and of each other (in sociological terms, the roles they play); and the sources of power and control that support various organizational forms.

6.1.1.2. Sociology of Groups and Classes. A second focus of our review here will regard the sociology of groups, including principally groups of ascription (that one is either born into or to which one is assumed to belong by virtue of one's position), but also those of affiliation (groups that one voluntarily joins, or comes to be connected with via one's efforts or work). Important here are the ways that education deals with such groups as those based on gender, class, and race, and how educational technology interacts with those groupings. While this topic has not been central in studies of educational technology, the review here will seek to suggest its importance and the value of further efforts to study it.

6.1.1.3. Sociology of Social Movements. Finally, we will need to consider the sociology of social movements and social change. Social institutions change under certain circumstances, and education is currently in a period where large changes are being suggested from a variety of quarters. Educational technology is often perceived as a harbinger or facilitator of educational change, and so it makes sense for us to examine the sociological literature on these questions and thus try to determine where and how such changes take place, what their relationships are to other shifts in the society, economy, or polity, etc.

Another aspect of education as a social movement, and of educational technology's place there, is what we might call the *role of ideology*. By ideology here is meant not an explicit, comprehensive, and enforced code of beliefs and practices to which all members of a group are held but rather a set of implicit, often vague, but widely shared set of expectations and assumptions about the social order. Essential here are such issues as the values that technology carries with it, its presumed contribution to the common good, and how it is perceived to interact with individuals' plans and goals.

6.1.1.4. Questions of Sociological Method. As a part of considering these questions, we will also examine briefly some questions of sociological method. Many sociological studies in education are conducted via surveys or questionnaires, instruments that were originally designed as sociological research tools. Inasmuch as sociologists have accumulated considerable experience in working with these methods, we need to note both the advantages and the problems of using such methods. Given especially the popularity of opinion surveys in education, it will be especially important to review the problem of attitudes vs. actions ("what people say vs. what they do").

A further question of interest for educational technologists has to do with the "stance" or position of the researcher. Most of the studies of attitudes and opinions that have been done in educational technology assume that the researcher stands in a neutral position, "outside the fray." Some examples from sociological research using the ethnomethodological paradigm are introduced, and their possible significance for further work on educational technology are considered.

The conclusion seeks to bring the discussion back specifically to the field of educational technology by asking how the effects surveyed in the preceding sections might play out in real school situations. How might educational technology affect the organization of classes, schools, and education as a social institution? How might the fates of particular groups (women, minorities) intersect with the ways educational technology is or is not used within schools? And finally, how might the prospects for long-term change in education as a social institution be altered by educational technology.

6.2 SOCIOLOGY AND ITS CONCERNS

6.2.1 A Concern for Collective Action

In the United States, most writing about education has had a distinctly psychological tone. This is in contrast with what is the case in certain other developed countries, especially England and western Europe, where there is a much stronger tradition of thinking about education, not merely as a matter of concern for the individual but also as a general *social* phenomenon, a matter of interest for the state and polity. Accordingly, it is appropriate that we review here briefly the principal focus of sociology as a field, and describe how it may be related to another field that in America has been studied almost exclusively through the disciplinary lenses of psychology.

Sociology as a discipline appeared during the 19th century in response to serious changes in the existing social structure. The industrial revolution had wrought large shifts in relationships among individuals, and especially in the relationships among different social groups. Marx's interest in class antagonisms, Weber's focus on social and political structure under conditions of change, Durkheim's investigations of the sense of "anomie" (alienation) seen as prevalent in the new social order—all these concerns were born of the shifts that were felt especially strongly as Western social life changed under the impact of the industrial revolution.

The questions of how individuals define their lives together, and how those definitions, once set in place and commonly accepted, constrain individuals' actions and life courses, formed the basis of early sociological inquiry. In many ways, these are the same questions that continue to interest sociologists today. What determines how and why humans organize themselves and their actions in particular ways? What effects do those organizations have on thought and action? And what limitations might those organizations impose on human action?

If psychology focuses on the individual, the internal processes of cognition and motives for action that individuals experience, then sociology focuses most of all on the ways people interact as members of organizations or groups, how they form new groups, and how their status as members of one or another group affects how they live and work. The "strong claim" of sociologists might be put simply as "settings have plans for us." That is, the social and organizational contexts of actions may be more important in explaining what people do than their individual motivations and internal states. How this general concern for collective action plays out is explored below in relation to each of three topics of general concern here: organizations, groups, and social change.

6.2.1.1. Sociology of Organizations. Schools and other educational enterprises are easily thought of as organizations, groups of people intentionally brought together to accomplish some specific purpose. Education as a social institution has existed in various forms over historical time, but only in the last 150 years or so has it come to have a distinctive and nearly universal organizational form. Earlier societies had ways to ensure that young people were provided with appropriate cultural values (enculturation), with specific forms of behavior and outlooks that would allow them to function successfully in a given society (socialization), and with training needed to earn a living

(observation and participation, formal apprenticeship, or formal schooling). But only recently have we come to think of education as necessarily a social institution characterized by specific organizational forms (schools, teachers, curricula, standards, laws, procedures for moving from one part of the system to another, etc.).

The emphasis here on education as a social organization leads us to three related subquestions that we will consider in more detail later. These include: (1) How does the fact that the specific organizational structure of schools is usually bureaucratic in form affect what goes on (and can go on) there, and how does educational technology enter into these relationships? (2) How are social roles defined in schools, and how does educational technology affect the definition of those roles? (3) How does the organizational structure of schools change, and how does educational technology interact with those processes of organizational change? Each of these questions will be introduced briefly here and treated in more depth in following sections.

6.2.1.1.1. Organizations and Bureaucracy. The particulars of school organizational structure are a matter of interest, for schools and universities have most frequently been organized as bureaucracies. That is, they develop well-defined sets of procedures for processing students, for dealing with teachers and other staff, and for addressing the public. These procedures deal with who is to be allowed to participate (rules for qualification, admission, assignment, and so forth), what will happen to them while they are part of the system (curricular standards, textbook selection policies, rules for teacher certification, student conduct, etc.), how the system will define that its work has been completed (requirements for receiving credit, graduation requirements, tests, etc.), as well as with how the system itself is to be run (administrator credentialing, governance structures, procedures for financial transactions within schools, relations among various parts of the system—accreditation, state vs. local vs. federal responsibility, etc.). Additional procedures may deal with such issues as how the public may participate in the life of the institution, how disputes are to be resolved, and how rewards and punishments are to be decided on and distributed (Bidwell, 1965). Educational organizations are thus participating in the continuing transition from what German sociologists called *gemeinschaft* to *gesellschaft,* from an earlier economic and social milieu defined by close familial bonds, personal relationships, and a small and caring community, to a milieu defined by ties to impersonal groups and large, bureaucratic organizations.

While bureaucratic forms of organization are not necessarily bad (and indeed were seen in the past century as a desirable antidote to personalized, corrupt, arbitrary social forms), the current popular image of bureaucracy is exceedingly negative. The disciplined and impersonal qualities of the bureaucrat, admired in the last century, are now frequently seen as ossified, irrelevant, a barrier to needed change.

A significant question may therefore be: What are the conditions that encourage bureaucratic systems, especially in education, to become more flexible, more responsive?

And since educational technology is often portrayed as a solution to the problems of bureaucracy, we need to ask about the evidence regarding technology and its impact on bureaucracies.

6.2.1.1.2. Organizations and Social Roles. To understand how organizations work, we need to understand not only the formal structure of the organization, the "organization chart." We also need to see the independent "life" of the organization as expressed and felt through such mechanisms as social and organizational roles. Roles have long been a staple of sociological study, but they are often misunderstood. A role is not merely a set of responsibilities that one person (say, a manager or administrator) in a social setting defines for another person (e.g., a worker, perhaps a teacher). Rather, it is better thought of as a set of interconnected expectations that participants in a given social setting have for their own and others' behaviors. Teachers expect students to act in certain ways; principals expect teachers to do thus and so; and teachers have similar expectations of principals. Roles, then, are best conceived of as "emergent properties" of social systems: They appear not in isolation but rather when people gather together and try to accomplish something together. Entire systems of social analysis (such as that proposed by George Herbert Mead [1934] under the rubric "symbolic interactionism") have been built on this basic set of ideas.

Educational institutions are the site for an extensive set of social roles, including those of teacher, student/pupil, administrator, staff professional, parent, future or present employer, and community member. Especially significant are the ways in which the role of the teacher may be affected by the introduction of educational technology into a school, or the formal or informal redefinition of job responsibilities following such introduction. How educational roles are defined and redefined, how new roles come into existence, and how educational technology may affect those processes, then, are all legitimate subjects for our attention here.

6.2.1.1.3. Organizations and Organizational Change. A further question of interest to sociologists is how organizations change. New organizations are constantly coming into being, old ones disappear, and existing ones change their form and functions. How this happens, what models or metaphors best describe these processes, and how organizations seek to ensure their success through time have all been studied extensively in sociology. There have been numerous investigations of innovation in organizations, as well as of innovation strategies, barriers to change, and so forth.

In education, these issues have been of special concern, for the persistent image of educational institutions has been one of unresponsive bureaucracies. Specific studies of educational innovation are therefore of interest to us here, with particular reference to how educational technology may interact with these processes.

6.2.1.2. Sociology of Groups. Our second major rubric involves groups, group membership, and the significance of group membership for an individual's life chances. Sociologists study all manner of groups: formal and informal,

groups of affiliation (which one joins voluntarily) and ascription (which one is a member of by virtue of birth, position, class), and so on. The latter kinds of groups, in which one's membership is not a matter of one's own choosing, have been of special interest to sociologists in this century. This interest has been especially strong since social barriers of race, gender, and class are no longer seen as immutable but rather as legitimate topics for state concern. As the focus of sociologists on mechanisms of social change has grown over the past decades, so has their interest in defining how group membership affects the life chances of individuals, and in prescribing what steps institutions (government, schools, etc.) might take to lessen the negative impact of ascriptive membership on individuals' futures.

Current discussion of education has often focused on the success of the system in enabling individuals to transcend the boundaries imposed by race, gender, and class (see also 9.5). The pioneering work by James Coleman in the 1960s (Coleman, 1966) on race and educational outcomes was critical to changing how Americans thought about integration of schools. Work by Carol Gilligan (Gilligan, Lyons & Hanmer, 1990) and others starting in the 1980s on the fate of women in education has led to a new awareness of the gender nonneutrality of many schooling practices (see 9.5.4, 10.4). The continuing importance of class is a topic of interest for a number of sociologists and social critics who frequently view the schooling system more as a mechanism for social reproduction than for social change (Apple, 1988; Giroux, 1981; Spring, 1989). These issues are of major importance to how we think about education in a changing democracy, and so we need to ask how educational technology may either contribute to the problems themselves or to their solution.

6.2.1.3. Sociology of Social Change and Social Movements. A third large concern of sociologists has been the issue of social stability and social change. The question has been addressed variously since the days of Karl Marx, whose vision posited the inevitability of a radical reconstruction of society based on scientific "laws" of historical and economic development, class identification, and class conflict via newly mobilized social movements. Social change is of no less importance to those who seek not to change but to preserve the social order. Talcott Parsons, an American sociologist of the middle of this century, is perhaps unjustly criticized for being a conservative, but he discussed in detail how particular social forms and institutions could be viewed as performing a function of "pattern maintenance" (Parsons, 1949, 1951).

Current concerns about social change are perhaps less apocalyptic today than they were for Marx, but in some quarters are viewed as no less critical. In particular, educational institutions are increasingly seen as one of the few places where society can exert leverage to bring about desired changes in the social and economic order. Present fears about "global economic competitiveness" are a good case in point. It is clear that for many policymakers, the primary task of schools in the current economic environment ought to be to produce an educated citizenry capable of competing with other nations. But other voices in education stress the importance of the educational system in conserving social values, passing on traditions. A variety of social movements have emerged in support of both these positions. Both positions contain a kernel that is essentially ideological—a set of assumptions, values, and positions as regards the individual and society. These ideologies are typically implicit and thus rarely are articulated openly. Nonetheless, identifying them is especially important to a deeper understanding of the questions involved.

It is reasonable for us to ask how sociologists have viewed social change, what indicators are seen as being most reliable in predicting how social change may take place, and what role social movements (organized groups in support of particular changes) may have in bringing change about. If education is to be viewed as a primary engine for such change, and if educational technology is seen by some as a principal part of that engine, then we need to understand how and why such changes may take place, and what role technology may rightly be expected to play. This raises in turn the issue of educational technology as a social and political movement itself and of its place vis-à-vis other organizations in the general sphere of education. The ideological underpinnings of technology in education are also important to consider. The values and assumptions of both supporters and critics of technology's use in education bear careful inspection if we are to see clearly the possible place for educational technology.

The following section offers a detailed look at the sociology of organizations, the sociology of school organization and of organizational roles, and the influences of educational technology on that organization. Historical studies of the impact of technology on organizational structures are also considered to provide a different perspective on how organizations change.

6.3 SOCIOLOGICAL STUDIES OF EDUCATION AND TECHNOLOGY

6.3.1 The Sociology of Organizations

Schools are many things, but (at least since the end of the 19th century) they have been organizations: intentionally created groups of people pursuing common purposes, and standing in particular relation to other groups and social institutions. Within the organization, there are consistent understandings of what the organization's purposes are, and participants stand in relatively well-defined positions vis-à-vis each other (e.g., the roles of teachers, student, parent, etc.). Additionally, the organization possesses a technical structure for carrying out its work (classes, textbooks, teacher certification), seeks to define job responsibilities so that tasks are accomplished, and has mechanisms for dealing with the outside world (PTA meetings, committees on textbook adoption, legislative lobbyists, school board meetings).

Sociology has approached the study of organizations in a number of ways. Earlier studies stressed the formal features of organizations and described their internal functioning and the relationships among participants within the bounds of the organization itself. Over the past 20 years or so, however, a new perspective has emerged, one that sees the organization in the context of its surrounding environment (Aldrich & Marsden, 1988). Major issues in the study of organizations using the environmental or organic approach include the factors that give rise to organizational diversity and those connected with change in the organization.

Perhaps it is obvious that questions of organizational change and organizational diversity are pertinent to the study of how educational technology has come to be used, or may be used, in educational environments, but let us use the sociological lens to examine why this is so. Schools as organizations are increasingly under pressure from outside social groups and from political and economic structures. Among the criticisms constantly leveled at the schools are that they are too hierarchical, too bureaucratized, and that current organizational patterns make changing the system almost impossible. (Whether these perceptions are in fact warranted is entirely another issue, one that we will not address here; see Carson, Huelskamp & Woodall, 1991.) We might reasonably ask whether we should be focusing attention on the organizational structure of schools as they are, rather than discussing desirable alternatives. Suffice it to say that massive change in an existing social institution, such as the schools, is difficult to undertake in a controlled, conscious way.

Those who suggest (e.g., Perelman, 1992) that schools as institutions will soon "wither away" are unaware of the historical flexibility of schools as organizations (Cuban, 1984; Tyack, 1974) and of the strong social pressures that militate for preservation of the existing institutional structure. The perspective here, then, is much more on how the existing structure of the social organizations we call *schools* can be affected in desirable ways, and so the issue of organizational change (rather than that of organizational generation) will be a major focus in what follows.

To make this review cohere, we will start by surveying what sociologists know about organizations generally, including specifically bureaucratic forms of organization. We will then consider the evidence regarding technology's impact on organizational structure in general, and on bureaucratic organization in particular. We will then proceed to a consideration of schools as a specific type of organization and concentrate on recent attempts to redefine patterns of school organization. Finally, we will consider how educational technology relates to school organization and to attempts to change that organization and the roles of those who work in schools.

6.3.1.1. Organizations: Two Sociological Perspectives. Much recent sociological work on the nature of organizations starts from the assumption that organizations are best studied and understood as parts of an environment. If organizations exist within a distinctive environment, then what aspects of that environment should be most closely examined? Sociologists have answered this question in two different ways: For some, the key features are the resources and information that may be used rationally within the organization or exchanged with other organizations within the environment; for others, the essential focus is on the cultural surround that determines and moderates the organization's possible courses of action in ways that are more subtle, less deterministic than the resources-information perspective suggests. While there are many exceptions, it is probably fair to say that the resources-information approach has been more often used in analyses of commercial organizations, and the latter, cultural approach used in studies of public and nonprofit organizations.

The environmental view of organizations has been especially fruitful in studies of organizational change. The roles of outside normative groups such as professional associations or state legislatures, for example, were stressed by DiMaggio and Powell (1983; see also Meyer & Scott, 1983), who noted that the actions of such groups tend to reduce organizational heterogeneity in the environment and thus inhibit change. While visible alternative organizational patterns may provide models for organizational change, other organizations in the same general field exert a counter-influence by supporting commonly accepted practices and demanding that alternative organizations adhere to those models, even when the alternative organization might not be required to do so. For example, an innovative school may be forced to modify its record-keeping practices so as to match more closely "how others do it" (Rothschild-Whitt, 1979).

How organizations react to outside pressure for change has also been studied. There is considerable disagreement as to whether such pressures result in dynamic transformation via the work of attentive leaders, or whether organizational inertia is more generally characteristic of organizations' reaction to outside pressures (Astley & Van de Ven, 1983; Hrebiniak & Joyce, 1985; Romanelli, 1991). Mintzberg (1979) suggested that there might be a trade-off here: Large organizations have the potential to change rapidly to meet new pressures (but only if they use appropriately their large and differentiated staffs, better forecasting abilities, etc.); small organizations can respond to outside pressures if they capitalize on their more flexible structure and relative lack of established routines.

Organizations face a number of common problems, including how to assess their effectiveness. Traditional evaluation studies have assumed that organizational goals can be relatively precisely defined, outcomes can be measured, and standards for success agreed upon by the parties involved (McLaughlin, 1987). More recent approaches suggest that examination of the "street-level" evaluation methods used by those who work within an organization may provide an additional, useful perspective on organizational effectiveness (Anspach, 1991). For example, "dramatic incidents," even though they are singularities, may define effectiveness or its lack for some participants.

6.3.1.2. Bureaucracy as a Condition of Organiza-

tions. We need to pay special attention to the particular form of organization we call *bureaucracy*, since this is a central feature of school environments where educational technology is often used. The emergence of this pattern as a primary way for ensuring that policies are implemented and that some degree of accountability is guaranteed lies in the 19th century (Peabody & Rourke, 1965; Waldo, 1952). Max Weber described the conditions under which social organizations would move away from direct, personalized, or "charismatic" control, and toward bureaucratic and administrative control (Weber, 1978).

The problem with bureaucracy, as anyone who has ever stood in line at a state office can attest, is that the organization's workers soon seem to focus exclusively on the rules and procedures established to provide accountability and control, rather than on the people or problems the bureaucratic system ostensibly exists to address (Herzfeld, 1992). The tension for the organization and those who work therein is between commitment to a particular leader, who may want to focus on people or problems, and commitment to a self-sustaining system with established mechanisms for ensuring how decisions are made and how individuals work within the organization, and which will likely continue to exist after a particular leader is gone. In this sense, one might view many of the current problems in schools and concerns with organizational reform (especially from the viewpoint of teachers) as attempts to move toward a more collegial mode of control and governance (Waters, 1993). We will return later to this theme of reform and change in the context of school bureaucratic structures when we deal more explicitly with the concepts of social change and social movements.

6.3.1.3. Technology and Organizations. Our intent

here is not merely to review what current thinking is regarding schools as organizations but also to say something about how the use of educational technology within schools might affect or be affected by those patterns of organization. Before we can address those issues, however, we must first consider how technology has been seen as affecting organizational structure generally. In other words, schools aside, is there any consensus on how technology affects the life of organizations, or the course of their development? While the issue would appear to be a significant one, and while there have been a good many general discussions of the potential impact of technology on organizations and the individuals who work there (e.g., Naisbitt & Aburdene, 1990; Toffler, 1990), there is remarkably little consensus about what precisely the nature of such impacts may be. Indeed, Americans seem to have a deep ambivalence about technology: Some see it as villain and scapegoat; others stress its role in social progress (Florman, 1981; Pagels, 1988; Segal, 1985; Winner, 1986).

Some of these concerns stem from the difficulty of keeping technology under social control once it has been introduced (Glendenning, 1990; Steffen, 1993, especially Chapters 3 and 5). Perrow (1984) suggests that current technological systems are so complex and "interactive" (showing tight relationship among parts) that accidents and problems cannot be avoided. They are, in effect, no longer accidents but an inevitable consequence of our limited ability to predict what can go wrong. Others, however, stress that technology is an essential part of human culture and that our images of technology would be better if elaborated to include the notion of "extending our humanity" (Rothenberg, 1993).

6.3.1.3.1. Historical Studies of Technology. As a framework for considering how technology affects or may affect organizational life, it may be useful to consider specific examples of earlier technological advances now seen to have altered social and organizational life in particular ways. A problem here is that initial prognoses for a technology's effects—indeed, the very reason a technology is developed in the first place—are often radically different from the ways in which a technology actually comes to be used. Few of those who witnessed the development of assembly-line manufacture, for example, had any idea of the import of the changes they were witnessing; although these shifts were perceived as miraculous and sometimes frightening, they were rarely seen as threatening the social status quo (Jennings, 1985; Marvin, 1988; see also 1.5).

Several specific technologies illustrate the ways initial intentions for a technology often translate over time into unexpected organizational and social consequences. The development of printing, for example, not only lowered the cost, increased the accuracy, and improved the efficiency of producing individual copies of written materials; it also had profound organizational impact on how governments were structured and did their work. Governments began to demand more types of information from local administrators and to circulate and use that information in pursuit of national goals (Boorstin, 1983; Darnton, 1984; Eisenstein, 1979; Febvre & Martin, 1958; Luke, 1989).

The telephone offers another example of a technology that significantly changed the organization of work in offices. Bell's original image of telephonic communication foresaw repetitive contacts among a few key points rather than the multipoint networked system we see today, and when Bell offered the telephone patents to William Orton, president of Western Union, Orton remarked, "What use could this company make of an electrical toy?" (Aronson, 1977). But the telephone brought a rapid reconceptualization of the workplace. After its development, the "information workers" of the day—newspaper reporters, financial managers, and so forth—no longer needed to be clustered together so tightly. Talking on the telephone also established patterns of communication that were more personal, less dense, and formal (de Sola Pool, 1977).

Chester Carlson, an engineer then working for a small company called Haloid, developed in 1938 a process for transferring images from one sheet of paper to another based on principles of electrical charge. Carlson's process, and the company that would become Xerox, also altered the organization of office life, perhaps in more local ways than the telephone. Initial estimates forecast only the "primary"

market for Xerox copies and ignored the large number of extra copies of reports that would be made and sent to a colleague in the next office, a friend, or someone in a government agency or university. This "secondary market" for copies turned out to be many times larger than the "primary market" for original copies, and the resulting dissemination of information has brought workers into closer contact with colleagues, given them easier access to information, and provided for more rapid circulation of information (Mort, 1989; Owen, 1986).

The impact of television on our forms of organizational life is difficult to document, though many have tried. Marshall McLuhan and his followers have suggested that television brought a view of the world that breaks down traditional social constructs. Among the effects noted by some analysts are the new position occupied by political figures (more readily accessible, less able to hide failures and problems from the electorate), changing relationships among parents and children (lack of former separation between adult and children's worlds), and shifts in relationships among the sexes (disappearance of formerly exclusively "male" and "female" domains of social action; Meyrowitz, 1985).

Process technologies may also have unforeseen organizational consequences, as seen in mass production via the assembly line. Production on the assembly line rationalized production of manufactured goods, improved their quality, and lowered prices. It also led to anguish in the form of worker alienation, and thus contributed to the development of socialism and Marxism, and to the birth of militant labor unions in the United States and abroad, altering forms of organization within factories and the nature of worker-management relationships (Boorstin, 1973; Hounshell, 1984; Smith, 1981. See also Bartky, 1990, on the introduction of standard time; and Norberg, 1990, on the advent of punch card technology).

6.3.1.3.2. Information Technology and Organizations. Many have argued that information technology will flatten organizational hierarchies and provide for more democratic forms of management. Shoshana Zuboff's study of how workers and managers in a number of corporate environments reacted to the introduction of computer-based manufacturing processes is one of the few empirically based studies to examine this issue (Zuboff, 1988). However, some have argued from the opposite stance that computerization in fact strengthens existing hierarchies and encourages top-down control (Evans, 1991). Still others (Winston, 1986) have argued that information technology has had minimal impact on the structure of work and organizations. Kling (1991) found remarkably little evidence of radical change in social patterns from empirical studies, noting that while computerization had led to increased worker responsibility and satisfaction in some settings, in others it had resulted in decreased interaction. He also indicated that computer systems are often merely "instruments in power games played by local governments" (p. 35; see also Danziger et al., 1986).

One significant reason for the difficulty in defining technology's effects is that the variety of work and work environments across organizations is so great (Palmquist, 1992). It is difficult to compare, for example, the record-keeping operation of a large hospital, the manufacturing division of a major automobile producer, and the diverse types of activities that teachers and school principals typically undertake. And even between similar environments in the same industry, the way in which jobs are structured and carried out may be significantly different. Some sociologists have concluded that it may therefore only make sense to study organizational impacts of technology on the micro level, i.e., within the subunits of a particular environment (Comstock & Scott, 1977; Scott, 1975, 1987).

Defining and predicting the organizational context of a new technology on such a local level have also proved difficult. It is extraordinarily complex to define the web of social intents, perceptions, decisions, reactions, group relations, and organizational settings into which a new technology will be cast. Those who work using this framework (e.g., Bijker, Hughes & Pinch, 1987; Fulk, 1993; Joerges, 1990; Nartonis, 1993) often try to identify the relationships among the participants in a given setting, and then on that basis try to define the meaning that a technology has for them, rather than focus on the impact of a particular kind of hardware on individuals' work in isolation.

A further aspect of the social context of technology has to do with the relative power and position of the actors involved. Langdon Winner (1980) argues that technologies are in fact not merely tools; they have their political and social meanings "built in" by virtue of the ways we define, design, and use them. A classic example for Winner is the network of freeways designed by civil engineer Robert Moses for the New York City metropolitan region in the 1930s. The bridges that spanned the new arterials that led to public beaches were too low to allow passage by city buses, thus keeping hoi polloi away from the ocean front, while at the same time welcoming the more affluent, newly mobile (car-owning) middle class. The design itself, rather than the hardware of bridge decks, roads, and beach access points, defined what could later be done with the system once it had been built and put into use. Similar effects of predisposition-through-design, Winner argues, are to be found in nuclear-power plants and nuclear-fuel reprocessing facilities (Winner, 1977, 1993).

An attempt to link the critical and positivist models of how technology interacts with social and political structures is provided by Street (1992). He proposes that subjecting to public scrutiny both the "hardware" side of technology and the fundamental assumptions that underlay its design and creation may lead to an improved way of handling the political decisions that necessarily now must be made with regard to implementation of particular technological systems.

6.3.1.3.3 Technology and Bureaucracy. One persistent view of technology's role within organizations is as a catalyst for overcoming centralized bureaucratic inertia (Rice, 1992; Sproul & Kiesler, 1991a). Electronic mail is widely reputed to provide a democratizing and leveling influence in large bureaucracies; wide access to electronic

databases within organizations may provide opportunities for whistle-blowers to identify and expose problems; the rapid collection and dissemination of information on a variety of organizational activities may allow both workers and managers to see how productive they are and where changes might lead to improvement (Sproull & Kiesler, 1991b). While the critics are equally vocal in pointing out technology's potential organizational downside in such domains as electronic monitoring of employee productivity and "deskilling"—the increasing polarization of the workforce into a small cadre of highly skilled managers and technocrats, and a much larger group of lower-level workers whose room for individual initiative and creativity is radically constrained by technology (e.g., Garson, 1989)—the general consensus (especially following the intensified discussion of the advent of the "information superhighway" in the early 1990s) seemed positive.

But ultimately the role of technology in an increasingly bureaucratized society may depend more on the internal assumptions we ourselves bring to thinking about its use. Rosenbrock (1990) suggests that we too easily confuse achievement of particular, economically desirable ends with the attainment of a more general personal, philosophical, or social good. This leads to the tension that we often feel when thinking about the possibility of replacement of humans by machines. Rosenbrock (1990) asserts that:

> Upon analysis it is easy to see that "assistance" will always become "replacement" if we accept [this] causal myth. The expert's skill is defined to be the application of a set of rules, which express the causal relations determining the expert's behavior. Assistance then can only mean the application of the same rules by a computer, in order to save the time and effort of the expert. When the rule set is made complete, the expert is no longer needed, because his skill contains nothing more than is embodied in the rules (p. 167).

But when we do this, he notes, we lose sight of basic human needs and succumb to a "manipulative view of human relations in technological systems" (p. 159).

6.3.1.4. Schools as Organizations. One problem that educational sociologists have faced for many years is how to describe schools as organizations. Early analyses focused on the role of school administrator as part of an industrial production engine: the school. Teachers were workers, students—products, and teaching materials and techniques—the means of production. The vision was persuasive in the early part of this century when schools, as other social organizations, were just developing into their current forms.

But the typical methods of analysis used in organizational sociology were designed to provide a clear view of how large industrial firms operated, and it early became clear that these enterprises were not identical to public schools. Their tasks were qualitatively different; their goals and outcomes were not equally definable or measurable; the techniques they used to pursue their aims were orders of magnitude apart in terms of specificity. Perhaps most importantly, schools operated in a messy, public environment where problems and demands came not from a single central location but seemingly from all sides; they had to cater to the needs of teachers, students, parents, employers, and politicians, all of whom might have different visions of what the schools were for.

It was in answer to this perceived gap between the conceptual models offered by classical organizational sociology and the realities of the school that led to the rise among school organization theorists of the "loose-coupling" model. According to this approach, schools were viewed as systems that were only loosely linked together with any given portion of their surroundings. It was the diversity of schools' environment that was important, argued these theorists. Their view was consistent with the stronger emphasis given to environmental variables in the field of organizational sociology in general starting with the 1970s.

The older, more mechanistic vision of schools as mechanisms did not die, however. Instead, it lived on and gained new adherents under a number of new banners. Two of these—the "Effective Schools" movement and "outcome-based education"—are especially significant for those working in the field of educational technology, because they are connected with essential aspects of our field. The effective-schools approach was born of the school reform efforts that started with the publication of the report on the state of America's schools, A Nation at Risk (National Commission, 1983). That report highlighted a number of problems with the nation's schools, including a perceived drop in standards for academic achievement (but note Carson et al., 1991). A number of states and school districts responded to this problem by attempting to define an "effective school." The definitions varied, but there were common elements: high expectations, concerned leadership, committed teaching, involved parents, and so forth. In a number of cases these elements were put together into a "package" that was intended to define and offer a prescription for good schooling (Mortimer, 1993; Fredericks & Brown, 1993; Purkey & Smith, 1983; Rosenholtz, 1985; Scheerens, 1991).

A further relative of the earlier mechanistic visions of school improvement was seen during the late 1980s in the trend toward definition of local, state, and national standards in education (e.g., National Governors' Association, 1986, 1987) and in the new enthusiasm for "outcome-based" education. Aspects of this trend become closely linked with economic analyses of the schooling system, such as those offered by Chubb and Moe (1990).

There were a number of criticisms and critiques of the effective-schools approach. The most severe of these came from two quarters: those concerned about the fate of minority children in the schools, who felt that these children would be forgotten in the new drive to push for higher standards and "excellence" (e.g., Dantley, 1990; Boysen, 1992) and those concerned with the fate of teachers who worked directly in schools, who were seen to be "deskilled" and ignored by an increasingly top-down system of educational reform (e.g., Elmore, 1992). These factions, discontented by the focus on results and apparent lack of attention to

individual needs and local control, have served as the focus for a "second wave" of school restructuring efforts that have generated such ideas as "building-based management," school site councils, teacher empowerment, and action research.

Some empirical evidence for the value of these approaches has begun to emerge recently, showing, for example, that teacher satisfaction and a sense of shared community among school staff are important predictors of efficacy (Lee, Dedrick & Smith, 1991). Indications from some earlier research, however, suggest that the school effectiveness and school restructuring approaches may in fact simply be two alternative conceptions of how schools might best be organized and managed. The school effectiveness model of centrally managed change may be more productive in settings where local forces are not sufficiently powerful, well organized, or clear on what needs to be done, whereas the locally determined course of school restructuring may be more useful when local forces can in fact come to a decision about what needs to happen (Firestone & Herriott, 1982).

How to make sense of these conflicting claims for what the optimal mode of school organization might be? The school effectiveness research urges us to see human organizations as rational, manageable creations, able to be shaped and changed by careful, conscious action of a few well-intentioned administrators. The school restructuring approach, on the other hand, suggests that organizations, and schools, are best thought of as collectivities, groups of individuals who, to do their work better, need both freedom and the incentive that comes from joining with peers in search of new approaches. The first puts the emphasis on structure, central control, and rational action; the latter on individuals, community values, and the development of shared meaning.

A potential linkage between these differing conceptions is offered by James Coleman, the well-known sociologist who studied the issue of integration and school achievement in the 1960s. Coleman (1993) paints a broad picture of the rise of corporate forms of organization (including notably schools) and concomitant decline of traditional sources of values and social control (family, church). He sees a potential solution in reinvesting parents (and perhaps by extension other community agents) with a significant economic stake in their children's future productivity to the state via a kind of modified and extended voucher system. The implications are intriguing, and we will return to them later in this chapter as we discuss the possibility of a sociology of educational technology.

6.3.1.5. Educational Technology and School Organization.

If we want to think about the sociological and organizational implications of educational technology as a field, we need something more than a "history of the creation of devices." Some histories of the field (e.g., Saettler, 1968) have provided just that. But while it is useful to know when certain devices first came on the scene, it would be more helpful in the larger scheme of things to know why school boards, principals, and teachers wanted to buy those devices, how educators thought about their use as they were introduced, what they were actually used for, and what real changes they brought about in how teachers and students worked in classrooms and how administrators and teachers worked together in schools and districts. It is through thousands of such decisions, reactions, perceptions, and intents that the field of educational technology has been defined.

As we consider schools as organizations, it is important to bear in mind that there are multiple levels of organization in any school: the organizational structure imposed by the state or district, the organization established for the particular school in question, and the varieties of organization present in both the classroom and among the teachers who work at the school. Certainly there are many ways of using technology that simply match (or even reinforce) existing bureaucratic patterns: districts that use e-mail only to send out directives from the central office, for example, or large-scale central computer labs equipped with integrated learning packages through which all children progress in defined fashion.

As we proceed to think about how technology may affect schools as organizations, there are three central questions we should consider. Two of these—the overall level of adoption and acceptance of technology into schools (i.e., the literature on educational innovation and change), and the impact of technology on specific patterns of organization and practice within individual classrooms and schools (i.e., the literature on roles and role change in education)— have been commonplaces in the research literature on educational technology for some years. The third—organizational analysis of schools under conditions of technological change—is only now emerging.

6.3.1.5.1. The Problem of Innovation. We gain perspective on the slow spread of technology into schools from work on innovations as social and political processes. Early models of how new practices come to be accepted were based on the normal distribution; a few brave misfits would first try a new practice, followed by community opinion leaders, "the masses," and finally a few stubborn laggards. Later elaborations suggested additional factors at work: concerns about the effects of the new approach on established patterns of work, different levels of commitment to the innovation, and so on (Rogers, 1962; Hall & Hord, 1984; Hall & Loucks, 1978. See also 23.7.7, Chapter 37).

If we view technologies as innovations in teachers' ways of working, then there is evidence they will be accepted and used if they buttress a teacher's role and authority in the classroom (e.g., Godfrey, 1965, on overhead projectors), and disregarded if they are proposed as alternatives to the teacher's presence and worth (e.g., early televised instruction, programmed instruction in its original Skinnerian garb; Cuban, 1986). Computers and related devices seem to fall somewhere in the middle: They can be seen as threats to the teacher, but also as helpmates and liberators from drudgery (Kerr, 1991). Attitudes on the parts of teachers

and principals toward the new technology have been well studied, both in the past and more recently regarding computers (e.g., Honey & Moeller, 1990; Pelgrum, 1993). But attitude studies, as noted earlier, rarely probe the significant issues of power, position, and changes in the organizational context of educators' work, and the discussion of acceptance of technology as a general stand-in for school change gradually has become less popular over the years. Scriven (1986), for example, suggested that it would be more productive to think of computers not simply as devices but rather as new sources of energy within the school, energy that might be applied in a variety of ways to alter teachers' roles.

Less attention has been paid to the diffusion of the "process technology" of the instructional development/ instructional design process. There have been some attempts to chart the spread of notions of systematic thinking among teachers, and a number of popular classroom teaching models of the 1970s (e.g., the "Instructional Theory into Practice," or ITIP, approach of Madeline Hunter) seemed closely related to the notions of ID. While some critics saw ID as simply another plot to move control of the classroom away from the teacher and into the hands of "technicians" (Nunan, 1983), others saw ID providing a stimulus for teachers to think in more logical, connected ways about their work, especially if technologists themselves recast ID approaches in a less formal way so as to allow teachers leeway to practice "high influence" teaching (Martin & Clemente, 1990; see also Shrock, 1985; Shrock & Higgins, 1990). More elaborated visions of this sort of application of both the hardware and software of educational technology to the micro- and macro-organization of schools include Reigeluth and Garfinkle's (1992) depiction of how the education system as a whole might change under the impact of new approaches (see also Kerr, 1989a, 1990a).

6.3.1.5.2. Studies of Technology and Educational Roles. What has happened in some situations with the advent of contemporary educational technology is a quite radical restructuring of classroom experience. This has not been simply a substitution of one model of classroom life for another but rather an extension and elaboration of what is possible in classroom practice. The specific elements involved are several: greater student involvement in project-oriented learning and increased learning in groups, a shift in the teacher's role and attitude from being a source of knowledge to being a coach and mentor, and a greater willingness on the parts of students to take responsibility for their own learning. Such changes do not come without costs; dealing with a group of self-directed learners who have significant resources to control and satisfy their own learning is not an easy job. But the social relationships within classrooms can be significantly altered by the addition of computers and a well-developed support structure. (For further examples of changes in teachers' roles away from traditional direct instruction and toward more diverse arrangements, see Davies, 1988; Hardy, 1992; Hooper, 1992; Hooper & Hannafin, 1991; Kerr, 1977, 1978; Laridon, 1990a, 1990b; McIlhenny, 1991; also 35.1. For a discussion of changes in the principal's role, see Wolf, 1993.)

Indeed, the evolving discussion on the place of ID in classroom life seems to be drawing closer to more traditional sociological studies of classroom organization and the teacher's role. One such study suggests that a "more uncertain" technology (in the sense of general organization) of classroom control can lead to more delegation of authority, more "lateral communication" among students, and increased effectiveness (Cohen, Lotan & Leechor, 1989). The value of intervening directly in administrators' and teachers' unexamined arrangements for classroom organization and classroom instruction was affirmed in a study by Dreeben and Barr (1988).

6.3.1.5.3. The Organizational Impact of Educational Technology. If the general conclusion of some sociologists (as noted above) that the organizational effects of technology are best observed on the microlevel of classrooms, offices, and interpersonal relations, rather than the macrolevel of district and state organization, then we would be well advised to focus our attention on what happens in specific spheres of school organizational life. It is not surprising that most studies of educational technology have focused on classroom applications, for that is the image that most educators have of its primary purpose. Discussions of the impact of technology on classroom organization, however, are rarer. Some empirical studies have found such effects, noting especially the change in the teacher's role and position from being the center of classroom attention to being more of a mentor and guide for pupils. This shift, however, is seen as taking significantly longer than many administrators might like, typically taking from 3 to 5 years (Kerr, 1991; Hadley & Sheingold, 1993; see also 13.6.7, 14.8.2).

Some models of application of technology to overall school organization do suggest that it can loosen bureaucratic structures (Hutchin, 1992; Kerr, 1989b; McDaniel, McInerney & Armstrong, 1993). Examples include the use of technology to allow teachers and administrators to communicate more directly, thus weakening existing patterns of one-way, top-down communication; and networks linking teachers and students, either within a school or district, or across regional or national borders, thus breaking the old pattern of isolation and parochialism and leading to greater collegiality (Tobin & Dawson, 1992). Linkages between schools, parents, and the broader community have also been tried sporadically, and results so far appear promising

There have been some studies that have focused on administrators' changed patterns of work with the advent of computers. Kuralt (1987), for example, described a computerized system for gathering and analyzing information on teacher and student activity. Special educators have been eager to consider both instructional and administrative uses for technology, with some seeing the potential to facilitate the often-cumbersome processes of student identification and placement through better application of technology (Prater & Ferrara, 1990). Administrators concerned about facilitating contacts with parents have also found solutions using technology to describe assignments, provide support-

ive approaches, and allow parents to communicate with teachers using voice mail (Bauch, 1989). However, improved communication does not necessarily lead to greater involvement, knowledge, or feelings of "ownership" on the parts of educators. In a study of how schools used technology to implement a new budget planning process in school-based management schools, Brown (1994) found that many teachers simply did not have the time or the training needed to participate meaningfully in budget planning via computer.

6.3.1.5.4. Educational Technology and Assumptions about Schools as Organizations. There is clearly no final verdict on the impact educational technology may have on schools as organizations. In fact, we seem to be faced with competing models of both the overall situation in schools and the image of what role educational technology might play there. On the one hand, the advocates of a rational-systems view of school organization and management—the effective-schools devotees—would stress technology's potential for improving the flow of information from administration to teachers, and from teachers to parents, for enabling management to collect more rapidly a wider variety of information about the successes and failures of parts of the system as they seek to achieve well-defined goals.

A very different image would come from those enticed by the vision of school restructuring. They would likely stress technology's role in allowing wide access to information, free exchange of ideas, and the democratizing potentials inherent in linking schools and communities more closely.

Is one of these images more accurate than the other? Hardly, for each depends on a different set of starting assumptions. The rational-systems adherents see society (and hence education) as a set of more or less mechanistic linkages, and efficiency as a general goal. Technology, in this vision, is a support for order, rationality, and enhanced control over processes that seem inordinately "messy." The proponents of the "teledemocracy" approach, on the other hand, are more taken by organic images, view schools as institutions where individuals can come together to create and recreate communities, and are more interested in technology's potential for making the organization of the educational system not necessarily more orderly, but perhaps more diverse.

These images and assumptions, in turn, play out in the tasks each group sets for technology: monitoring, evaluation, assurance of uniformity (in outcomes if not methods), and provision of data for management decisions on the one hand; communication among individuals, access to information, diversification of the educational experience, and provision of a basis on which group decisions may be made, on the other. We shall discuss the implications of these differences further in the concluding section.

6.4 THE SOCIOLOGY OF GROUPS

American sociologists have recently come to focus more and more on groups that are perceived to be in a position of social disadvantage. Racial minorities, women, and those from lower socioeconomic strata are the primary examples. The sociological questions raised in the study of disadvantaged groups include: How do such groups come to be identified as having special, unequal status? What forms of discrimination do they face? How are attitudes about their status formed, and how do these change among the population at large? And what social or organizational policies may unwittingly contribute to their disadvantaged status? Because these groupings of race, gender, and class are so central to discussions of education in American society, and because there are ways that each intersects with educational technology, they will serve as the framework for the discussion that follows.

For each of these groups, there is a set of related questions of concern to us here. First, assuming that we wish to sustain a democratic society that values equity, equal opportunity, and equal treatment under law, *are we currently providing equal access to educational technology in schools?* Second, when we do provide access, are we providing access to the *same kinds of experiences?* In other words, are the experiences of males and females in using technology in schools of roughly comparable quality? Does one group or the other suffer from bias in content of the materials with which they are asked to work, or in the types of experiences to which they are exposed? Third, are there *differing perspectives on the use of the technology that are particular to one group or the other?* The genders, for example, may in fact experience the world differently, and therefore their experiences with educational technology may be quite different. And finally, so what? That is, *is it really important that we provide equality of access to educational technology*, bias-free content, etc., or are these aspects of education ultimately neutral in their actual impact on an individual's life chances?

6.4.1 Minority Groups

The significance of thinking about the issue of access to education in terms of racial groupings was underlined in studies beginning with the 1960s. Coleman's (1966) landmark study on the educational fate of American school children from minority backgrounds led to a continuing struggle to desegregate and integrate American schools, a struggle that continues. Coleman's findings—that African-American children were harmed academically by being taught in predominantly minority schools, and that Caucasian children were not harmed by being in integrated schools—provided the basic empirical justification for a whole series of federal, state, and local policies encouraging racial integration and seeking to abolish de facto segregation. This struggle continues, though in a different vein. As laws and local policies abolished de facto forms of segregated education, and access was guaranteed, the need to provide fully valuable educational experiences became more obvious.

6.4.1.1. Minorities and Access to Educational Technology.

The issue of minority access to educational technology was not a central issue before the advent of computers in the early 1980s. While there were a few studies that explicitly sought to introduce minority kids to media production techniques (e.g., Culkin, 1965; Schwartz, 1987; Worth & Adair, 1972), the issue did not seem a critical one. The appearance of computers, however, brought a significant change. Not only did the machines represent a higher level of capitalization of the educational enterprise than had formerly been the case, they also carried a heavier symbolic load than had earlier technologies, being linked in the public mind with images of a better future, greater economic opportunity for children, and so forth. Each of these issues led to problems vis-à-vis minority access to computers.

Initial concerns about the access of minorities to new technologies in schools were raised in Becker's studies (1983), which seemed to show not only that children in poor schools (schools where a majority of the children were from low-socioeconomic-status family backgrounds) had fewer computers available to them but also that the activities they were typically assigned by teachers featured rote memorization via use of simple drill-and-practice programs, whereas children in schools with a wealthier student base were offered opportunities to learn programming and to work with more flexible software.

This pattern was found to be less strong in a follow-up set of studies conducted a few years later (Becker, 1986), but it has continued to be a topic of considerable concern. Perhaps school administrators and teachers became concerned and changed their practices, or perhaps there were simply more computers in the schools a few years later, allowing broader access. Nonetheless, other evidence of racial disparities in access to computing resources in schools was collected by Doctor (1991), who noted continuing disparities. In 1992, the popular computer magazine *Macworld* (Borrell, 1992; Kondracke, 1992; Piller, 1992) devoted an issue (headlined "America's Shame") to these questions, noting critically that this topic seemed to have slipped out of the consciousness of many of those in the field of educational technology, and raising in a direct way the issue of the relationship (or lack of one) between government policy on school computer use and the continuing discrepancies in minority access (see also 9.5.5).

If the issue of minority access to computing resources was not a high priority in the scholarly journals, it did receive a good deal of attention at the level of federal agencies, foundations, state departments of education, and local school districts. States such as Kentucky (Pritchard, 1991), Minnesota (McInerney & Park, 1986), New York (Webb, 1986), and a group of southern states (David, 1987), all identified the question of minority access to computing resources as an important priority. Additionally, national reports and foundation conferences focused attention on the issue in the context of low minority representation in math and science fields generally (Cheek, 1991; Kober, 1991). Madaus (1991) made a particular plea regarding the increasing move towards high-stakes computerized testing and its possible negative consequences for minority students.

The issue for the longer term may well be how educational technology interacts with the fundamental problem of providing not merely access but also a lasting and valuable education, something many minority children are clearly not receiving at present. The actual outcomes from use of educational technology in education may be less critical here than the symbolic functions of involvement of minorities with the hardware and software of a new era, and the value for life and career chances of their learning the language associated with powerful new forms of "social capital." We shall have occasion to return to this idea again below as part of the discussion of social class.

6.4.1.2. Gender

6.4.1.2.1. Gender and Technology. With the rise of the women's movement, and in reaction to the perceived "male bias" of technology generally, technology's relationship to issues of gender is one that has been explored increasingly in recent years. One economic analysis describes the complex interrelationship among technology, gender, and social patterns in homes during this century. Technological changes coincided with a need to increase the productivity of household labor. As wages rose, it became more expensive for women to remain at home, out of the workforce, and labor-saving technology, even though expensive, became more attractive, at first to upper-middle-class women, then to all. The simple awareness of technology's effects was enough, in this case, to bring about significant social changes (Day, 1992). Changes in patterns of office work by women have also been intensively considered by sociologists (Kraft & Siegenthaler, 1989; see also 1.12, 10.4).

6.4.1.2.2. Gender and Education. Questions of how boys' and girls' experiences in school differ have come to be a topic of serious consideration. Earlier assertions that most differences were the result of social custom or lack of appropriate role models have been called into question by the work of Gilligan and her colleagues (Gilligan, 1982; Gilligan, Ward & Taylor, 1988) which finds distinctive differences in how the sexes approach the task of learning in general, and faults a number of instructional approaches in particular (see also 9.5.4).

6.4.1.2.3. Gender and Access to Technology in Schools. Several scholars have raised the question of how women are accommodated in a generally male-centric vision of how educational technology is to be used in schools (Becker, 1986; Damarin, 1991; Kerr, 1990b; Turkle, 1984). In particular, Becker's surveys (1983, 1986) found that girls tended to use computers differently, focusing more on such activities as word processing and collaborative work, while boys liked game playing and competitive work. Similar problems were noted by Durndell and Lightbody (1993), Kerr (1990b), Lage (1991), Nelson and Watson (1991), and Nye (1991). Specific strategies to reduce the effect of gender differences in classrooms have been proposed (Neuter, 1986). The issue has also been addressed through national and international surveys of computer education

practices and policies (Reinen & Plomp, 1993; Kirk, 1992).

There is much good evidence that males and females differ both in terms of amount of computer exposure in school and in terms of the types of technology-based activities they typically choose to undertake. Some studies (Ogletree & Williams, 1990) suggest that prior experience with computers may determine interest and depth of involvement with computing by the time a student gets to higher grade levels. In fact, we are likely too close to the issues to have an accurate reading at present; the roles and expectations of girls in schools are changing, and different approaches are being tried to deal with the problems that exist. There have been some questions raised about the adequacy of the research methods used to unpack these key questions. Kay (1992), for example, found that scales and construct definitions were frequently poorly handled. Ultimately, the more complex issue of innate differences in social experience and ways of perceiving and dealing with the world will be extraordinarily difficult to unknot empirically, especially given the fundamental importance of initial definitions and the shifting social and political context in which these questions are being discussed.

Nonetheless, the question of how males and females define their experiences with technology will continue to be an important one. Ultimately, the most definitive factor here may turn out to be changes in the surrounding society and economy. As women increasingly move into management positions in business and industry, and as formerly "feminine" approaches to the organization of economic life (team management styles, collaborative decision making) are gradually reflected in technological approaches and products (computer-supported collaborative work, "groupware"), these perspectives and new approaches will gradually make their way into schools as well.

6.4.2 Social Class

Surprisingly little attention has been paid to the issue of social class differences in American education. Perhaps this is because Americans tend to think of their society as "classless," or that all are "members of the middle class." Despite some current thinking that suggests the continuing importance of class as a defining variable in American society, class and issues of access to education based on class considerations are little analyzed.

6.4.2.1. Class and Access to Educational Technology.
Only one study identified for this review addressed directly the question of access to computer technology and social class. Persell and Cookson (1987) found that computer knowledge represents a "new form of cultural capital," and that faculty and administration at elite boarding schools, in adopting new technologies, tend to think less about instructional uses and more about the need to master new technologies as a general strategy for social reproduction and protection of their own class interests.

6.4.2.1.1. Access to Information Under New Social

Conditions. If social class has been little studied, there have nonetheless been serious concerns raised about equity in access to information more generally under the new kinds of conditions that computerized information services make possible. For example, Kerr (1983) noted that certain kinds of information became less accessible when print-based information was transformed into electronic form, a concern also raised by Schiller (1976, 1981). While de Sola Pool (1983) saw the spread of new systems for information dissemination and retrieval as encouraging democracy, Doctor (1992) was concerned about existing and predicted problems in making such systems available to residents of rural areas, as well as the poor, minorities, the elderly, and the disabled.

Questions such as these are ultimately questions of policy and values. Will we be willing to pay more for services so that those less fortunate can have access at reduced or no cost? Will schools be given special access privileges if the information superhighway is eventually built? There are no answers at present, but these are significant issues that bear further examination.

6.5 EDUCATIONAL TECHNOLOGY AS SOCIAL MOVEMENT

An outside observer reading the educational technology literature over the past half century (perhaps longer) would be struck by the messianic tone in much of the writing. Edison's enthusiastic pronouncement about the value of film in education in 1918, that "soon all children will learn through the eye, not the ear" was only the first in a series of visions of technology-as-panacea. And, although their potential is now seen in a very different light, such break-throughs as instructional radio, dial-access audio, and educational television once enjoyed enormous support as "solutions" to all manner of educational problems (Cuban, 1986; Kerr, 1982).

Why has this been, and how can we understand educational technology's role over time as catalyst for a "move-ment" toward educational change, for reform in the status quo? To develop a perspective on this question, it would be useful to think about how sociologists have studied social movements. What causes a social movement to emerge, coalesce, grow, and wither? What is the role of organized professionals vs. laypersons in developing such a move-ment? What kinds of changes in social institutions do social movements bring about, and which have typically been beyond their power? How do the ideological positions of a movement's supporters (educational technologists, for example) influence the movement's fate? All these are areas in which the sociology of social movements may shed some light on educational technology's role as catalyst for changes in the structure of education and teaching.

6.5.1 The Sociology of Social Movements

Sociologists have viewed social movements using a number of different perspectives: movements as a response to social strains, as a reflection of trends and directions throughout the society more generally, as a reflection of individual dissatisfaction and feelings of deprivation, and as a natural step in the generation and modification of social institutions (McAdam, McCarthy & Zald, 1988). Much traditional work on the sociology of mass movements concentrated on the processes by which such movements emerged, how they recruited new members, defined their goals, and gathered the initial resources that would allow them to survive.

More recent work has focused attention on the processes by which movements, once organized, contrive to ensure the continued existence of their group and the long-term furtherance of its aims. Increasingly, social problems that in earlier eras were the occasion for short-lived expressions of protest by groups that may have measured their life spans in months are now the foci for long-lived organizations, for the activity of "social movement professionals," and for the creation of new institutions (McCarthy & Zald, 1973). This process is especially typical of those "professional" social movements where a primary intent is to create, extend, and preserve markets for particular professional services.

But while professionally oriented social movements enjoy some advantages in terms of expertise, organization, and the like, they also are often relatively easy for the state to control. In totalitarian governments, social movements have been controlled simply by repressing them. But in democratic systems, state and federal agencies, and their attached superstructure of laws and regulations, may in fact serve much the same function, directing and controlling the spheres of activity in which a movement is allowed to operate, offering penalties or rewards for compliance (e.g., tax-exempt status).

6.5.1.1. Educational Examples of Social Movements. While we want to focus here on educational technology as a social movement, it is useful to consider other aspects of education that have recently been mobilized in one way or another as social movements. Several examples are connected with the recent (1983 to date) efforts to reform and restructure schools. As noted above, there are differing sets of assumptions held by different sets of actors in this trend, and it is useful to think of several of them as professional social movements. One such grouping might include the Governors' Conference, Education Council of the States, and similar government-level official policy and advisory groups with a political stake in the success of the educational system. Another such movement might include the Holmes Group, NCREST (the National Center for the Reform of Education, Schools and Teaching), the National Network for Educational Renewal, and a few similar centers focused on changing the structure of teacher education. A further grouping would include conservative or liberal "think tanks" such as the Southern Poverty Law Center, People for the American Way, or the Eagle Forum, having a specific interest in the curriculum, the content of textbooks, and the teaching of particularly controversial subject matter (sex education, evolutionism vs. creationism, values education, conflict resolution, racial tolerance, etc.). We shall return later to this issue of the design of curriculum materials and the roles technologists play therein.

6.5.1.1.1. Educational Technology as Social Movement. To conceive of educational technology itself as a social movement, we need to think about the professional interests and goals of those who work within the field, and those outside the field who have a stake in its success. There have been a few earlier attempts to engage in those kinds of analyses: Travers (1973) looked at the field in terms of its political successes and failures and concluded that most activities of educational technologists were characterized by an astonishing naiveté as regards the political and bureaucratic environments in which they had to try to exist. Hooper (1969), a BBC executive, also noted that the field had failed almost entirely to establish a continuing place for its own agenda. Of those working during the 1960s and 1970s, only Heinich (1971) seemed to take seriously the issue of how those in the field thought about their work vis-à-vis other professionals. Of the critics, Nunan (1983) was most assertive in identifying educational technologists as a professionally self-interested lobby.

The advent of microcomputers changed the equation considerably. Now, technology-based programs moved from being perceived by parents, teachers, and communities as expensive toys of doubtful usefulness to being seen increasingly as the keys to future academic, economic, and social success. One consequence of this new interest was an increase in the number of professional groups interested in educational technology. Interestingly, the advantages of this new status for educational technology did not so much accrue to existing groups such as the Association for Educational Communication and Technology (AECT) or the Association for the Development of Computer-Based Instructional Systems (ADCIS), but rather to new groups such as the Institute for the Transfer of Technology to Education of the American School Board Association, the National Education Association, groups affiliated with such noneducational organizations as the Association for Computing Machinery (ACM), groups based on the hardware or applications of particular computer and software manufacturers (particularly Apple and IBM), and numerous academics and researchers involved in the design, production, and evaluation of software programs. There is also a substantial set of cross-connections between educational technology and the defense industry, as outlined in detail by Noble (1989, 1991). The interests of those helping to shape the new computer technology in the schools became clearer following publication of a number of federal and foundation-sponsored reports in the 1980s and 1990s (e.g., *Power On!*, 1988).

Teachers themselves also had a role in defining educational technology as a social movement. A number of studies of the early development of educational computing in schools (Hadley & Scheingold, 1993; Olson, 1988; Sandholtz, Ringstaff & Dwyer, 1991) noted that a small number of knowledgeable teachers in a given school typically assumed the role of "teacher-computer buffs," willingly becoming the source of information and inspiration for other teachers. It may be that some school principals and superintendents played a similar role among their peers, describing not specific ways of introducing and using computers in the classroom but general strategies for acquiring the technology, providing for teacher training, and securing funding from state and national sources. A further indication of the success of educational technology as a social movement is seen in the widespread acceptance of levies and special elections in support of technology-based projects, and in the increasing incidence of participation by citizen and corporate leaders in projects and campaigns to introduce technology into schools.

6.5.1.1.2. Educational Technology and the Construction of Curriculum Materials. Probably in no other area involving educational technologists has there been such rancorous debate over the past 20 years as in the definition and design of curricular materials. Textbook controversies have exploded in fields such as social studies (Ravitch & Finn, 1987) and natural sciences (e.g., Nelkin, 1977); the content of children's television has been endlessly examined (Mielke, 1990); and textbook publishers have been excoriated for the uniformity and conceptual vacuousness of their products (Honig, 1989).

Perhaps the strongest set of criticisms of the production of educational materials comes from those who view that process as intensely social and political, and who worry that others, especially professional educators, are sadly unaware of those considerations (e.g., Apple, 1988; Apple & Smith, 1991). Some saw "technical," nonpolitical curriculum specification and design as quintessentially American. In a criticism that might have been aimed at the supposedly bias-free, technically neutral instructional design community, Wong (1991) noted:

> Technical and pragmatic interests are also consistent with an instrumentalized curriculum that continues to influence how American education is defined and measured. Technical priorities are in keeping not only with professional interests and institutional objectives, but with historically rooted cultural expectations that emphasize utilitarian aims over intellectual pursuits (p. 17).

Technologists have begun to enter this arena with a more critical stance. Ellsworth and Whatley (1990) considered how educational films historically have reflected particular social and cultural values. Spring (1992) examined the particular ways that such materials have been consciously constructed and manipulated by various interest groups to yield a particular image of American life. The new study of Channel One by DeVaney and her colleagues (1994) indicates the ways in which the content selected for inclusion serves a number of different purposes and the interests of a number of groups, not always to educational ends.

All of these examples suggest that technologists may need to play a more active and more consciously committed role regarding the selection of content and design of materials. This process should not be regarded as merely a technical or instrumental part of the process of education but rather as part of its essence, with intense political and social overtones. This could come to be seen as an integral part of the field of educational technology, but doing so would require changes in curriculum for the preparation of educational technologists at the graduate level.

6.5.1.1.3. The Ideology of Educational Technology as a Social Movement. The examples above suggest that educational technology has had some success as a social movement, and that some of the claims made by the field (improved student learning, more efficient organization of schools, more rational deployment of limited resources, etc.) are attractive not only to educators but also to the public at large. Nonetheless, it is also worth considering the ideological underpinnings of the movement, the sets of fundamental assumptions and value positions that motivate and direct the work of educational technologists (see also 2.2, 3, 9.7.2, 10.2.3).

There is a common assumption among educational technologists that their view of the world is scientific, value neutral, and therefore easily applicable to the full array of possible educational problems. The technical and analytic procedures of instructional design ought to be useful in any setting, if correctly interpreted and applied. The iterative and formative processes of instructional development should be similarly applicable with only incidental regard to the particulars of the situation. The principles of design of CAI, multimedia, and other materials are best thought of as having universal potential. Gagné (1987) wrote about educational technology generally, for example that:

> . . . fundamental systematic knowledge derives from the research of cognitive psychologists who apply the methods of science to the investigation of human learning and the conditions of instruction (p. 7).

Rita Richey (1986), in one of the few attempts to integrate the diverse conceptual strands that feed into the field of instructional design, noted that:

> Instructional design can be defined as the science of creating detailed specifications for the development, evaluation, and maintenance of both large and small units of subject matter (p. 9).

The focus on science and scientific method is marked in other definitions of educational technology and instructional design as well. The best known text in the field (Gagné, Briggs & Wager, 1992) discusses the systems approach to instructional design as involving:

> . . . carrying out of a number of steps beginning with an analysis of needs and goals and ending with an evaluated system of instruction that demonstrably succeeds in meeting accepted goals. Decisions in each of the individual steps are based on empirical evidence, to the extent that such evidence allows. Each step leads to decisions that become "inputs" to the next step so that the whole process is as solidly based as is possible within the limits of human reason (p. 5).

Gilbert (1978, p. 81), a pioneer in the field of educational technology in the 1960s, supported his model for "behavioral engineering" with formulas:

We can therefore define behavior (*B*), in shorthand, as a product of both the repertory [of skills] *and* environment: $B = E \cdot P$

The assumption undergirding these (and many other) definitions and models of educational technology and its component parts, instructional design and instructional development, is that the procedures the field uses are scientific, value neutral, and precise. There are likely several sources for these assumptions: the behaviorist heritage of the field and the seeming control provided by such approaches as programmed instruction and CAI; the newer turn to systems theory (an approach itself rooted in the development of military systems in World War II) to provide an overall rationale for the specification of instructional environments; and the use of the field's approaches in settings ranging from schools and universities to the military, corporate and industrial training, and organizational development for large public-sector organizations.

In fact, there is considerable disagreement as to the extent to which these seemingly self-evident propositions of educational technology as movement are in fact value-free and universally applicable (or even desirable). Some of the most critical analysis of these ways of thinking about problems and their solution are in fact quite old.

Lewis Mumford, writing in 1930 about the impact of technology on society and culture, praised the "matter of fact" and "reasonable" personality that he saw arising in the age of the machine. These qualities, he asserted, were necessary if human culture was not only to assimilate the machine but also to go beyond it:

> Until we have absorbed the lessons of objectivity, impersonality, neutrality, the lessons of the mechanical realm, we cannot go further in our development toward the more richly organic, the more profoundly human (1962, p. 363).

For Mumford, the qualities of scientific thought, rational solution to social problems, and objective decision making were important, but only preliminary to a deeper engagement with more distinctively human (moral, ethical, spiritual) questions.

Jacques Ellul, a French sociologist writing in 1954, also considered the relationship between technology and society. For Ellul, the essence of "technical action" in any given field was "the search for greater efficiency" (1964, p. 20). In a description of how more efficient procedures might be identified and chosen, Ellul notes that the question is one

> . . . of finding the best means in the absolute sense, on the basis of numerical calculation. It is then the specialist who chooses the means; he is able to carry out the calculations that demonstrate the superiority of the means chosen over all the others. Thus a science of means comes into being—a science of techniques, progressively elaborated (p. 21).

"Pedagogical techniques," Ellul suggests, make up one aspect of the larger category of "human techniques," and the uses by "psychotechnicians" of such techniques on the formation of human beings will come more and more to focus on the attempt to

... restore man's lost unity, and patch together that which technological advances have separated [in work, leisure, etc.]. But only one way to accomplish this ever occurs to [psychotechnicians], and that is to use technical means. . . . There is no other way to regroup the elements of the human personality; the human being must be completely subjected to an omnicompetent technique, and all his acts and thoughts must be the objects of the human techniques (p. 411).

For Ellul, writing in what was still largely a precomputer era, the techniques in question were self-standing procedures monitored principally by other human beings. The possibility that computers might come to play a role in that process was one that Ellul hinted at, but could not fully foresee. In more recent scholarship, observers from varied disciplinary backgrounds have noted the tendency of computers (and those who develop and use them) to influence social systems of administration and control in directions that are rarely predicted and are probably deleterious to feelings of human self-determination, trust, and mutual respect. The anthropologist Shoshana Zuboff (1988), for example, found that the installation of an electronic mail system may lead not only to more rapid sharing of information but also to management reactions that generate on the part of workers the sense of working within a "panopticon of power," a work environment in which all decisions and discussion are monitored and controlled, a condition of transparent observability at all times.

Joseph Weizenbaum, computer scientist at MIT and pioneer in the field of artificial intelligence, wrote passionately about what he saw as the difficulty many of his colleagues had in separating the scientifically feasible from the ethically desirable. Weizenbaum (1976) was especially dubious of teaching university students to program computers as an end in itself:

When such students have completed their studies, they are rather like people who have somehow become eloquent in some foreign language, but who, when they attempt to write something in that language, find they have literally nothing to say (p. 278).

Weizenbaum is especially skeptical of a technical attitude toward the preparation of new computer scientists. He worries that if those who teach such students, and see their role as that of

... a mere trainer, a mere applier of "methods" for achieving ends determined by others, then he does his students two disservices. First, he invites them to become less than fully autonomous persons. He invites them to become mere followers of other people's orders, and finally no better than the machines that might someday replace them in that function. Second, he robs them of the glimpse of the ideas that alone purchase for computer science a place in the university's curriculum at all (p. 279).

Similar comments might be directed at those who would train educational technologists to work as "value-free" creators of purely efficient training.

Another critic of the "value-free" nature of technology is Neil Postman, who created a new term—Technopoly—to describe the dominance of technological thought in American society. This new world view, Postman (1992) observed,

... consists of the deification of technology, which means that the culture seeks its authorization in technology and finds its satisfactions in technology, and takes its orders from technology. This requires the development of a new kind of social order. . . . Those who feel most comfortable in Technopoly are those who are convinced that technical progress is humanity's supreme achievement and the instrument by which our most profound dilemmas may be solved. They also believe that information is an unmixed blessing, which through its continued and uncontrolled production and dissemination offers increased freedom, creativity, and peace of mind. The fact that information does none of these things—but quite the opposite—seems to change few opinions, for such unwavering beliefs are an inevitable product of the structure of Technopoly (p. 71).

Other critics also take educational technology to task for what they view as its simplistic claim to scientific neutrality. Richard Hooper, a pioneer in the field and longtime gadfly, commented that:

Much of the problem with educational technology lies in its attempt to ape science and scientific method. . . . An arts perspective may have some things to offer educational technology at the present time. An arts perspective focuses attention on values, where science's attention is on proof (p. 11).

Michael Apple (1991), another critic who has considered how values, educational programs, and teaching practices interact, noted that:

The more the new technology transforms the classroom into its own image, the more a technical logic will replace critical political and ethical understanding (p. 75).

Similar points have been made by Sloan (1985) and by Preston (1992). Postman's assertion that we must

... refuse to accept efficiency as the pre-eminent goal of human relations . . . not believe that science is the only system of thought capable of producing truth . . . [and] admire technological ingenuity but do not think it represents the highest possible form of human achievement (p. 184).

necessarily sounds unusual in the present context. Educational technologists are encouraged to see the processes they employ as beneficent, as value-free, as contributing to improved efficiency and effectiveness. The suggestions noted above that there may be different value positions, different stances toward the work of education, are a challenge, but one that the field needs to entertain seriously if it is to develop further as a social movement.

6.5.1.1.4. Success of Educational Technology as a Social Movement. If we look at the field of educational technology today, it has enjoyed remarkable success: Legislation at both state and federal levels includes educational technology as a focus for funded research and development; the topics the field addresses are regularly featured in the public media in a generally positive light; teachers, principals, and administrators actively work to incorporate educational technology into their daily routines; and citizens pass large bond issues to fund the acquisition of hardware and software for schools.

What explains the relative success of educational technology at this moment as compared with 2 decades ago? Several factors are likely involved. Certainly the greater capabilities of the hardware and software in providing for diverse, powerful instruction are not to be discounted, and the participation of technologists in defining the content of educational materials may be important for the future. But there are other features of the movement as well. Gamson (1975) discusses features of successful social movements and notes two that are especially relevant here.

As educational technologists began to urge administrators to take their approaches seriously in the 1960s and 1970s, there was often at least an implied claim that educational technology could not merely supplement but actually supplant classroom teachers. In the 1980s, this claim seems to have disappeared, and many key players (e.g., Apple Computer's Apple Classroom of Tomorrow [ACOT] project, GTE's Classroom of the Future, and others) sought to convince teachers that they were there not to replace them but to enhance their work and support them. This is in accordance with Gamson's finding that groups willing to coexist with the status quo had greater success than those seeking to replace their antagonists.

A further factor contributing to the success of the current educational technology movement may be the restricted, yet comprehensible and promising, claims it has made. The claims of earlier decades had stressed either the miraculous power of particular pieces of hardware (that were in fact quite restricted in capabilities) or the value of a generalized approach (instructional development/design) that seemed both too vague and too like what good teachers did anyway to be trustworthy as an alternative vision. In contrast, the movement to introduce computers to schools in the 1980s, while long on general rhetoric, in fact did not start with large promises but rather with an open commitment to experimentation and some limited claims (enhanced remediation for poor achievers, greater flexibility in classroom organization, and so on). This too is in keeping with Gamson's findings that social movements with single or limited issues have been more successful than those pushing for generalized goals or those with many subparts.

It is likely too early to say whether educational technology will ultimately be successful as a social movement, but the developments of the past dozen or so years are promising for the field. There are stronger indications of solidity and institutionalization now than previously, and the fact the technology is increasingly seen as part of the national educational, economic, and social discussion bodes well for the field. The increasing number of professionally related organizations, and their contacts with other parts of the educational, public policy, and legislative establishment are also encouraging signs. Whether institutionalization of the movement equates easily to success of its aims, however, is another question. Gamson notes that it has traditionally been easier for movements to gain acceptance from authorities and other sources of established power than actually to achieve their stated goals. Educational technologists must be careful not to confuse recognition and achievement of status for their work and their field with fulfillment of the mission they have claimed. The concerns noted above about the underlying ideology that educational technology asserts—value neutrality, use of a scientific approach, pursuit of efficiency—are also problematic, for they suggest that educational technologists may need to think still more deeply about fundamental aspects of their work than has been the case to date.

6.6 A NOTE ON SOCIOLOGICAL METHOD

The methods typically used in sociological research differ considerably from those usually employed in educational studies, and particularly from those used in the field of educational technology. Specifically, the use of two approaches in sociology—surveys and participant observation—differs sufficiently from common practice in educational research that it makes sense for us to consider them briefly here. In the first case, survey research, there are problems in making the inference from attitudes to probable actions that are infrequently recognized by practitioners in education. In the second case, participant observation and immersion in a cultural surround, the approach has particular relevance to the sorts of issues reviewed here, yet is not often employed by researchers in educational technology.

6.6.1 Surveys: from Attitudes to Actions

Survey research is hardly a novelty for educators; it is one of the most commonly taught methods in introductory research methods courses in education. Sociologists, who developed the method in the last century, have refined the approach considerably, and there exist good discussions of the process of survey construction that are likely more sophisticated than those encountered in introductory texts in educational research. These address nuances of such questions as sampling technique, eliciting high response rates, and so forth (e.g., Hyman, 1955, 1991). For our purposes here, we include all forms of surveys; mailed questionnaires, administered questionnaires, and in-person or telephone interviews (see also 41.2).

An issue often left unaddressed in discussions of the use of survey research in education, however, is the difficulty of making the inference that if a person holds an attitude on a particular question, that the attitude translates into a likelihood of engaging in related kinds of action. For example, it frequently seems to be taken for granted that if a teacher believes that all children have a right to an equal education, then that teacher will work to include children with disabilities in the class, will avoid discriminating against children from different ethnic backgrounds, and so forth.

Unfortunately, the evidence is not particularly hopeful that people do behave in accord with the beliefs that they articulate in response to surveys. This finding has been borne out in a number of different fields, from environmental protection (Scott & Willits, 1994), to smoking and health (van Assema, Pieterse & Kok, 1993), to sexual behavior (Norris & Ford, 1994), to racial prejudice (Duckitt, 1992–93). In all these cases, there exists a generally accepted social stereotype of what "correct" or "acceptable" attitudes are: One is supposed to care for the environment, refrain from smoking, use condoms during casual sex, and respect persons of different racial and ethnic backgrounds. Many people are aware of these stereotypes and will frame their answers on surveys in terms of them even when their actions do not reflect those beliefs. There is, in other words, a powerful inclination on the part of many people to answer in terms that the respondent thinks the interviewer or survey designer wants to hear.

This issue has been one of constant concern to methodologists. Investigators have attempted to use the observed discrepancies between attitude and action as a basis for challenging people about their actions and urging them to reflect on the differences between what they have said and what they have done. But some studies have suggested that bringing these discrepancies to people's attention may have effects opposite to what is intended; that is, consistency between attitudes and behavior is reduced still further (Holt, 1993).

6.6.1.1. Educational Attitudes and Actions.

The problem of discrepancies between attitudes and actions is especially pronounced for fields such as those noted above, where powerful agencies have made large efforts to shape public perceptions and, hopefully, behaviors. To what extent is it also true in education, and how might those tendencies shape research on educational technology? Differences between attitudes and actions among teachers have been especially problematic in such fields as special education (Bay & Bryan, 1991) and multicultural education (Abt-Perkins & Gomez, 1993), where changes in public values, combined with recent legal prescriptions, have generated powerful expectations among teachers, parents, and the public in general. Teachers frequently feel compelled to express beliefs in conformity to those new norms, whereas their actual behavior may still reflect unconscious biases or unacknowledged assumptions.

Is technology included among those fields where gaps exist between expressed attitudes and typical actions? There are occasions when teachers do express one thing and do another as regards the use of technology in their classrooms (McArthur & Malouf, 1991). Generally teachers have felt able to express ignorance and concerns about technology: Numerous surveys have supported this (e.g., Dupagne & Krendl, 1992; Savenye, 1992). Most studies of teacher attitudes regarding technology, however, have asked about general attitudes toward computers, their use in classrooms, and so on. But there have been few studies where attitudes toward technology are correlated to actual use.

As schools and districts spend large sums on hardware, software, and in-service training programs for teachers, the problem of attitudes and actions may become more serious. The amounts of money involved, combined with parental expectations, may lead to development of the kinds of strong social norms in support of educational technology that some other fields have already witnessed. If expectations grow for changes in patterns of classroom and school organization, such effects might be seen on several different levels. Monitoring these processes could be important for educational technologists.

6.6.2 Participant Observation

The research approach known as *participant observation* was pioneered not so much in sociology as in cultural anthropology, where its use became one of the principal tools for helping to understand diverse cultures (see also 40.2.2). Many of the pioneering anthropological studies of the early years of this century by such anthropologists as Franz Boas, Clyde Kluckhohn, and Margaret Mead used this approach, and it allowed them to demonstrate that cultures until then viewed as "primitive" in fact had very sophisticated world views, but ones based on radically different assumptions about the world, causality, evidence, and so on (Berger & Luckmann, 1966). The approach, and the studies that it permitted anthropologists to conduct, led to more complex understandings about cultures that were until that time mysteries to those who came into contact with them.

The attempts of the participant observer to both join in the activities of the group being studied and to remain in some sense "neutral" at the same time were, of course, critical to the success of the method. The problem remains a difficult one for those espousing this method, but has not blocked its continued use in certain disciplines. In sociology, an interesting outgrowth of this approach in the 1960s was the development of ethnomethodology, a perspective that focused on understanding the practices and world views of a group under study with the intent to use these very methods in studying the group (Garfinkel, 1967; Boden, 1990). Ethnomethodology borrowed significant ideas from the symbolic interactionism of G. H. Mead and also from the phenomenological work of the Frankfurt School of sociologists and philosophers. Among its propositions were a rejection of the importance of theoretical frameworks imposed from the outside and an affirmation of the sense-making activities of actors in particular settings. The approach was always perceived as controversial, and its use resulted in a good-many heated arguments in academic journals. Nonetheless, it was an important precursor to many of the ethnological approaches now being seriously used in the study of educational institutions and groups.

6.6.2.1. Participant Observation Studies and Educational Technology. The literature of educational technology is replete with studies that are based on surveys and questionnaires, and on a smaller number of recent works that take a more anthropological approach. Olsen's (1988) and Cuban's (1986) work are among the few that really seek to study teachers, for example, from the teacher's own perspective. Shrock's (1985) study with faculty members in higher education around the use of instructional design offers a further example. But there could easily be more of this work, studies that might probe teachers' thought practices as they were actually working in classrooms, or as they were trying to interact with peers in resolving some educational or school decision involving technology. Similar work with principals and administrators could illuminate how their work is structured and how technology affects their activities. Also, studies from the inside of how schools and colleges cope with major educational technology-based restructuring efforts could be enormously valuable. What the field is missing, and could profit from, are studies that would point out for us how and where technology is and is not embedded into the daily routines of teachers, and into the patterns of social interaction that characterize the school and the community.

6.7 TOWARD A SOCIOLOGY OF EDUCATIONAL TECHNOLOGY

6.7.1 Organizations and Educational Technology

The foregoing analysis suggests that there is sociological dimension to the application of educational technology that may be as significant as its impacts in the psychological realm. But if this is true, as an increasing number of scholars seem to feel (see, e.g., Cuban, 1993), then we are perilously thin on knowledge of how technology and the existing organizational structure of schools interact. And this ignorance, in turn, makes it difficult for us either to devise adequate research strategies to test hypotheses or to predict in which domains the organizational impact of technology may be most pronounced. Nonetheless, there are enough pieces of the puzzle in place for us to hazard some guesses.

6.7.1.1. The Micro-Organization of School Practice. Can educational technology serve as a catalyst for the general improvement of students' experience in classrooms? Improve student learning, ensure teacher accountability, provide accurate assessments of how students are faring vis-à-vis their peers? For many in the movement to improve school efficiency, these are key aspects of educational technology, and a large part of the rationale for its extended use in schools. For example, Perelman (1987, 1992) makes the vision of improved efficiency through technology a major theme of his work. This also is a principal feature of Chris Whittle's arguments for privatized, more efficient schools in the Edison Project. On the other hand, enthusiasts for school restructuring through teacher empowerment

and site-based management see technology as a tool for enhancing community and building new kinds of social relationships among students, between students and teachers, and among teachers, administrators, and parents (see also 35.1, 35.5).

6.7.1.1.1. Technologies and the Restructuring of Classroom Life. The possibilities here are several, and the approaches that might be taken are therefore likely orthogonal. We have evidence that technology can indeed improve efficiency in some cases, but we must not forget the problems that earlier educational technologists encountered when they sought to make technology, rather than teachers, the center of reform efforts (Kerr, 1989b). On the other hand, the enthusiasts for teacher-based reform strategies must recognize the complexities and time-consuming difficulties of these approaches, as well as the increasing political activism by the new technology lobbies of hardware and software producers, business interests, and parent groups concerned about perceived problems with the school system generally and teacher recalcitrance in particular.

Computers already have had a significant impact on the ways in which classroom life can be organized and conducted. Before the advent of computers, even the teacher most dedicated to trying to provide a variety of instructional approaches and materials was hard-pressed to make the reality match the desire. There were simply no easy solutions to the problem of how to organize and manage activities for 25 or 30 students. Trying to get teachers in training to think in more diverse and varied ways about their classroom work was a perennial problem for schools and colleges of education (see, e.g., Joyce & Weil, 1986).

Some applications of computers—use of large-scale Integrated Learning Systems (ILSs), for instance—support a changed classroom organization, but only within relatively narrow confines (and ones linked with the status quo). Other researchers have cast their studies in such a way that classroom management became an outcome variable. McLellan (1991), for example, discovered that dispersed groups of students working on computers could ease, rather than exacerbate, teachers' tasks of classroom management in relatively traditional settings.

Other studies have focused on the placement of computers in individual classrooms vs. self-contained laboratories or networks of linked computers. The latter arrangements, noted Watson (1990), are "in danger of inhibiting rather than encouraging a diversity of use and confidence in the power of the resource" (p. 36). Others who have studied this issue seem to agree that dispersion is more desirable than concentration in fostering diverse use.

On a wider scale, it has become clear that using computers can free teachers' time in ways unimaginable only a few years ago. Several necessary conditions must be met: Teachers must have considerable training in the use of educational technology; they must have a view of their own professional development that extends several years into the future; there must be support from the school or district; there must be sufficient hardware and software; and there should be a flexible district policy that gives teachers the chance to develop a personal style and a feeling of individual ownership and creativity in the crafting of personally significant individual models of what teaching with technology looks like (see, for examples, Lewis, 1990; Newman, 1990a, 1990b, 1991; Olson, 1988; Ringstaff, Sandholz & Dwyer, 1991; Sheingold & Hadley, 1990; Wiske, 1988).

6.7.1.1.2. Educational Organization at the Middle Range: Teachers Working with Teachers. A further significant result of the wider application of technology in education is a shift in the way educators (teachers, administrators, specialists) collect and use data in support of their work. Education has long been criticized for being a "soft" discipline, and that has in many cases been true. But there have been reasons: Statistical descriptions of academic achievement are not intrinsically easy to understand, and simply educating teachers in their use has never been easy; educational data have been seen as being more generalizable than they likely are, but incompatible formats and dissimilar measures have limited possibilities for sharing even those bits of information that might be useful across locations; and educators have not been well trained in how to generate useful data of their own and use it on a daily basis in their work (see also 35.8).

In each of these areas, the wider availability of computers and their linkage through networks can make a significant difference in educational practice. Teachers learn about statistical and research procedures more rapidly with software tools that allow data to be presented and visualized more readily. Networks allow sharing of information among teachers in different schools, districts, states, or even countries. Combined with the increased focus today on collaborative research projects that involve teachers in the definition and direction of the project, this move appears to allow educational information to be more readily shared. And the combination of easier training and easier sharing, together with a reemphasis on teacher education and the development of "reflective practitioners," indicates how teachers can become true "producers and consumers" of educational data. There is evidence that such changes do in fact occur, and that a more structured approach to information sharing among teachers can develop, but only over time and with much support (Sandholz, Ringstaff & Dwyer, 1991). Budin (1991) notes that much of the problem in working with teachers is that computer enthusiasts have insisted on casting the issue as one of training, whereas it might more productively "emphasize *teaching* as much as computing" (p. 24).

What remains to be seen here is the extent to which the spread of such technologies as electronic mail and wide access to networked information will change school organization. The evidence from fields outside of education has so far not been terribly persuasive that improved communication is necessarily equivalent to better management, improved efficiency, or flatter organizational structures. Rather, the technology in many cases merely seems to amplify processes and organizational cultures that already exist. It seems most likely that the strong organizational and cultural expectations that bind schools into certain forms will not be easily broken through the application of technology. Cuban (1993), Sheingold and Tucker (1990), and Cohen (1987) all suggest that these forms are immensely strong and supported by tight webs of cultural and social norms that are not shifted easily or quickly. Thus, we may be somewhat skeptical about the claims by enthusiasts that technology will by itself bring about a revolution in structure or intraschool effectiveness overnight. Its effects are likely to be slower and to depend on a complex of other decisions regarding organization taken within schools and districts.

6.7.1.1.3. The Macro-Organization of Schools and Communities. A particularly salient aspect of education in America and other developed nations is the linkage presumed to exist between schools and the surrounding community. Many forms of school organization and school life more generally are built around such linkages: relationships between parents and the school, between the schools and the workplaces of the community, between the school and various social organizations. These links are powerful determinants of what happens, and what may happen in schools, not so much because they influence specific curricular decisions, or because they determine administrative actions, but rather because they serve as conduits for a community's more basic expectations regarding the school, the students and their academic successes or failures, and the import of all of these for the future life of the community.

This is another domain in which technology may serve to alter traditional patterns of school organization. A particular example may be found in the relationships between schools and the businesses that employ their graduates. It is not surprising that businesses have for years seen schools in a negative light; the cultures and goals of the two types of institutions are significantly different. What is interesting is what technology does to the equation. Schools are, in industry's view, woefully undercapitalized. It is hard for businesses to see how schools can be so "wastefully" labor-intensive in dealing with their charges. Thus, much initial enthusiasm for joint ventures with schools and for educational reform efforts that involve technology appears, from the side of business, to be simply wise business practice: Replace old technology (teachers) with new (computers). This is the initial response when business begins to work with schools.

As industry-school partnerships grow, businesses often develop a greater appreciation of the problems and limitations schools have to face. (The pressure for such collaboration comes from the need on the part of industry to survive in a society that is increasingly dominated by "majority minorities," and whose needs for trained personnel are not adequately met by the public schools.) Classrooms, equipped with technology and with teachers who know how to use it, appear more as "real" workplaces. Technology provides ways of providing better preparation for students from disadvantaged backgrounds, and thus is a powerful support for new ways for schools and businesses to work together.

The business community is not a unified force by any means, but the competitiveness of American students and American industry in world markets is an increasing concern. As technology improves the relationship between schools and the economy, the place of the schools in the community becomes correspondingly strengthened.

Relationships between schools and businesses are not the only sphere in which technology may affect school-community relations. There are obvious possibilities in allowing closer contacts between teachers and parents, and among the various social service agencies that work in support of schools. While such communication would, in an ideal world, result in improvements to student achievement and motivation, recent experience suggests that many parents will not have the time or inclination to use these systems, even if they are available. Ultimately, again, the issues are social and political, rather than technical, in nature.

6.8 CONCLUSION: EDUCATIONAL TECHNOLOGY IS ABOUT WORK IN SCHOOLS

Contrary to the images and assumptions in most of the educational technology literature, educational technology's primary impact on schools may not be about improvements in learning or more efficient processing of students. What educational technology may be about is the work done in schools: how it is defined, who does it, to what purpose, and how that work connects with the surrounding community. Educational technology's direct effects on instruction, while important, are probably less significant in the long run than the ways in which teachers change their assumptions about what a classroom looks like, feels like, and how students in it interact when technology is added to the mix. Students' learning of thinking skills or of factual material through multimedia programs may ultimately be less significant than whether the new technologies encourage them to be active or passive participants in the civic life of a democratic society. If technology changes the ways in which information is shared within a school, it may thus change the distribution of power in that school and thereby alter fundamentally how the school does its work. And finally, technology may change the relationships between schools and communities, bringing them closer together.

These processes have already started. Their outcome is not certain, and other developments may eventually come to be seen as more significant than some of those discussed here. Nonetheless, it seems clear that the social impacts of both device and process technologies are in many cases more important than the purely technical problems that technologies are ostensibly developed to solve. As many critics note, these developments are not always benign and may have profound moral and ethical consequences that are rarely examined. What we need is a new, critical sociology

of educational technology (see 9.6), one that considers how technology affects the organization of schools, classrooms, and districts; how it provides opportunities for social groups to change their status; and how it interacts with other social and political movements that also focus on the schools. There are a few indications that such a perspective is emerging. Boyd (1991) and Webb (1991) offered a picture of educational technology as embedded in a cultural surround. And Hlynka and Belland (1991) provided a collection rich in new, critical approaches.

Much more is needed. Our view of how to use technologies is often too narrow. We tend to see the future, as Marshall McLuhan noted, through the rear-view mirror of familiar approaches and ideas from the past. In order to allow the potential inherent in educational technology to flourish, we need to shift our gaze and try to discern what lies ahead, as well as behind. As we do so, however, we must not underestimate the strength of the social milieu within which educational technology exists, or the plans that it has for how we may bring it to bear on the problems of education. A better-developed sociology of educational technology may help us refine that vision.

REFERENCES

Abt-Perkins, D. & Gomez, M.L. (1993). A good place to begin—examining our personal perspectives. *Language Arts 70*(3), 193–202.

Aldrich, H.E. & Marsden, P.V. (1988). Environments and organizations. *In* N.J. Smelser, ed. *Handbook of sociology,* 361–92. Newbury Park, CA: Sage.

Anspach, R.R. (1991). Everyday methods for assessing organizational effectiveness. *Social Problems 38*(1), 1–19.

Apple, M.W. (1988). *Teachers and texts: a political economy of class and gender relations in education.* New York: Routledge.

— (1991). The new technology: is it part of the solution or part of the problem in education? *Computers in the Schools 8*(1/2/3), 59–79.

— & Christian-Smith, L., eds. (1991). *The politics of the textbook.* New York: Routledge.

Aronson, Sidney H. (1977). Bell's electrical toy: what's the use? The sociology of early telephone usage. *In* I. de Sola Pool, ed. *The social impact of the telephone,* 15–39. Cambridge, MA: MIT Press.

Astley, W.G. & Van de Ven, A.H. (1983). Central perspectives and debates in organization theory. *Administrative Science Quarterly 28,* 245–73.

Bartky, I.R. (1989). The adoption of standard time. *Technology and Culture 30*(1), 25–56.

Bauch, J.P. (1989). The TransPARENT model: new technology for parent involvement. *Educational Leadership 47*(2), 32–34.

Bay, M. & Bryan, T.H. (1991). Teachers' reports of their thinking about at-risk learners and others. *Exceptionality 2*(3), 127–39.

Becker, H. (1983). *School uses of microcomputers: reports from a national survey.* Baltimore, MD: Johns Hopkins University, Center for the Social Organization of Schools.

— (1986). *Instructional uses of school computers.* Reports from the 1985 national study. Baltimore, MD: Johns Hopkins

University, Center for the Social Organization of Schools.

Berger, P.L. & Luckmann, T. (1966). *The social construction of reality; a treatise in the sociology of knowledge.* Garden City, NY: Doubleday.

Bidwell, C. (1965). The school as a formal organization. *In* J. March, ed. *Handbook of organizations,* 972–1022. Chicago, IL: Rand McNally.

Bijker, W.E., Hughes, T.P. & Pinch, T., eds. (1987). *The social construction of technology: new directions in the sociology and history of technology.* Cambridge, MA: MIT Press.

Boden, D. (1990). The world as it happens. *In* G. Ritzer, ed. *Frontiers of social theory,* 185–213). New York: Columbia University Press.

Boorstin, D.J. (1973). *The Americans: the democratic experience.* New York: Random House.

— (1983). *The discoverers.* New York: Random House.

Borrell, J. (1992, Sep.). America's shame: how we've abandoned our children's future. *Macworld 9*(9), 25–30.

Boyd, G. (1991). The shaping of educational technology by cultural politics and vice versa. *Educational and Training Technology International 28*(2), 87–95.

Boysen, T.C. (1992). Irreconcilable differences: effective urban schools versus restructuring. *Education and Urban Society 25*(1), 85–95.

Brown, J.A. (1994). Implications of technology for the enhancement of decisions in school-based management schools. *International Journal of Educational Media 21* (2), 87–95.

Budin, H.R. (1991). Technology and the teacher's role. *Computers in the Schools 8*(1/2/3), 15–25.

Carson, C.C., Huelskamp, R.M. & Woodall, T.D. (1991, May 10). *Perspectives on education in America.* Annotated briefing—3d draft. Albuquerque, NM: Sandia National Labs, Systems Analysis Division.

Cheek, D.W. (1991). *Broadening participation in science, technology, and medicine.* University Park, PA: National Association for Science, Technology, and Society. Available as ERIC ED No. 339671.

Chubb, J.E. & Moe, T.M. (1990). *Politics, markets, and America's schools.* Washington, DC: The Brookings Institution.

Cohen, D.K. (1987). Educational technology, policy, and practice. *Educational Evaluation and Policy Analysis 9* (2), 153–70.

Cohen, E.G., Lotan, R.A. & Leechor, C. (1989). Can classrooms learn? *Sociology of Education 62*(1), 75–94.

Coleman, J. (1993). The rational reconstruction of society. *American Sociological Review 58,* 1–15.

— (1966). *Equality of educational opportunity.* Washington, DC: U.S. Department of Health, Education, and Welfare; Office of Education.

Comstock, D.E. & Scott, W.R. (1977). Technology and the structure of subunits: distinguishing individual and work-group effects. *Administrative Science Quarterly 22,* 177–202.

Cuban, L. (1984). *How teachers taught: constancy and change in American classrooms, 1890-1980.* New York: Longman.

— (1986). *Teachers and machines: the classroom use of technology since 1920.* New York: Teachers College Press.

— (1993). Computers meet classroom: classroom wins. *Teachers College Record 95*(2), 185–210.

Culkin, J.M. (1965, October). Film study in the high school. *Catholic High School Quarterly Bulletin.*

Damarin, S.K. (1991). Feminist unthinking and educational technology. *Educational and Training Technology International 28*(2), 111–19.

Dantley, M.E. (1990). The ineffectiveness of effective schools leadership: an analysis of the effective schools movement from a critical perspective. *Journal of Negro Education 59* (4), 585–98.

Danziger, J.N. & Kraemer, K.L. (1986). *People and computers: the impacts of computing on end users in organizations.* New York: Columbia University Press, 1986.

Darnton, R. (1984). *The great cat massacre and other episodes in French cultural history.* New York: Basic Books.

David, J.L. (1987). *Annual report, 1986.* Jackson, MS: Southern Coalition for Educational Equity. Available as ERIC Report ED 283924.

Davies, D. (1988). Computer-supported cooperative learning systems: interactive group technologies and open learning. *Programmed Learning and Educational Technology 25* (3), 205–15.

Day, T. (1992). Capital-labor substitution in the home. *Technology and Culture 33*(2), 302–27.

de Sola Pool, I. (1983). *Technologies of freedom.* Cambridge, MA: Harvard University Press.

— ed. (1977). *The social impact of the telephone.* Cambridge, MA: MIT Press.

DeVaney, A., ed. (1994). *Watching Channel One: the convergence of students, technology & private business.* Albany, NY: State University of New York Press.

DiMaggio, P.J. & Powell, W.W. (1983). The iron cage revisited: institutional isomorphism and collective rationality in organizational fields. *American Sociological Review 48,* 147–60.

Doctor, R.D. (1991). Information technologies and social equity: confronting the revolution. *Journal of the American Society for Information Science 42*(3), 216–28.

— (1992). Social equity and information technologies: moving toward information democracy. *Annual Review of Information Science and Technology 27,* 43–96.

Dreeben, R. & Barr, R. (1988). Classroom composition and the design of instruction. *Sociology of Education 61*(3), 129–42.

Duckitt, J. (1992–93). Prejudice and behavior: a review. *Current Psychology: Research and Reviews 11*(4), 291–307.

Dupagne, M. & Krendl, K.A. (1992). Teachers' attitudes toward computers: a review of the literature. *Journal of Research on Computing in Education 24*(3), 420–29.

Durndell, A. & Lightbody, P. (1993). Gender and computing: change over time? *Computers in Education 21*(4), 331–36.

Eisenstein, E. (1979). *The printing press as an agent of change* (2 Vols.). New York: Cambridge University Press.

Ellsworth, E. & Whatley, M.H. (1990). *The ideology of images in educational media: hidden curriculums in the classroom.* New York: Teachers College Press.

Ellul, J. (1964). *The technological society.* New York: Knopf.

Elmore, R. F. (1992). Why restructuring won't improve teaching. *Educational Leadership 49*(7), 44–48.

Evans, F. (1991). To "informate" or "automate": the new information technologies and democratization of the workplace. *Social Theory and Practice 17*(3), 409–39.

Febvre, L. & Martin, H-J. (1958). *The coming of the book: the impact of printing, 1450-1800.* London: Verso.

Firestone, W.A. & Herriott, R.E. (1982). *Rational bureaucracy or loosely coupled system? An empirical comparison of two images of organization.* Philadelphia, PA: Research for Better Schools. Available as ERIC Report ED 238096.

Florman, Samuel C. (1981). *Blaming technology: the irrational search for scapegoats.* New York: St. Martin's.

Fredericks, J. & Brown, S. (1993). School effectiveness and principal productivity. *NASSP Bulletin 77*(556), 9–16.

Fulk, J. (1993). Social construction of communication technology. *Academy of Management Journal 36*(5), 921–50.

Gagné, R.M. (1987). *Educational technology: foundations.* Hillsdale, NJ: Erlbaum.

—, Briggs, L. & Wager, W. (1992). *Principles of instructional design,* 4th ed. Fort Worth, TX: Harcourt, Brace.

Gamson, W. (1975). *The strategy of social protest.* Homewood, IL: Dorsey.

Garfinkel, H. (1967). *Studies in ethnomethodology.* Englewood Cliffs, NJ: Prentice Hall.

Garson, B. (1989). *The electronic sweatshop: how computers are transforming the office of the future into the factory of the past.* New York: Penguin.

Gilbert, T. (1978). *Human competence: engineering worth performance.* New York: McGraw-Hill.

Gilligan, C. (1982). *In a different voice: psychological theory and women's development.* Cambridge, MA: Harvard University Press.

—, Lyons, N.P. & Hanmer, T.J. (1990). *Making connections: the relational worlds of adolescent girls at Emma Willard School.* Cambridge, MA: Harvard University Press.

—, Ward, J.V. & Taylor, J.M., eds. (1988). Mapping the moral domain: a contribution of women's thinking to psychological theory and education. Cambridge, MA: Harvard University Press.

Giroux, H.A. (1981). *Ideology, culture & the process of schooling.* Philadelphia, PA: Temple University Press.

Glendenning, C. (1990). *When technology wounds: the human consequences of progress.* New York: Morrow.

Godfrey, E. (1965). *Audio-visual media in the public schools, 1961–64.* Washington, DC: Bureau of Social Science Research. Available as ERIC ED No. 003 761.

Hadley, M. & Sheingold, K. (1993). Commonalties and distinctive patterns in teachers' integration of computers. *American Journal of Education 101*(3), 261–315.

Hall, G. & Hord, S. (1984). Analyzing what change facilitators do: the intervention taxonomy. *Knowledge 5*(3), 275–307.

— & Loucks, S. (1978). Teacher concerns as a basis for facilitating and personalizing staff development. *Teachers College Record 80*(1), 36–53.

Hardy, V. (1992). Introducing computer-mediated communications into participative management education: the impact on the tutor's role. *Education and Training Technology International 29*(4), 325–31.

Heinich, R. (1971). *Technology and the management of instruction.* Monograph No. 4. Washington, DC: Association for Educational Communications and Technology.

Herzfeld, M. (1992). *The social production of indifference: exploring the symbolic roots of western bureaucracy.* New York: Berg.

Hlynka, D. & Belland, J.C., eds. (1991). *Paradigms regained: the uses of illuminative, semiotic and post-modern criticism as modes of inquiry in educational technology.* Englewood Cliffs, NJ: Educational Technology.

Holt, D.L. (1993). Rationality is hard work: an alternative interpretation of the disruptive effects of thinking about reasons. *Philosophical Psychology 6*(3), 251–66.

Honey, M. & Moeller, B. (1990). *Teachers' beliefs and technology integration: different values, different understandings.* Technical Report No. 6. New York: Bank Street College of Education, Center for Technology in Education.

Honig, B. (1989). The challenge of making history "come alive." *Social Studies Review 28*(2), 3–6.

Hooper, R. (1969). A diagnosis of failure. *AV Communication Review 17*(3), 245–64.

— (1990). Computers and sacred cows. *Journal of Computer Assisted Learning 6*(1), 2–13.

Hooper, S. (1992). Cooperative learning and CBI. *Educational Technology: Research & Development 40*(3), 21–38.

— & Hannafin, M. (1991). The effects of group composition on achievement, interaction, and learning efficiency during computer-based cooperative instruction. *Educational Technology: Research & Development 39*(3), 27–40.

Hounshell, D.A. (1984). *From the American system to mass production, 1800-1932: the development of manufacturing technology in the United States.* Baltimore, MD: Johns Hopkins University Press.

Hrebiniak, L.G. & Joyce, W.F. (1985). Organizational adaptation: strategic choice and environmental determinism. *Administrative Science Quarterly 30,* 336–49.

Hutchin, T. (1992). Learning in the 'neural' organization. *Education and Training Technology International 29*(2), 105–08.

Hyman, H.H. (1955). Survey design and analysis: Principles, cases, and procedures. Glencoe, IL: Free Press.

— (1991). *Taking society's measure: a personal history of survey research.* New York: Sage.

Jennings, H. (1985). *Pandaemonium: the coming of the machine as seen by contemporary observers, 1660-1886.* New York: Free Press.

Joerges, B. (1990). Images of technology in sociology: computer as butterfly and bat. *Technology and Culture 31*(1), 203–27.

Joyce, B. & Weil, M. (1986). *Models of teaching,* 3d ed. Englewood Cliffs, NJ: Prentice Hall.

Kay, R. (1992). An analysis of methods used to examine gender differences in computer-related behavior. *Journal of Educational Computing Research 8*(3), 277–90.

Kerr, S.T. (1977). Are there instructional developers in the school? A sociological look at the development of a profession. *AV Communication Review.*

— (1978) Consensus for change in the role of the learning resources specialist: order and position differences. *Sociology of Education 51,* 304–23.

— (1982). Assumptions futurists make: technology and the approach of the millennium. *Futurics 6*(3, 4), 6-11.

— (1983). Videotex and education: current developments in screen design, data structure, and access control. *Machine-Mediated Learning 1*(3), 217–53.

— (1989). Pale screens: teachers and electronic texts. *In* P. Jackson and S. Haroutunian-Gordon, eds. *From Socrates to software: the teacher as text and the text as teacher,* 202–23. 88th NSSE Yearbook, Part I. Chicago, IL: University of Chicago Press.

— (1989). Technology, teachers, and the search for school reform. *Educational Technology Research and Development 37*(4), 5–17.

— (1990). Alternative technologies as textbooks and the social imperatives of educational change. *In* D.L. Elliott & A.

Woodward, eds. *Textbooks and schooling in the United States,* 194–221. 89th NSSE Yearbook, Part I. Chicago, IL: University of Chicago Press.

— (1990). Technology: education: justice: care. *Educational Technology* 30(11), 7–12.

— (1991). Lever and fulcrum: educational technology in teachers' thinking. (1991). *Teachers College Record* 93(1), 114–36.

— & Taylor, W., eds. (1985). Social aspects of educational communications and technology. *Educational Communication and Technology Journal* 33(1).

Kirk, D. (1992). Gender issues in information technology as found in schools: authentic/synthetic/fantastic? *Educational Technology* 32(4), 28–35.

Kling, R. (1991). Computerization and social transformations. *Science, Technology, and Human Values* 16(3), 342–67.

Kober, N. (1991). *What we know about mathematics teaching and learning.* Washington, DC: Council for Educational Development and Research. Available as ERIC ED No. 343793.

Kondracke, M. (1992, Sep.). The official word: how our government views the use of computers in schools. *Macworld* 9(9), 232–36.

Kraft, J.F. & Siegenthaler, J.K. (1989). Office automation, gender, and change: an analysis of the management literature. *Science, Technology, and Human Values* 14(2), 195–212.

Kuralt, R.C. (1987). The computer as a supervisory tool. *Educational Leadership* 44(7), 71-2.

Lage, E. (1991). Boys, girls, and microcomputing. *European Journal of Psychology of Education* 6(1), 29–44.

Laridon, P.E. (1990a). The role of the instructor in a computer-based interactive videodisc educational environment. *Education and Training Technology International* 27(4), 365–74.

Laridon, P.E. (1990b). The development of an instructional role model for a computer-based interactive videodisc environment for learning mathematics. *Education and Training Technology International* 27(4), 375–85.

Lee, V.E., Dedrick, R.F. & Smith, J.B. (1991). The effect of the social organization of schools on teachers' efficacy and satisfaction. *Sociology of Education* 64, 190–208.

Lewis, R. (1990). Selected research reviews: classrooms. *Journal of Computer Assisted Learning* 6(2), 113–18.

Luke, C. (1989). *Pedagogy, printing, and Protestantism: the discourse on childhood.* Albany, NY: SUNY Press.

Madaus, G.F. (1991). *A technological and historical consideration of equity issues associated with proposals to change our nation's testing policy.* Paper presented at the Ford Symposium on Equity and Educational Testing and Assessment, Washington, DC, Mar. 1992. Available as ERIC ED No. 363618.

Martin, B.L. & Clemente, R. (1990). Instructional systems design and public schools. *Educational Technology: Research & Development* 38(2), 61–75.

Marvin, C. (1988). When old technologies were new: thinking about electric communication in the late nineteenth century. New York: Oxford University Press.

McAdam, D., McCarthy, J.D. & Zald, M.N. (1988). Social movements. *In* N.J. Smelser, ed. *Handbook of sociology,* 695–737. Newbury Park, CA: Sage.

McArthur, C.A. & Malouf, D.B. (1991). Teachers' beliefs, plans, and decisions about computer-based instruction. *Journal of Special Education* 25(1), 44–72.

McCarthy, J.D. & Zald, M.N. (1973). *The trend of social movements in America: professionalization and resource mobilization.* Morristown, NJ: General Learning.

McDaniel, E., McInerney, W. & Armstrong, P. (1993). Computers and school reform. *Educational Technology: Research & Development* 41(1), 73–78.

McIlhenny, A. (1991). Tutor and student role change in supported self-study. *Education and Training Technology International* 28(3), 223–28.

McInerney, C. & Park, R. (1986). *Educational equity in the third wave: technology education for women and minorities.* White Bear Lake, MN: Minnesota Curriculum Services Center. Available as ERIC ED No. 339667.

McLaughlin, M.W. (1987). Implementation realities and evaluation design. *Evaluation Studies Review Annual 12,* 73–97.

McLellan, H. (1991). Teachers and classroom management in a computer learning environment. *International Journal of Instructional Media* 18(1), 19–27.

Mead, G.H. (1934). *Mind, self & society from the standpoint of a social behaviorist.* Chicago, IL: University of Chicago Press.

Meyer, J.W. & Scott, W.R. (1983). *Organizational environments: ritual and rationality.* Beverley Hills, CA: Sage.

Meyrowitz, J. (1985). *No sense of place: the impact of electronic media on social behavior.* New York: Oxford University Press.

Mielke, K. (1990). Research and development at the Children's Television Workshop. [Introduction to thematic issue on "Children's learning from television."] *Educational Technology: Research & Development* 38(4), 7–16.

Mintzberg, H. (1979). *The structuring of organizations.* Englewood Cliffs, NJ: Prentice Hall.

Mort, J. (1989). *The anatomy of xerography: its invention and evolution.* Jefferson, NC: McFarland.

Mortimer, P. (1993). School effectiveness and the management of effective learning and teaching. *School Effectiveness and School Improvement* 4(4), 290–310.

Mumford, L. (1963). *Technics and civilization.* New York: Harcourt, Brace.

Naisbitt, J. & Aburdene, P. (1990). *Megatrends 2000: ten new directions for the 1990s.* New York: Morrow.

Nartonis, D.K. (1993). Response to Postman's Technopoly. *Bulletin of Science, Technology, and Society* 13(2), 67–70.

National Commission on Excellence in Education (1983). *A nation at risk: the imperative for educational reform.* Washington, DC: U.S. Government Printing Office.

National Governors' Association. (1986). *Time for results. the governors' 1991 report on education.* Washington, DC: Author.

— (1987). *Results in education, 1987.* Washington, DC: Author.

Nelkin, D. (1977). *Science textbook controversies and the politics of equal time.* Cambridge, MA: MIT Press.

Nelson, C.S. & Watson, J.A. (1991). The computer gender gap: children's attitudes, performance, and socialization. *Journal of Educational Technology Systems* 19(4), 345–53.

Neuter computer (1986). New York: Women's Action Alliance, Computer Equity Training Project.

Newman, D. (1990a). *Opportunities for research on the organizational impact of school computers.* Technical Report No. 7. New York: Bank Street College of Education, Center for Technology in Education.

— (1990b). *Technology's role in restructuring for collaborative learning.* Technical Report No. 8. New York: Bank Street College of Education, Center for Technology in Education.

Newman, D. (1991). *Technology as support for school structure and school restructuring.* Technical Report No. 14. New York: Bank Street College of Education, Center for Technology in Education.

Noble, D. (1989). Cockpit cognition: education, the military and cognitive engineering. *AI and Society 3,* 271–96.

— (1991). *The classroom arsenal: military research, information technology, and public education.* New York: Falmer.

Norberg, A.L. (1990). High-technology calculation in the early 20th century: punched card machinery in business and government. *Technology and Culture 31*(4), 753–79.

Norris, A.E. & Ford, K. (1994). Associations between condom experiences and beliefs, intentions, and use in a sample of urban, low-income, African-American and Hispanic youth. *AIDS Education and Prevention 6*(1), 27–39.

Nunan, T. (1983). *Countering educational design.* New York: Nichols.

Nye, E.F. (1991). Computers and gender: noticing what perpetuates inequality. *English Journal 80*(3), 94–95.

Ogletree, S.M. & Williams, S.W. (1990). Sex and sex-typing effects on computer attitudes and aptitude. *Sex Roles 23* (11-12), 703–13.

Olson, John. (1988). *Schoolworlds/microworlds: computers and the culture of the classroom.* New York: Pergamon.

Owen, D. (1986, Feb.). Copies in seconds. *The Atlantic,* 65-72.

Pagels, H.R. (1988). *The dreams of reason: the computer and the rise of the sciences of complexity.* New York: Simon & Schuster.

Palmquist, R.A. (1992). The impact of information technology on the individual. *Annual Review of Information Science and Technology 27,* 3–42.

Parsons, T. (1949). *The structure of social action.* Glencoe, IL: Free Press.

— (1951). *The social system.* Glencoe, IL: Free Press.

Peabody, R.L. & Rourke, F.E. (1965). The structure of bureaucratic organizations, 802–37. *In* J. March, ed. *Handbook of organizations.* Chicago, IL: Rand McNally.

Pelgrum, W.J. (1993). Attitudes of school principals and teachers towards computers: does it matter what they think? *Studies in Educational Evaluation 19*(2), 199–212.

Perelman, L.J. (1992). *School's out: hyperlearning, the new technology, and the end of education.* New York: Morrow.

— (1987). *Technology and transformation of schools.* Alexandria, VA: National School Boards Association, Institute for the Transfer of Technology to Education.

Perrow, C. (1984). *Normal accidents: living with high-risk technologies.* New York: Basic Books.

Persell, C.H. & Cookson, P.W., Jr. (1987). Microcomputers and elite boarding schools: educational innovation and social reproduction. *Sociology of Education 60*(2), 123–34.

Piller, C. (1992, Sep.). Separate realities: the creation of the technological underclass in America's schools. *Macworld 9*(9), 218–31.

Postman, N. (1992). *Technopoly: the surrender of culture to technology.* New York: Knopf.

Power on! (1988). Washington, DC: Office of Technology Assessment, U.S. Congress.

Prater, M.A. & Ferrara, J.M. (1990). Training educators to accurately classify learning disabled students using concept instruction and expert system technology. *Journal of Special Education Technology 10*(3), 147–56.

Preston, N. (1992). Computing and teaching: a socially-critical review. *Journal of Computer Assisted Learning 8,* 49–56.

Pritchard Committee for Academic Excellence. (1991). *KERA Update. What for . . .* Lexington, KY: Author. Available as ERIC ED No. 342058.

Purkey, S.C. & Smith, M.S. (1983). Effective schools: a review. *Elementary School Journal 83,* 427–54.

Ravitch, D. & Finn, C.E. (1987). *What do our 17-year-olds know?* New York: Harper & Row.

Reigeluth, C.M. & Garfinkle, R.J. (1992). *Educational Technology 32*(11), 17–23.

Reinen, I.J. & Plomp, T. (1993). Some gender issues in educational computer use: results of an international comparative survey. *Computers and Education 20*(4), 353–65.

Rice, R.E. (1992). Contexts of research on organizational computer-mediated communication. *In* M. Lea, ed. *Contexts of computer-mediated communication,* 113–44. New York: Harvester.

Richey, R. (1986). *The theoretical and conceptual bases of instructional design.* New York: Kogan Page.

Ringstaff, C., Sandholtz, J.H. & Dwyer, D.C. (1991). *Trading places: when teachers utilize student expertise in technology-intensive classrooms.* ACOT Report 15. Cupertino, CA: Apple Computer.

Rogers, E. (1962). *Diffusion of innovations,* 3d ed., 1983. New York: Free Press.

Romanelli, E. (1991). The evolution of new organizational forms. *Annual Review of Sociology 17,* 79–103.

Rosenbrock, H.H. (1990). *Machines with a purpose.* New York: Oxford University Press.

Rosenholtz, S.J. (1985). Effective schools: interpreting the evidence. *American Journal of Education 94,* 352–88.

Rothenberg, D. (1993). *Hand's end: technology and the limits of nature.* Berkeley, CA: University of California Press.

Rothschild-Whitt, J. (1979). The collectivist organization: an alternative to rational bureaucracy. *American Sociological Review 44,* 509–27.

Saettler, Paul. (1968). *A history of instructional technology.* New York: McGraw-Hill.

Sandholtz, J.H., Ringstaff, C. & Dwyer, D.C. (1991). *The relationship between technological innovation and collegial interaction.* ACOT Report 13. Cupertino, CA: Apple Computer.

Savenye, W. (1992). Effects of an educational computing course on preservice teachers' attitudes and anxiety toward computers. *Journal of Computing in Childhood Education 3*(1), 31-41.

Scheerens, J. (1991). Process indicators of school functioning: a selection based on the research literature on school effectiveness. *Studies in Educational Evaluation 17*(2-3), 371–403.

Schiller, H.I. (1976). *Communication and cultural domination.* White Plains, NY: International Arts and Sciences Press.

— (1981). *Who knows: information in the age of the Fortune 500.* Norwood, NJ: Ablex.

Schwartz, Paula A. (1987). *Youth-produced video and television.* Unpublished doctoral dissertation. New York: Teachers College, Columbia University.

Scott, D. & Willits, F.K. (1994). Environmental attitudes and behavior: a Pennsylvania survey. *Environment and Behavior 26*(2), 239–60.

Scott, T., Cole, M. & Engel, M. (1992). Computers and education: a cultural constructivist perspective. *In* G. Grant, ed. *Review of research in education,* 191-251, Vol. 18. Washington, DC: American Educational Research Association.

Scott, W.R. (1975). Organizational structure. *Annual Review of Sociology 1,* 1–20.

— (1987). *Organizations: rational, natural, and open systems.* Englewood Cliffs, NJ: Prentice Hall.

Scriven, M. (1986 [1989]). Computers as energy: rethinking their role in schools. *Peabody Journal of Education 64*(1), 27–51.

Segal, Howard P. (1985). *Technological utopianism in American culture.* Chicago, IL: University of Chicago Press.

Sheingold, K. & Hadley, M. (1990, Sep.). *Accomplished teachers: integrating computers into classroom practice.* New York: Bank Street College of Education, Center for Technology in Education.

Sheingold, K. & Tucker, M.S., eds. (1990). *Restructuring for learning with technology.* New York: Center for Technology in Education; Rochester, NY: National Center on Education and the Economy.

Shrock, S.A. (1985). Faculty perceptions of instructional development and the success/failure of an instructional development program: a naturalistic study. *Educational Communication and Technology 33*(1), 16–25.

Shrock, S. & Higgins, N. (1990). Instructional systems development in the schools. *Educational Technology: Research & Development 38*(3), 77–80.

Sloan, D. (1985). *The computer in education: a critical perspective.* New York: Teachers College Press.

Smith, M.R. (1981). Eli Whitney and the American system of manufacturing. *In* C.W. Pursell, Jr., ed. *Technology in America: a history of individuals and ideas,* 45–61. Cambridge, MA: MIT Press.

Solomon, G. (1992). The computer as electronic doorway: technology and the promise of empowerment. *Phi Delta Kappan 74*(4), 327–29.

Spring, J.H. (1989). *The sorting machine revisited: national educational policy since 1945.* New York: Longman.

— (1992). *Images of American life: a history of ideological management in schools, movies, radio, and television.* Albany, NY: State University of New York Press.

Sproull, L. & Kiesler, S.B. (1991a). *Connections: new ways of working in the networked organization.* Cambridge, MA: MIT Press.

— & — (1991b). Computers, networks, and work. *Scientific American 265*(3), 116–23.

Steffen, J.O. (1993). *The tragedy of abundance.* Niwot, CO: University Press of Colorado.

Street, J. (1992). *Politics and technology.* New York: Guilford.

Tobin, K. & Dawson, G. (1992). Constraints to curriculum reform: teachers and the myths of schooling. *Educational Technology: Research & Development 40*(1), 81–92.

Toffler, A. (1990). *Powershift: knowledge, wealth, and violence at the edge of the 21st century.* New York: Bantam/Doubleday.

Trachtman, L.E., Spirek, M.M., Sparks, G.G. & Stohl, C. (1991). Factors affecting the adoption of a new technology. *Bulletin of Science, Technology, and Society 11*(6), 338–45.

Travers, R.M.W. (1973). Educational technology and related research viewed as a political force. *In* R.M.W. Travers, ed. *Second handbook of research on teaching,* 979–96. Chicago, IL: Rand McNally.

Turkle, S. (1984). *The second self.* New York: Simon & Schuster.

Tyack, D.B. (1974). *The one best system: a history of American urban education.* Cambridge, MA: Harvard University Press.

van Assema, P., Pieterse, M. & Kok, G. (1993). The determinants of four cancer-related risk behaviors. *Health Education Research 8*(4), 461–72.

Waldo, D. (1952). The development of a theory of democratic administration. *American Political Science Review 46,* 81–103.

Waters, M. (1993). Alternative organizational formations: a neo-Weberian typology of polycratic administrative systems. *The Sociological Review 41*(1), 54–81.

Watson, D.M. (1990). The classroom vs. the computer room. *Computers in Education 15*(1-3), 33–37.

Webb, M.B. (1986). *Technology in the schools: serving all students.* Albany, NY: Governor's Advisory Committee for Black Affairs. Available as ERIC ED No. 280906.

Weber, M. (1978). *Economy and society.* G. Roth & C. Wittich, eds. Berkeley, CA: University of California Press.

Weizenbaum, J. (1976). *Computer power and human reason.* New York: Freeman.

Winner, L. (1977). *Autonomous technology.* Cambridge, MA: MIT Press.

— (1980). Do artifacts have politics? *Daedalus 109*(1), 121–36.

— (1986). *The whale and the reactor: a search for limits in an age of high technology.* Chicago, IL: University of Chicago Press.

— (1993). Upon opening the black box and finding it empty—social constructivism and the philosophy of technology. *Science, Technology, and Human Values 18*(3), 362–78.

Winston, B. (1986). *Misunderstanding media.* Cambridge, MA: Harvard University Press.

Wiske, M.S., Zodhiates, P., Wilson, B., Gordon, M., Harvey, W., Krensky, L., Lord, B., Watt, M. & Williams, K. (1988). *How technology affects teaching.* ETC Publication Number TR87-10. Cambridge, MA: Harvard University, Educational Technology Center.

Wolf, R.M. (1993). The role of the school principal in computer education. *Studies in Educational Evaluation, 19*(2), 167–83.

Wong, S.L. (1991). Evaluating the content of textbooks: public interests and professional authority. *Sociology of Education 64*(1), 11–18.

Worth, S. & Adair, J. (1972). *Through Navajo eyes: an exploration in film communication and anthropology.* Bloomington, IN: Indiana University Press.

Zuboff, S. (1988). *In the age of the smart machine: the future of work and power.* New York: Basic Books.

7. CONSTRUCTIVISM: IMPLICATIONS FOR THE DESIGN AND DELIVERY OF INSTRUCTION[1]

Thomas M. Duffy   Donald J. Cunningham

INDIANA UNIVERSITY

> *Instruction should be designed to support a dialogue between the child and his or her future; not a dialogue between the child and the adult's history. Adult wisdom does not provide a teleology for child development.*
>
> — Adapted from Griffin and Cole's discussion (1984) of the zone of proximal development.

7.1 INTRODUCTION[1]

Constructivism! The increase in frequency with which this word appears in the discourse of educational research, theory, and policy is truly remarkable. Unfortunately much of the discussion is at the level of slogan and cliché, even bromide. "Students should construct their own knowledge" is being reverentially chanted throughout the halls of many a school/college/department of education these days, and any approach that is other than constructivist is characterized as promoting passive, rote, and sterile learning. For example, consider Rogoff's (1994) description of what she calls the *adult-run* model of how learning occurs:

> . . . learning is seen as a product of teaching or of adults' provision of information. Adults see themselves as responsible for filling children up with knowledge, as if children are receptacles and knowledge is a product. . . . [The] children are seen as receivers of a body of knowledge, but not active participants in learning. The children have little role except to be receptive, as if they could just open a little bottle cap to let adults pour the knowledge in. In this adult-run model, adults have to be concerned with how to package the knowledge and how to motivate the children to make themselves receptive (p. 211).

We wonder how many, if any, educators would recognize themselves in this description.[2] Perhaps the proponents of programmed instruction? Skinner would certainly reject the aspersion:

> A good program of instruction guarantees a great deal of successful action. Students do not need to have a natural interest in what they are doing, and subject matters do not need to be dressed up to attract attention. No one really cares whether PacMan gobbles up all those little spots on the screen. . . . What is reinforcing is successful play, and in a well-designed instructional program students gobble up their assignments (1984, p. 949).

Skinner goes on to describe a classroom in which the students are so volubly engaged with the instruction on their "teaching machine" that they don't even look up when the teacher makes distracting noises by jumping up and down on the teacher's platform at the front of the room.

It may be time to move beyond the paradigm debates of the last few years for precisely the reason that the tendency to sort the various approaches into "Good Guys" and "Bad Guys" (Cunningham, 1986) has not led in profitable directions. Skinner and his advocates see themselves as virtuous as any constructivist (see 2.5.2)! The debates have focused on *method*, as in whether we should use a problem-based method, or cooperative groups, or hypermedia databases, or programmed instruction, etc. For some, the paradigm issue

---

[1]The development of this paper was supported in part through T. M. Duffy's contract with the North Central Regional Education Laboratory. The views expressed in this paper, however, do not necessarily reflect the views of the Laboratory.

[2]Modesty prevents us from mentioning our own tendency toward this sort of hyperbole!

has reached the status of the utterly irrelevant; we should ignore theoretical issues and simply pick the methods that *work*, that reliably and efficiently lead to student learning.

What we see as crucial in these debates, however, is scarcely acknowledged: a fundamental difference in world view, disagreement at the level of *grounding assumptions*, the fundamental assumptions underlying our conception of the teaching-learning process. It must be recognized that grounding assumptions are always *assumed*, that they can never be proved unambiguously true or false. We may and certainly will provide evidence and try to persuade you that our assumptions are reasonable and those to which you should commit. An important part of our argument will be that these assumptions lead to demonstrably different goals, strategies, and embodiments of instruction, even when there are some superficial similarities to instruction derived from different assumptions.

An immediate difficulty confronts us, however. The term *constructivism* has come to serve as an umbrella term for a wide diversity of views. It is well beyond our purposes in this chapter to detail these similarities and differences across the many theories claiming some kinship to constructivism. However, they do seem to be committed to the general view that (1) learning is an active process of constructing rather than acquiring knowledge, and (2) instruction is a process of supporting that construction rather than communicating knowledge. The differences, some quite pronounced, are in definitions of such terms as *knowledge*, *learning*, and *construction*, and about the processes appropriate for supporting learning. For example, within Rogoff's (1994) distinction between three instructional approaches—(1) adult-run (transmission from experts to novices), (2) children-run (individual or collaborative discovery), or (3) community of learners (transformed participation in collective sociocultural experience)—one can see possibilities of both constructivist and nonconstructivist instruction. So, for example, reciprocal teaching (e.g., Palinscar & Brown, 1984) is often cited as a constructivist teaching strategy, yet it is very much teacher led. Similarly, group problem-based learning interventions (Savery & Duffy, 1995) might focus on the individual achievement of prescribed learning outcomes rather than on any sort of pattern of collective participation.

As the quote from Skinner suggests, everyone agrees that learning involves activity and a context, including the availability of information in some content domain. Traditionally in instruction, we have focused on the information presented or available for learning and have seen the activity of the learner as a vehicle for moving that information into the head. Hence the activity is a matter of processing the information. The constructivists, however, view the learning as the activity in context. The situation as a whole must be examined and understood in order to understand the learning. Rather than the content domain sitting as central, with activity and the "rest" of the context serving a supporting role, the entire gestalt is integral to what is learned.

An implication of this view of learning as constructed in the activity of the learner is that the individual can only know what he or she has constructed—and we cannot "know" in any complete sense of that term what someone else has constructed. This implication has led to considerable debate among many individuals seeking to understand constructivism. In particular we hear the reaction that constructivism leads inevitably to subjectivism, to a relativism where anyone's constructions are as good as any one else's and where we are unable to judge the value or truth of constructions with any degree of certainty. As will be detailed below, constructivists typically substitute some notion of viability for certainty; that is, we judge the validity of someone's knowledge, understanding, explanation, or other action, not by reference to the extent to which it matches reality but, rather, by testing the extent to which it provides a viable, workable, acceptable action relative to potential alternatives. As Bruner has noted, asking the question "How does this view affect my view of the world or my commitments to it, surely does not lead to 'anything goes.' It may lead to an unpacking of suppositions, the better to explore one's commitments" (1990, p. 27).

A second concern has been that the idiosyncrasies of constructions lead to an inability to communicate. That is, how can we possibly talk to one another if our world constructions (meanings) are idiosyncratic based on our experience. Indeed, the lack of shared meaning can make communication very difficult for two people from very different cultures. Simple language translations do not do the trick; rather we must develop cultural understandings before we can communicate adequately, a lesson the business community has already learned in this increasingly global economy. For those of us who share a common culture, however, the communication is not that difficult. Indeed, cultures are defined by a set of common experiences and the agreement of a common set of values based on those experiences. As Bruner (1990) puts it, culture forms minds, and minds make value judgments.

But don't we have shared meaning within the culture? Is it possible to have shared meaning? We can only evaluate whether meaning is shared by testing the compatibility of our individual meanings: exploring implications, probing more deeply. Of course, no matter how much we probe, we can never be sure that the meaning is shared.[3] Thus, rather than assuming a shared meaning, within the constructivist framework there is a seeking of compatibility, a lack of contradiction between views (Rorty, 1989). We probe at deeper and deeper levels to determine where or if our understandings begin to diverge. There are two important implications of this constructivist framework. First, we do

---

[3]Though we are sure all of our readers have had the experience of wondering whether our conversational partner "really" understands what we are saying. We have this experience most often in discussing educational theory and concepts. No matter how often our conversational partners states that they understand and even make statements indicative of understanding, we wonder if they really understand the "full" or deeper meaning and implications of what we are saying.

not assume that we must have a common meaning, but rather we actively seek to understand the different perspectives. Second, from a learning perspective, we do not assume that the learner will "acquire" the expert's meaning, and hence we do not seek a transmission approach to instruction. Rather we seek to understand and challenge the learner's thinking.

The common ground of constructivism could be summarized by von Glasersfeld's statement: "Instead of presupposing knowledge is a representation of what exists, knowledge is a mapping, in the light of human experience, of what is feasible" (1989, p. 134).

7.1.1 A Brief Historical and Philosophical Context

Current research and theory in learning and instruction has far too often been presented in an historical framework, with a consequence that we fail to learn about the complexity of the issues and the potential pitfalls from previous work (Cuban, 1991). Constructivism certainly has a long history in education and philosophy, and there is much to be learned from that history. However, a review of that history could easily be a book in and of itself. As a consequence of the space available, it is with apologies that we can only offer a brief reference to these historical contexts.

Von Glasersfeld (1989) attributes the first constructivist theory to an Italian philosopher, Giambattista Vico, in the early 18th century. As described by Von Glasersfeld, "one of Vico's basic ideas was that epistemic agents can know nothing but the cognitive structures they themselves have put together . . . 'to know' means *to know how to make*." (1989, p. 123). While Vico has received little attention in current constructivist theory building, there are several 20th-century philosophers who provide significant epistemological grounding for the current constructivist views. Kuhn (1970), the later Wittgenstein (Malcomb, 1986), and Rorty (1991) are all frequently cited for their basic argument that knowledge is a construction by individuals and is relative to the current context (community), rather than representing some correspondence to external reality.

Kuhn (1970), of course, has made this point most strongly in considering theory and research in science. His *Structure of Scientific Revolution* (Kuhn, 1970) provided the grounding for a major paradigm shift in science toward a "best description" view of theory rather than an approximation to the "truth." In essence, he argued that the meaning of our vocabulary resides in our theory rather than outside of it. Thus, there is no metavocabulary that sits independent of theory, and, as such, it is impossible to translate between theories. That is, theories provide their own lens into the world, with each theory providing a different lens (or perspective). For example, Kuhn argues that there is no independent way to reconstruct phrases like "really there." All "facts" are theory laden.

Wittgenstein (Malcom, 1986) took a similar position in his study of language, forsaking his initial logical positivist position (i.e., that words can be fully defined by their correspondence to objects) to argue for the total context dependency of meaning. Hence, he argued that as we crisscross the landscape of contexts for a word, it will continually become richer and richer in meaning.

The pragmatic theory of Richard Rorty (1991) has played a particularly significant role in the theoretical work of those constructivists most interested in the cognitive development of the individual in society. Rorty's pragmatism holds that "knowledge is not a matter of getting it right but rather acquiring habits of action for coping with reality" (1991, p. 1). Thus, rather than seeking "truth" by correspondence to the real world, we seek viability, i.e., explanations that are viable in the world as we understand it. We are always seeking to increase the viability of our understanding, both by improving our account of specific events or experiences and by interweaving our explanations, thus weaving a web of understanding.

Rorty argues that viability is culturally determined; knowledge and understanding are ethnocentric, and viability is established through obtaining unforced agreement within the community.[4] Thus knowledge (or fact) and opinion are distinguished not by their "truth" value, but rather by the ease with which one can obtain agreement in the community. Rorty points out that if we can set aside the desire for objectivity, we can change our self-image from one of "finding" to one of "making." Knowledge is in the constructive process rather than a finding: The culture defines and is defined by what it agrees is "known."

While Rorty describes the construction of knowledge as the seeking of unforced agreement within the community, the focus is not so much on the agreement as it is on the dialogical process involved in seeking understanding:

> We cannot, I think, imagine a moment at which the human race could settle back and say, "Well, now that we've arrived at the Truth we can relax." We should relish the thought that the sciences as well as the arts will *always* provide a spectacle of fierce competition between alternative theories, movements, and schools. The end of human activity is not rest, but rather richer and better human activity (Rorty, 1991, p. 39).

For example, science is not "better" than the arts or everyday problem-solving activity because it is discovering the truth, but rather because it has rules of discourse that support and focus on the seeking of unforced agreement (Bereiter, 1994). As Rorty puts it, ". . . the only sense in which science is exemplary is that it is a model of human solidarity" (1991, p. 39). Bereiter (1994) has argued that

---

[4] *Community* simply refers to the fact that knowledge is socially determined: Someone must agree with your assertion before it is counted as knowledgeable. To the extent that you increase the size of the community that is in unforced agreement, you have accounted for or accommodated more alternative perspectives, and hence you have expanded the web of understanding. Thus, in seeking unforced agreement, while we may start small, in our circle of colleagues, we are constantly seeking a wider spectrum of the community to come into some level of agreement with our propositions.

this "solidarity" rests in four key commitments in science. These are commitments to :

- Work toward common understanding satisfactory to all.
- Frame questions and propositions in ways that permit evidence to be brought to bear on them.
- Expand the body of collectively valid propositions.
- Allow any belief to be subject to criticism if it will advance the discourse.

To say that we think we are going in the right direction is simply to say that we can look back on the past and describe it as progress. That is, rather than moving closer to the truth, we are able to interweave and explain more and more. Rorty claims, for example, that the pragmatists' distinction between knowledge and opinion, ". . . is simply the distinction between topics on which agreement is relatively easy to get and topics on which agreement is relatively difficult to get" (1991, p. 23).

Philosophy is only one discipline that has relevance to constructivism in its application to instruction. There are views from a wide range of other disciplines that reflect the epistemological and methodological stances that are compatible with constructivism that we simply do not have the space to pursue in this chapter, e.g., semiotics (Cunningham, 1992), biology (Maturana & Varela, 1992), structuralism (Hawkes, 1977), and postmodernism (Lemke, 1994; Hlynka & Belland, 1991).

The philosophers, themselves, generally did not directly address the educational implications of their views. Rather, we see parallel developments in pedagogical theory and practice. Thus, while Vico published his work in the early 18th century, in the middle part of that century (1760) Jean Jaques Rousseau published *Émile* (Rousseau, 1955), a treatise on education in which he argued that the senses were the basis of intellectual development and that the child's interaction with the environment was the basis for constructing understanding (Page, 1990). Thus Rousseau emphasized learning by doing with the teacher's role being that of presenting problems that would stimulate curiosity and promote learning. Rousseau's views were in direct opposition to the existing educational framework in which the focus was on study and memorization of the classics. His treatise came shortly before the French Revolution and served as the basis for educational reform in France after the revolution.

John Dewey (1916, 1929, 1938) was perhaps the greatest proponent of situated learning and learning by doing. Dewey, like Rousseau, reacted against the traditional educational framework of memorization and recitation and argued that "education is not preparation for life, it is life itself." Also like Rousseau, Dewey was responding to the need for restructuring education to meet the changing needs of society, in this case the start of the Industrial Age in America and the demands of industrial technology. Dewey argued that life, including the vocations, should form the basic context for learning. In essence, rather than learning vocations, we learned science, math, literature, etc., through vocations (Kliebard, 1986). This is similar to the

current argument for "anchored instruction" in which the learning of any subject is anchored in a larger community or social context (CTGV, 1992).

Most importantly, learning was organized around the individual rather than around subject-matter topics and predetermined organizations of domains. Dewey emphasized perturbations of the individual's understanding as the stimulus for learning (Rochelle, 1992). In essence, the learner's interest in an issue had to be aroused, and learning was then organized around the learner's active effort to resolve that issue. Dewey's focus was on an inquiry-based approached to learning, for he saw scientific inquiry as a general model for reflective thinking (Kliebard, 1986). This is not to say that the learners were to learn the scientific method as a fixed procedure, but rather that they were to learn the problem-solving skills and informal reasoning associated with scientific work (see, for example, Bereiter, 1994).

In concluding this discussion of Dewey, we would like briefly to address the role of the teacher in this discussion of constructivist theory. While the focus of Rousseau, Dewey, and current constructivist educational theory is on the student's struggle with a problem, this should not be taken to suggest that there is no role for the teacher beyond developing and presenting problems. Indeed, as will be evident throughout this chapter, the teacher plays a central role, a role that we suspect is more central than in most instructional design frameworks. Dewey provides an eloquent statement on the issue:

> There is a present tendency in so-called advanced schools of educational thought . . . to say, in effect, let us surround pupils with materials, tools, appliances, etc., and let the pupils respond according to their own desires. Above all, let us not suggest any end or plan to the students; let us not suggest to them what they shall do, for that is unwarranted trespass upon their sacred intellectual individuality, since the essence of such individuality is to set up ends and means. Now, such a method is really stupid, for it attempts the impossible, which is always stupid, and it misconceives the conditions of independent thinking (Dewey in Page, 1990, p. 20).

Alfred North Whitehead also argued for a pedagogy reflective of the current constructivist theories. In his essay on the *Aims of Education*, Whitehead argued:

> Education is the acquisition of the art of the utilization of knowledge. . . . Interrelated truths are utilized *en bloc*, and the various propositions are employed in any order, and with any reiteration. Choose some important application of your theoretical subject; and study them concurrently with the systematic theoretical disposition (1929, p. 4).

Whitehead goes on to contrast this view of education with the prevailing approach:

> You take a textbook and make them learn it. . . . The child then knows how to solve a quadratic equation. But what is the point of teaching a child to solve a quadratic equation? There is a traditional answer to this question. It runs thus: The mind is an instrument; you first sharpen it and then use it. . . . solving the quadratic equation is part of sharpening

the mind. Now there is enough half-truths in that to have made it live through the ages. But for all its half-truths, it emphasizes a radical error which stifles the genius of the modern world. It is one of the most fatal, erroneous, and dangerous conceptions ever introduced into the theory of education. The mind is never passive; it is a perpetual activity. You cannot postpone its life until you have sharpened it. Whatever interest attaches to your subject matter must be evoked here and now; whatever powers you are strengthening in the pupil must be strengthened here and now; whatever possibilities of mental life your teaching should impart must be exhibited here and now. That is the golden rule of education, and a very difficult rule to follow (1929, pp. 5–6).

Like Rousseau and Dewey, Jerome Bruner saw learning in the activity of the learner (1966, 1971). In particular he emphasized discovery learning, focusing on the process of discovery in which the learner sought understanding of some issue. Within this context, Bruner emphasized that the issues or questions that guide the discovery process must be personally and societally relevant. Bruner's development of the social studies curriculum, *Man: A Course of Study* (MACOS), perhaps best exemplifies his theory. In designing this social studies curriculum for upper elementary students, Bruner and Dow summarize their overarching pedagogical view as:

> It is only in a trivial sense that one gives a course to "get something across," merely to impart information. There are better means to that end than teaching. Unless the learner also masters himself, disciplines his tastes, deepens his world view, the "something" that is gotten across is hardly worth the effort of transmission (undated, p. 3).

From that perspective, Bruner (1966) and his colleagues designed a social studies course that has as its goals that pupils:

- Have respect for and confidence in their powers of mind and extend that power to thinking about the human condition
- Are able to develop and apply workable models that make it easier to analyze the nature of the social world
- Develop a sense of respect for man as a species and to leave with a sense of the unfinished business of man's evolution

It should be clear from these goals that in Bruner's framework, knowledge is not in the content but in the activity of the person in the content domain. That is, the active struggling by the learner with issues *is* learning. Thus it was important for Bruner to begin the MACOS curriculum with the unknown as a means of stimulating the child's curiosity: In this case, it involved the study of baboon communities and the culture of the Nestlik Eskimos. This unknown was then related to the known, the child's familiar culture (family, school, etc.) in exploring the tool-making activities, language, social organizations, etc., as a mechanism for understanding both the unknown and the known. With this basic sequencing, the instructional methods used included: inquiry, experimentation, observation, interviewing, literature

search, summarizing, defense of opinion, etc. (Hanley, Whitla, Moo & Walter, 1970). As this list suggests, the students were very much involved in the construction of their understanding, and the social interaction in the classroom was essential to that constructive process.

Bruner paid particular attention to aiding teachers in adapting to this new approach. In addition to extensive workshops, there was a variety of support materials. Video of students participating in sample lessons provided visual images of the patterns of activity that were being sought and highlighted problems. Model lessons were designed to address particularly difficult concepts; reading material for the teacher provided a "lively" account of the nature of the unit, discussing the "mystery" and why it impels curiosity and wonder; and a guide presented "hints" to teachers as to the kind of questions to ask, contrasts to invoke, and resources to use.

Evaluations of the MACOS curriculum indicated that it was successful in promoting inquiry and interpersonal interaction, increasing the children's confidence in expressing ideas and their ability to attend, and increasing the children's enjoyment of social studies (Hanley et al., 1970; Cole & Lacefield, 1980). The difficulty came in the acceptance of an inquiry-driven curriculum that did not "cover the basic content." Some teachers expressed concern that there was a neglect of traditional skills; and there was a fairly widespread public concern that the students should actually be exposed to diverse perspectives and be involved in inquiry that examined the basics tenets of our culture (Dow, 1975; Conlan, 1975). We suspect this to be a continuing struggle in any inquiry-based approach to instruction. Indeed, in spite of his tremendous philosophical influence on education, Dewey's schools were similarly short lived. Kliebard (1986) proposes that, as with Bruner's MACOS curriculum, teachers and the community felt uncomfortable with the lack of a well-defined content that students will "have" when they leave school, and thus the inquiry approach became increasingly constrained by detailed content specifications.

7.1.2 Current Views

Beyond this common framework of learning as situated in activity, constructivism has come to serve as an umbrella for a wide diversity of views. These views may lend particular emphasis to the role of the teacher as a manager or coach, as in reciprocal teaching (Palinscar & Brown, 1984) and many other apprentice frameworks. Alternatively, they may focus on the student and his or her ownership of the learning activity, as for example in the design of problem-based learning curricula (Savery & Duffy, 1995), in using student query as a mechanism for defining curriculum (Scardamalia & Bereiter, 1991), or any of the variety of other learner-centered approaches (see, for example, Brooks & Brooks, 1993). Finally, an increasingly dominant constructivist view focuses on the cultural embeddedness of learning, employing the methods and framework of

TABLE 7-1.   CONTRASTS BETWEEN THE INDIVIDUAL COGNITIVE AND THE SOCIOCULTURAL CONSTRUCTIVIST VIEWS (adapted from Cobb, 1993)

	Cognitive Constructivist	Sociocultural Constructivist
The mind is located:	in the head	in the individual-in-social interaction
Learning is a process of:	active cognitive reorganization	acculturation into an established community of practice
Goal is to account for:	the social and cultural basis of personal experience	constitution of social and cultural processes by actively interpreting individuals
Theoretical attention is on:	individual psychological processes	social and cultural processes
Analysis of learning sees learning as:	cognitive self-organization, implicitly assuming that the child is participating in cultural practices	acculturation, implicitly assuming an actively constructing child
Focus of analyses:	building models of individual students' conceptual reorganization and by analyses of their joint constitution of the local social situation of development	individual's participation in culturally organized practices and face-to-face interactions
In looking at a classroom, we see:	an evolving microculture that is jointly constituted by the teacher and students	instantiation of the culturally organized practices of schooling
In looking at a group, we stress:	the heterogeneity and eschew analyses that single out pre-given social and cultural practices	the homogeneity of members of established communities and to eschew analyses of qualitative differences

cultural anthropology to examine how learning and cognition are distributed in the environment rather than stored in the head of an individual (Engstrom, 1993; Cole & Engstrom, 1993; Saxe, 1992; Cunningham & Knuth, 1993).

Cobb (1994a, 1994b) has attempted to characterize this diversity as representing two major trends that are often grouped together: individual cognitive and sociocultural (see Table 7-1). The individual cognitive approach derives from Piagetian theory (Piaget, 1977) and is closely associated with the current writings of Ernst von Glasersfeld (1984, 1989, 1992) and Cathy Fosnot (1989). This view emphasizes the constructive activity of the individual as he or she tries to make sense of the world. Learning is seen to occur when the learner's expectations are not met, and he or she must resolve the discrepancy between what was expected and what was actually encountered. Thus, the learning is in the individual's constructions as he or she attempts to resolve the conflict, or, alternatively put, individuals literally construct themselves and their world by accommodating to experiences. The conflict in Piagetian terms is known as *disequilibration*, but Dewey refers to the same stimulus as a *perturbation*. The first author has

preferred the more neutral term *puzzlement* (Savery & Duffy, 1995). From this perspective, the importance of the teacher and other students is as a source of perturbation or puzzlement as a stimulus for the individual's learning. As von Glasersfeld (1989) notes, people, by far, offer the most effective and ready-at-hand source of perturbation of a learner's current understanding. Hence, within this framework, the focus is on the individual within the group, and cognition occurs in the head of the individual. In studying learning, we examine the impact of culture on the individual psychological processes.

In contrast to the von Glasersfeld/Piaget focus on individual constructions, the sociocultural approach emphasizes the socially and culturally situated context of cognition. Drawing on the insights of such theorists as Vygotsky, Leont'ev, and Bakhtin (e.g., see Wertsch, 1991), this approach examines the social origins of cognition, for example, the impact of an individual's appropriation of language as a mediating tool to construct meaning. Collective actions become the focus, as in Rogoff's (1994, p. 209) learning communities, where "learning occurs as people participate in shared endeavors with others, with all playing active but often asymmetrical roles in sociocultural activity." It is the changes of ways in which one participates in a community which are crucial, not individual constructions of that activity. Likewise, Driver and her colleagues (Driver, Asoko, Leach, Mortimer & Scott, 1994, p. 4) characterize learning science as "being initiated into ideas and practices of the scientific community and making these ideas and practices meaningful at an individual level." Learning, then, is a process of acculturation, and thus the study of social and cultural processes and artifacts is central.

While Cobb (1994b) argues that these two approaches are complimentary, we are not of one mind on this matter. While we will not argue the case here, it does seem that there is a contradiction between a position that posits development as increasingly abstract and formal constructions of reality, and another that views reality as a constructive process embedded in sociocultural practices with the possibility of acting on and transforming reality within the context of those practices.

With this background in hand, the next two sections detail some of the grounding assumptions that characterize our approach to constructivism, in order to better position the examples and recommendations to follow.

7.2 METAPHORS OF THE MIND

In 1980, George Lakoff and Mark Johnson published a book titled *Metaphors We Live By* (see also Lakoff, 1987; Johnson, 1987) in which they present a strong case that the way in which we perceive and think about a situation is a function of the metaphors we have adopted for and use in that situation. For example, Marshall (1988) has argued convincingly that the dominant metaphor in many schools is "School Is Work." We speak of students needing to *work* harder on their studies, to complete their home*work*, to earn a grade, and so forth. Teachers are trained to *manage* their classes and are often held *accountable* in terms of their *productivity*. These metaphors not only structure the way we think about schools, they also help create the world of the school. It is these metaphors, these grounding assumptions, that we want to examine.

To begin, we want to examine perhaps the most fundamental metaphor of all, our metaphor of mind. There have been many conceptions of mind throughout the history of philosophical and psychological inquiry (Gardner, 1985). Skipping lightly over several centuries of blank slates, wax tablets, telephone switchboards, and so forth, we want to summarize briefly two modern metaphors of mind before presenting our alternative.

7.2.1 Mind as Computer

First is the notion of "mind as computer" (MAC), the basic premise underlying early traditional artificial intelligence, but also much of instructional design and development. MAC assumes that the mind is an instantiation of a Turing machine, a symbol manipulation device (e.g., Newell &

Simon: *General Problem Solver,* 1972). In this view, every cognitive process is algorithmic in the same sense that computer processes are algorithmic; i.e., the mind works by processing symbols according to rules. These symbols are entirely abstract and independent of any given individual's experience of them; i.e., the operation of the mind is completely independent of the person in whom it is contained. Meaning is mapped onto these symbols via our experiences in the world. Our understanding of the world is formed from a process of discovering reality "out there," interacting with it, and transferring that understanding into the mind, forming internal representations that determine our subsequent interactions with the environment. Symbols (or concepts) derive their meaning from their capacity to match (to a greater or lesser extent) aspects of reality. Any individual's internal representation will certainly depart from reality, but it does seem necessary to assume that, in principle, there must exist a conceptual framework that is entirely general and neutral, a single correct, completely objective way of representing the world. Learning is a process of information acquisition, processing according to innate or acquired rules, and storage for future use.

7.2.2 Mind as Brain

More recently cognitive scientists have proposed a metaphor of "mind as brain" (MAB), a view variously called *connectionism* or *parallel distributed processing* (see, for example, Rumelhart & McClelland, 1986). Connectionist models assume that symbols are learned consequences of particular experiences or interactions in the world, which are then mapped on or distributed across neural-like networks. Connectionism seeks to avoid the limitations of the MAC view and capitalize on precisely the experiential character of human concepts. It also deliberately links with our emergent knowledge of brain function; e.g., the brain would have to do massively parallel processing to accomplish even the most ordinary cognitive act, let alone the serial operations proposed by MAC models. Connectionism is the notion that intelligence emerges from the interactions of large numbers of simple processing units. Representations are not localized in some general-purpose symbol; rather they are distributed throughout a network of simple processing units according to patterns of activation that have emerged as a result of experience. Unlike MAC models, knowledge is not stored as a static copy of a pattern in long-term memory, with no real difference between what is retrieved and stored in working memory. Representation is an active process. What is stored in connectionist models are connection strengths between units that allow these patterns to be recreated (reconstructed). Consequently, learning is

> a matter of finding the right connection strengths so that the right pattern of activation will be produced under the right circumstances . . . , as a result of tuning of connections to capture the interdependencies between activations that the network is exposed to in the course of processing" (Rumelhart & McClelland, 1986, p. 32).

MAC and MAB models are alike in that both characterize mind as separate from the environment and as information processing bound within individuals. A major difference is that knowledge is a matter of storage and retrieval according to rules in the MAC view, but a function of distributed connection strengths and network activation for the MAB position. It is this difference that sets the stage for the possibility of some fresh thinking about the teaching/learning process.

7.2.3 Mind as Rhizome

The alternative we wish to propose here builds on the MAB metaphor but moves the mind out of the head and deliberately blurs or obliterates such common distinctions as environment/individual, inside/outside, and self/other. We will label our view "mind as rhizome" (MAR), a metaphor inspired by Umberto Eco (1984, p. 81; see also Deleuze & Guattari, 1983). A rhizome is a root crop, a prostrate or underground system of stems, roots, and fibers whose fruits are tubers, bulbs, and leaves. A tulip is a rhizome as is rice grass, even the familiar crab grass. The metaphor of rhizome specifically rejects the inevitability of such notions as hierarchy, order, node, kernel, or structure. The tangle of roots and tubers characteristic of rhizomes is meant to suggest a form of mind where:

- Every point can and must be connected with every other point, raising the possibility of an infinite juxtaposition.
- There are no fixed points or positions, only connections (relationships).
- The structure is dynamic, constantly changing, such that if a portion of the rhizome is broken off at any point it could be reconnected at another point, leaving the original potential for juxtaposition in place.
- There is no hierarchy or genealogy contained as where some points are inevitably superordinate or prior to others.
- The rhizome whole has no outside or inside but is rather an open network that can be connected with something else in all of its dimensions.

The notion of a rhizome is a difficult one to imagine, and any attempt to view it as a static picture risks minimizing its dynamic, temporal, and even self-contradictory character. Eco (1984) has labeled the rhizome as "an inconceivable globality" to highlight the impossibility of any global, overall description of the network. Since no one (user, scientist, or philosopher) can describe the whole, we are left with "local" descriptions, a vision of one or a few of the many potential structures derivable from the rhizome. Every local description of the network is an hypothesis, an abduction (see Shank, 1987) constantly subject to falsification. To quote Eco:

> Such a notion . . . does not deny the existence of structured knowledge; it only suggests that such a knowledge cannot be recognized and organized as a global system; it provides only "local" and transitory systems of knowledge which

can be contradicted by alternative and equally "local" cultural organizations; every attempt to recognize these local organizations as unique and "global"—ignoring their partiality—produces an *ideological* bias (1984, p. 84).

This last statement emphasizes the point that we are not proposing the metaphor of rhizome for an individual mind, but to *minds* as distributed in social, cultural, historical, and institutional contexts. Except as a degenerate case, there is no such thing as a single mind, unconnected to other minds or to their (collective) social-cultural constructions. Thinking, or whatever we choose to call the activity of mind, is always dialogic, connected to another, either directly as in some communicative action or indirectly via some form of semiotic mediation: signs and/or tools appropriated from the sociocultural context.

Wertsch (1991), drawing inspiration from Vygotsky and Bakhtin, has argued this case very well (without invoking the metaphor of the rhizome), and we will present his view more fully. For our purposes here, we want to stress the potential connectivity implied by the MAR metaphor. We are connected to other people individually but also collectively, as in the speech communities or social languages in which we are all embedded. We are connected to the sociocultural milieu in which we operate, a milieu characterized by the tools (computers, cars, television, and so forth) and signs (language, mathematics, drawing, etc.), which we may appropriate for our thinking. Thus thinking is not an action that takes place within a mind within a body, but rather at the connections, in the interactions. But it is worth saying again that this thinking is always "local," always a limited subset of the potential (unlimited) rhizomous connections.

Learning, then, is neither a matter of discriminating the symbols of the world and the rules for manipulating them nor of activating the right connections in the brain. It is, rather, a matter of constructing and navigating a local, situated path through a rhizomous labyrinth, a process of dialogue and negotiation with and within a local sociocultural context. Although this analogy fails if pushed too far, the connectivity we have in mind is a bit like the World Wide Web (WWW). While the "results" of a connection to WWW is experienced via an interface with one's local workstation, that experience is possible only as a result of connections with many (potentially an infinite number of) servers all over the world. The local workstation both contributes to (constructs) and is constructed by its connections.

7.3 METAPHORS WE TEACH BY

Given this background, we are now in a position to present and justify some of the grounding assumptions of our version of constructivism. We have separately (e.g., Cunningham, Knight & Watson, 1994; Savery & Duffy, 1995; Duffy, 1995) and jointly (Cunningham, Duffy & Knuth, 1992) offered such assumptions before, but never within the context of a model of "mind as rhizome." This addition has helped clarify our own thinking and, we hope, the readers'.

7.3.1 All Knowledge Is Constructed; All Learning Is a Process of Construction

In accord with the MAR metaphor, all knowledge is local, a slice through the rhizome. Since all connections are, in principle, possible, we must stress that we are not talking about a partial or incomplete version of the "truth," the world as it is unmediated by sensation, perception, or cognition. Elsewhere we have talked about the concept of *umwelt* (Cunningham, 1992), a term coined by Jacob von Uexküll (1957) and discussed in his brilliant paper "A Stroll Through the Worlds of Animals and Men." In brief, the term means phenomenal world or self-world, the worlds that organisms individually and collectively create and that then serve to mediate their experience in the world. It is these structures that determine a world view, the things we notice and ignore, the things that are important to us and not important, the means by which we organize our lives. This umwelt, determined jointly by species-specific factors, the sociocultural history of the community, and particular experiences of the organism in a given environment, characterizes that organism's behavior.[5]

In humans, this process of construction (or *semiosis*, as we prefer to call it) is unique in the universe as we know it. Structures are created which go beyond the immediate experience of the cognisizing organism. Words, pictures, mathematics, bodily movements, and the like generate structures of knowledge and objects that need have no basis in the "real" world and which can be manipulated independent of any such world. According to Deely (1982), it is the intervention of language that allows humans to engage in this particular type of semiosis. Through language, we create culture: institutions such as religions, governments, armies, schools, marriage rites, science, and so forth. Culture, in turn, impacts our lives by determining what is important and what is not, what makes sense and what does not. The culture then makes these constructions available to the young and to new initiates for appropriation and use in transforming their participation in that culture.

Learning, then, becomes a matter of changes in one's relation to the culture(s) to which one is connected—with the gradual transformation of one's means of constructing one's world as a function of the change in membership in that culture. Lave and Wenger (1991) discuss this in terms of legitimate peripheral participation: a transformation from newcomer to old timer. These cultures can be conceived at various levels (e.g., caregiver, family, school, church, ethnic community, vocation, nationality, etc.), activities (working, playing, talking, eating, etc.), tools (hammers, computers, televisions, cars, etc.) and signs (language, music, art, etc.). A complete explication of such a view goes well beyond our purposes for this chapter, but it is necessary to stress again the constructedness of our knowledge and the need to provide experience to learners of that constructedness and the means by which they can participate in that process. This will be detailed in the sections to follow.

7.3.2 Many World Views Can Be Constructed; Hence There Will Be Multiple Perspectives

We and other constructivists are often accused of advocating a kind of naive relativism or constructivist extremism. Since we argue that all knowledge is constructed, it is assumed that we must therefore accept the claim that every individual constructs his or her own meaning, untroubled by the realities of the real world or contact with other individuals. For example, Schwen, Goodrum, and Dorsey (1993) propound that they "find the extreme view of all knowledge being relevant to personal experience, and therefore idiosyncratic, too impractical and anarchic to be useful" (p. 6). But such a fundamental misconstrual of our position precisely illustrates our second principle and is nicely captured by Eco (1984, p. 12): "A world view can conceive of anything except an alternative world view."

As the MAR metaphor makes clear, knowledge is a construction, not by an individual in some pristine, autistic isolation but by participants in a community that simultaneously transforms and is transformed by such participation. What we choose to call *knowledge* is a consensus of beliefs, a consensus open to continual negotiation (Rorty, 1991). Such a process does not mean that the community will inevitably and perpetually debate whether the sea is blue or green, whether the word *dog* will continue to refer to a four-legged, domesticated, carnivorous canine, whether the Earth orbits the sun, or whether God is dead. A pervasive and largely benign effect of the structure of knowledge that we construct from the rhizome is that we tend to use those structures through which the world makes good sense to us, that seem "right." And we tend to assume that others see things in roughly the same way we do, that our world view is constructed as largely invisible. Providing experience that elevates our world view to a conscious level typically entails bringing up alternative views for comparison, as when we study cultures different from our own.

---

[5]It is important to distinguish the concept of umwelt from the more familiar concept of environment, for it is here where differences between MAR and other views are most striking. An environment is a physical setting that impacts the organism and serves as a source of stimulation. As such, it can be conceived independently of the organism in question and in fact is usually spoken of as an entity that exists for a multitude of different organisms. This separation of organism and environment is a fundamental tenet of most method and theory in instructional psychology, in particular, and psychology, in general. The umwelt of an organism, however, is not independent of the organism; in fact, it exists only in relation to the organism. In a famous example, von Uexküll (1957) described the various umwelten created by a tree: a rough-textured and convoluted terrain for a bug, a menacing form for a young child, a set of limbs for a nesting bird, and so on. In all these cases, the environment of the tree was the same; that is, the bark, the height, the limbs were "available" to each of the organisms, yet their experience of them was quite different.

In a classroom with which we have worked (Cunningham, 1994), the teacher is exchanging material (stories, letters, photographs, HyperCard stacks, etc.) with a similar classroom in Northern Ireland. The children in both cultures are constantly surprised by the differences that have been revealed, from simple things like the way a date is written or the likelihood that the family owns a car, to the extreme, as when the children in Northern Ireland talk about the "Troubles" (the sectarian violence). The children in both cultures are invited to put themselves in the perspective of the other and examine their own cultural practices based on this new perspective. What would it be like to live in a town where army patrols can be seen several times a day? To come upon a policeman with a cocked semiautomatic weapon? On the other hand, what is it like to live in a culture where person-on-person crime is common (such crimes are rare in Northern Ireland in comparison to the U.S.)? Even a term like *integrated school* has fundamentally different meanings in the two communities.

The "reality" of multiple perspectives should be a cause for celebration and optimism, not for fear that we will sink into some kind of utter subjectivism. Those who hold MAC view of mind expect and encourage acceptance and closure of a world view, while the MAB and MAR metaphors anticipate and encourage debate. It is this engagement with others, this establishment of the need to continually expand our web of understanding, that creates the awareness of multiple perspectives.

7.3.3 Knowledge Is Context Dependent, So Learning Should Occur in Contexts to Which It Is Relevant

Speaking of debate, this is a principle about which the authors have debated long and enthusiastically. While we are in sympathy with views of our colleagues concerning the need to situate (e.g., Brown, Collins & Duguid, 1989) or anchor (CTGV, 1992) learning in authentic, relevant, and/or realistic contexts, we disagree about why this is important. One of us (DJC) draws inspiration from the systems theoretic view of Maturana and Varela (1992), who argue that to say that someone *knows* something is to make the claim that she is acting effectively in a particular context. Thus to claim that Stephen W. Hawking knows science is to assert as valid that he behaves effectively in the domains of action that are accepted by the scientific community, a community that he in fact helps create. Knowledge is effective action. The contexts within which one can act effectively is an empirical matter. (See also Lave & Wenger, 1991.)

It is on the point of that empirical matter and its practical implications that the authors part company. The other author (TMD) agrees that to know something means that the individual can act effectively in a particular context. The concern is not with knowledge but with learning and, perhaps most importantly, with the issue of transfer. That is, if I want to prepare myself to be a scientist, what sort of

learning activity must I engage in and in what sort of environment? It would seem that the general statement of this question—i.e., how do we prepare ourselves to act effectively in particular contexts?—is central to our development as individuals and as a society. It is certainly central to the instructional design community.

Thus the question of context is really a question about what aspects of the context must be represented if the learning (knowledge) is to be used (elicited?) in other contexts. TMD discusses this issue at length elsewhere (Honebein, Duffy & Fishman, 1993). In brief, the focus is on the qualitative character of the metacognitive and cognitive processing and the skills required. The physical character of the environment is relevant only to the extent it impacts the character of the "thinking" and skill requirements.

This entire issue of learning and transfer raises a problem for both authors and for most constructivist theory. It has been labeled the "learning paradox" by Fodor (1980) and Bereiter (1985). The MAR view, and more generally the sociocultural constructivist's view, stresses the distribution of cognition in the environment. While Vygotsky discusses the internalization of social experience (with the implication that knowledge is internalized and hence stored), more recent sociocultural theorists have suggested that a better translation of the original Russian is "appropriation" rather than "internalization" (Rogoff, 1990). In this way, the concept of distributed cognition (the rhizome distributed across minds and cultural artifacts) would seem to be preserved. However, as Ann Brown, Ash, Rutherford, etc. (1993) have noted, this shift in terminology does not resolve the learning paradox.

We certainly do not have the solution to the learning paradox, and our own debate will continue. DJC worries that a view that posits abstract, generalizable operations, divorced from the contexts within which they were developed, will lead back to a MAC metaphor, while TMD worries that the focus on knowing fails to help us move forward on the critical issues of learning and the design of learning environments. Stay tuned.

7.3.4 Learning Is Mediated by Tools and Signs

In many ways, this assumption lies at the heart of constructivism as we view it. Wertsch (1994) agrees, asserting that any adequate theory of higher mental processes (i.e., beyond perception and involuntary attention) must be grounded in the notion of mediated action. Vygotsky (1978, p. 57) has argued that children's development proceeds on the basis of appropriating mediational means from the sociocultural milieu: "Every function in the child's cultural development appears twice: first, on the social level, and later, on the individual level; first, between people, then inside the child. . . . All the higher functions originate as actual relations between individuals." Vygotsky has proposed two mediational means: tools (technical tools) and signs (semiotic tools). The distinction is a slippery one, and particular examples often move back and forth between (even straddle) the two categories. But consider a hammer as a prototype example of a technical tool. How does the appropriation of this tool from the sociocultural milieu mediate action? As the needs of the culture encouraged the invention of a hammer as a more efficient means of driving posts into the ground or joining two boards, the hammer itself altered the very nature of carpentry itself. While it is true that the goal of driving a nail into a board is mediated by the use of a hammer, the invention of the hammer has radically altered the character of the structures we build (e.g., shelters built without the aid of a hammer tend to be less angular). Thus the invention of a tool and its use by members doesn't simply facilitate forms of action that would occur anyway; the tool changes the form, structure, and character of the activity.

If this is true for hammers, consider how substantial is the influence of more modern technological tools like automobiles, computers, video, etc. (see 20.4 for other examples). The word processor on which we write hasn't merely helped us to be more efficient in our professional writing as we did it 25 years ago. The nature of that writing process has changed radically. Culture creates the tool, but the tool changes the culture. Participants in the culture appropriate these tools from their culture to meet their goals and thereby transform their participation in the culture.

The computer is a good example of a mediational means that has aspects of both tool and sign. During the time and place where Vygotsky was writing, tools were used almost exclusively for physical labor, to manipulate physical objects in the environment. Signs, on the other hand, are mediational means used for cognitive functioning, and certainly word processors influence the writer as well as the written product. Language, of course, was the semiotic means about which Vygotsky wrote the most, but he also included numbers, algebraic notation, mnemonic techniques (his famous knot in a string to remember something), diagrams, maps, musical notation, etc. In fact these means are very reminiscent of the multiple intelligences proposed by Howard Gardner (e.g., 1993): linguistic, musical, logical-mathematical, spatial, bodily-kinesthetic, interpersonal and intrapersonal.[6] All these are not simply alternative means of expressing some underlying meaning but

rather semiautonomous systems for constructing meaning. They too have been invented by culture to address some need of the culture, but by their use actively transform the culture. It is the action produced by these mediational means that is crucial. Thus, humans "play an active role in using and transforming cultural tools and their associated meaning system." (Wertsch, 1994, p. 204). Wertsch goes on to argue that the "essence of mediated action is that it involves a kind of tension between the mediational means as provided in the sociocultural setting, and the unique contextualized use of these means in carrying out particular, concrete actions" (Wertsch, 1994, p. 205). In other words, all distinctly human instances of learning are constructions situated within a context that employs some form of mediational means, tools, and/or signs.

7.3.5 Learning Is an Inherently Social-Dialogical Activity

This assumption is actually a part of the previous one, but since Vygotsky and his followers have emphasized language as a mediational means above all others,[7] we felt it warranted separate treatment. Certainly the central position of language and dialogue in human culture and cognition can hardly be overemphasized.

In many educational applications commonly characterized as constructivist (e.g., reciprocal teaching, problem-based learning, collaborative groups, etc.), one finds a strong emphasis on dyadic or group discussion: talk, talk, talk! Even in applications like hypermedia systems that are intended for single users, the interface often models a dialogic structure, as in querying a database to solve a problem (Knuth, 1992), or actually includes means for synchronous or asynchronous dialogue among users (Duffy, 1995; Duffy & Knuth, 1990). Why this emphasis on dialogue?

A child is born into a sociocultural milieu that functions on the basis of some socially organized processes: operations, objects, and structures. As the child acts in this context, she is exposed to these means by which the community mediates its activities. Caregivers use language to interact with the child and intuitively coordinate these linguistic actions with the child's behavior. The child then appropriates this language tool to further influence and control her social interactions, but by adopting this mediational sign has transformed her ability to influence her *own* actions within her developing spheres of action. According to Wertsch: "The incorporation of mediational means does not simply facilitate action that could have occurred without them; instead, as Vygotsky (1981) noted, 'by being included in the process of behavior, the psychological tool alters the entire flow and structure of mental functions' " (1991, p. 137).

---

[6]While we are attracted by Gardner's view of multiple semiotic systems, we are not enamored with his view of education as the assessment of intellectual ability and the matching of instruction to the ability pattern of the student (Gardner, 1993, pp. 10–11). This seems to us to compound the error of assuming that one or two scores on an intelligence test can define the appropriate instruction for a child. One, two, seven, or a hundred, the error is in assuming that a score on a decontextualized task has relevance to learning out of the school context. We prefer Charles Morris's (1946) exhortation: "Training in the flexible use of signs means gaining the ability to enter into fruitful interaction with persons whose signs differ from one's own, 'translating' their signs into one's own vocabulary and one's own signs into their vocabulary, adapting discourse to the unique problems of diverse individuals interacting in unique situations" (p. 246).

---

[7]Wertsch (1991) speculates that Vygotsky's own cultural background (he grew up in a Jewish-Russian family with considerable intellectual stimulation) and the grounding of much of his work in the formal instruction of literacy accounts for this emphasis.

A primary way in which mental functions are altered by the mediation of language signs is that knowledge, and thereby learning, becomes a social, communicative, and discursive process, inexorably grounded in talk. James Wertsch (1991) has been particularly influential in arguing this case by presenting the views of a contemporary of Vygotsky, M. M. Bakhtin. Bakhtin focused his analysis on the utterance, or the shared activity of speech communication—that is, voice. In other words, he stresses the social functions of the linguistic sign, its use as a mediational means to express and share meanings within a social language community. Bakhtin has coined a wonderful term, *ventriloquation*, which is the process by means of which one individual (or voice) speaks through the voices or the language of a social community. In a very real sense, the way in which a student comes to manifest the effective behavior of a community (e.g., the community of scientists) is to speak with the voice of that community (e.g., to talk like a scientist). Paulo Freire's (1993) work has also stressed the importance of voice and dialogue as a means for action within a sociocultural context.

7.3.6 Learners Are Distributed, Multidimensional Participants in a Sociocultural Process

Perhaps the most "revolutionary" aspect of the MAR metaphor is the concept of a distributed mind and its corollary, a distributed self. Displacing the individual from the central position in cognitive action is, we suspect, a shift on a par with displacing the earth from the center of the universe. And yet more and more books and articles with titles like *Socially Shared Cognition* (Resnick, Levine & Teasley, 1991), *Distributed Cognitions* (Salomon, 1993), and *Distributed Decision Making* (Rasmussen, Brehmer & Leplat, 1991) are appearing. Lave and Wenger (1991) use the term *whole person* to characterize this conception of self, where learning is not a matter of a person's internalizing knowledge but a matter of a person's transforming his participation in a social community. The whole person defines as well as is defined by this participation. Lave and Wenger (1991, p. 53) describe identities as "long-term, living relations between persons and their place and participation in communities of practice."

Hutchins (1991) proposes a simple thought experiment to illustrate this idea. Look around where you are right now reading this and try to find something that "was not either produced or delivered to its present location by the cooperative efforts of humans working in socially organized groups" (p. 284). Unless your environment is strikingly different from ours, we think you will have difficulty identifying anything. Of course, your inclination is to declare those objects as different from you, as something other than self, but are they not really part and parcel of the means by which you participate in the communities that produced them? Isn't that your identity?

We won't belabor the point, but it should be clear that a distributed concept of self shifts the activity of learning to the connections one has with communities, to the patterns of participation, and away from efficient internalization of knowledge. Here then is another reason why so many constructivist applications employ discussion and dialogue in groups. Learning is not the lonely act of an individual, even when it is undertaken alone. It is a matter of being initiated into the practices of a community, of moving from legitimate peripheral participation to centripetal participation in the actions of a learning community (Lave & Wenger, 1991).

In anticipation of a common criticism, we would like to stress that the notion of distributed self does not remove self-agency from the learning process. It is sometimes argued that in models like this, the needs of the individual are sacrificed to the demands of the community. We admit that this is a danger, but no more so than the danger of indoctrination inherent in the process of internalization of knowledge transmitted from teacher or lesson to the learner. The important element missing in our model thus far, that of reflexivity, will reinforce the importance of self-agency (see 7.3.7).

7.3.7 Knowing How We Know Is the Ultimate Human Accomplishment

This last principle is the most important and probably the least controversial. We can't think of a single model of the teaching/learning process that would not stress the importance of self-awareness of learning and knowing. Certainly the extensive literature on metacognition (e.g., Flavell, 1979), thinking skills (e.g., Baron & Sternberg, 1987), theory of mind (e.g., Wellman, 1990), etc., within cognitive psychology are all pointed to the development of self-monitoring and self-control of the learning process. Even Skinner (1968, pp. 172–73) encourages learners to analyze the contingencies (see 2.2.1.3.1) that control their behavior and deliberately manipulate them so as to become self-reliant and self-managing (he even uses the word *freedom* to characterize this process!).

Where we differ, of course, is our account of the teaching/learning processes of which one should be aware! Many models of metacognition stress the development of strategies of efficient processing: primarily storage and retrieval (e.g., Bornstein, 1979). Programs in thinking skills frequently focus on the problem-solving process and train students to use systematic analytical procedures like Bransford and Stein's (1984) IDEAL problem solver or Sternberg's (1987) metacomponents. While we are unaware of any particular applications derived specifically from the MAB metaphor, we suspect that they would emphasize the process of perceptual tuning, perhaps in the sense of Donald Schon's (1987) reflective practitioner developing the ability to "see as."

We prefer the term *reflexivity*, which means directed, or turned back upon itself, or self-referential. To be reflexive about the principles cited above is to direct them back on your own efforts to learn, teach, and know. As specified in the principles above, we regard all learning as a social, dialogical process of construction by distributed, multidimensional selves using tools and signs within contexts created by the various communities with which they interact. This, we believe, is an entirely natural process of which we are ordinarily no more aware than we are of breathing or of our heartbeat. Our process of construction is directed toward creating a world that makes sense to us, one that is adequate for our everyday functioning. We are generally unaware of the beliefs we have adopted or created to live and teach by, but raising them to awareness can have salutary effects. Umberto Eco put the matter this way:

> To speak about "speaking," to signify signification, or to communicate about communication cannot but influence the universe of speaking, signifying, and communicating (1976, p. 29).

How do beliefs change? How do we become aware of them? When we are confronted with some experience not accounted for by our existing beliefs, we invent a new set of beliefs or revise an existing one, a process we have elsewhere referred to as *abduction* (Cunningham, 1992). This new structure will provide a context within which the surprising experience is a matter of course (i.e., it makes sense). Abduction is instigated when we are in a condition of inadequacy or uncertainty that arises from experience; hence it is naturally embedded in a relevant context (is situated or anchored). Thus when we experience or are shown a situation where our existing beliefs are inadequate, our awareness of our own state of knowing is enhanced. This is the essence of reflexivity.

Further awareness of the cultural origin and mediated nature of our beliefs allows us to explore varieties of belief structures. A reflexive analysis of the metaphors by which we live and teach will allow us to reconsider them. If we are not satisfied with the metaphor of "school is work," let's try another: "school as consulting service." Under this model, the school might be seen as a community resource where the teachers, students, equipment, and facilities are placed at the service of members of the community who may bring problems and issues to be addressed. Teachers and more experienced students mentor the younger ones during problem-solving projects geared toward the betterment of the community of which all are a part. But if this metaphor proves unuseful, try another!

Finally, we believe that via reflexivity, and in a manner not possible in other models, learners have real control over and responsibility for their beliefs. An awareness of the principles of constructivism listed above demands a strong sense of responsibility for the state of the world in which we find ourselves. If many world views are possible, then our choice of participation in the community that holds a particular view requires both a commitment to and a responsibility to respect the views of others. We have within our capability the constant renewal of our world view. Human reflection is the key to understanding and creating anew a world in which we coexist with others. Someone else's world view, her belief structure, can be as legitimate as our own. To coexist, a broader perspective is necessary,

one in which both parties cooperate to bring forth a common world where many perspectives are valid.

7.4 REEXAMINING SOME KEY CONCEPTS

In this section we would like to review some of the key concepts in instructional design and instructional methods, examining them from our constructivist perspective. In this discussion, it should be clear that methods can be implemented in many different ways, and how a method is implemented and what is the focus in that implementation is reflective of one's views of learning.

7.4.1 Discovery Learning

Discovery learning has a long and complex history in education (see Dewey, 1929; Bruner, 1961; Page, 1990). While it reached its heyday as a pedagogical framework in the 1960s, the generality of the term allows it to be applied to any learning environment in which the student is actively involved in problem solving (Bruner, 1961).

Discovery learning in its original formulation focused on the learning process, the goal being to develop inquiry skills in a content domain, an appreciation of inquiry as a way of approaching issues, and an appreciation of the complex issues in a domain. This view of defining what is learned in terms of the interrelationship of process and content is perhaps best exemplified in Bruner's design of the social studies curriculum, MACOS (Bruner, 1966; Bruner & Dow, undated). However, in its implementation over the years, in the form of the "new math," "open classroom," and other movements, discovery learning was employed as a method for acquiring content. The content goals remained the same as for other learning environments—knowledge was still seen as an entity—but the strategy for acquisition changed to one of "discovery."

The consequence of this view of discovery is that the students' inquiry is not honored. Rather, the learner has to discover the answer that the teacher already knows. Needless to say, learners quickly discover that the goal is not inquiry or exploration of a domain but rather discovering what the teacher wants them to discover. Rather than learner centered, the instruction is quite clearly teacher centered.

This view of discovery is perhaps an unfortunate consequence of the metaphor; "to discover" suggests that there is something (knowledge) hidden away, and our job is to find and acquire it. An alternative view of discovery is to think of it in terms of "invention," a personal construction, rather than as a discovery of what exists. From this perspective, we take as the goal of instruction not the acquisition of a specific, well-defined bit of content but rather the ability to learn in a content domain. Learning to learn—including the ability to ask questions, evaluate one's strategies, and develop answers to questions in the content domain—is the goal in this view of discovery learning (Brown et al., 1993). Such a goal requires a unity of process and content; both are integral and inseparable in developing the ability to work and think in the content domain. In this learning-to-learn view of discovery learning, the knowledge is in the learner's activity rather than being in the text. Thus it is a view that is fully consistent with the constructivist viewpoints.

In summary, if the goal is simply to learn a well-defined content—definition and procedures—then a discovery approach is not necessary. The learner should simply be told the answers and either given a memory (job) aid or required to memorize it. However, if the goal is to be able to use the information in a content domain, to be able to think in the content domain, to be able to invent defensible understandings, then the discovery method is appropriate.

7.4.2 Zone of Proximal Development

Vygotsky (1978, p. 86) defines the zone of proximal development (Zo-ped) as "the distance between the actual developmental level of a child as determined by independent problem solving and the level of potential development as determined through problem solving under adult guidance or in collaboration with more capable peers." In other words, we are describing a form of "joint" cognition, where the tutor provides support or scaffolding for the individual until the individual appropriates the knowledge or skill and brings it under his conscious control for his own use. The support is progressively withdrawn and, as the students take over more and more responsibility in a problem-solving situation, they become self-regulated and independent.

We would broaden the focus in two interrelated ways. First, there is a matter of perspective. Rather than talking about what we do to an individual, we would prefer to discuss the affordances of the environment. Thus, we can look more broadly at the environment to determine how the environment is designed to be supportive of the individual in relation to accomplishing some task. Neither the student nor the teacher "owns" the Zo-ped; rather, it is something that is established dynamically. From an instructional design perspective, this shifts the focus from what we teach to how we design a learning environment that will support the learner as he or she may request support, and can be discarded by that learner when it is no longer required.

Second, our broader view of the Zo-ped looks at the full cultural context of the individual's learning environment. Cole (1985) has characterized the Zo-ped as "where culture and cognition create each other." We can think of the Zo-ped in terms of what an individual can do as a function of being a part of a specific culture that would not be possible if he or she were not a part of that culture, and, as Cole's remark suggests, the changes in the individual, in turn, change the culture. Thus the full sociohistorical context is a part of the Zo-ped for development. An implication of this is that we can look at what a Zo-ped affords in any cultural context by simply looking at the difference between newcomers and old-timers in that community (Lave & Wenger, 1991).

This view has interesting implications for the distinction between learning and instruction (see, e.g., Heinich, Molenda & Russell, 1993) where instruction is defined as particular context for learning in which we purposefully organize the environment to achieve particular learning objectives. In the view we are discussing, there are a wide range of social situations that are designed to promote learning of particular goals. In our view, these social contexts are instructional environments. They differ from what we normally describe as instruction simply because we typically conceive of instruction as the formalized delivery or transmission of information. However, there are designed formal and informal social structures that teach the newcomer the rules and procedures of conduct. For example, Lave and Wenger (1991) describe the design of AA meetings such that individuals stand up and share stories. They provide a very nice analysis of this "instructional strategy" and its impact on newcomers. More generally, we could examine any community and look at the structure of the community as well as the effect that structure has on how we learn to behave. Some instructional designers might want to argue that such an environment is not designed, and hence it is not instructional. However, we would argue very strongly that it is designed to achieve particular ends. Simply try to change the structure of the community (the tacit rules) and see how the members would react. And of course, anyone who fails to learn is redirected in a manner analogous to any training program.

7.4.3 Scaffolding

Success in the Zo-ped requires support for learning, and that support is called the *scaffolding*. Indeed, the Zo-ped is defined in terms of the scaffolding or affordances of the environment. Scaffolding includes the support of other individuals, any artifacts in the environment that afford support, as well as the cultural context and history the individuals bring to the Zo-ped. We will discuss the role of the teacher in greater detail in the next two sections. At this point, we simply wish to clarify the general notion of the power relationship within the Zo-ped.

The scaffolding metaphor implies a rigid structure that is used to construct. That is, the placing of the scaffold presupposes much of the character of the structure being built. In our mind, this is an unfortunate choice of metaphors since it suggests a guiding and teaching of the learner toward some well-defined (structural) end. This "structural" metaphor of a scaffold is consistent with the objectivist view of instruction in which the teacher arranges the environment (including the teaching activities) to help the learner acquire the prespecified "knowledge." This view of scaffolding presents the Zo-ped as a teaching environment rather than as a learning environment. It is a model of transmission, the "objects" that provide the support/scaffold form the individual.

From our perspective, the Zo-ped and the scaffolding must be viewed as a learning environment—as supporting the growth of the learner. Griffin and Cole provide what we feel is an excellent contrast of the learning vs. teaching concept of scaffolding in the Zo-ped: "a Zo-ped is a dialogue between the child and his future; it is not a dialogue between the child and the adult's past" (1984, p. 62).

7.4.4 Cognitive Apprenticeship

The influential papers of Resnick (1987) and Brown, Collins, and Duiguid (1989) led to a renewal of interest in apprenticeship as a design for learning environments. The focus, however, shifted from physical job skills to the development of cognitive skills. The result was a focus on authentic learning environments where the cognitive demands in the learning are qualitatively the same as the cognitive demands of the environment for which the instruction was preparatory.

We fully agree with the focus on authentic cognitive demands. Indeed, this is consistent with our emphasis that the learning is in the activity of the learner, and hence we must examine the activity and the full sociocultural context in which it occurs. In traditional instruction, the learner's cognitive activity is centered on the development of strategies for determining what the text and the teacher are signaling as important, processing and remembering the information, and for evaluating test items to determine correct answers. These are all skills preparatory for more schooling—it is a cognitive apprenticeship for schooling—but not for much else (Honebein, Duffy & Fishman, 1993). Engaging learners in cognitive and metacognitive activities that involve the authentic use of information is a central goal in our instructional design.

While we agree with the focus on authentic cognitive activity, there are other aspects in the development of the concept of cognitive apprenticeship with which we are less sanguine. Our primary concern is that there has been a focus on cognitive apprenticeship as a "master-apprentice" relationship with an implicit view that the core of the apprenticeship is the master teaching the apprentice. Indeed, the most often-cited examples of cognitive apprenticeship are reciprocal teaching (Palinscar & Brown, 1984) and modeling "thinking like a mathematician" (Schoenfeld, 1991), both of which focus almost exclusively on a knowledgeable master working with the less-knowledgeable learner. This model of cognitive apprenticeship is more in line with the MAB or even with the MAC models of mind. It focuses on the individual cognitive activity (Kang, 1995).

Lave and Wenger (1991) present a view of cognitive apprenticeship more in line with our MAR model of mind. Rather than the master-apprentice relationship being central, Lave and Wenger examine the full sociocultural context of which the individual is a part. They discuss apprenticeship as being a legitimate peripheral participant in a social context. By this they mean that the individual is legitimately a participant but is only playing a partial role in the context. There is not a master who assigns tasks or who monitors the apprentice's behavior. Rather, the apprentice

begins to assume responsibilities, testing his or her ability to assume roles and responsibilities in that environment. The full cultural context—the artifacts as well as the experts (or old-timers)—afford the learner support (scaffold) as the learner attempts to take on these responsibilities. Lave and Wenger note that in most apprentice environments there is little direct teaching between master and apprentice.

In addition to decentering the "master" in the apprenticeship environment, Lave and Wenger argue that it is not so much that apprenticeship is the "best" learning environment; it is simply that it is a prevalent learning environment. In addition to formal apprenticeship, most informal learning can be interpreted from the perspective of "apprenticing" (see 20.3.1). In most new contexts, we first observe and then begin to take on some responsibilities in a group we wish to become an integral part of. Lave and Wenger provide several excellent examples of both formal and informal apprenticeships as a means to illustrate their concept of legitimate peripheral participation and to begin to analyze some of the critical variables in successful apprenticeships.

In summary, from an instructional design perspective, the apprentice environment is one way to view the design of a learning environment. However, in doing so the emphasis is not on master-apprentice but rather on the learner as a member of a larger community of practice who, through legitimate peripheral participation and the affordances of the environment, begins to assume greater responsibility in that community of practice. Thus our design must provide the learner access to that community of practice and provide the tools that will support the learner in assuming his or her role in that practice. The instructional principles outlined in the previous section provide the guidance in designing such an environment.

7.4.5 Coaching

We no longer teach, but rather we coach—we have moved from the sage on the stage to the guide on the side. The coach provides the scaffold for the learner. This is becoming common rhetoric in instructional theory, and the constructivist "movement" has been a primary stimulus for this shift in the teacher/trainer role. It is not so much that the teacher is seen as less important, rather the role of the teacher changes so that the focus is on aiding or providing the scaffolding for the learners rather than telling the learner. We fully appreciate this goal of decentering the teacher as the fount of knowledge. However, our concern is that the shift is a shift in method rather than a shift in the conceptual framework underlying the method—a trivial rather than a radical constructivist shift in von Glasersfeld's (1989) terms.

By a shift in method, we mean that while the method has moved from sage on the stage to guide on the side, the guide is still the fount of knowledge. He or she still possesses the knowledge the student is to acquire. It is a unidirectional relationship in which the student observes and mimics or follows the instructions of the coach. The coach, in turn, models the behavior or provides the answers. We coach the learner by giving the learner our knowledge, which is to be replicated. This is in large part consistent with the cognitive apprentice model advocated by Brown et al. (1989). Of course, this view is not much different from the traditional view of learning. Knowledge is still this entity to be transmitted from coach to learner—a new instructional method, but the same view of learning and knowledge.

Within our MAR constructivist framework, the coach-learner relationship is bidirectional. The skills and knowledge of both coach and learner are attended to and honored. Fosnot (1989) describes this as a mentor-protégé relationship in which the mentor begins by seeking to understand and expand the learner's or protégé's current conceptions. Thus both mentor and protégé are seeking to understand the other's views. Rather than the end goal being that the learner can replicate the coach's behavior or follow the coach's directions, it is that the mentor and learner come to an agreement even if it is an agreement to disagree. That is, the learner may not mimic the coach, but the deviations are knowledgeable deviations that the learner can defend and the coach can respect.

We can see for ourselves, and hopefully illustrate for the reader, the implications of these two points of view in our interactions with students and, oftentimes, even in our interactions with each other as we discuss research and theory. The most "natural" approach to an issue-based discussion is to have generated one's own point of view, one's own answer to the question on the table. Then, in conversing (coaching) student or colleague, we listen to see how what they say matches our conceptualization, and we catalogue the matches and the mismatches. Our response, then, is a question or comment that helps the learner understand our different points of view and encourages them to accept the alternative. This is the coaching framework that calls for the learner or colleague to mimic our point of view.

The alternative framework—the mentoring approach—would have us listening to the student or colleague to understand his or her point of view. We would then ask questions to help us clarify those aspects that we did not understand. Only after we felt a reasonable understanding of that alternative view would we engage in a discussion to try to understand and perhaps resolve the differences. But it may well be that the alternatives are compatible and each is acceptable. Fosnot has offered the following prescription for coaching preservice teachers within the constructivist framework, a prescription that is a method reflective of the underlying theory. It should be noted that while it is similar to the Socratic method, the acknowledgment of defensible alternative perspectives provides the deviation from the mimic aspect of the Socratic method:

1. The mentor learns the protégé's point of view through careful listening and probing.
2. The mentor teaches by inquiring at the "leading edge" of the protégé's thinking and by attempting to facilitate disequilibrium.
3. The mentor constructs a line of inquiry meaningful to the protégé, and the protégé constructs a line of reasoning meaningful to the mentor.

4. The mentor acknowledges that the protégé has the intellectual freedom to adopt and modify the pedagogical orientation of his or her choice (Fosnot, 1989, p. 97).

7.4.6 Context

In instructional and educational research, we have traditionally viewed context as a variable in our research. Context can be decomposed into components, and those components can be manipulated. The context sits separate from the individual and can be manipulated independently of the individual. This is an objectivist view of context more fitting of the MAC model of mind (see footnote 4, p. 172).

The constructivist view of context we would argue for has the context as a dynamic whole, including the individual and the sociohistorical context. The mind as rhizome provides one metaphor for this view, where elements can be pointed to much as the tubers, but in the context of the whole we cannot identify, where one element leaves off and another begins. Birdwhistell offers an analogous metaphor to explain this view of context:

> . . . sometimes I like to think of a rope. The fibers that make up the rope are discontinuous; when you twist them together, you do not make them continuous, you make the thread continuous . . . even though it may look in a thread as though each of those particles are going all through it, that isn't the case . . . that's essentially the descriptive model (Birdwhistell as cited in McDermott, 1980).

7.4.7 Learner Control

Learner control is a concept that was introduced in relation to computer-based instruction (see 23.9). At issue is how much or what type of control should be given to the learner during the learning process? The alternatives are learner control, computer control, or shared control. What is it that is controlled? Basically the control decision has to do with the pacing of the information presented, the sequence of the information, and the actual content (Milheim & Martin, 1991).

This is perhaps the epitome of an objectivist view of learning. The content of instruction is almost totally divorced from learning activity except as it is related to "processing" variables for "inputting" information. Learning is the input and mastery of particular content, the ability to repeat it, apply it, discriminate it where "it" is well defined. The ability of the person to think in the domain—to evaluate his understanding, judge relevance, and make decisions of what he needs toward what end—is irrelevant. Indeed, the irrelevance of thinking to the learning activity is reflected in this summary statement of the general view of learner control in instructional design and the state of our research findings:

> The notion of learner control has long held *intuitive* appeal for developers of computer-assisted instruction, but

its apparent *potential for improving learning* has never been experimentally established" (emphasis added, Goforth, 1994, p. 1).

And what is the intuitive appeal? It would seem that the belief is that learners should know best what they need, and so learning will be more efficient if they are in control. It has nothing to do with the thinking process being an integral part of knowing. As Ross and Morrison (1989) note, the notion of giving the learners control of their learning activities is based on two assumptions: learners know what is best for them, and they are capable of acting appropriately on that knowledge. If the learner does not meet either of these assumptions, then control of "learning" is given to the computer so that learning can occur "efficiently."

The concept of learner control is similar to the concept of teacher-centered instruction in the noncomputer environment. That is, rather than supporting learners in developing control of their own learning and hence of being able to think in a domain, the teacher-centered and computer-controlled instructional approaches take responsibility away from the learner. However, in teacher control, it is primarily a control of the content and the basic learner task. In computer-control literature, the control is far more pervasive in that the computer takes over even the minute decision making. We find the title of a recent paper on control instructive as to the importance of this variable on the dynamics of a learning environment: I Lost Control (and My Students Found It) (Schleper, 1993).

7.4.8 Assessment

Traditionally, assessment is an activity undertaken after learning is accomplished: Communicate some knowledge, then test to see if the knowledge has been successfully stored by the learner; demonstrate and coach a skill, then test to see if student can perform skill, etc. A great deal of technology of testing is devoted to enhancing the congruence of the testing context and the learning context. That is, is the test a reliable and valid measure of the extent to which learning has occurred? This approach also seeks to minimize factors that could contaminate test results. For example, a test that simply required the student to repeat answers to questions asked during learning would not be valid. Likewise, if the student were assisted in any way in completing the test, by a person or tool like a calculator, the results would likely be judged as invalid.

Generally speaking, the world of educational measurement adopts physical measurement as a model where a measurement tool quite different from the variable itself is applied: A ruler is applied to measure height, a micrometer is applied to measure thickness, etc. By analogy, an intelligence test measures intelligence but is not itself intelligence; an achievement tests measures a sample of a learned domain but is not itself that domain. Like micrometers and rulers, intelligence and achievement tests are tools (metrics) applied to the variables but somehow distinct from them.

The situation within constructivism is quite different. A rapidly growing literature (e.g., Shavelson, Baxter & Pine,

1992; Belak, Newman, Adams, Archbald, Burgess, Raven & Romberg, 1992; Gifford & O'Connor, 1992; Mabry & Stake, 1994; Linn, Baker & Dunbar, 1990) is introducing such terms as *performance assessment*, *portfolios*, *authentic assessment*, etc., and beginning the process of building a technology of assessment based on constructivist principles such as those proposed in this paper. The distinction between learning and testing is certainly blurred if not rejected in these attempts. For instance, Ann Brown and her colleagues (1993) describe "dynamic assessment," a procedure that shares many characteristics with reciprocal teaching. It too is an example of "assisted learning" (see also Tharp & Gallimore, 1988), where the assessor establishes a zone of proximal development with the student to scaffold new learning as well as assess. Later in the assessment/teaching process, the teacher/assessor withdraws prompts when it is felt that the child can perform independently. Thus, if learning is in the connections, in the activity itself, then learning *is* the test. If the aim of a reading teacher, for example, is to have the child develop the skill of asking questions about reading materials, then the "test" is embedded in the teaching/learning context: Can the student now ask effective questions while reading, whereas previously she was only able to do so with the teacher's support and scaffolding? Or if the aim of the medical school faculty is to have students diagnose and prescribe treatment (and be able to defend their decisions), the test is embedded within the activity, not distinct from it. Ironically, perhaps, when traditional measurement techniques are used in situations such as these, where their applicability is questionable, the scores often show performance at least as good as traditional instruction (Albanese & Mitchell, 1993; Hubbard Welsh, Iatridis, Ficklin & Vaughn, 1994).

Additionally, performance assessment specialists are beginning to develop methods of large-scale assessment of complex performances (e.g., teacher certification—see Delandshire & Petrosky, 1994) that are authentic, discursive, semiotic, and reflexive. It is becoming increasingly clear that assessment that is sympathetic to constructivist principles will require new conceptions of such traditional concepts as reliability and validity (see, for example, Messick, 1989) and of the sorts of evidence that will be helpful in making assessment decisions like who should be employed, hired, admitted to university, and so forth. Of all the areas we have identified, this may be the one that is most underdeveloped (and under development) at this point in time.

7.4.9 Collaborative Learning

Collaborative learning and cooperative learning (see Chapter 35): Everyone wants it. It is *the* instructional strategy, perhaps the strategy of the decade. But why do we have students working together in groups? This is perhaps an area where one's metaphor for learning can most clearly be seen in its impact on the implementation of a strategy. The use of groups may simply be used as an alternative instructional strategy, with little change in the learning goals from traditional didactic instruction (Slavin, 1990; Johnson & Johnson, 1990). The guidelines for using cooperative groups focuses on structural and management variables like the gender distribution, number of participants, etc., and how to ensure that everyone does the work. From this perspective, groups are used for reasons that include providing variation in the classroom activity, teaching students how to cooperate and work together, sharing work loads and hence permitting larger projects, and to promote peer tutoring.

Groups also work on problems in the constructivist environment, and the goal in that work is to share alternative viewpoints and challenge as well as help develop each alternative points of view (Cunningham, Duffy & Knuth, 1993; Savery & Duffy, 1995; Sharan & Sharan, 1992). As we noted previously, learning is an inherently social-dialogical process. Hence, our reason for using groups is to promote the dialogical interchange and reflexivity. Our emphasis in providing guidance on the use of groups is how to promote that dialogical interchange among group members. We emphasize the importance of supporting collaborative informal reasoning about problems and reflectivity on the learning process.

7.4.10 Computers and Media

Any Rip van Winkle who has just awakened after 10 years would undoubtedly be overwhelmed by the incredible changes in both the character and the pervasiveness of technology in our society. Video has moved out of the "professional production" limitation and out of the television and movie theaters to become a general medium available for the viewing and analysis of any event. The latest multimedia computers can store enormous amounts of information, present it via sound, text, video, graphics, etc., interact with users in modes that seem evermore natural and complex, and accomplish this with information and people distributed worldwide.

Given the widespread adoption of this technology in education and training, we will consider its role in education in some detail. Most often, technology is adopted by teachers and instructional designers as a "teaching tool," that is, to provide more effective and efficient delivery of instruction and hence more effective and efficient learning. According to this view, the video medium provides richer examples of concepts and principles, and thus we are able to teach the learner better how to execute a procedure, teach to discriminate between examples and nonexamples, etc. Computer technology permits us to build student and expert models (see 19.2.3) so that we can more effectively present problems to the learner and identify and remediate misconceptions (Psotka, Massey & Mutter, 1988). And, of course, the richness of the technology permits us to provider a richer and more exciting (entertaining?) learning environment that will better engage the student in learning the material being presented.

We, on the other hand, want to focus on the technology as a tool for the learner rather than as a tool for the teacher.

Let us hasten to clarify, however, that we do not mean to simply substitute "learner" for "teacher" in the previous paragraph: The computer is not, or not only, a tool for the learner to acquire the content or skill more efficiently. Rather, our concern is the new understandings and the new capabilities that are possible through the use of technology. Pea (1985, 1993), in contrasting these two views, describes the first as using technology as a tool simply to amplify what we were doing before (so that we can do it more efficiently and effectively), while the latter is seen as augmenting cognitive activity and thereby leading to a reorganization and extension of our cognition.

One impact of the augmentation view is to examine how the tools may permit the learner to attend to higher-level representations by "off-loading" basic cognitive demands. For example, the use of the word processor permits easy reorganizing of text and hence permits the writer to explore alternative organizations, ways of expressing ideas, etc. It also dramatically impacts the nature of the interaction in collaborative writing activities. Similarly, the calculating functions permit many new foci in mathematics teaching (NCTM, 1989).

In addition to off-loading basic cognitive tasks, the technology may offer genuinely *new* representations or views of phenomena that would not otherwise be possible, and hence provide *new* understandings. Pea (1993) has noted that contribution of scientific visualization techniques to the understanding of particular phenomena (see, e.g., Keller & Keller, 1993). Hay (1994) and Soloway, Guzdial, and Hay (1994) are bringing those visualization techniques into the classroom as a strategy for aiding learners in developing new and richer representations of scientific as well as everyday phenomena. In a related vein, the Vanderbilt group has used video to capture complex activities in ways that allow learners to analyze those complexities and examine the interrelationships (LTGV, 1992). We might also point to the impact of video technology (the ease of recording as well as the ease of random access to and annotation of the video records) on our understanding of dynamic events like teaching and small-group collaboration (Jordan & Henderson, 1994; Brown, 1994).

Within this "augmentation" view, the MAB and MAR models of cognition offer different interpretations or understandings of the technology. The "mind as brain" view, with its focus on the individual mind, sees the computer as enhancing the individual's cognition, focusing on what he or she "knows." As Salomon, Perkins, and Globerson (1991) describe it, it is the effects of computing on the individual's cognitive skills that will impact cognitive performance outside of the computing environment. The effect of computing is an effect that endures beyond the computing, and, as such, this view suggests that knowledge (the residue effect) resides outside of the activity; it is an entity in the head.

From a MAR viewpoint, the technology is seen as an integral component of the cognitive activity. As discussed previously, cognition is distributed in the environment such that an understanding of cognition requires an examination of the activity in the environment. Bateson's famous example of the blind man provides what is to us a very clear example of distributed cognition: how it is impossible to separate tools from cognition:

> Suppose I am a blind man, and I use a stick. I go tap, tap, tap. Where do I start? Is my mental system bounded at the handle of the stick? Is it bounded by my skin? Does it start halfway up the stick? Does it start at the tip of the stick? (1972, p. 459).

The answer to this, of course, depends on the activity of the blind man. In the case of navigating the world, the stick is an integral part of the cognition. However, when Bateson's blind man sits at a computer, the stick's relationship to his cognition has totally changed, and it is keyboards and mouses that become relevant. Cognition is distributed among the artifacts in the activity.

This view of distributed cognition significantly impacts how we think about the role of technology in education and training.[8] The focus is not on the individual in isolation and what he or she knows, but on the activity in the environment (see Table 7-1). It is the activity—focused and contexualized—that is central. Furthermore the task of the learner is no longer seen as static—the computer as applied to the task—but rather it is dynamic: The computer opens new opportunities and makes available new learning activities. As Pea (1993) has noted, our goal becomes one of expanding cognition, not of reallocating cognitive activity as a division of labor.

A good example of the use of technology to expand cognition is found in George Landow's (1992) argument for the design and use of hypermedia (see 21.4). Landow has been perhaps the most outspoken advocate of hypermedia technology, for he sees it as a medium that permits critical theorists to realize and test their views as never before possible. His views on the important relation between hypertext and critical theory is clear in the following statements:

> A paradigm shift, I suggest, has begun to take place in the writings of Jacques Derrida and Theodor Nelson, of Roland Barthes and Andries van Dam. I suspect that one name in each pair will be unknown to most of my readers. . . . [However] all four, like many others who write on hypertext or literary theory, argue that we must abandon conceptual systems founded on ideas of center, margins, hierarchy, and linearity, and replace them with ones of multilinearity, nodes, links, and networks. Almost all parties to this paradigm shift, which marks a revolution in human thought, see electronic writing as a direct response to the strengths and weaknesses of the printed book. This response has profound implications for literature, education, and books. . . . Using hypertext, we will have, or now already have, a new laboratory . . . in which to test their ideas. . . . [While] critical theory promises to theorize hypertext, hypertext promises to embody

and thereby test aspects of theory, particularly those concerning textuality, narrative, and the roles or functions of reader and writer (1992, pp. 2–3).

> . . . hypertext has much in common with some major points of contemporary literary theory and semiological theory, particularly with Derrida's emphasis on de-centering (see 10.5) and with Barthe's conception of the readerly vs. the writerly text. In fact hypertext creates an almost embarrassingly literal embodiment of both concepts (1992, pp. 33–34).

In essence, Landow is arguing that hypertext can be used to empower the reader to see and use text in new ways and in particular to support multilineal thinking. A goal of critical theory is to permit the reader his or her own center for investigation, not only in terms of starting points but also in terms of the consideration of the information and the paths along which those considerations might lead (see 9.2, 10.5.3). Thus a major goal in critical theory is to decenter the author and the text, to unconstrain the linkages of ideas from the linear flow of text and from the "container" of the book covers, and to place the authority for constructing and evaluating ideas in the reader and his or her collaboration with other readers.

We would suggest, with the proliferation of information in this information age, that such decentering will become essential to successful problem solving and thought in many domains. Success will increasingly depend on exploring interrelationships in an information-rich environment rather than on accepting the point of view of one author who pursued one set of relationships and presents conclusions reflecting his or her implicit biases. While we tend to think of books as "natural" ways of representing information and ideas, Landow reminds us that it is an artificial structure that may not serve our present needs:

> "The structure of books," Tom McArthur reminds us, "is anything but 'natural'—indeed, it is thoroughly *un*natural and took all of 4,000 years to bring about. The achievement of the Scholastics, preeminently among the world's scribal elites, was to conventionalize the themes, plots, and shapes of books in a truly rigorous way" (Landow, 1992, p. 57).

In essence, the design of the text imposed order on fragmented knowledge and ideas. Hypertext would remove the textual imposition of order, and, Landow argues, the reader would create his or her own order based on scientific, historical, cultural, or any other thematically coherent focus. The consistency of Landow's view of hypertext with our constructivist MAR model is clear:

> The hypertextual dissolution of centrality, which makes the medium such a potentially democratic one, also makes it a model of a society of conversations in which no one conversation, no one discipline or ideology, dominates or founds the others. It is thus the instantiation of what Richard Rorty terms the edifying philosophy, the point of which is to keep the conversation going rather than to find the objective truth" (Landow, 1992, p. 78).

Within Landow's framework, the diversity of "multilinearity" of a hypertext is critical, as is the availability of search tools and the ability of the reader to create his or her own links and nodes so as to find and create links and nodes

---

[8] Our focus here is on technology, but of course the view applies to other individuals in the environment, e.g., the role of collaboration, and the entire sociocultural context of the activity.

in the process of constructing reader-centered themes. Landow (1989a, 1989b) illustrates the educational realization of his view of hypertext in the teaching of his undergraduate and graduate courses in literature where students work in a hypertext database consisting of thousands of nodes and linking to other hypertext databases. Student's assignments establish themes for which they must construct alternative interpretations, e.g., as to how two authors or two passages are similar, which may involve issues of the social or cultural characteristics of the time, early experiences of the authors, the formalities of plot development, etc. Rather than there being a "true" reason or interpretation, Landow encourages his students to recognize the multicausality and the importance of focus on interpretation.

Landow's use of hypertext in his literature courses provides an example of the use of technology to augment cognition and in the evolution of the learning task that the technology permitted. This is a considerably different view from that of a traditional "instructional" view of hypertext where the concern is whether the student will cover the material and where tools are designed to restrict access until prerequisites are "covered" or to guide the student through prespecified paths. In concluding this discussion, we would like to describe briefly two additional examples of this "constructivist" view of effective uses of technology.

First, a most obvious example is the use of the Internet and other wide-area networks to promote collaboration (see 14.1, 14.2, and 14.7). We have multiple examples of the use of the network to create international as well as scientific collaboration to help students take a less parochial view of issues, to help them to see and evaluate multiple perspectives, and to engage them in more authentic research activities (see, e.g., Roupp, 1993). On a more local level, Harasim (1993) has demonstrated the use of the Internet as a vehicle to promote collaboration among students in a distance education course. Most distance education programs use technology, if it is available, to deliver instruction, emphasizing the transmission of the content rather than collaboration. In contrast, Harasim made the dialogic central in her distance education course. Materials were distributed via the mail, and the Internet was used for formal seminar discussions and for informal exchanges in a virtual café. Just as would be expected in any on-site seminar, students were expected to discuss the seminar topic, and grading was based in part on their contribution to that discussion. There was no formal, didactic instruction.

Finally, Strategic Teaching Framework,[9] (STF) provides an example of the use of multimedia in teacher education that honors the teacher as problem solver or researcher (Duffy, 1995). The goal of STF is to aid teachers in adopting a learner-centered, problem-solving, collaborative approach to learning, i.e., an approach based on constructivist principles. Typical technology-based approaches to teacher change

use video to present alternative scenarios that the teacher can respond to and then receive the "correct" response, or scenarios illustrating "the" correct method by examples and nonexamples. STF, in contrast, views teaching holistically rather than as a set of discrete methods. Additionally, it is designed under the assumption that adopting a learner-centered view requires a conceptual change in addition to the development of new strategies. Finally, it was assumed that teachers must construct and test their own understanding of methods and that construction must arise from their own evaluation of teaching.

This framework led to the design of STF based on the metaphor of visiting an ongoing classroom. If a teacher wanted to adopt new approaches to teaching, he or she would visit the classroom of experienced teachers, observe their teaching, ask questions, and explore different aspects of their approach. There would be multiple points of view expressed about what was important in the teaching process, and the teacher-learner would have to evaluate those perspectives. The teacher-learner would return to his or her classroom, test the strategies and views, and then, in an iterative process, return to the "mentors" classroom to observe more and ask additional questions. Ideally this teacher would be part of a community of teachers, all attempting to restructure their teaching, and the constructive dialogue would occur among members of this community.

STF, then, does not teach; rather it is a resource for learning. It consists of videos of classrooms the teacher-learner can visit. These are not brief scenarios, but rather an entire class episode, typically 50 minutes long. As teacher-learners sit in on the class, they may ask for points of view as to what is important instructionally at any particular point in the video. The learners have multiple perspectives available: the teacher they are observing, an experienced teacher-educator, or a researcher. Furthermore, the comments may address management, teaching, or assessment issues. Just as with the classroom video, none of the perspectives is scripted. They are straightforward comments from each "expert" as to what she or he thinks is important at that particular point in the class. Thus, this is an authentic interaction, both in visiting the classroom and in soliciting perspectives. While there is more to STF (a whole library of resources), this brief description illustrates the use of multimedia and, in particular, the richness of video, as a tool for the learner focused on constructing understanding rather than as a tool for the teacher (or instructional developer) to transmit knowledge.

7.5 AN INSTRUCTIONAL MODEL

In concluding this chapter we will describe problem-based learning, an instructional model that we feel exemplifies the constructivist theory represented by our MAR metaphor. There are numerous instructional models popular today that focus on "problems." Case-based learning, modeled after the traditions of business and law school (Christensen, 1987; Spizzen & Hart, 1985; Stevens, 1983), is perhaps the most

---

[9]The development of Strategic Teaching Framework is a joint effort of Indiana University and the North Central Regional Education Laboratory.

widespread and popular approach to problem-centered instruction (Greenwood & Parkay, 1989; Merseth & Lacey, 1993; Sykes & Bird, 1992; Wasserman, 1993). In this approach, instruction is centered around a description of some event that took place and that is relevant to the professional activities of the learners: an instructional scenario for teachers, a legal case for lawyers, etc. In business and industry, the instructional models for using problems are goal-based scenarios (Collins, 1994; Nowakowski, 1994) and action learning (Froiland, 1994). Both begin with a problem—a goal- or action-oriented decision the individual must make—but while the goal-based scenario model (see 20.33) uses problems from the past or specially created problems, action learning focuses on a real problem currently requiring action by one or more of the learners. It is, in essence, just-in-time training. Finally, at the elementary education level, the "problems" in the project-based learning model (Katz & Chard, 1989) involve a multidisciplinary (subject matter) exploration of a topic (e.g., trains) in which the students examine the topic from multiple perspectives over a week or more.

Problem-based learning as a specific instructional model was first implemented in medical education in the early 70s (see 20.3.4) and, like the models listed above, it too is based on presenting problems for the students to work on. It is not our goal to try to contrast the instructional models represented by cases/goals/projects/actions/problems. Indeed, there is so much variation in the implementation of each of these models that there is likely to be as much similarity between some implementations from different models than there is between different implementations within the same model (see, e.g., Barrows, 1986; Froiland, 1994; Williams, 1992).

A central theme to our chapter has been that an instructional designer's grounding assumptions about knowledge and learning are primary determinants of the instruction that is designed. So it is here. While there is widespread agreement as to the role of problems in instruction, the agreement is not so great in terms of the learning goals or assumptions about learning that surround the use of problems. We can identify five strategies for using problems that reflect different assumptions about either what is to be learned or how learning occurs.

1. *The Problem as a Guide.* Here the problem serves as a concrete reference point to focus the learner's attention. Reading assignments are given along with the case, and the readers are told to think of the reading in terms of the case. The case gives meaning to the reading assignment. This is similar to the study skill strategy of presenting questions at the start of the chapter to guide reading.

2. *The Problem as an Integrator or Test.* Here the problem is presented after the assigned readings are completed and perhaps even after they are discussed. The goal is to apply the knowledge from reading to the case to see how well the readings were understood and to aid the transfer process from learning to application. This is similar to presenting study or review questions at the end of the chapter.

3. *The Problem as an Example.* Here the problem is simply another bit of instructional material and is integrated in the reading. It is used to illustrate some particular point, and this is likely to be done through lecture or "teaching" as it is through student discussion. The focus is on the principle, concept, or procedure illustrated in the problem.

4. *The Problem as a Vehicle for Process.* Here the focus on critical thinking in relation to the problem is central. The problem becomes a vehicle for training thinking skills. Thus, heuristics for problem analysis are taught in relation to the problem. The goal is to develop thinking skills, not only to solve the problem.

5. *The Problem as a Stimulus for Authentic Activity.* Here the focus is on developing the skills related to solving the problem as well as other problems like it. Rather than "teaching" the skills, the skills are developed through working on the problem, i.e., through authentic activity. The "skills" here include physical skills, gathering and bringing knowledge in the domain to bear on the problem, and metacognitve skills related to all aspects of the problem-solving process.

It is this last use of problems, the problem as a stimulus for authentic activity, that is our focus. It is the approach developed by Howard Barrows for medical education in the early 70s and which he has continued to develop and refine (Barrows, 1985, 1992, 1994). This approach is founded on the goal of engaging and supporting the learner in activities that reflect the demands of professional practice. Rather than "teaching" the student in the sense of presenting or even assigning information, the goal is to support the student's learning. From our perspective, the focus is rightly on the activity of the learner in the content domain. That is, it is impossible to describe what is learned in terms of the activity alone or in terms of the content alone. It is not that students are learning critical-thinking skills, self-directed learning skills, or collaborative learning skills, nor is it that they are learning "the" content domain. Rather, it is the activity in relation to the content that defines learning: the ability to think critically in that content domain, to collaborate with peers and use them to test ideas about issues, and the ability to locate information related to the issues and bring it to bear on the diagnosis.

We should emphasize that while problem-based learning (PBL) has been developed for professional training, it clearly has generality to all levels of education. A grounding assumption is that we do not learn in a content domain simply to acquire information but rather to bring that information to bear on our daily lives. Thus, consistent with the goals advocated by Dewey (1916, 1938), the argument in PBL is that learning in school should model and prepare us for the self-directed learning we will need to do to be effective participants in our community and to be effective in our profession. For example, in working with high schools, Barrows and Myers (1993) designed problems that related to the flooding in the Midwest in 1993, the action that government should take to monitor asteroids in space, and an analysis of how the geography of the Middle East impacts the conflicts between nations in that area.

The problems Barrows and Myers generated for the high school level may sound very much like topics that might be used in *theme-based instruction.* Indeed, PBL is theme based in the sense that learning is organized around the problem rather than around subject matter. However, once again we must emphasize that the critical characteristic for us is that the teacher in PBL does not teach students what they should do/know and when they should do/know it. Rather, the teacher is there to support the students in developing their critical-thinking skills, self-directed learning skills, and content knowledge in relation to the problem. The teacher must honor and support the students' thinking rather than impose structure on it. (We note, of course, that honoring the students' thinking will include challenging that thinking.)

7.5.1 The PBL Process

Problem-based learning can perhaps best be understood through a brief description of the learning/instructional process as implemented by Barrows (1985, 1992, 1994) in a medical school. When students enter the medical school, they are divided into groups of five, and each group is assigned a facilitator. The students are then presented a problem in the form of a patient entering with presenting symptoms. The students' task is to diagnose the patient and be able to provide a rationale for that diagnosis and recommended treatment.

The students begin the problem "cold"—they do not know what the problem will be until it is presented. They discuss the problem, generating hypotheses based on whatever experience or knowledge they have, identifying relevant facts in the case, and identifying learning issues. The learning issues are topics of any sort that are deemed of potential relevance to this problem and which the group feels they do not understand as well as they should. A session is not complete until each student has an opportunity to reflect verbally on his or her current beliefs about the diagnosis (i.e., commit to a temporary position) and assume responsibility for particular learning issues that were identified. Note that there are no prespecified objectives presented to the students. The students generate the learning issues (objectives) based on their analysis of the problem.

After the session, the students all engage in self-directed learning. There are no assigned texts. Rather the students are totally responsible for gathering the information from the available medical library and computer database resources. Additionally, particular faculty are designated to be available as consultants (as they would be for any physician in the real world). The students may go to the consultants seeking information.

After self-directed learning, the students meet again. They begin by evaluating resources: what was most useful and what was not so useful. They then begin working on the problem with this new level of understanding. Note that they do not simply tell each other what they learned. Rather,

they use that learning in reexamining the problem. This cycle may repeat itself if new learning issues arise. Problems in the medical school program last anywhere from a week to 3 weeks.

Assessment at the end of the process is in terms of peer evaluation and self-evaluation. There are no tests in this medical school curriculum. The assessment includes self- and peer evaluation (with suggestions for improvement) in three areas: self-directed learning, problem solving, and skills as a group member. While the students must pass the Medical Board exam after 2 years, this is outside of the curriculum structure.[10] However, tests as part of the PBL curriculum are not precluded. For example, one high school teacher we know who uses the PBL approach designs traditional tests based on what the students have identified as learning issues. Thus, rather than a prespecification of what is to be learned, the assessment focuses on the issues the learners have identified.

7.5.2 Key Issues in Designing PBL Instruction

7.5.2.1. Task Analysis. In designing a problem-based learning curriculum, as with any curriculum, we must begin with an analysis of what must be learned. However, in doing this, the developer must combine identification of the *key* concepts, procedures, etc., with an analysis of the professional (or "good citizen") use of those concepts. Identification of key concepts is a matter of expert statements of what is most important for students to "know." In both the Ohio University Business School (Milter & Stinson, 1993) and the Southern Illinois University Medical School (Barrows, 1985), this involved going to faculty teaching the traditional courses and asking them to identify the key things a student should learn in their course. This naturally requires extensive negotiation and specification. However, it does not involve the analysis of that key information into underlying learning requirements. That is, the task analysis stops at the top level and only identifies key concepts. What must be understood about the key concepts is defined through the professional activity that calls for their use; that is, it is defined in the activity of the learner. In the medical profession, the activity has to do with diagnosing and treating patients with presenting symptoms. In the business school, the professional activity has to do with business analysis and decision making.

There are two points we wish to emphasize here. First, this analysis does not preclude any type of learning activity—memorization of a list or extensive practice of a skill may be necessary—but it should arise out of the need to use the

---

[10]PBL students do as well as traditional students in a variety of discipline areas on standard or board-qualifying exams. The PBL students seem to retain their knowledge longer after the exam than students in traditional classes (Albanese & Mitchell, 1993).

information in authentic tasks. Second, what must be learned includes not only information in the content domain but also metacognitive, collaborative, and other skills as are necessary for participating in authentic activity.

At Indiana University we have recently introduced an undergraduate minor in Corporate and Community Educa-tion (CCE) (Duffy, 1994). The goal of the minor is to devel-op the skills related to carrying out effective informal edu-cation related to community and professional needs. As part of the minor, the students take three core courses, all of which use a problem-based learning approach that involves the students in authentic educational problems. The skills

---

TABLE 7-2.   PRELIMINARY ANALYSIS OF THE SKILLS AND KNOWLEDGE REQUIRED IN THE CORPORATE AND COMMUNITY EDUCATION PROGRAM AT INDIANA UNIVERSITY

I. Analyzing problems. Given a potential corporate or community education problem, how effective are you in analyzing that problem, deciding what needs to be done, and developing a plan of action? This includes your ability to:

- Work collaboratively in a group as both a leader and a group member, carrying your weight in the problem-solving activity, and listening to and respecting alternative points of view.
- Think critically about a problem, analyzing it into subproblems with some rationale.
- Evaluate alternative perspectives and prioritize the perspectives on the problem, including the perspectives of the various stakeholders.
- Design a work strategy addressing the sequence of activity, time requirements, and resource requirements.
- Use project-planning tools to manage your work.
- Monitor and adjust strategies as needed.

II. Managing your learning. Given the analysis of a problem, how well can you identify and refine learning issues, locate resources relevant to those issues, and use those resources to obtain the information that will bear on the problem? This includes your ability to:

- Identify potentially relevant types of information resources and evaluate the usefulness of the resources after learning.
- Allocate the time necessary to achieve your self-directed learning objective.
- Sort through many relevant documents that express multiple perspectives, identifying relevant information and developing criteria for determining what information to use.

III. Use of information resources. Given a learning issue, how efficiently can you use the variety of information repositories to identify and obtain potentially relevant information? This includes your ability to:

- Locate and acquire information or expertise from the library, experts, and using electronic resources like e-mail, World Wide Web, and Newsreaders.
- Reformulate your learning issue in a way appropriate to searching, using the particular information resource, i.e., ability to develop key words, restrict searches, identify related topics, etc.

IV. Conduct audience/need analysis. Given a potential corporate or community education requirement, how well can you use the various strategies for evaluating the information needs? This includes your ability to:

- Determine what information needs to be collected about the audience.
- Design and evaluate alternative information collection strategies, e.g., phone interviewing, mail survey, door-to-door interview, questionnaires, etc.
- Implement an actual information collection strategy including determining strategies for sampling and accessing people.
- Analyze and summarize the results of the audience and needs analysis to make recommendations on information needs and delivery strategies.

V. Designing and delivering usable information. Given the need to educate a group on some issue, how well can you use the nec-essary tools to design and deliver information that meets the information need? This includes your ability to:

- Develop a rationale for a delivery strategy, content specification, and content layout to meet the information need.
- Apply rhetorical, graphic design, document design, interface design, instructional design, speech communication, teaching, and adult literacy principles as appropriate to the preparation of the document.
- Use the various computer- and video-based tools as appropriate to the design and delivery.

VI. Assess effectiveness of your performance and your products. The goal here is to develop the ability to monitor and adjust as necessary your performance in each of the five areas described above. More generally, this goal can be phrased as one of becoming a reflective practitioner and includes your ability to:

- Reflect on your activities and evaluate strengths and weakness and, based on that, develop strategies to increase your effectiveness.
- Ability to solicit and use feedback from others on your performance.
- Ability to design and implement strategies for evaluating your products and for using that evaluation to assess alternative design or development approaches.

and knowledge identified as critical in the CCE program and which guide the development of the problems in each of the core courses are outlined in Table 7-2.[11] These are the skills and knowledge that the students should develop over the course of the program.

7.5.2.2. Problem Generation. The content for the course rests in the problem that is generated. It determines what the students must learn. There are two guiding forces in developing problems. First, the problems must raise the concepts and principles relevant to the content domain (as defined by the task analysis). Second, the problems must be "real." There are three reasons for this. (1) Because the students are open to explore all dimensions of the problem there is considerable difficulty in creating a rich problem with a consistent set of information. (2) Real problems tend to engage learners more; there is a larger context of familiarity with the problem. (3) Students want to know the outcome or current status of the problem and tend to be disenfranchised when told it is not a real problem.

In the case of the medical school, a real problem means the case is based on a real patient, not necessarily a current patient, but not someone fictitious for whom symptoms are made up. In the business curriculum, this means that the problem is a current business problem; e.g., 3 years ago a problem that was meant to engage the students in particular concepts was "Should AT&T buy NCR?" The parallel problem last year was "Should Merck buy Medico?" (Stinson, 1994). For our corporate and community education course, the first problem,[12] one that will consume an entire semester, is stated as follows:

> About 15 years ago in Bloomington, a sludge byproduct of Westinghouse's manufacturing process was distributed around the community as a mulch rich in nitrogen. However, it was soon determined that the sludge was contaminated with PCBs, a chemical thought to be a significant carcinogen. The sludge has been gathered into piles and covered with tarps or concrete, though there are thought to be numerous sites around the county that are still contaminated.
>
> For the last 15 years there have been numerous proposals as to how to dispose of the PCBs, but no action as yet has been taken. Interestingly, the public has been apathetic about this potentially very serious issue. This past summer the EPA set up eight, 2-hour public meetings to discuss disposal of the PCBs. However, because of lack of response, they cut it back to two meetings, and then only 14 people showed up at one of those meetings. Another forum held this November was also sparsely attended. In both cases, the meetings received minimal press coverage.
>
> As responsible members of this community we are concerned that the PCBs are still scattered around Bloomington after all these years, and the public does not seem to care. We are going to design educational materials that will:

- Provide the information the citizens need to make a reasonable decision or to discuss alternatives that will lead to cleaning up the PCBs
- Present that information in such a way that the citizens will be motivated to actively participate in decision making regarding the PCBs.

7.5.3.3. The Learning Sequence. In this sequence, problem-based learning cycles go through two types of learning activities: collaborative problem analysis sessions and self-directed learning. The collaborative problem analysis session usually occurs with small groups of about five, supported by a facilitator. However, with modifications, this can be a mixture of large- and small-group activities (Milter & Stinson, 1993). In our corporate and community education program, we will use a jigsaw model. In the first stage of the jigsaw, the focus is on developing content expertise related to the problem area—PCBs in the case of the problem outlined above. The whole class will first work to identify learning issues in the content area, and then small groups assume responsibility for particular issues. They develop expertise on those issues and then share that expertise in large-group problem solving where all the expertise is brought to bear on the problem. Then as the class moves to the second stage of identifying the instructional strategy and designing the product, the groups will be redefined so that product development groups will consist of students having content expertise on different issues.

The sessions are student-run, problem-solving sessions in which hypotheses and action plans are generated, along with facts that support or refute the hypotheses and learning issues that must be addressed after the session. The learning goals underlying the design of these sessions include developing informal or hypothetico-deductive reasoning skills, reflective and metacognitive skills, and collaborative skills and content knowledge as other members of the group bring their content knowledge to bear on the problem.

In self-directed learning, the students seek and use resources that will address the issues they need to learn about. This is considerably different from learning activities in traditional instruction, where the reading is assigned by the instructor and the task is to learn what is in the text. In the PBL format, the students are learning how to identify, locate, and evaluate information resources as well as use those resources as tools in solving problems, rather than as ends in and of themselves. Interestingly, at all levels of schooling, the problem-based learning tends to lead the learners to primary sources, with secondary sources like textbooks being rejected as too vague or not current (Barrows, personal communications; Duffy & McMahon, 1992).

7.5.3.4. Facilitator Role. In his discussion of the tutorial process, Barrows states:

> The ability of the tutor to use facilitory teaching skills during the small-group learning process is the major determinant of the quality and success of any educational method aimed at (1) developing students' thinking or reasoning skills (problem solving, metacognition, critical thinking) as they learn, and (2) helping them to become independent and

[11]We would like to thank Doug Harper, Karen St. Rain, John Savery, Chuck Palenik, Melanie Harper, and Larry Mikulecky for their help in developing this skill and knowledge analysis.

[12]We would like to thank John Savery and Hugh Kremer for their contributions in developing this problem.

self-directed (learning to learn, learning management). Tutoring is a teaching skill central to problem-based, self-directed learning" (1992, p. 12).

Throughout a session the facilitator models higher-order thinking by asking questions that probe students knowledge deeply. To do this, the facilitator constantly asks Why? What do you mean? How do you know that's true? The facilitator's interactions with the students remain at a metacognitive level, and he or she avoids expressing an opinion or giving information to the students.

A second facilitator role is to challenge the learner's thinking. The facilitator (and hopefully the other students in this collaborative environment) will constantly ask: Do you know what that means? What are the implications of that? Is there anything else? Superficial thinking and vague notions do not go unchallenged. During the first few PBL sessions, the facilitator challenges both the level of understanding and the relevance and completeness of the issues studied. Gradually, however, the students take over this role themselves as they become self-directed learners.

7.5.3.5. Assessment. Assessment must be in the context of the problem the students are working on. There are numerous strategies for accomplishing this. Mildred Jackson, a high school science teacher at Choctaw County High School in Butler, Alabama, uses problem-based learning for the majority of her science instruction—with the reading materials being located by the students based on their learning issues. That is, there is no assigned reading. Butler simply uses for her testing what the students identify as learning issues. The text may be multiple choice, essay, or short answer; the critical characteristic is that it is generated from the students' learning issues.

Barrows relies entirely on student self- and peer assessment. However, the assessment is ongoing, rather than just being an end of the semester rating. Thus, while the students may be easy on one another initially, as they continue working on problems, they clearly begin to provide ratings and feedback to fellow group members more reflective of their contributions.

We also rely heavily on peer and self-assessment in the corporate and community education program. As noted in Table 7-2, the abilities to self-assess and to provide constructive feedback to team members are explicit learning goals, and this is not only an assessment process but also a learning process. Every other week, students assess themselves in terms of their skills as a problem solver, as a self-directed learner, and as a team member. They are provided guidance on the skills and knowledge development issues (Table 7-2) they should be considering in each of these categories. They also evaluate themselves by describing their learning over the last two weeks.

The self-evaluations are distributed to the instructor and to the team members. During the following week (the alternating weeks), the team members will provide feedback to the other team members as to how they performed—that is, they will examine the self-assessments for each team member and offer feedback, including suggestions on how they

might improve their performance. These peer evaluations are sent to the instructor, who integrates them and presents them to the individual students, thus providing anonymity in the peer evaluation process. While we would prefer open evaluations, we recognize that it is something we must work toward over the course of the curriculum.

The Indiana University Northwest Medical Center presents an interesting variation on the assessment strategy. While it has a PBL program, because it is part of a larger system, it was required to administer unit tests every 6 weeks that "covered" the subject-matter focus for that period. In discussions the first author had with the instructors, they reported that students worked hard and enjoyed the problems, but that after each problem some of the students would pester the instructor, asking, "That was all very good, but what do I really have to know for the test?" This became an ongoing problem for the instructors. In response, the dean of the center took the test development out of the hands of the instructors. Rather than developing a test, they purchased the unit test from another medical school, a different test each time so that even the instructors did not know what school the tests came from.[13]

7.6 LEARNING IN THE RHIZOME

In his popular novel *The Name of the Rose*, Umberto Eco (1983) describes a medieval library, a labyrinth of passages, stairways, and chambers filled with books. The library is a rhizome (as much as any actual existent thing can represent "an inconceivable globality"!), and learning is illustrated by Brother William, the main character of the novel, feeling and groping his way through the library. As Brother William constructs a path (or pattern of connections) through the library, one of only many possible paths, he is transforming his means of participating in the community of scholars, both those using the library (constructing their own paths) and those who have written manuscripts contained therein. Brother William is moving from legitimate peripheral to centripetal participation, learning the activities that will allow him to be effective in that community. In our view, he is *not* acquiring and internalizing, *not* building an abstract mental representation of the library and its contents.

Our responsibility as educators and instructional designers has traditionally been conceived of as efficient communication and motivation, as individuals knowledgeable in a subject-matter domain and/or skilled in communicating that content and provoking interest in it. The systematic approaches to design of instruction which dominate our field are disposed to find empirically valid, tried, and true methods for accomplishing those ends.

---

[13]We do not have the performance scores for students on these tests. However, before the PBL program, the Northwest students' performance on the MCAT exam was average for the eight-campus Indiana University system. After 2 years of the PBL program, the average performance of the Northwest students exceeded that of the other seven campuses (Albanese & Mitchell, 1993; Hubbard Welsh, Eatridis, Ficklin & Vaughn, 1994).

Under the assumptions discussed in this paper, however, educators and instructional designers become guides or supports for students as they struggle with constructing their connections to and with a sociocultural context. Rather than empirically validated generalizations about effective instructional strategies, constructivists look to develop support structures embedded in the problem tasks themselves, tools that may both support and transform participation, and outcomes, the attainment of which are their own reward. As Lakoff (1987) has put it:

> How we understand mind . . . matters for what we value in ourselves and others—for education, for research, for the way we set up human institutions, and most important for what counts as a humane way to live and act . . . If we fully appreciate the role of the imaginative aspects of reason, we will give them full value, investigate them more thoroughly, and provide better education in using them. Our ideas about what people can learn and should be learning, as well as what they should be doing with what they learn, depend on our concept of learning itself. It is important that we have discovered that rational thought goes well beyond the literal and the mechanical. It is important because our ideas about how human minds should be employed depend on our ideas of what a human mind is (Lakoff, 1987, p. xvi).

REFERENCES

Albanese, M. A. & Mitchell, S. (1993). Problem based learning: a review of the literature on its outcomes and implementation issues. *Academic Medicine 68*, 52–81.

Baron, J. & Sternberg, R., eds. (1987). *Teaching thinking skills.* New York: Freeman.

Barrows, H.S. (1986). A taxonomy of problem based learning methods. *Medical Education 20*, 481–86.

— (1992). *The tutorial process.* Springfield, IL: Southern Illinois University School of Medicine.

— (1994). *Practice-based learning: problem-based learning applied to medical education.* Springfield, IL: Southern Illinois University Medical School.

— & Myers, A.C. (1993). *Problem-based learning in secondary schools.* Unpublished monograph. Springfield, IL: Problem-Based Learning Institute, Lanphier High School and Southern Illinois University Medical School.

— (1985). *How to design a problem-based curriculum for the preclinical years.* New York: Springer.

Bateson, G. (1972). *Steps to an ecology of mind.* New York: Ballentine.

Bednar, A., Cunningham, D.J., Duffy, T. & Perry, D. (1991). Theory into practice: how do we link? *In* Anglin, G., ed. *Instructional technology: past, present and future,* 88-101. Englewood, CO: Libraries Unlimited.

Bereiter, C. (1985). Toward a solution of the learning paradox. *Review of Educational Research 55*, 201–26.

— (1994). Implications of postmodernism for science, or, science as progressive discourse. *Educational Technology 29*, 3–12.

Berlak, H., Newman, F., Adams, E., Archbald, D., Burgess, T., Raven, R. & Romberg, T. (1992). *Toward a new science of educational testing and assessment.* New York: SUNY Press.

Bornstein, A. (1979). *Memory.* Dubuque, IA: Kendall/Hunt.

Bransford, J. & Stein, B. (1984). *The IDEAL problem solver.* New York: Freeman.

Brooks, J. & Brooks, M. (1993). *In search of understanding: the case for constructivist classrooms.* Alexandria, VA: Association for Supervision and Curriculum Development.

Brown, J.S., Collins, A. & Duguid, P. (1989). Situated cognition and the culture of learning. *Educational Researcher 18*, 32–42.

Brown, Ann, Ash, D., Rutherford, M., Nakagawa, K., Gordon, A. & Campione, J. (1993). Distributed expertise in the classroom. *In* G.Salomon, ed. *Distributed cognitions.* New York: Cambridge University Press.

Bruner, Jerome (1961). The act of discovery. *Harvard Educational Review 31*, 21–32.

— (1966). *Towards a theory of instruction.* Cambridge, MA: Harvard University Press.

— (1971). The process of education revisited. *Phi Delta Kappan 20*, 18–21.

— (1990). *Acts of meaning.* Cambridge, MA: Harvard University Press.

— & Dow, Peter (undated). *Man: a course of study: a description of an elementary social studies curriculum.* Cambridge, MA: Educational Development Center.

Christensen, C.R. (1987). *Teaching and the case method: test, cases, and readings.* Boston, MA: Harvard Business School.

Cobb, P. (1994a). *Where is the mind? Constructivist and sociocultural perspectives on mathematical development.* Paper presented at the annual meeting of the American Educational Research Association, New Orleans, LA.

— (1994b). Where is the mind? Constructivist and sociocultural perspectives on mathematical development. *Educational Researcher 23*, 13–20.

Cognition and Technology Group at Vanderbilt (1992). Technology and the design of generative learning environments. *In* T. Duffy & D. Jonassen, eds. *Constructivism and the technology of instruction: a conversation.* Hillsdale, NJ: Erlbaum.

Cole, Henry G. & Lacefield, Warren (1980). *MACOS: its empirical effect versus its critics.* Paper presented at the annual meeting of the American Educational Research Association. Montreal, Quebec.

Cole, M. & Engestrom, Y. (1993). A cultural-historical approach to distributed cognition. *In* G. Salomon, ed. *Distributed cognitions.* New York: Cambridge University Press.

— (1985). The zone of proximal development: where culture and cognition create each other. *In* J. Wertsch, ed. *Culture, communication and cognition: Vygotskian perspectives.* New York: Cambridge University Press.

Collins, A. (1994). Goal-based scenarios and the problem of situated learning: a commentary on Andersen Consulting's design of goal-based scenarios. *Educational Technology 34*, 30–32.

Conlan, John (1975). MACOS: the push for a uniform national curriculum. *Social Education*, 388–92.

Cuban, L. (1991). Informal reasoning and instruction: a commentary. *In* J. F. Voss, D. Perkins & J. Segal, eds. *Informal reasoning and education.* Hillsdale, NJ: Erlbaum.

Cunningham, D.J. (1986). Good guys and bad guys. *Educational Communication and Technology Journal 34*, 3–7.

— (1991). Assessing constructions and constructing assessments. *Educational Technology 31*,(5) 13–17.

— (1991). In defense of extremism. *Educational Technology 31*(9), 26–27.

— (1992). Beyond educational psychology: steps toward an educational semiotic. *Educational Psychology Review 4*, 165–194.

— (1992). Everything said is said by someone. *Educational Psychology Review 4*, 261–67.

— (1994). Discussion and dialogue in education for mutual understanding. *In* S. Gamagi, ed. *Assimilation, pluralism and multiculturalism*, 195-205. Armidale, Australia: University of New England Press.

—, Duffy, T. & Knuth, R. (1993). The textbook of the future. *In* C. McKnight, A.Dillon & J. Richardson, eds. *Hypertext : a psychological perspective*, 19–50. Chichester: Horwood.

— and Knuth, R. (1993). Tools for constructivism. *In* T. Duffy, J. Lowyck & D. Jonassen, eds. *Designing environments for constructive learning*, 163–88. Berlin: Springer.

—, Knight, B. & Watson, K. (1994). Instructional prescriptions can be hazardous to your pedagogy. *Journal of Accelerative Learning and Teaching 19*, 17–44.

—, McMahon, H. & O'Neill, W. (1992). Bubble dialogue: a new tool for instruction and assessment. *Educational Technology Research and Development 40*, 59–67.

Deely, J. (1982). *Introducing semiotic*. Bloomington, IN: Indiana University Press.

Delandshere, G. & Petrosky, A. (1994). Capturing teachers' knowledge: performance assessment,(a) and post-structuralist epistemology, (b) from a post-structuralist perspective, (c) and post-structuralism, (d) none of the above. *Educational Researcher 23*, 11–18.

Deleuze, G. & Guattari, F. (1983). Rhizome. *In* G. Deleuze & F. Guattari, eds. *On the line*. New York: Semiotext(e).

Dewey, John (1916). *Democracy and education*. New York: Macmillan.

— (1929) *My pedagogical creed*. Washington, DC: Progressive Education Association.

— (1938). *Experience and education*. New York: Macmillan.

Dow, Peter (1975). MACOS revisited: a commentary on the most frequently asked questions about "Man: a course of study." *Social Education*, 388–96.

Driver, R., Asoko, H., Leach, J., Mortimer, E. & Scott, P. (1994). Constructing scientific knowledge in the classroom. *Educational Researcher 23*, 5–12.

Duffy, Thomas M. (1994). Corporate and community education: achieving success in the information society. Unpublished paper. Bloomington, IN: Indiana University.

— (1995). Strategic teaching frameworks: an instructional model for complex, interactive skills. *In* C. Dills & A. Romiszowski, eds. *Instructional development state of the art, Vol. 3: Paradigms*. Englewood Cliffs, NJ: Educational Technology.

Duffy, Thomas M. & Jonassen, D., eds. (1992). *Constructivism and the technology of instruction: a conversation*. Hillsdale NJ: Erlbaum.

— & Knuth, R. (1990). Hypermedia and instruction: where is the match? *In* D. Jonassen and H. Mandl, eds. *Designing hypermedia for learning*. Heidelberg, FRG: Springer.

—, Lowyck, J. & Jonassen, D., eds. (1993). *Designing environments for constructivist learning*. Heidelberg: Springer.

— & McMahon, Teresa (1992). The Buddy System project: four case studies. Unpublished technical report prepared for the Buddy System Project office. Bloomington IN: Indiana Univeristy, School of Education.

Eco, U. (1976). *A theory of semiotics*. Bloomington, IN: Indiana University Press.

— (1983). *The name of the rose*. William Weaver, trans. New York: Harcourt, Brace.

— (1984). *Semiotics and the philosophy of language*. Bloomington, IN: Indiana University Press.

Edelson, Daniel & O'Neil, K. (1994). *The CoVis Collaboratory Notebook: computer support for scientific inquiry*. Paper presented at the Annual Meeting of the American Educational Research Association, New Orleans, LA.

Flavell, J. (1976). Metacognitive aspects of problem solving. *In* L. Resnick, ed. *The nature of intelligence*. Hillsdale, NJ: Erlbaum

Fodor, J. (1980). On the impossibility of acquiring more "powerful structures." *In* M. Piattelli-Palmerini, ed. *Language and learning: the debate between Jean Piaget and Noam Chomsky*, 142–62. Cambridge, MA: Harvard University Press.

Forman, E., Minick, N. & Stone, C., eds. (1993). *Contexts for learning*. New York: Oxford University Press.

Fosnot, C.T. (1989). *Enquiring teachers enquiring learners. a constructivist approach to teaching*. New York: Teacher's College Press.

Freire, P. (1993). *The pedagogy of the oppressed* (rev. ed.) New York: Continuum.

Froiland, P. (1994). Action learning: taming real problems in real time. *Training 37*, 27–33.

Gardner, H. (1993). *Frames of mind: the theory of multiple intelligences*. New York: Basic Books.

Gardner, J. (1985). *The mind's new science*. New York: Basic Books.

Gifford, B. & O'Connor, M., eds. (1992). Changing assessments: alternative views of aptitude, achievement and instruction. Boston: Kluwer.

Goforth, D. (1994). Learner control = decision making + information. *Journal of Educational Computing Research 11*, 1–26.

Greenwood, G. & Parkay, F.W. (1989). *Case studies for teacher decision making*. New York: Random House.

Griffin, P. & Cole, M. (1984). Current activity for the future: the zo-ped. *In* B. Rogoff & J. Wertsch, eds. *Children's learning in the zone of proximal development*. San Francisco: Jossey-Bass.

Hanley, J.P., Whitla, D.K., Moo, E.W. & Walter, A.S. (1970). *Curiosity/competence/community: an evaluation of man: a course of study*. Cambridge, MA: Educational Development Center.

Harasim, Linda (1993). Collaborating in cyberspace: using computer conferences as a group learning environment. *Interactive Learning Environments 3*, 119–30.

Hawkes, T. (1977). *Structuralism and semiotics*. Berkeley, CA: University of California Press.

Hay, K.E. (1994). *Towards the learner-centered design paradigm: powerful tools for investigating weather within the Children's Museum*. Unpublished paper. Indianapolis, IN: Indiana University, School of Education.

Heinich, R., Molenda, M. & Russell, J. (1993). *Instructional media and the new technology of learning*, 4th ed. New York: Macmillan.

Honebein, P., Duffy, Thomas M. & Fishman, B. (1993). Constructivism and the design of learning environments: context and authentic activities for learning. *In* Thomas M. Duffy, Joost Lowyck & David Jonassen, eds. *Designing environments for constructivist learning*. Heidelberg: Springer.

Hubbard Welsh, L., Iatridis, P., Ficklin, F. & Vaughn, S. (1994, Oct.). The first four years of implementing a problem-based curriculum: an evaluation. Paper presented at the 33d annual meeting of the Research in Medical Education Conference, Boston, MA.

Hutchins, E. (1991). The social organization of distributed cognition. *In* L. Resnick, J. Levine & S. Teasley, eds. *Perspectives on socially shared cognition*. Washington, DC: American Psychological Association.

Hlynka, D. & Belland, J. (1991). *Paradigms regained*. Englewood Cliffs, NJ: Educational Technology.

Johnson, D.W. & Johnson, R.T. (1990). Cooperative learning and achievement. *In* S. Sharan, ed. *Cooperative learning: theory and practice*. New York: Praeger.

Johnson, M. (1987). *The body in the mind*. Chicago, IL: University of Chicago Press.

Kang, I. (1995). *Constructivist principles and the design of instruction: a case study of an associate instructor training program*. Unpublished doctoral dissertation. Bloomington, IN: School of Education, Indiana University.

Katz, L.G. & Chard, S.C. (1989). *Engaging children's minds: the project approach*. Norwood, NJ: Ablex.

Kliebard, H. (1986). *The struggle for the American curriculum: 1893-1958*. Boston, MA: Routledge.

Knuth, R. (1992). *Hypermedia and learning: the case of Intermedia*. Unpublished doctoral dissertation, Bloomington, IN: Indiana University.

Kuhn, T. (1970). *The structure of scientific revolutions*, 2d ed. Chicago, IL: University of Chicago Press.

Lakoff, G. (1987). *Women, fire and dangerous things*. Chicago, IL: University of Chicago Press.

— & Johnson, M. (1980). *Metaphors we live by*. Chicago, IL: University of Chicago Press.

Landow, G. (1989a). Course assignments in hypertext: the example of Intermedia. *Journal of Research on Computing in Education 21*, 340–65.

Landow, G. (1989b). Hypertext in literary education, criticism, and scholarship. *Computers and the Humanities 23*, 173–98.

— (1992). *Hypertext: the convergence of contemporary critical theory and technology*. Baltimore, MD: Johns Hopkins University Press.

Lave, J. & Wenger, E. (1991). *Situated learning*. New York: Cambridge University Press.

Lemke, J, (1990). *Talking science: language, learning and values*. New York: Ablex.

— (1994). Semiotics and the deconstruction of conceptual learning. *Journal of Accelerative Learning and Teaching 19*, 67–110.

Linn, R., Baker, E. & Dunbar, S. (1990). Performance based assessment: expectations and validation criteria. *Educational Researcher 20*, 15–21.

Mabry, L. & Stake, R. (1994). Aligning measurement with education. *Educational Researcher 23*, 33–34.

Malcom, N. (1986). *Wittgenstein: nothing is hidden*. Cambridge, MA: Blackwell.

Marshall, H. (1988). Work or learning: implications of classroom metaphors. *Educational Researcher 17*, 9–16.

Maturana, H.R. & Varela (1992). *The tree of knowledge: the biological roots of human understanding*. Boston, MA: Shambhala.

McDermott, D. (1980). Profile of Ray Birdwhistell. *The Kinesis Report 2*, 1–16.

Merseth, K.K. & Lacey, A. (1993). Weaving a stronger fabric: the pedagogical promise of hypermedia and case methods of teacher education. *Teacher and Teacher Education 9*, 283–99.

Messick, S. (1989). Validity. *In* R. Linn, ed. *Educational Measurement*, 3d ed. New York: Macmillan.

Milheim, W. & Martin, B. (1991). Theoretical basis for the use of learner control: three different perspectives. *Journal of Computer Based Instruction 18*, 99–105.

Milter, R.G. & Stinson, J.E. (1993). Educating leaders for the new competitive environment. *In* G. Gijselaers, S. Tempelaar, S. Keizer, eds. *Educational innovation in economics and business administration: the case of problem-based learning*. London: Kluwer.

Moll, L., ed. (1990). *Vygotsky and education*. New York: Cambridge University Press.

Morris, C. (1946). *Signs, language and behavior*. New York: Prentice Hall.

National Council of Teachers of Mathematics (1989). *Curriculum and evaluation standards for school mathematics*. Reston, VA: Author.

— (1991). *Professional standards for teaching mathematics*. Reston, VA: Author.

Newell, A. & Simon, H. (1972). *Human problem solving*. Englewood Cliffs, NJ: Prentice Hall.

Newman, D., Griffin, P. & Cole, M. (1989). *The construction zone: working for cognitive change in school*. New York: Cambridge University Press.

Nowakoski, A. (1994) Reengineering education at Andersen Consulting. *Educational Technology 34*, 3–8.

Page, Marilyn (1990). *Action learning: historical and contemporary perspectives*. Unpublished doctoral paper, Amherst, MA: University of Massachusetts (Eric: ED 338389).

Palinscar, A. & Brown, A. (1984). Reciprocal teaching of comprehension fostering and comprehension monitoring. *Cognition and Instruction 1*, 117–75.

Pea, Roy (1985). Beyond amplification: using the computer to reorganize mental functioning. *Educational Psychologist 20*, 167–82.

Perry, W. (1970). *Forms of intellectual and ethical development in the college years: a scheme*. New York: Holt.

Piaget, Jean (1977). *The development of thought: equilibration of cognitive structures*. New York: Viking.

Psotka, J. Massey, L.D. & Mutter, S. (1988). *Intelligent tutoring systems: lessons learned*. Hillsdale, NJ: Erlbaum.

Rasmussen, J., Brehmer, B. & Leplat, J., eds. (1991). *Distributed decision making: cognitive models for cooperative work*. Chichester: Wiley.

Resnick, L. Learning in school and out. *Educational Research 16*, 13–20.

—, Levine, J. & Teasley, S., eds. (1991). *Perspectives on socially shared cognition*. Washington, DC: American Psychological Association.

Rochelle, J. (1992). *Reflections on Dewey and technology for situated learning*. Paper presented at annual meeting of the American Educational Research Association, San Francisco, CA.

Rogoff, B. (1990). *Apprenticeship in thinking*. New York: Oxford University Press.

— (1994). Developing understanding of the idea of communities of learners. *Mind, Culture and Activity 1*, 209–29.

Rorty, Richard (1991). Objectivity, relativism, and truth: philosophical papers, Vol. 1. Cambridge, MA: Cambridge University Press.

Ross, S. & Morrison, G. (1989). In search of a happy medium in instructional technology research: issues concerning external validity, media replications, and learner control. *Educational Technology Research and Development 37*, 19–33.

Roup, R. (1993). *LabNet: toward a community of practice.* Hillsdale, NJ: Erlbaum.

Rousseau, J. (1955). *Emile.* New York: Dutton (original work published 1762).

Rumelhart, D. & McClelland, J. (1986). *Parallel distributed processing.* Cambridge, MA: MIT Press.

Salomon, G., ed. (1993). *Distributed cognitions.* New York: Cambridge University Press.

Salomon, G., Perkins, D. & Globerson, T. (1991). Partners in cognition: extending human intelligence with intelligent technologies. *Educational Research 20*, 2–9.

Savery, J. & Duffy, T. (1995). Problem based learning: an instructional model and its constructivist framework. *Educational Technology.*

Saxe, G. (1992). Studying children's learning in context: problems and prospects. *Journal of the Learning Sciences 2*, 215–34.

Scardamalia, M. & Bereiter, C. (1991). Higher levels of agency for children in knowledge building: a challenge for the design of new knowledge media. *The Journal of the Learning Sciences 1*, 37–68.

—, —, Brett, C., Burtis, P.J., Calhoun & Lea, N.S. (1992). Educational applications of a networked communal database. *Interactive Learning Environments 2*, 45–71.

Schleper, D. (1993) I lost control (and my students found it.) *Perspectives in Education and Deafness 11*, 12–15 .

Schon, D.A. (1987). *Educating the reflective practitioner.* San Francisco, CA: Jossey-Bass.

Schoenfeld, A. (1991). On mathematics and sense making: an informal attack on the unfortunate divorce of formal and informal mathematics. *In* J.F. Voss, D. Perkins & J. Segal, eds. *Informal reasoning and education.* Hillsdale, NJ: Erlbaum.

Schwen, T., Goodrum, D. & Dorsey, L. On the design of an enriched learning and information environment (ELIE). *Educational Technology 31*, 5–9.

Shank, G.D. (1987) Abductive strategies in educational research. *The American Journal of Semiotics 5*, 275–90.

Sharan, Y. & Sharan, S. (1992). *Expanding cooperative learning through group investigation.* New York: Teachers College Press.

Shavelson, R., Baxter, G. & Pine, P. (1992). Performance assessments: political rhetoric and measurement reality. *Educational Researcher 4*, 22–27.

Skinner, B. (1968). *The technology of teaching.* New York: Appelton-Century-Crofts.

— (1984). The shame of American education. *American Psychologist 39*, 947–54.

Slavin, R. (1990). *Cooperative learning: theory, research and practice.* Boston, MA: Allyn & Bacon.

Soloway, E., Guzdial, M. & Hay, K.E. (1994). Learner-centered design: the challenge for HCI in the 21st century. *Interactions 1*, 36–48.

Spizizen, G. & Hart, C. (1985). Active learning and the case method: theory and practice. *Cornell Hotel and Restaurant Administration Quarterly, 26*, 63–633.

Sternberg, R. (1987). Teaching intelligence: the application of cognitive psychology to the improvement of intellectual skills. *In* J. Baron & R. Sternberg, eds. *Teaching thinking skills.* New York: Freeman.

Stevens, R. (1983). *Law school: legal education in America from the 1830's to the 1980's.* Chapel Hill, NC: University of North Carolina Press.

Stinson, J.E. (1994). *Can digital equipment survive?* Paper presented at the 6th International Conference on Thinking, Boston, MA.

Suchman, L.A. (1987). *Plans and situated actions.* New York: Cambridge University Press.

Sykes, G. & Bird, T. (1992). Teacher education and the case idea. *In* G. Grant, ed. *Review of research in education*, Vol. 18. Washington, DC: American Educational Research Association.

Tharp, R. & Gallimore, R. (1988). *Rousing minds to life.* New York: Cambridge University Press.

Van der Veer, R. & Valsiner, J. (1991). *Understanding Vygotsky.* Cambridge, MA: Blackwell.

von Glasersfeld, E. (1984). An introduction to radical constructivism. *In* P. Watzlawick, ed. *The invented reality*, 17–40. New York: Norton.

— (1989). Cognition, construction of knowledge, and teaching. *Synthese 80*, 121–40.

— (1992). Constructivism reconstructed: a reply to Suchting. *Science and Education 1*, 379–84.

von Uexkull, J. (1957). A stroll through the worlds of animals and men. *In* C. Schiller, ed. *Instinctive behavior: the development of a modern concept.* New York: International Universities Press.

Vygotsky, L. (1962). *Thought and language.* Cambridge, MA: MIT Press.

— (1978). *Mind in society.* Cambridge, MA: Harvard University Press.

— (1981) The instrumental method in psychology. *In* J. Wertsch, ed. *The concept of activity in Soviet psychology.* Armouk, NY: Sharpe.

Wasserman, S. (1993). *Getting down to cases.* New York: Teachers College Press.

Wellman, H. (1990). *The child's theory of mind.* Cambridge, MA: MIT Press.

Wells, G. & Chang-Wells, G. (1992). *Constructing knowledge together.* Portsmouth, NH: Heinemann.

Wertsch, J. (1985). *Vygotsky and the social formation of mind.* Cambridge MA: Harvard University Press.

Wertsch, J. (1991). *Voices of the mind: a sociocultural approach to mediated action.* Cambridge, MA: Harvard University Press.

Wertsch, J. (1994). The primacy of mediated action in socio-cultural studies. *Mind, Culture, and Activity 1*, 202–08.

Whitehead, Alfred North (1929). *The aims of education and other essays.* New York: Free Press.

Williams, S.M. (1992). Putting case-based instruction into context: examples from legal and medical education. *Journal of the Learning Sciences 2*, 367–427.

8. MEDIA AS LIVED ENVIRONMENTS: THE ECOLOGICAL PSYCHOLOGY OF EDUCATIONAL TECHNOLOGY

Brockenbrough S. Allen   Richard G. Otto

SAN DIEGO STATE UNIVERSITY

We are rapidly moving towards an era in which most everyday activity will be shaped by environments that are not only *artificial*—most humans now live in cities—but also *mediated*. In developed countries, emotional and cognitive activity in all levels and segments of society is increasingly vested in information-rich venues supported by television, radio, phone, and computer networks. Even in remote areas of the world, peasants watch satellite broadcasts and play battery-operated video games. And in the depths of the Amazon River basin, primitive tribes use small videocams to document territorial encroachments and the destruction of rain forest habitat.

The narrow bandwidth of midcentury media technologies, however, has engendered a paradigm in which people think of *media* primarily as *channels* for sending and receiving symbols and messages (see 4.3, 4.4). Derivatives of this notion liken knowledge to content or even to a commodity that can be stored, transmitted, and received. The utility of this channel communications metaphor is being challenged by emerging computer-based media technologies that function less like books, journals, films, and broadcasts and more like workshops, laboratories, offices, and studios. These new venues for working, playing, teaching, and learning allow and often require exploratory action and ambulatory perception and thus are not entirely consistent with models of cognition that treat perception primarily as *reception*.

Indeed, the ergonomic utility of many contemporary human-computer interfaces is based on metaphors and mechanics that invite users to participate in worlds populated by semiautonomous objects and agents, ranging from buttons and windows to sprites and computer personas. Attempts to model user engagement with these worlds as processing of symbols, messages, and discourse are limited because the channel communications metaphor fails to specify many of the modalities by which humans as organisms understand their surroundings. These modalities include locating, tracking, identifying, grasping, moving, and modifying objects (see 31.2.2.2). There is a profound but not always obvious difference between receiving communication and acquiring information through such modalities.

8.1 OVERVIEW

Our chapter explores the metaphor of media as lived environments. A *medium* can be considered an environment to the extent that it supports both the perception of opportunities for acting and some *means* for acting. This ecological perspective can help us understand how media users exercise their powers of perception, mobility, and agency within the constraints imposed by particular media technologies and within the conventions established by various media cultures.

The chapter explores paradigms for linking the work of ecological psychologists with the concerns of researchers, designers, and developers who are responsible for understanding and improving the person-environment fit. It examines ways in which ecological psychology might inform the design of products and systems that are efficient in the sense that they promote wise use of human cognitive resources and humane in the sense that they enable authentic modes of being.

The metaphor of media as environments helps us to reconsider trade-offs between the cost of (a) *external* storage and processing of information in the form of realia[1] or media and the cost of (b) *internal* storage and processing of information as *Mental-Internal Representations of Situations.*[2] As a matter of convenience, we will use MIROS throughout this chapter as a general alternative to the super-abundance of terms for internal representations, including stimulus-response mechanisms, memories, images, associations, schemata, models, propositions, productions, and neural networks.

As will be argued later in greater detail, many MIROS are quite incomplete, functioning as *complements to* rather than *substitutes for* the external representation of situations provided by media and realia. Investment of organic resources in improved perception, whether such perception is acquired through learning or by natural selection, is an important alternative to construction of more complete MIROS, because improved perception allows organisms to use information reflected in the structure of the environment, information maintained at no biological cost to the organism. Environments rich in information related to the needs, goals, or intentions of an organism favor development of enhanced perception. In the long run, environments lacking such information favor development of enhanced MIROS. This trade-off between internal and external storage and processing provides a basis for coordinating media with MIROS so that they can "share the work" of representing situations (see 2.3.3).

The actions afforded by media environments are not always the same as those afforded by imaginary or real environments represented by media. Media technologies can partially overcome dislocations in time through storage of information and dislocations in space through transmission of information. Opportunities for perceiving and acting on media, however, are rarely identical to the opportunities for perceiving and acting on corresponding realia or MIROS.

Controversies that treat media as mere conveyances of symbols and messages often neglect differences in actions enabled, respectively, by media, realia, and MIROS. The pages of a book on human anatomy, for example, afford examination of the structures of the human body, as does a film of an autopsy. Each of these two types of media environments, however, offers radically different possibilities for exploratory action. The anatomy book affords systematic surveys of body structure through layouts and cross sections, while the film affords observation of the mechanics of the dissection process.

The advantages of storage and transmission provided by media technologies have to be weighed against some loss in *verity* (Thurman & Mattoon, 1994) and functional fidelity. Older technologies such as print and film have well-established conventions for helping end users reconstitute missing circumstances and points of view. Prominent among these conventions are the cues and explicit directions that accompany two-dimensional pictures and that serve to guide viewers in constructing the MIROS required for interpretation and understanding. These conventions, which we will examine in a later section of the chapter, help us understand how perception in mediated environments can substitute for hypothetical actions.

Emerging technologies challenge us to rethink conventional ideas about learning from and with media by reminding us that we humans are embodied beings with a long heritage of interactions in complex spatiotemporal and quasi-social environments—a heritage much older than our use of symbols and language. Like other organisms whose capabilities are shaped by niche or occupation, our modes of perception are adapted to opportunities for action in the environment. The conclusion of this chapter examines problems that can result when media technologies so degrade opportunities for integrating action with perception that users face a restricted range of options for moral thought and behavior.

8.2 BACKGROUND

Many important issues in ecological psychology were first identified by J. J. Gibson, a perceptual psychologist whose powerful, incomplete, and often misunderstood ideas have played a seminal role in technologies for simulating navigable environments. Although we do not entirely agree with Gibson's theories, which were still evolving when he died in 1979, his work serves as a useful framework for examining the implications of ecological psychology for media design and research.

We provide here, as an advance organizer, a verbatim list of phenomena that Gibson identified in personal notes as critical to the future of ecological psychology (J. J. Gibson, cited in Reed, 1971/1982, p. 394):

1. Perceiving environmental layout (inseparable from the problem of the ego and its locomotion)
2. Perceiving the objects of the environment (including their texture, color, shape—and including their affordances)
3. Perceiving events (and their affordances)
4. Perceiving other animals and persons ("together with what they persistently afford and what they momentarily do")
5. Perceiving the expressive responses of other persons
6. Perceiving by communication or speech
7. Knowledge mediated by artificial displays, images, pictures, and writing
8. Thought as mediated by symbols
9. Attending to sensations

---

[1]Realia (Latin, *realis,* relating to things): (a) objects that may be used as teaching aids but were not made for the purpose and (b) real things, actual facts, especially as distinct from theories about them (*1987 Compact Edition of the Oxford English Dictionary, Volume III Supplement*). Oxford, England: Oxford University Press.

[2]A situation can be defined as a structured relation between two or more objects. A MIROS is a mental representation of such a structured relationship. If perception is understood to be *acquisition of information* about the environment, percepts are not considered to be MIROS.

10. Attending to structure of experience (aesthetics)
11. Cultivating cognitive maps by traveling and sight-seeing

According to Gibson (1971/1982), everyday living depends on *direct perception*, perception that is independent of internal propositional or associational representations—perception that guides action intuitively and automatically. Direct perception, for example, guides drivers as they respond to subtle changes in their relationship to roadway centerlines. Direct perception adjusts the movements required to bring cup to lip and guides the manipulation of tools such as pencils, toothbrushes, and scalpels. Direct perception is tightly linked in real time with ongoing action.

Perhaps the most widely adopted of Gibson's (1979) contributions to the descriptive language of ecological psychology are his concepts of *affordances* (roughly, opportunities for action) and *effectivities* (roughly, capabilities for action). Natural selection gradually tunes a species' effectivities to the affordances associated with its niche or "occupation." Thus are teeth and jaws the effectivities that permit killer whales to exploit the "grab-ability" of seals; and so are wings the effectivities that allow birds to exploit the air.

In contrast to direct perception, indirect perception operates on intermediaries such as diagrams, symbols, words, and propositions that inform an organism or agent about a world or environment via indexical bonds (Nichols, 1991) with that environment. Following verbal directions to locate a hidden object is a good example of indirect perception. Indirect perception permits, even promotes, reflection and deliberation.

Gibson acknowledged the importance to human thought of such intermediaries as symbols and language-based propositions. He was skeptical, however, about claims that general cognitive processes can be modeled in terms of such intermediaries, and he argued that models that relied excessively on symbols and propositions would inevitably neglect critical relationships between perceiving and acting.

Although Gibson (1977/1982) did not develop a complete theory of *mediated* perceiving (see 7.3.4)—that is, perception through intermediaries such as pictures and text—he posited that such intermediaries are effective because they are "tools for perceiving by analogy with tools for performing" (p. 290). Careful appraisal of this idea reminds us that in the Gibsonian world view, everyday perceiving cannot be separated from acting. Therefore, there is no contradiction in the assertion that "tools for perceiving" might serve as analogs for action. Static media such as text, diagrams, pictures, and photos have traditionally achieved many of their most important informative effects by substituting acts of perception for acts of exploration.

Every media technology from book to video to computer simulation, however, imposes profound constraints on representation or description of real or imaginary worlds (see 12.3.1) and requires trade-offs as to which aspects of a world will be represented. Even museums, as repositories of "unmediated," authentic artifacts and specimens, must live within the technical limitations of display technologies that favor some modalities of perception over others—looking in lieu of touching, for instance.

8.3 NATURAL AND CULTURAL DYNAMICS OF INFORMATION AND MEDIA TECHNOLOGIES

What distinguishes contemporary humans from our pre-Ice Age ancestors is that our adaptations are primarily cultural. Many of the processes of natural selection that shaped *Homo sapiens* have been superseded by much faster mechanisms of adaptation. The human evolutionary clock may have slowed for the moment in some respects, because selection pressure can be accommodated by technical and social means rather than natural selection.

As Donald (1992) argues, the information age extends previous trends in the evolution of human cognition. His reconstruction of the origins of the modern mind makes the credible claim that the unfolding drama of our distinctly human neurological capacity has been characterized primarily by externalization of information, first as gestures and rudimentary songs, later as high-speed articulate speech, and eventually as visual markings that enabled storage of information in stable nonbiological systems.

Norman (1993) has succinctly captured this theme of information externalization in the title of his trade book, *Things That Make Us Smart*. He argues that the hallmark of human cognition lies not so much in our ability to reason or remember but rather in our ability to construct external cognitive artifacts and to use these artifacts to compensate for the limitations of our working and long-term memories. Norman defines cognitive artifacts as artificial devices designed to maintain, display, or operate on information in order to serve representational functions.

As Greeno (1991) notes, "a significant part of what we call 'memory' involves information that is in situations . . . rather than just in the mind of the behaving individual" (p. 265). Indeed, a sizable body of literature describes some profound limitations of internal representations, or in our terms, MIROS, that is, Mental-Internal Representations of Situations (see, for example, Carroll & Olson, 1988; Craik, 1943; di Sessa, 1983, 1988; D. Gentner & D. R. Gentner, 1983; D. Gentner & Stevens, 1983; Greeno, 1989; Johnson-Laird, 1983; Larkin & Simon, 1987; Lave, 1988; Payne, 1992; Rouse & Morris, 1986; Wood, Bruner & Ross, 1976; Young, 1983; see also 12.3.1.2). These works suggest that without the support of external devices or representations, MIROS are typically simplistic, incomplete, fragmentary, unstable, difficult to run or manipulate, lacking in firm boundaries, easily confused with one another, and generally unscientific.

8.3.1 Thermodynamic Efficiency of Externalization

There is reason to believe that the scope and complexity of MIROS are constrained by the thermodynamics of information storage and processing in biological systems (see 3.1.35). Seemingly lost in 3 decades of discussion on the problems of internal representation is Hawkins's (1964) insight that *external* representations can confer gains in *thermodynamic* efficiency.

> The capacity to learn is an externalization of function, the creation outside the cell nucleus of a new way of acquiring and storing vital information. The nucleus has its limitations, of information capacity and rate of evolution. . . . The point of innovation is that the code description of a machine [cell] that learns, that acquires information from and about the environment, can be small compared with what the machine [cell] learns. . . . When such a step occurred in the evolution of animal species, an essential limitation upon all previous evolution was removed: The self-reproducing molecule was no longer burdened with the organism's entire stock of information. The importance of such a step is comparable to that of the beginning of life itself . . . (pp. 272–73).

This line of argument is based partly on the work of Shannon and Weaver (1949), the mathematicians who applied thermodynamic analysis to technical problems such as the coding of messages, transmission of messages over channels, the maximum rate of signal transmission over given channels, and the effects of noise. Hawkins (1964) reasoned from Shannon and Weaver's theoretical treatment of information that learning, whether the system that learns be machine or human, ultimately confers its benefits through increased thermodynamic efficiency.

> In the conditioned reflex and in the switching mechanism that is the basis of the large digital computer, the essential thermodynamic condition is again the availability of free energy for the performance of entropy-reducing, order-increasing work. The switching mechanisms transmit flows of energy larger than the incoming signals that direct their behavior. Through reinforcement and inhibition, relatively simple stimuli come to release complex responses adapted to the character and behavior of the environment. The patterning of such responses represents, vis-à-vis the environment, a lowered entropy of arrangement (p. 273).

The externalization of information beyond the limits of the cell nucleus referred to by Hawkins is only one of the first of many strategies that life has evolved for increasing thermodynamic efficiency. Even greater gains accrue if an organism can off-load the work of information storage and processing to the environment itself and thus reduce the biological costs associated with maintaining and processing in neural networks. Unfortunately, explanatory models in the cognitive sciences still emphasize relatively complete mental representations rather than models that account for representation as distributed between the environment and the brain. As Zhang and Norman (1994) argue, this traditional approach to cognition

> . . . often assumes that representations are exclusively in the mind (e.g., as propositions, schemas, productions, mental images, connectionist networks, etc.). External objects, if

they have anything to do with cognition at all, are at most peripheral aids. For instance, written digits are usually considered as mere memory aids for calculation. Thus, because the traditional approach lacks a means of accommodating external representation in its own right, it sometimes has to postulate complex internal representations to account for the complexity of behavior, much of which, however, is merely a reflection of the complexity of the environment (p. 88).

All things being equal, we might expect investment of organic resources in improved perceptive capabilities to be a more effective strategy for organisms than construction of elaborate MIROS. Regardless of whether improved perception is acquired through learning or natural selection, it allows organisms to more effectively exploit information reflected in the structure of the environment—information that is maintained at no direct biological cost to the organism.

Yet all things are not equal: A number of factors determine how biological resources are divided between perceptual capabilities and MIROS. These factors include the niche or occupation of the organism, the availability in the environment of information related to the niche, the biological costs of action requisite to information acquisition, the costs of developing and maintaining perceptual organs, and the costs of developing and maintaining the MIROS. In addition, when information acquisition involves exploration or investigation by the organism, there is a cost of opportunities forgone: Moving or adjusting sensory organs to favor selection of information from one sector of the environment may preclude, for some time, selection of information from other sectors.

Consider how these factors operate at the extremes to favor development of, respectively, perception and MIROS in two hypothetical groups of people concerned with navigation in a high-security office building. The first group are ordinary workers who move into a building and after a short time are able to navigate effectively using an environment rich in information such as signage, landmarks, changes in color schemes, and the like.

If the building is well designed, it is unlikely the workers will invest much mental effort in remembering the actual details of the spatial layout. "Why bother?" they might ask. "It's obvious; you just keep going until you find a familiar landmark or sign, and then you make your next move. We don't need a mental model because we can see where to go." Norman and Rumelhart (1975) have demonstrated that living in buildings for many months is no guarantee that inhabitants will be able to draw realistic floor plans. In fact, such residents often make gross errors in their representation of environmental layouts—incorrectly locating the position of doors, balconies, and furniture.

Returning to the high-security building, suppose a second group, more nefarious and temporary, are commandos hired to steal company secrets in the same building during the dead of night when visual information about the environment is not so easily obtained. Each use of flashlights would entail risk of discovery (a kind of cost) and each act of exploration or orientation would increase the possibility of being caught. In preparing for their raid, therefore, the commandos might be willing to spend a great deal of time familiarizing themselves with the layout of a building they may raid only once. "Sure," they might say, "we have to invest a lot of mental resources to memorize floor plans, but it's an investment that pays off in saved time and reduced risk."

8.3.2 Coupling and Information Transfer

Perception, in the view of ecological psychologists, cannot be separated from action: Perceiving involves selecting and attending to some sources of information at the expense of others. Human eyes, for instance, are constantly flicking across the visual field in rapid eye movements called *saccades.* Natural environments cannot be easily modeled in terms of communications channels, because such environments typically contain numerous independent sources of information. Organisms attend to these sources selectively, depending on the relevance of the information to their needs and intentions. To use inadequately the communications metaphor, organisms constantly switch channels. Moreover, most organisms employ networks of sensors in multiple sense modalities and actively manipulate their sensor arrays. It is unclear how we should think of such sensor networks in a way that would be consistent with Shannon and Weaver's rigorous technical meaning for *channel* in which they model information flow as a single stream of serial bits (see 4.4.2).

According to Gibson's paradigm (1979), the information contained in situations is "picked up" or selected rather than "filtered" as suggested by the metaphors associated with many popular models of memory and perception. In the context of thermodynamics, selective perception of the environment confers benefits similar to the switching mechanisms of learning referred to above by Hawkins: Organisms expend small amounts of energy attending to those aspects of the environment that might yield large returns.

Hawkins extended another Shannon and Weaver insight by noting that some kind of coupling is a necessary condition for duplication or transmission of patterns. He argued that the idea of coupling—widely misinterpreted by communications and media theorists to mean mechanical, deterministic coupling—was used by Shannon and Weaver to refer to thermodynamic (probabilistic, stochastic) coupling. Thermodynamic coupling is a many-to-many form of linkage, a concept of coupling that not only accounts for the possible gains in efficiency but also preserves the ancient Greek sense of information as transference of form:

> Man's physical coupling with his environment is not that of an intrinsic source of energy, but is weaker, more purely thermodynamic. He controls his environment by subtle changes in its order, so that the streams of natural process

flow in new channels. But the control runs both ways. Competence is derived from acceptance of the de facto order of things. The potter who shapes the clay has long been the image of a godlike power, but this is not the perception the potter has of himself. He must be sensitive to the properties of the mix and to its responses to firing in shape and color and texture. The potter is as much transformed by his art as the clay is (Hawkins, 1964, p. 310).

As Maturana (1978) notes, information conceived as transfer of pattern or form implies that

> . . . learning is not a process of accumulation of representations of the environment; it is a continuous process of transformation of behavior through continuous change in the capacity of the nervous system to synthesize it. Recall does not depend on the indefinite retention of a structural invariant that represents an entity (an idea, image, or symbol) but on the functional ability of the system to create, when certain recurrent conditions are given, a behavior that satisfies the recurrent demands or that the observer would class as a reenacting of a previous one (p. 45).

Behavior so informed by the environment represents a lowered entropy—that is, a greater orderliness of arrangement. Chaotic, disorganized, and arbitrary aspects of an organism's activity are ameliorated by attention and intention directed towards aspects of the environment that are related to the organism's ecological niche. The orderliness and organization of behavior that results from niche-related attention and intention can be characterized as intelligence. Such intelligence is thermodynamically efficient because it leverages the expenditure of small amounts of biological energy (Gibbs Free Energy) to guide much larger flows of energy in the external environment.

Media users benefit from this thermodynamic leverage when they expend modest attentional resources to acquire information about how to control large amounts of energy. A speculator who makes a quick killing on Wall Street after reading a stock quote is making thermodynamically efficient use of media technology.

To summarize the preceding discussion of coupling and information transfer, one should understand that the extension of human cognitive capacity through media technologies reflects broader evolutionary trends characterized by increasing externalization of information storage and processing. Such externalization increases thermodynamic efficiency, reducing the organic costs of cognition by distributing the "work" of representing situations between humans and their external environment. Indeed, one arguable way to define higher-order learning is by the degree to which it permits individuals to benefit from externalization of information storage and processing. This can be conceptualized as *literacy* or, more generally, we propose, as *mediacy*. Both literacy and mediacy are qualities of intelligence manifested by the facility with which an individual is capable of perceiving and acting on mediated information. Bruner and Olson (1977–78) invoke this concept of mediacy succinctly when they define intelligence as "skill in a medium."

8.3.3 Simplicity and Complexity

Ecology in general is concerned with predicting and explaining how matter and energy are transferred and organized by members of biological communities. Since transfer and organization of matter and energy are ultimately governed by thermodynamics rather than purely mechanical exchanges, ecological sciences eschew purely deterministic explanation (one-to-one, reversible couplings) in favor of stochastic, probabilistic explanation (many-to-many, nonreversible couplings). Stochastic description and analysis is based on information transfer and formalized by measures of entropy or organized complexity.[3] Information is thought of roughly as a measure of *level of organization* or relatedness. Entropy is a measure of degrees of freedom (von Bertalanffy, 1967; Gatlin, 1972) or *opportunities for action*. So viewed, complex systems can be said to offer more freedom of action than simple systems because complex systems (see 3.1.1.1.1) are more highly organized, with more and higher-level relations. Complex biosystems, for example, encompass more species and support longer food chains than simple biosystems; tropical rain forests afford more freedom of action, more opportunities to hunt and gather than does arctic tundra. To change the context, a city offers many more opportunities for human action—different types of work, recreation, and socializing—than does even the largest cattle ranch.

Extremely simple systems can be said to offer no opportunities for action because (a) there is no organization—all is chance and chaos or (b) organization is rigid—all relations are absolutely determined. A square mile of ocean surface is simple and chaotic, whereas a square mile of sheer granite cliff is simple and rigid. Rigid systems compel, yet they do not enable.

---

[3]Here thermodynamics (or bioenergetics) sets the boundary conditions. Yet real events are controlled by rate processes (barriers, compartments, enzymes, etc.) that are both biotic and abiotic. As Hawkins notes, ". . . the reality of chance is not contravened by the hypothesis of exact, deterministic laws of motion, for these do not give a complete account of physical systems, which also have a certain number of degrees of freedom represented by spatio-temporal variables . . . the nondynamical premises of thermodynamics are of the kind—namely, premises of probability—that complement the laws of motion. . . . The most remarkable consequence of this development (Maxwell & Boltzmann's kinetic theory of heat) was that entropy reappeared in the new theory, not as a phenomenological variable measurable in the heat laboratory but as a parameter of the probability law describing the statistical behavior of large systems of particles, and was definable far outside the experimental range of ordinary calorimetry. As a result, thermodynamics received an extension of the range of phenomena to which it could be applied, becoming a truly universal science. The dimensionless variable (entropy) reappeared in the formulation of statistical mechanics as a nonmechanical variable—namely, as a parameter of the probability law characterizing the phase-space distribution of the system being described. In the meaning of this parameter was hidden the final explanation of the apparent contradiction between the symmetry of time direction in dynamics and its asymmetry in thermodynamics (1964, p. 194).

8.4 A MULTIPLICITY OF MEDIA

Amidst dramatic changes enabled by convergent computing and telecommunications technologies, there are fundamental shifts in concepts associated with the word *media*. Many conventional connotations of this term originated during the early 1900s in the concerns of advertisers who wanted to use newspapers and radio to reach mass markets. The term *medium* has been applied variously to:

1. Storage surfaces such as tapes, discs, and papers
2. Technologies for receiving, recording, copying, or playing messages
3. Human communication modalities such as text, diagrams, photos, or music
4. Physical and electronic infrastructures such as broadcast networks or cyberspace
5. Cultures of creation and use such as sports media, edutainment, the paparazzi, and "cyburbia" (Allen, 1991, p. 53)

These forms of usage are broadly consistent with a more general concept of a medium as "something intermediate in nature or degree [or] an intervening substance, as air, through which a force acts or an effect is produced" (Random House/Reference Software, 1993). This notion of intermediacy underlies technical usage and popular imagination of media as channels for sending and receiving messages. Intermediacy was also implicit in the metaphors of cognitivists in the 1970s and 1980s that characterized human cognition as information processing in which symbols flow through registers and processing modules in a progression of transformations akin to serial computation. A logical extension of this kind of thinking is that the way for humans to work with computers is to communicate with them through symbols and language-based discourse, including verbal commands.

This chapter is grounded in an emerging paradigm in which a *medium* is conceptualized as "the element that is the natural habitat of an organism [or] surrounding objects, conditions, or influences; environment" (Random House/Reference Software, 1993). This media-as-environments metaphor is certainly relevant in an era where electronic information pervades virtually every aspect of everyday life. Our perceptions of the planet are influenced by worldwide "supermedia" events (Real, 1989) even as we are surrounded by "info-cocoons" patched together from components such as facsimile machines, computers, copiers, cellular phones, radios, TVs, and video games. Public awareness of virtual realities and other immersive environments (see Chapter 15) has grown steadily since the early 1990s as these technologies have been popularized in films and amusement parks, and as they have been more widely used in architecture, medicine, aviation, and other disciplines.

Developers of computer-based environments of all types, and especially interactive multimedia, rely increasingly on object-oriented design and object-oriented programming (Martin, 1993). Object technologies challenge the media-as-channels and media-as-conveyors (R. E. Clark, 1983) metaphors because the objects—files and segments of code—contain instruction sets that endow the objects with varying degrees of behavioral autonomy.

Similarly, it is difficult to model as communication the kind of user interactions that typify graphical user interfaces (GUI) as employed by the Macintosh or Windows operating systems. When a user drags a folder into a trashcan icon, does the user intend to "communicate" with the computer? Possibly. When the trashcan icon puffs up after receiving the file, does the user interpret this as evidence of the trashcan's intention to communicate? Possibly. Yet the act of tossing an actual file into a *real* trashcan would not normally be interpreted as the result of some intent to communicate with the trashcan but rather as an intent to dispose of the file. And the presence of the file in the trashcan would not normally be interpreted by the tosser as the result of some intention of the trashcan to communicate its status as "containing something." What is the difference between virtual file tossing and real file tossing? To well-adapted computer users, both virtual and real trashcans have similar dispositional properties: From the user's point of view, trashcans are not receivers of messages but receivers of unwanted files.

GUIs and similar environments also challenge conventional notions of symbols. In conventional usage, the meaning of a symbol is determined by its referents—that is, a symbol refers to a set of objects or events. Letters in this sense refer to sounds, numerals refer to quantities, and isobars on a weather map refer to readings of air pressure. In arranging letters to spell a word, however, one is not voicing actual sounds; in arranging numerals to represent a mathematical operation, one is not manipulating actual quantities of objects; and in estimating the distance between isobars, one is not sensing the wind.

The dispositional properties of computer icons and tools set them apart from conventional symbols (see 5.4.4.2) because icons and tools afford opportunities for direct action. Double-clicking on a selected file icon does not *symbolize* the action of opening the selected file. Rather, it *is* the action of opening the file; the double-click causes the operating system to execute the code associated with the selected object. Clicking on a selected file does not symbolize file opening anymore than toggling a light switch symbolizes activation of the light bulb.

However useful engineers may find the communications metaphor in rationalizing the logic of information flows within hardware and software subsystems, questions about the research and design of contemporary user interfaces cluster at the level of object perception and manipulation precisely because perception and manipulation of objects invokes powerful cognitive abilities that are also used in many everyday activities: locating, tracking, and identifying objects; grasping and moving them; altering the properties of the objects, or "switching" them from one modality to another.

The means by which users carry out such activities in a GUI are often partially or completely removed from language-based communication: Pointing, dragging, and pushing allow the user to perceive and to continuously adjust virtual tools or other devices without using propositions or commands such as "erase selected file." Ecological psychologists recognize that, in spite of their apparent modernity, such activities represent very ancient modes of unified action-perception that are shared by many organisms: Every predator worthy of the name must be able to locate, track, identify, grasp, move, and modify objects. The cognitive faculties used by an artist who cuts objects from a complex computer-based drawing and saves them in her electronic library have much in common with the faculties employed by a wolf who snatches white rabbits from a snowfield and buries them until spring.

Contemporary, object-oriented regimes for interface design result in complex communities of semiautonomous entities—windows, buttons, "hot spots," and other objects—that exchange messages with each other, usually by means that are invisible to the user. Thus, the user is in a very real sense only one of many agents who populate and codetermine events in cyberspace. Increasingly, human computer users are not the only senders and receivers of messages but are, rather, participants in arenas that have been likened to theaters (Laurel, 1986) and living communities ("vivaria"; Kay, cited in Rheingold, 1991, p. 316).

8.5 AN ECOLOGY OF PERCEPTION AND ACTION

Perceiving is an achievement of the individual, not an appearance in the theater of his consciousness. It is a keeping-in-touch with the world, an experiencing of things, rather than a having of experiences. It involves awareness-of instead of just awareness. It may be awareness of something in the environment or something in the observer or both at once, but there is no content of awareness independent of that of which one is aware. This is close to the act psychology of the 19th century except that perception is not a mental act. Neither is it a bodily act. Perceiving is a psychosomatic act, not of the mind or of the body but of a living observer (J. J. Gibson, 1979, p. 239).

8.5.1 Integrated Perception and Action

Dominated by information-processing theories, the recent history of perceptual psychology has emphasized research paradigms that attempt to constrain action and to isolate sensation from attention and intention. This predilection for ignoring codeterminant relations between perception and action has resulted in a relatively weak foundation for the design of new media products and a limited basis for understanding many traditional media forms.

Ulric Neisser's (1976) perceptual cycle—which frankly acknowledges the influence of both J. J. Gibson and his spouse, Eleanor Gibson—serves as a simplified framework for examining the relationship between action and perception in mediated environments. Neisser (1976) was concerned with the inability of information-processing models to explain phenomena associated with attention, unit formation, meaning, coherence, veridicality, and per-

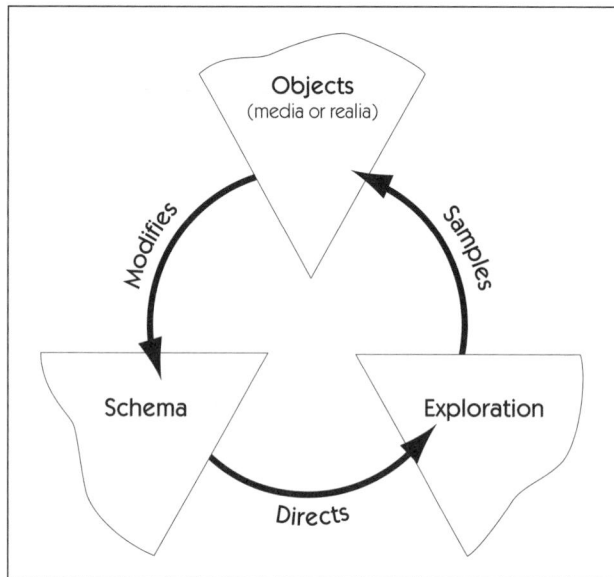

Figure 8-1. Neisser's Perceptual Cycle (modified from Neisser, 1976, p. 21). In the language of ecological psychologists, an organism selectively samples available information in accord with the demands of its niche. An organism's perceptions are tuned to the means that the environment offers for fulfilling the organism's intentions.

ceptual development. Information-processing models of the 1970s typically represented sensory organs as fixed and passive arrays of receptors. How, then, Neisser asked, would such models explain why different people attend to different aspects of the same situation? How would information-processing models help to explain why even infants attend to objects in ways that suggest the brain can easily assign to *things* stimuli obtained through distinct sensory modalities? How would information-processing models explain the remarkable ability of the brain to respond to scenes as if they were stable and coherent, even though the act of inspecting such scenes exposes the retina to rapidly shifting and wildly juxtaposed cascades of images?

The Neisser-Gibson alternative to the information-processing models adds the crucial function of exploration. This addition, reflected in Neisser's Perceptual Cycle (Fig. 8-1) reflects the fact that organisms *selectively sample* available information in accord with the demands of their niches and, further, that organisms' perceptual capabilities are tuned to the means that their accustomed environment offers for fulfilling the organisms' intentions.

Neisser's emphasis on exploratory perception reminds us that schemata can never be entirely complete as representations of realia. Schemata are not, in Neisser's opinion, to be thought of as templates for conceptualizing experience but rather as plans for interacting with situations. "The schema [is] not only the plan but also the executor of the plan. It is a pattern of action as well as a pattern for action" (Neisser, 1991, pp. 20–21).

The idea of the action-perception cycle, which is similar in some respects to early cybernetic models (see 3.1.2.5), can also be fruitfully thought of as a dialectic in which action and perception are codeterminant. In visual tracking, for example, retinal perception is codeterminant with eye movement (see Clancey, 1993, and Churchland, 1986, on tensors as neural models of action-perception dialectics).

Neisser's use of *schemata* and *plans* echoes a multiplicity of meanings from Kant (1781, 1966) to Bartlett (1932) to Piaget (1971) to Suchman (1987). His meaning is close to what we will define as *actionable mental models*. An actionable mental model integrates perception of the environment with evolving plans for action, including provisions for additional sampling of the environment. Actionable mental models draw not so much on memories of how the *environment* was structured in the past as they draw on memories of how past actions were related to past perceptions. Rather than mirroring the workings of external reality, actionable models help organisms attend to their perceptions of the environment and to formulate intentions.

Our use of actionable mental models assumes first that mental models are rarely self-sufficient (see D. Gentner & Stevens, 1983). That is, mental models cannot function effectively (are not "runnable") without access to data about a situation. Actionable mental models, in other words, must be "situated" (Collins, Brown & Newman, 1989; Greeno, 1994) in order to operate.

Ecological psychology assumes that much if not most of the information required to guide effective action in everyday situations is directly perceivable by individuals adapted to those situations. It seems reasonable to assume that natural selection in favor of cognitive efficiency (Gatlin, 1972; Minsky, 1985; von Foerster, 1986) will work against the development and maintenance of complex MIROS if simple MIROS will contribute to survival equally well. That is, the evolution of cognitive capacities will not favor unnecessary repleteness in mental models or the neurological structures that support them even when such models might be more truthful or veridical according to some "objective" standard of representation.

In many cases, MIROS cannot serve (or do not serve efficiently) as equivalents for direct perception of situations in which the environment does the "work" of "manipulating itself" in response to the actions of the perceiver. It is usually much easier, for instance, to observe how surroundings change in response to one's movement than it is to construct or use MIROS to predict such changes.

Even when humans *might* employ more complete MIROS, it appears they are often willing to expend energy manipulating things physically to avoid the effort of manipulating such things internally. Lave (1988) is on point in her discussion of a homemaker responsible for implementing a systematic dieting regime. After considering the effort involved in fairly complex calculations for using fractional measures to compute serving size, the homemaker, who had some background in higher mathematics, simply formed patties of cottage cheese and manipulated them physically to yield correct and edible solutions.

There are trade-offs between elaborate and simple MIROS. Impoverished environments are likely to select *against* improvement of elaborate sensory and perceptual faculties and may even favor degradation of some of these faculties: We can assume that the blindness of today's cave fish evolved because eyes contributed little to the survival of their sighted ancestors. It seems reasonable to assume that, in the long run, the calculus of natural selection balances resources invested in perception against resources invested in other means of representing the environment.

In any case, for reasons of parsimony in scientific explanation (in the tradition of Occam's razor), descriptions of MIROS—which are of necessity usually hypothetical— should not be any more complex than is necessary to explain observed facts. Accounting for observed behavior, then, with the simplest possible MIROS will assume that organisms attend to the environment directly because this is often more economical and more reliable than maintaining models of the environment or "reasoning" about it.

8.5.1.1. Perception.
Gibson's seminal works (1966 and 1979, for example) established many of the theories, principles, concepts, and methods employed by contemporary ecological psychologists. Developed over a 35-year span of research on the problems of visuospatial perception, his "ecological optics" now serves as a framework for extending the ecological approach to other areas of psychology. The implications of Gibson's research extend beyond the purely theoretical: He was instrumental in producing the first cinematic simulation of flying using model airplanes and model landing fields. Gibson's novel conception of the retinal image[4] substituted dynamic, flowing imagery of the mobile observer for the static, picturelike image of classical optics and inspired techniques of ground plane simulation and texture gradients that are the basis for many electronic games.

8.5.1.2. Invariants.
In developing his radical ecological optics, Gibson (1979) focused on the practical successes of an organism's everyday behavior as it lives in and adapts to its environment. He was particularly concerned with characteristics and properties of the environment that supported such success.

Generalizing this interest, ecological psychologists investigate "the information transactions between living systems and their environments, especially as they pertain to perceiving situations of significance to planning and execution of purposes activated in an environment" (Shaw, Mace & Turvey, 1986, p. iii). Ecological psychologists focus on ordinary everyday perceiving as a product of active and immediate engagement with the environment.

An organism selectively "picks up" information in its habitat when such information is related to its ecological niche. In this context, it is useful to think of *habitat* as roughly equivalent to address, and *niche* as roughly equiva-

lent to occupation. The perceptual capabilities of organisms are tuned to opportunities for action required to obtain enough energy and nutrients to reproduce.

"Attunement to constraints" (attributed to Lashley, 1951, by Gibson, 1966) thus reflects the most fundamental type of information that an organism can obtain about its environment. With this in mind, ecologists such as von Foerster (1986) contend that "one of the most important strategies for efficient   adjustment   to   an   environment   is the detection of invariance or unchanging aspects of that environment" (p. 82). The detection of invariances— constrained and predictable relations in the environment— simplifies perception and action for any organism. As we shall argue, detection of invariances is also critical to successful adaptation by humans to any mediated environment.

8.5.1.3. A Simple Experiment.
As an example of the importance of detecting invariants, consider the human visual system as it is often presented in simple models. Millions of rods and cones in the retina serve as a receptor array that transmits nerve impulses along bundled axons to an extensive array of neurons in the primary visual cortex called V1. Neurons in V1 are *spatiotopically mapped*, i.e., laid out in fields that preserve the integrity of the information captured by the retina. Neurons in V1 transmit to specialized centers that process color, form, and motion. Yet there is much more to seeing than the processing of retinal imagery. Seeing also integrates complex systems that focus lenses, dilate irises, control vergence and saccades, and enable rotation of the head and craning of the neck.

Perception by the visual system of invariants in the environment can be thrown into complete confusion by interfering with the brain's detection of head and eye movement. You may want to try this simple experiment: Close your left eye and cock your head repeatedly to the left 2 or 3 inches. Proprioceptors in your neck muscles allow the brain to assign this jerkiness to movements of your head rather than to changes in the environment. Without this natural ability to assign movement of retinal images to self-induced changes in head position, simply turning to watch an attractive person would "set one's world spinning."

Now close your left eye again and, keeping the right eye open, gently press on the left eyeball several times from the side. Under these abnormal conditions, your visual system now assigns roughly the same amount of eyeball jerkiness to radical movement of the environment itself.

Under normal circumstances, the brain does not attribute variation in retinal images resulting from head or eye movement to changes in the environment. Rather, an elaborate system of proprioceptive and locomotor sensors operates automatically in concert with retinal data to generate a framework of perceptual invariants against which true environmental change can be detected.

It is important to note that the concept of perceptual invariance does not necessarily imply a lack of change in the environment, but rather that the organism is able to detect reliable patterns in the change and therefore able to use the patterns as a background for less predictable

---

[4]"The natural retinal image consists of a binocular pair of ordinal structures of adjacencies and of successive transpositions and transformations of region of texture delimited by steps or margins, which are characterized by gradients and changes in gradients" (Reed on Gibson, 1988, p. 136).

variation. Tide pool animals, for instance, are superb at detecting underlying patterns in the apparent chaos of the surf and adjusting their activity patterns to these fluctuations.

8.5.1.4. Perception of Invariants: Some Implications for Media Design. The idea of a framework of invariants is very useful in the design, management, and utilization of media environments because it reminds us that

> . . . it is not necessarily better to throw more graphics techniques, more rendering power, or more artificial intelligence into the scene. These are not necessarily going to give us a better artificial world. The quantity of what goes into your artificial world is not what makes it better or more interesting; it is the quality of what goes into it. What defines quality for this activity are these environmental invariants, which drive the human perceptual system. We can think of it as though the levels of detail had a weighting system attached, telling us how important that *type* of detail is or that *level* of detail. If these details are not associated with perceptual invariants, then the weighting factor is small. Often you can remove certain kinds of detail from an image and people cannot perceive the difference. On the other hand, if the detail has a tight link to some kind of perceptual invariant, then the weighting factor is high. . . . (Gardner, 1987, pp. 106–07).

While Gibson's work in the 1970s met with skepticism from his contemporary psychologists, he generated even in his day a considerable following among human-factors engineers and ergonomicists. He is now read widely by virtual-world and interface designers. The central concern for these designers is how to engineer the relationship between perceptual variants and perceptual invariants so as to optimize the user's ability to perceive and act in complex, information-rich environments.

> Gibsonian psychology points to perceptual invariants that enrich our depth and distance perception. Many of the invariants relate to the ever-existent, textured, ground surface of our environment. . . . The strongest invariants are the ratios, gradients, calibration references, and optical flows tied to motion parallax, surface texture, the ground plane, and ego perception. By enabling the same perceptual invariants that people use to navigate the real world, the creator can construct a world that encourages exploration (Gardner, 1987, pp. 107–09).

8.5.2 Perceptual Learning

Gibson did not believe that sensory inputs are "filtered" or processed by propositional or symbolic schemes. Rather, he strongly favored a bottom-up paradigm in which exploratory actions rather than propositions drive processes of selective perception. Yet none of Gibson's ideas preclude *learning* to perceive directly, as when children come to understand that they must automatically respond to icy-slick sidewalks with flat-footed caution. Nor did Gibson deny the importance of reasoning about perceptions, as when a mountaineer carefully analyzes the complex textures of an ice-covered cliff in order to plan an ascent. Nevertheless, consistent with his view that action, not conception, drives perception, Gibson

believed that learning entails the tuning of attention and perception, not the conforming of percepts to concepts. Such perceptual learning is, in the words of Gibson's spouse, Eleanor, essentially

> . . . an increase in the ability of an organism to get information from its environment, as a result of practice with the array of stimulation provided by the environment. This definition implies that there are potential variables of stimuli which are not differentiated within the mass of impinging stimulation, but which may be, given the proper conditions of exposure and practice. As they are differentiated, the resulting perceptions become more specific with respect to stimulation, that is, in greater correspondence with it. There is a change in what the organism can respond to. The change is not acquisition or substitution of a new response to stimulation previously responded to in some other way, but is rather responding in any discriminating way to a variable of stimulation not responded to previously. The criterion of perceptual learning is thus an increase in specificity. What is learned can be described as detection of properties, patterns, and distinctive features (E. J. Gibson, 1969, p. 77).

8.5.2.1. Propositional vs. Nonpropositional Learning. Gibson's (1979) research on visual perception in everyday situations rather than laboratory situations led him to think of perceiving as a process in which organisms acquire information directly, without the mediation of propositional reasoning. Hochberg (1974) thinks that one of Gibson's most important ideas is that

> . . . there exist higher-order variables of stimulation to which the properties of the objects and events that we perceive are the direct and immediate response . . . [thus] the properties of the perceived world . . . are not the end products of associative processes in which kinesthetic and other imagery come to enrich two-dimensional and meaningless visual sensations with tri-dimensional depth and object meaning (Hochberg, p. 17).

Gibson sometimes used the term *associative thought* in ways that implied propositional reasoning. We have therefore substituted the latter in this chapter when we discuss his ideas in order to avoid confusion with current usage of the term *associative,* which is broadly inclusive of a variety of neurological processes. In any case, a brief review of the controversy regarding propositional and nonpropositional reasoning seems in order here (for more, see Vera & Simon, 1993, and Clancy's 1993 reply).

Cognitive psychologists and computer scientists have long used symbols and propositions to model human thought processes. Anderson's widely influential ACT* model (1983) is typical of rigorous efforts in the 1980s to use propositional logic to model learning. The ACT* model converts declarative knowledge—that is, knowledge that can be stated or described—into production rules through a process of *proceduralization.* The resulting *procedural knowledge* (roughly, skills) is highly automatic and not easily verbalized by learners.

Gordon (1994) offers this simplified example of how Anderson's (1983) notion of proceduralization might be used to model the way an agent learns to classify an object

(p. 139; content in brackets added):

IF the figure has four sides
    and sides are equal
    and sides are touching on both ends
    and four inner angles are 90°
    and figure is black
THEN classify as [black] square.

Such instructions might have some value as a script for teaching students about logic, or perhaps even as a crude strategy for teaching them to recognize squares. Yet even the most sophisticated computer models fail almost entirely when they attempt to use this kind of reasoning to recognize pattern and contexts that are very easy for animals and humans.

There are other reasons to doubt assertions that the brain represents perceptual skills as propositions or production rules. While declarative knowledge (language and propositions) is obviously useful for teaching perceptual skills, the ultimate mechanisms of internal representation need not be propositional. The observation that propositions help people learn to recognize patterns could be explained, for example, by a model in which propositional frameworks are maintained by the brain merely as temporary scaffolding ("private speech"; see Berk, 1994) that supports repeated rehearsal required for perceptual development. Once the perceptual skills have been automated, the brain gradually abandons the propositional representations and their arguable encumbrance of processing speed. It then becomes difficult for learners to verbalize "how" they perceive.

Having decided that perceptual learning is not directly dependent on internalized propositions or production rules, many cognitive scientists have turned to models of nonsymbolic representation. We suspect that Gibson would have found in these emerging models considerable support for many of his ideas about indirect perception.

Kosslyn and Koeing (1992), for instance, offers an excellent treatment of the ways in which connectionist models can explain the details of perceptual processing. Connectionist models (see A. Clark, 1989) employ networks of processing units that learn at a *subsymbolic level*. These networks (also called *neural networks*) can be trained, without using formal rules or propositions, to produce required outputs from given inputs, because the processing units mathematically adjust the weighting of connections through repeated trials. Neural nets are superior to proposition-based programs at learning tasks such as face recognition.

A trained subsymbolic network cannot be analyzed or dissected to yield classical rules or symbols, because the learned information is represented as weighted connections rather than as propositions. The learned information is not stored as symbols or bits of code located at specific sites. Rather, it is represented by the overall fabric of connections. Subsymbolic processing networks can, however, serve as *substrates* for conventional symbolic processing and therefore have some potential for modeling forms of human thought that do rely on symbols and language.

8.5.2.2. Affordances. In Gibson's view, sensory information alone is insufficient for guiding and controlling the activities of living organisms:

> The variables of sensory discrimination are radically different from the variables of perceptual discrimination. The former are said to be dimensions like quality, intensity, extensity, and duration, dimensions of hue, brightness, and saturation, of pitch, loudness, and timbre, of pressure, warm, cold, and pain. The latter are dimensions of the environment, the variable of events and those of surfaces, places, objects, of other animals, and even of symbols. Perception involves meaning; sensation does not . . . (J. J. Gibson, 1974/1982, p. 351).

Selective perception generates much more information about an experienced event than can be obtained by sensation alone because the organism is informed during selection by traces of its activities relating to location, orientation, and other conditions. In all but extreme laboratory settings, organisms employ the natural means available to them for locomotion in and manipulation of their environment—both to obtain additional information and to act on that information. For Gibson (1979), perception and action were inextricably coupled in a seamless cycle. To describe this coupling, he introduced the concepts of *affordances* (opportunities for action) and *effectivities* (capabilities for action).

Affordances are functional, meaningful, and persistent properties of the environment (J. J. Gibson, 1979), "nested sets of possibilities" (Turvey & Shaw, 1979, p. 261) for activity towards which the organism is oriented by its perceptual history and heritage. In active perceiving, "the affordances of things is what gets attended to, not the modalities, qualities, or intensities of the accompanying sensations . . . " (J. J. Gibson, 1977/1982, p. 289).

> If ecological information specifies the affordances of things . . . then it does not specify abstract physical properties of the classical sort (for example, the three Cartesian dimensions), but rather ecologically relevant properties such as texture, resistance to deformation, and manipulability. Both kinds of properties may be real, but it is the functional properties, the affordances, that we animals are aware of directly . . . (Reed, 1988, p. 232).

Thus, an affordance is, roughly speaking, a pathway for action that enhances the survivability of an organism in its niche—an *opportunity* for action

> . . . such as support by a firm surface, grasping by a limb of a tree, or mating by an animal of the opposite sex. Gibson claimed that affordances such as these are specified by the structure of light reflected from objects, and are directly detectable. There is therefore no need to invoke representations of the environment intervening between detection of affordances and action; one automatically leads to the other (Bruce & Green, 1990, p. 382).

Affordances simultaneously enable some possibilities and constrain others, and they make actions more predictable and replicable.

> Speaking more humanely, we do not in any sense reduce the statistical variety of nature when we are engaged in learning the fixed patterns, the constancies of nature. Rather, it is nature that reduces the statistical variety in us.

Our subsequent behavior becomes more predictable to an outside observer who knows the order of nature because it comes to be more closely coupled to, and defined by, that order. We have acquired, in Spinoza's phrase, more "aptness of the body" because our ideas are less "mutilated and confused" (Hawkins, 1964, p. 239).

Mediated habitats encompass a range of affordances and effectivities related to cognitive artifacts such as the book, the calculator, and the television. Such artifacts can do some of the work of storing and transforming information, and this work may therefore lessen the user's need to construct or maintain more complex MIROS. In addition, such artifacts can provide

> ... affordances for reasoning. ... [which] are properties of representation in relation to a person's or group's abilities to use the representations to make inferences. Reasoning is an activity that transforms a representation, and the representation affords that transformational activity. Abilities for reasoning activities include knowing the operations to perform on the notational objects in the representation and understanding the semantic significance of the objects and operations (Greeno, Moore & Smith, 1993, p. 109).

In the Gibsonian (1979) paradigm, affordances are opportunities for action rather than physical artifacts or objects. Nevertheless, it is useful to think of sets or suites of affordances as bundled in association with tools or devices (see 24.2). The affordance of "browse-ability" is itself composed of clusters of affordances; one exploits the turnability of a book's pages in order to exploit the readability of their text. We can characterize the phone by its "handle-ability," "dial-ability," "answer-ability," "listening-to-ability," and "talking-into-ability," affordances that in some cases serve multiple goals or ends. The complete action pathway for realizing the opportunity afforded by the telephone for talking to someone at a distance must be perceived, though not necessarily all at once, and "unpacked" through the effectivities of a human agent. Interface designers refer to this unpacking as *entrainment*.

One of the reasons Gibson argued that direct perception is independent of reasoning is because, by definition, the properties of an affordance are persistent, even invariant. They are the knowns of the problem: the "climb-ability" of a branch for the squirrel, the "alight-ability" of a rock for the seagull, the "grab-ability" of a deer for the wolf. Such affordances are perceived automatically as the result of repeated engagement with consistent circumstances, "hard wired" in the form of durable connections between dendrites (see Crutcher, 1986; Kupferman, 1991).

It may seem peculiar or contrived to use *climb-ability* as an alternative to the familiar forms of the verb *to climb*. The grammar of most human languages is, after all, centered on action in the form agent-action-object or agent-object-action. Organizing propositions in terms of action, however, is a serious limitation if one wants to describe mediated environments as complex fields of potentialities. The language of affordances and effectivities refocuses attention on how the environment structures activity rather than on descriptions of activity per se.

In the calculus of planning and action, detection of the invariant properties of affordances allows some aspects of a problem to be stipulated or assumed, freeing cognitive resources to attend to the unknowns, those aspects of the environment subject to change: Is this branch thick enough? Are the waves too frequent? Is the buck too big?

The capacity to detect and respond to affordances results from repeated engagement with sets of circumstances that over time—in the life of the individual or the species—are consistent enough to induce automaticity (Sternberg, 1977) in perception and action. Affordances influence the interaction of the organism with its environment, not only by enabling and constraining action but also by entraining the organism's perceiving and acting in predictable and repeatable sequences.

As a general rule, it can be assumed that organisms will not squander sensory or cognitive resources on aspects of the environment that have no value as affordances, because natural selection (or learning) will have effectively blinded them to objects and phenomena they cannot exploit. "We see the world not as *it is* but as *we are*," in the words of the Jewish epigram. To paraphrase this from a Gibsonian perspective, we see the world not as it is, but as we can use it.

8.5.2.3. Effectivities.   Effectivities (or capabilities; Greeno, Smith & Moore, 1993) are intentional, meaningful properties of a perceiving organism that trigger, guide, and control ongoing activities directed towards exploitation of the inherent possibilities of affordances (Turvey, Shaw, Reed & Mace, 1982). An effectivity encompasses the structure, functionality, and actions that might enable the organism to pursue what is, roughly speaking, in human terms, a goal (see 3.1.4.5). Using its "climber things," the squirrel exploits the climb-ability of the branch to escape a predator. Using its "alighter things," the seagull exploits the alight-ability of the rock for rest. Using its "grabber things," the wolf exploits the grab-ability of the deer to obtain nutrients.

> Taken together, geometrical, kinetic, and task constraints constitute a description of a person's effectivities. ... Geometrical and kinetic constraints are intrinsic to physical properties of the actor and can be directly measured/ calculated with respect to an external frame of reference (i.e., height, weight). Task constraints are more functional and "psychological." They include all of the intentional, goal-directed considerations that encourage the person to perform one action rather than another (Mark, Dainoff, Moritz & Vogele, 1991, pp. 484–85).

Affordances and effectivities are neither specific organs of perception nor specific tools of execution. Rather, they are emergent properties produced by interactions between the perceiver and its environment.

A well-tuned relationship between affordances (opportunities) and effectivities (abilities) generates a dialectic that, Csikszentmihalyi (1990) argues, is experienced by humans as highly satisfying. He calls this dialectic the "flow experience" (p. 67).

Affordances and effectivities are mutually grounded in

and supported by both the regularities of the physical structure of the environment and by the psychosomatic structure of the perceiver. It is meaningless to consider whether an object affords action without also considering the nature of corresponding effectivities that some organism might employ to exploit that affordance to achieve the organism's intentions: A flat, 3-feet-tall rock affords convenient sitting for a human but not for a bull elephant.

Indeed, meaning, of perhaps a quite fundamental sort, is extant in the relationship of organisms to their environments. Here is our working definition of *ecological meaning*:

> Those clusters of perceptions associated with the potential *means*—that is, affordances and effectivities—by which an organism might realize its intentions.

Our definition does not assume that organisms are conscious or that they use semantics or syntax, nor does it necessarily assume that organisms are purposeful. Our definition does assume, however, that all organisms engage in activities that can be characterized as intentional or goal oriented.

Many biologists and psychologists would criticize these notions of intentionality or goal orientedness, especially when they are applied to simpler forms of life. Intentionality implies teleological thinking, and such critics typically hold teleology in disrepute because it has been associated with doctrines that seek in natural systems evidence of deliberate design or purpose—vitalism and creationism, for example.

A narrower conception of intentionality and goal orientedness, however, is very convenient in the study of self-organizing and cybernetic systems (see 3.1.2.5) in which

> . . . feedback mechanisms are characterized by the fact that the input is controlled by the output, and thus stabilizes the output, or makes the performance relatively independent from disturbing influences. One can consider the stability of the output as the "goal" of the system. To turn the argument around, whenever a behavior in biology is described as goal directed, i.e., teleological, it is very likely that a feedback mechanism is involved (Gregory, 1989, p. 176).

When ecological psychologists attribute intentions and goals to nonhumans, they typically do so in the more limited sense associated with functional maintenance of homeostasis—or in Maturana's (1980) terms, *autopoesis*—rather than as an attribution of deliberate design or purpose (see 3.1.3.5).

8.5.2.4. Unification of Effectivities and Affordances.
A curious phenomenon emerges in humans when effectivities engage with affordances: The affordances often seem to disappear from awareness. Winograd and Flores (1986) cite Heidegger's example of hammering a nail:

> To the person doing the hammering, the hammer as such does not exist. It is part of the background of *readiness-to-hand* that is taken for granted without explicit recognition or identification as an object. It is part of the hammerer's world, but is not present [to awareness] any more than are the tendons of the hammerer's arm (p. 36).

The disappearance of an affordance from awareness signals the psychological unification of the effectivity with the corresponding affordances. One can think of this unification as an extension of the effectivity by the affordance or as a "path" for action-perception. In everyday activity, the very "routine-ness" and familiarity of such paths makes them invisible to the organism. Thus, another metaphor for directness of action-perception is transparency. The organism perceives and acts *through* the unified effectivity-affordance (arm and hammer) and is therefore only aware of the object of perception and action (the nail).

> The hammer presents itself as a hammer only when there is some kind of breaking down or *readiness-to-hand*. Its "hammerness" emerges if it breaks or slips from grasp or mars the wood, or if there is a nail to be driven and the hammer cannot be found. . . . As observers, we may talk about the hammer and reflect on its properties, but for the person engaged in . . . unhampered hammering, it does not exist as an entity (Winograd & Flores, 1986, p. 36).

In terms of ecological psychology, we can think of Heidegger's concepts of *breakdown* and resulting *unreadiness-to-hand* as a partial decoupling of an effectivity from its corresponding affordance. Breakdowns "serve an extremely important cognitive function, revealing to us the nature of our practices and equipment, making them 'present-to-hand' to us, perhaps for the first time. In this sense they function in a positive rather than a negative way" (Winograd & Flores, p. 78).

8.5.2.5. Everyday Learning and Media Environments.
For J. J. Gibson, the ordinary world of everyday learning and perception is

> . . . not the world of physicists. It is far larger than atoms and far smaller than galaxies. It is the geological environment of ground, water, earth, and sky, and it is the evolved world of flora and fauna. The substances and surfaces of the ground and the animate and inanimate things above it need to be described at their own level, if we are to understand what animals are aware of. Equally important, the energy fields in the medium of the air (or water) exist at an ecological level and contain information about the furnishings of our habitat. These sources of information in stimulation must therefore be studied ecologically, not physically. Psychology must begin with ecology, not with physics and physiology, for the entities of which we are aware and the means by which we apprehend them are ecological (Reed, 1988, p. 230).

The popularity of Donald Norman's (1988) book, *The Psychology of Everyday Things*, which shares key ideas with Gibson's work, testifies to an increased awareness by the general public that media engineers and scientists must look beyond the merely physical properties and attributes of systems. In an age of knowledge workers and postindustrialism, human habitats and artifacts must accommodate mentality as well as physicality, and support creativity as well as consumption. Cognitive ergonomics (Zuccermaglia, 1991) is just as important as corporal ergonomics (Mark, Dainoff, Moritz & Vogele, 1991): Both depend to a considerable extent on understanding fundamental human capabilities that were tuned long ago by ecological circumstances.

Yet if new media are to support the development and utilization of our uniquely human capabilities, then we must acknowledge that the most widely distributed human asset is the ability to learn in everyday situations through a tight coupling of action and perception.

> Covariations of tactile, auditory, visual, and other sensory inputs are normal concomitants of most action, and must be presumed to provide most of our normal clues for the integrated perception of our environments. The detection and analysis of covariation is thus the main function required of the relevant cortical network. Given this, the system has all it needs by way of an internal representation of the tactile world-as-perceived for the organization of relevant action. The state of conditional readiness for action using other dimensions of the effector system, such as walking, can be derived directly from this representation, without any need for an explicit "map" (MacKay, 1991, p. 84).

Emerging media systems and technologies appear headed toward a technical renaissance that could free media products from constraints that now limit the agency of end users: the limited symbology and dimensionality of paper and ink, the shadows captured and cast from a single point of view in photographs and films, the fixed sequences and pacing of analog broadcast technology.

Saba (1988), for example, argues that the virtual contiguity afforded by integrated telecommunications systems (incorporating venues such as two-way video conferences and distributed or networked multimedia) transforms possibilities for participation in communities of production and learning. In his view, the convergence of media technologies, techniques for multitasking, and sharing of tools for communication reduces the transactional distance between participants and reduces dependence on communication through explicit discourse.

8.6 ECOLOGICAL VS. EMPIRICAL APPROACHES

> Instead of . . . [assuming that] perception is some kind of *internal operation* of the brain (the seat of the mind) on the signals from the world, e.g., interpretation, addition, supplementation, or organization, but in any case a "processing" of the input . . . I suggest that the act of perceiving is one of becoming aware of the environment, or picking up of information about the environment, but that nothing like a *representation* of the environment exists in the brain or the mind which could be in greater or lesser correspondence with it—no "phenomenal" world which reflects or parallels the "physical" world (J. J. Gibson, 1974/1982, pp. 371–72).

Gibson (1979) found himself at odds with both the fading metaphors of behaviorists, who often likened the brain to a mechanical device, and the emergent metaphors of the cognitivists, who frequently spoke of the brain as a computer. One of his important insights was that *actions* involved in detecting and selecting information are, like *orienteering* (the use of a map and compass to navigate between checkpoints along an unfamiliar course) just as important to subsequent understanding of what is perceived as the processing of sensory stimuli.

Gibson's ideas about the importance of orientation led him to question the mind-body dualism of behaviorists and cognitivists , which dualismassumes the mind is a mechanical device or a computer and is therefore separable from mental phenomena (see 2.1, 7.2). Essentially, Gibson converted this ontological dualism into a useful methodological distinction:

> The aim of a perceptual experiment was no longer to ascertain what hypothetical processes converted inadequate inputs into percepts, but rather what stimulus variables specified what perceptions (J. J. Gibson, 1979, p. 25).

This methodological innovation regarding stimulus variables led Gibson to the

> . . . novel distinction between *literal* and *schematic perception*. When psychophysical experiments are arranged so that a subject "will make the best observations of which he is capable," perception is usually accurate and veridical, yielding what Gibson called the literal visual world. When one's experimental method involves "impoverished, ambiguous, or equivocal stimulation" with constraints on observation, such as brief exposure time, one obtains schematic perception of the visual world. Schematic perception is often inaccurate and erroneous, but, Gibson insisted, "the alterations and distortions might have been eliminated if the conditions of observation had been different" (Gibson, 1950, p. 217). The effects of perceptual habits and social custom on perceiving were assimilated by Gibson to the concept of schematic perception: The origin of perceptual error lies, not in mistaken processes of imagination, but in a mixture of inadequate stimulus conditions and the human tendency to adopt the customs of the group, even when they are less than fully adaptive (Reed, 1988, pp. 184-185).

Perhaps Gibson's (1979) most serious doubt about information-processing models was that such models focus on the organism's *analysis* of stimulus information at the expense of the organism's activities in *detecting and selecting* stimulus information. Thus, information-processing models tend to minimize the *context* of stimuli—their locality, temporality, and relatedness to other factors in the environment and in the organism.

8.6.1 Direct Perception, Context Sensitivity, and Mechanicalism

> The modern theory of automata based on computers. . . has the virtue of rejecting mentalism, but it is still preoccupied with the brain instead of the whole observer in his environment. Its approach is not ecological. The metaphor of

inputs, storage, and consulting of memory still lingers on. No computer has yet been designed which could learn about the *affordances* of its surroundings (J. J. Gibson, 1974/1982, p. 373).

Despite significant improvements in sensor and computing technologies, artificial-intelligence (AI) systems have been unable to emulate everyday tasks performed by animals and people, because AI technologies lack sufficient means for selecting and encoding contextual and situational variables (Winograd & Flores, 1986) and because artificial intelligence is not embodied (Johnson, 1987). As McCabe (1986) notes, " 'Context sensitivity' is the bane of all associationistic models" (p. 26).

In the process of reinventing the concept of retinal imagery that underlies his radical theoretical postulates concerning perception, Gibson (1966) implicitly relied on the context and situatedness of ambulatory vision. In his empirical research, he paid particular attention to the boundary conditions that affect and constrain visual perception in everyday living. This investigatory focus led Gibson to findings that he could not explain within the paradigms of the positivist tradition that convention had imposed on his discipline. Thus, Gibson was forced to rethink much of what psychologists had previously supposed about perception and to propose a new approach as well as new theoretical concepts and definitions.

The problem is that positivism relies almost exclusively on the traditional physicist's characterization of reality as matter in motion in a space-time continuum. This "mechanicalism" of Newtonian physics and engineering is allied with sensationalism, a set of assumptions permeating philosophy, psychology, and physiology since the modern era. Roughly speaking, sensationalism maintains that only that which comes through the senses can serve as the basis for objective scientific knowledge. Sensations, however, as Gibson (1966) consistently argued, are not specific to the environment: They are specific to sensory receptors. Thus, sensations are *internal states* that cannot be used to ensure the objectivity of mechanistic descriptions.

Conventional psychology relies on sensationalism and mechanicalism to treat perception as a mental process applied to sensory inputs from the real world. This treatment of perception, however, fails to bridge the gap between (a) incomplete data about limited physical properties such as location, color, texture, and form, and (b) the wider, more meaningful "ecological awareness" characterized by perception of opportunities for action.

The grand irony of the Cartesian tradition in psychology is that it forces on proponents of the mechanistic schools of thought concepts from the mentalist tradition, and vice versa. Recently this Cartesianism has cloaked itself in the computer metaphor of information processing; nonetheless, many of the most prominent neuroscientists of this century have been forced by their mechanistic account of perception into an outright mind-body dualism. What has been left out of the picture altogether in 20th-century psychology, as

Gibson makes clear, is the active self observing its surroundings (Reed, 1988, p. 201).

Ecological psychologists employ "geodesics" (Kugler, Shaw, Vincente & Kinsella-Shaw, 1991, p. 414) to complement mechanistic systems of description based on Cartesian metrics. Examples of geodesics are least work, least time, least distance, least action, and least resistance. Ecological psychology conceives of these action pathways as "streamlines" through the organism's niche structure and environmental layout rather than simple traversals of Cartesian space.

Geodesics are constrained by factors such as gravity, vectors associated with the arc of an organism's appendages or sensory organs, and energy available for exertion. For a simple example of geodesics, consider how cowpaths are created by animals avoiding unnecessary ascents and descents on an undulating landscape: In addition to serving as records of travel through Cartesian space, the paths reflect cow energy expenditure and the ability of the cows to detect constraints imposed by gravity.

Geodesics are essentially a thermodynamic construct, and as such they can be applied to human activity in media environments. Optimal perceiving and acting in mediated environments does not necessarily follow boxes, frames, or other contrivances based on arbitrary grids imposed in the Cartesian tradition—pages, tables, rules, keyboards, screens, and the like. True optimums for action and perception must be measured in terms of cognitive and corporal ergonomics rather than the metrical efficacy assumed by a one-grid-fits-all-organisms approach. Designing keyboards to conform to a grid may simplify circuitry and manufacture, but such keyboards may strain the human wrist.

Media designers and researchers can use geodesic analysis to study how users interact with print and computer-based media by, for example, tracking the extent to which users recognize opportunities for action afforded by features such as headers, indexes, icons, "hot buttons," and modal dialog boxes. In terms of thermodynamic efficiency, skilled use of shortcuts and navigational aids to wend one's way through a media environment is similar to the challenge faced by the cows: What pathway of action yields the desired result with the least expenditure of energy?

8.6.2 Situation and Selectivity

In place of a sensation-based theory of perception, Gibson (1974/1982) proposed a theory based on situations and selectivity: Perception entails the detecting of information, not the having of sensations. Rather than assuming a hypothetical perceiver, Gibson opted for a real, everyday perceiver, with all the possibilities and limitations implied by the ordinary. He situated this perceiver in an environment populated by ordinary, everyday people, living organisms, and natural as well as artificial affordances, rather than imagining the perceiver in an objectively accessible world defined and measured by conventional, mechanistic physics.

Gibson also appropriated familiar terms to create a new ecological vocabulary designed to complement the lexicon of physics (Reed, 1988):

1. Substances, surfaces, and media as complements for matter
2. Persistence and change as complements for space and time
3. Locomotion as a complement for motion
4. Situatedness in a niche as a complement for location in space and time

Gibson's (1979) development of ecological theory began with studies of the properties of surfaces. He identified several issues that have since proved important to designers of virtual realities and simulations.

> First, a surface is not *discrete* like a detached object, and thus surfaces are not denumerable. Instead, a surface is nested within superordinate surfaces. Second, a surface does not have a *location* as an object does, a locus in space. Instead, it is part of what I call the environmental *layout*; it is situated relative to the other surfaces of the habitat underlaid by the ground, the surface of support (J. J. Gibson, 1979, p. 351).

8.6.3 Alternatives to Traditional Empiricism

The idea of environmental layouts serves as a useful example of the tension between the mechanistic approach and the ecological approach. "Environmental layout" reflects a persistent concern expressed in the writings of ecological psychologists: The very successful systems of formal description and analysis employed by classical physics have been misapplied in describing the fields of action and perception available to organisms. There is little doubt that descriptions derived from classical physics are well suited to disciplines such as mechanical engineering and even biomechanics. Nevertheless, if we infer from thermodynamic principles that opportunities for action are ultimately determined by complexity of organization rather than space and time per se (see earlier discussion), then the usefulness of space-time grid maps for analyzing and explaining organic behavior is only partial. More useful are environmental layout maps that indicate opportunities and pathways for action and perception.

Critics such as Fodor and Pylyshyn (1981) have questioned the empirical foundations of ecological psychology, demanding that its new lexicon be verified within the conventions of laboratory-bound experimentalism. Yet, ecological psychologists such as Koffka (1935), Johansson (1950), Lashly (1951), McCabe (1986), and Turvey, Shaw, Reed, and Mace (1981) share with field biologists and anthropologists doubts about excessive reliance on laboratory experiments for gathering data relevant to the study of complex interactions between organisms and their environments.

Experimental psychologists often seem to feel that context effects are to be controlled and eliminated from an experiment if at all possible. This, we would argue, is a mistake. One can indeed suggest that some of the most serious conceptual errors in the history of psychology—errors that misled researchers for decades—began with naive attempts to remove phenomena from their natural contexts. We would argue rather that context effects are impossible to eliminate and that we should not wish to eliminate them totally, but only to study them. There is no zero point in the flow of contexts. They are not incidental phenomena that confound our careful experiments: They are *quintessential* in psychology. There is no experience without context (Barrs, 1988, p. 176).

Like many other life scientists, Gibson (1979) had to defend his ideas against some fairly vociferous opponents. Many of his defenses were polemical, and in our reading of his work we have learned to tolerate an imprecision in terminology and syntax that unfortunately left his ideas and arguments open to misunderstanding and marginal criticism. Without, then, either defending or exonerating his rhetoric, we offer our summary of Gibson's views on empiricism:

1. Empiricism can be distinguished from objectivism.
2. Eschewing objectivist theories of description need not imply abandonment of the scientific method, only rejection of unwarranted extensions in which the observations of a hypothetical observer are elevated to the status of a "God's-eye view" (Putnam, 1981).
3. The risks of misunderstanding inherent in cultural relativism, objectivism, and scientism can be ameliorated if reports of empirical observations are taken as instructions to others about how to replicate or verify findings and experiences rather than as veridical descriptions of reality (Winograd & Flores, 1986). We would add that when the authenticity of mediated representations is doubtful, the most ethical policy is to ensure that users can obtain instructions about how to replicate or verify represented objects and events. Lacking such instructions, users should be able to access information about the provenance of the representations.

8.7 INDIRECT PERCEPTION, MEDIATED PERCEPTION, AND DISTRIBUTED COGNITION

> Our species has invented various aids to perception, ways of improving, enhancing, or extending the pickup of information. The natural techniques of observation are supplemented by artificial techniques, *using tools for perceiving by analogy with tools for performing* (J. J. Gibson, 1977/1982, p. 290; emphasis added).

If the great advantage that direct perception confers on organisms lies in an improved ability to detect affordances, a secondary benefit is that direct perception underlies "all less direct kinds of apprehension or cognition" (J. J. Gibson, 1977/1982, p. 289). Although he never developed a theory of indirect perception, Gibson clearly considered it an important topic, and he recognized degrees of directness and indirectness. His writing on this issue, which consists mostly of unpublished notes, is inconsistent—as if he were still vacillating or cogitating about the idea.

Indirect perception is assisted perception: "the pickup of the invariant in stimulation after continued observation" (J. J. Gibson, 1979, p. 250). "The child who sees directly whether or not he can jump a ditch is aware of something more basic than is the child who has learned to say how wide it is in feet or meters" (J. J. Gibson, 1977/1982, p. 251).

Reed (1988, p. 315) points out that Gibson's preliminary efforts to distinguish direct and indirect forms of perception assumed that (a) ambient energy arrays within the environment (e.g., air pressure, light, gravity) provide the information that specifies affordance properties, and (b) the availability of these arrays has shaped the evolution of perceptual systems. Gibson thought that the exploratory actions of an organism engaged in perceiving energy arrays evidences the organism's "awareness" that stimulus information specifies affordance properties relevant to the requirements of the organism's niche.

On the other hand, Gibson recognized that instruments, pictures (see 26.2.3), and language can also be used to select, modify, and represent energy arrays.

> Knowledge that has been put into words or, similarly, into numbers can be said to be *explicit*. It is rather different from the knowledge got by direct perception, by the simpler instruments, and by pictures. Not all information about the world can be put into words and numbers. Sometimes there are no words for what can be seen and captured in a picture. Is this because no verbal description is possible, or only because it has not yet been formulated? (J. J. Gibson, 1977/1982, p. 291).

Gibson (1977/1982) argued that symbols (i.e., *notational symbols* in Goodman's 1976 sense) are quite different from pictures and other visual arrays. Gibson believed that symbols constitute perhaps the most extreme form of indirect perception because:

> . . . their meanings are attached by association. The meaning of an alphanumeric character or a combination of them fades away with prolonged visual fixation, unlike the meaning of a substance, surface, place, etc. . . . They make items that are unconnected with the rest of the world. Letters can stand for nonsense syllables (but there is no such thing as a nonsense place or a nonsense event) (p. 293).

Gibson, like other ecological psychologists, recognized the intellectual and constructive nature of indirect perception and, particularly, the important role that indirect perception plays in the creation and use of language.

> Perceiving helps talking, and talking fixes the gains of perceiving. It is true that the adult who talks to a child can educate his attention to certain differences instead of others. It is true that when a child talks to himself he may enhance the tuning of his perception to certain differences rather than others. The range of possible discriminations is unlimited. Selection is inevitable. But this does not imply that the verbal fixing of information distorts the perception of the world. The . . . observer can always observe more properties than he can describe (J. J. Gibson, 1966, p. 282).

We argued earlier that human beings and other organisms benefit from thermodynamic leverage when they can off-load information storage and processing to nonbiological systems. Such off-loading requires improved perception—more reliable access to external information. It is not always easy, however, to estimate the costs associated with, respectively, internal representation and external representation, because the information is allocated dynamically. For example, after repeatedly forgetting some information item, one might decide to write it down (external, mediated representation) or, alternatively, to make a deliberate effort to memorize it (internal representation). Wise computer designers and users similarly attempt to optimize storage and processing of information between *internal* mechanisms (fast, but energy-consuming and volatile CPUs and RAMs) and *external* media (slow but energy efficient and stable CD-ROMs and backup tapes).

Where human beings are concerned, such dynamic allocation of storage and processing can be modeled as *distributed cognitive tasks*, defined by Zhang and Norman (1994) as "tasks that require the processing of information across the internal mind and the external environment" (p. 88). Zhang and Norman conceive of a *distributed representation* as a set of representations with (a) *internal* members, such as schemas, mental images, or propositions, and (b) *external* members such as physical symbols and external rules or constraints embedded in physical configurations. *Representations* are abstract structures with referents to the represented world.

Zhang and Norman (1994) propose a theoretical framework in which internal representations and external representations form a "distributed representational space" that represents the abstract structures and properties of the task in "abstract task space" (p. 90). They developed this framework to support rigorous and formal analysis of distributed cognitive tasks and to assist their investigations of "representational effects [in which] different isomorphic representations of a common formal structure can cause dramatically different cognitive behaviors" (p. 88). Figure 8-2 freely adapts elements of the Zhang-Norman framework (1994, Fig. 1, p. 90) by substituting MIROS for "internal representational space" and by further dividing external representational space into media (media space) and realia (real space).

We do not propose in this chapter to define rigorously mutually exclusive categories for media and realia. There are many types of hybrids. Museums, for example, often integrate realia with explanatory diagrams and audio. Recursion is also a problem: A portrait of George Washington is of interest as a physical artifact and also as a mediated representation of a real person; a spreadsheet program may include representations of itself in on-line multimedia tutorials. Our modification of the Zhang-Norman framework distinguishes real space from media space nevertheless, because there are often considerable differences between the affordance properties of realia and the affordance properties of media.

Our adaptation of the Zhang-Norman model does not assume that corresponding elements in media space, real

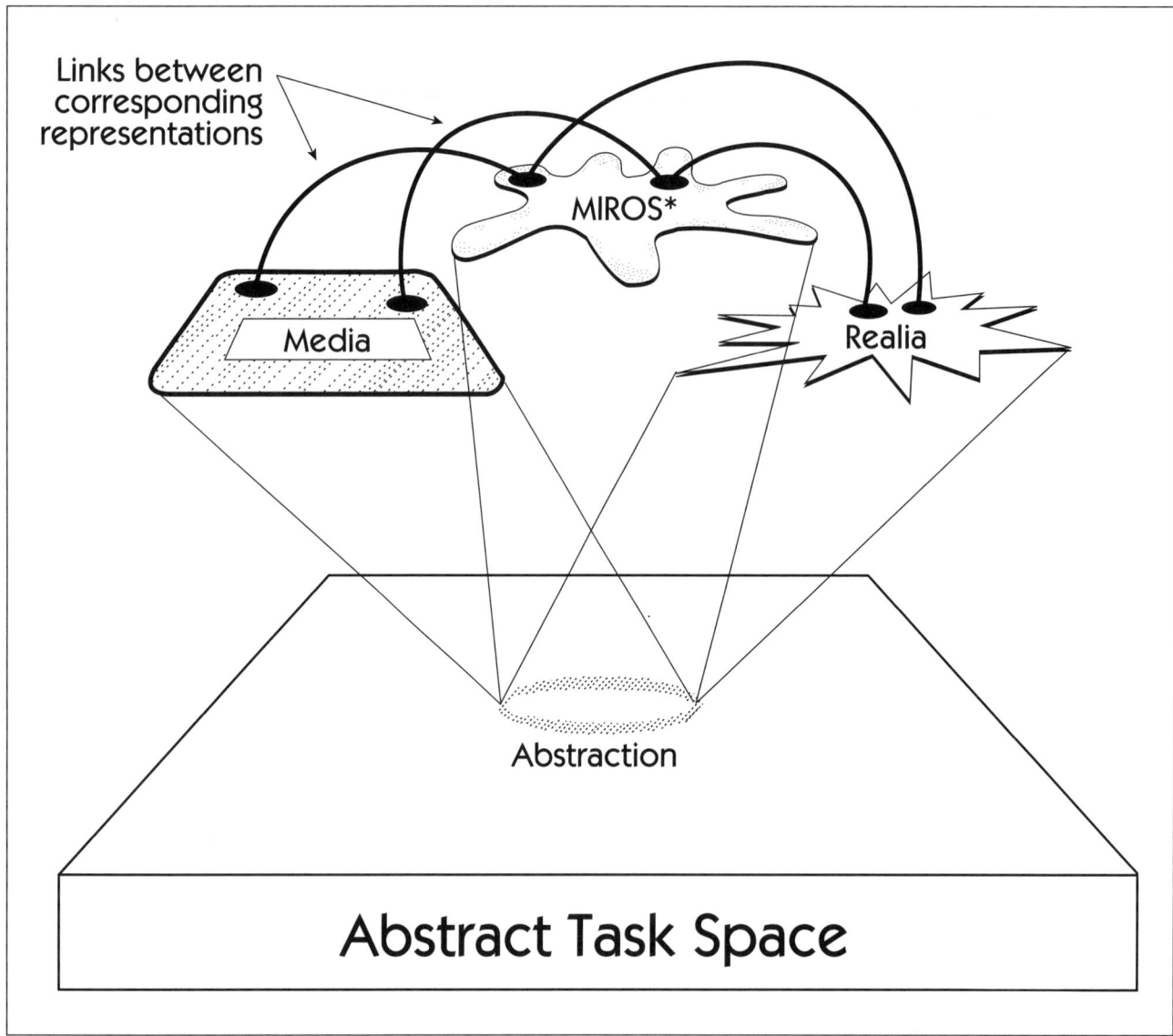

Figure 8-2. A framework for distributing cognition among media, realia, and mental-internal representations of situations (MIROS). Freely adapted from Zhang and Norman (1994, p. 90), this framework subdivides external representational space into *media space* (media) and *real space* (realia). The framework does not assume that corresponding elements in the three spaces will necessarily be isomorphic in function or structure. On the contrary, there are usually profound differences.

space, and internal representational space will necessarily be isomorphic in function or structure. On the contrary, there are often profound differences between the way corresponding information is structured in each space. Furthermore, as we argued earlier, MIROS vary in completeness and complexity. As Zhang and Norman (1994) demonstrated in their study of subjects attempting to solve the Tower of Hanoi problem, incongruent internal and external representations can interfere with task performance if critical aspects of the task structure are dependent on such congruence.

Whatever the degree of correspondences between the structures of media, MIROS, and realia, external representations allow individuals to distribute some of the burden of storing and processing information to nonbiological sys-

tems—thus presumably improving thermodynamic efficiency. A key to intelligent interaction with a medium is to know how to optimize this distribution, to know when to manipulate a device, when to look something up (or write something down), and when to keep something in mind.

Of course media and realia can also support construction of MIROS that function more or less independently of interactions with external representational space. Salomon (1979, p. 234) used the term *supplantation* to refer to internalization of external representations as when the arithmetic operations of an abacus are internalized by expert abacus users. Salomon saw such learning by observation, not as a simple act of imitation or copying but as a process of elaboration involving recoding and mastery of constituent acts.

Distributed cognition points the way to the design of more efficient systems for supporting learning and performance. Yet the new representational systems offered by emergent computer and telecommunications technologies will challenge media researchers and designers to develop better models for determining which aspects of a given situation are best allocated to media or realia, and which are best allocated to MIROS.

8.8 AN ECOLOGICAL APPROACH TO UNDERSTANDING MEDIA

As mediated perception extends and substitutes for direct perception, so do the affordance properties of mediated environments extend and substitute for the affordance properties of real environments. End users therefore must be guided by implicit conventions or explicit instructions that help them to select or construct MIROS that can substitute for the missing affordances.

8.8.1 Analogs for Acting

Every media technology from book to video to computer simulation imposes profound constraints on representation of real or imaginary worlds and requires trade-offs as to which aspects of a world will be represented.

A topographical map, for instance, represents three-dimensional land forms on a two-dimensional surface. Such maps are constructed through electromechanical processes, aided by human interpreters, in which numerous aerial photos taken from different angles are reconciled to yield a single image. This process captures some of the normal affordance properties available to the aerial observer—shadings, textures, angles, and occlusions, for instance—as well as the ways the values for these properties change in response to observer movement. The original affordance information—the climbability and walkability of the terrain, for example—is re-presented as a flat image that indicates elevation through contour intervals and ground cover or other features through color coding. Much of the information detected by the aerial observer is thus available vicariously to map viewers, *provided* that the viewers can use the affordances of the map—contours, color coding, legends, grids—in concert with their mental models of map viewing to imagine the affordances of the actual terrain. Thus,

Media + MIROS ≈ Realia

Many activities of everyday living are generally intuitive and relatively automatic because perceived affordances can be immediately exploited with minimal mental effort and because consequences can be immediately perceived. This tight linkage of action and perception in real time characterizes the praxis that enables much unschooled learning.

The collapsed affordance structures of many mediated environments, however, transform the means by which

users can exercise their powers of perception, mobility, and agency: Scanning a photo is not the same as scanning a scene, although ecological psychologists will argue that much is similar about the two acts. The lack of certain affordances in mediated representations may even promote reflection by reducing cognitive load: Viewing a scene vicariously through a photo frees one of the need to monitor or respond to immediate events: A topographical map can be read at leisure; there is no need to attend to the immediate passage of land forms under the reconnaissance airplane.

8.8.2 The Importance of Being There (or Not)

Gibson's (1977/1982) partial insights about visual displays remind us that, like other apes, human beings have well-developed faculties for managing information about objects and spaces when that information is derived through locomotor and stereoscopic functions.

8.8.2.1. Depiction. Pictorial representations of complex environments often pose extreme problems for writers of captions or other information about spatial relations. Picture captions also impose on readers task-irrelevant cognitive-processing burdens such as referencing figures in the text by cited numbers or hunting through the text of the caption to find relevant descriptions. Inspection of a typical illustration and its caption from *Gray's Anatomy* (Gray, 1930, p. 334) makes it clear that, lacking information about the hypothetical viewpoint of the artist, and lacking information about the more subtle relationships between the components depicted in the drawing, viewers will be unable to construct a suitable MIROS (Mental-Internal Representation of Situations) to complement the mediated representations (see Fig. 8.3).

Fortunately, anatomists have developed a rich lexicon for describing spatial relationships between viewers of an illustration and the objects portrayed by the illustration. For example, the text description matched to the preceding figure from *Gray's* reads:

> *The Ligamentum Teres Femoris*—The ligamentum teres femoris is a triangular, somewhat flattened band implanted by its apex into the antero-superior part of the fovea capitis femoris; its base is attached by two bands, one into either side of the acetabular notch, and between these bony attachments it blends with the transverse ligament. It is ensheathed by the synovial membrane, and varies greatly in strength in different subjects; occasionally only the synovial fold exists, and in rare cases even this is absent (p. 334).

Using only propositions to tell people about how to construct a MIROS for a three-dimensional structure may be a misappropriation of cognitive resources if better means are feasible—a physical or pictorial model, for instance. The issue is partly a matter of instructional intent: Designers of an anatomy course might decide to use, say, animated 3-D renderings of a situation—with orienting zooms and pans—to teach gross structure. If the goal is to teach spatial nomenclature as preparation for dissection through a spatial

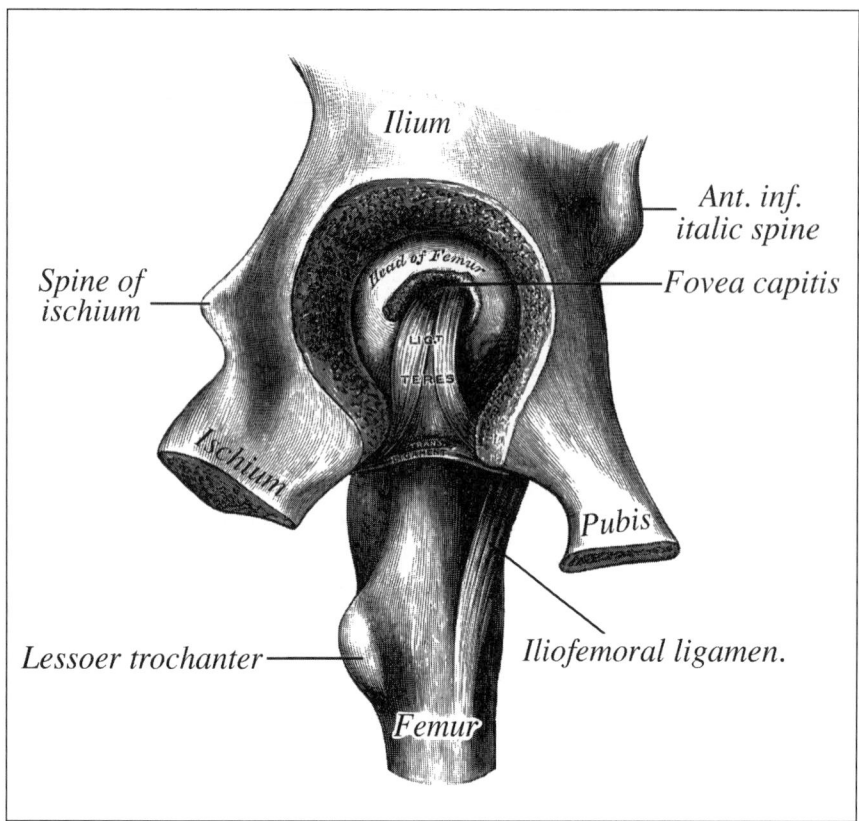

Figure 8-3.   A drawing from *Gray's Anatomy* (Gray, 1930, p. 334).

structure, however, the designers might select a strategy in which there is less emphasis on explicit visual representation of operations and more emphasis on narration. The two approaches are not mutually exclusive.

8.8.2.2. Photography.   Consider the camera as a tool for capturing photographic images: A photograph excludes large quantities of information that would have been available to bystanders at the scene who could have exercised their powers of exploratory action, ranging from gross-motor movements to tiny adjustments in eye lenses. In capturing the image, the photographer chooses to take the picture from a single viewpoint in space and time—a viewpoint that is but one of a number of possible viewpoints that are in principle infinite.

Even though a subsequent user of the photograph might be able to manipulate the position and orientation of the photo itself, take measurements of the objects as they are depicted, and engage in selective visual exploration, such exploration is an imperfect surrogate for ambulatory perception at the original scene. Both the user's perception of the depictions in photographs and the user's interpretation of these depictions require prior knowledge about the conventions of photographic culture as well as knowledge of the ways in which photography distorts situational factors such as orientation, distance, texture, hue, contrast, and shadows. The user's ability to perceive and interpret the photo may be enhanced if he or she can integrate information in the photo with adjunct verbal information such as captions, scales, and dates that, however inadequately,

support development of MIROS complementary to the actual situation.

8.8.2.3. Cinematography.   Although cinematography can record the transformation of imagery that results from camera movement through multiple viewpoints, cinematographs, like photographs, evoke mediated perceptions in the end user that are fundamentally decoupled from the kind of action that would have been possible in the actual situation. In other words, attention is partially decoupled from intention: The viewer can attend to changes in imagery but is unable to effect changes through exploratory action. Several studies have shown, in fact, that interfering with proprioception and ambulation retards adaptation by mammalian visual systems. For example, when experimenters require human subjects to view their surroundings through an inverting prism apparatus, the subjects adapt to the upside-down imagery after several weeks, achieving a high degree of functionality and reporting that their vision seems "normal" again (Rock, 1984). This adaptation does not occur, however, if the experimenters restrict the subjects' tactile and proprioceptive experience or their ability to engage in self-controlled locomotion.

In a study more directly related to use of media in education and training, Baggett (1983) found that subjects who were denied an opportunity to explore the parts of a model helicopter were less effective at a parts assembly task than subjects who explored the parts in advance, even though both types of subjects saw a videotape depicting the assembly process before performing the task.

Conventional cinematography substitutes dynamism for dimensionality by recording the way perspective views of objects transform in response to camera movements, collocating information on a single plane. Cinematic dynamism provides information about perspective, which always implies a single point of view or movement along a path. More importantly, cinema portrays invariant structure, the environment of many observers,

> through such devices as multiple points of view, glimpses of the surrounding of a scene (establishing shots). . . . It is important in editing a film to splice sequences in such a way that this invariant information is not destroyed by the sequence. For example, one must avoid splicing together two views of the same scene taken from opposite parts of the layout, for this would make the left side of the first sequence suddenly transform—without any information about the observer's path—into the right side. Ecological optics, with its emphasis on flow, might very well provide a scientific basis for the empirical, trial-and-error practices of film editing (Reed, 1988, p. 291).

8.8.3 Collapsing Multivariate Data

The problems of cinematography reflect the central challenge for authors and designers of most media products: How to collapse multivariate data into flat, two-dimensional displays while optimizing the ability of the end user to exploit the affordances of the displays.

As Tufte explains in *Envisioning Information* (1992), techniques for collapsing multivariate data involve constraints as well as opportunities. On the one hand,

> . . . nearly every escape from flatland demands extensive compromise, trading off one virtue against another; the literature consists of partial, arbitrary, and particularistic solutions; and neither clever idiosyncratic nor conventionally adopted designs solve the inherent general difficulties of dimensional compression. Even our language, like our paper, often lacks immediate capacity to communicate a sense of dimensional complexity. Paul Klee wrote to this point: "It is not easy to arrive at a conception of a whole which is constructed from parts belonging to different dimensions. And not only nature, but also art, her transformed image is such a whole. . . . For with such a medium of expression, we lack the means of discussing in its constituent parts an image which possesses simultaneously a number of dimensions" (p. 15).

On the other hand, as Tufte richly illustrates, the trade-offs necessary to successful compression of a data set with four or five variables, such as a map with an integrated train schedule, can work to the end user's advantage if the sacrificed data would have been confusing or superfluous.

8.8.4 Media and MIROS

> To describe the evolutions or the dances of these gods, their juxtapositions and their advances, to tell which came into line and which in opposition, to describe all this with-

out visual models would be labor spent in vain.—Plato, *The Timaeus*

Regardless of the medium and whether its representational constraints affect spatial and temporal dimensions or other properties such as form, color, and texture, authors of mediated representations must always sacrifice options for exploratory action that would have been available to unimpeded observers or actors in the represented situation. Media cannot represent realia in all their repleteness. Therefore, what is critical is this: that enough information be provided so that users can construct useful actionable mental models according to their needs and goals.

The short film *Powers of Ten* (C. Eames & R. Eames, 1977/1986) offers another neatly constrained example of language as an aid to interpreting mediated representations. Created by the office of Charles and Ray Eames to help viewers grasp "the relative size of things in the universe," *Powers of Ten* opens with a viewpoint somewhere in the dark void of intergalactic space, initiating a trip that ends in the nucleus of a carbon atom, $9\frac{1}{2}$ minutes later in Chicago.

Such a visual experience would be meaningless for most viewers without an audio narration about how to interpret the rapidly changing imagery—which includes diverse depictions ranging from galaxies, to the solar system, to Lake Superior, to a cell nucleus. The book version of *Powers of Ten* (Philip Morrison & Phylis Morrison, 1982) displays 42 frames from the film, supplemented by elaborative text and supplementary photos. The authors use a set of "rules" to describe the film's representation of situations, including propositions such as:

Rule 1. The traveler moves along a straight line, never leaving it.

Rule 2. One end of that line lies in the darkness of outermost space, while the other is on the Earth in Chicago, within a carbon atom beneath the skin of a man asleep in the sun.

Rule 3. Each square picture along the journey shows the view one would see looking toward the carbon atom's core, views that would encompass wider and wider scenes as the traveler moves further away. Because the journey is along a straight line, every picture contains all the pictures that are between it and the nucleus of the carbon atom. . . .

Rule 4. Although the scenes are all viewed from one direction, the traveler may move in either direction, going inward toward the carbon atom or outward toward the galaxies. . . .

Rule 5. The rule for the distance between viewpoints [is that]. . . each step is *multiplied* by a fixed number to produce the size of the next step: The traveler can take small, atom-sized steps near the atom, giant steps across Chicago, and planet-, star-, and galaxy-sized steps within their own realms (pp. 108–10).

The Morrison rules might be taken as an invitation to propositional reasoning. Yet the rules can also be usefully construed as instructions for constructing a MIROS that complements and partially overlaps the work of representation carried out by the film. Rule 2, for example, provides a framework for the reader to imagine moving back and forth on the straight line connecting the starting point (outermost space) and ending point (carbon nucleus), thus substituting for the action of the imaginary camera dollying across outer and finally inner space. Rule 3 describes the way in which each square picture encompasses a wider or narrower scene.

Rules 2 and 3 can also be directly perceived in the film itself by attending to the symmetricalness of image flow as various objects and structures stream from a fixed center point and move at equal rates toward the edge of the visual field. The film also indicates movement by depicting changes in the texture gradients of star fields and other structures. Such cues to both movement and direction epitomize the appropriation by filmmakers and other media producers of visual processing capabilities that are widespread among vertebrates, and as common among human beings as a jog on a forest trail or a drive down a two-lane highway.

What cannot be obtained through direct perception from either the film or the photos, however, is information indicating deceleration of the hypothetical camera as it dollys towards Earth. Rule 5, which concerns the logarithm governing the speed of motion, cannot be perceived directly because (a) the camera motion simulates a second-order derivative (deceleration rather than speed), and (b) the objects flowing past the camera are largely unfamiliar in everyday life and therefore have little value as scalars.

8.9 MEDIA AS ARENAS FOR UNIFIED PERCEPTION AND ACTION

The trend towards evermore rapid and extensive externalization of cognitive functions in nonbiological media leaves us paradoxically as creatures with an ancient and largely fixed core of perception-action modalities surrounded by rapidly fluctuating and increasingly powerful technological augmentation frameworks. Thus, whether emergent media technologies serve human beings well depends on the extent to which they honor ancient human capabilities for perceiving and acting, capabilities that are grounded in the fundamental ecological necessities of long ago.

8.9.1 Transformation and Alienation

While glib marketers of computer-based media tantalize us with vast fields of electronic action and apparently unlimited degrees of freedom, skeptics (W. Gibson, 1984; Mander, 1978; McKibbin, 1989) have served up warnings of isolation, manipulation, and diminished authenticity that can be traced back through McLuhan (1965) to Rousseau's (1764/1911) classic treatise on alienation from nature.

Much public discussion of the limitations and negative effects of so-called *passive media* such as television implic-

itly acknowledges both the epistemological and moral dimensions of mediated experience. For example, the hope that multimedia technology will redress the problems of an obese couch-potato nation that mindlessly surfs television channels in search of sex and violence is partly based on the assumption that somehow interactivity will empower viewers with more choices and promote a greater awareness and understanding of nature and culture. Yet what is interactivity and how do the ways we interact with media model the ways we interact with nature or culture? To begin to answer such questions we need to examine the relationship between perception and action—both in real worlds and in the artificial worlds represented by media systems and products.

The hope of human history has often been that technological augmentation would make us into gods or angels, or at least make us superior to enemies and aliens. Media technologies and the cognitive artifacts associated with them have played a special role in this regard by offering the seductive possibility of transformation: more than mere augmentation, a permanent acquisition of special knowledge and experience through recorded sounds and images. Yet receiving the word or beholding a revelation, whether real or artifactual, without active and appropriate participation risks distorted understanding and resultant alienation. Recognition of such risks underlay the prohibition of graven images that has figured strongly in Judaic, Islamic, and Bhuddist religious traditions.

In Christianity, doubts about religious imagery peaked in the eighth century with the radical proscriptions of the iconoclasts, who wanted to eliminate all religious depictions as demonic; such doubts helped to dampen Western artistic exploration until the Renaissance.

For human beings and all organisms, integration of action with perception is a necessary but not sufficient condition for living well. "Perception is the mechanism that functions to inform the actor of the means the environment affords for realizing the actor's goals" (Turvey, Shaw, Reed & Mace, 1982, p. 378). Perceptual faculties languish and degrade when they are decoupled from opportunities for action. Separated from action, perception cannot serve as a basis for formulating hypotheses and principles, for testing models and theories, for choosing alternatives, or for exploring consequences.

Indeed, Eleanor Gibson (1994) has reviewed a growing body of evidence that strongly suggests that without opportunities for action, or appropriate substitutes for action, perception does not develop at all or takes on wildly distorted forms. Behavioral capabilities likewise languish and degrade when they are decoupled from perception. "Action is the mechanism that functions to select the means by which goals of the actor may be effected" (Turvey, Shaw, Reed & Mace, 1982, p. 378). Deprived of information concerning opportunities for action, perception alone results in ritualistic performance unrelated to any real task and hence any realizable goal.

It is worth noting in this context that *sin* in the original Christian sense of the word meant *to miss the mark*, implying a failure that cannot be assigned to either action or perception alone. A similar understanding of the incompleteness of perception isolated from action can be found in other traditions, notably Zen (see, for example, Herrigel's 1953 classic *Zen and the Art of Archery*). Many meditative disciplines teach integration of perception and action by training students to unify attention (perception) and intention (action), using exercises such as "following one's breathing."

8.9.2 Caves and Consciousness

We need to move from our exclusive concern with the logic of processing, or reason, to the logic of perception. Perception is the basis of wisdom. For 24 centuries we have put all our intellectual effort into the logic of reason rather than the logic of perception. Yet in the conduct of human affairs perception is far more important. Why have we made this mistake? We might have believed that perception did not really matter and could in the end be controlled by logic and reason. We did not like the vagueness, subjectivity, and variability of perception and sought refuge in the solid absolutes of truth and logic. To some extent the Greeks created logic to make sense of perception. We were content to leave perception to the world of art (drama, poetry, painting, music, dance) while reason got on with its own business in science, mathematics, economics, and government. We have never understood perception. Perceptual truth is different from constructed truth. —Edward de Bono, *I am right—You are wrong: From rock logic to water logic* (1991, p. 42).

Among the ancient perplexities associated with the human condition, the relationship between perception, action, and environment has endured even as technical context and consciousness have continued to evolve. In the annals of Western civilization, Plato's Allegory of the Cave (Plato, *The Republic*) remains one of the most elegant and compelling treatments of the central issues. Chained and therefore unable to move, his cave-dwelling prisoners came to perceive shadows cast on the walls by firelight as real beings rather than phantasms. Why? Plato argues that this profound misperception resulted from external as well as internal conditions. First, consider the external conditions: If we take the liberty of imagining that the prisoners were rigidly bound and deprived of ambulatory vision, then they were probably (a) denied the cues of motion parallax that might have indicated the two-dimensionality of the shadows; (b) suffering from degraded stereopsis and texture recognition due to lighting conditions; and (c) incapacitated in their ability to investigate the source of illumination or its relationship to the props that were casting the shadows that captured their imagination.

Many readers of Plato's allegory have been tempted to assume that they would not personally be fooled in such a situation, leading us to consider the internal conditions: With a rudimentary knowledge of optics and common-sense understanding of caves, it might have been possible for the prisoners to entertain plausible alternatives to their belief that the shadows were real beings. For the prisoners

to entertain such an alternative, however, would have required that they be able to construct a model of the situation that would be "runnable," that is, serve as an internal analog for the physical actions of inspecting the layout of the cave, the pathways of light, and so on. In our interpretation, what doomed the prisoners to misperception was not only that they were constrained from exploratory action but also that they were unable to integrate working mental models with what they saw.

Plato's allegory involves both epistemological and moral dimensions. Epistemology considers problems involved in representing knowledge and reality (knowing-perceiving), whereas moral philosophy considers problems involved in determining possible and appropriate action (knowing-acting). Plato reminds us that perceiving and acting are complementary and inseparable: The prisoners cannot perceive appropriately without acting appropriately, and they cannot act appropriately without perceiving appropriately.

Alan Kay (1991) summarizes our thoughts about this dilemma as it applies to contemporary education:

Up to now, the contexts that give meaning and limitation to our various knowledges have been all but invisible. To make contexts visible, make them objects of discourse, and make them explicitly reshapable and inventable. These are strong aspirations very much in harmony with the pressing needs and on-rushing changes of our own time. It is therefore the duty of a well-conceived environment for learning to be contentious and even disturbing, seek contrasts rather than absolutes, aim for quality over quantity, and acknowledge the need for will and effort (p. 140).

Who knows what Plato would say about the darkened cavelike structures we call *movie theaters* and *home entertainment centers*, where patrons watch projections cast upon a wall or screen, only dimly aware of the original or true mechanics of the events they perceive? Our ability to interpret the shadowy phantasms of modern cinema and television is constrained not only by collapsed affordances of cinematography—two-dimensional, fixed-pace sequencing of images—but also by the lack of affordances for exercising action and observing consequences. We also often lack the mental models that might allow us to work through in our minds alternatives that are not explored on the screen. Even when we possess such models, it is often impossible to "run" them, due to interference from the relentless parade of new stimuli and the unconscious inhibition that attends most movie watching: Reflect too much on what you observe and you will be left behind as the medium unfolds its representations at a predetermined pace.

8.10 RESTATEMENT OF THEMES IN THIS CHAPTER

Widespread metaphors that liken media to channels for conveying messages do not lend themselves well to explanations of how human beings interact with mediated representations. Nor can they entirely explain how mind and media interact with each other to generate complex and dynamic cognitive phenomena that neither mind nor media can alone support.

Thinking of media as channels for sending and receiving symbols has often led by extension to the conclusion that perception is a process of *reception* and that cognition is the processing of symbols and language-based propositions. However, many interactions of mind and media are not easily explained in terms of channels and symbols, because humans, like most organisms, understand their environments through exploratory action and active perception. Successful design of products and services for emergent media technologies will depend in part on the extent to which such products and services honor modalities of integrated action-perception grounded in the necessities of survival and reproduction and tuned to opportunities for action in ecological niches.

Ecological psychology assumes that thermodynamic laws govern the structure and function of living communities and that successful strategies for living must be in accord with these laws. An organism's thermodynamic efficiency is partly a function of the means by which the organism obtains information about its environment and the strategies by which it uses this information to influence or control energy and matter. Living communities generate "organized complexity" by leveraging relatively small amounts of information to influence or exploit larger flows of energy and matter. Information storage and processing in turn require energy and matter, and this requirement can be thought of metaphorically as a cost to organisms, or as an investment.

The most widespread and common systems for storing and processing information on this planet are based on DNA. Yet DNA-based information systems are fundamentally limited in capacity and rate of evolution. While nervous systems offer the advantage of greatly increased flexibility for storing and processing information about the environment, such systems also impose biological costs. Off-loading information storage and processing to systems that are external to the organism can reduce this cost.

From the standpoint of cognitive theory, the environment can be considered a generator of information about itself, and perception the means of obtaining this information. In general, natural selection appears to favor investment of resources by a species in systems for detecting, selecting, and perceiving information in the environment when the cost of obtaining such information is less than the cost of generating or obtaining equivalent information from sources internal to the organism. Investing resources in improved perception is a means of obtaining information about the environment while minimizing investment in biological mechanisms for internal information processing.

The most important information an organism can derive from perception is information about invariant or unchanging aspects of the environment, for example, gravitational fields. Invariants anchor perception and action by function-

ing as "knowns" in decision-making or problem-solving processes. Action-perception related to invariants is often highly automatic, and in human beings is typically processed unconsciously.

Natural selection tunes perceptual processes to affordances or opportunities for action associated with an organism's ecological niche or occupation. Since selection similarly tunes effectivities or capabilities for action to opportunities, perception in most organisms is strongly associated with action. Indeed, a fundamental tenet of ecological psychology is that divorcing the study of perception from the study of action leads to a distorted understanding of attentional and intentional processes in organisms. Although cybernetic models often treat the relationship between action and perception as cyclic, a more appropriate alternative in many cases is to treat this relationship as covariant or codeterminant.

Human evolution has been accompanied by an increasing reliance on external information storage and processing. Social routines and gestures probably allowed early human beings to "off-load" much of their individual information processing to external venues associated with group activity—sharing the work of cognition with artifacts as well as with other human beings. However, it seems unlikely that human beings used language in the form of high-speed articulate speech to externalize information until the last few hundred thousand years. External storage became even more stable and reliable with the advent of markings, glyphs, and alphabets.

Modern minds can be arguably characterized as much by their dependence on tools and artifacts as by any purely internal mental process. Indeed, it appears that thinking and reasoning in today's artifact- and media-rich societies are best viewed as emergent functions of distributed cognitive systems in which the work of information storage and processing is shared between realia, media, and Mental-Internal Representations of Situations (MIROS).

It seems reasonable, therefore, to assume that much everyday cognition and many important modalities of thought are governed not by purely internal mental models of the way the world works but rather by open models that require a constant flux of data about how action is related to perception. Much conventional thinking about media technolgies has been strongly influenced by traditions of empirical research that have divorced the study of perception from the study of action. These traditions treat perception as the processing of symbols and cognition as the analysis of propositions. Yet many emerging computer environments for learning, work, and play invoke modalities of action-perception in which dispositional and enactive properties of objects take precedence over the purely symbolic meaning of such objects. Typically, these environments offer opportunities for action in which users realize their intentions by manipulating objects rather than by constructing language-based commands. Some of the most powerful and effective strategies for using interactive media, however, employ mixed modalities in which language and symbol-based communication operate in concert with object-oriented manipulation.

Although older media formats such as print and cinematography do not support a high degree of object manipulation, these formats invoke human capacities for integrating perception and action by selectively substituting perception components *for* action components. Verbal descriptions, for example, can serve as surrogates for action by informing viewers of how and where photographic images were captured. By reducing the action component, photographs create opportunities for reflection and deliberation that may not have been available to observers at the original scene. In contrast, cinematographs substitute the dynamics of camera movement for the real or imaginary actions of observers. Such dynamism may suppress reflection and deliberation.

As we acknowledge media for their potential as arenas for action, as means for exploring the relation between acting and perceiving, researchers and designers will begin to address strategies for modulating and varying these opportunities in order to support specific educational purposes and functions. Yet only by respecting our fundamental evolutionary heritage as organisms whose cognitive capacities are grounded in ecological necessitycan we hope to build media environments that allow us to live well as human beings.

REFERENCES

Allen, B.S. (1991). Virtualities. *In* B. Branyan-Broadbent & R. K. Wood, eds. *Educational Media and Technology Yearbook 17,* pp. 47–53.

Baars, B.J. (1988). *A cognitive theory of consciousness.* Cambridge, England: Cambridge University Press.

Baggett, P. (1983). *Learning a procedure for multimedia instructions: the effects of films and practice* (Eric No. ED239598). Boulder, CO: Colorado University Institute of Cognitive Science.

Balzano, G.J. & McCabe, V. (1986). An ecological perspective on concepts and cognition. *In* V. McCabe & G.J. Balzano, eds. *Event cognition,* 133–58. Hillsdale, NJ: Erlbaum.

Bartlett, F.C. (1932). *Remembering.* Cambridge, England: Cambridge University Press.

Berk, L.E. (1994). Why children talk to themselves. *Scientific American 271*(5), 78–83.

Bruce, V. & Green, P. (1990). *Visual perception: physiology, psychology, and ecology,* 2d ed. Hillsdale, NJ: Erlbaum.

Bruner, J.S. & Olson, D.R. (1977–78). Symbols and texts as tools for the intellect. *Interchange 8,* 1–15.

Carroll, J.M. & Olson, D.R. (1988). Mental models in human-computer interaction. *In* M. Helander, ed. *Handbook of human-computer interaction.* Amsterdam: Elsevier.

Churchland, P.S. (1986). *Neurophilosophy: towards a unified theory of the mind-brain.* Cambridge, MA: MIT Press.

Clancey, W.J. (1993). Situated action: a neuropsychological interpretation. *Cognitive Science 17,* 87–116.

Clark, A. (1991). *Microcognition: philosophy, cognitive science, and parallel distributed processing.* Cambridge, MA: MIT Press.

Clark, R.E. (1983). Reconsidering research on learning from

media. *Review of Educational Research 53,* 445–59.

Collins, A., Brown, J.S. & Newman, S.E. (1989). Cognitive apprenticeship: teaching the crafts of reading, writing, and mathematics. *In* L.B. Resnick, ed. *Knowing, learning, and instruction: essays in honor of Robert Glaser,* 453–94. Hillsdale, NJ: Erlbaum.

Craik, K. (1943). *The nature of explanation.* Cambridge, England: Cambridge University Press.

Crutcher, K.A. (1986). Anatomical correlates of neuronal plasticity. *In* J.L. Martinez & R.P. Kesner, eds., *Learning and memory: A biological view.* New York: Academic.

Csikszentmihalyi, M. (1990). *Flow: the psychology of optimal experience.* New York: Harper Perennial.

De Bono, E. (1991). *I am right—you are wrong: from rock logic to water logic.* New York: Viking/Penguin.

di Sessa, A. (1983). Phenomenology and the evolution of intuition. *In* D. Gentner & A.L. Stevens, eds., *Mental models.* Hillsdale, NJ: Erlbaum.

— (1988). Knowledge in pieces. *In* G. Froman & P. Pufrall, eds. *Constructivism in the computer age.* Hillsdale, NJ: Erlbaum.

Donald, M. (1991). *Origins of the modern mind: three stages in the evolution of culture and cognition.* Cambridge, MA: Harvard University Press.

Eames, C. & Eames, R. (producers) (1986). Powers of ten: a film dealing with the relative size of things in the universe and the effect of adding another zero. *In* M. Hagino (executive producer) & Y. Kawahara (producer/director), *The world of Charles and Ray Eames* (videodisc), Chap. 3. Tokyo: Pioneer Electronic Corporation. (Original work published 1977.)

Fodor, J.A. & Pylyshyn, S.W. (1981). How direct is visual perception? Some reflections on Gibson's ecological approach. *Cognition 9,* 139–96.

Gardner, H. (1987). *The mind's new science: a history of the cognitive revolution.* New York: Basic Books.

Gatlin, L.L. (1972). *Information theory and the living system.* New York: Columbia University Press.

Gentner, D. & Gentner, D.R. (1983). Flowing waters or teeming crowds: mental models of electricity. *In* D. Gentner & A.L. Stevens, eds. *Mental models.* Hillsdale, NJ: Erlbaum.

— & Stevens, A.L., eds. (1983). *Mental models.* Hillsdale, NJ: Erlbaum.

Gibson, E.J. (1969). *Principles of perceptual learning and development.* New York: Appleton-Century-Crofts.

— (1994). Has psychology a future? *Psychological Science 5,* 69–76.

Gibson, J.J. (1950). *The perception of the visual world.* Boston, MA: Houghton Mifflin.

— (1960). The concept of stimulus in psychology. *American Psychologist 17,* 23–30.

— (1966). *The senses considered as perceptual systems.* Boston, MA: Houghton Mifflin.

— (1971/1982). A note on problems of vision to be resolved. *In* E. Reed & R. Jones, eds. *Reasons for realism: selected essays of James J. Gibson,* 391–96. Hillsdale, NJ: Erlbaum. (Unpublished manuscript, spring, 1971.)

— (1974/1982). A note on current theories of perception. *In* E. Reed & R. Jones, eds. *Reasons for realism: selected essays of James J. Gibson,* 370–73. Hillsdale, NJ: Erlbaum. (Unpublished manuscript, Jul. 1974.)

— (1977/1982). Notes on direct perception and indirect apprehension. *In* E. Reed & R. Jones, eds. *Reasons for realism:*

selected essays of James J. Gibson, 289–93. Hillsdale, NJ.: Erlbaum. (Unpublished manuscript, May 1977.)

— (1979). *The ecological approach to visual perception.* Boston, MA: Houghton Mifflin.

Gibson, W. (1984). *Neuromancer.* New York: Berkeley Publications Group.

Goodman, N. (1976). *Languages of art.* Indianapolis, IN: Bobbs-Merrill.

Gray, H. (1930). *Anatomy of the human body,* 22d ed. New York: Lea & Febiger.

Greeno, J.G. (1989). Situations, mental models, and generative knowledge. *In* D. Klahr & K. Kotovsky, eds. *Complex information processing.* Hillsdale, NJ: Erlbaum.

— (1991). Mathematical cognition: accomplishments and challenges in research. *In* R.R. Hoffman & D.S. Palermo, eds. *Cognition and the symbolic processes: applied and ecological perspectives,* 255–81. Hillsdale, NJ: Erlbaum.

— (1994). Gibson's affordances. *Psychological Review 101,* 336–42.

—, Smith, D.R. & Moore, J.L. (1993). Transfer of situated learning. *In* D. Detterman & R. Sternberg, eds. *Transfer on trial: intelligence, cognition, and instruction.* Norwood, NJ: Ablex.

Gregory, R.L. (1987). *The Oxford companion to the mind.* Oxford, England: Oxford University Press.

Hawkins, D. (1964). *The language of nature: an essay in the philosophy of science.* San Francisco, CA: Freeman.

Herrigel, E. (1953). *Zen in the art of archery* (R.F.C. Hull, trans.). New York: Pantheon.

Hochberg, J. (1974). Higher-order stimuli and inter-response coupling in the perception of the visual world. *In* R.B. MacLeod & H.L. Pick, Jr., eds. *Perception: essays in honor of James J. Gibson,* 17–39. Ithaca, NY: Cornell University Press.

Johansson, G. (1950). *Configurations in event perception.* Uppsala, Sweden: Almqvist & Wiksell.

Johnson, M. (1987). *The body in the mind: the bodily basis of meaning, imagination, and reason.* Chicago, IL: The University of Chicago Press.

Johnson-Laird, P.N. (1983). *Mental models.* Cambridge, England: Cambridge University Press.

Kant, I. (1781/1966). *The critique of pure reason,* 2d ed. (F. Max Muller, trans.). New York: Anchor.

Kay, A. (1991). Computer networks and education. *Scientific American 265*(3), 138–48.

Koffka, K. (1935). *Principles of gestalt psychology.* New York: Harcourt, Brace.

Kosslyn, S.M. & Koeing, O. (1992). *Wet mind: the new cognitive neuroscience.* New York: Free Press.

Kugler, P.N., Shaw, R.E., Vicente, K.J. & Kinsella-Shaw, J. (1991). The role of attractors in the self-organization of intentional systems. *In* R.R. Hoffman & D.S. Palermo, eds. *Cognition and the symbolic processes: applied and ecological perspectives,* 371–87. Hillsdale, NJ: Erlbaum.

Kupfermann, I. (1991). Learning and memory. *In* E.R. Kandel, J.H. Schwartz & T.S. Jessell, eds. *Principles of neural science,* 3d ed. Norwalk, CN: Appleton & Lange.

Larkin J. & H. Simon (1987). Why a diagram is (sometimes) worth ten thousand words. *Cognitive Science 11,* 65–100.

Lashly, K.S. (1951). The problem of serial order in behavior. *In* L.A. Jeffress, ed. *Cerebral mechanism in behavior.* New York: Hafner.

Laurel, B.K. (1986). *The art of human-computer interface design.* Reading, MA: Addison-Wesley.

Lave, J. (1988). *Cognition in practice.* Cambridge, England: Cambridge University Press.

MacKay, D.M. (1991). *Behind the eye.* Cambridge, MA: Blackwell.

Mander, J. (1978). *Four arguments for the elimination of television.* New York: Quill.

Mark, L.S., Dainoff, M.J., Moritz & Vogele, D. (1991). An ecological framework for ergonomic research and design. *In* R.R. Hoffman & D.S. Palermo, eds. *Cognition and the symbolic processes: applied and ecological perspectives,* 477–507. Hillsdale, NJ: Erlbaum.

Martin, J. (1993). *Principles of object-oriented analysis and design.* Englewood Cliffs, NJ: Prentice Hall.

Maturana, H.R. & Varela, F.J. (1980). *Autopoesis and cognition: the realization of the living.* Dordrecht, The Netherlands: Reidel.

— (1978). Biology of language: the epistemology of reality. *In* G.A. Miller & E. Lenneberg, eds. *Psychology and biology of language and thought: essays in honor of Eric Lenneberg.* New York: Academic.

McCabe, V. (1986). The direct perception of universals: a theory of knowledge acquisition. *In* V. McCabe & G.J. Balzano, eds., *Event cognition,* 29–44. Hillsdale, NJ: Erlbaum.

— & Balzano, G.J., eds. (1986). *Event cognition.* Hillsdale, NJ: Erlbaum.

McKibbin, B. (1989). *The end of nature.* New York: Random House.

McLuhan, M. (1965). *Understanding media: the extensions of man.* New York: Bantam.

Minsky, M. (1985). *Society of mind.* New York: Simon & Schuster.

Morrison, Philip & Morrison, Phylis (1982). *Powers of ten.* New York: Freeman.

Neisser, U. (1976). *Cognition and reality.* San Francisco, CA: Freeman.

Neisser, U. (1991). Direct perception and other forms of knowing. *In* R.R. Hoffman & D.S. Palermo, eds. *Cognition and the symbolic processes: applied and ecological perspectives,* 17–33. Hillsdale, NJ: Erlbaum.

Nichols, B. (1991). *Representing reality: issues and concepts in documentary.* Bloomington, IN: Indiana University Press.

Norman, D.A. (1988). *The psychology of everyday things.* New York: Basic Books.

— (1993). *Things that make us smart.* Reading, MA: Addison-Wesley.

— & Rumelhart, D.E. (1975). *Explorations in cognition.* San Francisco, CA: Freeman.

Payne, S.J. (1992). On mental models and cognitive artifacts. *In* Y. Rogers, A. Rutherford & P. Bibby, eds. *Models in the mind: theory, perspective, and application.* New York: Academic.

Piaget, J. (1971). *Biology and knowledge: an essay on the relations between organic regulations and cognitive processes.* Chicago, IL: University of Chicago Press.

Putnam, H. (1981). *Reason, truth and history.* Cambridge, England: Cambridge University Press.

Real, M.R. (1989). *Super media: a cultural studies approach.* Newbury Park, CA: Sage.

Reed, E.S. & Jones, R., eds. (1982). *Reasons for realism: selected essays of James J. Gibson.* Hillsdale, NJ: Erlbaum.

— (1988). *James J. Gibson and the psychology of perception.* New Haven, CT: Yale University Press.

Reference Software [computer software] (1993). *Random House-Webster's electronic dictionary & thesaurus.* New York: Random House.

Rheingold, H. (1991). *Virtual reality.* New York: Simon & Schuster.

Rock, I. (1984). *Perception.* New York: Scientific American Library.

Rosch, E. (1978). Principles of categorization. *In* E. Rosch & B.B. Lloyd, eds. *Cognition and categorization.* Hillsdale, NJ: Erlbaum.

Rouse, W.B. & Morris, N.M. (1986). On looking into the black box: prospects and limits in the search for mental models. *Psychological Bulletin 100,* 349–63.

Rousseau, J.J. (1764/1911). *Emile* (B. Foxley, trans.). New York: Dutton.

Saba, F. (1990). Integrated telecommunications systems and instructional transactions. *In* M.G. Moore, ed. *Contemporary issues in American distance education,* 344–52. Oxford, England: Pergamon.

Salomon, G. (1979). *Interaction of media, cognition, and learning.* San Francisco, CA: Jossey-Bass.

Shannon, C. & Weaver, W. (1949). *The mathematical theory of communication.* Urbana, IL: University of Illinois Press.

Shaw, R.E. & Hazelett, W.M. (1986). Schemas in cognition. *In* V. McCabe & G.J. Balzano, eds. *Event cognition.* Hillsdale, NJ: Erlbaum.

—, Mace, W.M. & Turvey, M.T. (1986). Resources for ecological psychology. *In* V. McCabe & G.J. Balzano, eds. *Event cognition.* Hillsdale, NJ: Erlbaum.

—, Turvey, M.T. & Mace, W.M. (1982). Ecological psychology: the consequences of a commitment to realism. *In* W. Wiemer & D. Palermo, eds. *Cognition and the symbolic processes II.* Hillsdale, NJ: Erlbaum.

Sternberg, R.J. (1977). *Intelligence, information processing and analogical reasoning.* Hillsdale, NJ: Erlbaum.

Suchman, L.A. (1987). *Plans and situated actions: the problem of human-machine communications.* Cambridge, England: Cambridge University Press.

Tufte, E.R. (1992). *Envisioning information.* Cheshire, CN: Graphic.

Turvey, M.T. & Shaw, R.E. (1979). The primacy of perceiving: an ecological reformulation of perception for understanding memory. *In* L. Nilsson, ed. *Perspectives on memory research: essays in honor of Uppsala University's 500th anniversary.* Hillsdale, NJ: Erlbaum.

—, —, Reed, E.S. & Mace, W.M. (1981). Ecological laws of perceiving and acting: in reply to Fodor and Pylyshyn. *Cognition 9,* 373–415.

Varela, F.J., Thompson, E. & Rosch, E. (1991). *The embodied mind: cognitive science and human experience.* Cambridge, MA: MIT Press.

Vera, A.H. & Simon, H.A. (1993). Situated action: a symbolic interpretation. *Cognitive Science 17,* 7–48.

von Bertalanffy, L. (1967). *Robots, men, and minds.* New York: Braziller.

von Foerster, H. (1986). From stimulus to symbol. *In* V. McCabe & G.J. Balzano, eds. *Event cognition: an ecological perspective,* 79–91. Hillsdale, NJ: Erlbaum.

Winograd, T. & Flores, F. (1986). *Understanding computers and cognition: a new foundation for design.* Norwood, NJ: Ablex.

Wood, D.J., Bruner, J.S. & Ross, G. (1976). The role of tutoring in problem solving. *Journal of Child Psychology and Psychiatry 17,* 89–100.

Young, R.M. (1983). Surrogates and mappings: two kinds of conceptual models for interactive devices. *In* D. Gentner & A.L. Stevens, eds. *Mental models.* Hillsdale, NJ: Erlbaum.

Zhang, J. & Norman, D.A. (1994). Representations in distributed cognition tasks. *Cognitive Science, 18,* 87–122.

Zucchermaglia, C. (1991). Towards a cognitive ergonomics of educational technology. *In* T.M. Duffy, J. Lowyck & D.H. Jonassen, eds. *Designing environments for constructive learning.* New York: Springer.

9. CRITICAL THEORY AND EDUCATIONAL TECHNOLOGY

Randall G. Nichols   Vanessa Allen-Brown

UNIVERSITY OF CINCINNATI

9.1 INTRODUCTION*

Writing about critical theory is interesting and challenging when several critical theories exist, and they are ever-changing. For people who believe in verities, these changes can be exceedingly problematic. However, many critical theorists revel in the struggle it takes to become familiar with diverse, contradictory, and even conflicting theories and meanings. Helping educators interested in educational technology to understand and adopt critical theory may be even more challenging, since the typical experiences of these educators do not include much conscious attention to critical theory.

Partly in response to this lack, one of the goals of this chapter is to help readers understand critical theory by staying within a somewhat foreshortened conception of it. Thomas McCarthy's (1991) description of the main aspects of critical theory implies the conception the authors of this chapter have in mind:

- Critical theory challenges the notion of pure reason, showing its changeability depending on the culture, the history, and the power in which it is embedded.
- Critical theory rejects the "Cartesian picture of an autonomous rational subject" who is capable of controlling the world.
- Critical theory emphasizes the practical over the theoretical, but the two are inseparable.
- Knowledge is not disembodied from the test of existence, though a distanced or objectivating understanding of knowledge is needed.
- Established human sciences, scientifically trained experts, and rationalization are all closely analyzed by critical theorists.

- Critical theory's major purpose is to make problematic what is taken for granted in culture, so that a degree of social justice can be had by those who are oppressed (p. 43).

At this point, some readers are noting that the view just presented is not all that foreshortened. Perhaps it is more accurate to say this chapter addresses critical theory a la the Frankfurt School and Jürgen Habermas, and it crosses theoretic borders into critical theories that are feminist, postmodern, poststructural, deconstructionist, and critical pedagogical. However, this chapter leaves a good deal of the study of these latter views—particularly the postmodern—to the chapter by Yeaman and Hlynka, in this volume (see Chapter 10).

9.1.1 Critical, Educational Technology and Language

Note that *critical* is not meant to indicate a theory that examines only the negative. Critical theories seek to reveal the contradictions, social inequalities, and dominances; to this extent they can be called *negative*. However, it might be more accurate to say that because critical theories run contrary to that which oppresses people, the theories usually are positive and hopeful.

Educational technology, as it is used here, refers to media and hardware and the conscious, systematic application of technologies such as the processes of instructional design. But it also indicates more than this mundane description. Educational technology includes the ways in which technology gets into learning and schooling without anyone taking much formal notice. A number of authors (e.g, Apple, 1986; Bowers, 1993; Damarin, 1994; Koetting, 1994; Schrage, 1994; Taylor & Johnsen, 1986) argue that infusions of technology into learning and schooling are not guided so much by conscious, empirical, theoretical knowledge about learning as much as they are by so-called

---

*Many thanks to Elizabeth Ellsworth, Long Tran, Lauryne Alexis-Boyd, Andrew Yeaman, and Sharon Nichols for their valuable help with this chapter.

progressive, productive, and revolutionary mentalities that have many deleterious and often hidden effects. These manifestations of educational technologies are cultural phenomena in that they are widespread and largely taken for granted. It is these cultural manifestations of educational technology to which we also are referring.

The authors also acknowledge from the outset that the language of critical theory is at times difficult to understand. Goodman (1992) says that the language is needlessly abstract and jargon laden. It often seems to be aimed at building individual careers by criticizing the work of others, and it emphasizes the ways in which people are oppressed and despairing. Later in the chapter, we indicate refutations of these claims but, for now, note that we try to use less-difficult language where possible, and we have no illusion that the language is always easy to understand.

9.1.2 Limits of the Chapter

The scope of this chapter does not allow for an exhaustive examination of the ideas, people, places, or actions related to the several decades of critical theorizing in education and elsewhere. For fuller views and histories, readers should examine authors such as Yeaman and Hlynka (see Chapter 10) and Arato and Gebhardt (1978); Aronowitz and Giroux (1991); Bernstein (1976); Ellul (1964, 1990); Foucault (1976); Giroux (1983a, 1991); Giroux and McLaren (1994, 1994a); Grundy (1987); Held (1980); Hoy and McCarthy (1994); Ingram and Simon-Ingram (1991); Jay (1973); Lather (1991); Luke and Gore (1992); Marcus and Tar (1984); Martin, Gutman, and Hutton (1988); McCarthy (1978, 1991); Roderick (1986); Wexler (1991); and Young (1990). The first several pages, at least, of Yeaman's (1994a) "Deconstruction and Visuals: Is This a Telephone?" also provide a very good introduction to various histories, versions, and examples of critical theories.

Note, too, that most of the works in this chapter represent obvious critical-theory pieces, referring directly to aspects of critical theory or authors in the field, for example. However, other works appear because they are about oppression, freedom, technology as philosophy, and/or research that reflects an approach used by critical theorists. That is, several works fulfill the spirit of critical theory and, so, are included.

One more limitation: This chapter is not as much an example of critical theory as it is a review of critical theories. The authors are trying to describe and analyze this complex and, we think, noble enterprise, but we are not trying necessarily to bring our own critical analysis to bear, except inasmuch as our own subjectivities unavoidably inform our writing.

Despite these limits, and because critical theory speaks to many conceptions of educational technology outside the mainstream, critical theory is worth examining in some detail to establish its value in making educational technology more fully understood, meaningful, and even emancipatory.

9.1.3 Chapter Overview

After an introduction to several of the thinkers, ideas, and works associated with critical theories, an examination of the relationships of critical theories to education is presented. This is followed by an exposition of the work that has been done in the area of critical theory as that work relates to educational technology. Near the end, the chapter turns to problems associated with critical theories and, so, with critical theories about educational technology. The chapter ends by suggesting ideas to help educational technologists proceed with being critical theorists and by explaining why doing so is important.

9.2 FOUNDATIONS OF CRITICAL THEORY

The Institute for Social Research (the Frankfurt School) was founded in 1923 in Frankfurt, Germany. Its *Journal of the Institute for Social Research* published Horkheimer's "Traditional and Critical Theory" in 1937, which may be taken as the formal birth date of the institute's school of critical theory. Its most prominent early members included Theodor Adorno, Erich Fromm, Jürgen Habermas, Max Horkheimer, and Herbert Marcuse (Ingram & Simon-Ingram, 1991). McLaren (1994a) suggests that Michael Apple, Paulo Freire, Henry Giroux, Maxine Greene, Bell Hooks, and Jonathan Kozol, among others, represent current critical theorists:

> Ingram and Simon-Ingram (1991) state that early critical theory has been variously characterized as a radical social theory (or sociology), a sophisticated form of cultural criticism combining Freudian and Marxist ideas, and a utopian style of philosophical speculation deeply rooted in Jewish and German idealism. For their own part, critical theorists saw themselves as responding to the historical events of the day. The changing composition and direction of the European labor movement and the evolution of Soviet communism and Western capitalism attracted their attention initially. They later expanded their focus to include the decline of patriarchy in the nuclear family; the psychosocial dynamics underlying authoritarian, anti-Semitic and fascist tendencies; and the rising potential for totalitarian mind control in the mass production and consumption of "culture" (p. xix).

Carr and Kemmis (1986) point out that the early critical theorists also saw positive science being applied indiscriminately:

> Science had become an ideology, a culturally produced and socially supported, unexamined way of seeing the world which shapes and guides social action. As such, science's role had become one of legitimating social action by providing "objective fact" to justify courses of action. Questions of values underlying these courses of action were believed to be beyond the scope of science and were thus left unexamined. Scientific results merely distinguished more effective courses of action from less effective ones and explained how outcomes occurred—not whether they should be allowed to occur. Far from being a relentless

inquiry into the nature and conduct of social life, science was in danger of taking forms of social life for granted and reflecting only on "technical" issues (p. 132).

In the face of an historical division of rational inquiry either into scientific, fact-based analysis or into the existential, poetic, religious nature of existence,

The intellectual project of critical theory thus required recovering from early philosophy the elements of social thought which uniquely concerned the values, judgments, and interests of humankind, and integrating them into a framework of thought which could provide a new and justifiable approach to social science (Carr & Kemmis, 1986, p. 132).

So, the critical theorists were concerned not only with disclaiming rationality, science, and the technical altogether but rather with returning them to balance with other aspects of life, such as moral perspectives.

The early critique of capitalism, hinted at above, is related to Marxist theory. This relationship can sometimes evoke negative reactions in those unfamiliar with critical theory. However, most early critical theorists were forced to analyze the Marxist orientation and move away from it. Giroux's (1983b) analysis helps us to understand this history:

It is particularly in the rejection of certain doctrinal Marxist assumptions, developed under the historical shadow of totalitarianism and the rise of the consumer society in the West, that Horkheimer, Adorno, and Marcuse attempted to construct a more sufficient basis for social theory and political action. Certainly such a basis was not to be found in standard Marxist assumptions such as: the notion of historical inevitability; the primacy of the mode of production in the shaping of history; and the notion that class struggle as well as the mechanisms of domination take place primarily within the confines of the labour process . . . the focus of the Frankfurt School's research downplayed the area of political economy and emphasized instead the issue of how subjectivity was constituted, as well as the issue of how the spheres of culture and everyday life represented a new terrain of domination (p. 10).

Despite this move away from Marxism, capitalism remains an important issue for many critical theorists. Habermas, for example, believes that capitalist societies oppose democracy, partly by discouraging rational communication and encouraging destructive beliefs in "bourgeois ideologies revolving around competitive achievement, possessive individualism, familial privatism, and consumerism" (Ingram & Simon-Ingram, 1991, p. xxxii).

Within the field of education, too, analysis of capitalism occupies critical theorists (e.g., Bowles & Gintis, 1976; Feenberg, 1991; Greene, 1993; Liston, 1988). We hear McLaren (1994b): "Situated beyond the reach of ethically convincing forms of accountability, capitalism has dissolved the meaning of democracy into glossy aphorisms one finds in election campaign sound bites or a bargain basement sales [sic] in suburban shopping malls" (p. 192).

Critical theorists also suggest that modern social crises, say in education or government, are related to the intrusion of overly rational (scientific, analytical, technological), instrumental, means-ends philosophies that detract from reflection on our ultimate ends—ends related to good and bad, right and wrong. Over time, we have largely abandoned moral perspectives. Of course, critical theorists do not always agree with one another about specifics in the moral realm. Marcuse argues for a hedonism, where true "pleasures" are those that allow for the complete development of human intellectual and sensual faculties. On the other hand, Habermas (1983/1990) says that the best way to uncover universal moral principles is via rational argumentation, rational discourse.

Several methodologies are associated with the work of critical theorists (Popkewitz, 1990). Of these, the main method is "immanent critique, which proceeds through forcing existing views to their systematic conclusions, bringing them face to face with their incompleteness and contradictions, and, ultimately, with the social conditions of their existence" (Young, 1990, p. 18). To this end, strands of methods from disciplines such as psychology, economics, history, sociology, and philosophy have informed the research of critical theory. Horkheimer's interdisciplinary approach combined the objective, explanatory methods of traditional theory (science) with empathetic, subjective, and historical approaches. Marcuse used psychiatric theory to argue that under the imperative of capitalist production, societies have become less free and less happy. Habermas argues for the method of communicative action, where "rational justification must be conceived as a dialogical process of reaching agreement on contested statements" (Ingram & Simon-Ingram, 1991, p. xxvii).

Action research is a commonly used method which Grundy (1987) describes as social research aiming to help participants via improvement and involvement. *Improvement* often means that material contexts need to be bettered. *Involvement* means "it is always the knowledge generated from within the action research group which is to be regarded as the authentic and legitimate basis for action, not knowledge from 'outside' " (Grundy, 1987, p. 143). The process of action research is to spiral through action and reflection, planning and observation. Reflection and planning take place via discourse; action and observation are carried on via practice. Grundy points out that the underlying justifications for action research are "the interrelatedness of truth, justice, and freedom" (p. 144).

9.3 HABERMAS'S EPISTEMOLOGY

Habermas is one of today's best-known critical theorists, and he finds his way among the foregoing foundational issues by way of his epistemology about human interests, and the knowledge, medium, and science associated with each. Carr and Kemmis (1986, p. 136) schematize Habermas's epistemology in the following table:

Interest	Knowledge	Medium	Science
Technical	Instrumental (causal explanation)	Work	Empirical-analytical or natural sciences
Practical	Practical (under-standing)	Language	Hermeneutic or "interpretive" sciences
Emanci-patory	Emancipatory (reflection)	Power	Critical sciences

Ingram and Simon-Ingram (1991) summarize Habermas's thinking about the sciences and the interests as follows:

> The *empirical-analytic* sciences incorporate an objectifying experimental method that constitutes nature as a lawful system of interconnected facts. This method refines a pre-scientific mode of instrumental activity necessitated by a *technical* interest in controlling nature. The *historical-hermeneutic* sciences incorporate an interpretive method that constitutes social reality as a symbolic text comprising meaningful actions, artifacts, and events. The method of subjective understanding refines a prescientific mode of communication activity necessitated by a *practical* interest in coordinating action and establishing a common identity (or mutual understanding) between persons. Finally, the *critical social* sciences incorporate a reflective method that combines both objectifying (causal explanatory) and interpretive procedures in determining which social regularities are invariant and which are not. The critique of ideology refines a prescientific mode of critical self-examination necessitated by an *emancipatory* interest in achieving freedom from domination (p. xxx).

So, critical social sciences help individuals understand how their aims and purposes are subordinated to technical and practical interests such as science and technology. In this way, the critical sciences help people act to relieve oppression.

A major critique of Habermas's theories has been that they do not convincingly show they are free of ideologies and better than the empirical-analytical or hermeneutic sciences they wish to ameliorate. Habermas's response to these criticisms has been to develop his theory of communicative action, aspects of which are described succinctly by Ingram and Simon-Ingram (1991):

> Communication (speaking) is the primary vehicle by which personal and social identity is shaped and mutual understanding regarding a shared world is brought about. Language, Habermas argues, has evolved to the point where one can distinguish propositional (descriptive), interpersonal (prescriptive), and personal (expressive) uses. In everyday speech geared toward facilitating interaction . . . [*speech action*] all three uses are combined. For example, whenever I promise to do something I simultaneously assert (describe) something to be done, prescribe to myself an interpersonal obligation, and express a personal intention. Most important, what I say (describe, prescribe, and express) is tacitly accompanied by validity claims: to the

truth of what I assert to be the case, the rightness of what I prescribe, and the sincerity of what I express (p. xxxi).

The validity of any claims about truth, rightness, and authenticity is tested through argumentation, and only those arguments that meet (or could meet) with the approval of all affected by them can be considered acceptable. For Habermas (1981/1984), this is rational communication because agreement must be based on reasons, and those who participate could, under suitable circumstances, provide reasons for their expressions. Suitable conditions require that, among other things, there be no coercion (p. 17).

Habermas (1981/1984) calls this type of conversation a transcendental-pragmatic justification, in that the tacit in us and the rational in us meet in the taken-for-granted *lifeworld*. (See also Ihde, 1990, on the lifeworld.) Habermas says knowledge associated with the lifeworld "is an *implicit* knowledge that can not be represented in an infinite number of propositions; it is a *holistically structured* knowledge, the basic elements of which intrinsically define one another; and it is a knowledge that *does not stand at our disposition*, inasmuch as we can not make it conscious and place it in doubt as we please" (p. 336).

Though rational communicative action is thought of as a good thing, *rationalization* is questionable. Habermas argues that rationalization occurs when aspects of the lifeworld are made explicit. His thoughts on rationalization, then, run contrary to his statement that we cannot make the lifeworld "conscious and place it in doubt as we please." None the less, rationalization means that normative, value-vested contexts are transferred to rational yes/no positions. Habermas (1981/1987) gives this example: "Since the eighteenth century, there has been an increasingly pedagogical approach to child-rearing processes, which has made possible a formal system of education free from the imperative mandates of church and family" (p. 147).

As rationalization increases, societies become more complex, and mechanisms are developed to reduce the risks and failures involved in coordinating mutual understanding. These mechanisms are "delinguistified steering media" such as prestige, influence, power, money (and, sometimes, modern electronic mass media, the authors of this chapter would contend). Unfortunately, these media coordinate by either *condensing* or *replacing* mutual understanding (Habermas, 1981/1987, p. 181). Moreover, media such as money and power connect communication into complex networks for which no one feels responsible (p. 184). Environmental destruction and the overbureaucratization of educational systems can be explained as a result of capitalist growth and a "misuse" of power, which occur because of the false perception that only rational management must be applied to the environment and education (p. 293).

Actually, Habermas (1981/1987) also argues that neither the rationalization of the lifeworld nor the increases in system complexity are the worst characteristics of the modern crisis. The greatest difficulty is "an elitist splitting off of expert cultures from contexts of communicative action in daily life" (p. 330).

Habermas (1981/1987) does not think that media are always negative. He claims that some media can help mutual understanding when they encourage a trust in knowledge: "Media of this kind cannot uncouple interaction from the lifeworld context . . . because they have to make use of the resources of consensus formation in language" (p. 183).

Neither does Habermas (1974) altogether reject the rationality of the Enlightenment and the empirical-analytical sciences; like earlier critical theorists, he wants to develop a critical social science that lies somewhere between philosophy and science (p. 44). He believes that discovering universal knowledge, especially emancipatory knowledge, is possible through rational communicative action, though he can't say exactly when or how. This is important because, as we shall see shortly, this belief in universals runs contrary to the beliefs of many postmodernist, feminist, and deconstructionist theorists.

9.4 CRITICAL THEORY AND TECHNOLOGY

Critical theory and its relations to educational technology are examined later in the chapter, but by way of background, we look now at critical theory about technology in general.

Critical theories and technology have inseparable pasts, as evidenced in the Marxists' ideas about "mechanisms of control." Remember that many in the Frankfurt School believed that "science was in danger of taking forms of social life for granted and reflecting only on 'technical' issues" (Carr & Kemmis, 1986, p. 132). Marcuse believed that, as they were used predominantly, "industrial capitalism and the bureaucratization of society stripped humans of any claims to autonomy and undermined their critical expression with a functional language" (Daley, 1983). Lewis Mumford wrote extensively about technology and society in the 1920s and can be considered a critical theorist (Hughes & Hughes, 1990). In *The Illusion of Technique and Death of the Soul,* Barrett (1978, 1987, respectively) has written unique and penetrating philosophical and historical analyses of the relations of technology to freedom.

Of course, Habermas has criticized technology directly. His comments reflect the assessments of many critical theorists on this topic—especially those who wrestle with the question of the autonomous nature of technology (e.g., see Winner, 1977, *Autonomous Technology: Technics-out-of-Control as a Theme in Political Thought*). Habermas (1969) says:

> The quasi-autonomous progress of science and technology then appears as an independent variable on which the most important single system variable, namely, economic growth, depends. Thus arises a perspective in which the development of a social system seems to be determined by the logic of scientific-technical progress . . . the culturally defined self-understanding of a social lifeworld is replaced by . . . categories of purposive-rational action and adaptive behavior . . . The manifest domination of the authoritarian state gives way to the manipulative compulsions of technical-operational administration (p. 105).

Feminists, too, have written critically about technology in general. Stabile (1994), in *Feminism and The Technological Fix,* critiques the extremes of technomania and technophobia and tells how wider approaches to technology and socialist-feminist concerns give hope that all of us can survive the severe threats of capitalism. Wajcman's (1991) work in *Feminism Confronts Technology* is indicative of the depth, breadth, and high quality of analyses going on in this area. The book studies not only the differential effects of technology on men and women but also the ways society affects technologies, especially "advanced" societies. Wajcman also examines feminist critiques of workplace and reproductive, domestic, environmental, and masculine technologies. While much of the literature in these areas is about negative relations with technology, Wajcman also hopes to convince us

> that a recognition of the profoundly gendered character of technology need not lead to political pessimism or total rejection of existing technologies. The argument that women's relationship to technology is a contradictory one, combined with the realization that technology is itself a social construct, opens up fresh possibilities for feminist scholarship and action (p. x).

Like Wajcman, other critical theorists (who are not necessarily feminists) write about the positive potentials of rationality, science, and technology in general. Marcuse believed that technology had the potential to free people from repressive economies (Daley, 1983), though this potential is not often realized. Feenberg (1991), in *Critical Theory of Technology,* attempts to show how a critical theory can help form "a new technical code" that is dialectical, contextual, aesthetic, and humanly, socially, and ecologically responsible (p. 189).

9.5 CRITICAL THEORY AND EDUCATION

Though relatively few educators—including educational technologists—appear to concern themselves directly with critical theory (McLaren, 1994a), a number of influential educators are pursuing the theory in one or more of its current manifestations. Henry Giroux and Peter McLaren are among the best known of today's critical theorists, and we find critical theorists working across a spectrum of intellectual frames: postmodernism (Peters, 1995); critical pedagogy (Kanpol, 1994); power (Apple, 1993; Cherryholmes, 1988); teaching (Beyer, 1986; Gibson, 1986; Henricksen & Morgan, 1990; Simon, 1992; Weiler & Mitchell, 1992); curriculum (Apple, 1990; Giroux, Penna & Pinar, 1981; Beyer & Apple, 1988; Pinar, 1988; Castenell & Pinar, 1993); feminist pedagogies (Ellsworth, 1989a; Lather, 1991; Luke & Gore, 1992); teacher education (Sprague, 1992); mass media/communications studies (Hardt, 1993); vocational-technical studies (Davis, 1991); research summaries about critical theory (Ewert, 1991); and research using methods of the critical sciences (Carr & Kemmis, 1986; Grumet, 1992).

At least two publications attend in depth to Habermasian critical theory in education. Ewert (1991) has written a comprehensive analysis of the relationships of Habermasian critical theory to education, and in *A Critical Theory of Education,* Young (1990) tries to present a rather complete picture of Habermas's critical theory and its relations to education. Young says that critical theorists believe that extreme rationalization has

> lent itself to the further development of an alienated culture of manipulation. In the science of education, this led to a view of pedagogy as manipulation, while curriculum was divided into value-free subjects and value-based subjects where values were located decisionistically. The older view of pedagogy as a moral/ethical and practical art was abandoned (p. 20).

Young (1990) further points out that Habermas and other critical theorists believe that:

> We are on the threshold of a learning level characterised by the personal maturity of the decentered ego and by open, reflexive communication which fosters democratic participation and responsibility for all. We fall short of this because of the one-sided development of our rational capacity for understanding (p. 23).

Another seminal thinker who is responsible for several notions of critical theory in education is Paulo Freire. Freire's work, especially *Pedagogy of the Oppressed* (Freire, 1969), has been very influential in critical-education circles:

> Freire's project of democratic dialogue is attuned to the concrete operations of power (in and out of the classroom) and grounded in the painful yet empowering process of conscientization. This process embraces a critical demystifying moment in which structures of domination are laid bare and political engagement is imperative. This unique fusion of social theory, moral outrage, and political praxis constitutes a kind of pedagogical politics of conversation in which objects of history constitute themselves as active subjects of history ready to make a fundamental difference in the quality of the lives they individually and collectively live. Freire's genius is to explicate . . . and exemplify . . . the dynamics of this process of how ordinary people can and do make history in how they think, feel, act, and love (West, 1993, p. xiii).

9.5.1 Critical Theory Changes

Of course, critical theories of education are changing. Bennett and LeCompte (1990) and Wexler (1988) have good reports of the histories of these changes. In *Critical Theory and Educational Practice,* Giroux (1983a) looks at the work of earlier critical theorists and says they "did not develop a comprehensive theoretical approach for dealing with the patterns of conflict and contradictions that existed in various cultural spheres" (p. 33). He says they did not understand domination, American society, the working class, or the contradictory ways people view the world.

By 1991, Aronowitz and Giroux (1991) claim that Habermas sees postmodernism as "a threat to the foundations of democratic public life" (p. 61) and that, like its modernist predecessors, "Critical theory, left and right,

bemoans 'the eclipse of reason,' the 'closing of the American mind,' the 'culture of narcissism'" (p. 136). In other words, Habermas is too deeply rationalist, if his theory of communicative action and its dependence on rational communication are any indications. This is ironic, considering that earlier critical theorists contested the Enlightenment's great beliefs in rationality!

More recently, Fraser (1994) shows that Habermas's critical theory and conception of the public sphere (communicative action) prove inadequate for democracies in late capitalist societies. That is, critical theory should first

> render visible the ways in which social inequality taints deliberation within publics in late capitalist societies. Second, it should show how inequality affects relations among publics . . . how publics are differentially empowered or segmented, and how some are involuntarily enclaved and subordinated to others. Next, a critical theory should expose ways in which the labeling of some issues and interests as "private" limits the range of problems, and of approaches to problems, that can be widely contested in contemporary societies. Finally, our theory should show how the overly weak character of some public spheres in late capitalist societies denudes "public opinion" of practical force (p. 93).

9.5.2 Postmodernism

These accusations about Habermas indicate a clear evolution from (even a clear detachment from?) earlier critical theory to a postmodern view. Postmodern theories are more encompassing, according to Giroux (1991, p. 80), and McLaren (1994b) notes that

> the postmodern critique concerns itself with a rejection or debunking of modernism's epistemic foundations or metanarratives; a dethronement of the authority of the positivistic science that essentializes differences between what appear to be self-possessing identities, an attack on the notion of a unified goal of history, and a deconstruction of the magnificent Enlightenment swindle of the autonomous, stable, and self-contained ego that is supposed to be able to act independently of its own history, its own indigenist strands of meaning making and cultural and linguistic situatedness, and free from inscriptions in the discourses of, among others, gender, race, and class (p. 196).

This is to say that postmodernism resists dominant, oppressive cultures, and wants power shifted to groups of people struggling for power in their own lives (see 10.2, 10.5).

Though the references and the language are different, and the search for overly rationalistic, scientific-technical universals *may be,* dethroned, postmodern critical theory still is related to earlier critical theory, at least in terms of its formulation of knowledge as technical, practical, and emancipatory (McLaren, 1994a, p. 179). Further, just as earlier critical theorists do not rule out rationality altogether, Aronowitz and Giroux (1991) claim that:

> by combining the best insights of modernism and postmodernism, educators can deepen and extend what is generally

referred to as critical pedagogy. We need to combine the modernist emphasis on the capacity of individuals to use critical reason in addressing public life with a critical postmodernist concern with how we might experience agency in a world constituted in differences (p. 117).

9.5.3 Critical Pedagogy

Critical pedagogy is an educational version of postmodern critical theory (Kanpol, 1994). McLaren (1994a) says of it that:

> Critical pedagogy poses a variety of important counterlogics to the positivistic, ahistorical, and depoliticized analysis employed by both liberal and conservative critics of schooling—an analysis all too readily visible in the training programs in our colleges of education. Fundamentally concerned with the centrality of politics and power in our understanding of how schools work, critical theorists have produced work centering on the political economy of schooling, the state and education, the representation of texts, and the construction of student subjectivity (p. 167).

In researching the relationships between knowledge and power, thinkers like Apple and Giroux "attempt to develop an encompassing critical theory of education with resistance as its central theme" (Gibson, 1986, p. 59). Moreover, proponents of *resistance* desire a radical, hopeful, and action-oriented pedagogy. These qualities are evident in the writing of actors like Ira Shor (1986, 1987), in organizations such as The Goddard Institute on Teaching and Learning (Plainfield, VT) and The National Coalition of Educational Activists (Rosendale, NY), and newpapers such as *Rethinking Schools* (Milwaukee, WI). Also, the works of Simon (1992) and Kanpol (1994) are notable here. McLaren (1994a) says of critical pedagogy that:

> Teaching and learning should be a process of inquiry, of critique; it should also be a process of *constructing,* of building a social imagination that works within a language of hope. If teaching is cast in the form of . . . "a language of possibility," then a greater potential exists for making learning relevant, critical, and transformative. Knowledge is relevant only when it begins with the experiences students bring with them from the surrounding culture; it is critical only when these experiences are shown to sometimes be problematic (i.e., racist, sexist); and it is transformative only when students begin to use the knowledge to help empower others, including individuals in the surrounding community (p. 197).

9.5.4 Critical Feminism

9.5.4.1. General Theories. Contemporary feminism often is composed of theories of social transformation that describe women's lives in a hierarchial, structured, male-dominated society (see 10.4). Feminism supports and values women and women-centered perspectives, while advocating social, political, and economic equality for both women and men. Informed by postmodern critical theory,

feminism struggles to empower individuals and groups to participate in their liberation from oppressive structures within society; it challenges universal claims to truth and encourages the reconstruction of history. Various research traditions inform feminism and the development of feminist theories (Jagger, 1983; Weedon; 1987).

Of course, multiple versions of feminism exist. To put it too strictly, liberal feminists advocate the right of women to choose their role in society and in the home, as opposed to accepting sex-role stereotypes. Radical feminists advocate separatism as a political strategy to gain independence from patriarchal control and as a way to develop autonomy and empowerment. Socialist-feminists advocate a total transformation of the current social system that perpetuates racism, classism, and gender oppression. Socialist feminists propose the establishment of a social system that promotes

> full participation of men in childrearing; reproductive freedom for women, that is, the right to decide if and when to have children and under what conditions, together with the provision of the conditions necessary for the realization of the right of women to make these choices; the abolition of the privileging of heterosexuality, freedom to define one's own sexuality and the right of lesbians to raise children; the eventual abolition of the categories "woman" and "man," and the opening up of all social ways of being to all people (Weedon, 1987, p. 18).

The constructs of poststructuralism/postmodernism consist of several positions based on the writings of Derrida, Lacan, Dristeva, Althusser, and Foucault. The primary focus of the writings is on understanding language (see also 10.5). Thus, feminist poststructuralists encourage a dynamic mode of understanding oneself in the world through the interpretation and reinterpretation of language. Postmodern feminists "oppose a linear view of history that legitimates patriarchal notions of subjectivity and society" (Giroux, 1993, p. 61).

Womanist or black-feminist interpretations of feminism maintain that white, Western, privileged women have chosen to focus on sexual exploitation as the exclusive cause of oppression in the world and to ignore other forms of domination (Hooks, 1989; Collins, 1990; Moraga & Anzaldua, 1981). Black women's feminism is predicated on resistance to the "tridimensional phenomenon of race/class/gender oppression" (Cannon, 1988, p. 39). The absence of dialogue on this oppression led some black women to redefine their understanding of feminism and to accept Alice Walker's concept of womanist: "A black feminist or feminist of color." Walker's interpretation of feminism suggests that there is only a shade of difference between a womanist and a feminist, like purple is to lavender (Walker, 1983, p. ix).

Black feminists agree with Barbara Smith (1979) that this triad of race, class, and gender is a

> feminist issue [that is] easily explained by the inherent definition of feminism. Feminism is the political theory and practice to free all women of color, working-class women, poor women, physically challenged women, lesbians, old women, as well as white economically privileged hetero-

sexual women. Anything less than this is not feminism, but merely self-aggrandizement (B. Smith, 1979, quoted in Morage & Anzaldua, 1981, p. 61).

9.5.4.2. Pedagogical Theories. The intent of feminist pedagogy, like critical pedagogy, is to liberate. Through curriculum, discussions, and as agents of social change, feminist educators focus on the liberation of women from oppressive structures within society. Both feminists and critical pedagogists seek to empower students by affirming their race, class, and gender positions. They encourage students to reject any and all forms of oppression, injustice, and inequality. Students are taught to use their voices to prevent silencing by authoritarian social structures.

Socialist and poststructuralist feminists question critical pedagogy's Marxist ideology and its concept of emancipation. Marxist theory was traditionally concerned with male labor and production, while women's experiences were understood as part of oppression within their class position. Consequently, social feminists contend that Marxist and neo-Marxist theories are inadequate for gender analysis (Jagger, 1983; Lather, 1992a; Luke & Gore, 1992; Mackinnon, 1983; Weiler, 1988). Nicholson (1994) argues that Marxism is seen as "not only irrelevant to explaining important aspects of women's oppression but, indeed, as an obstacle in the attempt to develop such explanations" (p. 71). Nicholson also claims that similar arguments can be made against Marxism in movements against racism and in movements for gay and lesbians.

Not many works have been written about the relationship between feminist pedagogy and the "male inscribed liberation models of critical pedagogy" (Lather, 1992b, p. 129; Luke & Gore, 1992), but Luke (1992) suggests that because male authors of critical theory are at the center of its discourses, critical pedagogy is articulated from a male standpoint. Similarly, Ellsworth (1992) maintains that critical pedagogues consistently define empowerment in "ahistorical and depoliticized abstractions" (p. 99) which testify "to the failure of critical educators to come to terms with essentially paternalistic project of traditional education" (p. 99). Feminist discourses, unlike those of critical pedagogy, provide a context that encourages women to "conceptualize self-definitions." These definitions are "oppositional" to ones that may serve to subordinate women to men (p. 101).

Ellsworth also expresses concern for nonfeminist critical pedagogy's concept of "student voice," a construct that assumes that students are participating in a relationship of equal power, whereas individuals who are members of disadvantaged or subordinated social, racial, ethnic, or gender groups, may lack the critical-analysis skills necessary to participate in or even enter in critical-pedagogy dialogues.

Furthermore, in critical pedagogy, the assumption is made that the professor/teacher is committed to ending students' oppression. Yet no provisions are made in most critical pedagogy to problematize issues the professor/teacher brings to the classroom. Luke (1992) expresses a similar concern about empowerment and equal opportunity to speak in the classroom. She says that:

to grant equal classroom time to female students, to democratize the classroom speech situation, and to encourage marginal groups to make public what is personal and private does not alter theoretically or practically those gendered structural divisions upon which liberal capitalism and its knowledge industries are based (p. 37).

She agrees that possessing the "tools of critical thinking" will help women students to understand the masculine and feminine divisions of power and authority within the academy, but cautions that these same divisions

tend to render a feminist language of critique politically counterproductive for women, who still continue overwhelmingly to depend upon men for sanctioning of research topics, allocation of research funds, decreeing what knowledge counts as relevant and citeable for thesis examination, degree granting, promotion, and tenure (p. 38).

Gore (1992) proposes that the critical pedagogist's concept of teachers as agents of empowerment is problematic because it attributes extraordinary abilities to the teacher and may ignore the context of the teacher's work within patriarchal institutions. Weiler (1991) finds that women professors, like women students, struggle to understand the divisions of power and authority within the academy. Two questions seem to plague women. The first one "refers to the institutionally imposed authority of the teacher within a hierarchical university structure," where the

teacher in this role must give grades, is evaluated by administrators and colleagues in terms of expertise in a body of knowledge, and is expected to take responsibility for meeting the goals of an academic course as it is understood within the wider university (p. 460).

The second question refers to "the need for women to claim authority in a society that denies it to them" (p. 461). Kenway and Modra (1992) observe that power and authority do not appear to be outstanding issues for feminist school teachers. Another work on the subject of power and authority is Maher's (1987) "Toward a Richer Theory of Feminist Pedagogy." The topic of power and authority brings students, educators, and others face-to-face with issues relating to the feminist teacher as nurturer/mother, issues that are examined well by writers such as Noddings, (1984, 1991), Belenky et al. (1986), Grumet (1988), and Pagano (1992).

9.5.4.3. Pedagogical Strategies. Feminist teachers who are concerned with issues of authority, especially in the classroom, employ strategies that share the power of decision making with students (Bennett-deMarrais & LeCompte, 1994). These strategies are consistent with Schniedewind's fivefold "process goals" approach to pedagogy: (1) development of an atmosphere of mutual respect, trust, and community in the classroom; (2) shared leadership; (3) cooperative structures; (4) integration of cognitive and affective learning; and (5) action (Schniedewind, 1987, quoted in Kenway & Modra, 1992).

These kinds of process goals help to build communities and encourage involvement in democratic decision making and are consistent with other liberatory pedagogies.

Thompson and Disch (1992) explain that, as feminist teachers, they

> continually think about how [their] classes are going as communities. Other teachers obsess with lectures. We obsess about both the content we teach as well as the relationships among students and our relationships with both individuals and the group as a whole. We think carefully about how to express our anger when the class isn't taking responsibility to carry on meaningful discussion of the readings. We think carefully about how to address or resolve conflicts among particular pairs or groups of students. No two semesters are alike. The results of this kind of teaching cannot be predicted because the students have power, and we never know how they're going to challenge us, or how they're going to challenge each other (p. 9).

To ensure community and democratic decision making, feminist teachers function as facilitators and co-learners. They incorporate the use of journals, biographies, autobiographies, and narratives to encourage students to use their personal experiences to construct knowledge. As Thompson and Disch say (1992): "We assume that learning needs to be close to the heart, meaning that the course must move the learner and make a lasting impact on her or his life" (Thompson & Disch, 1992, p. 4).

Feminist educators are a diverse group. Remember that they, like most critical pedagogists, attempt to move educators and learners to action by prodding us with a most important question: Whose interests are served by education?

9.5.5 Critical Theory and Race

9.5.5.1. General Issues. The literature indicates that, in the United States, discussions based on race/ethnicity and education focus primarily on social class. Several researchers believe that improvement in an individual's social status will also improve her or his achievement in school. Others are suggesting that an examination of the larger population reveals that schooling and achievement are more closely tied to political issues.

Unfortunately, critical theorists must often counter researchers who develop scientific/biological theories to define the marginality experienced by racial/ethnic groups. McCarthy (1990) maintains that these scientific theories are inconclusive and do not adequately address the inequality experienced by racial minorities. Giroux (1992) believes that these theories are delusional and say too little about the power relations at the core of the discourse of white authority (p. 114). The acceptance of these biological/scientific theories is predicated on the ideology of racism.

Cornel West (1988) argues that Judeo-Christianity, science, and psychosexuality are the three central European traditions that support racism. Further, Africans are associated with bodily defecation, violation, and subordination. As such, Africans in the modern West "personify degraded otherness, exemplify radical alterity, and embody alien difference" (p. 118).

9.5.5.2. Race and Education-Related Issues. Critical educators utilize a variety of approaches to understand educational issues as they relate to race/ethnic minorities. For example, Ogbu and Matute-Bianchi (1986) examine specific school variables such as placement, counseling, teacher's behavior, and methods of testing as attempts to influence minority students' performance. Neo-Marxist sociologists such as Bowles and Gintis (1976) argue that schooling in the United States maintains the existing social class structure for the benefit of an economic elite.

McCarthy's (1990) alternative approach to race and education is related to work by authors such as Apple (1986, 1993), Apple and Weis (1983), and West (1988). McCarthy claims that this critical approach emphasizes the relationships between:

> (a) the structural and institutional arrangements of school knowledge and instrumental rules which constrain the educator and the educated alike, and (b) the self-affirming agency and capacities of social actors (teachers and students) to resist and transform the structural arrangements and relations that exist within educational settings and in the wider social milieu. (p. 7).

Giroux (1993) recommends a pedagogy that can retrieve and reconstruct possibilities for establishing the basis for a progressive vision that makes schooling for democracy and critical citizenship an unrealized yet possible reality (p. 118).

9.5.6 Critical Theory, Mass Media, and Popular Culture

Critical theorists also have begun to look at oppression and emancipatory action as they relate more broadly to technologies of mass media and other aspects of popular culture.

In *Ideology, Culture, and the Process of Schooling*, Giroux (1981) notes that forms of popular culture sometimes help to encourage rationalization of existence. The consolidation of culture by new technologies of mass communication, coupled with newly found social science disciplines such as social psychology and sociology, ushered in powerful, new modes of administration in the public sphere (p. 40).

Similarly, several nonprint media serve as wonderful examples of the kind of powerful views of culture a critical understanding can encourage. For instance, the film *Hungry for Profit* looks at ways corporate business has created among the largest of forced mass migrations of people in history. *America: What Went Wrong* (Moyers, 1992) explores the ways capital and politics have been used to the economic detriment of most Americans. *Manufacturing Consent: Noam Chomsky and the Media* shows how the U.S. government surreptitiously orchestrates information to avoid telling the public about its clandestine and democratically questionable activities against peoples worldwide.

Because of its profound relationships to society, politics, health, education, and so on, the technology of television has been the object of several print-based critical-theory analyses, though no one has, as far as we can find, summarized the work in this area. Several of these studies use notions of culture as their anchors (e.g., Dienst, 1991; Fehlman, 1992; Schwoch, White, Rilley & Scott, 1992) and intend to help viewers overcome the hidden intentions of TV. Note that we are not referring, here, to "critical viewing" or "critical thinking," which—in their cognitivist, rationalist, and individualist approaches—often foster technical interests rather than emancipatory ones.

At least one book critically examines representations of blacks (Hooks, 1992). Other studies (e.g., Poster, 1987–88; Wallace, 1994) bring a postmodern lens to the examination of media. For example, Aronowitz and Giroux (1991) claim that "in the age of instant information, global networking, and biogenetics, the old distinction between high and popular culture collapses, as the historically and socially constructed nature of meaning becomes evident, dissolving universalizing claims to history, truth, or class" (p. 115).

Just as Habermas and Marcuse, for example, do not believe that technology has only negative characteristics, not all education critical theorists find only harm in media. For example, Phelen's (1988) "Communing in Isolation," an article that alludes to critical theory, argues that mass media campaigns can successfully communicate messages when they use local celebrities, live meetings, and easily measured finite goals.

9.5.7 Critical Theory, Education, and Ecology

The topic of ecology in relation to critical theories of education comes up rarely. Feenberg (1991, p. 195) addresses it, and remember that Habermas (1981/1987) talks about the uses of media that inhibit communication such that "the destruction of urban environments as a result of uncontrolled capitalist growth, or the overbureaucratization of the educational system, can be explained as a 'misuse' of media" (p. 293).

Works by Bowers (1993) and Orr (1992) bear mentioning. Though neither book cites the Frankfurt School, McLaren, or "critical theory," for instance, they are included here because their topics are often the same as those in more commonly recognized critical theory (e.g., the predominance of science and technology over less objective aspects of life), and their methods are similar (critique of existing views' contradictory and oppressive conclusions). In other words, the works fulfill the spirit of critical theory.

Bowers (1993) argues that fundamental Western cultural assumptions of rationalism, progress, individualism, and consumerism found in schooling are detrimental to ecology. Bowers' arguments come up in later sections of this chapter on educational technology and ecology. Orr's (1992) *Ecological Literacy: Education and the Transition to a Postmodern World* posits that "there is no example of a society that was or is both technologically dynamic and environmentally sustainable. It remains to be seen how and whether these two can be harmonized" (p. 21). Perhaps the essence of Orr's dilemma is captured in a passage from his book's introduction:

The shortcomings of education reflect a deeper problem having to do with the way we define knowledge. "Research" has come to be the central focus and primary justification for the modern university. Some research is vital to our prospects, some of it is utterly trivial. Some of it may produce results that, given our present state of collective wisdom, is [sic] dangerous. A sizeable part of it is motivated by the fantasy of making an end run around constraints of time, space, nature, and human nature. It is, in short, part of the old project of dominating nature at whatever cost. Such distinctions are seldom made or even discussed. I happen to believe that our prospects depend more on the cultivation of political wisdom, moral virtue, and clear-headed self-knowledge than on gadgets. In any event, it is time to ask what we need to know to live humanely, peacefully, and responsibly on the earth and to set research priorities accordingly (p. xi).

Both Orr and Bowers spend considerable time discussing the ways education fosters ecologically dangerous technological effects, and they do so because of what many people think of as inherent and benign human characteristics such as inventiveness.

However, for the most part, few critical theorists are devoting their writing to issues of education and ecology.

9.6 CRITICAL THEORY OF EDUCATIONAL TECHNOLOGY

The balance of this chapter addresses critical theories as they relate to educational technology. The first relationships come from theorists previously mentioned in this chapter. Primarily though, the work of critical theorists more formally and closely tied to professional educational technology groups is surveyed.

Several of the critical theorists noted earlier assess the relationships of various sorts of technology to schooling and learning. They are interested not only in the obvious hardware and software of educational technology but also in technology as technique, bureaucracy, rationalization of the lifeworld, and so forth. For instance, remember that Habermas (1981/1987, p. 147) says that rationalization has created education systems that rely less on the normative mandates of the church or the family. He and other critical theorists think education systems have inhibited learners from reaching levels of maturity that foster communicative, democratic, or responsible learning (Young, 1990, p. 23).

McLaren (1994a), in *Life in Schools*, addresses the topic of "Technologizing Learning" when he concludes that in listening to experts who would have us reduce students to computer printouts by encouraging them to develop mechanistic cognitive styles, we perpetuate social inequality. In such circumstances "What we are left with is an emphasis on *practical* and *technical* forms of knowledge as opposed to . . . *transformative* knowledge" (p. 220).

Giroux (1981) uses Habermas's ideas of human interests to speak about technocratic rationalism, arguing that schools and teaching are governed by "the technical imperatives of rational engineering" (p. 10). Giroux (1988b) critiques the following assumptions of technical model of curriculum:

> (a) Theory in the curriculum field should operate in the interests of lawlike propositions that are empirically testable. (b) The natural sciences provide the "proper" model of explanation for the concepts and techniques of curriculum theory, design, and evaluation. (c) Knowledge should be objective and capable of being investigated and described in neutral fashion. (d) Statements of value are to be separated from "facts" and "modes of inquiry" that can and ought to be objective (p. 13).

This emphasis on objective, lawlike, valueless knowledge encourages people to ignore important aspects of schooling. Giroux (1981) says that "both intentionality and questions regarding the ethical and political nature of schools have been either ignored or dealt with reductively" (p. 10). As McLaren (1994a) puts it, "Teachers often emphasize classroom management procedures, efficiency, and 'how-to-do' techniques that ultimately ignore an important question: 'Why is knowledge being taught in the first place?'" (p. 177).

To resist these problems, Giroux (1986) advocates democratic practices, critical citizenship, and intellectual teachers. McLaren (1994a) says: "As teachers we need to collectively demythologize the infallibility of educational programmers and so-called experts, who often do nothing more than zealously impose their epistemological assumptions on unassuming teachers" (p. 219).

Feminists, too, are aware of educational technology and its effects. For example, Luke and Gore (1992) say that feminists are against "the technology of control" such as that found in many current liberal progressive discourses. Remember that Wajcman (1991) studies the differential effects of technology on men and women in society and suggests that technology may even foster feminist action and scholarship. A bit later in this chapter, Damarin (1990a) shows how, among other things, educational technology usurps classroom control and is biased against women teachers and students.

Note that, like other critical theorists, critical theorists concerned with educational technology are not always solely negative in their relations to technology (see 10.5.6). Just as Marcuse and Habermas believe that media can be used to enlighten and emancipate (even if often they are not used in these ways), and just as Giroux urges a hopeful "language of possibility," educational technology critical theorists can be positive. For instance, Ellsworth (1990) uses a form of critical pedagogy "that sees a special potential role for media in facilitating liberatory education" (p. 11).

Positive attitudes aside, few people attend to critical theory and its relations to educational technology. Such paucity is indicated by the fact that Saettler's (1990) history of educational technology does not reference any forms of critical theory. However, "Chapter 3—The Sources of Influence on Instructional Technology," in *Instructional Technology: Definition and Domains of the Field* (Seels & Ritchey, 1994), includes at least a passing reference to

postmodernist, feminist, and constructivist "Alternative Perspectives," as they are called by Ritchey and Seels (1994, p. 12). Nonetheless, some researchers *are* examining educational technology and critical theory, as we see in the next section.

9.7 TOPICS IN CRITICAL THEORY OF EDUCATIONAL TECHNOLOGY

The following sections of the chapter categorize and describe existing works about critical theory and educational technology, based on the topics from the first part of this chapter and on topics that emerge from this work itself. Many works cannot be categorized neatly because they speak to several issues; in such cases, works are categorized based primarily on "best fit" as judged by the authors of this chapter. The works cluster around the following issues:

- Foundational issues
- Societal relations
- Communication and media education
- Ethics
- Action research
- Ecology

9.7.1 Foundational Issues

This section addresses foundational issues related to critical theory and educational technology, including issues of philosophy, language, instructional design and development, computers, and visuals.

9.7.1.1. Philosophic Views. In "Philosophical Foundations of Instructional Technology," Koetting (1983a) has written one of the first works to explicitly relate critical theory to various manifestations of educational technology (see also 3.8.1). He focuses on epistemological questions in order to explicate their centrality in instructional technology and to suggest alternative theoretical understandings, practices, and modes of inquiry. This is accomplished, partly, by examining Habermas's three forms of science: the empirical-analytic, the historical-hermeneutic, and the critical. (See the schematic on Habermas's epistemology, noted earlier in this chapter.) Each has a primary interest in, respectively, technical control, mutual understanding in life, and emancipation. Each form of knowledge differs in its strategies and cognitive interests, which are deep anthropological interests human beings have in their self-formed historical contexts (McCarthy, 1978, p. 59).

Koetting (1983a) points out that "Educational technology . . . has its theoretical base within the framework of a scientific, behaviorally based model of rationality" (p. 8). Our uses of instructional design rely exclusively on an empirical, scientific model that is interested in control and that does not allow for any deviation from predetermined outcomes. This view is reductionist and simplistic and poses severe limits on knowledge and its formation. Koetting suggests that "we need to explore alternative ways of organizing curricula that acknowledge that students are capable of having views of the world" (p. 12). Thus, notions of epistemological ambiguity and diverse forms of communicating, learning, and conceiving of the world must be admitted to the field.

In a similar paper, Koetting (1983b) again refers to Habermas's knowledge types and suggests that the field of educational technology is rooted in a solely empirical view of knowledge. He says that expanding the field's theory base toward critical sciences would put us more in the mainstream of educational thought; help us examine more fully the languages of film, video, photography, and other media; and allow for more diverse and epistemologically appropriate educational outcomes, organizations, and research methods.

In *Paradigms Regained: The Uses of Illuminative, Semiotic, and Post-modern Criticism as Modes of Inquiry in Educational Technology,* Hlynka and Belland (1991a) note their association with the work of Habermas, saying the critical domain forms the basis of their book of readings (p. 7). Hlynka and Belland use *critical* to include connoisseurship, reconceptualism, semiotics, postmodernism, and poststructuralism.

In one chapter of *Paradigms Regained,* Murphy and Pardeck (1991) argue that educational technology advances a world view that denies the lifeworld and has adverse educational and social implications. The technological view fragments learning, is void of dynamism, and is monologic. Further, the technological view stifles communication, is more purely instrumental, and fosters lack of insight, imagination, and creativity. And it marginalizes morality. In contrast, education should return persons to a world of questions and

> the world of direct experience, and existential claim, which is the only type of world individuals can call their own. The world that educators must resurrect . . . is the "lived-world," the pre-objective world that is sustained by human praxis (p. 394).

In a speculative essay in Hlynka and Belland's (1991a) text, Nichols (1991) looks at Habermas's communication theory. After criticizing educational technologists' conceptions of knowledge, postpositivist philosophy, and disregard for the metaphysical, Nichols offers Habermas's theory of communicative action as a way of addressing these criticisms. Nichols concludes that educational technology is a system of purposive-rational action, that some educational technologists conceive of knowledge too narrowly, and that educational technologists generally do not operate consensually.

Elsewhere, Nichols (1993) draws direct and not very positive links between educational technology and its apparent ideology. He says a technical and practical ideology dominates over a democratic-communicative ideology. That is, students and teachers are not responsible for knowledge and education but for fulfilling the desires of others, especially the desires to have power and make money. We must critically study this dominance and actions

against it because such study can potentially encourage greater fulfillment of human communication, and freedom of communication is moral.

A work of note in a postmodern vein is "Postmodern Educational Technology" (Hlynka & Yeaman, 1992), in which the authors point out that the postmodern condition means questioning all dimensions of scientific approaches to technology use, recognizing there is no one best way to apply technology, and acknowledging that a postmodern approach can make a positive difference to the field of educational technology.

9.7.1.2. Language. In several works, researchers examine fundamental issues of language and their relationships to educational technology.

For example, Koetting and Januszewski (1991a, 1991b) argue that the Association for Educational Communications and Technology, in particular, focuses narrowly on empirical analytic science. They suggest, on the other hand, that new dialogue, new conceptions, and new languages of educational technology can emerge and affect praxis in the field. Nagel's sense of theory as a systematic analysis of a set of related concepts is helpful for these new aspects of the field, because this theory is both a conceptual analysis of words and normative statements of their uses.

The relations among language, critical theory, and educational technology are uncovered also in Winograd and Flores's (1986) *Understanding Computers and Cognition,* in which they "have shown how the projection of human capacities [like language] onto computational devices was misleading" (p. 174).

In *Hypertext: The Convergence of Contemporary Critical Theory and Technology,* Landow (1992) draws substantial parallels between postmodernism and hypertext. He claims that hypertext, like critical theory, encourages multilinearity and webbing, the blurring of distinctions between reader and writer, multivocality, intertextuality, and decentering. Multilinearity replaces

> the essentially linear fixed methods that had produced the triumphs of capitalism and industrialism with what are essentially poetic machines—machines that work according to analogy and association, machines that capture the anarchic brilliance of human imagination" (p. 18).

Postmodern conditions such as webbing and multivocality show us: (1) the historical connectedness of writing technology; (2) changes in the meanings of *literacy education, author,* and *narrative*; and (3) a democratized and liberated existence. Landow notes that the technology of writing, in whatever form, "is the greatest as well as the most destructive of all technologies" (p. 203), but mostly he is "excited" and looks forward to hypertext's appearance, particularly in that "it offers us a means of looking a short way into one or more possible futures" (p. 203).

9.7.1.3. Instructional Design and Development. Some publications in the area of critical theory and instructional design are subject/content specific (e.g., Stallings & Krasavage, 1986), but the generalized arguments that follow are more typical.

Nunan (1983) was among the first to critically "counter educational design," as he puts it, but of the works cited in this section, Streibel's (1991) may be the best known. In "Instructional Design and Human Practice: What Can We Learn from Habermas' Theory of Technical and Practical Human Interests?," Streibel (1991) shows that

> an instructional designer cannot rely on a technical approach to design. Rather, an instructional designer has to be guided by a practical human interest and support the instructional and learning processes that actually take place" (p. 8). Five implications follow for the designer: (1) Find ways to construct meaning in context. (2) Find ways to create resources that support meaning-making. (3) Give up designing teacher user-proof instruction. (4) Give up seeing everything in terms of skills; instead, see learning in terms of judgments, collective deliberation, and collective meaning making. (5) Participate directly in learning.

In *Computers in Education: Social, Political, and Historical Perspectives* (Muffoletto & Knupfer, 1993), we find the Streibel (1993b) piece called "Instructional Design and Human Practice: What Can We Learn from Grundy's Interpretation of Habermas' Theory of Technical and Practical Human Interests?" Streibel uses Grundy's work in curriculum studies to look at the effects of technical and practical interests on design and to recommend that designers leave some space for teachers and learners to construct their own senses of good instructional design.

Wilson (1989) examines the relationships of instructional design to ideological claims in education. He presents a heuristic that gives the relationship of instructional design to each of the claims according to: who designs learning, what is designed, the people for whom learning is designed, why learning is designed, and how designing should be done. He argues that the use of instructional design is ethically justified only if it meets the criteria most associated with the critical position.

9.7.1.4. Computers. As in other areas, not all people who find deleterious effects of educational computing are, strictly speaking, associated with critical theory, but they examine cultural and emancipatory effects of educational computing, and so can be called critical theorists. Such a researcher is Sutton (1991), who finds that computer uses in schools in the 1980s

> maintained and exaggerated existing inequalities in education input, processes of computer learning, and output. Poor, female, and minority students had less access to computers at home and, in addition, less access to computers at school. . . . Poor and minority students were more likely to use computers for drill and practice than were middle-class and white students, and females outnumbered males in word processing but were underrepresented in programming. Teachers, while concerned about equity, held attitudes which hindered access: They believed that better behaved students deserved computer time and that the primary benefit of computers for low-achieving students was mastery of basic skills. . . . Thus, children who were minority, poor, female, or low achieving were likely to be further behind after the introduction of computers in schools. . . .

These inequities were found in the U.S.A., Great Britain, Australia, Canada, and New Zealand (p. 494).

On the other hand, a few thinkers (e.g., Apple & Jungck, 1990) have analyzed explicit connections between educational computing and critical theories. In "A Critical Analysis of the Use of Computers in Education," Streibel (1988) is one of the first professionals to conduct such an analysis. He explores the educational uses of computers for drill-and-practice, tutorial, and simulation and programming. After alluding to Habermas's ideas about the social construction of knowledge, Streibel concludes that educational computing often embodies overly deterministic, behavioral, technological characteristics that limit personal responsibility for learning, mitigate against nonbehavioral goals of education, and leave the learner with "an underdeveloped intellectual agency within the qualitative, dialectical, and experiential domains of natural and social events" (Streibel, 1991).

In a later piece about "situated critical pedagogy," Streibel (1993b) addresses the role of emancipatory human interests, and he asks questions about praxis, situated critical pedagogy, interpretive processes, and emancipatory evaluation. To his earlier works, this one adds an interesting set of questions to educators about using computers in emancipatory ways: Do learners develop their own evaluative criteria in conjunction with fair educators? Is the discourse around computers comprehensible to learners? Are students participants in the construction of history and biography? Do evaluations result in appropriate individual and collective actions?

In "Culture, Power, and Educational Computing," Bromley (1992) analyzes the social, the artifactual, the historical, and the power relations of computers. He suggests that our computer uses tend toward individualism, the technical fix, domination of nature, efficiency, instructional systems thought, quantitative fixation, top-down thinking, positivism, and centralization. He shows how the social relations of progress, the military, and rationalization have contributed to these tendencies. He suggests that teachers be more responsible for computing and that a pedagogy that encourages student participation in decision making about computers will most help to make constructive uses of technologies. Bromley also explores the meanings of cybernetics in education.

As noted earlier, not every critical theorist concludes that technology is bound to be oppressive. The same holds for critical theorists in educational computing (e.g., Landow, 1992). Boyd (1987), for instance, uses critical theory to argue that computer conferencing may be a good technology for providing emancipative learning. Currently, students are emersed in schooling that is bureaucratic, domineering, and boring. Boyd suspects that computer-mediated conferences can be good, because everyone has an equal opportunity to have her or his arguments heard in such a conference. Though he thinks that education and computer-mediated conferences must aim for romance, precision, and generalization, Boyd believes that rational discourse of the kind that is possible via computers is most important if education is to be emancipative.

9.7.1.5. Visuals. Several researchers have used critical theory to examine educational uses of visuals. Given that the International Visual Literacy Association and its *Journal of Visual Literacy* have begun to accept presentations and publications of a critical theory nature (e.g., Lewis, 1991), perhaps such examinations are a growing trend.

Moore and Dwyer's (1994) *Visual Literacy: A Spectrum of Visual Learning* is a compilation of much of the latest thinking and research about the relations of visuals to teaching and learning, and several chapters in it are pertinent to critical theories. Two of the works, by DeVaney (1994a) and Nichols (1994), are discussed later in this chapter, but in "Representations: You, Me, and Them," Muffoletto (1994) argues that "The concerns of visual literacy go beyond questions of perceptions, production, and interpretation to questions of power and control over the formation of subjects" (p. 306) in the social world. He argues that the image is a social construction, and he wants the viewer to ask how social and taken-for-granted meanings accrue to that image. He also wants viewers to know how those who control images also control consciousness and who we think we are.

In a visually intriguing chapter called "Deconstruction and Visuals: Is This a Telephone?" Yeaman (1994a) shows readers how to resist dominant, and therefore oppressive, images. He uses visual examples, humor, and social analysis to examine conflicting senses and meanings in visuals and to show that images never mean what they say or say what they mean. In short, by deconstruction, Yeaman encourages readers to uncover the multiple meanings in visuals. His uncovering of the venerable Shannon and Weaver model of communication, for instance, takes us through layer after layer of meanings and, in doing so, helps us to see how the model is not "true."

9.7.2 Societal Relations

This section reviews works associated with critical approaches to understanding educational technologies and their societal relationships. Topics include social foundations, feminism, race, capitalism, and the military.

9.7.2.1. Social Foundations. Michael Apple is among the best known of those who think critically about social relations of educational technologies, particularly in the realm of the political/ideological. We can see his thought played out in works such as *Teachers and Texts: A Political Economy of Class and Gender Relations in Education* (1986), "Teaching and Technology: The Hidden Effects of Computers on Teachers and Students" (1988), and *Official Knowledge* (1993).

Apple (1993) stresses that teachers often have problems as curricula and teaching methods become more rationalized and economized:

We tend to think of technology in education as something of a "better mousetrap." Given a process/product curriculum

model that says that education is good if it gets us from point A to point B efficiently and cheaply, technology simply becomes one more means to get prechosen knowledge into the heads of students. . . . Films [and other technologies] are seen as better than dry text material or a lecture. Goals don't change. Only the means do. Film, in essence, becomes one more "delivery system" of official knowledge. The teacher sends; the student receives. "Banking" education goes on (p. 145).

Apple urges that one response to the conservative and technical agenda manifested in the banking metaphor is to help students be critical. He suggests that,

If we think of film not as a "delivery system" of prechosen messages, but as a form of aesthetic, political, and personal production, our entire orientation changes. If we think of it as a way that people help produce their own critical forms of visual literacy, this too forces major shifts in our perspective on the official politics of knowledge as well (p. 145).

Similarly, Koetting (1993) urges educators to examine technology through the lenses of social foundations and curriculum theory. He shows that schooling acts largely to maintain the status quo—not to encourage deep reform—by focusing on issues of economics, standardized tests, and the smooth functioning of society. He concludes that educational reform will not be substantive until we recognize that education is a political act; knowledge is socially constructed; and critical thinking is not simply cognitive but moral, social, and political.

In "Socio-cultural Methodology and Analysis of Historic and Current Instructional Materials" (Robinson, Wiegmann & Nichols, 1992), the authors attempt an unconventional approach to evaluating instructional materials, including video materials. They recommend asking a series of critical questions about who gains and who loses financially or politically or otherwise if a material is used.

Preston (1992), too, examines social perspectives in educational technology. After studying the social and ethical implications of educational computing in Queensland, Australia, he advocates a socially critical orientation for educational computing and technology, in which, for instance, teachers try to ensure that students are aware of social effects of computers; the computer is an empowering tool for students; benefits of computers are represented as a social good rather than solely an individual good; and questions of equity of access are addressed.

9.7.2.2. Feminism. Although many feminists do not want to be included very directly with several of the critical theorists noted already, feminists *are* encouraging self-consciousness and liberatory action that changes social and educational practices related to technology. In this way, at least, they are critical theorists.

Not a great amount altogether has been published in this area, but many topics are covered, ranging from various technological threats and promises for female teachers and students (Bohren, 1991); to media and sexism (Byerly, 1985); to the possibilities for critical theory in the field of educational technology (Jamison, 1994); to justice and caring (Kerr, 1990); to gender, languages, and computers (Rothschild, 1986); and to equity (Thurston, 1990). Other publications address issues of ethics and technological empowerment (Anderson, 1992, 1994) and action research and sex bias in media and materials (Clark, 1983).

Luke and Gore (1992) say that poststructuralist feminists "reject the self-certain subject, the truth of science and the fixity of language" (p. 5) and that "a poststructuralist feminist position takes issue with the technology of control" (p. 4). Rejection occurs "especially in liberal progressive discourses that make vocal claims to social justice on behalf of marginalized groups while denying their own technologies of power" (p. 7). So:

> Within this [feminist] foundation there is greater specificity about our pedagogical goals than currently exists for what is still an abstract, generalized discourse of critical pedagogy. . . . By locating our work in particular sites and with attention to specific practices, the possibilities for genuinely reshaping discursive and embodied relations in pedagogy seem within reach (p. 9).

One scholar for whom critical feminist pedagogy related to educational technologies is within reach is Suzanne Damarin (1988, 1991a, 1992a, 1992b). She is deeply analytical/critical of many forms and uses of educational technology (see also 10.4). In "Rethinking Equity: An Imperative for Educational Computing," Damarin (1989) discusses employment changes related to women in society, math anxiety, and computer anxiety; instructional and curriculum design; evaluation; and computer literacy as they relate to women's equity. In "Computers, Education, and Issues of Gender" (Damarin, 1990a) and in "Unthinking Educational Technology (Damarin, 1990)," she argues, among other things, that the theorizing of gender as a variable of consequence, valuing of women's experience as a scientific resource, and the positioning in the same plane as the researched can help us rethink educational technology. She also concludes that conventional research on the effectiveness of educational technology serves to take valuable control away from the teacher; students use technologies that are very sex biased; and women teachers and female students are denied access to much technology.

In "Rethinking Science and Mathematics Curriculum and Instruction: Feminist Perspectives in the Computer Era," Damarin (1991b) argues that computers can play a part in feminist reform of science and math curricula if feminism helps computers to move away from linear presentations of facts. Computers can open science and math to more women and more ideas. In "Women and Information Technology: Framing Some Issues for Education," Damarin (1992b) discusses views of the computer as superior human being, as cyborg, and as human-computer dyad, and she argues that these views have had less-than-positive effects on women and on at-risk and nonliterate students.

9.7.2.3. Race. Though, as a topic of study generally, the relationships of education and race are being explored relatively well and often (e.g., Castenell & Pinar, 1993),

very little has been written about issues of critical theories and race as they relate to educational technologies.

Exceptions include a work by Schwoch, White, Rilley, Scott, and Scott (1992) called "Drug Abuse, Race Relations, and the Prime Time News Program." The article analyzes a prime-time news report called *The Koppel Report—D.C./Divided City*, in which urban black males are portrayed as the major perpetrators of illegal drug trade. Racism and a rich history of blacks overcoming overwhelming problems are never addressed in the report. White responsibilities for these problems are never addressed, and Koppel "wipes away the earlier accusations of genocide and race/class struggle, as well as the implication of government and social institutions in maintaining racial inequalities" (p. 77). In opposition to these problems, the authors see positive signs in alternatives such as a greater ethnic diversity in programming, greater numbers of camcorders with which people produce and understand programs, and a more active critical viewership.

In a study called "Photographic Images of Blacks in Sexuality Texts," Whatley (1993; see also Whatley, 1990) concludes that, though publishers may be trying to represent blacks more positively in textbook photographs, in some books there is a tendency to emphasize the black man to the exclusion of the black woman, and "The possibilities for the sexuality of the black man become polarized into the dangerous pimp, or the good, loving father, without allowing for the full range of sexual expression allowed to whites" (p. 102).

9.7.2.4. Capitalism. As noted earlier, several critical theory studies examine the relations of capital to education generally (e.g., Bowles & Gintis, 1976; Liston; 1988; Feenberg, 1991). However, very few works concern themselves to any extended degree with critical theory and the relations of capital to educational technology. Most give the topic scant treatment (e.g., DeVaney, 1994d; Nichols, 1993; Bromley, 1992).

If more literature did exist, it likely would have the tenor of Apple's (1993) work in *Official Knowledge*:

> I must admit that when I am in Brazil, Thailand, and other countries doing educational and political work and participating with groups of people struggling to keep babies alive, to *find* enough food to eat, to even get a minimum of schooling for their children . . . I think that the relations that make up what we call capitalism are much more oppressive than other kinds of relations *in many situations* (p. 176).

In *Teachers and Texts: A Political Economy of Class and Gender Relations*, Apple (1986) has produced what may be the only book-length work to critically address educational technology and capitalism. In this empirical-critical work, Apple (1986) concludes that:

> The new technology is here. It will not go away. Our task as educators is to make sure that when it enters the classroom it is there for politically, economically, and educationally wise reasons, not because powerful groups may be redefining our major educational goals in their own image (p. 174).

In another of the very few works on this topic, a piece called *The Technical Fix: Education, Computers and Industry,* Robins and Webster (1989) claim that the root problem facing education is "the technocratic imagination which has come to dominate and deform education" (p. 256). They suggest that "Above all, it is necessary to appreciate the future of education as a political and ethical matter" and that "This political emphasis is about overcoming the stance of acceptance, accommodation, and adaptation involved in the commodification of education" (p. 274).

9.7.2.5. The Military. Except for relatively minor excursions into the topic (e.g., Bromley, 1992), as far as we can tell only Noble (1988, 1991) has written critically and at any length about the contradictions and social difficulties associated with the military's being responsible for so much of the technology found in education. In *The Classroom Arsenal: Military Research, Information Technology, and Public Education,* Noble (1991) talks about today's difficulties with public education and the potential for computer-based education (CBE) to fix those problems. He says:

> while appearing to address these problems in public education, CBE research actually participates in an entirely different enterprise, one with marginal or antithetical import for education. This is the design and engineering of man-machine systems. CBE research is thus, at best, an expensive distraction from the concerns of education.

At worst, the potential impact of CBE on education insomuch as it reflects a continuation of the momentum accumulated throughout its historical development, leads only to further fragmentation, decontextualization, and depersonalization of education" (p. 189).

9.7.3 Critical Media Education

This section describes critical studies related to feminist media literacy, media and popular culture, television and video production, and postmodern media analysis.

9.7.3.1. Feminist Media Literacy. Some feminist perspectives are showing up in the critical literature about educational media, including Whatley's (1991) "Raging Hormones and Powerful Cars: The Construction of Men's Sexuality in School Sex Education and Popular Adolescent Films," and Hooks's (1992) *Black Looks: Race and Representation.*

Ellsworth and Whatley's (1990) *The Ideology of Images in Educational Media* is representative of works in this area. It is a unique collection of works that explore:

> strategic understandings that ideological analyses make possible. It is intended to contribute to the strategies for interpretation available to educators as they define for themselves what is important to understand about mainstream educational media and what they must do with them in their particular contexts of struggle (p. 8).

In the first chapter of this text, Ellsworth (1990) points out that many educational films use conventions and viewing experiences that work against critical pedagogy, and that "media producers must stop creating images and narratives that invite viewers exclusively into physical, social, and ideological positions" where white patriarchal experts appear to know topics indisputably (p. 25).

9.7.3.2. Media Analysis and Popular Culture. Several authors (Giroux & Simon, 1992; McLaren, Hammer, Sholle & Reilly, 1995) have written critical examinations about media in general, the popular culture in which media occur, and education. In one such commentary, Giroux, Simon et al. (1989) study various forms of popular culture such as music and television to argue for a critical literacy that influences school curricula in terms of broadly democratic plurality. And the publication *Strategies* has been working toward media literacy for a long time, often from an overtly critical theory perspective (see, for example, "Schooling for Citizenship," 1992).

The kind of arguments found in *Media Knowledge: Readings in Popular Culture, Pedagogy, and Critical Citizenship* (Schwoch, White & Reilly, 1992) indicate how authors in this area want us to use critical perspectives to analyze film, television programs, advertising, and other forms of cultural representation. They say:

> A critical pedagogy of representation must establish the relativity of all forms of representations by situating them in historical and social constructions that both inform their content and structure their ideological parameters. Second, a pedagogy of representation must bring to light the strategies that are used to structure how texts are read, used, and received within particular contexts and practices. At stake here is understanding not only how power is inscribed in a pedagogy of representation but also how such a pedagogy can be used to disrupt the ideological, cultural, and political systems that both inscribe and contain them. This suggests that the practice of reading ideologies be connected to the production of political strategies informed by transformative ideologies. Third, a critical pedagogy of representation must be able to articulate between representations that operate in particular educational sites and representations that operate in other cultural sites around similar forms of address and relevancies. Fourth, a critical pedagogy of representation must take up as a form of ethical address which grounds the relationship between the self and others in practices that promote care and solidarity rather than oppression and human suffering. In this case, a pedagogy of representation cannot be disarticulated from the responsibility of both politics and ethics (p. xxix).

Ellsworth (1989b), in "Educational Media, Ideology, and the Presentation of Knowledge Through Popular Cultural Forms," notes that students and others construct intersections between popular cultural forms and education when educational media incorporate popular cultural forms for teaching. In this way, educational media make legitimate school knowledge by associating it with positive connotations about leisure, entertainment, pleasure, and so on. To resist this legitimizing, she argues for a "transformative media education" that helps students to understand media mechanisms and to develop skills aimed at social change.

A few authors also use critical approaches in the international arena (Trend, 1994) and in visual language (Goodman, 1992).

9.7.3.3. Television and Video Production. Critical theorists in education also address television in any of its several guises. Some researchers examine resistance to patriarchy in commercial television (Lee, 1991). Becker (1986) explores the grammar of television. Authors in DeVaney's (1994b) *Watching Channel One: The Convergence of Students, Technology, and Private Business* employ a variety of techniques for understanding the ethical, political, economic, social, and cognitive—as well as educational—dimensions of Channel One, which has been seen by millions of teens. DeVaney's (1994c, 1994d, respectively) "Introduction" and "Reading the Ads: Bacchanalian Adolescence" are examples of postmodern approaches to understanding Channel One. In the latter chapter, DeVaney concludes that:

> It is clear that the producers [of Channel One] borrowed production conventions or codes from two sources, namely, MTV and postmodern TV ads. However, parts of each of these TV formats are Rabelaisian in content and structure, because they build their messages upon the material base of the body, they both juxtapose unusual images with the fragmented body parts, and they valorize eating, drinking, and sexual activities. However, TV ads cannot completely abandon a structure that will appeal to those consumer-viewers accustomed to reading coherent modern text. So, the grotesque is eliminated and kept at bay, as it were, for the ultimate purpose of product sales" (p. 148).

Some writers advocate using media/video production to help people understand TV. For instance, Denski (1991) relates classroom experiences of trying to move theory into practice in order to break down various oppressive dichotomies—such as teacher/student—and foster empowerment, resistance, invention, and hope. Elsewhere, Higgins (1991) shows how video production is essentially a political act, how the structure of video is ideological and value laden, and how critical approaches may help students be conscious of these values and seek alternatives to them.

9.7.3.4. Postmodern Media Analysis. Kellner (1991) uses a postmodern approach to analyze media, and he wants to develop a critical media literacy so that people can "survive the onslaught of media images, messages, and spectacles which are inundating our culture" (p. 63). This requires that the distinction between "high" and "low" cultures be obliterated and that skills associated with deconstruction and reading of culture be learned. *Adbusters* (Vancouver, British Columbia) magazine is one place where these skills are put to use toward understanding advertising.

9.7.4 Ethics

Only a few writers (e.g., Anderson, 1992, 1994) address the relations of critical theories to educational technology and ethical or moral issues. DeVaney (1994a) does so in "Ethical Considerations of Visuals in the Classroom:

African-Americans and Hollywood Film." This work analyzes nonstereotypic images of African-American males so that those producing and using images in classrooms can show that the presence of blacks is rightfully constitutive of American life. Nichols (1994a), in "Considering Morals and Visuals (Beyond School)," lends a little attention to a postmodern view of images and ethics by noting that several postmodernist thinkers "are looking at the moral implications of mass media, including films and television. They are asking who is justified and empowered and who is delegitimized and 'othered' by mass media" (p. 375).

In "Critical Theory, Educational Technology, and Ethics: Helping Teachers Respond Meaningfully to Technology," Nichols (1993) concludes that educational technologies are ethically suspect, and in "Searching for Moral Guidance About Educational Technology," Nichols (1994b) suggests that educational technology is deleterious to education and the environment. Because educational technologists willfully neglect issues of educational inequality and ecology, because we inhibit democratic involvement by those affected by technology, we are morally suspect. He suggests that Habermas's notion of consensual communication can, in part, help to bring a more morally balanced educational technology.

9.7.5 Action Research

In education generally, many action research projects have been carried out (Carr & Kemmis, 1986; McKernan, 1993; McCutcheon & Jung, 1990; Tripp, 1990). In the area of educational technology, some researchers (Berlin & White, 1992; Kember & Gow, 1992; Tanner, 1992; Watt & Watt, 1991) use action research but appear largely to neglect issues of truth, justice, and freedom about educational technologies. Legitimate knowledge in these works appears more often to come from those doing the research than from those being researched. Further, some authors (e.g., Nosek & Yaverbaum, 1991; Oakes et al., 1985; Zeni, 1990) seem to support technologies uncritically; the research seems to have set out mostly to increase the infusion of technology and/or consumerism in education.

Other instances of action research appear to adhere to the characteristics noted earlier by Grundy and others. For instance, Morgan (1990) looks at distance education and concludes that qualitative evaluation has not much affected distance education, though it has the potential to do so. Harris (1986) proposes a shift from positivist to critical theoretical and hermeneutical epistemological foundations for research in library science. Calabrese and Acker (1987) argue for viewing the design of information systems from sociotechnical perspectives so that the systems might be practical. Leino (1991) describes a successful 5-year project in Finland where learning was to be more active and cooperative, learners were to be more self-responsible, school knowledge was to be integrated with students' social knowledge, and microcomputers were to be used effectively in this context.

9.7.6 Ecology

Few publications deal with critical theory as it applies to educational technology and ecological issues, though as this chapter is being written, the Professional Ethics Committee of the Association for Educational Communications and Technology is about to accept a new principle on this issue for its code of ethics. The principle encourages members to account for the ecological changes associated with their technology.

Elsewhere, Damarin (1990b) identifies links between educational technology and ecological damage. She elegantly fuses critical notions about domination and fragmentation with "ecology," and she suggests that:

> Ecofeminist considerations invite us to consider whether educational technology perceives the reality of "all aspects of human learning" as more like a freestanding machine than a living social organism, and to unthink this perception. How are educational technology practices of "analyzing problems and devising, implementing, evaluating, and managing solutions" rooted in more general notions of certainty, objectivity, and domination? How do these practices sanction the domination of both nature and women (and men)? (p. 4).

Nichols (1990) suggests several environmental and social catastrophes that will be exacerbated by educational technologies in that our uses of them support the

> destructive Western belief that humans should or can control most of our existence via increasingly dominant rational and technical descriptions and manipulations. . . . Reports of the Earth's declining condition make us clearer each day about the predicaments and dangers science and technology . . . have brought. In contrast, notions of a less rational-technical but balanced coexistence with the rest of the world, wherein our existence is dependent on leaving it free to influence us too, have slipped into a vague background knowledge for most Westerners.

More recently, Nichols (1994b) cites Bowers (1993) in order to say that:

> The ecologically suspect beliefs to which Bowers refers include progress, individualism, and rationalism. Each of these beliefs is often associated positively with educational technologies . . . [but] technology uses a lot of energy, most of it being carbon-based fuels that pollute. Also, just where does all the used plastic in computers go when it is discarded? (p. 42).

9.7.7 Related Works

Several individual pieces and collections of criticism of educational technology bear mentioning. These works are less directly related to versions of critical theory noted in previous sections of this chapter, but the authors hold to ideas such as emancipation, social justice, and ecological concern, and/or they exhibit the same critical attitudes about science, technology, and rationalization as found in works noted already.

Relatively early in the appearance of microcomputers in educational arenas, the *Teachers College Record* (Sloan, 1984) published a special issue raising critical questions about computers in education. Except for once in this issue (Simpson, 1984), critical theory is not mentioned; however, to the extent that the issue is one of the first times that scholars challenge the rationalization inherent in computing and force existing views of educational computing to their systematic and spurious conclusions, it is well worth citing.

A special issue of *The Journal of Thought* (Robinson, 1990) is noteworthy, and the February 1994 edition of *Educational Technology* (Yeaman, 1994b) magazine is worth rementioning, because they make critical, broad, and penetrating analyses of educational technology, and they appear to be the only professional publication theme issues devoted to the study of the ethical and societal dimensions of educational technologies.

A similar uniqueness also can been seen in individual works by authors such as Hlynka (1989); Kerr (1989), Kreuger, Karger, and Barwick (1988); and Yeaman (1990). In "Resisting Technological Momentum," Taylor and Johnsen (1986) say that our lack of understanding of technology:

> contributes to technological momentum and its pernicious effects. To overcome this condition, educators and young people will need to develop the vocabulary, definitions, concepts, and, equally important, the will to engage in a critical and extended study of technology (p. 219).

Bowers (1988, 1993), too, speaks eloquently to the ways education and rational-technical thinking are culpable when it comes to ecological threats (though, as noted in the next section, he would not want to be categorized with many of the critical theorists examined here). He concludes that middle-class culture, its schools, and its naive support of educational technologies combine to perpetuate ecologically destructive beliefs in the goodness of progress, individualism, and rationalism (Bowers, 1993, p. 15).

9.8 PROBLEMS WITH CRITICAL THEORIES OF EDUCATION

Critical theories are not without their critics. Perhaps the major criticism of them is that they fail to provide rational standards by which they can justify themselves, by which they can show themselves to be "better" than other theories of knowledge, science, or practice. Their ongoing problem has been to present a normative base for rationality that is not distorted by particular social ideologies (Held, 1983).

More bluntly, Gibson (1986) says that critical theories suffer from cliquishness, conformity, elitism, immodesty, anti-individualism, contradictoriness, uncriticalness, and naivety (p. 164). Perhaps this is the same sense that Hughes and Hughes (1990) have when they say of Habermas's theory of communicative action that it "says much about rational talkers talking, but very little about actors acting: Felt, perceptive, imaginative, bodily experience does not fit these theories" (p. 144).

Likewise, critical theories have been maligned for their dense language (Goodman, 1992). Philip Jackson's (1980) complaint still has appeal: "Terms like . . . *hermeneutics* get tossed around as though everybody but a fool is intimately familiar with their meaning" (p. 379). Counter arguments to these issues of language include claims that a call for clearer and more accessible language is anti-intellectual, a new "language of possibility" is needed, and oppressed peoples can understand and contribute to new languages.

Some feminist criticisms of critical theories have been especially powerful. Critical theories can be as narrow and oppressive as the rationalization, bureaucratization, and cultures they seek to unmask and change. Remember that Weiler (1991) said of Freire that he has a privileged position and believes in universals (p. 469). In one of the best-known analyses of critical pedagogists, Ellsworth (1989a) says they often are so tied to their vision of the truth that they fail to see themselves as one of many voices, and they fail to understand that their enlightening of the false consciousness of others may be a form of dominance, not liberation. Her comments and the vitriolic responses to them by McLaren and Giroux are given an enlightening reading in Lather's (1991) *Getting Smart*.

Further, Bowers (1993) points out that leaders for the emancipatory tradition in liberal education—Paulo Freire, Ira Shor, Henry Giroux, Maxine Greene—are remiss because they:

> always deal with social justice issues at an abstract level, and thus never engage the cultural complexity of specific political issues like how to deal with a group that may be the victims of racial prejudice and economic discrimination but who largely adopt the "right to life" stance on the abortion issue. . . . As slogans intended to provide a general focus of messianic energy, "resistance," "emancipatory power," "transformative intellectuals," and so forth, must remain ethereal and thus avoid the contradictions and splintering effects of the real world of politics (p. 111).

Bowers (1993) thinks critical pedagogists are particularly at fault for ignoring the ways in which their liberalism contributes to a declining ecology:

> [Their] vision and rhetoric promote those aspects of the Western mindset that is [sic] contributing to the degradation of the environment: the individual or group of individuals who would constitute the "state of collective autonomy" is still viewed as independent of the natural environment; critical reflection remains the only legitimate expression of intelligence, which excludes both traditional cultures and the complex of information exchanges that characterize an ecology; change is still understood in human and culturally specific terms that equate progress only with an expansion of the individual's sense of freedom. Understanding the interdependence of the human culture/natural habitat relationship in terms of what is sustainable over the long term . . . is simply not part of the Enlightenment vision of emancipation uncritically accepted by the followers of Dewey and Freire (p. 115).

9.9 PROBLEMS WITH CRITICAL THEORIES OF EDUCATIONAL TECHNOLOGY

It is no surprise that the criticisms outlined above also can be leveled at the critical theories of educational technology. In some instances, the written works and oral presentations of critical theorists in educational technology suffer from cliquishness, contradictoriness, naivety, and so on, and sometimes they fail to show how their ideas are any better or more reasonable than the theories they critique.

Much of the work of the critical educational technologists cited here is abstract and removed from doing the complex economic, social, political, educational, and personal work necessary to change any oppression related to educational technology. Put another way, the work usually does not take place in the lifeworld of learners.

Further, as Buckingham (1991) argues with regard to a critical-theory approach to media education and children, a rationalistic (i.e., critical-theory) approach to educational technology may fail to engage many learners' emotions and cultural experiences. Similarly, Goodman (1992) suggests that we develop various forms of a "language of critical imagery" because critical educators cannot continue to offer understandings at abstract levels.

There could be the claim, too, that forms of critical theory of educational technology are oppressive. Remember that Luke and Gore (1992) argue that critical pedagogists use "technologies of power" to marginalize women.

Finally, critical theorists of educational technology never have analyzed the extent to which they promote ecologically disturbing results. For instance, Landow's (1992) attraction to postmodern possibilities with computers is, in ecological terms, an attraction to using more of the Earth's resources to produce computers and, at the same time, produce more trash. It is bad enough that so few educational technologists ever look into the ways conventional educational technology philosophies, ideologies, and activities promote ecological degradation; but for educational technology critical theorists to omit looking at our own scholarship and the ways it offends ecology is, at best, ironic.

Except, perhaps, in the case of ignoring ecology, critical theorists of educational technology can refute these accusations. Critical theories may be better than others because they are contextualized and democratic. A few critical theorists (e.g., see several authors in DeVaney, 1994) are indeed working directly with the teachers and students affected by technology. Abstract rationalizing might be characteristic of theorists using a Habermasian sort of critical theory, but some postmodernists are evoking considerable concrete work and enthusiasm ("messianic energy"?) in people with whom they work.

9.10 SUMMARY

In this chapter, many of the critical-theory analyses of educational technologies (e.g., Streibel, 1986, 1991, 1993a, 1993b) reflect a longer-standing kind of critical analysis.

That is, they approach research from the point of view of "immanent critique, which proceeds through forcing existing views to their systematic conclusions, bringing them face to face with their incompleteness and contradictions, and, ultimately, with the social conditions of their existence" (Young, 1990, p. 18). Further, many of the studies (e.g., Koetting, 1983a, 1983b) use the Habermasian framework about sciences and their interests: empirical-analytic science (with a technical interest in control), historical-hermeneutic science (with a practical interest in mutual understanding), and critical sciences (with an interest in freedom). However, a few of the analyses approach educational technology studies more from postmodern (e.g., DeVaney, 1994b; Hlynka & Belland, 1991a; Landow, 1992), feminist (e.g., Damarin, 1989, 1990a, 1991a, 1994; Ellsworth, 1990), or critical pedagogical (e.g., Koetting, 1994) points of view, which often seek to understand the subjectivities of people being oppressed or ignored ("othered") in educational settings (see also 10.2, 10.5).

Though no great amount of them has been published, the written works produced so far in this area give people a solid start on working with and understanding critical theoretical analyses of some basic aspects of educational technology, especially aspects of the philosophies and the epistemologies of instructional design, computers, and educational technology generally. Many of the studies conclude that educational technology, instructional design, and computer uses are focused on knowledge and learning that are too analytical, empirical, cognitive, decontextualized, and instrumental. This is to say that the technologies are not used as wisely as possible. A few authors (e.g., Nichols, 1993, 1994b) go so far as to say that learners suffer and technologists are morally suspect because educational technologies are misused.

Several topics about critical theory and educational technology have received minimal attention. These topics include social relations, feminism and technology and media, media and popular culture generally, and television and video. Further, some topics have received virtually no attention from critical theorists. Such topics include language, visuals, race, capitalism, the military, politics, ethics, and ecology.

A majority of the critical-theory studies cited here find problems with educational technologies. This is probably a result of the lack of experience educational technologists have with this kind of research as well as the nature of critical theory, which is intent on showing inconsistencies, incompleteness, and oppressive social conditions. The approach initially is bound to lead to seemingly negative appraisals of the technology.

In time, one would expect the view and the tone of the studies to take on a somewhat more positive face, given the potential for critical theory to encourage democracy, emancipation, and equality, for example. At the moment in fact, there is a strain of optimism that computer and other technologies will enhance communication, democracy, postmodernism, and so forth (e.g., Boyd, 1991; Denski,

1991; Landow, 1992; Preston, 1992). This is not to say a completely supportive or positive position about educational technology would ever be the position of critical theorists of educational technology. Given the inherently detrimental characteristics of technology (e.g., Winner, 1977; Taylor & Johnsen, 1986; Nichols, 1990, 1991), as well as critical theorists' search for oppression, totally sunny reports are best left to the technologically illiterate, to technophiles, and to technology capitalists.

9.11 BEING CRITICAL EDUCATIONAL TECHNOLOGISTS

Only a few educators understand the purposes and approaches of critical theory and are using it. Few people understand that critical theorists are working with the relations of technology to issues of human understanding, freedom, and action (as opposed to narrower issues of cognition, technique, science, or the practical) in the realms of ecology, society, school, and culture. Most educational technologists are examining, say, visuals, but not from the point of view that asks *why* someone should learn the content of visuals. People are examining educational capital from the point of view that asks where to get more money for more computers, but not from the view that asks why supporters of educational computing are taking advantage of women, people of color, and poor people, as Sutton (1990) concludes. Instructional design is being examined, but not often from the view that asks how we use it to get students to unconsciously do as someone else wishes—and to do so, mostly, for reasons of power and profit. This limited view is apparently the case even with design theorists who support constructivist learning and other newer approaches to instructional design (such as those described in Hannafin & Hooper, 1992, p. 27).

Critical theories of educational technologies should be hopeful remedies to the kinds of problems with conventional stances toward technology identified in this chapter, and some readers may now be convinced that some version of critical theory is useful and enlightening and educative. What, then, could these hopeful people do by way of pursuing a critical theory of educational technology? Basic suggestions to this effect include:

• Educational technologists should use research methods embraced by critical theorists, as long as they are regulated by norms of noncoercive, democratic conversations. Action research in educational technology, for example, could move into the schools, where students and teachers should have primary responsibility for reports/activities associated with the research.

• Educational technologists should become more engaged with research about many foundational, essential, provocative, and morally pertinent issues that are largely unconscionably ignored. The issues include aspects of the philosophies and the epistemologies of instructional design and educational media generally. The issues include societal relations, feminism, and popular culture. Further issues include critical relations of educational technology to language, visuals, race, capitalism, the military, politics, ethics, and ecology. *The potential for fostering learners' social, educational, ecological, and democratic responsibilities and sensibilities related to technology generally and to educational technology specifically are enormous. Even more, our potential to engage individuals and cultures not directly related to education could be enhanced with critical-theory approaches to educational technology. After all, we are responsible to people of all walks of life.*

• Educational technologists should become critical pedagogists. Doing so holds tremendous prospects for engaging learners in meaningful education. Critical pedagogists should be guided by thoughts like McLaren's (1994a):

> Knowledge is relevant only when it begins with the experiences students bring with them from the surrounding culture; it is critical only when these experiences are shown to sometimes be problematic (i.e., racist, sexist); and it is transformative only when students begin to use the knowledge to help empower others, including individuals in the surrounding community (p. 197).

• Educational technologists should not be busy using technology to do things *to* and *for* learners. We should be busy asking learners to tell us what to do—and to tell us from philosophically, economically, politically, ecologically, and educationally informed subjective positions.

• Educational technologists should be developing greater amounts of nonprint forms of critical scholarship. Very few materials in forms other than print were found in researching scholarship for this chapter. Yet, multimedia critical approaches to understanding educational technologies would lead to understandings that are far more humanly accessible, widespread and, so, potentially freeing.

9.12 WHY APPROPRIATE CRITICAL THEORY?

If learning, teaching, and knowledge are culture bound, ever changing, and morally imbued, then we must admit that the critical theory described in this chapter will probably not exist in its present forms for much longer. Life changes. Current contentiousness and discussions about critical theories, learning, teaching, and knowledge indicate this changeability (see Anyon, 1994; Cherryholmes, 1994). Other theoretical views will eclipse critical theory; perhaps, as Winkler (1993) suggests, we already have entered an era of "post-theory" where "the day of high theory is dead" (p. A9). American critical theorists might be eclipsed by current French thinkers, who represent a pulling back from the excesses of postmodernism" (McMillen, 1994, p. A7), and who are diverse, leftist, and not very interested in politics. For them, democracy is taken for granted and, unlike some American theorists, they have undergone a process of self-criticism (McMillen, 1994, p. A7).

But whatever critical theory becomes, it will remain with us because people will always be subject to and, so, interested in oppression. Critical theory will always have the potential to open educational technologists to deeply important questions of self and community, the character of technology, freedom, and environmental sustenance. For example, what is implied is that technology may not always be oppressive or harmful, but because it is human, it is bound to be harmful sometimes. In what moral, democratic, educative ways can conscientization about the harmfulness of technology be fostered? How can we use critical approaches to help people understand to the fullest extent possible the ways in which all forms and relations of technology—capital, the military, science, technology, rationalization, education, educational biotechnology (Nichols, 1990, 1994b), and so on—affect the consciousness, conscientiousness, and freedoms of people and the environments in which we live.

Most importantly, perhaps, we need to try continually to understand *why* we use technologies in education. In struggling with this most important of questions, perhaps we can do justice to, say, that disinterested, slightly sarcastic learner at the back of the classroom who says, "Why do we have to learn this stuff?" That is the same critical question McLaren (1994a) asks, and when we can consistently have honest and open conversations (but not finished ones) with that learner about *why,* we will be on the road to more meaningful education. It may turn out that this sarcastic learner is less problematic to learning and society than students who naively and quietly accept cultural-technological forces in the classroom without wondering much about them.

Most importantly, it is moral to carry on conversations about the contributions educational technologies make to the problems of education, individuals, communities, and the ecology.

REFERENCES

Anderson, J. (1992). Ethics scenarios: a critical theory symposium. *In* M. Simonson, ed. The 1992 Proceedings of Selected Research Paper Presentations. Washington, DC: Association for Educational Communications and Technology.

— (1994, Feb.). The rite of right or the right of rite: moving towards an ethics of technological empowerment. *Educational Technology Magazine,* pp. 29–34.

Anyon, J. (1994). The retreat of Marxism and socialist feminism: postmodern and poststructural theories in education. *Curriculum Inquiry 24,* 115–33.

Apple, M.W. (1986). Teachers and texts: a political economy of class and gender relations in education. New York: Routledge & Kegan Paul.

— (1988). Teaching and technology: the hidden effects of computers on teachers and students. *In* L.E. Beyers & M.W. Apple, eds. *The curriculum: problems, politics, and possibilities,* 289–311. Albany, NY: SUNY Press.

— (1990). *Ideology and criticism.* New York: Routledge, Chapman & Hall.

— (1993). *Official knowledge: democratic education in a*

conservative age. New York: Routledge.

— & Jungck, S. (1990). "You don't have to be a teacher to teach this unit": teaching, technology, and gender in the classroom. *American Educational Research Journal 27*(2), 227–51.

— & Weis, L., eds. (1983). *Ideology and practice in schooling.* Philadelphia, PA: Temple University Press.

Arato, A. & Gebhardt, E. (1978). The essential Frankfurt School reader. New York: Urizen.

Aronowitz, S. & Giroux, H.A. (1991). *Postmodern education: politics, culture, and social criticism.* Minneapolis, MN: University of Minnesota Press.

Barrett, W. (1978). *The illusion of technique.* Garden City, NY: Anchor.

Barrett, W. (1987). *Death of the soul.* Garden City, NY: Anchor.

Becker, A.D. (1986). A teaching model for the grammar of television. *Journal of Visual and Verbal Languaging 6*(1), 41–47.

Belenky, M.F., Clinchy, B.M., Goldberger, N.R. & Tarule, J.M. (1986). Women's ways of knowing: the development of self, voice, and mind. New York: Basic Books.

Bennett, K.P. & LeCompte, M.D. (1990). *The ways schools work: a sociological analysis of education.* New York: Longman.

Berlin, D.F. & White, A.L. (1992, Apr.). *Action research as a solution to the problem of knowledge utilization.* Paper presented at the Annual Meeting of the American Educational Research Association, San Francisco, CA.

Bernstein, R. (1976). *The restructuring of social and political theory, part IV.* Philadelphia, PA: University of Pennsylvania Press.

Beyer, L.E. (1986). Critical theory and the art of teaching. *Journal of Curriculum and Supervision 1*(3), 221–32.

— & Apple, M.W., eds. (1988). *The curriculum: problems, politics, and possibilities.* Albany, NY: SUNY Press.

Bohren, J.L. (1991, Nov.). *Educational technology: threats and promises for female teachers and students.* Paper presented at the conference on Women, Technology, and Ethics: Defining the Issues of the 21st Century, Morehead, KY.

Bowers, C.A. (1988). *The cultural dimensions of educational computing.* New York: Teachers College Press.

— (1993). Education, cultural myths, and the ecological crisis: toward deep changes. Albany, NY: SUNY Press.

Bowles, S. & Gintis, H. (1976). *Schooling in capitalist America.* New York: Basic Books.

Boyd, G.M. (1991). Emancipative educational technology. *In* D. Hlynka & J. Belland, eds. *Paradigms regained: the uses of illuminative, semiotic, and post-modern criticism as modes of inquiry in educational technology,* 83–92. Englewood Cliffs, NJ: Educational Technology.

Bromley, H. (1992). Culture, power, and educational computing. *In* C. Bigum & B. Green, eds. *Understanding the new information technologies in education: a resource for teachers.* Geelong, Australia: Deakin University Press.

Buckingham, D. (1991, Apr.). *Media education: the limits of discourse.* Paper presented at the Annual Meeting of the American Educational Research Association, Chicago, IL.

Byerly, C.M. (1985). *Media and sexism (an instructional manual for secondary school teachers).* Olympia, WA: Washington Office of the State Superintendent of Public Instruction.

Calabrese, A.M. & Acker, S.R. (1987, May). *Information system design: a case study in the generation of innovations.* Paper presented at the Annual Meeting of the International Communication Association, Montreal, Quebec, Canada.

Cannon, K. (1988). *Black womanist ethics.* Atlanta, GA: Scholar.

Carr, W. & Kemmis, S. (1986). *Becoming critical. education, knowledge, and action research.* Philadelphia, PA: Falmer.

Castenell, L. & Pinar, W., eds. (1993). *Understanding curriculum as racial text: representations of identity and difference in education.* Albany, NY: SUNY Press.

Cherryholmes, C.H. (1988). *Power and criticism: poststructural investigations in education.* New York: Teachers College Press.

— (1994). Pragmatism, poststructuralism, and socially useful theorizing. *Curriculum Inquiry 24,* 193–213.

Clark, E.J. (1983, Mar.). *Improving the status of women in the third world: a challenge to adult educators.* Paper presented at the 27th Annual Conference of the Comparative and International Education Society, Atlanta, GA.

Collins, P.H. (1990). *Black feminist thought: knowledge, consciousness, and the politics of empowerment.* London, England: HarperCollins Academic.

Daley, P.J. (1983, Aug.). *Herbert Marcuse's critical theory of media.* Paper presented at the Annual Meeting of the Association for Education in Journalism and Mass Communication, Corvallis, OR.

Damarin, S.K. (1988). Issues of gender and computer-assisted instruction. *In* M. Simonson, ed. *The 1988 Proceedings of Selected Research Paper Presentations.* Washington, DC: Association for Educational Communications and Technology.

— (1989). Rethinking equity: an imperative for educational computing. *Computing Teacher 16*(7), 16–18.

— (1990a). Computers, education, and issues of gender. *Journal of Thought 25*(1&2), 81–98.

— (1990b). Unthinking educational technology. *In* M. Simonson, ed. *The 1990 Proceedings of Selected Research Paper Presentations,* 179–91. Washington, DC: Association for Educational Communications and Technology.

— (1991a). Feminist unthinking and educational technology. *Educational and Training Technology International 28*(2), 111–19.

— (1991b). Rethinking science and mathematics curriculum and instruction: Feminist perspectives in the computer era. Journal of Education 173(1), 107-123.

— (1992a). Feminisms, Foucault, and felicitous design. *In* M. Simonson, ed. *The 1992 Proceedings of Selected Research Paper Presentations.* Washington, DC: Association for Educational Communications and Technology.

— (1992b). Women and information technology: framing some issues for education. *Feminist Teacher 6*(2), 16–20.

— (1994, Feb.). Equity, caring, and beyond: can feminist ethics inform educational technology? *Educational Technology Magazine,* 34–39.

Davis, C. (1991). Vocational education project: planning in developing countries: a critical theory paradigm. *Journal of Industrial Teacher Education 28*(3), 35–45, Spring.

Denski, S.W. (1991). Critical pedagogy and media production: the theory and practice of video documentary. *Journal of Film and Video 43*(3), 3–17.

DeVaney, A. (1994a). Ethical considerations of visuals in the classroom: African-Americans and Hollywood film. *In* D.M. Moore & F.M. Dwyer, eds. *Visual literacy: a spectrum of visual learning,* 355–68. Englewood Cliffs, NJ: Educational Technology.

—, ed. (1994b). *Watching channel one: the convergence of*

students, technology, and private business. Ithaca, NY: SUNY Press.

— (1994c). Introduction. *Watching channel one: the convergence of students, technology, and private business,* 1–19. Ithaca, NY: SUNY Press.

— (1994d). Reading the ads: Bacchanalian adolescence. *In* A. DeVaney, ed. *Watching channel one: the convergence of students, technology, and private business,* 137–52. Ithaca, NY: SUNY Press.

Dienst, R.W. (1991). The worlds of television: theories of culture and technology. Dissertation Abstracts International. University Microfilms.

Ellsworth, E. (1989a). Why doesn't this feel empowering? Working through the repressive myths of critical pedagogy. *Harvard Educational Review 59,* 297–324.

— (1989b). Educational media, ideology, and the presentation of knowledge through popular cultural forms. *In* H.A. Giroux & R. Simon, eds. *Popular culture, schooling, and everyday life,* 47-60. Granby, MA: Bergin & Garvey.

— (1990). Educational films against critical pedagogy. *In* E. Ellsworth & M.H. Whatley, eds. *The ideology of images in educational media,* 10–26. New York: Teachers College Press.

— (1992). Why doesn't this feel empowering? Working through the repressive myths of critical pedagogy. *In* C. Luke & J. Gore, eds. *Feminisms and critical pedagogy,* 90–119. New York: Routledge.

— & Whatley, M.H., eds. (1990). *The ideology of images in educational media.* New York: Teachers College Press.

Ellul, J. (1964). *The technological society* (J. Wilkinson, trans.). New York: Knopf.

— (1990). *Technological bluff* (G. Bromiley, trans.). Grand Rapids, MI: Erdmann.

Ewert, G.D. (1991). Habermas and education: a comprehensive overview of the influence of Habermas in educational literature. *Review of Educational Research 61*(3), 345–78.

Feenberg, A. (1991). *Critical theory of technology.* New York: Oxford University Press.

Fehlman, R. (1992). Making meanings visible: critically reading TV. *English Journal 81*(7), 19–24.

Foucault, M. (1976). *The archeology of knowledge* (A.M. Sheridan Smith, trans.). New York: Harper & Row.

Fraser, N. (1994). Rethinking the public sphere: a contribution to the critique of actually existing democracy. *In* H.A. Giroux & P. McLaren, eds. *Between borders: pedagogy and the politics of cultural studies,* 74-98. New York: Routledge.

Freire, P. (1969). *Pedagogy of the oppressed* (Myra Bergman Ramos, trans.). New York: Continuum.

— (1993). Foreword. *In* P. McLaren & P. Leonard, eds. *Paulo Freire: a critical encounter,* ix–xii. New York: Routledge.

— & Faundez, A. (1989). *Learning to question: a pedagogy of liberation* (Tony Coates, trans.). New York: Continuum.

Gibson, R. (1986). *Critical theory and education.* London, England: Hodder & Stoughton.

Giroux, H.A. (1981). *Ideology, culture, and the process of schooling.* Philadelphia, PA: Temple University Press.

— (1983a). *Critical theory and educational practice* (Report No. ISBN-0-7300-0001-X). Victoria, Australia: Deacon University Press. (ERIC Document Reproduction Service No. ED 295 320.)

— (1983b). *Theory and resistance in education.* South Hadley, MA: Bergin & Garvey.

— (1988a). The hope of radical education: a conversation with Henry Giroux. *Journal of Education 170*(2), 91–101.

— (1988b). *Teachers as intellectuals.* New York: Bergin & Garvey.

— ed. (1991). *Postmodernism, feminism, and cultural politics: redrawing educational boundaries.* Albany, NY: SUNY Press.

— (1993). *Border crossings: cultural workers and the politics of education.* New York, NY: Routledge.

— & McLaren, P., eds. (1994). *Between borders: pedagogy and the politics of cultural studies.* New York: Routledge.

— Penna, A.N. & Pinar, W.F., eds. (1981). *Curriculum and instruction: alternatives in education.* Berkeley, CA: McCutchan.

— & Simon, R.I. (1989). *Popular culture, schooling, and everyday life.* Granby, MA: Bergin & Garvey.

— & — (1992). Schooling, popular culture, and a pedagogy of possibility. *In* K. Weiler & C. Mitchell, eds. *What schools can do: critical pedagogy and practice,* 217–36. Ithaca, NY: SUNY Press.

Goodman, J. (1992). Towards a discourse of imagery: critical curriculum theorizing. *The Educational Forum 56*(3), 269–89.

Gore, J. (1992). What we can do for you! What can "we" do for "you"? Struggling over empowerment in critical and feminist pedagogy. *In* C. Luke & J. Gore, eds. Feminisms and critical pedagogy, 54-73. New York: Routledge.

Greene, M. (1992). Foreword. *In* C. Luke & J. Gore, eds. *Feminisms and critical pedagogy,* ix–xi. New York: Routledge.

— (1993). Reflections on postmodernism and education. [Review of Towards a theory and practice of teacher cultural politics: continuing the postmodern debate.] *Educational Policy 7*(2), 106–11.

Grumet, M.R. (1988). Bitter milk: women and teaching. Amherst, MA: University of Massachusetts Press.

— (1992). Existential and phenomenological foundations of autobiographical methods. *In* W.F. Pinar & W.M. Reynolds, eds. *Understanding curriculum as phenomenological and deconstructed text,* 28–43. New York: Teachers College Press.

Grundy, S. (1987). Curriculum: product or praxis. Philadelphia, PA: Falmer.

Habermas, J. (1969). *Toward a rational society: student protest, science and politics.* Boston, MA: Beacon.

— (1971). *Knowledge and human interests.* Boston, MA: Beacon.

— (1974). *Theory and practice.* London: Heinemann.

— (1984). *The theory of communicative action: Vol. 1. reason and the rationalization of society* (T. McCarthy, trans.) Boston, MA: Beacon (original work published 1981).

— (1987). *The theory of communicative action: Vol 2. Lifeworld and system: a critique of functionalist reason* (T. McCarthy, trans.). Boston, MA: Beacon (original work published 1981).

— (1990). *Moral consciousness and communicative action* (C. Lenhart & S. Nicholsen, trans.). Cambridge, MA: MIT Press (original work published 1983).

Hannafin, M.J. & Hooper, S. (1992). Introduction to special issue. *Educational Technology Research and Development 40*(1), 47.

Hardt, H. (1993). Authenticity, communication, and critical theory. *Critical Studies in Mass Communications 10*(1), 49–69.

Harris, M.H. (1986). The dialectic of defeat: antimonies in research in library and information science. *Library Trends 34*(3), 515–31.

Held, D. (1980). *Introduction to critical theory: Horkheimer to Habermas.* Berkeley, CA: University of California Press.

— (1983). Frankfurt school. *In* T. Bottomore, ed. *A dictionary of Marxist thought,* 182–88. Cambridge, MA: Harvard University Press.

Henricksen, B. & Morgan, T., eds. (1990). *Reorientations: critical theories and pedagogies.* Urbana, IL: University of Illinois Press.

Higgins, J.W. (1991). Video pedagogy as political activity. *Journal of Film and Video 43*(3),18–29.

Hlynka, D. (1989). Applying semiotic theory to educational technology. *In* M. Simonson, ed. *The 1989 Proceedings of Selected Research Paper Presentations,* 179–91. Washington, DC: Association for Educational Communications and Technology.

— & Belland, J.C., eds. (1991a). *Paradigms regained: the uses of illuminative, semiotic, and post-modern criticism as modes of inquiry in educational technology.* Englewood Cliffs, NJ: Educational Technology.

— & Belland, J. (1991b). Introduction. Critical study of educational technology. *In* D. Hlynka & J. Belland, eds. *Paradigms regained: uses of illuminative, semiotic and post structural criticism as a mode of inquiry in educational technology,* 5–20. Englewood Cliffs, NJ: Educational Technology.

— & Chinlen, C. (1990). Technological visions. *Journal of Thought, 25*(1&2), 66–80.

— & Yeaman, A. (1992). Postmodern educational technology. *Eric Digest* EDO-IR-92-5. Syracuse, NY: ERIC clearinghouse on information resources. (ERIC Document Reproduction Service No. ED 348 042.)

Hooks, B. (1989). *Talking back: thinking feminist, thinking black.* Boston, MA: South End.

— (1992). *Black looks: race and representation.* Boston, MA: South End.

— (1994). Eros, eroticism, and the pedagogical process. *In* H.A. Giroux & P. McLaren, eds. *Between borders: pedagogy and the politics of cultural studies,* 113–18. New York: Routledge.

Hoy, D.C. & McCarthy, T. (1994). *Critical theory.* Cambridge, MA: Blackwell.

Hughes, T.P. & Hughes, A.C. (1990). *Lewis Mumford.* New York: Oxford University Press.

Ihde, D. (1990). *Technology and the lifeworld.* Bloomington, IN: Indiana University Press.

Ingram, D. & Simon-Ingram, J., eds. (1991). Critical theory: the essential readings. New York: Paragon.

Jackson, P.W. (1980). Curriculum and its discontents. *Curriculum Inquiry 1,* 28–43.

Jagger, A. (1983). Feminist politics and human nature. Sussex, England: Harvest.

Jamison, P.K. (1994, Feb.). The struggle for critical discourse: reflections on the possibilities of critical theory for educational technology. *Educational Technology Magazine,* 66-69.

Jay, M. (1973). *The dialectical imagination: a history of the Frankfurt School and the Institute of Social Research, 1923–1950.* London, England: Heinemann.

Kanpol, B. (1994). Critical pedagogy. South Hadley, MA: Bergin & Garvey.

Kellner, D. (1991). Reading images critically: toward a postmodern pedagogy. *In* H. A. Giroux, ed. *Postmodernism, feminism, and cultural politics: redrawing educational boundaries,* 60–82. Albany, NY: SUNY Press.

Kember, D. & Gow, L. (1992). Action research as a form of staff development in higher education. *Higher Education 23,* 297–310.

Kenway, J. & Modra, H. (l992). Feminist pedagogy and emancipatory possibilities. *In* C. Luke & J. Gore, eds. *Feminisms and critical pedagogy,* 138–66. New York: Routledge.

Kerr, S.T. (1989). Teachers and technology: an appropriate model to link research with practice. *In* M. Simonson, ed. *The 1989 Proceedings of Selected Research Paper Presentations,* 221–47. Washington, DC: Association for Educational Communications and Technology.

— (1990, Nov.). Education-justice: care or thoughts on reading Carol Gilligan. *Educational Technology Magazine,* 7–12.

Koetting, J.R. (1983a). *Philosophical foundations of instructional technology.* Paper presented at the annual meeting of the Association for Educational Communications and Technology, New Orleans, LA.

— (1983b). *Jürgen Habermas's theory of knowledge and human interests and educational technology: a theoretical investigation.* Unpublished manuscript.

— (1993). Educational technology, curriculum theory, and social foundations: toward a new language of possibility. *In* R. Muffoletto & N.N. Knupfer, eds. *Computers in education: social, political, and historical perspectives,* (129–39). Cresskill, NJ: Hampton.

— & Januszewski, A. (1991a). The notion of theory and educational technology: foundations for understanding. *Educational Training and Technology International 28*(2) 96–101.

—&— (1991b). Theory building and educational technology: foundations for reconceptualization. *In* M. Simonson, ed. *The 1991 Proceedings of Selected Research Paper Presentations,* 395–409. Washington, DC: Association for Educational Communications and Technology.

— (1994, Feb.). Postmodern thinking in a modernist cultural climate: the need for an unquiet pedagogy. *Educational Technology Magazine,* 55–56.

Kreuger, L., Karger, H. & Barwick, K. (1988). A critical look at children and microcomputers: some phenomenological observations. *Early Child Development and Care 32*(1-4), 69–82.

Landow, G.P. (1992). *Hypertext: the convergence of contemporary critical theory and technology.* Baltimore, MD: Johns Hopkins University Press.

Lather, P. (1991). *Getting smart: feminist research and pedagogy with/in the postmodern.* New York: Routledge.

— (1992a). Critical frames in educational research: feminist and post-structural perspectives. *Theory-Into-Practice 31*(1), 87–89.

— (1992b). Post-critical pedagogies: a feminist reading. *In* C. Luke & J. Gore, eds. *Feminisms and critical pedagogy,* 120–137. New York: Routledge.

Lee, J. (1991). Integrating popular culture into a pedagogy of resistance: students respond to the sitcom "Roseanne." *Feminist Teacher 5*(3), 19–24.

Leino, J. (1991). Dynamic knowledge in school: action research on instructional development with the aid of microcomputers (Research Bulletin 79). Helsinki, Finland: Helsinki University.

Lewis, C. (1991). Images and ideology: a theoretical framework for critical research in visual literacy. *Journal of Visual Literacy 11*(2), 9–34.

Liston, D.P. (1988). *Capitalist schools: explanation and ethics in radical studies of schooling.* New York: Routledge.

Luke, C. (1992). Feminist politics and radical pedagogy. *In* C. Luke & J. Gore, eds. *Feminisms and critical pedagogy,* 25–53. New York: Routledge.

— & Gore, J., eds. (1992). *Feminisms and critical pedagogy.* New York: Routledge.

Mackinnon, C. (1983). Feminism, Marxism, method and the state: an agenda for theory. *In* E. Abel & E. Abel, eds. *The signs reader: women, gender and scholarship,* 227–56. Chicago, IL: University of Chicago Press.

Maher, F. (1987). Toward a richer theory of feminist pedagogy: a comparison of "liberation" and "gender" models for teaching and learning. *Journal of Education 169*(3), 91–100.

Marcus, J. & Tar, Z. (1984). *Foundations of the Frankfurt School of Social Research.* New Brunswick, NJ: Transaction.

Martin, L.H., Gutman, H. & Hutton, D.H., eds. (1988). *Technologies of the self: a seminar with Michel Foucault.* Amherst, MA: University of Massachusetts Press.

McCarthy, C. (1990). *Race and curriculum: social inequality and the theories and politics of difference in contemporary research on schooling.* New York: Falmer.

McCarthy, T. (1978). *The critical theory of Jürgen Habermas.* Cambridge, MA: MIT Press.

— (1991). Ideals and illusions: on reconstruction and deconstruction in contemporary critical theory. Cambridge, MA: MIT Press.

McCutcheon, G. & Jung, B. (1990). Alternative perspectives on action research. *Theory-Into-Practice 29*(3), 144–51.

McKernan, J. (1993). Varieties of curriculum action research: constraints and typologies in American, British, and Irish projects. *Journal of Curriculum Studies 25,* 445–57.

McLaren, P., Hammer, R., Sholle, D. & Reilly, S. (1995). *Rethinking media literacy: a critical pedagogy of representation.* New York: Peter Lang.

— (1994a). *Life in Schools.* New York: Longman.

— (1994b). Multiculturalism and the postmodern critique: toward a pedagogy of resistance and transformation. *In* H. A. Giroux & P. McLaren, eds. *Between borders: pedagogy and the politics of cultural studies,* 192–224. New York: Routledge.

McMillen, L. (1994, Nov. 23). A new wave of French thinkers. *The Chronicle of Higher Education,* p. A7.

Moore, D.M. & Dwyer, F.M., eds. (1994). *Visual literacy: a spectrum of visual learning.* Englewood Cliffs, NJ: Educational Technology.

Morage, C. & Anzaldua, G., eds. (1981). *This bridge called my back: writings by radical women of color.* New York: Women of Color Press.

Moyers, B. (producer). (1992). *America: what went wrong? [film].* Public Broadcasting System, Alexandria, VA.

Morgan, A. (1990). Whatever happened to the silent scientific revolution? Research, theory, and practice in distance education (information analysis). Open University, England: Institute of Educational Technology.

Muffoletto, R. (1991). Technology and texts: breaking the window. *In* D. Hlynka & J.C. Belland, eds. *Paradigms regained: the uses of illuminative, semiotic, and postmodern criticism as modes of inquiry in educational technology,* 141–50. Englewood Cliffs, NJ: Educational Technology.

— (1994). Representations: you, me, and them. *In* D.M. Moore & F.M. Dwyer, eds. *Visual literacy: a spectrum of visual learning,* 295–310. Englewood Cliffs, NJ: Educational Technology.

— & Knupfer, N.N. (1993). *Computers in education: social, political, and historical perspectives.* Cresskill, NJ: Hampton.

Murphy, J.W. & Pardeck, J.T. (1985). The technological world-view and the responsible use of computers in education. *Journal of Education 167*(2), 98–117.

Nichols, R.G. (1990). Speculations on a catastrophic future, education, and technology. *Journal of Thought 25*(1 & 2), 126–42.

— (1991). Reconciling educational technology with the life-world: A study of Habermas' theory of communicative action. *In* D. Hlynka & J. Belland, eds. *Paradigms regained: uses of illuminative, semiotic and post structural criticism as a mode of inquiry in educational technology* 121–37. Englewood Cliffs, NJ: Educational Technology.

— (1993). Critical theory, educational technology, and ethics: helping teachers respond meaningfully to technology. *In* M. Simonson & K.O. Abu, eds. *The 1993 Proceedings of Selected Research Paper Presentations.* Washington, DC: Association for Educational Communications and Technology.

— (1994a). Considering morals and visuals (beyond school). *In* D.M. Moore & F.M. Dwyer, eds. *Visual literacy: a spectrum of visual learning,* 369–79. Englewood Cliffs, NJ: Educational Technology.

— (1994b, Feb.). Searching for moral guidance about educational technology. *Educational Technology Magazine,* 40–48.

Noble, D.D. (1988). Education, technology, and the military. *In* L.E. Beyers & M.W. Apple, eds. *The curriculum: problems, politics, and possibilities,* 241–58. Albany, NY: SUNY Press.

— (1991). *The classroom arsenal: military research, information technology, and public education.* Bristol, PA: Falmer.

Nosek, J.T. & Yaverbaum, G. (1991). Overcoming obstacles to university and industry synergy in information system education: lessons from action research. *Education for Information 9*(1), 3–19.

Nunan, T. (1983). *Countering educational design.* London: Croon Helm.

Oakes, J. (1985, Mar.). *Collaborative inquiry: a congenial paradigm in a cantankerous world.* Paper presented at the Annual Meeting of the American Educational Research Association, Chicago, IL.

Ogbu, J. & Matute-Bianchi, M. (1986). Understanding sociocultural factors in education: knowledge, identity, and school adjustment. In *Beyond language: social and cultural factors in schooling language minority students,* 73–142. Los Angeles, CA: Evaluation, Dissemination and Assessment Center, California State University.

Orr, D.W. (1992). Ecological literacy: education and the transition to a postmodern world. Albany, NY: SUNY Press.

Peters, M. (1995). *Education and the postmodern condition.* South Hadley, MA: Bergin & Garvey.

Phelen, J.M. (1988). Communing in isolation. *Critical Studies in Mass Communications 5*(4), 347–51.

Pinar, W. (1988). Introduction. *In* W.F. Pinar, ed. *Contemporary curriculum discourses,* 1–13. Scottsdale, AZ: Gorsuch Scarisbrick.

Popkewitz, T.S. (1990). Whose future? Whose past? Notes on critical theory and methodology. *In* E.G. Guba, ed. *The paradigm dialogue,* 46–66. Newbury Park, CA: Sage.

Poster, M. (1987). Foucault, the present and history. *Cultural Critique 8,* 105–21.

Preston, N. (1992). Computing and teaching: a socially-critical review. *Journal of Computer Assisted Learning 8*(1), 49–56.

Ritchey, R.C. & Seels, B. (1994). Defining a field: a case study of the development of the 1994 definition of instructional technology. *In* D.P. Ely & B.B. Minor, eds. *Educational media and technology yearbook—1994,* 2–17. Englewood, CO: Libraries Unlimited.

Robins, K. & Webster, F. (1989). The technical fix: education, computers and industry. New York: St. Martin's.

Robinson. R.S., ed. (1990) [special issue]. *Journal of Thought 25*(1&2).

— Wiegmann, B. & Nichols, R.G. (1992). Socio-cultural methodology and analysis of historic and current instructional materials. In *The 1992 Proceedings of the International Visual Literacy Association.* Blacksburg, VA: International Visual Literacy Association.

Roderick, R. (1986). *Habermas and the foundations of critical theory.* New York: St. Martin's.

Rothschild, J. (1986). *Turing's men, Turing's women, or Turing's person?: gender, languages, and computers.* Working paper. Wellesley College, Massachusetts Center for Research on Women.

Saettler, L.P. (1990). *The evolution of American educational technology.* Englewood, CO: Libraries Unlimited.

Schooling for citizenship. (1992). *Strategies 5*(4). San Francisco, CA: Strategies for Media Literacy.

Schrage, M. (1993, May 7). Beware the computer technocrats: hardware won't educate our kids. *Washington Post.*

Schwoch, J., White, M. & Reilly, S. (1992). *Media knowledge: readings in popular culture, pedagogy, and critical citizenship.* Albany, NY: SUNY Press.

Schwoch, J., White, M., Rilley, S. & Scott, R.B. (1992). Drug abuse, race relations, and the prime time news program. *In* J. Schwoch, M. White & S. Reilly, eds. Media knowledge: readings in popular culture, pedagogy, and critical citizenship, 63-79. Albany, NY: State University of New York Press.

Seels, B. & Ritchey, R.C. (1994). *Instructional technology: the definition and domains of the field.* Washington, DC: Association for Educational Communications and Technology.

Sholle, D. & Denski, S. (1994). *Media education and the (re)production of culture.* Westport, CT: Bergin & Garvey.

Shor, I. (1986). *Culture wars: school and society in the conservative restoration, 1969-1984.* Boston, MA: Routledge & Kegan Paul.

Shor, I. (1987). *Freire for the classroom: a sourcebook for liberating teaching.* Portsmouth, NH: Boyton/Cook.

Simon, R.I. (1992). *Teaching against the grain: texts for a pedagogy of possibility.* New York: Bergin & Garvey.

Simpson, B. (1984). Heading for the ha-ha. *Teachers College Record 85,* 622–30.

Sloan, D. (1984). On raising critical questions about computers in education. *Teachers College Record 85,* 539–47.

Sprague, J. (1992). Critical perspectives on teacher empowerment. *Communication Education 41*(2), 181–203.

Stabile, C.A. (1994). *Feminism and the technological fix.* Manchester & New York: Manchester University Press.

Stallings, J. & Krasavage, E. (1986, Jan.). Peaks, valleys, and plateaus in program implementation: a longitudinal study of a Madeline Hunter follow-through project. Paper presented at the family and research action V conference, Lubbock, TX.

Streibel, M.J. (1986). A critical analysis of the use of computers in education. *Educational Communications and Technology—A Journal of Theory, Research, and Development 34*(3) 137–61.

— (1991). Instructional design and human practice: what can we learn from Habermas's theory of technical and practical human interests? *In* M. Simonson, ed. *The 1991 Proceedings of Selected Research Paper Presentations.* Washington, DC: Association for Educational Communications and Technology.

— (1993a). Instructional design and human practice: what can we learn from Grundy's interpretation of Habermas's theory of technical and practical human interests? *In* R. Muffoletto & N.N. Knupfer, eds. *Computers in education: social, political, and historical perspectives,* 141–62. Cresskill, NJ: Hampton.

— (1993b, Mar.). Queries about computer education and situated critical pedagogy. *Educational Technology Magazine,* 22–26.

Sutton, R.E. (1991). Equity and computers in the schools: a decade of research. *Review of Educational Research 61,* 475–503.

Tanner, H. (1992). Developing the use of IT within mathematics through action research. *Computers and Education 18*(1-3), 143–48.

Taylor, P. (1993). The texts of Paulo Freire. Philadelphia, PA: Open University Press.

Taylor, W.D. & Johnsen, J.B. (1986). Resisting technological momentum. *In* J.A. Culbertson & L.L. Cunningham, eds. *Technology and education (85th yearbook of the National Society for the Study of Education),* 216–33. Chicago, IL: University of Chicago Press.

Thompson, B. & Disch, E. (1992). Feminist, anti-racist, anti-oppression teaching: two white women's experience. *Radical Teacher 41,* 4–10.

Thurston, L.P. (1989, Jun.). *Girls, computers, and amber waves of grain: computer equity programming for rural teachers.* Paper presented at the 11th Annual Conference of the National Women's Studies Association, Towson, MD.

Trend, D. (1994). Nationalities, pedagogies, and the media. *In* H.A. Giroux & P. McLaren, eds. *Between borders: pedagogy and the politics of cultural studies,* 225–41. New York: Routledge.

Tripp, D.H. (1990). Socially critical action research. *Theory-Into-Practice 29*(3), 158–166.

Wajcman, J. (1991). *Feminism confronts technology.* University Park, PA: Pennsylvania State University Press.

Wallace, M. (1994). Multiculturalism and oppositionality. *In* H.A. Giroux & P. McLaren, eds. *Between borders: pedagogy and the politics of cultural studies,* 180–91. New York: Routledge.

Walker, A. (1983). *In search of our mothers' garden.* New York: Harcourt, Brace.

Watt, M.L. & Watt, D.L. (1991, Apr.). *Classroom action*

research: a professional development opportunity for experienced teachers (draft). Paper presented at the Annual Meeting of the Educational Research Association, Chicago, IL.

Weedon, C. (l987). *Feminist practice and poststructuralist theory.* Oxford, England: Blackwell.

Weiler, K. (1988). *Women teaching for change.* South Hadley, MA: Bergin & Garvey.

— (1991). Freire and a feminist pedagogy of difference. *Harvard Educational Review 61,* 449–74.

— & Mitchell, C. (1992). What schools can do: critical pedagogy and practice. Ithaca, NY: SUNY Press.

West, C. (l988). Marxist theory and the specificity of Afro-American oppression. *In* Nelson & Grossberg, eds. *Marxism and the interpretation of culture,* 17–26. Urbana, IL: University of Illinois Press.

West, C. (1993). Preface. *In* P. McLaren & P. Leonard, eds. *Paulo Freire: a critical encounter,* xiii–xiv. New York: Routledge.

Wexler, P. (1988). Body and soul: sources of social change and strategies of education. *In* W.F. Pinar, ed. *Contemporary curriculum discourses* 201–22. Scottsdale, AZ: Gorsuch Scarisbrick.

— (1991). Critical theory now. Baltimore, MD: Taylor & Francis.

Whatley, M.H. (1990). The picture of health: how textbook photographs construct health. *In* E. Ellsworth & M.H. Whatley, eds. *The ideology of images in educational media,* 121–40. New York: Teachers College Press.

— (1991). Raging hormones and powerful cars: the construction of men's sexuality in school sex education and popular adolescent films. *In* H.A. Giroux, ed. *Postmodernism, feminism, and cultural politics: redrawing educational boundaries,* 119–44. Albany, NY: SUNY Press.

— (1993). Photographic images of blacks in sexuality texts. *In*

L.A. Castenell & W.F. Pinar, eds. *Understanding curriculum as racial text: representations of identity and difference in education,* 83–106. Albany, NY: SUNY Press.

Wilson, T. (1989, Mar.). *Who designs what, for whom, and how? Some preliminary thoughts on instructional design and educational ideologies.* Paper presented at the Annual Conference of the American Educational Research Association, San Francisco, CA.

Winkler, K.J. (1993, Oct. 13). Scholars mark the beginning of the age of "post theory." *The Chronicle of Higher Education,* p. A9.

Winner, L. (1977). *Autonomous technology: technics-out-of-control as a theme in political thought.* Cambridge, MA: MIT Press.

Winograd, T. & Flores, F. (1986). *Understanding computers and cognition.* Norwood, NJ: Ablex.

Yeaman, A.R.J. (1990). An anthropological view of educational communications and technology: beliefs and behaviors in research and theory. *Canadian Journal of Educational Communication 19*(3), 237–46.

— (1994a). Deconstruction and visuals: is this a telephone? *In* D.M. Moore & F.M. Dwyer. eds., *Visual literacy: a spectrum of visual learning,* 311–36. Englewood Cliffs, NJ: Educational Technology.

— ed. (1994b, Feb.). The ethical position of educational technology in society [special issue.]. *Educational Technology Magazine.* Englewood Cliffs, NJ: Educational Technology.

Young, R. (1990). *A critical theory of education: Habermas and our children's future.* New York: Teacher's College Press.

— (1991). Critical theory and classroom talk. Philadelphia, PA: Multilingual Matters.

Zeni, J. (1990). *WritingLands: composing with old and new writing tools.* Urbana IL: National Council of Teachers of English.

10. POSTMODERN AND POSTSTRUCTURAL THEORY

Andrew R. J. Yeaman
WESTMINSTER, COLORADO

Denis Hlynka
UNIVERSITY OF MANITOBA

Jane H. Anderson
JACKSONVILLE, OREGON

Suzanne K. Damarin
OHIO STATE UNIVERSITY

Robert Muffoletto
UNIVERSITY OF NORTHERN IOWA

10.1 READ ME FIRST (Andrew R. J. Yeaman)

10.1.1 How Chapter 10 Is Written

Form follows function in this chapter's intellectual commitment to the *uncertainty* of postmodern and poststructural theory. The *postmodernism* section makes this rationale explicit. Two invited essays follow and form the central part of the chapter. Their themes are broad but interrelated: *Realism and the Symbolic: Two Ways of Knowing,* and *Poststructural Feminism and Research in Educational Communications and Technology.* Although some readers will have, for example, prior knowledge of Foucault or Derrida, the last main section, *Postmodern and Poststructural Theory: Version 1.0,* refers to original sources and to authoritative collections. A short, concluding essay by the first author offers a summarizing contemporaneous perspective: *Envoi.*

10.1.2 How to Read Chapter 10

The sections of this chapter address deep subjects, but there is no intention of simplifying the complexity of those subjects. In no way is it suggested that readers lack sophistication and need some special sort of help in comprehension. Nevertheless, readers should be cautioned about the presence of metaphorical language in addition to the literal language more common throughout this handbook. The authors each write with their own words, and there should be no assumption that any précis can replace original work. Important ethical topics are marked out, but limits are not imposed on further research regarding social responsibility. There is no progressive development in exposition, and the sequence of the four middle sections as a narrative trope should be disregarded. Their postmodern, poststructural insights repeatedly demonstrate relevance to the future of theory and research in educational communications and technology.

10.2 POSTMODERNISM (Denis Hlynka)

Postmodernism? The very word, at first glance, seems out of place in a *Handbook of Research on Educational Communications and Technology.* But a closer look belies the claim. First attempts to come to grips with a definition of postmodernism are apt to lead to chaos. *Postmodernism* would seem to be a jargonistic term for anything new. To some, *postmodernism* should mean "after modernism." But if *modernism* means "contemporary," "now" or "current," then it would appear to be a contradiction of terms to have an "after-now," or "after-the-current-time," unless of course, one means "future." But postmodernism does *not* mean future.

Imagine two different approaches to the history and the study of educational technology. The first view is the traditional view. It sees educational technology as a study of how to improve teaching and learning through technology. This approach moves uneasily between a physical science paradigm and a behavioral science (see 2.2, 5.2) paradigm (Saettler, 1968).

The physical science paradigm focuses on the significant inventions of our time which seem to have a potential impact on the way teachers teach and learners learn. Moving linearly, this paradigm identifies the chalkboard, the still-picture camera, and the invention of photography, audiotape, the motion picture, television, videotape recording systems, and currently new information technologies of computers, telecommunications and the Internet. These are but a few of the inventions that have tried to change the classroom.

The behavioral science paradigm takes the same history, but from a psychological perspective. This view deemphasizes the hardware-software side and focuses instead on utilization. Typical chapters in this history might begin with Comenius's introduction of pictures into textbooks. Or perhaps the early tenets of behaviorism might set the stage for the principles of learning. Now the focus has moved towards making learning more effective and efficient. We do this by the science of control. Twentieth-century psychologists identified themselves as behaviorists, cyberneticists, cognitivists, and constructivists. Communication theory developed simultaneously from theories of individual communication models, to mass communication theories, to small group models. Educational technology was the pragmatic "educational" component of these theories, concepts, and ideas.

It is time to decenter all of this and to suggest a radically different view of educational technology, a view that perhaps doesn't yet exist. This view will eventually be classified as postmodern, although it might be described as simply following a different trajectory.

Suppose educational technology were an art form. The art objects produced are called *texts,* implying a semiotic perspective. These texts come in the forms of print, visuals, films, videotapes, computer software programs, and hypertext applications. The role of the educational technologist is the same as the role of any film critic, art critic, or television critic: to inform a target audience as to the introduction of a new text, to provide a critical commentary, to disclose to its audience how the text does what it does, and whether in the view of its critics, it is successful in doing what it does.

The history of such a field might begin with traditional modes of criticism. It would take ideas from the *New Critics* such as Wimsatt and Beardsley and provide a "close reading" of the text in question. *Semiotics,* the science of signs and sign systems, would provide a fruitful road to travel, beginning with Saussure's distinction of the signified and signifier, and continuing with Peirce's triadic object-interpretant-ground. Early semiotic instructional technology would be seen as a theoretical attempt to relate a specific object with a specific meaning. Our study would segue into the philosophy of *hermeneutics,* the art and science of interpretation. *Structuralism* would provide a way to hang many of these diverse trends together, as researchers search for meaning in structure. The products of educational technology clearly provide a structural model that becomes known as the *systems approach.*

Our hypothetical history would show the movement beyond structuralism into *poststructuralism.* Now, the search for transcendental signifieds would be suggested as impossible or irrelevant, and philosophers such as Derrida and Foucault would provide us with new ways of seeing, which allow us to deconstruct and reexamine the hegemony of an instructional message. Baudrillard would focus our attention on simulation, or using his own preferred word, the *simulacrum,* and show that in fact it is difficult to know what is real and what is imaginary. Indeed, Baudrillard would argue for the "precession of the simulacrum," in essence a deconstruction in which reality itself is deconstructed as we enter a world of "virtual" reality in cyberspace, a world that can be constructed through the application of computer technologies. Other strands would enter our thinking, too. A recognition of multiple ways of viewing would arise as we see the resurgence of cultures, and the rejection of the concept of empire. Ironic interplay of text would result as we become aware of the slipperiness of signifieds. Some critics would pull in one direction, others in other directions. A faint sense of the chaotic arises, and all seems about to fall in shambles. Yet, phoenixlike, out of the deconstruction comes reconstruction. We seem to start over, yet we are on a higher level, somewhat like Bruner's spiral curriculum. We approach all technologies with a healthy skepticism, recognizing on the one hand the benefits of such progress, but coupling that recognition with a wariness, and a careful search for alternatives. We recognize now that an instructional message is not the same for all learners or even for all teachers. The pragmatist sees use-value. The constructivist sees how meaning is made. The critical theorist sees an ideological hegemony.

We seem to live an educational world of unlimited semiosis, a state of chaos that nevertheless is curiously healthy, an environment that searches not for the one best way but for alternative ways of reaching different goals. Our method is eclectic; indeed our method is so diverse as to seem to have no common language. To some, the result is chaos, and is therefore inherently anarchistic. And yet, there is an ironic feeling that in disunity there is unity, out of many comes one, *e pluribis unum.* "The wisest of them all knows this only: that he knows nothing yet."

It remains to be said that such a history of educational technology, did it exist, would be given the same term used by the architects when they discovered similar axioms. It is the same term employed today by literary critics who explore disjunct styles of writing for a contemporary world. It is the same term that art historians prefer, as do social scientists, as do historians of science. That term is *postmodern.*

Educational technology today is not yet postmodern. But, ironically, educational technology is "always already" postmodern. It must be, as long are there are other voices with other ideas and other models out there waiting to be tried. The postmodern view will die when only one view is acceptable, when just one model can explain it all. And in a field as dynamic as educational technology, that should not even be a possibility.

This chapter will begin by defining the parameters of postmodernism, then examining the interface between educational technology and postmodernism. The literature reviewed will include the generic postmodern literature, as well as postmodern explorations that occur specifically within the domain of educational technology.

10.2.1 Postmodernism: A Definition

The concept of postmodernism is one that is still in flux and is a slippery one to capture. There are several ways into the maze of the postmodern world.

First, it is important to realize that postmodernism is not an ideology but rather a "condition." One does not opt to be a postmodernist; postmodernism has no project; postmodernism seeks no converts. Rather, the world can usefully be perceived within a postmodernist framework.

As such, the postmodern condition permeates all aspects of our contemporary society. Scientists write of postmodern science; literary theorists talk of postmodern literature. Postmodernism is found in architecture, literature, art, sociology, philosophy, education, and science.

Educational technologists do not have a choice as to whether or not they wish to "buy in" to the postmodern phenomenon. Very simply, postmodernism is.

The question, of course, becomes "is what"? One clear entry into the postmodern world is to return to the modernity/postmodernity opposition noted earlier. Postmodernism must be post to modernity. Now we can ask: "What is (or was) modernity?" Lyotard (1989) defines modernism as an activity that is legitimized by *metanarratives* or ultimate best ways. (Derrida's similar term is *transcendental signifieds*.) There would appear to be several defining characteristics of modernity: (1) an overriding faith and belief in science and technology, (2) a focus on the positive benefits of technology, and (3) a general assumption that progress is an inevitable and desirable outcome of modernist thinking (Hlynka & Yeaman, 1991)

Yet, even modernity is difficult to place precisely. Smart (1992, p. 144) has compiled several of the traditional hallmarks of modernity as including:

1. "St. Augustine's break with the classical conception of reason and reconstitution of the discourse of Western metaphysics"
2. The emergence of the "enlightenment" of the 18th century
3. The period of adventure characterized by voyages of discovery culminating in the discovery of the "new world" of the 15th and 16th centuries
4. The "age of reason" ushered in by the science of Galileo and Copernicus, resulting in the rise of the scientific method
5. The technological invention of printing in 1654 by Gutenburg

All of these are signs of modernity, summed up by Habermas as "the infinite progress of knowledge and . . . the infinite advance toward social and moral betterment" (Habermas, 1981, p. 4).

Postmodernism is suspicious and skeptical of the modernist vision and, at its extreme, totally rejects the perspective of modernity. If modernism is a search for metanarratives, then in Lyotard's words, postmodernism is an "incredulity towards [those] metanarratives." If to Habermas, modernity represents knowledge, then Lyotard argues that "the status of knowledge is altered as societies enter what is known as the postindustrial age and cultures enter what is known as the postmodern age" (1988, p. 3).

The defining characteristics of postmodernity would thus reject the tenets of modernity and replace them with (a) a belief in plurality, (2) a critical questioning of the benefits of technology, and (3) a questioning of "progress" as always inevitable, leading to a serious claim that "technological progress" may not be progress at all when examined by other yardsticks.

A variety of statements—not necessarily definitions—will give the flavor of the postmodern condition:

> Like the nightly news, whose quick camera cuts can juxtapose images of international violence with pitches for fabric softeners and headache remedies, the postmodern experience is best described as a perceptual montage (Solomon, 1988, p. 212).
>
> Simplifying to the extreme, I define postmodernism as incredulity towards metanarratives (Lyotard, 1988, p. xxiv).

Jencks (1986) thinks of postmodernism as "double coding." Postmodernism has also been linked to "the culture of late capitalism" (Jameson), the general condition of knowledge in times of information technology (Lyotard), the replacing of a modernist epistemological focus with an ontological one (McHale), and the substitution of the simulacrum for the real (Baudrillard) (Hutcheon, 1993).

> [A postmodernist will] develop actions, thought and desires by proliferation, juxtaposition and disjunction [and] . . . prefer what is positive and multiple, difference over uniformity, flows over unities, mobile arrangements over systems. Believe that what is productive and not sedentary, but nomadic (Foucault, 1984, p. xiii).
>
> A postmodern pedagogy . . . has as its basis a questioning of the assumptions of positivist science. It rejects the notion of a grand narrative and the notion that truth is to be found through the application of rational thought or enlightenment. It also recognizes multiple readings or interpretations of a text and values eclecticism rather than one method (Tinning, 1991, p. 11).

10.2.2 Postmodernism: The Connection with Educational Technology

Postmodernity is clearly a significant movement in the arts. Architecture, literature, and the fine arts in general can offer clear cases of postmodern production. To cross the line over to where educational technology sits is perceived as a difficulty by many. Education and educational technology as social sciences are more comfortable with psychological and sociological constructs such as cognitivism (Chapter 5), constructivism (Chapter 7), and the like. Yet, a careful scrutiny of the definitional literature of postmodernism reveals clear ties with technology. Thus, McDermott (1992) writes that "modernism can be seen as a reaction to the early twentieth-century instructional design machine age, and postmodernism to the age of computers and electronic information design." Her definition provides a useful jumping-in position for educational technologists. If technology is clearly integrated with the concept of postmodernism, then the term is important for educational technologists who are merely giving notice that by use of the adjective "educational," they mean to say that they are interested in those dimensions of technology that exist at the intersection of technology, the arts, and pedagogy. McDermott continues: "Postmodernism signaled an important shift away from technological optimism to a crisis of confidence in the benefits of technological progress." It is important to note that, in these views, postmodernism is not to be perceived as a negative, Luddite phenomenon, but rather a shift away from an overzealousness.

Duro and Greenhalg (1992) agree with McDermott's technology connection as a defining characteristic of postmodernism:

> Many of the shifts in consciousness that characterize postmodernism [are] the embracing of popular culture, the use of technology and the electronic media, multimedia events and feminism (p. 236).

Atkins (1990) has essentially argued in the same directions:

> The ecological revolt that dawned during the 1960s . . . signaled a loss of modern faith in technological progress that was replaced by postmodern ambivalence about the effects of that "progress" on the environment. Just as modern culture was driven by the needs to come to terms with the industrial age, so postmodernism has been fueled with desire for accommodation with the electric age (Atkins, 1990, p. 131).

From the above, it can be seen that the literature of postmodernism reflects a major concern with the influence of technology on society and culture. The corollary to that statement is that the topic of postmodernism cannot be ignored by educational technologists. The above writers set a clear place for the consideration of technology (and by extension, educational technology) within the rubric of the postmodern. If the place has been identified, it remains for the gap to be filled.

10.2.3 Two Models:
The World as Given; the World as Constructed

For a discussion of postmodernism, it is useful to identify and clarify two distinctly different and even contradictory ways of viewing educational technology. The first, and more traditional, is to see technology as part of a process for transmission of information. The second sees technology as a part of the construction of knowledge.

In the "transmission of knowledge" view, we theorize the existence of a sender, a channel of communication, a message, and a receiver. Perhaps the most noted versions of this approach are the Berlo (SMCR) model, and the Shannon Weaver Model. SMCR identifies sender-message-channel-receiver as the basic elements of communication, while the Shannon-Weaver model is a variant that uses only slightly different terminology. The Shannon-Weaver elements include information source, message, transmitter, signal, noise, receiver, and destination.

By this view, the role of educational technology is to transmit an instructional message in which the focus is on effectiveness and efficiency. The intent is that a given message is transmitted from a sender to a receiver with as high a degree of fidelity as possible.

Within educational technology, the most noted variant of this sender-receiver model designed to facilitate the development of instruction is known variously as *instructional development, instructional design,* or *instructional systems design.* Specific models proliferate, but the general model follows a define-develop-evaluate structure that sees the educational technologist proceeding through a series of steps that define the instructional transaction, develop the appropriate solution, and finally test whether the solution has indeed been effective. Much of the history of instructional development has been a series of attempts to "fine tune" this model.

There is however a totally different way of looking at the flow of information. This second model sees the communication process as involving not the transmission of some given quantity of information but instead as the making of meaning. Such a model is partly semiotic, partly structuralist, partly poststructuralist, and partly postmodernist.

The focus shifts by replacing the sender-message-channel-receiver model with an alternative: author-text-reader. The change may seem only cosmetic. After all the author is the sender, the message is in the text, and the receiver is the reader. But literary theorists analyze the model differently. A key question revolves around the issue of where ultimate authority or truth lies. Traditionally, one assumes that the author of a work is the ultimate authority. If anyone knows the "truth," surely it is the author. But it quickly becomes clear that there are situations where authorial intent is not enough. For example, in the most extreme case, the author may now be dead, making it impossible to ask the author what was meant by a particular phrase. Or the author may not be reachable, or may have written the text in a different context.

As a result, authority of the author is replaced by authority of the text. "Truth" now lies in the text itself, while the new task becomes one of interpretation. *Hermeneutics* is one of the terms used for the science of interpretation, and perhaps one of the most familiar examples is biblical studies. The "truth" is in the Bible; what is needed are individuals who can translate or interpret what the text really means.

Contemporary literary theory takes another step forward. Perhaps the authority lies not only in the author who wrote it, or in the text that says it, but in the reader who reads it. After all, each reader is unique. Each reader brings to a text his or her own background, interests, needs, and understandings. Such a view would explain why one reader will select a given text as important, while another reader will readily dismiss the same text as either useless, irrelevant, or even wrong. Ask yourself to name the greatest novel ever written. You may say *War and Peace.* Your colleague may suggest *Moby Dick.* A third will surprise you with *Gone with the Wind.* Reader response theory allows for multiple discourses and multiple options. To search for a "best novel" is a meaningless modernist trap, no different from the elusive search for the best medium of instruction.

Probably authority lies somewhere in between the three: author, text, and reader. Reader-response theory replaces a linear transmission model with an active constructivist model of information. Such a view is "postmodernist."

In educational technology, Eraut (1989) reiterates the basic opposition of what he terms the *positivist paradigm* vs. *interpretive paradigm.* He notes that "positivists believe in expertise; interpretivists believe in wisdom." In particular, he attempts to relate the two:

Positivist approaches are stronger in instructional design, and interpretive approaches in utilization. Positivist approaches are more readily found where there is political power and in large-scale developments, whereas interpretive approaches are found where there is little power and the enterprise is small scale and local. Positivist approaches are stronger in North America, interpretive approaches are stronger in Europe (p. 4).

These comments provide an entry into another significant issue, namely, that of the perceived neutrality of educational technology. The positivist/constructivist dichotomy presented above shows two approaches to the issue of neutrality. The positivist clearly supports a view where technology is neutral and the purpose of technology is to provide the most effective and efficient way of transmitting a given content. Technology is not supposed to get mixed up in the issues of what to transmit, or what to teach. That is the role of philosophers or teachers or subject-matter experts.

The constructivist or interpretivist view begins with a different assumption. The medium (or text or technology) is of necessity biased just as much as is the reader or the author. While most often educational technologists proceed from the assumption that educational technology is "value neutral," there have been some loud alternative voices. Harold Innis as early as 1951 titled his book *The Bias of Communication.* Marshall McLuhan became famous for his aphorism that recognized that a message is indistinguishable from its medium: "The medium is the message." Bowers (1988) subtitled his analysis of educational computing "Understanding the nonneutrality of technology." Belland (1991) has challenged the normal assumption of technology as tool with his "inverse tool" principle.

The discussion of technology as nonneutral makes sense, and indeed becomes an assumption, from a postmodern/constructivist viewpoint, while technology as neutral is an equally acceptable assumption from a positivist perspective.

10.2.4 Characteristics of Postmodern Educational Technology

This section will focus on those characteristics generally considered postmodern, and then place them within an educational-technology context. David Lodge (1977), writing about postmodern fiction, identifies five basic postmodern characteristics as contradiction, discontinuity, randomness, excess, and short circuit. Educational technologists may initially react to the considering of such characteristics within instructional design. Indeed, it might be argued that the five represent the antithesis of a well-thought-out instructional design system. For an instructional system to tolerate characteristics of contradiction, discontinuity, randomness, excess, and short circuit is certainly not a traditional view. Yet with closer inspection, one might reach a different conclusion. Open-ended "trigger films" feature contradiction. Hypertext (see 21.1) is based on discontinuity and randomness. Computer-assisted instruction (see 12.1) —by introducing more alternative paths of procedure, feedback loops, and remedial tracks—in essence produces "excess." Contemporary instructional software, by allowing a student to bypass detailed sections based on pretest results, is using "short-circuit." The Internet, by providing access to databanks of information and all the communication possibilities characterized by the expression "the information highway," may well exemplify all of Lodge's characteristics.

Beyer and Liston (1992), writing within the domain of educational theory, argue that the term *postmodern* "is said to capture the fractured world in which we now live" (p. 372). They go on to identify three postmodern characteristics as being: (1) "against metanarratives" (and therefore supporting "the preference for more local analysis"), (2) as being against representationalism ("a disavowal of the view that knowledge of the social world can be representational or systematic"), and (3) emphasizing a "concern for the 'other'" (supporting multiple and minority discourses).

Lather (1991) has identified five characteristics of the postmodern condition especially relevant to education. These deal with issues of: (1) forms of authority and knowledge, (2) concerns for the individual, (3) the material base, (4) view of history, and (5) place of community and tradition. Each of these can readily be expanded into an educational-technology context. The tentative discussion that follows exemplifies such analysis, which places issues of concern to educational technology within a postmodern structure.

10.2.4.1. Form of Authority. This is characterized by "participatory, dialogic, and pluralistic structures of authority" (Lather, p. 161). Educational technologists have long realized that a single author(ity) no longer applies in a mediated production. One needs only to watch the title credits of a major "blockbuster" Hollywood movie to realize that not one but hundreds of authorities can and do contribute to a final product. Such a list includes director, producer, scriptwriter, composer, casting director, cinematographer, actors, technicians, and many others. The authority of a single author is thus fragmented into hundreds of pieces. Although we traditionally have credited the director as holding ultimate intellectual ownership of a film or video product, contemporary thinking now accepts the multiplicity of contributions. Products deriving from the methodologies of instructional design may not have the vast numbers of a Hollywood production; nevertheless, a sophisticated product goes through significant trials, revisions, and reviews, and is considered a team effort far more than an individual effort. Indeed, contemporary instructional design implicitly and explicitly valorizes the team approach to the development of instructional systems, programs, and products. Such features are purely postmodern.

10.2.4.2. Concept of the Individual. The postmodern view presents the individual as a "de-centered subject culturally inscribed/constructed, contradictory, relational . . ." (Lather, p. 161). An important dilemma arises here. Should instructional designers aim at some "average" target audience member and assume that all users will have the same needs? Or should the program not only allow for individual needs but also in fact emphasize such differences? Traditional instructional development assumes an average student, and provides that student with a predetermined list of objectives. Yet contemporary constructivist theory has become very much aware of the needs of each individual student to create his or her own learning agenda. Technologies such as hypertext seem to encourage independent needs supported by a seemingly chaotic model instead of the more traditional linear model of curriculum presentation implying a single optimum path through a learning environment.

10.2.4.3. Material Base. The material base of a postmodern view is information. Many terms have been floated, all of which are relatively synonymous: the information age, information society, cybernetic society, electronic age, etc. Information has always been a starting point in any curriculum development exercise, and an early first step in instructional design is to determine what information is to be included within a given product. A postmodern view looks at information differently. There tends to be a suspicious distrust of information as final, and instead an understanding that while information characterized by the signified looks solid, it is in fact rapid, multiple, and shifting. When information is seen in this way, the importance of what goes into a product or course becomes less important, and the focus changes from content to process.

10.2.4.4. View of History. A postmodern view of history is "nonlinear, cyclic, indeterminate, discontinuous, contingent" (Lather, p. 161). Educational technology has only begun to explore its multiple histories. There is still only one standard history of educational technology (Saettler, 1968, 1990) that is essentially an American-based history. Indeed, it is significant that Saettler's original text was titled "*A History of Instructional Technology,*" while the revised edition was more modestly retitled "*The Evolution of American Educational Technology.*" We need to explore our other histories. Consider the following "alternative" histories of educational technology.

In Canada, educational technology has followed a unique path. The founding of a public broadcasting system (the Canadian Broadcasting Corporation) in 1939 provided a national communications link for a country widely separated by distance. This model was instituted some 30 years before the beginning of the American PBS network. Simultaneously in 1939 came the founding of a national film production unit, the National Film Board of Canada, an organization that brought the documentary tradition of John Grierson to its height. The aftermath of the Depression and the availability of a radio network allowed the formation of the Canadian Farm Forum, an interactive distance-education-by-radio experiment that brought farmers together across the country. Contemporary technological experiments in Canada include Telidon, a unique and powerful videotex system. Concordia University developed one of the largest graduate programs in educational technology, while scholars and practitioners were united by the Association for Media and Technology in Education in Canada and the *Canadian Journal of Educational Communication.* All of this activity was punctuated and underscored by an intellectual climate led by thinkers such as Marshall McLuhan, Harold Innis, and Northrop Frye.

Educational technology in Australia has tended to develop in the British tradition, with a distance-learning focus. A pioneering school of the air was provided to the isolated outback initially by John Flynn, the celebrated "flying doctor." Contemporary theoretic focus from Australia tends to be heavily based on critical theoretic, poststructural, and semiotic models.

British developments in educational technology are highlighted by several activities, including pioneering efforts in the development of film and television technology led by William Frieze-Greene, inventor of the first motion picture camera. This was followed by the development of a public system of broadcasting, the British Broadcasting Corporation. In computer communications, the British moved towards the production and introduction of a specific BBC computer for schools. In yet another direction, the entire concept of distant and open education was transformed with the development of the British Open University, a pioneer and leader in distance and correspondence education (see 13.2.2) based on the application of rigorous systematic instructional development.

Educational technology in India is highlighted by the SITE satellite project, promising education by satellite to every distant village. Educational technology developments in France placed that country at the forefront in telematics, while French intellectual theory brought about an entirely new focus with technological philosophers Jacques Ellul, Jean Baudrillard, and Jean Francois Lyotard. Educational technology in Eastern Europe, Asia, Africa, and South America is typically treated as beyond the concerns of our usual perspective.

These paragraphs serve only to highlight the diverse histories that together provide a vast and as yet essentially unexplored area of the growth of educational technology around the world. The postmodern view recognizes that there is not a single history, but that there are histories. These histories are not independent units, but interdependent and interrelated in sophisticated and complicated ways, resembling less a history, and more a genealogy in a Foucauldian sense.

10.2.4.5. Place of Community. A postmodern community begins with McLuhan's "global village" concept and extends to a "multinational hyperspace, difference without opposition, [and an international] ecopolitics" (Lather, p. 161). Educational technology is not a simple set of questions with right answers. Educational technology is a network of concerns, needs, and technological responses. Each community develops its own needs and focus. Yet within the local, autonomous community, technology recreates a new multinational community. As one example, today the Internet significantly supports e-mail, data transfer, and remote log-in on a regular and international basis. All of this will significantly change how we perceive both community and technology.

10.2.5 Postmodernism as Alternative Paradigms: Educational Connoisseurship

One major intellectual stream that a postmodern paradigm shift may lay claim to has been to suggest alternative modes of research and scholarship. Traditionally, educational technology has been treated as belonging to a scientific discourse. This means that the accepted modes of discursive practice have been grounded in a positivist philosophic mode.

Educational theory has long recognized both advantages and disadvantages of the positivist model grounded in a technical rationality. At the same time, a major alternative shift was to move from quantitative to qualitative modes. Hlynka and Belland (1991) have argued for yet a third, critical, discursive practice, stemming from the idea that educational technology may also be perceived as an art as well as a science.

The concept of criticism as a valid and useful approach to scholarship is, of course, not new. It flourishes most obviously in the study of the arts. Literary criticism, art criticism, and cinema studies have long and established critical histories.

Education and educational technology, both firmly grounded in quantitative, positivist, and systematic paradigms have been slow in accepting artistic paradigms as appropriate scholarship. Yet, the balance is in the process of being redressed. Pinar (1978) has labeled as "reconceptualist" those writers/researchers interested in that mode of thinking that conceptualizes education anew and privileges alternative modes of inquiry.

Huebner (1966) lays the groundwork for such analysis with his discussion of five basic foci for curriculum language. He argued that the five were *technical,* which provides a means-ends rationality to curriculum discourse; *political,* which focused on power and control; *scientific,* which attempts to maximize effectiveness and efficiency; *aesthetic,* which focuses on teaching and learning as an art; and the *ethical,* which examines the value of the educational act.

Following Huebner, John Mann (1968) presented what is generally considered one of the seminal papers leading the way for what Mann named *curriculum criticism.* Noting significant relationships between curriculum and fiction, he suggested that the curriculum critic should appropriately function as the equivalent of the literary critic. "As with the

literary critique," he pointed out, "the function of the curricular critique is to disclose its meanings, to illuminate its answers" (p. 77).

The metaphor was expanded upon by Willis (1975) and Kelly (1975). Eisner (1979) turned to art criticism for an extension of the model in a different direction and provided the literature with two terms that have since entered the everyday vocabulary of all curriculum evaluators, namely, educational connoisseurship and educational criticism. Connoisseurship, wrote Eisner "is the art of appreciation," while criticism" is the art of disclosure."

Vallance (1977) became interested in expanding Eisner's work to a description of curriculum materials, a task that becomes of special interest to educational technologists. Vallance's critical description of an instructional television series titled *The Great Plains Experience* provides a case study of what the model of educational criticism can offer. Essentially, Vallance argued that, while at a superficial level, everyone is a critic of curriculum materials. These conventional curriculum reviews

> deal either with surface features of the materials themselves or with the after effects of their use. But neither descriptions of the materials nor measures of their effectiveness really get at the heart of the matter. For neither addresses the question of what experience the curriculum materials make available to the student. The question is not a trivial one.

Criticism, to Vallance, is "the perception, analysis, interpretation, and portrayal of a work of art."

McCutcheon, in turn (1979, p. 5), notes that:

> the aim of educational criticism is to characterize, interpret, and appraise the nature of educational materials and settings and the nature of the curriculum and instruction taking place. Critics ask: "What is it like," "what does it mean," and "what is its merit?"

Eisner, within two editions of *The Educational Imagination,* provides a variety of examples of curriculum criticism.

Educational technology does not lag behind in the connoisseurship domain. Belland has long advocated a thoughtful, careful analysis of the programs and products of educational technology. One of the first steps, argues Belland (1991, p. 33), is that "instructional technologists need to experience the "classic works" in the field, especially instructional film." Some of those films, which should be familiar to every educational technologist, include Braverman's *American Time Capsule*; the U.S. Navy's *Film Tactics*; Lorenz's *The Plow That Broke the Plains*; McLaren's abstract experiments from Canada, including *Fiddle Dee Dee* and *Neighbors*; Flaherty's *Nanook of the North,* and countless others. To be unaware of the first halting attempts in informational, instructional, and what John Grierson termed *documentary* style, is to be uninformed as to the powerful early contributions of our field. In a rush towards a vague future, we sometimes forget that we do have a history, and that many of our contemporary experiments have been done before, in some different form or medium true, but, nevertheless, we are indeed grounded in a rich and illustrious past.

A connoisseur should be aware of our history, so that we do not always "reinvent the wheel." For example, a perusal of the various volumes of the *Encyclopedia of Educational Research* through the decades, dating from 1940 to the present, will reveal much of the contributions of educational technology. Belland et al. (1991) argue that a connoisseur who can communicate his or her depth of history, of art, of culture to others becomes a critic in the true sense of the word. He lists some six contributions of such educational criticism:

1. Criticism could help explain a technological object or process in terms of the quality of the relationship between its content and its form.
2. Criticism could help explain a technological object or process in terms of the relationship among the constituent parts and the whole.
3. Criticism may provide insight into the unifying themes and designs that help to hold the technological object or process together in all its richness and complexity.
4. Criticism may reveal the nature of the intimate experience that a well-informed, sensitive, and reflective critic has with the process or product of educational technology.
5. Criticism may reveal the grounds on which interpretations and judgments of the processes and objects of educational technology may rest, as well as the consequences the object and/or process may entail in human experience.
6. Criticism may serve to synthesize the knowledge derived from disparate research processes into more comprehensive theory.

Other examples of curriculum criticism dot the literature of educational technology. Belland and Taylor (1991) have experimented with a futuristic educational scenario for which Alger (1991) has prepared a "close reading" that is at once critical, aesthetic, and deconstructionist.

In similar vein, Moore and Garrison (1988) produced a two-page "joke" in ECTJ titled "The contribution of metaphysics to instructional technology," a paper that in many ways provides the ultimate example of an aesthetic response to the field of educational technology posed within a deliberate aesthetic frame of minimalism. Hlynka (1989) has provided a careful reading and deconstructive analysis of Moore and Garrison, showing their document to be full of meaning far beyond the apparent simplicity of the original "empty" paper.

10.2.6 Postmodern Methodologies: Derrida and Foucault

Novices in postmodern analysis tend to look for algorithms to focus their methodological direction. On the other hand, postmodernists resist the notion of algorithmization. By stating a precise procedure, one is defeating a basic postmodern perspective that there is no one best way to proceed. To state a procedure precisely is in fact to provide

a "transcendental signified," an ultimate meaning, and a preferred way. This is what postmodernism argues against. For this reason, the following algorithmic notes are presented with some hesitation.

Perhaps one of the major concepts of postmodern theory is that of *deconstruction,* a term associated with Jacques Derrida. Deconstruction is meant to provide a close reading of a text, but a close reading with a difference. The first step in deconstruction is to identify the "traditional" binary oppositions where the first term is the term normally valorized, while the second term is in opposition. Thus we have good/bad, nature/technology, male/female, and so on. The next step is to attempt to reverse the oppositions. That is, by analysis and argument, one shows that in fact the second term, usually devalued, should in fact be valued. An example: Some binary oppositions representing modernity might include these:

form/antiform	centering/decentering
design/chance	boundary/intertext
hierarchy/anarchy	root/rhizome
finished work/happening,	cause/trace
"found" art	
paradigm/syntagm	linear/nonlinear

Now, it should be recognized that in each case, it is the first term that is the "valorized" term. Within the idea of modernity, the key concepts are form, design, hierarchy, etc. Deconstruction takes some (not necessarily all) of the oppositions and shows how the "other" is equally valid. Take, for example, the second opposition from the above list: design/chance. From a modernist perspective, design is the favored mode. Yet on the other hand, does not the concept of design tend to limit and constrain? Teachers teach by designed lesson plan. But it is often argued that the truly effective teacher can capture the moment, bring contemporary happenings into the classroom, and relate all of these to the subject under discussion. This requires an aleatoric model, an ability to use randomness, and an effort to change direction on the spot. In fact, "designed" lessons more often than not lead to uninspired teaching and dull classrooms.

Thus the valorization of *design* deconstructs under close scrutiny, and we see that for *design* to work, one needs to incorporate some opportunity for chaos or *antidesign*. In fact *antidesign* is "always already" present in a good design. The moment one accepts the importance of design, one must recognize that antidesign must be present to prevent design from becoming static. Ultimately, the stated opposition no longer makes sense, and this identified dimension of modernity (design/chance) has been deconstructed.

Eagleton (1983, p. 133) has algorithmized Derrida's approach in a concise and useful statement:

> Derrida's own typical habit of reading is to seize on some apparently peripheral fragment in the work—a footnote, a recurrent minor theme or image, a casual allusion—and work it tenaciously through to the point where it threatens to dismantle the oppositions which govern the text as a whole.

The tactic of deconstructive criticism [is] to show how texts come to embarrass their own ruling systems of logic.

Although deconstruction is associated with Derrida, the idea has been around for a long time in other guises. Marshall McLuhan (1988) has presented a strikingly similar model within his presentation of what he called the *laws of media.* McLuhan argued that if one is to determine fully the effect of a given medium, one needs to ask four basic questions modeled after Karl Popper's falsifiability principle. McLuhan's four questions posed about media are as follows:

What does it enhance or intensify?
What does it render obsolete or displace?
What does it retrieve that was previously obsolesced?
What does it produce or become when pressed to an extreme?
(McLuhan & McLuhan, p. 7)

The result is a useful set of guidelines that has nevertheless not been systematically examined by researchers. The contemporary postmodern reincarnation and extension of McLuhan is found in the work of Baudrillard.

Deconstructionist methodologies have appeared in the literature of educational technology in recent years. Yeaman (1992) has summarized the impact of deconstruction on educational media. Hlynka (1989, 1991, 1992) has provided several deconstructionist readings. Curtis (1988) has deconstructed visual statements, while Magnusson and Osborne (1990) have provided an interesting deconstructionist reading of the concept of modular instruction. Suchting (1992) has provided a careful deconstruction of constructivist thinking.

Just as Derridian analyses provide a deconstructionist approach to analysis, so a Foucauldian analysis provides a focus on power connections. Michel Foucault is the "other" major personality in postmodern methodologies. Grounded in power issues and poststructural historiography, Foucault provides an alternative model towards asking postmodern questions. Cherryholmes (1988, p. 107) has algorithmized Foucault in the form of eleven questions as follows:

1. Who is authorized to speak?
2. Who listens?
3. What can be said?
4. What remains unspoken?
5. How does one become authorized to speak?
6. What utterances are rewarded?
7. What utterances are penalized?
8. Which categories, metaphors, modes of descriptions, explanation, and argument are valued and praised; which are excluded and silenced?
9. What social and political arrangements reward and deprive statements?
10. Which metaphors, modes of argumentation, explanation, and description are valued?
11. Which ideas are advanced as foundational to the discourse?

Foucauldian analyses are also in evidence in contemporary educational technology research. Damarrin (1994) has coupled feminist theories to the theories of Foucault, while McBride (1989) has provided a useful Foucauldian analysis of mathematical discourse in the classroom. Taylor and Swartz (1991) discuss the ramifications in educational technology to the statement "knowledge is not value neutral." In particular, issues of equity become significant.

10.2.7 Postmodernism as a Theoretic Underpinning for Hypertext

New information technologies have resulted in a variety of new forms of communication. Among the most popular of these is *hypertext* (see 21.1). Landow (1992) defines *hyptertext* as "blocks of text and the electronic links that join them." *Hypermedia,* by extension, would be blocks of media and the electronic links that join them, where the "blocks of media" might be presented as still visuals or as motion visuals with Quicktime or Linkway. The term *hypermedia* is often (but not always) synonymous with the current use of the term *multimedia.* One of the more popular versions of hypertext is *HyperCard,* which is the popular Macintosh utility allowing students (and others) to create and use hypertext documents within a Macintosh environment.

Computer programmers and others have been intrigued for perhaps a decade as to the potential of hypertext as a teaching/learning tool. Only recently have theoreticians (Landow, 1992; Ulmer, 1991; Burnett, 1993) drawn attention to the fact that the intellectual theory that undergirds the technology of hypertext is in fact postmodernism.

Ulmer (1991) suggests that Derrida's concept of grammatology provides a useful framework for hypermedia studies. Derrida has coined the term *grammatology* to suggest a study or science of writing. Derrida's grammatology is grounded in the idea that writing is devalued and seen as inferior to speech. Further, written reference is unstable. This creates a "difference" such that a text must always defer to something else. To Ulmer (1991), grammatology proves a theoretic frame of reference

free of the absolute commitment to the book apparatus that constrains research conducted within the frame of critique. The challenge of grammatology against all technological determinism, is to accept responsibility for inventing practices for institutionalizing electronic technologies.

In particular, Ulmer focuses on the card index metaphor that HyperCard so readily simulates as a perfect simulacrum for postmodern theories. It is an idea for which art critic and philosopher Walter Benjamin (1979) has previously set the stage:

Today, the book is already, as the present mode of scholarly production demonstrates, an outdated mediation between two different filing systems. For everything that matters is to be found in the card box of the researcher who wrote it, and the scholar studying it assimilates it into his own card index (p. 78).

Burnett (1993, p. 1) follows with the same general argument:

> What distinguishes hypermedia is that it posits an information structure so dissimilar to any other in human experience that it is difficult to describe as a structure at all. It is nonlinear and therefore may seem as alien wrapping of language when compared to the historical path written communication has traversed; it is explicitly nonsequential, neither hierarchical nor rooted in its organizational structure and therefore may appear chaotic and entropic (p. 1).

The most extended analysis to date of hypermedia as postmodern theory stems from Landow (1992). Using postmodern concepts of intertextuality, multivocality, decentering, and nonlinearity, Landow argues that "what is perhaps most interesting about hypertext, though, is not that it may fulfill certain claims of structuralist and post-structuralist criticism but that it provides a rich means of testing them" (p. 11). Indeed, he argues that "hypertext has much in common with some major points of contemporary literary and semiological theory, particularly with Derrida's emphasis on decentering and Barthes' conception of the readerly versus the writerly text." In fact, hypertext creates an almost embarrassingly literal embodiment of both concepts" (pp. 33–34).

To reiterate: It is argued that hypertext, one of the key products/concepts of contemporary educational technology, is grounded in postmodern theory. To work with hypertext, one of necessity must have a working acquaintance with postmodernism. It is a challenge that deserves to be taken seriously by more educational technology researchers.

10.2.8 Postmodern Texts

What makes an effective text? Traditional instructional design advocates such design guidelines as clarity, statement of objectives, verification of content, and so on. Yet, as one can guess from the above discussion of hypertext, there is already a postmodern view that sees texts differently. Spring (1991) provides guidelines from his personal experience:

> The postmodern textbook should avoid the presentation of information in a neutral language. Knowledge is not neutral. By presenting the reader with a compendium of information, the modern textbook, in contrast to the postmodern textbook, conveys the impression that scholars agree on a particular body of knowledge. . . . The postmodern textbook should . . . present the reader with a multiplicity of views of a given field of knowledge (p. 197).

Traditional instructional design guidelines assume that the reader will interact with the author in a linear mode. However, contemporary research is beginning to offer alternatives to linearity, even within traditional texts.

A particularly interesting example of attempts to move traditional text into nonlinear modes is the domain of children's literature. Two areas will be mentioned here: (1) interactive fiction and (2) postmodern writing for children.

Educational technologists have become interested in interactive fiction in a traditional textual mode. Probably the most commercially known product is the "choose your own adventure" books. In addition, educational technology research has made some significant forays into the field. For example, Norton (1992) has examined the literary concept of discourse as created by computers. Desilets (1989) suggested that interactive fiction is oriented to problem-solving strategies and therefore engages the interest of students. McLellan (1992) has qualitatively studied children's reactions to interactive stories presented within a HyperCard mode. The conclusions support the hypothesis that children can adapt to the interactive HyperCard mode of presentation. Even children's picture books, normally produced within a fairly standard presentation model, have begun to take a deliberate postmodern turn. Whether young children can understand all—or even some—of the subtleties is open for research. Two examples are David Macaulay's *Black and White* (1990) and Catherine Brighton's *Five Secrets in a Box* (1989).

10.2.8.1. Black and White. *Black and White* illustrates postmodern characteristics of multiple discourses and uses the strategy of resisting closure. The large-format picture book for primary school age children physically divides the book into four stories. But rather than presenting the stories sequentially, they are presented simultaneously. The first story, "Seeing Things," is presented in the upper-left quadrant of each two-page spread and tells of a young boy taking a train trip. The second story, "Problem Parents," is placed in the lower-left quadrant. "A Waiting Game," located in the upper-right quadrant, tells of passengers at a station waiting for a train. The lower-right quadrant story is called "Udder Chaos" and deals with a herd of Holstein cows blocking a train track.

Three of the stories are in full color, while one, "Problem Parents," is illustrated in sepia. The book is full of intertextual references to the other stories. In addition, the visuals must be examined carefully for further intertextual (intervisual?) content. Children may choose to read the four stories all at once, or they may choose to read each story separately. The entire book is prefaced with what the author calls a "warning."

> This book appears to contain a number of stories that do not necessarily occur at the same time. Then again, it may contain only one story. In any event, careful inspection of both words and pictures is recommended.

The result is a delightful children's picture book that challenges nearly all our assumptions of what children's books should be like. It also poses some interesting questions on the limits of understanding of young children which deserves future research.

10.2.8.2. Five Secrets in a Box. *Five Secrets in a Box* (Brighton, 1987), on the other hand, at first appears to be a simple story about the real daughter of Galileo. It is perhaps a discussion of girls and science. But once the original text is read, the young reader is presented with at least three alternative texts, each of which subtly or radically changes the meaning of the original simple story. One of these alternative texts is placed in the inside front cover, as a kind of preface, but not labeled as such. This text seems to explain the main picture story but adds substantial detail missing from the main text. A second alternative text is found on the inside back cover as a kind of postscript or epilogue that provides radically new content and changes the potential meaning of the story once again. Even the back flyleaf provides new information that adds to the story. Some information, such as the fact that Galileo was never married, is deliberately hidden from the reader. Finally, the visuals that support the text are themselves instructive. For example, the written text never sets the scene in Pisa, Italy, nor refers directly to the famous leaning tower story where Galileo drops light and heavy objects to test his theory of gravitation. Yet the visuals clearly picture the famous leaning tower on several pages. This requires an intertextuality that forces a very young reader to reach beyond the book itself for more complete information.

Thus once again, we have a postmodern text aimed clearly at very young children which violates all traditional rules of storytelling and in so doing features multiple contradictory texts and messages.

10.2.9 Postmodern Explorations in Educational Technology

The literature of postmodern educational technology that began as a trickle in the 80s has suddenly become a flood in the 90s. While single papers abound, special issues of journals seems to provide an effective avenue dissemination. Leading the way was the Research and Theory Division of AECT with a special issue of its in-house newsletter in 1989 edited by Koetting, consisting of a half-dozen postmodern and critical papers . The following year saw a special issue of the *Journal of Thought* edited by Robinson. The 1991 text *Paradigms Regained* presented some 26 scholars attempting to define a common place for postmodern, semiotic, illuminative, and critical theory studies within the broad rubric of educational technology. A 1993 book edited by Muffoletto and Knupfer extended the exploration specifically into the computer realm. The February 1994 issue of *Educational Technology* edited by Yeaman provided yet another dozen papers of postmodern commentary related to the ethics of educational technology. Deconstructive studies are found in the work of Yeaman (1994a, 1994b) and Hlynka (1991). Feminist approaches are represented by Anderson (1994) and Damarin (1994, 1991, 1989). The concept of an educational cyborg is found in Jamison (1994) and Yeaman (1994c).

10.2.10 Conclusions: Future Directions

As it becomes clear that postmodernism does not espouse a particular cause but is merely a "condition," researchers should more willingly add postmodern tools to their research toolbox. Postmodernism is able to provide a theoretic support and foundation for the following:

1. Nonlinear thinking (as in hypertext studies)
2. Multivocality and alternative paradigm research, providing a move away from the concept of a transcendental signified (as in increased acceptance of qualitative research)
3. Aesthetic/critical approaches to scholarship
4. Close readings and deconstructive readings to provide careful and thoughtful analyses of the role of information technology
5. Intertextual relationships
6. Decentering strategies which will assist the researcher in defocusing on traditional questions and refocusing in new and revealing ways
7. A closer relationship between the sciences and the arts, and between fictional and nonfictional modes of analysis and presentation

REFERENCES

Alger, C. (1991). Kelly and his/her world: where did we go wrong? *In* D. Hlynka, & J. Belland, eds. *Paradigms regained: the uses of illuminative, semiotic and postmodern criticism as modes of inquiry in educational technology.* Englewood Cliffs, NJ: Educational Technology.

Anderson, J. (1994). The rite of right or the right of rite: moving toward an ethics of technological empowerment. *Educational Technology 34* (2) 29–34.

Apple, M. (1986). *Teachers and texts: a political economy of class and gender relations in education.* New York: Routledge & Kegan Paul.

Atkins, R. (1990). *Artspeak: a guide to contemporary ideas, movements, and buzzwords.* New York: Abbeville.

Baker, P. & Belland J. (1988). Visual-spatial learning: issues in equity. In *Proceedings of selected research paper presented at the annual conference of the Association for Educational Communications and Technology,* New Orleans, LA.

Baudrillard, J. (1991). The precession of simulacra. *In* D. Hlynka, & J. Belland, eds. *Paradigms regained: the uses of illuminative, semiotic and postmodern criticism as modes of inquiry in educational technology.* Englewood Cliffs, NJ: Educational Technology.

Barthes, R. (1985). Day by day with Roland Barthes. *In* M. Blonsky, ed. *On Signs.* Baltimore, MD: John Hopkins University Press.

Belland, J. (1991). Developing connoisseurship in educational technology. *In* D. Hlynka, & J. Belland, eds. *Paradigms regained: the uses of illuminative, semiotic and postmodern criticism as modes of inquiry in educational technology.* Englewood Cliffs, NJ: Educational Technology.

— Duncan, J. & Deckman, M. (1991). Criticism as methodology for research in educational technology. *In* D. Hlynka, & J. Belland, eds. *Paradigms regained: the uses of illuminative, semiotic and postmodern criticism as modes of inquiry in educational technology.* Englewood Cliffs, NJ: Educational Technology.

— & Taylor, W. Kelly's Education. *In* D. Hlynka & J. Belland, eds. *Paradigms regained: the uses of illuminative, semiotic and postmodern criticism as modes of inquiry in educational technology.* Englewood Cliffs, NJ: Educational Technology.

Benjamin, W. (1978). Reflections: essays, aphorisms, autobiographical writing. New York: Schochen.

Beyer, L. & Liston, D. (1992). Discourse or moral action? A critique of postmodernism. *Educational Theory 42* (4) 371–393.

Bowers, C.A. (1988). *The cultural dimensions of educational computing: understanding the non-neutrality of technology.* New York: Teacher's College Press.

Brighton, C. (1987). *Five secrets in a box.* Toronto, Canada: Fitzhenry & Whiteside.

Burnett, K. (1993). Towards a theory of hypertextual design. *Postmodern Culture 3*(2). Available on Internet Gopher.

Cherryholmes, C. (1988). *Power and criticism: poststructural investigations in Education.* New York: Teacher's College Press.

Chinien, C. & Hlynka, D. (1993). Formative evaluation of prototypical products: from expert to connoisseur. *Educational and Training Technology International 30* (1), 60–66.

Curtis, D. (1988). Deconstructing visual statements to improve visual and oral expression. *Reading Psychology 9* (4), 483–494.

Damarin, S. (1989). Rethinking equity: an imperative for educational computing. *The Computer Teacher 16* (4), 16–18.

— (1991). Feminist unthinking and educational technology. *Educational and Training Technology International 28* (2), 111–19.

— (1992). Feminism, Foucault and felicitous design. *Proceedings of selected research and development presentations at the convention of the Association for Educational Communications and Technology.*

— (1994). Equity, caring and beyond: can feminist ethics inform educational technology? *Educational Technology 34* (2), 34–39.

— (1988). Issues of gender and computer-assisted instruction. Paper presented at the annual conference of the Association for Educational Communications and Technology, New Orleans, LA.

Desilets, B. (1989). Reading, thinking and interactive fiction. *English Journal 78* (3), 75–77.

Dixon, S (1992). Indians, cowboys, and the language of museums. *Akwe:kon-Journal 9* (1), 16–27.

Duro, P. & Greenhalgh, M. (1992). *Essential art history.* London: Bloomsbury.

Eagleton, T. (1983). *Literary theory: an introduction.* Oxford, England: Blackwell.

Eco, U. (1989) *Foucault's pendulum.* San Diego, CA: Harcourt, Brace, Jovanovich.

— (1990). *The limits of interpretation.* Bloomington, IN: Indiana University Press.

— (1992). *Interpretation and overinterpretation.* Cambridge, England: Cambridge University Press.

Eisner, E. (1977). Educational connoisseurship and educational criticism: their forms and functions in educational evaluation. *Teacher's College Record* (78), 3.

— (1979). *The educational imagination.* New York: Macmillan.

— (1985). *The educational imagination,* 2d ed. New York: Macmillan.

Ellsworth, E. (1987). Fiction as proof: critical analyses of the form, style and ideology of educational dramatization films. Paper presented at the annual conference of the Association for Educational Communications and Technology, Atlanta, GA.

Ellul, J. (1990). *The technological bluff.* Grand Rapids: Erdmans.

Eraut. M. (1989). *The international encyclopedia of educational technology.* Oxford, England: Pergamon.

Erdman, B. (1987). An historical analysis of form, style and instructional design in teaching films. Paper presented at the annual conference of the Association for Educational Communications and Technology, Atlanta, GA.

Foucault, M. (1984). *In* P. Rabinow, ed. *The Foucault reader.* London: Harmondsworth.

Franklin, U. (1990). *The real world of technology.* Montreal, Canada: Canadian Broadcasting Corporation.

Gablik, S. (1984). *Has modernism failed?* London: Thames & Hudson.

Gage, N.L. (1989). The paradigm wars and their aftermath: a historical sketch of research on teaching since 1989. *Teachers College Record 91* (2), 135–49.

Habermas, J. (1981) Modernity versus postmodernity. *New German Critique,* No. 22.

Harvey, D. (1980). *The condition of postmodernity: an enquiry into the origins of cultural change.* Cambridge, England: Blackwell.

Hlynka, D. & Belland, J. (1991). *Paradigms regained: the uses of illuminative, semiotic and postmodern criticism as modes of inquiry in educational technology.* Englewood Cliffs, NJ: Educational Technology.

— (1988). Reconceptualizing educational technology. Paper presented at the annual conference of the Canadian Society for the Study of Education, Windsor, Ontario, Canada.

— (1989). Much ado about educational technology: a response to Moore and Garrison. *Journal of Visual Literacy 9* (1).

— (1991). Making waves with educational technology: a deconstructionist reading of Ted Aoki. *Journal of Curriculum Theorizing 9* (3), 27–38.

— (1991). Postmodern excursions into educational technology. *Educational Technology 31*(6), 27–30.

— & Nelson, B. (1985). Educational technology as metaphor. *Programmed Learning and Educational Technology.*

— & Yeaman, A.R.J. (1992). *Postmodern educational technology* (ERIC Digest No. EDO-IR-92-5). (ERIC Document Reproduction Service No. ED 348 042.)

Huebner, D. (1966). Curriculum language and classroom meaning. *In* J. MacDonald & R. Leeper, eds. *Language and meaning.* Washington, DC: ASCD.

Hutcheon, L (1993). Postmodernism. *In* I. Makaryk, ed. *Encyclopedia of contemporary literary theory: approaches, scholars, terms,* 612. Toronto, Canada: University of Toronto Press.

Innis, H. (1951). *The bias of communication.* Toronto, Canada: University of Toronto Press.

Jamison, P.K. (1994a). Contradictory spaces: pleasure and the seduction of the cyborg discourse [617 lines]. *Electronic Journal on Virtual Culture* [On-line serial], *2* (1).

Jencks, C. (1986). *What is postmodernism?* New York: St. Martin's.

Jennings, E. (1992). The text is dead; long live the techst. *Postmodern Culture 2*(3). Available on Internet Gopher.

Kelly, E. (1975). Curriculum criticism and literary criticism: comments on the analogy. *Curriculum Theory Network 5* (2), 98–106.

Koetting, J.R., ed. (1989). *Research and theory. AECT-RTD Newsletter 13* (3), special issue.

— & Januszewski, A. (1991). The notion of theory and educational technology: foundations for understanding. *Educational and Training Technology International 28* (2), 96–101.

Landow, G. (1991). *Hypertext: the convergence of contemporary critical theory and technology.* Baltimore, MD: Johns Hopkins University Press.

Lather, P. (1991) *Getting smart: feminist research and pedagogy with/in the postmodern.* New York: Routledge.

Lodge, D. (1977). *The modes of modern writing: metaphor, metonymy and the typology of modern literature.* Ithaca, NY: Cornell University Press.

Lyotard, J. (1988). *The postmodern condition: a report on knowledge.* Minneapolis, MN: University of Minnesota Press.

Macaulley, D. (1990). *Black and white.* Boston, MA: Houghton Mifflin.

Magnusson, K. & Osborne, J. (1990). The rise of competency-based education: a deconstructionist analysis. *The Journal of Educational Thought 24* (1), 5–13

Mann, J. (1968). Curriculum criticism. *Curriculum Theory Network,* (71), 27–40.

Marchand, P. (1989). *Marshall McLuhan: the medium and the messenger.* Toronto, Canada: Random House.

Martin, B. (1988). The ethics of equity in instructional design. Paper presented at the annual conference of the Association for Educational Communications and Technology.

McBride, M. (1989). A Foucauldian analysis of mathematical discourse. *For the Learning of Mathematics 9* (1), 40–46.

McCutcheon, G. (1979). Educational criticism: methods and applications. *Journal of Curriculum Theorizing 1*(2), 5-12.

— (1981). Educational criticism: reflections and reconsiderations. *Journal of Curriculum Theorizing 4* (1), 171–76.

McDermott, C. (1992). *Essential design.* London: Bloomsbury.

McLellan, H. (1992). Narrative and episodic story structure in interactive stories. In *Proceedings of selected research and development presentations at the convention of the Association for Educational Communications and Technology,* ED348012.

McLuhan, M. & McLuhan, E. (1988). *Laws of media: the new science.* Toronto, Canada: University of Toronto Press.

Moore, D. & Garrison, J. (1988). The contribution of metaphysics to instructional technology: an existentialist perspective based on Sartre's *Being and Nothingness. Educational Communications and Technology Journal 36* (1), 33–34.

Muffoletto, R. & Knupfer, N., eds. (1993). *Computers in education: social, political and historical perspectives.* Cresskill, NJ: Hampton.

Nichols, R. (1990). Reconciling educational technology with the lifeworld: a study of Habermas' theory of communicative action. *Ohio Media Spectrum 42* (3), 32–39.

Norton, P. (1992). When technology meets the subject-matter disciplines in education. Part 2: understanding the computer as discourse. *Educational Technology 32* (7), 36–46.

Peirce, C.S. (1991). *Peirce on signs: writings on semiotic.* J. Hoopes, ed. Chapel Hill, NC: University of North Carolina Press.

Pinar, W. (1975). *Curriculum theory: the reconceptualists.* Berkeley, CA: McCutchan.

Robinson, R., ed. (1990). *Journal of Thought 25* (1 & 2), special issue on educational technology.

Rose, M. (1991). *The postmodern and the post-industrial.* Cambridge, England: Cambridge University Press.

Saettler, P. (1968). *A history of instructional technology.* New York: McGraw-Hill.

— (1990). *The evolution of American educational technology.* Englewood CO: Libraries Unlimited.

Saussure, F. (1983). *Course in general linguistics.* C. Bally & A. Sechehay, eds. London: Duckworth.

Smart, B. (1992). *Modern conditions, postmodern controversies.* London: Routledge.

Solomon, J. (1988). *The signs of our times: the secret meanings of everyday life.* New York: Harper & Row.

Spring, J. (1991). "Textbook writing and ideological management: a postmodern approach." *In* P. Altback et al., ed. *Textbooks in American society: politics, policy and pedagogy,* 185–98. Albany, NY: State University of New York Press.

Suchting, W.A. (1992). Constructivism deconstructed. *Science and Education 1,* 223–54.

Taylor, W. & Swartz, J. (1991). Whose knowledge? *In* D. Hlynka, & J. Belland, eds. *Paradigms regained: the uses of illuminative, semiotic and postmodern criticism as modes of inquiry in educational technology.* Englewood Cliffs, NJ: Educational Technology.

Tinning, R. (1991). Teacher education pedagogy: dominant discourses and the process of problem setting. *Journal of Teaching in Physical Education 11,* 1–20.

Ulmer, G. (1991). Grammatology hypermedia. *Postmodern Culture 1* (2). Available on Internet Gopher.

Vallance, E. (1975). *Aesthetic criticism and curriculum description.* Unpublished Ph.D. dissertation, Stanford University, CA.

Vallance, E. (1977) The landscape of the "Great Plains Experience." *Curriculum Inquiry 2* (7), 87–105.

Willis, G. (1978). *Qualitative evaluation: concepts and cases in curriculum criticism.* Berkeley, CA: McCutcheon.

Wimsatt, W.K. & Beardsley, M.C. (1954). *The verbal icon: studies in the meaning of poetry.* Lexington, KY: University of Kentucky Press.

Yeaman, A.R.J. (1992). Deconstruction and educational media. In *Proceedings of selected research and development presentations at the convention of the Association for Educational Communications and Technology.* (ERIC Document Reproduction Service, No. ED347 973.)

— (1994a). Deconstructing modern educational technology. *Educational Technology 34* (2), 15–24.

— (1994b). Cyborgs are us. *Electronic Journal on Virtual Culture* [On-line serial], *2* (1).

— (1994c). Where in the world is Jacques Derrida? A true fiction with an annotated bibliography. *Educational Technology 34* (2), 57–64.

10.3 REALISM AND THE SYMBOLIC: TWO WAYS OF KNOWING (Robert Muffoletto)

10.3.1 What is Educational Technology?

1. Educational technology is nothing until we say it is. From that position it is a social condition living within a dynamic history.
2. Educational technology is a way of thinking about education, instruction, curriculum, students, etc., rooted in positivism and science.
3. Educational technology is about control.
4. Educational technology has its own discourse and world view that has grown out of the enlightenment.
5. Again, educational technology is nothing until we say it is.

Our field is now beginning to address issues concerning multimedia, virtual reality, and global networking. The instrumentality of accomplishing our goals is complex enough, but we must also address the social, political, and epistemological questions usually ignored in our field. You cannot be simply a designer and producer of instructional messages without being concerned and involved with issues concerning meanings, voices of authority, and ideological reproduction. Inquiries concerning truth, meaning, consciousness, and notions of "self" are basic to our field. Without such questions, we may not realize that we are part of the system, and that the system is part of us. In this essay, I begin to address the notion of "truth" through two guiding paradigms I term as *realism* and the *symbolic*. The notion of truth is critical to those us who work in the fields of educational technology and instructional system design, because by the very acts we attempt to accomplish, we position ourselves and construct the users/learners.

What we understand as "real," "unreal," and "virtually real" is dependent on where we stand in relationship to what we believe is out there. Let me put it an other way: It may not be a question of conscious belief; either it, something called *reality,* is there or it is not. If you believe it is there, there is no point in thinking about it. On the other hand, what we know and what there is may not be the same. In any case, all we really have to work with are representations of the external and internal worlds we create. How we treat those representations, as a correspondence to reality or as flirtations with realism, defines ourselves as subjects and not as objects. Who we think or believe we are centers on how and what we believe we know. It comes down to a question of beliefs and unquestioned assumptions about knowing; an epistemology.

A paradigm, as a way of knowing, as a platform for defining and limiting understanding and fixing a world view that determines and legitimates actions, providing structures for understanding what is natural and correct, guides, directs, and limits what we think. If a paradigm defines what is natural and correct, it also defines what is unnatural and not correct (Kuhn, 1962). Paradigms define social relations as a constellation providing "shared ways of seeing the world, of working" (Popkewitz, 1984, p. 3) in the world. In this manner, paradigms are social constructs that suggest "a frame of reference which reflects a whole series of assumptions about the nature of the social world and the way it might be investigated" (Burrell & Morgan, 1979). Paradigms, as frameworks for thought and practice, as a system of values and beliefs about what is, are not neutral. They are born, maintained, and reflect human social and historical interest (Habermas, 1968). As Popkewitz (1987) suggests, a paradigm provides us with a "world view or framework of knowledge and beliefs through which we see and investigate the world" (p. 193). Frameworks and structures begin to define relationships and meanings within the limitations of itself. Adherence to ways of thinking about the world do more than define the world. Ways of thinking *are* the world.

My interest here is in the ways in which a paradigm defines objects as subjects, and how social realities and subjectivities are reproduced and maintained as a function of representation as a discourse within a paradigm. To accomplish this, I will refer to what I will term the *realist/functional* (classic realism) paradigm and the *symbolic/interpretive* (symbolic) paradigm.

10.3.2 Realism

Educational technology, instructional technology, and instructional systems exist within a realist/functional paradigm defined by positivism, capitalism, progressivism, structuralism, and classic realism. How our field has come to define effectiveness and efficiency, as well as forms of accountability, exist within that paradigm. The definitions and representations of reality, as legitimated by the paradigm, begin to define the discourse that in the end defines you and me. Discourse practices, language in use from a realist perspective, emerges from an ideology of realism. The correspondence between representation and what it refers to involves shared assumptions about reality, ourselves, and others who exist within it (Belsey, 1980; Cherryholmes, 1988; Rorty, 1991). Realism as an ideology operates as a discourse that interpolates human beings as subjects (Therborn, 1980).

"Culture and society, in the structural universe, are anonymous, objectified thought systems; they are systems of behavior and thought that no individual human has authored or intended" (Crick, 1991, p. 161). From this, perspective reality can be known and expressed through systems or relationships of representations or signs. In both realism and structuralism, there is an assumed system or structured correspondence between representation and reality. Furthermore, realism and structuralism decenters human interest where "significance, intelligibility, meaning are properties of systems, not a matter of human will, subjectivity, or intention" (Crick, 1991, p. 161). Realism suggests that "the social world external to the individual cognition is a real world made up of hard, tangible, and relatively immutable structures. . . . For the realist, the world exists independently of an individual's appreciation of it" Burrell & Morgan, 1979, p. 4).

As an alternative, poststructuralism offers a way of understanding, of knowing the world. Poststructuralism recognizes the authorship, voice, and the intentionality of various ways of knowing (Goodman, 1978; Rorty, 1991). It begs the question of meaning and significance. It positions language as discourse that benefits human interest (Cherryholmes, 1988).

The two opposing ways of understanding the world, structuralist and poststructuralist, are found within the dialects of realism and the symbolic. Realism, as discussed above, emerges from positivism, and holds that we can know reality through representations. From a realist perspective, the correspondence between representation and reality is not something that individuals create; it exists outside human intent, whereas the symbolic rests on the interpretive and constitutive acts of social performers.

Understanding the external world as an artifact, as a social construction "willed into existence through intentional acts . . . man [sic] is shown to live in a world created through consciousness" (Burrell & Morgan, 1979, p. 233). But how those relationships come to hold meaning does not exist outside the social world or any discourse as positivism and realism suggests. The meanings and their constructed relationships are the result, from a poststructuralist perspective, of historical social conditions. Semiotics and postsemiotics, as models for understanding the communication process, may be helpful in understanding the dialects of realism and the symbolic (Barthes, 1964; Cassirer, 1955; Hawkes, 1977; Norris, 1982; Weedon, 1987; Wollen, 1969).

As realism positions the individual in relationship to "a" reality, the symbolic positions the individual as a reflective participant in the social and historical discourse. A semiotic model, one that positions the sign as a referent to a known "truth," standing in place of what it refers to, runs counter to postsemiotics, where there exist many interpretations, many truths. From a realist perspective, the sign is what it depicts. The photograph of Uncle Joe does more than stand in place of Uncle Joe: It is Uncle Joe.

Semiotics, as a science of signs, positions all forms of language as a signifying system. Visual representations like photographs, illustrations, and drawings are part of that signifying system. Communication is the signifying system in practice. When we view an educational film or look at a textbook illustration, we are engaged in a process of signification, a process of meaning construction that from a realist perspective is fixed within a structure of relationships and other meanings. These structures and relationships over time become codified into reified systems of significance.

We come to know and understand the world and our position in it through the representations, the stories, we have at hand. The stories we read, hear, and see define who we are by the nature of the discourse employed. If those representations appear to be natural, like the language we use, they also appear to be objective and neutral, free of human intervention (Belsey, 1980). Realism and semiotics provide the view that the world is something we are born into; it is known and knowable. Language and significance is something we learn, not create. Meaning is reified, and the social and historical construction of relationships and intentions becomes transparent. What we see, what we hear and speak, what we know, all appear to be natural and real. From a realist semiotic structuralist perspective, there is no difference between the reality of the world and how we talk about it or picture it. Reality is reality.

Reification and realism go hand in hand in masking the authorship of the messages experienced by both producers and readers of constructed representations. It is through the use of the existing codes of realism that makes illusion plausible. The power of the realist text is to make itself appear to be real and natural. Through various modes of experience, the realist text seems more like day-to-day life and not the appearance it really is.

The correspondence between the understood world (one being real, accessible, and knowable) and the realistic representations of it have interesting implications for educational technology. If the world is as it is depicted, then what I have experienced is the "truth" (Rorty, 1991). How people, places, and objects are talked about, and are presented in relationship to each other and others, either confirm or contradict what I know about the world. If I believe in the objectivity and neutrality of what I see, I never question what I know or what the experts tell me (Muffoletto, 1993). What I know is what I know.

For me, the existence of the representation is not the question. The question that I feel should concern those working in the field of educational technology is the nature of signification. What does the text mean, to whom, and why? Positivism, structuralism, realism, and semiotics all present a way of seeing and understanding the world through representations. There is no questioning of the storyteller, or even the recognition of a storyteller. The world is as you are told.

10.3.3 Symbolism

Symbolism, as I use it here, fits more comfortably into an interpretive paradigm, one that is poststructural and postsemiotic. Postsemiotics departs from the notion of "a" truth or "a" reality; nothing is natural. Language, discourse, institutions, pictorial representations, and auditory reconstructions are social products, embedded with social purposes and human interest. The symbolic/interpretative paradigm of poststructuralism and postsemiotics attempts to deconstruct the nature and implications of naturalism. In doing so, poststructuralism rejects the notion of "a" reality, "a" truth, and a natural correspondence between representation and truth. In rejecting the acceptance of "a" truth, poststructuralism replaces the realist positivist point of view by recontextualizing signification, offering alternative and oppositional readings, thus creating other realities (Goodman, 1978).

Poststructuralism and symbolic interpretation recognizes the individual as a socially and historically constructed subject. It rejects realism and embraces constructivism (see 7.2, 7.3). Poststructuralism constructs a world that is the result of a consciousness, the consciousness of the individual. It is a consciousness that is itself the result of social and historical interactions. These interactions, reflective and critical, look to issues of power, control, and benefit in the analysis of messages, educational or otherwise.

Before I move on to a discussion of representation and subjectivity, it should become apparent that the differences between the two paradigms make them incompatible. One positions reality as something out there to be discovered, a preexisting world with established truths. The other argues for many possible realities, constructed by the consciousness of the individual. Here the world and truth(s) are not waiting to be discovered, but to be created. To understand one or the other, one must believe what the paradigm presents (Rorty, 1991).

10.3.4 Representations

Standing in place of something else, referents, representations, signs (indexes), emblems, etc., and particularly realistic images (icons), not only refer to a point in time and place but also refer to a relationship between the producer of the representation and the "object" referred to. Representations also refer to the perceived viewer as a reader or receiver (this at times may be the producer themselves) (Berger, 1972; Fish, 1980; Monaco, 1977). The difference between readers and receivers is a critical one. Readers actively produce meaning, their own meanings out of perceived experiences or texts (Attridge, Bennington & Young, 1987; Holub, 1984; Freund, 1987; Weedon, 1987). The term *receiver* has historically placed the individual in a more passive role in the communication process. Sometimes the receiver was to provide feedback, but at all times the receiver was to reproduce the intended message sent by the sender. Receivers were never empowered to create their own meanings of value and worth. It was the job of the sender to design a message that would produce the desired outcomes. Using the term *receivers,* the sender was empowered. The use of the term *reader* empowered individuals and valued their understanding.

Representations as a constructed experience, a text to be read—and this includes all types of messages—cannot be anything but intentional. Texts are produced as part of a history of interrelated texts and constructed experiences.

Meanings are produced and reproduced as a result of social and power relationships. The individual, and our notions about what it means to be an individual, is a result of those institutional affiliations (Berger & Luckmann, 1966; Bronowski, 1965; Eagleton, 1976; Popkewitz, 1991). Again, the producer of any representation is its first constructed reader. Readers are constructed so that messages may be designed to speak to them. Whether it is Whittle's "Channel One" (DeVaney, 1994) or who "I" think you are, the organization and presentation of any message is a result of the speaker's notion of whom they think they are talking to. To understand this connection between producer and reader, it must be positioned within existing institutional and knowledge power relationships. How a representation comes to be meaningful to both producer and reader is in the end a result of historical social, political, economic relationships and contests (Freund, 1987; Holub, 1984).

10.3.5 Receiver or Reader

It is necessary at this point to turn briefly to the notion of the individual as subject. It may suffice for now to suggest that who or what we think "we" are is socially constructed. How we think about ourselves and others is the result of our experiences with various ideological texts, representations, and discourses (Belsey, 1980; Berger, 1963; Berger & Luckmann, 1966; Berger, Berger & Kelner, 1973; Muffoletto, 1991, 1993). Social institutions—like families, religions, and education—inform the individual as to whom he or she is through the repetition of stories. Mass media and educational media as experienced phenomena present numerous narratives that inform us and position us in relationships to others and social institutions. In light of experiences and discourses that are controlled by others, we come to think of ourselves as autonomous individuals, when actually the "I" is a result of social, political, economic, and historical

factors. Ideology, sense making of the world, works to form and inform us (Ellsworth & Whatley, 1990; Popkewitz, 1991). This is no simple matter. The social construction of individuals as subjects is mediated through various forms of representations that consume the individual. This hegemonic process, as Feenberg (1991) suggests, is not imposed through struggle between self-actualized individuals but one that "is reproduced unreflectively by the standard beliefs and practices of the society" (p. 78) where individuals find themselves.

> The self-as-subject is a social construct whose place will vary according to the construction process. It is not a fixed-for-eternity entity but a moment in a relationship. How we are termed as individuals can therefore be framed as an ideological question, a matter of the position we occupy or believe we occupy within a social and cultural order (Nichols, 1981, p. 30).

How that self is formed, maintained, or changed is a result of repeated social experiences. I include within these social experiences the experiences of students and teachers with educational media and technology. These social experiences are representations and re-presentations of various encounters in the social world. For example, continuous experiences of women in submissive and powerless positions, acting out trivial roles, may, with other observed phenomena, affect the consciousness, a sense of self, of women and men and their perceived relationship to each other and the social order. If the vehicle for this example is codified in realism, the delivery of these continuous messages may become transparent, and the message eventually reified.

The struggle for control over minds and hearts of individuals is an ideological battle. Postsemiotics, as a form of discourse analysis, attempts to unpack the ideological framework of naturalism and realism to reveal its subjective and political nature. From the symbolic/interpretative paradigm, the representation or text is an experience created through the interaction of the intended text and the consciousness of the reader or viewer. The experienced text is the only text ever experienced. This experience is never fixed or natural, but is the result of social dynamics, agreements, and conflicts. Who we come to think we are is the result of experiencing various cultural and cross-cultural texts.

A word about the notion of interpretative communities in the formation of consciousness (Fish, 1980). How readers make sense out of their experiences, and their understanding of future experiences, may be understood in terms of history, power, and discourse. It is through historical experiences with representations as part of various discourses that we become subjects. If questions over authority and expertise are never raised, the meanings of experiences are told to us through various storytellers. The power and control over the meanings of experiences are given to us. This is not to suggest that there is no resistance to those imposed meanings. There are, and those whose resist are usually marginalized.

As individuals come to share like meanings, they form what Stanley Fish (1980) has referred to as "interpretive communities." These communities share some common understandings, visions, and projections. Because of this similarity of knowing, they form various levels of commonality. Individuals may hold, at different times, membership in various communities. Whether you are a student, a teacher, instructional designer, or parent, your understanding of experiences is determined by the horizons of that community. One's sense of self is maintained and reproduced by the continuous retelling of stories, always situating the listener in some relationship to the story.

We become what we know, and what we know we become. The sense of self, "who I am," is the result of interactions with voices of authority, constructed texts with intended meanings, and the ideological parameters of social likeness. In this manner, the individual is a social construction, a product of discourse and ideology.

Unlike the realist perspective, the symbolic recognizes the social existence of meaning, and the shifting horizons of self. As the symbolic suggests, meaning and truth must be unpacked. The problem is that in the deconstruction of meaning, meaning is never found, for once it is, it must again be unpacked. In this manner the individual is frozen—frozen because there is no ending to the process of deconstruction, of new meanings, and of new understandings.

There is no truth except for the moment.

REFERENCES

Attridge, D., Bennington, G. & Young, R. (1987). *Post-structuralism and the question of history.* New York: Cambridge University Press.

Barthes, R. (1964). *Elements of semiology.* New York: Hill & Wang.

Belsey, C. (1980). *Critical practice.* London: Methuen.

Berger, J. (1972) *Ways of seeing.* New York: Viking.

Berger, P.L. & Luckmann, T. (1966). *The social construction of reality: a treatise in the sociology of knowledge.* Garden City, NY: Doubleday.

— (1963). *Invitation to sociology: a humanistic perspective.* Garden City, NY: Doubleday.

—, Berger, B. & Kellner, H. (1973). *The homeless mind: modernization and consciousness.* New York: Vintage.

Bronowski, J. (1965). *The identity of man.* Garden City, NY: Natural History Press.

Burrell, G. & Morgan, G. (1979). *Sociological paradigms and organisational analysis: elements of the sociology of corporate life.* London: Heinemann.

Cassirer, E. (1955). *The philosophy of symbolic forms.* New Haven, CT: Yale University Press.

Cherryholmes, C.H. (1988). *Power and criticism: poststructural investigations in education.* New York: Teachers College Press.

Crick, M. (1991). Claude Levi-Strauss. *In* P. Beilharz, ed. *Social theory: a guide to central thinkers,* 160–67. Sydney, Australia: Allen & Unwin.

DeVaney, A. (1994). *Watching Channel One.* Albany, NY: SUNY Press.

Eagleton, T. (1976). *Criticism and ideology: a study in Marxist literary theory.* London: Verso.

Ellsworth, E. & Whatley, M.H.. (1990). *The ideology of images in educational media: hidden curriculums in the classroom.* New York: Teachers College Press.

Feenberg, A. (1991). *Critical theory of technology.* New York: Oxford University Press.

Fish, S. (1980). *Is there a text in this class? The authority of interpretive communities.* Cambridge, MA: Harvard University Press.

Freund, E. (1987). *The return of the reader: reader-response criticism.* London: Methuen.

Goodman, N. (1978). *Ways of worldmaking.* Indianapolis, IN: Hackett.

Habermas, J. (1968). *Knowledge and human interests.* Boston, MA: Beacon.

Hawkes, T. (1977). *Structuralism and semiotics.* Berkeley, CA: University of California Press.

Holub, R. C. (1984). *Reception theory: a critical introduction.* London: Methuen.

Kuhn, T.S. (1962). *The structure of scientific revolutions.* Chicago, IL: University of Chicago Press.

Monaco, J. (1977). *How to read a film: the art, technology, language, history and theory of film and media.* New York: Oxford University Press.

Muffoletto, R. (1991). Technology and texts: breaking the window. *Paradigms regained: the uses of illuminative, semiotic and post-modern criticism as modes of inquiry in educational technology.* Englewood Cliffs, NJ: Educational Technology.

— (1993). Machine as expert. *In* R. Muffoletto & N. Knupfer, eds. *Computers in education: social, political, and historical perspectives.* Cresskill, NJ: Hampton.

Nichols, B. (1981). *Ideology and the image: social representation in the cinema and other media.* Bloomington, IN: Indiana University Press.

Norris, C. (1982). *Deconstruction: theory and practice.* London: Methuen.

Popkewitz, T.S. (1984). *Paradigm and ideology in educational research: the social functions of the intellectual.* London: Falmer.

— (1987). *Critical studies in teacher education: its folklore, theory and practice.* London: Falmer.

— (1991). *A political sociology of educational reform: power/knowledge in teaching, teacher education, and research.* New York: Teachers College Press.

Rorty, R. (1991). *Objectivity, relativism, and truth.* Cambridge, England: Cambridge University Press.

Therborn, G. (1980). *The ideology of power and the power of ideology.* London: Verso.

Weedon, C. (1987). *Feminist practice and poststructuralist theory.* New York: Blackwell.

Wollen, P. (1969). *Signs and meaning in the cinema.* Bloomington, IN: Indiana University Press.

10.4 POSTSTRUCTURAL FEMINISM AND RESEARCH IN EDUCATIONAL COMMUNICATIONS AND TECHNOLOGY
(Jane H. Anderson and Suzanne K. Damarin)

We will know that the influence of poststructural feminism on educational communications and technology has arrived when handbooks like this no longer exist, when authorities no longer catalog the official view, and when the primary concerns of the field are no longer how best to produce efficient and effective learning materials but rather to speak with real live people of all genders, races, and classes, and to construct knowledge together. The idea of a handbook such as this, which tells people how to do research, we find troublesome. (Ironically, we are also glad to be included.) It is a form of institutionalization and attempts to lead people towards some issues and away from others. Would it not be better, we wonder, to provide a hypertext that shows many local examples of how many types of people find technology empowering and disempowering in a variety of situations? What are the purposes of standardization, hierarchy, fragmentation, and subjugation?

Most people know that feminist research is based in the lives of women (see also 1.12) and seeks, in one way or another, to improve the conditions of those lives. However, people, both women and men, may not know that there are several branches of feminism. The best-known branch, and the branch most frequently invoked in discussions of education, is liberal feminism: "Liberal feminism aims to achieve full equality of opportunity in all spheres of life without radically transforming the present social and political system" (Weedon, 1987, p. 5). Typical liberal feminist research deals with equity issues, such as whether male and female students have equal access to technology and/or how more women can be interested in computing as a career; reviews of research on gender equity and educational technology are abundant (e.g., Hawkins, 1987; Kay, 1992). Liberal feminism accepts unproblematically the political and theoretical assumptions of the dominant society and seeks to carve out for women a better place in a society that is otherwise unchanged. Other branches of feminism (e.g., socialist, Marxist, radical) disagree with these assumptions and believe that woman's position can be improved only with broader political and economic changes in the total society. Poststructural feminism, the branch of feminism that concerns us here, advocates societal change and shares with other poststructuralisms a turn away from projects that promote "progress" and the search for "truth."

Poststructural feminists are concerned with "how gender power relations are constituted, reproduced, and contested" (Weedon, 1987, p. vii). Poststructural feminists use poststructural concepts of language, subjectivity, social organization, and power in an effort to understand why women tolerate social relations that subordinate their interests to those of a masculinist culture (Weedon, 1987, p. 40). They/we also seek insights into the social mechanisms that convince people to adopt and act from particular attitudes.

Poststructural feminism challenges dominant masculinist views of knowledge by using strategies of opposition, resistance, and deconstruction. According to poststructuralism, theory is in the midst of a paradigm shift: The view of knowledge as objective and disinterested of social context is being replaced with a conception of knowledge as "constructed, contested, incessantly perspectival and polyphonic" (Lather, 1991, p. xx). Poststructural feminists seek to reveal patriarchal genealogies and delegitimize their centrality to society. Another aim of poststructural feminists

is to empower people who have been marginalized and to offer these people new ways of understanding the world. This work can entail both conversation (consciousness raising) and personal and political action to understand and to uproot the causes of powerlessness, systems of oppression, and women's complicity in them.

10.4.1 Language

Language, feminists claim, is never gender-free (Diamond & Quinby, 1988, p. xv).

For poststructuralists, experience has no inherent essential meaning, but the meaning of experience is produced and reproduced through the use of language. "Language enables people to think, speak, and give meaning to the world around them" (Weedon, 1987, p. 32). Like feminist linguists and radical feminists of the 1970s (Lakoff, 1975; Daly, 1978; Spender, 1980), poststructural feminists argue that language limits women by framing and inscribing their lives. Not only what is said, but what is unsaid and unheard, is subject to analysis. Poststructural feminists think the unthinkable and speak the unspeakable as strategies of resistance, opposition, and deconstruction.

In agreement with Michel Foucault and other poststructuralists, feminists note that discourses speak people. How people write, talk, and otherwise communicate about what they know, do, and believe reflects the ways they are shaped by particular discourse communities. The more people incorporate the language of a particular discourse community, the more power that discourse community has. For example, the languages of the AECT (1979) definition of educational technology, of "the learner" and of "components," of educational computing, and of hypertext, all inscribe the activities and potentialities of teachers and students, and thus "speak them" into a certain way of being. The ways in which the discourse of educational technology "speaks people" are discussed in the writings of Taylor and Johnsen (1986), Damarin (1991b), Anderson (1992), Bryson and deCastell (1994), and others. While these authors address the construction of language within educational technology, P. K. Jamison (1992) discusses the appropriation by the field of language developed outside it; by adopting/adapting the language of values, liberation, and empowerment from emancipatory pedagogy, educational technology denies its meaning and robs emancipatory educational reformers of their voices.

Poststructural feminists bring together Foucauldian and earlier feminist concerns with the political language of the body. They consider the ways in which women's bodies are positioned by discourses of gaze, spectacle, and pornography, and by the normalizing absorption of these discourses into the culture at large (Haraway, 1991). Some feminist poststructuralists within educational technology focus on the body politics within our field. For example, Ann DeVaney's work reveals the intrusion of pornographic imagery into educational television (DeVaney & Elenes,

1990) and of the discourse of woman as spectacle into computer software (DeVaney, 1993).

Recent work within postmodern feminism (e.g., Butler, 1990, 1991; Haraway, 1985, 1991) amplifies the language of "difference" while challenging the binary division associated with sex/gender. This development is important to the rethinking of research on gender and educational media and technology because most research in this area is based on the essentialist classification of students as male or female. Important work on this issue by Bryson and deCastell (1994) leads to rethinking of prior feminist research on educational computing (e.g., Turkle & Papert, 1990; Brunner, 1992). Many concepts that underlie instructional design (e.g., individualizing instruction, learning style) are associated with the sex/gender division. Consideration of these issues is closely related to concerns with subjectivity.

10.4.1.2. Subjectivity. One project of poststructural feminism is to deconstruct the liberal-humanist subject (the human entity) as a rational, unified, free, and self-determining individual. In contrast, poststructuralists view subjects as socially constructed; to the extent that media and technology contributes to social language, norms, and requirements, they also shape the postmodern subject. For poststructural feminists, "subjectivity" refers to "conscious and unconscious thoughts and emotions of the individual, her sense of herself and her ways of understanding her relation to the world" (Weedon, 1987, p. 32). Rather than considering individuals as having an essential being, poststructuralists see an individual's subjectivity as a site for disunity, conflict, struggle, and change. "Subjectivity is precarious, contradictory, and in process, constantly being reconstituted in discourse each time we think or speak" (Weedon, 1987, p. 33). Insofar as thoughts and emotions are constructed, mediated, and reinforced through language and discourse, subjectivity is derived from them; therefore, work such as DeVaney's (1994) is particularly important to understanding how educational media and technology influences, produces, and reproduces women's subjectivity.

In much of her work, Elizabeth Ellsworth (1987, 1988, 1990) addresses the interrelatedness of various aspects of education, media, diversity, and postmodern subjectivity, exploring at the interstices of these phenomena the dis-ease of the postmodern subject. Ellsworth uncovers ways in which the subjectivities of students and teachers affect, and are affected by, the use of educational media. Focusing on the language and normative practices of computing, Damarin (1991a, 1993b) suggests ways in which these affect subjectivity and identifies sites of disunity, resistance, and potential change. Damarin suggests that in postmodern times, simulation might replace the unified self as a metaphor for thinking about subjectivity.

In her radical critique of socialist feminism, Donna Haraway introduces the postmodern notion of the cyborg—part person, part machine—and describes the cyborgian displacement of modern by postmodern concepts and ways of being (1988, 1990, 1991). In the cyborg vision, representation gives way to simulation, work to text, mind to

artificial intelligence, perfection to optimization, cooperation to communications enhancement, and individual to replicon. Cyborgs construct subjectivity through strategies of resistance within an "informatics of domination" in which being "feminized means to be made extremely vulnerable; able to be disassembled, reassembled, exploited as a reserve labor force . . . leading an existence that always borders on the obscene, out of place, and reducible to sex" (Haraway, 1988 , p. 166).

As Haraway points out, cyborgian resistance requires the identification of strategic sites and often requires affiliation with unlikely co-conspirators. The strategic identification of such sites and partners within educational technology is an implicit goal of the work cited above. The cyborg is also influential in P. K. Jamison's critiques of educational technology (1991, 1992), and in Allecquerre Stone's (1993) discussion of subjectivity and virtual reality. As mainstream/malestream educational technology develops increasingly many and powerful uses of postmodern technologies, post-structural feminists within the field will continue to strive through research and practice to identify and open spaces in which women and other marginalized cyborgs/persons can construct subjectivities of power. As Haraway points out, because the networks of communications, multimedia, and virtual reality must be open in order for the powerful to exercise power, they are open to resistors and resistance as well.

10.4.1.3. Social Process. Consciousness-raising groups and activities, which were central to the women's liberation movement of the 60s and 70s, provided spaces for women to discuss their personal and public lives. These collective discussions led to the recognition of commonality in experiences and feelings. Through these discussions, women first questioned whether, and then concluded that, patriarchal and masculinist institutions were producing social and cultural practices that work against women's interests. Feminists' political drive to participate more actively in discussions and situations of gender, race, and class resulted. They engaged in political activity, often on the local level and around issues of community and family, under the banner "the personal is political."

Poststructural feminists reverse this binary link and argue that politics is personal: "This politics speaks to the ways that power operates at the most intimate levels of daily life" (Diamond & Quinby, 1988, p. xvi). Rejecting a politics of hierarchy and domination, they seek and create a politics that grows out of a concept of friendship and that suggests nonhierarchical and reciprocal relationships between people. Rejecting an ethics of justice and laws, they work toward defining an ethic of relation and care. They value dialogue over argument, and they recognize the worth and validity of individual views (Diamond & Quinby, 1988, pp. ix, x). Poststructural feminist educators, as theorists and practitioners, consider how to provide situations and spaces in which teachers and students can participate in reciprocal exchange, where teachers are no longer the disseminators of knowledge, authorities on subjects, or regulatory agents for an educational bureaucracy; instead, teachers facilitate learning experiences that allow students to participate in a variety of ways, with a multiplicity of voices, and in places where meaning and knowledge can be negotiated.

To date, feminist research on social process in educational technology and communication has dealt primarily with how technologies can provide more opportunities for social, collective, and reciprocal communication and exchange. Elizabeth Ellsworth (1987) writes about a course in racism and media that she offered at the University of Wisconsin because of racial tension on the Madison campus. As a final project, the students designed a group political statement to perform, show, or distribute on the topic of racism. Jane Anderson (1992) has considered how hypertext can be used in a course to decenter the authority of the teacher. Anderson suggests that hypertext design can provide for an electronic space where a collective, possibly anonymous, discussion can occur among the students on a subject without the directive energy of the teacher. Suzanne Damarin discusses similar issues in relation to the teaching of science (1991c) and also explores the potentialities of situated learning and cognition in relation to feminist practices and ideas (1993a, 1995).

10.4.1.4. Power/Institution.

For poststructural feminists, scientism, professionalism, technical rationality, and patriarchy have turned schooling into a machinery of social and cultural regulation (Gore, 1993). Education as an institution has helped to construct gender, race, and class differences. The language of efficiency, effectiveness, control, and predictable outcomes which dominates modern educational discourse has privileged an authority-based teacher/student relationship, process and goal-oriented teaching techniques, and activities that aim to turn people into self-regulatory individuals who don't question authority. By its definition (AECT, 1979), educational technology is complicit in these activities.

As part of the institutional machine, educational technology and communication has a history of promising tools and materials that can be used in any context, teach concepts quickly using scientific principles, and widen student vision beyond the limitations of the local classroom. These promises have appeal to educational groups that value concepts of scientific progress, professional power, civil control, and orderliness. In contrast, poststructural feminists tend to prefer educational practices that focus more on the local than on the institutional.

The influence of the military on education and educational technology is a particular concern for radical and poststructural feminists. As Sally Hacker (1989) and Cynthia Enloe (1988) argue, the military has developed as a masculinist and patriarchal institution (the integration of women into it, notwithstanding). The influences of West Point on Harvard, of military needs on engineering education, and of military codes of discipline and teaching on all educational institutions are documented by Hacker (1989). The fiscal and conceptual contributions of the armed ser-

vices to the educational design and development are well documented. Douglas Noble (1984, 1991) demonstrates how the move to mandate computer literacy instruction emanated from the Department of the Defense, and Paul Edwards' (1990) work analyzes the influences of the military on the development of computer technologies and their place in education. Carol Cohn's (1987) study of the language of the military reveals the boundedness of certain concepts to it.

Complementing the research that specifically addresses the influence of the military, Cornelia Brunner (1992) and colleagues examine differences in the ways in which women and men view technology and the types of technologies they would choose to construct. Findings to date indicate that men construct technologies with greater attention to enhancing power, while women seek technologies that promote human interaction. Linda Condron is interviewing women engineers concerning the ways they adapt and construct values within their workplaces (1993a, 1993b). As these and related researches are coming together, poststructural feminists use their findings to deconstruct practices in the institutions of education and educational technology.

Within educational technology and communications, feminist research on institutional power in the future might entail deconstructing the field or instructional design models to unravel what power groups are best served by particular instructional approaches (e.g., Damarin, 1991b). Poststructural feminists might also deconstruct their own teaching practices through collaborative study with their students and show how their interests are present in the teaching practices they use (Luke & Gore, 1992). Poststructural feminists claim that no instruction is innocent of the special interest of the teacher, but by foregrounding these special interests and how they shape practice, they feel they can open new space for understanding and change.

Like Foucault, feminist poststructuralist educators (e.g., Walkerdine, 1990; Gore, 1993) situate the academic study of pedagogy and public schooling within discourses of social regulation. They examine the effects on education of the political/patriarchal need for specifically skilled, obedient, and docile workers for the industrial age. As feminists they are particularly concerned with the ways in which schools and their discourses reproduce gender inequality; work such as Jane Gaskell's (1987) reveals how school requirements related to the mastery of technology devalues young women. Apple and Jungck (1990) address the related phenomenon of the deskilling of teachers through the introduction of (required) computer literacy units.

10.4.2 Research and Pedagogy: Focusing on Practice

Feminist scholarship has addressed and influenced all forms of academic research. Feminist historians studied and legitimized the use of diaries of "common folk" and oral histories as scholarly resources (Lerner, 1973); feminist literary and media critics have legitimized the reading of texts from positions of marginality (Spender, 1982). Because the dominant mode of scholarly research in education over the past several decades has been (quasi) scientific inquiry, feminist critique and philosophy of science are of particular interest to us here. Of the many feminist scientists and philosophers of science who have contributed insights relevant to educational research, the work of Sandra Harding (1986, 1987, 1991), Helen Longino (1987), and Donna Haraway (1988) is most pertinent. The following concepts, introduced and expanded by these theorists, are central to feminist research.

For these theorists, no research is objective in the sense traditionally claimed by scientists; a researcher cannot be in the position of "a god's-eye seeing everything from nowhere" (Haraway, 1991, p. 189). All research takes place from a position, and research should be conducted by one who stands in "the same critical plane" as the researched (Harding, 1987). Feminist research must attend to the concerns and lives of women (Harding, 1986; Longino, 1987, 1990). It should be carried out from the "feminist standpoint" (Harding, 1986, 1991, 1993); that is, it should begin with the lives and experiences of women. Like the proletarian standpoint of Marxism (Hartsock, 1983), and other standpoints of the less powerful, feminist standpoint epistemology yields objective "truths." Such research is argued to have "strong objectivity" (Harding 1991) as a result of its being conducted with less interest in preserving the status quo than mainstream/ malestream research. Thus, standpoint epistemology assumes that there are real objects in the world that we can study and understand. Haraway (1988) argues for a "radical objectivity" in which objects are conceived, not only as real but also as everchanging and as actors that act upon us, even as we act upon them.

Feminist postructuralist researchers borrow freely from the methods of standpoint epistemology without endorsing any form of objectivity. While they conduct research (primarily qualitative) beginning with the lives of women (or other marginalized groups), they recognize a need to report multiple interpretations of the data they have gathered and to interrogate and reveal their own positions in relation to multiple aspects of the study. Therefore, self-reflexivity is characteristic of feminist poststructuralist inquiry.

10.4.2.1. Self-Reflexivity. A leader in poststructuralist feminist research methodology, Patti Lather writes: "By *reflexive,* I mean those stories which bring the teller of the tale back into the narrative, embodied, desiring, invested in a variety of often contradictory privileges and struggles" (1991, pp. 128–29). Researchers are invested in what they study, what they select to report, and what meaning they find in the research situation. Self-reflexivity involves professional self-critique, in which the researchers own up to their values and how they are present in their work as interested people. Self-reflexive material gives readers a chance to learn how the personal interests of researchers might shape research questions, approaches, and findings. Susan Krieger (1991), in *Social Science and the Self:*

Personal Essays on an Art Form, writes about how the written products of research studies are more often about the researcher than anything else. For Krieger, doing research, interpreting it, and presenting it are projects of self-expression. When people are doing research, they are in a sense researching projections of themselves. For her, research can be a form of artistic expression. Krieger blurs the boundary between doing social science research and doing art.

Feminists (e.g., Bordo, 1987; Code, 1991; Keller, 1985) observe that historically only men were viewed as (or allowed to "be") rational. As a residue of this history, many people associate the language of rationality with the masculine, and the language marginalized or suppressed by rationalism —poetic language and the languages of mysticism, madness, and magic—with the feminine. In their research methodologies, several poststructuralist researchers honor and adopt the poetic (Richardson, 1993). Some feminists have long read the mystical and magical as credible (Lerner 1981, 1993), and worked towards the deconstruction of madness (Chesler, 1973; Mander & Rush, 1974; Millet, 1990). In this self-reflexive turn, these feminist women claim the power of the discourses assigned to them.

10.4.2.2. Pedagogy. For poststructural feminists in education, pedagogy is a central concern—it's where theory and practice meet. Poststructural feminists believe that pedagogy has a great affect on how gendered knowledge and experience are produced (Gore, 1993, p. 26). They advocate pedagogical styles that enable women and men to listen to themselves and each other, so that they might arrive at a better understanding of how different, variously capable, and socially responsible people are. They reject institutionalized pedagogical knowledge as being too technical and focused on method of teaching. Poststructural feminists also criticize critical pedagogists (such as Giroux, Freire, Apple, and McClaren) for being patriarchal and masculinist in their reverie of "emancipatory knowledges" (Luke & Gore, 1992).

Poststructural feminist pedagogy is more interested in locating the differences among gendered beings than the commonalities (Gore, 1993, p. 33; see also Britzman, 1991, 1993). Poststructuralist feminists argue against teaching practices that claim to be context-free and independent, and for teaching practice that maintains the specificity of a multifaceted situational learning event. For them/us, pedagogy should be rooted in the actual public and private lives of the women and men involved in the learning situation. The pedagogy should have elements of self-reflexivity, interactivity, and collaboration.

To date, most poststructural feminist research on pedagogy has been self-reflexive and has dealt with teaching undergraduates. This research uses journal entries, action research principles, and reflexive strategies to unpack how specific interests work for and against educational practices. In educational communications and technology, most media and software studies have shown how particular learning approaches tend to gender learning domains.

10.4.3 Our Theory/Our Practice: Self-Reflexive Notes

In writing this, we feel as though we have had to fragment and reduce the work of many people to bounded concepts; "in truth," the work we talk about aims to blur boundaries, to rupture the idea of a finely defined discipline. See the self-reflexive first paragraph of this feminist section. The issues we have spoken about are interrelated in complex ways, and we find it dangerous to single out and reduce them to specific subsections of a (part of a) paper. Language, subjectivity, power, institutions, social concerns, research, and pedagogy are everywhere, and they are deeply entailed in each other.

The work discussed here is the work of many people, only some of whom are acknowledged in this writing. We know there are many graduate students, teachers, and others whose course papers, diaries, and publications in remote places, and whose videos, software, songs, poems, and performances we wish we could have included. Much is still left to explore, and we believe it can be explored in many different ways. How can educational communications and technology transform social power and social relations so those who have been marginalized may have greater voice? How can educational communications and technology assist us so we might hear more clearly those who have been marginalized speaking with their own fine, strong voices?

REFERENCES

Anderson, Jane H. (1992, Apr.). *Connecting voices: feminist pedagogy and hypertext.* Paper presented at the meeting of the American Educational Research Association, San Francisco, CA.

Apple, Michael W. & Jungck, Susan (1990). "You don't have to be a teacher to teach this unit": teaching, technology, and gender in the classroom. *American Educational Research Journal 27* (2), 227–51.

Association for Educational Communication and Technology Task Force on Definition and Terminology. (1979). *Educational technology: definition and glossary of terms, Vol 1.* Washington, DC: AECT.

Bordo, Susan R. (1987). *The flight to objectivity: essays on Cartesianism and culture.* Albany, NY: SUNY Press.

Britzman, Deborah P. (1991). *Practice makes practice: a critical study of learning to teach.* Albany, NY: SUNY Press.

— (1993). Beyond rolling models: gender and multicultural education. *In* Sari Knopp Biklen & Diane Pollard, eds. *Gender and education: ninety-second yearbook of the National Society for the Study of Education,* 25–42. Chicago, IL: University of Chicago Press.

Brunner, Cornelia (1992, Apr.). *Gender and technological desire.* Paper presented at the meeting of the American Educational Research Association, San Francisco, CA.

Bryson, Mary & deCastell, Suzanne (1994). Telling tales out of school: modernist, critical, and postmodern "true stories" about educational computing. *Journal of Educational Computing Research 10,* 199–221.

Butler, Judith (1990). *Gender trouble: feminism and the subversion of identity.* New York: Routledge.

— (1991) Imitation and subordination. *In* Diana Fuss, ed. *Inside/out,* 13–31. New York: Routledge.

Chesler, Phyllis (1973). *Women & madness.* Garden City, NY: Avon.

Code, Lorraine (1991). *What can she know? Feminist theory and the construction of knowledge.* Ithaca, NY: Cornell University Press.

Cohn, Carol (1987). Sex and death in the rational world of defence intellectuals. *Signs 12* (4), 687–718.

Condron, L. (1993a). Women and the discourses of the visual: where are women in this picture? *In Visual literacy in the digital age: selected readings from the annual conference of the International Visual Literacy Association: 25th, Rochester, NY, Oct. 13–17, 1993.* (ERIC Document Reproduction Service No. ED 370 583.)

— (1993b). Women and technology: feminist perspectives. *Bulletin of Science, Technology & Society 13* (3), 139–41.

Daly, Mary (1978). *Gyn/ecology: the metaethics of radical feminism.* Boston, MA: Beacon.

Damarin, Suzanne K. (1991a). Feminist unthinking and educational technology. *Educational and Training Technology International 27* (4), 111–19.

— (1991b). Rethinking science and mathematics curriculum and instruction: feminist perspectives in the computer era. *Journal of Education 173* (1), 107–23.

— (1991c). Women and information technology: framing some issues for education. *Feminist Teacher 6* (2), 16–20.

— (1993a). Schooling and situated knowledge: travel or tourism? *Educational Technology 33* (3), 27–32.

— (1993b). Technologies of the individual: women and subjectivity in the age of information. *Research in Technology and Philosophy 13,* 185–200. [Special issue on Technology and Feminism, Joan Rothschild, ed.]

— (1995). The emancipatory potential of situated learning. *In* Hilary McLellan, ed. *Perspectives on situated learning.* Englewood Cliffs, NJ: Educational Technology.

DeVaney, Ann & Elenes, A. (1990). Square one: television and gender. *In* R.A. Braden, D.G. Beauchamp & J.C. Clark-Baca, eds. *Perceptions of visual literacy.* Conway, AR: International Visual Literacy Association.

— (1993). Reading educational computer programs. *In* R. Muffoletto & N. Knupfer, eds. *Computers in education: social, political, and historical perspectives,* 181–96. Cresskill, NJ: Hampton.

— (1994). *Watching channel one.* Albany, NY: SUNY Press.

Diamond, Irene & Quinby, Lee (1988). American feminism and the language of control. *In* I. Diamond & L. Quinby, eds. *Feminism and Foucault: reflections on resistance,* 193–206. Boston, MA: Northeastern University Press.

Edwards, Paul N. (1990). The army and the microworld: computers and the politics of gender. *Signs 16* (1), 102–27.

Ellsworth, Elizabeth (1987). Why doesn't this feel empowering? Working through the repressive myths of critical pedagogy. *Harvard Educational Review 59* (3), 297–324.

— (1988). Media interpretation as a social and political act. *Journal of Visual Literacy 8* (2), 27–38.

— (1990). *Teaching to support unassimilated difference.* Unpublished paper.

Enloe, Cynthia (1988). *Does khaki become you? The militarization of women's lives.* Boston, MA: Pandora.

Gaskell, Jane (1987). Gender and skill. *In* David W. Livingstone, ed. *Critical pedagogy and cultural power,* 137–53. South Hadley, MA: Bergin & Garvey.

Gore, Jennifer M. (1993). *The struggle of pedagogies: critical and feminist discourses as regimes of truth.* New York: Routledge.

Hacker, Sally (1989). *Pleasure, power, and technology.* Boston, MA: Unwin Hyman.

Haraway, Donna J. (1988). Situated knowledges: the science question in feminism and the privilege of partial perspective. *Feminist Studies 14* (3), 575–99.

— (1990). A manifesto for cyborgs: science, technology, and socialist feminism in the 1980's. *In* L.J. Nicholson, ed. *Feminism/postmodernism,* 190–233. New York: Routledge.

— (1991). *Simians, cyborgs, and women: the reinvention of nature.* New York: Routledge.

Harding, Sandra (1986). *The science question in feminism.* Ithaca, NY: Cornell University Press.

— (1987). The method question. *Hypatia: A Journal of Feminist Philosophy 2* (3), 19–35.

— (1991). *Whose science? Whose knowledge? Thinking from women's lives.* Ithaca, NY: Cornell University Press.

Hartsock, Nancy (1983). The feminist standpoint: developing the ground for a specifically feminist historical materialism. *In* S. Harding & M. Hintikka, eds. *Discovering reality: feminist perspectives on epistemology, metaphysics, methodology, and philosophy of science,* 283–310. Dordrecht, Holland: Reidel.

Hawkins, Jan. (1987). Computers and girls: rethinking the issues. *In* Karen Sheingold & Roy Pea, eds. *Mirrors of minds: patterns of experience in educational computing,* 242–57. New York: Ablex.

Jamison, P. K. (1991). An interview with Donna Haraway. *Feminist Teacher* 6(2), 3-15.

— (1992). *Tech(knowledge)y.* Paper presented at Bergamo Conference, Oct. 1992.

Kay, Robin H. (1992). Understanding gender differences in computer attitudes, aptitude, and use: an invitation to build theory. *Journal of Research on Computing in Education 25* (2), 159–71.

Keller, E.F. (1985). *Reflections on gender and science.* New Haven, CT: Yale University Press.

Krieger, Susan (1991). *Social science and the self: personal essays on an art form.* New Brunswick, NJ: Rutgers University Press.

Lakoff, Robin (1975). *Language and woman's place.* New York: Harper & Row.

Lather, Patti (1991). *Getting smart: feminist research and pedagogy with/in the postmodern.* New York: Routledge.

Lerner, Gerda (1973). *Black women in white America: a documentary history.* New York: Random House.

— (1986). *The creation of patriarchy.* New York: Oxford University Press.

— (1993). *The creation of feminist consciousness: from the Middle Ages to 1870.* New York: Oxford University Press.

Longino Helen. E. (Fall 1987). Can there be a feminist science? *Hypatia: A Journal of Feminist Philosophy 2* (3), 51—64.

— (1990). *Science as social knowledge.* Princeton, NJ: Princeton University Press.

Luke, Carmen & Gore, Jennifer, eds. (1992). *Feminisms and critical pedagogy.* New York: Routledge.

Mander, Anica Vesel & Rush, Anne Kent (1974). *Feminism as therapy.* New York: Random House.

Millet, Kate (1990). *The loony-bin trip.* New York: Simon & Schuster.

Noble, Douglas (1984). Computer literacy and ideology. *In* D. Sloan, ed. *The computer in education.: a critical perspective,* 64–76. New York: Teachers College Press.

— (1991). *The classroom arsenal: military research, information technology, and public education.* London: Falmer.

Richardson, Laurel (1993). The consequences of poetic representation: writing the other, rewriting the self. *In* Carolyn Ellis & M. Flaherty, eds. *Windows on lived experience,* 125–40. Newbury Park, CA: Sage.

Spender, Dale (1980). *Man made language.* New York: Routledge.

Spender, Dale (1982). *Women of ideas and what men have done to them: from Aphra Behn to Adrienne Rich.* London: Routledge & Kegan Paul.

Stone, Allecquerre Rosanne (1993). Will the real body please stand up? Boundary stories about virtual cultures. *In* Michael Benedikt, ed. *Cyberspace first steps.* Cambridge, MA: MIT Press.

Taylor, William D. & Johnsen, Jane B. (1986). Resisting technological momentum. *In* J.A. Culbertson & L.L. Cunningham, eds. *Microcomputers in education: eighty-fifth yearbook of the National Society for the Study of Education,* 216–33. Chicago, IL: University of Chicago Press.

Turkle, Sherry & Papert, Seymour (1990). Epistemological pluralism: styles and voices within the computer culture, *Signs 16* (1), 128–57.

Wajcman, Judy (1991). *Feminism confronts technology.* University Park, PA: Pennsylvania State University Press.

Walkerdine, Valerie (1990). *Schoolgirl fictions.* London: Verso.

Weedon, Chris (1987). *Feminist practice and poststructural theory.* Oxford, England: Blackwell.

10.5 POSTMODERN AND POSTSTRUCTIONAL THEORY: VERSION 1.0 (Andrew R. J. Yeaman)

Every philosophical colloquium necessarily has a political significance (Derrida, 1968/1982, p. 111).

This is not a work of fiction. Names, characters, places, and incidents are neither fictitious nor the products of the author's imagination. Any resemblance to actual persons, living or dead, events, or locales is entirely purposeful and intentional.

The purpose of this chapter is to present and explore theoretical work that is postmodern and poststructural. These contemporary ideas are advocated for their viability in obtaining understanding about educational communications and technology. Not only do they provide ecological sufficiency but also they raise ethical concerns. Although not all postmodern questions may be immediately answerable, the political act of poststructural analysis may in itself be humanizing.

The focus of postmodern, poststructural theory is for modern, structural research to reconceptualize itself towards acknowledgement of its assumptions, towards reflecting them inward, and towards consistency with those assumptions. Being postmodern indicates a historical, sociological point of view. Being poststructural indicates a strategy of analysis and knowing.

Given these provisions, readers may assume that the chapter is factual but wonder at the superfluous first paragraph. Looking again reveals something else is at play. The disclaimer inverts the conventional valuing of fact over fiction. That inversion draws attention to the politics of textuality, and all media, including educational communications and technology, in making a rhetorical distinction between truth and fabrication.

Neel explains the separation in *Plato, Derrida, and Writing*: "Establishing a split between creative and expository writing may be the essential maneuver in establishing the possibility of serious, referential, verifiable discourse. Such a division guarantees the existing hierarchy" (1988, p. 174). The unfortunate effect of this temporal stability is a form of intellectual impairment whereby certain texts may be classified as above analysis. Further, traditional understandings about reading make little contact with the practice of writing. Genres are not to be blurred together, and readers are not supposed to write. For example, Landow's instructional hypertexts based on critical theory (1992) are formally applied in ways supporting authority by transmitting approved data and opinions (Sosnoski, 1991).

What constitutes fact is a philosophical issue more dependent on who writes or speaks in a particular cultural setting than on style. Literary, imaginative, and fictive elements are inescapable aspects of factual narratives (White, 1978, 1987). The resemblance to novels like *Among Schoolchildren* (Kidder, 1989) or *The Double Helix* (Watson, 1968) indicates that border crossings are commonplace. Foucault's statement, "I am well aware that I have never written anything but fictions" (1980, p. 193), explains distance from received beliefs about what is perceived as true; "One 'fictions' history on the basis of a political reality that makes it true; one 'fictions' a politics not yet in existence on the basis of a historical truth." The postmodern, poststructural interrogation of the socially constructed textual etiquette of true facts and false fictions raises political questions:

- Who defines and writes the facts?
- Who is forbidden to write the facts?

For an immediate illustration, apply those questions of who may and who may not to one of the simplest and most frequently encountered sentences in education: PUPILS to whom this textbook is issued must not write on any page or mark any part of it in any way, consumable textbooks excepted.

10.5.1 Authorization in Progress—One Moment

Separating the author from the authority of a text requires acknowledging the political issues of knowledge and power. These directly affect the people who are both readers and authors: designers of instructional messages, developers of instructional systems, managers of learning resources such as librarians and media specialists, scholars and professors engaged in researching applications, and teachers and trainers in preservice and in-service programs. The social aspects of criticism provide the necessary perspective, but the critical position is a recent innovation in educational communications and technology (Belland, Duncan & Deckman, 1991).

There is much room for critical study, because unquestioning submission to authority or thoughtlessly following procedures prefers preconventional and conventional morality to the highest level of moral consciousness: the postconventional consideration of principles (Kohlberg, 1981, 1984). Neither utopian, nor accepting morality as scientifically proved, but towards recognizing technical, practical, and critical distinctions, Hlynka (1991, p. 44) quotes Knirk and Gustafson (1986, p. 33), with emphasis added on the key word: "Although an instructional technologist may have a voice in creating policy, he or she is primarily responsible for *implementing* policy decisions. . . . If an instructional technologist questions the goals, an interpretation should be provided by a representative of the policy-making body." To make a similar point about the basic assumptions of instructional design, Yeaman (1994f, p. 71) quotes Gagné, Briggs, and Wager (1988, p. 4): "We are not concerned here with 'mass' changes in opinion or capabilities, nor with education in the sense of 'diffusion' of information or attitudes within and among societies." The theoretical, philosophical foundation explained here reads all texts as political, especially those that deny any politics. This chapter asserts that the ethical responsibilities of practice and scholarship in educational communications and technology extend beyond functionalism.

10.5.2 Toward an Anthropology of Ourselves and the Politics of Knowledge

"Postmodernity" is the continuation of history beyond its end (Martin, 1992, p. 47).

Whereas Immanuel Kant offers the modern assumption that each person's life has an individual meaning over political circumstances, Martin Heidegger and Jean-Paul Sartre argue that if such humanistic beliefs require metaphysical faith, the anthropological question of the true human character remains unanswered and the purpose of life uncertain (Derrida, 1968/1982, p. 136). Derrida wrote under the political circumstances of intellectual authority overtly linked to bureaucratic authority when, in the late 1960s, French educational institutions revealed themselves as socializing agencies in the service of the state. University administrators called in police and militia to restore order with force (p. 114). Intelligentsia figures such as the structuralists Jean Piaget and Claude Lévi-Strauss, who said they were neutral scientists (Gardner, 1973, pp. 213–15), were seen as seeking national stability at the price of continued intolerance in the academy. The official answers to "Who are we and what is humanity?" evaded controversy and were restricted to authorized views from the Enlightenment *philosophes*. The resulting discourse of modernity had functioned to preserve the oppressive power of bureaucratic authorities. *Les Événements*, the Paris events of May 1968, drew disillusionment with Marxism and existentialism, both of which came to be viewed as unreasonably idealistic and the apolitical structuralist enterprise.

In contrast, Derrida's political position (1968/1982) was acceptable as representative of the Nouvelle Critique movement, along with Roland Barthes, Julia Kristeva, and Phillipe Sollers (Lamont, 1987). (See Barthes, 1966/1987, on the Nouvelle Critique dating back to the Liberation and distinct from Anglo-American New Criticism.) Derrida's appeal was in using learning from the classical tradition to reread authorized views and see through political circumstances. It is at this ongoing junction, where knowledge and power come together, where the logic of reason itself is interrogated, where philosophy becomes political, that postmodern and poststructuralist thought can be detected in rejecting modernity and structuralism and going beyond.

At the same time, a rewriting of Kant's end in autonomy is made possible by rereading in the shadow of political history (Martin, 1992, pp. 45–47). Political circumstances do make a difference. When they are ignored, the humanism is impure. For example, here is Sosnoski quoted out of context so as to seem to be following Descartes: "All theorizing is derived from the question 'Who am I?' To want to understand what you are doing is to want to understand who you are. . . . This question precipitates humanistic study. It is as important to students as it is to us. Like us, they are theorists" (1991, p. 284). In comparison, it is interest in Kant's importantly different question "What are we?" which exposes the state's power structures for being both individualizing and totalizing (Foucault, 1982a). In other words, what is political is reread and rewritten "in the general text of the modern crisis of representational thought and its mechanisms" (Jay, 1990, p. 78). As in the epigraph stating that all discussions are political (Derrida, 1968/1982, p. 111), the matter of autonomy remains the open question of the human identity (p. 136).

This chapter has been constructed with postmodern and poststructural theory's commitment to keeping questions open and to the resultant uncertainty. There should be consistency between the message and the way the message is presented, and this chapter is unlike a traditional research handbook chapter that has the linear, monolithic position of a metanarrative. Like an encyclopedia, several voices are required to show diversity as well as convergence, and any contradiction or overlap is intentional. This comes from Derrida's announcement that politics are inescapable (1968/1982, p. 111), and the conclusion: "One has nothing, from the inside where 'we are,' but the choice between two strategies" (p. 135):

> To attempt an exit and a deconstruction without changing terrain, by repeating what is implicit in the founding concepts

and the original problematic, by using what is implicit in the founding concepts and the original problematic, by using against the edifice the instruments or stones available in the house, that is, equally in language. . . . To decide to change terrain, in a discontinuous and irruptive fashion, by brutally placing oneself outside, and by affirming an absolute break and difference.

Derrida continues by explaining how these deconstructions are made possible: "A new writing must weave and interlace these two motifs of deconstruction. . . . One must speak several languages and produce several texts at once" (1968/1982, p. 135). There can be no single voice, no absolute knowledge, no perfect translation, and no expectation that anyone else thinks like ourselves. Freedom requires respect of the other, of truths other than the logic of white men, and meanings from others outside the West and those within but excluded: see Bannet (1989, pp. 222–23). Multivocality is a partial solution to these difficulties of identity, translation, and power. Concomitantly, there are fresh possibilities for social theory through widespread scholarship (see Derrida, 1994), and Martin proposes that "Derrida provides the basis for a new language of politics" (1992, p. 198).

In applying Derrida's declaration, scholars expert in postmodern and poststructural theory were invited to write essays for this chapter. The authors each describe positions that make and should continue to make significant contributions. The contributions give examples of practical situations and ways to proceed, and identify what is currently lacking in research and theory. The common intent is to make clear the value of postmodern and poststructural theory to research in educational communications and technology.

Like the postmodern and poststructural abandonment of the failed modern promises and failed revolutionary hopes of *Les Événements*, the work reported here resembles the politics that White (1987, pp. 104–05) reads in Foucault. Conservatism is not allowed to justify itself on the basis of tradition. Privatization of public resources by government for the public good is suspect. Liberal pleas for justice in the name of law and order seem ineffective and muddled: "The master's tools will never dismantle the master's house" (Lorde, 1979/1993). Leftists are recognized as tending towards utopian social science and naïve cultural idealism. Nevertheless, racism and xenophobia, heterosexism and homophobia, sexism, environmental destruction, and poverty are important to fight, among other instances of oppression, by giving specific support to radical, liberatory, critical pedagogy.

The position becomes apparent when the points of view in this chapter are seen as a whole rather than as a collection of parts. They coexist in their relationship to instructional systems development. They move educational communications and technology from being mostly psychological and management based to being more cultural and situated in society. The concerns are practical, but the writers also seek the meaning of a transformation towards nonreductionist theory.

10.5.3 Postmodern and Poststructural Theory as Criticism

Criticism is not science. Science deals with meanings; criticism produces them (Barthes, 1987, p. 79).

Critical theory indicates: "Un-American activities that employ a vocabulary and sometimes methods belonging to the history of ideas rather than strictly to the domain of literary criticism, such as those of phenomenology, structuralism, deconstruction, semiotics" (Spivak, 1985, p. 29). This fits well with Adams's belief that the Western tradition of critical theory, spanning more than 2,000 years of Western culture, will continue and not be dismissed by global acceptance of multicultural literature and thought (1992, p. v).

Critical theorizing in the tradition of the humanities is distinct and is the most intellectually important development in educational communications and technology (Yeaman, Nichols & Koetting, 1994). Through the way of knowing generally labeled criticism, humanistic study of communication aspects maintains the social relevance of the field. The design of instructional messages is seen as an artistic endeavor with sociopolitical consequences. The critical approach to instruction has a literary foundation that, as Geertz points out (1973, 1983), is appropriate for understanding culture by reading it.

In the context of the present chapter, *theory* means critical theory as it is widely applied in literary and philosophical studies: "The term *critical theory* is used here not in the narrow sense employed by the Frankfurt social critics but to include speculative writing about the nature of literature and the problems of critical discourse about it" (Adams, 1992, p. v). It is necessary for readers to compare critical theory in this chapter with how it is engaged in reference to the Frankfurt Institute for Social Research's *Kritische Theorie* by Koetting and Januszewski (1991), Streibel (1993), and Nichols's Chapter 9.

Contemporary literary works tend to be philosophical, while philosophical works tend to be literary. Each finds a complement in the other. Questions of philosophy as writing, and writing as philosophizing, occupy mutual ground. A typical title is *The Rhetoric of Interpretation and the Interpretation of Rhetoric* (Hernadi, 1989). This interdisciplinary work is given credibility by postmodern and poststructural endeavors acknowledging the interdependence of literary studies and philosophy.

Classes in statistical research design and educational psychology are unnecessary for carrying out humanistic research on this theoretical foundation. Neither a university position nor a Ph.D. is required for inquiry supported by critical literacy (Knoblauch & Brannon, 1993). What helps is a background in the humanities and considerable practice at the undergraduate level in reading, thinking, and writing. However, teachers being critical runs against the belief of many educational researchers that professor knows best (see Gibson, 1986, pp. 162–65 and 9.7.5). It contrasts the Leninist bias towards making academics dominant over others, which is not only upheld by Marxist social scientists

but also by positivists, empiricists, and liberals (Poster, 1984, pp. 76–78).

Some advice on how to become a critic explains, in part, what is criticism: Read anything and everything inside and outside the canon: novels, essays, poems, and criticism, and talk to other people about what you read. Learn about the social sciences: anthropology, history, sociology, and social psychology. Become acquainted with linguistics and philosophy. Experience the performing arts and various media such as cinema, and become literate about appreciation and production. Develop a sense of the past as contemporary stories about people in other cultures and different times. Become familiar with the methods and theories of historiography. None of this is to exclude learning about other domains such as mathematics, physics, or chemistry, and professional fields such as engineering, communications, business, or education.

There is much need for humanistic criticism to balance technoscience. Nearly all the scientists who have ever lived are alive today, and functionalist points of view have been strengthened by the exponential growth in the scientific establishment. Jay tells students (1990, pp. 336–37):

The worth of humanities courses lies precisely in the degree of their refusal of a technological, quantitative, absolutist, or correspondence model of truth. Here, on the contrary, is a laboratory for discovering the rules by which truths have been produced, the value systems these truths have supported, and the historical consequences of such discourses and institutions.

Criticism is necessary to comprehend the political mechanisms for deciding what is and is not real. With experience, it becomes apparent that the purification of language, much like Socrates rejecting the teaching of Lysias, is achieved by elevating expository writing above fiction. Neel explains it this way: "The really important disciplines—philosophy and math first, then history and literature—deal with ideas. The really practical disciplines—physics, biology, and chemistry first, then engineering, computer science, and business—describe the world and keep it running" (1988, p. 174). There is widespread complicity in neutralizing the power of writing towards maintaining a merely functional reality. Writing can be totalitarian and serve as an authoritarian stabilizer.

It should be understood that critical theory does not exist in isolation, representing the humanities alone, but is related to work in the social sciences in conceptual theorizing and qualitative investigation. There is considerable interdisciplinary crossover between critical theory and social theory. A comparison of recent anthologies from each area supports this relationship. Collected in *Social Theory: The Multicultural & Classic Readings* by Lemert (1993) are 88 writers. *Critical Theory Since Plato* by Adams (1971) has 102 selections from intellectuals, including saints, nobles, and professors, dating from antiquity to the middle of the 1960s. The authors also chosen by Lemert for *Social Theory* are Roland Barthes, Friedrich Engels, Sigmund Freud, and

Karl Marx. *Critical Theory Since 1965* by Adams and Searle (1986) has 56 selections from contemporaries. The authors also chosen by Lemert for *Social Theory* are Louis Althusser, Walter Benjamin, Jacques Derrida, Michel Foucault, Max Horkheimer, Jacques Lacan, Georg Lukács, Ferdinand de Saussure, and Claude Lévi-Strauss, whose essay on "The Structural Study of Myth" is the only duplicate text selection.

This is a cautious demonstration: Adams and Searle's 1986 collection went to press several years before Lemert's 1993 collection. Adams's second edition of *Critical Theory Since Plato* appeared in 1992 and contains more writings from outside the Western canon. To include unknowns along with greats is a current trend. Lemert points out (1993, p. 663) that there are less than obvious problems with representing theories and intellectual patterns with figures who are well known. Such exclusive modeling may contribute to political marginalization and to the narrowness of dogmatic tradition, but there is tremendous value in making a start. Although critical theory is not centered on political activists, economists, or present-day mainstream sociologists, Adams and Searle (1986) also overlap with Lemert's selections (1993) by making references to Roland Barthes, Simone de Beauvoir, Ruth Benedict, Emile Durkheim, Friedrich Engels, Frantz Fanon, Sigmund Freud, Erich Fromm, Harold Garfinkel, Charlotte Perkins Gilman, Erving Goffman, Jürgen Habermas, William James, V. I. Lenin, Jean-François Lyotard, Karl Mannheim, Karl Marx, Talcott Parsons, Richard Rorty, Georg Simmel, Gayatri Chakravorty Spivak, Max Weber, and Virginia Woolf.

The final score shows that 32 of Lemert's 88 social thinkers (1993) are also considered as major contributors to critical theory by Adams (1971) and Adams and Searle (1986).

Many of these authors are stimulating to read because they write with originality and brilliance seldom encountered in the education literature. This can be attributed to their more imaginative, creative, literary modes of thinking and expression through criticism. Ong, a long-established critic best known for an outstanding history of the relationship between mind and media (1982), provides a description of the analytical technique (1971, p. 1161):

> Although it is not to be equated with science, criticism is in some degree explanation, and has something of this same scientific bent. Unless it is to be itself a poem, criticism of a poem must involve some elucidation. Its ultimate object may be to introduce the reader more fully into the mystery which is the poem, but its technique will be to some extent "clear up" certain things.

An observation by a second-generation American poststructuralist gives an example of the use of criticism for the development of new knowledge (Johnson, 1980, p. xii):

> The "unknown" is not what lies beyond the limits of knowledge, some unreachable, sacred, ineffable point toward which we vainly yearn. It lies, rather, in the oversights and slip-ups that structure our lives in the same way that an *X* makes it possible to articulate an algebraic equation. . . .

It is not, in the final analysis, what you don't know that can or cannot hurt you. It is what you don't *know* you don't know that spins out and entangles "that perpetual error we call life."

Criticism results in "the critical work that thought brings to bear on itself" and is tested by writing essays (Foucault, 1985, pp. 8, 9). The intellectual tools, processes, and products of criticism are invoked by the full quotation:

> There are times in life when the question of knowing if one can think differently than one thinks, and perceive differently than one sees, is absolutely necessary if one is to go on looking and reflecting at all. People will say, perhaps, that these games with oneself would be better left backstage; or, at best, that they might properly form part of those preliminary exercises that are forgotten once they have served their purpose. But, then, what is philosophy today—philosophical activity, I mean—if it is not the critical work that thought brings to bear on itself? In what does it consist, if not in the endeavor to know how and to what extent it might be possible to think differently, instead of legitimating what is already known? (Foucault, 1985, pp. 8, 9).

The next section identifies important sources of postmodern and poststructural thinking. Starting with the writings cited here will reduce the confusion of encountering the unfamiliar. Readers seeking to understand postmodern and poststructural work in educational communications and technology will benefit by beginning their reading with the originals. Both terms are philosophical and political, but writers of varying quality and credentials use and misuse *postmodern* and *poststructural* as synonyms. Despite convergent interests in practical matters, postmodern theory tends to be more social, and poststructural theory is more literary in its points of view.

10.5.4 Reading the Postmodern

> We are at the end of what is called *The Modern Age.* Just as Antiquity was followed by several centuries of Oriental ascendancy, which Westerners provincially call *The Dark Ages,* so now *The Modern Age* is being succeeded by a post-modern period (Mills, 1959, pp. 165–66).

To explain what is meant by *modern* is to attempt describing the spirit of the industrial age sweeping across centuries, continents, and cultures. Nevertheless, the episteme of modernity as a historically constructed discursive practice may be expressed through such an archeological approach (Foucault, 1970/1972, pp. 190–92). As modern times have not yet fully passed, it may also be a mirror of contemporary ideals, too. The tone and jargon of a pair of electronic-mail postcards illuminates the discussion of modernity:

> Received your last two notes. Thanks! I am just now sitting down with a host of ideas for my part of the handbook. Will send you something soon, for your perusal. I had been looking for a captivating opening sentence or paragraph, and finally found the one I wanted. Of course, I may

change in midstream, but that is OK. I have been spending some time at the Winnipeg Art Gallery and reading about postmodernism in the fine arts. And now I have loads of (relevant) ideas!

My opening sentence? Here it is: "Postmodernism?" What do you think? Anyway, I am now working on the second sentence. (D. Hlynka, personal communication, March 15, 1993, 9:32 a.m.)

I suggest narrational framing:

"Postmodernism?" The other author replied by e-mail, "Not so much AFTER nor so much dogmatic ISM as a recognition of the MODERN that requires beginning with 'Postmodernism?'" (A. R. J. Yeaman, personal communication, Mar. 15, 1993, 11:12 a.m.)

The modern age was a way of conceptualizing Western history as the present in relation to the past. It was the time when Western society was industrializing and technoscience praised so highly that empirical thinking was applied to predicting what people would do. Certainty and control were gained at the price of losing understanding, and in the last 50 years vast numbers of people have been endangered by technology (Glendinning, 1990, pp. 18–20).

The general idea of Western civilization undergoing a course of evolutionary progress through scientific, technological developments preceded the influence of Auguste Comte, René Descartes, Benjamin Franklin, Immanuel Kant, and Claude Henri Saint-Simon, but is best expressed by their projects of enlightenment. Modernism is this belief in science, technology, and rationalization of productive activities for the good of all. Modern explanations of society in terms of solving human problems with factual knowledge, and this process leading to autonomy, have received varying degrees of acceptance, refinement, and rejection.

Writing in this decade, Ritzer presents McDonald's hamburger restaurants as the exemplar case of modernity (1993). Ritzer compares the systematicity of running fast-food business with the iron cage theory (Weber, 1905/1993) that rationalization results in inflexibility and false promises of improvement. Ritzer explains McDonaldization as the central bureaucratic process of modernity:

Formal rationality means that the search by people for the optimum means to a given end is shaped by rules, regulations, and larger social structures. . . . In effect, people no longer had to discover for themselves the optimum means to an end; rather, optimum means had already been discovered and were institutionalized in rules, regulations, and structures. People simply had to follow the rules, regulations, and dictates of the structure (p. 19).

Earlier Mills had parted with mainstream sociologists in the post–Second World War era by engaging in modern, self-reflective thinking (1959). Mills declares that the past two centuries of enlightenment have not achieved their objective and "The ideas of freedom and of reason have become moot; that increased rationality may not be assumed to make for increased freedom" (p. 167). A theoretical explanation is given:

Those in authority attempt to justify their rule over institutions by linking it, as if it were a necessary consequence, with widely believed-in moral symbols, sacred emblems, legal formulae. . . . Social scientists, following Weber, call such conceptions "legitimations," or sometimes "symbols of justification" (p. 36).

This early postmodern assessment meshes with the theory of metanarratives, determining what is knowledge in *The Postmodern Condition* (Lyotard, 1984). Although a common sociological and philosophical ground is shared with Habermas, who remains modern (1984, 1987), the interpretations are irreconcilable. (A balanced synopsis of the divergent positions is given by Toulmin (1990, pp. 172–74) in *Cosmopolis*. Deleuze's Foucauldian position on education is also postmodern and italicized in the original: "Just as the corporation replaces the factory, *perpetual training* tends to replace the *school,* and continuous control the examination" (1992, p. 5). This continues Deleuze's earlier work in collaboration with Guatarri (1983, 1987), where a sort of social masochism is identified and italicized: "*Training axiom—destroy the instinctive forces in order to replace them with transmitted forces*" (Deleuze & Guatarri, 1987, p. 155). The matter of cultural discontinuity is discussed further as a contemporary philosophical and political issue in *The Postmodern Explained* (Lyotard, 1992).

The idea of these times being postmodern, in that modern self-reflections show that rational societies have defeated their own ideals, is changing all areas of professional study and academic discipline. For example, an authoritative review chapter by Agger provides a recent account of influences on sociology (1991). Smart (1992) gives a detailed analysis including rereadings of McLuhan (1964) and Toffler (1980). A more global account is provided in a sequel (Smart, 1993). Postmodern thinking is applied in depth to education theory and practice by Lather in *Getting Smart* (1991). A brief overview for art educators is provided by MacGregor (1992). Qualitative scholarship on postmodern theory and its application deserves meticulous attention, and Mills's chapter "On Intellectual Craftsmanship" is highly recommended (1959, pp. 195–226).

Gore's AERA paper (1994) reports the work of a research group studying Foucault's (1977) analyses of power relations. Quasi-quantitative coding categories were developed for these activities as the mechanisms of schooling: surveillance, normalization, exclusion, distribution, classification, individualization, totalization, regulation, space, time, knowledge, and techniques or practices directed at the self by a researcher, a teacher, or a student (pp. 9, 10). The potential risk of "taming" Foucault (p. 24) is judged to be outweighed by the possibilities for fruitful theorizing and reconsidering practice.

Postmodern study of the same text is also demonstrated by a strikingly aware journal entry from a graduate seminar (B. Dallman, personal communication, Oct. 15, 1992). The seminar had been reading "The Means of Correct Training" (Foucault, 1984, pp. 188–205):

The day before I read this, I discussed the possibility of obtaining a waiver for the GRE with Marty [Tessmer]. After determining this was not likely, I felt disturbed but couldn't really articulate my feelings until reading this article. . . . It is as though the notion of disciplinary power was manifesting itself in higher education. . . . The notion of ritual and examination is a form of power that can repress individuals as well as empower them.

10.5.5 Reading the Poststructural

Structuralism, as it were, closed in Baltimore on opening night (Searle, 1986, p. 857).

The Ford Foundation provided funds for a massive 2-year program of seminars and colloquia to augment North American humanistic criticism and social science with French structuralist theory in cultural anthropology, semiology, sociology, and psychoanalysis, among other pertinent disciplines. Among the intellectuals flown across the Atlantic were stars, including Roland Barthes, Lucien Goldman, Jean Hyppolite, Jacques Lacan, and Tzvetan Todorov. See the proceedings edited by Macksey and Donato (1970/1972).

The commonly held structural belief was in language as the model of thought, that language is the model for everything including beliefs and behavior. Dreyfus and Rabinow (1982) quote the premier structuralist Claude Lévi-Strauss's *Totemism* (1963, p. 16). The ellipsis and the italicized emphases were added by Dreyfus and Rabinow (1982, p. xvi):

The method we adopt . . . consists in the following operations:

1. Define the phenomenon under study as a relation between two or more terms, real or supposed.
2. Construct a *table of possible permutations* between these two terms.
3. Take this table as the general object of analysis, which, at this level only, can yield necessary connections, the empirical phenomenon considered at the beginning being only one possible combination among others, the *complete system* of which must be reconstructed beforehand.

However, structuralism was being reconsidered from within for ignoring historical cultural practices. This was due to French interest in German phenomenology (see 38.2). Also see Greene (1994, pp. 429–30) and Hyppolite (1966/1972). One of the critics was Jacques Derrida, who had written on Husserl's phenomenological critique of science (1962/1989) after spending a year at Harvard in the late 1950s. Invited back to the United States for the first Ford Foundation meeting at Johns Hopkins University, Derrida (1966/1972, p. 258) quoted from Lévi-Strauss's *The Raw and the Cooked* (1964, p. 25): "Myths have no authors," and commented (italics in the original):

Thus it is at this point that ethnographic *bricolage* deliberately assumes its mythopoetic function. But by the same token, this function makes the philosophical or epistemo-

logical requirement of a center appear as mythological, that is to say a historical illusion.

In the discussion afterwards Derrida offered further clarification (1966/1972, p. 268):

How to define structure? Structure should be centered. But this center can be either thought, as it was classically, like a creator, or being, or a fixed and natural place; or also as a deficiency, let's say; or something which makes possible "free play," in the sense in which one speaks of the *jeu dans la machine,* of the *jeu des pièces,* and which receives—and this is what we call history—a series of determinations, of signifiers, which have no signifieds [*signifiés*] finally, which cannot become signifiers except as they begin from this deficiency.

Derrida was not alone among the European visitors in charting a revitalized trajectory for the humanities and the social sciences, and among other influential papers was Barthes' "To Write: An Intransitive Verb?" (1966/1972). Nonetheless, an important outcome was enthusiasm for Derrida among professors at prestigious universities in the United States where Derrida's ideas were soon disseminated (see Lamont, 1987). This was helped by Derrida's publishing three more books in the next year: *Speech and Phenomena* (1967/1973), *Of Grammatology* (1967/1976), and *Writing and Difference* (1967/1978). Derrida received visiting professor appointments, further scholarly sponsorship, and translation into English by advocates. Today Derrida is probably the world's most well-known and respected living philosopher. While it is still accepted that all cultural activities can possibly be read as if they were language, the roles of readers and authors—including anthropologists and humanities scholars—have changed now that Derrida has shown method to be uncertain.

Poststructuralism was the label generated by the Americans to account for what had happened. Roudinesco reveals the deep feelings, undercurrents, and personalities involved at the critical event in 1966 (1990, pp. 407–13). More than routine academic conflict had surfaced. Subsequently, Piaget's *Structuralism* invokes only Barthes' earlier work, does not mention Derrida, and gives Foucault, probably Derrida's most cogent professor, a makeover (1968/1970). Piaget first disparages Foucault for lack of method and then assimilates Foucault as a constructivist (pp. 128–35). Ironically *Le Structuralisme* was published the same year as *Les Événements* when the students' slogan was "Structuralism is dead" (Gardner, 1973, p. 214).

Two excellent anthologies of Derrida's writings are available by Attridge (1992) and Kamuf (1992). They include intelligent commentaries. Along with a distrust of formal method as in structuralism smuggling in the meaning it discovers, Derrida reinterpreted Saussurian difference between signs with a neologism: *différance,* whereby one thing is partly defined by the other but is nevertheless present while being omitted. The politics of *différance* recognize the patriarchal marginalization of women and racial minorities. The word most associated with Derrida is

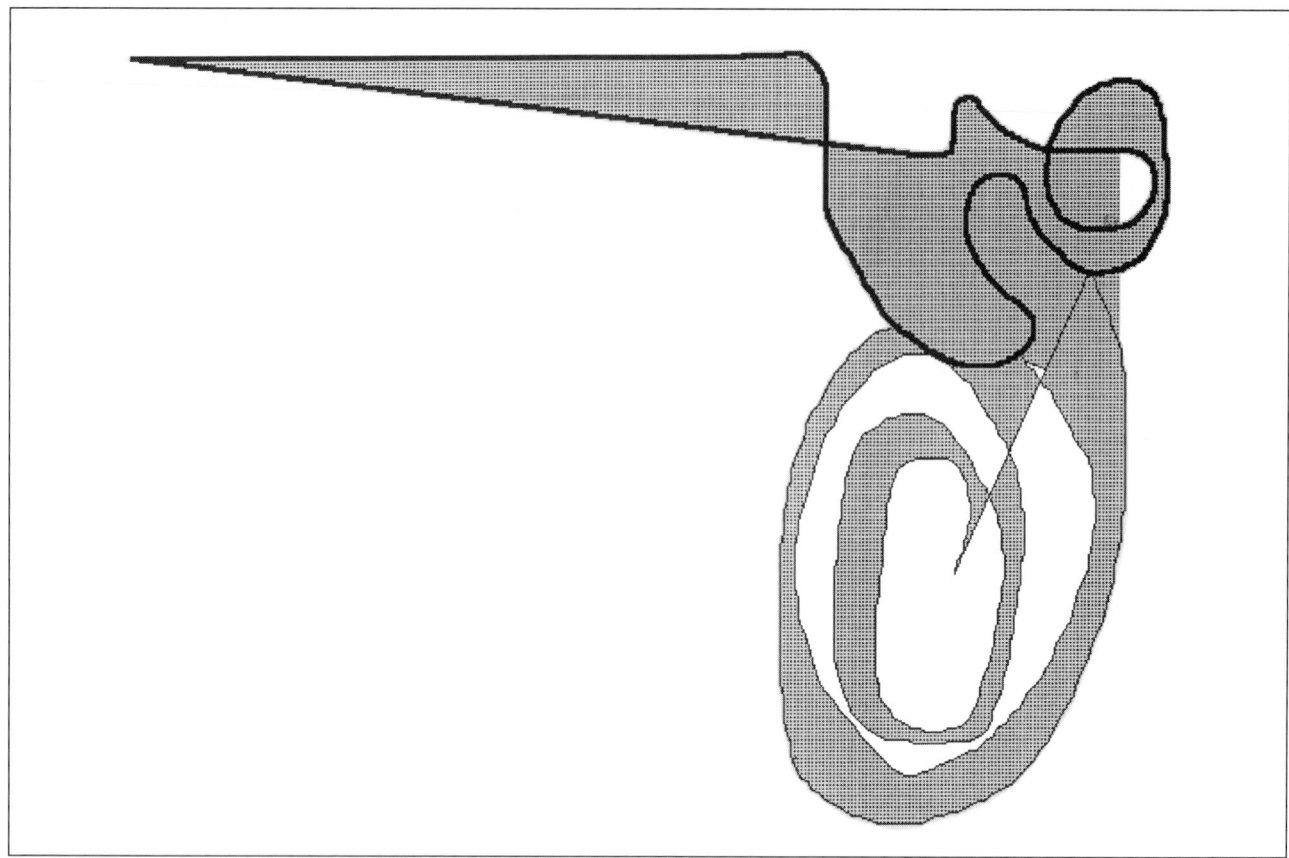

Figure 10-1.   This is an example of a signifier with nothing signified (except to signify that there can be a signifier with nothing signified except to signify that there can be a signifier with nothing signified except to signify that there can be a signifier . . .). (Original caption; Illustration by Andrew Yeaman.) From "Deconstruction and visuals: Is this a ~~telephone~~?" by Andrew R. J. Yeaman, p. 325, in D. M. Moore & F. M. Dwyer, eds. *Visual literacy: a spectrum of visual learning.* Copyright © 1994 by Educational Technology Publications. Reprinted with permission.

deconstruction, which is a term from Heidegger for the examination of foundational issues [see Hlynka & Yeaman, (1992) and Yeaman (1994c, 1994d, 1994e)]. Curiously, a "desire to domesticate deconstruction" into a professorial method tends to thwart its playful implications for theories of meaning (Lather, 1992, p. 132).

There has been widespread diffusion of Derrida's poststructural work; see, for example, *Deconstructive Criticism* by Leitch (1983); *What Is Deconstruction?* by Norris and Benjamin (1988); and *Deconstruction: Omnibus Volume* by Papadakis, Cooke, and Benjamin (1990). Self-scrutiny has been inspired in areas of knowledge unwittingly shaped by structuralism. As a result, there are occurrences of postmodern resistance. For a scholarly example, see Figures 10-1 and 10-2, which apply poststructural thinking to visual literacy and visual communication. Using a can of spray paint to write Robert Mapplethorpe AIDS Research Center on a university building named for U.S. Senator Robert Dole is only renaming, but it may be a theoretical beginning (Martin, 1992, p. 181). For social examples of political impact, see Penley (1991) and Treichler (1991), whose work on technology addresses women and HIV/AIDS,

respectively. Similarly, Poovey's argument for deconstruction as a feminist analytic tool refuses to allow deconstruction to become academically bland and apolitical (1988). Cherryholmes's *Power and Criticism* provides a poststructural review of education theory and practice (1988). Structuralist foundations exposed include Mager's behavioral objectives (1962/1984) and Bloom's taxonomy (Bloom, Engelhart, Furst, Hill & Krathwohl, 1956).

Foucault was not present at the eventful conference in Baltimore but was mentioned several times. "The Discourse on Language," Foucault's first public lecture at the Collège de France, will be helpful to anyone interested in learning about the demands of intellectual critique after structuralism (1970/1972, pp. 215–37).

When looking at art, art theory, and criticism as this century ends, a poststructural conclusion is inevitable: "What is clear is that Barthes and Derrida are the *writers,* not the critics, that students now read" (Krauss, 1986, p. 295). When looking at reading and writing, the massive long-term profits of the Ford Foundation's investment in criticism, and the subsequent transition from structural to poststructural theory, may be judged by this report in

Figure 10-2. A shoe? (Original caption; photograph by Robert Muffoletto.) This signifier is a photograph of an object like a shoe, possibly a hiking boot or a work boot. It is displayed on a box as if in an art class. It might be in a store but is not marked for sale and it looks worn. Who wears this shoe or boot? Conjectures like these follow Van Gogh's paintings that were labeled as shoes but appeared to depict boots; see Derrida (1987). Also see Foucault (1982b) on Magritte's drawing *Ceci n'est pas une pipe.* Perhaps what is signified here is the uncertainty of any signification; see Muffoletto (1994a). From the series titled "Mentioned." Copyright © 1989 by Robert Muffoletto. Reprinted with permission. Also published in "Representations: You, Me, and Them" by Robert Muffoletto, p. 304, in D. M. Moore & F. M. Dwyer, eds. *Visual literacy: a spectrum of visual learning.* Copyright © 1994 by Educational Technology Publications.

De Vaney's AECT conference paper (1989, pp. 21-22):

> In American schools, deconstruction is a political force to be reckoned with. Not only has its theory and practice infiltrated many English, foreign-language, and other humanities departments in institutions of higher learning, but officers in the powerful Modern Language Association and the National Council of Teachers of English are prominent American deconstructionists. . . . As educational technologists, interested in classroom practice, it then becomes of interest and concern to us.

Consequently the receivers of messages are changing as a result of poststructural theory spreading out through titles such as *Textual Power: Literary Theory and the Teaching of English* (Scholes, 1985); *The Art of Wondering: A Revisionist Return to the History of Rhetoric* (Covino, 1988); the MLA's *Contending with Words: Composition and Rhetoric in a Postmodern Age* (Harkin & Schilb, 1991); and the NCTE's books introducing teachers to deconstruction (Crowley, 1989) and to reader-response theories (Beach, 1993). Further, prominent traditionalists are amicable and intellectually receptive; see the interviews with Northrop Frye and Harold Bloom in *Criticism in Society* (Saluszinsky, 1987), as well as *Doing Things with Texts: Essays in Criticism and Critical Theory* (Abrams, 1989) and *The Electronic Word: Democracy, Technology, and the Arts* (Lanham, 1993).

In particular, these developments in rhetoric affect English teaching everywhere at all levels. The most visible group under pressure is the estimated 33,000 composition instructors and professors employed in the United States for the purpose of passing on the lore of how to write properly to 3-million adult students per term (Crowley, 1990, p. 139). In practice, not only is the writing and reading of memos and reports influenced but also the conduct of business, law, and politics.

Far from believing facts are facts and that facts are all that matters, or that nothing matters anymore because anything means any other thing, it is possible to reach past commonsense traditions about communication. The ambiguity of noise has a necessary function as part of making sense. Idealized and impersonal qualities such as unity, coherence, and linearity may conceal the power of the author as authority. Conventions of writing may seek to define the readers in professional class terms. However, readers may rewrite a text by deconstructing its social values. On realizing these possibilities, a gain in literacy is predictable. Whether or not there is an increase in media analysis skills, designers of instruction will need to consider the ethics of their own intentions and reconsider the altered profile of their audiences. Despite that "From the 17th century onward, the Western world has associated *truth* with *absolute, simple, scientific, truths,*" and that "Schools see themselves as preparing students to be trouble-free parts of the American industrial machine." Covino argues in a dramatization: "The best workers will be those who can create and analyze different patterns of information, those who are not locked into a limited format for thinking and writing" (1990, pp. 246–47). The future effect of poststructural thinking is checked by Gerbner's constraint: "No school or culture educates children for some other society. Giving teachers a messianic mission and having schools soak up all the dreams and aspirations citizens have for their children doom the enterprise to failure" (1974, p. 496). Nevertheless, it may be that poststructural learners will be less intellectually docile as classroom students and less malleable, after graduation, when exposed to new employee training (Yeaman, 1994c).

10.5.6 Postmodern and Poststructural Criticism in Educational Communications and Technology

The ongoing dilemma for educational communications and technology is that a sense of naïve realism about technoscience may lead to utopian justifications. It is a predicament that technological systematization can, over time, result in excessively rigid procedures. These may negate the original assumptions but have become dogmatic tradition. [Despite being incommensurable with postmodern and poststructural theory, Bowers (1988, 1993) is cited here for support because of shared concern.] Towards understanding itself better, the field requires more nonreductionist, interpretive, qualitative investigations into education and training situations. Persistent rethinking based on postmodern and poststructural theory is needed to ask "Who benefits from this application of technoscience?" and "What are the rational foundations of that which is regarded as reason?"

This position is documented and reinforced by chapters and articles in a special issue of *Research & Theory: AECT-RTD Newsletter* on reflective and critical points of view (Koetting, 1989); *The Ideology of Images in Educational Media: Hidden Curriculums in the Classroom* (Ellsworth & Whatley, 1990); a double issue of the *Journal of Thought* focusing on the social and cultural aspects of educational media (Robinson, 1990); *Paradigms Regained: The Uses of Illuminative, Semiotic and Post-modern Criticism as Modes of Inquiry in Educational Technology* (Hlynka & Belland, 1991); an ERIC Digest on *Postmodern Educational Technology* (Hlynka & Yeaman, 1992); *Computers in Education: Social, Political, and Historical Perspectives* (Muffoletto & Knupfer, 1993); *Visual literacy: A Spectrum of Visual Learning* (Moore & Dwyer, 1994); and *Watching Channel One: The Convergence of Students, Technology, and Private Business* (De Vaney, 1994c).

10.5.6.1. A Representative State-of-the-Art Study.
Consider *Watching Channel One* as an exemplary investigation (De Vaney, 1994c). The contributors range across the theory spectrum, but all report reputable findings about the broadcast of news television into schools, along with mandatory commercials. Authentic details have been gathered. The commercial force behind putting Channel One in schools was the same corporation that placed advertising posters in dentists' and physicians' waiting rooms. The California and North Carolina state legal debates over the

ethics of selling of students' instructional time make a dynamic comparison. Wiring was installed in some schools in ways that violated electrical code. The standards for high-quality broadcasting that had initially been shown to school boards and administrators, but apparently were not maintained once the contracts were signed, are reprinted in *Watching Channel One*.

There are postmodern and poststructural chapters. While the field descriptions and survey data take the readers into the schools, the poststructural media analyses help readers understand the television programming. An immediate contrast with teacher-centered lecture is apparent in the fast pacing of the show. A mind experiment gives immediate results: No one can rapidly read superficial, unrelated news facts from note cards, one topic per card, to a class and be said to fulfill the role of a teacher. Televising the same presentation of headlines, read from a teleprompter in a sensational voice by an actress or an actor, is offered as education.

De Vaney's chapter on "Reading the Ads" connects with some far-reaching implications (1994b). Both the Channel One program and the commercials communicate in the MTV style and are produced especially for the student audience. They are postmodern and "display the 'relieved state' which a product is supposed to produce, without presenting the prior state which a product is supposed to relieve" (p. 144). These ads work by conveying "a fractured narrative with fragmented images of a trouble-free, often celebratory life." Rather than the limited descriptive capabilities of content analysis for analyzing these postmodern ads, a poststructural reading is preferred. A Pringles ad is carefully read as a text about encouraging the consumption of corn chips. The effectiveness of the reading comes from verbalizing the fractured narrative and the fragmented images. The result is that the Pringles commercial's fascinatingly effective erotic metaphor is revealed. While teenagers cannot stop themselves from absorbing information via this medium, efforts should be made to teach them how to be visually literate so they can read the screen as they would read a text. The need to promote conscious understanding of media is a worthwhile message and is a valuable product of research. It should converge with the interest in poststructural analysis in English classrooms. For related work, also see De Vaney's inquiry into the racism and sexism of an award-winning, best-selling educational computer program (1993) and discussion of the ethical problems surrounding the portrayal of African-Americans in feature films (1994a).

10.5.6.2. Where Poetics and Politics Meet.
The work of Ulmer is seldom cited in educational communications and technology, but it provides a meaningful postmodern and poststructural bridge from the humanities (1985). There are few connections between these two areas, but there is potential for rapport. How media is understood has long been a research topic of educational communications and technology. How people can learn to understand and use media not only presents a fruitful area for investigation but also has a different politics.

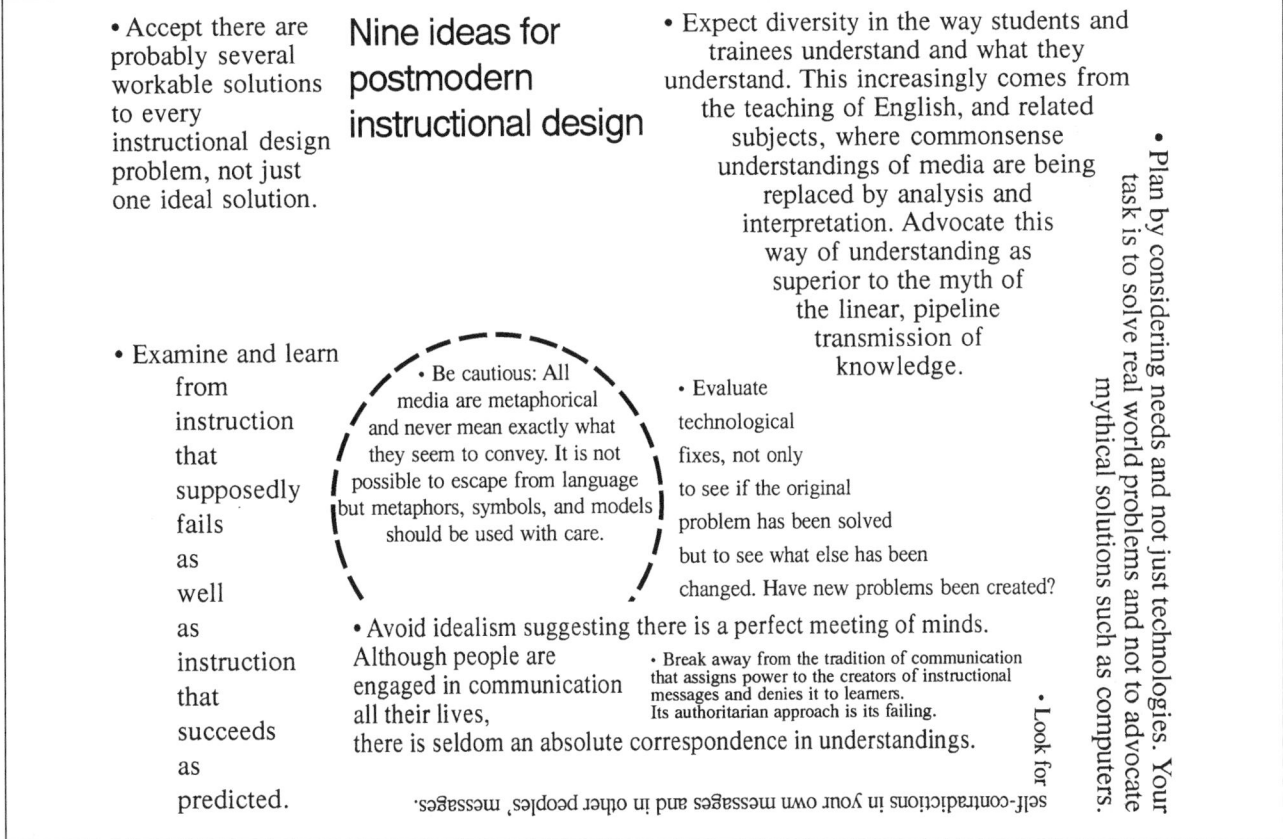

Figure 10-3. Nine ideas for postmodern instructional design. (Illustration by Andrew Yeaman.) From "Deconstructing Modern Educational Technology" by Andrew R. J. Yeaman, *Educational Technology* (Vol. 34, No. 2), Feb. 1994, p. 21. Copyright © 1994 by Educational Technology Publications. Reprinted with permission.

As an English professor, Ulmer is located at the point where poetics and politics meet. Ulmer explores the use of media literacy skills for personal expression to combat the reductionist ideologies of realism and individualism (1994). Ulmer suggests novel ways that students in English classes can use media, particularly video, that are self-expressive and freeing: "Write a mystory bringing into relation your experience with three levels of discourse. . . . Arrange the entries to highlight the chance associations that appear among the three levels" (1989, p. 209). Work on grammatology and hypermedia (Ulmer, 1992) influenced Hlynka's creation of a hypertext on poststructuralist literary theory, information technology, and ethnic studies (1993).

10.5.6.3. Ethics and Social Responsibility. A special issue of *Educational Technology* in February 1994 addressed the ethical position of educational communications and technology in society. The articles examine the ethics of the field as social responsibility and seek to encourage more interest in cultural analysis. The introductory essay by Yeaman, Nichols, and Koetting (1994) explains that the papers come from two research and theory symposia where presenters applied critical theory to provide insight into foundational aspects of the field. The sessions took place at the AECT Conferences in Washington, D.C., in 1992, and in New Orleans in 1993. The

declared socially responsible ethic of educational communications and technology is to facilitate humane learning, but that goal is rarely discussed, perhaps due to the emphasis on performance and function. Questions about facilitating humane learning neither dominate the literature nor the conferences: What is humane learning? Why is humane learning believed to be important? How can humane learning be achieved? What is the role of educational communications and technology in humane learning?

The authors appearing in the special issue share roots in an intellectual genealogy from which they develop ethical conscience through a humanities approach. They are part of an invisible college centered around the educational communications and technology programs at the Ohio State University and the University of Wisconsin-Madison. Their articles are based in the humanistic, nonpositivistic theories of criticism and include the critical theory of the Frankfurt school, feminist theory, and postmodern and poststructural theory.

Yeaman deconstructs two modern beliefs of educational technology: the telephone metaphor for communication and the systems approach to instruction (1994c). Yeaman ends with a draft agenda for a postmodern educational technology. See Figure 10-3 for the suggestions about instructional design.

According to Muffoletto (1994c), accepting the social agenda of technology results in conducting education through business management procedures. Muffoletto asks: Who will be in charge of restructuring technology in education? Distinctions are made between rethinking education and rethinking schools, between technology in education and educational technology. Educational reform unjustly blames teachers for society's problems and may cause teachers to be replaced with machines.

In "The Rite of Right or the Right of Rite: Moving Towards an Ethics of Technological Empowerment," Anderson puts forward the position that educational technology does not need professional ethics so much as it needs a sense of ethics that goes beyond control and consensus (1994).

Damarin states that women's issues are different issues (1994). The core issue of equity is not so much giving women equal access to the privileges of traditional power structures but giving women equal power through their own privileges. Damarin asks if instructional systems can encompass the feminist ethic of caring.

Nichols declares that there is no clear dividing line between educational technology and educational biotechnology, which intrudes into people's bodies and into the world ecology (1994). This link is first explored through Habermas's theoretical framework. Nichols goes on to describe Rorty's liberal irony that accepts immutable differences between people, despite the possibility of moral progress through a common understanding of cruelty. Then Nichols turns to Barrett in looking beyond rationality and the shared abhorrence of pain. In striving for moral will, faith in the spiritual is necessary through rituals such as prayer. However, a contradiction appears: Should one seek to be willful or will-less? Nichols concludes that there is an implied hope for conversation to continue.

In "Marginalizing Significant Others: The Canadian Contribution to Educational Technology," Hlynka points out that a sort of perceptual deficiency has concealed the importance of Canadian intellectuals (1994).

Muffoletto questions the ethics of social reality founded on the cultural values of industry and science (1994b). Information, how it is represented, and how learning takes place, are all shaped by that social reality. Critical theory is essential to school reform that recognizes those modern assumptions and strives to put democracy into practice.

Koetting views schooling as a political arena for social ethics and gives guidance towards the practice of critical pedagogy (1994).

In "Where in the World Is Jacques Derrida?" the branching text introduces Derrida's ideas according to readers' preferences and needs: facts, poetics, pragmatics, and further reading (Yeaman, 1994e).

10.5.6.4. Postmodern Cyborgs. The assertion that there is no clear division between people and their artifacts cannot be trivialized and dismissed. Scientists and technologists must look to anthropologists, historians, and sociologists to comprehend their own work. Field studies and library studies of research show that far from technoscientific

knowledge being the unveiled truth about nature, it is influenced by cultural factors such as normative pressures, economic motivations, linguistic competencies, and technologies for instrumentation and implementation (Locke, 1992). This is a typical instance of the processes of systematization, industrialization, mechanization, computerization, and the legitimation of knowledge affecting the question of identity discussed earlier in this chapter. Warnings about robotism and slavery (Fromm, 1955) were not effective, and automatization is probably not reversible. Although the cyborgs concept is expressed in popular culture as science fiction, there is an underlying social reality (Haraway, 1991, pp. 149–81) that returns to the issue of fact versus fiction mentioned previously.

Investigative work on postmodern cyborgs is a current object of research in educational communications and technology. The critical approaches of poststructural theory are being applied in the writing of humanistic essays. An informal network has been formed internationally as the Cyborg Collective. Formal presentations about the new species are made at conferences, and the work is receiving publication.

Bromley delivered "Do Cyborg Dreams Emancipate Sheep?" at Bergamo in 1992. Bromley describes school restructuring in terms of cybernetics, the production of student cyborgs, and uses the benefits employers receive from computers being placed in schools as a channel for exploring how education is rapidly becoming part of the global economy.

Damarin's 1994 AERA paper "Would You Rather Be a Cyborg or a Goddess? On Being a Teacher in a Postmodern Century" relates directly to Haraway's "Cyborg Manifesto" (1991). Damarin's feminist work on the cyborg theme is a continuation of "Technologies of the Individual: Women and Subjectivity in the Age of Information," which appeared in *Research in Philosophy and Technology* (1993) and recent writings such as "Women and Information Technology" (1992) and "Feminist Unthinking and Educational Technology" (1991).

In the Modern Machines and Postmodern Cyborgs session at the 1994 AECT conference in Nashville, there were cyborg papers given by Anderson (1994), Jamison (1994a), and Yeaman (1994b). The papers by Jamison (1994a) and by Yeaman (1994b) were submitted to *The Electronic Journal on Virtual Culture* for masked review and were accepted for refereed publication.

The paper "Cyborgian Orgasm: A Mythology of Educational Organizational Bliss" deals with the technology-serving people fantasy, the human-versus-technology dilemma, and the transcendence to a human-technology merger through cyborgs (Anderson, 1994). Anderson draws on the social construction and representation of computers in education to present a postmodern reading of pictures, essays, and focus group discussions by 100 undergraduate teacher education majors. The "Cyborgian Orgasm" paper concludes by asking educators to explore critically educational possibilities afforded by new technologies and broaden the discussion that associates the use of technology with progress.

In Jamison's "Contradictory Spaces: Pleasure, Comedy and the Seduction of the Cyborg Discourse," the cyborg image acts to deconstruct the finality of meaning in instructional development (1994a). Jamison argues that the examination of the cyborg as a discourse of pleasure, comedy, and seduction provides educators the opportunity to pursue questions of meaning, relationship, and contradiction:

1. What tension lies in a discourse that envisions machines as facilitators of social relationships?
2. If social reality and experience are the basis for education, how is the meaning of memory, time, body, movement, and expression represented in the cyborg discourse?
3. How do cyborgs name social reality?
4. How do cyborgs symbolize the paradox of human visions of social and machine reality?
5. How does the cyborg suggest contradictory meanings about education and technology?
6. What motifs in the cyborg discourse represent the contradictory themes of power and empowerment in social reality?
7. How does the cyborg discourse form a representation that is either like a human being or unlike one? What does this representation come to mean in education?
8. How does the cyborg teach? How does the cyborg design? How does the cyborg name education?
9. How do pleasure and comedy assist the reconceptualization of instructional development?
10. How does the cyborg discourse assist the reconceptualization of instructional development?

The "Cyborgs Are Us" article shows that the aesthetics of criticism can bring about awareness of cyborg fictions as a social anaesthetic (Yeaman, 1994b). Another purpose is to demonstrate writing as a way of exploring the social reality of cyborgs. Several genres are employed: A science fiction story tells readers "All My Teachers Were Cyborgs"; a poem with puns provides the "Concluding Summery: A Virtual Idyll"; factual third-person narrative prose follows the tabloid headline "Do Motherboards Bake Apple Pies?"; and scholarly first-person writing is used for the case study reporting of "Three Cases of Cyborgization." The analysis sections are autobiography, which is a genre recommended for qualitative research in education; see Gates (1991), Grumet (1990, 1992), and hooks (1990). This cyborg work continues from poststructural criticism of computer anxiety empiricism as mythmaking (Yeaman, 1993). Among the results were several provocative observations towards creating resistance (Yeaman, 1994a, pp. 70–71):

- Computers are sold to schools, as to any other customer, by corporations whose central concern is to produce profits.
- Computers in schools increase public knowledge about how to use computers, and that increase facilitates sales and the rate of adoption.
- Computers are vehicles for social stratification.

- Computers are not easy to use and are difficult to learn to use well.
- Computers do not always work well.
- Computers are not always useful.
- Computers can be a hindrance to getting things done.
- Computers-to-students ratios are a false measure of the quality of education.

The convergence of educational communications and technology with information technology may match this projected history of computers in education (Yeaman, 1994a, p. 71):

Somewhere between 1980 and 2030, a point would be reached where computers existed among all classes. It is hardly a coincidence that this diffusion should occur at the exact moment when the developments of the information revolution would demand a greater computerization of labor.

The "Cyborgs Are Us" investigation (Yeaman, 1994b) is followed by a case study about the social construction of instructors as cyborgs (Yeaman, 1995). Media analysis of a video about the dangers of television carts leads to its identification as propaganda. However, the psychological use of guilt to ensure compliant behavior only explains part of the video's effect. In the social context there are questions about who identifies "risk," who is "responsible," and why instructors have become fused with equipment and systems and made into cyborgs. Control is being internalized.

Poststructural techniques are particularly appropriate here. They function well in demystifying modern myths and can untangle the rhetoric of systems to show how technologies are socially constructed (Pinch, Ashmore & Mulkay, 1992). A question is also raised about what the safety video might have been like if the people affected had been allowed to make decisions about the instructional messages and format, as in the advocacy work of the Århus industrial designers such as Bødker, Greenbaum, and Kyng (1991).

10.6 Conclusion

Now, what I want is, *Facts*. Teach these boys and girls nothing but Facts. Facts alone are wanted in life. Plant nothing else, and root out everything else. You can only form the minds of reasoning animals upon Facts; nothing else will ever be of any service to them. This is the principle on which I bring up my own children, and this is the principle on which I bring up these children. Stick to Facts, sir! (Dickens, *Hard Times,* 1854/1990, p. 8).

With these words, Thomas Gradgrind, a fictitious Victorian schoolmaster with excessive cultural literacy values, helps conclude this chapter section. Aside from the detailed analysis presented by Whaley (1989), it is enough to declare that Gradgrind's educational philosophy is:

1. Authoritarian, fanatical, and bullying in its application
2. Rigid, abstract, and barren in quality
3. Materialistic and commercial in its orientation. (Lodge, 1969, p. 90)

In opposing the undeserved reverence for authorized facts, the postmodern and poststructural theories explored in this chapter are valuable to the designers of instructional messages and to other professionals in educational communications and technology. Without considering criticism, the field is only the institutional processing of students and trainees with machines and programs. The functionality should be redirected to enable freedom and respect for others. Application of the humanistic critical theories of the postmodern and the poststructural may provide the necessary perspective. The current consequences of postmodern, poststructural concern for the field are political, cultural, and interpretive (Jamison, 1994b, 1996).

Topics for continued investigation include who is doing what to whom, the expression of power relationships with signs, and the problem with language as a model for how minds and societies function. Criticism can address these egalitarian issues and create new knowledge from humanistic points of view. The critical epistemology transcends the nonneutrality of technoscience by regarding the technologies of education as communication and culture.

REFERENCES

Abrams, M.H. (1989). *Doing things with texts: essays in criticism and critical theory,* M. Fischer, ed. New York: Norton.

Adams, H., ed. (1971). *Critical theory since Plato.* San Diego, CA: Harcourt, Brace, Jovanovich.

— (1992). *Critical theory since Plato* (rev. ed.). Orlando, FL: Harcourt, Brace, Jovanovich.

— & Searle, L., eds. (1986). *Critical theory since 1965.* Tallahassee, FL: Florida State University Press.

Agger, B. (1991). Critical theory, poststructuralism, postmodernism: their sociological relevance. *Annual Review of Sociology 17,* 105–31.

Anderson, J. (1994). The rite of right or the right of rite: moving towards an ethics of technological empowerment. *Educational Technology 34* (2), 29–34.

— (1994, Jan.). *Cyborgian orgasm: a mythology of educational organizational bliss.* Paper presented at the meeting of the Association for Educational Communications and Technology, Nashville, TN.

Attridge, D., ed. (1992). *Acts of literature.* New York: Routledge.

Bannet, E.T. (1989). *Structuralism and the logic of dissent: Barthes, Derrida, Foucault, Lacan.* Urbana, IL: University of Illinois Press.

Barthes, R. (1972). To write: an intransitive verb? *In* R. Macksey & E. Donato, eds. *The structuralist controversy: the languages of criticism and the sciences of man,* 134–56. Baltimore, MD: Johns Hopkins University Press. (Original work published 1966.)

— (1987). *Criticism and truth* (K.P. Keuneman, trans. & ed.). Minneapolis, MN: University of Minnesota Press. (Original work published 1966.)

Beach, R. (1993). *A teacher's introduction to reader-response theories.* Urbana, IL: National Council of Teachers of English.

Belland, J.C., Duncan, J.K. & Deckman, M. (1991). Criticism as a methodology for research in educational technology. *In* D. Hlynka & J.C. Belland, eds. *Paradigms regained: the uses of illuminative, semiotic and post-modern criticism as modes of inquiry in educational technology: a book of readings,* 151–64. Englewood Cliffs, NJ: Educational Technology.

Bloom, B.S., Engelhart, M.D., Furst, E.J., Hill, W.H. & Krathwohl, D.R. (1956). *Taxonomy of educational objectives: the classification of educational goals. Handbook 1: cognitive domain.* New York: McKay.

Bødker, S., Greenbaum, J. & Kyng, M. (1991). Setting the stage for design as action. *In* J. Greenbaum & M. Kyng, eds. *Design at work: cooperative design of computer systems,* 139–54. Hillsdale, NJ: Erlbaum.

Bowers, C.A. (1988). *The cultural dimensions of educational computing: understanding the non-neutrality of technology.* New York: Teachers College Press.

— (1993). *Education, cultural myths, and the ecological crisis: toward deep changes.* Albany, NY: State University of New York Press.

Bromley, H. (1992, Oct.). *Do cyborg dreams emancipate sheep? (With apologies to Philip K. Dick.)* Paper presented at the Bergamo Conference on Curriculum Theory and Practice, Dayton, OH. (ERIC Document Reproduction Service No. ED 358 824.)

Cherryholmes, C.H. (1988). *Power and criticism: poststructural investigations in education.* New York: Teachers College Press.

Covino, W.A. (1988). *The art of wondering: a revisionist return to the history of rhetoric.* Portsmouth, NH: Boynton/Cook.

— (1990). *Forms of wondering: a dialogue on writing, for writers.* Portsmouth, NH: Boynton/Cook.

Crowley, S. (1989). *A teacher's introduction to deconstruction.* Urbana, IL: National Council of Teachers of English.

— (1990). *The methodical memory: invention in current-traditional rhetoric.* Carbondale, IL: Southern Illinois University Press.

Damarin, S.K. (1991). Feminist unthinking and educational technology. *Educational and Training Technology International 28,* 111–19.

— (1992). Women and information technology: framing some issues for education. *Feminist Teacher 6* (2), 16–20.

— (1993). Technologies of the individual: women and subjectivity in the age of information. *Research in Philosophy and Technology 13,* 183–98.

— (1994). Equity, caring, and beyond: can feminist ethics inform educational technology? *Educational Technology 34* (2), 34–39.

— (1994, Apr.). *Would you rather be a cyborg or a goddess? On being a teacher in a postmodern century.* Paper presented at the meeting of the American Educational Research Association, New Orleans, LA.

De Vaney, A. (1989, Jan.). *The application of reader theories to issues in educational technology.* Paper presented at the meeting of the Association for Educational Communications and Technology, Dallas, TX.

— (1993). Reading educational computer programs. *In* R. Muffoletto & N.N. Knupfer, eds. *Computers in education: social, political, historical perspectives,* 181–96. Cresskill, NJ: Hampton.

— (1994a). Ethical considerations of visuals in the classroom: African-Americans and Hollywood film. *In* D.M. Moore & F.M. Dwyer, eds. *Visual literacy: a spectrum of visual learning,* 355–368. Englewood Cliffs, NJ: Educational Technology.

— (1994b). Reading the ads: the bacchanalian adolescence. *In* A. De Vaney, ed. *Watching channel one: the convergence of students, technology, and private business,* 137–52. Albany, NY: State University of New York Press.

—, ed. (1994c).*Watching channel one: the convergence of students, technology, and private business.* Albany, NY: State University of New York Press.

Deleuze, G. (1992). Postscript on the societies of control. *Oct. 34,* 3–8.

— & Guatarri, F. (1983). *Anti-Oedipus: capitalism and schizophrenia* (R. Hurley, M. Seem & H.R. Lane, trans.). Minneapolis, MN: University of Minnesota Press. (Original work published 1972.)

— & Guatarri, F. (1987). *A thousand plateaus: capitalism and schizophrenia* (B. Massumi, trans.). Minneapolis, MN: University of Minnesota Press. (Original work published 1980.)

Derrida, J. (1972). Structure, sign, and play in the discourse of the human sciences. *In* R. Macksey & E. Donato, eds. *The structuralist controversy: the languages of criticism and the sciences of man,* 247–72. Baltimore, MD: Johns Hopkins University Press. (Original work published 1966.)

— (1973). *Speech and phenomena and other essays on Husserl's theory of signs* (D.B. Allison, trans.). Evanston, IL: Northwestern University Press. (Original work published 1967.)

— (1976). *Of grammatology* (G.C. Spivak, trans.). Baltimore, MD: Johns Hopkins University Press. (Original work published 1967.)

— (1978). *Writing and difference* (A. Bass, trans.). Chicago, IL: University of Chicago Press. (Original work published 1967.)

— (1982). The ends of man. In *Margins of philosophy,* 109–36 (A. Bass, trans.). Chicago, IL: University of Chicago Press. (Original work published 1968.)

— (1987). *The truth in painting* (G. Bennington & I. McLeod, trans.). Chicago: University of Chicago Press. (Original work published 1978.)

— (1989). *Edmund Husserl's "Origin of geometry": an introduction* (rev. ed.) (J.P. Leavey, Jr., trans.). Lincoln, NE: University of Nebraska Press. (Original work published 1962.)

—(1994). *Specters of Marx: the state of the debt, the work of mourning, and the new international* (P. Kamuf, trans.). New York: Routledge. (Original work published 1993.)

Dickens, C. (1990). *Hard times: an authoritative text: backgrounds, sources, and contemporary reactions: criticism,* 2d ed. G. Ford & S. Monod, eds. New York: Norton. (Original work published 1854.)

Dreyfus, H.L & Rabinow, P. (1982). *Michel Foucault: beyond structuralism and hermeneutics: with an afterword by Michel Foucault.* Chicago, IL: University of Chicago Press.

Ellsworth, E. & Whatley, M.H., eds. (1990). *The ideology of images in educational media: hidden curriculums in the classroom.* New York: Teachers College Press.

Foucault, M. (1972). *The archeology of knowledge and the discourse on language* (A.M. Sheridan Smith, trans.). New York: Pantheon. (Original work published 1970.)

— (1977). *Discipline and punish: the birth of the prison* (A. M. Sheridan Smith, trans.). New York: Pantheon.(Original work published 1975.)

— (1980). *Power/knowledge: selected interviews and other writings, 1972-1977* (C. Gordon, ed. & C. Gordon, L. Marshall, J. Mepham & K. Soper., trans.). New York: Pantheon.

— (1982a). Afterword: the subject and power. *In* H.. Dreyfus & P. Rabinow. *Michel Foucault: beyond structuralism and hermeneutics: with an afterword by Michel Foucault,* 208–26. Chicago, IL: University of Chicago Press.

— (1984). The Foucault reader (P. Rabinow, ed.). New York: Pantheon.

Foucault, M. (1985). *The use of pleasure: Vol. 2 of the history of sexuality* (R. Hurley, trans.). New York: Vintage.

— (1955). *The sane society.* New York: Holt, Rinehart & Winston.

Gagné, R.M., Briggs, L.J. & Wager, W.W. (1988). *Principles of instructional design,* 3d ed. New York: Holt, Rinehart & Winston.

Gardner, H. (1973). *The quest for mind: Piaget, Lévi-Strauss, and the structuralist movement.* New York: Knopf.

Gates, H.L., Jr., ed. (1991). *Bearing witness: selections from African-American autobiography in the twentieth century.* New York: Pantheon.

Geertz, C. (1973). *The interpretation of cultures: selected essays.* New York: Basic Books.

— (1983). *Local knowledge: further essays in interpretive anthropology.* New York: Basic Books.

Gerbner, G. (1974). Teacher image in mass culture: symbolic functions of the "hidden curriculum." *In* D.R. Olson, ed. *Media and symbols: the forms of expression, communication, and education: the 73d yearbook of the National Society for the Study of Education: Part 1,* 470–97. Chicago, IL: University of Chicago Press.

Gibson, R. (1986). *Critical theory and education.* London: Hodder & Stoughton.

Glendinning, C. (1990). *When technology wounds: the human consequences of progress.* New York: Morrow.

Gore, J.M. (1994, Apr.). *Power and pedagogy: an empirical investigation of four sites.* Paper presented at the meeting of the American Educational Research Association, New Orleans, LA.

Greene, M. (1994). Epistemology and educational research: the influence of recent approaches to knowledge. *In* L. Darling-Hammond, ed. *Review of research in education: 20,* 423–64. Washington, DC: American Educational Research Association.

Grumet, M.R. (1990). On daffodils that come before the swallow dares. *In* E.W. Eisner & A. Peshkin, eds. *Qualitative inquiry in education: the continuing debate,* 101–20. New York: Teachers College Press.

— (1992). Existential and phenomenological foundations of autobiographical methods. *In* W.F. Pinar & W.M. Reynolds, eds. *Understanding curriculum as phenomenological and deconstructed text,* 28–43. New York: Teachers College Press.

Habermas, J. (1983). Modernity: an incomplete project. *In* H. Foster, ed. *The anti-aesthetic: essays on postmodern culture,* 3–15. Seattle, WA: Bay Press.

— (1984). *The theory of communicative action: Vol. 1: reason and the rationalization of society* (T. McCarthy, trans.). Boston, MA: Beacon Press. (Original work published 1981.)

— (1987). *The theory of communicative action: Vol. 2: lifeworld and system: a critique of functionalist reason* (T. McCarthy, trans.). Boston, MA: Beacon Press. (Original work published 1981.)

Haraway, D.J. (1991). *Simians, cyborgs, and women: the reinvention of nature.* New York: Routledge.

Harkin, P. & Schilb, J., ed. (1991). *Contending with words: composition and rhetoric in a postmodern age.* New York: Modern Language Association of America.

Hernadi, P., ed. (1989). *The rhetoric of interpretation and the interpretation of rhetoric.* Durham, NC: Duke University Press.

Hlynka, D. (1991). Applying semiotic theory to educational technology. *In* D. Hlynka & J.C. Belland, eds. *Paradigms regained: the uses of illuminative, semiotic and post-modern criticism as modes of inquiry in educational technology: a book of readings,* 37–50. Englewood Cliffs, NJ: Educational Technology. (Also in ERIC No. ED 308 805.)

— (1993). *Hypertext and ethnic studies: an exploration of the convergence of contemporary poststructuralist literary theory and information technology within the domain of ethnic studies.* Paper presented at the meeting of the Canadian Ethnic Studies Association.

— (1994). Marginalizing significant others: the Canadian contribution to educational technology. *Educational Technology 34* (2), 49–51.

— & Belland, J.C., eds. (1991). *Paradigms regained: the uses of illuminative, semiotic and post-modern criticism as modes of inquiry in educational technology: a book of readings.* Englewood Cliffs, NJ: Educational Technology.

— & Yeaman, A.R.J. (1992). *Postmodern educational technology* (ERIC Digest No. EDO-IR-92-5). (ERIC Document Reproduction Service No. ED 348 042.)

hooks, b. (1990). *Yearning: race, gender, and cultural politics.* Boston, MA: South End.

Hyppolite, J. (1972). The structure of philosophic language according to the "Preface" to Hegel's *Phenomenology of the mind. In* R. Macksey & E. Donato, eds. *The structuralist controversy: the languages of criticism and the sciences of man,* 157–85. Baltimore, MD: Johns Hopkins University Press. (Original work published 1966.)

Jamison, P.K. (1994a). Contradictory spaces: pleasure and the seduction of the cyborg discourse. *Electronic Journal on Virtual Culture* [On-line serial], *2* (1). Available e-mail: listserv@kentvm.kent.edu Message: get jamison v2n1

— (1994b). The struggle for critical discourse: reflections on the possibilities of critical theory for educational technology. *Educational Technology 34* (2), 66–69

— (1996). How is instructional development a social practice?: instructional development in a postmodern world. *In* C. Dills & A. Romiszowski, eds. *Instructional design: the state of the art: Vol. 3.* Englewood Cliffs, NJ: Educational Technology.

Jay, G.S. (1990). *America the scrivener: deconstruction and the subject of literary history.* Ithaca, NY: Cornell University Press.

Johnson, B. (1980). *The critical difference: essays in the contemporary rhetoric of reading.* Baltimore, MD: Johns Hopkins University Press.

Kamuf, P., ed. (1992). *A Derrida reader: between the blinds.* Chicago, IL: University of Chicago Press.

Kidder, T. (1989). *Among schoolchildren.* New York: Avon.

Knirk, F.G. & Gustafson, K.L. (1986). *Instructional technology.* New York: Holt, Rinehart & Winston.

Knoblauch, C.H. & Brannon, L. (1993). *Critical teaching and the idea of literacy.* Portsmouth, NH: Boynton/Cook.

Koetting, J.R., ed. (1989). *Research & theory: AECT-RTD Newsletter 13*(3) (special issue).

— (1994). Post-modern thinking in a modernist cultural climate: the need for an unquiet pedagogy. *Educational Technology 34*(2), 55–56.

— & Januszewski, A. (1991). The notion of theory and educational technology: foundations for understanding. *Educational and Training Technology International 28,* 96–101.

Kohlberg, L. (1981). *Essays on moral development: Vol. 1: the philosophy of moral development.* San Francisco, CA: Harper & Row.

— (1984). *Essays on moral development: Vol. 2: the psychology of moral development; the nature and validity of moral stages.* San Francisco, CA: Harper & Row.

Krauss, R.E. (1986). *The originality of the avant-garde and other modernist myths.* Cambridge, MA: MIT Press.

Lamont, M. (1987). How to become a dominant French philosopher: the case of Jacques Derrida. *American Journal of Sociology 93,* 584–622.

Landow, G.P. (1992). *Hypertext: the convergence of contemporary critical theory and technology.* Baltimore, MD: Johns Hopkins University Press.

Lanham, R.A. (1993). *The electronic word: democracy, technology, and the arts.* Chicago, IL: University of Chicago Press.

Lather, P. (1991). *Getting smart: feminist research and pedagogy with/in the postmodern.* New York: Routledge.

— (1992). Post-critical pedagogies: a feminist reading. *In* C. Luke & J. Gore, eds. *Feminisms and critical pedagogy,* 120–37. New York: Routledge.

Lemert, C., ed. (1993). *Social theory: the multicultural and classic readings.* Boulder, CO: Westview.

Leitch, V.B. (1983). *Deconstructive criticism: an advanced introduction.* New York: Columbia University Press.

Lévi-Strauss, C. (1963). *Totemism.* Boston, MA: Beacon.

— (1964). *Le cru et le cuit.* Paris: Plon. (Published in translation in 1969 as *The raw and the cooked.* New York: Harper & Row.)

Locke, D. (1992). *Science as writing.* New Haven, CT: Yale University Press.

— (1969). The rhetoric of *Hard Times. In* P.E. Gray, ed. *Twentieth century interpretations of Hard Times: a collection of critical essays,* 86–105. Englewood Cliffs, NJ: Prentice Hall.

Lorde, A. (1993). The master's tools will never dismantle the master's house. *In* C. Lemert, ed. *Social theory: the multicultural and classic readings,* 485–87. Boulder, CO: Westview. (Original work published 1979.)

Lyotard, J. (1984). *The postmodern condition: a report on knowledge.* Minneapolis, MN: University of Minnesota Press. (Original work published 1979.)

— (1992). *The postmodern explained.* Minneapolis, MN: University of Minnesota Press. (Original work published 1988.)

MacGregor, R.N. (1992). *Post-modernism, art educators, and art education* (ERIC Digest). (ERIC Document Reproduction Service No. ED 348 328.)

Macksey, R. & Donato, E., eds. (1972). *The structuralist controversy: the languages of criticism and the sciences of man.* Baltimore, MD: Johns Hopkins University Press. (Original work published 1970.)

Mager, R.F. (1984). *Preparing instructional objectives,* 3d ed. Belmont, CA: David S. Lake. (Original work published 1962.)

Martin, B. (1992). *Matrix and line: Derrida and the possibilities of social theory.* New York: State University of New York Press.

McLuhan, M. (1964). *Understanding media: the extensions of man.* New York: McGraw-Hill.

Mills, C.W. (1959). *The sociological imagination.* New York: Oxford University Press.

Moore, D.M. & Dwyer, F.M. (1994). *Visual literacy: a spectrum of visual learning.* Englewood Cliffs, NJ: Educational Technology.

Muffoletto, R. (1994a). Representations: you, me, and them. *In* D.M. Moore & F.M. Dwyer, eds. *Visual literacy: a spectrum of visual learning,* 295–310. Englewood Cliffs, NJ: Educational Technology.

— (1994b). Schools and technology in a democratic society: equity and social justice. *Educational Technology 34* (2), 52–54.

— (1994c). Technology and restructuring education: constructing a context. *Educational Technology 34* (2), 24–28.

— & Knupfer, N.N. (1993). *Computers in education: social, political, and historical perspectives.* Cresskill, NJ: Hampton.

Neel, J. (1988). *Plato, Derrida, and writing.* Carbondale, IL: Southern Illinois University Press.

Nichols, R.G. (1994). Searching for moral guidance about educational technology. *Educational Technology 34* (2), 40–48.

Norris, C. & Benjamin, A. (1988). *What is deconstruction?* New York: St. Martin's.

Ong, W.J. (1971). A dialectic of aural and objective correlates. *In* H. Adams, ed. *Critical theory since Plato,* 1159–66. San Diego, CA: Harcourt Brace, Jovanovich.

Ong, W.J. (1982). *Orality and literacy: the technologizing of the word.* London: Methuen.

Papadakis, A., Cooke, C. & Benjamin, A. (1990). *Deconstruction: omnibus volume.* New York: Rizzoli.

Penley, C. (1991). Brownian motion: women, tactics, and technology. *In* C. Penley & A. Ross, eds. *Technoculture,* 135–61. Minneapolis, MN: University of Minnesota Press.

Piaget, J. (1970). *Structuralism* (C. Maschler, trans. & ed.). New York: Basic Books. (Original work published 1968.)

Pinch, T., Ashmore, M. & Mulkay, M. (1992). Technology, testing, text: clinical budgeting in the U.K. National Health Service. *In* W.E. Bijker & J. Law, eds. *Shaping technology/building society: studies in sociotechnical change,* 265–89. Cambridge, MA: MIT Press.

Poovey, M. (1988). Feminism and deconstruction. *Feminist Studies 14* (1), 51–65.

Poster, M. (1984). *Foucault, Marxism and history: mode of production versus mode of information.* Cambridge, UK: Polity.

Ritzer, G. (1993). *The McDonaldization of society: an investigation into the changing character of contemporary social life.* Newbury Park, CA: Pine Forge/Sage.

Robinson, R.S., ed. (1990) (special issue). *Journal of Thought 25* (1 & 2).

Roudinesco, E. (1990). *Jacques Lacan & Co.: a history of psychoanalysis in France, 1925–1985* (J. Mehlman, trans.). Chicago, IL: University of Chicago Press. (Original work published 1986.)

Saluszinsky, I. (1987). *Criticism in society.* New York: Methuen.

Scholes, R. (1985). *Textual power: literary theory and the teaching of English.* New Haven, CT: Yale University Press.

Searle, L. (1986). Afterword: criticism and the claims of reason. *In* H. Adams & L. Searle, eds. *Critical theory since 1965,* 856–72. Tallahassee, FL: Florida State University Press.

Smart, B. (1992). *Modern conditions, postmodern controversies.* London: Routledge.

— (1993). *Postmodernity.* London: Routledge.

Sosnoski, J.J. (1991). Students as theorists: collaborative hypertextbooks. *In* J.M. Cahalan & D.B. Downing, eds. *Practicing theory in introductory college literature courses,* 271–90. Urbana, IL: National Council of Teachers of English.

Spivak, G.C. (1985). Reading the world: literary studies in the 1980s. *In* G.D. Atkins & M. Johnson, eds. *Writing and reading differently: deconstruction and the teaching of composition and literature,* 27–37. Lawrence, KS: University Press of Kansas.

Streibel, M.J. (1993). Instructional design and human practice: what can we learn from Grundy's interpretation of Habermas' theory of technical and practical human interests? *In* R. Muffoletto & N.N. Knupfer, eds. *Computers in education: social, political, historical perspectives,* 141–62. Cresskill, NJ: Hampton.

Toffler, A. (1980). *The third wave.* New York: Morrow.

Toulmin, S. (1990). *Cosmopolis: the hidden agenda of modernity.* New York: Free Press.

Treichler, P.A. (1991). How to have theory in an epidemic: the evolution of AIDS treatment activism. *In* C. Penley & A. Ross, eds. *Technoculture,* 57–106. Minneapolis, MN: University of Minnesota Press.

Ulmer, G.L. (1985). *Applied grammatology: post(e) pedagogy from Jacques Derrida to Joseph Beuys.* Baltimore, MD: Johns Hopkins University Press.

—(1989). *Teletheory: grammatology in the age of video.* New York: Routledge.

— (1992). Grammatology (in the stacks) of hypermedia, a simulation: or, when does a pile become a heap? *In* M.C. Tuman, ed. *Literacy online: the promise (and peril) of reading and writing with computers,* 139–64. Pittsburgh, PA: University of Pittsburgh Press.

— (1994). *Heuretics: the logic of invention.* Baltimore, MD: Johns Hopkins University Press.

Watson, J. (1968). *The double helix.* New York: Mentor.

Weber, M. (1993). The spirit of capitalism and the iron cage. *In* C. Lemert, ed. *Social theory: the multicultural and classic readings,* 110–14. Boulder, CO: Westview. (Original work published 1905.)

Whaley, T. (1989). The Dickensian image of the school teacher. *In* P.W. Jackson & S. Haroutunian-Gordon, eds. *From Socrates to software: the teacher as text and the text as teacher: Eighty-ninth yearbook of the National Society for the Study of Education: Part 1,* 36–59. Chicago, IL: University of Chicago Press.

White, H. (1978). *Tropics of discourse: essays in cultural criticism.* Baltimore, MD: Johns Hopkins University Press.

— (1987). *The content of the form: narrative discourse and historical representation.* Baltimore, MD: Johns Hopkins University Press.

Yeaman, A.R.J. (1993). The mythical anxieties of computerization: a Barthesian analysis of a technological myth. *In* R. Muffoletto & N.N. Knupfer, eds. *Computers in education: social, political, historical perspectives,* 105–28. Cresskill, NJ: Hampton.

— (1994a). Analysis of computers in education as a cultural field. *In* D.P. Ely & B.B. Minor, eds. *Educational media and technology yearbook: Vol. 20,* 70–72. Englewood, CO: Libraries Unlimited.

— (1994b). Cyborgs are us [1,409 lines]. *Electronic Journal on Virtual Culture* [On-line serial], *2* (1). Available e-mail: listserv@kentvm.kent.edu Message: get yeaman v2n1

— (1994c). Deconstructing modern educational technology. *Educational Technology 34* (2), 15–24.

— (1994d). Deconstruction and visuals: is this a telephone? *In* D.M. Moore & F.M. Dwyer, eds. *Visual literacy: a spectrum of visual learning,* 311–36. Englewood Cliffs, NJ:

Educational Technology.

— (1994e). Where in the world is Jacques Derrida? A true fiction with an annotated bibliography. *Educational Technology 34* (2), 57–64.

— (1994f). Where is the wisdom we have lost in knowledge? *Educational Technology 34* (2), 70–72.

— (1995, Feb.). *A poststructural analysis of David's legacy: the social construction of risk, responsibility, and cyborgs.* Paper presented at the meeting of the Association for Educational Communications and Technology, Anaheim, CA.

—, Nichols, R.G. & Koetting, J.R. (1994). Critical theory, cultural analysis, and the ethics of educational technology as social responsibility. *Educational Technology 34* (2), 5–13.

10.7   ENVOI (Andrew R. J. Yeaman)

Chapter 10 ends, by way of an *envoi,* with a personal voice. As remarked in the introductory section, there is some difference between metaphorical and supposedly straightforward language. It is a theme that has been present throughout, and it resurfaces in this contemporaneous essay.

10.7.1   Apple Pie with Mustard

References to Derrida, Foucault, poststructural, and postmodern are becoming no more unusual in current academic prose than the salt, pepper, and sugar found on cafeteria tables. These names and terms represent general concepts. Like condiments, they have specific functions, are used in established rituals, and convey general meanings. They may be applied ungrammatically by people who have not yet learned the appropriate cultural associations. Like pouring salt into a cup of coffee, Latour's insightful exploration of modern scientific knowledge is marred by overreacting to extreme postmodern criticisms (1993). It is Jean Baudrillard in particular whom Latour overrates as representing all postmodern thinkers in not only totally condemning science but also accepting media representations as the only tangible reality. [An article by Baudrillard (1975/1991) has been included in the book of educational technology readings edited by Hlynka & Belland.] Like shaking sugar onto a plate of french fries, Papert spices up structuralist thinking derived from Piaget with "It is necessary to do a little deconstruction . . ." (1993, p. 136). In contrast, Turkle's (1995) connections to Baudrillard, Derrida, Foucault, and Lyotard make sense, but it is reasonable to question how much readers to whom these ideas are new will be able to comprehend. Just as foreign students may at first scoop chocolate pudding onto their plates of roast beef, Webster assembles various postmodernisms (1995, p. 175). [Webster's list seems derived from Poster's response to postindustrial totality (1990), which aligns Baudrillard with television and consumption, Foucault with digitization, Derrida with hypertext, and Lyotard with the politics of computerization.] Abstractions from quite different thinkers have been sampled by Webster as if they come from a smorgasbord at a technoboosters' conference for social, technological, and

aesthetic change. However, in Derrida, Foucault, and Lyotard, the emphasis remains on the activities that Webster values: cultural continuity, the persistence of history, and the undiminished importance of seeking to understand rhetoric and power.

These generalizations deserve to be read cautiously, like a browser's hypertextual path. There is at present no intellectual cartographer who has thoroughly mapped the positions of Adorno, Barthes, Benjamin, Derrida, Foucault, Habermas, Horkheimer, Lacan, Lévi-Strauss, Lyotard, Marcuse, and Sartre, among other important contemporary thinkers. The chart would show relationships in terms of points of agreement, disagreement, and indifference such as May (1995) answering Dews (1987) on the left. It would show theories in terms of influence and interaction over time such as Derrida (1994) responding to Fukuyama on the right (1992). The enterprise is complex and could not be undertaken without reading, verifying, and cataloging many diverse works. It would be worthwhile but as, in all visual and verbal representations, much would necessarily remain undecidable (Yeaman, 1995b).

Oversimplifications continue. The following example shows how postmodern, poststructural seasoning in educational communications and technology can be no better than sprinkling salt and pepper on the pages. Tossing in a postmodern reference can be no different from serving apple pie with mustard.

Wright's creed seems to be that school library media specialists must convince everyone to computerize now and forever (1993). The message of *The Challenge of Technology: Action Strategies for the School Library Media Specialist* is along the lines of: Promise people anything to get them to cooperate because technological changes are unavoidable, necessary, and for the good of all. [For diverging views see Crawford & Gorman (1995), Stoll (1995), and Talbott (1995) among other authorities critical of library automation as technolust.]

Wright writes: "Postmodern critics are concerned that technology will allow meaningful consideration of only that which can be treated objectively and computerized, treating all other aspects as meaningless" (1993, p. 14) and then refers to Damarin (1991). In suggesting strategies for taming "philosophic critics" and "postmodern critics," Wright misrepresents Damarin as a reductionist who believes culture is shaped by the tools available. Wright patronizingly accommodates Damarin: "This philosophical criticism is helpful where it raises questions about any technological drift toward dehumanizing the educational process" (1993, p. 15). Wright misses Damarin's point by completely leaving out the "feminist unthinking-rethinking-energizing-transforming of educational technology" (Damarin, 1991, p. 111).

The structure of Wright's writing (1993) draws comment beyond the fact that sentences are quoted from Damarin (1991) out of order. Wright's page 14 parallels Damarin's article (1991). Wright follows Damarin in quoting a definition of educational technology as solutions that are more than hardware (AECT, 1977, p. 1) but bypasses Damarin's criticism that the sources of the problems are unspecified. Next, Wright incorporates another quotation exactly the same as that used by Damarin: "The underlying premise of modern automation is a profound distrust of thinking human beings" (Garson, 1988, p. 261). Wright takes this for speculation and does not seem to know that Garson writes about work, not school, and that Garson's words are a summary statement from a data-driven book of case studies, interviews, and reflections on site visits. After a couple of more sentences, Wright acknowledges Damarin's work but not the feminist thesis: In a cultural mesh valuing males over females, educational technologies may be gender biased and should be reconsidered.

The photograph on the front cover of *The Challenge of Technology* shows three girls in computer training for carpal tunnel syndrome. The computer station is set up too high for the girl at the keyboard who has her wrists pressed against the sharp edge of the table. That Wright (1993) has no comment to make on this obvious problem confirms Goodall Jr.'s fieldwork in highly technological industries: "Technology is sorcery, word-magic, the secret tongues of a burgeoning civil religion. It is something its adherents *believe* in rather than do" (1994, p. 167).

Although it is not illegal to eat your apple pie with mustard, nor with ketchup and pickles, it is possible to rethink the social aspects of design processes. More of the people affected can participate in planning without being sidetracked and silenced. There is a very positive review by Napper in *ETR&D* (1994) of *Design at Work*, edited by Greenbaum and Kyng (1991). Although mostly influenced by Frankfurt School critical theory, rather than Derrida and Foucault, the procedures demonstrated in the book are an excellent alternative to unreflective, uncritical, technological illiteracy and infatuation with whatever is new.

10.7.2 Coda: What on Earth Is Going to Happen Next?

In this chapter, Hlynka and Muffoletto write about paradigms. They are not making sociohistorical statements but are employing figurative conventions for engaging readers. If you are tempted to read explanation for events into Hlynka and Muffoletto's paradigms, you should disregard that feeling. As much as Nicholas Copernicus wrote to Pope Paul III in 1543, in regard to establishing a system that agrees with the phenomena (Kuhn, 1957, 1966, pp. 136–38), there are about a dozen competing theories of sociotechnical change at this time (Bijker, 1995, pp. 303-04). In addition, there are theories available from other disciplines such as anthropology, history, and sociology. The explanatory power of paradigms is deficient much as the Copernican solar system is deficient when compared with astrophysics. A descriptive model is being offered but without explaining why planets formed and spin around the sun or why scientists' beliefs orbit around points of consensus.

The positivist idea of paradigms lacks currency and is approaching intellectual bankruptcy. Popularizers aim at both predicting and shaping the future (Tapscott & Caston, 1993). Popularizers admit that their broad applications to the human condition are utilitarian (Barker, 1992, pp. 38–40). Popularizers combine the authority of the Ancient Greek etymology of paradigms with instances from history and science so they can sell books and seminars for managers (Covey, 1991). Through a poverty of understanding, the paradigm myth is a modern, structuralist grand narrative. On the grounds that nature is adequately reflected in the mirror of mind, it justifies the unfolding of the truth through society as it stands today. Invoking the paradigm metaphor gives reassurance that there is a subject to be examined, but it is not a productive explanation; see Robinson (1990, 1995) and Yeaman (1989, 1990a) for further discussion of the overreliance on empiricism in this sociocultural and creative profession.

When Hlynka and Muffoletto write about paradigms, it is not to offer a social theory but to describe their views and preferences. The academic timbre of the second half of the 20th century is revealed. There are days when it still seems almost impossible to express oneself in a college of education except in language inflected with a scientific tone of certainty. Ironically, to discuss paradigms introduces postpositivist uncertainty (Lather, 1991; Yeaman, 1990b). For example, there is as much literary theory in the creation and consumption of hypertext as underlies Advent calendars, job aids, and traditional scholarly prose containing references and footnotes. The link between communication technology and the humanities is congruent because scholarly work has always been hypertextual. Engineers writing technical reports and academic philosophers in the third millennia of philosophy both need to reference those who have written before. Not only may the concepts be deep but also there are connections to reading other texts. In business, research, and the academy, making a connection between literary theory and hypertext serves to benefit those particular groups of social actors in the 1990s. Behind the smooth facade of textbook facts is the uneven reality of knowledge being relativistically shaped by personality clashes and the politics of negotiation, and produced through the social causation of material and economic circumstances. Scientific pretensions are detected and uncovered when interrogation shifts to the deconstruction of frames of meaning.

10.7.3 Postmodernisms and Poststructuralisms

As in Agger's review of sociology (1991), intertextuality blurs the boundaries between educational communications and technology and other disciplines. Jurisdictions over territory may be renegotiated with theory. In this context, the contribution of postmodern and poststructural theory appears not in a new social theory but as a sensibility modulating existing theories. It is demonstrated by the refocusing of measurement and evaluation, one of the most conservative areas in the educational research establishment (Moss, 1994, 1995). No posturing about an age of revelations is necessary. Despite social change there is continuity in culture. The present-day computerization of society and the medieval cathedralization of society should share the same explanations. While its definitions may develop and overlap with other fields, educational communications and technology continues as "a web of beliefs, activities, and products" (Yeaman, 1995d, p. 73).

10.7.4 Cadenza

Anderson and Damarin's feminist section in this chapter has an overtly self-reflective, political position: Instructional technologies should be evaluated on their ability to introduce ethical perspectives consistent with social ideals. Note that their reference list contains first names in order to improve the visibility of women.

A sea change in theory and practice is already underway in educational communications and technology from being technical to becoming more ethically minded. If people are to know for themselves instead of in obedience to authority, then instruction should be assessed for implicit values (Yeaman, 1995c). A similar development has taken place in composition studies where there is a resurgence of interest in rhetoric (Jarratt, 1991). Postmodern, poststructural, critical theory (along with constructivism) enlarges the "debate about the purpose and role of education in designing and delivering instruction" so that "social, ethical, and cultural responsibilities must be addressed" (Walster, 1995, p. 254). The ECT Foundation has established an award to sponsor and recognize such qualitative work in educational communications and technology (Yeaman, 1995a). The renewed focus on purpose acknowledges that there truly are real-world problems to solve. For instance, the diversity issues facing the United States in the next decade may be comparable in severity to the dilemmas experienced by the South African people in the 1970s.

The tools for postmodern rethinking and poststructural criticism are already present. If you missed them, turn back into the pages of this chapter. Designing, managing, and delivering good instruction is different from creating instruction that is materially and intellectually beneficial for people. The ethical question we should always ask is not about doing our work well but "Are we doing good?"

REFERENCES

Association for Educational Communications and Technology (1977). *The definition of educational technology.* Washington, DC: AECT.

Agger, B. (1991). Critical theory, poststructuralism, postmodernism: their sociological relevance. *Annual Review of Sociology 17,* 105–31.

Barker, J.A. (1992). *Paradigms: the business of discovering the future.* New York: HarperBusiness. [Original title: *Future edge.*]

Baudrillard, J. (1991). The precession of simulacra (P. Foss & P. Patton, trans.). *In* D. Hlynka & J.C. Belland, eds. *Paradigms regained: the uses of illuminative, semiotic and post-modern criticism as modes of inquiry in educational technology: a book of readings,* 441–80. Englewood Cliffs, NJ: Educational Technology. (Reprinted from *Art & Text 11,* 1983, Sep.) (Original work published 1975.)

Bijker, W.E. (1995). *Of bicycles, bakelites, and bulbs: toward a theory of sociotechnical change.* Cambridge, MA: MIT Press.

Covey, S.R. (1991). *Principle-centered leadership.* New York: Simon & Schuster.

Crawford, W. & Gorman, M. (1995). *Future libraries: dreams, madness, and reality.* Chicago, IL: American Library Association.

Damarin, S.K. (1991). Feminist unthinking and educational technology. *Educational and Training Technology International 28* (2), 111–19.

Derrida, J. (1994). *Specters of Marx: the state of the debt, the work of mourning, and the new international* (P. Kamuf, trans.). New York: Routledge. (Original work published 1993.)

Dews, P. (1987). *Logics of disintegration: post-structuralist thought and the claims of critical theory.* London: Verso.

Fukuyama, F. (1992). *The end of history and the last man.* New York: Avon.

Garson, B. (1988). *The electronic sweatshop: how computers are transforming the office of the future into the factory of the past.* New York: Simon & Schuster.

Goodall, Jr., H.L. (1994). *Casing a promised land: the autobiography of an organizational detective as cultural ethnographer* (expanded ed.). Carbondale, IL: Southern Illinois University Press.

Greenbaum, J. & Kyng, M., eds. (1991). *Design at work: cooperative design of computer systems.* Hillsdale, NJ: Erlbaum.

Jarratt, S.C. (1991). *Rereading the Sophists: classical rhetoric refigured.* Carbondale, IL: Southern Illinois University Press.

Kuhn, T.S. (1966). *The Copernican revolution: planetary astronomy in the development of western thought.* Cambridge, MA: Harvard University Press. (Original work published 1957.)

Lather, P. (1991). *Getting smart: feminist research and pedagogy with/in the postmodern.* New York: Routledge.

Latour, B. (1993). *We have never been modern* (C. Porter, trans.). Cambridge, MA: Harvard University Press. (Original work published 1991.)

May, T. (1995). *The moral theory of poststructuralism.* University Park, PA: Pennsylvania State University Press.

Moss, P.A. (1994). Can there be validity without reliability? *Educational Researcher 23* (2), 5–12.

— (1995). Themes and variations in validity theory. *Educational Measurement: Issues and Practice 14* (2), 5–13.

Napper, V.S. (1994). [Review of the book *Design at work: cooperative design of computer systems*]. *ETR&D 42* (1), 97–99.

Papert, S. (1993). *The children's machine: rethinking school in the age of the computer.* New York: Basic Books.

Poster, M. (1990). *The mode of information: poststructuralism and social context.* Chicago, IL: University of Chicago Press.

Robinson, R.S. (1990). Viewpoint. *Journal of Thought 25* (1 & 2), 143–47.

— (1995). Qualitative research: a case for case studies. *In* G.J. Anglin, ed. *Instructional technology: past, present, and future,* 2d ed., 330–39. Englewood, CO: Libraries Unlimited.

Stoll, C. (1995). *Silicon snake oil: second thoughts on the information highway.* New York: Doubleday.

Talbott, S.L. (1995). *The future does not compute: transcending the machine in our midst.* Sebastopol, CA: O'Reilly.

Tapscott, D. & Caston, A. (1993). *Paradigm shift: the new promise of information technology.* New York: McGraw-Hill.

Turkle, S. (1995). *Life on the screen: identity in the age of the internet.* New York: Simon & Schuster.

Walster, D. (1995). Using instructional design theories in library and information science education. *Journal of Education for Library and Information Science 36* (3), 239–48.

Webster, F. (1995). *Theories of the information society.* London: Routledge.

Wright, K.C. (1993). *The challenge of technology: action strategies for the school library media specialist.* Chicago, IL: American Library Association.

Yeaman, A.R.J. (1989). A postcognitivist view of educational communications and technology. *RTD Newsletter 13* (3), 21–24. (Research and Theory Division, AECT.)

— (1990a). An anthropological view of educational communications and technology: beliefs and behaviors in research and theory. *Canadian Journal of Educational Communication 19,* 237–46.

— (1990b). Empirical fact or social fact? *Proceedings of selected research paper presentations at the 1990 Annual Convention of the Association for Educational Communications and Technology,* 711–24. (ERIC Document Reproduction Service No. ED 323 958.)

— (1995a). ECT foundation establishes a new award for qualitative scholarship. *Tech Trends 40* (4), 43–44.

— (1995b). A headline functioning as a graphic element as well as a verbal cue. *The Visual Literacy Review 25* (3), 4.

— (1995c). Reflections on the teaching of ethics. *Tech Trends 40* (2), 12.

— (1995d). [Review of the book *Instructional technology: past, present, and future,* 2d ed.] *ETR&D 43* (4), 73–76.

II

HARD TECHNOLOGIES: MEDIA-RELATED RESEARCH

Robert B. Kozma, Center for Technology in Learning

Associate Editor

11. RESEARCH ON LEARNING FROM TELEVISION

Barbara Seels   **Louis H. Berry**   **Karen Fullerton**   **Laura J. Horn**

UNIVERSITY OF PITTSBURGH

This chapter[1] summarizes a body of literature about instructional technology that is unique not only in its depth but also in its breadth and importance. A recent search of articles in the Educational Clearinghouse on Information Resources (ERIC) since 1966 yielded 17,500 citations on television; while a similar search in *Psychology Abstracts* produced 1,882 citations about television since the mid–1980s. It is fitting, therefore, that there be a chapter in this handbook which reviews how instructional technology has used research on television as well as how the field has contributed to this body of research.

11.1 NATURE OF THE CHAPTER

In order to address research on learning from television,[2] it is necessary to define this phrase. For the purposes of this chapter, learning is defined as changes in knowledge, understanding, attitudes, and behavior due to the intentional* or incidental effects* of television programming. Thus, learning can occur intentionally as a result of programming that is planned to achieve specific instructional outcomes or incidentally through programming for entertainment or information purposes.

Three elements of the television viewing system* are covered: the independent variable or stimulus, mediating variables, and the resulting behavior or beliefs. The television viewing experience* is based on the interaction of these three components of the viewing system, which are usually described as programming, environment, and behavior. Each of these elements encompasses many variables; for example, message design* and content are programming variables. Viewer preferences and habits are environmental variables that mediate. Individual differences are also mediating variables in that they affect behavior. Learning and aggressive or cooperative behaviors are dependent variables.

For this review to serve an integrative function, it was necessary to be selective in order to comprehensively cover many areas. Several parameters were established to aid in selectivity. The first decision was that film and television research would be integrated. Although they are different mediums, their cognitive effects are the same. The technologies underlying each medium are quite different; however, for instructional purposes, the overall appearance and functions are essentially the same, with television being somewhat more versatile in terms of storage and distribution capabilities. Furthermore, films are frequently converted to television formats, a fact that blurs the distinction even more. Research on learning from television evolved from research on learning from motion pictures. Film research dominated until about 1959 when the Pennsylvania State University studies turned to research on learning from television. Investigations related to one medium will be identified as such; however, effects and other findings will be considered together. Classic research on both film and television is reviewed.

Nevertheless, relatively little space is devoted to film research because an assumption was made that there were other reviews of this early research, and its importance has diminished. It seemed more important to emphasize contributions from the last 20 years, especially since

[1] The authors would like to acknowledge the significant contribution that our reviewers have made to this article: Keith Mielke, senior research fellow, Children's Television Workshop; Marge Cambre, associate professor, Ohio State University; and Dave Jonassen, professor, Pennsylvania State University. In addition, Mary Sceiford of the Corporation for Public Broadcasting and Ray McKelvey of the Agency for Instructional Technology gave valuable advice. Barbara Minor assisted with searching through the resources of the Educational Clearinghouse on Information Resources (ERIC). Many students at the University of Pittsburgh also helped with the research.

[2] A glossary of terms related to learning from television is given at the end of the chapter. The first time a term defined in the glossary appears, it will be marked with an asterisk.

they are overwhelming the consumer of this literature by sheer volume.

Another decision was that although some important international studies would be reported, the majority of studies covered would be national. This was essential because the international body of literature was gargantuan. Those who wish to pursue international literature are advised to start with a topic that has existing cross-cultural bibliographies, such as the *Sesame Street Research Bibliography* (1989) available from Children's Television Workshop (CTW).

In addition, it was necessary to determine what to include and exclude in relation to the other chapters in the handbook. All distance learning (see Chapter 13) and interactive multimedia studies (see Chapter 29) were excluded because other chapters cover the newer technologies. Some media literacy* will be covered because it is a very important variable in learning from television. Nevertheless, it is assumed that aspects of visual literacy (i.e., visual learning and communication) will be covered throughout the handbook (see Chapters 16 and 26), not just in this chapter.

It was further decided that a variety of methodological approaches would be introduced, but that discussion should be limited because the final section of this handbook covers methodologies (see Chapters 39 to 42). Methodological issues, though, will be addressed throughout this chapter.

Our final decision was that this chapter would make a comprehensive effort to integrate research from both mass media* (see sections 4.4.1 to 6) and instructional television.* Although other publications have done this, generally one area dominates, and consequently the other is given inadequate attention. It was our intent to start the process of integrating more fully the literature from mass media and instructional television.

11.1.1 Relevance to Instructional Technology

Research on learning from television encompasses more than formal instruction. This body of research addresses learning in home as well as school environments. Many of the findings are relevant to the instructional technologist; for example, research on formal features* yields guidelines for message design (see Chapter 26). Instructional technologists can both promote students' learning to regulate and reinforce their own viewing* and educate parents and teachers about media utilization.

In addition, instructional technologists are also responsible for recommending and supporting policy that affects television utilization. The literature provides support for policy positions related to (a) control of advertising and violence* (see 11.7.4, 11.2.3), (b) parent and teacher training (see 11.5.3.5, 11.7.2.1), (c) provision of special programming (see 11.7), and (d) media literacy education (see 11.8.2).

Researchers in instructional technology can determine gaps in the theoretical base by using reviews such as this. In the future, more research that relates variables studied by psychologists to variables studied by educators will be required in order to identify guidelines for interventions and programming.

11.1.2 Organization of the Chapter

The chapter is organized chronologically and categorically in order to cover both research on the utilization of television in education and mass-media research on television effects. The beginning of the chapter chronologically traces the evolution of research in this area. Other sections, which are organized by subject, review theoretical and methodological issues and synthesize the findings. A glossary of terminology related to television research is given at the end of this chapter.

The chapter starts with a historical overview. After this introductory background, the chapter turns to sections organized categorically around major issues, some of which are independent or mediating variables, and others of which are effects. The first section synthesizes research on message design and mental processing. It reviews how formal features* affect comprehension* and attention.* The next issue section deals with the effects of television on school achievement. Turning to what is known about the effects of the family, viewing context, viewing environments,* and coviewing* are reviewed next. The effects of television on socialization* are explored through attitudes, beliefs, and behaviors. The next section covers programming and its utilization in the classroom and home. The final section covers theory on media literacy and mediation* through critical viewing skills.* The organization of the chapter follows this outline:

1. Historical overview
2. Message design and cognitive processing*
3. School achievement
4. Family-viewing context
5. Attitudes, beliefs, and behaviors
6. Programming and utilization
7. Critical-viewing skills
8. Glossary of terms

It was necessary to approach the literature broadly in order to synthesize effectively. Despite the disparity in types of research and areas of focus, most of the studies provided information about interactions that affect learning from television.

11.2 HISTORICAL OVERVIEW

Much research on the effects of television is contradictory or inconclusive, but that doesn't make the research useless, wasteful, or futile. We need to know as much as we can about how children learn, and conscientious research of any kind can teach us, if nothing else, how to do *better* research (Rogers & Head, 1983, p. 170).

As Fred Rogers and Barry Head suggest, to use research on television, one needs a historical perspective. The purpose of this section is to provide that perspective. It will briefly explain the evolution of the technologies, important historical milestones, the evolution of the research, and the variety of methodological approaches used. After reading this section, you should be able to place the research in historical context and understand its significance.

11.2.1 Contributors to the Literature

This large body of research is the result of individuals, organizations, and fields with constituencies naturally interested in the effects of television. The disciplines that are most dedicated to reflecting on learning from television are education, communications, psychology, and sociology. Within education, the fields of educational psychology, cognitive science, and instructional technology have a continuing interest. Educational psychology and cognitive science have focused on mental processing. Instructional technology has made its greatest contributions to television research through the areas of message design, formative evaluation,* and critical-viewing skills.

11.2.1.1. Organizations. Groups associated with research on television operate in diverse arenas. Government institutions, such as the National Institute of Mental Health (NIMH), the Educational Resources Clearinghouse on Information Resources (ERIC), and the Office of Research in the Department of Education have been the catalyst for many studies. Government has influenced research on television through hearings and legislation on violent programming and commercials for children. Government legislation also created the Public Broadcasting System (PBS).

Many universities have established centers or projects that pursue questions about the effects of television. These include the Family Television Research and Consultation Center at Yale University, the Center for Research on the Influence of Television on Children at the University of Kansas, the National Center for Children and Television at Princeton, and Project Zero at Harvard University. Foundations have supported research in the areas of media effects and instructional television, including the Spencer, Ford, and Carnegie Foundations. Public service organizations such as Action for Children's Television and church television awareness groups have spurred policy and research.

Research and development (R&D) organizations, such as the Southwest Educational Development Laboratory, have generated curricula on critical-viewing skills. Children's Television Workshop (CTW), the producer of *Sesame Street,* is an R&D organization that not only develops programming but also does research on the effects of television.

11.2.1.2. Review Articles and Books. Despite such long-term efforts, much of the literature on television lacks connection to other findings (Clark, 1983, 1994; Richey, 1986). The conceptual theory necessary to explain the relationship among variables is still evolving. Because of this, consumers of the literature are sometimes overwhelmed and unable to make decisions related to interactions in the television viewing system of programming, environment, and behavior.

Comprehensive and specialized reviews of the literature are helpful for synthesizing findings. Individual studies contribute a point of view and define variables, but it takes a review to examine each study in light of others. Fortunately, there have been many outstanding reviews of the literature. For example, Reid and MacLennan (1967) and Chu and Schramm (1968) did comprehensive reviews of learning from television that included studies on utilization. Aletha

Huston (1972) wrote a chapter for the National Society for the Study of Education (NSSE) yearbook on *Early Childhood Education* entitled "Mass Media and Young Children's Development" which presented a conceptual framework for studying television's effects. In 1975, the Rand Corporation published three books by George Comstock which reviewed pertinent scientific literature, key studies, and the state of research. Jerome and Dorothy Singer reviewed the implications of research for children's cognition, imagination, and emotion (Singer & Singer, 1983). In that article, they described the trend toward studying cognitive processes and formal features. By 1989, the American Psychological Association had produced a synthesis of the literature titled *Big World, Small Screen.*

Other reviews have concentrated on special areas like reading skills (Williams, 1986); cognitive development (Anderson & Collins, 1988); instructional television (Cambre, 1987); and violence (Liebert & Sprafkin, 1988). Lawrence Erlbaum Publishers offers a series of volumes edited by Dolf Zillmann and Jennings Bryant on research and theory about television effects.

Light and Pillemer (1984) argue against the single decisive-study approach and propose reviews around a specific research question that starts by reporting the main effects, then reports special circumstances that affect outcomes, and finishes by reporting special effects on particular types of people. This integrated research strategy is especially appropriate for reviews of research on television effects.

11.2.2 Evolution and Characteristics of the Technologies

The evolution of the technologies of motion pictures and television during the latter part of the 19th century and early 20th century can be described in terms of media characteristics, delivery systems, and communication functions. It is also important to know the terminology essential to understanding research descriptions and comparisons. This terminology is given in the glossary at the end of this chapter.

11.2.2.1. Functional Characteristics. These media characteristics of film and television are primarily realism or fidelity, mass access, referability, and, in some cases, immediacy. Producers for both of these technologies wanted to make persons, places, objects, or events more realistic to the viewer or listener. The intent was to ensure that the realistic representation of the thing or event was as accurate as possible (i.e., fidelity). The ability to transmit sounds or images to general audiences, or even to present such information to large groups in theaters, greatly expanded access to realistic presentations. In the case of television, the characteristic of immediacy allowed the audience to experience the representation of the thing or event almost simultaneously with its occurrence. The notion of "being there" was a further addition to the concept of realism. As these various forms of media developed, the ability to record the representations for later reference became an important characteristic. Viewers could not only replay events previously recorded but could also refer to specific aspects or segments of the recording time and time again for study and analysis. Each of these characteristics has driven or directed the use of film or television for instructional purposes.

11.2.2.2. Delivery Systems. The State University of Iowa began the first educational television* broadcasts in 1933. Educational broadcasting quickly grew, with several universities producing regular programming and commercial stations broadcasting educational materials for the general population. During the 1950s and 60s, other technical innovations emerged that expanded the flexibility and delivery of educational television. These included the development in 1956 of magnetic videotape* and videotape recorders, the advent of communications satellites* in 1962, and the widespread growth of cable television in the 1960s and 70s. Delivery systems encompass both transmission and storage capabilities. The various means whereby the message* is sent to the intended audience differ in terms of the breadth of the population who can access the message. These means of transmission include broadcast television,* communications satellite, closed-circuit television* (CCTV), cable access television* (CATV), and microwave relay links.*

Broadcast television programming is generally produced for large-scale audiences by major networks and, with the exception of cable or microwave relay agreements, can be received free of charge by any viewer with a receiver capable of receiving the signal. Satellite communication has the capability of distributing the television signal over most of the populated globe. Closed-circuit television is produced for limited audiences and for specified educational purposes. Cable television often presents programming produced by public television organizations, public service agencies, or educational institutions for educational purposes. Today, many of the microwave relay functions have been replaced by satellite relays; however, this transmission medium is still used to distribute closed-circuit programming within prescribed areas such as school districts.

11.2.2.3. Storage Media. In the beginning, television productions were often stored in the form of kinescopes,* which are rarely, if ever, used today, although some early television recording may still exist in kinescope form. Today, most video programs are stored on videotape cassette format, which is convenient and is produced in a variety of tape widths. Videotape permits a large number of replays; however, it can deteriorate after excessive use.

11.2.2.4. Communications Functions. From an instructional point of view, the most important factor in the development of any of these technologies is not the technical aspect of their development but rather the impact of the medium on the audience. Terms that relate to communications functions include instructional television (ITV), educational television (ETV), mass media, incidental learning, and intentional learning. Today, ITV programming is often transmitted by satellite to a school where it is either recorded and used when convenient or used immediately and interactively through a combination of computers and telecommunications. Educational television programming

is typically not part of a specific course of study and may be directed to large and diverse groups of individuals desiring general information or informal instruction.

The distinction between mass media and educational television is frequently difficult to make since most educational television programming is distributed via broadcast television, the primary mass-media mode. What differentiates mass media from educational television is the notion of intended purpose. With educational television, intentional effects are achieved through purposeful intervention to achieve educational objectives. Incidental effects, on the other hand, typically result from mass-media or entertainment-oriented programming.

11.2.3 Legislative Milestones

The history of research on television effects has been tied to important government policy actions (Wood & Wylie, 1977). In the 1930s the government declared air channels to be public property and created the Federal Communications Commission (FCC) to regulate systems such as radio. After lengthy hearings, in 1952 the Federal Communications Commission reserved 242 television channels for noncommercial, educational broadcasting.

11.2.3.1. The 1950s and 60s. The first congressional hearings on violence and television occurred in 1952. In 1954, hearings were held to investigate the link between television and juvenile crime. When he was doing his Bobo doll social-psychology experiments in the early 1960s, Albert Bandura published an article in *Look* magazine entitled "What Television Violence Can Do to Your Child." This article popularized the term "TV violence."

In 1964, Newton Minow assumed the chair of the FCC. He would prove to be a strong commissioner, remembered for his statement that television was "a vast wasteland." By 1965, advertisers had discovered that they could reach young children with advertisements for toys, candy, and cereal more cheaply and effectively on Saturday mornings than in prime time. Also in the 1960s, Congress created the Public Broadcasting System (PBS) and the Corporation for Public Broadcasting (CPB). By the end of the 1960s, the National Commission on the Causes and Prevention of Violence had issued a report stating that exposure to violence on television increased rates of physical aggression.* This led to the Surgeon General's appointing a committee to study the effects television programs have on children. The decade concluded by the Supreme Court's upholding the fairness doctrine, which required stations to give equal time to political candidates.

11.2.3.2. The 1970s. The decade of the 1970s started with a ban on cigarette advertising on television, which had been initiated after the Surgeon General's report that there was a relationship between cancer and smoking. In 1972, the Surgeon General issued a report on violence that alleged that there was also a causal link between violent behavior and violence on television and in motion pictures. This first major government report on television and violence

(NIMH, 1972) consisted of five volumes of reports and papers gathered through an inquiry process directed by the National Institute of Mental Health (NIMH). To prepare for this report, NIMH was empowered to solicit and fund a million dollars worth of research on the effects of television violence (Liebert & Sprafkin, 1988). By 1975, the FCC had received 25,000 complaints about violent or sexually oriented programs on television. As a consequence, in 1975 the Ford Foundation, the National Science Foundation, and the Markle Foundation cosponsored a major conference on television and human behavior. The Supreme Court ruled that the FCC could regulate hours in which "indecent" programming could be aired.

11.2.3.3. The 1980s. In 1982, the National Institute of Mental Health confirmed the link between television and aggression and stated that "violence on television does lead to aggressive behavior by children and teenagers who watch the programs" (NIMH, 1980, p. 6); thus television was labeled a cause of aggressive behavior. In 1985, the American Psychological Association (APA) publicly concluded that violence can cause aggressive behavior and urged broadcasters to reduce violence. As the decade ended, the FCC decided that the Fairness Doctrine was no longer necessary because there was no longer a scarcity of stations and that it was perhaps unconstitutional. Congress passed a bill to reinstitute the doctrine, but the President vetoed it. The President also vetoed legislation that would place limits on advertising during children's programs. In 1989, Congress passed the Television Violence Act granting television executives the authority to hold discussions on the issues of television violence without violating antitrust laws.

11.2.3.4. The 1990s. This brings us to the current decade, which started with Congress's passing the Children's Television Act that requires limits on advertising and evidence that stations provide programming to meet children's needs. This is the first legislation to establish the principle that broadcasters have a social responsibility to their child audiences. The advantage of this approach is that it avoids the thorny issue of censorship. The bill became a law without presidential signature. Congress established the National Endowment for Children's Television to provide resources for production of quality children's programming as well as the Television Decoder Circuitry Act, which requires all new sets to have closed-caption capability. Over presidential veto, Congress approved the Cable Television Consumer Protection and Competition Act to regulate the cable industry. In 1993, the National Research Council of the National Academy of Sciences published a comprehensive report on the causes of violence in American society, entitled "Understanding and Preventing Violence," which addressed the role of television. The Senate Commerce Committee held hearings on television violence during which Senator Hollings complained that Congress has been holding hearings on television violence for 40 years. The idea of "V-chip" legislation to require the technology in all sets to block showing of programs rated violent was introduced at these hearings. The Telecommunications Act of 1996 required that this V-chip be installed on all new television

sets. This landmark legislation had other important provisions, including one for discounted service rates for telecommunication lines into schools, especially for lines for compressed video and the Internet (Telecommunications Act of 1996). This overview of societal concerns about television documents the impetus for much research.

11.2.4 Historical Evolution of the Research

The first major research initiatives in both film and television began in the 1950s and 1960s. Research foci and variables of interest, as well as the social orientation of research, have changed considerably over the years.

Bowie (1986) reviewed research on learning from films and grouped the research into three phases:

1. Research on whether films can teach (1910–1950)
2. Research on how films teach (1940–1959)
3. Research on who learns from films (1960–1985)

Research from the last phase includes a great many experimental studies. The results of these experimental studies can be grouped in these areas: (a) use of films to teach higher-level cognitive skills, (b) effects of film viewing on individual learning, and (c) effects of film viewing on self-concept. Bowie concluded that the literature reviewed in these three areas suggests that:

- Films are effective in teaching inquiry learning and problem solving.
- Unstructured films are more effective for teaching problem solving.
- Films are effective in teaching observation skills and attention to detail.
- Low-aptitude students tend to benefit more from films.
- Films tend to be more effective for field-independent students.
- Films can positively influence self-concept.

Research on learning from films also served as a basis for research on instructional television.

Television research began with attention being devoted almost solely to its instructional effectiveness in formal instructional environments. The types and foci of research evolved into more varied agendas that considered not only the formal instructional implications of television but also the social, psychological, and instructional effects of broadcast television in less formal environments.

Sprafkin, Gadow, and Abelman (1992) describe the research on television as falling into three distinct chronological phases. The first of these they refer to as the "medium-orientation phase," in which television was seen as a powerful instructional tool that required research to describe its effectiveness. At this point, little attention was devoted to assessing the interaction of the media with developmental or individual differences in the viewers. The second phase that Sprafkin et al. describe is the "child orientation phase," in which research focused more closely on the relationship of television to young viewers' individual characteristics and aptitudes. Media effects were thought to be due to a child's mental-processing characteristics, not to programming. They termed the third phase the *interaction phase,* in which television effects were seen as complex three-way interactions between characteristics of the medium (such as type of content), the child or viewer variables (such as age), and factors in the viewing environment (such as parents and teachers). These three phases correspond approximately to the three eras of film and television research: the period of comparative media research (see 39.5.4) during the 1950s and early 1960s (Greenhill, 1967); the media effects and individual differences research of the late 1960s through the 1970s (Anderson & Levin, 1976; Wright & Huston, 1983); and the interaction research characterized by the work of Salomon (1979, 1983) during the later 1970s through the present time.

The purpose of this section is to chronicle the evolution of these research trends and describe the nature of the research associated with each phase. In doing so, we will attempt to relate the trends to methodologies and variables.

11.2.4.1. Research Prior to 1965. Before the mid-1950s, the vast majority of research was focused on the effects of instructional films,* usually in controlled educational or training environments, both in formal education and in military and industrial training. This period was marked primarily by the widely quoted Instructional Film Research Program conducted at the Pennsylvania State University. This program was initiated under the auspices of the U.S. Naval Training Devices Center to study a variety of variables related to the use of instructional films for personnel-training purposes. One report issued through this research project summarized and evaluated over 200 film research studies from 1918 until 1950 (Hoban & Van Ormer, 1950). The major focus of the Instructional Film Research Program, however, was the conduct of an extensive series of experiments that compared instruction delivered via film with "conventional" or "face-to-face instruction." Within these comparisons, researchers also investigated the effects of various production techniques, the effect of film-based instruction on learner attitudes, and the effectiveness of various applications of instructional films (Carpenter & Greenhill, 1956; Greenhill, 1967). This series of studies represents one of the first, and certainly most extensive, attempts to evaluate thoroughly the effectiveness of the medium. The findings of these studies, however, indicated no significant differences in most cases and have been criticized for a number of methodological procedures (Greenhill, 1967).

Typical among the studies conducted in this program were those that sought to compare the relative effectiveness of motion-picture–based instruction with conventional classroom instruction. A study by VanderMeer (1949) compared ninth-grade biology students taught by: (1) sound films, (2) sound films plus study guides, and (3) standard lecture-demonstration classroom instruction. No significant differences were found across all groups on either immediate or three-month-delayed achievement testing, although the film-only group showed a shorter completion time. This

study is quite characteristic of most of these film studies in that no significant differences were found across both the experimental and control groups. Other studies focused on the relative effectiveness of instructional films for teaching performance skills and generally found no significant difference or only slight benefit from the film treatment (Greenhill, 1967). The effects of production variables were also of interest to researchers, and the relative effects of such variables as inserted questions, variants in the sound track, color versus monochrome, animation versus still pictures, and the use of attention-gaining and directing devices were all studied, albeit with few, if any, significant differences across groups.

The period between the mid-1950s and the mid-1960s was characterized by a great deal of instructional television research by a group of researchers at the Pennsylvania State University, reconstituted as the Instructional Television Research Project (Carpenter & Greenhill, 1955), as well as by other individuals (Hagerstown Board of Education, 1959; Holmes, 1959; Kumata, 1956; Niven, 1958; Schramm, 1962). These projects and summaries of research included literally hundreds of studies covering many content areas and many different age groups. In most cases, the summary reports issued by these researchers or projects provided fairly comprehensive descriptions of the general findings and conclusions. As with the film research initiatives, the television research projects focused strongly on comparative research designs and similarly resulted in "no significant differences." Few studies reported findings entirely supportive of television, and conversely few found television instruction to be less effective than conventional classroom instruction. The finding of no significant difference was seen by Greenhill (1967) as a positive result because it implied that television could be a reasonable alternative to classroom instruction and consequently, for reasons of administrative, fiscal, and logistical benefit, could be a more desirable choice of instructional method.

The comparative studies of television conducted during this time were later criticized on methodological grounds by Stickell (1963) and Greenhill (1967). Stickell analyzed 250 comparisons and determined that only 10 were "interpretable" methodologically. Those 10 had employed random assignment of subjects, control of extraneous variables, and application of appropriate tests of significance in which the underlying assumptions of the test were met. Of the studies Stickell found to be "interpretable," none revealed significant differences.

The majority of these early comparative studies were designed to compare various forms of televised instruction to a vaguely specified standard known as "face-to-face instruction," "conventional," or "traditional classroom instruction" (Carpenter & Greenhill, 1956; Lumsdaine, 1963). Instructional techniques and formats included (a) a single instructor teaching the same content, (b) a "live instructor" teaching a class while the same class was being televised to a remote class, (c) a number of different instructors teaching the same general lesson as the televised lesson, and (d) kinescope recordings of a lesson augmented by various, instructor-led activities. In most cases, there was little or no means of equating the instructional formats being used in terms of instructor equivalence, content congruence, or environmental similarity (Greenhill, 1967; Wilkinson, 1980; Williams, Paul & Ogilvie, 1957). Among the large number of comparative studies, there are many that simply compared the medium with some standard of live classroom instruction, while a smaller proportion made comparisons with the audio message only, comparisons of film versus kinescope, and television versus an in-studio classroom (Kumata, 1956).

As mentioned, this matter was further complicated by the fact that the vast majority of the studies, in both film and television, produced results of "no significant difference" (Greenhill, 1967; Stickell, 1963). This finding, when considered in conjunction with the general comparative nature of the research, makes it difficult to draw specific conclusions or recommendations from most of these comparative studies. Other methodological problems also plagued this early research, including: lack of equivalence of experimental groups, confounding of variables, and statistical analysis procedures that were not powerful enough to detect differences that may have been present (Greenhill, 1967).

In terms of group equivalence, two problems were apparent. First, groups were rarely pretested to determine if prerequisite knowledge was approximately equivalent. Second, little attention was given to ensuring equivalence of assignment to experimental groups. In some cases, correlative data such as IQ scores or grade point averages were used as matching variables, but because of the use of intact classes, randomization was rarely employed to assign subjects (Chu & Schramm, 1968; Stickell, 1963). Because the variables of televised instruction and conventional instruction were not clearly defined, it was almost impossible to separate other mediating variables related to production methods, technologies, viewing and teaching environments, viewer characteristics, and content organization. The result was often a serious confounding of many variables, only some of which were of interest. In terms of statistical analysis, t and F tests were used only occasionally, and analysis of covariance procedures were employed rarely because adjusting variables were infrequently assessed (Stickell, 1963). Additionally, content-related factors and objectives as well as types of learning were often not addressed or confounded (Miller, 1968).

Other more carefully defined variables continued to be investigated during this time, including: technical or production variables such as color, camera techniques, and attention-gaining and directing devices (Ellery, 1959; Harris, 1962; Kanner & Rosenstein, 1960; Schwarzwalder, 1960); pedagogical variables, such as inserted questions and presentation modes (Gropper & Lumsdaine, 1961; Rock, Duva & Murray, 1951); and variables in the viewing environment, such as viewing angle, group size, and distractions (Carpenter & Greenhill, 1958; Hayman, 1963; McGrane & Baron, 1959). In addition, attitudes toward televised instruction and the use of television to teach procedural skills were studied (Hardaway, Beymer &

Engbretson, 1963; Pasewark, 1956).

Later studies, conducted during the 1960s and early 1970s, focused more specifically on individual variables, media characteristics, and the interaction between viewer characteristics and television effects. These studies typically employed the aptitude-treatment-interaction paradigm (see 22.3.3 to 22.2.7) described by Cronbach and Snow (1976) and were intended to explore specific effects of television on particular individuals. These designs were inherently more precise and more powerful and consequently enabled researchers to identify the effects of individual variables as well as the interaction of variables and other factors (Levie & Dickie, 1973).

During this time period, studies employed quantitative experimental methods almost exclusively to evaluate the relative effectiveness of film and televised instruction in generally controlled environments such as laboratories, studios, classrooms, and schools. Researchers did not have the resources or research interest to investigate or describe specific effects on larger or noncontrolled populations, such as the effect of incidental learning resulting from noneducational broadcast television.

11.2.4.2. Research from 1965 On. After 1965, research focus was increasingly directed toward mass media and social effects. The formation of Children's Television Workshop (CTW) in the late 1960s directed research interest to formal features and formative evaluation (Polsky, 1974). The 1970s were also devoted to research on the relationship between televised violence and aggression. With the 1980s, a change from the behavioral to cognitive paradigm in psychology stimulated further research on mental processing (see 5.4.1 to 5.4.4) and formal features. Some research questions have persisted from the 1960s until the present, such as effect on school achievement and aggression. Research evolved from a focus on specifying variables to describing the relationships and interactions among variables. More-varied research agendas have considered not only the formal instructional implications of television but also the social, psychological, and instructional effects of broadcast television in various, less-formal environments (Comstock & Paik, 1987; Huston et al., 1992).

11.2.5 Methodological Approaches

Historically, research on television has employed four methodologies: experimental, qualitative, descriptive, and developmental (see Chapters 39 to 42). There has been a general chronological correspondence between certain methodologies and research foci, for example, between comparative studies and instructional effectiveness and between correlational studies and school achievement. For this reason, it is important to understand that research related to television has, over the years, come to address more than simply the effects of televised instruction on learning. Evolving societal demands brought about the need for different methodological approaches to study the disparate effects of television on types of viewers, on variations in viewing environments, on socialization effects, and on interaction with programming variables (Cambre, 1987). Such a broad base of research agendas has necessitated reliance on research methodologies other than those of a traditional empirical nature.

The vast majority of current television research reflects these four methodological approaches: experimental, qualitative, descriptive, and developmental. This section deals with these various research methodologies with regard to their purposes, strengths, and weaknesses as they apply to film and television research.

11.2.5.1. Experimental Methodology.

Early research in television effects utilized traditional experimental designs (see Chapter 39), albeit with different levels of robustness and precision. The era of film and television research conducted during the 1940s through the mid-1960s, which has been referred to as the period of comparative research studies (see 39.5.4) generally used traditional experimental designs, such as those described by Campbell and Stanley (1963). Although many of these studies were methodologically weak in that they did not employ randomization of groups, pretests, or control groups, and have been subsequently criticized for these reasons (Greenhill, 1967; Stickell, 1963), it is important to note that there were many methodologically rigorous studies conducted during this period which continue to provide useful insights, not only into the comparative effects of television and traditional classroom instruction but also into the effects of specific variables, such as color, inserted questions, and presentation techniques (Greenhill, 1967; Reid & MacLennan, 1967). During the period of time from the mid-1960s through the 1970s, other empirical studies were prompted by (a) better design conceptualization such as the aptitude treatment interaction paradigm, (b) more robust statistical analysis techniques, and (c) greater attention to the individual characteristics of the medium, the child, and the viewing environment. Increasingly, research moved from the laboratory or classroom to the home and social environment. Two types of experimental studies that compare variables are common in research on television: laboratory and field experiments. The former has advantages when comparing theories, testing hypotheses, and measuring effects; the latter is suited to checking the results of laboratory experiments in real-life settings (Comstock, 1980). An example of a laboratory experiment would be three treatments (i.e., violent first segment, violent last segment, and nonviolent segment) given to three randomly assigned groups who are given written instruments assessing recall.* An example of a field experiment would be randomly assigning children to watch specific television shows at home and then administering attitude surveys and comprehension measures.

The major advantage of the laboratory experiment is that random assignment of subjects to specific treatment conditions can control for the effect of other variables. The disadvantage is that there is no certainty that the setting is realistic. The major disadvantage of the field experiment is that it produces little consistent evidence because control of variables is less rigorous. Nevertheless, one can be more confident in how realistic the findings are with a field experiment; however, realism and validity are gained at the expense of control of variables and the possibility of drawing causal conclusions. Laboratory research, on the other hand, generally allows one to draw cause-effect conclusions about interactions.

11.2.5.2. Qualitative Methodology.

Qualitative research methodology (see Chapter 40) includes approaches that typically use nonexperimental methods, such as ethnography or case studies, to investigate important variables that are not easily manipulated or controlled and which emphasize the use of multiple methods for collecting, recording, and analyzing data (Seels & Richey, 1994). Although case histories have been used frequently in television research, ethnographic studies are becoming more common. The trend towards qualitative research emerged after new research questions began to be asked about the mediating effect of the home context for television viewing (Leichter et al., 1985). Often with qualitative research, the purpose is hypothesis generating rather than hypothesis testing. Unlike survey methodology, qualitative research cannot present a broad picture because it concentrates on single subjects or groups, although longitudinal studies can describe how groups or individuals change over time. There is no attempt at representative sampling as in survey research. Examples of case studies abound in literature on early ITV and ETV projects. Ethnographic studies have been conducted by photographing or videotaping the home environment, which mediates television viewing (Allen, 1965; Lewis, 1993). An example of a recent ethnographic study on learning from television is the *Ghostwriter* study conducted by CTW (Children's Television Workshop, October 1994). *Ghostwriter* is an after-school literacy* program that encompasses a mix of media including television and utilizes outreach programs with community organizations. Ethnographic techniques were used to gather data on wide variations in observed phenomena in disparate settings. For example, case studies were done at Boys' and Girls' Clubs in Los Angeles and Indianapolis and at Bethune Family Learning Circle in Baltimore.

11.2.5.3. Descriptive Methodology.

Studies in this category (see Chapter 41) include survey research such as demographic, cross-cultural, and longitudinal, in addition to content and meta-analyses.* The common denominator among such studies is the use of survey techniques for the purpose of reporting characteristics of populations or samples.

Survey research uses samples of group populations to study sociological and psychological variables. To do this, data can be collected by personal or telephone interview, questionnaires, panels, and structured observation. Demographic research uses facts and figures collected by others, such as the census bureau or television information offices. Cross-cultural studies based on surveys use factual data about groups to draw generalizations.

There are many longitudinal* and cross-sectional* studies in the body of literature on learning from television. Sometimes these are based on qualitative research, sometimes on quantitative research, and sometimes on both. The longitudinal method can reveal links between earlier and later behavior and changes in individuals over time, but the changes may be the result of many factors not just developmental maturation. Cross-sectional studies can demonstrate age differences in behavior by observing people of different ages at one point in time. They provide information about change over time in cohort groups but not change in individuals. A sequential* method combines the cross-sectional and longitudinal approaches by observing different groups on multiple occasions. Obviously, the more variables are controlled in each of these methods, the more reliably results can be interpreted. If there is not sufficient control of variables, the results from a cross-sectional study can conflict with the results of a longitudinal study. The longitudinal method is more extensively used, perhaps because it is easier and less expensive.

Parallel longitudinal studies in Australia, Finland, Israel, Poland, and the United States (Heusman & Eron, 1986, cited in Huston et al., 1992) revealed a pattern of involvement with violence related to amount of television viewing. The amount of violence viewed at age 8 predicted aggression at age 18 and serious criminal behavior at age 30. Because this was a relational study, however, it could not be determined whether more violence was viewed because of the viewer's personality or whether violent programming affected the viewer through desensitization* or some other mechanism (Eron, 1982; Huesmann, Eron, Lefkowitz & Walder, 1984, cited in Huston et al., 1992). Milesky, Kessler, Stripp, and Reubens (1982) conducted a similar study and concluded that other research did not support the hypothesis. On the other hand, methodology experts who examined other studies supported the hypothesis on violence and aggression (Cook, Kendzencky & Thomas, 1983, cited in Huston et al., 1992).

Content analyses are used to determine variables such as (1) the number of violent, anti- or prosocial incidents in a program; (2) characteristics of roles* given ethnic groups, gender, age, or occupations portrayed; and (3) values presented on television, such as in commercials. Meta-analyses, which use statistical techniques for synthesis of the literature, and integrated research studies, which use comprehensive surveys and graphic comparison of the literature, are used to draw conclusions from multiple studies on a research question.

11.2.5.4. Developmental Methodology. Formative evaluation as a research methodology (see Chapter 42) developed in response to a need for procedures to systematically try out and revise materials during a product development process (Cambre, 1987). It is one of the major contributions of television research. According to Flagg (1990), "The goal of formative evaluation is to inform the decision-making process during the design, production, and implementation stages of an educational program with the purpose of improving the program" (p. 241). The techniques used in formative evaluation of television programs are important areas of competency for instructional technologists. Formative evaluation studies pose research questions rather

than hypotheses, and techniques employed range from oral reports and videotaping reactions to short questionnaires. Evaluation models incorporate phases, such as pre- and postproduction, in the research process.

An example of formative evaluation studies on television is the AIT report on the development of a lesson in the form of a program entitled "Taxes Influence Behavior" (Agency for Instructional Television, 1984). Students were questioned about attention to the program, interest, story believability, character perceptions, storyline comprehension, and program objectives. Teachers were asked about the program's appeal, curriculum fit, objectives, and utilization. Revisions and recommendations for teachers were based on the data collected.

It was Children's Television Workshop (CTW) that pioneered techniques for formative and summative evaluation* (Flagg, 1990). After specifying message design variables and then investigating the effect of these variables on psychological phenomena such as attention, CTW developed techniques for investigating relationships formatively, so that designs could be changed, and summatively, so that effects on behavior could be reported. In doing so, CTW forever put to rest the assumption that one style of television is best for all young children (Lesser, 1974) and the assumption that television was not an interactive enough medium to teach intellectual skills to young children.

Periodic bibliographies issued by CTW document not only the research done there but also research related to CTW productions. Sammur (1990) developed a "Selected Bibliography of Research on Programming at the Children's Television Workshop" that annotated 36 formative, summative, and theoretical research studies on the four educational children's television series produced by CTW. The CTW research program reflects the systematic application of design, development, and evaluation procedures that is necessitated by the expense of producing for sophisticated educational technologies.

11.2.6 Summary

Film research during the 1950s contributed an identification of variables, especially variables related to message design. However, much of this research was methodologically flawed. Therefore, today it is useful primarily for the model it set for television research and the variables it identified. During the 1960s, television research emphasized comparative studies and frequently focused on message design variables.

The 1970s were a period of transition in that there was a move from ITV to ETV research, and a move from comparative studies to the study of specific variables and effects via the aptitude treatment interaction paradigm. There was also a methodological shift to qualitative, descriptive, and developmental studies in addition to traditional empirical studies.

During the 1980s and 90s variables began to be categorized into a viewing system consisting of programming, environment, and behavior, all of which interrelated. We turn now from a chronological consideration of the historical context of film and television research to findings in the major areas of interest to researchers.

11.3 MESSAGE DESIGN AND COGNITIVE PROCESSING

The vast majority of early instructional films and television programs were essentially documentary works that were developed by commercial, noneducational producers. At this early point in the evolution of instructional technology, little attention was given to the use of instructional techniques or design principles. Similarly, the technology of film or television was still in its infancy, and few, if any, editing or special visual effects were available to the producers of such materials. In light of this, it is not surprising that most of the earlier research focused on simple comparisons between the technology and some form of standard instruction. Since the two technologies did not incorporate many of the production elements that have become part of their unique symbol system as we understand them today, little attention was given to assessing the effects of specific media characteristics on student learning.

11.3.1 The Evolution of Message Design

During the period of the Pennsylvania State University film studies, however, some research was directed at determining how the intentional incorporation of instructional techniques and media characteristics interacted with learner achievement from the materials. The variables studied included: the use of inserted questions, color, subjective camera angle, sound track modifications, and the use of visual cueing devices (Greenhill, 1956; Hoban & van Ormer, 1951). Similar studies were further conducted on instructional television in the late 1950s and early 1960s, generally on adult audiences in controlled environments (Chu & Schramm, 1967; Greenhill, 1967). From this time on, a growing number of researchers have investigated, in increasingly greater levels of detail, the instructional effectiveness of television productions incorporating specialized features that are intended to facilitate learning. The process of specifying and organizing these components has come to be called *message design* (see 26.1).

Fleming and Levie (1993) define an instructional message as "a pattern of signs (words, pictures, gestures) produced for the purpose of modifying the psychomotor, cognitive, or affective behavior of one or more persons" (p. x). Grabowski (1991) describes message design as "planning for the manipulation of the physical form of the message" (p. 206). The concept of message design was not used in the literature until the 1970s, although the general principles of message design were being synthesized from research on perception, psychology, and instruction. Early researchers focused primarily on visual perception (Norberg, 1962,

1966; Knowlton, 1966; Fleming, 1967); however, later researchers addressed auditory and print media as well. Fleming and Levie (1978, 1993) first defined the term *message design* and comprehensively articulated its general principles for instructional designers. Today, the concept of message design in television includes all of the scripting, production, and editing decisions that are made separate from the actual content of the program.

The design of the instructional television message (see 11.7.3.4) has become increasingly important as a greater understanding of instructional and cognitive principles has emerged from the study of learning and psychology, and with the growing sophistication of television production technology, particularly in broadcast television. The intentional use of various video effects such as zooms, cuts, dissolves, and the designer's manipulation of program pacing and use of various audio and graphic effects became a standard procedure among instructional designers wishing to maximize the effectiveness of television programming. For the most part, however, these production effects* were not systematically investigated, and, consequently, the television producer had few reliable research guidelines on which to base production decisions.

During the mid-1970s, Aletha Huston and John Wright used the term *formal features* to collectively describe the various production techniques employed in designing and producing the television message (Huston & Wright, 1983). They describe television as being distinguished by its unique forms, rather than simply by the content of the programming. These researchers and their associates at the University of Kansas began a systematic investigation of the formal attributes* or features of television, particularly with respect to how these techniques interact with cognitive processes, such as attention and comprehension (Rice, Huston & Wright, 1982).

By the late 1970s, much of the television research focused on how children view television and those processes that relate to attention and comprehension of the televised information. This era of research can be best characterized as the conjunction of interest in both the developmental aspects of learning and in cognitive processing of information. Two events in the area of children's television prompted this research: the initial success of *Sesame Street* and associated programming by the Children's Television Workshop (Mielke, 1990), and the increased criticism of television and its alleged negative effects by a number of popular writers (Mander, 1978; Postman, 1982; Winn, 1977).

With the advent of The Children's Television Workshop and *Sesame Street,* a number of researchers began to explore the value of using many of these production techniques. These studies were typically formative in nature, intended for in-house use to assess the adequacy of particular techniques, and consequently did not appear regularly in the research literature (Sammur, 1990). Thus, researchers began to focus on those unique features that promote children's attention and comprehension during television viewing. In this research, the cognitive effects of formal features such as pacing, audio cues, camera effects, animation, and editing techniques were also explored with regard to the role that they played in attention and comprehension (Meyer, 1983).

During this time, public interest was also drawn to the possible negative effects of television programming on children. In addition to the continuing public concern for the effects of television violence on children, interest increased into the possibly debilitating effects on children's cognitive-processing abilities. In her book, *The Plug-in Drug,* Winn (1977) charged that television and the formal features inherent in the programming were causing excessive cognitive passivity* and depressed processing capabilities.*

Organized research, which was prompted by these events and criticisms, investigated the general effects on both attention and comprehension, as well as on the specific effects of television's formal production features in a fairly comprehensive manner. Such research has given us a remarkably thorough understanding of how television promotes cognitive activities (Anderson & Collins, 1988).

As interest in the cognitive aspects of children's television grew, hypotheses were developed to account for these effects in a broad manner, irrespective of particular types of programming. While a number of these theoretical perspectives are unconfirmed, they have provided the impetus and base for substantial, systematic research.

11.3.2 The Effects of Television on Cognitive-Processing Abilities

Television has been both lauded and criticized for the ways in which it presents information to the viewer, irrespective of the information itself (Anderson & Collins, 1988). It is this area, that of the relationship between the ways in which information is presented on television and the effect of that presentation on the cognitive-processing abilities of the viewer, which has continued to attract a great deal of theoretical as well as supporting research interest (Huston et al., 1992).

11.3.2.1. Theoretical Orientations. One critical view that has persisted over the years, despite contrary research findings, is that the television image and associated presentation effects are cognitively debilitating (Mander, 1978; Winn, 1977). The central assertion of this viewpoint is that the rapidly changing television image—enhanced by production features such as cuts, zooms, animation, and special effects—is cognitively mesmerizing. This is hypothesized to result in cognitive passivity, shortened attention spans, and, paradoxically enough, hyperactive behavior (Winn, 1977; Dumont, 1976, cited in Winn, 1977). Such a view is more conjecture than substantiated fact or articulated theory and has been drawn substantially from subjective observation rather than from extensive empirical research. The notion, however, has appealed to many who associate these behavioral manifestations with general, adult entertainment forms of television and who are more critical of the content of television programming rather than the presentation formats. It should be noted

that most researchers in the area of cognitive science and educational technology have not supported these assertions, which remain, to a large degree, open to definitive and methodologically rigorous research (Anderson & Collins, 1988).

11.3.2.2. Empirical Research. For the most part, research related to this aspect of television effects has been drawn from studies done in the area of advertising and marketing or in electroencephalography (EEG). Krugman (1970, 1971) compared the EEGs of subjects viewing rear-projected visual images and those of subjects reading, and concluded that television viewing resulted in different brain wave patterns than did reading. It is important to note that these studies were conducted on a single subject and only used the subject's EEG obtained while browsing a magazine as a baseline index. The length of time the EEG was recorded was also only 15 minutes, and readings were taken at only one location on the head. The two brain wave patterns of interest were the alpha rhythm, which is associated with an inactive or resting-brain state, and the beta rhythm, which is usually indicative of cognitive activity. These experiments were repeated by Krugman, using actual television images with similar results (Krugman, 1979). Similar findings were produced by several other researchers who indicated that television viewing produced more alpha activity than reading, which resulted in greater beta activity (Appel, Weinstein & Weinstein, 1979; Fetherman, Frieser, Greenspun, Harris, Schulman & Crown, 1979; Walker, 1980; Weinstein, Appel & Weinstein, 1980). In these cases, alpha activity was associated with periods of low cognitive activity, which was interpreted to be the mesmerizing effect described by critics.

Drawing from the work of Krugman (1979), Emery and Emery (1975, 1980) criticized television images as "habituating" because the continuously scanned image emitted an overload of light-based information, potentially resulting in an overload of the processing system. This claim was substantially refuted, however, in studies by Silberstein, Agardy, Ong, and Heath (1983), who, in methodologically rigorous experiments with 12-year-old children, found no differences in brain wave activity between projected text and text presented on the television screen. Furthermore, differences were found between text presented on the television screen and documentary or interview programming; whereas no differences were found between the two types of programming. A third interesting finding was that both the text and interview program produced right- and left-hemisphere effects, while the documentary alone resulted in greater right-hemisphere activity. A comprehensive and critical review of most of the EEG research was published by Fite (1994). In this report, Fite found virtually no substantiation of the detrimental effects of television evidenced by EEG-based studies.

Focusing specifically on viewer attention, Rothshild, Thorson, Reeves, Hirsch, and Goldstein (1986) found that alpha activity dropped immediately following the introduction of a scene change or formal feature in the program material, which in these studies were commercial advertisements. Winn (1977) has further criticized children's television and *Sesame Street,* in particular, for contributing to shortened attention spans and hyperactive behavior. A study by Halpern (1975) has been frequently cited as providing evidence that programming such as *Sesame Street* contributed to hyperactive and compulsive behavior. This study has been seriously criticized on methodological grounds by Anderson and Collins (1988), and the findings have not been successfully replicated by Halpern. Other studies related to children's concentration and tolerance for delay reported moderate decreases in tolerance for delay associated with action programs (Friedrich & Stein, 1973) and actually increased concentration resulting from television viewing among children rated as low in imagination (Tower, Singer, Singer & Biggs, 1979). Anderson, Levin, and Lorch (1977) investigated the effect of program pacing on attention, activity, and impulsivity levels and found no differences in 5-year-old children's degree of activity, impulsivity, or perseverance levels. Salomon (1979), however, found that *Sesame Street* viewing, when compared to other general types of children's programming, produced a decrease in perseverance in a laboratory task. This effect may have been related to differences in the audience's age and the intended target age of the *Sesame Street* programming and the relative ease of the task.

11.3.3 The Television Symbol System or Code

For the most part, research into the cognitive effects of television has focused more specifically on how televised information is processed rather than on how television affects cognitive processing abilities (Anderson & Collins, 1988). This research is based on theory related to both the symbol system or formal features used in television and the ways that information is attended to and comprehended (see 26.4.3).

11.3.3.1. The Role of Filmic Codes in Processing. One of the most universal views of television as a medium was described by McLuhan (1964) when he suggested that the formal attributes of a medium, such as television, influence how we think and process information. Furthermore, McLuhan put forth the idea that different media present information in unique ways that are idiosyncratic to the individual medium. Goodman (1968) and Gardner, Howard, and Perkins (1974) further elaborated on the function of such symbol systems,* implying that similarities between the symbol system and mental representations of the content will facilitate comprehension of the instructional message. More recently, Kozma (1991) suggests that different media are defined by three characteristics: the technology,* the symbol systems employed, and the methods of processing information. Of these, the symbol system is crucial to the mental processing of the person interacting with the medium. The individual symbol systems may be idiosyncratic to the particular medium and consequently may need to be learned by the user. This thesis has been elaborated on by Gavriel Salomon, who has attempted to

test it empirically with regard to television (Salomon, 1972, 1974; Salomon, 1979; Salomon & Cohen, 1977). He suggested that different symbol systems or codes can represent information in different ways during encoding in memory, making it necessary to process the information in unique ways. Salomon contended that children learn to interpret these "filmic codes,"* which can be incorporated into cognitive activities in two ways (Salomon, 1979). The first function of symbolic or filmic codes is that they can call on or activate cognitive skills within the learner and can become internalized into the learner's repertoire of processing skills (Salomon & Cohen, 1977). In this way, such production features as montage* or cuts can activate respective cognitive processes such as inferencing and sequencing. The second role of filmic codes lies in the assumption that these codes, which model cognitive processes, can actually "stand in" for or "supplant" the cognitive skills themselves, thereby facilitating learning (Salomon, 1974). In this manner, features such as zooms and dissolves can be used to model the cognitive skills they represent and consequently enhance the processing skills of the viewer.

Rice, Huston, and Wright (1983) further differentiated the types of representation within the television code into three levels. These include at the most basic level, literal visual or auditory portrayal of real-world information. At the second level are media forms and conventions that have no real-world counterpart, such as production effects and formal features. The third level consists of symbolic code that is not distinctive to the television medium. These third-level codes consist of linguistic, nonlinguistic, and auditory code such as language, which may be used to "double encode" or describe the visual codes presented on the screen. Of the three, the media forms and conventions are of most interest to the researcher because they are idiosyncratic to the media of television and film and relate most specifically to the child's processing of the television message (Rice, Huston & Wright, 1983).

11.3.3.2. Research on Filmic Codes. There is not a great deal of empirical work related to the cognitive effects of television code. However, the work of Gavriel Salomon constitutes the most comprehensive series of empirical studies focused on the symbol system and code of television. Drawing on his theoretical position, he devised a series of experiments that explored the use of filmic codes to both model or supplant cognitive skills and to call on or activate specific cognitive skills. He conducted the first group of studies with Israeli eighth-graders to determine if the camera effect of zooming could indeed model the relation of the part to the whole (Salomon, 1974). The results indicated that the children exposed to the experimental treatment performed significantly better than did those students either shown the individual close-up and overall pictures or those receiving no treatment. In this case, the use of explicit modeling of the cognitive skill improved the student's ability to focus attention on the detailed parts of the overall display. A second experiment, using fewer visual transformations, was not as effective as the first, possibly indicating that extensive modeling of these skills is necessary for this effect to occur. In a third experiment, Salomon confirmed that the internalization of the filmic codes could enhance the cognitive skills of the viewer by presenting scenes where the three-dimensional unfolding of an object was compared with the same representation in two dimensions. In this case, the three-dimensional animation effect modeled the cognitive analog of mentally unfolding the object from three dimensions to two dimensions more effectively than did simple presentation of the two-dimensional object. A study conducted by Rovet (1983) using a spatial rotation task with third-grade children further confirmed Salomon's findings, although conclusive confirmation of this theory has not been provided through research.

The second assertion made by Salomon suggested that filmic codes could also activate or "call upon" specific cognitive skills. In a series of studies, Salomon (1979) tested this hypothesis on groups of preschool, second-grade, and third-grade Israeli students using *Sesame Street* programming as the content. After 6 months, the groups of school-aged children demonstrated significantly higher comprehension scores. This was interpreted by Salomon to indicate that students were able to learn the meanings of the filmic codes, and in so doing activated the respective cognitive skills. However, the effects were limited to the older children and have been qualified by Salomon to suggest that these mental skills can be activated by the appropriate filmic codes, but are not necessarily always activated in this manner.

11.3.4 Children's Attention to Television

The effect of the television symbol system on learning has been addressed through two areas of cognitive processing: attention and comprehension. For each of these areas, we discuss theoretical approaches and empirical research.

11.3.4.1. Reactive/Active Theory. Two approaches to understanding the way in which children attend to television have emerged. These positions include the reactive theory,* which generally views the child as passive and simply a receptor of information or stimuli delivered by the television, and the active theory,* which suggests that children cognitively interact with the information being presented as well as with the viewing environment (Anderson & Lorch, 1983). These two viewpoints generally parallel theoretical orientations to human information processing in that early concepts of the human information-processing system were reasonably linear and viewed attention as a relatively receptive process where the learner merely reacted to stimuli that were perceived (Atkinson & Shiffrin, 1968). Later conceptions of how we process information took the position that we are active participants in selecting and processing incoming stimuli (Anderson, 1980).

The first theoretical orientation, the reactive theory, is derived from Bandura's Social Learning Theory* (Bandura, 1977). In this conceptualization, the salient formal features of the television programming gain and maintain the viewer's attention. Continued attention and comprehension

occur more or less automatically as the child's information-processing system functions reactively. Singer (1980) describes this process as one where the continually changing screen and auditory patterns create an ongoing series of orienting reflexes in the viewer. Key to this orientation is the role of the viewer as a passive, involuntary processor of information that is absorbed from the screen. The reactive theory of attention to television is supported by little direct research, with most of the foundation for the theory being based on the early human information-processing theories such as those described by Atkinson and Shiffrin (1968, 1971), Broadbent (1959), and Neisser (1967). The work of Singer (1980) included little direct research relative to this perspective, but rather drew on what was, at that time, a popular theory of memory that described the human information-processing system as one in which information was processed in the sensory store, received further processing in short term memory, and was then transferred to long-term memory, all without a great deal of active or purposeful selection, processing, or coding by the learner.

It is generally accepted today that the reactive theory requires much revision, particularly with regard to the learner's role in initiating and actively processing new information in relation to prior knowledge. For these reasons, little substantiation of the theory can be put forth, especially in light of the support that current research provides to the opposing theory, the active theory.

The alternative theory, the active theory, defines the child as an active processor who is guided by previous knowledge, expectations, and schemata* (Anderson & Lorch, 1983). In this way, the child does not merely respond to the changing stimuli presented, but rather actively applies strategies based on previous experience with the content and formal features, personal knowledge structures, and available cognitive skills. Key to this view is the assumption that the child will apply existing schemas to the perception and processing of the televised information. Anderson and Lorch (1983) suggest that a number of premises underlie the functioning of the active theory. These include consideration of competing stimuli, the need to maintain a reasonable level of stimulus unfamiliarity, the role of auditory cues to refocus attention, and the effect of attentional inertia* to maintain cognitive involvement (Anderson, Alwitt, Lorch & Levin, 1979). Additionally, a key component of the active theory is the role of viewing schemata, which Anderson and Lorch suggest develop through increased interaction with television forms, as well as with general cognitive growth.

The notion of representational codes or formal features and their role and effects in the processing of television information has become an area of particular interest and the central focus of much research regarding how children attend to and process the television message. Formal features are defined by Anderson and Collins as characteristic attributes of the medium, which can be described without reference to specific content. In reality these include, but are not limited to, the visual features of zooms, camera movements, cuts and dissolves, montage techniques, animation, ellipses, program pace, and special visual effects, as well as the auditory features of music, sound effects, and unusual voices. A fairly comprehensive taxonomy of formal features has been developed by the research group at the Center for Research on the Influence of Television on Children (CRITC) (Huston & Wright, 1983; Rice, Huston & Wright, 1983).

Two constructs related to the visual message and the forms of television have emerged and become important to an understanding of how these forms function in the processing of the television message. These constructs, which include visual complexity or the amount and degree of change of information (Watt & Welch, 1983; Welch & Watt, 1982) and perceptual salience* or those attributes of the stimulus that increase its intensity, contrast, change, or novelty (Berlyne, 1960; Rice, Huston & Wright, 1983), relate to both quantitative and qualitative characteristics of the message. Researchers associated with each of these positions have developed or adapted models that can be used to conceptualize the effects of these attributes on the message and how it is processed by the viewer. Watt and Welch employed an information theory model for entropy to explain the relationship between static and dynamic complexity and learning from television content (Watt & Welch, 1983; Welch & Watt, 1982). Rice, Huston, and Wright (1982) presented a model that described the relationship between attention and stimulus complexity. For the most part, however, the effects of the formal features of television have been considered with regard to the particular cognitive processes or skills with which they are associated, attention and comprehension, and consequently, they are best examined from that perspective.

11.3.4.2. Research on Attention. The variable of attention to the television program has received extensive research interest, of which the most comprehensive group of studies has been conducted by Daniel Anderson and his associates at the University of Massachusetts. This group of researchers was the first to propose that the process of attending to television programming was active rather than simply a reaction to the stimuli presented.

One of the first questions relative to attention to television is a qualification of exactly what attention is and how it can appropriately be measured. Anderson and Field (1983) describe five methodologies that may constitute an effective measure of this attention. These include: (a) visual orientation, the physical orientation of the viewer toward the television screen; (b) eye movements and fixations; (c) comprehension and recognition testing, which measures attention through inferences drawn from objective recognition and comprehension tests; (d) interference methods, which pinpoint attention as that time when a viewer responds to and removes some form of interfering information from the message; and (e) physiological measures that include cardiac, galvanic skin response, and electroencephalographic records of arousal. Of these, the most frequently employed have been visual orientation and the use of recognition and comprehension tests.

Anderson and Field (1983) identify a number of settings and contexts for viewing that impinge on the attentional process. They differentiate between the home-viewing environment and laboratory settings in terms of the accuracy of data obtained. Home viewing generally results in overly inflated estimates of attentional time (Bechtel, Achelpohl & Akers, 1972). The use of monitoring cameras revealed that attention does not continue for long periods of time but rather consists of frequent interruptions, conversations, distractions,* and the viewer's exits and returns to the room (Allen, 1965; Anderson, 1983). Allen used time-lapse movie cameras, and Bechtel, Achelpohl, and Akers videotaped in the home. The results of these studies appear consistent, indicating that children up to age 10 averaged about 52% of the time in the viewing room actually attending to the program, while children aged 11 to 19 years showed an average attention of about 69% (Bechtel et al., 1972). In all cases, attention to children's programs was substantially higher than to adult-level programming, although this may not remain true today because of changes in programming and the increased viewing sophistication of children. In laboratory settings, where more control over outside distractions could be maintained, it was found that children still were frequently distracted and demonstrated only sporadic attention to the program (Becker & Wolfe, 1960). In several studies, preschool children were observed to look at and away from the television 150 to 200 times per hour (Alwitt, Anderson, Lorch & Levin, 1980; Anderson & Levin, 1976; Field, 1983). The length of "looks" were also seen as important characteristics of attention. Anderson, Lorch, Smith, Bradford, and Levin (1981) found that looks of more than 30 seconds were infrequent and that the majority of look lengths were less than 5 seconds.

The viewing context was also identified as an influential factor in attention. Sproull (1973) suggested that toys and other activities were strong attention-diverting stimuli, in the absence of which attention rose to 80%. Studies by Lorch, Anderson, and Levin (1979) concluded that attention is strategic in children, because audio cues were used heavily to monitor program content and indicate instances when attention should be redirected to the television. The presence of other children with whom they could discuss the program and use as models of attention were also shown to be strong factors contributing to attentional control (Anderson et al., 1981).

The factor of viewer age has frequently emerged as a variable of significance, particularly with regard to determining at what age children begin to attend to and comprehend the content of the television program. Very young children (6 to 12 months of age) appear to direct attention to the television screen about half the time in controlled situations (Hollenbeck & Slaby, 1979; Lemish & Rice, 1986), with a dramatic increase between 12 and 48 months (Anderson & Levin, 1976). In their study, Anderson and Levin observed an increase in look lengths by a factor of 4 at approximately 30 months of age. Other researchers have reported similar findings (Carew, 1980; Schramm, Lyle & Parker, 1961).

Attention appears to increase continuously beyond this age to about 12 years, at which point it plateaus (Alwitt et al., 1980; Anderson, 1983; Anderson, Lorch, Field, Collins & Nathan, 1986; Anderson, Lorch, Field & Sanders, 1981; Calvert, Huston, Watkins & Wright, 1982).

The unique role of the formal features of television has been the focus of much research on children's attention. Such features include both visual and auditory production effects that are integral to the television program composition and presentation. Formal features have significant implications for attention, comprehension, and, as has been discussed previously, modeling and activating cognitive skills. In terms of attention, the research has indicated that only some formal features, specifically special visual effects, changes in scene, character change, and high levels of action, are reasonably effective at eliciting attention, while conventional camera effects such as cuts, zooms, and pans have substantially less power to gain attention (Rice, Huston & Wright, 1983). The visual feature that most inhibited attention was the long zoom effect. Other program components, such as animation, puppets, and frequent changes of speaker, while not actually production features, were also found to promote attention. Those components that decreased attention were live animals, song and dance, and long speeches (Alwitt et al., 1980; Anderson & Levin, 1976; Calvert, Huston, Watkins & Wright, 1982).

Several researchers have observed that the sound track of the television program plays a major role in attention, particularly in gaining the attention of the nonviewing child (Anderson & Field, 1983). With respect to the generalized use or effect of the audio track to direct attention, Lorch et al. (1979) found that auditory attention parallels visual attention* and increases with age at a rate similar to that of visual attention. When the audio message was experimentally degraded so as to be unintelligible, either through technical reversal or substitution, children at ages 2, 3 1/2, and 5 years evidenced significant drops in attention to *Sesame Street* programs, with the most significant drop being observed with the older children (Anderson, Lorch, Field & Sanders, 1981). It has also been reported that children employ the audio message to monitor the program for critical or comprehensible content, which they can then attend to visually (Anderson & Lorch, 1983). Auditory attention to television is, to a large degree, mediated by the formal attributes of the auditory message, including type, age, and gender of voice, and the novelty of particular sound, sound effects, or music. Research conducted by Alwitt et al. (1980) revealed that certain audio effects were effective in gaining attention from nonviewing children. These included auditory changes, sound effects, laughter, instrumental music, and children's, women's, and "peculiar" voices; while men's voices, individual singing, and slow music inhibited attention (Anderson & Lorch, 1983). The researchers concluded that auditory devices such as those described cued the children that an important change was taking place in the program which might be of interest, thereby prompting attention. They also reported that audio effects

do not appear to have any significant effect before the age of 24 to 30 months, which parallels approximately the beginning of general attending behavior noted previously.

When all types of formal features, both visual and auditory, are considered in terms of their ability to facilitate attention, it becomes apparent that those which are most obvious are generally most effective (Wright, Huston, Ross, Calvert, Rolandelli, Weeks, Raeissi & Potts, 1984). These researchers contend that the more perceptually salient a feature is, such as fast action or pace, the more effectively it will gain attention. This was partially confirmed in research they describe in which those programs identified as high in feature saliency also had larger viewing audiences. Interestingly, *Sesame Street*, which has a high viewership and attention-gaining-power, has been found to be slower paced (in terms of shot length) than other entertainment programs (Bryant, 1992). Evidence was also found which suggests that violence per se is not necessarily attention gaining, but rather the high saliency of formal features in violent programs may be responsible for the higher viewer numbers (Huston & Wright, 1983; Wright et al., 1984; Wright & Huston, 1982).

The differential effects of both visual and auditory formal features have been cited by several researchers as significant evidence supporting the active theory of attention to television (Anderson & Field, 1983; Rice, Huston & Wright). They contend that for the reactive theory to be an apt descriptor of children's attentional behavior, all formal features should be effective at virtually all ages, because they should all automatically elicit an orienting reaction due to their movement, stimulus change, or salient visual patterns. Since the research consistently identifies only certain features at particular ages as attention gaining and conversely finds that other features are inhibiting to attention, this hypothesis is strongly rejected (Anderson & Field, 1983). With regard to the active theory, they describe the viewing child as actively and selectively in command of his or her own attentional strategies. For this reason, the child could be expected to respond differentially to the various stimuli and features, which is the case made by current research findings (Hawkins, Kin & Pingree, 1991). Alwitt et al. (1980) conclude:

> An attribute (feature) comes to have a positive or negative relationship to attention, we hypothesize, based on the degree to which it predicts relevant and comprehensible content. A child can thus use an attribute to divide attention between TV viewing and other activities: Full attention is given when an attribute is predictive of understandable content and terminated when an attribute predicts irrelevant, boring, and incomprehensible content (p. 65).

11.3.5 Children's Comprehension of Television

Anderson and Field (1983) explain that formal features perform two significant functions: First, they mark the beginning of important content segments, and second, they communicate producer-intended concepts of time, space, action, and character (Anderson & Field, 1983). The notion that the formal features, which comprise such television effects as montage, are able to convey changes in time, place, or movement is integral to a viewer's ability to comprehend story content and plot as well as simply to gain or hold attention. It is in the area of comprehension that formal features appear to play the most important role.

11.3.5.1. Relationship of Comprehension to Attention.
The basic theory related to children's comprehension of television relates to and derives from theoretical bases for attention (Anderson & Lorch, 1983). They cite the reactive theory for suggesting that once attention has been gained, comprehension will automatically follow as a natural consequence. Interestingly, Singer (1980) and Singer and Singer (1982), proponents of the reactive theory, suggest that the rapid pace or delivery of most television messages that gain or hold attention, may not permit the viewer to process adequately the information at a deep enough level to ensure high levels of comprehension. The active theory, on the other hand, maintains that attention itself is directed by children's monitoring* of the program for comprehensible content, which serves as a signal to focus more direct attention to the message (Anderson & Lorch, 1983). To represent the relationship, Rice, Huston, and Wright (1982) offered the attentional model presented in Figure 11-1. In this model, both high and low levels of comprehensibility inhibit attention. At the high end (incomprehensibility), the content is complex and not understood by the child and consequently elicits little interest or attention. At the low end (boredom), the content is familiar and lacking in information, making it less attention gaining. In this way, comprehension is interpreted to drive attention (Rice, Huston & Wright, 1983).

A good deal of the theory related to the formal features of television has relevance for the area of comprehension as

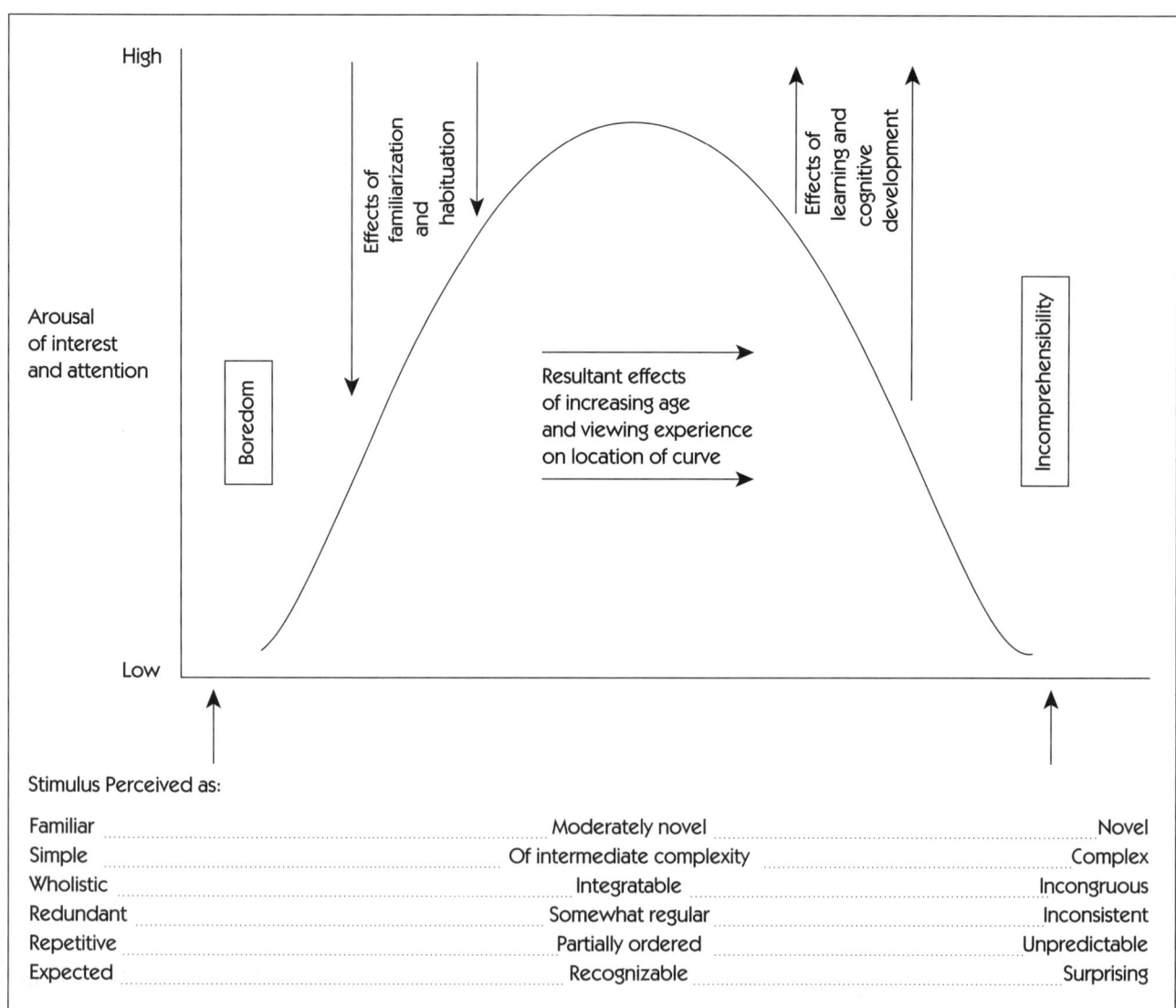

Figure 11-1.   A model of developmental changes in interest and attention. (From Rice, Huston & Wright, 1982.)

well as attention. Of particular interest is the concept of montage, one of the formal features previously described. A montage is a series of scenes interrupted by special effects such as cuts, dissolves, changes in point of view, and overlays, the purpose of which is to show various shifts in time, place, or personal point of view. Such actions call on the viewer to maintain a sequence of events, infer changes of scene or time, and to relate or integrate individual scenes to one another (Anderson & Field, 1983). In this way, any two scenes can be joined together to generate a new idea or suggest a relationship that has not been explicitly shown.

Piaget (1926) suggested that younger children (under 7 years) were limited in story comprehension because of weak seriation abilities and the inability to infer and comprehend transformations between events in a story which differ temporally. These limitations reduce the ability to develop complete schemas and consequently impair comprehension. Inconsistencies across theories such as these, however, have produced a dilemma among researchers concerning the ability of children to comprehend fully information presented in this manner via television (Wartella, 1979).

11.3.5.2. Research on Comprehension. Substantial research has addressed the interrelationship between comprehension and attention and the resultant support of the active theory suggested by Anderson and Lorch (1983). Lorch et al. (1979) compared different experimental attention situations in terms of recall of *Sesame Street* content by 5-year-olds. Their findings revealed that variations in the amount of attention a child demonstrated did not differentially affect comprehension scores. However, a significant positive correlation was found between the comprehension scores and the amount of attention exhibited during the specific program content that was related to the comprehension test items. These findings were further supported in research reported by Krull and Husson (1979) and Pezdek and Hartman (1981) who also identified the significance of audio cues in promoting comprehension as well as directing visual attention. A later study, however, by Anderson, Lorch, Field, and Sanders (1981, study 2), which controlled for extraneous confounding effects of formal features inserted in the programs, produced data that fully supported the earlier findings of Lorch et al. (1979). All in all, these studies provided strong support for the active theory over the reactive theory, in that attention appeared to be significantly directed by the comprehensibility of the program content.

Understandably, the role of formal features in comprehension is directly related to the active theory of television viewing. Anderson and Field (1983) suggest that the employment of formal features in a montage serve the purposes of the producers of the program to convey or infer changes in time, space, action, or point of view. They further contend that the active comprehension hypothesis is consequently supported, in that if children did not actively make the inferences, they would perceive the program as meaningless segments of video and would, therefore, not attend to it.

The earliest research on comprehension of film montage suggested that young children were incapable of comprehending the elements of montage (Piaget, 1926). Empirical research supported these contentions (Baron, 1980; Noble, 1975; Tada, 1969). In these cases, assessment of children's comprehension was made via verbal explanations of what had occurred, a process that has been criticized as being extremely difficult for younger children (Smith, Anderson & Fisher, 1985). In research that employed nonverbal testing methods such as reconstructing the story using dolls and the original television sets, these researchers found that children aged 3 and 5 years showed substantial comprehension of program content. It is interesting to note that no differences were found between treatments that employed the formal features of pans, zooms, fades, and dissolves and those treatments that relied solely on still photographic representation. Montage that incorporated formal features was apparently not necessary for comprehension of the story. Rather, children were able to comprehend the message presented via either montage or still pictures with equal ability. In a second experiment, Smith et al. (1985) examined the effects of specific montage elements in terms of the outcomes (ellipsis, spatial relationships, character point of view, and simultaneity of action) intended by the producer. In this case, both 4- and 7-year-olds demonstrated good comprehension via the nonverbal evaluation technique, with 7-year-old children showing greater comprehension. The researchers attribute this result to a greater amount of life experience on the part of the older children. A later study conducted by Huston and Wright (1989) indicated that formal features used in montage, such as those used to depict distorted perceptions, memory flashbacks, and instant replays were not comprehended well by school age children. Anderson and Collins (1988) have generally concluded that the features incorporated in montage are well comprehended by children, particularly those who are older and have greater prior experience and knowledge. Anderson and Field (1983) contend that the results of these studies indicate that young children make frequent, active inferences as they interpret montage effects in television programming. Furthermore, they suggest that this fact provides strong support for the active-comprehension hypothesis.

The comprehension of longer segments of programming that necessitated integration and inferencing skills was investigated by Lorch, Bellack, and Augsbach (1987). In two experiments, they determined that both 5-year-olds and 4- and 6-year-olds were capable of selectively recalling 92% of ideas that were central to the television stories. Much lower recall rates were found for incidental or noncentral information. In an earlier study, however, Calvert, Huston, Watkins, and Wright (1982) found that children recalled central content that was presented by means of highly salient formal features better than that which used low-salience features. In studies in which the programming content was of much longer duration, such as in commercially broadcast programs, older viewers were generally able to discriminate central content better than younger viewers (Collins, 1983). Collins further suggested that an inability to make inferences contributed to comprehension difficulties, although this research was conducted using entertainment programming that was intended primarily for adult audiences. Anderson and Collins (1988) concluded, however, that the poor comprehension of both central and implied content should be attributed primarily to less-developed knowledge bases rather than to any cognitive disability. More recent research (Sell, Ray & Lovelace, 1995) suggests, however, that repeated viewing of the program results in improved comprehension by 4-year-old children. They attribute this effect to more complete processing of the formal features that enabled children to focus on essential information critical to understanding the plot.

11.3.6 Summary and Recommendations

Two theoretical orientations have emerged with regard to the cognitive processing of television program content and the effect of the formal production features on that processing. The earlier, reactive theory suggested that the child was a passive entity that could only react to the stimuli being presented. A number of writers accepted this theory and employed it to further describe the viewer as not only passive but also mesmerized by the flickering stimuli presented on the screen. Only modest data, however, reflect a negative effect of certain types of television programming on attention and cognitive processing, and virtually no reliable research confirms the strong, deleterious effects claimed by a number of popular writers and critics of television.

A second opposing position, the active theory (or the active comprehension theory), drew on more contemporary cognitive views of the learner and described the child as actively exploring and analyzing the program content being presented. This theory suggests that attention to the television program is not a reaction to stimuli but rather a monitoring and comprehension process to identify meaningful content requiring more directed attention.

Research has generally supported the active hypothesis, describing the attentional and comprehension processes as highly interrelated, with comprehension being a precondition to attention. Comprehension is further facilitated through the effects of formal features that function as elements of montage to infer meaningful changes in space, time, and point of view.

The television image has been shown to incorporate a unique symbol system that has certain specifiable capabilities it shares with no other medium. The modes of symbolic representation in television exist as a singular language that must be learned by the child. The specific effects of formal features have received substantial research attention with regard to both attention and comprehension processes, as well as to their ability to model and activate cognitive skills. The importance of formal features as they interact with content has also been underscored by many findings; however, their interaction with other variables has not been pursued sufficiently by researchers. Any research agenda should include continuing investigation of formal features, especially their complex interactions with other variables.

The simple act of a child viewing television has been demonstrated not as a response to stimuli but as a complex, purposeful cognitive activity that becomes progressively sophisticated as the child matures to adulthood. The cognitive effects of such activity have far-reaching consequences for both formal and informal educational activities.

11.4 SCHOLASTIC ACHIEVEMENT

Television viewing has gained the widespread reputation of being detrimental to scholastic achievement. This perception of many teachers, parents, and researchers stems primarily from the negative statistical relationship sometimes found between amount of time spent watching television and scholastic performance (Anderson & Collins, 1988). The relationship between television and scholastic achievement is much more complicated and complex than such a simple inverse relationship suggests (Beentjes & Van der Voort, 1988; Comstock & Paik, 1987, 1991; Neuman, 1991). A review of the research on scholastic achievement, focusing particularly on that produced since the early 1980s, reveals the likelihood of many interacting variables influencing the impact of television.

This section of the chapter will first discuss some theoretical assumptions and major theories about television's impact on scholastic achievement, including a brief review of the body of research and methodological issues. A summary of the intervening variables that have been studied with regard to the television/achievement association and the current conclusions about that relationship will follow.

11.4.1 Theoretical Assumptions

Research on television's impact on scholastic achievement hinges on two assumptions. The first is the belief that an objective measurement of television viewing can be obtained. The second concerns the assessment and measurement of achievement. The methods used to gather data on both are similar.

Television viewing is often defined by hours of viewing per day or week. This information is primarily gathered through self-reporting instruments or parental diaries. Rarely is a distinction made about how the student is relating to the television set, whether or not others are in the room, or if there are concurrent activities being performed. A few studies record the type of programming watched, but again, these data are usually gathered from the subjects within a self-reporting context instead of by direct observation.

Scholastic achievement is overwhelmingly defined in the literature as reading. Reading assessments in the form of achievement tests on vocabulary and comprehension are the primary source of comparison. Some studies measure other school-related achievement such as mathematics but commonly discuss their study results mainly in terms of the reading scores. While this may be limiting in terms of our understanding of scholastic achievement, it has allowed for more comprehensive meta-analyses and comparisons between studies than otherwise would have been possible.

11.4.2 Major Theories

Research in this arena of television's effects has had two major thrusts. Researchers first sought to discover if there was an association between television and scholastic achievement. Many, having concluded that there was such an association, expanded their studies to search for the nature of the relationship. A number of theories attempt to explain and account for the often conflicting and confusing results of studies.

11.4.2.1. Frameworks for Theory. Hornik (1981) suggested a number of hypotheses for the relationship between television viewing and achievement. Television may (a) replace study time, (b) create expectation for fast-paced activities, (c) stimulate interest in school-related topics, (d) teach the same content as schools, (e) develop cognitive skills that may reinforce or conflict with reading skills, and (f) provide information concerning behaviors. Except for the first hypothesis, Reinking and Wu (1990), in their meta-analysis of studies examining television and reading achievement, found little research systematically investigating Hornik's theories.

Beentjes and Van der Voort (1988) grouped potential theories by impact. The facilitation hypothesis asserts a positive association, while the inhibition hypothesis asserts a negative association, and the no-effect hypothesis asserts no association. They found the most support for the inhibition hypothesis but noted that heavy viewers, socially advantaged children, and intelligent children are most vulnerable to the negative impact of television.

In her book *Literacy in the Television Age,* Neuman (1991) examined four prevailing perspectives of the television/achievement relationship: the displacement theory,* the information-processing theory, the short-term gratifications theory, and the interest stimulation theory. Her analysis of the evidence supporting and refuting each of these hypotheses is one of the most accessible and comprehensive to date. She also includes practical suggestions to help parents and teachers delineate situations where television can be beneficial for scholastic achievement and literacy development. Through Neuman's framework, we can examine the body of literature on the association between television viewing and scholastic achievement.

11.4.2.2. Displacement Theory. The displacement theory emerged in the late 1950s out of studies demonstrating that children watch many hours of television weekly. The displacement hypothesis* has been proposed by many theorists and critics to explain the effect of television viewing on other activities. This hypothesis states that "television influences both learning and social behavior by displacing such activities as reading, family interaction, and social play with peers" (Huston et al., 1992, p. 82). Since children are not spending those hours doing something else, television is displacing other activities. Theorists suggested that the negative relationship sometimes found between television

and achievement occurs because the activities being replaced are those that would enhance school performance (Williams, 1986). This theory is the most consistently present construct in achievement research.

Research supports the displacement hypothesis to some extent. The functional displacement hypothesis* holds that one medium will displace another when it performs some of the functions of the displaced medium (Himmelweit, Oppenheim & Vince, 1958, cited in Comstock & Paik, 1991). Therefore, television does displace other activities, but mostly similar activities such as use of other media (Huston et al., 1992). "Moreover, when children watch television together, their play is less active—that is, they are less talkative, less physically active, and less aggressive than during play without television" (Gadberry, 1974, cited in Huston et al., 1992, p. 86).

Trend studies, which analyze the change in scholastic (reading) achievement over the decades of television's diffusion into everyday life (Stedman & Kaestle, 1987; M. Winn, 1985), have generally supported the displacement theory. Their results provided weak evidence of the existence of a negative television/achievement relationship, since societal changes during the time periods studied include much more than the advent of television.

Another type of longitudinal research design uses surveys to measure a link between television viewing and achievement using measures of the same subjects' media use and achievement (Gaddy, 1986; Gortmaker, Salter, Walker & Dietz, 1990; Ritchie, Price & Roberts, 1987). Gaddy's analysis of 5,074 high school students during their sophomore and their senior years attempted to ascertain whether television viewing was impacting achievement by replacing more enriching activities. He found no significant correlations when other variables were controlled. Nor did television viewing rates predict 2-year reading-skill changes. Gaddy hypothesized that other researchers have found significant results due to their failure to consider important intervening variables.

The displacement theory received more rigorous support from quasi-experimental studies typified by the analysis of the impact of television's introduction into a community or the comparison of children in households with and without a television set (Greenstein, 1954; Hornik, 1978). Corteen and Williams's 1986 study of three British Columbia communities, one without television (Notel), one with a single television channel (Unitel), and one with multiple channels (Multitel), is a classic example of this design. In the first phase, the 217 children in the communities attending grades 2, 3, and 8 were tested for reading fluency before Notel received television transmissions. Two years later, when the children were in grades 4, 5, and 10, they were retested. In phase 2, 206 new second-, third-, and eighth-graders were tested. In a connected data-gathering activity, a reading assessment of vocabulary and comprehension was administered to students in grades 1 through 7 in all three communities 6 months after television came to Notel.

The cross-sectional and longitudinal analyses of these data sets produced very complex findings: (a) Over the 2 years, those Notel children who started the study in second and third grades showed gains in reading fluency that were not significantly different from their Unitel and Multitel counterparts; (b) the eighth-graders showed less progress if they lived in Notel; (c) phase 1 second- and third-graders had higher fluency scores than phase 2 second- and third-graders; and (d) Notel's second- and third-grade scores were higher than those in Unitel and Multitel on the assessment of reading comprehension and vocabulary.

Corteen and Williams's somewhat conflicting results also epitomize the difficulty and complexity of studies of television effects. Although not unequivocal, as a whole their data suggested that television may hinder the development in reading skills for children at certain ages (Beentjes & Van der Voort, 1988).

A number of correlational studies, which focused on the same two variables—amount of time spent watching television and cognitive development as measured by reading achievement test scores—have also found support for the displacement theory. However, the data, on the whole, from such simple correlational studies have been shown to be conflicting, finding negative, positive, or no significant relationship between television viewing and reading achievement (Bossing & Burgess, 1984; Quisenberry & Klasek, 1976; Zuckerman et al., 1980). Further analysis of more recent studies with larger sample sizes suggests that the relationship is likely to be curvilinear rather than linear, with achievement rising with light television watching (1 to 2 hours per day), but falling progressively with heavier viewing (Anderson et al., 1986; Fetler, 1984; Searls et al., 1985).

This curvilinear view of the negative association between television and achievement has been addressed by researchers using meta-analysis, a technique that attempts to discover trends through arithmetic aggregation of a number of studies. A key study of this type is Williams, Haertel, Haertel, and Walberg's 1982 analysis of 23 studies that examined the relationship between scholastic achievement and television viewing. The results of these meta-analyses were the basis for Comstock and Paik's discussion of scholastic achievement (1991). The five large-scale studies that became their major sources include:

1. The 1980 California Assessment Program (including Fetler & Carlson, 1982) that measured 282,000 sixth-graders and 227,000 twelfth-graders for mathematics, reading, and writing achievement, and for television viewing.
2. The 1980 High School and Beyond study (Keith, Reimers, Fehrman, Pottebaum & Aubey, 1986) that compared 28,000 high school seniors' television viewing in terms of achievement scores in mathematics and reading.
3. The 1983–1984 National Assessment of Educational Progress data (Anderson, Mead & Sullivan, 1988) that described the relationship between viewing and reading for 100,000 fourth-, eighth- and eleventh-graders across 30 states.

4. Neuman's synthesis of eight state reading assessments that included measures of attitudes toward television representing nearly 1 million students from fourth-through twelfth-grades (1988).
5. Gaddy's data from several thousand students who were studied during their sophomore and senior years (1986). A small average negative effect was obtained for the relationship between television and scholastic achievement by Williams and his associates. Interestingly, effects were slightly positive for lighter viewers (up to 10 hours weekly) and grew increasingly negative as students' viewed more television.

Comstock and Paik (1991) noted that for students who are not fluent in English, the opposite is true, with some important qualifications: (a) Family socioeconomic status has a stronger negative correlation with achievement than the negative correlation between television viewing and achievement; (b) as socioeconomic status rises, the inverse association between amount of television viewed and achievement increases; (c) this relationship is stronger for older students; and (d) for low-socioeconomic-status families there is only a slight rise in achievement associated with television viewing, especially for younger students.

A number of researchers augmented our understanding of the characteristics of television's impact on scholastic achievement by controlling for variables suspected of intervening (Anderson, Mead & Sullivan, 1988; Fetler & Carlson, 1982; Keith, Reimers, Fehrmann, Pottebaum & Aubey, 1986; Morgan, 1982; Morgan & Gross, 1980; Neuman, 1988; Potter, 1987; Ridley-Johnson, Cooper & Chance, 1982). In these studies, one or more third variables, often intelligence and socioeconomic status, are controlled. As a result, the relationship measured between achievement and television is not confounded by the third variable. For instance, controlling for intelligence tends to reduce the degree of negative association. However, the relationship remains intact for certain viewers and some content, such as adventure or entertainment programs (Beentjes & Van der Voort, 1988). Data from this form of research permit more precise analysis of variables that are involved in the complex interaction of television watching and scholastic achievement.

Neuman argued that the two pieces of evidence needed to validate the displacement theory, proof that other activities are being replaced and a demonstration that those activities are more beneficial to scholastic achievement than television, have not been adequately established in the literature (Neuman, 1991). Neither leisure reading at home nor homework activities have been consistently found to be displaced by television. Instead, functionally equivalent media activities such as movies or radio seem to be affected by television viewing (Neuman, 1991). Since other activities have not been proved to be more beneficial than television, Neuman finds the displacement theory unsubstantiated. The body of literature on achievement supports the need for a much more complex and sophisticated model than the simplistic one represented by pure displacement theory. Another trend in achievement research identified by Neuman is information-processing theory that examines the ways television's symbol system impacts mental processing. This theory was discussed in the section on message design and cognitive processing.

11.4.2.3. Short-Term Gratification Theory. Short-term gratification theory deals primarily with affective and motivational components of the learner: enthusiasm, perseverance, and concentration. Proponents of this theory, many of whom are teachers, believe that television's ability to entertain a passive viewer has "fundamentally changed children's expectations toward learning, creating a generation of apathetic spectators who are unable to pursue long-term goals" (Neuman, 1991, p. 105). They argue that students have come to believe that all activities should be as effortless as watching television and that students' attention spans are shorter due to such fast-paced programming as *Sesame Street* (Singer & Singer, 1983). This issue was presented in the section on mental processing and will be discussed in the section on "Programming and Utilization."

Writers in the 1970s claimed that the children's program *Sesame Street* had a number of undesirable unintended effects, namely, increased hyperactivity (Halpern, 1975) and reinforced passivity (Winn, 1977), especially when compared to its slower-paced competition *Mister Rogers' Neighborhood* (Tower, Singer, Singer & Biggs, 1979, cited in Neuman, 1991). These unintended effects gave credence to the short-term gratification theory and the general bias against the television medium. However, further investigations shed doubt on the accuracy of these conclusions (Anderson, Levin & Lorch, 1977; Neuman, 1991) by discovering that individual differences, family-viewing context, and other intervening variables were interacting within the association between television and achievement.

Salomon's theory of amount of invested mental effort (AIME*) suggested that children approach television as an "easy" source of information and, therefore, tend not to expend much mental effort to understand, process, and remember the information in television programs (Salomon, 1983, 1984). He explained that this caused most to perform below their capabilities unless they were specifically directed or encouraged to learn from the source. He further speculated that this "effort-free" experience became the expectation for other sources of information as well.

Gaddy's (1986) theory of diminishing challenge concurred with the concept that as children grow older they find television less cognitively challenging; thus, they need less effort to understand the information. Typical teenagers will spend less time watching television. Gaddy concluded that those who continue to watch at high levels are therefore spending an inordinate amount of time in cognitive "laziness."

11.4.2.4. Interest Stimulation Theory. The fourth trend in achievement research discussed by Neuman is the interest stimulation theory. This hypothesis suggests that television can potentially spark a student's interest in or imagination about a topic, fostering learning and creativity.

Examples of television's initiating interest, as demonstrated by increased reading and study around a topic, can be taken from most of our lives. For instance, after the broadcast of the miniseries *Roots,* Fairchild, Stockard, and Bowman (1986) reported that 37% of those sampled indicated increased interest and knowledge about issues of slavery. Similarly, Hornik (1981) has shown that adult book sales will boom after a special program airs on television. Morgan (1980) found that children who watch more television when they are younger are likely to read more when they are older. While this phenomenon has been measured, the arousal of interest and generation of incidental knowledge about subjects broadcast on television has been described as fleeting (Comstock & Paik, 1991; Leibert & Sprafkin, 1988; Neuman, 1991).

Neuman (1991) summarized three reasons to account for the ephemeral nature of incidental learning from ordinary entertainment viewing. First, most people who casually view television lack the intention to learn. Therefore, they do not engage in active cognitive processing of the material. Second, the redundancy of plot and character and the low intellectual level in most television programming increases the likelihood that any information intended for learning was previously mastered. Finally, unless the material has direct relevance to the viewer, any incidental information learned is quickly forgotten due to lack of reinforcement and practice. She suggests a series of concomitant strategies of parental and teacher mediation that can activate, broaden, and focus television's potential to stimulate interest in school-related topics under natural home-viewing conditions (Neuman, 1991).

11.4.2.5. Theories Related to Imagination. The idea of television as a stimulator of imagination and creativity has been an area of debate among scholars and researchers. Admittedly, studying the imagination is a difficult prospect at best. Techniques to do so have ranged from observations and self-reports to imagination tests using inkblots or inventories to teacher and parental descriptions. In his work *Art, Mind and Brain: A Cognitive Approach to Creativity* (1982), Howard Gardner recounts observations and research that support the idea that television is a rich medium for imaginative activity. "The child's imagination scoops up these figures from the television screen and then, in its mysterious ways, fashions the drawings and stories of his own fantasy world" (p. 254). He purports that television stimulates the sensory imagination of the young much more successfully than it generates the abstract, conceptual lines of thought important to older viewers' creativity.

Other researchers have found evidence of television's stimulation of imaginative play. Alexander, Ryan, and Munoz (1984) found brothers who used television-generated conversation to initiate fantasy play. James and McCain (1982) recorded children's play at a daycare center and observed that many games created by those children were taken from television characters and plots. They noted that the themes occurring in such television-activated play were similar to those in play not stimulated by television. Commercials in particular have been demonstrated in certain circumstances to contribute to imaginative activity (Greer, Potts, Wright & Huston, 1982; Reid & Frazer, 1980.)

A considerable amount of research in the area of television's impact on the imagination of the viewer, particularly that of children, has been conducted by Jerome and Dorothy Singer and various associates. They have concluded that television can present general information, models for behavior, themes, stories, and real and make-believe characters who are incorporated into creative play (Singer & Singer, 1981, 1986). This process is not guaranteed, nor is it always positive. Rather, a pattern emerges of a conditional association between television and developing imagination.

The first condition is the type of programming viewed. A number of studies have linked high-violence action adventure programs to decreased imagination, and low-violence situation comedies or informative programs with increased imagination (Huston-Stein, Fox, Greer, Watkins & Whitaker, 1981; J. Singer & Singer, 1981; Singer, Singer & Rapaczynski, 1984; Zuckerman, Singer & Singer, 1980). Singer and Singer have also argued that the pacing of television can impact the amount of imaginative play, with slower, carefully designed programs, such as *Mister Rogers' Neighborhood,* generating conditions for optimal creative thought and play (Singer & Singer, 1983). Dorothy Singer reported two studies on the effect of *Sesame Street* and *Mister Rogers' Neighborhood* on children's imagination (Friedrich & Stein, 1975, cited in Singer, 1978; Tower, Singer, Singer & Biggs, 1978). *Mister Rogers' Neighborhood* produced a significant increase in imagination. *Sesame Street* did not.

The type of programming watched may also affect the nature of fantasy activities. Rosenfeld, Huesmann, Eron, and Torney-Purta (1982) used J. Singer and Antrobus's (1972) Imaginal Processes Inventory to categorize types of fantasy. They found three types: (a) fanciful play around fairy tales and implausible events, (b) active play around heroes and achievement, and (c) aggressive negative play around fighting, killing, and being hurt. Children, chiefly boys, who demonstrated aggressive negative fantasy were those who tended to watch violent action adventure programs regularly (Singer & Singer, 1983). McIlwraith and Schallow (1982, 1983) and Schallow and McIlwraith (1986, 1987) investigated various media effects on imaginativeness in children and undergraduates and found connections between programming genre and type of imaginative thinking. For instance, pleasant, constructive daydreams came from watching drama, situation comedies, or general entertainment programs.

The second condition of television's association with imagination is the amount of time spent viewing television. Heavy viewers have been shown to be less imaginative (Peterson, Peterson & Carroll, 1987; Singer & Singer, 1986; Singer, Singer & Rapaczynski, 1984). Children who watch television many hours weekly tend to also exhibit traits within their fantasies similar to those who watch

action adventure programs. This is evidenced by the fact that they tend to be aggressive and violent in their play (Singer & Singer, 1983).

The final condition within the television and imagination association is that of mediation or family viewing context. Singer, Singer, and Rapaczynski's (1984) study found parental attitudes* and values about imagination to be a stronger indicator of child imaginativeness than type or amount of television viewing. D. Singer and Singer's (1981) year-long examination of 200 preschoolers within three treatment groups found that the greatest gains in imaginativeness were associated with adult mediation. The first group had television exposure and teacher-directed lesson plans designed around 2- to 3-minute televised segments intended to improve the child's cognitive, social, and imaginative skills. The second group received the specialized lesson plans without television exposure. The final group received the ordinary school curriculum. The results from the first group showed gains in imagination and other social skills such as leadership and cooperation.

Though the results of these studies examining television's effects on imagination are not universal, they reveal a pattern of conditional benefit. Children who are exposed to a limited amount of television, who watch carefully selected programs in terms of content and pacing, and who engage in conversations with adults who mediate that exposure are likely to use their television experience as a springboard to positive, creative, and imaginative activities.

11.4.2.6. Future Directions for Theory. Neuman (1991) concluded that we need a conceptual model to account for (a) the many uses for television, (b) the "spirited interplay" between various media including television, (see 8.4), and (c) the impact of television on scholastic achievement. The writings of Comstock and Paik (1991), Beentjes and Van der Voort (1988), and Reinking and Wu (1990) support the need for a conceptual model that links research variables. The difficulty researchers have encountered in finding consistent, definitive evidence about the magnitude and shape of an association and a functional description of such an association between television viewing and scholastic achievement may be due to the presence of negative bias toward television. Additionally, there is the aforementioned difficulty of the lack of a conceptual model that adequately explains the complex interactions of variables such as age, socioeconomic status, family viewing context, and intelligence.

11.4.3 Methodological Concerns

While many early studies found significant negative correlations between television viewing and achievement, reviewers (Beentjes & Van der Voort, 1988; Hornik, 1981; Neuman, 1991; Reinking & Wu, 1990) note that severe flaws in design shed doubt on the veracity of those early findings. These include: (a) small sample size, (b) lack of control for intervening variables, (c) less-powerful analysis techniques, (d) relative inattention to the content of programming, and (e) unreliable self-reporting instruments, whereas subsequent studies with larger sample sizes, better controls, and more rigorous analysis have continued to discover consistently significant relationships between television viewing and scholastic achievement (Anderson et al., 1986; Fetler & Carlson, 1982; Gaddy, 1986; Keith et al., 1986; Neuman, 1988).

Ritchie, Price, and Roberts (1987) postulated that television may have the most profound impact during the preschool years. Another concern they raise is the question of long-term exposure to the effects of television. This is a dilemma for researchers which can be addressed by more rigorous longitudinal studies.

Neuman (1991) itemized additional concerns about the television and achievement literature: (a) The majority of the research lacks a driving theory; (b) many studies purport to be qualitative but are actually anecdotal; (c) scholastic achievement has been narrowly defined and measured, focusing on reading achievement scores; and (d) due to an assumption that print is the intellectually superior medium, a negative bias pervades the literature.

11.4.4 Intervening Variables

A brief look at the variables that have been studied for their potential differential effects throughout the research will help illustrate the complexity of the interaction between the individual and television in terms of subsequent scholastic achievement.

11.4.4.1. Age. As with many other variables, there is conflicting evidence regarding how the variable of age affects scholastic achievement. The literature suggests that the negative correlation between television viewing and achievement is stronger for older students, which implies that older students may replace study time with television viewing, while younger children are monitored more closely by parents with regard to studying (Anderson et al., 1986; Neuman 1988; Roberts, Bachen, Hornby & Hernandez-Ramos, 1984; Searls, Mead & Ward, 1985).

11.4.4.2. Gender. Studies comparing the effects of television viewing on the scholastic achievement of boys and girls have produced conflicting findings. Morgan and Gross (1980) found a negative relationship for boys between television viewing and scholastic achievement. In contrast, Williams, Haertel, Haertel, and Walberg's (1982) meta-analysis identified a negative relationship for girls.

11.4.4.3. Intelligence. Morgan (1982) and Morgan and Gross (1980) found that the negative association between television and achievement was strongest for children of higher abilities. They found no significant effect for low- and medium-levels of intelligence. As with older children, television may have a greater impact on highly intelligent students because it displaces more cognitively stimulating activities (Beentjes & Van der Voort, 1988).

11.4.4.4. Home-Viewing Environment. Researchers have found that television-watching and leisure-reading patterns of children often reflect those of their parents (Morgan, 1982; Neuman, 1986). Many factors of the home environment are statistically significant indicators of television watching, especially for younger children (Roberts et al., 1984). Behavioral patterns of leisure reading and television watching seem to persist into adulthood (Reinking & Wu, 1990; Ritchie et al., 1987).

11.4.4.5. Reading Skills. Research on various levels of reading skill is inconclusive, due mainly to the habit of measuring reading skill with one overall score (Beenjes & Van der Voort, 1988). Corteen and Williams (1986) found a connection to comprehension, but not vocabulary, in their study of three Canadian towns.

11.4.4.6. Socioeconomic Status. Although heavy viewers universally have lower scholastic achievement, for light and moderate viewers socioeconomic status seems to have a place in the interaction. Contrary to high socioeconomic-status children who demonstrate a negative correlation, low socioeconomic-status children can improve achievement with television viewing (Anderson et al., 1986; Fetler, 1984; Searls et al., 1985). Combined with findings on the effect of intelligence, many scholars have reached a conclusion that supports the displacement theory in specific situations.

> The pattern invites a proposition: television viewing is inversely related to achievement when it displaces an intellectually and experientially richer environment, and it is positively related when it supplies such an environment (Comstock & Paik, 1987, p. 27).

11.4.4.7. Type of Programming Watched. Purely entertaining television programming such as cartoons (see 11.7.1.3), situation comedies, and adventure programs (see 11.5.5.2) have a negative correlation with school achievement (Neuman, 1981; Zuckerman, Singer & Singer, 1980). News programs (see 11.7.3) and other highly informative shows, on the other hand, have a positive relationship to achievement (Potter, 1987).

11.4.4.8. Various Levels of Viewing Time. Many studies have found different levels of viewing time (see 11.5.5.1) to be an important element in television's relationship to achievement (Anderson et al., 1986; Fetler, 1984; Neuman, 1988; Potter, 1987; Searls et al., 1985). In their discussion of Williams et al. (1982), Comstock and Paik concluded that there is a good possibility of curvilinearity at the intermediate and primary grades, especially for households of lower socioeconomic status or using English as a second language (1987, 1991). For these groups, television can have a beneficial effect at moderate levels of viewing.

One of the problems of interpreting studies of the effect of viewing time on achievement is that the content or context of that viewing time is often ignored, yet may have an effect. For example, in the early evaluations of *Sesame Street,* viewing time was positively correlated with learning outcomes when it was measured as an approximation of "time on task." If a more undifferentiated measure of viewing time—one unconnected with the content of sequences or programs—had been used, the findings may have been different. What is the relationship of intentional- and incidental-learning conditions to the interaction of viewing time and achievement? Is it important to distinguish between viewing as a primary activity and viewing as a secondary activity? Questions such as these need to be raised when researchers study the interaction of viewing time and achievement.

11.4.5 Summary and Recommendations

Few researchers today doubt that there is a relationship between television viewing and scholastic achievement. The debate centers instead around the nature of that association. Regardless of the seeming disparity of results, some patterns are emerging:

1. Heavy television viewers of all intellectual abilities and home environments tend to have lower scholastic achievement and demonstrate less imaginativeness when compared to their lighter-viewing peers. This effect is especially severe among students with high IQs and otherwise stimulating home environments.
2. For light-to-moderate viewers, a number of intervening variables come into play: age, ability, socioeconomic status, home-viewing environment, and type of programming watched. It has been shown that light television viewing may increase scholastic performance for children of lower abilities and lower socioeconomic status.
3. Within certain stages of intellectual and emotional development, television viewing can have a greater impact on achievement.
4. Parental attitudes and viewing patterns* are strong indicators of the child's current and future television viewing and its effect on scholastic achievement.
5. Home-viewing environment and adult mediation of viewed material are significantly related to the incidental and intentional learning and imaginative play that comes from television viewing.

There has been a call by many for television to cease being seen as intrinsically bad or good (Gomez, 1986; Hatt, 1982; Neuman, 1991; Reinking & Wu, 1990). The perception of television as detrimental has colored the attitudes of researchers and educators alike, Jankowski said:

> It is a source of constant amazement to me that the television set, an inert, immobile appliance that does not eat, drink, or smoke, buy or sell anything, can't vote, doesn't have a job, can't think, can't turn itself on or off, and is used only at our option, can be seen as the cause of so much of society's ills by so many people in education (cited in Neuman, 1991, p. 195).

The last decade of research has shown that the relationship of television viewing to scholastic achievement is a complex proposition with many interacting variables, not just a simple, negative relationship. The impact of this medium on achievement remains far from clear. However, research continues to improve our understanding of how each individual may be influenced by television.

Future research should seek to avoid these obvious problems while building on the body of literature available. Emphasis on mulitvariate relationships through correlation and on meta-analyses seems the most direct route to increasing our understanding of the nature of the television/achievement relationship.

11.5 FAMILY-VIEWING CONTEXT

By the late 1970s, two reviews of research on child development had concluded that television was more than a communicator of content because it organized and modified the home environment (Atman & Wohlwill, 1978; Majoriebanks, 1979). Conversely, it was known that the home environment organized and modified television viewing. For example, Frazer (1976) found that the family routine established the viewing habits* of preschoolers, not vice versa. Today we know that demographic differences, such as ethnicity (Tangney & Feshbach, 1988) and individual differences, such as genetics (Plomin, Corley, DeFries & Fulker, 1990), also influence the family-viewing context. This section deals with variables that mediate the effects of television in the home setting, including the home environment, coviewing, and viewing habits. For "television viewing occurs in an environmental context that influences what and when viewing occurs, as well as the ways in which viewers interpret what they see" (Huston et al., 1992, p. 98).

11.5.1 Variables That Mediate

The variables in the family context for television viewing can be grouped into three categories: (a) the environment, which encompasses the number and placement of sets, the toys and other media available, options for other activities, rules for viewing, and parental attitudes and style; (b) coviewing, which includes the nature and frequency of interactions, the effect of attitudes, and the effect of age and roles; and (c) viewing habits, which are based on variables such as amount of viewing, viewing patterns or preferences, and audience involvement.* These variables interact to create a social environment that mediates the effects of viewing.

Mediating variables can be separated into two types of variables: direct and indirect. Direct mediating variables are those that can be controlled, such as the situation or habits. Indirect mediating variables are those that are fixed, such as educational or socioeconomic level.

The research on television as a socializing agent is extensive and will be discussed later in this chapter. Although research on family context abounds, many findings are contradictory or inconclusive. Nevertheless, there is enough research to suggest some important interactions.

One approach to visualizing the relationship between program variables (e.g., formal features, content), context variables (e.g., environment, habits, coviewing), and outcome variables (e.g., attention, comprehension, attitudes) was presented by Seels in 1982 (see Fig. 11-2).

Another approach to conceptualizing visually the relationship of some of these mediating variables to exposure and outcomes was presented by Carolyn A. Stroman (1991) in Figure 11–3, which appeared in the *Journal of Negro Education.*

11.5.2 Theoretical Assumptions

At the level of operational investigation of these variables, assumptions are made that affect the questions researched, methodologies used, and interpretation of findings. One such issue is how television viewing should be defined. As discussed in the message design and cognitive-processing section, classic studies by Allen (1965) and Bechtel, Achelpohl, and Akers (1972) found there was a great deal of inattention while the television set was turned on. If viewing is defined as a low level of involvement, i.e., nothing more then being in the room when the television set is on, the result is estimates of the big role of television in children's lives. When estimates of viewing by 5-year-olds made from parent-kept viewing diaries and time-lapse video recordings are compared, diaries yield estimates of 40 hours a week and time-lapse video recordings analyzed for attentive viewing yield 3 1/2 hours a week (Anderson, Field, Collins, Lorch & Nathan, 1985, cited in Comstock & Paik, 1987). Viewing is often defined as "including entering and leaving the room while intermittently monitoring what is unfolding on the screen" (Comstock & Paik, 1991, p. 19).

On the other hand, current research on mental activities that occur during the television experience suggests that a great deal of mental activity can occur while viewing. Comstock and Paik (1991) suggest that a distinction be made between monitoring (paying attention to audio, visual, and social cues that indicate the desirability of attention to the screen) and viewing (paying attention to what is taking place on the screen).

The issue of whether the viewer is active or passive arises from differing conceptions of viewing and from the fact that research has established that the viewer can be either, depending on programming and the mediating variables. Comstock and Paik (1991) cite several classic and recent studies that established a high level of mental activity despite an often low level of involvement (Bryant, Zillmann & Brown, 1983; Huston & Wright, 1989; Krendl & Watkins, 1983; Krull, 1983; Lorch, Anderson & Levin, 1979; Meadowcroft & Reeves, 1989; Thorson, Reeves & Schleuder, 1985). As previously noted in the section on message design and cognitive processing, the notion of hypnotic watching of television has been largely discredited (Anderson & Lorch, 1983; Bryant & Anderson, 1983).

Three studies by Argenta, Stoneman, and Brody (1986), Wolf (1987), and Palmer (1986) reinforce this conclusion. Wolf and Palmer interviewed children about their viewing to determine interest, thoughtfulness, and insight. Their study, therefore, is susceptible to the biases of self-reporting. Argenta et al. analyzed the visual attention of preschoolers

to cartoons, *Sesame Street,* and situation comedies. They observed social interaction, viewing, and use of toys. With *Sesame Street* and situation comedies, attention was divided among social interaction, viewing, and toys. Only with cartoons did social interaction decrease. "The image of children mesmerized in front of the television set, forsaking social interaction and active involvement with their object environment, held true for only one type of programming, namely, cartoons" (Argenta et al., p. 370). Thus, findings will differ depending on how viewing is defined.

Another assumption is that incidental learning and intentional learning are separate during the television experience. Yet, if an adult reinforces or intervenes while coviewing a program for children, intentional learning will increase. And if a child learns indirectly through informative programming, incidental learning will increase. The nature of the television experience today, especially with cable and videocassette recorder (VCR) technology, may be that incidental and intentional learning happen concurrently and may even interact or reinforce each other. Coviewing with discussion may be a way to join incidental and intentional learning. In an article on "Family Contexts of Television," Leichter et al. (1985) point out that ways of representing and thinking about time may be learned from the television experience. Children can incidentally learn to recognize the hour or the day from the programming schedule. They can intentionally learn time concepts by watching *Mister Rogers' Neighborhood* and *Sesame Street.*

A methodological assumption underlying much research on the television viewing environment is the acceptability of self-reporting instruments and diaries. Although these techniques are valid, often they need to be compared with research results from other methodologies. This may be especially true in television research, because self-reporting techniques are used so extensively, particularly in studies on the family-viewing context.

11.5.3 The Television Viewing Environment

The television viewing environment is part of the television viewing system, which results in a television viewing experience. This section will next address several categories and subcategories of mediating variables starting with the viewing environment.

11.5.3.1. Number and Placement of Sets. Leichter and her colleagues (1985) discuss the temporal and spatial organization of the television viewing environment. According to Leichter et al., there are symbolic meanings associated with the placement of television sets in the home. In their discussion of the methodological approaches to the study of family environments, they stress the need "to obtain a detailed picture of the ways in which television is interwoven with the underlying organization of the family" (p. 31). They decided that ethnographic or naturalistic data gathering through a variety of observation techniques was best. Therefore, they used participant observation, interviewing, recording of specific behaviors, and video and audio recording of interactions. To gather data over a suffi-

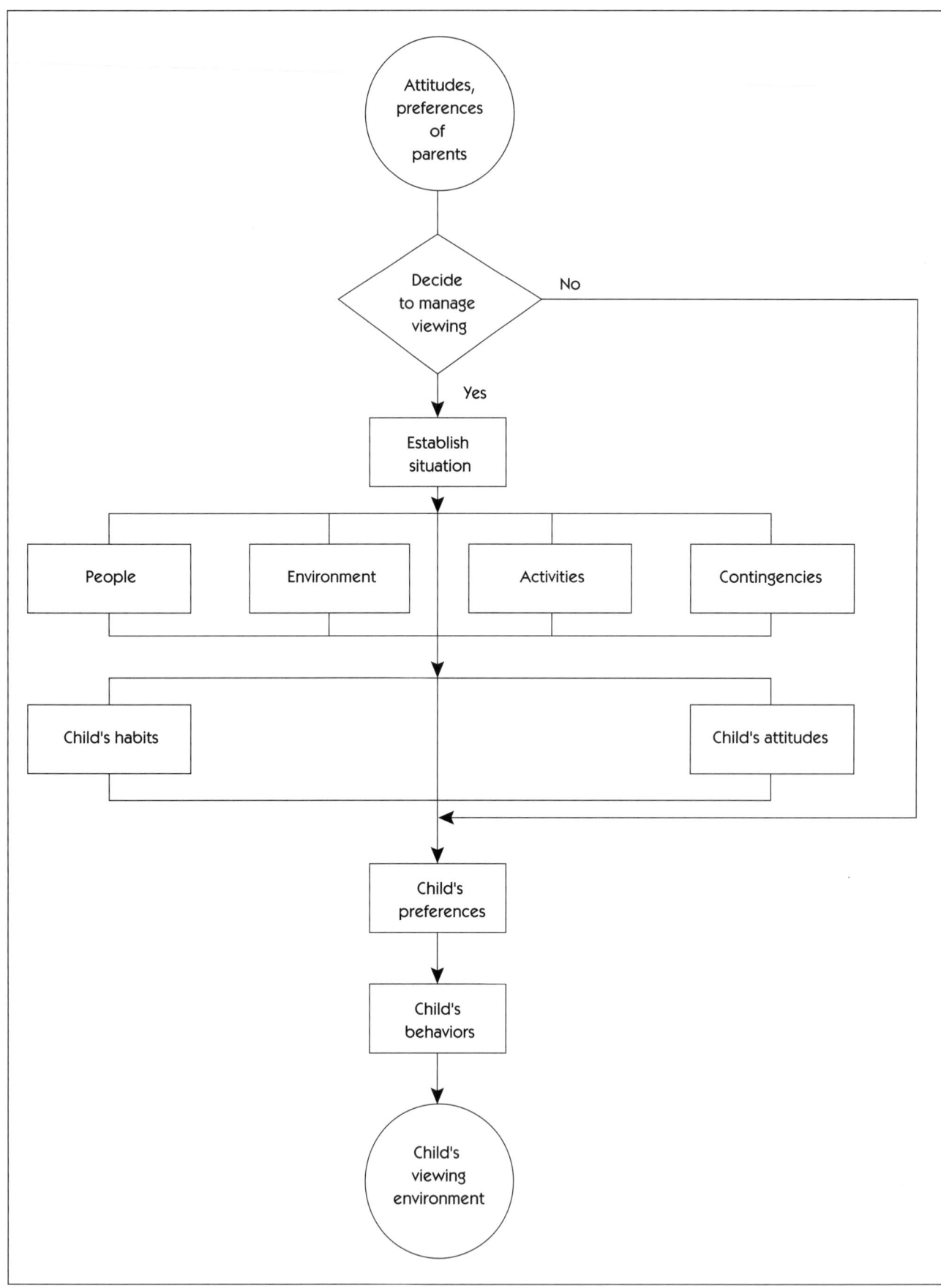

Figure 11-2.   Relationship among variables in the family-viewing context. (From Seels, 1982.)

cient time span, one observer moved in with the family. Leichter and her colleagues generated research questions through a study of three families followed by a study of ten families. They compared the data generated with a similar

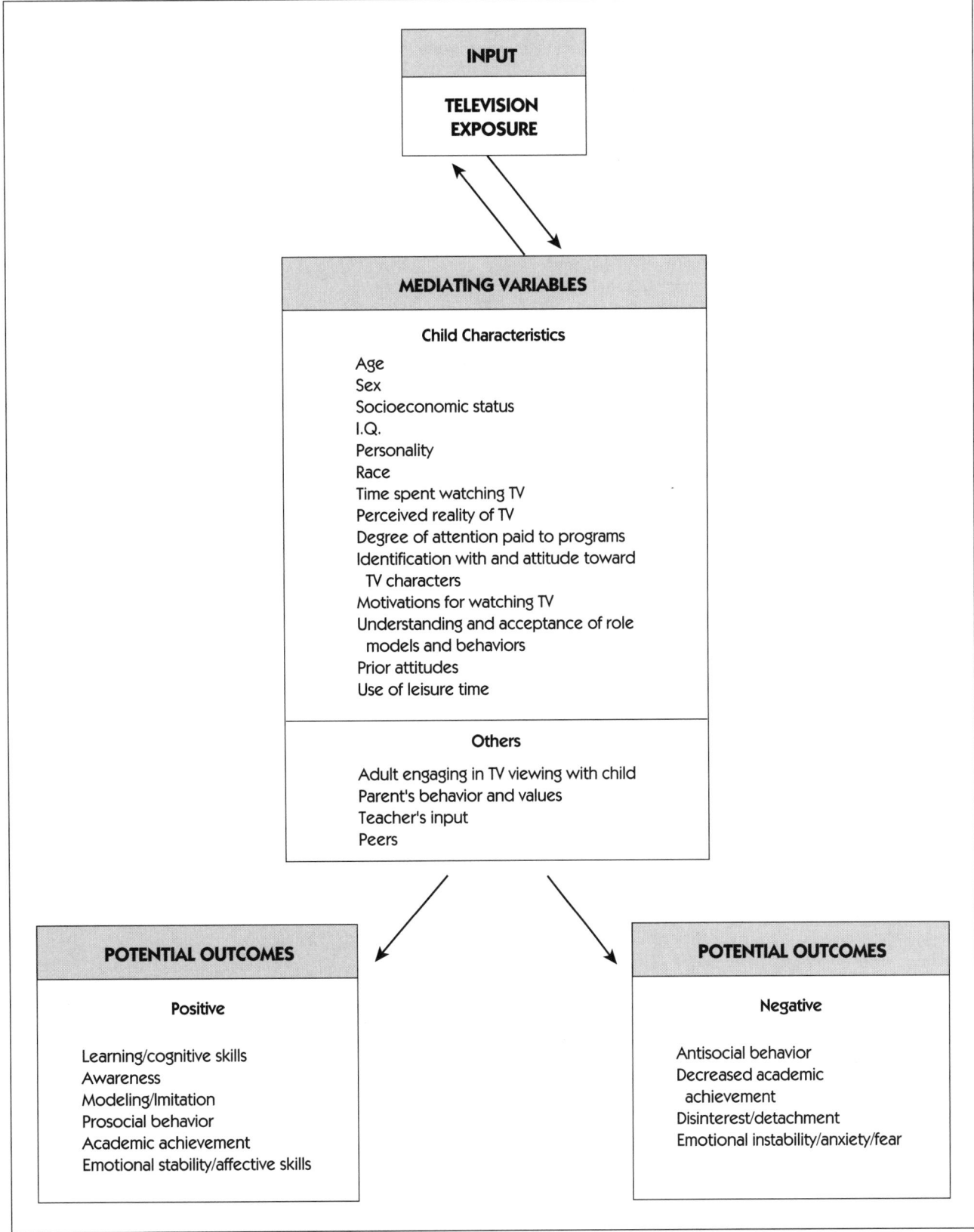

Figure 11-3. Hypothesized model for understanding television's socializing impact. (From Stroman, 1991.)

cross-cultural study done in Pakistan (Ahmed, 1983) and concluded that placement varies with the architecture of the home and with family perceptions. As a result, a set can be "fixed" or "static" in terms of its placement, just as individual position for viewing can be fixed or static. The area of placement can be close to traffic patterns or places of activity, or it can be set in out-of-the-way places reserved just for viewing. Where the set is placed may lead to conflict because of other activities.

Even though television is a "magnet," especially for young viewers, the physical design of the area where the set is placed can inhibit the amount of time spent viewing. This conclusion is supported by research on use of dormitory viewing areas in college (Preiser, 1970, cited in Ross, 1979). Young children engage in many other activities in the television area even if the television isn't in a desirable location for other activities (Rivlin, Wolfe & Beyda, 1973, cited in Ross, 1979).

Winn (1977) argues that the television should be put in an out-of-the-way area such as the basement in order to minimize its dominance. Others argue that the more centrally located the set, the more likely viewers will be influenced by other powerful variables such as coviewing.

One concept that could be used in research on placement is "household centrality."* Medrich et al. (1982, cited in Comstock & Paik, 1991) proposed that families can be classified on a dimension reflecting behavior and norms* that favor viewing. If there is high use by parents and children and there are few rules governing viewing, the household can be said to have "centrality" of television. Research is needed on the effect of placement of set(s) on centrality. Generally, if there is only one set, it is in a living or group recreational area. If there is a second set, it is usually placed in a bedroom (Leichter et al.,1985). The more central the location, the greater the likelihood that social interaction or coviewing will mediate the effects of television.

The majority of households in the United States have two or more sets, subscribe to cable, and own a VCR (Huston et al., 1992). Children in multiple-set homes tend to watch more television than those in single-set homes (Webster, Pearson & Webster, 1986). Christopher, Fabes, and Wilson (1989) found that parents who owned one television set tended to exert more control over their children's viewing than did parents owning multiple sets. They also found that parents who owned three or more sets were more positive about their children's watching television and spent twice as much time watching as those with fewer sets. Webster et al. (1986) cautioned that multiple sets could lead to decreased parent-child interactions.

Since additional sets are used to resolve conflicts over program choices, children may view more since they have more control over their own viewing. In sum, one obvious guideline is that young children should not have access to more sets than parents can monitor. The experience of resolving conflicts over who watches what can provide valuable lessons in sharing.

11.5.3.2. Availability of Toys. Children develop strategies for viewing, including strategies that allow for competing activities, such as playing with dolls (Levin & Anderson, 1976). Rapid television pacing has no effect on the number of toys used during a play period (Anderson, Levin & Lorch, 1977). Family rules govern the placement and use of toys during viewing. Some families forbid toys in the television room; others permit toys to be available during viewing (Leichter et al., 1985). Where the set is placed may affect the use of toys during viewing. If the set is in the living room where no toys are permitted, the use of toys as distractors or reinforcers during viewing will be less than if the set is in the playroom or recreation room where toys and games are available.

The availability of toys may distract young children from the television set. In a study by Lorch, Anderson, and Levin (1979), when attractive toys were available to 5-year-olds, attention to *Sesame Street* dropped from 87% to 44%. One of the methods employed in the earliest research on *Sesame Street* was to conduct formative evaluation by having children watch a sequence while seated at a table filled with toys. If the children played with the toys rather than watching, the sequence was deemed ineffective in holding attention. Among these now classic studies were studies by Lesser in 1972 and 1974, and by Lorch and his colleagues in the late 1970s. When Lorch, Anderson, and Levin (1979) showed a version of *Sesame Street* to two groups, one group of children surrounded by toys and one group with no toys in the environment, the children in the group without toys attended twice as much. However, there was no difference between the groups in comprehension of television content. Thus, toys may be seen as positive elements of the viewing environment in that they can reinforce viewing and provide a basis for interaction with others about television and other topics. On the other hand, toys can decrease attention, but this phenomenon does not seem to affect cognitive learning.

It is commonly believed that children learn about life through forms of play and social interaction (D. Winn, 1985). Although television can model prosocial forms of interaction, the time spent watching television results in less time for play, practice, and real interactions with other children or family members.

> Television has no sign on it: "Trespassers will be prosecuted." Television is living made easy for our children. It is the shortest cut yet devised, the most accessible back door to the grown-up world. Television is never too busy to talk to our children. Television plays with them, shares its work with them. Television wants their attention, needs it, goes to any length to get it (Shayon, 1950, p. 9).

It is likely that children watching television in an environment rich with toys and the opportunity for other activities will not be as mesmerized by television programming. Opportunities for elaboration, interaction, and creativity that extend the effect of the television stimulus should be richer in such an environment. However, research is not available at this time to support such suppositions.

11.5.3.3. Relationship to Other Activities. Television impacts other activities, and other activities impact television. A study on television's impact conducted by Johnson in 1967 (cited in Liebert & Sprafkin, 1988) showed that of those surveyed, 60% changed their sleep patterns, 55% altered meal times, and 78% used television as an electronic babysitter. Liebert and Sprafkin also cite a study by Robinson in 1972 that showed reductions in sleep, social gatherings away from home, leisure activities, conversation, household care, and newspaper reading.

Television is frequently secondary to other activities, or there is frequently another activity even when viewing is primary (Comstock, Chaffee, Katzman, McCombs & Roberts, 1978). Krugman and Johnson (1991) report that compared to traditional programming, VCR movie rental is associated with less time spent on other activities.

Parental mediation and the incorporation of other activities as adjuncts to the viewing process may be beneficial for children. Friedrich and Stein (1975) concluded that when adults provide discussion after viewing or read storybooks that summarize important concepts conveyed in programming, children increase their understanding of concepts and are able to generalize them to new situations better than children not provided with summaries. Singer, Singer, and Zuckerman (1981) reached the same conclusion when they had teachers lead discussions following viewing of prosocial programs.

Some families engage in orienting activities prior to viewing that lead to awareness of program options. According to Perse (1990), heavy viewers tend to use television guides and newspaper listings to select programs. They reevaluate during exposure by grazing* (quickly sampling a variety of programs using zapping* techniques with remote controls) while they are viewing.

Some studies have shown that television viewing reduces time devoted to other activities (Murray & Kippax, 1978; Williams, 1986). Murray and Kippax collected data from three towns in Australia: a no-television town, a low-television town, and a high-television town. The low-television town was defined as one receiving television for only 1 year, and the high as one receiving television for 5 years. Comparisons between the no-television town and the low-television town showed a marked decrease in other activities for all age levels when television was available. Television led to a restructuring of children's time use (Murray & Kippax, 1978; Himmelweit, Oppenheim & Vince, 1958, cited in Comstock & Paik, 1994). The displacement theory discussed in the section on school achievement attempts to explain the relationship of other activities to television viewing in the family context.

11.5.3.4. Rules for Viewing. The National Center for Educational Statistics conducted the National Education Longitudinal Study (NELS) of 1988. The study surveyed 25,000 eighth-graders, their parents, principals, and teachers.

A follow-up study was undertaken in 1990 when the same students were tenth-graders. Results of these surveys are given in two reports (National Center for Education Statistics, 1991; Office of Educational Research and Improvement, 1991). According to these reports, "69% of parents reported monitoring their eighth-grader's television viewing, 62% limited television viewing on school nights, and 84% restricted early or late viewing" (National Center for Educational Statistics, 1992, p. 1). These statistics are not as reassuring as one would hope.

> Two-thirds of the parents reported they *did* enforce rules limiting television viewing, while the same number of students reported their parents *did not* limit their television viewing. In fact, these eighth-graders spent almost 4 times as much time watching television each week as they did doing their homework (Office of Educational Research and Improvement, Fall 1991, p. 5).

Generally, research does not support the myth that children watch more television because their parents are absent. Even parents who are present rarely restrict children's viewing. The older the child, the less influence the parents have (Pearl, 1982). This pattern is disturbing in light of evidence that heavy viewers (4 hours a day or more) do less well in school and have fewer hobbies and friends (Huston et al., 1992). Gadberry (1980) did an experimental study in which parents restricted 6-year-olds to about half their normal viewing amount. When compared with a control group whose viewing was not restricted, the treatment group improved in cognitive performance and time spent on reading.

Parents who are selective viewers are more likely to encourage or restrict viewing and to watch with their children. Parents who believe television is a positive influence watch more television with children (Dorr et al., 1989). The least-effective position for parents to take is a laissez-faire one, because children whose parents neither regulate or encourage viewing watch more adult entertainment television, usually without an adult present. This puts children more at risk from the negative effects of television (Wright, St. Peters & Huston, 1990).

Lull (1990) describes the many roles television can play in family interaction. The roles are structural (time and activity cues) or relational (facilitation of either shared communication or avoidance of communication and demonstration of competence or authority). Thus, television is an important variable in how family members relate to each other. Using surveys, Bower (1988) has compared parents' use of rules for viewing in 1960, 1970, and 1980. The results indicated a trend toward an increase in the restrictions and prescriptions parents impose on viewing. This increase in rules about amount of viewing and hours for viewing was indicated for 4- to 6-year-olds and 7- to 9-year-olds. For younger children, this also included an increase in rules about changing the channel or "grazing." Bower found that the higher the educational level of parents, the more likely there were rules about viewing. This confirms the findings of Medrich et al., who also found that the likelihood of rules increased with parental education for all households, but African-American households at every socioeconomic level were less restrictive about television viewing (Bower, 1985; Medrich, Roizen, Rubin & Buckley, 1982, cited in Comstock & Paik, 1991).

Several studies discuss the effects of new technology, such as cable and VCRs, on parental restrictions. These studies are reviewed by Comstock and Paik (1991). Lin and Atkin (1989) found that several variables interact with rulemaking* for adolescent use of television and VCRs, including school grades, child media ownership, child age, and gender. They point out the difficulty in separating the research on rulemaking, parental mediation, and coviewing.

> Within this realm of parental guidance, the relationship between mediation and rulemaking is, itself, worthy of separate consideration. Few researchers have considered mediation (e.g., encouraging, discouraging, discussing viewing) apart from the notion of rulemaking (established guidelines about acceptable and/or prohibited behaviors). Those making mediation-rulemaking distinctions (Brown & Linne, 1976; Reid, 1979; Bryce & Leichter, 1983) found a fair degree of correspondence between the two. Although these two concepts may appear as indicators of the same general process, we maintain that they should be theoretically distinguished. Actual mediation isn't necessarily contingent upon established rules. Clearly, one can have mediation without making explicit rules (and vice versa) (Lin & Atkin, 1989, p. 57).

Still Lin and Atkin found that mediation and rule making were predicted by each other.

There is also the question of whether information or training can increase parental involvement. Greenberg, Abelman, and Cohen provided television guides that reviewed programs to parents who did not use them. However, the children used them to find programs with the warning "parental discretion is advised" so that they could watch them (Greenberg, Abelman & Cohen, 1990, cited in Comstock & Paik, 1991). The jury is out, however, on whether training can help parents guide children in using television wisely. There are many books available for parents, including the Corporation for Public Broadcasting's *Tips for Parents: Using Television to Help Your Child Learn* (1988); the more recent American Psychological Association's (APA) "Suggestions for Parents" (Huston et al., 1992); Chen's *The Smart Parent's Guide to KIDS' TV* (1994a); and the USOE Office of Educational Research and Improvement publication *TV Viewing and Parental Guidance* (1994).

There has been little training of parents and almost no research on the effectiveness of such training. There have been many materials for television awareness training, such as critical-viewing teaching materials, which have been evaluated formatively. These will be discussed later in this chapter.

11.5.3.5.   Parental Attitude and Style. Several studies found that parents did not mediate or enforce rules about

television viewing because they did not believe television was either a harmful or beneficial force (Mills & Watkins, 1982; Messaris, 1983; Messaris & Kerr, 1983, cited in Sprafkin, Gadow & Abelman, 1992). There is some research that reports that a parent's positive attitude towards television is an important mediator (Brown & Linne, 1976; Bybee, Robinson & Turow, 1982; Dorr, Kovaric & Doubleday, 1989). In 1991, St. Peters, Fitch, Huston, Wright, and Eakins concluded that attitudes about television were correlated with parents' regulation and encouragement of viewing. The next year, they reported that parents' negative attitudes about television were not sufficient to modify the effects of television viewing. To reach their conclusions, the researchers collected data from 326 children and their families through diaries, questionnaires, standardized instruments, and one-way mirror experiments. This research led to a finer delineation of the variable "parental attitude" toward television:

> Positive attitudes were positively associated with parents' encouragement of viewing certain types of programs. Negative attitudes were positively related to regulating children's television viewing. Those parents who both regulated and encouraged discriminating viewing had children who viewed less television than parents who were high on encouragement of viewing. However, the present analysis shows that while parents appear to criticize and regulate television's content because of its negative influence and coview violent programming (news and cartoons) with their children, parents may not be taking advantage of the opportunity to discuss the programs they watch with their children and moderate the effects of content either directly or indirectly. Parents' education and attitudes about television were not associated with children's social behavior towards others (St. Peters, Huston & Wright, 1989, p. 12).

Abelman found that parents who were more concerned with cognitive effects were more likely to discuss and criticize television content, whereas parents who were more concerned about behavioral effects were more likely to mediate by restricting viewing (Abelman, 1990, cited in Sprafkin, Gadow & Abelman, 1992). Earlier, Abelman and Rogers (1987) presented findings that compared the television mediation of parents of exceptional children. Parents of nonlabeled (no disability* identified) children were restrictive in style; parents of gifted children were evaluative in style; and parents of emotionally disturbed, learning-disabled, or mentally retarded children were unfocused in style. The actions of parents with restrictive styles included forbidding certain programs, restricting viewing, specifying viewing time, specifying programs to watch, and switching channels on objectionable programs. Parents with an evaluative style explained programs and advertising, evaluated character roles, and discussed character motivations and plot/story lines. Parents with an unfocused style were characterized by one or two of these actions: (a) coviewed with the child, (b) encouraged the use of a television guide, (c) used television as reward or punishment, and (d) talked about characters (Abelman & Rogers, 1987).

Singer and Singer and their colleagues have studied parental communication style as it interacts with television viewing and affects comprehension of television (Desmond et al., 1985, 1990; Singer, Singer & Rapaczynski, 1985, cited in Sprafkin et al., 1992). In a summary of these research findings, Desmond et al. (1990) suggest that "general family communication style may have been more critical than specific television rules and discipline for enhancing a range of cognitive skills, including television comprehension" (p. 302). Children are helped by an atmosphere that promotes explanation about issues instead of just comments on people and events. Similarly, Korzenny et al. conducted a study at Michigan State University to determine under what conditions children's modeling of antisocial portrayals on television was strongest. They found that parents who disciplined by reasoning and explanation had children who were less affected by antisocial content than children whose parents disciplined through power (Korzenny et al., 1979, cited in Sprafkin et al., 1992).

11.5.4 Coviewing as a Variable

Coviewing refers to viewing in a group of two or more, such as a child and parent or three adolescent peers. Since discussion has been shown in many studies to be an important variable in learning from television (Buerkel-Rothfuss, Greenberg, Atkin & Neuendorf, 1982, cited in Comstock & Paik, 1991; Desmond, Singer & Singer, 1990), one would expect coviewing to be a significant variable in the home-viewing context. Unfortunately, studies suggest that although coviewing is an important variable, there are few effects due to coviewing. The reasons for this conclusion will be explained in this section. Three categories will be discussed: the nature and frequency of interaction, the effect of attitudes, and the effects of age and roles.

11.5.4.1. Nature and Frequency of Interaction. Based on a review of several articles, Comstock and Paik (1991) speculate that the time adolescents and adults spend coviewing is declining. The greatest concern in the literature is that most parents don't spend time coviewing, and when parents do coview, their level of involvement is usually low. It is not just the amount of time spent coviewing; the type of interaction during coviewing is critical. Most conversation during coviewing is about the television medium itself, the plots, characters, and quality of programs (Neuman, 1982, cited in Comstock & Paik, 1991). These conversations help educate young viewers and make them more critical. According to Comstock and Paik, however, they are not as crucial as conversations that deal with the reality of the program or the rightness or wrongness of the behavior portrayed.

> The evidence suggests that parental mediation—when it employs critical discussions and interpretations of what is depicted and sets some guidelines on television use—can increase the understanding of television, improve judgments about reality and fantasy, and reduce total viewing (Comstock & Paik, 1991, p. 45).

Nevertheless, parental coviewing is not always a positive influence. Parents can give implicit approval to violence, prejudice, or dangerous behavior (Desmond, Singer & Singer, 1990, cited in Comstock & Paik, 1991). After surveying 400 second-, sixth-, and tenth-graders, Dorr, Kovaric, and Doubleday (1989, cited in Comstock & Paik, 1991) found that coviewing basically reflected habits and preferences, rather than parental mediation or conversational involvement. In 1989, Dorr et al. reported only weak evidence for positive consequences from coviewing. They concluded that coviewing is an imperfect indicator of parental mediation of children's viewing. In their review, they identify several methodological problems that make it difficult to use the literature, including differing definitions of coviewing, overestimates by parents, and the assumption that coviewing is motivated by parents' desire to be responsible mediators of childrens' interactions with television. They report that coviewing with young children is infrequent (Hopkins & Mullins, 1985, cited in Dorr et al., 1989). Moreover, several studies have found that parent-child coviewing decreases as the number of sets in the house increase (Lull, 1982; McDonald, 1986, cited in Dorr et al., 1989). Dorr and her colleagues investigated several hypotheses about coviewing using data from seven paper-and-pencil instruments given to both parents and children. Their subjects included 460 middle-class second-, sixth-, and tenth-grade children and one parent for each of 372 of these children. The results indicated that coviewing by itself had little relationship to children's judgment of reality. It did predict satisfaction with family viewing.

Thus, research shows that most coviewing takes place because parents and children have similar viewing interests and tastes. Little of the coviewing has been planned by the parent to aid with the child's understanding and comprehension of the show (MacDonald, 1985, 1986, cited in Dorr et al., 1989; Wand, 1968). Nevertheless, it is possible that coviewing may help parents deal with difficult issues. Through viewing scenarios on television, the child may discuss the television character's dilemma with a parent, or the child may simply accept the television portrayal as the appropriate solution.

11.5.4.2. Effect of Attitudes. Dorr and her colleagues also found that parental attitudes toward television were predictors of coviewing. Parents who were more positive coviewed with children more frequently. Coviewing also correlated moderately with parents' belief that children can learn from television and with parents' encouragement of viewing. They concluded that it has a greater effect when motivated by parents' determination to mediate television experiences. This is an important finding, because coviewing occurs least with those who need it most, young children. Children are willing to discuss television content with their parents. Gantz and Weaver (1984) found that children initiate discussions of what they view with their parents; however, children did not initiate discussions about programs unless the programs were coviewed.

11.5.4.3. Effect of Age and Roles. Coviewing is usually described in terms of whether the viewers are children, adolescents, or adults, and whether the social group is of mixed age or not. The usual roles referred to are siblings, peers, and parents.

Haefner and Wartella (1987) used an experimental design to test hypotheses about coviewing with siblings. By analyzing verbal interactions in coviewing situations, they determined that relatively little of the interaction helped younger children interpret the content. Some teaching by older siblings did occur but was limited to identifying characters, objects, words, and filmic conventions. The result was that older siblings influenced evaluation of characters and programs in general, rather than interpretation of content. Haefner and Wartella (1987) noted that other variables needed to be accounted for, such as gender, birth order, viewing style, and attitude, because they could affect differences in learning from siblings. Pinon, Huston, and Wright (1989) conducted a longitudinal study of family viewing of *Sesame Street* using interviews, testing sessions, and diaries with 326 children from ages 3 to 5 and 5 to 7. The presence of older children was found to reduce viewing, the presence of younger children to increase it. Alexander, Ryan, and Munoz (1984, cited in Pinon et al., 1989) found that younger children imitated the preferences of older children and that coviewing with older siblings promoted elaboration of program elements.

Salomon (1977) conducted an experimental study on mothers who coviewed *Sesame Street* with their 5-year-olds. He found:

> Mothers' co-observation significantly affected the amount of time that lower-SES children watched the show, as well as their enjoyment of the program, producing in turn an effect on learning and significantly attenuating initial SES differences. Co-observation effects were not found in the middle-class group, except for field dependency performance where encouragement of mothers accentuated SES differences (p. 1146).

Salomon speculated that the performance of lower-class children is more affected, because the mother as coviewer acts as a needed energizer of learning.

On the other hand, television viewing activity may restrict parent-child interaction. Gantz and Weaver (1984) reviewed the research on parent-child communication about television. They used a questionnaire to examine parent-child television viewing experiences. They report conflicting research, some of which revealed a decrease in family communication, and some of which revealed facilitation of communication. Generally, they found that when parents and children watched together, conversations were infrequent. Moreover, there seems to be a socioeconomic variable interacting with coviewing, because more effective mediation of the viewing experience occurs with higher socioeconomic and educational levels. When viewing occurs with the father present, he tends to dominate program selection (Lull, 1982, cited in Gantz & Weaver, 1984).

Hill and Stafford (1980) investigated the effect of working on the time mothers devote to activities such as childcare, leisure television viewing, and housework. The addition of one child increased the time devoted to housework by 6 to 7 hours a week. Mothers who worked took this time from personal care time, including sleep and television watching. Because early childhood may be an important time for the establishment of long-term patterns of television use, it becomes essential that parental patterns of viewing continue to include coviewing with children, even when family routine mandates changes.

Collett (1986) used a recording device to study coviewing. The device, a C-Box,* consisted of a television set and video camera that recorded the viewing area in front of the television. In addition, subjects were asked to complete a diary. He points out that:

> It is a sad fact that almost everything we know about television has come from asking people questions about their viewing habits and opinions, or from running them through experiments. The problem with asking people questions is that they may not be able to describe their actions reliably, or they may choose to offer accounts which they deem to be acceptable to the investigator (p. 9).

In 1988, Anderson and Collins examined the research literature on the relationship between coviewing by parents and critical-viewing skills programs, school achievement, and learning outcomes. The review concluded that there was little support for most of the beliefs about the negative influence of television on children. This opinion contrasts to some extent with conclusions of Haefner and Wartella (1987) and Winn (1977). Anderson and Collins concluded that adults can be helpful to children's comprehension through coviewing, but that it is not clear that interactions are common.

11.5.5 Viewing Habits

Another factor in the family viewing context is the viewing habits or patterns of the household. Because television viewing is often a social as well as a personal act, viewing habits both effect and are affected by other family variables. The factors that seem to emerge from research on viewing habits are the amount of viewing, viewing patterns, and audience involvement.

11.5.5.1. The Amount of Viewing. So far research related to this variable centers around the effects of heavy viewing. Estimates for the typical number of hours television is watched in the American home each day vary from 7 hours (Who are the biggest couch potatoes?, 1993) to 21 hours (Would you give up TV for a million bucks?, 1992). Those over age 55 watched the most; teenage girls, who averaged 3 hours a day, watched the least (Who are the biggest couch potatoes?, 1993). If heavy viewing is defined as more than 3 to 4 hours a day, many Americans are heavy viewers, which makes it difficult to research and draw conclusions about heavy viewing. Research does indicate that heavy viewing is associated with more negative feelings about life. Adults who watch television 3 or more hours daily are twice as likely to have high cholesterol levels as those who watch less than an hour daily, according to Larry Tucker, director of health promotion at Brigham Young University, who examined the viewing habits of 12,000 adults.

Children who are heavy viewers often have parents who are heavy viewers. Such parents are usually less educated and enforce fewer family rules about appropriate programs (Roderick & Jackson, 1985). The amount of viewing changes over a life span. Teenagers are relatively light viewers when compared with children and adults (Comstock & Paik, 1987). Some studies reported that children of mothers who work outside the home watch no more or less television than children of mothers at home (Webster, Pearson & Webster, 1986; Brown, Childers, Bauman & Koch, 1990); yet Atkin, Greenberg, and Baldwin (1991) summarized research that concluded that children view more in homes where the father is absent (Brown, Bauman, Lenz & Koch, 1987, cited in Atkin, Greenberg & Baldwin, 1991) and where the mother works (Medrich, Rozien, Rubin & Buckley, 1982, cited in Atkin, Greenberg & Baldwin, 1991).

Using a questionnaire, Roderick and Jackson (1985) identified differences in television viewing habits between gifted and nongifted viewers. More nongifted students were found to have their own television sets, which may account for the heavier viewing habits of nongifted students. Gifted students preferred different programs (educational, documentaries) from nongifted students (sitcoms, soaps, game shows). Gifted students were more likely to have VCRs in their home. They did not engage in the wishful thinking or fantasizing about television characters that was common with nongifted students. Roderick and Jackson had nongifted students respond in their classrooms and gifted students respond at home, which may have introduced bias.

The CPB participated in the 1993 Yankelovich Youth Monitor in order to answer some questions about viewing patterns in the 1990s (Corporation for Public Broadcasting, 1993). The Youth Monitor survey studied 1,200 children ages 6 to 17 with an in-home interview in randomly selected households. Today 50% of children have a television set in their bedroom. They watch 3 hours per weekday and 4 hours per weekend day. Less than 20% watch an hour or less per day. Viewing decreases as income increases. African-American and Hispanic children view the most. Television viewing is the number-1 activity in the hours between school and dinner time. Nearly half the children reported viewing television with their family each evening. This is especially true for children who watch public television.

11.5.5.2. Viewing Patterns. "Viewing patterns" refers to content preferences, but content does not dictate viewing, because, with few exceptions, other variables have more effect on preferences. This concept can be misleading, because, although there are few discernable patterns of preferences by program types, viewers would be unlikely to watch test patterns or the scrolling of stock market reports. Research supports the conclusion that viewers are relatively content indifferent.* Huston, Wright, Rice, Kerkman, and St. Peters (1990) conducted a longitudinal investigation of the development of television viewing patterns in early childhood, focusing on types and amounts of viewing from ages 3 to 7. They were interested in developmental changes resulting from maturation or cognitive development, individual and environmental variables affecting viewing patterns, and the stability of individual differences in viewing patterns over time. Viewing was measured from diaries kept by parents who were instructed to record as a viewer anyone who was present for more than one-half of a 15-minute interval when the television was on. While there were many individual differences, these differences tended to be stable over time. As they grew older, children watched programs that required more cognition, such as programs with less redundancy and increasing complexity. Nevertheless, the researchers concluded that family patterns and external variables are more important determinants of viewing than individual or developmental differences. They also found that boys watched more cartoons, action-adventure, and sports programs than did girls. Boys watched more television overall. Viewers of humorous children's programs evolve into viewers of comedy at a later age. Viewers of adventure stories become viewers of action-adventure by age 7. In comparison to this study, Lyle and Hoffman (1972, cited in Comstock & Paik, 1991) documented through questionnaires that preferences change with age.

Plomin, Corley, DeFries, and Fulker (1990) conducted a longitudinal study of 220 adopted children from age 3 to 5. Evidence for both significant genetic and environmental influences on television viewing patterns was found. Neither intelligence nor temperament was responsible for this genetic influence.

McDonald and Glynn (1986) examined adult opinion about how appropriate it is for children to view certain kinds of content. Telephone interviews were conducted with 285 respondents. Adults did not approve of crime-detective and adult-oriented programming for children.

Over 4 years, Frank and Greenberg (1979) conducted personal interviews with 2,476 people aged 13 years or older. They found support for their thesis that viewing audiences are more diverse than usually assumed. From the information collected, they constructed profiles of 14 segments of the television audience. Their study is an example of research that clusters variables. More of such research is needed, because so many variables interact in the television environment.

11.5.5.3. Audience Involvement. Research shows that selectivity and viewing motives can affect viewing involvement (Perse, 1990). Using factor analysis techniques with data generated from questionnaires, Perse investigated viewing motives classified as ritualistic* (watching for gratification) or instrumental* (watching for information). The study included four indications of audience involvement: (a) intentionality, or anticipating television viewing; (b) attention, or focused cognitive effort; (c) elaboration, or thinking about program content; and (d) engaging in distractions while viewing. Ritualistic television use, which indicates watching a broad variety of programs, is marked by higher selectivity before watching but lower levels of involvement while viewing. The study confirms the value of the Levy-Windahl Audience-Activity Typology (Levy &

Windahl, 1985, cited in Perse, 1990).

The Experience Sampling Method* was used to study media habits and experiences of 483 subjects aged 9 to 15 years (Kubey & Larson, 1990). Respondents carried electronic paging devices, and whenever contacted, they reported on their activities and subjective experiences. The utilization of three new forms of video entertainment (music videos, video games, and videocassettes) and traditional television was subsequently analyzed. Traditional television viewing remains the dominant video media form for preadolescents and adolescents. New video media are a relatively small part of their lives. However, the percentage of time spent alone with the new media is growing, perhaps because they offer chances for adolescents to be more independent of the family. Boys had more positive attitudes towards the new media. There could be many reasons for this, including gender differences or the content of the new media.

11.5.6 Summary and Recommendations

In 1978, Wright, Atkins, and Huston-Stein listed some characteristics of the setting in which a child views television:

- Presence of others who are better informed or who can answer questions raised by a child
- Behavior of others, who through well-timed comments and questions model elaboration of content
- Preparation of the child through previous reading, viewing, or discussion
- Opportunity to enact or rehearse, role play plots, characters, and situations viewed
- Distractions in the environment

Much is known today about each of these aspects of the family viewing context. In addition, new variables and interactions have been identified such as rulemaking, parental communication style, socioeconomic level, and ethnicity.

Nevertheless, many gaps exist in the research literature, especially about interactions. The well-supported conclusion that learning from television increases when an adult intervenes to guide and support learning even if the program is an entertainment (Johnston, 1987) suggests that much more needs to be done to relate the findings of mass-media research and research from instructional television and message design. Therefore, it is essential to relate findings about learning from television with findings about the family context for viewing* in order to design interventions that will ensure the positive benefits of television. Findings need to be related theoretically in order to develop recommendations for interventions.

St. Peters et al. (1991) summarize the situation:

> Whatever the effects of parental coviewing, encouragement, and regulation, it is clear that the family context is central to the socialization of young children's television use. Families determine not only the amount of television available to children, but the types of programs, and the quality of the viewing experience (p. 1422).

11.6 ATTITUDES, BELIEFS, AND BEHAVIORS

Since the early days of broadcast television, educators, parents, and legislators have been concerned about the effects of televised messages on the socialization of children. In 1987, a Louis Harris poll indicated that more than two-thirds of the adults surveyed were concerned about the effects of television on the values and behaviors of their children (Huston et al., 1992). Attention has also been directed to television's potential for cultivating prosocial behavior.* The cause-effect relationship between televised violence and violent behavior has not been conclusively supported by the research literature. Although there have been significant correlations in certain groups, such as those predisposed to aggressive behavior, the effects cannot be easily generalized to all children. As reported in the section on family viewing context, there are many mediating variables that influence the effects of television on attitudes and behaviors.

As in other areas of television research, methods vary between laboratory experiments, field studies, and surveys. Variables studied can include subject characteristics such as age, sex, ethnicity, socioeconomic status (SES), aggressive tendencies or predispositions, parental style, or amount of viewing. Other studies focus on the type of content that is presented, such as realistic, rewarded, or justified aggression. Still other studies focus on the influence of the physical and social context by manipulating variables such as parental approval (Hearold, 1986). More complex interactions may exist among these variables as well. Outcomes can be measured through observing spontaneous play, and through teacher and peer ratings, or through monitoring the intensity of responses that presumably produce pain. Treatments and behaviors can be delineated as antisocial, prosocial, or neutral.* As defined, each of these categories encompasses many variables.

During the 7 hours per day that the television set is typically turned on, it plays a subtle role as a teacher of rules, norms, and standards of behavior (Huston et al., 1992). This section will examine how television can impact beliefs and attitudes (see Chapter 34). It will also look at issues of desensitization, oversensitization,* and disinhibition.* Finally, it will review what has been learned about the effects of television on both antisocial and prosocial behavior.

11.6.1 Major Theories

Socialization is the process of learning over time how to function in a group or society. It is a set of paradigms, rules, procedures, and principles that govern perception, attention, choices, learning, and development (Dorr, 1982). Although there have been hundreds of studies that examine socialization effects, a consistent theoretical basis is lacking. Social learning theory, catharsis theory,* arousal or instigation theory, and cultivation theory are commonly cited when researchers examine the effects of television on attitudes, beliefs, and behaviors.

11.6.1.1. Social Learning Theory. Many studies of television effects are based on Bandura's social learning theory, which "assumes that modeling influences operate principally through their informative function, and that observers acquire mainly symbolic representations of modeled events rather than specific stimulus-response associations" (Bandura, 1971, p. 16). According to Bandura and Walters (1963), the best and most effective way to teach children novel ways of acting is to show them the behavior you want them to display. Children can imitate modeled behaviors almost identically (Bandura, Ross & Ross, 1961). Bandura (1971) states that although much social learning is fostered through observation of real-life models, television provides symbolic, pictorially presented models. Because of the amount of time that people are exposed to models on television, "such models play a major part in shaping behavior and in modifying social norms and thus exert a strong influence on the behavior of children and adolescents" (Bandura & Walters, 1963, p. 49).

Bandura and others conducted a series of studies known popularly as the "Bobo doll studies." In each of them, a child was shown someone assaulting a Bobo doll, a 5-foot-tall inflated plastic clown designed to be a punching bag. In some experiments, the model was in the room; in others, a film of either the model or a cartoon figure was projected onto a simulated television (Bandura, Ross & Ross, 1961, 1963; Liebert & Sprafkin, 1988). Different treatment groups saw the model receiving different consequences. A model acting aggressively was either rewarded, punished, or received no consequences. Some groups saw a nonaggressive model. After exposure, the children were observed playing with toys while their spontaneous imitative aggressions were counted by trained observers.

The results showed that (a) children spontaneously imitated a model who was rewarded or received no consequences; (b) children showed far more aggression than children in other groups when they observed an aggressive model who was rewarded; (c) children showed little tendency towards aggression when they saw either the aggressive model who was punished or a nonaggressive model who was inhibited; and (d) boys showed more imitative aggression than girls (Bandura, Ross & Ross, 1961, 1963; Bandura & Walters, 1963; Liebert & Sprafkin, 1988). Bandura found that children can learn an aggressive behavior but not demonstrate it until motivated to do so. After children were told they would receive treats if they could demonstrate what they had seen, children in all treatment conditions, even those who saw the model punished, were able to produce a high rate of imitation (Liebert & Sprafkin, 1988; Sprafkin, Gadow & Abelman, 1992; Wolf, 1975).

Although these studies provided evidence that modeled or mediated images can influence subsequent behavior, they are criticized for being conducted in laboratory conditions and for measuring play behavior toward a toy that was designed to be hit (Liebert & Sprafkin, 1988). Consequently, the results may not transfer to real-life situations. Environmental variables, such as parental approval or disapproval,

also played an important role in eliciting or inhibiting aggressive behavior in naturalistic settings (Bandura, Ross & Ross, 1963).

11.6.1.2. Catharsis Theory. In contrast to social learning theory, catharsis theory suggests that viewing televised violence reduces the likelihood of aggressive behavior (Murray, 1980). The basic assumption is that frustration* produces an increase in aggressive drive, and because this state is unpleasant, the person seeks to reduce it by engaging in aggressive acts or by viewing fantasy aggressions such as those seen in action-adventure television (Sprafkin, Gadow & Abelman, 1992). Children who view violence experience it vicariously and identify with the aggressive action, thereby discharging their pent-up aggression (Murray, 1980).

Scheff and Scheele (1980) delineate two conditions needed for catharsis*: stimuli that give rise to distressful emotion and adequate distancing from the stimuli. They suggest that characters in violent cartoons may provide enough distancing and detachment for catharsis to occur, but realistic violence may be too overwhelming to feel and subsequently discharge.

Since catharsis involves a particular type of emotional response, viewing television may or may not elicit that response, depending on characteristics of the stimuli, viewers, and other conditions (Scheff & Scheele, 1980). Feshbach and Singer (1971) took a slightly different theoretical approach to their investigations of the relationship between fantasy aggression and overt behavior. They state that specific types of fantasies can cause either arousal, which leads to an increase in activity, or inhibition, which, in turn, leads to drive reduction. In looking at the effects of televised violence over a 6-week period, they studied approximately 400 boys who were divided into two treatment groups based on whether they watched aggressive or nonaggressive television. Feshbach and Singer found no significant differences between these groups. However, when they analyzed the data by type of residential school (private versus boy's home), they found that in the boy's home the nonaggressive television group became more aggressive, while the aggressive television group became less aggressive. When they analyzed private schools, they found the opposite to be true. Thus, the catharsis theory was supported in the boy's-home setting only. Other factors such as the boy's resentment of not being allowed to watch preferred programming may have been more influential than the nonaggressive television treatment. The researchers also suggested that "violence presented in the form of fiction is less likely to reinforce, stimulate, or elicit aggressive responses in children than is violence in the form of a news event" (p. 158).

In general, catharsis theory has failed to receive support in studies on children (Liebert & Sprafkin, 1988) but has found support in studies on adolescents (Sprafkin, Gadow & Abelman, 1992). More research is needed on the effects on different populations. Scheff and Scheele (1980) cautioned that catharsis theory has never been adequately tested due to the lack of a careful definition and of systematic data collection. They recommended that studies be conducted that identify and separate viewers of violent programming who experience a cathartic emotional response from those who do not.

11.6.1.3. Instigation or Arousal Theory. Arousal theory* is related to catharsis theory only in its emphasis on an increase in a physiological state. But rather than reducing drives, this theory suggests that generalized emotional arousal can influence subsequent behaviors. Televised messages about emotion, sexuality, or violence can lead to "nonspecific physiological and cognitive arousal that will in turn energize a wide range of potential behaviors" (Huston et al., 1992, p. 36). For example, increased aggression following televised violence would be interpreted as the result of the level of arousal elicited by the program, not as a result of modeling (Liebert & Sprafkin, 1988). In over a dozen studies, Tannenbaum (1980) varied the content in film clips to include aggressive, sexual, humor, music, and content-free abstract symbols and movement. He compared subjects who viewed more-arousing (using physiological measures) though less-aggressive (in content) film clips to those who viewed less-arousing, more-aggressive clips. Subjects were required to make some form of aggressive or punitive response, usually the administration of alleged electric shocks. The subjects could only vary the intensity, frequency, or duration of the shocks. Tannenbaum found more aggression after subjects had seen the more-arousing though less-aggressive films. He cautions, however, that a necessary feature of these studies was a target (the researcher's accomplice) who had earlier angered the subjects and may have been considered as deserving an aggressive response.

This theory suggests that when aroused, people will behave with more intensity no matter what type of response they are called upon to make (Tannenbaum, 1980). An important implication of this theory is that behavior may be activated that is quite different from what was presented (Huston et al., 1992). Thus, arousal may stimulate a predisposition towards aggression.

Arousal levels can be measured by pulse amplitudes, a type of heart response measured by a physiograph (Comstock & Paik, 1991). With this method the measurement of effects is not influenced by extraneous factors, such as observer bias or counting errors.

11.6.1.4. Cultivation Hypothesis or Drip versus Drench Models. Cultivation theory (see 4.4.4.4) "predicts that the more a person is exposed to television, the more likely the person's perceptions of social realities will match those represented on television . . ."(Liebert & Sprafkin, 1988, p. 148). In other words, a person's view of the world will be more reflective of the common and repetitive images seen on television than of those actually experienced (Signorielli, 1991; Signorielli & Lears, 1992).

Television may influence viewers by the "drip model," the subtle accumulation of images and beliefs through a process of gradual incorporation of frequent and repeated messages (Huston et al., 1992). George Gerbner conducted a number of studies that demonstrated a cultivation effect; he found that individuals who watch greater amounts of television and therefore see more crime-related content develop beliefs about levels of crime and personal safety that reflect those risks as portrayed on television (Gunter, 1987).

Greenberg (1988, cited in Williams & Condry, 1989) asserted that critical images that stand out or are intense may contribute more to the formation of impressions than does the frequency of images over time. Huston et al. also found support for the "drench model" where single programs or series may have a strong effect when they contain particularly salient portrayals. For example, programs designed to counteract stereotypes,* such as *The Golden Girls,* can change children's attitudes and beliefs about older women.

The "drip versus drench models" illustrate a common problem in theory building. Even though the drip model is associated with cultivation theory, neither model explains the cognitive mechanisms that operate.

11.6.2 Attitudes and Beliefs

Television is just one of many sociological factors that influence the formation of beliefs and attitudes. Many of the poorest and most vulnerable groups in our society, such as children, the elderly, ethnic minorities, and women, are the heaviest users of television in part because it is used when other activities are not available or affordable (Huston et al., 1992; Stroman, 1991). In general, people with low incomes and with less formal education watch more television than people with high incomes and with higher education (Huston et al., 1992).

Liebert and Sprafkin (1988) reported that heavy viewers (those who watch more than 3 to 4 hours per day) are more likely than light viewers to have outlooks and perceptions congruent with television portrayals, even after controlling for income and education. They cautioned that some groups, such as adolescents with low parental involvement, are more susceptible than others. Huston et al. (1992) concluded that children and adults who watched a large number of aggressive programs also tended to hold attitudes and values that favored the use of aggression to resolve conflicts, even when factors such as social class, sex-role identity, education level, or parental behavior were controlled (see 4.4.4.3).

The beliefs and attitudes learned from television can also be positive. Bandura and Walters (1963) stated that exemplary models often reflect social norms and the appropriate conduct for given situations. Children can acquire a large number of scripts and schemes for a variety of social situations based on television prototypes (Wright & Huston, 1983). Television can also impact children's understanding of occupations with which they have no experience (Comstock & Paik, 1991). Viewing positive interactions of different ethnic groups on *Sesame Street* led to an increase in positive intergroup attitudes among preschool children

(Gorn, Goldberg & Kamungo, 1976, cited in Huston et al.) Unfortunately, many television producers continue to rely on stereotypes due to the desire to communicate images and drama quickly and effectively.

11.6.2.1. Stereotypes. A group is said to be stereotyped "whenever it is depicted or portrayed in such a way that all its members appear to have the same set of characteristics, attitudes, or life conditions" (Liebert & Sprafkin, 1988, p. 189). Durkin (1985) described stereotypes as being based on extreme characteristics attributed to the group, with usually negative values attached to that group. The less real-world information people have about social groups, the more inclined they are to accept the television image of that group. According to Gross (1991), nonrepresentation in the media maintains the powerless status of groups that possess insignificant material or power bases. He stated that mass media are especially powerful in cultivating images of groups for which there are few first-hand opportunities for learning.

Many studies assess stereotypes both quantitatively, with counts of how many and how often subgroups are portrayed, and qualitatively, with analyses of the nature and intent of the portrayals. "Recognition* refers to the frequency with which a group receives TV roles at all. Respect* refers to how characters behave and are treated once they have roles" (Liebert & Sprafkin, 1988, p. 187). Television can reflect and affect the position of groups in society, since the number and types of portrayals of a group symbolize their importance, power, and social value (Huston et al., 1992). For example, when Davis (1990) studied network programming in the spring of 1987, he concluded that television women are more ornamental than functional.

Huston et al. (1992) cautioned that "despite extensive documentation of television content, there is relatively little solid evidence about the effects of television portrayals on self-images, or on the perceptions, attitudes, and behaviors of other groups" (p. 33). As with other areas of television research, it may be too difficult to isolate the effects of television from other social effects. On the other hand, programs that are designed specifically to produce positive images of subgroups appear to be successful.

11.6.2.2. Gender Stereotypes. The effects of television in sex role* socialization is another area of concern (Signorielli & Lears, 1992). According to Durkin (1985), "The term sex role refers to the collection of behaviours or activities that a given society deems more appropriate to members of one sex than to members of the other sex" (p. 9). Television viewing is linked with sex-stereotyped attitudes and behaviors. Correlational studies show a positive relationship between amount of viewing and sex-stereotyped attitudes, and experimental studies demonstrate that even brief exposure to television can increase or decrease sex-stereotyped behaviors, depending on the type of program viewed (Lipinski & Calvert, 1985).

In the United States, women are portrayed on television as passive, dominated by men, deferential, governed by emotion or overly emotional, dependent, less intelligent than men, and generally weak (Davis, 1990; Higgs & Weiller, 1987; Liebert & Sprafkin, 1988; Signorielli & Lears, 1992). The percentage of starring characters who are women is 30% (Kimball, 1986).

The formal features of television can contribute to stereotyping by gender. Commercials aimed at women used soft background music and dissolves, and employed female narrators primarily for products dealing with female body care (Craig, 1991; Durkin, 1985; Signorielli & Lears, 1992; Zemach & Cohen, 1986), even though male narrators were used in 90% of all commercials (Zemach & Cohen, 1986). Commercials aimed at men more often incorporated variation in scenes, away-from-home action, high levels of activity, fast-paced cuts, loud and dramatic music and sound effects, and fantasy and excitement (Bryant & Anderson, 1983; Craig, 1991; Durkin, 1985).

Presenting a group in a way that connotes low status deprives that group of respect (Liebert & Sprafkin, 1988). Women were typically assigned marital, romantic, or family roles (Liebert & Sprafkin, 1988) and were depicted in subservient roles allocated to them by a patriarchal society (Craig, 1991). They were rarely shown to successfully combine marriage and employment (Signorielli, 1991). Davis (1990) also found that the television woman's existence was a function of youth and beauty. Women were younger than men by 10 years, and they disappeared from ages 35 to 50. They are 5 times more likely to have blond hair and are 4 times more likely to be dressed provocatively. They were also frequently defined by their marital or parental status.

Men were shown as major characters on average 3 times more often than women during prime time. A higher proportion of working women were portrayed in professional and entrepreneurial roles than actually existed. Furthermore, women rarely experienced problems with childcare, sex discrimination, harassment, or poverty (Huston et al., 1992).

Although many studies identified female role stereotypes, fewer examined male stereotypes and their characteristics (Craig, 1991; Langmeyer, 1989). In general, men on television tended to be active, dominant, governed by reason, and generally powerful (Liebert & Sprafkin, 1988). Meyers (1980) examined how men were portrayed in 269 television commercials. Her analysis found four main characteristics: authoritative-dominant, competitive/success hungry, breadwinner, or emotionless male. Commercials aimed at men are more likely to "stress the importance of being capable, ambitious, responsible, and independent and physically powerful, and of seeking accomplishment, physical comfort, and an exciting and prosperous life" (Scheibe & Condry, 1984, cited in Craig, 1991, p. 11).

Craig (1991) found that portrayals differed according to the time of day. For example, daytime television commercials that were aimed at women portrayed men from the perspective of home and family. Men appeared in the home, were hungry, were potential partners for romance, were rarely responsible for childcare, and were portrayed as husbands or celebrities (Craig, 1991). During the weekends, ads were "replete with masculine escapist fantasy" (Craig, p. 53). Men were primary characters 80% of the time and appeared in settings outside the home. In contrast, women were completely absent in 37% of the ads, and when they did appear, it was as sex objects or models 23% of the time.

In examining effects, heavy television viewing was associated with stronger traditional sex role development in boys and girls (Comstock & Paik, 1991; Gunter, 1986; Murray, 1980; Liebert & Sprafkin, 1988). Signorielli and Lears (1992) found a significant relationship between heavy television viewing and sex-stereotyped ideas about chores for preadolescent children. They found that children who watched more television were more likely to say that only girls should do the chores traditionally associated with women, and only boys should do those associated with men. Jeffery and Durkin (1989) found that children were more likely to accept a sex role transgression (i.e., a man doing domestic chores) when the character was presented as a powerful executive than when he was shown as a cleaner/custodian. When Kimball (1986) studied three Canadian communities, she found that 2 years after the introduction of television, children's perceptions relating to sex roles were more sex typed than before television was available. Although she recognized the influence of peers, parents, school, and other media, she concluded that the introduction of television to the Notel town added enough of an effect to produce an increase in sex stereotyping. Additionally, Bryant and Anderson (1983) reported that viewing public television (which contained less stereotyping than commercial television) was characteristic of children who made less stereotypical toy choices.

According to Dambrot, Reep, and Bell (1988), the role played by an actor or actress was more critical to viewers' perceptions than their sex. In their study examining crime action shows, they found that "viewers ascribe masculine traits to both female and male characters" (p. 399). When women were portrayed in nontraditional roles and situations, viewers did not attribute traditional stereotyped traits to them.

Hansen and Hansen (1988) studied the effect of viewing rock music videos on perception. Subjects who viewed stereotypic music videos were more likely to have a distorted impression of an interpersonal interaction than were subjects who viewed neutral videos. Although research on the effects of sex role portrayals suggests a link to beliefs about gender roles, Gunter (1986) cautioned that many studies do not account for other variables, such as the effect of parental role modeling, nor do they precisely measure what viewers actually watch.

Even in sports programming, television reinforced stereotypes (Higgs & Weiller, 1987; Weiller & Higgs, 1992). Commentators described men as strong, aggressive, and unstoppable. They used surnames and provided technical information about male athletes. On the other hand, in the limited coverage of women's sports, women were described by their pain and the difficulty of the competition, by their first names, and with derisive adjectives, such as "the best *little* center" in basketball (Higgs & Weiller, 1992, p. 11).

On a positive note, television altered expectations when it purposely deviated from stereotypic portrayals in order to change beliefs (Comstock & Paik, 1987; Gunter, 1986). Johnston and Ettema (1982) conducted summative evaluations of *Freestyle,* the 13-part public television program designed to change attitudes about sex roles among children aged 9 to 12. Their study included four experimental conditions spread among seven research sites. Although limited positive effects were seen with unstructured viewing, positive short-term and long-term effects were seen when the program was viewed in the classroom and discussion took place (Comstock & Paik, 1987; Durkin, 1985). Effects with home viewers were small and were found only for the heaviest viewers. Among female children who viewed the programs in school, however, there were significant changes in beliefs, attitudes, and interests. While there were few changes in boys' beliefs, attitudes, or interests, there were no cases of negative effect on males or females (Johnston & Ettema, 1982, cited in Johnson, 1987). The program was particularly successful in promoting greater acceptance of: (a) girls who displayed independence and abilities in athletics, mechanical activities, and leadership; (b) boys who were nurturing; and (c) men and women who chose nontraditional roles (Gunter, 1986; Johnston & Ettema, 1982). Overall, Johnston and Ettema concluded that the programs could impact children's beliefs and attitudes more than their interests in nontraditional pursuits.

11.6.2.3. Minority Stereotypes. The effects of television on beliefs and perceptions related to ethnicity have not received as much attention as those related to sex roles (Comstock & Paik, 1991). Because children are less likely to have contact with people of different racial or ethnic backgrounds, television may be the primary source of information about minorities (Takanishi, 1982; Williams & Condry, 1989). By 2080, Caucasians in the United States will no longer be the majority (Fitzgerald, 1992). In response to the United States being more racially integrated than at any other time in history, television is becoming more racially diverse.

According to Huston et al. (1992), television is particularly important for African-Americans because they watch more, have more favorable attitudes towards it, rely more on it for news and information, and perceive it as reflecting reality. Additionally, young, well-educated African-American adults are heavy viewers. Also, television may provide minority children with important information about the world that is not available to them in their immediate environment (Stroman, 1991); therefore, the effects may be greater.

Minority children on average spent more time watching television regardless of socioeconomic status (Comstock & Cobbey, 1982; Dorr, 1982) and ascribed more reality or credibility to television portrayals (Dorr, 1982). Stroman cited a study by Lee and Browne (1981) that reported that 26% of third- and fourth-graders and 15% of adolescents watched more than 8 hours of television per day. Since their families were less able to afford alternative forms of entertainment, African-American children relied more on television for entertainment and guidance and to learn about occupations (Stroman, 1991). The successful image of African-Americans on television was as far removed from reality as were negative portrayals (Wilson & Gutierrez, 1985, cited in Fitzgerald, 1992).

In the early days of television, African-Americans appeared in minor roles, frequently as servants or as comedians (Liebert & Sprafkin, 1988). According to Williams and Condry (1989), in the 1970s racism was more subtle. Black characters were younger and poorer, less likely to be cast in professional occupations, and dramatic or romantic roles, and often appeared in segregated environments. From their study of 1,987 network programs and commercials, they concluded that minorities were portrayed with blue-collar or public-service jobs, appeared as children, or appeared as perpetrators or victims of criminal and delinquent acts.

Ethnic identity* is the "attachment to an ethnic group and a positive orientation toward being a member of that group" (Takanishi, 1982, p. 83). Children are particularly vulnerable to negative portrayals of African-Americans. "Black children are ambivalent about their racial identity, and studies still show that many prefer whites, prefer to be white, and prefer white characters on television to characters like themselves" (Corner, 1982, p. 21). Graves (1982) cited several studies that demonstrated that preschoolers imitated televised Caucasian models more than African-American models, even when imitating toy selection. Other variables could be contributing to these studies, however. The results could be interpreted as relating more to the perceived status of the models than to their ethnicity (Comstock & Cobbey, 1982).

Although he criticized situation comedies for their portrayals of African-Americans as frivolous and stupid, Corner (1982) commented that these programs helped Caucasian third- through fifth-graders gain positive images of minorities, and many African-American children gained positive images about themselves. Graves (1982) found positive effects, including the acceptance and imitation of minority role models. Additionally, Mays and colleagues (1975) found that after viewing 16 episodes of *Vegetable Soup,* a program that featured the interactions of children of different ethnic backgrounds, children from 6 to 10 years expressed greater friendliness towards those differing in ethnicity (cited in Comstock & Paik, 1991). Mays and colleagues also found that those who were African-American expressed enhanced acceptance of their own ethnicity. Takanishi (1982) and Greenberg and Atkin (1982) cautioned that the effects of minority character portrayals were complicated by the different values, attitudes, and characteristics that children bring to viewing, as well as by social influences and the attributes of content.

According to Davis (1990) and Berry (1982), minority group portrayals have improved in terms of frequency. In 1987, African-Americans comprised 12.4% of television characters and 12.9% of the population (Davis, 1990). Although African-Americans were appearing more on television, segregation and isolation continued to be a problem (Berry, 1982). In 1980, cross-racial interactions appeared in only 2% of dramas and 4% of comedies (Weigel, Loomis & Soja, 1980, cited in Liebert & Sprafkin, 1988). In their study of 1987 network programming, Williams and Condry found that 40% of minorities were in segregated environments with no contact with whites. They did find an interesting trend in that cross-racial friendships among youth were commonplace. In contrast, they found that cross-racial relationships among adults were limited to job-related situations.

Audience-viewing patterns have the potential to counteract the negative effects of televised stereotypes. Greenberg and Atkin (1982) stated that African-American parents were more likely than Caucasian parents to sit down and watch television programs with their children, especially minority programs. Grayson (1979) and Stroman (1991) advised direct intervention by parents to reduce the impact of negative portrayals, including: (a) selectively viewing programs and excluding those that portray minorities in distorted or stereotyped roles; (b) looking for and coviewing programs that portray minorities in a positive, realistic, and sensitive manner; (c) viewing and discussing the program's applicability and relevance to real-life people and events; (d) providing exposure to content beyond television and to activities that will promote physical and intellectual growth, such as trips to zoos and museums; and (e) providing opportunities for children to be in real situations with minorities, elderly persons, and others.

Other minority groups were rarely portrayed. By the mid-1970s other subgroups complained to the networks about their portrayals, such as Arabs as terrorists or oil sheiks; Italians as Mafia hoodlums; Orientals as invaders, docile launderers, or karate experts; Chicanos/Hispanics as comics, banditos, or gang members; homosexuals as effeminate; and Native Americans as savages, victims, cowards, or medicine men (Davis, 1990; Williams & Condry, 1989; Willis, 1990). Relatively little is known about how television is used by other minority groups.

11.6.2.4. Elderly Stereotypes. As a group, the elderly have been under-represented on television, occupying no more than 3% of all roles (Bell, 1991; Huston et al., 1992; Liebert & Sprafkin, 1988). Of that number, men outnumbered women two to one and were likely to be more powerful, active, and productive. In a study of children's Saturday morning programs, Bishop and Krause (1984) found that over 90% of the comments made about the elderly were negative (cited in Liebert & Sprafkin, 1988). The elderly were also portrayed as unhappy and having problems they could not solve themselves. According to Davis and Davis (1986), they were shown as "more comical, stubborn, eccentric, and foolish than other characters. They are more likely to be treated with disrespect" (cited in Bell, 1991, p. 3).

This image of the elderly may be changing as the media recognize that one out of every six Americans is over 60 years of age, and marketing decisions begin to incorporate the elderly into television's prime time (Bell, 1991). According to Nielsen ratings, in 1989 the five most popular dramas for the over-age-55 audience featured older characters: *Murder She Wrote, The Golden Girls, Matlock, Jake and the Fatman,* and *In the Heat of the Night* (Bell, 1991). Bell found that they portrayed elderly who were at the center of the show as powerful characters, affluent, healthy, physically and socially active, quick witted, and admired. He concluded that while the elderly were portrayed better than they had been in the past, there were still problems. "When men appear with women, the old stereotypes of male prominence and power still operate" (Bell, 1991, p. 11). In his observation, these shows depicted two worlds: one where there were older women but no men, and one where there were older men with young women but no older women.

Some evidence exists for the potential of television to promote positive outcomes regarding the elderly. Keegan (1983) found that a planned program, *Over Easy,* which was designed to reach viewers over 55 years, was effective in fostering positive attitudes about aging (cited in Huston et al., 1992). Effects of images of the elderly need to be researched further and on different populations.

11.6.2.5. Disability Stereotypes.   According to the World Health Organization, disability is defined as "any restriction or lack (resulting from an impairment) of ability to perform an activity in the manner or within the range considered normal for a human being" (cited in Cumberbatch & Negrine, 1992, p. 5). Television tends to concentrate on the disability rather than on the individual aspects of the character portrayed. People with disabilities wish to be treated as ordinary people on television, not as superheroes or villains or with sentimentality. Cumberbatch and Negrine (1992) studied televised images of disability on programs produced in Great Britain from 1988 to 1989 and compared them to shows produced in the United States. By recording and coding 1,286 programs, they found that characters with disabilities were shown to have locomotor, behavioral, or disfigurement disabilities since these are visible. "The wheelchair has apparently become a ready symbol of the experience of disability, a shorthand for a variety of difficulties that someone suffering from disabilities may encounter" (Cumberbatch & Negrine, p. 136). They concluded that in feature films, characters with disabilities were stereotyped most commonly as criminals, as being barely human, or as powerless and pathetic. In British programs, they were portrayed as villains, moody, introverted, unsociable, or sad. In the United States, however, characters with disabilities were shown more positively and were more likely to be sociable, extroverted, moral, and nonaggressive. Research on the effects of portraying characters with disabilities is needed.

11.6.2.6. Sensitization and Inhibition Issues.   In addition to effects on stereotyping, studies suggest that some modeled behaviors can desensitize viewers, oversensitize viewers, or temporarily remove inhibitions (disinhibition effect). Variables include how victims' responses are portrayed as well as the type of behavior exhibited. Stein (1972) found that emotional arousal on exposure to violence declined with repeated exposure, but it was unclear if behavioral responses also declined (cited in Friedrich & Stein, 1973).

Repeated exposure to specific types of violent programming, especially sexual violence and sports, may result in some viewers becoming desensitized or disinhibited. Although exposure to erotic content does not appear to induce antisocial behavior,* research on sexual violence suggests that it can reinforce certain attitudes, perceptions, and beliefs about violence toward women (Huston et al., 1992). After seeing sexual assault modeled, men behave more punitively toward women than those shown sexual intimacy without aggression (Donnerstein, 1980, cited in Bandura, 1986).

> Showing women experiencing orgasmic pleasure while being raped stimulates greater punitiveness than if they are depicted expressing pain and abhorrence. Depictions of traumatic rape foster less aggression even though they are as arousing and more unpleasant than depictions of rape as pleasurable (Bandura, 1986, p. 295).

Bandura also states that since sexual modeling serves as a source of arousal and disinhibition, it can also heighten aggressiveness. Both male and female viewers who were massively exposed to pornography

> . . . regard hard-core fare as less offensive and more enjoyable, they perceive uncommon sexual practices as more prevalent than they really are, they show greater sexual callousness toward women, they devalue issues of importance to women, and they are more lenient toward rape offenses (Zillmann & Bryant, 1984, cited in Bandura, 1986, p. 294).

Although broadcast television is usually sexually suggestive rather than explicit, cable channels and videotape rentals can make violent and explicit sexual images readily available to children. Huston et al. (1992) call for more research to be done regarding the impact of these materials on children. Bandura (1986) expresses concern that while society exercises control over injurious actions, it presents discontinuities in the socialization of and boundaries for sexual behavior.

Although some viewers may become desensitized or disinhibited by what they watch on television, other viewers may become oversensitive. Television may cultivate or intensify distorted perceptions of the incidence of crime in the real world, especially for heavy viewers (Gunter, 1987; Gunter & Wakshlag, 1988; Murray, 1980; NIMH, 1982). Heavy viewers may think the world is more dangerous than it really is and perceive that the world is a mean and scary place (Liebert & Sprafkin, 1988). This may be the result of a circular effect where "greater fear of potential danger in the social environment may encourage people to stay indoors, where they watch more television, and are exposed to programmes which tell them things which in turn reinforce their anxieties" (Gunter & Wakshlag, 1988, pp. 208–209).

On the other hand, programs, such as crime dramas in which the antagonists end up being punished, can have the countereffect of providing comfort and reassurance in a just world (Gunter & Wakshlag, 1988). Gunter and Wober (1983) found a positive relationship between beliefs in a just world and exposure to crime drama programming (cited in Gunter, 1987).

The amount of viewing may be less important than the types of programs watched, the perception of and interpretation of content, and the actual level of crime where people live (Gunter, 1987). More detailed analyses are needed before causal conclusions can be drawn. Disinhibition effects that lead to increased aggressive behavior have also been observed. In a study conducted by Bandura and Walters (1963), experimental subjects were instructed to administer electrical shocks (simulated) to individuals who gave incorrect responses. In this study, subjects who were exposed to aggressive content (a scene of a knife fight) administered stronger electrical shocks than did their counterparts who were shown constructive or neutral films (Liebert & Sprafkin, 1988). They cautioned that many of the laboratory studies that supported disinhibition occurred in contrived circumstances with television segments that were taken out of context. They also found a trend for disinhibition effects among those who are initially more aggressive.

Some evidence exists that disinhibition also occurs when violence is viewed in real-life settings. For adults, disinhibition may be a factor in the increase in violence against women that occurs after football games. White, Katz, and Scarborough (1992) studied the incidence of trauma after National Football League games. Although Walker found that calls to women's shelters increased on the day that a team lost (cited in Nelson), White et al. found that women were more likely to be hospitalized for trauma from assaults on the day after a team won. They concluded that violence against women may be stimulated by some aspect of identification with an organization that dominates through violent behavior. "In a domestic context, the example of being successful through violent behavior may provide the male viewer with a heightened sense of power and may increase domination over his spouse or partner. This feeling of power can act to disinhibit constraints against violence" (White et al., p. 167). Additionally, calls to women's shelters increased in the first 4 to 5 hours after a Super Bowl game, with more calls being reported in some cities than on any other day of the year (Nelson, 1994). The director of a domestic abuse center stated that when men describe battering incidents that involve sports, "the men talk about being pumped up from the game" (p. 135). Other variables, such as intoxication, may confound these data.

11.6.3 Behaviors

A substantial body of research has been conducted relative to the positive and negative effects of television on behavior. Behavior patterns that are established in childhood and adolescence may affect the foundations for lifelong patterns that are manifested in adulthood (Huston et al., 1992). According to Wright and Huston (1983), "producers, advertisers, and broadcasters use violence in children's programming largely because they believe that dramatic content involving anger, aggression, threat, and conquest is essential to maintain the loyalty and attention of child audiences" (p. 838). The research on formal features has suggested alternative ways of maintaining attention, such as with high rates of child dialogue, high pace, auditory and visual special effects, salient music, and nonhuman speech (Wright & Huston, 1983). According to Hearold (1986), whether what is learned is put to use depends on a variety of factors:

> There must be the capability to perform the act, sufficient motivation, and some remembrance of what is viewed; performance also depends on the restraints present, including the perceived probability of punishment and the values held in regard to violence (p. 68).

Making definitive statements about the causes of behaviors or correlations between causes and effects is difficult because of inconsistencies in the labels for gross treatment effects. Antisocial and prosocial are broad terms that can represent diverse treatments or outcomes. There is also ambiguity in more specific terms such as frustration or aggression (Bandura & Walters, 1963).

In her meta-analysis of 230 studies that were conducted through 1977, however, Hearold (1986) made 1,043 treatment comparisons. Overall, she found a positive effect for antisocial treatments on antisocial behaviors and a positive effect for prosocial treatments on prosocial behaviors. When she looked at the most ecologically valid studies, Hearold found that effect sizes* continued to be positive, although they were lower. She cautions, however, that some of the differences may be understood by the intentionality of the treatments. For example, antisocial programs are generally created to entertain audiences, while prosocial programs have prosocial instruction as a goal. Other moderating variables can be the degree of acceptance of antisocial and prosocial behaviors.

11.6.3.1. Antisocial Outcomes. For decades, people have been concerned about the effect of television on antisocial behavior, particularly violence and aggression. Violence can be defined as "the overt expression of physical force against others or self, or the compelling of action against one's will on pain of being hurt or killed" (NIMH, 1972, p. 3). Aggression can be defined as an action intended to injure another person or object (Friedrich & Stein, 1973), but its designation as antisocial depends on the act as well as the circumstances and participants (NIMH, 1972). In observational studies, these antisocial acts include physical assault, nonverbal teasing, verbal aggression, commanding vigorously, tattling, injury to objects, and playful or fantasy aggression (Friedrich & Stein, 1973). Some laboratory studies use a "help-hurt" game in which the intensity, quantity, or length of pain-producing responses are measured when the subjects believe they are affecting another child or a researcher's accomplice.

Two decades of content analysis show that violence remains at approximately five violent acts per hour in prime-time television and at 20 to 25 acts per hour in children's Saturday morning programming. This translates into an average of 8,000 murders and over 100,000 acts of violence viewed by the time a child graduates from elementary school (Huston et al., 1992).

In 1994–1995, the National Cable Television Association funded the National Television Violence Study that went beyond counting the number of violent incidents portrayed on television. It identified important contextual factors, examined the presence of effect of ratings or content advisories, and explored the effectiveness of antiviolence television messages and public service announcements (Mediascope, 1996). Important contextual conclusions included:

- Perpetrators were unpunished in 73% of all violent scenes.
- The negative consequences of violence were not often portrayed.
- Handguns were used in 25% of violent interactions.
- On premium cable channels, 85% of the programs were violent, compared to public broadcasting channels with 18%.
- Movies were more likely to present violence in realistic settings than other program types.
- Children's programs were least likely to show the long-term consequences of violence.
- Violence was shown in a humorous context in 67% of children's programs.
- Only 4% of violent programs employed an antiviolence theme.

The study also found that "viewer discretion" advisories and "PG-13" or "R" ratings made programs more attractive for boys, particularly those aged 10 to 14, while the opposite was true for girls, especially those aged 5 to 9. Public service announcements and antiviolence programming were not effective in changing adolescents' attitudes about using violence to resolve conflict.

Antisocial outcomes have been shown to occur after exposure to antisocial programming. Although Huston et al.'s review of the literature stated that "there is clear evidence that television violence can cause aggressive behavior and can cultivate values favoring the use of aggression to resolve conflicts" (1992, p. 136), this statement should be treated with caution, because definitions of antisocial behavior, violence, and aggression can vary from study to study. Results can also vary depending on other variables such as age, sex, parenting style, or environmental cues. For example, Bandura and Walters' (1959) study of child-rearing practices found that parents of aggressive boys were more likely to encourage and condone aggression than the parents of nonaggressive boys (cited in Bandura & Walters, 1963). A predisposition for aggressiveness may also be a catalyst that produces increases in mediated behavior (Murray, 1980). Comstock and Paik (1987) list others factors that have been identified as heightening television's influence or contributing to viewers' antisocial behavior. These include the portrayal of violence as: (a) justified, rewarded, uncriticized, unpunished, or seemingly legal; (b) violence resulting in numerous victims or mass killings; (c) violence among friends or gang members; (d) viewers who are angered or provoked prior to viewing; and (e) viewers who are in a state of frustration or unresolved excitement after viewing (Comstock & Paik, 1987).

The accumulated research shows a positive correlation between viewing and aggression, i.e., "heavy viewers behave more aggressively than light viewers" (Huston et al., 1992, p. 54). But when a correlation is made between viewing televised violence and aggressive behavior, it does not mean that there is a causal relationship. Alternative explanations are possible, such as those who are more predisposed to aggression tend to watch more violent television.

Although experimental studies, such as the Bandura Bobo doll studies, have shown that aggression can increase after exposure to televised violence, the research hasn't proved that aggression demonstrated in laboratory settings transfers to real-life settings. Field studies show conflicting results, and naturalistic studies are frequently confounded by uncontrollable environmental factors.

In an effort to find more precise answers, a major endeavor was sponsored by the Surgeon General of the United States to study the effects of television on social behavior with a focus on the effects of televised violence on children and youth (NIMH, 1972). From 1969 to 1971, 23 independent projects were conducted, a number of which were field studies that showed correlations ranging from .0 to .30 (Atkin, Murray & Nayman, 1971). The end result was a very cautious report that stated, "On the basis of these findings . . . we can tentatively conclude that there is a modest relationship between exposure to television and aggressive behavior or tendencies . . ."(NIMH, 1972, p. 8). Only two of the studies showed +.30 correlations between earlier viewing and later aggression.

Finding positive correlations did not lead to statements of causality. The advisory committee cautioned that "a correlation coefficient of .30 would lead to the statement that 9% of the variance in each variable is accounted for by the variation in the other" (NIMH, 1972, p.167). They also wrote, "The majority of the values are trivially small, but the central tendency for the values is clearly positive. En masse, they indicate a small positive relationship between amount of violence viewing and aggressive behavior . . ." (NIMH, 1972, p. 168). They speculated that the correlations could be the result of any of three causal sequences: (a) viewing violence led to aggression, (b) aggression led to violence viewing, or that (c) both viewing and aggression were the products of some unidentified conditions. Such conditions could have included preexisting levels of aggression, underlying personality factors, or parental attitudes and behavior.

The committee found the experimental evidence to be weak and inconsistent. However, they felt there was a convergence of evidence for short-term causation of aggression among some children, but less evidence for long-term manifestations. They pointed out that the viewing-to-aggression sequence most likely applied to some children predisposed to aggressive behavior and that the manner in which children responded depended on the environmental context in which violence was presented and received (Atkin, Murray & Nayman, 1971–1972).

Overall, the Surgeon General's Advisory Committee concluded that there was a tentative indication of a causal relationship between viewing violence on television and aggressive behavior. Any relationship operated only on some children, those who were predisposed to be aggressive, and it operated only in some environmental contexts (NIMH, 1972).

In 1982, the NIMH published another report reviewing research conducted during the ensuing 10 years. In their summary, they concluded that the convergence of evidence supported the conclusion that there was a causal relationship between viewing televised violence and later aggressive behavior (NIMH, 1982). They cautioned that all the studies demonstrated group differences, not individual differences, and that no study unequivocally confirmed or refuted the conclusion that televised violence leads to aggressive behavior.

As stated earlier in this section, Hearold (1986) found similar results when she conducted a meta-analysis of studies conducted through 1977 which measured anti- or prosocial behavior or attitudes of subjects assigned to film or video treatment conditions. She included only those studies with valid comparison groups such as prepost comparison studies or those with control groups. Hearold found that the most frequently measured antisocial behavior was physical aggression, and concluded that positive findings have not been confined to a method, measure, or age group. While responses to television violence were undifferentiated by sex among young children under the age of 9, they became more differentiated with age as sex role norms were learned. Male-female differences were greatest for physical aggression in the later teen years when effect sizes for boys markedly increased, while those for girls decreased. When looking at outcome characteristics, Hearold found that physical aggression was a variable in 229 comparisons with a mean effect size of .31. She also found that when subjects were frustrated or provoked, the effect size increased (Hearold, 1986).

Other studies support the importance of individual predispositions and environmental contexts in predicting the negative effects of television. Because studying the effects of television in naturalistic settings is so complex, researchers called for a move away from determining if there are effects to seeking the explanations and processes responsible for causing effects (NIMH, 1982; Joy, Kimball & Zabrack, 1986). For example, Friedrich and Stein's (1973) study of 93 preschoolers found that children who were initially above average in aggression showed greater interpersonal aggression after exposure to aggressive cartoons than when exposed to neutral or prosocial programs. They also showed sharp declines in self-regulation such as delay tolerance and rule obedience. Children who were initially below average in aggression did not respond differently to the various treatment conditions.

In their longitudinal study, Joy, Kimball, and Zabrack (1986) found that after 2 years of exposure to television, children in the formerly Notel town were verbally and physically more aggressive than children in the Unitel and Multitel towns. They also found that boys were more aggressive than girls, and children who watched more television tended to be more physically aggressive. They speculate that this may have been due to a novelty effect rather than a cultivation effect.

Special populations of children can react to and use television differently from their nondisabled peers. When Sprafkin, Gadow, and Abelman (1992) reviewed field studies conducted with emotionally disturbed and learning disabled children, they found that these children demonstrated more physical aggression after viewing control material or cartoons with low levels of aggression than did nonlabeled children. However, in laboratory studies of exceptional children they found that children who are naturally more aggressive are more likely to be reactive to televised violence. Other variables may have impacted the results, including the use of nonaggressive, but highly stimulating or suspenseful, treatment materials.

There also seems to be a relationship between heavy viewing and restlessness. Studies conducted by Singer and colleagues and Desmond and colleagues (1990) found positive associations between heavy television viewing and greater restlessness for children whose parents were not involved in coviewing (cited in Comstock & Paik, 1991).

Most young children don't know the difference between reality and fantasy (NIMH, 1982). Some of the negative effects of violence and stereotypes may be attenuated if children can separate fiction from reality (Wright & Huston, 1983). Sprafkin, Gadow, and Dussault developed a test called the Perceptions of Reality on Television (PORT) to assess children's knowledge of the realism of people and situations shown on television (Sprafkin, Gadow & Abelman, 1992). It consists of showing a series of video excerpts about which children must answer questions. The PORT questions are based on judging the realism of aggressive content, nonaggressive content, and superhuman feats, on differentiating between the actor and the role played, and on differentiating between cartoons and nonanimated programs. PORT has been found to be a reliable and valid measure of children's perceptions of reality on television (Sprafkin, Gadow & Abelman, 1992). Research on the applicability of PORT to developing interventions in critical-viewing skills is needed.

At least three areas of concern arise from the literature on violence. The obvious ones are the relationship between television violence and aggression, even if the aggression is not directed against society, and the desensitization of children to pain and suffering (Smith, 1994). The less obvious one is the potential for effect on children who are sensitive and vulnerable and thus may become more fearful and insecure (Signorielli, 1991).

In response to these concerns, the United States Congress included in the Telecommunications Act of 1996 a requirement for television manufacturers to install an electronic device in every set that will be produced beginning in 1998. In order for this technology to work, the Telecommunications Act calls for programs to be rated and encoded according to their level of sex and violence. This device, popularly referred to as the "V-chip," enables parents to identify and block programming they determine is undesirable for their children (Telecommunications Act of 1996; Murray, 1995).

Alfred Hitchcock is reputed to have said, "Television has brought murder into the home, where it belongs" (Elkind, 1984, p. 103). Murders and crime occur about 10 times more frequently on television than in the real world. A third of all characters in television shows are committing crime or fighting it, most with guns. It becomes, therefore, a chicken-and-egg question. Does television programming include more violence because society is more violent, or does society become more violent because people are desensitized to violence through television? The answer is probably both. Too many factors interact for the extent of each influence to be determined.

When one examines violence in films the trend towards increased gore and explicit horror is easily documented. Rather than reflecting the content and meaning associated with myths and fairy tales, today's horror films are pure sensation with no serious content. In that aspect, they reflect our times, when so many have lives of pure sensation (Stein, 1982, cited in Elkind, 1984). If violence on television is controlled, children and adults will still be able to experience violence vicariously through other media, such as film, books, and recordings. Research on television suggests that the messages sent about violence do have an effect, but many factors can mediate these effects.

11.6.3.2. Prosocial Outcomes.   Although concerns about the negative effects of television are certainly valid, television also can be used to teach positive attitudes and behaviors. Prosocial behaviors include generosity, helping, cooperation, nurturing, sympathy, resisting temptation, verbalizing feelings, and delaying gratification (Friedrich & Stein, 1973; Rushton, 1982; Sprafkin, Gadow & Abelman, 1992). Liebert and Sprafkin (1988) divide prosocial behavior into two categories: altruism*—which includes generosity, helping, and cooperation—and self-control,* which includes delaying gratification and resisting the temptation to cheat, lie, or steal. However, children must be able to comprehend television content if prosocial messages are to be effectively conveyed.

Content analyses reveal an average of 11 to 13 altruistic acts per hour, 5 to 6 sympathetic behaviors, and less than 1 act of control of aggressive impulses or resistance to temptation (Liebert & Sprafkin, 1988). Although viewers are exposed to prosocial interpersonal behaviors, there are infrequent displays of self-control behaviors on television (Liebert & Sprafkin, 1988). Most of these prosocial behaviors appear in situation comedies and dramas.

In her meta-analysis, Hearold (1986) found 190 tests for effects of prosocial behavior. The average effect size for prosocial television on prosocial behavior (.63) was far higher than that for the effects of antisocial television on antisocial behavior (.30) (cited in Liebert & Sprafkin, 1988). "The most frequently measured prosocial behavior, altruism (helping or giving) had one of the strongest associations, with a mean effect size of .83" (Hearold, 1986, p. 105). Other noteworthy average effect sizes included .98 for self-control, .81 for buying books, .57 for a positive attitude toward work, and .57 for acceptance of others (Hearold, 1986). Due to these large effect sizes, Hearold called for more attention to and funding for production of prosocial programs for children.

One such program is *Mister Rogers' Neighborhood,* which has been lauded for its ability to promote prosocial behavior in preschool children. Field experiments showed that children increased self-control (Liebert & Sprafkin, 1988) and learned nurturance, sympathy, task persistence, empathy, and imaginativeness from viewing it (Huston et al., 1992). Positive interpersonal behavior was enhanced when viewing was supplemented with reinforcement activities such as role playing and play materials, especially for lower socioeconomic-status children (Huston et al., 1992; Sprafkin, Gadow & Abelman, 1992). After exposing children to 12 episodes of *Mister Rogers' Neighborhood* over a 4-week period, Stein and Friedrich (1972, cited in Murray, 1980) found that preschool children became more cooperative and willing to share toys and to delay gratification than children who watched antisocial cartoons. Friedrich and Stein (1973) also found that preschoolers showed higher levels of task persistence, rule obedience, and delay tolerance than subjects who viewed aggressive cartoons. These effects of increased self-regulatory behavior were particularly evident for children with above-average intelligence. Paulson (1974) reported that children who viewed *Sesame Street* programs designed to portray cooperation behaved more cooperatively in test situations than did nonviewers.

Sprafkin (1979) compiled the following results of research on other prosocial programs: *Sesame Street* improved children's racial attitudes towards African-Americans and Hispanics; *Big Blue Marble* caused fourth- through sixth-graders to perceive people around the world as being similar and "children in other countries as healthier, happier, and better off than before they had viewed the program" (p. 36); *Vegetable Soup* helped 6- to 10-year-olds become more accepting of children of different races; and finally, *Freestyle* helped 9- to 12-year-olds combat sex role and ethnic stereotyping in career attitudes.

Commercial television programs that reach larger audiences can also promote prosocial behavior. First-graders who viewed a prosocial *Lassie* episode were more willing to sacrifice good prizes to help animals seemingly in distress than a control group (Sprafkin, Liebert & Poulos, 1975, cited in Sprafkin, Gadow & Abelman, 1992). Children who viewed the cartoon *Fat Albert and the Cosby Kids* understood its prosocial messages and were able to apply them (Huston et al., 1992; Liebert & Sprafkin, 1988). Anderson and Williams (1983, cited in Stroman, 1991) found that after African-American children viewed an episode of *Good Times,* the children reported that they learned that street gangs are bad and that family members should help each other. Television can also explain to children how to handle fearful events, such as going to the dentist, or demonstrate that frightening situations aren't so bad (Stroman, 1991).

Forge and Phemister (1982) sought to determine whether a prosocial cartoon would be as effective as a live-model prosocial program. Forty preschool aged children were shown one of four different 15-minute videotapes. Subjects were then observed during 30 minutes of free play. The prosocial cartoon was as effective as the live-model program in eliciting prosocial behavior.

Unfortunately, some commercial superhero cartoons and crime/adventure programs may deliver prosocial or moral messages via characters who behave aggressively. Lisa, Reinhardt, and Fredriksen (1983, cited in Liebert & Sprafkin, 1988) used episodes of the cartoon *Superfriends* to compare a prosocial/aggressive condition to a purely prosocial condition. In their study of kindergarten, second-, and fourth-grade children, subjects were put in a situation where they could hurt or help another child within the context of a help-hurt game. They found that children exposed to a purely prosocial condition helped more than they hurt, tended to hurt less, and understood the plot and moral lesson significantly better than those in the prosocial/aggressive condition. Liebert and Sprafkin concluded that prosocial behavior should not be presented in an aggressive context.

Prosocial television has its critics, too. There are "legitimate moral objections to using a public medium to indoctrinate socially a whole nation of children" (Liebert & Sprafkin, 1988, p. 240). When Liebert and Sprafkin assisted with the production of an internationally broadcast public-service announcement that modeled cooperation by showing children sharing a swing, they were accused of trying to manipulate children's behavior and moral values and were told that their efforts could potentially be seen as "a highly objectionable form of psychological behavior control" (p. 243).

Although television can influence children and does so in an indiscriminate manner, an important question is whether anyone should purposely try to harness its power for specific socialization goals. Even so, Hearold (1986) makes a good point:

Although fewer studies exist on prosocial effects, the effect size is so much larger, holds up better under more stringent experimental conditions, and is consistently higher for boys and girls, that the potential for prosocial effects overrides the smaller but persistent negative effects of antisocial programs (p. 116).

11.6.4 Summary and Recommendations

Television can teach and change attitudes, values, beliefs, and behaviors, especially those considered prosocial. The beneficial effects of prosocial programming, especially for adolescents and adults, needs to be explored further.

Child-rearing practices are also a factor. Korzenny, Greenberg, and Atkin (1979, cited in Sprafkin, Gadow & Abelman, 1992) found that children of parents who disciplined with reasoning and explanation were less affected by antisocial content; children of parents who disciplined with power were most affected.

Many studies looked at behavior immediately following exposure to a short program. As research continues in these areas, it is important to examine the long-term and cumulative effects of exposure to television on attitudes, beliefs, and behaviors. As Schramm, Lyle, and Parker (1961) stated:

For some children, under some conditions, some television is harmful. For some children under the same conditions, or for the same children under other conditions, it may be beneficial. For most children, under most conditions, most television is probably neither particularly harmful nor particularly beneficial (cited in Hearold, p. 68).

It is also important to continue to identify those variables in the home, school, and society that are more important than television in the socialization of children. Rushton speculates that "television has become one of the most important agencies of socialization that our society possesses" (1982, p. 255). Many of the studies on socialization were based on content analyses, and detailed information was available about what was being portrayed (NIMH, 1982). Since television does appear to affect the world view of heavy users, research is needed to determine the long-term effects on viewers' attitudes, beliefs, and behaviors. Television violence can "work in subtle and insidious ways to adversely influence youth and society" (Liebert & Sprafkin, 1988, p. 135).

Although laboratory experiments do show a positive correlation between television violence and antisocial behavior, naturalistic studies are not as clear. In terms of causation, it appears that some populations in specific settings are sometimes affected. Many other factors—such as the characteristics of the viewers, friends and family, and environment—influence television effects. Research is moving away from determining if there is a relationship to determining the causes and nature of that relationship: "The concern is more with the kinds of violence, who commits violence, and who is victimized, because these portrayals may be critical mechanisms of social control" (NIMH, 1982, p. 41). It should be remembered that inferences of causation in violence studies are based on numerous correlational studies. One example of an area that should yield fruitful research is the interaction between formal features and the effects of television on aggression. If, as research indicates, aggression increases in the presence of specific formal features such as fast-paced action, regardless of the violence of the content, then researchers need to explore such interactions.

The television industry has recognized that it needs to play an active role in attempting to curb youth violence. In 1994, the Corporation for Public Broadcasting (CPB) partially funded "The National Campaign to Reduce Youth Violence." The goals of the campaign were (a) to focus on successful, community-based solutions, (b) to collaborate with multiple community resources and organizations, and (c) to involve youth in the problem-solving process (Head, 1994). Over an initial 2-year period, it hopes to have provided technical assistance with telecommunications services, two program series, and accompanying outreach programs. This campaign was designed to involve television, print, radio, government agencies, and community, educational, and industrial organizations. The purpose of the campaign is to identify and support interventions to counter the effects of violence on television.

11.7   PROGRAMMING AND UTILIZATION

We now turn to programming and its effects and to utilization studies. This section will critically review:

- Programming for preschoolers
- Programming for classrooms
- Programming for subject-matter teachers
- News programs
- Advertising on television
- Utilization studies

11.7.1   Programming for Preschoolers

11.7.1.1.   *Mister Rogers' Neighborhood.* Fred Rogers has stated that television can either facilitate or sabotage the development of learning readiness. According to Rogers, for a child to be ready to learn, the child must have at least six fundamentals: (a) a sense of self-worth, (b) a sense of trust, (c) curiosity, (d) the capacity to look and listen carefully, (e) the capacity to play, and (f) times of solitude. Television can help children develop the sense of uniqueness essential to their self-worth, or it can undermine this sense of uniqueness by teaching children to value things rather than people and by presenting stereotyped characters (Rogers & Head, 1963).

Rogers' program to develop learning readiness is the longest-running series on public television. Its goals are affective in that the programs are designed to increase self-esteem and valuing of self and others. Research shows that the program is successful in achieving these goals (Coates, Pusser & Goodman, 1976). Research has also shown that the program uses almost exclusively positive reinforcement to accomplish this goal (Coates & Pusser, 1975).

In 1992, McFarland found that the program helped childcare teachers and providers enhance the emotional development of preschool children. Parents had positive attitudes toward the use of quality children's programming in childcare. She found that while the behavior of adult childcare providers could be positively affected by watching *Mister Rogers' Neighborhood,* there were ambiguous effects for children's behavior. She concluded that Fred Rogers provided positive modeling that helped childcare providers to develop attitudes and behaviors that enhance the emotional development of preschool children. McFarland used a three-part study that included surveys, observations, and written feedback. Part 2 of the study used the programs plus accompanying materials for 5 months. To some extent, the success of the program is due to the use of supplementary materials, such as books, puppets, and tapes of songs on the show. Research has not determined the role of such materials in the instructional effectiveness of the program.

One issue that has been pursued in the research is the comparative effect of *Sesame Street* and *Mister Rogers' Neighborhood* on attention span. Studies on the effects of pacing on attention span are equivocal. Children who watched an hour of fast-paced programming were compared with children who watched an hour of slow-paced programming. No significant differences were found in effects on attention or perseverence. Two other studies showed that children who watched typical children's programming had increased impulsiveness and reduced perseverence. In another study, children who watched the slow-paced *Mister Rogers' Neighborhood* were found to be increasingly persistent in preschool activities (Anderson & Collins, 1988; Friedrich & Stein, 1973, cited in Huston et al., 1992). Anderson, Levin, and Lorch (1977) found no evidence that rapid television pacing had a negative impact on preschool children's behavior. Nor did they find a reduction in persistence or an increase in aggression or hyperactivity. Their research was an experiment using slow-paced and rapid-paced versions of *Sesame Street,* followed by a free-play period in a room full of toys.

11.7.1.2.   *Sesame Street.* In a series of classic studies of cognitive learning, Bogatz and Ball (1970, 1971) found that children who watched the most, learned the most, regardless of age, viewing or geographic location, socioeconomic status, or gender. Not only did children who watched gain basic skills in reading and arithmetic, they also entered school better prepared than their nonviewing or low-viewing peers. Encouragement to view was found to be an important factor in viewer gains. Paulson (1974) did an experiment to determine whether children learned social skills from watching. When tested in situations similar to those presented on the program, children who watched learned to cooperate more than children who did not. Reiser and his colleagues conducted two studies (1988, 1984) and concluded that cognitive learning increased when adults who watched *Sesame Street* with children asked them questions about letters and numbers and gave feedback.

More recent research on the relationship of viewing by preschool children to school readiness has been reported

(Zill, Davies & Daly, 1994). Zill et al. used data from the 1993 National Household Education Survey to determine who viewed the program and how regularly. Data from the survey were also examined to determine the relationship between viewing and (a) literacy and numeracy in preschool children, and (b) school readiness and achievement for early elementary students. The study found that the program reached the majority of children in all demographic groups including the "at risk" children. The findings revealed:

- Children of highly educated parents stopped watching the program earlier than children of less-educated parents.
- Children from disrupted families were more likely to watch the program.
- Children whose parents did not read to them regularly were less likely to watch the program.
- Children from low-income families who watched television showed more signs of emerging literacy than children from similar families who did not watch.
- Children who watched the program showed greater ability to read and had fewer reading problems in first and second grade.
- First- and second-graders who watched the program did not show less grade repetition or better academic standing.

The established value of *Sesame Street* for children in poverty is reviewed by Mielke (1994). In an article for a special issue of *Media Studies Journal* on "Children and the Media," he argued that the program is reaching and helping low-income children who have a narrower range of educational opportunities in the critical preschool years and that therefore it should be an important element in a national strategy for reaching our educational goals by the year 2000.

Recent research on CTW's educational programming is summarized in several documents that can be obtained from their research division, including:

- *"Sesame Street" Research Bibliography 1989–1994* (Petty, 1994a)
- *A review of "Sesame Street" Research 1989–1994* (Petty, 1994b)
- *"Sesame Street" Research Bibliography: Selected Citations to "Sesame Street" 1969–1989* (Research Division, CTW, June 1990)

The first of these documents provides an annotated bibliography. The second is a report of research in the areas of: (a) educational, cognitive, and prosocial implications; (b) effects of nonbroadcast materials; (c) formal features and content analyses; and (d) *Sesame Street* as stimulus material for other investigations. The third is also an annotated bibliography, but it covers research done both nationally and internationally.

11.7.1.3. Cartoons. Much of the discussion about the effects of cartoon programming has centered around the extent to which children of different ages assume that the fantasy presented in such shows is real. Fictional characters vary from realistic portrayals to superheros and heroines.

The photographic and dynamic qualities of television can make characters seem real. Children were shown photographs of television cartoon characters intermixed with photographs of familiar real people. Then, children were given tasks and asked questions designed to reveal their beliefs about these characters. There were 70 boys ages 5 to 12 participating. All the boys attributed unique physical characteristics to the characters, but the younger children generalized this uniqueness to other characteristics. For example, they believed a superhero could live forever because he was strong, or that he was happy because he could fly. Older children described the characters more realistically and were aware that physical ability doesn't ensure happiness. The study concluded that young children may miss important traits and consequences because visual effects heighten the physical dimension (Fernie, 1981, cited in Meringoff et al., 1983).

One of the problems with research on cartoons is that it is commonly done and reported within the Saturday morning children's programming context. A cartoon is typically a fantasy program with humor, mayhem, action, and drama. However, today realism is often mixed with animation, and there are many types of content represented in cartoons for children. Furthermore, religious training or calculus lessons can be put within an animated format that will influence children differently than will a Saturday morning entertainment cartoon. There has been much debate about whether cartoons are violent. All of these questions suggest that it is difficult to generalize from the research, because content becomes as important as format, and often these two variables are not separated, nor is their interaction studied.

11.7.2 Programming for Classrooms

After 40 years, the collective evidence that film and television can facilitate learning is overwhelming. This evidence is available for all forms of delivery, film, ITV, ETV, and mass media. It is reinforced by evaluation of programming prepared for these formats and delivered by newer delivery systems such as cable and satellite. The next section will review recent representative examples of this body of research. The section will be organized by these topics: general findings; video production*; educational series programming, including Children's Television Workshop productions; programming for subject-matter areas; satellite programming; and utilization studies.

11.7.2.1. General Findings. The findings reported here are the ones that are most important for futher research. In 1993, Katherine Cennamo critiqued the line of investigation initiated by Gavriel Salomon in the 1980s, with his construct of amount of invested mental effort, or AIME. Cennamo posed the question: Do learner's preconceptions of the amount of effort required by a medium influence the amount of effort they invest in processing such a lesson and consequently the quantity and quality of information they gain? Factors influencing preconceptions of effort required and actual effort expended were found to include characteristics of the task, media, and learners. In her summary, she noted that, in general, learners perceive television as a medium requiring little mental effort and believe they learn little from television. However, learners reported attending more closely to educational television programs than to commercial programs. The topic of the program also influenced preconceptions. She stated that in actuality, learning from television may be more difficult than learning from a single-channel medium because of its complexity. Learners achieved more from a lesson they were told to view for instructional reasons than from a lesson they were told to view for fun. This is consistent with many other findings about the importance of intentional use of the medium to help children learn, such as those reported in the Reiser et al. (1988, 1984) *Sesame Street* studies, which concluded that children learn more when an adult is present to guide and reinforce learning.

It is important to identify the types of learning that programs are designed to facilitate and the types of learning for which television can be used most effectively. Cennamo (1993) points out that the types of achievement tests used may not reveal mental effort or achievement in intended areas. For example, tests of factual recall cannot document increased mental effort or inferential thinking. Beentjes (1989) replicated Salomon's study on AIME and found that Dutch children perceived television to be a more difficult medium to learn from than did the American children in Salomon's study.

In 1967, Reid and MacLennan reviewed 350 instructional media comparisons and found a trend of no significant differences when televised instruction was compared to face-to-face instruction. However, their analysis of other uses of video instruction yielded different conclusions:

When videotapes were used in observation of demonstration teaching, teacher trainees gained as much from video observations as from actual classroom visits. In addition, when used in teaching performance skills—such as typing, sewing, and athletic skills—films often produced a significant increase in learning and an improvement in student attitudes (Cohen, Ebeling & Kulik, 1981, p. 27).

Another general finding is that the potential for television's effectiveness is increased when teachers are involved in its selection and utilization, and when teachers are given specialized training in the use of television for instruction (Graves, 1987). Teachers can integrate television in the curriculum, prepare students, extend and elaborate on content, encourage viewing, and provide feedback. They do this best if they themselves are prepared. If a distinction is made between television as a stand-alone teacher and television's capacity to teach when used by a teacher, the evidence indicates that although television can teach in a stand-alone format, it can teach more effectively when utilized by a competent teacher (Johnson, 1987). We turn now to the effects of specific programming used in classroom settings.

11.7.2.2. Film/Video Production. Interest in the effects

of production experience on students (see 9.7.3.3) started many years ago. In the early 1970s students learned how to produce Super 8-mm films. With easy access to half-inch videotape and portable equipment, they ventured into producing video. Since cable television has made more equipment, facilities, and training available, there has been an increase in video production by schools for educational purposes. Nevertheless, students have been producing programs for class assignments and school use since the 1960s. It is surprising, therefore, that there is very little research on the effects of video production by students on learning and attitudes. This may be due to the fact that most researchers are in university settings, and most video production is in school buildings, or to the difficulty of controlling variables in a field setting. Nevertheless, the effects of video production and the variables that mediate these effects are not being investigated. It may be that the strongest effects related to learning from television come from student productions, because the strongest commitment and identification is possible in these cases.

The Ford Foundation funded studies related to learning from film and television production. One such study reported on the effects of filmmaking on children (Sutton-Smith, 1976). Subjects attended a workshop on filmmaking. The researchers used the workshop to determine (a) the processes through which children of the same or different ages proceeded in the acquisition of filmmaking mastery, and (b) the perceptual, cognitive, and affective changes that resulted in the children. Observation, videotaping, and interviews were used for documentation. One interesting finding was that there were striking differences between younger and older children in filmmaking, despite repeated instruction in the same areas.

Young children tended not to make:

- Establishing shots
- Films about a major character
- Films about a group of characters
- Multiple scenes
- Markers in films (titles, ends, etc.)
- Story themes
- Story transitions
- Causal linkages
- Use of long shots, close-ups, pans, zooms, or changes in camera position
- Long films (18 seconds versus 65 seconds for older children)

Children 5 to 8 years old were considered young, and children 9 to 11 constituted the older group. It would be interesting to replicate this study today, because sophistication with the television code could generate different results.

Tidhar (1984, cited in Shutkin, 1990) researched the relationships between communication through filmmaking and the development of cognitive skills in children. She compared classes who studied scenario design, photography, and editing in different combinations and concluded that necessary mental skills for decoding film texts are developed during film production.

Those who encourage students to produce video assert that the process teaches them goal setting, creative problem solving, cooperative learning, interpersonal skills, and critical analysis skills. In addition, they claim the experience improves a student's self-esteem and self-concept. Furthermore, they contend that students who have trouble verbalizing or are "at risk" can succeed with this approach to learning when they can't in traditional classroom activities. There is little evidence to support such claims, because little research has been reported other than testimonials from teachers and students. Generally, the studies reported are subjective case histories that are likely to be both perceptive and biased. Another problem is that often intact classes are compared over long periods of time. Thus, lack of control of variables limits interpretation and confidence.

Barron (1985, cited in Shutkin, 1990) found that a comprehensive course for fifth-graders, involving both video production and media studies, led to the development of mental skills necessary for understanding television programming. Torrence (1985) reviewed research findings about the features that should be incorporated in school video production experiences. These features are offered through guidelines on message design and utilization factors. Laybourne (1981, cited in Valmont, 1995) states that children who make their own television productions become more critical viewers.

This assertion of an association between video production experience and media literacy is common in the literature, although few report studies that investigated the phenomena. Messaris (1994) addresses "production literacy," meaning competency in the production of images. He conducted a study in 1981 (cited in Messaris, 1994) that compared subjects with various levels of competency in filmmaking, from expert to apprentice to novice. They were shown a film containing both traditional naturalistic style (narrative) editing and experimental editing. All three groups ignored visual conventions in their interpretations of the traditional editing sequences and instead discussed the events in the film as if they actually occurred. With the experimental sequences, however, there were differences among the groups. The novices became confused and struggled to interpret. The apprentices and especially the experts discussed explicit intentions of the filmmaker and the visual conventions used. In a follow-up study (Messaris & Nielsen, 1989), the significance of production experience was confirmed. The researchers interpreted the findings as indications that production experience heightened awareness of manipulative conventions and intent and thus improved media literacy.

Shutkin (1990) has urged the development of a critical media pedagogy, because the adoption of video equipment in the schools is not politically neutral and, therefore, is potentially problematic. In support of his theoretical position, Shutkin offers a review of the research and theory around video production education and filmmaking. He points out that video production involves interpersonal and group process skills that can be researched, as well as other aspects of the communication process that suggest variables for researchers to pursue. Shutkin raises questions such as, "If video production is being used to lower the dropout rate, raise self-esteem, or develop technological skill, why are we not determining whether and how these results occur and what mediates the process?"

11.7.2.3. Educational Series Programming. The most important research on educational programs designed for home and classroom use comes from Children's Television Workshop (CTW). The contribution of this organization to television research is of such overwhelming importance that this section will devote much of its discussion to CTW. In 1990, Keith Mielke, senior research fellow at CTW, edited a special issue of *Educational Technology Research and Theory* devoted to CTW. In a case study of CTW, Polsky (1974) concluded that historical research supports the conclusion that systematic planning was the key to CTW's success.

CTW produced several series that were used in the classroom as well as broadcast to the home. Among these series were *Sesame Street*, which was used in some elementary schools, *Electric Company, 3-2-1 Contact*, and *Square One*. Research on *Sesame Street* has already been discussed; however, the research on each of the other series will be discussed separately in this section.

11.7.2.4. Electric Company. *Electric Company* was aimed at children in early elementary grades who were deficient in reading skills. It focused on blending consonants, chunking of letter groups, and scanning for patterns. Learning outcomes were supposed to be discrimination of vowels from consonants, scanning text for typical word structures, and reading for meaning by using context. The series was an experiment in using a video medium to teach decoding skills for a print medium.

Stroman (1991) stated that summative evaluations of *Sesame Street* and the *Electric Company* indicated that African-American children improve their cognitive skills after exposure to these programs. Graves (1982) pointed out the importance of adult coviewing. Learning increased and reading performance improved after children viewed these programs with an adult present. When teachers made sure children viewed, used additional learning materials, and provided practice, children learned these skills, with the greatest gains being made by the youngest children and children in the bottom half of the class. A comparison made with home viewing indicated that it was important to attract the viewers for a sufficient number of shows to have a measurable impact on reading skills. Research on the series suggested the difficulty of depending on the home as the context for learning (Johnson, 1987).

11.7.2.5. 3-2-1 Contact. *3-2-1 Contact* was designed to harness the power of television to convey to children the excitement and fascination of science. Its objective was to create a climate for learning about science, in other words to provide science readiness. It was aimed at 8- to 12-year-old children. After 2 years of research, CTW offered some surprising insights about 8- to 12-year-olds and television:

- They attended to stories where a problem was posed and resolved through relations between recurring characters, particularly those dealing with life and death themes.
- They attended primarily to the visual channel. A dense or abstract audio track overwhelmed them.
- They thought in terms of their personal experiences rather than abstractly.
- Boys favored action and adventure programs, while girls favored programs about warm, human relationships.
- They identified with and preferred the cast of members like themselves in terms of gender or ethnicity.
- They preferred role models who were somewhat older.
- They preferred the characters on the show who were competent or striving to be competent.
- They liked humor in sequences only when it was age and subject appropriate.
- They had a traditional image of scientists as middle-aged white males working in laboratories to invent or discover. However, younger scientists were often more impressive to these children than Nobel Prize winners.
- They needed a wrap-up at the end of the program to make connections and reinforce learning.

All of these findings were taken into account when the format and content of the program were determined (Iker, 1983). Research on the program indicated that significant gains occurred in comprehension and in interest and participation in science activities. However, there were no significant effects on career attitudes (Revelle, 1985; Research Communications, 1987, cited in Sammur, 1990). Gotthelf and Peel (1990) reported the steps CTW took to make the program, which was originally designed for home viewing, a more effective science teaching tool when used in school classrooms. Instructional technologists who read their article will be interested in the barriers that needed to be removed and the resources that needed to be provided. An annotated research bibliography on *3-2-1 Contact* is available from CTW (Research Division, CTW, n.d.).

11.7.2.6. Square One. This series was introduced in 1987 with the objective of addressing the national need for early positive exposure to mathematics. Its primary audience was intended to be 8- to 12-year-olds viewing at home. The content was to go beyond arithmetic into areas such as geometry, probability, and problem solving. However, the program was designed to be motivational rather than to teach cognitive skills. The program was used in classrooms. Chen, Ellis, and Hoelscher (1988) investigated the effectiveness of reformatted cassettes of the program. Chen et al. mention that previous studies of educational television identify two classes of barriers to school use: technological (i.e., obtaining equipment); and instructional (i.e., finding supplementary materials, designing lessons, and finding time). Teachers found the cassettes especially helpful in demonstrating

connections between mathematical ideas and real-world situations. The most researched variable related to this program is problem-solving outcomes. In studies done in the Corpus Christi, Texas, public elementary schools, viewers demonstrated more skill in problem solving than nonviewers. This was generally true in the research done on the effects of *Square One* (Debold, 1990; Hall, Esty & Fisch, 1990; Peel, Rockwell, Esty & Gonzer, 1987; Research Communications, 1989, cited in Sammur, 1990). In addition, viewers recalled aspects of mathematics presented on the show and displayed more positive attitudes and motivation towards science (Schauble, Peel, Sauerhaft & Kreutzer, 1987, as reported in Sammur, 1990; Debold, 1990). A five-volume report on a National Science Foundation study of the effects of the series reported an interesting finding:

> Across all of these themes, there were no substantive differences among the viewers' reactions as a function of their gender or socioeconomic status. The reactions described above came from both boys and girls and from children of different economic backgrounds (Fisch, Hall, Esty, Debold, Miller, Bennett & Solan, 1991, p. 13).

A research history and bibliography on *Square One* is available from CTW (Fisch, Cohen, McCann & Hoffman, 1993).

11.7.2.7. ThinkAbout. *ThinkAbout* was a series created by the Agency for Instructional Television in the early 1980s. It consisted of 60 15-minute episodes designed to strengthen reasoning skills and reinforce study skills. There were 13 program clusters on topics such as estimating, finding alternatives, and collecting information. The series was aimed at upper elementary students. Research on *ThinkAbout* is reported in a series of ERIC documents from the late 1970s and early 1980s (Carrozza & Jochums, 1979; Sanders & Sonnad, 1982).

Students who spent 2 hours a week watching the program improved their thinking skills to a very limited extent. Although the program added a new element to the classroom, research did not support its effectiveness (Sanders, 1983, cited in Johnson, 1987). Johnson also reported that the research itself was flawed in two ways. First, the criterion of effectiveness was performance on the California Test of Basic Skills, which was too general a test to provide a realistic measure of success. Secondly, the research was done after 1 year of uncontrolled use. There was no assurance that teachers had been trained to use the series as intended or that they did. This is documented by a series of case studies on how *ThinkAbout* was used in classrooms, which reported that the series was both used effectively and misused (Johnson, 1987). Over 80% of the teachers reported that the series presented complex ideas better than they could and that the programs stimulated discussion (Sanders, 1983, cited in Johnson, 1987).

Television series for classroom as well as home use have come from other sources. The British government funded the Open University, which has a library of over 3,000 instructional video programs keyed to courses. The British have also produced many series, such as *The Ascent of Man,* which are suitable for instructional purposes. Several series for secondary and postsecondary education in the United States have been funded by the Annenberg Foundation. Unfortunately, most of these fine series have neither been researched nor used in classroom settings.

11.7.2.8. Subject-Matter Instruction. Secondary teachers in subject-matter areas have used film and video to enhance their teaching. The areas in which they have been used most extensively are social studies and science.

Because television is the main source of news for most Americans, the area of social studies has a mandate to teach critical-viewing skills. In addition, television has become the primary medium for political campaigning in the United States. Thus, educating voters requires attention to television and its effects. Fortunately, there is plentiful research on learning from television news, some of which will be discussed later in this section (Hepburn, 1990). The other area in which research is available to help the social-studies teacher use television is economics. Huskey, Jackstadt, and Goldsmith (1991) conducted a replication study to determine the importance of economics knowledge to understanding the national news. Of the total news program, 13% (or 3 minutes) was devoted to economic stories, but knowledge of economic terms was essential to understand the stories (Huskey, Jackstadt & Goldsmith, 1991).

There are many studies on the effectiveness of using television and film to teach science and mathematics. Two recent interesting approaches need to be researched. One suggests that science fiction films and programming be used to teach science (Dubeck, Moshier & Boss, 1988); another uses teacher-training institutes for science, television, and technology to impact classroom teaching. This project is called the National Teacher Training Institutes for Science, Television and Technology. Managed by Thirteen/WNET, the New York City public television station, it is an alliance between education, business, and public television (Thirteen/WNET, 1992). The research was supported by Texaco Corporation. By the end of 1993, the Teacher Training Institutes will have reached 17,000 teachers and 2 million students. So far findings have been that students in classes exposed to ITV outperformed peers in non-ITV classes, that they scored higher on creative imagery and writing, that they are more confident in problem solving, and that they learn more in proportion to the time spent on ITV.

11.7.2.9. Satellite Programming. Programming delivered to the classroom via satellite can be divided into two categories: news programs and subject-matter courses. The most famous of the news programs is *Channel One,* but there are others, such as *CNN Newsroom,* which is broadcast by Ted Turner's news network (Wood, 1989). The courses are distributed from many sources, the most commonly known of which is the Satellite Educational Resource Consortium (SERC). Very little research has been done on courses distributed by satellite to schools, because this is a relatively recent phenomenon.

Zvacek (1992) compared three classroom news programs: *Channel One, CNN Newsroom,* and the front-end news segment of *Today.* Although each show followed a pattern of different segments, there was variability between the programs. She found differences in the proportion of time devoted to news and features, in the content of news stories, in the length of the news stories, in a national or international orientation, and in format. *Channel One* devoted slightly more time to features than did the other programs. *Today* spent more time on news than did the other programs. *CNN Newsroom* had more stories on world events and *Channel One* on national events. Late-breaking news often did not make it onto the pretaped school news programs. *Channel One* includes advertisements, while *CNN Newsroom* does not.

Some research has been done specifically on *Channel One.* Generally, the findings from different studies are consistent about these points:

- Viewers like the features more than the news.
- Viewers ignore the advertisements.
- Knowledge of current events does not improve significantly.
- The program is not integrated in the school curriculum; teachers do not prepare students for watching or discuss what was watched.
- Knowledge of geography and map reading is increased (Knupfer, 1994; Knupfer & Hayes, 1994; Thompson, Carl & Hill, 1992; Tiene, 1993, 1994).

There are many ethical and social issues associated with the use of *Channel One* in the schools. These issues arose because Whittle Communications offered free equipment to each school that would agree to require students to watch the news program for 10 minutes a day for 3 years. In exchange, a school received a satellite dish, two videocassette recorders, a color television set for every classroom, and all necessary internal wiring, installation, and servicing. Over 8 million teenagers in more than 12,000 schools currently view the program and its advertisements. The issues provoked by the acceptance of the program are explored in *Watching Channel One,* a book of research edited by Ann De Vaney (1994). In many ways, the book is an example of a postmodernist approach to research on television effects. As such it is interesting both for the methodologies incorporated and the ideas presented. In the book, John Belland raises questions such as whether it is ethical for educators to deliver a mass audience for advertisers, and whether the time invested is defensible even if used for a discussion of popular culture.

11.7.3 News Programs

Television news programs are essential sources of information for citizens of all countries. Because learning from television news programs is important, especially in a democracy, extensive research on learning from television news programs has been done nationally and internationally. Unfortunately, methodological problems have hampered researchers and limited the usefulness of this body of literature. For example, Robinson and Levy (1986) discredited the methodology of studies, which determined that television is the primary purveyor of news. Their criticism centered on poorly designed survey questions.

This section will address four variables after methodological issues are explained. Two of the variables will be independent variables: news item or story (content) characteristics and presentation variables.* One will be a mediating variable, viewer characteristics, and one will be a dependent variable, learning outcomes.

11.7.3.1. Methodological Issues. The major methodological issue is the confounding of variables. For example, it is difficult to determine to what extent differences in knowledge are affected by exposure to other media or by talking with family and friends. Without controls for other important variables, the independent effects of television news viewing on learning cannot be determined (Gunter, 1987). Another example is the confounding of two independent variables, content and presentation. It is difficult to determine whether effects are due to design or content factors or to an interaction of the two, because a message must incorporate both factors. This confounding is further complicated by additional mediating factors outside of television (Berry, 1983). Research that examines the relationship between dependence on newspapers or television for news and mediating factors, such as viewer characteristics or exposure to a variety of media, provides another example of the difficulty of controlling for confounding variables (Gunter, 1987).

A second major methodological issue is consistent with definitional issues reported in other sections, such as scholastic achievement and family context. It is difficult to make comparisons across studies, because variables are defined or interpreted differently. This is especially true with the variables of attention, recall, and comprehension. There are at least three distinct levels at which attention to news can be measured: (a) regularity of watching, (b) deliberateness of watching, and (c) degree of attentiveness to the screen (Berry, 1983). Recall can be free,* cued,* or aided, and can vary within each of these categories. Recall is sometimes incorrectly interpreted as comprehension of news stories.

An additional weakness in television news research is the generally narrow interpretation of the data without reference to a theoretical base. Consequently, it is difficult to relate the findings of different studies, and it's especially hard to relate them to what is known about learning in general. One reason for this is that research on television news is often done by those in mass-media areas who do not focus on theories of learning. This issue has been addressed from an information-processing perspective by Woodall, Davis, and Sahin (1983) in an article on news comprehension.

11.7.3.2. Viewer Characteristics. Educational level,

gender, intelligence, frequency of watching, interest, motivation, and knowledge of current events have all been found to be significantly related to learning from television news. Of these factors, the most significant seems to be knowledge of current events, because the other factors are only slightly related, or there are conflicting studies. Berry (1983) speculated on whether the importance of knowledge of current events is due to its correlation with education or its role as an indicator of ability to assimilate knowledge and thus retain it.

While there has been considerable interest in the effect of motivation on learning from television news, the evidence is not clear. Several studies claim to show motivational effects; however, there are not many studies that can be compared (Berry, 1983; Gunter, 1987). For example, differences in mean news recall from television bulletins were found to be greater in those with higher motivation than with higher educational level (Neuman, 1976). However, statistical controls for the effects of knowledge might change these results. Nevertheless, the finding that those who watch for information learn more than those who watch for purely entertainment is consistent with other research in education on learning from intentional set (Gantz, 1979, cited in Gunter, 1987).

Research on the effect of frequency of viewing is characterized by the same methodological problems as other research on learning from television news (Gunter, 1987). Cairns has studied comprehension of television news since 1980, using children from the North and South of Ireland and has found an interaction with age. Children aged 11 years who reported greater viewing frequency knew more about current events (Cairns, 1984, cited in Gunter, 1987). In 1990, Cairns reported research on how quantity of television news viewing influenced Northern Irish children's perceptions of local political violence. Based on a correlation between viewing frequency and perceptions that matched social reality, Cairns (1990) concluded that children's frequency of viewing affected comprehension. The findings on gender as they interact with learning from violent segments on television news will be discussed under the next topic, news item characteristics.

11.7.3.3. News Item Characteristics. This variable describes the content of news stories. Much of the research has centered around the effects of violent segments and the interaction of violent content with presentation and viewer variables. An important finding in the literature is that there is an interaction between gender and violence in television news. Visual presentation of violence affected how well females recalled the news. Violence negatively affected females recall of other contiguous, nonviolent news stories, but male subject recall was not affected similarly (Gunter, Furnham & Gietson, 1984; Furnham & Gunter, 1985, cited in Gunter, 1987).

This finding highlights an important aspect of the content of television news, its visuals. The visuals are important because they are selected by the producers and thus influence story interpretation, just as the words and announcer's tone do. Cognitive scientists have argued that imagery has an important role in memory. It is generally concluded that memory for pictures is better than memory for words (Fleming & Levie, 1993). The selection of dramatic visuals, therefore, can enhance or impair memory and comprehension.

Violence in a news story can increase interest. However, violent events can distract from attention and learning even though they heighten impact (Gunter, 1987). This finding is in contrast to findings that violent visuals are often remembered better. Gunter (1980) reported on Neuman's study of recall associated with economic news as compared with news of the war in Vietnam. Recall of the war news was much greater, probably due to the visuals used.

The organization of the message is also an important aspect of a news story. Cognitive frames of reference, known variously as schemata or scripts, which individuals utilize during learning, facilitate memory and comprehension. Thus, the absence of an organization compatible with the learner's schemata can contribute to poor comprehension and recall (Graber, 1984; Collins, 1979, cited in Gunter, 1987). Krendl and Watkins (1983) examined the components of a television narrative schema and the effect of set on learning. They concluded that the process of learning from television becomes a function of both the messages sent and the perceptual set with which the messages are received and interpreted. The groups with an educational set scored consistently higher than groups given an entertainment set. There were no significant differences between groups in understanding the plot; however, groups with an educational set had better recall and higher-level processing. Thus, the organization of the message seems to interact with motivation for watching.

Lang (1989) has studied the effects of chronological sequencing of news items on information processing. She hypothesized that a chronological organization would facilitate episodic processing and reduce the load on semantic memory, thereby reducing effort and increasing amount of information processed. This hypothesis was supported, in that chronological presentation of events was easier to remember than broadcast structure, which presented what is new followed by causes and consequences of the change.

11.7.3.4. Presentation Variables. Another term for these aspects of television news is *formal features*. With television news, research has centered around factors such as humor, recapping* and titles, narrator versus voice-over, and still and dynamic visuals (see 26.4.3). Kozma (1986) wrote a review article that examined the implications of the cognitive model of instruction for the design of educational broadcast television. In the article he reviews research related to pacing, cueing, modeling, and transformation that has implications for design of presentation features. By transformation he meant having the learner change knowledge in one form to another form, such as from verbal to visual form. He suggested that designers cue cognitive strategies for older learners and increase salience for younger learners.

Perloff, Wartella, and Becker (1982) and Son, Reese, and Davie (1987) investigated the use of recaps in television news. Both articles reported an increase in retention when the news was recapped. Son et al. (1987) speculated that this was due to time for rehearsal. Snyder (1994) analyzed scripts and stories used in television news and concluded that comprehension can be increased by captioning.

Edwardson, Grooms, and Pringle (1976) compared the effect of a filmed news story with the same story related by an anchorperson without visualization. They found that the filmed news story was remembered no better than the story told by the anchor. Slattery (1990) conducted an experiment to determine whether viewer evaluation of a news story would be influenced by visuals when the verbal information was held constant. Treatment number 1 used visuals both related and relevant to the information presented by the audio channel, i.e., visuals of a landfill when a landfill issue was presented. Treatment number 2 used only related visuals, i.e., a shot of a council meeting where an issue was discussed, instead of a visual of the home or people involved. Treatment number 3 consisted of audio information only; no visuals were used. The hypothesis was supported because the visuals influenced the interpretation of the news. Those in treatment number 1 found the story more interesting, important, informative, unforgettable, clear, and exciting than those in treatments number 2 or 3.

11.7.3.5. Learning Outcomes. The learning outcomes related to television news that have been investigated are attention, recall and retention, comprehension, and attitude change. Of these, the most researched areas are recall and comprehension. One important finding related to recall is that there are dramatic increases when cued or aided recall* is used (Neuman, 1976, cited in Gunter, 1987). Educational level is related to amount of recall. Stauffer, Frost, and Rybolt (1978, 1980, cited in Gunter, 1987) found that spontaneous recall was highest among educated subjects and lowest among illiterate subjects. It is not surprising that education and social class/occupational status were correlated with comprehension of television news (Trenaman, 1967, cited in Gunter, 1987). One must be careful when findings on recall and comprehension are reported, because sometimes measures of comprehension are actually measures of recall.

11.7.4 The Effects of Advertising

Ellen Notar (1989) argues that television is a curriculum, and as such it is the ultimate example of individualized instruction. She questions why we have left it almost entirely in the hands of the profitmakers and why children are not being taught to question the assumptions presented by advertising. She summarizes the situation:

Recently, I did an analysis of both programming and commercials aimed at children. Unbelievable results! The data were worse than an analysis I did in the late 1970s. Commercials were at least 12 to 14 minutes of each hour, repeated over and over again. The sound levels were higher than the regular programs. The messages were *violence solves problems, advertisers' products will make you happy, and popular, sugar products are selected by the best and the brightest.* The graphics, photography, and audio were invariably superior to the programs they surrounded, guaranteed to capture children's attention if program interest waned. Television advertiser's spend over $800 million a year on commercials directed at children under age 12! The average child watching television 4 hours a day sees more than 50 of these spots daily and about 18,000 per year! (p. 66).

11.7.4.1. Evolution of the Research Base.
Concern for the effects of advertising on television has a 30-year history. In 1977, the National Science Foundation (NSF) published a review of the literature on the effects of television advertising. The issues addressed are still controversial today:

1. Children's ability to distinguish television commercials from program material
2. The influence of format and audiovisual techniques on children's perceptions of commercial messages
3. Source effects and self-concept appeals in children's advertising
4. The effects of advertising containing premium offers
5. The effects of violence and unsafe acts in television commercials
6. The impact on children of proprietary medicine advertising
7. The effects on children of television food advertising
8. The effects of volume and repetition of television commercials
9. The impact of television advertising on consumer socialization
10. Television advertising and parent-child relations (National Science Foundation, 1977, p. ii)

The report considered both fantasy violence in commercials and commercials adjacent to violent programs. They concluded that there was relatively little violence in commercials, that the types of violence in commercials were rarely imitable, and that the duration of the violence was too short to suggest instigational effects on viewers. The question of definition arose again in regard to research on television; what should be interpreted as violence in commercials and in programming for children is still being debated.

The principal investigator for this report and some of his coinvestigators (Adler, Lesser, Meringoff, Robertson, Rossiter & Ward, 1980) subsequently published another review of the literature on the effects of television advertising. In 1987, Comstock and Paik recognized the importance of the issue for public-policy formation by reviewing its evolution, the points of contention, and the empirical evidence in a report commissioned by the ERIC Clearinghouse on Information Resources. In 1988, Liebert and Sprafkin reviewed the studies on effects of television violence and advertising on children. The areas they synthesized reflect the continuing issues: children's understanding of commercials, effects of common advertising tactics, concerns about products advertised, and training young consumers. A British

review of advertising effects of television (Young, 1990) brought attention to many variables that need to be investigated: for example, the effects of formal features used in advertising. In 1991, Comstock and Paik expanded their ERIC review into a book on *Television and the American Child* that reviewed empirical evidence in five areas related to television advertising: recognition and comprehension, harmfulness, parenting, programming, and program content.

The report of the American Psychological Association task force on television effects included a review of research on advertising around topics such as nutrition and health, advertising content and effects, and cognitive abilities necessary to process advertising (Huston et al., 1992). The members of the task force concluded that although the number of commercials increased due to federal deregulation in the early 1980s, many issues related to advertising were not addressed by the research. Some of these issues are the effects of (a) heavy viewing on materialistic values, (b) interruptions for commercials on attention span, (c) health-related commercials, and (d) individual differences in persuadability. Today, new issues have arisen that need to be investigated, because information is important for shaping public-policy positions. The effects of home shopping channels, infomercials, and *Channel One* are among these issues.

11.7.4.2. Consistent Findings.
Some findings have been consistent over these 30 years of research. The strongest is that the effects of television advertising diminish and change as the child ages. Attention to commercials decreases as children get older (Ward, Levinson & Wackman, 1972). Young children have difficulty distinguishing commercials from programming (Zuckerman, Ziegler & Stevenson, 1978), although this ability increases throughout the preschool years. Eventually by age 8, most viewers can make this distinction (Levin, Petros & Petrella, 1982). Kunkel (1988) found that children ages 4 to 8 were less likely to discriminate commercials from regular programming when a host-selling format was used, and that older children were more favorably influenced by commercials in this format. Television commercials influence children's food selections (Gorn & Goldberg, 1982), but the degree of influence is disputed (Bolton, 1983). The combined information seems to indicate that television commercials do have an effect on product selection that is limited when all aspects of a child's environment are taken into account. Nevertheless, young children may be affected greatly by television advertising and need help dealing with it.

Another finding of consistent importance over the years is the interrelationship of formal features and the effects of advertising. As early as the 1977 NSF report, there was speculation on this relationship. The report stated that the type of violence in children's commercials and programming almost always fell in the fantasy category. Thus, the impact of violence might vary according to the number of fantasy cues. Cartoons have at least three cues to indicate violence (animation, humor, and a remote setting); make-believe violence generally has two cues (humor and a remote setting); and realistically acted violence generally has only one cue (the viewer's knowledge that the portrayal is fictional). Real-life violence (i.e., news footage) has no cues to suggest fantasy. It easy to imagine a young child without media literacy becoming confused and misunderstanding such messages.

11.7.4.3. Important Findings. An important study, "A Longitudinal Analysis of Television Advertising Effects on Adolescents," was conducted by Moore and Moschis and reported in 1982. This study is mentioned because the effects of television advertising on a society of widely differing economic groups is another area that needs researching. Moore and Moschis concluded:

> In addressing the question of whether television advertising has a direct effect or is mediated through interpersonal processes, it was found that the family communication environment may perform such a mediating function. Specifically, television advertising appears to have some effects on the development of materialism* and traditional sex roles among those families which are not likely to discuss consumption matters with their children, apparently placing the child at the mercy of advertising, a finding consistent with previous research (Churchill & Moschis, 1979, p. 3).

Another important study was done by Jalongo in 1983. She investigated "The Preschool Child's Comprehension of Television Commercial Disclaimers."* She used "The Personal Interview Questionaire" (Blatt et al., 1971; Ward, 1972), which assessed general knowledge about television. Results indicated that linguistic ability was a poor predictor of paraphrase and standard/modified disclaimer scores. Scores reflecting general knowledge about television were the most effective predictors of disclaimer comprehension.

11.7.5 Utilization Studies

Research that investigates the use of instructional television, including factors such as (a) availability of equipment, programming, support personnel, and training; (b) attitudes towards television in the classroom and informally; and (c) the impact of instructional television, is grouped in a category called "utilization studies." There is a long tradition of utilization studies which dates back to the early 1950s when the FCC reserved channels for education and to film studies done earlier. Nevertheless, there are many gaps in this area of the literature. In a comprehensive review of ETV as a tool for science education, Chen (1994b) outlines the lack of research, especially developmental research, on the many science series broadcast nationally. Compared to the investment in production, minimal resources have been devoted to research on learning from most of these series.

The category "utilization studies" encompasses research on using television processes and resources for learning (Seels & Richey, 1994). This discussion of utilization research will cover several topics:

1. Variables investigated
2. Projects of historical interest
3. Studies from the Agency for Instructional Technology (AIT), formerly the Agency for Instructional Television

4. Studies from the Corporation for Public Broadcasting (CPB)
5. Other utilization studies

11.7.5.1. Variables Investigated. Chu and Schramm (1968) reviewed research on television before the ERIC Clearinghouse began to compile and organize the literature on learning from television. They summarized the variables that interacted with learning from instructional television. Today, many of these variables are being investigated under questions related to message design. The remaining variables are still pursued in the area of utilization studies. As identified by Chu and Schramm, these variables are:

- Viewing conditions, e.g., angle, context, grouping, interaction (see Chapter 36.)
- Attitudes towards ITV, e.g., students, teachers
- Learning in developing regions, e.g., visual literacy, resistance
- Educational level, e.g., elementary, adult
- Subject matter, e.g., health education, current events
- Relationship to other media, e.g., effectiveness, cost, integration.

Over the years, two of Chu and Schramm's variables have assumed increasing importance: the variable of effectiveness of instruction as measured by formative and summative evaluation, and the variable of impact on the individual, organization, and society.

11.7.5.2. Projects of Historical Interest. A good overview of the television utilization studies done in the 1950s, 60s, and 70s is obtained when projects in the Midwest, Hagerstown (Maryland), Samoa, and El Salvador are examined. Most of these projects received funding through Ford Foundation grants, local funds, and corporate equipment. Three districtwide patterns emerged. Studies revolved around investigation of the effectiveness of these patterns, which were (a) total instructional program presented by television teacher, (b) supplemented television instruction, and (c) television as a teaching aid. Total instruction meant that all curriculum was presented through television and the teacher acted as supervisor. With supplemented instruction, the teacher prepared the class and followed up after the program. Only part of the curriculum was presented through television. When television was used as a teaching aid, the classroom teacher just incorporated television into lessons, and use of television was more infrequent (Cuban, 1986).

The Hagerstown, Maryland, project was an early demonstration of supplemented television. Up to one-third of the school day was devoted to televised lessons, with teacher preparation and follow-up. From 1956 to 1961, the Fund for the Advancement of Education and corporations invested about $1.5 million in improving education in the Hagerstown schools through closed-circuit broadcasting. The initial experiment was a success, because costs were reduced while standardized test scores improved.

By the end of the experiment, over 70 production staff, including 25 studio teachers, telecast lessons in 8 different subjects at the elementary level and 15 subjects at the secondary level. All teachers were involved in the planning, because a team approach was used. Assessment of programs was continuous. Elementary students spent about 12% of their time with televised programs, the junior high students about 30% of their time, and high school students about 10% of their time. Fewer teachers were hired; however, master teachers were hired to teach televised classes. Student improvement was most dramatic when students who learned by television were compared with those in rural schools who did not receive televised lessons. Although standardized test scores were used to compare groups, there was no control for socioeconomic background. Still, when surveyed, parents, teachers, and administrators favored use of televised instruction.

Unfortunately, when funding was withdrawn after 5 years, problems began to arise because local resources were insufficient, especially for capital expenditures. This is a common pattern in utilization of instructional television. By 1983, the project had been reduced to a service department for the district, using a variety of technologies. The annual budget of $334,000 was justified, because all art and music lessons were offered through television, thus saving the cost of 12 itinerant teachers, a practice that would certainly be debated by aesthetic educators. Despite this and other exemplary supplemental television instruction projects, most schools used television simply as a teaching aid during this period (Cuban, 1986).

The Midwest Program of Airborne Instructional Television Instruction (MPATI) began in 1959 and continued in conjunction with the Purdue Research Foundation at Purdue University. Thirty-four courses were televised to 2,000 schools and 40,000 students through 15 educational television stations in 6 states. In addition, to reach schools not served by these stations, MPATI transmitted programs from an airplane circling at 23,000 feet over North-Central Indiana. Broadcasting began in 1961, with a cost of about $8 to 10 million annually (Seattler, 1968).

In contrast, television provided the total instructional program in American Samoa between 1964 and 1970. This approach was justified because the existing teaching staff and facilities were totally inadequate in 1961 when Governor H. Rex Lee was appointed. When Lee made restructure of the school system his top priority, Congress approved over $1 million in aid for the project. Soon four of every five students were spending one-quarter to one-third of their time watching televised lessons, especially in the elementary schools. The rest of the day was built around preparing for the televised lessons. The packets of material that accompanied the programs became the textbooks.

Researchers examined test scores before and after the introduction of television and found little difference in language scores, although slight advantages in reading and arithmetic were documented. There was little control for mediating variables. The English-speaking ability of the classroom teachers was generally poor, while English was the native language of television teachers. It is interesting, therefore, that the greatest advantage was found in the area of mathematics, not English language (Wells, 1976).

The project was initially reported a success, but by the early 1970s, objections to orienting the whole curriculum to televised lessons increased among students, teachers, and administrators, especially at grades 5 and above. By the eighth year of the project, students wanted less television, and teachers wanted more control over lessons. In 1973, policymakers shifted authority from the television studio to the classroom teacher and cut back the amount of television. In 1979, a utilization study conducted by Wilbur Schramm and his colleagues concluded that television's role had been reduced to supplemental or enrichment instruction, or at the high school level to little more than a teaching aid (Cuban, 1986).

In El Salvador, a major restructuring of education included the use of television to increase enrollment without a loss of quality. Overall educational reforms included (a) reorganization of the Ministry of Education, (b) teacher retraining, (c) curriculum revision, (d) development of new study materials, (d) development of more diverse technical program, (e) construction of new classrooms, (f) elimination of tuition, (g) use of double sessions and reduced hours to teach more students, (h) development of a new evaluation system, and (i) installation of a national television systems for grades 7 through 9. An evaluation project showed no advantage for the instructional television system. The only advantage was in the seventh grade. However, in the eighth and ninth grades, the nontelevision classrooms often obtained better scores. Positive scores during the first year of the reform were dismissed as due to the "halo effect," because scores diminished as novelty of the delivery method diminished (Wells, 1976). As with the Hagerstown project, however, an advantage was found for rural students (Hornik, Ingle, Mayo, McAnany & Schramm, 1973). Thus, "the consistent advantage of television seems to be in improving the test scores of rural students. One of the reasons for this improvement is that the technology provides for the distribution of the scarce resource of high-quality teaching ability" (Wells, 1976, p. 93).

Each of these projects generated related research and guidelines for practice. As television personnel learned about utilization, they shared their experience through handbooks for teachers on how to use television for instruction (Hillard & Head, 1976). Studies of process and impact were done. For example, Nugent (1977) reported a Nebraska State Department of Education field experiment that addressed whether teacher activities increased learning from television. She concluded that telelessons impacted learning, achievement in television classes was higher, and the nature of activities used had an affect on achievement but not the number of activities.

Tiffin (1978) used a multiple case study approach to analyze "Problems in Instructional Television in Latin America." After doing case studies on 8 of the 14 ITV systems in Latin America, critical subsystems were analyzed, especially in regard to conditions that were symptomatic of problems. Thus, problems and causes were traced until root causes were revealed. In many instances, these turned out to originate outside the ITV system. A hierarchy of casually interrelated problems, called a *problem structure,* was generated. Problems of utilization subsystems were analyzed. "In four cases the visual component of television was not being used and did not appear to be needed. If the television receiver were replaced by radio it appears unlikely that the measured learning outcomes would be appreciably effected" (Tiffin, 1978, p. 202).

Another project of historical significance is the research done by Educational Facilities Laboratories around the best use of space for the utilization of television. A nonprofit corporation established by the Ford Foundation, Educational Facilities Laboratories (EFL), encouraged research, experimentation, and dissemination about educational facilities. In their 1960 publication on "Design for ETV: Planning for Schools with Television," EFL recommended effective designs for seeing, hearing, and learning, and for group spaces. The issues of cost, equipment, and support were also discussed (Chapman, 1960).

11.7.5.3. Agency for Instructional Technology Studies.
AIT is a nonprofit U.S.-Canadian organization established in 1962 to strengthen education. AIT, which is located in Bloomington, Indiana, provides leadership and services through development, acquisition, and distribution of technology-based instructional materials. Although AIT's research program currently centers primarily around formative evaluation of materials, the organization has sponsored utilization studies. A few representative ones will be mentioned here. Dignam (1977) researched problems associated with the use of television in secondary schools, including equipment, scheduling, availability of programs, and teacher resistance. She reported a continuing debate about the extent to which teacher training should be emphasized in relation to systematic evaluation of utilization. Her report, which is based on a review of the literature, concluded that the relaxation of off-air taping regulations granted by some distributors eased scheduling and equipment difficulty, as did videocassette and videodiscs.

It Figures is a series of 28 15-minute video programs in mathematics designed for grade 4, in use since 1982. AIT (1984) did a survey of 117 teacher-users of this series. This survey gathered information on (a) teacher's backgrounds, (b) how teachers discovered and used the series, (c) perceived cognitive and attitudinal effects of the series, (d) teachers' reactions to the teacher's guide, and (e) overall reactions to the series. Seventy-six teachers responded that they perceived the series positively and used it in diverse ways. This is an example of an impact study.

AIT used a series of minicase studies to report on "Video at Work in American Schools" (Carlisle, 1987). This report takes the form of a compilation of experiences the author, Robert Carlisle, had during his travels through 12 states,

visiting applications of ITV. He talked to almost 160 people about television utilization and documented them and their projects through photographs. Carlisle concluded that access to equipment is no longer a sizable problem, nor is availability of programming, and the VCR has proved to be a very flexible tool for instruction. Nevertheless, the strength of the human support network behind the teacher was questionable.

1.7.5.4. Corporation for Public Broadcasting Studies.
Peter Dirr, director of the Catholic Telecommunications Network, did the first school use television studies for the Corporation for Public Broadcasting. Dirr and Petrone (1978) conducted a study in 1976–1977 that documented the pattern of greatest use of ITV in lower grades and diminishing use in higher grades. They used a stratified sample of 3,700 classroom teachers. This was the first indepth and rigorously conducted study of public school use since the introduction of television in schools (Cuban, 1986). Estimating based on data collected, they speculated that over 15 million students watched televised lessons daily. As is typical with most subsequent utilization studies, they investigated teacher attitudes, accessibility of equipment, and patterns of use in schools.

CPB sponsored two subsequent school utilization studies, one covering 1982–83 and another covering 1990–91. The research was conducted by CPB and the National Center for Education Statistics (NCES). The final report of the 1982–83 study compared the use of instructional television in 1977 and 1983 (Riccobono, 1985). This 1982–83 study surveyed the availability, use, and support (financial, personnel, and staff development) of instructional media in public and private elementary and secondary schools.

While the 1977 survey focused on television, this study was expanded by adding audio/radio and computers. Queries about instructional applications and equipment were directed to 619 superintendents, 1,350 principals, and 2,700 teachers. Responses were grouped by district size, wealth, and school level. The results indicated that although media use varied across districts and levels, almost all teachers had access to audio, video, and digital media. Over 90% of the districts offered in-service teacher training in media. The status of television for instruction remained relatively stable since 1977, except that fewer elementary teachers and more secondary teachers reported using television (CBP & NCES, 1984).

CPB sponsored the "1991 Study of School Uses of Television and Video," which surveyed almost 6,000 educators (CPB, n.d.). The results can be generalized to virtually all of the nation's public education system: 11,218 school districts, 72,291 public elementary and secondary schools, and 2,282,773 school teachers. The survey measured the use of instructional television and video, the availability of equipment and programming, and the support and resources devoted to instructional television. It replaced the audio/radio and computer component of the 1982–83 report with questions related to several new television-based technologies. The results of the survey show that instructional television is a firmly established teaching tool that is positively regarded by classroom teachers and increasingly well supported with equipment and programming. Programming availability was reported to be one source of frustration for teachers.

11.7.5.5. Other Utilization Studies. The major methodologies used for utilization studies have been experimentation and questionnaire survey. An example of an experimental design would be a study designed to investigate the relative effectiveness of three methods of instruction: conventional classroom instruction, televised instruction only, and a combination of classroom and televised instruction for teaching science content and vocabulary. A 1971 study done in the Santa Ana Unified School District reported no significant difference obtained by either classroom or televised instruction alone. The combination of televised and classroom instruction resulted in the greatest achievement (Santa Ana Unified School District, 1971). Such comparative studies have fallen into disfavor because they cannot be related to individual differences or mediating variables.

An example of a questionnaire approach is Turner and Simpson's (1982) study of the factors affecting the utilization of educational television in schools in Alabama. The researchers gathered information pertaining to five variables: (a) the percentage of students using ITV, (b) the ratio of students to videotape recorders, (c) ratio of students to television receivers, (d) ratio of students to color television receivers, and (e) students within districts using television. Scheduling was found to be the most important variable. This finding holds true in some cases today. Many districts that contracted for satellite telecourses when they were first offered were surprised to learn that some of the programs required one and a half of their regular periods and that students scheduled for such classes were therefore unable to take some regular classes.

Utilization studies (see 37.4) in the United States have focused on the availability of resources, attitudes towards ITV and ETV, and impact of programming. In comparison, utilization studies of television in developing countries have looked at resource issues from the perspective of the design and support of both educational and television systems.

11.7.6 Summary and Recommendations

Although a great deal of research has been done on programming for preschoolers and classrooms, there are major gaps in the literature. One such gap is in the effects of video production by students. Another area in which the research is confusing is that of newer programming genres for which it is difficult to compare findings. Contemporary varieties of advertising on television also present a very complex topic that warrants more research. Greater attention should be paid to the effects of genre differences and program formats, as well. It is important for researchers to investigate the interaction of the content and form of programming with other variables.

Many areas identified by research have not been adequately pursued, such as the effect of programs and utilization practices on rural children. Barriers to greater utilization are teachers' lack of knowledge about sources of programming for their subject-matter area and research on utilization. Utilization may be facilitated through "Cable in the Classroom," a nonprofit service of the cable television industry, which will offer educational programming for the classroom, curriculum-based support materials, and a clearinghouse for information on cable use in schools. Over 500 hours of high-quality programs will be delivered to schools each month, without commercial interruption (Kamil, 1992). Opportunities for research will arise as a result. KIDSNETT, a computerized clearinghouse concerned with programs for children preschool through high school, will be another source of information for researchers. Its "Active Database" has detailed information on 5,000 children's programs and public-service announcements and on 20,000 programs available for use in classrooms (Mielke, 1988).

11.8 CRITICAL-VIEWING SKILLS

To some extent, the critical-viewing skills movement was motivated by the gradual deregulation of the broadcasting industry. During the mid-1980s, as research turned more to the study of the interaction of variables, it became apparent that parents and teachers could have an important mediating role to play (Palmer, 1987; Sprafkin, Gadow & Abelman, 1992). This discussion of the critical-viewing skills movement will address (a) its relationship to the media literacy movement, (b) the assumptions underlying critical-viewing skills, (c) the goals adopted by the movement (see 16.6.2.2), (d) the curriculum projects developed to attain these goals, (e) the research findings on these projects, and (f) the impact of these projects. In an article on developmentally appropriate television, Levin and Carlsson-Paige (1994) suggested, "Now, the children who first fell prey to deregulated children's TV in 1984 are entering middle and high school; among them we see an alarming increase in violence" (p. 42). This inference is not easily supported in the literature, however, because there are other factors interacting with the effects of television. Nevertheless, violence has increased in society and on television. The authors point out that a content analysis of television programming reveals a:

- Dangerous, rather than secure world
- World where autonomy means fighting, and connectedness means helplessness, rather than a world of independent people helping each other
- World where physical strength and violence equal power, rather than a world where people have a positive effect without violence
- World with rigid gender divisions, rather than complex characters

- World where diversity is dangerous and dehumanizing and stereotyping abounds, rather than a world of respect where people enrich each others lives
- World where people are irresponsible and immoral, rather than a world where empathy and kindness pervade
- World full of imitative play, rather than creative, meaningful play

Based on this review and what is on television, it could be argued that this perception is biased towards negative effects. Nevertheless, there are plenty of instances of negative content to support this framework. Arguments about content on television and the role of mediation have stimulated efforts to emphasize media literacy.

11.8.1 Media Literacy

The media literacy debate encompasses issues around the role of content in relation to format and media literacy. It can be argued that today the medium dominates "symbol production and myth/reality dissemination in contemporary society" (Brown, 1991, p. 18). Others argue that to divorce content from examination of variables is illogical and self-defeating (K. W. Mielke, personal communication, Nov. 15, 1994). Another point of view is that television is decoded by a viewer drawing on a unique social and cognitive background, and thus the effects of television depend more on the receiver than on content or media literacy. The argument as to whether content should be controlled or taken into account in research is set in opposition to the development of media literacy, when probably both perspectives are important (Brown, 1991).

Worth raises another concern that reinforces the argument for attention to both content and media literacy.

Throughout the world, the air is being filled with reruns of "Bonanza" and ads for toothpaste, mouthwash, and vaginal deodorants. . . . If left unchecked, Bantuy, Dani, and Vietnamese children, as well as our own, will be taught to consume culture and learning through thousands of "Sesame Streets," taught not that learning is a creative process in which they participate, but rather that learning is a consumer product like commercials.

If left unchecked, we, and perhaps other nations like us, will continue to sell the technology which produces visual symbolic forms, while at the same time teaching other peoples our uses only, our conceptions, our codes, our mythic and narrative forms. We will, with technology, enforce our notions of what is, what is important, and what is right (Worth, 1981, p. 99, cited in Brown, 1991, p. 21).

A concern for receivership skills* developed from the perception that television was being used as a consumer product. Receivership skills "involve comprehending overt and hidden meanings of messages by analyzing language and visual and aural images, to understand the intended audiences and the intent of the message" (Brown, 1991, p.

70). Thus, an attempt is made to extend the tradition of teaching critical reading and critical thinking to include critical viewing.

Concern for media literacy is not new. When films were a prevalent audiovisual medium, there were many publications about the need for film literacy (Peters, 1961). A 1970 article by Joan and Louis Foresdale proposed film education to help students develop levels of comprehension and learn filmic code. As mentioned earlier under the topic filmic code, Salomon (1982) redirected attention to television literacy.* He theorized that comprehension occurred in two stages, both employing cognitive strategies for decoding and recoding. The first stage was specific television literacy dependent on knowing the symbol system associated with television viewing (see 16.4.2.1). The second stage required using general literacy skills to move to higher levels of learning. He also theorized that, except for small children, the general literacy skills were more important. He based his theory of a television symbol system on research conducted by himself and others (Salomon, 1982).

By the 1990s, books were available on television literacy (Neuman, 1991). Some of these came from the visual literacy movement, such as Messaris's *Visual "Literacy": Image, Mind, and Reality* (1994). In this book, he synthesizes research and practice in order to identify four aspects:

- Visual literacy is a prerequisite for comprehension of visual media.
- There are general cognitive consequences of visual literacy.
- Viewers must be made more aware of visual manipulation.
- Visual literacy is essential for aesthetic appreciation.

In responding to Clark's argument (1983, 1994) that media research tells us little, Kozma (1994) has brought attention to the centrality of media literacy for instructional technology research. Kozma argues that we need to consider the capabilities of media and their delivery methods as they interact with the cognitive and social processes by which knowledge is constructed. "From an interactionist perspective, learning with media can be thought of as a complementary process within which representations are constructed and procedures performed, sometimes by the learner and sometimes by the medium" (Kozma, 1994, p. 11). Thus, Kozma extends the attention directed to the interaction of media and mediating variables that began in the 1980s.

11.8.2 Critical-Viewing Education

During the 1980s, critical-viewing curricula were developed based on a number of underlying assumptions. These assumptions will be discussed next.

11.8.2.1. Assumptions about Critical Viewing. A significant assumption used in developing curricula on critical viewing was drawn from the analogy between positive television-viewing patterns and a balanced menu or diet. In fact, the terms "good TV diets" (O'Bryant & Corder-Bolz, 1978), "media diets" (Williams, 1986), "television diets" (Murray, 1980), and "balanced diet" (Searching for Alternatives, 1980) appeared frequently in the literature on television viewing. The assumption was that if television was watched in moderation and a variety of age-appropriate program genres were selected, the television experience would be positive. The only evidence we have found to support this assumption is the finding that moderate amounts of watching can increase school achievement. Other than indications that young children can become fearful or confused from watching adult programming, little evidence exists to support the need to view diverse and appropriate types of programs. Such research has not been done. It may be that individual or family differences justify an "unbalanced TV diet."

A second unstated assumption was that a critical viewer,* like a critical reader, would have the critical-thinking skills of an adult. But "the efficacy of children imitating adult reasoning remains untested" (Anderson, 1983, p. 320). Children, especially young children, process information concretely and creatively. Therefore, they may not benefit from more logical analyses. The critical viewer may be less like a critical reader and more like an art critic.

Another assumption was that the critical-viewing process had to have as its primary purpose education rather than entertainment. Consequently, viewers had to become more knowledgeable, and the best way to do this was through classroom curricula (Anderson, 1983). Critical-viewing curriculum projects had to meet the criteria of systematic instruction and the provision of a variety of audiovisual materials. For years, some anthropologists have argued that much visual literacy is learned naturally from the environment. Presumably, critical viewing could be learned in the home environment without instructional materials.

Primarily, the tests of these three assumptions were formative evaluations of the success of the educational interventions conducted in the name of critical-viewing skills curricula. While these efforts were found to improve learning, there was little other evidence to use. Nevertheless, positive reports from parents, teachers, experts, and students were given credence. On the other hand, the positive effects could be the result of maturation (Watkins, Sprafkin, Gadow & Sadetsky, 1988). Anderson (1980) has traced the theoretical lineage of critical-viewing curricula.

11.8.2.2. Goals for Critical-Viewing Curricula. Amy Dorr Leifer (1976) conducted a comparative study to identify critical evaluative skills associated with television viewing. Five skills were tentatively proposed:

1. Explicit and spontaneous reasoning
2. Readiness to compare television content to outside sources of information
3. Readiness to refer to industry knowledge in reasoning about television content
4. Tendency to find television content more fabricated or inaccurate

5. Less-positive evaluation of television content (Dorr, 1976, p. 14)

At the end of the 1970s, the U.S. Office of Education (USOE) sponsored a national project, *Development of Critical Television Viewing Skills in Students,* which was intended to help students become more active and discriminating viewers. Separate curricula were developed for elementary, middle-school, secondary-, and postsecondary-age students. Four critical television skills emphasized in the secondary curriculum were the ability to:

- Evaluate and manage one's own television-viewing behavior
- Question the reality of television programs
- Recognize the arguments employed on television and to counterargue
- Recognize the effects of television on one's own life (Lieberman, 1980; Wheeler, 1979)

In 1983 Anderson identified 11 objectives in 8 curriculum projects. He interpreted these as reflecting four goals common to all the projects. The goals were: (a) ability to grasp the meaning of the message; (b) ability to observe details, their sequence and relationships, and understand themes, values, motivating elements, plot lines, characters, and characterization; (c) ability to evaluate fact, opinion, logical and affective appeals, and separate fantasy and reality; and (d) the ability to apply receivership skills to understand inherent sources of bias (cited in Brown, 1991). The goals and objectives of the major critical-viewing skills projects are summarized by Brown (1991).

A common approach to attaining these goals was to include content on the various programming genre. Participants would be taught to distinguish types of programming and to use different analysis approaches with each. Brown (1991) reviews the various approaches to defining genre, such as types, classifications, and typology. Bryant and Zillmann (1991) dedicate Part II of their book of readings on *Responding to the Screen* to an in-depth analysis of research and theory on each genre and associated literacy issues including news and public affairs, comedy, suspense and mystery, horror, erotica, sports, and music television.

11.8.2.3. Critical-Viewing Skills Curricula. Over the years, there have been many curricula to develop television literacy, in addition to the USOE project curricula described above. In the United States, these curricula were developed by local television stations, national networks underwriting social research, school districts, research centers, and national coalitions. Most of these have been summarized by Brown in his book on major media literacy projects (1991). Some have been developed by companies (i.e., J. C. Penny's), some by researchers [i.e., the Critical Viewing Curriculum (KIDVID) and the Curriculum for Enhancing Social Skills Through Media Awareness (CESSMA)], some by practitioners (i.e., O'Reilly & Splaine, 1987), and some by nonprofit associations (i.e., Carnegie Corporation) or coalitions, such as Action for Children's Television. A few will be described here, especially those that have been summatively researched or that address unique populations or content.

The recommendations of Action for Children's Television (ACT) are summarized in *Changing Channels: Living (Sensibly) with Television* (Charren & Sandler, 1983). This is an example of an educational plan intended for general use rather than specifically for the classroom. A more current example of general recommendations is Chen's (1994a) *The Smart Parent's Guide to KIDS' TV.*

The Curriculum for Enhancing Social Skills Through Media Awareness (CESSMA) was designed to be used with educationally disabled and learning-disabled children to improve their prosocial learning from television. CESSMA was field tested in an elementary school for educationally disabled children on Long Island. The curriculum group significantly outperformed the control group on television knowledge. Children in the intervention group identified less with aggressive television characters than those in the control group. Nevertheless, there was no evidence that CESSMA significantly altered attitudes or behavior.

KIDVID has been used with gifted and learning-disabled children. It was designed to facilitate children's ability to recognize the prosocial content from a television program. The 3-week curriculum, originally developed for intellectually average and gifted children, was tested in intact fourth-grade classrooms using indices to measure the children's ability to identify and label the types of prosocial behaviors portrayed in commercial television programs. The curriculum was effective because all who participated were better able to recognize and label prosocial behaviors (Sprafkin, Gadow & Abelman, 1992).

Previously, in 1983, Abelman and Courtright had conducted a study on television literacy in the area of prosocial learning. In that study they found evidence that curriculum can be effective in amplifying the cognitive effects of commercial television's prosocial fare. They concluded:

> For children who rely on television information as an accurate source of social information, who spend the majority of their free time with the medium, and who are unable to separate television fantasy from reality, some form of mediation is imperative (p. 56).

A practitioner's approach to a curricula on television literacy for gifted learners was reported by Hunter (1992). This approach used video production to teach fifth- through eighth-graders. Students were divided into three treatment groups. One of the two critical-viewing treatment groups showed significant gains, while the control/no treatment group did not.

Another practitioner approach was reported by Luker and Johnston (1989). Teachers were advised to help adolescent social development by using television shows in the classroom with a four-step process:

> There are four steps to take after viewing a show: (1) Establish the facts of the conflict, (2) establish the perspectives of the central characters, (3) classify the coping style used by the main character, and (4) explore alternatives that the

main character could take and the consequences of each alternative both for the main character and the foil (p. 51).

They found that teachers were effective in completing the first two steps, but had greater difficulty with steps 3 and 4.

The effect of learning about television commercials was studied in an experiment by Donohue, Henke, and Meyer (1983). Two instructional units, one role-playing unit and one traditional, were designed to examine if young children can be taught general and specific intent of television commercials. Both treatment groups of 6- to 7-year-olds experienced significant increases in comprehension of commercials. The researchers concluded that:

> Through mediation via an instructional unit at the 7-year mark, the process of building defense mechanisms against the manipulative intent of countless television commercials can be considerably accelerated to the point where children are able to effectively and correctly assimilate commercial messages into their developing cognitive structures (p. 260).

Rapaczynski, Singer, and Singer (1980) looked at children in kindergarten through second grade. They introduced a curriculum designed to teach how television works, which was produced by simplifying the content of a curriculum intended for older children. Although a control group was not used, this curriculum intervention did appear to produce substantial knowledge gains. Another curriculum developed for kindergarteners and second-graders also was found to produce significant knowledge gains (Watkins, Sprafkin & Gadow, 1988). In this case, the study used another class at each grade level as nontreatment controls.

Currently, the Academy of Television Arts and Sciences is mounting a critical-viewing skills campaign. Its members offer free workshops using a videotape and exercises developed by Dorothy and Jerome Singer under the auspices of the Pacific Mountain Network in Denver.

11.8.2.4. Evaluation of the Curricula. The major thrust in critical-viewing skills came with the four curriculum development projects sponsored by the U.S. Office of Education at the end of the 1970s. Each project addressed a different age group. A final report on the development of the curriculum for teenagers was prepared by Lieberman (1980). The formative evaluation of the curriculum, which is reported in a series of Educational Resource and Information Clearinghouse (ERIC) documents, was done by the Educational Testing Service.

To evaluate the curriculum for teenagers, Educational Testing Service identified 35 reviewers representing various constituencies (Wheeler, 1979). Generally, the review revealed effective use of an instructional systems design and development process.

Based on his review of the literature, Brown (1991) presents 20 descriptive criteria for assessing critical-viewing skills curricula or projects. The criteria fall into these categories:

- Breadth: meaning social, political, aesthetic, and ethical perspectives

- Scope: meaning adaptibility and wide utilization
- Individuality and values: meaning reflecting diverse heritages and sensitization of viewers to their role
- Validity and reliability (accuracy): meaning based on research
- Cognition (developmental): meaning age-appropriate education
- Cognition (reasoning skills): meaning training in analysis and synthesis
- Pragmatics of media education: meaning incorporating the content and form of media literacy projects.

11.8.2.5. Impact of Critical-Viewing Projects. How effective have these curricula been across the country and over the years? Berger (1982) suggested that it would take 30 years before the results would be known. Bell (1984), however, concluded that several indicators pointed to the rapid demise of curricula on critical television viewing. Although he found little evidence that the curriculum materials produced under the aegis of the USOE had been assimilated into school curricula, he noted that the skills promoted have not been completely forgotten by instructional technologists. The impact of content and strategy was greater than the influence of the movement or subsequent use of the materials, many of which are no longer available. Bell also reported another troublesome indicator. The Boston University Critical Television Viewing Skills Project for adults, directed by the highly regarded Donis Dondis, dean of the School of Communication, was given the Golden Fleece award by Senator William Proxmire. This was his monthly prize for ridiculous and wasteful government spending. The lack of clear understanding of the need for such projects and their potential was clear in the statement he read in 1978:

> If education has failed to endow college students with critical facilities that can be applied to the spectrum of their lives, a series of new courses on how to watch television critically will not provide it (cited in Bell, 1984, p. 12).

11.8.2.6 Summary and Recommendations

From formative and summative evaluation and a few experimental studies, there is evidence that intervening with instruction on critical viewing increases knowledge of and sophistication about television. Ableman and Courtright (1983) summarize the situation well: ". . . television literacy curricula can be as much a social force as the medium itself" (p. 56).

The need for field research on the effects of interventions is documented by the paucity of literature on applying the findings of research through interventions. We know that children learn more from any form of television if adults intervene. The various ways of intervening need to be researched using methods other than formative evaluation. Systematic programs of intervention need to be developed and their impact measured.

11.9 CONCLUDING REMARKS

This chapter has dealt only with research on traditional forms of television (see 4.4.4.2) and instructional film. The research on newer technologies, such as interactive multimedia, has been left for others to review. Nevertheless, based on the literature surveyed, it would not be surprising to find that 20,000 research articles have already been published on learning from film and television. We have endeavored to identify the important variables that have surfaced from this mass of research. It was not possible to narrow this list of variables to any great extent, because most were relevant either to the design, development, or utilization functions of this field. Nor could we narrow the list by concentrating on research about film and television solely in the classroom, because instructional technology as a field has a responsibility to media literacy and learning in many environments. The review was not limited to research done within the field because, in this case, many disciplines contribute information useful to the practitioners and researchers in our field. Therefore, the chapter has traced the progress of research in many fields over decades and summarized the important variables related to areas of interest to our field. These areas are message design, mental processing, school achievement, family context for viewing, socialization, programming, utilization, and critical-viewing skills. Research in these areas has investigated independent variables, mediating variables, and effects. This chapter concludes with consideration of myths about learning from television in the light of this review.

Milton Chen (1994c), director for the Center for Education and Lifelong Learning at KQED in San Francisco, summarizes many myths about the effects of television. He argues that to conclude that television is primarily responsible for "turning kids into couch potatoes, frying their brains, shortening their attention spans, and lowering their academic abilities" is too simplistic. Indeed, there are several suppositions about the effects of television that seem mystifying in light of the research reviewed in this chapter.

The first myth is that television encourages mental and physical passivity. Research reveals a that great deal of mental activity takes place while viewing, some in reaction to programming and the rest in reaction to elements in the environment. In his essay on whether television stimulates or stultifies children, psychologist Howard Gardner (1982) argues that there is little if any support for the view that the child is a passive victim of television. Gardner says that, on the other hand, there is a great deal of evidence that the children are active transformers of what they see on television. He concludes that during the early childhood years, television is a great stimulator.

Similarly, it is often assumed that television has a negative effect on school achievement and reading. In reality, it has little effect if the home environment establishes rules that control the negative influences of television. In fact, for some students with difficulty in reading, it can provide another source of vocabulary and language development. Television can assist with reading and school readiness. A 1988 study by Anderson and Collins investigated the premise that television viewing has a detrimental effect on the cognitive development of children. They found that children comprehend programs produced for them, that they are cognitively active during learning, and that effect on reading achievement is small relative to other factors (Anderson & Collins, 1988). Generally, the evidence shows that moderate amounts of television viewing are positively related to academic achievement, while heavy viewing is negatively associated.

Another myth is that television is a great leveler because rich and poor alike watch the same programming. It is obviously an oversimplification to assume that all variables including socioeconomic ones are thus equalized by watching the same television programs. It would be more accurate to say that television can help provide a common conceptual framework for a community. Socioeconomic groups use television differently, and television has different effects on these groups. Lower-income children watching *Sesame Street* gained more in every area except knowledge of the alphabet (Zill, Davies & Daly, 1994). On the other hand, the more educated the family, the more likely there will be supervised use of television. Children who experience rules related to television viewing are likely to gain the most from the television experience. Television may be helpful to individuals from a lower socioeconomic class because it provides stimulation rather than displacing more valuable activities. Television has the potential both to positively and negatively affect minorities' self-concept (Stroman, 1991).

Another common belief is that television causes violent behavior. The research shows that while there is a relationship between television and aggression (see 4.4.4.3), the effects of this relationship vary depending on individual and environmental variables:

> In sum, the empirical and theoretical evidence suggests that in general the effects of television's content depend in part on the extent to which contradictory messages are available, understood, and consistent. In the case of sex role attitudes, messages from television are consistent and either absent or reinforced in real life, whereas in the case of aggressive behavior, most viewers receive contradictory messages from both sources. All viewers may learn aggression from television, but whether they will perform it will depend on a variety of factors. If we wish to predict behavior, that is, performance, we need to know something of the viewers' social milieu (Williams, 1986, p. 411).

It is true that research has shown that television has the potential to incite aggressive or antisocial behavior, to create problems resulting from advertising, and to portray characters in ways that foster stereotypes. Despite these potentially negative effects, television has the capability to educate, stimulate, persuade, and inform. Enough is known about how to use television positively to make a difference; however, the research has not led to successful interventions.

There are several reasons for this: the lack of conceptual theory relating findings, poor dissemination of findings, and little support for interventions.

What is most remarkable about the literature on learning from television is that the concerns haven't changed greatly in 40 years. Although the research questions have become more sophisticated as the medium evolved, the same issues—i.e., violence, commercialism, effect on school achievement—have continued. Yet, while interest in the negative aspects of television remains steady, efforts to increase positive effects seem more sporadic. Interventions are tried and discarded even if successful. The research on prosocial effects is reported and largely ignored. In fact, there is the danger that applying some of these findings could fuel a debate about "political correctness" that could lead to loss of funding. Perhaps the reason there seems to be less progress than warranted after 40 years is that the emphasis on negative effects has been more salient than efforts to ensure positive effects through interventions. Far more attention needs to be paid to the positive effects of television on learning and the potential for overcoming negative effects with these positive effects.

We would like to conclude by stressing the importance of emphasizing the positive through research on interventions, rather than through perpetuation of myths that emphasize negative effects. If this review has revealed anything, it is that the findings on learning from television are complex and so interrelated that there is a great danger of oversimplification before research can provide adequate answers to sophisticated questions. Other reviews, such as Signorielli's *A Sourcebook on Children and Television* (1991), have reached similar conclusions. It seems important, therefore, to urge action in areas where research or intervention is both needed and supported, but to caution about sweeping generalizations that create distortions that affect policy. Finally, we hope that by extending this review beyond the usual consideration of either mass media literature or literature from instruction to a review combining both, we have established support for increased attention to design factors and to interventions that affect utilization.

A conscious effort by teachers and parents to use television positively makes a difference. Discussion of programming, for example, enhances learning through elaboration and clarification. However, most parents who think they discuss television with their children do so only in a minimal way. Therefore, the belief that parents and teachers guide the use of television is a myth. Generally, they don't. Neither teachers nor parents are given assistance in developing the skills to intervene successfully in the television-viewing experience.

From the research, one can surmise that different variables are important at different points in the life span of viewers. Thus, research on preschool viewers concentrates on mental processing, imagination, and attention span, while research on school age viewers asks questions about television's effect on school achievement and language development. Research with adolescents turns to questions of violence and the learning of roles and prosocial behavior. Adult learners are questioned about attitude change and viewing habits. These foci cause discontinuities in the literature because the same research questions are not asked across all life span periods. Thus, we know very little about the mental processing of adults viewing television or the effect of television on adult achievement. One recommendation for a research agenda would be to ask the same questions about all life span periods.

In pursuing the same questions across different life span periods, researchers need to ensure that self-reporting instruments measure the same phenomena for each age studied. When data are collected through self-reporting measures such as interviews, questionnaires, and psychological tests, there are limitations to take into account. Self-reporting instruments are used less effectively with young children and those with language disabilities. Moreover, subjects of different ages may interpret questions differently due to comprehension or interest. In addition, respondents may try to present themselves in a positive or socially desirable manner, thus misleading the researcher (Sigelman & Shaffer, 1995).

Which brings us to final conclusions. The need to study research questions through a variety of methodologies appropriate to respective variables and through investigations of interactions among variables is apparent from this review. One can only hope that enough researchers become interested enough, especially those open to interdisciplinary research, to provide some of the answers society, teachers, and parents need.

11.10 GLOSSARY OF TERMS

Active Theory Describes the child as an active processor of information, guided by previous knowledge, expectations, and schemata (Anderson & Lorch, 1983).

Aggression An antisocial "behavior, the intent of which is injury to a person or destruction of an object" (Bandura, Ross & Ross, 1963, p. 10).

Aided Recall When interviewers probe for further detail by cuing (Gunter, 1987, p. 93).

AIME The amount of invested mental effort in nonautomatic elaboration of material (Salomon, 1981a, 1981b). Theory that the amount of invested mental effort that children apply to the television-viewing experience influences their program recall and comprehension (Sprafkin, Gadow & Abelman, 1992, p. 55).

Altruism The prosocial "unselfish concern for the welfare of others" (Neufeldt & Sparks, 1990, p. 18). Evidenced by generosity, helping, cooperation, self-control, delaying gratification, or resisting the temptation to cheat, lie, or steal.

Antisocial Behavior Behavior that goes against the norms of society, including "physical aggression, verbal aggression, passivity, stereotyping, theft, rule breaking, materialism, unlawful behaviors, or pathological behavior" (Hearold, 1986, p. 81).

Arousal Theory Contends that communication messages can evoke varying degrees of generalized emotional arousal and that this can influence any behavior an individual is engaged in while the state of arousal persists (Sprafkin, Gadow & Abelman, 1992, p. 79).

Attention The cognitive process of orienting to and perceiving stimuli. With regard to television research, this may be measured by visual orientation to the television or "looking" by eye movements, by electrophysiological activity, and by inference through secondary recall and recognition tests (Anderson & Collins, 1988). See Visual Attention.

Attentional Inertia "The maintenance of cognitive involvement across breaks or pauses in comprehension and changes of content" (Anderson & Lorch, 1983, p. 9).

Attribute A characteristic of programming, such as of advertising, e.g., uses hard-sell tone. See Formal Features.

Audience Involvement The degree to which people personally relate to media content; one dimension of the construct audience activity (Perse, 1990, p. 676). Indications of audience involvement include anticipating viewing (intentionality), attention (focused cognitive effort), elaboration (thinking about content), and engaging in distractions while viewing.

Broadcast Television Refers to any television signal that is transmitted over FCC-regulated and licensed frequencies within the bandwidth of 54 to 890 megaherz. Broadcast television messages may be received by home antenna, or they may be relayed via cable, satellite, or microwave to individual subscribers.

C-Box A recording device consisting of a television set and a video camera that records the viewing area in front of the television set.

Cable Access Television (CATV) Used to describe the distribution of broadcast, locally originated, or subscription television programming over a coaxial cable or fiber optic network. Such distribution frequently includes locally produced or syndicated programming intended for specialized audiences; also known as *narrowcasting*.

Catharsis Theory "Frustration produces an increase in aggressive drive because the state is unpleasant and the individual seeks to reduce it by engaging in either aggressive acts or fantasy aggression" (Sprafkin, Gadow & Abelman, 1992, p. 79).

Catharsis "The notion that aggressive impulses can be drained off by exposure to fantasy aggression . . ." (Liebert & Sprafkin, 1988, p. 75); drive reduction (Feshbach & Singer, 1971, p. 39).

Closed-Circuit Television (CCTV) Refers to the transmission of the television signal over a wire or fiber optic medium. The most important aspect of closed-circuit television for education is the ability to distribute a television signal within a school building or district. Also called *wire transmission* (which includes fiber optic transmission).

Cognitive Processing Refers collectively to the various mental processes involved in perception, attention, semantic encoding, and retrieval of information from memory. Typically used to describe activities associated with learning.

Cohort "A group of people born at the same time, either in the same year or within a specified, limited span of years" (Siegelman & Shaffer, p. 18).

Commercial Broadcast Stations Stations that are privately owned and supported primarily by commercial advertising revenues.

Communications Satellite Refers to the transmission and reception of a television signal via a geocentric communications satellite. This form of communication link involves the transmission of a television signal to a satellite (uplink) that is placed in a geocentric orbit (one that is synchronized with the rotation of the Earth so as to appear motionless over approximately one-third of the populated planet). The satellite then rebroadcasts the signal to dish-type receiver antennas at other geographic locations (downlink).

Comprehension The extraction of meaning; the first step in critically analyzing any presentation regardless of medium (Anderson, 1983, p. 318). Comprehension may include the ability to recall or recognize content information and to infer story sequence or plot.

Content Indifference The theory that content does not dictate viewing; that, with a few exceptions, other variables have more effect on preferences (Comstock & Paik, 1991, p. 5).

Coviewing Viewing television in the presence of others, for example, viewing in a group of two or more, such as with a parent, child, or peers.

Critical Viewer "One who can first grasp the central meaning of a statement, recognize its ambiguities, establish its relationship with other statements, and the like; one who plans television viewing in advance and who evaluates programs while watching" (Anderson, 1983, pp. 313–318).

Critical-Viewing Skills The competencies specified as objectives for television literacy curricula.

Cross-Sectional Method A research method that involves the observation of different groups (or cohorts) at one point in time.

Cued Recall Recall based on questions about specific program details (Berry, 1993, p. 359).

Desensitization A decline in emotional arousal or the decreased likelihood of helping victims of violence due to repeated exposure to violent programming.

Disability "Any restriction or lack (resulting from an impairment) of ability to perform an activity in the manner or within the range considered normal for a human being" (Cumberbatch & Negrine, 1992, p. 5).

Disclaimer Aural and/or visual displays designed to delineate an advertised item's actual performance and to dispel misconceptions that might be created by demonstration of a product (Jalongo, 1983, p. 6).

Disinhibition Temporary removal of an inhibition through the action of an unrelated stimulation.

Disinhibitory Effects "The observation of a response of a particular class (for example, an aggressive response) that leads to an increased likelihood of displaying other different responses that belong to the same class" (Liebert & Sprafkin, 1988, p. 71).

Displacement Hypothesis The notion that television influences both learning and social behavior by displacing such activities as reading, family interaction, and social play with peers (Huston et al., 1992, p. 82).

Displacement Theory Other activities are replaced by watching television.

Distractions Alternatives to television viewing such as toys, other children, music, or some combination of these.

Educational Television (ETV) Consists of commercial or public broadcast programming targeted at large audiences over wide geographic areas, with the express purpose of providing instruction in a content or developmental area.

Effect Size In meta-analysis studies, "The mean difference between treated and control subjects divided by the standard deviation of the control group" (Hearold, 1986, pp. 75–76). See Meta-analysis.

Ethnic Identity The "attachment to an ethnic group and a positive orientation toward being a member of that group" (Takanishi, 1982, p. 83).

Experience-Sampling Method The use of paging devices to gather data on television activities and experiences.

Exposure Measures Measures of hours of television watched per day or of watching specific content, e.g., frequency of watching news (Gunter, 1987, p. 125).

Family Context for Viewing An environmental context that influences what and when viewing occurs as well as the ways in which viewers interpret what they see (Huston et al., 1992, p. 99); created through the interaction of variables in the home setting that mediate the effects of television, including environment, coviewing, and viewing habits.

Filmic/Cinematic Code Describes the collective formal features of television as a symbol system unique to both film and television (Salomon, 1979).

Formal Features Program attributes that can be defined independently from the content of a program, such as action, pace, and visual techniques (Huston & Wright, 1983). Synonomous with Production Effects or Presentation Effects.

Formative Evaluation Gathering information on the adequacy of an instructional product or program and using this information as a basis for further development (Seels & Richey, 1994).

Free Recall Recall where viewers must recall all they can from a specified program [without cues] (Berry, 1983, p. 359).

Frustration A state caused by "delay in reinforcement" (Bandura & Walters, 1963, p. 116).

Functional Displacement Hypothesis One medium will displace another when it performs the function of the displaced medium in a superior manner (Comstock & Paik, 1991, p. 78).

Genre A category of programming having a particular form, content, and purpose as in comedy, news, drama, MTV.

Grazing Quickly sampling a variety of programs using remote controls while viewing.

Household Centrality Dimension reflecting behavior and norms that favor viewing (Comstock & Paik, 1991, p. 69).

Incidental Effects Those behavioral or cognitive outcomes that result as a byproduct of the programming. These are usually not planned and may be negative or positive in nature. They may result from observational learning, role modeling, pro- or antisocial messages, or attitude formation.

Instructional Films/Motion Pictures Motion pictures that have been designed to produce specific learning outcomes through the direct manipulation of the presentation format and sequence.

Instructional Television (ITV) Programming that has as its primary purpose the achievement of specified instructional objectives by students in school settings. In practice, it has usually referred to programming that is formally incorporated into a particular course of study and presented to intact classes or groups of students or trainees.

Instrumental Viewing Watching for information.

Intentional Effects Those mental processes or behaviors that occur as a direct result of organized instructional events or practices and that are generally expected to occur through the viewer's interaction with the television programming.

Kinescope Medium consisting of a motion picture recording of a live television program, in which the television frame rate was synchronized with the film frame rate.

Learning from Television Changes in knowledge, understanding, attitudes, and behaviors due to the intentional or incidental effects of television programming.

Literacy "One's ability to extract information from coded messages and to express ideas, feelings, and thoughts through them in accepted ways; the mastery of specific mental skills that become cultivated as a response to the specific functional demands of a symbol system" (Salomon, 1982, p. 7).

Longitudinal Method A research method that involves the observation of people or group repeatedly over time.

Mass Communication "The process of using a mass medium to send messages to large audiences for the purpose of informing, entertaining, persuading" (Vivian, 1991, p. 15).

Mass Media Delivery systems (i.e., television, newspapers, radio) that channel the flow of information to large and diverse audiences and that are characterized by unlimited access, and by the vast amount of noncontent-related (incidental) learning that occurs as a byproduct. Generally intended to provide entertainment-oriented programming. See Mass Communication.

Materialism "An orientation emphasizing possession and money for personal happiness and social progress" (Ward & Wackman, 1981, cited in Moore & Moschis, 1982, p. 9).

Media Dependency Relying on the media for information and guidance (Comstock & Paik, 1991, p. 143).

Media Literacy The ability to learn from media; capable of comprehending filmic code. See Literacy and Visual Literacy.

Mediation "Parents or teachers intervening in the television viewing experience by encouraging, discouraging, or discussing viewing" (Lin & Atkin, 1989, p. 54).

Mesmerizing Effect Describes a passive, hypnotic state in the viewer, presumably associated with reduced cognitive processing and high alpha activity (Mander, 1978).

Message "A pattern of signs (words, pictures, gestures) produced for the purpose of modifying the psychomotor, cognitive, or affective behavior of one or more persons" (Fleming & Levie, 1994, p. x).

Message Design "Planning for the manipulation of the physical form of the message" (Grabowski, 1991, p. 206).

Meta-analysis "A statistical approach to summarizing the results of many studies that have investigated basically the same problem" (Gay, 1992, p. 590). See Effect Size.

Microwave Relay Links Technology that employs a series of microwave transmission towers to transmit and relay the television signal. Such transmission is generally used in areas where cable distribution systems are not practical or where television network signals must be transmitted over long distances. Microwave relays are also used to transmit location broadcast signals from remote locations to the television studio for news or public-events coverage.

Monitoring Attention to audio, visual, and social cues as to the desirability of paying attention to the screen (Comstock & Paik, 1991, p. 23).

Montage Television sequence that incorporates formal features to imply changes in space, time, action, mental state, or character point of view (Anderson & Field, 1983, p. 76).

Neutral Behavior Behavior that observers would not describe as being antisocial or prosocial (Hearold, 1986, p. 81).

Norm Belief held by a number of members of a group, that the members ought to behave in a certain way in certain circumstances (Holmans, 1961, p. 6).

Oversensitization As a result of overexposure to televised violence, the belief that the world is mean and scary or that the incidence of crime and risk of personal injury are greater than they really are.

Parental Attitude "Parents' perceptions of television's impact on their children" (Sprafkin et al., 1992, p. 103).

Passivity Acted upon rather than acting or causing action.

Presentation Variables See Formal Features.

Processing Capabilities "The ability of a medium to operate on available symbol systems in specified ways; in general, information can be displayed, received, stored, retrieved, organized, translated, transformed, and evaluated" (Kozma, 1994, p. 11).

Production Effects See Formal Features.

Prosocial Behavior Behaviors that are socially desirable and that in some way benefit another person or society at large (Rushton, 1979, cited in Liebert & Sprafkin, 1988, p. 228). Includes behaviors such as generosity, helping, nurturing, or delaying gratification.

Public Stations Stations that derive their funding from government, public, and philanthropic sources. On such stations, commercial messages are either not aired or are used only for the recognition of the contributor.

Reactive Theory Describes the child as a passive, involuntary processor of information who simply reacts to stimuli (Singer, 1980).

Recall Memory for content and features from television viewing; can be cued or uncued.

Recapping Refers to repeating the most important facts; it is a source redundancy (Son, Reese & Davie, 1987, p. 208).

Receivership Skills "The comprehension of overt and hidden meanings of messages by analyzing language and visual and aural images, to understand the intended audiences and the intent of the message" (Brown, 1991, p. 70).

Recognition "Refers to the frequency with which a group receives TV roles at all" (Liebert & Sprafkin, 1988, p. 187).

Respect "Refers to how characters behave and are treated once they have roles" (Liebert & Sprafkin, 1988, p. 187).

Ritualistic Viewing Watching for gratification.

Roles "Refers to expectations about activities that are performed and to beliefs and values attributed to performers" (Birenbaum, 1978, pp. 128–129).

Rulemaking Establishing guidelines about acceptable and/or prohibited behavior (Lin & Atkin, 1989, p. 54); "also called restrictive mediation" (Atkin, Greenberg & Baldwin, 1991, p. 43).

Salience Highlighting certain components of the program for viewers through formal or production features; perceptual salience may elicit and maintain attention and influence comprehension by aiding in selection of content (Huston & Wright, 1983, p. 44).

Schemata "Conceptual frames of reference that provide organizational guidelines for newly encoded information about people and social or behavioral roles and events; they can be important mediators of learning" (Taylor & Crocker, 1981, cited in Gunter, 1987, p. 65).

Self-Control "Specific kinds of prosocial action, including a willingness to work and wait for long-term goals, as well as the ability to resist the temptation to cheat, steal, or lie" (Liebert & Sprafkin, 1988, p. 229).

Sequential Method A research method that combines cross-sectional and longitudinal approaches by observing different groups at multiple points in time.

Sex Role "Refers to the collection of behaviors or activities that a given society deems more appropriate to members of one sex than to members of the other sex" (Durkin, 1985, p. 9).

Social Learning Theory (1) Acquiring symbolic representations through observation. (2) Learning through imitation of observed behavior (Bandura & Walters, 1963).

Socialization Learning the values, norms, language, and behaviors needed to function in a group or society; socialization agents often include mass media, parents, peers, and the school (Moore & Moschis, 1982, p. 4). Learning over time how to function in a group or society by assimilating a set of paradigms, rules, procedures, and principles that govern perception, attention, choices, learning, and development (Dorr, 1982).

Stereotype "A generalization based on inadequate or incomplete information" (Stern & Robinson, 1994), "A group is said to be stereotyped whenever it is depicted or portrayed in such a way that all its members appear to have the same set of characteristics, attitudes, or life conditions" (Liebert & Sprafkin, p. 189).

Summative Evaluation "Involves gathering information on adequacy and using this information to make decisions about utilization" (Seels & Richey, 1994, p. 134).

Symbol Systems Sets of symbolic expressions by which information is communicated about a field of reference, e.g., spoken language, printed text, pictures, numerals and formulae, musical scores, performed music, maps, or graphs (Goodman, 1976, cited in Kozma, 1994, p. 11).

Technology "The physical, mechanical, or electronic capabilities of a medium that determine its function and, to some extent, its shape and other features" (Kozma, 1994, p. 11).

Television Literacy Understanding television programming, including how it is produced and broadcast, familiarity with the formats used, ability to recognize overt and covert themes of programs and commercial messages, and appreciation of television as an art form (Corder-Bolz, 1982, cited in Williams, 1986, p. 418). Also see Critical-Viewing Skills.

Video Production Producing television programming in the community or schools.

Videotape Format generally used today to record and play back video programming. It consists of an oxide-coated roll of acetate, polyester, or mylar tape on which a magnetized signal is placed.

Viewing Environment A social context created by the interaction of variables, such as the number and placement of sets, toys, and other media, other activities, rules, and parental communication.

Viewing Experience Result of interaction of programming, mediating variables, and outcomes; variously described as active or passive and positive or negative. See Viewing System.

Viewing Habits When and what children watch and for how long as determined by the amount of time a child spends in front of a television set, program preferences, and identification with characters (Sprafkin et al., 1992, p. 23).

Viewing Patterns Content preferences of viewers.

Viewing System Components of the viewing process, including programming, environment, and behavior and their interaction. See Viewing Experience.

Viewing Visual attention to what is taking place on the screen (Comstock & Paik, 1991, p. 22).

Violence "The overt expression of physical force against others or self, or the compelling of action against one's will on pain of being hurt or killed" (NIMH, 1972, p. 3).

Visual Attention "Visual orientation (eyes directed towards the screen) and visual fixation (precise location on the screen toward which eyes are directed given visual orientation)" (Anderson & Lorch, 1983, p. 2).

Visual Literacy The ability to understand and use images, including the ability to think, learn, and express oneself in terms of images (Braden & Hortin, 1982, p. 41). See Media Literacy.

Zapping Changing channels quickly using a remote control.

REFERENCES

Abelman, R. & Rogers, A. (1987). From "plug-in drug" to "magic window": the role of television in special education. Paper presented at the Seventh Annual World Conference on Gifted Education, Salt Lake City, UT.

— & Courtright, J. (1983). Television literacy: amplifying the cognitive level effects of television's prosocial fare through curriculum intervention. *Journal of Research and Development in Education 17* (1), 46–57.

Adler, R.P., Lesser, G.S., Meringoff, L.K., Robertson, T.S., Rossiter, J.R. & Ward, S. (1980). *The effects of television advertising on children: review and recommendations.* Lexington, MA: Lexington.

Agency for Instructional Television (1984). *Formative evaluation of "taxes influence behavior" (lesson #2) from "tax whys: understanding taxes," Research Report 91.* Bloomington, IN: Agency for Instructional Television. (ERIC Document Reproduction Service No. ED 249 974.)

— (1984, Jun.) *"It figures": a survey of users. Research report 91.* Bloomington, IN: Agency for Instructional Television. (ERIC Document Reproduction Service No. ED 249 975.)

Ahmed, D. (1983). *Television in Pakistan.* Unpublished doctoral dissertation. New York: Columbia University Teacher's College,

Alexander, A., Ryan, M. & Munoz, P. (1984). Creating a learning context: investigations on the interactions of siblings during television viewing. *Critical Studies in Mass Communication 1,* 345–64.

Allen, C.L. (1965). Photographing the TV audience. *Journal of Advertising Research 28* (1), 2–8.

Alwitt, L., Anderson, D., Lorch, E. & Levin, S. (1980). Preschool children's visual attention to television. *Human Communication Research 7,* 52–67.

Anderson, B., Mead, M. & Sullivan, S. (1988). *Television: what do national assessment results tell us?* Princeton, NJ: National Assessment of Educational Progress, Educational Testing Service. (ERIC Document Reproduction Service No. ED 277 072.)

Anderson, D.R. & Collins, P.A. (1988). *The impact on children's education: television's influence on cognitive development.* Washington, DC: U.S. Department of Education, Office of Educational Research and Improvement. (ERIC Document Reproduction Service No. ED 295 271.)

— & Levin, S.R. (1976). Young children's attention to "Sesame Street." *Child Development 47,* 806–11.

— & Lorch, E.P. (1983). Looking at television: action or reaction. *In* J. Bryant & D.R. Anderson, eds. *Children's understanding of television: research on attention and comprehension,* 1–34. San Diego, CA: Academic.

—, Levin, S.R. & Lorch, E.P. (1977). The effects of TV program pacing on the behavior of preschool children. *AV Communication Review 25,* 159–66.

Anderson, D. & Field, D. (1983). Children's attention to television: Implications for production. *In* M. Meyer, ed. *Children and the formal features of television,* 56–96. Munich: Saur.

—, Alwitt, L., Lorch, E. & Levin, S. (1979). Watching children watch television. *In* G. Hale & M. Lewis, eds. *Attention and cognitive development,* 331–61. New York: Plenum.

—, Levin, S. & Lorch, E. (1977). The effects of TV program pacing on the behavior of preschool children. *AV Communication Review 25,* 159–66.

—, Lorch, E., Field, D. & Sanders, J. (1981). The effects of TV program comprehensibility on preschool children's visual attention to television. *Child Development 52,* 151–57.

—, Lorch, E., Field, D., Collins, P. & Nathan, J. (1986). Television viewing at home: age trends in visual attention and time with television. *Child Development 57,* 1024–33.

—, Lorch, E., Smith, R., Bradford, R. & Levin, S. (1981). Effects of peer presence on preschool children's visual attention to television. *Developmental Psychology 17,* 446–53.

Anderson, J.A. (1980). The theoretical lineage of critical viewing curricula. *Journal of Communication 30* (3), 64–70.

— (1981). Receivership skills: an educational response. *In* M. Ploghoft & J.A. Anderson, eds. *Education for the television age,* 19–27. Springfield, IL: Thomas.

— (1983). Television literacy and the critical viewer. *In* J. Bryant & D.R. Anderson, eds. *Children's understanding of television: research on attention and comprehension,* 297–330. San Diego, CA: Academic.

Anderson, J.R. (1980). *Cognitive psychology and its implications.* San Francisco, CA: Freeman.

Appel, V., Weinstein, S. & Weinstein, C. (1979). Brain activity and recall of TV advertising. *Journal of Advertising Research 19* (4), 7–15.

Argenta, D.M., Stoneman, Z. & Brody, G.H. (1986). The effects of three different television programs on young children's peer interactions and toy play. *Journal of Applied Developmental Psychology 7,* 355–71.

Atkin, C.K., Murray, J.P. & Nayman, O.B. (1971–72). The surgeon general's research program on television and social behavior: a review of empirical findings. *Journal of Broadcasting 16* (1), 21–35.

Atkin, D.J., Greenberg, B.S. & Baldwin, T.F. (1991). The home ecology of children's television viewing: parental mediation and the new video environment. *Journal of Communication 41* (3), 40–52.

Atkinson, R.C. & Shiffrin, R.M. (1968). Human memory: a proposed system and its control processes. *In* K.W. Spence & J.T. Spence, eds. *The psychology of learning and motivation: advances in research and theory, Vol. 2,* 89–193. San Diego, CA: Academic.

Atman, I. & Wohlwill, J.F., eds. (1978). *Children and environment.* New York: Plenum.

Ball, S. & Bogatz, G.A. (1970). *The first year of Sesame Street: an evaluation.* Princeton, NJ: Educational Testing Service.

Bandura, A. (1965). Influence of models' reinforcement contingencies on the acquisition of imitative responses. *Journal of Personality and Social Psychology 1,* 585–95.

— (1971). Analysis of modeling processes. *In* Bandura, A., ed. *Psychological modeling: conflicting theories,* 1–62.

Chicago, IL: Aldine Atherton.

— (1977). *Social learning theory.* Englewood Cliffs, NJ: Prentice Hall.

— (1986). *Social foundations of thought and action: a social cognitive theory.* Englewood Cliffs, NJ: Prentice Hall.

— & Walters, R.H. (1963). *Social learning and personality development.* New York: Holt, Rinehart & Winston.

—, Ross, D. & Ross, S.A. (1961) Transmission of aggression through imitation of aggressive models. *Journal of Abnormal and Social Psychology 63* (3), 575–82.

—, — & — (1963). Imitation of film-mediated aggressive models. *Journal of Abnormal and Social Psychology 66* (1), 3–11.

Baron, L. (1980). What do children really see on television? Paper presented at the annual meeting of the American Educational Research Association, Boston, MA.

Baughman, J.L. (1985). *Television's guardians: the FCC and the politics of programming 1958–1967.* Knoxville, TN: University of Tennessee Press.

Bechtel, R.P., Achepohl, C. & Akers, R. (1972). Correlates between observed behavior and questionnaire responses on television viewing. *In* E.A. Rubinstein, G.A. Comstock & J.P. Murray, eds. *Television and social behavior: Vol. 4. Television in day-to-day life: patterns of use,* 274–344. Washington, DC: Government Printing Office.

Becker, S. & Wolfe, G. (1960). Can adults predict children's interest in a television program? *In* W. Schramm, ed. *The impact of educational television,* 195–213. Urbana, IL: University of Illinois Press.

Beentjes, J.W.J. (1989). Learning from television and books: a Dutch replication study based on Salomon's model. *Educational Technology Research and Development 37,* 47–58.

— & Van der Voort, T.H.A. (1988). Television's impact on children's reading skills: a review of research. *Reading Research Quarterly 23* (4), 389–413.

Bell, J. (1984). *"TV's sort of . . . just there": critical television viewing skills.* (ERIC Document Reproduction Service No. ED 249 945.)

— (1991, Jun.) *The elderly on television: changing stereotypes.* Paper presented at the Annual Visual Communication Conference, Brackenridge, CO. (ERIC Document Reproduction Service No. ED 337 836.)

Belland, J. (1994). Is this the news? *In* A. De Vaney, ed. *Watching channel one: the convergence of students, technology, and private business.* Albany, NY: SUNY Press.

Berger, A.A. (1982). Televaccinations. [Review of: *Television: a family focus; critical television viewing; inside television: a guide to critical viewing;* and *critical television viewing skills*]. *Journal of Communication 32* (1), 213–15.

Berlyne, D.E. (1960). *Conflict, arousal, and curiosity.* New York: McGraw-Hill.

Berry, C. (1983). Learning from television news: a critique of the research. *Journal of Broadcasting 27,* 359–70.

— (1982). Research perspectives on the portrayals of Afro-American families on television. *In* A. Jackson, ed. *Black families and the medium of television,* 147–59. Ann Arbor, MI: Bush Program in Child Development & Social Policy, University of Michigan.

Birenbaum, A. (1978). Status and role. *In* E. Sagan, ed. *Sociology: the basic concepts,* 128–39. New York: Holt, Rinehart & Winston.

Bogatz, G.A. & Ball, S. (1971). *The second year of Sesame Street: a continuing evaluation, Vols. 1,2.* Princeton, NJ: Educational Testing Service. (ERIC Document Reproduction Service Nos. ED 122 800, ED 122 801.)

Bolton, R.N. (1983). Modeling the impact of television food advertising on children's diets. *In* J.H. Leigh & C.R. Martin, Jr., eds. *Current issues and research in advertising.* Ann Arbor, MI: Graduate School of Business Administration, University of Michigan.

Bossing, L. & Burgess, L.B. (1984). *Television viewing: its relationship to reading achievement of third-grade students.* (ERIC Document Reproduction Services No. ED 252 816.)

Bower, R.T. (1985). *The changing television audience in America.* New York: Columbia University Press.

Bowie, M.M. (1986, Jan.). Instructional film research and the learner. Paper presented at the Annual Convention of the Association for Educational Communications and Technology, Las Vegas, NV. (ERIC Document Reproduction Service No. ED 267 757.)

Braden, R.A & Hortin, J.L. (1982). Identifying the theoretical foundations of visual literacy. *Journal of Visual/Verbal Languaging 2,* 37–42.

Bretl, D.J. & Cantor, J. (1988). The portrayal of men and women in U.S. television commercials: a recent content analysis and trends over 15 years. *Sex Roles 18* (9/10), 595–609.

Broadbent, D. (1958). *Perception and communication.* London: Pergamon.

Brown, J.A. (1991). *Television "critical viewing skills" education: major media literacy projects in the United States and selected countries.* Hillsdale, NJ: Erlbaum.

Brown, J.D., Childers, K.E. & Koch, C.C. (1990). The influence of new media and family structure on young adolescents' television and radio use. *Communication Research 17* (1), 65–82.

Brown, J.R. & Linne, O. (1976). The family as a mediator of television's effects. *In* R. Brown, ed. *Children and Television,* 184–98. Beverly Hills, CA: Sage.

Bryant, J. & Anderson, D.R., eds. (1983). *Children's understanding of television: research on attention and comprehension.* San Diego, CA: Academic.

— & Zillmann, D., eds. (1991). *Responding to the screen: reception and reaction processes.* Hillsdale, NJ: Erlbaum.

— (1992). Examining the effects of television program pacing on children's cognitive development. Paper presented at the U.S. Department of Health and Human Service, Administration for Children and Families' Conference on "Television and the preparation of the mind for learning: critical questions on the effects of television on the developing brains of young children," Washington, DC.

—, Zillmann, D. & Brown, D. (1983). Entertainment features in children's educational television: effects on attention and information acquisition. *In* J. Bryant & D.R. Anderson, eds. *Children's understanding of television: research on attention and comprehension,* 221–40. San Diego, CA: Academic.

Bryce, J.W. & Leichter, H.J. (1983). The family and television. *Journal of Family Issues 4,* 309–28.

Bybee, C., Robinson, D. & Turow, J. (1982). Determinants of parental guidance of children's television viewing for a special subgroup: mass media scholars. *Journal of Broadcasting 16,* 697–710.

Cairns, E. (1990). Impact of television news exposure on children's perceptions of violence in Northern Ireland. *Journal of Social Psychology 130* (4), 447–52.

Calvert, S., Huston, A., Watkins, B. & Wright, J. (1982). The effects of selective attention to television forms on children's comprehension of content. *Child Development 53,* 601–10.

Cambre, M.A. (1987). *A reappraisal of instructional television.* ERIC Clearinghouse on Information Resources. Syracuse, NY: Syracuse University.

Campbell, D.T. & Stanley, J.C. (1963). *Experimental and quasi-experimental designs for research.* Chicago, IL: Rand McNally.

Carew, J. (1980). Experience and the development of intelligence in young children at home and in day care. *Monographs of the Society for Research in Child Development 45* (187), 1–89.

Carlisle, R.D.B. (1987). *Video at work in American schools.* Bloomington, IN: Agency for Instructional Technology.

Carpenter, C.R. & Greenhill, L.P. (1958). *Instructional television research. Report No. 2.* University Park, PA: Pennsylvania State University.

— & — (1955). *Instructional television research project number one: an investigation of closed circuit television for teaching university courses.* University Park, PA: Pennsylvania State University.

— &— (1956). *Instructional film reports, Vol. 2* (Technical Report No. 269-7-61). Port Washington, NY: Special Devices Center, U.S. Navy.

Carrozza, F. & Jochums, B. (1979, Apr.). *A summary of the "ThinkAbout" cluster evaluation: collection information.* Bloomington, IN: Agency for Instructional Television. (ERIC Document Reproduction Service No. ED 249 947.)

Cennamo, K.S. (1993). Learning from video: factors influencing learner's preconceptions and invested mental effort. *Educational Technology Research and Development 41* (3), 33–45.

Chapman, D. (1960). *Design for ETV: planning for schools with television* (rev. by F. Carioti, 1968). New York: Educational Facilities.

Charren, P. & Sandler, M. (1983). *Changing channels: living (sensibly) with television.* Reading, MA: Addison-Wesley.

Chen, M. (1994a). *The smart parent's guide to KIDS' TV.* San Francisco, CA: KQED.

— (1994b). Television and informal science education: Assessing the past, present, and future of research. *In* V. Crane, H. Nicholson, M. Chen & S. Bitgood, eds. *Informal science learning: what the research says about television, science museums, and community-based projects,* 15–60. Dedham, MA: Research Communications.

— (1994c). Six myths about television and children. *Media Studies Journal 8* (4), 105–14.

—, Ellis, J. & Hoelscher, K. (1988). Repurposing children's television for the classroom: teachers' use of "square one" TV videocassettes. *Educational Communications and Technology Journal 36* (3), 161–78.

Children's Television Workshop. (1994, Oct.). *Ghostwriter and youth-serving organizations: report to Carnegie Corporation of New York.* New York: Children's Television Workshop.

— (1989). Sesame Street research bibliography: selected citations relating to Sesame Street 1969–1989. New York: Author.

Christopher, F.S., Fabes, R.A. & Wilson, P.M. (1989). Family television viewing: implications for family life education. *Family Relations 38* (2), 210–14.

Chu, G. & Schramm, W. (1967). *Learning from television: what the research says.* Stanford, CA: Institute for Communications Research.

Clark, R.E. (1983). Reconsidering research on learning from media. *Review of Educational Research 53* (4), 445–59.

— (1994). Media will never influence learning. *Educational Technology Research and Development 42* (2), 21–29.

Coates, B. & Pusser, H.E. (1975). Positive reinforcement and punishment in "Sesame Street" and "Mister Rogers." *Journal of Broadcasting 19* (2), 143–51.

—, — & Goodman, I. (1976). The influence of "Sesame Street" and "Mister Rogers' Neighborhood" on children's social behavior in preschool. *Child Development 47,* 138–44.

Cohen, P.A., Ebeling, B. & Kulik, J. (1981). A meta-analysis of outcome studies of visual-based instruction. *Educational Communications and Technology Journal 29* (1), 26–36.

Collett, P. (1986). Watching the TV audience. Paper presented at the International Television Studies Conference, London. (ERIC Document Reproduction Service No. ED 293 498.)

Collins, W.A. (1983). Interpretation and inference in children's television viewing. *In* J. Bryant & D.R. Anderson, eds. *Children's understanding of television: research on attention and comprehension.* San Diego, CA: Academic.

Comstock, G. (1980). New emphases in research on the effects of television and film violence. *In* E.L. Palmer & A. Dorr, eds. *Children and the faces of television.* New York: Academic.

— & Cobbey, R.E. (1982). Television and the children of ethnic minorities: perspectives from research. *In* G.L. Berry & C. Mitchell-Kernan, eds. *Television and the socialization of the minority child,* 245–59. San Diego, CA: Academic.

— & Paik, H. (1987). *Television and children: a review of recent research.* (IR-71). Syracuse, NY: ERIC Clearinghouse on Information Resources.

— & — (1991). *Television and the American child.* San Diego, CA: Academic.

—, Chaffee, S., Katzman, N., McCombs, M. & Roberts, D. (1978). *Television and human behavior.* New York: Columbia University Press.

Corner, J. (1982). The importance of television images of black families. *In* A. Jackson, ed. *Black families and the medium of television,* 19–25. Ann Arbor, MI: Bush Program in Child Development & Social Policy, University of Michigan.

Corporation for Public Broadcasting & National Center for Educational Statistics. (1984, May). *School utilization study, 1982–83: executive summary.* Washington, DC: Author. (ERIC Document Reproduction Service No. ED 248 832.)

— (1988). *TV tips for parents: using television to help your child learn.* Washington, DC: Corporation for Public Broadcasting. (ERIC Document Reproduction Service No. 299 946.)

— (1993, Nov.). Kids and television in the nineties: responses from the Youth Monitor. *CPB Research Notes No. 64.*

— (n.d.). *Summary report: study of school uses of television and video 1990–1991 School Year.* Washington, DC: Author.

— (n.d.). *Technical report of the 1991 study of school uses of television and video.* Washington, DC: Author.

Corteen, R.S. & Williams, T.M. (1986). Television and reading skills. *In* T.M. Williams, ed. *The impact of television: a natural experiment in three communities,* 39–86. San Diego, CA: Academic.

Craig, R.S. (1991). *A content analysis comparing gender images*

in network television commercials aired in daytime, evening, and weekend telecasts. (ERIC Document Reproduction Service No. ED 329 217.)

Cronbach, L.J. & Snow, R.E. (1977). *Aptitudes and instructional methods.* New York: Irvington.

Cuban, L. (1986). *Teachers and machines: the classroom use of technology since 1920.* New York: Teachers College Press, Columbia University.

Cumberbatch, C. & Negrine, R. (1992). *Images of disability on television.* London: Routledge.

Dambrot, F.H., Reep, D.C. & Bell, D. (1988). Television and sex roles in the 1980's: do viewers' sex and sex role orientation change the picture? *Sex Roles 19* (5-6), 387–401.

Davis, D.M. (1990). Portrayals of women in prime-time network television: some demographic characteristics. *Sex Roles 23* (5-6), 325–31.

De Vaney, A., ed. (1994). *Watching channel one: the convergence of students, technology and private business.* New York: SUNY Press.

Debold, E. (1990). *Children's attitudes towards mathematics and the effects of square one: Vol. III. Children's problem-solving behavior and their attitudes towards mathematics: a study of the effects of square one TV.* New York: Children's Television Workshop.

Dee, J. (1985). *Myths and mirrors: a qualitative analysis of images of violence against women in mainstream advertising.* (ERIC Document Reproduction Service No. Ed 292 139.)

Desmond, R.J., Singer, J.L. & Singer, D.G. (1990). Family mediation: parental communication patterns and the influence of television on children. *In* J. Bryant, ed. *Television and the American family,* 293–310. Hillsdale, NJ: Erlbaum.

Dignam, M. (1977, Jun.). *Research on the use of television in secondary schools. Research report 48.* Bloomington, IN: Agency for Instructional Television. (ERIC Document Reproduction Service No. ED 156 166.)

Dirr, P. & Pedone, R. (1978, Jan.). A national report on the use of instructional television. *AV Instruction,* 11–13.

Donohue, T.R., Henke, L.L. & Meyer, T.P. (1983). Learning about television commercials: the impact of instructional units on children's perceptions of motive and intent. *Journal of Broadcasting 27* (3), 251–61.

Dorr, A. (1982). Television and its socialization influences on minority children. *In* G.L. Berry & C. Mitchell-Kernan, eds. *Television and the socialization of the minority child,* 15–35. San Diego, CA: Academic.

—, Kovaric, P. & Doubleday, C. (1989). Parent-child coviewing of television. *Journal of Broadcasting & Electronic Media 33* (1), 15–51.

Dubeck, L.W., Moshier, S.E. & Boss, J.E. (1988). *Science in cinema.* New York: Teachers College Press, Columbia University.

Dumont, M. (1976). [Letter to the editor]. *American Journal of Psychiatry,* 133.

Durkin, K. (1985). *Television, sex roles, and children.* Philadelphia: Open University Press.

Edwardson, M., Grooms, D. & Pringle, P. (1976). Visualization and TV news information gain. *Journal of Broadcasting 20* (3), 373–80.

Elkin, D. (1984). *All grown up and no place to go: teenagers in crisis.* Reading, MA: Addison-Wesley.

Ellery, J.B. (1959). *A pilot study of the nature of aesthetic experiences associated with television and its place in education.* Detroit, MI: Wayne State University.

Emery, M. & Emery, F. (1975). *A choice of futures: to enlighten and inform.* Canberra, Australia: Center for Continuing Education, Australian National University.

— & — (1980). The vacuous vision: the TV medium. *Journal of the University Film Association 32,* 27–32.

Eron, L.D. (1982). Parent child interaction: television violence and aggression of children. *American Psychologist 37,* 197–211.

Fairchild, H.H., Stockard, R. & Bowman, P. (1986). Impact of roots: EvideSce of the national survey of black Americans. *Journal of Black Studies 16,* 307–18.

Featherman, G., Frieser, D., Greenspun, D., Harris, B., Schulman, D. & Crown, P. (1979). Electroencephalographic and electrooculographic correlates of television watching. Final Technical Report. Hampshire College, Amherst, MA.

Feshbach, S. & Singer, R.D. (1971). *Television and aggression.* San Francisco, CA: Jossey-Bass.

Fetler, M. (1984). Television viewing and school achievement. *Journal of Communication 34* (2), 104–18.

— & Carlson, D. (1982). *California assessment program surveys of television and achievement.* New York: Annual Meeting of the American Educational Research Association, March. (ERIC Document Reproduction Services No. ED 217 876.)

Field, D. (1983). *Children's television viewing strategies.* Paper presented at the Society for Research in Child Development, biennial meeting, Detroit, MI.

Fisch, S.M., Hall, E.R., Esty, E.T., Debold, E., Miller, B.A., Bennett, D.T. & Solan, S.V. (1991). *Children's problem-solving behavior and their attitudes towards mathematics: a study of the effects of square one TV, Vol. V. Executive summary.* New York: Children's Television Workshop.

Fisch, S., Cohen, D., McCann, S. & Hoffman, L. (1993, Jan.). "Square one" TV: research history and bibliography. New York: Children's Television Workshop.

Fite, K.V. (1994). *Television and the brain: a review.* New York: Children's Television Workshop.

Fitzgerald, T.K. (1992). Media, ethnicity and identity. *In* P. Scannell, P. Schlesinger & C. Sparks, eds. *Culture and power: a media, culture & society reader,* 112–33. Beverly Hills, CA: Sage.

Flagg, B.N. (1990). *Formative evaluation for educational technologies.* Hillsdale, NJ: Erlbaum.

Fleming, M. & Levie, W.H., eds. (1978). *Instructional message design: principles from the behavioral sciences.* Englewood Cliffs, NJ: Educational Technology.

— & —, eds. (1993). *Instructional message design: principles from the behavioral sciences,* 2d ed. Englewood Cliffs, NJ: Educational Technology.

Fleming, M. (1967). Classification and analysis of instructional illustrations. *Audio-visual Communication Review 15* (3), 246–58.

Forge, K.L.S. & Phemister, S. (1982). Effect of prosocial cartoons on preschool children (unpublished report). (ERIC Document Reproduction Service No. ED 262 905.)

Forsdale, J.R. & Forsdale, L. (1970). Film literacy. *AV Communication Review 18* (3), 263–76.

Frank, R.E. & Greenberg, M.G. (1979). Zooming in on TV audiences. *Psychology Today 13* (4), 92–103, 114.

Frazer, C.F. (1976). A symbolic interactionist approach to child television viewing. Unpublished doctoral dissertation.

University of Illinois at Urbana, Champaign, IL.

Friedrich, L.K. & Stein, A.H., (1973). Aggressive and prosocial television programs and the natural behavior of preschool children. *Monographs of the Society for Research in Child Development 38* (4, serial no. 151).

Gadberry, S. (1980). Effects of restricting first-graders' TV-viewing on leisure time use, IQ change, and cognitive style. *Journal of Applied Developmental Psychology 1,* 45–58.

Gaddy, G.D. (1986). Television's impact on high school achievement. *Public Opinion Quarterly 50,* 340–59.

Gantz, W. & Weaver, J.P. (1984). Parent-child communication about television: a view from the parent's perspective. Paper presented at the annual convention of the Association for Education in Journalism and Mass Communication, Gainesville, FL. (ERIC Document Reproduction Service No. ED 265 840.)

Gardner, H. (1982). *Art, mind and brain: a cognitive approach to creativity.* New York: Basic Books.

— Howard, V.A. & Perkins, D. (1974). Symbol systems: a philosophical, psychological and educational investigation. *In* D. Olson, ed. *Media and symbols: the forms of expression, communication and education* (73d annual yearbook of the National Society for the Study of Education). Chicago, IL: University of Chicago Press.

Gay, L.R. (1992). *Educational research: competencies for analysis and application,* 4th ed. New York: Merrill.

Gomez, G.O. (1986, Jul.). *Research on cognitive effects of non-educational TV: an epistemological discussion.* London. International Television Studies Conference. (ERIC Document Reproduction Service No. ED 294 534.)

Goodman, N. (1968). *Languages of art.* Indianapolis, IN: Hackett.

Gorn, G.J. & Goldberg, M.E. (1982). Behavioral evidence of the effects of televised food messages on children. *Journal of Consumer Research 9,* 200–05.

Gortmaker, S.L., Salter, C.A., Walker, D.K. & Dietz, W.H. Jr. (1990). The impact of television viewing on mental aptitude and achievement: a longitudinal study. *Public Opinion Quarterly 54,* 594–604.

Gotthelf, C. & Peel, T. (1990). The Children's Television Workshop goes to school. *Educational Technology Research and Development 38* (4), 25–33.

Grabowski, B.L. (1991). Message Design: issues and trends. *In* G.J. Anglin, ed. *Instructional technology: past, present and future,* 202–12. Englewood, CO: Libraries Unlimited.

Graves, S.B. (1982). The impact of television on the cognitive and affective development of minority children. *In* G.L. Berry & C. Mitchell-Kernan, eds. *Television and the socialization of the minority child,* 37–69. San Diego, CA: Academic.

— (1987). *Final report on Newburgh, New York, sample.* New York: Children's Television Workshop.

Grayson, B. (1979). Television and minorities. *In* B. Logan & K. Moody, eds. *Television awareness training: the viewer's guide for family and community,* 139–44. New York: Media Action Research Center.

Gredler, M.E. (1992). *Learning and instruction: theory into practice,* 2d ed. New York: Macmillan.

Greenberg, B.S. & Atkin, C.K. (1982). Television, minority children, and perspectives from research and practice. *In* G.L. Berry & C. Mitchell-Kernan, eds. *Television and the socialization of the minority child,* 215–43. San Diego, CA: Academic.

Greenhill, L.P. (1967). Review of trends in research on instructional television and film. *In* J.C. Reid & D.W. MacLennan, eds. *Research in instructional television and film.* U.S. Office of Education.

— (1956). *Instructional film research program: final report.* University Park, PA: Pennsylvania State University.

Greenstein, J. (1954). Effects of television on elementary school grades. *Journal of Educational Research 48,* 161–76.

Greer, D., Potts, R., Wright, J. & Huston, A.C. (1982). The effects of television commercial from and commercial placement on children's social behavior and attention. *Child Development 53,* 611–19.

Gropper, G.L. & Lumsdaine, A.A. (1961). *The use of student response to improve televised instruction: an overview.* Pittsburgh, PA: American Institutes for Research.

Gross, L. (1991). Out of the mainstream: sexual minorities and the mass media. *In* M.A. Wolf & A.P. Kielwasser, eds. *Gay people, sex and the media,* 19–46. New York: Haworth.

Gunter, B. (1980). Remembering television news: effects of picture content. *Journal of General Psychology 102,* 127–33.

— (1986). *Television and sex role stereotyping.* London: Libbey.

— (1987). *Poor reception: misunderstanding and forgetting broadcast news.* Hillsdale, NJ: Erlbaum.

— (1987). *Television and the fear of crime.* London: Libbey.

— & Wakshlag, J. (1988). Television viewing and perceptions of crime among London residents. *In* P. Drummond & R. Paterson, eds. *Television and its audience: international research perspectives,* 191–209. London: BFI Books.

Haefner, M.J. & Wartella, E.A. (1987). Effects of sibling coviewing on children's interpretations of television programs. *Journal of Broadcasting & Electronic Media 31* (2), 153–68.

Hagerstown: The Board of Education (1959). *Closed circuit television: teaching in Washington County 1958–68.*

Halpern, W. (1975). Turned-on toddlers. *Journal of Communication 25,* 66–70.

Hansen, C.H. & Hansen, R.D. (1988). How rock music videos can change what is seen when boy meets girl: priming stereotypic appraisal of social interactions. *Sex Roles 19* (5–6), 287–316.

Hardaway, C.W., Beymer, W.C.L. & Engbretson, W.E. (1963). *A study of attitudinal changes of teachers and pupils of various groups toward educational television.* USOE Project No. 988. Terre Haute, IN: Indiana State College.

Harris, C.O. (1962). *Development of problem-solving ability and learning of relevant-irrelevant information through film and TV versions of a strength of materials testing laboratory.* USOE Grant NO. 7-20-040-00. East Lansing, MI: College of Engineering, Michigan State University.

Hatt, P. (1982). *A review of research on the effects of television viewing on the reading achievement of elementary school children.* (ERIC Document Reproduction Service No ED 233 297.)

Hawkins, R., Kin, Y. & Pingree, S. (1991). The ups and downs of attention to television. *Communication Research 18* (1), 53–76.

Hayman, J.L. Jr. (1963). Viewer location and learning in instructional television. *AV Communication Review 11,* 96–103.

Head, C. (1994, Nov.-Dec.). Partners against youth violence. *Focus,* 3–4.

Hearold, S. (1986). A synthesis of 1043 effects of television on social behavior. *In* G. Comstock, ed. *Public communication and behavior, Vol. 1,* 65–133. San Diego, CA: Academic.

Hepburn, M.A. (1990). Americans glued to the tube: mass media, information and social studies. *Social Studies Education 54* (4), 233–36.

Higgs, C.T. & Weiller, K.H. (1987, Apr.). The aggressive male versus the passive female: an analysis of differentials in role portrayals. Paper presented at the National Convention of the American Alliance for Health, Physical Education, Recreation, and Dance, Las Vegas, NV. (ERIC Document Reproduction Service No. ED 283 796.)

Hill, C.R. & Stafford, F.P. (1980). Parental care of children: time diary estimates of quantity, predictability, and variety. *The Journal of Human Resources 15* (2), 219–39.

Hilliard, R.L. & Field, H.H. (1976). *Television and the teacher.* New York: Hastings House.

Hoban, C.F. & VanOrmer, E.B. (1950, Dec.). *Instructional film research 1918–1959.* Technical Report No. 269-7-19. Port Washington, NY: U.S. Naval Training Devices Center.

Hollenbeck, A. & Slaby, R. (1979). Infant visual responses to television. *Child Development 50,* 41–45.

Holmes, P.D. (1959). *Television research in the teaching-learning process.* Detroit, MI: Wayne State University Division of Broadcasting.

Homans, G.C. (1961). *Social behavior: its elementary forms.* New York: Harcourt, Brace & World.

Hornik, R. (1978). Television access and the slowing of cognitive growth. *American Educational Research Journal 15,* 1–15.

— (1981). Out-of-school television and schooling: hypotheses and methods. *Review of Educational Research 51,* 193–214.

—, Ingle, H.T., Mayo, J.K., McAnany, E.G. & Schramm, W. (1973). *Television and educational reform in El Salvador: final Report.* Palo Alto, CA: Institute for Communication Research, Stanford University.

Huesman, L.R., Eron, L.D., Lefkowitz, M.M. & Walder, L.O. (1984). Stability of aggression over time and generations. *Developmental Psychology 20,* 1120–34.

Hunter, P. (1992). Teaching critical television viewing: an approach for gifted learners. *Roeper Review 15* (2), 84–89.

Huskey, L., Jackstadt, S.L. & Goldsmith, S. (1991). Economic literacy and the content of television network news. *Social Education 55* (3), 182–85.

Huston, A.C. & Wright, J.C. (1983). Children's processing of television: the informative functions of formal features. *In* J. Bryant & D.R. Anderson, eds. *Children's understanding of television: research on attention and comprehension,* 35–68. San Diego, CA: Academic.

—, Donnerstein, E., Fairchild, H., Feshbach, N.D., Katz, P.A., Murray, J.P., Rubinstein, E.A., Wilcox, B.L. & Zuckerman, D. (1992). *Big world, small screen: the role of television in American society.* Lincoln, NE: University of Nebraska Press.

—, Watkins, B.A. & Kunkel, D. (1989). Public policy and children's television. *American Psychologist 44* (2), 424–33.

—, Wright, J.C., Rice, M.L., Kerkman, D. & St. Peters, M. (1990). Development of television viewing patterns in early childhood: a longitudinal investigation. *Developmental Psychology 26* (3), 409–20.

— & — (1989). The forms of television and the child viewer. *In* G. Comstock, ed. *Public communication and behavior, Vol. 2,* 103–59. San Diego, CA: Academic.

Huston-Stein, A. (1972). Mass media and young children's development. *In* I. Gordon, ed. *Early childhood education. The 71st yearbook of the National Society for the Study of Education*, 180–202. Chicago, IL: University of Chicago Press.

Huston-Stein, A., Fox, S., Greer, D., Watkins, B.A. & Whitaker, J. (1981). The effects of TV action and violence on children's social behavior. *The Journal of Genetic Psychology 138*, 183–91.

Iker, S. (1983, Nov./Dec.). Science, children and television. *MOSAIC*, 8–13.

Jalongo, M.R. (1983). The preschool child's comprehension of television commercial disclaimers. Paper presented at the Research Forum of the Annual Study Conference of the Association for Childhood Education International, Cleveland, OH. (ERIC Document Reproduction Service No. ED 229 122.)

James, N.C. & McCain, T.A. (1982). Television games preschool children play: patterns, themes, and uses. *Journal of Broadcasting 26* (4), 783–800.

Jeffery, L. & Durkin, K. (1989). Children's reactions to televised counter-stereotyped male sex role behaviour as a function of age, sex, and perceived power. *Social Behaviour 4*, 285–310.

Johnson, J. (1987). *Electronic learning: from audiotape to videodisc.* Hillsdale, NJ: Erlbaum.

Johnston, J. & Ettema, J.S. (1982). *Positive images: breaking stereotypes with children's television.* Beverly Hills, CA: Sage.

Joy, L.A., Kimball, M.M. & Zabrack, M.L. (1986). Television and children's aggressive behavior. *In* T.M. Williams, ed. *The impact of television: a natural experiment in three communities*, 303–60. San Diego, CA: Academic.

Kamil, B.L. (1992). Cable in the classroom. *In* D. Ely & B. Minor, eds. *Educational Media Yearbook, Vol. 18.* Englewood, CO: Libraries Unlimited in cooperation with the Association for Educational Communications & Technology.

Kanner, J.H. & Rosenstein, A.J. (1960). Television in army training: color vs. black and white. *AV Communication Review 8*, 243–52.

Keith, T.Z., Reimers, T.M., Fehrmann, P.G., Pottebaum, S.M. & Aubey, L.W. (1986). Parental involvement, homework, and TV time: direct and indirect effects on high school achievement. *Journal of Educational Psychology 78* (5), 373–80.

Kimball, M.M. (1986). Television and sex-role attitudes. *In* T.M. Williams, ed. *The impact of television: a natural experiment in three communities*, 265–301. San Diego, CA: Academic.

Knowlton, J.Q. (1966). On the definition of "picture." *Audiovisual Communication Review 14* (2), 157–83.

Knupfer, N.N. (1994). Channel one: reactions of students, teachers and parents. *In* A. De Vaney, ed. *Watching channel one: the convergence of students, technology, and private business*, 61–86. Albany, NY: SUNY Press.

— & Hayes, P. (1994). The effects of the channel one broadcast on students' knowledge of current events. *In* A. De Vaney, ed. *Watching channel one: the convergence of students, technology, and private business*, 42–60. Albany, NY: SUNY Press.

Kozma, R.B. (1986). Implications of instructional psychology for the design of educational television. *Educational Communications and Technology Journal 34* (1), 11–19.

— (1991). Learning with media. *Review of Educational Research 61* (2), 179–211.

— (1994). *Will media influence learning? Reframing the debate. Educational Technology Research and Development 42* (2), 7–19.

Krendl, K.A., & Watkins, B. (1983). Understanding television: an exploratory inquiry into the reconstruction of narrative content. *Educational Communications and Technology Journal 31* (4), 201–12.

Krugman, D.M. & Johnson, K.F. (1991). Differences in the consumption of traditional broadcast and VCR movie rentals. *Journal of Broadcasting 35* (2), 213–32.

Krugman, H. (1970). *Electroencephalographic aspects of low involvement: implications for the McLuhan hypothesis.* Cambridge, MA: Marketing & Science Institute.

— (1979, January 29). The two brains: new evidence on TV impact. *Broadcasting,* p. 14.

— (1971). Brain wave measures of media involvement. *Journal of Advertising Research 11*, 3–9.

Krull, R. (1983). Children learning to watch television. *In* J. Bryant & D.R. Anderson, eds. *Children's understanding of television: research on attention and comprehension*, 103–23. San Diego, CA: Academic.

Kubey, R. & Larson, R. (1990). The use and experience of the new video media among children and young adolescents. *Communication Research 17* (1), 107–30.

Kumata, H. (1956). *An inventory of instructional television research.* Ann Arbor, MI: Educational Television and Radio Center.

Kunkel, D. (1988). Children and host-selling television commercials. *Communication Research 15* (1), 71–92.

Lang, A. (1989). Effects of chronological presentation of information on processing and memory for broadcast news. *Journal of Broadcasting and Electronic Media 33* (4), 441–52.

Langmeyer, L. (1989, Mar.). Gender stereotypes in advertising: a critical review. Paper presented at the annual meeting of the Southeastern Psychological Association, Washington, DC. (ERIC Document Reproduction Service No. ED 309 484.)

Lashly, K.S. & Watson, J.B (1922). *A psychological study of motion pictures in relation to venereal disease campaigns.* Washington, DC: U.S. Interdepartmental Social Hygiene Board.

Leichter, H.J., Ahmed, D., Barrios, J.B., Larsen, E. & Moe, L. (1985). Family contexts of television. *Educational Communication and Technology Journal 33* (1), 26–40.

Leifer, A.D. (1976). Factors which predict the credibility ascribed to television. Paper presented at the annual convention of the American Psychological Association, Washington, DC. (ERIC Document Reproduction Service No. ED 135 332.)

Lemish, D. & Rice, M. (1986). Television as a talking picture book: a prop for language acquisition. *Journal of Child Language 13*, 251–74.

Lesser, G.S. (1972). Language, teaching and television production for children: the experience from "Sesame Street." *Harvard Educational Review 42*, 232–72.

— (1974). *Children and television: lessons from "Sesame Street."* New York: Random House.

Levie, H.W. & Dickie, K.E. (1973). The analysis and application of media. *In* R.M.W. Travers, ed. *Second handbook of research on teaching,* 858–82. Chicago, IL: Rand McNally.

Levin, D.E. & Carlsson-Paige, N. (1994, Jul.). Developmentally appropriate television: putting children first. *Young Children 49* (5), 38–44.

Levin, S.R. & Anderson, D.R. (1976). "Sesame Street" around the world: the development of attention. *Journal of Communication 26* (2), 126–35.

—, Petros, T.V. & Petrella, F.W. (1982). Preschoolers' awareness of television advertising. *Child Development 53,* 933–37.

Lewis, C. (1993). The interactive dimension of television: negotiation and socialization in the family room. *Journal of Visual Literacy 13* (2), 9–50.

Lieberman, D. (1980). *Critical T.V. viewing workshops for high school teachers, parents, and community leaders [trainer's manual], Vol. II: workshop handouts.* San Francisco, CA: Far West Laboratory for Educational Research and Development. (ERIC Document Reproduction Service No. ED 244 585.)

— (1980). *Critical television viewing skills curriculum.* final Report (Oct. 1, 1979–Nov. 30, 1980. San Francisco, CA: Far West Laboratory for Educational Research & Development. (ERIC Document Reproduction Service No. ED 215 668.)

Liebert, R.M. & Sprafkin, J. (1988). *The early window: effects of television on children and youth,* 3d ed. New York: Pergamon.

Light, R.J. & Pillemer, D.B. (1984). *Summing up: the science of reviewing research.* Cambridge, MA: Harvard University Press.

Lin, C.A. & Atkin, D.J. (1989). Parental mediation and rule-making for adolescent use of television and VCRs. *Journal of Broadcasting & Electronic Media 33* (1), 53–67.

Lipinski, J.W. & Calvert, S.L. (1985). *The influence of television on children's sex typing.* (ERIC Document Reproduction Service No. ED 280 586.)

Lloyd-Kolkin, D., Wheeler, P. & Strand, T. (1980). Developing a curriculum for teenagers. *Journal of Communication 30* (3), 119–25.

Lorch, E.P., Anderson, D.R. & Levin, S.R. (1979). The relationship of visual attention to children's comprehension of television. *Child Development 50,* 722–27.

—, Bellack, D. & Augsbach, L. (1987). Young children's memory for televised stories: effects of importance. *Child Development 58,* 453–63.

Luker, R. & Johnston, J. (1989). Television in adolescent social development. *Education Digest 54* (6), 50–51.

Lull, J. (1990). Families' social uses of television as extensions of the household. *In* J. Bryant, ed. *Television and the American family,* 59–72. Hillsdale, NJ: Erlbaum.

Lumsdaine, A.A. (1963). Instruments and media of instruction. *In* N.L. Gage, ed. *Handbook of Research on Teaching,* 583–682. Chicago, IL: Rand McNally.

Mander, J. (1978). *Four arguments for the elimination of television.* New York: Morrow.

Marjoriebanks, K. (1979). *Families and their learning environments.* Boston, MA: Routledge & Kegan Paul.

McDonald, D.G. & Glynn, C.J. (1986). Television content viewing patterns: some clues from societal norms. Paper presented to the Mass Communication Division of the International Communication Association Annual Convention, Chicago, IL. (ERIC Document Reproduction Service No. ED 278 063.)

McFarland, S.L. (1992). *Extending "the neighborhood" to child care. Research report.* Toledo, OH: Public Broadcasting Foundation of Northwest Ohio. (ERIC Document Reproduction Service No. ED 351 136.)

McGrane, J.F. & Baron, M.L. (1959). A comparison of learning resulting from motion picture projector and closed circuit television presentations. *Society of Motion Picture and Television Engineers Journal 68,* 824–27.

McIlwraith, R.D. & Schallow, J. (1983). Adult fantasy life and patterns of media use. *Journal of Communication 33* (1), 78–91.

— & — (1982-83). Television viewing and styles of children's fantasy. *Imagination, Cognition and Personality 2* (4), 323–31.

McLuhan, M. (1964). *Understanding media: the extensions of man.* New York: McGraw-Hill.

Meadowcroft, J.M. & Reeves, B. (1989). Influence of story schema development on children's attention to television. *Communication Research 16* (3), 352–74.

Mediascope, Inc. (1996). *National television violence study: executive summary.* Studio City, CA: Author.

Meringoff, L.K., Vibbert, M.M., Char, C.A., Fernie, D.E., Banker, G.S. & Gardner, H. (1983). How is children's learning from television distinctive? Exploiting the medium methodologically. *In* J. Bryant & D.R. Anderson, ed. *Children's understanding of television,* 151–77. San Diego, CA: Academic.

Messaris, P. & Nielsen, K. (1989, Aug.). Viewers' interpretations of associational montage: the influence of visual literacy and educational background. Paper presented to the Association for Education in Journalism and Mass Communication, Washington, DC.

— (1994). *Visual literacy: image, mind, & reality.* Boulder, CO: Westview.

Meyer M. (1983). *Children and the formal features of television.* Munich: Saur.

Meyers, R. (1980, Nov.). An examination of the male sex role model in prime time television commercials. Paper presented at the annual meeting of the Speech Communication Association, New York. (ERIC Document Reproduction Service No. ED 208 347.)

Mielke, K., ed. (1990). Children's learning from television: research and development at the Children's Television Workshop [special issue]. *Educational Technology Research and Development 38* (4).

— (1988, Sep.). Television in the social studies classroom. *Social Education,* 362–64.

— (1994). "Sesame Street" and children in poverty. *Media Studies Journal 8* (4), 125–34.

Milavsky, J.R., Kessler, R.C., Stipp, H.H. & Reubens, W.S. (1982). *Television and aggression: a panel study.* San Diego, CA: Academic.

Miller, W.C. (1968, Dec.). Standards for ETV research. *Educational Broadcasting Review,* 48–53.

Moore, R.L. & Moschis, G.P. (1982). A longitudinal analysis of television advertising effects on adolescents. Paper presented at the annual meeting of the Association for Education in Journalism, Athens, OH. (ERIC Document Reproduction Service No. ED 219 753.)

Morgan, M. (1980). Television viewing and reading: does more equal better? *Journal of Communication 32,* 159–65.

— (1982, Mar.). More than a simple association: conditional patterns of television and achievement. Paper presented at the annual meeting of the American Educational Research Association, New York. (ERIC Document Reproduction Services No. ED 217 864.)

— & Gross, L. (1980). Television and academic achievement. *Journal of Broadcasting 24,* 117–232.

Murray, J.P. (1995, Spring). Children and television violence. *The Kansas Journal of Law & Public Policy,,* 7-15.

— (1980). *Television and youth: 25 years of research and controversy.* Boys Town, NE: Boys Town Center for the Study of Youth Development. (ERIC Document Reproduction Service No. ED 201 302.)

— & Kippax, S. (1978). Children's social behavior in three towns with differing television experience. *Journal of Communication 28* (1), 19–29.

National Center for Education Statistics. (1991). NELS-A profile of the American eighth grader (Stock No. 065-000-00404-6). Washington, DC: U.S. Government Printing Office.

— (1992, Sep.). *New reports focus on eighth graders and their parents* (Announcement NCES 92-488A). Washington, DC: Office of Educational Research & Improvement.

National Institute of Mental Health (NIMH) (1972). Television and growing up: the impact of televised violence. Report to the Surgeon General, U.S. Public Health Service, from the Surgeon General's Scientific Advisory Committee on Television and Social Behavior, U.S. Department of Health, Education, & Welfare; Health Services & Mental Health Administration. Rockville, MD: National Institute of Mental Health. [DHEW Publication No. 72-9090.]

— (1982). *Television and behavior: ten years of scientific progress and implications for the eighties* (Vol. 1: summary report). Rockville, MD: National Institute of Mental Health. [DHHS Publication no. 82-1195.]

National Science Foundation. (1977). *Research on the effects of television advertising on children: a review of the literature and recommendations for future research* (NSF/RA 770115). Washington, DC:U.S. Government Printing Office No. 0-246-412.

Neisser, U. (1967). *Cognitive psychology.* New York: Appleton-Century-Crofts.

Nelson, M.B. (1994). *The stronger women get, the more men love football: sexism and the American culture of sports.* New York: Harcourt, Brace.

Neufeldt, V. & Sparks, A.N., eds. (1990). *Webster's new world dictionary.* New York: Warner Books.

Neuman, S.B. (1986). Television reading and the home environment. *Reading Research and Instruction 25,* 173–83.

— (1988). The displacement effect: assessing the relation between television viewing and reading performance. *Reading Research Quarterly 23,* 414–40.

— (1991). *Literacy in the television age: the myth of the TV effect.* Norwood, NJ: Ablex.

Niven, H.F. (1958). Instructional television as a medium of teaching in higher education. Unpublished doctoral dissertation, Ohio State University.

Noble, G. (1975). *Children in front of the small screen.* Beverly Hills, CA: Sage.

Norberg, K. (1966). Visual perception theory and instructional communication. *Audio-visual Communication Review 3* (14), 301–17.

—, ed. (1962). Perception theory and AV education [supplement 5]. *Audio-visual Communication Review 10* (5).

Notar, E. (1989). Children and TV commercials "wave after wave of exploitation." *Childhood Education 66* (2), 66–67.

Nugent, G. (1977). *Television and utilization training: how do they influence learning?* Lincoln, NE: Nebraska University. (ERIC Document Reproduction Service No. ED 191 433.)

O'Bryant, S.L. & Corder-Bolz, C.R. (1978). Children and television. *Children Today.* DHEW Publication No. (OHDS) 79-30169. Washington, DC: U.S. Government Printing Office.

O'Reilly, K. & Splaine, J. (1987, May/Jun.). *Critical viewing: stimulant to critical thinking.* South Hamilton, MA: Critical Thinking. (ERIC Document Reproduction Service No. ED 289 796.)

Office of Educational Research and Improvement (1991). *The executive summary of "NAEP–the state of mathematics achievement"* (NCES Publication No. 91-1050). Washington, DC: Office of Educational Research & Improvement, U.S. Office of Education.

— (1991, Fall). Data indicate lack of parent involvement (No. ED/OERI 91-1). *OERI Bulletin,* 5.

— (1994, Oct.). *TV viewing and parental guidance.* Washington, DC: Office of Educational Research & Improvement, U.S. Office of Education.

Palmer, E.L. (1987). *Children in the cradle of television.* Lexington, MA: Lexington Books, Heath.

Palmer, P. (1986). *The lively audience.* Boston, MA: Allen & Unwin.

Pasewark, W.R. (1956). *Teaching typing through television.* Research Report No. 17. East Lansing, MI: Michigan State University.

Paulson, R.L. (1974). Teaching cooperation on television: an evaluation of Sesame Street social goals program. *AV Communication Review 22* (3), 229–46.

Pearl, D., Bouthilet, L. & Lazar, J., eds. (1982). *Television and behavior: ten years of scientific progress and implications for the eighties,* Vol. 2, technical reviews. Rockville, MD: National Institute of Mental Health. [DHHS Publication no. 82-1195.]

—, — & —, eds. (1982). *Television and behavior: ten years of scientific progress and implications for the eighties,* Vol. 1, summary report. Washington, DC: U.S. Government Printing Office.

Perloff, R.M., Wartella, E.A. & Becker, L.B. (1982). Increasing learning from TV news. *Journalism Quarterly 59,* 83–86.

Perse, E.M. (1990). Audience selectivity and involvement in the newer media environment. *Communication Research 17* (5), 675–97.

Peters, J.M.L. (1961). *Teaching about the film.* New York: International Document Service, Columbia University Press.

Peterson, C.C., Peterson, J.L. & Carroll, J. (1987) Television viewing and imaginative problem solving during preadolescence. *The Journal of Genetic Psychology 20* (1), 61–67.

Petty, L.I. (1994a, Sep.). *"Sesame Street" research bibliography 1989–1994.* New York: Children's Television Workshop.

— (1994b, Sep.). *A review of "Sesame Street" research 1989–1994.* New York: Children's Television Workshop.

Piaget, J. (1926). *The language and thought of the child.* New

York: Harcourt, Brace.

Pinon, M.F., Huston, A.C. & Wright, J.C. (1989). Family ecology and child characteristics that predict young children's educational television viewing. *Child Development 60,* 846–56.

Plomin, R., Corley, R., DeFries, J.C. & Fulker, D.W. (1990). Individual differences in television viewing in early childhood: nature as well as nurture. *Psychological Science 1* (6), 371–77.

Polsky, R.M. (1974). *Getting to Sesame Street: origins of the Children's Television Workshop.* New York: Praeger.

Postman, N. (1982). *The disappearance of childhood.* New York: Delacorte.

Potter, W.J. (1987). Does television viewing hinder academic achievement among adolescents? *Human Communication Research 14,* 27–46.

— (1990). Adolescents' perceptions of the primary values of television programming. *Journalism Quarterly 67* (4), 843–51.

Quisenberry, N. & Klasek, C. (1976). *The relationship of children's television viewing to achievement at the intermediate level.* Carbondale, IL: Southern Illinois University. (ERIC Document Reproduction Service No. ED 143 336.)

Rapaczynski, W., Singer, D.G. & Singer, J.L. (1982). Teaching television: a curriculum for young children. *Journal of Communication 32* (2), 46–55.

Reid, J.C. & MacLennan, D.W., eds. (1967). *Research in instructional television and film.* Washington, DC: U.S. Department of Health, Education, & Welfare.

Reid, L.N. (1979). Viewing rules as mediating factors of children's responses to commercials. *Journal of Broadcasting 23* (1), 15–26.

— & Frazer, C.F. (1980). Children's use of television commercials to initiate social interaction in family viewing situations. *Journal of Broadcasting 24* (2), 149–58.

Reinking, D. & Wu, J. (1990). Reexamining the research on television and reading. *Reading Research and Instruction 29* (2), 30–43.

Reiser, R.A., Tessmer, M.A. & Phelps, P.C. (1984). Adult-child interaction in children's learning from "Sesame Street." *Educational Communications and Technology Journal 32* (4), 217–33.

—, Williamson, N. & Suzuki, K. (1988). Using "Sesame Street" to facilitate children's recognition of letters and numbers. *Educational Communications and Technology Journal 36* (1), 15–21.

Research Division, Children's Television Workshop (n.d.). *"3, 2, 1 contact" research bibliography.* New York: Children's Television Workshop.

Riccobono, J.A. (1985). *School utilization study: availability, use, and support of instructional media, 1982–83, final report.* Washington, DC: Corporation for Public Broadcasting. (ERIC Document Reproduction Service No. ED 256 292.)

Rice, M., Huston, A. & Wright, J. (1982). The forms of television: effects on children's attention, comprehension, and social behavior. *In* D. Pearl, L. Bouthilet & J. Lazar, eds. Television and behavior: ten years of scientific inquiry and implications for the eighties: Vol. 2. Technical review, 24–38. Washington, DC: U.S. Government Printing Office.

—, — & — (1983). The forms of television: effects on children's attention, comprehension, and social behavior. *In* M.

Meyer, ed. *Children and the formal features of television,* 21–55. Munich: Saur.

Richey, R. (1986). *The theoretical and conceptual bases of instructional design.* London: Kogan Page.

Ridley-Johnson, R., Cooper, H. & Chance, J. (1982). The relation of children's television viewing to school achievement and I.Q. *Journal of Educational Research 76* (5), 294–97.

Ritchie, D., Price, V. & Roberts, D.E. (1987). Television, reading and reading achievement: a reappraisal. *Communication Research 14,* 292–315.

Roberts, D.F., Bachen, C.M., Hornby, M.C. & Hernandez-Ramos, P. (1984). Reading and television predictors of reading achievement at different age levels. *Communication Research 11,* 9–49.

Robinson, J.P. & Levy, M.R. (1986). *The main source: learning from television news.* Beverly Hills, CA: Sage.

Rock, R.T., Duva, J.S. & Murray, J.E. (1951). *The effectiveness of television instruction in training naval air reservists, instructional TV research reports* (Technical Report SDC 476-02-S2). Port Washington, NY: U.S. Naval Special Devices Center.

Roderick, J. & Jackson, P. (1985, Mar.). TV viewing habits, family rules, and reading grades of gifted and nongifted middle school students. Paper presented at the Conference of the Ohio Association for Gifted Children. (ERIC Document Reproduction Service No. ED 264 050.)

Rogers, F. & Head, B. (1963). *Mister Rogers talks to parents.* New York: Berkley Publishing Group and Family Communications.

Rosenfeld, E., Heusmann, L.R., Eron, L.D. & Torney-Purta, J.V. (1982). Measuring patterns of fantasy behavior in children. *Journal of Personality and Social Psychology 42,* 347–66.

Ross, R.P. (1979, Jun.). A part of our environment left unexplored by environmental designers: television. Paper presented at the annual meeting of the Environmental Design Research Association, Buffalo, NY. (ERIC Document Reproduction Service No. ED 184 526.)

Rothschild, M., Thorson, E., Reeves, B., Hirsch, J. & Goldstein, R. (1986). EEG activity and the processing of television commercials. *Communication Research 13,* 182–220.

Rovet, J. (1983). The education of spatial transformations. *In* D.R. Olson & E. Bialystok, eds. *Spatial cognition: the structures and development of mental representations of spatial relations,* 164–81. Hillsdale, NJ: Erlbaum.

Rushton, J.P. (1982). Television and prosocial behavior. *In* D. Pearl, L. Bouthilet & J. Lazar, eds. *Television and behavior: ten years of scientific progress and implications for the eighties,* Vol. 2: technical teviews, 248–57. Rockville, MD: National Institute of Mental Health. [DHHS Publication no. 82-1195.]

Salomon, G. (1972). Can we affect cognitive skills through visual media? An hypothesis and initial findings. *AV Communication Review 20* (4), 401–22.

— (1974). Internalization of filmic schematic operations in interaction with learner's aptitudes. *Journal of Educational Psychology 66,* 499–511.

— (1977). Effects of encouraging Israeli mothers to co-observe "Sesame Street" with their five-year-olds. *Child Development 48,* 1146–51.

— (1979). *Interaction of media, cognition, and learning: an exploration of how symbolic forms cultivate mental skills and affect knowledge acquisition.* San Francisco,

CA: Jossey-Bass.

— (1981a). Introducing AIME: the assessment of children's mental involvement with television. *In* H. Gardner & H. Kelly, eds. *Children and the worlds of television.* San Francisco, CA: Jossey-Bass.

— (1981b). *Communication and education: social and psychological interactions.* Beverly Hills, CA: Sage.

— (1982). Television literacy vs. literacy. *Journal of Visual Verbal Languaging 2* (2), 7–16.

— (1983). Television watching and mental effort: a social psychological view. *In* J. Bryant & D.R. Anderson, eds. *Children's understanding of television: research on attention and comprehension,* 181–98. San Diego, CA: Academic.

— (1984). Television is "easy" and print is "tough": the differential investment of mental effort in learning as a function of perceptions and attributions. *Journal of Educational Psychology 76,* 647–58.

— & Cohen, A.A. (1977). Television formats, mastery of mental skills, and the acquisition of knowledge. *Journal of Educational Psychology 69* (5), 612–19.

Sammur, G.B. (1990). Selected bibliography of research on programming at the Children's Television Workshop. *Educational Technology Research and Development 38* (4), 81–92.

Sanders, J.R. & Sonnad, S.R. (1982, Jan.). *Research on the introduction, use, and impact of the "ThinkAbout" instructional television series: executive summary.* Bloomington, IN: Agency for Instructional Television. (ERIC Document Reproduction Service No. ED 249 948.)

Santa Ana Unified School District (1971, Apr.). *The effect of instructional television utilization techniques on science achievement in the sixth grade.* Santa Ana, CA: Author. (ERIC Document Reproduction Service No. ED 048 751.)

Schallow, J.R. & McIlwraith, R.D. (1986–87). Is television viewing really bad for your imagination?: content and process of TV viewing and imaginal styles. *Imagination, Cognition and Personality 6* (1), 25–42.

Scheff, T.J. & Scheele, S.C. (1980). Humor and catharsis: the effect of comedy on audiences. *In* P.H. Tannenbaum, ed. *The entertainment functions of television,* 165–82. Hillsdale, NJ: Erlbaum.

Schramm, W. (1962). *What we know about learning from instructional television, educational television: the next ten years.* Stanford, CA: Institute for Communication Research.

—, Lyle, J. & Parker, E. (1961). *Television in the lives of our children.* Stanford, CA: Stanford University Press.

Schwarzwalder, J.C. (1960). *An investigation of the relative effectiveness of certain specific TV techniques on learning* (USOE Project No. 985). St. Paul, MN: KTCA-TV.

Searching for alternatives: critical TV viewing and public broadcasting. (1980, Summer) [special issue]. *Journal of Communication 30* (3).

Searls, D.T., Mead, N.A. & Ward, B. (1985). The relationship of students' reading skills to TV watching, leisure time reading and homework. *Journal of Reading 29,* 158–62.

Seattler, P. (1968). *A history of instructional technology.* New York: McGraw-Hill.

Seels, B. (1982). Variables in the environment for pre-school television viewing. *In* R.A. Braden & A.D. Walker, eds. *Television and visual literacy,* 53–67. Bloomington, IN: International Visual Literacy Association.

Seels, B.B. & Richey, R.C. (1994). *Instructional technology: the definition and domains of the field.* Washington, DC: Association for Educational Communications & Technology.

Sell, M.A., Ray, G.E. & Lovelace, L. (1995). Preschool children's comprehension of a "Sesame Street" video tape: the effects of repeated viewing and previewing instructions. *Educational Technology Research and Development 43* (3), 49–60.

Shayon, R.L. (1950, Nov. 25). The pied piper of video. *Saturday Review of Literature 33.*

Shutkin, D.S. (1990). Video production education: towards a critical media pedagogy. *Journal of Visual Literacy 10* (2), 42–59.

Sigelman, C.K. & Shaffer, D.R. (1995). *Understanding life-span human development.* Pacific Grove, CA: Brooks/Cole.

Signorielli, N. (1989). Television and conceptions about sex roles: maintaining conventionality and the status quo. *Sex Roles 21* (5–6), 341–60.

— (1991). *A sourcebook on children and television.* New York: Greenwood.

— (1991, Sep.). Adolescents and ambivalence toward marriage: a cultivation analysis. *Youth & Society 23,* 121–49.

— & Lears, M. (1992). Children, television, and conceptions about chores: attitudes and behaviors. *Sex Roles 27* (3–4), 157–69.

Silberstein, R., Agardy, S., Ong, B. & Heath, D. (1983). *Electroencephalographic responses of children to television.* Melbourne: Australian Broadcasting Tribunal.

Singer, J.L. & Antrobus, L.S. (1972). Dimensions of daydreaming and the stream of thought. *In* K.S. Pope & J.L. Singer, eds. *The stream of consciousness.* New York: Plenum.

— & Singer, D.G. (1981). *Television, imagination, and aggression: a study of preschoolers.* Hillsdale, NJ: Erlbaum.

— (1978). Television and imaginative play. *Journal of Mental Imagery 2,* 145–64.

— & Singer, J.L. (1981). Television and the developing imagination of the child. *Journal of Broadcasting 25,* 373–87.

—, — & Zuckerman, D.M. (1981). *Teaching television: how to use TV to your child's advantage.* New York: Dial.

—, Zuckerman, D.M. & Singer, J.L. (1980). Helping elementary school children learn about TV. *Journal of Communication 30* (3), 84–93.

—, — & — (1981). Teaching elementary school children critical television viewing skills: an evaluation. *In* M.E. Ploghoft & J.A. Anderson, eds. *Education for the television age,* 71–81. Athens, OH: Ohio University.

Singer, J. (1980). The power and limitations of television: a cognitive affective analysis. *In* P.H. Tannenbaum, ed. *The entertainment functions of television,* 31–65. Hillsdale, NJ: Erlbaum.

— & Singer, D.G. (1983). Implications of childhood television viewing for cognition, imagination and emotion. *In* J. Bryant & D.R. Anderson, eds. *Children's understanding of television: research on attention and comprehension,* 265–95. San Diego, CA: Academic.

— & — (1986). Family experiences and television viewing as predictors of children's imagination, restlessness, and aggression. *Journal of Social Issues 42,* 107–24.

—, — & Rapaczynski, W.S. (1984). Family patterns and television viewing as predictors of children's beliefs and aggression. *Journal of Communication 34* (2), 73–89.

Slattery, K.F. (1990). Visual information in viewer interpretation and evaluation of television news stories. *Journal of*

Visual Literacy 10 (1), 26–44.

Smith, M.E. (1994). Television violence and behavior: a research summary. *In* D.P. Ely & B. Minor, eds. *Educational Media and Technology Yearbook,* Vol. 20, 164–68. Englewood, CO: Libraries Unlimited.

Smith, R., Anderson, D. & Fischer, C. (1985). Young children's comprehension of montage. *Child Development 56,* 962–71.

Snyder, R. (1994). Information processing: a visual theory for television news. *Journal of Visual Literacy 14* (1), 69–76.

Son, J., Reese, S.D. & Davie, W.R. (1987). Effects of visual-verbal redundancy and recaps on television news learning. *Journal of Broadcasting and Electronic Media 31* (2), 207–16.

Sprafkin, J.N. (1979). Stereotypes on television *In* B. Logan & K. Moody, eds. *Television awareness training: the viewer's guide for family and community,* 33–37. New York: Media Action Research Center.

Sprafkin, J., Gadow, K.D., & Abelman, R. (1992). *Television and the exceptional child: the forgotten audience.* Hillsdale, NJ: Erlbaum.

Sproull, N. (1973). Visual attention, modeling behaviors, and other verbal and nonverbal metacommunication of pre-kindergarten children viewing Sesame Street. *American Educational Research Journal 10,* 101–14.

St. Peters, M., Fitch, M., Huston, A.C., Wright, J.C. & Eakins, D.J. (1991). Television and families: what do young children watch with their parents? *Child Development 62,* 1409–23.

—, Huston, A.C. & Wright, J.C. (1989, Apr.). Television and families: parental coviewing and young children's language development, social behavior, and television processing. Paper presented at the conference of the Society for Research in Child Development, Kansas City, KS.

Stedman, L.C. & Kaestle, C.F. (1987). Literacy and reading performance in the United States, from 1880 to the present. *Reading Research Quarterly 22,* 8–46.

Stern R.C. & Robinson, R.S. (1994). Perception and its role in communication and learning. *In* D.M. Moore & F.M. Dwyer, eds. *Visual literacy.* Englewood Cliffs, NJ: Educational Technology.

Stickell, D.W. (1963). A critical review of the methodology and results of research comparing televised and face-to-face instruction. Unpublished doctoral dissertation, The Pennsylvania State University.

Stroman, C.A. (1991). Television's role in the socialization of African American children and adolescents. *The Journal of Negro Education 60* (3), 314–27.

Sutton-Smith, B. (1976). *A developmental psychology of children's film making: annual report No. 1, 1974–75 and annual report No. 2, 1975–76.* New York: Ford Foundation. (ERIC Document Reproduction Service No. ED 148 330.)

Tada, T. (1969). Image-cognition: a developmental approach. *In* S. Takashima & H. Ichinohe, eds. *Studies of broadcasting.* Tokyo: Nippon Hoso Kyokai.

Takanishi, R. (1982). The influence of television on the ethnic identity of minority children: a conceptual framework. *In* G.L. Berry & C. Mitchell-Kernan, eds. *Television and the socialization of the minority child,* 81–103. San Diego, CA: *Academic.*

Talking with TV: a guide to starting dialogue with youth (1994). Washington, DC: The Center for Population Options.

Tangney, J.P. & Feshbach, S. (1988). Children's television-viewing frequency: individual differences and demographic correlates. *Personality and Social Psychology Bulletin 14* (1), 145–58.

Tannenbaum, P.H. (1980). Entertainment as vicarious emotional experience. *In* P.H. Tannenbaum, ed. *The entertainment functions of television,* 107–31. Hillsdale, NJ: Erlbaum.

Telecommunications Act of 1996, Pub. L., No. 104-S.652, Title V, Subtitle B, Sec. 551. Parental choice in television programming. [on-line]. Available: http://thomas.loc.gov/cgi-bin/query/z?104:S.652.enr:

Thirteen/WNET (1992). *Evaluation of thirteen/Texaco teacher train.* New York: Author.

Thompson, M.E., Carl, D. & Hill, F. (1992). Channel One news in the classroom: does it make a difference?. *In* M. Simonson, ed. *Proceedings of Selected Research & Development Presentations at the Convention of the Association for Educational Communications & Technology.* Washington, DC: AECT, Research and Theory Division. (ERIC Document Reproduction Service No. ED 348 032.)

Thorson, E., Reeves, B. & Schleuder, J. (1985). Message complexity and attention to television. *Communication Research 12,* 427–54.

Tiene, D. (1993). Exploring the effectiveness of the Channel One school telecasts. *Educational Technology 33* (5), 36–20.

— (1994). Teens react to Channel One: a survey of high school students. *Tech Trends 39* (3), 17–38.

Tiffin, J.W. (1978). Problems in instructional television in Latin America. *Revista de Tenologia Educativa 4* (2), 163–234.

Torrence, D.R. (1985). How video can help: video can be an integral part of your training effort. *Training and Development Journal 39* (12), 50.

Tower, R., Singer, D., Singer, J. & Biggs, A. (1979). Differential effects of television programming on preschooler's cognition, imagination and social play. *American Journal of Orthopsychiatry 49,* 265–81.

Turner, P.M. & Simpson, W. (1982, Mar.). *Factors affecting instructional television utilization in Alabama.* (ERIC Document Reproduction Service No. ED 216 698.)

Valmont, W.J. (1995). *Creating videos for school use.* Boston, MA: Allyn & Bacon.

VanderMeer, A.W. (1950, Jul.). *Relative effectiveness of instruction by films exclusively, films plus study guides, and standard lecture methods* (technical report No. SDC 269-7-13). Port Washington, NY: U.S. Naval Training Devices Center.

Vivian, J. (1991). *The media of mass communication.* Boston, MA: Allyn & Bacon.

Walker, J. (1980). Changes in EEG rhythms during television viewing: preliminary comparisons with reading and other tasks. *Perceptual and Motor Skills 51,* 255–61.

Ward, S., Wackman, D.B. & Wartella, E. (1975). *Children learning to buy: the development of consumer information processing skills.* Cambridge, MA: Marketing Science Institute.

Wartella, E. (1979). The developmental perspective. *In* E. Wartella, ed. *Children communicating: media and development of thought, speech, understanding,* 7–20. Beverly Hills, CA: Sage

Watkins, L.T., Sprafkin, J. & Gadow, K.D. (1988). Effects of a critical viewing skills curriculum on elementary school children's knowledge and attitudes about television. *Journal of Educational Research 81* (3), 165–70.

Watt, J. & Welch, A. (1983). Effects of static and dynamic

complexity on children's attention and recall of televised instruction. *In* J. Bryant & D.R. Anderson, eds. *Children's understanding of television: research on attention and comprehension,* 69–102. San Diego, CA: Academic.

Webster, J.G., Pearson, J.C. & Webster, D.B. (1986). Children's television viewing as affected by contextual variables in the home. *Communication Research Reports 3,* 1–7.

Weiller, K.H. & Higgs, C.T. (1992, Apr.). Images of illusion, images of reality: gender differences in televised sport—the 1980's and beyond. Paper presented at the National Convention of the American Alliance for Health, Physical Education, Recreation, & Dance, Indianapolis, IN. (ERIC Document Reproduction Service No. ED 346 037.)

Weinstein, S., Appel, V. & Weinstein, C. (1980). Brain activity responses to magazine and television advertising. *Journal of Advertising Research 20* (3), 57–63.

Welch, A. & Watt, J. (1982). Visual complexity and young children's learning from television. *Human Communication Research 8* (2), 13–45.

Wells, S. (1976). *Instructional technology in developing countries: decisionmaking processes in education.* New York: Praeger.

Wheeler, P. (1979). *Formative review of the critical television viewing skills curriculum for secondary schools, Vol. I: final report. Vol. II: teacher's guide: reviewers' suggested revisions* (OE Contract No. 300-78-0495). San Francisco, CA: Far West Laboratory for Educational Research & Development. (ERIC Document Reproduction Service No. ED 215 669.)

White, G.F., Katz, J. & Scarborough, K. (1992). The impact of professional football games upon violent assaults on women. *Violence and Victims 7* (2), 157–71.

Who are the biggest couch potatoes? (1993, May 23). *Parade Magazine,* p. 17.

Wilkinson, G.L. (1980). *Media in instruction: 60 years of research.* Washington, DC: Association for Educational Communications & Technology.

Williams, D.C., Paul, J. & Ogilvie, J.C. (1957). Mass media, learning, and retention. *Canadian Journal of Psychology 11,* 157–63.

Williams, M.E. & Condry, J.C. (1989, Apr.). Living color: minority portrayals and cross-racial interactions on television. Paper presented at the Biennial Meeting of the Society for Research in Child Development, Kansas City, MO. (ERIC Document Reproduction Service No. ED 307 025.)

Williams, P., Haertle, E., Haertel, G. & Walberg, H. (1982). The impact of leisure time television on school learning. *American Educational Research Journal 19,* 19–50.

Williams, T.M., ed. (1986). *The impact of television: a natural experiment in three communities.* San Diego, CA: Academic.

Willis, G. (1990). Stereotyping in TV programming: assessing the need for multicultural education in teaching scriptwriting. Doctoral dissertation, University of Pittsburgh.

Winn, D. (1985a). TV and its affect on the family. Paper presented at the annual Weber State College "Families Alive" Conference, Ogden, UT. (ERIC Document Reproduction Service No. ED 272 314.)

Winn, M. (1977). *The plug-in drug.* New York: Viking.

— (1985b). *The plug-in drug: television, children and the family.* New York: Viking.

Wolf, M.A. (1987). How children negotiate television. *In* T.R. Lindlof, ed. *Natural audiences: qualitative research of media uses and effects,* 58–94. Norwood, NJ: Ablex.

Wolf, T.M. (1975). Response consequences to televised modeled sex-inappropriate play behavior. *Journal of Genetic Psychology 127,* 35–44.

Wood, D.B. (1989, Sep. 29). Schoolroom newscasts-minus ads. *Christian Science Monitor,* pp. 10–11.

Wood, D.N. & Wylie, D.G. (1977). Educational telecommunications. Belmont, CA: Wadsworth.

Woodall, W.G., Davis, D.K. & Sahin, H. (1983). From the boob tube to the black box: television news comprehension from an information processing perspective. *Journal of Broadcasting 27* (1), 1–23.

Would you give up TV for a million bucks? (1992, Oct. 10). *TV Guide,* pp. 10–17.

Wright, J.C. & Huston, A.C. (1983). A matter of form: potentials of television for young viewers. *American Psychologist 38,* 835–43.

Wright, J.C., Atkins, B. & Huston-Stein, A.C. (1978, Aug.). Active vs. passive television viewing: a model of the development of information processing by children. Paper presented at the annual meeting of the American Psychological Association, Toronto. (ERIC Document Reproduction Service No. ED 184-521.)

—, St. Peters, M. & Huston, A.C. (1990). Family television use and its relation to children's cognitive skills and social behavior. *In* J. Bryant, ed. *Television and the American family,* 227–52. Hillsdale, NJ: Erlbaum.

— & Huston, A. (1989). Potentials of television for young viewers. *In* G.A. Comstock, ed. *Public communication and behavior,* Vol. 1. San Diego, CA: Academic.

Young, B.M. (1990). *Television advertising and children.* Oxford, England: Clarendon.

Zemach, T. & Cohen, A.A. (1986). Perception of gender equality on television and in social reality. *Journal of Broadcasting & Electronic Media 30* (4). 427–44.

Zill, N., Davies, E. & Daly, M. (1994, Jun.). *Viewing of "Sesame Street" by preschool children in the United States and its relationship to school readiness.* New York: Children's Television Workshop.

Zuckerman, D.M., Singer, D.G. & Singer, J.L. (1980). Television viewing, children's reading, and related classroom behavior. *Journal of Communication 30* (1), 166–74.

Zuckerman, P., Ziegler, M. & Stevenson, H.W. (1978). Children's viewing of television and recognition memory of commercials. *Child Development 49,* 96–104.

Zvacek, S.M. (1992, Feb.). All the news that's fit to watch in school. Paper presented at the annual meeting of the Association for Educational Communications & Technology, Washington, DC.

12. RESEARCH ON AND RESEARCH WITH EMERGING TECHNOLOGIES

Michael J. Hannafin
UNIVERSITY OF GEORGIA

Kathleen M. Hannafin
MEDICAL COLLEGE OF GEORGIA

Simon R. Hooper
UNIVERSITY OF MINNESOTA

Lloyd P. Rieber
UNIVERSITY OF GEORGIA

Asit S. Kini
TEXAS A&M UNIVERSITY

Few developments have piqued the interest of researchers as has the growth of computers in their various hybrid forms. A seemingly infinite range of methods and strategies has evolved to exploit the potential of these technologies. The problem has not been a scarcity of research. Literally thousands of studies related to computers and learning have been published during the past 3 decades. The problem has been one of making sense of the enormous, and growing, body of available research.

What, on balance, does this research tell us about computers, emerging technologies, and learning? Have problems and issues been clarified or obscured through these efforts? The purposes of this chapter are: (1) to examine research in computer-assisted learning systems over the past 30 years from an historical perspective, (2) to analyze critically contemporary computer-based instruction (CBI) research as it relates to issues of effectiveness, design, and individual differences, (3) to examine and analyze research on emerging computer-based learning systems, and (4) to identify problems, issues, and unresolved research questions related to the future of computer-aided learning.

It is important to note that we do not attempt to separate research on, or with, specific technologies, but view them as phases of an ongoing metamorphosis. Specific technologies have changed, and will continue to change continuously. However, the most compelling evolution has been in the manner in which their features have been utilized. The nature of computer-based learning has, arguably, undergone a far greater metamorphosis than the hardware technologies themselves (Baker-Albaugh, 1993).

12.1 EVOLUTION OF COMPUTER-BASED INSTRUCTION: HISTORICAL PERSPECTIVES

While the genesis of computers has been traced to the theoretical work of mathematicians such as Pascal, and events such as the processing of immigrants at Ellis Island, early hardware developments and applications were both extremely costly and predictably narrow in focus. The size, space, and costs associated with computers generally limited initial application to fields where resources were available and needs were significant. The computer's information management capabilities made it ideal for large-scale organization and retrieval of information, complex computations, and the like. Apart from simple management and analysis, comparatively little attention was paid to the role of computers in learning,

Once sufficient interest in computers and learning was generated, a host of related problems was encountered. Apart from cost, size, and space barriers, virtually no educational software was available. Available programming languages were, for the most part, designed to support data manipulation and business applications, rendering them cumbersome and limited in their educational utility. Computer hardware was, by contemporary yardsticks, extremely primitive, requiring batch-mode cards or electronic typewriters for input, remote printers (or, in later cases, low-resolution monochrome monitors) for output, and entire rooms to house the basic central processing unit. The decision to test the power of the computer for learning was no small commitment. It required that applications be developed from the ground up, including not only sound lesson design but also the hardware and software environments to support their creation.

Not surprisingly, then, early efforts were limited both in terms of pedagogy and usability. The criticism of early lessons as little more than electronic page-turners was, for the most part, well founded. Typical computerized lessons were often significantly poorer than alternatives in terms of their ability to represent images, provide direct access to various parts of a lesson, highlight and otherwise emphasize important information, and so on. Early efforts to replace existing media and teaching methods were singularly unsuccessful.

Initial research, particularly the Stanford Arithmetic Project in the mid-1960s, helped to legitimize the scientific study of computer-assisted learning. Attempts were made to define variables operationally, isolate learning effects, and otherwise control extraneous factors (within the limitations of the available mathematics software). The systems were primitive in current terms but reflected state-of-the-art, both with respect to the hardware available and the pedagogy enabled.

Clearly, a great deal has changed since the heyday of the Stanford Arithmetic Project. The technologies have changed dramatically both in size and form, and the underlying psychological and pedagogical underpinnings have evolved in many unforeseen ways. Still, these efforts were the genesis of present-day research in computer-based learning. Their contributions were due not to their similarity with contemporary approaches but to the commitment to disciplined inquiry. The debate shifted from a purely intellectual activity to one that could be advanced empirically.

A pivotal point in the early evolution of computers and learning came with the emphasis on human-computer interactions, heretofore awkward or impossible with the media and methods of the day. Spurred by the growing influence of behaviorists such as B. F. Skinner, few questioned the importance of overt responding and differential reinforcement to learning. The computer, through which learners could interact with lessons on an individual basis, was seen as a significant technological breakthrough to overcoming many problems associated with programmed instruction (see 2.3.4 and 19.2.1 for related discussions). Predictably, early lessons were influenced heavily by behavioral psychology: relatively small and discrete steps, overt responses, feedback, and differential branching in the form of drills and tutorials. Individual knowledge, in the form of stimulus-response-reinforcement (S->R->S^R) associations, could be engineered in the form of progressively linked chains (see 2.2). Many large-scale research and development efforts, including the University of Illinois PLATO project, as well as institutes at Florida State University and Penn State University, generated courseware on a significant scale based largely on these roots. For the most part, traditional experimental research paradigms dominated.

Beginning in the late 1960s, cognitive perspectives gained increased acceptance. Research and development shifted toward methods and strategies that induced desired cognitive processes. Strategies were designed to assist the learner in selecting appropriate information, organizing information into internally consistent concepts, and integrating new with existing knowledge, making it personally relevant and meaningful (see 5.3 through 5.5, 20.1). As alternative psychological and pedagogical perspectives emerged and hardware and software capabilities expanded, both the nature of computer-based learning systems and their underlying foundations metamorphosed. Contemporary research and development thrusts are now evident in areas such as user-centered learning, open-ended learning, and hypermedia (e.g., Horwitz & Barowy, 1994).

The evolution of computers in learning has not occurred in isolation. Rather, it is an interactive byproduct of ongoing developments in psychology, pedagogy, and technology (Atkins, 1993; Hannafin, 1992). At times, technology has been at the forefront of these developments, helping to shape our understanding by demonstrating heretofore untested teaching and learning methods. At other times, technology has enabled widely held notions about teaching and learning, perhaps "increasing the horsepower" of conventional methods. Whether leading or following, technology has assumed a prominent role.

To understand research, one must understand more than the myriad of often-conflicting findings resulting from idiosyncratic approaches employed in individual studies. To understand the research on computers, emerging technologies, and learning, one must attempt to assemble and organize, not merely to collect; to interpret rather than to simply report; to relate across studies and specific technologies, not merely to isolate findings. These are the goals of this chapter.

12.2 EFFECTIVENESS OF EMERGING TECHNOLOGIES

Few issues have the broad appeal of, yet remain as elusive as, the basic question: Did it work? Interest in testing the effectiveness, or lack thereof, of computer technologies has been long standing. Several approaches have been advanced. Some have attempted to identify the unique learning contributions of computer-based learning systems. Others have focused on the overall effectiveness of computer-based versus noncomputer-based learning systems, while still others have emphasized cost effectiveness. Not surprisingly, results have proved highly variable depending on the focus of the effort and the methods employed to address the question.

This section contains three subsections: cost effectiveness, findings from meta-analyses, and design research. The cost effectiveness subsection analyzes the ways in which technology-supported learning has been approached from a cost-benefit perspective. The meta-analysis subsection emphasizes research undertaken to address "big questions" about the effectiveness of computers. Finally, research is organized according to its implications for the design of computer-based learning systems.

12.2.1 Cost Effectiveness

The value of computers in instruction has been of considerable interest for some time [see Niemiec (1989) for a review of several cost effectiveness studies related to computer-based instruction]. Early in the evolution of computer-assisted instruction, it became clear that developing courseware and acquiring needed hardware would be an expensive proposition. Often, researchers used "cost-added" models, where the marginal gains associated with such systems were evaluated relative to the additional costs incurred in obtaining them [see, for example, the methods described by Levin & Meister (1986) and Niemeier, Blackwell & Walberg (1986) in *Kappan's* issue on the effects of computer-assisted instruction]. The approaches were often near-term in nature, with capital costs (computer hardware) and software associated with specific learning tasks evaluated over relatively short durations. Comparisons of recurring costs and maintenance were rare. Using cost-added models, the costs associated with computer-aided learning were rarely considered feasible.

Cost replacement approaches evolved to evaluate the relative costs associated with learning via "traditional" approaches—usually teacher-led, textbook-based methods—versus computer-aided methods. The underlying question of these approaches shifted from assessing the marginal gains using "add-on" technologies to one in which the costs and outcomes associated with the overall delivery system were evaluated. This was the essence of Bork's (1986) "grand experiment," in which he advocated that computer-intensive learning systems, designed for optimal impact versus educational convenience, be developed and tested fairly. Judgments as to the true value of computers versus traditional classroom-based teaching on learning could then be assessed, appropriate designs and models could be implemented, true costs (immediate, recurring, long term) associated with each could be identified, and the relative effectiveness of each method could be benchmarked without undue confounding.

Needless to say, these ideas have met with considerable resistance over the past 30 years. The political consequences of altering laws, revising policies and procedures related to teacher preparation and certification, and other educational traditions were, and remain to this day, formidable. The resistance is largely the product of concern over one possible model—total elimination and replacement of teachers—rather than a response to a widely held view. In truth, it is not yet known what roles, if any, teachers might play in truly alternative technology-based learning systems.

While Bork's proposed experiment has yet to be implemented on a significant scale, technology has become the centerpiece of many school reform initiatives. Collectively, educators have become more amenable to, and at the forefront of, technology in school reform. A wide range of innovative efforts has been reported, with roles for technology varying from primary delivery of new information via integrated learning systems, to knowledge-building tools,

to management of performance and educational decision making, to comprehensive multimedia in both teaching and learning. The promise is great; however, comparatively little hard data have been generated.

Cost effectiveness is arguably the most critical issue to reconcile from a purely pragmatic perspective. Yet, it may be the most fundamentally flawed in how it has been studied. Increased learning outcomes, even at moderate costs, are unlikely to engender much adoption and diffusion. Consumers seek additional value for their investments. They seek not simply to move marginally further along the same yardstick but to evolve different metrics and ways to measure. They seek to spend less, not more. The effectiveness of computers is unlikely to be assessed simply by comparing their costs with specific teaching methods and traditional learning outcomes. We need to evolve a more inclusive understanding of computer capabilities to support and alter the everyday lives of learners. Our approaches and evaluation models need to emphasize qualitative differences in areas such as the nature of learning via powerful learning technologies, logistical advantages gained by their use, and potential to access and employ varied resources. We need to evolve approaches that better represent the complexity of the problem posed, not approaches that unnecessarily and artificially simplify it. We need to better represent situational factors that influence what is considered to be cost effective in one setting but not another. In short, we need to better frame the real questions we want to address, consider how the uniquely important factors related to cost effectiveness need to be weighed, and develop models that provide data sensitive to the decisions being made. Until greater value, defined according to the situational needs of adopters and investors, can be garnered from significant technology investments, and the costs associated with them, reluctance to commit significant financial resources will likely continue.

12.2.2 Meta-Analyses

Meta-analysis is a statistical process whereby the findings of several studies, focusing on a common problem or topic, are pooled in an effort to draw inferences as to the meaning of a collective body of research. In effect, the goal is to answer "bigger" questions not readily addressed in a single study by aggregating data related to the question at hand across a large number of studies.

Early studies focused on "box score" approaches, which were used to determine the proportion of studies in which favorable results were reported. Several reviews indicated that varied forms of computer-assisted instruction (tutorials, simulations, drills) improved the arithmetic achievement of elementary students (Visonhaler & Bass, 1972) as well as students in elementary school through high school students (Edwards, Norton, Taylor, Weiss & Dusseldorp, 1975). Subsequent meta-analysis studies, which focused on computer drills and tutorials in arithmetic in elementary and secondary schools, also reported significant improvements in computational arithmetic skills, with effect sizes ranging from .37 to .42 standard deviations [see, for example, Burns (1981) and Hartley (1978)]. These reviews and analyses were based heavily on studies published prior to the micro-computer revolution beginning in the late 1970s.

Beginning in the early 1980s, several meta-analyses related to the effects of computers on learning were published by Kulik and his associates at the University of Michigan [see J. Kulik, C-L. Kulik & Cohen (1980) for an initial analysis, and Kulik & Kulik (1987) for a more recent analysis]. These studies included mainframe CAI studies as well as the emerging literature on microcomputer instruction. Significant, but generally declining, effect sizes have been reported for learning via computer-assisted instruction from elementary school [ranging from .47 in J. Kulik, C-L. Kulik & Bangert-Drowns (1985b)], to secondary school [.26 to .36 in Bangert-Drowns, J. Kulik & C-L. Kulik (1985)], to college [.26 in C-L. Kulik & J. Kulik (1986)] and adult learners [.42 in J. Kulik, C-L. Kulik & Schwalb (1986)]. The reported effects have also been quite similar between experimental and quasi-experimental studies, suggesting that, on balance, the findings are not simply artifacts of the specific research methods employed (cf. C-L. Kulik & J. Kulik, 1991).

What does all this tell us about the effectiveness of computer-based instruction? Unfortunately, we are left with more questions than answers. Richard Clark (1985), for example, also employed meta-analysis methods in computer-based instruction research, but in ways quite different from those of Kulik. Clark computed an initial apparent effect, then recalculated effect sizes after systematically eliminating confounding influences such as instructor-designer differences, design integrity, and so forth. Similar to his conclusions concerning the lack of media effects in general (Clark, 1983), he concluded that no evidence existed to support the inherent superiority of computer-assisted instruction to alternative approaches. [See J. Kulik, C-L. Kulik & Bangert-Drowns (1985a) for an interesting rejoinder.]

Other problems have surfaced as well. Often, studies that are quite dated have been utilized, so the actual nature of the delivery system is unclear. While researchers have often attempted to balance the influence of editorial gate-keeping in published research with use of nonjournal sources (e.g., dissertation studies), it has tended to further obscure interpretation. What domains were under study, using what strategies, and in what quantity and quality? Meta-analysis research attempts to determine whether or not computer-assisted instruction is effective, but fails to improve our understanding as to what constitutes effective computer-assisted instruction.

To many, the focus on whole-effect, meta-analysis research is misdirected. The "big question, big answer" goal often obscures potentially more important questions and issues. The issue, it is argued, should not be simply one of "if" computers are effective in promoting learning but how best to utilize them to redefine, support, or compliment teaching and/or learning efforts. The task is not simply one of replacing old media with computers, thereby "increasing the horsepower" of traditional methods, but unleashing the capabilities of both computer technologies and learners (Hannafin, 1992; Hooper & Hannafin, 1991). In the following section, we report design research, where the goal is to identify such methods and approaches.

12.2.3 Design of Computer-Based Instruction

12.2.3.1. Orienting the Learner. Learners often experience difficulty accessing important lesson content due to poorly integrated knowledge or the complexity of lesson presentations. Some are easily disoriented because of the lesson structure, while others are unable to deal with the cognitive demands associated with increased decision making in hypermedia learning environments (Jonassen, 1989). Furthermore, although computer-based instruction is often rich in opportunities for students to interact and receive feedback, designers often neglect to provide students with the support supplied by effective classroom teachers (Hawk, McLeod & Jonassen, 1985). To support the learner, orienting activities are often provided to establish expectancies for, and perspectives on, forthcoming lesson content.

Verbal-orienting activities perform two cognitive functions. They cue important lesson content and help to link new with existing knowledge. Hannafin and Hughes (1986), in extrapolating research and theory to the design of interactive video, outlined several distinctions between learning that results from using explicit objectives derived from behaviorist traditions and advance organizers based in cognitive traditions. Behavioral objectives (see 2.3.6), precise statements concerning anticipated learner behaviors following instruction, focus attention on specific lesson content. Advance organizers are more abstract and general, and help learners to establish an inclusive anticipatory framework for learning.

The specificity of the learning objective is inversely related to transfer. Specific orienting activities incorporated within interactive video instruction (e.g., preinstructional objectives, prequestions, etc.), for example, promote intended learning selectively by eliciting greater attention to highlighted information (Ho, Savenye & Haas, 1986). Students may use specific behavioral objectives to identify and learn information long enough to pass a related test. However, explicitly stated learning outcomes often limit students' ability to use new information in situations that are dissimilar to those in which initial learning occurred. In contrast, advance organizers tend to stimulate higher-level learning [see, for example, studies by Krahn & Blanchaer (1986) in the teaching of chemistry via computer simulation], but often fail to stimulate factual learning.

Orientation has evolved a different connotation in the study of hypermedia. Orientation is viewed as the individual's awareness of his or her location within a hypermedia system and the individual's capacity to respond meaningfully given these perceptions. The concept of disorientation, or of being "lost in hyperspace" (Edwards & Hardman, 1989), has been used to characterize the aimless state wherein users find themselves unable to determine where they are or what to do. Disorientation, in effect, is the product of insufficient initial orientation to the system and inadequate ongoing guidance in the nature and use of the system.

12.2.3.2. Presenting the Lesson. It is widely assumed that multimodal instruction enhances learning more than information presented from a single source. For example, many believe that presenting information via sound, picture, and text improves understanding. It is not surprising, therefore, that many believe that use of computers and other information technologies will inherently improve learning (see, for example, Clark, 1985). Well-documented research on cognitive resource allocation has established conclusively that more is not necessarily better when presenting stimuli. Individuals possess limited ability to process information presented simultaneously in multiple channels (e.g., aural, visual). Typically, one channel is largely ignored by learners since the messages cause undue competition for cognitive resources (Gavora & Hannafin, 1995). Once automated, however, individuals increase in their capacity to process messages in multiple channels, since the cognitive demands are drastically reduced.

In some cases multimodal presentations (see 29.3) may indeed improve learning. They are particularly likely to be beneficial when information is encoded via multiple coding mechanisms. Individuals possess multiple channels through which information may be encoded. For example, information presented in pictures may be encoded once as a picture and then again by the verbal description given to the picture. In contrast, text is encoded only once, via a verbal channel. Information that is processed more than once often adds to it retrievability. This so-called "dual-coding" of information (see 29.2.3.) essentially doubles the probability that it will be recalled (Paivio, 1979).

12.2.3.2.1. Illustrations. Visual representations can reveal the hierarchical structure of text and illustrate relationships (see, for example, Perkins & Unger, 1994, and see 16.11). They serve three important roles. First, they help to make explicit the structure of to-be-learned information, which reduces uncertainty and clarifies relationships among important lesson concepts. Next, they are readily recalled and, when associated with important content, tend to enhance recall of that information (Dunston, 1992). Finally, as Kenny (1993) concluded based on several studies of pictorial graphic organizers, pictures help learners to integrate lesson content during computer-based instruction (see 26.4).

Kenny also suggested that learners be encouraged to generate their own graphic organizers rather than simply viewing those created by other people. Whereas "given" graphic organizers may encourage learners to adopt passive (reactive) roles during instruction, learner-generated organizers involve searching a body of information to locate key concepts, thus they are inherently more proactive in nature.

12.2.3.2.2. Animation. Animation has been the focus of recent attention (see, for example, Park & Gittleman, 1992). Mayer and Anderson (1992) studied the influence of animation either as a support to, or replacement of, oral presentation methods. They examined how hypermedia features facilitate college students' sense-making of mechanical operations concepts. Consistent with dual-coding models of learning (see 29.2.3), animations paired with oral presentations proved more effective than either animation alone or oral presentations alone.

One system, *Space Shuttle Commander* (Rieber, 1992), utilizes animation both to illustrate basic physics concepts and to provide visual feedback for responses made by the student. Learners were encouraged to alter a number of attributes and values and to see the influence of their manipulations on objects in space. Animation, in this sense, provided not only coding support but also a feedback mechanism to illustrate the influence of learner choices in a Newtonian microworld.

Rieber (1990) also analyzed several studies on the effects of computer-based animation on the learning of science concepts and derived several conclusions for its use. In general, animation should be used when one or more of its attributes (e.g., attention gaining, demonstration, and reinforcement) can enhance learning. Rieber reported that manipulating systematically the attributes of animation significantly facilitated learning compared to providing static graphics or no graphics at all when such attributes were integral to the learning task, that is, when the animated object's attributes are consonant with the learning task.

However, the benefits of animation can easily be neutralized by unnecessary complexity, ineffective design, or poor cue attendance. The prior knowledge and expertise of the user may also influence the effects of animation: Novices (who are often poor cue attenders) are often unable to perceive cues highlighted through animation. In addition, learners may need to participate and actively locate important information rather than simply view animations. Finally, animation may be most effective when students are encouraged to interact with the animations; manipulation appears to have important affective and cognitive outcomes (see 26.4.3).

12.2.3.2.3. Fidelity. The term *fidelity* is commonly used to describe the extent to which computer-based instruction approximates the form and function of the stimuli it represents. Computerized, three-dimensional cockpit simulators, for example, are often of such high fidelity that users are unable to distinguish between flying the simulator and "real" flying. In contrast, aviation manuals on how to fly often employ line diagrams for features such as aircraft instruments. Students may learn basic principles by reading the manual but would be unlikely to confuse their knowledge with real flying.

Proponents of high-fidelity instruction often laud computer-based instruction for its capacity to reflect accurately "on-the-job" performance. Until recently, few researchers questioned the benefits of high-fidelity design. However, it is now widely believed that low-fidelity stimuli are often superior to high-fidelity stimuli, especially for novices. High-fidelity designs increase the number of stimuli to which students must attend and consequently place greater demands on working memory. These demands may lower performance when students possess little background knowledge.

Alessi (1988) proposed that the fidelity employed during computer-based instruction should increase as student performance improves. In other words, the importance of fidelity is determined largely by the expertise of the student. In the flying example, a novice is unlikely to learn to fly effectively by immediate immersion into a flight simulator, but may benefit considerably from a narrated video. In contrast, experienced pilots benefit more from experiencing the effects of complex physical phenomena in a flight simulator, wherein they may experiment in relative safety.

12.2.3.2.4. Screen Design and Display. Effective screen design appears to be as much art as science. Although several authors have generated screen design guidelines, empirical evidence supporting this advice has been scarce. Human factors research literature addresses the ergonomics of design and configurations for optimizing text processing, but guidance for improving learning is often based more on heuristics than proven cause-effect relationships (see 36.3.6).

Recent screen design researchers have examined the effects of varying information placement and access. Aspillaga (1991) compared the effects of three approaches to text display: overlapping important parts of graphic images, consistent placement, and random placement. Consistent usage and relevant text placement yielded higher achievement than random placement, suggesting that learners were cued to specific content and responses. Grabinger (1993) generated three "rules of thumb" to guide screen design: Divide the screen into consistently placed functional areas; use organizing techniques to illustrate the structure of a screen; and design screens that are interesting but not complex.

Recently, researchers have also examined the effects of information metered via windows (Billingsly, 1988). Window environments, which allow multiple files or applications to be displayed simultaneously, are generally either tiled and overlapped. Tiled windows are always visible and do not overlap, whereas overlapping windows allow foreground files to obscure background files. Bly and Rosenberg (1986) found that tiling systems helped learners to locate information significantly faster than did overlapping system. Students using the tiling system had fewer mental operations to perform than did students using the overlapping system. Moreover, results indicated that overlapping systems are better for experienced users, but that tiling systems may be easier for novices. Tasks that involve little window manipulation are accomplished more efficiently with tiled windows, and tasks that involve much window manipulation are more efficiently accomplished with overlapping windows.

Benshoof and Hooper (1993) also examined the effects of presenting information in tiled and overlapped windows.

High- and low-ability sixth-graders learned novel information and rules governing its use. Students were given the same information via tiled or overlapped window treatments, but those in the overlapping treatment had access to only one information source at a time. High-ability students in the overlapping-window treatment demonstrated higher achievement than did all other students. Apparently, overlapping induced the more able students to invest greater effort than did the tiled treatment.

Gender appears to affect preference for some screen design elements. For example, Jakobsdóttir, Krey, and Sales (1994) examined the effects of gender on boys' and girls' graphics preferences. Students in grades 2, 4, and 6 were asked to rate three groups of computer graphics: high female interest, high male interest, and equal interest (created by mixing elements of interest together). A significant interaction between picture type and gender was found, indicating that girls rated female-interest pictures highest, male-interest pictures lowest, and equal-interest pictures in between; the reverse was true for boys. Similarly, in a study examining the use of computer graphics among boys and girls, Freedman (1989) observed that fifth-grade girls were more concerned than were boys with using color, color combinations, and relationships among object shapes. Boys were more interested in movement, and sometimes conceptualized shapes as objects capable of violence.

Despite the intuitive appeal of using colorful displays in instructional materials, research has consistently failed to support the role of color as a primary instructional variable. Instead, the effect of color on learning appears to have, at best, secondary influences. Color is most effective when it supports other instructional strategies, such as organization of information and providing contrast between screen objects (Dwyer & Lamberski, 1982–1983). Related objects can be color coded and text structure can be highlighted to aid organization of important lesson content. However, care must be taken to avoid using color carelessly or unnecessarily, since the distraction potential of color can be quite high (Hannafin & Peck, 1988; Rieber, 1994).

Much of the past research on illustrations has focused on presenting information to learners. Emerging technologies offer unique capabilities for learners to do more than "watch"; learners can create, organize, highlight, colorize, and compare their own illustrations with those of peers, or even against those of experts. *Science Vision,* for example, allows students to "construct" their own computer representations of a roller coaster, and to test their designs against their own goals, those of an expert, or advanced specifications that require fine-tuned understanding (Tobin & Dawson, 1992). The Cognition and Technology Group at Vanderbilt's *Jasper* series utilizes video images not only to capture and maintain attention but also to establish contexts within which key problem-solving information is embedded. In still other instances, the presentation features evolve dynamically as learners make decisions and progress, providing stimuli that is uniquely sensitive to the individual user's actions. This ability to personalize, share, and revise individual interpretations is a powerful asset for expressing conceptual knowledge and its relationships.

12.2.3.3. Encoding Support. The impact of encoding support on student performance may be best understood within a meaningful learning conceptual model. Mayer (1993) outlined three phases through which learners must progress in order for learning to become meaningful. First, learners must select relevant information from that presented to them. Second, they must organize the information into a coherent outline. Finally, they must relate the outline to a structure or event with which they are familiar. When the first phase is not met, no learning occurs. When only the first phase is met, rote learning occurs. When the first two phases are met, nonmeaningful and inflexible learning occur. Meaningful learning occurs only when the third phase has been reached. Mayer's framework is consistent with Wittrock's generative learning model (Wittrock, 1990), which emphasizes improving learning by stimulating deeper processing (see 31.1.1). Generative learning stresses forming connections among information to be learned and linking these associations with each learner's knowledge and experiences (see 31.2).

Encoding support will be effective to the extent that it helps learners to select, organize, and integrate learning experiences within mental models that have been clearly formulated in memory (Bliss, 1994). To some degree, the specific activity must, by definition, be idiosyncratic because everyone differs in what is clearly understood. However, to a larger extent, the nature of the activity that brings about cognitive transformation may vary little from person to person. In this section, we address two key approaches for supporting encoding: personalizing instruction and designing interaction strategies.

12.2.3.3.1. Personalizing Instruction. Personalizing instruction involves integrating personally relevant information to help each learner associate unfamiliar lesson content with his or her own background and interests. Several benefits have been associated with personalized instruction. Miller and Kulhavy (1991) hypothesized that personalization improves memory by increasing the strength of association between lesson content and the personalized content. Additionally, Lopez and Sullivan (1991) suggested that the self-referencing associated with personalization reduces the cognitive demands of processing ongoing instruction.

Ross and his associates personalized computer-based instructional materials by adapting specific examples and questions to personal experience. Ross and Morrison (1988) suggested that difficulties with math story problems are not necessarily due to deficient computation skills. Rather, students are often unable to understand story problems that are situated in unfamiliar contexts. In contrast, they noted that students have little difficulty solving similar problems in which the story is closely associated with their everyday experiences. To test this hypothesis, Ross and Anand (1987, Anand & Ross, 1987) examined the effects of modifying computer-based mathematics learning materials to elementary school students' interests. Students demon-

strated higher achievement and better attitudes after receiving mathematics problems that included personal information. However, Ross and Morrison (1988) cautioned against overusing personalized materials. They warned that the effects of personalization may be due, in part, to a novelty effect that might diminish over time.

Personalizing efforts have evolved during the past decade from early notions of integrating personally relevant information into lessons, to providing contexts focused on relevant learner experiences and interests. Research in situated learning and everyday cognition, for example, has suggested that people think very differently in formal (e.g., classrooms) versus everyday contexts (e.g., supermarkets) (Choi & Hannafin, 1995; Collins, 1993). As these areas continue to evolve, alternative design strategies will need to be developed and refined.

12.2.3.3.2. Interaction Methods. Though lauded by many for its ability to handle user inputs, there is little consensus with regard to the design of human–computer interactions. Indeed, disagreement even exists about the meaning of the term *interactive* as applied to emerging technologies. Researchers have described fundamentally different perspectives on the roles of interactions, ranging from facilitating lesson navigation to supporting encoding of specific lesson context. Floyd (1982), for example, emphasized production of an overt response that subsequently differentiated lesson branching in his application to interactive video. Others emphasize response frequency in terms of either duration or lesson density [see, for example, Bork (1985)].

Gavora and Hannafin (1995) described a conceptual model for the design of human–computer interactions. In their definition, cognitive restructuring is integral to the definition of interaction, not the mere presence of overt responses. Indeed, the authors argued that it is common for physical responses to be made during computer-based instruction which fail to reflect, or initiate, learner thoughtfulness and intent. Successful interactions have cognitive as well as physical requirements and are mediated by the quantity and quality of effort. Interactions cause the differential allocation of cognitive resources in accordance with the learner's familiarity with the domain under study. As critical aspects of the domain become familiar, the associated cognitive processes become automated, requiring few or no cognitive resources. Conversely, complex, unfamiliar domains require significant resource allocations for even small details. The lack of familiarity and perceived complexity cause competition for limited cognitive resources— a problem that must be managed through interaction. In unfamiliar domains, complexity is managed by initially inducing simple, discrete interactions. These relatively modest responses eventually become automated. Once facility is attained, the amount and complexity of the interactions can be increased.

Research on interaction methods may be among the most critical. For example, new and largely unexplored possibilities have emerged with developments in virtual reality. Input methods have changed radically, from almost exclusively typing-via-keyboard to mice, touchscreens, joysticks, voice recognition, and optical scanning. Increased interest in open-ended, user-centered learning systems, construction and manipulation, and authentic learning all bode significant potential, and problems, for interaction design. The domain of possibilities has broadened substantially, yet little research has been advanced which might guide their design.

12.2.3.4. Detecting, Correcting Errors. One activity that appears to promote effective learning is error correction. Error identification helps learners recognize inadequacies in their mental models and stimulates deeper understanding. Allen, Lipson, and Fisher (1989) developed the EPOSODE model, which involves embedding errors in CBIV lessons. Successful error detection is followed by feedback, after which students are often required to classify the errors, to describe the consequences of an error, or to explain how the errors could be corrected. Finally, students observe a corrected video segment before proceeding. The computer provides advantages that are difficult, or impossible, to achieve with other media. Errors that remain undetected can be repeated by replaying the video segment, using slow-motion or freeze-frame capabilities, or by playing a video segment in reverse from the point of an error. Moreover, error isolation can be enhanced through the computer's graphic overlay capabilities. [See, also, GUIDON, an intelligent tutoring system, designed to stimulate learning through error detection (Clancy, 1986), and TORUS, a diagnostic system designed to address mathematics misconceptions (Woodward & Howard, 1994).]

Recently, Bangert-Drowns, Kulik, Kulik, and Morgan (1991) noted that, counterintuitively, feedback often failed to benefit, and sometimes even lowered, performance. However, in their meta-analysis, they noted that mindfulness and the nature of feedback were critical. Feedback must be used mindfully to be effective. Feedback is unlikely to benefit, and may even diminish, learning when students simply reproduce correct answers. The nature of feedback is strongly related to its impact on learning (see 32.5.4): Simply providing a statement concerning the accuracy of a response is less effective than providing some degree of elaboration (see 32.5).

Kulhavy and Stock (1989) outlined two feedback components necessary to improve learning in computer-based instruction: verification and elaboration (see 32.4). *Verification* indicates the accuracy of a response; *elaboration* refers to additional information made available to the student. Not surprisingly, several studies have indicated that elaborative feedback is more effective than simple knowledge of correct results. For example, a study of college undergraduates using CBI found that students demonstrated higher posttest achievement after receiving information related to the accuracy of a response, the correct response, and a brief explanation about the correct answer compared to simply receiving a statement as to the accuracy of a response (Pridemore & Klein, 1991). However, increases in achievement were accompanied by increases in reading time, suggesting that elaboration may also have improved the quantity of instruction. The effect of feedback on retrieval increases as error rates increase, as more opportunities for receiving elaborations are provided.

Litchfield (1993) noted that response certitude is essential in understanding the value of feedback. Individuals with little or no response confidence or certainty are unlikely to benefit significantly from feedback during interactive video instruction—or any instruction for that matter (see 32.4.1). Others have described the varied ways in which feedback can be applied with emerging technologies (Hannafin, Hannafin & Dalton, 1993). Feedback can be used to clarify key elements of the response-learning task itself (present consequences of responses, demonstrate impact in context, reinforce specific lesson content, approximate sensory aspects). Feedback can also be employed to provide strategic information (diagnosis, prescription, performance to date, management, learning processes) as well as affective information. It is clear that the nature of feedback has evolved considerably since the initial text-based emphasis, broadening substantially its implications for emerging technologies.

Research on error detection and correction has mostly focused on feedback. In general, research indicates that feedback is a valuable tool for correcting errors; it is timely, meaningful, and relevant. Emerging technologies offer a wide range of possibilities for delivering feedback to learners. Future research is likely to focus on determining how, when, and what types of feedback best promote desired ends.

12.2.3.5. Lesson Sequencing. While effective control is central to effective CBI, beliefs concerning who should control lesson-sequencing decisions vary according to several factors. To some, the computer should adapt dynamically to modify lesson content to match students' individual needs. Proponents of this approach use CBI to present carefully crafted, individually relevant lesson content to learners. The computer can control the presentation order of a lesson, the amount and complexity of information presented, the nature of feedback, and all related decisions. In other words, the computer allows the creation of environments in which students complete optimal instructional sequences, according to external judgments, to achieve predetermined educational goals.

To others, however, the computer presents the opportunity for student-centered learning. Learners can control a wide variety of instructional variables including access to lesson content, the context in which instruction is situated, the presentation stimuli, the option to select additional content, the amount of practice to complete, the difficulty of content and related questions, and the amount of advice to be provided during instruction (Schwier, 1992). In effect, the computer encourages learners to build relationships among lesson concepts through exploration, experimentation, and manipulation.

12.2.3.5.1. Learner vs. Designer Control. Perhaps no single topic has received as much attention by researchers as that of locus of instructional control. The question of where lesson execution control should reside—program or learner—remains a source of controversy and debate. The most externally metered program control option is completely linear. It involves presenting identical content to all students, in the same order, and with the same strategies, depth, and complexity. In practice, however, such an approach often proves inefficient and is usually a poor candidate for computer-based lessons. Within any group of students, individual needs vary widely. Instructional support needed by the most able students is likely to differ greatly from that needed for the weakest students.

The benefits and liabilities of learner control are well documented (see 33.5) [see, for example, reviews by Steinberg (1977, 1989; see 33.5]. Learner control has been found to stimulate achievement and improve attitudes and motivation (Kinzie, 1990; Kinzie & Berdel, 1990; Lepper, 1985; Pollock & Sullivan, 1990). Kohn (1993) noted that learner control improved self-attribution, achievement, and behavior. On the other hand, learners have also proved poor judges of their learning needs, often seeking information that is not needed or terminating lessons prematurely (Hannafin, 1984).

Linear lessons, and all program-controlled instruction for that matter, are inherently structured. The nature of the structure either limits or manages individual variability. Linear structures provide no opportunity for students to engage selectively in activities deemed uniquely appropriate, emphasizing instead activities thought to be of greatest value to all. Generally, complete program control has been effective for domain novices and for tasks with explicit performance requirements (Chung & Reigeluth, 1992). Highly structured environments are likely to be especially limiting for high-ability and high prior-knowledge students.

Differences in learner preferences, knowledge, and styles are often accommodated by varying learner control. In cases of optimal learner control, students individually identify what they will study and seek and revisit lesson segments as they evolve new representations. Doing so involves exploring learning environments many times and from many different perspectives (Spiro, Feltovich, Jacobson & Coulson, 1991).

The issue of learner control appears to be particularly germane in the design of hypermedia learning environments (see 21.3). Hypermedia presents two critical problems for designers. First, many students may have difficulty navigating in hypermedia environments: They tend to become easily disoriented (Park & Hannafin, 1993). Second, when given unaided access to information, students may experience difficulties locating and linking information to build meaningful cognitive structures.

Despite the wealth of learner control research, Reeves (1993) suggested that much of it is little more than "pseudoscience." He argued that researchers often fail to employ consistent working definitions across experiments. Most of the research on learner control has been conducted on artificially controlled drill and practice and tutorial programs with the imposition of measured lesson control. In practice, however, diverse classes of computer software are associated with different levels of control. He suggested that research methodologies often lack internal and external validity. Instructional treatments are often too brief for

students to learn how to exercise effective learner control. The materials used are often unrelated to the regular curriculum and irrelevant to students, so the amount of effort invested in a task is often not representative of normal behavior. Reeves also noted that experimental analyses are often suspect. Small sample sizes, for example, suggest that the underlying assumptions of some statistical analyses have been violated; researchers often ignore the causes of high experimental attrition. Finally, few studies are grounded in psychological theory; few researchers have established a solid theoretical base for their studies.

Although locus of instructional control has been researched extensively, continued efforts are important due to changing nature of "control" now afforded to both designers and learners. With the advent of hypermedia and hypertext, structured or linear approaches to design are no longer the only options. Radical reconceptualizations have occurred related to how we think about, and design for, software control. Design strategies that maximize the learning potentials of open-ended environments, as well as learners, will likely redefine learner vs. designer control issues into the 21st century.

12.2.3.5.2. Adapting Instruction.   Adaptive control provides an alternative to either rigid program control or unassisted learner control. Adaptive control adjusts instruction to meet individual needs based on user traits (Boyd & Mitchell, 1992) and ongoing performance (Tennyson, 1984). It is tacitly assumed that the designer can better determine domain needs than the individual. This perspective is problematic from at least two perspectives. First, in many cases designers cannot effectively diagnose and prescribe, in advance, instructional remedies. Second, prescriptive models may do little to develop learners who are capable of making effective, independent instructional decisions (see 22.3, 22.4).

One approach to adapting instruction involves using mathematical equations to adjust the amount of instruction, the number of examples, display time, and other relevant factors. Ross and Morrison's (1988) model involves three steps: identifying variables that affect lesson performance, collecting data to generate equations that can be used to estimate achievement, and generating criteria to link students' performances with anticipated outcomes. The method produces equations that, when used in concert with ongoing lesson data, adapt instruction according to individual performance and need.

Tennyson and Christensen's (1988) method differs in its monitoring of student needs. Their approach involves greater computer "judgment" of learner needs and needed branching. The prescriptions generated during a lesson are similar to those employed by classroom teachers: They determine appropriate lesson content density, monitor and adapt instructional strategies, and manage the instructional process. Using multivariate analyses, the Minnesota Adaptive Instructional System (MAIS) diagnoses individual needs to prescribe instruction, adapts prescriptions to reflect ongoing lesson performance, and continuously updates its decision-making system. The system generates data on several variables that are used to modify instruction (see 19.2.3).

The adaptation abilities of the technology—the capacity to change lesson sequences, difficulty level, and pace according to unique learner needs—is among the longest standing of assets. From its early days, the computer has been touted as possessing extraordinary potential to accommodate vastly different learning styles, rates, and background knowledge. Yet, as the focus of teaching and learning continues to shift, contemporary approaches emphasize learner empowerment over "smart" computers. Many now believe that it is more important to create systems for learners to recognize metacognitively when they fail to comprehend, and seek support accordingly, than to create lessons that supplant these capabilities [see, for example, Salomon, Perkins & Globerson (1991)]. A very different kind of adaptation will be required from those that empower only the computer with the capacity to adapt.

12.2.3.5.3. Advising Learners. One of the underlying assumptions of many hypermedia systems is that students will actively explore their learning environments. In practice, however, students are often unable to benefit from the freedom associated with hypermedia (Santiago & Okey, 1992). Students may be unable, or unwilling, to explore unfamiliar computer-based environments. However, they may benefit from the expert guidance delivered via the computer, which is often referred to as *advisement.*

Advisement performs two important functions in lesson execution. First, it can either augment or supplant metacognitive processing. As an augmenting resource, it can be used by capable learners as a kind of "second opinion" to reference against individual beliefs; as a supplanting resource, it can free the learner from the cognitive burdens associated with self-regulated learning in order to focus more completely on lesson content (Hannafin, Hall, Land & Hill, 1994). By providing information concerning ongoing lesson performance, the amount of instruction needed to optimize learning, and information to guide effective navigation, students can guide their on-task behavior and model effective study strategies.

Advisement may be particularly useful for reluctant, or passive, learners. Lee and Lehman (1993), working with college undergraduates on hypermedia and videodisc technologies, found that active learners consistently selected more information, spent longer on task, and demonstrated higher achievement on a posttest than did passive learners. However, when cues were provided in the form of suggestions to elicit elaborations, passive students selected more elaborated lesson content and spent longer on task. The investments of effort and time appear to stimulate higher achievement scores, while advisement cues appear to supplement deficient metacognitive strategies.

In a more general sense, emerging technologies must continue to expand their capacity to facilitate the learner's efforts rather than to advise on how to attain what the lesson's designer has deemed important. Facilitation, in this sense, addresses a more learner-centered question: How can the unique intents of each learner be supported? This poses a very perplexing problem for researchers and designers: How can systems be created capable of supporting needs and intents that cannot be fully known in advance? This is a most intriguing problem, one for which research is sorely needed.

12.2.3.5.4. Hypertext/Hypermedia Linking. One key to successful sequencing in computer-based environments is to connect to information that can be readily assimilated by the learner (see 21.4). Many systems, especially hypermedia systems, permit students to access parts of a lesson that may only be tangentially related. For example, students may have access to information that is related literally rather than semantically or conceptually. Students may link to information related in literal structure but not in contextual meaning (Gall & Hannafin, 1994; Jonassen, 1989).

Following literal rather than semantic links is more likely to occur among students with limited related prior knowledge. Given control over lesson sequence, students with high domain knowledge readily connect conceptually related ideas. In contrast, students with little domain knowledge tend to connect literal definitions and examples rather than make conceptually advanced associations (Nelson & Palumbo, 1992).

Linking in hypertext/hypermedia is among the most significant capabilities that have effected design to date. These capabilities make it possible for individuals to access information in tightly controlled or open-ended manners, literally enabling lessons of unlimited variations. Designers can now provide tools that aid thinking, personalizing, connecting, and interacting with vast amounts of information (see, for example, Bliss & Ogborn, 1989; Horwitz & Fuerzeig, 1994; Reader & Hammond, 1994). The challenge for researchers is to study how, when, and if tools and resources are managed successfully by learners, and how the decision making of users can be supported.

12.2.3.6. Motivation. Kinzie (1990) suggested that two motivational constructs, intrinsic and continuing motivation, are important for maintaining the participation necessary to flourish in CBI environments. Intrinsic motivation describes the state that exists when individuals participate in an activity for the gratification generated by the activity itself. Continuing motivation is evident when students choose to return to a lesson without the presence of external motivators (see, for example, Seymour, Sullivan, Story & Mosley, 1987). Some computer-based learning environments, such as simulations and games, seem to be inherently motivating, especially for children (Malone, 1981; Rieber, 1992).

Keller and Suzuki (1988) adapted and elaborated a motivational model for CBI design. ARCS is an acronym that represents four categories: attention, relevance, confidence, and satisfaction. *Attention gaining* is often the easiest phase of the motivation process and addresses strategies to arouse and sustain performance. *Relevance* addresses how instruction helps students achieve their personal goals. Lessons that relate to prior or anticipated experiences are likely to increase motivation. *Confidence* refers to the degree to which students believe that they will succeed at a given task. Students who believe that personal success is achievable and a function of their effort are more likely to succeed than those who lack confidence or who attribute success to luck or some other uncontrollable factors. *Satisfaction* refers to students' perceptions about the outcomes of instruction. In general, lessons are more motivating when students feel appropriately rewarded for their efforts.

Keller and Suzuki identified three key factors: motivational objectives, learner characteristics, and learner expectations. The setting of motivational objectives is important in designing and evaluating CBI. Motivational objectives are too frequently assessed simplistically using students' responses to questionnaires and task performance. That is, students are often assumed to be motivated if they respond favorably to surveys or if they perform well on achievements tests. Alternative measures, such as task persistence, indicators of continuing motivation, and increased confidence and relevance, may be better indicators of student motivation.

A careful analysis of learner characteristics can help designers assess the motivational strategies needed. For example, students may require little additional motivation when they already perceive the content as important and relevant. However, students who lack confidence or perceive little relevance require more focus on motivational strategies. In their attempts to stimulate student interest, CBI designers must ensure that lessons do not inadvertently lower student motivation. Lessons that include irritating routines or that fail to demonstrate minimum visual standards may reduce motivation, regardless of the quality of the instructional content.

Malone and Lepper (1987) developed a taxonomy of intrinsic motivation based on a survey of computer-game preferences among elementary school children. They classified motivation into four categories: challenge, control, curiosity, and fantasy. *Challenge,* the level of difficulty, is optimized when balance exists between activities that are easy and hard. Challenging activities establish attainable goals (which may be determined by the student), maintain a level of uncertainty, and generate clear feedback that is frequent, informative, and encouraging.

Control of one's environment is fundamental to intrinsic motivation. The amount of control that learners exercise depends on the degree to which students' actions affect the range of outcomes. High levels of control empower students. Malone and Lepper (1987) suggest that control in CBI is promoted by strategies such as varying lesson presentations and feedback according to individual needs, and allowing students to choose lesson sequence and instructional difficulty (or at least appear as if they have chosen). However, they warn that although autonomy increases motivation, too little lesson structure may result in learners becoming frustrated and unmotivated.

Few would argue with the proposition that ensuring initial motivation, maintaining interest during instruction,

and encouraging continuing interest in the subject under study (and the tools with which it is studied) are as critical to the success of computer-based instruction as to any form of instruction. Although occasional evidence is found to the contrary (for example, Kinzie & Sullivan, 1989), it seems unlikely that simply receiving instruction via computer will prove inherently motivating to learners—especially over time (see Clark, 1983, 1985). Interestingly, researchers and designers have garnered considerable input as to what motivates individuals in noneducation settings. The explosion of arcade–like home computer games, for example, underscored how challenge and competition help to initiate and sustain engagement. There remains much to be learned, however. As systems become increasingly connected, and the learner's electronic "window to the world" is opened dramatically, we face a different challenge. The diverse resources available through high-powered information retrieval systems, such as NETSCAPE™ and MOSAIC™, lack unifying methods, approaches, and structures. One resource may prove captivating; others may prove boring. Since no single publisher accounts for the myriad of resources, and the nature and quality may prove very uneven in any given instance, we need to find ways to simplify learner's task while eliciting, maintaining, and continuing interest in both topic and the system (cf. Lepper & Gurtner, 1989).

12.2.3.7. Applying Knowledge and Skills. Retrieving and using knowledge and skill are inextricably tied to encoding: One cannot retrieve what has not yet been learned. The ability to retrieve is a function of the quality and nature of initial encoding, the presence of cues (internally generated or externally supplied) that trigger appropriate processes, and the application of strategies to identify and restructure information. The ability to apply such knowledge and skill, however, is mediated by the context in which they were learned and their utility.

12.2.3.7.1. Problem Solving. Perhaps no process better illustrates the role and value of retrieval than problem solving (see 23.5.2). Lambrecht (1993) outlined three approaches to teaching problem solving for, and with, computer-based learning: general, integrated, and immersed. General problem solving is sometimes referred to as *cognitive strategy training.* The effectiveness of general problem-solving skills appears to improve when students learn self-regulation metacognitive skills. Delclos and Harrington (1991), for example, compared three treatments used to complete a computer problem-solving task: general problem solving, general problem solving with embedded self-monitoring activities, and a control activity. Results indicated that the monitored problem-solving group solved more complex problems in less time than did other treatments. Self-regulation training helps students transfer learning to more difficult problems within the same domain.

Similarly, King (1991) found that embedding strategic questions helped to guide fifth-graders through computer-based problem-solving activities. Students in a guided group were given strategic questions during the problem-solving process. Students in an unguided treatment were directed to interact with their partners, and those in a control group were given no instructions on how to interact. After completing four computer programs on general problem solving, students in the guided questioning group performed best on tests of general problem solving. Strategic prompting apparently helped to focus intragroup interaction, which promoted successful problem solving.

The arguments supporting general approaches to problem solving are intuitively appealing: If generalizable strategies exist, they should be taught directly to make students more effective problem solvers. However, the power of general problem-solving approaches has not been established conclusively. Indeed, the generalizability of problem-solving skills is often believed to be inversely related to their effectiveness: the more specific the strategy, the less generalizable to different problems; the more general a problem-solving technique, the less powerful for specific problems (Perkins & Salomon, 1989).

Integrated approaches attempt to teach problem-solving skills within realistic learning contexts. Kozma (1987) suggested that computer-based cognitive tools (see 24.2) can teach problem-solving strategies by modeling cognitive processes. Some writing programs, for example, model such critical-writing processes as to identify topics, to structure writing, and to edit and revise, which help students internalize and apply the basic steps involved in writing (Kozma, 1991a).

In contrast, some have argued that domain-specific knowledge is prerequisite to effective problem solving. According to Pea and Kurland (1987), one needs to acquire strong background and proficiency within a given domain to become a proficient problem solver. If so, then differences between experts and novices may be attributable to the magnitude of their domain knowledge rather than to knowledge of problem-solving strategies (Perkins & Salomon, 1989).

Another problem-solving approach, immersion, focuses more on the nature of the learning experience than the processes involved in problem solving. Advocates propose that students learn to become effective problem solvers when they are immersed in solving real-life problems. Students acquire problem-solving skills in the "culture" in which problems exist. When concepts are used (or learned for the first time), they acquire new meanings; that is, the learning context becomes a part of the concept. Utility, therefore, is a function of the diversity of contexts in which concepts are used (Prawat, 1991).

Technology's potential to stimulate problem solving lies principally in its ability to manage processing resources and to encourage effective problem representation and transfer. Problem solving often involves managing large quantities of data that must be maintained and manipulated. The cognitive load associated with these tasks can divert attention from the problem-solving task. Computers can augment the learner's problem-solving capabilities by managing available data and performing requisite transformations and calculations (Pea, 1992).

The transformational capabilities of the computer facilitate problem representation by helping to clarify relationships between symbolic representations and physical events. Kozma (1991b) described two studies in which the computer helped students to form more accurate mental representations of physical phenomena. In one study (Mokros & Tinker, 1987) seventh- and eighth-grade students, exposed to computer-based sensors for 3 months, were better able to interpret graphs. Apparently, transforming information from electronic sensors into their graphical representations helped to clarify the relationships between symbols and the real world. Similarly, Brasell (1987) reported that instantaneous feedback generated by motion sensors in a microcomputer-based laboratory helped twelfth-grade students to associate physical motion with appropriate graphs.

Emerging technologies increase the ways (and combination of ways) designers can present and display problems for learners. Atkins and Blisset (1992), for example, applied the realistic images available through interactive video to the development of problem-solving skills. Additionally, technologies offer a variety of ways learners can directly interact and experiment with problems and their variables. Systems can encourage learners to be more active in their problem solving. For example, through direct manipulation and experimentation, learners often discover important underlying processes, principles, and logic that result in problems or alter the problems in important ways. These design strategies allow learners to model more than simple procedures or gain additional practice; they help them develop insight into the nature as well as cause of problems. Future research in problem solving should continue to explore various design strategies for problem solving, as well as help to clarify how virtual worlds and realities can be used to enhance these thinking skills.

12.2.3.7.2. Transfer. Much has been written regarding the capacity to apply knowledge and skill to similar versus dissimilar circumstances. Clark and Voogel (1985) described this as a "near" versus "far" transfer continuum. Near transfer involves the application of previously acquired knowledge to problems of similar, or nearly identical, contexts; far transfer involves application to circumstances dissimilar to, or wholly unlike, the contexts in which knowledge and skill were initially acquired. According to Clark and Voogel, antagonism exists between initial acquisition and transfer contexts: Learning under explicitly structured approaches generally tends to facilitate near transfer, while more conceptually oriented learning tends to promote far transfer.

Similarly, Salomon and Perkins (1989) described how the nature of an instructional strategy is likely to impact transfer. Low-road (near) transfer occurs when students can immediately apply learned information or skills in situations that differ slightly from those in which initial learning occurred. High-road (far) transfer occurs when students apply learning in diverse contexts. Although technology can stimulate learning of both, low- and high-road transfer appear to require different instructional conditions. High-road transfer of problem-solving skills, for example, is stimulated by practicing in diverse contexts until automaticity has been achieved in enabling skills and processes.

Kozma (1991b) described technology's potential to facilitate the transition from novice to expert. Computers can help students incorporate complex phenomena, which are not usually included, into their mental models. White (1984) used computer microworld environments to represent abstract, physical phenomena in diverse ways. High school science students who used a microworld environment for less than 1 hour demonstrated improved conceptual understanding of important lesson principles and significant improvement on transfer tests.

White (1992) extended this research during a 2-month study. Students interacted regularly with a computer microworld incorporating several features of Newtonian physics. During the study, participants not only interacted with the microworld but also tested the authenticity of several potential principles governing the system. Following the study, the experimental group outperformed the control group on a transfer test. Interestingly, the activities engaged in by students during the study appeared to stimulate mindful abstraction, the conditions required for high-road transfer (Salomon & Perkins, 1989).

The growth of interest in constructs such as situated cognition, everyday thinking, and anchored instruction reflects considerable interest in the utilization or application of knowledge and skill in contexts in which they have meaning (Choi & Hannafin, 1995). Transfer—especially far transfer—involves the ability to access and utilize knowledge acquired from one context to another. It is fundamental to virtually all conceptions of learning and performance, yet research on transfer has often proved discouraging. How much of our present "school knowledge" and "academic skill" can be situated effectively, and will situated learning contexts improve the productive value of what is learned? Will the cost and effort required to create authentic learning environments be justified by improved transfer? Will high-cost environments yield high gain, in terms of transfer? These are significant issues, issues that must be studied if substantial commitments to alternative systems are to become a reality.

12.2.3.8. Contextual Factors. Context has become the cornerstone of contemporary research in areas such as situated cognition, cognitive apprenticeships, authentic learning, and anchored instruction (see 23.5.1.1; Brown, Collins & Duguid, 1989; Chiou, 1992; Choi & Hannafin, 1995; Cognition and Technology Group at Vanderbilt, 1992a, 1992b, 1993, 1994). Cognitive processes and context are viewed as inextricably related, suggesting that knowledge is rooted fundamentally in the context in which it is acquired (see 7.3.3). This has led many researchers to disdain the decontextualized teaching and instructing methods that dominate traditional approaches.

Technology has played a significant role in establishing contexts for learning. Perhaps the best-known applications

have been in simulations, where to-be-learned content and processes are represented in ways deemed to capture important contextual information and processes (see, for example, the physics simulation described by Lewis, Stern & Linn, 1993). Many have focused on high-fidelity images that capture substance, processes, and affective elements of real-life events. Harless (1986), for example, developed a voice-activated interactive videodisc simulation on emergency room (ER) intake and treatment procedures. Video vignettes orient users, in this case medical interns, to the circumstances surrounding potential ER patients. The circumstances range from "real" symptoms and related medical histories to contrived symptoms and histories often provided for personal versus medical reasons. The interns must decide whether or not to admit the patients and what course of treatment should be followed. A range of paths are possible, depending upon the diagnoses and treatment plans prescribed. The context, in effect, is that of the typical emergency room, complete with potentially life-threatening illnesses, unanticipated complications, and cost accumulation.

Context has been studied in other ways as well. Dalton and Hannafin (1987) compared the effects of interactive video lessons designed to emphasize specific knowledge (i.e., isolation of key terms, definitions, and explicit cueing) or contextual elements (i.e., important concepts retained, and presented, within authentic circumstances) on declarative knowledge and problem solving by junior high school students. Contextual approaches yielded comparable recall of declarative knowledge but significantly greater application to problems than did specific knowledge-cueing strategies. Breuer and Kummer (1990) applied process-learning approaches, wherein lesson content was embedded successfully within computer simulations in vocational education. In both studies, content was successfully embedded within, rather than disembodied from, the contexts that gave it meaning.

12.2.3.8.1. Grouping.   Recent studies suggest that students often complete CBI as effectively, and in some cases more effectively, with a partner than alone (Repman, 1993; Repman, Rooze & Weller, 1991). Mevarech, Silber, and Fine (1991), for example, examined the effects of paired and individual use of an integrated learning system (ILS). The ILS was designed to teach basic numeric skills. The system individualized instruction by diagnosing individual difficulties and prescribing possible solutions. After completing two 20-minute sessions over approximately 2 months, sixth-grade students working alone showed no benefits compared to those working with a partner. Grouping resulted in higher achievement across learners and lower math anxiety for the least able students.

Recently, researchers also compared the performance of students who completed computer-based tutorials alone versus in cooperative learning groups (see 35.9). Students often learn more effectively and enjoy instruction more when collaborating than when studying alone at the computer (Hooper, Temiyakarn & Williams, 1993; Hooper, 1992b;

Johnson, Johnson & Stanne, 1985, 1986). Johnson and Johnson (1989) identified several important learning and social benefits associated with cooperative learning. From a cognitive perspective, cooperative learning produces higher achievement and productivity than do competitive or individualistic environments, and the results are strongest for complex learning rather than for cognitively low-level learning. One reason for the increased productivity may be that cooperative learning maintains higher levels of student engagement than do other approaches. Increased engagement apparently reflects improved attitudes and perceptions of belonging that are often associated with cooperative learning. Following collaboration with peers in cooperative groups, students often feel more liked, are more concerned for each other's well-being, and enjoy academic work more than after working alone. Consequently, students are willing to remain on task for longer periods of time.

Many cognitive benefits can be gained by working alongside a partner; cooperative learning appears to be particularly effective for improving student achievement (see 35.5). Cooperative learning is designed to deepen understanding of complex lesson content through student interaction and modeling. Students working in groups are made interdependent by controlling individual and group rewards, encouraging group development, stimulating appropriate intragroup interaction, and maintaining high personal accountability for individual and group performance (Hooper, 1992a).

Contextual factors have demonstrated their potency for enhancing both the encoding and retrieving of information. As new technologies continue to evolve, richer capabilities for designing contexts will be developed. During the past decade, research on cooperative learning has suggested many important grouping distinctions. Design strategies have been developed which support the needs of both cooperative learning and other kinds of grouping. Future researchers need to investigate new ways for learners to model cooperative strategies as well as track accountability in very personalized ways.

12.2.4 Evolution in Perspective

Thus far, we examined research on cost effectiveness, learning effectiveness, and design. Although it needs to be examined using new metrics, we concede that, redefined or not, cost should always be a concern. Cost is an especially contentious issue as resources for education become scarce and increasingly politicized.

Three other findings seem especially significant. First, how technological capabilities are utilized is more critical than the capabilities themselves. Simply put, more is not necessarily better. Designers must be aware of the cognitive demands their systems place on learners and thoughtfully apply techniques that support, not interfere with, learner effort. Next, design must be rooted in research on teaching

and learning; the tools and resources provided must support the learner's efforts (Salomon, 1993). Finally, emerging technologies have made it easier than ever to create learning systems, while simultaneously making it more complex to design effectively. For example, while technologies have increased the designer's ability to create and present rich contexts for learning, the prospect of designing contexts that are authentic, reasonably situated, appropriately anchored, well guided and supported, and motivational is no easy task. It is far easier to create something with great cosmetic appeal than an integrated learning system that is consistent with available research and theory (see, for example, Koen, 1985). So much is possible, yet we know so little about many fundamental design and development issues.

Emerging technologies have also altered the design process itself (see, for example, Collins, 1993). Emerging design methods, often adapted from other disciplines (e.g., engineering), no longer limit designers to traditional linear approaches. For example, rapid prototyping allows designers to quickly produce functional models of far more elaborate designs. These models not only help developers envision full-scale models and lesson functionality but also promote greater en-route design experimentation and creativity. Again, the dilemma is balancing *what should be produced, against what can be produced.*

Finally, research on design most clearly indicates that traditional design strategies have focused on *how and what to teach* rather than *empowering to learn*. These differing views ultimately affect how designs are operationalized, evaluated, and researched. While a great deal of useful research has been conducted related to traditional design methods, research on designs that empower learners is relatively rare. Developing, testing, and researching alternative design methods may be among the most daunting of tasks facing future researchers.

Although past instructional technology research has contributed to a better understanding of the effects of particular technologies on learning, it has done little to help us relate such findings to critically important contexts such as schools and classrooms (Kozma, 1991b). We have a better understanding of the parts, but are comparatively naive about the whole. As we approach the 21st century, our research needs to reflect a more integrated approach to teaching, learning, and technology.

12.3 EMERGING CONSTRUCTS AND LEARNING SYSTEMS

Whereas traditional approaches to computer-based learning have been rooted in behavioral learning principles, contemporary approaches are more often rooted in cognitive learning theories. They focus not on the *product* technology of the computer but on the *idea technologies* afforded by the computer (Hooper & Rieber, 1995). Idea technologies tend to emphasize constructivist orientations to learning (see 24.3; Papert, 1981, 1993; Schwartz, Yerushalmy & Wilson, 1993; White, 1993).

Contemporary research with emerging technologies centers on the cognitive impact of people working in partnership with technology rather than studying the effects of technology on learning (see, for example, Perkins, 1985). This research can best be understood when classified as effects *of* versus *with* the computer on cognition (Salomon, Perkins & Globerson, 1991). Research on the effects of the computer *on* cognition attempts to determine if "cognitive residue" results as a consequence of the interaction between the individual and computer, such as an increase in general problem-solving ability or mathematical reasoning. Research *with* technology focuses on how human processing changes in distinct, qualitative ways when an individual is engaged in an intellectual activity using the computer as a tool. Taken interactively, an intellectual partnership is formed between the individual and the technology; the resulting changes to cognition cannot be understood when the individual or the technology are considered apart (see also 24.3).

A simple, yet profound, example of this intellectual partnership is evident in how human memory has been altered qualitatively with a relatively primitive technology: the pencil. The storage and retrieval strategies one uses to perform routine memorization are qualitatively different in cultures where writing instruments are universally available throughout one's life. Although computers are a long way from being as ubiquitous as pencil and paper, some researchers believe that computers offer a similar potential due to the unique processing support capabilities they provide. An emphasis on learning *with* media, as opposed to learning *from* media, may help to resolve some of the debate and controversy surrounding media research over the past 50 years [see, for example, Clark (1983) versus Kozma (1991b)].

This section focuses on learning systems and environments that have emerged based on contemporary psychological and pedagogical perspectives.

12.3.1 Psychological Constructs

12.3.1.1. Learning as the Active Construction of Knowledge. Most contemporary cognitive psychologists hold that learning consists of individual constructions of knowledge (see 7.4, 23.4.1.2). Learning is a personal event that results from sustained and meaningful engagement with one's environment (Bruner, 1961, 1985, 1986). This view also holds that learning cannot be viewed apart from the social and cultural contexts in which it occurs (Prawat & Floden, 1994). In education, the historical roots of constructivism are most heavily founded in developmental psychology and social learning theories. Educational practices encourage "equilibration" through the enabling processes of assimilation and accommodation described by

Piaget (1952), and Vygotsky's (1978) construct of the zone of proximal development (Fowler, 1994). In some studies, researchers have even equated the computer as a scaffolding tool supporting readers as they enter, and maneuver within, the zone of proximal development (Salomon, Globerson & Guterman, 1989).

No single learning system design results from constructivist philosophies of learning [see Tobin (1993) for a collection of applications in science education]. Indeed, the notion that one person should design or plan a learning experience for another is antithetical to constructivism (Jonassen, 1991). Cognitive apprenticeships and anchored instruction, however, reflect ways in which instructional practice might change to accommodate the shift in learning from reception to construction (see Chapter 23). That these approaches lend themselves to widely varying interpretations is both an advantage and disadvantage. The literature is replete with innovative strategies for nurturing the construction process, but there are also many conflicts about the directions constructivist education should take (Strommen & Lincoln, 1992). Discovery-based, context-driven approaches are well suited to ill-structured domains, whereas traditional, directed instructional methods may be more appropriate in well-structured domains (Tripp, 1992).

12.3.1.2. Situated Cognition and Generative Learning. Two theoretical frameworks rooted in the principles advanced by Piaget and Vygotsky, situated cognition and generative learning (see 23.4.5, 31.1.1), are particularly promising for technologically enhanced learning environments (see, for example, Cognition and Technology Group at Vanderbilt, 1991). Situated cognition theory holds that learning should occur in environments that closely resemble those in which experts work. The most meaningful and useful kinds of learning are believed to be those embedded in activities that make deliberate use of social and physical contexts: "Activity, concept, and culture are interdependent. No one can be totally understood without the other two. Learning must involve all three" (Brown, Collins & Duguid, 1989, p. 33). Learning environments that support situated cognition closely resemble the apprenticeship system common in the craft professions (e.g., plumbing, carpentry, and tailoring) as well as professions that require extensive schooling (e.g., medical, dental, and legal). Likewise, learning about other subject matter in cognitive domains, such as mathematics, physics, and language arts, are often enabled through cognitive apprenticeships (Choi & Hannafin, 1995).

Current computing environments allow for a wide range of generative learning strategies to be incorporated into courseware (Jonassen, 1988). Generative learning models (see 31.3) suggest that meaningful learning results when the learner actively and consciously relates prior knowledge to new material and creates understandings based on these relationships (Wittrock, 1974, 1978; Wetzel, 1993). The role of instruction is to support activities and strategies that learners may use to generate meaning, and even to supply mechanisms if the learner is unable to do so on his or her own (such as in the case of very young children or novices). Generative learning requires learners to be proactive and mindful as they search for meaning by continually relating new information to what they already know. Generative activities include paraphrasing, summarizing, outlining, analytic reasoning, and mental imagery.

The work on computer-supported intentional learning environments (CSILE) by Marlene Scardamalia and her associates is one of the most extensive attempts to date to produce a computer system that facilitates generative learning (Scardamalia, Bereiter, McLean, Swallow & Woodruff, 1989). CSILE uses an instructional approach called *procedural facilitation* to support higher-order thinking skills. CSILE gives students tools and a context for making learning skills overt while providing just enough structure to enable cognitive processing, though such structure is reduced as students become more mature in their learning habits. CSILE permits students to enter information into a common database in a variety of representations (such as text, graphics, time-lines, etc.). As a shared database, students are able to enter newly discovered information while at the same time are prompted to describe points of confusion and enter questions they might have. Students are also encouraged to evaluate and refine each other's entries. CSILE makes students responsible for their learning while providing them with tools and strategies that support metacognitive processes, such as goal setting, elaboration, and self-evaluation. Early research with CSILE has produced very promising, though largely anecdotal, results.

12.3.1.3. Microworlds.
A microworld represents the simplest case of a domain that is still recognizable by an expert in the domain. As a learner becomes more proficient, the microworld can become more complex and sophisticated. Most importantly, the learner decides how to structure and direct the microworld according to individual needs.

Microworlds tend to focus on conceptual and qualitative understanding within relatively narrow and limited sets of interrelated constructs. This is an especially important departure from traditionally quantitative domains, such as mathematics and physics. Traditional instruction often enables students to calculate accurately the mathematics of motion problems without changing student's fundamental conceptions or "personal theories" of physical science (diSessa, 1988, 1993; Roschelle, 1991; Roschelle & Greeno, 1987). Carefully designed physics microworlds, many with gamelike features, have been found to qualitatively alter students' conceptions of physics problems (White, 1984, 1992, 1993).

Computer-based microworlds provide opportunities for students to explore and experience phenomena intuitively and formulate hypotheses that may run counter to intuition (diSessa, 1982). Using well-conceived microworlds, children as young as sixth-graders demonstrate better qualitative understanding of physics, and comparable calculation capabilities, as their twelfth-grade counterparts (White &

Fredericksen, 1987, as cited in Striley, 1988). The aims of such systems are often fundamentally different from traditional, objectivist aims; the methods required for their study must reflect these basic differences.

12.3.2 Emerging Learning Systems

Concrete applications of constructivism to educational practice have become increasingly prevalent [see, for example, STELLA described by Steed (1992)]. Some have detailed ways to alter dramatically classroom practices from instruction to construction using traditional media and materials (see Fosnot, 1989). However, several important developmental projects have resulted that utilize the computational and processing power of computers to create, or alter, learning environments. In this section, we describe four noteworthy systems, each of which has been studied extensively, that utilize technology in innovative ways to support the construction on personal understanding: Logo MicroWorlds, Jasper Woodbury, Voyage of the Mimi, and Citizen Kane.

12.3.2.1. Logo MicroWorlds.
Early research on Logo yielded conflicting results and interpretations, though the most consistently positive results were in the affective domain (Clements, 1985). Children using Logo often reported positive attitudes, were enthusiastic about learning, and improved in their motivation to cooperate in groups (e.g., Burnet & Higginson, 1984; Hawkins, Sheingold, Gearheart & Berger, 1982).

Among the most contentious issues was whether Logo influenced general cognitive skills, such as problem solving (see 24.5.1). Several notable studies indicated no improvements in problem-solving from using Logo (Pea, 1987; Pea & Kurland, 1984), whereas others reported successes (Clements & Gullo, 1984; Kynigos, 1993; Resnick, 1990; Soloway, Lockhead & Clement, 1982). The source of these discrepancies likely were rooted in the different research approaches. For example, Clements and Gullo (1984) studied the effects of Logo programming over a wide range of issues including cognitive style, metacognitive ability, and cognitive development. Nine children were provided Logo programming experience, while nine other children were provided traditional computer-related instructional activities. The Logo children showed increases in metacognition, whereas the control group did not. In contrast, Pea and Kurland (1984) tested the learners' capacity to solve specific related problems rather than general ones, such as problem planning. Consistent with the bulk of research on generalized problem solving, Logo failed to yield favorable results, suggesting that improvements, if they occur, may be of an exceedingly broad nature.

Inconsistent transfer of cognitive skills may also be attributable to different approaches to studying transfer (see, for example, Lehrer & Littlefield, 1993). According to Salomon and Perkins (1989), many unsuccessful Logo studies were concerned with low-road transfer. This is not surprising, since young students rarely attain very sophisticated programming skill with Logo, even after 2 years (Leron, 1985). Successful studies, such as reported by Clements and Gullo (1985), emphasized high-road transfer. Students received guidance and structure as they worked with Logo as compared to the free discovery methods often misattributed to Papert.

Papert (1987) contended that early research on Logo effects was fundamentally misguided, since Logo, like the constructivist philosophy on which it is based, must be viewed holistically. Context, culture, and activity must be viewed together; reducing the experience to its individual parts necessarily changes the nature of the experience. Logo, Papert asserts, is but one knowledge tool in the student's culture. Hypotheses related to the effects *of* Logo *on* learners are akin to hypotheses related to the effects of hammers and wood on building good houses.

Recent research with current generations of Logo, such as MicroWorlds Project Builder, MicroWorlds Language Art, and MicroWorlds Math Links, focuses on a special interpretation of constructivism that Papert calls *constructionism.* Papert chose the term *constructionism* because of the emphasis placed on building artifacts of understanding, such as children building their own games to learn about fractions (Harel, 1990, 1991; Harel & Papert, 1991; Kafai, 1994). Each MicroWorlds system extends underlying Logo vocabulary, syntax, and primitives with a variety of tools, color palettes, shapes, animation, fonts, and other features to make use more readily apparent and intuitive. The constructionist philosophy reflected within each system remains essentially the same as the early versions of Logo. The means for empowering learners, however, evolved to make transparent the tool uses of the computer in constructing artifacts of their understanding.

12.3.2.2. Jasper Woodbury.

The Jasper project (see also 23.5.1.1) is primarily video based, featuring both videotape and videodisc versions, though recent efforts have extended the materials to other multimedia contexts (Marsh & Kumar, 1992). Though traditional computer technology is not central to the project, the importance of microprocessor technology in accessing segments in the video scenarios, rapidly and precisely, is integral to its design. The Jasper series represents an application of constructive approaches to learning, specifically generative learning and anchored instruction (Cognition and Technology Group at Vanderbilt, 1992a, 1992b).

The Jasper series uses brief vignettes to present a complex problem to be solved. The episodes use real-life drama to present a "macro context" for students to engage in problem solving. The purpose of the macro context is to anchor instruction, and situate cognition, in a context that is perceived as real and meaningful (Choi & Hannafin, 1995; Eylon & Linn, 1988). The video presents the problem context or goal, such as how to transport a wounded eagle from a remote site as quickly as possible under a number of situational constraints. All information necessary to solve the problem is embedded in the video, which students can play repeatedly to search for, and extract, relevant information. However, students are not prompted in explicit ways to the embedded information, nor are they told how to solve the problem. Instead, they must generate their own tentative solutions, test them, and revise their approach and theory accordingly (see 23.5.1).

In addition, analogs and extensions are available to challenge students to transfer their problem-solving skills to other contexts and to make flexible their knowledge representations. Analog problems change various parameters of the original video episode, such as the wind conditions on the day of the eagle's rescue. Extension problems challenge students to integrate their knowledge of the problem in the video to other curriculum areas, such as Lindbergh's flight across the Atlantic.

Students using the Jasper Series demonstrated significant gains in storywriting, vocabulary usage, and acquisition of relevant subject matter. In addition, they demonstrated better transfer of complex problem solving when provided with the anchored instruction. Those given the anchored instruction scored equally well on standardized achievement tests, despite the fact that the Jasper series was not designed to promote the kind of learning that these tests typically measure (Cognition and Technology Group at Vanderbilt, 1993, 1994).

12.3.2.3. The Voyage of the Mimi.

A similar use of video to anchor, or situate, learning is found in *The Voyage of the Mimi,* a multimedia curriculum package developed at the Bank Street College of Education. Mimi integrates print, video, and computer materials in learning about science and mathematics. Video is used to present a realistic, fictional account of the adventures of the crew of the Mimi, a ship hired by a team of scientists to study humpback whales (additional Mimi voyages have also been produced using contexts such as Mayan archaeology). This context is used throughout the Mimi curriculum to teach about problem solving in mathematics and science. The Mimi video shows scientists at work using mathematics and science as vital tools for understanding and helping whales. The video is likewise used to invite the viewer to become involved in the same knowledge through the interactive computer materials.

The Mimi's computer materials provide students with a wide variety of interactive activities, such as simulations and games, that parallel the adventures of the Mimi's crew. The computer materials are organized around four modules: maps and navigation, ecosystems, whales and environments, and introduction to computing. The printed materials provide paper-and-pencil problems and activities for students to complete. The Mimi materials were developed to be sufficiently flexible to provide teachers with multiple levels of entry to the materials in their classrooms (Martin, 1987). Teachers can select to use some or all of the materials to augment or replace an existing curriculum. The materials and activities support a wide range of learning outcomes and can be used individually or in cooperative groups.

12.3.2.4. Citizen Kane. *Citizen Kane* is a multimedia learning system adapted by Rand Spiro and his colleagues from Orson Wells's classic movie of the same title. It was an effort to create an environment within which understanding of complex concepts could be accomplished flexibly. Cognitive flexibility theory (see 23.4.1.3) addresses the problem of learning simple versus complex knowledge by having students use interactive multimedia (i.e., computer-controlled videodisc using hypertext principles) to reveal multifaceted issues (Spiro & Jehng, 1990). Cognitive flexibility theory describes the knowledge structures that learners need to interpret and analyze complex and novel situations. Certain domains, such as literary criticism, appear to demand cognitively flexible learners. The first half of *Citizen Kane* introduces the basic characters and plot. The final half of the original movie was edited to allow various scenes to be juxtaposed. These scenes were theme related and provided students a model and environment with which to manipulate and understand the complex nature of the characters and the movie.

12.3.3 Reflections on Emerging Learning Systems

Contemporary applications of technologies have shifted the teaching-learning paradigm dramatically. There has been unprecedented attention to the student's role in the instructional process. Indeed, even the term *instruction* is considered a pejorative to some in describing emerging learning systems. Whereas designers have traditionally focused on what subject matter to teach and how best to teach it (e.g., presentation and sequencing strategies), emerging learning systems place greater responsibility on the learner. As a result, many long-standing notions about teaching, learning, and design have changed.

The role of the computer has changed from a transmitter of knowledge to a tool that aids in the construction of knowledge (see, for example, Forman & Pufall, 1988). Motivational considerations have also shifted, though not always for the better. Some designers emphasize high-interest activities in order to arouse students, often to the detriment of the learning activity (see, for example, Coleman, Koballa & Crawley, 1992).

The shift away from a subject-matter focus and conventional design wisdom has not been without debate and detractors. Diverse interpretations and views exist as to what such transitions mean to instructional technology (see, for example, Duffy & Jonassen, 1992; Kember & Murphy, 1990; Perkins, 1992). While R&D has thrived, there has been comparatively little impact in the "real world." School curriculum is still largely focused on basic skills and formal subject-matter information [see Raghavan & Glaser (1995) for an interesting alternative]. Many still feel that the computer's role is to support, or even duplicate, accepted instructional practices. To many, increased focus on learning processes over outcomes is seen as inappropriate and ill advised. However, recent examples, such as CSILE and Jasper, provide well-rooted, empirically grounded systems and clearer distinctions and benefits between the use of technology to promote learning of fixed knowledge versus learner empowerment. Unfortunately, strongly rooted efforts remain the exception, not the rule.

The learning systems we presented depart from traditional educational technology–instructional design applications in three major ways. First , they represent a shift away from traditional notions of learning from media to more contemporary notions of learning with media. The tools and resources described here present a fundamentally different approach to teaching and learning. For example, many tools and resources support direct and active learner manipulation and organization of information in order promote deeper or different understandings. Second, the aforementioned systems are firmly rooted in contemporary research and theory on teaching and learning and focus on the construction of knowledge rather than the transmission of information. For example, microworlds not only assist students in solving problems but also help learners think about, experience, and manipulate problems in order to develop expertise, modify knowledge, or change personal beliefs (Resnick, 1991). Third, the functional features support, extend, and enhance the processes of teaching, learning, and thinking. Ill-structured domains, of which there are many, require tools that support varied perspectives, encourage the student to analyze from a variety of points of view, and avoid artificial simplification of complex concepts for the sake of expedience. Easier is not necessarily better.

This review not only illustrates the potential of emerging technologies to redefine many of our traditional notions about teaching, learning, and technology, but it punctuates the need for researchers to continue to develop, assess, and evaluate these new constructs and systems. Research is needed to understand better how to optimize the capabilities of learners *and* technologies, as well as to conceptualize how emerging technologies can be utilized to improve classrooms and schools.

12.4 INTO THE 21st CENTURY

Perhaps the greatest difference between contemporary and traditional technology research is the shift to thinking and learning processes versus outcomes. Research has evolved to emphasize learning *with* media and developing technology to support and optimize thinking, learning, and teaching processes. Several trends have emerged, though often their initial impetus derives from outside the educational technology–instructional design field.

Based on trends in research on teaching, learning, and educational technology, four categories of future research have been identified: new design methods, tools for thinking and learning, classroom applications, and expanded theory and research. Eleven research thrusts, embedded within the four categories, are likely to dominate educational technology research into the 21st century.

12.4.1 New Design Methods

12.4.1.1. Development of Alternative Design Strategies. Emerging technologies have increased dramatically the toolkit for designing learning environments. New technologies have enabled the creation and testing of design strategies heretofore considered unknown or impractical (Perkins & Unger, 1994; see Chapter 23). Alternatives have already been implemented based on the visions and models of researchers and theorists. For example, emerging technologies have helped to build rich scenarios for problem-based teaching and learning. Learning has been anchored within familiar, meaningful contexts, providing cognitive apprenticeships and authentic learning experiences (see for example, Cognition and Technology Group at Vanderbilt, 1992a, 1992b; Eylon & Linn, 1988). Efforts to discover strategies that unleash, versus harness, human and technological capabilities will continue to emerge.

12.4.1.2. Rapid Prototyping of Innovative Designs and Strategies. Although emerging technologies offer significant potential for improving teaching and learning, they also complicate design and development considerably. Often technology obscures the balance between what *should be* and *what could be* produced. Prototyping allows the rapid construction and testing of design concepts (Gayeski, 1991; Henson & Knezek, 1991). Unlike traditional design models, rapid prototyping does not require full specification prior to development. Instead, it focuses on the creation of working models of a limited scale, which are, themselves, modified through successive iterations. Rapid prototyping offers a flexible, nonlinear approach to design, making it especially well suited for developing products of unknown initial design (Tripp & Bichelmeyer, 1990). This provides an important alternative to traditional design processes because it reduces "blind" detailing and costs associated with planning while emphasizing design creativity and flexibility. Future research is needed to understand better the strengths, limitations, and cost effectiveness of such alternative design processes (see Jones, Li & Merrill, 1992).

12.4.1.3. Hybridization of Analog Technologies into Digital Formats. The transition from analog to digital formats is accompanied by problems of storage, image fidelity, access time, manipulability, and portability. With increased digital storage capacity, comprising billions of data points, the cognitive burden associated with navigating, retrieving, sorting, and thinking must be addressed. If carefully managed by designers and/or learners, powerful alternatives can be provided to support learning; if not

thoughtfully designed, however, the cognitive burdens can be substantial. Future research will emphasize not simply the development of new digital formats but how they can best be organized, configured, and accessed to support teaching, learning, and thinking.

12.4.2 Tools for Thinking and Learning

12.4.2.1. Tools and Resources That Aid in the Construction of Knowledge. Whereas tools and resources traditionally focused on mastery of external bodies of knowledge via on-line, direct instruction, contemporary notions focus on facilitating knowledge construction by relating new ideas to personal knowledge, beliefs, and experiences (see 23.4.1, 24.2, 24.3). Construction involves the creation, or revision, of how one thinks or reasons. Therefore, knowledge construction via tools and resources is not simply additive in nature but also allows the learner to alter the manner in which knowledge is represented and manipulated (see, for example, Derry & Lajoie, 1993; Jonassen, 1996; Scardamalia et al., 1989; White & Fredericksen, 1987, as cited in Striley, 1988). Emerging computer technologies have the capacity to augment needed intellectual endeavors as well as supplant unnecessary cognitive resources previously required. Future research will shed light on the varied ways this can be accomplished.

12.4.3 Classroom Applications

12.4.3.1. Innovative Classrooms and Reinvented Schools. Emerging technologies have recently spawned the creation of powerful incubators for innovative classrooms and reinvented schools. While emerging technologies have played important roles in these change processes, researchers need to become immersed in mediating issues, such as research on effective schools, school change, and the adoption and diffusion of innovation. The path to innovative, reinvented schools is not simply one of designing an idealized technology-enhanced learning environment, but one of understanding the history and culture of formal schooling. Future research should continue to emphasize not only how emerging technologies can support learning but also how to develop both idealistic *and* realistic visions given the social and political realities of schools, students, and communities.

12.4.3.2. Optimization of Both Learner and Technological Capabilities. In order to optimize technological capabilities, we need to understand better what technologies do best: process, present, store, and retrieve information and images on demand. These capabilities can be managed to engage students in thinking and learning while concurrently supporting specific teaching strategies. Optimization of human capabilities, however, where individuals are empowered to reflect deeply about meaning problems, is also critical. Students can solve problems within authentic contexts, manipulate information in real, compressed, or slowed time, and engage in activities designed to promote critical thinking (see 23.4).

12.4.4 Theory and Research

12.4.4.1. Integrated Views of Teaching, Learning, and Technologies. Traditional instructional technology research has focused on media issues such as hardware and software design, automation of instructional practices, learner control, and so forth. Often these issues have been studied in isolation from the contexts within which teaching and learning occur. Integrated approaches help researchers identify and understand the role of context in relating findings to educational practice. Future research will continue to integrate media issues within the diverse contexts of teaching and learning, and focus on alternative strategies for conceptualizing, organizing, and managing learning processes. This approach is important not only because it addresses pressing educational needs but also because it bridges gaps in everyday practice. Research will emphasize the complexity of learning in context rather than the simplicity of decontextualized learning.

12.4.4.2. Clarification of Relationships Among Teaching, Learning, and Technology. Often research has examined teaching, learning, or technology as discrete, separate elements. It has become increasingly important to clarify the interdependent nature of these elements. Research on teaching, learning, and technological processes will help researchers to understand better *how, when, why, and for what purposes* elements should be combined. It will also help develop rationales and beliefs for designing and developing learning systems. The outcomes of this research should produce better ways for teachers to teach, students to learn, and technologies to support the processes of teaching, learning, and thinking.

12.4.4.3. Redefinition of Research Problems and Assessment Methods. New designs require new assessment methods. Emerging technologies offer a wide range of capabilities for designing, as well as assessing, process outcomes (Clark, 1994; see 23.4.6). Yet, for the most part, these capabilities have been underutilized, and the methods for assessing impact have gone undeveloped. Emerging technologies have the capability to not only address existing questions but also to redefine the questions themselves. As implementations raise new, often novel questions and issues, research methods will need to evolve accordingly. Ideally, as we garner a greater sense of power as researchers, we will better shape the future of such applications.

12.4.4.4. The Study of Expertise. The study of expertise is concerned with how individuals acquire understanding and insight and become increasingly self-sufficient. In effect, it is the developmental process through which novices become more capable in a domain (see, for example, Spiro & Jehng, 1990; White, 1984). Its study focuses on the tasks confronting new learners in complex domains, the initial beliefs they derive, and how beliefs are modified through experience. Expertise reflects the products of experiences and the derivation of domain and strategic knowledge. The study of expertise presents unique opportunities. We need a better understanding of how individuals become increasingly capable and how technologies can provide experiences that are representative of varied phases in the expertise continuum.

12.4.4.5. Evolution of New, Integrated Theories. As the instructional technology knowledge base builds, researchers need to connect the research and theory from allied disciplines. This will require IT researchers to be more closely aligned with disciplines such as mathematics and science education, teacher preparation, psychology, computer science, and so forth. This linkage will provides a vehicle for IT researchers to understand and benefit from others research while also building IT theory, knowledge, and expertise.

12.5 SUMMARY AND CONCLUSIONS

As technologies have become more sophisticated, research on teaching, learning, and technology has become more complex. Recent interests have shifted to understanding how the processes of teaching, learning, and thinking are influenced by technologies and how these elements combine to form contexts for learning. As interests have shifted, many traditional notions regarding design and instruction have also changed; many have been described in this chapter. This shift from *learning from media* to *learning with media* has been welcome in emerging technology research and will only strengthen into the 21st century.

REFERENCES

Alessi, S.M. (1988). Fidelity in the design of instructional simulations. *Journal of Computer-Based Instruction 15* (2), 40–7.

Allen, B.S., Lipson, J.I. & Fisher, K.M. (1989). EPOSODE: enhanced procedural orchestration through student observation and detection of errors. *Machine-Mediated Learning 3*, 147–67.

Anand, P.G. & Ross, S.M. (1987). Using computer-assisted instruction to personalize arithmetic materials for elementary school children. *Journal of Educational Psychology 79*, 72–8.

Aspillaga, M. (1991). Screen design: location of information and its affect on learning. *Journal of Computer-Based Instruction 18* (3), 89–92.

Atkins, M. (1993). Theories of learning and multimedia applications: an overview. *Research Papers in Education 8* (2), 251–71.

Atkins, M. & Blissett, G. (1992). Interactive video and cognitive problem-solving skills. *Educational Technology 32* (1), 44–50.

Baker-Albaugh, P. (1993). Definitions of interactive learning: what we see is not what we get. *Journal of Instruction Delivery Systems 7* (3), 36–9.

Bangert-Drowns, R.L., Kulik, J.A. & Kulik, C-L. (1985). Effectiveness of computer-based education in secondary schools. *Journal of Computer-Based Instruction 12* (3), 59–68.

Bangert-Drowns, R.L., Kulik, C-L., Kulik, J.A. & Morgan, M. (1991). The instructional effect of feedback in test-like events. *Review of Educational Research 61,* 213–38.

Becker, H.J. (1985). Men and women as computer-using teachers. *Sex Roles 13,* 137–48.

Benshoof, L.A. & Hooper, S. (1993). The effects of single- and multiple-window presentation on achievement during computer-based instruction. *Journal of Computer-Based Instruction 20,* 113–7.

Billingsly, P.A. (1988). Taking panes: issues in the design of windowing systems. *In* M. Helender, ed. *Handbook of Human-Computer Interaction,* 413–36. North-Holland: Elsevier.

Bliss, J. (1994). From mental models to modelling. *In* H. Mellar, J. Bliss, R. Boohan, J. Ogborn & C. Tompsett, eds. *Learning with artificial worlds: computer based modelling in the curriculum,* 27–32. London: Falmer.

Bliss, J. & Ogborn, J. (1989). Tools for exploratory learning. *Journal of Computer-Assisted Learning 5,* 37–50.

Bly, S.A. & Rosenberg, J.K. (1986). A comparison of tiled and overlapping windows. *Proceedings of the Human Factors in Computing Systems Conference,* 101–06. New York: Association for Computing Machinery.

Bork, A. (1985). *Children, computers, and the future of education.* Irvine, CA: Educational Technology Center, University of California, Irvine.

— (1986). Let's test the power of interactive technology. *Educational Leadership 43* (6), 36–37.

Boyd, G. & Mitchell, P. (1992). How can intelligent CAL better adapt to learners? *Computers and Education 18,* 23–28.

Brasell, H. (1987). The effect of real-time laboratory graphing on learning graphic representations of distance and velocity. *Journal of Research in Science Teaching 24,* 385–95.

Breuer, K. & Kummer, R. (1990). Cognitive effects of process learning with computer-based instruction. *Computers in Human Behavior 6,* 69–81.

Brown, J.S., Collins, A. & Duguid, P. (1989). Situated cognition and the culture of learning. *Educational Researcher 18* (1), 32–42.

Bruner, J.S. (1961). The act of discovery. *Harvard Educational Review 31* (1), 21–32.

— (1985). Models of the learner. *Educational Researcher 14* (6), 5–8.

— (1986). *Actual minds, possible worlds.* Cambridge, MA: Harvard University Press.

Burns, P. (1981). A quantitative synthesis of research findings relative to the pedagogical effectiveness of computer-assisted instruction in elementary and secondary schools. *Dissertation Abstracts International 42,* 2946A.

Chiou, G. (1992). Situated learning, metaphors, and computer-based learning environments. *Educational Technology 32* (8), 7–11.

Choi, J. & Hannafin, M.J. (1995). Situated cognition and learning environments: roles, structures, and implications for design. *Educational Technology Research and Development 43* (2), 53–69.

Chung, J. & Reigeluth, C. (1992). Instructional prescriptions for learner control. *Educational Technology 32* (10), 14–20.

Clancy, W.J. (1986). From GUIDON to NEOMYCIN and HERACLES in twenty short lessons: ONR final report, 1979-1985. *AI Magazine 7* (3), 40–60.

Clark, R.E. (1983). Reconsidering research on learning from media. *Review of Educational Research 53* (4), 445–59.

— (1994). *Assessment of distance learning technology.* Hillsdale, NJ: Erlbaum.

— (1985). Evidence for confounding in educational computing research. *Journal of Educational Computing Research 1* (2), 137–48.

— & Voogel, A. (1985). Transfer of training principles for instructional design. *Educational Communications and Technology Journal 33,* 113–23.

Clements, D. (1985). Research on LOGO in education: is the turtle slow but steady, or not even in the race? *Computers in the Schools 2* (2/3), 55–72.

— & Gullo, D.F. (1984). Effects of computer programming on young children's cognition. *Journal of Educational Psychology 76,* 1051–58.

Cognition and Technology Group at Vanderbilt (1991). Technology and the design of generative learning environments. *Educational Technology 31* (5), 34–40.

— (1992a). The Jasper experiment: an exploration of issues in learning and instructional design. *Educational Technology Research & Development 40* (1), 65–80.

— (1992b). An anchored instruction approach to cognitive skills acquisition and intelligent tutoring. *In* J.W.R. & V. Shute, eds. *Cognitive approaches to automated instruction,* 135–70. Hillsdale, NJ: Album.

— (1993). Anchored instruction and situated cognition revisited. *Educational Technology* 52–70.

— (1994). From visual word problems to learning communities: changing conceptions of cognitive research. *In* K. McGilly, ed. *Classroom lessons: integrating cognitive theory and classroom practice.* Cambridge, MA: MIT Press/Bradford.

Coleman, D.C., Koballa, T.R. & Crawley, F.E. (1992). TLTG interactive videodisc physical science program: interest results of the 1988–1989 field test. *Journal of Educational Multimedia and Hypermedia 1* (2), 223–34.

Collins, A. (1993). *Design issues for learning environments.* New York: Center for Technology in Education (ERIC Document ED 357 733).

— (1994). Goal-based scenarios and the problem of situated learning: a commentary on Andersen Consulting's design of goal-based scenarios. *Educational Technology 34* (9), 30–2.

Dalton, D. & Hannafin, M. (1987). Effects of knowledge-versus context-based design strategies on information and application learning from interactive video. *Journal of Computer-Based Instruction 14,* 138–41.

Delclos, V. & Harrington, C. (1991). Effects of strategy monitoring and proactive instruction on children's problem-solving performance. *Journal of Educational Psychology 83,* 35–42.

Derry, S. & Lojoie, S. (1993). A middle camp for (un)intelligent computing: an introduction. *In* S. Lajoie & S. Derry, eds. *Computers as cognitive tools.* Hillsdale, NJ: Erlbaum.

diSessa, A. (1982). Unlearning Aristotelian physics: a study of knowledge-based learning. *Cognitive Science 6* (1), 37–75.

diSessa, A.A. (1988). Knowledge in pieces. *In* G. Forman & P. Pufall, eds. *Constructivism in the computer age,* 49–70. Hillsdale, NJ: Erlbaum.

— (1989). *Computational media as a foundation for new learning cultures* Technical Report-G5: University of California, Berkeley.

— (1993). Toward an epistemology of physics. *Cognition and Instruction 10* (2 & 3), 105-225.

Duffy, T.M. & Jonassen, D.H., eds. (1992). *Constructivism and the technology of instruction: a conversation.* Hillsdale, NJ: Erlbaum.

Dunston, P.J. (1992). A critique of graphic organizer research. *Reading Research and Instruction 31* (2), 57–65.

Dwyer, F. & Lamberski, R. (1982-83). A review of the research on the effects of the use of color in the teaching-learning process. *International Journal of Instructional Media 10,* 303–28.

Edwards, D. & Hardman, L. (1989). "Lost in hyperspace": cognitive mapping and navigation in a hypertext environment, 105–25. *In* R. McAleese, ed. *Hypertext: theory into practice.* London: BSP.

Edwards, J., Norton, S., Taylor, S., Weiss, M. & Dusseldorp, R. (1975). How effective is CAI? A review of the research. *Educational Leadership 33,* 147–53.

Eylon, B. & Linn, M. (1988). Learning and instruction: an examination of four research perspectives in science education. *Review of Educational Research 58* (3), 251–301.

Floyd, S. (1992). Thinking interactively. *In* S. Floyd & B. Floyd, eds. *Handbook of interactive video.* White Plains, NY: Knowledge Industries.

Forman, G. & Pufall, P., eds. (1988). *Constructivism in the computer age.* Hillsdale, NJ: Erlbaum.

Fosnot, C.T. (1989). *Enquiring teachers, enquiring learners: a constructivist approach for teaching.* New York: Teacher's College Press.

Fowler, R.C. (1994, Apr.). *Piagetian versus Vygotskian perspectives on development and education.* Paper presented at the annual meeting of the American Educational Research Association, New Orleans, LA.

Freedman, K. (1989). Microcomputers and the dynamics of image making and social life in three art classrooms. *Journal of Research on Computing in Education 21,* 290–98.

Gall, J. & Hannafin, M.J. (1994). A framework for the study of hypertext. *Instructional Science 22,* 207–32.

Gavora, M. & Hannafin, M.J. (1995). Perspectives in the design of human-computer interactions: issues and implications. *Instructional Science 22,* 445–77.

Gayeski, D.M. (1991). Rapid prototyping: a new model for developing multimedia. *Multimedia Review,* Fall, 18–23.

Grabinger, R.S. (1993). Computer screen designs: viewer judgments. *Educational Technology Research and Development 41* (2), 35–73.

Hannafin, M.J. (1984). Guidelines for using locus of instructional control in the design of computer-assisted instruction. *Journal of Instructional Development 7* (3), 6–10.

— (1992). Emerging technologies, ISD, and learning environments: critical perspectives. *Educational Technology Research and Development 40* (1), 49–63.

— Hall, C., Land, S. & Hill, J. (1994). Learning in open-ended environments: assumptions, methods, and implications. *Educational Technology 34* (8), 48–55.

—, Hannafin, K.M. & Dalton, D.W. (1993). Feedback and emerging instructional technologies. *In* J. Dempsey & G. Sales, eds. *Feedback and interactive instruction,* 263–86. Englewood Cliffs, NJ: Educational Technology.

— & Hughes, C.W. (1986). A framework for incorporating orienting activities in computer-based interactive video. *Instructional Science 15,* 239–55.

— & Peck, K.L. (1988). *The design, development, and evaluation of instructional software.* New York: Macmillan.

Harel, I. (1990). Children as software designers: a constructionist approach for learning mathematics. *Journal of Mathematical Behavior 9* (1), 3–93.

— (1991). *Children designers: interdisciplinary constructions for learning and knowing mathematics in a computer-rich school.* Norwood, NJ: Ablex.

— & Papert, S. (1991). Software design as a learning environment. *In* I. Harel & S. Papert, eds. *Constructionism,* 41–84. Norwood, NJ: Ablex.

Harless, W. (1986). An interactive videodisk drama: the case of Frank Hall. *Journal of Computer-Based Instruction 13,* 113–16.

Hartley, S. (1978). Meta-analysis of the effects of individually paced instruction in mathematics. *Dissertation Abstracts International 38* (7-A), 4003.

Hawk, P., McLeod, N.P. & Jonassen, D.H. (1985). Graphic organizers in texts. *In* D.H. Jonassen, ed. *The technology of text: principles for structuring, designing, and displaying text,* Vol. 2, 158–85. Englewood Cliffs, NJ: Educational Technology.

Hawkins, J., Sheingold, K., Gearhart, M. & Berger, C. (1982). Microcomputers in schools: impact on the social life of elementary classrooms. *Journal of Applied Developmental Psychology 3,* 361–73.

Henson, K.L. & Knezek, G.A. (1991). The use of prototyping for educational software development. *Journal of Research on Computing in Education 24* (2), 230–39.

Ho, C., Savenye, W. & Haas, N. (1986). The effects of orienting objectives and review on learning from interactive video. *Journal of Computer-Based Instruction 13,* 126–29.

Hooper, S. (1992a). Cooperative learning and computer-based instruction. *Educational Technology Research and Development 40* (3), 21–38.

—(1992b). The effects of peer interaction on learning during computer-based mathematics instruction. *Journal of Educational Research 85,* 180–89.

— & Hannafin, M. (1991). Psychological perspectives on the design of emerging instructional technologies: a critical analysis. *Educational Psychologist 26,* 69–95.

— & Rieber, L.P. (1995). Teaching with technology. *In* A. Ornstein, ed. *Theory and practice of teaching,* 154–70. New York: Allyn & Bacon.

Horwitz, P. & Barowy, B. (1994). Designing and using open-ended software to promote conceptual change. *Journal of Science Education and Technology 3* (3), 161–85.

— & Feurzeig, W. (1994). Computer-aided inquiry in mathematics Education. *Journal of Computers in Mathematics and Science Teaching 13* (3), 265–301.

Hooper, S., Temiyakarn, C. & Williams, M.D. (1993). The effects of cooperative learning and learner control on high- and average-ability students. *Educational Technology Research and Development 41* (2), 5–18.

Jakobsdóttir, S., Krey, C.L. & Sales, G.S. (1994). Computer graphics: preferences by gender in grades 2, 4 and 6. *Journal of Educational Research 88,* 91–100.

Johnson, D.W. & Johnson, R.T. (1989). *Cooperation and competition: theory and research.* Edina, MN: Interaction.

Johnson, R.T., Johnson, D.W. & Stanne, M.B. (1985). Effects of cooperative, competitive, and individualistic goal structures on computer-assisted instruction. *Journal of Educational Psychology 77*, 668–77.

—, Johnson, D.W. & Stanne, M.B. (1986). Comparison of computer-assisted cooperative, competitive, and individualistic learning. *American Educational Research Journal 23*, 382–92.

Jonassen, D.H. (1996). *Computers in the classroom: mindtools for critical thinking.* Columbus, OH: Prentice Hall.

— (1991). Objectivism versus constructivism: do we need a new philosophical paradigm? *Educational Technology Research and Development 39* (3), 5–14.

— (1988). Integrating learning strategies into courseware to facilitate deeper processing. *In* D.H. Jonassen, ed. *Instructional designs for microcomputer courseware,* 151–81. Hillsdale, NJ: Erlbaum.

— (1989). *Hypertext/hypermedia.* Englewood Cliffs, NJ: Educational Technology.

Jones, M.K., Li, Z. & Merrill, M.D. (1992). Rapid prototyping in automated instructional design. *Educational Technology Research & Development 40* (4), 95–100.

Kafai, Y. (1994). *Minds in play.* Hillsdale, NJ: Erlbaum.

Keller, J. & Suzuki, K. (1988). Using the ARCS motivation model in courseware design. *In* D. Jonassen, ed. *Instructional designs for microcomputer courseware,* 401–34. Hillsdale, NJ: Erlbaum.

Kember, D. & Murphy, D. (1990). Alternative new directions for instructional design. *Educational Technology 30* (8), 42–47.

Kenny, R. (1993). *The effectiveness of instructional orienting activities in computer-based instruction.* Paper presented at the annual convention of the Association for Educational Communications and Technology, New Orleans, LA.

King, A. (1991). Effects of training in strategic questioning on children's problem-solving performance. *Journal of Educational Psychology 83*, 307–17.

Kinzie, M.B. (1990). Requirements and benefits of effective interactive instruction: learner control, self-regulation, and continuing motivation. *Educational Technology Research and Development 38* (1), 5–21.

— & Berdel, R.L. (1990). Design and use of hypermedia systems. *Educational Technology Research and Development 38* (3), 61–68.

— & Sullivan, H.J. (1989). Continuing motivation, learner control, and CAI. *Educational Technology Research and Development 37* (2), 5–14.

Koen, B.V. (1985). *Definition of the engineering method.* Washington, DC. American Society for Engineering Education.

Kohn, A. (1993). Choices for children: why and how to let students decide. *Phi Delta Kappan,* Sep., 9–20.

Kozma, R.B. (1987). The implications of cognitive psychology for computer-based learning tools. *Educational Technology,* Nov., 20–25.

— (1991a). The impact of computer-based tools and embedded prompts on writing process and products of novice and advanced college writers. *Cognition and Instruction 8* (1), 1–27.

— (1991b). Learning with media. *Review of Educational Research 61*, 179–211.

Krahn, C. & Blanchaer, M. (1986). Using an advance organizer to improve knowledge application by medical students in computer-based clinical simulations. *Journal of Computer-Based Instruction 13*, 71–4.

Kulhavy, R.W. & Stock, W.A. (1989). Control of feedback in computer-assisted instruction. *Educational Technology Research and Development 39* (4), 27–32.

Kulik, J.A. & Kulik, C-L. (1987). Review of recent research literature on computer-based instruction. *Contemporary Educational Psychology 12*, 222–30.

Kulik, C-L. & Kulik, J.A. (1991). Effectiveness of computer-based instruction: an updated analysis. *Computers and Human Behavior 7*, 75–94.

Kulik, C-L. & Kulik, J.A. (1986). Effectiveness of computer-based education in colleges. *AEDS Journal,* 81–108.

— & Kulik, J.A. & Schwalb, B. J. (1986). Effectiveness of computer-based adult education: a meta-analysis. *Journal of Educational Computing Research 2* (2), 235–52.

Kulik, J.A., Kulik, C-L. & Bangert-Drowns, R. (1985a). The importance of outcome studies: a reply to Clark. *Journal of Educational Computing Research 1*, 381–88.

—, Kulik, C-L. & Bangert-Drowns, R. (1985b). Effectiveness of computer-based education on elementary pupils. *Computers in Human Behavior 1*, 59–74.

—, — & Cohen, P. (1980). Effectiveness of computer-based college teaching: a meta-analysis of findings. *Review of Educational Research 50*, 525–44.

Kynigos, C. (1993). Children's inductive thinking during intrinsic and Euclidean geometrical activities in a computer programming environment. *Educational Studies in Mathematics 24* (2), 177–97.

Lambrecht, J.J. (1993). Applications software as cognitive enhancers. *Journal of Research on Computing in Education 25* (4), 506–20.

Lee, Y.B. & Lehman, J.D. (1993). Instructional cueing in hypermedia: a study with active and passive learners. *Journal of Educational Multimedia and Hypermedia 2* (1), 25–37.

Lehrer, R. & Littlefield, J. (1993). Relationships among cognitive components in Logo learning and transfer. *Journal of Educational Psychology 85* (2), 317–30.

Lepper, M.R. (1985). Microcomputers in education: motivational and social issues. *American Psychologist 40*, 1–18.

— & Gurtner, J. (1989). Children and computers: approaching the twenty-first century. *American Psychologist 44*, 170–78.

Leron, U. (1985). Logo today: vision and reality. *Computing Teacher,* Feb., 26–32.

Levin, H. & Meister, G. (1986). Is CAI cost-effective? *Phi Delta Kappan 67*, 745–49.

Lewis, E., Stern, J. & Linn, M. (1993). The effects of computer simulations on introductory thermodynamics understanding. *Educational Technology 33* (1), 45–58.

Litchfield, B. (1993). Feedback and certitude in interactive videodisc programs. *In* J. Dempsey & G. Sales, eds. *Interactive instruction and feedback,* 229–61. Englewood Cliffs, NJ: Educational Technology.

Lopez, C.L. & Sullivan, H.J. (1991). Effects of personalized math instruction for Hispanic students. *Contemporary Educational Psychology 16*, 95–100.

Malone, T.W. (1981). Toward a theory of intrinsically motivating instruction. *Cognitive Science 4*, 333–69.

— & Lepper, M.R. (1987). Making learning fun: a taxonomy of intrinsic motivations for learning. *In* R.E. Snow & M.J. Farr, eds. *Aptitude, learning, and instruction: cognitive and affec-*

tive process analysis, Vol. 3, 223–53. Hillsdale, NJ: Erlbaum.

Marsh, E.J. & Kumar, D.D. (1992). Hypermedia: a conceptual framework for science education and review of recent findings. *Journal of Educational Multimedia and Hypermedia 1* (1), 25–37.

Martin, L.M.W. (1987). Teachers' adoption of multimedia technologies for science and mathematics instruction. *In* R.D. Pea & K. Sheingold, eds. *Mirrors of minds: patterns of experience in educational computing,* 35–56. Norwood, NJ: Ablex.

Mayer, R.E. (1993). Problem-solving principles. *In* M. Fleming & W.H. Levie, eds. *Instructional message design: principles from the behavioral and cognitive sciences,* 2d ed., 253–82. Hillsdale, NJ: Educational Technology.

Mayer, R.E. & Anderson, R. (1992). The instructive animation: helping students build connections between words and pictures in multimedia learning. *Journal of Educational Psychology 84,* 444–52.

McNiff, K. (1982). Sex differences in children's art. *Journal of Education 164,* 271–89.

Mevarech, Z.R., Silber, O. & Fine, D. (1991). Learning with computers in small groups: cognitive and affective outcomes. *Journal of Educational Computing Research 7,* 233–43.

Miller, D.C. & Kulhavy, R.W. (1991). Personalizing sentences and text. *Contemporary Educational Psychology 16,* 287–92.

Mokros, J. & Tinker, R. (1987). The impact of microcomputer-based labs on children's ability to interpret graphs. *Journal of Research in Science Teaching 24* (4), 369–83.

Nelson, W. & Palumbo, D. (1992). Learning, instruction, and hypermedia. *Journal of Educational Multimedia and Hypermedia 1,* 287–99.

Niemeier, R., Blackwell, M. & Walberg, H. (1986). CAI can be doubly effective. *Phi Delta Kappan 67,* 750–1.

Niemiec, R. (1989). Comparing the cost-effectiveness of tutoring and computer-based instruction. *Journal of Educational Computing Research 5,* 395–407.

Paivio, A. (1979). *Imagery and verbal processes.* Hillsdale, NJ: Erlbaum.

Papert, S. (1981). Computer-based microworlds as incubators for powerful ideas. *In* R. Taylor, ed. *The computer in the school: tutor, tool, tutee,* 203–10. New York: Teacher's College Press.

— (1987). Computer criticism vs. technocentric thinking. *Educational Researcher 16* (1), 22–30.

— (1993). *The children's machine: rethinking school in the age of the computer.* New York: Basic Books.

Park, I. & Hannafin, M.J. (1993). Empirically-based guidelines for the design of interactive multimedia. *Educational Technology Research and Development 41* (3), 63–85.

Park, O. & Gittleman, S. (1992). Selective use of animation and feedback in computer-based instruction. *Educational Technology Research and Development 40* (4), 27–38.

Pea, R.D. (1987). The aims of software criticism: reply to Professor Papert. *Educational Researcher 16* (5), 4–8.

— (1992). Augmenting the discourse of learning with computer-based learning environments. *In* M.L.E. DeCorte & L. Verschaffel, eds. *Computer-based learning environments and problem solving,* 313–44. New York: Springer.

— & Kurland, D.M. (1984). *Logo programming and the development of planning skills* (Report No. 16). New York: Bank Street College.

— & Kurland, D.M. (1987). Cognitive technologies for writing. *Review of Research in Education 14,* 227–326.

Perkins, D.N. (1992). Technology meets constructivism: do they make a marriage? *Educational Technology 31* (5), 18–23.

— (1985). The fingertip effect: how information-processing technology shapes thinking. *Educational Researcher 14* (7), 11–17.

— & Salomon, G. (1989). Are cognitive skills context bound? *Educational Researcher 18* (1), 16–25.

— & Unger, C. (1994). A new look at representations for mathematics and science learning. *Instructional Science 22* (1), 1–37.

Piaget, J. (1952). *The origins of intelligence in children.* New York: Basic Books.

Pollock, J. & Sullivan, H. (1990). Practice mode and learner control in computer-based instruction. *Contemporary Educational Psychology 15,* 251–60.

Prawat, R.S. (1991). The value of ideas: the immersion approach to the development of thinking. *Educational Researcher 20* (2), 3–10.

— & Floden, R.E. (1994). Philosophical perspectives on constructivist views of learning. *Educational Psychologist 29* (1), 37–48.

Pridemore, D. & Klein, J. (1991). Control of feedback in computer-assisted instruction. *Educational Technology Research and Development 39* (4), 27–32.

Raghavan, K. & Glaser, R. (1995). Model-based analysis and reasoning in science: the MARS curriculum. *Science Education 79* (1), 37–61.

Reader, W. & Hammond, N. (1994). Computer-based tools to support learning from hypertext: concept mapping tools and beyond. *Computers and Education 22* (1), 99–106.

Reeves, T.C. (1993). Pseudoscience in computer-based instruction: the case of learner control research. *Journal of Computer-Based Instruction 30* (2), 39–46.

Repman, J. (1993). Collaborative, computer-based learning: cognitive and affective outcomes. *Journal of Educational Computing Research 9,* 149–63.

Repman, J., Rooze, G. & Weller, H. (1991). Interaction of learner cognitive style with components of hypermedia-based instruction. *HyperNEXUS: Journal of Hypermedia and Multimedia Studies 2* (1), 30–33.

Resnick, M. (1990). MultiLogo: a study of children and concurrent programming. *Interactive Learning Environments 1* (3), 153–70.

— (1991). Children and artificial life. *In* I. Harel & S. Papert, eds. *Constructionism,* 379–90. Norwood, NJ: Ablex.

— (1991). Overcoming the centralized mindset: towards an understanding of emergent phenomena. *In* I. Harel & S. Papert, eds. *Constructionism,* 204–14. Norwood, NJ: Ablex.

Rieber, L.P. (1990). Animation in computer-based instruction. *Educational Technology Research and Development 38* (1), 77–86.

— (1991). Animation, incidental learning, and continuing motivation. *Journal of Educational Psychology 83,* 318–28.

— (1992). Computer-based microworlds: a bridge between constructivism and direct instruction. *Educational Technology Research and Development 40* (1), 93–106.

— (1994). *Computers, graphics, and learning.* Madison, WI: Brown & Benchmark.

Roschelle, J. (1991, Apr.). *Microanalysis of qualitative physics:*

opening the black box. Paper presented at the annual meeting of the American Educational Research Association, Chicago, IL (ERIC Document ED338 490).

— & Greeno, J.G. (1987). *Mental models in expert physics reasoning.* Washington, DC: Office of Naval Research (ERIC Document 285 736).

Ross, S.M. & Anand, P.G. (1987). A computer-based strategy for personalizing verbal problems in teaching mathematics. *Educational Communications and Technology Journal 35,* 151–62.

— & Morrison, G.R. (1988). Adapting instruction to learner performance and background variables. *In* D. Jonassen, ed. *Instructional designs for microcomputer courseware,* 227–45. Hillsdale, NJ: Erlbaum.

Salomon, G. (1993). On the nature of pedagogic computer tools: the case of the writing partner. *In* S. Lajoie & S. Derry, eds. *Computers as cognitive tools.* Hillsdale, NJ: Erlbaum.

—, Globerson, T. & Guterman, E. (1989). The computer as zone of proximal development: internalizing reading-related metacognitions from a reading partner. *Journal of Educational Psychology 81* (4), 620–27.

— & Perkins, D.N. (1989). Rocky roads to transfer: rethinking mechanisms of a neglected phenomenon. *Educational Psychologist 24* (2), 113–42.

—, Perkins, D.N. & Globerson, T. (1991). Partners in cognition: extending human intelligence with intelligent technologies. *Educational Researcher 20* (3), 2–9.

Santiago, R. & Okey, J. (1992). The effects of advisement and locus of control on achievement in learner-controlled instruction. *Journal of Computer-Based Instruction 19,* 47–53.

Scardamalia, M. Bereiter, C., McLean, R.S., Swallow, J. & Woodruff, E. (1989). Computer-supported intentional learning environments. *Journal of Educational Computing Research 5* (1), 51–68.

Schwartz, G., Yerushalmy, M. & Wilson, B., eds. (1993). *The Geometric Supposer: what is it a case of?* Hillsdale, NJ: Erlbaum.

Schwier, R. (1992). *A taxonomy of interaction for instructional multimedia.* Paper presented at the Annual Conference of the Association for Media and Technology in Education in Canada.

Seymour, S.L., Sullivan, H.J., Story, N.O. & Mosley, M.L. (1987). Microcomputers and continuing motivation. *Educational Communications and Technology Journal 35* (1), 18–23.

Soloway, E., Lockhead, J. & Clement, J. (1982). Does computer programming enhance problem-solving ability? Some positive evidence on algebra word problems. *In* R. Seidel, R. Anderson & B. Hunter, eds. *Computer literacy,* 171–85. New York: Academic.

Spiro, R.J., Feltovich, P., Jacobson, M. & Coulson, R. (1991). Cognitive flexibility, constructivism, and hypertext: random access instruction for advanced knowledge acquisition in ill-structured domains. *Educational Technology 31* (5), 24–33.

— & Jehng, J. (1990). Cognitive flexibility and hypertext: theory and technology for the nonlinear and multidimensional traversal of complex subject matter. *In* D. Nix & R.J. Spiro, eds. *Cognition, education, and multimedia: exploring ideas in high technology,* 163–205. Hillsdale, NJ: Erlbaum.

Steed, M. (1992). Stella: a simulation construction kit: cognitive process and educational implications. *Journal of Computers in Mathematics and Science Teaching 11* (1), 39–52.

Steinberg, E.R. (1977). Review of student control of learning in computer-assisted instruction. *Journal of Computer-Based Instruction 3* (3), 84–90.

— (1989). Cognition and learner control: a literature review. *Journal of Computer-Based Instruction 16* (4), 117–21.

Striley, J. (1988). Physics for the rest of us. *Educational Researcher 17* (6), 7–10.

Strommen, E. & Lincoln, B. (1992). Constructivism, technology, and the future of classroom learning. *Education and Urban Society 24,* 466–76.

Tennyson, R. (1984). Application of artificial intelligence methods to computer-based instructional design: the Minnesota Adaptive Instructional System. *Journal of Instructional Development 7* (4), 17–22.

— & Christensen, D. (1988). MAIS: an intelligent learning system. *In* D. Jonassen, ed. *Instructional designs for microcomputer courseware,* 247–74. Hillsdale, NJ: Erlbaum.

Tobin, K.G., ed. (1993). *The practice of constructivism in science education.* Washington, DC: AAAS.

— & Dawson, G. (1992). Constraints to curriculum reform: teachers and the myths of schooling. *Educational Technology Research and Development 40* (1), 81–92.

Tripp, S.D. (1992). A skills matrix and its implications. *Performance and Instruction 31* (6), 28–31.

— & Bichelmeyer, B. (1990). Rapid prototyping: an alternative instructional design strategy. *Educational Technology Research & Development 38* (1), 31–44.

Visonhaler, J. & Bass, R. (1972). A summary of ten major studies in CAI drill and practice. *Educational Technology 12,* 29–32.

Vygotsky, L.S. (1978). *Mind in society: the development of higher mental processes.* Cambridge, MA: Harvard University Press.

Wetzel, C.D. (1993). Generative aspects of the computer-based educational software system (CBESS). *Instructional Science 21,* 269–93.

White, B. (1984). Designing computer games to help physics students understand Newton's laws of motion. *Cognition and Instruction 1* (1), 69–108.

— (1992). A microworld-based approach to science education. *In* E. Scanlon & P. O'Shea, eds. *New directions in educational technology,* 227–42. New York: Springer.

— (1993). ThinkerTools: causal models, conceptual change, and science education. *Cognition and Instruction 10* (1), 1–100.

— & Frederiksen, J.R. (1987). *Causal model progressions as foundation for intelligent learning environments* (Technical Report No. 6686). Cambridge, MA: Bolt, Beranek & Newman).

Wittrock, M.C. (1990). Generative processes of comprehension. *Educational Psychologist 24,* 345–76.

— (1974). Learning as a generative process. *Educational Psychologist 11,* 87–95.

— (1978). The cognitive movement in instruction. *Educational Psychologist 13,* 15–29.

Woodward, J. & Howard, L. (1994). The misconceptions of youth: errors and their mathematical meaning. *Exceptional Children 61* (2), 126–36.

13. DISTANCE EDUCATION

Marina Stock McIsaac
ARIZONA STATE UNIVERSITY

Charlotte Nirmalani Gunawardena
UNIVERSITY OF NEW MEXICO

13.1 INTRODUCTION*

Distance education, structured learning in which the student and instructor are separated by time and place, is currently the fastest growing form of domestic and international education. What was once considered a special form of education using nontraditional delivery systems is now becoming an important concept in mainstream education.

Due to the rapid development of technology, courses using a variety of media are being delivered to students in various locations in an effort to serve the educational needs of growing populations. In many cases, developments in technology allow distance education programs to provide specialized courses to students in remote geographic areas with increasing interactivity between student and teacher. Although the ways in which distance education is implemented differ markedly from country to country, most distance learning programs rely on technologies that are either already in place or are being considered for their cost effectiveness. Such programs are particularly beneficial for the many people who are not financially, physically, or geographically able to obtain traditional education.

Distance education has experienced dramatic growth both nationally and internationally since the early 1980s. It has evolved from early correspondence education using primarily print-based materials into a worldwide movement using various technologies. The goals of distance education, as an alternative to traditional education, have been to offer degree-granting programs, to battle illiteracy in developing countries, to provide training opportunities for economic growth, and to offer curriculum enrichment in nontraditional educational settings. A variety of technologies have been used as delivery systems to facilitate this learning at a distance.

In order to understand how research and research issues have developed in distance education, it is necessary to understand the context of the field. Distance education relies heavily on technologies of delivery. Print materials (see Chapter 27), broadcast radio (see Chapter 28, 16.1), broadcast television (see 11.7), computer conferencing (see Chapter 13), e-mail, interactive video, satellite tele-communications, and multimedia computer technology (see 24.6) are all used to promote student-teacher interaction and provide necessary feedback to the learner at a distance. Because technologies as delivery systems have been so crucial to the growth of distance education, research has reflected rather than driven practice. Research in distance education has focused on media comparison studies (see 39.5.4), descriptive studies (see Chapter 41), and evaluation reports. Researchers have examined those issues that have been of particular interest to administrators of distance education programs, such as, student attrition rates, the design of instructional materials for large-scale distribution, the appropriateness of certain technologies for delivery of instruction, and the cost effectiveness of programs.

However, recent developments in interactive multimedia technologies that promise to facilitate "individualized" and "collaborative" learning (see Chapter 35) are blurring the distinctions between distance and traditional education. These technologies also have the capability of creating such new environments for learning as "virtual communities." Students in traditional settings are being given entire courses on CD-ROM multimedia disks through which they progress at their own pace, interacting with the instructor and other students on electronic mail or face-to-face according to their needs (Technology Based Learning, 1994). Through international collaboration, students around the world participate in cooperative learning activities, sharing information through the use of computer networks (Riel, 1993). In such cases, global classrooms may have participants from various countries interacting with each other at a distance. Many mediated educational activities allow students to participate in collaborative, authentic, situated learning activities (Brown & Palincsar, 1989; Brown, Collins & Duguid, 1989). In fact, the explosion of information technologies has brought learners together by erasing the boundaries of time and place for both site-based and distance learners.

*The authors would like to acknowledge the contributions of Rosalie Wells, John Barnard, and Angie Parker.

Research in distance education reflects the rapid technological changes in this field. Although early research was centered around media comparison studies (see 39.5.4), educators have recently become more interested in examining how the attributes of different media promote the construction of knowledge (Salomon, Perkins & Globerson, 1991). It is within the theoretical framework of knowledge construction and expert systems (Glaser, 1992) that some of the most promising research on mediated learning appears (Barrett, 1992; Harasim, 1993; Salomon, 1993).

This chapter traces the history of the distance education movement, discusses the definitions and theoretical principles that have marked the development of the field, and explores the research in this field which is inextricably tied to the technology of course delivery. A critical analysis of current research (1988–1993) in distance education was conducted for this chapter. Material for the analysis came from four primary data sources. The first source was an ERIC search, which resulted in over 900 entries. This largely North American review was supplemented with international studies located in the International Centre for Distance Learning (ICDL) database. The entries were then categorized according to content and source. Second, conference papers were reviewed which represented current, completed work in the field of distance education. Third, dissertations were obtained from universities which produced the majority of doctoral dissertations in Educational Technology doctoral programs. Finally, four journals were chosen for further examination because of their recurrent frequency in the ERIC listing. Those journals were *Open Learning, American Journal of Distance Education, Research in Distance Education,* and *Distance Education.*

13.2 HISTORY OF DISTANCE EDUCATION

Distance education is not a new concept. In the late 1800s, at the University of Chicago, the first major correspondence program in the United States was established in which the teacher and learner were at different locations. Before that time, particularly in preindustrial Europe, education had been available primarily to males in higher levels of society. The most effective form of instruction in those days was to bring students together in one place and one time to learn from one of the masters. That form of traditional educational remains the dominant model of learning today. The early efforts of educators like William Rainey Harper in 1890 to establish alternatives were laughed at. Correspondence study, which was designed to provide educational opportunities for those who were not among the elite and who could not afford full-time residence at an educational institution, was looked down on as inferior education. Many educators regarded correspondence courses as simply business operations. Correspondence education offended the elitist and extremely undemocratic educational system that characterized the early years in this country (Pittman, 1991). Indeed, many correspondence courses were viewed as simply poor excuses for the real thing. However, the need to provide equal access to educational opportunities has always been part of our democratic ideals, so correspondence study took a new turn.

As radio developed during the First World War and television in the 1950s (see 11.2.3), instruction outside of the traditional classroom had suddenly found new delivery systems. There are many examples of how early radio and television were used in schools to deliver instruction at a distance. Wisconsin's School of the Air was an early effort, in the 1920s, to affirm that the boundaries of the school were the boundaries of the state. More recently, audio and computer teleconferencing have influenced the delivery of instruction in public schools, higher education, the military, business, and industry. Following the establishment of the Open University in Britain in 1970, and Charles Wedemeyer's innovative uses of media in 1986 at the University of Wisconsin, correspondence study began to use developing technologies to provide more effective distance education.

13.2.1 Correspondence Study to Distance Education

In 1982, the International Council for Correspondence Education changed its name to the International Council for Distance Education to reflect the developments in the field. With the rapid growth of new technologies and the evolution of systems for delivering information, distance education, with its ideals of providing equality of access to education, became a reality. Today there are distance education courses offered by dozens of public and private organizations and institutions to school districts, universities, the military, and large corporations. Direct satellite broadcasts are produced by more than 20 of the country's major universities to provide over 500 courses in engineering delivered live by satellite as part of the National Technological University (NTU). In the corporate sector, more than $40 billion a year are spent by IBM, Kodak, and the Fortune 500 companies in distance education programs.

What, exactly, are the prospects and promises of distance education? Desmond Keegan (Keegan, 1980) identified six key elements of distance education:

- Separation of teacher and learner
- Influence of an educational organization
- Use of media to link teacher and learner
- Two-way exchange of communication
- Learners as individuals rather than grouped
- Educators as an industrialized form

Distance education has traditionally been defined as instruction through print or electronic communications media to persons engaged in planned learning in a place or time different from that of the instructor or instructors. The traditional definition of distance education is slowly being eroded as new technological developments challenge educators to reconceptualize the idea of schooling and lifelong learning. At the same time, interest in the unlimited possibilities of individualized distance learning is growing with the development of each new communication technology. Although educational technologists agree that it is the systematic design of instruction that should drive the development of distance learning, the rapid development of computer-related technologies has captured the interest of the public and has been responsible for much of the limelight in which distance educators currently find themselves. Although the United States has seen rapid growth in the use of technology for distance education, much of the pioneering work has been done abroad.

13.2.2 Open Learning in the U.K.

The establishment of the British Open University in the United Kingdom in 1969 marked the beginning of the use of technology to supplement print-based instruction through well-designed courses. Learning materials were delivered on a large scale to students in three programs: undergraduates, postgraduates, and associate students. Although course materials were primarily print based, they were supported by a variety of technologies. No formal educational qualifications have been required to be admitted to the British Open University. Courses are closely monitored and have been successfully delivered to over 100,000 students. As a direct result of its success, the Open University model has been adopted by many countries in both the developed and developing world (Keegan, 1986). Researchers in the United Kingdom continue to be leaders in identifying problems and proposing solutions for practitioners in the field (Harry, Keegan & Magnus, 1993). The International Centre for Distance Learning, at the British Open University, maintains the most complete holdings of literature in both research and practice of international distance learning. Research studies, evaluation reports, course modules, books, journal articles, and ephemeral material concerning distance education around the world are all available through quarterly accessions lists or on line.

13.2.3 Distance Education in the United States

The United States was slow to enter the distance education marketplace, and when it did, a form of distance education unique to its needs evolved. Not having the economic problems of some countries or the massive illiteracy problems of developing nations, the United States nevertheless had problems of economy of delivery. Teacher shortages in areas of science, math, and foreign language combined with state mandates to rural schools produced a climate, in the late 80s, conducive to the rapid growth of commercial courses such as those offered via satellite by the TI-IN network in Texas and at Oklahoma State University. In the United States, fewer than 10 states were promoting distance education in 1987. A year later, that number had grown to two-thirds of the states, and by 1989 virtually all states were involved in distance learning programs. Perhaps the most important political document describing the state of

distance education has been the report done for Congress by the Office of Technology Assessment in 1989 called *Linking for Learning* (Office of Technology Assessment, 1989). The report gives an overview of distance learning, the role of teachers, and reports of local, state, and federal projects. It describes the state of distance education programs throughout the United States in 1989 and highlights how technology was being used in the schools. Model state networks and telecommunication delivery systems are outlined with recommendations given for setting up local and wide-area networks to link schools. Some projects, such as the Panhandle Shared Video Network and the Iowa Educational Telecommunications Network, serve as examples of operating video networks that are both efficient and cost effective.

13.2.4 Distance Education as a Global Movement

In Europe and other Western countries, a global concern was beginning to emerge. In a recent report, the 12 members of the European Association of Distance Teaching Universities proposed a European Open University to begin in 1992. This is in direct response to the European Parliament, the Council of Europe, and the European Community (Bates, 1990). In this report, articles from authors in nine European countries describe the use of media and technology in higher education in Europe and reflect upon the need for providing unified educational access in the form of a European Open University to a culturally diverse population.

Telecommunication networks now circle the globe, linking people from many nations together in novel and exciting ways. As the borders of our global community continue to shrink, we search for new ways to improve communication by providing greater access to information on an international scale. Emerging communication technologies, and telecommunications in particular, provide highly cost-effective solutions to the problems of sharing information and promoting global understanding between people. In today's electronic age, it is predicted that the amount of information produced will increase exponentially every year. Since economic and political power is directly related to access to information, many educators like Takeshi Utsumi, president of GLOSAS (Global Systems Analysis and Simulation) have worked to develop models of the "Global University" and the "Global Lecture Hall" which provide resources allowing less-affluent countries to keep up with advances in global research and education (Utsumi, Rossman & Rosen, 1990).

In the developing world, since the 1950s, the population has doubled to over 5 billion people, most of whom want to be literate and want greater educational opportunities for themselves and their children. The majority of this expanding population is in Asia, where there are massive problems of poverty, illiteracy, and disease. In most developing countries, such as Bangladesh, distance education offers the promise of a system of information distribution through which new ideas, attitudes, and understanding might begin to ooze through the layers of the disadvantaged environments (Shah, 1989). Drawing upon the well-known model of the British Open University, countries such as Pakistan, India, and China have combined modern methods of teaching with emerging technologies in order to provide low-cost instruction for basic literacy and job training. Turkey has recently joined those nations involved in large-scale distance learning. Only 12 years old, their distance education program has enrolled almost 1 million students and is the sixth largest distance education program in the world (Demiray & McIsaac, 1993).

Because of the economies of size and distribution, both industrialized and developing countries have embarked on distance education programs. In the early 1980s, record numbers of students in developing countries have gained access to higher education through distance education programs (Rumble & Harry, 1982). In many cases, local experts are not available to develop original programs in the language and culture of the people. For this reason, the majority of educational programs are either used intact from the host country or are superficially translated with very few adaptations to the local culture. When this is done, the results are often unsuccessful. The cultural values of the program designer become dominant, desirable, and used as the standard. There are many examples of programs from North America, Australia, Great Britain, and Europe that were purchased but never used in Africa and Asia because the material was not relevant in those countries. Because the appropriate design of instructional material is a critical element in its effectiveness, the issue of "who designs what and for whom" is central to any discussion of the economic, political, and cultural dangers that face distance educators using information technologies (McIsaac, 1993). There have been a variety of efforts to identify theoretical foundations for the study of distance education. Thus far, there has been little agreement about which theoretical principles are common to the field and even less agreement on how to proceed in conducting programmatic research.

13.3 THEORY OF DISTANCE EDUCATION

The development of new technologies has promoted an astounding growth in distance education, both in the number of students enrolling and in the number of universities adding education at a distance to their curriculum (Garrison, 1990). While the application of modern technology may glamorize distance education, literature in the field reveals a conceptually fragmented framework lacking in both theoretical foundation and programmatic research. Without a strong base in research and theory, distance education has struggled for recognition by the traditional academic community. Distance education has been described by some (Garrison, 1990; Hayes, 1990) as no more than a hodgepodge of ideas and practices taken from traditional classroom settings and imposed on learners who just happen to be separated physi-

cally from an instructor. As distance education struggles to identify appropriate theoretical frameworks, implementation issues also become important. These issues involve the learner, the instructor, and the technology. Because of the very nature of distance education as learner-centered instruction, distance educators must move ahead to investigate how the learner, the instructor, and the technology collaborate to generate knowledge.

Traditionally, both theoretical constructs and research studies in distance education have been considered in the context of an educational enterprise that was entirely separate from the standard, classroom-based, classical instructional model. In part to justify, and in part to explain, the phenomenon, theoreticians like Holmberg, Keegan, and Rumble explored the underlying assumptions of what it is that makes distance education different from traditional education. With an early vision of what it meant to be a nontraditional learner, these pioneers in distance education defined the distance learner as one who is physically separated from the teacher (Rumble, 1986), has a planned and guided learning experience (Holmberg, 1986), and participates in a two-way structured form of distance education that is distinct from the traditional form of classroom instruction (Keegan, 1988). In order to justify the importance of this nontraditional kind of education, early theoretical approaches attempted to define the important and unique attributes of distance education.

Keegan (1986) identifies three historical approaches to the development of a theory of distance education. Theories of autonomy and independence from the 1960s and 1970s, argued by Wedemeyer (1977) and Moore (1973), reflect the essential component of the independence of the learner. Otto Peter's (1971) work on a theory of industrialization in the 1960s reflects the attempt to view the field of distance education as an industrialized form of teaching and learning. The third approach integrates theories of interaction and communication formulated by Bääth (1982, 1987), and Daniel and Marquis (1979). Using the postindustrial model, Keegan presents these three approaches to the study and development of the academic discipline of distance education. It is this concept of industrialized, open, nontraditional learning that, Keegan says, will change the practice of education.

Wedemeyer (1981) identifies essential elements of independent learning as greater student responsibility, widely available instruction, effective mix of media and methods, adaptation to individual differences, and a wide variety of start, stop, and learn times. Holmberg (1989) calls for foundations of theory construction around the concepts of independence, learning, and teaching:

> Meaningful learning, which anchors new learning matter in the cognitive structures, not rote learning, is the center of interest. Teaching is taken to mean facilitation of learning. Individualization of teaching and learning, encouragement of critical thinking, and far-reaching student autonomy are integrated with this view of learning and teaching (Holmberg, 1989, p. 161).

Holmberg summarizes his theoretical approach by stating that :

> Distance education is a concept that covers the learning-teaching activities in the cognitive and/or psycho-motor and affective domains of an individual learner and a supporting organization. It is characterized by non-contiguous communication and can be carried out anywhere and at any time, which makes it attractive to adults with professional and social commitments (Holmberg, 1989, p. 168).

Garrison and Shale (1987) include in their essential criteria for formulation of a distance education theory the elements of noncontiguous communication, two-way interactive communication, and the use of technology to mediate the necessary two-way communication.

13.3.1 Theoretical Constructs

Recently, a wider range of theoretical notions has provided a richer understanding of the learner at a distance. Four such concepts are transactional distance, interaction, learner control, and social presence.

13.3.1.1. Transactional Distance.   Moore's (1990) concept of "transactional distance" encompasses the distance that, he says, exists in all educational relationships. This distance is determined by the amount of dialogue that occurs between the learner and the instructor, and the amount of structure that exists in the design of the course. Greater transactional distance occurs when an educational program has more structure and less student-teacher dialogue, as might be found in some traditional distance education courses. Education offers a continuum of transactions from less distant, where there is greater interaction and less structure, to more distant, where there may be less interaction and more structure. This continuum blurs the distinctions between conventional and distance programs because of the variety of transactions that occur between teachers and learners in both settings. Thus distance is not determined by geography but by the relationship between dialogue and structure.

Saba and Shearer (Saba & Shearer, 1994) carry the concept of transactional distance a step farther by proposing a system dynamics model to examine the relationship between dialogue and structure in transactional distance. In their study, Saba and Shearer conclude that as learner control and dialogue increase, transactional distance decreases. It is not location that determines the effect of instruction but the amount of transaction between learner and instructor. This concept has implications for traditional classrooms as well as distant ones. The use of integrated telecommunication systems may permit a greater variety of transactions to occur, thus improving dialogue to minimize transactional distance.

13.3.1.2. Interaction.   A second theoretical construct of recent interest to distance educators, and one that has received much attention in the theoretical literature, is that of interaction. Moore (1989) discusses three types of interaction essential in distance education. Learner-instructor

interaction is that component of his model that provides motivation, feedback, and dialogue between the teacher and student. Learner-content interaction is the method by which students obtain intellectual information from the material. Learner-learner interaction is the exchange of information, ideas, and dialogue that occur between students about the course, whether this happens in a structured or nonstructured manner. The concept of interaction is fundamental to the effectiveness of distance education programs as well as traditional ones. Hillman, Hills, and Gunawardena (1994) have taken the idea of interaction a step farther and added a fourth component to the model learner-interface interaction. They note that the interaction between the learner and the technology that delivers instruction is a critical component of the model, which has been missing thus far in the literature. They propose a new paradigm that includes understanding the use of the interface in all transactions. Learners who do not have the basic skills required to use a communication medium spend inordinate amounts of time learning to interact with the technology and have less time to learn the lesson. For this reason, instructional designers must include learner-interface interactions that enable the learner to have successful interactions with the mediating technology.

13.3.1.3. Control.   A third theoretical concept receiving attention in the distance education literature is that of independence and learner control. Studies that examine locus of control (Altmann & Arambasich, 1982; Rotter, 1989) conclude that students who perceive that their academic success is a result of their own personal accomplishments have an internal locus of control and are more likely to persist in their education. Students with an external locus of control feel that their success, or lack of it, is due largely to events such as luck or fate outside their control. Thus, externals are more likely to become dropouts. Factors of control that influence dropout rate have been of concern to distance educators as they search for criteria to predict successful course completion. Baynton (1992) developed a model to examine the concept of control as it is defined by independence, competence, and support. She notes that control is more than independence. It requires striking a balance among three factors: a learner's independence (the opportunity to make choices), competence (ability and skill), and support (both human and material). Baynton's factor analysis confirms the significance of these three factors and suggests other factors that may affect the concept of control and which should be examined to portray accurately the complex interaction between teacher and learner in the distance learning setting.

13.3.1.4. Social Context.   Finally, the social context in which distance learning takes place is emerging as a significant area for research. Theorists are examining how the social environment affects motivation, attitudes, teaching, and learning. There is a widespread notion that technology is culturally neutral, and can be easily used in a variety of settings. However media, materials, and services are often inappropriately transferred without attention being paid to the social setting or to the local recipient culture (McIsaac,

1993). Technology-based learning activities are frequently used without attention to the impact on the local social environment. Computer-mediated communication attempts to reduce patterns of discrimination by providing equality of social interaction among participants who may be anonymous in terms of gender, race, and physical features. However, there is evidence that the social equality factor may not extend, for example, to participants who are not good writers but who must communicate primarily in a text-based format (Gunawardena, 1993). It is particularly important to examine social factors in distance learning environments where the communication process is mediated and where social climates are created that are very different from traditional settings. Feenberg and Bellman (1990) propose a social factor model to examine computer networking environments that create specialized electronic social environments for students and collaborators working in groups.

One social factor particularly significant to distance educators is social presence, the degree to which a person feels "socially present" in a mediated situation. The notion is that social presence is inherent in the medium itself, and technologies offer participants varying degrees of "social presence" (Short, Williams & Christie, 1976). Hackman and Walker (1990), studying learners in an interactive television class, found that cues given to students such as encouraging gestures, smiles, and praise were social factors that enhanced both students' satisfaction and their perceptions of learning. Constructs such as social presence, immediacy, and intimacy are social factors that deserve further inquiry.

13.3.2 Toward a Theoretical Foundation

Although there have been numerous attempts to formulate a theory base for the field, American distance education remains "chaotic and confused. There is no national policy, nor anything approaching a consensus among educators of the value, the methodology or even the concept of distance education" (Moore, 1993). Shale (1990) calls for theoreticians and practitioners to stop emphasizing points of difference between distance and traditional education, but instead to identify common educational problems. Distance education is, after all, simply education at a distance with common frameworks, common conceptual concerns, and similar research questions relating to the social process of teaching and learning. Many distance educators are beginning to call for a theoretic model based on constructivist epistemology (Jegede, 1991). Technological advances have already begun to blur the distinction between traditional and distance educational settings. Time and place qualifiers are no longer unique. The need to test assumptions and hypotheses about how and under what conditions individuals learn best leads to research questions about learning, teaching, course design, and the role of technology in the educational process. As traditional education integrates the use of interactive, multimedia technologies to enhance

individual learning, the role of the teacher changes from knowledge source to knowledge facilitator. As networks become available in schools and homes to encourage individuals to become their own knowledge navigators, the structure of education will change, and the need for separate theories for distance education will blend into the theoretical foundations for the mainstream of education.

More than 35% of the literature reviewed reported the need for developing a central, theoretical framework on which future distance education development can be based. While numerous journal articles and conference presentations discussed the lack of theoretical framework in the field, most of the work was descriptive rather than research oriented. However, several writers have contributed to theory formulation.

Verduin and Clark (1991) offer a rationale by suggesting that confusion over distance education terminology may be to blame. In response to this theoretical void, Gibson (1990) suggests borrowing a theory from existing disciplines. Miller (1989) concurs by suggesting that "it is important that the study of distance education be informed by work done in other disciplines" (p. 15). Boyd and Apps (1980) struggle with the idea of borrowing a theory, as they see the important issue being the development of a clearly defined structure, function, purpose, and goal for distance education. "We must ask ourselves what erroneous assumptions we may be accepting when we borrow from established disciplines to define distance education" (pp. 2–3). Furthermore, borrowing extensively from other fields in order to define and solve problems allows the field to define the borrowed field (Gibson, 1990) In an effort to define theoretically the field of distance education, the literature advances three strategies. Deshler and Hagen (1989) advocate a multidisciplinary and interdisciplinary approach resulting in a diversity of perspectives. They caution that anything short of this approach may "produce theory that suffers from a view that is narrow, incomplete, discipline-based and restricted . . . to a predominant view of reality" (p. 163).

A second approach is advocated by Hayes (1990), who supports the work of Knowles (1984) and Brookfield (1986). Hayes emphasizes that theoretical development relative to adult learning must be distinct from youth learning. While past experiences may occasionally interfere with an adult's openness to new learning experiences, the majority of literature views experience as a resource for new learning. Knowles (1984), for example, supports an andragogical, learner-focused foundation in his belief that "adults draw on previous experiences in order to test the validity of new information" (p. 44). A third strategy for theory development from an international perspective has been proposed by Sophason and Prescott (1988). They caution that certain lines of questioning are more appropriate in some countries than in others, thus the emanating theory "may have a particular slant" (p. 17). A comparative analysis strategy would undoubtedly be influenced by cultural bias and language barriers (Pratt, 1989). Pratt further indicates that understanding different culturally related beliefs about the nature of the individual and society may be critical in defining appropriate distance education theories. Pratt clarifies his belief through a description of how differences in societies' historical traditions and philosophies can contribute to differing orientations toward self-expression and social interactions within educational settings.

Although these three strategies for the advancement of a theoretical foundation for distance education are repeated in current literature, Ely (1992) foresees a road block to the theoretical progression. "What seems to be needed is an unclouded understanding of distance education. This includes the audience, setting, and delivery methodologies" (p. 43). Loesch and Foley (1988) concur and ask for further research in this area in their statement that only when a clear understanding of distance education becomes available can concise questions be developed that can lead to establishment of theory. Evans and Nation (1992) contribute some of the most thoughtful and insightful comments on theory building when they suggest that we examine broader social and historic contexts in our efforts to extend previously narrow views of theories in open and distance education. They urge us to move toward deconstruction of the instructional industrialism of distance education, and toward the construction of a critical approach that, combined with an integration of theories from the humanities and social sciences, can enrich the theory building in our field.

Although there has been no central theoretical framework to guide research in distance education, there have been a number of important studies that have examined the interactions of technologies with learning, course design, and instruction. Because of the heavy use of technology in distance education, it is appropriate to examine its role in this context.

13.4 DISTANCE LEARNING TECHNOLOGIES

Until the advent of telecommunications technologies, distance educators were hard pressed to provide for two-way, real-time interaction, or time-delayed interaction between students and the instructor or among peers. In the correspondence model of distance education, which emphasized learner independence, the main instructional medium was print, and it was usually delivered using the postal service. Interaction between the student and the instructor usually took the form of correspondence of self-assessment exercises that the student completed and sent to the instructor for feedback. Formal group work or collaborative learning was very rare in distance education, even though attempts have been made to facilitate group activities at local study centers. Also, traditionally, distance education courses were designed with a heavy emphasis on learner independence and were usually self-contained. With the development of synchronous (two-way, real-time interactive) technologies, such as audio teleconferencing, audio graphics conferencing, and videoconferencing, it is now possible to link learners and instructors who are geographically separated for real-time interaction. However, the type of interaction that takes place is usually on a one-to-one basis, between one learner

and another and between one learner and the instructor at one particular time. These technologies are not very suitable for promoting cooperative learning between groups of learners located at different sites. Also, the synchronous nature of these technologies may not be suitable or convenient for many distance learners.

The asynchronous (time delayed) feature of computer-mediated communications (CMC; see 14.2.3), on the other hand, offers an advantage in that the CMC class is open 24 hours a day, 7 days a week, to accommodate the time schedules of distance learners. Although CMC systems may be either synchronous (real time) or asynchronous (time delayed), it is asynchronous CMC, because of its time-independent feature, that is an important medium for facilitating cooperative group work among distance learners.

Current developments in digital communications and the convergence of telecommunications technologies, exemplified by international standards such as ISDN (Integrated Services Digital Network), make available audio, video, graphic, and data communication through an ordinary telephone line on a desktop workstation. Therefore, as we look at distance learning technologies today and look to the future, it is important to think in terms of integrated telecommunication systems rather than simply video vs. audio vs. data systems. More and more institutions that teach at a distance are moving toward multimedia systems integrating a combination of technologies both synchronous and asynchronous that meets learner needs. Therefore, while in the 1970s and 1980s many distance education institutions throughout the world used print as a major delivery medium, by the year 2000 many institutions will probably have adopted telecommunications-based systems for the delivery of distance education. This does not necessarily mean that print will no longer be used in distance education. It is more likely that print will be used as a supplementary medium in most telecommunications-based systems, and better ways of communicating information through print will be investigated and incorporated into the design of study guides and other print-based media.

In order to describe the technologies used in distance education, we have selected "The 4-Square Map of Groupware Options" that was developed by Johansen et al. (1991) which is based on recent research in groupware (see Fig. 13-1). This model seemed most suitable to our purpose, because we see distance education moving from highly individualized forms of instruction, as in correspondence education, to formats that encourage teaching students as a group and collaborative learning among peers. The "4-square map of groupware option" model is premised on two basic configurations that teams must cope with as they work: time and place. Teams or groups of people who work together on a common goal deal with their work in the same place at the same time as in face-to-face meetings, and sometimes they must work apart in different places and at different times, as in the use of asynchronous computer conferencing. They also need to handle two other variations: being in different places at the same time, as in the use of telephones for an audio teleconference, and at the

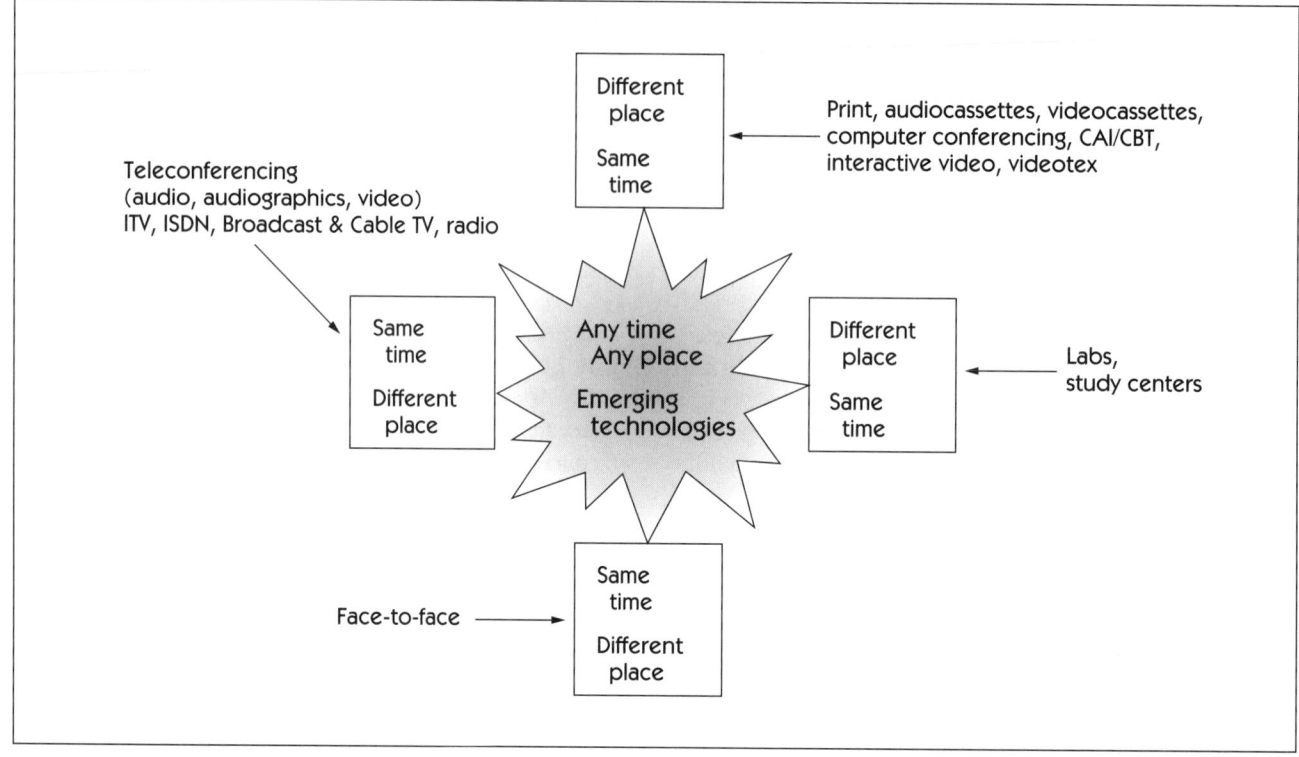

Figure 13-1.   The 4-square map of distance education technology options. (Adapted from R. Johansen et al., 1991, p. 16.)

same place at different times, as in workplaces, study centers, or laboratories. Based on these configurations, the 4-square model classifies four types of technologies that support the group process: (1) same time/same place, (2) different time/different place, (3) same time/different place, and (4) same place/different time. These four categories are used for describing technologies that currently support distance teaching and learning.

While we use the 4-square model to discuss the major distance education technologies currently being used, we feel that this model does not lend itself very well to discussing new and future developments in integrated telecommunications. Since these integrated systems incorporate many of the features that we classify separately in the 4-square model, we have decided to describe new and future developments in a separate section titled "Future Directions and Emerging Technologies" (p. 417).

13.4.1 Same Time/Same Place Instruction

Same time/same place group interaction is the most familiar format of face-to-face meetings. Certain objectives in distance education programs can only be met by meeting face-to-face. The British Open University, which teaches entirely at a distance, brings students on campus during the summer to participate in laboratory experiments. When course objectives require the careful demonstration, observation, practice, and feedback of such life-threatening procedures as a surgical procedure, it is important to organize face-to-face meetings. In a face-to-face setting,

accepted practices are modified only slightly to accommodate electronic media. Basic technologies that facilitate a face-to-face meeting involve an overhead projector, a flip chart, electronic blackboard, or a projection system that displays computer screens via a LCD monitor. At the more sophisticated end are desktop workstations for each group member which run on special software that helps the group to brainstorm, generate ideas, rank solutions, and vote. Also, a record of the group process can be produced at the conclusion of the groups' activities. IBM's Decision Conference Center in Bethesda, Maryland, employs such sophisticated groupware to facilitate group decision-making processes. However, innovative approaches are now being adopted to design laboratory work at a distance by using technologies—as in the dissection of a fetal pig experiment that was designed by the University of Maine using a combination of two-way interactive television—videotape, and group work at sites.

13.4.2 Same Time/Different Place Instruction

There are two kinds of same time/different place instruction: (1) a meeting through a telecommunications medium or teleconferencing during which participants who are separated by geographic distance can interact with each other simultaneously, and (2) the use of noninteractive media such as open broadcast television and radio to instruct a vast number of students at the same time without the ability of the students to call back and interact with the originators of the program.

Teleconferencing can be classified into four separate categories depending on the technologies that they use: audio teleconferencing, audiographics teleconferencing, video teleconferencing, and computer conferencing. There are two types of computer conferencing: synchronous computer conferencing, when two or more computers are linked at the same time so that participants can interact with each other, and asynchronous computer conferencing, when participants interact with each other at a time and place convenient to them. Asynchronous computer conferencing is described under different time/different place instruction.

The four major types of teleconferencing vary in the types of technologies, complexity of use, and cost. However, they have several features in common: All of them use a telecommunication channel to mediate the communication process, link individuals or groups of participants at multiple locations, and provide for live, two-way communication or interaction. One advantage of teleconferencing systems is that they can link a large number of people who are geographically separated. If satellite technology is used for the teleconference, there is no limit to the number of sites that can be linked through the combination of several communications satellites. In order to participate in a teleconference, participants usually have to assemble at a specific site in order to use the special equipment necessary for a group to participate in the conference. The only exceptions are (1) audio teleconferences that can link up any individual who has access to a telephone; (2) computer conferences that can link up individuals, their computers, and modems at home; or (3) direct broadcast satellites that can deliver information directly to participant's homes. However, if more than two people are present at a participating site then it is necessary for the participants to gather at a location equipped with teleconferencing equipment in order to participate in a teleconference. This may restrict access for some learners. In terms of control, participants will have control over the interaction that takes place in a teleconference only to the extent that the instructional design allows for it. However, if the teleconference is taped for later review, students will have more control in the use of the conference.

The unique advantage of teleconferences is that they provide for two-way interaction between the originators and the participants. Teleconferences need to be designed to optimize the interaction that takes place during the conference. Interaction needs to be thought of not only as interaction that occurs during the teleconference but pre- and postconference activities that allow groups to interact. Monson (1978) describes four design components for teleconferences: humanizing, participation, message style, and feedback. Humanizing is the process of creating an atmosphere that focuses on the importance of the individual and overcomes distance by generating group rapport. Participation is the process of getting beyond the technology by providing opportunities for the spontaneous interaction between participants. Message style is presenting what is to be said in such a way that it will be received, understood, and remembered. Feedback is the process of getting information about the message, which helps the instructor and the participants complete the communications loop. Monson (1978) offers excellent guidelines for incorporating these four elements into teleconferencing design. The symbolic characteristics and the interfaces that are unique to each medium are discussed, along with the description of each technology.

13.4.2.1. Audio Teleconferencing. Audio teleconferencing or audioconferencing is voice-only communication. Even though it lacks a visual dimension, audio teleconferencing has some major strengths: It uses the regular telephone system, which is readily available and a familiar technology; it can connect a large number of locations for a conference; the conferences can be set up at short notice; and it is relatively inexpensive to use when compared with other technologies.

The interconnection medium for an audio teleconference is usually the telephone, which can incorporate microwave, satellite, fiber optic, or coaxial cable transmission. The conference call between three or more persons at different locations is the simplest type of audio teleconferencing. For multipoint teleconferencing among three or more sites, an audio bridge is required to enable sites to interact clearly. The bridge links the telephone lines together so that parties at each location can hear and talk to each other. Olgren and Parker (1983) observe that there are many system options for audio teleconferencing, but the most common forms are: (1) user-initiated conference calls or ("ad lib" teleconferencing), (2) operator-initiated or dial-up or (dial-out) teleconferencing, (3) dial-in or meet-me teleconferencing, and (4) dedicated audio networks.

In order to facilitate group-to-group communication, audio teleconferencing requires the use of some type of amplified telephone equipment with a loudspeaker and microphones. The equipment may be built into the room or may be portable. Audio teleconferencing equipment can be described as simplex, quasi-duplex, or full-duplex, depending on the kind of interactivity and interruptibility of the conference connection.

Olgren and Parker (1983) observe that one should keep in mind that voice communication is the backbone of any teleconferencing system, with the exception of computer conferencing. Sophisticated video or graphics equipment can be added to any audio system. But it is the audio channel that is the primary mode of communication. If the audio is of poor quality, it will have a negative impact on users of even the most sophisticated graphics and video technologies. This is very important to keep in mind, because the evaluation of interactive television systems have shown (Dillon, Gunawardena & Parker, 1992) that the most often-cited technical problem in television systems is the poor audio quality. While expensive investments have been made in video and graphics systems, very little attention has been paid to the improvement of audio quality in video and audiographics conferencing systems.

Audio teleconferences can be enhanced by adding a visual component to the conference by mailing ahead of time printed graphics, transparencies, or a videocassette to be used during the conference. Each site must be equipped with an overhead projector and a VCR if such graphical or video support is used.

13.4.2.2. Audiographics Conferencing.
Audiographics systems use ordinary telephone lines for two-way voice communication and the transmission of graphics and written material. Audiographics add a visual element to audio teleconferencing while maintaining the flexibility and economy of using telephone lines. Audio teleconferencing is now combined with written, print, graphics, and still or full-motion video information. Most audiographics systems use two telephone lines, one for audio and one for the transmission of written, graphic, and video information.

Currently, the simplest audiographics system is the addition of a fax machine using a second telephone line to an audio teleconference. Printed information can be exchanged during the conference using the fax machine so that visuals can be shared between sites. As a result of recent developments in computer, digital, and video compression technology, fairly sophisticated computer-based audiographics systems are available in the market. These systems combine voice, data, graphics, and digitized still video to create a powerful communications medium. The PC-based systems have specially designed communications software that control a scanner: graphics tablet, pen, and key board; and video camera, printer, and a modem.

One of the key advantages of an audiographics system is the ability to use the screen-sharing feature of the system. Participants at different sites can use different colored pens to create a graphic on the same screen at the same time. This feature enables the use of collaborative learning methods that involve learners at the remote locations. Since each site is most often equipped with the same types of equipment, it is possible to originate instruction from any location. The systems allow for a higher degree of interaction than one-way video and two-way audio systems. If the system is equipped with a video camera, it is possible to bring video footage to the class or show three-dimensional objects. High-resolution, full-color still video images can quickly be transmitted through dial-up telephone lines. Some systems have incorporated a keypad device that is used for polling participant's opinions and feedback. When the instructor asks a multiple-choice question, participants can use the keypad to key in their response. A central computer tabulates these responses, and the instructor gets an instantaneous statistical summary of the entire group's responses, as well as how each site responded. This is a good way of soliciting and getting feedback from the participants, so that the instructor can adjust his or her presentation depending on the responses received.

Because audiographics systems use regular telephone lines, they are much more cost effective than full-motion video systems. Participants need to be present at locations equipped with the systems in order to participate in a conference, and this may be inconvenient to some learners.

The systems enable the transmission of audio, graphics, data, and still-video information and create a moderate sense of social presence. The human-interface depends to a large degree on the type of communications software that has been designed for the system. Most graphic systems can be mastered by novices with about 1 hour's training on the system.

13.4.2.3. Video Teleconferencing.
Video teleconferencing systems transmit voice, graphics, and images of people. They have the advantage of being able to show an image of the speaker, three-dimensional objects, motion, and preproduced video footage. The teleconference can be designed to take advantage of the three symbolic characteristics of the medium: iconic, digital, and analog, where the iconic or the visual properties of the medium which is television's foremost strength can be manipulated to convey a very convincing message. Because of its ability to show the images of people, video teleconferences can create a "social presence" that closely approximates face-to-face interaction. Video teleconferencing systems are fully interactive systems that either allow for two-way video and audio, where the presenters and the audience can see and hear each other, or one-way video and two-way audio, where the audience sees and hears the presenter, and the presenter hears only the audience. During a video teleconference, audio, video, and data signals are transmitted to distant sites using a single combined channel, as in the use of a fiber-optic line or on separate channels. Audio is most often transmitted over a dial-up telephone line. The transmission channel can be analog or digital; signals can be sent via satellite, microwave, fiber optics, or coaxial cable, or a combination of these delivery systems.

The term *video teleconferencing* has become popular as an ad hoc one-time, special-event conference that usually connects a vast number of sites in order to make the conference cost effective. A video teleconference is usually distinguished from interactive instructional television (ITV), which is generally used to extend the campus classroom and carries programming for a significant length of time, such as a semester. ITV may use the same transmission channels as a video teleconference but is distinguished from video teleconferencing because of its different applications: video teleconferencing, an ad hoc conference, and ITV extending the classroom over a longer period of time.

Video teleconferences can be classified into two broad areas according to the technology used for transmission: full-motion video teleconferencing or compressed (or near-motion) video teleconferencing. Full-motion video teleconferencing uses the normal TV broadcast method or an analog video channel that requires a wideband channel to transmit pictures. The range of frequencies needed to reproduce a high-quality motion TV signal is at least 4.2 million Hz (4.2 MHz). The cost of a full-motion video teleconference is therefore extremely high. In the 1970s, conversion of the analog video signal to a digital bit stream enabled the first significant reductions in video signal bandwidth, making video conferencing less cost prohibitive.

Therefore, in compressed video, full video information is compressed by a piece of technology known as a Codec, in order to send it down the narrower bandwidth of a special telephone line. The compressed video method is cheaper and more flexible than the TV broadcast method.

13.4.2.4. Full-Motion Video Teleconferencing. *Full-motion video teleconferencing* became popular with the advent of satellite technology. For the past decade, educational developers have provided credit courses via satellite television over networks such as the National Technological University (for graduate engineering course), the Arts & Sciences Teleconferencing Service at Oklahoma State University, the TI-IN Network in Texas (for advanced placement high school courses). Both remote and urban schools and businesses have found these educational services valuable enough for their students and employees to make the investment in satellite hardware and tuition fees. Standard C- or Ku-band satellite TV signals can be received by consumer-level hardware costing well under $2,000. For a producer of educational programming, satellite delivery is still more economical than any other format for point-to-multipoint video transmission. Video compression standards and the introduction of fiber-optic cable infrastructure by many telephone and cable companies promises to make terrestrial line transmission of video much cheaper in the near future.

There are, however, at least two reasons that satellite television will probably remain available and, in fact, increase in the foreseeable future. First, there are still many remote areas of the world, even in North America, where telephone service, if it exists at all, is supported by antiquated technology barely able to provide a usable audio or data signal, let alone carry video. These remote areas simply need to point a relatively inexpensive satellite dish—powered by solar panels, batteries, or generators—at the appropriate satellite to receive its signal. Additionally, new higher-powered satellites are making it unnecessary to use today's large unwieldy satellite dishes. The new generation of Ku-band satellite is already offering direct broadcast service (DBS) to European households. These receivers, known as VSATs (or very small aperture terminals), are no larger than 1 to 3 feet in diameter and currently cost less than $500.

The proliferation of smaller, less-expensive satellite television reception technology, along with the continued launching of new, higher-powered satellites, will ensure a continuing niche for this technology to deliver instructional video and data to even the remotest areas of the world that lack other information infrastructure.

Fiber optics is gaining in popularity as a transmission medium for video teleconferencing. Fiber optics is a transmission technology using an attenuated glass fiber hardly thicker than a human hair, which conducts light from a laser source. A single glass fiber can carry the equivalent of 100 channels of television or 100,000 telephone calls, and even more capacity is possible by encasing many fibers within a cable. Fiber optics offers several advantages: It can carry a tremendous amount of data at high transmission speeds; it

does not experience signal degradation over distance as does coaxial cable; and it is a multipurpose system that can transmit video, audio, data, and graphics into the school through a single cable. A single fiber-optic cable can carry over a billion bits per second, enabling several video teleconferences to run simultaneously. Many companies, universities, and states in the United States are building fiber-optic transmission networks to carry voice, data, and video.

Video teleconferencing can also use digital or analog microwave systems or dial-up digital transmission lines. Current developments center on converging the different transmission channels and using a combination of telecommunications channels, satellites, fiber optics, microwaves, and coaxial cables to deliver full-motion video teleconferencing.

13.4.2.5. Compressed Video Teleconferencing. Video-compression techniques have greatly reduced the amount of data needed to describe a video picture, and have enabled the video signal to be transmitted at a lower and less-expensive data rate. The device used to digitize and compress an analog video signal is called a *video codec,* short for COder/DEcoder, which is the opposite of a modem (MOdulator/DEModulator). Reduction of transmission rate means trade-offs in picture quality. As the transmission rate is reduced, less data can be sent to describe picture changes. Lower data rates yield less resolution and less ability to handle motion. Therefore, if an image moves quickly, the motion will "streak" or "jerk" on the screen.

Currently most compressed video systems use either T-1 or half a T-1 channel. In a T-1 channel, video is compressed at 1.536 Mbps, which is the digital equivalent of 24 voice-grade lines. Many users of T-1 codecs opt for transmission at 768 kbps, which is half a T-1 channel. The difference in video quality between transmission at 768 kbps and 1.536 Mbps is slight, but the cost savings are significant. With the proliferation of fiber-optic networks, some private video teleconferencing networks are taking advantage of high-quality 45-Mbps transmission. Digital video compression technology has allowed video teleconferencing to become less cost prohibitive. It is not as cost effective as audio teleconferencing and audiographics teleconferencing, but it may soon compete with more-sophisticated audiographics systems with future developments in video compression technology.

13.4.2.6. Desktop Video Teleconferencing. Future developments in video teleconferencing will move toward integrated desktop video teleconferencing combining audio, video, and data. A fusion of network, personal computer, and digital video has produced the field of desktop videoconferencing. Saba (1993) observes that several telecommunications companies have introduced integrated systems (voice, video, and data) that reside in a desktop computer and provide two-way synchronous communications with voice, image, and file-transfer and screen-share capabilities. This technology allows users to see each other, speak to each other, transfer application files, and work together on such files at a distance. Most systems do not require advanced digital communications technologies such as ISDN to operate. For those wanting to utilize ISDN, it is possible to purchase an ISDN card, while most systems are now being designed to work with telecommunications standards such as ISDN.

Education can use this technology as a method of presenting class material and forming work groups, even though they may be at a considerable distance from each other. An instructor could conceivably present material to the entire class either "live" or through delivery of an audio file to each student's electronic mail account. Students could then work together in real time if they wished to share information over telephone lines.

In one current example, German officials are making use of desktop videoconferencing to form what has been dubbed a "virtual government." As planing progresses to move offices from Bonn, the current capital, to Berlin, planners meet regularly using on-line workstations rather than traveling to meetings. The results provide faster interaction at a much lower cost (Merwyn, 1993).

As more technologies begin to dovetail, desktop video-conferencing becomes laptop videoconferencing. The use of cellular telephone technology combined with high-speed laptop modems will make it possible for people to hold meetings and work group sessions whether they are at home, in an office, or on the beach.

13.4.2.7. Interactive Instructional Television (ITV).

Interactive instructional television (ITV) systems usually use a combination of "instructional television fixed service" (ITFS) and point-to-point microwave. They can transmit either two-way video and two-way audio, or one-way video and two-way audio, to several distant locations. The advantage of combining ITFS and microwave is that microwave is a point-to-point system, while ITFS is a point-to-multipoint system. Therefore, large geographical areas can be covered by the combination of the two technologies. Microwave connects one location to another electronically with its point-to-point signals, while ITFS distributes that signal to several receiving stations around a 20-mile radius. In the U.S., several states such as Iowa and Oklahoma support statewide networks that use a combination of ITFS, microwave, satellite, fiber optics, and coaxial cable.

In an ITFS and microwave television system, the course delivered over the system originates from a "studio class-room" on the campus. The classroom is specially designed to facilitate the extension of a conventional class through television. The audio feedback permits interaction between the teacher and students at distant locations. If a student viewing the class at a remote location has a question, he or she asks it through a talkback system, and it is heard by both on-campus and off-campus class members. The talk-back system uses either the telephone or FM microwave technology, called *radio talkback*.

Interactive instructional television systems also use satellite, fiber optics, or compressed video to extend the traditional classroom. However, these systems are currently

not as cost effective as systems that comprise of ITFS and point-to-point microwave.

13.4.2.8. Integrated Services Digital Network (ISDN).

ISDN is a new international telecommunications standard that offers a future worldwide network capable of transmitting voice, data, video, and graphics in digital form over standard telephone lines or fiber-optic cable. ISDN transmits media using digital rather than analog signals. In order to move toward a global network, ISDN promises end-to-end digital connectivity, multiple services over the same transmission path, and standard interfaces or conversion facilities for ubiquitous or transparent user access. Saba (1988) points out ISDN's applications for distance education: convergence, multitasking, and shared communications. Convergence refers to the convergence on audio, video, and data media in an integrated telecommunication system. Instruction is possible through voice, data, graphics, and video images. Multitasking refers to the variety of telecomputing capabilities that are available to the learner through integrated telecommunication systems based on minicomputers or microcomputers. Learners can gain access to on-line databases worldwide and explore multimedia libraries comprising of digital sound, text, and images. The shared communications feature allows the teacher and a group of learners separated by distance to work interactively on the same screen, sharing graphics, text, or data at the same time. Therefore, it is possible to solve a problem together or draw a graphic together, even though a group of learners may be at different geographic locations. Currently available audiographics systems and desktop video teleconferencing systems provide for the features that will be available in a more user-friendly and cost-effective manner with the development of ISDN systems.

13.4.2.9. Broadcast Television and Radio.

Broadcast television (see 11.7) and radio (see 28.1.6.1) fall under the classification of same-time/different-place instruction. The difference between broadcast television and radio and the previously discussed technologies under the same category is that broadcast television and radio do not provide for real-time, two-way interaction between presenters and participants. These media, however, can be used to instruct a vast number of students at the same time, even though the students do not have the ability to call back and clarify a statement or ask a question in real time. Many distance education institutions in developing countries, as well as institutions in developed countries such as the British Open University, use broadcast television and radio extensively to deliver programming to a large number of distant learners.

In the United States, while television—both open-broadcast cable and ITV—is the most popular media for delivering distance education, radio remains an underutilized medium (Gunawardena, 1988). It is in the developing countries that radio programming has been produced to either support and supplement print-based materials or to carry the majority of the course content.

In the United States, the most common pattern of open-broadcast use for delivering distance education is for an institution to make arrangements with the Public Broadcasting Service (PBS) and/or a commercial television station to distribute the educational programming (see 11.7). One of the limitations of this type of distribution is that educational programming is confined to broadcast schedules predetermined by the broadcasting station, which may not be times convenient for students taking the course.

Bates (1984) observes that broadcasts are ephemeral, cannot be reviewed, are uninterruptable, and are presented at the same pace for all students. A student cannot reflect on an idea or pursue a line of thought during a fast-paced program without losing the thread of the program itself. A student cannot go over the same material several times until it is understood.

Therefore, it is difficult for the learner to integrate or relate broadcast material to other learning. Hence, the need for broadcast programming to be accompanied by support materials in the form of prebroadcast notes and follow-up exercises and activities. Research at the British Open University has indicated that "most students find it impossible to take notes while viewing, and those that do are usually very dissatisfied with their notes" (Bates, 1983, p. 61). Access to a videotape of the broadcast, however, will alleviate these problems by giving the learner control over the medium, with the ability to stop and rewind sections that were not clear.

Despite its ability to reach a large section of the student population, open-broadcast television is a one-way communication medium. It does not provide for interaction (two-way communication) between the student and the teacher and lacks flexibility and ability to respond to student feedback. Since students cannot question the instructor to clarify problems, and since professional broadcast production "makes the learner dependent on 'responsible' broadcasting" (Bates, 1983, p. 61), this system of distribution can encourage passive acceptance of the instruction. To make the system interactive, open-broadcast distribution requires an added system to provide either an audio or audio-video return circuit.

13.4.2.10. Cable Television. In the United States, cable television began in remote rural areas, expanded into the suburbs, and has now penetrated into large urban areas. Cable has evolved from a way of improving reception in rural areas to a technology capable of providing many channels and even two-way video communication. Microwave relays have enabled cable operators to pick up signals from television stations too distant to be picked up over the air. Satellite interconnection of cable systems makes possible the importation of programming from virtually any part of the world. Today, cable technology is readily available and reaches a large number of homes and apartment units in the United States.

Where cable can provide access to a large section of the population of a given geographic area, it can be used to distribute distance education. Cable can be used to replay programming offered over open-broadcast television, usually at more convenient times for the students than open-broadcast schedules, or used as a means of delivering nationally distributed television programs, where terrestrial broadcasting facilities are not available.

Interactive cable in most cases is not two-way video. It is one-way video with telephone feedback from the viewer to the instructor, or a technology that provides viewers with one-way video and one-way audio feedback combined with keypads or polling devices with which they can transmit impulses to a central computer in response to questions posed by the instructor. Student responses, such as "yes," "no," "do not understand," "slow down," etc., are immediately summarized by a central computer for the instructor, and often for the viewing audience, thereby adding an element of interaction to the experience.

13.4.3 Different Time/Same Place Instruction

This type of instruction usually takes place in a lab or study center where distance learners gather at different times to interact with instructors, tutors, and other students. Certain types of instructional objectives can only be successfully met by arranging for learners to conduct an experiment in a lab and observing this experiment for evaluation purposes. Local study centers are used by major distance teaching universities such as the British Open University to support the distance learner by offering meetings with tutors, discussion with peer groups, and library facilities. A survey of distance teaching institutions in the United States (Gunawardena, 1988) found that only 41% of the total number of institutions surveyed used local study centers. The types of services provided by most of the institutions were student access to media equipment such as videocassette players and microcomputers, and library facilities such as books, tapes, and cassettes, rather than arrangements for tutor-student interaction.

13.4.4 Different Time/ Different Place Instruction

The technologies used in this category are further classified as those that transmit one-way information such as print, audio- and videocassettes, and those that provide for interaction. Technologies that provide for interaction are divided into two groups: (1) those that permit interaction between the instructor and the learner, and among groups of learners such as computer-mediated communication (CMC) (see Chapter 14); and (2) those that provide learner-machine interaction as in computer-assisted instruction (CAI)/computer-based training (CBT) (see 12.2.3) and interactive video and videotex. CAI/CBT, interactive video, and videotex are highly individualized learning experiences that can be designed to give learners control over their learning. Since the technologies that provide learner-machine interaction are discussed elsewhere in this book, they will not be discussed in this chapter.

13.4.4.1. Print. Until the beginning of the 1970s and the advent of two-way telecommunications technologies, print and the mail system were the predominant delivery medium for distance education. Correspondence study relied primarily on print to mediate the communication between the instructor and the learner. Currently, many distance education institutions in developing countries use print-based correspondence study as the main distance education medium, as the use of communications technologies is often cost prohibitive. Garrison (1990) refers to print-based correspondence study as the first generation of distance education technology. It is characterized by the mass production of educational materials, and Peters (1983) describes it as an industrial form of education. The difficulty with correspondence education has been the infrequent and inefficient form of communication between the instructor and the students. Also, it was difficult to arrange for peer interaction in correspondence-based distance education. The development of broadcast technologies and two-way interactive media have mitigated the limitations of correspondence study, especially in relation to facilitating two-way communication. However, print remains a very important support medium for electronically delivered distance education. Printed study guides have become a very important component of electronic distance education. In a survey of distance teaching institutions in the United States that use television as a main delivery medium, Gunawardena (1988) found that a majority of institutions cited the study guide, which provides printed lesson materials and guidelines for studying, the most important form of support for distance learners. A study guide can steer and facilitate the study of correspondence texts, television programs, and other components in a distance education course. A study guide, if well designed, can provide the integration between various media components and activate students to read and or listen to presentations of various kinds, to compare and criticize them, and to try to come to conclusions of their own. In a study guide or correspondence text, simulated conversation can be brought about by the use of a conversational tone, advance organizers, mathemagenic (see 30.4, 30.6) devices such as directions, and underlining, self-assessment, and self-remediation exercises.

13.4.4.2. Audiocassettes. Audiocassettes afford the learner control over the learning material, because learners can stop, rewind, and fast-forward the tape. They offer great flexibility in the way they can be used, either at home or while driving a car. Since audiocassettes are a fairly cost-effective medium, they are easily accessible to students. Audiocassettes can be used to tape lectures or can be specially designed with clear stopping points in order to supplement print or video material. For example, in order to facilitate student learning, audiocassettes can be used to describe diagrams and abstract concepts that students encounter in texts. An audiocassette can be used to record the sound portion of a television program if a videocassette

recorder is not available, and an audiocassette can provide a review of a television program in order to assist students to analyze the video material. The audiocassette can also be used to provide feedback to student assignments and is a very useful medium to check student pronunciation when languages are being taught at a distance. Audiocassettes can be an excellent supplementary medium to enrich print or other media and can provide resource material to distance learners. Since they can be produced and distributed without much cost, audiocassettes are also a very cost-effective medium for use in distance education.

13.4.4.3. Videocassettes. Videocassettes are like broadcast television in that they combine moving pictures and sound, but unlike broadcast television, videocassettes are distributed differently and viewed in different ways. An institution using videocassettes for distribution of video material to distant learners can use them as (a) a copy technology for open-broadcast, satellite, or cablecast programming; (b) a supplementary medium, for instance, providing the visual component for educational material carried over audio teleconferencing networks; (c) a specially designed video program that takes advantage of the cassette medium, e.g., its stop/review functions, so that students can be directed at the end of sequences to stop and take notes on, or discuss, what they have seen and heard.

An important advantage in using videocassettes is that students can exercise "control" over the programming by using the stop, rewind, replay, and fast-forward features to proceed at their own pace. Videocassettes are also a very flexible medium allowing students to use the cassettes at a time that is suitable to them. Bates (1987) observed that the "videocassette is to the broadcast what the book is to the lecture" (p. 13).

If videocassettes are designed to take advantage of their "control" characteristics and students are encouraged to use the "control" characteristics, then there is opportunity for students to interact with the lesson material. Students can repeat the material until they gain mastery of it by reflecting on and analyzing it. The control features that videocassettes afford the learner give course designers the ability to integrate video material more closely with other learning materials, so that learners can move between lesson material supplied by different media. "The ability to create 'chunks' of learning material, or to edit and reconstruct video material, can help develop a more-questioning approach to the presentation of video material. Recorded television therefore considerably increases the control of the learner (and the teacher) over the way video material can be used for learning purposes" (Bates, 1983, pp. 61–62).

Bates (1987) discusses the implications of the "control" characteristics for program design on videocassettes: (a) use of segments, (b) clear stopping points, (c) use of activities, (d) indexing, (e) close integration with other media (e.g., text, discussion), and (f) concentration on audiovisual aspects.

When videocassettes are used in a tutored video instruction (TVI) program, where tutors attend video-playback sessions at workplaces or study centers to answer questions and to encourage student discussion, students can take advantage of the features of a lecture (on videocassette) and a small-group discussion, which gives them the opportunity for personal interaction available in on-campus instruction.

13.4.4.4. Computer-Mediated Communication (CMC). CMC supports three types of on-line services: electronic mail (e-mail), computer conferencing, and on-line databases (see Chapter 14). In e-mail systems, a message is routed by the system to the addressee's mailbox on the host computer and remains there until it is read by the addressee. This message can be read, replied to, left in the mailbox for later perusal, saved to the hard disk on the microcomputer, deleted, or forwarded to someone else. Most e-mail systems have a bulletin board feature that allows users to read and post messages and documents to be seen by all. However, the messages in the bulletin board system are not linked to each other and provide for only a very limited form of group communication.

Computer conferencing systems, on the other hand, provide a conferencing feature in addition to e-mail, which supports group and many-to-many communication. In these systems, messages are linked to form chains of communication, and these messages are stored on the host computer until an individual logs on to read and reply to messages. Most conferencing systems offer a range of facilities for enhancing group communication and information retrieval. These include directories of users and conferences, conference management tools, search facilities, polling options, cooperative authoring, the ability to customize the system with special commands for particular groups, and access to databases (Kaye, 1989). Databases can be made available on the same host computer used for an e-mail or computer conferencing system, or users can access public or private databases resident on other computers. Some of the well-known computer conferencing systems are: EIES, PARTI, CAUCUS, CONFER, COSY, VAX NOTES, and TEAMATE. Recent developments in groupware, the design of software that facilitates group processes especially in the CMC environment, will have a tremendous impact on facilitating group work between participants who are separated in time and place.

The key features of computer conferencing systems that have an impact on distance education are the ability to support many-to-many interactive communication and the asynchronous (time-independent) and place-independent features. It offers the flexibility of assembling groups at times and places convenient to participants. The disadvantage, however, is that since on-line groups depend on text-based communication, they lack the benefit of nonverbal cues that facilitate interaction in a face-to-face meeting. Levinson (1990) notes that research into education via computer conferencing must be sensitive to the ways in which subtle differences in the technology can impact the social educational environment. "The importance of social factors suggests that 'computer conferencing' may be a better name

for the process than is 'computer-mediated communication'; the term 'conferencing' accentuates the inherent 'groupness' of this educational medium" (p. 7). Harasim (1989) emphasizes the necessity to approach on-line education as a distinct and unique domain. "The group nature of computer conferencing may be the most fundamental or critical component underpinning theory building and the design and implementation of on-line educational activities" (p. 51). Gunawardena (1993) reviews research related to the essentially group or socially interactive nature of computer conferences, focusing on factors that impact collaborative learning and group dynamics.

Globaled, a project that linked graduate classes in six universities—San Diego State University, Texas A&M University, University of New Mexico, University of Oklahoma, University of Wisconsin-Madison, and the University of Wyoming—to engage in the discussion of research related to distance education, is an example of the potential of computer conferencing to link students and instructors in learning communities (Gunawardena, Campbell Gibson, Cochenour, Dean, Dillon, Hessmiller et al., 1994). While the six major participating universities conducted research projects and moderated the discussions of their findings on Globaled, several interested students and faculty from other U.S. and overseas universities, including the Pennsylvania State University and the University of Wollongong in Australia, participated in the discussions. The Globaled community had approximately 90 participants. Globaled was premised on a learner-centered collaborative learning model in which the learner would be an active participant in the learning process involved in constructing knowledge through a process of interaction and discussion with learning peers and instructors.

13.5 FUTURE DIRECTIONS AND EMERGING TECHNOLOGIES

The field of distance education is in the midst of dynamic growth and change. The directions that distance education takes will depend on such factors as the development of new media and computing technologies, different methods of group learning and information gathering, and the development of government telecommunications policies.

While the phenomenal growth of electronic networks (exemplified by recent public attention to the Internet) has provided the primary technological thrust, several other emerging technologies also promise to drastically change the landscape of education, in general, and distance education, in particular.

13.5.1 Electronic Networks

The past few years have produced an explosion of electronic information resources available to students, teachers, library patrons, and anyone with a computer. Millions of pages of graphics and text-based information can be accessed directly on-line through hundreds of public, private, and commercial networks, including the biggest network of all: the Internet. The Internet is, in fact, a collection of independent academic, scientific, government, and commercial networks providing electronic mail and access to file servers with free software and millions of pages of text and graphic data that even thousands of elementary and secondary students are now using (McIsaac & Barnard, 1995).

For example, Mosaic and Netscape are two applications that have been made available on the Internet by the World Wide Web project, which enables users to browse around databases and supercomputers on the Internet using a hypermedia format. The World Wide Web project is a distributed hypermedia environment that originated at CERN with the collaboration of a large international design and development team that continues to work informally on the project to bring about new innovations on the Internet. Mosaic and Netscape, World Wide Web applications, are Internet-based global hypermedia browsers that allow you to discover, retrieve, and display documents and data from all over the Internet. For example, using these interfaces, learners can search the databases in museums all over the world that are connected to the Internet by navigating in a hypermedia format. Browsing tools such as these help learners explore a huge and rapidly expanding universe of information and gives them the powerful new capabilities for interacting with information.

The Clinton-Gore administration came into office with plans for developing a new U.S. high-speed electronic network that will vastly extend the capabilities of current Internet services to learners through an information superhighway. The plan, *The National Information Infrastructure: Agenda for Action* (U.S. Department of Commerce, 1993), is ambitious and will have far-reaching effects on education by expanding access to information.

The Clinton administration has proposed a federal assistance program to help schools acquire the hardware necessary to access the Internet. The plan would include providing matching grants to schools through the Commerce Department to buy computers and other telecommunications equipment needed to provide access to the Internet and any new information infrastructure. Plans are to include all levels of education, and to create a federal task force to provide telecommunications standards for education (West, 1993).

The fiber-optic infrastructure in the United States that will provide the backbone of the NII is rapidly expanding through both public and commercial efforts. Fiber optics are capable of carrying much greater bandwidth technologies, such as full-motion video. These lines can provide two-way videoconferencing, on-line multimedia, and video programming on demand. Iowa, for example, has installed nearly 3,000 miles of fiber-optic cable linking 15 community colleges and 3 public universities with a 48-channel interactive video capability (Suwinski, 1993).

The ultimate goal of electronic networks is, as Christopher Dede (Dede, 1991) puts it, to "widen the bandwidth of communication" between people regardless of their locations. Virtual communities of learners and educators are already sharing information resources, which are growing exponentially over the Internet and will grow even faster with a more extended international information infrastructure. Global "virtual libraries" are now emerging through connections between university research libraries (Rossman, 1992). These shared on-line public databases form the beginning of a comprehensive worldwide knowledge resource that is becoming available to anyone with access to a network gateway.

13.5.2 CD-ROM

CD-ROM is one of the most promising of the rapidly emerging technologies for education. An ever-increasing amount of text, graphic, and even full-motion video data is being recorded and distributed on CD-ROM. There is also a constantly expanding hardware base for CD-ROM as more and more personal computers are being shipped with CD-ROM drives and people are retrofitting PCs with the drives. As digital video compression improves, CD-ROM, or a similar optical-storage format, could replace videotape and laser discs as the most popular medium for distributing full-motion video programming, films, and telecourses.

Current versions of CD-ROMs hold about 600 Mb of digitized information. Most multimedia applications are CD-ROM–based, since video, audio, and graphic files require enormous amounts of storage space. An example of a popular CD-ROM title is the *Compton's Multimedia Encyclopedia,* which provides both the traditional text and still images along with animation and video. Essentially a hypermedia database, the encyclopedia allows random access to any of its material guided by the interests of the user.

A good example of how CD-ROM can affect education is the creation of a graduate media design course developed by the College of Education at Arizona State University. With the help of a grant from the Intel Corporation, this course was redesigned and transferred to CD-ROM. The entire class and all supporting materials are now available to students and Intel trainers to learn at their own pace and in any setting (Technology Based Learning, 1994). If it is now possible to offer a graduate course completely packaged on one CD-ROM, then virtually any other academic course could be designed, developed, and produced for this medium.

There are currently nearly 4,000 CD-ROM titles listed in media directories. Although heralded as the wave of the future for years, CD-ROM has languished as a technology while suffering a "chicken-or-the-egg" problem. CD-ROM titles grew slowly because there was only a small installed hardware base. Meanwhile, many people were hesitant to buy CD-ROM drives until more titles were offered. Recently, however, the market has begun to snowball as faster, less-expensive drives are being installed by manufacturers, and the CD-ROM developers are finding a rapidly expanding market for their products.

13.5.3 Personal Digital Assistants

Apple's introduction of personal digital assistants (PDAs) has opened a new realm of freedom and power for computing and telecommunications users that could well have important implications for educational users. PDAs provide a screen that can interpret what is written on it with a stylus and convert that to text. These handheld devices currently are used to send and receive fax messages via cellular telephone technology, store calendars, store telephone numbers, and dial them for voice communications, and the devices can send and receive data with the user's desktop computer.

PDAs offer convenient audio and data storage for the relatively small amounts of information that professionals working in the field need. Although they are used for writing notes and keeping track of schedules, their future value may be more in the order of complete wireless telecommunications devices.

Combined with the rapid proliferation of cellular telephone service in the United States, these technologies can free learners from the need to be tied to a particular hard-wired location to access information. Additionally, a consortium of major telecommunications, electronics, and aerospace firms is currently planning a global satellite network that would offer direct telephone service without the need for satellite dishes to literally any location on Earth. This could provide not only voice but also direct-data and fax access to anyone anywhere utilizing PDA technology. How viable this will be for remote populations depends on the cost for this service, but the technology could soon be in place.

With the profusion of microprocessor technology in offices, homes, cars, and all forms of electronics, PDAs could someday become the ultimate remote control allowing people to access records on home or office computers and control functions of electronics in these locations using cellular-phone technology.

What we see in all of these technologies is that once-separate devices are now merging to form information appliances that eventually will allow users to communicate seamlessly with each other, control home and office environments, and, most importantly of all, access most of the world's information, whether in text, audio, or visual form, at any place and any time.

13.5.4 Virtual Reality

Virtual reality (VR) (see 15.3) offers the promise of training future students in ways that currently are far too dangerous or expensive. Virtual reality combines the power of computer-generated graphics with the computer's ability to monitor massive data inflows in real time to create an enclosed man/machine interactive feedback loop. VR participants, wearing visors projecting the computer images, react to what they see, while sensors in the visor and body suit send information on position and the head and eye movement of the wearer. The computer changes the scene to follow the wearer and gives the impression of actually moving within an artificial environment.

Medical students wearing a virtual-reality visor and data suit could perform any operation on a computer-generated patient and actually see the results of what they are doing. Pilots could practice maneuvers as they do now in trainers, but with far more realism. The U.S. Defense Department has already used primitive networked versions in their SIMNET training. This network connects and controls training simulators in the U.S. and Europe, so that hundreds of soldiers can practice armored maneuvers while the computer reacts to their judgments and allows them to see each other's moves as if they were all together (Alluisi, 1991).

Beyond practical training needs, virtual reality could put students on a street in ancient Rome, floating inside of a molecule, or flying the length of our galaxy. Many scientists are now beginning to understand the power of visualization in understanding the raw data they receive. Virtual reality will be used by students and professionals alike to interpret and understand the universe.

Individuals interacting in a virtual world will undoubtedly create unanticipated communities and possibly even new and unique cultures. There are concerns, however. Dede (1992) warns that "the cultural consequences of technology-mediated physical social environments are mixed." While providing a wider range of human experience and knowledge bases, these environments can also be used for manipulation and to create misleading depictions of the world.

13.5.5 Video Servers/Digital Video

The next step in the delivery of full-motion video is the advent of reasonably priced video servers. Video servers are essentially nothing more than a large hard drive fast enough to play back the digitized video signal. With current compression techniques, 1 minute of full-motion video and audio requires about 6 Mb of storage space.

One impressive example of how video servers are already being used for education is the Holocaust Museum in Washington, D.C. Museum visitors have instant random access to 35 hours of documentary film stored on a 60-gigabyte-drive array from any one of 25 touchscreen kiosks (Lauriston, 1993). With the installation of greater bandwidth telecommunications lines, it is possible that in the near future students and researchers anywhere could have access to this and thousands of other global video servers from their desktops. A local area network within the museum provides a graphical front-end user interface at several kiosks for simultaneous patron access to any of the material.

Such servers could also provide access to filmed or videotaped footage for military trainers, flight simulators, or other industrial types of training needs. It also becomes possible, as video compression becomes more efficient and digital storage capacity becomes larger and less expensive, to place more and more of the historical visual archives of the 20th century in an accessible format on demand.

Indeed, we believe that the trumpeted phenomena of 500- and 600-channel cable television will be short lived, if in fact it ever is implemented. Instead, consumers and learners will need only one channel into their homes. They will have access to thousands of video databases to order up telecourses, documentary footage, movies, shows, and news over fiber-optic cable.

Dialing into these resources should be no more difficult than calling a phone number. The main challenge will be how to navigate this sea of visual resources. Artificial-intelligence software will be needed that will track all of the databases, their contents, and, most importantly, that will be able to learn what the users needs and interests are.

Current federal programs are providing funds to the National Science Foundation and NASA to develop the technology for turning massive amounts of audio, text, and visual databases into on-line "digital libraries" (Polly, 1993). Setting national standards and formats for these data could open the floodgates to the digitizing and subsequent public access to enormous amounts of information beginning with government agencies such as the National Archives, the Library of Congress, and the collections of the Smithsonian museums.

13.5.6 Personal Computers

Personal computers are not new as technology, but they are rapidly evolving into new areas. During the past decade, PCs have been used in education to run tutorials and teach students to use the big three: word processing, database management, and spreadsheets. Now personal computers are poised to explode into new areas.

PCs will provide the hub for new electronic information appliances. These will control incoming video over cable and fiber-optic lines, handle both incoming and outgoing electronic mail over the Internet and the newer National Information Infrastructure, and even search globally for text, audio, graphic, and video files needed by the user. Children in many schools are already piloting some of these computer-based uses by navigating the Internet to find files, downloading information from the networks, and electronically copying and pasting reference material from network resources to their papers. They are also discovering the ease of communicating with their peers around the world through their computers.

As more people migrate to laptop computers, the additional portability makes it possible to carry all files, papers, financial records, and any other text-based materials. New software is making communication, writing, publishing, and learning easier. Further miniaturization and increased power of microprocessors will help control everything from cooking to telecommunications. As protocols are standardized so that they can work together, one personal network can become seamless as processors control fax, copying, and telecommunications functions, as well as environment

and power utilization. Combining them with data storage devices like CD-ROM makes it possible to create more educational support for personal computers.

These new technologies can lead to more empowerment and thus more learner control of instruction for distance education students who have access to them. Access, however, may turn out to be the key problem. The Internet is currently paid for by federal government funds and its constituent members. Students at institutions on the network rarely have to pay for their accounts. Will this change when more and more commercial interests take part?

Students in developing countries with limited assets may have very little access to these technologies and thus fall further behind in terms of information infrastructure. On the other hand, new telecommunications avenues such as satellite telephone service could open channels at reasonable cost to even the remotest areas of the world. One very encouraging sign from the Internet's rapidly developing history is not only the willingness but also the eagerness with which networkers share information and areas of expertise. Networks have the potential of providing a broad knowledge base to citizens around the world, and those networks will offer opportunities for expanded applications of distance education. Research is just beginning to indicate how these newer technologies can benefit learners.

13.6 RESEARCH RELATED TO MEDIA IN DISTANCE EDUCATION

Much of the early research in distance education focused on comparisons between delivery media such as television, video, or computer and traditional face-to-face teaching. Other research compared the effectiveness of one distance delivery medium over another. Most of these media comparison studies (see 4.3.4.2) found no significant differences (NSD) in learning (Boswell, Mocker & Hamlin, 1968; Chu & Schramm, 1967; Chute, Bruning & Hulick, 1984; Hoyt & Frye, 1972; Kruh, 1983; Whittington, 1987). Critiquing these early media comparison studies, Spenser (1991) points out that they tended to report comparative statistics that gave no indication of the size of differences, if any, between the types of instruction. Conclusions tended to be based on the presence or absence of a statistically significant result. "When groups of research were reviewed there was a tendency to use a 'box score' tally approach, frequently resulting in a small number of studies favoring the innovation, a similar number favoring the traditional approach, and the vast majority showing NSD" (p. 13).

Whatever methods have been used to report the results of media comparison studies and their instructional impact, these studies have yielded very little useful guidance for distance education practice. This prompted Clark (1984) to make the following observation: "Learning gains come from adequate instructional design theory and practice, not from the medium used to deliver instruction" (p. 3).

Although Clark's statement has been debated (Kozma, 1994), educational technologists agree that the quality of the instructional design has a significant impact on learning. It is time, therefore, to move away from media comparison studies that often yield no significant differences and begin to examine factors such as instructional design, learning and instructional theory, and theoretical frameworks in distance education, which when applied to learning, might account for significant differences in levels of performance. The questions that need to be asked are not which medium works best, but rather how best to incorporate media attributes into the design of effective instruction for learning. Studies that compare two different instructional designs using the same medium may yield more useful results for practice than simple media comparisons. Little research has been done to examine what happens in the learning process when students interact with various technologies.

Research in the area of distance education falls into areas of traditional and exploratory research. Traditional research occurs within the field and is reported in the distance education literature. Exploratory research is often interdisciplinary and found in related literature. It is frequently the result of interest in educational application of newer technologies in various related disciplines.

The traditional research literature in distance education is brief and inconclusive. Both quantitative and qualitative studies have generally lacked rigor. Driven by practice, much research has taken the form of program evaluation, descriptions of individual distance education programs, brief case studies, institutional surveys, and speculative reports. Although well-reported case studies offer valuable insights for further investigation, the literature in distance education lacks rich qualitative information or programmatic experimental research that would lead to testing of research hypotheses. Also, because of the international nature of the field, research is reported in international journals, many of which are not peer reviewed. A number of research reports are generated by governmental agencies and institutions responsible for large-scale distance delivery programs. These may be proprietary and are often not readily available.

Much traditional research in distance education has focused on issues of technology. More than 23% of the literature reviewed concerned issues related to technology and the role of the distance educator. As we said, most of those related to technology were media comparison studies that resulted in no significant difference. Issues concerning new technological advancements were most frequently a concern of North American writers.

13.6.1 Research Development

Scholars have approached the question of distance education research in a variety of ways. Coldeway (1990) notes that researchers in the field have not tested the various theories that have been advanced, and hypotheses have not been identified for experimental research. He calls for the development of a research base using, for example, Keller's Personalized System of Instruction to build a baseline of data for distance education research. Shale (1990) comments that research within the field is not productive because the field has limited itself to studies of past and present practices that look at "distance" as the significant concept. He calls for an examination of broader issues in education that look at communication technologies as part of education at a distance. He cautions that:

> In sum, distance education ought to be regarded as education at a distance. All of what constitutes the process of education when teacher and student are able to meet face-to-face also constitutes the process of education when teacher and student are physically separated (p. 334).

This view has not been popular within the distance education community. However, it has become apparent that more significant research dealing with variables that affect distance learners is being done outside of distance education than within it. Model studies, often exploratory, are appearing not within traditional distance education literature, but across disciplines where researchers are examining the interaction of learners with newly developing technologies. Nonetheless, there are a number of significant research studies both in traditional and exploratory areas of distance education.

A few recent studies have attempted to examine learning style variables and the media and methods used in distance education. Davie (1987) conducted a study of the interaction of learning styles (as measured by the Kolb instrument) and computer-mediated communication (see Chapter 14), and noted the need to conduct similar studies using larger samples and the importance of examining the relationship of learning style to student achievement. Gunawardena and Boverie (1992) conducted a study that examined the interaction of learning styles and media, method of instruction, and group functioning in distance learning classes that used audiographics conferencing as the predominant delivery medium. The learning style instrument used for this study was the Kolb LSI (1985). The major finding of this study was that learning styles do not impact how students interact with media and methods of instruction, their instructor, or other learners. But learning styles do affect satisfaction with activities involving other learners. Accommodators appear the most satisfied and Divergers the least satisfied with class discussions and group activities. Class type, whether students were on campus or off campus, rather than learning styles impacted student satisfaction with media, methods, learner-instructor interaction, learner-learner interaction, group satisfaction, goal setting, and group climate. The results of this study cannot be generalized because of the small sample in the distance class. The authors suggest that further research involving larger samples is necessary to validate these results.

13.6.2 Research and Technology

Garrison (1990) begins the discussion of technology with this statement:

> Distance education is inexorably linked to the technology of delivery. It can be seen as a set of instructional methods based largely on mediated communication capable of extending the influence of the educator beyond the formal institutional setting for the purpose of benefiting the learner through appropriate guidance and support. Without technology, a future for distance education does not exist (p. 45).

Most distance education programs today require the use of technology, and many authors (Baker, 1989; Clark, 1989; Stubbs & Burnham, 1990) are calling for revised evaluation techniques. In 1983, Clark startled the educational community with his statement that there is nothing intrinsic to technology that makes the slightest difference to student achievement. Hoko (1986) agreed with Clark in his hypothesis that there is no distinct advantage to one medium over another. Six years later, however, Clark (1989) called for an evaluation plan to determine both the basic needs of students and instructors and the technological components that mesh with those needs. Baker (1989) went a step further by saying that the evaluation process must be ongoing. As each new technology emerges, evaluation of that technology should be done prior to and throughout its implementation.

Stubbs and Burnham (1990) take a slightly different view. They argue that most media evaluation models like the Reiser and Gagne model (Reiser & Gagne, 1983) do not deal with critical dimensions of distance education. In distance education, media provide primary rather than secondary materials for learning. Winn (1990) suggests that the technology chosen for instruction may not affect the eventual achievement outcome, but "it greatly affects the efficiency with which instruction can be delivered" (p. 53). Distance education developers, worldwide, face the challenge of selecting the most efficient medium for delivery of instruction. Wagner (1990) believes that as technologies become more complex—i.e., interactive television, computer-based instruction, and teleconferencing—the need to be more accountable and effective when selecting and utilizing instructional delivery systems becomes increasingly more important.

Early distance education programs relied primarily on print materials for instruction. This format is still the medium of choice in places like Spain and Latin America where the cost of broadcast television is considered prohibitive (Garrido, 1991). Numerous texts and didactic guides are published yearly by the National University for Distance Education (NUDE) located in Spain. In addition to the print material, Spain and Latin America now supplement the printed material with a series of daily radio broadcasts from Radio Nacional de España. Spain and Latin America are not alone in their widespread use of print material. Garrido's article also includes Venezuela, which only recently insti-

tuted, on a limited basis, both television and audiocassette delivery systems to supplement text-based instruction. Costa Rica has a similar program in operation (Garrison, 1990). While many countries must rely on print to disseminate instruction, Turkey and other developing countries with large communication infrastructures already in place use broadcast television (McIsaac, 1990). As distance education increases worldwide, the need for continued modern delivery systems will continue (Winn, 1990).

Much of the literature originating in the United States, though not in other countries, discusses the advancement of technology to facilitate the delivery of distance education. Computer-assisted learning (CAL) (see 12.23) and computer conferencing (see Chapter 14) lead the list for the number of articles. One reason may be that CAL and computer conferencing have allowed a shift from individualized, self-directed learning to collaborative learning (Lauzon & Moore, 1989). Additionally, Lauzon and Moore report that CAL meets the diverse needs and characteristics of adult learners by providing the opportunity for the learner to control and pace the instruction. Qualitative research by Cheng, Lehman, and Armstrong (1991) supports the effectiveness of CAL and reports CAL to be "an effective teletraining device for academic institutions" (p. 63). Abrioux (1991), however, sees CAL as a somewhat questionable technological application. His research on language acquisition foreshadowed a need for student-to-student and student-to-instructor interaction. Abrioux also questions the cost effectiveness of CAL in terms of student achievement. While CAL was once viewed as one student working with material presented by one computer, advances in technology have allowed linkage of many computers and many students. This linkage is often entitled *computer conferencing.*

In their discussion of computer conferencing, Davie and Wells (1991) support the need for interaction. They describe one of computer conferencing's most frequently cited characteristics as being its many-to-many capability. Computer conferencing is an ideal communication tool for bridging time and space among those who share similar interests. Lauzon and Moore (1989) note that computer conferencing is "effective in removing the barriers of time and space as constraints on communication" (p. 40). Their article goes on to describe "on-line communities that will be instrumental in the realization of a 'learning society' by transforming current distance education systems into on-line educational communities" (p. 40). Harasim (1990) observes that because of the democratic openness of the computer conference environment, all students have an equal opportunity to contribute. Although the majority of literature on computer conferencing is positive, Harasim continues her response to computer conferencing by pointing out several opposing features. She reports that class members have difficulty reading the computer screens and following a variety of on-line, visual cues. She also cautions that distance educators should review the amount of material students are required to read both on and off the computer screen. While these comments are precautionary and important to both students and instructors in distance education, an overall view of the literature indicates that the positive benefits of CAL and computer conferencing appear to outweigh the disadvantages.

A second technology often cited in current literature is interactive television with two-way audio and two-way video capabilities. Although the majority of literature reviewed interactive projects within the United States, Collis (1991) reports from the DELTA Project (Developing European Learning Through Technological Advance) that nearly all of the countries involved expressed a need for modern interactive technology in Europe's future distance education projects. A further comment calls for teamwork and interaction. "The learning system should be capable of supporting team work in the classroom or between learners at different locations, enabling work material to be exchanged between and displayed at other locations (von Stachelsky, 1991, p. 9). Canada has joined the United States and the countries involved with the DELTA Project in selecting interactive television technology because of its interactive modality for students and instructors (Helm, 1989). The term *interaction* in the literature does not exclusively refer to a two-way technologically mediated exchange. Cost factors, coupled with lack of access to the necessary components of interactive television, have led several institutions to give "interactive" a less mechanically oriented definition. The Ontario Institute for Studies in Education (Harasim, 1990), Nova University (Scigliano, Joslyn & Levin, 1989), and the Dutch Open University (Meurs & Bouhuijs, 1989) all facilitate interaction by combining face-to-face meetings with computer-assisted learning (Davie & Wells, 1991). Regardless of how interaction is defined, its importance cannot be underestimated, especially in the realm of distance education (Harasim, 1990).

Television, another often cited technology, is becoming a widely used medium due to the availability of satellites, both in Europe and China. China's satellite television-based multimedia education system is the largest in the world (Gao, 1991). Gao continues by stating that, with a population of 1.2 billion people, Chinese satellite television is the only technology capable of reaching so many people and meeting their educational needs. Germany's academic Society for Adult Further Education based in Stuttgart also uses satellite television to disseminate instruction throughout Germany (Hawkridge, 1991).

Technologies come in many packages, says Garrison (1989), but each must be scrutinized for its effect on the achievement of the learner, for its costs, and for the environmental conditions necessary for its implementation. Administrators of distance education should not attend exclusively to the issues related to technology. Research is needed to identify how technology interacts with students and how it affects teaching and learning.

Areas of interest to researchers in distance education have been categorized in a variety of ways. The International Centre for Distance Learning (ICDL) at the British Open University, the largest single database of distance learning literature, has divided topics in distance education into theory, student psychology and motivation, administration and support, curriculum development, teaching materials and resources, and institutions and staff.

13.6.3 Research and Students

Although studies focusing on learners have received attention in the literature (18%), it is largely descriptive. Research-based articles, however, can be found in works by Tovar (1989), Wilkinson and Sherman (1990), and Baynton (1992). Aslanian and Brickell's (1988) qualitative research offers a very extensive profile of the distance education student in America. Their findings are congruent with international programs, although the international research is generally empirical. Nearly one-fourth of the literature reviewed about students calls for student-instructor interaction in order to decrease anxiety and increase motivation. The need for interaction is additionally associated with the selection and implementation of specific media within the distance education course.

As a form of nontraditional education, distance education serves mainly adults, and those adult students possess unique needs, motivations, goals, and self-concepts. In a qualitative study with 1,000 adults, Aslanian and Brickell (1988) developed a profile of an adult distance education learner. They found that, in general, the students are married (61%), female (58%), part-time students (80%), employed full time (71%), and paying for their own schooling (60%). Of the adults surveyed, 75% were between the ages of 25 and 44 years of age. Apt and Enert (1983) compiled student characteristics at six open-learning programs and found similar results. International results were found to be congruent in work done by Van Enckevort, Harry, Marin, and Schultz (1987) at four European distance education universities. Administration, instructors, and curriculum designers must take the needs of the adult student population into account when proposing theoretical and andragogically based instruction designed for distance education programs (Verduin & Clark, 1991).

The adult student generally enters the learning environment, whether traditional or distant, with a high degree of motivation (Ehrman, 1990). Knowles's (1984) learner-focused theory of andragogy suggests that much intentional learning activity of adults is motivated by their desire to move from their current level of proficiency to a new, higher level. Verduin and Clark (1991) agree with both Knowles and Ehrman: "Discrepancies between adults' current level and desired proficiency level directly affect motivation and achievement in both learning activities and life roles" (p. 25).

Although adults possess a high degree of motivation, the technology associated with distance education, coupled with the distance separating the student and instructor, leads to high degrees of anxiety. Anxiety in learning has occasionally been described as helpful, but more often treated in terms of its negative affects (Aggasiz, 1971). A negative view of anxiety comes from Darke (1988), who believes that anxiety can debilitate cognitive processing. The importance of student anxiety cannot be underestimated in facilitating two-way interaction between students and instructors in the distance education setting. The painful anxieties that learners experience in any instructional setting tend to be exacerbated when that learning is mediated by technology (Garrison, 1989).

Other distance education researchers (Keegan, 1988; Lewis, 1988) have questioned the need for too much student/instructor interaction. They see a large amount of interaction as inhibiting the independence of the learner. Although distance education is premised on creating the potential for greater independence for the learner, it is often "just as confining and inflexible as other forms of education" (Lewis, 1988, p.9). Sewart (1987) suggests that distance education students, perhaps, have greater freedom, but with that freedom comes responsibilities. Freedom demands that the student make a number of important decisions that would normally be made for him:

> It is an interesting and perhaps sometimes infuriating paradox; this provision of flexibility to cater for individuals needs inevitably results in increasing complexity of administrative and organizational procedures which may present the student with problems (Sewart, 1987, p. 168).

13.6.4 Instruction and Learner Support

The issue of learner support has received wide attention in distance education. The research, however, has been varied and inconclusive. After examining 107 articles to determine whether there were predictors of successful student support, Dillon and Blanchard (1991) conclude that the reported research was mixed. They propose a model to examine the support needs of the distance student, related to institutional characteristics, course content, and the technology. In a study analyzing learner support services in a statewide distance education system, Dillon, Gunawardena, and Parker (1992) outline the function and effectiveness of one learner support system and make recommendations for examining student program interactions. Feasley (1991) comments that although research on student support falls largely into the evaluation category, there are some very useful case studies and institutional surveys such as reports issued by FernUniversitat and National Home Study Council which summarize statistics about student services for a number of institutions. Wright (1991) comments that the largest number of studies related to student support have been conducted outside the United States with large distance education programs. The student support activities reported are preenrollment activities and tutorial services, as well as counseling and advising services.

In addition to student support, several ethical and administrative issues related to students are repeated in the current literature as well. The mediation of technology coupled with the distance between instructor and student poses questions related to admission, counseling, and retention. Reed and Sork (1990) provide evidence that admission criteria and intake systems should take into account the unique demands of the adult learner (i.e., motivation, anxiety, interactions, and learning style). Nelson (1988) states that admission requirements should consider the effects of the individual's cognitive styles, as these often affect student achievement in programs characterized by mediated communications and limited personal contact.

Combined with the institutions' responsibilities related to admissions procedures is the responsibility of counseling students into and out of programs where the learner and advisor are physically separated (Reed & Sork, 1990). Herein two issues arise. First, the nearly impossible task of understanding the life situation of the learner when distance and time interfere with communication makes counseling a difficult task at best. Second, the monetary requirements of the distance education institution and the well-being of the student who may or may not be advised into a distance education environment must be considered. Reed and Sork (1990) observe that students counseled out of distance education represent a loss of revenue. Counseling in a traditional setting requires expertise in a number of psychological and academic areas. However, counseling from a distance is a highly complex process that calls for a variety of methods, materials, and a knowledge of adult learner characteristics (Verduin & Clark, 1991).

The recent literature has offered various profiles of the distance education student. Counseling professionals should review the research on student needs and develop new methodologies for assisting students at a distance. Additional research is called for in all areas of student interaction with the learning environment.

13.6.4.1. Learning and Characteristics of Learners.

The study of learning and characteristics of learners engages the largest number of researchers and includes studies of learning styles, attitudes, personality, locus of control, motivation, and attrition. Included are general studies about cognition and metacognition, as well as specific studies related to the particular needs of the distance learner. Many studies have been single-group evaluations, few with randomization of subjects or programmatic investigations. Some exploratory research has involved a small number of participants in short interventions. Although these efforts yield interesting insights, they have not helped solve the problem of isolating and testing variables that might predict academic success. Often, experimental studies use thin descriptions and do not provide deep contextual information. Similarly, descriptive studies often lack generalizability and are not qualitatively rich.

Research reports that do appear in the literature are often inconclusive. Reports in the literature suggest that some combination of cognitive style, personality characteristics, and self-expectations can be predictors of success in distance education programs. It appears that those students who are most successful in distance learning situations tend to be independent, autonomous learners who prefer to control their own learning situations.

Characteristics besides independence which appear to be predictors of success are high self-expectations and self-confidence (Laube, 1992), academic accomplishment (Coggins, 1988; Dille & Mexack, 1991), and external locus of control (Baynton, 1992). Another motivation that reportedly influences academic persistence is the desire to improve employment possibilities (von Prummer, 1990). Research findings suggest that it is the combination of personal (such as learning style), environmental, and social factors that must be taken into account when predicting academic success in distance learning programs.

Verduin and Clark (1991) examined learning styles within the distance education setting and reviewed the research done on learning styles by Canfield in 1983. Canfield developed a learning style inventory that conceptualized learning styles as composed of preferred conditions, content, mode, and expectancy scores. Verduin and Clark (1991) believe this information can be helpful to educators in planning courses for students who will receive the instruction from a distance. They indicate that an understanding of how individual learners approach learning may make it possible for the distance educator to see a pattern of learning styles and plan or adjust course presentations accordingly. They conclude by saying that adults may or may not learn more easily when the style of presentation matches the students' learning style, but when the two do match, the students report being more satisfied with the course.

Perhaps the most interesting work in cognition appears outside the traditional confines of the distance education literature. Research that examines the interaction of learners and delivery media is currently being conducted with multimedia. These studies examine learning and problem solving in asynchronous, virtual environments in which the learner is encouraged to progress and interact with learning materials in a very individual way. In the Jasper experiment (see 12.3.2.2), for example, math problems are anchored in authentic real-world situations portrayed on videodisc (Van Haneghan, Barron, Young, Williams, Vye & Bransford, 1992). It was hypothesized that the attributes of videodisc, which allow the portrayal of rich audio and visual images of a problem situation, would enhance the problem-solving abilities of learners. Research results showed significant gains for the video-based group over the text-based group, not only in solving the original Jasper problems but also in identifying and solving similar and related problems. The rich video-based format context was found to simulate a real-world context for problem solving (Van Haneghan et al., 1992). In a similar vein, the Young Children's literacy project uses a Vygotsky scaffolding approach to support the construction of mental model-building skills for listening and storytelling (Cognition & Technology Group at Vanderbilt, 1991). Programs like Jasper and the Young Children's literacy project provide robust sensory environments for developing metacognitive strategies and participating in critical thinking. These cognitive approaches to teaching abstract thinking skills have found fertile ground in the design and development of multimedia programs.

Individualized instruction delivered in multimedia settings has begun to blur the distinction between distance education and traditional education. The use of computer technologies to enhance thinking has generated interest in all areas of the curriculum. Researchers are examining ways to decontextualize classroom learning by anchoring and situating problems to be solved as real-life events (Brown, Collins & Duguid, 1989). Collaborative interactions between learner and technology have caused cognitive psychologists to reexamine the effects of computer technology on intellectual performance. Salomon, Perkins, and Globerson (1991) call on educators to investigate the learning activities that new technologies promote. They argue that it is this collaborative cognitive processing between intelligent technology and learner which may have the potential for affecting human intellectual performance.

The authors make the distinction between effects *with* technology, in which the learner enters into a partnership in which the technology assumes part of the intellectual burden of processing information (calculator), and effects *of* technology (see 24.3.5) and related transfer of skills. The former role of technology is what has been referred to by Pea (1993) as *distributed cognition* (see 24.3.8). The distributed model of cognition has its roots in the cultural-historical tradition and is reflected in the work of Luria (1979) and Vygotsky (1978). This view of the distribution of cognition from a cultural-historical perspective maintains that learning is not an individual process but is part of a larger activity that involves the teacher, pupil, and cultural artifacts of the classroom. Knowledge does not reside with an individual alone but is distributed among the tools and artifacts of the culture. The technologies of today have created graphic interfaces that offer symbiotic and virtual environments distributed between human and machine.

One example of such a symbiotic environment is a computer conference network called the WELL. It is a "virtual community" where people meet, converse, and socialize. This "digital watering hole for information-age hunters and gatherers" has developed into a unique social and communication phenomenon (Rheingold, 1993). It functions as café, beauty shop, town square, pub, lecture hall, and library. In short, it is a network of communications in cyberspace, a true virtual community. The social and cultural ramifications of this type of community, which functions in cognitive and social space rather than geographic space, has vast implications for research in distance education.

These new learning environments are distance learning settings, and they prompt researchers to ask further questions:

How do these environments enhance cognitive activities? Which personal learning-style factors are important to consider in designing interactive materials for effective instruction? Can we predict which program elements are likely to enhance student learning?

13.6.5 Course Design and Communications

A number of research studies have been conducted around the issues of designing course material for distance education. A brief review of the literature reveals that the most frequently expressed concern in courses designed for distance learners has to do with providing the learner with adequate feedback (Howard, 1987; McCleary & Eagan, 1989). Learner feedback is listed as one of the five most important considerations in course design and instruction, and it is identified by Howard as the most significant component in his model for effective course design.

Other major issues that relate to course design are effective instructional design, selection of appropriate media based on instructional needs, basic evaluation, and programmatic research. There appears to be little reported systematic research in this area because of the time and costs involved in conducting such large-scale projects. McCleary and Egan (1989) examined course design and found that their second and third courses received higher ratings as a result of improving three elements of course design, one of which was feedback. In a review of the research, Dwyer (1991) proposes the use of instructional consistency/congruency paradigms when designing distance education materials in order to pair content of material with level of learners' ability. Others suggest models combining cognitive complexity, intellectual activity, and forms of instruction for integrating the use of technology in course delivery.

Although consideration is given in the literature to elements of course design such as interactivity, student support, media selection, instructional design issues, and feedback, little research has been reported other than evaluative studies. Few are generalizable to global situations. Although course design is a primary component of large-scale international distance education programs, little attention has been paid to the underlying social and cultural assumptions within which such instruction is designed. Critical theorists have examined how teaching materials and classroom practices reflect social assumptions of validity, authority, and empowerment. Although the thread of critical theory (see Chapter 9) has woven its way through the fabric of the literature in education, nowhere is it more important to examine educational assumptions underlying course design than in distance education.

Courses designed for distance delivery often cost thousands of dollars to produce and reach hundreds of thousands of students. Not only are hidden curricula in the classroom well documented, there is a growing body of evidence in the literature which critically analyzes the impact of social norms on the production of educational media. In their book, Ellsworth and Whatley (1990) examine the ways in which particular historical and social perspectives combine to produce images in educational media that serve the interests of a particular social and historical interpretation of values. Distance learning materials are designed to rely heavily on visual materials to maintain student interest. Film, video, and still photography should no longer be viewed as neutral carriers of information. In a seminal book of readings, Hlynka and Belland (1991) explore critical inquiry in the field of educational technology as a third paradigm, equally as important as the qualitative and quantitative perspectives. This collection of essays encourages instructional designers to examine issues in educational media and technology using paradigms drawn from the humanities and social sciences and sociology and anthropology.

The examination of issues concerning the use of technology is especially important when designing courses for distance education. There are six factors that are particularly critical and need to be considered. In order to distinguish the characteristics of the communications technologies currently being used in distance education, it is necessary to adopt a classification system, although any classification system may not remain current for very long with the constant development of new technologies.

13.6.5.1. Media and Course Design.

Several classification models have been developed to describe the technologies used in distance education (Barker, Frisbie & Patrick, 1989; Bates, 1991; Johansen, Martin, Mittman & Saffo, 1991). In a recent attempt to classify the media used in distance education, Bates (1993) notes that there should be two distinctions. The first is that it is important to make a distinction between "media" and "technology." Media are the forms of communication associated with particular ways of representing knowledge. Therefore, each medium has its unique way of presenting knowledge and organizing it, which is reflected in particular formats or styles of presentation. Bates (1993) notes that in distance education, the most important four media are text, audio, television, and computing. Each medium, however, can usually be carried by more than one technology. For example, the audio medium can be carried by audiocassettes, radio, and telephone, while the television medium can be carried by broadcasting, videocassettes, videodiscs, cable, satellite, fiber optics, ITFS, and microwave. In other words, a variety of different technologies may be used to deliver one medium. The second distinction is the one between primarily one-way and primarily two-way technologies. One-way technologies, such as radio and broadcast television, do not provide opportunities for interaction, while two-way technologies, such as videoconferencing or interactive television, allow for interaction between learners and instructors and among learners themselves.

For the purpose of this chapter, we would like to expand on a definition adopted by Willen (1988), who noted that where distance teaching and learning are concerned, three characteristics have proved critical to the optimization of the study situation: (a) the ability of the medium to reach all learners, or provide access; (b) the flexibility of the medium; and (c) the two-way communication capability of the medium. We feel that it is necessary to expand these three characteristics to include three others: the symbolic characteristics of the medium, the social presence conveyed by the medium, and the human-machine interface for a particular technology. Whatever classification system is used to describe the technologies, we feel that six important characteristics need to be kept in mind in the adoption and use of these technologies for distance education:

1. *Delivery and access*: the way in which the technology distributes the learning material to distance learners and the location to which it is distributed—homes, places of work, or local study centers. Student access to technologies in order to participate in the learning process is an important consideration.

2. *Control*: the extent to which the learner has control over the medium (the extent to which the medium provides flexibility in allowing the students to use it at a time and place and in a manner which suits them best). For example, the advantage of using videocassettes over broadcast television is that students can exercise "control" over the programming by using the stop, rewind, replay, and fast-forward features to proceed at their own pace. Videocassettes are also a very flexible medium allowing students to use the cassettes at a time that is suitable to them.

3. *Interaction*: the degree to which the technology permits interaction (two-way communication) between the teacher and the student, and among students. Technologies utilized for distance education can be classified as one-way transmission, or two-way interactive technologies. One-way transmission media include printed texts and materials, radio programs, open broadcast or cablecast television programs, and audiocassettes and videocassettes. Technologies that permit two-way interaction can be classified as either synchronous (real-time communication) or asynchronous (time-delayed communication) systems (see 14.2.3). Audio teleconferencing, audiographics teleconferencing, video teleconferencing, interactive television, and real-time computer chatting—when two or more computers are linked so that participants can talk to each other at the same time—are synchronous technologies that permit real-time, two-way communication. Computer-mediated communications (CMC)—including electronic mail (e-mail), bulletin boards, and computer conferencing—when used in a time-delayed fashion, are asynchronous technologies that permit two-way communication (see Chapter 14).

4. *Symbolic (or audiovisual) characteristics of the medium*: Salomon (1979) distinguishes between three kinds of symbol systems: iconic, digital, and analog. Iconic systems use pictorial representation; digital systems convey meaning by written language, musical notation, and mathematical symbols; and analog systems are made up of continuous elements that nevertheless have reorganized meaning and forms, such as voice quality, performed music, and dance. Television, for example, uses all three coding systems to convey a message. Salomon (1979) observes that it is the symbol system that a medium embodies rather than its other characteristics that may relate more directly to cognition and learning. "A code can activate a skill, it can short-circuit it, or it can overtly supplant it" (Salomon, 1979, p. 134).

5. *The social presence created by the medium*: Telecommunication systems, even two-way video and audio systems that permit the transmission of facial expressions and gestures, create social climates that are very different from the traditional classroom. Short et al. (1976) define social presence as the "degree of salience of the other person in the interaction and the consequent salience of the interpersonal relationships . . ." (p. 65). This means the degree to which a person is perceived as a "real person" in mediated communication. They define social presence as a quality of the medium itself, and hypothesize that communications media vary in their degree of social presence, and that these variations are important in determining the way individuals interact. The capacity of the medium to transmit information about facial expression, direction of looking, posture, dress, and nonverbal vocal cues, all contribute to the degree of social presence of a communications medium. Two concepts associated with social presence are "intimacy" and "immediacy." Short et al. (1976) suggest that the social presence of the communications medium contributes to the level of intimacy, which depends on factors such as physical distance, eye contact, smiling, and personal topics of conversation. They observe that the use of television rather than audio-only communication makes for greater intimacy, other things being equal. Immediacy is a measure of the psychological distance that a communicator puts between himself or herself and the object of his or her communication. A person can convey immediacy or nonimmediacy nonverbally (physical proximity, formality of dress, and facial expression) as well as verbally. Therefore, social presence can be conveyed both by the medium—video can convey a higher degree of social presence than audio—and by the people who are involved in using the medium for interaction—instructors who humanize the classroom climate may convey a higher degree of social presence than those who do not. A recent study (Gunawardena, Campbell Gibson, Cochenour, Dean, Dillon, Hessmiller et al., 1994) examines the concept of social presence in distance education and analyzes student perceptions of two media: audiographics and computer conferencing.

6. *Human-machine interface for a particular technology that takes into consideration how the equipment interfaces with the end users*: The learner must interact with the interface or the technological medium in order to interact with the content, instructor, and other learners. This may include an activity, such as pushing the press-to-talk bar on some microphones, or learning to use a graphics tablet to communicate graphically in an audio-graphics system. With the rapid growth of new telecommunications technologies, ergonomics (design of human-machine interfaces) has become an important area of research and development within the broader area of research related to human factors. The kinds of interfaces the technology employs has implications for the kind of training or orientation that both teachers and students must receive in order to be competent users of the medium.

When selecting technologies for a distance learning program, or when designing instruction for distance learning, these six factors need to be kept in mind. They are not entities in and of themselves but interact with each other to make up the total environment in which a specific medium operates. Figure 13-2 indicates this interaction.

The evolution of geographic space into cyberspace has profound implications for communication, instruction, and the design of the instructional message.

13.6.5.2. Course Design and the International Market. Issues that examine course design in distance education cross geographic boundaries. Courses that are produced in North America are exported across the world. There is a widespread belief that Western technologies, particularly the computer, are culturally neutral and can be used to modernize traditional societies. When distance education programs are delivered to developing countries, cultural differences are often dealt with by simply translating the existing software, or by writing new software in the local language. What remains is still instruction based on a set of cultural assumptions emphasizing the view that Western technology and science represent the most advanced stage in cultural evolution. This rationalist, secularist, and individualist philosophy remains at the tacit level and suggests that, for any country, true modernization relies on the scientific method and the adoption of culture-free technology. The imported technology boasts capabilities based on assumptions that are frequently in direct opposition to traditions and social practices in the local culture.

Critical theorists (see Chapter 9), and others, have engaged in the debate over obvious discrepancies between the ideal Western view of life and the reality of deteriorating social fabric, loss of traditional values, high crime and drug rates, and other visible social ills. The Western view of modernization and progress have not been universally accepted as ideal. However, by embracing new communication technologies, non-Western countries are buying into a new set of cultural assumptions. The danger is that this may occur at the cost of their own indigenous traditions.

UNESCO has argued that when urban, individualistic images of life are part of the cultural agendas of Western media, people in developing countries will aspire to these to be modern. The long-term effects of technological innovations on cultural traditions have not yet been well documented. It may be that, in racing to embrace modernism and technological innovations, social and traditional patterns of life will be altered to the extent that local traditions may be irrevocably changed. The cultural values of individualism, secularism, and feminism are not all recognized as desirable in other cultures that place higher values on religion, group efforts, and well-defined gender roles (McIsaac, 1993). Course materials designed with a particular cultural bias embedded in the instruction may have a negative effect on learning.

Moral issues surrounding loss of local culture can result from wholesale importation of foreign values. At the minimum, educators engaged in technology transfer should analyze local social customs and consider those customs, whenever possible. Such social conventions as extended hospitality, differing perceptions of time, and the perceived importance of the technology project can all affect the credibility of the program and, ultimately, its success (McIsaac & Koymen, 1988).

Course designers should first determine the underlying assumptions conveyed by the educational message being designed. Designers should consider the social and political setting in which the lessons will be used. They should determine whether the instructional design model has implicit cultural and social bias. And, finally, tacit messages and hidden agendas should be examined and eliminated wherever possible so that course materials do not reflect particular ideological points of view. Distance education research in course design should include programs of social research that explore the effects of technological innovations on cultural traditions.

13.6.6 Issues Related to Teaching

Studies that examine teaching in distance education address the developing role of the instructor, the need for decreasing resistance as traditional educators begin to use distance delivery systems, and, finally, faculty attitude toward the use of technology. Altered roles for faculty who teach in distance education settings is a common thread found throughout the literature. Sammons (1989) sees a need for definition of the role of teacher. He stresses that without this definition, prepackaged, mass distribution of education will result. Holmberg's (1989) theory of guided didactic conversation suggests that a relationship exists between the faculty's role in the conversation and student performance. Smith's (1991) qualitative study places students' involvement at the center of the foundation for distance education

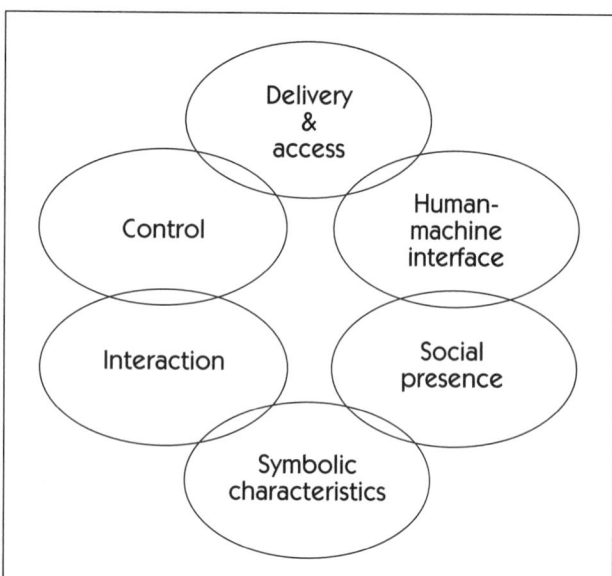

Figure 13-2. Factors impacting selection and use of distance education technologies.

teaching activities. The extent to which faculty roles are modified by the distance education environment is related to how the technology is used (Dillon & Walsh, 1992).

Some educators express concern that the use of packaged television courses creates negative consequences for mediated instruction. Sammons (1989) notes that the teaching role is an interactive, social process and questions whether presenting a telecourse or mass producing learning material for presentation at a distance is teaching. Peters (1983) lends an organizational perspective in his comparison of distance teaching to an industrial enterprise. He reports on the mass production of learning materials, mechanization, automation, quality control, and other operational activities. According to Peters, the teacher need not teach in a personal, face-to-face mode but rather should provide cost-effective instruction that can reach large numbers of students.

The emergence of increasingly student-centered learning activities of the 1970s, facilitated by technology in the 1980s, is contributing to an evolution of the role of faculty in the 1990s (Beaudoin, 1990). In particular, the increase in distance education enrollment will profoundly impact faculty members' instructional roles. Rather than transmit information in person, many faculty will have to make the adjustment to monitoring and facilitating the work of geographically distant learners (Bates, 1991). Faculty accustomed to the more conventional teaching roles will be required to accommodate new skills and assume expanding roles (Kember & Murphy, 1990).

This role shift from the European model of teacher as the exclusive source of information to one of facilitator is a difficult and threatening situation for most teachers. The role of teacher is not becoming obsolete but instead is being transformed (Beaudoin, 1990). Educators, and in particular those in distance educational environments, must be proficient at both delivery of content and the operation of the technology. Beaudoin goes on to point out that the teacher's role in the 90s is becoming one of facilitator and bridge between student and the learning source (i.e., computer, television).

With new technologies being capable of delivering instruction, teachers are entering into a partnership with the technology. Garrison (1989) notes that while the teacher must be aware of the external aspects of learning, those related to the technology, it is the internal cognitive aspects of the learning experience that remain in the hands of the teacher. Ramsden (1988) sees the role of the distance education instructor as including the challenge of dialogue and interaction. "Machines," Ramsden says, "transmit information as if it were an unquestionable truth" (p. 52). The teacher's role, which must include dialogue, is to challenge the seemingly unquestionable truths and to elicit meaning for the student.

Dillon and Walsh (1992) see a lack of research focus on the role adaptations of faculty, and they recommend future research on this topic. In their review of current literature, Dillon and Walsh found only 24 of 225 articles on faculty roles. Research by Garrison (1990) indicates that educators are resistant to adaptation and to introduction of technology into previously designed classes. The literature suggests that faculty attitudes improve as experience with distance education increases, and as faculty become more familiar with the technology. Taylor and White (1991) support this idea in their findings of positive attitudes from faculty who have completed the first distance education class, but their study also indicates a faculty preference for face-to-face traditional teaching. The reason most often cited in their qualitative study is lack of student interaction. Additionally, Taylor and White found through interviews and surveys that faculty agree that distance teaching is not appropriate for all content areas or for all students.

There is a lack of training opportunity in distance education which could help faculty overcome anxieties about technology and might improve teacher attitudes. Most teacher in-service programs that deal with technology teach how to operate equipment, with little attention paid to the more important aspects of how to incorporate technology into instruction. Virtually none addresses the concept and practice of distance education as a unique enterprise with different techniques of instruction from the traditional classroom.

In addition to conducting research on the emerging roles of faculty involved in distance education activities, studies are needed to examine faculty attitudes. Many teachers have a natural concern that technology will replace them in the classroom. It is important, says Hawkridge (1991), for teachers in training to be stimulated to a positive attitude toward technology as a means of enhancing the quality of the human interaction, and not to see technology as a dehumanizing influence. Hawkridge is joined by other researchers who call for future study in the area of instructor role development. As technology becomes a means for future educational delivery, a new view of the profession of teaching may need to be developed.

13.6.7 Policy and Management

State and national policies on the use of telecommunication technologies for distance education have been slow to develop in the United States. Many other countries have had well-developed national plans for the implementation of distance education delivery systems over large geographic areas. Countries in which education is centralized at the national level are often those with the largest distance education enterprises. Countries in Asia, the Middle East, Latin America, and Europe which have national policies for the development of distance education often use communication infrastructures that are already in place to deliver massive programs over broadcast media (McIsaac, Murphy & Demiray, 1988). As is the case with the area of learner support, the literature in theory and policy management is concerned largely with institutional evaluation studies that are extremely useful to countries looking for prototype models for establishing large-scale programs, but the literature does not offer testable hypotheses or rich, detailed qualitative analyses. These international evaluation reports of large-scale distance education projects raise issues of national educational priorities, funding sources, and policy determination.

In the United States, the most significant early study to be done on a large scale was Linking for Learning (Office of Technology Assessment, 1989). This report was the first to examine national and state telecommunication initiatives and make recommendations for a plan of action, based on needs of state and local schools. Because distance education in the United States is not supported by a central educational authority as in other countries, development of national and state policy is slower in developing. Key policy issues now receiving attention include: funding, equal access to high-quality education, effectiveness of educational systems, licensing of distance education programs, and equal access to delivery systems (Dirr, 1991). Donaldson (1991) calls for application of organization theory to issues of management and administration in distance education.

Finally, we might ask what conclusions we can draw from the collection of research studies in this rapidly growing area. It seems evident that research has been conducted from many perspectives and in many disciplines. As the body of research studies grows, methods such as meta-analysis can help us analyze the growing body of information. Meta-analysis, the application of qualitative and quantitative procedures for the purpose of integrating, synthesizing, and analyzing various studies, would be particularly useful (McIsaac, 1990). Sophason and Prescott (1988) believe that single studies cannot expect to provide definitive answers to theoretical questions. Instead, a method such as meta-analysis is needed to identify underlying trends and principles emerging from the research.

13.7   INTERNATIONAL ISSUES

Distance learning delivery systems, particularly those that rely on telecommunications, have benefited from the economic growth of the industry. In 1990 alone, telecommunication equipment and services accounted for $350 billion and employed 2.8 million workers. The communication industry in OECD countries has recently become an extremely profitable and competitive business with public telecommunication operators developing new integrated services digital networks (ISDNs) and satellite services. It is predicted that the increased development of high-definition television (HDTV) and mobile communications will be matched with increased deregulation and privatization of networks, increasing competition and lowering costs.

In many countries, although the existing communication infrastructure is old and dysfunctional, newer technologies are developing which will provide for the flow of information to the majority of the population through distance education delivery systems (McIsaac, 1992). This is particularly true in the newly emerging eastern European countries

where previous communication suppliers were sparse or nonexistent. In these situations, the newer cellular radio technologies, which can handle a greater number of users than previous fixed-link networks, may provide the answer. Such mobile technologies can be put in place with less cost than wired networks and, in addition, occupy a very small spectrum of the radio frequencies.

Although the future of new technological developments promises increased accessibility to information at low cost, this access is not without its own pitfalls. Economic power remains largely within the hands of developed countries. From an economic point of view, some disadvantages include the selection of a costly technological solution when a simpler and existing technology might suffice. Technology that must be used over long physical distances with primitive and unreliable electricity and telephone services is not in the best interest of the developing country. The most important consideration for the majority of developing countries is economic independence. It is in many of the economically developing countries that the largest distance learning projects are undertaken. A top educational priority for many such countries is to improve the cost effectiveness of education and to provide training and jobs for the general population. Researchers across the globe are calling for the establishment of national priorities for research in areas such as distance education (Jegede, 1993).

Research-based distance education programs face a number of obstacles around the world. The lack of financial resources available for conducting adequate needs assessment in many countries, particularly prior to embarking on a massive distance education plan, is a common problem (McIsaac, 1990). In many cases, investing money in research is perceived to be unnecessary and a drain from areas in which the money is needed. Time is an additional problem, since programs are often mandated with very little start-up time. In the interest of expedience, an existing distance learning program from another country may be used and revised, but many times this does not adequately answer the needs of the specific population.

One solution to the lack of adequate resources available locally has traditionally been the donation of time and expertise by international organizations to help in developing project goals and objectives. The criticism of this approach is that visiting experts seldom have adequate time to become completely familiar with the economic, social, and political factors influencing the success of the project. A second, and more appropriate solution, has been to train local experts to research, design, and implement sound distance learning programs based on the needs of the particular economy.

Distance education and its related delivery systems are often called upon to support national educational priorities and the current political system. One goal of education, particularly in developing countries, is to support the political organization of the country and to develop good citizens. Distance education programs that endorse this priority will have greater chance for success. National political philosophies and priorities are found reflected in the diversity of distance education programs around the world. These programs conform to prevailing political, social, and economic values. Research, particularly of the applied variety, is essential to avoid the trial-and-error approach that costs international distance education projects millions of dollars.

13.8 SUMMARY AND RECOMMENDATIONS

Distance education programs will continue to grow both in the United States and abroad. One of the reasons for this growth is related to the ever-growing global need for an educated workforce, combined with financial constraints of established educational systems. Distance education offers lifelong learning potential to working adults and will play a significant part in educating societies around the world. Distance education will become of far greater importance in the United States in the years ahead because it is so cost efficient and because it allows for independent learning by working adults. If society is to cope with this growing need for an educated workforce, distance education must continue to make its place in the educational community.

Although distance education has been difficult to establish in a number of European countries, influential networks are being established to facilitate future growth. The European Association of Distance Teaching Universities (EADTU) has combined with Eurostep (which organizes educational television across Europe using satellite) and the Budapest Platform (providing satellite television to central and eastern countries) to develop a system of distance education programs throughout Europe. Distance education programs will become major components facilitating economic progress throughout the world.

Future research should focus on establishing theoretical frameworks as a basis for research and should examine the interactions of technology with teaching and learning. Researchers should address issues of achievement, motivation, attrition, and control.

Distance education is no longer viewed as a marginal educational activity. Instead, it is regarded internationally as a viable and cost effective way of providing individualized instruction. Recent developments in technology are erasing the lines between traditional and distance learners as more students have the opportunity to work with multimedia designed for individual and interactive learning. Print once was the primary method of instructional delivery but is now taking a backseat to modern interactive technologies.

The content of future research should:

- Move beyond media comparison studies.
- Examine the characteristics of the distance learner and investigate the collaborative effects of media attributes and cognition.
- Explore the relationship between media and the socio-cultural construction of knowledge.
- Identify course design elements effective in interactive learning systems.
- Contribute to a shared international research database.
- Examine the cultural effects of technology and courseware transfer in distance education programs.

Research methodologies should:

- Avoid microanalyses.
- Progress beyond early descriptive studies.
- Generate a substantive research base by conducting longitudinal and collaborative studies.
- Identify and develop appropriate conceptual frameworks from related disciplines such as cognitive psychology, social learning theory, critical theory, communication theory, and social science theories.
- Conduct thorough qualitative studies that identify the combination of personal, social, and educational elements that create a successful environment for the independent learner.
- Combine qualitative and experimental methodologies, where appropriate, to enrich research findings.

Technology may be driving the rapid rise in popularity of distance education, but it is the well-designed instructional situation that allows the learner to interact with the technology in the construction of knowledge. It is the effective interaction of instructor, student, and delivery system that affords distance education its prominence within the educational community. Distance education can offer the opportunity for a research-based, practical, integration of technology, instruction and instructor creating a successful educational package.

REFERENCES

Abrioux, D. (1991). Computer assisted language learning at a distance: an international survey. *The American Journal of Distance Education* 5(1), 3–14.

Aggasiz, E.C. (1971). Society to encourage studies at home. *In* O. Mackenzie, ed. *The changing world of correspondence study,* 239–45. University Park, PA: University Press.

Alluisi, E.A. (1991). The development of technology for collective training: SIMNET, a case history. *Human Factors* 33(3), 343–62.

Altmann, H. & Arambasich, L. (1982). A study of locus of control with adult students. *Canadian Counselor 16* (2), 97–101.

Apt, L.R. & Enert, C. (1983). Students in distance education programs. In *Profiles Conference.* Oslo, Norway.

Arger, G. (1990). Distance education in the third world: critical analysis of the promise and reality. *Open Learning* 5(2), 9–18.

Aslanian, C. & Brickell, H.M. (1988). *Americans in transition: life changes as a reason for learning.* New York: New York Entrance Examination Board.

Baker, E.L. (1989). Technology assessment: policy and methodological issues. In *Proceedings of the 2d Intelligent Tutoring*

Systems Research Forum, 151–58. U.S. Air Force.

Barker, B.O., Frisbie, A.G. & Patrick, K.R. (1989). Broadening the definition of distance education in light of the new telecommunications technologies. *The American Journal of Distance Education 3*(1), 20–9.

Barnard, J. (1992). Multimedia and the future of distance learning technology. *Educational Media International 29*(3), 139–44.

Barrett, E., ed. (1992). *Sociomedia: multimedia, hypermedia and the social construction of knowledge.* Cambridge, MA: MIT Press.

Bates, A.W. (1983). Adult learning from educational television: the open university experience. *In* M.J.A. Howe, ed. *Learning from television: psychological and educational research,* 57–77. London: Academic.

— (1984). Broadcast television in distance education: a worldwide perspective. *In* A. W. Bates, ed. *The role of technology in distance education,* 29–41. London: Croom Helm.

— (1987). *Television, learning and distance education.* Milton Keynes, U.K.: Open University Press, Institute of Educational Technology.

— (1990). *Media and technology in European distance education.* Milton Keynes, U.K.: Open University Press.

— (1991). Third generation distance education: the challenge of new technology. *Research in Distance Education 3* (2), 10–5.

Bates, T. (1993). Theory and practice in the use of technology in distance education. *In* D. Keegan, ed. *Theoretical principles of distance education,* 213–33. London: Routledge.

Baynton, M. (1992). Dimensions of control in distance education: a factor analysis. *The American Journal of Distance Education 6*(2), 17–31.

Bääth, J. (1982). Distance students' learning—empirical findings and theoretical deliberations. *Distance Education 3*(1), 6–27.

Beaudoin, M. (1990). The instructor's changing role in distance education. *The American Journal of Distance Education 4*(2), 21–9.

Bloom, B. (1956). *Taxonomy of educational objectives: the classification of educational goals.* New York: Longman.

Boswell, J.J., Mocker, D.W. & Hamlin, W.C. (1968). Telelecture: an experiment in remote teaching. *Adult Leadership 16*(9), 321-22, 338.

Boyd, R. & Apps, J. (1980). *Redefining the disciplining of adult education.* San Francisco, CA: Jossey-Bass.

Brew, A. & Wright, T. (1990). Changing teaching styles. *Distance Education 11*(2), 183–212.

Brindley, J. & Jean-Louis, M. (1990). Student support services: the case for a proactive approach. *Journal of Distance Education V*(1), 71–2.

Brookfield, S.D. (1986). *Understanding and facilitating adult learning.* San Francisco, CA: Jossey-Bass.

Brown, J.S., Collins, A. & Duguid, P. (1989). Situated cognition and the culture of learning. *Educational Researcher 18*(1), 32–42.

Brown, A.L. & Palincsar, A.S. (1989). Guided, cooperative learning and individual knowledge acquisition. *In* L.B. Resnick, ed. *Knowing, learning and instruction: essays in honor of Robert Glaser,* 393–452. Hillsdale, NJ: Erlbaum.

Burge, L. (1988). Beyond andragogy: some explorations for distance learning design. *Journal of Distance Education 3*(1), 5–23.

—, Snow, J. & Howard, J. (1989). Interactive libraries: dimensions of interdependence. *In* A. Tait, ed. *Proceedings of the Conference on Interaction and Independence: Student Support in Distance Education and Open Learning.* Cambridge, U.K.: Open University Press.

Burge, E.J. & Howard, J.L. (1990). Audio-conferencing in graduate education: a case study. *The American Journal of Distance Education 4*(2), 3–13.

Campbell-Gibson, C. (1990). Questions and research strategies: one researcher's perspective. *The American Journal of Distance Education 4*(1), 69–81.

Carl, D.R. (1989). A response to Greville Rumble's "On defining distance education." *The American Journal of Distance Education 3*(3), 65–7.

Cheng, H., Lehman, J. & Armstrong, P. (1991). Comparison of performance and attitude in traditional and computer conference classes. *The American Journal of Distance Education 5*(3).

Chu, G.C. & Schramm, W. (1967). *Learning from television: what the research says.* Washington, D.C.: National Association of Educational Broadcasters.

Chute, A.G., Bruning, K.K. & Hulick, M.K. (1984). *The AT&T Communications National Teletraining Network: applications, benefits and costs.* Cincinnati, OH: AT&T Communication Sales and Marketing Education.

Clark, R.E. (1984). Research on student thought processes during computer-based instruction. *Journal of Instructional Development 7*(3), 2–5.

— (1989). Evaluating distance learning technologies. *Paper presented at the Invitation of the United States Congress* Office of Technology Assessment, Washington, DC.

— (1994). Media will never influence learning. *Educational Technology Research and Development 42*(2), 21–29.

Coggins, C.C. (1988). Preferred learning styles and their impact on completion of external degree programs. *The American Journal of Distance Education 2*(1), 25–37.

Cognition and Technology Group at Vanderbilt (1991). Integrated media: toward a theoretical framework for utilizing their potential. *Multimedida Technology Seminar,* 1–21. Washington, DC.

Coldeway, D. (1990). Methodological issues in distance education research. *In* M.G. Moore, ed. *Contemporary issues in American distance education,* 386–96. Oxford: Pergamon.

Collis, B. (1991). Telecommunications-based training in Europe. *The American Journal of Distance Education 5*(2), 31–40.

Daniel, J. & Marquis, C. (1979). Interaction and independence: getting the mixture right. *Teaching at a Distance 15,* 25–44.

Darke, G.S. (1988). Proficiency in adult learning. *Contemporary Psychology 3*(5), 372–84.

Davie, L.E. (1987). Learning through networks: a graduate course using computer conferencing. *Canadian Journal of University Continuing Education 13*(2), 11–26.

— & Wells, R. (1991). Empowering the learner through computer-mediated communication. *The American Journal of Distance Education 5*(1), 15–23.

Dede, C.J. (1991). Emerging technologies: impacts on distance learning. *Annals of the American Academy of Political and Social Science* (514), 146–58.

— (1992). The future of multimedia: bridging to virtual worlds. *Educational Technology* (32), 54–60.

Demiray, U. & McIsaac, M.S. (1993). Ten years of distance

education in Turkey. *In* B. Scriven, R. Lundin & Y. Ryan, eds. *Distance education for the twenty-first century,* 403–06. Oslo, Norway: International Council for Distance Education.

Deshler, D. & Hagan, N. (1989). Adult education research: issues and directions. *In* S. Merriam & P. Cunningham, eds. *The handbook of adult and continuing education,* 147–67. San Francisco, CA: Jossey-Bass.

Dille, B. & Mezack, M. (1991). Identifying predictors of high risk among community college telecourse students. *The American Journal of Distance Education 5*(1), 24–35.

Dillon, C.L. & Aagaard, L. (1990). Questions and research strategies: another perspective. *The American Journal of Distance Education 4*(3), 57–65.

— & Blanchard, D. (1991). Education for each: learner driven distance education. *Second American Symposium on Research in Distance Education.* University Park, PA.

—, Gunawardena, C.N. & Parker, R. (1992). Learner support: the critical link in distance education. *Distance Education 13*(1), 29–45.

— & Walsh, S.M. (1992). Faculty: the neglected resource in distance education. *The American Journal of Distance Education 6*(3), 5–21.

Dirr, P. (1991). Research issues: state and national policies in distance education. *Second American Symposium on Research in Distance Education.* University Park, PA: Pennsylvania State University.

Donaldson, J. (1991). Boundary articulation, domain determination, and organizational learning in distance education: practice opportunities and research needs. *Second American Symposium on Research in Distance Education.* University Park, PA: Pennsylvania State University.

Duffy, T.M. & Jonassen, D.H., eds. (1992). *Constructivism and the technology of instruction: a conversation.* Hillsdale, NJ: Erlbaum.

Dwyer, F. (1991). A paradigm for generating curriculum design oriented research questions in distance education. *Second American Symposium on Research in Distance Education.* University Park, PA: Pennsylvania State University.

Ehrman, M. (1990). Psychological factors and distance education. *The American Journal of Distance Education 4*(1), 10–24.

Ellsworth, E. & Whatley, M. (1990). *The ideology of images in educational media: hidden curriculums in the classroom.* New York: Teachers College Press.

Ely, D. (1992). *Trends in educational technology.* Syracuse, NY: ERIC Clearinghouse on Information Resources.

Evans, T. & Nation, D. (1989). Reflecting on the project. *In* T. Evans & D. Nation, eds. *Critical reflections on distance education.* London: Falmer.

— & Nation, D. (1992). Theorising open and distance education. *Open Learning* (Jun.), 3–13.

Feasley, C. (1991). Does evaluation = research lite? *Second American Symposium on Research in Distance Education.* University Park, PA: Pennsylvania State University.

Feenberg, A. & Bellman, B. (1990). Social factor research in computer-mediated communications. *In* L.M. Harasim, ed. *Online education: perspectives on a new environment,* 67–97. New York: Praeger.

Freeman, R. (1990). Open learning: taking stock. *Open Learning 5*(3), 3–9.

Gao, F. (1991). The challenge of distance education in China. *The American Journal of Distance Education 5*(2), 54–58.

Garrido, J.L. (1991). Overview of Spanish and Latin American distance higher education. *The American Journal of Distance Education 5*(2), 64–68.

Garrison, D.R. & Baynton, M. (1987). Beyond independence in distance education: the concept of control. *The American Journal of Distance Education 1*(1), 3–15.

— & Shale, D. (1987). Mapping the boundaries of distance education: problems in defining the field. *The American Journal of Distance Education 1*(1), 7–13.

— (1989). *Understanding distance education: a framework for the future.* London: Routledge.

— (1990). An analysis and evaluation of audio teleconferencing to facilitate education at a distance. *The American Journal of Distance Education 4*(3), 13–24.

Gibson, C.C. (1990). Questions and research strategies: one researcher's perspectives. *The American Journal of Distance Education 4*(1), 69–81.

Gilcher, K.W. & Johnstone, S.M. (1988). *A critical review of the use of audiographic conferencing systems by selected educational institutions.* College, Park, MD: The University of Maryland, University College, Office of Instructional Telecommunications.

Glaser, R. (1992). Expert knowledge and processes of thinking. *In* D.F. Halpern, ed. *Enhancing thinking skills in the sciences and mathematics,* 63–76. Hillsdale, NJ: Erlbaum.

Greeno, J. (1989). Situations, mental models, and generative knowledge. *In* D. Khahr & K. Kotovsky, eds. *Complex information processing.* Hillsdale, NJ: Erlbaum.

Gunawardena, C.N. (1988). New communications technologies and distance education: a paradigm for the integration of video-based instruction. Unpublished doctoral dissertation. University of Kansas

— (1990). The integration of video-based instruction. *In* D.R. Garrison & D. Shale, eds. *Education at a distance: from issues to practice,* 109–122. Malabar, Fl: Krieger.

— (1990). Integrating telecommunication systems to reach distance learners. *The American Journal of Distance Education 4*(3), 38–46.

— (1991). Collaborative learning and group dynamics in computer-mediated communication networks. *The Second American Symposium on Research in Distance Education.* University Park: PA: Pennsylvania State University.

— (1992). Changing faculty roles for audiographics and online teaching. *American Journal of Distance Education 6* (3), 58–71.

— & Boverie, P.E. (1992). Interaction of learning style and media, method of instruction, and group functioning in distance learning. *Proceedings of the Eighth Annual Conference on Distance Teaching and Learning,* 65–69. Madison, WI: University of Wisconsin, Madison.

— (1993). The social context of online education. *Proceedings of the Distance Education Conference,* Portland, OR.

—, Campbell Gibson, C., Cochenour, J. et al. (1994). Multiple perspectives on implementing inter-university computer conferencing. *Proceedings of the Distance Learning Research Conference,* 101–117. San Antonio, TX: Texas A&M University, Dept. of Educational Human Resources.

Hackman, M.Z. & Walker, K.B. (1990). Instructional communication in the televised classroom: the effects of system design and teacher immediacy on student learning and satisfaction. *Communication Education 39*(3), 196–209.

Harasim, L.M. (1989). Online education: a new domain.

In R. Mason & A. Kaye, eds. *Mindweave,* 50–62. Oxford, England: Pergamon.

— (1990). Online education: an environment for collaboration and intellectual amplification. *In* L.M. Harasim, ed. *Online education: perspectives on a new environment,* 39–64. New York: Praeger.

—, ed. (1993). *Global networks.* Cambridge, MA: MIT Press.

Harry, K. & Rumble, G. (1982). *The distance teaching universities.* New York: St. Martin's.

— Keegan, D. & Magnus, J., eds. (1993). *Distance education: new perspectives.* London: Routledge.

Hart, G. (1990). Peer learning and support via audio-conferencing in continuing education for nurses. *Distance Education 11*(1), 308–19.

Hawkridge, D. (1991). Challenging educational technologies. *Educational and Training Technology International 28* (2), 102–10.

Hayes, E. (1990). Adult education: context and challenge for distance educators. *The American Journal of Distance Education 4*(1), 25–38.

Helm, B. (1989). Distance learning using communication technologies in Canada. *In* R. Sweet, ed. *Post secondary distance education in Canada,* 45–98. Quebec: Athabasca University Press.

Hillman, D.C., Willis, D.J. & Gunawardena, C.N. (1994). Learner-interface interaction in distance education: an extension of contemporary models and strategies for practitioners. *The American Journal of Distance Education 8*(2), 30–42.

Hlynka, D. & Belland, J., eds. (1991). *Paradigms regained: the uses of illuminative, semiotic and post-modern criticism as modes of inquiry in educational technology.* Englewood Cliffs, NJ: Educational Technology.

Hodgson, V.E. (1986). The interrelationship between support and learning materials. *Programmed Learning and Educational Technology 23*(1), 56–61.

Hoko, A. (1986). What is the scientific value of comparing automated and human instruction? *Educational Technology 26*(2), 18.

Holmberg, B. (1986). *Growth and structure of distance education.* London: Croom Helm.

— (1989). *Theory and practice of distance education.* London: Routledge.

Howard, D.C. (1987). Designing learner feedback in distance education. *The American Journal of Distance Education 1*(3), 24–40.

Hoyt, D.P. & Frye, D. (1972). *The effectiveness of telecommunications as an educational delivery system.* Manhattan, KS: Kansas State University.

Jegede, O. (1991). Constructivist epistemology and its implications for contemporary research in distance learning. *In* T. Evans & P. Juler, eds. *Second research in distance education seminar.* Victoria, Canada: Deakin University Press.

— (1993). *Distance education research priorities for Australia: a study of the opinions of distance educators and practitioners.* Adelaide: University Press of South Australia.

Johansen, R., Martin, A., Mittman, R. & Saffo, P. (1991). *Leading business teams: how teams can use technology and group process tools to enhance performance.* Reading, MA: Addison-Wesley.

Jonassen, D.H. (1985). Interactive lesson designs: a taxonomy. *Educational Technology 25*(6), 7–17.

—, Campbell, J.P. & Davidson, M.E. (1994). Learning with media: restructuring the debate. *Educational Technology Research and Development 42*(2), 31–39.

Kantor, R.J., Moore, A.L. & Bransford, J.D. (1993). *Extending the impact of classroom-based technology: the satellite challenge series.* American Educational Research Association Annual Conference. Atlanta, GA.

Kaye, A. (1989). Computer-mediated communication and distance education. *In* R. Mason & A. Kaye, eds. *Mindweave,* 3–21. Oxford, England: Pergamon.

Keegan, D. (1980). On defining distance education. *Distance Education 1*(1), 13–36.

— (1986). *The foundations of distance education,* 2d ed. London: Routledge.

— (1988). Problems in defining the field of distance education. *The American Journal of Distance Education 2*(2), 4–11.

—, ed. (1993). *Theoretical principles of distance education.* London: Routledge.

Kember, D. & Murphy, D. (1990). A synthesis of open, distance and student centered learning. *Open Learning 5*(2), 3–8.

Kirkup, G. & von Prummer, C. (1990). Support and connectedness: the needs of women distance education students. *Journal of Distance Education V*(2), 9–31.

Knowles, M.S. (1980). *The modern practice of adult education: from pedagogy to andragogy.* New York: Cambridge Books.

— (1984). *Andragogy in action.* San Francisco, CA: Jossey-Bass.

Kozma, R.B. (1991). Learning with media. *Review of Educational Research 61*(2), 179–211.

— (1994). Will media influence learning? Reframing the debate. *Educational Technology Research and Development 42*(2), 7–19.

Kruh, J. (1983). Student evaluation of instructional teleconferencing. *In* L. Parker & C. Olgren, eds. *Teleconferencing and electronic communications,* Vol. 2. Madison, WI: University of Wisconsin-Extension, Center for Interactive Programs.

Laube, M.R. (1992). Academic and social integration variables and secondary student persistence in distance education. *Research in Distance Education 4*(1), 2–5.

Lauriston, R. (1993). Serving up video. *NewMedia 3*(11), 52–57.

Lauzon, A.C. & Moore, M. (1989). Enhancing accessibility to meaningful learning opportunities: a pilot program in online education at the University of Guelph. *Research in Distance Education 3*(4), 2–5.

Levinson, P. (1990). Computer conferencing in the context of the evolution of media. *In* L. Harasim, ed. *Online education: perspectives on a new environment,* 3–14. New York: Praeger.

Lewis, R.J. (1988). Instructional applications of information technologies: a summary of higher education in the west. Western Interstate Conference for Distance Education. Boulder, CO.

— (1990). Open learning and the misuse of language: a response to Greville Rumble. *Open Learning 5*(1), 3–8.

Loesch, T. & Foley, R. (1988). Learning preference differences among adults in traditional and non-traditional baccalaureate programs. *Adult Education Quarterly 38,* 224–33.

Luria, A.R. (1979). *The making of mind: a personal account of Soviet psychology.* Cambridge, MA: Harvard University Press.

Mackenzie, N., Postgate, R. & Scupham, J. (1975). *Open learning: systems and problems in post-secondary education.* Paris: UNESCO Press.

McCleary, I.D. & Eagan, M.W. (1989). Program design and evaluation: two-way interactive television. *The American Journal of Distance Education 3*(1), 50–60.

McIsaac, M.S., Murphy, K.L. & Demiray, U. (1988). Examining distance education in Turkey. *Distance Education 9* (1), 106–13.

— & Koymen, U. (1988). Distance education opportunities for women in Turkey. *International Council for Distance Education Bulletin 17*(May), 22–27.

— (1990). Problems affecting evaluation of distance education in developing countries. *Research in Distance Education 2*(3), 12–16.

— (1991). Toward an analysis of social issues and course design. *Second American symposium on research in distance education.* University Park, PA: Pennsylvania State University.

— (1992). Networks for knowledge: the Turkish electronic classroom in the twenty-first century. *Educational Media International 29*(3), 165–70.

— (1993). Economic, political and social considerations in the use of global computer-based distance education. *In* R. Muffoletto & N. Knupfer, eds. *Computers in education: social, political, and historical perspectives,* 219–32. Cresskill, NJ: Hampton.

Merrill, M.D., Li, Z. & Jones, M.K. (1990). Second generation instructional design (ID2). *Educational Technology 30* (2), 7–14.

Merwyn, A. (1993). Videoconferencing goes to work. *NewMedia 3*(11), 60–64.

Meurs, E. & Bouhuijs, P.A. (1989). Tele-education: an experiment on home computing at the Dutch Open University. *Open Learning 4*(1), 33–36.

Miller, G. (1989). Learning from other disciplines: distance education and the education of the whole person. *Research in Distance Education 1*(1), 15–17.

Monson, M. (1978). *Bridging the distance: an instructional guide to teleconferencing.* Madison, WI: Instructional Communications Systems, University of Wisconsin-Extension.

Moore, G.A.B. (1991). Course design and communication technology in distance education. *Second American symposium on research in distance education.* University Park, PA: Pennsylvania State University.

Moore, M.G. (1973). Toward a theory of independent learning and teaching. *Journal of Higher Education 44,* 66–69.

— (1987). Distance learning in the United States: the near future. *Distance Education 8*(1), 38–46.

— (1987). Homogenization of instruction and the need for research. *The American Journal of Distance Education 1*(2), 1–5.

— (1988). On a theory of independent study. *In* D. Stewart, D. Keegan & B. Holmberg, eds. *Distance education: international perspectives,* 68–94. London: Routledge.

— (1989). Three types of interaction. *The American Journal of Distance Education 3*(2), 1–6.

—, ed. (1990). *Contemporary issues in American distance education.* Oxford, England: Pergamon.

— (1990). Recent contributions to the theory of distance education. *Open Learning 5*(3), 10–15.

—, Thompson, M.M. & Dirr, P. (1991). *Report on the second American symposium on research in distance education.* University Park, PA: Pennsylvania State University.

— (1993). Is teaching like flying? A total systems view of distance education. *American Journal of Distance Education 7*(1), 1–10.

Nation, D., Paine, N. & Richardson, M. (1990). Open learning and the misuse of language: some comments on the Rumble/Lewis debate. *Open Learning 5*(2), 40–45.

Nelson, A. (1988). Making distance education more efficient. *ICDE Bulletin 18,* 18–20.

Office of Technology Assessment (1989). *Linking for learning.* Washington, DC: U.S. Government Printing Office.

Olgren, C.H. & Parker, L.A. (1983). *Teleconferencing technology and applications.* Norwood, MA: Artech House.

Pea, R. (1993). Practices of distributed intelligence and designs for education. *In* G. Salomon, eds. *Distributed cognitions: psychological and educational considerations,* 47–87. Cambridge, MA: Cambridge University Press.

Peters, O. (1971). Theoretical aspects of correspondence instruction. *In* O. Mackenzie & E.L. Christensen, eds. *The changing world of correspondence study.* University Park, PA: Pennsylvania State University.

— (1983). Distance teaching and industrial production: a comparative interpretation in outline. *In* D. Sewart, D. Keegan & B. Holmberg, eds. *Distance education: international perspectives,* 95–113. London: Croom Helm.

Pittman, V. (1991). Rivalry for respectability: collegiate and proprietary correspondence programs. *Second American symposium on research in distance education.* University Park, PA: Pennsylvania State University.

Polly, J.A. (1993). NREN for all: insurmountable opportunity. Available on e-mail:jpolly@nysernet,org.

Pratt, D.D. (1989). Culture and learning: a comparison of western and Chinese conceptions of self and individualized instruction. *30th Annual Adult Educational Research Conference.* Madison, WI.

Ramsden, P. (1988). *Studying learning: improved teaching.* London: Kogan Page.

Reed, D. & Sork, T.J. (1990). Ethical considerations in distance education. *The American Journal of Distance Education 4*(2), 30–43.

Reiser, R.A. & Gagne, R.M. (1983). *Selecting media for instruction.* Englewood Cliffs, NJ: Education Technology.

Rekkedal, T. (1993). Recent research on distance education in Norway. *Open Learning* (Feb.), 32–50.

Resnick, L.B., ed. (1989). *Knowing, learning and instruction: essays in honor of Robert Glaser.* Hillsdale, NJ: Erlbaum.

Rheingold, H. (1993). *The virtual community: homesteading on the electronic frontier.* New York: Addison-Wesley.

Riel, M. (1993). Global education through learning circles. *In* L.M. Harasim, ed. *Global networks,* 221–236. Cambridge, MA: MIT Press.

Ritchie, H. & Newby, T.J. (1989). Classroom lecture/discussion vs. live televised instruction: a comparison of effects on student performance, attitude and interaction. *The American Journal of Distance Education 3*(3), 36–45.

Rossman, P. (1992). *The emerging worldwide electronic university: information age global higher education.* Westport, CT: Greenwood.

Rotter, J. (1989). Internal versus external control of reinforcement. *American Psychologist 45*(4), 489–93.

Rubio, R.A. (1993). A researcher's strategy for promoting widespread usage of telecommunications. *Journal of Computers in Mathematics and Science Teaching 12*(3/4), 220–26.

Rumble, G. & Harry, K., eds. (1982). *The distance teaching universities.* London: Croom Helm.

— (1986). *The planning and management of distance education.* London: Croom Helm.

— (1989). On defining distance education. *The American Journal of Distance Education 3*(2), 8–21.

— (1989). 'Open learning,' 'distance learning' and the misuse of language. *Open Learning 4*(2), 28–36.

— (1990). Open learning and the misuse of language: a reply. *Open Learning 5*(3), 50–51.

Saba, F. (1988). Integrated telecommunications systems and instructional transaction. *The American Journal of Distance Education 2*(3), 17–24.

— & Twitchell, D. (1988). Research in distance education: a system modeling approach. *The American Journal of Distance Education 2*(1), 9–24.

— & Shearer, R. (1994). Verifying key theoretical concepts in a dynamic model of distance education. *American Journal of Distance Education 8*(1), 36–59.

Salomon, G. (1979). *Interaction of media, cognition and learning: an exploration of how symbolic forms cultivate mental skills and affect knowledge acquisition.* San Francisco, CA: Jossey-Bass.

—, Perkins, D. N. & Globerson, T. (1991). Partners in cognition: extending human intelligence with intelligent technologies. *Educational Researcher 20*(3), 2–9.

—, ed. (1993). *Distributed cognitions: psychological and educational considerations.* Cambridge, MA: Cambridge University Press.

Sammons, M. (1989). An epistemological justification for the role of teaching in distance education. *The American Journal of Distance Education 2*(3), 5–16.

Schlosser, C.A. & Anderson, M.L. (1994). *Distance education: review of the literature.* Washington, DC: Association for Educational Communication and Technology.

Scigliano, J.A., Joslyn, D.L. & Levin, J. (1989). ECR: an online classroom for the non-school learning environment. *T.H.E. Journal 16*(6), 63–67.

Sewart, D., ed. (1987). *Staff development needs in distance education and campus-based education: are they so different?* London: Croom Helm.

Shah, G. (1989). A distance education strategy for Bangladesh. *International Council for Distance Education Bulletin 19,* 9–14.

Shale, D. (1990). Toward a reconceptualization of distance education. *In* M.G. Moore, ed. *Contemporary issues in American distance education,* 333–343. Oxford, England: Pergamon.

Short, J., Williams, E. & Christie, B. (1976). *The social psychology of telecommunications.* London: Wiley.

Smith, F.A. (1991). Interactive instructional strategies: ways to enhance learning by television. *7th annual conference on distance teaching and learning.* Madison, WI.

Sophason, K. & Prescott, C. (1988). *The VITAL/THAI system: a joint development of computer assisted instruction systems for distance education.* Nonthaburi, Thailand: Sukothai Thammathirat University.

Spenser, K. (1991). Modes, media and methods: the search for educational effectiveness. *British Journal of Educational Technology 22*(1), 12–22.

Stubbs, S.T. & Burnham, B.R. (1990). An instrument for evaluating the potential effectiveness of electronic distance education systems. *The American Journal of Distance Education 4*(3), 25–37.

Suwinski, J.H. (1993). Fiber optics: deregulate and deploy. *Technos 2*(3), 8–11.

Taylor, J.C. & White, V.J. (1991). Faculty attitudes towards teaching in the distance education mode: an exploratory investigation. *Research in Distance Education 3*(3), 7–11.

Technology Based Learning (1994). *Instructional media design on CD-ROM.* Tempe, AZ: Arizona State University.

Tovar, M. (1989). Representing multiple perspectives: collaborative-democratic evaluations in distance education. *The American Journal of Distance Education 3*(2), 44–55.

U.S. Department of Commerce (1993). *The national information infrastructure: agenda for action.* Available online: FTP:ntia.doc.gov/pub/niiagenda.asc.

Utsumi, T., Rossman, P. & Rosen, S. (1990). The global electronic university. *In* M.G. Moore, ed. *Contemporary issues in American distance education,* 96–110. New York: Pergamon.

Van Enckevort, M., Harry, T., Marin, R. & Schultz, C. (1987). *A study of distance education student characteristics.* Telecommunications in Higher Education Conference, Baden Baden, Germany.

Van Haneghan, J., Barron, L., Young, M., Williams, S., Vye, N. & Bransford, J. (1992). The Jasper series: an experiment with new ways to enhance mathematical thinking. *In* D.F. Halpern, ed. *Enhancing thinking skills in the sciences and mathematics.* Hillsdale, NJ: Erlbaum

Verduin, J.R. & Clark, T.A. (1991). *Distance education: the foundations of effective practice.* San Francisco, CA: Jossey-Bass.

von Prummer, C. (1990). Study motivation of distance students: a report on some results from a survey done at the FernUniverität in 1987/88. *Distance Education 2*(2), 2–6.

von Stachelsky, F. (1991). *Corporate training by advanced telecommunication.* Telecommunication Based Training Systems Seminar, Madrid.

Vygotsky, L.S. (1978). *Mind in society: the development of the higher psychological processes.* Cambridge, MA: Harvard University Press.

Wagner, E. (1990). Looking at distance education through an educational technologist's eyes. *The American Journal of Distance Education 4*(1), 53–67.

Wagner, E.D. (1991). *Interaction in distance education: theoretical constructs affecting teaching and learning.* Forum for the Teaching of Distance Education. Norman, OK: University of Oklahoma.

Wedemeyer, C.A. (1977). Independent study. *In* A.S. Knowles, ed. *The international encyclopedia of higher education.* Boston, MA: Northeastern University.

— (1981). *Learning at the back door: reflections on nontraditional learning in the lifespan.* Madison, WI: University of Wisconsin.

Wells, R.A. (1990). *Computer-mediated communication for distance education and training: literature review and international resources.* Boise, ID: U.S. Army Research Institute.

West, P. (1993). School links to electronic highway proposed. *Education Week 12*(23), 27.

Weston, C. & Cranton, P.A. (1986). Selecting instructional strategies. *The Journal of Higher Education 57*(3), 259–88.

Whittington, N. (1987). Is instructional television educationally effective?: A research review. *The American Journal of Distance Education 1*(1), 47–57.

Wilkinson, T.W. & Sherman, T.M. (1990). Perceptions and actions of distance educators on academic procrastination . *The American Journal of Distance Education 4*(3), 47–56.

Willen, B. (1988). What happened to the Open University?: briefly. *Distance Education 9,* 71–83.

Winn, B. (1990). Media and instructional methods. *In* D.R. Garrison & D. Shale, eds. *Education at a distance: from issues to practice,* 53–66. Malabar, FL: Krieger.

Wright, S. (1991). Critique of recent research on instruction and learner support in distance education with suggestions for needed research. *Second American symposium on research in distance education..* University Park, PA: Pennsylvania State University.

14. COMPUTER-MEDIATED COMMUNICATION

Alexander J. Romiszowski
SYRACUSE UNIVERSITY

Robin Mason
OPEN UNIVERSITY

14.1 INTRODUCTION: VARIETIES OF CMC TECHNOLOGIES

14.1.1 Scope of This Chapter*

Computer-mediated communication (CMC) is a generic term now commonly used for a variety of systems that enable people to communicate with other people by means of computers and networks. Well-known examples of such systems include computer conferencing, electronic mail, discussion lists, and bulletin boards. However, there are yet other possible applications of CMC, both in the work environment and in education and training. In the work environment, a common and growing phenomenon is collaborative work by individuals or groups who are separated from each other by either time or distance. This has come to be called *computer-supported cooperative work* (CSCW) (Grief, 1988). In the education and training context, in addition to computer "conferencing," we can set up computer-mediated discussions of a more-focused nature as exemplified by the so-called virtual classroom (Hiltz, 1986, 1990), computer-mediated seminars and case study discussions (Romiszowski & DeHaas, 1989; Romiszowski, Jost & Chang, 1990), and computer-mediated job "performance support systems" (Gery, 1991). The variety of alternative modalities is large and growing. In this chapter we shall limit our discussion to those approaches that have been implemented for a few years and have therefore generated a reasonable quantity of research on their effectiveness and operational characteristics.

14.1.2 Out-of-Scope

We will exclude from our analysis the use of computer networks for accessing remote databases or library systems or for the transmission of large bodies of text that are not the basis for a person-to-person discussion and argument (e.g., on-line journals). We shall also exclude computer-assisted instruction (CAI), computer-based training (CBT), and other varieties of computer-assisted learning (see 12.2.3) in which the student interacts with the computer but not necessarily with other people. Similarly, we shall also exclude such systems as, for example, a group of four or five students all together at one time and place, using one computer to work collaboratively on some problem. As we move into the age of synergy between the cognitive sciences, computer sciences, and telecommunications, we are continually being faced with new possibilities for communication over distances. As an example, the recent movement towards multimedia computing has already found an application in computer-based audiographic conferencing systems (see 13.4.2.2) with multimedia support for visual communications and in desktop-video conferencing systems (see 13.4.2.6) that provide two-way digitized video communication between remote sites. Voice mail systems are also being applied in education and training contexts to enable asynchronous audio conferencing or multiway communication between people at remote sites (Bernard & Naidu, 1990; Romiszowski & Iskandar, 1992; Iskandar, 1994).

14.1.3 Partly-in-Scope

However, it is difficult to draw a precise line, as we have recently seen hybrid applications that involve a combination of computer-based instruction and computer-mediated discussions between students at a distance (e.g., Romiszowski & Chang, 1992, 1994). Similarly it is increasingly common to encounter systems that combine the use of information accessed from remote databases with CMC interchanges between users separated from each other by time or distance. Indeed, computer-based collaborative work almost invariably involves such a combination. Some authors see such hybrid "fourth-generation distance education systems" as playing a central role in future technology-based education (Lauzon & Moore, 1989).

---

*Early versions of this chapter were reviewed by Dan Eastmond, to whom the authors are grateful.

These new developments will also largely be excluded from this chapter, though occasionally they may be mentioned as future developments with implications for future research questions. Finally, although we do not explicitly exclude all applications of CMC in elementary and secondary school settings, we have tended to concentrate our review on the postsecondary levels, both in higher education and business training contexts.

14.2 CHARACTERISTICS OF CMC

A working definition of computer-mediated communication is "communication between different parties separated in space and/or time, mediated by interconnected computers." The computer network acts as a communication medium just as if it were a printed book containing text and graphics or a video broadcasting system. However, the computer brings certain characteristics to the communication process that the majority of previously available communication media did not offer.

14.2.1 Highly Interactive Communication

The first of these characteristics is the capability of supporting complex processes of interaction between the participants. The computer combines the permanent nature of written communication with the speed and to some extent the dynamicism of spoken telephone communication. Unlike the limited interactivity available in other forms of computer-based learning such as CAI, the possibilities for interaction and feedback are almost limitless, being a function of the creativity and personal involvement of the participants in the on-line discussion.

The feedback messages do not have to be preprepared and stored, as is the case with CAI. Also, the participants are able to some extent to express within their messages not only the bare content but also their personal viewpoints and, to a limited extent, the emotional overtones that may be present. Thus, the potential for interaction in a CMC system is both more flexible and potentially richer than in other forms of computer-based education.

14.2.2 Multi-Way Communication

Another aspect of the communication process is that it is essentially multiway communication. At the very least, the communication is two-way, as in the case of two people exchanging messages in an electronic-mail environment. More often, however, the communication is multiway, between all the participants of a group who may receive and respond to messages from all the other participants.

One point that should be considered is whether unlimited multiway communication is in fact always desirable within an educational situation. Many participants in computer conferencing have expressed frustration and disappointment with the difficulty they have had in sorting out relevant from irrelevant information, because there are so many participants contributing messages on a variety of different topics. One approach to creating some order in this chaos is through the development of special-purpose educational CMC software environments that may break down a complex conference into subthemes and issues held in separate "areas," as if in separate rooms in a convention center (for example, CoSy, PARTIcipate). Another approach is through the use of hypertext environments (see Chapter 22) that automatically link the incoming messages so that the users of the CMC system can get a clear idea of the structure of previous discussion. Such hypertext environments have also been applied to breaking down a large group of participants into small groups for intensive discussion, replicating in the on-line environment the classroom-based techniques of seminars or case study (Romiszowski & Chang, 1992; Chang, 1994). The latest windows-based conferencing systems allow participants to view a list of messages in a conference and then to point and click on those they wish to read. This facilitates greater selectivity for users than the old command line systems.

14.2.3 Synchronous or Asynchronous Communication

Finally, the communication process may have both synchronous and asynchronous characteristics. By synchronous communication, we understand communication between two or more people in real time, such as classroom-based, face-to-face discussion, or a telephone conversation. In asynchronous communication, the participants are not on-line at one and the same time, as in the case of correspondence by letter or fax. The interesting aspect of using the computer as a communication medium is that it is possible to use it at will both as a synchronous communication medium like a telephone or an asynchronous communication medium like a letter-writing or fax system, depending on what is ideally required by the particular situation (Rawson, 1990; Sheffield & McQueen, 1990). We will later explore these characteristics of synchronous and asynchronous communication in a computer-mediated environment, identifying potential benefits in different situations for each one of these modalities.

14.3 PERVASIVENESS OF CMC

14.3.1 Origins of CMC Networks

Computer-mediated communication is in fact one of the earlier modes in which computers have been used within the education process. Before CAI was more than an idea in the minds of certain researchers, computer networking and conferencing systems were already implemented, initially to facilitate communication among researchers. Indeed, it was in response to the fear of a possible war damaging the potential of researchers to continue to work that many of the major universities and government research institutions of the United States were linked by a network named ARPANET, which was so designed as to offer multiple communication paths between the various nodes or sites in the network (Elmer-Dewitt, 1994). The idea was that if certain sites were knocked out, the remaining sites could still communicate with each other independently of the particular geographic location of the disabled sites. This characteristic of the ARPANET system has been maintained in its successors such as Bitnet and Internet. Indeed, Internet is in effect a worldwide network of ARPANET-like local regional networks (Jacobson & Zimpfer, 1992).

14.3.2 Proliferation of the Networks

The linking of all regional networks to all the others creates multiple pathways of access from any one node in any one network to any other node in any of the other networks. This powerful web of electronic communication has become an indispensable tool for research and collaborative work in the scientific community. During the last year or so, the academic exclusivity of Internet has broken down as an ever-increasing number of commercial providers have opened access to anybody willing to subscribe. In 1994, the estimate of the size of Internet was in the region of 25 million connected computers, many of them with, of course, multiple users. This number is double the previous year's, and it is estimated that the number of users will continue to double annually for the foreseeable future (Elmer-Dewitt, 1994). It would seem that we are in the process of a major transformation of the communication habits and patterns of our society.

14.3.3 Corporate Uses of CMC

In the area of business communications, CMC has already become firmly established. Today, most of the major companies in the United States and Europe either rent or maintain their own data and personal communication networks so that all departments can communicate effectively and efficiently by electronic means. One aspect of increasing importance in these systems is the use of electronic mail, computer conferencing, and, increasingly, computer-supported collaborative work between individuals or groups who may be scattered in different regions of a country or even different continents. The "globalization" of business communication has become necessary for staying competitive.

An interesting aspect of the economics of this trend is illustrated by the growing tendency for North American telephone companies to offer low cost rates for business communication in Europe, given that much of the business day in Europe falls in a quiet period of early morning when telecommunication traffic in North America is at its lowest. Now, European companies are retaliating by adopting the same global marketing strategy rather than attempting to rely on (unenforceable) protective legislation. The tendency to this "whole world" view of telecommunications, coupled with the possibility of digitizing and storing messages for transmission at more convenient or more economical times, is transforming the whole sociopolitical structure of business communications and is now also beginning to impact on personal communications.

14.3.4 Educational Uses of CMC

In education, a particular growth area is the use of computer-mediated communication systems, not only for distance education when the participants are separated physically but also for more convenient communication on the same campus. Applications include institutions that utilize CMC as a principal mode of instruction and communication between tutors and students for whole courses, programs that run a few course units by means of CMC, and the use of CMC as a support medium for enrichment in otherwise conventional courses. However, such developments are not free of problems.

One of the problems identified in the educational uses of computer conferencing is that of teacher workload. Experiences from the NKI Electronic College in Norway show that teachers' main reservation about educational CMC is the open-ended demand on their time (Paulsen, 1992). As early as 1988, Hiltz noted that teaching an on-line course, at least the first time, was a bit like parenthood. "You are 'on duty' all the time, and there seems to be no end to the demands on your time and energy" (Hiltz, 1988, p. 31).

Nevertheless, many educators enthusiastic about the use of this new teaching medium have adapted strategies from small-group and interactive face-to-face techniques to the on-line world. Examples include seminars, learning partnerships, group projects, team presentations, simulations and role plays, peer counseling, and self-help groups. These and others are described in Miller (1991).

As economic realities shift towards ever-decreasing costs of electronic communication and ever-increasing costs of transport, space, lighting, heating, and teaching salaries, the tendency towards distance education methods, particularly electronically delivered distance education, is likely to increase yet further. In the light of this situation, it is important to verify to what extent the use of computer-mediated communication can be an effective alternative to conventional methods of teaching and learning. It is for these reasons that a review of current research on CMC and identification of potential future research questions is of particular importance at this time.

14.4 ISSUES IN CMC

14.4.1 Changing Technologies

One important trend already mentioned is the explosive rate at which new technologies for communication are being disseminated. The current multimedia and hypermedia developments have already been absorbed into CMC educational environments, producing systems that, at least in principle, have the potential for vastly improving the rather unstructured and text-based modes of communication that were the characteristic of earlier CMC systems. The incorporation of graphics, audio, video, and, in the future perhaps, even simulations of a virtual reality nature, which may all be transmitted across the digital information superhighways, is opening the potential for a much richer form of CMC. Most of the research completed so far is related to the earlier forms of text-based CMC. Some of these results may be equally valid within the future multimedia distance education systems. However, we may expect many new issues and research questions to emerge as these broadband, multimedia, multimodal communication systems link both people and remote databases into one seamless information and communication environment.

14.4.2 Replicate or Innovate

Another issue that is increasingly facing researchers and practitioners in the area of CMC is whether this medium should be considered as an alternative way of implementing previously well-tried teaching/learning strategies or whether the medium itself may lead to the implementation of novel strategies that previously were not used. Among the research and development work that has followed the line of replication of the past, a notable trend is illustrated by the "virtual classroom" methodologies that have been implemented and researched by Roxanne Hiltz and her collaborators (Hiltz, 1986, 1990). This work has focused on the replication of well-tried classroom-based teaching/ learning strategies in an asynchronous networked environment. Variations on the virtual classroom might include the virtual conference room (that is, computer conferencing), the virtual seminar room, and the virtual case study discussion room, each implying a specific set of teaching/learning strategies (Romiszowski, 1993).

An example of a somewhat novel approach is the trend towards the implementation of learner-controlled environments that may combine the use of information resources stored remotely as a hypermedia network of information, together with computer-supported collaborative project work between groups of individuals utilizing the CMC capabilities of the network. A nonconventional example of a popular use of CMC is to supplement conventional classroom-based instruction with group exercises or projects that participants "take home" but continue to interact with both teacher and colleagues through the medium of CMC while working on their projects. This approach, although not new with respect to its project work details, is novel in that it extends the possibilities for group interaction (Grabowski, Suciati & Pusch, 1990).

14.4.3 Technological Synergy

The third issue is the technological synergy between computer sciences, cognitive sciences, and telecommunications sciences, which is offering a host of possibilities such as artificial intelligence software that may act as an intelligent interface between remote databases in libraries and students or may in other ways facilitate the learning process. One possibility that is not yet a full reality is the capability of a computer-mediated communication system to handle instant translation so that group discussions may take place between participants from different countries, the groups using their own native languages in the process. Yet another area of current technological development that is yet to show its promise in practice is virtual reality or, in other words, the physical simulation of personal closeness and involvement in a particular environment. It is possible to imagine CMC systems of the future that will not be open to the criticism of the loss of nonverbal communication elements such as expression, gesture, or even touch. The applications of these new technological possibilities are yet unresearched. However, progress in the field is so rapid that it is not too early to consider some of the research issues that such new technological possibilities may pose.

14.4.4 Changing Theories and Philosophies

One notable current debate that impacts on the role of CMC in education is the "constructivism vs. objectivism" debate. The constructivist viewpoint (see Chapter 7) is often aligned with CMC and opposed to CAI, which is seen as an objectivist approach to teaching and learning (Cunningham, Duffy & Knuth, 1993; Kaye, 1992). The current vigor of this philosophical trend may be partly behind the growth in popularity of CMC systems, particularly in the humanities and philosophical subject areas.

Another, not so recent, debate that has been revived in relation to the use of CMC is the "humanism vs. mechanism" issue. The humanists see the personal interaction between people that CMC allows as an important element in the appropriate uses of computers in education. A similar debate on the "cognitive vs. behaviorist psychology" platform may lead to positions being taken either for or against the use of CMC (Morrison, 1989). Other groups of theorists argue for CMC from the social constructivist standpoint of learning as "conversation." In this viewpoint, the teaching/ learning process is seen as a form of conversation, whether real or in the mind of the learner, which leads to an "agreement" on the meaning of specific content. It is argued that CMC, through the provision of real opportunities for conversation, may be a more appropriate medium for the development of those types of learning objectives where a conversational approach is of particular importance, i.e., higher-order learning objectives associated with problem-solving and critical-thinking skills (Romiszowski & Corso, 1990). Yet other philosophical/theoretical viewpoints that have been brought to bear on the relevance and appropriateness of CMC are Habermas's theory of undominated communicative action (Boyd, 1990) and postmodernism (Soby, 1990).

All of these different theoretical and philosophical viewpoints are interesting but are largely unresearched. Some current research is beginning to address certain issues in this field, but much further research is necessary in order to validate the claims and counterclaims and to develop a robust set of principles for the selection, design, and use of CMC environments in education and training.

14.5   STATUS OF RESEARCH ON CMC

This section investigates the status of research to date on computer-mediated communication. It addresses such issues as the amount and quality of existing research findings, the sources of CMC information, various research methodologies being employed, the extent of theories and knowledge about CMC, and the difficulty of examining dynamic information technologies with static research tools.

14.5.1   Sources of CMC Information

Research surrounding CMC parallels the expansion of this technology. Journal articles begin appearing with frequency around 1984, although the roots of research in the field go back to the 1960s and earlier (Hiltz & Turoff, 1978). Regular academic conferences are convened, and several edited books devoted to CMC appear from the early 1980s (Kerr & Hiltz, 1982; Harasim, 1990; Kay, 1992; Mason & Kaye, 1989; Mason, 1993). Since 1990, scholars have developed several comprehensive bibliographies. Among these, Romiszowski (1991) and Burge (1992) each list approximately 400 references, from conferences proceedings, edited book chapters, professional papers, and journal articles.

Now there is a constant stream of conference proceedings and edited books appearing at the rate of several per year, some devoted to specific and others to general aspects of research and development in CMC. Notable among recent publications are the anthology on *Collaborative Learning through Computer Conferencing,* edited by Kaye (1992), the Proceedings of the Third Teleteaching Conference held in Trondheim, Norway, edited by Davies and Samways (1993), and the regular Conference Proceedings emanating from such universities as Wisconsin at Madison, United States; Guelph in Ontario, Canada; and the Open University in the United Kingdom.

Examination of these materials finds many of them to be anecdotal in nature, written by pioneers in implementing CMC technology for educational purposes, promoting the exciting educational possibilities of this new medium, and reporting case descriptions of their own experiences with these innovations. However, some basic research is underway; a 1992 survey found over 35 CMC studies completed or in progress (Cole, Beam, Karn & Hoad-Reddick, 1992). These authors report that the majority of studies came out of a quantitative/positivist paradigm. However, they argue, as does Mason (1992), that interpretist and critical-theory paradigms (see Chapter 9) may be more appropriate for studying the CMC environment. So far, few studies have been performed from these "neoqualitative" perspectives.

14.5.2   Principal Issues Investigated

As mentioned above, a large proportion of earlier writing and indeed some of current writing on CMC is exploring the potential of CMC rather than reporting hard research. As an example, among the 400 publications listed in the bibliography prepared by Romiszowski (1991), only some 10% to 15% were research studies. This compares to 25% on overviews, reviews, applications, trends, and policy; another 15% on design, development, and implementation strategies; 15% on the hardware, software, systems, and logistics; another 20% on aspects of networking, and hardware- and system-related issues; finally, some 15% on topics of database access and "computer-supported cooperative work."

The research papers can be further classified into several areas of interest as follows. First, there are issues of general concern such as the access to CMC and whether it has a democratizing or elitist impact on society; the quality of on-line information and its equivalence to printed material (particularly relevant in the case of on-line journals); the social impact of CMC on the users; methods of implementation and use in both distance education and in conventional courses; and research aspects of software capability, design, and utilization.

A second group of research interests can be generally referred to as "teaching and learning concerns." These include the content and objectives that may be treated by CMC, the process of interactivity and interaction as it occurs in CMC, appropriate learning strategies and tactics that may be employed in CMC, aspects of learner control or system control of CMC systems, and the effectiveness or other outcomes of CMC used for educational purposes.

A third group of research interests may be best referred to as "implementation concerns." These include aspects of student participation or nonparticipation and their attitudes, attitudes and participation styles of instructors and teachers using CMC, aspects to do with the implementation and administration of CMC systems, and logistic and planning aspects to do with staff and support systems.

The later sections of this chapter will follow the organization schema presented here to review the principal findings to date from the, as yet relatively sparse, research that has been performed in this area of educational technology.

14.5.3   Methods Being Used

Because of the difficulty of reaching CMC users, often separated by space or time, most research efforts to date involved survey research, either through electronic or conventionally distributed questionnaires (see, for example, Ryan, 1992; Grabowski, Suciati & Pusch, 1990; Phillips & Pease, 1987). Another relatively popular method is the evaluative case study (e.g., Phillips, 1990; Mason, 1990; Phillips, Santoro & Kuehn, 1988). However, many researchers recognize the value of automatic computer-based recording of communications transactions and have sought to capitalize on usage, interaction, and transcript information directly available from the conferences (Mason, 1992; Henri, 1992; Tucker, 1991; Levin, Kim & Riel, 1990). Harasim (1987) first used mainframe computer records to analyze student access times and dispersion of participation in a graduate computer conference. There is little use to date, in the study of CMC, of qualitative approaches based on observation and interviewing (either in person or over the telephone). This is so for several reasons: (a) the labor intensity of qualitative research study, (b) the expense and difficulty of contacting ex-CMC users, and (c) the newly emerging acceptance of qualitative research in education. Some recent studies, for example, Eastmond (1993) and Burge (1993), have, however, adopted such a methodology.

Nevertheless, the most glaring omission in CMC research continues to be the lack of analytical techniques applied to the content of the conference transcript. Given that the educational value of computer conferencing is much touted by enthusiasts, it is remarkable that so few evaluators are willing to tackle this research area. One of the pioneers in this field is Henri (1992), who presents an analytical framework to categorize five dimensions of the learning process exteriorized in messages: participation, interactions, social, cognitive, and metacognitive. Another is Mason (1992), who has attempted to draw up a typology of conference messages related to the educational values they display.

14.5.4 Extent of Theory/Knowledge Base

CMC scholarship tends to proudly acclaim the educational merits of this technology for a variety of reasons—access, collaboration, interactivity, self-direction, and experiential learning, to name a few—yet few of these are grounded in systematic, rigorous inquiry. Current CMC research, like much of that in distance education, focuses on narrow topics within specific institutional contexts and has not sought to generalize to wider contexts. Yet, slowly, the studies are appearing, some by the early promotional scholars and others to substantiate and refute their claims. The broad dimensions of CMC inquiry are laid out, yet few attempts to present theories or research-based models of any aspect of CMC study have emerged. Exceptions would be Burge's (1993) "power-load-margin" work, building on Howard McClusky's work, and Eastmond's (1993) "adult distance study through computer conferencing" (ADSCC) model. Paulsen (1993) and Moore (1991) have developed theories of distance education based on the attributes of computer conferencing, but these are yet waiting for experimental verification.

14.5.5 Moving–Target Difficulty

Exacerbating the research and theory-building endeavors is the continual flux of CMC technologies. Descriptive studies portray the dynamics of CMC at the present moment, but technological changes continually alter and enrich the instructional systems captured in the umbrella term CMC. However, as noted earlier (and in Eastmond's 1993 study), many conventional educational patterns are replicated on-line, either purposely (such as in the virtual or electronic-classroom efforts) or unintentionally, as educators seek to design appropriate instructional practices for CMC.

14.6 FINDINGS TO DATE

What do findings from research to date tell us about computer-mediated communication? This section presents findings from that research, addressing first the general concerns surrounding CMC use, and then looking at various contexts that use CMC: educational, organizational, and network contexts.

14.6.1 General Concerns

14.6.1.1. Equitable Access. Those who advocate the use of CMC, especially for distance education, argue that this technology allows for greater access at reduced costs by reaching rural areas, providing communication access for those who cannot attend class because of hectic life schedules, physical limitations, or institutional barriers (Dirr, 1990).

However, others counterargue that computer usage in general is accessible to wealthier, high-achieving male European-American students who live in urban areas (Faddis, 1985; Neuman, 1991; O'Connor, 1992). White (1991) reports how relatively few Americans have access to CMC technology. The situation in other developed countries (e.g., Britain) is similar (Kirkwood, 1993), while in the developing world, computer technology often significantly increases the gap between the "haves" and the "have-nots." Most CMC use is institutional, but, as Eastmond (1993) reports, CMC use often depends on adults' occupational status and socialization as to whether they value this sort of experience.

A policy study directed towards providing home-computing access to distance learners at the British Open University (Jones, Kirkup, Kirkwood & Mason, 1992) found that a rental policy of low cost for the necessary equipment was particularly important for women and less-advantaged students. They found that other family members rarely use CMC equipment, but that it requires large life-style changes and investment in time for learning the technology. Novice students required more help, leaning on tutors who often resented providing the necessary support. These studies were based on extensive survey questionnaires to British Open University students using computers for home-based learning as part of the university's home-commuting policy begun in 1988.

14.6.1.2. Information Quality. The larger the CMC network, the richer the resource for information exchange. However, depersonalization also occurs, and so individuals are less likely to know the position, background, and expertise of those with whom they communicate. This may call into question the credibility of the information and opinions that are gathered over the networks. In the case of some of the research on the British Open University's use of computer conferencing, there was concern that on-line messages held little important information (Grint, 1989), while others asserted that they do (Graddol, 1989). Eastmond (1992) claims that much of students' valuing of CMC activity stems from their conception of learning, corroborating in part Grint's (1989) argument of CMCs being perceived as trivial or not dependent on student's perceptions of the nature of technical information being objective, procedural, and concrete.

14.6.1.3. Social Impact in Distance Education.
Students' concern over their physical health surfaced in a couple of studies (Eastmond, 1993; Harasim, 1987), particularly with eye strain, but this did not seem to be a central issue with most CMC users. Some researchers expressed concern that CMC will build global networks while reducing proximate neighborhood and family ties, that CMC may alter peoples' work and communication patterns significantly and may dehumanize interpersonal interaction (Eastmond, 1992; Zuboff, 1988). Levinson (1990) counters (without a research basis) that the technologies are more genuine than we imagine in conveying human communication.

Few studies directly addressed on-line relationships. Boshier's (1988) investigation of computer conferences on listserves found that friendly relationships developed in spite of reduced cues, that participants became more casual and humorous over time, and that this medium invites more equitable participation. Phillips (1990) found that students who participated in an electronic "student lounge" maintained their attitude of positive potential for this medium after direct experience with it. They enjoyed chatting, and making friends and professional contacts, and felt less isolated.

Zuboff (1988) did extensive fieldwork and analysis over a 10-year period on the impact of computerization on companies, looking at manufacturing automation, clerical-work restructuring, the implementation of a database management system, and communications using computer conferencing. She describes worker alienation and the social breakdown of the workplace as new management styles emerged. A study with similar themes (Attewell & Rule, 1988) reviewed literature on organizational changes as a result of computerization.

14.6.1.4. Intellectual Impact on Conventional Courses.
The purpose of most of the uses of CMC is to reduce problems caused by large geographic distances between colleagues. However, some very important effects from local uses can also be realized. Kuehn (1988) suggests that electronic mail can extend classroom discussions, increase the ease of evaluating student assignments, increase the connectedness of students and faculty, and increase both the social as well as an intellectual impact from this means of communication. Muffo (1987) also suggests that personal communications themselves can change due to the

inclusion of computers, and particularly electronic mail, in the curriculum.

One of the problems observed by Grabowski (1990) was the need to increase opportunities for intellectual and social exchange among students. This includes new students who enter the program each semester and need to adjust to a new environment, establish new friends, adjust to a new pattern for studying, and juggle time for classes and life events, as well as seasoned students who are at the dissertation stage. Grabowski (1990) observed that there were several subpopulations of students: those who were heavy users of CMC, light users, one-time users, and those who did not use it at all. In order to evaluate the perceived usefulness, Grabowski mailed surveys to students who were currently enrolled, both users and nonusers. The principle findings can be summarized as follows:

- Full-time doctoral students without children are the most likely e-mail users.
- A high percentage of the users send e-mail to fellow students, friends, and faculty for the purpose of exchanging information or discussing ideas, and a lower number send e-mail to exchange social information.
- For nonusers, "no need" (40%) was reported most as the reason for nonuse. Technical skills (13%) and convenience (14%) were not as important.

From the data, there was very little indication of social impact, but a very high indication of intellectual impact among users, with 23% of the respondents either agreeing or strongly agreeing with the statement about social impact; whereas 73% agreed or strongly agreed with the statement about the impact on their intellectual life.

14.6.1.5. Software Capability and Design.
Opinions vary as to the significance of the software and its impact on the learning environment. For example, Eastmond contends that the "user-friendliness" and transparency of the system for enabling participants in CMC to use software features heavily impacts CMC experience and learning approaches taken with the media (Eastmond, 1992). While the first systems worked with a command-line interface, modern computer conferencing systems such as FirstClass support formatted messages, multimedia attachments to messages, and a point-and-click method of navigating from conference to conference. Educational users have developed tools for managing student assignments, taking polls of student opinion, and monitoring the level of student participation. Mason (1994), however, claims that there are greater influences in the learning environments than in the software:

Research is just beginning on the effects of these friendlier systems on the educational process. Will ease of learning and using the system lead to more active and interactive participants? While it is hard to expect anything but positive improvements, evaluators of conferencing applications have always concluded that the technology is not the problem. Social and pedagogical issues play by far the bigger part in the creation of a successful learning environment (Mason, 1994, pp. 51–52).

Ultimately, the aim of all CMC systems is that the user is most conscious of the content of the communication, not the equipment or the means of communication. In some sense, computer conferencing has a very long way to go in achieving transparency. Even with the newest software, the user still needs some awareness of telecommunications, some understanding of personal computing, and often a great deal of ingenuity with troubleshooting problems on their own equipment.

An example of the way the software capabilities may influence a student's success and the overall success of a CMC experience was identified by Romiszowski and DeHaas (1989) and Romiszowski and Jost (1989) in analyzing the dynamics of educational computer conferences of a seminarlike nature held within a typical electronic-mail environment. These studies identified two major problems experienced by both the participants and the CMC exercise organizers. The participants experienced a loss of the "sense of structure" of the discussion. The messages coming into their mailbox in a linear stream did not reflect the sequence of elaboration of arguments within the various parallel discussions that were going on in the seminar. The result of this was that participants typically recalled only the most recent messages and did not relate them clearly to earlier messages. At the end of the conference, it was found that participants varied considerably in terms of their overall general view of what has been discussed and decided on.

A second problem, which may be considered more a problem of the organizers of the CMC experience, was the problem of "loss of control" over what exactly would be discussed. Maybe partly as a consequence of the loss of a sense of structure on the part of the students, the students would tend to pick up on a recently circulated message and respond to that out of context, often leading the discussion into a completely new area. It was found that the task of bringing discussants back to the original topic was much more difficult in the CMC environment than would normally be the case in face-to-face discussion.

It was shown that these two problems were largely caused by the software environment within which the conferences were taking place by modifying this environment and demonstrating that both the problems were greatly diminished. Specific modifications used were the development of a structured discussion environment within a hypertext software package that would automatically create separate discussion areas for each topic and automatically create links between relevant messages that could later be followed with ease (Romiszowski & Chang, 1992).

14.6.2 Educational Issues

Educational CMC takes place within an institutional context, with learning as the desired outcome of this activity. This section focuses first on various learning concerns that surface with the use of this medium. Next, it shifts to address institutional concerns, such as students and their participation, instructors and teaching, administration and implementation, and staff and support issues.

14.6.2.1. Teaching/Learning Concerns

14.6.2.1.1. Content and Objectives. The characteristics of CMC, although changing rapidly, still shape the instructional and communication activities they support. Perhaps the most obvious question to arise is whether CMC, which is primarily text based, is equally suited for various subject matters. Florini (1990) suggests that subjects such as science, mathematics, and the arts do not lend themselves to CMC instruction because of its inability to convey audio, visual, and kinesthetic information. Wells (1992) surveyed the types of courses being taught at both the undergraduate and graduate levels in the following subject areas: computer science, foreign language, group performance skills, history, humanities, physics, statistics, education (various types), engineering, management, and media studies. Wells suggests that subject matter that involves discussion, brainstorming, problem solving, collaboration, and reflection is best suited to CMC.

14.6.2.1.2. Interactivity and Interaction Processes. Interactivity, that is, the capability of participants to receive specific feedback of any length to their contributions from any other member of a CMC discussion, is touted as a primary advantage of this medium (Moore, 1991; Harasim, 1989; Feenberg, 1989). Studies of message exchange patterns support the perspective that communication patterns are more democratic and group discussion oriented than would be found in classrooms or other telecommunications settings (Harasim, 1989; Levin, Kim & Riel, 1990; Siegal, Dubrovsky, Kiesler & McGuire, 1986). Eastmond (1993) suggested that CMC wasn't inherently interactive, but instead depended largely on participation frequency, timely contributions by members, and the nature of messages posted. Computer conference participants who got behind found the medium to be rather didactic and passive.

CMC has been proclaimed as uniquely suited for collaborative study (Harasim, 1989; Harasim, 1990b; Kaye, 1992). Eastmond (1993) found that a competitive model of computer conferencing was equally adaptable to study through CMC study, and the collaborative model did not work equally well for all students. Siegel et al. (1986) investigated the effects of CMC on communication efficiency, participation, interpersonal behavior, and group choice. They found that CMC groups interacted less and took longer in the decision-making process than similar groups in face-to-face discussion. On the other hand, the CMC group members tended to behave as equals, whereas there was evidence of social inequality and of unequal participation in the face-to-face group.

Romiszowski and Chang (1992) have performed several studies investigating techniques by which the CMC environment could promote the same level of cognitive processing and interactivity that may occur in a one-on-one tutorial between a student and an expert teacher. The strategy employed has been to use an initial, partially prepared exercise that invites a student to create a structural "picture" of all related elements that are seen to be relevant to the solution of a particular complex, multifaceted problem. This complex student response is then the basis of a CMC discussion that may take place either between student and tutor or between a group of students commenting on each others' alternative solutions. This adaptation of a methodology called "structural communication" has shown itself to be effective for implementing such interactive teaching methods as the Harvard Business Case methodology and, furthermore, reducing the amount of human facilitator or monitor interaction necessary to lead the exercise to a satisfactory conclusion (Romiszowski, 1990; Romiszowski & Chang, 1992; Chang, 1994).

14.6.2.1.3. Learning Strategies and Tactics.   Several researchers have looked at the learning strategies students employ when engaged in on-line study. Burge (1993) used structured, open-ended interviews to study how students think they learn through CMC. He found a set of learning strategies with similarities to both those proposed by cognitive psychologists and adult educators for other means of study, with the addition of a group of interpersonal and logistical factors for the "management of the metacontext of learning." Learning strategies he found students using fell into the following major categories: making choices, expression, group interaction, and the organization of information. Eastmond (1993) found distance students who took courses through computer conferencing to transfer learning-to-learn approaches from other instructional contexts. These transferred elements included study patterns, time scheduling, working with others, establishing attitudes, setting goals, seeking task and structure information, and demonstrating competence. However, the nature of this novel instructional context required them to develop idiosyncratic ways of dealing with the on-line learning environment. Some CMC-specific strategies they employed included dealing with multiple discussions, information overload, asynchronicity, textual ambiguity, and processing the on-line information and determining what contributions to make.

14.6.2.1.4. Learner Control and System Control. Some proponents of CMC see the principal use and value of the medium as an emancipatory communication medium, totally under control of the users, for whatever purpose they wish to use it. There is no doubt that such a medium of communication may be valuable in education and was a missing aspect in most conventional distance education systems of the past. The CMC-based common room/coffee-shop is a phenomenon to be welcomed. However, it seems difficult to support the argument that this is the only valid use of CMC systems in education.

CMC has also been promoted (Mason, 1988) as an excellent medium for self-directed learning as a defining characteristic of adult learning (Knowles, 1984). Self-direction manifests itself when students voluntarily elect to take a CMC-based course, determine how, when, and where they will study, and negotiate the learning activities and content focus they will pursue during the course. Eastmond (1993) found that distance students taking CMC courses

exhibited varying patterns of self-direction. They were confident about their abilities to manage their schedule and the study process to produce necessary learning results, but they wanted the assignments clearly set forth for them by the instructor.

There are also problems that need to be addressed when using CMC as an integral part of a course. Some of these spring from the *asynchronous* qualities of the communication process. Unlike face-to-face instruction, or real-time teleconferencing, in which the participants communicate during one fixed period of time, CMC allows one to choose *when* to respond to another participant's comment. This offers the benefit of allowing one to think out a more structured, more complex response, and the benefit of being able to participate at times that are personally convenient. This same factor can also generate communication difficulties. One problem is that it may promote procrastination, leaving the response for later, and, perhaps in some cases, failure to respond altogether. This adds to the complexity of the developing structure in that students may, at any time, be inputting new comments related to different stages of the development of the topic. Not only is the discourse "multilevel" in that several different topics may be in simultaneous discussion, but it is also "multispeed" (Romiszowski & DeHaas, 1989).

Another problem originates from the *distance* communication aspect of CMC. Although distance communication (see Chapter 13) allows one to participate in a discourse that may otherwise be impossible, it also introduces some difficulties of *control* of the discourse. The instructor loses some of the benefits offered by a face-to-face group situation. When the discussion drifts off the topic, it often takes longer, and is more difficult, to bring the group back on task. There is also the problem of knowing who is and is not participating. There is only knowledge of who is contributing. How can we know who is "lurking" in the system, so that we can try to draw them into the discourse (Romiszowski & De Haas, 1989)?

14.6.2.1.5. Outcomes and Their Evaluation. Assessment of student achievement in CMC courses versus those offered through correspondence or classroom formats is reported in only a few studies. Cheng, Lehman, and Armstrong (1991) compared achievement, attitudes, time-on-task, and interaction between groups involved in each of the three types of instructional formats for a graduate course about microcomputers. They found that the CMC group scored lower on achievement tests and attitudes than the other two groups, but time-on-task was the same. Completion rates were greatest for those attending class, but a study group at one CMC site improved completion rates there. In another study, Phelps et al. (1981) compare both the effectiveness and the costs of a computer-mediated communication course in the U.S. Army. In this study, the CMC students tended to score somewhat higher than those taking the conventional courses. However, the CMC courses had higher dropout rates. As regards costs, once the initial conversion and start-up costs are recovered, the CMC courses were found to cost 48% less than the equivalent conventional courses.

14.6.2.2. Implementation Concerns

14.6.2.2.1. Students and Participation. Just a few studies touch on the distance students' life situation, goals, and personal factors that affect their pursuit of a formal education. Robinson (1992) looked at demographic characteristics of distance students at a Canadian university and found that the majority of them were working women, pursuing an education part time. Most of them had prior university experience. Gibson (1991) found that self-confidence impacts student success in an external degree program. Factors that enhanced self-confidence in a learning context were instructor empathy, success in completing work, progress toward a goal, and students' perceived understanding of themselves and the educational process they were undergoing.

By studying the hard-copy transcripts of a computer conferencing course, Harasim (1987) plotted the participation patterns of the students. She found that the smallest group, full-time graduate students, used the system during the weekdays, but the majority of the class who worked full time Monday through Friday used the system most heavily on the weekends. Unsurprisingly, the heaviest usage on weekdays was in the evening, but participation was spread throughout the day on weekends.

Likewise, little research addresses distance students' perceptions of education and their distance learning. Manninen (1991) found class differences to affect participation in courses taught using computer conferencing. Middle-class students found it easier to access the computer network, and they discussed actively on the system. In contrast, working-class students contributed less in reactive responses, but their participation increased over time. Roberts (1990) found that distance university students held learning and career-oriented goals, not social and cultural ones. These students were self-confident, independent, achieving, and persistent. However, differences existed on goals and academic self-concept by gender, class, experience, and income level. Distance students were more confident and learning oriented than their conventional counterparts.

Several studies explored student perceptions of the on-line communications medium generally, not just computer conferencing. Grabowski, Suciati, and Pusch (1990) found that graduate students felt that e-mail was effective for exchanging social and academic information with their peers and professors. Those who chose not to use it did so because they felt no need for it, found access to the computer network inconvenient or unavailable, or simply had not learned the necessary skills for using the technology. Grint (1989) found that students thought it difficult to carry out conversations in asynchronous time and felt that they were overloaded with trivial information before being able to contribute. They were inhibited by their impression of a large, "lurking," anonymous audience who would read their contributions. Students perceived that unless they contributed facts, which was difficult in the new subject-matter area

they were studying, their additions to the conference were unimportant. Therefore, they disliked reading the opinions of other students on-line. Status and gender also affected participation among those he studied.

Harasim's (1987) research of two graduate courses taught through computer conferencing is probably the most telling about how students perceive this medium. Using both quantitative and qualitative approaches, she found that students spent longer on-line than they were required by the course, and they felt that this medium was effective. Students listed the advantages of computer conferencing as increased interaction, access to a group, the democratic environment it fostered, the convenience of access, their control over the instructional process, the motivation they had to participate, and the textual nature of the computer conferencing medium. The disadvantages they mentioned about this medium were the information overload they felt, the medium's asynchronicity, which caused delayed responses, difficulty they felt following on-line discussions, the loss of visual cues with this communication, increased access inconvenience, and health concerns about computer radiation.

Other studies support Harasim's conclusions while adding some additional insights. Hiltz (1986) found that students commented among themselves and more highly valued computer conferencing when it was a supplemental activity of the course and not the main medium of instruction. Students said that convenience was the greatest advantage of computer conferencing, but the awkwardness they felt in communicating with unknown persons was its greatest liability. Robinson (1992) found that convenience of access at the student's own time schedule was more important than the separation in proximity of distance learners. McCreary and Van Duren (1987) found that those of higher or lower status submit written contributions less frequently to computer conferences. Graduate students' participation was more active and horizontal (among fellow students) than was the on-line activity of undergraduates. Differences in content areas didn't affect participation. Scollon (1981) found that the Native Alaskan students she studied were easily confused by the excessive and scattered communication on-line. Instructors couldn't attend to the many students in the course (60 people), and the volume of communication was particularly difficult for everyone to process. The students welcomed a return to the audio cues of teleconferencing.

14.6.2.3. Instructors and Teaching.
The role of the computer conferencing teacher is quite different from the traditional classroom instructor or lecturer. Course design becomes more important, and preparation entails the structuring of conferences and topics, and the design of activities and small group work. During a computer conferencing course, the teacher must adopt the role of facilitator not content provider.

The facilitator needs to pay careful attention to welcoming each student to the electronic course, and reinforcing early attempts to communicate. In the first few weeks, I make sure that my notes in the conference specifically reference prior student notes. I send many individual messages to students suggesting resources and generally reaching out to students. The coaching function is key to easing the students' transition to computer-mediated communication (Davie, 1989, p. 82).

While the teacher's role is particularly time consuming in the initial phase of a computer conferencing course, it usually reduces as students take over the discussions. Nevertheless, some reports indicate that teachers spend up to twice as long, overall, to deliver a course via computer conferencing as they do to give a course by traditional means.

Given that CMC is so time consuming, why are so many teachers willing to teach electronically? The reason lies in the reported rewards: tremendous satisfaction in working towards the goal of developing independent, questioning learners. The literature abounds with comments from teachers recording their personal learning experience in adopting this medium (Gunawardena, 1992). One of the additional rewards for computer conferencing lies in the flexibility it gives them to work at their convenience, not at set times.

14.6.2.3.1. Administrators. Most small-scale uses of computer conferencing begin at grass-roots level with a few enthusiastic teachers, but its eventual acceptance within a large institution usually requires backing at the highest level.

Implementing a program of on-line teaching can raise major policy issues. For example, there is the question of incentives and remuneration of faculty who teach via telecommunications. Very few institutions currently acknowledge the extra effort and time involved in teaching via CMC, with additional payment. Furthermore, the academic promotion process does not adequately reward faculty for taking on teleconferencing duties. Lack of recognition continues to be a significant deterrent to growth and acceptance among faculty. This issue is bound up with the much more complex and long-term issue of whether the use of CMC saves organizations money.

There is growing acceptance of the notion that turning to CMC is not a route to major cost cutting but rather a means of extending access to courses, improving the quality of current provision, and meeting the need for flexible learning that cannot be accommodated otherwise.

14.6.2.3.2. Support Staff. Teaching via computer conferencing requires a high degree of familiarity with the system's features and architecture, and the training and support of teachers and students are critical aspects of any educational program using this medium. While it is relatively easy to train teachers and students to use a CMC system, it is much more difficult to teach the skill of moderating educational computer conferencing: how to promote discussion, devise activities, and encourage interaction. Experienced on-line teachers have written guidelines (Brochet, 1989; Kerr, 1986), but in the end, teachers have to find their own style through practice.

Institutions with large CMC programs often operate a help desk for queries about equipment and communications systems; smaller programs usually have to provide some

staff resource to give advice to students with technical difficulties. However, given the technical complications of the current telecommunications scene, some organizations adopt the policy of expecting students to turn to their local dealer for this support.

Managing and supporting equipment through its lifetime is another issue that some institutions face for the first time with telecommunications. For some organizations, a whole new unit and type of staff are necessary. Many underestimate the extent of this element of telecommunications. According to Maloy and Perry (1991), to understate the dollars required to operate, maintain, upgrade, and train to the system is to undercut its assimilation into the instructional process. When this happens, technology remains supplemental, making it even more vulnerable to cost reductions.

14.7 A LOOK TO THE FUTURE

14.7.1 Electronic Networks and Future Education and Training

The development of telecommunications and digital data transmission is revolutionizing the way business is performed. People are working and communicating ever more by means of computer-based workstations that support databases, electronic mail, and a host of other information tools.

As electronic communication networks become more ubiquitous, easier to use, and more powerful, the trend towards electronic, networked business communications will grow rapidly. As a result, people will spend an increasing proportion of their time at workstations and proportionately less at live meetings (Vallee, 1982; Zuboff, 1988).

This trend is also liable to spread to meetings with educational or human resource–development aims. The U.S. telephone company AT&T, for example, has already moved towards the massive use of teleconferencing in place of conventional classroom-based courses for most of its sales and management training needs. The major part of sales and management training in AT&T is now delivered by this method (in 1989, over 69,000 employees participated at least once in some form of teletraining), and results overall are considered to be quite satisfactory (Chute, 1990).

Of course, the rapid expansion in use of electronic teletraining is being driven, as always, not so much by effectiveness, but rather by economic factors. AT&T has reported an overall reduction of over 50% in the costs per student hour of training. This cost saving comes almost entirely from savings in travel and subsistence costs when employees participate in centrally organized "place-based" courses, as well as from reduced loss of productivity due to a reduction in the time that employees are away from their jobs (Chute, 1988, 1990).

14.7.2 New Forms of Education and Training

There are also other pressures, both organizational and philosophical, that are increasing the amount of autonomy, self-directedness, and responsibility that learners have in respect of their own education and development. From the philosophical side, there is the viewpoint that people should have more control over what they learn and how they learn it. These viewpoints are embodied in the principles of modern adult education, or andragogy. They also reflect earlier humanist traditions. They are further strengthened by the modern concepts of continuing or "permanent education," which spring from the realization that change in society, and particularly in the workplace, is now so fast that everyone is of necessity involved in a process of lifelong learning.

This need for updating may in some respects be very specific and personal for each individual. Hence the growing popularity of the "open learning" concept as a modular approach to education that can take anyone from wherever they are at present in a given domain to wherever they need or want to be, relatively independently of the needs or wants of other people (Paine, 1988).

Given the increasingly competitive nature of business in the international marketplace and the critical importance that access to and use of up-to-date information and methods play in a company's competitiveness, it is not surprising that the concept of human resources development as "self-development" is taking root. This concept sees keeping up-to-date and employable as the responsibility of every employee. The employer's responsibility is to make this possible, by helping to identify the needs of the individual and by facilitating access to the resources necessary to satisfy those needs. Doing so will call less frequently for lengthy courses organized either within the company or by outside providers, but will instead make much more use of networking, access to external databases and electronic libraries, small specialist group teletraining, and self-instruction in all its forms (Eurich, 1990).

As the trends outlined above expand through the business community, similar trends will be seen in relation to adult education, especially in the growing use of distance education in formal educational institutions. To some extent, similar economic factors may lead to a greater use of distance education and electronic networking as the prime delivery media for certain courses. More ubiquitous, however, will be the use of electronic communication media as support to conventional courses. This will be brought about partly by organizational and pedagogical benefits that such systems can offer conventional courses and partly because it will be seen to be the duty of education to use such systems in order to prepare its graduates for the realities of a workplace where they will be obliged to use them.

This last point really brings home the importance of examining now how to get high-quality educational experiences and effective learning from future networked communication systems. The particular focus should be on the effective implementation of group discussion or "conversational" methodologies on electronic telecommunications networks. This focus is particularly important, as we know much less about how to converse effectively on electronic networks than we do about electronic self-instruction. There is a long history and fairly developed technology of the design, development, and delivery-at-a-distance of self-study materials. There is much less known about the running of effective group discussion sessions at a distance.

Such teaching methods as seminars or case studies are traditionally implemented in small or medium-sized groups, led by skilled and experienced "facilitators." Much of the success of these teaching methods is ascribed to the facilitators and the skill with which they focus discussion; guide the approaches adopted by the participants; use natural group dynamics to stimulate interest, participation, and deep involvement; pull together what has been learned in the final debriefing discussion; and so on. Can such participatory discussion methods be effectively orchestrated at a distance? How might this be done?

14.7.3 Two Paradigms Compared

In order to answer these questions, let us review a little theory and also some of the research already available on this topic. It may help to compare and contrast two alternative paradigms, or perhaps philosophies, which are current in education: the "instructional" and the "conversational" paradigms. These are summarized in Table 14-1.

The instructional paradigm is the one that has driven much (though by no means all) of the research and development of the past 30 years that has been performed under the label of educational (or instructional) technology. The conversational paradigm may be seen as the basis of much of the work done on small-group study, group dynamics, experiential learning, and so on.

In relation to distance teaching specifically, one may notice at the bottom of Table 14-1 that the more conventional "study module" or typical correspondence model may serve as a good example of the instructional paradigm. Synchronous teleconferencing, both audio and video based, is on the other hand a good example of the conversational paradigm in action. CMC, however, is seen as being able to support both conversational and instructional procedures. For example, joint cooperation on the analysis and development of a hypertext document satisfies all the basic requirements of a conversation between the participants. The study of an on-line version of a maintenance manual for an airplane in order to learn a particular set of troubleshooting procedures satisfies the requirements of instruction. This versatility of CMC systems and their potential integration with on-line information sources such as hypertext makes them particularly interesting systems to study with a view to their rational adoption in education and training (Horn, 1989; Romiszowski, 1990).

14.7.4 Future Trends

The future of computer conferencing is undoubtedly one of great mergers: with synchronous media, with multimedia, and with the whole panoply of desktop facilities. Some would say, the sooner the better! While this merger is already happening at the leading edge with integrated text, sound, and graphics being exchanged on higher-speed

TABLE 14-1. TWO TEACHING PARADIGMS

Paradigm		"Instruction"	"Conversation"
Objectives:	(why?)	specific	general
(output)		predefined	negotiable
		products	processes
		standard	variable
Messages:	(what?)	designed	created
(input)	(when?)	preprepared	on-line
	(who?)	instructor	participants
	(whom?)	one-to-many	many-to-many
Interaction:	(process-focus)	behaviors	ideas
	(analysis)	criterion-ref.	content/structure
	(feedback)	corrective	constructive
	(complexity)	one-layer thick	interwoven layers
Distance education:		correspondence	teleconferencing,
(example)		courses	videoconferencing
			computer-mediated
			communication

modems, the growth area for CMC lies with the resources available over the Internet. The role of the on-line teacher will increasingly be that of guide to these resources. It will be interesting to see what needs computer conferencing fulfills with the advent of cheap audio and visual connections. If messages remain asynchronous (like telephone-answering machines), will text be relegated to formal papers and documents? Will the stimulation of voice and visual communication overcome learners' inertia and be more compelling to respond to than text?

Another trend predicted to continue is international on-line connections, for example, collaborations among students studying similar courses at different institutions. School children carrying out multicultural investigations are a powerful and inexpensive resource for extending the classroom walls.

> It would be naive to think that communication will automatically lead to greater knowledge, increased respect for individual and cultural differences, and a new appreciation of similarities. But a more peaceful world will not evolve without communication. The technology of CMC does not lead directly to the answers, but the dialogue it supports is a significant way for people to begin to embrace the common questions (Wells, 1993, p. 85).

As "pure" computer conferencing falls increasingly towards the trailing edge of technology, it will continue to find specialist uses in education and training. Old computer equipment will be perfectly adequate for textual communication, and could be used with those who currently cannot afford access. By comparison with multimedia conferencing, computer conferencing will be an inexpensive technology, which will continue to grow at the grass-roots level.

In the short term, conferencing systems with improved interfaces will find increasing markets, and learners will increasingly have to adapt to the interactive and collaborative paradigm they represent. However, this technology-led growth will eventually meet a new generation of users reared with the computer and schooled in international communication, and then tele-learning will become the norm rather than the exception.

14.8 A RESEARCH AGENDA

The previous section of the chapter looked at what the future may be holding in store. It presented scenarios based on technological change and its impact in the workplace and the home and the impact of those on technological change in educational institutions. It also looked at some aspects of future technological synergy that will be offering evermore powerful communication alternatives that may (or may not) have applicability in education and training systems.

The reason for putting this section prior to the research agenda is to indicate more clearly how the research issues listed in this section are linked to our vision of what the future possibly may hold in store. The driving objective behind the research agenda that follows is to try to be proactive and anticipative of technological change and its potential impact, both for the good and for the bad, on education and training systems.

The organizing principle for the following research agenda is a four-level planning model that considers separately, but in an integrated manner, the research issues that should be investigated in order to supply the answers we will need in order to:

1. Make sensible policy decisions regarding CMC.
2. Make effective strategic planning decisions.
3. Make tactical decisions within specific CMC projects.

4. Make good logistic decisions in relation to selection and use of the hardware and software that will be the tools of future CMC systems.

14.8.1 General Research: The Policy Level

Under this heading, perhaps one of the most important (and least practiced) forms of educational research is the "futures study." In some respects the scenario presented in the section called "A Look to the Future" is an example of a futures study. The need is for more rigorous futures research that may evaluate, in advance, the impact of potential changes in the workplace or in society that may be brought about by technological progress or other change.

These in turn should be evaluated in terms of two factors. The first factor is in terms of the direct impact of societal changes on education, that is, on the goals, the content, the delivery methods in the macro sense (for example, to what extent will the demand for distance education grow and in what sectors of the market?), and so on. Secondly, the study should investigate in what way new technological developments can offer solutions to some of education's current or anticipated future problems and challenges.

This particular area of research is especially prone to what we described earlier as the "moving-target difficulty," in that technological change is happening at such a rate that the prediction of futures may be considered to be a continuing task rather than a project that may be done once and for all during a particular decade. The implications of not evaluating the alternatives in advance, or of evaluating incorrectly, are potentially very great both in terms of misapplied project funding and in terms of possible disappointment with end results of an innovation.

This area of futures research cannot be undertaken exclusively from a technological or an end-user standpoint. Technology and the citizens of society exist within a complex system that has its economic, political, and other pressures and constraints. A very clear example of possible misjudgments can be seen in plans that have been undertaken over the last years on the assumptions that certain technological improvements will be available within certain time spans. In the mid- and late 1980s, millions of dollars were invested in the United States into the "education utility" concept on the assumption that within a year or two all schools will be networked with sufficient bandwidth in order to enable a provider of educational information located at a distance to offer better service than the established system of booksellers, printers, videotape producers, etc. The education utility would replace all these traditional informational providers with one central electronic database that would supply any information to anyone anywhere on demand, just as electricity or water is supplied, and then bill the end user at the end of the month for the information actually used, just as the electricity or water utilities bill (Gooler, 1986).

Nearly 10 years have gone by and the education utility concept has not become a reality on a grand scale, although there are numerous "mini-education utilities" that have been implemented by corporations or by certain states (for example, the state of Texas). The technology is here, but the political will and the economic pressures to make it available are not necessarily here. Therefore, futures research of the type suggested here must be a broad systemic approach to the analysis of all factors that may play a part in the actual shaping of the future that we may expect.

Another aspect of general research is to keep up with technological developments. At the present time, developments may focus on the potential integration of computer-mediated communication (which is most commonly used as an asynchronous communication medium), with synchronous technologies of audio conferencing and video conferencing. The technological possibilities exist to integrate these currently separate technologies, so that, for example, some of the distinctions that were made in Table 14-1 may take on a purely academic meaning. However, just how would such integration work, what would it depend on, what will be its capabilities, and what are the expected time-lines and costs for availability?

14.8.2 Organizational Research: The Strategic Level

If the previous category of general research can inform policy decisions in relation to CMC, then this next level of research would principally support strategic decisions in the context of overall planning of CMC systems and the integration of these systems into broader education and training systems. The research issues that require attention are ones related to overall educational system planning, with CMC seen as one component. For example, to what extent ought CMC be involved as a component in open learning systems or in other flexible learning programs? In the industrial-training context, to what extent and in what way can we utilize CMC systems as part of the tendency to develop electronic performance support systems that may enable the trainee to receive all necessary information both for learning and for reference at the workplace as and when required (Gery, 1991)? Alternatively, if the training continues to be off the job, can CMC be utilized to put into reality the concept of a "just-in-time-training" in its broadest sense?

Another important research agenda concerns strategies for effective dissemination of CMC in actual educational systems. The British Open University (OU) is currently engaged in finding answers to the research questions concerned with "scalability" of CMC. How can the undoubted successes of small-group educational computer conferencing be scaled up to large-distance education? So far this medium has only been used as a means of tutorial support on large courses, and this has been shown to have a number of major disadvantages. While some students valued electronic contact with their tutor and found that the medium reduced the isolation often reported by distance learners, the pedagogical benefits of this minimal use of the system proved fairly marginal. But more significantly, the success of even this low-level use of conferencing was shown to be highly dependent on the quality and quantity of the tutor input. This problem of tutor workload is a critical issue, where tutors are currently paid for only half-dozen hours of student contact throughout an entire course (Mason & Kaye, 1989).

The Open University has experimented with a number of small-scale uses of computer conferencing with 25 to 50 students. Many of these trials have involved the use of the conferencing system FirstClass. The results of these have shown how exciting and educationally valuable this medium can be (Mason, 1994b). However, it is the conclusion of those involved in many of these trials that no ideal model has yet been identified for applying these successes to large courses of 1,000 to 5,000 students. Some of the suggestions under consideration include: the extension and enhancement of peer learning groups; the use of "master classes," in which a few students interact with an expert while the remainder can read only; increased input from central academic staff who normally write courses rather than interact with students; the use of World Wide Web facilities integrated with conferencing facilities; and the development of a few specialist conferencing tutors rather than the expectation that all tutors will be trained and paid for conferencing duties. A variety of uses of conferencing are jumbled together among these suggestions, and it is important to distinguish them: conferencing used for teaching (the content of the course) and conferencing used for tutoring (supporting the student); conferencing used for course delivery (of articles, updating material, directives from the course team) and conferencing used for interaction (between students and teachers). While it is possible, perhaps even desirable, that the OU use conferencing for all these things, it is necessary to be clear on the objectives for each type of use. Over the next few years as the OU expands into continental Europe, extensive use will be made of computer conferencing, and many of these uses will be integrated with various forms of multimedia educational facilities, such as CD-ROM. During this period, the OU will be experimenting widely with a variety of large-scale conferencing models.

Apart from specific courses that use electronic communication as a teaching vehicle, the Open University is also setting an ambitious target for providing administrative access to students through computer networking. By 1996, the OU aims to make a wide range of services available on-line: inquiry and information services including on-line registration; induction material, library access, and support services; local call access and Internet connections for all students; and a network support environment package. While these facilities may not be innovative for campus-based universities, providing these systems for as many students spread as widely as OU students is a major undertaking. The benefits are perceived to be increased individual autonomy and control over the learning process, bringing the university to the home to a much greater extent than before, adding flexibility and tailorability to courses, and freeing the OU from the assumption that large student numbers are needed to achieve economies of scale.

14.8.3 Instructional Research: The Tactical Level

Perhaps one of the most important areas for tactical research at the moment is to investigate the potential applications and specific methodologies for collaborative learning. This research should look at the tools available and also the tools that would be desirable for collaborative learning. These may include shared workspaces, the sharing of documents, and even virtual-reality possibilities of being in almost physical contact with collaborators who are in reality at a distance.

A second area of important research for the future is the design and evaluation of specific CMC environments for the effective implementation of particular types of instructional activities. These may include simulation games, small-group discussions, group assignments, or case study discussions. These techniques, which are typically practiced in small-group discussion situations facilitated by a skilled expert, are among the techniques that are most valued for the development of critical thinking, problem solving, and other higher-order cognitive skills.

As society progresses into the age of technology, more of the routine tasks performed by human beings will be taken over by computers (whether they be physical tasks replaced by robots or intellectual tasks replaced by expert systems). The area for human employability will be ever-more restricted to those types of tasks that computer systems cannot perform effectively. Some of these will be tasks that are very reliant on interpersonal skills, empathy, and human contact. Others will be the tasks of the "knowledge worker," that is, the person who can perform intellectual tasks beyond the capability of computer software. Such knowledge work is characterized by the utilization of current knowledge for the creation of new knowledge. It is not so much problem solving as the formulation of problems that are worth solving. It is creativity; it is invention; it is leadership. As an ever-greater proportion of the jobs performed by human beings have these characteristics, there will be an ever-greater need for critical thinking and creativity skills and therefore an increasing need for educational methodologies and techniques that are effective at developing them.

Here we have a somewhat paradoxical situation in that as the scenario presented earlier would suggest, small-group face-to-face meetings will appear evermore expensive as compared with the falling costs of various telecommunications-based methodologies of communication. Therefore, we may be able to afford ever less (in terms of teaching methodologies) of what we require evermore—*unless* we can implement on CMC networks techniques for small-group discussion that will be able to substitute the small-group face-to-face techniques that we may not be able to afford. As an example, the work being performed by

Romiszowski and Chang (1992) and Chang (1994) is focused exactly on this particular set of research questions, concentrating in particular on the replication in a CMC environment of effective business case analysis and discussion methodologies.

14.8.4 Network Research: The Tool Level

We have proceeded through the levels of policymaking, strategic planning, and tactical decision making. The fourth area of research can be referred to as the logistics area, that is, research into the tools required in order to put our strategic and tactical plans into action. Very often in the field of new technological developments, the tools are the elements that appear first. Sometimes, too often in fact, the availability of the tools becomes the starting point for a project, and we follow the process of a "solution in search of a problem to solve," as opposed to a systemic and well-organized problem-solving approach.

It should be stressed that both of these alternative approaches are important in the research field. As new tools appear, such as for example desktop video, there is a need to explore their potential within certain areas of possible application. For example, in the area of education, and particularly computer-mediated communication, in what way is desktop video a new technology that will offer simply a reduced cost per hour of video conferencing, or will it offer certain potential for setting up tactical plans or even overall strategies that were not possible before with the technologies at our disposal? Of course, having set up these possible scenarios and going through the research stages of proving the concept and its viability, then comes the stage of turning the process around in order to verify to what extent there really is a market or a need for this potential new product.

The tools-related research should therefore be integrated very closely with the three upper levels of research that we have already outlined. There is an obvious need for keeping the policy, strategic, and tactical research abreast of the tools research so that we have rational plans for the utilization of specific new tools and technologies as they become available, rather than being swept away by the appearance of the tools without a chance for prior evaluation of whether we are traveling in the most appropriate direction.

REFERENCES

Attewell, P. & Rule, J. (1988). Computers and organizations: what we know and what we don't know. *In* I. Greif, ed. *Computer-supported cooperative work: a book of readings,* 557–579. San Mateo, CA: Kaufmann.

Bernard, R.M. & Naidu, S. (1990). Enhancing interpersonal communication in distance education: can voice-mail help? *Educational and Training Technology International (ETTI) 27*(3), 293–99.

Boshier (1988). Socio-psychological factors in electronic net-working. *Canadian Association for the Study of Adult Education: proceedings of the annual conference.* (ERIC Document Reproduction Service No. ED 299 461.)

Boyd, G. (1990). Appropriate uses of computer mediated communication systems for education: conferencing "R-PLACES." *Educational and Training Technology International (ETTI) 27*(3), 271–75.

Brochet, M. (1989). Effective moderation of computer conferences: notes and suggestions. *In* M. Brochet, ed. *Moderating Conferences,* 6.01–6.08. Guelph, Ontario: Computing Support Services, University of Guelph.

Burge, E.J. (1992). *Computer mediated communication and education: a selected bibliography.* Toronto, Canada: Distance Learning Office, Ontario Institute for Studies in Education.

— (1993). Students' perceptions of learning in computer conferencing: a qualitative analysis. Unpublished doctoral dissertation. University of Toronto, Toronto, Canada.

Chang, Echeol (1994). Investigation of constructivist principles applied to collaborative study of business cases in computer-mediated communication. Unpublished Ph.D. dissertation, Syracuse University.

Chapanis, A. (1988). Interactive human communication. *In* I. Greif, ed. *Computer-supported cooperative work: a book of readings,* 125–139. San Mateo, CA: Kaufmann.

Cheng, H., Lehman, J. & Armstrong, P. (1991). Comparison of performance and attitude in traditional and computer conferencing classes. *The American Journal of Distance Education 5*(3), 51–64.

—, Lehman, J. & Reynolds, A. (1991). What do we know about asynchronous group computer-based distance learning? *Educational Technology 31*(11), 16–19.

Chute, A.G., et al. (1988). Learning from teletraining. *American Journal of Distance Education 2*(3), 55–63.

— (1990). Strategies for implementing teletraining systems. *Educational & Training Technology International 27* (3), 264–70.

Cole, S.L., Beam, M., Karn, L. & Hoad-Reddick, A. (1992). *Educational computer-mediated communication: a field study of recent research.* Unpublished paper, Toronto, Canada: Ontario Institute for Studies in Education.

Cunningham, D.J., Duffy, T.M. & Knuth, R.A. (1993). The textbook of the future. *In* C. McKnight, ed. *Hypertext: a psychological perspective.* London: Horwood.

Davie, L. (1989). Facilitation techniques for the on-line tutor. *In* R. Mason & A.R. Kaye, eds. Mindweave: communication, computers and distance Education. Oxford, England: Pergamon.

Dirr, P.J. (1990). Distance education: policy considerations for the year 2000. *In* M.G. Moore, ed. *Contemporary issues in American distance education,* 397–406. New York: Pergamon.

Eastmond, D.V. (1992). Effective facilitation of computer conferencing. *Continuing Higher Education Review 56*(1&2), 23–34.

— (1993). Adult learning of distance students through computer conferencing. Ph.D. dissertation. New York: Syracuse University.

Elmer-Dewitt, P. (1994). Battle for the soul of the Internet. *Time 144*(4), 50–6.

Eurich, N.P. (1990). *The learning industry: education for adult workers*. Princeton, NJ: The Carnegie Foundation for the Advancement of Teaching.

Faddis, B. (1985). Computer equity. ERIC DIGEST. ERIC Clearinghouse on Information Resources, Syracuse University.

Feenberg, A. & Bellman, B. (1990). Social factor research in computer-mediated communications. *In* L.M. Harasim, ed. *Online education: perspectives on a new environment, 67–97.* New York: Pergamon.

— (1989). The written world: on the theory and practice of computer conferencing. *In* R. Mason & A.R. Kaye, eds. *Mindweave: communication, computers, and distance education, 22–39.* New York: Pergamon.

Florini, B.M. (1990). Delivery Systems for distance education: focus on commuter conferencing. *In* M.G. Moore, ed. *Contemporary issues in American distance education, 277–89.* New York: Pergamon.

Gery, G. (1991). *Electronic performance support systems.* New York: Weingarten.

Gibson, C.C. (1991). In for how long? Factors affecting persistence in the early months of distance learning. *Proceedings of the 7th Annual Conference on Distance Teaching and Learning 7,* 208–12.

Gooler, D.D. (1986). *The education utility: the power to revitalize education and society.* Englewood Cliffs, NJ: Educational Technology.

Grabowski, B. (1990). Social and intellectual exchange through electronic communications in a graduate community. *Instructional Developments 1*(1), 19–21.

—, Suciati, & Pusch, W. (1990). Social and intellectual value of computer-mediated communications in a graduate community. *Educational and Training Technology International 27*(3), 276–83.

Graddol, D. (1989). Some CMC discourse properties and their educational significance. *In* R. Mason & A.R. Kaye, eds. *Mindweave: communication, computers and distance education,* 236–41. Oxford, England: Pergamon.

Grief, I. (1988). *Computer-supported cooperative work: a book of readings.* San Mateo, CA: Kaufmann.

Grint, K. (1989). Accounting for failure: participation and non-participation in CMC. *In* R. Mason & A.R. Kaye, eds. *Mindweave: communication, computers and distance education,* 189–191. Oxford, England: Pergamon.

Gunawardena, C. (1992). Changing faculty roles for audiographics and online teaching. *The American Journal of Distance Education 6*(3), 58–71.

Gundry, J. (1992). Understanding collaborative learning in networked organizations. *In* A.R. Kaye, ed. *Collaborating learning through computer conferencing: the Najaden papers,* 167–78. New York: Springer.

Harasim, L.M. (1987). Teaching and learning on-line: issues in computer-mediated graduate courses. *Canadian Journal of Educational Communication 16*(2), 117–35.

— (1989). Online education: a new domain. *In* R. Mason & A.R. Kaye, eds. *Mindweave: communication, computers, and distance education,* 50–62. New York: Pergamon.

— (1990a). Bibliography on educational CMC. *In* L.M. Harasim, ed. *Online education: perspectives on a new environment.* New York: Praeger.

— (1990b). Online education: an environment for collaboration and intellectual amplification. *In* L.M. Harasim, ed. *Online education: perspectives on a new environment,* 229–64. New York: Praeger.

Harasim, L.M. (ed.). (1990c). *Online education: perspectives on a new environment.* New York: Praeger.

Hellerman, L. (1986). *Electronic messaging and conferencing with an emphasis on social use: an exploratory study, ED 177 061.*

Henri, F. (1992). Computer conferencing and content analysis. *In* A.R. Kaye, ed. Collaborative learning through computer conferencing: the Najaden papers, 115–36. New York: Springer.

Hiltz, S.R. (1986). The "virtual classroom": using computer-mediated communication for university teaching. *Journal of Communication 36*(2), 95–104.

— (1988). *Teaching in a virtual classroom.* Vol. 2: a virtual classroom on EIES: final evaluation report. Newark, NJ: New Jersey Institute of Technology.

— (1990). Evaluating the virtual classroom. *In* L.M. Harasim, ed. Online education: perspectives on a new environment, 133–83. New York: Praeger.

— & Turoff, M. (1978). The network nation: human communication via computer. New York: Addison-Wesley.

Horn, R.E. (1989). *Mapping hypertext.* Lexington, MA: The Lexington Institute.

Iskandar, H. (1994). The efficiency of different methods of providing feedback to distance learners in a developing country. Ph.D. dissertation thesis. New York: Syracuse University.

Jacobson, T. & Zimpfer, S. (1992). The global distribution of selected computer network resources. Paper presented at the Aug. 1992 Conference of the International Association for Mass Communication Research, Guaruja, Brazil.

Jones, A., Kirkup, G., Kirkwood, A. & Mason, R. (1992). Providing computing for distance learners: a strategy for home use. *Computers in Education 18*(1-3), 183–93.

Kaye, A.R., ed. (1992). *Collaborating learning through computer conferencing: the Najadn papers.* New York: Springer.

— (1992). Learning together apart. *In* A.R. Kaye, ed. *Collaborative learning through computer conferencing: the Najadn papers.* New York: Springer.

Kerr, E.B. (1986). Electronic leadership: a guide to moderating online conferences. *IEEE Transactions on Professional Communications PC29*(1), 12–8.

— & Hiltz, S. R. (1982). *Computer mediated communication.* New York: Academic.

Kiesler, S. (1992). Talking, teaching, and learning in network groups: lessons from research. *In* A.R. Kaye, ed. *Collaborative learning through computer conferencing: the Najaden papers,* 147–65. New York: Springer.

Kiesler, S., Siegel, J. & McGuire, T.W. (1988). Social psychological aspects of computer-mediated communication. *In* L.M. Harasim, ed. *Online education: perspectives on a new environment,* 185–214. New York: Praeger.

Kirkwood, A. (1993). Screens and their surroundings: learning at home with information and communication technologies. *In* G. David & B. Samways, eds. *Teleteaching: Proceedings of the IFIP TC3 Third Teleteaching Conference,* Trondheim, Norway; Amsterdam, North Holland.

Knowles, M.S. (1984). *The adult learner: a neglected species,* 3d ed. Houston, TX: Gulf.

Kuehn, S. (1988). *Discovering all the available means for computer assisted instruction: adapting available university facilities for the small to medium-sized course.* ED 294 284.

Lauzon, A.C. & Moore, G.A.B. (1989). A fourth generation

distance education system: integrating computer-assisted learning and computer conferencing. *The American Journal of Distance Education 3*(1).

Lea, M. & Spears, R. (1991). Computer-mediated communication, de-individuation and group decisionmaking. *International Journal of Man-Machine Studies 34,* 283–301.

Levin, J. A., Kim, H. & Riel, M.M. (1990). Analyzing instructional interactions on electronic message networks. *In* L. M. Harasim, ed. *Online education: perspectives on a new environment,* 185–214. New York: Praeger.

Levinson, P. (1989). Media relations: integrating computer telecommunications with educational media. *In* R. Mason & A.R. Kaye, eds. *Mindweave: communication, computers, and distance education,* 40–49. London, UK: Pergamon.

— (1990). Computer conferencing in the context of the evolution of media. *In* L.M. Harasim, ed. *Online education: perspectives on a new environment,* 3–14. New York: Praeger.

Malone, T.W., Grant, K.R., Lai, K., Rao, R. & Rosenblitt, D. (1988). Semistructured messages are surprisingly useful for computer-supported coordination. *In* I. Greif, ed. *Computer-supported cooperative work: a book of readings,* 311–31. San Mateo, CA: Kaufmann.

Maloy, W. & Perry, N. (1991). A navy video teletraining project: lessons learned. *The American Journal of Distance Education 5*(3).

Manninen, J. (1991). Computer conference on learning environment: experiences from computer-mediated facilitating. *Proceedings of the Nordisk Kongerence on Fjernundervisning.* Opplaering of Dataformidlet Kommunikasjon, Oslo, Norway, 81–85.

Mason, R. (1988). Computer conferencing: a contribution to self-directed learning. *British Journal of Educational Technology 19*(1), 28–41.

Mason, R. (1990). *Home computing evaluation: use of CoSy on DT200, 1989.* (CITE Report No. 99.) (ERIC Document Reproduction Service No. ED 320 541.)

— (1992). Methodologies for evaluating applications of computer conferencing. *In* A.R. Kaye, ed. *Collaborative learning through computer conferencing: the Najaden papers,* 105–16. New York: Springer.

—, ed. (1993). *Computer conferencing: the last word.* Victoria, BC: Beach Holme Publications.

— (1994a). *Using communications media in open and flexible learning.* London: Kogan Page.

— (1994b). Computer conferencing and the Open University. *CTISS File,* 17, 5–7.

— & Kaye, A.R., eds. (1989). *Mindweave: communication, computers, and distance education.* New York: Pergamon.

— & Kaye, T. (1990). Toward a new paradigm for distance education. *In* L.M. Harasim, ed. *Online education: perspectives on a new environment,* 15–38. New York: Praeger.

McCreary, E. & Brochet, M. (1992). Collaboration in international online teams. *In* A. R. Kaye, ed. *Collaborative learning through computer conferencing: the Najaden papers,* 69–85. New York: Springer.

McCreary, E.K. & Van Duren, J. (1987). Educational applications of computer conferencing. *Canadian Journal of Educational Communications 16*(2), 107–15.

Miller, A.J., ed. (1991). Applications of computer conferencing to teacher education and human resource development. Proceedings from an International Symposium on Computer Conferencing at the Ohio State University, Jun. 13–15.

Moore, M.G. (1991). Computer conferencing in the context of theory and practice of distance education. *Proceedings of the International Symposium on Computer Conferencing,* 1–9. Columbus, OH: Ohio State University.

Morrison, J.L. (1989). Impact of computer conferencing upon refining problem-solving skills. *Proceedings of the 31st International ADCIS Conference.* Association for the Development of Computer-based Instructional Systems (ADCIS).

Muffo, J. & Connor, M. (1987). *Unintended/unexpected outcomes of computer usage in higher education.* AIR Annual form Paper. ED 293 444.

Neuman, D. (1991, Dec.). Technology and equity. *ERIC Digest.* ERIC Clearinghouse on Information Resources, Syracuse University.

O'Connor, R.J. (1992, November 26). The great electronic divide. *Syracuse Herald Journal 1,* 16.

Paine, N. (1988). *Open learning in transition: an agenda for action.* London: Kogan Page.

Paulsen, M.F. (1992). The NKI electronic college: five years of computer conferencing in distance education. *In* M.F. Paulsen, ed. *From bulletin boards to electronic universities: distance education, computer-mediated communication, and online education.* The American Center for the Study of Distance Education, 2–17, University Park, PA.

— (1993). The hexagon of cooperative freedom: a distance education theory attuned to computer conferencing. *DEOS NEWS—The distance education online symposium 3*(2).

Phelps, R.H., Wells, R.A., Ashworth, R.L. & Hahn, H.A. (1991). Effectiveness and costs of distance education using computer-mediated communication. *The American Journal of Distance Education 5*(3), 7–19.

Phillips, A.F. & Pease, P.S. (1987). Computer conferencing and education: complementary or contradictory concepts? *The American Journal of Distance Education 1*(2), 44–52.

Phillips, C. (1990). Making friends in the electronic student lounge. *Distance Education 11*(2), 320–33.

Phillips, G.M., Santoro, G.M. & Kuehn, S.A. (1988). The use of computer mediated communication in training students in group problem-solving and decision-making techniques. *The American Journal of Distance Education 2*(1), 38–51.

Rawson, J.H. (1990). Simulation at a distance using computer conferencing. *Educational and Training Technology International (ETTI) 27*(3), 284–92.

Roberts, L.H. (1990). Educational goals and self-concepts of distance learners at Empire State College. Ph.D. dissertation, Nova University.

Robinson, R. (1992). Andragogy applied to the open college learner. *Research in Distance Education 4*(1), 10–13.

Romiszowski, A.J. (1990). Computer mediated communication and hypertext: the instructional use of two converging technologies. *Interactive Learning International 6,* 5–29.

— (1992). *Computer mediated communications: a selected bibliography* (ETSBS, No. 5). Englewood Cliffs, NJ: Educational Technology.

— (1993). Telecommunications in training. In *ASTD handbook of training technology,* American Society for Training and Development (ASTD).

— & Chang, E. (1992). Hypertext's contribution to computer-mediated communication: in search of an instructional model. *In* M. Giardina, ed. *Interactive multimedia learning environments.* Berlin: Springer.

— & — (1994). Alternative strategies for collaborative study of business cases by computer-mediated communication. *Instructional Developments 4*(1). Syracuse, NY: Syracuse University.

— & Corso, M. (1990). Computer mediated seminars and case studies. Paper presented at the 15th World Conference on Distance Education, Caracas, Venezuela. International Council for Distance Education (ICDE).

— & DeHaas, J. (1989). Computer-mediated communication for instruction: using E-mail as a seminar. *Educational Technology 24*(10).

— & Iskandar, H. (1992). New telecommunications and voice-mail technologies in distance education. *Proceedings of the 16th World Conference on Distance Education,* Bangkok, Thailand. International Council for Distance Education.

— & Jost, K. (1989). Computer conferencing and the distance learner: problems of structure and control. *Proceedings of the 5th Annual Conference on Teaching at a Distance,* Madison, WI, Aug. 8–10, 1989.

—, Jost, K. & Chang, E. (1990). Computer-mediated communication: a hypertext approach to structuring distance seminars. In *Proceedings of the 32d Annual ADCIS International Conference.* Association for the Development of Computer-based Instructional Systems (ADCIS).

Ryan, R. (1992). International connectivity: a survey of attitudes about cultural and national differences encountered in computer-mediated communication. *The Online Chronicle of Distance Education and Communication 6*(1).

Scollon, S. (1981, Dec.). *The teacher-student role in instructional telecommunications.* Paper presented at the Annual Meeting of the American Anthropological Association, Los Angeles, CA. (ERIC Document Reproduction Service No. ED 239 792.)

Sheffield, J. & McQueen, R.J. (1990). Groupware and management education: matching communication medium to task requirements. *Proceedings of the 3d Guelph Symposium on Computer Mediated Communication,* 181–82.

Siegel, J., Dubrovsky, V., Kiesler, S. & McGuire, T.W. (1986). Group processes in computer-mediated communication. *Organizational Behavior and Human Decision Processes 37,* 157–87.

Soby, M. (1990). The postmodern condition and distance education, computer conferencing and communicative competence. *Proceedings of the 3d Guelph Symposium on Computer Mediated Communication,* 112–20.

Tucker, R.W. (1991). Editor's desk: virtual assessment. *Adult Assessment Forum 1*(3), 3–4.

Vallee, J. (1982). *The network revolution: confessions of a scientist.* Berkeley, CA: And/Or Press.

Wells, R. (1992). *Computer-mediated communication for distance education: an international review of design, teaching, and institutional issues* (ACSDE Monograph No. 6). University Park, PA: The American Center for the Study of Distance Education.

— (1993). The use of computer-mediated communication in distance education: progress, problems and trends. *In* G. Davies & B. Samways, eds. Teleteaching. Proceedings of the IFIP TC3 3d Teleteaching Conference, Trondheim, Norway; North-Holland, Amsterdam.

White, C.S. (1991, May). Information technology and the informed citizen: new challenges for government and libraries. *ERIC DIGEST.* ERIC Clearinghouse on Information Resources, Syracuse University.

Zuboff, S. (1988). *In the age of the smart machine: the future of work and power.* New York: Basic Books.

15. VIRTUAL REALITIES

Hilary McLellan
MCLELLAN WYATT DIGITAL

15.1 INTRODUCTION

Virtual realities are a set of newly emerging educational technologies, less than a decade old (Hamit, 1993; Aukstalnis & Blatner, 1992; Helsel, 1992a, 1992b, 1992c; Middleton, 1992; Pimentel & Teixiera, 1992; Helsel & Roth, 1991; Rheingold, 1991). Virtual reality (VR) can be defined as a class of computer-controlled multisensory communication technologies that allow more intuitive interactions with data and involve human senses in new ways. Virtual reality can also be defined as an environment created by the computer in which the user feels immersed in the present (Jacobson, 1993a). This technology was devised to enable people to deal with information more easily. VR provides a different way to see and experience information, one that is dynamic and immediate. It is also a tool for model building and problem solving. VR is potentially a tool for experiential learning. The virtual world is interactive; it responds to the user's actions. Virtual reality evokes a feeling of immersion, a perceptual and psychological sense of being in the digital environment presented to the senses. The sense of presence or immersion is a critical feature distinguishing virtual reality from other types of computer applications.

Virtual reality is a new type of computer tool that adds vast power to scientific visualization. Buxton (1992, p. 27) explains that:

> Scientific visualization involves the graphic rendering of complex data in a way that helps make pertinent aspects and relationships within the data more salient to the viewer. The idea is to tailor the visual presentation to take better advantage of the human ability to recognize patterns and see structures.

However, as Erickson (1993) explains, the word *visualization* is really too narrow when considering virtual reality. *Perceptualization* is probably more appropriate. With virtual reality, sound and touch, as well as visual appearance, may be used effectively to represent data. Perceptualization involving the sense of touch may include both tactile feedback (passive touch, feeling surfaces and textures) and haptic feedback (active touch, where there is a sense of force feedback, pressure, or resistance) (Brooks, 1988; Hon, 1991; Dowding, 1991, 1992; Minsky, 1991; Marcus, 1994). The key to visualization is in representing information in ways that can engage any of our sensory systems and thus draw on our extensive experience in organizing and interpreting sensory input (Erickson, 1993).

The term *virtual reality* was coined by Jaron Lanier, one of the developers of the first immersive interface devices (Hall, 1990). *Virtual* often denotes the computer-generated counterpart of a physical object: a "virtual room," a "virtual glove," a "virtual chair." Other terms such as *virtual worlds, virtual environments,* and *cyberspace* are used as global terms to identify this technology. For example, David Zelter of the MIT Media Lab suggests that the term *virtual environments* is more appropriate than *virtual reality,* since virtual reality, like artificial intelligence, is ultimately unattainable (Wheeler, 1991). But *virtual reality* remains the most commonly used generic term (although many researchers in the field vehemently dislike this term).

Virtual reality provides a degree of interactivity that goes beyond what can be found in traditional multimedia programs. Even a sophisticated multimedia program, such as the Palenque DVI program, which features simulated spatial exploration of an ancient Mayan pyramid, is limited to predetermined paths. With a virtual world you can go anywhere and explore any point of view.

Virtual reality emerged as a distinctive area of computer interfaces and applications only during the 1980s. Any assessment of this technology must keep in mind that it is at a very early stage of development. To date there is very little research, especially concerning the educational implications of this technology. However, some exciting applications have been developed. Furthermore, researchers are beginning to collect valuable information about the usefulness of virtual reality for particular applications, including education and training. And a great deal of theory building has already been initiated concerning this emerging technology and its potentials in education and training.

15.2 HISTORICAL BACKGROUND

Woolley (1992) explains that, "Trying to trace the origins of the idea of virtual reality is like trying to trace the source of a river. It is produced by the accumulated flow of many streams of ideas, fed by many springs of inspiration." One forum where the potentials of virtual reality have been explored is science fiction (Bradbury, 1951; Harrison, 1972; W. Gibson, 1986; Stephenson, 1992; Sterling, 1994), together with the related area of scenario-building (Kellogg, Carroll & Richards, 1991).

The technology that has led up to virtual-reality technology—computer graphics, simulation, human-computer interfaces, etc.—has been developing and coalescing for over 3 decades. In the 1960s, Ivan Sutherland created one of the pioneering virtual-reality systems, which incorporated a head-mounted display (Sutherland, 1965, 1968) nicknamed "The Sword of Damocles" because of its strange appearance. Sutherland did not continue with this work because the computer graphics systems available to him at that time were very primitive. Instead, he shifted his attention to inventing many of the fundamental algorithms, hardware, and software of computer graphics (McGreevy, 1993). Sutherland's work provided a foundation for the emergence of virtual reality in the 1980s. His early work inspired others, such as Frederick P. Brooks, Jr., of the University of North Carolina, who began experimenting with ways to simulate accurately and display the structure of molecules. Brooks's work developed into a major virtual-reality research initiative at the University of North Carolina (Hamit, 1993; Rheingold, 1991; Robinett, 1991).

In 1961, Mortin Heilig, a filmmaker, patented Sensorama, a totally mechanical virtual-reality device (a one-person theater) that included three-dimensional, full-color film together with sounds, smells, and the feeling of motion, as well as the sensation of wind on the viewer's face. In the Sensorama, the user could experience several scenarios, including a motorcycle ride through New York, a bicycle ride, or a helicopter ride over Century City. The Sensorama was not a commercial success, but it reflected tremendous vision, which has now returned with computer-based rather than mechanical virtual-reality systems (Hamit, 1993; Rheingold, 1991).

During the 1960s and 1970s, the Air Force established a laboratory at Wright-Patterson Air Force Base in Ohio to develop flight simulators and head-mounted displays that could facilitate learning and performance in sophisticated, high-workload, high-speed military aircraft. This initiative resulted in the SuperCockpit, which allows pilots to fly ultra-high-speed aircraft using only head, eye, and hand movements. The director of the SuperCockpit project, Tom Furness, is now the director of the Human Interface Technology Lab at the University of Washington, a leading VR R&D center, and VR research continues at Wright-Patterson Air Force Base (Auburn, 1993; Stytz, 1993, 1994). Flight simulators have been used extensively and effectively for pilot training since the 1920s (Lauber & Fouchee, 1981; Woolley, 1992; Bricken & Byrne, 1993).

In the 1960s, GE developed a simulator that was adapted for lunar-mission simulations. It was primarily useful for practicing rendezvous and, especially, docking between the lunar excursion module (LEM) and the command module (CM). This simulator was also adapted as a city planning tool in a project at UCLA—the first time a simulator had been used to explore a digital model of a city (McGreevy, 1993).

In the 1970s, researchers at MIT developed a spatial data management system using videodisc technology. This work resulted in the *Aspen Movie Map* (MIT, 1981; Mohl, 1982), a recreation of part of the town of Aspen, Colorado, stored on an optical disk that gave users the simulated experience of driving through the town of Aspen, interactively choosing to turn left or right to pursue any destination (within the confines of the model). Twenty miles of Aspen streets were photographed from all directions at 10-foot intervals, as was every possible turn. Aerial views were also included. This photo-based experiment proved to be too complicated (i.e., it was not user-friendly), so this approach was not used to replicate larger cities, which entail a higher degree of complexity (Hamit, 1993).

Also in the 1970s, Myron Krueger began experimenting with human-computer interaction as a graduate student at the University of Wisconsin-Madison. Krueger designed responsive but nonimmersive environments that combined video and computer. He referred to this as *artificial reality*. As Krueger (1993, p. 149) explains,

> You are perceived by a video camera and the image of your body is displayed in a graphic world. The juxtaposition of your image with graphic objects on the screen suggests that perhaps you could affect the graphic objects. This expectation is innate. It does not need to be explained. To take advantage of it, the computer continually analyzes your image with respect to the graphic world. When your image touches a graphic object, the computer can respond in many ways. For example, the object can move as if pushed. It can explode, stick to your finger, or cause your image to disappear. You can play music with your finger or cause your image to disappear. The graphic world need not be realistic. Your image can be moved, scaled, and rotated like a graphic object in response to your actions or simulated forces. You can even fly your image around the screen.

The technologies underlying virtual reality came together at the NASA Ames Lab in California during the mid-1980s with the development of a system that utilized a stereoscopic head-mounted display (using screens scavenged from two miniature televisions) and the fiber-optic-wired glove interface device. This breakthrough project at NASA was based on a long tradition of developing ways to simulate the environments and the procedures that astronauts would be engaged in during space flights, such as the GE simulator developed in the 1960s (McGreevy, 1993).

15.3 DIFFERENT KINDS OF VIRTUAL REALTY

There is more than one type of virtual reality. Furthermore, there are different schemas for classifying various types of virtual reality. Jacobson (1993a) suggests that there are four types of virtual realities: (1) immersive virtual reality, (2) desktop virtual reality (i.e., low-cost home-brew virtual reality), (3) projection virtual reality, and (4) simulation virtual reality.

Thurman and Mattoon (1994) present a model for differentiating between different types of VR, based on several "dimensions." They identify a "verity dimension" that helps to differentiate between different types of virtual reality, based on how closely the application corresponds to physical reality. They propose a scale showing the verity dimension of virtual realities (see Fig. 15-1). According to Thurman and Mattoon (1994, p. 57),

> The two end points of this dimension—physical and abstract—describe the degree that a VR and entities within the virtual environment have the characteristics of reality. On the left end of the scale, VRs simulate or mimic real-world counterparts which correspond to natural laws. On the right side of the scale, VRs represent abstract ideas that are completely novel and may not even resemble the real world.

Thurman and Mattoon (1994) also identify an "integration dimension" that focuses on how human beings are integrated into the computer system. This dimension includes a scale featuring three categories: batch processing, shared control, and total inclusion. These categories are based on three broad eras of human-computer integration, culminating with VR—total inclusion. A third dimension of this model is interface, on a scale ranging between natural and artificial. These three dimensions are combined to form a three-dimensional classification scheme for virtual realities. This model provides a valuable tool for understanding and comparing different virtual realities.

Another classification scheme has been delineated by Brill (1993, 1994b). This model will be discussed in detail here. Brill's model features seven different types of virtual reality: (1) immersive first-person, (2) through the window, (3) mirror world, (4) Waldo world, (5) chamber world, (6) cab simulator environment, and (7) cyberspace. Some of Brill's categories of virtual reality are physically immersive and some are not. The key feature of all virtual-reality systems is that they provide an environment created by the computer or other media where the user feels present, that is, immersed physically, perceptually, and psychologically.

Virtual-reality systems enable users to become participants in artificial spaces created by the computer. It is important to note that not all virtual worlds are three dimensional. This is not necessary to provide an enriching experience. And to explore a virtual world, the user doesn't have to be completely immersed in it: first-person (direct) interaction, as well as second-person and third-person interaction, with the virtual world are all possible (Laurel, 1991; Norman, 1993), as the following discussion indicates.

15.3.1 Immersive First-Person

Usually when we think of virtual reality, we think of immersive systems involving computer interface devices such as a head-mounted display (HMD), fiber-optic-wired gloves, position-tracking devices, and audio systems providing 3-D (binaural) sound. Immersive virtual reality provides an immediate, first-person experience. With some applications, there is a treadmill interface to simulate the experience of walking through virtual space. And in place of the head-mounted display, there is the BOOM viewer from Fake Space Labs which hangs suspended in front of the viewer's face, not on it, so it is not as heavy and tiring to wear as the head-mounted display. In immersive VR, the user is placed inside the image; the generated image is assigned properties that make it look and act real in terms of visual perception and, in some cases, aural and tactile perception (Brooks, 1988; Trubitt, 1990; Begault, 1991; Markoff, 1991; Minsky, 1991; Gehring, 1992). There is even research on creating virtual smells; an application to patent such a product has been submitted by researchers at the Southwest Research Institute (Varner, 1993).

Children are already familiar with some of this technology from video games. Mattel's Power Glove™, used as an interface with Nintendo Games, is a low-cost design based on the DataGlove™ from VPL Research, Inc. The Power Glove™ failed as a toy, but it has achieved some success as an interface device in some low-cost virtual-reality systems, particularly in what are known as *homebrew* or *garage* virtual-reality systems (Jacobson, 1994). Inexpensive software and computer cards are available that make it possible to use the Power Glove™ as an input device with Amiga, Macintosh, or IBM computers (Eberhart, 1993; Stampe, Roehl & Eagan, 1993; Jacobson, 1994; Hollands, 1995).

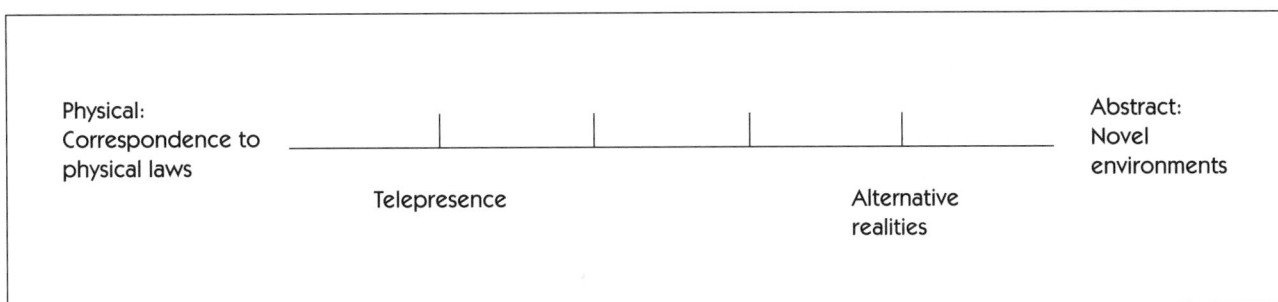

Figure 15-1. Thurston and Mattoon's verity scale for virtual reality. (Adapted from Thurston & Mattoon, 1994.)

15.3.2 Augmented Reality

A variation of immersive virtual reality is "augmented reality," where a see-through layer of computer graphics is superimposed over the real world to highlight certain features and enhance understanding. One application of augmented reality is in aviation, where certain controls can be highlighted, for example, the controls needed to land an airplane. And many medical applications are under development (Taubes, 1994b). Recently, for the first time, a surgeon conducted surgery to remove a brain tumor using an augmented reality system; a video image superimposed with 3-D graphics helped the doctor to see the site of the operation more effectively (Satava, 1993).

15.3.3 Through the Window

With this kind of system, also known as *desktop VR,* the user sees the 3-D world through the "window"" of the computer screen and navigates through the space with a control device such as a mouse. Like immersive virtual reality, this provides a first-person experience. One low-cost example of a Through the Window virtual reality system is the 3-D architectural design planning tool *Virtus WalkThrough,* which makes it possible to explore virtual reality on a Macintosh or IBM computer. Developed as a computer visualization tool to help plan complex high-tech filmmaking for the movie *The Abyss,* directed by James Cameron, *Virtus WalkThrough* is now used as a set design and planning tool for many Hollywood movies and advertisements, as well as architectural planning and educational applications. A similar, less-expensive and less-sophisticated program that is starting to find use in elementary and secondary schools is *Virtus VR* (Law, 1994; Pantelidis, n.d.).

Another example of Through the Window virtual reality comes from the field of dance, where a computer program called *LifeForms* lets choreographers create sophisticated human motion animations. *LifeForms* permits the user to access "shape" libraries of figures in sitting, standing, jumping, sports poses, dance poses, and other positions. *LifeForms* supports the compositional process of dance and animation so that choreographers can create, fine-tune, and plan dances "virtually" on the computer. The great modern dancer and choreographer Merce Cunningham has begun using *LifeForms* to choreograph new dances (Schiphorst, 1992). Using *LifeForms,* it is possible to learn a great deal about the design process without actually rehearsing and mounting a performance.

The field of forensic animation is merging with Through the Window VR (Baird, 1992; Hamilton, 1993). Here, dynamic computer animations are used to recreate the scene of a crime and the sequence of events, as reconstructed through analysis of the evidence (for example, bullet speed and trajectory can be modeled). These dynamic visualizations are used in crime investigations and as evidence in trials. The London Metropolitan Police use VR to document witnesses' descriptions of crime scenes. Similarly, the FBI uses *Virtus WalkThrough* as a training tool at the FBI Academy and as a site visualization tool in hostage crisis situations.

15.3.4 Mirror World

In contrast to the first-person systems described above, Mirror World (Projected Realities) provides a second-person experience in which the viewer stands outside the imaginary world, but communicates with characters or objects inside it. Mirror World systems use a video camera as an input device. Users see their images superimposed on or merged with a virtual world presented on a large video monitor or video-projected image. Using a digitizer, the computer processes the users' images to extract features such as their positions, movements, or the number of fingers raised. These systems are usually less expensive than total immersion systems, and the users are unencumbered by head gear, wired gloves, or other interfaces (Lantz, 1992). Four examples of a Mirror World virtual-reality system are: (1) Myron Krueger's "artificial reality" systems such as VIDEOPLACE; (2) the Mandala system from the Vivid Group, created by a group of performance artists in Toronto; (3) the InView system, which has provided the basis for developing entertainment applications for children, including a TV game show, and (4) Meta Media's wall-sized screen applications, such as shooting basketball hoops and experiencing what happens when you try to throw a ball under zero gravity conditions (Brill, 1995; O'Donnell, 1994; Wagner, 1994).

In Krueger's system, users see colorful silhouettes of their hands or their entire bodies. As users move, their silhouette mirror images move correspondingly, interacting with other silhouette objects generated by computer. Scale can be adjusted so that one person's mirror silhouette appears very small by comparison with other people and objects present in the VIDEOPLACE artificial world. Krueger suggests that:

> In artificial realities, the body can be employed as a teaching aid, rather than suppressed by the need to keep order. The theme is not "learning by doing" in the Dewey sense, but instead "doing is learning," a completely different emphasis (Krueger, 1993, p. 152).

The Mandala and InView systems feature a video camera above the computer screen that captures an image of the user and places this image within the scene portrayed on the screen using computer graphics. There are actually three components: (1) the scene portrayed (usually stored on videodisc), (2) the digitized image of the user, and (3) computer graphics–generated objects that appear to fit within the scene that are programmed to be interactive, responding to the "touch" of the user's image. The user interacts with the objects on the screen—for example, to play a drum or to hit a ball. (Tactile feedback is not possible with this technique.) This type of system is becoming popular as an interactive museum exhibit. For example, at the National Hockey Museum, a Mandala system shows you on the screen in front of the goalie net, trying to keep the "virtual" puck out of the net. Recently, a Mandala installation was completed for Paramount Pictures and the Oregon Museum of Science and Industry that is a simulation of Star Trek: The Next Generation's Holodeck.

> Users step into an actual set of the transporter room in the real world and view themselves in the "Star Trek virtual world" on a large screen in front of them. They control where they wish to be transported and can interact with the scene when they arrive. For example, users could transport themselves to the surface of a planet, move around the location, and manipulate the objects there. Actual video footage from the television show is used for backgrounds and is controlled via videodisc (Wyshynski & Vincent, 1993, p. 130).

Another application is an experimental teleconferencing project—Virtual Cities—for children developed by the Vivid Group in collaboration with the Marshal McLuhan Foundation (*Mandala VR News*, 1993). In this application, students in different cities around the world are brought into a networked common virtual environment using videophones.

The Meta Media VR system is similar to the Mandala and InView systems, but the image is presented on a really large wall-sized screen, appropriate for a large audience. Applications of this system, such as Virtual Hoops, are finding widespread use in entertainment and in museums (Brill, 1995). One fascinating aspect of this type of VR mirror world is that it promotes a powerful social dimension: people waiting in the bleachers for a turn at Virtual Hoops cheer the player who makes a hoop—it's very interactive in this way. And preliminary evidence suggests that learners get more caught up in physics lessons presented with this technology, even when they are only sitting in the audience (Wisne, 1994).

15.3.5 Waldo World

This type of virtual-reality application is a form of digital puppetry involving real-time computer animation. The name "Waldo" is drawn from a science fiction story by Robert Heinlein (1965). Wearing an electronic mask or body armor equipped with sensors that detect motion, a puppeteer controls, in real time, a computer animation figure on a screen or a robot.

One example of a Waldo World VR application is the Virtual Actors™ developed by SimGraphics Engineering (Tice & Jacobson, 1992). These are computer-generated animated characters controlled by human actors, in real time. To perform a Virtual Actor (VA), an actor wears a "Waldo" that tracks the actor's eyebrows, cheek, head, chin, and lip movements, allowing these features to control the corresponding features of the computer-generated character with their own movements. For example, when the actor smiles, the animated character smiles correspondingly. A hidden video camera aimed at the audience is fed into a video monitor backstage, so that the actor can see the audience and "speak" to individual members of the audience through the lip-synced computer animation image of the character on the display screen. This digital puppetry application is like the Wizard of Oz interacting with Dorothy and her companions: "Pay no attention to that man behind the curtain!"

The Virtual Actor characters include Mario in Real Time (MIRT), based on the hero of the Super Mario Nintendo games, as well as a Virtual Mark Twain. MIRT and the Virtual Mark Twain are used as an interactive entertainment and promotional medium at trade shows (Tice & Jacobson, 1992). Another Virtual Actor is Eggwardo, an animation character developed for use with children at the Loma Linda Medical Center (Warner & Jacobson, 1992; Warner, 1993). Neuroscientist Dave Warner (1993) explains:

> We brought Eggwardo into the hospital where he interacted with children who were terminally ill. Some kids couldn't even leave their beds, so Eggwardo's image was sent to the TV monitors above their beds, while they talked to the actor over the phone and watched and listened as Eggwardo joked with them and asked how they were feeling and if they'd taken their medicine. The idea is to use Eggwardo, and others like him, to help communicate with therapy patients and mitigate the fears of children who face surgery and other daunting medical procedures.

Another type of Waldo World has been developed by Ascension, using its Flock of Birds™ positioning system (Scully, 1994). This is a full-body Waldo system that is not used in real time but as a foundation for creating animated films and advertisements.

15.3.6 Chamber World

A Chamber World is a small virtual-reality projection theater controlled by several computers that gives users the sense of freer movement within a virtual world than the immersive VR systems and thus a feeling of greater immersion. Images are projected on all of the walls that can be viewed in 3-D, with a head-mounted display showing a seamless virtual environment. The first of these systems was the CAVE, developed at the Electronic Visualization Laboratory at the University of Illinois (Cruz-Nierna, 1993; DeFanti, Sandin & Cruz-Neira, 1993; Wilson, 1994). Another Chamber World system—EVE: Extended Virtual Environment—was developed at the *Kernforschungszntrum* (Nuclear Research Center) Karlsruhe in collaboration with the *Institut fur Angewandte Informatik* (Institute of Applied Informatics) in Germany (Shaw, 1994; Shaw & May, 1994). The recently opened Sony Omnimax 3-D theaters, where all members of the audience wear a head-mounted display in order to see 3-D graphics and hear 3-D audio, is another—albeit much larger—example of this type of virtual reality (Grimes, 1994).

The CAVE is a 3-D real-projection theater made up of three walls and a floor, projected in stereo and viewed with "stereo glasses" that are less heavy and cumbersome than many other head-mounted displays used for immersive VR (Cruz-Nierna, 1993; Wilson, 1994). The CAVE provides a first-person experience. As a CAVE viewer moves within the display boundaries (wearing a location sensor and 3-D glasses), the correct perspective and stereo projections of the environment are updated and the image moves with and surrounds the viewer. Four Silicon Graphics computers control the operation of the CAVE, which has been used for scientific visualization applications such as astronomy.

15.3.7 Cab Simulator Environment

This is another type of "first-person" virtual-reality technology that is essentially an extension of the traditional simulator (see 17.4). Hamit (1993) defines the cab simulator environment as:

> Usually an entertainment or experience simulation form of virtual reality, which can be used by a small group or by a single individual. The illusion of presence in the virtual environment is created by the use of visual elements greater than the field of view, three-dimensional sound inputs, computer-controlled motion bases, and more than a bit of theatre (p. 428).

Cab simulators are finding many applications in training and entertainment. For example, AGC Simulation Products has developed a cab simulator training system for police officers to practice driving under high-speed and dangerous conditions (Flack, 1993). SIMNET is a networked system of cab simulators that is used in military training (Hamit, 1993; Sterling, 1993). Virtual Worlds Entertainment has developed BattleTech, a location-based entertainment system where players in six cabs are linked together to play simulation games (Jacobson, 1993b). An entertainment center in Irvine, California, called Fighter Town features actual flight simulators as "virtual environments." Patrons pay for a training session where they learn how to operate the simulator, and then they get to go through a flight scenario.

15.3.8 Cyberspace

The term *cyberspace* was coined by William Gibson in the science fiction novel *Neuromancer* (1986), that describes a future dominated by vast computer networks and databases. Cyberspace is a global artificial reality that can be visited simultaneously by many people via networked computers. Cyberspace is where you are when you're hooked up to a computer network or electronic database—or talking on the telephone. However, there are more specialized applications of cyberspace where users hook up to a virtual world

that exists only electronically; these applications include text-based MUDs (Multi-User Dungeons or Multi-User Domains) and MUSEs (Multi-User Simulated Environments). One MUSE, Cyberion City, has been established specifically to support education within a constructivist learning context (Rheingold, 1993). Groupware, also known as computer-supported cooperative work (CSCW), is another type of cyberspace technology (Schrage, 1991; Miley, 1992; Baecker, 1993; Bruckman & Resnick, 1993; Coleman, 1993; Wexelblat, 1993).

Habitat, designed by Chip Morningstar and F. Randall Farmer (1991, 1993) at Lucasfilm, was one of the first attempts to create a large-scale, commercial, many-user, graphical virtual environment. Habitat is built on top of an ordinary commercial on-line service and uses low-cost Commodore 64 home computers to support user interaction in a virtual world. The system can support thousands of users in a single shared cyberspace. Habitat presents its users with a real-time animated view into an on-line graphic virtual world. Users can communicate, play games, and go on adventures in Habitat. There are two versions of Habitat in operation, one in the United States and another in Japan.

Similar to this, researchers at the University of Central Florida have developed ExploreNet, a low-cost 2-D networked virtual environment intended for public education (Moshell & Dunn-Roberts, 1993; Moshell & Hughes, 1993, 1994a, 1994b). This system is built on a network of 386 and 486 IBM PCs. ExploreNet is a role-playing game. Students must use teamwork to solve various mathematical problems that arise while pursuing a "quest." Each participant has an animated figure on the screen, located in a shared world. When one student moves her animated figure or takes an action, all the players see the results on the networked computers, located in different rooms, schools, or even cities. ExploreNet is the basis for a major research initiative.

CyberCity, an interactive graphical world, is currently being added as a section of CompuServe (Van Nedervelde, 1994). This is only one example of an increasing trend toward graphic interfaces in cyberspace, which is most clearly exemplified by graphical browses, such as MOSAIC. However, systems like CyberCity and Habitat are interactive virtual worlds rather than a hypertextual graphic user interface (GUI) system (see 21.4) like MOSAIC.

There is an electronically networked coffee house (Galloway & Rabinowitz, 1992). The Electronic Cafe International, headquartered in Santa Monica, California, links people at about 60 sites around the globe via video and computer for talk, music, and performance art conducted jointly by people at the various sites.

Another example of cyberspace is the Army's SIMNET system. Tank simulators (a type of cab simulator) are networked together electronically, often at different sites, and war games are played using the battlefield modeled in cyberspace. Participants may be at different locations, but they are "fighting" each other at the same location in cyberspace via SIMNET (Hamit, 1993; Sterling, 1993). Not only is the virtual battlefield portrayed electronically but also participants' actions in the virtual tanks are monitored, revised, and coordinated. There is virtual radio traffic. And the radio traffic is recorded for later analysis by trainers. Several battlefield training sites such as the Mojave Desert in California and 73 Easting in Iraq (the site of a major battle in the 1991 war) are digitally replicated within the computer so that all the soldiers will see the same terrain, the same simulated enemy, and friendly tanks. Battle conditions can be changed for different war game scenarios (Hamit, 1993; Sterling, 1993).

15.3.9 Telepresence/Teleoperation

The concept of cyberspace is linked to the notion of *telepresence,* the feeling of being in a location other than where you actually are. Related to this, *teleoperation* means that you can control a robot or another device at a distance. In the Jason project, children at different sites across the U.S. have the opportunity to teleoperate the unmanned submarine Jason, the namesake for this innovative science education project directed by Robert Ballard, a scientist at the Woods Hole Oceanographic Institute (EDS, 1991; Ulman, 1993; McLellan, 1995). An extensive set of curriculum materials is developed by the National Science Teachers Association to support each Jason expedition. A new site is chosen each year. In past voyages, the Jason project has gone to the Mediterranean Sea, the Great Lakes, the Gulf of Mexico, the Galapagos Islands, and Belize. The 1995 expedition will go to Hawaii.

Similar to this, NASA has implemented an educational program in conjuction with the "telepresence-controlled remotely operated underwater vehicle" (TROV) that has been deployed to Antarctica (Stoker, 1994). By means of a distributed computer control architecture developed at NASA, school children in classrooms across the U.S. can take turns driving the TROV in Antarctica.

Surgeon Richard Satava is pioneering telepresence surgery for gall bladder removal, without any direct contact from the surgeon after an initial small incision is made— a robot does the rest, following the movements of the surgeon's hands at another location (Satava, 1992; Taubes, 1994b). Satava believes that telepresence surgery can someday be carried out in space, on the battlefield, or in the Third World, without actually sending the doctor.

15.4 INTRODUCTION TO VIRTUAL REALITY APPLICATIONS IN EDUCATION TRAINING

Virtual reality appears to offer educational potentials in the following areas: (1) data gathering and visualization, (2) project planning and design, (3) design of interactive training systems, (4) virtual field trips, and (5) design of experiential learning environments. Virtual reality also offers many possibilities as a tool for nontraditional learners,

including the physically disabled and those undergoing rehabilitation who must learn (or relearn) communication and psychomotor skills (Pausch, Vogtle & Conway, 1991; Pausch & Williams, 1991; Knapp & Lusted, 1992; Warner & Jacobson, 1992; Delaney, 1993; Trimble, 1993; Murphy, 1994; Sklaroff, 1994). Virtual reality offers professional applications in many disciplines—robotics, medicine, scientific visualization, aviation, business, architectural and interior design, city planning, product design, law enforcement, entertainment, the visual arts, music, and dance—and concommitantly, virtual reality offers potentials as a training tool linked to these professional applications (Goodlett, 1990; Jacobson, 1992; Hyde & Loftin, 1993; Hughes, 1993; Donelson, 1994; Dunkley, 1994). For example, just as virtual reality is used as a tool by surgeons, it can be used by medical students training to become surgeons.

Originally designed as a visualization tool to help scientists, virtual reality has been taken up by artists as well. VR offers great potential as a creative tool and a medium of expression in the arts. Creative virtual-reality applications have been developed for the audio and visual arts. An exhibit of virtual-reality art was held at the Soho Guggenheim Museum in 1993, and artistic applications of VR are regularly shown at the Banff Center for the Arts in Canada (Stenger, 1991; Frenkel, 1994; Laurel, 1994; Teixeira, 1994a, 1994b). This trend is expanding (Krueger, 1991; Treviranus, 1993; Brill, 1995; Cooper, 1995). Virtual reality has been applied to the theater, including a venerable puppet theater in France (Coats, 1994). And virtual reality has a role to play in filmmaking, including project planning and special effects (Smith, 1993). This has important implications for education, as demonstrated by Bricken and Byrne's (1993) research (described later in this chapter), as well as other projects.

One of VR's most powerful capabilities in relation to education is as a data-gathering and feedback tool on human performance (Hamilton, 1992; Greenleaf, 1994; Lampton, Knerr, Goldberg, Bliss, Moshell & Blau, 1994; McLellan, 1994b). Greenleaf Medical has developed a modified version of the VPL DataGlove™ that can be used for performance data gathering for sports, medicine, and rehabilitation. For example, Greenleaf Medical developed an application for the Boston Red Sox that records, analyzes, and visually models hand and arm movements when a fast ball is thrown by one of the team pitchers, such as Roger Clemens. Musician Yo Yo Ma uses a virtual-reality application called a *hyperinstrument,* developed by MIT Media Lab researcher, Tod Machover, that records the movement of his bow and bow hand (Markoff, 1991). In addition to listening to the audio recordings, Yo Yo Ma can examine data concerning differences in his bowing during several performances of the same piece of music to determine what works best and thus how to improve his performance. NEC has created a prototype of a virtual-reality ski training system that monitors and responds to the stress/relaxation rate indicated by the skier's blood flow to adjust the difficulty of the virtual terrain within the training system

(Lerman, 1993; VR Monitor, 1993). Flight simulators can "replay" a flight or battle tank war game so that there can be no disagreement about what actually happened during a simulation exercise.

In considering the educational potentials of virtual reality, it is interesting to note that the legendary virtual-reality pioneer, Jaron Lanier, one of the developers of the DataGlove™, originally set out to explore educational applications of virtual reality. Unfortunately, this initiative was ahead of its time; it could not be developed into a cost-effective and commercially viable product. Lanier explains:

> I had in mind an ambitious scheme to make a really low-cost system for schools, immediately. We tried to put together something that might be described as a Commodore 64 with a cheap glove on it and a sort of cylindrical software environment (quoted in Ditlea, 1993, p. 10).

Subsequently, during the mid-1980s, Lanier teamed up with scientists at the NASA Ames Lab on the research and development project where immersive virtual reality first came together.

Another virtual-reality pioneer, Warren Robinett, designed the educational software program *Rocky's Boots* (see 12.3) (Learning Company, 1983) during the early 1980s. This highly regarded program, which provides learners with a 2-D "virtual world" where they can explore the basic concepts of electronics, was developed before virtual reality came into focus; it serves as a model for experiential virtual-reality learning environments.

Newby (1993, p. 11) points out that:

> Education is perhaps the area of VR which has some of the greatest potential for improvement through the application of advanced technology. The lack of funding to place VR systems (or, in many cases, more modest educational technology) in public K-12 schools is the major impediment in this area. There are almost no articles in the literature describing research and potential applications in progress which fall clearly in the domain of education in K-12 or college.

Nonetheless, a few secondary schools have started to use virtual-reality technology, including the Academy for the Advancement of Science and Technology in Hackensack, New Jersey, and the West Denton High School in Newcastle-on-Tyne in Great Britain, and Kelly Walsh High School in Natrona County, Wyoming. Gay (1994a) describes how immersive virtual reality was implemented in Natrona County "on a school budget" using public-domain software and other resources. And there have been experimental programs where children are introduced to virtual-reality technology, such as the programs by Bricken and Byrne (1993) and Merickel (1992), which are described later in this chapter. In addition, desktop VR applications featuring Virtus WalkThrough are used increasingly in K-12 schools.

East Carolina State University, in Greenville, North Carolina, has established a Virtual Reality and Education Lab (VREL), which has as its goals, "to identify suitable applications of virtual reality in education, evaluate virtual-reality software and hardware, examine the impact of virtual reality on education, and disseminate this information as broadly as possible" (Auld & Pantelidis, 1994, p. 29). Researchers at VREL have focused intensively on assembling and sharing information. For example, VREL regularly releases an updated bibliography concerning VR and education via the Internet. Veronica Pantelidis, co-director of VREL, has prepared several reports, including: *North Carolina Competency-Based Curriculum Objectives and Virtual Reality* (1993), *Virtus VR and Virtus Walk-Through Uses in the Classroom,* and *Virtual Reality: 10 Questions and Answers.* Related to this, there are currently two Internet listservs concerning VR and education: listserv@mcmuse.mc.maricopa.edu (subscribe cbnvee your name) and listserv@juvm.stjohns.edu (subscribe VirtEd your name). In addition, there are several published reference guides to virtual reality, including *Information Sources for Virtual Reality: A Research Guide,* by Robert Carande (1993); *Virtual Reality: A Selected Bibliography,* by Hilary McLellan (1992); and *Virtual Reality: An International Directory of Research Projects,* edited by Jeremy Thompson (1993).

Many museums are adopting virtual reality for displays as well as educational programs (Lantz, 1992; Britton, 1994; O'Donnell, 1994; Greschler, 1994; Wagner, 1994; Wisne, 1994; Brill, 1994b, 1994c, 1995). The Boston Computer Museum carried out a research project, funded by NSF, to study learners in an experiential learning environment (Gay, 1994b; Greschler, 1994). This research will be discussed in detail in this chapter (15.8.4). And other museum projects are providing useful information concerning effective design and implementation of educational VR applications, such as the social dimension of the Virtual Hoops application discussed earlier. Kellogg, Carroll, and Richards (1991) present a brilliant scenario of "A Natural History Museum Cyberspace," describing how interactive VR museum displays can be designed to support learning. Carl Loeffler of Carnegie Mellon University directs a project featuring the Networked Virtual Art Museum, an art museum that joins telecommunications and virtual reality (Loeffler, 1993; Brill, 1994a: Jacobson, 1994b; Holden, 1992).

Newby (1993, p. 11) points out

> . . . that VR for education, even if developed and proven successful, must await further commitment of funds before it can see widespread use. This situation is common to all countries where VR research is being undertaken, with the possible exception of Japan, which has followed through on an initiative to provide technological infrastructure to students.

So far, most educational applications of virtual reality have been developed for professional training in highly technical fields such as medical education, astronaut training, and military training (Merril, 1993, 1995; Eckhouse, 1993). In particular, military training has been an important focus for the development of virtual-reality training systems, since VR-based training is safer and more cost effective than other approaches to military training (Auburn, 1992; Fritz, 1991; Gambicki & Rousseau, 1993; Hamit, 1993; Sterling, 1993; Stytz, 1993, 1994; Dovey, 1994). It is important to note that the cost of VR technologies, while still expensive, has substantially gone down in price over the last few years. And options at the lower end of the cost scale such as garage VR and desktop VR are expanding. Also, at least one virtual-reality software program, Sense8's WorldToolKit, can be ported between different computer systems.

NASA has developed a number of virtual environment R&D projects, including the Hubble Telescope Rescue Mission training project, the Space Station Coupola training project, and the shared virtual environment where astronauts can practice reconnoitering outside the space shuttle for joint training, human factors, and engineering design (Dede, Loftin & Salzman, 1994; Loftin, 1993). And NASA researcher Bowen Loftin has developed the Virtual Physics Lab where learners can explore conditions such as changes in gravity (Loftin, Engleberg & Beneditti 1993a, 1993b, 1993c). Loftin et al. (1993a) report that at NASA there is a serious lag time between the hardware delivery and training since it takes time to come to terms with the complex new technological systems that characterize the space program. Virtual reality can make it possible to reduce the time lag between receiving equipment and implementing training by making possible virtual prototypes or models of the equipment for training purposes. Bowen Loftin, Christopher Dede, and other researchers are working on further initiatives concerning VR and education at the Johnson Space Center (Dede, 1990, 1992, 1993; Dede, Loftin & Salzman, 1994).

In terms of medical training, several companies have introduced surgical simulators (see 17.4) that feature virtual reality, including both visual and tactile feedback (Satava, 1992; Stix, 1992; Satava, 1993; Hon, 1993, 1994; Marcus, 1994; Merril, 1993, 1994, 1995; Brennan, 1994; Burrow, 1994; McGovern, 1994; Merril, Roy, Merril & Raju, 1994; Rosen, 1994; Spritzer, 1994; Taubes; 1994b; Weghorst, 1994). Merril (1993, p. 35) explains:

Anatomy is three-dimensional, and processes in the body are dynamic; these aspects do not lend themselves to capture with two-dimensional imaging. Now computer technology has finally caught up with our needs to examine and capture and explain the complex goings-on in the body. The simulator must also have knowledge of how each instrument interacts with the tissues. A scalpel will cut tissue when a certain amount of pressure is applied; however, a blunt instrument may not—this fact must be simulated. In addition the tissues must know where their boundaries are when they are intersecting each other.

Virtual-reality simulators are beginning to offer a powerful dynamic virtual model of the human body that can be used to improve medical education (Taubes, 1994b).

Related to this, virtual reality is under exploration as a therapeutic tool. For example, Lamson (1994) reports that the Kaiser-Permanente Medical Group in California is using virtual reality as a tool with patients who are afraid of heights. And Oliver and Rothman (1993) have explored the use of virtual reality with emotionally disturbed children. Knox, Schacht, and Turner (1993) report on a proposed VR application for treating test anxiety in college students. A virtual-reality application in dentistry has been developed for similar purposes: virtual reality serves as a "dental distractor," distracting and entertaining the patient while the dentist is working on the patient's teeth.

15.5 ESTABLISHING A RESEARCH AGENDA FOR VIRTUAL REALITIES IN EDUCATION AND TRAINING

Since virtual reality is such a new technology, establishing a research agenda, identifying the important issues for research, is an important first step in exploring its potential. So far, work in virtual reality has focused primarily on refining and improving the technology and developing applications. Many analysts suggest that VR research needs to deal with far more than just technical issues. Laurel (1992) comments: "In the last 3 years, VR researchers have achieved a quantum leap in the ability to provide sensory immersion. Now it is time to turn our attention to the emotional, cognitive, and aesthetic dimensions of human experience in virtual worlds." Related to this, Thurman (1993) recommends that VR researchers need to focus on instructional strategies, because "device dependency is an immature perspective that almost always gives way to an examination of the effects of training on learners, and thereby fine-tunes how the medium is applied." To date, not much research has been conducted to rigorously test the benefits—and limitations—of learning and training in virtual reality. This is especially true of immersive applications. And assessing the research that has been carried out must take into consideration the rapid changes and improvements in the technology: improved graphics resolution, lighter head-mounted displays, improved processing speed, improved position-tracking devices, and increased computer power. So any research concerning the educational benefits of virtual reality must be assessed in the context of rapid technological improvement.

Any research agenda for virtual realities must also take into consideration existing research in related areas that may be relevant. Many analysts (Henderson, 1991; Laurel, 1991; Biocca, 1992a, 1992b; Heeter, 1992; Pausch, Crea & Conway, 1992; Piantanida, 1993, 1994; Thurman & Mattoon, 1994) have pointed out that there is a strong foundation of research and theory building in related areas—human perception, simulation, communications, computer graphics, game design, multimedia, ethology, etc.—that can be drawn upon in designing and studying VR applications in education and training. Increasingly, research and development in virtual reality is showing an overlap with the field of artificial intelligence (Badler, Barsky & Zeltzer, 1991; Waldern, 1994; Taubes, 1994a). And Fontaine (1992) has suggested that research concerning the experience of presence in international and intercultural encounters may be valuable for understanding the sense of presence in virtual realities. This example in particular gives a good indication of just how broad the scope of research relevant to virtual realities may be.

Furthermore, research in these foundation areas can be extended as part of a research agenda designed to extend our understanding of the potentials of virtual reality. For example, in terms of research related to perception that is needed to support the development of VR, Moshell and Dunn-Roberts (1993) recommend that theoretical and experimental psychology must provide:

1. Systematic measurement of basic properties
2. Better theories of perception, to guide the formation of hypotheses—including visual perception, auditory perception, movement and motion sickness, and haptic perception (the sense of force, pressure, etc.)
3. Careful tests of hypotheses, which result in increasingly valid theories
4. Constructing and testing of input and output devices based on empirical and theoretical guidelines
5. Evaluation metrics and calibration procedures

Human factors considerations will need careful attention (Pausch, Crea & Conway, 1992; Piantanida, 1993, 1994). Waldern (1991) suggests that the following issues are vital considerations in virtual-reality research and development: (1) optical configuration, (2) engineering construction, (3) form, (4) user considerations, (5) wire management, and (6) safety standards. According to Waldern, the single most difficult aspect is user considerations, which includes anthropometric, ergonomic, and health and safety factors. Waldern explains: "If these are wrong, even by a small degree, the design will be a failure because people will choose not to use it." One issue that has come under scrutiny is the safety of head-mounted displays (HMDs), especially with long-term use. This issue will need further study as the technology improves. Wann, Rushton, Mon-Williams, Hawkes, and Smyth (1993) report:

> Everyone accepts that increased screen resolution is a requirement for future HMDs, but equally we would suggest that a minimum requirement for the reduction of serious visual stress in stereoscopic presentations is variable focal depth.

Thurman and Mattoon (1994, p. 56) comment:

> It is our view that VR research and development will provide a foundation for a new and effective form of simulation-based training. However, this can be achieved only if the education and training communities are able to conceptualize the substantial differences (and subsequent improvements) between VR and other simulation strategies. For example, there are indications that VR is already misinterpreted as a single technological innovation associated with head-mounted displays, or sometimes with input devices such as sensor gloves or 3-D trackballs. This is analogous to the mistaken notion that crept into the artificial intelligence (AI) and subsequently the intelligence tutoring system

(ITS) community in the not too distant past. That is, in its infant stages, the AI and ITS community mistakenly assumed that certain computer processors (e.g., LISP machines) and languages (e.g., Prolog) constituted artificial intelligence technology. It was not until early implementers were able to get past the "surface features" of the technology and began to look at the "deep structure" of the concept that real inroads and conceptual leaps were made."

This is a very important point for VR researchers to keep in mind.

It will be important to articulate a research agenda specifically relating to virtual reality and education. Fennington and Loge (1992) identify the following issues: (1) How is learning in virtual reality different from that of a traditional educational environment? (2) What do we know about multisensory learning that will be of value in determining the effectiveness of this technology? (3) How are learning styles enhanced or changed by VR? (4) What kinds of research will be needed to assist instructional designers in developing effective VR learning environments? Related to this, McLellan (1994b) argues that virtual reality can support all seven of the multiple intelligences postulated by Howard Gardner: linguistic, spatial, logical, musical, kinesthetic, and interpersonal and intrapersonal intelligences. VR researchers may want to test this notion.

A detailed research agenda concerning virtual reality as applied to a particular type of training application is provided by a front-end analysis that was conducted by researchers at SRI International (Boman, Piantanida & Schlager, 1993) to determine the feasibility of using virtual-environment technology in Air Force maintenance training. This study was based on interviews with maintenance training and testing experts at Air Force and NASA training sites and at Air Force contractors' sites. Boman et al. (1993) surveyed existing maintenance training and testing practices and technologies, including classroom training, hands-on laboratory training, on-the-job training, software simulations, interactive video, and hardware simulators. This study also examined the training-development process and future maintenance training and testing trends. Boman et al. (1993) determined that virtual environments might offer solutions to several problems that exist in previous training systems. For example, with training in the actual equipment or in some hardware trainers, instructors often cannot see what the student is doing and cannot affect the session in ways that would enhance learning.

> The most-cited requirements were the need to allow the instructor to view the ongoing training session (from several perspectives) and to interrupt or modify the simulation on the fly (e.g., introducing faults). Other capabilities included instructional guidance and feedback to the student and the capture of the playback of a session. Such capabilities should be integral features of a VE system (Vol. II, pp. 26–27).

Boman et al. (1993) report that the technicians, developers, and instructors interviewed for this study were all in general agreement that if the capabilities outlined above were incorporated in a virtual-environment training system, it would have several advantages over current training delivery methods. The most commonly cited advantages were availability, increased safety, and reduced damage to equipment associated with a simulated practice environment. Virtual reality was seen as a way to alleviate the current problem of gaining access to actual equipment and hardware trainers. Self-pacing was also identified as an advantage. For example, instructors could "walk through" a simulated system with all students, allow faster learners to work ahead on their own, and provide remediation to slower students. Boman et al. (1993) report that another potential benfit would be if the system enforced uniformity, helping to solve the problem of maintaining standardization of the maintenance procedures being taught.

Boman et al. (1993) report that some possible impacts of virtual environment simulations include:

1. Portraying specific aircraft systems
2. Evaluating performance
3. Quick upgrading
4. Avoiding many hardware fabrication costs
5. Disassembling in seconds the computer-generated VR model
6. Configuring the VR model for infrequent or hazardous tasks
7. Incorporating the VR model modifications in electronic form

Their findings indicate that: (1) A need exists for the kind of training virtual reality offers, and (2) virtual environment technology has the potential to fill that need. To provide effective VR maintenance training systems, Boman et al. (1993) report that research will be needed in three broad areas: (1) technology development to produce equipment with the fidelity needed for VR training, (2) engineering studies to evaluate functional fidelity requirements and develop new methodologies, and (3) training/testing studies to develop an understanding of how best to train using virtual-reality training applications. For example, Boman et al. (1993) recommend the development of new methods to use virtual-environment devices with simulations, including:

1. Evaluating methods for navigating within a simulated environment, in particular comparing the use of speech, gestures, and 3-D/6-D input devices for navigation commands
2. Evaluating methods for manipulating virtual objects, including the use of auditory or tactile cues to detect object collision
3. Evaluating virtual menu screens, voice, and hand gesture command modes for steering simulations
4. Evaluating methods for interaction within multiple-participant simulations, including methods to give instructors views from multiple perspectives (e.g., student viewpoint, God's-eye-view, panorama)
5. Having the staff from facilities involved in virtual-environment software and courseware development perform the studies on new methodologies

In sum, virtual environments appear to hold great promise for filling maintenance and other technical training needs, particularly for tasks for which training could not otherwise be adequate because of risks to personnel, prohibitive costs, environmental constraints, or other factors. The utility of virtual environments as more general-purpose maintenance training tools, however, remains unsubstantiated. Boman et al. (1993, Vol. IV, pp. 12–16) make a number of recommendations:

- Develop road maps for virtual-environment training and testing research.
- Identify and/or set up facilities to conduct virtual environment training/testing research.
- Conduct experimental studies to establish the effectiveness of VE simulations in facilitating learning at the cognitive process level.
- Develop effective principles and methods for training in a virtual environment.
- Assess the suitablity of VE simulation for both evaluative and aptitude-testing purposes.
- Develop criteria for specifying the characteristics of tasks that would benefit from virtual-environment training for media selection.
- Conduct studies to identify virtual-environment training system requirements.
- Develop demonstration systems and conduct formative evaluations.
- Conduct studies to identify guidelines specifying when and where virtual environment or other technologies are more appropriate in the total curriculum, and how they can be used in concert to maximize training efficiency and optimize the benefits of both.
- Develop integrated virtual-environment maintenance training system and curriculum prototypes.
- Conduct summative evaluation of system performance, usablity, and utility, and of training outcomes.

This study gives a good indication of the scope of the research still needed to assess the educational potentials of virtual realities. As this study indicates, a wide gamut of issues will need to be included in any research agenda concerning the educational potentials of VR. Virtual realities appear to hold great promise for education and training, but extensive research and development is still needed to refine and assess the potentials of this emerging technology.

15.6 THEORETICAL PERSPECTIVES ON VIRTUAL REALTIES

Already there has been a great deal of theory building as well as theory adapting vis-à-vis virtual reality. Theorists have looked to a broad array of sources—theater, psychology, ethology, perception, communication, computer science, and learning theories—to try to understand this emerging technology and how it can be applied in education and other fields.

15.6.1 Ecological Psychology Perspective— J. J. Gibson

The model of ecological psychology proposed by J. J. Gibson (1986) (see also 8.5) has been particularly influential in laying a theoretical foundation for virtual reality. Ecological psychology is the psychology of the awareness and activities of individuals in an environment (Mace, 1977; Gibson, 1986). This is a theory of perceptual systems based on direct perception of the environment. In Gibson's theory, "affordances" are the distinctive features of a thing which help to distinguish it from other things that it is not. Affordances help us to perceive and understand how to interact with an object. For example, a handle helps us to understand that a cup affords being picked up. A handle tells us where to grab a tool such as a saw. And door knobs tell us how to proceed in opening a door. Affordances provide strong clues to the operations of things.

Affordance perceptions allow learners to identify information through the recognition of relationships among objects or contextual conditions. Affordance recognition must be understood as a contextually sensitive activity for determining what will (most likely) be paid attention to and whether an affordance will be perceived. J. J. Gibson (1986) explains that the ability to recognize affordances is a selective process related to the individual's ability to attend to and learn from contextual information.

Significantly, Gibson's model of ecological perception emphasizes that perception is an active process (see 8.5.2). Gibson does not view the different senses as mere producers of visual, auditory, tactile, or other sensations. Instead he regards them as active, seeking mechanisms for looking, listening, touching, etc. Furthermore, Gibson emphasizes the importance of regarding the different perceptual systems as strongly interrelated, operating in tandem. Gibson argues that visual perception evolved in the context of the perceptual and motor systems, which constantly work to keep us upright, orient us in space, and enable us to navigate and handle the world. Thus, visual perception, involving head and eye movements, is frequently used to seek information for coordinating hand and body movements and maintaining balance. Similar active adjustments take place as one secures audio information with the ear and head system.

J. J. Gibson (1986) hypothesized that by observing one's own capacity for visual, manipulative, and locomotor interaction with environments and objects, one perceives the meanings and the utility of environments and objects, i.e., their affordances. McGreevy (1993) emphasizes that Gibson's ideas highlight the importance of understanding the kinds of interactions offered by real environments and the real objects in those environments. Some virtual-reality researchers (McGreevy, 1993; Ellis, 1991, 1992; Zeltner, 1992; Sheridan & Zeltner, 1993) suggest that this knowledge from the real world can inform the design of interactions in the virtual environment so that they appear natural and realistic, or at least meaningful.

Michael McGreevy, a researcher at the NASA Ames Lab, is studying the potential of virtual reality as a scientific visualization tool for planetary exploration, including virtual geological exploration. He has developed a theoretical model of the scientist in the virtual world as an explorer, based on J. J. Gibson's theory of ecological psychology. In particular, McGreevy links the Gibsonian idea, that the environment must "afford" exploration in order for people to make sense of it, to the idea that we can begin to learn something important from the data retrieved from planetary exploration by flying through the images themselves via immersive VR, from all different points of view. McGreevy (1993) explains:

> Environments afford exploration. Environments are composed of openings, paths, steps, and shallow slopes, which afford locomotion. Environments also consist of obstacles, which afford collision and possible injury; water, fire, and wind, which afford life and danger; and shelters, which afford protection from hostile elements. Most importantly, environments afford a context for interaction with a collection of objects.

As for objects, they afford

> grasping, throwing, portability, containment, and sitting on. Objects afford shaping, molding, manufacture, stacking, piling, and building. Some objects afford eating. Some very special objects afford use as tools, or spontaneous action and interaction (that is, some objects are other animals) (McGreevy, 1993, p. 87).

McGreevy (1993) points out that natural objects and environments offer far more opportunity for use, interaction, manipulation, and exploration than the ones typically generated on computer systems. Furthermore, a user's natural capacity for visual, manipulative, and locomotor interaction with real environments and objects is far more informative than the typically restricted interactions with computer-generated scenes. Perhaps virtual reality can bridge this gap. Although a virtual world may differ from the real world, virtual objects and environments must provide some measure of the affordances of the objects and environments depicted (standing in for the real world) in order to support natural vision (perceptualization) more fully.

Related to this, Rheingold (1991) explains that a wired glove paired with its representation in the virtual world which is used to control a virtual object offers an affordance—a means of literally grabbing on to a virtual world and making it a part of our experience. Rheingold explains:

> By sticking your hand out into space and seeing the hand's representation move in virtual space, then moving the virtual hand close to a virtual object, you are mapping the dimensions of the virtual world into your internal perception-structuring system (p. 144).

And virtual-reality pioneer Jaron Lanier (1992) has commented that the principle of head tracking in virtual reality suggests that when we think about perception —in this case, sight—we shouldn't consider eyes as "cameras" that passively take in a scene. We should think of the eye as a kind of spy submarine moving around in space, gathering information. This creates a picture of perception as an *active* activity, not a *passive* one, in keeping with J. J. Gibson's theory. And it demonstrates a fundamental advantage of virtual reality: VR facilitates active perception and exploration of the environment portrayed.

15.6.2 Computers-as-Theater Perspective—Brenda Laurel

Brenda Laurel (1990a, 1990b, 1991) suggests that the principles of effective drama can be adapted to the design of interactive computer programs and, in particular, virtual reality. Laurel (1990, p. 6) comments:

> Millennia of dramatic theory and practice have been devoted to an end that is remarkably similar to that of human-computer interaction design: namely, creating artificial realities in which the potential for action is cognitively, emotionally, and aesthetically enhanced.

Laurel has articulated a theory of how principles of drama dating back to Aristotle can be adapted to understanding human-computer interaction and the design of virtual reality.

Laurel's (1991) ideas began with an examination of two activities that are extremely successful in capturing people's attention: games and theater. She distinguishes between two modes of participation: (1) first person, direct participation; and (2) third person, watching as a spectator with the subjective experience of an outsider looking in, detached from the events.

The basic components of Laurel's (1991) model are:

1. Dramatic storytelling (storytelling designed to enable significant and arresting kinds of actions)
2. Enactment (for example, playing a VR game or learning scenario as performance)
3. Intensification (selecting, arranging, and representing events to intensify emotion)
4. Compression (eliminating irrelevant factors, economical design)
5. Unity of action (strong central action with separate incidents that are linked to that action, clear causal connections between events)
6. Closure (providing an end point that is satisfying both cognitively and emotionally so that some catharsis occurs)
7. Magnitude (limiting the duration of an action to promote aesthetic and cognitive satisfaction)
8. Willing suspension of disbelief (cognitive and emotional engagement)

A dramatic approach to structuring a virtual-reality experience has significant benefits in terms of engagement and emotion. It emphasizes the need to delineate and represent human-computer activities as organic wholes with dramatic structural characteristics. And it provides a means whereby people experience agency and involvement naturally and effortlessly. Laurel (1991) theorizes that engagement is similar in many ways to the theatrical notion of the "willing suspension of disbelief." She explains:

Engagement involves a kind of complicity. We agree to think and feel in terms of both the content and conventions of a mimetic context. In return, we gain a plethora of new possibilities for action and a kind of emotional guarantee (p. 115).

Furthermore,

> "Engagement is only possible when we can rely on the system to maintain the representational context" (p. 115).

Magnitude and closure are two design elements associated with enactment. Magnitude suggests that limiting the *duration* of an action has aesthetic and cognitive aspects as well as physical ones. Closure suggests that there should be an end point that is satisfying both cognitively and emotionally, providing catharsis.

> In simulation-based activities, the need for catharsis strongly implies that what goes on be structured as a whole action with a dramatic "shape." If I am flying a simulated jet fighter, then either I will land successfully or be blown out of the sky, hopefully after some action of a duration that is sufficient to provide pleasure has had a chance to unfold. Flight simulators shouldn't stop in the middle, even if the training goal is simply to help a pilot learn to accomplish some midflight task. Catharsis can be accomplished, as we have seen, through a proper understanding of the nature of the whole action and the deployment of dramatic probability. If the end of an activity is the result of a causally related and well-crafted series of events, then the experience of catharsis is the natural result of the moment at which probability becomes necessity (Laurel, 1991, p. 122).

Instructional designers and the designers of virtual worlds and experiences within them should keep in mind the importance of defining the "whole" activity as something that can provide satisfaction and closure when it is achieved.

Related to this theory of design based on principles of drama, Laurel has recently introduced the concept of "smart costumes" to describe characters or agents in a virtual world. She has developed an art project, PLACEHOLDER, that features smart costumes—a set of four animal characters—crow, snake, spider, and fish (Frenkel, 1994; Laurel, 1994). A person visiting the PLACEHOLDER world may assume the character of one of these animals and thereby experience aspects of its unique visual perception, its way of moving about, and its voice. For example, snakes can see the infrared portion of the spectrum, and so the system tries to model this: the space appears brighter to someone wearing this smart costume. The smart costumes change more than the appearance of the person within. Laurel (1991) explains that characters (or "agents") need not be complex models of human personality; indeed, dramatic characters are effective precisely because the they are less complex and therefore more discursive and predictable than human beings.

Virtual agents are becoming an increasingly important area of design in virtual reality, bridging VR with artificial intelligence (see 19.2.3.1). For example, Waldern (1994) has described how virtual agents based on artificial-intelligence techniques such as neural nets and fuzzy logic form a basis of virtual-reality games such as *Legend Quest.* Bates (1992) is conducting research concerning dramatic virtual characters. And researchers at the Center for Human Modeling and Simulation at the University of Pennsylvania are studying virtual agents in "synthetic-conversation group" research (Badler, Barsky & Zeltzer, 1991; Taubes, 1994a; Goodwin Marcus Systems, Ltd., n.d.). The virtual agent Jack™, developed at the Center for Human Modeling and Simulation, has been trademarked and is used as a 3-D graphics software environment for conducting ergonomic studies of people with products (such as cars and helicopters), buildings, and interaction situations, for example, a bank teller interacting with a customer (Goodwin Marcus Systems, n.d.). Researchers at the MIT Media Lab are studying ethology—the science of animal behavior—as a basis for representing virtual characters (Zeltner, 1992).

15.6.3 Spacemaker Design Perspective— Randal Walser

Randall Walser (1991, 1992) draws on ideas from film-making, performance art, and role-playing games such as Dungeons and Dragons to articulate his model of "spacemaking."

> The goal of spacemaking is to augment human performance. Compare a spacemaker (or world builder) with a filmmaker. Filmmakers work with frozen virtual worlds. Virtual reality cannot be fully scripted. There's a similarity to performance art. Spacemakers are especially skilled at using the new medium so they can guide others in using virtual reality (Walser, 1992).

Walser (1991) places the VR roles of spacemaker (designer) and cyberspace player (user) in the context of creative and performing artists, as shown in Figure 15-2.

Walser (1992) places virtual reality (or cyberspace, as he refers to VR) in the context of a full spectrum of media, including film as well as print, radio, telephony, television, and desktop computing. In particular, Walser compares cyberspace with desktop computing. Just as desktop computing, based on the graphic user interface and the desktop metaphor, created a new paradigm in computing, Walser proposes that cyberspace is based on still another new paradigm, which is shown in Figure 15-3.

Walser (1992) is particularly concerned with immersive virtual reality. He explains that in the desktop paradigm, computers are viewed as tools for the mind, mind as dissembodied intellect. In the new cyberspace paradigm, computers are viewed as engines for worlds of experience where mind and body are inseparable. Embodiment is central to cyberspace, as Walser (1992) explains:

> Cyberspace is a medium that gives people the feeling they have been bodily transported from the ordinary physical world to worlds of pure imagination. Although artists can use any medium to evoke imaginary worlds, cyberspace carries the various worlds itself. It has a lot in common with film and stage, but is unique in the amount of power it yields to its audience. Film yields little power, as it provides no way for its audience to alter screen images. The stage grants more power than film does, as stage actors can "play off" audience reactions, but the course of the action is still basically determined by a script. Cyberspace grants seemingly ultimate power, as it not only enables its audience to observe a reality, but also to enter it and experience it as reality. No one can know what will happen from one moment to the next in a cyberspace, not even the spacemaker (designer). Every moment gives each participant an opportunity to create the next event. Whereas film depicts a reality to the audience, cyberspace grants a virtual body and a role, to everyone in the audience.

Similar to Brenda Laurel, Walser (1992) theorizes that cyberspace is fundamentally a theatrical medium, in the broad sense that it, like traditional theater, enables people to

Creative artists		Performing artists
	writer	storyteller
	speechwriter	orator
	joke writer	comedian
	poet	bard
novelist	choreographer	dancer, mime
architect	composer	instrumentalist
sculptor	coach	athlete
painter	songwriter	singer
	playwright	stage actor
	filmmaker	film actor
user interface designer	dungeon master	D & D role player
	spacemaker	cyberspace player

Figure 15-2. Walser's media spectrum, including spacemaker and cyberspace player categories. (Adapted from Walser, 1991.)

Desktop paradigm	Cyberspace paradigm
mind	body
ideas	actions
creative arts	performing arts
products	performances

Figure 15-3. Walser's (1992) comparison of the desktop and cyberspace paradigms of media design.

invent, communicate, and comprehend realities by "acting them out." Walser explains that acting out roles or points of view is not just a form of expression, but a fundamental way of knowing.

15.6.4 Constructivist Learning Perspective—Meredith and William Bricken

Focusing primarily on immersive applications of VR, Meredith Bricken theorizes that virtual reality is a very powerful educational tool for constructivist learning (see 7.3), the theory introduced by Jean Piaget (Bricken, 1991; Bricken & Byrne, 1993). According to Bricken, the virtual-reality learning environment is experiential and intuitive; it provides a shared information context that offers unique interactivity and can be configured for individual learning and performance styles. Virtual reality can support hands-on learning, group projects and discussions, field trips, simulations, and concept visualization, all successful instructional strategies. Bricken envisions that within the limits of system functionality, it is possible to create anything imaginable and then become part of it.

Bricken speculates that in virtual reality, learners can actively inhabit a spatial multisensory environment. In VR, learners are both physically and perceptually involved in the experience; they perceive a sense of presence within a virtual world. Bricken suggests that virtual reality allows natural interaction with information. In a virtual world, learners are empowered to move, talk, gesture, and manipulate objects and systems intuitively. And according to Bricken, virtual reality is highly motivational: it has a magical quality.

> You can fly, you can make objects appear, disappear, and transform. You can have these experiences without learning an operating system or programming language, without any reading or calculation at all. But the magic trick of creating new experiences requires basic academic skills, thinking skills, and a clear mental model of what computers do (Bricken, 1991, p. 3).

Meredith Bricken points out that virtual reality is a powerful context in which learners can control time, scale, and physics. Participants have entirely new capabilities, such as the ability to fly through the virtual world, to occupy any object as a virtual body, to observe the environment

from many perspectives. Understanding multiple perspectives is both a conceptual and a social skill; virtual reality enables learners to practice this skill in ways that cannot be achieved in the physical world.

Meredith Bricken theorizes that virtual reality provides a developmentally flexible, interdisciplinary learning environment. A single interface provides teachers and trainers with an enormous variety and supply of virtual-learning "materials" that do not break or wear out. And as Bricken (1991) envisions it, virtual reality is a shared experience for multiple participants.

William Bricken (1990) has also theorized about virtual reality as a tool for experiential learning (see 24.3), based on the ideas of John Dewey and Jean Piaget. According to him,

> VR teaches active construction of the environment. Data is not an abstract list of numerals, data is what we perceive in our environment. Learning is not an abstract list of textbook words, it is what we do in our environment. The hidden curriculum of VR is: make your world and take care of it. Try experiments, safely. Experience consequences, then choose from knowledge" (Bricken, 1990, p. 2).

Like his wife Meredith Bricken, William Bricken's attention is focused primarily on immersive virtual reality. William Bricken (1990) suggests that virtual reality represents a new paradigm in the design of human-computer interfaces. Bricken's model of the new virtual-reality paradigm, contrasted with the "old" desktop-computing paradigm, is presented in Figure 15-4. This new VR paradigm is based on the transition from multiple points of view external to the human, to multiple points of view that the human being enters, like moving from one room to another. Related to this, William Bricken and William Winn (Winn & Bricken, 1992a, 1992b) report on how VR can be used to teach mathematics experientially.

15.6.5 Situated Learning Perspective—Hilary McLellan

McLellan (1991) has theorized that virtual reality–based learning environments can be designed to support situated

Desktop paradigm (old)	Virtual-reality paradigm (new)
symbol processing	reality generation
viewing a monitor	wearing a computer
symbolic	experiential
observer	participant
interface	inclusion
physical	programmable
visual	multimodal
metaphor	virtuality

Figure 15-4. William Bricken's (1990) comparison of the desktop and virtual-realty paradigms of media design.

learning (see 3.1.2, 7.4), the model of learning proposed by Brown, Collins, and Duguid (1989). According to this model, knowledge is situated; it is a product of the activity, context, and culture in which it is developed and used. Activity and situations are integral to cognition and learning. Therefore, this knowledge must be learned in context—in the actual work setting or a highly realistic or "virtual" surrogate of the actual work environment. The situated learning model features apprenticeship, collaboration, reflection, coaching, multiple practice, and articulation. It also emphasizes technology and stories.

McLellan (1991) analyzes a training program for pilots called Line-Oriented Flight Training (LOFT), featuring simulators (virtual environments) that exemplify situated learning. LOFT was introduced in the early 1980s in response to data showing that most airplane accidents and incidents, including fatal crashes, resulted from pilot error (Lauber & Foushee, 1981). Concommitently, these data showed that pilot error is linked to poor communication and coordination in the cockpit under crisis situations. So the LOFT training program was instituted to provide practice in team building and crisis management. LOFT teaches pilots and copilots to work together so that an unexpected cascade of small problems on a flight do not escalate into a catastrophe (Lauber & Foushee, 1981).

All six of the critical situated learning components—apprenticeship, collaboration, reflection, coaching, multiple practice, articulation of learning skills—are present in the LOFT training program (McLellan, 1991). Within the simulated flight, the environmental conditions are controlled, modified, and *articulated* by the instructor to simulate increasingly difficult conditions. The learning environment is contextually rich and highly realistic. *Apprenticeship* is present since the instructor decides on what array of interlocking problems to present on each simulated flight. The pilots must gain experience with different sets of problems in order to build the skills necessary for *collaborative teamwork and coordination.* And they must learn to solve problems for themselves: There is no instructor intervention during the simulated flights. *Reflection* is scheduled into the training after the simulated flight is over, when an instructor sits down with the crew to critique the pilots' performance. This involves *coaching* from the instructor as well. The simulation provides the opportunity for *multiple practice,* including practice where different factors are *articulated.* Related to this, it is noteworthy that many virtual-reality game players are very eager to obtain feedback about their performance, which is monitored electronically.

The LOFT training program emphasizes stories: stories of real disasters and simulated stories (scenarios) of crisis situations that represent all the possible kinds of technical and human problems that a crew might encounter in the "real world." According to Fouchee (1992), the pilots who landed a severely crippled United Airlines airplane in Sioux City, Iowa, several years ago, saving many lives under near-miraculous conditions, later reported in debriefing that they kept referring back to their LOFT training scenarios as

they struggled to maintain control of the plane, which had lost its hydraulic system. The training scenarios were as "real" as any other experience they could draw upon.

Another example of situated learning in a virtual environment is a program for corporate training in team building that utilizes the Virtual Worlds Entertainment (VWE) games (BattleTech, Red Planet, etc.), featuring networked simulator pods (Lakeland Group, 1994; McLellan, 1994a). This is a fascinating example of how an entertainment system has been adapted to create a training application. One of the advantages of using the VWE games is that it creates a level playing field. These virtual environments eliminate contextual factors that create inequalities between learners, thereby interfering with the actual learning skills featured in the training program, i.e., interpersonal skills, collaboration, and team building. Thus, McGrath (1994) reports that this approach is better than other training programs for team building. The Lakeland team training program suggests that virtual reality can be used to support learning that involves a strong social component, involving effective coordination and collaboration with other participants. Since both LOFT and the Lakeland Group training program are based on virtual environments (cab simulators), it remains to be seen how other types of virtual reality can be used to support situated learning. Mirror world applications in particular seem to offer potential for situated learning.

15.7 DESIGN MODELS AND METAPHORS

Developing design models and design metaphors will be an important aspect of theory building, research, and development (see also 7.2) in the emerging virtual-reality medium. A few models and design metaphors have emerged that are specifically for education and training.

Wickens (1993) and Wickens and Baker (1994) have proposed a model of virtual-reality parameters that must be considered for instructional design. These analysts suggest that virtual reality can be conceptualized in terms of a set of five features, which are shown in Figure 15-5. Any one of these five features can be present or absent to create a greater sense of reality. These analysts suggest that, based on these five elements, several justifications can be cited for using virtual reality as an educational tool. These justifications include: (1) motivational value, (2) transfer of learning environment, (3) different perspective, and (4) natural interface. According to Wickens and Baker (1994, p. 4),

> We may conceptualize the features of VR in terms of two overlapping goals: that of increasing the naturalness of the interface to reduce the cognitive effort required in navigation and interpretation, and that of creating dynamic interaction and novel perspective. It is important to keep the distinctions between these goals clear as we consider the conditions in which VR can facilitate or possibly inhibit learning. Specifically, we argue that those features of an interface that may reduce effort and increase performance, may actually reduce retention.

Based on this model, these analysts discuss the cognitive issues involved in using virtual reality for task performance and for learning applications. They suggest that virtual reality may prove useful for four types of educational tasks: (1) on-line performance, (2) off-line training and rehearsal, (3) on-line comprehension, and (4) off-line learning and knowledge acquisition. These four categories, and the examples of each category that the authors present, clearly reflect emerging training needs linked to high technology, as well as more traditional training needs.

On-line performance refers to systems where the virtual environment is providing the operator with direct manipulation capabilities in a remote, or nonviewable, environment —for example, the operation of a remote manipulator, such as an undersea robot, space shuttle arm, or hazardous waste handler, the control of a remotely piloted vehicle, or the task of navigating through a virtual database to obtain a particular item. Wickens and Baker (1994) suggest that three general human performance concerns are relevant in these environments: (a) Closed-loop perceptual motor performance should be good (that is, errors should be small, reactions should be fast, and tracking of moving targets should be stable); (b) situation awareness should be high; and (c) workload or cognitive efforts should be low.

Concerning off-line training and rehearsal, Wickens and Baker (1994) suggest that virtual environments may serve as a tool for rehearsing critical actions in a safe environment, in preparation for target performance in a less-forgiving one. According to Wickens and Baker (1994, p. 5),

> This may involve practicing lumbar injection for a spinal or epidural anesthesia, maneuvering a space craft, carrying out rehearsal flights prior to a dangerous mission, or practicing emergency procedures in an aircraft or nuclear power facility. The primary criterion here is the effective transfer of training from practice in the virtual environment to the "true reality" target environment.

In terms of on-line comprehension, Wickens and Baker (1994) explain that the goal of interacting with a virtual environment may be to reach insight or understanding regarding the structure of an environment. This type of application is particularly valuable for scientists and others dealing with highly abstract data. Finally, off-line learning and knowledge acquisition concerns the transfer of knowledge, acquired in a virtual environment, to be employed, later in a different, more abstract form (Wickens & Baker, 1994).

Wickens (1994, p. 17) cautions that:

> The goals of good interface design for the user and good design for the learner, while overlapping in many respects, are not identical. A key feature in this overlap is the concern for the reduction in effort; many of the features of virtual

	Less real	More real
1. Dimensionality	2-D	3-D
2. Motion	Static	Dynamic
3. Interaction	Open loop	Closed loop
4. Frame of reference	Outside-in (God's eye)	Inside-out (User's eye)
	World referenced	Ego referenced
5. Multimodal interaction (Enhanced sensory experience)	Limited	Multimodal

Figure 15-5. Five components of virtual reality. (Adapted from Wickens & Baker, 1994.)

1. Three-dimensional (perspective and/or stereoscopic) viewing vs. two-dimensional planar viewing. Three-dimensional viewing potentially offers a more realistic view of the geography of an environment than a 2-D contour map.
2. Dynamic vs. static display. A dynamic display appears more real than a series of static images of the same material.
3. Closed-loop (interactive or learner centered) vs. open-loop interaction. A more realistic closed-loop mode is one in which the learner has control over what aspect of the learning "world" is viewed or visited. That is, the learner is an active navigator as well as an observer.
4. Inside-out (ego referenced) vs. outside-in (world referenced) frame of reference. The more realistic inside-out frame of reference is one in which the image of the world on the display is viewed from the perspective of the point of ego reference of the user (that point which is being manipulated by the control).
5. Multimodal interaction (enhanced sensory experience). Virtual environments employ a variety of techniques for user input, including speech recognition and gestures, either sensed through a "data glove" or captured by camera.

reality may accomplish this reduction. Some of these features, like the naturalness of an interface which can replace arbitrary symbolic command and display strings, clearly serve the goals of both. But when effort-reduction features of virtual reality serve to circumvent cognitive transformations that are necessary to understanding and learning the relationships between different facets of data, or of a body of knowledge, then a disservice may be done (p. 17).

These design considerations must be kept in mind as virtual-reality concepts are introduced into education. Wickens also recommends that care should be taken to ensure redundancy of presentation formats, exploit the utility of visual momentum, exploit the benefits of closed-loop interaction, and use other principles of human factors design.

Wickens (1994) recommends that related human factors research concerning the characteristics of cognitive processes and tasks that may be used in a virtual environment should be taken into account. These factors include task analysis, including search, navigation, perceptual biases, visual-motor coupling, manipulation, perception and inspection, and learning (including procedural learning, perceptual motor skill learning, spatial learning and navigational rehearsal, and conceptual learning). And Wickens suggests that there are three human factors principles relevant to the design of virtual environments—consistency, redundancy, and visual momentum—which have been shown to help performance and, also, if carefully applied, facilitate learning in such an environment.

A design metaphor for representing the actions of the VR instructional developer has been proposed by researchers at Lockheed (Grant, McCarthy, Pontecorvo & Stiles, 1991). These researchers found that the most appropriate metaphor is that of a television studio, with a studio control booth, stage, and audience section. The control booth serves as the developer's information workspace, providing all the tools required for courseware development. The visual simulation and interactions with the system are carried out on the studio stage, where the trainee may participate and affect the outcome of a given instructional simulation. The audience metaphor allows passive observation and, if the instructional developer allows it, provides the trainee with freedom of movement within the virtual environment without affecting the simulation. For both the instructional developer and the student, the important spatial criteria are perspective, orientation, scale, level of visual detail, and granularity of simulation (Grant, McCarthy, Pontecorvo & Stiles, 1991).

15.8 VIRTUAL REALITIES RESEARCH AND DEVELOPMENT

15.8.1 Research on VR and Training Effectiveness

Regian, Shebilske, and Monk (1992) report on empirical research that explored the instructional potential of immersive virtual reality as an interface for simulation-based training. According to these researchers, virtual reality may

hold promise for simulation-based training because the interface preserves: (a) visual-spatial characteristics of the simulated world and (b) the linkage between motor actions of the student and resulting effects in the simulated world. This research featured two studies. In one study, learners learned how to use a virtual-control console. In the other study, learners learned to navigate a virtual maze.

In studying spatial cognition, it is useful to distinguish between small-scale and large-scale space (Siegal, 1981). Small-scale space can be viewed from a single vantage point at a single point in time. Large-scale space extends beyond the immediate vantage point of the viewer and must be experienced across time. Subjects can construct functional representations of large-scale space from sequential, isolated views of small-scale space presented in two-dimensional media such as film (Hochberg, 1986) or computer graphics (Regian, 1986). Virtual reality, however, offers the possibility of presenting both small-scale and large-scale spatial information in a three-dimensional format that eliminates the need for students to translate the representation from 2-D to 3-D. The resulting reduction in cognitive load may benefit training. Regian et al. (1992) investigated the use of immersive virtual reality to teach procedural tasks requiring performance of motor sequences within small-scale space (the virtual console) and to teach navigational tasks requiring configurational knowledge of large-scale space (the virtual maze).

In these studies, 31 subjects learned spatial-procedural skills and spatial-navigational skills in immersive virtual worlds accessed with head-mounted display and Dataglove™. Two VR worlds were created for this research: a virtual console and a virtual maze. Both were designed to support analogs of distinctly different tasks. The first was a procedural console-operations task and the second was a three-dimensional maze-navigation task. Each task involved a training phase and a testing phase. The console data show that subjects not only learned the procedure but also continued to acquire skill while being tested on the procedure, as the tests provided continued practice in executing the procedure. The maze data show that subjects learned three-dimensional, configurational knowledge of the virtual maze and were able to use the knowledge to navigate accurately within the virtual reality.

15.8.2 Research on Learners' Cognitive Visualization in 2-D and 3-D Environments

Merickel (1990, 1991) carried out a study designed to determine whether a relationship exists between the perceived realism of computer graphics images and the ability of children to solve spatially related problems (see Chapter 8). This project was designed to give children an opportunity to develop and amplify certain cognitive abilities: imagery, spatial relations, displacement and transformation, creativity, and spatially related problem solving. One way to enhance these cognitive abilities is to have students develop, displace, transform, and interact with 2-D and 3-D computer graphics models. The goal of this study was to determine if specially designed 2-D and 3-D computer graphics training would enhance any, or all, of these cognitive abilities.

Merickel reports that experiments were performed using 23 subjects between the ages of 8 and 11 who were enrolled in an elementary summer school program in Novato, California. Two different computer apparatuses were used: computer workstations and an immersive virtual-reality system developed by Autodesk, Inc. The students were divided into two groups. The first used microcomputers (workstations) equipped with AutoSketch and AutoCAD software. The other group worked with virtual-reality. The workstation treatment incorporated three booklets to instruct the subjects on how to solve five different spatial-relationship problems.

The virtual-reality system provided by Autodesk that was used in the virtual-reality treatment included an 80386-based MS-DOS microcomputer, a head-mounted display, and a VPL DataGlove™; a Polhemus 6D Isotrak positioning and head-tracking device; Matrox SM 1281 real-time graphics boards; and software developed at Autodesk.

The cyberspace part of the project began with classroom training in the various techniques and physical gestures required for moving within and interacting with cyberspace modes. Each child was shown how the DataGlove™ and the head-mounted display would feel by having them first try them on without being connected to the computer.

Merickel reports that after the practice runs, 14 children were given the opportunity to don the cyberspace apparatus and interact with two different computer-generated, 3-D virtual realities. The DataGlove™ had to be calibrated. Students looked around the virtual world of an office and, using hand gesture commands, practiced moving toward objects and "picked up" objects in the virtual world. Students also practiced "flying," which was activated by pointing the index finger of the hand in the DataGlove™.

The second cyberspace voyage was designed to have students travel in a large "outdoor" space and find various objects including a sphere, a book, a chair, a racquet, and two cube models—not unlike a treasure hunt. But this treasure hunt had a few variations. One was that the two cube models were designed to see if the students could differentiate between a target model and its transformed (mirrored) image. The students' task was to identify which of the two models matched the untransformed target model. Students were instructed to fly to the models and study them; they were also instructed to fly around the models to see them from different viewpoints before making a choice. Most students were able to correctly identify the target model.

Merickel reports that during this second time in cyberspace, most students were flying with little or no difficulty. Their gestures were more fluid and, therefore, so was their traveling in cyberspace. They began to relax and walk around more, even though walking movement is restricted by the cables that attach the DataGlove™ and head-mounted display to the tracking devices. Students began to turn or walk around in order to track and find various items. They appeared to have no preconceived notions or reserva-

tions about "traveling inside a computer." In sum, these children had become quite proficient with this cutting-edge technology in a very short time.

Merickel reports that four cognitive ability tests were administered to the subjects from both treatment groups. The dependent variable (i.e., spatially related problem solving) was measured with the Differential Aptitude Test. The three other measures (Minnesota Pager Form Board Test, Mental Rotation Test, and the Torrance Test of Creative Thinking) were used to partial out any effects that visualization abilities and the ability to manipulate mentally two-dimensional figures, displacement and transformation of mental images abilities, and creative thinking might have had on spatially related problem solving.

Merickel concluded that the relationships between perceived realism and spatially related problem solving were inconclusive, based on the results of this study, but worthy of further study. Furthermore, Merickel points out that the ability to visualize and mentally manipulate two-dimensional objects are predictors of spatially related problem-solving abilities. In sum, Merickel concluded that virtual reality is highly promising and deserves extensive development as an instructional tool.

15.8.3 Research on Children's Designing and Exploring Virtual Worlds

Winn (1993) presented an overview of the educational initiatives that are either underway or planned at the Human Interface Technology Lab at the University of Washington. One goal is to establish a learning center to serve as a point of focus for research projects and instructional development initiatives, as well as a resource for researchers in kinesthesiology who are looking for experimental collaborators. A second goal is to conduct outreach, including plans to bring virtual reality to schools as well as pre- and in-service teacher training. Research objectives include the development of a theoretical framework, knowledge construction, and data gathering about effectiveness of virtual reality for learning in different content areas and for different learners. Specific research questions include: (1) Can children build virtual-reality worlds? (2) Can children learn content by building worlds? (3) Can children learn content by being in worlds built for them?

Byrne (1992) and Bricken and Byrne (1993) report on a study that examined this first research issue: whether children can build VR worlds (see 7.4). This study featured an experimental program of weeklong summer workshops at the Pacific Science Center where groups of children designed and then explored their own immersive virtual worlds. The primary focus was to evaluate VR's usefulness and appeal to students 10 to 15 years old, documenting their behavior and soliciting their opinions as they used VR to construct and explore their own virtual worlds. Concurrently, the researchers used this opportunity to collect usability data that might point out system design issues particular to tailoring VR technology for learning applications.

Bricken and Byrne (1993) report that the student groups were limited to approximately 10 new students each week for 7 weeks. Participants were 10 years old and older. A total of 59 students 10 to 15 years old self-selected to participate over the 7-week period. The average age of students was 13 years, and the gender distribution was predominantly male (72%). The students were of relatively homogeneous ethnic origin; the majority were Caucasians, along with a few Asian-Americans and African-Americans. The group demonstrated familiarity with Macintosh computers, but none of the students had worked with 3-D graphics or had heard of VR before coming to the VR workshops. The Macintosh modeling software package, Swivel 3-D™, was used for creating the virtual worlds.

Each student research group had access to five computers for 8 hours per day. They worked in groups of two or three to a computer. They used a codiscovery strategy in learning to use the modeling tools. Teachers answered the questions they could; however, the software was new to them as well, so they could not readily answer all student questions. On the last day of each session, students were able to get inside their worlds using VR interface technology at the HIT Lab. (The desktop Macintosh programs designed by the children with Swivel 3-D™ were converted over for use on more powerful computer workstations.)

Bricken and Byrne (1993) report that they wanted to see what these students were motivated to do with VR when given access to the technology in an open-ended context. The researchers predicted that the participants would gain a basic understanding of VR technology. In addition, the researchers expected that in using the modeling software, this group might learn to color, cluster, scale, and link graphic primitives (cubes, spheres), to assemble simple geometric 3-D environments, and to specify basic interactions such as "grab a ball, fly it to the box, drop it in."

The participants' experience was designed to be a hands-on, student-driven collaborative process in which they could learn about VR technology by using it and learn about virtual worlds by designing and constructing them. Their only constraints in this task were time and the inherent limitations of the technology.

At the end of the week, students explored their worlds one at a time, while other group members watched what the participant was seeing on a large TV monitor. Although this was not a networked VR, it was a shared experience in that the kids "outside" the virtual world conversed with participants, often acting as guides. Bricken and Byrne (1993) report that the virtual worlds constructed by the students are the most visible demonstrations of the success of the world-building activity.

In collecting information on both student response and system usability, Bricken and Byrne (1993) reported that they used three different information-gathering techniques. Their goal was to attain both cross-verification across techniques and technique-specific insights. They videotaped student activities, elicited student opinions with surveys, and collected informal observations from teachers and researchers. Each data source revealed different facets of the whole process.

Bricken and Byrne (1993, p. 204) reported that the students who participated in these workshops

. . . were fascinated by the experience of creating and entering virtual worlds. Across the seven sessions, they consistently made the effort to submit a thoughtfully planned, carefully modeled, well-documented virtual world. All of these students were motivated to achieve functional competence in the skills required to design and model objects, demonstrated a willingness to focus significant effort toward a finished product, and expressed strong satisfaction with their accomplishment. Their virtual worlds are distinctive and imaginative in both conceptualization and implementation. Collaboration between students was highly cooperative, and every student contributed elements to their group's virtual world. The degree to which student-centered methodology influenced the results of the study may be another fruitful area for further research.

Bricken and Byrne (1993, p. 205) report that students demonstrated rapid comprehension of complex concepts and skills:

They learned computer graphics concepts (real time versus batch rendering, Cartesian coordinate space, object attributes), 3-D modeling techniques, and world design approaches. They learned about VR concepts ("what you do is what you get," presence) and enabling technology (head-mounted display, position and orientation sensing, 6-D interface devices). They also learned about data organization: Students were required by the modeling software to link graphical elements hierarchically, with explicit constraints; students printed out this data tree each week as part of the documentation process.

According to these researchers, this project revealed which of the present virtual-reality system components were usable, which were distracting, and which were dysfunctional for this age group. The researchers' conclusion is that improvement in the display device is mandatory. The resolution was inadequate for object and location recognition and hopeless for perception of detail. Another concern is with interactivity tools. This study showed that manipulating objects with the DataGlove™ is awkward and unnatural. Bricken and Byrne (1993) also report that the head-mounted display has since been replaced with a boom-mounted display for lighter weight and a less-intrusive cable arrangement.

In sum, students, teachers, and researchers agreed that this exploration of VR tools and technology was a successful experience for everyone involved (Byrne, 1992; Bricken & Byrne, 1993). Most important was the demonstration of students' desires and abilities to use virtual reality *constructively* to build expressions of their knowledge and imagination. They suggest that virtual reality is a significantly compelling environment in which to teach and learn. Students could learn by creating virtual worlds that reflected the evolution of their skills and the pattern of their conceptual growth. For teachers, evaluating comprehension and competence would become experiential as well as analytical, as they explored the worlds of thought constructed by their students.

15.8.4 Research on Learners in Experiential Learning Environments

Recently, an exciting experiential learning environment was developed at the Boston Computer Museum, using immersive virtual-reality technology (Gay, 1993, 1994a, 1994b; Greschler, 1994). The Cell Biology Project was funded by the National Science Foundation. David Greschler, of the Boston Computer Museum, explains that in this case, the NSF was interested in testing how VR can impact informal education (that is, self-directed, unstructured learning experiences). So an application was developed in two formats (immersive VR and flat-panel screen desktop VR) to study virtual reality as an informal learning tool. A key issue was: What do learners do once they're in the virtual world? In this application, participants had the opportunity to build "virtual" human cells and learn about cell biology. As Greschler explains, they looked at

> . . . the basics of the cell. First of all the cell is made up of things called organelles. Now these organelles, they perform different functions. Human cells: if you open most textbooks on human cells they show you one picture of one human cell and they show you organelles. But what we found out very quickly, in fact, is that there are different kinds of human cells. Like there's a neuron, and there's an intestinal cell, and there's a muscle cell. And all those cells are not the same at the basic level. They're different. They have different proportions of organelles, based on the kinds of needs that they have. For instance, a muscle cell needs more power, because it needs to be doing more work. And so as a result, it needs more mitochondrias, which is really the powerhouse. So we wanted to try to get across these basic principles.

In the Cell Biology Virtual World, the user would start by coming up to this girl within the virtual world who would say, "Please help me. I need neuron cells to think with, muscle cells to move with, and stomach cells to eat with." So you would either touch the stomach or the leg or the head and "you'd end up into the world where there was the neuron cell or the muscle cell or the intestinal cell and you would have all the pieces of that cell around you and marked and you would actually go around and build." You would go over, pick up the mitochondria, and move it into the cell. As Greschler (1994) explains, "there's a real sense of accomplishment, a real sense of building. And then, in addition to that, you would build this person." Greschler reports that before trying to compare the different media versions of the cell biology world,

> [The designers] sort of said, we have to make sure our virtual world is good and people like it. It's one thing to just go for the educational point of view, but you've got to get a good experience or else big deal. So the first thing we did,

we decided to build a really good world. And be less concerned about the educational components so much as a great experience.

That way, people would want to experience the virtual world, so that learning would occur.

A pilot virtual world was built and tested and improvements were made. Greschler reports:

> We found that it needed more information. There needs to be some sort of introduction to how to navigate in the virtual world. A lot of people didn't know how to move their hand tracker and so on. So what we did is we felt like, having revised the world, we'd come up with a world that was . . . I suppose you could say "Good." It was compelling to people and that people liked it. To us that was very important.

They defined virtual reality in terms of immersion, natural interaction (via hand trackers), and interactivity: The user could control the world and move through it at will by walking around in the head mount (within a perimeter of 10×10 feet).

Testing with visitors at the Boston Computer Museum indicated that the nonimmersive desktop group consistently was able to retain more information about the cells and the organelles (at least for the short term). This group retained more cognitive information. However, in terms of level of engagement, the immersive VR group was much stronger with that. They underestimated the amount of time they were in the virtual world by, on average, more than 5 minutes, far more than the other group.

In terms of conclusions, Greschler (1994) suggests that immersive virtual reality

> . . . probably isn't good for getting across factual information. What it might be good for is more general experiences; getting a sense for how one might do things like travel. I mean the whole idea [of the Cell Biology Project] is traveling into a cell. It's more getting a sense of what a cell is, rather than the facts behind it. So it's more perhaps like a visualization tool or something just to get a feel for certain ideas rather than getting across fact a, b, or c.

Furthermore,

> I think the whole point of this is it's all new. . . . We're still trying to figure out the right grammar for it, the right uses for it. I mean video is great to get across a lot of stuff. Sometimes it just isn't the right thing to use. Books are great for a lot of things, but sometimes they're just not quite right. I think what we're still trying to figure out is what is that "quite right" thing for VR. There's clearly something there—there's an incredible level of engagement. And concentration. That's, I think, probably the most important thing.

Greschler (1994) thinks that virtual reality will be a good tool for informal learning. "And my hope in fact is that it will bring more informal learning into formal learning environments because I think that there needs to be more of that. More open-endedness, more exploration, more exploratory versus explanatory."

15.8.5 Research on Attitudes Toward Virtual Reality

Heeter (1992, 1994) has studied people's attitudinal responses to virtual reality. In one study, she investigated how players responded to BattleTech, one of the earliest virtual-reality location-based entertainment systems. Related to this, Heeter has examined differences in responses based on gender, since a much higher proportion of BattleTech players are males (just as with videogames). Heeter conducted a study of BattleTech players at the Virtual Worlds Entertainment Center in Chicago.

In the BattleTech study, players were given questionnaires when they purchased playing times, to be turned in after the game (Heeter, 1992). A total of 312 completed questionnaires were collected, for a completion rate of 34%. (One questionnaire was collected per person; at least 45% of the 1,644 games sold during the sample days represented repeat plays within the sample period.) Different questionnaires were administered for each of three classes of players: novices, who had played 1 to 10 BattleTech games ($n = 223$); veterans, who had played 11 to 50 games ($n = 42$); and masters, who had played more than 50 games ($n = 47$).

According to Heeter (1992), the results of this study indicate that BattleTech fits the criteria of Czikszentmihalyi's (1990) model of "flow" or optimal experience:

1. Require learning of skills.
2. Have concrete goals.
3. Provide feedback.
4. Let person feel in control.
5. Facilitate concentration and involvement.
6. Be distinct from the everyday world ("paramount reality").

Heeter (1992, p. 67) explains:

BattleTech fits these criteria very well. Playing BattleTech is hard. It's confusing and intimidating at first. Feedback is extensive and varied. There are sensors; six selectable viewscreens with different information which show the location of other players (nearby and broader viewpoint), condition of your 'Mech, heat sensors, feedback on which 'Mechs are in weapon range (if any), and more. After the game, there is additional feedback in the form of individual scores on a video display and also a complete printout summarizing every shot fired by any of the six concurrent players and what happened as a result of the shot. In fact, there is far more feedback than new players can attend to.

According to Heeter (1992, p. 67),

BattleTech may be a little too challenging for novices, scaring away potential players. There is a tension between designing for novices and designing for long-term play. One-third of novices feel there are too many buttons and controls. Novices who pay to play BattleTech may feel intimidated by the complexity of the BattleTech controls, and some potential novices may even be so intimidated by that complexity that they are scared away completely. But

among veterans and masters, 14% feel there are too many buttons and controls, while almost 40% say it's just right.).

Heeter (1992) reports that if participants have their way, virtual reality will be a very social technology. The BattleTech data identify consistently strong desires for interacting with real human beings in addition to virtual beings and environments in virtual reality. Just 2% of respondents would prefer to play against computers only. But 58% wanted to play against human beings only, and 40% wanted to play against a combination of computers and humans. Respondents preferred playing on teams (71%) rather than everyone against everyone (29%). Learning to cooperate with others in team play was considered the most challenging BattleTech skill by masters, who estimated on average that it takes 56 games to learn how to cooperate effectively. Six players at a time was not considered enough. Veterans rated "more players at once" 7.1 on a 10-point scale of importance of factors to improve the game. More players was even more important to masters (8.1). In sum, Heeter concludes that "Both the commercial success of BattleTech and the findings of the survey say that BattleTech is definitely doing some things right and offers some lessons to designers of future virtual worlds."

Heeter (1992) reports that BattleTech players are mostly male. Masters are 98% male, veterans are 95% male, and novices are 91% male. BattleTech is not a child's game. Significant gender differences were found in reactions to BattleTech. Because such a small percentage of veterans and masters were female, gender comparisons for BattleTech were conducted only among novices. Specifically, 2% of masters, 5% of veterans, and 9% of novices were female. This small group of females who chose to play BattleTech might be expected to be more similar to the males who play BattleTech than would females in general. Even so, gender differences in BattleTech responses were numerous and followed a distinct, predictable stereotypical pattern. For example, on a scale from 0 to 10, female novices found BattleTech to be *less relaxing* (1.1 versus 2.9) and *more embarrassing* (4.1 versus 2.0) than did male novices. Males were more aware of where their opponents were than females were (63% versus 33%) and of when they hit an opponent (66% versus 39%). Female BattleTech players enjoyed blowing people up less than males did, although both sexes enjoyed blowing people up a great deal (2.4 versus 1.5 out of 7, where 1 is *very much*). Females reported that they did not understand how to drive the robot as well (4.6 compared to 3.1 for males where 7 is *not at all*). Of female novices, 57% said they would prefer that BattleTech cockpits have fewer than 100+ buttons and controls, compared to 28% of male novices who wanted fewer controls.

Heeter (1994) concludes: "Today's consumer VR experiences appear to hold little appeal for the female half of the population. Demographics collected at the BattleTech Center in Chicago in 1991 indicated that 93% of the players were male." At FighterTown the proportion was 97%.

Women also do not play today's video games. Although it is clear that women are not attracted to the current battle-oriented VR experiences, what women *do* want from VR has received little attention. Whether from a moral imperative to enable VR to enrich the lives of both sexes, or from a financial incentive of capturing another 50% of the potential marketplace, or from a personal curiosity about the differences between females and males, insights into this question should be of considerable interest.

In another study, Heeter (1993) explored what types of virtual-reality applications might appeal to people, both men and women. Heeter conducted a survey of students in a large-enrollment "Information Society" Telecommunications course at Michigan State University, where the students were willing to answer a 20-minute questionnaire, followed by a guest lecture about consumer VR games. The full study was conducted with 203 students. Of the 203 respondents, 61% were male. The average age was 20, ranging from 17 to 32. To summarize findings from this exploratory study, here is what women *do* want from VR experiences: They are strongly attracted to the idea of virtual travel. They would also be very interested in some form of virtual comedy, adventure, MTV, or drama. Virtual presence at live events is consistently rated positively, although not top on the list. The females in this study want very much to interact with other human beings in virtual environments, be it virtual travel, virtual fitness, or other experiences. If they play a game, they want it to be based mostly on exploration and creativity. Physical sensations and emotional experiences are important. They want the virtual-reality experience to have meaningful parallels to real life.

Heeter (1993) reported that another line of virtual-reality research in the Michigan State University Comm Tech Lab involves the development of virtual-reality prototype experiences demonstrating different design concepts. Data are collected from attendees at various conferences who try using the prototype.

15.8.6 Research on
Special Education Applications of VR

Virtual reality appears to offer many potentials as a tool that can enhance capabilities for the disabled in the areas of communication, perception, mobility, and access to tools (Pausch, Vogtle & Conway, 1991; Pausch & Williams, 1991; Warner & Jacobson, 1992; Marcus, 1993; Middleton, 1993; Treviranus, 1993; Murphy, 1994). Virtual reality can extend, enhance, and supplement the remaining capabilities of people who must contend with a disability such as deafness or blindness. And virtual reality offers potential as a rehabilitation tool. Delaney (1993) predicts that virtual reality will be instrumental in providing physical capabilities for persons with disabilities in the following areas:

1. Individuals with movement restricting disabilities could be in one location while their "virtual being" is in a totally different location. This opens up possibilities for participating in work, study, or leisure activities anywhere in the world, from home, or even a hospital bed

2. Individuals with physical disabilities could interact with the real world through robotic devices they control from within a virtual world

3. Blind persons could navigate through or among buildings represented in a virtual world made up of three-dimensional sound images. This will be helpful to rehearse travel to unfamiliar places, such as hotels or conference centers

4. Learning-disabled, cognitively impaired, and brain-injured individuals could control work processes that would otherwise be too complicated by transforming the tasks into a simpler form in a VR environment

5. Designers and others involved in the design of prosthetic and assistive devices may be able to experience the reality of a person with a disability. They could take on the disability in virtual reality, and thus experience problems firsthand, and their potential solutions.

At a conference on "Virtual Reality and Persons with Disabilities" that has been held annually in San Francisco since 1992 (sponsored by the Center on Disabilities at California State University Northridge), researchers and developers report on their work. This conference was established partly in response to the national policy, embedded in two separate pieces of legislation: section 504 of the Rehabilitation Act of 1973, and the Americans with Disabilities Act (ADA). Within these laws is the overriding mandate for persons with disabilities to have equal access to electronic equipment and information. The recently enacted American Disabilities Act offers potential as a catalyst for the development of virtual-reality technologies. Harry Murphy (1994), the director of the Center on Disabilities at California State University Northridge, explains that "Virtual reality is not a cure for disability. It is a helpful tool, and like all other helpful tools, television and computers, for example, we need to consider access." Murphy (1994, p. 59) argues that,

Virtuality and virtual reality hold benefits for everyone. The same benefits that anyone might realize have some special implications for people with disabilities, to be sure. However, our thinking should be for the general good of society, as well as the special benefits that might come to people with disabilities.

Many virtual-reality applications for persons with disabilities are under development, showing great promise, but few have been rigorously tested. One award-winning application is the Wheelchair VR application from Prairie Virtual Systems of Chicago (Trimble, 1993). With this application, wheelchair-bound individuals "roll through" a virtual model of a building such as a hospital that is under design by an architect who tests whether the design supports wheelchair access. Related to this, Dean Inman, an orthopedic research scientist at the Oregon Research Institute, is using virtual reality to teach kids the skills of driving wheel chairs (Buckert-Donelson, 1995).

Virtual Technologies of Palo Alto, California, has developed a "talking glove" application that makes it possible for deaf individuals to "speak" sign language while wearing a wired glove and have their hand gestures translated into English and printed on a computer screen, so that they can communicate easily with those who do not speak sign language. Similar to this, Eberhart (1993) has developed a much less powerful noncommercial system that utilizes the Power Glove™ toy as an interface, together with an Echo Speech Synthesizer. Eberhart (1993) is exploring neural networks in conjunction with the design of VR applications for the disabled. Eberhart trained the computer to recognize the glove movements by training a neural network.

Newby (1993) described another much more sophisticated gesture recognition system than the one demonstrated by Eberhart. In this application, a DataGlove™ and Polhemus tracker are employed to measure hand location and finger position to "train" for a number of different hand gestures. Native users of American Sign Language (ASL) helped in the development of this application by providing templates of the letters of the manual alphabet, then giving feedback on how accurately the program was able to recognize gestures within various tolerance calibrations. A least-squares algorithm was used to measure the difference between a given gesture and the set of known gestures that the system had been trained to recognize.

Greenleaf (1993) described the GloveTalker, a computer-based gesture-to-speech communication device for the vocally impaired that uses a modified DataGlove™. The wearer of the GloveTalker speaks·by signaling the computer with his or her personalized set of gestures. The DataGlove™ transmits the gesture signals through its fiber-optic sensors to the Voice Synthesis System, which speaks for the DataGlove™ wearer. This system allows individuals who are temporarily or permanently impaired vocally to communicate verbally with the hearing world through hand gestures. Unlike the use of sign language, the GloveTalker does not require either the speaker or the listener to know American Sign Language (ASL). The GloveTalker itself functions as a gesture interpreter. The computer automatically translates hand movements and gestures into spoken output. The wearer of the GloveTalker creates a library of personalized gestures on the computer that can be accessed to rapidly communicate spoken phrases. The voice output can be sent over a computer network or over a telephone system, thus enabling vocally impaired individuals to communicate verbally over a distance. The GloveTalker system can also be used for a wide array of other applications involving data gathering and data visualization. For example, an instrumented glove is used to measure the progress of arm and hand tremors in patients with Parkinson's disease.

The Shepherd School, the largest special school in the United Kingdom, is working with a virtual-reality research team at Nottingham University (Lowe, 1994). The Shephard School is exploring the benefits of virtual reality as a way

of teaching children with complex problems to communicate and gain control over their environment.

Researchers at the Hugh Macmillan Center in Toronto, Canada, are exploring virtual-reality applications involving Mandala and the Very Nervous System, a responsive musical environment developed by artist David Rokeby that is activated by movement so that it "plays" interactive musical compositions based on the position and quality of the movement in front of the sensor: the faster the motions, the higher the tones (Treviranus, 1993). Rokeby has developed several interactive compositions for this system (Cooper, 1995).

Salcedo and Salcedo (1993) of the Blind Children Learning Center in Santa Ana, California, report that they are using the Amiga computer, Mandala software, and a videocamera to increase the quantity and quality of movement in young children with visual impairments. With this system, children receive increased feedback from their movements through the musical sounds their movements generate. Related to this is the VIDI MICE, a low-cost program available from Tensor Productions, which interfaces with the Amiga computer (Jacobs, 1991).

Massof (1993) reports that a project is underway (involving collaboration by Johns Hopkins University, NASA, and the Veterans Administration) in which the goal is to develop a head-mounted video display system for the visually impaired that incorporates custom-prescribed, real-time image processing designed to enhance the vision of the user. A prototype of this technology has been developed and is being tested.

Nemire, Burke, and Jacoby (1993) of Interface Technologies in Capitola, California, report that they have developed a virtual-learning environment for physics instruction for disabled students. This application has been developed to provide an immmersive, interactive, and intuitive virtual-learning environment for these students.

Important efforts at theory building concerning virtual reality and persons with disabilities have been initiated. For example, Mendenhall and Vanderheiden (1993) have conceptualized two classification schemes (virtual reality versus virtual altered reality) for better understanding the opportunities and barriers presented by virtual-reality systems to persons with disabilities. And Marsh, Meisel, and Meisel (1993) have examined virtual reality in relation to human evolution. These researchers suggested that virtual reality can be considered a conscious reentering of the process of evolution. Within this reconceptualization of the context of "survival of the fittest," disability becomes far less arbitrary. In practical terms, virtual reality can bring new meaning to the emerging concepts of universal design, rehabilitation engineering, and adaptive technology.

Related to this, Lasko-Harvill (1993) commented:

In Virtual Reality the distinction between people with and without disabilities disappears. The difference between Virtual Reality and other forms of computer simulation lies in the ability of the participant to interact with the computer-generated environment as though he or she was actually inside of it, and no one can do that without what are called in one context "assistive" devices and another "user interface" devices.

This is an important comparison to make, pointing out that user interfaces can be conceived as "assistive technologies" for the fully abled as well as the disabled. Lasko-Harvill explains that virtual reality can have a leveling effect between abled and differently abled individuals. This is similar to what the Lakeland Group found in their training program for team building at Virtual Worlds Entertainment Centers (McGrath, 1994; McLellan, 1994a).

15.9 IMPLICATIONS

This emerging panoply of technologies—virtual realities—offers many potentials and implications. This chapter has outlined these potentials and implications, although they are subject to change and expansion as this very new set of educational technologies, virtual realities, develops. It is important to reiterate that since virtual realities as a distinct category of educational technology are less than a decade old, research and development are at a very, very early stage. And rapid technological improvements mean that existing research concerning virtual realities must be assessed carefully, since it may be rapidly outdated with the advent of improved technological capabilities such as graphics resolution for visual displays, increased processing speed, ergonomically enhanced, lighter-weight interface design, and greater mobility. Research and development programs are underway throughout the world to study the potentials of virtual-reality technologies and applications (Thompson, 1992). As yet, however, very little research on virtual realities as a tool for learning has been carried out. Thus there is a wealth of possibilities for research. As discussed in this chapter, the agenda for needed research is quite broad in scope. And as many analysts have pointed out, there is a broad base of research in related fields such as simulation and human perception that can and must be considered in establishing a research agenda for virtual reality overall, and concerning educational potentials of virtual reality in particular. Research can be expected to expand as the technology improves and becomes less expensive.

REFERENCES

Auburn, P. (1992, Jun. 1). Mission planning and debriefing using head-mounted display systems. *1992 EFDPMA Conference on Virtual Reality.* Washington, DC: Education Foundation of the Data Processing Management Association.

Aukstalnis, S. & Blatner, D. (1992). *Silicone mirage: the art and science of virtual reality.* Berkeley, CA: Peachpit.

Auld, L.W.S. & Pantelidis, V.S. (1994, Jan./Feb.). Exploring virtual reality for classroom use: The Virtual Reality and Education Lab at East Carolina University. *Tech Trends 39*(2), 29–31.

Badler, N.I., Barsky, B. & Zeltzer, D., eds. (1991). *Making them move: mechanics, control and animation of articulated figures.* San Mateo, CA: Kaufman.

Baecker, R.M., ed. (1993). *Readings in groupware and computer-supported cooperative work.* San Mateo, CA: Kaufman.

Baird, J.B. (1992, Sep. 6). New from the computer: 'cartoons' for the courtroom. *New York Times.*

Bates, J. (1992). Virtual reality, art, and entertainment. *Presence 1*(1), 133–38.

Begault, D.R. (1991, Sep. 23). *3-D sound for virtual reality: the possible and the probable.* Paper presented at the Virtual Reality '91 Conference. San Francisco, CA.

Biocca, F. (1992a). Communication within virtual reality: creating a space for research. *Journal of Communication 42*(4), 5–22.

— (1992b). *Communication design for virtual environments* Paper presented at the Meckler Virtual Reality '92 Conference. San Jose, CA.

Boman, D., Piantanida, T. & Schlager, M. (1993, Feb.). *Virtual environment systems for maintenance training.* Final report, Vol. 1–4. Menlo Park, CA: SRI International.

Bradbury, Ray (1951). The veldt. In *Illustrated man.* New York: Doubleday.

Brennan, J. (1994, Nov. 30). *Delivery room of the future.* Paper presented at the Virtual Reality Expo '94. New York.

Bricken, M. (1991). *Virtual reality learning environments: potentials and challenges.* Human Interface Technology Laboratory Technical Publication No. HITL-P-91-5. Seattle, WA: Human Interface Technology Laboratory.

— & Byrne, C.M., (1993). Summer students in virtual reality: a pilot study on educational applications of virtual reality technology. *In* Alan Wexelblat, ed. *Virtual reality: applications and explorations,* 199–218. Boston, MA: Academic.

Bricken, W. (1990). *Learning in virtual reality* (HITL Memo No. M-90-5). Seattle, WA: Human Interface Technology Laboratory.

Brill, L. (1995, Jan./Feb.). Museum VR: Part II. *Virtual Reality World 3*(1), 36–43.

— (1994a, Jan./Feb.). The networked VR museum. *Virtual Reality World 2*(1), 12–17.

— (1994b, May/Jun.). Metaphors for the traveling cybernaut—Part II. *Virtual Reality World 2*(3), 30–33.

— (1994c, Nov./Dec.). Museum VR: Part I. *Virtual Reality World 1*(6), 33–40.

— (1993). Metaphors for the traveling cybernaut. *Virtual Reality World 1*(1), q-s.

Britton, D. (1994, Dec. 1). *VR tour of the Lascaux Cave.* Paper presented at the Virtual Reality Expo '94. New York.

Brooks, F.P., Jr. (1988). Grasping reality through illusion: interactive graphics serving science. *In* E. Soloway, D. Frye & S. Sheppard. *CHI '88 Proceedings,* 1–13.

Brown, J.S., Collins, A. & Duguid, P. (1989). Situated cognition and the culture of learning. *Educational Researcher 18*(1), 32–42.

Bruckman, A. & Resnick, M. (1993, May). *Virtual professional community, results from the Media MOO Project.* Paper presented at the Third International Conference on Cyberspace (3Cybercon). Austin, TX.

Buckert-Donelson, A. (1995, Jan./Feb.). Dean Inman. *Virtual Reality World 3* (1), 23–26.

Burrow, M. (1994, Nov. 30). *Telemedicine.* Paper presented at the Virtual Reality Expo '94. New York.

Buxton, B. (1992). Snow's two cultures revisited: perspectives on human-computer interface design. *In* Linda Jacobson, ed. *CyberArts: exploring art and technology,* 24–38.

Byrne, C. (1992, Winter). Students explore VR technology. *HIT Lab Review,* pp. 6–7.

Carande, R.J. (1993). *Information sources for virtual reality: a research guide.* Westport, CT: Greenwood.

Coats, G. (1994, May 13). *VR in the theater.* Paper presented at the Meckler Virtual Reality '94 Conference. San Jose, CA.

Coleman, D.D., ed. (1993). *Groupware '93 Proceedings.* San Mateo, CA: Kaufman.

Connell, A. (1992, Sep. 18). *VR in Europe.* Preconference Tutorial. Meckler Virtual Reality '92 Conference. San Jose, CA.

Cooper, D. (1995, Mar.). Very nervous system. *Wired 3* (3), 1994.

Cruz-Nierna, C. (1993, May 19). *The cave.* Paper presented at the Meckler Virtual Reality '93 Conference. San Jose, CA.

Czikszentmihalyi, M. (1990). *Flow: the psychology of optimum experience.* New York: HarperCollins.

Dede, C., Loftin, R.B. & Salzman, M. (1994, Sep. 15). *The potential of virtual reality technology to improve science education.* Paper presented at the Conference on New Media for Global Communication from an East West Perspective. Moscow, Russia.

— (1993, May 7). *ICAT-VET conference highlights.* Paper presented at the 1993 Conference on Intelligent Computer-Aided Training and Virtual Environment Technology. Houston, TX.

— (1992, May). The future of multimedia: bridging to virtual worlds. *Educational Technology 32*(5), 54–60.

— (1990, May). Visualizing cognition: depicting mental models in cyberspace (abstract). *In* Benedikt, M., ed. *Collected abstracts from the 1st Conference on Cyberspace,* 20–21. Austin, TX: School of Architecture, University of Texas.

DeFanti, T.A., Sandin, D.J. & Cruz-Neira, C. (1993, Oct.). A 'room' with a view. *IEEE Spectrum 30*(10), 30–33.

Delaney, B. (1993, Fall). VR and persons with disabilities. *Medicine and Biotechnology: Cyberedge Journal Special Edition,* p. 3.

Ditlea, S. (1993, June). Virtual reality: how Jaron Lanier created an industry but lost his company. *Upside 5*(6), 8–21.

Donelson, A. (1994, Nov./Dec.). Fighting fires in virtual worlds. *Virtual Reality World 2*(6), 6–7.

Dovey, M.E. (1994, Jul.). Virtual reality: training in the 21st century. *Marine Corps Gazette 78*(7), 23–26.

Dowding, T.J. (1991, Sep. 23). *Kinesthetic training devices.* Paper presented at the Virtual Reality '91 Conference. San Francisco, CA.

— (1992, A self-contained interactive motorskill trainer. *In*: S.K. Helsel, ed. *Beyond the vision: the technology, research, and business of virtual reality: Proceedings of Virtual Reality '91, the Second Annual Conference on Virtual Reality, Artificial Reality, and Cyberspace.* Westport, CT: Meckler.

Dunkley, P. (1994, May 14). Virtual reality in medical training. *Lancet 343*(8907), 1218.

Eberhart, R. (1993, Jun. 17) *Glove Talk for $100.* Paper presented at the 1993 Conference on Virtual Reality and Persons with Disabilities. San Francisco, CA.

Eckhouse, J. (1993, May 20). Technology offers new view of world. *San Francisco Chronicle,* pp. A1, A15.

EDS (1991). *EDS: bringing JASON's vision home.* Dallas, TX: Author [brochure].

Ellis, S. (1991). Nature and origins of virtual environments: a bibliographical essay. *Computing Systems in Engineering 2*(4), 321–347.

—, ed. (1992). *Pictorial communication in virtual and real environments.* New York: Taylor & Francis.

Erickson, T. (1993). Artificial realities as data visualization environments. *In* Alan Wexelblat, ed. *Virtual reality: applications and explorations,* 1–22. Boston: Academic.

Fennington, G. & Loge, K. (1992, Apr.). Virtual reality: a new learning environment. *The Computing Teacher 20* (7), 16–19.

Flack, J.F. (1993, May 19). *First person cab simulator.* Paper presented at the Meckler Virtual Reality '93 Conference. San Jose, CA.

Fontaine, G. (1992, Fall). The experience of a sense of presence in intercultural and international encounters. *Presence 1*(4), 482–490.

Fouchee, C. (1992, Jan. 20). Personal communication.

Frenkel, K.A. (1994). A conversation with Brenda Laurel. *Interactions 1*(1), 44–53.

Fritz, M. (1991, Feb.). The world of virtual reality. *Training 28*(2), 45–50.

Gambicki, M. & Rousseau, D. (1993). Naval applications of virtual reality. *AI Expert Virtual Reality 93 Special Report.* 67–72.

Gay, E. (1994a, Nov./Dec.). Virtual reality at the Natrona County School System: building virtual worlds on a shoestring budget. *Virtual Reality World 2*(6), 44–47.

— (1994b, Winter). Is virtual reality a good teaching tool? *Virtual Reality Special Report. 1*(4), 51–59.

— (1993). VR sparks education. *Pix-Elation* (10), 14–17.

Galloway, I. & Rabinowitz, S. (1992). Welcome to "Electronic Cafe International": a nice place for hot coffee, iced tea, and virtual space. *In* L. Jacobson. *CyberArts: exploring art and technology,* 255–63. San Francisco, CA: Miller Freeman.

Gibson, J.J. (1986). *The ecological approach to visual perception.* Hillsdale, NJ: Erlbaum.

Gibson, W. (1986). *Neuromancer.* New York: Bantam.

Goodlett, J. Jr. (1990, May). Cyberspace in architectural education (abstract). *In* Benedikt, M., ed. *Collected abstracts from the 1st Conference on Cyberspace,* 36–37. Austin, TX: School of Architecture, University of Texas.

Goodwin Marcus Systems, Ltd. (n.d.). *Jack™: the human factors modeling system.* Middlewich, England: Goodwin Marcus Systems, Ltd. [brochure].

Grant, F.L., McCarthy, L.S., Pontecorvo, M.S. & Stiles, R.J. (1991). Training in virtual environments. *Proceedings of the 1991 Conference on Intelligent Computer-Aided Training,* 320–33. Houston, TX, Nov. 20–22, 1991.

Greenleaf, W. (1994, Nov. 30). *Virtual reality for ergonomic rehabilitation and physical medicine.* Paper presented at the Virtual Reality Expo '94. New York.

— (1993). Greenleaf data glove: the future of functional assessment. *Greanleaf News 2* (1), 6.

Greschler, D. (1994, Oct. 14). Personal communication.

Grimes, W. (1994, Nov. 13). Is 3-D Imax the future or another Cinerama? *New York Times.*

Hale, J. (1993). *Marshall Space Flight Center's Virtual Reality Applications Program.* Paper presented at the Intelligent Computer-aided Training and Virtual Environments (ICAT-VE) Conference. NASA Johnson Space Center, Houston, TX.

Hall, T. (1990, Jul. 8). 'Virtual reality' takes its place in the real world. *New York Times,* p. 1.

Hamilton, J. (1992, Oct. 5). Virtual reality: how a computer-generated world could change the world. *Businessweek* (3286), 96–105.

Hamit, F. (1993). *Virtual reality and the exploration of*

cyberspace. Carmel, IN: Sams.

Harrison, Harry (1972). Ever branching tree. *In* Anthony Cheetham, ed. *Science against man.* New York: Avon.

Heeter, C. (1994a, Mar./Apr.). Gender differences and VR: a non-user survey of what women want. *Virtual Reality World 2*(2), 75–85.

— (1994b, May 13). *Comparing child and adult reactions to educational VR.* Paper presented at the Meckler Virtual Reality '94 Conference. San Jose, CA.

— (1992). BattleTech masters: emergence of the first U.S. virtual reality subculture. *Multimedia Review 3*(4), 65–70.

Heinlein, Robert (1965). *Three by Heinlein: The puppet master; Waldo; Magic, Inc.* Garden City, NY: Doubleday.

Helsel, S.K. (1992a). Virtual reality as a learning medium. *Instructional Delivery Systems 6*(4), 4–5.

— (1992b). CAD Institute. *Virtual Reality Report 2*(10), 1–4.

— (1992c, May). Virtual reality and education. *Educational Technology 32*(5), 38–42.

— & Roth, J., eds. (1991). *Virtual reality: theory, practice, and promise.* Westport, CT: Meckler.

Henderson, Joseph (1990). Designing realities: interactive media, virtual realities, and cyberspace. *In* S. Helsel, ed. *Virtual reality: theory, practice, and promise,* 65–73. Westport, CT: Meckler.

— (1991, Mar.). Designing realities: interactive media, virtual realities, and cyberspace. *Multimedia Review 2*(3), 47–51.

Hochberg, J. (1986). Representation of motion and space in video and cinematic displays. *In* K. Boff, L. Kaufman & J. Thomas, eds. *Handbook of perception and human performance.* New York: Wiley.

Holden, L. (1992, Oct./Nov.). Carnegie Mellon's STUDIO for creative enquiry and the Interdisciplinary Teaching Network (ITeN) and Interactive Fiction and the Networked Virtual Art Museum. *Bulletin of the American Society for Information Science 19*(1), 9–14.

Hollands, R. (1995, Jan./Feb.). Essential garage peripherals. *Virtual Reality World 2*(1), 56–57.

Hon, D. (1994, Nov. 30). *Questions enroute to realism: the medical simulation experience.* Paper presented at the Virtual Reality Expo '94. New York.

— (1993, Nov. 30). *Telepresence surgery.* Paper presented at the New York Virtual Reality Expo '93. New York.

— (1991, Sep. 23). *An evolution of synthetic reality and tactile interfaces.* Paper presented at the Virtual Reality '91 Conference. San Francisco, CA.

Hughes, F. (1993, May 6). *Training technology challenges for the next decade and beyond.* Paper presented at the Intelligent Computer-aided Training and Virtual Environments (ICAT-VE) Conference. NASA Johnson Space Center, Houston, TX.

Hyde, P.R. & R.B. Loftin, eds. (1993). *Proceedings of the Contributed Sessions: 1993 Conference on Intelligent Computer-Aided Training and Virtual Environment Technology,* Houston, TX: NASA/Johnson Space Center.

Jacobs, S. (1191, Aug./Sep.). Modern-day storyteller, info, 24-25.

Jacobson, L. (1994a). *Garage virtual reality.* Carmel, IN: Sams.

— (1994b, Sep./Oct.). The virtual art world of Carl Loeffler. *Virtual Reality World 2*(5), 32–39.

— (1993a). Welcome to the virtual world. *In* Richard Swadley, ed. *On the cutting edge of technology,* 69–79. Carmel, IN: Sams.

— (1993b, Aug.). BattleTech's New Beachheads. *Wired 1* (3), 36–39.

—, ed. (1992). *CyberArts: exploring art and technology.* San Francisco, CA: Miller Freeman.

Johnson, A.D. & Cutt, P.S. (1991). Tactile feedback and virtual environments for training. *Proceedings of the 1991 Conference on Intelligent Computer-Aided Training,* 334. Houston, TX. Nov. 20–22, 1991

Karnow, (1993, Dec. 1). *Liability and emergent virtual reality systems.* Paper presented at the New York Virtual Reality Expo '93. New York.

Kellogg, W.A., Carroll, J.M. & Richards, J.T. (1991). Making reality a cyberspace. *In* M. Benedikt, ed. *Cyberspace: first steps,* 411–31. Cambridge, MA: MIT Press.

Knapp, R.B. & Lusted, H.S. (1992). *Biocontrollers for the physically disabled: a direct link from the nervous system to computer.* Paper presented at the Conference on Virtual Reality and Persons with Disabilities. San Francisco, CA, Jun. 15, 1992.

Knox, D., Schacht, C. & Turner, J. (1993, Sep.). Virtual reality: a proposal for treating test anxiety in college students. *College Student Journal 27*(3), 294–96.

Kreuger, M.W. (1991). *Artificial reality II.* Reading, MA: Addison-Wesley.

— (1993). An easy entry artificial reality. *In* Alan Wexelblat, ed. *Virtual reality: applications and explorations,* 147–62. Boston, MA: Academic.

Lakeland Group (1994). *Tomorrow's team today . . . team development in a virtual world*™. [brochure]. San Francisco, CA: Lakeland.

Lampton, D.R., Knerr, B.W., Goldberg, S.L., Bliss, J.P., Moshell, J.M. & Blau, B.S. (1994, Spring). The virtual environment performance assessment battery (VEPAB): development and evaluation. *Presence 3*(2), 145–57.

Lamson, R. (1994, Nov. 30). *Virtual therapy: using VR to treat fear of heights.* Paper presented at the Virtual Reality Expo '94. New York.

Lanier, J. (1992, Jul.). The state of virtual reality practice and what's coming next. *Virtual Reality Special Report/AI Expert.,* 11–18. San Francisco, CA: Miller Freeman.

Lantz, E. (1992). Virtual reality in science museums. *Instructional Delivery Systems 6*(4), 10–12.

Lasko-Harvill, A. (1993). *User interface devices for virtual reality as technology for people with disabilities.* Paper presented at the Conference on Virtual Reality and Persons with Disabilities. San Francisco, CA.

Lauber, J.K. & Foushee, H.C. (1981, Jan. 13–15). *Guidelines for line-oriented flight training.* Proceedings of a NASA/Industry workshop held at NASA Ames Research Center, Moffett Field, California. U.S. National Aeronautics & Space Administration, Scientific & Technical Information Branch.

Laurel, B. (1994, May 13). *Art issues in VR.* Paper presented at the Virtual Reality '94 Conference. San Jose, CA.

— (1992). Finger flying and other faulty notions. *In* L. Jacobson, *CyberArts: exploring art and technology,* 286–91. San Francisco, CA: Miller Freeman.

— (1991). *Computers as theater.* Reading, MA: Addison-Wesley.

— (1990a). On dramatic interaction. *Verbum 3*(3), 6–7.

— (1990b, Summer). Virtual reality design: a personal view. *Multimedia Review 1*(2), 14–17.

Law, L. (1994, Dec. 15). Personal communication.

Learning Company (1983). *Rocky's boots.* Freemont, CA: Author [computer software].

Lerman, J. (1993, Feb.). Virtue not to ski? *Skiing 45*(6), 12–17.

Loeffler, C.E. (1993, Summer). Networked virtual reality: applications for industry, education, and entertainment. *Virtual Reality World 1*(2), g–i.

Loftin, R.B. (1992). *Hubble space telescope repair and maintenance: virtual environment training.* Houston, TX: NASA Johnson Space Center.

—, Engelberg, M. & Benedetti, R. (1993a). Virtual environments for science education: a virtual physics laboratory. *In* P.R. Hyde & R. Bowen Loftin. *Proceedings of the Contributed Sessions: 1993 Conference on Intelligent Computer-Aided Training and Virtual Environment Technology,* Vol. I, 190.

—, Engelberg, M. & Benedetti, R. (1993b). Virtual controls for interactive environments: a virtual physics laboratory. *Proceedings of the Society for Information Display, 1993 International Symposium, Digest of Technical Papers 24,* 823–26.

—, Engelberg, M. & Benedetti, R. (1993c). Applying virtual reality in education: a prototypical virtual physics laboratory. *Proceedings of the IEEE 1993 Symposium on Research Frontiers in Virtual Reality,* 67–74.

Lowe, R. (1994, Mar./Apr.). Three UK case studies in virtual reality. *Virtual Reality World 2*(2), 51–54.

Mace, W.M. (1977). James J. Gibson's Strategy for perceiving: ask not what's inside your head, but what your head's inside of. *In* R. Shaw & J. Bransford, eds. *Perceiving, acting, and knowing: toward an ecological psychology.* Hillsdale, NJ: LEA.

Mandala VR News (1993, Fall/Winter). Future watch: interactive teleconferencing. *Mandala VR News,* 3. Toronto, Canada: The Vivid Group.

Marcus, B. (1994, May 12). *Haptic feedback for surgical simulations.* Paper presented at the Virtual Reality '94 Conference. San Jose, CA.

Marcus, S. (1993, June 17). *Virtual realities: from the concrete to the barely imaginable.* Paper presented at the 1993 Conference on Virtual Reality and Persons with Disabilities. San Francisco, CA.

Markoff, J. (1991, Feb. 17). Using computer engineering to mimic the movement of the bow. *New York Times,* p. 8F.

Marsh, C.H., Meisel, A. & Meisel, H. (1993, Jun. 17). *Virtual reality, human evolution, and the world of disability.* Paper presented at the 1993 Conference on Virtual Reality and Persons with Disabilities. San Francisco, CA.

Massachusetts Institute of Technology (1981). *Aspen movie map.* Cambridge, MA: Author [videodisc].

Massof, R. (1993, Jun. 17). *Low vision enhancements: basic principles and enabling technologies.* Paper presented at the 1993 Conference on Virtual Reality and Persons with Disabilities. San Francisco, CA.

McCarthy, L., Pontecorvo, M., Grant, F. & Stiles, R. (1993). Spatial considerations for instructional development in a virtual environment. *In* P.R. Hyde & R. Bowen Loftin. *Proceedings of the Contributed Sessions: 1993 Conference on Intelligent Computer-Aided Training and Virtual Environment Technology,* Vol. I, 180–89.

McLellan, H. (1995, Jan./Feb.). Virtual field trips: the Jason project. *Virtual Reality World 3* (1), 49-50.

McGovern, K. (1994, Nov. 30). *Surgical Training.* Paper presented at the Virtual Reality Expo '94. New York.

McGrath, E. (1994, May 13). *Team training at Virtual Worlds Center.* Paper presented at the Meckler Virtual Reality '94 Conference. San Jose, CA.

McGreevy, M.W. (1993). Virtual reality and planetary exploration. *In* Alan Wexelblat, ed. *Virtual reality: applications and explorations,* 163–98. Boston: Academic.

McKenna, Atherton & Sabiston (1990). *Grinning evil death.* Cambridge, MA: MIT Media Lab [computer animation].

McLellan, H. (1991, Winter). Virtual environments and situated learning. *Multimedia Review 2*(3), 25–37.

— (1992). Virtual Reality: A selected bibliography. Englewood Cliffs, NJ: Educational Technology.

— (1994a). The Lakeland Group: tomorrow's team today . . . team development in a virtual world. *Virtual Reality Report 4*(5), 7–11.

— (1994b). Virtual reality and multiple intelligences: potentials for higher education. *Journal of Computing in Higher Education 5*(2), 33–66.

Mendenhall, J. & Vanderheiden, G. (1993, Jun. 17). *Two classification schemes for better understanding the opportunities and barriers presented by virtual reality systems to persons with disabilities.* Paper presented at the 1993 Conference on Virtual Reality and Persons with Disabilities. San Francisco, CA.

Merickel M.L. (1990, Dec.). The creative technologies project: will training in 2D/3D graphics enhance kids' cognitive skills? *T.H.E. Journal,* 55–58.

— (1991). *A study of the relationship between perceived realism and the ability of children to create, manipulate and utilize mental images in solving problems.* Oregon State University. Unpublished doctoral dissertation.

Merril, J.R. (1993, Nov./Dec.). Window to the soul: teaching physiology of the eye. *Virtual Reality World 3*(1), 51–57.

— (1994, May 12). *VR in medical education: use for trade shows and individual physician education.* Paper presented at the Virtual Reality '94 Conference. San Jose, CA.

— (1995, Jan./Feb.). Surgery on the cutting-edge. *Virtual Reality World 1* (3&4), 51–56.

—, Roy, R., Merril, G. & Raju, R. (1994, Winter). Revealing the mysteries of the brain with VR. *Virtual Reality Special Report 1*(4), 61–66.

Middleton, T. (1993, Jun. 18). *Matching virtual reality solutions to special needs.* Paper presented at the 1993 Conference on Virtual Reality and Persons with Disabilities. San Francisco, CA.

— (1992). Applications of virtual reality to learning. *Interactive Learning International 8*(4), 253–57.

Miley, M. (1992). Groupware meets multimedia. *NewMedia 2*(11), 39–40.

Minsky, M. (1991, Sep. 23). *Force feedback: the sense of touch at the interface.* Paper presented at the Virtual Reality '91 Conference. San Francisco, CA.

Mohl, R.F. (1982). *Cognitive space in the interactive movie map: an investigation of spatial learning in virtual environments.* Massachusetts Institute of Technology. Unpublished doctoral dissertation.

Morningstar, C. & Farmer, F.R. (1993). The lessons of Lucasfilm's Habitat. *Virtual Reality Special Report/AI Expert,* 23–32. San Francisco, CA: Miller Freeman.

— & — (1991). The lessons of Lucasfilm's Habitat. *In* Michael Benedikt, ed. *Cyberspace: first steps,* 273–302. Cambridge, MA: MIT Press.

Moshell, J.M. & Dunn-Roberts, R. (1993). Virtual environments: research in North America. *In* Thompson, J., ed.

Virtual reality: an international directory of research projects, 3–26. Westport, CT: Meckler.

— & Hughes, C.E. (1994a, Jan.). *The virtual school.* Orlando, FL: Institute for Simulation and Training. Document JMM94.2.

— & — (1994b, Jan./Feb.). Shared virtual worlds for education. *Virtual Reality World* 2(1), 63–74.

— & — (1994c, Feb.). *The virtual academy: networked simulation and the future of education,* 6–18. Proceedings of the IMAGINA Conference. Monte Carlo, Monaco.

Murphy, H. (1994). The promise of VR applications for persons with disabilities. *In* Helsel, S., ed. *London Virtual Reality Expo '94: Proceedings of the 4th Annual Conference on Virtual Reality,* 55–65. London: Mecklermedia.

Nemire, Burke & Jacoby (1993, Jun. 15). *Virtual learning environment for disabled students: modular assistive technology for physics instruction.* Paper presented at the 1993 Conference on Virtual Reality and Persons with Disabilities. San Francisco, CA.

Newby, G. (1993, Feb.). Virtual Reality. Pre-publication draft of a chapter to be included in the *Annual Review of Information Science and Technology.*

Norman, D. (1993). *Things that make us smart.* Reading, MA: Addison-Wesley.

O'Donnell, T. (1994, Dec. 1). *The virtual demonstration stage: a breakthrough teaching tool arrives for museums.* Paper presented at the Virtual Reality Expo '94. New York.

Oliver, D. & Rothman, P. (1993, Jun. 17). *Virtual reality games for teaching conflict management with seriously emotionally disturbed (SED) and learning disabled (LD) children.* Paper presented at the 1st Conference on Virtual Reality and Persons with Disabilities. San Francisco, CA.

Pantelidis, V.S. (n.d.). *Virtus VR and Virtus WalkThrough uses in the classroom.* Unpublished document. Greenville, NC: Department of Library Studies and Educational Technology, East Carolina University.

— (1993). *North Carolina competency-based curriculum objectives and virtual reality.* Unpublished document. Greenville, NC: Virtual Reality and Education Laboratory, College of Education, East Carolina University.

— (1994). *Virtual reality and educators: information sources.* Unpublished document. Greenville, NC: Virtual Reality and Education Laboratory, School of Education, East Carolina University. (Note: This document is regularly updated.)

Pausch, R., Crea, T. & Conway, M. (1992). A literature survey for virtual environments: military flight simulator visual systems and simulator sickness. *Presence 1,* 344–63.

—, Vogtle, L. & Conway, M. (1991, Oct. 7). *One dimensional motion tailoring for the disabled: a user study.* Computer Science Report No. TR-91-21. Computer Science Department, University of Virginia. Charlottesville, VA.

— & Williams, R.D. (1991). *Giving CANDY to children: user-tailored gesture input driving an articulator-based speech synthesizer.* Computer Science Report No. TR-91-23. Computer Science Department, University of Virginia. Charlottesville, VA.

Piantanida, T. (1994a, Nov. 29). *Low-cost virtual-reality head-mounted displays and vision.* Paper presented at the Virtual Reality Expo '94. New York.

Piantanida, T. (1994b, Dec. 2). *Health and safety issues in home virtual-reality systems.* Paper presented at the Virtual Reality Expo '94. New York.

Piantanida, T. (1993). Another look at HMD safety. *CyberEdge Journal 3*(6), 9–12.

Pimentel, K. & Teixeira, K. (1992). *Virtual reality: through the new looking glass.* New York: McGraw-Hill.

Regian, J.W. (1986). *An assessment procedure for configurational knowledge of large-scale space.* Unpublished doctoral dissertation. University of California, Santa Barbara.

Regian, W. (1993, May 6). *Virtual reality—basic research for the effectiveness of training transfer.* Paper presented at the 1993 Conference on Intelligent Computer-Aided Training and Virtual Environment Technology 9 (CAT-VET).

—, Shebilske, W.L. & Monk, J.M. (1992). Virtual reality: an instructional medium for visual-spatial tasks. *Journal of Communication 42*(4), 136–49.

Rheingold, H. (1991). *Virtual reality.* Reading, MA: Addison-Wesley.

— (1993). *The virtual community: homesteading on the electronic frontier.* Reading, MA: Addison-Wesley.

Robinett, W. (1991, Fall). Electronic expansion of human perception. *Whole Earth Review,* 16–21.

Rosen, J. (1994, Nov. 30). *Telemedicine.* Paper presented at the Virtual Reality Expo '94. New York.

Salcedo, M. & Salcedo, P. (1993, Jun. 17). *Movement development in preschool children with visual impairments.* 1993 Conference on Virtual Reality and Persons with Disabilities. San Francisco, CA.

Satava, R.V. (1992, Jun. 9). *Telepresence surgery.* Paper presented at the 1992 EFDPMA Conference on Virtual Reality. Education Foundation of the Data Processing Management Association, Washington, DC.

Satava, R.V. (1993, May 6). *Virtual reality for anatomical and surgical simulation.* Paper presented at the Intelligent Computer-aided Training and Virtual Environments (ICAT-VE) Conference. NASA Johnson Space Center, Houston, TX.

Schiphorst, T. (1992). The choreography machine: a design tool for character and human movement. *In* Linda Jacobson, ed. (1992). *CyberArts: exploring art and technology,* 147–56. San Francisco, CA: Miller Freeman.

Schlager, M. & Boman, D. (1994, May 13). *VR in education and training.* Paper presented at the Meckler Virtual Reality '94 Conference. San Jose, CA.

Schrage, Michael (1991). *Shared minds: the new technologies of Collaboration.* New York: Random House.

Scully, J. (1994, Dec. 2). *Tracking technologies and virtual characters.* Paper presented at Virtual Reality Expo '94. New York.

Shaw, J. (1994). EVE: Extended virtual environment. *Virtual Reality World 2*(3), 59–62.

Shaw, J. & May, G. (1994). EVE: Extended virtual environment. *In* S. Helsel, ed. *London Virtual Reality Expo '94: Proceedings of the 4th annual conference on Virtual Reality,* 102–09. London: Mecklermedia.

Sheridan, T.B. & Zeltzer, D. (1993, Oct.). Virtual reality check. *Technology Review 96*(7), 20–28.

Siegal, A.W. (1981). The externalization of cognitive maps by childern and adults: in search of ways to ask better questions. *In* L. Liben, A. Patterson & N. Newcombe, eds. *Spatial representation and behavior across the life span,* 163–89. New York: Academic.

Sklaroff, S. (1994, Jun. 1). Virtual reality puts disabled students in touch. *Education Week 13*(36), 8.

Smith, D. (1993, May 19). *Through the window.* Paper presented at the Virtual Reality '93 Conference. San Jose, CA.

Spritzer, V. (1994, Nov. 30). *Medical modeling: the visible human project.* Paper presented at the Virtual Reality Expo '94. New York .

Stampe, D., Roehl, B. & Eagan, J. (1993). *Virtual reality creations.* Corta Madiera, CA: Waite.

Stenger, N. (1991, Sep. 23). *"Angels," or "Les Recontres Angeliques."* Paper presented at the Virtual Reality '91 Conference. San Francisco, CA.

Sterling, B. (1994). *Heavy weather.* New York: Bantam.

— (1993). War is virtual hell. *Wired 1*(1), 46–51+.

Stephenson, N. (1992). *Snow crash.* New York: Bantam.

Stix, G. (1992, Sep.). See-through view: virtual reality may guide physicians hands. *Scientific American,* 166.

Stoker, C. (1994, Jul.). Telepresence, remote vision and VR at NASA: from Antarctica to Mars. *Advanced Imaging 9* (7), 24–26.

Stytz, M. (1993, May 20). The view from the synthetic Battlebridge. *Virtual Reality* '93 Conference, San Jose, CA.

— (1994). An overview of U.S. military development in *VR.* New York Virtual Reality Expo '94 Conference. New York.

Sutherland, I.E. (1965). The ultimate display. *Proceedings of the IFIPS 2,* 506–08.

— (1968). A head-mounted three dimensional display. *Proceedings of the Fall Joint Computer Conference 33,* 757–64.

Taubes, G. (1994a, Jun.). Virtual Jack. *Discover 15*(6), 66–74.

— (1994b, Dec.). Surgery in cyberspace. *Discover 15* (12), 84–94.

Teixeira, K. (1994a, May/Jun.). Behind the scenes at the Guggenheim. *Virtual Reality World 2*(3), 66–70.

— (1994b, May 13). *Intel's IDEA Project and the VR art exhibit at the Guggenheim.* Paper presented at the Virtual Reality '94 Conference. San Jose, CA.

Thompson, J., ed. (1993). *Virtual reality: an international directory of research projects.* Westport, CT: Meckler.

Thurman, R.A. (1992, Jun. 1). *Simulation and training based technology.* Paper presented at the EFDPMA (Educational Foundation of the Data Processing Management Association) Conference on Virtual Reality.

— & Mattoon, J.S. (1994, Oct.). Virtual reality: toward fundamental improvements in simulation-based training. *Educational Technology 34*(8), 56–64.

Tice, S. & Jacobson, L. (1992). VR in visualization, animation, and entertainment. *In* Jacobson, L., ed. *CyberArts: exploring art and technology.* San Francisco, CA: Miller Freeman.

Treviranus, J. (1993, Jun. 17). *Artists who develop virtual reality technologies and persons with disabilities.* Paper presented at the 1993 Conference on Virtual Reality and Persons with Disabilities. San Francisco, CA.

Trimble, J. (1993, May 20). *Virtual barrier-free design ("Wheelchair VR").* Paper presented at the 1993 Conference on Virtual Reality and Persons with Disabilities. San Francisco, CA.

Trubitt, D. (1990, Jul.). Into new worlds: virtual reality and the electronic musician. *Electronic Musician 6*(7), 30–40.

Ulman, N. (1993, Mar. 17). High-tech connection between schools and science expeditions enlivens classes. *Wall Street Journal,* B1, B10.

Van Nedervelde, P. (1994, Dec. 1). *Cyberspace for the rest of us.* Paper presented at the Virtual Reality Expo '94. New York.

Varner, D. (1993). *Contribution of audition and olfaction to immersion in a virtual environment.* Paper presented at the 1993 Conference on Intelligent Computer-Aided Training and Virtual Environment Technology.

VR Monitor (1993, Jan./Feb.). VR si training system by NEC. *VR Monitor 2* (1), 9.

Wagner, E. (1994, Dec. 1). *Virtual reality at "the cutting edge."* Paper presented at the Virtual Reality Expo '94. New York.

Waldern, J.D. (1991). Virtuality: the world's first production virtual reality workstation. *In* Tony Feldman, ed. *Virtual Reality '91: impacts and applications. Proceedings of the 1st Annual Conference on Virtual Reality 91,* 26–30. London: Meckler.

— (1992, Jun. 1). *Virtual reality: the serious side.* Paper presented at the EFDPMA (Educational Foundation of the Data Processing Management Association) Conference on Virtual Reality.

— (1994). Software design of virtual teammates and virtual opponents. *In* S. Helsel, ed. *London Virtual Reality Expo '94: Proceedings of the 4th annual Conference on Virtual Reality,* 120–25. London: Mecklermedia.

Walser, R. (1991). *Cyberspace trix: toward an infrastructure for a new industry.* Internal paper. Advanced Technology Department. Autodesk, Inc.

— (1992, Jun. 1). *Construction in cyberspace.* Paper presented at the EFDPMA (Education Foundation of the Data Processing Management Association) Conference on Virtual Reality. Washington, DC.

Wann, J., Rushton, S., Mon-Williams, M., Hawkes, R. & Smyth, M. (1993, Sep./Oct.). *What's wrong with our head mounted display?,* 1–2. CyberEdge Journal Monograph. Sausalito, CA: CyberEdge.

Warner, D. (1993, May 20). *More than garage nerds and isolated physicians who make VR medical technology.* Paper presented at the Meckler Virtual Reality '93 Conference. San Jose, CA.

— & Jacobson, L. (1992, Jul.). Medical rehabilitation, cyberstyle. *Virtual Reality Special Report/AI Expert,* 19–22. San Francisco, CA: Miller Freeman.

Weghorst, S. (1994, Nov. 30). *A VR project: Parkinson disease.* Paper presented at the Virtual Reality Expo '94. New York.

Wexelblat, A. (1993). The reality of cooperation: virtual reality and CSCW. *In* Alan Wexelblat, ed. *Virtual reality: applications and explorations,* 23–44. Boston, MA: Academic.

Wheeler, D.L. (1991, Mar. 31). Computer-created world of 'virtual reality' opening new vistas to scientists. *The Chronicle of Higher Education 37*(26), A6+.

Wickens, C.D. (1993, Apr.). *Virtual reality and education.* Technical Report ARL-93-2/NSF-93-1 prepared for the National Science Foundation. Aviation Research Laboratory Institute of Aviation. University of Illinois at Urbana-Champaign, Savoy, IL.

— & Baker, P. (1994, Feb.). *Cognitive issues in virtual reality.* Human Perception and Performance Technical Report UIUC-BI-HPP-94-02. The Beckman Institute, University of Illinois at Urbana-Champaign, Urbana, IL. *In* W. Barfield & T. Furness, eds. (1995). *Virtual reality.* Oxford, England: Oxford University Press.

Wilson, D.L. (1994, Nov. 16). A key for entering virtual worlds. *Chronicle of Higher Education,* A19.

Winn, W. (1993, Dec. 1). *A discussion of the Human Interface Laboratory (HIT) and its educational projects.* Paper presented at the Virtual Reality Expo '93. New York.

— & Bricken, W. (1992a, Apr.). *Designing virtual worlds for use in mathematics education.* Paper presented at the Annual Meeting of the American Educational Research Association. San Francisco, CA.

— & — (1992b, Dec.). Designing virtual worlds for use in mathematics education: the example of experiential algebra. *Educational Technology 32*(12), 12–19.

Wisne, J. (1994, Dec. 1). *VR at the Ohio's Center of Science & Industry.* Paper presented at the Virtual Reality Expo '94. New York.

Woolley, B. (1992). *Virtual worlds: a journey in hype and hyperreality.* Oxford, England: Blackwell.

Wyshynski & Vincent, V.J. (1993). Full-body unencumbered immersion in virtual worlds. In Alan Wexelblat, ed. *Virtual reality: applications and explorations,* 123–46. Boston, MA: Academic .

Zeltner, D. (1992, Jun. 1). *Virtual environment technology.* Paper presented at the EFDPMA (Education Foundation of the Data Processing Management Association) Conference on Virtual Reality. Washington, DC.

III

SOFT TECHNOLOGIES: INSTRUCTIONAL AND INFORMATIONAL DESIGN RESEARCH

Robert D. Tennyson, University of Minnesota

Associate Editor

16. VISUAL LITERACY

Roberts A. Braden
CALIFORNIA STATE UNIVERSITY AT CHICO

There are two major impediments to research on visual literacy. The first is a lack of a widely accepted definition of the term *visual literacy* itself. The second, perhaps a consequence of the first, is a lack of a cohesive theory. We must confront the ever-present problem of identifying visual literacy itself before we can identify the body of visual literacy research. The visual literacy concept as an area of study has been plagued by an identity crisis from the outset. Skeptics doubt that visual literacy really exists.

16.1 DEFINITION

For one group of advocates, a literal definition of the term has led to investigation of visual languages with a one-for-one analogy with the reading and writing aspects of verbal literacy. For others, more inclusive definitions have led to the study of visualization in all of its aspects of communication and education. The definitional controversy has been so much a part of visual literacy that Cassidy and Knowlton wrote a major paper in 1983 entitled "Visual Literacy, a Failed Metaphor?" and in 1994 Moore and Dwyer included in their book a chapter titled "Visual Literacy: The Definition Problem" (Seels, 1994). Cassidy and Knowlton (1983) may have had trouble with the term because Knowlton (1966) had set for himself an *exclusive* definition. Seels and most others at this time favor a more *inclusive* attitude toward what constitutes the area of visual literacy.

As evidence that there is no common definition, we merely need to look at the titles of six recent books: *Visual Literacy: Image, Mind, & Reality* (Messaris, 1994); *Visual Literacy: A Conceptual Approach to Solving Graphic Problems* (Wilde & Wilde, 1991); *Introduction to Visual Literacy* (Curtiss, 1987); *Visual Literacy Connections to Thinking, Reading and Writing* (Sinatra, 1986); *Visual Literacy: A Spectrum of Visual Learning* (Moore & Dwyer, 1994); and *Art, Science & Visual Literacy* (Braden, Baca & Beauchamp, 1993).

Each of these books contains the term *visual literacy* in the title, but, how different are their basic assumptions. The

Messaris (1994) approached the subject—and thus defines and delimits it—from the communications field and particularly from the perspectives of film, television, and advertising. Wilde and Wilde (1991) have written a basic textbook for graphic artists that contains 15 graphic design exercises and 4 illustration exercises, with each exercise followed by examples of how the authors' students have solved those problems. Like the work of Curtiss, the Wildes work relates visual literacy more to art than to communication, and except in the graphic-design world, nobody would accept their assumed limited definition of *visual literacy*. Curtiss (1987) took a wide-ranging look, but primarily from the viewpoint of the fine artist. Sinatra's (1986) title includes the term, but his book is more about the acquisition of verbal literacy (reading). Moore and Dwyer (1994) have compiled an eclectic, comprehensive text, covering 22 aspects of visual literacy. Their particular delimiter (definitional bias) is *learning*: the ways that visuals and visualization affect the learning process. Finally, the Braden, Baca, and Beauchamp (1993) volume is just one of more than a dozen annual books of readings published by the International Visual Literacy Association. Similar to proceedings, these edited compilations include articles that have only one unifying thread: they all have something to do with seeing.

This chapter will attempt to deal with so-called *visual literacy research* that includes widely diverging topics of interest. With such an expanded conception of visual literacy, to describe all of the relevant research and to present all of the findings would take an entire volume, not a chapter. Thus, the thrust of this chapter will be to identify and categorize a large portion of the related literature and to elaborate on only selected studies.

16.2 THEORETICAL FOUNDATIONS OF VISUAL LITERACY

The concept of visual literacy was crystallized by John Debes (1968, 1969, 1970), but as Jonassen and Fork noted, "Visual literacy is eclectic in origin" (1975, p. 7). Debes

(1970) may or may not have coined the term *visual literacy*, but indeed he did provide its longest (and perhaps longest lasting) definition:

> Visual literacy refers to a group of vision competencies a human being can develop by seeing at the same time he has and integrates other sensory experiences. The development of these competencies is fundamental to normal human learning. When developed, they enable a visually literate person to discriminate and interpret the visible actions, objects, and/or symbols, natural or man made, that he encounters in his environment. Through the creative use of these competencies, he is able to communicate with others. Through the appreciative use of these competencies, he is able to comprehend and enjoy the masterworks of visual communication (p. 14).

In that early visual literacy work, "The Loom of Visual Literacy," Debes flirted with the idea of a visual language, and referred to the even earlier work of Chomsky (1957) on syntactic structures and the work of Paul Wendt (1962) who had written about the language of pictures. Colin Turbayne, an early visual literacy theorist (1962, 1969, 1970a, 1970b), explored the syntax of visual language (1970b) and concluded that, "Unhappily the code of visual language is chaotic" (p. 24). He was concerned that "Words are often ambiguous" (1970a, p. 115) and that for an object or image to have language utility, it must ". . . always suggest things in the same uniform way . . ." (p. 115). Turbayne, more than any other, laid the groundwork for an analogy of a visual language to verbal language. He wrote, "Just as a large part of learning to understand words consists in learning how to respond to them, so is it the case in learning how to see" (1970, p. 125). The notion that human beings can be taught (thus learn) "how to see" has been central to visual literacists ever since.

16.2.1 Dual Coding

In 1971, Paivio published his book, *Imagery and Verbal Processes*. In that work he introduced in print what has come to be known as the Dual Coding Theory (DCT) of memory and cognition (see 26.3, 29.2.3). Later, Paivio (1991) said that DCT evolved from his specific experiments on the role of imagery in associative learning (e.g., Paivio, 1963, 1965). Paivio isn't easy reading, and he is prone to take many pages to explain his theory, but nowhere does he state it simply. The closest that he comes is within a summary table (Paivio, 1991) where parsimony is essential:

> Cognition is served by two modality-specific systems that are experientially derived and differentially specialized for representing and processing information concerning nonverbal objects, events, and language (p. 258).

Not all theorists agree with the basic tenets of dual-coding theory. Miller and Burton (1994) characterize those who argue that imaging is encoded as neutral abstract propositions (as opposed to spatial and modality-specific encoding) as the "anti-image group" (e.g., Pylyshyn, 1981). Although there has been no direct conflict between cue summation theory (see 29.4) and dual coding theory, neither has there been any concerted attempt to reconcile the two theories into a more encompassing theorization.

Although dual-coding research is primarily within the province of the field of psychology, the implications for visual literacy are obvious. If, in fact, we do encode both visually and verbally, and if, in fact, the conceptual-peg hypothesis is true [an oversimplification of the hypothesis that verbal concepts are hung on nonverbal pegs in memory, that imagery is the effective variable in recall of concrete verbal information], then the visualization, visual thinking, and visual-verbal connections aspects of visual literacy are theoretically supported.

16.2.2 Theoretical Foundations

Hortin has done the most intensive study of the theoretical foundations of visual literacy. His dissertation (Hortin, 1980a) was subtitled *An Investigation of the Research, Practices, and Theories* [of visual literacy]. In that document and subsequent writings (Hortin 1980b, 1994; Braden & Hortin, 1982), he has agreed with Jonassen and Fork (1975), emphasizing the eclectic nature of the origins of the field of visual literacy and of the range of interests that find a common bond under that rubric. Like the pseudopod metaphor advanced by Debes (1970) as a description of the parameters of visual literacy, Hortin has portrayed visual literacy as a confluence of thought—incorporating linguistics, art, psychology, philosophy, and more.

Incidentally, the first researcher to characterize visual literacy as "a confluence of theories" was Johnson (1977). In his doctoral dissertation he wrote:

> I was disappointed to discover that visual literacy is really nothing more than a "confluence of theories," brought together to form a vague, unorganized concept that tries to explain the notion of "visual sequencing" (p. 141).

Visual sequencing is only one narrow aspect of visual literacy as it is viewed today. The point of view of the researcher is critical, of course. Hortin was fascinated by the metaphor of parallel languages, and concentrated much of his focus on the contributions of linguist Noam Chomsky (1957, 1964, 1968, 1975). However, Hortin's primary research interest was with "visual thinking," and therefore his interpretation of what constituted a confluence of theories was much broader than that of Johnson whose field was the English language.

While Johnson (1977) was delving into the nature of visual literacy as an approach to English instruction, Hocking (1978) was exploring the wider issue of the parameters of visual literacy. His study at the University of Colorado sought to determine visual literacy goals. The paper by Braden and Hortin (1982) also explored the boundaries of the field. Braden and Hortin also offered a shorter definition than that of Debes's. They refined Hortin's own earlier definition (Hortin, 1980a) and came up with this definition:

Visual literacy is the ability to understand and use images, including the ability to think, learn, and express oneself in terms of images (p. 169).

Seels (1994), in her chapter on the "visual literacy definition problem," uses the Braden-Hortin definition in her glossary, giving current support to defining the field in broader terms. Many other attempts have been made to examine the nature of visual literacy and to define the concept. Notable among them are the work of Case-Gant (1973), Lamberski (1976), Fork and Newhouse (1978), Sucy (1985), Sinatra (1988), Whiteside and Whiteside (1988), and the participants at the Twenty-second Annual Lake Okoboji Educational Media Leadership Conference (Cureton & Cochran, 1976).

Baca (1990) did the most recent and most comprehensive study to date, a delphi study in which visual literacy professionals collectively helped identify what is and what is not a part of visual literacy. After years of quibbling about the nature of visual literacy, Baca found that "There is a great deal of agreement regarding the basic tenets of visual literacy among the scholars who study it" (p. 74). Baca listed 186 accepted constructs of visual literacy. Those regarding definition included: "Visual literacy refers to the use of visuals for the purposes of communication, thinking, learning, constructing meaning, creative expression, [and] aesthetic enjoyment" (p. 65). Earlier, Baca and Braden (1990) had pointed out regarding the Braden-Hortin definition that "even that definition fails to directly address design, creativity, and aesthetics as they apply to visualization." The delphi study acknowledged the additions.

The primary contribution of the Baca study was that it affirmed the broad scope of interests that are subsumed under the visual literacy umbrella. The study also provided an organizational scheme for categorizing the constructs of the field, but it did not identify all of the legs of Debes's pseudopod. That is one objective of this chapter: to organize the research of the field into the subfields of visual literacy. Such a framework will help to clarify the focus of future visual literacy research and will aid future fledgling researchers to select an area for study.

A host of theories and diverging areas of specialization emerged in the dozen years immediately after the visual literacy movement was set in motion. Braden and Hortin (1982, p. 164) compiled a short list:

Some of the theories have dealt with: visual languaging (e.g., Ausburn & Ausburn, 1978; Debes, 1972, 1974: Turbayne, 1970b); visual thinking (e.g., Arnheim, 1969; Haber, 1970; Wileman, 1980); visual learning (e.g., Dwyer, 1978; Jonassen & Fork, 1978; Randhawa, Back & Meyers, 1977); hemispheric lateralization of the brain (e.g., Bogen, 1979; Ragan, 1977; Sperry, 1973); mental imagery (e.g., Fleming, 1977; Kosslyn & Pomerantz, 1977; Pylyshyn, 1973); levels of abstraction (e.g., Clark & Clark, 1976; Clark, 1978); cul-

tural interaction (Cochran, Younghouse, Sorflaten & Molek, 1980); and the interactive theories dealing with symbol systems and dual coding (e.g., Levie, 1978; Levie & Levie, 1975; Paivio, 1971, 1975, 1983; Salomon, 1972, 1979a).

The list was not meant to be all inclusive then, and certainly is incomplete another dozen years later. Clearly, there are many theories relevant to the area loosely called *visual literacy*. No one theory comes even close to encompassing all (or even one) of the others.

16.3 ESTABLISHING A VISUAL LITERACY RESEARCH AGENDA

In the past, others have attempted in sundry ways to facilitate the research of the visual literacy area. The first authors to undertake the task of building a framework for visual literacy research were Spitzer and McNerny (1975). Their emphasis was on operationally defining visual literacy so that others could proceed with research to support the operational definitions. An extensive study was made by Hocking to determine visual literacy goals, which in turn could become the basis for research (Hocking, 1978). At about the same time, Levie (1978a) offered the field a prospectus for instructional research on visual literacy. The link of instruction to visual literacy was important, and *the bulk of all visual literacy research has been done with learning and instruction in mind.*

Lida Cochran and her associates took a more pragmatic approach. The Cochran team held seminars and meetings with aspiring visual literacists and examined the possible avenues of visual literacy research. A direction for the field was recommended, and possibilities were outlined for a broader audience in their *Educational Communication and Technology Journal* article (Cochran et al., 1980). For those with a greater interest in the linguistic aspects of visual literacy, Hennis (1981) pointed out the need for research in the area of visual language. More recently, other authors have provided their conceptions of an agenda for visual literacy research. For example, Hartley (1987) addressed the role of print-based research in an era when we must accommodate to changes brought about by the emergence of electronic text.

Gnizak and Girshman (1984) turned the entire process on its head. Rather than concern themselves with doing research about visual literacy, they undertook an experiment in visualizing during the research process. They encouraged students to "define a pressing social problem in visual terms and thereby develop student abilities to analyze, to criticize, and finally to synthesize" (p. 207).

16.3.1 Levie's "Islands"

Levie (1987) lamented the fact that research on pictures was done in small topical islands, barely connected. He said that "an additional approach that brings together data and ideas from separate contexts could contribute much to our understanding of this pervasive, versatile mode of communication" (p. 27). *A list of Levie's "islands" is an outline of much of the research in visual literacy.* His selected bibliography to accompany that list is broken into categories and is exceptional, including sections for:

- Picture perception (6 bibliography entries)
- Theoretical approaches to picture perception (21 entries)
- Attention and scanning (40 entries)
- Interpreting figures and pictorial cues (40 entries)
- Perceiving global meaning (25 entries)
- Memory for pictures (6 entries)
- Memory models (25 entries)
- Recognition memory (44 entries)
- Recall (20 entries)
- Other types of memory research (27 entries)
- Learning and cognition (7 entries)
- The acquisition of knowledge (48 entries)
- Problem solving and visual thinking (26 entries)
- Acquisition of cognitive skills (32 entries)
- Media research (39 entries)
- Affective responses to pictures (95 entries; broken down further as follows: arousal and emotional impact, 17 entries; preferences, 22 entries; attitudes, 25 entries; and aesthetic responses, 31 entries)

Obviously, many of the topics above are included in the research agendas of other fields. What is remarkable is that so much research in sundry fields has been found to have visual literacy implications.

16.4 VISUAL VOCABULARY

Although Levie's summary of the research on pictures covers much of the research relevant to visual literacy, Baca's study reminds us that the use of "visuals" touches other areas, including thinking and learning, and constructing meaning. To construct meaning from visuals implies that in some way the constructed meaning can be "read" by persons who view it. The notion that images can be "read" implies the existence of at least a rudimentary visual language made up of vocabulary components.

16.4.1 Reading Pictures

Some authors have addressed the encoding of pictorial information directly. Stewig (1989) even titled his article "Reading Pictures." In Stewig's study, 28 fifth-grade students listened to the reading of three different versions of *The Three Little Pigs,* each version with a different set of illustrations. A rather complex 3-day procedure was adopted which involved letting students ask questions, having students make comparisons, and encouraging other interactions with the pictures and the stories. On the fourth day, students wrote what they liked best and why. Only 15 comments of 83 related to the story: content, plot, and book design. The other 68 comments referred to the pictures: color, style,

detail, brightness, medium, and size. One student wrote: "The pictures told the whole story themselves because they were so clear" (p. 79).

Other research has been done to examine how children interpret pictures (interpretation in this sense is a measure of how the students read the picture). Leslie Higgins has done three notable studies in this area (1978, 1979, 1980). The studies were based on her own model which posits that ". . . picture interpretation consists of two related and interdependent forms of behavior: observation and inference drawing" (Higgins, 1978, p. 216). She goes on to explain that "Inferring in the picture interpretation context carries understanding beyond an awareness of what is seen. . ." (p. 216). In her first experiment with 95 fifth- and sixth-graders, Higgins (1978) found that picture interpretation ability correlated highly with only one factor: *operational facility,* a characteristic that reflects Piaget's operational stages. In her second study, she set out to determine whether children can be taught to draw inferences from pictures (Higgins, 1979). Students who were given "thinking guides" prior to the picture interpretation tests did significantly better at making inferences. However, the guides did not help the students to better evaluate their inferences. In four experiments to assess literalism in the interpretation of pictures by children, Higgins (1980) found that many children in the 4- to 7-year-old range gather information that the pictures were not intended to convey. For example, in a picture in which only half a dog is shown (the other half being out of the frame), the child may conclude that the character (dog) has no head and only two legs. This phenomenon was found to be a maturational attribute that does not occur in older children. No evidence was given to indicate whether children grow out of this mistake-prone behavior simply by aging or whether learning is the change factor.

Ramsey (1989a, 1989b) suggests that "Artistic style may also be a powerful pictorial variable which primary-age children utilize as a yardstick in predicting the reality or fantasy of accompanying text content." She reports two of her own studies, done in 1982 and 1989, that demonstrate the wide range of interpretation skills already possessed by children that age.

Pettersson (1984, 1993) has approached the matter of reading pictures from the standpoint of picture readability. He first created a picture readability index called BLIX (a Swedish acronym) based on 19 picture variables that were ultimately collapsed into five rating (indexing) factors. Then he validated the index experimentally:

Experiments with ranking and rating of test-pictures showed that pictures with high BLIX-values were ranked and rated better than those with lower values by children as well as adults. Experiments with the actual making of pictures showed that despite detailed instructions on the execution of the visuals, there was still plenty of scope for individual creativity. It was also shown that informative pictures drawn so that their BLIX-ratings were high (more than 4.5 on a scale of 5.0) were to a large extent rated as aesthetically pleasing, rated as "suitable" or "very suitable" for teaching, and did not take more time to make than pictures with lower BLIX-ratings (1993, p. 158).

16.4.2 Visual Representation

The study of *visual representation* has generally fallen into five distinct areas of inquiry: (1) semiotics and film/video conventions; (2) signs, symbols, and icons; (3) images and illustration (including the survey by Levie discussed above); (4) multi-image; and (5) graphic representation. Each of those areas has its own growing research literature.

16.4.2.1. Semiotics and Film/Video Conventions. The literature of film is voluminous. Arnheim (1957) theorized about the nature of images in film and about film structure. He made popular the idea of film as art. Metz (1974), on the other hand, was concerned with the linguisitic attributes of film and the sign language (semiotics) used by filmmakers. He identified and categorized the visual building blocks of film imagery into a notational scheme that has since become the basis for reader theories. In that sense, semiotics has become the basis for analysis of "the language of film."

The educational media field was introduced to the concept of analyzing film by Pryluck and Snow (1975). Theirs was the linguistic approach. Corcoran (1981) was one of the first to deal with semiotics and film/video conventions in a way that is related to visual literacy. He pointed out that there are problems in the use of linguistic models or reader theories as they apply to reading the images of screen media. Others who have focused on the relationship of semiotics to visual literacy are Muffoletto (1982), Metallinos (1982, 1995a), and Gavriel Salomon (1979b, 1982, 1983, 1984). In his earlier work, Salomon (1979b) indicated that different symbol systems are employed by different media. Jack Solomon (1988) extended Salomon's logic by interpreting hidden signs within the environment at large.

The vast majority of the scholarly work in semiotics is theoretical and analytical-interpretive rather than experimental. Thus, Salomon (1979b) speaks of the differences between notational symbol systems and nonnotational ones, but research on labeled and nonlabeled illustrations is done by people outside the semiotics area, like Mayer (1989).

Monoco (1981) popularized the idea of interpreting film symbols as "reading" film. The latter research by Salomon (1983, 1984) has focused on demonstrating experimentally that it is much easier in terms of mental effort for an individual to view television than it is to read text. He characterized television as easy, and print as tough. This conclusion was consistent with his earlier lament (Salomon, 1979b), based on his interpretation of Samuels' (1970) study of children reading illustrated text: "Specifically, the employment of charts, graphs, or pictures could save mental effort and make the acquisition of knowledge more effective, but it will impede [reading] skill development" (p. 83). The implication that the availability of visuals and film may make learners lazy is obvious.

The primary scholarly interest in film semiotics has been directed toward film criticism. While many approaches to

film criticism have evolved, each with its advocates, it was not until 1994 that *a visual literacy approach to film criticism* was introduced (Metallinos, 1995). Whether the underlying theory of that approach will lead to supportive research is not yet clear.

Hefzalla (1987) has taken the position that the principle of visual primacy in film has led to the use of the visual element of film as a tool for communicating more than is actually shown. Thus film has an implying power [his term] more powerful than simple, literal linguistics. Related research has disproportionately focused on cinematic production variables: lighting, focus, shot selection, camera angle, image placement, camera movement, and such (e.g., McCain, Chilberg & Wakshlag, 1977; Metallinos & Tiemens, 1977; Kaha, 1993; Kipper, 1986). While many of these results are of interest to the visual literacy and instructional technology fields, the research is the primary province of those doing encoding research in the fields of mass communication and film studies.

Goodman (1968, 1977, 1978) contributed basic theory about symbol systems that had an influence on semiotics (Salomon, 1979a) and also added a cognitive (as contrasted to an aesthetic) dimension to the interpretation of art. In his "theory of symbols," he created a taxonomy of the major symbol systems used by human beings, including gestural and visual graphics systems. The theoretical literature on semiotics and symbol systems is rich. The research to validate the theories is, as yet, not so rich.

16.4.2.2. Signs, Symbols, and Icons. Scholarship concerning signs, symbols, and icons is interwoven with that of semiotics, but it also stands apart. The concepts are easily confused, and frequently the terms are used and misused interchangeably. Thus, to define *symbol*, Salomon (1979b) indicated that "most objects, marks, events, models, or pictures that serve as bearers of extractable knowledge are symbols" and that "Symbols serve as characters or coding elements . . ." (p. 29). By Salomon's definition, symbols subsume both signs and icons, which are at opposite ends of a continuum of abstractness and resemblance.

Historically there has been much disagreement over the nature, meaning, and definition of symbols (Sewell, 1994). Semiotic theorists have considered *sign* to be the more inclusive term, subsuming symbols, signals, indexes, and icons. Sewell (1994) helped bring focus to the *functional* nature of symbols this way:

> Symbols are classified into a three-tiered hierarchy along a concrete to abstract continuum as *pictorial symbols* that include 3-D models, photographs, and illustration drawings, *graphic symbols* that include image-related graphics, concept-related graphics, and arbitrary graphics, and *verbal symbols* that are the most abstract, since they have no graphic resemblance with the object to which they refer (p. 137).

Eisner (1970), too, was concerned with the element of resemblance of symbols to their referents. However, his taxonomy classified symbols into four classes that reflect more than the simple polarity of the continuum. His classes of symbols are: conventional symbols (abstract signs/symbols with finite referents), representational symbols (iconic symbols that faithfully depict their referents), connotative symbols (those that distort the image of the referent), and qualitative symbols (those that are neither signs nor icons per se, but rather are images that establish an atmosphere or evoke feelings). Theorists have quibbled over how and why symbols represent referents and over such points as the functional imperatives of symbols as either descriptive or depictive (Goodman, 1968; Salomon, 1979b). However, these issues have not been an object of research, and the categorization schemes serve research only as obvious variables to be used in all manner of visual representation studies.

Salomon has linked his interest in codes and symbols system with his concern for cognition and learning (1979a). In generalizing the results of four coding experiments, he reported "that at least three kinds of covert skills—singling out details, visualization, and changing points of view—can be affected by filmic coding elements" (Salomon, 1979b, p. 155).

Almost anything can be a *sign,* depending on how one defines the term. However, the common lay uses of the term have driven the research. Dewar and Ellis (1977) studied the perception of, and understanding of, traffic signs. Makett-Stout and Dewar (1981) evaluated the effectiveness of public information signs. They concluded that such signs communicate as individual symbols, but that they do not constitute a visual language. They also found that the proliferation of safety signs and symbols has resulted in the creation of several signs with identical meanings.

In a related analysis, Yeaman (1987) investigated the functions and content of signs in libraries. His taxonomy was austere, establishing only three basic categories of library signage: directional, locational, and informational. While his analysis included legibility concerns, font selection, and location considerations, it did not consider the use of symbolic, nonverbal signs.

Three recent studies have investigated how well people are able to read and interpret graphic signs, symbols, and icons (Griffin & Gibbs, 1993; Griffin, 1994; Griffin, Pettersson, Semali & Takakuwa, 1995). In the first of these studies (Griffin & Gibbs, 1993), subjects from the United States and Jamaica were asked to identify 48 widely used symbols. Subjects from both countries found some symbols to be confusing. Some symbols, though widely used, were found to be not widely understood. And there were significant differences in the recognition patterns between subjects of the two cultures. The study verified that signs are culture related. In a study that drew symbols from street signs, computer notation, and clip art, Griffin (1994) found that symbols used in business presentations were often misinterpreted or not understood. He found that image perception and understanding is relevant to context (verbal context can make visual symbols easier to interpret correctly). He also found that subjects make rapid judgments about the meaning of symbols because:

> They often do not look at the visual in great detail. Rather, they take a superficial look at the symbol and then make a determination of the meaning. Visual experts should not

rely on symbols to convey in-depth meaning or ideas which are critical to an outcome. *Symbols do not convey accurate meanings*" (p. 44, emphasis added).

The third study (Griffin, Pettersson, Semali & Takakuwa, 1995) was performed on subjects in four different countries, each country with its own distinct culture. The methods and results paralleled those of the 1993 Griffin and Gibbs study. The evidence of American culture was evident in the responses in other countries, particularly in Japan regarding computer-related symbols, but the overwhelming evidence was in favor of cultural differences being the predominant variable when symbol understanding was measured. An international symbol system based on intuitive interpretation of symbol meanings may not be possible until the world shares a common culture.

16.4.2.3. Images and Illustration. In the area of images and illustration, including pictorial research, we find important contributions by Alesandrini (1981, 1984), Duchastel (1978, 1980), Duchastel and Waller (1979), Knowlton (1966), Levie (1978, 1987), Levie and Lentz (1982), Pettersson (1989, 1993), and the text *The Psychology of Illustration, Volume 1, Basic Research,* by Willows and Houghton (1987).

First Knowlton (1966), then Alesandrini (1984), offered classification schemes for illustrations. Their categories are conceptually quite similar. Knowlton proposed three categories: realistic, analogical, and logical. Alesandrini also offered three categories: representational, analogical, and arbitrary. These categories have been useful tools for the field. Realistic or representational illustrations share a physical resemblance to the referent object or concept. Analogical illustrations show something other than the referent object and imply a similarity. Logical or arbitrary illustrations bear no resemblance to the referent object or concept but rather offer some organizational or layout feature that highlights a conceptual or logical relationship of the illustration's components to each other.

While *the results of research relevant to images and illustration are spread throughout this chapter,* special notice should be made of two chapters in the Willows and Houghton book that deal with the use of illustrations in children's learning. In one chapter, Pressley and Miller (1987) have reviewed the research on "Effects of Illustrations on Children's Listening Comprehension and Oral Prose Memory." In the other, Peek (1987) has brought together the research on "The Role of Illustrations in Processing and Remembering Illustrated Text." The information being too voluminous to be included here in toto, these chapters can only be touched on briefly, with closer examination commended to readers.

Pressley and Miller (1987) have explicitly written their review of the effects of illustration on children's memory as a reflection of Paivio's dual-coding theory. That theoretical bias reflects Pressley's (1977) own conclusion that enough research evidence had been gathered regarding illustrated text, so that "No more experiments are required to substantiate the positive effect of pictures on children's learning" (p. 613). In a summary and analysis of the issues related to research on illustrations in text, Duchastel (1980) agreed with that general conclusion.

Most of the research on illustrations has involved text-illustration relationships and comparisons or other linkages of visual to verbal material. Pressley and Miller (1987) point out that verbal cues have a greater effect on memory than visual cues, but:

> There can be little doubt from the available data, however, that if the picture and verbal cues [both] can be activated, they promote children's learning of stories relevant to verbal codes alone (p. 89).

Peek (1987) has reviewed the research on illustrated text regarding the role of illustrations in mental processing and remembering. She cites numerous authors who have made claims about the beneficial affective-motivational roles and functions of illustrations in texts. Pictures have been said to arouse interest, set mood, arouse curiosity, make reading more enjoyable, and to create positive attitudes toward subject content and toward reading itself. While acknowledging that a few studies support such claims, Peek's overall judgment is that:

> Although the proposed roles sound quite plausible, educational research has not come up with much evidence in support of these claims—perhaps because researchers consider the interest and enjoyment effects too obvious for serious investigation (p. 117).

Regarding cognitive effects of illustrations in text, Peek has concentrated on studies of retention effects. Her general conclusions are that "retention of depicted text information is facilitated, whereas unillustrated text is not," and "with growing delay, subjects tend to base their retention-test responses on what they have seen in the pictorial supplements" (p. 128). In other words, when pictures and text are used together, retention is facilitated, and pictures help delayed recall more than immediate recall.

Levie and Lentz (1982) have provided an outstanding review of the research on effects of illustrated text on learning. They summarized the results of 155 experimental comparisons of learning from illustrated versus nonillustrated text. Forty-six of those studies compared learning from illustrated text material versus from text alone:

> In all but 1 of these 46 cases, the group mean for those reading illustrated text was superior to that of the group reading text alone. . . . In 39 of the 46 comparisons, the difference was statistically significant . . . and the average group score for the illustrated-text groups was 36% better than for text-alone groups (p. 198).

The Levie and Lentz review also analyzed as a group those studies that dealt with learning a combination of illustrated and nonillustrated text information from illustrated text versus text alone. The studies included the earlier works prior to 1970 that had led many to conclude that pictures do not facilitate comprehension of text (see Samuels, 1970). However, when all of the studies were considered together, Levie and Lentz concluded:

> In summary, the diverse group of studies . . . indicates that when the test of learning is something other than a test of only illustrated text information or only nonillustrated text information, the addition of pictures should not be expected to hinder learning; nor should pictures always be expected to facilitate learning. Even so, learning is better with pictures in most cases (p. 206).

A third aspect of the Levie and Lentz review is its coverage of "some closely related research areas" (p. 214). Accordingly, theirs is the most comprehensive review available of the research on learning from illustrated text in all of its aspects. For that reason their nine conclusions are particularly noteworthy:

1. In normal instructional situations, the addition of pictorial *embellishments* will not enhance the learning of information in the text [emphasis added].
2. When illustrations provide text-redundant information, learning information in the text that is also shown in pictures will be facilitated.
3. The presence of text-redundant illustrations will neither help nor hinder the learning of information in the text that is not illustrated.
4. Illustrations can help learners understand what they read, can help learners remember what they read, and can perform a variety of other instructional functions.
5. Illustrations can sometimes be used as effective/efficient substitutes for words or as providers of extralinguistic information.
6. Learners may fail to make effective use of complex illustrations unless they are prompted to do so.
7. Illustrations usually enhance learner enjoyment, and they can be used to evoke affective reactions.
8. Illustrations may be somewhat more helpful to poor readers than to good readers.
9. Learner-generated imaginal adjuncts are generally less helpful than provided illustrations (pp. 225–26).

16.4.2.4. Multi-Image. Multimedia is an area whose current popularity has spurred both articles in the popular press and research interest. Romiszowski (1994) lauds "the motivation-enhancement role of multimedia that is a result of providing appropriate information through impactful presentations" (p. 12). However, multimedia has not yet become a research interest of visual literacists.

Before there was multimedia, there was multi-image, which was inadequately researched, although there was enough published over 30 years for it to be reviewed as a body of research by Burke and Leps (1989). Jonassen (1979) noted that "Research on multi-imagery generally has focused on the linear versus simultaneous presentation issue" (p. 291). The presentation of two or more images simultaneously (multi-image) has obvious implications on perception, encoding, and many other issues that remain areas of popular visual literacy concern.

Perrin (1969) provided a theory of multiple-image communication that posited that more information would be assimilated by viewers when multiple images were presented simultaneously on multiple screens. Perrin's theory was based on the assumption that viewers would mentally combine the images and consequently be able to make more and better comparisons. Perrin did not address the issue of information overload, which other scholars have considered to be either positive or negative, depending on the purpose of the multi-image presentation: positive when affective responses are sought, negative when cognitive learning is the purpose (Goldstein, 1975).

Goldstein (1975) reconsidered the relevant research on perception and applied those findings to the perception of multiple images. He cited Haber (1970) as concluding that "recognition memory for pictures is essentially perfect" and linked that to the findings of fixation studies:

> We know that once a picture receives only a few fixations, that the picture will be recognized later. The presentation should be slow enough to allow the necessary fixations, but, since our memory for pictures is excellent, overly long exposures are not necessary (p. 59).

Whiteside (1987) reviewed the four multi-image dissertations of Didcoct, Ehlinger; Tierney, and Toler. The studies covered single-image versus multi-image comparisons, picture recognition following a multi-image presentation, physiological and intellectual effects on subjects viewing multi-image, perception questions, and, of course, the effects of simultaneous versus sequential presentation on learning. Whiteside generalized that the majority of the studies (three of four) had not revealed significant differences. The other study (Toler, n.d.) found the effect of simultaneous presentation on visual discrimination tasks to be significantly higher scores than when the presentation was sequential. She also confirmed that "visuals" (visual learners) would outperform haptics, but that haptics would benefit most from multi-image presentation.

Like film, much of the scholarly writing in regard to multiple imagery has been devoted to aesthetics and criticism. Burke (1977) offered a scheme for multi-image criticism that considered the unique characteristics of the medium. In contrast, Seigler (1980) drew directly from film theory when he theorized about the montage effects of multiple images.

Although it would seem natural that multi-image would be the stage on which the competing cue summation and dual-coding theories would be compared, that has not happened. Jonassen's (1979) study comes close. In an experiment with seventh-grade students, one-screen, three-screen, and four-screen presentations were made of the same content. All treatment groups achieved substantial improvement on the criterion task, confirming the instructional effectiveness of the slide-tape medium. The one-screen presentation was a basic linear slide-tape. The three-screen presentation was a duplication of the one-screen presentation, except that additional examples of the concepts were shown concurrently alongside the basic set of slides. The four-screen presentation proved to be significantly more effective than the other treatments. That treatment used only the basic set of images, but kept previously shown slides in view as new images were introduced. The four-screen treatment was the only one that provided concurrent projection of both examples and nonexamples for the students to compare visually.

The paucity of multi-image research may be a function of a lack of a unifying theory of multi-image (Burke, 1991a). In two recent articles, Burke (1991a, 1991b) has provided a new theoretical framework for the study of multi-image that is consistent with classical film theory. His theory accommodates the differing spatial emphasis of painting, photography, cinema, video, and multi-image. With theory in place, perhaps elaborating research will follow.

16.4.2.5. Graphic Representation. Spread across several disciplines are many papers on graphic representation, such as those of Jonassen, Beissner and Yacci (1993), Bertoline, Burton, and Wiley (1992), Braden (1983), Whiteside and Whiteside (1988), Griffin (1989), Macdonald-Ross (1977a, 1977b, 1979), Moxley (1983), Pruisner (1992), Winn (1980, 1981, 1982, 1983, 1986, 1987), and Winn and Holiday (1982).

16.4.2.5.1. Graphics. Saunders (1994) identifies nine categories of graphics: "symbols (pictographic or abstract), maps, graphs, diagrams, illustrations or rendered pictures (realistic to abstract), photos (still or moving), three-dimensional models, graphic devices and elements (may also be considered as symbols, and composite graphics made up of two or more of the other types)" (p. 184). At first glance, two of those categories seem questionable, those of photos and 3-D models. However, Saunders explains that she refers to photos that have been digitized and are capable of artistic manipulation and to models constructed through computer graphics and animation. These then all fit within her definition: "Graphics may be simply defined as a *prepared form of visual message or a visual form of communication*" (p. 184). As noted previously, Alesandrini (1984) classified graphics much differently under three rubrics: representational, analogical, and arbitrary. Her classification has been widely used in the research literature.

Graphics have also been categorized according to instructional applications. Reiber (1994) classified graphic applications as cosmetic, motivation, attention gaining, presentation, and practice. He further noted that cosmetic and motivation applications served affective functions, and that the other three applications served cognitive functions.

Research on graphics is heavily interwoven with research on pictures, as reviewed by Levie (1987). Accordingly, most of Levie's "picture" conclusions are applicable to graphics. Thus, we might read his conclusions as follows:

> Overall, research on interpreting pictorial cues and features [graphic cues and features] demonstrates that although some fundamental skills such as object recognition are essentially innate, young children and adults without ample picture-viewing [graphics-viewing] experience have trouble decoding pictorial [graphic] information that is abstract, complex, or represented in culture-bound conventions—especially when the objects and concepts shown are unfamiliar (Levie, 1987, pp. 7, 8; brackets added).

However, this expansion of Levie's conclusions must be taken with a grain of caution. When the purpose of the visuals is exclusively to support *reading to learn,* the effects of pictures and representational illustrations are more effective than those of graphics (Levin, Anglin & Carney, 1987).

16.4.2.5.2. Charts, Graphs, and Diagrams. For a more extensive review and discussion of research on charts, diagrams, and graphs than is provided here, readers are referred to the chapter by Bill Winn in Houghton and Willows' *The Psychology of Illustration: Basic Research* (1987). In that review of research on charts, graphs, and diagrams, Winn (1987) summarized that usually, but not always, graphics have done more to improve performance of students with low ability than those with high ability. Studies that supported that conclusion included the study of the effects of complex flow diagrams on 10th-grade science learning by Holliday, Bruner, and Donais (1977) and the study of elementary and secondary school students solving illustrated math story problems by Moyer, Sowder, Threadgill-Sowder, and Moyer (1984). Both of those studies are "diagram" studies.

16.4.2.6. Diagrams. According to Saunders (1994), diagrams "include those visuals drawn to represent and identify parts of a whole, a process, a general scheme, and/or the flow of results of an action or process" (p. 185). Winn (1987) points out that:

> There is a disproportionate amount of research on what we have defined as "diagrams." There is very little on the instructional effectiveness of graphs, and not much more on charts (p. 168).

Diagrams have proved particularly effective in science instruction when used to show processes (Winn, 1987).

In a study that examined the effectiveness of two mathemagenic activities, study questions, and diagrams, Buttolph and Branch (1993) found a weak effect in favor of diagrams, but no significant difference between the treatment groups. However, their post hoc comparison led them to "suggest that diagrams have the potential to be more effective mathemagenic aids to learning than study questions . . ." (p. 25). Since the subjects in this study created their own diagrams with prompts, the results should be compared to those of Alesandrini's (1981) study that involved student creation of mathemagenic material. In that study, college students were given a science chapter to read and were assigned one of two study strategies. Students who wrote paraphrases were compared to students who drew pictures of the material. Alesandrini, too, found only weak (not significant) effects in favor of the drawing strategy.

16.4.2.7. Charts. As a graphic form, charts are characterized by the organization of information on the page in groupings that are set apart from each other by columns and rows (Winn, 1987). Thus defined, charts will be used with increasing frequency in the future due to their ease of creation with the spreadsheet and tables functions of modern computer software. The term *chart,* however, is used incorrectly to refer to many other graphic forms such as posters, pie *graphs,* bar *graphs,* and line *graphs,* as wall *charts,* pie *charts,* and so forth.

Winn (1987), in reviewing the studies of Decker and Wheatley (1982) and of Rabinowitz and Mandler (1983), concluded that students improve free recall if they take advantage of spatial grouping, and that this free recall is further facilitated if the cognitive elements are grouped according to a conceptual structure. Considering an even wider body of research, Winn (1987) said, "We can conclude from this research that even the simplest spatial organization of elements into meaningful clusters has the potential for improving learning" (p. 177).

16.4.2.8. Graphs. Graphs are used to show quantitative relationships. Different types of graphs show different functions; e.g., line graphs show sequence and trends, pie graphs show portions of a whole, and bar graphs show quantitative comparisons (Fry, 1983; Macdonald Ross, 1977b; Pettersson, 1993; Winn, 1987). A form of bar graph that is of particular interest to visual literacists is the isotype graph, wherein quantities are represented not by bars but by series of small representational drawings (Winn, 1987). The isotype is thus visually a combination of the graph and the illustration.

More than any other of the graphic forms, graphs are governed by design conventions, and organizations such as the American Statistical Association have gone so far as to prepare style sheets to codify those conventions (ASA, 1976; Tufte, 1983). Research to substantiate the unique teaching values of graphs, even the highly pictorial isotype graphs, is lacking.

16.4.2.8.1 Graphic Organizers. Closely related to the effects of graphic materials are the effects that occur when they are used in special ways. Early research on graphic organizers showed "little or no effect" (Levie & Lentz, 1982, p. 215). Therefore, it will not be discussed here. Bellanca (1990, 1992) has proposed two dozen graphic organizers as tools for teaching thinking. The organizers all have two things in common. First, each has a visual (or graphic) component. Second, each graphic component is meant to be the structural background for the display of words, phrases, or other verbal information. Unfortunately (for our purposes), the Bellanca works are trade books, written for elementary and secondary school teachers. No research evidence is presented to validate the effectiveness of these graphic patterns, although each is recommended for use in a particular type of learning situation. Black and Black (1990) also have written a trade book that suggests that thinking can be organized with graphic organizers. Again, there is no substantiating research evidence. Does this mean that scholars have no interest in this issue? Not at all. If we accept what Bellanca classifies as a *graphic organizer,* then we can say that some, not all, of the graphic organizers have received limited research attention.

In early studies that measured the effect of graphic organizers when used as teacher-directed, prereading activities, graphic organizers failed to significantly facilitate learning of content material (Smith, 1978). Moore and Readance in the first of two meta-analyses (1980) reported more positive results, indicating that there was, in fact, a small overall effect of graphic organizers on learning from text. They also noted a strong effect when graphic organizers were used as student-constructed postorganizers rather than preorganizers. The second Moore and Readance meta-analysis (1984) confirmed the results of the 1980 study and found that adults benefit more from graphic organizers than do children.

Moore and Readance (1984) also analyzed the affective effect on teachers. Teachers were reported themselves to be more confident, better organized, and more in control when they had prepared themselves to use graphic organizer strategies. "In essence, teachers believed that graphic organizers prepared them to help students cope with particular pieces of content" (p. 15).

Johnson, Toms-Bronowski, and Pittelman (1982) found semantic maps to be superior to traditional teaching methods when used to teach vocabulary. Sinatra, Berg, and Dunn (1985) used a graphical outline with learning-disabled students, with positive effects on learning comprehension.

Sinatra, Stahl-Gemake, and Berg (1984) presented vocabulary concepts through graphic networking to 27 disabled readers. Results were compared against a verbal-oriented readiness approach, yielding significantly higher comprehension scores in favor of the mapping approach. Sinatra (1984) introduced four different types of network outlines in an attempt to increase reading and writing proficiency. Using these semantic mapping techniques had no significant effect on quality of writing but did have significant effects on improving reading comprehension.

In a fourth study, Sinatra demonstrated that these same semantic mapping techniques could render significant improvement in writing over a short period of time when the graphic outline is used to help the student organize thoughts prior to writing.

Jonassen, Beissner, and Yacci (1993) take a narrower view of what constitutes a graphic organizer, limiting the category to structural overviews. As such, graphic organizers are visual aids that function as "organizers" in the sense of what Ausubel (1978) termed an *advance organizer.* So defined, the graphic usually takes the form of labeled nodes connected to unlabeled lines. Jonassen, Beissner, and Yacci recommend using graphic organizers with good or more mature students. They cite examples of graphic organizer research with significant increases in learning effects for science learning (Amerine, 1986), and for recall of social science passages (Boothy & Alvermann, 1984).

Eggen, Kauchuk, and Kirby (1978) examined the effects of graphic organizers on comprehending and producing hierarchies. They found a significant increase in comprehension for fourth-, fifth-, and sixth-grade students asked (and able) to draw a hierarchy of the information in a text. The ability to create hierarchical drawings was not a metacognitive skill possessed by all students at that developmental stage.

16.4.3 Color

Although color could be a subtopic of any or all of the five categories of visual representation above, the topic generates so much interest that it will be covered here separately. Dwyer and Lamberski (1983) reviewed the research literature on the use of color in teaching. Their reference list includes 185 items, most being reports of research. Their general conclusion was that "The instructional value of color appears highly dependent upon the complexity of the task in the materials and perceived response requirements by the learners" (p. 316). More specific conclusions were that:

- Color was found to be of value in nonmeaningful tasks, especially if other perceptual cues lacked physical form differences or were low in associative value.
- The application of color to meaningful tasks appeared related to the interaction between learner and materials.
- In externally paced materials (passive), color appeared to be secondary to other salient features.
- If the task in passive materials became confusing, especially in simultaneous audio and visual materials, the learner selectively attended to a preferred mode as the functional stimulus. However, in most adult learners, this preferred mode is verbal, though in some incidences an integrated verbal and visual strategy may be used.
- If color was central to the concept being presented and if students focused their attention on it, color facilitated learning.
- In unstructured situations, older learners . . . disregard . . . the potential contribution that could have been made by the relevant visual code.
- In structured situations . . . older learners appeared to have the encoding and rehearsal strategies necessary to use an integrated code system like color.
- Younger learners generally have been found to benefit from color cues in passive materials, due more to their motivational characteristics rather than to their identified cognitive functions.
- Color codes have been found to be ineffective in passive materials, apparently due to insufficient learner-material interactive time.
- Color codes have had more success in facilitating verbal performance in self-paced (active) materials.
- The value of color in retrieval tasks appears highly task related.
- Color cues appeared to facilitate recall of low-perceptual tasks which are highly visual [but not of more verbal tasks].
- Color codes have been found to facilitate achievement in complex self-paced tasks, particularly with criterion tasks that are visual in nature (p. 317).

There is continued interest in color. See, for example, the recent work of Pruisner (1992, 1993, 1994). Pruisner (1994) concluded that students *prefer* color-cued text, and that the use of color in graphics enhances learning. Pett (1994) reviewed the research on the use of white letters on colored backgrounds. Preferred background colors for both slides and CRTs were found to be blue and cyan. Medium-density backgrounds were found to provide greater legibility than either high or low density. Green and cyan provided high legibility with slides, but not on a CRT.

None of the research cited above has resulted in major new theory or in revelations of such a magnitude as to cause paradigm shift. Rather, the studies have resulted in the revelation of principles for image design and for instructional applications.

Four extraordinary books have been published which support research on illustration and graphic representation: the two books by Houghton and Willows/Willows and Houghton (1987) and the two books by Tufte (1983, 1990). While the latter are not research compendia, per se, Tufte's *The Visual Display of Quantitative Information* (1983) is scholarly, filled with principles drawn from the research, and is a definitive work on the subject. In a like manner, Tufte's *Envisioning Information* (1990) is a comprehensive, scholarly work that is a definitive book on how to use illustrations in support of concepts.

16.5 VISUALIZATION

Visualization is both something that we do for others and something that we do internally within our minds. The creative, do-it-for-others sense of visualization is covered in this chapter under other topics such as visual representation: How do we "visualize" ideas for transmission to others? Most of the how-do-we-visualize questions had been answered to the general satisfaction of the field until new, computer-associated questions arose. Revived interest now expresses itself in terms of screen design, icon design, figure-ground, and similar look-of-the-tube issues. Friedhoff (1989) has commented that "visualization, because of the computer, is emerging as a distinctive new discipline" (p. 16).

The more abstract, more problematic concept of visualization is related to mental imagery ("picture that in your mind"), visual mnemonics ("visualize a duck with a yellow bill turning pancakes as a means of remembering the name Bill Turner"), mental spatial manipulations ("look at this picture of a polygon, then picture in your mind what it would look like from the back side"), mental rehearsal ("imagine yourself cutting out the letter A"), and mental recall ("visualize the face of Abraham Lincoln").

Visualization and other visual skills are widely considered to be innate. Salomon's (1979a) study of the effects of television viewing on TV-naive children led him to conclude that visual skills will develop naturally as a result of exposure to visual media. However, there is no evidence that individuals will innately learn how and when to apply those skills or whether the skills will fully develop "naturally." Winn (1982a) concluded that:

. . . imagery can be used in some shape or form by most people. However, only some learners can be said to be 'mentally skilled' in its use" (p. 4) and also that, "In general, any basic visual process can be developed into a visual skill through practice, and any visual skill can be developed into a useful learning strategy through training (p. 17).

16.5.1 Mental Imaging and Recall of Mental Images

Clark (1978) constructed a graphic model of the auditory and visual memory system. The model shows separate paths for coding and storing verbal and spatial representations in memory, following the dual-coding theory of Paivio (1971). In that model is a visual-spatial system that processes visual imagery (see 26.2). To test the model and the assumption that multichannel presentation of instruction with its dual-coding possibilities would be superior to single-channel presentation, Clark (1978) designed an experiment utilizing highly visual subject content to be learned by college students. The auditory-visual treatment group scored significantly higher than all others, and the visual-only treatment was second.

Under ideal conditions, mental imagery has been demonstrated to be effective as an aid to prose learning (Lesgold, McCormick & Golinkoff, 1975; Levin, 1973; Pressley, 1976). Pressley (1976) found that when eight-year-olds were instructed on forming mental images, given practice at imaging, and were provided separate times for reading and imaging (as opposed to simultaneous reading/imaging), their memory of story content was significantly improved. Lesgold, McCormick, and Golinkoff (1975) established an imagery training procedure for third- and fourth-graders. In the procedure, students read a passage, then drew stick figure cartoons illustrating the passage's content.

> After extended training in drawing adequate "comic strips" to illustrate prose passages, performance in a paraphrase-recall-task improved, but only when explicit imagery instructions were given with the task (p. 663). . . . The need for direct imagery instructions in order to get the effect is consistent with general paired-associate findings that even adults show substantially better performance when given explicit imagery instructions than when left to their own devices (p. 666).

Other early studies clearly established that when learners are told how to process visual information, their performance improves (Kosslyn, 1980; J. R. Levin et al., 1974; Paivio & Foth, 1970; Simon, 1972).

Several studies confirm the finding that imagery strategies particularly aid poor readers and poor-learning populations (Levin, 1973; Paris, Mahoney & Buckhalt, 1974; Pressley, 1976). Being *instructed to visualize* is a factor in these studies. *Age* is also a factor in the research associated with these findings. Rohwer (1970) demonstrated that children 5 and 6 years old do not benefit from visual imagery instructions. Levin et al. (1973) found that children have acquired the requisite internal elaboration ability by age 7. However, Shimron (1974) is cited in Lesgold et al. (1975) as having found 6- and 7-year-olds still not able to profit from imagery instructions in prose-learning tasks.

16.5.2 Mnemonics

For centuries, people have used mnemonic imagery as an aid to memory. The research doesn't go back that far.

Atkinson (1975) wrote a seminal research paper that introduced the keyword *mnemonic strategy*. Atkinson's interest was in the value of mnemonic images to aid in learning second-language vocabulary. The keyword process is based on a simple two-stage process, First, a keyword is selected to represent the concept to be learned. Second, a visual image representing or using that keyword is created either by the student or the teacher to act as a mental proxy for the concept. Levin and Pressley (1978) used Atkinson's strategy, and it later became the focal point of a series of studies that demonstrated the effectiveness of the strategy for learning different kinds of subject matter (Levin et al., 1980, 1986, 1988; Pressley & Levin, 1981; Rosenheck et al., 1989). These experiments have demonstrated that the keyword technique is successful in aiding recall across a broad range of subject matter. Levin and Levin (1990), in discussing this series of studies, said that there is "a growing body of research that indicates that information acquired on the basis of mnemonic instruction is not just remembered better at the rote memory level. It is often applied better in a number of thinking contexts as well" (p. 315).

Another mnemonic technique that has proved to be useful for remembering people's names is the face-name mnemonic (Carney, Levin & Morrison, 1988). The process, developed by Carney in 1984, is similar to the keyword procedure in that it uses proxy images to stimulate recall, but it involves a third stage. First, a keyword is devised. Next, a prominent feature of the person's face is identified. Then, a visual image is generated which relates the facial feature to the keyword. Although Carney originated the procedure as an aid to remembering names, in the Carney, Levin, and Morrison (1988) experiments, the strategy was used to aid college students learn about art. The Carney team reported, "These three experiments demonstrate that the face-name mnemonic may be successfully extended to an ecologically valid task, the learning of artists and their paintings, such as one would find in an art appreciation class" (p. 120).

Still another derivative technique has been labeled by its creators as *mnemonomy* (Levin & Levin, 1990). The procedure combines the concept of figural taxonomy with that of visual mnemonics. That is, a scientific taxonomy is transformed into a "pictorial mnemonic (memory-enhancing) taxonomy" (p. 302). The Levins conducted three experiments using a botany mnemonomy. Subjects were college students. Mnemonomy students statistically outperformed their taxonomy counterparts in all experiments. The pictorial mnemonomy substantially enhanced students' ability to reconstruct the botany classification system. Mnemonic subjects were more fluent in their ability to navigate the plant classification system. Mnemonic subjects outperformed other subjects on tests of memory. In a surprise to the researchers, mnemonomy subjects statistically surpassed free-study students in related problem-solving ability.

16.6   VISUAL LEARNING/VISUAL TEACHING

The visual literacy movement has been tied to the field of education from the outset. While the research on visualiza-

tion has demonstrated that visual skills can be taught (Winn, 1982a, and others), there has been no standard approach to teaching visual skills. Although visual skills and visual literacy instruction in the schools is the exception rather than the rule, in several instances visual literacy courses have been introduced. Dake (1982) reviewed 50 visual literacy curricula representing all education levels. He concluded:

> Programs that propose to promote visual literacy come in an amazing variety of formats with significantly different content. Each program seems to have been uniquely formed around existing conditions, the support and facilities available, and the knowledge and dedication of personnel already on hand (p. 2).

As to the significantly different content that he mentioned, Dake went on to list 20 topics that could be found in the various curricula. The list is interesting because of its diversity and because several topics seem only remotely related to communicating visually.

1. Developing an understanding of visual media
2. Development of an awareness of communications (mass media) technology and its pervasiveness
3. Technical information on photography, video, etc.
4. The psychology and physiology of vision (These are organized with various levels of analysis of specific behaviors as well as holistic subjective content.)
5. The analysis, evaluation, and interpretation of visual communication
6. Aesthetics
7. How visual literacy contributes to the development of general intellectual skills
8. Developing [visual] learning skills
9. Developing positive self-concept, autonomy, and self-esteem
10. Learning attentiveness to concrete experiences
11. The blending of vision with other senses
12. Developing self-knowledge (The selectivity that goes into visual messaging reveals a great deal about the creator.)
13. Metaphoric thinking and language—development of meaning
14. The creative process
15. The nature of consciousness
16. Imagination
17. The relationship of visual literacy to concept development
18. Perception of patterns and classification (such as causation)
19. Body and object language
20. Exploring visual/verbal relations (p. 3)

Dake (1982) concluded that "the programs surveyed do not show a consistent relationship between visual literacy theory and research and the structure of the curricula." While he gathered and published information about 19 of the curricula, including evaluation information, no conclusive research conclusions can be drawn. (All of the programs were considered to be "successful," but evaluation evidence was more anecdotal than empirical.)

16.6.1 Realism and the Program of Systematic Evaluation

As noted earlier, Levie (1978) set a research agenda that had its focus on learning and cognition. Prior to that, Dwyer (1972) wrote his *Guide for Improving Visualized Instruction,* which made widely known that he and his associates had been involved in a series of related experimental studies employing similar instructional materials since 1965. That program of ongoing research came to be known as the Program of Systematic Evaluation (PSE), and the 1972 report covered the results of the first phase of that program. The second phase was reported in Dwyer's 1978 book, *Strategies for Improving Visual Learning.* In 1987, Dwyer edited a volume of more than 30 research papers selected from the then 150-odd PSE experiments (the number has since passed 200). Dwyer himself (1994) characterized the 1987 book as a report on phase 3 of PSE. *No other body of research rivals in size or scope the PSE series of experiments.* Recently, summaries of the PSE research have been made available (Dwyer, Dwyer & Canelos, 1989; Dwyer, 1994). The findings of PSE have resulted in dozens of principles for visualized instruction and for visual design. For example, here are 3 (of nearly 40) generalizations from Dwyer's latest overview (Dwyer, 1994):

- Boys and girls in the same grade level (high school) learn equally well from identical types of visual illustrations when they are used to complement oral instruction [a finding from phase 1 of PSE].
- The realism continuum for visual illustrations applied to externally paced instruction is not an effective predictor of learning efficiency of all types of educational objectives. An increase in the amount of realistic detail contained in an illustration will not produce a corresponding increase in the amount of information a student will acquire from it [a finding from phase 2 of PSE].
- Achievement is enhanced when embedded cueing strategies are integrated into computer-based instruction [a finding from phase 3 of PSE].

16.6.1.1. Realism Studies. Other areas of study associated with visual learning and visual teaching have included *realism studies,* which are closely related to the PSE program in thrust but not in method. For a sample of this area of inquiry, readers are referred to Knowlton (1966), Levie (1978), Levie and Lentz (1982), Wileman (1980, 1993), Beauchamp and Braden (1989), and Braden and Beauchamp (1987).

The two Wileman texts (1980, 1993) have provided (and updated) a typology for the realism continuum that has been adopted by several other authors (e.g., Pettersson, 1993; Braden, 1994). Knowlton (1966) proposed that images be categorized for purposes of study and research. His categorization scheme was based primarily on degrees of realism. Levie and Lentz (1982), while concentrating on the effects of illustration on text, digressed to discuss providing additional pictorial information.

Braden and Beauchamp (1987) proposed a 2×2 matrix model for the concurrent study of the visual realism continuum and the audible realism continuum. The extremes of both continua were labeled *verbal* and *nonverbal.* Thus, four separate slide-plus-tape instructional presentations

were prepared, each representing verbal and nonverbal extremes of visuals and sounds. Acknowledging that there is an aesthetic or affective component to interpretations at the abstract ends of both continua, they suggested an eclectic research approach to include both quantitative and qualitative methods in the investigation of the interactions of the two sets of variables. When the slide-plus-tapes were administered as instruction in a study with college students, significant cognitive and affective differences were found (Beauchamp & Braden, 1989). The following conclusions were drawn:

1. In a sight-plus-sound presentation, when verbal language is used to appeal to only one sense via either printed or spoken words, cognitive achievement is not significantly diminished.
2. Pictures used in a sight-plus-sound presentation prompt viewer recall from memory or experience of information not in the presentation.
3. Cognitive stimuli prompt immediate cognitive recall.
4. Visuals, especially photographs, prompt immediate positive affective responses to a presentation.
5. Music from a sight-plus-sound presentation, more so than visuals, prompts long-range, or delayed, positive affective responses.
6. Students are aware of "when" and "if" they are learning. Changing the delivery-of-instruction mode does not change this apparently innate sense of learning.
7. A desired change in attitude is prompted through the introduction of new concepts and ideas, not through the presentation itself (p. 38).

16.6.2. Perception and Critical Viewing Skills

16.6.2.1. Perception. Perception, narrowly defined, is awareness. Most of what we perceive is perceived visually—perhaps three-quarters or more (Barry, 1994; Hansen, 1987). Perception is sensing, and visual perception is seeing. Studies of perception at that level are beyond the scope of this chapter. Still, the relevance to visual literacy of perception more broadly defined is obvious. Barry (1994) defines perception as "the process by which we *derive meaning* from what we see, hear, taste, and smell" (p. 114, emphasis added). Seeing images and deriving meaning from them is both an act of perception and a necessary condition of visual literacy.

In his book on visual information, Pettersson (1993) includes a chapter on perception that assumes the broadest kind of definition of the term. Included in his chapter is a section on the physiological aspects of vision, including reference to studies of his own and of others about eye movements, fixations, and scanning as physical attributes of seeing-to-perceive. There is also a section on picture perception, again supported by reports of his own and others' research. In the smorgasbord of topics that he includes are subliminal reception, illusions, visual imagery, and a cognitive model of perception.

From the mass of research that Pettersson reviews and describes, he reached the following eclectic conclusions (among others):

- All visual experience is subject to individual interpretation.
- Perceived image content is different from intended image content.
- Even simple pictures may cause many different associations.
- A given set of basic elements can be combined to form completely different images.
- The design of a picture can be changed a great deal without any major impact on the perception of the image contents.
- Content is more important than execution or form.
- Picture readability is positively correlated with both aesthetic ratings and assessed usefulness in teaching.
- Legends should be written with great care. They heavily influence our interpretation of image content.
- To a large degree, readers see what they are told to see in an image.
- There seems to be no major difference between genders in interpretation of image contents.
- Students display poor pictorial capabilities.
- We must learn to read image content (p. 86).

Barry (1994) has written an elaborate piece on perceptual aesthetics and visual language. Although most of her chapter is expository and theoretical, she makes some interesting connections. For example, she brings together meaning and feeling and explains how the perceptual process serves as a link. She provides a useful conception of Gestalt psychology as a basis for aesthetic theory. Others who have concerned themselves with *visual aesthetics* are Arnheim (1979) and Curtiss (1987).

Winn (1993) has written a new two-part chapter on perception for the revised Fleming and Levie (1993) book of principles from the behavioral and cognitive sciences. In the Winn chapter, conclusions from the research are stated as principles, and each principle is then briefly explained. Many of the explanations cite the underlying research. In Part I, most of the 31 perception principles are generalized, but a few address visual perception directly. For example, these four *research-based principles* relate directly to visualization and visual literacy:

1.3. Distinguishing between figure and ground is one of the most basic perceptual processes. Early perceptual processes are active in figure-ground organization (p. 59).
1.5b. Whether people see the "big picture" or details first depends primarily, in vision perception, on the size of the visual angle, that is, on the size of the image relative to the whole visual field (p. 64).
1.6. A horizontal-vertical reference system seems to be fundamental to perceptual organization. There is also a natural tendency for people to partition images into left and right fields (p. 65).
2.5. If none of these factors [sequence, organization, or composition] comes into play, there is a tendency for literate viewers to "read" visual messages in the same way they read text—for English speakers, that means from left to right and top to bottom (p. 70).

Part II of Winn's chapter on perception principles contains a section on "The Perception of Pictures," with 12 principles, and a section on "The Perception of Diagrams, Charts, and Graphs," with 14 principles. All of these 26 research-based items are germane to visualization and visual literacy, and are commended to our readers.

16.6.2.2.   Critical-Viewing Skills. The need for instruction in critical TV-viewing skills has been taken for granted. The Far West Laboratory for Educational Research and Development sponsored a national program of TV Viewing Workshops in support of Ned White's (1980) high school curriculum (and textbook) entitled *Inside Television: A Guide to Critical Viewing.* Lieberman (n.d.), in the trainer's manual for those workshops, offered a rationale for teaching critical-viewing skills: "Students do require training to develop the ability to analyze and evaluate these [TV] messages, know the capabilities and limitations of the medium, and make conscious decisions about when and what to watch" (p. 3). She did *not* cite any research to justify the need for or the effectiveness of critical-viewing skill instruction, and her extensive bibliography does not include any references to such research; either none exists or it is fugitive literature.

Minneapolis was the first American city to adopt a city-wide program for teaching visual literacy skills across the curriculum, based on the assumption that to do so would develop creative and critical thinkers (Lacy, 1987). An 81-page curriculum document written by Lyn Lacy was published and distributed throughout the city (Lacy, 1989). The rationale stated in that document was not documented by research either, but its main points are of interest here. Regarding the teaching of thinking, the Minneapolis guidelines say that visual literacy and thinking:

1. Should both be taught throughout the curriculum
2. Should both be taught in relation to content
3. Should initially both be taught in sequential order but, once learned, neither are always used consciously and in sequence thereafter
4. Should both be taught as processes in themselves, so that students understand what they are doing and can apply processes elsewhere (Lacy, 1988, p. 34)

Another program for teaching critical-viewing skills is sponsored by the Washington [D.C.] Association for Television and Children (WATCH). This small association published a critical-viewing guide (Banta & Creighton, 1985) and collaborated with a local television station in the production of a regional critical-viewing project (Sutton, 1987). Like the other examples given, the rationale for the WATCH critical-viewing project was based on *values* rather than on research.

To summarize on this topic, intuition that students will profit from critical viewing may well be sound. However, longitudinal research on the effects of these programs is needed. A number of authors have concentrated on perception and critical-viewing skills (Adams & Hamm, 1987; Baron, 1985; Finn, 1980; Hefzallah, 1986, 1987; Lloyd-Kolkin, 1982; Watkins et al., 1988; White, 1980).

A dedicated group of scholars has investigated visuals and visualizing as functions of *learning strategies and learner styles* (Ausburn & Ausburn, 1978b; Canelos, 1980, 1983; Dwyer & Moore, 1992; Moore, 1986; Moore &

Dwyer, 1991; Moore & Bedient, 1986; Streibel, 1980; Ragan, 1978). Two approaches have been taken to investigating visuals as a function of learning styles. The first has focused on the differential effects when the learning style is based on the visual/haptic scale. According to Jonassen & Grabowski (1993):

> Visually oriented individuals acquaint themselves with the environment through their vision. . . . The individual with haptic tendencies is more concerned with body sensations experienced through a tactile and/or kinesthetic mode. . . . Visual and haptic learning styles are, theoretically, at opposite ends of a continuum of perceptual organization of the external environment (p. 177).

A much-used indicator of visual/haptic style has been field dependence. In 1991, Mike Moore reported the results of a program of eight research studies by him and his students at Virginia Tech involving field dependence-independence and a variety of media attributes. That program of research continues.

The other scale commonly used to identify individual differences involving visuals is that of visualizer/verbalizer. The important dimension used to identify the polarized ends of this spectrum is that visualizers are image oriented, whereas verbalizers are word oriented. Richardson (1977) established the link between the visualizer/verbalizer styles and brain hemisphericity and created the Verbal and Visual Learning Styles Questionnaire. The recent study by Kirby, Moore, and Shofield (1988) indicated that verbal ability as measured by Richardson's questionnaire was positively correlated with spatial relations and spatial visualization, but nothing else. Useful significant findings to date are few, the most important being that students whose styles are matched to the styles of teachers tend to do better (Moore, 1991), and when students' preferred learning mode is matched to the learning task, they also tend to do better (Riding & Burt, 1982).

While many individuals have shown an interest in teaching with visuals, only a few have chosen to explore the effects of both teaching with and testing with visuals. Most of the *visual testing* research has been done in conjunction with the PSE program (DeMelo, Sazbo & Dwyer, 1981; F. Dwyer & DeMelo, 1983; Szabo, 1981; Szabo, F. Dwyer & DeMelo, 1981; DeMelo & F. Dwyer, 1983; C. Dwyer, 1984, 1985; C. Dwyer & F. Dwyer, 1985). In general the results of that research are that visualized testing provides better assessment and strengthens retention from visualized instruction.

16.7 VISUAL THINKING

Visual thinking is the most abstract concept that draws attention from researchers of visual literacy. Arnheim (1969) was one of the first to use the term. His theory of visual thinking has dominated the later work of such popular writers as McKim (1972), Dondis (1973), and Paivio (1971, 1975). Hortin (1982a) stretched the concept to add the dimension of visual rehearsal as a strategy for employing visual thinking in the learning process, and introduced the concept of introspection (is that a form of metacognition?) to the discussion of visual thinking (Hortin 1982b). Hortin also looked at the ways we use imagery in our daily lives (1983), connections of mental imagery to instructional design (1984), and the use of both internal and external imagery as aids for problem solving (1985). As noted earlier, the Minneapolis Public Schools have initiated a program that attempts to teach visual thinking (Lacy, 1989).

Since each individual's thinking is idiosyncratic, the teaching of thinking and thinking skills is problematic and controversial. Salomon (1979b, reprinted 1994) set a theoretical base for discussions of visual thinking in his comments on symbol systems: "Symbols serve as *characters or coding elements . . .* (p. 29), [and] *. . . some coding elements of symbol systems can become internalized to serve as vehicles of thought* (p. 84).

Conclusions about visual thinking evolve in strange ways. For example, Richard Mayer participated in two very different studies. One related to conceptual models for teaching computer programming (Bayman & Mayer, 1988). The other involved cognitive processing during reading (Mayer, 1987). From the two studies, he concluded that "Illustrations may help readers build useful mental models" (Mayer, 1989, p. 240).

16.8 VISUAL LITERACY AND VERBAL LITERACY

A natural outgrowth of the "literacy" metaphor has been the level of interest by teachers of reading and researchers in the field of reading in the relationship of visual literacy to the teaching of reading. Mulcahy and Samuels (1987) have written an extensive history of the use of illustrations in American textbooks over the last 300 years. They point out that only as printing technology has progressed has it been practical for publishers of textbooks to be concerned with semantic and syntactic text parallels between the illustration and the context to the text. Having the right images in the right places in a textbook is a concern that is as new as the visual literacy movement itself.

Scholars who have concerned themselves with visual literacy and reading include Sinatra (1987), who offered a technique to use pictures as tools to teach writing as well as reading, Haber and Haber (1981), whose primary interest was in the reading process, and Levie and Lentz (1982), who addressed the issue more directly as one of "pictures and prose."

Not all of the research concerning the effects of pictures on reading has favored the use of visuals. Early studies of the concurrent use of text and pictures focused on whether readers would attend to the text or to the pictures (Chall, 1967; Samuels, 1967, 1970; Willows, 1978). The emphasis of the research was to determine whether and to what degree the presence of pictures distracted beginning readers. Not surprisingly, Willows (1978) found that second- and third-grade readers read more slowly when the text was in the presence of pictures. Both background pictures and pictures on the periphery were shown to be distracting. Willows found that related pictures aided encoding, but reported that finding in a way biased against pictures: "Unrelated pictures produced more interference than related pictures" (p. 258). (An example of a "related" picture was of a dog on which the word *cat* had been superimposed.)

Braun (1969) randomly assigned 240 kindergartners to picture and no-picture groups, with the subjects trying to learn sight vocabulary. In seven of eight comparisons, the no-picture group learned the vocabulary faster than the picture group. Samuels (1967) reported experimental results showing that poor beginning readers were distracted by pictures when trying to learn sight words as reading vocabulary. Samuels (1970), in a review of the research on the effects of pictures (in illustrated books), found that:

1. The bulk of the research findings on the effect of pictures on acquisition of a sight vocabulary was that pictures interfere with learning to read.
2. There was almost unanimous agreement that pictures, when used as adjuncts to the printed text, do not facilitate comprehension.
3. In the few studies done on attitudes, the concensus was that pictures can influence attitudes (p. 405).

In reaction to the notion that illustrations were not really very important in assisting instruction, both Denburg (1977) and Duchastel (1980) agreed that "it is not enough to examine whether illustrations can enhance learning; one must also examine why or how they can do so" (p. 283). Levin and Lesgold (1978) reviewed research on the effects of pictures on prose learning when the prose was presented orally. They concluded that "there is solid evidence that pictures facilitate prose learning" (p. 233). Rohwer and Harris (1975) found that the media effects on prose learning correlated with socioeconomic status (SES). Black students from a lower SES benefitted from pictures added to prose, while white students from a high SES did not.

Haring and Fry (1979) noted the contrast in the findings of Samuels and of Levin and Lesgold, and also noted that research since the Samuels review had been mixed on the effects of pictures on reading comprehension. They conducted four experiments with pictures and nonfictional text. They used single pictures to illustrate the main ideas in a newspaper article, and they used a group of pictures to illustrate each sentence. In all four experiments, the students who received the picture-supported information significantly outperformed students in the no-picture control group. Their broad conclusion was that "the pictures resulted in improved recall of both more and less important passage information" (p. 183).

Levin (1981) provided a theoretical structure for the study of prose-relevant pictures—one that went far beyond using pictures in basic reading texts. A year later, Levie and Lentz (1982) reviewed 46 studies that had compared learning from illustrated text to learning from text sans pictures. They reported "an overwhelming advantage for the inclusion of pictures" (p. 203).

Prose-relevant picture studies have addressed the question of long-term recall. These durability studies (Anglin, 1986, 1987; Peng & Levin, 1979) generally show that not only does the presence of pictures with prose aid in recall but also those effects endure over time. Peng and Levin used story-relevant pictures with second-graders and found persistent positive effects after 3 days. Anglin (1986, 1987) conducted similar experiments on adults. In his first study, significant durability effects were demonstrated after 24 days. In the second experiment, the durability of positive picture effects was shown to still exist after 55 days. The Levin and Berry (1980) study mentioned earlier also demonstrated that the effects of visual illustrations on children's recall of prose persisted 1, 2, and 3 days later.

Research has also been done on the recall effects of pictures that conflict in some way with the accompanying text (Peek, 1974; Pressley et al., 1983). Peek (1974) found that 7- to 9-year-old students who read stories with mismatched pictures did more poorly on a test of story content than did students who read the story without pictures. Pressley et al. found that "pictures mismatched with the prose content are unlikely to reduce children's prose recall substantially" (p. 141).

Brody (1981, 1982, 1983) has been concerned with pragmatic aspects of using pictures in textbooks. He conceded that his information was "pieced together from disparate studies which are only tangentially concerned with the picture-text relationship" (Brody, 1982, p. 315) when he made these suggestions:

1. Pictures should be referred to in the written narrative.
2. Captions can help students understand the relevance of the pictures.
3. Photographs and realistic detailed drawings are usually preferred to simpler formats such as line drawings. However, preference is not always related to student achievement.
4. Within limits, students will spend more time examining complex images.
5. Pictures containing dynamic images are generally more interesting than those which contain static images.
6. Placement of pictures should be based on the function the picture is to serve.

Hurt (1987) has also taken a pragmatic approach to visualization of texts. From his experiment with 180 undergraduate college students he concluded that:

. . . illustrations possessing literal representations are more effective than illustrations possessing analogical representation when the instructional function to be served is identification of properties of phenomenal information, and that illustrations possessing analogical representation are more effective than illustrations possessing literal representation when the instructional function to be served is clarification of nonphenomenal information (p. 94).

Special recognition needs to be given to the comprehensive review of pictures-in-reading-to-learn research done by Levin, Anglin, and Carney (1987). Their chapter in the Willows and Houghton (1987) text provides extraordinary coverage of the topic. As the framework for a meta-analysis, Levin, Anglin, and Carney adopted five of Levin's (1981) "functions" (decoration, representation, organization, interpretation, and transformation) that text-imbedded pictures serve in prose learning. Each function is explained and documented with numerous examples of the research relevant to that function. The meta-analysis covered 87 empirical studies, all of which are identified in a bibliographic appendix. Overall, the reported findings, based on average effect size, show positive effects for all functions except the decoration function. A comparison of the effectiveness of illustrations (pictures embedded in text) versus visual imagery (instructing students to visualize the text) demonstrated the greater strength of provided illustrations—again based on average effect size of the several studies. Levin, Anglin, and Carney (1987) supplement their meta-analysis with a set of "ten commandments of picture facilitation." These are a set of pragmatic suggestions and specific observations they have drawn from the review of the research literature. In spite of the stilted *shalt* and *shalt not* language, these prescriptions and proscriptions are valuable advice for producers of instructional text materials.

16.9 THE VISUAL-VERBAL RELATIONSHIP

When *visual literacy* was coined as a term, an early outcome was to suggest the existence or possibility of a visual language(s). From the beginning, comparisons have been made as if by second nature. Once we began to compare the communication aspects of imagery with written language, it was inevitable that the relationship between traditional verbal language and visuals would be explored. Sensory redundancy studies were one of the results of this natural progression of inquiry. Several researchers have explored the effects of visuals used alone and with written or spoken words. Some of the more interesting work along these lines has been done by Appelman (1993), Duchastel (1978), Braden (1983), Fleming (1987), and Dwyer (1988). A general conclusion would be that visuals and verbal materials when used together are in most cases stronger message carriers than when either is used alone.

Braden (1983) coined the terms *visual-verbal symbiosis* and *visual-verbal discontinuity.* Dwyer (1988) found a symbiotic relationship between verbal and visual literacy when the two were combined to facilitate student achievement. The concept of visual-verbal symbiosis is rooted in the idea that "visuals" support "verbals," and vice versa. Braden (1993, 1994) postulated that there are static and dynamic visuals and that they are found in 12 support relationships with each other and with static and dynamic verbal elements. Examples of each relationship are given in a 4 × 4 matrix (Braden, 1993, 1994) in what amounts to an expansion of the 2 × 2 audible-visual matrix of Beauchamp and Braden (1989). Research is needed to validate when, in the teaching-learning process, each of these relationships is most appropriate and to inform the field about the effects of

altering the degrees of visualization or verbalization in each of the relationships.

Pettersson (1993) has taken a more definitional approach to visual-verbal relationships. In an explication of his model on linguistic combinations, he discussed visual languages in which symbols and pictures are both visual. He terms a combination of visual and verbal languages as *verbo-visual,* divided into *oral-visual* and *lexivisual.* The term *verbo-visual* has caught on in the European scholarly community and is now coming into use by North American scholars (e.g., Metallinos, 1994; Zettl, 1994).

16.10 VISIBLE LANGUAGE: TEXT AS VISUALS

The field of typography deals with the design and appearance of printed text. Typographical research has delved into such matters as readability of letterforms with resulting principles for using upper- and lowercase letters together, letter spacing, line length or column width, hyphenation, justified vs. unjustified margins, and so forth (e.g., Davenport & Smith, 1965; Waller, 1979; McLean, 1980). Some of that research applies to visual literacy and its application to instruction and has been made widely available to the field by Hartley (1978, 1985) and Jonassen (1982, 1985). Misanchuk (1992) has shown how those same principles apply to amateur typography: desktop publishing. When visuals and verbal elements are used together, they become symbiotic (Braden, 1982), and in some forms the words or letters themselves become the visual message.

There is a distinction between text-as-visuals and text-in-visuals. Labels on diagrams, illustrations, or pictures are examples of text-in-visuals. Mayer (1989) conducted two experiments wherein effects of labeled illustrations on recall were compared to the effects of unlabeled illustrations. Students who read passages containing the labeled illustrations recalled more explanative information than did those who read passages with unlabeled illustrations. Mayer and Gallini (1990) found the use of visuals to be an effective presentation strategy when the visual material explains the information in the text. Mayer and Anderson (1991) conclude that "studies have shown that simultaneous presentation of illustrations and verbal labels in instructional texts resulted in better problem-solving transfer than did presenting illustrations without verbal labels" (p. 490).

16.11 ELECTRONIC VISUALS

16.11.1 Screen Design

Several studies have been conducted that investigated aspects of computer screen design. Grabinger has followed an ongoing line of research regarding display of text and other design elements on computer screens (1984, 1897, 1989, 1993). In 1989, he did a review of the research and provided guidelines that identified specific things that screen designers ought to do. His most recent work (Gra-binger, 1993) investigated viewer responses to screen designs, finding that adult viewers of instructional screens judged them primarily on two dimensions: organization and visual interest.

Hannafin and Hooper/Hooper and Hannafin (1986, 1988, 1989) also published a series of papers about screen design and layout. While their papers, much like the Gra-binger 1989 paper, were prescriptive, the most enduring contribution they make is less about screen design than about facilitating individual learning styles. The problem is that screens have changed since most of the research was done, e.g., that of Grabinger in 1984. Jones (1995) has stated the situation clearly: "Screen design literature is dated, and the existing guidelines do not allow for advances in computer technology" (p. 264). Jones went on to say, "there is a dearth of research into how the screen in a CBI program can incorporate a dynamic interface to promote the acquisition of knowledge to the end of promoting and improving human learning" (p. 266).

Duin (1988) followed the best guidance available at the time and created a "well-designed CAI program" that was tested against a poorly designed program and a control group that did not use CAI. While the experiment produced some positive results regarding student attitudes toward well-designed instruction, the resulting guidelines that emerged from the study seem more suited to monochrome screens than to today's high-resolution color monitors with powerful graphics capability.

Some research relevant to screen design, of course, will prove durable. For example, the study by Herbener, Van Tuber-gen, and Whitlow (1979) investigated the location of objects within the visual frame. That study only considered black-and-white images and did not include motion or attempts at three dimensionality, yet the findings are instructive:

> Subjects seem to consider images more active when the center of interest is higher in the frame. Subjects appear to rate images as slightly more potent when the center of interest is higher in the frame. When the center of interest is placed away from the geometric center of the frame, . . . subjects tend to rate the image more negatively. Not unex-pectedly, ratings on the verticality scale are higher when the center of interest is higher in the frame; but there is also the hint . . . that a given vertical position is seen as higher when it is horizontally centered (p. 87).

16.11.2 Computer Graphics

An advantage of computer graphics is that they can be drawn either statically or dynamically. Moreover, they can be called or dismissed interactively. Alesandrini (1987) reviewed the research relevant to computer graphics in learning and instruction. She introduced her chapter with the following caveat:

> The effects of computer graphics on learning and motiva-tion are only beginning to be explored. While many studies

have investigated the use of graphics in traditional instruc-tion, few studies have investigated graphics in CAI (com-puter-assisted instruction) or the instructional uses of graphics application software. Although the published find-ings are limited, many projects are currently underway to field-test the variety of uses of computer graphics (p. 159).

Indeed some of those studies are beginning to appear, but advances in computer technology are outpacing research on computer utilization. Among other enhanced capabilities of microcomputers is the ability to portray with ease graphic representations of conceptual networks. Con-sequently, the research questions have changed with the emerging technology, and we see studies like that of Allen, Hoffman, Kompella, and Sticht (1993) that examine com-puter-based mapping as a tool for curriculum development.

We find current researchers turning back to basic graph-ing skills research as they consider the possibilities of com-puter-generated visualization. For example, Drahuschak and Harvey (1993) wrote an article on computer-based graphing that posed the problem this way:

> The question we should ask now is this: Which instruction-al strategies will prove useful in developing critical think-ing skills within this emerging discipline of visualization? Research performed by McKenzie and Padilla (1984), Mokros and Tinker (1987), Talley (1973), and Sie-mankowski and MacKnight (1971) has concluded that in order to be successful in science two critical areas must be mastered: graphing abilities and spatial abilities. Visualiz-ing a data pattern in three-dimensional space once required a well-developed imagination. Fortunately, students today can augment their mental capabilities with the use of a computer system . . . (p. 3).

To place that quotation in context: McKenzie and Padilla (1984) found that formal operational thinkers tend to score higher in graphical achievement than concrete operational thinkers. Mokros and Tinker (1987) reported that experience in microcomputer labs enhanced children's ability to inter-pret graphs. Talley (1973) studied three-dimensional visual-ization, concluding that individuals who have better visualization skills perform at consistently higher levels of conceptualization. Siemankowski and MacKnight (1971) found science-oriented students to have greater three-dimensional visualization or spatial abilities than students who are not science oriented.

16.11.3 Animation

As computer technology advances and authoring systems become more friendly and powerful, computer special effects that were once esoteric are now becoming common-place. As a result, computer animation, which has long been around in computer-based instruction (CBI), but only as a rarity, is now a pervasive reality. Just as the incidence of animated CBI has increased, so has the research about it. Rieber (1989, 1990a, 1990b, 1991a, 1991b; Rieber, Boyce & Assad, 1990; Reiber & Hannafin, 1988; Reiber & Kini,

1991) has generated a flurry of research. Many others have contributed also, including those whose interest preceded the new technologies (Alesandrini, 1987; Cambre, Johnsen & Taylor, 1985; King, 1975; Moore, Norwocki & Simutis, 1979; Rigney & Lutz, 1975), and others in more recent times (Baek & Lane, 1988; Mayer & Anderson, 1991; Torres-Rodriquez & Dwyer, 1991). Reiber (1990a) has promoted the appropriate use of animation, but cautioned that "CBI designers . . . must resist incorporating special effects, like animation, when no rationale exists . . ." (p. 84).

The findings tend to be related to narrow research questions. For example, the results of the Cambre, Johnsen, and Taylor study "indicated that children learned from and liked both serious and humorous animations, especially those animations designed for older audiences" (p. 111) Reiber, Boyce, and Assad reported that "although animation did not affect learning, it helped decrease the time necessary to retrieve information from long-term memory and then subsequently reconstruct it in short-term memory" (p. 50). Mayer and Anderson (1991) performed two experiments involving college students. In one experiment, instruction with an animation and a concurrent verbal explanation was compared to instruction where the narration was given first, followed by the animation. In the second experiment, the same comparison was made, and other treatments were added to include students who saw the animation only, students who heard the words only, or students who had no instruction (control). Students in the words-with-animation treatment performed better than students who received any of the other treatments. Reiber (1991), in an experiment with fourth-graders, "showed that students successfully extracted incidental information from animated graphics without risk to intentional learning, but were also more prone to developing a scientific misconception" (p. 318). In a study utilizing college students as subjects, Torres-Rodriquez and Dwyer (1991) set out to assess the relative effectiveness of animation, zoom-in, and a combination of animation and zoom-in. Students were grouped according to high or low prior knowledge of the content. The researchers reported that:

. . . even though each treatment had been deliberately designed and positioned in the instructional sequence to instigate higher levels of information processing, when students were permitted to interact with their respective treatments for equal amounts of time insignificant results in student achievement occurred on the different criterion tests. Results also indicate that different visual enhancement strategies function differentially in reducing prior knowledge (high and low) between students within each group (p. 85).

While computer animation research can be covered in only a few paragraphs here, Reiber (1994) was able to devote an entire chapter to the subject. Considering the recency and thoroughness of his review, his conclusions are the best and latest word on the subject:

- Despite the popularity of animation among CBI designers and developers, little research is available on its effectiveness.

- Although animation can be a dramatic visual effect, research indicates that animation's effects on learning are quite subtle.
- Early animation research was heavily prone to confounding.
- In order for animation to be effective, there must be a need for external visualization of changes to an object over time (motion attribute) and/or in a certain direction (trajectory attribute).
- Children and adults vary in the degree to which they benefit from animated displays.
- Learners may need to be carefully cued to information contained in an animated display.
- Young children seem able to extract information incidentally from animated displays, although they may form misconceptions without proper guidance.
- Animation, as continuous visual feedback, is an important part of visually based simulations, although the role that animation plays in such activities cannot be isolated and studied apart from the activity itself.
- Research indicates that visually based simulations can be effective practice strategies, as compared to traditional questioning activities.
- Visually based simulations have shown to be intrinsically motivating for children in intermediate grades.
- Early research on using visually based simulations as inductive learning strategies indicates that adults are frequently uncomfortable with open-ended, discovery-based activities, especially when they perceive the learning environment to be formal or "school-like" in other ways (p. 169).

16.11.4 Graphic User Interfaces and Graphic Browsers

The graphical user interface (GUI) is changing the way computers are used. Much has been written about it in the trade press and even in a few scholarly works (e.g., Reiber, 1994). However, in spite of the fact that the GUI represents a shift from verbal access to, and verbal manipulation of, computers, no visual literacy research has been reported. Macintosh mavens have heralded the fact that learning new Mac applications is easy because they all share a similar look (share a common visual language). Shneiderman (1987) indicated that students tend to reject the use of computer applications that do not have an interface (appearance) they can understand.

GUI conventions include the use of standardized icons such as the trashcan, folders, a printer graphic, a paint brush, and a magnifying glass. Emerging CBI standards for GUI include general acceptance of right and left arrow buttons that allow students to go to the next frame or to return to the previous one, hooked arrows that let users return to the previous menu, and the ubiquitous question mark that can be clicked for on-screen help. Screen geography (location of elements) is partially standardized. There are drop-down menus and roll-ups that are activated by a mouse-controlled arrow. And each individual program has the potential to be accessed by easily learned "buttons," the key aspect of which is their visual recognizability. While usage has tended to standardize these conventions, research has not played a significant role.

Limited research has been done on the effectiveness and acceptability of buttons. Egido and Patterson (1988) studied the effects of buttons as browsers. They found that buttons that combined icons and words were superior to word buttons. In corporate research reported by Microsoft (Temple, Barker & Sloane, 1990), picture buttons (icons) were found by adult users to be preferred to other types of buttons.

Lucas & Tuscher (1993) conducted a study to determine whether adult button preferences applied to adolescents. They found that, like adults, early adolescent students preferred buttons that contained both "pictures" and words, but that they were more accurate when using word-only buttons.

The button and drag features of the GUI have made possible interactive CBI. Mays, Kibby, and Watson (1988) reported the development and evaluation of hypermedia instruction on the Macintosh that featured *learning by browsing*. In an experimental study that assessed learning as measured in a posttest, Tripp and Roby (1990) found that induced visual metaphors did not significantly increase learning of foreign-language vocabulary (Japanese). There was functional similarity in their work and that of Mays, Kibby, and Watson (1988) in that the students had visual browsing capability. Jones (1995), whose criticism of current screen design guidelines was mentioned earlier, has provided seven guidelines of his own for designing screens that facilitate browsing:

1. Provide selectable areas to allow users to access information.
2. Allow users to access information in a user-determined order.
3. Provide maps so that users can find where they are and allow provisions to jump to other information of interest from the map.
4. Provide users with feedback to let them know that they must wait when significant time delays are required for the program to access information.
5. Provide users with information that lets them know that they are making progress.
6. Arrange information in a nonthreatening manner so that users are not overwhelmed by the amount of information contained in a program.
7. Provide visual effects to give users visual feedback that their choices have been made and registered by the program (p. 267).

When the research catches up with the possibilities offered by the technology, these guidelines will have been empirically validated or rejected.

16.12 CONCLUSIONS

The research and scholarly literature of the field of visual literacy is voluminous. The bibliography of Clemente and Bohlin (1990), available from Educational Technology Publications, is 37 pages in length and contains about 400 entries from sources who, by and large, are not part of the visual literacy movement. In an attempt to map the field of visual communication—which is even broader than the field of visual literacy—Moriarty (1995, Oct.) has evolved a taxonomy of the literature. She analyzed the input of 37 visual communication scholars in setting her 13 categories and 90 subcategories. These she has used much as one would use a key word classification system to classify the 1,600-plus books and articles in her ever-growing bibliography.

Two bibliographies by Walker (1990, 1994) contain nearly 500 entries from 11 of the last 14 International Visual Literacy Association's books of readings (Braden & Walker, 1982; Braden & Walker, 1983; Walker, Braden & Dunker, 1984; Thayer & Clayton-Randolph, 1985; Miller, 1986; Braden, Beauchamp & Miller, 1987; Braden, Braden, Beauchamp & Miller, 1988; Braden, Beauchamp, Miller & Moore, 1989; Braden, Beauchamp & Baca, 1990; Beauchamp, Baca & Braden, 1991; Baca, Beauchamp & Braden, 1992; Braden, Baca & Beauchamp, 1993; Beauchamp, Braden & Baca, 1994; Beauchamp, Braden & Griffin, 1995). The IVLA books are not widely disseminated, so most have been made available through ERIC.

16.12.1 Visual Literacy Research: Where to Start

There is much research yet to be done. As mentioned, the literature about visuals and visual literacy is overwhelming. This author is asked from time to time where a neophyte researcher interested in visual literacy should start. The temptation is to answer, "with the meta-analyses and reviews of the literature" (e.g., Levie, 1987; Levie & Lentz, 1982, Moore & Readance, 1984; Winn, 1987), but that is not a very helpful response. The best advice would be to read carefully three books: those of Moore and Dwyer (1994), Pettersson (1993), and Willows & Houghton (1987). Add to that list the dissertation of Baca (1990), if it is easily available. Another recommended early read would be Dwyer's 1987 book, with its 37 articles describing PSE research. Then the new researcher should select the meta-analyses and reviews of the literature relevant to his or her personal interests.

The best advice regarding research methods would be to design quantitative studies rather than qualitative ones. The aesthetic aspects of pictures, film, and television are real. They are also the bait to encourage qualitative methods. However, visual literacy is seen somewhat as a field of inquiry that lacks rigor, and even an excellent qualitative visual literacy study would be greeted with a general lack of respect. In terms of need, research is overdue that addresses longitudinal image effects, electronic imagery related to visual literacy constructs, and interaction of cue summation theory and dual-coding theory (as complementary or conflicting).

Those interested in finding a research topic, who don't have the time to read all of the recommended books, would be well advised to consider Baca's (1990) list. Visual literacy research is needed to:

• Identify the learnable visual literacy skills

- Identify the teachable visual literacy skills
- Develop implementation of visual literacy constructs
- Validate implementation of visual literacy constructs
- Provide a rationale for visual literacy implementation in our society
- Provide a rationale for visual literacy implementation in our educational system
- Supplement research conducted in other fields, including psychology, education, learning, visual perception and eye movement studies, print literacy (p. 70)

Baca also lists a dozen or so other possible research options. As an eclectic field, visual literacy provides many avenues of investigation. Fortunately, many resources are already available to facilitate future scholarly activity.

REFERENCES

Adams, D.M. & Hamm, M. (1987). Teaching students critical viewing skills. *Curriculum Review 26* (3), 29–31.

Alesandrini, K.L. (1981). Pictorial-verbal and analytic-holistic learning strategies in science learning. *Journal of Educational Psychology 73, 358–68.*

— *(1984). Pictures and adult learning.* Instructional Science *13,* 63–77.

— (1987). Computer graphics in learning and instruction. *In* H.A. Houghton & D.M. Willows. *The psychology of illustration, Vol. 2: instructional issues.* New York: Springer.

Allen, B.S., Hoffman, R.P., Kompella, J. & Sticht, T.G. (1993). Computer-based mapping for curriculum development. *In* M.R. Simonson & K. Abu-Omar, eds. 15th Annual Proceedings of Selected Research and Development Presentations (RTD/AECT). Ames, IA: Iowa State University.

American Statistical Association (1976). JASA style sheet. *Journal of the American Statistical Association 71, 260–61.*

Amerine, F.J. (1986). *First things first.* Clearinghouse *59,* 396–97.

Anglin, G.J. (1986). Prose-relevant pictures and older learners' recall of written prose. *Educational Communication and Technology Journal 34 (2), 131–36.*

— *(1987). Effect of pictures on recall of written prose: how durable are picture effects?* Educational Communication and Technology Journal *35* (1), 25–30.

Appelman, R.L. (1993) The effects of congruency between structural & contextual dominance in image processing. Unpublished doctoral dissertation, Indiana University.

Arnheim, R. (1954). *Art and visual perception: a psychology of the creative eye.* Berkley, CA: University of California Press.

— (1969). *Visual thinking.* Berkeley and Los Angeles, CA: University of California Press.

— (1979). *Art and visual perception.* Los Angeles, CA: University of California Press.

Atkinson, R.C. (1975). Mnemotechnics in second-language learning. *American Psychologist 30, 821–28.*

Ausburn, L.J. & Ausburn, F.B. (1978a). *Visual literacy: background theory and practice.* Programmed Learning & Educational Technology *15,* 291–97.

— & Ausburn, F.B. (1978b). Cognitive styles: some information and implications for instructional design. *Educational Communications and Technology Journal 26,* 337–54.

Ausubel, D.P. (1978). *Educational psychology: a cognitive view.* New York: Holt, Rinehart & Winston.

Baca, J.C. (1990). Identification by concensus of the critical constructs of visual literacy: a delphi study. Unpublished doctoral dissertation, East Texas State University.

—, Beauchamp, D.W. & Braden, R.A., eds. (1992). *Visual communication: bridging across cultures.* Blacksburg, VA: International Visual Literacy Association. (ERIC Document Reproduction Service No. ED 352 932.)

— & Braden R.A. (1990, Feb.). A research approach to the identification, clarification, and definition of visual literacy and related constructs. Paper presented at the 1990 Annual Convention of the Association of Educational Communications and Technology, Anaheim, CA.

Baek, Y. & Layne, B. (1988). Color graphics, and animation in a computer-assisted learning tutorial lesson. *Journal of Computer-Based Instruction 15* (4), 131–35.

Banta, M.A. & Creighton, F.K. (1985). *WATCH: critical viewing guide.* Washington, DC: WATCH.

Baron, L.J. (1985). Televised literacy curriculum in action: a long-term study. *Journal of Educational Television 11* (1), 49–55.

Barry, A.M.S. (1994). Perceptual aesthetics and visual language. *In* D.M. Moore & F.M. Dwyer, eds. *Visual literacy: a spectrum of visual learning.* Englewood Cliffs, NJ: Educational Technology.

Bayman, P. & Mayer, R.E. (1988). Using conceptual models to teach BASIC computer programming. *Journal of Educational Psychology 80,* 291–98.

Beauchamp, D.G., Baca, J.C. & Braden, R.A. (1991). *Investigating visual literacy.* Conway, AR: International Visual Literacy Association. (ERIC Document Reproduction Service No. 352 051.)

— & Braden, R.A. (1989). An eclectic qualitative-quantitative research design for the study of affective-cognitive learning. *In* M.R. Simonson & D. Frey, eds. 11th Annual Proceedings of Selected Research Paper Presentations (RTD-AECT). Ames, IA: Association for Educational Communications and Technology, 57–68.

—, — & Baca, J.C. (1994). *Visual literacy in the digital age.* Blacksburg, VA: International Visual Literacy Association. (ERIC Document Reproduction Service No. ED 370 602.)

—, — & Griffin, R.E. (1995). *Imagery and visual literacy.* Blacksburg, VA: International Visual Literacy Association.

Bellanca, J. (1990). *The cooperative think tank: Graphic organizers to teach thinking in the cooperative classroom.* Palatine, IL: IRI/Skylight.

— (1992). *The cooperative think tank II: Graphic organizers to teach thinking in the cooperative classroom.* Palatine, IL: IRI/Skylight.

Bertoline, G.R., Burton, T.L. & Wiley, S.E. (1992). Technical graphics as a catalyst for developing visual literacy within general education. *In* J. Clark-Baca, D.G. Beauchamp & R.A. Braden, eds. *Visual communications: bridging across cultures.* Blacksburg, VA: International Visual Literacy Association.

Berry, L. & Dwyer, F.M. (1983). Interactive effects of color realism and learners' I.Q. in effectiveness of verbal instruction. *Perceptual and Motor Skills 54,* 1087–91.

Black, H. & Black, S. (1990). *Organizing thinking: graphic organizers, Book II.* Pacific Grove, CA: Critical Thinking Press & Software.

Bogen, J.E. (1979). Some educational aspects of hemispheric specialization. *In* D.J. Fork, J.J. Newhouse & J. Beauchemin, eds. Proceedings 11th annual conference on visual literacy. Bloomington, IN: Indiana University (IVLA).

Boothy, P.R. & Alvermann, D.E. (1984). A classroom training study: the effects of graphic organizer instruction on fourth graders' comprehension. *Reading World 23,* 325–39.

Braden, R.A. (1982, May). The outline graphic. Paper presented at the Association for Educational Communication and Technology annual convention, Dallas, TX. (ERIC Document Reproduction Service No. ED 238 413.)

— (1983). Visualizing the verbal and verbalizing the visual. *In* R.A. Braden & A.D. Walker, eds. *Seeing ourselves: visualization in a social context.* Blacksburg, VA: The International Visual Literacy Association, Inc. (ERIC Document Reproduction Service No. ED 233 677.)

— (1993). *In* R.A. Braden, J.C. Baca & D.G. Beauchamp, eds. *Art, science & visual literacy.* Blacksburg, VA: International Visual Literacy Association. (ERIC Document Reproduction Service, No. ED 363 280.)

— (1994). *In* D.M. Moore & F.M. Dwyer, eds. *Visual literacy: a spectrum of visual learning.* Englewood Cliffs, NJ: Educational Technology.

—, Baca, J.C. & Beauchamp. D.G., eds. (1993). *Art, science and visual literacy.* Blacksburg, VA: International Visual Literacy Association. (ERIC Document Reproduction Service No. ED 363 280.)

— & Beauchamp, D.G. (1987). Catering to the visual audience: a reverse design process. *In* R.A. Braden, D.G. Beauchamp & L.W. Miller. *Visible & viable: the role of images in instruction and communication.* Commerce, TX: International Visual Literacy Association. (ERIC Document Reproduction Service, No. ED 352 931.)

—, Beauchamp, D.G. & Baca, J.C. (1990). *Perceptions of visual literacy.* Conway, AR: International Visual Literacy Association. (ERIC Document Reproduction Service, No. ED 321 729.)

—, Beauchamp, D.G. & Miller, L.W. (1987). *Visible & viable: the role of images in instruction and communication.* Commerce, TX: International Visual Literacy Association. (ERIC Document Reproduction Service, No. ED 352 931.)

—, Beauchamp, D.G., Miller, L.W. & Moore, D.M. (1989). *About visuals: research, teaching, and applications.* Blacksburg, VA: International Visual Literacy Association. (ERIC Document Reproduction Service No. ED 311 865.)

—, Braden, B.D., Beauchamp, D.G. & Miller, L.W. (1988). *Visual literacy in life and learning.* Blacksburg, VA: International Visual Literacy Association.

— & Hortin, J.A. (1982). Identifying the theoretical foundations of visual literacy. *In* R.A. Braden & A.D. Walker. *Television and visual literacy.* Bloomington, IN: International Visual Literacy Association. (ERIC Document Reproduction Service No. ED 228 980.) Reprinted in *Journal of Visual/Verbal Languaging 2* (2), 37–42.

— & Walker, A.D., eds. (1982). *Television and visual literacy.* Bloomington, IN: International Visual Literacy Association. (ERIC Document Reproduction Service No. ED 228 980.)

— & Walker, A.D., eds. (1983). *Seeing ourselves: visualization in a social context.* Blacksburg, VA: The International Visual Literacy Association. (ERIC Document Reproduction Service No. ED 233 677.)

Braun, C. (1969). Interest loading and modality effects on textual response acquisition. *Reading Research Quarterly 4,* 428–44.

Brody, P.J. (1981). Research on pictures in instructional texts: the need for a broadened perspective. *Educational Communication and Technology Journal 29* (2), 93–100.

— (1982). Affecting instructional textbooks through pictures. *In* D.H. Jonassen, ed. *The technology of text.* Englewood Cliffs, NJ: Educational Technology.

— (1983). An analysis of pictures in middle-level life science textbooks. *International Journal of Instructional Media 10* (2), 113–21.

Burke, K. (1977). A pragmatic approach to criticism of multimedia. *Journal of Educational Technology Systems 6* (1), 57–76.

— (1991a). Windows and frames: another approach toward a theory of multi-image. Part I. *International Journal of Instructional Media 18* (3), 243–54.

— (1991b). Windows and frames: another approach toward a theory of multi-image. Part II. *International Journal of Instructional Media 18* (4), 313–25.

— & Leps, A.A. (1989). Multi-image research: a thirty-year retrospective. *International Journal of Instructional Media 16* (3), 181–95.

Buttolph, D. & Branch, R.C. (1993). Effect of diagrams and study questions as mathemagenic activities on learner achievement. *Journal of Visual Literacy 13* (1), 9–34.

Cambre, M.A., Johnsen, J.B. & Taylor, W.D. (1985). A formative research study of the effects of instructional animations. *International Journal of Instructional Media 12* (2), 111–26.

Canelos, J.J. (1980). Three types of learning strategies and their effects upon learning from visualized instruction consisting of varying stimulus complexity. *Research and Theory Division Instructional Communication and Technology Research Reports 10* (4), 16–21.

— (1983). The instructional effectiveness of three context-independent imagery learning strategies and visualized instruction of varying complexity. *Journal of Experimental Education 51,* 58–68.

Carney, R.N., Levin, J.R. & Morrison, C.R. (1988). Mnemonic learning of artists and their paintings. *American Educational Research Journal 25* (1), 107–25.

Case-Gant, A. (1973). *Visual literacy: an exciting environmental adventure.* Richmond, VA: Richmond Public Schools. (ERIC Document Reproduction Service No. ED 071 448.)

Cassidy, M.F. & Knowlton, J.Q. (1983). Visual literacy: a failed metaphor? *Educational Communication and Technology Journal 31* (2), 67–90.

Clark, E.D. (1978). Levels of abstraction: theoretical concept in explaining the place of visuals in instructional strategies. *In* D. Fork & J.J. Newhouse, eds. *Exploration and interpretation: theoretical approaches to the study of visual literacy and visual learning.* Philadelphia, PA: International Visual Literacy Association.

— & Clark, M.P. (1976). The theoretical context of visual literacy: understanding the nature of two types of knowledge. Paper presented at the annual conference of the International Visual Literacy Association. Nashville, TN. (ERIC Document Reproduction Service No. ED 138 977.)

Clark, R.L. (1978). Media, mental imagery, and memory. *Educational Communication and Technology Journal 26* (4), 355–63.

Clemente, R. & Bohlin, R.M. (1990). *Visual literacy: a selected bibliography.* Englewood Cliffs, NJ: Educational Technology.

Chall, J.S. (1967). *Learning to read: the great debate.* New York: McGraw-Hill.

Chomsky, N. (1957). *Syntactic structures.* Gravenhage, The Netherlands: Mouton.

— (1964). *Current issues in linguistic theory.* The Hague, The Netherlands: Mouton.

— (1968). *Language and mind.* New York: Harcourt, Brace.

— (1975). *The logical structure of linguistic theory.* New York: Plenum.

Cochran, L.M., Younghouse, P., Sorflaten, J. & Molek, R. (1980). Exploring approaches to researching visual literacy. *Educational Communications and Technology Journal 28* (4), 243–65.

Corcoran, F. (1981). Processing information from screen media: a psycholinguistic approach. *Educational Communication and Technology Journal 29* (2), 117–28.

Cureton, J.W. & Cochran, L.W. (1976). *Visual literacy (the last word). Summary report of the twenty-second Lake Okoboji educational media leadership conference.* Iowa City, IA: The University of Iowa. (ERIC Document Reproduction Service No. ED 135 360.)

Curtiss, D. (1987). *Introduction to visual literacy: a guide to the visual arts and communication.* Englewood Cliffs, NJ: Prentice Hall.

Dake, D.M. (1982). *Curriculums in visual literacy.* Ames, IA: Iowa State University.

Davenport, J.S. & Smith, S.A. (1965). Effects of hyphenation, justification, and type size on readability. *Journalism Quarterly 42,* 381.

Debes, J.L. (1968). Some foundations for visual literacy. *Audiovisual Instruction 13,* 961–64.

— (1969). The loom of visual literacy. *Audiovisual Instruction 14* (8), 25–27.

— (1970). The loom of visual literacy—an overview. *In* C.M. Williams, & J.L. Debes, eds. *Proceedings of the first national conference on visual literacy.* New York: Pitman.

— (1972, Mar.). Some aspects of the reading of visual languages. Paper presented at the National Conference on Visual Literacy, Cincinnati, OH. (ERIC Document Reproduction Service No. ED 079 974.)

— (1974, Nov.). Mind, languages, and literacy. Paper presented at the annual convention of the National Council of Teachers of English. New Orleans. (ERIC Document Reproduction Service No. ED 108 659.)

Decker, W.H. & Wheatley, P.C. (1982). Spatial grouping, imagery, and free recall. *Perceptual and Motor Skills 55,* 45–46.

DeMelo, H., Szabo, M. & Dwyer, F.M. (1981) Visual testing: an experimental assessment of the encoding specificity hypothesis. *In* M.R. Simonson & E. Hooper, eds. *Proceedings of selected research paper presentations.* AECT/RTD. Ames, IA: Iowa State University.

— & Dwyer, F.M. (1983). The effect of visual testing in assessing the instructional potential of variables associated with visualized instruction. *Journal of Instructional Psychology 10* (3), 126–38.

Denburg, S. (1977). The interaction of picture and print in reading instruction. *Reading Research Quarterly 12,* 176–89.

Dewar, R.E. & Ellis, J.G. (1977). The semantic differential as an index of traffic sign perception and comprehension.

*Human Factors 19,*183–89.

Didcot, study cited in Whiteside, 1987.

Dondis, D.A. (1973). *A primer of visual literacy.* Cambridge, MA: MIT Press.

Drahuschak, J. & Harvey, F.A. (1993). *Using computer-based graphic methods to enhance integrated science process skills.* I. Proceedings of the third international seminar on misconceptions and educational strategies in science and mathematics. Ithaca, NY: Cornell University.

Duchastel, P.C. (1978). Illustrating instructional texts. *Educational Technology 18* (11), 36–39.

— (1980). Research on illustrations in text: issues and perspectives. *Educational Communication and Technology Journal 28* (4), 283–87.

— & Waller, R. (1979). Pictorial illustration in instructional texts. *Educational Technology 19* (11), 20–23.

Duin, A.H. (1988). Computer-assisted instructional displays: effects on students' computing behaviors, prewriting, and attitudes. *Journal of Computer Based Instruction 15* (2), 48–56.

Dwyer, C.A. (1984) The effect of varied rehearsal strategies in facilitating achievement of different educational objectives as measured by verbal and visual testing modes. Unpublished Doctoral Dissertation, The Pennsylvania State University.

— (1985). The effect of varied rehearsal strategies in facilitating achievement of different educational objectives as measured by verbal and visual testing modes. *Journal of Experimental Education 54* (2), 73–84.

— & Dwyer, F.M. (1985) The effect of visualized instruction and varied rehearsal and evaluation strategies (verbal and visual) in facilitating students' long-term retention on tests measuring different instructional objectives. *Journal of Visual Verbal Languaging 5* (1), 7–15.

— (1972). *A guide for improving visualized instruction.* State College, PA; Learning Services.

— (1978). *Strategies for improving visual learning: a handbook for the effective selection, design, and use of visualized materials.* State College, PA: Learning Services.

— (1987). *Enhancing visualized instruction—recommendations for practitioners.* State College, PA: Learning Services.

— (1988). Examining the symbiotic relationship between verbal and visual literacy in terms of facilitating student achievement. *Reading Psychology 9,* 365–80.

— (1994). One dimension of visual research: a paradigm and its implementation. *In* D.M. Moore & F.M. Dwyer. *Visual literacy: a spectrum of visual learning.* Englewood Cliffs, NJ: Educational Technology.

—, Dwyer, C.A. & Canelos, J. (1989). An overview of the program of systematic evaluation (PSE). *In* R.A. Braden, D.G., Beauchamp, L.W. Miller & D.M. Moore, eds. *About visuals: research, teaching and applications.* Blacksburg, VA: International Visual Literacy Association. (ERIC Document Reproduction Service No. ED 311 865.)

— & DeMelo (1983). The effects of visual testing in assessing the instructional potential of variables associated with visualized instruction. *Journal of Instructional Psychology 10,* 126–40.

— & Lamberski, R.J. (1983). A review of the research on the effects of the use of color in the teaching-learning process. *International Journal of Instructional Media 10,* 303–28.

— & Moore, D.M. (1992). Effect of color on visually and verbally oriented tests with students of different field dependence levels. *Journal of Educational Systems Technology 20* (4), 311–20.

Eggen, P.D., Kauchak, D.P. & Kirk, S., (1978). The effect of hierarchical cues on the learning of concepts from prose materials. *Journal of Experimental Education 46*(4), 7–11.

Ehlinger, study cited in Whiteside, 1987.

Eisner, E.W. (1970). Media, expression and the arts. *In* G. Salomon & R.E. Snow, eds., *Commentaries on research in instructional media.* Bloomington, IN: Indiana University.

Finn, P. (1980). Developing critical television viewing skills. *Educational Forum 44,* 473–82.

Fleming, M. (1977). The picture in your mind. *AV Communication Review 25* (1), 43–62.

— (1987). Designing pictorial/verbal instruction: some speculative extensions from research to practice. *In* H.A. Houghton & D.M. Willows, eds. *The psychology of illustration, Vol. 2: instructional issues.* New York: Springer.

Fleming, M. & Levie, W.H., ed. (1993). *Instructional message design: principles from the behavioral and cognitive sciences, 2d ed.* Englewood Cliffs, NJ: Educational Technology.

Fork, D. & Newhouse, J.J. (1978). *Exploration and interpretation: theoretical approaches to the study of visual literacy and visual learning.* Philadelphia, PA: International Visual Literacy Association.

Friedhoff, R.M. (1989). *Visualization, the second computer revolution.* New York: Abrams.

Fry, E. (1983). *A theory of graphs for reading comprehension and writing communication.* New Brunswick, NJ: Rutgers University. (ERIC Document Reproduction Service No. 240 528.)

Gnizak, E. & Girshman, R. (1984). Visualizing research. *In* A.D. Walker, R.A. Braden & L.H. Dunker, eds. *Enhancing human potential.* Blacksburg, VA: International Visual Literacy Association, 207–12. (Out of print, accessible through ERIC Document Reproduction Service No. ED 246 843.)

Goldstein, E.B. (1975). The perception of multiple images. *AV Communication Review 23* (1), 34–68.

Goodman, N. (1968, 1976). *Languages of art.* Indianapolis, IN: Hacket.

— (1977). When is art? *In* D. Perkins & B. Leondar, eds. *The arts and cognition.* Baltimore, MD: Johns Hopkins University Press.

— (1978. *Ways of worldmaking.* Indianapolis, IN: Hacket.

Grabinger, R.S. (1984). CRT text design: psychological attributes underlying the evaluation of models of CRT text displays. *Journal of Visual Verbal Languaging 4* (1),

— (1987). Relationships among text format variables in computer generated text. *Journal of Visual Verbal Languaging 6* (3).

— (1989). Screen layout design: research into the overall appearance of the screen. *Computers in Human Behavior 5,* 175–83.

— (1993). Computer screen designs: viewer judgments. *Educational Technology Research and Development 41*(2), 35–73.

Griffin, R.E. (1989). Using graphs correctly: what are the basic elements for the language of graphs? *In* R.A. Braden, D.G. Beauchamp, L.W. Miller & D.M. Moore, eds. *About visuals: research, teaching, and applications.* Blacksburg, VA: International Visual Literacy Association. (ERIC Document Reproduction Service No. ED 311 865.)

— (1994) Using symbols in business presentations: how well are they understood? *In* D.G. Beauchamp, R.A. Braden &

J.C. Baca, eds. *Visual literacy in the digital age.* Blacksburg, VA: The International Visual Literacy Association. (ERIC Document Reproduction Service No. ED 370 602.)

— & Gibbs, W.J. (1993). International icon symbols: how well are these symbols understood? *In* R.A. Braden, J.C. Baca & D.G. Beauchamp, eds. *Art, science & visual literacy.* Blacksburg, VA: International Visual Literacy Association. (ERIC Document Reproduction Service No. ED 363 280.)

—, Petterson, R., Semali, L. & Takakuwu, Y. (1995). Using symbols in international business presentations. *In* D.G. Beauchamp, R.A. Braden & R.E. Griffin, eds. *Imagery and visual literacy.* Blacksburg, VA: International Visual Literacy Association.

Haber, R.N. (1970). How we remember what we see. *Scientific American 222* (5), 104–12.

— & Haber L.R. (1981). Visual components of the reading process. *Visual Language 15* (2).

Hannafin, M.J. & Hooper, S. (1989). An integrated framework for CBI screen design and layout. *Computers in Human Behavior 5,* 155–65.

Hansen, J. (1987). *Understanding video.* Newbury Park, CA: Sage.

Haring, M.J. & Fry, M.A. (1979). Effect of pictures on children's comprehension of written text. *Educational Communication and Technology Journal 27* (3), 185–90.

Hartley, J. (1978). *Designing instructional text.* London: Kogan Page.

— (1985). *Designing instructional text, 2d ed.* New York: Nichols.

— (1987). Designing electronic text: the role of print-based research. *Educational Communications and Technology Journal 35* (1), 3–17.

Hefzallah, I.M. (1986). The why of studying critical viewing. *International Journal of Instructional Media 13,* 93-103.

— (1987). *Critical viewing of television.* Lanham, MD: University Press of America.

Hennis, R.S. (1981). Needed: research in the visual language. *English Journal 70* (1), 79–82.

Herbener, G.F., Van Tubergen, G.N. & Whitlow, S.S. (1979). Dynamics of the frame in visual composition. *Educational Communication and Technology Journal 27* (2), 83–88.

Higgins, L.C. (1978). A factor analysis study of children's picture interpretation behavior. *Educational Communication and Technology Journal 26* (3), 215–32.

— (1979). Effects of strategy-oriented training on children's inference drawing from pictures. *Educational Communication and Technology Journal 27* (4), 281–90.

— (1980). Literalism in the young child's interpretation of pictures. *Educational Communication and Technology Journal 28* (2), 99–119.

Hocking, F.O. (1978). *A nationwide survey to determine visual literacy goals, constraints and factors influencing their selection.* Doctoral dissertation, University of Colorado. *Dissertation Abstracts International 39,* 2669A. (University Microfilm No. 78-20520.)

Holliday, W.G., Brunner, L.L & Donais, E.L. (1977). Differential cognitive and affective responses to flow diagrams in science. *Journal of Research in Science Teaching 14,* 129–38.

Hooper, S. & Hannafin, M.J. (1986). Variables affecting the legibility of computer generated text. *Journal of Instructional Development 9* (4), 22–28.

— & — (1988). Learning the ROPES of instructional design: Guidelines for emerging interactive technologies. *Educa-*

tional Technology 28 (7), 14–18.

Hortin, J.A. (1980a). Visual literacy—the theoretical foundations: an investigation of the research, practices, and theories. Doctoral dissertation, Northern Illinois University. *Dissertation Abstracts International,* 1981 (University Microfilms No. 81-11564).

— (1980b). Symbol systems and mental skills research: their emphasis and future. *Media Adult Learning 2* (2), 3–6.

— (1982a). Experimental phenomenology and visual literacy. *In* R.A. Braden & A.D. Walker, eds. *Television and visual literacy.* Bloomington, IN: International Visual Literacy Association. (ERIC Document Reproduction Service No. ED 228 980.)

— (1982b). Introspection and visual thinking for instructional technology. *Educational Technology 13,* 6.

— (1983). Imagery in our daily lives. *In* R.A. Braden & A.D. Walker, eds. *Seeing ourselves: visualization in a social context.* Blacksburg, VA: International Visual Literacy Association. (ERIC Document Reproduction Service No. ED 233 677.)

— (1984). Mental imagery and participatory instructional design. *In* A.D. Walker, R.A. Braden & L.H. Dunker, eds. *Visual literacy—Enhancing human potential.* Blacksburg, VA: International Visual Literacy Association (ERIC Document Reproduction Service No. ED 246 843.)

— (1985). Research on internal and external imagery for problem solving. *In* N.J. Thayer & S. Clayton-Randolph, eds. Bloomington, IN: International Visual Literacy Association.

— (1994). Perceptual, historical, and theoretical foundations of visual learning. *In* D.M. Moore & F.M. Dwyer, eds. *Visual literacy: a spectrum of visual learning.* Englewood Cliffs, NJ: Educational Technology.

— & Bailey, G.D. (1983). Visualization: theory and applications for teacher. *Reading Improvement 20* (1), 70–74.

Houghton, H.A. & Willows, D.M., eds. (1987). *The psychology of illustration, Vol. 2: instructional issues.* New York: Springer.

Hurt, J.A. (1987). Assessing functional effectiveness of pictorial representations used in text. *Educational Communication and Technology Journal 35* (2), 85–94.

Johnson, B.D. (1977). Visual literacy, media literacy, and mass communications for English instruction. Doctoral dissertation, Northwestern University. *Dissertation Abstracts International,* 1977, 38, 6581A. (University Microfilms No. 78-5287.)

Johnson, D.D., Toms-Bronowski, S. & Pittleman, S.D. (1982). *An investigation of the effectiveness of semantic mapping and semantic feature analysis with intermediate-grade-level children.* Madison, WI: Wisconsin Center for Educational Research.

Jonassen, D.H. (1979). Implications of multi-image for concept acquisition. *Educational Communication and Technology Journal 27* (4), 291–302.

—, ed. (1982). *The technology of text: principles for structuring, designing, and displaying text.* Englewood Cliffs, NJ: Educational Technology.

Jonassen, D.H., ed. (1985). The technology of text: principles for structuring, designing, and displaying text, Vol. 2. Englewood Cliffs, NJ: Educational Technology.

—, Beissner, K. & Yacci, M. (1993). *Structural knowledge: techniques for representing, conveying, and acquiring structural knowledge.* Hillsdale, NJ: Erlbaum.

— & Grabowski, B.L. (1993) *Handbook of individual differences, learning , and instruction.* Hillsdale, NJ: Erlbaum.

— & Fork, D.J. (1975). Visual literacy: a bibliographic survey. Paper presented at the Pennsylvania Learning Resources Association Annual conference, Hershey, PA. (ERIC Document Reproduction Service No. ED 131 837.)

— & — (1978). A constructive view of visual learning. *In* D.J. Fork & J.J. Newhouse, eds. Exploration and interpretation: theoretical approaches to the study of visual literacy and visual learning. Philadelphia, PA: International Visual Literacy Association.

Jones, M.G. (1995). Visuals for information access: a new philosophy for screen and interface design. *In* D.G. Beauchamp, R.A. Braden & R.E. Griffin, eds. *Imagery and visual literacy.* Blacksburg, VA: International Visual Literacy Association.

Kaha, C.W. (1993). Towards a syntax of motion. *Critical Studies in Mass Communication 10,* 339–48.

King, W. (1975). *A comparison of three combinations of text and graphics for concept learning.* San Diego, CA: Navy Personnel and Research Development Center. (ERIC Document Reproduction Service No. ED 112 936.)

— (1990). A comparison of three combinations of text and graphics for concept learning. (ERIC Document Reproduction Service No. ED 112 936.)

Kipper, P. (1986). Television camera movement as a source of perceptual information. *Journal of Broadcasting and Electronic Media 30,* 215–397.

Kirby, J., Moore, P. & Shofield, N. (1988). Verbal and visual learning styles, *Contemporary Educational Psychology 13,* 169–84.

Kosslyn, S.M. (1980). *Images and mind.* Cambridge, MA: Harvard University Press.

— & Pomerantz, J.(1977). Imagery, propositions, and the form of internal representations. *Cognitive Psychology 9,* 52–76.

Knowlton, J.Q. (1966). On the definition of "picture." *Audiovisual Communication Review 14,* 157–83.

Lacy, L. (1987). An interdisciplinary approach for students K-12 using visuals of all kinds. *In* R.A. Braden, D.G. Beauchamp & L.W. Miller, eds. *Visible & viable: the role of images in instruction and communication.* Commerce, TX: International Visual Literacy Association, 45-50. (ERIC Document Reproduction Service No. ED 352 931.)

— (1989). Look, think, act: Minneapolis Public Schools program in visual education. *In* R.A. Braden, D.G. Beauchamp & L.W. Miller, eds. *About visuals: research, teaching, and applications.* Blacksburg, VA: International Visual Literacy Association. (ERIC Document Reproduction Service No. ED 311 865.)

Lamberski, R.J. (1976). Visual literacy: emerging and diverging points of view. *AECT Research and Theory Newsletter 5* (3), 1 (visual literacy issue).

Lesgold, A.M., McCormick, C. & Golinkoff, R.M. (1975). Imagery training and children's prose learning. *Journal of Educational Psychology 67,* 663–67.

Levie, W.H. (1978). A prospectus for instructional research on visual literacy. *Educational Communications and Technology Journal 26* (1), 25–36.

— (1987). Research on pictures: a guide to the literature. *In* D.M. Willows & H.A. Houghton, eds. *The psychology of illustration, Vol. 1: basic research.* New York, Berlin, Heidelberg, London, Paris, Tokyo: Springer.

— & Lentz, R. (1982). Effects of text illustrations: a review of research. *Educational Communication and Technology Journal 30,* 195–232.

— & Levie, D. (1975). Pictorial memory processes. *AV Communication Review 23* (1), 81–95.

Levin, J.R. (1973). Inducing comprehension in poor readers: a test of a recent model. *Journal of Educational Psychology 65,* 19–24.

— (1981). On functions of pictures in prose. *In* F.J. Pirozzolo & M.C. Whittrock, eds. *Neuropsychological and cognitive processes in reading.* New York: Academic.

—, Anglin, G.J. & Carney, R.N. (1987) On empirically validating functions of pictures in prose. *In* D.M. Willows & H.A. Houghton. *The psychology of illustration, Vol. 1: basic research.* New York: Springer.

— & Berry, J.K. (1980). Children's learning of all the news that's fit to picture. *Educational Communication and Technology Journal 28* (3), 177–85.

—, Divine-Hawkins, P., Kerst, S. & Guttman, J. (1974). Individual differences in learning from pictures and words: the development and application of an instrument. *Journal of Educational Psychology 66,* 296–303.

— & Lesgold, A.M. (1978). On pictures in prose. *Educational Communication and Technology Journal 26* (3), 233–43.

—, Morrison, C.R., McGivern, J.E., Mastropieri, M.A. & Scruggs, T.E. (1986). Mnemonic facilitation of text-embedded science facts. *American Educational Research Journal 23,* 489–506.

—, Shriberg, L.K., Miller, G.E., McCormick, C.B. & Levin, B.B. (1980). The keyword method as applied to elementary school children's social studies content. *Elementary School Journal 80,*185–91.

Levin, M.E. & Levin, J.R. (1990). Scientific mnemonomies: methods for maximizing more than memory. *American Educational Research Journal 27* (2), 301–21.

—, Rosencheck, M.B. & Levin, J.R. (1988). Mnemonic text processing strategies. *Reading Psychology 9,* 343–63.

Lieberman, D. (n.d.). *Trainer's manual: critical T.V. viewing workshops, Vol. 1.* San Francisco, CA: Far West Laboratory.

Lloyd-Kolkin, D. (1982). Teaching students to become television viewers. *Journal of Educational Television 8,* 99–108.

Macdonald-Ross, M. (1977a). Graphics in text. *In* L.S. Shulman,, ed. *Review of research in education.* Itasca, IL: Peacock.

— (1977b). How numbers are shown: a review of research on the presentation of quantitative data in texts. *AV Communication Review 25,* 359–410.

— (1979). Scientific diagrams and the generation of plausible hypotheses: an essay in the history of ideas. *Instructional Science 8,* 223–34.

Mackett-Stout, J. & Dewar, R. (1981) Evaluation of symbolic public information signs. *Human Factors 23,* 139–51.

Mayer, R.E. (1987). Instructional variables that influence cognitive processing during reading. *In* B.K. Britton & S. Glynn, eds. *Executive control process in reading.* Hillsdale, NJ: Erlbaum.

— (1989). Systematic thinking fostered by illustrations in scientific text. *Journal of Educational Psychology 81* (2), 240–46.

— & Anderson, R.B. (1991). Animations need narrations: an experimental test of a dual-coding hypothesis. *Journal of Educational Psychology 83* (4), 484–90.

— & Gallini, J.K. (1990). When is an illustration worth ten thousand words? *Journal of Educational Psychology 82* (6), 715–26.

Mays, J.T., Kibby, M.R. & Watson, H. (1988). The development and evaluation of a learning-by-browsing system on the Macintosh. *Computers in Education 12* (1), 221–29.

McCain, T.A., Chilberg, J. & Wakshlag, J. (1977). The effect of cameral angle on source credibility and attraction. *Journal of Broadcasting 17,* 35–46.

McKenzie, D.L. & Padilla, M.J. (1984). *Effects of laboratory activities and written simulations on the acquisition of graphing skills by eight-grade students.* National Association for Research in Science Teaching, New Orleans, LA. (ERIC Document Reproduction Service No. ED 244 780.)

McKim, R.H. (1972). *Experiences in visual thinking.* Monterey, CA: Brooks/Cole.

McLean, R. (1980). *The Thames and Hudson manual of typography.* New York: Thames & Hudson.

Messaris, P. (1994). *Visual literacy: image, mind, and reality.* Boulder, CO: Westview.

Metallinos, N. (1982). Children's perception, retention and preference of asymmetrical composition in pictures. *In* R.A. Braden & A.D. Walker, eds. *Television and visual literacy.* Bloomington, IN: Indiana University. 33-44. (ERIC Document Reproduction Service No. ED 233 677.)

— (1992). Perceptual factors in the study of television aesthetics. *In* J.C. Baca, D.G. Beauchamp & R.A. Braden, eds. *Visual communications: bridging across cultures.* Blacksburg, VA: International Visual Literacy Association. (ERIC Document Reproduction Service No. ED 352 932.)

—, ed. (1994). *Verbo-visual literacy: understanding and applying new educational communication media technologies.* Montreal: 3Dmt Research and Information Center.

— (1995a). Approaches to visual communication media criticism and their application to television genres. *In* D.G. Beauchamp, R.A. Braden & R.E. Griffin, eds. *Imagery and visual literacy.* Blacksburg, VA: International Visual Literacy Association.

— (1995b). The syntax of moving images: principles and applications. *In* D.G. Beauchamp, R.A. Braden & R.E. Griffin, eds. *Imagery and visual literacy.* Blacksburg, VA: International Visual Literacy Association.

— & Tiemens, R.K. (1977). Asymmetry of the screen: the effect of left versus right placement of television images. *Journal of Broadcasting 21* (1).

Metz, C. (1974). *Language and cinema.* The Hague: Mouton.

Miller, H.B. & Burton, J.K. (1994). Images and imagery theory. *In* D.M. Moore & F.M. Dwyer, eds. *Visual literacy: a spectrum of visual learning.* Englewood Cliffs, NJ: Educational Technology.

Miller, L.W., ed. (1986). *Creating meaning.* Silver Spring, MD: International Visual Literacy Association.

Misanchuk, E.R. (1992). *Preparing instructional text: document design using desktop publishing.* Englewood Cliffs, NJ: Educational Technology.

Mokros, J.R. & Tinker, R.F. (1987). The impact of microcomputer-based labs on children's ability to interpret graphs. *Journal of Research in Science Teaching 24,* 369–83.

Monoco, J. (1981). *How to read a film: the art, technology, language, history, and theory of film media* (rev. ed.). New York: Oxford University Press.

Moore, D.M. (1986). Effects of field dependence-independence on size and type of visuals. *Journal of Educational Technology Systems 14,* 165–72, 198.

— (1991). Visual attributes and cognitive style: a program of research. *In* D.G. Beauchamp, J.C. Baca & R.A. Braden, eds. *Investigating visual literacy.* Blacksburg, VA: International Visual Literacy Association. (ERIC Document Reproduction No. ED 352 051.)

— & Bedient, D. (1986). Effects of presentation mode and visual characteristics on cognitive style. *Journal of Instructional Psychology 13,* 19–24.

— & Dwyer, F.M. (1991). Effect of color coded information on students' levels of field dependence. *Perceptual and Motor Skills 72,* 611–16.

— & Dwyer, F.M., eds. (1994). *Visual literacy: a spectrum of visual learning.* Englewood Cliffs, NJ: Educational Technology.

— & Readance, J.E. (1982). A meta-analysis of the effect of graphic organizers on learning from text. *In* M.L. Kamil & A.J. Moe, eds. *Perspectives in reading research instruction: Twenty-ninth yearbook of the National Reading Conference.* Milwaukee, WI: National Reading Conference.

— & Readance, J.E. (1984). A quantitative and qualitative review of graphic organizer research. *Journal of Educational Research 78* (1), 11–17.

Moore, M., Norwocki, L. & Simutis, Z. (1979). The instructional effectiveness of three levels of graphics displays for computer-assisted instruction. (ERIC Document Reproduction Service No. Ed 178 057.)

Moriarty, S.E. (1995, Oct.). Defining visual communication: mapping the field. Paper presented at the annual conference of the International Visual Literacy Association. Chicago, IL.

Moxley, R. (1983). Educational diagrams. *Instructional Science 12,* 147–60.

Moyer, J.C., Sowder, L., Threadgill-Sowder & Moyer, M.B. (1984). Story problem formats: drawn versus verbal versus telegraphic. *Journal of Research in Mathematics Education 15,* 342–51.

Muffoletto, R. (1982). The reading of pictures: a consideration for developing a critical model. *In* R.A. Braden & A.D. Walker, eds. *Television and visual literacy,* 147–56. Bloomington, IN: Indiana University.

Mulcahy, P. & Samuels, J.S. (1987). Three hundred years of illustrations in American textbooks. *In* H.A. Houghton & D.M. Willows, eds. *The psychology of illustrations, Vol. 2: instructional issues,* 1–52. New York: Springer.

Neisser, U. (1976). *Cognition and reality.* San Francisco, CA: Freeman.

Paivio, A. (1963). Learning of adjective-noun paired associates as a function of adjective-noun word order and noun abstractness. *Canadian Journal of Psychology 17,* 370–79.

— (1965). Abstractness, imagery, and meaningfulness in paired-associate learning. *Journal of Verbal Learning and Verbal Behavior 4,* 32–38.

— (1971). *Imagery and verbal processes.* New York: Holt, Rinehart & Winston.

— (1975). Perceptual comparisons through the mind's eye. *Memory and Cognition 3* (6), 635–47.

— (1983). The empirical case for dual coding. *In* J.C. Yuille, ed. *Imagery, memory, and cognition.* Hillsdale, NJ: Erlbaum.

— (1991). Dual coding theory: retrospect and current status. *Canadian Journal of Psychology 45* (3), 255–87.

— & Foth (1970). Imaginal and verbal mediators and noun concreteness in paired-associate learning: the elusive interaction. *Journal of Verbal Learning and Verbal Behavior 9,* 384–90.

Paris, S.G., Mahoney, G.J. & Buckhalt, J.A. (1974). Facilitation of semantic integration in sentence memory of retarded children. *American Journal of Mental Deficiency 78,* 714–20.

Peek, J. (1974). Retention of pictorial and verbal content of a text with illustrations. *Journal of Educational Psychology 66,* 880–88.

— (1987). The role of illustrations in processing and remembering illustrated text. *In* D.M. Willows & H.A. Houghton. *The psychology of illustration, Vol. 1: basic research.* New York: Springer.

Peng, C.Y. & Levin, J.R. (1979). Pictures and children's story recall: some questions of durability. *Educational Communication and Technology Journal 27* (1), 39–44.

Perrin, D.G. A theory of multiple-image communication. *AV Communication Review 17* (4), 368–82.

Pett, D. (1994). White letters on colored backgrounds: legibility and preference. *In* D.G. Beauchamp, R.A. Braden & J.C. Baca, eds. *Visual literacy in the digital age.* Blacksburg, VA: International Visual Literacy Association.

Pettersson, R. (1984). Picture legibility, readability, and reading value. *In* A.D. Walker, R.A. Braden & L.H. Dunker, eds. *Visual literacy: enhancing human potential.* Blacksburg, VA: The International Visual Literacy Association.

Pettersson, R. (1987). Image-word-image. *In* R.A. Braden, D.G. Beauchamp & L.W. Miller, eds. *Visible and viable: the role of images in instruction and communication.* Commerce, TX: International Visual Literacy Association.

— (1989). *Visuals for information, research and practice.* Englewood Cliffs, NJ: Educational Technology.

— (1993). *Visuals for information, research and practice, 2d ed.* Englewood Cliffs, NJ: Educational Technology.

Pressley, G.M., (1976). Mental imagery helps eight-year-olds remember what they read. *Journal of Educational Psychology 68* (3), 355–59

— (1977). Imagery and children's learning: putting the picture in developmental perspective. *Review of Educational Research 47,* 585–622

Pressley, M. & Levin, J.R. (1978) Learning via mnemonic pictures: analysis of the presidential process. *Educational Communication and Technology Journal 31* (3), 161–17.

— & Levin, J.R. (1981). The keyword method and recall of vocabulary words from definitions. *Journal of Experimental Psychology: Human Learning and Memory 7,* 72–76.

—, — & Delaney, H.D. (1982). The mnemonic keyword method. *Review of Educational Research 52* (1), 61–91.

—, —, Piggott, S., LeComte, M. & Hope, D.J. (1983). Mismatched pictures and children's prose learning. *Educational Communication and Technology Journal 31* (3), 131–43.

— & Miller, G.E. (1987). Effects of Children's listening comprehension and oral prose memory. *In* Willows & Houghton. *The psychology of illustration, Vol. 1: basic research.* New York: Springer.

Pruisner, P.A. (1992). The effects of a color code in graphic presentation and assessment on remembering visual material. *In* J.C. Baca, D.G. Beauchamp & R.A. Braden, eds. *Visual communications: bridging across cultures.* Blacksburg, VA: International Visual Literacy Association.

— (1993). The effect of color code used in graphics on the recall of verbal material. *In* R.A. Braden, J.C. Baca & D.G. Beauchamp, eds. *Art, science & visual literacy.* Blacksburg, VA: International Visual Literacy Association.

— (1994). From color code to color cue: remembering graphic information. *In* D.G. Beauchamp, R.A. Braden & J.C. Baca, eds. *Visual literacy in the digital age.* Blacksburg, VA: International Visual Literacy Association.

Pryluck, C. & Snow, R.E., (1975). Toward a psycholinguistics of cinema. *AV Communication Review 15,* 54–75.

Pylyshyn, Z. (1973). What the mind's eye tells the mind's

brain. *Psychological Bulletin 80,* 1–22.

— (1981). The imagery debate: analogue media versus tacit knowledge. *Psychological Review 88,* 16–45.

Rabinowitz, M. & Mandler, J.M. (1983). Organization and information retrieval. *Journal of Experimental Psychology: Learning, Memory, and Cognition 9,* 430–39.

Ragan, T.J. (1977). Visual literacy and the brain. (ERIC Document Reproduction No. ED 180 439.)

— (1978). Insights on visual capacities from perceptual and cognitive styles. (ERIC Document Reproduction Service No. ED 179 228.)

Ramsey, I.L. (1989a). Primary children's ability to distinguish between illustration styles. *Journal of Visual Literacy 9* (2), 69–82.

— (1989b). Children's responses to selected art styles. *Journal of Educational Research 83* (1), 46–52.

Randhawa, B.S., Back, K.T. & Meyers, P.J. (1977, Apr.). Visual learning. Paper presented at the annual convention of the Association for Educational Communication and Technology. (ERIC Document Reproduction Service No. ED 143 319.)

Reiber, L.P. (1989). The effects of computer animated elaboration strategies and practice on factual and application learning in an elementary science lesson. *Journal of Educational Computing Research 54* (4), 431–44.

— (1990a). Animation in computer-based instruction. *Educational Technology Research and Development 38* (1), 77–86.

— (1990b). Using animation in science instruction with young children. *Journal of Educational Psychology 82* (1), 135–40.

— (1991a). Effects of visual grouping strategies of computer animated presentations on selective attention in science. *Educational Technology Research and Development 39* (4), 5–15.

— (1991b). Computer animation, incidental learning, and continuing motivation. *Journal of Educational Psychology 83* (3), 318–28.

— (1994). *Computers, graphics, & learning.* Dubuque, IA: Brown & Benchmark.

—, Boyce, M. & Assad, C. (1990). The effects of computer animation on adult learning and retrieval tasks. *Journal of Computer-Based Instruction 17* (2), 46–52.

— & Hannifin, M. (1988). The effects of textual and animated orienting activities and practice on learning from computer-based instruction. *Computers in the Schools 5* (1/2), 77–89.

— & Kini, A. (1991). Theoretical foundations of instructional applications of computer-generated animated visuals. *Journal of Computer-Based Instruction 18* (3), 83–88.

Richardson, A. (1977). Verbalizer—visualizer: a cognitive style dimension. *Journal of Mental Imagery 1,* 109–26.

Riding, R.J. & Burt, J.M. (1982). Reading versus listening in children: the effects of extraversion and coding complexity. *Educational Psychology 2,* 47–58.

Rigney, J. & Lutz, K. (1975). The effects of interactive graphic analogies on recall of concepts in chemistry. (ERIC Document Reproduction Service No. ED 109 639.)

Rohwer, W.D., Jr. (1970). Images and pictures in children's learning: research results and educational implications. *Psychological Bulletin 73,* 393–403.

Rohwer, W.D. & Harris, W.J. (1975). Media effects on prose learning in two populations of children. *Journal of Educa-*

tional Psychology 67 (5), 651–57.

Romiszowski, A.J. (1994). Educational systems design implications of electronic publishing. *Educational Technology 34* (7), 6–12.

Rosencheck, M.B., Levin, M.E. & Levin, J.R. (1989). Learning botany concepts mnemonically: seeing the forest and the trees. *Journal of Educational Psychology 81,* 196–203.

Roupas, T.G. (1977). Information and pictorial representation. *In* D. Perkins & B. Leondar, eds. *The arts and cognition.* Baltimore, MD: Johns Hopkins University Press.

Salomon, G. (1972). Can we affect cognitive skills through visual media? *AV Communication Review 20* (4), 401–23.

— (1979a). Media and symbol systems as related to cognition and learning. *Journal of Educational Psychology 71,* 131–48.

— (1979b, reprinted 1994). *Interaction of media, cognition and learning: an exploration of how symbolic forms cultivate mental skills and affect knowledge acquisition.* San Francisco, CA: Jossey-Bass.

— (1982). Television literacy and television vs. literacy. *Journal of Visual/Verbal Literacy 2* (2), 7–16.

— (1983). Television watching and mental effort: a social psychological view. *In* J. Bryant & D.R. Anderson, eds. *Children's understanding of television.* New York: Academic.

— (1984). Television is "easy" and print is "tough": the differential investment of mental effort in learning as a function of perceptions and attributions. *Journal of Educational Psychology 76,* 647–58.

Samuels, J.J. (1967). Attentional process in reading: the effect of pictures on the acquisition of reading responses. *Journal of Educational Psychology 58* (6), 337–42.

— (1970). Effects of pictures on learning to read, comprehension and attitudes. *Journal of Educational Research 40* (3), 397–407.

Saunders, A.C. (1994). Graphics and how they communicate. *In* D.M. Moore & F.M. Dwyer, eds. *Visual literacy: a spectrum of visual learning.* Englewood Cliffs, NJ: Educational Technology.

Seels, B.A. (1994). Visual literacy: the definition problem. *In* D.M. Moore & F.M. Dwyer, eds. *Visual Literacy: a spectrum of visual learning.* Englewood Cliffs, NJ: Educational Technology.

Sewell, E.H., Jr. (1994). Visual symbols. *In* D.M. Moore & F.M. Dwyer, eds. *Visual literacy: a spectrum of visual learning.* Englewood Cliffs, NJ: Educational Technology.

Shepard, R. (1978). The mental image. *American Psychologist 33,* 125–37.

Siegler, R. (1980). Masquage: an extrapolation of Eisenstein's theory of montage-as-conflict to the multi-image film. *In* K. Burke, ed. *An anthology of multi-image.* Abington, PA: Association of Multi-Image.

Siemankowski, F.T. & MacKnight, F.C. (1971). Spatial cognition: success prognostication in college science courses. *Journal of College Science Teaching 1,* 56–59.

Simon, H.A. (1972). What is visual imagery? An information-processing interpretation. *In* L.W. Gregg, ed. *Cognition in learning and memory.* New York: Wiley.

Sinatra, R. (1984). Visual/spatial strategies for writing and reading improvement. *In* A.D. Walker & R.A. Braden, eds. *Visual literacy: enhancing human potential.* Blacksburg, VA: International Visual Literacy Association. (ERIC Document Reproduction Service No. ED 246 843.)

— (1986a). *Visual literacy connections to thinking, reading, and writing.* Springfield, IL: Thomas.

— (1986b). Effects of visual ordering on the writing process. *In* N.J. Thayer & S. Clayton-Randolph, eds. *Visual literacy: cruising into the future.* Bloomington, IN: International Visual Literacy Association.

— (1988). Use of graphics to conceptualize meaning in language arts CAI. *In* R.A. Braden, B.D. Braden, D.G. Beauchamp & L.W. Miller, eds. *Visual literacy in life and learning.* Blacksburg, VA: International Visual Literacy Association.

—, Stahl-Gemake, J. & Berg, D. (1984). Improving reading comprehension of disabled readers through semantic mapping. *The Reading Teacher 38,* 22–29.

—, Berg, D. & Dunn, R. (1985). Semantic mapping improves reading comprehension of learning disabled students. *Teaching Exceptional Children 17,* 310–14.

Smith, A.L. (1978). The structured overview: a pre-reading strategy. *In* J.L. Vaughn, Jr. & P.J. Gaus, eds. *Research on reading in secondary schools, Vol. 2.* Tucson, AZ: University of Arizona, Reading Department.

Solomon, J. (1988). *The signs of our time: semiotics, the hidden messages of environment.* Los Angeles, CA: Tarcher.

Sonderston, C. (1983). An evaluative and prescriptive look at graphic research. (ERIC Document Reproduction Service No, ED 261 385.)

Sperry, R.W. (1973). Lateral specialization of cerebral function in the surgically separated hemispheres. *In* F.J. McGuigan, ed. *The psychophysiology of thinking.* New York: Academic.

Spitzer, D.R. & McNerny, T.O. (1975). Operationally defining "visual literacy": a research challenge. *Audiovisual Instruction 20* (7), 30–31.

Stewig, J.W. (1989). Reading pictures. *Journal of Visual Literacy 9* (1), 70–82.

Streibel, M.J. (1980). The role of stimulus size on performance in the embedded-figures-test and in the rod-and-frame test and the implications of this role for the field-dependence-independence construct. Unpublished doctoral dissertation, The University of Wisconsin-Madison.

Sucy, J. (1985). Why do visual literacy projects fail? *In* N.J. Thayer & S. Clayton-Randolph, eds. *Visual literacy: cruising into the future,* 149–55. Bloomington, IN: International Visual Literacy Association.

Sutton, R.E. (1987). Watch: critical viewing guide for children. *In* R.A. Braden, D.G. Beauchamp & L.W. Miller, eds. *Visible & viable: the role of images in instruction and communication,* 51–54. Commerce, TX: International Visual Literacy Association.

Szabo, M., Dwyer, F.M. & DeMelo, H. (1981). Visual testing: visual literacy's second dimension. *Educational Communication and Technology Journal 29* (3), 177–87.

Talley, L.H. (1973). The use of three-dimensional visualization as a moderator in the higher cognitive learning of concepts in college level chemistry. *Journal of Research in Science Teaching 10,* 263–69.

Thayer, N.J. & Clayton-Randolph, S. (1985). *Visual literacy: cruising into the future.* Bloomington, IN: International Visual Literacy Association.

Tierney, study cited in Whiteside, 1987.

Toler, study cited in Whiteside, 1987.

Torres-Rodriquez, J. & Dwyer, F.M. (1991). The effect of time on the instructional effectiveness of varied visual enhancement strategies. *International Journal of Instructional*

Media 18 (1), 85–93.

Tripp, S.D. & Roby, W. (1990) Orientation and disorientation in a hypertext lexicon. *Journal of Computer-Based Instruction 17* (4), 120–24.

Tufte, E.R. (1983). *The visual display of quantitative information.* Cheshire, CT: Graphics.

— (1990). *Envisioning information.* Cheshire, CT: Graphics.

Turbayne, C.M. (1962). *The myth of metaphor.* New Haven, CT: Yale University Press.

Turbayne, C.M. (1969). Visual language from the verbal model. *The Journal of Typographic Research III* (4), 345–70.

— (1970a). *The myth of metaphor* (rev. ed.). Charleston, SC: University of South Carolina Press.

— (1970b). The syntax of visual language. *In* C.M. Williams & J.L. Debes, eds. *Proceedings of the first national conference on visual literacy.* New York: Pitman.

Walker, A.D., Braden, R.A. & Dunker, L.H., eds. (1984). *Visual literacy: enhancing human potential.* Blacksburg, VA: International Visual Literacy Association.

— (1990). Examining visual literacy, 1983–1989: a seven-year IVLA bibliography. *In* R.A. Braden, D.G. Beauchamp & J.C. Baca, eds. *Perceptions of visual literacy,* 131–60. Conway, AR: International Visual Literacy Association.

— (1994). International Visual Literacy Association. Readings Bibliography: 1990–1993. *In* D.G. Beauchamp, R.A. Braden & J.C. Baca, eds. *Visual literacy in the digital age.* Blacksburg, VA: International Visual Literacy Association.

Waller, R.H. (1979). Typographical access structures for education text. *In* P.A. Kolers, M.E. Wrolstad & H. Bouma. *Processing of visible language, Vol. 1.* New York: Plenum.

Watkins, L.T., Sprafkin, J., Gadow, K.D. & Sadetsky, I. (1988). Effects of a critical viewing skills curriculum on elementary school children's knowledge and attitudes about television. *Journal of Educational Research 81,* 165–70.

Wendt, P.R. (1962). The language of pictures. *In* S.I. Hayakawa, ed. *The use and misuse of language,* 175–83. Greenwich, CT: Fawcett.

White, N. (1980). *Inside television: a guide to critical viewing.* Palo Alto, CA: Science & Behavior.

Whiteside, H.C. (1987). Can multi-image presentations be affective and effective in education? *In* R.A. Braden, D.G. Beauchamp & L.W. Miller, eds. *Visible and viable: the role of images in instruction and communication.* Commerce, TX: International Visual Literacy Association.

Whiteside, A.J. & Whiteside, M.F. (1988). Case for "organizing word-visuals" to facilitate recall from text-based materials. *Reading Psychology 9,* 323–42.

Wileman, R.E. (1980). *Exercises in visual thinking.* New York: Hastings.

— (1993). *Visual communicating.* Englewood Cliffs, NJ: Educational Technology.

Wilde, J. & Wilde, R. (1991). *Visual literacy: a conceptual approach to solving graphic problems.* New York: Watson-Guptell.

Willows, D.M. (1978). A picture is not always worth a thousand words: pictures as distractors in reading. *Journal of Educational Psychology 70,* 255–62.

— (1979). Reading between the lines: selective attention in good and poor readers. *Child Development 45,* 408–15.

— & Houghton, H.A. (1987). *The psychology of illustration, Vol. 1: basic research.* New York: Springer.

Winn, W.D. (1980). The effect of block-word diagrams on the

structuring of science concepts as a function of general ability. *Journal of Research in Science Teaching 17,* 201–11.

— (1981). The effect of attribute highlighting and spatial organization on identification and classification. *Journal of Research in Science Teaching 18,* 23–32.

— (1982a). Visualization in learning and instruction: a cognitive approach. *Educational Communication and Technology Journal 30* (1), 3–25.

— (1982b). The role of diagrammatic representation in learning sequences, identification and classification as a function of verbal and spatial ability. *Journal of Research in Science Teaching 19,* 79–89.

— (1983). Perceptual strategies used with flow diagrams having normal and unanticipated formats. *Perceptual and Motor Skills 57,* 751–62.

— (1986). Knowledge of task, ability and strategy in the processing of letter patterns. *Perceptual and Motor Skills 63,* 726.

— (1987). Charts, graphs, and diagrams in educational materials. (Chap. 5). *In* D.M. Willows & H.A. Houghton, eds. *The psychology of illustration, Vol. 1: basic research.* New York: Springer.

— (1993). Perception principles. *In* M. Fleming & W.H. Levie, eds. *Instructional message design: principles from the behavioral and cognitive sciences, 2d ed.* Englewood Cliffs, NJ: Educational Technolgy.

— & Holliday, W.G. (1982). Design principles for diagrams and charts (Chap. 13). *In* D. Jonassen, ed. *The technology of text: principles for structuring, designing, and displaying text.* Englewood Cliffs, NJ: Educational Technology.

Yeaman, A.R.J. (1987). Effective communication and better access: improving the design of library signs. *In* R.A. Braden, D.G. Beauchamp & L.W. Miller, eds. *Visible and viable: the role of images in instruction and communication.* Commerce, TX: International Visual literacy Association. (ERIC Document Reproduction Service No. ED 352 931.)

Zettl, H. (1994). The age of pixels: a call for visual literacy. *In* N. Metallinos, ed. *Verbo-visual literacy: understanding and applying new educational communication media technologies.* Montreal, Canada: 3Dmt Research and Information Center.

17. EDUCATIONAL GAMES AND SIMULATIONS: A TECHNOLOGY IN SEARCH OF A (RESEARCH) PARADIGM

Margaret E. Gredler
UNIVERSITY OF SOUTH CAROLINA

17.1 INTRODUCTION

Educational games and simulations, unlike direct forms of instruction, are experiential exercises. That is, student teams may be racing each other to reach a pot of gold (game), sifting through an archeological site and analyzing the artifacts (simulation), or managing a financial institution for several months (simulation).

Games and simulations entered the broad educational scene in the late 1950s. Until the early 1970s, they were not part of the instructional design movement. Instead, these exercises were primarily developed by business and medical education faculty and sociologists who adapted instructional developments pioneered by the military services. Although popular in the public schools in the 1960s, games and simulations in United States classrooms declined with the advent of the basic-skills movement.

Currently, the increased power and flexibility of computer technology is contributing to renewed interest in games and simulations. This development coincides with the current perspective of effective instruction in which meaningful learning depends on the construction of knowledge by the learner. Games and simulations, which can provide an environment for the learner's construction of new knowledge, have the potential to become a major component of this focus.

The technology, however, faces two major problems at present. One is that comprehensive design paradigms derived from learning principles have not been available. Coupled with the variety of disciplines attempting to develop games and simulations, the result is a variety of truncated exercises often mislabeled as simulations. One study, for example, referred to a static computer graphic of a pegboard as a simulation. Another study that purported to be a simulation of decision making was a series of test questions about different situations in which the student was to assume that he or she was an administrator of special education. A third "simulation" simply provided preservice teachers practice in completing classroom inventory forms, supply requisition forms, and incident reports. These latter two examples are context-based problems, but they are not simulations.

These mislabeled exercises indicated the need for effective design models for games and simulations. Design models are the "soft technologies" that influence and activate the thought processes of the learners rather than the "hard technology" of the computer (Jonassen, 1988). Also, poorly developed exercises are not effective in achieving the objectives for which simulations are most appropriate—that of developing students' problem-solving skills. Finally, poorly developed games and simulations often have negative effects on students, some of which are discussed later in the chapter.

The second major problem for developers and users of games and simulations is the lack of well-designed research studies. Much of the published literature consists of anecdotal reports and testimonials. These discussions typically provide a sketchy description of the game or simulation and report only perceived student reactions.

Further, as indicated by Pierfy (1977), most of the research is flawed by basic weaknesses in both design and measurement. Some studies implemented games or simulations that were brief treatments of 40 minutes or less and assessed effects weeks later on midterm or final examinations. Intervening instruction, however, contaminates the results.

Another major design weakness is that most studies compare simulations to regular classroom instruction (lecture and/or classroom discussion). However, the instructional goals for which each can be most effective often differ. The lecture method is likely to be superior in transmitting items of information. In contrast, simulations have the potential to develop students' mental models of complex situations as well as their problem-solving strategies. Not surprisingly, a meta-analysis of 27 research studies (for the period 1969–1979) that met basic validity and reliability criteria found that simulations were not superior to lecture or discussion on information-oriented posttests (Dekkers & Donatti, 1981).

Among the measurement problems in reported studies is the failure to describe the nature of the posttests used to measure student learning. Some studies use essay questions, while others use some type of instructor-developed test with no reported validity or reliability information. In addition, some researchers provided the simulation group with additional problems to solve or information summaries that the other group did not receive.

Another problem is that comparison studies often are not sensitive to the student characteristics that interact with instruction to influence achievement. One study by Wentworth and Lewis (1973) identified three characteristics that mediated the instructional effects of a commercially developed simulation for junior college students in economics. Formulation of a stepwise regression model to identify the variables that predict achievement indicated that prior knowledge, ability, and the school attended were significant contributors to posttest achievement on a standardized economics test for students in the course-related simulation. In other words, like other forms of instruction, simulations and games are likely to be more effective with some students than with others.

Finally, the classroom research paradigm implemented in the 1960s and 1970s did not document the actual instructional processes associated with an innovation. Instead, the innovation was assumed to differ substantially from typical classroom instruction, and the innovation was compared with traditional practice. Subsequent analyses of the 1970s classroom research has indicated that, in many cases, instruction in the comparison classes shared key characteristics with the innovative classes (see House et al., 1978; Glass, 1979; Hall & Loucks, 1977). The result was a "no significant difference" finding in these comparisons.

Like other classroom research, studies that addressed games and simulations did not document the ways that students interacted with the subject matter and each other during a game or simulation. For example, although simulations are described as enhancing decision making, key questions unasked by the research are: For which student and in what ways? What tradeoffs between increased decision making and information load? And so on. At present, a few studies are beginning to investigate the dynamics of student interactions with games and simulations, and this research and the implications for design are discussed in this chapter.

Given the issues facing the gaming and simulation field, the purpose of this chapter is threefold. The chapter first presents and discusses a definitive framework for games and simulations that addresses the essential features of each type of exercise. Then the chapter discusses the research studies that have implications for instructional design. The chapter concludes with a discussion of recommended guidelines for research on games and simulations.

17.2 A DEFINITIVE FRAMEWORK

Games and simulations are often referred to as *experiential exercises* because they provide unique opportunities for students to interact with a knowledge domain. Two con-

cepts important in the analysis of the nature of games and simulations are surface structure and deep structure. Briefly defined, *surface structure* refers to the paraphernalia and observable mechanics of an exercise (van Ments, 1984). Examples in games are drawing cards, moving pieces around a board, and so on. An essential surface structure component in a simulation, in contrast, is a scenario or set of data to be addressed by the participant.

Deep structure, in contrast, may be defined as the psychological mechanisms operating in the exercise (Gredler, 1990, 1992a). Deep structure refers to the nature of the interactions (1) between the learner and the major tasks in the exercise, and (2) between the students in the exercise. Examples include the extent of student control in the exercise, the learner actions that are rewarded in the exercise or which receive positive feedback, and the complexity of the decision sequence in the exercise (e.g., linear or branching).

17.2.1 Deep-Structure Characteristics

A shared feature of games and simulations is that they transport the players (game) or participants (simulation) to another world. For example, children may be searching for vocabulary clues to capture a wicked wizard (game), and medical students may be diagnosing and treating a comatose emergency room patient (simulation).

Another similarity is that, excluding adaptations of simple games like Bingo, games and simulations are environments in which students are in control of the action. Within the constraints established by the rules, game players plan strategy in order to win, and simulation participants undertake particular roles or tasks in order to manage an evolving situation. Examples of evolving situations are managing a business and designing and managing research projects on generations of genetic traits.

The deep structure of games and simulations, however, varies in three important ways. First, games are competitive exercises in which the objective is to excel by winning. Players compete for points or other advances (such as moving forward on a board) that indicate they are outperforming the other players. In a simulation, however, participants take on either (1) demanding, responsible roles such as concerned citizens, business managers, interplanetary explorers, or physicians, or (2) professional tasks such as exploring the causes of water pollution or operating a complex equipment system. In other words, instead of attempting to win, participants in a simulation for the classroom are executing serious responsibilities, with the associated privileges and consequences. Jones (1984, 1987) refers to this characteristic of simulations as "reality of function."

A second difference is that the event sequence of a game is typically linear, whereas a simulation sequence is nonlinear. The player or team in a game responds to a stimulus, typically a content-related question, and either advances or does not advance, depending on the answer. This sequence is repeated for each player or team at each turn.

In a simulation, however, participants at each decision point face different problems, issues, or events that result in large measure from their prior decisions. In a computer-delivered simulation, this feature is referred to as *branching*.

A third difference between simulations and games is the mechanisms that determine the consequences to be delivered for different actions taken by the students in the exercise. Games consist of rules that describe allowable player moves, game constraints and privileges (such as ways of earning extra turns), and penalties for illegal (nonpermissable) actions. Further, the rules may be imaginative in that they need not relate to real-world events. In contrast, the basis for a simulation is a dynamic set of relationships among several variables that (1) change over time and (2) reflect authentic causal processes (i.e., the relationships must be verifiable). For example, in diagnostic simulations in which the student is managing the treatment of a patient, the patient's symptoms, general health characteristics, and selected treatment, all interact in predictable ways.

In addition to these three general characteristics, particular games and simulations also differ in the tasks established for students and the actions that are rewarded in the exercise. These specific differences are discussed later in the chapter.

17.2.2 Experiential and Symbolic Simulations

The broad category of instructional simulations consists of two principal types. One type, referred to as *experiential simulations,* establishes a particular psychological reality and places the participants in defined roles within that reality. The participants, in the context of their roles, execute their responsibilities in an evolving situation. Experiential simulations, in other words, are dynamic case studies with the participants on the inside (see 23.4.2).

Essential components of an experiential simulation are (1) a scenario of a complex task or problem that unfolds in part in response to learner actions, (2) a serious role taken by the learner in which he or she executes the responsibilities of the position, (3) multiple plausible paths through the experience, and (4) learner control of decision making (see Chapter 33).

Experiential simulations originally were developed to provide learner interactions in situations that are too costly or hazardous to provide in a real-world setting. Increasingly, however, they have begun to fulfill a broader function, that of permitting students to execute multidimensional problem-solving strategies as part of a defined role. The need for such exercises is indicated by several studies. For example, Willems (1981) found that students in law, social geography, science, and sociology often are unable to apply knowledge they had acquired to the task of solving problems. Further, de Mesquita (1992) found that 53% of school psychology students and graduates initially made an incorrect diagnosis in a school-referral problem involving a third-grader.

Experiential simulations are designed to immerse the learner in a complex, evolving situation in which the learner

is one of the functional components. The advent of computer technology, however, made possible the design of a different type of interaction exercise: a symbolic simulation. Briefly, a symbolic simulation is a dynamic representation of the functioning or behavior of some universe, system, set of processes, or phenomena by another system (in this case a computer). The behavior that is being simulated involves the interaction of two or more variables over time.

A key characteristic of symbolic simulations (like experiential simulations) is that they involve the dynamic interactions of two or more variables. An example of a symbolic simulation is a population-ecology simulation with 75 variables that represents global ecological processes for the 200-year period after 1900 (Forrester, 1971; Hinze, 1984). Another is a dynamic computer representation of a complex equipment system. The student, interacting with a symbolic simulation, may be executing any of several tasks, such as troubleshooting equipment or predicting future trends. However, the student remains external to the evolving events. Many computer exercises erroneously labeled as simulations do not meet this criterion, and this shortcoming arises from the misapplication of the term *simulated*. For example, simulated diamonds are imitation diamonds. Extrapolation of this concept to instructional development has led to the erroneous designation of imitations of objects or events as "simulations." An example is a brief Apple II computer program that purports to simulate plant growth. However, the program only presents an outline of a two-leafed plant that shoots up faster, slower, or not at all, depending on whether the student selects "full light," "half light," or "no light." The motion of the stilted graphic is a highly simplistic imitation of plant growth, but it is not a simulation. In other words, an animated graphic of some event is not necessarily a simulation.

Symbolic simulations differ from experiential simulations in two major ways. First, the learner is not a functional element of the situation. Instead, symbolic simulations are populations of events or interacting processes on which the learner may conduct any of several different operations. In other words, the deep structure of symbolic simulations is that the learner manipulates variables that are elements of a particular population. The purpose is to discover scientific relationships or principles, explain or predict events, confront misconceptions, and others. Potential instructional purposes for symbolic simulations are described by Riegeluth and Schwartz (1989) as explanation, prediction, solution, or procedure. Tennyson et al. (1987) differentiate simulations as task oriented or problem oriented.

The second major difference is the mechanisms for reinforcing appropriate student behaviors. The learner in an experiential simulation steps into a scenario in which consequences for his or her actions occur in the form of (1) other participants' actions or (2) changes in (or effects on) the complex problem that the learner is attempting to manage. The learner who is executing random strategies often quickly experiences powerful contingencies for such behavior, from the reactions of other participants to being exited from the simulation for inadvertently "killing" the patient.

The symbolic simulation, however, is a population of events or set of processes external to the learner. That is, there is not an assigned role that establishes a vested interest for the learner in the outcome. Although the learner is expected to interact with the symbolic simulation as a researcher or investigator, the exercise, by its very nature, cannot divert the learner from the use of random strategies.

One solution is to ensure, in prior instruction, that students acquire both the relevant domain knowledge and essential research skills. That is, students should be proficient in developing mental models of complex situations, testing variables systematically, and revising one's mental model where necessary. In this way, students can approach the symbolic simulation equipped to address its complexities, and the possibility of executing random strategies holds little appeal.

Table 17-1 summarizes the primary characteristics of games, experiential simulations, and symbolic simulations. Specific design rules and subtypes are discussed in the following sections.

17.3 ACADEMIC GAMES

As already indicated, games are competitive contests characterized by discrete plays or moves by the players. The objective is to win by any strategy permitted by the rules. Of importance in selecting games for classroom use are particular characteristics of the deep structure of the exercise. First, academic games should not sanction strategies that involve questionable ethics. The deep structure of Monopoly, for example, is such that a player is reinforced by attempting to bankrupt other players. Although an acceptable practice in a parlor game, reinforcing student strategies designed to bankrupt others is not appropriate in the public school classroom.

The deep structure of academic games should meet two requirements. First, chance or random factors should not contribute to winning. For example, some poor examples of computer games purport to develop students' spatial skills. However, they are merely two-dimensional puzzles that may be solved by guessing (Edens & Gredler, 1990).

Second, winning in academic games should depend solely on the application of subject-matter knowledge and/or problem-solving skills. Given this characteristic, games may be used for any of four general purposes in the classroom. They are (1) to practice and/or to refine knowledge/skills already acquired, (2) to identify gaps or weaknesses in knowledge or skills, (3) to serve as a summation or review, and (4) to develop new relationships among concepts and principles.

The academic skills that contribute to challenging classroom games are the intellectual skills (see 18.3.3) identified by Gagné (1977, 1985). They are discriminating, such as matching chemical formulas to names; concept learning, such as classifying paintings into styles or periods; and rule using, such as predicting consequences from events.

TABLE 17-1. PRIMARY CHARACTERISTICS OF GAMES AND SIMULATIONS

	Games	Simulations	
		Experiential	Symbolic
Setting:			
Students are transported to another world or environment	X	X	X
Purpose:			
Competition and winning	X		
Fulfilling a professional role		X	
Executing a professional task			X
Event sequence:			
Typically linear	X		
Nonlinear or branching		X	X
Mechanisms that determine consequences:			
Sets of rules (may be imaginative)	X		
Dynamic set of authentic causal relationships among two or more variables		X	X
Participant is a component of the evolving scenario and executes the responsibilities of his or her role		X	
Participant interacts with a database or sets of processes to discover scientific principles, explain or predict events, and confront misconceptions			X

One key characteristic of games is that, during the exercise, they alter two aspects of the classroom reward structure. They are the frequency of reinforcement and the immediacy of feedback (DeVries & Edwards, 1973). The player or team that successfully responds to the game stimulus, typically an academic question or problem, is reinforced immediately by advancing in the game. The student or team decision that is incorrect receives immediate feedback by not advancing in the exercise.

Manual games are limited in the amount and extent of feedback they can provide for learner actions. The data-processing capability of the computer, however, makes possible the development of sophisticated games in which students apply a broad base of knowledge to solve complex problems. A rare example of this type of game requires the student to apply his or her knowledge of social and economic institutions in 17th-century France to improve the social standing of a Frenchman of that century (Lougee, 1988). At each turn, the student has several options, such as attempting to establish a marriage contract, buying and selling grain, leasing land, and so on. The computer evaluates each choice made by the player and maintains a running score in the form of a social index.

Success in such a game requires players to direct and manage their thinking in an efficient and effective manner. Variables must be noted, likely consequences of actions must be considered in advance, and then a course of action must be developed. These capabilities are of the type referred to by Gagné (1977, 1985) as *cognitive strategies*. Thus, one advantage of computer games is that they have the potential to challenge students' thinking in a variety of ways.

17.4 EXPERIENTIAL SIMULATIONS

Like the player in an academic game, the participant in a simulation also applies a knowledge base. However, the simulation participant is facing a complex situation in which he or she is one of the components. Further, the situation evolves and changes in part in response to the participant's decisions and actions.

Within the category of experiential simulations, exercises may differ in (1) the nature of the participants' roles, (2) the types of decisions and interactions in the exercise, and (3) the nature of the relationships among the variables. That is, experiential simulations may be individual or group exercises, the focus may vary from executing professional expertise to experiencing a different cultural reality, and the relationships among the variables may be quantitative or qualitative. Four major types of experiential simulations are data management, diagnostic, crisis management, and social-process simulations (Gredler, 1992a).

17.4.1 Data Management Simulations

A participant in a data management simulation typically functions as a member of a team of financial managers or planners. Each team that is managing a company or institution allocates economic resources to any of several variables in order to achieve a particular goal. The long-range goal is to improve the status of the institution or company (Gredler, 1992a).

The simulation typically encompasses 12 to 18 business quarters (rounds) in which each team makes several short- and long-term investment and budgeting decisions. At the end of the business quarter (from 45 minutes to 2 to 3 hours), the decisions are analyzed by the computer, and each team receives an updated printout that indicates their institution's financial standing. The team analyzes the printout and makes the next set of decisions.

Although the team members interact in making decisions, the primary focus in data management simulations is on the interrelationships and trade-offs among quantifiable variables. In a bank management simulation, for example, participants are expected to address the relationships among profitability, liquidity, and solvency, and between profits and volume of business (Galitz, 1983).

Data management simulations are based on mathematical models that adjust parameter values as student inputs are made. The simulation designer specifies the set of equations that reflects the relationships among the variables. Depending on the complexity of the situation, the number of required equations may range from half a dozen to over 50.

17.4.2 Diagnostic Simulations

Originating in medical education, diagnostic simulations are currently found primarily in several health care fields, education, and psychology. Some diagnostic simulations are team exercises that require the discovery, evaluation, and interpretation of relevant data, as in an air accident investigation (Rolfe & Taylor, 1984). In the majority of examples, however, a student takes the role of a physician, nurse, psychologist, or teacher. The student selects and interprets data and selects corrective actions in the diagnosis and management of the patient's or client's problem.

The deep structure of diagnostic simulations consists of an evolving problem that requires sequential interrelated decisions. The sequential nature of the task links each decision to prior decisions and results. Therefore, as in real situations, errors may be compounded on top of errors as nonproductive diagnostic and solution procedures are pursued (Berven & Scofield, 1980).

Key components of diagnostic simulations are a sketchy description of a multifaceted problem, the prescribed role of the participant, and multiple plausible alternatives at each decision point (McGuire, Bashook & Solomon, 1976). Also, the problems are those that involve the consideration of more than a simple cause. Thus, they are not textbook problems. In an air accident investigation, for example, contributing factors are both human and mechanical (Rolfe & Taylor, 1984).

Of major importance is that the student who is unsure of the appropriate course of action can find plausible choices. The only feedback received by the student during the exercise is either the data he or she requested or the effects of a selected action on the situation. Further, the complications that the student must address will vary depending on his or her unique pattern of decisions (McGuire et al., 1976). Thus, a major purpose of many diagnostic simulations is to obtain a record of the student's progress through the multiple possible paths so as to differentiate adequate problem solvers from the students using ineffective approaches.

Figure 17-1 illustrates the various paths through a simulation for the diagnosis and management of a patient. Each of the major strategy decisions, e.g., take history, obtain laboratory data, and so on, is represented by a box on the simulation map. Within the major strategy choices, students may select from a number of plausible specific decisions. The map indicates the decisions to be made and those to be avoided, according to a panel of experts. Solid arrows indicate the route recommended by a panel of experts. As indicated by the map, the student is not terminated from the simulation unless he or she takes action that causes the patient's death.

Early examples of diagnostic simulations for individual students were multiple-branching exercises in booklet form. They have since been replaced by computer-delivered exercises, some of which accept voice input (see Distlehorst & Barrows, 1982; Pickell et al., 1986).

17.4.3 Crisis Management Simulations

A crisis management simulation begins with an unexpected event that threatens the welfare of an individual or a group and which must be quickly resolved. Key components of crisis-management simulations are the rapidly increasing time pressure and the need to prevent a major disaster of some sort.

Both political-crisis exercises, in which a country's security or welfare is threatened, and combat simulations are examples. Political-crisis exercises involve a small team of decision makers representing each country and interacting in a compressed time frame. Combat simulations used for training are either individual or team exercises, and these simulations have been revolutionized by advanced computer technology. Large-scale field maneuvers used to educate commanders and their staffs and some weapons systems training are currently conducted with discrete and networked computer simulations (Oswalt, 1993). A current project is creating a simulated environment that will permit military personnel to view the battlefield in three dimensions, including the capability to reconnoiter the terrain (Oswalt, 1993, p. 154).

17.4.4 Social-Process Simulations

The focus of data management, diagnostic, and crisis management simulations is on a complex task or problem in which human interactions play minor roles, if at all. The student behaviors of primary interest are the decisions made to address a complex cognitive problem. In contrast, the deep structure of social-process simulations is the interactions among the participants and the ways that one's beliefs, assumptions, goals, and actions may be questioned, hindered, or supported in interactions with others (Gredler, 1992a). Goals of social-process simulations are (1) to develop an understanding of a particular social organization or culture, (2) to help develop abilities to think and communicate in an unfamiliar situation (Jones, 1982), or (3) to help develop empathy for others by experiencing an aversive situation as others would, followed by reviewing and discussing one's beliefs and assumptions (Thatcher, 1983; Thatcher & Robinson, 1990).

Participants typically take roles with different interests, priorities, and responsibilities in one of the groups faced with conflicting issues or tasks. Among the examples of social-process simulations are (1) an economically deprived region that must address a proposed tourism development that will also have some negative effects, and (2) the writing, editing, and broadcasting of a radio news program as items continue to come in until air time.

Key components of social-process simulations are (a) a precipitating event or key task, (b) well-defined participant roles, (c) complicating factors, and (d) context (Gredler, 1992a). All of these components interact with each other to set in motion the interactions among participants that are the core of the simulation. Of major importance is that each role (1) must have a stake in the outcome of the exercise and (2) be one to which the participant can commit his or her thoughts and feelings; that is, the role must generate "reality of function."

17.4.5 Discussion: Experiential Simulations

Experiential simulations vary widely in the type of experience established for the learner and the type of causal model underlying the exercise. Data management simulations are most often team exercises in which the relationships among the variables to be manipulated are specified by sets of mathematical equations—a quantitative causal model (see Table 17-2).

In contrast, diagnostic, crisis management, and social-process simulations are based on qualitative causal models. That is, cause-effect contingencies are drawn from actual cases, and the optimal route through the simulation is verified by experts who are asked to work through the exercise. Social-process exercises, however, depend on the interactions of individuals as they react to different situations. Unless contingencies for different actions have been carefully embedded in the context and various roles, the exercise can take unexpected directions.

Of the four types, only the diagnostic simulation can be computer based. Decisions in the other types typically require team decision making, and computers cannot replicate social situations (Crookall, Coleman & Oxford, 1992).

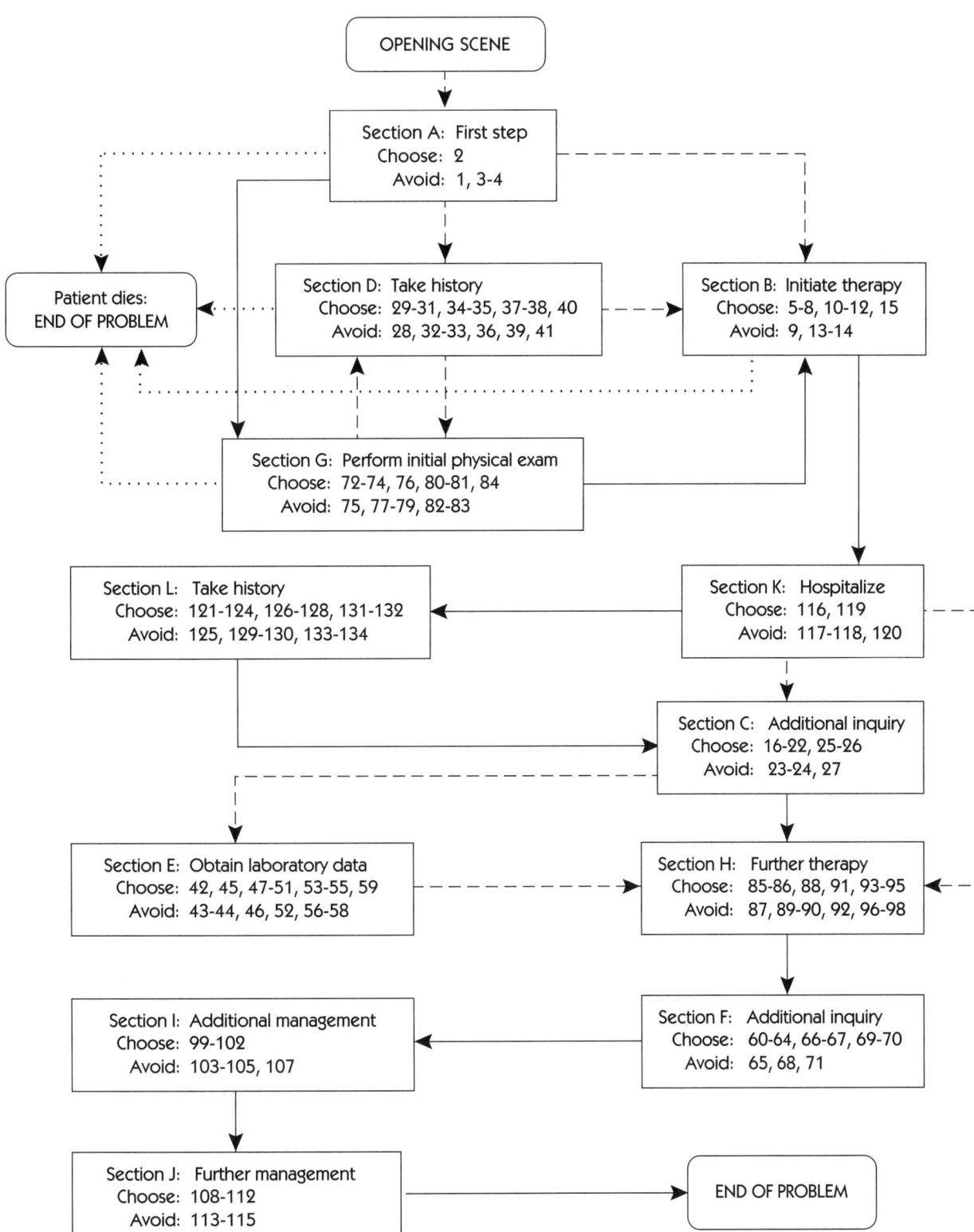

Figure 17-1.   Map of a simulation to diagnose and manage patient SL. Numbers in boxes refer to items to be chosen and to items to be avoided. Solid arrows indicate the route recommended by a panel of experts. Dashed arrows indicate alternate path; solution still possible. Dotted arrows indicate path to unsatisfactory termination. (Reprinted by permission of the Psychological Corporation.)

TABLE 17-2. SUMMARY OF EXPERIMENTAL SIMULATIONS

Type	Structure	Underlying Model	Task
Data management	Successive rounds of decision making; typically team based	Quantitative	Allocate economic resources to any of several variables to improve status of the institution or company
Diagnostic	An evolving complex problem that requires sequential interrelated decisions; typically an individual exercise	Qualitative	Select and interpret data and implement strategies in order to manage a complex, evolving problem
Crisis management	An escalating situation that threatens the welfare of a group or individual; may be individual or team based	Qualitative	Resolve the escalating situation under increasing time and other pressures
Social-process simulations	The interaction of a precipitating social task or event, well-defined participant roles, complicating factors, and context; team-based exercise	Qualitative	Resolve a social problem or issue that is accompanied by different priorities or goals of the associated roles

However, computer analyses of data generated by team members often serves as input to participant decisions.

Experiential simulations share several key characteristics. First, the learner is a functional component of the situation and experiences it from the inside. Second, the learner takes on serious responsibilities as a participant in an ongoing fluid situation. Third, the intent is for the participant to experience the effects of his or her decisions; i.e., the student's discipline problem becomes worse, a proposed compromise is repealed, and so on. Finally, experiential simulations also can provide opportunities for students to develop their cognitive strategies because the exercises require that they organize and manage their own thinking and learning.

17.5   SYMBOLIC SIMULATIONS

In contrast to experiential simulations, a symbolic simulation is a dynamic representation of the functioning or behavior of some universe, system, set of processes, or phenomena by another system (in this case, a computer). In other words, symbolic simulations are populations of events or sets of interacting processes. The role of the learner in relation to a symbolic simulation is typically that of a researcher or investigator. That is, the learner manipulates different variables in order to discover scientific relationships, explain or predict events, or confront misconceptions.

Symbolic simulations may be classified according to the nature of the variables and the nature of the interactions among them. Four types of symbolic simulations are cur-

rently in use that differ in these characteristics. They are data-universe simulations, system simulations, process simulations, and laboratory-research simulations.

17.5.1   Data Universe Simulations

A data universe simulation represents the behavior of sets of related elements that compose a population of continuing events. The simulation expresses the relationships among the variables through the use of mathematical equations. An example is the population ecology simulation described earlier. The simulation illustrates the effects of the 75 variables on population, capital investment, food production, pollution, and quality of life (Forester, 1971; Hinze, 1984). The output is a graph that illustrates the effects of continued turn-of-the-century trends on the five characteristics of civilizations. Trends also may be altered by the user and the effects observed.

The situation typically posed for the student in a data universe simulation is to test student-generated hypotheses about a large population of interrelated variables and outcomes. The goal is to discover relationships or trends among the variables. The purpose of a data universe simulation typically is to provide students with opportunities to discover scientific laws and principles, such as the laws of genetics (see 24.9 for a discussion of databases and cognitive tools).

Note that data universe simulations differ from other simulations that involve the manipulation of variables. First, students are functioning as researchers by testing their own hypotheses, reviewing the outcomes, and testing new hypotheses or continuing their research strategy. In other interactive exercises, students are often attempting to solve a problem that has been posed for them and/or they are working with a smaller database. For example, in a data management simulation, the student is executing specific role-related responsibilities in which the goal for the student or the team is to enhance the economic status of an institution or enterprise.

17.5.2 System Simulations

A system simulation demonstrates the functional relationships between the components of a physical or biological system (such as a small ecosystem) or a constructed system (such as complex equipment systems). Students learn about the particular system or solve problems involving the system by manipulating the components.

One important role for the interactive graphics and videodisc capability of current computer technology is to provide functional representations of complex systems that students can operate. An example is the steam plant system and subsystems developed for the U.S. Navy known as *STEAMER.* The exercise also includes a quantitative component so that the student can open and shut valves, turn components on and off, adjust throttles, and observe the effects on indicators, such as dials, thermometers, and digital readouts (Stevens & Roberts, 1983).

System simulations are often used to teach the operational principles of complex equipment composed of subsystems. They also are used to teach procedures and may, depending on the design of the simulation, develop students' cognitive strategies. The use of a simulation to teach maintenance procedures, for example, is the procedural simulation referred to by Riegeluth and Schwartz (1989).

Examples that develop students' cognitive strategies are the low-cost plywood M1 tank simulators and M2/3 fighting vehicles, each with its own microprocessor database of the terrain, graphics, and sound system developed in project SIMNET. Each "armored vehicle" is a system that generates the battle engagement environment required for the combat mission training of its crew. Each crew member sees a part of the virtual world defined by his line of sight (e.g., forward for the driver) (Alluisi, 1991, p. 350).

17.5.3 Process Simulations

The focus of a process simulation is a naturally occurring phenomenon in the physical, chemical, or biological realm (Riegeluth & Schwartz, 1987). Interactive graphics images can illustrate processes that are unobservable and/or are not easily experimented with in the classroom. Students can manipulate variables and attempt different tasks in order (1) to discover the relationships among the variables or (2) to confront their misconceptions.

Confronting student misconceptions about Newtonian mechanics is the goal of several process simulations devel-

oped in physical science (Flick, 1990; White, 1984). DiSessa (1982, 1985) and others note that students' intuitive knowledge about force, motion, and velocity derived from experience in a gravity-bound world often prevents students' construction of accurate mental models of physics principles. White (1984, 1995), for example, has designed several progressively more difficult gamelike tasks that require the student to perform several actions on a "spaceship" in a frictionless environment (space). Force, velocity, and speed are illustrated in the interactive exercises.

DiSessa (1982) identifies three important contributions of process simulations that represent physics principles. First, they provide students an opportunity to interact with phenomena at a qualitative level. Often, students only interact with quantitative problems in which getting the right answer typically becomes their goal. Second, students' fragmented and often naive knowledge of phenomena is challenged. Third, simulations can change the time scale of exercises from the 20 minutes or so per type to problems that can engage students in investigations that can span days or weeks.

17.5.4 Laboratory Research Simulations

Laboratory-research simulations are specific to courses that include laboratory sessions as part of the course work. Among them are biology, chemistry, physics, and, occasionally, physical science. These exercises provide visual and graphic components for students to manipulate, and they illustrate the results. Early examples of chemistry experiments used color microfiche images projected onto the back of a plasma panel with a PLATO IV system (Smith & Sherwood, 1976). Currently, computer laboratory simulations are making use of videodisc technology to expand the range and complexity of the experiments conducted by students.

These simulations differ from data-universe and process simulations in that they are a series of discrete problems. Because laboratory research exercises are a series of discrete experiments instead of a complex evolving problem, they are categorized by some theorists as problem-solving exercises in a simulated context (Gredler, 1992a). Nevertheless, the computer videodisc simulations provide realistic experimental reactions. Further, students can conduct experiments that involve hazardous or costly materials. Also, slow reactions that students may not ordinarily be able to observe may be sped up (and others may be slowed down). Moreover, experiments can be repeated (Smith & Jones, 1989).

17.5.5 Discussion: Symbolic Simulation

Symbolic simulations may be developed at any of several different levels of complexity. Data universe simulations are the most complex, in which a large population of events is represented and the causal models are quantitative. System simulations are less broad and may involve either quantitative or qualitative models of causality. Process simulations, in contrast, typically address specific interactive processes in the physical world that are often poorly understood by students. In addition to biological processes, the interactions of variables such as force, speed, and velocity are typical examples. Causal models for process simulations also may be quantitative or qualitative. Laboratory research simulations, in contrast, involve a series of discrete activities that are directed by students. Again, the causal models for the specific experiments may be quantitative or qualitative (see Table 17-3).

17.6 INSTRUCTIONAL DESIGN IMPLICATIONS DERIVED FROM RESEARCH

Many classroom games and simulations are developed for a particular class, and the key design variables often are not explicitly identified. Further, much of the research has investigated "variables of convenience," i.e., attitudes and content-related achievement (Wentworth & Lewis, 1972). Nevertheless, a few studies have investigated other effects of games and simulations that have implications for design.

17.6.1 Academic Games

One of the stated requirements for academic games is that advancement in the exercise and winning should be based on academic skills. A study conducted by Schild (1966) tested the premise that students learn those skills and strategies that are reinforced by the structure of the game, i.e., the skills essential for winning. He recorded the decisions made by four groups of players of the Parent-Child game, in which pairs composed of one parent and one child must negotiate appropriate child behaviors on five issues. The

"child" can damage the "parent's" score through consistent delinquency, and the "parent" can damage the "child's" score by excessive control and punishment. However, by round 4 of the game, most players had learned the optimal strategy essential to maximizing both the parent and child scores for their team. In other words, the teams had learned the optimal strategy for winning. The implication for game design is that game structure should be carefully constructed so that winning depends on strategies acceptable in the classroom and knowledge in the subject area.

Several studies on the classroom game Teams-Games-Tournaments (TGT) have implications for game design. A unique feature of TGT is that it alters both the task and reinforcement structure of the classroom. Most classrooms are highly competitive, with individual students competing for scarce reinforcements (DeVries & Edwards, 1973; DeVries & Slavin, 1978). In contrast, TGT introduces a cooperative task structure within teams and increases greatly the availability of reinforcement.

TGT organizes the class into teams of comparable achievement (e.g., one high achiever, two average achievers, and one low achiever), but each student competes at a three-person tournament table with students at the same ability level. Each student's score contributes to the overall team score. (Scores earned at the tournament are 6 points, high scorer; 4 points, middle scorer; and 2 points, low scorer.) Practice sessions also are scheduled a few days prior to the weekly or biweekly tournament.

Because the team score is dependent on the performance of all the team members, the game structure reinforces peer tutoring and cooperative learning during the practice sessions. In one study, the games/teams combination increased the amount of peer tutoring beyond that in either games/ indi-

TABLE 17-3. SUMMARY OF SYMBOLIC SIMULATIONS			
Type	**Structure**	**Underlying Model**	**Task**
Data universe	Represents a large population of events; may be individual or team based	Quantitative	To develop mental models about the interrelationships of variables and test the models
System	Demonstrates the functional relationships between the components of a physical or biological system or a constructed system (such as complex equipment systems)	Quantitative or qualitative	To explain or predict events in the system
Process	Represents specific interactive processes in the physical world	Quantitative or qualitative	To discover relationships among the variables and/or to confront misconceptions
Laboratory research	A series of student directed discrete experiments in simulated environments	Quantitative or qualitative	To become proficient in conducting specific experiments, documenting results, and conclusions

vidual reward or quizzes/team reward classes (DeVries & Edwards, 1973). Classes that participated in TGT (team reward) also perceived a decrease in both classroom competitiveness and course difficulty (measured by the Learning Environment Inventory, LEI). The researchers suggest that these perceptions are the result of the task interdependence of the game and the increased opportunities for reinforcement.

A review of 10 studies in which TGT was implemented in mathematics, language arts, and social-studies classes indicated consistent effects on achievement (measured by standardized tests) and mutual concern (measured by questionnaire scales adapted from the Learning Environment Inventory). Some of the studies compared TGT to regular classroom instruction, and others compared TGT to the traditional classroom and a modification of TGT in which higher- or lower-scoring students' scores were weighted more heavily. However, the modifications did not produce a greater effect on achievement than the original TGT.

Of importance for game design in general is the relationship between competition and cooperation. Competition is the essence of any game. However, the mutual dependence of students on each other reinforces cooperation, an important characteristic of a positive classroom environment.

17.6.2 Computer Games

A key issue in manual games is the influence of a game on classroom dynamics. In contrast, key issues in computer-delivered games are the mechanics of play and the observance of accepted instructional design principles. Many computer-delivered games, however, have not been developed by instructional designers. Instead, like the programmed instruction movement of the 1960s, various other groups have developed many of the products. Often, the computer software has not undergone formative or summative evaluation. Although reviews of software are available, few reviewers implement the materials with students. Moreover, evaluation checklists do not require the reviewer to conduct observations of student use (Vargas, 1986).

Observations of students using computer software indicate some problems with computer games in both game mechanics and principles of instructional design (Vargas, 1986; Gredler, 1992a). Briefly summarized, the game mechanics problems include inappropriate vocabulary for young students, inadequate directions, lengthy texts, and multistep directions with no opportunity for student practice and inappropriate use of graphics (Vargas, 1986; Gredler, 1992a). In addition, computer games often do not provide options for students to bypass tasks that are too complex or bypass items they are unable to answer. Since the only way for the player to continue in the game is to strike a key or type in a word, players are forced to enter random answers, which, of course, are evaluated by the computer as wrong (Gredler, 1992a).

In addition to the mechanics of play, frequent observations of students using computer software indicate two

instructional design problems. They are (1) inadequate stimulus control and (2) defective reinforcement contingencies. For example, the use of a question with several possible answers in which only one answer is accepted by the computer penalizes the student who selects a correct answer that is not included in the program. The task stimulus in such situations is inappropriate.

Two types of defective reinforcement contingencies have been observed during student use of computer software. First, the game or other exercise is often delayed because the keyboard is locked while stars twinkle, trains puff across the screen, or smiley faces wink or nod (Vargas, 1986, p. 75). A more serious problem occurs when the consequences that follow wrong answers are more interesting than the feedback for correct answers. In one computer exercise, for example, a little man jumps up and down and waves his arms after a wrong answer. Students, instead of solving the problems for the correct answers, randomly enter any answer in order to see the little man jump up and down (Gredler, 1992a).

Potential users of classroom computer games, therefore, should carefully review the exercises for several likely flaws. They are inappropriate vocabulary, too lengthy text, inadequate directions and branching, inadequate stimulus control, and defective reinforcement contingencies.

17.6.3 The Mixed—Metaphor Problem

Games are competitive exercises in which the objective is to win, and experiential simulations are interactive exercises in which participants take on roles with serious decision-making responsibilities. However, some developers have attempted to mix the two perspectives by assigning participants serious roles, placing them in direct competition with each other, and identifying the participants as winners or losers according to the individual's or team's performance. These exercises are sometimes referred to as *simulation games* and *gaming simulations.*

Games and experiential simulations, however, are different psychological realities, and mixing the two techniques is a contradiction in terms. Such exercises send conflicting messages to participants (Jones, 1984, 1987). They also can lead to bad feelings between participants who address their roles in a professional manner and those who treat the exercise as "only a game" (Jones, 1987).

Many exercises that otherwise would be classified as data management simulations are mixed-metaphor exercises. That is, student teams that each manage a "company" are placed in direct competition with each other with profitability as the criterion for winning. For example, in the Business Policy Game, the winning firm is the one with the highest return on investment. Further, in many classes, from 10% to 50% of the student's course grade depends on the team's performance.

Several problems recently have been identified with these exercises. Lundy (1985) observed that sometimes a team that is not doing well in later rounds attempts to "crash the system." Seeing no way to win, team members behave like game players and behave in such a way as to prevent others from winning. Other desperation plays are charging an astronomical price for a product in hopes of selling a few, and end-of-activity plays, such as eliminating all research and development or ordering no raw materials (Teach, 1990). Some teams, however, view the exercise as simply a situation in which to show their prowess. Golden and Smith (1991) describe these teams as "dogfighters" because their behavior resembles that found in the classic World War II aviation dogfight.

The major problem with such exercises, however, is that competition in the business world does not routinely result in one company's being declared a winner while others enter bankruptcy (Teach, 1990). Instead, companies strive for market share and alter their strategies based on feedback about market conditions and the success of their earlier efforts. Thus, the focus on being "the winner" distorts the simulation experience.

Some researchers have investigated the factors that contribute to team success in these exercises. Gentry (1980) investigated the relationships between team size (three to five members) and various attitudinal and performance variables in three undergraduate business classes. However, of the variables entered into the stepwise regression equation to predict team standing, he found that group performance was predicted better by the ability of the best student in the group rather than by a composite of the group's abilities. Thus, group performance was more a function of a group leader rather than knowledge and ability of group members.

In addition, Remus (1977) and Remus and Jenner (1981) found a significant correlation between the student's enjoyment of the exercise and final standing of their teams. Several students in one study also disagreed with statements that the exercise was a valuable experience and represented real-world decision making (Remus & Jenner, 1981). In summary, the observations of Teach (1990), Golden and Smith (1991) and Lundy (1985), and the findings of Remus and Jenner (1981), lend support to the findings of Schild (1966). Specifically, students will tend to enact those behaviors that are reinforced by winning. In simulation games, these actions may be counterproductive to the expected learning.

17.6.4 Experiential Simulations

The student in an experiential simulation takes on a serious role in an evolving scenario and experiences the privileges and responsibilities of that role in attempting to solve a complex problem or realize a goal. Four major types of experiential simulations are data management, crisis management, and diagnostic and social-process exercises. Of these four types, crisis management simulations are developed to meet preestablished criteria regarding the nature of the crisis and expected student reactions. Data related to the development of these exercises typically are not reported for public consumption. Moreover, data management and social-process

simulations often (1) are not standardized exercises and/or (2) do not provide student data other than posttest achievement on some instructor-developed instrument.

Many diagnostic simulations, in contrast, are standardized situations in which optimal sequential decisions in relation to the evolving problem have been identified. Further, research conducted on the analyses of problem-solving decisions in diagnostic simulations can serve as a model for analyzing students' cognitive strategies in other types of simulations. The first step is the evaluation of the range of possible decisions at each decision point by a group of experts. Each decision is classified in one of five categories that range from "clearly contraindicated" to "clearly indicated and important," and a positive or negative weight (e.g., -1 to -3 or +1 to +3) is assigned to each decision (McGuire & Babbott, 1967, p. 5). Then, the combination of choices that represent a skilled decision-making strategy are summed for a total numerical score. When the simulation is administered, the numerical score of each student decision is recorded. The extent of congruence between the student's total and the expert decisions is referred to as a *proficiency score.*

A study of the problem-solving skills in simulations with 186 fourth-year medical students analyzed students' proficiency scores and revealed four different problem-solving styles (McGuire & Bashook, 1967). The high scorers included two groups identified as (1) thorough and discriminating and (2) the "shotgun" group. Although both groups earned total problem-solving scores between 32 and 60, the "shotgun" group made many choices that were not warranted (high errors of commission). Similarly, two problem-solving patterns were identified in the low-scoring group (scores below 30). One, the constricted group, chose few desirable or undesirable actions. In contrast, the other group, the random problem solvers, chose few desirable actions, but they also chose many actions that were not warranted.

This method of analyzing the specific characteristics of student performance in diagnostic simulations is applicable to other types of simulations that address problem-solving strategies. First, optimal strategies through the complex task or problem are identified. Other plausible steps are then weighted according to the extent to which they are neutral (do not advance the problem solution) or are debilitating. Finally, the number of debilitating decisions made by both high and low scorers is tabulated to identify the problem-solving pattern.

Given the recent emphasis on students' constructing knowledge during learning, this model or a similar one can provide information to teachers about specific student difficulties. Also, the computer can tabulate both total and component scores on students as they work through the exercise.

17.6.5 Symbolic Simulations

A symbolic simulation is a dynamic representation of a universe, system, process, or phenomenon by another system. The behavior that is simulated involves the interaction of at least two variables over time. The student interacts with symbolic simulation from the outside, unlike the experiential simulation. The types of symbolic simulations are data universe, system, process, and laboratory-research simulations.

17.6.5.1. Data Universe Simulations. At present, few data universe simulations have been developed for instructional purposes. One example, however, is Jungck and Calley's (1985) Genetics Construction Kit (GCK). The software consists of two parts. One is a data universe that includes the complex behavior of 10 phenomena in classical Mendelian genetics. Operations that may be performed on this universe include crosses, comparisons of parental and filial generations, Chi-square analyses, and building up the number of progeny through successive experiments (Jungck & Calley, 1985). The second part develops "populations of organisms" for study that include combinations of the phenomena in the data universe (Stewart et al., 1992).

One study implemented GCK in the first 5 weeks of a 9-week high school genetics course. Students first completed an activity in which they built models to explain a "black-box" situation and then discussed the adequacy of their models for explaining the data. They worked in groups to research problems generated by GCK by building and testing models that appeared to explain the data (Stewart et al., 1992).

After 3 weeks, the researchers selected six students who had a good understanding of simple dominance and meiosis models. These students were presented individually with subsequent problems the others were studying in groups for 6 class days. Detailed analyses of their computer records and audio recordings of their "think-aloud" strategies indicated several findings. First, students revised their original explanatory models in most of the problems they encountered. Second, all but three of the final models were compatible with the data. Of these, half represented accepted scientific theory, and half represented an alternative perspective.

Third, and of primary importance to instructional design, the researchers documented a detailed and involved model-building process used by the students (see 12.3.1..1, 24.3.1). Among the actions initiated by the students were conducting experiments within the given field population, using an existing model to explain features of the data, using limitations of the proposed model to identify other possible causal factors, and bracketing cases of interest as a first step in revising the proposed model. Identification of the steps used by students in conducting research with other data universe simulations is a first step in developing instructional strategies for these simulations.

The variety of strategies that may be implemented by students when faced with a complex problem is illustrated by two different implementations of the genetics simulation CATLAB (Kinnear, 1982). The exercise permits students to construct a population of nonpedigree cats (up to 91 cats) and then to breed any two of the cats for any number of litters. In constructing the experimental population, the student chooses gender, tail or no tail, and color for each cat. If nonwhite is first chosen, then several options follow for both color and pattern. After the students complete their selec-

tions, the Apple II program provides rather stilted color images of the student's choices and the resulting litters.

One biology teacher reported that her students tended to breed cats without a plan (Vargas, 1986). The range of mixed characteristics in the resulting litters made it impossible for students to observe the relevant genetic principles. In addition, one student set about producing as many different-looking cats as possible. Vargas (1986, p. 742) concluded that the simulation *by itself* was no better than leaving a student unsupervised in a science laboratory to proceed by trial and error.

In contrast, Simmons and Lunetta (1993) implemented a three-part instructional strategy with three expert and eight novice problem solvers using CATLAB. The subjects were first directed to explore various traits with cats. In phase 2, the researcher had a brief discussion with each subject about his or her actions and rationale. Phase 3 required the subjects to investigate and determine the inheritance pattern of the orange and tabby striping trait.

The original intent of the study was to identify differences between expert and novice problem solvers in their interactions with the simulation. However, this dichotomy was too restrictive to explain the patterns of problem solving found in the data (Simmons & Lunetta, 1993). Instead, three levels of problem-solving performance were found. The highest level, successful problem solvers, consisted of two experts and two novices. This group (1) used systematic procedures, (2) developed valid reasons for their results, and (3) generated correct answers. They also had the highest percentage of correct responses (75%–100%). The second level, the transitional or less-successful problem solvers, consisted of one expert and three novices. Of their responses, 60% to 70% were correct. This group also used less-systematic procedures and generated some invalid explanations. In addition, they did not rule out alternative explanations that could account for their conclusions. The third level consisted of the unsuccessful problem solvers (five novices). These students exhibited the most random approaches to the problem and did not use valid scientific explanations. They typically used circular definitions to justify their actions (Simmons & Lunetta, 1993). From 35% to 45% of their responses were correct.

Analysis of the videotapes of the subjects indicated that successful problem solvers applied integrated knowledge during the process. Unsuccessful subjects, however, were unable to use domain-specific knowledge to describe their observations and were unable to detect the features of genetics concepts and principles in the data (Simmons & Lunetta, 1993). They also exhibited misunderstandings about the nature of probability. The findings of the study, which indicate three levels of problem solving, suggest that successful performance requires more than an advanced knowledge of the subject matter (Simmons & Lunetta, 1993). That is, both novices and experts exhibited a variety of strategies that ranged from least to most successful.

Data universe simulations lend themselves to several types of cognitive tasks. However, they are likely to be unsuccessful unless students have developed a systematic strategy for approaching the task and also are able to apply an integrated knowledge base of concepts and principles.

17.6.5.2. System Simulations. Developers of complex equipment simulations typically establish performance standards for students and refine the simulation until those standards are met. Essential terms and definitions are typically taught prior to student engagement with the simulation.

Developing the skills of analysis and prediction in other system simulations with several variables presents a different instructional design problem. Students' prediction skills in relation to one system, water pollution, were investigated by Lavoie and Good (1988). In the system, five variables (temperature, waste type, dumping rate, type of treatment, and type of body water) affected oxygen and waste concentration of the water.

After a short period to explore the simulation, the 14 students read background material on water pollution that described some of the effects among the variables. They next worked through several exercises with the computer simulation which involved choosing preselected parameters and observing the effects on a given dependent variable. The students then were given three prediction problems to solve.

Problem-solving ability on the prediction problems was related to three factors: high or moderate initial knowledge, high academic achievement, and cognitive performance at the Piagetian stage of formal operational thinking. Unsuccessful students tended to have both low initial knowledge and low academic ability and to be at the Piagetian stage of concrete operational thinking.

One of the key differences between the Piagetian stages of concrete and formal reasoning is that concrete thinkers typically are able to manipulate systematically only one or two variables at a time. Given a more complex situation, they change several independent variables at a time and, therefore, cannot observe the effects of any one variable (Piaget, 1972; Gredler, 1992b). In contrast, formal operational thinkers are capable of developing hypotheses that systematically test the influence of several variables on an outcome. Analysis of the videotapes of the students confirmed that they executed the strategies consistently with their level of Piagetian reasoning.

In addition, the unsuccessful students expressed dissatisfaction and lack of interest at various times during the learning sequence (Lavoie & Good, 1988, p. 342). They also conducted, on average, 50% fewer simulation runs, took fewer notes than successful students, and spent less time reviewing and evaluating their predictions than the successful subjects. Further, a postexercise interview revealed that the unsuccessful students had more misconceptions about solubility and the relationships among oxygen, bacteria, and waste than the successful students.

The researchers also identified 21 behavioral tendencies that differed between successful and unsuccessful problem solvers. Others, in addition to those already mentioned, are that successful problem solvers made fewer errors in reading graphs, relied on information learned during the lesson

to make predictions, and understood the directions and information in the lesson. The implications for instructional design are clear. Systems in which several independent variables influence the values of two or more dependent variables are complex situations for students. Simulations of such systems should include preassessments of students' level of both Piagetian thinking and knowledge level. Students at the concrete level of thinking and/or with low subject knowledge should be directed to other materials prior to interacting with the simulation. Like the data universe simulations, a requisite skill is the capability of applying an integrated knowledge base to an unfamiliar situation.

17.6.5.3. Process Simulations. Often, naturally occurring phenomena are either unobservable or are not easily subject to experimentation. Examples include Newton's laws of motion, photosynthesis, and complex atomic reactions. Process simulations that can use symbols to represent the interactions of unobservable variables and which are subject to student manipulation can be useful instructional devices.

White (1984) designed and tested a series of exercises using symbols to confront students' misconceptions of Newton's laws of motion and conservation of momentum. A series of 10 exercises was designed that required students to conduct progressively more difficult operations on a spaceship in outer space (frictionless environment). Among the misconceptions addressed by the exercises is the intuitive belief that objects always go in the direction they are kicked (White, 1984).

Thirty-two students who had studied PSSC physics participated in the study. The 18 students in the experimental group and the 14 students in the control group did not differ significantly on the pretest problems. From 1/3 to 1/2 of the students demonstrated misconceptions about the effects in some of the basic questions. Posttest data indicated that the group that interacted with the simulation significantly improved their performance.

However, on the exercise involving prediction of the effects of an orthogonal impulse, the simulation exercise led to as many students changing from right pretest answers to wrong posttest answers as changed from wrong to right. Further, many of the exercises could be solved by simple heuristics, such as, "if one impulse (force or thrust) is not enough, try two" (White, 1984). The use of such strategies supports Kozma's (1992) concern that abstract symbols may not have a referent in another domain for the students (p. 206). That is, students may learn to operate directly on the objects without developing an understanding of the underlying principles.

Among the subsequent improvements to the exercise (White, 1994) are (1) additional structure, including "laws" to be tested in the simulation, (2) the addition of real-world transfer problems, and (3) the inclusion of other symbols to focus on important concepts. An example of an additional symbol is the use of a "wake" behind the spaceship to illustrate a change in velocity. Kozma (1992) reports that White (1994) found significant improvement on the transfer problems and significantly higher performance of students in a

2-month curriculum using the simulation than students in two regular physics classes.

A long-standing problem in education is the issue of overcoming students' misconceptions that are based on their limited everyday experience and intuitions. That is, students may be able to verbalize a phenomenon accurately, but when faced with a real-world problem, they revert to out-of-school knowledge as a basis for conceptualizing the situation (Alexander, 1992). Process simulations can be a powerful instructional tool to provide the repeated experiences that Piaget (1970) first identified as essential in overcoming these problems. However, careful attention to both symbol selection and links to laws and principles is required.

17.6.5.4. Laboratory Research Simulations. Laboratory research simulations consist of a series of discrete qualitative and quantitative experiments that students may direct in a specific subject area. Several studies have compared computer-based simulations with "wet labs" in chemistry and biology courses. The results, however, are confounded by one group or the other receiving extra materials, such as summary sheets, or written problems to solve following instructions.

One development, however, is a series of experiments for introductory college chemistry courses. The experiments were revised based on student comments during formative evaluation and then placed into a comparison group pilot study. The laboratory simulations use a single-screen system that permits computer text and graphics to be superimposed on video images. Components of the system are a personal computer, a video interface card, a videodisc player, and a television monitor. This system is more expensive than other configurations; however, an advantage is that students can respond to text questions while the images remain on the screen.

In the pilot study, 103 students were randomly assigned to a lab-only group, videodisc-only group, or videodisc-plus-lab group. Six interactive videodisc workstations were available on a self-scheduled basis for the students using the computer software. On a brief seven-point posttest, the difference between the means of the videodisc group and the laboratory group was 1.03 standard deviation units. Significant differences were also found between the means of the anonymously graded laboratory reports (videodisc-plus-lab = 31.04 and lab-only = 26.44). Also, students in the laboratory group were more likely to rely on the rote citation of examples in the lab manual even when these examples did not fit the data (Smith, Jones & Waugh, 1986).

17.6.6 Discussion

Research on games and simulations indicates three major areas that are essential for effective design: (1) the task-reinforcement structure, (2) the role of prior knowledge, and (3) the complexity of problem solving.

17.6.6.1. Task Reinforcement Structure. Both games and simulations alter the reinforcement structure of the classroom because they expand the opportunities for students to earn reinforcement. Because winning is a powerful reinforcer, games must be carefully designed so that inappropriate strategies are not learned. Although teams-games-tournaments reinforces cooperation and peer tutoring, other games reinforce guessing and the selection of wrong answers.

The major task for game players is to win, whereas the task for simulation participants is to execute serious responsibilities identified by the nature of the simulation (experiential) or by the accompanying instruction (symbolic simulation). To mix games and simulations establishes conflicting tasks, i.e., defeating other participants or executing a role with identified responsibilities.

In contrast, experiential simulations establish particular tasks or goals for participants and provide contingencies in the form of changes in the complex problem or the actions of other participants. Designers of symbolic simulations, however, face particular problems. That is, simply providing a data universe, a system, or interacting processes is a necessary but not sufficient condition for a successful or meaningful problem-solving experience. For example, if the student's decisions result in a colorful screen display, the exercise reinforces random search strategies as well as thoughtful student choices.

Moreover, in the absence of prior instruction on conducting research in multivariate open-ended situations, some students will be unsuccessful. As indicated in one study, the unsuccessful students became frustrated and lost interest. Instead of a reinforcing exercise, the simulation becomes a form of punishment for the student's effort. One solution is to teach model-building strategies so that students become proficient in using them to solve broad open-ended problems. Another is to program the exercise such that random selection of variables initiates a message that suspends the simulation and routes the student to particular information sources for assistance, such as the teacher or particular instructional materials.

17.6.6.2. The Role of Prior Knowledge. Although the research on data universe, system, and process simulations is limited, the studies indicate the importance of prior knowledge on successful performance. Prior achievement level typically serves as an indicator of prior knowledge; however, this variable alone is insufficient to predict problem-solving performance. The research identifies two types of prior knowledge that appear to be essential in some simulations. One is domain-specific knowledge that must be integrated into a coherent whole. (Fragmented or partial knowledge is insufficient.) In one study, for example, unsuccessful students held several misconceptions about key topics.

A second type of knowledge essential for success is a systematic strategy for addressing a multifaceted situation. Students who had been taught to use models to explain data and to revise their models to account for new data were successful in conducting genetics research in a data universe simulation.

The capability of developing hypothetical models of a complex situation was found to be important in another study. In a system simulation involving the interactions of several variables, formal Piagetian reasoning (as opposed to concrete reasoning) also was found to be essential. Of interest is that formal operational thinkers are capable of developing hypothetical models that are then tested systematically. In contrast, concrete operational thinkers can successfully manipulate only one or two variables at a time.

The implication for instructional design is that the identification of essential prerequisites, long an important design principle, involves at least two areas for some simulations. First, major concepts in the subject domain that are essential to manipulating variables or conducting research using the simulation should be identified. Level of academic achievement or a description of completed courses is insufficient to indicate essential prerequisite knowledge. In other words, variables identified in artificial-intelligence approaches to computer-based learning—i.e., problem-solving skill, aptitude, and ability (Tennyson & Park, 1987)—must be specified for the different types of simulations.

Second, the level of the task in terms of the number and nature of the variables to be manipulated also should be identified. Simulations that illustrate the interactive effects of several variables are more complex in terms of the reasoning strategies required for student success. Prior instruction in systematically manipulating variables may be required.

17.6.6.3. The Complexity of Problem Solving.

Understanding problem solving in a variety of contexts is a major focus in cognitive theories of learning (Gredler, 1992b). Research on simulations suggests implications for these perspectives. One theoretical perspective, Gagné's conditions of learning, identifies five distinct categories of learning that differ in instructional requirements for successful learning. One of these domains is cognitive strategies, which consists of the skills essential to the student's management of his or her thinking and learning (Gagné, 1977, 1985). Cognitive strategies, however, may vary widely among students. Analyses of students' decisions in a diagnostic simulation, for example, indicated that successful students ranged from thorough and discriminating to the "shotgun" group, which chose many unwarranted actions. Analyses of students' strategies in a data universe simulation indicated 21 behavioral tendencies that differed between successful and unsuccessful problem solvers.

Another concern in terms of strategies acquired by the learner is that situational heuristics rather than generalizable principles may be learned. Thus, simulation design must incorporate links to the relevant theoretical framework.

Information-processing theories, another cognitive perspective, focus on the differences between expert and novice problem solvers. Research in several subject areas has identified general characteristics of both types of problem solvers (see Glaser & Chi, 1988). The expert/novice dichotomy, however, may oversimplify differences among individuals. One study, for example, found a continuum of capabilities from least to most successful that varied along the dimensions of (1) extent of integrated knowledge and (2) level of strategic reasoning.

A third cognitive development is that of constructivism (see Chapter 7). At present, no single constructivist theory of instruction has been developed (Driscoll, 1994). A basic tenet of constructivism, however, is that knowledge is a construction by the learner. That is, the learner interprets information in terms of his or her particular experience and constructs a knowledge base from these interpretations.

Beyond this common tenet, constructivism is interpreted by different proponents in somewhat different ways. Two of these views are particularly relevant for simulations. One view is based in part on Piaget's (1970) theory of cognitive development, which states that logical thinking develops from (1) the learner's confrontation with his or her misconceptions about the world and (2) the resulting reorganization of thinking on a more logical level. Thus, instruction should place learners in situations in which they must face the inconsistencies in their naive models of thinking. The process simulation discussed earlier that incorporates principles of Newtonian mechanics is an example.

Another perspective in constructivism is the view that authentic tasks with real-world relevance and utility should replace isolated decontextualized demands (Brown et al., 1989; Jonassen, 1991; Driscoll, 1994). Such tasks are particularly important in ill-structured domains such as medicine, history, and literature interpretation in which problems or cases require the flexible assembly of knowledge from a variety of sources (Spiro et al., 1991). Examples are diagnostic simulations in which students face complex, authentic, and evolving problems that they must attempt to understand and manage to a successful conclusion. Some data universe and system simulations, if accompanied by appropriate instruction, can also address the requirements of this constructivist view.

One concern that has been raised in relation to placing students in complex situations requiring many steps is that such tasks may overwhelm the less-capable learner (Dick, 1991, p. 42). In other words, the gap may be too great between the learner's capabilities and the tools and information provided in the exercise. The system simulation on water pollution is an example. The unsuccessful students lacked both basic knowledge related to the situation and systematic strategies for addressing multifactor problems, and expressed dissatisfaction and lack of interest several times during the activity.

In summary, the research on simulations indicates the varieties of cognitive strategies enacted by students in complex situations, and the range of differences between expert and novice problem solvers, and it offers a mechanism for empirically validating major concepts in constructivism.

17.7 RECOMMENDATIONS FOR FUTURE RESEARCH

Early research on games and simulations typically compared the particular interactive exercise with regular classroom instruction on information-oriented achievement tests.

These "apples and oranges" comparisons did not yield definitive information about the effectiveness of the innovations. Further, key processes in the innovation often were not documented, student characteristics that may interact with the exercise in different ways were not investigated, and outcome measures often were poorly described.

Conducting definitive research on games and simulations, however, requires more than the specification of additional variables and the description of student interactions and outcome measures. Specifically, if an exercise is poorly designed, documentation of implementation and outcomes contributes little to an understanding of the potential of the innovation (Gredler, 1996). A three-step strategy is essential to conducting useful research on games and simulations. The steps are: (1) Document the design validity of the innovation; (2) verify the cognitive strategy and/or social interaction processes executed by students during the exercise in small-group tryout (formative evaluation) and redesign where necessary; and (3) conduct follow-up research on specific processes and effects (see Chapters 39 to 42 for specific approaches to research).

17.7.1 Document Design Validity

Several issues important in design validity for both games and simulations are: (1) a reliance on a knowledge domain and subject-area expertise, (2) the exclusion of chance or random strategies as a means to success, and (3) the avoidance of mixed-metaphor exercises and zero-sum games.

Particularly important for simulations is the analysis of the mode of delivery and the causal model for events in the exercise. Specifically, social-process simulations cannot be delivered by the computer; however, any of the symbolic simulations are legitimate computer-based exercises.

The causal model for the simulation, whether quantitative or qualitative, should reflect verifiable processes and interrelationships, not random events. Some early computer-based exercises inadvertently established Russian-roulette situations for students in which the criteria for successful management are unknown to the participants. Students repeatedly assign values to a limited number of variables in the absence of a knowledge base and await the outcome. In such exercises, the students play against the odds established by the house (the computer program) instead of a real-world causal model (Gredler, 1992a).

Often, careful analysis is required to identify these variable-assignment exercises. An example is *Lemonade Stand*. First, students repeatedly assign values to only three variables. Thus, the same limited number of decisions is made again and again. The three variables are: (1) the number of glasses of lemonade one wishes to sell, (2) selling price per glass, and (3) amount of advertising expenditures. After students input their selections, the program compares them with the preprogrammed model and informs them of the amount of profit or loss for that day. Sometimes this figure is accompanied by the statement that the weather was cloudy and rainy that day; thus, little or no profit was earned.

The inadequacy of the causal model also is noted by Vargas (1986). The exercise omits important considerations, such as the components of the lemonade (how much sugar and lemon to use in the brew), location of the stand, and the fact that few people would set up a stand in rainy weather. Thus, the exercise leads the prospective user to expect more than it delivers (p. 742). Further, the exercise is simply a guessing game for students as they attempt to discover the variable weightings that were selected by the programmer.

A much more useful exercise would be one that engages the students in planning for a lemonade stand in which weather data for past years as well as information on pedestrian traffic patterns, costs of resources, and so on are available. In this way, students' cognitive strategies may be facilitated.

17.7.2 Verification of Cognitive Strategy and/or Social Interaction Processes

A game or simulation that meets design criteria should then be implemented with a small group of students to determine the actual behaviors that it precipitates. This practice is a long-standing and accepted tenet of instructional design. However, many computer products marketed for schools do not undergo this test of effectiveness.

Important information can be obtained in tryouts of a game or simulation with answers to these questions: Do the students become frustrated and lose interest because the exercise is too difficult for them? Does success depend on skills other than those intended by the designers? What unanticipated behaviors do students execute during the exercise? What are learner attitudes toward the game or simulation?

Particularly important is the issue of task difficulty. A symbolic simulation that challenges the learner's naive conceptions or requires sophisticated research strategies beyond the learner's level of expertise is one that places high cognitive demand on the learner. Such a situation, in which the learner may be thrashing around with few resources for resolution, may generate reactions such as, "Why don't you just tell me what you want me to know?" (Perkins, 1991, p. 20).

Small-group tryout, in other words, is essential for determining whether intended processes and effects occur and the nature of unintended effects. Logistical difficulties in implementing the exercise also may be identified.

The researcher or designer then makes adjustments in the context for implementation, support materials for the exercise, or level of prerequisite knowledge and strategy use specified for the exercise, and implements the game or simulation with another small group. One alteration for a symbolic simulation, for example, may be to implement the exercise with a two-member team rather than as an individual exercise. In an experiential simulation, penalties for certain irresponsible actions may be added or the rules altered in order to deter unethical behavior.

17.7.3 Conduct Follow-up

Experiential exercises that meet design and formative evaluation criteria may then be further tested in group implementations. However, the type of research that is conducted on the exercise depends in part on the nature of the exercise and the purpose for which it was developed. Exercises that are designed to develop particular skills and capabilities traditionally provided by an existing instructional approach may be compared for effectiveness to that approach. For example, laboratory research simulations were developed for a viable option to the traditional "wet-lab" experience. In such a situation, comparisons of student performance between the computer-based and laboratory-based experiments on laboratory reports and posttests are logical. Also, system simulations that substitute learner operation of system components by computer-managed videodiscs may be compared to equipment-based instruction.

Similarly, business colleges often implement both data management simulations and case studies to provide students with experience in managing the finances of a company. Given similar goals, comparison research with these two types of exercises is legitimate. However, an important component of the research is to identify the types of student abilities, attitudes, and skills that interact with the exercises.

Other simulations, in contrast, typically address an instructional need that is not currently met by other forms of instruction. Diagnostic simulations, for example, were developed originally to bridge the gap between course work and hospital internships for medical students. Also, data universe and process simulations provide opportunities for students to conduct extended research and to confront their misconceptions and inadequate mental models. Such opportunities are not available in typical instructional situations.

For such simulations, a series of related exploratory studies is needed to determine the range and variety of reasoning and thinking strategies implemented by students and the effects. This research can make use of both quantitative and qualitative data. Pretests of domain knowledge and reasoning skills may be administered and then matched to the problem-solving strategies used by the students during the simulation and to other information to develop profiles of student interactions with these complex exercises.

Qualitative data in the form of analyses of students' problem-solving efforts may be obtained by (1) requesting students to verbalize their thoughts as they work through the exercise and by (2) videotaping the sessions. Transcriptions of the videotapes are then analyzed and coded to identify the specific steps implemented by each of the students. Semistructured individual interviews with students after their session(s) with the simulation can shed light on their noncognitive reactions to the experience.

Such research is time consuming and painstaking. However, strategy-based games and experiential and symbolic simulations offer opportunities for learning that are qualitatively different from those of direct instruction. The challenge is to develop the associated knowledge base for complex student-directed learning.

REFERENCES

Alexander, P. (1992). Domain knowledge: evolving themes and emerging concerns. *Educational Psychologist 27*(1), 33–51.

Alluisi, E.A. (1991). The development of technology for collective training: SIMNET, a case history. *Human Factors 33*(3) 343–62.

Berven, N.L. & Scofield, M.E. (1980). Evaluation of clinical problem-solving skills through standardized case-management simulations. *Journal of Counseling Psychology 27*(2), 199–208.

Blake, R.P. & Mouton, J.S. (1961). Reactions to intergroup competition under win-lose conditions. *Management Science 7*, 420–35.

Brown, J., Collins, A. & Dugnid, P. (1989). Situated cognition and the culture of learning. *Educational Researcher 17*, 32–44.

Crookall, D., Coleman, D. & Oxford, R. (1992). Computer-mediated language learning environments. *CALL 5*(1–2), 93–120.

Dekkers, J. & Donatti, S. (1981). The integration of research studies on the use of simulation as an instructional strategy. *Journal of Educational Research 74*, 424–27.

deMesquita, P. (1992) Diagnostic problem-solving: method or guesswork? *Journal of School Psychology 50*, 269–91.

DeVries, D.L. & Edwards, K.J. (1973). Learning games and student teams: their effects on classroom processes. *American Educational Research Journal 10*(4), 307–18.

— & Slavin, R.E. (1978). Teams-games-tournaments (TGT): review of ten classroom experiments. *Journal of Research and Development in Education 12*(1), 28–38.

Dick, W. (1991). An instructional designer's view of constructivism. *Educational Technology 31*(5), 41–44.

diSessa, A. (1982) Unlearning Aristotelian physics: a study of knowledge-based learning. *Cognitive Science 6*(1), 37–75.

— (1985). Learning about knowing. *In* E. Klein, ed. *Children and computers: new directions for child development 28*, 97-124. San Francisco, CA: Jossey-Bass.

Distlehorst, L.H. & Barrows, H.S. (1982). A new tool for problem-based self-directed learning. *Journal of Medical Education 57*, 486–88.

Driscoll, M. (1994). *Psychology of learning for instruction.* Needham Heights, MA: Allyn & Bacon.

Edens, K. & Gredler, M. (1990). A further analysis of computer-based simulations. *Simulations/Games for Learning 19*(2), 76–81.

Flick, L.B. (1990). Interaction of intuitive physics with computer simulated physics. *Journal of Research in Science Teaching 27*(3), 219–31.

Forrester, J. (1971). *World dynamics.* Cambridge, MA: Wright Allen.

Gagné, R. (1977). *The conditions of learning,* 3d ed. New York: Holt.

— (1985). *The conditions of learning,* 4th ed. New York: Holt.

Galitz, L.C. (1983). Interbank: a bank management simulation exercise. *Journal of Banking and Finance 7*, 355–82.

Gentry, (1980). Cognitive structures of business game players. *Simulation and Games 11*(4), 451–60.

Glaser, R. & Chi, M. (1988). Overview. *In* M. Chi, R. Glaser & M. J. Farr, eds. *The nature of expertise,* xv–xxxvi. Hillsdale, NJ: Erlbaum.

Glass, G.E. (1979). Policy for the unpredictable (uncertainty research and policy). *Educational Researcher, 8* (9), 12–14.

Golden, P.A. & Smith, J.R. (1991). A simulation director's perspective. *Simulation and Gaming 1,* 84–85.

Gredler, M. (1995). *Program evaluation.* New York: Macmillan.

— (1992a). *Designing and evaluating games and simulations: a process approach.* London: Kogan Page.

— (1992b). *Learning and instruction: theory into practice,* 2d ed. New York: Macmillan.

Gredler, M. (1990). Analyzing deep structure in games and simulations. *Simulation/Games for Learning 20* (3), 329–34.

Hall, G. & Loucks, S. (1977). A developmental model for determining whether the treatment is actually implemented. *American Educational Research Journal 14*(3), 263–76.

Hinze, K.E. (1984). Using a population-ecology simulation in college courses. *Collegiate Microcomputer 2*(1), 61–63.

House, E.R., Glass, G., McLean, L. & Walker, D.F. (1978). No simple answer: critique of the follow-through evaluation. *Harvard Educational Review 48*(2), 128–60.

Jonassen, D.H. (1991). Evaluating constructivist learning. *Educational Technology 31*(9), 28–33.

— (1988). Integrating learning strategies into courseware to facilitate deeper processing. *In* D.H. Jonassen, ed. *Instructional designs for microcomputer courseware,* 151–81. Hillsdale, NJ: Erlbaum.

Jones, K. (1982). *Simulations in language teaching.* Cambridge, MA: Cambridge University Press.

— (1984). Simulations versus professional educators. *In* D. Jaques & E. Tipper, eds. *Learning future with games and simulations,* 45–50. Loughborough, England: SAGSET/ Loughborough University of Technology.

— (1987). *Simulations: a handbook for teachers and trainers.* London: Kogan Page.

Jones, G.L. & Keith, K.D. (1983). Computer clinical simulations in health sciences. *Journal of Computer-Based Instruction 9*(3), 108–14.

Jungck, J.R. & Calley, J. (1985). Strategic simulations and post-Socratic pedagogy: constructing computer software to develop long-term inference through experimental inquiry. *American Biology Teacher 47,* 11–15.

Kozma, R.B. (1992). Learning with media. *Review of Educational Research 61*(2), 179-211.

Lavoie, D.R. & Good, R. (1988). The nature and use of prediction skills in a biological computer simulation. *Journal of Research and Science Teaching 25*(5), 335–60.

Lougee, C. (1988). The would-be gentleman: a historical simulation of the France of Louis XIV. *History Microcomputer Review 4*(1),

Lundy, J. (1985). The effects of competition in business games. *In* M. van Ments & K. Hearnden, eds. *Effective Use of Games and Simulation,* 199–208. Loughborough, England: SAGSET/Loughborough University of Technology.

McGuire, C. & Babbott, D. (1967). Simulation technique in the measurement of problem-solving skills. *Journal of Educational Measurement 4*(1), 1–10.

McGuire, C., Solomon, L.M. & Bashook, P.G. (1976). *Construction and use of written simulations.* New York: Psychological Corporation.

Oswalt, I. (1973). Current applications, trends, and organizations in U.S. military simulation and gaming. *Simulation and Gaming 24*(2), 153–89.

Perkins, D. (1991). What constructivism demands of the learner.

Educational Technology 31(9), 19–21.

Piaget, J. (1970). Piaget's theory. *In* P.H., ed. *Carmichael's manual of psychology,* 703–32. New York: Wiley.

— (1972). Intellectual evolution from adolescence to adulthood. *Human Development 15,* 1–12.

Pickell, G.C., Medal, D., Mann, W.S. & Staeheler, R.J. (1986). Computerizing clinical patient problems: an evolving tool for medical education. *Medical Education 20,* 201–203.

Pierfy, D.A. (1977). Comparative simulation game research: stumbling blocks and steppingstones. *Simulation and Games 8*(2), 255–68.

Remus, W. (1977). Who likes business games? *Simulation and Games 8,* 64–68.

— & Jenner, S. (1981). Playing business games: expectations and realities. *Simulation and Games 12,* 480–88.

Riegeluth, C.M. & Schwartz, E. (1989). An instructional theory for the design of computer-based simulations. *Journal of Computer-Based Simulations 16*(1), 1–10.

Rolfe, J. & Taylor, F. (1984). In the hot seat: an accident investigation management simulation. *In* D. Jaques and E. Tipper, eds. *Learning for the future with games and simulations,* 149–64. Loughborough, England: SAGSET/ Loughborough University of Technology.

Schild, E.O. (1966). The shaping of strategies. *American Behavioral Scientist 10*(3), 1–4.

Smith, S.G. & Sherwood, B.A. (1976). Educational uses of the PLATO computer system. *Science 192,* 334–52.

— & Jones, L.L. (1986). The video laboratory—a new element in teaching chemistry. *Perspectives in computing 6* (2), 20–26.

— & — (1989). Images, imagination, and chemical reality. *Journal of Chemical Education 66* (1), 8–11.

—, — & Waugh, M.L. (1986). Production and evaluation of interactive videodisc lessons in laboratory instruction. *Journal of Computer-Based Instruction 13.*

Simmons, P.E. & Lunetta, V.N. (1993). Problem-solving behaviors during a genetics computer simulation: beyond the expert/novice dichotomy. *Journal of Research in Science Teaching 30*(2), 153–73.

Spiro, R., Feltovich, P., Jacobson, M. & Coulson, R. (1991). Cognitive flexibility, constructivism and hypertext: random access instruction for advanced knowledge acquisition in ill-structured domains. *Educational Technology 31*(5), 24–33.

Stewart, J., Hafner, R., Johnson, S. & Finkel, E. (1992). Science as model building: Computers and high-school genetics. *Educational Psychologist 27*(3), 317–36.

Teach, R.D. (1990). Profits: the false prophet in business gaming. *Simulation and Gaming 21*(1), 12–16.

Tennyson, R. (1987). MAIS: an educational alternation of ICAI. *Educational Technology 27*(5), 22–28.

— & Park, O. (1987). Artificial intelligence and computer-based learning. *In* R. M. Gagne, ed. *Instructional technology: foundations,* 319–42. Hillsdale, NJ: Erlbaum.

—, Thurlow, R. & Brewer, K. (1987). Problem-oriented simulations to improve higher-order thinking strategies. *Computers in Human Behavior 3,* 151–65.

Thatcher, D. (1983). A consideration of the use of simulation for the promotion of empathy in the training of the caring professions: *me the slow learner,* a case study. *Simulation/Games for Learning 13*(1), 10–16.

— & Robinson, J. (1990). *me the slow learner*: reflections eight years on from its original design. *Simulation/Games for Learning 20*(3), 264–75.

Vanments, M. (1984). Simulation and game structure. *In* D. Thatcher & J. Robinson, eds. *Business health and nursing education*, 51–58. Loughborough, England: SAGSET.

Vargas, J.S. (1986). Instructional design flows in computer-assisted instruction. *Phi Delta Kappan 64,* 738–44.

Wentworth, D.R. & Lewis, D.R. (1973). A review of research on instructional games and simulations. *Social Education 37,* 432–40.

— & — (1972). An evaluation of a simulation game for teaching introductory economics. *The Journal of Experimental Education 42*(2), 87–96.

White, B.Y. (1984). Designing computer games to help physics students understand Newton's laws of motion. *Cognition and Instruction 1* (1), 69–108.

— (1994). A microworld-based approach to science education. *In* E. Scanlon & T. O'Shea, eds. *New directions in educational technology.* New York: Springer.

Williems, J. (1981). Problem-based group teaching: a cognitive science approach to using available knowledge. *Instructional Science 10,* 5–21.

18. CONDITIONS-BASED MODELS FOR DESIGNING INSTRUCTION

Tillman J. Ragan   Patricia L. Smith

UNIVERSITY OF OKLAHOMA

18.1 INTRODUCTION

One of the most influential and pervasive theories underlying instructional design are the propositions that: (a) There are identifiably different types of learning outcomes, and (b) the acquisition of these outcomes requires different internal and external conditions of learning.[1] In other words, this theory suggests that all learning is not qualitatively the same, that there are learning outcomes across contents, contexts, and learners that have significant and identifiable similarities in their cognitive demands on the learner. Further, each learning outcome category has significant and identifiable differences in its cognitive demands from the demands of other learning outcome categories. Finally, as this family of theories is instructional in nature, they propose that these distinctive cognitive processing demands can be supported by equally distinctive instructional methods, strategies, tactics, or conditions.

These propositions underlie what Wilson and Cole (1991) terms a "conditions-of-learning" paradigm of instructional design. Models of instructional design that follow a conditions-based theory are predicated upon the seminal principles of Robert Gagné (1966): (a) Learning can be classified into categories that require similar cognitive activities for learning (Gagné termed these "internal conditions of learning"); and, therefore, (b) within these categories of learning, similar instructional supports are needed to facilitate learning (Gagné termed these "external conditions of learning").

The influence of a conditions-based perspective can be found in the task analysis, strategy development, assessment, and evaluation procedures of conditions-based instructional design models. However, the point at which the conditions-based perspective has the greatest influence and most unique contribution is on the development of instructional strategies. According to conditions-based models, when designing instructional strategies, instructional designers must determine the goals of instruction, categorize these goals as to outcome category, and select strategies that have been suggested as being effective for this category of learning outcome (or devise strategies consistent with the cognitive processing demands of the learning task).

Examples of conditions-based models of design have been authored by Gagné (1985) and Gagné, Briggs, and Wager (1988), Merrill (1983), Reigeluth (1979), Merrill and Li (1990), and Smith and Ragan (1993). Other authors, though they may not posit a complete approach to instructional design or "model," have suggested conditions-based approaches to strategy design (e.g., Horn, 1976; Landa, 1983). Interestingly, several of these explications (Jonassen, Grabinger & Harris, 1991; West, Farmer & Wolf, 1991) present the instructional processes first and then suggest the learning outcomes for which these strategies might be appropriate.

The purpose of this chapter is to describe the evolution of the conditions-based perspective, exemplify and compare conditions-based models, and examine the assumptions of the conditions-based model both theoretically and empirically. These assumptions are:

1. Learning goals can be categorized as to learning outcome or knowledge type.
2. Learning outcomes can be represented in a predictable prerequisite relationship.
3. Acquisition of different outcome categories requires different internal processes (or, different internal processes lead to different cognitive outcomes).
4. Different internal processes are supported by identifiably different instructional processes (or, different instructional processes lead to different internal processes).

---

[1] We refer here to "conditions of learning" as described by Gagné (1985) as external conditions of learning, that is, those instructional supports that are designed to promote learning, rather than instructional conditions as described by Reigeluth and Merrill (1978), which are primarily learner and learning context variables.

18.2 EVOLUTION OF THE CONDITIONS-BASED THEORY

The first full statement of a conditions-based theory of instruction appears to have been by R. M. Gagné in the early 1960s.[2] However, there was a considerable amount of conjecture within this paradigm by a variety of researchers prior to Gagné. In addition, Gagné and others have developed a conditions-based theory along a variety of lines of thought until the present day. In this section, we will review work leading to the conditions model, discuss Gagné's early and evolving conceptions, and review various lines of research in the conditions-based tradition which have appeared subsequent to Gagné's first work (see also 1.6, 5.2).

18.2.1 Early Work Leading to Conditions-Based Thinking

Among the earliest writing that specifically addresses the need to beware of overgeneralization of knowledge about learning, Carr (1933) cautioned that conclusions that are valid for one category of learning may not be valid for others. The categories of which Carr spoke were not within a formally defined taxonomy or system, but rather they were reflected in the different experimental tasks, research procedures, and measures employed in different studies.

Interest in devising useful categories of learning persisted over the decade, and Melton wrote in the learning theory chapter in the 1941 *Encyclopedia of Educational Research* (Melton, 1941) of efforts to develop a psychologically based taxonomy of learning outcomes. During this same period, Tolman (1949) described six categories of learning, and Woodworth (1958) described five categories.

The behaviorist movement lent a rigor and precision to the study of learning that is perhaps difficult to appreciate today (see 1.4.4, 1.4.5, 2.2.2.3). When one looks at the work of some behaviorist learning researchers, one finds compelling (if not esoteric) evidence that there are different kinds of learning with different conditions for their attainment. Wickens (1962) described Spence's studies of animal learning involving both aversive conditioning and approach behaviors:

> Spence (1956) has used the same approach in differentiation of the instrumental avoidance situation of the type represented by the eyelid conditioning from an approach learning represented by an animal scurrying down a runway for its daily pellet. Spence is quite specific: The antecedent of H (the intervening variable leading to the running response) in the latter case is a function only of n and not of incentive magnitude; in the former, it—the intervening

variable H—is a function of n and also of magnitude of the UCS. This conclusion leads him to describe the excitatory component of behavior, E, as being a function of two intervening variables, H and D, insofar as classical aversive conditioning is concerned, while the excitatory component of runway behavior requires, for him, three intervening variables, H, D, and K (Wickens, 1962, p. 81).

Another specification of differences in learning tasks is seen in Bloom's taxonomy (Bloom, Englehart, Furst, Hill & Krathwohl, 1956). This group's thinking about the need for a taxonomy of educational outcomes originated at an informal meeting of college examiners at the 1948 meeting of the American Psychological Association, at which "interest was expressed in a theoretical framework that could be used to facilitate communication among examiners" (Bloom et al., 1956, p. 4). The taxonomy arose not from a synthesis of research but in response to a collective need for standardization of terminology.

Applications of Bloom's taxonomy, however, have frequently assumed a stature similar to that of psychologically based approaches. For example, a study by Kunen, Cohen & Solman (1981) investigated the cumulative hierarchical assumption of Bloom's taxonomy. The study concluded that there is "moderately strong support for the assumption that the taxonomy represents a cumulative hierarchy of categories of cognitive operations" (p. 207). The tasks used in the study involved recall of knowledge, recall of applications, recall of words related to a synthesis task, and so forth ("the dependent variable was the number of critical words correctly free recalled," p. 207). As all of the tasks appear to involve recall, we have some doubt about the validity of conclusions supporting a hierarchy of cognitive operations. Furst's (1981) review of research on Bloom's taxonomy leveled a great deal of criticism of the taxonomy in terms of its lack of cumulative hierarchical structure. It seems clear that the taxonomy's uses have exceeded its original design and purpose.

18.2.2 Military and Industry Training Researchers

In the 1950s and 1960s (and continuing to the present), a substantial amount of research and development related to learning and instruction has been conducted by the military services and industry (see also 1.10). Edling and associates pointed out that this group of scientists in military and industrial settings was large for its work to be so unfamiliar to many educators. Indeed, in 1963 the Army's HumRRO employed 100 "training psychologists" of whom 65 were Ph.D.s, and the Air Force Training and Research Center at one time employed 168 psychologists of whom 100 held Ph.D.s (Edling et al., 1972, p. 94).

Among the contributions of these researchers were some "relatively sophisticated taxonomies of learner tasks," such as those developed by Cotterman (1959), Demaree (1961), Lumsdaine (1960), Miller (1962), Parker and Downs (1961),

---

[2] A full statement of Gagné's conditions model appears in Gagné, "Problem Solving," in A.W. Melton's 1964 edited work, *Categories of Learning*. The paper on which the chapter is based was delivered in a symposium convened by Melton in January 1962, for the purpose of exploring "the interrelationship of different categories of learning" (Melton, 1964, p. vii).

Stolurow (1963), and Willis (1961). Gagné's work, also perceived of evolving within this context, was seen to be "particularly powerful" (Edling, 1972, p. 95).

Of these taxonomies, Miller's treatment of learning types illuminates the idea of "task analysis" as it was viewed in the 1950s and early 1960s (Miller, 1953, 1954, 1956, 1962). Miller, employed by IBM, proposed that an "equipment task analysis" description "should include analysis of perceptual, short-term recall, long-term recall, decision-making and motor processes implied by the initial equipment task analysis" (Smode, 1962, p. 435). Miller reflected the mainstream approach by focusing on job tasks, although it is clear that consideration of cognitive processes greatly influenced much of his analysis scheme's structure and content.

Much of the progress in defining learning tasks made by the military and corporate researchers may be attributed to their employer's demands. Increasingly, technical training requirements in the military and in industry were placing high demands on the skills of training designers to develop instruction in problem solving, troubleshooting, and other expertise-related tasks. Bryan (1962) discussed the pertinence of troubleshooting studies to the topics of transfer, concept formation, problem solving, decision making, thinking, and learning. To perhaps exaggerate a bit, one can envision academic colleagues running rats in the laboratories, while their counterparts who were employed by the military and large corporations were struggling with issues of human learning and skilled performance. This pressure to describe complex learning (often felt by academics as well) forced behaviorally trained psychologists to consider cognitive issues long before the mainstream, and produced a unique blend of "neobehaviorism" with what we might call "precognitive" psychology. As we view Gagné's work and its evolution, this blend and transition will be clearly illustrated.

18.2.3 Academic Learning Psychologists

The thinking of academic psychologists about types of learning are well represented in a 1964 volume edited by A. W. Melton, *Categories of Human Learning.* In chapters by N. H. Anderson, E. J. Archer, G. E. Briggs, J. Deese, W. K. Estes, P. M. Fitts, R. M. Gagné, D. A. Grant, H. A. Kendler, T. S. Kendler, G. A. Kimble, A. W. Melton, L. Postman, B. J. Underwood, and D. D. Wickens, concerns and progress toward understanding varieties of human learning are discussed. Two of these contributions will be discussed here for the information they contain on state of the art and as illustrations of the categories defined within this period.

Underwood (1964) discussed possible approaches to a taxonomy of human learning, proposing how it would be possible "to express the relationships among research findings for all forms of human learning" (p. 48). Underwood noted that a single, grand unified theory did not yet exist in which a master set of statements and relationships could lead to deductions of findings in each of the various areas of interest in learning research. A second approach that

Underwood suggested in the absence of a grand unified theory was to attempt to

express the continuity for all human learning . . . in terms of phenomena produced by comparable operations. Thus, can the operations defining extinction in eyelid conditioning be duplicated in verbal learning, in motor learning, in concept formation, and so on, and, if so, do the same phenomena result from these operations? (p. 48).

Underwood (p. 48) noted that a difficulty in doing such cross-category research is that the differences among tasks make it physically impossible to manipulate them in comparable manners:

For example, it would seem difficult to manipulate meaningfulness on a pursuit rotor in the same sense that this variable is manipulated in verbal learning. Or, what operations in problem solving are comparable to variations in intensity of the conditioned stimulus in classical conditioning?

Underwood later described a technique for determining the similarity of learning in different situations. That technique is illustrated in work by Richardson (1958) in which "A descriptive difference between concept formation and rote verbal learning can be stated in terms of the number of identical responses to be associated with similar stimuli" (p. 49). The number of responses to a stimulus associated with a concept-learning task was different from the number of responses to the same stimulus when it was part of a rote-learning task, reflecting a lack of "continuity" between the two types of tasks.

In a seminal chapter in *Categories of Human Learning,* Melton (1964) pointed out that neither the physical structures of the human organism nor its cognitive processes themselves (such as motivational, perceptual, and performance processes) provide guidance for a taxonomy of learning, as such structures would provide in classifying physical attributes. Of the need for a conditions-based approach, Melton (1964, p. 327) bemoans the lack of articulation between training design questions and knowledge about learning:

When one is confronted with a decision to use massed or distributed practice, to insist on information feedback or not to insist on it, to arrange training so as to maximize or minimize requirements for contiguous stimulus differentiation, etc., and (one) discovers that the guidance received from experimental research and theory is different for rote learning, for skill learning, and for problem solving, taxonomic issues become critical and taxonomic ambiguities become frustrating, to say the least.

A strong element of formalism, in addition to the practical concerns noted in the quote above, seems to shape Melton's thinking, which is illustrative for the time in which he was writing. Melton wrote at length about a "taxonomy" of learning from the standpoint of taxonomies themselves and how they come about in science. A persistent theme is how the "primitive categories" will end up being used—to what extent they will be used and how they can conceivably be modified. The primitive categories, reflected to a large extent by chapter topics in the book, are rather long-standing areas of research and theory interest in learning psychology: conditioning, rote learning, probability learning, skills learning, concept learning, and problem solving. Apparently, Melton expected that all of these topics should, as organized in some appropriate and meaningful way, be related to one another in a taxonomic, hierarchical structure. One may notice, coincidentally perhaps, that Gagné's first edition of *Conditions of Learning* included a set of learning types that were, unlike those found in more recent editions, in toto a taxonomic list, in which each category in the classification scheme was prerequisite to the others (with the exception of the first category, classical conditioning). In later versions of the types of learning, Gagné included many categories that he did not propose as being in hierarchical relationship (only the learning types within the intellectual skills category are proposed as hierarchical in more current versions.)

18.3 CONTRIBUTIONS OF R. M. GAGNÉ

As R. M. Gagné is generally identified as the primary originator of a conditions-based model of instructional design, an understanding of his evolution of thought becomes foundational to understanding the theory that extends beyond his contribution.

18.3.1 Precursors to Gagné's Conditions-Based Theory

In a review of factors that contribute to learning efficiency for a volume on programmed instruction sponsored by the Air Force Office of Scientific Research, Gagné and Bolles noted that "the learning tasks that have been most intensively studied by psychologists have been of an artificial "laboratory" variety; relatively little is known about learning in real life situations" (Gagné & Bolles, 1959, pp. 13–14). In 1962, as one who worked as a researcher in an academic setting, then as a researcher and research director in a military setting, and finally back in the academic setting, Gagné reflected on military training research in an article entitled "Military Training and Principles of Learning."

Training research in the 1950s (see 1.10) put Gagné in touch with a wide variety of instructional problems, representing a wide variety of learning tasks. Illustrative studies in the literature are Gagné (1954), "An Analysis of Two Problem Solving Activities," involving troubleshooting and interpretation of aerial photographs, and Gagné, Baker, and Wylie (1951), "Effects of an Interfering Task on the Learning of a Complex Motor Skill," involving manipulations of controls similar to aircraft controls. In a review of problem solving and thinking, Gagné pointed out the relevance of troubleshooting studies to issues in concept formation (Gagné, 1959). Wide and vigorous participation in research on learning and instruction in the military environment,

along with his thorough and rigorous background as a learning psychologist, may have created the dissonance that motivated Gagné to develop the concepts of types of learning outcomes, learning hierarchies and events of instruction, and conditions of learning.

18.3.2 Development of Types of Learning

In his chapter on problem solving for Melton's *Categories of Human Learning,* Gagné (1964) presents a table entitled "A Suggested Ordering of the Types of Human Learning," in which he proposed the following six types of learning: response learning, chaining, verbal learning (paired associates), concept learning, principle learning, problem solving (p. 312). He did not cite a previous publication of his here, so this may be the first appearance of his types-of-learning scheme. This is not to say that he had not engaged in much previous thought and writing on important differences between forms of learning. However, the pulling together of types of learning to form a totally inclusive scheme containing mutually exclusive elements appears to have taken place around the time the "Categories of Learning" symposium was taking place, early in 1962.

Gagné's thinking on types of learning is illustrated by his discussion of problem solving as a form of learning. In the following, he points out how problem solving, as a form of learning, differs from other forms of learning:

> . . . the learning situation for problem solving never includes performances which could, by simple summation, constitute the criterion performance. In conditioning and trial-and-error learning, the performance finally exhibited (blinking an eye, or tracing a path) occurs as part of the learning situation. In verbal learning, the syllables or words to be learned are included in the learning situation. In concept learning, however, this is not always so, and there is consequently a resemblance to problem solving in this respect. Although mediation experiments may present a concept during learning which is later a part of the criterion performance, many concept learning experiments do not use this procedure. Instead they require the S to respond with a performance scored in a way which was not directly given in learning (the stating of an abstraction such as "round" or "long and rectangular"). Similarly, the "solution" of the problem is not presented within the learning situation for problem solving. Concept formation and problem solving are *nonreproductive* types of learning (Gagné, 1964, p. 311).

Perhaps the first full and complete statement of the types of learning conception appeared in the first edition of *The Conditions of Learning* (Gagné, 1965). In that work, Gagné began by reviewing learning theory and research, such as that by James, Dewey, Watson, Thorndike, Tolman, Ebbinghaus, Pavlov, and Köhler. To introduce the idea of types of learning, Gagné presents the notion of "learning prototypes": "Throughout the period of scientific investigation of learning there has been frequent recourse to certain typical experimental situations to serve as prototypes for learning" (p.18). The differences in kinds of learning among these prototypes is seen in the inability to "reduce" one variety to another, although many attempts have been made" (p. 18). To clarify how these distinctive forms of learning have come to be lumped together as one form, Gagné (pp. 18–19) pointed out:

> These learning prototypes all have a similar history in this respect: each of them started to be a representative of a particular variety of learning situation. Thorndike wanted to study animal association. Pavlov was studying reflexes. Ebbinghaus studied the memorization of verbal lists. Köhler was studying the solving of problems by animals. By some peculiar semantic process, these examples became prototypes of learning, and thus were considered to represent the domain of learning as a whole, or at least in large part.

Gagné (1965) presented eight types of learning in the first edition, in a strict hierarchical relationship. All types but the first, signal learning (classical conditioning), have prerequisite relationships with one another. The eight types of learning, with corresponding researcher links, were:

1. Signal learning (Pavlov, 1927)
2. Stimulus-response learning (Thorndike, 1989; Skinner, 1938; Kimball, 1961)
3. Chaining (Skinner, 1938; Gilbert, 1962)
4. Verbal association (Underwood, 1964)
5. Multiple discrimination (Postman, 1961)
6. Concept learning (Kendler, 1964)
7. Principle learning (Gagné, 1964)
8. Problem solving (Katona, 1940; Maier, 1930)

Regarding the distinctions between these types, Gagné describes support for some of the distinctions (Gagné, 1965, p. 59). Table 18-1 summarizes that discussion.

Later editions of *Conditions of Learning* modified the list of types of learning considerably. Although the second edition (Gagné, 1970) reflected no change in the number or labeling of the eight types of learning, by the third edition (Gagné, 1977) information-processing theories were added to the treatment of learning prototypes, and a large section was added on information processing along with recasting the types of learning (see 5.4.1). The information-processing perspective, present in the third edition, was not part of the first or second edition, even though earlier work reflected a strong information-processing background

(Gagné 1962c). Surprisingly, while Gagné's primary base was shifting from behavioral to cognitive in the third edition, task characteristics, rather than psychological processes, begin to guide the form and content of the types of learning. In Gagné's fourth edition (1985), a hierarchical, prerequisite relationship is limited to four subcategories of one major category, intellectual skills. The types of learning in the fourth edition are:

1. Intellectual skills
   discriminations
   concepts
   rules
   problem solving
2. Cognitive strategies
3. Verbal information
4. Motor skills
5. Attitudes

Gagné's descriptions of the categories of problem solving and cognitive strategies have continued to evolve in recent years. For example, in Gagné and Glaser (1987), "problem solving" was combined into one category along with cognitive strategies. Inspection of the text reveals that, in fact, domain-specific problem solving was meant here, along with strategies for learning and strategies for remembering (see pp. 66–67). The evaluation of Gagné's problem-solving category can also be noted in his fourth edition of *Conditions of Learning,* in which problem solving was moved out of the intellectual skills category as higher-order rules and appears to have become a category separate from both the rule-based learning of intellectual skills and the domain-general category of cognitive strategy.

Gagné and Merrill (1990) described an approach to the integration of multiple learning objectives for larger, longer-term efforts that are unified through "pursuit of a comprehensive purpose in which the learner is engaged, called an enterprise" (p. 23). A learning enterprise may be defined as "a purposive activity that may depend for its execution on some combination of verbal information, intellectual skills, and cognitive strategies, all related by their involvement in the common goal" (p. 25). The storage of enterprises is discussed in terms of mental models (Gentner & Stevens, 1983), schemata (Rummelhart & Norman, 1978), and work models (Bunderson, Gibbons, Olsen & Kearsley, 1981). Three kinds of enterprise schemata are described: denoting, manifesting, and discovering. Disappointingly, all of their examples are of individual learning, not of sets of them.

What do these categories of learning represent? Gagné described the types of learning outcomes as "learned dispositions," "capabilities," or "long-term memory states" (p. 245), qualities that reside within the learner. He further described two of these categories, verbal information and intellectual skills, as having distinctly different memory storage systems. Gagné and White (1978) provided an empirical basis for the "verbal information" knowledge to be stored as propositional networks. They further described rule using as stored in

---

TABLE 18-1. SUMMARY OF THE ETIOLOGY OF LEARNING TYPES

Type 1 distinct from type 2:	Thorndike, 1989
	Skinner, 1938
	Hull, 1934
Type 3 as a distinct form:	Skinner, 1938
	Hull, 1943
Type 5 distinct from type 6:	Mowrer, 1960b
	Harlow, 1959

hierarchical skill structures, which they at that time called *intellectual skills.*

More recently, Gagné (1985) has described verbal information learning as stored as propositional networks or schemata. He describes rules, including defining rules or concepts, as stored as "If . . . then" productions. He does not suggest how problem-solving capabilities themselves are stored, although he implied that they are interconnections of schemata and productions. Nor does he explicitly conjecture regarding the storage mechanisms of attitudes, motor skills, or cognitive strategies.

As the concept of types of learning evolved from its neobehaviorist beginnings to a more cognitive orientation seen in the fourth edition of *Conditions of Learning,* the research basis for differences in conditions for their achievement appears to have been largely lost. Although the concept remains as intuitively valid as ever to many instructional technologists, direct support in the literature is shockingly absent. Kyllonen and Schute (1989) describe Gagné's types of learning as a "rational taxonomy," being developed via proposing "task categories in terms of characteristics that will foster or inhibit learned performance" (p. 120). The drawback to such an approach is that its basis does not lie in psychological processes and, therefore, such processes are unsystematically considered.

18.3.3 Development of the Learning Hierarchies Concept

A study by Gagné and Brown (1961) revealed thinking that led directly to Gagné's conceptions of learning hierarchies and types of learning. Here, in the context of programmed instruction, Gagné and Brown were concerned with the acquisition of meaningful "conceptual" learning, as compared with the rote memorization or association learning that characterized the work of Holland and Skinner:

> . . . from an examination of representative published examples of programs (e.g., Holland, 1959; Skinner, 1958), it is not immediately apparent that they are conveying "understanding" in the sense of capability for inducing transfer to new problem situations. They appear to be concerned primarily with the usages of words in a variety of stimulus contexts" (p. 174).

The phenomenon of transfer appears to have been central to Gagné and Brown's concerns, both of transfer from prerequisite learnings to higher-level outcomes (sometimes termed *vertical transfer*) and in terms of transfer from the learning situation to later application (sometimes termed *lateral transfer*). Although a great deal of attention is given to the study's programmed instruction format in the report, it is clear that the authors' interests were focused on a question of vertical transfer to problem solving (the particular learning task would now be considered relational rule use).

In Gagné and Brown (1961), the authors described a study with a programmed instruction lesson teaching concepts (see 2.3.4) related to number series: the terms *value* and

number. After a common introduction to the fundamental concepts, the study employed three treatment methods to teach application of the concepts to finding the key to number series problems: (1) rule & example (R&E), (2) discovery (D), and (3) guided discovery (GD). The authors considered issues such as "size of step" and others of interest in programmed-instruction research of the day. However, they concluded that "some aspect of what has been learned . . . is of greater effect than how it has been learned" (p. 181). The difference in "what" as supplied by the three treatments was that the guided discovery method required use of previously learned concepts in a new context.

Although all three methods were effective in teaching learners to solve numerical series problems, the GD and D methods were superior to the R&E method, with the GD method being the most effective of all. The inferiority of the R&E method was attributed to the fact that it did not *require* learners to practice the application of concepts to a problem situation. In other conditions, learners could make the application but were believed to have, in general, not applied the concepts to the problem situation.

A postscript: It is ironic perhaps that in this early study, one that employed programmed instruction methods and reflects Gagné's thinking at that time very much as a neobehaviorist, the instructional strategies labeled "discovery" and "guided discovery" were found to provide superior instruction. It should be noted that the "discovery" method used was more structured than what many today might construct: A good amount of supplantive instruction on prerequisites preceded the "discovery" condition.

Gagné's first references to "learning hierarchies" appears in articles published in 1962: a report of a study, "Factors in Acquiring Knowledge of a Mathematical Task," and another study, "The Acquisition of Knowledge," which involved similar learning tasks. These reports were preceded by a study by Gagné and Paradise (1961) which formed a foundation for the latter studies. In 1961, Gagné and Paradise found support for the proposition that transfer of learning from subordinate sets of learning tasks could account for performance in a terminal learning task. In a subsequent study, Gagné, Mayor, Garstens, and Paradise (1962) sought to extend and confirm the validity of the idea of the "learning hierarchy."

Gagné, Mayor, Garstens, and Paradise (1962) sought to test effects of three factors that should mediate the effectiveness of learning hierarchies: (a) identifiability, which roughly translates into "acquisition of prerequisite concepts"; (b) recallability, stimulated in the study by cueing and repetition of prerequisite concepts; and (c) integration, in this study provided by what Gagné and Briggs later termed "provision of learning guidance," which was directed toward assisting the learner in applying concepts to problem situations. Two variables, used in various combinations, served to modify a basic learning program: repetition (high and low) and guidance (high and low). The posttest supplied information about achievement of not only the terminal task (adding integers) but also the 12 prerequisite learning sets, each scored as "pass" or "fail." These data were analyzed to supply evidence of the effects of the treatments on transfer. Success in final task achievement correlated highly with the number of subordinate tasks successfully achieved for both of the two terminal learning tasks (.87 and .88). Patterns of transfer among the subordinate tasks also conformed to theoretical predictions.

In "The Acquisition of Knowledge," Gagné began by explicating the concept of a "class of tasks," differentiating the idea from "a response" by noting that in acquiring useful knowledge, it is inadequate to consider knowledge as a set of responses, since, when applied, it is impossible to identify from each specific response which skills, such as multiplication or punctuating compound sentences, the responses imply: "Any of an infinite number of distinguishable stimulus situations and an equal number of responses may be involved" (1962, p. 229).

18.3.4 Research Confirming Learning Hierarchies

In 1973, Gagné described the idea of learning hierarchies and noted that learning hierarchies have the following characteristics: (a) They describe "successively achievable intellectual skills, each of which is stated as a performance class"; (b) they do not include "verbal information, cognitive strategies, motivational factors, or performance sets"; and (c) each step in the hierarchy describes "only those prerequisite skills that must be recalled at the moment of learning" to supply the necessary "internal" component of the total learning situation (pp. 21–22).

Gagné also described several studies on the validation of learning hierarchies. A fundamental way to accomplish this is to look at differences in transfer between groups that attain and groups that do not attain hypothesized prerequisites. Gagné, Mayor, Garstens, and Paradise (1962, Table 3, p. 9) is cited as an example providing positive evidence from such an approach. Other validation studies were reported, each looking in one way or another at the validity of a particular learning hierarchy—in other words, at the extent to which the hierarchy was a true description of prerequisite relationships among hypothesized subtasks. As a set, these studies can be seen to present evidence to the validity of the concept of learning hierarchies. The studies are summarized in Table 18-2.

In addition to the above, studies by Gagné and associates commonly cited to support the learning hierarchies hypothesis include: Gagné, 1962; Gagné and Paradise, 1961; Gagné, Mayor, Garstens, and Paradise, 1962; Gagné and Bassler, 1963; Gagné and Staff, University of Maryland Mathematics Project, 1965.

It should be noted that in "Factors in Acquiring Knowledge of a Mathematical Task" and in "The Acquisition of Knowledge," Gagné dealt primarily with learning hierarchies, not yet with the idea that different types of learning might require different instructional conditions. The thrust of Gagné's ideas at this point was toward the organization and sequence of instruction, not toward the form of encounter.

18.3.5 Development of Events of Instruction and Conditions of Learning

18.3.5.1. Events of Instruction. In "The Acquisition of Knowledge" (Gagné, 1962), in addition to presenting the "learning hierarchies" concept, Gagné also introduced a precursor to the nine events of instruction. The description is of four functions that a theory of knowledge acquisition must account for:

1. Required terminal performance
2. Elements of the stimulus situation
3. High recallability of learning sets
4. Provision of "guidance of thinking"

Another foundation for the events of instruction was Gagné's thinking on the idea of internal and external conditions of learning, which is fundamental to the thesis of the first edition of *Conditions of Learning* in 1965. Internal and external conditions are defined (p. 21), and discussion of each of the types of learning is organized essentially along lines of internal and external conditions for achievement of that type of learning. To summarize his descriptions of these two types of conditions: Internal conditions were primarily described as learners' possession of prerequisite knowledge, and external conditions were viewed as instruction.

The first edition of *Conditions of Learning* (Gagné, 1965) did not have a discussion of the "events of instruction" in the

TABLE 18-2. RESULTS OF STUDIES ON HIERARCHIES

Author(s)	Date	Learning Task	Results
Wiegand	1970	inclined plane	transfer demonstrated
Nicholas	1970	not stated	replicated Wiegand
Coleman & Gagné	1970	exports comparison	too much mastery by ctrl. gp., but > transfer to prob. solv. found
Eustace	1969	concept "noun"	hypothesized sequence better
Okey & Gagné	1970	chemistry	lng. hier. revis. > orig. ver.
Resnick et al.	1971	double classification	successfully predicted outcomes
Caruso & Resnick	1971	replication	Resnick et al., 1971, confirmed
Wang et al.	1972	math curriculum	several dependency sequen. found

same fashion as the term later came to be used—as a listing intended to be inclusive, reflecting events that must occur, and if not supplied by instruction, generated by learners. The treatment in *Conditions of Learning,* under the heading "External Events of Instruction," included discussion of (a) control of the stimulus situation (strategy prescriptions varied with types of learning), (b) verbally communicated "directions" (directing attention, conveying information about expected performance, inducing recall of previously learned entities, and guidance in learning by discovery), and (c) feedback from learning.

The "events of instruction" conception may be more directly attributable to L. J. Briggs's work than Gagné's, although the two collaborated extensively on it. For example, Briggs, Campeau, Gagné, and May's (1967) handbook for "multimedia design of instruction" uses nearly all the elements of what was to become the "events of instruction" within its examples, but it does not present a list of the events (see Briggs, 1967, pp. 53–73; May & Briggs, 1967, pp. 74–138). In another chapter in that manual, Briggs, Gagné, and May noted (p. 45) as "instructional functions of stimuli," the following:

1. Set a goal in terms of performance desired.
2. Direct attention.
3. Present instructional content (also stimuli).
4. Elicit response.
5. Provide feedback.
6. Direct the next effort.
7. Help the student evaluate his performance.

Also noted here under "other special functions of stimuli" are: (a) providing the degree of cueing or prompting desired, (b) enhancing motivation, (c) aiding the student in recall of relevant concepts, (d) promoting transfer, and (e) inducing generalizing experiences (Briggs, Gagné & May, 1967, p. 45). Between the two lists, the events-of-instruction formulation appears to have been taking shape.

The first edition of *The Conditions of Learning* (Gagné, 1965) contained a section called "component functions of the instructional situation" that, except for the label, was to be virtually identical in conception and content to the "events of instruction" seen in later editions of *The Conditions of Learning,* as well as in Gagné & Briggs, *Principles of Instructional Design* (1974). The eight functions were: (a) presenting the stimulus, (b) directing attention and other learner activities, (c) providing a model for terminal performance, (d) furnishing external prompts, (e) guiding the direction of thinking, (f) inducing transfer of knowledge, (g) assessing learning attainments, and (h) providing feedback. With *Principles of Instructional Design* (Gagné & Briggs, 1974), the full Events of Instruction Model was first presented and fully discussed. Table 18.3 presents the Events of Instruction along with cross-reference to other sections in this handbook which relate to each section.

18.3.5.2. Conditions of Learning. Completing Gagné's contribution to conditions-based theory are his discussion of the internal and external conditions of learning that support

each type of learning outcome. "Internal conditions" are those cognitive processes that support the acquisition of particular categories of learning outcomes. "External conditions" are those instructional conditions provided by teacher, materials, or other learners that can facilitate the internal conditions necessary for learning. These external conditions, too, vary according to type of learning. Not surprisingly, given Gagné's transition from behavioral to cognitive theory bases, he developed the external conditions model first.

As an instructional psychologist, Gagné was particularly interested in the external conditions that might occur or could be provided to "activate and support" the internal processing necessary for learning to occur (1985, p. 276). In fact, Gagné defined the purpose of instructional theory as "to propose a rationally based relationship between instructional events, their effects on learning processes, and the learning outcomes that are produced as a result of these processes" (1985, p. 244). Therefore, Gagné derived the external events from the internal events of information processing. (See Table 18.3.)

Gagné particularized the general external events, the "events of instruction," that begin to be described in his work in 1962 to specific prescriptions for external conditions for each type of learning, event by event, for each of the categories of learned capability. Much of these external conditions are logically derived from the intersection of the function of the external event (those cognitive processes that it supports) and the nature of the learned capability.

In "Domains of Learning" (1972), Gagné argued very specifically for a conditions-based theory but did not present research directly on it; rather, he presented arguments about the nature of different learning domains, buttressed often in a general fashion by research. The five domains—motor skills, verbal information, intellectual skills, cognitive strategies, and attitudes—are the level at which he argued that there is a difference in how they should be taught, particularly in terms of (a) the kind and amount of practice required and (b) the role of meaningful context. Additional criteria as means by which types of learning can be contrasted with regard to instructional concerns appear in a 1984 article, "Learning Outcomes."

In Gagné and White's 1978 article, two general domains of learning outcome were discussed: (a) knowledge stating and (b) rule application. References used to support the distinctness of these two domains include Gagné (1972) and Olson and Bruner (1974).

In 1987, Gagné and Glaser (1987) developed a review that included a brief survey of Gagné's early work, learning as cognition, importance of short-term memory, learning complex performances, knowledge organization for problem solving, mental models, and self-regulation. Table 18-4 (on p. 550), reproduced from that review, provides an excellent summary of hypothesized differential learning conditions for types of learning (see 5.3.5.4).

18.3.5.3. Internal Conditions of Learning. Gagné suggested that, for each category or subcategory of learning

TABLE 18-3. CROSS-REFERENCED GAGNÉ-BRIGGS (1974) EVENTS OF INSTRUCTION

Event	Handbook Cross-Reference
1. Gain attention	31.3.1, 34
2. Inform learner of objective	30.6.2
3. Stimulate recall of prerequisite learning	22.3.4.4
4. Presenting stimulus material	7.4, 11.3, 12.2.3, 13.4, 26–28, 31
5. Providing learning guidance	
6. Eliciting performance	30.6.1
7. Providing feedback	32
8. Assessing performance	7.47, 23.4.6
9. Enhancing retention and transfer	23.5.2.1

capability to be acquired, certain internal conditions were necessary. By 1985, Gagné described these internal conditions as two kinds: (a) prerequisite knowledge, which is stored in long-term memory, and (b) particular cognitive processes that bring this old knowledge and new knowledge together and store it in a retrievable form. Gagné described these cognitive processes using an information-processing model: attention, selective perception, semantic encoding, retrieval, response organization, control processes, and expectancies.

It should be noted that in Gagné's detailing of the internal conditions of each type of learning, the major internal condition that he described was prerequisite knowledge. For example, Gagné specifies the internal conditions for rule learning to be knowledge of (the ability to classify previously unencountered instances and noninstances of) component concepts. This may be because the research base for the identification of the specific internal conditions for each learning capability was inadequate or because as an instructional theorist, his predominant interest was the external conditions that could support the generalized information-processing mechanism and those internal conditions necessary prior to the initiation of new learning.

Gagné (1984) suggested that the internal events that may differ most across learning capabilities are "(a) the substantive type of relevant prior knowledge, (b) manner of encoding into long-term storage, (c) requirement for retrieval and transfer to new situations" (p. 514). Therefore, in his 1985 edition of *Conditions of Learning,* he pointed out that the events that may differ most significantly from learning category to learning category are those corresponding to the above three internal events: These external events are (a) stimulating recall of prior knowledge, (b) providing learning guidance, and (c) enhancing retention and transfer.

18.4 EXAMPLES OF CONDITIONS-BASED MODELS

Robert Gagné provided the intellectual leadership for a conditions-based theory of instruction. A number of scholars followed in his tradition by developing more detailed prescription of the external conditions that will support different types of learning.

The two texts edited by Reigeluth in the 1980s, *Instructional Design Theories and Models* (1983) and *Instructional Theories in Action* (1987), clearly delineate a number of models that we would describe as conditions-based models of design. (Some of the models in this text, such as those by Scandura, Collins & Keller, we would not describe as full conditions-based models, as they do not describe the cognitive and instructional conditions for more than one learning type.) It is not the purpose of this chapter to replicate the thorough discussions of the conditions-based models presented in Reigeluth (1983, 1987). However, we will briefly discuss and compare the models, because it is through the comparisons that many of the major issues regarding conditions-based models are revealed and exemplified. We will also briefly review research and evaluation studies that have examined the effectiveness of the model as a whole or individual features of the model. We have also included in our discussion some "models" not presented in Reigeluth's texts. Some examples provided are arguably not *instructional design models* at all (such as the work of Horn, 1976; Resnick, 1967; West, Farmer & Wolf, 1991), but all employ, reflect, or extend the *conditions-based theory* propositions listed in the introduction of this chapter in one important way or another.

18.4.1 Gagné and Gagné, Briggs, and Wager

We have thoroughly described Gagné's conditions-based theory of instruction elsewhere in this chapter. This theory was the basis of an instructional design model presented in Briggs's *Instructional Design: Principles and Applications* (1977) and *Principles of Instructional Design* (Gagné & Briggs, 1974, 1979; Gagné, Briggs & Wager, 1988, 1992).

Research examining the validity of Gagné's theory are of two types: those that have examined the validity of Gagné's instructional theory as a cluster of treatment variables and those that have examined the individual propositions of the theory as separate variables. Research of the latter type will be discussed later in this chapter. A few studies have attempted to evaluate the overall value of instruction based on Gagné's theory or portions of Gagné's theory that are not central to the conditions-based theory. We will describe several examples of studies of this first type. Goldberg (1987), Marshall (1987), Mengel (1986), and Stahl (1979) compared "traditional" textbook or teacher-led instruction to print-based or teacher-led instruction designed according to Gagné's principles. These studies were across age groups and subject matters. Mengal and Stahl found significant differences in learning effects for the versions developed according to Gagné's principles, and for Goldberg and Marshall no significant difference in treatments. Although we believe such gross comparison studies to be essential to the development of research in an area, they suffer from some of the same threats to validity of conclusions as other comparison studies. In particular, it is unclear that the "traditional" versions did not include some features of Gagné's principles and that the "Gagnétian" versions were fully consistent with these principles. Research that has examined the principles from Gagné's instructional design models that are directly related to propositions of his theory will be discussed in a later section of this chapter.

18.4.2 Merrill: Component Display Theory

Merrill's (1983) Component Display Theory (CDT), an extension of Gagné's theory, is a conditions-based theory of instructional design, as he prescribed instructional conditions based on types of learning outcomes desired.

18.4.2.1. Types of Learned Capabilities. Merrill classified learning objectives (or capabilities) along two dimensions: performance level (remember, use, or find) and content type (facts, concepts, principles, or procedures). So, there are conceivably 12 distinct categories of objectives that his model addresses. Instead of having a declarative knowledge category, as Gagné does, which would include remembering facts, concept definitions, rule statements, and procedural steps, Merrill makes separate categories for each of these types of declarative knowledge. Similarly, instead of having a single cognitive strategies category as Gagné does, through his intersection of the two dimensions, Merrill proposes "find" operations for each of the content types: Find a fact, find a concept, find a rule, and find a procedure.

Merrill provided a rationale for his categorization scheme based on "some assumptions about the nature of subject matter" (p. 298). The rationale for content type is based on five operations that he proposes can be conducted on subject matter: identity (facts), inclusion and intersection (concepts), order (procedures), and causal operations (principles). He derived his performance levels from assumptions regarding differences in four memory structures: associative, episodic, image, and algorithmic. His performance levels derive from the associative (remember: verbatim and paraphrased) and algorithmic (use and find) memory structures. Merrill does not explicitly address the internal processes that accompany the acquisition of each of these categories of learning types.

18.4.2.2. External Conditions of Learning. Merrill described instructional conditions as "presentation forms" and classified these forms as primary and secondary. Primary presentation forms have two dimensions: content (generality or instance) and approach (expository or inquisitory). Secondary presentation forms are types of elaborations that may extend the primary presentations: context, prerequisite, mnemonic, mathemagenic help, representation or alternative representation, and feedback. Merrill's model then further describes for each category of capability" a unique combination of primary and secondary presentation forms that will most effectively promote acquisition of that type of objective" (p. 283).

18.4.2.3. Research on Component Display Theory. Researchers have examined component display theory in

---

TABLE 18-4. GAGNÉ AND GLASSER'S LEARNING CATEGORIES AND CONDITIONS SUMMARY

Effective Learning Conditions for Catagories of Learned Capabilities

Type of Capability	Learning Conditions
Intellectual skill	Retrieval of subordinate (component) skills Guidance by verbal or other means Demonstration of applic. by student; precise feedback Spaced reviews
Verbal information	Retrieval of context of meaningful information Performance of reconstructing new knowledge; feedback
Cognitive strategy (problem solving)	Retrieval of relevant rules & concepts Successive presentation (usually over extended time) of novel problem situations Demonstration of solution by student

Attitude	Retrieval of information and intell. skills relevant to targeted
	    personal actions
	Establishment or recall of respect for human model
	Reinforcement for personal action either by successful
	    direct experience or vicariously by observation of respected person

Motor Skill	Retrieval of component motor chains Establishment or recall of executive subroutines Practice of total skill; precise feedback (Gagné & Glaser, 1987, p. 64)

two ways: evaluation in comparison to "traditional" approaches and examination of individual strategy variations within component display theory. We briefly describe examples of both types of research.

In research across a range of content, age groups, and learning tasks, researchers have examined the effectiveness of instruction following design principles proposed by component display theory to existing or "traditional" instruction. For example, Keller (1982) compared more conventional mathematics instruction in both expository and discovery formats to instruction following a "modified discovery" approach suggested by CDT. Keller found no significant effects on acquisition of set theory concepts, concluding that is was important to learning that the generality be presented explicitly, but less important whether this generality was presented prior to or following presentation of examples. In contrast, Stein (1982) found a superiority of CDT for concept learning among eighth-grade learners, comparing four treatments: expository prose, expository prose plus adjunct questions, CDT with only primary presentation forms, CDT with both primary and secondary presentation forms. She found that both CDT versions were significantly more effective in promoting students' ability to recognize previously presented instances of these concepts and to generalize the concept to previously unencountered instances. In addition, she found that this effect was more pronounced for the more difficult concepts. In a similar prose study, Robinson (1984) found a CDT version of a lesson on text editing to be significantly superior (on recall of the procedure, marginally on use of the procedure [$p = .11$]) to two other versions of prose instruction: one version with summarizing examples, one version with inserted questions. Van Hurst (1984) found a similar positive effect of materials revised using CDT principles when compared with the existing instructional materials in Japanese language learning. The CDT version was found to promote significantly greater achievement and more positive affect and confidence than the original version.

Researchers have also examined individual variables in component display theory. For example, Keller (1985) examined the relative benefits of generality alone, best example alone, or both generality and best example on learning graphing concepts and procedures. She found that the combined treatment was superior for remembering the steps in the procedure. None of the treatments was superior for using the procedure (only practice seemed to be critical). Further, the combined condition was superior for promoting finding a new procedural generality. Chao (1983) also examined the benefits of two expository versions of CDT (generality, example, practice, generality/generality, example, practice) and two discovery treatments (examples, practice/examples, practice, generality) on application and transfer of concepts and principles of plate tectonics. Unlike Chao and similar to her earlier comparisons of expository and discovery sequences (1982), Keller found no statistically significant difference in the participants' performance on application or transfer measures. Although

order of generality, example, and practice may not be found to affect performance, Sasayama (1984) found that for a procedure-using learning task, a rule-example-practice treatment had superior effects on learning than a rule-only, example-only, or rule-example treatment.

Many of the weaknesses of Merrill's model are similar to those of Gagné's, such as lack of an explicit and empirically validated tie between internal processes and external events. However, Merrill's model conjectures even less on internal processes. It is also less complete, as his model addresses only the cognitive domain, does not fully delineate the instructional conditions for the "find" (cognitive strategies) category, and does not have a category for complex learning reflected in what is often called "problem solving." A strength of CDT may be its evolution to fit with the demands of designing intelligent CAI systems, as noted by Wilson (1987).

18.4.3 Reigeluth: Elaboration Theory

Reigeluth and his associates (Reigeluth, Merrill & Wilson, 1978; Reigeluth & Darwazeh, 1982; Reigeluth & Rogers, 1980; Reigeluth & Stein, 1983) developed the elaboration theory as a guide for developing macrostrategies for large segments of instruction, such as courses and units. The elaboration theory is conditions based in nature as it describes (a) "three models of instruction and (b) a system for prescribing those models on the basis of the goals for a whole course of instruction" (p. 340). His theory specifies a general model of selecting, sequencing, synthesizing, and summarizing content in a simple to more complex structure. The major features of the general model are an epitome at the beginning of the instruction, levels of elaboration of this epitome, learning-prerequisite sequence within level of elaboration, a learner-control format, and use of analogies, summarizers, and synthesizers.

The conditions-based nature of the model is obtained from Reigeluth's specification of three differing structures—conceptual, procedural, or theoretical—which are selected based on the goals of the course. Reigeluth further suggested that conceptual structures are of three types: parts, kinds, or matrices (combinations of two or more conceptual structures). He described two different kinds of procedural structures: procedural order and procedural decision. Finally, he subdivided theoretical structures into two types: those that describe natural phenomena (descriptive structures) and those that affect a desired outcome (prescriptive structures).

The nature of the epitome, sequence, summarizers, perquisites, synthesizers, content of elaborations will vary depending on the type of knowledge structure chosen, which was based on the goals of the course. For example, if the knowledge structure is conceptual, the epitome will contain a presentation of the most fundamental concepts for the entire course. If the structure is procedural, the epitome should present the most fundamental or "shortest path" procedure. Reigeluth recommended use of Merrill's component display theory as the guideline for designing at the micro or lesson level within each elaboration cycle.

In recent years, Reigeluth (1992) has placed more emphasis on the importance of using a simplifying conditions method (SCM) of sequencing instruction than on the sequencing and structuring of instruction based on one of the major knowledge structures. The simplifying conditions method suggests that designers "work with experts to identify a simple case that is as representative as possible of the task as a whole" (p. 81). This task should serve as the epitome of the course with succeeding levels of elaborating "relaxing" the simplifying conditions so that the task becomes more and more complex. The theory still retains some of its conditions-based orientation, though, as Reigeluth has suggested, different simplifying conditions structures need to be developed for each of the kinds of knowledge structures he described (Reigeluth & Rogers, 1980; Reigeluth, 1987).

18.4.3.1. Research on Elaboration Theory. As with the previous models, some research has evaluated the effectiveness of instruction based on the principles of elaboration theory in comparison to instruction designed based on other models. Examples of this type of research are Beukhof (1986), who found that instructional text designed following elaboration theory prescriptions were more effective than "traditional" text for learners or learners with low prior knowledge. In contrast, Wagner (1994) compared instruction on handling hazardous materials designed using the elaboration theory to materials designed using structural learning theory (Scandura, 1983). She found that although it took longer for learners to reach criterion performance with the structured learning materials, they performed significantly better on the delayed posttest than learners in the elaboration theory group. Wedman and Smith (1989) compared text designed according to Gagné's prescriptions and following a strictly hierarchical sequence to text designed according to the elaboration theory. They found no significant differences in either immediate or delayed principle application (photography principles). Nor did they find any interactions with a learner characteristic, field independence/dependence. In another study using the same materials, Smith and Wedman (1988) found some subtle differences between the read-think-aloud protocols of participants from the same population who were interacting with the two versions of the materials. They found that participants interacting with the elaborated version (a) required less time per page than the hierarchical version, (b) made more references to their own prior knowledge, (c) made fewer summarizing statements, (d) used mnemonics less often, and (e) made about the same types of markings and nonverbal actions as participants interacting with the hierarchical version. They concluded that although instruction designed following the two different approaches may evoke subtle processing differences, these differences are not translated into differences in immediate and delayed principle application, at least within the 2 hours of instruction that this study encompassed. As Reigeluth pro-

poses that the elaboration theory is a macrostrategies theory, effective for the design of units and courses, and recommends component display theory as a microdesign strategy for lessons, it is perhaps not surprising that researchers have not uniformly found positive effects of the elaboration theory designs with their shorter instruction.

Researchers have also examined design questions regarding individual variables within elaboration theory, such as synthesizers, summarizers, nonexamples in learning procedures, and sequencing. Table 18-5 below summarizes the findings of several of these studies.

18.4.3.2. Evaluation of Elaboration Theory. Elaboration theory is a macrostrategy design theory that was much needed in the field of instructional design. Throughout the evolution of elaboration theory, Reigeluth has proposed design principles that maintained a conditions-based orientation. Due to the strong emphasis on learning hierarchy analysis, until Reigeluth's work many designers had assumed that instruction should proceed from one enabling objective to another from the beginning to the end of a course. Reigeluth suggested a theoretically sound alternative for designing large segments of instruction. It is unfortunate that researchers in the field have not found it pragmatically possible to evaluate the theory in comparison to alternatives with course-level instruction.

In light of advances in cognitive theory, Wilson and Cole (1992) suggested a number of recommendations for revising elaboration theory. These suggestions include (a) deproceduralizing the theory; (b) removing unnecessary design constraints (including the use of primary structures, which form the basis of much of the conditions-based aspect of elaboration theory); (c) basing organization and sequencing decisions on what is known by the learners as well as content structure; and (d) assuming a more "constructivist stance" toward content structure and sequencing (p. 76). Reigeluth (1992) responded to these recommendations in an admirable way: Regarding the deproceduralization of the elaboration theory, he pointed out that he agreed that the theory itself should not be proceduralized, but that he has always included in his discussions of ET ways to operationalize it. Reigeluth proposes that he has already removed "unnecessary design constraints" (the second Wilson & Cole recommendation) by replacing the "content structure" approach by the simplifying conditions method. This approach may more nearly reflect Reigeluth's original intentions for the elaboration theory. However, it does not eliminate the underlying conditions-based principle (which we interpret Wilson & Cole to be recommending), as the method for identifying simplified conditions seems to vary according to whether the instructional goal is conceptual, theoretical, or procedural. Reigeluth concurs with Wilson and Cole's recommendation to take the learners' existing knowledge into account in the elaboration theory, although beyond some revision in the sequencing of conceptual layers (from the middle out, rather than top down), he does not propose that this will be formalized in his theory. Regarding the recommendation that he assume a more "constructivist stance," Reigeluth concurs that this may be important in ill-structured

TABLE 18-5. STUDIES EXAMINING ELABORATION THEORY VARIABLES

Author(s)	Date	Variables	Findings
McLean	1983	Types of synthesizers : visual, verbal, both, none	Visual > verbal or none for remembering relationships Visual & verbal > none for remembering relationships
Chao & Reigeluth	1983	Types of synthesizers: visual/verbal, lean or rich	NSD for visual/verbal rich> lean for remember level
Van Patten	1983	Location of synthesizers: internal, external (pre), external (post)	NSD
Carson & Reigeluth	1983	Location of synthesizers	Post > pre
Tilden	1985	Types of summarizers	GPA X summarizer interaction (richer better for low GPA)
Carson & Reigeluth	1983	Sequencing of content: gen. to detail/ detail to gen.	Gen. to detail > detail to gen.
Van Patten	1983	Sequencing of content: gen. to detail/ simple to complex	NSD
Bentti, Golden & Reigeluth	1983	Non-egs in teaching procedures	Greater divergence of non-egs > less & diverg. Clearly labeled non-egs > nonlabeled
Garduno	1984	Presence/absence of non-egs in teaching procedures	NSD
Marcone & Reigeluth	1988	Non-egs in egs or generalities in teaching procedures	non-egs in generality > non-egs in eg form
Beissner & Reigeluth	1987	Integration of content structures	Can be effective
Jackson	1993	Presence/absences of ET elements	Not all equally effective
English & Reigeluth	1994	Formative research of ET	Suggestions for sequencing and construction of epitome

domains, which the elaboration theory does not currently address. However, he insightfully suggests, "People individually construct their own meanings, but the purpose of instruction—and indeed of language and communication itself—is to help people to arrive at shared meanings" (p. 81).

18.4.4 Landa

In terms of learning outcome types, Landa's (1983) algoheuristic theory of instruction, or "Landamatics," makes a distinction between knowledge and skills (ability to apply knowledge): categories that seem to be equivalent to declarative and procedural knowledge. According to Landa, learners acquire *knowledge* about objects and operations. Objects are known as a perceptive image, i.e., as a mental image or as a concept. A concept can be expressed as a proposition, but it is not necessary that a concept be expressed in order to be known. There are other kinds of propositions such as definitions, axioms, postulates, theorems, laws, and rules which can form a part of knowledge. Operations (action on an object)

are transformations of either real material objects or their mental representations (images, concepts, propositions). A skill is the ability to perform operations. Operations that transform material objects are motor operations. Operations that transform materials objects are cognitive operations. Operations can be algorithmic, "a series of relatively elementary operations that are performed in some regular and uniform way under defined conditions to solve all problems of a certain class" (p. 175), or heuristic, operations for which a series of steps can be identified but are not so singular, regularized, and predictable as algorithms. Algorithmic operations appear similar to Merrill's conception of procedures, and the heuristic operations appear similar to Smith and Ragan's treatment of procedural rules and Gagné's problem solving (higher-order rule). A critical aspect of Landa's model is the importance that he ascribes to the verification of hypothetical description of algorithmic or heuristic process through observation, computer simulation, or error analysis. Such empirical validation is present in specifics of design models in task analysis but is generally missing in conditions-based models with regard to a generalized hypothetical cognitive task analysis for each class of outcomes that can be directly related to prescriptions for external conditions of learning.

Landa's theory suggests how to support processes that turn knowledge into skills and abilities, a transition that provides much of the substance of Anderson's (1985) ACT* theory. He suggests the following conditions for teaching individual operations:

1. Check to make sure that the learners understand the meaning of the procedure.
2. Present problem that requires application of the procedure.
3. Have the student name the operation or preview what should be done to execute the operation.
4. Present next problem.
5. Practice until mastery.

Although he suggests a procedure for teaching students to discover procedures (algorithms), he points out that this process is difficult and time consuming.

18.4.4.1. Research and Evaluation. Research on Landa's model is not as readily available in the literature as the previously reviewed models. However, Landa has reported some evaluation of his model in comparison with more "conventional" training. Landa (1993) estimated that he has saved Allstate $35 million in costs due to (a) many times fewer errors (up to 40 times fewer), (b) tasks performed up to 2 times faster, and (c) workers' confidence level several times higher.

18.4.5 Smith-Ragan

Rather than developing a new conditions-based model, Smith and Ragan (1993) sought to exemplify and elaborate Gagné's theory. To address what they perceived to be limitations in most conditions-based models, they postulated a generalized cognitive process necessary for the acquisition of each of the different learning capabilities. With regard to the external conditions of learning, Smith and Ragan suggested that events of instruction as Gagné portrayed them insufficiently considered learner-generated and learner-initiated learning. Smith and Ragan restated the events so that they could be perceived as either learner-supplied, in the form of learning strategies, or instruction-supported, in the form of instructional strategies.

Smith and Ragan also proposed a model for determining the balance between instructional strategies (instruction-supplied events) and learning strategies (learner-supplied events) based on context, learner, and task variables. They also proposed that there is a "middle ground" between instruction supplied, supplantive (also know as *mathemagenic*) events (see 30.6), and learner-initiated events (see 33.2), in which the instruction facilitates or prompts the learner to provide the cognitive processing necessary to an instructional event.

18.4.5.1. Research and Evaluation. Smith (1992) cited theoretical and empirical bases for some of the learner-task-context-strategy relationships proposed in the COGSS

model, which forms the basis of the balance between instruction-supplied and learner-generated events. In this presentation she proposed an agenda for validation of the model.

18.4.6 Tennyson and Rasch

Tennyson and Rasch (1988) described a model of how instructional prescriptions might be tied to cognitive learning theory. This work was preceded by a short paper by Tennyson (1987) which contained the key elements of the model. In this paper, part of a symposium on Clark's "media as mere vehicles" assertions, Tennyson discussed how one might "trace" the links between different treatments that media might supply and different learning processes. He described six learning processes (three storage processes: declarative knowledge, procedural knowledge, and conceptual knowledge; and three retrieval processes: differentiating, integrating, and creating) which he paired with types of learning objectives, types of knowledge bases, instructional variables, instructional strategies, and computer-based enhancements.

Tennyson and Rasch (1988a, b) and Tennyson (1990) suggested that kinds of learning should refer to types of "memory systems." As with the previous conditions-based models, Tennyson and Rasch employed an information-processing model as their foundation and suggested the main types of knowledge to be: (a) declarative, which is stored as associative networks or schemata and relates to verbal information objectives; (b) procedural, which relates to intellectual skills objectives; and (c) contextual, which relates to problem-solving objectives and knowing when and why to employ intellectual skills. Five forms of objectives are described as requiring distinct cognitive activity (verbal information, intellectual skills, conditions information, thinking strategies, and creativity). In discussing the relationships among the types of knowledge, Tennyson and Rasch noted that contextual knowledge is based on "standards, values, and situational appropriateness. . . . Whereas both declarative and procedural knowledge form the amount of information in a knowledge base, contextual knowledge forms its organization and accessibility" (Tennyson & Rasch, 1988a, p. 372).

In terms of instructional conditions, for declarative knowledge they recommended expository strategies, such as worked examples, which provide information in statement form on both the context and structure of information and question/problem repetition, which presents selected information repeatedly until the student answers or solves all items at some predetermined level of proficiency. For procedural knowledge, they recommended practice strategies in which learners apply knowledge to unencountered situations and some monitoring in terms of evaluation of learner responses and advisement. To teach contextual knowledge, they suggested problem-oriented simulation techniques. And for complex problem situations, they recommended a simulation in which the consequences of decisions update the situational conditions and proceed to make the next iteration more complex.

An interesting element is a prescription of learning time for the different types of learning: 10% for verbal information, 20% for intellectual skills, 25% for conditional information, 30% for thinking strategies, and 15% for creativity. One intent of this distribution was to reflect Goodlad's (1984) prescription of a reversal of traditional classroom practice from 70% of instructional time devoted to declarative and procedural knowledge and only 30% to conceptual knowledge and cognitive abilities. Although such general proportions may serve to illuminate general curriculum issues, specification of percentages of time to types of learning, regardless of consideration of other factors in a particular learning situation, may find limited applicability to instructional design.

18.4.6.1. Research and Evaluation. Tennyson and Rasch's model has not yet been subjected to evaluation and research. In terms of the extension of conditions-based models, some issues do emerge. Although other theorists propose this conditional knowledge, it is unclear whether the addition of a contextual type of learning will enhance the validity of the model. It is possible that such knowledge is stored as declarative knowledge that is in some way associated with procedural knowledge, such as in a mental model or problem schema. The suggestion of time that should be allocated to each type of learning is intriguing, as it attempts to point out the necessity of emphasis on higher-order learning. However, the basis for determination of the proportion of time that should be spent on each type of outcome remains unclear.

18.4.7 Merrill, Li, and Jones—ID2

In reaction to a number of limitations that they perceived in existing instructional design theories and models (including Merrill's own), Merrill, Li, and Jones (1990a, 1990b) have set about to construct a "second-generation theory of instructional design." One of the specific goals of its developers is to expedite design of an automated ID system, "ID Expert," and thereby expedite the instructional design process itself. Ultimately, the developers hope that the system will possess both authoring and delivery environments that grow from a knowledge and rule base. Of all the models described in this chapter, ID2 is the most ambitious in its goal to thoroughly prescribe the instructional conditions for each type of learning. The ID2 model is being developed to (a) analyze, represent, and guide instruction to teach integrated sets of knowledge and skill; (b) produce pedagogic prescriptions about selection and sequence; and (c) be an open system that can respond to new theory. This model has retained its conditions-based orientation. Indeed, Merrill and his associates (p. 8) have elaborated on the relationships between outcomes and internal/external conditions:

> (a) A given learned performance results from a given organized and elaborated cognitive structure, which we will call a mental model. Different learning outcomes require different types of mental models; (b) the construction of a mental model by a learner is facilitated by instruction that explicit-

ly organizes and elaborates the knowledge being taught, during the instruction; (c) there are different organizations and elaborations of knowledge required to promote different learning outcomes.

Within ID2, outcomes of instruction are considered to be enterprises composed of entities, activities, or processes, which might loosely be interpreted as concepts, procedures, and principles, respectively. Merrill and his associates have spent a vast amount of effort describing the structure of knowledge relating to these types of knowledge and how these types of knowledge relate to each other.

Merrill and associates have described a number of conditions (external conditions or instructional methods) that can be placed either under either system or learner control. These conditions are described as "transactions" of various classes. Evidence of Merrill's component display theory can be found in the prescriptions for these transactions. To create this system based on his ID2, Merrill and his colleagues (1991, 1992a, b, c) have attempted to identify the decisions that designers must make regarding the types of information to build into the system and the methods by which this information can be made available to learners. This analysis is incredibly detailed in and of itself. For example, Table 18-6 summarizes the "responsibilities" of the transactions that may be made available in instruction, the "methods" that make up these responsibilities, and the range (or parameters) of these methods. Merrill et al. have made similar analyses of information that may be made available to learners when learning entities, activities, or processes. In addition to detailing the options of pedagogy and information that can be made available in instruction, the developers of a system may also establish the "rules" by which system choices may be made as to which of these options to present to learners.

18.4.7.1. Research and Evaluation. Parts of the system been evaluated by Spector and Muraida (1991) and by Canfield and Spector (1991). For example, one of the major evaluation questions has been: "Can the target audience of novice designers use the system, and can this system expedite instructional design activities?" In Spector and Muraida's study, investigating the utility of the system to expedite design, eight subjects participated in 30 hours of instruction in which they learned to use the system and developed 1 hour of instruction. The results indicated that all subjects who remained in the study were able to complete a computer-based lesson using the support of a portion of the system.

As yet there are no comparison data with more conventional design processes. In their effort to carefully explicate necessary knowledge for learning and instruction, as well as the means by which these interact with each other, the developers have created a model that is quite complex. One benefit of the model is that its complexity reflects and makes concrete much of the complexity of the instructional design process. Unfortunately, it seems that terminology has shifted during development. ID2 is not without its critics. Among criticisms frequently leveled are its utility when used by novices, the lack of evidence of theory base, issues regarding

TABLE 18-6. SUMMARY OF ID2 INSTRUCTIONAL TRANSACTION RESPONSIBILITIES

Method	Parameters
Select knowledge	Selection control (learner, system)
Partition knowledge	Partition control (learner, system) Focus (entire entity or component of entity) Levels (amount of knowledge cluster below focus to include) Coverage (all, user identifies)
Portray knowledge	Portrayal control (learner, system) View (structural, physical, functional) Mode (language, symbolic, literal) Fidelity (low to high)
Amplify knowledge	Ancillary information control (learner, system) Ancillary information mode (verbal, audio) Pronunciation availability (no, system, learner) Pronunciation mode (verbal, audio) Component function availability (no, learner, system) Component function mode (verbal, audio) Component description availability (no, learner, system) Component description mode (verbal, audio) Component aside available (no, learner, system) Component aside mode (verbal, audio)
Sequence knowledge	Sequence control (learner, system)
Route learner	Segment sequence control (learner, system) Segment sequence type (elaboration, cumulation, accrual, learner) Depth (depth first, breadth first) Accrual (all, isolated part, replacement) Priority (chronological, frequency, criticality, familiarity)
Guide advancement	Shift segment on (learner, repetitions, practice, criterion, assessment criterion) Repetitions Criterion
Manage interaction	Management control (learner, system)
Prioritize interactions	Strategy control (learner, system) interaction strategy type (overview, familiarity, basic, mastery, basic-remediation, mastery-remediation, learner)
Expedite acquirement	Shift interaction on (learner, repetitions, criterion, response time, elapsed time) Repetition Criterion Response time Elapsed time
Enact interactions	Enactment control (learner, system)
Overview knowledge	Overview control (learner, system) Overview view (structure, + focus, + level 1) Structure format (tree, browser)
Present knowledge	Presentation display element control (learner, system) Presentation display element availability (label, function, properties) Presentation display element timing (untimed, n seconds) Presentation display element sequence (order, simultaneous, sequential)
Enable practice	Practice formats (locate, label, function, properties) Practice format sequence (sequential, simultaneous) Response mode (recall, recognize) Response timing (untimed, n seconds) Practice format control (learner, system) Response repetition (n, contingent) Component order (learner, same, random) Feedback availability (yes, no) Feedback type (intrinsic, correct ans., right-wrong, attn. focusing, designer specific) Feedback control (learner, system) Feedback timing (immediate, schedule, delayed) Feedback schedule type (fixed interval, variable interval, fixed ratio, variable ratio)
Assess knowledge	

sufficient agreement to generate strategies, and the likelihood of sameness of results in multiple applications.

18.4.8 Other Applications of Conditions-Based Theory

Although they have not sought to develop complete instructional design models, a number of notable scholars within and outside the instructional design field have utilized a conditions-based theory as a basis for much of their work. We will briefly describe four of these examples; they illustrate how pervasive and influential the conditions-based theory has been.

18.4.8.1. Jonassen, Grabinger, and Harris. Jonassen, Grabinger, and Harris (1991) developed a decision model for selecting strategies and tactics of instruction based on three levels of decisions: (a) scope (macro/micro); (b) instructional event (prepare learner, present information, clarify ideas, provide practice, and assess knowledge); and (c) learning outcome. Levels (b) and (c) are similar to the decisions patterns suggested by Gagné and Gagné and Briggs.

Jonassen, Grabinger, and Harris recommended making decisions regarding instructional tactics based on three major categories of learning outcomes: intellectual skills (concept or rule), verbal information, or cognitive strategy (iconic, verbal/digital). They suggested prescriptions for instructional events based on the learning outcome—for example, for the event of preparing the learning by supporting recall of prior knowledge of intellectual skills through presenting a verbal/oral comparative advance organizer, adapting content of instruction to learners' prior knowledge, and reviewing prerequisite skills and knowledge. This work has been elaborated into a more complete outcomes-based model for formatively evaluating instruction (Jonassen & Tessmer, 1996).

18.4.8.2. Horn. Horn's approach to text design has many elements of a design model and clearly employs a conditions-based set of assumptions. Horn's work, called *structured writing,* presents a highly prescriptive approach to the design of instructional and informative text. In addition to format concerns, Horn proposed different treatments for different types of learning. The types of learning he identified are procedures (which explain how to do something and in what order to do it); structure (about physical things, objects that have identifiable boundaries); classification (which shows how a set of concepts is organized); process (which explains how a process or operation works, how changes take place in time); concepts (which define and give examples and nonexamples of new aspects of the subject matter), and facts (which give results of observations or measurements without supporting evidence) (Horn, 1976, p. 17). Horn described differential conditions for text presentation by identifying what elements (or "blocks") each presentation relating to a particular type of learning (or "map") must have. Horn differentiated between necessary and optional elements for each type of learning.

18.4.8.3. West, Farmer, and Wolf. West, Farmer, and Wolf (1991) referred to three kinds of knowledge: (a) declarative, which is stored in propositional networks that may be semantic or episodic and may structured as data or state schemata; (b) procedural knowledge that is order-specific and time-dependent (p. 16), and (c) conditional knowledge, which is knowing when and why to use a procedure (similar to Tennyson & Rasch's "contextual knowledge"). They describe "cognitive strategies" that can support the acquisition of each of these learning types, which the instructional designer plans instruction to activate. In contrast to Gagné, who typically portrays cognitive strategies as instructional strategies, supplied by instruction, and in contrast to Smith and Ragan (1993), who portray the primary load of information processing as something that should shift between learner and instruction depending on circumstances, West, Farmer, and Wolf imply that strategies are always provided by the learner. These cognitive strategies are chunking, frames (graphic organizers, concept mapping, advance organizer, metaphor, rehearsal, imagery, and mnemonics). In terms of prescriptive or conditions-based models, West, Farmer, and Wolf prescribe the strategies as effective to support acquisition of all types of knowledge. However, they also use Gagné's five domains as types of outcomes for prescribing the appropriateness of each strategy, which is somewhat confusing, as procedural knowledge and intellectual skills, which are usually considered to refer to the same capabilities, are not given the same prescriptions for strategies. Our evaluation is that their prescriptions are for the declarative portion of higher-order knowledge types.

18.4.8.4. E. Gagné. Unlike most instructional models, E. Gagné's work (1993) is primarily descriptive, rather than prescriptive. E. Gagné based her conditions-based propositions on J. Anderson's (1990) cognitive theories of learning, and placed her theory base within the information-processing theories. She subscribed to Anderson's types of knowledge: declarative and procedural. Gagné described the representations of declarative knowledge as propositions, images, linear orderings, and schemas (which can be composed of propositions, images, and linear orderings). Procedural knowledge is represented as a production system, which can result in domain-specific skills, domain-specific strategies, and, to a limited degree, domain-general strategies.

Although the majority of her text is more descriptive than prescriptive, E. Gagné utilized the conditions-based theory as she discussed the internal processes required in the acquisition of each of the types of knowledge and the instructional support that can promote this acquisition. She described instructional support as increasing the probability that required processes will occur, or making learning easier or faster.

A strength of E. Gagné's formulation is her description of internal processes. In addition, she provides empirical evidence of effectiveness of instructional support conditions.

18.5 AN EXAMINATION OF THE PROPOSITIONS OF A CONDITIONS-BASED THEORY

As noted in introduction to this chapter, the primary propositions of conditions-based theory can be summarized to four main assertions: (a) Learning goals can be categorized as to learning outcome or knowledge type; (b) related to (a), different outcome categories require different internal conditions (or, one can view the proposition as "different internal conditions leading to different cognitive outcomes"); (c) outcomes can be represented in a prerequisite relationship; (d) different learning outcomes require different external conditions for learning. In this section, issues relating to each of the primary propositions will be discussed.

18.5.1 Learning Outcomes Can Be Categorized

What is meant by a learning outcome? The meaning we attribute to "outcomes" differs depending on whether we perceive these outcomes as external (as a category of task or goal) or internal (as an acquired capability, perhaps supported by a unique memory system). Gagné (1985) clearly described his classification system of outcomes as "acquired capabilities," an internal definition. Merrill (1983) has described his outcome categories as "performances," "categories of objectives," and "learned capabilities," rather a mix of internal and external connotations. Reigeluth's categorization is of "types of content," which somewhat implies the categorized of an external referent. Landa describes his kinds of knowledge as "psychological phenomena," suggesting an internal orientation. Clearly, there is no consensus even within the models described in this chapter as to what the term *learning outcomes* actually implies. Indeed, the evidence to support the validity of each category system would vary in its type and complexity, depending on whether the phenomena are viewed as entities "out there" that can be pinned down and observed, or "within," where we only see circumstantial evidence of their presence.

The statement "learning outcomes can be categorized" is both a philosophical and psychological assertion. Indeed, both philosophers, such as Ryle (1949), and psychologists, such as Anderson (1990), have posited ways to categorize knowledge. Interestingly, Ryle and Anderson agreed on a similar declarative/procedural classification system. Certainly, instructional theorists have suggested a variety of category systems. (However, most are compatible with the declarative/procedural classification. Gagné certainly adds additional categories to these: attitude, motor skill, and, perhaps, cognitive strategies. Tennyson and Rasch add a third class of learning, contextual knowledge.) For each group, the philosopher, the psychologist, and the instructional theorist, the evidence for the "truth" of the proposition would vary. For philosophers, this is an epistemological question, and the manner for determining its truth would depend on the philosophic school to which a particular philosopher

ascribes. We will not pursue this approach for determining the validity of our assertion directly.

Reigeluth (1983) suggests a utility criterion for determining whether a categorization system is appropriate:

> When we say concepts are human-made and arbitrary, we mean phenomena can be conceptualized (i.e., grouped or categorized) in many alternative ways. . . . Practically all classification schemes will improve our understanding of instructional phenomena, but concepts are not the kind of knowledge for which instructional scientists are looking, except as a stepping stone. Instructional scientists want to determine *when* different methods should be used—they want to discover principles of instruction—so that they can prescribe optimal methods. But not all classification schemes are equally useful for forming highly reliable and broadly applicable principles. . . . The same is true of classes of instructional phenomena: Some will have high *predictive usefulness* and some will not. The challenge to our discipline is to find out which ones are the most useful (pp. 12–13).

The psychologist would want empirical evidence that the categories are distinct, which leads to our second proposition.

18.5.2 Different Outcome Categories Require Different Internal Conditions

Most of the models within the conditions-based theory propose that learning categories are different in terms of cognitive-processing demands and activities. All of the major seven design models described in this chapter appear to make this assumption, to a greater or lesser degree. Although all models in this chapter suggest that a general information-processing procedure occurs in learning, they also suggest that this processing significantly and predictably differs for each of the categories of learning that they have identified. For example, R. Gagné suggested that in particular the cognitive processes of retrieval of prior knowledge, encoding, and retrieval and transfer of new learning would differ significantly in nature, depending on the type of learning goal. Indeed, several of the model developers, including Tennyson and Rash (1988), R. Gagné (1985), Merrill (1983), and Smith and Ragan (1993), postulated different memory structures for different types of learning outcomes.

A slightly different statement of the proposition allows for a closer relationship to the first proposition (outcomes can be categorized): Different internal conditions lead to different cognitive outcomes. This more descriptive (and less prescriptive) assertion seems to be supported by additional educational theorists. For example, both Anderson (1990) and E. Gagné (1993) propose that different cognitive processes lead to declarative and procedural learning. They also propose that these two types of learning have different memory systems, schemata for declarative knowledge and productions for procedural learning. They both provide some empirical evidence that these cognitive processes and storage systems are indeed unique to the two types of learning.

We must point out that even if connectionists (Bereiter, 1991) are correct, that there is only one memory system (neural networks) and only one basic cognitive process (pattern recognition), this does not necessarily preclude the possibility of different types of learning capabilities. For example, there may be generalized activation patterns that represent certain types of learning.

18.5.3 Outcomes Can Be Represented in a Prerequisite Relationship

Gagné's work on learning hierarchies would appear to be sufficient to confirm this assumption rather resoundingly, as reported previously in this chapter. In addition to work by Gagné and others working directly in his tradition, research by individuals working from entirely different frames of reference appears also to solidly confirm this assumption.

Although early learning hierarchy research appeared highly confirmatory, R. T. White developed an important review of learning hierarchy research in the early 1970s (White, 1973). In this review, studies validating the idea of learning hierarchies were sought. Due to methodological weaknesses, White found no studies that were able to validate a complete and precise fit between a proposed learning hierarchy and optimal learning: "All of the studies suffered from one or more of the following weaknesses: small sample size, imprecise specification of component elements, use of only one question per element, and placing of tests at the end of the learning program or even the omission of instruction altogether" (White, 1973, p. 371).

In research following White's review, research that applied his recommendations to correct methodological weaknesses, a series of studies providing confirmation of the learning hierarchy formulation were published. (White 1974a, b, c; Linke, 1973) These results led Gagné to conclude: "The basic hypothesis of learning hierarchies is now well established, and sound practical methods for testing newly designed hierarchies exist" (White & Gagné, 1974, p. 363). Other research from what may be considered within the Gagné tradition which appears to confirm the learning hierarchy hypothesis includes Resnick, 1967; Resnick and Wang, 1969; Merrill, Barton, and Wood, 1970; and Linke, 1973.

Work on learning hierarchies from outside the Gagné tradition or a conditions theory perspective includes studies by Winkles, Bergan, and associates, and Kallison. Winkles (1986) investigated the learning of trigonometry skills with a learning hierarchy validation study identifying both lateral and vertical transfer. Two experiments with eighth- and ninth-grade students involved instructional treatments described as "achievement with understanding" and "achievement only." Results reported "achievement with understanding treatment is better for the development of lateral transfer for most students, and of vertical transfer for the more mathematically able students, whereas the differences between the treatment groups on tests of achievement and retention of taught skills are not significant. A small amount of additional instruction

on vertical transfer items produces much better performance under both treatments" (p. 275).

Bergan, Towstopiat, Cancelli, and Karp (1982), also not working from the conditions tradition, reported a study that provided what appears to be a particularly interesting form of confirmation of the learning hierarchy concept and some insights into rule learning:

> This investigation examined ordered and equivalence relations among hierarchically arranged fraction identification tasks. The study investigated whether hierarchical ordering among fraction identification problems reflects the replacement of simple rules by complex rules. A total of 456 middle-class second-, third-, and fourth-grade children were asked to identify fractional parts of sets of objects. Latent class techniques reveal that children applied rules that were adequate for simple problems but had to be replaced to solve more complex problems (Bergan, Towstopiat, Cancelli & Karp, 1982, p. 39).

In a follow-up study to the 1982 work, Bergan, Stone, and Feld (1984) employed a large sample of elementary-age children in their learning of basic numerical skills. Students were presented with tasks that required rules of increasing complexity. The researchers were again studying the replacement of relatively simple rules with more complex extensions of them:

> Hypotheses were generated to reflect the assumption of hierarchical ordering associated with rule replacement. In addition, restrictive knowledge and variable knowledge perspectives were evaluated. Latent-class models were used to test equivalence and ordered relations among the tasks. The results provided evidence that the development of counting skills is an evolving process in which parts of a relatively simple rule are replaced by features that enable the child to perform an increasingly broad range of counting tasks. The results also suggested that rule replacement in counting plays an important role in the development of other math skills. The results also give support for the restrictive knowledge perspective, lending credence to the stair-step learning theory (Bergan, Stone & Feld, 1984, p. 289).

An unusual and indirect, but interesting and suggestive, view of the importance of hierarchies in learning intellectual skills is found in a study by Kallison (1986), who varied sequence (proper vs. manipulated, i.e., reasonable vs. modified to disrupt clarity) and explicitness of lesson organization (organization of lesson explained/organization hidden). In the disrupted sequence treatment, even though care was taken to make an unclear presentation, the hierarchical nature of content relationships was preserved. Four treatments resulted and were used with three ability levels (2 × 2 × 3). In the study, 67 college students were taught intellectual skills: numeration systems, base 10 and base 5, and how to convert from one system to the other. Although sequence modification did *not* affect achievement substantially, the explicitness of lesson organization explicit did significantly impact achievement, with the more explicit lesson structure promoting better learning. Kallison found no aptitude-treatment interactions.

Kallison was careful to point out that although the sequence was altered, nothing got in the way of learning prerequisites. He modified sequence in such a way that learning hierarchies were not interfered with, only the reasonableness or "clarity" of the lesson organization: Where care was taken *not* to violate learning hierarchy principles, sequence could be disrupted, and it did not impact on learning, even with unclear presentation. As the learning task clearly involves intellectual skills, Gagné's principle of sequencing according to learning hierarchies was not violated. Although there is considerable evidence to validate learning hierarchies already, an unusual confirmation could be obtained by replicating Kallison's study with an additional condition of sequence modified in such a way as to violate learning hierarchy principles but maintain "clarity."

In another unusual test of the validity of the idea that learning tasks can be productively cast in a prerequisite relationship, Yao (1989) sought to test Gagné's assumption that in a validated learning hierarchy, some learners should be able to skip some elements based on their individual abilities. A valid learning hierarchy represents the most probable expectation of greatest learning for an entire sample. In a carefully designed experiment, Yao confirmed that some individuals could successfully skip certain prerequisites, and she found a treatment by ability interaction regarding the pattern of skipping in which certain forms of skipping can be less detrimental for high-ability learners than for low-ability learners. However, as the theory predicts, the treatment that skipped prerequisites was less effective for both low- and high-ability learners (as a group).

18.5.4 Different Learning Outcomes Require Different External Conditions

In an effort to find evidence in support of this basic tenant of the conditions theory, we engaged in a survey of research, looking across a wide scope. The following research is presented in an effort to survey the evidence. The reader may find a dizzying variety of approaches and perspectives reflected. Studies and reviews on the following topics will be briefly presented to illustrate the variety of standpoints from which evidence may be found in general support of the conditions model: interaction between use of objectives and objective type, goal structure and learning task, advance organizers and learning task, presentation mode (e.g., visual presentation) and learning task, evoked cognitive strategies and learning outcomes, expertise and learning hierarchies, teacher thinking for different types of learning, adjunct questions and type of learning, feedback for different types of learning, and provided versus evoked instructional support for different types of learning. What follows, then, is a sample of studies that lend support—in varying ways from varying standpoints—to the theory that different instructional outcomes may best be achieved with differing types of instructional support.

18.5.4.1. Interaction of Use of Objectives and Objective Type. Hartley and Davies (1976) subjected to further

examination a review by Duchastel and Merrill (1973) on the effects of providing learners with objectives. Although the original Duchastel and Merrill review found no effect, Hartley and Davies found that "behavioral objectives do not appear to be useful in terms of ultimate posttest scores, in learning tasks calling for knowledge and comprehension. On the other hand, objectives do appear to be more useful in higher-level learning tasks calling for analysis, synthesis, and evaluation" (p. 250). They also note a report by Yellon and Schmidt (1971) which pointed out a possible interference effect from informing students of objectives in problem-solving tasks by reducing the amount of reasoning required.

18.5.4.2. Goal Structure and Learning Task. Johnson and Johnson (1974) found in a review of research on cooperative, competitive, and individualistic goal structures that goal structure interacted with learning task. "Competition may be superior to cooperative or individualistic goal structures when a task is a simple drill activity or when sheet quantity of work is desired on a mechanical or skill-oriented task that requires little if any help from another person" (p. 220). They cite Chapman and Feder, 1917; Clayton, 1964; Clifford, 1971; Hurlock, 1927; Julian and Perry, 1967; Maller, 1929; Miller and Hamblin, 1963; Phillips, 1954; Sorokin, Tranquist, Parten, and Zimmerman, 1930; and Tripplet, 1897. All findings do not clearly distinguish a grouping-by-outcomes (declarative/procedural) condition. For example, Smith, Madden, and Sobel, 1957; Yuker, 1955, found that memorization learning is also enhanced by cooperative work.

On the other hand, Johnson and Johnson pointed out: "When the instructional task is some sort of problem-solving activity, the research clearly indicates that a cooperative goal structure results in higher achievement than does a competitive goal structure" (p. 220). They cite Almack, 1930; Deutsch, 1949a; Edwards, DeVries, and Snyder, 1972; Gurnee, 1968; Husband, 1940; Jones and Vroom, 1964; Laughlin and McGlynn, 1967; O'Connel, 1965; Shaw, 1958; Wodarski, Hamblin, Buckholdt, and Feritor, 1971.

18.5.4.3. Visual Presentation Mode and Learning Task. Dwyer and Parkhurst (1982) present a multifactor analysis (three methods × four outcomes × three ability levels-reading comprehension). This analysis did not concentrate on different types of objectives, but apparently because different contents were used, the authors could draw this conclusion: "The results of this study indicated that (a) different methods of presenting programmed instruction are not equally effective in facilitating student achievement of all types of educational objectives" (p. 108). There were four measures, which were taken to represent four different types of learning outcome: (a) a drawing test involving generation of drawings given labels for parts of the heart such as aorta, pulmonary valve, and so forth; (b) identification test: a multiple-choice test of matching nature on various heart parts; (c) a terminology test consisting of 20 multiple-choice items on knowledge of facts, terms, and definitions; and (d) a comprehension test of 20 multiple-choice items that involved looking at the position of a given heart part during a specified moment in its functioning.

Analysis of the interactions among the different outcomes was not presented in the 1982 study; however, in what appears to be a follow-up study, Dwyer and Dwyer (1987) report the analyses of interactions. The authors conclude that "all levels of depth of processing are not equally effective in facilitating student achievement of different instructional objectives" (Dwyer & Dwyer, 1987, p. 264). In Dwyer's studies, tasks requiring "different levels of processing" appear to these reviewers as generally reflecting differing ways of eliciting declarative knowledge learning, yet meaningful differences among learning tasks were seen and reported by the authors of the studies.

18.5.4.4. Evoked Cognitive Strategies and Learning Outcomes.

Kiewra and Benton (1987) report a study that investigated relationships among note taking, review of instructor's notes, and use of higher-order questions and their effect on learning of two sorts: factual and higher order. Subjects were college students in a college class setting. Half of the class was in a condition in which they took notes themselves and reviewed them, and the other half reviewed notes provided by the instructor. At the conclusion of the class, additional practice questions of a "higher-order" nature were provided to half of each group. An interaction between methodology and learning outcomes was reported. "Students who listed and reviewed the instructor's notes achieved more on factual items than did note takers, and . . . higher-order practice questions did not differentially affect test performance" (p. 186).

A study along lines similar to Kiewra and Benton's (1987) study was conducted by Shrager and Mayer (1989), in which some students were instructed to take notes and others were not so instructed, as both groups watched videotaped information. The researchers predicted that the "note taking would result in improved problem-solving transfer and semantic recall but not verbatim recognition or verbatim fact retention for low-knowledge learners, but would have essentially no effects on test performance for high-knowledge learners" (p. 263). This prediction was confirmed, supporting similar findings by Peper and Mayer (1978, 1986), who used the same design but different contents, automotive engines, and statistics. This study is somewhat confounded in treatment and learner characteristics. Degree of declarative knowledge and the stage of transition from declarative to procedural (Anderson, 1990) is often the distinction between novice and expert. Instead of indicating that declarative knowledge and procedural knowledge require different instructional conditions, the study may reveal, instead, that novice learners need more direct and explicit learning guidance in employing cognitive strategies that more knowledgeable learners will do on their own.

There is no doubt that properly applied to the proper task, the mnemonic keyword technique is a powerful one in assisting learning: "The evidence is overwhelming that the use of the keyword method, as applied to recall of vocabulary definitions, greatly facilitates performance. . . . In short, keyword methods effects are pervasive and of impressive magnitude" (Pressley, Levin & Delaney, 1982,

pp. 70–71). The strategy, like many others, is a task-specific one: In other words, it makes no sense to apply it to other-than appropriate tasks. Levin (1986) elaborates on this principle and brings to bear an enormous amount of research from him and his associates on particular cognitive strategies (learning strategies) that have considerable power in improving learning.

18.5.4.5. Expertise and Learning Hierarchies.

The utility and validity of learning hierarchies within authentic contexts has been studied by Dunn and Taylor (1990) and Dunn and Taylor (1994). In these studies, hierarchical analyses were performed on the activities of language arts teachers (1990) and medical personnel (1994). Development of expertise is encouraged to take place from "task-relevant" experience, assisted by advice strategies developed from hierarchical analysis.

18.5.4.6. Adjunct Questions.

Hamilton (1985) provides a review of research on using adjunct questions (see 30.61) and objectives in instruction. The review contains different sections on research with use of adjunct questions with different types of learning, leading to conclusions that vary with type of learning in question.

18.5.4.7. Practice.

Some inconsistency is found in the results of studies looking at interaction of practice and types of learning. Hannafin and Colamaio (1987) found a significant interaction between practice and type of learning. Scores on practiced items were higher than nonpracticed items for each type of learning, but the effects were proportionately greatest for factual learning and least influential for procedural learning. However, in a study by Hannafin, Phillips, and Tripp (1986), opposite results were obtained, in which practice was more helpful for factual learning than for application learning. Slee (1989), in a review of interactive video research, noted that a lack of adequacy in lesson materials may confound these studies, as they both used the National Gallery of Art Tour videodisc, which was noted to have insufficient examples and practice available.

Rieber (1988) investigated effects of practice and animations on learning of two types: factual learning and application learning in a CBI lesson. The study looked at both immediate learning and transfer to other learning outcomes. Main-effect differences were not observed between either different elaboration treatments or practice. However, a significant interaction was found between learning outcome and transfer, in which the lesson promoted far transfer for factual information but did not facilitate far transfer for application learning. Another interaction was observed between practice and learning outcome, in which practice improved students application scores more than factual scores. As with studies by Hannafin and associates, unintended attributes of lesson materials may have confounded the study; in this case, as reported by the researcher, the lesson materials may have been too difficult.

18.5.4.8. Feedback for Different Types of Learning.

Getsie, Langer, and Glass (1985) provided a meta-analysis of research on feedback (reinforcement versus punishment) and discrimination learning. They concluded that punishment is an effective form of feedback for discrimination learning: "Punishment is clearly superior to reward only, with effect sizes ranging from .10 to .31" (p. 20). The authors also concluded that reward is the least effective: "First, the most consistent finding is that compared to punishment or reward plus punishment, reward is the least efficient form of feedback during discrimination learning" (p. 20). Although discrimination learning was not compared with other forms of learning, we predict that this conclusion should not be generalized to other forms of learning (e.g., to provide punishment as feedback for practice in learning relational rules, as compared with informative feedback) or to other forms of feedback, such as levels of informational feedback.

Smith and Ragan (1993b) present a compilation of research and practice recommendations on designing instructional feedback for different learning outcomes. Using the Gagné types of learning construct as a framework, they present feedback prescriptions for different categories of learning task. They conclude that "questions regarding the optimal content of feedback . . . really revolve around the issue of the match between the cognitive demands of the learning task; the cognitive skill, prior knowledge, and motivations of the learners; and constraints, such as time, within the learning environment" (p. 100).

An interesting insight into feedback and different types of learning is provided by a meta-analysis of research on feedback by Schimmel (1983). In attempting to explain the major inconsistencies in findings, Schimmel speculated such different characteristics of the instructional content as "different levels of difficulty in recall" (p. 11).

18.5.4.9. Provided vs. Evoked Instructional Support for Different Types of Learning. Husic, Linn, and Sloane (1989) report a study involving effects of different strategies for different types of learning. The content was learning to program in Pascal. Two different college classes were studied, a beginning class in which the learning task was characterized as "learning syntax" (perhaps analogous to rule using) and an advanced class that concentrated on "learning to plan and debug complex problems" (perhaps analogous to problem solving). The abstract of the report showed that:

> Programming proficiency varied as a function of instructional practices and class level. Introductory students benefited from direct instruction, and AP students performed better with less direct guidance and more opportunities for autonomy. Characteristics of effective programming instruction vary depending on the cognitive demands of courses (Husic, Linn & Sloane, 1989, p. 570).

18.6 CONCLUSIONS

There are some conclusions we would draw from this review:

1. It appears that conditions models have a long history of interest in psychology, educational psychology, and instructional technology. This history illustrates work that may not be widely known among instructional technologists today; work that can be instructive as to the actual base and significance of the conditions approach. Perhaps we will see fewer erroneous statements in our literature about what is known regarding types of learning, learning hierarchies, and conditions of learning.

2. There appears to be continuing interest in this area, due to its utility in helping specify instructional strategies and also due to the sizable gaps and inconsistencies that exist in current formulations and research on and with them. We have described in this chapter many fruitful areas for further research.

3. We have reached a conclusion about the work of R. M. Gagné which we would like to share, and suggest that readers examine their own conclusions from reading. We find Gagné's work cast within so much that preceded it and which follows it to remain both dominating in its appeal and utility and, paradoxically, heavily flawed and in need of improvement. The utility and appeal of this work appears to derive greatly from the solid scholarship and cogent writing that Gagné brought to bear, as well as his willingness to change the formulation to keep up with changing times and new knowledge. Many of the gaps and flaws, in keeping with the paradox, appear to be a product of the very changes that he made to keep up with current interests. We believe those changes to be in the main beneficial, but see a clear need for systematic and rigorous scholarship on issues opened by those changes.

4. We still see utility in thinking of learning as more than one kind of thing, especially for practitioners. It is too easy, in the heat of practitioner's struggles, to slip to the assumption that all knowledge is declarative (as is so often seen in the learning outcomes statements of large-scale instructional systems) or all problem solving (as is so often assumed in the pronouncements of pundits and critics of public education), and, as a result, fail to consider either the vast arena of application of declarative knowledge or the multitude of prerequisites for problem solving. It is unhelpful to develop new systems of types of learning for the mere purpose of naming. Improvements in categorization schemes should be based on known differences in cognitive processing and required differences in external conditions.

5. There is substantial weakness in the tie from categories of learning to external conditions of learning. What is missing is the explication of the *internal* conditions involved in acquisition of different kinds of learning. The research on transition from expert to novice and of artificial-intelligence research that attempts to describe knowledge of experts should be particularly fruitful in helping us fill this void. Perhaps this void is a result of failure to have a sufficient emphasis on qualitative research in our field.

6. There is research to support the conclusion that different external events of instruction lead to different kinds of learning, especially looking at the declarative/procedural level. What appears lacking is any systematic body of research directly on the central tenant, not just of conditions models but of practically anyone who would attempt to

teach much less design instruction: What is the relationship between internal learner conditions and subsequent learning from instruction? Such a topic seems a far cry from studies that would directly inform designers as to procedures and techniques, yet such a great deal seems to hinge on that one question. With more insight into it, many quibbles and debates may disappear, and the work of translation into design principles may begin at a new level of efficacy.

REFERENCES

Alexander, P.A., Schallert, D.L. & Hare, V.C. (1991). Coming to terms: how researchers in learning and literacy talk about knowledge. *Review of Educational Research 61* (3), 315–43.

Anderson, J.R. (1985). *Cognitive psychology and its implications,* 3d ed. New York: Freeman.

Ausubel, D.P. & Robinson, F.G. (1969). *School Learning.* New York: Holt.

Barnes, B.R. & Clawson, E.V. (1975). Do advance organizers facilitate learning? Recommendations for further research based on an analysis of 32 studies. *Review of Educational Research 45* (2), 637–59.

Beissner, K. & Reigeluth, C.M. (1987). *Multiple strand sequencing using elaboration theory.* (ERIC Document Reproduction Service No. ED 314 065.)

Bentti, F., Golden, A. & Reigeluth, C.M. (1983). *Teaching common errors in applying a procedure.* (IDD&E Working Paper No. 17.) Syracuse University, School of Education. (ERIC Document Reproduction Service No. ED 289 464.)

Bereiter, C. (1985). Toward a solution of the learning paradox. *Review of Educational Research 55* (2), 201–26.

Bergan, J.R., Stone, C.A. & Feld, J.K. (1984). Rule replacement in the development of basic number skills. *Journal of Educational Psychology 76* (2), 289–99.

—, Towstopiat, O., Cancelli, A.A. & Karp, C. (1982). Replacement and component rules in hierarchically ordered mathematics rule learning tasks. *Journal of Educational Psychology 74* (1), 39–50.

Beukhof, G. (1986, Apr.). *Designing instructional texts: interaction between text and learner.* Paper presented at the annual meeting of the American Educational Research Association, San Francisco, CA. (ERIC Document Reproduction Service No. ED 274 313.)

Bloom, B.S., Englehart, M.D., Furst, E.J., Hill, W.H. & Krathwohl, D.R. (1956). *Taxonomy of educational objectives: the classification of educational goals, handbook 1: cognitive domain.* New York: McKay.

Brien, R. & Duchastel, P. (1986). Cognitive task analysis underlying the specification of instructional objectives. *Programmed Learning and Educational Technology 23* (4), 363–70.

Briggs, G.E. (1962). The generality of research on transfer functions. *In* A.W. Melton, *Categories of human learning,* 286–92. New York: Academic.

Briggs, L.J. (1967). An illustration of the analysis procedure for a group of objectives from a course in elementary science. *In* L.J. Briggs, P.L. Campeau, R.M. Gagné & M.A. May, eds. *Instructional media: a procedure for the design of multi-media instruction, a critical review of research,*
and suggestions for future research, 53–73. Pittsburgh, PA: American Institutes for Research.

— (1968). *Sequencing of instruction in relation to hierarchies of competence* (Monograph No. 3). Pittsburgh, PA: American Institutes for Research.

—, ed. (1977). *Instructional design: principles and applications.* Englewood Cliffs, NJ: Educational Technology.

—, Campeau, P.L., Gagné, R.M. & May, M.A., eds. (1967). *Instructional media: a procedure for the design of multi-media instruction, a critical review of research, and suggestions for future research.* Pittsburgh, PA: American Institutes for Research (final report prepared by the Instructional Methods Program of the Center for Research and Evaluation in Applications of Technology in Education, submitted to U.S. Department of Health, Education, & Welfare).

—, Gagné, R.M. & May, M.A. (1967). A procedure for choosing media for instruction. *In* L.J. Briggs, P.L. Campeau, R.M. Gagné & M.A. May, eds. *Instructional media: a procedure for the design of multi-media instruction, a critical review of research, and suggestions for future research,* 28–52. Pittsburgh, PA: American Institutes for Research.

Bryan, G.L. (1962). The training of electronics maintenance technicians. *In* R. Glaser, ed. *Training research and education,* 295–321. Pittsburgh, PA: University of Pittsburgh Press.

Burns, R.B. & Lash, A.A. (1986). *American Educational Research Journal 23* (3), 393–414.

Campbell, V.N. (1964). Self-direction and programmed instruction for five different types of learning objectives. *Psychology in the Schools 1* (4), 348–58.

Carr, H.A. (1933). The quest for constants. *Psychological Review 40,* 514–22.

Carson, C.H. & Reigeluth, C.M. (1983). *The effects of sequence and synthesis on concept learning using a parts-conceptual structure.* (IDD&E Working Paper No. 22.) Syracuse University, School of Education. (ERIC Document Reproduction Service No. ED 288 518.)

Caruso, J.L. & Resnick, L.B. (1971). *Task sequence and over-training in children's learning and transfer of double classification skills.* Paper presented at the meeting of the American Psychological Association, Miami, FL.

Case, R. (1978). A developmentally based theory and technology of instruction. *Review of Educational Research 48* (3), 439–463.

Chi, M.T.H., Glaser, R. & Farr, M.J., eds. (1988). *The nature of expertise.* Hillsdale, NJ: Erlbaum.

Chao, C.I. (1983). *Effects of four instructional sequences on application and transfer.* (IDD&E Working Paper No. 12.) Syracuse University, School of Education. (ERIC Document Reproduction Service No. ED 289 461.)

— & Reigeluth, C.M. (1986). *The effects of format and structure of synthesizer of procedural-decision learning* (IDD&E Working Paper, No. 22.) Syracuse University, School of Education. (ERIC Document Reproduction Service No. ED 289 469.)

Coleman, L.T. & Gagné, R.M. (1970). Transfer of learning in a social studies task of comparing-contrasting. *In* R.M. Gagné, ed. *Basic studies of learning hierarchies in school subjects.* Final Report, April, University of California, Berkeley, Contract No. OEC-4-062940-3066, U.S. Office of Education.

Cooper, G. & Sweller, J. (1987). Effects of schema acquisition and rule automation on mathematical problem-solving transfer. *Journal of Educational Psychology 79* (4), 347–62.

Cotterman, T.E. (1959). *Task classification: an approach to partially ordering information on human learning.* Technical Note WADC TN 58-374. Wright Patterson Air Force Base, Ohio: Wright Development Center.

Demaree, R.G. (1961). *Development of training equipment planning information.* ASD TR 61-533. Aeronautical Systems Division, Wright-Patterson Air Force Base, Ohio (AD 267 326).

Derry, S.J. & Murphy, D.A. (1986). Designing systems that train learning ability: from theory to practice. *Review of Educational Research 56* (1), 1–39.

Duchastel, P.C. & Merrill, P.F. (1973). The effects of behavioral objectives on learning: a review of empirical studies. *Review of Educational Research 75,* 250–66.

Dunn, T.G. & Taylor, C.A. (1990). Hierarchical structures in expert performance. *Educational Technology Research & Development 38* (2), 5–18.

— & — (1994). *Learning analysis in ill-structured knowledge domains of professional practice.* Paper presented at American Educational Research Association, New Orleans, LA.

Dwyer, C.A. & Dwyer, F.M. (1987). Effect of depth of information processing on students' ability to acquire and retrieve information related to different instructional objectives. *Programmed Learning and Educational Technology 24* (4), 264–79.

Dwyer, F.M. & Parkhurst, P.E. (1982). A multifactor analysis of the instructional effectiveness of self-paced visualized instruction on different educational objectives. *Programmed Learning and Educational Technology 19* (2), 108–18.

Edling, J.V., Hamreus, D.G., Schalock, H.D. Beaird, J.H., Paulson, C.F. & Crawford, J. (1972). *The cognitive domain: a resource book for media specialists.* Contributions of behavioral science to instructional technology, Handbook 2. Washington, DC: Gryphon House.

Eigen, L.D. & Margulies, S. (1963). *Response characteristics as a function of information level.* New York: Center for Programmed Instruction.

English, R.E. & Reigeluth, C.M. (1994, Apr.). *Formative research on sequencing instruction with the elaboration theory.* Paper presented at the annual meeting of the American Educational Research Association, New Orleans, LA.

Eustace, B.W. (1969). Learning a complex concept a differing hierarchical levels. *Journal of Educational Psychology 60,* 449–52.

Faw, H.W. & Waller, T.G. (1976). Mathemagenic behaviors and efficiency in learning from prose materials: review, critique, and recommendations. *Review of Educational Research 46* (4), 691–720.

Fitts, P.M. (1962). Perceptual-motor skill learning. *In* A.W. Melton, *Categories of Human Learning,* 243–85. New York: Academic.

Fodor, J.A. (1980). Fixation of belief and concept acquisition. *In* M. Piattelli-Palerini, ed. *Language and learning: the debate between Jean Piaget and Noam Chomsky,* 142–49. Cambridge, MA: Harvard University Press.

Foshay, W.R. (1983). Alternative methods of task analysis: a comparison of three techniques. *Journal of Instructional Development 6* (4), 2–9.

Frase, L.T. (1968). The effect of question location, pacing, and mode upon retention of prose material. *Journal of Educational Psychology 58,* 244–49.

Furst, E.J. (1981). Bloom's taxonomy of educational objectives for the cognitive domain: philosophical and educational issues. *Review of Educational Research 51* (5), 441–54.

Gagné, E., Yekovich, C.W. & Yekovich, F.R. (1993). *The cognitive psychology of school learning,* 2d ed. New York: HarperCollins.

Gagné, R.M. (1954). Training devices and simulators: some research issues. *American Psychologist 9,* 95–107. *In* R.M. Gagné (1989), *Studies of Learning,* 77–96. Tallahassee, FL: Learning Systems Institute.

— (1959). Problem solving and thinking. *Annual Reviews of Psychology 10,* 147–72.

— (1962a). The acquisition of knowledge. *Psychological Review 69,* 355-65. *In* R.M. Gagné (1989), *Studies of Learning,* 229–42. Tallahassee, FL: Learning Systems Institute.

— (1962b). Military training and principles of learning. *American Psychologist 17,* 83-91. *In* R.M. Gagné (1989), *Studies of Learning,* 141–53. Tallahassee, FL: Learning Systems Institute.

— (1962c). Human functions in systems. *In* R.M. Gagné, ed. *Psychological principles in system development.* New York: Holt.

— (1964). Problem solving. *In* A.W. Melton, *Categories of human learning,* 293–323. New York: Academic.

— (1965a). The analysis of instructional objectives for the design of instruction. *In* R. Glaser, ed. *Teaching machines and programmed learning II: data and directions,* 21–65. Washington, DC: National Education Association. *In* R.M. Gagné (1989), *Studies of Learning,* 251–86. Tallahassee, FL: Learning Systems Institute.

— (1965b). *The conditions of learning.* New York: Holt.

— (1967). Curriculum research and the promotion of learning. *In* R. Stake, ed. *Perspectives of curriculum evaluation.* AERA monograph series on curriculum evaluation, No. 1. Chicago, IL: Rand McNally.

— (1972). Domains of learning. *Interchange 3,* 1–8.

— (1973). Learning and instructional sequence. *In* F.N. Kerlinger, ed. *Review of research in education,* Vol. 1., 3–33. Itasca, IL: Peacock.

— (1974). Educational technology and the learning process. *Educational Researcher 3* (1), 3–8.

— (1984). Learning outcomes and their effects: useful categories of human performance. *American Psychologist 39,* 377–85.

— (1985). *The conditions of learning and theory of instruction,* 4th ed. New York: Holt.

— & Bassler, O.C. (1963, Jun.). A study of retention of some topics of elementary non-metric geometry. *Journal of Educational Psychology 54,* 123–31.

— & Bolles, R.C. (1959). Review of factors in learning efficiency. *In* E. Galanter, ed. *Automatic teaching: the state of the art,* 13–53. New York: Wiley.

—& Briggs, L.J. (1974). *Principles of instructional design.* New York: Holt.

— & Briggs, L.J. (1979). *Principles of instructional design,* 2d ed. Fort Worth, TX: Harcourt, Brace.

— & Brown, L.T. (1961). Some factors in the programming of conceptual learning. *Journal of Experimental Psychology 62,* 313–21. *In* R.M. Gagné (1989). *Studies of learning,* 173–85. Tallahassee, FL: Learning Systems Institute.

— & Glaser, R. (1987). Foundations in learning research. *In*

R.M. Gagné, ed. *Instructional technology foundations,* 49–83. Hillsdale, NJ: Erlbaum.

— & Merrill, M.D. (1990). Integrative goals for instructional design. *Educational Technology Research & Development 38* (1), 23–30.

— & Paradise, N.E. (1961). Abilities and learning sets in knowledge acquisition. *Psychological Monographs 75* (14) (Whole No. 518.)

— & Rohwer, W.D., Jr. (1969). Instructional psychology. *Annual Review of Psychology 20,* 381–418.

— & Smith, E.C., Jr. (1962). A study of the effects of verbalization on problem solving. *Journal of Experimental Psychology 63,* 12–18. *In* R.M. Gagné (1989), *Studies of Learning,* 187–96. Tallahassee, FL: Learning Systems Institute.

— & White, R.T. (1978). Memory structures and learning outcomes. *Review of Educational Research 48* (2), 187–222.

Gagné, R.M. & Staff, University of Maryland Mathematics Project (1965). Some factors in learning non-metric geometry. *Monographs of Society for Research in Child Development 30,* 42–49.

Gagné, R.M., Baker, K.E. & Wylie, R.C. (1951). Effects of an interfering task on the learning of a complex motor skills. *Journal of Experimental Psychology 41,* 1–9. *In* R.M. Gagné (1989). *Studies of Learning,* 63–74. Tallahassee, FL: Learning Systems Institute.

—, Briggs, L.J. & Wager, W.W. (1988). *Principles of instructional design,* 3d ed. Fort Worth, TX: Harcourt, Brace.

—, Briggs, L.J. & Wager, W.W. (1992). *Principles of instructional design,* 4th ed. Fort Worth, TX: Harcourt, Brace.

—, Mayor, J.R., Garstens, H.L. & Paradise, N.E. (1962). Factors in acquiring knowledge of a mathematical task. *Psychological Monographs 76* (7). (Whole No. 526.) *In* R.M. Gagné (1989), *Studies of Learning,* 197–227. Tallahassee, FL: Learning Systems Institute.

Gardner, M.J. (1985). Cognitive psychological approaches to instructional task analysis. *In* E. Gordon, ed. *Review of Research in Education 12,* 157–96. Washington, DC: American Educational Research Association.

Garduno, A.O. (1984). *Teaching common errors in applying a procedure.* (IDD&E Working Paper No. 18.) (ERIC Document Reproduction Service No. ED 289 465.)

Getsie, R.L., Langer, P. & Glass, G.V. (1985). Meta-analysis of the effects of type and combination of feedback on children's discrimination learning. *Review of Educational Research 55* (4), 49–22.

Gilbert, T.F. (1962). Mathetics: the technology of education. *Journal of Mathetics 1,* 7–73.

Glaser, R. & Resnick, L.B. (1972). Instructional psychology. *Annual Review of Psychology 23,* 207–76.

— & Glanzer, M. (1958). *Training and training research.* Pittsburgh, PA: American Institutes for Research.

Goldberg, N.S. (1987). An evaluation of a Gagné-Briggs based course designed for college algebra remediation. *Dissertation Abstracts International 47* (12), 4313. (University Microfilms No. AAC87-06313.)

Goodlad, R. (1984). *Crisis in the classroom.* San Francisco, CA: Freeman.

Greeno, J.G. (1978). *A study of problem solving. In* R. Glaser, ed. Advances in instructional psychology, Vol. 1. Hillsdale, NJ: Erlbaum.

Greeno, J.G. (1980). Some examples of cognitive task analysis with instructional implications. *In* R. Snow, P. Federico & W.

Montague, eds. *Aptitude, learning, and instruction, Vol. 2: cognitive process analysis of learning and problem solving,* 1–21. Hillsdale, NJ: Erlbaum.

Gregg, L.W. (1976). Methods and models for task analysis in instructional design. *In* D. Klahr, ed. *Cognition and instruction,* 109–116. Hillsdale, NJ: Erlbaum.

Gustafson, K.L. (1981). *Survey of instructional development models with an annotated ERIC bibliography.* Syracuse, NY: ERIC Clearinghouse on Information Resources.

Haertel, G.D., Walberg, H.J. & Weinstein, T. (1983). Psychological models of educational performance: a theoretical synthesis of constructs. *Review of Educational Research 53* (1), 75–92.

Hamilton, R.J. (1985). A framework for the evaluation of the effectiveness of adjunct questions and objectives. *Review of Educational Research 55* (4), 47–85.

Hannafin, M.J. (1983). Fruits and fallacies of instructional systems: effects of an instructional systems approach on the concept attainment of Anglo and Hispanic students. *American Educational Research Journal 20* (2), 237–49.

Hannafin, M.J. & Colamaio, M.E. (1987). The effects of locus of instructional control and practice on learning from interactive video. Paper presented at annual meeting of the Association for Educational Communications and Technology, Atlanta, GA. *In* M.L. Simonson & S. Zvacek, eds. *Proceedings of selected research paper presentations,* 297–312. Ames, IA: Iowa State University.

—, Phillips, T.L. & Tripp, S.D. (1986). The effects of orienting, processing, and practicing activities on learning from interactive video. *Journal of Computer-Based Instruction 13* (4), 134–39.

Hartley, J. & Davies, I.K. (1976). Preinstructional strategies: the role of pretests, behavioral objectives, overviews, and advance organizers. *Review of Educational Research 46* (2), 239–65.

Hoffman, C.K. & Medsker, K.L. (1983). Instructional analysis: the missing link between task analysis and objectives. *Journal of Instructional Development 6* (4), 17–23.

Horn, R.E. (1976). *How to write information mapping.* Lexington, MA: Information Resources.

Hunkins, F.P. (1969). Effects of analysis and evaluation questions on various levels of achievement. *Journal of Experimental Education 38,* 45–58.

Husic, F.T., Linn, M.C. & Sloane, K.D. (1989). Adapting instruction to the cognitive demands of learning to program. *Journal of Educational Psychology 81* (4), 570–83.

Johnson, D.W. & Johnson, R.T. (1974). Instructional goal structure: cooperative, competitive, or individualistic. *Review of Educational Research 44* (2), 213–40.

—, Grabinger, R.S. & Harris, N.D. (1991). Analyzing and selecting instructional strategies and tactics. *Performance Improvement Quarterly 4* (2), 77–97.

—, Hannum, W.H. & Tessmer, M. (1989). *Handbook of task analysis procedures.* New York: Praeger.

Jonassen, D.H. & Tessmer, M. (1996). An outcomes-based taxonomy for the design, evaluation, and research of instructional systems. *Training Research Journal 1* (3).

Kallison, J.M. (1986). Effects of lesson organization on achievement. *American Educational Research Journal 23* (2), 337–47.

Katona, G. (1940). *Organizing and memorizing.* New York: Columbia University Press.

Keller, B.H. (1986). The effects of selected presentation forms using conceptual and procedural content from elementary mathematics (component display theory, concept learning and development model, best example). *Dissertation Abstracts International 47*(05), 1591. (University Microfilms No. AAC86-17320.)

Keller, B. & Reigeluth, C.H. (1982). *A comparison of three instructional presentation formats.* (IDD&E Working Paper No. 6.) Syracuse University, School of Education. (ERIC Document Reproduction Service No. ED 288 516.)

Kendler, H.H. (1962). The concept of the concept. *In* A.W. Melton, *Categories of human learning,* 211–36. New York: Academic.

Kennedy, C.K, Esque, T. & Novak, J. (1983). A functional analysis of task analysis procedures for instructional design. *Journal of Instructional Development 6* (4), 10–16.

Kiewra, K.A. & Benton, S.L. (1987). Effects of notetaking, the instructor's notes, and higher-order practice questions on factual and higher-order learning. *Journal of Instructional Psychology 14* (4), 186–94.

Kimble, G.A. (1961). *Hilgard and Marquis' "Conditioning and learning."* New York: Appleton-Century-Crofts.

Krathwohl, D.R., Bloom, B.S. & Masia, B.B. (1964). *Taxonomy of educational objectives, the classification of educational goals, handbook II: effective domain.* New York: McKay.

Kulik, J.A. & Kulik, C.L.C. (1988). Timing of feedback and verbal learning. *Review of Educational Research 58* (1), 79–97.

Kunen, S., Cohen, R. & Solman, R. (1981). A levels-of-processing analysis of Bloom's taxonomy. *Journal of Educational Psychology 73,*(2), 202–11.

Landa, L.N. (1983). The algo-heuristic theory of instruction. *In* C.M. Reigeluth, ed. *Instructional-design theories and models,* 163–211. Hillsdale, NJ: Erlbaum.

— (1993). Landamatics ten years later: an interview with Lev N. Landa. *Educational Technology 32* (6), 7–18.

Lawton, J.T. & Wanska, S.K. (1977). Advance organizers as a teaching strategy: a reply to Barnes and Clawson. *Review of Educational Research 47* (2), 233–244.

Leinhardt, G. & Greeno, J.G. (1986). The cognitive skill of teaching. *Journal of Educational Psychology 78* (2), 75–95.

—, Zaslavsky & Stein, F.S. (1990) Functions and graphing. *Review of Educational Research 60,* 1.

Levin, J.R. (1986). Four cognitive principles of learning strategy instruction. *Educational Psychologist 2* (1 & 2), 3–17.

Li, Z. & Merrill, M.D. (1990). ID Expert 2.0: design theory and process. *Educational Technology Research & Development 39* (2), 53–69.

Linke, R.D. (1973). *The effects of certain personal and situation variables on the acquisition sequence of graphical interpretation skills.* Doctoral dissertation, Monash University.

Locatis, C. & Park, O. (1992). Some uneasy inquiries into ID expert systems. *Educational Technology Research and Development 40* (3), 87–94.

Lumsdaine, A.A. (1960). Design of training aids and devices. *In* J.D. Folley, ed. *Human factors methods for system design.* Pittsburgh, PA: American Institutes for Research.

Lumsdaine, A.A. (1962). Experimental research on instructional devices and materials. *In* R. Glaser, ed. *Training research and education,* 247–94. Pittsburgh, PA: University of Pittsburgh Press.

Maier, N.R.F. (1930). Reasoning in humans: I. on direction. *Journal of Comparative Psychology 10,* 115–43.

Marcone, S. & Reigeluth, C.M. (1988) Teaching common errors in applying a procedure. *Educational Communications and Technology Journal 36* (1), 23–32.

Markle, S. (1975). They teach concepts, don't they? *Educational Researcher 4,* 3–9.

Marshall, J.M. (1986). A comparative study of two instructional methods employed in teaching nutrition among culturally diverse adolescents: teacher-oriented lecture and student-oriented instructional design. *Dissertation Abstracts International 47* (08), 2901. (University Microfilms No. AAC86-19212.)

Mayer, R.E. (1975). Different problem solving competencies established in learning computer programming with and without meaningful models. *Journal of Educational Psychology 68,* 143–50.

— (1976). Integration of information during problem solving due to a meaningful context of learning. *Memory & Cognition, 4,* 603–608.

— (1979). Can advance organizers influence meaningful learning? *Review of Educational Research 49* (2), 371–83.

McLean, L. (1983). *The effects of format of synthesizer on conceptual learning.* (IDD&E Working Paper No. 13.) (ERIC Document Reproduction Service No. ED 289 462.)

Melton, A.W. (1941). Learning. *In* W.S. Monroe, ed. *Encyclopedia of educational research,* 667–86. New York: Macmillan.

— (1964). The taxonomy of human learning: Overview. *In* A.W. Melton, ed. *Categories of human learning,* 325–39. New York: Academic.

—, ed. (1964). *Categories of human learning.* New York: Academic.

Mengel, N.S. (1986). The acceptability and effectiveness of textbook materials revised using instructional design criteria. *Journal of Instructional Development 9* (2), 13–18.

Merrill, M.D. & Boutwell, R.C. (1973). Instructional development: methodology & research. *In* F.N. Kerlinger, ed. *Review of research in education,* Vol. 1, 95–131. Itasca, IL: Peacock.

— (1983). Component display theory. *In* C.M. Reigeluth, ed. *Instructional-design theories and models,* 279–333. Hillsdale, NJ: Erlbaum.

—, Barton, K. & Wood, L.E. (1970). Specific review in learning a hierarchical imaginary science. *Journal of Educational Psychology 61,* 102–09.

—, Jones, M.K. & Li, Z. (1992). Instructional transaction theory: classes of transactions. *Educational Technology 32* (6), 12–26.

—, — & — (1990a). Limitations of first generation instructional design. *Educational Technology 30* (1), 7–11.

—, — & — (1990b). Second generation instructional design. *Educational Technology 30* (2), 7–14.

—, — & — (1991). Instructional transaction theory: an introduction. *Educational Technology 31* (6), 7–12.

—, — & — (1992). Instructional transaction shells: responsibilities, methods, and parameters. *Educational Technology 32* (2), 5–26.

—, — & — Chen-Troester, J. & Schwab, S. (1992). Instructional transaction theory: knowledge relationships among processes, entities, and activities.

Miller, R.B. & Folley, J.D., Jr. *A study of methods for determining skills, knowledge and ability requirements for maintenance of newly developed equipment.* Pittsburgh, PA: American Institutes for Research.

Miller, R.B. (1953). *A method for man-machine task analysis.* Technical Report 53-137. Wright-Patterson Air Force Base, OH: Wright Air Development Center.

— (1954). *Psychological considerations in the design of training equipment.* Technical Report 54-563. Wright-Patterson Air Force Base, OH: Wright Air Development Center.

— (1956, Apr.). *A suggested guide to position-task description.* Technical Memorandum ASPRL-TM-56-16. Lowry AFB, CO: Armament Systems Personnel Research Laboratory, Air Force Personnel and Training Research Center.

— (1962). Analysis and specification of behavior for training. *In* R. Glaser, ed. *Training research and education,* 31-62. Pittsburgh, PA: University of Pittsburgh Press.

Nicholas, J.R. (1970). *Modality of verbal instructions for problems and transfer for a science hierarchy.* Doctoral dissertation, University of California, Berkely, 1970.

Okey, J.R. & Gagné, R.M. (1970). Revision of a science topic using evidence of performance on subordinate skills. *Journal of Research in Science Teaching 7,* 321–25.

Palumbo, D.B. (1990). Programming and problem solving. *Review of Educational Research 60* (1), 65–89.

Parker, J.F. & Downs, J.E. (1961). *Selection of training media.* ASD TR 61-473. Aeronautical Systems Division, Wright-Patterson Air Force Base, OH. (AD 271 483).

Pavlov, I.P. (1927). *Conditioned reflexes.* (G.V. Anrep., trans.) London, England: Oxford University Press.

Peper, R.J. & Mayer, R.E. (1978). Notetaking as a generative activity. *Journal of Educational Psychology 70,* 514–22.

— & Mayer, R.E. (1986). Generative effects of note-taking during science lectures. *Journal of Educational Psychology 78,* 34–38.

Peverly, S.T. (1991). Problems with the knowledge-based explanation of memory and development. *Review of Educational Research 61* (1), 71–93.

Phenix, P.H. (1964), *Realms of meaning,* Chap. 22. New York: McGraw-Hill.

Phillips, D.C. & Kelly, M.E. (1975). Hierarchical theories of development in education and psychology. *Harvard Educational Review 45,* 351–75.

Posner, G.P. & Rudnitsky, A.N. (1978). *Course design: a guide to curriculum development for teachers.* New York: Longman.

— & Strike, K.A. (1976). A categorization scheme for principles of sequencing content. *Review of Educational Research 46* (4), 665–90.

Postman, L. (1961). The present status of interference theory. *In* C.N. Cofer, ed. *Verbal learning and verbal behavior.* New York: McGraw-Hill.

Pressley, M. Levin, J.R. & Delaney, H. (1982) The mnemonic keyword method. *Review of Educational Research 52* (1), 61–91.

Rabinowitz, M. & Mandler, J.M. (1983). Organization and information retrieval: human learning and cognition. *Journal of Experimental Psychology: Learning, Memory and Cognition 9,* 430–39.

Reigeluth, C.M & Darwazeh, A.N. (1982). The elaboration theory's procedures for designing instruction: a conceptual approach. *Journal of Instructional Development 5,* 22–32.

— & Curtis, R.V. (1987). Learning situations and instructional models. *In* R.M. Gagné, ed. *Instructional Technology Foundations,* 175–206. Hillsdale, NJ: Erlbaum.

— (1979). In search of a better way to organize instruction: the elaboration theory. *Journal of Instructional Development 6,* 40–46.

— (1983) Current trends in task analysis: the integration of task analysis and instructional design. *Journal of Instructional Development 6* (4), 24–30.

— (1983). Instructional design: what is it and why is it? *In* C.M. Reigeluth, ed. *Instructional design theories and models,* 3–36. Hillsdale, NJ: Erlbaum.

— (1992). Elaborating the elaboration theory. *Educational Technology Research and Development 40* (3), 80–86.

— & Rogers, C.A. (1980). The elaboration theory of instruction: prescriptions for task analysis and design. *NSPI Journal 19,* 16–26.

— & Stein, F.S. (1983). The elaboration theory of instruction. *In* C.M. Reigeluth, ed. *Instructional design theories and models,* 335–82. Hillsdale, NJ: Erlbaum.

Resnick, L.B. (1967). Design of an early learning curriculum. Working paper 16, Learning Research and Development Center, University of Pittsburgh.

— (1976). Task analysis in instructional design: some cases from mathematics. *In* D. Klahr, ed. *Cognition and instruction,* 51–80. Hillsdale, NJ: Erlbaum.

— & Wang, M.C. (1969). Approaches to the validation of learning hierarchies, *Proceedings of the 18th Annual Regional Conference on Testing Problems.* Princeton, NJ: Educational Testing Service.

—, Siegel, A.W. & Kresh, E. (1971). Transfer and sequence in learning double classification skills. *Journal of Experimental Child Psychology 11,* 139–49.

Richardson J. (1958) The relationship of stimulus similarity and number of responses. *Journal of Experimental Psychology 56,* 478–84.

Rickards, J.P. (1979). Adjunct postquestions in text: a critical review of methods and processes. *Review of Educational Research 49* (2), 181–96.

Robinson, E.R.N. (1984). The relationship between the effects of four instructional formats and test scores of adult civilian and military personnel when learning to use a text editor. (Doctoral dissertation, University of Southern California, 1984.) *Dissertation Abstracts International 45,* 3311.

Rothkopf, E.Z. & Bisbicos, E. (1967). Selective facilitative effects of interspersed questions on learning from written material. *Journal of Educational Psychology 58,* 56–61.

Ryder, J.M. & Redding, R.E. (1993). Integrating cognitive task analysis in instructional systems development. *Educational Technology Research and Development 41* (2), 75–96.

Sasayama, G.M.D. (1985). Effects of rules, examples and practice on learning concept-classification, principle-using, and procedure-using tasks: a cross-cultural study. *Dissertation Abstracts International,* 46 (01), 65. (University Microfilms No. AAC85-05584.)

Scandura, J.M. (1983). Instructional strategies based on the structural learning theory. *In* C.M. Reigeluth, ed. *Instructional-design theories and models: an overview of their current status,* 213–246. Hillsdale, NJ: Erlbaum.

Schimmel, B.J. (1983). A meta-analysis of feedback to learners in computerized and programmed instruction. Paper presented to Annual Meeting of the American Educational Research Association, Montreal, Canada, Apr. 11–14, 1983. (ERIC Document Reproduction Service No. ED 233708.)

Shrager, L. & Mayer, R.E. (1989). Note-taking fosters generative learning strategies in novices. *Journal of Educational Psychology 81* (2), 263–64.

Sigel, I.E., Roeper, A. & Hooper, F. (1966). A training procedure for acquisition of Piaget's conservation of quantity: a pilot study and its replication. *British Journal of Educational Psychology 36,* 301–11.

Sjoberg, L. Hoyer, B. & Olsson, I. (1970). Teaching conservation of weight by means of verbal instructions. *Scandinavian Journal of Psychology 11,* 266–73.

Skinner, B.F. (1938). *The behavior of organisms; an experimental analysis.* New York: Appleton-Century-Crofts.

Slee, E.J. (1989). A review of the research on interactive video. Paper presented at annual meeting of the Association for Educational Communications and Technology, Dallas, TX. *In* M.L. Simonson & D. Frey, eds. *Proceedings of selected research paper presentations,* 150–66. Ames, IA: Iowa State University.

Smith, P.L. & Ragan, T.J. (1993a). *Instructional design.* New York: Macmillan.

— & Ragan, T.J. (1993b). Designing instructional feedback for different learning outcomes. *In* J.V. Dempsey & G.C. Sales, eds. *Interactive instruction and feedback,* 75–103. Englewood Cliffs, NJ: Educational Technology.

— & Wedman, J.F. (1988, Feb.). *The effects of organization of instruction on cognitive processing.* Paper presented at the annual convention of the Association for Educational Communications and Technology, New Orleans, LA.

Smode, A.F. (1962). Recent developments in training problems, and training and training research methodology. *In* R. Glaser, ed. *Training research and education,* 429–495. Pittsburgh, PA: University of Pittsburgh Press.

Spector, J.M. & Muraida, D.J. (1991). Evaluating instructional transaction theory. *Educational Technology 31* (10), 29–35.

Stahl, R.J. (1979, Apr.). *Validating a modified Gagnean concept-acquisition model: the results of an experimental study using art-related content.* Paper presented at annual meeting of the American Educational Research Association, San Francisco, CA. (ERIC Document Reproduction Service No. ED 168 942.)

Stein, F.S. (1982). Beyond prose and adjunct questions: a comparison with a designed approach to instruction. *Dissertation Abstracts International,* 43 (09), 2880. (University Microfilms No. AAC82-29019.)

Stolurow, L.M. (1961). *Teaching by machine.* Washington, DC: U.S. Department of Health, Education, and Welfare, Office of Education.

Stolurow, L.M. (1964). *A taxonomy of learning task characteristics.* AMRL-TDR-64-2, Aerospace Medical Research Laboratories, Wright-Patterson Air Force Base, OH (AD 433 199).

Tennyson, R.D. (1981). Use of adaptive information for advisement in learning concepts and rules using computer-assisted instruction. *American Educational Research Journal 18,* 425–38.

— (1987). Computer-based enhancements for the improvement of learning. Paper presented at annual meeting of the Association for Educational Communications and Technology, Atlanta, GA. *In* M.L. Simonson & S. Zvacek, eds. *Proceedings of selected research paper presentations,* 25–38. Ames, IA: Iowa State University.

— (1990). Instructional design theory: advancements from cognitive science and instructional technology. Paper presented at annual meeting of the Association for Educational Communications and Technology, Dallas, TX. *In* M.L. Simonson & D. Frey, eds. *Proceedings of selected research paper presentations,* 610–30. Ames, IA: Iowa State University.

— & Park, O. (1980). The teaching of concepts: a review of the instructional design literature. *Review of Educational Research 50,* 55–70.

— & Cocchiarella, M.J. (1986). An empirically based instructional design theory for teaching concepts. *Review of Educational Research 56* (1), 40–71.

— & Merrill, M.D. (1971). Hierarchical models in the development of a theory of instruction. *Educational Technology 11,* 27–31.

— & Rasch, M. (1988a). Linking cognitive learning theory to instructional prescriptions. *Instructional Science 17,* 369–85.

— & — (1988b). Instructional design for the improvement of learning and cognition. Paper presented at annual meeting of the Association for Educational Communications and Technology, Atlanta, GA. *In* M.L. Simonson & S. Zvacek, eds. *Proceedings of selected research paper presentations,* 760–75. Ames, IA: Iowa State University.

—, Elmore, R.L. & Snyder, L. (1992). Advancements in instructional design theory: contextual module analysis and integrated instructional strategies. *Educational Technology Research & Development 40* (2), 9–22.

—, Welsh, J.C., Christensen, D.L. & Hajovy, H. (1985). Interactive effect of information structure sequence of information and process learning time on rule learning using computer-based instruction. *Educational Communications and Technology Journal 33* (3), 213–23.

Thorndike, E.L. (1898). Animal intelligence: an experimental study of the associative processes in animals. *Psychology Review Monograph Supplement 2* (4) (Whole No. 8).

Tilden, D.V. (1985). The nature of review: components of a summarizer which may increase retention (instructional design). *Dissertation Abstracts International 45* (12), 159. (University Microfilms No. AAC85-00771.)

Tolman, E.C. (1949). There is more than one kind of learning. *Psychological Review 56,* 144–155. (In Wickens, 1962, p. 80; also noted in Gagné, 1965)

Training Psychology Branch, Behavioral Sciences Laboratory, Aerospace Medical Laboratory (1960). *Uses of task analysis in deriving training and training equipment requirements.* Technical Report 60–593. Wright-Patterson Air Force Base, OH: Wright Air Development Center.

Tyler, R.W. (1949). Achievement testing and curriculum construction. *In* G. Williamson, ed. *Trends in student personnel work,* 391–407. Minneapolis, MN: University of Minnesota Press.

Underwood, B.J. (1962). The representativeness of rote verbal learning. *In* A.W. Melton, *Categories of human learning,* 47–78. New York: Academic.

— (1964). Laboratory studies of verbal learning. *In* E.R. Hilgard, ed. *Theories of learning and instruction,* 133–52. Sixty-third Yearbook. Chicago, IL: National Society for the Study of Education.

Van Patten, J.E. (1984). The effects of conceptual and procedural sequences and synthesizers on selected outcomes of instruction. *Dissertation Abstracts International 44* (10), 2973. (University Microfilms No. AAC84-00790.)

Von Hurst, E.M. (1984). The effectiveness of component display theory in the remediation of self-instructional materials for Japanese learners. Doctoral dissertation, University of Southern California, 1984. *Dissertation Abstracts International 45,* 794.

Wagner, K.K. (1994). A comparison of two content sequencing theories applied to hypertext-based instruction (elaboration theory, structural learning theory). *Dissertation Abstracts International 54* (11), 101. (University Microfilms No. AAC94-13334.)

Wang, M.C., Resnick, L.B. & Boozer, R.F. (1972). The sequence of development of some early mathematics behaviors. *Child Development 43.*

Wedman, J.F. & Smith, P.L. (1989). An examination of two approaches to organizing instruction. *International Journal of Instructional Media 16* (4).

West, C.K., Farmer, J.A. & Wolf, P.M. (1991). *Instructional design: implications for cognitive science.* Englewood Cliffs, NJ: Prentice Hall.

White, R.T. (1973). Research into learning hierarchies. *Review of Educational Research 43* (3), 361–75.

— (1973). A limit to the application of learning hierarchies. *Australian Journal of Education 17,* 153–56.

— (1974a). A model for validation of learning hierarchies. *Journal of Research in Science Teaching 11,* 1–3.

— (1974b). Indexes used in testing the validity of learning hierarchies. *Journal of Research in Science Teaching 11,* 61–66.

— (1974c). The validation of a learning hierarchy. *American Educational Research Journal 11,* 121–36.

— & Gagné, R.M. (1974). Past and future research on learning hierarchies. *Educational Psychologist 11,* 19–28. *In* R.M. Gagné (1989), *Studies of learning,* 361–73. Tallahassee, FL: Learning Systems Institute.

Wickens, D.D. (1962). The centrality of verbal learning: comments on Professor Underwood's paper. *In* A.W. Melton, *Categories of human learning,* 79–87. New York: Academic.

Wiegand, V.K. (1969). *A study of subordinate skills in science problem solving.* Doctoral dissertation, University of California at Berkeley, 1969.

— (1970). A study of subordinate skills in science problem solving. *In* R.M. Gagné, ed. *Basic studies of learning hierarchies in school subjects.* Final Report, Apr., University of California, Berkeley, Contract no. OEC-4-062940-3066, U.S. Office of Education.

Wilcox, W.C., Merrill, M.D. & Black, H.B. (1981). Effect of teaching a conceptual hierarchy on concept classification performance. *Journal of Instructional Development 5* (1), 8–13.

Willis, M.P. & Peterson, R.O. (1961). *Deriving training device implications from learning theory principles: I. guidelines for training device design, development, and use.* TR: NAVTRADEVCEN 784-1. Port Washington, NY: U.S. Naval Training Device Center.

Wilson, B.G. (1987). Computers and instructional design: component display theory in transition. Paper presented at annual meeting of the Association for Educational Communications and Technology, Atlanta, GA. *In* M.L. Simonson & S. Zvacek, eds. *Proceedings of selected research paper presentations,* 767–82. Ames, IA: Iowa State University.

— & Cole, P. (1992). A critical review of elaboration theory. *Educational Technology Research and Development 40* (3), 63–79.

Winkles, J. (1986). Achievement, understanding, and transfer in a learning hierarchy. *American Educational Research Journal 23* (2), 275–1288.

Woodworth, R.S. (1958). *Dynamics of behavior.* New York: Holt.

Yao, K. (1989). Factors related to the skipping of subordinate skills in Gagné's learning hierarchies. Paper presented at annual meeting of the Association for Educational Communications and Technology, Dallas, TX. *In* M.L. Simonson & D. Frey, eds. *Proceedings of selected research paper presentations,* 661-74. Ames, IA: Iowa State University.

Yellon, S.L. & Schmidt, W.H. (1971). *The effect of objective sand instructions on the learning of a complex cognitive task.* Paper presented at the meeting of the American Educational Research Association, New York.

19. INTELLIGENT TUTORING SYSTEMS: PAST, PRESENT, AND FUTURE

Valerie J. Shute
**ARMSTRONG LABORATORY
BROOKS AIR FORCE BASE, TEXAS**

Joseph Psotka
**U.S. ARMY RESEARCH INSTITUTE
ALEXANDRIA, VIRGINIA**

19.1 INTRODUCTION

Many aspects of intelligent tutoring systems (ITS) are addressed in a search for answers to the following main questions: (a) What are the precursors of ITS? (b) What does the term mean? (c) What are some important milestones and issues across the 20+ years of ITS history? (d) What is the status of ITS evaluations? (e) What is the future of ITS? Let's start with an historical perspective.

19.2 PRECURSORS OF ITS

19.2.1 Early Mechanical Systems

Charles Babbage (early 1800s) is typically credited with being the first to envision a multipurpose computer. He dreamed of creating an all-purpose machine, which he called the *analytic engine*. However, because of the technological constraints of the time, he was never able to build his dream, although he did succeed in building a difference engine, an automatic (mechanical) means of calculating logarithm tables.

The notion of using "intelligent machines" for teaching purposes can be traced back to 1926 when Pressey built an instructional machine teeming with multiple-choice questions and answers submitted by the teacher (see 2.3.4.2). It delivered questions, then provided immediate feedback to each learner:

> The somewhat astounding way in which the functioning of the apparatus seems to fit in with the so-called "laws of learning" deserves mention in this connection. The "law of recency" operates to establish the correct answer in the mind of the subject, since it is always the *last* answer which is the right one. The "law of frequency" also cooperates; by chance the right response tends to be made most often, since it is the *only* response by which the subject can go on

to the next question. Further, with the addition of a simple attachment, the apparatus will present the subject with a piece of candy or other reward upon his making any given score for which the experimenter may have set the device; that is the "law of effect" also can be made, automatically (see 2.2.1.3), to aid in the establishing of the right answer (Pressey, 1926, p. 375).

While the above system was definitely clever for its time, it could not be construed as intelligent as it was mechanically set with prespecified questions and answers. So, although it was inflexible, this system did incorporate contemporary learning theories and pedagogical strategies into its design (e.g., giving out candy for correct responses).

General-purpose digital computers arose in the mid-1900s, paving the way for truly (artificially) intelligent machines. Basically, these computers consisted of a numerical central processor whose mechanism was electronic, not mechanical, and based on a binary, not decimal, system. They were also characterized by having a built-in ability to make logical decisions, and a built-in device for easy storage and manipulation of data.

During this period of computer infancy, Alan Turing (1912–1954, British mathematician and logician) provided a major link between these modern, digital computing systems and thinking. He described a computing system capable of not only "number crunching" but symbolic manipulation as well. He also developed what is now known as the "Turing test," a means of determining a machine's intelligence. The test consists of an individual asking questions, in real-time, of both a human being and a computer. The interrogator attempts, in any way possible, to figure out which is which via conversations over the communication links. The Turing test has particular relevance to intelligent tutoring systems. The core concept behind the test is whether a reasonable person can distinguish between a computer and a person based solely on their respective responses to whatever questions or statements the interrogator renders. Thus, for a computer to pass the test, it would need to communicate like a human being, which is a nontrivial goal. This line of inquiry has challenged and occupied researchers for more than 20 years, and continues to play a prominent role in the development of ITS (see Merrill, Reiser, Ranney & Trafton, 1992). Other communication-related research includes devising knowledge structuring and hypertext techniques within ITS to provide answers to the many possible questions that students could pose to the system. So, the success of this ITS enterprise really can be measured in a way that is similar to the Turing test: How well can the ITS communicate? We should point out, however, that the goal of ITS is to communicate its embedded knowledge effectively, not necessarily in an *identical* manner as human teachers. In fact, some teachers have great difficulty achieving the effective communication goal themselves.

Concurrent with the gradual emergence of computers on the scene (circa 1950s), educational psychologists began reporting in the literature that carefully designed, individualized tutoring produces the best learning for the most people (e.g., Bloom, 1956; Carroll, 1963; Crowder, 1959; Glaser, 1976; Skinner, 1957; see 35.2). Thus, it was quite a natural development to apply computers to the task of individualized teaching. From the 1970s to the present, ITS has been heralded as the most promising approach to delivering such individualized instruction (e.g., Burton & Brown, 1982; Lewis, McArthur, Stasz & Zmuidzinas, 1990; Shute & Regian, 1990; Sleeman & Brown, 1982; Wenger, 1987; Woolf, 1988; Yazdani & Lawler, 1986). We'll now review what led to the development of "intelligent" computerized instruction.

19.2.2 Programmed Instruction and Computer-Assisted Instruction

In the early 1960s, programmed instruction (PI) was educationally fashionable (see 2.3.4, 22.4.1). This kind of pedagogy related to any structured, goal-oriented instruction. According to Bunderson (1970), PI required the program designer to specify input and output in terms of entering skills and terminal behaviors of the learner. In performing a task analysis, the designer determined the subproblems or component behaviors, as well as their relationships. As learners were led through the problems in the curriculum (lockstep), overt responses were obtained at every step. Incorrect responses were immediately corrected, and learners were always informed of their solution accuracy before moving on to some other content area. Most supporters of the PI technology strongly believed that it would enhance learning, particularly for low-aptitude individuals. However, evidence supporting this belief was underwhelming (see Cronbach & Snow, 1981).

In general, PI refers to any instructional methodology that utilizes a systematic approach to problem decomposition and teaching (e.g., Briggs, Campeau, Gagné & May, 1967; Gagné, 1965; see 2.3.4, 22.4.1). In some cases, PI was embedded in a computer program, known as *computer-assisted instruction* (CAI or computer-based training, CBT). Some similarities between PI and CAI are that both have well-defined curricula and branching routines (intrinsic branching for PI, conditional branching for CAI). A major distinction between the two is that CAI is administered on a computer (see 12.1).

Computer-assisted instruction also evolved from Skinnerian stimulus-response psychology: ". . . the student's response serves primarily as a means of determining whether the communication process has been effective and at the same time allows appropriate corrective action to be taken" (Crowder, 1959). In other words, at every point in the curriculum, the computer program evaluates whether the student's answer is right or wrong and then moves the student to the proper path. Built-in remediation loops tutor students who are attempting to answer a question incorrectly. If learners answer correctly, they are moved ahead in the curriculum. Figure 19-1 illustrates a typical flow of events in CAI.

The teacher constructs all branching in the program, ahead of time. The normal CAI procedure presents some material to be learned, followed by a problem to be solved that represents a subset of the curriculum. Problem solution tests the learner's acquisition of the knowledge or skill being instructed at that time. The student's answer is compared to the correct answer, then the computer gives appropriate feedback. If the answer is correct, a new problem is selected and presented. If the student answers incorrectly, remediation is invoked that reviews the earlier material, presents simpler problems that graduate to the depth of the original material, and so forth. Remediation usually requires some attempt to find the source of the error and to treat it specially.

As can be seen in Figure 19-1, there are several places where this simple model may be expanded to create more flexibility and, hence, render it adaptive to individual learners. For instance, various mastery criteria can be imposed, where subjects have to answer a certain proportion of items correctly before moving on. Failure to reach a criterion would force the student back into remediation mode (see "If incorrect" branch) where a different problem is presented, rather than the problem that caused the error.

19.2.3 Intelligent Computer-Assisted Instruction

To distinguish between simple versus more adaptive CAI (i.e., "intelligent" computer-assisted instruction, ICAI), Wenger (1987) pointed out that actually there is no explicit demarcation between the two. Instead, there's a continuum, from linear CAI to more complex branching CAI, to elementary ICAI, to autonomous (or stand-alone) ICAI. This continuum is often misconstrued as representing a worse-to-better progression. Yet, for some learning situations and for some curricula, using fancy programming techniques may be like using a shotgun to kill a fly. If a drill-and-practice environment is all that is required to attain a particular instructional goal, then that's what should be used.

COMPUTER-ASSISTED INSTRUCTIONS

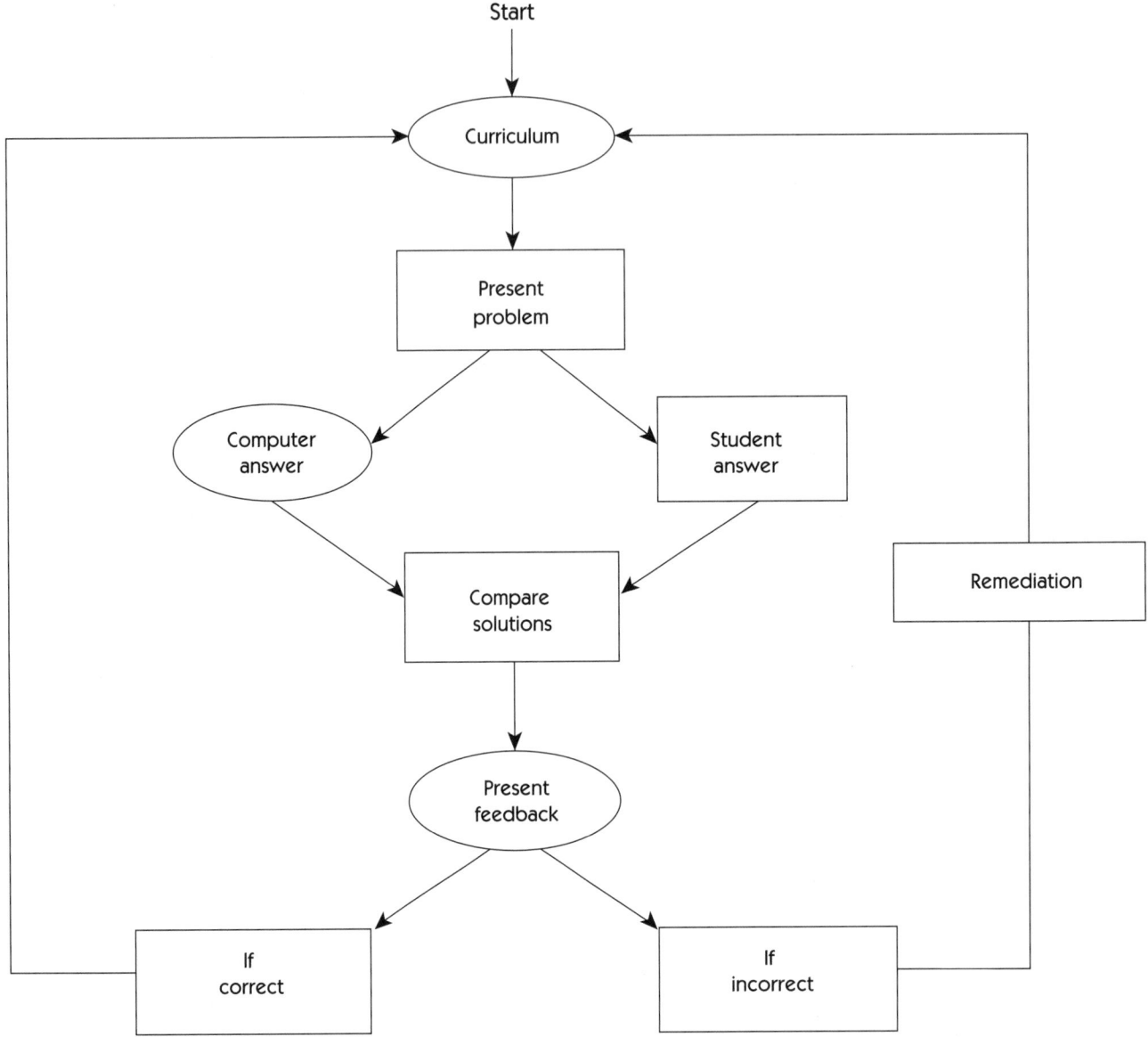

Figure 19-1. Computer-assisted instructions: boxes = program actions; ellipses = canned program knowledge.

Suppose you wanted to build a computerized instructional system to help second-graders learn double-digit addition. If student A answered the following two problems as: 22 + 39 = 61, and 46 + 37 = 83, you'd surmise (with a fair amount of confidence) that A understood, and could successfully apply, the "carrying procedure." But consider some other responses. Student B answers the same problems with 51 and 73; student C answers with 161 and 203; and student D answers with 61 and 85. Simple CAI systems may be incapable of differentiating these incorrect solutions, and remediation would require all three students to redo the specific unit of instruction. But a big problem with this approach is that, typically, there is little difference between the remedial and original instruction. That means

that a student who didn't get it right the first time may not get it right the next time if the same instruction and similar problems are used.

A more sensitive (or *intelligent*) response by the system would be to diagnose/classify B's answer as a failure to carry a 1 to the tens column, C's answer as the incorrect adding of the ones column result (11 and 13) to the tens column, and D's as a probable computational error in the second problem (mistakenly adding 6 + 7 = 15 instead of 13). An intelligent system would remediate by specifically addressing each of the three qualitatively different errors.

19.2.3.1. Artificial Intelligence and Cognitive Psychology. How can a computer system be programmed to perform intelligently? This question drives the empirical and engineering research in a field called *artificial intelligence* (AI). The simplest definition is that, "Artificial intelligence is the study of mental faculties through the use of computational models" (Charniak & McDermott, 1985, p. 6). One of the main objectives of AI is to design and develop computer systems that can solve the same kinds of activities that we deem intelligent (e.g., solving a math problem like the one illustrated above, understanding natural language, programming a computer to perform some function(s), maneuvering an aircraft through obstacles, planning a wedding reception, and so forth; see also 22.4.4). There are far too many AI applications to delineate in this chapter. For our purposes, AI techniques relevant to ITS include those dealing with the efficient representation, storage, and retrieval of knowledge (i.e., a large collection of facts and skills—correct and buggy versions), as well as the effective communication of that information. In addition, AI techniques can include inductive and deductive reasoning processes that allow a system to access its own database to derive novel (i.e., not programmed) answers to learners' queries.

Cognitive psychology also provides part of the answer to the question of how to get a computer to behave intelligently by examining issues related to the representation and organization of knowledge types in human memory. Research in this area provides detailed structural specifications for implementation in intelligent computer programs. Cognitive psychology also addresses the nature of errors, a critical feature in the design of intelligent systems to assist learners during the learning process (see 12.2.3, 32.5.3).

19.2.3.2. The Nature of Errors. The idea that students and trainees make mistakes that have to be corrected is fundamental to teaching and learning. Something so fundamental ought to be strongly resistant to change, so it is really quite surprising how the idea of a mistake or error has undergone radical change over the past 2 decades of ITS development. The traditional view of errors encompassed many kinds—from inexplicable accidents, to deliberate inaccuracies—but the most widely held view was that remedial errors stemmed from inaccurate or insufficient knowledge. Remediation then corrected the mistake by providing the correct knowledge or overriding the inaccuracy. The first major shift that occurred in this view began with the development of a theoretical position that errors arose because of complex organizations in knowledge structures that were not wrong, in the traditional sense, but represented the best a student could have at that stage of cognitive development. These developmentally appropriate knowledge structures were called *misconceptions,* and they were soon analyzed in a broad range of sciences (e.g., Aristotelian versus Newtonian physics, studies of heat and temperature) and practical training environments (automobile repair, radar maintenance).

This view of error was explicated in great detail in a series of analyses and experiments by Barbara White and John Frederiksen (1987) in their QUEST system for analyzing levels of understanding of electrical functioning into graduated mental models. Their analyses were actually implemented as qualitative models of the electrical activity in automobile ignition circuits. Simple models, or models that occur developmentally early in the growth of knowledge, were not only incomplete; they were also wrong or inconsistent in basic ways. They could not easily be transformed into more complete models. Yet, the simple models effectively captured the knowledge of novices as they moved on the road to expertise, so it is not clear if these models could have been improved at that stage of development. Thus, it appeared that error or inconsistency was necessary in the growth of knowledge.

As they demonstrated, it took a great deal of effort to conduct error analysis with sufficient scope and detail to be able to arrive at such complete models. It is perhaps for this reason that no other example comes close to duplicating their feat. Yet, the intellectual implications of graduated mental models as the basis for misconceptions and error is stunningly apparent for whoever next decides to pick up the challenge and analyze knowledge structures into such progressive systems.

An alternative conception of error that has developed contemporaneously with the misconception literature is that of a *buggy algorithm.* Work in this area began with Burton and Brown's seminal simulation—*How the West Was Won*—where certain strategic and algorithmic bugs were identified in student play. A specific program was written, DEBUGGY, that attempted to identify and remediate these bugs (Brown & Burton, 1978; Burton, 1982). Unlike the work on misconceptions and graduated mental models, bugs were simpler deconstructions in smaller semantic networks of skills.

This analysis of errors has had a productive life of its own in the work of Soloway (catalogs of bugs, Johnson & Soloway, 1984), Sleeman (mal-rules, Sleeman, 1987), and VanLehn (impasses, VanLehn, 1990). It continues strongly in the model-tracing technology of John Anderson's various tutors (e.g., Anderson, 1993) where bug catalogs or lists of errors are embedded in specific production system rules that manage all interactions between the student and tutor. Anderson has proclaimed a much broader view to encompass not only errors but also all cognitive skills. His position is, simply stated, that cognitive skills are realized by production rules. Not only errors, but all skills as well, are decomposable into unitary rules that fit into a grand cognitive architecture dominated by production rules.

VanLehn's work on *impasses* extends this buggy conception of errors by analyzing the ways these errors are generated (VanLehn, 1990). Oversimplifying his analysis somewhat, VanLehn's framework can be described by saying that bugs are the result of unsuccessful attempts to extend existing rules to apply to novel situations (repairs). These repairs can be modeled and predicted by impasse theory to predict students bugs and problem solving. Usually the repairs are simple actions, such as removing an action step in the production rules, substituting an operator, or deleting a variable.

The final view of errors that has evolved along with ITS sees the error as a result of insufficient support given to the student. When a student learns a new skill or body of knowledge, it is through the support of teachers, students, or other parts of the environment. This environment acts as a general scaffolding to strengthen the student's first new skills or knowledge structures (Palincsar & Brown, 1984). It also provides the context that makes the skills or knowledge meaningful. Some of this scaffolding lies literally in the minds of the other students or teachers, or more precisely, between the minds of everyone. As a kind of social group think, the ideas and scaffolding are part of the total situation (Brown, Collins & Duguid, 1989) and so it has been called *situated cognition.* If the environment is literally part of the skills and knowledge, then changing it abruptly can actually change student thinking and lead directly to errors.

This fascinating research related to different kinds of errors owes its existence directly to the practical and theoretical developments that ITS has spawned. All have real import for the design of instruction, but at the moment, they are still very distant from each other and show no real signs of converging into a common theoretical framework.

19.2.3.3. Summary. Branching is a fundamental aspect of PI, CAI, and ICAI. It recognizes the fact that knowledge is interrelated in many complex ways, and there may be multiple good paths through the curriculum. AI programming techniques empower the computer to manifest intelligence by going beyond what's explicitly programmed, understanding student inputs, and generating rational responses based on reasoning from the inputs and the system's own database.

In the example just provided, prior to teaching double-digit addition, the system could first ascertain if the learner was skilled (to the point of automaticity) with single-digit addition, drilling the learner across a variety of problems, and noting accuracy and latency for each solution. Subsequently, it may be effective to introduce: (a) double-digit addition without the carrying procedure (23 + 41), (b) single- to double-digit addition (5 + 32), or (c) single-digit addition to 10 (7 + 10). Each of these curriculum elements is warranted, and some are easier to grasp than others. However, for more complex knowledge domains, such as history, or the scientific debate over the extinction of dinosaurs, the complexity of alternatives is beyond enumeration. And it is the complexity of this branching that really provides a qualitative break between older forms of PI and CAI and newer ITS. Not only is the branching in ITS complex, it is also algorithmic and not enumerated, predefined, or hand crafted. With this qualitative increase in complexity comes a flexibility of interaction and potential for communication that, better than anything else before, begins to qualify for the word *intelligent.*

Another aspect of computer intelligence deals with the identification and remediation of errors (bugs) in a learner's knowledge structure or performance. The simple illustration with four hypothetical students shows the possible power of adding AI to instructional software that can recognize bugs or misconceptions via: (a) a bug catalog that specifically recognizes each mistake (e.g., Johnson & Soloway, 1984),

(b) a set of mal-rules that define the kinds of mistakes possible with this set of problems (e.g., Sleeman, 1987), or (c) a set of production rules that specifically anticipate all alternative problem solutions and can respond to each one (e.g., Anderson, 1993; VanLehn, 1990). Each of these will be discussed in more detail in the section of this chapter outlining the 20-plus years of history of ITS. First, we need to operationalize some terms.

19.3 INTELLIGENT TUTORING SYSTEMS DEFINED

While many researchers in the field view ICAI and ITS as interchangeable designations, we make a subtle distinction between the two: ITS represents a more specific type of ICAI, due to the attributes discussed below.

19.3.1 Early Specifications of ITS

An early outline of ITS requirements was presented by Hartley and Sleeman (1973). They argued that ITS must possess: (a) knowledge of the domain (expert model), (b) knowledge of the learner (student model), and (c) knowledge of teaching strategies (tutor). It is interesting to note that this simple list has not changed in more than 20 years (see Lajoie & Derry, 1993; Polson & Richardson, 1988; Psotka, Massey & Mutter, 1988; Regian & Shute, 1992; Sleeman & Brown, 1982).

All of this computer-resident knowledge marks a radical shift from earlier "knowledge-free" CAI routines. Furthermore, the ability to diagnose errors and tailor remediation based on the diagnosis represents a key difference between ICAI and CAI. Figure 19-2 illustrates these knowledge components and their relations within a generic ITS. Each of these ITS components will be discussed, in turn.

19.3.2 ITS Components and Relationships

A student learns from an ITS primarily by solving problems—ones that are appropriately selected or tailormade—that serve as good learning experiences for that student. The system starts by assessing what the student already knows, the *student model.* The system concurrently must consider what the student needs to know, the *curriculum* (also known as the *domain expert*). Finally, the system must decide which curriculum element (unit of instruction) ought to be instructed next and how it shall be presented, the *tutor* or inherent teaching strategy. From all of these considerations, the system selects, or generates, a problem, then either works out a solution to the problem (via the domain expert) or retrieves a prepared solution. The ITS then compares its solution, in real time, to the one the student has prepared and performs a diagnosis based on differences between the two.

Feedback is offered by the ITS based on such student-advisor considerations as how long it's been since feedback

INTELLIGENT TUTORING SYSTEM

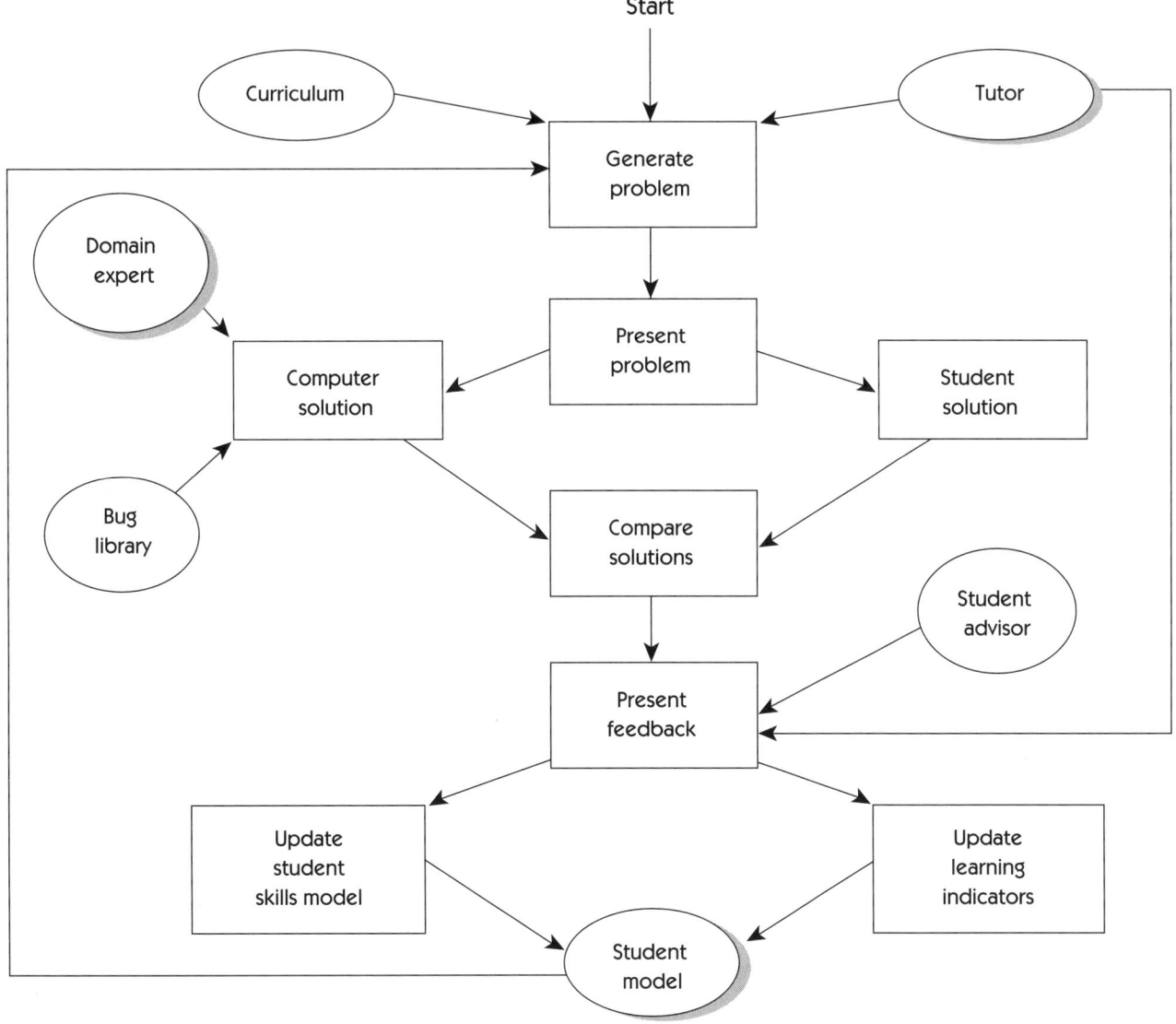

Figure 19-2.   Intelligent tutoring system: boxes = program decisions & actions; ellipses = program knowledge bases; shaded ellipses = core ITS components.

was last provided, whether the student already received some particular advice, and so on. After the feedback loop, the program updates the student skills model (a record of what the student knows and doesn't know) and increments learning progress indicators. These updating activities modify the student model, and the entire cycle is repeated, starting with selecting or generating a new problem (see 32.3).

Not all ITS include these components, and the problem-test-feedback cycle does not adequately characterize all systems. However, this generic depiction does describe many current ITS. Alternative implementations exist, representing conceptual as well as practical differences in their design. For example, the standard approach to building a student model involves representing emerging learner knowledge

and skills. The computer responds to updated observations with a modified curriculum that is minutely adjusted. Instruction, therefore, is very much dependent on individual response histories. But an alternative approach involves assessing *incoming* knowledge and skills, either instead of, or in addition to, emerging knowledge and skills. This alternative enables the curriculum to adapt to both persistent and/or momentary performance information as well as their interaction (see Shute, 1993a, 1993b, 1995). In fact, many have argued that incoming knowledge is the single most important determinant of subsequent learning (e.g., Alexander & Judy, 1988; Dochy, 1992; Glaser, 1984).

Other kinds of systems may not even have a tutor/coach present. For example, the strength of microworlds (exploratory environments) resides in the underlying simulation and explicit interfaces in which students can freely conduct experiments and obtain results quickly and safely (see 12.3). This is a particularly attractive feature for domains that are hazardous, or do not frequently occur in the real world. Furthermore, these systems can be intrinsically motivating, in terms of generating interesting complexities that keep students interested in continuing to explore, while giving them sufficient success to prevent frustration.

19.3.3 The "I" in ITS

Our working definition of computer-tutor intelligence is that the system must *behave* intelligently, not actually *be* intelligent, like a human being. More specifically, we believe that an intelligent system must be able to: (a) accurately diagnose students' knowledge structures, skills, and/or styles using principles, rather than preprogrammed responses, to decide what to do next; and then (b) adapt instruction accordingly (e.g., Clancey, 1986; Shute, 1992; Sleeman & Brown, 1982). Moreover, the traditional intelligent tutoring system ". . . takes a longitudinal, rather than cross-sectional, perspective, focusing on the fluctuating cognitive needs of a single learner over time, rather than on stable inter-individual differences" (Ohlsson, 1986, pp. 293–294).

In order to obtain a rough idea of the degree of consensus among researchers in the ITS community, 20 experts were asked to summarize, in a couple of sentences, their ideas on what the "I" in ITS meant. Following are the different responses received (in alphabetical order, and slightly edited, for readability).

Ton de Jong: "Intelligent" in ITS stands for the ability to use (in a connected way) different levels of abstraction in the representation of the learner, the domain, and the instruction. The higher the range of abstraction, the higher the intelligence. The phrase "in a connected way" implies that one should be able to go from specific (e.g., log files) to abstract (e.g., learner characteristics), as well as the other way around (e.g., from general instructional strategies to a specific instructional transaction).

Sharon Derry: An intelligent instructional system can observe what the student is doing during problem solving and/or has done over a series of problem-solving sessions, and from this information draw inferences about the student's knowledge, beliefs, and attitudes in terms of some theory of cognition. A system can be intelligent whether or not it makes instructional decisions based on this information, but if it *doesn't* use such information in instructional decision making, then I don't think of it as a tutoring system, but rather a tool that has some diagnostic capabilities.

Wayne Gray: I concede a wide latitude on the application of the term "ITS" in regard to instructional systems. However, at some level and to some degree, there should be some sort of "cognitive modeling" technology involved. The modeling can be of an ideal student, instructor, or grad-

er, or of a less-than-ideal problem solver as in the "student models" that are often built up in ITS. To be intelligent, a system has to incorporate and use a model for making decisions about what to do at any given point during learning.

Lee Gugerty: Intelligent tutoring involves: (a) explicit modeling of expert representations and cognitive processes; (b) detection of student errors; (c) diagnosis of students' knowledge (correct, incorrect, and missing); (d) instruction adapted to students' knowledge state (via problem selection, hints, feedback, and explicit didactic instruction); and (e) doing all of the above in a timely fashion as the student solves problems (not post hoc).

Pat Kyllonen: An "intelligent" tutoring system is one that uses AI programming techniques or principles. However, what is considered AI (as opposed to standard) programming changes over time (e.g., expert systems used to be archetypal AI systems but are now found in $100 PC software packages). For me, two features separate ITS software from conventional CAI. One is the existence of a student model. What the student knows cannot be recorded directly but must be inferred by the system, based on a pattern of successes or failures by the student and an "understanding" of what knowledge problems in the curriculum call upon. Another feature is the existence of "coaches," "demons," or "bug libraries" that can observe a student's behavior and either diagnose the behavior in terms of the student's current knowledge structure or suggest corrections to that behavior.

Susanne Lajoie: The "I" in ITS means that the computer can provide adaptive forms of feedback to the learner based on a dynamic assessment of the student's "model" of performance. Intelligent feedback means that the assessment of the learner is ongoing, the feedback is appropriate to that particular learner in the context of where an impasse has been encountered, and it is not canned but generated on the spot, based on student needs.

Alan Lesgold: "Intelligent" means that the system uses inference mechanisms to provide coaching, explanation, or other information to the student performing a task. Further, it implies that this information is tuned to the context of the student's ongoing work and/or a model of the student's evolving knowledge.

Matt Lewis: An "intelligent" tutoring system contains, at a minimum, a reasonably general simulation of human problem solving in direct service of communicating knowledge and, like a good human tutor, separates domain knowledge from pedagogical knowledge. The simulation might solve domain-specific problems in the target instructional domain (e.g., a humanlike approach and solution to the problem of writing a fugue) or solve pedagogical problems (e.g., error diagnosis and attribution, or selection of appropriate response).

Wes Regian: An ITS differs from CAI in that: (a) instructional interactions are individually tuned at run time to be as efficient as possible, (b) instruction is based on cognitive principles, and (c) at least some of the feedback is generated at run time, rather than being all canned. It is not particularly important to me what language the system is written in, whether or not the system is in any sense arguably aware of anything, and whether its decisions are rendered in a manner that is the same as a human decision.

Frank Ritter: The "I" in ITS usually indicates that a single knowledge-based component has been added that helps a tutoring system perform one aspect of its performance in a better way. This can be in lesson scheduling, providing examples of domain knowledge in action, or providing domain knowledge for comparison with a student's behavior. What it *should* mean is that it does the whole job intelligently. The systems are usually not systems in the full sense of the word; they tend to be prototypes, with whole parts missing.

Derek Sleeman: "Intelligent" tutoring systems need to have motivating learning environments, to communicate effectively, and to render dynamic decisions about appropriate control strategies. Since the 1960s, we've seen that the same material delivered on various systems differentially invoke motivation; thus we need to confirm the factors that impact a learner's motivation. Next, communication can only occur when there's a shared world view. In conventional dialogues, human beings dynamically tailor their language to the person to whom they are speaking, but computers are not yet so adaptable. Finally, control implies which of the partners in the dialogue will take the initiative, and it's often necessary to change control during an interaction, depending on the social setting, the student's motivation, and the level of incoming knowledge.

Elliot Soloway: The intent of the "I" in ITS was to explicitly recognize that a tutoring system needs to be exceedingly flexible in order to respond to the immense variety of learner responses. CAI, as the forerunner of ITS, didn't have the range of interactivity needed for learning. In fact, the movement from ICAI to ITS was to further distance the new type of learning environments from the rigidity of CAI.

Sig Tobias: "Intelligent," in an ITS context, means that the program is flexible in the method and sequence with which instructional materials are presented to the student. Furthermore, the system is capable of adapting instructional parameters to student characteristics by using data collected prior to, or during, instruction for such decisions. Finally, it suggests that the instructional system can advise the student regarding options most likely to be successful for the student.

Kurt VanLehn: "Intelligent" means that at least one of the three classic modules is included in the tutoring system. That is, the machine has either a subject-matter expert, a diagnostician/student modeler, or an expert teacher. Just as in any AI system, an expert system with only 10 production rules is intelligent only in that it holds the possibilities for expansion; a 100-rule system is moderately intelligent; and 1,000+ rules means you're really getting there.

Beverly Woolf: My view of tutor intelligence includes the following elements: (a) mechanisms that model the thinking processes of domain experts, tutors, and students;

(b) environments that supply world-class laboratories within which students can build and test their own reality; and (c) a computer partner that facilitates the aha! experience, recognizes the student's intention, and aids and advises the student. An intelligent environment would also support complex discoveries.

As seen in this nonrandom sample of responses about what constitutes intelligence in an ITS, just about everyone agrees that the most critical element is real-time *cognitive diagnosis* (or student modeling). The next most frequently cited feature is *adaptive remediation* (see 22.5). And while some maintain that remediation actually comprises the "T" in intelligent tutoring systems, our position is that the two components (diagnosis and remediation), working in concert, make up the intelligence in an ITS (see our working definition, above). Consider the case where a system diagnoses a student's skill level, but makes no effort to rectify any faulty behaviors. Can that system really be classified as intelligent? Theoretically, perhaps, but practically, no. Other characteristics of intelligence appear less frequently in these responses (e.g., canned vs. generated problems and feedback, degree of learner control in the environment, and presence of awareness).

The degree of agreement among responders was actually surprising given the diversity of respective research interests and backgrounds (computer scientists, psychologists, educators). But this degree of consensus was not always there. Until fairly recently, the field was not only esoteric but also quite fractionated; people disagreed about the definition of "intelligence" in a computer tutor. To understand the current congruence, we need to jump back briefly in time to see the evolution of intelligent tutoring systems, from the late 1960s to the present (mid-1990s).

19.4 THE 20–YEAR HISTORY OF ITS

Instead of discussing individual tutoring systems that spanned this period, we present salient characteristics of systems appearing at various points in time, illustrating with exemplar tutors. For excellent discussions of individual intelligent tutoring systems, see the following books: Bierman, Breuker & Sandberg, 1989; Goodyear, 1991; Lajoie & Derry, 1993; Lawler & Yazdani, 1987; Nickerson & Zodhiates, 1988; Polson & Richardson, 1988; Psotka, Massey & Mutter, 1988; Regian & Shute, 1992; Self, 1988; Sleeman & Brown, 1982; and Wenger, 1987. The issues, by decade, that will be discussed can be seen in Table 19-1.

19.4.1 Up through the 1970s: Defining the Issues

Hardware and software have evolved at an astounding rate over the past 20 years. To put things in perspective, consider the 1970s: "Pong" was the rage (i.e., a simple black-and-white computerized table tennis game) and 8K random access memory (RAM) the norm for a PC. Computer-

TABLE 19-1. IMPORTANT ISSUES RELATED TO ITS DEVELOPMENT

1970s	1980s	1990s
Problem Generation	Model Tracing	Learner Control
Simple student modeling	More buggy-based systems	Individual vs. collaborative Learning
Knowledge representation	Case-based reasoning	Situated learning vs. information processing
Socratic tutoring	Discovery worlds	Virtual reality
Skills & strategic knowledge	Progression of mental models	
Reactive learning environments	Simulations	
Buggy library	Natural language processing	
Expert systems & tutors	Authoring systems	
Overlay models/genetic graph		

administered instruction developed before the 1970s was inflexible and didactic because the systems had very limited capabilities (i.e., memory capacity and computational speed) for adaptive diagnosis and feedback. Furthermore, ". . . the only theory available to guide instructional development was behavior theory, which poorly matched the cognitive goals of education" (Lesgold, 1988, p. iii; see 2.2). Over time, researchers in AI and cognitive psychology joined forces, and together provided a basis for a new generation of computer-based teaching programs. Some of the research issues that dominated the 70s are discussed below (see 5.23).

19.4.1.1 Real-Time Problem Generation. The earliest systems to incorporate some now "classic" ITS elements were programs that generated problems and learning tasks, representing a big departure from the canned problems stored in CAI databases (see also 7.5.2). For example, Uhr (1969) developed a computer-based learning system that created, in real time, simple arithmetic problems and vocabulary recall tasks. The next major advance in this area came in the form of computer programs that generated problems that had been tailored to the knowledge and skill level of a particular student, thus providing the foundation for student modeling.

19.4.1.2. Simple Student Modeling. The Basic Instructional Program (BIP) develops procedural skills required in learning the programming language BASIC (Barr, Beard & Atkinson, 1976). It did so by selecting problems based on what the student already knew (past performance), which skills should be taught next, and its analysis of the skills required (problems in the curriculum). Exercises were dynamically and individually selected per person (from a pool of 100 sample problems). Then teaching heuristics were applied to the student model to identify skills to be taught, and exercises were selected that best involved those skills. Selection of appropriate exercises was based on information contained in a network called the Curriculum Information Network (CIN), relating tasks in the curriculum to issues in the domain knowledge. Thus, a programming task in the tutor was represented in terms of its component skill

requirements. Based on a task analysis, BIP knew that the component skills needed for solving a particular programming problem included such skills as: initialize numeric variable, use for-next loop with literal as final value, and so forth. Moreover, each task tapped a number of skills.

19.4.1.3. Knowledge Representation. Classic CAI used pages of text to represent knowledge, but with little psychological validity. In contrast, Carbonell's (1970) SCHOLAR program (often credited with being the first true ITS) used a semantic net to represent domain knowledge (South American geography) as well as the student model. Nodes in the network had tags to indicate whether the concept was known to the student. This novel application of semantic network as a general structure of knowledge representation supported mixed-initiative dialogs with students. Not only could the computer ask questions of the student but the student also could, theoretically, ask questions of the computer. One major limitation of this semantic knowledge representation was the difficulty of representing procedural knowledge (see 5.3).

19.4.1.4. Socratic Tutoring. Carbonell's research spawned another line of work concerned with enabling systems to engage in Socratic dialogues, believed to involve the learner more actively in the learning process. Collins (1977) outlined a set of tutorial rules for Socratic tutoring that were incorporated into a system called WHY (Stevens & Collins, 1977). For example, consider the following IF/THEN string: IF the student gives an explanation of one or more factors that are not sufficient, THEN formulate a general rule for asserting that the given factors are sufficient, and ask the student if the rule is true (Collins, 1977, pp. 343–344). Instead of semantic nets, the domain knowledge (rainfall) was stored in a "script hierarchy" containing information about stereotypical sequences of events.

19.4.1.5. Skills and Strategic Knowledge. Another attempt to stimulate thought among students (rather than being passive recipients of information) was the focus of a group of researchers at Xerox PARC in the mid- to late-1970s. For instance, WEST (Burton & Brown, 1976) was developed to help students learn/practice skills involved in the manipulation of arithmetic expressions. The goal was to move around a game board (*How the West Was Won*) and either advance the maximum number of squares, land on and thus "bump" an opponent back some fixed amount of squares, or take a shortcut. Not only was basic arithmetic skill involved but also strategic knowledge was required. The system was attentive to all levels of knowledge and skill, but the "coach" was somewhat unobtrusive, sitting in the background monitoring the student's moves, intervening only when it was clear that the student was floundering. Then the coach would make a few suggestions to enhance student skills. WEST's coaching goals were accomplished by focusing on the strategy used to construct a move (viz.,"issue-based" tutoring).

19.4.1.6. Reactive Learning Environments.
In reactive learning environments, the system responds to learners' actions in a variety of ways that extend understanding and help change entrenched belief structures using examples that challenge the learner's current hypotheses. An early, excellent example of this kind of environment was SOPHIE (Sophisticated Instructional Environment), designed to assist learners in developing electronic troubleshooting skills (see Brown & Burton, 1975; Brown, Burton & deKleer, 1982). For instance, in SOPHIE I, learners located faults in a broken piece of equipment. They could ask SOPHIE questions in English (e.g., to obtain values of various measurements taken on the device). SOPHIE I included three main components: a mathematical simulation, a program to understand a subset of natural language, and routines to set up contexts, keep history lists, and so on. A student, troubleshooting a simulated piece of equipment, could offer a hypothesis about what was wrong. SOPHIE I reacted to the request by comparing the hypothesis to the measurements entered by the student. SOPHIE II extended the environment of its predecessor by adding an articulate expert based on a prestored decision tree for troubleshooting the power supply that was annotated with schema for producing explanations. SOPHIE III represented a significant advance; it contained an underlying expert based on a causal model rather than on a mathematical simulation. The importance of this change is that, in SOPHIE I, the simulator worked out a set of equations not using humanlike, causal reasoning, so it wasn't possible for the system to explain its decision in any detail. But SOPHIE III did employ a causal model of circuits to deal with the student feedback deficiency. Research with SOPHIE spawned a lot of later research in troubleshooting, reactive learning environments, and articulate experts.

19.4.1.7. Buggy Library.
Brown and Burton (1978) also developed BUGGY, a frequently cited example of a system employing a "buggy" library approach to the diagnosis of student errors. BUGGY was a framework for modeling misconceptions underlying procedural errors in addition and subtraction where students' errors were represented as the results of "bugs" (errors) in an otherwise correct set of procedures. DEBUGGY (Burton, 1982) was developed as an off-line version of the system based on the BUGGY framework's using the pattern of errors from a set of problems to construct an hypothesis concerning a bug, or combination of bugs, from the library that generated the errors. IDEBUGGY (Burton, 1982) was an on-line version of BUGGY, diagnosing the student's procedure bit-by-bit while giving the learner new problems to solve. The major limitation of these kinds of systems was the inability to anticipate all possible misconceptions. Moreover, bugs could appear transient as they were being repaired.

19.4.1.8. Expert Systems and Tutors.
MYCIN (Shortliffe, 1976) was a rule-based expert system for diagnosing certain infectious diseases such as meningitis. GUIDON (Clancey, 1979) was constructed to interface with MYCIN for tutoring, interactively presenting the rules in the knowledge base to a student. This tutoring operated as follows: GUIDON described case dialogues of a sick patient to the student in general terms. The student had to adopt the role of a physician and ask for information that might be relevant to the case. GUIDON compared the student's questions to those that MYCIN would have asked, and then responded accordingly.

19.4.1.9. Overlay Models/Genetic Graph.
The definition of an overlay model is one of a novice-expert difference model representing missing conceptions. It's typically implemented as either an expert model annotated for missing items, or an expert model with weights assigned to each element in the expert knowledge base. To illustrate how it works, consider WUSOR (Stansfield, Carr & Goldstein, 1976), the name of the on-line coach for the game WUMPUS (Yob, 1975). The WUMPUS player had to traverse through successive caves to locate the hiding Wumpus. Many dangers faced the player (e.g., pits, bats), but the problem could be solved by applying logical and probabilistic reasoning to information obtained along the way. The goal of the game was to shoot an arrow into the Wumpus' hiding spot before you were killed. WUSOR evolved through (at least) three generations, each with a progressively more sophisticated student model. The first version had only an expert and advisor and did not try to diagnose the learner's state of knowledge. The next version (II) incorporated an overlay model (Carr & Goldstein, 1977) where the expertise was represented as rules, and the student's knowledge state was a subset of the expert's knowledge. Goldstein (1979) made the final transformation to WUSOR (III) by including the genetic graph, combining overlay modeling (rule-based representation) with a learner-oriented set of links between curricular elements. *Genetic* related to the notion of knowledge being evolutionary, and *graph* denoted the relationships between parts of knowledge expressed as links in a network. A genetic graph could represent type of links (e.g., generalization, analogy, refinement) as well as deviation links (i.e., buggy rules as opposed to simply absent ones).

The 1970s were marked by experimental systems that bore little resemblance to one another. During the following decade, systems became less idiosyncratic, but there was still a lot of diversity in the field.

19.4.2 1980s: Standardized Approaches and Environments

The 1980s were characterized by enormous growth and momentum in the ITS field. By the mid-1980s, the development of tutors greatly exceeded their evaluations; everyone wanted to participate in the excitement of building ITS, but few cared to test their system's efficacy (Baker, 1990; Littman & Soloway, 1988; see 12.2, 39.4). Sleeman (1984) attempted to focus research efforts by outlining four main problems with ITS at the time:

1. *Feedback specificity.* Instructional feedback was often not sufficiently detailed for a particular learner.
2. *Nonadaptability.* Systems forced students into their own conceptual framework rather than adapting to a particular student's conceptualization.
3. *Atheoretical foundation.* Tutoring strategies used by the systems lacked a theoretical cognitive foundation.
4. *Restrictive environment.* User interaction and exploration was too restricted.

These main criticisms were addressed, to varying degrees, during the 1980s.

19.4.2.1. Model Tracing.
Anderson and his colleagues at Carnegie-Mellon University developed a model-tracing approach to tutoring based on production systems as a way of modeling student behavior. The model-tracing approach has been employed in a variety of tutoring systems, such as the LISP tutor (Anderson, Boyle & Reiser, 1985) and the geometry tutor (Anderson, Boyle & Yost, 1985). Model tracing provides a powerful way both to validate cognitive theories (e.g., Anderson, 1987) and to deliver low-level, personalized remediation. The approach works by delineating many hundreds of production rules that model curricular "chunks" of cognitive skill. A learner's acquisition of these chunks is monitored (i.e., the student model is traced), and departure from the optimal route is immediately remediated.

In theory (and practice), the model-tracing approach for the geometry and LISP tutors is so complete that it captures an enormous percentage of all students' errors. A major drawback is that this approach does not allow students to commit those errors themselves. As soon as there is a misstep, the tutor cries "foul" and stops the student from doing anything else until the correct step is taken. As Reiser points out (e.g., Reiser, Ranney, Lovett & Kimberg, 1989), the student is not only prevented from following these mistakes to their logical conclusion (and getting hopelessly confused) but also prevented from obtaining an insight into the mistake (i.e., that the mistake is obvious). These are some of the best learning experiences students can have, but they appear to be blocked by the model-tracing approach.

Model tracing challenges the first criticism (feedback specificity). That is, the grain size of feedback is as small as you can get (i.e., the production level), thus providing the most detailed, specific feedback possible. However, in some cases (i.e., for certain students or particular problems), this level of feedback may be too elemental; the *for-*

est is lost for the trees. Next, as mentioned above, the systems can adapt to a wide range of student conceptualizations, challenging the second (nonadaptability) criticism. The approach also demolishes the third criticism (atheoretical foundation), as it was explicitly based on Anderson's cognitive theory (ACT*). The positive features of this approach, however, are achieved at the expense of the fourth (restrictive environment) criticism. That is, the model-tracing approach is restrictive. To accomplish the necessary low-level monitoring and remediation of this approach, the learner's freedom has to be curtailed. So, learning by one's mistakes is out (which is often a powerful way to learn). A final drawback of this approach is that, while it works very well in modeling procedural skill acquisition, it does not work well for domains that are ill-structured, or that are not rule-based (e.g., creative writing, economics, Russian history).

19.4.2.2. More Buggy-Based Systems.
During this time period, a plethora of tutors was developed based on the "buggy" library approach (see BUGGY, above). While these systems do provide very specific feedback about the nature of the learner's error (countering criticism 1, feedback specificity), the system response is dependent on the program's ability to match the student's error with that of a stored "bug." Along these same lines, as with model tracing (because only stored bugs are acknowledged), novel bugs are ignored; thus there is no way to update the buggy library or adapt to the learner's current conceptualization (criticism 2, nonadaptability). This approach is theoretically based on the notion of cognitive errors in specific procedures, impasse learning, and repair theory (VanLehn, 1990), countering criticism 3 (atheoretical foundation). Finally, these systems constrain the learner somewhat less than the model-tracing approach; thus, it is a response to criticism 4 (restrictive environment).

A good illustration of a system based on the buggy approach is PROUST (Johnson, 1986; Littman & Soloway, 1988), designed to diagnose nonsyntactic student errors in Pascal programs. The system works by locating errors in students' programs where they compute various descriptive statistics such as the minimum and maximum values, and averages. The major drawback of this system is that it is implemented off line. In other words, the tutor has access to a final product on which to base its diagnosis of student errors: Completed student programs are submitted to PROUST, which prints out the diagnosis (Johnson & Soloway, 1984).

A parallel "buggy" research project involved a system called PIXIE (Sleeman, 1987), an on-line ITS based on the Leeds Modeling System (LMS), a diagnostic model for determining sources of error in algebra problem solving due to incorrect procedural rules or "mal-rules." While some may equate mal-rules with buggy rules, they differ in a fundamental way. Sleeman created them by postulating a set of basic buggy rules from which higher-order mal-rules could be generated from the structure of the knowledge base itself. Mal-rules are inferred from basic principles and bugs; they are at a level of abstraction above bugs. In fact, John Anderson makes the same point about his model-tracing procedures. Because of the complexity of his model-tracing pro-ductions, many productions fire or are used over and over again in contexts for which they were not first generated, and so they too take on a kind of abstract or general quality in his framework. The major problem with LMS is that it only diagnoses the incorrect rules; it does not remediate.

19.4.2.3. Case-Based Reasoning.

Another category of systems emerging at this time came from case-based rea-soning (CBR) research (Schank, 1982; Kolodner, 1988). Proponents of this approach suggest that the goal of ITS should be to teach cases and how to index them. Given that the student, not the program, is the one doing the indexing, this system affords the learner greater freedom and pro-motes a more adaptive learning environment (countering criticisms 4, restrictive environment, and 2, nonadaptabili-ty, respectively). Furthermore, whereas the model-tracing tutors work poorly in ill-structured domains, CBR works well in those areas (e.g., politics, philosophy). This trade-off, however, can result in less specific feedback to learners (criticism 1, feedback specificity).

These CBR systems also perform well in domains where there are too many rules, or too many ways in which rules can be applied (e.g., programming, game playing). CBR suggests *approximate* answers to complex problems, there-by limiting how many rule combinations should be explored. There are two main processes involved with CBR: indexing (labeling new experiences for future retrieval) and adaptation (changing a retrieved case to fit a current situation). Further, two kinds of indices are required: concrete and abstract. Concrete indices refer to objects and actions usually directly mentioned in the case, while abstract indices refer to more general characteriza-tions. The "indexing problem" deals with ways to deter-mine the correct abstract and concrete indices for cases. How one indexes new cases determines what cases one will compare the inputs against. Using a general index, one can retrieve a case even when it shares no specific details with the current situation.

Schank has made some very provocative statements about the human mind as a storyteller, and about the need to encapsulate knowledge into stories, not into hierarchical data structures like semantic networks. But his procedures have yet to lead to any of the other strong characteristics of ITS that we emphasize in this paper: student models, teach-ing models, bugs, and so on. Instead, they exist as very gen-erative and interesting systems. As such, they have something in common with microworlds; that is, people enjoy exploring them and can learn from them, particularly those regarding ill-structured and complex domains. How-ever, when students don't learn, or manifest some miscon-ception(s), the very same looseness of structure and organization in these systems prevents them from determin-ing why, and doing something about it. Finally, according to Riesbeck and Schank (1990), case-based reasoning (CBR) serves as a *model* of cognition and learning. But, while these systems present a provocative and well-conceived approach that has many practical and obvious merits, they cannot be said to possess a solid theoretical foundation (criticism 3, atheoretical foundation). A major limitation of this approach includes the problem of anticipating and representing a suf-ficient number of cases to be cataloged.

19.4.2.4. Discovery Worlds.

With just a few excep-tions, learning from computers in the 1960s and 1970s was characterized by inflexible presentations of didactic materi-al. But an opposition movement arose in the 1970s that gained steam in the 1980s; it resulted in the development of discovery learning environments (see 7.4.1). These com-puterized systems (typically a computer simulation envi-ronment with simple interface and tools) were designed to make it possible for students to acquire various knowledge and skills on their own. For example, students could learn LOGO (Papert, 1980; see 12.3.2, 24.5) or Newton's laws of motion (White, 1984) within discovery (or micro) worlds. Typically, feedback was "natural" or implicit, not specifi-cally explained to the learner (relating to criticism 1, feed-back specificity).

One of the main strengths of these systems was their great adaptability to a range of different learners (counter-ing criticism 2, nonadaptability). Students were free to explore and act within the microworld as they chose; with the ramifications of their actions immediately revealed, countering criticism 4 (restrictive environment). This move-ment was based on the theoretical premise that in discovery learning, one can radically alter the perceptual relationship between the learner and the knowledge or skills to be acquired, thus addressing criticism 3 (atheoretical founda-tion). This position was epitomized by Piaget (1954), who stated that ". . . an education which is an active discovery of reality is superior to one that consists merely in providing the young with ready-made wills to will with, and ready-made truths to know with."

A major drawback of these systems is that not all per-sons are skilled in the requisite inquiry behaviors necessary to achieve success in these environments (see Shute & Glaser, 1990). That is, to be successful, an individual should be able to: formulate efficient experiments; state, confirm, and/or negate hypotheses; appropriately relate hypotheses and experiments; plan future experiments and tests; engage in self-monitoring; and so on.

19.4.2.5. Progression of Mental Models.

White, Fred-eriksen, and their colleagues (Frederiksen, White, Collins & Eggan, 1988; White & Frederiksen, 1987; White & Horowitz, 1987) incorporated ideas from: (a) AI research on mental models and (b) qualitative reasoning to develop QUEST (Qualitative Understanding of Electrical System Troubleshooting) as well as "Thinker Tools." This approach, like model tracing, above, is thus theoretically grounded (in opposition to criticism 3, atheoretical foundation).

These systems work by motivating students to want to learn by pointing out errors and inconsistencies in their cur-rent beliefs. Then students are guided through a series of microworlds, each more complex than the one preceding, toward the objective of more precise mental models (see 5.3.7) of the evolving subject matter (e.g., electrical concepts or Newtonian mechanics). Finally, students formalize their developing mental models by evaluating a set of laws describing phenomena in the microworld; then they apply the selected law to see how well it predicts real-world events.

These systems promote learning, neither completely free nor overly restricted (relating to criticism 4, restrictive environment), that resides about halfway between true discovery environments and model-tracing environments. A programmed series of mental models produces higher-level feedback compared to, for example, feedback at the production level (addressing criticism 1, feedback specificity). Finally, the systems can adapt to a wide range of learner misconceptions (challenging criticism 2, nonadaptability).

19.4.2.6. Simulations.   Graphical simulations have become more central to the ITS enterprise as the power of computers has grown. Along with increasing computational power, software systems have grown more complex; object-oriented systems can now mimic devices of great complexity and interactivity. Simulations are useful wherever real objects are involved in a learning or training task, and they provide many benefits over real devices. Not only are they less dangerous, less messy, and exactly replicable; simulations are inspectable and self-explanatory in ways that real objects cannot be. Simulations not only display aggregate behavior, but they also are decomposable into constituents that mimic novice or expert mental models. This decomposability of graphic displays and simulations mimics the power of productions in expert systems for creating natural chunks that promote learning (see 17.4).

Early ITS, like SOPHIE, could generate only very simple line drawings. A dramatic increase in the power of graphic simulations took place with Steamer (Hollan, Hutchins & Weitzman, 1984) and the use of personal LISP machines. These machines could generate interactive graphics with animated components. It was not long before this graphical power became available for ITS on smaller personal computers that could be used in industrial and educational settings. Of course, more powerful systems that were developed in the 1980s, like Hawk MACH-III, could expand the number of components and complexity of the animations by orders of magnitude (Kurland, Granville & MacLaughlin, 1992). Using object-oriented constructions, MACH-III made each part of complex radar systems inspectable and self-explanatory. For teaching troubleshooting, each decomposable part of the radar device could even explain its role in the troubleshooting sequence for any fault that had been created in the system. Given this power and complexity, these systems were stretched to their limits and brought to their knees by additional requirements for student models, curriculum sequences, and hypertext interfaces. Even though these computer simulations were forced to operate at the edge of their acceptability, an official Army evaluation verified the many benefits of simulation-based training systems (Farr & Psotka, 1992).

Depending on the level that a simulated device has been decomposed to, and the degree of learner response regarding manipulations and ensuing ramifications, feedback could attain various levels of detail (criticism 1, feedback specificity). Furthermore, as simulations become typically very reactive to learner actions, they can serve as a direct challenge to the second criticism (nonadaptability). Simulations, similar to discovery worlds, also leave quite a bit of freedom to explore and manipulate simulated objects and devices (countering criticism 4, restriction environments). However, the drawback of these systems is that a solid theoretical basis is lacking (criticism 3, atheoretical foundation). Simulation research in the 1980s spurred later work that attempted to incorporate pedagogical strategies into the simulation-based systems. Moreover, related developments continue to evolve in complexity with the addition of virtual-reality interfaces to three-dimensional models and simulations (Acchione-Noel & Psotka, 1993).

Two other areas of research and development gained prominence at this time: natural language processing (NLP) and authoring shells. While these research spheres were important in relation to ITS research, they could be applied within a variety of tutor types. For example, NLP could be used to communicate information to the learner (or accept input from the learner) in model-tracing tutors, discovery worlds, and so forth. And authoring shells could be built for the development of a range of tutoring systems. Because of this openness, the following two ITS-related issues won't be discussed in relation to our four criticisms, listed earlier.

19.4.2.7. Natural Language Processing (NLP).   This technology was an important part of ITS right from the beginning. SOPHIE, in fact, was built on a powerful and original NLP technique developed by Richard Burton; it was called *Semantic Grammar.* Representing a powerful combination of carefully selected keywords with algorithms that searched the context for meaningful variables and objects, it worked surprisingly well, given its relative simplicity. Since communication is such an important element of ITS (see Wenger, 1987, for emphasis), it is not surprising that NLP technologies have been used in several ITS for discourse networks (Woolf, 1988) and especially for language instruction (Yazdani, 1990; Psotka, Holland & Kerst, 1992). The development of powerful, efficient Prolog compilers and languages on PCs has led to the implementation of some interesting instructional grammars that can handle discourse in English or other languages, and provide multimedia instruction in advanced language concepts and grammar, as well as simple vocabulary and verb declension. The potential addition of animations and immersion into virtual environments adds a bright new prospect to the old goal of *immersive* language learning.

19.4.2.8. Authoring Systems.   The creation of computer-based environments to facilitate the design and development of ITS has been an important and continuing thread of research. The goal of authoring systems is to give relative computer novices a software toolkit to take advantage of the power of computers for designing instruction. An example of one powerful graphic authoring system developed over the last decade is that by Towne and Munro (1992).

Quite powerful CBT systems have been made available over the years. Research, beginning in the 1980s, attempted to adapt such systems as authoring shells for developing ITS. Miller and Lucado (1992) were among the first to integrate the power of CBT authoring environments with the technology of ITS. Their prototype system was the harbinger of many more powerful combinations of traditional CBT and next-generation ITS technologies. Most recently, DARPA has funded a unique consortium of Apple Computer, textbook publishers such as Houghton-Mifflin, and ITS experts Beverly Woolf and John Anderson to begin the development of next-generation authoring tools for instruction and training

The relative quiescence of the 80s transitioned into the current state of ITS affairs, marked by a perception of instability and controversy.

19.4.3 1990s: Great Debates

The four hot ITS topics right now may be broadly characterized as: (a) How much learner control should be allowed in systems? (b) Should learners interact with ITS individually or collaboratively? (c) Is learning situated, unique, and ongoing, or is it more symbolic, following from an information-processing model? (d) Does virtual reality (VR) uniquely contribute to learning beyond CAI, ITS, or even multimedia? There are, of course, proponents and opponents to each of these positions.

19.4.3.1. Degree of Learner Control. The debate over the amount of learner control that should be a part of the learning process has raged for many years (see 7.4.6, 12.2.3.5, 14.6.2, 22.5.5, 23.7.2, Chapter 33). On the one hand, some have argued that discovering information on one's own is the best way to learn (e.g., Bruner, 1961). On the other hand, structure and direction have been stressed as the important ingredients in the promotion of student learning (e.g., Ausubel, 1963). The same debate has appeared in the ITS arena. Two differing perspectives, representing the ends of this continuum, have arisen in response to the issue of the optimal ITS learning environment. One approach is to develop a computerized environment containing assorted tools, and allow learners freedom to explore and learn independently (e.g., Collins & Brown, 1988; Shute, Glaser & Raghavan, 1989; White & Horowitz, 1987). Advocates of the opposing position argue that it is more effective to develop straightforward learning environments with no digressions permitted (e.g., Anderson, Boyle & Reiser, 1985; Corbett & Anderson, 1989; Sleeman, Kelly, Martinak, Ward & Moore, 1989). This disparity between perspectives becomes more complicated because the issue is not just which is the better learning environment, but which is the better environment for whom, a classic aptitude-treatment interaction question (see 22.3.3; Cronbach & Snow, 1981). There are, undoubtedly, temporal aspects to this issue as well. For instance, it may be more efficient to learn a new cognitive skill initially by direct instruction, then later by greater exploration. In this way, learners can better control their own learning process.

Merrill, Reiser, Ranney, and Trafton (1992) investigated how human tutors dealt with the issue of learner control.

They compared human- to computer-tutoring techniques, and found that, while expert human tutors did sometimes act like model tracers, they actually maintained a "delicate balance" between (a) allowing students freedom and control and (b) giving students sufficient guidance. In general, pedagogical research findings differ with regard to the amount of learner control to allow in automated systems (e.g., Fox, 1991; Lepper, Aspinwall, Mumme & Chabay, 1990; Merrill, Reiser & Landes, 1992). In addition to the temporal factor cited above, this issue of learner control is also greatly dependent on other variables, such as the subject matter being instructed, the desired knowledge or skill outcome, incoming aptitudes, and so on (see Kyllonen & Shute, 1989, for a complete discussion of these interacting variables). That is, if the desired learning outcome is a smoothly executed skill, it may be more efficient to instruct certain learning tasks with direct instruction and plenty of practice. But if the desired learning outcome is a functional mental model of relevant principles, an exploratory environment (complete with various components such as on-line circuits, ammeters, and resistors) perhaps is optimal to achieve that educational objective.

Most current computer-administered instructional systems do not foster self-reliance in students or encourage them to seek new information on their own. To rectify this deficit, Barnard, Erkens, and Sandberg (1990) propound the building of more flexible systems packaging communication expertise as a separate component. With less learner initiative, it's much easier to interpret input, but at what cost to learning outcome? In Japan, research is being conducted along these lines. The concept and development of ITS is becoming merged with interactive learning environments (ILE) to produce what is referred to as a "bi-modus learning environment" (BLE) (Otsuki, 1993). Whereas the main strength of ITS is its ability to derive a student model based on the identification of acquired rules, its main weakness is the inability to help learners acquire new knowledge by themselves. In contrast, students in an ILE can extract and comprehend rules induced from a complex domain, but the ILE cannot explicitly identify a student's misconceptions or tutor them in terms of their comprehension level. Thus the two (ITS and ILE) are complementary to one another, and BLE represents combining the strengths of each.

Another way to increase learner control has been suggested by Bull, Pain, and Brna (1993). Their intriguing alternative to traditional student modeling (that of replacing the burden of the ITS) is to produce accurate representations of the learner's knowledge state; the learner is empowered with greater control, e.g., to construct and repair the model. Bull and associates contend that their model will result in a more accurate representation of the learner's beliefs, and thus be more highly regarded by the student. The learner is expected to benefit through the reflection necessary to accomplish this modeling task. Unfortunately, no data have yet been collected about the efficacy of this novel approach.

"Coached practice environments" (i.e., Sherlock I and II) represent yet another way to provide control during learning by combining apprenticeship training with intelligent instructional systems (Lajoie & Lesgold, 1992; Lesgold, Eggan, Katz & Rao, 1992; see 7.4.5). These systems support greater learner initiative because the apprentice learns by doing (singularly or collaboratively); knowledge is anchored in experience; and the coach provides knowledge within an applicable context. Intelligent systems are developed with many of the characteristics of human apprenticeships, and performance can be easily assessed. Through replay and comparisons with the expert performance, this approach also supports trainee analysis of performance.

Salomon (1993) supports the trend of moving away from building traditional ITS and towards the design of systems as cognitive tools. He sees cognitive tools manipulated by students as instruments that promote constructive thinking, transcending cognitive limitations, and making it possible for students to engage in cognitive operations they wouldn't otherwise have been capable of. Some ITS programs make most diagnostic and tutorial decisions for the student; therefore they are not really cognitive tools because "they are not designed to upgrade students' intelligent engagements" (p. 180). Also in accordance with the notion of computers as learning tools, learners should have the option to alter the degree of control themselves, from none (e.g., didactic environment) to maximum (e.g., discovery environment), as necessary.

By shifting toward increased learner control, are individuals who are not very active or exploratory by nature being penalized or handicapped? Shute and Glaser (1990) investigated individual differences in learning from a discovery environment (Smithtown) and found that individuals who demonstrated systematic, exploratory behaviors (e.g., recording baseline data, limiting the number of changed variables) were significantly more successful in Smithtown compared to those who revealed less systematic behaviors. On the basis of that finding, they hypothesized in a different study (using an electricity tutor) that high-exploratory individuals would learn more from an inductive environment (than from a more directed, applied environment), and less-exploratory learners would benefit from a supportive, applied environment (compared to an inductive one). A person's exploratory level was quantified based on certain indices (e.g., number of tries and length of time spent changing a resistor value, using the on-line voltmeter or ammeter). Subjects were randomly assigned to one of two learning environments, and the data were analyzed, post hoc. The hypothesized learning style by aptitude treatment interaction (ATI) (see 22.3.3) was supported by the data (Shute, 1993b). So, discovery learning environments do not suit everyone equally well. For some, they provide a really bad fit. To determine whether this kind of learner style by treatment interaction is replicable, Shute (1994) conducted a *confirmatory* test of the same ATI, reported above. Subjects were placed a priori in one of two environments based on the decision rule obtained from the previous study. And, in fact, the ATI was confirmed (see 11.4.4, 22.3.6, and 33.6 for more on ATIs).

In conclusion, a midpoint between too much and too little learner control is probably the best bet as far as optimal ITS learning environment. Furthermore, this milestone should not be fixed, but should change in response to learners' evolving needs. Finally, learners should have some input into the design of the environment, as well.

Our next debate addresses the issue of whether learning alone is better or worse than learning in conjunction with others where "others" may mean other human beings, or with a computer acting as a "partner" in the learning process). As with everything relating to learning, there is probably no clear-cut answer to this question: Is there no "overall" superior way to learn? Rather, it is almost certain that interactions exist, where solo learning may be superior for certain topics (e.g., rote memorization of multiplication tables) or for particular learner types (e.g., highly motivated individuals). Collaborative learning may be more effective for other domains or persons. While we don't specifically address these interactions in the following discussions, they should be kept in mind (also refer to Chapter 6, 7.4.8, 23.4.4, Chapter 35).

19.4.3.2.   Individual vs. Collaborative Learning. Traditionally, ITS have been designed as single-learner enterprises. Bloom (1984) and others have presented compelling evidence that individualized tutoring (using human tutors) engenders the most effective and efficient learning across an array of domains (see also Shute & Regian, 1990; Woolf, 1988). Furthermore, intelligent tutoring systems *epitomize* this principle of individualized instruction. In his often-cited 1984 paper, Bloom presented a challenge to instructional researchers that has been called the "two sigma problem." The goal is to achieve two standard-deviation improvements with tutoring over traditional instruction methods. So far, this goal has yet to be attained using individualized ITS.

An alternative approach to individualized instruction is collaborative learning, the notion that students, working together, can learn more than by themselves, especially when they bring complementary, rather than identical, contributions to the joint enterprise (Cummings & Self, 1989). Collaboration is defined as a process by which "individuals negotiate and share meanings relevant to the problem-solving task at hand" (Teasley & Roschelle, 1993, p. 229), and is distinct from cooperation, which relates to the division of labor required to achieve some task.

Two empirical questions relevant to this chapter include: (a) Are two heads better than one? (b) Can intelligent computer systems support collaborative learning endeavors? Recently, research is beginning to shed light on both of these questions. For example, many researchers have shown impressive student gains in knowledge and skill acquisition from collaborative learning environments (e.g., Brown & Palincsar, 1989; Lampert, 1986; Palincsar & Brown, 1984; Scardamalia, Bereiter, McLean, Swallow & Woodruff, 1989; Schoenfeld, 1985). Furthermore, the few studies of the effectiveness of collaborative learning in computer-based learning environments have also been positive (e.g., Justen, Waldrop & Adams, 1990; Katz & Lesgold, 1993; Papert, 1980).

There are basically two ways of implementing collaborative learning environments using computers: (a) A small group of learners interact with a single intelligent computer system, or (b) the computer system itself serves as the "partner" in the collaboration. The first way (i.e., a small group using one computer) represents an extension of the research on collaborative learning in classrooms. In this case, some of the issues that need to be addressed have been outlined by Teasley and Roschelle (1993). The system must be able to: (a) introduce and accept knowledge into a joint problem-solving space, (b) monitor ongoing activities for evidence of divergences in meaning, and (c) repair divergences that impede the progress of the collaboration. The difference between this list and general modeling issues in ITS is that it deals with a student model that's built on a joint, rather than single, problem-solving space. The second way of implementing collaboration (i.e., assigning the computer as the learner's partner) represents an intriguing twist on the notion of collaborative learning. To illustrate, Cummings and Self (1989) proposed a collaborative intelligent education system (IES) that engages the learner in a partnership. Here, the computer serves as a collaborator, not as an authoritarian instructor. In both cases, a student model still must be derived, either that of an individual or a group.

Additional research and controlled studies must be conducted in order to test the relative efficacy of collaborative versus individualized instruction. For a variety of reasons (e.g., greater range of shared knowledge, resource limitations, etc.), the notion of collaborative learning environments is appealing. There are a lot of unanswered research questions that need to be addressed, however. Some of these (listed in Katz & Lesgold, 1993) include: What parts of the curriculum should be learned collaboratively, and what parts learned individually? What teaching methods should be used to achieve the instructional goals, and how should they be sequenced to optimize learning? What should the computer tutor do while students work on problems? What additional roles could the computer coach perform? This area of research is also likely to shed light on the interactions mentioned earlier. We now present the third hot topic, namely, the nature of learning and its impact on ITS design.

19.4.3.3. Situated Learning Controversy. To supporters, this is not just a trend but a radically new perspective (or philosophy) that supports the integration of ". . . psychological theories of physical and cognitive skills, uniting emotions, reasoning, and development, in a neurobiologically grounded way" (Clancey, 1993, p. 98). It has also been referred to in the literature as "situated action" and "situated cognition." Recently, several prominent journals have devoted entire issues to the debate concerning the value of situated learning compared to the more standard paradigms (e.g., ACT*, SOAR): 1993 *Cognitive Science 17* (1), and 1993 *Journal of Artificial Intelligence and Education 4* (1) (see 12.3.1.2, 8.7, 8.9).

Obviously, one's belief in either situated cognition or the traditional information-processing model has implications for the design of ITS. To illustrate this distinction, first consider Greeno's summary of situated cognition's perspective on where knowledge resides: "Rather than thinking that knowledge is in the minds of individuals, we could alternatively think of knowledge as the potential for situated activity. On this view, knowledge would be understood as a relation between an individual and a social or physical situation, rather than as a property of an individual" (Greeno, 1989, p. 286). Next, consider the nature of knowledge from the information-processing perspective. Anderson's (1983) ACT* theory proposed two fundamental forms of knowledge: *procedural,* represented in the form of a production system, and *declarative,* represented in the form of a node-link network of propositions (see 5.4, 29.2). Both representations are believed to operate within long-term and short-term memory structures.

These two positions present quite different views on how learning, or knowledge acquisition, occurs. In the first case (situated cognition), learning is a process of creating representations, inventing languages, and formulating models *for the first time.* Learning is ongoing, occurring with every thought, perception, and action, and is situated in each unique circumstance. Situated cognition argues for an instructional system rich with explicit tools and varied exemplars that can support and extend learners' discovery processes. "Insight is more likely when the problematic situation is so arranged that all necessary aspects are open to observation" (Bower & Hilgard, 1981, p. 319).

The second position (information processing) sees learning as progressing from declarative knowledge, to procedural skills, to automatic skills, dependent on: enablers (i.e., what one already knows and can transfer to new situations) and mediators (i.e., cognitive processes determining what one can acquire, such as working-memory capacity and information-processing speed; e.g., Anderson, 1983, 1987; Kyllonen & Christal, 1990). Thus, learning refers to the addition and restructuring of information to a database, in accordance with specific learning mechanisms (e.g., knowledge compilation, transfer). To facilitate learning, one must build a system that can (a) analyze the initial state of knowledge and skill, (b) describe the desired or end state of knowledge and skill (learning outcome), and (c) present material and problems that will transition a learner from initial to desired state. This kind of tutoring system is based on a well-defined curriculum that's been so arranged to promote knowledge/skill acquisition (or facilitate transition from current to goal state).

It may be that these two positions are mutually exclusive. That is, knowledge either resides internally in one's head or externally in the environment. Alternatively, it may be that there is some overlap, whereby some forms of knowledge are stored and some are derivable from the current situation. In a preliminary attempt to bridge the gap between situated- and traditional-learning models, Shute and Gawlick-Grendell (1994) have recently developed a series of statistics modules, *Stat Lady.* Learning is situated within various gaming environments (e.g., "Stat Craps"). The theoretical postulates are that learning is a constructive process, enhanced by experiential involvement with the subject matter, that is, situated in real-world examples and problems. Furthermore, the system has a well-defined curriculum in accordance with popular learning theory.

According to constructivism, learners actively construct new knowledge and skills, either from what they already know (information-processing premise) or from what resides in the environment (situated cognition stance; see Chapter 7). Both positions would probably agree that learners do not come to a learning situation with a *tabula rasa,* but rather as active-pursuers (not passive-recipients) of new knowledge (e.g., Bartlett, 1932; Collins, Brown & Newman, 1989; Drescher, 1991; Edelman, 1987; Piaget, 1954). Both positions also support the premise that the construction process can be enhanced by environments supporting experiential learning. Research in this area has shown that knowledge derived experientially tends to be more memorable than passively received knowledge, because the experience ("doing" rather than "receiving") provides cognitive structure, and is intrinsically motivating and involving (e.g., Friedman & Yarbrough, 1985; Harel, 1991; Harel & Papert, 1991; Shute & Glaser, 1991; Spencer & Van Eynde, 1986). Finally, when instruction is situated (or anchored) in interesting and real-world problem-solving scenarios, that also is believed to enhance learning (Brooks, 1991; Brown, Collins & Duguid, 1989; Clancey, 1992; Collins, Brown & Newman, 1989; Lave & Wenger, 1991; Suchman, 1987; The Cognition & Technology Group at Vanderbilt, 1992).

The Cognition and Technology Group at Vanderbilt (1992) has also been working on developing a pedagogical approach to situated cognition. They define "anchored instruction" as an attempt to actively engage learners in the learning process by situating instruction in interesting and real-world problem-solving environments. Rather than teaching students how to solve particular problems, these systems teach generalizable skills, helpful across a variety of problem-solving situations. The major goal of this type of instruction is to create authentic-feeling environments in which one can explore and understand problems and opportunities experienced by experts in a domain, and learn about the tools these experts use. This group has developed a series of adventures for middle-school students focusing on math problem formulation and problem solving. These are the "Adventures of Jasper Woodbury" series (see 23.5.1.1). The goal of the project is to facilitate broad transfer to other domains, embodying several design principles: (1) video-based presentation, (2) narrative format, (3) generative learning, (4) embedded data design, (5) problem complexity, (6) pairs of related adventures, and (7) links across the curriculum.

One of the major problems with this whole debate over situated cognition versus traditional information-processing models is that the former position simply has not tested its underlying hypotheses at this time, while the latter has enjoyed decades of solid research. Vera and Simon (1993), rebutting Clancey's support paper(s) for situated learning, stated, "Clancey leaves us with philosophy (whether correct or not is another matter), but with precious little science" (p. 118). And that appears to be true. Because cognitive psychology is an empirical science, studies need to be conducted that examine claims made by any new position (see 42.5.2). For instance, supporters of our final "hot topic" of the 90s (virtual reality, or VR) claim that this new technology can improve learning by virtue of fully immersing the learner in the learning process (learning by saturation). But is there any veracity to this claim? It is certainly testable. The relationship between experience, learning, and pedagogy is a briar patch of thorny questions. Recent theoretical harangues on the nature of situated learning have laid a kind of groundwork for VR by arguing for an epistemology of learning based on experience.

19.4.3.4. Virtual Reality and Learning. A collection of technologies, known as virtual reality (VR), has recently been exciting the instructional-technology community. This new technology refers collectively to the hardware, software, and interface technologies available to the user interested in experiencing certain aspects of a simulated three-dimensional environment. The simulated aspects of the environment ("world") currently include a stereoscopic, low-to-medium fidelity visual representation displayed on a head-mounted display system. Using head-tracking technologies, one can update the display in accordance with head and body motions. This feature, along with the stereo disparity of the images on the two screens (one for each eye), supports the illusion of moving around in three-dimensional space (for more, see Chapter 15).

Unquestionably, VR changes the relationships between learning and experience, highlighting the role of perception (particularly visual) in learning. Experience is both social and perceptual, and VR epitomizes the notion of experiential learning. Many systems are now being developed that have demonstrated the success of the experiential approach. The current question is: Does VR represent the next logical, developmental step in the design of instructional systems? In other words, does the immersion experience (i.e., extra fidelity and related cost) significantly improve learning and performance beyond the more traditional pedagogical approaches?

Recently, there have been some empirical data collected on the relative success of VR in terms of instructional effectiveness as well as skill transfer to the real world. For instance, Regian, Shebilske, and Monk (1992) showed that people can, indeed, learn to perform certain tasks from virtual environments (e.g., console operations and large-scale spatial navigation). Next, knowledge and skill acquired in a VR have been shown to transfer to performance in the real world. Regian, Shebilske, and Monk (1993) found that: (a) VR console operations training can transfer/facilitate real-world console operations performance; and (b) VR spatial navigation training successfully transfers to real-world spatial navigation. In contrast to the Regian et al. (1993) findings, however, those reported by Kozak, Hancock, Arthur, and Chrysler (1993) showed *no* evidence for transfer of a "pick and place" task from VR to the real world. However, the criterion task used in that study was quite easy; thus, the conclusions may actually be inconclusive. So, even with the relatively poor fidelity and interface currently available in VR technology, there is some evidence for its efficacy and potential as a serious learning/training environment (see 15.8).

Another positive example of VR's potential for training was presented by Psotka (1993), who argued that VR creates one uniform point of view on any representation that overcomes the conflicts and cognitive load of maintaining two disparate points of view (Sweller, 1988). The reduced cognitive overhead resulting from the single "egocenter" in a VR should expedite information access and learning (see 15.6). Central to this perceptual experience of VR is the poorly understood phenomenon of immersion or presence. Preliminary insight based on the SIMNET experience (Psotka, 1993) provides not only personal testimonials to the motivating and stimulating effects of the social and vehicle-based immersion of synthetic environments but also preliminary effectiveness data on its potency for learning and training. That is, even though SIMNET provides an impoverished perceptual simulation of a tank in action, the cues from interactive communications among crew members, as well as the auditory and visual cues of the simulated sights, provide gut-wrenching and sweaty believability. What's more, the evidence clearly shows a level of training effectiveness (even without a curriculum) that is superior to many other classroom- and simulation-based efforts (Bessemer, 1991). Research is continuing on how to make this training more effective by including surrogate crew members and intelligent semiautomated forces in the environments. The need to involve dismounted infantry, not just tanks and vehicles, is creating a research base for better computational models of agents and coaches (Badler, Phillips & Webber, 1992).

Virtual reality shows promise in the construction of microworlds for physics and other science instruction. For instance, Loftin and Dede (1993) are creating a Virtual Physics Laboratory from the base facilities of a VR world created for NASA astronaut training. In their virtual laboratory, students can conduct experiments in a virtual world where everyday accidents, structural imperfections, and extrinsic forces, such as friction, can be completely controlled or eliminated. Balls that bounce with complete determinism can be measured accurately at all times and places, and can even leave visible trails of their paths. The effects of gravity can be controlled, and variations of gravity can be experienced visually, and, perhaps, even kinesthetically.

Although the perceptual aspects of experience are clearly important, it is easy to assume that there are no difficulties to learning from existing visual representations and simulations, like photographs, graphs, and static drawings. It is easy to downplay and overlook difficulties in modern learning environments. Most of us are experts at interpreting visual representations on printed pages (figures, graphs, photographs, icons, drawings, and prints), but it's easy to forget the difficulty we once experienced as we tried to interpret scatterplots and line graphs. We know from many studies that those difficulties never completely go away. For younger learners, they may be even more pronounced. VR can remove these difficulties to a degree and make information more accessible through the evolutionarily prepared channels of visual and perceptual experience. As to the question of whether the delivered "bang" is worth the bucks, the jury is still out.

We now turn our attention away from these controversies, and toward the analysis of a collection of ITS that have been systematically evaluated and reported in the literature. The purpose of this section is to provide a flavor for evaluations that have been conducted, rather than to review all possible evaluations.

19.5 ITS EVALUATIONS

> Building a tutor and not evaluating it is like building a boat and not taking it in the water. We find the evaluation as exciting as the process of developing the ITS. Often, the results are surprising, and sometimes they are humbling. With careful experimental design, they will always be informative (Shute & Regian, 1993, p. 268).

Which systems instruct effectively? What makes them effective? One might think that increasing the personalization of instruction (e.g., model tracing) would enhance learning efficiency, and in the process improve both the rate and quality of knowledge and skill acquisition. But results cited in the literature on learning, in relation to increased computer adaptivity, are equivocal. In some cases, researchers have reported no advantage of error remediation in relation to learning outcome (e.g., Bunderson & Olsen, 1983; Sleeman, Kelly, Martinak, Ward & Moore, 1989). In others, some advantage has been reported for more personalized remediation (e.g., Anderson, Conrad & Corbett, 1989; Shute, 1993a; Swan, 1983).

If, however, more researchers conducted controlled ITS evaluations, this issue would be easier to resolve. But, in addition to the availability of relatively few reported evaluations of ITS, there has been little agreement on a standard approach for designing and assessing these systems (see 39.5). Results from six ITS evaluations will now be presented.

19.5.1 Six ITS Evaluations

A few examples of systematic, controlled evaluations of ITS reported in the literature include: the LISP tutor (e.g., Anderson, Farrell & Sauers, 1984), instructing LISP programming skills; Smithtown (Shute & Glaser, 1990, 1991), a discovery world that teaches scientific inquiry skills in the context of microeconomics; Sherlock (Nichols, Pokorny, Jones, Gott & Alley, 1995; Lesgold, Lajoie, Bunzo & Eggan, 1992), a tutor for avionics troubleshooting; Bridge (Bonar, Cunningham, Beatty & Weil, 1988; Shute, 1991), teaching Pascal programming skills; *Stat Lady,* instructing statistical procedures (Shute & Gawlick-Grendell, 1993), and the Geometry tutor (Anderson, Boyle & Yost, 1985), providing an environment in which students can prove geometry theorems. Results from these evaluations show that these tutors *do* accelerate learning with, at the very least, no degradation in outcome performance compared to appropriate control groups.

19.5.1.1. The LISP Tutor.
Anderson and his colleagues at Carnegie-Mellon University (Anderson, Farrell & Sauers, 1984) developed a LISP tutor that provides students with a series of LISP programming exercises and tutorial assistance as needed during the solution process. In one evaluation study, Anderson, Boyle, and Reiser (1985) reported data from three groups of subjects: human-tutored, computer-tutored (LISP tutor), and traditional instruction (subjects solving problems on their own). The time to complete identical exercises were: 11.4, 15.0, and 26.5 hours, respectively. Furthermore, all groups performed equally well on the outcome tests of LISP knowledge. A second evaluation study (Anderson, Boyle & Reiser, 1985) compared two groups of subjects: students using the LISP tutor and students completing the exercises on their own. Both received the same lectures and reading materials. Findings showed that it took the group in the traditional instruction condition 30% *longer* to finish the exercises than the computer-tutored group. Moreover, the computer-tutored group scored 43% *higher* on the final exam than the control group. So, in two different studies, compared to traditional instruction, the LISP tutor was apparently successful in promoting faster learning with no degradation in outcome performance.

In a third study using the LISP tutor to investigate individual differences in learning, Anderson (1990) found that when prior, related experience was held constant, two "metafactors" emerged. These two metafactors, or basic learning abilities, included an *acquisition* factor and a *retention* factor. Not only did these two factors explain variance underlying tutor performance, they also significantly predicted performance on a paper-and-pencil midterm and final examination.

A fourth study with the LISP tutor concerns the usefulness of productions for analyzing learning. In analyzing student performance on the first six problems in Chapter 3 of the LISP tutor, Anderson (1993, p. 32) discovered uneven, unsystematic trends in learning. One problem was relatively easy, and the next might be relatively more difficult. However, by decomposing the problems into their constituent production rules, Anderson was able to convert the chaos of these results into very systematic program solution learning curves, for both time and accuracy. He analyzed performance on individual production rules across problems. Because productions were reused, and others newly introduced in each problem, he could plot performance in terms of the number of opportunities each production rule had for contributing to an additional unit of LISP code. This simplifying transformation demonstrates that knowledge is acquired in terms of production rules, and that if we are to understand how learning cognitive skills is to be explained, our analysis of the task and data ought to be conducted in terms of production rules.

19.5.1.2. Smithtown.
Shute and Glaser (1991) developed an ITS designed to improve an individual's scientific inquiry skills within microworld environment for learning principles of basic microeconomics. In one study (Shute, Glaser & Raghavan, 1989), three groups of subjects were compared: a group interacting with Smithtown, an introductory economics classroom, and a control group. The curriculum was identical in both treatment groups (i.e., laws of supply and demand). Results showed that while all three groups performed equivalently on the pretest battery (around 50% correct), the classroom and the Smithtown groups showed the same gains from pretest to posttest (26.4% and 25.2%, respectively); they significantly outperformed the control group. Although the classroom group received more than twice as much exposure to the subject matter as did the Smithtown group (11 vs. 5 hours, respectively), the groups did not differ on their posttest scores. These findings are particularly interesting because the instructional focus of Smithtown was not on economic knowledge, per se, but rather on general scientific inquiry skills, such as hypothesis testing.

19.5.1.3. Sherlock.
"Sherlock" is the name given to a tutor that provides a coached practice environment for an electronics troubleshooting task (Lesgold, Lajoie, Bunzo & Eggan, 1990). The tutor teaches troubleshooting procedures for problems associated with an F-15 manual avionics test station. The curriculum consists of 34 troubleshooting scenarios with associated hints. A study was conducted evaluating Sherlock's effectiveness using 32 trainees from two separate Air Force bases (Nichols, Pokorny, Jones, Gott & Alley, 1995). Pre- and posttutor assessment used verbal troubleshooting techniques as well as a paper-and-pencil test. Two groups of subjects per Air Force base were tested: (1) subjects receiving 20 hours of instruction on Sherlock, and (2) a control group receiving on-the-job training over the same period of time. Statistical analyses indicated that there were no differences between the treatment and the control groups on the pretest (means = 56.9 and 53.4, respectively). However, on the verbal posttest as well as the paper-and-pencil test, the treatment group (mean = 79.0) performed significantly better than the control group (mean = 58.9) and equivalent to experienced technicians with several *years* of on-the-job experience (mean = 82.2). The average gain score for the group using Sherlock was equivalent to almost 4 years of experience.

19.5.1.4. Pascal ITS ("Bridge").
An intelligent programming tutor was developed to assist novice programmers in their designing, testing, and implementing Pascal code (Bonar, Cunningham, Beatty & Weil, 1988). The goal of this tutor is to promote conceptualization of programming constructs or "plans" using intermediate solutions. A study was conducted with 260 subjects who spent approximately 12 hours learning from the Pascal ITS (see Shute, 1991). Learning efficiency rates were estimated from the time it took subjects to complete the curriculum. This measure involved both speed and accuracy, since subjects could not proceed to a subsequent problem until they were com-

pletely successful in the current one. To estimate learning outcome (i.e., the breadth and depth of knowledge and skills acquired), three criterion posttests were administered measuring retention, application, and generalization of programming skills.

The Pascal curriculum embodied by the tutor was equivalent to about half a semester of introductory Pascal. That is, the curriculum equaled about 7 weeks or 21 hours of instruction time. Adding 2 hours per week for computer laboratory time (conservative estimate), the total time spent learning a half-semester of Pascal the traditional way would be at least 35 hours. In the study discussed above, subjects completed the tutor in considerably less time (i.e., mean = 12 hours, SD = 5 hours, normal distribution). So, on average, it would take about 3 times as long to learn the same Pascal material in a traditional classroom and laboratory environment as with this tutor (i.e., 35 vs. 12 hours).

While all subjects finished the Pascal ITS curriculum in less time compared to time needed to complete the curriculum under traditional instructional methods, there were large differences in learning rates found at the end of the tutor. For these subjects (having no prior Pascal experience), the maximum and minimum completion times were 29.2 and 2.8 hours, a range of more than 10:1. In addition, while all 260 subjects successfully solved the various programming problems in the tutor's curriculum, their learning outcome scores reflected differing degrees of achievement. The mean of the three criterion scores was 55.8% (SD = 19, normal distribution). The range from the highest to the lowest score, 96.7% to 17.3%, represented large between-subject variation at the conclusion of the tutor. To account for these individual differences in outcome performance, Shute (1991) found that a measure of working memory capacity, specific problem-solving abilities (i.e., problem identification and sequencing of elements), and some learning style measures (i.e., asking for hints and running programs) accounted for 68% of the outcome variance.

19.5.1.5. Stat Lady. Two studies have been conducted to date with *Stat Lady*. One study (Shute, Gawlick-Grendell & Young, 1993) tested the efficacy of learning probability from *Stat Lady* in relation to a traditional lecture and a no-treatment control group. Results showed that both treatment groups learned significantly more than the control group, yet there was no difference between the two treatment groups in terms of pretest to posttest improvements after 3 hours of instruction. The results were viewed as very encouraging because not only was the lecture a more familiar learning environment for these subjects but also the professor administering the lecture had more than 20 years experience teaching this subject matter, while this was *Stat Lady's* first teaching assignment. When test items were separated into declarative and procedural categories, they found that: (a) Students using *Stat Lady* acquired significantly more declarative knowledge than the other groups, but (b) when procedural skill acquisition was assessed, the lecture group prevailed. Finally, a significant aptitude-treatment interaction was obtained where high-aptitude subjects

learned significantly more from *Stat Lady* than from the lecture environment, but for low-aptitude subjects, there was no difference in learning outcome by condition. Together, these results suggest that a teacher-computer combination maximizes learning.

The second study (Shute & Gawlick-Grendell, 1994) compared learning from *Stat Lady* vs. learning from a paper-and-pencil Workbook version of the identical curriculum, and addressed the question: What does the computer contribute to learning? Findings showed that *Stat Lady* learners performed at least as well (and in some cases, much better) on the outcome tests compared to the Workbook group, again despite the presence of factors strongly favoring the traditional condition. Specifically, they found that (a) *Stat Lady* was clearly the superior environment for high-aptitude subjects; (b) *Stat Lady* subjects acquired significantly more declarative knowledge than the Workbook subjects; and (c) regardless of aptitude, the majority of learners found the *Stat Lady* condition to be significantly more enjoyable and helpful than the Workbook condition.

19.5.1.6. Anderson's Geometry Tutor. The geometry tutor (Anderson, Boyle & Yost, 1985) provides an environment for students to prove geometry theorems. The system monitors student performance and jumps in as soon as a mistake is made. The skill this system imparts is how to prove geometry theorems that someone else has provided. Schofield and Evans-Rhodes (1989) conducted a large-scale evaluation of the tutor in place within an urban high school. Six geometry classes were instructed by the tutor (in conjunction with trained teachers), and three control geometry classes taught geometry in the traditional manner. The researchers closely observed the classes using the geometry tutor and traditional instruction for more than 100 hours. One of the really nice and intriguing results of Schofield and Evans-Rhodes's (1989) evaluation of this tutor was the counter-intuitive reversal of its effects. Although the geometry tutor was designed to individualize instruction, one of its pragmatic and unintended side effects was to encourage students to share their experiences and cooperatively solve problems. Since their experiences with the geometry tutor was so carefully controlled by the immediate feedback principles of its operations, the tutor guaranteed that students' experiences were much more uniform and similar than was the case for normal classrooms. As a result, students could more easily share experiences and make use of one another's experiences and problem-solving strategies. The practical result was a great deal of cooperative problem solving.

19.5.2 Conclusions from the Six Evaluation Studies

These evaluation results all appear very positive regarding the efficacy of ITS; however, there is always a selection bias involved with the publication of unambiguous evidence of successful instructional interventions. We are familiar with other (unpublished) tutor-evaluation studies that were conducted but were "failures." However, the general positive trend is viewed as encouraging, especially given the enormous differences among the six tutors in design structure as well as evaluation methods. The findings indicate that these systems do accelerate learning with no degradation in final outcome.

Obviously, principled approaches to both the design and evaluation of ITS are badly needed before we can definitively judge the merits of these systems. Some principled approaches are beginning to emerge. For example, Kyllonen and Shute (1989) outlined a taxonomy of learning skills that has implications for the systematic *design* of ITS. They hypothesized a multidimensional interaction predicting learning outcome as a function of type of learning/instructional environment, type of knowledge/skill being instructed, subject matter, and characteristics of the learner (e.g., aptitude, learning style). With a few modifications to this taxonomy, Regian and colleagues at the Armstrong Laboratory are currently trying to fill in the cells in the matrix through systematic, empirical studies designed to assess performance across a range of these aforementioned dimensions. Their goal is to map instructional and knowledge-type variables to learning.

In terms of systematic approaches to *evaluating* ITS, Shute and Regian (1993) suggested seven steps for ITS evaluation: (1) Delineate goals of the tutor. (2) Define goals of the evaluation study. (3) Select the appropriate design to meet defined goals. (4) Instantiate the design with appropriate measures, number, and type of subjects and control groups. (5) Make careful logistical preparations for conducting the study. (6) Pilot test tutor and other aspects of the study. (7) Plan primary data analysis concurrent with planning the study. These principles may also be employed as a framework for organizing, discussing, and comparing ITS evaluation studies.

19.6 FUTURE ITS RESEARCH AND DEVELOPMENT

What is possible for the future includes ample computing resources for every student . . . tapping electronically many resources outside the classroom. It includes the idea of a personal factotum that could serve as a knowledgeable intermediary . . . to bridge the gap between the classroom and the external world. . . . Virtual field trips linking libraries and museums will have their holdings available in electronic (or photonic) form . . ."(Nickerson, 1988, p. 312).

We've seen where ITS research and development has been, and we've discussed a few of the systems that have been evaluated in controlled studies. We'll now examine some of the conceivable futures for these systems. Given the diversity of researchers in the area, and the great differences among learners, there will be, in reality, many different streams of research co-occurring, and the most likely future is probably a composite of them all.

19.6.1 Future 1: Immersive Learning Environments Evolve from ITS

Alden (age 11) walks into his cubicle at school and excitedly puts on his VR bodysuit. Today's itinerary (jointly produced by Alden and his main teacher) is teeming with new learning adventures. After taking a Dramamine, he boards a boat heading up the Nile. This trip (and his on-line tour guide) will help him learn about East Africa's geography, flora, and fauna as he cruises, observes, hears, and smells things along the world's longest river. When the trip concludes, he plans on visiting Olduvai Gorge for some archeological excavations (after all, he's already in Africa). Specifically, Alden will get a chance to help dig out some early human remains. Then, for a change of pace, Alden and his VR pal Rafael, who lives in Mexico City, will meet in a happenin' space station they programmed together. They are learning each others' language and culture: Rafael speaks English and helps Alden learn Spanish, while Alden speaks Spanish and assists Rafael with his English. Following a real lunch (not a virtual one, as all this learning makes one hungry), Alden concludes his day on an artistic note. He's creating a VR masterpiece representing his interpretation of the classical score "The Wall," by the noted composer Roger Waters, designing virtual sculptures, their choreography, and musical arrangement.

This imagined future using "immersive learning environments" can attain its instructional goals as follows. As a ghost presence, the tutor in these new systems can interact with a student through digital speech, through text that floats in the air, or through replays. As an embodied presence, the tutor can vary in reality from a stick figure to a realistic mannequin, with facial expressions and voice. The possibilities for realistic guidance that is as believable and as forceful as a real tutor may be quite difficult to achieve, but it can be dramatic in implications. The believability of these new systems hinges on the quality of the immersive experience they provide. The differences between an immersive learning environment and its 2-D simulation counterpart depends on the results of immersion and in the different ways that students can interact with the world. Instead of moving a mouse or a joystick, learners can move their own hands to pick something up (see 8.5.2). Although they might not feel the object accurately, there are enough cues to provide the *sensation* of picking things up. First, they see it happening, and vision clearly dominates other senses to provide a compelling illusion. Contact and force can be provided realistically with expensive force-feedback devices, or suggestively with sounds, such as a ping that denotes collision or touching (see 13.5.4, Chapter 15, 29.5).

VR also opens the opportunity for providing handicapped or disabled people an experience of unfettered motion, or new interfaces to control the world with minimal movements. It can make invisible forces like gravity and air pressure visible and, hence, more comprehensible to students. For instance, Minstrell (1988) pointed out that high school students go through a period of misconceptions during which they confuse gravity and air pressure; so that when air is pumped out of a bell jar, objects inside it are expected to become lighter or even float. VR offers an opportunity for doing a set of experiments in which the forces of gravity and air pressure could be made visible through graphic icons, such as colored arrows or textures. As the gas is removed from a bell jar, it could be visible as a colored gas flowing out. Students could actually reach into the bell jar and manipulate the objects as the gas is removed. They could even adopt the point of view, or frame of reference, of an object *inside* the bell jar and experience the change in forces directly. Making these forces visible in a multitude of lifelike and believable environments may have profound effects on children's understanding of science.

It should be noted that the same problems that plague ITS are relevant to VR. That is, the emphasis needs to perhaps shift away from omnipotent VR systems, toward a collection of specific minisystems and goals (e.g. teach the knowledge of *X,* the skill of *Y,* and provide the kinesthetic feedback for *Z*).

19.6.2 Future 2: Traditional ITS Disappear; Specific Cognitive Tools Dominate

Whitney (age 14) arrives in her classroom and takes a seat at her learning station, a large comfortable desk with an embedded computer. The touch screen is divided into many different areas that have distinct functions (e.g., graphics, spreadsheet, sound analyzer, dozens of databases). From the front of the class, a visiting detective (serving as the day's teacher) accesses the international police database (IPD) and obtains details surrounding a grisly murder that happened the previous month in a small Italian city. She electronically transmits all of the information to the students, which includes electronic photographs of the physical evidence (e.g., the body and the weapon), psychological profiles of the victim and 11 suspects, recorded interviews, alibis and motives, phone logs, and so on. The students have to engage in a variety of coordinated cognitive activities to solve the murder mystery. Whitney first brings up the psychological profile of the dead man. After reading the file, she notes in her electronic scratch pad that the victim had a history of drug abuse and depression. On another part of her 25-inch screen, she accesses a 3-D photo of the victim, zooms in on his arms, and sees evidence of two recent intravenous injections. The pathology report from the coroner's office concluded that the victim died from a gunshot wound to his heart, but traces of a narcotic substance were also found in his body. Playing the interview tapes on her "stress analyzer," Whitney discovers that two of the suspects are clearly lying. Throughout the day, puzzle pieces slowly come together, the detective-teacher offers a few suggestions, and, finally, Whitney figures out whodunit (with .93 probability of accuracy).

In this vision of the future, "omnipotent" intelligent tutoring systems have been replaced by collections of specialized educational or cognitive tools: technological devices that help people to perform cognitive tasks (i.e., help them know, think, or learn). For example, simulators, smart spreadsheets, and extensive databases are cognitive

tools available within classrooms. Apprenticeship training is envisioned as the main source of imparting skill, in conjunction with the supplemental simulator and associated tools for the apprentice to employ during learning. The training situations relate to real-world events, thus placing learning within a meaningful context.

One reason that ITS may disappear in the future is that, while many researchers agree that intelligence in an ITS is directly a function of the presence of a student model, the student model may, in fact, be the wrong framework around which to build good learning machines. Derry and Lajoie (1993) presented six reasons why the student modeling paradigm is problematic: (1) In complex domains, the student model cannot specify all possible solution paths. (2) One cannot determine or induce all possible "buggy" behaviors. (3) "Canned" text is antithetical to principles of tutorial dialog. (4) Reflection and diagnosis should be performed by the *student,* not the tutor. (5) Implementing the student modeling approach is very difficult, technically. (6) Model tracing is only applicable to procedural learning, but the focus should be on critical thinking and problem solving.

A second factor that could contribute to the decline of ITS is that the term *intelligent tutoring system* is associated with philosophical issues relating to the nature of intelligence. Many people associate intelligence with awareness and, since no AI system could be said to have achieved awareness, these people would not grant that any ITS had ever been developed. Nevertheless, dozens of "intelligent" tutoring systems have been routinely reported in the literature, and even more discussed at conferences. So, the name (and hence, the whole enterprise) may be inappropriate or misleading. Simply put, ITS may promise too much, deliver too little, and constitute too restrictive a construct. Gugerty (1993) summed it up best:

> There is a sense in which the goals of traditional intelligent tutoring systems are both too ambitious and too narrow. Most traditional ITS . . . are designed to provide tutoring in a stand-alone setting. . . . This ambitious goal requires that the ITS handle all aspects of the very difficult task of tutoring, including expert problem solving, student diagnosis, tailoring instruction to changing student needs, and providing an instructional environment. . . . On the other hand, the goal of developing very intelligent stand-alone ITS is narrow in the sense that it limits our conception of how intelligence can be incorporated into computer-based training and education (p. 3).

As a parallel, consider what happened in the field of robotics. First-generation robots were constructed out of pure research curiosity. Then, after the initial flurry of excitement in the 1960s and early 1970s died down, emphasis shifted from building single-system robots to more emphasis on building component parts. This trade-off was due to the problems associated with designing a system that has general-purpose problem-solving skills versus one with more focused expertise. The next generation of robots, arising from the work being done on the individual parts, may resolve this conflict by becoming an expert in a given domain, but also possessing a wide repertoire of general problem-solving skills. The same applies for ITS. Rather than attempting to build an omnipotent tutor, a more fruitful approach might be to create a coherent collection of computerized tools (i.e., a divide-and-conquer strategy) (see 12.4, Chapter 24).

19.6.3 Future 3: Distance Learning

Curtis (age 9) rolls out of bed, greets his parents (already at work in their cubicles), eats breakfast, glances at the sleet falling outside, then ambles over to his computer for his morning curriculum. Curtis "goes to school" in his home. When he logs onto the Public School System, he first checks his mail, then receives a menu of options for the morning's learning project: Would he like to learn about *Tyrannosaurus Rex,* the politics leading up to World War II, or what caused the California earthquake of 1994? All he has to do is tap into the appropriate database, travel to the correct geographical region and time period, and interact with these respective environments through the multimedia systems. The respective databases all include on-line hosts to narrate events and answer questions, movies to depict a range of relevant topics (from mundane to crucial), and simulators to allow Curtis to experiment within the different worlds. After choosing *T. Rex* as his learning project, the host narrates some basic declarative information (e.g., when they existed and for how long, size of the dinosaur, diet, mating habits, other coexisting plants and animals), then Curtis uses the simulator to manipulate geological events to see their ramifications on the dinosaur. The first thing he does is to reverse the advancing Ice Age (introducing a global warming trend in its place), and then sees its implications not only on the survival of the lizard king but also on the evolution of other plants and animals on the planet. Periodically, the host asks for some predictions, Curtis responds, and receives feedback from the host. On occasion, other students in the same module communicate their findings and questions to him over the network lines.

As can be seen, this future is attractive for a lot of reasons. With distance learning, one can allow learners to stay at home or at some other convenient learning location (saving time and transportation costs) and connect to a rich network of information and training software, available across an information superhighway (see Chapter 13). To achieve this future, expert systems—spanning a huge array of possible domains—are needed that present comprehensive information, as well as provide thought-provoking questions, and respond to student-directed queries. The network should also allocate nodes to which one's peers can be connected, thus providing for collaborative learning opportunities. Notice that this distance-learning future is not limited to accessing declarative knowledge from databases. Rather, software (e.g., simulators) should also be accessible to practice skill in any specific domain.

In this future, it is possible to access quickly on-line, digital-rich *libraries* with virtually limitless realms/databases for our personal learning pleasure. And while the educational horizon will invariably include VR technology as an important instructional medium (see Future 1), it will be just one of many media.

Finally, to attain this future and the metaphor and promise of the library as a knowledge space (i.e., the epitome of Carbonell's dream and the hypertext vision), we must first make a fundamental change on how we think about education. Our narrow conception of education (e.g., "school"), only relevant for those between ages 5 and 18, is no longer appropriate. Education should be for everyone, all ages, and available in all places.

19.6.4 Future 4: Individualized Learning Is Out; Collaborative Learning Is In

Sierra, Nicole, Fernando, Sasha, Kevin, and Uri comprise "team 3." They are between the ages of 18 to 22 (college sophomores). In their sociology class, there are two professors and five teams, each team reflecting an optimal mixture of aptitude, gender, learning styles, personality types, and ethnic backgrounds. They are all geared up for their on-line VR lesson on "racial prejudice." The six students are transported to Birmingham, Alabama, on a hot August day in 1951. In reality, only Sasha and Kevin are African-American, but in this lesson, all six kids are transformed into "Negroes" (as they're called in 1951). The lesson requires them to take a city bus to a "Whites Only" park that has a nice public swimming pool, try to swim in the pool, then go home to their impoverished residences on the outskirts of town. Problems arise immediately in this compelling simulation when they board the bus. Automatically, they all sit down in the front seats; after all, there are only four other riders on the bus, sitting in the middle section. The white bus driver rudely informs them to "move to the back" whereupon Sierra (team 3's outspoken leader) politely asks "Why?" When she gets slapped for her impudence, Nicole starts to cry. But Sierra persists. Then the bus driver utters some very ugly sentiments about them all, based solely on their skin color. They see by his reddening face and posture that he's about to strike out again, so they collectively decide to move quickly to the back of the bus. During the ride to the park, they discuss their experiences (what they feel, what they could have done differently, what caused this state of affairs, etc.). Sasha and Kevin contribute valuable information to the discussion from personal tales related to them by their grandparents and great-grandparents. Finally they arrive at the park, and things really go downhill from there. They're not allowed to enter the park or swim in the pool, they're called "dirty" and worse, and the simulation makes them all painfully aware of racial prejudice. Afterward, team 3 reviews and discusses all of the events, and their professors provide information, as needed, about the historical roots of racial prejudice leading up to the situation they encountered in their lesson.

The motivating force driving this future is the belief that collaborative learning is superior to individualized learning (se also Chapter 35). That is, learning may be invaluably enhanced from conversations with those who have differing opinions, backgrounds, or skills; know more about some topic; or who can ask perceptive, thought-provoking questions. Basic research is being conducted in cognitive and social psychology that seeks answers to questions pertaining to the optimal compositions of learner groups. Some of these research questions include: Is it better to mix genders, or have more homogeneous groupings? When establishing groups based on aptitude levels, is it better to match highs with highs, or a high with a low? What are the optimal coordinations of affective characteristics (e.g., passive with gregarious)? And what other cognitive/social considerations should be made (e.g., letting individuals self-select their group vs. being assigned)? According to Resnick and Johnson (1988), sociological studies show that most people prefer personal sources of information, and computers can enhance such communications. For more information on this topic, see Shute, Lajoie, and Gluck (in press).

Technology is evolving to the point where computer systems can routinely contain learning environments that support a high level of social interaction. This important technology facilitates effective learning, especially within the classroom. The atmospheres in the classrooms containing the connected computerized environment are boisterously controlled, similar to what Feurzeig (1988) found in a collaborative mathematics course that was ". . . more like a beehive than a math class" (p. 117). These collaborative classrooms can even support networked VR, which means that students, trainees, and experts can interact between schools and remote sites, and that trainees and instructors can share the same experience. Learners can work collaboratively on the same project. On the other hand, different students can work on the same project at the same time, without awareness of each other's presence, but with some invisible instructor lurking over their shoulders. The number of combinations are staggering, and their learning/training potential is unknown.

The other person in the networked world could also be an autonomous agent, or cyborg, part real and part synthetic. This idea raises a whole new set of possibilities for a computer coach, explanations, and guidance. "Social interface agents" (Thorisson, 1993) have progressed steadily as information about how to direct gaze, when to use paraverbals (hmmm, uh . . .) and when to take turns in a dialogue, all become better understood. Improvements in modeling human actions and planning (e.g., Badler, Phillips & Webber, 1992), including natural language interaction, will soon lead to the development of virtual agents that can coach and guide learners' actions within carefully planned learning activities. Some of these interactions are already available in a text form (Curtis & Nichols, 1993). These virtual agents focus on students' errors by offering experts' stories (Kedar, Baudin, Birnbaum, Osgood & Bareiss, 1993). Networked digital spaces, such as digital libraries, demand new techniques for navigating through these complex spaces without getting lost. Issues of how to maintain a sense of location (Benedikt, 1991) and how to best use these environments to support memory with the method of loci (Neisser, 1987) need more research.

As shown in the above illustration, VR provides a new saliency on the notion that some things (such as race and gender) are constructed, and that we can become what we play, argue about, and build. For instance, text-based VR already invites the participation of women and girls in social interactions in ways that adventure games like dungeons and dragons did not (Turkle, 1993). Turkle points out that MUDs (i.e., multiuser dungeons) are easily used for gender swapping. When gender roles are switched, sexist expectations and overt demands that might be ignored in daily life become highly visible and reactive, and they are openly discussed. The MUD then becomes an evocative object for a richer understanding, not only of sexual harassment but also of the social construction of gender.

19.6.5 Future 5: The ITS Approach Continues; Becoming Truly Intelligent

Ken (age 10) arrives at the math lab where he sits in front of a computer that is going to help him learn to solve algebra word problems better. Today's focus is on those troublesome distance-rate-time problems. After stating his name, the computer accesses Ken's records, flagging his salient strengths and weaknesses (i.e., not only his higher-level aptitudes but also the low-level productions that he's acquired and not yet acquired). Beginning with a review of concepts and skills that he learned the day before, the ITS generates a problem that is just a little bit out of his grasp. The ITS then works out the correct solution to the problem, along with an alternative solution that Ken is very likely to come up with based on its student model of him. In fact, he solves the problem exactly as the tutor predicted. As part of its student model of him, the ITS "knows" to instruct Ken with an emphasis on a graphical representation of the problem to clarify the discrepancy between the correct and incorrect solutions and facilitate the formation of a functional mental model. Thus, the tutor presents two animated trains appearing on opposite sides of the screen that converge at a point almost in the middle of the screen. They travel at different rates of speed. The problem statement stays up at the top of the screen, and the tutor points out, as it periodically pauses the simulation, what elements should be attended to and when. Ken states that he understands the mapping between the explicated mental model, the appropriate equation, and the relevant parts of the word problem. So the ITS presents an isomorphic word problem. This time he solves it correctly, without any supplemental graphics. Ken exercises an option to play around with some trains, missiles, and boats on his own for a while to test his emerging understanding. He views his "score" of curricular elements acquired, and seems a little frustrated about his progress, but the ITS reassures him that he is proceeding at a reasonable rate. Instruction and learning continue.

For ITS to evolve to the point seen in the above scenario, more controlled research must be conducted in three areas of intelligence: the domain expert, the student model, and the tutor. First, the subject matter must be understood by the computer well enough for the embedded expert to draw inferences or solve problems in the domain. Next, the system must be able to deduce a learner's approximation of that knowledge. Finally, the tutorial strategy must be intelligent to the point where an on-line tutor can implement strategies to reduce the differences between the expert and student performance (Burns & Capps, 1988).

Solutions to problems involving difficult AI, psychology, and pedagogy will emerge from research endeavors that yield information about effective and efficient ways to (a) represent, utilize, and communicate domain knowledge; (b) represent an individual's evolving knowledge state (for both declarative knowledge and procedural skill); and (c) instruct the material most effectively for a particular learner. Some specific research questions include: How can computers better understand natural language (input as well as output)? What kinds of inference mechanisms can optimally model students' knowledge status? How can computers be programmed to understand "semilogical" reasoning (including intuitions, pet theories, prior experiences)? What are the specific characteristics of learners who perform better in certain types of learning environments and not in others? Are certain domains better suited for specific instructional methods? When should feedback be provided, what should it say, and how best should it be presented? How much learner control should be allowed?

Some additional limitations of current ITS have already been mentioned (e.g., student models cannot specify all possible solution paths in complex domains; model tracing is only suitable for procedural learning). One possible solution would be to use a kind of model-tracing approach for instructing well-defined procedural skills, using an underlying expert and student model that are primarily rule based. And for instructing declarative information or complex, ill-structured domains, the ITS may include a knowledge base that is a semantic net with extensive indexing (like CBR).

Whatever future ultimately evolves from ITS, the fields of AI, education, and psychology have profited enormously from the contributions made in the ITS arena. Learning theories have been tested; individual differences issues have been validated against complex, real-world learning tasks (e.g., ITS, in contrast to artificial laboratory tasks); AI programming techniques have been refined; different instructional approaches have been compared; controlled studies have been conducted of aptitude-treatment interactions; and so forth. So, in terms of research vehicles, ITS are greatly underestimated. But for purposes of education, their time may be limited; maybe not.

19.7 CONCLUSIONS

Before the computer age, the prevailing instructional approach was sufficient (e.g., one teacher transmitting information to about 30 students), but we now reside in a computerized world. Initial implementations of CAI mirrored this pedantic approach, and, to some extent, so does the currently popular model-tracing approach in sophisticated ITS. Do we need to change our educational philosophies or systems?

We have most of the components necessary to advance educational reform. Not only is there great need for change, but also there are powerful, affordable technologies available to support it. Missing are definitive answers to the psychological controversies cited earlier. Basic research is actively being pursued to resolve these issues. For example, studies are beginning to find consistently that higher-order thinking skills are not acquired through didactic approaches (i.e., straight conveyance of facts) but rather through learners' active involvement with the subject matter. This "constructivist" view of learning allows students to achieve intellectual accomplishments not possible under more traditional pedagogical approaches (Collins, Brown & Newman, 1989; Resnick, 1987).

Table 19-2 contrasts old versus new approaches to instruction (from Means, Blando, Olson, Middleton, Morocco, Remz & Zorfass, 1993). The table provides a clear direction for ITS research and implementation. That is, to get from "old" to "new," we need to open up learning environments that promote increased learner initiative and between-learner collaboration. We should assess learning as it transfers to authentic tasks, not standardized tests, and attempt to establish connections across various fields so topics are not learned in isolation of one another. As technologies emerge and advance, we can fit them into this framework. Furthermore, additional research is needed to validate the goodness of the new over the old approach to teaching-learning.

Look around you. Computer technologies have dramatically transformed the workplace, communications, and commercial activities, as well as the entire business community. But education remains status quo. We need to harness the computer's potential and find ways to employ it in

TABLE 19-2. OLD VERSUS NEW APPROACHES TO INSTRUCTION

Old	New
Teacher-directed activities	Student-directed explorations
Didactic teaching	Interactive modes of instruction
Short instruction on a single subject	Extended, multidisciplinary instruction
Individual work	Collaborative work
Teacher as knowledge dispenser	Teacher as facilitator
Ability groupings	Heterogeneous groupings
Assessment of factual knowledge and discrete skills	Performance-based assessment

promoting educational change. Are current and prevalent ITS adequate for our purposes—now and in the 21st century (just right around the corner)? We believe that, as currently implemented, these systems may have asymptoted in utility. A philosophical shift has been suggested in this chapter, away from stand-alone instructional devices and toward using tools to aid in the more collaborative learning process. There are actually very few ITS in place in schools, yet they exist in abundance in research laboratories. We need to move on.

As we've discussed here, reform can proceed along a number of pathways (perhaps in parallel). For instance, computer graphics are getting better every day; we can now develop three-dimensional virtual environments where individuals can interact with any artificial world we choose to program (or purchase). Satellite transmissions can relay data to very distant locations; learners from different parts of the globe can access distal data, or even get together and jointly experience and solve various problems. Cognitive tools abound (e.g., simulators, hypertext/hypermedia formats, etc.), and we seem to be ready to recast our convictions about ITS. Rather than trying to create all-knowing, all-purpose teaching machines, a more fruitful approach may be to develop specific computerized tools. These tools can be specific for a given domain, or general purpose, applicable across domains. To paraphrase a well-known quotation: A person who is given a fish will eat for a day, but a person who learns how to fish will eat for a lifetime.

We can see the seeds of discontent growing. Go to any ITS-related conference and notice how researchers in the field have begun to discontinue using the term "ITS." Instead, in a show of semantic squirming, they refer to advanced automated instructional systems (formerly, ITS) as: interactive learning environments, cognitive tutors, individualized teaching systems, computer-assisted learning, automated instructional support systems, computer-based learning environments, immersive tutoring systems, knowledge communications systems, computer tools, and so on.

Not only is the ITS construct too ambitious, but there is no universally accepted definition of what comprises computer intelligence. While our working definition of intelligence is fairly specific, there exists a wide range of criteria in the literature related to computer-tutor intelligence. For instance, some say that for an automated instructional system to earn the label *intelligent,* it must demonstrate the ability to learn by showing an evolving knowledge base. Yazdani and Lawler (1986) asserted, "No system which is too rigid to learn should be called intelligent" (p. 201). Others have argued that intelligent systems must provide for learner control during the learning process (Papert, 1980; Scardamalia et al., 1989). Still others (e.g., MacKenzie, 1990) suggest that we reserve the word *intelligent* to describe only those systems showing truly impressive advances (e.g., intuition, empathy). Are these even realistic goals?

The fields of AI, psychology, and education have all greatly benefited from ITS research. But to continue, much more *systematic* research is needed to achieve some of the great potential offered by these systems. One suggestion is to begin a coordinated stream of systematic ITS research and development, altering specific features of existing systems and evaluating the results of those changes in accordance with a principled approach. According to Self (1989), "Once a sounder foundation for ITS has been specified, it becomes possible to identify the elements of a theory of ITS. These elements lie within (formal) AI, in areas such as belief logics, reason maintenance, metalevel architectures, and discourse models, areas from which ITS research has been divorced" (p. 244). Intelligent tutoring systems, as we now know them, may not exist 20 years from now, but we're on the right path, the motives are commendable, and the learner will ultimately profit.

As we began this review of ITS with the evolution of computer technology, so do we end it. ITS and related, developing technologies for education and training are constrained by two important factors: (a) the cost and power of computers, and (b) the pragmatic and theoretical knowledge of how best to employ them. Every month, computers are dramatically decreasing in cost and increasing in power, these changes bearing directly on consumer knowledge and application of the technology. While discussion of the interaction between these two factors goes beyond the scope of this chapter, we can make straightforward predictions about upcoming hardware and software developments. The Mips (millions of instructions per second) curve is already converging on a Bips (billions of instructions per second) curve in an exponential explosion that knows no limits. Desktop computers with 100 Mips are currently available, and this raw horsepower makes a qualitative difference in computing possibilities. Soon, powerful systems will be available in notebook- and calculator-sized formats that fit into our hands, shirt pockets, and purses. Further, software tools enable us to learn from, and perform within, all major domains, such as algebra, biology, physics, art history, computer science, home economics, psychology, botany, calculus, accounting, and even manufacturing, medicine, and engineering. With our fingertips, we will be able to retrieve information, translate foreign languages, complete our tax returns, work out investment portfolios, analyze sales trends, and so forth. Software will be everywhere with embedded "assistants" to explain, critique, provide on-line support and coaching, and perform all of the ITS activities outlined in this chapter. Society stands at the edge of all this. Although the time-line for these exciting developments is uncertain, we do know that the research conducted so far is just a drizzle in comparison with the deluge to come.

REFERENCES

Acchione-Noel, S. & Psotka, J. (1993). *MACH III: past and future approaches to intelligent tutoring.* Proceedings of the 1993 Conference on Intelligent Computer-Aided Training and Virtual Environment Technology, Houston, TX.

Alexander, P.A. & Judy, J.E. (1988). The interaction of domain-specific and strategic knowledge in academic performance. *Review of Educational Research* 58(4), 375–404.

Anderson, J.R. (1983). *The architecture of cognition.* Cambridge, MA: Harvard University Press.

— (1987). Skill acquisition: compilation of weak-method problem solutions. *Psychological Review 94,* 192–210.

— (1990). Analysis of student performance with the LISP tutor. *In* N. Fredericksen, R. Glaser, A. Lesgold & M. Shafto, eds. *Diagnostic monitoring of skill and knowledge acquisition.* Hillsdale, NJ: Erlbaum.

— (1993). *Rules of the mind.* Hillsdale, NJ: Erlbaum.

—, Boyle, C. & Reiser, B. (1985). Intelligent tutoring systems. *Science 228,* 456–62.

—, Boyle, C. & Yost, G. (1985). The geometry tutor. In *Proceedings of IJCAI-85,* pp. 1-7. Los Angeles, CA: IJCAI.

—, Conrad, F.G. & Corbett, A.T. (1989). Skill acquisition and the LISP tutor. *Cognitive Science 13*(4), 467–505.

—, Farrell, R., & Sauers, R. (1984). Learning to program in LISP. *Cognitive Science 8,* 87–129.

Ausubel, D.P. (1963). *The psychology of meaningful verbal learning: an introduction to school learning.* New York: Grune & Stratton.

Badler, N.I., Phillips, C.B. & Webber, B.L. (1992). *Virtual humans and simulated agents.* New York: Oxford University Press.

Baker, E.L. (1990). Technology assessment: Policy and methodological issues. *In* H.L. Burns, J. Parlett & C. Luckhardt, eds. *Intelligent tutoring systems: evolutions in design.* Hillsdale, NJ: Erlbaum.

Barnard, Y.F., Erkens, G. & Sandberg, J.A.C. (1990). Interaction in intelligent tutoring systems. *Journal of Structural Learning 10*(3), 197–213.

Barr, A., Beard, M. & Atkinson, R.C. (1976). The computer as a tutorial laboratory: the Stanford BIP Project. *International Journal of Man-Machine Studies 8,* 567–96.

Bartlett, F.C. (1932). *Remembering: a study in experimental and social psychology.* London, England: Cambridge University Press.

Benedikt, M., ed. (1991). *Cyberspace: first steps.* Cambridge, MA: MIT Press.

Bessemer, D.W. (1991). *Transfer of SIMNET training in the army officer basic course.* (ARI Technical Report #120.) Alexandria, VA: U.S. Army Research Institute for the Behavioral and Social Sciences.

Bierman, D., Breuker, J. & Sandberg, J., eds. (1989). *Artificial intelligence and education: synthesis and reflection.* Springfield, VA: IOS.

Bloom, B.S. (1956). Taxonomy of educational objectives: the classification of educational goals. *In* B.S. Bloom, ed. *Cognitive domain, handbook 1.* New York: McKay.

— (1984). The 2 sigma problem: the search for methods of group instruction as effective as one-to-one tutoring. *Educational Researcher 13*(6), 4-16.

Bonar, J., Cunningham, R., Beatty, P. & Weil, W. (1988). Bridge: intelligent tutoring system with intermediate representations (technical report). Pittsburgh, PA: University of Pittsburgh, Learning Research & Development Center.

Bower, G.H. & Hilgard, E.R. (1981). *Theories of learning.* Englewood Cliffs, NJ: Prentice Hall.

Briggs, L.J., Campeau, P.L., Gagné, R.M. & May, M.A. (1967). *Instructional media: a procedure for the design of multi-media instruction, a critical review of research and suggestions for further research.* Pittsburgh, PA: American Institutes for Research.

Brooks, R.A. (1991).   Intelligence without representation. *Artificial Intelligence 47,* 139–59.

Brown, A.L. & Palincsar, A.S. (1989). Guided, cooperative learning and individual knowledge acquisition. *In* L.B. Resnick, ed. *Knowing, learning, and instruction: essays in honor of Robert Glaser,* 393–451. Hillsdale, NJ: Erlbaum.

Brown, J.S. & Burton, R.R. (1975). Multiple representations of knowledge for tutorial reasoning. *In* D.G. Bobrow & A. Collins, eds. *Representation and understanding,* 311–49. New York: Academic.

— & — (1978). *An investigation of computer coaching for informal learning activities.* Technical Report, Defense Advanced Research Projects Agency, Human Resources Lab., Lowry AFB, CO.

—, Collins, A. & Duguid, P. (1989). Situated cognition and the culture of learning. *Educational Researcher 18*(1), 32–42.

—, Burton, R.R. & deKleer, J. (1982). Pedagogical natural language, and knowledge engineering techniques in SOPHIE I, II, and III. *In* D. Sleeman & J.S. Brown, eds. *Intelligent tutoring systems,* 227–282. New York: Academic.

Bruner, J.S. (1961). The act of discovery. *Harvard Educational Review 31,* 21–32.

Bull, S., Pain, H. & Brna, P. (1993). Collaborative student modelling: cooperation between the student and system [summary]. *In* P. Brna, S. Ohlsson & H. Pain, eds. *Proceedings of AI-ED '93: World Conference on Artificial Intelligence in Education,* 547.

Bunderson, C.V. & Olsen, J.B. (1983). *Mental errors in arithmetic skills: their diagnosis in precollege students* (final project report, NSF SED 80-125000). Provo, UT: WICAT Education Institution.

Burns, H.L. & Capps, C.G. (1988). Foundations of intelligent tutoring systems: an introduction. *In* M.C. Polson & J.J. Richardson, eds. *Foundations of intelligent tutoring systems,* 1–19. Hillsdale, NJ: Erlbaum.

Burton, R.R. (1982). Diagnosing bugs in a simple procedural skill. *In* D.H. Sleeman & J.S. Brown, eds. *Intelligent tutoring systems,* 157–183. New York: Academic.

— & Brown, J.S. (1976). A tutoring and student modeling paradigm for gaming environments. *In* R. Colman & P. Lorton, Jr., eds. *Computer Science and Education. ACM SIGCSE Bulletin 8*(1), 236–46.

— & — (1982). An investigation of computer coaching for informal learning activities. *In* D. Sleeman & J.S. Brown, eds. *Intelligent tutoring systems.* London, England: Academic.

Carbonell, J.R. (1970). AI in CAI: an artificial intelligence approach to computer-assisted instruction. *IEEE Transactions on Man-Machine Systems 11*(4), 190–202.

Carr, B. & Goldstein, I.P. (1977). *Overlays: a theory of modeling for computer-aided instruction.* AI Lab Memo 406 MIT, Cambridge, MA.

Carroll, J. (1963). A model of school learning. *Teachers College Record 64,* 723–33.

Charniak, E. & McDermott, D. (1985). *Introduction to artificial intelligence.* Reading, MA: Addison-Wesley.

Clancey, W.J. (1979). Tutoring rules for guiding a case method dialogue. *International Journal of Man-Machine Studies 11* (9), 25–49.

— (1986). *Intelligent tutoring systems: a tutorial survey.* (Report No. KSL-86-58.) Stanford, CA: Stanford University Press.

— (1992). Representation of knowing: in defense of cognitive apprenticeship. *Journal of Artificial Intelligence in Education*

3, 139–68.

— (1993). Situated action: a neuropsychological interpretation response to Vera and Simon. *Cognitive Science 17,* 87–116.

Cognition and Technology Group at Vanderbilt (1992). An anchored instruction approach to cognitive skills acquisition and intelligent tutoring. *In* J.W. Regian & V.J. Shute, eds. *Cognitive approaches to automated instruction,* 135–70, Hillsdale, NJ: Erlbaum.

Collins, A. (1977). Processes in acquiring knowledge. *In* R.C. Anderson, R.J. Spiro & W.E. Montague, eds. *Schooling and the acquisition of knowledge,* 339–63. Hillsdale, NJ: Erlbaum.

— & Brown, J.S. (1988). The computer as a tool for learning through reflection. *In* H. Mandl & A. Lesgold, eds. *Learning issues for intelligent tutoring systems,* 1–18. New York: Springer.

—, — & Newman, S.E. (1989). Cognitive apprenticeship: teaching the craft of reading, writing, and mathematics. *In* L.B. Resnick, ed. *Cognition and instruction: issues and agendas.* Hillsdale, NJ: Erlbaum.

Corbett, A.T. & Anderson, J.R. (1989). Feedback timing and student control in the LISP intelligent tutoring system. *In* D. Bierman, J. Brueker & J. Sandberg, eds. *Artificial intelligence and education: synthesis and reflection,* 64–72. Springfield, VA: IOS.

Cronbach, L.J. & Snow, R.E. (1981). *Aptitudes and instructional methods: a handbook for research on interactions.* New York: Irvington.

Crowder, N.A. (1959). Automatic tutoring by means of intrinsic programming. *In* E. Galanter, ed. *Automatic teaching: the state of the art.* New York: Wiley.

Cummings, G. & Self, J. (1989). Collaborative intelligent educating systems. *In* D. Bierman, J. Brueker & J. Sandberg, eds. *Artificial intelligence and education: synthesis and reflection,* 73–80. Springfield, VA: IOS.

Curtis, P. & Nichols, D.A. (1993). MUDs grow up: social virtual reality in the real world. *Proceedings of the 3d annual Cyberspace Conference,* Austin, TX.

Derry, S.J. & Lajoie, S.P. (1993). A middle camp for (un)intelligent instructional computing: an introduction. *In* S.P. Lajoie & S.J. Derry, eds. *Computers as cognitive tools,* 1–11. Hillsdale, NJ: Erlbaum.

Dochy, F.J.R.C. (1992). *Assessment of prior knowledge as a determinant for future learning.* Heerlen: Open University of the Netherlands.

Drescher, G.L. (1991). *Made-up minds: a constructivist approach to artificial intelligence.* Cambridge, MA: MIT Press.

Edelman, G.M. (1987). *Neural Darwinism: the theory of neuronal group selection.* New York: Basic Books.

Farr, M.J. & Psotka, J. (1992). Introduction. *In* M.J. Farr & J. Psotka, eds. *Intelligent instruction by computer: theory and practice.* Washington, DC.: Taylor & Francis.

Feurzeig, W. (1988). Apprentice tools: students as practitioners. *In* R.S. Nickerson & P.P. Zodhiates, eds. *Technology in education: looking toward 2020.* Hillsdale, NJ: Erlbaum.

Fox, B.A. (1991). Cognitive and interactional aspects of correction in tutoring. *In* P. Goodyear, ed. *Teaching knowledge and intelligent tutoring,* 149–72. Hillsdale, NJ: Ablex.

Frederiksen, J.R., White, B.Y., Collins, A. & Eggan, G. (1988). Intelligent tutoring systems for electronic troubleshooting. *In* J. Psotka, L.D. Massey & S.A. Mutter, eds. *Intelligent tutoring systems: lessons learned,* 351–68. Hillsdale, NJ: Erlbaum.

Friedman, P.G. & Yarbrough, E.A. (1985). *Training strategies from start to finish.* Englewood Cliffs, NJ: Prentice Hall.

Gagné, R.M. (1965). *The conditions of learning.* New York: Holt.

Glaser, R. (1976). The processes of intelligence and education. *In* L.B. Resnick, ed. *The nature of intelligence,* 341–52. Hillsdale, NJ: Erlbaum.

—(1984). Education and thinking: the role of knowledge. *American Psychologist 39*(2), 93–104.

Goldstein, I.P. (1979). The genetic graph: a representation for the evolution of procedural knowledge. *International Journal of Man-Machine Studies 11,* 51–77.

Goodyear, P., ed. (1991). *Teaching knowledge and intelligent tutoring.* Norwood, NJ: Ablex.

Greeno, J.G. (1989). Situations, mental models, and generative knowledge. *In* D. Klahr & K. Kotovsky, eds. *Complex information processing: the impact of Herbert A. Simon,* 285–318. Hillsdale, NJ: Erlbaum.

Gugerty, L. (1993). *Non-diagnostic intelligent tutoring systems: learning collaboratively without student models.* Manuscript submitted for publication.

Harel, I. (1991). *Children designers.* Norwood, NJ: Ablex.

— & Papert, S. (1991). *Constructionism.* Norwood, NJ: Ablex.

Hartley, J.R. & Sleeman, D.H. (1973). Towards more intelligent teaching systems. *International Journal of Man-Machine Studies 2,* 215–36.

Hollan, J.D., Hutchins, E.L. & Weitzman, L. (1984). STEAMER: an interactive inspectable simulation-based training system. *The AI Magazine 2,* 15–27.

Johnson, W.L. (1986). *Intention-based diagnosis of novice programming errors.* Research notes in artificial intelligence. Los Altos, CA: Kaufmann (copublished with Pitman, London).

— & Soloway, E.M. (1984). PROUST: knowledge-based program debugging. In *Proceedings of the Seventh International Software Engineering Conference,* 369–80, Orlando, FL.

Justen, J.E., Waldrop, T.M. & Adams, T.M. (1990). Effects of paired versus individual user computer-assisted instruction and type of feedback on student achievement. *Educational Technology 30*(7), 51–53.

Katz, S. & Lesgold, A. (1993). The role of the tutor in computer-based collaborative learning situations. *In* S.P. Lajoie & S.J. Derry, eds. *Computers as cognitive tools,* 289–318. Hillsdale, NJ: Erlbaum.

Kedar, S., Baudin, C., Birnbaum, L., Osgood, R. & Bareiss, R. (1993). Ask how it works: an interactive intelligent manual for devices. *Proceedings of INTERCHI,* 171–72, Amsterdam.

Kolodner, J.L., ed. (1988). *Proceedings of the First Case-Based Reasoning Workshop.* Los Altos, CA: Kaufmann.

Kozak, J.J., Hancock, P.A., Arthur, E.J. & Chrysler, S.T. (1993). Transfer of training from virtual reality. *Ergonomics 36*(7), 777–84.

Kurland, L.C., Granville, R.A. & MacLaughlin, D.M. (1992). Design, development, and implementation of an intelligent tutoring system for training radar mechanics to troubleshoot. *In* M.J. Farr & J. Psotka, eds. *Intelligent instruction by computer: theory and practice,* 205–238. Washington, DC: Taylor & Francis.

Kyllonen, P.C. & Christal, R.E. (1990). Cognitive modeling of learning abilities: a status report of LAMP. *In* R. Dillon & J.W. Pellegrino, eds. *Testing: theoretical and applied issues,* 112–37. San Francisco, CA: Freeman.

— & Shute, V.J. (1989). A taxonomy of learning skills. *In* P.L. Ackerman, R.J. Sternberg & R. Glaser, eds. *Learning and individual differences,* 117-63. New York: Freeman.

Lajoie, S.P. & Derry, S.J., eds. (1993). *Computers as cognitive tools.* Hillsdale, NJ: Erlbaum.

— & Lesgold, A. (1992). Apprenticeship training in the workplace: a computer-coached practice environment as a new form of apprenticeship. *In* M. Farr & J. Psotka, eds. *Intelligent instruction by computer: theory and practice,* 15–36. New York: Taylor & Francis.

Lampert, M. (1986). Knowing, doing, and teaching multiplication. *Cognition and Instruction 3*(4), 305–42.

Lave, J. & Wenger, E. (1991). *Situated learning: legitimate peripheral participation.* Cambridge, MA: Cambridge University Press.

Lawler, R.W., & Yazdani, M. (1987). *Artificial intelligence and education.* Norwood, NJ: Ablex.

Lepper, M.R., Aspinwall, L., Mumme, D. & Chabay, R.W. (1990). Self-perception and social perception processes in tutoring: subtle social control strategies of expert tutors. *In* J.M. Olson & M.P. Zanna, eds. *Self inference processes: the sixth Ontario symposium in social psychology,* 217–37. Hillsdale, NJ: Erlbaum.

Lesgold, A. (1988). Toward a theory of curriculum for use in designing intelligent instructional systems. *In* H. Mandl & A. Lesgold, eds. *Learning issues for intelligent tutoring systems,* 114–37. New York: Springer.

—, Eggan, G., Katz, S. & Rao, G. (1992). Possibilities for assessment using computer-based apprenticeship environments. *In* J.W. Regian & V.J. Shute, eds. *Cognitive approaches to automated instruction,* 49–80. Hillsdale, NJ: Erlbaum.

—, Lajoie, S.P., Bunzo, M. & Eggan, G. (1992). A coached practice environment for an electronics troubleshooting job. *In* J. Larkin, R. Chabay & C. Sheftic, eds. *Computer-assisted instruction and intelligent tutoring systems: establishing communication and collaboration.* Hillsdale, NJ: Erlbaum.

Lewis, M.W., McArthur, D., Stasz, C. & Zmuidzinas, M. (1990). Discovery-based tutoring in mathematics. *AAAI Spring Symposium Series.* Stanford University, Stanford, CA.

Littman, D. & Soloway, E. (1988). Evaluating ITSs: the cognitive science perspective. *In* M.C. Polson & J.J. Richardson, eds. *Foundations of intelligent tutoring systems,* 209–42. Hillsdale, NJ: Erlbaum.

Loftin, B. & Dede, C. (1993). Described in surreal science. *Scientific American,* Feb., p. 103.

MacKenzie, I.S. (1990). Courseware evaluation: where's the intelligence? *Journal of Computer Assisted Learning 6,* 273–85.

Means, B., Blando, J., Olson, K., Middleton, T., Morocco, C.C., Remz, A.R. & Zorfass, J. (1993). *Using technology to support education reform.* Washington, DC: U.S. Government Printing Office.

Merrill, D.C., Reiser, B.J. & Landes, S. (1992). *Human tutoring: pedagogical strategies and learning outcomes.* Paper presented at the Annual Meeting of the American Educational Research Association, San Francisco, CA.

—, Reiser, B.J., Ranney, M. & Trafton, G.J. (1992). Effective tutoring techniques: a comparison of human tutors and intelligent tutoring systems. *The Journal of the Learning Sciences.*

Miller, M.L. & Lucado, S.R. (1992). Integrating intelligent tutoring, computer-based training, and interactive video in a prototype maintenance trainer. *In* M.J. Farr & J. Psotka, eds. *Intelligent instruction by computer: theory and practice,* 127–50. Washington, DC: Taylor & Francis.

Minstrell, J. (1988). Teachers' assistants: what could technology make feasible? *In* R.S. Nickerson & P.P. Zodhiates, eds. *Technology in education: looking toward 2020.* Hillsdale, NJ: Erlbaum.

Neisser, U. (1987). A sense of where you are: functions of the spatial module. *In* P. Ellen & C. Thinus-Blanc, eds. *Cognitive processes and spatial orientation in animal and man, Vol. II: neurophysiology and developmental aspects,* 293–310. Boston, MA: Martinus Nijhoff.

Nichols, P., Pokorny, R., Jones, G., Gott, S.P. & Alley, W.E. (1995). *Evaluation of an avionics troubleshooting tutoring system.* Technical Report, Armstrong Laboratory, Human Resources Directorate, Brooks AFB, TX.

Nickerson, R.S. (1988). Technology in education: possible influences on context, purposes, content, and methods. *In* R.S. Nickerson & P.P. Zodhiates, eds. *Technology in education: looking toward 2020.* Hillsdale, NJ: Erlbaum.

— & Zodhiates, P.P., eds. (1988). *Technology in education: looking toward 2020.* Hillsdale, NJ: Erlbaum.

Ohlsson, S. (1986). Some principles of intelligent tutoring. *Instructional Science 14,* 293–326.

Otsuki, S. (1993). Intelligent environment for discovery learning. *In* P. Brna, S. Ehlsson & H. Pain, eds. *Proceedings from Artificial Intelligence in Education,* 15–20. Charlottesville, VA: AACE.

Palincsar, A.S. & Brown, A.L. (1984). Reciprocal teaching of comprehension-fostering and comprehension-monitoring activities. *Cognition and Instruction 1,* 117–75.

Papert, S. (1980). *Mindstorms: children, computers, and powerful ideas.* New York: Basic Books.

Piaget, J. (1954). *The construction of reality in the child.* New York: Ballentine.

Polson, M.C. & Richardson, J.J., eds. (1988). *Foundations of intelligent tutoring systems.* Hillsdale, NJ: Erlbaum.

Pressey, S.L. (1926). A simple apparatus which gives tests and scores-and-teaches. *School and Society 23,* 373–76.

Psotka, J. (1993, May). *Virtual egocenters as a function of display geometric field of view and eye station point.* Proceedings of 2d Conference on Intelligent Computer Aided Instruction and Synthetic Environments, Houston, TX.

—, Holland, M. & Kerst, S. (1992). The technological promise for second language intelligent tutoring systems in the 21st century. *In* M. Swartz & M. Yazdani, eds. *Intelligent tutoring systems for foreign language learning: the bridge to international communication.* Berlin: Springer.

—, Massey, L.D. & Mutter, S.A. (1988). *Intelligent tutoring systems: lessons learned.* Hillsdale, NJ: Erlbaum.

Regian, J.W. & Shute, V.J., eds. (1992). *Cognitive approaches to automated instruction.* Hillsdale, NJ: Erlbaum.

—, Shebilske, W. & Monk, J. (1992). A preliminary empirical evaluation of virtual reality as an instructional medium for visual-spatial tasks. *Journal of Communication 42* (4), 136–49.

Regian, J.W., Shebilske, W. & Monk, J. (1993). *VR as a training tool: transfer effects.* Unpublished manuscript. Armstrong Laboratory, Brooks Air Force Base, TX.

Reiser, B.J., Ranney, M., Lovett, M.C. & Kimberg, D.Y. (1989). Facilitating students' reasoning with causal explanations and visual representations. *In* D. Bierman, J. Breuker & J. Sandberg, eds. *Artificial intelligence and education: synthesis and reflection,* 228–35. Springfield, VA: IOS.

Resnick, L.B. (1987). *Education and learning to think.* Washington, DC: National Academy.

Resnick, L.B. & Johnson, A. (1988). Intelligent machines for intelligent people: cognitive theory and the future of computer-assisted learning. *In* R.S. Nickerson & P.P. Zodhiates, eds. *Technology in education: looking toward 2020.* Hillsdale, NJ: Erlbaum.

Riesbeck, C.K. & Schank, R.C. (1990). From training to teaching: techniques for case-based ITS. *In* H. Burns, C. Luckhardt & J. Parlett, eds. *Knowledge architectures in intelligent tutoring systems.* Orlando, FL: Academic.

Salomon, G. (1993). On the nature of pedagogic computer tools: the case of the *writing partner. In* S.P. Lajoie & S.J. Derry, eds. *Computers as cognitive tools,* 179–96. Hillsdale, NJ: Erlbaum.

Scardamalia, M., Bereiter, C., McLean, R.S., Swallow, J. & Woodruff, E. (1989). Computer-supported intentional learning environments. *Journal of Educational Computing Research 5*(1), 51–68.

Schank, R.C. (1982). *Dynamic memory: a theory of learning in computers and people.* Cambridge, MA: Cambridge University Press.

Schoenfeld, A.H. (1985). *Mathematical problem solving.* New York: Academic.

Schofield, J.W. & Evans-Rhodes, D. (1989) Artificial intelligence in the classroom. *In* D. Bierman, J. Breuker & J. Sandberg, eds. *Artificial intelligence and education: synthesis and reflection,* 238–43. Springfield, VA: IOS.

Self, J.A., ed. (1988). *Artificial intelligence and human learning: intelligent computer-aided instruction.* London, England: Chapman & Hall.

— (1989). The case for formalising student models (and intelligent tutoring systems generally). *In* D. Bierman, J. Breuker & J. Sandberg, eds. *Artificial intelligence and education: synthesis and reflection,* 244. Springfield, VA: IOS.

Shortliffe, E.H. (1976). *Computer-based medical consultations: MYCIN.* Amsterdam, Holland: Elsevier.

Shute, V.J. (1991). Who is likely to acquire programming skills? *Journal of Educational Computing Research 7,* 1–24.

— (1992). Aptitude-treatment interactions and cognitive skill diagnosis. *In* J.W. Regian & V.J. Shute, eds. *Cognitive approaches to automated instruction,* 15–47. Hillsdale, NJ: Erlbaum.

— (1993-a). A macroadaptive approach to tutoring. *Journal of Artificial Intelligence and Education 4*(1), 61–93.

— (1993b). A comparison of learning environments: all that glitters . . . *In* S.P. Lajoie & S.J. Derry, eds. *Computers as cognitive tools,* 47–74. Hillsdale, NJ: Erlbaum.

— (1994, Apr.). *Discovery learning environments: appropriate for all?* Paper presented at the American Educational Research Association, New Orleans, LA.

— (1995). SMART: Student modeling approach for responsive tutoring. *User Modeling and User-Adapted Interaction 5,* 1–44.

— , Lajoie, S.P. & Gluck, K.A. (in press). Individualized and group approaches to training. To appear in S. Tobias & D. Fletcher, eds., *Handbook on training.*

— & Gawlick-Grendell, L.A. (1994). *What does the computer contribute to learning?* Manuscript submitted for publication.

—, — & Young, R. (1993, Apr.). *An experiential system for learning probability: Stat Lady.* Paper presented at the American Educational Research Association, Atlanta, GA.

— & Glaser, R. (1990). A large-scale evaluation of an intelligent discovery world: Smithtown. *Interactive Learning Environments (1),* 51–76.

— & — (1991). An intelligent tutoring system for exploring principles of economics. *In* R.E. Snow & D. Wiley, eds. *Improving inquiry in social science: a volume in honor of Lee J. Cronbach,* 333–66. Hillsdale, NJ: Erlbaum.

—, — & Raghavan, K. (1989). Inference and discovery in an exploratory laboratory. *In* P.L. Ackerman, R.J. Sternberg & R. Glaser, eds. *Learning and individual differences,* 279–326. New York: Freeman.

—, Lajoie, S.P. & Gluck, K.A. (in press). Individualized and group approaches to training. To appear in S. Tobias & D. Fletcher, eds. *Handbook on training.*

— & Regian, J.W. (1990). Rose garden promises of intelligent tutoring systems: blossom or thorn? *Proceedings from the Space Operations, Applications and Research Symposium,* Albuquerque, NM.

— & — (1993). Principles for evaluating intelligent tutoring systems. In a special evaluation issue of *Journal of Artificial Intelligence & Education 4*(3), 245–71.

Skinner, B.F. (1957). *Verbal behavior.* Englewood Cliffs, NJ: Prentice Hall.

Sleeman, D.H. (1984). *Intelligent tutoring systems: a review* (Report No. IR011683). Stanford, CA: Stanford University, School of Education & Department of Computer Science. (ERIC Document Reproduction Service No. ED 257 450.)

— (1987). PIXIE: a shell for developing intelligent tutoring systems. *In* R. Lawler & M. Yazdani, eds. *AI and education: learning environments and intelligent tutoring systems,* 239–65. Norwood, NJ: Ablex .

— & Brown, J.S. (1982). *Intelligent tutoring systems.* London, England: Academic.

—, Kelly, A.E., Martinak, R., Ward, R.D. & Moore, J.L. (1989). Studies of diagnosis and remediation with high school algebra students. *Cognitive Science 13*(4), 551–68.

Spencer, R.W. & Van Eynde, D.F. (1986, Fall). Experiential learning in economics. *Journal of Economic Education,* 289–94.

Stansfield, J.C., Carr, B. & Goldstein, I.P. (1976). Wumpus advisor I: a first implementation of a program that tutors logical and probabilistic reasoning skills. *AI Lab Memo 381.* MIT, Cambridge, MA.

Stevens, A.L. & Collins, A. (1977). The goal structure of a Socratic tutor. In *Proceedings of the National ACM Conference,* Seattle, WA, 256–63. New York: Association for Computing Machinery.

Suchman, L.A. (1987). *Plans and situated actions.* Cambridge, MA: Cambridge University Press.

Swan, M.B. (1983). *Teaching decimal place value: a comparative study of conflict and positively-only approaches* (Research Rep. No. 31). Nottingham, England: University of Nottingham, Sheel Center for Mathematical Education.

Sweller, J. (1988). Cognitive load during problem solving: effects on learning. *Cognitive Science 12,* 257–85.

Teasley, S.D. & Roschelle, J. (1993). Constructing a joint problem space: the computer as a tool for sharing knowledge. *In* S.P. Lajoie & S.J. Derry, eds. *Computers as cognitive tools,* 229–58. Hillsdale, NJ: Erlbaum.

Thorisson, K.R. (1993). Dialogue control in social interface agents. *Proceedings of INTERCHI,* 139–40. Amsterdam, Holland.

Towne, D.M. & Munro, A. (1992). Two approaches to simulation composition for training. *In* M.J. Farr & J. Psotka, eds.

Intelligent instruction by computer: theory and practice, 105–25. Washington, DC: Taylor & Francis.

Turkle, S. (1993, May). Constructions and reconstructions of the self in virtual reality. *Proceedings of the 3d annual Cyberspace Conference,* Austin, TX.

Uhr, L. (1969). Teaching machine programs that generate problems as a function of interaction with students. *Proceedings of the 24th National Conferences,* 125–34.

VanLehn, K. (1990). *Mind bugs: the origins of procedural misconceptions.* Cambridge, MA: MIT Press.

Vera, A.H., & Simon, H.A. (1993). Situated action: reply to William Clancey. *Cognitive Science 17*(1), 117–33.

Wenger, E. (1987). *Artificial intelligence and tutoring systems.* Los Altos, CA: Kaufmann.

White, B.Y. (1984). Designing computer games to help physics students understand Newton's laws of motion. *Cognition and Instruction 1*(1), 69–108.

— & Frederiksen, J.R. (1987). Qualitative models and intelligent learning environments. *In* R. Lawler & M. Yazdani, eds. *AI and education,* 281–305. Norwood, NJ: Ablex.

— & Horowitz, P. (1987). *Thinker tools: enabling children to understand physical laws* (Report No. 6470). Cambridge, MA: Bolt, Beranek & Newman.

Woolf, B.P. (1988). Intelligent tutoring systems: a survey. *In* H. Schrobe, ed. *Exploring artificial intelligence,* 1–44. Palo Alto, CA: Kaufmann.

Yazdani, M. & Lawler, R.W. (1986). Artificial intelligence and education: an overview. *Instructional Science 14,* 197–206.

Yob, G. (1975, Sep./Oct.). Hunt the Wumpus. *Creative Computing,* 51–54.

20. COGNITIVE TEACHING MODELS

Brent G. Wilson
UNIVERSITY OF COLORADO AT DENVER

Peggy Cole
ARAPAHOE COMMUNITY COLLEGE

20.1 COGNITIVE TEACHING MODELS

Educational psychology and instructional design (ID) have had a long and fruitful relationship (Dick, 1987; Merrill, Kowallis & Wilson, 1981). Educational psychologists like Gagné and Glaser have always shown an interest in issues of design (Gagné, 1968; Glaser, 1976); indeed, they helped establish instructional design as a field of study (see 18.3) (Gagné, 1987; Lumsdaine & Glaser, 1960). In recent years, a growing number of cognitive psychologists have shown a renewed interest in design issues and have tested out their ideas by developing prototype teaching models. These teaching models differ from most educational innovations in that they are well grounded in cognitive learning theory. Examples include John Anderson's intelligent tutors (Anderson, 1987) and Brown and Palincsar's reciprocal teaching method for teaching reading (for a research review, see Rosenshine & Meister, 1994). Wilson and Cole (1991) reviewed a number of these prototype teaching models and related them to current ID theory. This chapter continues that agenda by reviewing a number of additional teaching models and drawing implications for the design of instruction.

Specifically, the purpose of the chapter is to:

1. Argue that the development and validation of teaching models is a legitimate research method and has been an important vehicle for advancing knowledge in learning and instruction.
2. Show how the development of cognitive teaching models compares to the development of traditional ID theory.
3. Review a number of cognitive teaching models, and discuss a few in detail.
4. Look for insights from these cognitive teaching models that relate to instructional design.
5. Identify issues for future research.

20.1.1 Instructional Psychology and Design: An Historical Overview

To provide a context for interpreting the chapter, consider the historical overview provided in Table 20-1.

The field of instructional design developed in the 1960s and early 1970s at a time when behaviorism still dominated mainstream psychology. ID shared those behaviorist roots and at the time was closer to mainstream psychology. ID theorists such as Gagné, Briggs, Merrill, and Scandura all were educational psychologists. With the cognitive revolution of the 1970s, instructional psychology differentiated itself from ID and drifted more to the cognitive mainstream, leaving ID relatively isolated with concerns of design. In a review of instructional psychology in 1981, Lauren Resnick (who only a few years earlier had developed Gagné-style learning hierarchies) observed:

> An interesting thing has happened to instructional psychology. It has become part of the mainstream of research on human cognition, learning, and development. For about 20 years the number of psychologists devoting attention to instructionally relevant questions has been gradually increasing. In the past 5 years this increase has accelerated so that it is now difficult to draw a clear line between instructional psychology and the main body of basic research on complex cognitive processes. Instructional psychology is no longer basic psychology *applied* to education. It is fundamental research *on* the processes of instruction and learning (Resnick, 1981, p. 660).

In her review, Resnick acknowledged that mainstream instructional psychologists had focused on issues of performance modeling and cognitive task analysis, neglecting the challenge of devising effective instructional strategies, models, and interventions. Even so, she did not look to the ID community to fill the need because "Instructional design theory . . . , which is directly concerned with prescribing

**TABLE 20-1. THE CHANGING RELATIONSHIP BETWEEN INSTRUCTIONAL PSYCHOLOGY
AND ID FROM THE 1960s TO THE PRESENT**

Dominant paradigm	Behavioral psychology	Information processing psychology	Knowledge construction/ social mediation
Status of ID	ID emerging	ID engaged in theory/model development	ID engaged in redefinition
Status of instructional psychology	Behaviorist	Moves toward cognitive mainstream	Follows mainstream towards constructivism
Relationship between ID and instructional psychology	ID and instructional psychology closely aligned	ID and instructional psychology diverge	ID and instructional psychology engaged in more dialogue
Time period	1960–75	1976–1988	1989–present

interventions, has developed without much reference to cognitive psychology" (Resnick, 1981, p. 693). Hence, she excluded ID theory entirely from her review. Of course, the ID community was active during this time, with even some attempt at integrating cognitive psychology into their methods (e.g., Low, 1981; Merrill, Wilson & Kelety, 1981; Merrill, Kowallis & Wilson, 1981)—Resnick and other mainstream psychologists just weren't reading them! This polarization between ID and psychology continued through the 1980s. In spite of efforts to move ID into the cognitive mainstream, psychologists and designers continued to move in different circles and speak somewhat different languages (see 5.5). Psychologists viewed designers with suspicion because of the eclectic and ad hoc nature of the ID theory base and because of the field's concern for stimulus design over cognitive processes. Likewise, the ID literature often ignored developments in cognitive theory, resulting in theory that was generally divorced from state-of-the-art learning theory (e.g., Reigeluth, 1983, 1987).

Only recently, with the vigorous dialogue on constructivism and situated learning, have psychologists and designers resumed a substantive conversation (Duffy & Jonassen, 1992; *Educational Technology,* Apr. 1993 special issue on situated learning; Wilson, 1995). Psychologists such as Bransford, Perkins, Scardamalia, and Lesgold, who have taken on the challenge of design, have run up against many of the same problems addressed by traditional ID theories. At the same time, the perspectives of psychologists have stimulated reflection and renewal within the ID community. The net result of this interplay is a renewed recognition of the importance of design, as well as an array of new designs that take into account new technologies and theories of learning.

20.1.2 The Role of Teaching Models in Research

Like other scientists, instructional psychologists develop theories and models describing the world, then use accepted methods of inquiry to test and revise those theories. Examples of appropriate research methods include controlled experiments in laboratory settings as well as ethnographic and qualitative studies in field settings. Another legitimate method of testing out concepts and strategies is to develop a prototype teaching model and assess its overall effectiveness in different settings. A teaching model incorporates a complex array of learning/instructional factors into a single working system. For example, John Anderson tested out his ideas of procedural learning by developing intelligent tutoring systems (see 19.4) in LISP programming, geometry, and algebra (Anderson, 1987; Lewis, Milson & Anderson, 1988). Ann Brown and her colleagues (Brown, Campione & Day, 1981; Brown & Palincsar, 1989) developed reciprocal teaching as a means of testing their research-based findings in metacognition.

The development and tryout of practical teaching models would not normally come to mind as a method of "research," yet surely such design and implementation efforts yield important new knowledge about the viability of cognitive theories and models. Perhaps such practical projects could be termed *inquiry* even if they do not fit the traditional connotation of *research.* When researchers become interested in the problem of how people learn complex subject matters in realistic learning settings, practical tryout of programs and methods fills a role that no amount of theorizing or isolated-factor research can provide.

Teaching models can derive from direct empirical observation. Collins and Stevens (1982, 1983) closely observed teachers who used a Socratic dialogue approach and, based on the observed patterns, developed an instructional framework for inquiry teaching. Duffy (1995) developed a hypermedia tool to help preservice teachers to select relevant instructional strategies. The tool displays real-life segments of master teachers' lessons, then offers critiques from a number of perspectives, including those of the observed teachers. It also provides an electronic notepad for each preservice teacher to reflect on strategies used in the teaching episodes. While one could argue that Duffy's work is merely a neutral tool for displaying observed teaching performances, the tool embodies an underlying teaching model that is heavily grounded in actual teaching performances (see 7.3.3, 7.4.1). Such "bottom-up" approaches can complement the heavy influence of "top-down" learning theory as a basis for the design of teaching models.

In summary, the development of teaching models constitutes a unique combination of theory construction and empirical testing. Theoretical abstractions must be carried to a new level of specificity as they become instantiated into an effective teaching program. At the same time, promising theory must be tested against the demands of real-world settings. Thus the development and testing of teaching models helps triangulate findings from more traditional research methods and ensures a relevance to the practice of teaching.

In the review of models below, we have purposefully selected a range of models to illustrate the diversity found in the instructional psychology literature. We conclude with a discussion of goals and methods for instruction aimed at bringing some order to the diversity.

20.2 IMPROVING TRADITIONAL INSTRUCTION: COGNITIVE LOAD THEORY

For a number of years, John Sweller, an Australian psychologist from the University of New South Wales, has examined instructional implications of a model of memory called *cognitive load theory,* which is based on a straightforward reading of information-processing concepts of memory, schema development, and automaticity of procedural knowledge:

- Human working memory is limited; we can only keep in mind a few things at a time. This poses a fundamental constraint on human performance and learning capacity.
- Two mechanisms to circumvent the limits of working memory are: (1) schema acquisition, which allows us to chunk information into meaningful units, and (2) automation of procedural knowledge.

The first mechanism deals primarily with processing and understanding information; the second deals with the acquisition of skills. Each mechanism helps us overcome the limits of working memory by drawing on our long-term memories, which are very detailed and powerful.

Sweller's model of instructional design is based on these concepts:

1. Our limited working memories make it difficult to assimilate multiple elements of information simultaneously.

2. When multiple information elements interact, they *must* be presented simultaneously. This imposes a heavy cognitive load on the learner of the information and threatens successful learning.

3. High levels of element "interactivity" and their resulting cognitive load can be inherent in the content; e.g., learning language grammar inherently involves more element interactivity than simple vocabulary learning. However, weak methods of presentation and instruction may result in unnecessarily high overhead. An example would be to present a student a figure whose understanding requires repeated consultation of the text. The extra work required in decoding and translating the figure competes with the content for precious working-memory resources as the learner attempts to comprehend the material.

Cognitive load theory leads to some specific predictions for student learning:

- Simple content—i.e., content with relatively few intrinsic interactive elements—is not threatened by weak instructional methods. Learners are generally able to fit the demands of content and instruction within their working memories in such cases.
- Content containing high levels of interactivity among its elements cannot be learned effectively through weak instructional methods, that is, methods that require extra processing by learners. The demands of content and/or the method exceed the limits of the learner's working memory, and learning does not occur.

Sweller's cognitive load theory has led to a number of instructional prescriptions, including:

- Carefully analyze the attention demands of instruction. Sweller's method defines *elements* and then counts the number of elements in instructional messages. Processing troubles arise when the learner must attend to too many different elements at the same time.
- Use single, coherent representations. These should allow the learner to focus attention rather than split attention between two places, e.g., between a diagram and the text or even between a diagram with labels not located close to their referents (Chandler & Sweller, 1991; see discussion in Sweller & Chandler, 1994, pp. 192–193).
- Eliminate redundancy. Redundant information between text and diagram have been shown to decrease learning. (See Saunders & Solman, 1984; Reder & Anderson, 1982; Lesh, Landau & Hamilton, 1983; and Schooler & Engstler-Schooler, 1990, for research on redundant information on other tasks.)
- Provide for systematic problem-space exploration instead of conventional repeated practice (Pierce, Duncan, Gholson, Ray & Kamhi, 1993).
- In multimedia instruction, present animation and audio narration (and/or text descriptions) simultaneously rather than sequentially (Mayer & Anderson, 1991, 1992; Mayer & Sims, 1994).
- Provide worked examples as alternatives to conventional problem-based instruction (Paas & Van Merriënboer, 1994; Carroll, 1994; in the area of analogical reasoning tasks, see Robins & Mayer, 1993, and Pierce et al., 1993).

In the section below, we present an overview of research on worked examples to illustrate the implications of cognitive load theory for instruction. For more discussion of the other instructional strategies briefly listed above, refer to Sweller (1989) and Sweller and Chandler (1994).

20.2.1 Worked Examples

Conventional models of instruction in many domains involve the presentation of a principle, concept, or rule, followed by extensive practice on problems applying the rule. This approach at first glance seems like common sense—providing ample skills practice is "learning by doing." However, cognitive load theory suggests that such instructional approaches may actually be hurting learners' understanding of the subject matter.

Sweller and Cooper (1985) examined the cognitive-load effects of methods for teaching algebra to high school students. They hypothesized that when learners confront a conventional end-of-chapter practice exercise, they devote too much attention to the problem goal and to relatively weak search strategies such as means-end analysis. Students already know how to use general search strategies to solve problems; what they lack is the specific understanding of how cases relate to the general rule.

Sweller and Cooper hypothesized that learners might benefit from studying worked examples until they have "mastered" them, rather than working on conventional practice problems as soon as they have "obtained a basic familiarity with new material" (p. 87). The authors developed an alternative teaching model that emphasized the study of worked examples. After learners acquire a basic understanding of the algebraic principle, they study a series of examples; then the teacher answers any questions the learners have. When the learners indicate they understand the problems, they are required to explain the goal of each sample problem and to identify the mathematical operation used in each step of the problem. The teacher provides assistance to any learners who have difficulty with the questions. Then the learners complete similar problems, repeating them until they are solved with no errors; if too much time elapses, the teacher provides the answer.

Sweller and Cooper found that in the worked-examples model, acquisition of knowledge was significantly less time consuming than in the conventional practice-based model. Furthermore, learners required significantly less time to solve similar problems (i.e., problems identical in structure) and made significantly fewer errors than did their counterparts. There were no significant group differences in solving novel problems. Thus learning was more efficient with no discerned loss in effectiveness. The authors concluded that "the use of worked examples may redirect attention away from the problem goal and toward problem-state configurations and their associated moves" (p. 86).

Sweller (1989) summarizes his position toward problem solving and learning by arguing that:

a. Both schema acquisition and rule automation are the building blocks of skilled problem-solving performance.
b. Paradoxically, a heavy emphasis on conveying problem solving is not the best way to acquire schemas or facilitate rule automation, because the means-end strategy commonly used focuses attention inappropriately and imposes a heavy cognitive load.
c. Alternatives to conventional problem solving such as . . . worked examples must be carefully analyzed and, if necessary, modified to ensure that they, too, do not inappropriately direct attention and impose a heavy cognitive load.

d. For the same reasons as for point c, the format of instructional materials should be organized to minimize the need for students to attend to and mentally integrate disparate sources of information (Sweller, 1989, p. 465, reformatted).

Sweller's critics might claim that students under the worked-example treatment were indeed actively engaging in problem-solving and practice activities, but that the nature of the practice shifted from traditional word problems to the study of worked examples. Instead of engaging in a multitask activity (e.g., translating the word problem into one or more formulas, and performing calculations), the task narrowed to articulating the goal of the worked example and the appropriate mathematical operation. Sweller would likely agree with the critic. The point of the research is to suggest that not all "problem-solving" activities are equally effective. Some problem-solving activities actually leave learners at a loss, forcing them to resort to "weak" problem-solving methods—which they already know—rather than "strong" or domain-specific methods—which they are trying to learn. Bereiter and Scardamalia (1992) discuss this issue:

> In novel situations, where no strong methods have been devised, weak methods are all anyone has. We use them all the time, whenever we are stumped. But just because everyone uses them, could hardly survive without doing so, and therefore practices them extensively, there is reason to question the value of teaching them. Teaching problem-solving skills may be an illusion, like teaching babies to talk (Bereiter & Scardamalia, 1992, p. 528).

If our goal is to teach students certain well-defined domains such as algebra or physics, then giving them problems requiring extensive use of "weak" methods may be counterproductive and may even interfere with learning the domain.

20.2.1.1. Worked Examples and Self-Explanations. One limitation of the Sweller and Cooper study was that only indirect inferences could be made concerning learners' cognitive processes. Chi and her colleagues (e.g., Chi, Bassok, Lewis, Reimann & Glaser, 1989; Chi, de Leeuw, Chiu & LaVancher, 1991; Chi & VanLehn, 1991) addressed this issue in the area of college-level physics. They analyzed the think-aloud protocols of good and poor problem solvers to identify the cognitive processes learners used in studying worked examples in physics. Learners in the study did not differ significantly in their prior knowledge of physics; instead, good and poor problem solvers were identified by their performance on objective tests.

Chi's worked examples differed from those used by Sweller and Cooper (1985) in significant ways. Sweller and Cooper presented worked-example sheets that were not part of a text and that included no verbal commentary. By contrast, the physics examples were part of the text and included step-by-step verbal commentary, although the learners had to infer the "why's and wherefore's" of each step.

Self-explanations were one kind of student response to the worked examples. "A self-explanation is a comment about an example statement that contains domain-relevant information over and above what was stated in the example line itself" (p. 69). Chi et al. (1989) found that good problem solvers generated more self-explanations than poor problem solvers, and that poor problem solvers used the examples rotely as prompts for solving subsequent problems. Chi and VanLehn (1991) conjectured that "the act of self-explaining may make the tacit knowledge . . . more explicit and available for use" (p. 101). They identified two general sources for self-explanations: "deduction from knowledge acquired earlier while reading the text part of the chapter, . . . [and] generalization and extension of the example statements" (p. 69).

In an intervention study, Chi et al. (1991) found that high-ability and average-ability students benefited equally from being prompted to generate self-explanations. This finding counters other research on strategy training, which has found that such training generally benefits low-ability students while it doesn't benefit and may even interfere with the performance of high-ability students (e.g., Brown & Campione, 1981). These discrepant findings might be partially explained by the fact that the earlier studies tended to teach skills rather than strategies (see Duffy & Roehler, 1989, for a discussion of the confusion about skills and strategies).

20.2.1.2. Summary.   Cognitive load theory bears a strong resemblance to traditional instructional-design theories (Reigeluth, 1983, 1987). The prescriptions for instruction require a careful task analysis that especially considers the memory load implications of different content combinations and instructional methods. The emphasis on well-defined content, worked examples, and careful doses of presented information is reminiscent of Merrill's (1983; Merrill & Tennyson, 1977) Rule-Example-Practice prescriptions for teaching concepts and procedures. The emphasis on careful control over presentation and pacing, and the strongly positive gains attributable to managing cognitive load, serve as prudent reminders of the importance of task and memory variables.

20.3 CONTEXTUALIZING INSTRUCTION: COGNITIVE APPRENTICESHIPS

Collins, Brown, and colleagues (e.g., Collins, Brown & Newman, 1989; Collins, 1991) developed an instructional model derived from the metaphor of the apprentice working under the master craftsperson in traditional societies, and from the way people seem to learn in everyday informal environments (Lave, 1988). The *cognitive apprenticeship* model rests on a somewhat romantic conception of the "ideal" apprenticeship as a method of becoming a master in a complex domain (Brown, Collins & Duguid, 1989). In contrast to the classroom context, which tends to remove knowledge from its sphere of use, Collins and Brown recommend establishing settings where worthwhile problems can be worked with and solved. The need for a problem-solving orientation to education is apparent from the difficulty schools are having in achieving substantial learning outcomes (Resnick, 1989).

Emulating the best features of apprenticeships is needed because, as Gott (1988a) noted, lengthy periods of apprenticeship are becoming a rarity in industrial and military settings. She termed this phenomenon the *lost apprenticeship* and noted the effects of the increased complexity and automation of production systems. First, the need is growing for high levels of expertise in supervising and using automated work systems; correspondingly, the need for entry levels of expertise is declining. Workers on the job are more and more expected to be flexible problem solvers; human intervention is often most needed at points of breakdown or malfunction. At these points, the *expert* is called in. Experts, however narrow the domain, do more than apply canned job aids or troubleshooting algorithms; rather, they draw on the considerable knowledge they have internalized and use it to solve problems flexibly in real time (Gott, 1988b).

Gott's second observation relates to training opportunities. Now, at a time when more problem-solving expertise is needed due to the complexity of systems, fewer on-the-job training opportunities exist for entry-level workers. There is often little or no chance for beginning workers to acclimatize themselves to the job, and workers very quickly are expected to perform like seasoned professionals. True apprenticeship experiences are becoming relatively rare. Gott calls this dilemma—more complex job requirements with less time on the job to learn—*the "lost" apprenticeship* and argues for the critical need for cognitive apprenticeships and simulation-type training to help workers develop greater problem-solving expertise.

20.3.1 Features of Cognitive Apprenticeships

The Collins-Brown model of cognitive apprenticeship (see 7.4.4) incorporates the following instructional strategies or components.

1. **Content:** *Teach tacit, heuristic knowledge as well as textbook knowledge.* Collins et al. (1989) refer to four kinds of knowledge:

• Domain knowledge is the conceptual, factual, and procedural knowledge typically found in textbooks and other instructional materials. This knowledge is important, but often is insufficient to enable students to approach and solve problems independently.

• Heuristic strategies are "tricks of the trade" or "rules of thumb" that often help narrow solution paths. Experts usually pick up heuristic knowledge indirectly through repeated problem-solving practice; slower learners usually fail to acquire this subtle knowledge and never develop competence. There is evidence to believe, however, that at least some heuristic knowledge can be made explicit and represented in a teachable form (Chi, Glaser & Farr, 1988).

• Control strategies are required for students to monitor and regulate their problem-solving activity. Control strategies have monitoring, diagnostic, and remedial components; this kind of knowledge is often termed *metacognition* (Paris & Winograd, 1990).

• Learning strategies are strategies for learning; they may be domain, heuristic, or control strategies, aimed at learning. Inquiry teaching to some extent directly models expert learning strategies (Collins & Stevens, 1983).

2. **Situated learning:** *Teach knowledge and skills in contexts that reflect the way the knowledge will be useful in real life.* Brown, Collins, and Duguid (1989) argue for placing all instruction within "authentic" contexts that mirror real-life problem-solving situations. Collins (1991) is less forceful, moving away from real-life requirements and toward problem-solving situations: For teaching math skills, situated learning could encompass settings "ranging from running a bank or shopping in a grocery store to inventing new theorems or finding new proofs. That is, situated learning can incorporate situations from everyday life to the most theoretical endeavors" (Collins, 1991, p. 122).

Collins cites several benefits for placing instruction within problem-solving contexts:

• Learners learn to apply their knowledge under appropriate conditions.

• Problem-solving situations foster invention and creativity.

• Learners come to see the implications of new knowledge. A common problem inherent in classroom learning is the question of relevance: How does this relate to my life and goals? When knowledge is acquired in the context of solving a meaningful problem, the question of relevance is at least partly answered.

• Knowledge is stored in ways that make it accessible when solving problems. People tend to retrieve knowledge more easily when they return to the setting of its acquisition. Knowledge learned while solving problems gets encoded in a way that can be accessed again in similar problem-solving situations.

3. **Modeling and explaining:** *Show how a process unfolds and tell reasons why it happens that way.* Collins (1991) cites two kinds of modeling: modeling of processes observed in the world and modeling of expert performance, including covert cognitive processes. Computers can be used to aid in the modeling of these processes. Collins stresses the importance of integrating both the demonstration and the explanation during instruction. Learners need access to explanations as they observe details of the modeled performance. Computers are particularly good at modeling covert processes that otherwise would be difficult to observe. Collins suggests that truly modeling competent performance, including the false starts, dead ends, and backup strategies, can help learners more quickly adopt the tacit forms of knowledge alluded to above in the section on content. Teachers in this way are seen as "intelligent novices" (Bransford et al., 1988). By seeing both process modeling and accompanying explanations, students can develop "conditionalized" knowledge, that is, knowledge about when and where knowledge should be used to solve a variety of problems.

4. **Coaching:** *Observe students as they try to complete tasks and provide hints and helps when needed* (see 7.4.5). Intelligent tutoring systems sometimes embody sophisticated coaching systems that model the learner's progress and provide hints and support as practice activities increase in difficulty. The same principles of coaching can be implemented in a variety of settings. Bransford and Vye (1989) identify several characteristics of effective coaches:

• Coaches need to monitor learners' performance to prevent their getting too far off base, but leaving enough room to allow for a real sense of exploration and problem solving.

• Coaches help learners reflect on their performance and compare it to the performance of others.

• Coaches use problem-solving exercises to assess learners' knowledge states. Misconceptions and buggy strategies can be identified in the context of solving problems.

• Coaches use problem-solving exercises to create the "teachable moment."

5. **Articulation:** *Have students think about their actions and give reasons for their decisions and strategies, thus making their tacit knowledge more explicit.* Think-aloud protocols are one example of articulation. Collins (1991) cites the benefits of added insight and the ability to compare knowledge across contexts. As learners' tacit knowledge is brought to light, that knowledge can be recruited to solve other problems.

6. **Reflection:** *Have students look back over their efforts to complete a task and analyze their own performance.* Reflection is like articulation, except it is pointed backwards to past tasks. Analyzing past performance efforts can also influence strategic goal-setting and intentional learning (Bereiter & Scardamalia, 1989). Collins and Brown (1988) suggest four kinds or levels of reflection:

• *Imitation* occurs when a batting coach demonstrates a proper swing, contrasting it with your swing.

• *Replay* occurs when the coach videotapes your swing and plays it back, critiquing and comparing it to the swing of an expert.

• *Abstracted replay* might occur by tracing an expert's movements of key body parts such as elbows, wrists, hips, and knees, and comparing those movement to your movements.

• *Spatial reification* would take the tracings of body parts and plot them moving through space.

The latter forms of reflection seem to rely on technologies—video or computer—for feasible implementation.

7. **Exploration:** *Encourage students to try out different strategies and hypotheses and observe their effects.* Collins (1991) claims that through exploration, students learn how to set achievable goals and to manage the pursuit of those goals. They learn to set and try out hypotheses, and to seek knowledge independently. Real-world exploration is always an attractive option; however, constraints of cost, time, and safety sometimes prohibit instruction in realistic settings. Simulations are one way to allow exploration; hypermedia structures are another.

8. **Sequence:** *Present instruction in an ordering from simple to complex, with increasing diversity, and global before local skills.*

• *Increasing complexity.* Collins et al. (1989) point to two methods for helping learners deal with increasing complexity. First, instruction should take steps to control the complexity of assigned tasks. They cite Lave's study of tailoring apprenticeships: Apprentices first learn to sew drawers, which have straight lines, few pieces of material, and no special features like zippers or pockets. They progress to more complex garments over a period of time. The second method for controlling complexity is through scaffolding. In this case the cases or content remains complex, but the instructor provides the needed scaffolding for initial performances and gradually fades that support.

• *Increasing diversity* refers to the variety in examples and practice contexts.

• *Global before local skills* refers to helping learners acquire a mental model of the problem space at very early stages of learning. Even though learners are not engaged in full problem solving, through modeling and helping on parts of the task (scaffolding), they can understand the goals of the activity and the way various strategies relate to the problem's solution. Once they have a clear "conceptual map" of the activity, they can proceed to developing specific skills.

The three teaching models presented below illustrate various features of the cognitive apprenticeship model. The first two are computer-based environments: Sherlock and goal-based scenarios. The third model is the problem-based learning environment developed by medical educators at the University of Illinois. All three models build instruction around problems or cases that are authentic to real-life situations, within which learners learn the details of a subject matter.

20.3.2 Sherlock

What happens when you combine extensive cognitive-task analysis of a well-defined, technical domain with a situated-learning philosophy and a teaching model based on intelligent tutoring systems (ITS)? Sherlock is an example of such a teaching tool. Sherlock is a computer-coached practice environment developed by Alan Lesgold and colleagues (e.g., Lajoie & Lesgold, 1992; Lesgold et al., 1988; Lesgold, Lajoie, Bunzo & Eggan, 1992) to develop the troubleshooting skills of Air Force electronics technicians. Sherlock was specifically designed to teach the most difficult parts of the troubleshooter's job. Learners are presented a number of troubleshooting problems requiring two kinds of activities:

- The student solves the problem, requesting advice from the intelligent tutor/coach as necessary.
- The student reviews a record of his/her problem-solving activity, receiving constructive critique from the coach (Gott, Lesgold & Kane, 1996).

Sherlock serves not only as an instructional environment and an assessment device but also as a laboratory for instructional research (Lajoie & Lesgold, 1992). Assessment is interwoven with instruction so that coaching is highly individualized. This is achieved using expert systems technology to create two types of student modeling using expert systems technology: a competency model that is updated throughout the program, and a performance model. Together, they provide the basis for diagnosing learner problems and selecting appropriate instructional mediation relating to goals, operators, methods, and strategies.

A central feature of Sherlock is its intelligent hyperdisplay:

When *Sherlock* constructs a schematic diagram to help illustrate the advice it is providing, that diagram is organized to show expert understanding about the system with which the trainee is working. . . . What is displayed is approximately what a trainee would want to know at that time, but every display component is "hot" and can be used as a portal to more detail or explanation (Gott et al., 1995).

Sherlock's diagrams are dynamic; that is, they are assembled at any point in the program to be sensitive to immediate conditions. The diagrams are adjusted so that conceptually central components are afforded the most space; diagram boxes and circuit paths are color coded to reflect the learner's prior knowledge about them.

Gott, Hall, Pokorny, Dibble. and Glaser (1992) studied Sherlock learning environments to find out how students made flexible use of their knowledge in novel situations:

Time and again we observed [successful] learners access their existing mental models of equipment structure . . . and their schema of the troubleshooting task. . . . They then used these models as flexible blueprints to guide their performance as they crafted solutions to new problems. Their prior models became interpretive structures, and when these models were inadequate, better learners flexibly used them as the basis for transposed and elaborated structures that could accommodate the novel situations. They were ready and willing to construct new knowledge that was grounded in their existing representational and functional competence (Gott et al., 1996, pp. 37–38).

The current incarnation of the program, Sherlock 2, includes a number of refinements aimed at facilitating students' development of device models and transfer of knowledge. Consistent with the cognitive apprenticeship model, students have a variety of supports and reflective tools available to them:

To complement coached learning by doing, we have developed a collection of tools for postperformance reflection. One provides an intelligent replay of the trainee's actions. A trainee can "walk through" the actions he just performed while solving the problem. In addition, he can access information about what can in principle be known about the system given the actions replayed so far. . . . Also, he can ask what an expert might have done in place of any of his actions, get a critique of his action, and have his action evaluated by the system. . . . Further, there is an option for side-by-side listing of an expert solution and the trainee's most recent effort (Gott et al., 1996, p. 35).

One key to Sherlock's success is the extensive and sophisticated cognitive task analysis that provided "critical information necessary for developing the appropriate student models of proficiency" (Lajoie & Lesgold, 1992, p. 381). The program addresses eight dimensions of proficiency proposed by Glaser, Lesgold, and Lajoie (1987) and based on research on expert-novice differences (Lajoie & Lesgold, 1992):

1. Knowledge organization & structures
2. Depth of underlying principles
3. Quality of mental models
4. Efficiency of procedures
5. Automaticity to reduce attentional demands
6. Procedural knowledge
7. Procedures for theory change
8. Metacognitive skills

According to Gott et al. (1996, p. 36), the Sherlock team's approach to task analysis is similar but distinguishable from traditional instructional-design approaches. "What is different is that the structure of learning tasks is more authentic, rooted in the needs of practice (or simulated practice) rather than being derived directly from task analysis structure. . . ."

Research has found that learners who used Sherlock improved dramatically in their troubleshooting skills, during training as well as on a posttest (Lesgold et al., 1988; Nichols, Pokorny, Jones, Gott & Alley, 1995). Sherlock 2 yielded effect sizes on posttest measures ranging from .87 to 1.27 (Gott et al., 1996).

20.3.3   Goal-Based Scenarios

Roger Schank and colleagues at the Institute for the Learning Sciences have developed an architecture for the design of learn-by-doing courses and simulations (Schank, Fano, Bell & Jona, 1993/1994). *Goal-based scenarios* constitute an approach to the design of intelligent tutoring systems (ITS) that combine elements of simulation, case-based reasoning, and traditional ITS modeling techniques. Riesbeck (1996, p. 52) describes the concept of a goal-based scenario:

> In a [goal-based scenario], a student is given a role to play, e.g., owner of a trucking company or chief scientist at a nuclear research installation, and interesting problems to solve or goals to achieve. The role and problems should be of real interest to the student, e.g., feeding the world, getting rich, or flying a rocket to the moon, not artificial word problems. . . .

The student engages in a simulation in order to solve the defined problem or achieve the goal. Typically the student interacts with simulated agents and objects within a simulated environment. A goal-based scenario differs, however, from traditional simulations in a number of respects. For example:

> When the student gets stuck or in trouble, a tutor, in video form, appears to offer advice, tell stories, and so on. The stories come from a multimedia archive of texts and video interviews of experts in that domain, telling personal experiences similar to the student's simulated situation. These stories are also organized for browsing in a structure we call *ASK networks* (Ferguson et al., 1991, cited in Riesbeck, 1996, p. 52).

ASK networks are systems for indexing and archiving stories in a way that makes them useful within the goal-based scenario. Stories are brought into the simulation as the need arises, with the indexing sensitive to the learner's progress and other local conditions.

Three goal-based scenarios that have been developed are briefly reported below.

20.3.3.1.   Broadcast News. High school students collaborate to produce their own simulated TV news broadcast. "The student first sees a brief introduction informing him or her that he or she will be working on a newscast for a particular day in history . . . [say] May 21, 1991. The student is then given a rough draft of a news story that requires revisions so it can go on the air" (Schank et al., 1993/94, p. 309).

Students often lack the historical or political knowledge to understand the draft script, so they consult tools and resources within the program that provide a context for understanding the script.

The student then needs to revise the script and prepare it for broadcast. Rather than personally rewriting the draft, the student submits specifications for revision back to the writers. The program's experts can provide support and advice through this process. As in real life, two experts' feedback, in fact, may conflict with each other, forcing the student to decide how to interpret suggestions and incorporate them into the revised script.

> After the student gives final approval to a story, he or she can then choose to play the role of anchorperson for the newscast as well. The program then acts as a teleprompter and editing booth. The student reads the story as the text rolls by on the screen. A video camera controlled by the computer records the student as he or she plays the role of anchor; the computer also supplies the video accompanying the story. A complete videotape of the student's newscast is ready as soon as the newscast ends (Schank et al., 1993/94, pp. 309-10).

The student can watch the tape and compare it with a professional network newscast covering the same event. This comparison fosters reflection and discussion about the process and decisions made.

20.3.3.2.   Sickle Cell Counselor. This is an interactive hypermedia exhibit designed for the Museum of Science and Industry in Chicago (Bell, Bareiss & Beckwith, 1993/94; Schank et al., 1994, pp. 310-11). The user assumes a role of genetic counselor advising couples of the genetic risks of their upcoming marriage. The student is able to run simulated lab tests, interact via interactive video with the couple, collect data from the couple, and offer advice. Research indicated that museum visitors spent considerably more time with the exhibit than for other exhibits and learned something about genetics (based on both self-report and performance on pre- and posttests).

20.3.3.3.   YELLO. This is a program designed to teach telephone operators how to sell Yellow Pages advertising (Kass, Burke, Blevis & Williamson, 1993/94). The program follows a framework designed for the teaching of complex social skills. Of particular interest is the interjection of stories into the practice section. The program tracks student performance and retrieves a "story" that matches the student's performance profile, based on a sophisticated indexing scheme. The story—a real-life recounting by an experienced practitioner—is then provided to the student to strengthen motivation and make the task meaningful, as well as to correct the performance.

Schank et al. (1993/1994) outline the principal components of goal-based scenarios, along with criteria for good design. The following four components form the basis of a goal-based scenario.

20.3.3.4. Mission. The mission is the overall goal of the goal-based scenario. A scenario's mission may relate to *process* skills or *outcome achievement* skills. Process skills (e.g., running a trucking company, flying a plane, being a bank teller, etc.) lend themselves to role-play scenarios where the learner assumes the role of a character and learns the knowledge and skills related to that role. Outcome achievement skills (e.g., troubleshooting an engine or building a bridge) lend themselves to a scenario focusing on a specific task or achieving a particular result. By accomplishing the task, the student learns relevant skills along the way.

20.3.3.5. Mission Focus. Schank et al. (1993/94) refer to the mission focus as "the underlying organization" of the activities engaged in by students (p. 327). They identified four mission foci:

- *Explanation.* Students are asked to account for phenomena, predict outcomes, diagnose systems, etc. Sickle Cell Counselor has an explanation mission focus.
- *Control.* Students are asked to run an organization or maintain and regulate a functioning system. Examples of a control focus would be managing a software project or running a nuclear power plant (Schank et al., 1993/94, p. 331).
- *Discovery.* Students enter a microworld and explore the features available. They may be asked to infer the microworld's governing principles or participate in activities available. YELLO offers an example of this type of mission focus.
- *Design.* Students create or compose some product or create the design specifications for some artifact. An example would be Broadcast News.

20.3.3.6. Cover Story. The cover story provides the specifics of the student's role and the surrounding context. Schank et al. (1993/94) suggest designing a cover story around something the student might like to do (e.g., be President of the United States or fly an airplane) or something the student would have some strong feeling for (e.g., investigate the Chernobyl accident site, help a person threatening suicide). The details of the story are worked out in the design of the cover story, including the "setup" (explanations to students about why the scenario is important, specification of tools available in solving problems, etc.) and the "scenes" (the specific physical settings encountered in the story).

20.3.3.7. Scenario Operations. Specification of scenario operations is the final stage of a goal-based scenario design. Scenario operations are the discrete, specific responses required of students engaged in the program. Examples might include "adjusting a parameter with a dial, issuing a directive in a social simulation, answering a question, using a tool to shape part of an artifact, searching for a piece of information, and deciding between two alternatives" (Schank et al., 1993/94, p. 336).

In many ways, Schank's work continues the tradition of developing instructional simulations (see 17.4, 17.5), popular forms since the advent of computer-based instruction in the 1960s, including models of role playing, control of dynamic systems, and task performance. Schank's contribution has been in the development of a sound theoretical model based on cognitive memory research, and in the creation of a design laboratory that follows a well-defined development model in creating working products. The costs of developing full-blown goal-based scenarios undoubtedly remain high, but they signal important progress in the design of instructional systems.

20.3.4 Problem-Based Learning

As noted above, intelligent tutoring systems rely on extensive and sophisticated cognitive task analysis to develop expert and student models; moreover, they are usually designed for individual learners. Like Sherlock, they tend to address well-structured problems in well-structured domains and build on a broad base of content knowledge. Problem-based learning (PBL) addresses ill-structured problems and/or ill-structured domains. Koschmann, Myers, Feltovich, and Barrows (1994) stressed the distinction between an ill-structured domain (see 7.5, 23.5.1.3), as characterized by Spiro, Coulson, Feltovich, and Anderson (1988), "in which no single concept, or even a small number of conceptual elements, is sufficient for capturing the workings of a typical instance of knowledge application" (Koschmann et al., 1994, p. 231), and an ill-structured problem:

> . . . defining the problem requires more information than is initially available—the nature of the problem unfolds over time; there is no single, right way to get that information; as new information is obtained, the problem changes; decisions must be made in the absence of definitive knowledge; and there may never be certainty about having made the right decision (Barrows & Feltovich, 1987, as summarized by Koschmann et al., 1994, p. 231).

Problem-based learning integrates the learning of content and skills, utilizes a collaborative environment, and emphasizes "learning to learn" by placing most of the responsibility for learning on the learner rather than providing a sophisticated predesigned instructional system (see 7.5, 23.5.1.3).

The PBL model has been implemented in several areas of higher education, including medicine, business, education, architecture, law, engineering, and social work, as well as in high school (Savery & Duffy, 1996). However, the best known applications of PBL are in medical schools, where it was developed in the 1950s, and whose graduates face particularly ill-structured problems in an ill-structured and ever-expanding domain that requires lifelong learning skills. (See, e.g., Williams, 1992; Savery & Duffy, 1996, and Koschmann et al., 1994, for critical overviews of the use of PBL in medical schools.) More than 100 medical programs include a PBL option (Duffy, 1994). PBL combines the teacher-directed case method that is used extensively in law and business schools with the discovery-learning philosophy of Jerome Bruner (Lipkin, 1989; Schmidt, 1989).

During the first 2 years of medical school, students in a PBL curriculum work in small self-directed groups to learn simultaneously content (basic science knowledge) and skills (the procedural skills of examining and diagnosing patients, and metacognitive skills such as monitoring their comprehension, identifying their learning needs, identifying and using resources efficiently, and reflecting on procedural and metacognitive skills). In lieu of traditional lectures and laboratory exercises, the problem-based curriculum presents a series of authentic patient problems; groups of five to seven students work intensely for about a week on each problem, diagnosing and learning to understand its causes. Authenticity is critical in motivating students and in avoiding the "construction of fictional problems . . . [with] symptoms that cannot coexist" (Williams, 1992, p. 404).

The facts of the problem are presented, just as they were initially to a doctor, as an incomplete set of symptoms that must be evaluated and explained. For practical reasons, the presentation is usually simulated on paper or by an actor trained as a patient. The facts of the complete case are contained in a problem-based learning module (Barrows, 1985; Distlehorst & Barrows, 1982), which "is designed to allow for free inquiry, providing responses for any question, examination, or laboratory test an examiner might request for the actual patient" (Koschmann et al., 1994, p. 241) without cueing any factors that are critical to the case (Savery & Duffy, 1995). A tutor facilitates students' negotiation of five recursive stages of the problem-based methodology (Koschmann et al., 1994):

1. *Problem formulation.* Students isolate important facts from their rich context, identify the problem, and generate hypotheses.
2. *Self-directed learning.* Group members identify and address information needed to evaluate hypotheses. This list of needed information sets the learning agenda. For example, they might research basic biological mechanisms that might underlie a patient's problems, question or "examine" the patient, review results of tests they "order," and consult with the medical faculty.
3. *Problem reexamination.* Group members bring to bear their findings from their self-directed learning activities—adding, deleting, or revising hypotheses as warranted.
4. *Abstraction.* This is an articulation process (cf. Collins, Brown & Newman, 1989) during which members

compare and contrast cases, forming cognitive connections to increase the utility of the knowledge gained in specific contexts.
5. *Reflection.* At this point the group debriefs the experience and identifies areas for improvement in their learning processes.

The role of the tutor, according to Barrows (1992), is critical to "the success of any educational method aimed at (1) developing students' thinking or reasoning skills (problem solving, metacognition, critical thinking) as they learn, and (2) helping them to become independent, self-directed learners . . ." (p. 12). The tutor must not provide minilectures or suggest solutions but help each member of the group internalize effective metacognitive strategies by monitoring, modeling, coaching, and fading. This role includes

> not only moving students through the various stages . . . but also monitoring group process and the participation of individuals within it, guiding the development of the clinical reasoning process by strategically questioning the rationale underlying the inquiry strategy of the group or individuals, externalizing self-questioning and self-reflection by directing appropriate questions to individuals or the group as a whole, and evaluating each student's development (Koschmann et al., 1994, p. 243).

The tutor externalizes higher-order thinking that students are expected to internalize, by asking students to justify not only their inferences (e.g., "How do you know that's true?") but also any question they ask the patient (Savery & Duffy, 1995; Williams, 1992). Thus the students learn to identify and challenge superficial thinking and vague notions. In PBL, the tutor carefully monitors each student's development and forces him or her to remain an active learner.

Medical students appear to be very positive about the approach, particularly in their first year. However, many issues are still to be addressed. Because so much of the work is group oriented, PBL cannot guarantee that the student will do his or her own thinking. As Koschmann et al. (1994) noted:

> Teaching methods that depend on group interaction often experience what is termed *the polling problem*; the opinions of individuals vary as a function of the order in which their views are gathered. Contributions of less dominant members may be suppressed or contaminated by the more dominant members; convictions of any single individual in the group may be inappropriately influenced by other members; individuals can find means to hide or ride on the coattails of other group members. The polling problem, therefore, can result in the suppression of ideas, reducing the multiplicity of viewpoints expressed (p. 243).

Compared to the computer-based programs reviewed above, PBL is relatively ill-defined; that is, students' specific interactions cannot be prespecified. Because of this, good design and successful implementation become intertwined: Design must happen constantly throughout the course of students' activities. The instructor must remain vigilant to ensure that less-dominant members still have a voice within the group. Reluctant learners need to be monitored and encouraged to participate. Thus, more than some forms of controlled instruction, PBL depends on high-quality implementation by skilled instructors and participants.

PBL is also time consuming. Problem-based activities can become tedious and boring, especially for students who have already internalized the clinical reasoning process. These complaints lead one to ask: Is it essential that students discover or seek out primary sources in the library for every case? Or might learning be just as effective but more efficient if hypermedia programs consolidated answers to relevant questions to reduce the temporal and cognitive loads, at least for some of the cases? A careful analysis to identify the specific activities most valuable in generating new knowledge seems in order (cf. Collins's epistemic games, described below).

Indeed, faculty have begun to modify PBL programs. For example, faculty at the University of New Mexico School of Medicine designed focused cases "to solve these problems by encouraging learning on a single topic rather than leading to the generation of multiple, diverse hypotheses" (Williams, 1992, pp. 403–04). Koschmann et al. (1994) are developing computer-assisted programs to augment PBL, several of which directly or indirectly reduce cognitive load. These programs will facilitate:

- Students' expression of their honest viewpoints
- "A retrievable record of the group's deliberations for previously studied cases" (p. 247)
- The tutor's monitoring of the development of each person's progress
- The collection of authentic cases
- The selection of cases appropriate to the needs of the students
- Students' communicating outside group meetings
- Students' access to learning resources
- Students' access to information in their notes

Koschmann et al. (1994) are designing programs that utilize groupware (Stefik & Brown, 1989), hypertext/hypermedia (Conklin, 1987; see Chapter 21), database technologies (see 24.9), and electronic mail.

20.4 TOOLS FOR KNOWLEDGE-BUILDING COMMUNITIES

In an article on the design of collaborative learning environments, Pea (1994) describes three metaphors of communication:

1. Communication as *transmission of information*. This is the dominant idea that communication conveys a message over time and distance from one person to another.

2. Communication as *ritual*. This refers to the participation and fellowship involved in the sharing of certain forms of expression. Participation in the performing arts such as dance, theater, and music, either as a performer or as an audience member, involves ritualistic aspects of communication. The content of the message is often less important than the medium and style of expression, informing the audience and strengthening the common bond of group membership. Ritual communication emphasizes the sharing and communal functions of communications, allowing groups to maintain a sense of identity and coherence.

3. Communication as *transformation*. Both the "sender" and "receiver" of information are transformed as they share a goal of learning and knowledge generation. Participants in transformative communication open themselves up and expect change to occur as part of the process. Communication thus serves as a stimulus to inquiry, observation, and reflection. Transformative communication combines aspects of knowledge sharing and group collaboration, with an emphasis on new experience and learning (Pea, 1994, pp. 287–88).

Transformative styles of communication are characteristic of learning communities, whether in schools, classrooms, workgroups, or families. Pea (1994, p. 289) notes that a number of researchers are presently moving from a cognitive-science base toward a social-cognition framework in their attempt to understand the symbols and discourses of learning communities. Cognitive apprenticeships (see 7.4.4) are an example, as are Brown's (1994) *communities of learning* and Scardamalia and Bereiter's (1994) *knowledge-building communities*. The common notion is that groups of people share a goal of building meaningful knowledge representations through activities, projects, and discussion.

Transformative communication seems not to be emphasized in Sherlock or Schank's case-based scenarios. The goal is not mutual change between communicating parties, but more computer-directed change in the student. Similarly, the PBL model expects the students to be transformed, playing roles of both senders and receivers, but the tutor is expected to remain basically detached, monitoring, coaching, and externalizing higher-order thinking. A transformative or learning-community view would suggest that the instructor is a part of the learning community and should be an active, learning participant in the community.

The models described below are designed as tools or helps to support knowledge-building communities.

20.4.1 Epistemic Games

What do learning communities do? Collins and colleagues (Collins & Ferguson, 1993; Morrison & Collins, 1996) would respond that learning communities generate new knowledge by participating in certain defined cultural patterns or forms. The products of this work they call *epistemic forms* and adhere to defined structures accepted by the community. Epistemic forms contain new knowledge. Working together to generate these forms is called participating in *epistemic games*. The game is the set of rules or conventions that can be followed in generating a given epistemic form.

Collins and Ferguson (1993) suggest three important types of epistemic games, along with several subcategories shown in Table 20-2:

1. *Structural* analysis games. What are the components or elements of a system?

2. *Functional* analysis games. How are the elements in a system related to each other?

3. *Process* analysis games. How does the system behave?

Each of these general game types is found in every subject matter. Additional knowledge-building games and activities are found in Collins and Ferguson (1993) and in Jonassen, Bessner, and Yacci (1993). Domain-specific games take on very specific forms, for example, designing a research study or developing a time-line for a project. As games become more domain-specific, they typically become more valuable to participants of that work area.

Morrison and Collins (1995) argue the following:

1. Our culture supports numerous ways of constructing knowledge—some domain-specific, and some more general.

2. These different ways of constructing knowledge, which we call *epistemic games,* are culturally patterned.

3. Different contexts (communities of practice) support different ways of knowing, and therefore different kinds of epistemic games. People are more or less fluent epistemically, depending largely on their contextual experiences, i.e., the sorts of subcultures and communities of practice in which they have participated.

4. An important goal of school is to help people become epistemically fluent, i.e., be able to use and recognize a relatively large number of epistemic games.

5. A key question to ask about particular environments is whether they tend to foster (or inhibit) epistemic fluency . . . (Morrison & Collins, 1995).

The epistemic-game framework can serve as a language for describing learning activities within constructivist learning environments (see 23.3, 23.4) (Wilson, 1996).

According to Collins and Ferguson (1993, pp. 27–28), the playing of epistemic games exhibits the following characteristics:

1. There are *constraints* to playing. In playing a list game, for example, the items listed should be *similar* (that is, on the same scale or level) and yet *distinct* from one another. The lists should be *comprehensive* in their coverage (that is, leaving nothing important out), yet *brief* and succinct. These constraints can serve as the rules or criteria we use to judge the quality or appropriateness of a new list.

2. There are *entry conditions* that define when and where game playing is appropriate and worthwhile. The list game, for example, becomes appropriate in response to a question such as "What is involved in *X*?" or "What is the nature of *X*?" where *X* can be decomposed or analyzed in simple fashion.

3. Allowable *moves* are the actions appropriate during the course of the game. List moves include adding a new item, consolidating two items, and rejecting or removing an item from consideration.

4. Players occasionally may *transfer* from one game to another. For example, a list game may shift to a hierarchy game when the structure of list elements begins to assume a form containing subcategories.

5. Game playing results in the generation of a defined epistemic form, e.g., lists, hierarchies, processes, etc.

The Collins framework of epistemic games and forms provides a structure and language to articulate what learning communities do when they work together to generate new knowledge. Such a framework can become useful to understanding classroom and workgroup processes, but it also can serve a prescriptive or heuristic role for teachers and designers. Many teachers complain that they want to teach critical thinking, but they have failed to find a suitable set of strategies.

Epistemic games can be useful to teachers in either of two ways:

1. Using the framework as a diagnostic or interpretive device. Existing learning activities can be interpreted from an epistemic-game perspective, providing valuable insights into processes and interactions.

2. Targeting game playing as a learning objective. Our students (Sherry & Trigg, 1996) are presently developing learning materials aimed at teachers, encouraging them to engage students directly in epistemic games.

While empirical research in this area is only in beginning stages, epistemic game playing seems a promising way to think about knowledge-generating activities. It provides a needed link between cultural forms and cognitive-epistemic points of view. Research must address many questions, such as the extent to which the games encourage knowledge generation rather than rote learning, and the types and amount of scaffolding that are desirable in various learning situations. One could imagine students mindlessly developing a list or guessing at causes where no new knowledge was generated. Rules need to be developed for playing games in a way that is conducive to knowledge generation.

20.4.2 Tabletop

Tabletop (Hancock & Kaput, 1990a; Hancock & Kaput, 1990 b; Hancock, Kaput & Goldsmith, 1992; Kaput & Hancock, 1991) is a computer-based tool that allows users to manipulate numerical data sets. By combining features of what Perkins (1992a) calls symbol pads and construction kits, Tabletop provides a "general purpose environment for building, exploring, and analyzing databases" (Hancock et al., 1992, p. 340).

The program allows the user to construct a conventional row-and-column database (see 24.9) and then to manipulate the data by imposing constraints on the data with animated icons. Double clicking on an icon displays the complete record for that icon. Summary computations can be represented in a variety of formats, including scatter plots, histograms, cross tabulations, Venn diagrams, and other graphs.

Tabletop is a product of two major design goals: intelligibility and informativeness. Hancock et al. (1992) compare the role of the individual icons, which allow the learner to identify with them physically, to the role of the Turtle in Papert's Logo programming language. They theorize that the icons provide a "pivotal representation in which kinesthetic/indi-

TABLE 20-2. AN OUTLINE OF SEVERAL TYPES OF EPISTEMIC GAMES (from Collins & Ferguson, 1993).

Catalogue of Games

Structural Analysis Games

List	Make a list of answers to a specific question.
Spatial decomposition	Break an entity down into nonoverlapping parts and specify topographical relations between them.
Temporal decomposition	Make a list of sequential stages of a process.
Compare & contrast	Compare salient features of entities.
Cost-benefit	Identify the pros and cons of choices.
Primitive elements	Characterize a set of phenomena by their makeup or component elements.
Cross products	Compare listed items across a set of dimensions or attributes.
Axiom systems	Diagram the relationships between a set of formulas and their rules of inference.

Functional Analysis Games

Critical-event	Identify causes leading to an event, or the consequences derived from an event.
Cause & effect	Use critical-event analysis, distinguishing between causes and preconditions. Each effect of a cause can become a cause of a new effect.
Problem centered	Break an event stream into problems and actions taken to solve them. The side effects of the solution may cause new problems.
AND/OR graphs	Create a causal chain diagram showing the logical AND and OR relationships between links in the chain.
Form and function	Distinguish between an object's structure and its purpose.

Process Analysis Games

Systems-dynamics	Model a system showing how the contributory variables increase and decrease, and how they affect the system via feedback.
Aggregate behavior	Model a system showing how the interactive events between the components affect the behavior of the system.
Constraints	Model a system by creating a set of equations that describe system behavior.
Situation-action	Model a situation by a set of rules to apply in various cases. The situation can change because the world changes, or an agent takes action.
Trend/cyclical	Model the relationships between variables by showing how each changes over a period of time. Variable behavior can be linear, exponential, cyclical, or growth.

vidual understanding can . . . be enlisted as a foundation for developing visual/aggregate-understanding" (p. 346).

Intelligibility and accessibility are also supported by other aspects of the program. For example, the user constructs and can modify graphs through a series of reversible steps and always has the full database in view. Thus, the user can observe the effect each new constraint has on each member of the database (a feature that also contributes to the program's informativeness).

The intelligibility and informativeness of the program support the learner in negotiating meaning in a real-world iterative process of construction, question asking, and inter-

pretation. Hancock et al. (1992) describe a case in which a student used Tabletop to graph a hypothesis about data that had not yet been entered in the database.

Tabletop was initially piloted on students aged 8 to 15, and with students aged 11 to 18. The pilot studies provided insight into the kinds of questions, problems, and thinking processes that students engage in during all phases of data modeling and confirmed Hancock et al.'s (1992) belief that data creation and data analysis are inextricably intertwined. The description of the thinking students engaged in clearly reveals that in the "data definition phase" the students were drawing on the "raw data" of their individual experiences.

Tabletop was clinically tested on an eighth-grade class and a combined fifth- and sixth-grade class in six units during one school year. Clinical observation clearly demonstrated that Tabletop can help students develop their understanding of many kinds of graphs. However, students were less successful in:

a. Using that graph to characterize group trends
b. Constructing the graph in order to generate, confirm, or disconfirm a hypothesis
c. Connecting the graph with the data structures necessary to produce it
d. Embedding the graph in the context of a purposeful, convergent project (pp. 361–62)

Tabletop is not designed to be a self-contained program for developing skills and concepts in data modeling. Indeed, the developers envision it as a tool in a collaborative learning environment (see 7.4.9, 23.4.4), with students helping each other and receiving appropriate scaffolding and coaching from the teacher, as in a cognitive apprenticeship model (7.4.4, 20.3.1). In the pilot and clinical tests of the program, students sometimes were unable to perceive—even with some coaching and scaffolding—that they could not create particular graphs because they had not coded the data in a relevant way. Because of time constraints, the teacher sometimes scaffolded learning by adding a relevant data field "between sessions" (Hancock, Kaput & Goldsmith, 1992, p. 350). Although the researchers imply that it would have been preferable for the students to discover the solution for themselves, research must still address the issue of whether, when, and how much scaffolding of this sort is beneficial.

As noted above, while Tabletop was generally effective in helping students understand a variety of graphs, it was less effective in helping students use the graphs to support general conclusions. Like Duffy and Roehler (1989), Hancock, Kaput, and Goldsmith (1992) found that learning and incorporating new strategies into one's repertoire requires much time. They concluded that 1 year was insufficient time for students to develop "authentic, well-reasoned data-modeling activities" (p. 353). Even after a year, students' projects lacked coherence and purpose, beginning "without clear questions, and end[ing] without clear answers" (p. 358).

Two lessons can be learned from Tabletop. First, it is an excellent example of a tool that allows ideas and content elements to be manipulated, tested, explored, and reflected upon. Students working with Tabletop have a qualitatively different experience than they would completing exercises at the back of the chapter. Second, students using these kinds of tools need well-designed supports, meaningful goals and projects, and carefully attending teachers to realize the tool's potential. Even when conditions are favorable and care is given to design and support, students cannot be expected to reach higher levels of schema acquisition and problem-solving skill simply by having experience with the tool. Learning environments that allow projects, data manipulation, and exploration require continuing attention to design in order for students to achieve learning gains (See Jonassen, 1996, for a discussion of other tools useful to learning communities.)

20.5 COMPUTER-SUPPORTED INTENTIONAL LEARNING ENVIRONMENTS (CSILE)

Scardamalia, Bereiter, McLean, Swallow, and Woodruff (1989) observe:

There has been a history of attempts in computer-assisted instruction to give students more autonomy or more control over the course of instruction. Usually these attempts presupposed a well-developed repertoire of learning strategies, skills, and goals, without providing means to foster them (p. 51).

Scardamalia and Bereiter envision a computer-based learning environment wherein students can learn and exercise these metacognitive skills, giving the name *computer-supported intentional learning environments* to "environments that foster rather than presuppose the ability of students to exert intentional control over their own learning . . ." (Scardamalia et al., 1989, p. 52). In a series of studies, Scardamalia and Bereiter (1992) found that children were capable of generating impressive higher-order questions about a new subject, based on their interest and background knowledge. These questions could then be used to guide students' research and exploration of the topic. Intentional learning environments are designed to support the high-level, knowledge-generating activity resulting from this question-asking process.

The authors have developed a model computer program referred to as CSILE (for computer-supported intentional learning environment), the acronym denoting the specific program developed in the laboratory. While CSILE exhibits a number of design features, for space reasons we focus on the program's foundation and philosophy. In an early report, Scardamalia et al. (1989) suggest 11 principles that should guide the design of intentional learning environments:

1. Make knowledge-construction activities overt.
2. Maintain attention to cognitive goals.
3. Treat knowledge lacks in a positive way.
4. Provide process-relevant feedback.
5. Encourage learning strategies other than rehearsal.
6. Encourage multiple passes through information.
7. Support varied ways for students to organize their knowledge.
8. Encourage maximum use and examination of existing knowledge.
9. Provide opportunities for reflectivity and individual learning styles.
10. Facilitate transfer of knowledge across contexts.
11. Give students more responsibility for contributing to each other's learning.

While many of these principles also are similar to traditional instructional-design prescriptions (e.g., Reigeluth, 1983), there is additional emphasis on knowledge construction consistent with the cognitive apprenticeship model and other constructivist learning theories.

More recently, Scardamalia and Bereiter describe three ideas that are foundational to intentional learning environments:

1. *Intentional learning.* Ng and Bereiter (1991) observed students learning computer programming and found three kinds of goals:

- Performance goals, i.e., task completion goals.
- Instructional goals, i.e., the goals articulated by the instructor and the learning materials.
- Learning goals, i.e., the specific goals for learning brought to the situation by the learner. Learning goals usually overlap but do not equate to performance or instructional goals.

Intentional learning depends on students having learning goals and finding successful avenues to learn based on those goals.

2. *The process of expertise.* Scardamalia and Bereiter argue for a view of expertise in process terms rather than strictly as a performance capability. As people gain experience in a domain, simple tasks become routinized, freeing up mental resources for other tasks. If those newly available resources are *reinvested* back into learning more about the domain, then more and more difficult problems can be mastered. This process of expertise is equally characteristic of serious students and seasoned experts "working at the edges of their competence" (Scardamalia & Bereiter, 1994, p. 266). To become experts, students must demonstrate a disposition and commitment to engage in systematic intentional learning, in addition to having the brute cognitive capacity to learn.

3. *Restructuring schools as knowledge-building communities.* Scardamalia and Bereiter (1994) contrast what we call *static* from dynamic learning communities.[1] Students in static communities adapt to the environment, but once adapted, "one becomes an old timer, comfortably integrated into a relatively stable system of routines . . . (pp. 266–67). Traditional schools and even child-centered, individualized instruction are often static in this sense. In contrast, a dynamic learning community requires constant readaptation to other community members. Sports and businesses are examples. "[T]he accomplishments of participants keep raising the standard that the others strive for" (p. 267). In the sciences, for example, the collective knowledge base is continually changing. The challenge in these environments is to continue growing, adapting, and contributing along with the rest of the community. Dynamic knowledge-building communities engage in the kind of transformative communica-

tion suggested by Pea (1994; see discussion above). In large part, the goal of the CSILE research agenda is to find ways to help classrooms and schools become dynamic knowledge-building communities in this respect.

Central to intentional learning environments is the cultivation of a collective knowledge base, explicitly represented in CSILE as a computer database. This knowledge base allows the creation and storage of numerous forms of representation-text, graphics, video, audio—as well as the linking of items together via a hypermedia structure. The knowledge base is built up over a period of time in response to students' questions and their subsequent investigations and reports.

Another key feature of CSILE is the "publication" process, similar to the review process of academic journals:

> Students produce notes of various kinds and frequently revise them. When they think they have a note that makes a solid contribution to the knowledge base in some area, they can mark it as a candidate for publication. They then must complete a form that indicates, among other things, what they believe is the distinctive contribution of their note. After a review process (typically by other students with final clearance by the teacher), the note becomes identified as published. It appears in a different font, and users searching the database may, if they wish, restrict their search to published notes on the topic they designate (Scardamalia & Bereiter, 1994, p. 279).

Thus CSILE emulates in many respects the activities of scholarly knowledge-building communities. Attempts at applying a CSILE-like model to higher education classrooms are reported in Grabinger (Chapter 23).

Like problem-based learning, the CSILE model provides a concrete framework for designers and teachers seeking to break out of traditional conventions and incorporate constructivist principles of instructional design. Two remaining issues for consideration are:

- *Matching intentional learning activities to prespecified curriculum objectives.* Every learning environment exists within a larger system of curriculum expectations and learning needs. A student may want to study *X* while the teacher thinks that *Y* would be a better choice. Meanwhile, the school district has a policy insisting on *Z* as the proper content. Negotiating between student-generated study questions and the surrounding system is an important consideration.

- *Maintaining motivation.* As in every learning environment, designers of intentional environments must develop methods for encouraging thoughtful collaboration while avoiding the damaging effects of competition. Cultivating a cooperative, open spirit among participants requires attention to group dynamics and the chemistry between individuals and within working groups. Maintaining motivation could be a challenge within an environment of widely diverging competencies and expectations.

20.6 CONCLUSION

In our previous review of cognitive teaching models (Wilson & Cole, 1991), we were surprised by the diversity of

---

[1]Scardamalia and Bereiter use the terms *first-order* and *second-order environments.* We have used the terms *static* and *dynamic* to suggest more concretely their differences.

approach and method. In this review, key differences again should be acknowledged between the various models. Cognitive load theory adopts a no-nonsense approach to the efficient and effective teaching of defined content. The packaged computer-based learning environments (Sherlock and the case-based scenarios) are highly effective, controlled environments that filter out much of the world's complexity and provide learners with an authentic-enough environment conducive to learning. The problem-based learning model is simpler in design yet more ambitious in the sense that it departs more radically from established instructional methods. Finally, the tools and models related to learning communities become almost antimodels in the sense that so much is left to the participants, both instructors and students.

In view of the substantial differences between models, generalizing across them is a difficult task. Several key points of reflection, however, are offered below.

1. *Learning from implementation as well as design.* There is no doubt that developing and trying out coherent models can yield important outcome information. Knowing, for example, that reciprocal teaching produces, on average, effect sizes of .32 on standardized tests and .88 on locally developed measures (Rosenshine & Meister, 1994) conveys a sense of confidence and reliability for users of the method. At the same time, some of the most valuable lessons learned may come from the real-world experience gained in setting up and administering a program. The implementation can be just as important as the theory-guided design.

An example may be taken from the 1970s research in computer-assisted instruction. One program, the TICCIT project, was shown by an NSF evaluation to achieve its objectives more successfully than traditional classroom instruction (Merrill, Schneider & Fletcher, 1979). The program failed, however, in getting students to stay with the program; the dropout rate was unacceptably high when compared to traditional classrooms. In this case, the actual development and tryout of working models produced knowledge that would not have been anticipated ahead of time.

Another example is Clancey's Guidon-Manage research in intelligent tutoring systems (see 19.3, 19.4), or ITS (1993). In a remarkable example of self-reflection, Clancey concludes: "After more than a decade, I felt that I could no longer continue saying that I was developing instructional programs for medicine because not a single program I worked on was in routine use . . ." (p. 7). What did Clancey learn from his research? Apart from his contribution to intelligent tutoring technologies, he learned that research in a laboratory differs from research in the field. "*[R]esearchers must participate in the community they wish to influence . . .* (p. 9, italics retained). "As ITS matures, some members of our research community must necessarily broaden their goals from developing representational tools to *changing practice*—changing how people interact and changing their lives . . . (p. 9, italics retained). Clancey then reflects on how he might approach the

Guidon-Manage research differently today:

- Participating with users in multidisciplinary design teams versus viewing teachers and students as my subjects
- Adopting a global view of the context . . . instead of delivering a program in a . . . box
- Being committed to provide cost-effective solutions for real problems versus imposing my research agenda on another community
- Facilitating conversations between people versus only automating human roles
- Relating . . . ITS computer systems to . . . everyday practice . . . versus viewing models . . . as constituting the essence of expert knowledge that is to be transferred to a student
- Viewing the group as a psychological unit versus modeling only individual behavior (Clancey, 1993, p. 17)

Although the specific research agenda is different, Clancey's lessons learned apply very well to cognitive teaching models. Developers of teaching models need to stay close to the context of use and include implementation within their domain of interest.

Like the TICCIT and Guidon projects, outcomes of research are sometimes negative, for example, the failure of young students to learn abstract concepts via Tabletop, or the tendency for some experienced medical students to become bored with PBL activities. We believe that these negative findings can become extremely useful as formative evaluation data, feeding back into future implementations of the model.

Norman (1993) speaks of the power of representation as a stimulus to scientific progress. Repeatedly in the history of science, revolutionary strides are made when a new technology is developed that allows a repicturing of problems in a domain. By analogy, a similar kind of progress is made possible by research on teaching models. Through the careful articulation and construction of actual working methods, new perspectives are made possible. An actual product, once created, may be examined from a variety of angles and for a variety of purposes, many perhaps unintended by the creator. Determining exactly "what is learned" from research of this type may be difficult to articulate yet remain extremely valuable to the scientific and practitioner communities.

2. *Deciding on a model is closely tied to the curriculum question.* Perkins (1992b) warns of a common fallacy implied by the statement: "What we need is a new and better method. If only we had improved ways of inculcating knowledge or inducing youngsters to learn, we would attain the precise . . . outcomes we cherish" (p. 44). Instead, Perkins believes that "given reasonably sound methods, the most powerful choice we can make concerns not method but curriculum—not how we teach but what we choose to try to teach" (p. 44). This comment suggests that a fundamental step in instructional design involves the serious consideration of learning goals. A variety of constituencies should be included in this process, including sponsors and members of the learning community

itself. Once consensus is reached about the *kind* of learning being sought, certain teaching models become unfeasible while others become more attractive.

A basic lesson learned from observing schools is that two teachers may be covering the same ostensive curriculum while what *really* is taught differs radically between them. And what any two students learn in the same teacher's class may differ just as radically. At its base, the constructivist movement in education involves curriculum reform, a rethinking of what it means to know something. A constructivist curriculum is reflected in many of the models reviewed in this chapter. Thus, if a commitment is made toward rethinking curriculum to expand the roles of knowledge construction and learning communities, then a corresponding commitment needs to be made in rethinking learning activities. Deciding on a teaching model is not a value-neutral activity. Recognizing this puts the selection of a teaching model squarely into the political realm of policymaking. New issues become important, such as access, equity, representation, voice, and achieving consensus amid diverse perspectives.

As Reigeluth (1983) acknowledges, curriculum and instruction cannot be completely separated. There is a tendency among many institutions to give lip service to higher-order outcomes while maintaining teaching methods that specifically suppress such outcomes. Medical schools that teach students to simply memorize and take tests are an example. Another example is a military school whose mission statement prizes "creativity" in students, yet whose teaching methods and authoritarian culture strictly reinforce conformity and transmission of content.

3. *Deciding on a teaching model and making decisions within that framework are highly situated activities.* The success of a given implementation will depend more on the local variables than on the general variables contained in the various models described above. Put another way, "the devil is in the details." There is a way to succeed and a way to fail using a whole host of teaching models. All the models reviewed above can succeed if properly implemented. Teachers and students must see the sense of what they are doing, come to believe in the efficacy of the program, and work hard to ensure that the right outcomes are achieved.

This situational perspective conflicts with traditional views. Thinking of instructional design as a technology would lead us to think that a situation gets analyzed, which leads to a technical fix to be implemented, which leads either to a measured solution to the problem or a revision in the fix for the next cycle of intervention. A situated view of instructional design would lead to a different process:

A. A learning community examines and negotiates its own values, desired outcomes, and acceptable conventions and practices.

B. The learning community plans for and engages in knowledge-generating activities within the established framework of goals, conventions, and practices.

C. Members of the learning community, including both teachers and students, observe and monitor learning and make needed adjustments to support each other in their learning activities.

D. Participants occasionally reexamine negotiated learning goals and activities for the purpose of improving learning and maintaining a vital community of motivated learners. This may lead to new goals and methods and cultural changes at all levels, from cosmetic to foundational.

This situated, community-oriented view of instruction takes a more holistic view to the design of instruction. The community is opportunistic in addressing "design" issues at any stage of planning and implementation. Community members, including students, have a voice in determining what happens to them in instruction. In return, they must show the needed commitment and disposition to behave responsibly and in support of learning.

If community members have participated in the establishment of a program, they are more likely to believe in it. If they believe in the program, the chances of success increase dramatically. As Perkins (1992b) suggests, even very imperfect instructional methods can work if the commitment is made to work together and ask the right questions in designing curriculum.

4. *Each teaching model is a particular blend of costs and outcomes.* Some kind of costs-benefits analysis—implicit or explicit—happens in designing educational programs. Surveying our teaching models reveals that some have demonstrably high development costs. Sherlock has taken a decade of patient research to achieve its present form. Once developed, however, the prototype model may be replicated at a reasonable cost. Other models, such as problem-based learning, may pose heavy demands in terms of time in the curriculum. Instructional designers (or learning-community members) must then face the question of how and whether to implement such resource-demanding teaching methods into an existing system and curriculum.

Every decision to adopt one teaching model over another involves such weighing of pros and cons. However, while costs may be objectively measured and estimated, learning benefits are notoriously difficult to reduce down to a number. This inequity of measurability results in a common bias: The cost differences become exaggerated, while the potential benefits, because they are harder to measure, tend to be undervalued or ignored. Comparison of alternative teaching models must give full consideration to qualitative differences in learning outcomes, in addition to the more visible cost differences in time and money.

Some ideas may be borrowed and inexpensively incorporated into related products or programs. For example, if an instructor becomes excited by Schank's case-based scenarios, she may choose to incorporate case histories and classroom simulations into her teaching. While the resulting lessons may bear only a passing resemblance to the computer-based scenarios, they are heavily influenced by Schank's principles of case-based, interactive instruction. Many of the principles discussed above, including those of cognitive apprenticeships and intentional learning communities, can be efficiently adapted into instruction in a number of ways, depending on local circumstances and resources.

5. *Instruction should support learners as they become efficient in procedural performance and deliberate in their self-reflection and understanding.* Virtually all of the teaching models under review—Sweller's research notwithstanding—emphasize the grounding of instruction in complex problems, cases, or performance opportunities. Yet organizing instruction around problems and cases should not mask the importance of perception, reflection, and metacognitive activity. Indeed, these two aspects of human performance (problem solving and perception) can be seen as inherently complementary and equally necessary. Contrary to the suggestion of Dreyfus and Dreyfus (1986), experts are more than mere automatic problem solvers. Rather, experts become experts through a progressive series of encounters with the domain, each involving an element of routine performance and a corresponding element of reflection and deliberation. This is the process of expertise spoken of by Scardamalia and Bereiter (1994) and discussed above.

Prawat (1993) makes this point well. While there is a tendency among cognitive psychologists to make problem solving central to all cognition, Prawat reminds us that schemas, ideas, and perceptual processes hold an equally important place. *Learning how to see* is as important as solving a problem once we do see. Principles of perception—whether from ecological psychology (Allen & Otto, Chapter 8), connectionism, or aesthetics—need to have a place within successful teaching models. This includes teaching students how to represent problems and situations, but also how to appreciate and respond to the aesthetic side of the subject, how to reflect upon one's actions, and how to "raise one's consciousness" and recognize recurring themes and patterns in behavior and interactions.

6. *Successful programs must seek to make complex performance do-able while avoiding the pitfalls of simplistic proceduralization.* The art of "scaffolding" complex performance is a key problem area that surprisingly is still not well understood. How does a coach entice a young gymnast to perform just beyond her capacities, overcoming the fear and uncertainty that normally accompany new performances? How does the coach know just when and where to step in, preserving the integrity of the task (and the learning) while not letting the athlete fall on her head? These are questions of appropriate scaffolding or support for learning. Once a teacher begins believing the constructivist agenda and the importance of authentic, meaningful tasks, then the challenge of supporting novice performance within a complex environment becomes a central concern. As Sweller's research makes clear, poorly supported problem-solving activities force learners to rely on weak methods that they already know. Appropriate and wise scaffolding makes problem-solving activities more efficient because learners stayed focused within the critical "development" zone between previously mastered knowledge and skills beyond their reach.

Developing a technology for optimizing this kind of support is an area in need of further research and development.

This same concept of scaffolding can be directed to the implementation of the teaching model itself. Instructional designers and teachers need proper supports and aids in designing according to a particular model or tradition. At the same time, they should be cautioned against simplistically "applying" a model in a proceduralized or objectivist fashion. Postmodernists would say that in such cases, the model "does violence" to the situation. The complexities of a situation should not be reduced down to the simple maxims of a teaching model. Any model that is forced on a situation and made to fit will lead inevitably to unintended negative consequences. The negative fallout will happen at those points of disjuncture or lack of fit between model and situation. As we have stressed, the details of the situation need to be respected and taken into account when adapting a model to a situation.

This, perhaps, is a more appropriate way of thinking about implementation: Rather than *applying* a particular teaching model, a teacher necessarily *adapts* that model to present circumstances. Learning how to adapt abstractions to concrete realities is a worthy task for both students and teachers, and, indeed, may lie at the heart of some forms of expertise.

Each of these points is worthy of continued research. As psychologists continue to develop models for teaching that embody their best thinking and theories, the field of instructional design will have opportunities for reflection and growth as they reexamine their own models and methods. Our hope is that the dialogue may continue to flourish and expand, resulting in a "transformation" of both communities.

REFERENCES

Anderson, J.R. (1987). Methodologies for studying human knowledge. *Behavioral and Brain Science 10,* 467–77.

Barrows, H.S. (1985). *How to design a problem-based curriculum for the years.* New York: Springer.

— (1992). *The tutorial process.* Springfield, IL: Southern Illinois University School of Medicine.

— & Feltovich, P.J. (1987). The clinical reasoning process. *Journal of Medical Education 21,* 86–91.

Bell, B., Bareiss, R. & Beckwith, R. (1993/94). Sickle cell counselor: a prototype goal-based scenario for instruction in a museum environment. *The Journal of the Learning Sciences 3* (4), 347–86.

Bereiter, C. & Scardamalia, M. (1992). Cognition and curriculum. *In* P. Jackson, ed. *Handbook of research on curriculum,* 517–42. New York: Macmillan.

Brown, A.L. (1994). The advancement of learning. *Educational Researcher 23* (3), 4–12.

— & Campione, J.C. (1981). Inducing flexible thinking: a problem of access. *In* M. Friedman, J.P. Das & N. O'Connor, eds. *Intelligence and learning ,* 515-29. New York: Plenum.

—, — & Day, J.D. (1981). Learning to learn: on training students to learn from texts. *Educational Researcher 10* (2), 14–21.

— & Palincsar, A.S. (1989). Guided, cooperative learning and individual knowledge acquisition. *In* L.B. Resnick, ed. *Knowing, learning, and instruction: essays in honor of Robert Glaser.* Hillsdale, NJ: Erlbaum.

Carroll, W.M. (1994). Using worked examples as an instructional support in the algebra classroom. *Journal of Educational Psychology 86* (3), 360–67.

Chandler, P. & Sweller, J. (1991). Cognitive load theory and the format of instruction. *Cognition and Instruction 8,* 293–332.

Chi, M.T.H., de Leeuw, N., Chiu, M-H & LaVancher, C. (1991). *The use of self-explanations as a learning tool.* Pittsburgh, PA: The Learning Research and Development Center, University of Pittsburgh.

— & VanLehn, K.A. (1991). The content of physics self-explanations. *The Journal of the Learning Sciences 1* (1), 69–105.

— & Bassok, M. (1989). Learning from examples via self-explanations. *In* L.B. Resnick, ed. *Knowing, learning, and instruction: essays in honor of Robert Glaser,* 251–82. Hillsdale, NJ: Erlbaum.

—, Bassok, M., Lewis, M. W., Reimann, P. & Glaser, R. (1989). Self-explanations: how students study and use examples in learning to solve problems. *Cognitive Science 13,* 145–82.

—, de Leeuw, N., Chiu, M-H & LaVancher, C. (1991). *The use of self-explanations as a learning tool.* Pittsburgh PA: The Learning Research and Development Center, University of Pittsburgh.

— & VanLehn, K.A. (1991). The content of physics self-explanations. *The Journal of the Learning Sciences 1* (1), 69–105.

Clancey, W.J. (1993). Guidon-Manage revisited: a socio-technical systems approach. *Journal of Artificial Intelligence in Education 4* (1), 5–34.

Collins, A., Brown, J.S. & Newman, S.E. (1989). Cognitive apprenticeship: teaching the crafts of reading, writing, and mathematics. *In* L.B. Resnick, ed. *Knowing, learning, and instruction: essays in honor of Robert Glaser.* Hillsdale, NJ: Erlbaum.

— & Stevens, A.L. (1983). A cognitive theory of inquiry teaching. *In* C.M. Reigeluth, ed. *Instructional-design theories and models: An overview of their current status,* 247–78. Hillsdale, NJ: Erlbaum.

Conklin, J. (1987). Hypertext: a survey and introduction. *IEEE Computer 20* (9), 17–41.

Dick, W. (1987). A history of instructional design and its impact on educational psychology. *In* J.A. Glover & R.R. Ronning, eds. *Historical foundations of educational psychology,* 183–200. New York: Plenum.

Distlehorst, L.H. & Barrows, H.S. (1982). A new tool for problem-based self-directed learning, *Journal of Medical Education 57,* 466–88.

Dreyfus, H.L. & Dreyfus, S.E. (1986). *Mind over machine: the power of human intuition and expertise in the era of the computer.* New York: Free Press.

Duffy, T.M. (1995). Strategic teaching framework: an instructional model for learning complex, interactive skills. *In* C. Dills & A. Romiszowski, eds. *Perspectives on instructional design.* Englewood Cliffs NJ: Educational Technology.

— (1994, Oct. 22). *Workshop on problem-based learning.* Denver, CO: University of Colorado at Denver.

— & Jonassen, D.H., eds. (1993). *Constructivism and the technology of instruction: a conversation.* Hillsdale, NJ: Erlbaum.

Duffy, G.G. & Roehler, L.R. (1989). Why strategy instruction is so difficult and what we need to do about it. *In* C. McCormick, G. Miller & M. Pressley, eds. *Cognitive strategy research: from basic research to educational applications,* 133–54. New York: Springer.

Gagné, R.M. (1968). Learning hierarchies. Presidential Address of APA Division 15. *Educational Psychologist 6* (1), 1–9.

—, ed. (1987). *Instructional technology: foundations.* Hillsdale, NJ: Erlbaum.

Glaser, R., Lesgold, A. & Lajoie, S.P. (1987). Toward a cognitive theory for the measurement of achievement. *In* R. Ronning, J. Glover, J.C. Conoley & J.C. Witt, eds. *The influence of cognitive psychology on testing, Buros/Nebrasks Symposium on measurement: Vol. 3,* 41–85. Hillsdale, NJ: Erlbaum.

— (1990). The reemergence of learning theory within instructional research. *American Psychologist 45* (1), 29–39.

— (1976). Components of a psychology of instruction: toward a science of design. *Review of Educational Research 46,* 1–24.

Gott, S.P. (1988a, April). *The lost apprenticeship: a challenge for cognitive science.* Paper presented at the meeting of the American Educational Research Association, New Orleans, LA.

— (1988b). Apprenticeship instruction for real-world tasks: the coordination of procedures, mental models, and strategies. *In* E.Z. Rothkopf, ed. *Review of Research in Education 15,* 97–169.

—, Hall, E.P., Pokorny, R.A., Dibble, E. & Glaser, R. (1992). A naturalistic study of transfer: adaptive expertise in technical domains. *In* D.K. Detterman & R.J. Sternberg, eds. *Transfer on trial: intelligence, cognition, and instruction,* 258–88. Norwood, NJ: Ablex.

—, Lesgold, A. & Kane, R.S. (1996). Tutoring for transfer of technical competence. *In* B.G. Wilson, ed. *Constructivist learning environments: case studies in instructional design,* 33–48. Englewood Cliffs, NJ: Educational Technology.

Hancock, C.M. & Kaput, J. (1990a). *Annual report of hands on data* (NSF MDR-#8855617). Cambridge, MA: TERC.

— & — (1990b). Computerized tools and the process of data modeling. *In* G. Booker, P. Cobb & T.N. deMendicuti, eds. *Proceedings of the 14th International Conference on the Psychology of Mathematics Education,* Vol. 3, 65–172. Mexico: The Program Committee of the 14th PME Conference.

Hancock, J.J., Kaput, L.T. & Goldsmith, L.T. (1992). Authentic inquiry with data: critical barriers to classroom implementation. *Educational Psychologist 27* (3), 337–64.

Jonassen, D.H. (1996). *Computers in the classroom: mindtools for critical thinking.* New York: Macmillan.

—, Bessner, K. & Yacci, M. (1993). *Structural knowledge: techniques for representing, conveying, and acquiring structural knowledge.* Hillsdale, NJ: Erlbaum.

Kaput, J.J. & Hancock, C.M. (1991). Cognitive issues in translating between semantic structure and formal record structure. *In* F. Furinghetti, ed. *Proceedings of the 15th International Conference on the Psychology of Mathematics Education,* Vol. 2, 237–44. Genova, Italy: Dipartimento di Matematica dell' Università de Genova.

Kass, A., Burke, R., Blevis, E. & Williamson, M. (1993/94). Constructing learning environments for complex social skills. *The Journal of the Learning Sciences 3* (4), 387–427.

Koschmann, T.D. (1994). Toward a theory of computer support for collaborative learning. *The Journal of the Learning Sciences 3* (3), 219–25.

—, Myers, A.C., Feltovich, P.J. & Barrows, H.S. (1994). Using technology to assist in realizing effective learning and instruction: a principled approach to the use of computers in collaborative learning. *The Journal of the Learning Sciences 3* (3), 227–64.

Lajoie, S.P. & Lesgold, A.M. (1992). Dynamic assessment of proficiency for solving procedural knowledge tasks. *Educational Psychologist 27* (3), 365–84.

— & — (1989). Apprenticeship training in the workplace: computer coached practice environment as a new form of apprenticeship. *Machine-Mediate Learning 3,* 7–28.

Lave, J. (1988). *Cognition in practice: mind, mathematics and culture in everyday life.* Cambridge, England: Cambridge University Press.

Lesgold, A., Lajoie, S., Bunzo, M. & Eggan, G. (1992). A coached practice environment for an electronics troubleshooting job. *In* J. Larkin & R. Chabay, eds. *Computer assisted instruction and intelligent tutoring systems: establishing communications and collaboration,* 201–38. Hillsdale, NJ: Erlbaum.

Lesh, R., Landau, M. & Hamilton, E. (1983). Conceptual models and applied mathematical problem solving research. *In* R. Lesh & M. Landau, eds. *Acquisition of mathematical concepts and processes,* 263–343. New York: Academic.

Lewis, M.W., Milson, R. & Anderson, J.R. (1988). Designing an intelligent authoring system for high school mathematics ICAI: the teacher apprentice project. *In* G.P. Kearsley, ed. *Artificial intelligence and instruction: applications and methods,* 269–301. New York: Addison-Wesley.

Lipkin, M. (1989). Education of doctors who care. *In* H.G. Schmidt, M. Lipkin, Jr., M.W. de Vries & J.M. Greep, eds. *New directions for medical education,* 3–16. New York: Springer.

Low, W.C. (1981). Changes in instructional development: the aftermath of an information processing takeover in psychology. *Journal of Instructional Development 4* (2), 10–18.

Lumsdaine, A.A. & Glaser, R. (1960). *Teaching machines and programmed learning.* Washington, DC: National Educational Association.

Mayer, R.E. & Anderson, R.B. (1991). Animations need narrations: an experimental test of a dual-coding hypothesis. *Journal of Educational Psychology 83* (4), 484–90.

— & Anderson, R.B. (1992). The instructive animation: helping students build connections between words and pictures in multimedia learning. *Journal of Educational Psychology 84* (4), 444–52.

— & Sims, V.K. (1994). For whom is a picture worth a thousand words? Extensions of a dual-coding theory of multimedia learning. *Journal of Educational Psychology 86* (3), 389–401.

Merrill, M.D. (1983). Component display theory. *In* C.M. Reigeluth, ed. *Instructional-design theories and models: an overview of their current status,* 282–333. Hillsdale, NJ: Erlbaum.

—, Kowallis, T. & Wilson, B.G. (1981). Instructional design in transition. *In* F. Farley & N. Gordon, eds. *Psychology and education: the state of the union.* Chicago, IL: McCutcheon.

—, Schneider, E. & Fletcher, K. (1979). *TICCIT.* Englewood Cliffs, NJ: Educational Technology.

—, Wilson, B.G. & Kelety, J.C. (1981). Elaboration theory and cognitive psychology. *Instructional Science 10,* 217–35.

— & Tennyson, R. (1977). *Teaching concepts: an instruction-al design guide,* 1st ed. Englewood Cliffs, NJ: Educational Technology.

Morrison, D. & Collins, A. (1996). Epistemic fluency and constructivism. *In* B.B. Wilson, ed. *Learning environments,* 107–19.

Ng, E. & Bereiter, C. (1991). Three levels of goal orientation in learning. *The Journal of the Learning Sciences 1* (3), 243–71.

Nichols, P., Poknorny, R., Jones, G., Gott, S.P. & Alley, W.E. (1995). Evaluation of an avionics troubleshooting tutoring system. AL/HR TR-94–XX. Brooks AFB, TX.

Paas, F.G.W.C. & Van Merriënboer, J.J.G. (1994). Variability of worked examples and transfer of geometrical problem-solving skills: a cognitive-load approach. *Journal of Educational Psychology 86* (1), 122–33.

Pea, R.D. (1994). Seeing what we build together: distributed multimedia learning environments for transformative communications. *The Journal of the Learning Sciences 3* (3), 285–99.

Perkins, D.N. (1992a). Technology meets constructivism: do they make a marriage? *In* T.M. Duffy & D.H. Jonassen, eds. *Constructivism and the technology of instruction,* 45–55. Hillsdale, NJ: Erlbaum.

— (1992b). Smart schools: from training memories to educating minds. New York: Free Press.

Pierce, K.A., Duncan, M.K., Gholson, B., Ray, G.E. & Kamhi, A.G. (1993). Cognitive load, schema acquisition, and procedural adaptation in nonisomorphic analogical transfer. *Journal of Educational Psychology 85* (1), 66–74.

Prawat, R.S. (1993). The value of ideas: problems versus possibilities in learning. *Educational Researcher 22* (6), 5–16.

Reder, L. & Anderson, J. (1982). Effects of spacing and embellishment on memory for main points of a text. *Memory and Cognition 10,* 97–102.

Reigeluth, C.M., ed. (1983). *Instructional-design theories and models: an overview of their current status.* Hillsdale, NJ: Erlbaum.

—, ed. (1987). *Instructional theories in action: lessons illustrating selected theories and models .* Hillsdale, NJ: Erlbaum.

Riesbeck, C.K. (1996). Case-based teaching and constructivism: carpenters and tools. *In* B.G. Wilson, ed. *Constructivist learning environments: case studies in instructional design,* 49–61. Englewood Cliffs, NJ: Educational Technology.

Resnick, L.B. (1981). Instructional psychology. *Annual Review of Psychology 32,* 659–704.

Robin, S. & Mayer, R.E. (1993). Schema training in analogical reasoning. *Journal of Educational Psychology 85* (3), 529–38.

Rosenshine, B. & Meister, C. (1994). Reciprocal teaching: a review of the research. *Review of Educational Research 64* (4), 479–530.

Saunders, R. & Solman, R. (1984). The effect of pictures on the acquisition of a small vocabulary of similar sight-words. *British Journal of Educational Psychology 54,* 265–75.

Savery, J.R. & Duffy, T.M. (1996). Problem based learning: an instructional model and its constructivist framework. *In* B.G. Wilson, ed. *Constructivist learning environments: cases studies in instructional design,* 135–48. Englewood Cliffs, NJ: Educational Technology.

Scardamalia, M., Bereiter, C., McLean, R.S., Swallow, J. & Woodruff, E. (1989). Computer-supported intentional learning environments. *Journal of Educational Computing Research 5* (1), 51–68.

— & — (1991). Higher levels of agency for children in knowledge building: a challenge for the design of new knowledge media. *The Journal of the Learning Sciences 1* (1), 37–68.

— & — (1994). Computer support for knowledge-building communities. *The Journal of the Learning Sciences 3* (3), 265–83.

Schank, R.C., Fano, A., Bell, B. & Jona, M. (1993/1994). The design of goal-based scenarios. *The Journal of the Learning Sciences 3* (4), 305–45.

Schmidt, H.G. (1989). The rationale behind problem-based learning. *In* H.G. Schmidt, M. Lipkin, Jr., M.W. de Vries & J.M. Greep, eds. *New directions for medical education,* 105–11. New York: Springer.

Schooler, J. & Engstler-Schooler, T. (1990). Verbal overshadowing of visual memories: some things are better left unsaid. *Cognitive Psychology 22,* 36–71.

Sherry, L. & Trigg, M. (1996). Epistemic forms and epistemic games. *Educational Technology 36* (3), 38–44.

Stefik, M. & Brown, J.S. (1989). Toward portable ideas. *In* M. Olson, ed. *Technological support for work group collaboration,* 147–66. Hillsdale, NJ: Erlbaum.

Sweller, J. (1989). Cognitive technology: some procedures for facilitating learning and problem solving in mathematics and science. *Journal of Educational Psychology 81* (4), 457–66.

Sweller, J. & Cooper, G.A. (1985). The use of worked examples as a substitute for problem solving in learning algebra. *Cognition and Instruction 2* (1), 59–89.

Sweller, J. & Chandler, P. (1994). Why some material is difficult to learn. *Cognition and Instruction 12* (3), 185–233.

Williams, S.M. (1992). Putting case-based instruction into context: examples from legal and medical education. *The Journal of the Learning Sciences 2* (4), 367–427.

Wilson, B.G., ed. (1996). *Constructivist learning environments: case studies in instructional design.* Englewood, Cliffs, NJ: Educational Technology.

— & Cole, P. (1991). A review of cognitive teaching models. *Educational Technology Research & Development 39* (4), 47–64.

21. USER-CENTERED DESIGN OF HYPERTEXT/HYPERMEDIA FOR EDUCATION

Cliff McKnight
LOUGHBOROUGH UNIVERSITY
OF TECHNOLOGY

Andrew Dillon
INDIANA
UNIVERSITY

John Richardson
LOUGHBOROUGH UNIVERSITY
OF TECHNOLOGY

21.1 WHAT IS HYPERTEXT; WHAT IS HYPERMEDIA?

The prefix *hyper* usually means "more than," so we may begin by asking what is it that hypertext has that makes it more than text (see 24.6.1). The simple answer to this is that as well as text, hypertext has "links." The text is usually organized into chunks, units, or "nodes," as they have come to be known, and the links form connections between certain nodes.

There are no "rules" about how big a node should be or what it should contain. Similarly there are no rules governing what gets linked to what. Hence, there can be many different kinds of hypertext in the same way that there are many different kinds of text. Furthermore, hypertext allows the concept of "document" to be extended since, logically, entire documents can be treated as nodes and linked together to form a single hypertext.

The concept of links between units of information has a history almost as old as writing itself. Think of a footnote marker in a text: It links the main text with the footnote text, although in this case the marker is a static link—the reader must make the movement between text and footnote. In hypertext, the links are active: Selecting the link moves the reader to the linked text in some way. It is this dynamic aspect of presentation that is the principal difference between text and hypertext. An alternative term for hypertext which never gained the same currency was *interactive documentation* (Brown, 1986), and a recent paper used the term *responsive text* (Hillinger, 1990).

If hypertext isn't a new idea, why has it recently become so popular? In fact, hypertext has been an idea waiting for technology to catch up with it. In order to implement active links, it is necessary to use a dynamic display medium such as a computer screen. Hence, in the 1960s in the research laboratories, several groups started using large mainframe computers in order to explore the potential of hypertext. Advances in computer technology have led to the development of the minicomputer and the microcomputer, making considerable computer power available to the individual user: the personal computer with so-called "user friendly" interfaces. On such computers, "popular" hypertext becomes feasible.

Hypermedia is presented as a further development of hypertext. As computers have moved from being able to present little more than uppercase text to being able to present information in a variety of communication media—sound, graphics, video—so it is possible to link these media together using hypertext techniques, hence the term *hypermedia*. However, in the same way that a book can contain text, drawings, tables, photographs, or even pop-up models, so the distinction between hypertext and hypermedia is somewhat arbitrary. We will use either term to refer to a set of nodes of information that are dynamically linked.

By way of example, consider how information relating to the European Union (EU) could be presented. At the top level, the reader could be presented with a map of Europe and then be able to select various aspects of the EU or any particular member state for more information (see Fig. 21-1). This may take the form of a more detailed map showing the major cities that, when selected, showed some information about the city. Alternatively, the reader may be offered other information about the country, such as the currency, culture, audioclips of common words in the language such as *please* and *thank you,* and so forth (see Figure 21-2). The city maps could offer sites of interest such as museums, local transport details, entertainment sites such as theaters, or even restaurants and pubs; they could include videoclips of the major tourist sites, on the beach or at the disco. Now the tourist "brochures" can feature live action and be interactive in a way that the present printed chapter cannot.

21.2 THE GENESIS OF HYPERTEXT

We do not intend this section to be a general overview of everything that has gone before. The reader who is interested in such a description would do well to read Jeff Conklin's excellent review (Conklin, 1987), followed by Jakob Nielsen's popular book (Nielsen, 1990). Rather, we would like to present some of the historical highlights as being representative of three different conceptual stances, and we represent each of these by an influential figure in the field. These are:

- The human being as possessor of a cognitive system based on association: the view of Vannevar Bush
- Technology as an augmenter of the human intellect: the personal philosophy of Doug Engelbart
- The need for a flexible and usable access mechanism to the world of interrelated information: the dream of Ted Nelson

The article most often cited as the modern birthplace of hypertext is Vannevar Bush's "As We May Think" (Bush, 1945). Bush was appointed the first director of the Office of Scientific Research and Development by President Roosevelt in 1941. He saw clearly the problems associated with the ever-increasing volumes of information that were the product of the Second World War research and technology initiatives:

There is a growing mountain of research. But there is increased evidence that we are being bogged down today as specialization extends. The investigator is staggered by the findings and conclusions of thousands of other workers—conclusions which he cannot find time to grasp, much less to remember, as they appear. Yet specialization becomes increasingly necessary for progress, and the effort to bridge between disciplines is correspondingly superficial.

It surprises many people to learn that this statement was made 50 years ago—the information explosion is not such a modern phenomenon after all! To cope with this plethora of information, Bush conceived the *memex,* a device " . . . in which an individual stores his books, records, and communications, and which is mechanized so that it may be consulted with exceeding speed and flexibility." More than a simple repository, the memex was based on the principle of association, the notion that all facts, concepts, and ideas are linked in the mind, and that any one knowledge chunk can act as a stimulus or trigger to remember another.

In devising a supporting technology of this kind, Bush sought to create a means of information storage and retrieval that was intuitive to the user by virtue of its similarity to the workings of the mind. The appeal to intuitive operation predates many of the arguments that have subsequently emerged in the design of information technology. For Bush, it was suffi-

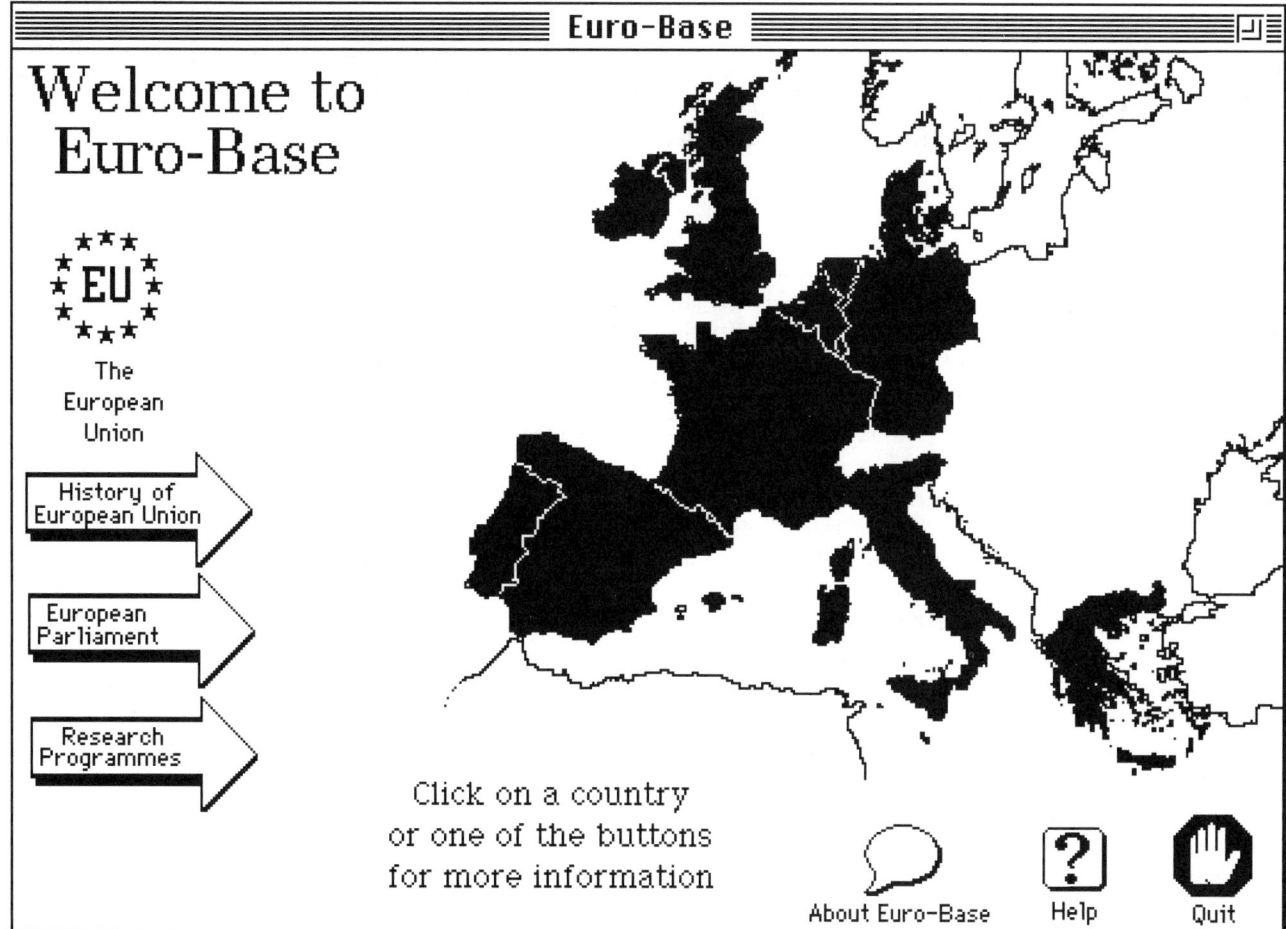

Figure 21-1. The top level of the Euro-Base hypertext, a wealth of information at the click of a button.

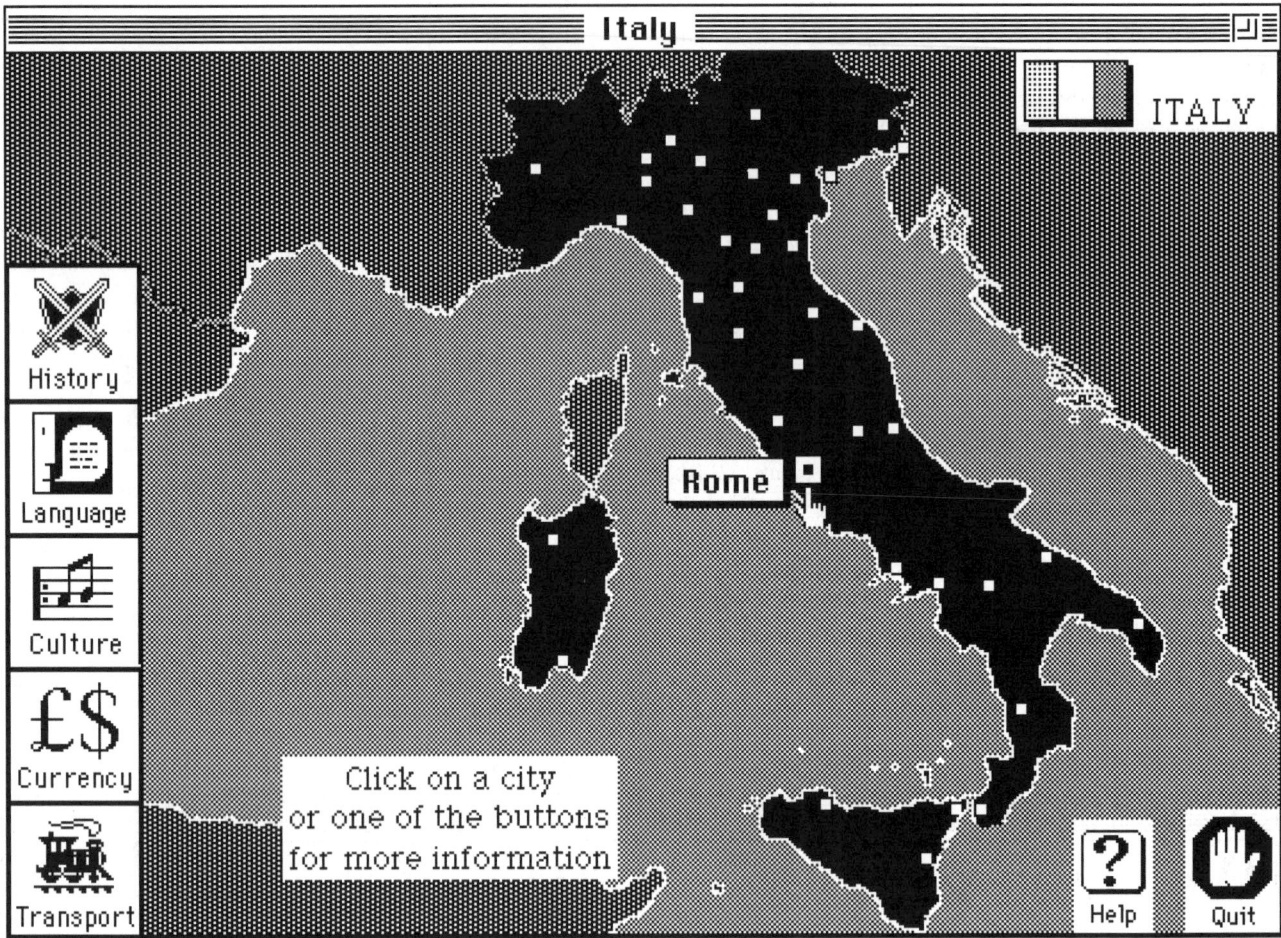

Figure 21-2.   See and hear the sights and sounds of Europe.

cient that a principle such as association—at that time a current view of the human cognitive system—would satisfy the organizational requirements of information users, an approach to design that is also neatly mirrored in current human factors thinking. However, given the volume of information a person might need to handle and what we now know about the vagaries of human association (e.g., Howe, 1980), it appears unlikely to us that such a principle alone could act as a sufficient design constraint on a hypermedia system.

These objections aside, it is interesting that Bush viewed the need for system design in such a user-centered manner. Unfortunately, the technology of the day was not as developed as the ideas: Bush conceived of the memex as being microfilm based. Hence, his ideas lay dormant for at least 2 decades, waiting for the technology to catch up. However, it is still commonplace to hear hypertext spoken of as a "natural" information system and a viable model of the human mind.

Whereas Bush (and others) sought to devise systems based on cognitive equivalence, Doug Engelbart has been developing his conception of hypertext since the early 1960s by placing his emphasis on the augmenting or amplifying of human intellect (cf. Engelbart , 1963), as reflected in the naming of his system as *Augment*. Engelbart's first implementation was NLS (oN Line System), which was

meant as an environment to serve the working needs of his Augmented Human Intellect Research Center at Stanford Research Institute. This was a computer-based environment containing all the documents, memos, notes, reports, and so forth, in addition to supporting planning, debugging, and communication. As such, NLS can be seen as one of the earliest attempts to provide a hypertext environment in which computer-supported collaborative work (CSCW) could take place.

Engelbart's pragmatic position is less concerned with modeling the information-processing tendencies of the human being than with extending them, although to some extent such a position is logically determined by an image of the mind that one is trying to enhance or augment. In conceptualizing the technology in this way, Engelbart espoused the notion of hypertext as some form of cognitive artifact, extending the capabilities of the human being and offering the potential to attain performance levels in information tasks which would be difficult or impossible to achieve without hypertext. This is not dissimilar to McLuhan's ideas of technologies as extensions of human faculties, for example, wheels as an extension of legs (McLuhan, 1964), ideas that had their own philosophical roots in the "personal knowledge" work of Michael Polanyi (1957).

The actual term *hypertext* is attributed to Ted Nelson, who called his dream system *Xanadu*—a "docuverse" in which the entire literature of the world is linked, a "universal instantaneous hypertext publishing network" (Nelson, 1988). In Xanadu nothing ever needs to be written twice; a document is built up of original, or *native,* bytes and bytes that are *transclusions,* a term that implies the transfer and inclusion of part of one document into another. However, an important aspect of Xanadu is that the transclusion is virtual, with each document containing links to the original document rather than to copies of its parts.

While Nelson's view may appear to be the most ambitious, in many ways his advocacy of this form of system is the most realistic, since it rests less on contemporary assumptions drawn from the psychological theories of the day and more on the requirement for a technology to provide rapid, easy access to the world of information. At an abstract level, the World Wide Web developed by Tim Berners-Lee and colleagues at CERN (Berners-Lee et al., 1994) comes close to realizing Nelson's dream, since it allows links between documents anywhere in the world (or at least anywhere with a connection to the Internet).[1] Indeed, this may be the route through which some of the ideas behind Xanadu will now be instantiated. When Autodesk, the CAD company, purchased Xanadu in 1988, there was hope that an actual product would be developed. However, 5 years and reputedly $5 million later, Autodesk has abandoned the project, and the Xanadu name is back with Nelson who, at the Hypertext '93 conference, was talking about "Xanadu Light" based on existing tools such as Gopher and Telnet.

The three views represented here are not mutually exclusive; it is possible to advocate a hypertext system that provides ready access to all information and therefore allows users to perform new tasks. Indeed, there is a fine line between these idealized positions, and it is not possible, or indeed very useful, to describe any particular contemporary system (or system designer's viewpoint) in terms of one or any of them. However, the fact that different views can proliferate illustrates the point that *hypertext* is not a unitary concept, not a single thing that can be defined any more precisely than in terms of nodes and links. It is for this reason that hypertext software packages with completely different "look and feel" (cf. Guide and HyperCard) can be produced and still claim to embody the concept of hypertext.

The corollary to this is that we should not expect any particular hypertext system to be ideal in all task situations. It is not surprising that Conklin's (1987) historical survey of hypertext systems groups them in a largely task-based way. He uses four categories: macroliterary systems, which center on the integration and ready accessibility of large volumes of information; problem exploration systems, which are designed to allow the interactive manipulation of information; systems for structured reading/browsing/reference; and, finally, systems that might have been applied to a specific application but whose real purpose in construction had been the experimental investigation of hypertext technology itself.

As we shall attempt to demonstrate here, the pedagogic implications of hypertext rest on a mixture of these three underlying philosophies. However, a major weakness of the field has been the inadequate theoretical explication of the nature of learning that hypertext systems might support. In particular, an oversimplistic acceptance of the naturalistic argument advocated by Bush remains, even if the models of the mind subscribed to by contemporary learning theorists (e.g., Greeno et al., 1978) are more sophisticated than the principle of association current in Bush's time. Consequently, the field lacks a dominant theoretical perspective that can draw on significant empirical support, and much of the literature in the field is rhetorical in style, reflecting the preparadigmatic nature of the field.

21.3 HYPERTEXT AND LEARNING

For over 40 years, technological "solutions" have been offered to the teaching profession in order to improve their effectiveness, ranging from programmed text and teaching machines through to the modern fascination with computers. Areas such as computer-based learning (CBL) or computer-aided instruction (CAI) aim to provide some of the functions of the teacher (see 2.3.2, 12.1, 19.2.2). The technologist's dream, of course, was the provision of a workstation for every learner so that they may proceed at their own pace, and to some extent the dream remains today. However, between the earliest teaching machines and the latest hypermedia environments, there has been a radical shift in prevailing pedagogy, from the repetitive reinforcement schedules of the behaviorists through the cognitivist movement and latterly the constructivists. Each movement has sought to make the technology its own and can make a case for the use of hypertext in its own terms (see 2.2.1, 5.5, Chapter 7).

It is not our intention to expound these arguments here. Suffice it to say that few theorists of any philosophical persuasion within the learning discipline have been able to specify a distinctive learning environment within the technology that uniquely supports their position. Indeed, critics of the old behaviorist teaching machines characterized the technology as betraying a crude, mechanistic model of learning where teaching reduces simply to optimizing the presentation of material—a criticism not lessened in any way by improvements in technology per se.

Within education, hypertext has been seen by some as a valuable new constructivist tool (see 7.1) for supporting teachers and students (Cunningham, Duffy & Knuth, 1993), whereas others have seen it as simply a fancy new "jug" (Whalley, 1993). There is merit in both positions, but

---

[1] At the detailed level, there are still numerous important differences between Xanadu and the World Wide Web, the former including consideration of, for example, copyright payment, storage and usage charging, addressing to the character level, typed links, and, of course, transclusions.

for us the crucial point is that the argument is currently showing no sign of resolution, since neither side's claims have been subjected to sufficient empirical testing.

The perceived advantages of hypertext as an educational medium are usually ascribed to its nonlinear property. This is often contrasted with the assumed linearity of traditional text, for example: "In contrast [to hypertext] most standard text documents are constructed to be read *linearly, from beginning page to ending page*" (van den Berg & Watt, 1991, p. 118).

We have discussed the myth of linear text at length elsewhere (McKnight, Dillon & Richardson, 1991). Suffice it to say that most texts are *not* constructed to be read from beginning to end. This becomes blatantly obvious after the briefest of observations of people using "standard" text documents—e.g., journal articles, course textbooks, encyclopedias, and newspapers. How are you reading the book you are holding? Did you reach this page after reading all the preceding pages, or did you browse the contents and flick through and glance at some chapters before deciding which to read now? Even within this chapter, you may have glanced at the references first (have we referred to your work?), skipped sections (maybe you are not interested in the historical roots of *hypertext*), and so forth. Apart from the novel, very few texts are constructed to be read linearly in their entirety. As we have pointed out elsewhere, even the novel may be used in many nonlinear ways in, say, a literature class in tertiary education (Dillon & McKnight, 1990).

Hypertext has certainly become a popular term to be bandied about in education, not surprisingly since it is relatively new, technically impressive, and, until the novelty wears off, often fun to use. A brief search of the literature from 1989 to 1993, using the search terms *hypertext* OR *hypermedia* AND *learning* will yield over 100 references. The issues covered and the disciplines and journals represented are many: using multimedia with Navajo children to alleviate problems of cultural learning style, in *Reading and Writing Quarterly*; monitoring hypertext users, in *Interacting with Computers*; hypertext in cognate-language learning, in the *Journal of Computer Assisted Learning*; opportunities for hypertext in interactive learning, in the *Journal of the American Society for Information Science*.[2]

Unfortunately for present purposes, very few of these report on the systematic evaluation of hypertext in an educational setting. By *systematic evaluation,* we mean the empirical testing of real users interacting with the artifact in an ecologically valid task. The vast majority either say how wonderful hypertext is or might be, or describe some hypertext-based courseware in detail without evaluating its effectiveness. Some even equate Apple's HyperCard with hypertext, assuming that if it is built in the former, it must

be an example of the latter (e.g., Horton, Boone & Lovitt, 1990). Although these authors do perform an evaluation, their results provide evidence for computer-aided instruction rather than hypertext.

One of the earliest attempts to evaluate hypertext's potential in a learning environment was that reported by Beeman et al. (1987). Their paper reports on attempts to use the Intermedia hypertext system in two of Brown University's existing courses—an English literature course and a plant cell biology course. The evaluation of the effect of introducing hypertext was far from easy. Each of the courses was closely observed by a team of social scientists, once prior to the introduction of the hypertext and once when the hypertext materials were in use. Instructors and students were interviewed several times throughout the evaluation; a group of students was asked to keep diaries of their activities during the time the courses were taught; and the use of a specially set up computer laboratory by both students and instructors was monitored.

At first sight the effects of introducing hypertext seem to have been positive. Beeman et al. report a small positive correlation ($r = 0.29$ at 0.05 level of confidence) between high Intermedia use and high grades. However, they also report an unexpected finding that suggests that improvements may not have been attributable to the introduction of hypertext per se, but rather to factors related to its introduction. Because the Intermedia workstations were not ready in time, the professor in charge of the English course was forced to teach the course without using the system but having already prepared the Intermedia material. The result of this was that he changed the way he taught the course and subsequently felt that students grasped "pluralistic" reasoning styles better than in previous years. Furthermore, the students were more satisfied with the course than in previous years. This suggests that the need to rethink the course design may have been the major contributor to the improvement in grades. A professor who has taught the same course for years may not be as "inspiring" as he used to be, but interest may well be rekindled and communicated to the students by having to redesign the course for a new medium.

A further difficulty in making any strong statements about the apparent improvements in grades is also raised by Beeman. By themselves, the studies offer no evidence that the style of thinking fostered in these two courses transfers to other courses. As Beeman points out, students are generally good at adapting to teachers because they are interested in doing well. Hence, their results may indicate a course-specific adaptation rather than a genuine change in thinking style. However, it would be extremely difficult to test such an hypothesis, since it would involve the comparative evaluation of students across many courses.

The Beeman studies are an excellent illustration of the difficulties involved in assessing the effect of introducing not only hypertext but any new teaching technique or technology into an educational context. The Hawthorne effect, so-called because of the industrial context in which it was first *systematically* observed, is just as likely to appear in an

---

[2] Note that we are not concerned here with information retrieval from hypertext, a topic large enough to merit a separate chapter. The reader interested in exploring this topic is referred to Smeaton (1991) as a convenient starting point.

educational setting. Furthermore, Beeman's most interesting conclusion was that the significant learning effects observed through the use of Intermedia were more pronounced for the people involved in producing the materials rather than for students using the system, apparently substantiating the adage that "the best way to learn something is to teach it!"

Despite the topic of learning having formed a major section of psychology for many years, we still know very little about the cognitive processes of learning. As psychologists we recognize this as a parlous state of affairs, since many people recognize the ability to learn as a key attribute of human behavior. From the outset, psychology has sought to define, explain, and predict learning, from associative principles to laws of effect, from principles of reinforcement to cognitive skill acquisition, from mental model acquisition to constructivism. However, as Norman (1980) states boldly, "it has all come to nought." Learning, once the backbone of psychology, is now rarely found as a major component of psychology degrees but resides in specialized subdisciplines such as education. While this might be interpreted as a position of strength engendered by the subject's inherent importance, such a position is hard to justify in the absence of similar developments for other major psychological issues such as thinking, memory, perception, social interaction, and so forth. In effect, 100 years of studying learning has provided little by way of systematic knowledge for ensuring desirable learning outcomes. Hence, evaluating the interactive technology to support this process is by no means straightforward.

Hammond (1989) claims that we seem to be good at providing some appropriate environments for learning:

> . . . in teaching a child to talk, the parent merely needs to give appropriate stimulation at appropriate times; details of intermediate states of knowledge and the processes of acquisition can safely be left to the child and to the research psychologist (p. 172).

This comment is telling in that it suggests that "merely" providing the appropriate stimulation at the right time might have the desired results (a rather Skinnerian perspective for such a cognitivist to take, though with obvious Chomskian resonance!), with the learners themselves doing the rest. If this really is the best we can do, then psychology's role is less to worry about the nature of learning than to concentrate on the provision of suitable environments . . . and hypertext may be one such environment.

Hammond and Allinson (1989) suggest that hypertext can provide the basis for an exploratory learning system, but that by itself it is insufficient, needing to be supplemented by more directed guidance and access mechanisms. In order to investigate this suggestion, they conducted an experiment in which all subjects used the same material held in a hypertext form, but with differing guidance and access facilities available. The baseline group had a basic hypertext with no additional facilities, while other groups had either a map or index or guided tours available, and a final group had all three facilities (map, index, tours) available. Half of the sub-

jects were given a series of questions to answer while accessing the material (a directed task), while the other half were instructed to make use of the material to prepare for a subsequent multiple-choice test (an exploratory task).

Perhaps surprisingly, Hammond and Allinson report no reliable differences between task conditions for the three groups, which had a single additional facility, although in all three groups the facilities were used to a substantial extent. However, in the group having all three facilities available, there was a significant task-by-facility interaction. Those subjects performing the exploratory task made little use of the index but significant use of the tours, while those performing the directed task made little use of the tours and far more use of the index. Thus, Hammond and Allinson argue that after only 20 minutes, subjects were able to employ the facilities in a task-directed manner.

The additional facilities also allowed more accurate overviews of the available material and resulted in a higher rate of exposure to new rather than repeated information. However, there were no significant differences in task performance between groups. Hammond and Allinson attribute this lack of difference to the fact that neither of the tasks required any strategic organization of the material, and they therefore caution against extrapolating such results to situations other than simple rote learning of relatively unstructured material. Indeed, even the subjective judgments of the subjects—that the system was easy to use, getting lost was not a major problem, and the system was rated as "better than a book"— should be viewed in the light of the fact that the hypertext used was very small (consisting of only 39 information screens), and subjects only used the system for a maximum of 20 minutes. Although it discusses "learning support environments" and is clearly aimed at an educational context, Hammond and Allinson's work provides a contrast to the Beeman study in that its strength is its controlled, experimental nature, whereas the strength of Beeman's work is its applied, "real world" nature. Both types of study have a role to play in the attempt to discover the effects of hypertext in education.

Stanton and Stammers (1990) suggest that the reasons why a nonlinear environment might be superior are that it (a) allows for different levels of prior knowledge, (b) encourages exploration, (c) enables subjects to see a subtask as part of the whole task, and (d) allows subjects to adapt material to their own learning style. In their experiments (1989, 1990), one set of subjects was given the freedom to access a set of training modules in any order, while another set of subjects was presented with the modules in a fixed order. They reported that performance was significantly improved when subjects trained in the nonlinear condition. Although such comparisons may provide valid experimental designs, extrapolating the results to realistic learning situations is difficult, particularly in higher education where students are rarely forced to access material in a rigid, predetermined order. Hence, the results may reflect the advantage not so much of nonlinear environments but rather of giving the learner some degree of control over the learning environment—a return to the more straightforward notion of providing accessible material and letting the learners "get on with it" themselves.

It could be argued that a hypertext environment does provide for greater learner control and therefore possesses advantages over traditional paper-based learning materials. However, this suggests two equally plausible interpretations: greater control over the user's access to the hypertext's contents by way of the links provided by the author/designer, or greater control by users because they are free to follow the pathways of their choice—an option that is allegedly more difficult with printed text. The second option seems more optimistic and attractive, but experience does not give much encouragement. Given the option of following their own path through a hypertext courseware or taking a path suggested by the tutor, how many are likely to follow their own inclinations? Furthermore, how many tutors would put as much energy into generating paths through the hypertext which support a stance antithetical to their own? Students using hypertext courseware will tend to follow the paths provided by the course tutor or hypertext author. If either of these possibilities is true, then a hypertext courseware may prove more constraining than the books it replaces, which can be opened at any page.

In principle, the whole of a book or journal volume is available to the reader simply by turning page after page, whereas in hypertext, the learner is at the mercy of the author, reliant on his having provided suitable links (see 12.2.3.5.4). Even if learners are given the facility to add their own links, they must have seen the nodes at both ends of the link in order to make the judgment that a link is desirable. This makes the process of adding links seem a little more "hit-and-miss" than it is usually described.

Although the notion of control is an important one in education, it is far from clear that hypertext provides the learner with more control than traditional media. While Duchastel (1988) states that computers promote interaction through a manipulative style of learning where the student reacts to the information presented, the fact that the learner is using a mouse to select items and move through the information space does not make the process any more "active" than consulting an index, turning the pages of a book, underlining passages, and writing notes in the margin. In the main part, interactivity in education comes, as it has done for over 2,000 years, from verbal discourse.

If current hypertext systems appear to provide greater opportunities for learner control and best support exploratory styles of learning, this may in part explain the excessive zeal among their proponents for the importance of these aspects of learning. Romiszowski (1990) provides a welcome degree of caution:

> There is, however, some doubt as to whether all these process-oriented aspects of hypertext systems are necessarily "a good thing" in all manner of learning situations. The research on learner control of the learning process is, to say the least, mixed. There is much evidence to suggest that learners, when free to select their own strategies, do not always select wisely" (p. 322).

This echoes earlier suggestions that the majority of students are not able to set learning objectives for themselves and study autonomously (Bunderson, 1974; O'Shea & Self, 1983). Many undergraduate programs start with study skill courses.

A heavy emphasis on exploratory learning for younger students may soon, if not already, be seen as yet another progressive enthusiasm that flowered in the 1960s. Today it is more likely to be seen as just one useful tool in the teacher's armory—perhaps a stimulus and motivator to be used at regular intervals between sessions of more structured classwork.

At the other end of the student age spectrum, access to a wide-ranging and richly interconnected hypermedia database may be of real interest to, say, the fledgling humanities Ph.D. candidate who is trying to identify common factors that have influenced a diverse range of human activities. The term *fledgling* is used intentionally, since who else will incorporate primary documents that are accessed so very rarely (unless thesis requirements are changed to dictate that all referenced material is incorporated into the hypertext "canon"!) Undergraduates will probably still feel so overwhelmed by the extent of their workload that following associative flights of fancy, rather than sticking to the prescribed texts of the reading list, will seem at best a luxury if not sheer folly. As Whalley (1990) points out: "The hypertext reader might flit between the trees with greater ease and yet still not perceive the shape of the wood any better than before."

The scientific principle of parsimony, of adopting the most simple explanation, is worth applying to learning and the new media. "Pluralistic reasoning" to some is "confused thinking" to others, and given the far-from-certain results of much cognitive psychological work on mental representations and knowledge construction, as well as the ongoing revisionism in the educational field, we might best consider hypertext as an information-accessing medium and the learner as a seeker of information before positing elaborate notions of thinking style that prove difficult to validate empirically.

Adopting such a perspective allows us to shift our concern from theorizing about the mental activity of learning to designing an information environment that can support task performance. We will return to this point later, but before outlining an approach that could help improve the design of hypertexts, we will review some of the studies that have actually attempted, with varying degrees of success, to evaluate hypertext systems in an educational context.

In a study by Gordon and Lewis (1992), 80 subjects read a tutorial about a state-of-the-art hi-fi videocassette recorder in either a linear format or one of two hypertext formats (unconstrained network or constrained structure). They were then asked to summarize the tutorial, answer a series of questions, and solve two problems using the hi-fi VCR to perform particular tasks. For the factual questions, subjects using the linear form of the information scored significantly higher than either of the hypertext groups, which did not differ from each other. For the problem-solving tasks, subjects using the constrained hypertext performed equivalently to the linear subject, with the free network subjects performing significantly worse. The authors conclude that: "If it is critical that students learn the details of material in a document, the instructor cannot rely on the student to hypertext [sic] through the information and acquire it; linear formats should probably be retained" (p. 307). It is a pity that these authors did not include a condition in which subjects used the traditional paper manual.

A study by Higgins and Boone (1990) compared the effectiveness of a hypertext study guide used either in combination with or instead of lectures. Forty ninth-grade students (mean age 14.6 years) enrolled in a course in Washington State history took part. Of the 40, there were 10 with learning disabilities, 15 remedial students, and 15 regular students. They were randomly allocated to the three conditions of (1) lecture alone, (2) lecture plus study guide, and (3) study guide alone. Their results led them to conclude that "The hypertext computer study guide is as effective an instructional medium for students with learning disabilities, remedial students, and regular education students as a well-prepared lecture, as measured by recall and retention of information both factual and inferential" (p. 539). They drew identical conclusions for the combination of study guide and lecture and suggested that the study guide could provide some students with the practice necessary to increase quiz performance. Strangely, the authors appear not to have considered subjective preference. If there was not much to choose between them in terms of outcome, then the more attractive system has a major advantage in terms of student motivation, especially with less able students.

Despite our criticism above of van den Berg and Watt's (1991) view of text linearity, the study reported in their paper is worthy of consideration. In a design similar to that of Higgins and Boone (1990), they compared the effectiveness of a hypertext document containing material on introductory statistics and hypothesis testing. In a "competitive" condition, a random sample of 28 students used the hypertext during a 6-week period when they did not attend lectures, while the remaining 81 students continued to attend lectures. In a "supplementary" condition, 30 randomly selected students were given the hypertext to use at their discretion, while the remaining 72 were not allowed access to it. In the "replacement" condition, the hypertext served as the sole source of instruction, and there were no accompanying lectures. These conditions were run over three consecutive semesters; subjects were senior-level communications sciences majors.

Interestingly, although there were no significant differences in the objective performances of the groups, the subjective acceptance of hypertext was highest in the supplementary condition and lowest in the competitive condition. The authors suggest that subjects in the competitive condition may have been influenced by the contrast between being left to their own devices compared with the guidance they perceived the control group receiving. They conclude that the most suitable use for hypertext might be as a replacement for in-person instruction where teaching is not available.

Jonassen, one of the most prolific of authors in the field of hypertext and learning, recently reported on a series of three studies attempting to evaluate hypertext (Jonassen, 1993). In terms of structural knowledge acquisition, Jonassen was forced to conclude that his results called into question "the ability of learners to engage in meaningful learning rather than information retrieval from hypertext, especially in the context of a learning environment" (p. 165). Far from being the "natural" learning environment that somehow reflects semantic memory, Jonassen suggests that "A fair evaluation of learning from hypertext can only come from hypertext-literate learners who have developed a useful set of strategies for navigating and integrating information from hypertext" (p. 165).

Marchionini and Shneiderman (1988) have suggested that hypertext is more suited to browsing than directed retrieval tasks. Following from this suggestion, Jones (1989) hypothesized that more incidental learning would occur in a browsing task than in a task requiring the use of an index. The argument advanced by Jones was that the links in a hypertext node represent an embedded menu and that the context provided by the node should encourage the connection of the ideas at either end of the link. In other words, the learner's semantic net is more likely to be elaborated or more learning is likely to occur.

Two groups of subjects were used in Jones's experiment. Both groups used the same hypertext database, but one group was shown how to browse through the information using the links and were explicitly instructed not to use the index, while the other group were instructed in the use of the index and were not informed about the active nature of the highlighted words on screen (which were described to them as "clues to other index entries"). Subjects were given 5 questions to answer from the database, but afterwards were given 10 questions to measure incidental learning.

Although Jones's argument has intuitive appeal, her experiment failed to support her hypothesis. No significant differences were observed in terms of performance on the incidental learning questions. It is possible that the nature of the questions given to the subjects to answer from the database did not encourage incidental learning. This is certainly suggested by the low overall success level of subjects on the incidental learning test—the *highest* mean number correct for any group was 1.56. Even in the five target questions, taking all groups together, no question was answered correctly by more than half of the subjects. This suggests that the task was not particularly sensitive to the effect of the experimental manipulations, and hence we can do little more than agree with Jones that "much more research is needed."

In total, these studies illustrate the problems that befall most evaluations of hypertext in education: difficulties in controlled experimentation, difficulties in finding ecologically valid tasks, difficulties in describing process and difficulties of defining—let alone measuring—the outcomes of learning. Marchionini (1990) sums it up: "The essential problem of evaluating highly interactive systems is in measuring both the quality of the interaction as well as the product of learning. Evaluations of hypermedia-based learning must address the process of learning and the outcomes of learning" (p. 20.6).

If there has been inadequate evaluation of the hypertext systems that have been implemented, does this prevent the design of a new generation of improved hypertext systems? We answer this question both Yes and No! There can be no possibility of progress without reliable and convincing evaluation, but there are certain established ways to improve the design of the initial system. These are the views underlying user-centered system design and the view of hypertexts and their users as one form of system.

21.4 USER-CENTERED DESIGN

User-centered design has emerged as the prevalent technological design philosophy (see 12.4.1) in recent years in response to an increased awareness that interactive computer-based systems often failed to achieve the goals of their designers, especially in relation to user requirements and consequently user satisfaction. The conceptual theory has been recast in more operational terms as enhancing a system or product's "usability" with measurable objectives such as speed of learning, reduction in error, task efficiency, and effectiveness in and reduction in need of support requirements.

To understand the usability issues underlying hypertext, it is helpful to conceptualize the system in terms of four basic factors: the users, their tasks, the information space in which the task is being performed, and the environment or context in which all these interact.

21.4.1 The Users

Users vary tremendously in terms of the skills, habits, intentions, and numerous other attributes that they bring to the computer when interacting with hypertext. Information technology's rapid development over the last decade and its penetration into almost every sphere of human activity has raised new challenges in terms of design assumptions. It can no longer be assumed that users will be trained computer scientists or IT professionals who have experience of a wide range of systems or applications. User interfaces, particularly in educational and public access applications, must be designed with the assumption that some users may well bring no previous computing knowledge with them to the interface. Since contemporary thinking rightly stresses that technology should be designed with the users' needs in mind, an essential first stage of user-centered design methods is the analysis of users' skills and requirements.

21.4.2 The Tasks

The tasks that can be performed with documents are also extremely variable. People read texts for pleasure, to solve problems, to stimulate ideas, or to monitor developments, for example. Since such interactions also vary widely in terms of time, effort, and skill involved, then when we consider the development of a new information presentation medium, we must also determine the nature of the tasks it is intended to

support if we are to avoid catch-all phrases or claims such as "hypermedia is better than paper."

21.4.3 The Information Space

These first two terms are relatively self-explanatory, but *information space* is a more vague term, by which is meant the document, database, texts, and so forth on which the user works (see 26.5.2). An information space could therefore be as small as a single text fragment or as large as an on-line database, national archive, or university library. It is the presence of a boundary rather than the size or number of items which defines the concept. The information spaces currently in existence are numerous (just think of all the types of documents that are available in the paper domain), but these are likely to be overrun with new forms of information space in the hypermedia world when graphics, sound, video, and immersive graphics eventually appear. Information type can be shown to interact with both users and tasks; i.e., people utilize information differently depending on its type, their experience, and what they want from it (Dillon et al., 1989).

21.4.4 The Centrality of Context

Of course all three basic factors come together to provide some context—the scenario in which certain users interact with particular information to perform specific tasks (see 12.3.1.2) . In embracing user-centered principles for design, it is essential that the contextual variables are clearly specified. A doctoral student and a solicitor may both be searching an on-line database for references to relevant material, but one may be looking for *any* relevant item while the other may be looking for a specific supporting case. To assume that this is the same task, or that these users are equivalent and could be supported by the same system would be simplistic and lead to the sort of confused reasoning that posits "hypertext is better (or worse!) than paper." Such statements betray a naive acceptance of commonality of purpose and ability on the part of all potential users and is almost certain to lead to lack of usability in systems design.

21.4.5 Usability and Hypertext

Jonassen (1990) recognizes the central connection between hypertext design and user requirements: "The most significant problem in creating hypermedia is deciding how to structure the information. The answer to this question depends, in part, upon how the hypermedia will be used" (p. 12). Wright (1990) also supports a strongly user-centered approach to hypertext design for educational applications. In response to the rhetorical question as to "what really matters?" in hypertext design, she gives an unequivocal answer: "The answer will nearly always depend upon the task that the learner is engaged in. This task will determine the functionality required by the learner . . ." (p. 171).

For some learning tasks, minimal requirements might seem obvious: CD-quality sound for poetry and language students, high-resolution screens for students of the visual arts, and large-format screens for designers. Yet even these would hardly ensure learning and at best could only be considered the starting point for a user-centered design. However, for many learning contexts the functional requirements are not even that specifiable, particularly when interface and information structures are at issue. The only solution is a fine-grained task analysis that cannot only determine the functionality but also the particular instantiation that is most appropriate for the range of users. As Wright points out, there are often many ways in which a function can be provided—just think of the number of ways in which a database can be searched.

The microcomputer has been justifiably celebrated as a real general-purpose tool. Ironically, the hypertext designer may have to constrain the computer in order to empower the user. While the computer can be programmed to undertake highly complex transformations on abstract data structures, the majority of users are more inclined to think in terms of simple transformations on more "concrete" or familiar data structures.

It may seem that we are arguing for a different hypertext instantiation for every learning context based on a new and detailed task analysis. Without a backward look at existing user models of data structures, this would probably be a recipe for chaos. Evidence for this suggestion comes directly from the evolution of our most successful information technology—the printed book.

We have had nearly 500 years experience of using printed textbooks, and they not only support a wide range of applications but users also have such a strong mental model of their generic structure and organization that they can successfully adopt an equally wide range of usage strategies. What we understand as the book's standard structure, both physical and organizational, evolved over time, and readers' models also developed and accommodated these changes. However, the enduring success of the book as an artifact is largely due to a faithful adherence to common user expectations—change took place but only very slowly.

While it is clear that hypertext can support activities impossible or very difficult to perform with paper, we must be sure that we introduce such designs in order to improve our support of, or to enable, valid learning tasks. It is not sufficient that we can browse a million pages on our desktop, or link 100 articles together for rapid retrieval at the click of a mouse button: such capabilities are only important in terms of their utility to human learners. Yet there are few signs that most learning scenarios require such support, and little knowledge on how we might best provide it in terms of usability, even if it were required.

21.4.6 Beyond Media Differences—Information Structures and Knowledge Representation

It is clear that readers form mental representations of a paper document's structure in terms of spatial location (Lovelace & Southall, 1983) and overall organization. Dillon (1991), for example, has shown that experienced academic journal readers can predict the location within an article of isolated selections of material from it with a high degree of accuracy, even when they cannot read the target material in detail. Such representations or models are derived from years of exposure to the information type or can be formed in the case of spatial recall from a quick scan of the material. Such models or superstructural representations (van Dijk & Kintsch, 1983; see 5.3.7) are useful in terms of predicting where information will be found or even what type of information is available. Consideration of existing models is vital in the design of new versions so as to avoid designing against the intended users' views of how the information should be organized.

The qualitative differences between the models readers possess for paper and electronic documents can easily be appreciated by considering what you can tell about either at first glance. A paper text is extremely informative. When we open a hypertext document, however, we do not have the same amount of information available to us. We are likely to be faced with a welcoming screen that might give us a rough idea of the contents (i.e., subject matter) and information about the authors/developers of the document, but little else.

Hypertext may appear to be a completely new presentation format and therefore free to establish new user models based on the radically new technology. Unfortunately for the creative system designer, the current generation of potential users approach the new technology with expectations that are grounded in print. This is not surprising when the primary content of most hypermedia systems is, and may well continue to be, text. It may be electronic rather than printed, but that can be a minor difference to the user.

Some researchers have accepted this legacy and constructed hypertext systems that rest heavily on not only the conceptual structure but the physical format as well. Benest's (1990) hypertext system employs a realistic on-screen representation of an open book with pages that can be "turned." The system was not designed, or developed, with the benefit of empirical studies, but it is intuitively appealing and an impressive achievement in its time.

In contrast, the SuperBook developed at Bellcore and described comprehensively by Landauer et al. (1993) has benefited from exhaustive user studies (see 30.11.1). SuperBook incorporates a number of familiar print conventions but does not attempt to reinvent the printed book on screen. Instead, development effort has been directed to enhancing the application's intelligent features in a manner that users can employ effectively. In comparative trials, SuperBook has proved superior to printed texts in terms of speed and accuracy for search-type tasks—but only after repeated tests and redesigns on the basis of those tests (see 12.4.1.2).

What is important to note is that experienced readers have acquired expectations of how information spaces are organized, and we need to be aware of this in our designs. It is precisely because such models of information are often ignored that we read so much of the navigation problem for users of hypertext (see Dillon, McKnight & Richardson, 1993).

21.5 CONCLUSIONS

If there is little reliable evidence (yet) to support the claims that hypertext systems can really support alternative and superior modes of learning, and we have few effective means of measuring the process of learning anyway, what does that leave us? Three compatible options are available: a reduction in expectations, a switch from process to outcome, and a concentration on an evolutionary approach to development, building on user models rather than trying to make a step-function change: Mao's thousand-mile march started with the first step!

A reduction in expectations is probably now due, given the amount of hype that has accompanied the popularization of hypermedia. As any marketing executive will tell you, a certain amount of hype is necessary in order to stand out against the background noise. However, now that hypermedia has gained a certain amount of acceptance, we can afford to be a little more realistic in our expectations.

A switch from process to outcome might seem reasonable, given our arguments to the effect that psychology does not have a good understanding of the process. Unfortunately, it is no simple matter to measure "learning" as an outcome. Notwithstanding the fact that the education system lumbers on, those involved in the system continue to search for ways that truly reflect meaningful changes in learners as a result of their experiences with the system. It is somewhat ironic that the current emphasis within the British tertiary education system is on measuring the quality of teaching, yet we do not have a philosophically defensible measure of learning against which to judge the teaching function.

Our own preference, as the foregoing has hopefully argued convincingly in favor of, is for an evolutionary approach to system development. However, we take a proactive view of evolution rather than see it as a simple environmental winnowing. We believe that, rather than generating many systems and relying on the "survival of the fittest," it is possible to design "the fittest" for any context by utilizing user-centered, task-based design grounded in an empirical methodology. While we have certain sympathies with the humanistic emphases of the constructivist movement (see 7.4), we find the general scientific approach more fruitful. When the constructivists have achieved as much as the scientists, we may be persuaded otherwise. After all, the essence of science is a mind open to data. For now, the debate continues.

REFERENCES

Beeman, W.O., Anderson, K.T., Bader, G., Larkin, J., McClard, A.P., McQuilian, P. & Shields, M. (1987). Hypertext and pluralism: from lineal to non-lineal thinking. *Proceedings of Hypertext '87,* 67–88. University of North Carolina, Chapel Hill.

Benest, I.D. (1990). A hypertext system with controlled hype. *In* R. McAleese & C. Green, eds. *Hypertext: state of the art,* 52–63. Oxford, England: Intellect.

Berners-Lee, T., Cailliau, R., Luotonen, A., Nielsen, H.F. & Secret, A. (1994). The World-Wide Web. *Communications of the ACM 37* (8), 76–82.

Brown, P.J. (1986). Interactive documentation. *Software—Practice and Experience 16* (3), 291–99.

Bunderson, C.V. (1974). The design and production of learner-controlled software for the TICCIT system: a progress report. *International Journal of Man-Machine Studies 6,* 479–92.

Bush, V. (1945). As we may think. *Atlantic Monthly,* 176/1, 101–08.

Conklin, J. (1987). Hypertext: an introduction and survey. *IEEE Computer,* 17–41.

Cunningham, D.J., Duffy, T.M. & Knuth, R.A. (1993). The textbook of the future. *In* C. McKnight, A. Dillon & J. Richardson, eds. *Hypertext: a psychological perspective,* 19–49. Chichester, England: Horwood.

Dillon, A. (1991). Readers' models of text structures: the case of academic articles. *International Journal of Man-Machine Studies 35,* 913–25.

— & McKnight, C. (1990). Towards a classification of text types: a repertory grid approach. *International Journal of Man-Machine Studies 33,* 623–36.

—, — & Richardson, J. (1993). Space—the final chapter *or* why physical representations are not semantic intentions. *In* C. McKnight, A. Dillon & J. Richardson, eds. *Hypertext: a psychological perspective,* 169–91. Chichester, England: Horwood.

—, Richardson, J. & McKnight, C. (1989). The human factors of journal usage and the design of electronic text. *Interacting with Computers 1* (2), 183–89.

Duchastel, P. (1988). Display and interaction features of instructional texts and computers. *British Journal of Educational Technology 19* (1), 58–65.

Engelbart, D.C. (1963). A conceptual framework for the augmentation of man's intellect. *In* P.W. Howerton & D.C. Weeks, eds. *Vistas in information handling,* 1–29. Vol. 1. London: Cleaver-Hume.

Gordon, S. & Lewis, V. (1992). Enhancing hypertext documents to support learning from text. *Technical Communication,* 305–08.

Greeno, J.G., Carlton, T.J., DaPolito, F. & Polson, P.G. (1978). *Associative learning: a cognitive analysis.* Engelwood Cliffs, NJ: Prentice Hall.

Hammond, N. (1989). Hypermedia and learning: who guides whom? *In* H. Maurer, ed. *Computer assisted learning,* 167–81. Berlin, Germany: Springer.

— & Allinson, L. (1989). The travel metaphor as design principle and training aid for navigating around complex systems. *In* D. Diaper & R. Winder, eds. *People and computers III.* Cambridge, England: Cambridge University Press.

Higgins, K. & Boone, R. (1990). Hypertext computer study guides and the social studies achievement of students with learning disabilities, remedial students, and regular education students. *Journal of Learning Disabilities 23* (9), 529–40.

Hillinger, M. (1990). Responsive text: a training environment for literacy and job skills. In *Proceedings of the Human*

Factors Society 34th Annual Meeting, 1422–25. Santa Monica, CA: The Human Factors Society.

Horton, S.V., Boone, R.A. & Lovitt, T.C. (1990). Teaching social studies to learning disabled high school students: effects of a hypertext study guide. *British Journal of Educational Technology 21*(2), 118–31.

Howe, M.J.A. (1980). *The psychology of human learning.* New York: Harper & Row.

Jonassen, D.H. & Grabinger, S. (1990). Problems and issues in designing hypertext/hypermedia for learning. *In* D.H. Jonassen & H. Mandl, eds. *Designing hypermedia for learning,* 3–25. Heidelberg, Germany: Springer.

— (1993). Effects of semantically structured hypertext knowledge bases on users' knowledge structures. *In* C. McKnight, A. Dillon & J. Richardson, eds. *Hypertext: a psychological perspective,* 153–68. Chichester, England: Horwood.

Jones, T. (1989). Incidental learning during information retrieval: a hypertext experiment. *In* H. Maurer, ed. *Computer assisted learning,* 235–51. Berlin, Germany: Springer.

Landauer, T., Egan, D., Remde, J., Lesk, M., Lochbaum, C. & Ketchum, D. (1993). Enhancing the usability of text through computer delivery and formative evaluation: the SuperBook project. *In* C. McKnight, A. Dillon & J. Richardson, eds. *Hypertext: a psychological perspective,* 71–136. Chichester, England: Horwood.

Lovelace, E.A. & Southall, S.D. (1983). Memory for words in prose and their locations on the page. *Memory and Cognition 11* (5), 429–34.

Marchionini, G. (1990). Evaluating hypermedia-based learning. *In* D.H. Jonassen & H. Mandl, eds. *Designing hypermedia for learning,* 355–73. Heidelberg, Germany: Springer.

— & Shneiderman, B. (1988). Finding facts versus browsing knowledge in hypertext systems. *IEEE Computer,* Jan., 70–80.

McKnight, C., Dillon, A. & Richardson, J. (1991). *Hypertext in context.* Cambridge, England: Cambridge University Press.

McLuhan, M. (1964). *Understanding Media.* London, England: Routledge & Kegan Paul.

Nelson, T.H. (1988, Jan.). Managing immense storage. *Byte,*

225–38.

Nielsen, J. (1990). *Hypertext and hypermedia.* Boston, MA: Academic.

Norman, D.A. (1980). Twelve issues for cognitive science. *Cognitive Science 4,* 1–33.

O'Shea, T. & Self, J. (1983). *Learning and teaching with computers.* Brighton, England: Harvester.

Polanyi, M. (1957). *Personal knowledge.* Cambridge, England: Cambridge University Press.

Romiszowski, A.J. (1990). The hypertext/hypermedia solution—but what exactly is the problem? *In* D.H. Jonassen & H. Mandl, eds. *Designing hypermedia for learning,* 321–54. Heidelberg, Germany: Springer.

Smeaton, A.F. (1991). Retrieving information from hypertext: issues and problems. *European Journal of Information Systems 1,* 239–47.

Stanton, N.A. & Stammers, R.B. (1989). A comparison of structured and unstructured navigation through a computer based training package for a simulated industrial task. Paper presented to the Symposium on Computer Assisted Learning—CAL 89, University of Surrey, England.

— & — (1990). Learning styles in a non-linear training environment. *In* R. McAleese & C. Green, eds. *Hypertext: state of the art,* 114–20. Oxford, England: Intellect.

van den Berg, S. & Watt, J.H. (1991). Effects of educational setting on student responses to structured hypertext. *Journal of Computer-Based Instruction 18* (4), 118–24.

van Dijk, T.A. & Kintsch, W. (1983). *Strategies of discourse comprehension.* New York: Academic.

Whalley, P. (1990). Models of hypertext structure and learning. *In* D.H. Jonassen & H. Mandl, eds. *Designing hypermedia for learning,* 61–67. Heidelberg, Germany: Springer.

— (1993). An alternative rhetoric for hypertext. *In* C. McKnight, A. Dillon & J. Richardson, eds. *Hypertext: a psychological perspective,* 7–17. Chichester, England: Horwood.

Wright, P.(1990). Hypertexts as an interface for learners: some human factors issues. *In* D.H. Jonassen & H. Mandl, eds. *Designing hypermedia for learning,* 169–84. Heidelberg, Germany: Springer.

22. ADAPTIVE INSTRUCTIONAL SYSTEMS

Ok-choon Park
U.S. ARMY RESEARCH INSTITUTE

A central and persisting issue in educational technology is the provision of instructional environments and conditions that can comply with individually different educational goals and learning abilities. Instructional approaches and techniques that are geared to meet the needs of the individually different student are called *adaptive instruction* (Corno & Snow, 1986). More specifically, adaptive instruction refers to educational interventions aimed at effectively accommodating individual differences in students while helping each student develop the knowledge and skills required to learn a task. Adaptive instruction is generally characterized as an educational approach that incorporates alternative procedures and strategies for instruction and resource utilization and has the built-in flexibility to permit students to take various routes to, and amounts of time for, learning (Wang & Lindvall, 1984). Glaser (1977) described three essential ingredients of adaptive instruction. First, it provides a variety of alternatives for learning and many goals from which to choose. Second, it attempts to utilize and develop the capabilities that an individual brings to the alternatives for his or her learning and to adjust to the learner's particular talents, strengths, and weaknesses. Third, it attempts to strengthen an individual's ability to meet the demands of available educational opportunities and develop the skills necessary for success in the complex world.

Adaptive instruction has been interchangeably used with *individualized instruction* in the literature (Wang & Lindvall, 1984; Reiser, 1987). However, they are different depending on specific methods and procedures employed during instruction. Any type of instruction presented in a one-on-one setting can be considered individualized instruction. However, if that instruction is not flexible enough to meet the student's specific learning needs, it cannot be considered adaptive. Similarly, even though instruction is provided in a group environment, it can be adaptive if it is sensitive to the unique needs of each student as well as the common needs of the group. Ideal individualized instruction should be adaptive, since instruction will be most powerful when it is adapted to unique needs of each individual. It can be easily assumed that the superiority of individualized instruction over group instruction reported in many studies (e.g., Bloom, 1984; Kulik, 1982) is due to the adaptive nature of the individualized instruction.

The long history of thoughts and admonition for adapting instruction to individual student's needs has been documented by many researchers (e.g., Corno & Snow, 1986; Federico, 1980; Reiser, 1987; Tobias, 1989). Since at least the fourth century BC, adapting has been viewed as a primary factor for the success of instruction (Corno & Snow, 1986), and adaptive instruction by tutoring was the common method of education until the mid-1800s (Reiser, 1987). Even after graded systems were adopted, the importance of adapting instruction to individual needs was continuously emphasized. For example, Dewey, in his 1902 essay, "Child and Curriculum," deplored the current emphasis on a single kind of curriculum development that produced a uniform, inflexible sequence of instruction that ignored or minimized the child's individual peculiarities, whims, and experiences (1902/1964). Nine years later, Thorndike (1911) argued for a specialization of instruction that acknowledged differences among pupils within a single class as well as specialization of the curriculum for different classes. Since then, various approaches and methods have been proposed and attempted to provide adaptive instruction to individually different students (see Reiser, 1987, for early systems).

Particularly since Cronbach (1957) declared that a united discipline of psychology not only will be interested in organism and treatment variables but also will be concerned with the otherwise ignored interactions between organism and treatment variables, numerous studies have been conducted to investigate what kinds of student characteristics and background variables should be considered in adapting instruction to individuals and how instructional methods and procedures should be adapted to those characteristics and variables (Cronbach, 1971; Cronbach & Snow, 1977; Federico, 1980; Snow & Swanson, 1992). It is surprising, however, to realize how little scientific evidence has been accumulated for such adaptations and how difficult it is to provide guidelines to practitioners for making such adaptations.

This chapter has four objectives: (a) selectively to review systematic efforts for establishing and implementing adaptive instruction, (b) to discuss theoretical paradigms and research variables studied to provide theoretical bases and development guidelines of adaptive instruction, (c) to discuss problems and limitations of the current approach to adaptive instruction, and (d) to propose a response-sensitive approach to the development of an adaptive instruction.

22.1 ADAPTIVE INSTRUCTION: THREE APPROACHES

The efforts to develop and implement adaptive instruction have taken different approaches based on the aspects of instruction that are intended to adapt to different students. The first approach is to adapt instruction on a macrolevel by allowing different alternatives in selecting only a few main components of instruction such as instructional goals, depth of curriculum content, delivery systems, etc. Most adaptive instructional systems developed as alternatives to the traditional lock-step group instruction in school environments have taken this approach. In this macro-approach, instructional alternatives are mostly selected on the basis of the student's instructional goals, general ability, and achievement levels in the curriculum structure. The second approach is to adapt specific instructional procedures and strategies to specific student characteristics. Since this approach requires the identification of the most relevant learner characteristics (or aptitudes) for the instruction and the selection of instructional strategies that best facilitate the learning process of the students who have the aptitudes, it is called *aptitude-treatment interactions* (ATI). The third approach is to adapt instruction on a microlevel by diagnosing the student's specific learning needs during instruction and providing instructional prescriptions for the needs. Since this microapproach is designed to guide the student's ongoing learning process throughout the instruction, the diagnosis and prescription are often continuously performed from the analysis of the student's performance on the task.

The degree of adaptation is determined by how sensitive the diagnostic procedure is to the specific learning needs of each student and how much the prescriptive activities are tailored to the learner's needs. Depending on the available resources and constraints in the given situation, the instruction can be designed to be adaptive using a different combination of the three approaches. However, the student in an ideal micro-adaptive system is supposed to achieve his or her instructional objective by following the guidance that the system provides. The rapid development of computer technology has provided a powerful tool for developing and implementing micro-adaptive instructional systems more efficiently than ever before. Thus, in this chapter micro-adaptive instructional systems and the related issues are

reviewed and discussed more thoroughly than macro-adaptive systems and ATI approaches.

22.2 MACRO-ADAPTIVE INSTRUCTIONAL SYSTEMS

Early attempts to adapt the instructional process to individual learners in school education were certainly macrolevel because the students were simply grouped or tracked by grades or scores from ability tests. This homogeneous grouping had minimal effect because the groups seldom received different kinds of instructional treatments (Tennyson, 1975). In the early 1900s, however, a number of adaptive systems were developed to better accommodate different student abilities. As examples, Reiser (1987) described the Burke plan, Dalton plan, and Winnetka plan that were developed in the early 1900s. The main adaptive feature in these plans was that the student was allowed to go through the instructional materials at her or his own pace. The notion of mastery learning was also fostered in Dalton and Winnetka plans (Reiser, 1987).

Since macro-adaptive instruction is frequently used within a class to aid the differentiation of teaching operations over larger segments of instruction, it often involves a repeated sequence of "recitation" activity initiated by teachers' behaviors in classrooms (Corno & Snow, 1983). For example, a typical pattern of teaching is: (a) explaining or presenting specific information, (b) asking questions to monitor student learning, and (c) providing appropriate feedback for the student's responses.

Several macro-adaptive instructional systems developed in the 1960s are briefly reviewed below.

22.2.1 Keller Plan

In 1963, Keller and his associates (Keller, 1968, 1974) at Columbia University developed a macro-adaptive system called the *Keller plan* in which the instructional process was personalized for each student. The program incorporated four unique features: (a) requiring mastery of each unit before moving to the next unit, (b) allowing self-learning pace, (c) using textbooks and workbooks as the primary instructional means, and (d) using student proctors for evaluating student performance and providing feedback. The Keller plan was used at many colleges and universities throughout the world (Reiser, 1987) during the late 1960s and early 1970s.

22.2.2 Audio-Tutorial System

In 1961, the Audio-Tutorial System (Postlethwait, Novak & Murray, 1972) was developed at Purdue University by applying audiovisual media, particularly audiotape. The unique feature of this audio-tutorial approach was a tutorial-like instruction using audiotapes, along with other media like texts, slides, models, etc. This approach was effectively used for teaching college science courses (Postlethwait, 1981).

22.2.3 PLAN

In 1967, Flanagan and his associates (Flanagan, Shanner, Brudner & Marker, 1975) developed a Program for Learning in Accordance with Needs (PLAN) to provide students with options for selecting different instructional objectives and learning materials. For the selected instructional objective(s), the student needed to study a specific instructional unit and demonstrate the mastery before advancing to the next unit for other objective(s). In the early 1970s, more than 100 elementary schools participated in this program.

22.2.4 Mastery Learning Systems

A popular approach to individualized instruction was developed by Bloom and his associates at the University of Chicago (Block, 1980). In this mastery learning system, virtually every student achieves the given instructional objectives by having sufficient instructional time and materials for her or his learning. "Formative" examination is given to determine whether the student needs more time to master the given unit, and "summative" examination is given to determine mastery. The mastery learning approach was widely used in the United States and several foreign countries. The basic notion of mastery learning, initially proposed by Carroll (1963), is still alive at many schools and other educational institutes. However, the instructional adaptiveness of this mastery learning approach is mostly limited to the "time" variable.

22.2.5 IGE

A more comprehensive macro-adaptive instructional system, called Individually Guided Education (IGE), was developed at the University of Wisconsin in 1965 (Klausmeier, 1975, 1976). In IGE, instructional objectives are first determined for each student based on his or her academic-ability profile, which includes diagnostic assessments in reading and mathematics, previous achievements, and other aptitude and motivation data. Then, to accommodate different student-learning abilities and styles, the teacher determines necessary guidance for each student, and selects alternative instructional materials (e.g., text, audiovisuals, group activities, etc.) and interactions with other students. The goals and implementation methods of this program could be changed to comply with the school's educational assumptions and institutional traditions (Klausmeier, 1977). However, an evaluation study by Popkewitz, Tabachnick, and Wehlage (1982) reported that the implementation and maintenance of IGE in existing school systems were greatly constrained by the school environments.

22.2.6 IPI

The Individually Prescribed Instructional System (IPI) was developed by the Learning Research and Development Center (LRDC) at the University of Pittsburgh in 1964 to provide students with adaptive instructional environments (Glaser, 1977). In IPI, the student was assigned to an instructional unit within a course according to the student's performance on a placement test given before the instruction. Within the unit, a pretest was given to determine which objectives the student needed to study. Learning materials required to master the instructional objectives were prescribed. After studying each unit, students took a posttest to determine their mastery of the unit. The student was required to master specific objectives for the instructional unit before advancing to the next unit.

22.2.7 ALEM

The LRDC extended IPI with more various types of diagnosis methods, remedial activities, and instructional prescriptions. The extended system is called the Adaptive Learning Environments Model (ALEM) (Wang, 1980). The main functions of ALEM include: (a) instructional management for providing learning guidelines on the use of instructional time and resources materials, (b) guidance for parental involvements at home in learning activities provided at school, (c) a procedure for team teaching and group activities, and (d) staff development for training teachers to implement the system (Corno & Snow, 1983). An evaluation study (Wang & Walberg, 1983) reported that 96% of teachers were able to establish and maintain the ALEM in teaching economically disadvantaged children (kindergarten through grade 3), and that the degree of its implementation was associated with students' efficient use of learning time and with constructive classroom behaviors and processes.

22.2.8 CMI Systems

Well-designed computer-managed instructional (CMI) systems have functions to diagnose student learning needs and prescribe instructional activities appropriate for the needs. For example, the Plato Learning Management (PLM) System at Control Data Corporation had functions to give a test on different levels of instruction: an instructional module, lesson, course, and curriculum. An instructional module was designed to teach one or more instructional objectives; a lesson consisted of one or more modules; a course consisted of one or more lessons; and a curriculum had one or more courses. The PLM can evaluate each student's performance on the test and provide specific instructional prescriptions. For example, if a student's score has not reached the mastery criterion for a specific instructional objective on the module test, the PLM assigns a learning activity or activities for the student. After studying the learning activities, the student is required to take the test again. When the student demonstrates the mastery of all objectives in the module, the student is allowed to move to the next module. Depending on the instructor or instructional administrator's choice, the student can complete the lesson, course, or curriculum by taking only corresponding module tests, although the student may be required to take additional summary tests on the lesson level, course level, and curriculum level. In either case, this test-evaluation-assignment process is continued until the student demonstrates the mastery of all the objectives, modules, lessons, courses, and curriculum. In addition to the test-evaluation-prescription process, the PLM provides several other features important in adapting instruction to the student's needs and ability: (a) the instructor is allowed to choose appropriate objectives, modules, lessons, and courses in the curriculum for each student to study; (b) the student can decide the sequence of instructional activities by choosing a specific module to study; (c) frequently, more than one learning activity is associated with an instructional objective, and the student has the option to choose which activity or activities to study; and (d) since most learning activities associated with the PLM are instructor-free, the student can choose the time to study it and progress at his or her own pace.

As described above in the PLM functions, well-designed CMI systems provide many important macro-adaptive instructional features. While the value of a CMI system has been well understood, its actual use has been limited due to the need for a central computer system that allows the instructor to monitor and control the student's learning activities at different locations and different times. However, the dramatic increase of personal computer (PC) capability and the simple procedure to make linkages among PCs make it easy to provide a personalized CMI system.

Ross and Morrison (1988) developed a macro-adaptive system combining some of the basic functions of CMI (e.g., prescription of instruction) and some of the features of micro-adaptive models (e.g., prediction of student learning needs). Unlike the PLM, this system was designed primarily for providing adaptive instruction rather than managing the instructional process. However, the student's learning needs are diagnosed only from preinstructional data, and a new instructional prescription cannot be generated until the next unit of instruction begins. This system consisted of three basic steps: First, variables for predicting the student's performance on the task are selected (e.g., measures of prior knowledge, reading comprehension, locus of control, and anxiety). Second, a predictive equation is developed using multiple regression analysis. Third, instructional prescription (e.g., necessary number of examples estimated to learn the task) was selected based on the student's predicted performance. This system was developed by simplifying a micro-adaptive model (trajectory/multiple regression approach) described in a later section.

The macro-adaptive instructional programs described above are representative examples that have been instantiated and used in existing educational systems. As mentioned at the beginning of this chapter, macro-adaptive instruction, except for CMI systems, has been a common practice in many school classrooms for a long time, although the adaptive procedures have been mostly unsystematic and primitive with the magnitude of adaptation widely different among teachers. Thus, several different models have been proposed to examine analytically the different levels and methods of adaptive instruction and to provide guidance for developing adaptive instructional programs.

22.3 MACRO-ADAPTIVE INSTRUCTIONAL MODELS

22.3.1 A Taxonomy of Macro-Adaptive Instruction

Corno and Snow (1983) developed a taxonomy of adaptive instruction to provide systematic guidance in selecting instructional mediation (i.e., activities) depending on the objectives of adaptive instruction and student aptitudes. Corno and Snow distinguished two different objectives of adaptive instruction: (a) aptitude development necessary for further instruction such as cognitive skills and strategies useful in later problem solving and effective decision making, and (b) circumvention or compensation for existing sources of inaptitude needed to proceed with instruction. They categorized aptitudes related to learning into three types: (a) intellectual abilities and prior achievement, (b) cognitive and learning styles, and (c) academic motivation and related personality characteristics. (For in-depth discussions about aptitudes in relation to adaptive instruction, see Federico, 1980; Cronbach & Snow, 1977; Snow, 1986; Snow & Swanson, 1992; Tobias, 1987.) Corno and Snow categorized instructional mediation into four types, from the least intrusive form of mediation to the most intrusive one: (a) activating, which mostly calls forth students' capabilities and capitalizes on learner aptitudes as in discovery learning; (b) modeling; (c) participant modeling; and (d) short-circuiting, which requires step-by-step direct instruction. This taxonomy gives a general idea of how to adapt instructional mediation for the given instructional objective and student aptitude. According to Corno and Snow (1983), this taxonomy can be applied to both levels of adaptive instruction (macro and micro). For example, the activating mediation may be more beneficial for more intellectually able and motivated students, while the short-circuiting mediation may be better for the intellectually low-end students. However, this level of guidance does not provide specific information about how to develop and implement an adaptive instruction. More specifically, it does not suggest how to perform ongoing learning diagnosis and instructional prescriptions during the instructional process.

22.3.2 Macro-Adaptive Instructional Models

While Corno and Snow's taxonomy represents possible ranges of adaptation of instructional activities for the given instructional objective and student aptitudes, Glaser's (1977) five models provide specific alternatives for the design of adaptive instruction.

Glaser's first model is an instructional environment that provides limited alternatives. In this model, the instructional objective and activity to achieve the objective are fixed. Thus, if the student does not have appropriate initial competence to achieve the objective with the given activity, he or she is designated as a poor learner and is dropped out. Only students who demonstrate the appropriate initial state of competence are allowed to participate in the instructional activity. If the student does not demonstrate the achievement of the objective after the activity, the student is allowed to repeat the same activity or is dropped out.

The second model provides an opportunity to develop the appropriate initial competence for students who do not have it. However, no alternative activities are available. Thus, students who do not achieve the objective after the activity should repeat the same activity or drop out.

The third model accommodates different styles of learning. In this model, alternative instructional activities are available, and students are assessed whether they have the appropriate initial competence for achieving the objective through one of the alternatives. However, there are no remedial activities for the development of the appropriate initial competence. Thus, if the student does not have initial competence appropriate for any of the alternative activities, she or he is designated as a poor learner. Once an instructional activity is selected based on the student's initial competence, the student should repeat the activity until achieving the objective or drop out.

The fourth model provides an opportunity to develop the appropriate initial competence and accommodate different styles of learning. If the student does not have the appropriate initial competence to achieve the objective through any of the alternative instructional activities, a remedial instructional activity is provided to develop the initial competence. If the student has developed the competence, an appropriate instructional activity is selected based on the nature of the initial competence. The student should repeat the selected instructional activity until achieving the objective or drop out.

The last model allows students to achieve different types of instructional objectives or different levels of the same objective depending on their individual needs or ability. The basic process is the same as the fourth model, except that the student's achievement is considered successful if any of the alternative instructional objectives (e.g., different type or different level of the same objective) are achieved.

Glaser (1977) described six conditions necessary for instantiating adaptive instructional systems: (a) the human and mental resources of the school should be flexibly employed to assist in the adaptive process; (b) curricula should be designed to provide realistic sequencing and multiple options for learning; (c) open display and access to information and instructional materials should be provided; (d) testing and monitoring procedures should be designed to provide information to teachers and students for decision making; (e) emphasis should be placed on developing abilities in children that assist them in guiding their own learning; and (f) the role of teachers and other school personnel should be the guidance of individual students.

Glaser's conditions suggest that the development and implementation of an adaptive instructional program in an existing system are complex and difficult. This might be the primary reason why most macro-adaptive instructional systems have not been used as successfully and widely as hoped. However, computer technology provides a powerful means to overcome at least some of the problems encountered in the planning and implementing of adaptive instructional systems.

22.3.3 APTITUDE-TREATMENT INTERACTION MODELS

Cronbach (1957) suggested that facilitating educational development in a wide range of students would require a wide range of environments suited to the optimal learning of the individual student. For example, instructional units covering available content elements in different sequences would be adapted to differences among students. Cronbach's strategy proposed prescribing one type of sequence (and even media) for a student of certain characteristics, while another learner of differing characteristics would receive an entirely different form of instruction. This strategy has been termed *aptitude-treatment interaction* (ATI). Cronbach and Snow (1977) defined *aptitude* as any individual characteristic that increases or impairs the student's probability of success in a given treatment, and defined *treatment* as variations in the pace or style of instruction. Potential interactions are likely to reside in two main categories of aptitudes for learning (Snow & Swanson, 1992): (1) cognitive aptitudes, and (2) conative and affective aptitudes. Cognitive aptitudes include: (a) intellectual ability constructs mostly consisting of fluid analytic reasoning ability, visual spatial abilities, crystallized verbal abilities, mathematical abilities, memory space, and mental speed; (b) cognitive and learning styles, and (c) prior knowledge. Conative and affective aptitudes include: (a) motivational constructs such as anxiety, achievement motivation, and interests; and (b) volitional or action-control constructs such as self-efficacy.

To provide systematic guidelines in selecting instructional strategies for individually different students, Carrier and Jonassen (1988) proposed four different types of matches based on Salomon's (1972) work: (a) remedial for providing supplementary instruction to learners who are deficient in a particular aptitude or characteristic, (b) capitalization/preferential for providing instruction in a manner that is consistent with a learner's preferred mode of perceiving or reasoning, (c) compensatory for supplanting some processing requirements of the task for which the learner may have a deficiency, and (d) challenge for stimulating learners to use and develop new modes of processing.

22.3.4 Aptitude Variables and Instructional Implications

To find linkages between different aptitude variables and learning, numerous studies have been conducted (see Cronbach & Snow, 1977; Gagné, 1967; Gallangher, 1994; Snow, 1986; Snow & Swanson, 1992; Tobias, 1983, 1989, 1994). Since the detailed review of ATI research findings is beyond the scope of this chapter, a few representative aptitude variables showing relatively important implications for adaptive instruction are briefly presented below.

22.3.4.1. Intellectual Ability. General intellectual ability consisting of various types of cognitive abilities (e.g., crystallized intelligence such as verbal ability, fluid intelligence such as deductive and logical reasoning, and visual perception such as spatial relations) (see Snow, 1986) is suggested to have interaction effects with instructional supports. For example, more structured and less complex instruction (e.g., expository method) may be more beneficial for students with low intellectual ability, while less-structured and more complex instruction (e.g., discovery method) may be better for students with high intellectual ability (Snow & Lohman, 1984). More specifically, Corno and Snow (1986) suggested that crystallized ability may relate to, and benefit in interaction with, familiar and similar instructional methods and content, whereas fluid ability may relate to and benefit from learning under conditions of new or unusual methods or content.

22.3.4.2. Cognitive Styles. Cognitive styles are characteristic modes of perceiving, remembering, thinking, problem solving, and decision making. They do not reflect competence (i.e., ability) per se but, rather, the utilization (i.e., style) of competence (Messick, 1994). Among many different dimensions of cognitive style (e.g., field dependence versus field independence, reflectivity versus impulsivity, haptic versus visual, leveling versus sharpening, cognitive complexity versus simplicity, constricted versus flexible control, scanning, breadth of categorization, tolerance of unrealistic experiences, etc.), field-dependent versus field-independent and impulsive versus reflective styles have been considered to be most useful in adapting instruction. The following are instructional implications of these two cognitive styles that have been considered in ATI studies.

Field-independent persons are more likely to be: (a) self-motivated and influenced by internal reinforcement, and (b) better at analyzing features and dimensions of information and for conceptually restructuring it. In contrast, field-dependent persons are more likely to be: (a) concerned with what others think and affected by external reinforcement, and (b) accepting of given information as it stands and more attracted to salient cues within a defined learning situation. These comparisons imply some ATI research. For example, studies showing significant interactions revealed that field-independent students achieved best with deductive instruction, and field-dependent students performed best in instruction based on examples (Davis, 1991; Messick, 1994).

Reflective persons are likely to: (a) take more time to examine problem situations and make fewer errors in their performance, (b) exhibit more anxiety over making mistakes on intellectual tasks, and (c) separate patterns into different features. In contrast, impulsive persons have a tendency to: (a) show greater concern about appearing incompetent due to slow responses and take less time examining problem situations, and (b) view the stimulus or information as a single, global unit.

As some of the instructional implications described above suggest, these two cognitive styles are not completely independent of each other (Vernon, 1973).

22.3.4.3. Learning Styles. Efforts for matching instructional presentation and materials with the student's preferences and needs have produced a number of different learning styles (Schmeck, 1988). For example, Pask (1976, 1988) identified two learning styles: (a) a holist, who prefers a global task approach, a wide range of attention, reliance on analogies and illustrations, and construction of an overall concept before filling in details, and (b) a serialist, who prefers a linear task approach focusing on operational details and sequential procedures. Students who are flexible employ both strategies and are called *versatile learners* (Messick, 1994). Marton (1988) distinguished between students who are conclusion oriented and take a deep-processing approach to learning and students who are description oriented and take a shallow-processing approach. French (1975) identified seven perception styles (print oriented, aural, oral-interactive, visual, tactile, motor, and olfactory) and five concept formation approaches (sequential, logical, intuitive, spontaneous, and open). Dunn and Dunn (1978) classified learning stimuli into four categories (environmental, emotional, sociological, and physical) and identified several different learning styles within each category. The student's preference in environmental stimuli can be quiet or noisy sound, bright or dim illumination, cool or warm temperature, and formal or informal design. For emotional stimuli, students may be motivated by self, peer, or adult (parent or teacher), and more or less persistent, and more or less responsible. For sociological stimuli, students may prefer learning alone, with peers, with adults, or through a variety of ways. Preferences in physical stimuli can be auditory, visual, or tactile/kinesthetic. Kolb (1971, 1977) identified four learning styles and a desirable learning experience for each style: (a) Feeling or enthusiastic students may benefit more from concrete experiences; (b) watching or imaginative students prefer reflective observations; (c) thinking or logical students are strong in abstract conceptualizations; and (d) doing or practical students like active experimentation. Hagberg and Leider (1978) also developed a model for identifying learning styles, which is similar to Kolb's.

Each of the learning styles reviewed above provides some practical implications for designing adaptive instruction. However, there is not yet sufficient empirical evidence to support the value of learning styles, and no reliable methods for assessing the different learning styles developed.

22.3.4.4. Prior Knowledge. Glaser and Nitko (1971) suggested that the behaviors that need to be measured in adaptive instruction are those that are predictive of immediate learning success with a particular instructional technique. Since prior achievement measures relate directly to the instructional task, they should therefore provide a more valid and reliable basis for determining adaptations than other aptitude variables.

The value of prior knowledge in predicting the student's achievement and needs of instructional supports has been demonstrated in many studies (e.g., Ross & Morrison, 1988). Research findings showed that the higher the level of prior achievement, the less the instructional support required to accomplish the given task (e.g., Abramson & Kagen, 1975; Salomon, 1974; Tobias 1973; Tobias & Federico, 1984; Tobias & Ingber, 1976). Furthermore, prior knowledge has a substantial linear relationship with interest in the subject (Tobias, 1994).

22.3.4.5. Anxiety. Many studies showed that students with high test anxiety performed poorly on tests in comparison to students with low test anxiety (see Sieber, O'Neil & Tobias, 1977; Tobias, 1987). Since research findings suggest that high anxiety interferes with the cognitive processes that control learning, procedures for reducing the anxiety level have been investigated. For example, Deutsch and Tobias (1980) found that highly anxious students who had options to review study materials (e.g., videotaped lessons) during learning showed a higher achievement than other highly anxious students who did not have the review option. Under an assumption that anxiety and study skills have complementary effects, Tobias (1987) proposed a research hypothesis in an ATI paradigm: "Test-anxious students with poor study skills would learn optimally from a program addressing both anxiety reduction and study skills training. On the other hand, test-anxious students with effective study skills would profit optimally from programs emphasizing anxiety reduction without the additional study skill training" (p. 223). However, more studies are needed to investigate specific procedures or methods for reducing anxiety before guidelines for adaptive instructional design can be made.

22.3.4.6. Achievement Motivation. Motivation is an associative network of affectively toned personality characteristics such as self-perceived competence, locus of control, anxiety, etc. (McClelland, 1965). Thus, understanding and incorporating the interactive roles of motivation with cognitive process variables during instruction is important. However, little research evidence is available for understanding the interactions between the affective and cognitive variables, particularly individual differences in the interactions.

Although motivation as the psychological determinant of learning achievement has been emphasized by many researchers, research evidence suggests that it has to be activated for each task (Weiner, 1990). According to Snow (1986), students achieve their optimal level of performance when they have an intermediate level of motivation to achieve success and to avoid failure. Nicholla, Jagacinski, and Miller (1986) suggested that intrinsically motivated students engage in the task more intensively and show better performance than extrinsically motivated students. However, some studies showed opposite results (e.g., Frase, Patrick & Schumer, 1970). The contradictory findings suggest possible interaction effects of different types of motivation with different students. For example, the intrinsic motivation may be more effective for students who

are strongly goal oriented, like adult learners, while extrinsic motivation may be better for students who study because they have to, like many young children.

Entwistle's (1981) classification of student-motivation orientation provides more hints for adapting instruction to the student's motivation state. He identified three types of students based on motivation-orientation styles: (a) meaning-oriented students, who are internally motivated by academic interest; (b) reproducing-oriented students, who are extrinsically motivated by fear of failure; and (c) achieving-oriented students, who are primarily motivated by hope for success. The meaning-oriented students are more likely to adopt a holist learning strategy that requires deep cognitive processing, while the reproduction-oriented students tend to adopt a serialist strategy that requires relatively shallow cognitive processing (Schmeck, 1988). The achieving-oriented students are likely to adopt either type of learning strategy depending on the given learning content and situation.

However, the specific roles of motivation in learning have not been well understood, particularly in relation to the interactions with the student's other characteristics, task, and other learning conditions. Without understanding the interactions between motivation and other variables, including instructional strategies, simply adapting instruction to the student's motivation may not be useful.

Recently, Tobias (1994) examined student interest in a specific subject and its relations with prior knowledge and learning. Interest, however, is not clearly distinguishable from motivation because interest seems to originate or stimulate intrinsic motivation, and external motivators (e.g., reward) may stimulate interest.

22.3.4.7. Self-Efficacy. Self-efficacy influences people's intellectual and social behaviors, including academic achievement (Bandura, 1982). Since self-efficacy is a student's evaluation of his or her own ability to perform a given task, the student may maintain widely varying senses of self-efficacy, depending on the context (Gallagher, 1994). According to Schunk (1991), self-efficacy changes with experiences of success or failure in certain tasks. A study by Hoge, Smith, and Hanson (1990) showed that feedback from teachers and grades received in specific subjects were important factors for the student's academic self-efficacy. Although many positive aspects of high self-esteem have been discussed, few studies have been conducted to investigate the instructional effect of self-efficacy in the ATI paradigm. Zimmerman and Martinez-Pons (1990) suggested that students with high verbal and mathematical self-efficacy used more self-regulatory and metacognitive strategies in learning the subject. Although it is clear that self-regulatory and metacognitive learning strategies have a positive relationship with students' achievement, this study seems to suggest that the intellectual ability is a more primary factor than self-esteem in the selection of learning strategies. More research is needed to find factors contributing to the formation of self-esteem, relationships between self-efficacy and other motivational and cognitive variables influencing learning processes, and strategies for modifying self-efficacy. Before studying these questions, investigating specific instructional strategies for low and high self-efficacy students in an ATI paradigm may not be fruitful.

In addition to variables discussed above, many other individual difference variables (e.g., locus of control, cognitive development stages, cerebral activities and topological localization of brain hemisphere, personality variables, etc.) have been studied in relation to learning and instruction. Few studies, however, provided feasible suggestions for adapting instruction to individual differences in these variables.

22.3.5 A Taxonomy of Instructional Strategies

Although numerous learning and instructional strategies have been studied (e.g., O'Neil, 1978; Weinstein, Goetz & Alexander, 1988), selecting a specific strategy for a given instructional situation is difficult because its effect may be different for different instructional contexts. It is particularly true for adaptive instruction. Thus, instructional strategies should be selected and designed with the consideration of many variables uniquely involved in a given context. To provide a general guideline for selecting instructional strategies, Jonassen (1988) proposed a taxonomy of instructional strategies corresponding to different processes of cognitive learning. After identifying four stages of the learning process (recall, integration, organization, and elaboration) and related learning strategies for each stage, he identified specific instructional activities for facilitating the learning process. Also, he identified different strategies for monitoring different types of cognitive operations (i.e., planning, attending, encoding, reviewing, and evaluating).

Park (1983) also proposed a taxonomy of instructional strategies (Table 22-1) for different instructional stages or activities (i.e., preinstructional strategies, knowledge presentation strategies, interaction strategies, instructional control strategies, and postinstructional strategies). However, these taxonomies are identified from the author's subjective analysis of learning/instructional processes and do not provide direct or indirect suggestions for selecting instructional strategies in ATI research or adaptive instructional development.

22.3.6 Limitations of Aptitude-Treatment Interactions

In the 3 decades since Cronbach (1957) made his proposal, relatively few studies have found consistent results to support the paradigm and made little contribution to either instructional theory or practice. As several reviews of ATI research (Berlinger & Cohen, 1983; Cronbach & Snow, 1977; Tobias, 1976) have pointed out, the measures of intellectual abilities and other aptitude variables were used in a large number of studies to investigate their interactions with a variety of instructional treatments. However, no convincing evidence was found to suggest that such individual differences were useful variables for differentiating alternative treatments for subjects in a homogeneous age group, although it was believed that the individual difference measures were correlated substantially with achievement in most school-related tasks (Glaser & Resnick, 1972; Tobias, 1987).

The unsatisfactory results of ATI research have prompted researchers to reexamine the paradigm and assess its effectiveness. A number of difficulties in the ATI approach are viewed by Tobias (1976, 1987, 1989) as a function of past reliance on what he terms the *alternative abilities* concept. Under this concept, it is assumed that instruction is divided into input, processing, and output variables. The instruction methods, which form the input of the model, are hypothesized to interact with different psychological abilities (processing variables), resulting in certain levels of performance (or outcomes) on criterion tests. According to Tobias, however, several serious limitations of the model often prevent the occurrence of the hypothesized relations. The limitations are:

1. The abilities assumed to be most effective for a particular treatment may not be exclusive; consequently, one ability may be used as effectively as another ability for instruction by a certain method (see Cronbach & Snow, 1977).
2. Abilities required by a treatment may shift as the task progresses so that the ability becomes more or less important for one unit (or lesson) than for another (see Burns, 1980; Federico, 1983).
3. ATIs validated for a particular task and subject area may not be generalizable to other areas. Research has suggested that ATIs may well be highly specific and vary for different kinds of content (see Peterson, 1977; Peterson & Janicki, 1979; Peterson, Janicki & Swing, 1981).
4. ATIs validated in laboratory experiments may not be applicable to actual classroom situations.

Another criticism is that ATI research has tended to be overly concerned with exploration of simple input/output relations between measured traits and learning outcomes. According to this criticism, a thorough understanding of the psychological process in learning a specific task is a prerequisite to the development theory on the ATIs (DiVesta, 1975). Since individual difference variables are difficult to measure, the test validity can also be a problem in attempting to adapt instruction to general student characteristics.

22.3.7 Achievement-Treatment Interactions

To reduce some of the difficulties in the ATI approach, Tobias (1976) proposed an alternative model, achievement-treatment interactions (see 33.9.1). While the ATI approach stresses relatively permanent dispositions for learning as assessed by measures of aptitudes (e.g., intelligence, personality, and cognitive styles), achievement-treatment interactions represent a distinctly different orientation, emphasizing task-specific

TABLE 22-1. A TAXONOMY OF INSTRUCTIONAL STRATEGIES (PARK, 1984; SEIDEL, PARK & PEREZ, 1988). (THE LISTING OF INSTRUCTIONAL STRATEGIES IN THIS TABLE IS NOT EXHAUSTIVE, AND THE CLASSIFICATIONS ARE ARBITRARILY MADE.)

1. Preinstructional Strategies

  1. **Instructional objective**
    Terminal objectives and enabling objectives
    Cognitive objectives vs. behavioral objectives
    Performance criterion and condition specifications

  2. **Advance organizer**
    Expository organizer vs. comparative organizer
    Verbal organizer vs. pictorial organizer

  3. **Overview**
    Narrative overview
    Topic listing
    Orienting questions

  4. **Pretest**
    Types of test (e.g., objective: true-false, multiple choice, matching, etc. vs. subjective: short answer, essay, etc.)
    Order of test item presentation (e.g., random, sequence, response-sensitive, etc.)
    Item replacement (e.g., with or without replacement of presented items)
    Timing (e.g., limited vs. unlimited)
    Reference (e.g., criterion-reference vs. norm-reference)

2. Knowledge Presentation Strategies

  1. **Types of knowledge presentation**
    Generality (e.g., definition, rules, principles, etc.)
    Instance: diversity and complexity (e.g., example and nonexample problems)
    Generality help (e.g., analytical explanation of generality)
    Instance help (e.g., analytical explanation of instance)

  2. **Formats of knowledge presentation**
    Enactive, concrete physical representation
    Iconic, pictorial/graphic representation
    Symbolic, abstract verbal, or notational representation

  3. **Forms of knowledge presentation**
    Expository, statement form
    Interrogatory, question form

  4. **Techniques for knowledge acquisition**
    Mnemonic
    Metaphors and analogies
    Attribute isolations (e.g., coloring, underlining, etc.)
    Verbal articulation
    Observation and emulation

3. Interaction Strategies

  1. **Questions**
    Level of questions (e.g., understanding/idea vs. factual information)
    Time of questioning (e.g., before or after instruction)
    Response mode required (e.g., selective vs. constructive; overt vs. covert)

  2. **Hints and prompts**
    Formal, thematic, algorithmic, etc.
    Scaffolding (e.g., gradual withdraw of instructor supports)
    Reminder and refreshment

  3. **Feedback**
    Amount of information (e.g., knowledge of results, analytical explanation, algorithmic feedback, reflective comparison, etc.)
    Time of feedback (e.g., immediate vs. delayed feedback)
    Type of feedback (e.g., cognitive/informative feedback vs. psychological reinforcing)

4. Instructional Control Strategies

  1. **Sequence**
    Linear
    Branching
    Response-sensitive
    Response-sensitive plus aptitude-matched

  2. **Control options**
    Program control
    Learner control
    Learner control with advice
    Condition-dependent mixed control

5. Postinstructional Strategies

  1. **Summary**
    Narrative review
    Topic-listing
    Review questions

  2. **Postorganizer**
    Conceptual mapping
    Synthesizing

  3. **Posttest**
    Types of test (e.g., objective: true-false, multiple choice, matching, etc. vs. subjective: short answer, essay, etc.)
    Order of test item presentation (e.g., random, sequence, response-sensitive, etc.)
    Item replacement (e.g., with or without replacement of presented items)
    Timing (e.g., limited vs. unlimited)
    Reference (e.g., criterion-reference vs. norm-reference)

---

variables relating to prior achievement and subject-matter familiarity. This approach stresses the need to consider interactions between prior achievement and performance on the instructional task to be learned. Prior achievement can be assessed rather easily and conveniently through administration of pretests or through analysis of students' previous per-

formance on related tasks. Thus, it eliminates many potential sources of measurement error, which has been a problem in ATI research, since the type of abilities to be assessed would be, for the most part, clear and unambiguous.

Many studies (e.g., see Tobias 1973, 1976; Tobias & Federico, 1984) confirmed the hypothesis that the lower the level of prior achievement is, the more the instructional support is required to accomplish the given task, and vice versa. However, a major problem in the ATI approach, that learner abilities and characteristics fluctuate during instruction, is still unsolved in the achievement-treatment interaction. The treatments investigated in the studies of this approach were not generated by systematic analysis of the kind of psychological processes called upon in particular instructional methods, and individual differences were not assessed in terms of these processes (Glaser, 1972). In addition to the inability to accommodate shifts in the psychological processes active during or required by a given task, the achievement-treatment interaction has another problem: In this model, some useful information might be lost by discounting possible contribution of factors such as intellectual ability, cognitive style, anxiety, motivation, etc.

22.3.8 Cognitive Processes and ATI Research

The limitation of aptitudes measured prior to instruction in predicting the student's learning needs suggests that the cognitive processes intrinsic to learning should be paramount considerations in adapting instructional techniques to individual differences. However, psychological testing developed to measure and classify people according to abilities and aptitudes has neglected to identify the internal processes that underlie such classifications (Federico, 1980).

According to Tobias (1982, 1987), learning involves two types of cognitive processes: (a) macroprocesses that are relatively molar processes, such as mental tactics (Derry & Murphy, 1986), and deployed under student's volitional control; and (b) microprocesses that are relatively molecular processes, such as the manipulation of information in short-term memory, and are less readily altered by students. Tobias (1989) assumed that unless the instructional methods examined in ATI research induce students with different aptitudes to use different types of macroprocesses, the expected interactions would not occur. To validate this assumption, Tobias (1987, 1988) conducted a series of experiments in rereading comprehension using CBI. In the experiments, students were given various options to employ different macroprocesses through the presentation of different instructional activities (e.g., adjunct questions, feedback, various review requirements, instructions to think of the adjunct question while reviewing, rereading with external support, etc.). In summarizing the findings from the experiments, Tobias (1989) concluded that varying instructional methods does not lead to the use of different macrocognitive processes or to changes in the frequency with which different processes are used. Also, the findings showed little evidence that voluntary use of macrocognitive processes are meaningfully related to student characteristics such as anxiety, domain-specific knowledge, or reading ability. Although some of these findings are not consistent with previous studies that showed a high correlation between prior knowledge and the outcome of learning, they explain the reasons for the inconsistent findings in ATI research.

Based on the results of the experiments and the review of relevant studies, Tobias (1989) suggested that

> Researchers should not assume student use of cognitive processes, no matter how clearly these appear to be required or stimulated by the instructional method. Instead, some students should be trained or at least prompted to use the cognitive processes expected to be evoked by instructional methods, whereas such intervention should be omitted for others (p. 220).

This suggestion requires a new paradigm for ATI research that specifies not only student characteristics and alternative instructional methods for teaching students with different characteristics but also strategies for prompting the student to use the cognitive processes required in the instructional methods. This suggestion, however, would make ATI research more complex without being able to produce consistent findings. For example, if an experiment did not produce the expected interaction, it would be virtually impossible to find out whether the result came from the ineffectiveness of the instructional method or the failure of the prompting strategy to use the instructional method.

22.3.9 Learner Control

An alternative approach to adaptive instruction is learner control (see 33.2) that gives learners full or partial control over the process or style of instruction they receive (Snow, 1980). Individual students are different in their abilities for assessing the learning requirements of a given task, their own learning abilities, and instructional options available to learn the given task. Therefore, it can be considered within the ATI framework, although the decision-making authority required for the learning assessment and instructional prescription is changed to the student from the instructional agent (human teacher or media-based tutor).

Snow (1980) divided the degree of learner control into three levels depending on the imposed and elected educational goals and treatments: (a) complete independence, self-direction, and self-evaluation; (b) imposed tasks, but with learner control of sequence, scheduling, and pace of learning; and (c) fixed tasks, with learner control of pace. Numerous studies have been conducted to test the instructional effects of learner control and specific instructional strategies that can be effectively used in learner-control environments (see 33.2) The results have provided some important implications for developing adaptive systems: (a) Individual differences play an important role in the success of learner control strategy; (b) some learning activities performed during the instruction are closely related to the effectiveness of learner control; and (c) the learning activities and effects of learner control can be predicted from the premeasured aptitude variables (Snow, 1980). For example, a study by Shin, Schallert, and Savenye (1994) showed that limited learner control and advisement during instruction were more effective for low-prior-knowledge students, while high-prior-knowledge students did equally well in both full or limited learner-control environments with or without advisement. These results suggest that learner control should be considered both a dimension along which instructional treatments differ and a dimension characteristic of individual differences among learners (Snow, 1980). However, research findings in learner control are not consistent (see 33.5.4), and many questions remain to be answered in terms of the learner-control activities and metacognitive processes. For example, more research is needed in terms of learner-control strategies related to assessment of knowledge about the domain content, ability to learn, selection and processing of learning strategies, etc.

22.3.10 An Eight-Step Model for Designing ATI Courseware

As reviewed above, findings in ATI research suggest that it is premature or impossible to assign students with one set of characteristics to one instructional method and those with different characteristics to another (Tobias, 1987). However, faith in adaptive instruction using the ATI model is still alive because of the theoretical and practical implications of ATI research.

In spite of the inconclusive research evidence and many unresolved issues in the ATI approach, Carrier and Jonassen (1988) proposed an eight-step model to provide practical guidance for applying the ATI model to the design of computer-based instructional (CBI) courseware. The eight steps are: (1) Identify objectives for the courseware; (2) specify task characteristics; (3) identify an initial pool of learner characteristics; (4) select the most relevant learner characteristics; (5) analyze learners in the target population; (6) select final differences (in the learner characteristics); (7) determine how to adapt instruction; and (8) design alternative treatments. This model is basically a modified systems approach to instructional development (Gagné & Briggs, 1979; Dick & Carey, 1985). This model proposes to identify specific learner characteristics of the individual student for the given task, in addition to their general characteristics. For the use of this model, Carrier and Jonassen (1988) listed important individual variables that influence learning. They are (a) aptitude variables, including intelligence and academic achievement; (b) prior knowledge; (c) cognitive styles; and (d) personality variables, including intrinsic and extrinsic motivation, locus of control, anxiety, etc. (see p. 205 in Carrier & Jonassen, 1988). For instructional adaptation, they recommended several types of instructional matches: (a) remedial, (b) capitalization/preferential, (c) compensatory, and (d) challenge.

This model seemingly has practical value. Without theoretically coherent and empirically traceable matrices that link the different learner variables, the different types and levels of learning requirements in different tasks, and different instructional strategies, however, the mere application of this model may not produce results much different

from that of nonadaptive instructional systems. ATI research findings suggest that varying instructional methods does not necessarily invoke different types or frequencies of cognitive processing required in learning the given task, nor are individual difference measures consistently related to such processing (Tobias, 1989). Furthermore, the application of Carrier and Jonassen's (1988) model in the development and implementation of courseware would be very difficult because of the amount of work required in identifying, measuring, and analyzing the appropriate learner characteristics and in developing alternative instructional strategies.

22.4 MICRO-ADAPTIVE INSTRUCTIONAL MODELS

Although the research evidence has failed to show the advantage of the ATI approach for the development of adaptive instructional systems, research for finding aptitude constructs relevant to learning, learning and instructional strategies, and their interactions continues. However, the outlook is not optimistic for the development of a comprehensive ATI model or set of principles for developing adaptive instruction that is empirically traceable and theoretically coherent in the near future. Thus, some researchers have attempted to establish micro-adaptive instructional models using on-task measures rather than pretask measures. On-task measures of student behavior and performance, such as response errors, response latencies, and emotional states, can be valuable sources for making adaptive instructional decisions during the instructional process. Such measures taken during the course of instruction can be applied to the manipulation and optimization of instructional treatments and sequences on a much more refined scale (Federico, 1983). Thus, micro-adaptive instructional models using on-task measures are likely to be more sensitive to the student's needs.

A typical example of micro-adaptive instruction is one-on-one tutoring. The tutor selects the most appropriate information to teach based on his or her judgment of the student's learning ability, including prior knowledge, intellectual ability, and motivation. Then, the tutor continuously monitors and diagnoses the student's learning process and determines the next instructional actions. The instructional actions could be questions, feedback, explanations, or others that maximize the student's learning. Although the instructional effect of one-on-one tutoring has been fully recognized for a long time and empirically proven (Bloom, 1984; Kulik, 1982), few systematic guidelines have been developed. That is, most tutoring activities are determined by the tutor's intuitive judgments about the student's learning needs and ability for the given task. Also, one-on-one tutoring is virtually impossible for most educational situations because of the lack of both qualified tutors and resources.

As the one-on-one tutorial process suggests, the essential element of micro-adaptive instruction is the ongoing diagnosis of the student's learning needs and the prescription of instructional treatments based on the diagnosis. Holland (1977) emphasized the importance of the diagnostic and prescriptive process by defining adaptive instruction as a set of processes by which individual differences in student needs are diagnosed in an attempt to present each student with only those teaching materials necessary to reach proficiency in the terminal objectives of instruction. Landa (1976) also said that adaptive instruction is the diagnostic and prescriptive processes aimed at adjusting the basic learning environment to the unique learning characteristics and needs of each learner. According to Rothen and Tennyson (1978), the diagnostic process should assess a variety of learner indices (e.g., aptitudes and prior achievement) and characteristics of the learning task (e.g., difficulty level, content structure, and conceptual attributes). Hansen, Ross, and Rakow (1977) described the instructional prescription as a corrective process that facilitates a more appropriate interaction between the individual learner and the targeted learning task by systematically adapting the allocation of learning resources to the learner's aptitudes and recent performance.

Instructional researchers or developers have different views about the variables, indices, procedures, and actions that should be included in the diagnostic and the prescriptive processes. For example, Atkinson (1976) says that an adaptive instructional system should have the capability of varying the sequence of instructional action as a function of a given learner's performance history. According to Rothen and Tennyson (1977), a strategy for selecting the optimal amount of instruction and time necessary to achieve a given objective is the essential ingredient in an adaptive instructional system. This observation suggests that different adaptive systems have been developed to adapt different features of instruction to learners in different ways.

Micro-adaptive instructional systems have been developed through a series of different attempts beginning with programmed instruction to the recent application of artificial intelligence (AI) methodology for the development of intelligent tutoring systems (ITS) (see 19.3 to 19.5).

22.4.1 Programmed Instruction

Skinner has generally been considered the pioneer of programmed instruction (see 2.3.4). However, 3 decades earlier than Skinner (1954, 1958), Pressey (1926) used a mechanical device to assess a student's achievement and to provide further instruction in the learning process. The mechanical device, which used a keyboard, presented a series of multiple-choice questions, and required the student to respond by pressing the appropriate key. If the student pressed the correct key to answer the question, the device would present the next question. However, if the student pressed a wrong key, the device would ask the student to choose another answer without advancing to the next question. Using Thorndike's (1913) "Law of Effect" as the theoretical base for the teaching methodology incorporated in his mechanical

device, Pressey (1927) claimed that its purpose was to ensure mastery of a given instructional objective. If the student correctly answered two questions in succession, mastery was accomplished, and no additional questions were given. The device also recorded responses to determine whether the student needed more instruction (further questions) to master the objective. According to Pressey, this made use of a modified form of Thorndike's "Law of Exercise." Little's (1934) study demonstrated the effectiveness of Pressey's testing-drill device against a testing-only device.

Skinner (1954) criticized Pressey's work by stating that it was not based on a thorough understanding of learning behavior. However, Pressey's work contained some noticeable instructional principles (see 2.3.4.2). First, he brought the mastery learning concept into his programmed instructional device, although the determination of mastery was arbitrary and did not consider measurement or testing theory. Second, he considered the difficulty level of the instructional objectives, suggesting that more difficult objectives would need additional instructional items (questions) for the student to reach mastery. Finally, his procedure exhibited a diagnostic characteristic in that, although the criterion level was based on intuition, he determined from the student's responses whether or not more instruction was needed.

Using Pressey's (1926, 1927) basic idea, Skinner (1954, 1958) designed a teaching machine to arrange contingencies of reinforcement in school learning (see 2.3.4.1). The instructional program format used in the teaching machine had the following characteristics: (a) It was made up of small, relatively easy-to-learn steps; (b) the student had an active role in the instructional process; and (c) positive reinforcement was given immediately following each correct response. In particular, Skinner's (1968) linear programmed instruction emphasized an individually different learning rate. However, the programmed material itself was not individualized since all students received the same instructional sequence (Cohen, 1963). In 1959, Pressey criticized this nonadaptive nature of the Skinnerian programmed instruction.

The influx of technology influenced Crowder's (1959) procedure of intrinsic programming with provisions for branching able students through the same material more rapidly than slower students, who received remedial frames whenever a question was missed (see 2.3.4.2). Crowder's intrinsic program was based totally on the nature of the student's response. The response to a particular frame was used both to determine whether the student learned from the preceding material and to determine the material to be presented next. The student's response was thought to reflect her or his knowledge rate, and the program was designed to adapt to that rate. Having provided only a description of his intrinsic programming, however, Crowder revealed no underlying theory or empirical evidence that could support its effectiveness against other kinds of programmed instruction. Because of the difficulty in developing tasks that required review sections for each alternative answer, Crowder's procedure was not widely used in instructional situations (Merrill, 1971).

In 1957, Pask described a perceptual motor training device in which differences in task difficulty were considered for different learners. The instructional target was made progressively more difficult until the student made an error, at which point the device would make the target somewhat easier to detect. From that point, the level of difficulty would build again. Remediation consisted of a step backward on a difficulty dimension to provide the student with further practice on the task. Pask's (1960a, 1960b) Solartron Automatic Key-board Instructor (SAKI) was capable of electronically measuring the student's performance and storing it in a diagnostic history that included response latency, error number, and pattern. On the basis of this diagnostic history, the machine prescribed exercises to be presented next and varied the rate and amount of material to be presented in accordance with the proficiency. Lewis and Pask (1965) demonstrated the effectiveness of Pask's device by testing the hypothesis that adjusting difficulty level and amount of practice would be more effective than adjusting difficulty level alone. Though the application of the device was limited to instruction of perceptual motor tasks, Pask (1960a) described a general framework for the device which included instruction of conceptual as well as perceptual motor tasks.

As described above, most of early programmed instruction methods relied primarily on intuition of the school learning process rather than on a particular model or theory of learning, instruction, or measurement. Although some of the methods were designed on a theoretical basis (for example, Skinner's teaching machine), they were primitive in terms of the adaptation of the learning environment to the individual differences of students. However, programmed instruction did provide some important implications for the development of more sophisticated instructional strategies made possible by the advance in computer technology.

22.4.2 Micro-Adaptive Instructional Models

Using computer technology, a number of micro-adaptive instructional models have been developed. An adaptive instructional model differs from programmed instruction techniques in that it is based on a particular model or theory of learning, and its adaptation of the learning environment is rather sophisticated, while the early programmed instruction was primarily based on intuition and its adaptation was primitive. Unlike macro-adaptive models, the micro-adaptive model uses the temporal nature of learner abilities and characteristics as a major source of diagnostic information on which an instructional treatment is prescribed. Thus, an attribute of a micro-adaptive model is its dynamic nature as contrasted with a macro-adaptive model. A typical micro-adaptive model includes more variables related to instruction than a macro-adaptive model or programmed instruction. It thus provides a better control process than a macro-adaptive model or programmed instruction in responding to the student's performance in reference to type

of content and behavior required in a learning task (Merrill & Boutwell, 1973).

As described by Suppes, Fletcher, and Zanottie (1976), most micro-adaptive models use a quantitative representation and trajectory methodology. The most important feature of a micro-adaptive model relates to the timeliness and accuracy with which it can determine and adjust learning prescriptions during instruction. A conventional instructional method identifies how the student answers but does not identify the reasoning process that leads the student to that answer. An adaptive model, however, relies on different processes that lead to given outcomes. Discrimination between the different processes is possible when on-task information is used. The importance of the adaptive model is not that the instruction can correct each mistake, but that it attempts to identify the psychological cause of mistakes and thereby lower the probability that such mistakes will occur again.

Several examples of micro-adaptive models are described in the following section. Although some of these models are a few decades old, an attempt was made to provide a rather detailed review because the theoretical bases and technical (nonprogramming) procedures used in these models are still relevant and valuable in identifying research issues related to adaptive instruction and in designing future adaptive systems. Particularly, having considered that some theoretical issues and ideas proposed in these models could not be fully explored because of the lack of computer power at that time, the review may provide some valuable research and development agenda.

22.4.2.1. Mathematical Model. According to Atkinson (1972), an optimal instructional strategy must be derived from a model of learning. In mathematical learning theory, two general models describe the learning process: a linear (or incremental) model and an all-or-none (or one-element) model. From these two models, Atkinson and Paulson (1972) deducted three strategies for prescribing the most effective instructional sequence for a few special subjects, like foreign-language vocabulary (Atkinson, 1968, 1974, 1976; Atkinson & Fletcher, 1972).

In the linear model, learning is defined as the gradual reduction in probability of error by repeated presentations of the given instructional items. The strategy in this model orders the instructional materials without taking into account the student's responses or abilities, since it is assumed that all students learn with the same probability. Because the probability of student error on each item is determined in advance, prediction of his or her success depends only on the number of presentations of the items.

In the all-or-none model, learning an item is not all gradual but occurs on a single trial. An item is in one of two states, a learned state or an unlearned state. If an item in the learned state is presented, the correct response is always given; however, if an item in the unlearned state is presented, an incorrect response is given unless the student makes a correct response by guessing. The optimal strategy in this model is to select for presentation the item least likely to be in the learned state, because once an item has been learned, there is no further reason to present it again. If an item in the unlearned state is presented, it changes to the learned state with a probability that remains constant throughout the procedure. Unlike the strategy in the linear model, this strategy is response sensitive. A student's response protocol for a single item provides a good index of the likelihood of that item's being in the learned state (Groen & Atkinson, 1966). This response-sensitive strategy used a dynamic programming technique (Smallwood, 1962). The dynamic programming technique is a method for finding an optimal strategy by systematically varying the number of learning stages and obtaining an expression that gives the return for a process with n stages as a function of the return for a process with $n - 1$ stages. The operational function in a deterministic process of the all-or-none strategy is $Wn = T(Wn - 1, dn - 1)$, where W is the student's state in learning, n is the stage, and d is the decision (Groen & Atkinson, 1966). In this strategy, the items should be presented at well-spaced intervals, because it is not effective under the condition of massed presentation (Dear, Silberman, Estavan & Atkinson, 1967).

This all-or-none model does not depend on the values of its parameters. In other words, such parameters as the probability of changing an item in the unlearned state to the learned state with a presentation of the item, probability of making a correct response by guessing, and the initial error probability are constant throughout all stages because of the assumption that items and students are homogeneous.

On the basis of Norman's (1964) work, Atkinson and Paulson (1972) proposed the random-trial incremental model, a compromise between the linear and all-or-none models. The instructional strategy derived for this model is parameter dependent, allowing the parameters to vary with student abilities and item difficulty. This strategy determines which item, if presented, has the best expected immediate gain, using a reasonable approximation (Calfee, 1970). The initial parameter of a subject-item (π_{ij}) is estimated with an analysis of variance model: $E(\pi_{ij}) = m = a_i + d_j$, where m is the mean, a_i is the probability of student i, and d_j is the difficulty of item j. Because this equation cannot generate the probabilities of the parameters ($0 < \pi_{ij} < 1$), it is transformed in a logistic equation through an algebraic operation and a logarithmic procedure (see Atkinson & Paulson, 1972). The logistic equation is *logit* $\pi_{ij} = \mu + A_i + D_j$, where μ is the mean, A_i is the ability of student i applied across all items, and D_j is the difficulty of item j applied across all students. This logistic equation reduces the number of parameters for N items $\times$ S subjects to $N + S$ parameters. The subject and item effects (A_i and D_j are estimated by standard analysis of variance procedures. Using the estimated student and item effects, the logit μ_{ij} is transformed back to obtain the final estimates of the original student-item parameter.

Atkinson and Crothers (1964) assumed that the all-or-none model provided a better account of data than the linear model, and that the random-trial increments model was better than either of them. This assumption was supported by testing the effectiveness of the strategies (Atkinson, 1976).

The all-or-none strategy was more effective than the standard linear procedure for spelling instruction, while the parameter-dependent strategy was better than the all-or-none strategy for teaching foreign vocabularies (Lorton, 1972).

In the context of instruction, cost-benefit analysis is one of the key elements in a description of the learning process and determination of instructional actions (Atkinson, 1972). In the mathematical adaptive strategies, however, it is assumed that the costs of instruction are equal for all strategies, since the instructional formats and the time allocated to instruction are all the same. If both costs and benefits are significantly variable in a problem, then it is essential that both quantities be estimated accurately. Smallwood (1970, 1971) treated this problem by including a utility function into the mathematical model. The utility function, $U_a(k, h)$, specifies the immediate value accrued if alternative a is presented to a student with response history (h), and k is the response elicited. The terminal utility function is $U_o(h)$, which describes the utility associated with terminating the instruction for a student with a past history h. Smallwood's (1971) economic teaching strategy is a special form of the all-or-none model strategy, except that it can be applied for an instructional situation in which the instructional alternatives have different costs and benefits.

Recently, Townsend (1992) and Fisher and Townsend (1993) applied a mathematical model to the development of a computer simulation and testing system for predicting the probability and duration of student responses in the acquisition of Morse code classification skills. The mathematical adaptive model, however, has never been widely used, probably because the learning process in the model is oversimplified and the applicability is limited to a relatively simple range of instructional contents.

There are criticisms of the mathematical adaptive instructional models. First, the learning process in the mathematical model is oversimplified when implemented in a practical teaching system. Yet it may not be so simple to quantify the transition probability of a learning state and the response probabilities that are uniquely associated with the student's internal states of knowledge and with the particular alternatives for presentation (Glaser, 1976). Although quantitative knowledge can be obtained about how the variables in the model interact, reducing computer decision time has little overall importance if the system can handle only a limited range of instructional materials and objectives, such as foreign-language vocabulary items (Gregg, 1970). Also, the two-state or three-state or n-state model cannot be arbitrarily chosen because the values for transitional probabilities of a learning state can change depending on how one chooses to aggregate over states. The response probabilities may not be assumed equally likely in a multiple-choice test question. This kind of assumption would hold only for homogeneous materials and highly sophisticated preliminary item analyses (Gregg, 1970).

Another disadvantage of the mathematical adaptive model is that its estimates for the instructional diagnosis and prescription cannot be reliable until a significant amount of student and content data are accumulated. For example, the parameter-dependent strategy supposes to predict the performance of other students or the same student on other items from the estimates computed by the logistic equation. However, the first students in an instructional program employing this strategy do not benefit from the program's sensitivity to individual differences in students or items because the initial parameter estimates must be based on data from these students. Thus, the effectiveness of this strategy is questionable unless the instructional program continues over a long period of time.

Atkinson (1972) admitted that the mathematical adaptive models are very simple, and the identification of truly effective strategies will not be possible until the learning process is better understood. However, Atkinson (1972, 1976) contended that an all-inclusive theory of learning is not a prerequisite for the development of optimal procedures. Rather, a model is needed that captures the essential features of that part of the learning process being tapped by a given instructional task.

22.4.2.2. Trajectory Model: Multiple Regression Analysis Approach.

In a typical adaptive instructional program, the diagnostic and prescriptive decisions are frequently made based on the estimated contribution of one or two particular variables. The possible contributions of other variables are ignored. In a trajectory model, however, numerous variables can be included with the use of a multiple regression technique to yield what may be a more powerful and precise predictive base than is obtained by considering a particular variable alone.

The theoretical view in the trajectory model is that the expected course of the adaptive instructional trajectory is determined primarily by generic or trait factors that define the student group. The actual proceeding of the trajectory is dependent on the specific effects of individual learner parameters and variables derived from the task situation (Suppes, Fletcher & Zanotti, 1976). Using this theoretical view, Hansen, Ross, and Rakow (1977; Ross & Rakow, 1982; Ross & Morrison, 1988) developed an adaptive model that reflects both group and individual indices and matches them to appropriate changes both for predictions on entry and adjustments during the treatment process. The model was developed to find an optimal strategy for selecting the appropriate number of examples in a mathematical rule-learning task.

The procedures Hansen et al. used to develop an adaptive system using the trajectory model are as follows:

(a) Learning and test materials were prepared (for example, the instructional unit consisted of 10 basic algebra rules) and the predictive input database was obtained from two measures of personality variables (locus of control and trait anxiety), one measure of general aptitude related to the task (math and verbal), and one measure of a subject familiarity (pretest). Upon completion of the pretest, the subject was given the programmed manual and task instructions. After working through the manual, the student took the posttest, which was matched to the pretest in the number of

items, format, and level of difficulty. The measures of the four entry variables and the posttest score provided the predictive database for the formulation of adaptive grouping.

(b) With the cluster analysis technique, students who had similar characteristics according to the predictive database are clustered in one of a reasonably small number of mutually exclusive groups. The purpose of grouping was to aggregate students so that those within a group were relatively homogeneous among themselves and relatively different from students in other groups. Hansen et al. assumed that for instructional purposes, approximately three to five groups best characterize the cultural and psychological characteristics of the group which are to be differentially treated.

(c) The new students who would receive the adaptive treatments were classified into one of the groups by discriminant analysis. This is a method used to seek the linear combination of variables that will maximize the difference between the groups relative to the difference within the groups.

(d) Multiple regression analysis was used to derive differential predictions about the number of instructional items (examples) to assign to the student. From regression equations based on group parameter characteristics, initial performance estimates were derived for all subjects. In order to derive a decision rule for converting the performance estimate on the test into the prescription example number, a quasi-standard score (Z score) procedure was employed. To systematize matching of the Z score to example prescriptions, the latter were treated as whole numbers on a score continuum having a median number and a range from the minimum to the maximum number of examples for learning each rule. For example, minimum = 2, median = 6, and maximum = 10. A student who had a predicted score close to the mean ($Z = 0$) on a given rule received a prescription of the median number of examples. If the student was predicted to be performing below or above the mean, he or she received more or fewer examples. For example, for a student who was below one standard deviation from the mean, nine examples were given. This decision rule was arbitrary.

(e) The initial prescription derived from the group characteristics were redefined during instruction on the basis of the student's performance on the immediately preceding rule posttest (termed *minitest*). The decision rule employed in making this refinement was again arbitrary. For example, two examples were added following the rule prescription for a minitest score of 0; one example was added for a minitest score of 1; one example was subtracted for a minitest score of 3; two examples were subtracted for a minitest score of 4; no adjustment was made for a minitest score of 2. These adjustments were made only on the next rule in the sequence. To maintain the arbitrarily established boundaries of minimum and maximum, the prescriptions were not limited to vary beyond the minimum or maximum number of examples regardless of the minitest performance.

Hansen et al. (1977) assessed their trajectory adaptive model with a validation study that supported the basic tenets of the model. A desirable number of groups (four) with differential characteristics was found, and the outcomes were as predicted: superior for the adaptive group, highly positive for the cluster group, and poorest for the mismatched groups. The outcome of regression analysis revealed that the pretest yielded the largest amount of explained variance within the regression coefficient. The math reading comprehension measures seemed to contribute to the assignment of the broader skill domain involved in the learning task. However, the two personality measures varied in terms of directions as well as magnitude.

This regression model is apparently helpful in estimating the relative importance of different variables for instruction. However, it does not seem to be a very useful adaptive instructional strategy. Even though many variables can be included in the analysis process, the evaluation study results indicate that only one or two are needed in the instructional prescription process because of the inconsistent or negligible contribution of other variables to the instruction. Unless the number of students to be taught is large, this approach cannot be effective since the establishment of the predictive database in advance requires a considerable number of students, and this strategy cannot be applied to those students who make up the initial database. Furthermore, a new predictive database has to be established whenever the characteristics of the learning task are changed. Transforming the student's score, as predicted from the regression equation, into the necessary number of examples does not have strong justification when a quasi-standard score procedure is used. The decision rules for adjustment of instructional treatment during on-task performance as well as for the initial instructional prescription are entirely arbitrary. Since regression analyses are based on group characteristics, shrinkage of the degrees of freedom due to reduced sample size may raise questions about the value of this approach.

To offset the shortcoming of the regression model that is limited to the adaptation of instructional amount (e.g., selection of the number of examples in concept or rule learning), Ross and Morrison (1988) attempted to expand its functional scope by adding the capability for selecting the appropriate instructional content based on the student's interest and other background information. This contextual adaptation was based on empirical research evidence that the personalized context based on an individual student's interest and orientation facilitates the student's understanding of the problem and learning of the solution. A field study demonstrated the effectiveness of the contextual adaptation (Ross & Anand, 1986).

Ross and Morrison (1988) further extended their idea of contextual adaptation by allowing the system to select different densities (or "detailedness") of textual explanation based on the student's predicted learning needs. The predicted learning needs were estimated using a multiple regression model described above. A preliminary evaluation study showed the superior effect of the adaptation of contextual density over a standard contextual density condition or learner-control condition.

The Ross and Morrison's approaches for the contextual adaptation alone cannot be considered micro-adaptive systems because they do not have the capability of performing the ongoing diagnosis and prescription generation during the task performance. Their diagnostic and prescriptive decisions are made on the basis of preinstructional data. The contextual adaptation approach, however, can be a significant addition to a micro-adaptive model like the regression analysis approach that has a limited function for adapting the quality of instruction, including the content. Although we presume that the contextual adaptation approaches were originally developed with the intent to be incorporated in the regression analysis model, the incorporation has not yet been fully accomplished.

22.4.2.3. Bayesian Probability Model. The Bayesian probability model employs a two-step approach for adapting instruction to individual students. After the initial assignment of the instructional treatment is made on the basis of preinstructional measures (e.g., pretest scores), the treatment prescription is continuously adjusted according to student on-task performance data.

To operationalize this approach in CBI, a Bayesian statistical model was used. The Bayes's theorem of conditional probability seems appropriate for the development of an adaptive instructional system because it can predict the probability of mastery of the new learning task from student preinstructional characteristics and then continuously update the probability according to the on-task performance data (Rothen & Tennyson, 1978; Tennyson & Christensen, 1988). Accordingly, the instructional treatment is selected and adjusted.

The functional operation of this model is related to guidelines described by Novick and Lewis (1974) for determining the minimal length of a test adequate to provide sufficient information about the learner's degree of mastery of behavior being tested. Novick and Lewis's procedure uses a pretest on a set of objectives. From this pretest, the initial prior estimate of a student's ability per objective is combined in a Bayesian manner with information accumulated from previous students to generate a posterior estimate (using the beta, β, distribution) of the student's probability of mastery of each objective. This procedure generates a table of values for different test lengths for the objectives and selects an appropriate number of test items from this table that seem adequate to predict mastery of each objective. Rothen and Tennyson (1978) modified Novick and Lewis's (1974) model in such a way that a definite rule or algorithm selects an instructional prescription from the table of generated values. In addition, this prescription is updated according to individual student's on-task learning performance. The implementation of this procedure requires the establishment of three parameters:

(a) An estimate is made of the student's initial ability based on prior knowledge. The beta distribution is used to characterize this information in probabilistic terms. This involves making an initial estimate of probability by administering a pretest and comparing the score to historically accumulated data (i.e., information collected from previous students). Rothen and Tennyson used the procedure described by Novic and Jackson (1974) in the selection of a particular beta distribution to characterize prior briefs. Novick and Lewis (1974) suggested using a prior distribution, $\beta(a, b)$, which assign a probability slightly greater than .5 to the region above the criterion level set in advance to determine the mastery of the given objective.

(b) A criterion level (π_o) for the objective is set. To decide on a student's attainment of mastery, it is necessary to select a minimum acceptance probability that a student's true level (π) exceeds or is equal to the criterion. For a test of length n with a student's score of x, a value of π_o must be selected such that the probability $(\pi \geq \pi_o / x, n) \geq .5$. This is equivalent to at least a 50% certainty that the student's level of functioning is above π_o.

(c) The loss ratio (R) is defined as the disutilities associated with a false advance to a false retain decision. R refers to the relative losses associated with advancing a learner whose true level of functioning is below π_o and retaining a learner whose true level exceeds π_o.

Specification of these parameters, $\beta(a, b)$, R, and π_o affects the minimum necessary instructional presentation. As the prior distribution approaches unity, the length of instructional presentation decreases. A large loss ratio increases the length of instructional presentation to allow the possibility of high posterior probability of mastery. If the criterion level approaches 1, the instructional length is increased to provide adequate information about a student's level of functioning in the interval of the criterion.

The amount of instruction is selected by establishing the operating level for the student. The operating level is updated with each on-task response and compared to the posterior distribution. If the student's operating level is greater than or equal to the posterior probability, the student is judged to have correctly mastered the objective, and no further instruction is given. If the student's operating level is below that generated from the posterior distribution, his or her posterior distribution is used as a prior distribution with the same parameters for the criterion level and loss ratio as before. A new instructional presentation is then generated. This procedure is applied iteratively until either the student is judged to have mastered the objective or the instructional materials pool is exhausted.

Studies by Tennyson and his associates (see Tennyson & Christensen, 1988) demonstrated the effectiveness of the Bayesian probabilistic adaptive model in selecting the appropriate number of examples in concept learning. Posttest scores showed that the adaptive group was significantly better than the nonadaptive groups. Particularly, students in the adaptive group required significantly less learning time than students in the nonadaptive groups. This model was also effective in selecting the appropriate amount of instructional time for each student based on her or his on-task performance (Tennyson & S. Park, 1984; Tennyson, Park & Christensen, 1985).

If the instructional system uses mastery learning as its primary goal (Glaser, 1963) and adjustment of the instructional treatment is critical for learning, this model may be ideal. Another advantage of this model is that no assumption

regarding the instructional item homogeneity (in content or difficulty) is needed. A questionable aspect of the model, however, is whether or not variables other than prior achievement and on-task performance can be effectively incorporated. Tennyson and Rothen (1977) used a task-related aptitude measure (logical reasoning ability) in deciding the loss ratio and included a response-confidence measure in weighting the on-task performance score. However, these procedures were employed without a theoretical base. Another difficulty of this model is how to make a prior-distribution from the pretest score and historical information collected from previous students. Although Hambleton and Novick (1973) suggested the possibility of using the student's performance level on other referral tasks for the historical data, until enough historical data are accumulated, this model cannot be utilized. Also, the application of this model is limited to rather simple tasks such as concept and rule learning.

Park and Tennyson (1980, 1986) extended the function of the Bayesian model by incorporating a sequencing strategy in the model. Park and Tennyson (1980) developed a responsive-sensitive strategy for selecting the presentation order of examples in concept learning from the analysis of cognitive learning requirements in concept learning (Tennyson & Park, 1982). Studies by Park and Tennyson (1980, 1986) and Tennyson, Park, and Christensen (1985) showed that the response-sensitive sequence was not only more effective than nonresponse-sensitive strategy but also reduced the necessary number of examples that the Bayesian model predicted for the student. Also, Park and Tennyson's studies found that the value of the pretask information decreases as the instruction progresses. In contrast, the contribution of the on-task performance data to the model's prediction increases as the instruction progresses.

22.4.2.4. Structural and Algorithmic Approach. The optimization of instruction in Scandura's (1973, 1977a, 1977b, 1983) structural learning theory consists of finding optimal trade-offs between the sum of the values of the objectives achieved and total time required for instruction. Optimization will involve balancing gains against costs (a form of cost-benefit analysis). This notion is conceptually similar to Atkinson's (1976) and Atkinson and Paulson's (1972) cost-benefit dimension of instructional theory, Smallwood's (1971) economic teaching strategy, and Chant and Atkinson's (1973) optimal allocation of instructional efforts.

In structural learning theory, structural analysis of content is especially important as a means of finding optimal trade-offs. According to Scandura (1977a, 1977b), the competence underlying a given task domain is represented in terms of sets of processes, or rules for problem solving. Analysis of content structure is a method for identifying those processes.

Given a class of tasks, the structural analysis of content involves (a) sampling a wide variety of tasks, (b) identifying a set of problem-solving rules (R) for performing the tasks (as an ideal student in the target population might use), (c) identifying parallels among the rules and devising higher-order rules that reflect these parallels, (d) constructing more basic rule sets that incorporate higher-order and other rules, (e) testing and refining the resulting rule set on new problems, and (f) extending the rule set when necessary so that it accounts for both familiar and novel tasks in the domain. This method may be reapplied to the obtained rule set and repeated again as many times as desired. Each time the method is applied, the resulting rule set tends to become more basic in two senses: first, the individual rules become more simple, and second, the new rule set as a whole has greater generating power for solving a wider variety of problems.

Once a basic rule set $B(R_m)$ has been identified, and if B can be considered the student's entering knowledge from assessment of prior knowledge, it is possible to determine whether or not given problems might be solved by applying rules to other available rules, and, correspondingly, which rules might be learned (derived) as a result. The rule set that might be learned (at a given stage) by the student with exact knowledge of the rules in B is denoted as B^2. The rule set immediately learnable, given the rules in B^{n-1}, is denoted B^n. Each rule in B^n represents a unit of knowledge that might be acquired by the student whose entry knowledge (B) includes only the initial rules (R_m). In general, B^n will be a far more encompassing and powerful rule set than the initial rule set R_m from which B^n is derived. The ability to solve problems associated with B^n comes about gradually as a result of solving sequences of simple problems associated with $B, B^2, \ldots, B^{n-1}$.

Hence, given any random selection of problems from the domain and a set of rules available in the learner's knowledge, it is possible to determine algorithmically which of the problems might be learned at any given stage and which problems require further instruction (e.g., in the form of prior problem-solving experience). In turn, this makes it possible to arrange the problems algorithmically in a learnable order. In general, it would be impossible or impractical to teach directly all of the solution rules contained in B^n.

The algorithmic sequence can be determined by computer alone, without the student's involvement. The operational procedure of the computer program is as follows: The program takes as input the initial set of rules, which is available in the student's knowledge, and an arbitrary list of problems. It then attempts the given problem in turn. Solved problems are added to a learnable sequence, and rules derived from solving problems are added to the rule set. Failed problems are retained on a failing problem list and reattempted after all problems are solved, or until the number of failed problems reaches a prespecified limit. This process has the effect of reordering presented problems so that each problem is solvable on its first presentation. That is, the program outputs may be used to discard redundant problems, to rearrange problems, or to add intermediate problems so that unsolved problems become solvable.

According to Scandura (1977a) and Wulfeck and Scandura (1977), the instructional sequence determined by this algorithmic procedure is optimal. This algorithmically designed sequence was superior to learner-controlled and random sequences in terms of the performance scores and the problem solution time (Wulfeck & Scandura, 1977). Also, Scandura and Durnin (1977) reported that a testing method based on the algorithmic sequence could assess the student's performance potential more accurately with fewer test items and less time than a domain-reference generation procedure and a hierarchical item generation procedure.

Since the algorithmic sequence is determined only by the structural characteristics of given problems and the prior knowledge of the target population (not individual students), the instructional process in structural learning theory is not adaptive to individual differences of the learner. Stressing the importance of individual differences in his structural learning theory, Scandura (1977a, 1977b, 1983) states that what is learned at each stage depends both on what is presented to the learner and what the learner knows. Based on the algorithmic sequence in the structural learning theory, Scandura and his associates (Scandura & E. Scandura, 1988) developed a rule-based CBI system. However, there has been no combined study of algorithmic sequence and individual differences that might show how individual differences could be used to determine the algorithmic sequences.

Landa's (1976) structural psychodiagnostic method may be well combined with Scandura's algorithmic sequence strategy to adapt the sequential procedure to individual differences that would emerge as the student learns a given task using the predetermined algorithmic sequence. According to Landa (1976), the structural psychodiagnostic method can identify the specific defects in the student's psychological mechanisms of cognitive activity by isolating the attributes of the given learning task which define the required actions and then by joining these attributes with the student's logical operations.

22.4.2.5. Other Micro-Adaptive Models. For the last 2 decades, some other micro-adaptive instructional systems have been developed to optimize the effectiveness or efficiency of instruction for individual students. For example, McCombs and McDaniel (1981) developed a two-step (macro and micro) adaptive system to accommodate the multivariate nature of learning characteristics and idiosyncratic learning processes in the ATI paradigm. McComb and McDaniel identified the important learning characteristics (e.g., reading/reasoning and memory ability, anxiety, and curiosity, etc.) from the results of multiple stepwise regression analyses of existing student performance data. To compensate for the student's deficiencies of the learning characteristics, they added a number of special-treatment components to the main track of instructional materials. For example, to assist low-ability students in reading comprehension or information-processing skills, schematic visual organizers were added. However, most systems like McComb and McDaniel's are not included in this review because they do not have true on-task adaptive capability, which is the most important criterion to be qualified as a micro-adaptive model. In addition, these systems are task dependent, and the applicability to other tasks is very limited, although the basic principles or ideas of the systems are plausible.

22.4.3 Treatment Variables in Micro-Adaptive Models

As reviewed above, micro-adaptive models are primarily developed to adapt two instructional variables: amount of content to be presented and presentation sequence of content. The Bayesian probabilistic model and the multiple regression model are designed to select the amount of instruction needed to learn the given task. Park and Tennyson (1980, 1986) incorporated sequencing strategies in the Bayesian probability model, and Ross and his associates (Ross & Anand, 1986; Ross & Morrison, 1986) investigated strategies for selecting content in the multiple regression model. Although these efforts showed that other instructional strategies could be incorporated in the model, they did not change the primary instructional variables and the operational procedure of the model. The mathematical model and the structural/algorithmic approach are designed mainly to select the optimal sequence of instruction. According to the Bayesian model and the multiple regression approach, the appropriate amount of instruction is determined by individual learning differences (aptitudes, including prior knowledge) and the individual's specific learning needs (on-task requirements). In the mathematical model, the history of the student's response pattern determines the sequence of instruction. However, an important implication of the structural/algorithmic approach is that the sequence of instruction should be decided by the content structure of the learning task as well as the student's performance history.

The Bayesian model and the multiple regression model use both pretask and on-task information to prescribe the appropriate amount of instruction. Studies by Tennyson and his associates (Tennyson & Rothen, 1977; Park & Tennyson, 1980) and Hansen et al. (1977) demonstrated the relative importance of these variables in predicting the appropriate amount of instruction. Subjects who received the amount of instruction selected based on the pretask measures (e.g., prior achievement, aptitude related to the task) needed less time to complete the task and showed higher performance level on the posttest than subjects who received the same amount of instruction regardless of individual differences. In addition, some studies (Hansen et al., 1977; Ross & Morrison, 1988) indicated that only prior achievement among pretask measures (e.g., anxiety, locus of control, etc.) provides consistent and reliable information for prescribing the amount of instruction. However, subjects who received the amount of instruction selected based on both pretask measures and on-task measures needed less time and showed higher test scores than subjects who received the amount of instruction based on only pretask measures. The results of the response-sensitive strategies studied by Park and Tennyson (1980, 1986) suggest that the predictive power of the pretask measures, including prior knowledge, decreases, while that of on-task measures increases as the instruction progresses.

As reviewed above, a common characteristic of micro-adaptive instructional models is response sensitivity. For response-sensitive instruction, the diagnostic and prescriptive processes attempt to change the student's internal state of knowledge about the content being presented. Therefore, the optimal presentation of instructional stimulus should be determined on the basis of the student's response pattern.

Response-sensitive instruction has a long history of development from Crowder's (1959) simple branching program to Atkinson's mathematical model of adaptive instruction. Until the late 1960s, technology was not readily available to implement the response-sensitive diagnostic and prescriptive procedures as a general practice outside the experimental laboratory (Hall, 1977). Although the recent development of computer technology has made the implementation of this kind of adaptive procedures possible and allowed for further investigation of their instructional effects, as seen in the descriptions of microadaptive models, they have been mostly limited to simple tasks that can be easily analyzed for quantitative applications.

However, the AI methodology has provided a powerful tool for overcoming the primary limitation of micro-adaptive instructional models, so the response sensitive procedures can be utilized for more broad and complex domain areas.

22.4.4 Intelligent Tutoring Systems

Intelligent tutoring systems (ITS) are adaptive instructional systems developed with the application of AI methods and techniques. ITSs are developed to resemble what actually occurs when student and teacher sit down one-on-one and attempt to teach and learn together (see 19.3). As in any other instructional systems, ITSs have components representing content to be taught, the inherent teaching or instructional strategy, and mechanisms for understanding what the student does and does not know. In ITSs, these components are referred to as the *problem-solving* or *expertise module, student-modeling module,* and *tutoring module.* The expertise module evaluates the student's performance and generates instructional content during the instructional process. The student-modeling module assesses the student's current knowledge state and makes hypotheses about his or her conceptions and reasoning strategies employed to achieve the current state of knowledge. The tutorial module usually consists of a set of specifications for the selection of instructional materials the system should present and how and when they should be presented. AI methods for the representation of knowledge (e.g., production rules, semantic networks, and scripts frames) make it possible for the ITS to generate the knowledge to present the student based on his or her performance on the task rather than selecting the presentation according to the predetermined branching rules. Methods and techniques for natural language dialogues allow much more flexible interactions between the system and student. The function for making inferences about the cause of the student's misconceptions and learning needs allows the ITS to make qualitative decisions about the learning diagnosis and instructional prescription, unlike the micro-adaptive model in which the decision is entirely based on quantitative data. (For a detailed description of the ITS components and the AI methods used in the systems, see Chapter 19.)

Furthermore, ITS techniques provide a powerful tool for effectively capturing human learning and teaching processes. It has apparently contributed to a better understanding of cognitive processes involved in learning specific skills and knowledge (see 19.4). Some ITSs have not just demonstrated their effects for teaching specific domain contents but also provided research environments for investigating specific instructional strategies and tools for modeling human tutors and simulating human learning and cognition (Seidel & Park, 1994; see also 19.5). However, there are criticisms that ITS developers have failed to incorporate many valuable learning principles and instructional strategies developed by instructional researchers and educators (Park, Perez & Seidel, 1987). Cooperative efforts among experts in different domains, including learning/instruction and AI, are required to develop more powerful adaptive systems using the ITS methods and techniques (Park & Seidel, 1989; Seidel, Park & Perez, 1988). However, theoretical issues of how to learn and teach with emerging technology, including AI, would continue to remain the most challenging problem.

22.5 APTITUDES, ON-TASK PERFORMANCE, AND RESPONSE-SENSITIVE ADAPTATION

As reviewed above, micro-adaptive systems, including ITS, demonstrate the power of on-task measures in adapting instruction to students' learning needs that are individually different and constantly changing, while ATI research has shown few consistent findings. Because of the theoretical implications, however, efforts for selectively applying aptitude variables in adaptive instruction is continuing. It has been suggested to integrate some aptitude variables in the micro-adaptive system. For example, Park and Seidel (1989) recommended to include several aptitude variables in the ITS student model and use them in the diagnostic and tutoring processes.

22.5.1 A Two-level Model of Adaptive Instruction

To integrate the ATI approach in a micro-adaptive model, Tennyson and Christensen (1985, 1988; also see Tennyson & Park, 1987) have proposed a two-level model of adaptive instruction. This two-level model is partially based on the findings of their own research in adaptive instruction over the last 2 decades. First, this computer-based model allows the computer tutor to establish conditions of instruction based on learner aptitude variables (cognitive, affective, and memory structure) and context (information) structure. Second, the computer tutor provides moment-to-moment adjustment of instructional conditions by adapting the amount of information, example formats, display time, sequence of instruction, instructional advisement, and embedded refreshment and remediation. The microlevel of adaptation takes place based on the student's on-task performance, and the procedure is response-sensitive (Park & Tennyson, 1980). The amount of information to be presented and the time to display the information on the computer screen are determined through the continuous decision-making process of the Bayesian adaptive model based on on-task performance data. The selection and presentation of other instructional strategies (sequence of examples, advisement, and embedded refreshment and remediation) are determined based on the evaluation of the on-task performance. However, the response-sensitive procedure used in this micro-adaptation level has two major limitations, as discussed in the Bayesian adaptive instructional model: (a) problems associated with the quantification process in transforming the learning needs into the Bayesian probabilities, and (b) the capability of handling only limited types of learning tasks (e.g., concept and rule learning).

For variables to be considered in the macro-adaptive process, Tennyson and Christensen (1988) identified the types of learning objectives, instructional variables, and the enhancement strategies for different types of memory structure (i.e., declarative knowledge, conceptual knowledge, and procedural knowledge), and cognitive processes (storage and retrieval). However, the procedure for integrating components of learning and instruction are not clearly demonstrated in their Minnesota Adaptive Instructional System.

22.5.2 On-Task Performance and Response-Sensitive Strategies

Studies reviewed in the micro-adaptive models demonstrated the superior diagnostic power of on-task performance measure to pretask measures and the stronger effect of response-sensitive adaptation to ATI or nonadaptive instruction. These results indicate the relative importance of the response-sensitive strategy compared to ATI methods. The student's on-task performance or response to a given problem is the reflection of the integrated effect of all the variables, identifiable or unidentifiable, involved in the student's learning and response-generation process. As discussed earlier, a shortcoming of the ATI method is adapting instructional processes to one or two selected aptitude variables in spite of the fact that learning results from the integrated effects of many identifiable or unidentifiable aptitude variables and their interactions with the complex learning requirements of the given task. Some of the aptitude variables involved in the learning process could be stable in nature, while others could be temporal. Identifying all of the aptitude variables and their interactions with the task-learning requirements is practically impossible.

Research evidence shows that some aptitude variables (e.g., prior knowledge, interest, intellectual ability) (Tobias,

1994; Whitener, 1989) are important predictors in selecting instructional treatments for individual students. However, some studies (Park & Tennyson, 1980, 1988) suggest that the predictive value of aptitude variables decreases as the learning process continues, because the involvement of other aptitude variables and their interactions may increase as learning occurs. For example, knowledge the student has learned in the immediately preceding unit becomes the most important factor in learning the next unit, and motivational level for learning the next unit may not be the same as in learning the last unit. Thus, the general intellectual ability measured prior to instruction may not be as important in predicting the student's performance and learning requirements for the later stage or unit of the instruction as it was for the initial stage or unit.

In a summary of factor analytic studies of human abilities for learning, Fleishman and Bartlett (1969) provided evidence that the particular combinations of abilities contributing to performance change as the individual works on the task. Dunham, Guilford, and Hoepner (1968) also found that definite trends in ability factor loading can be seen as a function of stage of practice on the task. According to Fredrickson (1969), changes in the factorial composition of a task might be a function of the student's employing cognitive strategies early in the learning task and changing the strategies later in the task. Because the behavior of the learner changes during the course of learning, including the learner's strategies, abilities that transfer and produce effects at one stage of learning may differ from those effective at other stages.

22.5.3 Diagnostic Power of Aptitudes and On-Task Performance

As discussed above, the change of aptitudes during the learning process suggests that the diagnostic power of premeasured aptitude variables for assessing his or her learning needs, including instructional treatments, decreases as the learning continues. In contrast, the diagnostic power of on-

task performance increases because it reflects the most updated and integrated reflection of aptitude and other variables involved in the learning. In contrast, the student's on-task performance in the initial stage of learning may not be as powerful as in the later stage of learning because of the student's lack of understanding about the nature of the task, specific learning requirements in the task, and his or her ability related to the learning of the task. Therefore, during the initial stage of instruction, specific aptitude variables like prior knowledge and general intellectual ability may be more valuable than on-task performance or response in prescribing the best instructional treatment for the student.

The decrease in predictive power of the premeasured aptitude variables and the increase in that of on-task performance can be represented as Figure 22-1.

22.5.4 Response-Sensitive Adaptation

Figure 22-1 suggests that an adaptive instructional system should be a two-stage approach: (a) adaptation to the selected aptitude variable, and (b) response-sensitive adaptation. In the two-stage approach, the student will initially be assigned to the best instructional alternative for the aptitude measured prior to instruction, and then response-sensitive procedures will be applied as the student's response patterns emerge to reflect his or her knowledge or skills on the given task. A representative example of this two-stage approach is the Bayesian adaptive instructional model. In this model, the student's initial learning needs are estimated from the student's performance on a pretest, and the estimate is continuously adjusted by reflecting the student's on-task performance (i.e., correct or incorrect response to the given question). As the process for estimating student learning needs continues in this Bayesian model, the value of the pretest performance data becomes less important, and the most recent performance data become more important.

The response-sensitive procedure is particularly important because it can determine and adjust learning prescriptions

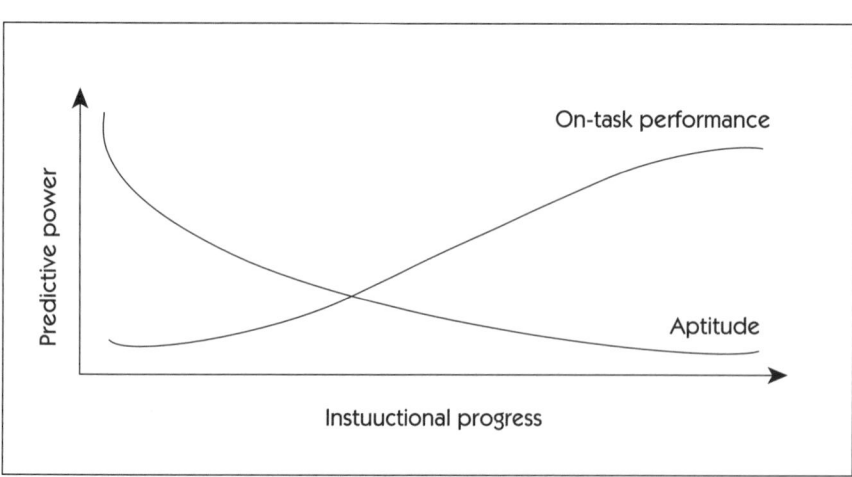

Figure 22-1. Predictive power of aptitudes and on-task performance.

with timeliness and accuracy during instruction. The focus of a response-sensitive approach is that the instruction should attempt to identify the psychological cause of the student's response and thereby lower the probability that similar mistakes will occur again rather than merely correcting each mistake. The effect of a response-sensitive approach (e.g., Atkinson, 1968; Park & Tennyson, 1980, 1986) has been empirically supported. Also, some of the successful ITSs (e.g., SHERLOCK) diagnose the student learning needs and generate instructional treatments entirely based on a student's response to the given specific problem without an extensive student-modeling function.

Development of a response-sensitive system requires procedures for obtaining instant assessment of student knowledge or abilities and alternative methods for using those assessments to make instructional decisions. Also, the learning requirements of the given task, including the structural characteristics and difficulty level, should be assessed continuously with an on-task analysis. Without considering the content structure, the student's response reflecting his or her knowledge state about the task cannot be appropriately analyzed, and a reasonable instructional treatment cannot be prescribed. The importance of the content structure of the learning task was well illustrated by Scandura's (1973, 1977a, 1977b) Structural Analysis and Landa's (1970, 1976) Algo-Heuristics approaches.

To implement a response-sensitive strategy in determining the presentation sequence of examples in concept learning, Tennyson and Park (1980) recommended analyzing on-task error patterns from the student's response history and content and structural characteristics of the task. Many ITSs have incorporated functions to make inferences about the cause of a student misconception from the analysis of the student's response errors and the content structure and to instantly generate instructional treatment (i.e., knowledge) appropriate for the misconception (see Chapter 19).

22.5.5 On-task Performance and Adaptive Learner-Control

A similar curve to the instructional diagnostic power of aptitudes (Fig. 22-1) can be applied in predicting the effect of the learner-control approach. In the beginning stage of learning, the student's familiarity with the subject knowledge and its learning requirements would be relatively low, and the student would not be able to choose the best strategies for learning. However, as the process of instruction and learning continues and external or self-assessment about the student's own ability is repeated, her or his familiarity with the subject and ability to learn it would increase. Thus, as the instruction progresses, the student would be able to make better decisions in selecting strategies for learning the subject. This argument is supported by research evidence that the strong effect of learner-control strategies are mostly found in relatively long-term studies (Seidel, Wagner, Rosenblatt, Hillelsohn & Stelzer, 1978; Snow, 1980), while

scattered effects are found usually in short-term experiments (Carrier, 1984; Ross & Rakow, 1981).

The speed, degree, and quality of obtaining the self-regulatory ability in the learning process, however, would be different between students (Gallangher, 1994), because learning is an idiosyncratic process influenced by many identifiable and unidentifiable individual difference variables. Thus, an on-task adaptive learner control, which gradually gives the learner the options for controlling the instructional process based on the progress of the learner's on-task performance, should be better than non- or predetermined adaptive learner control, which gives the options without considering individual differences or is based on aptitudes measured prior to instruction. An on-task adaptive learner control will decide not only when is the best time for giving the learner-control option but also what kind of control options (e.g., selection of contents, learning activities, etc.) should be given based on the student's on-task performance. When the learner-control options are given adaptively, the concern that learner control may guide the student to put in less effort (Clark, 1984) would not be a serious matter.

22.6 INTERACTIVE COMMUNICATION IN ADAPTIVE INSTRUCTION

The response-sensitive strategies in CBI have been mostly applied to simple student-computer interactions such as multiple-choice, true-false, and short-answer types of question-asking and responding processes. However, AI techniques for natural language dialogues have provided an opportunity to apply the response-sensitive strategy in a manner requiring much more in-depth communications between the student and computer (see 19.2.3). For example, many ITSs have a function to understand and generate natural dialogues during the tutoring process. Although the AI method of handling natural languages is still limited and its development is relatively slow, it is certain that future adaptive instructional systems, including ITS, will have a more powerful function for handling response-sensitive strategies.

The development of a powerful response-sensitive instructional system using emerging technology, including AI, requires a communication model that depicts the process of interactions between the student and tutor. As Wenger (1987) defined, the development of an adaptive instructional system is the process of software engineering for constructing a knowledge communication system that causes and/or supports the acquisition of one's knowledge by someone else, via a restricted set of communication operations.

22.6.1 Process of Instructional Communication

To develop a communication model for instruction, the process of instructional communication should first be understood. Seidel and his associates (Seidel, Compton,

Kopstein, Rosenblatt & See, 1969) divided instructional communication into teaching and assessment channels existing between the instructor and student. (Fig. 22-2 is adopted from Seidel et al. with modifications.) Through the teaching channel, the instructor presents the student communication materials via the interface medium (e.g., computer display). The communication materials are generated from the selective integration of the instructor's domain knowledge expertise and teaching strategies based on information he or she has about the student. The student reads and interprets the communication materials based on the student's own current knowledge and the perceived instructor's expectation. The student's understanding and learning of the materials is communicated through his or her response or questions. The questions and responses by the student through the interface medium are read and interpreted by the instructor. Seidel et al. (1969; Seidel, 1971) called the communication process from the student to the instructor the *assessment channel.* Through this process, the instructor updates or modifies his or her information about the student and generates new communication materials based on the most up-to-date information. The student's knowledge successively approximates to the state that the instructor plans to accomplish or expects.

The model of Seidel and his associates (1969) describes the general process of instruction. However, it does not explain how to assess the student's questions or responses and generate specific communication materials. Since specific combinations of questions and responses between the student and instructor occurring in the teaching and assessment process are mostly task-specific, it is difficult to develop a general model for describing and guiding the process.

22.6.2 Diagnostic Questions and Instructional Explanations

Most student-system interactions in adaptive instruction consist of questions that the system asks to diagnose the student's learning needs and explanations that the system provides based on the student's learning needs. Many studies have been conducted to investigate classroom discourse patterns (see Cazden, 1986) and the effect of questioning (Farrar, 1986; Hamaker, 1986; Redfield & Rouseau, 1981). However, few principles or procedures for asking diagnostic questions in CBI or ITS have been developed. Most diagnostic processes in CBI and ITS take place from the analysis of the student's on-task performance. For assessing the student's knowledge state and diagnosing his or her misconceptions, two basic methods have been used in ITS (see also 19.3.2): (a) overlay method for comparing the student's current knowledge structure with the expert's, and (b) buggy method for identifying specific misconceptions from a precompiled list of possible misconceptions. In both methods, the primary source for identifying the student's knowledge structure or misconceptions is the student's on-task performance data.

From the analysis of interactions between graduate students tutoring undergraduates in research methods, Graesser

(1993) identified a five-step dialogue pattern to implement in an ITS. They are: (a) Tutor asks question; (b) student answers question; (c) tutor gives short feedback on answer quality; (d) tutor and student collaboratively improve on answer quality; and (e) tutor assesses the student's understanding of the answer. According to Graesser's observation, tutor questions were primarily motivated by curriculum scripts and the process of coaching student's idiosyncratic knowledge deficits. This five-step dialogue pattern suggests only a general nature of tutoring interactions rather than specific procedures for generating interactive questions and answers.

Collins and Stevens (1982, 1983) generated a set of inquiry techniques from analyses of teachers' interactive behaviors in a variety of domain areas. Nine of their most important strategies are: (a) selecting positive and negative examples; (b) varying cases systematically; (c) selecting counter examples; (d) forming hypotheses; (e) testing hypotheses; (f) considering alternative predictions; (g) entrapping students; (h) tracing consequences to a contradiction; and (i) questioning authority. Although these techniques are derived from the observation of classroom teachers' behaviors rather than experienced tutors, they provide valuable implications for producing diagnostic questions.

Brown and Palincsar (1982, 1989) emphasize expert scaffolding (see 7.4.3) and Socratic dialogue techniques in their reciprocal teaching (see also 23.4.1.3.4). While the expert scaffolding provides guidance for the tutor's involvement or provision of aids in the learning process, the Socratic dialogue techniques suggest what kinds of questions should be asked to diagnose the student's learning needs. Five ploys are important to present in the diagnostic questions: (a) Systematic varied cases are asked to help the student focus on relevant facts; (b) counter examples and hypothetical cases are asked to question the legitimacy of the student's conclusions; (c) entrapment strategies are presented in questions to lure the student into making incorrect predictions or premature formulations of general rules based on faulty reasoning; (d) hypothesis identifications are forced by asking the student to specify his or her work hypotheses; and (e) hypothesis evaluations are forced by asking the student's prediction (Brown & Palincsar, 1989).

Leinhardt's (1989) work provides important implications for generating explanations for the student's misconceptions identified from the analysis of on-task performance or response. She identified two primary features in expert teachers' explanations: (a) explicating the goal and objectives of the lessons, and (b) using parallel representations and their linkages. A model of explanation that she developed from the analysis of an expert tutor's explanations in teaching algebra subtraction problems shows that explanations are generated from various relations (e.g., pre-, co- and postrequisite) between the instructional goal and content elements and the constraints for the use of the learned content.

As the above review suggests, efforts for generating the principles of tutoring strategies (diagnosis and explana-

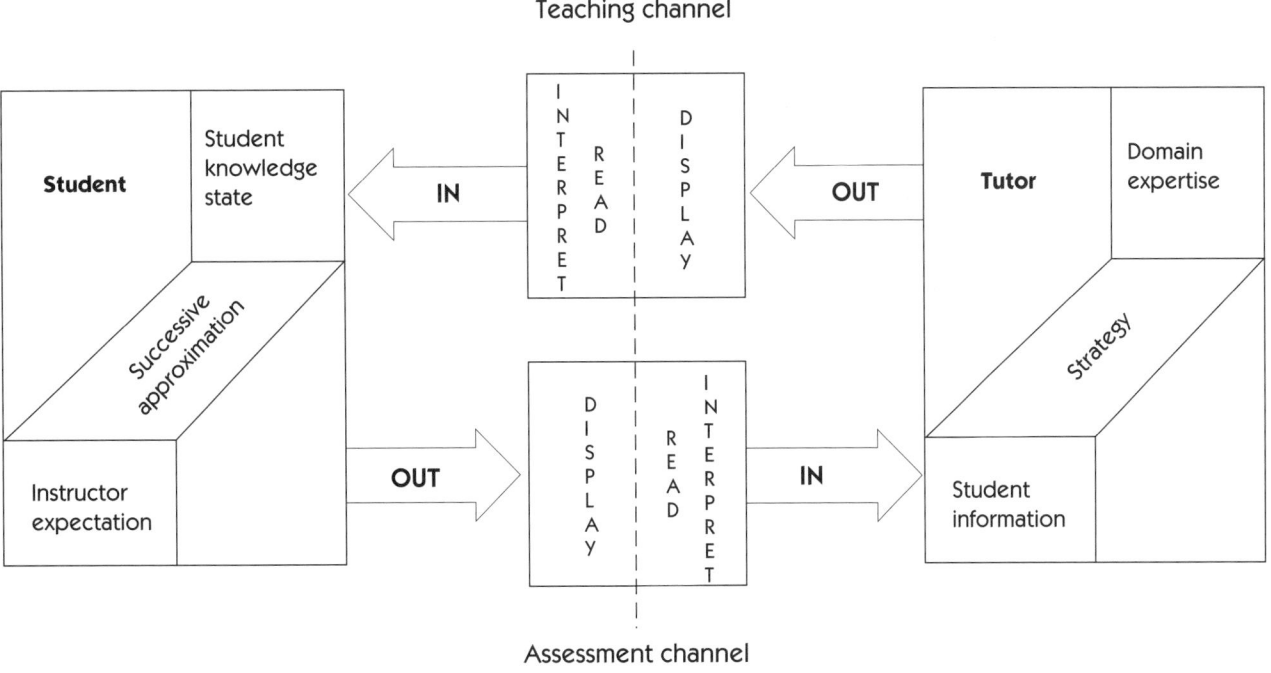

Figure 22-2. Process of instructional communication. (Adapted from Siedel et al., 1969.)

tions) have continued from the observation of human tutoring activities (e.g., Berliner, 1991; Borko & Livingston, 1989; Leinhardt, 1989; Putnam, 1987), and from simulation and testing of tutoring processes in ITS environments (Ohlson & Rees, 1991; see Chapter 19.) However, specific principles and practical guidelines for generating questions and explanations in an on-task adaptive system have yet to be developed.

22.6.3 Generation of Tutoring Dialogues

Once the principles and patterns of tutoring interactions are defined, they should be implemented through interactions (particularly, dialogues) between the student and system. However, the generation of specific rules for tutoring dialogues is an extremely difficult task. After having extensively studied human tutorial dialogues, Fox (1993) concluded that tutoring languages and communication are indeterminate, because a given linguistic item (including silence, face and body movement, and voice tones) is in principle open to an indefinite number of interpretations and reinterpretations. She argues that indeterminacy is a fundamental principle of interaction and that tutoring interactions should be nonrule governed. Also, she says that tutoring dialogues should be contexualized, and the contexualization should be tailored to fit exactly the needs of the student at the moment. The difficulty of developing tutoring dialogues in an adaptive system suggests that the development of future adaptive systems should focus on the application of the advantageous features of computer tech-

nology for the improvement of the tutoring functions of the adaptive system rather than simulating human tutoring behaviors and activities. As discussed earlier, however, AI methods and techniques have provided a much more powerful tool for developing and implementing flexible interactions required in adaptive instruction than traditional programming methods used in developing ordinary CBI programs. Also, the development of computer technology, including AI, continuously provides opportunities to enrich our environment for instructional research, development, and implementation.

22.7 A MODEL OF ADAPTIVE INSTRUCTIONAL SYSTEMS

In the above section, I emphasized the importance of on-task performance or a response-sensitive approach in the development of adaptive instructional systems. However, a complete adaptive system should have the capability to update continuously every component in the instructional system based on the student's on-task performance and the interactions between the student and system. However, almost all adaptive instructional systems, including ITSs, have been developed with emphasis on a few specific aspects or functions of instruction. Therefore, we present a conceptual model for developing a complete adaptive instructional system (Fig. 22-3). This model is adopted from the work of Seidel and his associates (Seidel, 1971), with consideration of recent developments in learning and instructional psychology and computer technology (Park, Perez & Seidel, 1987).

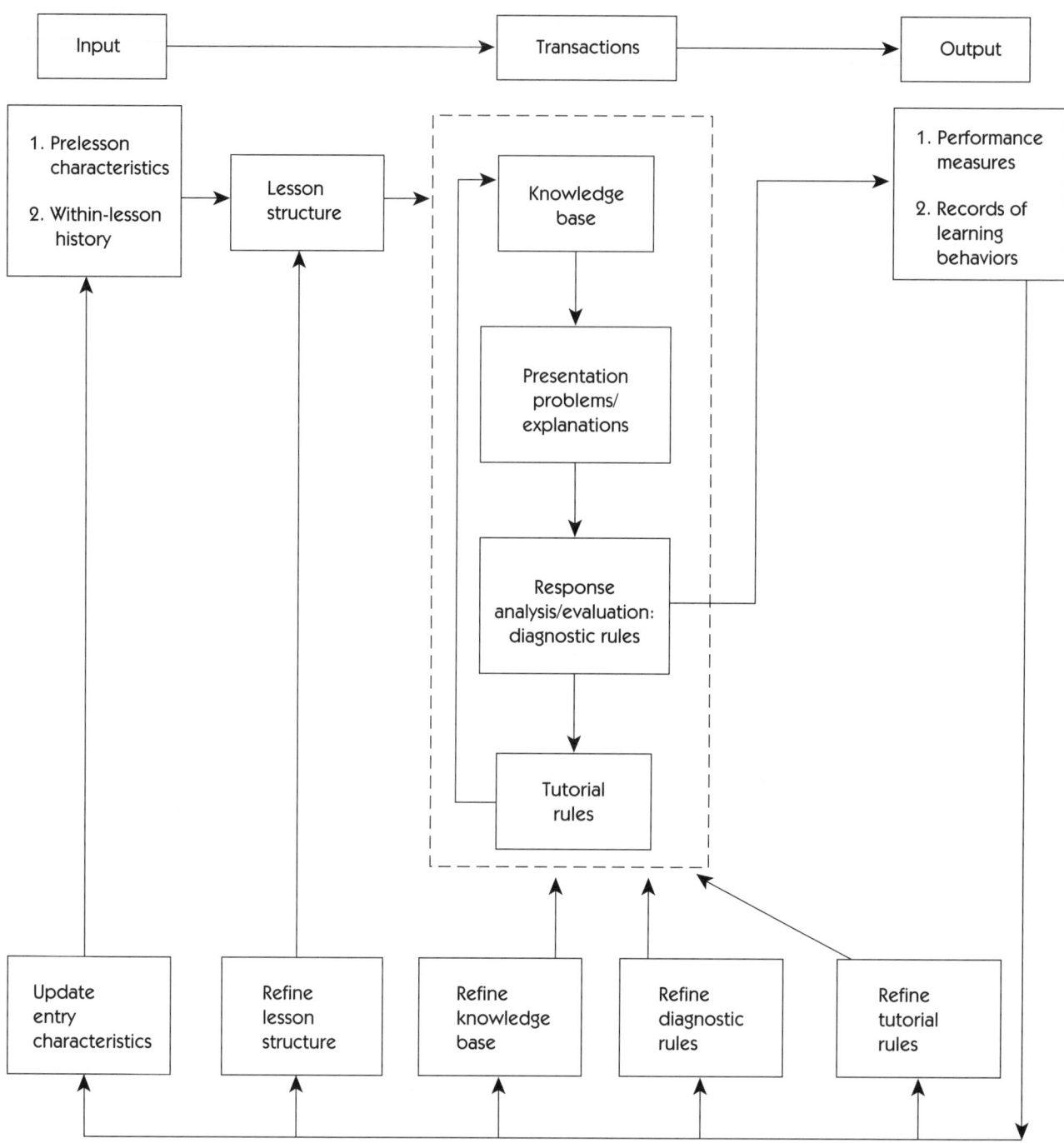

Figure 22-3. A model of adaptive instruction (Park et al., 1987). (Originally adapted from Seidel, 1971.)

This model does not provide specific procedures or technical guidelines for developing an adaptive system. However, we think that the cybernetic metasystem approach used in the model is generalizable as a guide for developing a more effective and efficient control process required in adaptive instructional systems. The model illustrates what components an adaptive system should have and how those components should be interrelated in an instructional process. Also,

the model shows what specific self-improving or updating capabilities the system may need to have.

As Figure 22-3 shows, this model divides the instructional process into three stages: input, transactions, and output. The input stage basically consists of the analysis of the student's entry characteristics. The student's entry characteristics include not only his or her within-lesson history (e.g., response history) but also prelesson characteristics.

The prelesson characteristics may include information about the student's aptitudes and other variables influencing his or her learning. As discussed earlier, the aptitude variables measured prior to instruction will be useful for the beginning stage of instruction but will become less important as the student's on-task performance history is accumulated. Thus, the within-lesson history should be continuously updated using the evaluation information of the performance (i.e., output measures).

The transaction stage consists of the interactions between the student and system. In the beginning stage of the instruction, the system will select problems and explanations to present based on the student's entry characteristics, mainly the premeasured aptitudes. Then, the system will evaluate the student's responses (or any other student input such as questions or comments) to the given problem or task. The response evaluation provides information for diagnosing the student's specific learning needs and for assessing overall performance level on the task. The learning needs will be inferred according to diagnostic rules in the system. Finally, the system will select new display presentations and questions for the student according to the tutorial rules. The tutorial rules should be developed in consideration of different learning and instructional theories (e.g., see Snelbecker, 1974; Reigeluth, 1983), research findings (e.g., see Gallangher, 1994; Weinstein & Mayer, 1986), expert heuristics (Jonassen, 1988), and response-sensitive strategies discussed in the earlier section of this chapter.

The output stage mainly consists of performance evaluation. The performance evaluation may include not only the student's overall achievement level on a given task and specific performance on the subtasks but also the analysis of complete learning behaviors related to the task and subtasks. According to the performance evaluation and analysis, the instructional components will be modified or updated. The instructional components to be updated may include contents in the knowledge base (including questions and explanations), instructional strategies, diagnostic and tutorial rules, the lesson structure, and entry characteristics. If the system does not have the capability to modify or update some of the instructional components automatically, the human monitor may be required to perform that task.

22.8 CONCLUSION

Adaptive instruction has a long history (Reiser, 1987). However, systematic effort aimed at developing adaptive instructional systems was not made until the early 1900s. The effort for developing adaptive instructional systems has taken different approaches: macro-adaptive, ATI, and micro-adaptive. Macro-adaptive systems have been developed to provide more individualized instruction on the basis of the student's basic learning needs and abilities determined prior to instruction. The ATI approach is to adapt instructional methods, procedures, or strategies to the student's specific aptitude information. Micro-adaptive systems have been developed to diagnose the student's learning needs and provide optimal instructional treatments during the instructional transaction process.

Some macro-adaptive instructional systems seemed to be positioned as an alternative educational system because of their demonstrated effectiveness. However, most of the macrosystems were discontinued without much success because of the difficulty associated with the development and implementation of the systems, including curriculum development, teacher training, resource limitation, and organizational resistance. Numerous studies have been conducted to investigate ATI methods and strategies because of ATI's theoretical appealing and practical application possibilities. However, the results are not consistent and have provided little implications for developing an adaptive instructional system.

Using computer technology, a number of different micro-adaptive instructional systems have been developed. However, their applications have been mostly in laboratory environments because of the limitation of their functional capability to handle the complex transaction processes involved in the learning of various types of tasks by many different students.

Another contribution to the limited success of adaptive instructional systems can be attributed to the unverified theoretical assumptions that were used for the development of the systems. Particularly, ATI, including the achievement and treatment interactions, has been used as the theoretical bases for many ATI studies. However, the variability of ATI research findings suggests that the theoretical assumptions used in ATI research may not be valid, and the development of a complete taxonomy of all likely aptitudes and instructional variables may not be possible. Even if it is possible to develop such a taxonomy, its instructional value will be limited because learning will be influenced by many variables, including aptitudes. Also, the instructional value of aptitude variables measured prior to instruction becomes less important as the instruction progresses. In the meantime, the student's on-task performance (i.e., response to the given problem or task) becomes more important for diagnosing the student's learning needs (see Fig. 22-1) because on-task performance is the integrated reflection of many verifiable and unverifiable variables involved in the learning.

Therefore, I propose an on-task performance and treatment interaction approach. In this approach, response-sensitive methods will be used as the primary strategy. Many studies (e.g., Atkinson, 1974; Park & Tennyson, 1980, 1986) demonstrated the effects of response-sensitive strategies. However, the application of the response-sensitive strategy has been limited to simple tasks such as vocabulary acquisition and concept learning because of the technical limitations of handling the complex interactions involved in learning more sophisticated tasks such as problem solving. However, ITSs developed in the last 2 decades have demonstrated that technical methods and tools are now available for the development of more sophisticated response-sensitive systems. Unfortunately, this technical development has not significantly contributed to an intellectual breakthrough in the field of learning and instruction. Thus, no principles or systematic guidelines for developing questions and explanations necessary in the response-sensitive strategy have been developed. In this chapter, I reviewed several studies that provide some valuable suggestions for the development of response-sensitive strategies, including asking diagnostic questions and providing explanations (Collins & Stevens, 1983; Brown & Palinscar, 1989; Leinhardt, 1983). Further research for asking diagnostic questions and providing explanations is needed for the development of response-sensitive adaptive systems.

Since response-sensitive diagnostic and prescriptive processes should be developed on the basis of many different types of information available in the system, I propose to use a complete model of adaptive instructional systems described by Park et al. (1987). This model consists of input, transactions, and output stages, and components directly required to implement the response-sensitive strategy are in the transaction stage of instruction.

To develop an adaptive instructional system using this model will require a multidisciplinary approach because it will need expertise from different domain areas such as learning psychology, cognitive science or knowledge engineering, and instructional technology (Park & Seidel, 1989). However, with the current technology and our knowledge of learning and instruction, the development of a complete adaptive instructional system like the one presented in Figure 22-3 may not be possible in the immediate future. It is expected that cognitive scientists will further improve the capabilities of current AI technology such as natural language dialogues and inferencing processes for capturing the human reasoning and cognitive process. In the meantime, the continuous accumulation of research findings in learning and instruction will make a significant contribution to instructional researchers' and developers' efforts for developing more powerful adaptive instructional systems.

REFERENCES

Abramson, T. & Kagen, E. (1975). Familiarization of content and different response modes in programmed instruction. *Journal of Educational Psychology 67*, 83–88.

Atkinson, R.C. (1968). Computerized instruction and the learning process. *American Psychologist 23*, 225–39.

— (1972). Ingredients for a theory of instruction. *American Psychologist 27*, 921–31.

— (1974). Teaching children to read using computer. *American Psychologist 29*, 169–78.

— (1976). Adaptive instructional systems: some attempts to optimize the learning process. *In* D. Klahr, ed. *Cognition and instruction*. New York: Wiley.

— & Crothers, E.J. (1964). A comparison of paired-associate learning models having different acquisition and retention axioms. *Journal of Mathematical Psychology 2*, 285–315.

— & Fletcher, J.D. (1972). Teaching children to read with computer. *The Reading Teacher 25*, 319–27.

— & Paulson, J.A. (1972). An approach to the psychology of instruction. *Psychological Bulletin 78*, 49–61.

Bandura, A. (1982). Self-efficacy mechanism in human agency. *American Psychologist 37*, 122–48.

Berliner, D.C. (1991). Educational psychology and pedagogical expertise: new findings and new opportunities for thinking about training. *Educational Psychologist 26*, 145–55.

— & Cohen, L.S. (1973). Trait-treatment interaction and learning. *Review of Research in Education 1*, 58–94.

Block, J.H. (1980). Promising excellence through mastery learning. *Theory and Practice 19*, 66–74.

Bloom, B.S. (1984). The 2 sigma problem: the search for methods of group instruction as effective as one-to-one tutoring. *Educational Researcher 13*, 4–16.

Borko, H. & Livingston, C. (1989). Cognition and improvisation: differences in mathematics instruction by expert and novice teachers. *American Educational Research Journal 26*, 474–98.

Brown, A.L. & Palincsar, A.S. (1989). Guided, cooperative learning and individual knowledge acquisition. *In* L. Resnick, ed. *Knowledge, learning, and instruction: essays in honor of Robert Glaser*. Hillsdale, NJ: Erlbaum .

— & Palincsar, A.S. (1982). Reciprocal teaching of comprehension strategies: a natural history of one program for enhancing learning. *In* J.D. Day & J. Borkowski, eds. *Intelligence and exceptionality: new directions for theory, assessment and instructional practice*. Norwood, NJ: Ablex.

Burns, R.B. (1980). Relation of aptitude learning at different points in time during instruction. *Journal of Educational Psychology 72*, 785–97.

Calfee, R.C. (1970). The role of mathematical model in optimizing instruction. *Scientia: Revue Internationale de Sythese Scientifique 105*, 1–25.

Carrier, C. (1984). Do learners make good choices? *Instructional Innovator 29*, 15–17, 48.

— & Jonassen, D.H. (1988). Adapting courseware to accommodate individual differences. *In* D. Jonassen, ed. *Instructional designs for microcomputer courseware*. Hillsdale, NJ: Erlbaum .

Carroll, J.B. (1963). A model of school learning. *Teachers College Record 64*, 723–33.

Cazden, C.B. (1986). Classroom discourse. *In* M.C. Wittrock, ed. *Handbook of research on teaching, 3d ed.* New York: Macmillan.

Chant, V.G. & Atkinson, R.C. Optimal allocation of instructional effort to interrelated learning strands. *Journal of Mathematical Psychology 10*, 1–25.

Clark, R. (1984). Research on student thought processes during computer-based instruction. *Journal of Instructional Development 7*, 2–5.

Cohen, I.S. (1963). Programmed learning and the Socratic dialogue. *American Psychologist 17*, 772–75.

Collins, A. & Stevens, A. (1983). A cognitive theory of inquiry teaching. *In* C.M. Reigeluth, ed. *Instructional-design theories and models: an overview of their current status*. Hillsdale, NJ: Erlbaum .

— & — (1982). Goals and strategies of effective teachers. *In* R. Glaser, ed. *Advances in instructional psychology, Vol. 2*. Hillsdale, NJ: Erlbaum .

Corno, L. & Snow, E.R. (1986). Adapting teaching to individual differences among learners. *In* M.C. Wittrock, ed.

Handbook of research on teaching, 3d ed. New York: Macmillan.

Cronbach, L.J. (1957). The two disciplines of scientific psychology. *American Psychologist 12,* 671–84.

— (1971). How can instruction be adapted to individual differences? *In* R.A. Weisgerber, ed. *Perspective in individualized learning.* Itasca, IL: Peacock.

— & Snow, R.E. (1977). *Aptitudes and instructional methods: a handbook for research on interactions.* New York: Irvingston.

Crowder, N.W. (1959). *Automatic tutoring: the state of art.* New York: Wiley.

Davis, J.K. (1991). Educational implications of field dependence-independence. *In* S. Wapner & J. Demick, eds. *Field dependence-independence: cognitive style across the life span,* 149–76. Hillsdale, NJ: Erlbaum .

Dear, R.E., Silberman, H.F., Estavan, D.P. & Atkinson, R.C. (1967). An optimal strategy for the presentation of paired-associate items. *Behavioral Science 12,* 1–13.

Derry, S.J. & Murphy, D.A. (1986). Designing systems that train learning ability: from theory to practice. *Review of Educational Research 56,* 1–39.

Deutsch, T. & and Tobias, S. (1980). *Prior achievement, anxiety, and instructional method.* Paper presented at the annual meeting of the American Psychological Association, Montreal, Canada.

Dewey, J. (1964/1902). The child and the curriculum. *In* R.D. Archambault, ed. *John Dewey on education: selected writings.* New York: Modern Library.

Dick, W. & Carey, L. (1985). *The systematic design of instruction, 2d ed.* Glenview, IL: Scott, Foresman.

DiVesta, F.J. (1975). Trait-treatment interactions, cognitive processes, and research on communication media. *AV Communication Review 23,* 185–96.

Dunn, R. & Dunn, K. (1978). *Teaching students through their individual learning styles: a practical approach.* Reston, VA: Reston.

Dunham, J.L., Guilford, J.P. & Hoepner, R. (1968). Multivariate approach to discovering the intellectual components of concept learning. *Psychological Review 75,* 206–21.

Entwistle, N. (1981). *Styles of learning and teaching.* New York: Wiley.

Flanagan, J.C., Shanner, W.M., Brudner, H.J. & Marker, R.W. (1975). An individualized instructional system: PLAN. *In* H. Talmage, ed. *Systems of individualized education.* Berkeley, CA: McCutchan.

Farrar, M.T. (1986). Teacher questions: the complexity of the cognitive simple. *Instructional Science 15,* 89–107.

Federico, P. (1980). Adaptive instruction: trends and issues. *In* R.E. Snow, P. Federico, W.E. Montague, eds. *Aptitude, learning and instruction, Vol. 1: cognitive process analyses of aptitude.* Hillsdale, NJ: Erlbaum.

Fisher, D.F. & Townsend, J.T. (1993). *Models of Morse code skill acquisition: simulation and analysis.* Research Product 93-04, Alexandria, VA: U.S. Army Research Institute.

Fleishman, E.A. & Bartlett, C.J. (1969). Human abilities. *Annual Review of Psychology 20,* 349–80.

Fox, B.A. (1993). *The human tutoring dialogue project: issues in the design of instructional systems.* Hillsdale, NJ.: Erlbaum.

Frase, L,T., Patrick, E. & Schumer, H. (1970). Effect of question position and frequency upon learning from text under different levels of incentives. *Journal of Educational Psychology 61,* 52–56.

Fredrickson, C.H. (1969). Abilities, transfer and information retrieval in verbal learning. *Multivariate Behavioral Research Monographs,* 2.

French, R.L. (1975). Teaching strategies and learning processes. *Educational Considerations 3,* 27–28.

Gagné, R.M. (1967). *Learning and individual differences.* Columbus, OH: Merrill.

— & Briggs, L.J. (1979). *Principles of instructional design, 2d ed.* New York: Holt.

Gallangher, J.J. (1994). Teaching and learning: new models. *Annual Review of Psychology 45,* 171–95.

Glaser, R. (1972). Individual and learning: the new aptitudes. *Educational Researcher 6,* 5–13.

— (1976). Cognitive psychology and instructional design. *In* D. Klahr, ed. *Cognition and instruction.* New York: Wiley.

— (1977). *Adaptive education: individual diversity and learning.* New York: Holt.

— & Nitko, A.J. (1971). Measurement in learning and instruction. *In* R.L. Thorndike, ed. *Educational Measurement, 2d ed.* Washington, DC: American Council of Education.

— & Resnick, L.B. (1972). Instructional psychology. *Annual Review of Psychology 23,* 207–76.

Graesser, A.C. (1993). *Questioning mechanisms during tutoring, conversation, and human-computer interaction* Office of Naval Research technical report, 93-1. Memphis, TN: Memphis State University.

Gregg, L.W. (1970). Optimal policies of wise choice? A critique of Smallwood's optimization procedure. *In* W.H. Holtzman, ed. *Computer-assisted instruction, testing and guidance.* New York: Harper & Row.

Groan, G.J. & Atkinson, R.C. (1966). Models for optimizing the learning process. *Psychological Bulletin 66,* 309–20.

Hagberg, J.O. & Leider, R.J. (1978). *The inventures: excursions in life and career renewal.* Reading, MA: Addison-Wesley.

Hall, K.A. (1977). A research model for applying computer technology to the interactive instructional process. *Journal of Computer-Based Instruction 3,* 68–75.

Hamaker, C. (1986). The effects of adjunct questions on prose learning. *Review of Educational Research 56,* 212–42.

Hambleton, R.K. & Novick, M.R. (1973). Toward an integration of theory and method for criterion-referenced tests. *Journal of Educational Measurement 10,* 159–70.

Hansen, D.N., Ross, S.M. & Rakow, E. (1977). *Adaptive models for computer-based training systems* (annual report to Navy Personnel Research and Development Center). Memphis, TN: Memphis State University.

Hoge, D., Smith, E. & Hanson, S. (1990). School experiences predicting changes in self-esteem of sixth- and seventh-grade students. *Journal of Educational Psychology 82,* 117–27.

Holland, J.G. (1977). Variables in adaptive decisions in individualized instruction. *Educational Psychologist 12,* 146–61.

Jonassen, D.H. (1988). Integrating learning strategies into courseware to facilitate deeper processing. *In* D.H. Jonassen, ed. *Instructional designs for microcomputer courseware.* Hillsdale, NJ: Erlbaum.

Keller, F.S. (1968). "Goodbye Teacher. . . ." *Journal of Applied Behavior Analysis 1,* 79–89.

— (1974). Ten years of personalized instruction. *Teaching of Psychology 1,* 4–9.

Klausmeier, H.J. (1975). IGE: an alternative form of schooling. *In* H. Talmage, ed. *Systems of individualized education.*

Berkeley, CA: McCutchan.

— (1976). Individually guided education: 1966–1980. *Journal of Teacher Education 27,* 199–205.

— (1977). Origin and overview of IGE. *In* H.J. Klausmeier, R.A. Rossmiller & M. Saily, eds. *Individually guided elementary education: concepts and practice.* New York: Academic.

Kolb, D.A. (1971). *Individual learning styles and the learning process.* Cambridge, MA: MIT Press.

— (1977). *Learning style inventory: a self-description of preferred learning modes.* Boston, MA: McBer.

Kulik, J.A. (1982). Individualized systems of instruction. *In* H.E. Mitzel, ed. *Encyclopedia of educational research, 5th ed.* New York: Macmillan.

Landa, L.N. (1970). *Algorithmization in learning and instruction.* Englewood Cliffs, NJ: Educational Technology.

— (1976). *Instructional regulation and control.* Englewood Cliffs, NJ: Educational Technology.

Leinhardt, G. (1989). Development of expert explanation: an analysis of a sequence of subtraction lessons. *In* L. Resnick, ed. *Knowledge, learning, and instruction: essays in honor of Robert Glaser,* 67–124. Hillsdale, NJ: Erlbaum .

Lewis, B.N. & Pask, G. (1965). The theory and practice of adaptive teaching systems. *In* R. Glaser, ed. *Teaching machines and programmed learning II.* Washington, DC: National Educational Association.

Little, K.L. (1934). Results of use of machines for testing and for drill, upon learning in educational psychology. *Journal of Experimental Education 3,* 45–49.

Lorton, P. (1972). *Computer-based instruction in spelling: an investigation of optimal strategies for presenting instructional material* (unpublished doctoral dissertation). Palo Alto, CA: Stanford University.

Marton, F. (1988). Describing and improving learning. *In* R.R. Schmeck, ed. *Learning strategies and learning styles.* New York: Plenum.

McClelland, D.C. (1965). Toward a theory of motive acquisition. *American Psychologist 33,* 201–11.

McCombs, B.L. & McDaniel, M.A. (1981). On the design of adaptive treatments for individualized instructional systems. *Educational Psychologist 16,* 11–22.

Merrill, M.D. (1971). *Instructional design: reading.* Englewood Cliffs, NJ: Prentice Hall.

— & Boutwell, R.C. (1973). Instructional development: methodology and research. *In* F. Kerlinger, ed. *Review of research in education.* Itasca, IL: Peacock.

Messick, S. (1994). The matter of style: manifestations of personality in cognition, learning and teaching. *Educational Psychologist 29,* 121–36.

Norman, M.F. (1964). Incremental learning on random trials. *Journal of Mathematical Psychology 2,* 336–50.

Novic, M.R. & Jackson, P.H. (1974). *Statistical methods for educational and psychological research.* New York: McGraw-Hill.

— & Lewis, C. (1974). *Prescribing test length for criterion-referenced measurement — I: Posttests* (ACT Technical Bulletin No. 18). Iowa City, IO: American College Testing Program.

Ohlson, S. & Rees, E. (1991). The function of conceptual understanding in the learning of arithmetic procedures. *Cognition and Instruction 8,* 103–79.

O'Neil, H.F., Jr. (1978). *Learning strategies.* New York: Academic.

Park, O. (1983). *Instructional strategies: a hypothetical taxonomy* (Technical Report No. 3). Minneapolis, MN: Control Data Corporation.

—, Perez, R.S. & Seidel, R.J. (1987). Intelligent CAI: old wine in new bottles or a new vintage? *In* G. Kearsley, ed. *Artificial intelligence and instruction: applications and methods.* Boston, MA: Addison-Wesley.

— & Seidel, R.J. (1989). A multidisciplinary model for development of intelligent computer-assisted instruction. *Educational Technology Research and Development 37,* 72–80.

— & Tennyson, R.D. (1980). Adaptive design strategies for selecting number and presentation order of examples in coordinate concept acquisition. *Journal of Educational Psychology 78,* 499–505.

— & — (1986). Computer-based response-sensitive design strategies for selecting presentation form and sequence examples in learning of coordinate concepts. *Journal of Educational Psychology 78,* 153-–58.

Pask, G. (1957). Automatic teaching techniques. *British Communication and Electronics 4,* 210–11.

— (1960a). Electronic keyboard teaching machines. *In* A.A. Lumsdaine & R. Glaser, eds. *Teaching machines and programmed learning I.* Washington, DC: National Educational Association.

— (1960b). Adaptive teaching with adaptive machines. *In* A.A. Lumsdaine & R. Glaser, eds. *Teaching machines and programmed learning I.* Washington, DC: National Educational Association.

— (1976). Styles and strategies of learning. *British Journal of Educational Psychology 46,* 128–48.

— (1988). Learning strategies, teaching strategies, and conceptual or learning style. *In* R.R. Schmeck, ed. *Learning strategies and learning styles,* 83–100. New York: Plenum.

Peterson, P.L. (1977). Review of human characteristics and school learning. *American Educational Research Journal 14,* 73–79.

— & Janicki, T.C. (1979). Individual characteristics and children's learning in large-group and small-group approaches. *Journal of Educational Psychology 71,* 677–87.

—, — & Swing, S. (1981). Ability × treatment interaction effects on children's learning in large-group and small-group approaches. *American Educational Research Journal 18,* 453–73.

Popkewitz, T.S., Tabachnick, B.R. & Wehlage, G. (1982). *The myth of educational reform: a study of school response to a program of change.* Madison, WI: University of Wisconsin Press.

Postlethwait, S.N. (1981). A basis for instructional alternatives. *Journal of College Science Teaching 21,* 44–46.

—, Novak, J. & Murray, H.T. (1972). *The audio-tutorial approach to learning, 3d ed.* Minneapolis, MN: Burgess.

Pressey, S.L. (1926). A simple apparatus which gives tests and scores and teaches. *School and Society 23,* 373–76.

— (1927). A machine for automatic teaching of drill material. *School and Society 25,* 1–14.

— (1959). Certain major educational issues appearing in the conference on teaching machines. *In* E.H. Galanter, ed. *Automatic teaching: the state of art.* New York: Wiley.

Putnam, R.T. (1987). Structuring and adjusting content for students: a study of live and simulated tutoring addition. *American Educational research Journal 24,* 13–48.

Redfield, D.L. & Rousseau, E.W. (1981). A meta-analysis of experimental research on teacher questioning behavior.

Review of Educational Research 51, 237–45.

Reigeluth, C.M. (1983). *Instructional-design theories and models: an overview of their current status.* Hillsdale, NJ: Erlbaum .

Reiser, R.A. (1987). Instructional technology: a history. *In* R. Gagné, ed. *Instructional technology: foundations.* Hillsdale, NJ: Erlbaum.

Ross, S.M. (1983). Increasing the meaningfulness of quantitative materials by adapting context to student background. *Journal of Educational Psychology 75,* 519–29.

— & Anand, P. (1986). *Using computer-based instruction to personalize math learning materials for elementary school children.* Paper presented at the annual meeting of the American Educational Research Association, San Francisco, CA.

— & Morrison, G.R. (1988). Adapting instruction to learner performance and background variables. *In* D. Jonassen, ed. *Instructional designs for microcomputer courseware,* 227–43. Hillsdale, NJ: Erlbaum .

— & Rakow, E.A. (1981). Learner control versus program control as adaptive strategies for selection of instructional support on math rules. *Journal of Educational Psychology 73,* 745–53.

— & — (1982). Adaptive instructional strategies for teaching rules in mathematics. *Educational Communication and Technology Journal 30,* 67–74.

Rothen, W. & Tennyson, R.D. (1978). Application of Bayes' theory in designing computer-based adaptive instructional strategies. *Educational Psychologist 12,* 317–23.

Salomon, G. (1972). Heuristic models for the generation of aptitude treatment interaction hypotheses. *Review of Educational Research 42,* 327–43.

— (1974). Internalization of filmic schematic operations in interaction with learner's aptitudes. *Journal of Educational Psychology 66,* 499–511.

Scandura, J.M. (1973). *Structural learning I: theory and research.* New York: Gordon & Breach Science.

Scandura, J.M. (1977a). *Problem solving: a structural/ processes approach with instructional implications.* New York: Academic.

— (1977b). Structural approach to instructional problems. *American Psychologist 32,* 33–53.

— (1983). Instructional strategies based on the structural learning theory. *In* C.M. Reigeluth (1983). *Instructional- design theories and models: An overview of their current status,* 213–49. Hillsdale, NJ: Erlbaum

— & Scandura, A.B. (1988). A structured approach to intelligent tutoring. *In* D.H. Jonassen, ed. *Instructional designs for microcomputer courseware.* Hillsdale, NJ: Erlbaum .

— & Durnin, J.H. (1977). Assessing behavior potential: test of basic theoretical assumptions. *In* J.M. Scandura, ed. *Problem solving: a structural/processes approach with instructional implications.* New York: Academic.

Schmeck, R.R. (1988). Strategies and styles of learning: an integration of varied perspectives. *In* R.R. Schmeck, ed. *Learning strategies and learning styles.* New York: Plenum.

Schunk, D.H. (1991). Self-efficacy and academic motivation. *Educational Psychologist 26,* 207–31

Seidel, R.J. (1971). *Theories and strategies related to measurement in individualized instruction.* Professional paper 2-72, Alexandria, VA: Human Resources Research Organization.

—, Compton, J.G., Kopstein, F.F., Rosenblatt, R.D. & See, S. (1969). *Project IMPACT: description of learning and pre- scription for instruction.* Professional paper 22-69, Alexandria, VA: Human Resources Research Organization.

— & Park, O. (1994). An historical perspective and a model for evaluation of intelligent tutoring systems. *Journal of Educational Computing Research 10,* 103–28.

—, — & Perez, R. (1989). Expertise of ICAI: development requirements. *Computers in Human Behaviors 4,* 235–56.

—, Wagner, H., Rosenblatt, R.D., Hillelsohn, M.J., & Stelzer, J. (1978). Learner control of instructional sequencing within an adaptive tutorial CAI environment. *Instructional Science 7,* 37–80.

Shin, E.C., Schallert, D.L. & Savenye, W.C. (1994). Effects of learner control, advisement, and prior knowledge on young students' learning in a hypertext environment. *Educational Technology Research and Development 42,* 33–46.

Shute, V.J. & Psotka, J. (1995). Intelligent tutoring systems: past, present and future. *In* D. Jonassen, ed. *Handbook of research on educational communications and technology.* New York: Scholastic.

Sieber, J.R., O'Neil, H.F. Jr. & Tobias, S. (1977). *Anxiety, learning and instruction.* Hillsdale, NJ: Erlbaum.

Skinner, B.F. (1954). The science of learning and the art of teaching. *Harvard Educational Review 24,* 86–97.

— (1968). *The technology of teaching.* New York: Appleton- Century-Crofts.

— (1958). The teaching machines. *Science 128,* 969–77.

Smallwood, R.D. (1962). *A decision structure for teaching machines.* Cambridge, MA: MIT Press.

— (1970). Optimal policy regions for computer-directed teaching systems. *In* W.H. Holtzman, ed. *Computer-assisted instruction, testing and guidance.* New York: Harper & Row.

— (1971). The analysis of economic teaching strategies for a simple learning model. *Journal of Mathematical Psychology 8,* 285–301.

Snelbbecker, G.E. (1974). *Learning theory, instructional theory, and psychoeducational design.* New York: McGraw-Hill.

Snow, E.R. (1980). Aptitude, learner control, and adaptive instruction. *Educational Psychologist 15,* 151–58.

— (1986). Individual differences and the design of educational program. *American Psychologist 41,* 1029–39.

— & Lohman, D.F. (1984). Toward a theory of cognitive aptitude for learning from instruction. *Journal of Educational Psychology 76,* 347–76.

— & Swanson, J. (1992). Instructional psychology: aptitude, adaptation, and assessment. *Annual Review of Psychology 43,* 583–626.

Suppes, P., Fletcher, J.D. & Zanottie, M. (1976). Models of individual trajectories in computer-assisted instruction for deaf students. *Journal of Educational Psychology 68,* 117–27.

Tennyson, R.D. (1981). Use of adaptive information for advisement in learning concepts and rules using computer- assisted instruction. *American Educational Research Journal 73,* 326–34.

— & Christensen, D.L. (1988). MAIS: an intelligent learning system. *In* D. Jonassen, ed. *Instructional designs for micro- computer courseware,* 247–74. Hillsdale, NJ: Erlbaum .

— & Park, O. (1987). Artificial intelligence and computer- based learning. *In* R. Gagné, ed. *Instructional technology: foundations.* Hillsdale, NJ: Erlbaum .

—, — & Christensen, D.L. (1985). Adaptive control of learning time and content sequence in concept learning using computer-based instruction. *Journal of Educational*

Psychology 77, 481–91.

— & Park, S. (1984). Process learning time as an adaptive design variable in concept learning using computer-based instruction. *Journal of Educational Psychology 76,* 452–65.

— & Rothen, W. (1977). Pretask and on-task adaptive design strategies for selecting number of instances in concept acquisition. *Journal of Educational Psychology 69,* 586–92.

Thorndike, E.L. (1911). *Individuality.* Boston, MA: Houghton Mifflin.

— (1913). *The psychology of learning: educational psychology II.* New York: Teachers College Press.

Tobias, S. (1973). Review of the response mode issues. *Review of Educational Research 43,* 193–204.

— (1976). Achievement-treatment interactions. *Review of Educational Research 46,* 61–74.

— (1982). When do instructional methods make a difference? *Educational Researcher 11,* 4–9.

— (1987). Learner characteristics. *In* R. Gagné, ed. *Instructional technology: foundations.* Hillsdale, NJ: Erlbaum

— (1988). Learner characteristics. *In* R. Gagné, ed. *Instructional technology: foundations.* Hillsdale, NJ: Erlbaum .

— (1989). Another look at research on the adaptation of instruction to student characteristics. *Educational Psychologist 24,* 213–27.

— (1994). Interest, prior knowledge, and learning. *Review of Educational Research 64,* 37–54.

— & Ingber, T. (1976). Achievement-treatment interactions in programmed instruction. *Journal of Educational Psychology 68,* 43–47.

— & Federico, P.A. (1984). Changing aptitude-achievement relationships in instruction: a comment. *Journal of Computer-Based Instruction 11,* 111–12.

Townsend, J.T. (1992). *Initial mathematical models of early Morse code performance.* Research Product 93-04, Alexandria, VA: U.S. Army Research Institute.

Vernon, P.E. (1973). Multivariate approaches to the study of cognitive styles. *In* J.R. Royce, ed. *Multivariate analysis and psychological theory,* 125–41. New York: Academic.

Wang, M. (1980). Adaptive instruction: building on diversity. *Theory into Practice 19,* 122–28.

— & Lindvall, C.M. (1984). Individual differences and school learning environments. *Review of Research in Education 11,* 161–225.

— & Walberg, H.J. (1983). Adaptive instruction and classroom time. *American Educational Research Journal 20,* 601–26.

Wenger, E. (1987). *Artificial intelligence and tutoring systems: computational and cognitive approaches to the communication of knowledge.* Los Altos, CA: Kaufmann.

Weiner, B. (1990). History of motivational researcher in education. *Journal of Educational Psychology 82,* 616–22.

Weinstein, C.F. & Mayer, R. (1986). The teaching of learning strategies. *In* M.C. Wittrock, ed. *Handbook of research on teaching, 3d ed.* New York: Macmillan.

—, Goetz, E.T. & Alexander, P.A. (1988). *Learning and study strategies.* San Diego, CA: Academic.

Whitener, E.M. (1989). A meta-analytic review of the effect on learning of the interaction between prior achievement and instructional support. *Review of Educational Research 59,* 65–86.

Wulfeck, W.H. II. & Scandura, J.M. (1977). Theory of adaptive instruction with application to sequencing in teaching problem solving. *In* J.M. Scandura, ed. *Problem solving: a structural/processes approach with instructional implications.* New York: Academic.

Zimmerman, B.J. & Martinez-Pons, M. (1990). Student differences in self-regulated learning: relating grade, sex, and giftedness to self-efficacy and strategy use. *Journal of Educational Psychology 82,* 51–59.

23. RICH ENVIRONMENTS FOR ACTIVE LEARNING

R. Scott Grabinger

UNIVERSITY OF COLORADO AT DENVER

23.1 CHAPTER PURPOSES

In today's complex world, simply knowing how to use tools and knowledge in a single domain is not enough to remain competitive. People must also learn when to use tools and knowledge in new domains and different situations. Industry specialists report that people at every organizational level must be creative and flexible problem solvers (Lynton, 1989). Even members of the "blue-collar" workforce must demonstrate advanced levels of problem-solving skills to attain and retain employment. This requires the ability to apply experience and knowledge to address novel problems. Consequently, learning to think critically, to analyze and synthesize information to solve technical, social, economic, political, and scientific problems, and to work productively in groups are crucial skills for successful and fulfilling participation in our modern, competitive society.

This chapter has two main goals: First, I describe and organize the common elements of rich environments for active learning, or REALs, including the theoretical foundations and instructional strategies to provide a common ground for discussion. REALs are based on constructivist values and theories including "collaboration, personal autonomy, generativity, reflectivity, active engagement, personal relevance, and pluralism" (Lebow, 1993, p. 5). REALs provide learning activities that, instead of transferring knowledge to students, engage students in a continuous collaborative process of building and reshaping understanding as a natural consequence of their experiences and interactions with the world in authentic ways (Forman & Pufall, 1988; Fosnot, 1989; Goodman, 1984). Advocating a holistic approach to education, REALs reflect the assumption that the process of knowledge and understanding acquisition is "firmly embedded in the social and emotional context in which learning takes place" (Lebow, 1993, p. 6), Second, I look at some of the research conducted with various implementations of REALs. I examine the research methodologies used, the topics investigated, and close with suggestions for future research directions.

23.2 NEED FOR EDUCATIONAL CHANGE

23.2.1 Changing Society

Education is receiving increasing pressure from changing global economic circumstances and complex societal needs. Yet, according to Lynton (1989, p. 23), "At this time . . . education is far from fully contributing to the economic well-being of this country" [United States]. Public and private institutions are demanding employees who can think critically and solve a range of problems, yet they claim that those people are difficult to find.

Education, to its credit, is neither deaf to the plea nor ignorant of the need. Calls for restructuring the way students learn come from a variety of institutions including the American Association for the Advancement of Science (1989) and the National Council of Teachers for Mathematics (1989). Educators agree that we must help students learn to solve problems and think independently (Bransford, Sherwood, Hasselbring, Kinzer & Williams, 1990; Feuerstein, 1979; Linn, 1986; Mann, 1979; Resnick & Klopfer, 1989; Segal, Chipman & Glaser, 1985). The challenge for educators is to develop strategies that teach content in ways that also teach thinking and problem-solving skills (Bransford et al., 1990).

22.2.2 Weaknesses within the Current System

There is considerable evidence that today's students are not particularly strong in the areas of thinking and reasoning (Bransford, Goldman & Vye, 1991; Nickerson, 1988; Resnick, 1987). Bransford (1990, pp. 115–16) states that the "basic problem is that traditional instruction often fails to produce the kinds of transfer to new problem-solving situations

The author wishes to thank Joanna Dunlap for help with the initial conceptualization of this chapter, and Karen Norum, Dawn Buckingham-Hull, and James Teslow for research assistance. All are outstanding doctoral students at the University of Colorado at Denver.

that most educators would like to see." Neither do children often experience in the classroom the kinds of problems that make knowledge relevant to them (Collins, Brown & Holum, 1991). "They [students] treat knowledge as ends rather than as a means to important ends" (Bransford et al., 1990, p. 117). Students treat new information as facts to be memorized and recited back rather than as tools to solve problems relevant to their own needs.

23.2.2.1. Inert Knowledge. Research shows that knowledge learned but not explicitly related to relevant problem solving remains inert (CTGV, 1993c; Perfetto, Bransford & Franks, 1983; Whitehead, 1929). Knowledge acquired in abstract circumstances without direct relevance to the needs of learners is not readily available for application or transfer to novel situations (for a review of transfer research, refer to Butterfield & Nelson, 1989; Clark & Voogel, 1985). The Cognition and Technology Group at Vanderbilt (CTGV) (CTGV, 1993c) specifies the following flaws in our conventional approaches to schooling and teaching that lead to inert knowledge:

1. In the constant battle of breadth versus depth, breadth usually always wins. We (educators) tend to fill our students with facts and leave no time for dealing with topics in depth. "Students who rely on memorized algorithms for solving problems typically do not perform as well on transfer problems as do students who rely on an understanding of the underlying concepts" (Robertson, 1990, p. 253).

2. In our desire to cover as much material as possible, we focus our instructional activities on abstract decontextualized basic skills, concepts, and technical definitions that we believe have broad applicability and that are unaffected by the activities or environments in which they are acquired and used (Brown, Collins & Duguid, 1989). However, when we do this, students do not learn when to apply those skills or within what kinds of contexts they work. We do this despite a large body of evidence that indicates that abstracted skills are seldom transferred from one domain to another (Butterfield & Nelson, 1989; Clark & Voogel, 1985).

3. When we do provide practice for our students, we give them arbitrary, uninteresting, unrealistic problems to solve. The example of story problems in math is overused. We can also find examples of oversimplified, unrealistic problems in the sciences, language arts, and social studies. Again, we do this in the mistaken belief that we must emphasize decontextualized skills that are applicable everywhere.

4. We treat students passively for 12 to 16 years, rarely giving them the opportunity to take responsibility for their own learning, to explore ideas of their own choosing, to collaborate with one another or with teachers, or to make valuable contributions to the learning of others. They do not learn to take charge of their own learning, nor do they learn the skills necessary to become life-long learners and daily problem solvers.

I add a couple of more items not cited in the CTGV article to the list of conventional educational practices:

5. Students are not evaluated in authentic ways. After teaching in decontextualized ways, we test in the same ways. We do not look at actual performance but use complex paper-pencil tests to measure the quantity of knowledge learned.

6. Finally, our current school practices often have negative effects on the morale and motivation of students. Perelman (1992, p. 72) states that "Students are forced to compete to achieve as much as they can within the periods of time allotted for each activity. This design requires that most students fail or do less well most of the times so that a minority of them can be labeled 'excellent.' The main functional focus of the system is not 'learning,' it is 'screening out' "(p. 72).

We have created an evaluation, testing, and grading substructure that helps perpetuate the system. Education is often a "game" that teaches our students to focus on tests and grades rather than on problem solving in a risk-free environment. The best students learn early on that they succeed best by working by themselves as quickly as possible. They learn to "beat" the tests.

23.2.2.2. Erroneous Assumptions. We begin to change these conventional practices by calling into question some of our basic assumptions. Berryman (1991) says that the educational practices described above stem from five erroneous assumptions about learning that have governed education since the beginning of the industrial age. He holds that we often assume incorrectly that:

1. People easily transfer learning from one situation to another if they have learned the fundamental skills and concepts.

2. Learners are "receivers" of knowledge in verbal forms from books, experts, and teachers.

3. Learning is entirely behavioristic, involving the strengthening of bonds between stimuli and correct responses (see 2.2).

4. Learners are blank slates ready to be written on and filled with knowledge.

5. Skills and knowledge are best acquired independent of realistic contexts for use.

To begin to address the issues of transfer and instructional methods to meet employer and societal needs, reasoning and problem-solving skill development must be an integrated part of an interdisciplinary program of study in education (Lynton & Elman, 1987), a program or environment that places students in situations where they can practice solving problems in a meaningful and constructive manner.

23.2.3 We Need to Look at Other Ways

One view of an alternative framework comes from researchers who are beginning to emphasize the importance of anchoring or situating instruction in meaningful problem-solving environments . . . (CTGV, 1993c, p. 81).

The Cognition and Technology Group at Vanderbilt (1993c) is a leader in describing alternative frameworks of instruction and schooling. The group posits the following necessary changes: first, we as educators must establish *new goals for learning.* We must move from emphasizing decontextualized reading and computational skills to developing independent thinkers and learners who engage in lifelong learning. This does not mean that we abandon the important skills of reading and computation; instead, we should be teaching reading and computation within more situated contexts that demonstrate the value of those skills.

Second, in contrast to our long operative conventional assumptions (see above), we must base our teaching on *new assumptions about the nature of thinking, learning, and instruction.* We must accept that:

> . . . the mere accumulation of factual or declarative knowledge is not sufficient to support problem solving. In addition to factual or declarative knowledge, students must learn why, when, and how various skills and concepts are relevant (CTGV, 1993c, p. 79).

Effective problem solving and thinking are not based solely on motivation and knowledge of thinking strategies but also on well-organized and indexed content knowledge. Learners must have rich knowledge structures with many contextual links to help them persevere with complex problems. Therefore, to compare new assumptions about learning with the aforementioned old assumptions, we propose the following changes (see also Table 23-1 for a summary):

1. People transfer learning from one like situation to another with difficulty. Learning is more likely to be transferred from complex and rich learning situations. Learning activities must help students think deeply about the content in relevant and realistic contexts (CTGV, 1993c).

2. Learners are "constructors" of knowledge in a variety of forms and from peers in addition to experts and teachers. They take an active role in forming new understandings and are not just passive receptors.

3. Learning is cognitive and involves the processing of information and the constant evolution and creation of knowledge structures. We must focus on and make visible thinking and reasoning processes as well as content. We are not suggesting abandoning the teaching of content to teach only thinking and reasoning, because "knowledge of concepts, theories, and principles empowers people to think effectively" (Bransford et al., 1990, p. 115). (See Chapter 5 for a more extensive discussion of cognitions and Chapter 21 for a discussion of cognitive learning models.)

4. Learners bring their own needs and experiences to a learning situation and are ready to act according to those needs. We must incorporate those needs and experiences into instructional strategies to help students take ownership and responsibility for their own learning.

5. Skills and knowledge are best acquired within realistic contexts. Morris (1979) calls this *transfer appropriate processing.* Transfer appropriate processing means that students must have the opportunity to practice and learn the outcomes that are expected of them under realistic or authentic conditions.

6. Assessment of students must take more realistic and holistic forms utilizing projects and portfolios and deemphasizing standardized testing. Educators are increasingly aware that conventional achievement and intelligence tests do not measure the ability of people to perform in everyday settings and adapt to new situations (CTGV, 1993c).

A discussion of the foundations for these assumptions, their implementation, and research issues makes up the rest of this chapter.

TABLE 23-1. OLD VERSUS NEW ASSUMPTIONS ABOUT LEARNING

Old Assumptions	New Assumptions
1. People transfer learning with ease by learning abstract and decontextualized concepts.	1. People transfer learning with difficulty, needing both content and context learning.
2. Learners are receivers of knowledge.	2. Learners are active constructors of knowledge.
3. Learning is behavioristic and involves the strengthening of stimulus and response.	3. Learning is cognitive and in a constant state of growth and evolution.
4. Learners are blank slates ready to be filled with knowledge.	4. Learners bring their own needs and experiences to learning situations.
5. Skills and knowledge are best acquired independent of context.	5. Skills and knowledge are best acquired within realistic contexts.
	6. Assessment must take more realistic and holistic forms.

23.3 RICH ENVIRONMENTS FOR ACTIVE LEARNING

23.3.1. Definition of REALs

We must implement a number of strategies to adopt the new assumptions about thinking, learning, instruction, and achievement. The adoption of these strategies creates learning environments that we call *rich environments for active learning* (REALs), which are comprehensive instructional systems that:

- Are evolving from constructivist philosophies and theories
- Promote study and investigation within authentic (i.e., realistic, meaningful, relevant, complex, and information-rich) contexts
- Encourage the growth of student responsibility, initiative, decision making, and intentional learning
- Cultivate an atmosphere of cooperative learning among students and teachers
- Utilize dynamic, generative learning activities that promote high-level thinking processes (i.e., analysis, synthesis, problem solving, experimentation, creativity, and examination of topics from multiple perspectives) to help students integrate new knowledge with old knowledge and thereby create rich and complex knowledge structures
- Assess student progress in content and learning to learn through realistic tasks and performances

It is important to note that two of the most critical features of learning environments are integration and comprehensiveness (Hannafin, 1992). Hannafin describes *integration* as a process of linking new knowledge to old and modifying and enriching existing knowledge. Integration enhances the depth of learning to increase the number of access points to that information. Goldman states that

> These environments are designed to invite the kinds of thinking that help students develop *general* skills and attitudes that contribute to effective problem solving, plus acquire *specific* concepts and principles that allow them to think effectively about particular domains (Goldman et al., 1992, p. 1).

Comprehensiveness refers to the importance of linking learning in broad, realistic contexts rather than decontextualizing and compartmentalizing knowledge. REAL learning strategies, then, guide and mediate an individual's learning and support the learner's decision making (Hannafin, 1992). Themes are used to help organize learning around contexts that focus on problem solving or projects that link concepts and knowledge to focused activities within the environment (Hannafin, 1992).

23.3.1.1. What a REAL Isn't. Because the term *learning environment* is broadly and carelessly used in educational literature to describe everything from schools to classrooms to computer microworlds to learning activities to air conditioning and furniture, I'll try to clarify what a

REAL isn't before examining the attributes in more detail. I attempt to make the case that a REAL is a more accurate description of what people generally mean when they use *learning environment.*

First, a REAL is not a delivery technology like video, CD-ROM, or audiotapes. Clark (1994) defines *delivery technologies* as those that draw on resources and media to deliver instruction and affect the cost and access of instruction. Media technologies can be integral components of REALs. However, a REAL is not limited to any specific media but instead is an assortment of methods and ideas that help cause learning. Clark's point is important from a research standpoint because instructional methods are often confounded with media in research, and he argues strongly and convincingly that it is instructional methods, not media, that influence learning. He contends that any necessary teaching method can usually be designed in more than one media. Although there are varying degrees of acceptance and disagreement with Clark's point of view (e.g., Jonassen, 1994b; Kozma, 1994), a REAL is a set of instructional methods designed on the assumptions that media are tools for students and teachers to use and that the learning that occurs within the environment is founded on the activities and processes that encourage thinking and reasoning, not the media that deliver information.

Second, do not confuse REALs with computer-based microworlds or learner support environments (LSEs) (Allinson & Hammond, 1990). Computer-based microworlds are computer programs that are designed to apply constructivist theories. Examples include case-based applications, simulations, intentional learning environments, and some hypermedia resources. Developers of microworlds often refer to their programs as learning environments because they often attempt to simulate on a smaller simplified scale realistic environments. However, I contend that this limits the concept of learning environment. Learning environments, and especially REALs, are much more comprehensive and holistic than individual computer applications. Although some computer-based applications use constructivist ideas quite admirably [see especially the *Strategic Teaching Framework* (Duffy, 1992; Duffy, 1996)] and the *Transfusion Medicine Modules* (Ambruso & The Transfusion Medicine Group, 1994), they are not learning environments in the sense that REALs are. To create REALs, teachers must involve their students, parents, administrators, and colleagues in planning and implementing strategies that encourage student responsibility, active knowledge construction, and generative learning activities on a large scale and in a variety of methods and forms. Microworlds may play a role in a REAL through the delivery of information, practice, finding and presenting information, stimulation of high-level thought processes, promotion of collaboration, or exploration. However, REALs involve many more activities and demand much more flexibility than can probably ever be contained in a single computer program. A REAL is an environment that "includes the content taught, the pedagogical methods employed, the sequencing of learning activities, and the sociology of learning" (Collins et al., 1991, p. 6).

Therefore, what are the critical attributes of REALs? The next section of this chapter discusses each of the main attributes in its definition: (a) the application of constructivist ideas, (b) authentic, generative learning activities, (c) student responsibility and initiative, (d) collaboration, (e) higher-level thinking skills and metacognition, and (f) authentic assessment strategies. I will illustrate each attribute with examples of functioning REALs from the areas of anchored instruction, problem-based learning (PBL), case-based learning, reciprocal teaching, and teacher education.

23.4 THE MAIN ATTRIBUTES OF REALS

23.4.1 Constructivist Influences

23.4.1.1. Historical Antecedents. REALs (i.e., constructivist learning environments, information-rich learning environments, or interactive learning environments) are not new to education. We can go back to Socrates (470–390 BC) and see that he used problems and questions to guide students to analyze and think about their environments (Coltrane, 1993). Rousseau prescribed using direct experience (Farnham-Diggory, 1992). In the early 1900s, John Dewey (1910) proposed student-directed reforms and experiential learning. Bruner (1961) advocated discovery or inquiry learning around realistic problems. The notion that students should learn through practice, application, and apprenticeship has been with us for centuries. It wasn't until the industrial age, when we needed places to store children until old enough to work on assembly lines, that we began trying to mass produce replicable results. Yet, the last 5 to 10 years have seen renewed emphasis on reforming schools and teaching practices to replace our production lines with classrooms that teach people to think and to solve problems. This current effort at renewal revolves around a set of ideas and theories referred to as *constructivism.*

23.4.1.2. Characteristics of Constructivism. The class of theories that guides the development of REALs is called *constructivist theories* (see 7.3; Bednar, Cunningham, Duffy & Perry, 1991; Bransford & Vye, 1989; Clement, 1982; Duffy & Bednar, 1991; Minstrell, 1989; Perkins, 1991; Resnick & Klopfer, 1989; Scardamalia & Bereiter, 1991; Schoenfeld, 1989; Spiro, Feltovich, Jacobson & Coulson, 1991). I shall, for background, provide only a brief description. Fundamentally, constructivism asserts that we learn through a continual process of constructing, interpreting, and modifying our own representations of reality based on our experiences with reality (Jonassen, 1994c). Learning includes a social component and conceptual growth comes from sharing perspectives and modifying our internal representations in response to that sharing (Bednar et al., 1991). Wheatley (1992) summarizes these ideas and emphasizes the importance of active involvement in the environment:

Learning (innovation) is fostered by information gathered from new connections; from insights gained by journeys into other disciplines or places; from active, collegial networks and fluid, open boundaries. Learning (innovation) arises from ongoing circles of exchange where information is not just accumulated or stored but created. Knowledge is generated anew from connections that weren't there before. When this information self-organizes, learning (innovation) occurs, the progeny of information-rich, ambiguous environments (p. 113).

There are several important characteristics of the constructivist view of learning that govern our design of REALs. First is the notion that knowledge is not a product to be accumulated but an active process in which the learner attempts to make sense out of the world (Gurney, 1989) that is under constant evolution. Brown, Collins, and Duguid (1989) illustrate this idea:

A concept, for example, will continually evolve with each new occasion of use, because new situations, negotiations, and activities inevitably recast it in a new, more densely textured form. So a concept, like the meaning of a word, is always under construction (Brown et al., 1989, p. 33).

A second characteristic is the notion that people conditionalize their knowledge in personal ways (Gurney, 1989). That is, they acquire knowledge in forms that enable them to use that knowledge later (Bransford et al., 1990). Bransford (1990, p. 122) states that ". . . there are large differences between knowing something and spontaneously thinking to do it or use it when one is engaged in an actual problem-solving situation." Knowledge is "indexed" to the contexts in which we encounter it. We are unlikely to use knowledge that is decontextualized because it has no relevance for us. A person who indexes and conditionalizes knowledge knows when to apply that knowledge. A person who learns in a decontextualized way often is not aware that he or she has the applicable knowledge to solve a problem. Students must acquire concepts and theories in ways that help them use the information later on and appreciate the value of that information. Brown, Collins, and Duguid (1989, p. 36) describe this process as "indexicalizing knowledge." They mean that rich involvement in realistic and relevant problem solving enables learners to develop many broad and deep indexicalized representations that enable them to apply more spontaneously knowledge to new situations because they can compare a known and relevant situation with a new situation. The more links there are across related knowledge structures, the more likely students are to apply that knowledge. The more closely the learning context resembles the actual context, the better people will perform. Tulving and Thompson (1973) refer to this as *encoding specificity,* which holds that successful retrieval of information is enhanced when cues relevant to later retrieval of that information are encoded along with the material learned. It is important to note that constructivists contend that these rich links cannot be developed in decontextualized learning activities; rather learning must be placed in realistic contexts that provide cognitive conflict or puzzlement and determine the organization and nature of what is learned (Savery & Duffy, 1994).

White (cf. Robertson, 1990) theorizes that there are two kinds of links that need to be developed while learning: internal and external. Internal associations are connections among the criterial attributes of a principle. Internal associations reflect the learner's understanding of the concept. External associations refer to connections between the principle and everyday experiences or context and indicate the "usability" of a concept. Learning to solve problems requires both kinds of links. Our schools are good at building the internal links, but poor at providing the external links.

The third major characteristic of constructivism is the importance of collaboration and the social negotiation of meaning. Common understandings and shared meanings are developed through interaction among peers and teachers. This is the cultural aspect of knowledge.

> The activities of a domain are framed by its culture. Their meaning and purpose are socially constructed through negotiations among present and past members. Activities thus cohere in a way that is, in theory, if not always in practice, accessible to members who move within the social framework. These coherent, meaningful, and purposeful activities are authentic, according to the definition of the term we use here (Brown et al., 1989, p. 34).

This social aspect of constructivism is important on an individual level as well as cultural level, for collaborative interactions allow us to test the viability of our understandings, theories, and conjectures (Savery & Duffy, 1994).

23.4.1.3. REAL Example: Cognitive Flexibility Theory. Cognitive flexibility theory (CFT) implements many of the ideas of constructivism (Jacobson & Spiro, 1992; Spiro et al., 1991), particularly focusing on the development of conditionalized and indexicalized knowledge structures.

> Essentially, the theory states that cognitive flexibility is needed in order to construct an ensemble of conceptual and case representations necessary to understand a particular problem-solving situation. The idea is that we cannot be said to have a full understanding of a domain unless we have the opportunity to see different case representations (Borsook & Higginbotham-Wheat, 1992, p. 63).

CFT attempts to teach content in ill-structured domains, that is, in domains where the knowledge base is so vast and complex that multiple solutions to problems are possible and likely. There are no clear-cut answers in ill-structured domains, so simple algorithms often fail. Ill-structured domains include law, medicine, and education. Therefore, CFT emphasizes the following instructional strategies to help learners develop rich and deep knowledge structures (Jacobson, 1994):

1. CFT uses several cases and rich examples in their full complexity. One of the tenets of CFT is to avoid oversimplifying knowledge and examples because it leads to future misunderstandings that are difficult to change.

2. CFT uses multiple forms of knowledge representation, providing examples in several kinds of media. CFT encourages students to look at knowledge in several ways and from several perspectives.

3. CFT links abstract concepts to case examples and brings out the generalizable concepts and strategies applicable to other problems or cases.

4. To avoid the mistakes of oversimplification, CFT presents a number of examples to make apparent, rather than hide, the variability of concepts and themes within the domain.

Although CFT does not emphasize the collaborative nature of knowledge construction, its strategies include opportunities for social negotiation of meaning. We examine further on in the chapter other examples of REALs that place a high emphasis on cooperative learning.

23.4.2 Authentic Learning Contexts

The second characteristic of a REAL is that learning takes place within an authentic context. An authentic task, activity, or goal provides learning experiences as realistic as possible given the age and maturation level of the students and other environmental constraints, including safety and expense. The most important feature of this definition is to understand that "realistic experience" includes more than the situation; it includes both the context and the tasks that a learner performs (Honebein, Duffy & Fishman, 1993). *Those tasks must be realistic in terms of the cognitive, physical, and social requirements.* A realistic context includes as much fidelity as possible to what students will encounter outside school in terms of tools, complexity, and interactions with people (Williams & Dodge, 1992).

Authenticity is important to REALs for three reasons. First, it encourages students to take ownership of the situation and their own learning. Realistic problems hold more relevance to students needs and experiences, because they can relate what they are learning to problems and goals that they see every day. Second, it develops deeper and richer (indexicalized and conditioned) knowledge structures leading to a higher likelihood of transfer to novel situations. Finally, it encourages collaboration and negotiation. Complex problems require a team approach that provides natural opportunities for learners to test and refine their ideas and to help each other understand the content.

23.4.2.1. REAL Example: Anchored Instruction. One of the ways to create authentic instruction in a REAL is to anchor that instruction on a realistic event, problem, or theme (CTGV, 1990, 1992a, 1992b, 1993a, 1993d). Anchored instruction is fixed within a real-world event that is appealing and meaningful to students (Bransford et al., 1990). Anchored instruction involves complex contexts that require students to solve interconnected subproblems. Students share multiple perspectives, solutions, and processes (CTGV, 1992b). "At the heart of the model is an emphasis on the importance of creating an anchor or focus to generate interest and enable students to identify and solve problems and pay attention to their own perception and comprehension of these problems" (Bransford et al., 1990, p. 123).

In anchored learning situations, students develop component skills and objectives in the context of meaningful, realistic problems and problem-solving activities. These complex contexts are called *macrocontexts* (Williams & Dodge, 1992, p. 373). The primary goal of anchored instruction (and REALs) is to overcome the problem of inert knowledge. For example, students in an instructional design and development class work in teams with actual clients to develop instruction that will be delivered to another group of students. They must define the problem, identify resources, set priorities, and explore alternative solutions—the same skills and abilities that are required during realistic, outside-of-the-classroom problem-solving and decision-making activities. This is in direct contrast to the way students develop component skills and objectives in a more traditional classroom environment by working simplified, compartmentalized, and decontextualized problems. Simply stated, it is the difference between providing meaningful, authentic learning activities and "I'm never going to use this" activities.

Anchored instruction shares many features of programs that are case based and problem based (Barrows, 1985; Spiro et al., 1991; Williams & Dodge, 1992). The idea is to let learners experience the intellectual changes that experts feel when modifying their own understandings from working with realistic situations (CTGV, 1992b).

Effective anchors are intrinsically interesting, fostering ownership, and help students notice the features of problem situations that make particular actions relevant (Bransford et al., 1990, p. 123). The CTGV (1991) uses the following design principles when creating anchored instruction. First, they use a video-based presentation format because of the dramatic power of the medium and because of the use of multiple modalities, realistic imagery, and omnipresence in our culture. Second, they present a problem using actors and a narrative format for interest. Third, the problem solution requires a generative learning format in which students must identify pertinent information in the fourth feature, embedded data design. Fifth, the problem is complex with the possibility of multiple solutions and perspectives and requiring a team approach. Sixth, they use pairs of similar problems in different contexts to enrich the indexicalization of knowledge structures. Finally, they attempt to draw links across the curriculum to enhance the relevance of the problem.

There are several advantages to organizing curricula and learning around anchors and then progressing to hands-on projects (CTGV, 1993a). First, it is more practical and manageable for teachers to create anchors in the classroom than to try to arrange all of the resources, planning, and meetings around actual community-based projects. Second, the chance to work through one or more anchored problems prepares students for actual problems they may undertake at a later time. Third, anchors provide a common experi-

ence and knowledge base that helps students share information with each other and with community members.

One of the CTGV's projects in anchored instruction is the *Jasper Woodbury* series (CTGV, 1992b). Jasper is a video-based series designed to promote problem posing, problem solving, reasoning, and effective communication. Each of Jasper's adventures is a 15- to 20-minute story in which the characters encounter a problem that the students in the classroom must solve before they are allowed to see how the movie characters solved the problem. The Jasper series helps students learn to break a problem into parts, generate subgoals, find and identify relevant information, generate and test hypotheses, and cooperate with others.

23.4.3 Student Responsibility and Initiative

Information-rich learning environments are not designed as much as assembled, informally by individual learners. Hence they are constructivist in an almost literal sense of the term (Yacci, 1994, p. 1).

The third characteristic of REALs is that they are student centered. Student-centered learning environments place a major emphasis on developing intentional learning and lifelong learning skills. These skills include the abilities for self-reflection and metacognition.

23.4.3.1. Intentional Learning. Scardamalia and her colleagues noticed that passive or immature learners have certain characteristics that prevent them from becoming skillful problem solvers (1989). First, immature learners tend to organize their mental activities around topics rather than goals, promoting decontextualization and failing to see the relevance of the activity to their lives. Second, they tend to focus on surface features and do not examine a topic in depth. Third, they work straight ahead; that is, they tend to work until a task is finished. They do not take time to examine the quality of their work, nor do they make revisions in their work or thinking. Finally, they think of learning in an additive fashion rather than transforming and enriching their existing knowledge structures.

These characteristics are, in essence, the product of the conventional kind of schooling that we described earlier in the chapter. These behaviors prevent students from transferring their knowledge to new problems because they have learned in a decontextualized context and have learned with strategies that are decontextualized. They do not see the applicability of what they learned. Palincsar (1990, p. 37) states that:

To achieve transfer, it is necessary to attend to the context in which instruction and practice occur; transfer is likely to occur to the extent that there are common elements between the situation in which the children are learning this tactic and the situations in which such a tactic would be useful (p. 37).

Palincsar, Scardamalia, and Bereiter are leading proponents of the conviction that students must be taught to take more responsibility for their own learning to enhance the likelihood of transfer. They refer to this concept as *intentional learning,* or "those cognitive processes that have learning as a goal rather than an accidental outcome" (Bereiter & Scardamalia, 1989, p. 363). Palincsar and Klenk (1992) state that "Intentional learning, in contrast to incidental learning, is an achievement resulting from the learner's purposeful, effortful, self-regulated, and active engagement." To be intentional learners, students must learn to learn as well as learn to accrue knowledge. Learning to learn involves the teaching of generic skills as much as it does occupational or domain-specific skills. Teaching, too, takes on a revised role, for to teach for intentional learning means to cultivate those general abilities that facilitate lifelong learning (Palincsar, 1990). The main skills involved in teaching students to be more intentional are questioning, self-reflection, and metacognition, "or the awareness and ability to monitor and control one's activity as a learner" (Brown, Bransford, Ferrara & Campione, 1983, p. 212).

23.4.3.2. Questioning.   Scardamalia and Bereiter (1991) believe that one of the first steps in developing intentional learners is by helping students take more executive control over what they decide to learn through the development of questioning skills. They point out that in a typical classroom, teachers ask the questions and that the question-generation and asking processes involve important high-level thinking skills and executive control decisions. Adults ask questions based on their needs, but teachers ask questions of students based on the teacher's perceptions of student needs. The students, therefore, do not ask questions related to their needs and do not learn to perform the analysis activities related to question generation. Research by Scardamalia and Bereiter (1991) indicate that students can learn to ask questions to guide their knowledge building, thus assuming a "higher level of agency" and more ownership for their learning. In a student-centered REAL, students are given more executive control over their learning to enable them to take more ownership, to find more relevance and authenticity, and to learn lifelong learning skills.

In addition to questioning, other intentional behaviors include goal setting, managing time, and setting priorities. Each of these helps students learn to manage their own learning and become more independent in the learning process. This independence leads to more ownership as the students discover that they are able to pursue their own needs and uncover information that is important to them.

23.4.3.2. Self-Reflection.   A second skill in intentional learning is self-reflection. "*Self-reflection* implies observing and putting an interpretation on one's own actions, for instance, considering one's own intentions and motives as objects of thought" (Von Wright, 1992, p. 61). Von Wright writes that self-reflection involves the abstraction of meaning and is an interpretative process aimed at the understanding of reality. To understand the world in different ways involves modifying our conceptions of the world and our place in the world. It involves thinking about reality in alternative ways.

Von Wright (1992) goes on to describe two levels of reflection. One level of reflection has to do with the ability to reflect about features of the world in the sense of considering and comparing them in mind and thinking about on ways of coping in familiar contexts. This involves learning to think about implications and consequences of actions. A second level of reflection is the ability to think about one's self as an intentional subject of one's own actions and to consider the consequences and efficacy of those actions. This involves the ability to look at one's self in an objective way and to consider ways of changing to improve performance. The second level of reflection also involves metacognitive learning skills.

23.4.3.3. Metacognitive Skills.   "Metacognitive skills refer to the steps that people take to regulate and modify the progress of their cognitive activity: to learn such skills is to acquire procedures which regulate cognitive processes" (Von Wright, 1992, p. 64). Metacognitive skills include taking conscious control of learning, planning and selecting strategies, monitoring the progress of learning, correcting errors, analyzing the effectiveness of learning strategies, and changing learning behaviors and strategies when necessary (Ridley, Schutz, Glanz & Weinstein, 1992). These abilities interact with developmental maturation and domain expertise. Immature learners can't to do this; they may have learned a single strategy, such as memorization, and then attempt to apply that to all situations.

Studies show that use of metacognitive strategies can increase learning skills and that independent use of these metacognitive strategies can be gradually developed in people (Biggs, 1985; Brown, 1978; Weinstein, Goetz & Alexander, 1988). Blakely and Spence (1990) describe several basic strategies for developing metacognitive behaviors:

1. Students should be asked to identify consciously what they "know" as opposed to "what they don't know."
2. Students should keep journals or logs in which they reflect on their learning processes, thinking about what works and what doesn't.
3. Students should manage their own time and resources, including estimating time requirements, organizing materials, and scheduling the procedures necessary to complete an activity
4. Students must participate in guided self-evaluation through individual conferences and checklists to help them focus on the thinking process.

23.4.3.4. REAL Example: Reciprocal Teaching.   One of the manifestations of a REAL that emphasizes the development of intentional learning skills is reciprocal teaching. The context of reciprocal teaching is social, interactive, and holistic. Palincsar and Klenk (1992) used reciprocal teaching with at-risk first-grade students to develop reading skills. Palincsar and Klenk describe reciprocal teaching as:

> . . . an instructional procedure that takes place in a collaborative learning group and features guided practice in the flexible application of four concrete strategies to the task of text comprehension: questioning, summarizing, clarifying, and predicting. The teacher and group of students take turns leading

discussions regarding the content of the text they are jointly attempting to understand (Palincsar & Klenk, 1992, p. 213).

These strategies are the kinds of intentional learning strategies that encourage self-regulation and self-monitoring behaviors.

The relationship of reciprocal teaching to REALs is founded on three theoretical principles based on the work of Vygotsky (1978) as described by Palincsar and Klenk (1992). The first principle states that the higher cognitive processes originate from social interactions. This is consistent with the constructivist theories described above. The second principle is Vygotsky's *zone of proximal development* (ZPD). Vygotsky (p. 86) described the ZPD as "the distance between the actual developmental level as determined by independent problem solving and the level of potential development as determined through problem solving under adult guidance, or in collaboration with more capable peers." Reciprocal teaching is designed to provide a zone of proximal development in which students, with the help of teachers and peers, take on greater responsibility for learning activities. Finally, Vygotsky's third principle advocates that learning take place in a contextualized, holistic activity that has relevance for the learners. In other words, we revisit the notion of authentic learning or anchored instruction.

How, then, does reciprocal teaching work? The process begins with a text that a class reads silently, orally, or read-along, depending on the skill level of the students. Following each segment, a dialogue leader (students take turns) asks questions that deal with content or "wonderment" issues. The questions often stimulate further inquiry. The other students respond to the questions, raise their own questions, and, in cases of disagreement or confusion, reread the text. The discussion leader is responsible for summarizing and synthesizing the reading and discussion and clarifying the purpose of the reading. The leader also generates and solicits predictions about the upcoming text to prepare for meaningful reading of the next segment. The teacher must model the appropriate behavior and provide scaffolding to sustain the discussion. (The preceding description is taken from Palincsar & Klenk, 1992.) The students, then, are involved in the higher-level thinking and decision-making activities usually within the realm of the teacher. With the help of the teacher, students share a zone of proximal development where they can learn questioning, summarizing, clarifying, and predicting activities so integral to metacognitive awareness.

Finally, why does reciprocal teaching work? Collins, Brown, and Holum (1991) posit the following reasons for its success (and, in a broader view, for the success of REALs):

1. The reciprocal teaching model engages students in activities that help them form a new conceptual model of the task of reading. They see reading as a process that involves reflection and prediction rather than just the recitation of words. They learn to make what they are reading relevant to their needs and to monitor their progress and strive for clarification.

2. Teacher and student share a problem context while the teacher models expert strategies that the students learn to use independently.

3. Scaffolding is crucial in the success of reciprocal teaching. "Most importantly, it decomposes the task as necessary for the students to carry it out, thereby helping them to see how, in detail, to go about it" (Collins, Brown & Holum, 199, p. 11).

4. The students play both the roles of producer and critic. They learn cognitive activities that go beyond producing something for the teacher. They learn the self-monitoring activities and thinking processes involved in critiquing and improving their work.

23.4.4 Cooperative Learning

The fourth characteristic of REALs acknowledges the transactional nature of knowledge and suggests that a shift be made to focus on social practice, meaning, and patterns (Roth, 1990). "All cooperative learning methods share the idea that students work together to learn and are responsible for one another's learning as well as their own" (Slavin, 1991, p. 73; see 35.3). Working in peer groups helps students refine their knowledge through argumentation, structured controversy, and reciprocal teaching. Additionally, students are more willing to take on the extra risk required to tackle complex, ill-structured, authentic problems when they have the support of others in the cooperative group. Cooperative learning and problem-solving groups also address students' needs for scaffolding during unfamiliar learning and problem-solving activities; therefore, with the support of others in the group, students are more likely to achieve goals they may not have been able to meet on their own. Constructivists argue that cooperative learning and problem-solving groups facilitate generative learning. Some of the generative activities that students engage in cooperative groups include (Brown et al., 1989):

1. *Collective problem solving.* Groups give rise synergistically to insights and solutions that would not come about individually.

2. *Displaying multiple roles.* Group participation means that the members must understand many different roles. They also may play different roles within the group to gain additional insights.

3. *Confronting ineffective strategies and misconceptions.* Teachers do not have enough time to hear what students are thinking or how they are thinking. Groups draw out, confront, and discuss both misconceptions and ineffective strategies.

4. *Providing collaborative work skills.* Students learn to work together in a give-and-take interaction rather than just dividing the workload.

Research indicates that cooperative learning, when implemented properly, is highly successful. Slavin (1991) provides the following four summary statements regarding research findings in cooperative learning:

1. Successful cooperative learning strategies always incorporate the two key elements of group goals and individual accountability.

2. When both group goals and individual accountability are used, achievement effects are consistently positive. His review found that 37 of 44 experimental/ control comparisons of at least 4 weeks' duration found significantly positive effects, with none favoring traditional methods.

3. Positive achievement effects are present to about the same degree across all grade levels (2–12), in all major subjects, and in urban, rural, and suburban schools. Effects are equally positive for high, average, and low achievers.

4. Positive effects of cooperative learning are consistently found on such diverse outcomes as self-esteem, intergroup relations, acceptance of academically handicapped students, attitudes toward school, and ability to work cooperatively.

23.4.4.1. REAL Example: Problem-Based Learning.

Another manifestation of REALs is problem-based learning (PBL) (see 7.5, 20.3.4). PBL is "the learning that results from the process of working toward the understanding or resolution of a problem" (Barrows & Tamblyn, 1980, p. 18). It found initial acceptance in the medical field and has grown to become a major learning system for a number of medical, law, and business schools. PBL reflects the REAL attribute that knowledge is constructed rather than received, for it is based on the assumption that knowledge arises from work with an authentic problem (Coltrane, 1993). Benor (1984) states that:

"Problem-based learning in the context of medical education means self-directed study by learners who seek out information pertinent to either a real-life or a simulated problem. The students have to understand the problem to the extent that its constituents can be identified and defined. The learners have then to collect, integrate, synthesize, and apply this information to the given problem, using strategies that will yield a solution" (p. 49).

How does problem-based learning work? We begin with Coltrane's description of the three fundamental theoretical principles of PBL:

1. Work on the problem begins with activating prior knowledge to enable students understand the structure of the new information. We also saw this principle used in the discussion about intentional learning that emphasized that students must ask themselves what they do know about a subject.

2. We also see the continual reference to the necessity for transfer in PBL, for when the learning context is similar to the situation in which the learning is to be applied, learning transfer is more likely to occur.

3. Learners must have opportunities to elaborate on the information presented at the time of learning in order to enhance their understanding. This is one of the main purposes for using cooperative learning strate-

gies in REALs and was also seen as a part of reciprocal learning.

Savery and Duffy (1994) describe four characteristics of PBL. First, PBL environments include the learning goals of realistic problem-solving behavior, self-directed learning, content knowledge acquisition, and the development of metacognitive skills.

Second, Savery and Duffy state that PBLs are based on problems that are generated because they raise relevant concepts and principles that are authentic. Problems must be authentic because it is difficult to create artificial problems that maintain the complexity and dimensions of actual problems. Recall that we also encountered the need for complexity in the REAL example of cognitive flexibility theory and anchored instruction. Realistic problems also have a motivational effect. They tend to engage learners more because they want to know the outcome of the problem.

Third, the actual presentation of the problem is a critical component of PBLs. Problems are encountered before any preparation or study has occurred (Barrows, 1980). The problem must be presented in a realistic way that encourages students to adopt and take ownership for the problem (Barrows, 1980; Savery & Duffy, 1994). The data must be embedded in the problem presentation (refer back to the example of anchored instruction) but must not highlight the critical factors in the case. Students must make their own decisions about what is critical and what is not because that is cognitively authentic: It reflects actual job performance (Savery & Duffy, 1994).

Fourth, the facilitator has a crucial role comparable to the roles described in anchored instruction and reciprocal teaching. The facilitator interacts with the students at a metacognitive level, helping them ask the right questions and monitor their own progress. Facilitators avoid expressing opinion, giving information, or leading to a correct answer. Their role is to challenge the students (from Savery & Duffy, 1994).

Cooperative learning is a critical component of PBL, for it is used from the beginning through the end of the problem-solution process. The group listens to the problem presentation together. They analyze the problem's components, recall what they know, hypothesize, consider possible resources, and choose directions to go. They test and help each other. They work together on the solutions and reach consensus on final actions. The entire process from beginning to end is cooperative. Cooperative learning is also used for its motivational factors.

Problem discussion also increases motivation by gaining and maintaining student interest (attention), by relating the learning to student needs or helping students to meet personal goals (relevance), by providing conditions conducive to student success (confidence), and through the motivation provided by that mastery of the task(s) (satisfaction) (Coltrane, 1993, pp. 12, 13).

The PBL is the epitome of the REAL constructive learning process. Students work with problems in a manner that fosters reasoning and knowledge application appropriate to their levels of learning. In the process of working on the problem and with their peers, students identify areas of learning to guide their own individualized study. The skills and knowledge acquired by this study are applied back to the problem to evaluate the effectiveness of learning and to reinforce learning. The learning that has occurred in work with the problem and in individualized study is summarized and integrated into the student's existing knowledge structure.

23.4.5 Generative Learning Activities

The fifth requirement of REALs is that students engage in generative learning activities (see 31.1.1). People who learn through active involvement and use tools build an "increasingly rich implicit understanding of the world . . ." (Brown et al., 1989, p. 33). Generative learning requires that students "engage in argumentation and reflection as they try to use and then refine their existing knowledge as they attempt to make sense of alternate points of view" (CTGV, 1993b, p. 16). Studies indicate that knowledge is more likely to be active and used when acquired in a problem-solving mode rather than in a factual-knowledge mode (Adams et al., 1988; Lockhart, Lamon & Gick, 1988). The concept of generative learning is an extension of the concept of constructing learning. Students cannot construct their own learning without generating something through active involvement.

Generative learning requires a shift in the traditional roles of students and instructors. Students become investigators, seekers, and problem solvers. Teachers become facilitators and guides, rather than presenters of knowledge. For example, rather than simply learning what objectives and goals are, students in a teacher education class generate lesson plans and objectives and then manipulate and revise them to solve new teaching problems. In generative learning, students *apply* the information they learn. Generative learning activities require students to take static information and *generate* fluid, flexible, usable knowledge. Generative learning, then, means that students are involved heavily with projects and creating solutions to authentic problems. A REAL model that relies heavily on projects is cognitive apprenticeship.

23.4.5.1. REAL Example: Cognitive Apprenticeship. Cognitive apprenticeship is modeled after the traditional apprenticeship (see 20.3) way of learning arts and crafts. It incorporates elements of traditional apprenticeship and modern schooling. In apprenticeship, learners see products *and processes* of work. In traditional apprenticeship, the processes of an activity are visible and involve learning a physical and outwardly observable activity (Collins et al., 1991). The expert shows an apprentice how to perform a task, then watches and coaches as the apprentice practices portions of the task, and finally turns over more and more responsibility to the apprentice until the apprentice can perform the task alone (Collins et al., 1991). Traditional apprenticeship deals with processes that are easily visible

because they involve skills and producing products.

The goal of cognitive apprenticeship is to make processes that are normally invisible visible. In schooling, the process of thinking is usually invisible to both students and teachers. For example, the practices of problem solving, reading comprehension, and computation are not visible processes (Collins et al., 1991). Brown, Collins, and Duguid (1989) point out that the term *cognitive apprenticeship* emphasizes that apprenticeship techniques can reach beyond observable physical skills to the kinds of cognitive skills associated with learning in schools. In a cognitive apprenticeship environment, the teacher attempts to make visible the thinking processes involved in performing a cognitive task. The teacher first models how to perform a cognitive task by thinking aloud. Then the teacher watches, coaches, and provides scaffolding as the students practice portions of the task. Finally, he or she turns over more and more responsibility to students and fades coaching and scaffolding until they can perform the task alone. "Cognitive apprenticeship supports learning in a domain by enabling students to acquire, develop, and use cognitive tools in authentic domain activity" (Brown et al., 1989, p. 39).

The differences between traditional and cognitive apprenticeship (Collins et al., 1991) are important because they indicate where the effort must be placed on instruction design of learning activities. First, in traditional apprenticeship the task is easily observable. In cognitive apprenticeship, the thinking must be deliberately brought into the open by the teacher, and the teacher must help the students learn to bring their thinking into the open. Second, in traditional apprenticeship, the tasks come from the world, and learning is situated in the workplace. In cognitive apprenticeship, the challenge is to situate the abstract goals of school curriculum in contexts that make sense to students. Third, in traditional apprenticeship, the skills learned are inherent in the task. In schooling, students learn skills that are supposed to move across to different tasks. In cognitive apprenticeship, the challenge is to present a range of tasks to encourage reflection and to identify common transferable elements across tasks. The goal is to help students generalize and transfer their learning.

Cognitive apprenticeship and generative learning are closely linked, because the process of making cognitive processes visible means that students must create or generate things that represent those processes. Teachers must create work and tasks that represent the process of solving a problem, writing, or computation in addition to products. To examine the development of student thinking, an English teacher may ask for questions, themes, concept maps, and outlines before students begin writing. Math teachers are often notorious for telling students, "I want to see your work, not just the answer," so they can look for errors in the thinking process.

The elements of cognitive apprenticeship are present in the examples we have already examined. One of the purposes of reciprocal teaching, which we have already examined, is to teach children to perform some of the tasks of the teacher. Students watch the teacher model the tasks and then practice performing those tasks under the guidance of the teacher. In the Jasper series, students must demonstrate visible signs of the whole problem-solving process by asking questions, forming plans, finding resources, breaking a problem into its parts, and testing possible solutions with each other. In problem-based learning, the students work under the guidance of the teacher to solve real problems.

Generative learning is one of the simplest features of a REAL. It simply demands that students produce something of value. It is probably the most exciting part of a REAL, because students work on projects and tasks that are relevant to them and to their peers. It keeps students busy and happy while helping them learn. It also creates some unique assessment problems, which we will examine next.

23.4.6 Authentic Assessment

The sixth and final REAL attribute is authentic assessment. Conventional schooling relies heavily on standardized and paper/pencil tests to measure the quantity of knowledge that students have accrued. Traditional tests, written reports, and grading schemes are inappropriate measures (Frederiksen & Collins, 1989), are time consuming to administer and score (Williams & Dodge, 1992), and are not always good indicators of how students will perform in actual problem-solving conditions. Williams also states that students are often assessed on skills different from ones that are taught and experience problem-solving assessments that tend to be subjective. Testing and assessment must recognize the importance of the organization of the knowledge base and its connectedness to contexts.

Wiggins (1989) contrasts authentic tests, which he describes as contextualized, complex intellectual challenges with multiple-choice measures that he describes as fragmented and static. According to Wiggins, authentic tests include the following criteria:

1. The intellectual design features of tests and evaluation tasks must emphasize realistic complexity, stress depth more than breadth, include ill-structured tasks or problems, and require students to contextualize content knowledge.
2. Standards of grading and scoring features should include complex multifaceted criteria that can be specified and that are reliable across multiple scorers. What constitutes a high level of performance should be explainable to students and teachers *before* they take the test. Teachers often claim that criteria are subjective; however this is seldom the case, for most criteria can be described with some thoughtful effort.
3. Tests and evaluations must be diverse and recognize the existence of multiple kinds of intelligences. In terms of fairness and equity, evaluations and assessments should allow students to use their strengths within areas that their interests lie.

23.4.6.1.   REAL Example: Learning in Design. Carver, Lehrer, Connell, and Erickson (1992) elaborate on this

theme by proposing an extensive list of behaviors needed by students in a REAL. In their particular manifestation of a REAL, they consider the classroom a design community in which students design instruction for other students, documentaries for local media, and other exhibits for the community. Their program has the same goals of high-level thinking, reflection, and transfer as other REALs:

> The instructional virtues of these design experiences include the opportunity to develop and coordinate a variety of complex mental skills, such as decomposing a topic into subtopics, gathering data from a variety of sources, organizing diverse and often contradictory information, formulating a point of view, translating ideas into a presentation targeted at a particular audience, evaluating the design, and making revisions based on the evaluations (Carver et al., 1992, p. 386).

Again, there are several parallels with the other examples that we have discussed. Their REAL focuses on complex mental skills; analyzing, comparing, and manipulating information; working on authentic, community-based tasks; and working with others.

To fairly evaluate students working in this environment, teachers need a clear specification of skills students need for design tasks and prescriptions for how teachers can effectively support their skills (see also Agnew, Kellerman & Meyer, 1992). Specification of skills and prescriptions of support are two parts of assessment that must be linked for fair assessment. If a skill cannot be supported by the teacher or some kind of scaffolding technique, then it cannot be fairly evaluated. It may, in fact, be outside the zone of proximal development and beyond the current capability of the student. One of the teacher's jobs in a REAL is to specify skills and performances that can be supported so that the student can grow in ability. Carver et al. (1992) break the important behaviors for their environment into:

1. Project management skills, including creating a timeline, allocating resources, and assigning team roles
2. Research skills, including determining the nature of the problem, posing questions, searching for information, developing new information, and analyzing and interpreting information
3. Organization and representation skills, including choosing the organization and structure of information; developing representations (text, audio, and graphics); arranging structure and sequence; and juggling constraints
4. Presentation skills, including transferring their design into media and catching and maintaining audience interest
5. Reflection skills, including evaluating the process and revising the design

Their criteria work for their learning environment. Other models may need to revise some of the specifics, though the five main categories provide an excellent starting place in specifying skills targeted for assessment. Goldman's (1994) discussion of assessment in the CTGV Jasper series suggests the following assessment areas: assessment of complex mathematical problem solving (math is the content domain of Jasper), measures of group problem-solving performance, assessment of extensions into other areas of the content area, and assessment of cross-curricular extensions. While conducting an assessment for a REAL is more work than conventional assessment, it is also an integral part of the learning process rather than a periodic quantifiable measure. Authentic assessment provides feedback and information that is useful for planning future learning.

23.4.6.2. Assessment of the REAL. There is yet another dimension to the issue of assessment: evaluation of the environment. To examine this, I'll look at another example of a REAL, case-based learning (CBL). "Case-based teaching exploits the basic capacity for students to learn from stories and the basic desire of teachers to tell stories that are indicative of their experiences" (Shank, 1990, p. 231). In case-based learning, teachers first teach students what they need to know to become interested in the case that will be examined. This, incidentally, is the prime difference between case-based learning and problem-based learning.

> PBL problems differ from the typical case history in that they [PBL teachers] do not (initially) provide or synthesize all the information needed to solve the problem. In PBL, the problem is presented first, before students have learned basic science or clinical concepts, not after (Albanese & Mitchell, 1993, p. 53).

The information in CBL is presented to students in the form of stories. Students work with each other to analyze the stories or cases to abstract rules, heuristics, or practices that may be transferable to other cases. In CBL, the information is present within the case; students do not have to pursue other resources or individualized plans to learn more information as they do in PBL. Again, the main attributes of REALs are present: constructing knowledge, personal responsibility, cooperative learning, authentic context, and generative learning activities.

Williams (1992) developed a framework for comparing and evaluating methods of case-based instruction in the areas of teaching and learning and materials and curriculum. She poses 10 questions to guide the evaluation of case-based instruction (pp. 375–76):

Teaching and Learning
1. Does instruction begin with a problem to be solved?
2. Does the teacher model expert problem solving in the context of a complex problem?
3. Are students given the opportunity to engage actively in solving problems, and does the teacher provide specific immediate feedback while students are solving problems?
4. What type of scaffolding is used to support students as they solve problems?
5. Does instruction emphasize metacognitive strategies as well as domain knowledge?
6. Are there frequent opportunities for both teacher and students to assess how well learning is progressing?

Is the type of assessment used appropriate for measuring the skills that are taught?

Materials and Curriculum
7. Are the problems authentic; that is, are they ones that would be solved by practitioners?
8. Are the problems realistically complex? Do their solutions involve multiple steps? Are the settings rich and detailed? Are multiple skills and concepts linked to each problem?
9. Are the problems presented in a way that makes complexity manageable, for example, using a story format, presenting them on video, and providing all relevant data?
10. Are problems sequenced to support students' needs at different stages of learning?

These questions apply to all REALs, not just case-based learning implementations. This common utility of these evaluation questions is another example of how much each of the examples of REALs that we have examined hold in common.

23.4.6.3. Evaluation Techniques. Assessment in REALs means that we have to consider more varied techniques. Neuman (1993), in her work with the Perseus hypermedia program, suggests several alternatives. First, she suggests that teachers use more observations, including evaluator observations of performance processes, think-alouds by students, and automatic transaction monitoring. Second, she suggests using interviews of students, instructors, and staff using both questionnaires and focus groups. Finally, she suggests the use of document and product analysis including assignments, syllabi, essays, journals, paths, reports, documentation, and presentations.

The issue of assessment is one of the more complex attributes of REALs because it is multidimensional. Assessment involves simultaneous assessment of both students and the environment. It also represents more than any other single attribute the depth of change necessary to implement a REAL. The move from paper/pencil tests to portfolio analysis, observations, interviews, and document analysis more than any single attribute signals the radical difference between REALs and conventional instruction.

23.4.7 Conclusion of REAL Characteristics Section

We have looked at each of the six main characteristics of REALs: (1) constructivist heritage, (2) authentic instruction, (3) student responsibility, (4) collaborative learning, (5) generative learning activities, and (6) authentic assessment. Each characteristic of REALs builds on and uses the other. None is mutually exclusive; one is no more important than another: You cannot talk about one feature without incorporating the other. In effect, the characteristics of REALs mirror the comprehensive and integrated nature of REALs. The characteristics are symbiotic, with one feature both supporting and needing the others to create a successful, rich environment for active learning. In the next section, we examine some of the research related to the effectiveness of REALs.

23.5 RESEARCH AND REALS

Current research issues within the field of REALs center on their overall effectiveness, methodological issues in conducting research, and making cognitive processes visible. Research conducted in the field parallels the development of REALs. REALs have developed in theory and implementation from content area teaching strategies used occasionally to integrated and comprehensive strategies guiding a whole curriculum. Research has evolved from comparing REALs with conventional teaching to studies focusing on how learners think and perform differently using REAL strategies. In the following literature survey, we begin with a look at the overall effectiveness of REALs and then move on to narrower issues related to learning and implementation.

23.5.1 REAL vs. Conventional Instruction

Research comparing REALs with conventional instruction is generally quite favorable, finding REALs equal or superior to conventional instruction in teaching both problem-solving skills and content. I summarize several studies below that examine the overall effectiveness of a particular implementation of a REAL. Some are more successful than others. In my review, I attempt to bring out some of the methodological issues related to conducting research with REALs and suggest future research opportunities.

23.5.1.1. The Jasper Series. In one of the most extensive comparisons of a REAL versus conventional instruction, James Pellegrino and his CTGV colleagues (1991) tested the Jasper series in 16 schools in 9 states. Two teachers and a corporate support person had responsibility for implementing the program over the course of the 1990–1991 school year at each site. Teams received intensive 2-week training in the program before implementation. The CTGV group developed assessment strategies to evaluate Jasper's main goals for students: (1) to develop critical mathematical problem solving and reasoning skills, (2) to develop an appreciation of mathematics as a realistic part of their world and everyday problem solving, and (3) to develop various sets of specific mathematical knowledge and skills.

Pellegrino's group made a thorough attempt to measure changes in children's mathematical skills and attitudes over the course of a year. They used a battery of paper/pencil tests administered at the beginning and end of the school year to examine basic math concepts and content, attitudes toward math, word problem–solving skills, and higher-level problem-solving skills. Mini versions of these tests were administered at midyear. The Jasper classes were compared to children in classes that did not use the Jasper program.

23.5.1.1.1. Math Attitudes. The CTGV team used a 35-item questionnaire that covered 11 different categories about attitudes and exploration and attribution behaviors. Although the reliabilities were low on the attitude scales (probably because of too few items), Jasper groups had more improved attitudes toward math at the end of the year compared to the control groups, believing that math was more fun and interesting than they did at the beginning of the year. However, despite the improved attitudes, Jasper students showed no greater desire to study or explore math than the control groups. Nor did the Jasper students attribute any more of their success to their own abilities than they did at the beginning of the year, for they still saw the teacher as the main force guiding their learning. It seems difficult to assess attributional and exploration behavior from a test. Future research might examine growth behaviors related in independence and personal responsibility to see if Jasper affects the development of intentional learning using observational techniques to supplement test instruments.

23.5.1.1.2. Basic Math Concepts. The Jasper content covered time and distance, area, perimeter, and volume, fraction/decimal conversion, representation of fractions, and units of money, weight, and length. The Jasper students received no explicit instruction in these concepts, because the Jasper teams believed that Jasper provided a strong context in which students could anchor their learning of the concepts. Pellegrino used paper/pencil tests and word problems to examine students' skills. No main effects or interactions were found for gender. On tests of basic math abilities for decimals, fraction/decimals conversion, and area/perimeter/volume, Jasper students had significantly larger increases in performance across the school year than the control groups. The study also used word problems to test "near transfer" of Jasper problem-solving skills. The word problems were a mix of one-step, two-step, and multistep problems. The Jasper group significantly outperformed the control group on all three problem types at year end, demonstrating greater problem-solving skills.

23.5.1.1.3. Planning Skills. One of the main goals of both Jasper and REALs is to teach students to become better problem solvers. Pellegrino et al., in the thoroughness that characterizes this study, created experimental planning problems to assess higher-level planning, subgoal comprehension, and calculation ability for the two Jasper subject areas: trip planning and sampling for business plans. The Jasper students were significantly more skilled at identifying the goal of the problem and in breaking the problem down into the smaller components or subgoals that lead to the solution.

23.5.1.1.4. Standardized Achievement Test Scores. Realizing that no innovation will be adopted in schools if it does not deal with the political realities of standardized testing, Pellegrino compared the standardized achievement scores of Jasper to the control group. This was a difficult task, and results were difficult to interpret, because not all of the sites had scores to compare, and five different tests were used across the sites. The Jasper students tended to perform slightly better than the control group, but not significantly so. Results are probably always going to be difficult to interpret because of the differences between the purposes of testing and the purposes of the instructional strategies used in REALs. However, the issue of standardized testing will not go away, and more structured studies need to be conducted.

23.5.1.1.5. Strengths and Weaknesses. Although experimental researchers may consider this study as "too uncontrolled" to be generalizable, I hold the contrary belief. This study is one of the most thorough and objectively reported that we have read in this field. It is a broad study using many schools and teachers incorporating qualitative and quantitative measures. Rather than trying to control every single factor within the classroom, it treated those factors as natural elements of the study. (I will examine later a study that tried to control too many factors.) When the researchers found anomalies in the quantitative results, they used their observations of the classrooms to find explanations. One of their most significant strengths is their effort to find out why their students scored as they did, not just what their students scored, although the researchers themselves criticize their measurement instruments as lacking sensitivity for this kind of research. They also need to rely less on paper-and-pencil tests and test the students in the way that Jasper works, in a team approach to problem solving. They also did not measure the effect of group participation or the growth individuals showed in their ability to work within groups. Finally, the reactions of administrators, colleagues, and parents to the program need examination.

23.5.1.2. Stoiber's Research in Teacher Education. Most research with REALs begins from a desire to develop instructional strategies that help students become more thoughtful and cognitively flexible so that they can perform better in realistic problem-solving situations. Often, the standard we hold our students to is that of the expert job performer. It is the expert's behavior that we wish to teach to our students. For example, Stoiber (1991) states that expert teachers are more thoughtful and have more developed knowledge structures to support reasoning and problem solving when managing classrooms. They also have a highly developed sense of responsibility for student motivation and achievement in the learning environment. In a study at the university level with preservice teacher education students, Stoiber found that a REAL strategy was more effective in developing reflective teachers than conventional instruction. Stoiber looked at 67 students in a teacher education program who had no experience in classroom teaching or management. The students were divided into technical, reflective, and control groups. Instruction in classroom management concepts was conducted over ten 50-minute sessions that met weekly.

23.5.1.2.1. Technical Condition. The technical approach is based on an orientation that portrays learning as acquiring concepts, principles, and techniques. The instructor emphasized prescribed principles using a review-lecture-student participation format. Modeling and role playing were also used.

23.5.1.2.2. Reflective Condition. The reflective approach, on the other hand, stresses the construction of concepts and principles based on existing knowledge structures. In the reflective condition, students analyzed classroom cases that focused on cognitive functions corresponding to three stages of teaching: preteaching (planning), interactive teaching, and postteaching. In the preteaching phase, students used self-inquiry methods to activate prior knowledge. They constructed mental representations of classrooms, including situations, decisions, actions, and outcomes visualizing situations and asking themselves what they would do in certain circumstances. In the interactive phase, students would "think aloud" while solving classroom case situations to help them become more conscious of the steps or strategies undertaken during classroom management. The postteaching phase involved self-evaluation comparing goals, intents, and images of teaching to teaching outcomes.

23.5.1.2.3. Control Condition. In the control condition, students were instructed in education practices not related to classroom management. Students received excerpts of readings on an unrelated topic and examined vignettes and wrote short responses.

23.5.1.2.4. Instrumentation. Stoiber was creative in her measurement of student behaviors. She examined pedagogical reasoning and problem-solving performances. To examine pedagogical reasoning, she individually administered a video-stimulated interview of participants.

> This measure examined participants pedagogical reasoning by stimulating their thinking about classroom management. The participants viewed a videotape of four classroom situations depicting classroom management problems (e.g., children whispering during a test, children not paying attention) role-played by an elementary teacher and her students. Each classroom problem vignette consisted of a classroom management incident prior to the teacher intervention. At the end of each videotape segment, participants were asked what action they would take if they were the teacher. Then to assess their pedagogical abilities, they were asked: "Why did you decide on this particular action/response?" (Stoiber, 1991, p. 134).

Interviews were audiotaped and coded for pedagogical reasoning by two advanced graduate students. The students' reasons were rated on a three-point scale: (1) contains no or limited reasons, (2) contains adequate or specific reasons supporting viewpoint or decision, and (3) contains elaborate or ethical reasons. Interviews were also coded for expressions of teacher responsibility related to (a) student affect, (b) student cognition, and (c) learning environment.

She measured problem-solving performance by examining student ability to solve management problems assessed using video-stimulated interview. Students watched a teacher deal inappropriately with the problem and were asked, "What suggestions would you offer for improving outcome?" Interview responses were coded in terms of five problem-solving strategies: (a) problem identification (identification or clarification of the problem), (b) generating alternative plans and solutions, (c) reflecting on the consequences of the plan's actions, (d) self-awareness and metacognitive activity during the interview, and (e) evaluative skills for reflecting on and critiquing teaching. Finally, they completed a problem-solving inventory.

23.5.1.2.5. Results. In the pedagogical reasoning analysis, the students in the reflective condition showed more expertlike behavior than those in the technical or control conditions. Their reasons for supporting their suggested actions were rated higher than were technical or control groups. They reported significantly more concern about student affect/attitudes more often than technical condition and mentioned being responsible for student cognitive performance significantly more often than control condition. They took significantly more responsibility for a positive learning environment than either technical or control groups.

The reflective group was also more sophisticated in its problem-solving skills. The reflective group offered significantly more suggestions for alternative ways to handle the videotape situation than either other condition. The reflective group reflected significantly more often on the consequences of their decisions than the control group and reported significantly more alternatives for evaluating teaching practices than both the technical or control groups. The reflective group also exhibited more metacognitive awareness for improving poor pedagogical practices than the technical group and reported more frequently perceptions of themselves as solving problems in a manner associated with success than did the technical and control groups.

"The results of this study provide evidence that preservice teachers are capable of constructing concepts and developing the cognitive abilities needed to make sense of challenging classroom situations" (Stoiber, 1991, p. 137). Like the previous Jasper study, Stoiber's study is an excellent example of research with REALs. It combines qualitative and quantitative observations that not only measure the effects of the reasoning and problem solving skills but also explains why one group is more expertlike than another. However, like the Jasper study, we still need to see if this kind of development transfers to actual performance on the job.

23.5.1.3. Problem-Based Learning. Wilson and Cole, in Chapter 22, provide an extensive review of problem-based learning (PBL). I briefly summarize a review of PBL research in medical education by Coltrane (1993) to examine its overall effectiveness as a learning environment. The research on PBL is less conclusive than the research reported in the last two studies. Coltrane (1993) found too little data to determine conclusively that PBL is superior to conventional instruction in preparing physicians, though she found PBL at least equal to conventional instruction. The question of whether PBL is equal to or better than conventional instruction is important. REALs are usually viewed as more expensive in terms of time, effort, and resources than conventional, didactic instruction. Should PBL or REALs be adopted if they are not better than conventional instruction? Coltrane reports that Berkson (1993), in a meta-analysis of 12 PBL studies, found no direct advantage of one medical curriculum over another (PBL vs. regular). On the other hand, Mennin et al. (1993) found that PBL students outperformed conventional students in the later years of

their study when self-directed, less-structured, and more independent learning experiences were encountered in their residencies. This last finding is critical, because, like the two previously discussed studies, it finds that PBL students improve the problem-solving skills that are a major component of high-quality, diagnostic performance. We also point out that the PBL research is more concerned with content acquisition than intentional learning and specific cognitive processes.

The concern for content coverage is also a concern of teachers thinking about adopting REAL teaching strategies. Teachers fear that their students will sacrifice breadth of content if they focus on the opportunity for depth that REALs afford. There is also the concern that the new teaching strategies will not prepare students for standardized achievement tests. However, the data in this area are generally positive. Dolmans (1993) found that PBL learning activities covered an average of 64% of intended course content. However, the coverage actually increased when students generated learning issues in response to their own needs, because half of those issues were judged relevant to course content. In terms of covering prescribed objectives, Rangachari (1991) found that students brainstorming about PBL problems identified and exceeded all of the faculty objectives. Blumberg and colleagues (1990) found adequate consistency between student issues and objectives generated by faculty. Coulson and Osborne (cf. Coltrane, 1994) discovered that PBL student groups identified an average of 61% of faculty objectives deemed essential.

So, although the research on problem-based learning does not conclusively find that REAL strategies are better than conventional teaching in all regards, it does lend strong support. PBLs are at least equal to conventional instruction and probably better as the need for problem-solving and independent learning skills grow. Content and learning objective coverage may not be as systematic; however, research indicates that it is more than adequate.

23.5.1.4. Reciprocal Teaching. Another research question for REALs is whether they are useful for populations with special needs. Palincsar and Klenk (1992) investigated the effect of their intentional learning environment, reciprocal teaching, with young, at-risk children. "Young children with learning disabilities typically encounter difficulty with academic tasks requiring intentional effort and effective use of metacognitive skills—qualities that competent readers and writers possess" (Palincsar & Klenk, 1992, p. 211). Special education teachers often deal with these problems with greater decontextualization, isolating basic skills and drilling and practicing without context. However, Palincsar and Klenk contend that such instruction contributes to limited notions of literacy and fails to teach elements of intentional learning. So, they developed the reciprocal teaching strategies to place reading within a more meaningful context and to teach the intentional learning skills many learning-disabled children do not use.

Reciprocal teaching emphasizes the social nature of learning with a focus on students learning many of the executive control functions usually considered the exclusive province of the teacher. Reciprocal teaching helps students learn these skills through appropriate questioning and dialogues about reading materials (see earlier in this chapter for a more detailed description of reciprocal teaching). The primary academic goal of Palincsar's program is to improve reading and listening-comprehension skills. In reciprocal teaching, students and teachers take turns leading discussions about the content of a text that they are trying to understand. The strategies used encourage the self-regulation and self-monitoring behaviors that promote intentional learning. Baseline studies indicate that at-risk students score typically below the 40th percentile in achievement and about 30% correct on independent measures of text comprehension on entering a reciprocal teaching study (Brown & Palincsar, 1989; Palincsar, 1990; Palincsar & Brown, 1989). After 3 months of instruction using reciprocal teaching, 80% met the criteria for success (75% to 80% correct) on measures of comprehension, recall, ability to draw inferences, ability to state the gist of material read, and application of knowledge acquired from the text. The students, both primary and middle school, maintained those gains 6 months later.

In another study (Palincsar & Klenk, 1992), results show that children with learning disabilities benefit significantly "from strategy instruction occurring within classroom cultures that support collaborative discourse, the flexible application of comprehension strategies, and appropriate, meaningful opportunities for reading and writing" (p. 211). In this study, which we will examine in detail, Palincsar and Klenk used 6 teachers and 30 first-grade children who typically scored below the 35th percentile on a standardized test of listening and comprehension. The children worked with a set of texts covering related science concepts.

23.5.1.4.1. Pretests. The study began with a pretest to measure comprehension and knowledge of the science principles. The comprehension test was administered by reading a passage aloud to a student and then asking questions. This testing procedure was used regularly throughout the study. At the time of the pretest, the experimental and control children attained 47% correct. In identifying the theme of the passage, 29.2% of the experimental students were successful compared to 27.2% of the control group. A classification and sorting task was used to assess the children's ability to identify and use the analogy underlying the various topics. The teachers presented the children with pictures and asked them to put the pictures that go together in one pile and the other pictures in another pile. At the pretest, 43% (37% control) of the sorting decisions by the experimental groups were based on physical characteristics of the objects, and only 13% (14% control) were based on thematic characteristics.

23.5.1.4.2. Methodology. After the pretest, one passage was read to the students each day for 20 days. The basis of the procedure was reciprocal dialogues (see the actual article for sample dialogues). The children and teacher took turns leading discussions in which they questioned one another about the content of the passage. The group summarized the content, generated predictions about upcoming text, and clarified ambiguous information.

23.5.1.4.3. Results. The children in the experimental group made outstanding progress in 20 days. After the first 10 days of instruction, the experimental group attained 49.9% (37.7% control) correct on the comprehension measures. During the second 10 days, they attained 70.6% (39.5% control) correct. In their ability to identify the theme of the passage, the experimental group was correct 45.5% (14.9% control) during the first 10 days. During the second 10 days, this rose to 63.9% correct (10.5% control). On the classification task, the experimental group attained 53.1% correct (27% control) during the first half and 76.6% correct (17.3% control) during the second half.

Palincsar's and Klenk's work is another model study—difficult and complicated, but valid and authentic. They designed the study carefully, trained the teachers, and conducted measurements that indicated thought and development in the students, not just knowledge acquisition. The measurements and tasks were authentic and fit within the normal range of classroom activities. Their study was thorough and included the most important dimensions of reciprocal teaching: discourse patterns among students and teachers, playfulness, the role of the teacher, and the role of the text. Palincsar and Klenk managed to conduct research with REALs in the most unobtrusive and authentic way possible.

23.5.1.5. Meaning Versus Algorithmic Math Teaching. In a year-long study of 40 eighth-grade mathematics classrooms comparing teaching with meaning, teaching with algorithmic strategies, and conventional teaching strategies, Sigurdson and Olson (1992) found significant effects for teaching with meaning. Both the algorithmic teaching and meaning strategies were considered innovative treatments. They defined algorithmic teaching as teaching math emphasizing computational performance and automatic application of mathematical rules. They defined "teaching with meaning" as "teaching in context." Students used physical and pictorial objects to represent mathematical concepts, placed concepts in familiar applications, and performed mathematical interpretations. The conventional classrooms were control groups using typical strategies. Included in their study was a long-term training program to help teachers learn either the algorithmic or meaning strategies, though the training program ran concurrently with the classroom treatments. Reported results are based only on the teachers who were considered successful implementers of the strategies.

The results of the study are a bit difficult to interpret, because they make a distinction between class ability and student ability, the relevance of which is hard to understand. It is also difficult to find the results that were "significant" over those that "showed trends." However, generally, the students in the classes of teachers who successfully implemented the teaching-with-meaning strategies had the highest achievement at the end of the year on a posttest. The above-average classes showed much greater gains in performance under the meaning strategies, while the below-average performed equally poorly under all strategies. In terms of individual abilities, higher-level students performed well under any strategy, while the middle-level ability students did better with the meaning strategy. The lower-level students did poorly with all strategies. Sigurdson's and Olson's study is a complex study fraught with all of the confounding problems of doing research in this area: individual ability levels, different classes, different teaching styles, the difficulty in achieving consistency among treatment classes, teacher training, and teacher cooperation. They may have had poorer results with the lower-ability students because their definition of "meaning" and "context" was severely limited. The teaching-with-meaning activities, though aimed at a deeper understanding of the concepts, lacked the authenticity level found in the Jasper series. The training program may have also had a negative effect on class achievement because some teachers may have grasped and implemented the strategies before others. The significance of their study is in the questions raised related to individual differences and abilities.

23.5.2 Narrower Issues

The above findings show that REALs work in a general way. Jasper teaches math and problem-solving skills. Stoiber's teacher education program taught preservice teachers to be more reflective and creative in solving classroom management problems. Problem-based learning covers the content and teaches problem-solving skills. Reciprocal teaching places reading in context and teaches students to be more reflective and metacognitively aware while reading. Teaching math with meaning is more successful for some learners than an algorithmic approach. Now I examine some more specific issues related to the effectiveness of REALs, including problem solving and transfer, tutors and content expertise, attitude toward content, and effects on cognitive structure.

23.5.2.1. Problem Solving and Transfer. One of the main assertions of REAL developers is that REALs improve problem-solving skills and enhance the likelihood that learning transfers to new situations. To accomplish this goal, REAL strategies do three things: (1) They make relevant problem-solving skills explicit; (2) they use context and authenticity to avoid the problem of inert knowledge; and (3) they have students deal with complex problems in complex ways.

23.5.2.1.1. Making Skills Explicit. Susan Williams and her colleagues at Vanderbilt (1992) found that without prior instruction in "what-if" thinking, students often have difficulty in knowing which aspects of their previous knowledge should remain intact and be used in a new problem. In her study, Jasper and control students watched a Jasper adventure. The Jasper students received instruction in the Jasper program, and the control students worked in a traditional math curriculum. Following instruction, students received a what-if problem related to the Jasper program. (A what-if

program changed some variables in the original Jasper program.) Students were asked to talk aloud while solving the problem. The protocols were analyzed for the number of subgoals (16 necessary) attempted and the type of reasoning used. The Jasper students attempted to solve more subgoals than the control students. The Jasper work had made the problem-solving process more visible to them.

23.5.2.1.2. Inert Knowledge. The Jasper students in Williams's study also tried to make use of the declarative knowledge from the previous computations by applying it to the new problems. They may not have been right in their application, but the knowledge they learned provided a context for them to work in and did not remain inert. It helped them become active problem solvers. A number of other studies (Asch, 1969; Bransford et al., 1990; Brown et al., 1989; Gick & Holyoak, 1983; Ross, 1984; Stein, Way, Benningfield & Hedgecough, 1986) have found that when subjects are not explicitly informed about the relevance of knowledge to a problem, they do not use the knowledge—it remains inert. Bransford (1990) found that students who received statements that explicitly related acquired knowledge to problem statements were more likely to use that information during problem solving than subjects who did not receive statements drawing explicit links to the problem and their knowledge. Explicitly stating these relationships in the problem presentation helped students understand how information permitted a solution to that problem. Prior information that was recalled was then used more spontaneously.

23.5.2.1.3. Complexity. Real-world problems, that is, problems outside the classroom, are usually complex, requiring multiple substeps to solve. Yet, in classrooms, we have a tendency to limit problems to one or two steps. Students do not learn how to deal with multistep problems. The best way to teach complex problem solving, then, is to have students deal with complex problems in authentic contexts (CTGV, 1993d).

23.5.2.1.4. Far and Near Transfer. The Cognition and Technology Group at Vanderbilt (1993d) found that making processes explicit, drawing explicit relationships with existing knowledge, and using natural complexity improved problem-solving skills faciliates transfer. In one study, the CTGV examined a high-achieving fifth-grade math class for near transfer. Students were assigned to a Jasper instruction group or a word problem group. They were given tests to assess learning and transfer before and after four 1-hour instructional sessions. Students in the Jasper group scored much better on a mastery test of the Jasper program. The transfer test assessed transfer from Jasper to a highly similar problem. Students watched the transfer video and then solved the problem while talking aloud during an interview procedure. Their interviews were scored on whether they mentioned, attempted, or solved the major subproblems of the problem. The Jasper students scored higher than the word problem students. More than 75% of the Jasper-instructed group solved at least one of the top-level goals, compared with less than 20% of the word problem groups. These findings are also supported by

Van Haneghan et al. (1992), Goldman with CTGV (1991), and Goldman et al. (1991).

In a second study by the CTGV, the groups were tested on another transfer problem that was not isomorphically the same as the instructional problem—a far-transfer problem. Again the Jasper students scored significantly higher than the word-problem students. Jasper students mentioned, attempted, and solved a greater number of subproblems, even though the problem-solving steps were not the same as those encountered in the instructional program. This suggests that the Jasper-instructed students may have learned a general heuristic from the instruction.

On the whole, these findings suggest optimism about the value of REALs in teaching general problem-solving skills and transfer ability. Yet, there is still much work to do related to transfer. The distinction between near and far transfer is a continuum and not a dichotomy. The problem type, learner experience and intelligence, and problem context all play roles in determining what is near or far. What is far for one student may be near for another. What about transfer outside the classroom and across the curriculum? How successful are students in completely new environments? Are Jasper students able to apply anything they know to social studies, language arts, or science? The question of transfer is really the bottom line of REAL research. We justify REALs because our students are currently poor at transferring what they know. Are we improving?

23.5.2.2. Tutors and Content Expertise. REALs change teachers' roles by making teachers a greater part of the process of learning rather than the delivery of information. Teachers are often seen as equal participants in the learning process with students. This raises questions regarding their content expertise. Do teachers who are learning along with the students need to be experts in the content area? Or, since teachers are learning along with the students, do they only need to be experts in the learning process? The problem-based learning literature sheds some light on these questions.

Coltrane's (1993) review of PBL studies supports the contention that tutors should be experts in content. Students guided by content-expert tutors achieved better learning outcomes and spent more time on self-directed learning when their teachers were content experts. Expert tutors generated twice as many learning issues that were 3 times more congruent with case objectives than nonexpert tutors. However, Coltrane also found a disadvantage to expert tutors. Expert tutors tended to retain too much control of the learning process: They are more directive, speak more frequently and for longer periods, and more directly answered student questions, though they do suggest more discussion topics than nonexperts. Silver (1991) found that groups with expert tutors are less likely to be student directed.

It appears that good training of teachers may remedy the difficulties. Content knowledge balanced by an ability to "let go" and surrender control may be the best choice.

23.5.2.3. Attitude Toward Content Area. The Pellegrino et al. (1991) study (described above) found that students who used the REAL Jasper series had improved attitudes toward mathematics. In another, more loosely structured program, Myers (1992) studied the effects of using *The Voyage of the Mimi* in middle-school classes on female students. Mimi is a program that uses thirteen 15-minute video segments about a scientific expedition to study the Humpback whale. One of Mimi's main goals is to help integrate science across math, language arts, science, and social studies curricula boundaries promoting higher-level thinking activities. Students using the Mimi adventure spent the first period of the day viewing the day's adventure and then left for their other classes, rotating in and out of math, science, English, and social studies classrooms. The math teacher used a Mimi module on maps and navigation to study map making, measurement, distances, latitude and longitude, triangulation, rations, and time-and-distance problems. The science classes studied the scientific method, food chains, and food webs. The English teacher had students keep journals, pretending to be a Mimi crew member. They also studied ethics of whaling, communication, and poetry. The social studies teacher conducted research on endangered species, paleontology, evolution, codes, and land forms.

The observer and teachers were struck by the enthusiasm students showed to studying Mimi-related subjects. Anchoring the study of the content areas into a realistic context was highly motivating. To study attitudes of female students toward the math and science content, Myers administered before-and-after attitude questionnaires. Myers administered the postexercise questionnaire 2 weeks following the unit. The prequestionnaire showed no difference in attitudes towards math and science between male and female students. The postquestionnaire showed no improvement from the start of the exercise till the end for the female students.

There are several possible reasons for this. First, the study lasted only 2 weeks, which is hardly enough time to effect lasting attitude change (see Chapter 34 for a discussion of media and attitude change). Secondly, in Myers' view, the teachers tried to maintain their traditional approach to instruction, adhering to behavioral objectives and county and state guidelines. They became more flexible through the unit, but were as much "guinea pigs" as the students. Third, he conducted no advance training for the teachers. If they were unprepared to change their attitudes, it is hardly reasonable to expect a great change among the students. Finally, I question the integrative nature of the study. The students had a common topic, but moved from class to class in a compartmentalized way. That is hardly an integrative approach to instruction, for in most integrative approaches, the teachers work together and in teams with their students. So, the effects of REALs on student attitudes toward content is still an open issue.

23.5.2.4. Cognitive Structure. The theoretical models of Ausubel (1968) and Gagné and White (1978) suggest that "connections" among propositions, images, episodes, and intellectual skills within a person's cognitive structure promote understanding and transfer. "These models also imply that, to understand new concepts, one must anchor the new concepts to existing structures" (Robertson, 1990, pp. 253–54). However, as David Jonassen (Jonassen, 1994a) is fond of saying, "The cerebra-scope has not yet been invented," so a clear picture of a person's cognitive structures that support conceptual understanding does not exist. However, research to visually approximate these cognitive structures has been conducted using pathfinder and multidimensional scaling analyses.

One of these methods uses cognitive maps representing the perceived relationships among several pairs of concepts associated with a specific topic using pathfinder techniques. Dunlap and Grabinger (1992) examined the effect of working within a computer-supported learning environment on participants' knowledge structures about learning environments. They conducted a class that studied the attributes of REALs. At the beginning of the class, they used KNOT-Mac (Interlink, 1990) to rate the degree of relatedness among 17 concepts about REALs. The KNOT-Mac program uses pathfinder analysis techniques to produce a map representing the user's knowledge structure. At the end of the class, the students rated the same 17 concepts. Average maps representing the class starting map, class ending map, and an experts' map were compared for similarity and complexity. Their findings indicate that after working within the learning environment the participants' ending map (the average map for the whole class) became much more complex and sophisticated than the average beginning map. However, the class map did not replicate the average experts' map. This was to be expected, since the experts had worked with the concepts in different ways and for a longer period of time than the students.

One of the unexpected benefits of using the maps was that the students became involved in analyzing their maps. First, they tended to ask, "Is my map right or wrong?" assuming the map was some kind of test. After being convinced that the map was no test, they began to ask themselves why certain concepts were linked and other weren't. They wanted to refine their understanding of the concepts.

Robertson (1990) implemented REAL strategies to teach physics problems related to Newton's second law. He used strategies to contextualize the students' learning to ensure that both internal and external associations were among the criteria attributes of a principle. Internal associations are connections among the criteria attributes of a principle. External associations refer to connections between the principle and everyday experiences or context. He used student-generated concept maps to help analyze the understandings that students had of Newton's second law and the related concepts. Robertson gave students practice with a number of problems. One set of problems was highly similar and another set was both similar and varied, requiring further transfer. The similar problems focused on internal connections, while the varied problems helped students make additional external connections. Using the maps, he rated the level of understanding students had of the system, looking at both internal and external connections. He found that 86.5% of variance for predicting success in solving the physics problems could be attributed to system-concept understanding developed through practice with several kinds of problems. The maps and problem performance indicated that students who practiced with both similar and varied problems to develop external and internal connections were more successful. The maps helped indicate and show visually the kinds of connections they made.

Pathfinder networks and concept maps can provide visual data to help interpret and analyze the progress of student thinking processes. They are complex and difficult to use and subject to student resistance because they take much time to generate. But, when used carefully and with student acceptance, they can be quite revealing and a valuable qualitative research tool.

23.5.3 Research Conclusion

On the whole, research into implementations of REALs shows positive effects for the REAL strategies. These positive effects show across ages, abilities, and content areas. However, research into the implementation of REALs is still young and developing. At the same time that teachers are trying to change their classrooms from the teaching of decontextualized skills to the teaching of lifelong learning skills in context, educational research is struggling to move from a history of decontextualized experimental studies to more qualitative kinds of research within the natural context of the classroom. Both teachers and researchers have a lot to learn in terms of methodology in each area.

23.6 METHODOLOGICAL ISSUES

Performing studies with REALs is raising two important issues in instructional technology research methodology. First, the movement from experimental research methods to qualitative research methods is affecting the way in which researchers conduct their studies and report their results. Second, the field of instructional technology has had a fixation on performing research about media rather than about methods and learning. (Part VII of this text covers these issues and others in a more thorough manner.)

23.6.1 Experimental versus Qualitative Issues

Much of the current debate in educational research centers on experimental versus qualitative and naturalistic strategies. While I see the value for both kinds of research, I argue that professional researchers need to expand their conceptualizations of research methodologies when investigating the effects of REALs. Bissex (1987, p. 12) holds that

> The assumption of external and controllable causation would seem to underlie all studies based on experimental and control groups. Yet observational studies of children's language development and preschool literacy have revealed children to be creators rather than mere recipients of their learning (p. 12).

Bissex's statement mirrors the same issues we presented at the beginning of the chapter when discussing conventional versus REAL teaching strategies. A conventional classroom is didactic, based on the assumption that learners receive their learning from a controlling teacher. A REAL classroom is founded on the assumption that learners are the managers and creators of their own learning under the guidance of a teacher. She goes on to argue that experimental research focuses on issues of *teaching* and control, while observational studies focus on issues of *learning* and internal processes. It seems logical, then, to expect that new teaching methods demand new research methods.

Another factor in the methodological debate is the issue of generalizability. Bissex again argues that experimental research has limited generalizability because of the artificial nature of controls placed on treatment interventions. Experimental researchers try to isolate some factors and eliminate others; however, this is does not reflect the natural events within classrooms. Qualitative research, including observational and case study methods, forms more generalizable theories because the results are based on natural classroom and learning events that encompass many of the factors that influence learning and student behavior.

Bissex also argues that researchers must come to know the people they are working with quite closely. This is contrary to experimental studies where the researcher attempts to maintain distance from the subjects for fear of contaminating the results of the experiment. In observational techniques, researchers must take time to see their students in many situations and gain their confidences to gain valid and realistic perspectives of how the many factors in instruction are affecting the learners.

Again, I state that there is a role for both kinds of methodologies, usually within the same study. However, we do hold that Bissex's comments are valid and present good reasons for adopting more qualitative research methodologies. REAL classrooms are complex, with many factors in operation. They are, in essence, uncontrollable. To understand what is happening with students and teachers in the classroom, we cannot isolate or eliminate variables because we would be destroying the natural environment. The results would be meaningless.

For an example of some the above ideas, I can examine the 1992 study by Sigurdson and Olson that we cited earlier. While it has some interesting findings in the area of individual differences, it is also fraught with the difficulties and weaknesses inherent in conducting experimental research in a classroom. The purpose of their study was to compare three teaching approaches: one emphasizing meaning, another emphasizing other skills and procedures in mathematics, and the third using a traditional approach. Although their basic problem is worth investigating, we believe that they severely limited the generalizability of their results by using the experimental approach. To attempt for consistency among treatment groups and teachers, they varied seatwork but tried to keep homework, class talk, and questioning the same. This artificially constrains the use of the meaning-treatment methods. It is also unlikely that all of those factors were controlled adequately among several for an experimental study, thereby confounding the results. (In fact, they had to throw out some results because some teachers did not follow the program adequately.) They used a posttest and a retention test composed of multiple-choice questions covering computation, comprehension, and problem-solving questions. All treatment groups took the same test. Again, this is a necessity in an experimental study, but hardly reflective of actual classrooms. REALs use authentic assessment strategies, matching assessment with the objectives and methods. It is unlikely that an actual classroom using a meaning approach would use conventional testing strategies. The experimental nature of the study violates a teaching principle of evaluating in ways that match the ways students are taught. So, although they found some differences among the groups, the generalizability of those findings is limited because of the artificial constraints placed on the teaching and assessment methods.

23.6.2 Media Versus Method

Another major research issue, especially for instructional technologists, is the question of media versus method. Clark (1994) states that instructional methods are confounded with media, and it is instructional methods that influence learning, not the media. He contends that media are simply interchangeable delivery platforms whereby any necessary teaching method can be designed in a variety of media. Clark states that:

> . . . if learning occurs as a result of exposure to any media, the learning is caused by the instructional method embedded in the media presentation. Method is the inclusion of one of a number of possible representations of a cognitive process or strategy that is necessary for learning but which students cannot or will not provide for themselves (p. 26).

I agree with Clark and believe that our instructional technology research needs to focus more on processes and less on media. One need only attend conferences fairly regularly to see that our field runs through fads or favorite media in cycles. At the time of this writing, hypermedia and multimedia are popular applications and foci of research. Yet both are simply kinds of media used to support instructional methods.

Researchers and developers sometimes argue that certain kinds of media encourage different kinds of reasoning. For example, researchers using hypermedia applications sometimes claim that hypermedia affects learners' reasoning and processing activities because of the nonlinear construction of hypermedia applications (Nielsen, 1990). Yet the media are the same used in other applications. If hypermedia or multimedia encourage a specific kind of reasoning, it is because of the methods designed in the program, such as using hypermedia to apply cognitive flexibility theory (Borsook & Higginbotham-Wheat, 1992; Jacobson & Spiro, 1991; Jonassen, Ambruso & Olesen, 1992). Clark

(1994) would contend, then, that cognitive flexibility could be applied equally well to other media, including video, text, or illustrations. If studies that show that a specific medium or set of media attributes cause learning, then they are at the same time confounded because the study has failed to control for instructional method. Instructional method is always present, while a medium or media attributes are surface features that are replaceable.

This is an important issue for instructional technologists because it delineates what is important in a learning environment. Whether a REAL is supported by technology or not is not important. Research that focuses on the use of specific media diverts attention from what is actually important in a REAL, the instructional methods that permit students to take initiative for their own learning within authentic contexts. Clark (1994) describes this as an economic issue:

> The question is critical because if different media or attributes yield similar learning gains and facilitate achievement of necessary performance criteria, then in a design science or an instructional technology, we must always choose the *less expensive* way to achieve a learning goal. I must also form out theories around the underlying structural features of the *shared properties* of the interchangeable variables and not base theory on the irrelevant surface features (p. 22).

23.6.3 Methodology Strategies

Research strategies, then, need to emphasize learning processes. Therefore we need to develop and to find strategies that let us examine the cognitive processes of learning rather than just the products. Below, we describe several strategies worth noting, hopefully to entice you into doing further research into their applicability to your own research programs.

23.6.3.1. Think-Alouds.   One strategy gaining increasing use is think-aloud protocols. Ericsson and Simon (1984) demonstrated that protocol analysis can produce detailed, quantifiable, and reproducible data on human thought processes. Think-alouds ask learners to literally think aloud while solving a problem. This illuminates their understanding of concepts and the presence of any misconceptions. Pellegrino et al. (1991), Stoiber (1991), and Palincsar and Klenk (1992) all used some form of think-alouds in the reviews above.

23.6.3.2. Written-Question Generation.   Torney-Purta (1990) describes the use of question generation techniques. Torney-Purta asked students to generate four questions dealing with a problem. The questions indicate the depth of understanding and often illuminate cause-and-effect relationships. Students that generate what-if questions usually indicate a deeper understanding of the content because they can wonder about variables and the relationship of one to another.

23.6.3.3. Ranking and Classification Techniques. Another technique used by Torney-Purta (1990) is a ranking or classification task. She asked students to rank items within a group according to a specific dimension and to give reasons for the rankings (combining the think-aloud protocol). Classification indicates depth of understanding

of the dimensions used for ranking and can point up misconceptions. Palincsar and Klenk (1992) also used a classification technique to study reciprocal teaching. Students sorted pictures into two piles and talked aloud to explain why one picture belonged with the others. This indicated the kind of dimension (i.e., physical or thematic) that students were using and the depth of understanding related to the text they read.

23.6.3.4. Concept Maps.   Robertson (1990) and Dunlap and Grabinger (1992) have shown that concept maps, generated either by students or by computer programs, can also represent the depth of understanding and complexity of understanding of related concepts. They provide a tool for students to compare and analyze their own thinking. The maps could be combined with think-alouds by having students try to explain their own conceptions.

23.6.3.5. Analysis of Recordings.   Stoiber (1991) used an individual video-stimulated interview technique. She had students reflect on a videotaped performance to examine their ability to use concepts and understandings to critique the tape. The interviews indicated how creative the students were in applying classroom management techniques.

23.6.3.6. Dependent Measures and Assessment Foci. What do the above strategies aim to measure? In general terms, I present four complexities defined by Torney-Purta (1990). These "complexities" (generalized the author; the original article focused on social studies) define areas in which we hope any REAL is successful. These areas, then, provide assessment goals and emphases for research studies. They suggest dependent measures and assessments to measure the effectiveness of REALs and the growth of students' problem-solving abilities.

1. Students with complex structures should be able to visualize or access a variety of different solutions to a problem. A research study could give students opportunities to explore different options and observe how the thinking of the student changes as a result of the exploration and experimentation.

2. Students with complex knowledge structures can see constraints on the effectiveness of possible solutions. Pellegrino et al. (1991) discovered that students experienced in multiple-step problem solving could identify constraints within the context more easily than students who did not have the same experience. They used think-alouds to monitor student processes.

3. Students with complex scripts as a structure for understanding a domain can see the relevance of potential actions. They can pose questions and hypotheses that represent the depth of the domain. Students who can do this can ask what-if questions and have also developed a sense of experimentation and wonderment.

4. Students with complex structures are able to rank or categorize definable groups along a complex set of dimensions. Learners must indicate depth of understanding in evaluations, and a classification task is good way to visualize that depth.

Torney-Purta's complexities are indications of the effectiveness of REALs in developing problem-solving skills. Ultimately, we must examine student performance with authentic problems both close in and removed from the original learning situation.

23.7 RESEARCH ISSUES AND QUESTIONS

What, then, are some of the issues that need investigation in REALs? In actuality, it is everything. At this stage, nothing has been done too much or too well. However, I consider the following topics particularly important.

23.7.1 Individual Differences

Sigurdson's and Olson's (1992) study raises a question found in other ability research. They found that the students in the top one-third of the class responded almost as well to algorithmic-practice teaching as to meaning teaching. The best students learn in spite of what we do to them. The middle one-third of students responded well to teaching with meaning, while the lowest one-third did not respond well to either of treatment. Can this effect be replicated in other studies? Can low-ability students benefit from REALs, or are REALs only for higher abilities or intelligence levels? If REALs are limited to the higher-ability students, are the methodologies inherent in REALs the reason for successful learning, or is it the ability inherent in the successful students?

23.7.2 Learner Control

Individual differences are closely related to questions of learner control. Learner control is one of the main issues related to teaching students to become intentional learners. They must develop metacognitive skills to make good control decisions. Can we specify those metacognitive skills? What can we do to help students develop those skills? For example, Arnone, Grabowski, and Rynd (1994) found that high-curious primary-age children function better given more learner control than low-curious children. Do the high-curious children possess greater intellectual curiosity or ability? How do they use their curiosity? What do they do differently in terms of learning processes?

23.7.3 Scaffolding and Support

An important part of teaching students to be intentional learners is providing them with the appropriate scaffolding and support to help them move toward more independence. The CTGV (1993) state that:

> We need to carefully explore issues of how best to provide support for comprehension and learning. We suspect that there is a need to consider [interactive media] designs that function as scaffolds rather than always providing an option for full support (p. 78).

We need to identify the skills students need to perform independently to help them develop lifelong learning skills. Yes, we know in general what independent learners do, but we need to break those general skills into operational skills that teachers can work with. Brown (1989, p. 40) asserts that "one of the particularly difficult challenges for research . . . is determining what should be made explicit in teaching and what should be left implicit."

Many of the research strategies described above are aimed at examining reflective processes by making them visible. What can be done to increase students' ability to reflect both on the problem and on their own problem-solving and learning processes? In part, this is related to providing scaffolding and support, for support must go beyond tools and strategies for learning content; it must also include tools and strategies for learning the processes of learning and developing metacognitive awareness.

Research into scaffolding and support should also be directed at teachers. How can developers of REALs support their implementation and adoption in the classroom? Using REALs means radical changes, and it is difficult to make those changes without support. The CTGV is trying out electronic networks and teleconferencing in helping teachers develop the skills necessary to change and to use REALs in the classroom. What tools and strategies do we need to prepare for teachers?

23.7.4 Learning

Learning is still the *raison d'être* for REALs. Williams (1992) suggests that we investigate methods that help students abstract general principles from the study of cases and problems. What can teachers do to help students abstract general principles from context specific learning? She also suggests that we measure not only content-based learning but also improvement in skills related to learning to learn. I must expand our concern from how much students learn to the inclusion of how people learned what they learned. This leads directly to assessment issues.

23.7.5 Assessment

We should assess learning in ways that are authentic, manageable, and supported by parents and administrations. Assessment strategies must examine what content people learned, the strategies employed in learning, and what students can do with the knowledge. Williams (1992) describes the following problems with current assessment strategies: First, students are often assessed on skills different from the ones they are taught; second, written tests of problem-solving performance are time consuming to administer and score; and third, assessment of problem-solving performance tends to be subjective. I made a number of suggestions related to assessment in the first half of the paper, but those options are probably only the beginning of new ways of assessing learning. Research needs to be conducted on all of those options to identify the most efficient and effective ways to apply them.

Peer assessment is also an area needing more research. Peer assessment is another way for students to assume more responsibility for their learning and for each other's learning within the learning community. Rushton, Ramsey, and Rada (1993) studied a group of 32 undergraduate students who participated in a peer assessment exercise. Contrary to expectations, the marks awarded by the peers were remarkably similar to those awarded by the tutors. Despite this, the majority of the students were extremely skeptical of peer assessment, preferring traditional teacher-based assessment. Rushton, Ramsey, and Rada's results need to be replicated, and we need to find ways to increase student assessment.

23.7.6 Technology and Research

You may have noticed something conspicuous in its absence, especially in a book on research in instructional technology—the absence of any discussion about technology in its hardware form. If you go back and look at the definition of REALs, you won't even find the word *technology* in the definition. Although we argued earlier that research needs to focus on methods and not media, this does not preclude research into technology to determine its potential usefulness and ways to integrate instructional methods within technology. (Part II of this text deals with a number of hard technologies and media-related research.) REALs are gaining more attention because technology has developed to an extent that helps teachers give more time to individuals, and because it provides tools to help learners become more independent. In the past, AV delivery systems depended on discrete audio and visual channels that transmitted separate message content. These constraints encouraged people to think about their designs as tools, either audio or video (Allen, 1994). Allen states that thinking in terms of information channels is artificial:

> Humans in unmediated environments do not seem to frame their perceptions or actions in terms of information channels; rather, they appear to organize both their perception and their reasoning in terms of objects and agents of action. In spite of separate pathways for sensory information dictated by different cranial nerves for vision, olfaction, and audition, our capabilities of perception, memory, and language integrate across sensory modalities and our minds attend to avenues for exploration and action (p. 34).

Therefore, the human-machine relationship is more than discrete sensory inputs. The machines are tools that facilitate processes. So, how can we design machines to help people learn and think? Does this mean that machines need to replicate human processes or that machines support processes? Can we use machines to help make the thinking and learning processes visible and more accessible? Allen (1994) says that "I need to think more about how to design media systems as livable environments, and this will

require much rethinking about what it means for humans to be intimate with their media machines" (p. 34).

Besides the nature of technology and its interfaces, we need to look at specific tool uses for technology. (For a much more detailed treatment of this topic, see Chapter 25.) Lajoie (1993) describes four uses for cognitive tools in learning environments: (1) to support cognitive processes, (2) to share the cognitive load by providing support for lower-level cognitive skills, (3) to allow learners to engage in learning activities normally out of reach, and (4) to allow learners to generate and test hypotheses. These uses are related to scaffolding and metacognitive issues, and again emphasize the importance of working with technology in the context of a strategy rather than as the cause of learning.

23.7.7 The Process of Change

The implementation of REALs means radical change in most classrooms and schools. Change is always difficult, even when supported strongly by the parties involved. (Chapter 37 discusses diffusion and adoption of educational technology.) Kirsner and Bethell (1992) describe one high school teacher's attempt to change her mathematics teaching in ways that are consistent with the National Council of Teachers of Mathematics. Although they found that a professional development school provided a relatively supportive environment, the teacher would have benefited from more consistent support as she struggled with pedagogical and content-related issues. Schools are set up to support one style of teaching. "Calls for change of any kind are seen as impositions or disturbances to be quelled as soon as possible, as unreasonable attempts to change the rules in the middle of the game" (Hodas, 1993, p. 7). In fact, Van Haneghan (1992) lists five reasons for failure or difficulties in implementing REAL strategies, and each can be dealt with through effective change management processes:

1. Curriculum developers fail to realize that their curricula involve more than materials. They must include methods and resources, too. Teachers have little time, so we must provide them with as many tools as possible to facilitate the change to a REAL classroom.
2. Curriculum developers fail to adequately train and provide support to teachers when a curriculum becomes widespread. Many teachers are interested in new techniques but need strategies and support to be successful. They must have colleagues whom they can talk to, either personally or electronically.
3. Curriculum developers fail to provide ways to integrate the program into the curricular goals of particular schools and teachers. Developers must recognize that their curriculum is not isolated but must fit within a system. Support must be provided to fit the new curriculum within the "old" school.
4. Assessment is a long-neglected issue, and developers fail to develop adequate assessment tools. Developers must not expect teachers to automatically develop

new assessment strategies. Teachers need new ideas and tools for this topic, too.

5. Curriculum developers assume that curricula are developed in a top-down manner. They often dictate to teachers what they should or should not do. But teachers are more likely to adopt something from a grass roots movement than top-down fiat. They need to see the benefit and buy into the new program.

What can we do to support teachers who wish to try another style? What strategies can we provide teachers? How can we gain student, collegial, administrative, and parental support? Recall, too, that students are probably the most important group involved in this change, especially older students in high schools and colleges. These older students have learned to "play the game" with years of practice. The further they advance in education, the more successful they are at the game. Our own experiences in adopting REALs have shown significant initial resistance from students. They have to learn a new set of rules. Responsibility is risky, and they need to know that the risk is not going to be punished. This is an area of research interest that needs much work but is often not pursued by our technologically oriented field. I need to expand our field and promote research into the instructional change process.

23.8 CONCLUSION

In this chapter, I have defined REALs, looked at research into the effectiveness of REALs, and discussed several issues awaiting research. There have been a number of several recurring themes in our discussion of REALs. First is the importance of transfer. REALs are used to facilitate transfer to new situations and to meet the complaint from employers and schools that students cannot use what they know. Second is the importance of context in learning. Decontextualized learning causes inert knowledge. Even though a new context may be different from the context in which students learned, it is more likely that the students will try to apply what they know. They may be wrong, but what they've learned is the necessity for trying new things and analyzing what is right or wrong. They have created indexes that relate to real problems, not abstract, meaningless problems. Fourth is the importance of self-reflection and metacognitive awareness. A lifelong learner is by definition reflective and metacognitively aware. Lifelong learners try alternatives, look for multiple solutions, and, most importantly, try to optimize their solutions. They look for alternatives rather than a single way for solving problems. Finally, the attributes of REALs are interdependent and symbiotic. A REAL is a set of interlocking strategies designed to promote the learning of content and learning. Some manifestations of REALs may emphasize one attribute over another, but you will find evidence of each attribute in cognitive flexibility, anchored instruction, problem-based learning, intentional learning, reciprocal teaching, and so on.

Rich environments for active learning are one way of looking at and applying constructivist principles to learning. REALs are one attempt to bring together thoughts, ideas, and theories in a way that will help teachers at all levels develop classroom environments that foster higher-level thinking skills, especially reflection, problem solving, flexible thinking, and creativity. I owe our students a return on their investments. One way to make that return is by adopting methods and roles that help our students not only learn content but also learn skills that will make them lifelong learners.

REFERENCES

Adams, L., Kasserman, J., Yearwood, A., Perfetto, G., Bransford, J. & Franks, J. (1988). The effects of facts versus problem-oriented acquisition. *Memory & Cognition 16,* 167–75.

Agnew, P., Kellerman, A. & Meyer, J. (1992). *Constructing multimedia: solutions for education.* Paper presented at the 34th Annual International Conference of the Association for the Development of Computer-Based Instructional Systems, Norfolk, VA.

Albanese, M.A. & Mitchell, S. (1993). Problem-based learning: a review of literature on its outcomes and implementation issues. *Academic Medicine 68* (1), 52–81.

Allen, B.S. (1994). Multiplicity of media: changing paradigms for working and learning in multimedia environments. *Educational Technology 34* (4), 33–34.

Allinson, L. & Hammond, N. (1990). Learning support environments: rationale and evaluation. *Computers in Education 15* (1), 137–43.

Ambruso, D. & The Transfusion Medicine Group (1994). *Transfusion medicine modules* [computer programs]. Denver, CO: Bonfils Blood Center.

American Association for the Advancement of Science. (1989). *A project 2061 report on literacy goals in science, mathematics, and technology.* Washington, DC: AAAS.

Arnone, M.P., Grabowski, B.L. & Rynd, C.P. (1994). Curiosity as a personality variable influencing learning in a learner controlled lesson with and without advisement. *Educational Technology Research and Development 42* (1), 5–20.

Asch, S.E. (1969). A reformulation of the problem of associations. *American Psychologist 24,* 92–102.

Ausubel, D.P. (1968). *Educational psychology: a cognitive view.* New York: Academic.

Barrows, H.S. (1985). *How to design a problem-based curriculum for the preclinical years.* New York: Springer.

— & Tamblyn, R.M. (1980). *Problem-based learning: an approach to medical education.* New York: Springer.

Bednar, A.K., Cunningham, D., Duffy, T.M. & Perry, J.D. (1991). Theory into practice: how do we link? *In* G.J. Anglin, ed. *Instructional technology: past, present, and future,* 88–101. Englewood, CO: Libraries Unlimited.

Benor, D.E. (1984). An alternative, non-Brunerian approach to problem-based learning. *In* H.G. Schmidt & M.L.d. Volder, eds. *Tutorials in problem-based learning: new directions in training for the health professions,* 48–58. Assen/Maastrict: Van Gor Cum.

Bereiter, C. & Scardamalia, M. (1989). Intentional learning as a goal of instruction. *In* L.B. Resnick, ed. *Knowing, learning, and instruction: essays in honor of Robert Glaser,* 361–92. Hillsdale, NJ: Erlbaum.

Berkson, L. (1993). Problem-based learning: have the expectations been met? *Academic Medicine 68* (10), S79–S88.

Berryman, S.E. (1991). Designing effective learning environments: cognitive apprenticeship models. *ERIC Document 337 689,* 1–5.

Biggs, J.B. (1985). The role of metalearning in study processes. *British Journal of Educational Psychology 55,* 185–212.

Bissex, G.L. (1987). Why case studies? *In* G.L. Bissex & R. Bullock, eds. *Seeing for ourselves: case study research by teachers of writing,* 7–19. Portsmouth, NH: Heinemann.

Blakey, E. & Spence, S. (1990). Developing metacognition. *ERIC Document 327 218,* 1–4.

Blumberg, P., et al. (1990). Roles of student-generated learning issues in problem-based learning. *Teaching and Learning in Medicine 2* (3), 149–54.

Borsook, T.K. & Higginbotham-Wheat, N. (1992). *The psychology of hypermedia: a conceptual framework for R & D.* Paper presented at the 1992 National Convention of the Association for Educational Communications and Technology, Washington, DC.

Bransford, J., Goldman, S.R. & Vye, N.J. (1991). Making a difference in peoples' abilities to think: reflections on a decade of work and some hopes for the future. *In* L. Okagaki & R.J. Strnberg, eds. *Directors of development: influences on children,* 147–80. Hillsdale, NJ: Erlbaum.

— & Vye, N.J. (1989). A perspective on cognitive research and its implications for instruction. *In* L. Resnick & L.E. Klopfer, eds. *Toward the thinking curriculum: current cognitive research,* 173–205. Alexandria, VA: ASCD.

—, Sherwood, R.D., Hasselbring, T.S., Kinzer, C.K. & Williams, S.M. (1990). Anchored instruction: why we need it and how technology can help. *In* D. Nix & R. Spiro, eds. *Cognition, education, and multimedia: exploring ideas in high technology,* 115–41. Hillsdale, NJ: Erlbaum.

Brown, A.L. (1978). Knowing when, where, and how to remember: a problem of metacognition. *In* R. Glaser, ed. *Advances in instructional psychology.* Hillsdale, NJ: Erlbaum.

—, Bransford, J.D., Ferrara, R.A. & Campione, J.C. (1983). Learning, remembering, and understanding. *In* J.H. Flavell & E.M. Markman, eds. *Vol. 3, Handbook of child psychology: cognitive development,* 177–266. New York: Wiley.

— & Palincsar, A.S. (1989). Guided, cooperative learning and individual knowledge acquisition. *In* L.B. Resnick, ed. *Knowing and learning: issues for a cognitive psychology of learning. Essays in honor of Robert Glaser,* 393–451. Hillsdale, NJ: Erlbaum.

Brown, J.S., Collins, A. & Duguid, P. (1989). Situated cognition and the culture of learning. *Educational Researcher,* Jan.-Feb., 32–42.

Bruner, J.S. (1961). The act of discovery. *Harvard Educational Review,* 21–32.

Butterfield, E. & Nelson, G. (1989). Theory and practice of teaching for transfer. *Educational Technology Research and Development 37* (3), 5–38.

Carver, S.M., Leherer, R., Connell, T. & Erickson, J. (1992). Learning by hypermedia design: issues of assessment and implementation. *Educational Psychologist 27* (3), 385–404.

Clark, R.E. (1994). Media will never influence learning. *Educational Technology Research and Development 42* (2), 21–29.

Clark, R.E. & Voogel, A. (1985). Transfer of training principles for instructional design. *Educational Communication and Technology Journal 33* (2), 113–25.

Clement, J. (1982). Algebra word problem solutions: thought processes underlying a common misconception. *Journal of Research in Mathematics Education 13,* 16–30.

Cognition and Technology Group at Vanderbilt (CTGV) (1990). Anchored instruction and its relationship to situated cognition. *Educational Researcher 19* (6), 2–10.

— (1991). Technology and the design of generative learning environments. *Educational Technology 31,* 34–40.

— (1992a). Anchored instruction in science and mathematics: theoretical basis, developmental projects, and initial research findings. *In* R.A. Duschl & R.J. Hamilton, eds. *Philosophy of science, cognitive psychology, and educational theory and practice,* 244–73. New York: SUNY Press.

— (1992b). The Jasper Series as an example of anchored instruction: theory, program description, and assessment data. *Educational Psychologist 27*(3), 291–315.

— (1993a). Anchored instruction and situated cognition revisited. *Educational Technology 13* (3), 52–70.

— (1993b). Designing learning environments that support thinking. *In* T.M. Duffy, J. Lowyck & D.H. Jonassen, eds. *Designing environments for constructive learning,* 9–36. New York: Springer.

— (1993c). Integrated media: toward a theoretical framework for utilizing their potential. *Journal of Special Education Technology 12* (2), 76–89.

— (1993d). The Jasper series: theoretical foundations and data on problem solving and transfer. *In* L.A. Penner, G.M. Batsche, H.M. Knoff & D.L. Nelson, eds. *The challenges in mathematics and science education: psychology's response,* 113–52. Washington, DC: American Psychological Association.

Collins, A., Brown, J.S. & Holum, A. (1991). Cognitive apprenticeship: making thinking visible. *American Educator* (Winter), 6–11, 38–46.

Coltrane, L. (1993). An overview of problem-based learning in medical education. Class paper.

Dewey, J. (1910). *How we think.* Boston, MA: Heath.

Dolmans, D.H.J.M. (1993). Problem effectiveness in a course using problem-based learning. *Academic Medicine 68* (3), 207–13.

Duffy, T.M. (1992). *The strategic teaching framework.* Bloomington, IN: Interactive Software.

— (1996). Strategic teaching framework: an instructional model for learning complex, interactive skills. *In* C. Dill & A. Romiszowski, eds. *Encyclopedia of educational technology.* Englewood, NJ: Educational Technology.

— & Bednar, A.K. (1991). Attempting to come to grips with alternative perspectives. *Educational Technology 31* (9), 12–15.

Dunlap, J.C. & Grabinger, R.S. (1992). *A comparison of conceptual maps constructed after using computer-based learning environments.* Paper presented at the 34th Annual International Conference of the Association for the Development of Computer-Based Instructional Systems, Norfolk, VA.

Ericsson, K.A. & Simon, H.A. (1984). *Protocol analysis: verbal reports as data.* Cambridge, MA: MIT Press.

Farnham-Diggory, S. (1992). *Cognitive processes in education,* 2d ed. New York: HarperCollins.

Feuerstein, R. (1979). *Instrumental enrichment.* Baltimore, MD: University Park.

Forman, G. & Pufall, P., eds. (1988). *Constructivism in the computer age.* Hillsdale, NJ: Erlbaum.

Fosnot, C. (1989). *Inquiring teachers, inquiring learners: a constructivist approach for teaching.* New York: Teacher's College Press.

Frederiksen, J.R. & Collins, A. (1989). A systems approach to educational testing. *Educational Researcher 18,* 27–32.

Gagné, R.M. & White, R.T. (1978). Memory structures and learning outcomes. *Review of Educational Research 48,* 187–222.

Gick, M.L. & Holyoak, K.J. (1983). Schema induction and analogical transfer. *Cognitive Psychology 15,* 1–38.

Goldman, S.R. & Cognition and Technology Group at Vanderbilt. (1991). *Meaningful learning environments for mathematical problem solving: the Jasper problem-solving series.* Paper presented at the Fourth European Conference for Research on Learning and Instruction, Turku, Finland.

—, Pellegrino, J.W. & Bransford, J. (1994). Assessing programs that invite thinking. *In* E. Baker & J. Harold F. O'Neill, eds. *Technology assessment in education and training,* pp. x–y. Hillsdale, NJ: Erlbaum.

—, Petrosino, A., Sherwood, R.D., Garrison, S., Hickey, D., Bransford, J.D. & Pellegrino, J.W. (1992). *Multimedia environments for enhancing science instruction.* Paper presented at the NATO Advanced Study Institute on Psychological and Educational Foundations of Technology-Based Learning Environments, Kolymbari, Greece.

— Vye, N.J., Williams, S.M., Rewey, K. & Pellegrino, J.W. (1991). *Problem space analyses of the Jasper problems and student's attempts to solve them.* Paper presented at the American Educational Research Association, Chicago, IL.

Goodman, N. (1984). *Of mind and other matters.* Cambridge, MA: Harvard University Press.

Gurney, B. (1989). Constructivism and professional development: a stereoscopic view. *ERIC Document ED 305 259,* 1–28.

Hannafin, M.J. (1992). Emerging technologies, ISD, and learning environments: critical perspectives. *Educational Technology Research and Development 40* (1), 49–63.

Hodas, S. (1993). *Technology refusal and the organizational culture of schools* [electronic journal]: School of Education, Leadership and Policy Studies, University of Washington.

Honebein, P.C., Duffy, T.M. & Fishman, B.J. (1993). Constructivism and the design of learning environments: context and authentic activities for learning. *In* T.M. Duffy, J. Lowych & D.H. Jonassen, eds. *Designing environments for constructive learning.* Hillsdale, NJ: Erlbaum.

Interlink (1990). KNOT-Mac: knowledge network organizing tool for the Mac. Las Cruces, NM: Interlink.

Jacobson, M.J. (1994). Issues in hypertext and hypermedia research: toward a framework for linking theory-to-design. *Journal of Educational Multimedia and Hypermedia 3* (2), 141–54.

— & Spiro, R.J. (1991). *Hypertext learning environments and cognitive flexibility: characteristics promoting the transfer of complex knowledge.* Paper presented at the International Conference on the Learning Sciences, Evanston, IL.

— & — (1992). *Hypertext learning environments, cognitive flexibility, and the transfer of complex knowledge: an empirical investigation.* Paper presented at the Annual Meeting of the American Educational Research Association, San Francisco, CA.

Jonassen, D.H. (1994a). The cerebra-scope. Personal communication.

— (1994b). Sometimes media influence learning. *Educational Technology Research and Development 42* (2).

— (1994c). Thinking technology: toward a constructivist design model. *Educational Technology 34* (3), 34–37.

—, Ambruso, D.R. & Olesen, J. (1992). Designing a hypertext on transfusion medicine using cognitive flexibility theory. *Journal of Educational Multimedia and Hypermedia 1* (3), 309–21.

Kirsner, S.A. & Bethell, S. (1992). *Creating a flexible and responsive learning environment for general mathematics students* (92-7). National Center for Research on Teacher Learning, Michigan State University.

Kozma, R. (1994). Media attributes. *Educational Technology Research and Development 42* (2).

Lajoie, S.P. (1993). Computer environments as cognitive tools for enhancing learning. *In* S. Lajoie & S. Derry, eds. *Computers as cognitive tools,* 261–88. Hillsdale, NJ: Erlbaum.

Lebow, D. (1993). Constructivist values for instructional systems design: five principles toward a new mindset. *Educational Technology Research and Development 41* (3), 4–16.

Linn, M.C. (1986). *Establishing a research base for science education: challenges, trends, and recommendations.* (Report of a National Science Foundation national conference.) University of California.

Lockhart, R.S., Lamon, M. & Gick, M.L. (1988). Conceptual transfer in simple insight problems. *Memory & Cognition 16,* 36–34.

Lynton, E. (1989). *Higher education and American competitiveness.* National Center on Education and the Economy.

Lynton, E. & Elman, S. (1987). *New priorities for the university.* San Francisco, CA: Jossey-Bass.

Mann, L. (1979). *On the trail of process: a historical perspective on cognitive processes and their training.* New York: Grune & Stratton.

Mennin, S.P., Friedman, M., Skipper, B., Kalishman, S. & Snyder, J. (1993). Performances on the NBME I, II, and III by medical students in the problem-based learning and conventional tracks at the University of New Mexico. *Academic Medicine 68* (8), 616–24.

Minstrell, J.A. (1989). Teaching science for understanding. *In* L.B. Resnick & L.E. Klopfer, eds. *Toward the thinking curriculum: current cognitive research,* 129–49. Alexandria, VA: ASCD.

Morris, C.D., Bransford, J.D. & Franks, J.J. (1979). Levels of processing versus transfer appropriate processing. *Journal of Verbal Learning and Verbal Behavior 16,* 519–33.

Myers, R.J. (1992). *Interdisciplinary multimedia learning using anchored instruction.* Paper presented at the 34th Annual Conference of the Association for the Development of Computer-Based Instructional Systems, Norfolk, VA.

National Council of Teachers of Mathematics (1989). *Curriculum and evaluation standards for school mathematics.* Reston, VA: NCTM.

Neuman, D. (1993). *Evaluation of the Perseus project.* Paper presented at the 1993 National Conference of the Association for Educational Communications and Technology, New Orleans, LA.

Nickerson, R.S. (1988). On improving thinking through instruction. *Review of Research in Education 15,* 3–57.

Nielsen, J. (1990). *Hypertext and hypermedia.* Boston, MA: Academic.

Palincsar, A.S. (1990). Providing the context for intentional learning. *Remedial and Special Education 11* (6), 36–39.

— & Brown, A.L. (1989). Classroom dialogues to promote self-regulated comprehension. *In* J. Brophy, ed. *Teaching for meaningful understanding and self-regulated learning,* Vol. 1, pp. 35–72. Greenwich, CT: JAI.

— & Klenk, L. (1992). Fostering literacy learning in supportive contexts. *Journal of Learning Disabilities 25* (4), 211–25.

Pellegrino, J.W., Hickey, D., Heath, A., Rewey, K., Vye, N.J. & Vanderbilt, CTGV (1991). *Assessing the outcomes of an innovative instructional program: the 1990–1991 implementation of the "Adventures of Jasper Woodbury"* (Tech. Rep. No. 91-1): Vanderbilt University, Learning Technology Center.

Perelman, L.J. (1992). *Living in the gap between old and new: managing transition.* Paper presented at the Technology in Education Conference, Steamboat Springs, CO.

Perfetto, B.A., Bransford, J.D. & Franks, J.J. (1983). Constraints on access in a problem solving context. *Memory and Cognition 11,* 24–31.

Perkins, D.N. (1991). What constructivism demands of the learner. *Educational Technology 31* (9), 19–21.

Rangachari, P.K. (1991). Design of a problem-based undergraduate course in pharmacology: implications for the teaching of physiology. *Advances in Physiology Education 5* (1), s14–s21.

Resnick, L. (1987). *Education and learning to think.* Washington, DC: National Academy Press.

Resnick, L.B. & Klopfer, L.E., eds. (1989). *Toward the thinking curriculum: current cognitive research.* Alexandria, VA: ASCD.

Ridley, D.S., Schutz, P.A., Glanz, R.S. & Weinstein, C.E. (1992). Self-regulated learning: the interactive influence of metacognitive awareness and goal-setting. *Journal of Experimental Education 60* (4), 293–306.

Robertson, W.C. (1990). Detection of cognitive structure with protocol data: predicting performance on physics transfer problems. *Cognitive Science 14,* 253–80.

Ross, B.H. (1984). *Remindings and their effects in learning a cognitive skill.* New York: Academic.

Roth, W.M. (1990). Collaboration and constructivism in the science classroom. *ERIC Document 318 631,* 1–39.

Rushton, C., Ramsey, P. & Rada, R. (1993). Peer assessment in a collaborative hypermedia environment. *Journal of Computer-Based Instruction 20* (3), 75–80.

Savery, J.R. & Duffy, T.M. (1994). Problem based learning: an instructional model and its constructivist framework. *Educational Technology* (Aug.).

Scardamalia, M. & Bereiter, C. (1991). Higher levels of agency for children in knowledge building: a challenge for the design of new knowledge media. *The Journal of the Learning Sciences 1* (1), 37–68.

—, —, McLean, R.S., Swallow, J. & Woodruff, E. (1989). Computer-supported intentional learning environments. *Journal of Educational Computing Research 5* (1), 51–68.

Schoenfeld, A.H. (1989). Teaching mathematical thinking and problem solving. *In* L.B. Resnick & L.E. Klopfer, eds. *Toward the thinking curriculum: current cognitive research,* 83–103. Alexandria, VA: ASCD.

Segal, J., Chipman, S. & Glaser, R., eds. (1985). *Thinking and learning skills: Relating instruction to basic research.,* Vol.

1. Hillsdale, NJ: Erlbaum.

Shank, R.C. (1990). Case-based teaching: four experiences in educational software design. *Interactive Learning Environments 1* (4), 231–53.

Sigurdson, S.E. & Olson, A.T. (1992). Teaching mathematics with meaning. *Journal of Mathematical Behavior 11,* 37–57.

Silver, M. & Wilkerson, L. (1991). Effects of tutors with subject expertise on the problem-based tutorial process. *Academic Medicine 66* (5), 298–300.

Slavin, R.E. (1991). Synthesis of research on cooperative learning. *Educational Leadership 48* (5), 71–82.

Spiro, R.J., Feltovich, P.L., Jacobson, M.J. & Coulson, R.L. (1991). Cognitive flexibility, constructivism, and hypertext: random access instruction for advanced knowledge acquisition in ill-structured domains. *Educational Technology 31* (5), 24–33.

Stein, B.S., Way, K.R., Benningfield, S.E. & Hedgecough, C.A. (1986). *Constraints on spontaneous transfer in problem-solving tasks.* Cookeville, TN: Tennessee Technological University.

Stoiber, K.C. (1991). The effect of technical and reflective preservice instruction on pedagogical reasoning and problem solving. *Journal of Teacher Education 42* (2), 131–39.

Torney-Purta, J. (1990). Measuring performance in social studies in an authentic fashion. *ERIC Document ED 347 120.*

Tulving, E. & Thompson, D.M. (1973). Encoding specificity and retrieval processes in episodic memory. *Psychological Review 80,* 352–73.

Van Haneghan, J., Barron, L., Young, M., Williams, S., Vye, N. & Bransford, J. (1992). The Jasper series: an experiment with new ways to enhance mathematical thinking. *In* D.F. Halpern, ed. *Enhancing thinking skills in the sciences and mathematics,* 15–38. Hillsdale, NJ: Erlbaum.

Von Wright, J. (1992). Reflections on reflection. *Learning and Instruction* (2), 59–68.

Vygotsky, L.S. (1978). *Mind in society.* Cambridge, MA: Harvard University Press.

Weinstein, C.E., Goetz, E.T. & Alexander, P.A. (1988). *Learning and study strategies: issues in assessment, instruction, and evaluation.* San Diego, CA: Academic.

Wheatley, M. (1992). *Leadership and the new science.* San Francisco, CA: Berrett-Koehler.

Whitehead, A.N. (1929). *The aims of education and other essays.* New York: Macmillan.

Wiggins, G. (1989). A true test: toward more authentic and equitable assessment. *Phi Delta Kappan 70,* 703–13.

Williams, M.D. & Dodge, B.J. (1992). *Tracking and analyzing learner-computer Interaction.* Paper presented at the 1992 National Conference of the Association for Educational Communications and Technology, New Orleans, LA.

Williams, S.M. (1992). Putting case-based instruction into context: examples from legal and medical education. *The Journal of the Learning Sciences 2* (4), 367–427.

—, Bransford, J.D., Vye, N.J., Goldman, S.R. & Carlson, K. (1992). *Positive and negative effects of specific knowledge on mathematical problem solving.* Paper presented at the Annual Conference for the American Educational Research Association, San Francisco, CA.

Yacci, M. (1994). *A grounded theory of information–rich learning environments.* Paper presented at the Annual International Conference of the Association for the Development of Computer-based Instructional Systems, Nashville, TN.

24. LEARNING *WITH* TECHNOLOGY: USING COMPUTERS AS COGNITIVE TOOLS

David H. Jonassen
PENNSYLVANIA STATE UNIVERSITY

Thomas C. Reeves
UNIVERSITY OF GEORGIA

24.1 INTRODUCTION

Human progress can be investigated in many ways. One insightful approach is to study the nature and quality of the tools people have discovered, invented, and refined over the centuries. The most common understanding of tools focuses on them as external implements, i.e., the levers, pulleys, and simple machines that have enabled physically weak human beings to change the course of mighty rivers, build giant edifices, and create ever-more complicated machines. A more theoretical perspective of tools recognizes that some tools are powerful without having a tangible physical substance, in the sense that a hammer does. Pea (1985) refers to these tools as *cognitive technologies,* and Salomon, Perkins, and Globerson (1991) call them *technologies of the mind.* In this chapter, we prefer the term *cognitive tools* (Kommers, Jonassen & Mayes, 1992) and elsewhere *mindtools* (Jonassen, 1996). Cognitive tools refer to technologies, tangible or intangible, that enhance the cognitive powers of human beings during thinking, problem solving, and learning. Written language, mathematical notation, and, most recently, the universal computer are examples of cognitive tools. This chapter focuses on computer-based cognitive tools, including common software applications and interactive learning environments, and their effects in the context of human learning.

Our emphasis on the uses and effects of computers and related technologies as cognitive tools is distinctly different from that of most of the other chapters in this handbook, in which technologies are primarily considered as forms of "media." Despite efforts to change the focus of the debate (cf. Jonassen, Campbell & Davidson, 1994), long-standing arguments about the relative effectiveness of media continue (cf. Clark, 1994; Kozma, 1994). Whether one sides with those who believe that media have little or no effects on learning or with those who promote its unique instructional

effectiveness, such arguments are limited by narrow definitions of media as conveyors of information, communicators of knowledge, or tutors of students. We regard the "technology as instructional communications" perspective (see Chapter 4), although admittedly widespread throughout education and training, to be inherently flawed because it fails to recognize learners as active constructors of knowledge (Duffy & Jonassen, 1992; see Chapters 7 and 23).

Grounded in this limited perspective, most research studies reported in the other chapters in this handbook treat students as perceivers or recipients of knowledge encoded in various forms of instructional media. In essence, these studies and the technology applications investigated in them are about "educational communications," i.e., the deliberate and intentional act of communicating content to students, with the assumption that they will learn something "from" these communications (see Chapter 4). In educational communications, information or knowledge is encoded visually or verbally in the symbol systems enabled by various technologies. During the "instructional" process, students perceive the messages encoded in the media, e.g., in video, and occasionally "interact" with the technology, e.g., in computer-based instruction. Interaction is normally operationalized in terms of student input to the technology, some form of answer judging, and a response in the form of some message previously encoded in the media. Technologies as conveyors of information have been used for centuries to "teach" students, whereas interactive technologies began to be introduced early in the 20th century to "engage" students in the learning process (Cuban, 1986).

Educational communications and the technologies in which they are encoded are conceived, analyzed, and designed by educational specialists (often referred to as *educational* or *instructional technologists*). Historically, educational media have been developed by teams of educational technologists, including instructional designers, media producers, and media managers, in collaboration with other types of specialists, e.g., subject-matter experts and teachers. These teams often employ systematic instructional design models (cf. Dick & Carey, 1990; Gagné, Briggs & Wager, 1987) to guide their efforts to analyze, develop, produce, and evaluate instruction. Design decisions made by these teams are purported to be informed by the kinds of educational communications and media research represented throughout this handbook, and some theorists even claim to be on the verge of automating the instructional design process based on existing learning theory and research (cf. Merrill, Li & Jones, 1990; Spector, Polson & Muraida, 1993).

24.2 COMPUTERS AS COGNITIVE TOOLS

By contrast, this chapter represents a departure from the central emphasis in this handbook on media and technology as vehicles for educational communications. Instead, we focus on the applications of technologies, primarily computers, as cognitive tools. This chapter is about computer-based cognitive tools and learning environments that have been adapted or developed to function as intellectual partners to enable and facilitate critical thinking and higher-order learning. Examples of cognitive tools include (but are not necessarily limited to):

- Databases
- Spreadsheets
- Semantic networks
- Expert systems
- Multimedia/hypermedia construction software
- Computer-based conferencing
- Collaborative knowledge construction environments
- Computer programming languages
- Microworlds

The cognitive tools perspective is distinctly different from traditional conceptions of instructional technologies. In cognitive tools, information is not encoded in predefined educational communications that are then used to transmit knowledge to students. With cognitive tools, the instructional design processes referred to above are eliminated. Instead of specialists such as instructional designers using technology to constrain students' learning processes through prescribed communications and interactions, the technologies are taken away from the specialists and given to learners to use as media for representing and expressing what they know. Learners themselves function as designers using technologies as tools for analyzing the world, accessing information, interpreting and organizing their personal knowledge, and representing what they know to others.

As important as it is to distinguish the "cognitive tools" perspective from the traditional educational media approach, it is also important to highlight differences between this conception of technology and earlier perspectives of using computers to support learning that have not

been successful. Ever since Taylor (1980) presented his classic model of the roles of computers in education as "tutor, tool, and tutee," many educators and commercial entrepreneurs have predicted that computers would revolutionize education through one or more of these roles. In reality, none of these approaches has lived up to its promise.

In recent years, advocates of computer-based instruction and intelligent tutoring systems (ITS) who represent the computer-as-"tutor" perspective have begun to acknowledge the lack of impact they have had on mainstream education and training (cf. Lajoie & Derry, 1993; Shlechter, 1991). At least part of this failure stems from the overly restrictive perspective of students as perceivers or recipients of educational communications that characterizes the research in this field. Another factor contributing to the lack of success of ITS is that the technical difficulties inherent in building student models and facilitating humanlike communications have been greatly underestimated by proponents of the "tutor" model (see 19.5).

The computer-as-"tool" approach has also disappointed many of its proponents, although there have been some successes when tools have been embedded within innovative pedagogy such as a whole-language approach to literacy development (cf. Bruce & Rubin, 1993). In many cases, software tools such as word-processing, spreadsheet, database, and computer-aided design (CAD) programs have failed to improve teaching and learning significantly because they have been largely relegated to the service of a traditional "instructivist" pedagogy. Goodlad (1984) and others have described the teacher-directed, text- and workbook–dominated curriculum that has characterized educational practice for decades. Instead of being employed as cognitive tools to solve challenging problems, pursue personal learning goals, or accomplish authentic tasks, computer tools have often been regarded as objects for study themselves and subjected to the same deadly instructivist pedagogy that has stymied intellectual growth by most students in more traditional areas such as science, mathematics, and social studies. Consider, for example, computer-aided design (CAD) software, which has revolutionized professional practices and dramatically increased productivity in engineering, architecture, and other design fields. Industrial arts teachers (now called *technology educators*) have enthusiastically adopted CAD software into their classrooms and computers labs, but instead of engaging students in authentic tasks, they usually "teach" students the command sets for the software outside of any meaningful contexts. Not surprisingly, students end up failing to perceive the relevance and value of such programs within the design professions or their own lives. As pointed out by Salomon et al. (1991), "No important impact can be expected when the same old activity is carried out with a technology that makes it a bit faster or easier; the activity itself has to change" (p. 8).

The results of the "tutee" role for computers in education, despite the almost religious fervor with which it has been embraced in some circles (cf. Papert, 1980), have also been much less spectacular than promised (see 12.3.2.1).

According to the computer-as-"tutee" approach, students develop higher-order thinking skills and creativity by teaching the computer to perform tasks, e.g., draw a picture, through the use of "friendly" programming languages such as Logo (Papert, 1980) and microworlds such as Karel the Robot (Popyack, 1989). Studies aimed at investigating the effects of Logo (cf. Pea & Kurland, 1987) have failed to demonstrate the cognitive advantages promised by Papert and others. Defenders of the "tutee" approach would maintain that the implementations of Logo investigated in most studies were too brief and unfocused. To be sure, many applications of Logo and other microworlds described in the literature seem to lack the "mindful engagement" that Salomon and Globerson (1987) argue is necessary for learning. As shown in greater detail below, more intensive applications of Logo, wherein students are engaged in meaningful tasks over longer periods of time, have demonstrated more impressive cognitive effects (cf. Harel, 1991; Papert, 1993).

24.3 WHY COGNITIVE TOOLS?

The history of educational communications and technology includes numerous examples of failed innovations and unfulfilled promises. Cognitive tools could become yet another casualty in the difficult struggle to improve teaching and learning unless it has a strong foundation of theory and practical principles to support it. In the following section, we briefly describe constructivist learning theory and related principles (see also Chapter 7) for its implementation. Considered together, constructivism and its attendant principles constitute a strong rationale for using technology as cognitive tools.

24.3.1 Knowledge Construction, Not Reproduction

Learning theory is in the midst of a revolution. Constructivist learning theory is gradually gaining the same respect and attention long accorded to instructivist learning theories such as behaviorism (Duffy & Jonassen, 1992), though not without a struggle (cf. Phillips, 1995). Constructivism is concerned with the process of how we construct meaning and knowledge in the world as well as with the results of the constructive process. How we construct knowledge depends on what we already know, our previous experiences, how we have organized those experiences into knowledge structures such as schemata and mental models, and the beliefs that we use to interpret the objects and events we encounter in the world. Cognitive tools can help us as learners organize, restructure, and represent what we know.

Constructivists (cf. von Glaserfeld, 1989) maintain that we construct our own reality through interpreting our experiences in the world. From the constructivist perspective, the ultimate nature of reality, or whether it even exists, does not matter as much as our unique and shared constructions

of reality. According to constructivism, the teacher cannot map his or her own interpretations of the world onto the learner, because they do not share a set of common experiences and interpretations. Reality (or at least what we know and understand of it) resides in the mind of each knower who interprets the external world according to his or her own experiences, beliefs, and knowledge. Learners are able to comprehend a variety of interpretations and to use them in arriving at their own unique interpretations of the world. The mind filters input from the world in making its interpretations, and therefore we each conceive of the external world somewhat differently.

Whereas instructivists emphasize the transmission of standardized interpretations of the world by teachers and the educational communications they employ, as well as standardized assessments to test the degree to which students' understandings match the accepted interpretations, constructivists are more interested in creating learning environments wherein learners use cognitive tools to help themselves construct their own knowledge representations. Cognitive tools and the goals, tasks, culture, resources, and human collaboration integral to their use enable learners to engage in active, mindful, and purposeful interpretation and reflection. In traditional instruction, *active* refers to stimulus, response, feedback, and reinforcement conditions that help students mirror accepted views of reality, whereas in constructivist learning environments, *active* learners participate and interact with the surrounding environment to create their own interpretations of reality.

24.3.2 Designers as Learners

Ironically, the people who seem to learn the most from the systematic instructional design of instructional materials are the designers themselves. Jonassen, Wilson, Wang, and Grabinger (1993) reported this discovery while developing expert systems advisors that were intended to supplant the thinking required by instructional designers. The process of articulating their knowledge about the process of instructional design forced them to reflect upon their knowledge in a new and meaningful way. Following the old adage that the surest way to learn about subject matter is to have to teach it, the process of designing and producing instructional materials as performed by designers of educational communications enables instructional designers to understand content much more deeply than the students whose thinking will be constrained and controlled by the very materials they are developing. It follows that empowering learners to design and produce their own knowledge representations and educational communications is a powerful learning experience.

24.3.3 Learners as Designers

Langer (1989) and others (cf. Salomon & Globerson, 1987) have reminded us of the importance of mindfulness in learning. Students learn and retain the most from thinking in meaningful (mindful) ways. Some of the best thinking results when students try to represent what they know. Representing knowledge as a mindful task can be enabled by cognitive tools such as hypermedia construction software or electronic spreadsheets. Such cognitive tools require students to think in meaningful ways to use the application's capabilities and features to represent what they know. Just as electronics troubleshooters cannot work effectively without the use of tools such as probes and oscilloscopes, students cannot learn deeply or mindfully without access to cognitive tools that help them assemble and represent knowledge. In short, the real power of computers to improve education will only be realized when students actively use them as cognitive tools rather than passively perceive them as tutors or repositories of information.

24.3.4 Experiential and Reflective Thinking

Norman (1983) distinguishes between two forms of thinking: experiential and reflective. Experiential thinking evolves from our experiences in the world; it is reflexive and occurs automatically. We experience something in the world and react to it; e.g., we see a red light and brake the car. Reflective thinking, on the other hand, requires more careful deliberation. We encounter a complex situation, think about it, reflect on stored knowledge, make inferences about it, determine implications, and reason about it. Reflective thought is the careful, deliberate kind of thinking that helps us make sense of what we have experienced and supports our construction of what we know. For example, consider the reflective thought required by major decisions in life concerning career, family, and health. Reflective thinking often requires external support, including books, computers, or other people. Norman contends that computers support reflective thinking when they enable users to compose new knowledge by adding new representations, modifying old ones, and comparing the two. Cognitive tools should be readily accessible to learners to support reflective thinking within the context of learning.

24.3.5 The Effects of Learning *with* and *of* Technology

Salomon, Perkins, and Globerson (1991) make an important distinction between the effects of learning *with* and *of* technology:

> First, we distinguish between two kinds of cognitive effects: Effects *with* technology obtained during intellectual partnership with it, and the effects *of* it in terms of the transferable cognitive residue that this partnership leaves behind in the form of better mastery of skills and strategies (p. 2).

Cognitive tools are important in both respects. With respect to the "with" effects, we agree with Salomon et al. (1991) that "the cognitive effects with computer tools greatly depend on the mindful engagement of learners in the

tasks afforded by these tools" (p. 2). We think that educators should empower learners with cognitive tools and assess their abilities in conjunction with the use of these tools.

Such a development will entail a new conception of ability as an "intellectual partnership" between the learner's mind and various cognitive tools. Although some might worry that this partnership makes learners too dependent on the technology to perform without it, we must recognize that many contemporary performances are meaningless without the technologies that enable them. Allowing students to demonstrate their learning in collaboration with cognitive tools may be attacked by certain authorities with heavy investments in the existing system, but we should remember that such attacks have occurred in the face of every innovation. For example, Plato criticized written language as a technology that would weaken human memory. Just as we would not assess the ability of an artist without allowing the use of brushes, paint, and other media, we should not assess contemporary intellectual abilities without the tools of contemporary intellectual practices, including books and computers (Salomon et al., 1991). Indeed, our very conception of knowledge must change. For example, Simon (1987) maintains that we should move from a conception of knowledge as possession of facts and figures to one of knowledge as the ability to retrieve information from databases and use it to solve problems.

Postmodernists and other critical theorists (see Chapters 9 and 10) worry about our eventual evolution into cyborgs (Yeaman, 1994). Although we do not share this concern, we recognize that there are many important intellectual abilities that should be performed and accessed without the aid of cognitive tools. This is where Salomon et al.'s (1991) delineation of the learning effects *of* technology become so important:

> Until intelligent technologies become as ubiquitous as pencil and paper—and we are not there yet by a long shot—how a person functions away from intelligent technologies must be considered. Moreover, even if computer technology became as ubiquitous as the pencil, students will still face an infinite number of problems to solve, new kinds of knowledge to mentally construct, and decisions to make, for which no intelligent technology would be available or accessible (p. 5).

Salomon et al. (1991) argue that the existing research, largely experimental, "has demonstrated more what transferable effects the partnership with computer tools and programs *can be made* to have than the effects it actually does have under more natural conditions of daily employment" (pp. 6, 7). Whether cognitive tools leave the "cognitive residue" that they are predicted to leave in practical educational settings is the focus of some of the research reported in this chapter.

24.3.6 Meaningful versus Easy Learning

One of the false promises of many previous instructional innovations has been to make learning fun and easy

(Cuban, 1986). Cognitive tools make no such promise, either for learners or teachers. Instead, cognitive tools and interactive learning environments activate complex cognitive learning strategies and critical thinking. These computer-based tools not only extend the mind, they have the potential also to reorganize mental functioning (Pea, 1985) and engage learners in high-level generative processing of information (Wittrock, 1974). In generative processing, deeper information processing results from activating appropriate mental models, using them to interpret new information, assimilating new information back into those models, reorganizing the models in light of the newly interpreted information, and using the newly aggrandized mental models to explain, interpret, or infer new knowledge (Norman, 1983). Knowledge acquisition and integration, according to these perspectives, is a constructive process involving "mindful" cognitive effort (Langer, 1989; Salomon & Globerson, 1987). When using cognitive tools, learners engage in knowledge construction rather than knowledge reproduction.

Cognitive tools actively engage learners in creating knowledge that reflects their comprehension and conceptualization of information and ideas rather than absorbing predetermined presentations of objective knowledge. Cognitive tools are learner controlled, not teacher controlled or technology driven. For example, when students construct databases, they are constructing their own conceptualization of the organization of the content domain. Cognitive tools are not designed to reduce information processing, that is, make a task easier, as has been the goal of instructional design as a field and many previous instructional innovations. Nor are they "fingertip" tools (Perkins, 1993) that learners use naturally, effortlessly, and effectively. Rather, cognitive tools are essential components of a learning environment in which learners are required to think harder about the subject-matter domain being studied or the task being undertaken and to generate thoughts that would be impossible without these tools.

As noted above, cognitive tools are reflection tools that amplify, extend, and even reorganize human mental powers to help learners construct their own realities and complete challenging tasks. However, the enormous potential of cognitive tools can only be realized within a constructivist framework for learning. Moreover, the nature and source of the task becomes paramount in such an environment. Past failures of "tool" approaches to using computers in education can be largely attributed to the relegation of the tools to traditional academic tasks set by teachers or the curriculum within the context of outmoded instructivist pedagogy. Cognitive tools are best used by students to represent knowledge and solve problems within the context of pursuing investigations that are relevant to their own lives. Those investigations are ideally elicited or supported by a constructivist learning environment (Duffy, Lowyck & Jonassen, 1993). Cognitive tools are less likely to be effective when used to support only teacher-controlled or curriculum-driven tasks.

24.3.7 (Un)intelligent Tools

Education communications too often try to do the thinking for learners, to act like tutors and guide learning. During the last decade, the most exalted form of educational communications systems have been called *intelligent tutoring systems* (ITS) (Chapter 19; Polson & Richardson, 1988). ITS possess some degree of "intelligence," usually in the form of expert and student models that are used to make instructional decisions about how much and what kind of instruction learners need. In the face of the disappointing results of ITS, some experts suggest that "the appropriate role for a computer is not that of a teacher/expert but rather that of a mind-extension 'cognitive tool'" (Derry & Lajoie, 1993, p. 5). Cognitive tools, as we conceive them, are *un*intelligent tools, relying on the learner to provide the intelligence, not the computer. This means that planning, decision making, and self-regulation are the responsibility of the learner, not the technology. Cognitive tools can serve as powerful catalysts for facilitating these skills, assuming that they are used in ways that promote reflection, discussion, and collaborative problem solving.

24.3.8 Distributed Cognitive Processing

Cognitive technologies may be provided by any medium that helps learners transcend the limitations of their minds, such as limits on memory, thinking, or problem solving (Pea, 1985). The most pervasive cognitive technology is language. Imagine trying to learn to do something complex without the use of language. Language amplifies the thinking of the learner. Computers may also function as cognitive tools for amplifying and reorganizing the ways that learners think.

Computer-based cognitive tools can function as intellectual partners that share the cognitive burden of carrying out tasks (Salomon, 1993). When learners use computers as partners, they off-load some of the unproductive memorizing tasks to the computer, allowing themselves to think more productively. Perkins (1993) claims that learning does not result from solitary, unsupported thinking by learners. Cognitive tools enable us to allocate to ourselves the responsibility for the cognitive processing we do best, while we allocate to the technology the processing that it does best.

Rather than focusing on microlevel decisions about message design and media presentation features on a computer screen, researchers should seek to reveal the nature of interactions and collaborations between the learner and the computer. Unfortunately, most of the research in our field has investigated how we can use the limited capabilities of the computer to present information and judge learner input (neither of which computers do well) while asking learners to memorize information and later recall it on tests (which computers do with far greater speed and accuracy than humans; see Chapter 39). The cognitive tools approach assumes that we will assign cognitive responsibility to the part of the learning system that does it best. The learner should be responsible for recognizing and judging patterns of information and then organizing it, while the computer should perform calculations, store information, and retrieve it on the learner's command. When cognitive tools function as intellectual partners, the performance of the learner is enhanced, leaving some "cognitive residue" in the learner that may transfer in situations where the learner encounters the tool again or even to situations where the tool is inaccessible (Salomon, 1993).

24.3.9 Summary of the Foundations for Cognitive Tools Research

The following principles sum up the foundations for the research findings reviewed in the rest of this chapter:

- Cognitive tools will have their greatest effectiveness when they are applied within constructivist learning environments.
- Cognitive tools empower learners to design their own representations of knowledge rather than absorbing knowledge representations preconceived by others.
- Cognitive tools can be used to support the deep reflective thinking that is necessary for meaningful learning.
- As a form of cognitive technology, cognitive tools have two kinds of important cognitive effects, those that are *with* the technology in terms of intellectual partnerships and those that are *of* the technology in terms of cognitive residue that remains after the cognitive tools are used.
- Cognitive tools enable mindful, challenging learning, rather than the effortless learning promised but rarely realized by other instructional innovations.
- The source of the tasks or problems to which cognitive tools are applied should be learners, guided by teachers and other resources in the learning environment.
- Ideally, tasks or problems for the application of cognitive tools should be situated in realistic contexts, with results that are personally meaningful for learners.
- Cognitive tools do not contain preconceived intelligence in the sense that intelligent tutoring systems are claimed to possess, but they do enable intellectual partnerships in the form of distributed cognitive processing.

24.4 OVERVIEW OF THE CHAPTER

In the remainder of this chapter, we describe the use of different cognitive tools for engaging learners in critical thinking, knowledge representation, and problem solving. We begin with computer programming languages as cognitive tools because these languages, especially Logo, were among the earliest applications of the "cognitive tools" perspective and because more research has been done with programming languages than with other types of cognitive tools. We then describe research conducted with hypermedia/multimedia authoring systems, semantic networking,

and expert systems, three cognitive tools that have attracted much attention in recent years. Lastly, we review the limited research conducted with databases and spreadsheets, popular software applications that, although creative teachers have adopted them as cognitive tools for years, have been the focus of relatively little research.

24.5 COMPUTER PROGRAMMING LANGUAGES AS COGNITIVE TOOLS

24.5.1 What Are Computer Programming Languages?

Computers are essentially high-speed calculators that are able only to accept and move around electronic signals. Their power and any intelligence that can be ascribed to them are implicit in the programs that operate them. Many different kinds of programs can be entered into computers to control what they do. At the lowest level, many of a computer's electronic components (the ROM and EPROM chips) have "hard-wired" programs that are encoded into the logic of the physical connections themselves. The electronic programs that actually drive the computer describe memory locations to which combinations of high and low voltage charges (zeroes and ones) should be moved or ways to manipulate the charges that correspond to larger numbers that represent higher-level information. Programmers use higher-level assembly language programs to activate these machine language programs. Assembly language programs are comprised of low-level commands to move information around the machine.

Programming most often refers to the use of higher-level, procedural languages, like BASIC and Pascal. These languages are the ones that are most often taught to students in schools. Computer programming languages consist of sets of keywords and commands that are interpreted or compiled by other assembly language programs through the programming language editors into machine code that ultimately "runs" the computer. Combinations of commands define programming structures. Procedural languages have only three major types of programming structures: list, repetition, and decision (selection) structures. *List structures* describe linear sequences of operations that are performed by the computer every time the list routine is invoked. *Repetition structures* (loops) are sets of operations that are repeated by the computer. The same set of operations may be repeated a specific number of times or until a certain numerical state exists, or while a certain numerical state exists. Repetition structures are often embedded within each other, so that loops of operations run inside other loops, which run inside still other loops. *Selection structures* describe the causal, decision-making operations in a program. These statements are typically written in IF-THEN-ELSE format; that is, if a specific conditions exists, do one sequence of operations. If another condition exists, do another sequence of operations. If neither condition exists (ELSE), do something else. Decisions can be combined to provide complex options. There are many ways these structures can be written and combined in order to solve computational problems.

Selecting and sequencing programming commands in order to solve some computational problem is a very complex process. Taylor (1991) defines the process of computer programming in five steps: problem definition, algorithm design, code writing, debugging, and documentation. According to Pea and Kurland (1984), programming consists of similar subtasks, such as understanding the problem, designing and planning the program, coding the program, and comprehending and debugging the program.

For many years, people have theorized that learning to program is an activity that develops higher-order thinking skills (Taylor, 1980). The languages that have most often been taught to learners in American schools in hopes of developing reasoning and thinking skills are BASIC, Pascal, and LOGO. A microcomputer version of the artificial intelligence (AI) language, Prolog, is often taught in European schools.

24.5.1.1. BASIC.
The development of BASIC (Beginner's All-purpose Symbolic Instruction Code) accompanied the rapid growth of computing in the 1960s. It was developed at Dartmouth University as a standard, introductory procedural programming language. Although very popular in the "computer literacy" movement of the 1980s, BASIC has been phased out of many educational programs in recent years. The primary complaint about BASIC is its inherently unstructured nature. BASIC code is written in the numerical sequence in which it will be executed. The flow of any BASIC program is controlled by GOTO statements that refer to the line number of the statement to be executed. Unless a careful and very structured approach to writing BASIC code is used, the order of operations can become very confused through unrestricted use of flow control statements. Newer versions of BASIC are inherently more structured and powerful.

24.5.1.2. Pascal.
Unlike BASIC, Pascal is an inherently structured programming language that requires that programmers identify all of the variables, procedures, and functions that they intend to use in the program. The purpose of this requirement is to produce more organized, better-structured programs. Since its introduction in 1971, Pascal, named for the French mathematician, has become the language that is often taught first to computer science students. Pascal, like LOGO (described below), enables programmers to define subprograms, including functions and procedures, and then to call them whenever they are needed. This feature avoids having to repeat sections of the code within the program. Another advantage of Pascal is the flexibility of its control structures, which are used to define subtasks or program modules. Repetition structures, such as REPEAT-UNTIL and WHILE-SO, and selections structures, such as IF-THEN-ELSE and CASE, are straightforward and easy to use.

24.5.1.3. LOGO.
LOGO is a simplified language created at the Massachusetts Institute of Technology (MIT) by Seymour Papert (1980) to engage children in the construction of microworlds. The part of the LOGO language that is used most often consists of geometric commands that are sent to a turtlelike object on the computer screen to draw objects on the screen. (A cybernetic turtle that moves along the floor and draws onto a piece of paper under the turtle is also sometimes used in classrooms with very young children.) Children use LOGO to "teach" the turtle to draw objects by writing Pascal-like procedures. Children learn to combine those procedures into larger procedures that draw more complex scenes containing those objects. The syntax of the language is simplified enough to allow learners to explore and experiment with creating scenes (called *microworlds*). The main ideas that are fostered by LOGO are procedures, nesting procedures, and recursion (having a procedure call itself).

In addition to turtle graphics, LOGO contains a set of list-processing commands that are equivalent to the AI language, LISP. Learners use these commands and the procedures acquired through turtle graphics to create poems or conversations with each other. Although LOGO is syntactically much easier than BASIC or Pascal, it still requires the understanding of very abstract concepts, such as variables, procedures, and recursion. A more recent development is the integration of LOGO, the programming language, with Lego, the toy building blocks. With LOGO-Lego, children build physical structures (e.g., a windmill) with Lego pieces and activate them with LOGO commands.

24.5.1.4. Prolog.
Prolog (PROgramming in LOGic) was developed as an artificial-intelligence language for solving problems that involve objects and their relationships stated in terms of declarative logic. That is why it is so often used to write programs representing human knowledge structures. It is interactive and conversational. Programming in Prolog consists of declaring facts about objects and their relationships, defining rules about those objects and relationships (like inheritance), and asking questions about those objects and relationships.

Micro-Prolog (Prolog for microcomputers) programs are made up of sentences that state objects and their relationships. These objects and relationships are added to the program individually. Prolog allows the user to ask true-false and search questions about the database that has been developed. The power of Prolog is afforded by its use of conditional, rule-based logic. Using simple building blocks, Prolog can be used to develop complex databases of information. What makes Prolog especially useful as a cognitive tool is its focus on knowledge representation.

24.5.1.5. Other Languages.
Other procedural languages, like C and its derivatives, and AI languages like LISP, are also taught to students, though certainly not with the degree of regularity of those described above. The trends in programming include a diminished interest in procedural languages like BASIC and Pascal, and a translation of those and other procedural languages into "object-oriented programming systems" (OOPS). Rather than procedures and functions as sequences of actions, in OOPS, these are treated as reusable objects that can be combined like building blocks to construct a program. The program or the

user sends messages to these objects. These objects respond according to the message sent. The building block approach is especially important in defining screen objects like scroll bars, windows, buttons, icons, and menus in window-type environments that comprise the user interface to the program. So when the user points and clicks at an icon, the icon object responds depending on its location and program. Languages like Smalltalk were originally designed as OOPS environments; however, object-oriented versions of procedural languages like BASIC (Microsoft's Visual BASIC), Pascal (Borland's Delphi), and C (Borland's C++) are preferred by most programmers today. OOPS languages can help to promote critical thinking as well as programming efficiency because of their inherent structure and more clearly defined interfaces and usage declarations. OOPS may encourage more effective collaboration in defining interfaces, and the skills students learn may be more marketable since most businesses are using object-oriented versions of popular programming languages. Probably the most commonly used object-oriented language in schools is HyperTalk, the scripting language that is used with HyperCard, though object-oriented versions of most computer languages are now available.

24.5.2 How Are Computer Programming Languages Used as Cognitive Tools?

Proponents of programming have argued that learning to program requires that learners think in an organized, systematic way about the problems they are attempting to solve, and that the thinking skills acquired while learning to program transfer to other nonprogramming problem situations. Before considering the cognitive effects of programming, we briefly review research on the cognitive requirements of learning to program.

Programming is a complex task. It involves many aspects of problem solving, such as problem decomposition, selecting appropriate information, assigning variables, identifying plausible solutions, applying programming structures, debugging code, and so on. McCoy (1990) showed that learning to program requires five skills: general strategy, planning, logical thinking, variables, and debugging.

Complex skills like these require different forms of intelligence. Cafolla (1987–88) found that the strongest predictors of learning to program were verbal reasoning, level of cognitive development, and mathematical reasoning. Additionally, analogical reasoning ability is strongly related to the ability to write subprocedures among high school students learning to program in LOGO (Clement, Kurland, Mawby & Pea, 1986). Computer programming is also dependent on various cognitive controls and styles of learners (Jonassen & Grabowski, 1993). Students who are field independent perform better in computer programming classes than field-dependent learners; i.e., field-independent students are more analytical thinkers. In fact, field independence, logical reasoning, and direction-following skills were found to be highly correlated with programming skills among college students (Foreman, 1988).

Computer programming is also subject to developmental differences among learners. Fourth-graders were far less able than older students to understand and use variables because of the level of abstraction, the dynamic nature of the values of variables, the degree of complexity in using variables, and the level of reasoning required (Nachmias, 1986). This means that computer programming may be introduced at the upper elementary level, but that abstract concepts in programming must wait until later. Even college students experience difficulties in learning to program. Among undergraduates, Fischer (1986) found that programming skill in a course was highly correlated to formal operational reasoning (from Piaget), especially the classification of abstract concepts, control structures, and top-down programming. Formal operational reasoning ability is also essential for the use of some of the other cognitive tools, especially expert systems.

Computer programming has long been associated with mathematics. It has often been assumed that skilled mathematicians make competent programmers, because the same kinds of logical reasoning are required. This is partially true; however, programming computers is more directly related to analytical reasoning. Chin and Zecker (1985) found that programming ability was not, as expected, related to math ability, but rather internal locus of control was a much better predictor. On the other hand, Nowaczyk (1983) found that mathematics and English course performance, previous computer experience, and logic and algebraic word problem performance were significantly correlated to programming performance among college students. Being able to break down problems and search and select relevant information and solutions to the problem are most important for learners. Many people, including scientists, engineers, and mathematicians, are analytic, while many people are not. Most people can learn to function more analytically, but it is not easy. Programming is difficult because it requires thinking that learners are not often called on to perform.

24.5.3 What Learning Outcomes Result from Using Computer Programming Languages as Cognitive Tools?

Most of the educational research on computer programming has assessed how much the logical reasoning required to program computers generalizes or transfers to other nonprogramming problems. The assumptions of most of this research is that the analytic thinking required to program will naturally make learners better problem solvers in other settings. Learning to program has been shown to have a variety of effects on learners' thinking in different settings, although the research findings are inconsistent. Ahmed (1992) reviewed 21 studies and found that half of the studies showed some positive effects of learning to program;

half did not. Much of this research focuses on the cognitive residue from learning to program. Some studies found positive correlations. Liao and Bright (1991) conducted a meta-analysis of research on the effects of computer programming on cognitive outcomes and found that the large majority of studies concluded that students who learned to program scored higher on various cognitive tests than those who did not, although the differences were not large. For example, students who learned six weeks of BASIC performed better on mathematical-thinking skills, including programming ability, generalization, and understanding variables, than the control group (Oprea, 1988). This was especially true for shorter programming courses rather than longer ones and for learning LOGO rather than BASIC or Pascal.

Most of the cognitive outcomes research was conducted on learning to use LOGO for building microworlds. While LOGO was designed as an experimental tool for building microworlds, it also uses a procedural programming language. The cognitive residue from these experiences varies. Clements (1985) conducted a thorough review of LOGO research and concluded that almost all children can learn to program in LOGO. LOGO is especially effective in encouraging prosocial behavior, positive self-image, and positive attitudes toward learning. However, the cognitive gains from LOGO apply mainly to LOGO-related learning. Clements also found that programming does facilitate some problem-solving behaviors, and LOGO may facilitate the development of some cognitive skills such as classifying, seriating, and conserving. Clements and Gullo (1984) found that learning to program in LOGO improved 6-year-olds' reflectivity, divergent thinking, and metacognitive ability, when compared to a group receiving computer-assisted instruction. After one year of LOGO experience, fifth- and sixth-graders performed better on LOGO-related problem solving, general problem solving, and the mental rotation of geometric figures, a spatial reasoning ability (Miller, Kelly & Kelly, 1988). However, Pea and Kurland (1984) found that LOGO programmers were no better at planning skills than control group students, and no differences in the ability to visualize and draw designs resulted from learning to program among fourth- and fifth-graders (Williamson & Ginther, 1992). Kurland, Pea, Clement, and Mawby (1986) found that after studying programming for a year, LOGO programming experience did not transfer to other domains with similar properties. Jansson (1987) conducted three studies that showed no benefit of learning to program on conditional reasoning tasks.

The equivocal results of learning to use LOGO is partially a result of the teaching methods used with LOGO. Although it was intended to be used as an experiential, discovery-learning tool, too often LOGO was taught by direct teaching. Swan and Black (1990) found that explicitly teaching problem-solving strategies and applying them to solve problems in LOGO was more effective than providing only LOGO programming practice, teaching the strategies *with* concrete manipulables, or traditional problem-solving instruction. That

is, learning to program is facilitated by practice in programming. But programming was not the primary purpose of LOGO. Harel (1991) maintains that one reason for the failure of LOGO skills to transfer to other domains is that teachers have often treated "LOGO as an object of knowledge in itself, rather than as a tool for acquiring other learning" (p. 37). Harel also complains that in most of the negative studies of the effects of learning LOGO, "children did not have time to learn LOGO in any depth" (p. 84). However, even if the sustained study of programming can be demonstrated to improve the ability of students to perform on some critical-thinking tests, the gains may not be worth the time and effort required to learn to program.

Harel's (1991) Instructional Software Design Project (ISDP) represents a unique effort to use programming as a cognitive tool within a software design context. Harel claims that the ISDP combines Papert's "constructionist" theory (1993) with Perkins "knowledge as design" pedagogy (1986). In the ISDP research study conducted by Harel for her doctoral dissertation, 17 fourth-grade students used LOGO for a semester to create software products that were intended to teach fractions to third-grade students. Her study combined quantitative, qualitative, and comparative research methods to investigate the effects of this "learners as designers" approach.

Harel (1991) reports that the fourth-grade students spent an average of 70 hours working on their software design projects. While the particular nature of the software projects was left open, there were two important requirements for students in the program: (1) writing in a "Designer's Notebook" every day and (2) attending periodic "Focus Sessions" about software design, LOGO programming, and fractions. A teacher and the researcher were available at all times to help the students with their design efforts. Although each of the students produced a separate software product, collaboration among the students was encouraged.

Harel compared the differences in LOGO skills and fractions knowledge between the 17 students in the ISDP and 34 other students in two classes who were studying LOGO and fractions via "a traditional teaching method" (p. 263). No significant differences were found in pretests among the three classes. Harel reports that "In general, the 17 children of the experimental class did better than the other 34 children on all posttests (fractions and LOGO)" (p. 272). Although not all differences were statistically significant, the general trend was quite positive in terms of specific learning outcomes as measured by multiple measures, including paper-and-pencil tests, computer exercises, videotaped observations, and interviews.

The major part of Harel's (1991) study is a detailed description of the activities and metacognition of one student, "Debbie," over the 4-month period of the project. Harel wrote that her detailed analysis of Debbie's work as well as her observations of other students indicated that "Throughout ISDP, the students were constantly involved in metacognitive acts: learning by explaining, creating, and discussing knowledge representations, finding design strategies, and reflecting on all of the above" (p. 359). In addition to positive cognitive effects in terms of metacognition, Harel concluded that the ISDP students acquired enhanced cognitive flexibility, better control over their problem solving, and greater confidence in their thinking abilities. She notes, however, that the study did not include any direct measures of thinking skills, but her own interpretations of the students' metacognition and problem-solving processes were based on observations and analysis of documentation such as their Designer's Notebooks.

Thinking is always somewhat dependent on the nature of the problem or the content. Programming clearly requires learners to think deeply. However, this deep thinking does not necessarily transfer to other content or problems as much as educational experiences that are focused on content-dependent problem-solving skills. The transfer of programming logic could probably be enhanced by direct instruction that models how to apply programming skills to other problems rather than teaching the language and only later applying it to solving problems. Harel's (1991) study provides an exemplary approach to the integration of learning programming into a design and problem-solving environment. Kafai's (1995, 1996) studies of students using LOGO to create games for other students is a creative continuation of the research carried out by Harel. Interestingly, Kafai found that the students designing games using LOGO did not perform as well as a control group of students using LOGO to design instruction in the manner used in Harel's ISDP.

In light of the results described above, a question rises: Why have the results of learning to program been so inconsistent and generally disappointing to the advocates of this approach? The answer may be found in both the nature of the cognitive tools themselves and the different approaches to applying them. Some cognitive tools such as databases, spreadsheets, and even hypermedia/multimedia authoring systems described later in this chapter share a common set of attributes (Jonassen, 1996). They are readily available, generic applications; they are affordable; they are used to represent knowledge in content domains; they are applicable across different subject domains; they engage critical thinking in learners; they facilitate transfer of learning; they are simple, powerful formalisms; and they are reasonably easy to learn.

This latter criterion is the most problematic for computer programming. Programming in most computer languages requires learning as many as 100 different commands, knowing when and how to embed those commands into programming structures, and, most problematic and especially time consuming, a lot of syntax that constrains both of these. After a semester-long Pascal course in high school, students made errors using virtually every Pascal construction (Sleeman, Putnam, Baxter & Kuspa, 1986). Punctuation, spaces, order of operations, and a host of other syntactical requirements add hundreds and even thousands of rules that must be learned and faithfully used before programs run without error. Unlike traditional human languages, where the meaning of speech or writing can usually

be determined regardless of misspellings, placement, or usage errors, computers are unforgiving. A single error can prevent a program from running, despite the fact that many beginning programming students believe that computers have the reasoning power of human beings in comprehending language (Sleeman et al., 1986).

The primary conclusion of programming research is that the cognitive overhead (the amount of mental effort required to use programming languages) mitigates the ability of the learner to use computer programming as an easy and effective means for solving problems or representing what the learner knows, which is the goal of using cognitive tools in the first place. After 2 years of programming instruction, many students have only rudimentary understanding of programming ideas (Kurland, Pea, Clement & Mawby, 1986). Until programming skills become automated (which requires years of experience to occur), more effort is required to program the computer than to represent the knowledge or solve the problem. There is little doubt, however, that computer programming is among the most flexible and powerful of the cognitive tools for those who are skilled programmers. It is the requirement of these complex skills that calls into question the utility of computer programming as a cognitive tool.

This argument against programming as a robust cognitive tool is being mitigated by newer computer-programming environments, like Think Pascal and Think C, that have syntax error detection and correction routines built in. These routines identify syntax errors when they are made, thereby reducing the cognitive load and responsibilities on the learner. They also automatically format the code by indenting where necessary. Newer programming languages, such as Visual BASIC, Delphi, and Visual C, provide even more sophisticated code-generating routines, so that the programmer needs only to identify the program structure and the variables, and the environment is able to generate the necessary programming code. These languages are especially effective for producing user interfaces by automating the creation dialog boxes, windows, and so on. These types of environments represent major improvements in simplifying the programming process, allowing the programmer to act as a designer who focuses on the problem-solving task more than on writing code. However, to what extent does this replacement affect the thinking that the programmer is required to do? These environments definitely enhance code generation, but do they support critical thinking? Additional research must be done before we can answer this question.

In addition to differences in the nature of various cognitive tools, the approach to using them obviously has a major impact on their effectiveness. When cognitive tools become objects of study in and of themselves, as seems to be the case in many studies of the effects of programming, they cannot be expected to have major effects on higher-order thinking skills. However, where these tools are applied to meaningful and personally rewarding tasks, they may have much more impressive results. Despite the cognitive demands of learning programming, there may be nothing inherently wrong in the use of programming as cognitive tools if the context in which programming is learned captures the attention, intrinsic motivation, and commitment of learners.

24.6 HYPERMEDIA/MULTIMEDIA AUTHORING SYSTEMS AS COGNITIVE TOOLS

24.6.1 What Are Hypermedia and Multimedia?

The concept of hypermedia is founded on the earlier notion of hypertext, i.e., the nonsequential, nonlinear method for organizing and displaying text (Jonassen, 1989). It was designed to enable the reader to access information from a text in ways that are more meaningful for the reader, based on the assumption that the organization that the reader imposes on a text is more meaningful (to the reader) than that of the author (Nelson, 1980). Hypermedia is an extension of hypertext that integrates graphics, animation, audio, and video with text.

The most pervasive characteristic of hypermedia is the node that consists of chunks or fragments of text or other media. The most common metaphor for a node is a card, as in HyperCard (Apple Computer, 1984). Nodes are the basic unit of information storage, and may consist of a page of text, a graphic, a sound bite, a video clip, or even an entire document. While studying a hypermedia knowledge base, learners can access any node, depending on their interests or needs. In many hypermedia systems, nodes can be amended or modified by the learner. The learner may add to, delete, or change the information in a node or create his or her own unique nodes of information. In short, a hypertext can be a dynamic knowledge base that continues to grow, representing new and different points of view.

The organization of a hypermedia knowledge base, that is, the interrelationships between the nodes, is defined by the links that interconnect the nodes. Links in hypermedia systems are typically associative; that is, they describe associations between the nodes they connect. While looking at a node, the user's attention may be drawn to a link (usually identified by buttons or hot spots on the screen). If the user activates the link by clicking on a button or hot spot with a mouse or other pointing device or pressing an associated keyboard key, the user will be linked to another node of information. Having arrived at the new node related to the previous link, the user may wish to return to the node from which he or she came or to go to yet another node. The links in hypermedia transport the user through the information space to the nodes that are selected, enabling the user to move through the knowledge base. The node structure and the link structure form a network of ideas in the knowledge base—structures and networks that may be very rich.

Multimedia are just that: multiple media or the integration of more than one medium into some form of communication. Most often, multimedia refers to the integration of media such as text, sound, graphics, animation, video, imaging, and spatial modeling into a computer system (von Wodtke, 1993). Multimedia in other forms, such as slide-tape presentations and interactive video, have been available for a long time. The term has gained popularity recently with the advent of high-resolution monitors, sound and video compression cards, increased random-access memory, and larger storage media for personal computers. Employing relatively inexpensive desktop computers, users are now able to capture sounds and video, manipulate audio and images to achieve special effects, synthesize audio and video, create sophisticated graphics including animation, and integrate them all into a single multimedia presentation. Individuals with very little experience are becoming their own multimedia artists, producers, and publishers.

Multimedia presentations are engaging because they are multimodal. In other words, multimedia can stimulate more than one sense at a time, and in doing so may be more attention getting and attention holding. Futurists and industry leaders, as well as many educators, often promote the idea that multimodal access is essential when teaching today's video generation (cf. Perelman, 1992). Not surprisingly, others have begun to question the benefits of multimedia and related technologies (cf. Stoll, 1995).

Nielsen (1990) attempts to clarify the difference between multimedia and hypermedia:

> . . . even though many hypertext systems are in fact hypermedia systems and include many multimedia effects, the fact that a system is multimedia based does not make it hypertext. The mixture of text and graphics is not enough in itself. Many multimedia systems are based mostly on displaying various films clips to a passive user who does not get to navigate an information space. Only when users interactively take control of a set of dynamic links among units of information does a system get to be a hypertext (p. 10).

Although hypermedia affords many options to users, some very significant problems have plagued hypermedia users. The most commonly acknowledged problem is navigation. Hypermedia documents often contain thousands of nodes, each with multiple links to other nodes. It is easy for users to get lost in that morass of information. Users become disoriented, unaware of the route they took, or how to find their way out of the hypertext or to another topic of interest.

A related problem is how and where do users access information in the hypertext. Most hypertexts provide an array of options to the user but typically fail to provide suggestions about where the user should begin. The user's initial access to the hypertext may greatly affect the user's understanding of the information contained in it. Another problem is a lack of orientation as to how much of the hypertext the user has accessed and how much remains to be revealed.

Perhaps the greatest concern related to using multimedia and hypermedia to facilitate learning is the problem learners face in integrating the information acquired in a hypertext into their own knowledge structures (Jonassen,

Beissner & Yacci, 1993). As learners navigate through the hypertext, how can they best relate new information to what they already know and what they have learned from the hypermedia? How do learners develop their own knowledge structures and use them to accommodate the new information? One aspect seems clear, i.e., the creation of new knowledge structures must be applied within a personally meaningful context to a relevant problem or task. Learners don't automatically create new knowledge structures simply by browsing hypermedia resources (Jonassen & Wang, 1993).

24.6.2 How Are Hypermedia/Multimedia Authoring Systems Used as Cognitive Tools?

A solution to the problems of navigating and integrating information in hypermedia is not to think of hypermedia as a form of instruction to learn *from,* but rather to look at hypermedia as a tool for constructing and learning *with* (Jonassen, Myers & McKillop, 1996). In other words, we advocate the use of hypermedia as a cognitive tool. Learners may create multimedia databases that reflect their own perspectives on, or understanding of, ideas. Or learners may collaborate with other learners to develop a classroom or school hypermedia knowledge base. We contend that students are likely to learn more by constructing hypermedia instructional materials than by studying hypermedia created by others. Of course, hypermedia created by others (such as World Wide Web sites) can provide excellent resources for students in the process of creating their own hypermedia.

Hypermedia and multimedia construction is predicated on the idea of knowledge as design (Perkins, 1986), which refocuses the educational process away from one of knowledge as information and the teacher as transmitter of that knowledge to one of teachers and students as collaborators in the knowledge construction process. One way to promote this design process is to place learners in the role of instructional software designers (Harel, 1991). Rather than reading textbooks and solving workbook problems, students must define and constantly refine the nature of a problem they have identified, reconstruct their knowledge to solve that problem, and represent their solution in hypermedia (Lehrer, 1993).

Designing multimedia presentations is a complex process that engages many skills in learners. Carver, Lehrer, Connell, and Ericksen (1992) suggest some of the major thinking skills that learners need to use as designers:

Project Management Skills
- Creating a timeline for the completion of the project
- Allocating resources and time to different parts of the project
- Assigning roles to team members

Research Skills
- Determining the nature of the problem and how research should be organized

- Posing thoughtful questions about structure, models, cases, values, and roles
- Searching for information using text, electronic, and pictorial information sources
- Developing new information with interviews, questionnaires, and other survey methods
- Analyzing and interpreting all the information collected to identify and interpret patterns

Organization and Representation Skills
- Deciding how to segment and sequence information to make it understandable
- Deciding how information will be represented (text, pictures, movies, audio, etc.)
- Deciding how the information will be organized (hierarchy, sequence) and how it will be linked

Presentation Skills
- Mapping the design onto the presentation and implementing the ideas in multimedia
- Attracting and maintaining the interests of the intended audiences

Reflection Skills
- Evaluating the program and the process used to create it
- Revising the design of the program using feedback

While the engagement of each of these skills has yet to be empirically validated in a series of studies, there is no doubt that constructing hypermedia and multimedia programs represents a complex combination of skills. Verifying these skills and their effects on thinking should become a major research agenda in the years to come.

24.6.3 What Research Supports the Use of Hypermedia/Multimedia Authoring Systems as Cognitive Tools?

One of the principles stated above for the implementation of cognitive tools is: "Ideally, tasks or problems for the application of cognitive tools should be situated in realistic contexts with results that are personally meaningful for learners." Beichner (1994) reports on a project where these conditions were met in a unique way. The subjects in this study were seventh- and eight-grade students enrolled in a middle school located on the grounds of a large, metropolitan zoo. The school is a magnet school emphasizing the study of science to which students are admitted based on a lottery. A primarily qualitative, observational investigation was conducted over a 2-year period while the students worked cooperatively to create interactive displays for a touch-sensitive multimedia kiosk for the zoo.

Several categories emerged out of the qualitative analysis of the data, which included extensive videotapes, interviews, observations, and student-created materials. The students' strong appreciation that they were preparing multimedia materials for a real audience emerged as the core category in the analysis. Additional positive findings were:

(1) Students demonstrated great concern for accuracy in their displays; (2) students quickly assumed the major responsibility for content and editing decisions, despite the fact that the original task of designing the displays had been structured for them by the teacher; (3) students accessed wide ranges of science materials and sources to find the content they desired; and (4) their commitment to and enthusiasm for the project remained very high. On the negative side, the project failed to integrate its activities into the larger curriculum in the school or to attract the participation of teachers other than the computer coordinator. The bottom line was that by establishing an environment where creative thinking about content is combined with real-world assignments, students learned the content, enjoyed the learning process, and recognized that they have created something worthwhile.

Lehrer (1993) describes the development, use, and results of a hypermedia construction tool called Hyper-Author that was used by eighth-graders to design their own lessons about the American Civil War. This study exemplifies the principle that: "Cognitive tools empower learners to design their own representations of knowledge rather than absorbing knowledge representations preconceived by others." As Perkins (1986) maintains, knowledge is a process of design and not something to be transmitted from teacher to student. Thus, students should be engaged in "HyperComposition" by designing their own hypermedia (Lehrer, 1993). The process requires learners to transform information into dimensional representations, determine what is important and what is not, segment information into nodes, link the information segments by semantic relationships, and decide how to represent ideas. This is a highly motivating process because authorship results in ownership of the ideas in the presentation.

Students in the Lehrer (1993) study were high- and low-ability eighth-graders who worked at the hypermedia construction tasks for one class period of 45 minutes each day over a period of several months. The students worked in a media center of the school's library where they had access to a color Macintosh computer, scanner, sound digitizer, HyperAuthor software, and numerous print and nonprint resources about the Civil War. An instructor was also available to coach students in the conceptualization, design, and production of the hypermedia programs. Students created programs reflecting their unique interests and individual differences. For example, they created hypermedia about the role of women in the Civil War, the perspectives of slaves toward the war, and "not-so-famous people" from that period.

According to Lehrer (1993): "The most striking finding was the degree of student involvement and engagement" (p. 209). Both high- and low-ability students became very task oriented, increasingly so as they gained more autonomy and confidence with the cognitive tools. At the end of the study, students in the hypermedia group and a control group of students who had studied the Civil War via traditional classroom methods during the same period of time were given an identical teacher-constructed test of knowledge. No significant test differences were found. Lehrer conjectured that "these measures were not valid indicators of the extent of learning in the hypermedia design groups, perhaps because much of what students developed in the design context was not anticipated by the classroom teacher" (p. 218). However, a year later, when students in the design and control groups were interviewed by an independent interviewer unconnected with the previous year's work, important differences were found. Students in the control group could recall almost nothing about the historical content, whereas students in the design group displayed elaborate concepts and ideas that they had extended to other areas of history. Most importantly, although students in the control group defined history as the record of the facts of the past, students in the design class defined history as a process of interpreting the past from different perspectives. In short, the hypermedia "design approach lead to knowledge that was richer, better connected, and more applicable to subsequent learning and events" (p. 221).

Lehrer, Erickson, Love, and Connell (1994) conducted another study with ninth-grade students who were using HyperAuthor to develop hypermedia about World War I, lifestyles between 1870 and 1920, immigration, and imperialism. They found similar results to the aforementioned Civil War project: (1) Students' on-task behavior increased over time; (2) students perceived the benefits of planning and transforming stages of development; and (3) they developed generalizable skills such as taking notes, finding information, coordinating their work with other team members, writing interpretations, and designing presentations.

The Highly Interactive Computing Environments (HI-CE) Group at the University of Michigan has developed a multimedia composition tool called MediaText (Hays, Weingard, Guzdial, Jackson, Boyle & Soloway, 1993). They believe that rather than using media to deliver instruction to learners, learners should use the media to generate their own instruction and, in so doing, learn more about the content. The HI-CE group has studied high school students creating MediaText stories, biographies, or instructional aids, as well as multimedia essays. Students have learned to use techniques such as mentioning, directives, titling, and juxtaposition to integrate their documents. They have found that as students' experiences with MediaText increase, their documents become more integrated rather than merely annotated text. Students have been very enthusiastic about being constructionists (Papert, 1993), believing that they are learning more because they understand the ideas better.

The ACCESS (American Culture in Context: Enrichment for Secondary Schools) Project (Spoehr, 1994; Spoehr & Shapiro, 1991) focuses on the subject matter commonly taught in high school, such as United States history, American literature, and American studies. The project began with teachers assembling a collection of textual, pictorial, audio, and video materials to supplement their courses. Initially, students simply used the materials for information retrieval. Students who made more extensive use of the conceptual organization built into the system benefited more than the students who used the system like a linear electronic book. The researchers found that hypermedia's effectiveness depends on the extent to which students can internalize the important conceptual structures in a subject matter as they browse.

Eventually, the ACCESS project orientation shifted from teacher-created hypermedia materials to student-generated hypermedia documents. To make it easier for students to create hypermedia projects, the ACCESS user interface was improved. Students generally produce several small hypermedia documents of increasing size and complexity early in the school year to become familiar with the authoring process. Later, they generally take on one or more major research projects, the results of which are presented as hypermedia.

According to Spoehr (1994), the structures that students impose on their hypermedia knowledge vary. A few students (5% to 10%) typically underutilize the power of the hypermedia and use a linear format (i.e., one overview card followed by a linear series of screens). Most students produce more interesting organizational types, including the "star," in which the entry point is an overview containing buttons to two or more subtopics, each of which appears as a linear sequence, and the "tree," in which one or more main branches off the initial overview in the program are subdivided into further subtopics that are then organized as linear sequences or divided into sub-subtopics. Students utilizing the "tree" organization (about 25% of the students) generally show more sophisticated understanding of the topic than students using the "star" structure.

There are many ways that the ACCESS Project students appear to benefit from their experiences as hypermedia authors, most of which fall into the category of superior knowledge representation and higher-order thinking skills. Spoehr (1993) reports that students who build and use hypermedia apparently develop a proficiency in organizing knowledge about a subject in a more expertlike fashion. For example, they are able to represent multiple linkages between ideas and organize concepts into meaningful clusters. In turn, these superior knowledge representations support more complex arguments in written essays. Most importantly, the conceptual organization skills acquired through building hypermedia are robust enough to allow students to generalize these skills to content that they acquire from other sources.

The studies described above, especially the research of Lehrer (1993) and Spoehr (1994), illustrate the need to investigate the effects of using hypermedia and multimedia as cognitive tools on the development of the higher-order thinking skills of students. In turn, focusing on higher-order outcomes requires an emphasis on alternative approaches to assessment (Mitchell, 1992; Reeves & Okey, 1996). Higher-order learning outcomes such as the ability to frame and resolve ill-defined problems or the tendency to exhibit intellectual curiosity are rarely directly observable. These types of outcomes can only be inferred from students' performance on a range of alternative assessments (Neimeyer,

1993). Alternative cognitive assessments will most likely be quite different from traditional testing procedures that assess lower-level knowledge and skills. Research focused on the higher-order outcomes of cognitive tools such as hypermedia/multimedia construction software must proceed hand in hand with the development of reliable, valid, and feasible cognitive assessments (Worthen, 1993).

24.7 SEMANTIC NETWORKING AS COGNITIVE TOOLS

24.7.1 What Are Semantic Networks?

A new genre of cognitive tools, semantic networking tools, has appeared in recent years. Programs such as SemNet (Fisher, 1990, 1992), Learning Tool (Kozma, 1987, 1992), and TextVision (Kommers, 1989) are cognitive tools that provide visual and verbal screen tools for developing concept maps, otherwise known as *cognitive maps* (see Fig. 24-1). Cognitive maps are spatial representations of ideas and their interrelationships that are stored in memory. These tools enable learners to interrelate the ideas they are studying as multidimensional networks of concepts, to label the relationships between those concepts, and to describe the nature of the relationships between all of the ideas in the network.

Semantic networks are representations of human memory structures. The cognitive theory underlying semantic networks maintains that human memory is organized semantically, that is, according to meaningful relationships between ideas in memory. These ideas, known as *schemas,* are arranged in networks of interrelated ideas known as *semantic networks.* Semantic networking programs are computer-based, visualizing tools for representing semantic networks. Perhaps the best-known theory of semantic networks is active structural networks (Quillian, 1968). These are mental structures composed of nodes (representing schemas) and ordered relationships or links connecting them. The nodes are instances of concepts or propositions, and the links describe the prepositional relationship between the nodes. In computer-based semantic networks, nodes are represented as information blocks or cards and the links as labeled lines (see Fig. 24-1).

The purpose of semantic networks is to represent the organization of ideas that someone knows about some phenomenon (e.g., baseball) or the underlying organization of ideas in a content domain (e.g., sociology). Semantic networks function as cognitive tools by engaging learners in analyzing the structural relationships among the content being studied. They can also be used as evaluation tools for assessing changes in thinking by learners (Preece, 1976). If we agree that a meaningful representation of memory is a semantic network, then learning can be thought of as a reorganization of semantic memory. Producing semantic networks reflect those changes in semantic memory, since the networks describe what a learner knows. In this way, semantic networking programs can be used to reflect knowledge acquisition.

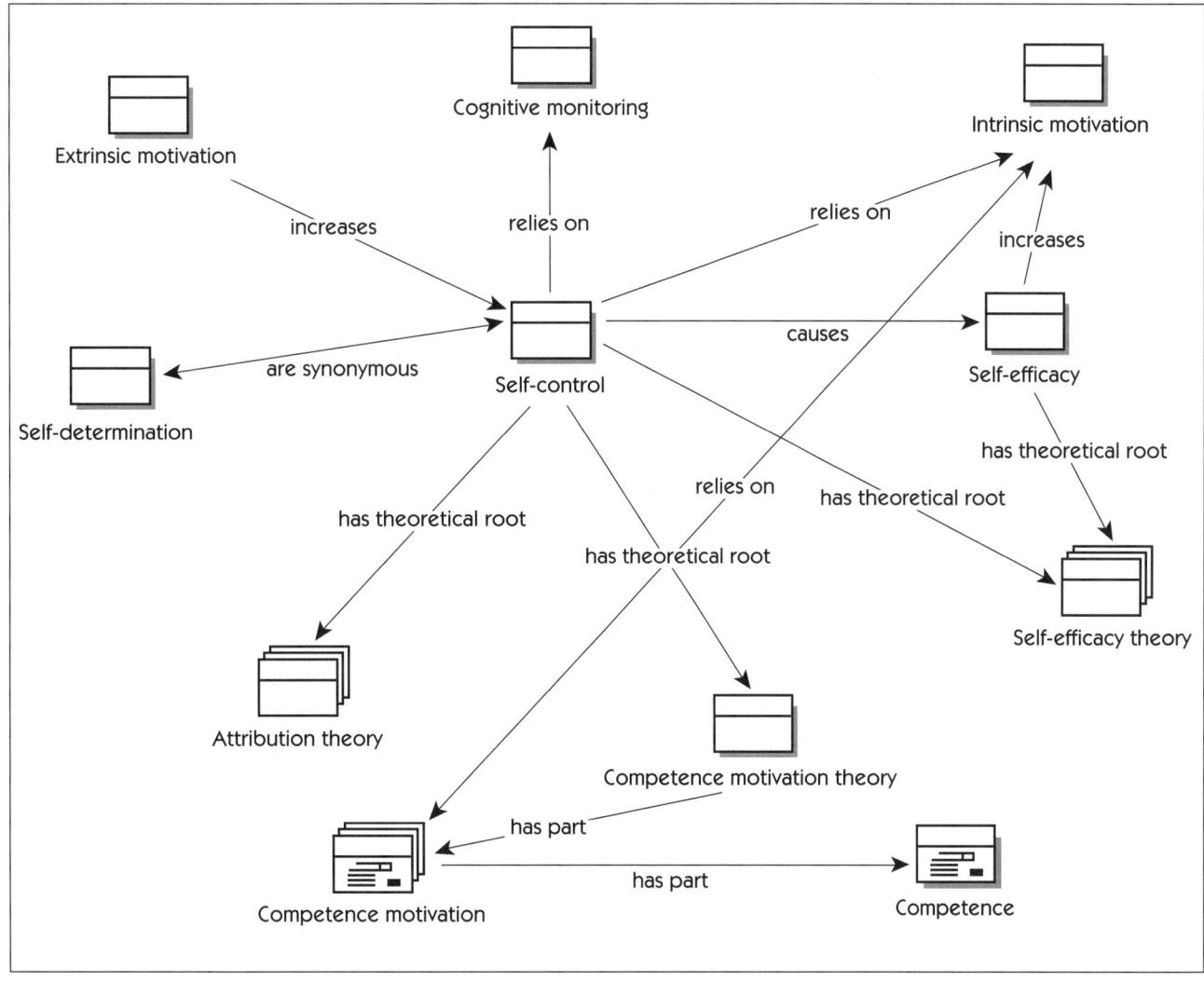

Figure 24-1.   Semantic network of concepts in motivation theory.

24.7.2 How Are Semantic Networks Used as CognitiveTools?

Semantic networking aids learning by requiring learners to analyze the underlying structure of ideas they are studying. The process of creating semantic networks engages learners in an analysis of their own knowledge structures, which helps them integrate new knowledge into existing knowledge structures. The result is that the knowledge that is acquired can be used more effectively. Kozma (1987, 1992), one of the developers of the semantic networking tool Learning Tool, believes that semantic networks are cognitive tools that amplify, extend, and enhance human cognition. Constructing computer-based semantic nets engages learners in (1) the reorganization of knowledge through the explicit description of concepts and their interrelationships; (2) deep processing of knowledge, which promotes better remembering, retrieval, and the ability to apply knowledge in new situations; (3) relating new concepts to existing concepts and ideas which improves understanding (Davis, 1990); and (4) spatial learning through the spatial representation of concepts

within an area of study (Fisher, Faletti, Patterson, Lipson, Thornton & Spring, 1990).

24.7.3 What Research Supports the Use of Semantic Networks as Cognitive Tools?

The usefulness of semantic nets and concepts maps is perhaps best indicated by their relationships to other forms of higher-order thinking. They have been significantly related to formal reasoning in chemistry (Schreiber & Abegg, 1991) and reasoning ability in biology (Briscoe & LeMaster, 1991; Mikulecky, 1988). Semantic networks can also provide a useful evaluation tool for measuring the acquisition of knowledge. In a geometry class, concept maps were used to evaluate teaching outcomes and to monitor student progress in the course (Mansfield & Happs, 1991).

An important research agenda in learning psychology focuses on the expert-novice distinction, comparing student knowledge representation with teacher or expert representations. Research has shown that during the process of learning, the learner's knowledge structure begins to resemble the knowledge structures of the instructors, and the degree of similarity is a good predictor of classroom examination performance (Diekhoff, 1983; Shavelson, 1972, 1974; Thro, 1978). Instruction, then, may be conceived of as the mapping of subject-matter knowledge (usually that possessed by the teacher or expert) onto the learner's knowledge structure. Semantic nets are a way of measuring that convergence.

Using compared Pathfinder nets (Schvaneveldt, 1990), researchers have also shown that semantic nets are related to course examination performance (Goldsmith, Johnson & Acton, 1991). In a study examining the use of generating computer-based semantic networks in a computer programming course, Feghali (1991) found that students who built nets scored better in course tests; however, the differences were not statistically significant. More and better research of this type is needed to verify a consistent relationship between particular criteria for evaluating semantic nets and traditional measures of course performance, such as exams, research papers, or case studies. That research needs to relate semantic net construction with different cognitive outcomes, not just test performance. In fact, traditional test results may be the least effective variable to investigate. Tests of transfer to performance environments would be more useful dependent variables.

Another potentially important area of research with semantic networks involves changes in knowledge structures of learners as an outcome of learning. Constructing semantic networks and cognitive maps has been shown to be an accurate means for representing cognitive structure (Jonassen, 1987). That is, semantic networking helps learners to map their own cognitive structure. This affords researchers a powerful tool for verifying other learning effects. In a more recent study, Jonassen (1993) showed that building semantic networks in a course resulted in more consistent, hierarchical, and coherent knowledge structures than building expert systems in the same course. Semantic networks are a powerful knowledge analysis and integration tool that also provides means for assessing knowledge structures. Schema-based theories of learning (Rumelhart, 1980; Rumelhart & Ortony, 1977) suggest that learning is, at least in part, a reorganization of the learner's knowledge structure. Semantic network tools provide powerful assessment tools for evaluating those changes in knowledge structure.

24.8 EXPERT SYSTEMS AS COGNITIVE TOOLS

24.8.1 What Are Expert Systems?

Expert systems are computer-based tools that are designed to function as intelligent aids to decision making in all sorts of tasks. Early expert systems, such as MYCIN, were developed to help physicians diagnose bacterial infections with which they were unfamiliar. Prominent expert systems have also been developed to help geologists decide where

to drill for oil, fire fighters decide how to extinguish different kinds of fires, computer sales technicians how to configure computer systems, and employees to decide among a large number of company benefits alternatives. Problems whose solution includes recommendations based on a variety of decisions are good candidates for expert systems.

Expert systems have evolved from research in the field of artificial intelligence (AI). AI is a field of computer science and cognitive science that focuses on the development of both hardware innovations and programming techniques that enable machines to perform tasks that are regarded as intelligent when done by people. *Intelligence* is the capacity to learn, reason, and understand. *Artificial* means simulated. So, in other words, AI researchers and expert system builders attempt to develop programs that simulate the human capability to reason and to learn. *Simulated* means only imitating a real object or event. AI programs, including expert systems, may perform functions that resemble human thinking, such as decision making. In reality though, AI programs are just computer programs; they only imitate a human activity within a narrowly defined situation.

An expert system, then, is a computer program that simulates the way human experts solve problems—an artificial decision maker. For example, when we consult an expert (e.g., doctor, lawyer, teacher) about a problem, the expert asks for current information about our condition, searches his or her knowledge base (memory) for existing knowledge that can be related to elements of the current situation, processes the information (thinks), arrives at a decision, and presents his or her solution. Like a human expert, an expert system (computer program) is approached by an individual with a problem. The system queries the individual about the current status of the problem, searches its own knowledge base (stored previously) for pertinent facts and rules that reflect the knowledge of an expert, processes the information, arrives at a decision, and reports the solution to the user.

Most expert systems consist of several components, including the knowledge base, inference engine, and user interface. The knowledge base consists of facts and rules that are programmed into the system by the designer. For example, an expert system designed to diagnose cars that will not start might include facts and rules such as:

Fact: Battery supplies voltage to ignition.
Fact: Ignition routes voltage to solenoid.
Rule: IF ignition is on,
       AND solenoid is not engaged,
       THEN battery is dead,
       OR ignition switch is faulty.

The expert system inference engine is programmed into the system and acts on the knowledge base and current problem data to generate solutions. It sets a goal and then collects information from the knowledge base in order to yield a solution. When the knowledge base does not contain enough information, the inference engine asks the user to supply the missing information. The inference engine continues to seek information until it is able to reach a solution which the system then presents to the user. The inference engine is the logic unit in the expert system. The part of the expert system that makes it a cognitive tool is the knowledge base. Building the knowledge base requires the designer to articulate the expertise that the system provides, not only in the form of facts but also rules. Identifying the causal relationships and procedural knowledge underlying a knowledge domain necessarily engages designers of expert systems in higher-order thinking.

24.8.2 How Are Expert Systems Used as Cognitive Tools?

When analyzing outcomes from building and using expert-systems, a distinction must be drawn between using an existing expert system rule base to support decision making and building an expert system. The former is the most common application. Although expert systems are primarily used in businesses as advisors that control production processes or in certain professions to assist practitioners in decision making, they also have many applications in education. Chandler (1994) describes the development of an expert-system design to help teachers plan science education lessons. Considerable research has focused on developing expert-system advisors to help teachers identify and classify learning disabled students (cf. Fuchs, 1992). Expert-system advisors have been developed to guide novices through the instructional development process (Tennyson & Christensen, 1991) or to assist students in selecting the correct statistical test (Karake, 1990; Saleem & Azad, 1992). With this type of application, professional knowledge engineers produce expert-system knowledge bases that are accessed by users when they need advice in making decisions (Bossinger & Milheim, 1993). However, simply using existing knowledge bases to get advice does not engage users as deeply as building a knowledge base to reflect their own thinking (Wideman & Owston, 1993). Querying a knowledge base to help solve a problem involves primarily comprehension of the problem and its factors; the application of some predetermined rules for solving the problem is often hidden from the user within the expert system itself.

Expert systems can also function as cognitive tools (Kommers, Jonassen & Mayes, 1992). Trollip, Lippert, Starfield, and Smith (1992) believe that the development of expert systems results in deeper understanding because they provide an intellectual environment that demands the refinement of domain knowledge, supports problem solving, and monitors the acquisition of knowledge. Building expert systems requires the developer to model explicitly the knowledge of the expert (Starfield, Smith & Bleloch, 1990). This entails identifying declarative knowledge (facts and concepts), structural knowledge (the knowledge of the interrelationships of ideas in memory), and procedural knowledge (how to apply the former). In fact, building expert systems is one of the few formalisms for depicting procedural knowledge. Psychologists usually represent procedural knowledge as a series of IF-THEN rules (Gagné,

1985); such a representation mode is obviously well suited to expert-system codification. As learners identify the IF-THEN structure of a domain, they will tend to understand the nature of decision-making tasks better, and this deeper understanding should make subsequent practice opportunities more meaningful. This is not to suggest that the mere development of an expert system necessarily leads learners to acquire the compiled procedural knowledge of a domain. Students could correctly identify many of the IF-THEN rules involved in flying an airplane, but actually acquiring the procedural expertise to fly would still require extended practice opportunities in realistic performance settings.

When expert systems are used as cognitive tools, the roles of teachers and students change dramatically. Students as knowledge engineers assume a more active role in acquiring prerequisite knowledge and focusing and directing interactions with the teacher, who assumes the role of expert (Morrelli, 1990). This frees the teacher from having to motivate students and allows them to respond as an expert to student probing concerning the more demanding and interesting aspects of various problems. Students must analyze the knowledge domain (identifying outcomes, factors, and values for those factors) and then synthesize rules and rule sequences. Morrelli argues that interaction between active, self-directed learners and a supportive, articulate teacher is an excellent model for learning science. We agree.

24.8.3 What Research Supports the Use of Expert Systems as Cognitive Tools?

Much of the research with the use of expert systems has focused on teachers and students as users of predefined rule bases. For instance, students who used an expert system to select the most appropriate statistical analysis procedure were more accurate in their selections and also retained the information better than students who used traditional computer-assisted instruction (Marcoulides, 1988). Grabinger and Pollock (1989) used expert systems to direct students to evaluate their own projects. Students who generated their own feedback with the help of expert systems produced a greater number of criteria in subsequent exercises and favored the method to teacher-only feedback. As described earlier, using expert systems supplants (provides or substitutes knowledge that is not known) thinking and therefore does not necessarily engage users in thinking critically about the content they are studying.

The use of expert systems as cognitive tools is relatively recent. Trollip and Lippert (1987) found that the analysis of subject matter required to develop expert systems is so deep and so incisive that learners develop a greater comprehension of their subject matter. They reported that building expert system rule bases engages learners in analytical reasoning, elaboration strategies such as synthesis, and metacognition. Lippert (1988, 1989), among the early advocates of expert systems as cognitive tools, argued that asking students to construct small rule bases is a valuable method for teaching problem solving and knowledge structuring for students from sixth grade to adults. Not only do learners solve problems, they also engage in metacognitive reflection on their problem solving while constructing rule bases (Trollip & Lippert, 1988). Developing the knowledge base requires learners to isolate facts, variables, and rules about the relationships between content in a domain. Developing rule bases as a cognitive tool represents a constructivist application of expert systems (Jonassen, Wilson, Wang & Grabinger, 1993).

A small body of research has validated the use of expert systems as cognitive tools. Lai (1992) found that when nursing students developed medical expert systems, they developed enhanced reasoning skills and acquired a deeper understanding of the subject domain. Lippert (1988) described the development of rule bases to solve problems about forces by six freshmen physics students who used an expert-system shell to create questions, decisions, rules, and explanations pertaining to classical projectile motion. The students developed more refined, domain-specific knowledge due to greater degrees of elaboration during encoding and greater quantity of material processed in an explicit, coherent context, and therefore in greater semantic depth (Lippert & Finley, 1988). Students identified factors such as kind of force acting on an object (e.g., gravitational or centripetal), motion of the object (e.g., free fall, circular, or sliding), velocity of the object, and so on. The decisions that students defined were based on the laws that affect the motion and the formulas that should be applied. Students reported meaningful learning from evaluating their own thought processes, more enthusiasm for learning, and the learning of content that they were not expected to master.

Knox-Quinn (1992) reported that MBA (masters of business administration) students who developed knowledge bases on tax laws in an accounting course were consistently engaged in higher-order thinking, such as classifying information, breaking down content, organizing information, and integrating and elaborating information. All of the students who developed rule bases showed substantial gains in the quantity and quality of declarative and procedural knowledge and improved their problem-solving strategies. Students who built expert systems reasoned similarly to experts.

Like most cognitive tools, the research base on expert systems is very limited. However, with the increased interest in constructivist applications of expert systems and other computer tools, the research base should grow dramatically. We predict that future research will continue to verify the cognitive and metacognitive effects of learners functioning as knowledge engineers.

24.9 DATABASES AS COGNITIVE TOOLS

24.9.1 What Are Databases?

Databases are computerized record-keeping systems that were designed originally to replace paper-based information retrieval systems. A database consists of one or more files,

each of which contains information in the form of a set of records (e.g., an individual's bank account information). Each record in a database is divided into fields, which describe the class or type of information contained therein. The same type of information is stored in each field in each record. An address database for a professional association might contain many records, each with information such as names and addresses of the members. These records are systematically broken down into fields (subunits of each record) that define a common pattern of information. For example, an address database might contain six fields, one each for the name, street address, city, state, zip code, and telephone number. The content and arrangement of each field is standardized within the records so that the computer will "know" which part of the record to search for to locate a particular kind of information. Database management systems (DBMS) provide the capability for managing, searching, and sorting information in a database as well as creating and defining new database files. Having defined the data structure, information can be entered into or deleted from the file. File management functions enable the user to make permanent copies of the information in the database.

The most important functions of DBMS are the organization tools that help us answer queries about information in the database. These tools include the search functions we can use to search through the database to find specific information. We can search the entire database or by specific fields, using Boolean combinations of search terms, such as AND, OR, and NOT. The other organizational tool that is used extensively is the sort function that enables us to rearrange the contents of the database, usually in ascending or descending order. Essentially, DBMS allow us to store information in an organized way and to locate or arrange the order of information to help us answer queries about the information in it. Most applications of databases support administrative purposes such as maintaining records of dues paid by members of a professional association. However, we can use the same functions to analyze and enter subject-matter content into databases, which can then be searched and sorted to answer specific questions about the content or to seek interrelationships and inferences among the content records. In short, databases may be used as cognitive tools.

24.9.2 How Are Databases Used as Cognitive Tools?

The organized and defined nature of a database facilitates the acquisition or collection of information and the analysis of content domains through the breaking down of information into its constituent parts. Therefore, knowledge databases can function as cognitive tools. McCurry and McCurry (1992) described the use of database software to classify types of seashells. Rooze (1988–89) emphasized the value of databases in social studies classes in terms of their placing students in active rather than passive roles. Rooze maintained that the creation of databases allows students to determine what information to collect and to organize seemingly unrelated bits of information into meaningful categories. Rooze reported that the teacher must guide the development of categories and search procedures if the students are going to be able to use the database effectively, and recommended a "Concept Development Strategy" and an "Interpretation of Data Strategy" in the development and uses of databases.

Knight and Timmins (1986) also recommended the use of databases to meet the objectives of history instruction. Pon (1984) described the use of database software as an inquiry tool to aid higher-order thinking in a fourth-grade American Indian studies course. Watson and Strudler (1988–89) described a lesson based on Taba's Inductive Thinking Model that teaches higher-order thinking using databases. Watson and Strudler concluded that building databases involves analyzing, synthesizing, and evaluating information, all clearly important critical-thinking skills.

24.9.3 What Research Supports the Use of Databases as Cognitive Tools?

The use of databases as cognitive tools has generated no formal research, and as a result, only anecdotal evidence exists to support their efficacy. However, the opportunities for assessing the effects of building and using databases is extensive. The following paragraphs describe some of the issues that can be researched.

There are several basic activities involved in developing and using knowledge databases in education, each of which engages a different combination of cognitive processes. The simplest application is filling in an existing database by searching for information that fits into the data structure. For instance, a database comparing the social and economic development of different countries might include fields such as gross national product (GNP), population, infant mortality rate, personal income, literacy rate, defense spending, and so forth. Students could consult reference sources to locate information to contribute to the database.

Querying the databases they have created also supports learning. Learners can use the database to answer or construct questions about the information in it, such as:

1. What is the relationship between the average income and literacy rate? Which country is different from others with a high literacy rate? How will recent events affect that country?
2. If you knew nothing about these countries except what is in the database, in which one would you want to live? Why?
3. How are infant mortality rate and literacy related to GNP?
4. Which are the most socially advanced countries? Based on which criteria?

Querying a database is a two-stage process: understanding the query and then following database-specific procedures for answering the query (Schlager, 1991).

Even more intellectual engagement may result from identifying a content domain, sensing an information need, and developing a data structure for accommodating the information to be included and the kinds of questions that need to be asked. A large number of critical-thinking skills are required to construct and use knowledge-oriented databases. The necessity for conducting research on databases as cognitive tools is considerable. Opportunities in this area are nearly unlimited at many levels of education and training.

We were unable to locate any formal empirical research to validate the use of databases as a cognitive tool. Many educators have practiced using databases as cognitive tools, but none that we are aware of have researched the effects. We would expect that constructing databases would certainly enhance recall and retention of information. We would also expect that building databases would improve students' ability to comprehend domain knowledge as well as draw inferences and implications from information. There is great research potential here for future researchers.

24.10 SPREADSHEETS AS COGNITIVE TOOLS

24.10.1 What Are Spreadsheets?

Spreadsheets are computerized, numerical record-keeping systems that were originally designed to replace paper-based accounting systems. Essentially, a spreadsheet is a grid, table, or matrix of empty cells with columns identified by letters and rows identified by numbers. Each cell may contain values, formulas, or functions. Numerical or textual data can be entered into each cell. Functions consist of mathematical or logical operations that also act on the values of the different cells, such as sum or average. Other functions automatically match values in cells with other cells, look-up values in a table of values, or create an index of values to be compared with other cells.

Spreadsheets have three primary functions: storing, calculating, and presenting information. Information, usually numerical, can be filed by a spreadsheet program into a particular location (the cell). This enables that information to be accessed and retrieved efficiently. Most importantly, spreadsheets support calculation functions. The numerical contents of any combination of cells can be mathematically related in just about any way the user wishes. Cells can be added, multiplied, and factored in any combinations of ways. Most spreadsheets provide mathematical functions such as logarithms and trigonometric functions. Contemporary spreadsheet software such as Microsoft Excel also includes sophisticated tools for generating tables and graphs.

Most spreadsheets support the entering of values with functions such as replication, whereby the program will fill in formulas in cells by replicating a formula in another cell. During spreadsheet construction, the author is not required to copy a similar formula over and over again in different cells. The spreadsheet can change the formula relative to the position of the cell as well. Many spreadsheet programs also allow users to write "macros," i.e., procedures for automating a series of spreadsheet functions by using a single command.

Spreadsheets were originally developed to support business decision-making and accounting operations. They are especially useful for answering "what if" questions; e.g., what if interest rates increased by 1%? Changes need to be made in only one location, and the spreadsheet automatically recalculates all of the affected values. Spreadsheets are powerful problem-solving tools. However, the difficulty in using spreadsheets for problem solving depends on the amount of abstractness and information processing the problem contains (Leon-Argyla, 1988).

24.10.2 How Are Spreadsheets Used as Cognitive Tools?

Spreadsheets may be used as a cognitive tool for amplifying and reorganizing mental functioning. Spreadsheets completely restructured the work of budgeting for managers and business people around the globe, enabling planners to be hypothesis testers (playing "what if?" games) rather than calculators (Pea, 1985). The unique power of spreadsheets is sometimes credited with spurring the remarkable growth of microcomputers, starting with the development of the Visicalc spreadsheet in 1978 (Ditlea, 1984).

In the same way that spreadsheets have qualitatively changed the accounting process, they can change any educational process that involves working with quantitative information. The Working Group for Technology of the National Curriculum Commission (1990) charged with framing the national curriculum in Great Britain has recognized the role of spreadsheets as tools that enable students "to use information technology to explore patterns and relationships and to form and test sample hypotheses."

Spreadsheets are rule-using tools that require that users become rulemakers (Vockell & van Deusen, 1989). Calculating values in a spreadsheet requires that the user identify relationships and patterns among the data that he or she wants to represent in the spreadsheet. Next, those relationships must be modeled mathematically, using rules to describe the relationships in the model. Building spreadsheets requires abstract reasoning by the user, thereby matching one of the important goals of cognitive tools.

Spreadsheets support problem-solving activities. Given a problem situation with complex quantitative relationships, spreadsheets can be used to represent those relationships. The "what if?" thinking that is best supported by spreadsheets is essential to decision analysis (Sounderpandian, 1989). Such reasoning requires learners to consider implications of conditions or options, thereby engaging higher-order thinking.

Identifying values and developing formulas to interrelate them in spreadsheets enhance learners' understanding of the algorithms used to compare them and also the mathematical

models used to describe content domains. Students understand calculations (both antecedents and consequents) because they are actively involved in identifying the interrelationships between the components of the calculation. Spreadsheet construction and use demonstrate all steps of problem solutions, showing the progression of calculations as they are performed. The spreadsheet process models the mathematical logic that is implied by calculations. Making the underlying logic obvious to learners should improve their understandings of the interrelationships and procedures.

Numerous educators have explored the use of spreadsheets as cognitive tools. Spreadsheets have frequently been used in mathematics classes for such purposes as a calculator to demonstrate multiplicative relationships in elementary mathematics (Edwards & Bitter, 1989); for root finding in precalculus using synthetic division, bisection methods, and Newton's method (Pinter-Lucke, 1992); for helping students to understand the meaning of large numbers (e.g., a million) by comparing quantities to everyday things (Parker & Widmer, 1991); for solving elementary mathematical story problems in math classes (Verderber, 1990); for implementing linear system algorithms for solving advanced mathematical formulas (Watkins & Taylor, 1989); and for implementing Polya's problem-solving plan with arithmetic problems (Sgroi, 1992).

Spreadsheets have often been used to manifest quantitative relationships in various chemistry and physics classes, such as calculating the dimensions of a scale model of the Milky Way to demonstrate its intensity (Whitmer, 1990); solving complex chemistry problems such as wet and dry analysis of flue gases, which may be expanded to include volumetric flow rate, pressure, humidity, dew point, temperature, and combustion temperature in a mass and balances course (Misovich & Biasca, 1990); modeling the stoichiometric relationships in chemical reactions and calculating how many bonds are broken, the energy required to break bonds, and the new masses and densities of the products and reagents in the reactions (Brosnan, 1990); calculating the force needed to lift various weights in various level positions (Schlenker & Yoshida, 1991); solving rate equation chemical kinetics problems in a physical chemistry course (Blickensderfer, 1990); calculating and graphing quantum mechanical functions such as atomic orbitals to simulate rotational and vibrational energy levels of atomic components in a physical chemistry class (Kari, 1990); solving challenging science problems, including incline plane simulations and converting protein into energy (Goodfellow, 1990); solving physics laboratory experiments such as time, displacement, velocity, and their interrelationships using a free-fall apparatus (Krieger & Stith, 1990); and estimating and comparing the relative velocities of different dinosaurs (Karlin, 1988).

Spreadsheets are also useful in supporting social studies instruction, such as representing Keynesian vs. classical macro-economical models including savings-investment and inflation-unemployment relationships (Adams & Kroch, 1989); supporting decision analysis by helping users to find the best use of available information, as well as evaluating any additional information that can be obtained (Sounderpandian, 1989); interrelating demographic variables in population geography using population templates (Rudnicki, 1990); tracking portfolio performance in a stock-trading simulation (Crisci, 1992); and creating and manipulating economic models (e.g., balance of payments, investment appraisal, elasticity, and cost benefit analysis) in an economics course (Cashian, 1990).

Spreadsheets have been used in other disciplines as well. They have supported ecology education in the analysis of field data about tree species (Sigismondi & Calise, 1990) and the analysis of lunchroom trash to help students make projections of annual waste accumulation for an Earth Day project (Ramondetta, 1992). Spreadsheets have even been used to facilitate student grading of peer speech performances, providing a high level of motivation for students (Dribin, 1985).

It is sometimes useful to provide guided activities and problems to structure the use of spreadsheets. For example, to support higher-level thinking skills such as collecting, describing, and interpreting data, Niess (1992) provided students with a spreadsheet with wind data from various towns. Wind directions (NE, SW, WSW) described rows of data, with the percentage of days for each month of the year representing columns. She then asked students to use the spreadsheet to answer queries, such as:

- Are the winds more predominant from one direction during certain months? Why do you think this is the case?
- In which months is the wind the calmest?
- Which wind direction is the most stable during the year?

24.10.3 What Research Supports the Use of Spreadsheets as Cognitive Tools?

As with databases, there has been very little empirical study of the effects of using spreadsheets as cognitive tools. A few studies have examined the effects of different instructional treatments on learning to use spreadsheets (Charney, Reder & Kusbit, 1990; Kerr & Payne, 1994; Tiemann & Markle, 1990). These studies were not investigating the cognitive requirements or effects of using spreadsheets. Rather they were interested in the effects of different computer-based tutorial treatments, and spreadsheets happened to be the content or skill being learned. Baxter and Oatley (1991) compared the effectiveness of two different spreadsheet packages. Not surprisingly, the users' prior experience levels with spreadsheets was far more important to learning than the usability of the software package. These studies provide few insights about the effectiveness of spreadsheets as cognitive tools.

In one of the rare studies investigating spreadsheets as cognitive tools, Sutherland and Rojano (1993) were interested in how prealgebra students could use spreadsheets to represent and solve algebra problems. This study was conducted simultaneously in Britain and Mexico and took place over a

5-month period. During that time, students moved from a strict cause-effect local numerical notion of algebraic relationships to general rule-governed relationships that could be symbolized both in the spreadsheet and in algebraic notation. Another study used spreadsheets in community college math classes to help students solve linear and nonlinear equations problems (Hulse, 1992). Nonsignificant increases in mathematics achievement and decreases in numerical computation anxiety were reported; however, this study was so methodologically flawed by short treatment times and the use of inappropriate measures of achievement that it would be difficult to generalize the results.

All of the literature that we found provides accounts of how to use spreadsheets in various curricular application, along with some occasional anecdotal support for their use. For instance, Kari (1990) reported from several years of student use that students can learn both spreadsheet construction as well as physical chemistry concepts when provided with partially completed spreadsheets or spreadsheet templates. So the use of spreadsheets as cognitive tools remains speculative. Research on the cognitive outcomes from using spreadsheets is needed before we can conclude that they can function as generalizable cognitive tools.

24.11 CONCLUSIONS

We have presented a strong rationale for the application of cognitive tools in education, described a number of alternative approaches to using cognitive tools, and provided evidence that supports the uses of these cognitive tools in specific contexts. Support for some cognitive tools, such as programming languages, was found to be inconsistent. We also reported that very little research has been done to investigate the premise that cognitive tools based on common software such as databases and spreadsheets have beneficial effects on the development of higher-order thinking skills.

The overall finding that (1) learners develop critical-thinking skills as authors, designers, and constructors of knowledge and (2) learn more in the process than they do as the recipients of knowledge prepackaged in educational communications presents a major challenge for researchers in our field. For starters, this finding throws into question the value of much of the research reported elsewhere in this handbook. The findings of traditional educational communications research, already narrow in scope and limited in generalizability, may ultimately have little or no relevance in a world transformed by constructivist learning theory.

24.11.1 Future Research with Cognitive Tools

If nothing else, the research described in this chapter illustrates the need for sustained research agendas regarding the cognitive effects of cognitive tools, such as the studies carried out by Harel (1991), Kafai (1995), and other associates of Seymour Papert at MIT, rather than the isolated short-term "pseudoscience" studies carried out in many educational communications and technology research areas such as learner control research (Reeves, 1993). Our hope is that the research studies reported above will inspire an improved research agenda for our field that will eventually reform educational practice.

There are hopeful signs of change within the educational research community, as evidenced in a recent theoretical paper by Ackermann (1994):

> An increasing number of software designers, cognitive scientists, and educators have come to the view that experience is actively constructed and reconstructed through direct interaction with the world, and that, indeed, knowledge is experience. According to this view, a learner is not an empty vessel to be filled, or a passive listener to be filled in. Knowledge is not a mere commodity to be transmitted from one person to another. It is not an entity to be emitted at one end, encoded, stored, retrieved, and reapplied at the other. The conduit metaphor is progressively fading away, and is being replaced by the more recent toolmaker paradigm. . . . Children are perceived as the active builders of their own cognitive tools, comprising both mental capacities and external mediations that prolong those mental capacities. Constructivism is in the air . . . (pp. 13, 14).

We share in Ackermann's enthusiasm for these changes, and also in the caution she issues later in her paper that "'Hands-on' won't do without 'heads-in'" (p. 15). We view cognitive tools as affording learners unparalleled opportunities for heads-in learning within constructivist learning environments. Cognitive tools, as described in this paper and elsewhere (cf. Jonassen, 1996), represent a vehicle for both educational restructuring and a research agenda that will have significant impact on the restructuring process. We invite others to join us in this quest. To further that quest, we would make some recommendations about methodologies that should be used the:

24.11.1.1.   Multiple Assessments. The cognitive processes engaged by cognitive tools are complex and cannot be adequately assessed using a single type of measuring device. We recommend assessing the products of using cognitive tools as evidence of the thinking engaged by them. Criteria for evaluating those outcomes have not been verified, though many are suggested by Jonassen (1996). For instance, for evaluating semantic networks that are produced by students, a researcher might assess the:

- Number of nodes (breadth of the net)
- Number of instances (extent of the net)
- Ratio of instances to concepts (integratedness or embeddedness of concepts)
- Centrality of each node
- Depth (hierarchicalness) of the net
- Number of links (parsimony or economy of connections)
- Consistency in use of links
- Number of "dead-end" nodes (linked to only one other concept)
- Ratio of the number of links to the number of nodes

Other products of learning might include traditional tests (objective form), essays (look at the use of structural knowledge in the essays), speeches and presentations, and, most importantly, measures of transfer of learning. Cognitive tools should benefit learning transfer, so it is important to include assessments of problem solving in different domains or contexts, as well as in the domain being studied. These measures must assess the ability of learners to solve original problems, diagnose situations, draw implications or inferences from problem situations, or predict the result of changes in any problem situation.

In addition to assessing products of learning, it is important to assess the process as well. This can be accomplished by observing students as they work with cognitive tools and assessing variables such as effortful time-on-task, level of collaboration, or creativity. Research focused on how learners construct mental models may be especially fruitful (Jih & Reeves, 1992; Seel & Dinter, 1995). We recommend carefully analyzing the mix of methods employed by Lehrer (1993), Lehrer et al. (1994), and Spoehr (1992, 1993, 1994) in their investigation of learning from producing hypermedia knowledge bases. These are exemplary studies.

24.11.1.2.   Qualitative Methodologies. In order to assess the complexities and subtleties of knowledge construction, it is essential to use qualitative as well as quantitative assessment strategies. It is impossible and even inappropriate to hypothesize all of the cognitive outcomes of using cognitive tools. The processes are too rich and unpredictable. Qualitative methodologies are elaborated in Chapters 40 and 41.

24.11.1.3.   Meaningful Contexts and Assignments. Knowledge that is acquired in classrooms is "inert" in part because the purpose and context for learning such knowledge often has no relevance to learners whatsoever. The use of cognitive tools will likely result in greater learning if they are used in the context of solving some kind of problem that is meaningful to the learners. However, the meaningfulness of the context may also provide a researchable variable. Comparing the effects of cognitive tools used in a meaningful context with the use of cognitive tools as an adjunct memorization aid might provide some illuminating results.

24.11.1.4.   Multiple Evaluations. In addition to using multiple-assessment methods, the evaluations made from those assessments should also vary. Comparing the learner's knowledge or interpretations with the expert's or teacher's may be reasonable in some contexts. After all, research has shown that during the process of learning, the learner's knowledge structure increasingly resembles the knowledge structures of the instructors, and the degree of similarity is a good predictor of classroom examination performance (Diekhoff, 1983; Shavelson, 1974; Thro, 1978). Given an instructivist context where the purpose of instruction is to get the learner to think like the teacher, researchers may wish to determine the extent of the learner's knowledge growth and compare it to that of the teacher or expert. In such a context, the products of using cognitive tools can provide evidence in a pretest-posttest fashion of how much the learner has learned.

However, from a constructivist perspective, it is always necessary to assess the learner's unique perspective in addition to making any external comparisons. Understanding the sense that learners make from studying any content domain may be far more informative than comparing the student's knowledge to that of the teacher or expert. With this in mind, it is often useful and illuminating to allow learners to create multiple products (perhaps using different tools) with reference to the same content or problem. Some learners may be better able to express themselves through multimedia, others through more abstract tools such as spreadsheets or databases.

24.12 A FINAL WORD

We perceive major differences between the types of studies we advocate for investigating computers as cognitive tools (cf. Harel, 1991; Lehrer, 1993) and the morass of pseudoscience research studies endemic in the field of educational communications and technology (Reeves, 1993). In the first examples, pedagogical models grounded in robust cognitive learning theories have been identified, and, subsequently, powerful technologies have been used to implement these models. In the latter, the power of various forms of technology to instruct has been assumed, and reductionist experiments were conducted to detect the effects on students. Further, in Harel's (1991) and Lehrer's (1993) studies, students with authentic needs experienced powerful learning opportunities over a period of weeks and months. By contrast, in most pseudoscience studies, undergraduates earn "extra credit" for less than an hour of their time spent using some form of mediated "treatment" that has little or no relevance for them. The ethics of conducting the latter types of reductionist experiments in education should be more closely examined.

In a landmark paper, Salomon (1991) describes the contrast between analytic and systemic approaches to educational research. Salomon claims that this analytic-systemic contrast transcends the "basic versus applied" or "quantitative versus qualitative" arguments that so often dominate debates about the relevancy of educational research. Salomon concludes that the analytic and systemic approaches are complementary, arguing that "the analytic approach capitalizes on precision, while the systemic approach capitalizes on authenticity" (p. 16).

While we agree with Salomon in theory, the dominance of pseudoscience in educational communications and technology research threatens to invalidate this complementarity in practice. Many of those who engage in analytic research approaches consistently violate the basic premises of the empirical paradigm they espouse, especially with respect to the testing of meaningful hypotheses derived from strong theory (Reeves, 1993). The question must be asked: Can society continue to afford the conduct of atheoretical analytical research in education on the scale reported elsewhere in this volume? We think not. Educational com-munications and technology require a much more valid body of systemic and analytical research grounded in sound theory than currently exists. Although limited in scope, we believe that the research focused on the effects of using computers as cognitive tools described in this chapter points the way toward a more valid and socially responsible research agenda for the 21st century.

REFERENCES

Ackermann, E. (1994). Direct and mediated experience: their role in learning. *In* R. Lewis & P. Mendelsohn, eds. *Lessons from learning.* Amsterdam: North-Holland.

Adams, F.G. & Kroch, E. (1989). The computer in the teaching of macroeconomics. *Journal of Economic Education 20* (3), 269–80.

Ahmed, A.M. (1992). *Learning to program and its transference to student's cognition.* (ERIC Document No. ED 352261.)

Apple Computer (1984). *HyperCard* [Computer software]. Cupertino, CA: Apple Computer.

Baxter, I. & Oatley, K. (1991). Measuring the learnability of spreadsheets in inexperienced users and those with previous spreadsheet experience. *Behaviour & Information Technology 10* (6), 475–90.

Beichner, R.J. (1994). Multimedia editing to promote science learning. *Journal of Educational Multimedia and Hypermedia 3* (1), 55–70.

Blickensderfer, R. (1990). Learning chemical kinetics with spreadsheets. *Journal of Computers in Mathematics and Science Teaching 9* (4), 35–43.

Bossinger, J. & Milheim, W.D. (1993). The development and application of expert systems: a national survey. *Educational Technology 33* (7), 7–17.

Briscoe, C. & LeMaster, S.U. (1991). Meaningful learning in college biology through concept mapping. *American Biology Teacher 53* (4), 214–19.

Brosnan, T. (1990). Using spreadsheets in the teaching of chemistry: two more ideas and some limitations. *School Science Review 71* (256), 53–59.

Bruce, B. & Rubin, A. (1993). *Electronic quills: a situated evaluation of using computers for writing in classrooms.* Hillsdale, NJ: Erlbaum.

Cafolla, R. (1987–88). Piagetian formal operations and other cognitive correlates of achievement in computer programming. *Journal of Educational Psychology 16* (1), 45–57.

Carver, S.M., Lehrer, R., Connell, T. & Ericksen, J. (1992). Learning by hypermedia design: issues of assessment and implementation. *Educational Psychologist 27* (3), 385–404.

Cashian, P. (1990). Spreadsheet investigations in economics teaching. *Economics 26* (110), 73–84.

Chandler, T.N. (1994). The science education advisor: applying a user-centered design approach to the development of an interactive case-based advising system. *Journal of Artificial Intelligence in Education 5* (3), 283–318.

Charney, D., Reder, L. & Kusbit, G.W. (1990). Goal setting and procedure selection in acquiring computer skills: a comparison of tutorial, problem solving, and learner exploration. *Cognition & Instruction 7* (4), 323–42.

Chin, J.P. & Zecker, S.G. (1985). Personality and cognitive factors influencing computer programming performance. Paper presented at the Annual Meeting of the Eastern Educational Research Association, Boston, MA (ERIC Document No. ED 261666).

Clark, R.E. (1994). Media will never influence learning. *Educational Technology Research and Development 42* (2), 21–29.

Clement, C.A., Kurland, D.M., Mawby, R. & Pea, R.D. (1986). Analogical reasoning and computer programming. *Journal of Educational Computing Research 2* (4), 473–85.

Clements, D.H. (1985). Research in Logo in education: is the turtle slow but steady or not even in the race? *Computers in the Schools 2* (2–3), 55–71.

— & Gullo, D.F. (1984). Effects of computer programming on young children's cognition. *Journal of Educational Psychology 76,* 1051–58.

Crisci, G. (1992, Jan.). Play the market! *Instructor 101* (5), 68–69.

Cuban, L. (1986). *Teachers and machines: the classroom use of technology since 1920.* New York: Teachers College Press.

Davis, N.T. (1990). Using concept mapping to assist prospective elementary teachers in making meaning. *Journal of Science Teacher Education 1* (4), 66–69.

Derry, S.J. & Lajoie, S.P. (1993). A middle camp for (un)intelligent instructional computing: an introduction. *In* S.P. Lajoie & S.J. Derry, eds. *Computers as cognitive tools,* 1–11. Hillsdale, NJ: Erlbaum.

Dick, W. & Carey, L. (1990). *The systematic design of instruction,* 3d ed. Glenview, IL: Scott, Foresman/Little, Brown.

Diekhoff, G.M. (1983). Relationship judgments in the evaluation of structural understanding. *Journal of Educational Psychology 75,* 227–33.

Ditlea, S., ed. (1984). *Digital deli.* New York: Workman.

Dribin, C.I. (1985, Jun.). Spreadsheets and performance: a guide for student-graded presentations. *The Computing Teacher 12* (9), 22–25.

Duffy, T.M. & Jonassen, D.H., eds. (1992). *Constructivism and the technology of instruction: a conversation.* Hillsdale, NJ: Erlbaum.

—, Lowyck, J. & Jonassen, D.H., eds. (1993). *Designing environments for constructive learning.* Berlin: Springer.

Edwards, N.T. & Bitter, B.G. (1989, Oct.). Teaching mathematics with technology. *Arithmetic Teacher 37* (2), 40–44.

Feghali, A.A. (1991). A study of engineering college students' use of computer-based semantic networks in a computer programming language class (doctoral dissertation, Purdue University). *Dissertation Abstracts International 53* (3), 701.

Fischer, G.B. (1986). *Computer programming: a formal operational task.* Paper presented at the Annual Symposium of the Piaget Society, Philadelphia, PA (ERIC Document No. ED 275316).

Fischer, K.M. (1992). SemNet: a tool for personal knowledge construction. *In* P. Kommers, D. Jonassen & T. Mayes, eds. *Cognitive tools for learning.* Berlin: Springer.

— (1990). Semantic networking: new kid on the block. *Journal of Research in Science Teaching 27* (10), 1001–18.

—, Faletti, J., Patterson, H., Thornton, R., Lipson, J. & Spring, C. (1990). Computer assisted concept mapping. *Journal of College Science Teaching 19* (6), 347–52.

Foreman, K.H.D. (1988). Cognitive style, cognitive ability, and the acquisition of initial programming competence. *In* M.R. Simonson & J.K. Frederick, eds. *Proceedings of selected research papers presented at the Annual Meeting of the Association for Educational Communications and Technology,* New Orleans, LA.

Fuchs, L.S. (1992). Effects of expert system consultation within curriculum-based measurement using a reading maze task. *Exceptional Children 58* (5), 436–50.

Gagné, E. (1985). *The cognitive psychology of school learning.* Boston, MA: Little, Brown.

Gagné, R.M., Briggs, L.J. & Wager, W. (1987). *Principles of instructional design,* 3d ed. New York: Holt, Rinehart & Winston.

Goldsmith, T.E., Johnson, P.J. & Acton, W.H. (1991). Assessing structural knowledge. *Journal of Educational Psychology 83,* 88–96.

Goodfellow, T. (1990). Spreadsheets: powerful tools in science education. *School Science Review 71* (257), 47–57.

Goodlad, J.I. (1984). *A place called school: prospects for the future.* New York: McGraw-Hill.

Grabinger, R.S. & Pollock, J. (1989). The effectiveness of internally generated feedback with an instructional expert system. *Journal of Educational Computing Research 5* (3), 12–15.

Harel, I., ed. (1991). *Children designers: interdisciplinary constructions for learning and knowing mathematics in a computer-rich school.* Norwood, NJ: Ablex.

— & Papert, S. (1990). Software design as a learning environment. *Interactive Learning Environments 1* (1), 1–32.

Hays, K.E., Weingard, P., Guzdial, M., Jackson, S., Boyle, R.A. & Soloway, E. (1993, Jun.). *Students as multimedia authors.* Paper presented at ED-MEDIA '93, Orlando, FL.

Hulse, J.W. (1992). A comparison of the effects of spreadsheet use and traditional methods on student achievement and attitudes in selected collegiate mathematics topics (doctoral dissertation, University of South Dakota). *Dissertation Abstracts International 45* (8), 2723.

Jansson, L.C. (1987). Computer programming and logical reasoning. *School Science and Mathematics 87* (5), 371–79.

Jih, H.J. & Reeves, T.C. (1992). Mental models: a research focus for interactive learning systems. *Educational Technology Research and Development 40* (3), 39–53.

Jonassen, D.H. (1996). *Computers in the classroom: mindtools for critical thinking.* Columbus, OH: Prentice Hall.

— (1993). Changes in knowledge structures from building semantic net versus production rule representations of subject content. *Journal of Computer Based Instruction 20* (4), 99–106.

— (1989). *Hypertext/hypermedia.* Englewood Cliffs, NJ: Educational Technology.

— (1987). Assessing cognitive structure: verifying a method using pattern notes. *Journal of Research and Development in Education 20* (3), 1–14.

— (1984). The electronic notebook: integrating learning strategies into courseware to raise the level of processing. *In* G. Mills & B. Alloway, eds. *Aspects of educational technology.* London: Kogan Page.

—, Beissner, K. & Yacci, M.A. (1993). *Structural knowledge: techniques for representing, conveying, and acquiring structural knowledge.* Hillsdale, NJ: Erlbaum.

—, Campbell, J.P. & Davidson, M.E. (1994). Learning with media: restructuring the debate. *Educational Technology Research and Development 42* (2), 31–39.

— & Grabowski, B.L. (1993). *Handbook of individual differences, learning, and instruction.* Hillsdale, NJ: Erlbaum.

—, Myers, J.M. & McKillop, A.M. (1996). From constructivism to constructionism: learning with hypermedia/multimedia rather than from it. *In* B. Wilson, ed. *Constructivist learning environments, 93–106.* Englewood Cliffs, NJ: Educational Technology.

—, Wilson, B.G., Wang, S. & Grabinger, R.S. (1993). Constructivistic uses of expert systems to support learning. *Journal of Computer Based Instruction 20* (3), 86–94.

Kafai, Y.B. (1995). *Minds in play: computer game design as a context for children's learning.* Hillsdale, NJ: Erlbaum.

— (1996). Gender differences in children's constructions of video games. *In* Patricia M. Greenfield & Rodney R. Cocking, eds. *Interacting with video, 39–66.* Norwood, NJ: Ablex.

Karake, Z.A. (1990). Enhancing the learning process with expert systems. *Computers and Education 14* (6), 495–503.

Kari, R. (1990). Spreadsheets in advanced physical chemistry. *Journal of Computers in Mathematics and Science Teaching 10* (1), 39–48.

Karlin, M. (1988, Feb.). Beyond distance = rate * time. *The Computing Teacher 15* (5), 20–23.

Kerr, M.P. & Payne, S.J. (1994). Learning to use a spreadsheet by doing and by watching. *Interacting with Computers 6* (1), 3–22.

Knight, P. & Timmins, G. (1986). Using databases in history teaching. *Journal of Computer Assisted Learning 2* (2), 93–101.

Knox-Quinn, C. (1992, Apr.). *Student construction of expert systems in the classroom.* Paper presented at the Annual Meeting of the American Educational Research Association, San Francisco, CA.

Kommers, P.A.M. (1989). *TextVision* [computer software]. Enschede, Netherlands: Twente University.

Kommers, P., Jonassen, D.H. & Mayes, T., eds. (1992). *Cognitive tools for learning.* Berlin: Springer.

Kozma, R.B. (1994). Will media influence learning? Reframing the debate. *Educational Technology Research and Development 42* (2), 7–19.

— (1992). Constructing knowledge with Learning Tool. *In* P. Kommers, D. Jonassen & T. Mayes, eds. *Cognitive tools for learning.* Berlin: Springer.

— (1987). The implications of cognitive psychology for computer-based learning tools. *Educational Technology 27* (11), 20–25.

Krieger, M.E. & Stith, J.H. (1990, Sep.). Spreadsheets in the physics laboratory. *The Physics Teacher 28* (6), 378–84.

Kurland, D.M., Pea, R.D., Clement, C. & Mawby, R. (1986). A study of the development of programming ability and thinking skills in high school students. *Journal of Educational Computing Research 2* (4), 429–55.

Lai, K.W. (1992, Mar.). *Acquiring expertise and cognitive skills in the process of constructing an expert system: a preliminary study.* Paper presented at the Annual Meeting of the American Educational Research Association, San Francisco, CA.

Lajoie, S.P. (1990, Apr.). *Computer environments as cognitive tools for enhancing mental models.* Paper presented at the Annual Meeting of the American Educational Research Association, Boston, MA.

— & Derry, S.J., eds. (1993). *Computers as cognitive tools.* Hillsdale, NJ: Erlbaum.

Langer, E.J. (1989). *Mindfulness.* Reading, MA: Addison-Wesley.

Lehrer, R. (1993). Authors of knowledge: patterns of hypermedia design. *In* S.P. Lajoie & S.J. Derry, eds. *Computers as cognitive tools, 197–227.* Hillsdale, NJ: Erlbaum.

Lehrer, R., Erickson, J. & Connell, T. (1994). Learning by designing hypermedia documents. *Computers in Schools 10* (1–2), 227–54.

Leon-Argyla, E.R. (1988). A study of spreadsheet problem solving and testing for problem solving ability (doctoral dissertation, Michigan State University). *Dissertation Abstracts International 49* (10), 3005.

Liao, Y.K.C. & Bright, G.W. (1991). Effects of computer programming on cognitive outcomes. *Journal of Educational Computing Research 7* (3), 251–68.

Lippert, R.C. (1989). Expert systems: tutors, tools, and tutees. *Journal of Computer-Based Instruction 16* (1), 11–19.

— (1988). An expert system shell to teach problem solving. *Tech Trends 33* (2), 22–26.

— & Finley, F. (1988, Apr.). *Student's refinement of knowledge during the development of knowledge bases for expert systems.* Paper presented at the Annual Meeting of the National Association for Research in Science Teaching, Lake of the Ozarks, MO (ERIC Document No. ED 293872).

Mansfield, H. & Happs, J. (1991). Concepts maps. *Australian Mathematics Teacher 47* (3), 30–33.

Marcoulides, G.A. (1988). An intelligent computer-based learning program. *Collegiate Microcomputer 6* (2), 123–26.

McCoy, L.P. (1990). Literature related to learning problem solving in mathematics and computer programming. *School Science and Mathematics 90* (1), 48–60.

McCurry, N. & McCurry, A. (1992, Apr.). Science: database programs and the study of seashells. *The Computing Teacher 19* (7), 32–34.

Merrill, M.D., Li, Z. & Jones, M.K. (1990). Second generation instructional design (ID2). *Educational Technology 30* (2), 7–14.

Mikulecky, L. (1988). *Development of interactive programs to help students transfer basic skills to college level science and behavioral sciences courses.* Bloomington, IN: Indiana University (ERIC Document No. ED 318469).

Miller, R.B., Kelly, G.N. & Kelly, J.T. (1988). Effects of Logo computer programming experience on problem solving and spatial relations ability. *Contemporary Educational Psychology 13,* 348–57.

Misovich, M. & Biasca, K. (1990). The power of spreadsheets in a mass and energy balance course. *Chemical Engineering Education 24,* 46–50.

Mitchell, R. (1992). *Testing for learning: how new approaches to evaluation can improve American schools.* New York: Free Press.

Morrelli, R. (1990). The student as knowledge engineer: a constructivist model for science education. *Journal of Computing in Higher Education 2* (1), 78–102.

Nachmias, R. (1986, Apr.). *Variables—an obstacle to children learning computer programming.* Paper presented at the Annual Meeting of the American Educational Research Association, San Francisco, CA (ERIC Document No. ED 290459).

National Curriculum Commission. (1990). *Technology in the national curriculum.* London: National Curriculum Commission.

Neimeyer, G.J. (1993). *Constructivist assessment: a casebook.* Newbury Park, CA: Sage.

Nelson, T. (1980). Replacing the printed word: a complete literary system. *In* S.H. Lavingston, ed. *Proceedings of the IFIP Congress, 1013–23.* Amsterdam: North-Holland.

Nielsen, J. (1990). *Hypertext & hypermedia.* Boston, MA: Academic Professional.

Niess, M.L. (1992, Mar.). Math: winds of change. *The Computing Teacher 19* (6), 32–35.

Norman, D.A. (1983). Some observations on mental models. *In* D. Gentner & A.L. Stevens, eds. *Mental models.* Hillsdale, NJ: Erlbaum.

Nowaczyk, R.H. (1983, Mar.). *Cognitive skills needed in computer programming.* Paper presented at the Annual Meeting of the Southeastern Psychological Association, Atlanta, GA (ERIC Document No. ED 236466).

Oprea, J.M. (1988). Computer programming and mathematical thinking. *Journal of Mathematical Behavior 7,* 15–190.

Papert, S. (1993). *The children's machine: rethinking school in the age of the computer.* New York: Basic Books.

Papert, S. (1980). *Mindstorms: children, computers and powerful ideas.* New York: Basic Books.

Parker, J. & Widmer, C.C. (1991, Sep.). Teaching mathematics with technology: how big is a million? *Arithmetic Teacher 39* (1), 38–41.

Pea, R.D. (1985). Beyond amplification: using the computer to reorganize mental functioning. *Educational Psychologist 20* (4), 167–82.

— & Kurland, D.M. (1987). On the cognitive effects of learning computer programming. *In* R.D. Pea & K. Sheingold, eds. *Mirrors of minds: patterns of experience in educational computing,* 147–77. Norwood, NJ: Ablex.

Perelman, L.J. (1992). *School's out: hyperlearning, the new technology, and the end of education.* New York: Morrow.

Perkins, D.N. (1993). Person-plus: a distributed view of thinking and learning. *In* G. Salomon, ed. *Distributed cognitions: psychological and educational considerations,* 88–110. Cambridge, UK: Cambridge University Press.

— (1986). *Knowledge as design.* Hillsdale, NJ: Erlbaum.

Phillips, D.C. (1995). The good, the bad, and the ugly: the many faces of constructivism. *Educational Researcher 24* (7), 5–12.

Pinter-Lucke, C. (1992). Rootfinding with a spreadsheet in pre-calculus. *Journal of Computers in Mathematics and Science Teaching 11* (1), 85–93.

Polson, M.C. & Richardson, J.J., eds. (1988). *Foundations of intelligent tutoring systems.* Hillsdale, NJ: Erlbaum.

Pon, K. (1984, Nov.). Databasing in the elementary (and secondary) classroom. *The Computing Teacher 12* (3), 28–30.

Popyack, J.L. (1989). *Karel* [computer software]. Santa Barbara, CA: Intellimation.

Preece, P.F.W. (1976). Mapping cognitive structure: a comparison of methods. *Journal of Educational Psychology 68* (1), 1–8.

Quillian, M.R. (1968). Semantic memory. *In* M. Minsky, ed. *Semantic information processing,* 43–67. Cambridge, MA: MIT Press.

Ramondetta, J. (1992, Apr./May). Using computers: learning from lunchroom trash. *Learning 20* (8), 59.

Reeves, T.C. (1993). Pseudoscience in computer-based instruction: the case of learner control research. *Journal of Computer-Based Instruction 20* (2), 39–46.

— & Okey, J. (1996). Alternative assessment for constructivist learning environments. *In* B. Wilson, ed. *Constructivist learning environments,* 191–202. Englewood Cliffs, NJ: Educational Technology.

Rooze, G.E. (1988-89). Developing thinking with databases: what's really involved? *Michigan Social Studies Journal 3* (1), 25–26.

Rudnicki, R. (1990). Using spreadsheets in population geography classes. *Journal of Geography 89* (3), 118–22.

Rumelhart, D.E. (1980). Schemata: the building blocks of cognition. *In* R.J. Spiro, B.C. Bruce & W.F. Brewer, eds. *Theoretical issues in reading comprehension: perspectives from cognitive psychology, linguistics, artificial intelligence, and education.* Hillsdale, NJ: Erlbaum.

— & Ortony, A. (1977). The representation of knowledge in memory. *In* R.C. Anderson, R.J. Spiro & W.E. Montague, eds. *Schooling and the acquisition of knowledge.* Hillsdale, NJ: Erlbaum.

Saleem, N. & Azad, A.N. (1992). Expert systems as a statistics tutor on call. *Journal of Computers in Mathematics and Science Teaching 11* (2), 179–91.

Salomon, G. (1993). On the nature of pedagogic computer tools: the case of the writing partner. *In* S.P. Lajoie & S.J. Derry, eds. *Computers as cognitive tools,* 179–96. Hillsdale, NJ: Erlbaum.

— (1991). Transcending the qualitative-quantitative debate: the analytic and systemic approaches to educational research. *Educational Researcher 20* (6), 10–18.

— & Globerson, T. (1987). Skill may not be enough: the role of mindfulness in learning and transfer. *International Journal of Educational Research 11,* 623–38.

— Perkins, D.N. & Globerson, T. (1991). Partners in cognition: extending human intelligence with intelligent technologies. *Educational Researcher 20* (3), 2–9.

Schlager, M.S. (1991). *An analysis of database querying as a cognitive skill.* Doctoral dissertation, University of Colorado at Boulder, 1991.

Schlenker, R.M. & Yoshida, S.J. (1991, Feb.). A clever lever endeavor: you can't beat the spreadsheet. *The Science Teacher 58* (2), 36–39.

Schreiber, D.A. & Abegg, G.L. (1991, Apr.). *Scoring student-generated concept maps in introductory college chemistry.* Paper presented at the Annual Meeting of the National Association for Research in Science Teaching, Lake Geneva, WI (ERIC Document No. 347055).

Schvaneveldt, R.W., ed. (1990). *Pathfinder associative networks: studies in knowledge organization.* Norwood, NJ: Ablex.

Seel, N.M. & Dinter, F.R. (1995). Instruction and mental model progression: learner-dependent effects of teaching strategies on knowledge acquisition and analogical transfer. *Educational Research and Evaluation 1* (1), 4–35.

Sgroi, R.J. (1992, Mar.). Systematizing trial and error using spreadsheets. *Arithmetic Teacher 39* (7), 8–12.

Shavelson, R.J. (1974). Methods for examining representations of subject matter structure in students' memory. *Journal of Research in Science Teaching 11* (3), 231–49.

— (1972). Some aspects of the correspondence between content structure and cognitive structure in physics instruction. *Journal of Educational Psychology 63* (3), 225–34.

Shlechter, T.M., ed. (1991). *Problems and promises of computer-based training.* Norwood, NJ: Ablex.

Sigismondi, L.A. & Calise, C. (1990). Integrating basic computer skills into science classes: analysis of ecological data. *The American Biology Teacher 52* (5), 296–301.

Simon, H.A. (1987). Computers and society. *In* S.B. Kiesler & L.S. Sproul, eds. *Computing and change on campus,* 4–15. New York: Cambridge University Press.

Sleeman, D., Putnam, R.T., Baxter, J. & Kuspa, L. (1986). Pascal and high school students: a study of errors. *Journal of Educational Computing Research 2* (1), 6–10.

Sounderpandian, J. (1989). Decision analysis using spreadsheets. *Collegiate Microcomputer 7* (2), 157–63.

Spector, J.M., Polson, M.C. & Muraida, D.J., eds. (1993). *Automating instructional design: concepts and issues.* Englewood Cliffs, NJ: Educational Technology.

Spoehr, K.T. (1994). Enhancing the acquisition of conceptual structures through hypermedia. *In* K. McGilly, ed. *Classroom lessons: integrating cognitive theory and classroom practice.* Cambridge, MA: MIT Press.

— (1993, Apr.). *Profiles of hypermedia authors: how students learn by doing.* Paper presented at the Annual Meeting of the American Educational Research Association, Atlanta, GA.

— (1992, Apr.). *Using hypermedia to clarify conceptual structures: illustrations from history and literature.* Paper presented at the Annual Meeting of the American Educational Research Association, Atlanta, GA.

— & Shapiro, A. (1991). *Learning from hypermedia: making sense of a multiply-linked database.* (ERIC Document No. ED 333864.)

Starfield, A.M., Smith, K.A. & Bleloch, A.L. (1990). *How to model it: problem solving for the computer age.* New York: McGraw-Hill.

Stoll, C. (1995). *Silicon snake oil: second thoughts on the information highway.* New York: Doubleday.

Sutherland, R. & Rojano, T. (1993). A spreadsheet approach to solving algebra problems. *Journal of Mathematical Behavior 12* (4), 353–83.

Swan, K. & Black, J.B. (1990, Apr.). *Logo programming, problem solving, and knowledge-based instruction.* Paper presented at the Annual Meeting of the American Educational Research Association, Boston, MA (ERIC Document No. ED 349968).

Taylor, K.A. (1991). *An annotated bibliography of current literature dealing with the effective teaching of computer programming in high schools.* (ERIC Document No. 338217.)

Taylor, R., ed. (1980). *The computer in the school: tutor, tool, tutee.* New York: Teachers College Press.

Tennyson, R.D. & Christensen, D.L. (1991). Automating instructional systems development. *In* M.R. Simonson, ed. *Proceedings of selected research presentations at the Annual Conference of the Association for Educational Communications and Technology,* 885–915. Washington, DC: Association for Educational Communications & Technology.

Thro, M.P. (1978). Relationships between associative and content structure of physics concepts. *Journal of Educational Psychology 70* (6), 971–78.

Tiemann, P.W. & Markle, S.M. (1990). Effects of varying interactive strategies provided by computer-based tutorial for a software application program. *Performance Improvement Quarterly 3* (2), 48–64.

Trollip, S. & Lippert, R. (1988). Constructing knowledge bases: a promising instructional tool. *Journal of Computer-Based Instruction 14* (2), 44–48.

—, Lippert, R., Starfield, A. & Smith, K.A. (1992). Building knowledge bases: an environment for making cognitive connections. *In* P. Kommers, D. Jonassen & T. Mayes, eds. *Cognitive tools for learning.* Berlin: Springer.

Verderber, N.L. (1990). Spreadsheets and problem solving with AppleWorks in mathematics teaching. *Journal of Computers in Mathematics and Science Teaching 9* (3), 45–51.

Vockell, E. & van Deusen, R.M. (1989). *The computer and higher-order thinking skills.* Watsonville, CA: Mitchell.

von Glaserfeld, E. (1989). An exposition of constructivism: why some like it radical. *In* R.B. Davis, C.A. Maher & N. Noddings, eds. *Constructivist views on the teaching and learning of mathematics.* Athens, GA: JRME Monographs.

von Wodtke, M. (1993). *Mind over media: creative thinking skills for electronic media.* New York: McGraw-Hill.

Watkins, W. & Taylor, M. (1989). A spreadsheet in the mathematics classroom. *Collegiate Microcomputer 7* (3), 233–39.

Watson, J. & Strudler, N. (1988-89). Teaching higher-order thinking skills with databases. *The Computing Teacher 16* (4), 47–50, 55.

Whitmer, J. C. (1990, Oct.). Modeling the Milky Way: spreadsheet science. *The Science Teacher 57* (7), 19–21.

Wideman, H.H. & Owston, R.D. (1993). Knowledge base construction as a pedagogical activity. *Journal of Educational Computing Research 9* (2), 165–96.

Williamson, J.D. & Ginther, D.W. (1992). Knowledge representation and cognitive outcomes of teaching Logo to children. *Journal of Computing in Childhood Education 3* (3-4), 303–22.

Wittrock, M.C. (1974). Learning as a generative activity. *Educational Psychologist 11,* 87–95.

Worthen, B.R. (1993). Critical issues that will determine the future of alternative assessment. *Phi Delta Kappan 74* (6), 444–56.

Yeaman, A.R.J. (1994). Deconstructing modern educational technology. *Educational Technology 34* (2), 15–24.

25. TECHNOLOGIES FOR INFORMATION ACCESS IN LIBRARY AND INFORMATION CENTERS

Dian Walster

UNIVERSITY OF COLORADO AT DENVER

25.1 INTRODUCTION

Information access is a physical, psychological, social, cultural, and political issue. It involves more than calling up an item record on an on-line system or pointing to a book on a shelf and saying, "Ah, the small green book has everything I need" (Moholt, 1988). It is all the relationships that exist when users access information. Library and information science (LIS) researchers study users and information and how users access information. The relationships involve cognitive, affective, and physical components. They are moderated by cultural, sociological, and economic factors. They are subject to the constraints of technology, science, and education. This review focuses on LIS literature and research. It examines the theoretical and philosophical foundations for research in information access and discusses changes in focus and methodology.

25.2 CATEGORIES OF RESEARCH IN INFORMATION ACCESS

To organize the literature and provide a viewfinder, categories of research in information access were created. Research on information access is divided into three segments: users, access, and information. Each of these is discussed separately by looking at foundational research and inquiry. These three areas were identified using the basic question that initiated this review: How do people access information? In attempting to answer the question, an initial analysis revealed that researchers look at three separate issues: users, access, and information.

Users, both collectively and individually, engage in particular activities. The user plays a significant role in establishing and maintaining the problem situation. Various attributes and characteristics of users who want access to information are considered by researchers. Access is the second part of the research problem.

Access refers both to the technologies that provide access and to the factors that may enhance or limit access. Therefore, research in this area not only looks at technological capabilities but also at the impact of space, time, and culture.

Information is the goal of access, in the sense that information is what users want to access. What constitutes information and how information is constructed and stored creates the research foundation for this information access area.

Researchers studying users look at beliefs, behaviors, and needs. They attempt to describe user characteristics and variables important to information access. They examine ways to change users to create more efficient access. Researchers who study access look at technologies of access. They examine features related to mechanical technologies and social environments impacting user access. They may also study the system of information access, but from a system rather than user point of view. Information researchers study the characteristics and construction of information. They are interested in how information is represented, how the retrieval process is managed, and barriers to information access.

25.2.1 Users

Users initiate the information access process. Users can be students in a school library media center, engineers in a chemical corporation, agronomy professors on site in the field, doctors in their offices, or children at the zoo. Anyone looking for information is a user. There is a causal relationship between users and the other two pieces of the model. Without the initial problem, question, query, significant imbalance, or need, neither information nor a way to access it is necessary. Characteristics and issues related to users of information are essential to understanding information access. Research about users has generally focused in three areas:

720

- User studies
- Information seeking
- Information skills

User studies address such issues as different types of user groups, information needs of various people, and general characteristics of users that may impact information need. Information-seeking research examines the cognitive processes and search strategies that individuals use to access information. It often looks at differences between search intermediaries and end users. Information seeking can be considered a subset of cognitive characteristics. The concept of information skills focuses on knowledge and processes users need to improve information access effectiveness. This area has models of information skills development and research on the search process as a learning strategy.

25.2.2 Access

Access requires a user and a point of access. An access point could be a computer, a reference book, a phone directory, another person, a cage at the zoo, or any of a variety of other physical things. At some place in time, the user and the access point come together. An access point is a physical location. (*Question*: If a person accesses his or her own information, i.e., thinks about something, is there a physical access point? Are there other access instances where there is no way of construing physicalness?)

The access point is accompanied by physical factors that interact with the action of access. The point exists within near space: a work space, a library space, a classroom niche, a government waiting room, a kitchen with a telephone. This near space has physical, psychological, and social characteristics that influence access. The near space is surrounded by a room, a building, a facility, or a type of finite environment. The surrounding space is designed, developed, and maintained. It also interacts with characteristics of the user trying to access information. The space that contains the access point is located in a geographical relationship to the user. If the access point is a computer in the individual's bedroom, this is a close geographical relationship. If the access point is located at the university library, 50 miles away, this is a distant geographical relationship. Each of these factors has research and theory implications for information access in library and information centers.

Research in information access falls into three general areas: (1) research on the mechanical technologies of access points, such as on-line public access catalogs (OPACs), electronic mail (e-mail), on-line search services, and their associated social technologies, such as interface design and screen design; (2) research on the physical and social issues that impact the immediate use of an access point such as handicapped access, facilities design, and sign systems; and (3) research on larger issues that affect the use of the access point, such as public policies for use and geographic availability. LIS research on access to information

is drawn from different theoretical backgrounds such as social and cognitive psychology, human factors, computer programming, and educational technology. Much of the research in this area is in the developmental stage for library and information centers.

25.2.3 Information

Access is only as useful as the information that is accessed. In general, information is defined by LIS researchers in the broadest terms to include antelopes and books and computers and rocks (Buckland, 1991). As raw information, access is focused on the relationship between the individual and the information source. A child watching an antelope eating at the zoo could be considered to be accessing from an information center. The zoo is a repository of live natural history information. Another type of information is that which is constructed into different formats. Databases (see 24.9), semantic nets (24.7), indexing and cataloging, and expert systems (see 24.8) are all forms of information construction. Access to constructed information may be different than access to raw information. Information is also affected by the influence of public policies and cultural norms on what information is made available and to whom. Researchers, such as Dervin (1992), suggest that information should be considered subjective: a personal construction created by human observers.

Information is used, analyzed, and made available in four different contexts: (1) as basic content or reality, (2) as this reality constructed in large sets, (3) as filtered by political and social constraints, and (4) as constructed by the individual. Research on information encompasses a broad scope and complexity. It has technical and social implications. For example, does the content of information influence access to information? Does mathematics literature have an inherently different structure for searching and sorting than poetry? This chapter will focus on the organizational structures developed in LIS to sort, categorize, and aid in the retrieval of information.

25.3 CHAPTER OVERVIEW

Each of the three areas of research in information access are now examined in depth: users, access, and information.

- Research and methodological issues are discussed.
- Analyses of significant studies are provided.
- Directions for future research are considered.

In addition, three longitudinal research projects that integrate users, access, and information are reviewed at length. The final section of the chapter summarizes LIS research and briefly discusses implications of access issues in library and information centers for research in educational communications and technology.

This chapter has three limitations for readers to consider: subject content, time frame, and scope of literature reviewed.

The subject content is the literature and research of library and information science related to information access. By focusing on one subject content domain, it is possible to identify patterns in the research. These can be matched with research in compatible areas such as educational communication and technology. The time frame is approximately a 15-year span beginning in 1980. Some earlier work is examined, and reviews of research that cover earlier periods are included. The scope is reviews of research as the first focus, and specific studies secondarily. Reviews of research provide foundations for exploring patterns. Specific studies provide exemplars and point to new research areas.

25.3.1 RESEARCH ON USERS

User research has undergone significant changes in the past 25 years. It has moved from a field that primarily studied identifiable groups and focused on system-centered questions to a field that looks at individuals and focuses on user-centered behavior and questions. The current foundations encompass communications theory, social psychology, and cognitive psychology. Methodology is moving from sociological surveys toward qualitative techniques such as case studies, ethnographic research, and grounded theory. Quantitative methods from communications theory and cognitive psychology are also being applied.

Research about users has formed a significant part of the research in library and information science (Krikelas, 1983). Emphasis on user groups predominated the early research efforts (Hewins, 1990) and still accounts for a large portion of research. Because of the specific characteristics and problems of groups in different content areas, the research literature on user groups is scattered among many content areas from medical science to agronomy research. A research trend is to explore characteristics of individual users rather than focus on specific content groups. Since the late 1970s, suggestions for focusing on individuals in practical contexts has become prevalent (Wersig & Windel, 1985; Wilson, 1981, 1984). Research on how people, whether collectively or individually, fit into information access can be divided into three areas:

- *User studies,* which include characteristics of users, information on how different user groups function, and identification of user needs
- *Information seeking,* which includes cognitive processes used to access information, user search strategies, and differences between end users and search intermediaries
- *Information skills,* which include creating models of information skills functions and developing research on the information search process

25.3.1.1.   User Studies.   The most important body of literature on user studies is the review series appearing in the *Annual Review of Information Science and Technology*

(ARIST) since 1966. These reviews provide an overview of a research area over an extended period of time.

1966	Menzel	1972	Lin & Garvey
1967	Herner & Herner	1974	Martyn
1968	Paisley	1978	Crawford
1969	Allen	1986	Dervin & Nilan
1970	Lipetz	1990	Hewins
1971	Crane		

They show the development of a field study over more than 25 years. Earlier reviews detail how user studies began. Later reviews build on earlier reviews by evaluating their ideas and analysis schemes. In the beginning, these reviews appeared every year, then every 2 years, and most recently on an unscheduled basis with 4 to 8 years between reviews. Krikelas (1983) believes this may be due to erratic and all-encompassing definitions of what user studies constitute. Bates (1971), for example, includes catalog use, use of reference services, use of library materials, and general library attendance, in addition to information-gathering habits of scientists.   To examine current trends in user studies and definitions, this section elaborates on the two latest review articles (Dervin & Nilan, 1986; Hewins, 1990). An analysis of issues of concern related to user studies completes this section.

Dervin and Nilan (1986) review 1978 to approximately 1986, almost 8 years. They include all user studies since the previous review (Crawford, 1978).   They approximate 300 overall citations related to users but narrow their focus to conceptualizations that drive the research. Past reviews have shown that the field may have conceptual limitations. Menzel (1968) explains that theory from the social sciences should drive user research. Crane (1971), Crawford (1978), Lin & Garvey (1972), and Paisley (1968) discuss the development of theory or conceptual frameworks within the context of user studies. Lipetz (1970) focuses on a methodological issue: improving predictive value. Allen (1969), Herner and Herner (1967), and Martyn (1974) ask for methodological choice and attitudinal perspectives.

Dervin and Nilan (1986) say the current literature, 1978–86, has a number of critical essays calling for reassessments of the type of research and a particular concern for conceptualization. They see two distinct areas: need for theory and need for better definitions and premises. They believe that definition is preliminary to theory and should be developed first. They state that innovative work in the time frame of the review does concentrate on definition.

Four research changes for user studies are identified. The first is to increase the match between information systems and users to serve the client better. This would result in greater accountability and fewer underserved clients. Their second research change would focus on user needs and uses. This would result in the user as a central issue for research, not the system or the technology. Their third research change would redesign the system to look more closely at person-machine links. Their fourth research change would focus on the technology of user access.

Dervin and Nilan (1986) also discuss their beliefs about changes in user studies research. Much of the work is the same as before (looking at users in terms of systems), but some research seems to represent a different direction (looking specifically at users). A common systems study looks at the degree that a user has actually used a system or systems, identifies barriers to the use of the system, or identifies satisfaction with attributes of the system. This research has also looked at demographics, sociological components, and life-style tasks. Problems with these types of studies have included ill-defined terminology and terms used interchangeably. They suggest that this systemic emphasis results in six approaches to needs assessment:

1. How much do users use the system?
2. How aware are users of the system?
3. What do users like and dislike?
4. What are the users priorities for information?
5. What are users interests, activities, and group involvement?

Researchers trying to change user studies suggest an alternative approach. Dervin and Nilan (1986, pp. 13–16) develop seven categories to contrast differences between the traditional and alternative approaches they believe are beginning to take hold in user research:

1. Objective vs. subjective information
2. Mechanistic, passive vs. constructivist, active users
3. Trans-situationality vs. situationality
4. Atomistic vs. wholistic views of experience
5. External behavior vs. internal cognitions
6. Chaotic vs. systematic individuality
7. Quantitative vs. qualitative research

Hewins's (1990) review updates Dervin and Nilan (1986) and reasserts the belief that research has shifted from sociological to psychological. Hewins's review states that Dervin and Nilan proposed a change from traditional empirical studies to user studies that provides rational frameworks and systematic bases for methods and definitions. Hewins restates Dervin and Nilan's belief that three new approaches are emerging: (1) user values, (2) sense making, and (3) anomalous states of knowledge (ASK). These new approaches focus on identifying user characteristics rather than on measuring system performance. In addition, Hewins says studies from the past have a common framework in that they are sociological or system based. The study of groups and the design of appropriate systems formed the foundation for the earlier work in user studies.

Hewins (1990) believes that few innovative methods have been developed, because questionnaires and surveys are still the norm. Dervin and Dewdney's (1986) time-line–critical-events approach is described as a new and interesting methodology. The National Library of Medicine's (1988) solution development record, a variation on critical-incident methods, is also discussed. In summary, Hewin (1990) states that new cognitively based approaches include categorization techniques, long- and short-term memory, learning styles, motivation, personality types, and semantic factors. The need for more interdisciplinarity is discussed.

After reading both Hewins (1990) and Dervin and Nilan (1986), it is apparent that a change is taking place in the study of users, systems, and their interaction. This seems to reflect general changes taking place in the way educational researchers and scholars view research. There has been more emphasis on qualitative methodology, a swing from behavioral to cognitive psychology, and a greater tolerance for deriving theory from a broad spectrum of research areas.

User surveys, the most common method of data collection in user studies, are reviewed by Verhoeven (1990) and reflect some of the same issues discussed by Dervin and Nilan. Both methodological and conceptual problems with the user survey are discussed. Issues such as incomparable results, lack of generalizability, and confounding methods are examined. In a general review of research findings from surveys over time, Verhoeven reports the following:

- In public libraries, adult users are well educated; 20% of the population accounts for most of the adult use.
- Younger library users used public libraries almost exclusively for course work.
- On-line catalogs are popular.
- Microfilm has been dissatisfying to people who wear glasses.
- People who do not use libraries have no need or no time.
- Friends and colleagues are preferable to libraries for seeking information.
- Considerable variability exists in information-seeking behavior. One persons' easy search can be most difficult for another (p. 391).

New approaches to the user survey can be divided into two general areas: (1) improving surveying techniques, (2) finding new directions (Verhoeven, 1990). The first type of researcher turns to surveys as a research area. The attempt is to find out why traditional surveys do not work. The next step would be to use this knowledge to design better surveys. The second approach looks at a different aspect. Traditional surveys were predominantly questionnaires that examined user satisfaction and user interaction with specific researcher-generated services. A new research focus is to identify the situations that prompted the user need. The information problem is examined from the user rather than the system perspective. Verhoeven defines the first approach as positivistic and the second approach as phenomenological. The ongoing conflict between the two methods is summarized in this way:

> Some commentators believe that, although the phenomenologists have destroyed positivist underpinnings, they have proffered little to put in their place. . . . On the other hand, there are those who find it not unreasonable to continue asking library users about their experience with libraries . . . (p. 394).

Applegate (1993) is one of the researchers suggesting a new method for determining user needs. Three models of user satisfaction are evaluated in the 1993 article: (1) material satisfaction model, (2) emotional satisfaction model–simple path, and (3) emotional satisfaction model–multiple path. In material satisfaction models, measures of product performance such as recall and precision are the determiners of user satisfaction. This can often lead to false positive conclusions where the product performs well but users are not necessarily satisfied. Simple-path emotional models are built on measuring users levels of satisfaction through direct and indirect questions to the user such as, "Are you satisfied with the results of your search?" Again, a false positive can result. Users express satisfaction but have received poor results from the search. The multiple-path model uses both user satisfaction responses and additional factors such as setting and expectations.

These three models have implications for research in user satisfaction. Applegate (1993) suggests that researchers should clearly specify what definition of satisfaction they are measuring. Secondly, more standardized instruments for data collection are recommended. Finally, multipath models such as that described above are suggested as explaining more complexity in user satisfaction.

There also appear to be other areas where user studies research could direct greater effort. One of the issues Hewins (1990) addresses is that studies which are site, system, or service specific and that do not contribute to method, theory, or model building are not covered in the review. On the surface this seems reasonable. On the other hand, this may not fully represent local knowledge and the development of grounded theory. Informal and formal case studies can provide valuable information about site-specific user characteristics and needs. From the description, it is difficult to know what was not included in this review. However, further use of techniques that gather and develop theory from local knowledge, such as action research (see 9.7.5), might prove useful for research in user studies.

User-need studies look at the user and what she or he brings to the situation. The studies also need to examine social constraints, cultural influences, and the effects of demographic variables such as age, gender, and class. Chen and Herndon (1982) is one of the landmark research studies in user needs. One issue from the Chen and Herndon study that is still relevant today is underserved populations. They found two especially relevant groups to consider: (1) users who are not using library and information center services, and (2) users who are not able to use library and information center services. For example, in their survey many elderly users were not able to answer the questions asked, so their information needs were not known. A more recent study by Metoyer-Duran (1993b) demonstrates that for minority populations, the source of information can serve as gatekeeper to access for both the individual and the community.

Reneker (1993) sums up the basic problems with user studies in this way:

> [This research] leaves one with little more than a sense of what kinds of materials are used by specific groups of

scholars, researchers, or students. Most of these studies attempt to relate specific variables to particular pieces of information-seeking tasks or behaviors (p. 488).

The previous research of user studies was focused on systems and founded in sociological traditions both theoretical and methodological. The reason ARIST reviews in this area are becoming fewer and farther between may be that a new area of research is emerging which combines aspects of users with other research issues. Research focusing on the individual user rather than on groups is discussed in the "information seeking" section that follows.

25.3.2 Information Seeking

Information seeking is an active process: ". . . it begins when someone perceives that the current state of possessed knowledge is less than that needed. . . . [It] ends when that perception no longer exists" (Krikelas, 1983, p. 7). Researchers who study information seeking are looking at more than the specific user variables that relate to the system as described in the user studies above. Information-seeking researchers want to know the individual strategies and techniques users employ to look for and find answers. They are asking complex questions and using theories and methods that can provide breadth and depth to the answers. Two theoretical positions are foundational in information-seeking research: communication theory (Dervin, 1983a, 1983b, 1989b) and cognitive psychology (Belkin, 1990; Ingwersen, 1992; Reneker, 1993). In addition, two types of users are commonly considered by the information-seeking researcher: the end user and the search intermediary. End users are individuals who want to answer their own questions and use the information resources independently. Intermediaries are trained librarians who interpret users' questions and problems. Information seeking and search strategies can be different depending on who is seeking and searching.

The sense-making theory of Brenda Dervin and colleagues is founded in communication research and builds on constructivist principles (Savolainen, 1993). Its strength is that it is a programmatic research effort conducted over time, systematically examining problems and issues in information seeking and use (Dervin, 1983b, 1989a, 1989b). It focuses on a user-centered rather than a system-centered approach. In sense-making theory, sense-making behavior is considered to be communicating behavior. The theory has been tested over a series of 40 empirical case studies of information seeking and use. (A detailed discussion of Dervin's research is found in a later section of this chapter.)

A new trend in information-seeking research uses qualitative approaches, specifically ethnography (see 40.2; Reneker, 1993) and grounded theory (see 40.2.1; Ellis, 1993; Ellis, Cox & Hall, 1993). This research attempts to examine complex issues and provide information on the nature and effects of information seeking. These researchers want to go beyond superficial or surface layers. Reneker (1993), in a study of information seeking among academics, used a set of 2,050 information-seeking incidents as a foundation for analysis. These activities were drawn from personal, social, scholarly, academic, work-related, political, and other arenas. Conclusions from the study showed that information seeking is a part of daily tasks and relationships. It can result both from an articulation of a need and from available information.

Ellis (1993) and Ellis et al. (1993) used grounded theory to examine, respectively, the information-seeking patterns of academic researchers and to compare researchers in the physical and social sciences. The results of their research are the outlining of different categories to represent information-seeking patterns for four content specialists: social scientists, physicists, chemists, and English literature researchers. After analysis, the following six categories were developed for social scientists: starting, changing, browsing, differentiating, monitoring, and extracting. For physicists, five categories were identified: initial familiarization, chasing, source prioritization, maintaining awareness, and locating. The study of chemists identified eight categories: starting, changing, browsing, differentiating, monitoring, and extracting (the same as the social scientists), plus verifying and ending. The English literature researchers resulted in six categories also: starting, surveying, chaining, selection and sifting, assembly, and dissemination. Ellis states that even though different terminology and slightly differing numbers of categories were identified, they can be considered to represent fundamentally the same activities.

Another information-seeking research area focuses on information seeking within the context of electronic technologies. Marchionini, Dwiggins, Katz, and Lin (1993) exemplify studies conducted in this area. They review four previous studies and discuss implications for various types of users. They describe information seeking as a problem-solving activity and look at both content area experts and search intermediaries. They focus on five factors: an information seeker, an information problem/setting, a knowledge domain, a search system, and a set of outcomes. They conclude that content experts focused on search strategies that emphasized content, while search intermediaries were problem driven.

New studies (Reneker, 1993; Ellis, 1993) in information seeking are quoting the Dervin and Nilan (1986) review of user studies literature to verify that a paradigm shift has occurred. To date, no one has actually validated the assertion with an analysis of the literature or articulated the common components of the new paradigm. It seems that one statement has been influential in directing the beliefs of other researchers. These beliefs need to be confirmed through further analysis and study. With the exception of the Dervin sense-making studies, there are few longitudinal studies creating a body of sustained knowledge. Each researcher creates unique categories of the seeking process. Attempts to integrate the various points of view or to discuss the commonalities and differences between the results would be a valuable addition to the information-seeking literature. Research studies based on these common categories or focusing on the impact of theoretical differences could help extend the knowledge base of information-seeking research.

25.3.3 Information Skills

Information skills research is primarily undertaken within the context of school library media centers. It seeks to ". . . define the nature and scope of information processes" (Eisenberg & Spitzer, 1991, p. 265). Scholarly activity in this arena can be divided between model development and information skills process research. Cutlip (1988), Eisenberg and Berkowitz (1990), Irving (1985), Loertscher (1988), and Stripling and Pitts (1988) fall into the first category. Kuhlthau (1983, 1988, 1993b) is an example of a researcher with a systematic program in information skills: the information search process.

Kuhlthau has explored stages of the information search process through use of qualitative research methods to build grounded theory. Both affective and cognitive aspects of the process were developed based on longitudinal observations and interviews with high school students, public library users, and others. (A detailed discussion of Kuhlthau's work can be found in a later section of this chapter.)

Bartolo and Smith (1993) used Kuhlthau's information search process (ISP) theoretical model in a study of manual and on-line search methods in university journalism classes. The focus was on interdisplinarity, and the method was an eclectic mix of techniques. They found that: "the superior performance of the on-line group over the manual group supports the authors' hypothesis that on-line search methods are more effective than manual search methods in helping researchers handle the challenges of interdisciplinary work . . ." (p. 351).

Work in information skills and the development of research studies and a research agenda is emerging. Treasure Mountain Research Retreat 5 (Barron, Grover & Loertscher, 1994) shows future directions for information skills research including: further model development, longitudinal studies of integrating information skills with content areas, and alternative assessment measures.

25.3.4 Summary of Issues Related to User Research

Many of the early studies within user research are descriptive. They delineate characteristics of users and their needs. The populations of focus were groups of users such as chemists, doctors, and agronomists. The subject of focus was how the systems were used by these groups. Over time the emphasis shifted to look at more complex issues and began to examine the cognitive strategies of individuals. Models of user search strategies were created. Currently, the emphasis has shifted again to a qualitative focus. There are attempts to derive models from behavior rather than creating models to fit behavior. The greatest needs in user research are to integrate the results from studies and to develop long-term research agendas and projects. The work of Brenda Dervin and Carol Kuhlthau provide exemplars of longitudinal research based in strong theory and methodology.

There are also problem areas and questions that need to be more fully addressed in user research. Issues of use of libraries and information centers by social class (see 6.4.2), ethnicity, gender (see 9.5.4), and age are still underrepresented in the research. Characteristics of these users and issues of effectiveness, access, and satisfaction could use more concentrated study. Younger children are also underrepresented as subjects of research. Emphasis seems to be predominantly in academic settings or with professional people. Studying users of library and information centers may focus on the available pool rather than on the possible pool. Extending the populations studied to nonlibrary users and nontraditional information users, and focusing on people as well as institutions and systems, could increase the range and usefulness of user needs research.

Ongoing research issues in user studies include identifying what is user research, defining terms, and differentiating between a system in which users are a component and research that concentrates on users. Researchers who focus on specific user characteristics such as information search strategies or the information skills process often incorporate access issues into their research. This section has identified the specific issues related to users who influence the research process. In the next section, patterns related to the access of information are explored. This chapter identifies common components in each area first. It examines how theory and methods are being applied to solving specific problems related to users, access, and information. Comparing similarities, differences, and potential for future studies can isolate trends and commonalities for application to library and information center problems.

25.4 RESEARCH ON ACCESS

Research on access in the context of this chapter focuses on the point of access and the surrounding environment. Current research emphasizes electronic technologies, the design of those technologies, and users' beliefs about the technologies. However, issues of workspace, facilities use, and public policies must also be considered part of access research. Access has technical and social issues impacting on how users access information. Scholarly literature in the context of access relates to design, implementation, and planning. Discussions of access issues often iterate what has been done and result in prescriptions based on logic, common sense, or rationality (e.g., Vickery & Vickery, 1993). These writings are the application of local knowledge to solving general problems such as choosing workstation locations, providing effective sign systems, or deciding on the location for a new library building. Access research also draws on theory from other disciplines and applies findings from human factors, human-computer interaction, cognitive science, and cognitive ergonomics to library and information center problems.

While research on users has been a significant component of library research for many years, LIS research on access issues is a growing field. Researchers are exploring theoretical foundations and developing research agendas.

Much of the research has focused on aspects of technologies such as on-line public access catalogs and on-line search services. The range of potential research questions in access is also influenced by the research on users. Issues that may influence access include all of those characteristics, needs, and components that were part of user research. This review focuses on research and issues that are founded in LIS literature. Some sections include discussions of directions for future research rather than results of research. There are still many unknowns about access point issues and how the environment impacts information use.

Research on access and the components that affect access can be divided in four areas:

1. *The access point,* which includes interface and screen design aspects of human computer interaction and common access technologies
2. *The work and use space,* which focuses on decisions about using an access point and use of the space for working once chosen
3. *The building and facilities space,* which looks at physical access issues such as handicapped access and cognitive issues such as sign systems
4. *The outside environment,* which could look at physical access issues such as geographic availability and public policy or social issues

25.4.1 The Access Point

The point at which the user and the gateway to information come into contact is referred to in this chapter as the access point. Two aspects of research on the access point will be examined: the human-computer access point interface and the technologies of access. The technologies of access discussed include:

- On-line public access catalogs (OPACs or PACs)
- On-line search services (e.g., DIALOG, BRS, Internet)
- CD-ROMs and optical media
- Full-text databases, including hypermedia and multimedia applications

The focus in this section on the technologies of access will be the way in which they relate to the user. In the following section on information, the internal construction of information stored in the technologies will be discussed. This section then examines cognitive aspects of access, while the information section looks at engineering and mechanical aspects of access, specifically the storage and retrieval of information.

25.4.1.1. Human-Computer Interactions to Access Information. Users can access information directly. They can read a book, view a videotape, listen to a recording, go to the zoo, or enjoy a painting in a museum. These are direct-access interactions between a user and a specific item. This section looks at interactions that have been created to help users access large bodies of collected information. There are two predominating areas of literature in human-computer interaction. The first is advice, models based on practice, and examples of what seems to work. The second is psychologically based research, examining aspects of the interaction but specifically focusing on cognitive components of the user interface (see 21.4). This review examines the second type of literature, psychologically based research founded in LIS. The predominant research foundation for design and development in LIS is cognitive science.

Allen (1991) reviews the research implications of cognitive science in LIS for the design of information systems such as access points (for earlier reviews of cognition, human-computer interaction, and LIS, see Borgman, 1984, 1986; Daniels, 1986). The beginnings of cognitive research in LIS are believed to have originated in the International Workshop on the Cognitive Viewpoint in Ghent, 1977 (Belkin, 1990). From these origins, a design and research agenda was developed which continues to influence the development of user interfaces and human-computer interactions in LIS. This program is to improve information access and information transfer by developing models of users' knowledge that can be integrated with information system structures. The focus is on the point at which the user and the system come into contact: the access point.

Four types of knowledge related to users and cognitive models are suggested by Allen (1991): world knowledge, system knowledge, task knowledge, and domain knowledge. Each of these has implications for the interactions between users and systems. In addition, cognitive processes such as cognitive load, learning, memory, and problem solving are discussed and related to user knowledge. The methods used to research these issues are drawn directly from cognitive science. For example, Hancock-Beaulieu (1990) used interviewing and think-aloud protocol analysis in a problem-solving situation related to on-line catalog searching. Users adapted their search strategies and proceeded through a number of different stages in their attempts to interact with the public catalog system. The implications for design of access technologies from this study include developing on-line help for initially constructing a search strategy.

Allen (1991, pp. 23–24) concludes the review of cognitive research in LIS by identifying significant research issues for ongoing implementations:

- The need through further research efforts to increase the understanding of how cognitive processes, such as cognitive load, contribute to information behavior
- A continuing focus and ongoing research on knowledge-based information retrieval and the creation of prototype systems
- The development and testing of interface designs to guide search strategy creation and intelligent tutoring systems
- Greater emphasis in applying understandings of domain and task knowledge to increase the quality of information retrieval systems

Allen's review examined the agenda setting and research foundations of cognitive science in the design and development of LIS access points. The research discussed below looks specifically at the interface design and draws on the literature from human factors and ergonomics.

Shneiderman (1987) laid out three types of human-computer interaction: commands, menus, and direct manipulation. Research has compared and contrasted these interactions. Results have been mixed and inconclusive. Smith (1988) found that a menu improved performance with both novice and experienced users. Spavold (1990), working with 9- to 11-year-olds, also found that menus were more effective than command modes, as did Canter, Powell, Wishheart, and Roderick (1986) when studying novice users. However, Paap and Roske-Hofstrand (1988), in summarizing studies of menu-based vs. command interfaces, conclude that novice users find commands more natural than menus. Taylor (1986) offered a choice, and 60% chose the menu mode, which shows preferences but does not confirm effective access.

The mixed results reported above could be due to comparisons of command languages with menus exhibiting different features. Menus have changed and developed over time, with features becoming both more complex and simpler depending on the application. Research issues related to menus include: order of reading (MacGregor & Lee, 1987a, 1987b), vertical position (Allen, 1983), depth and breadth (Lee & MacGregor, 1985), size of categories represented (Paap & Roske-Hofstrand, 1988), and categorical rather than alphabetical presentation (Hollands & Merikle, 1987). Research comparisons need to take into account these and other features as significant variables when comparing menus with command languages.

Direct manipulation is a more recent interaction category. It includes characteristics such as continuous representation of the object and physical actions that show an impact on the object that is both immediately visible and reversible. Ziegler and Fahnrich (1988), in a review of empirical studies, indicate that using a mouse to manipulate objects can cause problems for novice users. Chiang (1989) compares commands, menus, and direct manipulation, and concludes that direct manipulation may help overcome both conceptual and mechanical problems.

Another ongoing research area in human-computer interfaces is the creation of evaluation mechanisms. Nielsen and Molich (1989) report a heuristic evaluation process for user interfaces. Chin, Diehl, and Norman (1988) discuss the development of QUIS (Questionnaire for User Interaction Satisfaction), which has demonstrated reliable results over time. Hartson and Hix (1989) discuss the impact of rapid prototyping on ongoing interface evaluation. Gomoll (1990) lays out the 10 steps used at Apple Computer for observing user/computer interactions.

Shaw (1991) provides an overall review of the human-computer interface in information retrieval for LIS applications. The general principles of interface design are discussed, including display features, modes of interactions, and help/system messages. Research related to these three areas is examined, and implications for LIS research are discussed. Specific interfaces for information retrieval are also identified. Implications of these systems, such as on-line searching, CD-ROM, and on-line catalogs, are discussed in the following section.

25.4.2 Technologies of Access

Within LIS, the longest tradition of research on technologies of access relates to on-line search services and on-line public access catalogs (OPACs). It is only within the last few years that research has extended to other technologies such as CD-ROMs and more optically based information platforms. In addition, full-text access—including hypermedia/multimedia applications with sound, visuals, and moving images—is an emerging area. Internet (an example of an on-line search service with particular features) will also result in research related to access technologies.

25.4.2.1. On-Line Public Access Catalogs (OPACs).
OPACs were replacements for card catalogs. They began as card catalogs represented on a computer screen. Initially OPAC interfaces were not much different from those associated with traditional card catalogs. Due to economic conditions and user preferences, OPACs have developed features different from card catalogs. Some OPACs are incorporating on-line search services, electronic encyclopedias, and other full-text and multimedia applications. Research compares different types of OPACs, looks at similar features, and creates generalizations for the further development of better OPACs (Cochrane & Markey, 1985; Matthews, 1986).

Larson (1991) reviews research related to subject searching in the on-line public-access catalog (OPAC). Lack of effective subject access is identified as a primary problem with OPACs. The needs of users for subject searching are examined. Subject searching accounts for more than half of all searches in on-line catalogs, and two problems are most common. Search failure occurs when users fail to identify information relevant to the questions they wish answered. Information overload occurs when the responses to a question are overwhelming in number. Four forms of enhancements for OPACs are recommended to improve subject access: classification changes, subject heading revisions, keyword searching improvements, and special indexes such as subject thesauri. Earlier reviews summarizing aspects of OPAC research and study include Borgman (1986), Cochrane and Markey (1983), Lunde and Copeland (1989), and Markey (1984).

On-line public access catalogs (OPACs) draw together many issues of relevance to researchers in LIS. OPACs are used to study user behavior, human-computer interfaces, information retrieval mechanisms, and record design (Yee, 1991). Earlier in this chapter, research about user behavior and interface design was discussed. Later in this chapter, research related to information retrieval and record sets will be discussed. This section examines research in how OPACs perform as a system and how users interpret their interactions with the system. The focus of these research studies is on the OPAC. It includes issues such as users perceptions and beliefs on how well OPACs work.

Early studies of OPACs included Hildreth's (1982) study of the computer-human interface as a window. It investigated aspects of the technology. Matthews, Lawrence, and Ferguson (1983), in a classic study for the Council of Library Resources (CLR), analyzed user requirements and behavior. The study determined users' attitudes and levels of satisfaction about on-line catalogs. Replications of the CLR study included Steinberg and Metz (1983) at Virginia Tech and Baldwin, Ostrye, and Selton (1988) at the University of Wyoming.

A problem with card catalog studies was location, specific findings, and methods. The sites and the instruments were unique. It was difficult to draw conclusions and generalizations from the data collected. The CLR research provided a standard data collection instrument that could be used across situations and ensured that all users responded to the same set of questions (Broadus, 1983).

OPAC user research has consistently applied two methods: surveys and questionnaires (e.g., Matthews et al., 1983) and transaction log analysis (e.g., Kaske, 1988; Nielsen, 1986; Peters, 1989; Tolle, 1983). Focus groups (e.g., Markey, 1983), protocol analysis (e.g., Sullivan & Seiden, 1985), and observation (e.g., Solomon, 1993) have also been used. The survey questionnaire is the most popular research method for studying on-line catalog use in LIS (Peters, 1991). Surveys measure what users know, believe, and think about OPACs. Surveys can also ask for reports of behavior.

Actual behavior at an OPAC is most often measured through the use of transaction log analysis. This type of analysis can be accomplished at the macro- or microlevel. Macro-analysis combines information about OPAC usage and patterns (e.g., Kaske, 1988). Micro-analysis looks at how individual users make choices and the patterns of their searches (e.g., Tolle, 1983). Discussion of the merits and problems with transaction analysis constitutes a significant scholarly area in OPAC research (e.g., Cochrane & Markey, 1983; Crawford, 1987; Hildreth, 1985; Markey, 1983; Weiskel, 1986).

Research has included aspects of the technology and information about beliefs of the users related to OPACs. Research on the technology of OPACs has resulted in a mixture of findings:

> . . . the computer as an information retrieval tool solved some problems (e.g., keyword access to individual terms in author, title, and subject-heading fields), created others (e.g., inability to browse subjects, titles, and authors), and left some untouched (e.g., the provision of subject headings in the catalog that correspond to the language of users) (Solomon, 1993, p. 245).

Users studies have been more consistent in findings. Most library users report that they accept and like on-line catalogs (Peters, 1991).

Two studies of OPAC use are discussed to demonstrate trends in OPAC research. Solomon (1993) conducted a naturalistic study of elementary children's use of an OPAC. It is an example of qualitative research methods and theory that are beginning to be seen in many aspects of LIS research. Dalrymple and Zweizig (1992) completed a factor analysis of affective data gathered in comparing traditional card catalog use with OPAC use. It is an example of applying a quantitative analysis not generally used in LIS research to studying information access.

Research examining children's OPAC usage is limited (e.g., Borgman, Gallagher, Krieger & Bower, 1990; Borgman, Ballagher, Walter & Rosenberg, 1991; Marchionini, 1989; Edmonds, Moore & Balcom, 1990; Walter & Borgman, 1991). Solomon's (1993) study is the most in-depth analysis of issues about children's OPAC usage and information retrieval patterns to date. The results of the study are based on approximately 900 transactions performed by about 500 students over the course of a school year. Recommendations for adding features that enhance children's OPAC use were suggested.

Solomon (1993) observed occasions of success using the OPAC (66% of the transactions) and occasions where breakdown occurred. Three factors contributing to success were: finding assistance, applying search strategies, and using common terms. Breakdown exhibited more complex situations including knowledge, rules, and skills breakdowns. Each of these three areas were further analyzed into specific categories.

The process of OPAC searching was also examined, including initiating actions, intentions, opening moves, and search strategies. Specific examples from the observations and extended analyzes of these categories were provided. For example, it was found that first-graders were more likely to use assistance as a search strategy than sixth-graders. Based on this study, Solomon (1993, p. 263) suggests that information retrieval systems for children should provide:

- Specific user tools (e.g., subject domains and their underlying content structures)
- General user mechanisms (e.g., navigation tools to explore a subject heading domain)
- Management tools (e.g., interactive programs to add locally generated cross-references

Dalrymple and Zweizig (1992) compared card catalog use with use of an OPAC. There were 20 subjects in each group, and each group was assigned the same problems to solve. After completing searches, subjects evaluated the results of the search and filled out an attitude questionnaire. Separate factor analysis solutions on the 11 attitude questions were completed for each group. The on-line catalog group yielded two strong factors: benefits, which explained 54% of the variance, and frustration, which explained 31% of the variance. The card catalog group analysis resulted in similar factors: frustration, which explained 27% of the variance, and benefits, which explained 43% of the variance.

In addition, these attitudinal dimensions were compared with reformulation behavior (trying the search in different ways), user beliefs about the results of their searches, and perseverance measures. Reformulation showed a positive relationship in the on-line group, with feelings about benefits of the system. Perseverance (spending longer times on the searches) showed a relationship with feelings of frustration for both groups.

The consistency of dimensions across groups, even though loadings as first and second factors were reversed, has implications for future research design. If benefits and frustrations are important components of users' attitudes toward information access with OPACs, they could be built into research designs to increase understanding of user behavior. Dalrymple and Zweizig (1992) suggest applying this research direction to search behavior, information systems design, and bibliographic instruction.

25.4.2.2. Other Access Technologies: On-Line Services, CD-ROM, Full Text, Multimedia. OPACs are an access technology unique to library and information center environments. The first OPACS were designed, developed, and sold by libraries. Today private vendors are the primary developers of OPACs. Researchers can examine different questions through the use of OPACs, such as information access, information retrieval, and user behavior. At one time, the research was applied directly to the design of OPACs. Now the research is used by developers in the design of other types of access technology including: on-line search services, CD-ROM and optical media, full-text databases, multimedia and hypermedia, and Internet.

Historically each of these other access technologies could be considered unique, like OPACs, with special features assigned to each technology. However, technological features are merging across technologies, and even OPACs have full-text and multimedia features. Some resources are available in different formats, such as ERIC on-line, ERIC on CD-ROM, and ERIC as paper index or electronic encyclopedias, which can be paper, CD-ROM, or accessed on an OPAC. The processes and strategies needed to access the information stored in these merging technologies are more similar than they are different.

Shaw's (1991) review examines research aspects related to these different technologies. On-line searching is particularly sensitive to issues of front-end and menu development. CD-ROM also has research questions surrounding interface diversity and different possibilities for front-end access. In addition, CD-ROM has large graphics storage capabilities and has design and research problems related to retrieval of visual and moving images. Full-text databases are also seen to have front-end scftware research implications for interfaces with the user. Another research agenda with full-text databases is comparison of electronic systems with their paper counterparts. Joseph, Steinberg, and Jones (1989) compared a print and on-line version of an army manual. They found that initially new users preferred the print index and table of contents. However, after experience with the on-line system, most users preferred the keyword search option from the electronic access. Two studies discussed below are also examples of comparisons of print and electronic access.

Shaw (1991) concludes the review by summarizing the issues and problems of research in human-computer interaction in LIS:

- Research in human-computer interactions is cross-disciplinary and requires searching a variety of resources for converging information.
- Significant gaps exist in understanding the relative value of interface features such as graphical interfaces and command-mode interactions. The research shows contradictory findings.
- The impact of cognitive styles, eye-hand coordination, and previous experience could be intervening variables to help understand the contradictory findings.
- There are differences among researchers about how and what to study related to human-computer interfaces in information environments (pp. 178–179).

Another significant factor in electronic-access technologies has been the change from their use by professional search intermediaries to their use by searchers who wish the information. The design and implementation of information resources whether on-line, CD-ROM, full text, or multimedia now considers the novice as well as the trained professional. This requires research on user interfaces, search strategies, and expert systems. The systems and features that worked for professionals who were willing to learn command languages and technical process such as Boolean strategies are not effective for end users (Mischo & Jounghyoun, 1987). With remote access and a home market, vendors need to develop features that help novices complete sophisticated and complex searches as end users. Recent research related to users and intermediaries has included: individual differences (Borgman, 1989), interactions between users and intermediaries (Kuhlthau, Spink & Cool, 1992; Saracevic, Mokros & Su, 1990), remote users (Kalin, 1991), search moves (Wildemuth, de Bliek, He & Friedman, 1992; Fidel, 1990), and user behaviors (Belkin, Chang, Downs, Saracevic & Zhao, 1990; Wildemuth, Jacob, Fullington, de Bleik & Friedman, 1991).

Research using CD-ROMs as the interface device is becoming more prevalent in LIS. Marchioni (1989; Marchionini & Liebscher, 1991) reported results on the use of electronic encyclopedias on CD-ROM. Marchionini (1989) examined elementary children searching on a full-text encyclopedia delivered via CD-ROM. Older searchers were more successful and took less time than younger searchers. Looking at search patterns showed that novices used highly interactive strategies. Marchionini and Liebscher (1991) looked at undergraduate student's mental models (see 5.3.7). These models were used to make quickly the transition from paper encyclopedias to a variety of electronic encyclopedias. Balaraman (1991) described a preliminary study examining the impact of individual differences on novice users of CD-ROMs. Large, Beheshti, Breuleux, and Renaud (1994) compared elementary students' use of a print and a CD-ROM encyclopedia. Four questions of differing complexity were searched by the students. The time

it took to complete the searches was approximately equal for both print and CD-ROM. Both groups exhibited good skills in choosing appropriate search terms. Students seemed able to use the CD-ROM interface with only a short training session.

Other electronic access devices that are of interest to LIS researchers include: computer conferencing (Rosenbaum & Snyder, 1991), electronic mail (Gluck, Coliz & Rosenbaum, 1991; Tsai, 1992), hypertext (Grumling, 1992; Marchionini, et al., 1990), Internet (Dillon, 1993), multimedia (Schamber, 1991), videotext (Case, 1991), and voice mail (Rice & Danowski, 1991).

25.4.3 The Work and Use Space

The environment immediately surrounding the access point has two implications for users. When approaching the access point (i.e., an OPAC, a CD-ROM, an Internet terminal, or a paper index), users make choices about whether or not they want to be in that space. Some characteristics of the immediate environment may interact positively with users' choice to try an access point, and others may create barriers or problems. Once at work or using an access point, the characteristics of the space, which enhance or inhibit ongoing use of the access technology, also will interact with the individual user.

Issues related to the first aspect of the access point environment, initial choice, have to do with affective considerations, physical necessities, and cultural preferences. The colors of the space, the height of the ceiling, the lighting, and the size of the space could influence users' affective responses. Particularly, types of physical spaces are necessary for effective use by disabled users, exceptionally tall or short people, children, and the aged. Cultural and personal preferences could affect how users react to very crowded spaces or very wide open spaces.

The use of access point space for work related to information access is also important to understanding what affects users. For example, provision of a sufficient writing area for taking notes, writing down citations, or opening indexes is critical to effective use of the access tool. Lighting and air quality may also impact use of the access space, particularly for users who work for long periods of time in one space. Long-term use of computer terminals also has implications for screen placement, keyboard height, chair design, and flexibility to rearrange and change the space.

There is little research in LIS about these aspects of information access (see 36.3). Most literature related to the use of access points or space is prescriptive or descriptive rather than research oriented. Suggestions are made for where to place OPACs in the overall library scheme, such as close to the entryway, by the reference desk, or next to the card catalog. Explanations of how particular libraries chose the color scheme for their children's room or the furniture for their CD-ROM stations are also part of the literature. Research either quantitatively or qualitatively based could be a valuable asset to understanding which aspects of the work and use space are significant factors in users' information access. Theories and methods from human factors research, such as the person-environment fit theory, could be effectively applied to use and workspace research.

25.4.4 The Building and Facilities Space

The immediate environment is critical in users' choice of a particular access point once a library or information center has been entered. It interacts with the user choosing the reference librarian, the OPAC, the CD-ROM, the card catalog, browsing, or any of a number of possible access points in a library or information center. The overall building and facility may impact whether or not a user chooses an access point in a library or information center or goes elsewhere.

Research on the relationship of buildings and facilities to information access is another area in which research is emerging. The following issues could be considered in conducting this research:

- Impact of physical access—not only disabled access but also elderly, children, and others
- Affective impressions of the building and its "friendliness"
- Sign systems and way finding, including maps
- Architectural design and its interaction with cultural and sociocultural preferences
- Availability of public transportation
- Parking space and ease of accessibility

25.4.5 The Outside Environment

Geographical access to a library or information center is also a critical component in use of the access point. Geographic access begins to interact with social and cultural factors particularly related to economics and class. Libraries are often built and maintained where they are supported by a strong economic or tax base. Some areas, particularly in urban environments, are considered to be safer for locating libraries than other areas. In rural areas, the available money may allow for only a few libraries within a large geographical area. These factors mean that some users may not have the money or the experience to travel to the sources of information. It may also mean that some users may never see the library as part of their neighborhood or social environment.

Making information available via remote access has become a way to meet user needs, as discussed above. State libraries have developed mail services for users who do not have easy access to a local library or information center. Phone reference services are available in most public and academic libraries. Newer technologies such as Internet, dial-in access to OPACs, and proprietary services such as America Online, Compuserve, and Prodigy are all attempts to widen access. The proposal for a national electronic highway is also a possible method for increasing access to information. Research stills needs to be conducted both on the issues of geographical access described above and whether or not remote access technologies will make a difference in socioeconomic equality for information access.

25.4.6 Summary of Issues Related to Research in Access

OPAC research is the strongest component of access research in LIS. User preferences, menu development, search strategies, and interactions between users and technologies have been essential to the OPAC research agenda. This research also uses a variety of methods including surveys, questionnaires, attitude studies, experimental research, and naturalistic inquiry. Theoretical foundations are primarily psychological, looking at the interaction of cognition and OPAC features or the social psychology of individual responses to OPACs. Research on OPACs can examine features and processes of interest to the use of other electronic technologies. As features merge in the new technologies, issues such as screen design, direct manipulation, subject access, and remote connections can be studied across technologies. The foundational research in OPACs can be used as a guide to the research in access to other technologies.

Literature and research related to cognition and technological access is spread across a wide interdisciplinary content spectrum and must be accessed using many different search terms (see 24.6):

> . . . cognitive engineering, cognitive ergonomics, computer-human interaction/interface (CHI), convivial computing, cooperative interface, human-computer interaction/interface (HCI), person-machine interface, software ergonomics, usability engineering, user friendly/cordial/oriented/centered, and user interface (Shaw, 1991, pp. 178–179).

This broad coverage of literature and research can result in difficulty accessing significant and relevant information on a specific aspect of human-computer interaction and its cognitive relationships. Another problem in cognitive research in LIS is generalizability of findings compared to applicability (Allen, 1991, p. 18). Research focusing on existing systems may lack generalizability, while research on more general cognitive processes may have limited applicability.

Another way to conceptualize access is to think of issues in terms of social technologies and mechanical technologies. The mechanical technologies are the things themselves: the physical hardware, desks, circulations stations, buildings, and parking spaces that people must use in order to access information. The social technologies are the processes that interact with the mechanical technologies. They are socially and culturally engineered features of access and include such things as interface design, human computer interaction, user preferences, and social acceptability. In examining LIS research and scholarly writing about access, an interesting pattern emerges. With the exception of OPACs, the design of the things is generally not part of LIS. The mechanical technologies are created by structural engineers, physicists, computer scientists, and human factors engineers. LIS research on mechanical technologies is conducted to provide information for others or to help find instructional solutions to increase effective access to mechanical technologies. It is the social technologies that interact and result in the use of the access technologies that is the focus of LIS research.

25.5 RESEARCH ON INFORMATION

In this section, information is examined as a tangible entity and a tangible process (Buckland, 1991, p. 6). The focus is on information as a thing that requires processing and organizing to provide access. Access to knowledge as enhanced or restricted by public policies and private usage is also discussed. Early work on information in LIS tended to be structural, with the focus on mathematics, linguistics, and logic representation. More recently, other aspects of information have become prevalent in the research. Searching for pictorial information, representing audio data in a database, and finding moving images have become part of the information substructure. These have enlarged the foundations used to understand, construct, and interpret information. This review examines three general areas that relate to the tangible aspects of information: (1) What is information? (2) How is information organized? (3) How is information controlled? Issues such as group uses of information, using information to generate knowledge or to become informed, and information seeking are discussed in other sections of this chapter.

25.5.1 What Is Information?

This section defines information in terms of its use in the access process and looks at common characteristics of information as discussed within LIS. Because of its position in this review, information is seen as it relates to users and access issues. The information presented in this section builds on that presented in other sections. Order of presentation can affect interpretation of information. The linear presentation suggests that users come first, then access, and then information. It implies a causal chain of events. Another reviewer could have presented information research first, then users, and finally access issues. One of the constituents of information might be relative position in the information access sequence.

The characteristics of information that are important in the context of information access as discussed in this chapter have to do with the ability to organize, structure, and retrieve information. Each type of information—textual, visual, moving, iconic—will have different characteristics that interact with the need to store and retrieve information. Until recently, most major information storage and retrieval systems focused almost exclusively on retrieval via words and numbers. Even pictorial information was assigned indexing terms (words) to aid in retrieving maps, pictures, and slides.

The addition of computers has changed both information that is stored and its organization and retrieval. This has implications for characteristics of information that are considered essential to represent in storage systems. Another change that has occurred is the storage of entire documents or other original materials, as opposed to surrogate representations (e.g., bibliographic citations, abstracts). Until recently, libraries, document rooms, museums, or other large facilities were required for storage of original materials. The characteristics of information that were important to represent had to do with physical descriptions, subject or content representation, and methods of retrieval. With new electronic capabilities to store original materials, the range of characteristics that must be considered and the organizational sophistication necessary for retrieval are more complex.

Another aspect of understanding what constitutes information has to do with philosophical assumptions about the nature of human beings and their relationship to information. One position among researchers is that information does not exist without human construction. No matter what the storage medium, the organizational structure, or the retrieval mechanisms, there is no meaning until an individual creates meaning. Among researchers who deal exclusively with information, mathematical representations, and database structures, there would be those who agree and those who disagree with this assumption.

One of the difficulties in discussing information is the need to tie information to the retrieval system employed. Often the structure of the database or storage system is designed with specific retrieval capabilities. Some ways to access information are not possible due to the original system design. For example, the Colorado Alliance of Research Libraries (CARL) only allows keyword access. There is no subject access capability. Searches for a subject such as *library research* include all the materials that have the keywords *library* and *research*. This could be "The *Library* of *Research* in Primate Behavior." Another system would allow the retrieval of only information that had the subject heading *library research*. Systems restrictions can create problems in information access. Retrieval systems must interface with humans and must respond to human logic and needs. Information storage systems must function within the limitations and physical characteristics of the hardware used. These two needs are not necessarily compatible. The limitations of the hardware can be imposed on the retrieval system rather than the system being designed to meet retrieval needs. This basic incompatibility creates dilemmas for researchers (Peters, 1991). Should the limitations of the system be researched and suggestions for improvement created? Should the needs of the user be explored and instruction developed to improve the users skills to access the system? Should some other combinations of factors be employed in the research process? The construction of information and its storage systems have implications for both users and access.

The concepts of value, utility, relevance, pertinence, and acceptability are also characteristics of information. It is possible to store all types of information. Everything from a child's finger painting on the refrigerator to a holographic image of a lion to complete sound and three-dimensional virtual reality of the Globe theater has the potential to be stored and retrieved. What actually is saved, the characteristics stored, the features considered unnecessary, and the method of storage have to do with decisions of value, utility, relevance, and acceptability. The decisions are affected by economic factors about who will pay for the initial storage, the long-term care, and the retrieval and maintenance costs. Information is sorted and discarded before it is ever stored. The characteristics of what should be saved related to what could be saved need to be considered.

To summarize what constitutes information: It is things (symbols, ideas, knowledge, wisdom, antelopes); it is the characteristics of those things (names, places, dates, subjects, content, values); and it is the process that is used to make decisions about which of those things actually are important or useful information (storing, saving, making available, selling).

25.5.2 How Is Information Organized?

Larson (1991) developed a four-part explanation of the functional components of an on-line public access catalog (OPAC) which described the steps that come between users and information:

- User interface
- Database management system interface
- Database management system
- Database

In a more generic sense, these four components can be used to account for all forms of information organization and will be used to guide the review of literature that follows.

Description of the user interface and associated research was discussed earlier in this chapter. It will be referred to here as it has bearing on information organization. Generically, the *user interface* must be conceptualized as human-human interactions, human-computer interactions, and all other forms of socially constructed human-information interactions (e.g., human beings using indexes, bibliographies, tables of contents, telephones, hypermedia nodes, Veronicas, Archies, gophers, and virtual-reality devices). The user interface is exactly what the user sees, hears, touches, and tries to interpret.

The *database system management interface* is hidden to the user. In an on-line public access catalog, it is the software that translates the information from the user interface into commands the system database manager can understand and handle. In human terms, the reference librarian could be considered a system management interface. The reference librarian helps the user interpret the language and structure of a system such as Social Sciences Citation Index or the Library of Congress Classification system.

In an OPAC, the *database system manager* is the software and sets of algorithms, rules, or heuristics that search the database and retrieve information. In noncomputer applications, sets of rules, algorithms, or heuristics that organize and provide a view into information could be considered system managers. For example, the Anglo-American Cataloging Rules II Revised, the Dewey Decimal Classification System, Library of Congress Subject Headings or any indexing system provides structure and process windows into specific bodies of information.

The *database* (storage system) in an OPAC consists of information chosen to represent a collection of materials. This information is stored in some predefined structure, with limitations on the type and extent of characteristics that can be included. All other information storage systems such as libraries, on-line databases, CD-ROMs, laser discs, videotapes, or maps have structures that limit storage possibilities. Only certain information is chosen to be included in an information set. Limited characteristics or values related to that information are provided to help retrieve the information. (Even in full-text databases, there are limitations on how much and what is included and how it may be searched.) Some predefined structure for storage is developed. The storage medium and technical process limitations on the structure also have implications for retrieval. In the next three sections, organizational schemes, structures and research related to systems interfaces, the systems themselves, and the storage of information are explored.

25.5.3 The System Manager Interface

Vickery and Vickery (1993, p. 160) review and describe many prototype and operational interfaces. Their conclusion demonstrates the variety of techniques that information science has contributed to system management interfaces. Listed below are techniques and examples of interfaces:

- Technique: Thesaurus relations and classification hierarchies
  Systems: MAI, CITE NLM, INSERM INTERFACE, TOME SEARCHER, METACAT, BIBLIOGRAPHY MANAGER, CANSEARCH, CIRCE, EDOR, DIANEGUIDE/NLA
- Technique: Stoplists
  Systems: FASIT, CITE NLM, TOME SEARCHER, CIRCE, METACAT, LEXIQUEST
- Technique: Recognition of suffixes and stemming
  Systems: FASIT, CITE NLM, ERLI/MINITEL, METACAT, BIBLIOGRAPHY MANAGER, DIANEGUIDE/NLA
- Technique: Formation of Boolean search statements
  Systems: TOME SEARCHER, CANSEARCH, EURISKO, DIANEGUIDE/NLA
- Technique: Manipulation of Boolean search statements
  Systems: QUESTQUORUM, CIRT
- Technique: Near matching of search terms rather than exact
  Systems: CIRCE, METACAT

- Technique: Calculation of term relevance, document weighting and ranking
  Systems: CITE NLM, CIRT, SABRE
- Technique: Query amendment by relevance feedback
  Systems: CIRCE, EURISKO
- Technique: Co-occurence of terms within documentary items
  Systems: LEXIQUEST, ESA ZOOM

The purpose of the system manager interface is to release human searchers from routine and technical acts of searching that can be effectively automated. Different system interface managers can be created for different users, such as expert searchers, end users, and novice users. Expert search intermediaries need system interfaces that help them access unfamiliar systems and databases. Experts have strong search skills but may need aid in applying those skills to new systems. End users and novice users are more likely to need system interfaces that aid them in choosing and using search strategies. End users need their natural-language queries translated into system language. Novice users need help in learning how to search. Expert systems are being developed as system management interfaces to provide multiple approaches for all levels of users. Specific examples of these systems are discussed in the next section on system managers.

25.5.4 The System Manager

The *system manager interface* and the *system manager* are conceptualized as performing different functions. Their definitions provide a viewfinder for thinking about information retrieval at different levels of mechanical access. In reality the differences can be difficult to separate. Functions are becoming merged due to technical advances and innovations. A program with the appearance of a system management interface may also serve as a system manager, and the reverse. The previous section briefly reviewed system interface techniques applied to information retrieval. This section details information retrieval research. A brief review of information retrieval history is followed by examining the two most prevalent retrieval methods: statistical/probabilistic and cognitive. Expert systems, hypermedia, and future issues in information retrieval conclude the discussion.

Scholars of information retrieval date its beginning to the early 1950s. The Cranfield projects (reviewed in Ellis, 1990, pp. 3–14) were early information retrieval research programs. They developed operationalizations for three dependent variables that are still used in retrieval research. These measures are recall, precision, and relevance. Relevance measures whether an item retrieved contains information to meet the search request (see Eisenberg, 1988; Park, 1993). Recall and precision are ratios that relate to relevance (see Buckland & Gey, 1994). Recall is the ratio of all relevant items in a data set to the number of relevant items that were actually retrieved by the search. For example, if a database contained 20 items about frogs, and 10 of those were

retrieved during a search, the recall for frogs would be .5. Precision is the ratio of the total number of documents retrieved to relevant items retrieved. For example, if a search resulted in 40 items, and 10 of those items were about frogs, the precision for frogs would be .25.

In the period following the Cranfield projects until the 1980s, intense debate in information retrieval surrounded the concept of relevance. Relevance is a judgment about whether or not a particular item meets the search request. Personal and economic factors can influence the judgment about an item's relevance. For example, in a study to test a new proprietary system that would automate the assignment of indexing terms, two differing judgments of relevance were found (reviewed in Ellis, 1990, pp. 1–3). The company's representatives found that the items retrieved were relevant. The representatives from professional indexing found the items retrieved less relevant. Each of these parties had personal and economic values attached to the outcomes. The company wanted to sell its product. The professional indexers may have seen the product as a threat to their livelihood. Another explanation would be that each group had different set points or standards about how much information was necessary in an item to achieve relevance. In relevance judgments, issues of variability (how much information is necessary for an item to be considered relevant) and consistency (can different individuals apply the criteria in the same way?) are critical and can effect judgments about what is relevant. Saracevic (1970, 1975) provides extensive reviews of the relevance controversy during the 1960s and early 1970s.

Current information retrieval research focuses in two areas: statistics and probability research (for an overview of issues see Belkin & Croft, 1987, and Fidel, 1987) and cognitive research (for reviews of current issues see Ingwersen, 1992, and Jacobs, 1993). Statistics and probability research uses techniques such as automated indexing, classification, searching, and abstracting. Statistics and probability measures are based on matching the query as expressed in the search statement with the representations in the database searched (query needs). They look at physical representations, mathematical probabilities, and logical rules. Cognitive research creates models of users (see 5.3.6), develops expert systems (see 24.8.1), and applies other methods to help the users match their needs with the system. Other techniques looking at the integration of users and information systems include user modeling, expert systems, and hypermedia applications (see 21.1). User modeling involves creating a representation of the user to interact with the system. Expert systems are designed to help the user understand and interact with the system more effectively. Hypermedia applications are designed to improve browsing, navigation, and user interaction capabilities (e.g., Chang & Rice, 1993; Newby, 1990).

Statistical and probability efforts can be divided in two types of retrieval techniques: exact matching and partial matching. Exact matching indicates that the search request and the items found in the database or retrieval set are identical.

Techniques such as Boolean searching, full text, and string matching represent exact matching. Most operational information retrieval systems are based on exact matching techniques.

Partial matching techniques are those where the retrieved documents or their representatives are not a complete match with the search request. Belkin and Croft (1987, p. 112) provide a schematic classification system that depicts types of partial match techniques and their relationships. The most frequently studied partial match techniques are: (1) networking techniques that look at groups of documents and include clustering, browsing and spreading activation, and (2) individual techniques that examine one item at a time and include fuzzy set, vector space, and probability techniques.

Networking Techniques
- Document clustering: Closely linked documents are relevant to the same requests (e.g., Willett, 1988).
- Browsing: User browses through nodes and connections in a network (e.g., Croft & Thompson, 1987).
- Spreading activation: Similar to browsing, but the system rather than the user activates parts of the network and their relationships (e.g., Cohen & Kjeldsen, 1987; Lee, Kim & Lee, 1993).

Individual Techniques

- Fuzzy set: Integrates Boolean queries with ranking techniques (e.g., Bookstein, 1985).
- Vector space: Represents documents by weighted term in dimensional space where each dimension corresponds to an index term (e.g.. Buckley & Lewit, 1985; Wilbur, 1992).
- Probability ranking principle: Similar to vector space, attempts to estimate how relevant a document will be to a search request (e.g., Bookstein, 1983; Croft, 1986).

Cognitive-based research in information retrieval looks at the interaction of the user and the information system. The attempt is to create, via system enhancements or changes, a better representation of the user request. Allen (1994) is an example of this type of research. Two experiments on the relationships between users' cognitive abilities and information system features were conducted. In each experiment, systems that included different approaches to the design of information were explored. In addition, cognitive abilities of participants were tested and randomly assigned to the different systems. A general linear modeling statistic (a statistic that combines features of ANOVA and linear regression) was used to test the hypothesis that there would be an interaction between system design and individual differences in cognitive ability. In one study, results showed an interaction between logical reasoning and order of presentation of references. In the other study, no interaction was discovered between perceptual speed and the way index terms were presented in browsable displays. Allen (1994) interprets these results for the overall design of information systems. System designers may wish to consider different orders of presentation as user-selected options to take into account the logical reasoning differences. On the other hand, since the browsable

displays showed no impact on search precision, other factors may be more relevant in the choice of browsing displays.

Belkin's anomalous states of knowledge (ASK) model (Belkin, 1980; Belkin, Oddy & Brooks, 1982a, 1982b) is an example of cognitive user modeling in LIS research. ASK looks at a network of associations between items on a database. Two aspects are critical: (1) the author's decision to communicate and (2) the users' decision to search and the decision that a particular item meets the search need. ASK relates to the second component. The searcher is aware of an anomaly in his or her state of knowledge about a problem or issue. The searcher examines items from a knowledge structure to interact with the searcher's request. This process continues until the ASK is resolved.

Two features underlie this cognitive approach to information retrieval: (1) construction of a model of the user of the system and (2) derivation of this model from cognitive characteristics of the user (Ellis, 1990, p. 67). The searcher interacts with a database via the creation of a model of her or his perceptions and requirements. In theory, conceptual associations are at the foundation of the model constructed. In reality, term associations are more likely to be used. Most of the research and development in this area are prototypes rather than operational systems.

Expert systems (see 24.8) and expert system intermediaries are more likely to be operational systems than user-modeling prototypes. Some expert systems have user-modeling components and some do not. Most expert systems are founded on assumptions about cognition and the user of the system (for reviews see Borko, 1987; Croft, 1987; Hawkins, 1988; Smith, 1987). Brooks says, "The influence of expert systems has shifted [information retrieval] research from a paradigm concerned largely with retrieval algorithms to one in which users, retrieval heuristics, knowledge, and human-computer interaction are key themes" (1987, p. 379). Expert systems have been influential in adding the users' perspective to information retrieval research. Expert systems engage users in dialogue to acquire a detailed request model or provide multiple retrieval techniques. Expert systems are used for query formulation, database selection, retrieval in subject domains, user modeling, and knowledge acquisition (Drenth et al., 1991).

Drenth et al. (1991) suggest three categories of expert systems that are under development in LIS: search advisors, intelligent front ends, and intelligent intermediaries. Search advisors teach users how to accomplish such tasks as search an on-line system. Intelligent front ends provide search tactics, search formulations, selection of terms, selection of databases, and search strategies. Intelligent intermediaries draw on knowledge of users and search tactics to interpret and elaborate search requests. They also use conceptual knowledge from the database or storage system. Information retrieval expert systems are primarily intelligent intermediaries (see Gauch, 1992, for an introduction to intelligent information retrieval). They serve to bridge the system gaps between the user and the stored information. Examples of expert system development in LIS include

Croft and Thompson, 1987; Fox, 1987; Gauch and Smith, 1993; Khoo and Poo, 1994; Shute and Smith, 1993.

I3R (Croft & Thompson, 1987) is an example of an intelligent intermediary expert system in information retrieval. I3R (Intelligent Intermediary for Information Retrieval) is a prototype system that optimizes the system's picture of the user's information need. It uses both probabilistic and clustering algorithms for retrieval. It also adds browsing, domain knowledge, and natural language processing. It is a multiple retrieval strategy system including both statistical and cognitive techniques. The system tries to build an accurate picture of the user's request by incorporating query analysis, domain knowledge, and browsing. This is then used with probabilistic and cluster retrieval techniques to retrieve documents through an inference process. User evaluation and further browsing provide a feedback loop to refine the request model and lead to more retrieval.

Multimedia- and hypermedia-based retrieval have looked at two functions: (1) integrating database management and information retrieval systems into a single model and (2) applying hypermedia as a browsing interface (retrieval by association). Agosti (1993) suggests that these new hypermedia retrieval models need to incorporate the concept of navigation as well as direct search. In one navigation model, Arents and Bogaerts (1993) developed a concept-based retrieval system that includes three-dimensional index navigation and semantic hyperindexing. They indicate that this type of navigation based on concept indexing could result in more effective retrieval of information in hypermedia environments.

Other LIS approaches to retrieval in hypermedia environments include plausible inference, subject browsing, and the use of classification systems. In most hypertext systems, retrieval can be accomplished through browsing or searching. In a plausible inference system (Lucarella & Zanzi, 1993), these two strategies are combined to increase retrieval effectiveness and search efficiency. Pollard, on the other hand, suggests improving efficiency in hypertext through the use of subject thesauri as navigational aids. The outcome is improved access to the subject content of the bibliographic database. Rada, Wang, and Birchall (1993) use a similar thesaurus approach in the development of their MUCH (Many Using and Creating Hypertext) system. Aboud, Chrisment, Razouk, Sedes, and Soule-Dupuy (1993) suggest the application of another traditional method from LIS to increase effective use of hypermedia. They describe a navigation approach that uses classification processess with the graphical interface. Selected nodes are ordered through their relevance, thus favoring some entry points in the database over others. This could reduce the disorientation to users in browsing space.

LIS retrieval research within hypermedia environments also addresses problems such as full-text retrieval, application of search strategies, and user interactions. Full-text databases create special problems for information retrieval via hypermedia methods. Browsing-based hypermedia systems may provide ease of access for beginners, but they often perform poorly with large document bases (Dunlop & van Rijsbergen, 1993). Dunlop and van Rijsbergen (1993)

conducted experiments to test a hybrid variation on the problems of browsing from large databases and retrieval through multimedia access. They used the results of the experiments to design a prototype system that minimizes the negative effects. Croft and Turtle (1993) examine another retrieval issue in hypertext: search strategies. They designed a probabilistic model based on inference nets. Results showed this retrieval strategy to be as effective as the more standard spreading activation technique. Belkin, Marchetti, and Cool (1993) designed a user interface that focused on user interactions for retrieval of bibliographic information. It used a two-level hypertext model and many different search strategies to increase interactions with users.

Whether the research is statistical/probabilistic or cognitive, whether the applications are expert systems, hypermedia, or another system, research in information retrieval has four ongoing areas of concentration:

- Operational systems compared to experimental systems
- Effectiveness of the different retrieval techniques
- Use of multiple strategies as opposed to a single-strategy search
- Retrieving information other than text

Belkin and Croft (1987) discuss the relationship between currently operational systems and experimental techniques. They ask ". . . why has the experimental experience had little effect on the operational environment?" (p. 112). It appears that most operational retrieval processes are based on exact-match retrieval and use Boolean, string searching, or full-text match as their basis. Suggestions for why new techniques are not applied include cost, time, and the need to learn to use new systems. In addition, the experimental techniques often have been tried on limited data sets and have not shown their effectiveness for large-scale database application. The addition of expert systems and hypermedia applications to LIS has increased the operational systems that used alternative retrieval methods.

All retrieval techniques seem to have certain areas where they are more effective. This leads to the belief that since current systems function, there is no need to add the time and cost of the experimental techniques. On the other hand, often experimental or theoretical techniques perform better than those in current use. Salton, Fox, and Vorhees (1986) found that, in general, partial-match techniques have been shown to respond better than exact match. One suggested reason is that cumulative results mask the effects of individual queries in comparison experiments. Information retrieval techniques are ways of comparing the search query with the document (or item) to be retrieved. Representations of items (e.g., citations, abstracts) interact with retrieval techniques and influence the retrieval of relevant items.

One of the consistent findings across retrieval research is that use of multiple retrieval strategies are more effective than use of a single strategy (e.g., Saracevic & Kantor, 1988b). Expert systems are one method for providing users with access to multiple retrieval strategies. Ongoing issues in this research are how to choose the strategies that will be accessed for any particular search and which strategies should be made available (Belkin & Croft, 1987).

New areas of retrieval that go beyond text and document retrieval are being explored, particularly in expert system, multimedia, and hypermedia environments. Other research areas include: pattern recognition, image matching, numerical representation, and chemical structures. A complete listing of new research areas in information storage and retrieval is provided at the end of the "Information Storage and Structure" section.

25.5.5 Information Storage and Structure

Information storage is a highly technical area of research and development in LIS. Because of its complexity and depth, the literature and research of how materials are stored will not be extensively addressed in this review. Key issues are briefly discussed below. Interested readers can find entry points to the literature in the following: Burt and Kinnucan, 1990; Fox, Levitin, and Redman, 1994; Lancaster and Warner, 1993; Meadows, 1992; Pao, 1989; Soergel, 1985; Tremblay, 1985; Wiederhold, 1987.

The storage of information is related to characteristics of the information such as format, size, and retrieval needs. These characteristics can interact with the different types of information storage:

- Information representations (e.g., subject headings, descriptive cataloging, bibliographic citations, sound bytes, thesauri, abstracts)
- Original materials (e.g., books, videotapes, maps, speeches, holograms)

An OPAC, an on-line search service such as ERIC, and a bibliographic index such as *Psychology Abstracts* could be considered storage of representations of original materials. A library, a full-text database, a CD of Martin Luther King's speeches, or a museum could be considered storage of original materials.

Creating, organizing, and storing representations of information is a core area of LIS. The development of rules, procedures, algorithms, heuristics, and other organizational structures has been a cornerstone of LIS research development since the profession began. Before computers, this work was in the form of card catalogs, indexes, and abstracts. Some of the conventions from these earlier structures have been translated into use with computerized storage. Some processes, such as the Anglo American Cataloging Rules II (AACRII), have well-established conventions for describing and representing the information housed in libraries and information centers. Others such as subject analysis and content code (cataloging) of materials have no equivalent to the AACRII conventions. Research issues in this area include: models of data structure (e.g., linear, relational, hierarchical, network), semantic nets, indexing, subject analysis (including automated analysis), natural and artificial language, and information representation.

Storage of original materials is advancing with changes in electronic technologies. Mechanical access media such as microfilm and microfiche are being replaced by electronic media such as laser discs and computer discs. There are technical implications about length of storage, speed of access, and cost of replication. Research in storage of original materials includes such issues as: knowledge base construction, access to very large databases, database construction, information construction, storage of nontextual information, hypermedia and multimedia, and data compression.

The 1994 request for proposal for a digital library initiative from the National Science Foundation and the Advanced Research Projects Agency laid out three areas for future research: capturing data, advanced algorithms, and networked databases. The details of this proposal are provided below as an overview of future research areas for information storage and retrieval.

1. Capturing data of all forms and categorizing and organizing electronic information in a variety of formats

- Optical character reader (OCR) page layout
- Speech recognition, audio segmentation, broadcast capture
- Graphics understanding (image, drawing, graphs)
- Indexing, interpretation, classification, and cataloging of electronic information
- Multilingual indexing
- Hypermedia structuring and linking
- Graphical interfaces
- Browsing technology

2. Advanced software and algorithms for browsing, searching, filtering, abstracting, summarizing, and combining large volumes of data, imagery, and all kinds of information

- Retrieval theories and models for data, metadata, information, knowledge bases, evaluation methods
- Formal structures of documents and texts, query languages
- Feature-based image analysis and classification, pattern recognition
- Spatial-temporal feature indexing of video
- Filtering, routing, alerting and selection, dissemination of information
- Natural language analysis
- Adaptive learning systems
- Pictorial feature recognition, image classification
- Multiscale displays, zooming
- Data visualization, interactive visualization control, simulation to improve visualization
- Navigation, hypermedia, metaphors, virtual reality

3. Research on networking protocols and standards needed to ensure the ability of the digital network to accommodate high volume and worldwide distribution

- Network security
- Protocol design
- Data compression

- Scalability for large numbers of simultaneous users
- Knowbots, agents, mediators, intelligent gatekeepers
- Personalized interactive news, magazine, and journal services
- Modeling and simulating usage
- Collaboration technology

25.5.6 How Is Information Controlled?

In a democratic society, we prefer to believe that information is not controlled, that access to any type of information is available to every citizen. Yet we all know cases where information is not available for reasons of government security, because no one thought it was important enough to distribute widely, because it would limit sales, or because the library or information agency was required to remove the item due to complaints. Even in a democratic society, there are controls placed on both the information that is made available and the access to that information. It is in balance, understanding, and constant vigilance that those controls do not become repressive. One significant control on information is economic. The availability of information can be limited by the cost of making it available.

Three issues that have social, economic, and cultural implications to information access are discussed. Public policies about information availability and information gatekeepers are explored. Access through United States government resources is examined. Proprietary aspects of information access are discussed. The control of information can have positive and negative connotations. Control can limit, reduce, and provide barriers. Control can also add access points, increase public awareness of information availability, and raise questions for consideration and reflection.

25.5.6.1. Public Policy. Libraries and public information agencies are an example of a U.S. public policy for making information easily available to all of its members. These agencies are the results of ongoing policies and cultural belief systems that indicate free access to all types of information is important. Through research on users, user needs, user feelings, and user beliefs, library and information centers try to balance services, facilities, and materials to make the most available to the most people. This public policy to provide information and access to all citizens is an example of a positive element. Other elements, however, can serve to hamper this general policy. Local policies such as library hours, information center location, type of access (e.g., telephone reference, electronic access), and services for special populations can provide barriers and constraints to all members of a community sharing equal access to information resources. Economic issues can also limit access to information in libraries and information centers. Selection and collection development policies are created to take into account the economic necessities, but they can also limit what is made available. For example, with limited funding, a school library media center may restrict purchases to curriculum-related items. Students with special inter-

ests in personal reading or viewing may not be able to find items of interest in their school library media center.

Cheryl Metoyer-Duran (1993a, 1993b, 1993c) describes another aspect of control: gatekeepers. Gatekeepers are individuals who influence the access of others to information. In a large body of literature, gatekeepers are considered to form the function of restricting access to information and providing negative controls. Metoyer-Duran suggests that gatekeepers, particularly in ethno-linguistically different communities, can improve access to information for community members.

25.5.6.2. United States Government Access. The United States government is a special case of information collection, storage, and dissemination. One purpose of government is to educate and inform the people it serves. It tries to do this through information dissemination that is economically viable. There is also a need to protect national security and other sensitive areas of government. Hernon and McClure divide government information into two types: (1) public information, which they define as that collected or developed by the government, not classified personal or proprietary; and (2) private information, which is for use only by the government for reasons of a privacy right or statutory obligation (1987, pp. 6–7).

Public service, economic constraints, and legal obligations create conflicting values and needs that influence the collection, storage, and dissemination of government information. Three emerging areas of research and discussion related to government information are discussed below: electronic information, access for special-needs populations, and economic conflicts. While the discussion for this review centers on U.S. federal government access, the issues discussed are equally relevant to local and state government information. For further research on government access to information, see: access (Hernon & McClure, 1988), electronic information (Hernon & McClure, 1993), federal statistics (Sy & Robbin, 1990), Internet (Kalhin, 1991; Lynch & Preston, 1990), National Resources in Education Network—NREN (McClure, Bishop, Doty, & Rosenbaum, 1991), privatizing government information (Stewart, 1990), and technology and information policies (Ballard, 1987).

A new issue in government access to information is electronic availability (Hernon & McClure, 1993). Government agencies are attempting to reduce cost and increase information access through electronic availability such as government files through Internet and alternative formats such as microfiche and CD-ROM. Sprehe (1992) suggests that federal agencies will need to organize and administer public access to maintain the greatest benefit to the user with the least disruption to the agency.

Other issues related to government access include information availability to special populations. Marshall (1992) suggests a number of issues related to the print disabled (blind and others who cannot read print). Information needs to be formatted in specific ways in order for it to be read by speech synthesizers or translated into Braille copy. There may be limited access that relates to hardware, software, and standards. Economic constraints to access also exist. Certain products are too expensive to purchase and translate (e.g., the Federal Register). Significant barriers to access to government information by print-disabled persons are created.

The cost for government agencies to gather, organize, and disseminate information is both in real dollars and resolving conflicts created by agency policies. Different groups have needs that may conflict in regard to the price of government information and the ease of accessibility. A summary of economic problems and issues associated with access to electronic government information is provided by Hernon and McClure (1993, p. 76):

- Librarians want to increase access but limit cost.
- Budgeters want to decrease the federal deficit and increase revenue.
- Economists want marginal cost pricing in order to maximize efficiency.
- Lawyers want precedents and consistency with other laws.
- Political scientists want an equitable process for setting prices.
- Researchers and scientists want data available, they want to know the format, and they are not much interested in prices.
- Statisticians want to maintain the integrity and accuracy of the data.
- Computer specialists want controls to ensure efficient use (e.g., price controls).
- Computer users want friendliness and flexibility in access.

While these economic factors were developed to account for differing needs around electronic access, they also are relevant to information access in general. Information has differing values and meanings to groups and individuals. For some, cost is a serious consideration in accessing information. For others, cost is unimportant, but the nature of the information's storage is critical (e.g., Braille, computer tape, hologram). For still others, it is the policy issues that regulate the dissemination of information that is crucial. Information needs can conflict and create confusion and dissent in policy development and implementation of access procedures.

25.5.6.3. Proprietary Interests. Services such as the Internet are resulting in mixtures of public and proprietary information sources that may have conflicting values, beliefs, and needs about who accesses information, what information is made available, and how much it costs. Some recent information scenarios illustrate conflicting values in information access between proprietary and public interests. The first scenario is an example of a conflict between public access to information and the proprietary use and sale of government information. The second scenario is related to public access to proprietary information. Both examples can be interpreted to respond to different public and private needs and pressures.

In the mid-1980s, a lobbying campaign by information industries resulted in information produced directly by government agencies becoming a commodity for sale to private companies (Smith, 1985). Private firms organize, package, and sell government information. This in itself is not a problem. The problem occurs because government versions of the same information, which used to be free to the public, now are difficult and sometimes impossible to obtain. Proprietary and public interests are in conflict.

Another example of conflict between proprietary and public interests is reported by Pfaffenberger (1990, p. 12). A librarian for the AFL-CIO attempted to search a DIALOG database produced by Dun & Bradstreet. The AFL-CIO had paid all the appropriate subscription and on-line fees for usage of DIALOG databases. They were denied access to the Dun & Bradstreet database. Dun & Bradstreet had sent a list to DIALOG indicating approximately 240 groups that were not allowed access. These groups were predominantly labor, consumer, and environmental organizations. There is a conflict between a proprietary organization's right to limit sales of its product and a strong societal belief that information should be available to everyone.

Services such as Internet provide access to both free and private information. Issues of who should have access to the proprietary and public information will continue to be part of a debate about information control. In addition, other issues are being raised about certain groups of people and their access to information. For example, should students be allowed free access to all resources of Internet, including the sexual and incendiary?

Doctor (1992) summarizes many of the research issues related to information technology and social equity. Five areas are discussed (p. 45): (1) the relationship between society and technology, (2) implementations of democracy and control relationships, (3) social justice and social equity, (4) information needs, sources, and uses, and (5) mass information delivery systems such as high-capacity computer networks. A common theme related to research in technology and society is the nature of their interactions. No technology is free of social pressures for its application and use. Technology and society are interdependent. These interactions can be seen in such research questions as: How is equity of access to technology achieved? What are implications of cultural lag in the workplace?

In discussing power and control in a democracy, Doctor (1992) addresses social justice and the distribution of power. Information-based power is considered as one of the possible outcomes of increasing technological implementation. Disparities in wealth and information access can also be seen to affect other aspects of social justice and social equity. "The gap between the wealthiest people in America and the poorest is increasing. Disparities in income, and therefore in the ability to acquire information resources, are worsening" (p. 54).

Doctor (1992) discusses the impact of mass information systems in terms of the distribution of information resources across society. Federal funding has helped some community-based agencies, including libraries, experiment with different types of information and referral systems. More recently, computer technologies are affecting the interactive delivery of information. Doctor suggests that there are two basic types of systems: specialist based and consumer based. Specialist-based systems are services such as DIALOG, BRS, and CompuServe. Consumer-based systems are services such as library-based community information systems, free-nets, Prodigy, and telephone company gateway systems. However, few of these current systems serve the daily information needs of the poor. "They are designed to serve upper- and upper-middle-income groups; only incidentally do some effectively reach down to middle- and lower-income groups" (p. 79). Doctor suggests that the development of programs to ensure distribution of resources to the one-third of the population that is information poor is both a research and a professional challenge.

25.5.7 Summary of Research Issues Related to Information

Information retrieval processes that interface with the storage of information are a substantive research area in information access. Two methods predominate in information retrieval: statistical/probabilistic and cognitive. Statistical and probability techniques focus on the development of management systems. They look at improving technological processes and retrieval functions. Cognitive retrieval efforts attempt to create models of users and develop interfaces for storage systems. They look at translating user needs into useful system retrieval methods. An example of cognitive research is the provision of multiple search strategies via an expert system interface.

Early cognitive research in information retrieval focused on developing prototype models. More recently, expert system intermediaries and hypermedia interfaces have been put into operation and their effects studied. The problems associated with applying both the prototypes and the operational systems to large databases are still under consideration. In addition, research to integrate sound, pictorial, and three-dimensional and moving images into the interface and retrieval processes is beginning. Issues such as image classification, spatial-temporal indexing of video, and hypermedia structuring are becoming part of the research of LIS. Merging features in electronic technologies are beginning to indicate that future research will focus on the processes— such as interface design, retrieval strategies, and knowledge construction—rather than on the specifics of technologies such as CD-ROM, OPACs, or on-line search services.

Technical considerations are one component of information research in LIS. Social, political, and economic issues that affect public policy and information access are another area of research and development. What gets stored must be considered. Who has access to the stored information is part of the decision-making process for building information structures. Information has inherent meaning and value. Suf-

ficient mechanical storage and retrieval by technical means does not necessarily meet the meaning and value needs of users. Some researchers concentrate on improving storage and retrieval mechanisms, technologies, and process. Other researchers focus on social, political, and economic issues (see 13.6.1) that affect information access. A future research direction might be to integrate the technical and social aspects of information into a wholistic research agenda.

25.6 INTEGRATING USERS, ACCESS, AND INFORMATION: THREE LONGITUDINAL STUDIES

Research suggesting linkages between users, access, and information supplies the meaning to information access. Examining each of the research areas of users, access, and information is one way to compare and contrast the existing state of knowledge about information access. However, at some point, all three areas need to be integrated into a meaningful process. Finding out that something exists, one definition of access, does not imply that the information is meaningful or useful. Access does not even necessarily imply retrieval of the information. In a limited sense, access might simply indicate that a given item or piece of information exists. In this section, three long-term research projects that examine the relationships between users, access, and information are examined in detail, namely the work of:

1. Tefko Saracevic and associates on information seeking and retrieval
2. Brenda Dervin and associates on sense making in information access
3. Carol Kuhlthau on the information search process

These projects are similar in that they are longitudinal; they address all three aspects of information access discussed in this chapter; and they focus on the process of information access. They are substantially different in methodology, theoretical orientation, process focus, and population studied. Taken together, these three research projects represent the most substantive and influential work on information access in LIS.

25.6.1 Information Seeking and Retrieval

The information-seeking and retrieval project of Tefko Saracevic and associates discussed below began in 1980 with the development of a model and a research methodology (Derr, 1982, 1984, 1985a, 1985b; Pao, 1983; Saracevic, 1980, 1983, 1984, 1985). The model has five components: user, question, searcher, search, and items retrieved. Each of these components is measured in multiple ways, including Likert scaling, categorical variables, standardized tests, and numbers of items. The methodology is quantitative and uses traditional regression and analysis of variance techniques. However, ". . . regression analysis and analysis of variance proved to be disappointing in uncovering significant relationships" (Saracevic, Kantor, Chamis & Trivison, 1988, p. 213). The use of the cross-product ratio, traditionally found in biomedical research, was a more powerful statistical method for application in LIS research on information seeking and retrieval. The results of the application of this technique are detailed in the study described below.

Between 1985 and 1987, Saracevic et al. (1987, 1988) conducted an extensive research study on the model's five components and obtained significant results using the cross-product ratio statistic. The study consisted of 40 research questions submitted by 40 different academic and industrial workers. These questions were researched by 36 experienced users of DIALOG. In addition, the same 40 questions were researched in four different ways by three project researchers. This resulted in a total of 200 outside searches on the 40 questions, and 360 project searches on the 40 questions. A total of 5,411 unique items were identified as solutions to the problems posed in the 40 questions. Of these, 1,343 were judged as relevant, 1,448 as partially relevant, and 1,620 as not relevant by the original question askers.

Each of the five components of the model was operationalized with multiple measures. Use of the cross-product ratio resulted in significant effects for the following aspects of the model's components:

- Of the four measures for *users* (problem, intent, public knowledge, and internal knowledge), only problem and public knowledge showed a significant positive impact on retrieving relevant items.
- Of the five measures for *questions* (domain, clarity, specificity, complexity, and presuppositions), low clarity, low specificity, high complexity, and many suppositions showed a significant positive impact on retrieving relevant items.
- Of the four measures for *searchers* (Remote Associations Test-RAT, Symbolic Reasoning Test-SRT, Learning Style Inventory-LSI, and search experience), only high RAT scores and high Abstract Conceptualization on the LSI showed a significant positive impact on retrieving relevant items. Concrete Experience on the LIS was negatively related to retrieving relevant items.
- Of the six measures of *search tactics and efficiency* (commands, iterative cycles, search terms, preparation time, on-line time, and total time), high numbers of cycles, low numbers of search terms, below-average preparation time, and below-average total time showed a significant positive impact on the retrieval of relevant items.
- Of the six indicators of *item retrieval* (relevant, partially relevant, not relevant, evaluated items, not evaluated items, and total items), if the number of relevant, partially relevant, and total items were high, then there was a significant positive impact on the retrieval of relevant items.

In addition to examining relationships to relevance, this study also looked at all categories described above as related to precision and recall. These measures are both traditionally used in overall macrowise retrieval research. While there were some significant findings for these categories, the more important information was gained from the microwise item analysis discussed above related to relevance. This study made no attempt to aggregate the effects of the variables, which showed positive relationships to relevance, precision, and recall.

One of the most significant results of this study was from pairwise comparisons of all 200 outside searches done for the 40 questions. This resulted in 800 pairs of comparisons examining the overlap of terms selected for searching and items retrieved by searchers. The overlap of search terms was relatively low. In 56.4% of the cases, the agreement was less than 25% (Saracevic & Kantor, 1988a, p. 204). In item retrieval, 69% of the items were retrieved only once. If an item was retrieved more than once, it was more likely to be relevant. The odds of an item retrieved once being relevant was 10:10. The odds of an item retrieved by five different searchers being relevant was 57:10.

This research project has implications for all three areas of information access discussed in this chapter: users, access, and information. In terms of access, the project demonstrates the importance of questions and users on the development of access points and interfaces. Interactions—whether between a search intermediary as described in this study or a system such as an OPAC, an expert system, or an on-line database—require sophistication in interpreting users' questions. The use of keywords from a question was the least effective search method found in this study. The most effective method was information compiled from a number of searchers using different terms and search strategies.

In terms of information, this study clearly demonstrated the lack of overlap in the use of search terms and the retrieval of relevant information. This has strong implications for indexing, database construction, and information organization. There is not a simple correspondence in choosing an exactly correct term or series of terms to solve a complex problem. Information structures that restrict the ability of searchers to create complex and iterated searches reduce the possibilities for effective information problem solving.

In terms of users, implications from the searcher's strategies can be applied to developing instruction for individual users as well as professional searchers. The use of many search terms and concrete linear strategies resulted in retrieving fewer relevant items. Focusing instruction on developing word association skills and abstract conceptualizations of information problems could improve user's solutions to information problems and increase feelings of satisfaction.

The Saracevic information-seeking and retrieval project developed a model and implemented a quantitative statistic new to information science research: the cross-product ratio. Testing the model is a step toward theory building. The project created hypotheses and questions that need to be tested further and used to develop an information-seeking and retrieval theory. Saracevic and Kantor state in the conclusion of the 1988 report that the theory still needs to be developed. They suggest the need for a theory of information seeking and retrieving that has the following characteristics:

- Be part of a broad theory of human information behavior
- Not use computer logic as a model because it is inadequate
- Incorporate both context and content of information in addition to syntax and logic
- Incorporate individual differences in patterns
- Be dynamic and interactive rather than linear and unidimensional
- Account for both human-human and human-computer interactions
- Allow for dynamic changes over time (Saracevic & Kantor, 1988b, p. 213)

25.6.2 Sense-Making Theory

The longitudinal research projects of Brenda Dervin and associates (Atwood & Dervin, 1982; Dervin, 1983, 1989a, 1989b; Dervin & Clark, 1987; Dervin, Johnson & Nilan, 1982) uses both qualitative and quantitative measures. It is based in communication theory and examined populations of different ethnicities, age groups, and sociocultural backgrounds. The studies have been performed with other information agencies as well as libraries. Dervin's work focuses on process and identifies the user as the foundational element in that process.

In the literature, this body of work is generally called *sense-making theory.* Dervin describes her work in this way: "Some people call sense making a theory, others a set of methods, others a methodology, others a body of findings. In the most general sense it is all of these" (Dervin, 1992, p. 61).

Dervin's sense-making research covers 40 projects over 17 years (Dervin, 1992). They include Asian, Hispanic, Afro-American, and Anglo populations, as well as teenagers, preschoolers, and adults. Subjects range from blood donation to politics to completing class assignments. Information agencies include libraries, health organizations, and government bodies. These series of projects are quite possibly the broadest and most wide ranging in LIS related to information access.

The foundation of sense making is a series of assumptions about information and communication. Sense making is founded on the assumption of discontinuity: discontinuity in time, in space, between people, and within an individual. Dervin conceptualizes this discontinuity as a gap. In information access, the goal is for the individual to create a bridge from the problem situation and over the gap through the use of information resources. This process is depicted as a triangle, with the points being situation, gap, and helps (or resources). Sense making can be applied to intrapersonal, interpersonal, small group, organizational, telecommunications, databases, societal, or other information use and information-seeking environments.

Three aspects of information drive both sense-making theory and the implementation of specific methods:

1. Information is constructed by the individual.
2. Information use, therefore, must center on the perspective of the actor.
3. Processes and behavioral strategies and tactics are the focus of research.

Methods develop from these three foundations in the following ways. A person constructs information through a series of steps to bridge gaps. A discontinuity occurs when the step stops. This is the point at which the researcher needs to acquire information about what processes and strategies are being used by the individual. Dervin has developed a set of interview techniques to help understand and obtain appropriate information. The foundational interview method is called the *micro-moment time-line interview.* A respondent is asked to recall what happened (the situation), what the gap was, and what the goal was (or the help that was needed). This type of interview results in detailed, time-focused information related to all points of the sense-making triangle. Three other interview techniques have also been developed but are not as intensive and focus on more specific issues. The abbreviated time-line interview is used to concentrate on one point of the triangle and elicit specific information about that factor. The help chain looks at the help point of the triangle. The question is asked: How did the library, the book, the video, etc., help? With each response, the interviewee is asked again: And how did that help? The question is repeated until the respondent feels his or her answer is completed. Message queing is the third focused interview technique. Respondents focus specifically on the gap-bridging or gap-defining portion of the sense-making environment.

Information gathered from the interviews is analyzed in both qualitative and quantitative ways. One of the primary methods, however, is content analysis. Results of studies provide data for both hypothesis testing of aspects of sense-making theory and data to inform and help solve the problem of practice on which the research study is based. Dervin's goals are both the development of theory and the solving of problems of practice. Each is equally important to the use of sense making (Dervin, 1992).

In a study for the California State Library (Atwood & Dervin, 1982), content analysis was used to classify how individuals identified and described gaps. The hypothesis tested was that the nature of a gap would be consistent across race. It was found that race did not predict information seeking in terms of questions asked. Race did interact with the channels and sources individuals used to get answers. The practice component of the California study provided descriptive information on need, questions, barriers, strategies, and successes of the people interviewed to help the California State Library develop and deliver services of value to users and potential users of all races.

A theory-building result across studies was the identification and naming of categories of stops, gap definings, and helps. Stops included such components as barriers, spin-outs, and washouts. Gap definings have related to self, others, objects, actions, and events. Help categories included creating ideas, acquiring skills, calming down, and reaching goals. These categories were consistent across populations and problem situations.

Dervin's research has implications for all three areas of information access discussed in this chapter. In terms of users, this is a strong, theoretically based explanation of how users access information, deal with problems of access, and identify helps and resources. It provides the necessary foundation to develop hypotheses within a framework and test those hypotheses about users with validated and reliable methods that are directly cogent to the theory.

In terms of access, the results of these studies have implications for the design and development of user interfaces and human reference interactions. One of the particularly interesting cross-situational and cross-participant stops identified is the idea of someone (or something) leading the individual down a road they do not wish to travel. No matter how correct that road may seem to the computer, the reference librarian or the teacher who is trying to lead it becomes a stop to the individual with the problem. The need for flexibility and using the paths of the questioner should be integrated into human-human interactions and human-computer interactions.

In terms of information, an example from a study of blood donors (Dervin et al., 1982) demonstrates information issues that were addressed by the sense-making research. A series of different predictors were compared to see how donors wanted information to help them. They wanted and needed different information at different steps in the donation process. Sometimes they wanted details. Sometimes they wanted reassurance and no details. Different donors might also want information from different sources. To the question, "Will I faint?" one donor might want a doctor's response, while another might want statistical counts of how many people faint, and a third might want information from a previous donor. The solution in this instance was to construct a computerized question-answering system that could be accessed at the five points identified by donors as gaps or stop points. Typical questions were displayed on the screens, and a variety of question-answering strategies was made available, including responses from various sources such as doctors, statistics, and previous donors.

25.6.3 Information Search Process

The research projects of Carol Kuhlthau (Kuhlthau, 1983, 1988, 1989, 1993a, 1993b, 1993c) were qualitative and resulted in the creation of grounded theory about the information search process. The research looks at information access in instructional environments. The purposes of Kuhlthau's work are to develop a theory of the information search process and to provide guidelines for instruction in

this process (Kuhlthau, 1993c). This research concentrates on process and identifies the user as the foundational element in that process.

Kuhlthau's (1983) research began as a test of Kelly's personal construct theory. Kuhlthau explored the stages of the information search process and believed that ". . . the search process is, in itself, a process of construction" (Kuhlthau, 1988, p. 233). All of Kuhlthau's studies use field-based qualitative research methods to build grounded theory about the information search process. The original high school study (1983) was followed with further studies varying the population and refining the theory. Across-studies (Kuhlthau, 1989) looked at high school students, college students, high-, middle-, and low-achieving high school seniors, and academic and public library users. The final theory is a three-by-seven matrix of stages by process. The three states are feelings, thoughts, and actions. The seven stages are: task initiation, topic selection, prefocus exploration, focus formulation, information collection, search closure, and starting writing. For each of the three stages, a continuum of activities is developed along the seven processes. For example, feelings range from uncertainty to relief, thoughts from ambiguity to specificity, and actions from seeking relevant information to seeking pertinent information.

Kuhlthau used these studies and the grounded theory to create a principle of uncertainty for information seeking (1993a). This principle has six corollaries and seeks to integrate the cognitive processes of information seeking with affective considerations. In the 1993a article, Kuhlthau clearly indicates the constructivist focus of her information-seeking research and examines the influences of Dewey, Kelly, and Bruner on the development of the principle's conceptual framework. The basic uncertainty principle represented by this research is stated as: "Uncertainty is a cognitive state which commonly causes affective symptoms of anxiety and lack of confidence" (Kuhlthau, 1993a, p. 347). The six corollaries to this principle are: the process corollary, the formulation corollary, the redundancy corollary, the mood corollary, the prediction corollary, and the interest corollary. This principle and the associated corollaries are a strong conceptual framework for further research in information needs and uses.

Kuhlthau's research has implications for all three areas of information access discussed in this chapter: users, access, and information. In terms of users, Kuhlthau's work is highly focused on the impact of mood and internal affect on the process of seeking and finding information. She clearly delineates cycles that users can refer to and gauge their own feelings. The user's feelings of helplessness or frustration can be acknowledged as part of the information-seeking process.

Both Dervin and Saracevic also addressed affective issues. Saracevic looked at user satisfaction with items received to answer questions posed. Dervin examined users' perceptions of institutional images. Dervin also considered feelings, emotions, and affect as part of the process that may be gap defining or barrier producing. The differences between Saracevic, Dervin, and Kuhlthau are in degree of focus. Kuhlthau's work relies the most heavily on the impact of feelings on behavior.

In terms of access, Kuhlthau's grounded theory provides observations on the information-seeking process. It appears that information may not be as important as an individual's state of mind at the time the information is accessed. Information accessed early in the seeking process may be considered too difficult, not relevant, or unintelligible. At later stages of the seeking process, the same information, from the same access point, under the same delivery conditions, could be perceived differently. In designing access systems, the different states of users when they access the system, either human or machine, need to be taken into consideration.

In terms of information, the notion of value-free information comes into play. Often databases, indexing systems, and other forms of information organization assume that information can be sorted into value-free categories and structures. Individuals carry values and feelings into the information search process. Those beliefs interact with information structures no matter how they were constructed. A related idea from Kuhlthau's work is the difference between relevant information and pertinent information. Most information structures are designed to provide relevant but not necessarily pertinent information. Pertinence is a measure of value.

25.6.4 Comparing Three Longitudinal Information Access Projects

Each of the three projects discussed above has applications to user, access, and information research. They each use distinct methodologies, focus on process, and take the user as their center of study. In addition, these researchers have continued their projects over 10 years or longer. There is longevity and growing complexity in their ideas and theoretical positions. They have set ideas out, tested them, and refined and revised.

These three projects demonstrate three different organizational structures for conducting research. Dervin's projects include both qualitative and quantitative methods and are based in communication theory. Kuhlthau's qualitative methods and grounded theory provide an examination of personal and affective characteristics. Saracevic demonstrates how a quantitative method from another research area can be successfully adapted for use in LIS. All three projects use constructivist assumptions in thinking about users' behaviors and beliefs. They acknowledge the role of the user in constructing information. They also demonstrate that quantitative, qualitative, and a combination of quantitative and qualitative methods can all be successfully used to understand differing aspects of information access.

Taken together these three longitudinal research projects suggest the range of theory use, methodological differences, and organizational foundations that can be applied to studying the overall process of information access, including users, access, and information.

25.7 CONCLUSION

The categories of research presented in this chapter looked at issues related to foundational components associated with information access: users, access, and information. Other organizational structures could be equally useful in understanding the research of information access. For example, each theoretical position such as cognitive psychology, information processing, or human factors could be examined for how it is used within the context of information access. The areas that the theoretical position is applied to could be looked at for consistencies, inconsistencies, and general patterns. Another approach would be to examine methodology. Are certain methods used more frequently in certain content areas related to information access? Are they accompanied by a single theoretical framework? Is theory developed from the method? Is a new theory generated for use with a particular method? This chapter focused on reviewing information access from the point of view of content. Other methods could be used to look at processes, theories, or methodologies.

When information is structured, modeled, or defined, some of its inherent reality is lost. The map is not the place. The picture is not the person. The signature is not the signer. The social artifacts are not the reality . . . and the environment requires agreement among the players about the rules and the playing field. This chapter set up a clearly defined playing field and rationally designed rules for inclusion or exclusion of information. The results are patterns of research, theory, and methods applied to solving problems in information access related to users, access, and information in LIS.

25.7.1 Summary of Information Access Research Issues from LIS

User research addresses needs, characteristics, and strategies of the user of access services in libraries and information centers. It attempts to understand cognitive, affective, and learning issues about the people who wish access to information. Current user research can be characterized in the following ways:

- User research moved from sociological to psychological foundations.
- The emphasis on groups of users changed to an emphasis on individuals.
- Quantitative, qualitative, and combinations of quantitative and qualitative research are part of user studies.
- User needs and their search processes are being combined through information-seeking research. The emphasis is on cognitive search strategies.

Access, in this chapter, is defined as the point at which the user meets the information system. It is characterized by physical, social, and technical components. Physical issues associated with access include workspace, remote access, building and facilities design, and geographic availability.

Social issues include public policies and laws, cultural factors, and users' attitudes and beliefs. Technical issues include interface design, human computer interaction, and attributes of the technologies. Access research can be characterized in the following ways:

- Access research related to the use of OPACs can be applied to understanding emerging technologies such as CD-ROM, Internet, and full-text databases.
- Methods commonly used in OPAC research are surveys and questionnaires and transaction log analyses.
- Areas such as workspace use, the interaction of facilities, remote access, and geographic accessibilities could use methods and theory from human factors such as person-environment fit.
- Human-computer interaction, interface design, and evaluation research from other content areas is applied to research in the technologies of information access in libraries and information centers.
- New technologies such as CD-ROM, multimedia, and Internet demonstrate merging of features from more-established technologies. Continuing research on common issues such as front-end design, menus and commands, direct manipulation, and graphics retrieval could benefit all access technologies.

Information research examines both the structure and content of information. It looks at how to define and categorize information and the processes used to retrieve information that are not transparent to the user. Information research considers barriers and constraints related to who has access to what kinds of information at what cost. Information research can be characterized in the following ways:

- Cognitive science is a theoretical foundation for information retrieval and storage research.
- Research in information retrieval strategies that connect the user interface and the information storage system uses statistical/probabilistic and cognitive methods.
- Expert systems that provide multiple search strategies can be applied across information technologies such as CD-ROM, hypermedia, and multimedia.
- Information storage looks at both original information and information representations in all formats.
- Research on policy issues related to government and private ownership and access is a growing concern in LIS.

Longitudinal studies such as those by Dervin, Kuhlthau, and Saracevic can contribute to understanding how users, access, and information issues are an integrated process. Different theoretical foundations and methodologies can be applied to studying information access with positive results. Each provides a viewfinder on the overall process. One significant contribution to information access research would be the development of models based on theory which integrate components from various research projects. The following models have been created and perhaps could form a foundation for comparison and examination of crucial aspects of the information access process:

- Bates (1986), subject access in on-line catalogs
- Belkin (1980), anomalous states of knowledge
- Brown (1991), information-seeking behavior
- Dervin (1992), user sense making
- Fidel & Soergel (1983), conceptual framework for bibliographic retrieval
- Hert (1992), information retrieval interfaces
- Kuhlthau (1993a), information search process
- Meadow (1992), information retrieval
- Saracevic et al. (1988), information seeking and retrieval

25.7.2 Relevance of Information Access Research to Educational Communication and Technology

In a wide-ranging review of literature and research, Palmquist (1992) discusses issues relevant to the impact of information technology on the individual. The emphasis on how computer-based technologies affect the individual is particularly relevant to the research of educational communication and technology (ECT). The individual's need for social experience is a critical element of education and instruction. One of the ongoing criticisms of computerization of instruction is the potential for mechanizing and dehumanizing the learner. The effect of electronic technologies in isolating individuals is reviewed by Palmquist. Topics such as electronic dating, intolerance of boredom, and computer hackers are investigated. In addition, Palmquist reviews issues of cultural shifts, the use of television to acquire synthetic culture, and dissolution of identifiable roles due to increased information access. Other areas for examination include the individual at home and the individual in the community. These social impacts of computer use on the individual can provide an arena for further discussion and evaluation in ECT research.

The social environment of the workplace has been particularly affected by information technology (Palmquist, 1992). One group of researchers sees social interactions becoming minimized due to technologies like e-mail, fax, teleconferencing, and group-decision support systems. Other researchers see these new technologies as increasing cohesiveness and decreasing group tensions and difficult problem situations. De-skilling is a common concern among researchers looking at information technology and jobs. The quality of worklife and job satisfaction are also part of the complexity of changes that information technology is bringing. The area of instructional design and development within ECT may wish to examine these social influences on the training environment.

Palmquist (1992) concludes by indicating that the overall impact of information technologies on the individual is still primarily unknown. Many of the technologies are new and still novel. Their influences cannot be accurately assessed. There is evidence that household management may be improved by computering technology, but it also results in an increase in loneliness and lack of social integration. Information technology can both enhance and detract from job satisfaction and the overall quality of worklife. Integrating some of the questions and problems posed by Palmquist into the research of ECT could provide an added social dimension to understanding the impact of access technologies on users and their acquisition of knowledge.

Library and information science literature related to information access can also contribute specific understandings, methods, and theory for consideration by ECT researchers. The strengths of traditional LIS research for ECT to consider are: information-seeking strategies, on-line public access research methods, and information retrieval techniques. Each of these three areas has built a tradition of theory, research methodology, and ongoing findings that could be added to the existing knowledge within ECT. LIS research complements and adds to the research of ECT. Two new LIS research areas could provide relevant theory and methodology for ECT researchers: social construction of technology (Case, 1991; Pfaffenberger, 1990) and information gatekeepers (Metoyer-Duran, 1993a, 1993b, 1993c). Social construction of technology looks at the relationships between technology, principle actors, social artifacts, and the process of integrating technology into the environment. Metoyer-Duran's work on information gatekeepers demonstrates the positive effects of community and individual involvement with information in ethno-linguistically diverse communities.

25.7.3 Conclusions

There are strengths and areas for further development in LIS research about information access. Information access is an interdisciplinary and growing research area because it cuts across psychological, sociological, political, economic, and technical issues. The technicalities of information retrieval that are related to computers and mathematics cannot be separated from the social issues about who will be allowed access and at what cost. The human factor design issues of how to create effective interfaces cannot be separated from the needs, preferences, and changing strategies of the user over time and space. The effect of users with special needs and interests cannot be separated from the technological limitations created by the economic environment. The increasing number of access tools and multiple methods for accessing information cannot be separated from the instructional and educational needs of the user. The issues of information access are related and interdependent. Some researchers and research areas will focus on different pieces in greater or lesser depth, but it is important to look at larger issues and draw together the research from various areas at points in time. This chapter attempts to make the research of LIS more accessible to educational communication and technology researchers.

REFERENCES

Aboud, M., Chrisment, C., Razouk, R., Sedes, F. & Soule-Dupuy, C. (1993). Querying a hypertext information sys-

tem by the use of classification. *Information Processing & Management 29*, 387–96.

Agosti, M. (1993). Hypertext and information retrieval. *Information Processing & Management 29*, 283–85.

Allen, B.L. (1991). Cognitive research in information science: implications for design. *Annual Review of Information Science and Technology 26*, 3–38.

— (1994). Cognitive abilities and information system usability. *Information Processing & Management 30*, 177–92.

Allen, R.B. (1983). Cognitive factors in the use of menus and trees: an experiment. *IEEE Journal on Selected Areas in Communications 1*, 333–36.

Allen, T.J. (1969). Information needs and uses. *Annual Review of Information Science and Technology 4*, 1–29.

Applegate, R. (1993). Models of user satisfaction: understanding false positives. *RQ 32*, 525–39.

Arents, H.C. & Bogaerts, W.F.L. (1993). Concept-based retrieval of hypermedia information: from term indexing to semantic hyperindexing. *Information Processing & Management 29*, 373–86.

Atwood, R. & Dervin, B. (1982). Challenges to sociocultural predictors of information seeking: a test of race versus situation movement state. *Communication Yearbook 5*, 549–69.

Balaraman, K. (1991). End-user studies in a CD-ROM environment: work in progress. *Proceedings of the 54th Annual Meeting of the American Society for Information Science 28*, 283–94.

Baldwin, D.A., Ostrye, A.T. & Shelton, D.W. (1988). University of Wyoming catalog survey. *Technical Services Quarterly 5*, 15–26.

Ballard, S. (1987). Federal science and technology information policies: an overview. *In* C.R. McClure & P. Hernon, eds. *Information policies in the 1980s*, 195–225. Norwood, NJ: Ablex.

Barron, D., Grover, R. & Loertscher, D. (1994). Future scenarios for school library media programs. *Proceedings of Treasure Mountain Research Retreat 5*. Brown County, IN, Nov. 8, 1994.

Bartolo, L.M. & Smith, T.D. (1993). Interdisciplinary work and the information search process: a comparison of manual and online searching. *College and Research Libraries 54*, 344–53.

Bates, M. (1971). *User studies: a review for librarians and information scientists*. U.S. Office of Education (ED 047 738).

— (1984). Fallacy of the perfect thirty-item online search. *RQ 24*, 43–50.

— (1986). Subject access in online catalogs: a design model. *Journal of the American Society for Information Science 37*, 357–76.

Belkin, N.J. (1980). Anomalous states of knowledge as a basis for information retrieval. *Canadian Journal of Information Science 5*, 133–43.

— (1984). Cognitive models and information transfer. *Social Science Information Studies 4*, 111–29.

— (1990). Cognitive viewpoint in information science. *Journal of Information Science: Principles and Practice 16*, 11–16.

—, Chang, S., Downs, T., Saracevic, T. & Zhao, S. (1990). Taking account of user tasks, goals and behavior for the design of online public access catalogs. *Proceedings of the 53d Annual Meeting of the American Society for Information Science 27*, 69–79.

— & Croft, W.B. (1987). Retrieval techniques. *Annual Review of Information Science and Technology 22*, 109–45.

—, Marchetti, P.G. & Cool, C. (1993). Braque: design of an interface to support user interaction in information retrieval. *Information Processing & Management 29*, 225–44.

—, Oddy, R.N. & Brooks, H.M. (1982a). ASK for information retrieval I: background and theory. *Journal of Documentation 38*, 61–71.

—, — & — (1982b). ASK for information retrieval II: results of a design study. *Journal of Documentation 38*, 145–64.

Bookstein, A. (1983). Outline of a general probabilistic retrieval model. *Journal of Documentation 39*, 63–72.

— (1985). Probability and fuzzy-set applications in information retrieval. *Annual Review of Information Science and Technology 20*, 117–52.

Borgman, C.L. (1984). Psychological research in human-computer interaction. *Annual Review of Information Science and Technology 19*, 33–64.

— (1986). Human-computer interaction with information retrieval systems: understanding complex communication behavior. *Progress in Communication Sciences 7*, 91–122.

— (1989). All users of information retrieval systems are not created equal: an exploration into individual differences. *Information Processing & Management 25*, 237–51.

—, Gallagher, A.L., Krieger, D. & Bower, J. (1990). Children's use of an interactive catalog of science materials. *Proceedings of the 53d Annual Meeting of the American Society for Information Science 27*, 55–68.

—, —, Walter, V.A. & Rosenberg, J. (1991). Science library catalog project: comparison of children's searching behavior in hypertext and keyword search system. *Proceedings of the 54th Annual Meeting of the American Society for Information Science 28*, 162–69.

Borko, H., ed. (1987). Expert systems and library and information science (special issue). *Information Processing & Management 23*, 75–154.

Bouazza, A. (1989). Information user studies. *Encyclopedia of Library and Information Science 44*, 144–64.

Boyce, B.R. & Kraft, D.H. (1985). Principles and theories in information science. *Annual Review of Information Science and Technology 20*, 153–78.

Broadus, R.N. (1983). Online catalogs and their users: a review article on the CLR study of online catalogs. *College and Research Libraries 44*, 458–67.

Brooks, H.M. (1987). Expert systems and intelligent information retrieval. *Information Processing & Management 23*, 367–82.

Brown, M.A. (1991). General model of information-seeking behavior. *Proceedings of the 54th Annual Meeting of the American Society for Information Science 28*, 9–14.

Buckland, M. (1991). *Information and information systems*. New York: Greenwood.

— & Gey, F. (1994). Relationship between recall and precision. *Journal of the American Society for Information Science 45*, 12–19.

Buckley, C. & Levit, A.F. (1985). Optimization of inverted vector searches. *Association for Computing Machinery's 8th Annual Special Interest Group in Information Retrieval*, Jun. 5–7, 97–110.

Burt, P.V. & Kinnucan, M.T. (1990). Information models and modeling techniques for information systems. *Annual Review of Information Science and Technology 25*, 175–208.

Canter, D., Powell, J., Wishart, J. & Roderick, C. (1986). User navigation in complex database systems. *Behaviour & Information Technology 5*, 249–57.

Case, D.O. (1991). Example of the social construction of information technologies: videotext in the United States and Europe. *Proceedings of the 54th Annual Meeting of the American Society for Information Science 28*, 139–49.

Chang, S. & Rice R.E. (1993). Browsing: a multidimensional framework. *Annual Review of Information Science and Technology 28*, 231–76.

Chen, C. & Hernon, P. (1982). *Information seeking*. New York: Schuman.

Chiang, K. & Eng, W. (1989). Library interfaces: NOTIS and beyond. *In* M. Dillon, ed. *American Society for Information Science 18th Mid-Year Meeting*, May 21–24/5.

Chin, J.P., Diehl, V.A. & Norman, K.L. (1988). Development of an instrument measuring user satisfaction of the human-computer interface. *In* E. Soloway, D. Frye & S.B. Sheppard, eds. *Proceedings of the Association for Computing Machinery's Special Interest Group on Computer and Human Interaction*, May 15–19, pp. 213–18.

Cochrane, P.A. & Markey, K. (1983). Catalog use studies—since the introduction of online interactive catalogs: impact on design for subject access. *Library and Information Science Research 5*, 337–63.

— & — (1985). Catalog use studies—since the introduction of online interactive catalogs: impact on design for subject access. *In* P.A. Cochrane, ed. *Redesign of catalogs and indexes for improved online subject access*, 159–84. Phoenix, AZ: Oryx.

Cohen, P.R. & Kjeldren, R. (1987). Information retrieval by constrained spreading activation in semantic networks. *Information Processing & Management*.

Crane, D. (1971). Information needs and uses. *Annual Review of Information Science and Technology 6*, 1–39.

Crawford, S. (1978). Information needs and uses. *Annual Review of Information Science and Technology 13*, 61–81.

Crawford, W. (1987). *Patron access issues for online catalogs*. Boston, MA: Hall.

Croft, W.B. (1986). Boolean queries and term dependencies in probabilistic retrieval models. *Journal of the American Society for Information Science 37*, 71–77.

— (1987). Approaches to intelligent retrieval. *Information Processing & Management 23*, 249–54.

— & Thompson, R.H. (1987). I3R: a new approach to the design of document retrieval systems. *Journal of the American Society for Information Science 38*, 389–404.

— & Turtle, H.R. (1993). Retrieval strategies for hypertext. *Information Processing & Management 29*, 313–24.

Cutlip, G. W. (1988). *Learning and information: skills for the secondary classroom and library media program*. Englewood, CO: Libraries Unlimited.

Dalrymple, P.W. & Zweizig, D.L. (1992). Users' experience of information retrieval systems: an exploration of the relationship between search experience and affective measures. *Library and Information Science Research 14*, 167–81.

Daniels, P.J. (1986). Cognitive models in information retrieval: an evaluative review. *Journal of Documentation 42*, 272–304.

Derr, R.L. (1982). Classification of questions in information retrieval by conceptual presupposition. *Proceedings of the 45th American Society for Information Science Annual Meeting 19*, 69–71.

— (1984). Information seeking expressions of users. *Journal of the American Society for Information Science 35*, 124–28.

— (1985a). Concept of information in ordinary discourse. *Information Processing & Management 21,* 489–500.

— (1985b). Questions: definitions, structure, and classification. *RQ 24,* 186–90.

Dervin, B. (1983a). Information as user construct: the relevance of perceived information needs to synthesis and interpretation. *In* S.A. Ward & L.J. Reed, eds. *Knowledge structure and use: implications for synthesis and interpretation,* 153–83. Philadelphia, PA: Temple University Press.

— (1983b). Overview of sense-making research: concepts, methods and results to date. *Annual Meeting of the International Communication Association,* Dallas, TX: May 1983.

— (1989a). Audience as listener and learner, teacher and confidante. *In* R. Rice & C. Atkins, eds. *Public Communication Campaigns,* 67–86. Newbury Park, CA: Sage.

— (1989b). Users as research inventions: how research categories perpetuate inequities. *Journal of Communication 39,* 216–33.

— (1992). From the mind's eye of the user: the sense-making qualitative-quantitative methodology. *In* J.D. Glazier & R.R. Powell, eds. *Qualitative Research in Information Management,* 61–84. Englewood, CO: Libraries Unlimited.

— & Clark, K. (1987). Asking significant questions: alternative tools for information need and accountability assessments by libraries. *Report to California State Library,* July 1987.

— & Dewdney, P. (1986). Neutral questioning: a new approach to the reference interview. *RQ 25,* 506–13.

—, Jacobson, T.L. & Nilan, M.S. (1982). Measuring aspects of information seeking: a test of a quantitative/qualitative methodology. *Communication Yearbook 6,* 419–44.

— & Nilan, M. (1986). Information needs and uses. *Annual Review of Information Science and Technology 21,* 3–33.

— et al. (1982). Improving predictors of information use: a comparison of predictor types in a health communication setting. *Communication Yearbook 5,* 806–30.

Dillon, M., Jul, E. & Burge, M. (1993). Assessing information on the Internet: toward providing library services for computer-mediated communication: results of an OCLC research project. *Internet Research 3,* 54–89.

Doctor, R.D. (1992). Social equity and information technologies: moving toward information democracy. *Annual Review of Information Science and Technology 27,* 43–96.

Doszkocs, T.E., Reggia, J.A. & Lin, X. (1990). Connectionist models and information retrieval. *Annual Review of Information Science and Technology 25,* 209–60.

Doty, P. (1992). Electronic networks and social change in science. *Proceedings of the 55th Annual Meeting of the American Society for Information Science 29,* 185–91.

Drenth, H., Morris, A. & Tseng, G. (1991). Expert systems as information intermediaries. *Annual Review of Information Science and Technology 26,* 113–54.

Dunlop, M.D. & van Rijsbergen, C.J. (1993). Hypermedia and free text retrieval. *Information Processing & Management 29,* 287–98.

Eastman, C. (1985). Database management systems. *Annual Review of Information Science and Technology 20,* 91–116.

Edmonds, L., Moore, P. & Balcom, K.M. (1990). Effectiveness of an online catalog. *School Library Journal 36,* 28–32.

Efthimiadis, E. (1990). Online searching aids: a review of front ends, gateways and other interfaces. *Journal of Documentation 46,* 218–62.

Eisenberg, M.B. (1988). Measuring relevance judgment. *Information Processing & Management 24,* 373–89.

— & Berkowitz, R.E. (1990). *Information problem solving: the big six skills approach to library and information skills instruction.* Norwood, NJ: Ablex.

— & Spitzer, K.L. (1991). Information technology and services in schools. *Annual Review of Information Science and Technology 26,* 243–85.

Ellis, D. (1984). Theory and explanation in information retrieval research. *Journal of Information Science 8,* 25–38.

— (1989a). Behavioural approach to information retrieval system design. *Journal of Documentation 45,* 171–212.

— (1989b). Behavioural model for information retrieval system design. *Journal of Information Science 15,* 237–47.

— (1990). *New horizons in information retrieval.* London, England: Library Association.

— (1993). Modeling the information-seeking patterns of academic researchers: a grounded theory approach. *Library Quarterly 63,* 469–86.

—, Cox, D. & Hall, K. (1993). Comparison of the information seeking patterns of researchers in the physical and social sciences. *Journal of Documentation 49,* 356–69.

Ensor, P. (1992). Knowledge level of users and nonusers of keyword/Boolean searching on an online public access catalog. *RQ 31,* 60–74.

Evens, M. (1989). Computer-readable dictionaries. *Annual Review of Information Science and Technology 24,* 85–118.

Fidel, R. (1987). *Database design for information retrieval, a conceptual approach.* New York: Wiley.

— (1990). Online searching styles. *Proceedings of the 53d Annual Meeting of the American Society for Information Science 27,* 98–103.

— & Soergel, D. (1983). Factors affecting online bibliographic retrieval: a conceptual framework for research. *Journal of the American Society for Information Science 34,* 163–80.

Fox, C., Levitin, A. & Redman, T. (1994). Nature of data and its quality dimensions. *Information Processing & Management 30,* 9–19.

Fox, E.A. (1987). Development of the CODER system: a testbed for artificial intelligence methods in information retrieval. *Information Processing & Management 23,* 341–66.

— (1988). Optical disks and CD-ROM: publishing and access. *Annual Review of Information Science and Technology 23,* 85–124.

Gauch, S. (1992). Intelligent information retrieval: an introduction. *Journal of the American Society for Information Science 43,* 175–92.

— & Smith, J.B. (1993). Expert system for automatic query reformation. *Journal of the American Society for Information Science 44,* 124–36.

Gluck, M., Coliz, J. & Rosenbaum, H. (1991). Study comparing electronic mail and voice messaging channels. *Proceedings of the 54th Annual Meeting of the American Society for Information Science 28,* 150–55.

Gomoll, K. (1990). Some techniques for observing users. *In* B. Laurel, ed. *Art of human-computer interface design,* 85–90. Reading, MA; Addison-Wesley.

Griffiths, A., Luckhurst, H.C. & Willett, P. (1986). Using interdocument similarity information in document retrieval systems. *Journal of the American Society for Information Science 37,* 3–11.

Grumling, D.K. (1992). Managing information about cataloging conventions using hypertext. *Proceedings of the 55th Annual Meeting of the American Society for Information Science 29*, 150–53.

Hancock-Beaulieu, M. (1990). Evaluating the impact of an online library catalogue on subject searching behavior. *Journal of Documentation 46*, 318–38.

Hartson, H.R. & Hix, D. (1989). Human-computer interface development: concepts and systems for its management. *ACM Computing Surveys 21*, 5–92.

Hawkins, D.T. (1988). Applications of artificial intelligence (AI) and expert systems for online searching. *Online 12*, 31–43.

Herner, S. & Herner, M. (1967). Information needs and uses in science and technology. *Annual Review of Information Science and Technology 2*, 1–34.

Hernon, P. & McClure, C.R. (1987). *Federal information policies in the 1980's: conflicts and issues.* Norwood, NJ: Ablex.

— & — (1993). Electronic U.S. government information: policy issues and directions. *Annual Review of Information Science and Technology 28*, 45–110.

Hert, C.A. (1992). Exploring a new model for understanding information retrieval interactions. *Proceedings of the 55th Annual Meeting of the American Society for Information Science 29*, 72–75.

— & Nilan, M.S. (1991). User-based information retrieval system interface evaluation: an examination of an on-line public access catalog. *Proceedings of the 54th Annual Meeting of the American Society for Information Science 28*, 170–77.

Hewins, E.T. (1990). Information need and use studies. *Annual Review of Information Science and Technology 25*, 45–172.

Hildreth, C.R. (1982). *Online public access catalogs. the user interface.* Dublin, OH: OCLC.

— (1985). Online public access catalogs. *Annual Review of Information Science and Technology 20*, 233–86.

— (1989). *Intelligent interfaces and retrieval methods for subject searching in bibliographic retrieval systems.* Washington, DC: Library of Congress.

Hollands, J.G. & Merikle, P.M. (1987). Menu organization and user expertise in information search tasks. *Human Factors 29*, 577–86.

Ingwersen, P. (1987). Towards a new research paradigm in information retrieval. *In* I. Wormell, ed. *Knowledge engineering: expert systems and information retrieval,* 150–89. London, England: Taylor Graham.

— (1992). *Information retrieval interaction.* London, England: Taylor Graham.

Irving, A. (1984) *Study and information skills across the curriculum.* London, England: Heinemann.

Jacobs, P.S., ed. (1993). *Text-based intelligent systems: current research and practice in information extraction and retrieval.* Hillsdale, NJ: Erlbaum.

Kahin, B. (1991). Information policy and the Internet: toward a public information infrastructure in the United States. *Government Publications Review 18*, 451–72.

Kalin, S.W. (1991). Searching behavior of remote users: a study of one online public access catalog (OPAC). *Proceedings of the 54th Annual Meeting of the American Society for Information Science 28*, 178–85.

Kaske, N.K. (1988). Variability and intensity over time of subject searching in an online public access catalog. *Information Technology and Libraries 7*, 273–87.

Katzer, J. & Snyder, H. (1990). Toward a more realistic assessment of information retrieval performance. *Proceedings of the 53d Annual Meeting of the American Society for Information Science 27*, 80–85.

Khoo, C.S.G. & Poo, D.C.C. (1994). Expert system approach to online catalog subject searching. *Information Processing and Management 30*, 223–38.

Krikelas, J. (1983). Information-seeking behavior: patterns and concepts. *Drexel Library Quarterly 19*, 5–20.

Kuhlthau, C.C. (1983). *Library research process: case studies and interventions with high school seniors in advanced placement English classes using Kelly's theory of constructs.* Princeton, NJ: Rutgers University. Unpublished doctoral dissertation.

— (1988). Developing a model of the library search process: cognitive and affective aspects. *RQ 28*, 232–42.

— (1989). Information search process: a summary of research and implications for school library media programs. *School Library Media Quarterly 18*, 19–25.

— (1993a). Principle of uncertainty for information seeking. *Journal of Documentation 49*, 339–55.

— (1993b). Implementing a process approach to information skills: a study identifying indicators of success in library media programs. *School Library Media Quarterly 22*, 11–18.

— (1993c). *Seeking meaning: a process approach to library and information services.* Norwood, NJ: Ablex.

—, Spink, A. & Cool, C. (1992). Exploration into stages in the information search process in online information retrieval: communication between users and intermediaries. *Proceedings of the 55th Annual Meeting of the American Society for Information Science 29*, 67–71.

Lancaster, F.W., Elliker, C. & Connell, T.H. (1989). Subject analysis. *Annual Review of Information Science and Technology 24*, 35–84.

— & Warner, A.J. (1993). *Information retrieval today.* Arlington, VA: Information Resources.

Large, A., Beheshti, J., Breuleux, A. & Renaud, A. (1994). Comparison of information retrieval from print and CD-ROM versions of an encyclopedia by elementary school students. *Information Processing and Management 30*, 449–513.

Larson, R.R. (1991). Between Scylla and Charybdis: subject searching in the online catalog. *Advances in Librarianship 15*, 175–236.

Lee, E. & MacGregor, J. (1985). Minimizing user search time in menu retrieval systems. *Human Factors 27*, 157–62.

Lee, J.H., Kim, M.H. & Lee, Y.J. (1993). Information retrieval based on conceptual distance in IS-A hierarchies. *Journal of Documentation 49*, 188–207.

Lin, N. & Garvey, W.D. (1972). Information needs and uses. *Annual Review of Information Science and Technology 7*, 1–37.

Lipetz, B. (1970). Information needs and uses. *Annual Review of Information Science and Technology 5*, 1–32.

Loertscher, D. (1988). *Taxonomies of the school library media program.* Englewood, CO: Libraries Unlimited.

Lucarella, D. & Zanzi, A. (1993). Information retrieval from hypertext: an approach using plausible inference. *Information Processing & Management 29*, 299–312.

Lunde, D.B. & Copeland, N.S. (1989). Online catalog use studies: part II. *Library Hi Tech Bibliography 4*, 99–112.

Lynch, C.A. & Preston, C.M. (1990). Internet access to information resources. *Annual Review of Information Science and Technology 25*, 263–312.

MacGregor, J.N. & Lee, E.S. (1987a). Menu search: random or systematic? *International Journal of Man-Machine Studies 26*, 627–31.

— & — (1987b). Performance and preference in videotex menu retrieval: a review of the empirical literature. *Behaviour & Information Technology 6*, 43–68.

Marchionini, G. (1989). Information-seeking strategies of novices using a full-text electronic encyclopedia. *Journal of the American Society for Information Science 40*, 54–66.

—, Dwiggins, S., Katz, A. & Lin, X. (1993). Information seeking in full-text end-user-oriented search systems: the roles of domain and search expertise. *Library and Information Science Research 15*, 35–69.

— & Liebscher, P. (1991). Performance in electronic encyclopedias: implications for adaptive systems. *Proceedings of the 54th Annual Meeting of the American Society for Information Science 28*, 39–48.

Markey, K. (1983). Thus spake the OPAC user. *Information Technology and Libraries 2*, 381–87.

— (1984). *Subject searching in library catalogs: before and after the introduction of online catalogs.* Dublin, OH: OCLC.

Marshall, S. (1992). Key to access. *Government Insider 2*, 14–16.

Martyn, J. (1974). Information needs and uses. *Annual Review of Information Science and Technology 9*, 1–23.

Matthews, J.R., ed. (1986). *Impact of online catalogs.* New York: Schuman.

—, Lawrence, G.S. & Ferguson, D.K., eds. (1983). *Using online catalogs: a nationwide survey.* New York: Schuman.

McClure, C.R., Bishop, A., Doty, P. & Rosenbaum, H. (1991). *National research in education network: research and policy perspectives.* Norwood, NJ: Ablex.

—, Ryan, J. & Moen, W.E. (1992). Identifying and describing federal information inventory/locators systems: preliminary findings and key issues. *Proceedings of the 55th Annual Meeting of the American Society for Information Science 29*, 110–19.

McCone, G.K. & Starr, D.O. (1990). Document delivery using image transmission over Internet: a pilot project at the National Agricultural Library. *Proceedings of the 53d Annual Meeting of the American Society for Information Science 27*, 36–38.

Meadows, C.T. (1992). *Text information retrieval systems.* San Diego, CA: Academic.

Menzel, H. (1966). Information needs and uses in science and technology. *Annual Review of Information Science and Technology 1*, 41–69.

Metoyer-Duran, C. (1993a). *Gatekeepers in ethnoliguistic communities.* Norwood, NJ: Ablex.

— (1993b). Information and referral process in culturally diverse communities. *RQ 32*, 359–71.

— (1993c). Information gatekeepers. *Annual Review of Information Science and Technology 28*, 111–49.

Mischo, W.H. & Jounghyoun, L. (1987). End-user searching of bibliographic databases. *Annual Review of Information Science and Technology 22*, 227–63.

Moholt, P. (1988). Research issues in information access. In *Rethinking the library in the information age–Vol. II: issues in library research: proposals for the 1990s*, 93–97. Washington, DC: Office of Library Programs, Department of Education.

National Library of Medicine. (1988). *Survey of individual users of MEDLINE on the NLM system.* Bethesda, MD: National Library of Medicine. (NTIS # PB89-133722.)

Newby, G.B. (1991). Navigation: a fundamental concept for information systems with implications for information retrieval. *Proceedings of the 54th Annual Meeting of the American Society for Information Science 28*, 111–17.

—, Nilan, M.S. & Duvall, L.M. (1991). Toward a reassessment of individual differences for information systems: the power of user-based situational predictors. *Proceedings of the 54th Annual Meeting of the American Society for Information Science 28*, 73–81.

Nielsen, B. (1986). What they say they do and what they do: assessing online catalog use interaction through transaction monitoring. *Information Technology and Libraries 5*, 28–34.

Nielsen, J. & Molich, R. (1990). Heuristic evaluation of user interfaces. *Proceedings of the Association for Computing Machinery's Special Interest Group on Computer and Human Interaction*, Apr. 1–5, 249–56.

O'Neill, E.T. & Vizine-Goetz, D. (1988). Quality control in online databases. *Annual Review of Information Science and Technology 23*, 125–56.

Paap, K.R. & Roske-Hofstrand, R.J. (1988). Design of menus. In M. Helander, ed. *Handbook of Human-Computer Interaction*, 105–35. Amsterdam, The Netherlands: North-Holland.

Paisley, W. (1968). Information needs and uses. *Annual Review of Information Science and Technology 3*, 1–30.

Palmer, J. & Harding, S. (1992). Can information users be classified like books? *Library and Information Science Research News 15*, 12–16.

Palmquist, R.A. (1992). Impact of information technology on the individual. *Annual Review of Information Science and Technology 27*, 3–42.

Pao, M.L. (1983). Specificity of terms in questions. *Proceedings of the 46th American Society for Information Science Annual Meeting 20*, 26-27.

Pao, M.L. (1989). *Concepts of information retrieval.* Englewood, CO: Libraries Unlimited.

Park, T.K. (1993). Nature of relevance in information retrieval: an experimental study. *Library Quarterly 63*, 318–51.

Peters, T. (1989). When smart people fail: an analysis of the transaction log of an online public access catalog. *Journal of Academic Librarianship 15*, 267–73.

Peters, T. (1991). *Online catalog: a critical examination of public use.* Jefferson, NC: MacFarland.

Pfaffenberger, B. (1990). *Democratizing information: online databases and the rise of end-user searching.* Boston, MA: Hall.

Pollard, R. (1993). Hypertext-based thesaurus as a subject browsing aid for bibliographic databases. *Information Processing & Management 29*, 345–57.

Rada, R., Wang, W. & Brichall, A. (1993). Retrieval hierarchies in hypertext. *Information Processing & Management 29*, 359–71.

Rasmussen, E.M. (1992). Parallel information processing. *Annual Review of Information Science and Technology 27*, 99–130.

Reneker, M.H. (1993). Qualitative study of information seeking among members of an academic community: methodological issues and problems. *Library Quarterly 63*, 487–507.

Rice, R.E. & Danowski, J.A. (1991). Comparing comments and semantic networks about voice mail. *Proceedings of the 54th Annual Meeting of the American Society for Information Science 28*, 134–38.

Rohde, N.F. (1986). Information needs. *Advances in Librarianship 14*, 49–73.

Rorvig, M.E. (1988). Psychometric measurement and information retrieval. *Annual Review of Information Science and Technology 23*, 157–90.

Rosenbaum, H. & Snyder, H. (1991). Investigation of emerging norms in computer mediated communications: an empirical study of computer conferencing. *Proceedings of the 54th Annual Meeting of the American Society for Information Science 28*, 15–23.

Salton, G. (1986). *Automatic text processing: the transformation, analysis and retrieval of information by computers.* Reading, MA: Addison-Wesley.

Salton, G., Fox, E.A. & Vorhees, E.M. (1986). Advanced feedback methods in information retrieval. *Journal of the American Society for Information Science 36*, 200–10.

Saracevic, T. (1970). Ten years of relevance experimentation: a summary and synthesis of conclusions. *Proceedings of the American Society for Information Science 7*, 33–36.

Saracevic, T. (1975). Relevance: a review of a framework for thinking on the notion in information science. *Journal of the American Society for Information Science 26*, 321–43.

— (1980). Research project on classification of questions in information retrieval—preliminary work. *Proceedings of the 43d American Society for Information Science Annual Meeting 17*, 146–48.

— (1983). On a method for studying the structure and nature of requests in information retrieval. *Proceedings of the 46th American Society for Information Science Annual Meeting 20*, 22–25.

— (1984). Measuring the degree of agreement between searchers. *Proceedings of the 47th Annual Meeting of the American Society for Information Science 21*, 227–30.

— (1985). Information retrieval. *In* E.H. Brenner & T. Saracevic, eds. *Indexing and searching in perspective*, 4:1–4:29. Philadelphia, PA: National Federation of Abstracting and Indexing Services.

— (1991). Individual differences in organizing, searching and retrieving information. *Proceedings of the 54th Annual Meeting of the American Society for Information Science 28*, 82–86.

— & Kantor, P. (1988a). Study of information seeking and retrieving: II. users, questions, and effectiveness. *Journal of the American Society for Information Science 39*, 177–96.

— & — (1988b). Study of information seeking and retrieving: III. searchers, searches, and overlap. *Journal of the American Society for Information Science 39*, 197–216.

—, Kantor, P., Chamis, A. & Trivison, D. (1987). *Experiments on the cognitive aspects of information seeking and retrieving.* Final Report for National Science Foundation Grant IST-8505411. Washington, DC: National Technical Information Service Educational Research Information Center (ED 281530).

—, —, — & — (1988). Study of information seeking and retrieving: I. background and methodology. *Journal of the American Society of Information Science 39*, 161–76.

—, Mokros, H. & Su, L. (1990). Nature of interaction between users and intermediaries in online searching: a qualitative analysis. *Proceedings of the 53d Annual Meeting of the American Society for Information Science 27*, 47–54.

Savolainen, R. (1993). Sense-making theory: reviewing the interests of a user-centered approach to information seeking and use. *Information Processing & Management 29*, 13–28.

Schamber, L. (1991). Users' criteria for evaluation in a multimedia environment. *Proceedings of the 54th Annual Meeting of the American Society for Information Science 28*, 126–33.

Schwartz, C. & Eisenmann, L.M. (1986). Subject analysis. *Annual Review of Information Science and Technology 21*, 37–62.

Shaffer, C.A. (1992). Data representation for geographic information systems. *Annual Review of Information Science and Technology 27*, 135–72.

Shaw, D. (1991). Human-computer interface for information retrieval. *Annual Review of Information Science and Technology 26*, 55–195.

Shneiderman, B. (1986). Designing menu selection systems. *Journal of the American Society for Information Science 37*, 57–70.

— (1987). *Designing the user interface: strategies for effective human-computer interaction.* Reading, MA: Addison-Wesley.

Shute, S.J. & Smith, P.J. (1993). Knowledge-based search tactics. *Information Processing & Management 29*, 29–45.

Smith, D. (1985). Commercialization and privatization of government information. *Government Publications Review 12*, 45.

Smith, L.C. (1987). Artificial intelligence and information retrieval. *Annual Review of Information Science and Technology 22*, 41–78.

Smith, T.W. (1988). *Assessing the usability of user interfaces: Guidance and online help features.* Tucson, AZ: University of Arizona. Unpublished doctoral dissertation. (University Microfilms International # ADG88-09947.)

Soergel, D. (1985). *Organizing information: principles of database and retrieval systems.* San Diego, CA: Academic.

Solomon, P. (1992). On the dynamics of information system use: from novice to ? *Proceedings of the 55th Annual Meeting of the American Society for Information Science 29*, 162–69.

— (1993). Children's information retrieval behavior: a case analysis of an OPAC. *Journal of the American Society for Information Science 44*, 245–64.

Sowizral, H.A. (1985). Expert systems. *Annual Review of Information Science and Technology 20*, 179–200.

Spavold, J. (1990). Child as naive user: a study of database use with young children. *International Journal of Man-Machine Studies 32*, 603–25.

Spink, A. & Saracevic, T. (1992). Sources and use of search terms in online searching. *Proceedings of the 55th Annual Meeting of the American Society for Information Science 29*, 249–55.

Sprehe, T.J. (1992). Online public access to federal agency computers. *Government Information Quarterly 9*, 199–203.

Steinberg, D. & Metz, P. (1984). User response to and knowledge about an online catalog. *College and Research Libraries 45*, 66–70.

Stewart, R.K. (1990). *Access and efficiency in Reagan-era information policy: a case study of the attempt to privatize the National Technical Information Service.* Seattle, WA: University of Washington. Unpublished doctoral dissertation. (University Microfilms International # 9104302.)

Stripling, B.K. & Pitts, J.M. (1988). *Brainstorms and blueprints: teaching library research as a thinking process.* Englewood, CO: Libraries Unlimited.

Sullivan, P. & Seiden, P. (1985). Educating online catalog users: the protocol assessment of needs. *Library Hi Tech 3*, 11–19.

Sy, K. & Robbin, A. (1990). Federal statistical policies and programs: how good are the numbers? *Annual Review of Information Science and Technology 25,* 3–54.

Taylor, R.A. (1986). *Using multiple dialog modes in a user-system interface to accommodate different levels of user experience: an experimental study.* Austin, TX: University of Texas at Austin Unpublished doctoral dissertation. (University Microfilms International # 87-06113.)

Tolle, J.E. (1983). Understanding patrons' use of online catalogs: transaction log analysis of the search method. *Proceedings of the 46th Annual Meeting of the American Society for Information Science 20,* 167–71.

Tremblay, J. & Sorenson, P. (1985). *Introduction to data structures with new applications.* New York: McGraw-Hill.

Tsai, B. (1992). Effectiveness measurement of electronic mail communications within a special professional community. *Proceedings of the 55th Annual Meeting of the American Society for Information Science 29,* 75–85.

Verhoeven, S.M. (1990). User surveys. *Encyclopedia of Library and Information Science 45,* 373–99.

Vickery, B. & Vickery, A. (1993). Online search interface design. *Journal of Documentation 49,* 103–87.

Vigil, P.J. (1986). Software interface. *Annual Review of Information Science and Technology 21,* 63–86.

Walter, V.A. & Borgman, C.L. (1991). Science library catalog: a prototype information retrieval system for children. *Youth Services in Libraries 4,* 159–66.

Warner, A.J. (1987). Natural language processing. *Annual Review of Information Science and Technology 22,* 79–108.

Warner, J. (1992). Retrieval performance tests in relation to online bibliographic searching. *Proceedings of the 55th Annual Meeting of the American Society for Information Science 29,* 231–41.

Weiskel, T.C. (1986). Libraries as life-systems: information, entropy and coevolution on campus. *College and Research Libraries 47,* 545–63.

Wersig, G. & Windel, G. (1985). Information science needs a theory of "information actions." *Social Science Information Studies 5,* 11–23.

Westbrook, L. (1993). User needs: a synthesis and analysis of current theories for the practitioner. *RQ 32,* 541–49.

White, H.D. & McCain, K.W. (1989). Bibliometrics. *Annual Review of Information Science and Technology 24,* 119–86.

Wiederhold, G. (1987). *File organization for database design.* New York: McGraw-Hill.

Wilbur, W.J. (1992). A retrieval system based on automatic relevance weighting of search terms. *Proceedings of the 55th Annual Meeting of the American Society for Information Science 29,* 216–20.

Wildemuth, B.M., de Bliek, R., Friedman, C.P. & Dekker, H. (1991). Measures of success in searching a full-text fact base. *Proceedings of the 53d Annual Meeting of the American Society for Information Science 27.*

—, de Bliek, R., He, S. & Friedman, C.P. (1992). Search moves made by novice end users. *Proceedings of the 55th Annual Meeting of the American Society for Information Science 29,* 154–61.

—, Jacob, E.K., Fullington, A., de Bliek, R. & Friedman, C.P. (1991). Detailed analysis of end-user search behaviors. *Proceedings of the 54th Annual Meeting of the American Society for Information Science 28,* 302–12.

Willett, P. (1988). Recent trends in hierarchic document clustering: a critical review. *Information Processing and Management 24,* 577–97.

Wilson, T.D. (1981). On user studies and information needs. *Journal of Documentation 37,* 3–15.

— (1984). Cognitive approach to information seeking behavior and information use. *Social Science Information Studies 4,* 197–204.

Yee, M.M. (1991). System design and cataloging meet the user: user interfaces to online public access catalogs. *Journal of the American Society for Information Science 42,* 78–98.

Ziegler, J.E. & Fahnrich, K.P. (1988). Direct manipulation. *In* M. Helander, ed. *Handbook of human-computer interaction,* 123–33. Amsterdam, The Netherlands: North-Holland.

IV

INSTRUCTIONAL MESSAGE DESIGN RESEARCH

Frank M. Dwyer, Pennsylvania State University

Associate Editor

26. VISUAL MESSAGE DESIGN AND LEARNING: THE ROLE OF STATIC AND DYNAMIC ILLUSTRATIONS

Gary J. Anglin
UNIVERSITY OF KENTUCKY

Robert L. Towers
EASTERN KENTUCKY UNIVERSITY

W. Howard Levie*
INDIANA UNIVERSITY

The use of illustrations in instructional materials is pervasive (Feaver, 1977; Slythe, 1970). With the proliferation of illustrations in instructional materials, it becomes increasingly important to investigate their effects on student learning. A substantial research literature has already accumulated concerning the role of illustrations in instructional materials. The purpose of this chapter is to introduce researchers in instructional message design to the primary theories of picture perception and to provide a survey and critique of the visual message design research that incorporates static and dynamic (animated) illustrations.

26.1 SCOPE

The effective use of illustrations (pictures, charts, graphs, and diagrams) in instructional materials is an important facet of instructional message design (see 9.7, 16.4.2). Fleming (1993) defines a message as "a pattern of signs (words, pictures, gestures) produced for the purpose of modifying the psychomotor, cognitive, or affective behavior of one or more persons" (p. x). We define pictures as illustrations that have some resemblance to the entity that they stand for, while nonrepresentational graphics, including charts, graphs, and diagrams, are more abstract but do use spatial layout in a consequential way (Knowlton, 1966; Levie & Dickie, 1973; Rieber, 1994; Winn, 1987). Levie (1987) has suggested that there are at least four lines of research on illustrations: (a) picture perception, (b) memory for pictures, (c) learning and cognition, and (d) affective responses to pictures. In this chapter we will first present several theories of picture perception and a brief discussion of selected memory models that have been used to describe how words and pictures are encoded. Next, knowledge acquisition studies incorporating static and dynamic pictures will be reviewed. Finally, we will critically analyze the literature and offer suggestions for future research and practice based on results of primary research and all literature reviews discussed in the chapter. Given the magnitude of the literature, our own expertise, and the economics of publishing, we have only reviewed comparative-experimental research studies (see Chapter 39). Visual message design studies completed using other research methods are certainly reasonable and appropriate. There are many variables to consider when designing visual instructional messages. Our system of classification represents only one perspective on the literature. We have reviewed a wide range of studies, but we do not claim that the review is exhaustive (see 5.2).

26.2 PICTURE PERCEPTION

26.2.1 Theories of Picture Perception

When is a surface with marks on it a "picture?" How do pictures carry meaning? What kinds of meaning can pictures carry (see 8.8.2, 15.8)? Is there a grammar of picturing? Is picture perception essentially innate, or is it a skill that must be learned?

Questions such as these have provoked conjecture from philosophers, psychologists, art historians, semioticians, and computer scientists. It is a fascinating, disputatious literature, one with implications for researchers in educational communication and technology—although widely neglected.

This section of the chapter provides a concise introduction to the major scientific theories of picture perception. To set the discussion of modern theories in historical context, the article begins with a description of the theory of linear perspective developed during the Italian Renaissance. Then two major conflicting theories are introduced: James J. Gibson's resemblance theory, in which meaning is

---

* Prior to Dr. Howard Levie's untimely death, he contributed to this chapter, both through his writing and his mentoring of the senior author.

based on the picture's resemblance to the visual environment, and E. H. Gombrich's constructivist theory, in which meaning is based on pictorial conventions. Next, a compromise position by Margaret Hagen is described. Then a third major theory is presented: Rudolph Arnheim's Gestalt approach, followed by the views of Julian Hochberg, who is in opposition to Arnheim, and John M. Kennedy, who supports Arnheim.

Next the discussion shifts to two approaches from the field of semiotics: James Knowlton's analysis of the iconic sign, and Nelson Goodman's theory of symbol systems. Finally, some emerging approaches from cognitive science are noted, exemplified by David Marr's computational theory of vision.

Only the gist of each approach is presented, but suggestions for further reading are provided. Overviews to the area can be found in several edited books containing chapters on a wide range of issues: Crozier and Chapman (1984), Hagen (1980b, 1980c), Mitchell (1980), Nodine and Fisher (1979), Olson (1974), and Perkins and Leondar (1977).

26.2.2 Renaissance Perspective Theory: Brunelleschi

The technique of linear perspective by which three-dimensional scenes are represented on two-dimensional surfaces has its origins in ancient Greek architecture and scene design. It was not until 1420, however, that a theoretical basis for the technique was elucidated by Filippo Brunelleschi of Florence. The technique involves using the pattern of light rays emanating from a natural scene. The artists draws the composition that is projected onto a picture plane—a cross section of the straight lines connecting the artist's viewpoint with the objects in the scene. Accordingly, our ability to understand pictures is due to the optical equivalence between pictures and their real-world referents. Because the picture is an optical surrogate for the scene, picture perception is thought to be straightforward and essentially automatic.

But there are problems with this theory. According to the theory, a picture will be perceived accurately only when the person viewing the picture assumes the point of observation taken by the artist. Viewing the picture from a different position should result in distorted perception—an outcome that does not occur in practice. For example, when we look at a portrait from an oblique angle we do not conclude that the person portrayed actually has an elongated head. We take notice of our orientation to the picture surface and judge shapes as though our viewpoint were perpendicular to the picture [although modest distortion due to oblique viewing may occur (Goldstein, 1987)].

Another problem is that successful pictures often violate perspective theory. For example, artists rarely obey the rules of perspective in the vertical dimension. When a tall building is seen from ground level, the rules of three-point perspective stipulate that the sides of the building should be drawn as converging lines. Such drawings are usually judged to look unnatural. On the other hand, when artists

violate perspective in the third dimension, the "error" is visually noticed only by those few who are attuned to watch for it. Another violation is that artists often use more than one station point. Often each major figure in a picture is drawn from a different station point, a fact that goes unnoticed by most viewers. On the other hand, pictures drawn from a single station point can look distorted if the station point is very close to the subject. Yet another problem—and there are several more—is that the shapes on the picture plane are ambiguous since they can be the result of the projections of more than one three-dimensional object.

Thus the techniques of pictorial composition used in post-Renaissance Western culture often disobey the geometric rules of perspective. In practice, pictures are very rarely the optical equivalence of the sense they represent, and Renaissance perspective theory cannot serve as an adequate explanation of picture perception.

Detailed treatments of the geometry of perspective are provided by Hagen (1986) and Kubovy (1986). Other commentary on this topic can be found in Greene (1983), Haber (1979), Penrice (1980), and Pirenne (1970).

26.2.3 Resemblance Theory: James J. Gibson

The laws of linear perspective were the starting point for Gibson's resemblance theory of picture perception (sometimes called *projective theory* or the "*direct perception*" approach). Although modified somewhat by his final position on the status of pictures (Gibson, 1979), Gibson's best known definition of *picture* is: "A picture is a surface so treated that a delimited optic array to a point of observation is made available that contains the same kind of information that is found in the ambient optic arrays of an ordinary environment" (Gibson, 1971, p. 31).

But what is this "kind of information" that is found in both the picture and environment? According to Gibson it is something beyond the static lines and shapes in the picture; it is a higher-order kind of information consisting of formless, timeless invariants. The concept of an invariant is described by Gibson:

> When a young child sees the family cat at play, the front view, side view, rear view, top view, and so on are not seen, and what gets perceived is the invariant cat. Hence, when the child first sees a picture of a cat, he is prepared to pick up the invariants, and he pays no attention to the frozen cartoon. It is not that he sees an abstract cat, or a conceptual cat, or the common features of the class of cats; what he gets is the information for the persistence of that peculiar, furry, mobile layout of surfaces (Gibson, 1979, p. 271).

These stable, enduring structures that are picked up from the environment are also present in the optic array provided by a picture, and are used to interpret the picture. An example of an invariant is the texture of surfaces such as sand or fur. Such textures are represented in photographs, and act as optical gradients that guide judgments of distances (Gibson & Bridgeman, 1987). Although it is not equally clear how we are able to perceive the invariant shapes of the objects in a picture (e.g., what does an "invariant cat" look like?), Gibson uses the concept to avoid some of the problems of perspective theory (e.g., how can we identify an object in a picture if it is depicted from a point of view we have never seen?). Nevertheless, Gibson's theory of pictorial representation is based primarily on the optical correspondence of the picture and the environment, and it is the structure of the stimulus that is the driving force in picture perception.

For recent discussions of Gibson's work see Cutting (1982, 1987), Fodor and Pylyshyn (1981), Natsoulas (1983), Reed and Jones (1982), Rogers and Costall (1983), and Wilcox and Edwards (1982).

26.2.4 Constructivism: E. H. Gombrich

Perception, as Neisser (1976) puts it, is where reality and cognition meet. Whereas Gibson assigns the major role in this meeting to reality, constructivists such as Gombrich emphasize the role of cognition. Pictures do not "tell their own story," Gombrich argues, the viewer must *construct* a meaning (see also 7.3.1).

Pictures will be interpreted differently depending on the attitude taken by the eye of the beholder. What we see, or think we see, is filtered through a variety of mental sets and expectations. For example, briefly shown playing cards in which hearts are colored black are sometime seen as purple (Bruner & Postman, 1949).

One special class of expectations consists of the artistic conventions in common use. Gombrich (1969) traces the history of Western art, showing how cultural and technological changes have altered the criteria for pictorial realism. What is judged to be a "good likeness" is a function of the conventions and drawing techniques that now look "wrong" and amateurish to our modern eye.

A more pervasive example of a system of pictorial convention in use today is the outline drawing. The use of lines to represent the edges of objects is a substantial departure from nature. The objects in the world are not bounded by lines, and it is due to convention that we perceive outline drawings as depicting shapes rather than arrangements of wires. Whereas the convention that shapes can be represented by outlines is a rapidly acquired understanding, the ability to interpret some conventions such as implied motion cues may require extensive experience or even direct instruction (Levie, 1978).

Such conventions are not arbitrary. Artists are not free to adopt any technique they choose. In fact, the history of naturalistic art can be thought of as a series of innovations in the technique of approximating what is seen by viewing the environment. But Gombrich argues that realism in art is more than just an effort to record the optical data present in nature. The artists must produce an "illusion of reality" that matches the viewer's concept (schema) of what a picture of a given kind *should* look like. And how are these schemata acquired? By repeated exposure to the art of the day. These

schemata then function as the standards for judging reality in subsequent picture viewing.

Such schemata can also affect our perceptions of nature. "We not only believe what we see: to some extent we see what we believe" (Gregory, 1970, p. 86). Our experience with art may lead us to look at the natural environment in new ways. For example, the sensitive museum visitor may note that the pastel patches of impressionist paintings can be observed in nature as well. So the ways of representing nature can become ways of seeing nature. Similarly, artists vacillate between painting what they see in nature and seeing in nature what they paint on canvas.

One controversial claim by Gombrich (1972) is that pictures lack the "statement function" of words. For example, he argues that the statement "The cat sits on the mat" cannot be directly pictured. A picture of a cat on a mat depicts a particular cat in a particular environment as seen from a particular viewpoint. An equivalent verbal message would be something like: "There is a cat seen from behind." Gombrich would not, however, propose that pictures are a poor source of ideas. Indeed, the conceptual richness of pictorial representation is a central theme of his work.

For further comment on this approach, see Blinder (1983), Carrier (1983), Gregory (1973, 1981), Heffernan (1985), and Katz (1983).

26.2.5 A Generative Theory: Margaret Hagen

Is picture perception primarily a bottom-up process as Gibson claims, or a top-down process as Gombrich claims? Hagen (1978, 1980a) provides a generative theory of representation that suggests a reconciliation: "Meaning is not given by the head to the unstructured stimulus, nor is it given by the stimulus to the unstructured head. The relation between the two is reciprocal and symmetrical" (1980a, p. 45).

In developing her thesis, Hagen describes differences between how we perceive the natural world and how we perceive "the world within the picture." For example, as compared to natural perception, picture perception compresses the perceived third dimension and increases the awareness of the angle among objects (the spread). Thus, picture perception has a special character that is based partly on ecological geometry (the natural perspective of the visual environment), and partly on the creativity or generativity of the perceiver.

Recently Hagen (1986) has provided a category system for describing the geometrical foundations of many styles of representational art: early Egyptian art, Roman murals, Northwest Coast Indian art, Japanese art, Mayan art, and ice age cave art, to name just a few. For example, there are several options for the location of the artist's station point. It can be close to the subject of the picture, at a moderate distance, or at optical infinity, in which case vanishing points and the convergence of parallel lines (e.g., railroad tracks meeting at the horizon) are obviated. Also, the system can involve the use of a single station point or multiple station points. Hagen observes that each system of depiction is "correct" when judged according to its assumptions. Thus in evaluating the art of other times and cultures, we must reject the premise that the prevailing post-Renaissance system of Western art is the only valid system for representing reality, a position also taken by Arnheim.

26.2.6 A Gestalt Approach: Rudolf Arnheim

According to Arnheim, picture perception is not primarily an act of direct perception as Gibson claims, nor is it a response to changing conventions as Gombrich claims. Picture perception is primarily a matter of organizing the lines and other elements of a picture into shapes and patterns according to innate laws of structure. Arnheim (1954) applies the principles of Gestalt psychology to the study of art. He shows how the laws of organization (e.g., the rules of grouping, the laws of simplicity and good continuation) can be found in the art of many periods. Meaning, he argues, has always been embodied in the Gestalt, the whole which is greater than the sum of its parts. Picture making is also derived from Gestalt principles:

> The urge to create simple shapes . . . cannot be explained as an urge to copy nature; it can be understood only when one realizes that perceiving is not passive recording but understanding, that understanding can take place only through the conception of definable shapes. For this reason art begins not with attempts to duplicate nature, but with highly abstract general principles that take the form of elementary shapes (Arnheim, 1986, pp. 161–162).

Arnheim observes that our judgment of the art of other times and cultures suffers from "a prejudice generated by the particular conventions of Western art since the Renaissance" (Arnheim, 1986, p. 159). Furthermore, current technique is so pervasive that we assume that it is the only correct way to make pictures. But the techniques of unfamiliar art styles are not, as sometimes supposed, due to lack of skill or accidentally acquired convention; nor are they deliberate distortions devised for some artistic purpose. Each style is based on an internally consistent system of solutions to visual problems, solutions that are no more in need of justification than contemporary technique.

Arnheim (1969) is also known for his advocacy of "visual thinking." He rejects the belief that reasoning occurs only through the use of language. In fact, he argues that thinking occurs primarily through abstract imagery. Arnheim champions the role of art in education and stresses the importance of teaching students to become fluent in thinking with shapes.

Another recurrent theme in Arnheim's work is the nature of abstraction. Representational art involves one kind of abstraction. Portraits, for example, are more abstract than their real-world referents. In such cases, "abstractness is a means by which a picture interprets what it portrays" (Arnheim, 1969, p. 137). On the other hand, pictures may be less abstract than the concepts they symbolize. For example, the silhouette of a cow on a roadside sign, although quite abstract, is still less abstract than the concept "cattle crossing." Arnheim (1974) discusses some of the problems faced by educators in determining the most effective kind and level of abstraction to use in instructional illustrations.

Although Gestalt ideas have been eschewed by cognitive psychologists, recent discoveries in visual anatomy and physiology and the study of perceptual organization have attracted some renewed interest in the area (Hoffman & Dodwell, 1985; Kubovy, 1981, #1056).

26.2.7 Picture Perception as Purposive Behavior: Julian Hochberg

Hochberg opposes the Gestalt approach, arguing that "the whole stimulus configuration cannot in general be taken as the effective determinant for perception" (Peterson & Hochberg, 1983, p. 192). Here is why: All aspects of a picture cannot be perceived in a single glance. Vision is sharp only in a small central area of the visual field—an area about the size of your thumbnail when held at arm's length. On the retina of the eye, acuity falls off rapidly from this area (the fovea). Since detailed discriminations are possible only on the fovea, it is necessary to scan pictures in order to take in all the details. Scanning does not occur in smooth sweeps, but rather as a series of very rapid jumps called *saccades* and brief stops called *fixations*—normally about one-third second each. The information obtained from these separate fixations must be integrated into a mental map. Thus "at any given time most of the picture as we perceive it is not only the retina of the eye, nor on the plane of the picture—it is in the mind's eye" (Hochberg, 1972). So the whole is not perceived directly, as Arnheim claims; it is the result of synthesis based on the analysis of parts. These interactions between the picture, eye movements, and cognitions, are "highly skilled sequential purposive behaviors" that are, according to Hochberg, the keys to understanding picture perception.

Hochberg (1979, 1980) describes how certain techniques used in painting can be thought to mimic the workings of the visual system. For example, in some of Rembrandt's paintings most of the canvas is blurred; only a few areas are rendered in sharp detail, simulating what is registered by the eye in a series of fixations. Similarly, techniques used in impressionistic paintings (which Hochberg calls "painting for parafoveal viewing"), pointillist paintings, and Op Art (Vitz & Glimcher, 1984) mirror processes of the human perceptual system.

Another issue discussed by Hochberg concerns the question of which picture of an object is the "best" picture. Hochberg uses the term *canonical form* to refer to "the most readily recognized and remembered view or 'clean up' version of some form or object" (Hochberg, 1980, p. 76). Canonical form preserves the most distinctive features of an object and eliminates noninformative features. Another factor in determining canonical form is the point of view from which an object is depicted.

26.2.8 A Mentalistic Approach: John M. Kennedy

Kennedy is supportive of Arnheim's approach and opposed to Gibson and Gombrich. He argues that we will learn very little about how pictures are perceived by studying the optical geometry of naturalistic art. Understanding picture perception should begin with the realization that pictures are made by people trying to communicate to receivers who are themselves intelligent perceivers striving to grasp the sender's intent. Pictures are made to communicate ideas, not just show scenes. To exemplify his approach, Kennedy discusses the pictorial metaphor:

> Imagine a picture of a businessman with as many arms as an octopus, each hand holding a telephone. Or imagine a picture of a bride looking into a mirror and seeing a harried housewife. These pictures violate the laws of physics; they break the rules that Gibson called on. . . . And they do so precisely because the artist wants to put across ideas: that business men are overworked; that present bliss gives rise to future stress (Kennedy, 1985, p. 38).

Metaphoric pictures present two meanings, one false, the other intended. Understanding the perception of such pictures requires a "mentalistic analysis" in which assumptions are made about the experience and mental processes of the sender and the receiver. "The person who makes the metaphor expects the recipient to notice both meanings, and expects the recipient to know which was intended, and expects the recipient to know what the maker expected from the recipient" (Kennedy, 1984b, p. 901). Kennedy also argues that pictorial cues such as implied motion cues can be conceived of as metaphor rather than as pictorial convention.

As a historical footnote, Kennedy was Gibson's student at Cornell, and at one time followed in his footsteps, writing a survey of the field that was based largely on Gibsonian ideas (1974). But a decade later, Kennedy would write: "Regrettably scientific psychology as found in our universities can never be anything more than a trivial pursuit. By its very nature it is incapable of profound insights into humankind" (Kennedy, 1984a, p. 30). Although this represents a dramatic change in philosophy on Kennedy's part, the attack on a competing approach is by no means unusual. The picture perception literature is an intellectual battlefield delightfully seasoned with charge and countercharge. Theorists are robustly combative in attacking opposing views while defending their own.

26.2.9 A Semiotic Approach: James Knowlton

The theories discussed so far approach the topic from points of view related to visual perception, either by way of perceptual psychology or through the analysis of visual art. The next two theories have a different starting point; they derive from a concern with symbol using in general, thus placing the discussion of picture perception in a broader context.

The boundaries of semiotics—the science of signs—are wide and indistinct. The domain includes questions of the meaning of as well as the communication of meaning. Among the central figures in this field are Cassirer (1944), Morris (1946), Pierce (1960), and Sebeok (1976). For further commentary on the contribution of semiotics to picture perception see Cassidy (1982), Eco (1976), Holowka (1981), Langer (1976), Sless (1986), and Veltrusky (1976).

Here, however, we will focus on the theorist in this tradition who speaks most directly to our present concerns with visual message design research: James Knowlton. Knowlton (1964, 1966) develops a metalanguage for talking about pictures beginning with the term *sign*. A sign is a stimulus intentionally produced for the purpose of making reference to some other object or concept. A key distinction is that between digital signs and iconic signs. Digital signs bear no resemblance to their referents. For example, the physical appearance of the signs "man" and "hombre" do not in any way look like their referent. Examples of digital signs are words, numbers, Morse code, Braille, and semaphore. Iconic signs, on the other hand, are not arbitrary in their appearance. In some way, iconic signs include drawings, photographs, maps, and blueprints.

Usually pictures are thought to resemble their referents in terms of visual appearance. Resemblance can, however, take other forms. Knowlton broadens the concept of "picture" to include "logical pictures" and "analogical pictures." Logical pictures resemble their referents in terms of the relationships between elements. An electrical writing schematic, for example, bears no visual resemblance to the piece of apparatus it represents; it is a picture of the pattern of connections between elements. Flowcharts and diagrams are other examples of logical pictures. In analogical pictures, the intent is to portray a resemblance in function. For example, a pictorial analogy could be made between a suit of armor and an insect's exoskeleton. Thus Knowlton's definition of "resemblance" goes far beyond Gibson's concept in which resemblance is based on the optical equivalence of pictures and their referents. And, even when resemblance is based on physical appearance, the resemblance of a picture to its referent can, according to Knowlton, be slight. Sometimes a simple silhouette will do the job. Additionally, the ways in which resemblance functions in pictorial communication often depend on factors that are extrinsic to the picture itself:

> Resemblance does not designate a single relation between pictures and their subjects; it designates the members of a fairly comprehensive class of relations—a class whose boundaries are not clear. And relations of resemblance are not always immediately evident to the uneducated eye. Knowing how to look at a picture is required to discern the ways it resembles its subject. Knowledge of other matters may be required as well—pictorial conventions, referential connections, historical, scientific, or mythical lore that sets the context of the work. Such matters are not taken in at a glance (Elgin, 1984, p. 919).

The most extreme and controversial position on the role of resemblance is taken by Goodman. He asserts that resemblance between picture and nature is not necessary, and that "A picture is realistic to the extent that it is correct under the accustomed system of representation" (Goodman, 1978, p. 130).

26.2.10 Symbol Systems Theory: Nelson Goodman

Goodman (1976) has devised a detailed theory of symbol systems. A symbol system consists of a set of inscriptions (e.g., phonemes, numbers) organized into a scheme that correlates with a field of reference. For example, musical staff notation consists of five horizontal lines on which notes and other marks are placed that correlate with a musical performance. As another example, maps consist of lines, shapes, and symbols that correlate with a musical performance. Also, maps consist of lines, shapes, and symbols that correlate with roads, boundaries, and landmarks. Thus the analysis of a symbol system involves an examination of (1) the scheme of representation, (2) the field of reference, and (3) the rules of correspondence between the two.

Goodman provides several conceptual tools that can be used for analyzing symbol systems. One key concept is *notationality*. Notationality is the degree to which the elements of a symbol system are distinct and are combined according to precise rules. Music is high in notationality. The notes on the scale are distinct in terms of pitch and duration, and the rules for combining them are clear. Mathematics systems are also high in notationality; each number is distinct and the rules for "making statements" are precise. Pictures, on the other hand, are nonnotational. The "elements" of picturing are overlapping, confusable, and lacking in syntax. The lines and shadings that pictures are built from are without limit, and the ways they are combined to produce a symbol are undefined.

Notationality is an aspect of symbol using that may have implications for human information processing. Gardner (1982) speculates that "a case can be made that the left hemisphere of the human brain is relatively more effective than the right at dealing with notational symbol systems, . . . while the right hemisphere is more at ease in dealing with . . . nonnotational systems" (p. 59).

Another key concept in Goodman's theory is repleteness. Some symbol schemes, such as most pictures, are replete (or dense), whereas other schemes, such as printed words, are lacking in repleteness. The degree of repleteness is an index of how many aspects of a scheme are significant. In printed text, changes in the typeface, boldness, ink color, and other physical parameters do not necessarily alter meaning in any significant way. Drawings, on the other hand, are relatively replete, since several aspects of the marks in a drawing are often critical. Paintings are very high in repleteness. "Everything about a painting is part of it—design, coloration, brush stroke, texture, and so on. A painting is unrepeatable in the strict sense of the term" (Kolers, 1983, p. 146).

Goodman distinguishes three primary functions of symbol systems. Symbols can represent concepts by denoting or depicting them. Symbols can *exemplify* ideas or qualities by providing a sample of the concept. And symbols can *express* affective meaning (emotions).

Symbol systems differ in respect to the ease with which they can perform the functions of representation, exemplification, and expression. For example, music, although richly expressive, has no literal denotation. Music in the absence of a title or lyrics is not "about" anything. Number systems are limited in a different way. Numbers represent quantities, but they normally have no expressive function. Most pictorial systems are versatile. Line drawings, photographs, and representational paintings can depict, exemplify, and express forcefully.

Pictures exemplify qualities such as color and shape through the possession and presentation of them. The qualities exemplified are properties of the picture. Pictures express through "metaphorical exemplification", the figurative possession and presentation of emotion. For example, when a picture expresses sorrow, the feeling can be said to be "in the picture." We must, however, learn how to decode the expressive features of pictorial systems. "Emotions are everywhere the same; but the artistic expression of them varies from age to age and from one country to another" (Goodman, 1976, p. 90).

For other comments on Goodman's theory see Coldron (1982), Gardner, Howard, and Perkins (1974), Roupas (1977), Salomon (1979a, 1979b), and Scruton (1974).

26.2.11   Cognitive Science: David Marr

Artificial-intelligence research on computer vision is a rapidly developing area that may contribute to understanding picture perception by humans. One focus of this work involves determining the computations that are required in order to program a computer to see. To do this, it is necessary to specify the nature of the visual input, to describe how this input is transformed into data that can be handled by a computer, and to enumerate the computations that are carried out on-line to produce solutions to visual problems. Such problems include the detection of shape contours and surface textures.

A central figure in this area is David Marr. Marr's (1982) theory of vision involves the analysis of visual input through a series of stages that culminates the meaningful interpretation of an image. In Marr's theory, an initial analysis involves the detection of features such as boundaries. These determinations are used to construct a "primal sketch" that distinguishes the sections of the display. From these sections, surface data such as shading are used to define the simple three-dimensional shapes in the scene. Finally, "generalized cones" form the basis for the representation and recognition of complex shapes such as animals.

Marr (1982) asserts that since the early days of the Gestalt school "students of the psychology of perception have made no serious attempts at an overall understanding of what perception is" (p. 9). Some psychologists are equally skeptical of the reciprocal value of Marr's work. Kolers (1983), for example, comments that "Although the study of human perceiving may continue to inform the study of machine vision, it remains to be seen whether students of computer vision will teach us much about human perceiving" (p. 160). For comments on Marr's work and other recent approaches to computer vision, see Connell and Brady (1987), Fischler and Firschein (1987), Gregory (1981), Jackendoff (1987), Kitcher (1988), Kolers and Smythe (1984), Lowe (1987), and Rosenfeld (1986).

A theory that is closely related to Marr's approach has been proposed by Biederman (1985, 1987). Biederman describes a process by which an object in a two-dimensional image can be recognized. The process uses a set of primitive elements: 36 generalized-cone components called *geons*. These geons are derived from the combination of only five aspects of the edges of objects (e.g., curvature and symmetry). The process of interpreting a picture involves detecting the edge elements in an image, generating the resulting geons, combining these geons to produce meaningful forms, and matching them to known forms in the visual environment. Only 36 geons are needed for the perception of all possible images, a situation that is analogous to speech perception in which only 44 phonemes are needed to encode all the words in the English language. Biederman invokes evidence showing that the recognition of objects is robust across a wide range of viewing conditions (e.g., occluded views) and viewpoints (e.g., rotations in depth). Biederman's theory would appear to be in opposition to most other theorists who contend that it makes little sense to talk of a "vocabulary" and "grammar" of picturing.

Another area that should be mentioned is neurophysiology. Kosslyn (1986, 1987) suggests how neurophysiology might be combined with AI computational theory to yield a more complete understanding of vision. After all, Kosslyn observes, perception and cognition are something the brain does. The extreme belief regarding the potential importance of neurophysiology is expressed by Kitcher (1988): "Ultimately, all phenomena currently regarded as psychological will either be explained by neurophysiology or not at all" (p. 10).

26.2.12 Implications for Media Researchers: An Example

Picture perception theorists have challenged many of our orthodox beliefs about pictures. For example, consider the question of what constitutes "realism" in pictures. In the media research literature, realism is generally defined as a matter of faithfully copying nature. A picture is said to be "realistic" to the degree that it mirrors the visual information provided by the real-world referent, and researchers studying the effects of pictorial realism have manipulated "realism cues" such as amount of detail, color, and motion. The outcomes of this research have been frequently disappointing.

Picture perception theorists have offered alternatives to the simple "copy theory" of realism. Although Gibson's

approach stresses the fidelity of picture to referent, he adds the qualification that a successful picture copies the *invariant* visual information in nature—the optical data about reality that remains constant across time and across different views of an object. Goodman (1976) contends that realism is ". . . not a matter of copying but of conveying. It is more a matter of 'catching a likeness' than of duplicating— in the sense that a likeness lost in a photograph may be caught in a caricature" (p. 14). For Gombrich, the criteria for realism are not in nature, but in the perceiver's head in the form of expectations for what pictures of a given type "should" look like. These expectations are built up during extensive experience with the prevailing pictorial system and function as the standards for judging realism. Arnheim argues that perceptions of realism are relative to pictorial style, and are particularly influenced by how a style represents what we know about an object (conceptual reality) as compared to what the object looks like (perceptual reality). Marr and Biederman propose bottom-up theories that focus on the match between abstract elementary forms in pictures and their referents.

Thus contrasting the copy theory of pictorial realism with those of picture perception theorists, the copy theory emphasizes the exact visual match between pictures and referents, whereas theorists emphasize the nature of departures of picture from reality: surface level vs. deeper semantic, psychological, stimulus only vs. contribution of perceiver also.

26.3 MEMORY MODELS

There is significant evidence that generally memory for pictures is better than memory for words. This consistent finding is referred to as the *picture superiority effect*. At least three significant theoretical perspectives have been used to explain the "picture superiority effect," including: (1) the dual-code model (see 16.2.1, 29.2.3), (2) the single-code model, and (3) the sensory-semantic model (see Fig. 26-1).

Proponents of the dual-coding theory argue that there are two interdependent types of memory codes, verbal and nonverbal, for processing and storing information (Paivio, 1971, 1978, 1990, 1991).

The verbal code is a specialized system for processing and storing verbal information such as words and sentences. The nonverbal system "includes memory for all nonverbal phenomenon, including such things as emotional reactions. This system is most easily thought of as a code for images and other 'picture-like' representations (although it would be inaccurate to think of this as pictures stored in the head)" (Rieber, 1994, p. 111). If it is assumed, as Paivio does, that the dual coding of pictures in verbal and nonverbal memory is more likely to occur for pictures than words, then the "picture superiority effect" could be explained using dual-coding theory.

Proponents of a single-code model argue that visual information is transformed into abstract propositions stored

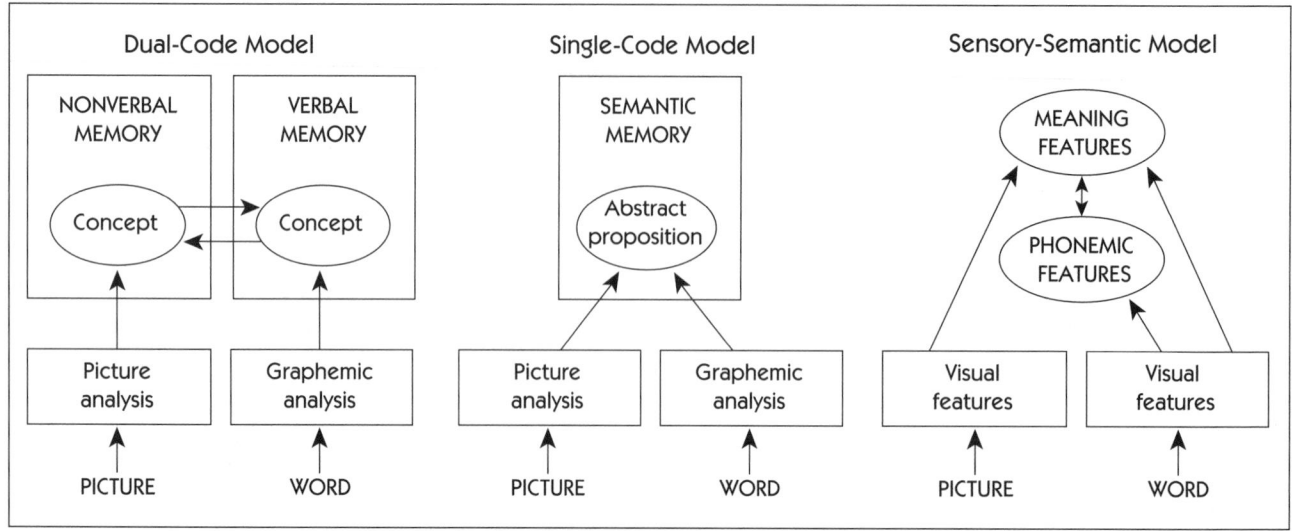

Figure 26-1. Three prominent models of encoding words and pictures. From "Picture-word differences in decision latency: a test of common-coding assumptions" by J. te Linde, 1982, *Journal of Experimental Psychology: Learning, Memory, and Cognition 8,* pp. 585, 586. Copyright 1982 by American Psychological Association. Adapted by permission. Also from "Learning to order pictures and words: a model of sensory and semantic encoding": by D. L. Nelson, V. S. Reed & C. L. McEvoy, 1977, *Journal of Experimental Psychology: Human Learning and Memory 3,* p. 486. Copyright 1977 by the American Psychological Association. Adapted by permission. Also from "Research on pictures: a guide to the literature" by W. Howard Levie, 1982. *In* D. M. Willows & H. A. Houghton, eds. *The psychology of illustration: basic research,* p. 1. Copyright 1982 by Springer-Verlag, New York. Reprinted by permission.

in semantic memory (Anderson, 1978; Kieras, 1978; Kosslyn, 1980, 1981; Pylyshyn, 1981; Rieber, 1994; Shepard, 1978). Advocates for a single-code model argue that pictures activate a single semantic memory system differently than do words. Individuals "provided with pictures just naturally spend more time and effort processing pictures" (Rieber, 1994, p. 114).

Picture superiority can also be explained using a sensory-semantic model (Nelson, 1979). There may be a more distinctive sensory code for pictures, or the probability that pictures will be processed semantically is greater than that for words (Levie, 1987; Nelson, Reed & Walling, 1976; Smith & Magee, 1980). In many cases researchers in educational communications and technology have neglected the work that has been done concerning memory models.

26.4 PICTURES AND KNOWLEDGE ACQUISITION

26.4.1 Literature Search and Reviews

Through various on-line and manual literature searches, 2,196 primary research studies, reviews, books, conceptual papers, and magazine articles were identified, collected, and catalogued. The literature search was limited to the categories of static and dynamic pictures and knowledge acquisition. Many of the documents collected were not

appropriate for the current review. For example, numerous papers reported the results of memory recognition studies including pictures. In addition, several studies were not included because of methodological flaws such as failing to include a control group or appropriate statistics. Many of the papers identified were not primary research studies or theoretical in nature. A total of 132 primary research studies were included across the two categories (static illustrations, dynamic graphics) used for the review. We first report the results of earlier literature reviews. Then an abridged guide to the literature will be presented.

26.4.2 Static Pictures and Knowledge Acquisition

In this section, we first present a summary of earlier reviews of the literature concerning the role of static pictures in the acquisition of knowledge. Second, we discuss the results of our literature search and summary. A similar approach will be used for dynamic pictures and knowledge acquisition.

26.4.2.1. Static Pictures and Knowledge Acquisition: Literature Reviews. Spaulding (1955) reviewed 16 research studies using pictorial illustrations conducted between 1930 and 1953. Based on the findings of the 16 studies, Spaulding concluded that illustrations: (a) are effective interest-getting devices; (b) help the learner interpret and remember the content of the illustrated text; (c) are more effective in realistic color than black-and-white, but the amount of effectiveness might not always be significant; (d) will draw more attention if they are large; and (e) should conform to eye movement tendencies.

Samuels (1970) reviewed a series of 23 studies that investigated the effects of pictures on learning to read words, on reading comprehension, and on reader attitudes. Samuels's review covered a time span from 1938 to 1969. The studies reviewed included such treatments as: (a) learning to read words in isolation with and without pictures, (b) acquiring a sight-vocabulary with and without pictures, (c) using pictures as a response alternative in a reading program, and (d) using pictures as prompts. Samuels concluded that: (a) Most studies show that, for acquisition of a sight-vocabulary, pictures interfere with learning to read; (b) the majority of studies indicate that pictures used as adjuncts to printed text do not facilitate comprehension; and (c) pictures can influence attitudes. Many of the studies reviewed by Samuels were narrowly focused on the use of illustrations to learn to decode words in isolation. Illustrations used in the context of learning to read have generally not proved to facilitate learning.

An analysis of the pictorial research in science instruction has also been conducted (Holliday, 1973). The general conclusions reached by Holliday concerning the effect of pictures on science education were that: (a) Pictures used in conjunction with related verbal material can aid recall of a combination of verbal and pictorial information; (b) pictures will facilitate learning if they relate to relevant criterion test items; (c) pictorial variables such as embellishment, size, and preference are complex issues; and there are almost infinite interrelationships between picture types, presentation formats, subject content, and individual learner characteristics.

Concannon (1975) reviewed a number of studies on the effects of illustrations in children's texts (mainly basal readers). Concannon summarized the results of her review with the single conclusion that when pictures are used as motivating factors, they do not contribute significantly to helping a young reader decode the textual information.

Levin and Lesgold (1978, pp. 234–235) reviewed studies of prose learning with pictures and concluded that pictures do facilitate prose learning when five ground rules are adhered to, including:

1. Prose passages are presented orally.
2. The subjects are children.
3. The passages are fictional narratives.
4. The pictures overlap the story content.
5. Learning is demonstrated by factual recall.

While Levin and Lesgold (1978) focused on oral prose, they also suggest that pictures may benefit individuals reading for comprehension.

Schallert (1980) reviewed a number of research studies and presented the case for and against pictures in instructional materials. In the case against pictures, Shallert reviewed the work of Samuels (1967, 1970) and others. Shallert states that "the most convincing evidence against

the use of illustrations in children's text has been marshaled by Samuels" (p. 505). Shallert noted that many of the early reviews completed by Samuels, Concannon, and others reported that the use of pictures serving as motivating factors do not facilitate a child's ability to decode text information. Shallert indicated that some of the reasons the pre-1970 studies did not identify picture effects were: (a) The primary emphasis in the word acquisition treatments were speed and efficiency; with the words being spoken aloud, pictures used in that context are of little value; (b) the illustrations used in many studies were not meant to convey new information and were only used as adjuncts to the text; (c) many illustrations used in basal readers vaguely relate to the contextual information in the text; and (d) the effects of illustrations on long-term memory were not measured in these earlier studies.

In the case supporting positive picture effects, Shallert (1980) reviewed a series of studies that covered the time period from 1972 to 1977. The general conclusions reached by Schallert were that pictures can help subjects: (a) learn and comprehend text when the pictures illustrate information central to the text, (b) when they represent new content important to the overall message being presented, (c) when they help depict the structural relationships covered by the text, and (d) if the illustrated information contributes more than a simple second rehearsal of the text.

Readence and Moore (1981) conducted a meta-analytic review of the literature on the effect of experimenter-provided adjunct pictures on reading comprehension. The 16 studies reviewed included 2,227 subjects and incorporated a total of 122 measures of association between the use of adjunct pictures and reading comprehension. The overall results across all studies revealed only minimal positive effects on reading text and subsequent reading comprehension when using adjunct pictures. The magnitude of picture effects were more substantial for university subjects who read text containing adjunct pictures.

One of the most comprehensive reviews of the effects of illustrated text on learning was done by Levie and Lentz (1982). The Levie and Lentz (1982) review compared three separate areas concerning the role of illustration in learning: (a) learning illustrated text information, (b) learning nonillustrated text information, and (c) learning using a combination of illustrated and nonillustrated text information. Studies included in the Levie and Lentz review cover a time period from 1938 to 1981. Levie and Lentz also present a functional perspective, which could be used to explain how illustrations might function to facilitate learning. Functional frameworks will be covered in detail in a later section of this chapter.

Summarizing the results across all studies included in their review, Levie and Lentz (1982) drew three primary conclusions: (a) Learning will be facilitated when the information in the written text is depicted in the illustrations; (b) learning of text material will not be helped nor necessarily hindered with illustrations that are not related to the text; and (c) when the criterion measure of learning includes both illustrated and nonillustrated text information, a modest improvement may often result from the addition of pictures.

Using Levin's (1981) framework to classify pictures according to the function they serve in prose learning, Levin, Anglin, and Carney (1987) conducted a meta-analysis of the pictures in prose studies. The reviewers concluded that for pictures (not mental images), serving a representation, organization, interpretation, or transformation function yielded at least moderate degrees of facilitation. A substantial effect size was identified for the transformation function.

One of the most significant programs of research on visual learning has been conducted by Dwyer and his associates (Dwyer, 1972, 1978, 1987; Levie & Lentz, 1982; Rieber, 1994). The research program is unique in several ways. The studies in the Dwyer series used similar stimulus materials. In particular, the stimulus materials included a 2,000-word prose passage describing the parts, locations, and functions of the human heart along with various types of visual materials including line drawings, shaded drawings, and photographs in black and white and in color. The materials were delivered in a number of formats and combinations including: written prose with illustrations, a slide-tape program with audio and television, and computer-based. In addition, a rationale was provided for the inclusion of visual illustrations in the treatments. If the information tested in a particular section of the text material was not difficult for the student (did not require external visualization), visual information would not be included and tested for this section of the text. Several types of criterion measure were developed by Dwyer and his associates, including a drawing test, an identification test, a terminology test, and a comprehension test. The research has been conducted with over 48,000 students (Dwyer, 1972, 1978, 1987).

Levie and Lentz (1982) conducted a meta-analysis using the treatments developed by Dwyer and presented in a text format or programmed booklet. All studies included in the meta-analysis included a text-only condition. Based on 41 comparisons of treatments with text-plus-prose, with text only using four criterion measures (drawing test, identification test, terminology test, comprehension test), Levie and Lentz (1982) report that 36 comparisons favor illustrated text, and 4 favor text alone (see Appendix Table 26-1).* As with other reviews of literature discussed, one conclusion that can be drawn from the work of Dwyer and his colleagues is that visuals are "effective some of the time under some conditions" (Rieber, 1994, p. 132). Space limitations do not permit a more detailed discussion of the Dwyer series (Dwyer, 1972, 1978, 1987).

26.4.2.2. Guide to the Literature: Static Illustrations. Based on our literature search, 90 studies investigating the role of static pictures in knowledge acquisition were identified (see 12.2). The 90 studies were conducted with more than 13,528 subjects ranging from elementary school children to adults (see Appendix Table 26-3.) All of the studies static visual illustrations of various types with a prose-only

included at least one comparison of learning with prose and treatment. A number of the studies included written prose materials, while other included prose presented orally. It should be noted that many of the studies summarized included other comparisons irrelevant to this review, and they are not discussed. In the 118 experiments included in the 90 studies, 102 significant effects for treatments including text and visual illustrations vs. text only were identified. The results of the "box score" summary indicate that static visuals can have a positive effect on the acquisition of knowledge by students. The treatments used were varied, and many of the studies were not based on a particular theoretical perspective. In many of the studies, it was not possible to identify the role or function of the visual illustrations in the instructional treatments. Examples of visuals and criterion measure items should more regularly be included in published studies. It was also difficult to determine what type of information was tested using the criterion measures in many of the studies. The reliability coefficients of the criterion measures were infrequently reported in the studies reviewed. In addition, few of the studies have been replicated. Notable exceptions are the research programs of Dwyer and Levin. A more detailed summary of each study is reported in Appendix Table 26-2. The studies by Dwyer and his associates that are reported in Table 26-1 are not duplicated in Table 26-3.

Based on our review of reviews of the literature and our own literature summary concerning the role of visual illustrations and knowledge acquisition, we still agree with a conclusion stated by Levie (1987) that:

> It is clear that "research on pictures" is not a coherent field of inquiry. An aerial view of the picture research literature would look like a group of small topical islands with only a few connecting bridges in between. Most researchers refer to a narrow range of this literature in devising their hypotheses and in discussing their results. Similarly, authors of picture memory models, for example, take little notice of theories of picture perception (Levie, 1987, p. 26).

One of the primary reasons much of the research on the role of visual illustrations in knowledge acquisition is not easily integrated is that the role or function of the pictures and illustrations in the instructional treatments are not identified. We feel that it is critically important to determine, in advance of conducting research, the particular functions of the visual illustrations.

26.4.2.3. The Use of Functional Frameworks in Static Visual Research. In spite of the considerable amount of research concerning how static visuals facilitate learning, many empirical research studies reflect an unclear perception on the part of researchers of the manner in which illustrations function in facilitating learning. A number of researchers have provided a variety of functional frameworks that may provide assistance in classifying static visuals into meaningful functional categories (Alesandrini, 1984; Brody, 1984; Duchastel & Waller, 1979; Levie & Lentz, 1982; Levin, 1981; Levin et al., 1987). We will provide a brief summary of several functional frameworks.

---

*All tables are gathered in an appendix at the end of the chapter.

Two taxonomies have been proposed which take a morphological approach (what an illustration physically looks like) to picture classification (Fleming, 1967; Twyman, 1985). But classifying the role of pictures on the basis of "form" rather than "function" has not proved to be very useful (Duchastel & Waller, 1979). According to Duchastel and Waller, what is needed is not a taxonomy of illustrations but a grammar of illustrations that provides a functional set of principles that relate illustrations to the potential effects they may have on the learner.

Duchastel (1978) identified three general functional roles of illustrations in text: (a) an attentional role, (b) a retentional role, and (c) an explicative role. The attentional role relies on the fact that pictures naturally attract attention. The retentional role aids the learner in recalling information seen in an illustration, and the explicative role explains, in visual terms, information that would be hard to convey in verbal or written terms (Duchastel & Waller, 1979). Duchastel and Waller (1979) concluded that the explicative role of illustrations provides the most direct means with which to classify the role of illustrations in text. Seven subfunctions of explicative illustrations were identified by Duchastel and Waller (1979, pp. 21–24). These explicative subfunctions are:

1. *Descriptive.* The role of the descriptive function is to show what an object looks like physically.
2. *Expressive.* The expressive role is to make an impact on the reader beyond a simple description.
3. *Constructional.* The intent of the constructional role is to show how the parts of a system form the whole.
4. *Functional.* The functional role allows a learner to follow visually the unfolding of a process or the organization of a system.
5. *Logico-mathematical.* The purpose of this role is to show mathematical concepts through curves, graphs, etc.
6. *Algorithmic.* The algorithmic role is used to show action possibilities.
7. *Data display.* The functional role of data display is to allow quick visual comparison and easy access to data such as pie charts, histograms, dot maps, or bar graphs.

An alternative functional framework offered by Levie and Lentz (1982) suggests a functional framework that includes classifying illustrations in text based on how they impact a learner in attending, feeling, or thinking about the information being presented. Their framework contains four major functions: (a) attentional, (b) affective, (c) cognitive, and (d) compensatory. The attentional function attracts or directs attention to the material. The affective function enhances enjoyment or in some other way affects emotions and attitude. Illustrations serving a cognitive function facilitate learning text content through improving comprehension, improving retention, or providing additional information. The last functional role identified by Levie and Lentz is the compensatory role used to accommodate poor readers. Levie and Lentz, after reviewing a large number of studies containing 155 experimental comparisons of learning, have found much empirical support for the utility of their functional framework. Such a framework can help researchers sort out the functions that illustrations perform and can be used to identify the ways illustrations should be designed and used for specific cases (Levie & Lentz, 1982).

A functional framework that has proved to be useful in explaining differences in research studies concerning pictures and prose is provided by (Levin, 1981). Levin contended that different types of text-embedded pictures serve five prose learning functions. The five functions identified by Levin are: (a) decoration, (b) representation, (c) organization, (d) interpretive, and (e) transformation. The decoration function is associated with text-irrelevant pictures (e.g., pictures used to make a written text more attractive) and does not represent the actors, objects, and activities happening in the text. Representational pictures are associated with text-relevant pictures and do represent the actors, objects, and activities happening in the text. The role of organizational pictures is to provide an organizational structure giving the text more coherence. Interpretational pictures serve to clarify passages and abstract concepts or ideas that are hard to understand. Transformational pictures are first, unconventional, and not often found in traditional textbooks. Transformational pictures are designed to have a direct impact on a learner's memory (e.g., pictures used as a mnemonical aid serve a transformation function).

After reviewing the frameworks offered by Duchastel, Levin, Levie and Lentz, and others, Brody (1984) suggests that many of the specific functions identified within these frameworks do not clarify how pictures function in instructional settings. First, some functions are too broad or general in nature and add little to gaining an understanding of the instructional roles served by visuals. As an example, Brody contends that a single picture can increase comprehension in multiple ways such as gaining attention, repeating information, offering new information, and providing additional examples. A broad functional role such as increasing prose comprehension does not provide an adequate explanation of how a picture is to be used to affect prose comprehension (Brody, 1984). Brody (1984) also suggests that many previously defined functional roles of pictures are often too narrow in their view. In an effort to ameliorate the limitations of previously identified functional roles of pictures, Brody offers his own set of representative instructional functions served by illustrations. Brody's approach to creating a potentially more useful functional framework was to identify functions in terms of what occurs during the instructional process. Another prime objective was to make the functional framework as general as possible in scope, that is, to make the functions independent of the specific form of instruction, content area, or types of learning skills being taught. Brody identified 20 representative instructional functions served by pictures. A potential problem with Brody's classification system for determining the role of illustrations in instructional materials is that it already contains a large number of categories. To extend his classification scheme further would make it less practical for identifying the role of pictures in either research or instructional design practice.

Alesandrini (1984) states that some of the previous functional frameworks dealt only with representational pictures, that is, pictures that represent the actors, objects, and activities taking place in the text. Alesandrini notes that other frameworks also include arbitrary or nonrepresentational roles of pictures such as graphs and flowcharts in the functional mix. Alesandrini offers a functional framework based on how instructional pictures convey meaning. Based on previous work by Grooper and Knowlton, Alesandrini classifies the role of instructional pictures into three functions: (a) representational, (b) analogical, and (c) arbitrary. Representational pictures can convey information in a direct way through tangible objects or concepts, or indirectly by the portrayal of intangible concepts that have no physical existence. Photos and drawings, or models and manipulatives, are examples of representational illustrations. Analogical pictures convey meaning by acting as a substitute and then implying a similarity for the concept or topic being presented. Arbitrary pictures (sometimes referred to as *logical pictures*) are highly schematized visuals that do not look like the things they represent but are related in some conceptual or logical way. Arbitrary illustrations include schematized charts and diagrams, flowcharts, tree diagrams, maps, and networks.

26.4.2.4. Static Visuals and Knowledge Acquisition: Conclusions. Based on the conclusions of our review of earlier literature reviews and the studies we summarized in Tables 26-1 and 26-3, we conclude that static visual illustrations can facilitate the acquisition of knowledge when they are presented with text materials. However, the facilitative effects of illustrations are not present across all learning situations. It is very difficult to integrate the results across all studies due to the lack of connections (theoretical or functional) between many of them. We do offer the following broad conclusions regarding the effects of illustrated visuals on learning: (a) Illustrated visuals used in the context of learning to read are not very helpful; (b) illustrated visuals that contain text-redundant information can facilitate learning; (c) illustrated visuals that are not text-redundant neither help nor hinder learning; (d) illustration variables (cueing) such as size, page position, style, color, and degree of realism may direct attention but may not act as a significant aid in learning; and (e) there is a curvilinear relationship between the degree of realism in illustrations and the subsequent learning that takes place.

There has been substantial progress in understanding how static illustrations affect the learning process. However, much remains to be done. Validations for many of the functional frameworks summarized in this chapter need to be completed. Theory-based studies that are informed by both memory research and theories of picture perception are lacking. Specific studies incorporating a particular theory of picture perception and a particular memory model need to be conducted. Theory-based research will provide us with a deeper understanding of the mechanisms that contribute to the effectiveness or ineffectiveness of static illustrations in instructional materials. It is also not clear how students use illustrations in instructional materials or that they even know

how to use them. A number of methods, including eye movement measurements, student surveys, and simply questioning students while they are using visual illustrations, will provide useful data on how students use or do not use illustrations. These data will be complimentary to the results of the recall and comprehension studies already completed. In addition, studies are needed that attempt to identify effective strategies for using illustrations included in instructional materials. Assuming that strategies for effectively using illustrations are identified, studies will then be needed that consider effective ways to train students to use these strategies. The issue of what constitutes "realism" in illustrations also needs to be reconsidered in light of the theories of picture perception discussed in this chapter. Many of the criterion measures (recall or comprehension tests) are administered immediately after the presentation of the instructional treatments. It is also important to determine if the illustration effects identified in many of the studies reviewed in this chapter are durable over time. Finally, few of the studies reviewed systematically controlled for the type of text or picture included. Perhaps the effects of illustrations on learning will vary according to the type of prose passage or picture used.

26.4.3 Dynamic Pictures and Knowledge Acquisition

In this section, we first review the early research on the effect of dynamic visuals on learning (see also 1.5, 16.11). Next we will summarize more recent reviews of the literature concerning the role of dynamic visual displays and knowledge acquisition. Finally, we present the results of our literature search and analysis.

26.4.3.1. Dynamic Pictures and Knowledge Acquisition: Literature Reviews. Early studies examining the effects of dynamic visuals on learning can be found in instructional film research. Freeman (1924) summarized 13 research studies that compared the effectiveness of various forms of visual instruction. The treatment formats used in the 13 studies included film, slides, lectures, still pictures, prints, live demonstrations, and stereographs. The motion treatments in these studies included the use of action pictures, animated drawings, and maps or cartoons. Based on the results of the 13 studies, it was concluded that motion or animated sequences in film are effective when (a) motion is a critical attribute of the concept being presented, and (b) motion is used to cue or draw the viewer's attention to the material being presented. It should be noted that the methodologies used in the 13 studies do not meet current standards for conducting comparative experimental research. A number of other investigators have conducted instructional film research that examined the effect of dynamic visuals on learning (Lumsdaine, Sultzer & Kopstein, 1961; May & Lumsdaine, 1958; Weber, 1926). Several conclusions can be drawn based on the early research on the role of dynamic visuals in instructional materials, including that (a) animation (motion) can lead to positive learning effects if it is a critical attribute of the concept(s) being presented, (b) animation (motion) can increase learning of a complex procedural task, and (c) motion or action used primarily to enhance the realism of the presentation does not appear to have a significant effect on learning. It should be noted that the conclusions drawn are based on a limited number of studies in which the motion variables were not usually tightly controlled.

Rieber (1990) summarized the results of 13 empirical studies investigating the role of animated graphics in computer-based instruction. Significant effects for animated treatments were found in 5 of the primary research studies reviewed. Based on the results of the 13 studies reviewed, Rieber presented three design recommendations for the use of animated visuals in instructional materials, including that: (a) "animation should be incorporated only when its attributes are congruent to the learning task" (Rieber, 1990, p. 79); (b) "evidence suggests that when learners are novices in the content area, they may not know how to attend to relevant cues or details provided by animation" (Rieber, 1990, p. 82); and (c) "animation's greatest contributions to CBI may lie in interactive graphic applications (e. g., interactive dynamics)" (Rieber, 1990, p. 82).

As discussed in the review of static visuals, a number of frameworks have been provided to classify static visual material. A similar functional approach would be appropriate for dynamic visual research. Rieber (1990) suggests that "generally, animation has been used in instruction to fulfill or assist one of three functions: attention-gaining, presentation, and practice" (p. 77).

More recently, Park and Hopkins (1993, p. 19) identified five important instructional roles of animated visuals:

1. As an attention guide, the animated visual can serve to guide and direct the subject's attention.
2. As an aid for illustration, dynamic visuals can be used as an effective aid to represent the structural and functional relations among components in a domain of knowledge.
3. As a representation of domain knowledge, movement and action can be used to effectively represent certain domain knowledge.
4. As a device model for forming a mental image, graphical animation can be used to represent system structures and functions that are not directly observable (e.g., blood flowing through the heart).
5. As a visual analogy or reasoning anchor for understanding abstract and symbolic concepts or processes, animation can make abstract and symbolic concepts (e.g., velocity) become more concrete and directly observable.

When both the characteristics of the domain knowledge and the characteristics of the subjects require one or more of the five instructional roles described above to be used, then animated visuals will most likely be effective (Park & Hopkins, 1993).

Using their functional framework, Park and Hopkins produced a research summary of 25 studies investigating the effects of dynamic versus static visual displays. The delivery medium for 17 of the studies was computer-based instruction, while the delivery medium for the remaining 8 studies was film or television. Fourteen of the studies yielded significant effects for dynamic visual displays. However:

> The research findings do not consistently support the superior effect of dynamic visual displays. The conflicting findings seem to be related to the different theoretical rationales and methodological approaches used in various studies (Park & Hopkins, 1993, p. 427).

One of the most interesting and rigorous programs of research on the effect of animation on learning has been conducted by Rieber (Rieber, 1989, 1994). The animation research conducted by Rieber included students across age groups, with realistic instructional content (Newton's laws of motion) and higher-level learning outcomes. As with the static visual research of Dwyer and his associates, the Rieber series of studies used animated graphics only when there was a need for external visualization. Results from the Rieber series are mixed and do not support the use of animated graphics across the board.

In summary, conclusions drawn from early reviews of the animation research literature are mixed. Rieber (1990) states that "the few serious attempts to study the instructional attributes of animation have reported inconsistent results. . . . CBI designers . . . must resist incorporating special effects, like animation, when no rationale exists" (p. 84).

26.4.3.2. Guide to the Literature. Forty-two studies were located which included at least one animation treatment. Information concerning the author, treatments, subjects, and results is reported in Table 26-5. Initially, we attempted to classify the animated treatments according to the function they performed (Park & Hopkins, 1993). However, we later abandoned the approach due to lack of specific information concerning the treatments. It was also difficult to classify many of the animated treatments as performing a single role using the classification system.

From the group of 42 studies, a total 45 comparisons were identified which included at least one animation treatment. Significant animation effects were identified in 21 of these comparisons. Animated treatments used by investigators have included various visual content such as animated illustrations, diagrams and visuals, real-time motion graphics, dynamic spatial visualization graphics, and animated interactive maps with blinking dots. General content areas covered by these studies include general science, physics, geometry, mathematics, statistics, and electronics. Subjects for these experiments ranged from mature adults to primary school children in the first, second, and third grade. A variety of tests were used to measure learning outcomes, including (a) learning of facts, concepts, and procedures; (b) problem solving and visual thinking; and (c) acquisition of cognitive skills that are primarily spatial or perceptual in nature.

How can the mixed results of the animation research be interpreted? Based on these "box score" results only, one could conclude that the use of animated graphics does not facilitate learning. However, methodological issues need to be considered. For example, in many of the studies it was not indicated if it was determined that there was a need for external visuals, static or dynamic. Perhaps reading text alone is adequate. In addition, many of the investigators did not provide a rationale for why motion is needed to either indicate changes over time or changes in direction. Text or text-plus-static graphics may be the optimal treatment if motion is not required. Many of the research reports reviewed did not specifically indicate that the animated sequences were text relevant or at least congruent with the text information presented. Also, both the information tested and the test type are critical considerations when investigating the learning effects for both static and animated graphic displays. It was not always possible to determine if the information tested was presented only in the animation, only in the animated sequence, or presented in both. It was also difficult to determine the function of the animated sequences. Using the lessons learned from static graphic research, more attention needs to be given to the functional role of animated sequences in research studies.

Such methodological problems call into question the results of these studies reporting insignificant animation effects. We believe that the comments of Rieber, and of Park and Hopkins, are still timely and appropriate. Rieber (1990) stated that "while speculative explanations for these studies which did not produce effects have been offered, many rival hypotheses linger rooted in general procedural flaws such as poor conceptualization of the research problem or inappropriate implementation of methods" (p. 84).

In a later review of the literature, Park and Hopkins (1993, p. 439) suggested that:

> Probably the most profound discrepancy separating the research is theoretical in nature. One important difference between studies which found significant effects of DVDs [dynamic visuals] and studies which found no such effects is that the former were guided by theoretical rationales which derived the appropriate uses for dynamic and static features of visual displays and their presumed effect. Accordingly, learner variables, the learning requirements in the task, and/or the medium characteristics were appropriately coordinated in most of the studies that found significant effects.

As is the case for static graphics, it is clear that facilitative effects are not present for animated treatments across all learning situations.

26.4.3.3. Dynamic Visuals and Knowledge Acquisition: Conclusions. Unlike research pertaining to static visuals, which encompass many additional studies and dozens of treatment conditions, research on the effects of dynamic visuals is very limited. The early research lacked appropriate controls, so that the specific effects of animation on learning cannot be determined. Results from the limited number of completed studies of the effect of dynamic visuals on learning are mixed. As discussed earlier, a number of the studies are methodologically flawed. Thus, the verdict is still out on the effect of animated treatments on student learning.

More work needs to be completed concerning the functions of animated visuals in learning materials. Contributions of Rieber, and of Park and Hopkins, have provided a starting point for further work. Refinement and validation of the functional frameworks suggested by Rieber, and by Park and Hopkins, are needed. In addition, it has not been demonstrated if or how learners use an animated sequence in the learning process. The effect of experience, prior knowledge, and aptitude patterns on the effective use of dynamic visual displays needs to be considered. Also, will students who are naive to specific instructional content be able to determine that an animated sequence indicates changes over time or changes in direction, and relate these changes to the specific content they are learning? Perhaps students need specific training on how to use animated sequences for learning. In almost all of the animation studies we reviewed, students in an animated treatment condition received visualized instruction (an animated sequence) and then were tested verbally. It is an open question whether a verbal test covering content displayed in a visual animated sequence measures the learning that has occurred. Also, many animated sequences particularly in simulations include a significant amount of information incidental to the particular purpose of the instructional package. Studies investigating the effect of such animated treatments on incidental learning are needed. Few of the animation studies we reviewed considered the effects of developmental level on learning. Animated treatments may differentially affect older vs. younger students. Finally, as discussed earlier, Rieber has suggested that animation may be most effective in computer-based instruction when used in interactive graphic applications. Much work needs to be done in this promising area of inquiry. In any case, future research investigating the effect of dynamic visual displays on learning should: (a) be based on a functional framework (i.e., Rieber, Park & Hopkins), (b) include content for which external visual information is needed and which requires the illustration of motion or the trajectory of an object, and (c) control for the effect of static graphics.

While some progress had been made, it is apparent that we know very little about the effect of dynamic visual displays on student learning. Given the proliferation of visual information in instructional material, it is imperative that the most effective strategies for using animated visuals be determined. Relative to the production of static visuals and text materials, the cost of producing animated sequences is high. Caraballo-Rios (1985) stated that "insisting on the use of computer animation in cases where it is not absolutely necessary should be considered an extravagance" (p. 4). Many additional theory-based studies, including a range of content areas, audiences, treatment conditions, and learner characteristics, are needed.

26.5 CONCLUSIONS

We have briefly reviewed theories of picture perception and memory models. Then a survey of existing studies and reviews concerning the effect of static and dynamic visuals on learning was presented. Significant progress has been made concerning our understanding of the effect of static and animated visuals on learning. Several problems are evident in the research reviewed. First, for both static and animated graphics, the research is fragmented and sporadic. Notable exceptions are the research programs of Dwyer, Levin, and Rieber. Second, the animation research is very limited in scope. Third, many of the researchers in instructional communication and technology have neglected the work on memory models and theories of picture perception. Future research related to visual learning should derive from theories of picture perception and incorporate memory models. Fourth, the functional roles of visuals in instructional materials need to be further clarified. There is much that we do not know about how to design effective visual messages. Future research strategies should be selected carefully to ensure that we continue to make significant progress.

REFERENCES

Alesandrini, K.L. (1984). Pictures and adult learning. *Instructional Science 13*, 63–77.

Anderson, J.R. (1978). Arguments concerning representations for mental imagery. *Psychological Review 85*, 249–77.

Arnheim, R. (1954). *Art and visual perception: a psychology of the creative eye*. Berkeley, CA: University of California Press.

— (1969). *Visual thinking*. Berkeley, CA: University of California Press.

— (1974). Virtues and vices of the visual media. *In* D.R. Olsen, ed. *Media and symbols: the forms of expression, communication, and education. The 73d Yearbook of the National Society for the Study of Education*, 180–210. Chicago, IL: University of Chicago Press.

— (1986). *New essays on the psychology of art*. Berkeley, CA: University of California Press.

Biederman, I. (1985). Human image understanding: recent research and a theory. *Computer Vision, Graphics, and Image Processing 32*, 29–73.

— (1987). Recognition by components: a theory of human image understanding. *Psychological Review 94*, 115–47.

Blinder, D. (1983). The controversy over conventionalism. *Journal of Aesthetics and Art Criticism 41* 253–64.

Brody, P.J. (1984). In search of instructional utility: a function-based approach to pictorial research. *Instructional Science 13*, 47–61.

Bruner, J.S. & Postman, L. (1949). On the perception of incongruity: a paradigm. *Journal of Personality 18*, 206–23.

Caraballo-Rios, A.L. (1985). An experimental study to investigate the effects of computer animation on the understanding and retention of selected levels of learning outcomes. (Doctoral dissertation, The Pennsylvania State University, 1985.) Dissertation Abstracts International, 46, 1494A.

Carrier, D. (1983). Gombrich on art historical explanations. *Leonardo 16*, 91–96.

Cassidy, M.F. (1982). Toward integration: education, instructional technology, and semiotics. *Educational Communication and Technology Journal 30*, 75–89.

Cassirer, E. (1944). *An essay on man*. New Haven, CT: Yale University Press.

Coldron, J. (1982). Peltz on Goodman on exemplification. *Journal of Aesthetic Education 16*, 88–93.

Concannon, S.J. (1975). Illustrations in books for children: review of research. *The Reading Teacher 29*, 254–56.

Connell, J.H. & Brady, M. (1987). Generating and generalizing models of visual objects. *Artificial Intelligence 31*, 159–83.

Crozier, W.R. & Chapman, A.J., eds. (1984). *Cognitive processes in the perception of art*. Amsterdam, The Netherlands: Elsevier.

Cutting, J.E. (1982). Two ecological perspectives: Gibson vs. Shaw and Turvey. *American Journal of Psychology 95* (2), 199–222.

— (1987). Perception and information. *Annual Review of Psychology 38*, 61–90.

Duchastel, P.C. & Waller, R. (1979, Nov.). Pictorial illustration in instructional texts. *Educational Technology,* 20–25.

— (1978). Illustrating instructional texts. *Educational Technology 11*, 36–39.

Dwyer, F.M. (1972). *A guide for improving visualized instruction*. State College, PA: Learning Services.

— (1978). *Strategies for improving visual learning*. State College, PA: Learning Services.

—, ed. (1987). *Enhancing visualized instruction—recommendations for practitioners*. State College, PA: Learning Services.

Eco, U. (1976). *A theory of semiotics*. Bloomington, IN: Indiana University Press.

Elgin, C.Z. (1984). Representation, comprehension, and competence. *Social Research 51* (4), 905–25.

Feaver, W. (1977). *When we were young: two centuries of children's book illustration*. London, England.: Thames & Hudson.

Fischler, M. & Firschein, O., eds. (1987). *Readings in computer vision: issues, problems, principles, and paradigms*. Palo Alto, CA: Kaufmann.

Fleming, M. (1967). Classification and analysis of instructional illustrations. *AV Communication Review 15* (3), 246–58.

— (1993). Introduction. *In* M. Fleming & W.H. Levie, eds. *Instructional message design: principles from the behavioral and cognitive sciences*, p. x. Englewood Cliffs, NJ: Educational Technology.

Fodor, J.H. & Pylyshyn, Z.W. (1981). How direct is visual perception? Some reflections on Gibson's "ecological approach." *Cognition 9*, 139–96.

Freeman, F.N., ed. (1924). *Visual education: a comparative study of motion pictures and other methods of instruction*. Chicago, IL: University of Chicago Press.

Gardner, H. (1982). *Art, mind, and brain: a cognitive approach to creativity*. New York: Basic Books.

—, Howard, V.A. & Perkins, D. (1974). Symbol systems: a philosophical, psychological, and educational investigation. *In* D.R. Olson, ed. *Media and symbols: the forms of expression, communication, and education. 73d Yearbook of the National Society for the Study of Education*, pp. 27–55. Chicago, IL: University of Chicago Press.

Gibson, J.J. (1971). The information available in pictures. *Leonardo 4*, 27–35.

— (1979). *The ecological approach to visual perception*. Boston, MA: Houghton Mifflin.

— & Bridgeman, B. (1987). The visual perception of surface texture in photographs. *Psychological Review 49*, 1–5.

Goldstein, E.B. (1987). Spatial layout, orientation relative to the observer, and perceived projection in pictures viewed at an angle. *Journal of Experimental Psychology: Human Perception and Performance 13* (2), 256–66.

Gombrich, E.H. (1969). *Art and illusion: a study in the psychology of pictorial representation.* Princeton, NJ: Princeton University Press.

— (1972). The visual image. *Scientific American 227* (3), 82–96.

Goodman, N., ed. (1976). *Languages of art: an approach to a theory of symbols,* 2d ed. Indianapolis, IN: Hackett.

— (1978). *Ways of worldmaking.* Indianapolis: Hacket.

Greene, R. (1983). Determining the preferred viewpoint in linear perspective. *Leonardo 16,* 97–102.

Gregory, R.L. (1970). *The intelligent eye.* New York: McGraw-Hill.

— (1973). *Eye and brain.* New York: McGraw-Hill.

— (1981). Questions of pattern and object perception by man and computer. *In* J. Long & A. Baddeley, eds. *Attention and performance IX,* pp. 97–116. Hillsdale, NJ: Erlbaum.

Haber, R.N. (1979). Perceiving the layout of space in pictures: a perspective theory based upon Leonardo da Vinci. *In* C.F. Nodine & D.F. Fisher, eds. *Perception and pictorial representation,* 84–99. New York: Praeger.

Hagen, M.A. (1978). An outline of an investigation into the special character of pictures. *In* H.L.J. Pick & E. Saltzman, eds. *Modes of perceiving and processing information,* 23–38. New York: Wiley.

— (1980a). Generative theory: a perceptual theory of pictorial representation. *In* M.A. Hagen, ed. *The perception of pictures, Vol. 2,* 3–46. New York: Academic.

—, ed. (1980b). *The perception of pictures, Vol. 1, Alberti's window: the projective model of pictorial information.* New York: Academic.

—, ed. (1980c). *The perception of pictures, Vol. 2, Durer's devices: beyond the projective model of pictures.* New York: Academic.

— (1986). *Varieties of realism: geometries of representational art.* New York: Cambridge University Press.

Heffernan, J.A. (1985). Resemblance, signification, and metaphor in the visual arts. *Journal of Aesthetics and Arts Criticism 44* (2), 167–80.

Hochberg, J. (1972). The representation of things and people. *In* E.H. Gombrich, J. Hochberg & M. Black, eds. *Art, perception, and reality,* 47–94. Baltimore, MD: Johns Hopkins Press.

— (1979). Some of the things that paintings are. *In* C.F. Nodine & D.F. Fisher, eds. *Perception and pictorial representation,* 17–41. New York: Praeger.

— (1980). Pictorial functions and perceptual structures. *In* M.A. Hagen, ed. *The perception of pictures, Vol. 2,* 47–93. New York: Academic.

Hoffman, W.C. & Dodwell, P.C. (1985). Geometric psychology generates the visual Gestalt. *Canadian Journal of Psychology 39,* 491–528.

Holliday, W.G. (1973). Critical analysis of pictorial research related to science education. *Science Education 57* (2), 201–14.

Holowka, T. (1981). On conventionality of signs. *Semiotica 33,* 79–86.

Jackendoff, R. (1987). On beyond zebra: the relation of linguistic and visual information. *Cognition 26,* 89–114.

Katz, S. (1983). R.L. Gregory et al.: The wrong picture of the picture theory of perception. *Perception 12,* 269–79.

Kennedy, J.M. (1974). *A psychology of picture perception.* San Francisco, CA: Jossey-Bass.

— (1984a). Gombrich and Winner: schema theories of perception in aesthetics. *Visual Arts Research 10* (2), 30–36.

— (1984b). How minds use pictures. *Social Research 51* (4), 885–904.

— (1985). Arnheim, Gestalt theory and pictures. *Visual Arts Research 11,* 23–44.

Kieras, D. (1978). Beyond pictures and words: alternative information processing models for imagery effects in verbal memory. *Psychological Bulletin 85,* 532–54.

Kitcher, P. (1988). Marrs's computational theory of vision. *Philosophy of Science 55,* 1–24.

Knowlton, J.Q. (1964). *A socio- and psycho-linguistic theory of pictorial communication.* Bloomington, IN: Indiana University.

— (1966). On the definition of "picture." *AV Communication Review 14,* 157–83.

Kolers, P.A. (1983). Perception and representation. *Annual Review of Psychology 34,* 129–66.

— & Smythe, W.E. (1984). Symbol manipulation: alternatives to the computational view of mind. *Journal of Verbal Learning and Verbal Behavior 23,* 289–314.

Kosslyn, S.M. (1980). *Image and mind.* Cambridge, MA: Harvard University Press.

—(1981). The medium and the message in mental imagery: a theory. *Psychological Review 88,* 46–66.

— (1986). Toward a computational neuropsychology of high-level vision. *In* T.J. Knapp & L.C. Robertson, eds. *Approaches to cognition: contrasts and controversies,* 223–42. Hillsdale, NJ: Erlbaum.

— (1987). Seeing and imagining in the cerebral hemispheres: a computational approach. *Psychological Review 94* (2), 148–75.

Kubovy, M. (1986). *The psychology of perspective and Renaissance art.* New York: Cambridge University Press.

Langer, S. (1976). *Philosophy in a new key,* 3d ed. Cambridge, MA: Harvard University Press.

Levie, W.H. (1978). A prospectus for instructional research on visual literacy. *Educational Communication and Technology Journal 26,* 25–36.

— (1987). Research on pictures: a guide to the literature. *In* D.M. Willows & H.A. Houghton, eds. *The psychology of illustration: Vol. 1: Basic research,* 1–50. New York: Springer.

— & Dickie, K.E. (1973). The analysis and application of media. *In* R.M.W. Travers, ed. *Second handbook of research on teaching,* 858–82. Chicago, IL: Rand McNally.

— & Lentz, R. (1982). Effects of text illustrations: a review of research. *Educational Communication and Technology Journal 30* (4), 195–232.

Levin, J.R. (1981). On the functions of pictures in prose. *In* F.J. Pirozzolo & M.C. Wittrock, eds. *Neuropsychological and cognitive processes in reading,* 203–28. New York: Academic.

—, Anglin, G.J. & Carney, R.N. (1987). On empirically validating functions of pictures in prose. *In* D.M. Willows & H.A. Houghton, eds. *The Psychology of illustration,* 51–80. New York: Springer.

— & Lesgold, A.M. (1978). On pictures in prose. *Educational Communication and Technology Journal 26,* 233–43.

Lowe, D.G. (1987). Three-dimensional object recognition from single two-dimensional images. *Artificial Intelligence 31,* 355–95.

Lumsdaine, A.A., Sultzer, R.L. & Kopstein, F.F. (1961). The effect of animation cues and repetition of examples on learning from an instructional film. *In* A.A. Lumsdaine, ed.

Student response in programmed instruction, 241–69. Washington, DC: National Research Council.

Marr, D. (1982). *Vision: a computational investigation into the human representation and processing of visual information.* San Francisco, CA: Freeman.

May, M.A. & Lumsdaine, A.A. (1958). *Learning from films.* New Haven, CT: Yale University Press.

Mitchell, W.J.T., ed. (1980). *The languages of images.* Chicago, IL: University of Chicago Press.

Morris, C.W. (1946). *Signs, language and behavior.* Englewood Cliffs, NJ: Prentice Hall.

Natsoulas, T. (1983). What are the objects of perceptual consciousness? *American Journal of Psychology 96* (4), 435–67.

Neisser, U. (1976). *Cognition and reality.* San Francisco, CA: Freeman.

Nelson, D.L. (1979). Remembering pictures and words: appearance, significance, and name. *In* L.S. Cermak & F.I.M. Craik, eds. *Levels of processing in human memory,* 45–76. Hillsdale, NJ: Erlbaum.

—, Reed, V.S. & Walling, J.R. (1976). The pictorial superiority effect. *Journal of Experimental Psychology: Human Learning and Memory 2,* 523–28.

Nodine, C.F. & Fisher, D.F., eds. (1979). *Perception and pictorial representation.* New York: Praeger.

Olson, D.R., ed. (1974). *Media and symbols: the forms of expression, communication, and education. 73d yearbook of the National Society for the Study of Education.* Chicago, IL: University of Chicago Press.

Paivio, A. (1971). *Imagery and verbal processes.* New York: Holt.

— (1978). A dual coding approach to perception and cognition. *In* J. &. H.L. Pick & E. Saltzman, eds. *Modes of perceiving and processing information,* 39–51. Hillsdale, NJ: Erlbaum.

— (1990). *Mental representations: a dual coding approach,* 2d ed. New York: Oxford University Press.

— (1991). Dual coding theory: retrospect and current status. *Canadian Journal of Psychology 45,* 255–87.

Park, O. & Hopkins, R. (1993). Instructional conditions for using dynamic visual displays: a review. *Instructional Science 22,* 1–24.

Penrice, L. (1980). The background to perspective. *Information Design Journal 1,* 190–203.

Perkins, D.N. & Leondar, B., eds. (1977). *The arts and cognition.* Baltimore, MD: Johns Hopkins University Press.

Peterson, M.A. & Hochberg, J. (1983). Opposed-set measurement procedure: a quantitative analysis of the role of local cues and intention in form perception. *Journal of Experimental Psychology: Human Perception and Performance 9,* 183–93.

Pierce, C.S. (1960). *The icon, index, and symbol (1902): collected papers.* Cambridge, MA: Harvard University Press.

Pirenne, M.H. (1970). *Optics, painting, and photography.* Cambridge, MA: Cambridge University Press.

Pylyshyn, Z.W. (1981). The imagery debate: analogue media versus tacit knowledge. *Psychological Review 88,* 16–45.

Readence, J.E. & Moore, D.W. (1981). A meta-analytic review of the effect of adjunct pictures on reading comprehension. *Psychology in the Schools 18,* 218–24.

Reed, E. & Jones, R., eds. (1982). *Reasons for realism: selected essays of James J. Gibson.* Hillsdale, NJ: Erlbaum.

Rieber, L.P. (1989). A review of animation research in computer-based instruction. *In* Proceedings of selected research papers presented at the annual meeting of the Association for Educa-

tional Communications and Technology, Dallas, TX, Feb. 1–5 (ERIC Document Reproduction Service No. 308-832).

Rieber, L.P. (1990). Animation in computer-based instruction. *Educational Technology Research and Development 38* (1), 77–86.

— (1994). *Computers, graphics, and learning.* Madison, WI: WCB Brown & Benchmark.

Rogers, S. & Costall, A. (1983). On the horizon: picture perception and Gibson's concept of information. *Leonardo 16,* 180–82.

Rosenfeld, A. (1986). *Human and machine vision II.* New York: Academic.

Roupas, T.G. (1977). Information and pictorial representation. *In* D. Perkins & B. Leondar, eds. *The arts and cognition,* 48–79. Baltimore, MD: Johns Hopkins Press.

Salomon, G. (1979a). *Interaction of media, cognition, and learning: an exploration of how symbolic forms cultivate mental skills and affect knowledge acquisition.* San Francisco, CA: Jossey-Bass.

— (1979b). Media and symbol systems as related to cognition and learning. *Journal of Educational Psychology 71,* 131–48.

Samuels, S.J. (1967). Attentional process in reading: the effect of pictures on the acquisition of reading responses. *Journal of Educational Psychology 58* (6), 337–42.

— (1970). Effects of pictures on learning to read, comprehension and attitudes. *Review of Educational Research 40,* 397–407.

Schallert, D.L. (1980). The role of illustrations in reading comprehension. *In* B. Spiro & W.F. Brewer, eds. *Theoretical issues in reading comprehension,* 503–23. Hillsdale, NJ: Erlbaum.

Scruton, R. (1974). *Art and imagination.* New York: Harper & Row.

Sebeok, T.A. (1976). *Contributions to the doctrine of signs: studies in semiotics, Vol. 5.* Bloomington, IN: Indiana University Press.

Shepard, R.N. (1978). The mental image. *American Psychologist 33,* 125–37.

Sless, D. (1986). Reading semiotics. *Information Design Journal 4,* 179–89.

Slythe, R.M. (1970). *The art of illustration 1750-1900.* London: Library Association.

Smith, M.C. & Magee, L.E. (1980). Tracing the time course of picture-word processing. *Journal of Experimental Psychology: General 109,* 373–92.

Spaulding, S. (1955). Research on pictorial illustration. *AV Communication Review 3,* 35–45.

Twyman, M. (1985). Using pictorial language: a discussion of the dimensions of the problem. *In* T.M.D. & R. Waller, eds. *Designing usable texts,* 245–312. New York: Academic.

Veltrusky, J. (1976). Some aspects of the pictorial sign. *In* L. Matejka & I.R. Titunik, eds. *Semiotics of art,* 245–64. Cambridge, MA: MIT Press.

Vitz, P.C. & Glimcher, A.B. (1984). *Modern art and modern science.* New York: Praeger.

Weber, J.J. (1926). Three important studies on the use of educational films. *In* A.P. Hollis, ed. *Motion pictures for instruction,* 162–96. New York: Century.

Wilcox, S. & Edwards, D.A. (1982). Some Gibsonian perspectives on the ways that psychologists use physics. *Acta Psychologica 52,* 147–63.

Winn, B. (1987). Charts, graphs, and diagrams in educational materials. *In* D.M. Willows & H.A. Houghton, eds. *The psychology of illustration,* 152–93. New York: Springer.

APPENDIX TABLES

TABLE 26-1. SUMMARY MATRIX OF STUDIES BY DWYER AND HIS ASSOCIATES*

Study	Learners (N)	Drawing Test			Identification Test			Terminology Test			Comprehension Test		
		Better Version	Effect Size	Mean IT / Mean TA	Better Version	Effect Size	Mean IT / Mean TA	Better Version	Effect Size	Mean IT / Mean TA	Better Version	Effect Size	Mean IT / Mean TA
Dwyer (1967)	College (86)	IT	.35	1.14	IT	.34	1.09	IT	.23	1.06	IT	.02	1.00
Dwyer (1968)	9th grade (141)	IT	.82	1.28	IT	.57	1.24	TA	-.10	.96	TA	-.17	.94
Delayed retest	9th grade (129)	IT	.36	1.09	IT	.42	1.14	IT	.27	1.06	IT	.50	1.18
Dwyer (1969)	College (175)	IT	1.23	1.37	IT	.67	1.17	IT	.80	1.16	NSD	—	—
Dwyer (1972)	College (266)	IT	.43	1.12	IT	.26	1.07	IT	.16	1.04	IT	.11	1.03
Dwyer (1975)	College (587)	IT	.82	1.16	IT	.47	1.13	IT	.52	1.11	TA	-.04	.99
Arnold & Dwyer (1975)	10th grade (185)	—	—	—	—	—	—	IT	.77	1.27	IT	.90	1.22
Joseph (1978)	10th grade (414)	IT	.41	1.07	IT	.14	1.02	TA	-.12	.98	IT	.01	1.00
Delayed retest	10th grade	IT	.24	1.03	IT	.13	1.02	IT	.47	1.10	IT	.23	1.04
de Melo (1980)	High school (48)	—	—	—	IT	.23	1.11	IT	.34	1.18	IT	.36	1.15
Pictorial test	High school (48)	—	—	—	IT	1.42	1.72	IT	1.11	1.50	IT	.52	1.23

IT = illustrated text; TA = text alone; NSD = no significant difference; dashes indicate that the value was not provided in the published report.
* Reprinted from *Educational Communication and Technology Journal* by permission of the Association for Educational Communications and Technology. Copyright 1984 by AECT.

TABLE 26-2. REFERENCE LIST FOR DWYER SERIES REVIEWED BY W. HOWARD LEVIE

Arnold, T.C. & Dwyer, F.M. (1975). Realism in visualized instruction. *Perceptual and Motor Skills 40*, 369–70.

de Melo, H.T. (1981). Visual self-paced instruction and visual testing in biological science at the secondary level. (Doctoral dissertation, Pennsylvania State University, 1980.) *Dissertation Abstracts International 41*, 4954A.

Dwyer, F.M., Jr. (1967). The relative effectiveness of varied visual illustrations in complementing programmed instruction. *Journal of Experimental Education 36*, 34–42.

— (1968). The effectiveness of visual illustrations used to complement programmed instruction. *The Journal of Psychology 70*, 157–62.

— (1969). The effect of varying the amount of realistic detail in visual illustrations designed to complement programmed instruction. *Programmed Learning and Educational Technology 6*, 147–53.

— (1972). The effect of overt responses in improving visually programmed science instruction. *Journal of Research in Science Teaching 9*, 47–55.

— (1975). On visualized instruction effect of students' entering behavior. *The Journal of Experimental Education 43*, 78–83.

Joseph, J.H. (1979). The instructional effectiveness of integrating abstract and realistic visualization. (Doctoral dissertation, Pennsylvania State University, 1978). *Dissertation Abstracts International 39*, 5907A.

TABLE 26-3. SUMMARY MATRIX OF RESEARCH RESULTS FOR STATIC VISUALS

Appendix 3 Study	Treatments	Content	Subjects	Dependent Variable(s)	Prose Type	Results
Alesandrini & Rigney (1981)	1. Verbal + interactive graphics expansion	Science (battery cell)	Undergraduate (98)	1. 37-item verbal test 2. 27-item picture recognition test	Written	SD
Experiment 1.0	2. Verbal + computer game 3. Verbal + verbal expansion					
Experiment 2.0	4. Verbal + game 1. Verbal + pictorial review 2. Verbal + verbal review	Same (50)	Undergraduate	1. 60-item verbal test 2. 27-item picture recognition test	Same (verbal)	NSD
Alesandrini (1981)	1. Pictorial + learning strategy (3) 2. Verbal + learning strategy (3) 3. Verbal (read twice)	Science (battery cell)	College (383)	A 60-item test of: (a) Knowledge (b) Comprehension (c) Application 12-item multiple-choice test Immediate and 28-day delay	Written	SD (picture) SD (holistic learning strategy) SD (immediate) NSD (delayed)
Anglin & Stevens (1986)	1. Prose + pictures 2. Prose only	Science (water clock)	Undergraduate (42)		Written	
Anglin (1986) Experiment 1.0	1. Prose + picture 2. Prose only	3 human interest stories	Graduate (52)	Consisted of 15 short-answer paraphrase questions; immediate and 14-day delay	Written	SD (immediate & delayed)
Experiment 2.0	Same	Same	Graduate (47)	Same, except delay increased to 28 days	Same	SD (immediate & delayed)
Anglin (1987)	1. Prose + picture 2. Prose	3 human interest stories	Graduate (30)	Recall Test had 15 paraphrase questions on text-redundant information, 5 short-answer questions on text-only information (immediate & 55-day delayed recall)	Written	SD for text-redundant information on immediate & delayed NSD for text-only information
Arnold & Brooks (1976)	1. Verbal + pictorial integrated organizer 2. Verbal + pictorial nonintegrated organizer 3. Verbal + verbal integrated organizer 4. Verbal + verbal nonintegrated organizer	8 organizationally complex paragraphs about unusual situations	Elementary school (32)	1. Total responses 2. Inferential responses 3. Recall responses 4. Correct responses	Oral	SD dependent on age & organizer type
Beck (1984)	1. Prose + pictorial cues 2. Prose + textual cues 3. Prose + combinational cues 4. Prose + noncues	12 passages & pictures based on carnivorous plants	Elementary school (256)	Recall 1-day delayed multiple-choice test	Written	SD for combinational cueing only

TABLE 26-3. Continued

Appendix 3 Study	Treatments	Content	Subjects	Dependent Variable(s)	Prose Type	Results
Bender & Levin (1978)	1. Story + illustrations 2. Story + generate visual images 3. Story (listen twice) 4. Story (listen once)	20-sentence fictitious story	Mental-retarded children (96)	Recall scores 10 verbatim + 10 paraphrase questions	Oral	SD (illustrations) NSD other 3 conditions
Bernard, Petterson & Ally (1981)	1. Verbal organizer 2. Contextual image (picture) 3. No organizer control 4. Placebo control	800-word passage about function of the brain	Undergraduate (104)	Recognition. 18 paraphrase & nonparaphrase questions Immediate & delayed testing (2 weeks)	Written	SD for both verbal & image organizers NSD between them
Bieger & Glock (1984)	1. Ten combinations of text + pictures by information type 2. Nothing control Information types: nonoperational, contextual, spatial, operational + contextual, operational + spatial	2 assembly tasks (hand truck & wall hanging)	Undergraduate (120)	1. Mean assembly times 2. Mean number of assembly errors	Written	SD depending on information type
Bluth (1973)	1. Prose + illustrations 2. Prose only	2 different cloze passages of 126 words each	Elementary school (80)	Cloze test measure of comprehension	Written	SD (good readers)
Borges & Robins (1980)	1. Story + appropriate context picture 2. Story + partial context picture 3. Story + no picture	Character motivation story	Undergraduate (120)	1. Recall based on 14 idea units 2. Mean comprehension rating	Oral	SD Appropriate > Partial > No picture
Bransford & Johnson (1972) Experiment 1.0	1. No context 1 (heard prose passage) 2. No context 2 (heard prose passage twice) 3. Context after (picture after passage) 4. Partial context (partial picture before passage) 5. Context before (picture before passage)	Fictitious prose passage	High school (50)	1. Mean comprehension 2. Mean recall score	Oral	SD context picture before passage
Covey & Carroll (1985)	1. Text + line drawings 2. Text only	3 expository science passages of approximately 300 words each	Elementary school (132)	Recognition using 36-item multiple-choice test	Written	SD
Dean & Enemoh (1983)	1. Pictures before reading text 2. Pictures after reading text 3. Text only	Difficult geology passage containing 262 words	Undergraduate (90)	Total number of "idea units" recalled	Written	SD picture before passage

TABLE 26-3: *Continued*

Appendix 3 Study	Treatments	Content	Subjects	Dependent Variable(s)	Prose Type	Results
DeRose (1976)	1. Prose + experimenter-provided illustration 2. Prose + instructions to summarize 3. Prose + experimenter-provided summary 4. Prose + instructions to image 5. Prose-only control	A 490-word passage from a social studies textbook	Middle school (192)	14 short-answer questions	Written	SD for experimenter provided illustrations
Digdon, Pressley & Levin (1985)	1. Object picture + no imagery instruction 2. Partial picture + no imagery instruction 3. Object picture + imagery instruction 4. Partial picture + imagery instruction 5. Object picture + partial picture + imagery instruction 6. Object picture + partial picture + no imagery instruction 7. Prose + imagery instruction 8. Prose + no imagery instruction	Two 10-sentence prose stories	Young children (160)	Set of cued recall questions	Oral	SD for object + partial pictures with and without imagery instruction
Duchastel (1980)	(Illustrations conveyed the topical ideas) 1. Prose only 2. Prose + illustrations	A 750-word prose passage on energy	High school (77)	Retention by: 1. summary 2. free recall 3. 30 short answers	Written	NSD
Duchastel (1981)	1. Prose + illustrations 2. Prose only	A 1,700-word history passage	High school (77)	1. Topical recall 2. Cued recall (36 questions) Immediate & 2-week delay	Written	SD on 2-week delay only (recall test)
Durso & Johnson (1980) Experiment 1.0	1. Words (verbal orienting task) 2. Pictures (verbal orienting task) 3. Words (imaging orienting task) 4. Pictures (imaging orienting task) 5. Words (referential orienting task) 6. Pictures (referential orienting task) (Pictures were line drawings of each of the 140-word concepts)	Contained 140 words, each a concept, chosen from Kucera & Francis word norms	Undergraduate (120)	A response of either a picture or word was taken as an indication that the item remembered as having been present during acquisition	Oral	SD for the verbal orienting tasks only
Experiment 2.0	Same	Same	Undergraduate (60)	Free recall of the items presented:	Same	Same
Gibbons et al. (1986)	1. Prose + visuals 2. Prose only	Dolls as actors performing in several settings	Young children (96)	1. Free recall 2. Reconstruction of story content	Oral	SD audiovisual condition
Goldberg (1974)	1. Prose (incidental information) + illustrations 2. Prose (incidental information)	Spelling and grammar exercise	Elementary school (216)	Incidental information: 12 recognition and 12 recall questions	Written	SD
Goldston & Richman (1985)	1. Prose + partial pictures during study 2. Prose + partial sentence repetition during study 3. Prose only	10-sentence narrative story	Elementary school (288)	Cued-recall measures	Oral	SD for partial pictorial cues

TABLE 26-3: Continued

Appendix 3 Study	Treatments	Content	Subjects	Dependent Variable(s)	Prose Type	Results
Guttmann, Levin & Pressley (1977) Experiment 1.0	1. Imagery + prose 2. Partial pictures + prose 3. Complete pictures + prose 4. Prose only	2 short stories each with a person, object, and thing	Young children & elementary school (240)	Cued recall 20 questions	Oral	SD Kindergarten for complete pictures only, SD 3d-graders for imagery = partial = complete SD 2d-graders for complete> partial> imagery> control
Hannafin (1988)	1. Pictures + oral 2. Pictures 3. Prose only	Fictitious children's story	Elementary school (168)	Recall test containing 24-item short answers of abstract and concrete items Immediate and 1-week delayed	Oral	SD oral + pictures immediate & delayed
Haring & Fry (1979)	1. Top-level + lower-level pictures + prose 2. Top-level pictures + prose 3. Prose only (text redundant line drawings)	A 360-word version of "Mercury and the Woodcutter"	Elementary school & middle school (150)	Free recall of both level of idea units Immediate and 5-day delayed	Written	SD for top-level idea units for both immediate and delayed
Hayes & Readence (1983)	1. Two line drawings + prose + no instructions 2. Two line drawings + prose + instructions to pay careful attention to pictures 3. Prose + instruction to form images 4. Prose + no instructions	Four 400-word prose passages from illustrated educational texts	Middle school (108)	1. Mean score on information recalled 2. Mean proportion of inferences per information unit recalled	Written	SD of both illustrated conditions NSD between illustrated conditions
Hayes & Readence (1982)	1. Two line drawings + prose + no instructions 2. Two line drawings + prose + instructions to pay careful attention to pictures 3. Prose + instruction to form images 4. Prose + no instructions	Four 300-word science texts about simple machines	Middle school (82)	Student success at working study problems with text available	Written	SD illustrated text with or without instructions

TABLE 26-3. *Continued*

Appendix 3 Study	Treatments	Content	Subjects	Dependent Variable(s)	Prose Type	Results
Hayes & Henk (1986)	1. Pictures only 2. Pictures + prose 3. Prose only (5 simple line drawings)	How to tie a "bowline" knot	High school (102)	Nonverbal applied performance Immediate and 2-week delayed	Written	SD pictures + prose & pictures, immediate testing only NSD between them
Holliday (1975)	1. Textbook-like illustrations + verbal 2. verbal	Verbal prose (23 pages) about plant growth hormones	High school (80)	Verbal comprehension 30-item multiple choice administered orally	Oral	SD
Holliday & Harvey (1976)	1. Adjunct labeled line drawings + prose 2. Prose only	Biology lesson on density, pressure & Archimedes' principal	High school (61)	Verbal quantitative (nonpictorial), multiple-choice test	Written	SD
Holmes (1987)	1. Prose + picture 2. Pictures 3. Prose only	15 passages of 150–200 words each; material from popular magazines	Elementary school, middle school (116)	25 inferential questions	Written	SD Pictures + text > pictures > prose NSD Pictures vs. prose
Jagodzinska (1976)	1. Prose + schematic correspondent illustration 2. Prose + realistic correspondent illustration 3. Prose + schematic supplement illustration 4. Prose + realistic supplement illustration 5. Prose Note: Above instructional conditions crossed with two text types (essential & nonessential) giving 10 total conditions	2 versions of a biology lesson	Middle school (200)	1. Reproduction (amount of material reproduced) 2. Text organization. Both immediate & delayed 2-week testing	Written	SD depending on picture type and its relationship to the text type

TABLE 26-3. Continued

Appendix 3 Study	Treatments	Content	Subjects	Dependent Variable(s)	Prose Type	Results
Jahoda et al. (1976) Experiment 1.0	1. Pictures + prose 2. Pictures 3. Prose only 4. Control	Expository text designed to be culturally free	Middle school, high school, (938) Scotland India Ghana Kenya	Recall scores 10 pictorial or verbal questions of picture & text-redundant information	Written	SD for pictures + text NSD pictures alone vs. text alone
Jonassen (1979)	1. Prose + 1-screen presentation 2. Prose + 3-screen presentation 3. Prose + 4-screen presentation 4. Prose only	Biology lesson on 4 plant types	Middle school (363)	Criterion test of a verbal and visual classification exercise Immediate & 2-week delay	Oral	SD 4-screen condition on visual classification Immediate & delayed
Koenke & Otto (1969)	1. Prose + illustrations (both specifically relevant and generally relevant to passage) 2. Prose only	Three 198-word passages from *Readers Digest*	Elementary school, middle school (60)	Comprehension of main ideas	Written	SD (both picture types) 6th-graders only
Koran & Koran (1980)	1. Picture before text 2. Picture after text 3. Text only	Science lesson on hydrologic cycle	Middle school (84)	23-item completion consisting of transformed and paraphrase questions	Written	SD for 7th-graders regardless of picture placement NSD for 8th-graders
Lesgold & DeGood & Levin (1977)	1. Prose + subject illustrated story using cutouts on a background 2. Prose + coloring simple figures in a booklet	16 prose stories, 4 of each type (50 vs. 100 words; 1 vs. 2 locations)	Elementary school (32)	Free and cued-recall scores	Oral	SD
Lesgold et al. (1975) Experiment 1.0	1. Prose + subjects made up illustrations from cutouts (some potentially interfering) 2. Prose + subjects copied or colored geometric forms during illustration phase	5 single episode stories of 30–50 words each	Elementary school (24)	Oral recall	Oral	NSD
Experiment 2.0a	1. Prose + subjects made up illustrations from fewer cutouts than experiment #1 2. Prose + subjects copied or colored geometric forms during illustration phase	3 stories of 5 sentences each	Elementary school (48)	Oral recall, both free and cued	Same	SD

TABLE 26-3. Continued

Appendix 3 Study	Treatments	Content	Subjects	Dependent Variable(s)	Prose Type	Results
Experiment 2.0b	1. Prose + experimenter-provided pictures 2. Prose + subjects copied or colored geometric forms during illustration phase	Same as 2a	Elementary school (24)	Same as 2a	Same	SD for both picture conditions NSD between the 2 picture conditions
Experiment 3.0	1. Prose + experimenter-provided pictures 2. Prose + subjects made up illustrations from fewer cutouts than experiment #1 2. Prose + subjects copied or colored geometric forms during illustration phase	Same as 2a	Elementary school (36)	Same as 2a	Same	SD for experimenter-provided pictures only
Levin & Berry (1980) Experiment 1.0	1. Prose + 1-colored, main idea line drawing per passage 2. Prose only	5 human interest and novelty stories, from local newspapers, of approximately 100 words each	Elementary school (50)	6 short-answer paraphrase questions per passage (30 total). Half the questions about information in the pictures, the other half about information not in pictures.	Oral	SD for pictured information
Experiment 2.0	Same (change was in time of testing only)	A 6th passage added	Elementary school (37)	Same but testing took place on 3-day delayed basis	Same	SD
Experiment 3a	1. Single main idea picture + prose 2. Prose + prompt (verbal analog of main idea for each passage)	Same	Elementary school (36)	16 main-idea questions	Same	SD
Experiment 3b	1. One main idea picture/passage + prose 2. Prose + no prompting	Same as 3a	Elementary school (36)	16 main-idea questions plus 24 nonmain-idea questions	Same	SD (both question types)
Levin (1976) Experiment 2.0	1. Prose + experimenter-provided culminating pictures 2. Prose + experimenter-provided nonculminating pictures 3. Repetition condition (passage repeated once) 4. Activity control (passage + nonrelevant coloring activity) 5. Nonactivity control (passage only)	3 single-episode stories of 30 to 75 words each	Elementary school (61)	Cued-recall, 5 short-answer questions	Oral	SD
Experiment 3.0	Same (minus the activity control condition)	Two 10-sentence passages	Elementary school (64)	Cued-recall, 10 questions/story	Same	SD

TABLE 26-3. Continued

Appendix 3 Study	Treatments	Content	Subjects	Dependent Variable(s)	Prose Type	Results
Levin et al. (1983) Experiment 1.0	1. Prose + colored mnemonic illustrations 2. Prose only	Learn the numerical order of 10 U.S. presidents	Middle school (46)	1. Total recall 2. Serial-position profile 3. Response latencies	Oral	NSD on total recall
Experiment 2.0	Same + additional study trials added	Same	Middle school (40)	Same + name recall added	Same	NSD on total recall
Experiment 3.0	Same + 3 study trials added	Same	High school (32)	Total recall scores only	Same	SD
Levin et al. (1982) Experiment 1.0	1. Keyword context (word list + contextually explicit colored "keyword" illustration) 2. Control condition (word list + experimenter read aloud + use own strategy)	Learn meanings of 12 challenging vocabulary words	Elementary school (30)	Total number of words defined correctly	Oral	SD
Experiment 2.0	1. Keyword context (word list + contextually explicit colored "keyword" illustration) 2. Picture context (colored illustration of words definition + read definition aloud) 3. Experiential context (read 3 sentences with definition + application question with word) 4. Control condition (word list + experimenter read aloud + use own strategy)	14 words to learn	Elementary school (64)	Same	Same	SD Keyword context best Picture better than experiential
Levin et al. (1983) Experiment 1a & 1b	1. Prose + organized mnemonic "keyword" picture 2. Prose + organized single picture 3. Prose + separate pictures 4. Prose + subjects use own learning strategy	Short prose passages about distinguishing attributes of fictitious towns	Middle school (178)	1. Total number of attributes remembered via matching questions 2. Clustering score	Oral	SD organized mnemonic "keyword" NSD separate picture
Experiment 2a & 2b	Same without organized separate picture condition (# 2 above)	Same	Middle school (113)	Subject responses of (a) verbatim correct (b) essence correct	Same	SD organized mnemonic NSD separate picture
Levin et al. (1986) Experiment 1.0	1. Text + mnemonic pictures 2. Text + summary using fact mapping 3. Text + free study instructions	A 540-word text about minerals organized around "names"	Middle school (53)	Names and attributes recall testing	Written	SD for mnemonic pictures
Experiment 2.0	Same	Same except text organized around "attributes"	Middle school (115)	Same	Same	SD for mnemonic pictures

TABLE 26-3. *Continued*

Appendix 3 Study	Treatments	Content	Subjects	Dependent Variable(s)	Prose Type	Results
Mange & Parknas (1962) Experiment 1.0	1. Picture information slide + picture test slide 2. Picture information slide + word test slide 3. Word slide + picture test slide 4. Word slide + word test slide	Biology lesson on plant types	Middle school (228)	Retention of pictorial or verbal information	Written	SD When retention measured by pictorial testing
Experiment 2.0	Same	Same	College (81)	Same	Same	SD (same condition)
Experiment 3.0	1. Prose + filmstrip 2. Prose	Lesson on Greenland	Middle school (192)	Retention using both verbal and pictorial questions	Same	SD (same condition)
Main & Griffiths (1977)	1. Printed text + printed and pictorial supplement 2. Printed text + audio and pictorial supplement 3. Printed text + printed supplement 4. Printed text (control)	12 passages from a chapter on weather	Adult (120)	1. Vocabulary test 2. 100-item sentence completion part 3. 55-item multiple-choice section	Written Oral	SD all experimental group vs. control NSD between experimental groups
Mayer (1989) Experiment 1.0	1. Text + illustrations including labels 2. Text only	Vehicle braking systems	College (34)	95 idea units of both explanative and nonexplanative information	Written	SD on recall of explanative information
Experiment 2.0	1. Text + labeled illustrations 2. Text + nonlabeled illustrations 3. Text only	Same	College (44)	Same	Same	SD on recall of explanative information for labeled illustrations
McCormick et al. (1984)	1. Related text + separate mnemonic illustrations 2. Related text + integrated mnemonic illustration 3. Noninterference control (read 3 unrelated passages) 4. Interference control (read 3 related but potentially interfering passages)	3 fictitious biographical stories	College (160)	11 short-answer recall questions	Written	SD for integrated mnemonic illustrations

TABLE 26-3. *Continued*

Appendix 3 Study	Treatments	Content	Subjects	Dependent Variable(s)	Prose Type	Results
McCormick & Levin (1984) Experiment 1.0	1. Text + mnemonic pictures (keyword-paired) 2. Text + mnemonic pictures (keyword-chained) 3. Text + mnemonic pictures (keyword-integrated) 4. Simple control (text + additional study each sentence) 5. Cumulative control (text + cumulative study of all sentences)	4 fictitious biographies	Middle school (220)	20 cued-recall questions	Written	SD for all 3 mnemonic conditions but NSD between them
Experiment 2.0	Same except delete condition # 2 above	Same	Middle school (82)	Name-attribute recognition test both immediate and 2-day delayed	Same	SD for keyword conditions both immediate & delayed
Miller (1938)	1. Prose + illustrations 2. Prose only	3 stories from basal readers	Elementary school (600)	Comprehension	Written	NSD
Moore (1975)	1. Illustrations + prose together 2. Illustrations before prose 3. Illustrations after prose 4. Prose only	Text on learning time from a sundial	Elementary school (63)	Comprehension—20-item multiple choice	Written	NSD
Nugent (1982) Experiment 1.0	1. Visuals + print + audio 2. Visuals + print 3. Visuals + audio 4. Print + audio 5. Visuals 6. Print 7. Audio 8. Control	Film about factual life of a cheetah	Elementary school, middle school (201)	23 multiple-choice comprehension test	Oral	NSD single media SD dual media SD 3 media
O'Keefe & Solman (1987) Experiment 1.0 & 2.0	1. Complex pictures before prose 2. Complex pictures after prose 3. Normal pictures before prose 4. Normal pictures after prose	Stories about 470 words in length	Elementary school (118)	Recall of semantic & logical network of story information	Written	NSD
Peeck (1974)	1. Prose + pictures 2. Pictures 3. Prose only	Passage from "Rupert Bear" story	Elementary school (71)	40-item retention test Immediate, 1-day & 1-week delayed testing	Written	SD immediate & delayed testing
Peng & Levin (1979)	1. Prose + colored line drawings 2. Prose only	Two 10-sentence narrative stories	Elementary school (64) questions both immediate and 3-day delayed	Cued-recall using paraphrase & verbatim	Oral	SD immediate & delayed testing

TABLE 26-3. Continued

Appendix 3 Study	Treatments	Content	Subjects	Dependent Variable(s)	Prose Type	Results
Popham (1969)	1. Cartoon embellished tape/slide version 2. Unembellished tape/slide version 3. Programmed text version	Program developed for public school administrators	College (175)	1. Cognitive achievement (58 items) 2. Anonymous response (4 items)	Written Oral	NSD SD
Pressley, Pigott & Bryant (1982) Experiment 1	1. Prose + completely matched picture 2. Prose + actor action picture 3. Prose + actor static picture 4. Prose + mismatched picture/object incorrect 5. Prose + incorrect object picture 6. Prose only	2 lists of concrete sentences	Young children	Correct recall responses	Oral	SD
Experiment 2	1. Prose + completely matched picture 2. Prose + actor action/object correct picture 3. Prose + actor static/object picture 4. Prose only	Same	Young children (52)	Same	Same	SD Matched pictures > action object > prose only NSD action object & static object
Pressley et al. (1983) Collapsed experiments 1, 2, 2A, 3 & 3A	1. Prose + matched pictures 2. Prose + mismatched pictures 3. Prose only Note: Above basic conditions were combined with explicit or nonexplicit instructions regarding picture-text relationships	33 concrete sentences or 6 moderately difficult stories	Elementary school (414)	1. Cued-recall questions 2. Picture recognition in some instances	Written Oral	SD in all cases for matched pictures NSD for mismatched pictures vs. prose only
Rankin & Culhane (1970)	1. Typed format text with no illustrations 2. Printed format text with illustrations	A passage from "Pioneer Life in America"	Middle school (57) High school (22)	50-item cloze comprehension test	Written	NSD
Rasco et al. (1975) Experiment 1.0	1. Prose + drawings + instructional strategy 2. Prose + drawings 3. Prose + instructional strategy 4. Prose only	2,511-word prose passage	Undergraduate (91)	35-item test with 28-true/false, 1 constructed response & 6 multiple-choice questions on the verbal information in the text	Written	NSD
Experiment 2.0 Experiment 3.0	Same Same	Same 2 shorter passages (429 words & 633 words)	High school (80) Elementary school (93)	Same 20 multiple-choice questions on verbal information	Same Same	NSD SD Prose + strategy + pictures

TABLE 26-3. Continued

Appendix 3 Study	Treatments	Content	Subjects	Dependent Variable(s)	Prose Type	Results
Reid, Briggs & Beveridge (1983)	1. Prose + colored illustrations 2. Prose + black & white illustrations 3. Prose only	Specifically written science topic "Structure and Function of the Mammalian Heart"	Middle school (338)	1. Cloze test immediately 2. Objective test items 15 minutes delayed	Written	SD for pictures on objective test NSD for pictures on cloze testing
Rice, Doan & Brown (1981)	1. Prose + pictures 2. Prose only	Prose story "Little Bear"	Elementary school (60)	Reading comprehension with a 11-item test	Written	SD
Riding & Shore (1974)	1. Prose + visuals 2. Prose only	Prose passage "A Story of Rhodpis" containing 185 words	High school (100)	Recall test with 43 questions	Oral	SD
Rohwer & Matz (1975)	1. Prose + pictures 2. Prose only	Prose containing 3 passages	Elementary school (128)	Total number of assertions correctly verified	Oral	SD
Rohwer & Harris (1975)	1. Oral prose + written prose + pictures 2. Written prose + pictures 3. Oral prose + pictures 4. Oral prose + written prose 5. Pictures only 6. Oral prose only 7. Written prose only	Passages about 2 types of monkeys	Elementary school (186)	1. Short answers 2. Free-recall 3. Verification of statements in text	Oral Written	SD oral + pictures was superior
Royer & Cable (1976)	1. Abstract passage + illustrations 2. Unembellished abstract passage 3. Abstract passage with analogues 4. Concrete passage 5. Unrelated prose (control)	Science lesson on heat flow & electrical conductivity	College (80)	Recall of "idea units"	Written	SD
Ruch & Levin (1977)	1. Partial test (partial pictures with each question) 2. Partial study (look at partial pictures during narrative) 3. Repetition (each sentence twice in succession) 4. Control (listened to text once)	Two 10-sentence narrative passages	Elementary school (112)	Cued-recall: 10 verbatim 10 paraphrase	Oral	SD (relative to other 3 conditions) for partial pictures during study on paraphrase questions only

TABLE 26-3. *Continued*

Appendix 3 Study	Treatments	Content	Subjects	Dependent Variable(s)	Prose Type	Results
Ruch & Levin (1979) Experiment 1.0	1. Reinstated picture condition (prose + partial picture at onset of passage and at question time) 2. Partial picture condition (prose + partial picture at onset of each passage) 3. Prose only	2-sentence narrative passage that makes reference to an object	Elementary school (48)	Set of 10 "Wh" questions containing both paraphrase & verbatim information	Oral	SD for reinstated picture condition only
Experiment 2.0	1. Reinstated descriptions (prose + partial picture at onset of passage & 2-sentence verbal description prior to each question) 2. Reinstated pictures (prose + partial pictures both during story and questions) 3. Partial pictures only during story presentation 4. Prose only	Same plus 2-sentence verbal description developed for each picture added	Elementary school (42)	Same	Same	SD reinstated pictures > reinstated descriptions
Rusted & Coltheart (1979b)	1. Prose + simple line drawings 2. Prose only	2 sets of concrete nouns plus a short prose passage	Elementary school (32)	Mean recall, recognition & pronunciation scores	Written	SD
Rusted & Coltheart (1979a) Experiment 1.0	1. Prose + line drawings 2. Prose only	6 short factual passages of highly unusual plant or creatures	Elementary school (72)	Free recall both immediate and 5–7-minute delayed	Written	SD both immediate and delayed testing
Experiment 2.0	1-3. Prose + 3 picture types 4-6. 3 picture types alone 7. Prose Picture types: (a) line drawing, (b) colored drawing, (c) color & background	Same	Elementary school (100)	Number of features recalled both immediate & delayed testing	Same	SD independent of picture type both immediate and delayed testing
Rusted & Hodgson (1985)	1. Text + text-relevant and text-nonrelevant pictures 2. Text only	1 factual & 1 fictitious passage	Middle school (40)	Oral recall scores	Written	SD for factual/expository text
Scruggs, et al. (1985)	1. Mnemonic-instruction (10 interactive illustrations) 2. Direct-study (realistic colored illustration) 3. Free-study (text only)	Passage describing 8 North American minerals	High school + LD (56)	Recall of mineral attributes	Written	SD mnemonic condition

TABLE 26-3. Continued

Appendix 3 Study	Treatments	Content	Subjects	Dependent Variable(s)	Prose Type	Results
Sewell, Jr. & Moore (1980)	1. Cartoon text (text + 43 cartoon embellishments) 2. Visual only (cartoons embellishment) 3. Audio/visual (audio + slides of cartoons) 4. Audio only 5. Printed text only	Cartoon strip used as passage	College (150)	Comprehension using 25-item multiple-choice test	Written Oral	SD audio/visual
Sherman (1976)	1. Graphic partial before passage 2. Graphic partial after passage 3. Graphic complete before passage 4. Graphic complete after passage 5. Verbal partial before passage 6. Verbal partial after passage 7. Verbal complete before passage 8. Verbal complete after passage	Eight, 70-word paragraphs (both concrete & abstract versions)	High school (144)	Free recall Total words, idea units, and thematic intrusions recalled	Written	SD for all graphics vs. all verbal conditions
Shriberg et al. (1892) Experiment 1.0	1. Prose + pictures plus (colored "keyword" line drawings + 2 additional pieces of incidental information) 2. Prose + pictures (colored "keyword" line drawings) 3. Prose (12 passages)	Twelve 3-sentence passages about famous people	Middle school (48)	12 sets test questions relating to passages	Written	SD for pictures NSD between picture conditions
Experiment 2.0	1. Prose + pictures plus (colored "keyword" line drawings + 4 additional pieces of incidental information) 2. Imagery + name & keyword pages 3. Prose (12 passages)	Same	Middle school (48)	Same	Same	SD
Silvern (1980)	1. Picture (listen + picture) 2. Play (listen + pretend in story) 3. Repetition (listen twice) 4. Control (listen once)	2 stories, each 10 sentences long	Young children (40)	Comprehension using 10 "Wh" questions	Oral	NSD
Snowman & Cunningham (1975)	1. Pictures before relevant text 2. Pictures after relevant text 3. Pictures & questions before relevant text 4. Pictures & questions after relevant text 5. Questions before relevant text 6. Questions after relevant text 7. Text with no adjunct aids	A 2,189-word fictitious passage	Undergraduate (63)	Recall of specific factual information for both practiced and nonpracticed items	Written	NSD (with respect to type of adjunct aid)
Stone & Glock (1981)	1. Prose + text redundant line drawings 2. Text redundant line drawings 3. Text only	Directs for assembly of a "hand truck" toy	Undergraduate (90)	1. Number of assembly errors 2. Comprehension of reading the instructions	Written	SD (drawing + text)

TABLE 26-3. Continued

Appendix 3 Study	Treatments	Content	Subjects	Dependent Variable(s)	Prose Type	Results
Strommes & Nyman (1974)	1. Prose + mnemonic illustrations preceding each sentence 2. Prose only	Two 30-sentence stories of connected discourse	High school (30)	Immediate paced recall with pictures or empty frames; paced and free recall 1-year delayed	Written	SD for immediate but NSD for delayed testing
Talley (1989)	1. Basal text + basal pictures 2. Story grammar + story grammar pictures 3. Literature + pictures 4. Basal text 5. Story grammar 6. Literature	4 stories from basal readers	Elementary school (72)	1. Comprehension questions 2. Recall measures	Written	SD for picture conditions
Thomas (1978)	1. Color photographs + text 2. Simplified line drawings + text 3. Text only	Prose from a science textbook	Elementary school (108)	1. Literal comprehension 2. Inferential comprehension	Written	NSD
Towers (1994) Experiment 1.0	1. Prose only 2. Prose + static visuals	Weather patterns	College (69)	10 short-answer paraphrase questions	Written	SD
Experiment 2.0	same	Same	College (64)	13 short-answer paraphrase questions + 4 comprehension questions	Same	NSD
	Note: These 2 experiments also contained an animated treatment not included in this summary					
Vernon (1953) Series 1 & 2	1. Prose + photographs 2. Prose + graphs (series 1.0 only) 3. Prose only	Expository short stories of 700–800 words each	High school (62) (major points)	Oral recall of verbal information	Written	NSD
Vernon (1954) Experiment 1.0	1. Prose + pictures 2. Prose only	Text from 2 small books of 755 & 940 words in length	Elementary school & middle school (24)	6 fairly general questions related to text on recall measures	Written	NSD
Experiment 2.0	1. Prose + pictures cutout from book 2. Prose + 4 simple line drawings 3. Text + photographs	Text taken from book "The Shape of of Things"	Elementary school (60)	1. Number of items remembered 2. Question to test understanding	Oral	NSD
Vye et al. (1986)	1. Sentence + picture 2. Picture 3. Sentence Note: 1. Above instructional conditions crossed with elaboration type (precise, imprecise), crossed with retrieval cue (verbal, pictorial) yielding 12 total instructional conditions	20 precise-sentences & 20 imprecise sentences	Undergraduate (168)	Cued recall	Oral	SD for sentence + picture condition superior

TABLE 26-3. *Continued*

Appendix 3 Study	Treatments	Content	Subjects	Dependent Variable(s)	Prose Type	Results
Waddill, McDaniel & Einstein (1988) Experiment 1.0	1. Prose + detailed pictures 2. Prose + relational pictures 3. Prose only	2 text types, a narrative fairy tale & an expository text	College (172)	1. Comprehension 2. Free recall 3. Cued recall	Written	SD dependent on text type and picture type
Experiment 2.0	Same + subjects instructed to attend to the type of information not normally encoded from each text type	Same	College (72)	Same	Same	SD dependent on text type and picture type
Weintraub (1960)	1. Prose + pictures 2. Pictures only 3. Prose only	3 stories from selected basal readers	Elementary school (104)	Questions dealing with comprehension	Written	NSD
Weisberg (1970)	1. Prose + advanced organizer (graph) 2. Prose + advanced organizer (map) 3. Prose + advanced organizer (verbal) 4. Prose + no advanced organizer	Earth science concepts	Middle school (96)	40 questions, verbal multiple choice of knowledge content	Written	SD Map > graph > verbal > prose
Woolridge et al. (1982)	1. Partial pictures during prose & question phases 2. Partial pictures during question phase 3. Partial pictures during prose phase 4. Prose only	Two 10-sentence narrative paragraphs	Elementary school (80)	Two 10-sentence narrative paragraphs	Oral	SD

NSD = nonsignificant difference; SDS = significant static graphics effect

TABLE 26-4. STUDIES LISTED IN THE MATRIX FOR STATIC VISUALS

Alesandrini, K.L. (1981). Pictorial-verbal and analytic-holistic learning strategies in science learning. *Journal of Educational Psychology 73*, 358–68.

— & Rigney, J.W. (1981). Pictorial presentation and review strategies in science learning. *Journal of Research in Science Teaching 18* (5), 465–74.

Anglin, G.J. (1986). Prose-relevant pictures and older learners' recall of written prose. *Educational Communication and Technology Journal 34* (3), 131–36.

— (1987). Effect of pictures on recall of written prose: how durable are picture effects? *Educational Communication and Technology Journal 35* (1), 25–30.

— & Stevens, J.T. (1986). Prose-relevant pictures and recall from science text. *Perceptual and Motor Skills 63* (3), 1143–48.

Arnold, D.J. & Brooks, P.H. (1976). Influence of contextual organizing material on children's listening comprehension. *Journal of Educational Psychology 68*, 711–16.

Beck, C.R. (1984). Visual cueing strategies: pictorial, textual, and combinational effects. *Educational Communication and Technology Journal 32*, 207–16.

Bender, B.G. & Levin, J.R. (1978). Pictures, imagery, and retarded children's prose learning. *Journal of Educational Psychology 70*, 583–88.

Bernard, R.M., Petersen, C.H. & Ally, M. (1981). Can images provide contextual support for prose? *Educational Communication and Technology Journal 29*, 101–08.

Bieger, G.R. & Glock, M.D. (1984). Comprehending spatial and contextual information in picture-text instructions. *Journal of Experimental Education*, 181–88.

Bluth, L.F. (1973). A comparison of the reading comprehension of good and poor readers in the second grade with and without illustration. (Doctoral dissertation, University of Illinois at Urbana-Champaign, 1972.) *Dissertations Abstracts International 34*, 637A.

Borges, M.A. & Robins, S.L. (1980). Contextual and motivational cue effects on the comprehension and recall of prose. *Psychological Reports 47*, 263–68.

Bransford, J.D. & Johnson, M.K. (1972). Contextual prerequisites for understanding: some investigations of comprehension and recall. *Journal of Verbal Learning and Verbal Behavior 11*, 717–26.

Covey, R.E. & Carroll, J.L. (1985). *Effects of adjunct pictures on comprehension of grade six science texts under three levels of text organization.* Paper presented at the annual meeting of the Evaluation Network/Evaluation Research Society, San Francisco, CA Oct. 10–13 (ERIC Document Reproduction Service No. 259-946).

Dean, R.S. & Enemoh, P.A. (1983). Pictorial organization in prose learning. *Contemporary Educational Psychology 8*, 20–27.

DeRose, T. (1976). *The effects of verbally and pictorially induced and imposed strategies on children's memory for text.* Wisconsin Research and Development Center for Cognitive Learning, The University of Wisconsin. Madison, WI (ERIC Document Reproduction Service No. 133-709).

Digdon, N., Pressley, M. & Levin, J.R. (1985). Preschoolers' learning when pictures do not tell the whole story. *Educational Communication and Technology Journal 33*, 139–45.

Duchastel, P.C. (1980). Test of the role in retention of illustra-

tions in text. *Psychological Reports 47*, 204–06.

— (1981). Illustrations in text: a retentional role. *Programmed Learning and Educational Technology 18*, 11–15.

Durso, F.T. & Johnson, M.K. (1980). The effects of orienting tasks on recognition, recall, and modality confusion of pictures and words. *Journal of Verbal Learning and Verbal Behavior 19*, 416–29.

Gibbons, J., et al. (1986). Young children's recall and reconstruction of audio and audiovisual narratives. *Child Development 57*(4), 1014–23.

Goldberg, F. (1974). Effects of imagery on learning incidental material in the classroom. *Journal of Educational Psychology 66*, 233–37.

Goldston, D.B. & Richman, C.L. (1985). Imagery, encoding, specificity, and prose recall in 6-year-old children. *Journal of Experimental Child Psychology 40*, 395–405.

Guttmann, J., Levin, J.R. & Pressley, M. (1977). Pictures, partial pictures, and young children's oral prose learning. *Journal of Educational Psychology 69*, 473–80.

Hannafin, M.J. (1988). The effects of instructional explicitness on learning and error persistence. *Contemporary Educational Psychology 13*, 126–32.

Haring, M.J. & Fry, M.A. (1979). Effect of pictures on children's comprehension of written text. *Educational Communication and Technology Journal 27*, 185–90.

Hayes, D.A. & Henk, W.A. (1986). Understanding and remembering complex prose augmented by analogic and pictorial illustration. *Journal of Reading Behavior 18* (1), 63–77.

— & Readance, J.E. (1983). Transfer of learning from illustration-dependent text. *Journal of Educational Research 76*, 245–48.

— & Readance, J.E. (1982). Effects of cued attention to illustrations in text. *In G.A. Niles & L.A. Harris, eds. New inquiries in reading research and instruction*, 60–63. Rochester, NY:

Holliday, W.G. (1975). The effects of verbal and adjunct pictorial-verbal information in science instruction. *Journal of Research in Science Teaching 12*, 77–83.

— & Harvey, D.A. (1976). Adjunct labeled drawings in teaching physics to junior high school students. *Journal of Research in Science Teaching 13*, 37–43.

Holmes, B.C. (1987). Children's inferences with print and pictures. *Journal of Educational Psychology 79* (1), 14–18.

Jagodzinska, M. (1976). The role of illustrations in verbal learning. *Polish Psychological Bulletin 7*, 95–104.

Jahoda, G., Cheyne, W.M., Deregowski, J.B., Sinha, D. & Collingsbourne, R. (1976). Utilization of pictorial information in classroom learning: a cross cultural study. *AV Communication Review 24*, 295–315.

Jonassen, D.H. (1979). Implications of multi-image for concept acquisition. *ECTJ 27* (4), 291–302.

Koenke, K. & Otto, W. (1969). Contribution of pictures to children's comprehension of the main idea in reading. *Psychology in the Schools 6*, 298–302.

Koran, M.L. & Koran, J.J.J. (1980). Interaction of learner characteristics with pictorial adjuncts in learning from science text. *Journal of Research in Science Teaching 17* (5), 477–83.

Lesgold, A.M., DeGood, & Levin, J.R. (1977). Pictures and

TABLE 26-4. *Continued*

---

young children's prose learning: a supplementary report. *Journal of Reading Behavior 9*, 353–60.

—, Levin, J.R., Shimron, J. & Guttmann, J. (1975). Pictures and young children's learning from oral prose. *Journal of Educational Psychology 67*, 636–42.

Levin, J.R. (1976). What have we learned about maximizing what children learn? In J.R.L. & V.L. Allen, eds. *Cognitive learning in children: theories and strategies*, 105–34. New York: Academic.

— & Berry, J.K. (1980). Children's learning of all the news that's fit to picture. *Educational Communication and Technology Journal 28*, 177–85.

—, McCormick, C.B., Miller, G.E., Berry, J.K. & Pressley, M. (1982). Mnemonic versus nonmnemonic vocabulary-learning strategies for children. *American Educational Research Journal 19*, 121–36.

—, Morrison, C.R., McGivern, J.E., Mastropieri, M.S. & Scruggs, T.E. (1986). Mnemonic facilitation of text-embedded science facts. *American Educational Research Journal 23*, 489–506.

—, et al. (1983). Learning via mnemonic pictures: analysis of presidential process. *Educational Communication and Technology Journal 31* (3), 161–73.

—, Shriberg, L.K. & Berry, J.K. (1983). A concrete strategy for remembering abstract prose. *American Educational Research Journal 20* (2), 277–90.

Magne, O. & Parknas, L. (1962). The learning effects of pictures. *British Journal of Educational Psychology 33*, 265–75.

Main, R.E. & Griffiths, B. (1977). Evaluation of audio and pictorial instructional supplements. *AV Communication Review 25* (2), 167–79.

Mayer, R.E. (1989). Systematic thinking fostered by illustrations in scientific text. *Journal of Educational Psychology 81* (2), 240–46.

McCormick, C.B. & Levin, J.R. (1984). A comparison of different prose-learning variations of the mnemonic keyword method. *American Education Research Journal 21*, 379–98.

—, Levin, J.R., Cykowski, F. & Danilovics, P. (1984). Mnemonic strategy reduction of prose-learning interference. *Educational Communication and Technology Journal 32*, 154–52.

Miller, W.A. (1938). Reading with and without pictures. *Elementary School Journal 38*, 676–82.

Moore, A.M. (1975). Investigation of the effect of patterns of illustrations on third graders' comprehension of information. (Doctoral dissertation, Kent State University, 1974.) *Dissertation Abstracts International 36*, 1275A.

Nugent, G.C. (1982). Pictures, audio, and print: symbolic representation and effect on learning. *Educational Communications and Technology Journal 30* (3), 163–74.

O'Keefe, E.J. & Solman, R.T. (1987). The influence of illustrations on children's comprehension of written stories. *Journal of Reading Behavior 19* (4), 353–77.

Peeck, J. (1974). Retention of pictorial and verbal content of a text with illustrations. *Journal of Educational Psychology 66*, 880–88.

Peng, C.Y. & Levin, J.R. (1979). Pictures and children's story recall: some questions of durability. *Educational Communi-cation and Technology Journal 27*, 179–92.

Popham, W.J. (1969). Pictorial embellishments in a tape-slide instructional program. *AV Communication Review 17* (1), 28–35.

Pressley, M., Levin, J.R., Pigott, S., LeComte, M. & Hope, D.J. (1983). Mismatched pictures and children's prose learning. *Educational Communication and Technology Journal 31*, 131–43.

Pressley, M., Pigott, S. & Bryant, S.L. (1982). Picture content and preschoolers' learning from sentences. *Educational Communication and Technology Journal 30*, 151–61.

Rankin, E.F. & Culhane, J.W. (1970). One picture equals 1,000 words? *Reading Improvement 7*, 37–40.

Rasco, R.W., Tennyson, R.D. & Boutwell, R. . (1975). Imagery instructions and drawings in learning prose. *Journal of Educational Psychology 67*, 188–92.

Reid, D.J., Briggs, N. & Beveridge, M. (1983). The effect of pictures upon the readability of a school science topic. *British Journal of Educational Psychology 53*, 327–35.

Rice, D.R., Doan, R.L. & Brown, S.J. (1981). The effects of pictures on reading comprehension, speed and interest of second grade students. *Reading Improvement 18*, 308–12.

Riding, R.J. & Shore, J.M. (1974). A comparison of two methods of improving prose comprehension in educationally subnormal children. *British Journal of Educational Psychology 44*, 300–03.

Rohwer, W.D. & Matz, R.D. (1975). Improving aural comprehension in white and in black children. *Journal of Experimental Child Psychology 19*, 23–36.

— & Harris, W.J. (1975). Media effects of prose learning in two populations of children. *Journal of Educational Psychology 67*, 651–57.

Royer, J.M. & Cable, G.W. (1976). Illustrations, analogies, and facilitative transfer in prose learning. *Journal of Educational Psychology 68*, 205–09.

Ruch, M.D. & Levin, J.R. (1977). Pictorial organization versus verbal repetition of children's prose: evidence for processing differences. *AV Communication Review 25*, 269–80.

— & Levin, J.R. (1979). Partial pictures as imagery-retrieval cues in young children's prose recall. *Journal of Experimental Child Psychology 28*, 268–79.

Rusted, J. & Coltheart, M. (1979a). Facilitation of children's prose recall by the presence of pictures. *Memory and Cognition 7* (5), 354–59.

— & Coltheart, V. (1979b). The effect of pictures on the retention of novel words and prose passages. *Journal of Experimental Child Psychology 28*, 516–24.

— & Hodgson, S. (1985). Evaluating the picture facilitation effect in children's recall of written texts. *British Journal of Educational Psychology 55* (3), 288–94.

Scruggs, T.E., Mastropieri, M.A., Levin, J.R. & Gaffney, J.S. (1985). Facilitating the acquisition of science facts in learning disabled students. *American Educational Research Journal 22*, 575–86.

Sewell, E.H. & Moore, R.L. (1980). Cartoon embellishments in informative presentations. *Educational Communication and Technology Journal 28*, 39–46.

Sherman, J.L. (1976). Contextual information and prose comprehension. *Journal of Reading Behavior 8*, 369–79.

TABLE 26-4. *Continued*

Shriberg, L.K., Levin, J.R., McCormick, C.B. & Pressley, M. (1982). Learning about "famous" people via the keyword method. *Journal of Educational Psychology 74,* 238–47.

Silvern, S.B. (1980). Play, pictures, and repetition: mediators in aural prose learning. *Educational Communication and Technology Journal 28,* 134–39.

Snowman, J. & Cunningham, D.J. (1975). A comparison of pictorial and written adjunct aids in learning from text. *Journal of Educational Psychology 67,* 307–11.

Stone, D.E. & Glock, M.D. (1981). How do young adults read directions with and without pictures? *Journal of Educational Psychology 73,* 419–26.

Stromnes, F.J. & Nyman, J. (1974). Immediate and long-term retention of connected concrete discourse as a function of mnemonic picture-type sequence and context. *Scandinavian Journal of Psychology 15,* 197–202.

Talley, J.E. (1989). The effect of pictures and story text structure on recall and comprehension. (Doctoral dissertation, Auburn University, 1988.) *Dissertation Abstracts International 49,* 2604A.

Thomas, J.L. (1978). The influence of pictorial illustrations with written text and previous achievement on the reading comprehension of fourth grade science students. *Journal of Research in Science Teaching 15,* 401–05.

Towers, R.L. (1994). The effects of animated graphics and static graphics on student learning in a computer-based instructional format. (Doctoral dissertation, University of Kentucky, 1994.) Unpublished.

Vernon, M.D. (1953). The value of pictorial illustration. *British Journal of Educational Psychology 23,* 180–87.

— (1954). The instruction of children by pictorial illustration. *British Journal of Educational Psychology 24,* 171–79.

Vye, N.J., Bransford, J.D., Symons, S.E. & Acton, H. (1986). *Constraints on elaborations in visual domains.* Paper presented at the meeting of the American Educational Research Association, San Francisco, CA, Apr. 1986.

Waddill, M.A. & McDaniel, MA. (1988). Illustrations as adjuncts to prose: a text-appropriate processing approach. *Journal of Educational Psychology 80*(4), 457–64.

Weintraub, S. (1960). The effect of pictures on the comprehension of a second-grade basal reader. (Doctoral dissertation, University of Illinois, 1960.) *Dissertation Abstracts International 21,* 1428.

Weisberg, J.S. (1970). The use of visual advance organizers for learning earth science concepts. *Journal of Research in Science Teaching 7,* 161–65.

Woolridge, P., Nall, L., Hughes, L., Rauch, T., Stewart, G. & Richman, C.L. (1982). Prose recall in first-grade children using imagery, pictures, and questions. *Bulletin of the Psychonomic Society 20,* 249–52.

TABLE 26-5. SUMMARY OF STUDY RESULTS FOR DYNAMIC VISUALS

Study	Treatment	Subjects	Results*
Alesandrini & Rigney (1981)	Exp. #1. mode (all-verbal vs. verbal-pictorial) × practice (review with dynamic graphics vs. no-review)	College (96)	DVD
	Exp. #2. mode (all-verbal) × practice (review with dynamic graphics vs. no-review)	College (50)	DVD
Avons (1983)	Graphic simulation (active vs. passive)	Middle school, & high school (108)	NSD
Baek & Layne (1988)	(Color vs. B/W) × (text vs. static vs. animation)	High school (119)	DVD
Beichner (1990)	Technique (videograph or traditional) vs. view (witnessed a real motion event or did not)	High school & college (237)	NSD
Blake (1977)	(Still slides) vs. (animated cueing arrows) vs. (full motion film)	College (84)	Mixed
Brasell (1987)	Standard -MBL (real time graphing) vs. delayed-MBL or (delayed graphing) vs. (paper only) vs. (test only)	High school (93)	DVD
Caputo (1982)	(Dynamic graphics enhanced CAI) vs. (verbal CAI) vs. (checklist CAI)	College (72)	DVD
Caraballo (1985)	(Control) vs. (text only) vs. (text + still) vs. (text + still + animation)	College (80)	NSD
Caraballo-Rios (1985)	(text) × (text + still) vs. (text + still + animation)	College (109)	NSD
Chien (1986)	(Hands on simulation) vs. (animated interactive graphics)	Elementary school (72)	NSD
Collins et. al. (1978)	(Unlabeled map) vs. (static labeled map) vs. (interactive dynamic map with blinking dots)	High school & college (18)	DVD
Hativa & Reingold (1987)	(Static graphics + no sound + monochrome) vs. (sound + animation + color)	Middle school (92)	DVD
Johnson (1985)	(Interactive dynamic computer graphics) vs. (static computer graphics)	High school (165)	DVD
King (1975)	(Text) vs. (text + still) vs. (text + still + dynamic)	Adult (45)	NSD
Kinzer et al. (1989)	(Expository text only) vs. (simulation using animation)	Elementary school (52)	SDT
Klein (1986)	Rule type (temporal vs. spatial) vs. mode (nonanimated graphics vs. animated graphics)	College (38)	Mixed

TABLE 26-5. *Continued*

Study	Treatment	Subjects	Results*
Laner (1954)	(Static film strip) vs. (full motion picture film)	Adult (75)	NSD
Laner (1955)	(Text + static diagrams) vs. (full motion film)	Adult (50)	NSD
Lumsdaine et al. (1961)	(Nonanimated film) vs. (animated film)	Adult (1300)	DVD
Mayer & Anderson (1991)	Exp. #2. (words with animation) vs. (animation only) vs. (words only) vs. (no treatment)	College (48)	DVD
Mayton (1990)	(Static + no cueing) vs. (static + imagery cueing) vs. (animation + imagery cueing)	College (72)	DVD
McCloskey & Kohl (1983)	(No motion) vs. (dynamic rotations) vs. (dynamic trajectories)	College (90)	NSD
McCuistion (1990)	(Static visuals) vs. (dynamic visuals)	College (137)	NSD
Moore et al. (1979)	(Alphanumeric & schematics) vs. (line drawings) vs. (animation)	Adult (90)	NSD
Myers (1990)	(Traditional classroom) vs. (dynamic interactive graphics)	College (52)	DVD
Park & Gittelman (1992)	(Type of feedback) x (static vs. animated)	College (90)	DVD
Peters & Daiker (1982)	(Program with no animation) vs. (CAI program with animation)	College (35)	NSD
Ponick (1987)	(Nonanimated graphics) vs. (animated graphics)	College (71)	DVD
Reed (1985)	(Animated single dot) vs. (animated two dots)	College (180)	Mixed
Rieber & Hannafin (1988)	(Text) vs. (animation) vs. (text + animation) vs. (none) vs. (animation) vs. (text + animation)	Elementary school (111)	NSD
Rieber (1989)	Practice type × (no graphics) vs. (static graphics) vs. (animation)	SC (192)	NSD
Rieber (1990)	Practice type × (no graphics) vs. (static graphics) vs. (animated graphics)	Elementary school (119)	DVD
Rieber, Boyce & Assad (1990)	Visual elaboration × (no graphic) vs. (static graphics) vs. (animation) × (practice order)	College (141)	NSD
Rieber (1991)	(Static graphics) vs. (animation) × (practice order)	Elementary school (70)	DVD
Rigney & Lutz (1976)	(Written description only) vs. (verbal statement plus animation)	College (40)	DVD
Roshal (1961)	Motion (yes vs. no) × show hands (yes vs. no) × active participation (yes vs. no)	Adult (3314)	DVD
Spangenberg (1973)	Exp. #1. (motion sequence) vs. (set of still photo's)	Adult (40)	DVD
	Exp. #2. (motion sequence) vs. (motion sequence + cueing arrows) vs. (static) vs. (static + cueing arrows)	Adult (80)	DVD
Spangler (1994)	Traditional instruction vs. static graphics vs. animated graphics	College (57)	NSD
Swezey et al. (1991)	(Video motion) vs. (static 35-mm slides)	Children (120)	NSD
Thompson & Riding (1990)	(Static diagram no computer) vs. computer (static or animated diagrams)	College (108)	DVD
Towers (1994)	Exp. #1. prose only vs. prose + static vs. prose + animated	College (49)	SDS
	Exp. #2. prose only vs. prose + static vs. prose + animated	College (64)	NSD
Zavotka (1987)	(Tested only no snimation) vs. (3-D animated projection)	College (101)	Mixed

*NSD = nonsignificant differences; Mixed = mixed effects reported; DVD = significant differences for dynamic visual displays; SDT text = significant difference for static text treatment; SDS = significant differences for static graphics.

TABLE 26-6. STUDIES LISTED IN THE MATRIX FOR DYNAMIC VISUALS

Alesandrini, K.L. & Rigney, J.W. (1981). Pictorial presentation and review strategies in science learning. *Journal of Research in Science Teaching 18* (5), 465–74.

Avons, S.E., Beveridge, M.C., Hickman, A.T. & Hitch, G.J. (1983). Teaching journey graphs with microcomputer animation. *Human Learning 2,* 93–105.

Baek, Y.K. & Layne, B.H. (1988). Color, graphics, and animation in a computer-assisted learning tutorial lesson. *Journal of Computer-Based Instruction 15* (4), 131–35.

Beichner, R.J. (1990). The effect of simultaneous motion presentation and graph generation in a kinematics lab. *Journal of Research in Science Teaching 27* (8), 803–15.

Blake, T. (1977). Motion in instructional media: some subject-display mode interactions. *Perceptual and Motor Skills 44,* 975–85.

Brasell, H. (1987). The effect of real-time laboratory graphing on learning graphic representations of distance and velocity. *Journal of Research In Science Teaching 24* (4), 385–95.

Caputo, D.J. (1982). An analysis of the relative effectiveness of a graphics-enhanced microcomputer-based remedial system in a university basic mathematical skills deficiency removal plan. (Doctoral dissertation, University of Pittsburgh, 1981.) *Dissertation Abstracts International 42,* 3482A.

Caraballo, J.N. (1985). The effect of various visual display modes in computer-based instruction and language background upon achievement of selected educational objectives. (Doctoral dissertation, The Pennsylvania State University, 1985.) *Dissertation Abstracts International 46* (6), 1494A.

Caraballo-Rios, A.L. (1985). An experimental study to investigate the effects of computer animation on the understanding and retention of selected levels of learning outcomes. (Doctoral dissertation, The Pennsylvania State University, 1985.) *Dissertation Abstracts International 46,* 1494A.

Chien, S.C. (1986). The effectiveness of animated and interactive microcomputer graphics on childrens' development of spatial visualization ability/mental rotation skills. (Doctoral dissertation, Ohio State University, 1986.) *Dissertation Abstracts International 47,* 1601A.

Collins, A., Adams, M.J. & Pew, R.W. (1978). Effectiveness of an interactive map display in tutoring geography. *Journal of Educational Psychology 70* (1), 1–7.

Hativa, N. & Reingold, A. (1987). Effects of audiovisual stimuli on learning through microcomputer-based class presentation. *Instructional Science 16,* 287–306.

Johnson, M.K. & Kim, J.K. (1985). Do alcoholic Korsakoff's syndrome patients acquire affective reactions? *Journal of Experimental Psychology 11* (1), 22–36.

King, W.A. (1975). *A comparison of three combinations of text and graphics for concept learning.* (Report No. NPRDC-TR-76-16.) San Diego, CA: Navy Personnel Research and Development Center. (ERIC Document Reproduction Service No. ED 112 936.)

Kinzer, C.K., Sherwood, R.D. & Loofbourrow, M.C. (1989). Simulation software vs. expository text: a comparison of retention across two instructional tools. *Reading Research and Instruction 28* (2), 41–49.

Klein, D. (1986). Conditions influencing the effectiveness of animated and non-animated displays in computer assisted instruction. (Doctoral dissertation, University of Illinois at Urbana, Champaign, IL, 1985.) *Dissertation Abstracts International 46,* 1878A.

Laner, S. (1954). The impact of visual aid displays showing a manipulative task. *The Quarterly Journal of Experimental Psychology 6,* 95–106.

— (1955). Some factors influencing the effectiveness of an instructional film. *British Journal of Psychology 46,* 280–94.

Lumsdaine, A.A., Sultzer, R.L. & Kopstein, F.F. (1961). The effect of animation cues and repetition of examples on learning from an instructional film. *In* A.A. Lumsdaine, eds. *Student response in programmed instruction,* 241–69. Washington, DC: National Research Council.

Mayer, R.E. & Anderson, R.B. (1991). Animations need narrations: an experimental test of a dual-coding hypothesis. *Journal of Educational Psychology 83*(4), 484–90.

Mayton, G.B. (1990). The effects of the animation of visuals on the learning of dynamic processes through microcomputer-based instruction. (Doctoral dissertation, The Ohio State University, 1990.) *Dissertation Abstracts International 51,* 4097A.

McCloskey, M. & Kohl, D. (1983). Naive physics: the curvilinear impetus principle and its role in interactions with moving objects. *Journal of Experimental Psychology: Learning, memory, and cognition 9*(1), 146–56.

Mccuistion, P.J. (1990). Static vs dynamic visuals in computer-assisted instruction. (Doctoral dissertation, Texas A&M University, 1989.) *Dissertation Abstracts International 42,* 4409A.

Moore, M.V., Nawrocki, L.H. & Simutis, Z.M. (1979). *The instructional effectiveness of three levels of graphics displays for computer-assisted instruction* (No. ARI-TP-359). Arlington, VA: Army Research Institute for the Behavioral and Social Sciences (ERIC Document Service No. ED 178 057).

Myers, K.N. (1990). An exploratory study of the effectiveness of computer graphics and simulations in a computer-student interactive environment in illustrating random sampling and the central limit theorem. (Doctoral dissertation, Florida State University, 1990.) *Dissertation Abstracts International 51,* 441A.

Park, O. & Gittelmen, S. (1992). Selective use of animation and feedback in computer-based instruction. *Educational Technology Research and Development 40,* 27–38.

Peters, H.J. & Daiker, K.C. (1982). Graphics and animation as instructional tools: a case study. *Pipeline 7* (1), 11–13.

Ponick, D.A. (1987). Animation used as a logical organizer in visualization for concept learning. (Doctoral dissertation, University of Minnesota, 1986.) *Dissertation Abstracts International 47,* 3300A.

Reed, S.K. (1985). Effect of computer graphics on improving estimates to algebra word problems. *Journal of Educational Psychology 77* (3), 285–98.

Rieber, L.P. (1989). The effects of computer animated elaboration strategies and practice on factual and application learning in an elementary science lesson. *Journal of Educational Computing Research 5* (4), 431–44.

— (1990). Using computer animated graphics in science instruction with children. *Journal of Educational Psychology 82* (1), 135–40.

— (1991). Animation, incidental learning, and continuing motivation. *Journal of Educational Psychology 83* (3), 318–28.

TABLE 26-6. *Continued*

—, Boyce, M.J. & Assad, C. (1990). The effects of computer animation on adult learning and retrieval tasks. *Journal of Computer-Based Instruction 17* (2), 46–52.

— & Hannafin, M.J. (1988). Effects of textual and animated orienting activities and practice on learning from computer-based instruction. *Computers in the Schools 5* (1/2), 77–89.

Rigney, J.W. & Lutz, K.A. (1976). Effect of graphic analogies of concepts in chemistry on learning and attitude. *Journal of Educational Psychology 68* (3), 305–11.

Roshal, S.M. (1961). Film mediated learning with varying representations of the task: viewing angle, portrayal of demonstration, motion, and student participation. *In A.A. Lumsdaine, ed. Student response in programmed instruction,* 155–75. Washington, DC: National Research Council.

Spangenberg, R. (1973). The motion variable in procedural learning. *AV Communication Review 21,* 419–36.

Spangler, R.D. (1994). The effects of computer-based animated and static graphics on learning to visualize three-dimensional objects. (Doctoral dissertation, University of Kentucky, 1994.) Unpublished.

Swezey, R.W., Perez, R.S. & Allen, J.A. (1991). Effects of instructional strategy and motion presentation conditions on the acquisition and transfer of electromechanical troubleshooting skills. *Human Factors 33* (3), 309–23.

Thompson, S.V. & Riding, R.J. (1990). The effect of animated diagrams on the understanding of a mathematical demonstration in 11-to-14-year-old pupils. *British Journal of Educational Psychology 60,* 93–98.

Towers, R.L. (1994). The effects of animated graphics and static graphics on student learning in a computer-based instructional format. (Doctoral dissertation, University of Kentucky, 1994.)

Zavotka, S.L. (1987). Three-dimensional computer animated graphics: a tool for spatial skills instruction. *Educational Communication and Technology Journal 35* (3), 133–44.

TABLE 26-7. SUMMARY TABLE FOR PRIMARY RESEARCH STUDIES INCLUDED IN THE LITERATURE SURVEY

	Total Number	Subjects*					Prose Type		Results†	
		Y	H	U	G	A	Written	Oral	SD	NSD
Static Pictures										
Studies	90	9217	1362	2700	129	120	61	34	81	33
Experiments	118						73	48	102	36
Animation										
Studies	42	690	429	1991	—	4994	42	0	19	18
Experiments	45						45	0	21	18

*Y = Young children, elementary, and middle school; H = High school; U = Undergraduate; G = Graduate; A = Adult

†SD = Significant differences; NSD = Nonsignificant differences.

Mixed effects were identified in four animation studies.

27. TEXT DESIGN

James Hartley
UNIVERSITY OF KEELE, U.K.

This chapter is divided into six sections as follows:

1. Some typographical considerations
2. Text layout: structure and access
3. Text difficulty
4. Text design for readers with special needs
5. How textbooks are used
6. Future directions in textbook design

My aim in each section has been to present a particular argument, supported by references to empirical research. In addition, I hope that these references will enable interested readers to follow up the issues raised more widely, should they wish. Regrettably, I have decided that there is no one clear theoretical perspective that I could take in writing this chapter so, accordingly, none is offered. References to particular paradigms in text design are, however, made where appropriate.

One important aspect of text design that is omitted in this chapter is that of the design and positioning of elements such as tables, diagrams, and figures. These issues are discussed in Chapters 16 and 26.

27.1 SOME TYPOGRAPHICAL CONSIDERATIONS

27.1.1 Page Sizes

Printed materials come in many shapes and sizes. There are no specific rules or guidelines that might suggest to writers, designers, or printers why they should choose one page size in preference to any other. The research literature on legibility and textbook design offers little help, for page size is not an issue that features in many books on text design. Why then do I choose to start this chapter by discussing page sizes?

Many people expect a chapter on textbook design to begin with issues such as type sizes, typefaces, and line lengths. However, it is important to realize that the choices for these variables are already constrained by earlier decisions. Clearly, we do not expect to find large type sizes in a pocket dictionary or a single column of print in a daily newspaper. These examples are extreme, but they illustrate the point. The choice of page size comes first, and this affects the choices that are available for subsequent decisions.

The size of the page (and, these days, the electronic screen) determines the size of the overall visual display. The reader needs to be able to scan, read, and focus on both the gross and the fine details of this display (see 16.11). The size of the page (or screen) constrains the decisions that writers and designers make about these details.

The choice of an appropriate page size is not always easy. A number of factors contribute to decisions about which size to employ. Perhaps the most important one is some knowledge of how the information is going to be used. Others are reader preferences, the costs of production and marketing, basic paper sheet sizes, and, more generally, the need to conserve resources and avoid waste (Hartley, 1994a; Spencer, 1969).

27.1.2 Standard Page Sizes

The page sizes that we commonly see are cut from much larger basic sheets that have been folded several times. The present-day variety in page sizes results from the manufacturers using different sizes for their basic printing sheets and folding them in different ways. If the basic printing sheets were all one standard size, however, and the method of folding them allowed for little if any wastage at the cutting stage, then great economies could be achieved.

The need to rationalize paper sizes has long been discussed in the history of information printing. In 1798, for example, the French government prescribed a standard for official documents based on the proportion of width:height as 1:1.41, with a basic printing sheet of 1 square meter in area. In 1911, Wilhelm Oswald proposed the ratio 1:1.414 (that is, $1:\sqrt{2}$) as the "world format." In 1922, the German standard, DIN 476, was published. For this standard, the ratio of width:height as $1:\sqrt{2}$ was retained, with a basic printing sheet size of 1 square meter. This German standard, together with the A, B, and C series of sizes, was adopted in 1958 by the International Organization for Standardization (ISO). Today the ISO series is recommended by the 50 or more national standards bodies that together make up the ISO.

The dimensions of the sizes in the ISO A series are set out below. In the United Kingdom, the A series is used widely, especially the A4 and A5 sizes.

ISO SERIES OF TRIMMED PAPER SIZES

A Series	
Designation	**Size (mm)**
A0	841 × 1189
A1	594 × 841
A2	420 × 594
A3	297 × 420
A4	210 × 297
A5	148 × 210
A6	105 × 148
A7	74 × 105
A8	52 × 74
A9	37 × 52
A10	26 × 37

The unifying principle of the ISO-recommended range of sizes is that a rectangle with sides in the ratio of $1:\sqrt{2}$ can be halved or doubled to produce a series of rectangles, each of which retains the proportions of the original. A rectangle of any other proportion will generate geometrically similar rectangles only at every other point in the process of halving or doubling (see Fig. 27-1).

As the pages of a book are made by folding the larger basic printing sheet in half—once, twice, three times, or more—all the pages made from a standard-size basic sheet will be in the ratio of $1:\sqrt{2}$. Basic sheets that do not conform to this standard do not exhibit this property of geometric similarity when folded, and this can create waste.

We may note at this point, of course, that documents can be arranged in a vertical (portrait) or horizontal (landscape) style and bound at the top (notebook style) or on the left. These variations allow for a variety of page layouts (see Fig. 27-2).

It is considerations such as these that come first when designing instructional text. When these decisions have been made (but not necessarily finalized), the designer can begin to think more about the details of typography. The next step is to consider the widths of the columns and the margins.

27.1.3 Margins

In many books, the margins appear to be planned like a picture frame around a rectangle of print. Tinker (1965) reported that the space devoted to margins in this way could sometimes occupy as much as 50% of the page. However, if we take a functional approach rather than an aesthetic one, it seems to be fairly well agreed that a margin of about 10 mm is necessary at the top and the bottom of the page. However, the inner or binding edge margin is a special case. Here, thought needs to be given to factors that suggest the need for

a wider margin. For example, the printed page may be copied at some time and the copies punched for filing with other material. The binding system itself may involve the punching of pages, or it may be of the kind that causes some part of the edge of the page to be hidden from view. Indeed, the binding system may be such that text or diagrams printed too close to the binding edge may curve inwards and be difficult to read. So, since text appears on both the front and the back of the page, a margin of about 25 mm is usually necessary for both the left- and the right-hand margins.

27.1.4 Column Widths

The choice of column widths also depends on the size of the page, the widths of the margins, and the nature of the text. For printed text, it is normal to consider one, two, or even three columns of print (depending on the page size). A decision to use three columns of print may be appropriate for text that is not very complex (typographically speaking). Other variations, such as one wide column and one narrow one, are possible with larger page sizes, and this is sometimes useful to consider when planning the size and positioning of illustrative materials (see Misanchuk, 1992, for a fuller discussion).

27.1.5 Type Sizes

Several researchers have made suggestions concerning appropriate type sizes for reading matter and have given advice on related issues such as line length and line spacing. Tinker (1963, 1965) and Watts and Nisbet (1974) provide good summaries of the earlier literature in this respect, and Black (1990) provides a more up-to-date account.

Unfortunately much of the early research was not very helpful to designers of instructional text. This was principally because the variables such as type size, line length, and interline space were not studied in the "real-life" context of instructional material. Most early researchers, for example, considered issues of type size with short, simple settings of continuous prose (e.g., see Paterson & Tinker, 1929). Furthermore, the generalizations that emerged from this research did not take into account the difficulties that arose from the fact that different typefaces with the same designated type sizes do not, in fact, look the same.

There are many different measurement systems used in the printing industry, but, with the advent of desktop publishing, these will undoubtedly be rationalized. One measure that is likely to remain, however, is that of the "point." (A point measures 0.0138 inches.) Typical type sizes in textbooks are 10, 11, and 12 point. The "small print" (in legal documents, for example) may be 6 or 8 point, but this is too small for most people to read with ease. Larger sizes (such as 14, 18, and 24 point) are used for headings and display purposes. In this text, the typographic setting of the text is 10 point on 12 point. This indicates that there is an extra space of 2 points between the lines of print to facilitate reading. The main text headings are set in 11-point bold, and the chapter headings in 22-point bold.

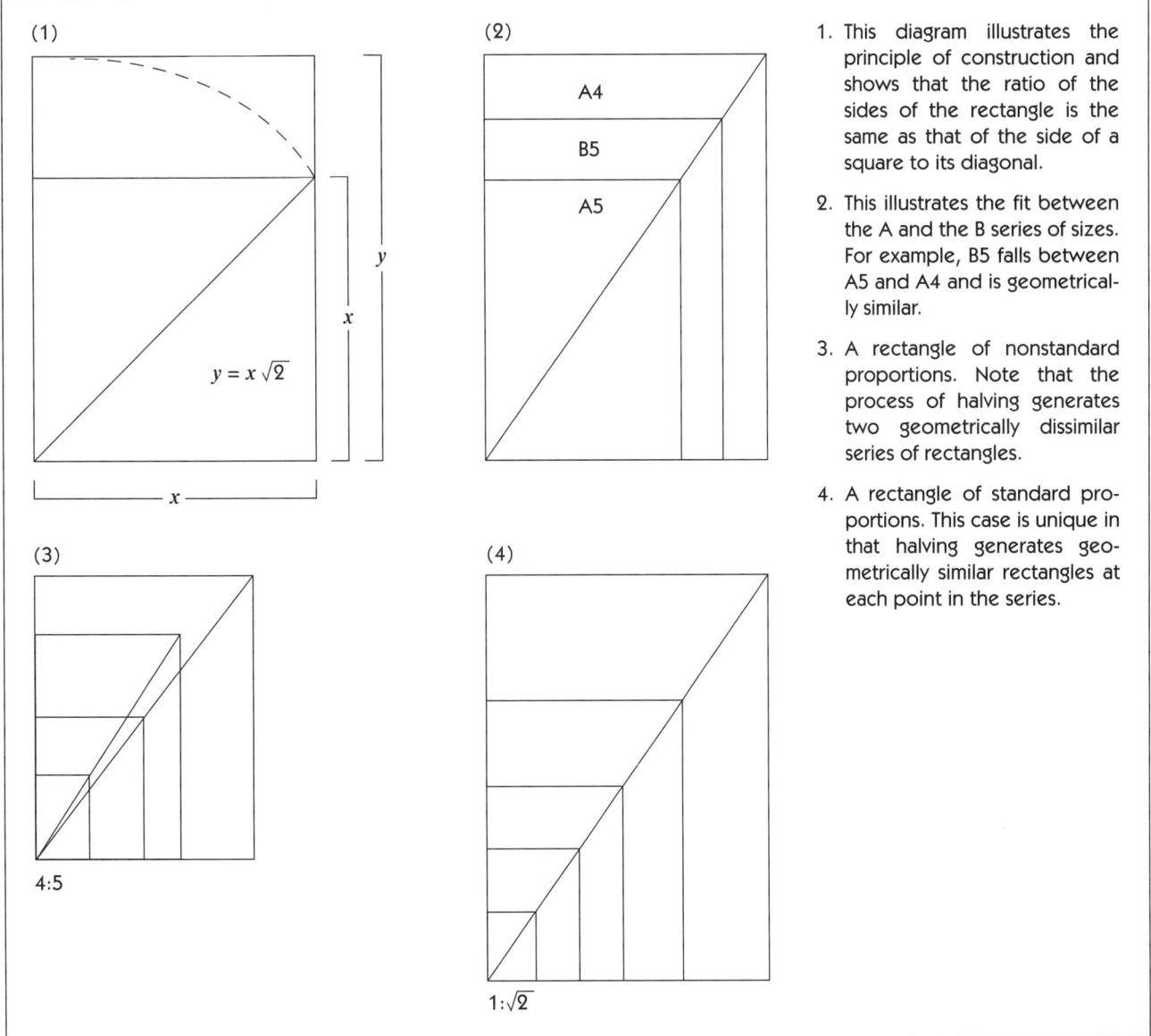

(1)

$y = x \sqrt{2}$

(2)

A4

B5

A5

(3)

4:5

(4)

$1:\sqrt{2}$

1. This diagram illustrates the principle of construction and shows that the ratio of the sides of the rectangle is the same as that of the side of a square to its diagonal.

2. This illustrates the fit between the A and the B series of sizes. For example, B5 falls between A5 and A4 and is geometrically similar.

3. A rectangle of nonstandard proportions. Note that the process of halving generates two geometrically dissimilar series of rectangles.

4. A rectangle of standard proportions. This case is unique in that halving generates geometrically similar rectangles at each point in the series.

Figure 27-1. The principles underlying the recommended page sizes of the International Standards Organization.

However, as noted above, a confusing aspect of past research in this field has been the tendency to recommend the use of specific type sizes without proper regard for the fact that the specified size of a particular typeface (say 12 point) does not refer to the size of the image of the printed characters as seen by the reader. The specified size refers instead to the original depth of space that was required by a line of metal type when it was set with minimum line-to-line spacing. Letters were originally carved on the top of the metal shanks that took up this space. Consequently, the size and style of the letters on top of a shank could vary, although the measure of the shank always remained the same.

Figure 27-3, for instance, shows the same sentence printed in one size of type but in five different typefaces. As can be seen, at best, type size is but a first approximation to image size.

The effect is more dramatic when whole paragraphs, rather than single sentences, are considered. This particular paragraph is printed in 10-point Times Roman. The following paragraph is printed in 10-point Bookman to illustrate the effect.

It is not my intention here to recommend specific type sizes for use in printing instructional materials. However, I would like to outline one approach to the problem of choosing a type size for a text. At root, this concerns choosing a maximum permissible line length that, when related to the type size, will not obstruct the proper and sensible phrasing of the information.

Designers need to examine their text carefully to look for problems that can arise if they choose too large a typeface. For example, in childrens' reading books, the maximum per-

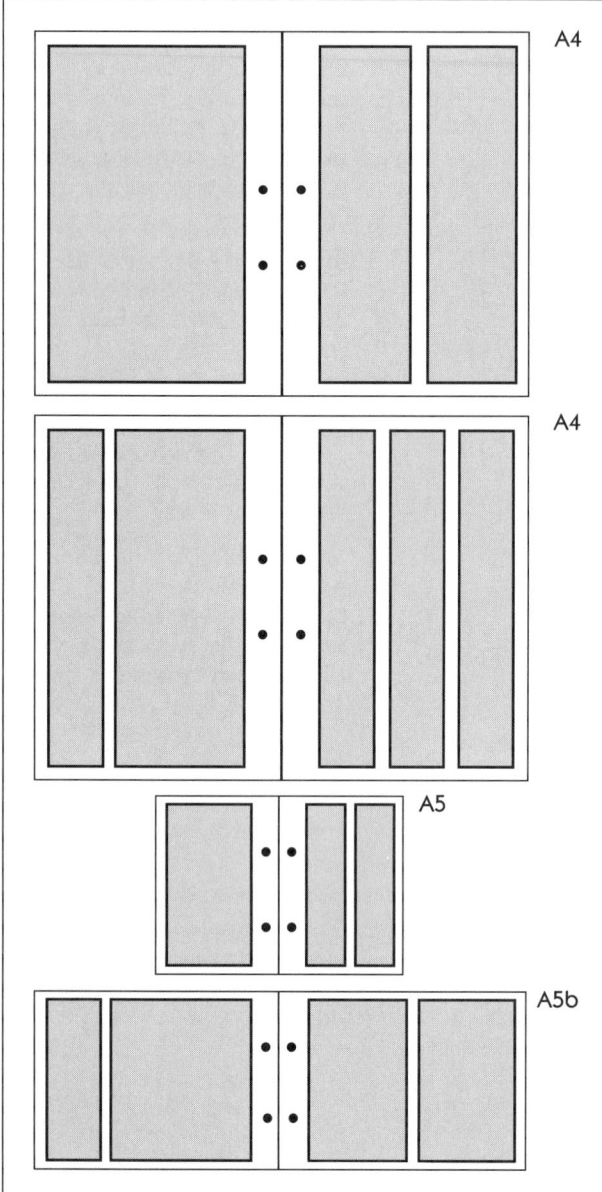

Figure 27-2. How a standard-size sheet can be arranged to provide a variety of page layouts.

This is 12-point Times Roman

This is 12-point Palatino

This is 12-point Helvetica

This is 12-point Century Schoolbook

This is 12-point Bookman

Figure 27-3. How different typefaces with the same designated type size actually differ in size.

missible line length is often limited by the use of large type sizes to three or four words long. Often, in this case, it is difficult to group syntactically the words in the lines. Indeed, some children think that sentences are completed at the end of each line (Raban, 1982). Thus, as shown in the Bookman paragraph, one of the primary dimensions to be considered when thinking about type sizes is the width of the character groups and syntactically structured word strings, and not the vertical dimension of the characters per se.

27.1.6 Typefaces

One particular source of confusion for novice designers is how to choose an appropriate typeface from the bewildering range of typefaces currently available. For example, one encyclopedia of typefaces published in 1930 listed over 2,350 entries. Today, it is estimated that by now there must be several thousand typefaces available. Many desktop systems offer their users a huge variety of choice, so how does one decide?

In practice, as Black (1990) points out, choosing a typeface really means:

1. Considering the purpose of the text
2. Making sure that the chosen sizes and weights required for the text (e.g., light, medium, bold) are available
3. Making sure that the character set contains not only the commonly used signs but also any additional special characters called for by the text
4. Considering how well particular typefaces will withstand repeated copying

Certain typefaces seem more appropriate in some situations than others. Neither Gothic, for example, nor Balloon would seem very helpful for instructional text. Typefaces such as these have emotional connotations (see Lewis & Walker, 1989; Tannenbaum, Jacobson & Norris, 1964), and Spencer (1969) provides a review of earlier studies in this respect. Certainly some readers have personal preferences (see Misanchuk, 1992). These individual differences suggest that it may be wiser to stick to conventional and familiar typefaces than to employ idiosyncratic ones. Black (1990) provides a useful full-length treatment of these issues.

One way of classifying familiar typefaces is in terms of those that have serifs (finishing strokes at the ends of letters) and those that do not (sans serifs). For example, this paragraph is printed in Times Roman, a face with serifs. The following paragraph is printed in Futura, a sans-serif face, to illustrate the effects.

The available research gives no clear guidance on which typefaces are best. Some designers recommend that faces with serifs be used for the body of the text and that faces without serifs be used for headings or for other purposes (such as to differentiate examples from the body of the text). Others consider that typefaces without serifs are more legible in the smaller sizes (e.g., 6 and 8 point) and go on to argue that such sans-serif typefaces are better for text that is not intended for continuous reading (e.g., reference works, tables, catalogs, etc.). Others suggest that sans-serif faces are more appropriate for older readers.

Berger (1991), Black (1990), Misanchuk (1992), and Spencer (1969) review the relevant literature in this field. They conclude that one has to make decisions here that are based on good practice and common sense. I would add, too, that there are so many different typefaces within each group (serif or sans serif) that it makes little sense to generalize in terms of comparing faces with serifs with those without them; it is far better to consider how different typefaces compare and to specify which ones are being discussed.

27.1.7 Capital Letters

Words printed in capital letters contain less-distinctive information per unit of space than do words set in lowercase characters of the same type size (Tinker & Paterson, 1928).

THUS IT IS GENERALLY BELIEVED THAT WHOLE PARAGRAPHS OF TEXT SET IN CAPITAL LETTERS ARE MORE DIFFICULT TO READ THAN ARE PARAGRAPHS SET IN NORMAL UPPER- AND LOWERCASE LETTERS. THE USE OF STRINGS OF WORDS IN CAPITALS FOR MAIN HEADINGS (OR SMALL CAPITALS FOR SECONDARY HEADINGS) MAY BE SATISFACTORY BECAUSE SUCH HEADINGS ARE NORMALLY SURROUNDED BY SPACE THAT AIDS THEIR PERCEPTION. ON THE WHOLE, THOUGH, THE USE OF CAPITAL LETTERS SHOULD BE KEPT TO A MINIMUM. APART FROM SPECIALIZED USE IN MATHEMATICAL WORK, CAPITAL LETTERS ARE BEST RESERVED FOR THE FIRST LETTER OF A SENTENCE (INCLUDING HEADINGS), AND FOR THE FIRST LETTER OF PROPER NOUNS (see Tinker, 1965).

27.1.8 Italicized Letters

Sloping or "italic" characters were originally introduced into printed books in the 16th century as a means of setting more characters to the line, the style of letters being more compressed than the vertically drawn and rounded forms of the normal lowercase character set. Again, it is commonly believed that continuous italic text is harder to read than the more conventional typographic settings. (See Misanchuk, 1992, for further discussion.) Today, italicized characters are often used in instructional text for emphasizing words, for book titles when these appear in the text or in bibliographic references, and sometimes for setting summaries or abstracts.

27.1.9 Color

Color can be used in textbooks in many different ways. Sometimes, for example, colored headings are used simply to make the text more appealing. In other situations, subtexts may be set in a different color in order to differentiate them from the main content.

There is actually a considerable amount of research on the effectiveness of color in printed instructional text (see Dwyer, 1978; Tinker, 1965), and this is an issue that is also prominent in current work with multimedia (e.g., see Clarke, 1992, and Chapter 29). As it happens, there appear to be few clear generalizations that one can make, but it does seem that:

- Readers have color preferences.
- Readers like additional color.
- Color can help learning (see Dwyer, 1978).
- Extra colors have to be used sparingly and consistently if they are not to confuse the readers.
- Certain combinations of colored inks on colored papers are more legible than others. Thus, for example, black ink on white or yellow paper is generally preferable to red ink on these colors, and black ink on dark-red or purple paper is generally to be avoided. (See Clarke, 1992; Dwyer, 1978; and 16.4.3 for further details.)

It must be remembered that young readers, of course, cannot be expected to know automatically why any change from the traditional norm has taken place. This particularly applies to the printing of individual words in bold, capitals, italic, or in color. Early readers need to be taught these conventions. And, in addition, we need to remember that all of these devices need to be used sparingly, as they can lose their significance when they are used in combination or to excess (see, e.g., Foster, 1979; Hartley, 1993a; Hershberger & Terry, 1965; Welsh et al., 1993).

Finally, we should also note in this section that it is not wise to present readers with text that continually changes its size, its spacing, and its typeface. A brief rule of thumb might be that there is no need to use three or more additional cues when one or two at most will do.

27.1.10 Spacing the Text

One of my main arguments in this chapter is that the way in which the designer uses the space on the page greatly affects how easily the reader can understand and retrieve the information from it. Although the text is important— one cannot do without it—I want to argue that the clarity of the text can be enhanced by a rational and consistent use of the "white space" (Hartley, 1994a).

But first a bit more history. Most people today know what a textbook looks like and how it is arranged. But, as Small (1997) points out, books originally began as vertical rolls. The concept of a page did not exist, and there were no page breaks or page numbers. Furthermore, in Classical Greek times, there were no breaks between words, sentences, or even paragraphs. (The paragraph as a unit of text on the page did not appear until the 16th century.) Cross-references were very vague, like "see above" and "see below." The letters forming the words were of the same height and often of the same width. Line lengths were equal, and words were wrapped around the ends of lines without hyphenation. Figure 27-4 simulates what such text used to look like. It is clear to our

---

BOOKXXXIVCONTENTSCOPPERMETALKINDSOFCOPPERC
ORINTHIANDELIANAEGINETANONBRONZEDININGCOUC
HESONCANDELABRAONTEMPLEDECORATIONSOFBRON
ZEFIRSTBRONZEIMAGEOFAGODMADEATROMEONTHEO
RIGINALSTATUTESA

Book XXXIV. Contents: Copper metal. Kinds of copper:
Corinthian, Delian, Aeginetan. On bronze dining
couches; on candelabra; on temple decorations of
bronze; first bronze. . . .

Figure 27-4. Shown schematically in the top illustration is the original way of presenting Classical Greek text. The bottom illustration shows the conventional way of presenting text today. Note that the original text would also have been in handwriting, which would have made it even more difficult to read. [Figure based on illustrations from Small (1997) and reproduced with permission.]

modern eyes that punctuation and spacing, together with upper- and lowercase letters, make such text easier to read.

Space thus plays an important role in clarifying text. It is space that separates letters from each other. It is space that separates words from each other. It is space (with punctuation) that separates phrases, clauses, and paragraphs from each other; and it is space (with headings and subheadings) that separates subsections and chapters from one another.

There is some evidence from eye movement research that shows that these spatial cues are important aids to understanding text. It is argued, for instance, that with increasing maturity and experience, readers come to rely more heavily on such spatial cues to enhance their reading and search efficiency (Fisher, 1976). It has been found that the beginning of a line—and not its end—has a marked effect on eye movement fixations, and that text which starts in an irregular manner, such as poetry, produces more regressive fixations (look-backs) than does regularly spaced text (Carpenter & Just, 1977).

In this chapter, I maintain that consistent spacing helps readers to:

1. See redundancies in the text and thus to read faster
2. See more easily which bits of the text are personally relevant for them
3. See the structure of the document as a whole
4. Grasp its organization

27.1.10.1 Vertical Spacing. The spacing of a page can be considered from both a vertical and a horizontal point of view. Let us consider vertical spacing first. The argument here is that the underlying structure of complex text can be made more apparent to the reader by the consistent and planned use of vertical spacing. In practice, this means that predetermined increments of line space can be used consistently to separate out such components of the text as sentences, paragraphs, and sub- and major headings.

One simple way of using line space in this way is to use it in a proportional system. One can, for example, separate paragraphs by one line space; separate subheadings from paragraphs by two extra lines above and one below; and one can separate main headings from text by four extra lines above and two below. With more complex text, one can even start each sentence on a new line within each paragraph.

What is the effect of such an approach? Figure 27-5a shows a traditionally spaced piece of text, and Figure 27-5b shows a revised version using the system described above. Such a proportional system is an effective way of determining that the amount of space between the component parts of a piece of text is consistent throughout the work. Other systems (not proportional, but equally consistent) can be used. Indeed, for even more complex text, one might wish to introduce indentation into the text to convey further substructure.

Research has shown that readers usually prefer lengthy paragraphs to be set in a more open manner (e.g., see Hartley, Trueman & Burnhill, 1980). Readers thus generally prefer text set in the style of Figure 27-5b to that of Figure 27-5a.

Finally, in this section on spacing the text, we should note that if the vertical spacing between the components of the text is to be consistent throughout the text, then this leads to the idea that the text will have what is called a *floating baseline*. This means that, in contrast to the method used in this handbook, the text does not stop at the same place on every page, irrespective of its content. With a floating baseline, the stopping point on each page is determined by the content and the structure of the text rather than by the need to fill the page.

General

This section describes the care, maintenance, and inspection of insulating rubber blankets. This section is reissued to delete reference to the KS-13602 cleaner; this has been superseded by the B cleaning fluid (AT-8236).

Description

An insulating rubber blanket is made of flat, flexible sheets of black rubber. These sheets do not contain either beaded edges or eyelets. The blankets are approximately 36 inches square, $1/10$ inch thick, and weigh approximately 7 pounds. The electrical, weather, and chemical resistance properties of the blanket are very good.

Rubber-stamped on each blanket is a "return for test" date. Blankets must be returned for testing by that date to the Western Electric Company or other authorized agent. The blankets should be returned in rolls ($3^1/_2$ inches in diameter) and wrapped properly so as to avoid damage. A replacement blanket will be made available when a blanket is returned for testing.

Figure 27-5a. A traditionally spaced piece of text.

General

This section describes the care, maintenance, and inspection of insulating rubber blankets.
This section is reissued to delete reference to the KS-13602 cleaner; this has been superseded by the B cleaning fluid (AT-8236).

Description

An insulating rubber blanket is made of flat, flexible sheets of black rubber.
These sheets do not contain either beaded edges or eyelets.
The blankets are approximately 36 inches square, $1/_{10}$ inch thick, and weigh approximately 7 pounds.
The electrical, weather, and chemical resistance properties of the blanket are very good.

Rubber-stamped on each blanket is a "return for test" date.
Blankets must be returned for testing by that date to the Western Electric Company or other authorized agent.
The blankets should be returned in rolls ($3^{1}/_{2}$ inches in diameter) and wrapped properly so as to avoid damage.
A replacement blanket will be made available when a blanket is returned for testing.

Figure 27-5b. A revised version of Figure 27-5a with a proportionally based spacing system.

As a rule of thumb, we can say that each page of the text should have a specified number of lines, plus or minus two. This flexibility allows the designer to accommodate "widows" and "orphans"—where a page starts with the last line of a previous paragraph or ends with a heading or the first line of a new paragraph—without changing the underlying spacing of the text. In traditional settings, as in this chapter, the internal spacing is sometimes stretched or squeezed to force the text to finish at the same point on each page. Normally this has little effect in pages of continuous prose, but Hartley (1991) provided an illustration of where such a policy could mislead the reader.

27.1.10.2. Horizontal Spacing. One can consider the horizontal spacing of text in much the same way as we have considered the vertical spacing. That is to say we can also look to see how we can use the horizontal spacing to separate and to group components of the text, and how we can vary the stopping point of horizontal text in accord with its content, rather than using arbitrary rules about line lengths.

In this handbook, all the lines of text are set "justified." This means that all of the lines within the columns are of equal width, and that the columns have straight left- and right-hand edges. These straight edges are achieved by varying the spacing between the words on each line and, occasionally, by hyphenating or breaking words at the ends

of the lines. Indeed, in text that has very narrow columns (e.g., in newspapers or advertising copy), the spaces between the letters forming the words are also often varied in order to force the text to fit a given length of line.

A different approach to setting the text is to provide a consistent space between each word. Such a procedure produces "unjustified" text, i.e., the same amount of space between each word, and usually no word breaks (or hyphenation) at the ends of lines. Consequently, the text has a ragged right-hand edge.

There has been much debate over the relative merits of justified and unjustified text. Muncer et al. (1986) and Misanchuk (1992) provide representative reviews, and Kinross (1994) provides an interesting historical footnote. It would appear that it does not matter much which setting is used as far as understanding conventional text is concerned: The decision concerning which format to use is largely a matter of choice. There is some evidence, however, that unjustified text might be more helpful for less-able readers, be they younger children or older adults (see Hartley, 1994b).

Nonetheless, it is doubtful whether the studies reviewed by Muncer et al. and by Misanchuk fully considered all of the possible advantages of unjustified text. One clear advantage is that one does not have to fill up each line with text; one can consider (as with vertical spacing) where best to end each line. With unjustified text, for instance, it is possible to specify that no line should end with the first word of a new sentence, or that if the last word on a line is preceded by a punctuation mark, then this last word should be carried over to the next line. And, of course, it is possible to consider the starting points of each line too. Figure 27-6a shows a piece of justified text; Figure 27-6b shows what happens to this text when space is used to show the underlying structure of the text. Research has shown that readers often recall more from text set in the manner shown in Figure 27-6b than they do from text set in the manner of Figure 27-6a (see Jandreau & Bever, 1992, for a review of this literature). And, curiously enough, when asked to write out their recalls of short texts set in these different formats, most readers write them out in the formats they are presented with (Hartley, 1993b).

27.1.10.3. Combining Vertical and Horizontal Spacing. So far I have discussed vertical and horizontal spacing as though they are separate issues—which, of course, they are not. For all texts, interrelated decisions need to be taken

---

Now the sons of Jacob were twelve. The sons of Leah; Reuben, Jacob's firstborn, and Simeon, and Levi, and Judah, and Issachar, and Zebulun. The sons of Rachel; Joseph, and Benjamin: And the sons of Bilhah, Rachel's handmaid; Dan, and Naphtali. And the sons of Zilpah, Leah's handmaid; Gad, and Asher. These are the sons of Jacob, which were born to him in Padan-aram.

Figure 27-6a. A piece of text with a traditional *justified* setting.

Now the sons of Jacob were twelve.
The sons of Leah;
    Reuben, Jacob's firstborn,
    and Simeon, and Levi, and Judah,
    and Issachar, and Zebulun.
The sons of Rachel;
    Joseph, and Benjamin:
And the sons of Bilhah, Rachel's handmaid;
    Dan, and Naphtali.
And the sons of Zilpah, Leah's handmaid;
    Gad, and Asher.
These are the sons of Jacob, which were born
to him in Padan-aram.

Figure 27-6b. The same text with an *unjustified* setting. Note here that in this case both the settings of the beginnings and the endings of the lines are determined by syntactic considerations. Normally, of course, it is only the endings of the lines that are unjustified.

which depend on the nature of the text. If the text consists of nothing but continuous prose, then (on a smallish page) a single-column structure with normal paragraph indentation may be perfectly acceptable. If, however, the text consists of numerous small elements, many of which start on new lines, then using traditional indentation to denote new paragraphs can be misleading. It is for reasons such as these that I generally advocate the use of line spacing rather than indentation to denote the start of new paragraphs in instructional text (Hartley, Burnhill & Davies, 1972).

If the text contains a mixture of text, diagrams, instructions, and other typical material, then one has to think much harder about the appropriate way of presenting it. The key point here, of course, is that instructional text should not be designed on a "let's put this here" basis for every page. Decisions concerning the vertical and the horizontal spacing of the full text have to be made in advance of keyboarding it, and these decisions have to be adhered to throughout. Many designers advocate using what is called a "typographical reference grid" in this respect (e.g. see Crouwel,1979; Hartley, 1994a; Miles, 1987; Swann, 1989.) Using such a procedure—in which spacing decisions are mapped out in terms of grid modules—leads to a regular and consistent layout that will not confuse the reader.

27.2 TEXT LAYOUT: STRUCTURE AND ACCESS

So far I have discussed matters of typography that I believe help readers to find their way around a text and to grasp its underlying structure. I now turn to discuss those devices that are specifically used by writers and designers to further help readers in this respect. I have called this section "structure and access" because these devices—perhaps unwit-

tingly—both clarify the structure of the text and also help the readers gain access to it. Readers do not simply read instructional text from the beginning to the end: they skim, search, reread, etc. Devices that help them do this include titles, contents pages, summaries, outlines, headings, and subheadings, and numbering systems. In addition, authors use such linguistic devices as "signals" to help readers follow the organization of their arguments (Waller, 1979).

27.2.1 Titles

Titles aim to describe the content of a text in the fewest words possible; but these are often supplemented with a subtitle. Such succinct descriptions help to focus attention and expectations, and studies have shown that titles affect the readers' perception and interpretation of ambiguous text (e.g., Bransford, 1979). However, it is to be hoped that instructional text will not be ambiguous! So one would hardly expect titles to have much effect on the comprehension of instructional text, although they may aid later recall of what the text was about. Unfortunately, I know of no research on typographic variables connected with the setting of titles (e.g., type sizes, typefaces, weights, etc.) and none on the more interesting problems of using different title formats (e.g., statements, questions, quotations).

27.2.2 Summaries

Summaries in text can have different positions and roles. Beginning summaries tell the readers what the text is about; they help the readers decide whether or not they want to read it, and they help the readers who do read it to organize their subsequent reading. Interim summaries summarize the argument so far, and indicate what is to come. End summaries list or review the main points made, and thus aid the recall of important points in the text. End summaries can use the more technical vocabulary introduced in the text; beginning summaries might not. Research on the effectiveness of author-provided summaries has been reported by Hartley and Trueman (1982), Reder and Anderson, (1980), and Sherrard (1988). Research on the effectiveness of reader-generated summaries has been reported by, among others, Annis (1985) and Kirby and Pedwell (1991).

Summaries can be typeset in many different ways: in medium, bold, or italic, in large or small type, boxed in, etc. There is no research to my knowledge on the effect of such typographic variables in this context, although there is some indication that readers dislike journal abstracts set in a smaller type size than the main body of the text (Hartley, 1994c).

27.2.3 Outlines

Outlines can have much the same function as a summary, although it is likely that outlines depict the structure of the text more clearly. Often outlines are provided in a graphic form, sometimes in the form of a tree diagram or flowchart (Guri-Rozenblit, 1989). Such displays facilitate understanding and recall in at least two ways. Firstly, readers can see the organizing structure of the text all at once. Secondly, readers can follow different routes within this structure—comparing and contrasting different parts—in the order of their choice: The argument is no longer linear, and it is not obscured by lengthy paragraphs of text. Research reviewing the effectiveness of outlines has been reported on and summarized by Glover and Krug (1988); Glynn, Britton, and Muth (1985); Hall, Dansereau, and Skaggs (1992); and Lambiotte and Dansereau (1992).

27.2.4 The Role of Boxes

Authors frequently seek to extend the reader's comprehension of the main ideas in instructional text by including supporting material, such as examples, anecdotes, and bibliographies. Often one way of handling such material is to treat the information as a figure, to box it off from the main body of the text, and to use a different typeface and/or typographic setting. Presumably the idea here is that, by being separated from the main text, the information in the box is seen as separate and adjunct, and that it is less likely to interfere with either the author's presentation or the reader's comprehension of the main ideas.

Some authors have provided interesting comments on the problems of dealing with this ancillary material (e.g., Armbruster & Anderson, 1985; Schumacher, 1985), but I know of no research inquiry into the effectiveness of such procedures. However, if one examines what writers and reviewers of instructional text have to say on the matter, one can discern some unease among them. Consider, for example, this extract from James Thomas's (1984) review of four introductory psychology textbooks:

> On the negative side the text includes many boxed inserts presenting "Critical Issues" and "Applications." I object to this common approach for two reasons. First, these inserts disrupt the logical flow of the running text. If the application or issue is important enough for it to be boxed, why not include it in the running text and avoid breaking the reader's train of thought? Second, the boxed inserts exaggerate the importance of single, nonreplicated research findings. In many cases, these boxes report unusual, unexpected, or sensational research or applications that have not been adequately evaluated. Their appearance in an introductory textbook, especially in a highlighted position, seems to legitimize these findings and applications, whereas they should still be regarded as tentative. These concerns apply to three of the texts under review."

27.2.5 Headings

Headings may be written in the form of questions, statements, or (like here) with one- or two-word labels. Headings may be placed in the margin or in the body of the text.

In a series of experiments with 12- to 14-year-old school children, Mark Trueman and I investigated the role of different kinds of heading (questions versus statements) and their position (marginal versus embedded). We concluded that headings significantly aided search, recall, and retrieval, but that the position and the kinds of heading that we used had no significant effects with the texts that we employed (Hartley & Trueman, 1985). More studies still need to be carried out on factors such as the:

- Nature of the text (technical versus semiliterary)
- Frequency of headings
- Typographic denotation of headings of different levels (primary, secondary, tertiary)

Additional research indicating the effectiveness of headings has been provided by Spyridakis and Standal (1987), Townsend et al. (1990), and Wilhite (1989)

27.2.6 Questions

Questions may be interspersed in the text itself, or presented in a list at the end of a chapter to provide material for exercises. There is some indication that readers ignore questions given at the ends of chapters, so it might be more appropriate to consider how best they can be embedded in the text. It appears that factual questions, placed in a passage before paragraphs of relevant material, often lead to specific learning, whereas similar questions placed in the passage after the relevant content will sometimes lead to more general learning as well (see Allington & Weber, 1993; Hamaker, 1986; Hamilton, 1985). The level of difficulty of these questions, too, may be important (Allington & Weber, 1993; Armbruster & Ostertag, 1993; see also 30.6, 31.2.13).

Some of our earlier research suggested that headings in the form of questions were particularly suitable for less-able readers, but our more recent (better-designed) studies failed to confirm this (see Hartley & Trueman, 1985). None the less, it might be important to consider headings in this form for certain texts.

27.2.7 Sequencing

There has been little research on the sequencing of sentences or paragraphs within instructional text, apart from work with programmed instruction (see Chapter 20). Some of this work suggested that violations in natural sequences provided little difficulty for most readers. However, just what is a "natural sequence"? Posner and Strike (1978) contrast 17 different ways to show that sequencing is not a simple matter, and Van Patten et al. (1986) develop these issues further.

There are some situations, however, where we might all agree that the sequence used is unhelpful. Take, for example, this odd sequence of instructions I once found for using an electric razor:

1. To gain access to the heads for cleaning, press the button on the side of the appliance (see Fig. 4).
2. To remove the razor from its packaging. . . .

Readers find it easier to follow a sequence in which the events match the temporal order in which they occur. Compare "Before the machine is switched on, the lid must be closed and the powder placed within its compartment" with "The powder must be placed in its compartment and the lid closed before the machine is switched on."

27.2.8 Sequencing Lists

It is fairly common in instructional writing to find sentences containing embedded lists of items such as this:

Five devices that aid the reader are (i) skeleton outlines for each chapter, (ii) headings in the text, (iii) an end summary, (iv) a glossary for new technical terms, and (v) a comprehensive subject and author index.

However, research suggests that readers prefer text that has such lists or numbered sequences spaced out and separated, rather than run on in continuous prose. The above example would be better thus:

Five devices that aid the reader are:

- Skeleton outlines for each chapter
- Headings in the text
- An end summary
- A glossary for new technical terms
- A comprehensive subject and author index

27.2.9 Numbers in Text

Numbers are often used to signal the structure of a piece of text. Lorch and Chen (1986) showed that when making a series of points within paragraphs it was helpful to list and enumerate them. Commentators suggest that it is best to use Arabic numbers when there is an order or sequence in the points being made: "Bullets," as used above, are perhaps more appropriate when each point is of equal value.

The structure and organization of a piece of text can often be made clearer for the reader by the use of numbered paragraphs. Such numbering systems can be used to organize information in many different ways, e.g., the heading numbers in this book. There has been little research on the effectiveness of such systems. Many people undoubtedly feel that they are valuable, particularly for reference purposes. But such systems can be abused if they are overdone, and they can lead to extraordinary confusion (see Smith & Aucella, 1983; Waller, 1980).

27.2.10 Verbal Quantifiers

When numerical data are presented in text, prose descriptions often seem more comfortable to readers than do actual numbers. Everyday words that act as rough quantifiers, e.g., "nearly half the group," seem adequate for most purposes and are handled with reasonable consistency by most people (Moxey & Sanford, 1993). Young children, of course, may have greater difficulties with some of these terms (Badzinski, Cantor & Hoffner, 1989).

Research by Hartley, Trueman, and Rodgers (1984) suggested that the following phrases can be used with confidence with adults:

Numerical Value	Suitable Phrases to Be Conveyed
above 85%	almost all of . . .
60–75%	rather more than half of . . .
40–50%	nearly half of . . .
15–35%	a part of . . .
under 10%	a very small part of . . .

None the less, it may be better (or at least clearer for the reader) if more exact verbal equivalents of numbers are given. For example:

Numerical Value	Suitable Phrases to Be Conveyed
100%	all of . . .
75%	three-quarters of . . .
50%	half of . . .
25%	a quarter of . . .
0%	none of . . .

Verbal descriptions of probabilities are also more comfortable for most people than are actual probability statements. People are less consistent, however, in their interpretations of verbal descriptions of probability than they are in their interpretations of verbal descriptions of quantity (Moxey & Sanford, 1993). If precision is required, actual quantities can be given with a verbal quantifier. For example, one can say "nearly half the group—43%—said . . ." or "There was a distinct chance ($p < 0.06$) that. . . ."

27.2.11 Signaling

A rather different way of making text organization more explicit is to use verbal "signals." Signals have been defined by Meyer, Young, and Bartlett (1989) as "noncontent words that serve to emphasize the conceptual structure or organization of the passage." Words and phrases such as *however*, *but*, or *on the other hand* signal to the reader that some form of comparison is to be made. Similarly, words and phrases such as *firstly*, *secondly*, "three reasons for this are . . ., a better example, however, would be. . ." signal the structure of the argument (and comparisons with subsections). Likewise, words and phrases such as *therefore*, *as a result*, *so that*, *in order to*, *because* signal causal relationships. Studies have shown that such signals help readers grasp the underlying structure of the author's argument (e.g., see Rice, Meyer & Miller, 1989). However, there may be some confusion in the future over the use of the term *signal*. I now find it being used to cover devices such as headings, overviews, and summaries (Lorch, Lorch & Inman, 1993).

27.2.12 Conclusions

This section on structure and access has shown that there is a good deal of research available on the variety of methods used to help readers grasp the structure of a text and to gain access to it. However, most of this research is uncoordinated and atheoretical. Most researchers focus on one device or another, and few consider the effects of several such devices in combination. Few, too, carry out lengthy programs of research that aim to investigate systematically the myriad factors affecting the effectiveness of particular devices. (Some exceptions to this criticism are Dwyer's work on illustrations, Dansereau's work on outlines, Meyer's work on signals, and possibly my own on headings.) Such theories as there are are thus buried below a welter of specific instances rather than being subjected to any rigorous analysis that might, in the long term, lead to deeper understanding.

27.3 TEXT DIFFICULTY

A separate area of research relevant to text design concerns itself with assessing how difficult a text might be for its intended readers and, indeed, whether or not difficulty per se is a bad thing. The title of a book by Chall and Conard (1991) puts the question succinctly: *Should Textbooks Challenge Students? The Case for Easier or Harder Books*. The area of text difficulty has been examined from numerous points of view (e.g., see Davison & Green, 1987; Schriver, 1989). Here I want simply to report on some of the issues and findings.

Again, if we start with an historical perspective, it is probably true to say that the instructional materials of today are not only more spaciously arrayed but also contain shorter paragraphs, shorter sentences, and shorter words than did texts published some 50 years ago. What can research tell us about these features of text difficulty?

27.3.1 Paragraph Lengths

Few researchers have commented on the effects of long chapters and long paragraphs on readability. It would seem, other things being equal, that short chapters, and short paragraphs within them, will make a text easier to read. In addition, the ways in which new paragraphs are denoted may be important. One problem is knowing how best to format paragraphs without unduly breaking the readers' flow. In an early study, Hartley, Burnhill, and Davies (1978) suggested that different methods of paragraph denotation can affect

the speed and accuracy of location and access, as well as the recall of information.

27.3.2 Sentence Length

It is generally considered that long sentences—such as this present one—are difficult to understand because they often contain a number of subordinate clauses that, because of their parenthetical nature, make it difficult for readers to bear all of their points in mind and, in addition, because there are often so many of them, make it harder for readers to remember the first part of the sentence when they are reading the last part. Long sentences overload the memory system; short sentences do not.

I once wrote:

> As a rule of thumb, sentences less than 20 words long are probably fine. Sentences 20 to 30 words long are probably satisfactory. Sentences 30 to 40 words long are suspect, and sentences containing over 40 words will almost certainly benefit from rewriting.

Perceptive readers will notice that many of my sentences in this chapter contain more than 30 words—but at least they have been scrutinized! Furthermore, the sentence above ignores the advice given by many other commentators (e.g., see Berger, 1993) that sentences (and paragraphs) should vary in length if they are to entertain the reader.

27.3.3 Word Length

Long words, like long sentences, also cause difficulty. It is easier to understand short, familiar words than technical terms that mean the same thing. If, for example, you wanted to sell thixotropic paint, you would probably do better to call it nondrip! One author on style quoted a letter writer in *The Times* who asked a government department how to obtain a book. He was "authorized to acquire the work in question by purchasing it through the ordinary trade channels"—in other words "to buy it." Concrete words and phrases are shorter and clearer than abstract ones.

27.3.4 Difficult Short Sentences

It does not necessarily follow, of course, that passages written in short sentences and short words will always be better understood. Alphonse Chapanis (1965, 1988) provides many examples of short pieces of text that are difficult to understand. The one I like best is the notice that reads:

> PLEASE
> WALK UP ONE FLOOR
> WALK DOWN TWO FLOORS
> FOR IMPROVED ELEVATOR SERVICE

People interpret the notice as meaning "to get on the elevator I must either walk up one floor, or go down two floors," or even "to get on the elevator I must first walk up one floor and then down two floors." When they have done this, they find the same notice confronting them! What this notice means, in effect, is "Please, don't use the elevator if you are only going a short distance." Chapanis's articles are well worth studying. They are abundantly illustrated with short sentences that are hard to understand and (in some cases) potentially lethal.

27.3.5 Ambiguities

Many short (and indeed many long) sentences can turn out to be ambiguous. Consider "Then roll up the three additional blankets and place them inside the first blanket in the canister." Does this sentence mean that each blanket should be rolled inside the other, or that three rolled blankets should be placed side by side and a fourth one wrapped around them? (An illustration would clarify this ambiguity.)

Ambiguities, or at least difficulties, often result from the use of abbreviations or acronyms (strings of capital letters that form words, e.g., PLATO). I once counted over 20 such acronyms in a two-page text distributed by my university computer center. Chapanis (1988) provides additional examples, also from the field of computing. The meanings of acronyms may be familiar to the writer, but they need to be explained to the reader. Furthermore, readers easily forget what an author's abbreviations stand for when they are not familiar with the material.

27.3.6 Clarifying Text

Generally speaking, text is usually easier to understand when:

1. Writers produce few sentences containing more than two subordinate clauses. The more subordinate clauses or modifying statements there are, the more difficult it is to understand a sentence. Consider, for example, the problems posed for an anxious student by this examination rubric: "Alternative C: Answer four questions including at least one from at least two sections (1-5)."
2. Writers use the active rather than the passive voice. Compare the active form, "We found that the engineers had a significantly higher interocular transfer index than did the chemists" with the passive form, "For the engineers, as compared with the chemists, a significantly higher interocular transfer index was found."
3. Writers use positive terms (e.g., "more than," "heavier than," "thicker than") rather than negative ones (e.g., "less than," "lighter than," "thinner than"). Compare "The rain is heavier today" with "The rain was lighter yesterday."
4. Writers avoid negatives, especially double or triple ones. Negatives can often be confusing. I once saw, for example, a label fixed to a machine in a school workshop which read, "This machine is dangerous: It is not to be used only by the teacher." Harold Evans (1972) provides another example. Compare "The figures provide no indication that costs would have not been

lower if competition had not been restricted" with "The figures provide no indication that competition would have produced higher costs." Negative qualifications can be used, however, for particular emphasis and for correcting misconceptions. Negatives can make imperatives (e.g., "Do not . . . unless . . .") easier to understand.

5. Writers personalize texts. In one study that Cathryn Brown and I conducted we compared two medical audiotapes. The first tape began:

Welcome to the Health Department's Medical Directory. This tape is about multiple sclerosis: what causes it, and what you can do about it.

The second tape began:

Welcome to the Health Department's Medical Directory. My name is Nick and I want to tell you about multiple sclerosis. I am able to do this because I am suffering from the disease. In this tape I will tell you about what causes multiple sclerosis and what you can do about it.

Both tapes contained the same information, but while the first tape was formal, the second tape conveyed the information in a more personal way. Students listening to this tape recalled more information from it than they did from the first one. Similar results have been reported by Rook (1987). Personalizing instruction, of course, can take many forms. It is possible to insert the appropriate names of people and places in computer-generated texts, and problems can be tailored to students' backgrounds. For example, the same mathematical problems can be presented in different contexts for nursing, teaching, and psychology students (e.g., see Davis-Dorsey, Ross & Morrison, 1991). Again, age and ability differences are important considerations in this field. Bracken (1982), for example, found that personalizing stories helped less-able fourth-graders but had no effect with those of average ability.

6. Writers make text more interesting. Lively examples and anecdotes cannot fail to make the text more memorable—or can they? Research has indicated that vivid anecdotes and the like can indeed make text more interesting, but this is often at a cost. Apparently many readers tend to recall these "seductive details" at the expense of the main information in the passage (Renninger, Hidi & Krapp, 1992).

27.3.7 Measuring Text Difficulty

There are many readability formulas available that attempt to predict the age at which the reader, on average, will have the necessary reading skills and abilities to understand a piece of text. Most readability formulas are not in fact as accurate at predicting this as one might wish, but the figures that they provide do give a rough guide. Typical readability formulas combine two main measures (with a constant) to predict reading age. These are: (1) the average number of words per sentence, and (2) the average length of the words in these sentences (usually measured in syllables). Thus, the longer the sentences and the more complex the vocabulary, the more difficult the text is rated.

Many readability formulas can be calculated by hand. One of the simplest, the Gunning Fog Index, is as follows:

- Take a sample of 100 words.
- Calculate the average number of words per sentence in the sample.
- Count the number of words with three or more syllables in the sample.
- Add the average number of words per sentence to the total number of words with three or more syllables.
- Multiply the result by 0.4.

The result is the (American) reading grade level.

A better-known formula, but one that is harder to calculate by hand, is the Flesch Reading Ease (RE) formula. This is:

$RE = 206.835 - 0.846w - 1.015s$, where w = number of syllables per 100 words; s = average number of words per sentence.

In this case, the higher the RE score, the easier the text.

The relationship between RE, difficulty, and suggested reading ages is as follows:

RE Value	Description of Style	Required Reading Skill
90–100	Very easy	5th grade
80– 90	Easy	6th grade
70– 80	Fairly easy	7th grade
60– 70	Standard	8th–9th grade
50– 60	Fairly difficult	10th–12th grade
30– 50	Difficult	13th–16th grade
0– 30	Very difficult	College graduate

Today, with word-processing systems, it is much easier to apply the more complex readability formulas. For example, the readability program on my word processor can be applied to text to provide three sets of readability data derived from three different formulas. When this program was run on some 50 sentences of this chapter, the outcomes were as follows:

	Formula	Reading Age
1	Flesch	15–16 years
2	Kincaid	15 years
3	Gunning	18 years

It can be seen that the predictions from the four formulas vary slightly and only give a rough estimate of reading difficulty. Such readability formulas have other obvious limitations. Some short sentences are difficult to understand (e.g., "God is grace"). Some technical abbreviations are short (e.g., DNA) but difficult for people unfamiliar with them. Some long words, because of their frequent use, are quite familiar (e.g. *communication*). The order of the words, sentences, and paragraphs is not taken into account, nor are the effects of other aids to understanding such as illustrations, headings,

numbering systems, and typographical layout. Also, most importantly, the readers' motivation and prior knowledge of the topic are not assessed. All of these factors affect text difficulty. (See Davison & Green, 1987, for a fuller discussion.)

Nonetheless, despite these problems, readability formulas can be useful tools for having a quick look at the likely difficulty of text that is being produced, and also—provided you use the same measure—for comparing the relative difficulty of two or more pieces of text. Comparison studies of original and revised texts have shown advantages for more-readable text in:

- Examination questions
- Scientific papers
- School textbooks
- Correspondence materials
- Job aids
- Medical instructions
- Insurance policies
- Legal documents
- Fairy tales! (Britton et al., 1993)

The difficulty with readability measures arises when people attempt to use them to change the way text is written. Text that has short, choppy sentences can be difficult to read (Armbruster & Anderson, 1985). Critics of readability formula have had fun producing "more readable" versions of such famous texts as the Declaration of Independence or the Lord's Prayer to highlight the limitations of readability formulas in these respects. Davison and Green (1987) provide one of the best critiques of readability formulas currently available. Studies by Beck and her colleagues are also interesting to note in this connection (e.g., Beck, McKeown & Worthy, 1995; Loxterman, Beck & McKeown, 1994). Here the more-readable texts in these studies score as less readable on readability formulas.

27.3.8 Revising Written Text

There are numerous guidelines on how to write clear text and also on how to revise one's own text, or text written by someone else (e.g., see Bellquist, 1993; Kahn, 1991). In my own work with 11- to 13-year-old school children, I have used the guidelines given in Figure 27-7. These guidelines are based on theoretical work conducted by psychologists and others on the nature of the writing process.

27.3.8.1. Computer-Aided Revision. Several computer programs have now been developed to help writers revise both technical and conventional text (e.g., see Hartley, 1992). Many of these programs were originally designed to be run when the text had been written, to analyze it and to make suggestions for improvement. Today, however, we may expect writers to use such programs concurrently with their writing. Such programs point to potential difficulties and offer on-screen advice. Figure 27-8 provides an illustration of the advice given to an author who had a "dangling modifier" in her text.

One typical suite of such programs at the time of writing is Grammatik 5. The number of facilities available is currently

1. Read the text through.
2. Read the text through again but this time ask yourself:
   - What is the writer trying to do?
   - Who is the text for?
3. Read the text through again, but this time ask yourself:
   - What changes do I need to make to help the writer?
   - How can I make the text clearer?
   - What changes do I need to make to help the reader?
   - How can I make the text easier to follow?
4. To make these changes you may need to make:
   - Big or global changes (e.g., rewrite sections yourself).
   - Small or minor text changes (e.g., change slightly the original text). You will need to decide whether you are going to focus first on global changes or first on text changes.
5. Global changes you might like to consider in turn are:
   - Resequencing parts of the text
   - Rewriting sections in your own words
   - Adding in examples
   - Changing the writer's examples for better ones
   - Deleting parts that seem confusing
6. Text changes you might like to consider in turn are:
   - Using simpler wording
   - Using shorter sentences
   - Using shorter paragraphs
   - Using active rather than passive tenses
   - Substituting positives for negatives
   - Writing sequences in order
   - Spacing numbered sequences or lists down the page (as here)
7. Keep reading your revised text through from start to finish to see if you want to make any more global changes.
8. Finally, repeat this whole procedure some time after making your initial revisions (say 24 hours), and do it without looking back at the original text.

Figure 27-7. Guidelines for revising text.

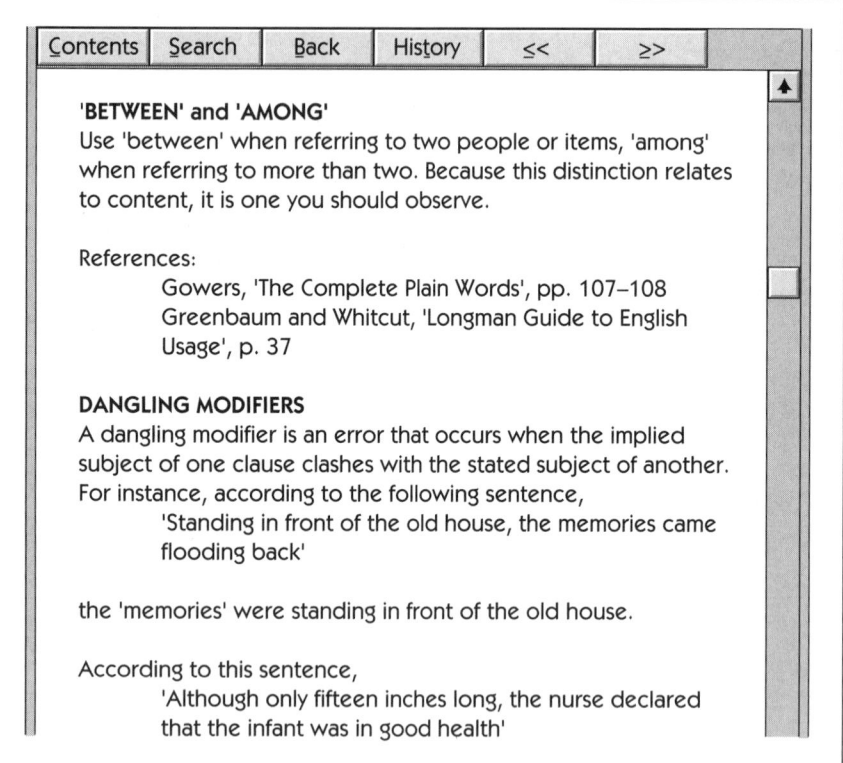

Figure 27-8. Grammatik's tutorial system.

being expanded, but Figure 27-9 lists some of them. One difficulty here is whether the novice writer can cope with all the information provided. Another appears to be that writers often need to understand sophisticated grammar in order to follow the advice offered by the authors of such programs!

Evaluation studies of different programs are now beginning to appear (e.g., see Kohut & Gorman, 1995).

In 1984, I published a report of how useful one such set of computer-aided writing programs (The Writer's Workbench) had been to me in revising a particular article.

I compared the suggestions made by nine colleagues with the suggestions made by the computer programs. The human and the computer aids to writing differed in two main ways. My colleagues were more variable than the computer programs: Different colleagues picked on different things to comment on. None made comments in all of the (14) categories of comments that I derived in the inquiry. The computer programs were more thorough and more consistent than my colleagues, but this was over a narrower range of (six) categories. The programs picked up every misspelling; they drew attention to every sentence that was over 30 words long; they indicated that I had missed out a bracket, but did not say where; and they provided me with 85 suggestions for better wording! Thus the computer programs were excellent at doing the donkey work of editing; my colleagues excelled at using their knowledge to point out inconsistencies, errors of fact, and to suggest better examples. The final version of the article thus benefitted from the combined use of both sources of information.

Programs that indicate grammatical errors:

- Adjective errors
- Adverb errors
- Article errors
- Clause errors
- Comparative/super-lative use
- Double negatives
- Incomplete sentences
- Noun phrase errors

- Object of verb errors
- Possessive misuse
- Preposition errors
- Pronoun errors
- Sequence of tense errors
- Subject-verb errors
- Tense changes
- etc.

Programs that indicate mechanical errors:

- Spelling errors
- Capitalization errors
- Double word
- Ellipsis misuse
- End-of-sentence punctuation errors
- Incorrect punctuation

- Number style errors
- Question mark errors
- Quotation mark misuse
- Similar words
- Split words
- etc.

Programs that indicate stylistic errors:

- Long sentences
- Wordy sentences
- Passive tenses
- End-of-sentence prepositions
- Split infinitives
- Cliched words/phrases
- Colloquial language
- Americanisms

- Archaic language
- Gender-specific words
- Jargon
- Abbreviation errors
- Paragraph problems
- Questionable word usage
- etc.

Figure 27-9. A sample of computer programs available in Grammatik 5 from Apple Macintosh.

In 1993, I replicated this study with a journalist colleague (Dorner & Hartley, 1993). The conclusions that we reached were much the same, despite the advances made in computer-aided writing programs.

27.4 TEXT DESIGN FOR READERS WITH SPECIAL NEEDS

In this section, I turn to consider issues of text design for two sets of readers with special needs: the elderly and the visually impaired. These two sets of people can, of course, overlap.

27.4.1 Instructional Text and Older Readers

The proportion of older people in society has gradually been increasing throughout the 20th century. Life expectancy at birth in the U.K. has increased by 50% in this century, and 4 in every 10 British adults are now over 50. In the United States, currently 12% of the population is 65 years of age or older, and the number of Americans over the age of 65 years is expected to double to 65 million by 2030. Thus people are living longer, and the number of elderly people in the community is getting larger. Consequently, there are more older people reading traditional texts, and more texts being produced especially for them.

The research on the effects of aging can be described in terms of three overlapping areas: physiological, cognitive, and social. Physiological research looks at the biology of aging and its physiological correlates. Most people, for example, experience a sharp decline in eyesight. Cognitive research on aging focuses on changes in memory, learning, and judgment. Such effects have implications for work on text design. Social research on aging examines how, for example, societies expect their older members to function. Studies of "ageism," for example, focus on how commonly held attitudes and beliefs about what old people should and should not do determine to a considerable extent what, in fact, they do do.

It is difficult to summarize in a few lines the main findings of studies of aging and their implications for text design. (Fuller expositions can be found in Birren & Schaie, 1990, or Craik & Salthouse, 1992.) Here, for the sake of argument, I would like to suggest two main points that I think it is helpful to bear in mind when thinking about these issues. These are:

- Working memory capacity (i.e., information held and used in ongoing tasks) declines as people get older.
- The more difficult the task and the older the person, the more disproportionately difficult the task becomes.

Studies of memory for text suggest that a number of possibilities can occur (Meyer et al., 1989). Evidence has been provided in different studies indicating that older people:

- Remember the main ideas but forget the details
- Remember the details but forget the main ideas
- Forget both the main ideas and the details

These different outcomes may result from different investigators focusing on different issues in their studies. The findings suggest that older people may not have much difficulty reading or working with text that is relatively simple (in terms of its typography) or familiar to them. However, text that is typographically complex and which deals with unfamiliar material (like how to operate a video recorder) may cause middle-aged and older people considerable problems.

Thus, one might not expect differences between older and younger readers when the verbal ability of the readers is high, when they have good prior knowledge, and when the texts are well presented. However, as Meyer et al. (1989) suggest, differences might well be expected to emerge with less-able readers, less-familiar materials, and poorly designed text.

27.4.1.1. Improving Typographically Simple Layouts.
Generally speaking, the literature reviewed above suggests that text will be easier for older people to use if their perceptual and memory-processing loads are reduced. I would want to argue that this can be achieved by, for example:

- Using larger type sizes
- Using more readable text
- Using clearer layouts
- Clarifying the structure of the text by, for example, using summaries, headings, and "signals"

Unfortunately, there are insufficient studies in this area to support or reject these hypotheses. In a separate review (Hartley, 1994b), I have summarized the results from some 16 studies that examined varied aspects of text design with older participants. These studies used what I called relatively simple typographic layouts: mainly continuous run-on prose. Table 27-1 shows how, except for the area of type size, there are insufficient studies for anyone to make any clear generalizations from their findings.

TABLE 27-1. THE NUMBER OF STUDIES WITH OLDER PEOPLE FOUND FOR EACH ASPECT OF TEXT DESIGN LISTED IN THE TEXT

Number of Studies	Text Design Feature
5	Type size
2	Unjustified text
2	Underlining
2	Improving readability
2	Advance organizers
1	Questions in text
1	Signals
1	Text structure and organization

However, all five studies on type size did suggest that larger type sizes were more suitable for older readers. It appears that—ignoring my earlier caveats about measuring type sizes—that 12- or 14-point type seems more appropriate for older readers.

The two studies with unjustified text suggested that there were advantages for unjustified text with *less-able*

older readers when the line lengths were short (seven to eight words).

The two studies on underlining and the two on advanced organizers had mixed results: one positive and one neutral in each case. The two studies on improving readability showed that this had no effect with age. However, there were age effects for the studies with questions, signals, and variations in text structure: Older readers did less well than younger ones, but high-ability readers were helped by the textual variable being considered.

My review highlighted three issues in this research:

1. There were ability effects rather than age effects in about half of these studies. The more-able participants did better than less-able ones, irrespective of age.
2. Less than half of the 16 studies used a control group of younger participants: Most were done with a single group of older persons. So it was not possible to see if the variable in question was additionally helpful (or not) for older readers.
3. Very few of the investigators reported working with text that was appropriately designed for visually impaired older readers (although one or two did check that their participants could read the texts). Thus, one might argue, many of the older readers in these studies were probably working under an additional handicap.

27.4.1.2. Typographically Complex Texts.
So far I have discussed research with older readers and texts that have had a relatively simple typographic structure. I now turn to consider more complex materials. These include, for example, bus and train schedules, labels on medicine bottles, food packaging, and government forms. Regrettably, there are very few studies in this context.

Six studies that I did find suggested, as noted earlier, that more complex text presents greater difficulties for older readers. These studies involved readers completing income tax forms (James, Lewis & Allinson, 1987), following diagrams (Lipman & Caplan, 1992), using an analogous model (Caplan & Schooler, 1990), reading prescription information (Morrell, Poon & Park, 1990), following instructions for completing assembly-type tasks (Morrell & Park, 1993), and using flowcharts to aid decision making (Michael, 1988).

In these studies, the younger participants always did better than the older ones, and the devices used to aid the readers here proved more helpful for the younger readers than for the older ones in the studies by Caplan and Schooler (1990), Lipman and Caplan (1992), Morrell and Park (1993), and Michael (1988). Indeed, I drew the tentative conclusion in my review that devices used to help readers in these situations actually *hindered* older readers.

Clearly, more work needs to be done in this area of instructional design. One useful suggestion that did emerge from these papers was that it might be wise to ensure that older people are included in initial evaluation studies of textual materials. It can be argued that designing a text for an older reader may not confuse a younger one. However, designing a text for a younger reader may confuse an older one.

27.4.2 Text Design for the Visually Impaired

During 1986/87, the U.K. Royal National Institute for the Blind (the RNIB) conducted a survey of the needs of blind and partially sighted adults in Britain, and a final report was published in 1991 (Bruce et al., 1991). A similar report on the needs of blind and partially sighted children was published in 1992 (Walker et al., 1992). And although these reports describe the situation in the U.K., we can anticipate that the problems are similar in other developed countries and worse in developing ones.

The 1991 U.K. report indicated that there were approaching 1 million (960,000) blind and partially sighted adults in Great Britain, many more than those actually registered (239,000). The prevalence rates (for those registered) were as follows:

3 per 1,000 among 16- to 59-year-olds
23 per 1,000 among 60- to 74-year-olds
152 per 1,000 among those over 75 years of age

Thus, one person in seven aged 75 or over was blind or partially sighted, and this prevalence rate was almost certainly higher among those over 80 and those over 85.

It is, of course, important to realize that the great majority of these people are not completely blind but are, in fact, partially sighted. The RNIB 1991 report estimated that only 20% of "blind" people are completely blind (and this number includes people who can perceive light but nothing more). Thus, 80% of the blind have varying degrees of visual impairment, and, as we shall see below, many can read large print.

Similar findings were presented in the 1992 report on blind and partially sighted children. It was estimated that there were at least 10,000 children in Great Britain with significant visual impairments, and possibly as many as 25,000. As many as 80% of the children in the sample were reported to have had their sight problem from birth.

For some children (and adults for that matter), spectacles, contact lenses, and other magnifying devices mean that they can in fact read and write using print rather than Braille. In this children's sample:

- Over 80% used tape recordings for learning and/or entertainment.
- 40% could read normal-sized print.
- 63% were using microcomputers in school.
- 36% were using microcomputers at home.
- 90% liked listening to the radio and listening to and watching television.

The RNIB reports point out that the needs of blind and partially sighted are complex. Many of them have additional disabilities, and many cannot use Braille or computers because of additional learning or physical difficulties.

27.4.2.1. Large Print. The RNIB considers that 10-point type (as used in this handbook) is too small for many readers, not just the blind and partially sighted. They recommend 12-point type for most documents and 14 point as the minimum type size for material intended for the blind and partially sighted. Other recommendations are given in

Figure 27-10. Similar guidelines have been produced in the United States by the American Association of Retired Persons (1986) and by the Civil Rights Division of the U.S. Department of Justice (1988). These guidelines share some common characteristics: They make good sense but occasionally imply too strongly that they are based on known research findings.

It is important to remember, as noted earlier, that with large print the width of the text expands, as well as the depth. This may make it difficult to perceive the syntactical groupings of words if the page size stays the same. So, simply enlarging a text may not always be a sensible solution to the problem: One might take the opportunity to reconsider its design (see Hartley, 1994a).

- Contrast. There needs to be good contrast between the type and the paper on which it is printed or photocopied. Contrast is affected by paper color, print color, type size, and weight. Black type on white or yellow paper gives a very good contrast. Pale-colored papers provide better contrast than dark ones. Black or very dark-colored print can be used if the paper is very pale. The print should not run across photographs or illustrations.
- Type sizes. 14 or 16 point is acceptable when printing for the partially sighted (see the text).
- Type weights. Avoid light typefaces, especially in small sizes. Medium and bold type weights are more appropriate in this context.
- Typefaces. Most typefaces in common use are suitable. Avoid bizarre or indistinct typefaces. Numbers need to be printed clearly: Blind and partially sighted people can easily misread 3, 5, and 8 in some faces, and even 0 and 6.
- Capital letters. Avoid long strings of text in capital letters; they are harder to read than lowercase.
- Line lengths. These, ideally, should be in the range of 50 to 65 characters. Blind and partially sighted people may prefer shorter lines than this. Avoid hyphenation at the ends of lines.
- Spacing. Keep to regular word spacing: Do not stretch or condense lines of type; that is, avoid justified type settings. Allow the line spacing to be equivalent to the type size plus the word spacing. Use a line space between paragraphs, and use space to show the underlying structure of the text. Additional lines or "rules" may help keep separate unrelated sections. Do not fit text around illustrations. (It is also worth noting that blind and partially sighted people often need more generous space on forms for handwritten responses, as their handwriting tends to be larger than average.)
- Paper. Print on glossy paper can be difficult to read. Very thin papers also cause problems, because text can show through from the reverse.

Figure 27-10. Recommendations to follow when designing text for the visually impaired. Guidelines adapted from RNIB (1993). *See It Right: Clear Print Guidelines.* Fact Sheet 2. Reproduced with permission of the RNIB.

There have been few actual studies of designing printed texts for the partially sighted. Those that have been carried out have mainly been concerned with the setting of children's reading books rather than with material for adults. Shaw (1969) provides a good review of the earlier literature and reports on a detailed study with adults. Shaw asked her participants to read aloud short passages that varied in typefaces (Gill & Plantin), type sizes (from 10 point to 24 point), weight (bold and medium), and various spatial settings (see Fig. 27-11).

Shaw reported that an increase in type size achieved a 16% improvement in reading performance, an increase in weight 9%, and a change from Plantin (a serif face) to Gill Sans (a sans-serif face) a 4% improvement. (This typeface change was particularly helpful for readers over 50 years of age.) These results must, of course, be considered with caution in view of the fact that the participants were asked to read the texts out loud and that the texts themselves, as shown in Figure 27-11, were very odd.

27.4.3 Presenting Text in Braille

The Braille system—in which each character is conveyed by one of six embossed dots in a 2×3 matrix—is well known to many and is illustrated in Figure 27-12. Braille text was originally produced on thick card, but today it is more likely to be produced by a thermoform system with heated, paper-thin, plastic sheets. This system also allows one to produce tactile maps and line drawings.

To the sighted reader, a page of Braille may look like a large and cumbersome equivalent of a piece of conventionally printed text. But this would be naive. Completely blind readers cannot see the top and the bottom of the page simultaneously; they have to work out which is which. They cannot see headings and subheadings at a glance. They cannot see at a glance how many paragraphs there are on the page, and thus how dense the text is. They cannot tell until they start whether the language of the text is going to be easy or difficult. To discover what is there, blind readers must start at the beginning and work through to the end without knowing (for the most part) when the end is coming.

In this chapter, I have described how instructional text can be improved by paying attention to the typographic layout, to the wording or language of the text, and to the use of headings, summaries, numbering systems, and other such devices. Much of the research I have described would seem applicable to the setting of Braille text. Despite the fact that many Braille texts seem to be devoid of clear spatial cues—perhaps because of the assumption that there is no need to include space because blind people cannot see it—it would

---

Face: GILL
Weight: ROMAN
Size: 12 POINT

Main floors escape special loads. Foreign glories arrange careful bills. Returning fathers concern large merchants. Valuable shadows know frequent corn. Lower money beats straight diseases. Last oils enjoy

Spacing: "normal"

Wild life claims perfect witnesses. Loud beauties move demanding chairs. Sad wages attract silent populations. Exact spaces please ideal dinners. Appointed plates see lost farms. Deep newspapers expect square

Spacing: extra space between letters and words

Next season allows set companions. Modern banks paint vain trade. Brave adventures marry extreme churches. Ancient machinery shoots future currents. Important stories take late posts. Black clubs seize twenty

Spacing: extra space between words only

Noble ways sing other bread. Long stores perform second teeth. Religious fashions compose wide factories. Excellent officials appear usual towns. Sorry coals walk five defences. Numerous flowers speak wrong

Spacing: extra space between lines only

Figure 27-11. An example of the materials used in Shaw's experiment. (Figure reproduced with permission of the U.K. Library Association.)

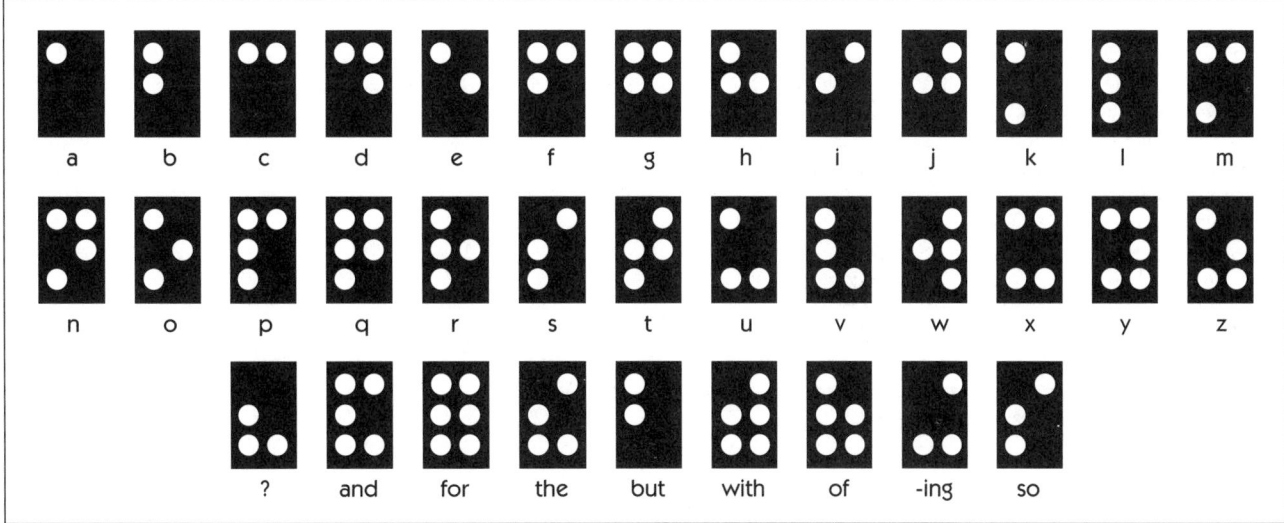

Figure 27-12. The Braille code.

seem to me that the structure of Braille texts could be clarified by the methods discussed above. My observations of skilled Braille readers indicate that they can indeed "look ahead" by quickly scanning (with both forefingers), and that they welcome devices such as headings (Hartley, 1989).

Blind readers require practical information (e.g., telling them how long an article is going to be) and contextual information (e.g., the use of overview summaries). If headings are numbered and phrased in the form of questions (e.g., who, what, when, where, why, how), then blind and visually impaired readers can read with such questions in mind, and they will know when they have reached the end of particular sections. Overview summaries and headings enable readers to "look ahead" more easily and thus to reduce their memory load while reading.

In addition, it might also be profitable to think of how one can convey information differently without the array of typographical devices available in printed text. In Figure 27-13, for instance, I contrast the traditional sequence used in presenting references in a scientific journal with what might be appropriate in a Braille version. In Version A—the traditional setting—the text is continuous, and different sections of the references are denoted by different typographic cues. In Braille versions of this material, it is conventional to follow this continuous sequence of the printed version. In Version B, however, I have shown how by resequencing the elements, and by placing the key elements on different lines, the text is easier to search, even though it has no typographic cues. Clearly making changes such as these may be costly in terms of the additional space required, but such changes may be more cost effective if readers find the resulting text easier to read.

At present, of course, we do not know whether respacing traditional Braille settings would be of value to blind readers: It may make little difference to those blind from birth. However, it is likely that those who become blind in later life and who wish to learn to read Braille do carry with

them a repertoire of expectations about text layout that is currently not realized in Braille.

27.5 HOW TEXTBOOKS ARE USED

In this penultimate section I want to turn from discussing textbook design, where design is taken to be the equivalent of typography and layout, to considering the situation where design is taken to be synonymous with manipulation. In short, I am interested in how one might use the knowledge we have gained from the studies described in the earlier sections in order to manipulate text so that learners can read and use text more effectively.

One aspect of this research that is of interest here is to find out what readers actually value in different text design features, both separately and in combination. For example, Thompson and Maniam (two of my undergraduates) asked a group of university students to indicate their preferences for four various designs for tabular layouts presented by Ehrenberg (1977) and illustrated in Hartley (1994a). Strong support was found for Ehrenberg's personal judgments. In another study, Kim Little (another undergraduate) asked 87 adolescents aged between 12 and 16 for their preferences for various features of the design of textbooks. Table 27-2 indicates the results. Access structures were clearly appreciated, but devices that required work (tables, graphs, questions, and suggestions for further reading) were clearly not so popular. (See also Weiten, Guadagno & Beck, 1996.) Such findings have implications for textbook writers, particularly those who want to encourage deeper text processing and/or improve the quality of textbooks (e.g., Jones, 1988).

There has been surprisingly little research on how students and teachers actually use textbooks, and on which features they appreciate. Newton (1984) describes some early British studies with university students and with teacher-trained college students reading science textbooks. In his 1984 report, he outlines the results he obtained from

Version A	Version B
Kanski, J. J. and Packard, R. B. S., **Cataract and Lens Implant Surgery**, Churchill Livingstone, 1985, 60pp, £26.00, ISBN 0 443 03205.	Cataract and Lens Implant Surgery, Kanski, J. J. and Packard, R. B. S. Churchill Livingstone, 1985, 60pp, £26.00, ISBN 0 443 03205.
Gilbert, P., **Mental Handicap: a practical guide for social workers**, Community Care, 1985, 130pp, pbk £3.95, ISBN 0617 00447 1.	Mental Handicap: a practical guide for social workers, Gilbert, P. Community Care, 1985, 130pp, pbk £3.95, ISBN 0617 00447 1.
Dechesne, B. H. H, Pons, C. and Schellen, A. M. C. M. (eds.), **Sexuality and Handicap: problems of motor handicapped people**, Woodhead-Faulkner, 1985, 234pp, pbk £19.95, ISBN 0 85941 231 8.	Sexuality and Handicap: problems of motor handicapped people, Dechesne, B. H. H, Pons, C. and Schellen, A. M. C. M. (eds.), Woodhead-Faulkner, 1985, 234pp, pbk £19.95, ISBN 0 85941 231 8.
Holloway, C. and Otto, S., **Getting Organised**, Bedford Square Press, 1985, 70pp, pbk £4.95, ISBN 0 7199 1162 1.	Getting Organised, Holloway, C. and Otto, S., Bedford Square Press, 1985, 70pp, pbk £4.95, ISBN 0 7199 1162 1.

Figure 27-13. Version A shows an excerpt from a list of references as typically presented in the *British Journal of Visual Impairment.* Version B shows the same text using space rather than typographic cueing to show the structure of the entries in the list. The argument is that Version B would be more helpful in a Braille setting than Version A.

examining how 12th-grade pupils used textbooks in physics, chemistry, and biology. Basically Newton found that, in these British studies, it was rare for students to read the complete texts. It appeared that on average just over one-third of the physics text was read, slightly less than half of the chemistry text, and just over one-half of the biology text. In all cases, it was common for the texts to be read after the appropriate lessons rather then before them, and there were great variations in the amounts read by individual students. The main uses that the students made of the texts were to help them answer specific questions, to help

them revise, and to provide supplementary reading. Newton concludes that the main role of the textbook in this study was to act as "a surrogate teacher" and a provider of supplementary reading.

There have been more detailed reports, with case histories, of how students use distance learning materials (e.g., see Marland et al., 1984, 1990, 1992). These studies have tended to focus on how such students allocate their time, what sections they read (or don't read), and in what order they carry out the assignments requested of them. Marland et al. (1990) draw attention to the fact that different groups of students in their

TABLE 27-2. THE RANK ORDER OF PREFERENCES FOR FEATURES IN TEXTBOOKS (RESPONDENTS WERE ASKED TO INDICATE WHETHER THEY FOUND THE FEATURES LISTED AS HELPFUL, MADE NO DIFFERENCE, OR UNHELPFUL IN THEIR READING OF TEXTBOOKS)

		% Endorsing ($N = 87$)		
Rank	Feature	Helpful	No Difference	Unhelpful
1	Headings	71	28	1
2	A section to tell you what the chapter is about	69	29	2
2	Short chapters	68	29	3
4	Cartoons	68	25	7
5 =	Use of color to show important points	63	34	2
5 =	Use of underlining to show important points	63	34	2
7	Photographs	63	30	7
8	Spacious layout	54	39	7
9	Subheadings	53	41	6
10	Tables	48	40	11
11	A section to remind you what the chapter was about	47	45	6
12	Graphs	44	43	14
13	Questions at the end of each chapter	41	46	13
14	Suggestions for further reading	40	47	13

study paid attention to different features. Some focused on the course objectives, but others never looked at them; very few paid much attention to the headings. Tables, however, were inspected closely; some students were bemused by author-provided underlining; and there was little indication that any of the students sought to develop a broad, integrated understanding of the text (see also Chapter 13). Studies by Macdonald-Ross and Scott (1995) have examined the reading skills of large samples of students entering the British Open University. The results suggest that many entering students have difficulties with academic text. Findings such as these have implications for text design, which will be discussed below.

Clearly, how teachers use textbooks in class is also an important consideration. Three American studies (Alverman, 1989; Hinchman, 1987; and Zahorik, 1991) suggest that teachers, overall, appear to have three different ways of using textbooks in class. These are to provide:

- Authoritative content
- Basic material that they can embellish
- Material for discussion

Zahorik found that over 80% of the teachers in his sample said they would use a textbook when teaching a particular lesson, but over 40% said they would not have their pupils read it from cover to cover. Other investigators also provide more detailed accounts, with case histories, of how teachers use textbooks in class (e.g., DiGisi & Willett, 1995; Freeman & Porter, 1980; Garner & Alexander, 1994; Roth & Anderson, 1988).

As noted above, Newton (1984) indicates that textbooks in the United Kingdom are sometimes used as "surrogate teachers." He suggests that such a use tends to restrict the ways in which textbooks are written and designed. Authors, he writes, "can assume nothing" and "the expositional style adopted has tended to give the reader a passive role."

There is some evidence to support these notions. Schallert, Alexander, and Goetz (1988) examined the strategies designed to help students process text that had been used by the authors of five popular introductory psychology and biology textbooks. The categories listed by Schallert et al. are shown in Table 27-3, together with approximate estimates of their amount of use. Schallert et al. concluded that, despite the presence of these cues, the authors generally required little effort and activity from their readers. Schallert et al. write:

> Pictures and graphs were provided. Directed imagery, where an author might ask readers to imagine or construct a mental representation, was never used in our sample. Summaries were provided, but readers were not asked to summarize for themselves. . . . The most effort-demanding cues that were used with any substantial frequency were questions to be answered by the reader. These were usually found at the ends of chapters and may have been easily overlooked during studying.

The quality of these questions, too, may leave something to be desired (Armbruster & Ostertag, 1993; Turner, 1989).

Such a passive view of studying appears to be fairly commonplace among textbook authors. That view neglects the fact that readers vary enormously in their reasons for studying, in their ability and motivation, and in their methods of approach (see, e.g., Carbo, Dunn & Dunn, 1986; Lorch, Lorch & Klusewitz, 1993).

One particular distinction currently receiving much attention in Europe is that between "surface" and "deep" approaches to studying and reading (Entwistle, 1992; Marton & Saljo, 1984). Surface readers skim the text, retain isolated facts, and are not concerned with the overall structure or argument of the text. Deep readers, on the other hand, search for the underlying structure of the text, question it, relate ideas in the text to their own prior knowledge and experience, and so on. Table 27-4 suggests how these different study strategies may manifest themselves.

This distinction between deep and surface learning, of course, is only one of many similar ones. Whatever the

TABLE 27-3. STRATEGIES USED BY AUTHORS OF FIVE PSYCHOLOGY AND FIVE BIOLOGY INTRODUCTORY TEXTBOOKS
(Data based on Schallert, Alexander & Goetz, 1988)

Proportion of Use:		Strategies Used by Authors
Psychology Textbooks	Biology Textbooks	
45%	29%	Cues that direct the reader's attention (e.g., objectives, questions, boldfaces, italics)
25%	31%	Cues to signal content and organization (e.g., headings, summaries, overviews, outlines, intertextual references, text to graphic references)
10%	22%	Cues that help the reader to elaborate (e.g., examples, paraphrases, applications, marginal comments)
5%	11%	Cues to support the communication (e.g., tables, graphs, referenced drawings, photographs)
3%	5%	Cues that relate text material to familiar information (e.g., familiar quotes, allusions to common experiences and comparisons)
6%	2%	Cues that arouse and motivate the reader (e.g., humor, unreferenced illustrations, photographs)

TABLE 27-4. OUTLINES OF STUDY ORIENTATIONS
(Reproduced with permission of P. Marland)

Characteristics	Study Orientations	
	X	**Y**
Motivation	Intrinsic, professional • Improve teaching • Improve self-knowledge • Develop understanding of teaching • Get more out of course • Put more effort into course (not concerned about grades)	Extrinsic • Obtain graduate qualifications • Achieve higher status • Get salary increment • Enhance employment prospects

Study strategies	Optimizing
	• Read beyond course materials
	• Process material three times
	• Generate own questions
	• Use textual material to evaluate
	  own teaching whenever appropriate
	  or interested
		Satisficing
		• Select textual material for study
		  that is relevant to assessment
		• Process material once
		• Complete minimal requirements
		• Use textual material to evaluate
		  own teaching when required
		• Evaluate ideas in text when required

Student role	• Diverge from assigned or
	  implied student role when
	  necessary, appropriate
		• Fulfill assigned or implied role

General characteristics	Information processing is
	generally deep
	
	Student is:
	• More professionally oriented
	• Not text bound
	• An optimizer (that is, tries
	  to get the most out of study)
		Information processing is generally
		surface unless otherwise required
		
		Student is:
		• Assessment oriented
		• Text bound
		• A satisficer (that is, is satisfied
		  with getting by on what is required
		  by assessment)

terminology used, the question being raised here is how can one design instructional text encourage readers to take a deeper and a more active approach to reading? One answer, I think, is to identify successful learning strategies for reading, and to write the text in such a way that it encourages readers to practice them.

If, as Newton (1984) suggests, we consider a book as a device to think with, and if we consider that active participation is more likely to foster understanding than is a passive role, then we must consider how, as textbook designers, we might achieve this. Newton suggests, for example, that we can use self-test questions ("not necessarily difficult ones"), outlines, and advance organizers to help pupils enter into a dialogue with the author. Also, he suggests that pupils can be encouraged to use the materials provided in an active way (for example, by constructing tables and drawing diagrams). Marland et al. (1990), in their study of distance learning materials, similarly suggest that their findings have implications for text design. They write:

> It may be helpful if writers were to: reduce the scope of the content to allow for more in-depth study of the text; be explicit about the expectations as to study strategies to be employed, level or quality of student response, and types of cognitive processes to be used when completing the in-text activity; structure the text in such a way that emphasizes a cumulative,

interactive organic view of learning rather than a view of learning as the acquisition of isolated bits of knowledge; design assessment activities that require reinterpretation and integration of substantial chunks of content; use outcomes of in-text activities as prerequisite knowledge for further study; and make completion of some in-text activities compulsory.

In a paper I wrote in 1987, I listed 13 such strategies that writers, teachers, and students might use that would encourage deeper text processing. Jones (1988) similarly describes a curriculum with such learning strategies embedded within it. Thus Newton, Marland, Jones, and I are arguing, along with others (e.g., Armbruster & Anderson, 1985; Rowntree, 1992), for what we call more *coherent* texts. Such texts are written for specific groups of readers; they use language with which the readers are familiar; they include experiences that readers share; they provide meaningful examples; they ask readers questions as they go along—not just in the headings or at the end (see Walczyk & Hall, 1989)—and they provide examples and problems that readers actually have to work through in order to follow the exposition. Such texts, too, can be supplemented by other kinds of reading materials (see Lapp, Flood & Ranck-Buhr, 1995).

I have provided elsewhere two chapters that illustrate how writers can use questions that readers have to answer in order to understand the following exposition (Hartley,

1985, 1986) and other examples of more complete texts in this vein, including Bransford's (1979) *Human Cognition*, Gagne's (1984) *The Cognitive Psychology of School Learning*, and Lockwoods' (1992) *Activities in Self-Instructional Texts*. Given the preponderance of textbooks in our schools, changing the ways in which we write them can make a major improvement in instructional practice.

27.6 FUTURE DIRECTIONS IN TEXTBOOK DESIGN

In the previous sections, I have described a good deal of research on textbook design. Much of this research, however, as I noted particularly in 27.3, is uncoordinated and atheoretical. Most researchers focus on one particular feature of text design, few consider the effects of several features in combination, and few carry out carefully developed programmatic studies.

Furthermore, most researchers work within a particular framework. Researchers with a leaning towards a cognitive approach (see Chapter 5), for instance, might look, for example, at how prior knowledge affects the usefulness of headings (e.g., Wilhite, 1989). In contrast, researchers following a constructivist approach (see Chapter 7) might focus on how getting readers to generate their own outlines, headings, or questions might be more advantageous than their simply reading those provided by authors (e.g., see Foos, Mora & Tkacz, 1994; Jonassen, Hartley & Trueman, 1986; Speigel & Barufaldi, 1994). This distinction between author- and reader-provided devices occurs in research on summaries, outlines, headings, and underlining. Presumably, too, depending on one's point of view, it affects how one writes instructional text.

Furthermore, we need to remember that textbooks are constantly evolving. Weiten and Wight (1992) provide a good example of this in their historical analysis of introductory textbooks in psychology. Currently, British textbooks lag behind American ones in this evolutionary process. British textbooks use far less color and far fewer graphics. Handbooks—such as this one—also suffer from this problem. In 5 to 10 years, however, our school children and our university students will be familiar with multimedia, interactive compact discs (see Chapters 12, 14, 15, 24) that they will read on colorful computer screens. Textbooks, *as we currently know them*, may become a thing of the past.

Some people (e.g., Jonassen, 1992; Schlosser, 1994) have already predicted the demise of the textbook and described current textbooks as obsolete. Although I think they go too far, I do agree that the physical nature of textbooks may change. New technology already allows visually handicapped students to print out text in the type sizes and typefaces that they prefer. Perhaps, in the future, readers will be able to order textbooks with their preferred fonts, type sizes, line lengths, margins, etc. And, similarly, textbooks may be read on screens in whatever configuration the reader chooses. I am indebted to Thomas Anderson for the sugges-

tion that, with the help of computer publishing, perhaps students can opt to design their own specialized textbooks by choosing not only their preferred typefaces and type sizes but choosing also between, for example, (1) inserted questions or not, (2) summaries listed before or after the chapter prose, (3) concept maps or outlines, (4) embedded or marginal headings, (5) headings written as statements or questions, and (6) particular chapters from the ones available. These choices would depend on the use that was to be made of the textbook. In other words, Anderson suggests that the future directions of textbook design may be more under the control of the readers than the authors (see Chapter 33). Research in textbook design may never answer the question "Which typeface/type size/line length is best?" for every individual occasion, but it may allow us to present readers of the future with an appropriate menu from which to choose.

ACKNOWLEDGEMENTS

I am grateful to my reviewers, Thomas Anderson, Gary Morrison, and David Jonassen for helpful comments, and to Margaret Woodward for assistance with the technical presentation of this chapter.

REFERENCES

A.A.R.P. (1986). *Truth about aging: guidelines for accurate communications.* Washington, DC: American Association of Retired Persons.

Allington, R.L. & Weber, R. (1993). Questioning questions in teaching and learning from text. *In* B.K. Britton, A. Woodward & M. Binkley, eds. *Learning from textbooks: theory and practice,* 47–68. Hillsdale, NJ: Erlbaum.

Alverman, D. (1989). Teacher-student mediation of content area texts. *Theory into Practice 27,* 142–47.

Annis, L.F. (1985). Student-generated paragraph summaries and the information-processing theory of prose learning. *Journal of Experimental Education 54,* 4–10.

Armbruster, B.B. & Anderson, T.H. (1985). Producing "considerate" expository text: or easy reading is damned hard writing. *Journal of Curriculum Studies 17,* 247–74.

— & Ostertag, J. (1993). Questions in elementary science and social studies textbooks. *In* B.K. Britton, A. Woodward & M. Binkley, eds. *Learning from textbooks: theory and practice,* 69–94. Hillsdale, NJ: Erlbaum.

Badzinski, D.M., Cantor, J. & Hoffner, C. (1989). Children's understanding of quantifiers. *Child Study Journal 19 (4),* 241–58.

Beck, I.L., McKeown, M.G. & Worthy, J. (1995). Giving a text voice can improve students' understanding. *Reading Research Quarterly 30 (2),* 220–38.

Bellquist, J.E. (1993). *A guide to grammar and usage for psychology and related fields.* Hillsdale, NJ: Erlbaum.

Berger, A.A. (1993). *Improving writing skills: memos, letters, reports and proposals.* Newbury Park, CA: Sage.

Berger, S. (1991). *The design of bibliographies: observations, references and examples.* London: Mansell.

Birren, J.E. & Schaie, K.W., eds. (1990). *Handbook of the psychology of aging.* San Diego, CA: Academic.

Black, A. (1990). *Typefaces for desktop publishing: a user guide.* London: Architecture Design and Technology Press.

Bracken, B.A. (1982). Effect of personalized basal stories on the reading comprehension of fourth-grade poor and average readers. *Contemporary Educational Psychology 7,* 320–24.

Bransford, J.D. (1979). *Human cognition.* Belmont, CA: Wadsworth.

Britton, B.K., Woodward, A. & Binkley, M., eds. (1993). *Learning from textbooks: theory and practice.* Hillsdale, NJ: Erlbaum.

Bruce, I., McKennell, A. & Walker, E. (1991). *Blind and partially sighted adults in Britain*: the RNIB Survey, Vol. 1. London: HMSO.

Caplan, L.J. & Schooler, C. (1990). The effects of analogical training models and age on problem-solving in a new domain. *Experimental Aging Research 16* (3), 151–54.

Carbo, M., Dunn, R. & Dunn, K. (1986). *Teaching students to read.* Englewood Cliffs, NJ: Prentice Hall.

Carpenter, P.A. & Just, M.A. (1977). Reading comprehension as the eyes see it. *In* M.A. Just & P.A. Carpenter, eds. *Cognitive processes in comprehension,* 109–39. Hillsdale, N.J: Erlbaum.

Chall, J.S. & Conard, S.S. (1991). *Should textbooks challenge students? The case for easier or harder books.* New York: Teachers College Press.

Chapanis, A. (1965). Words, words, words. *Human Factors 7* (1), 1–17.

— (1988). "Words, words, words" revisited. *International Review of Ergonomics 2,* 1–30.

Clarke, A. (1992). *The principles of screen design for computer based learning materials,* 2d ed. Moorfoot, Sheffield, U.K.: Employment Department.

Craik, F.I.M. & Salthouse, T.A., eds. (1992). *The handbook of aging and cognition.* Hillsdale, NJ: Erlbaum.

Crouwel, W. (1979). Typography: a technique of making text legible. *In* P.A. Kolers, M.E. Wrolstad & H. Bouma, eds. *Processing of visible language,* Vol. 1, 151–64. New York: Plenum.

Davis-Dorsey, J.D., Ross, S.M. & Morrison, G.R. (1991). The role of rewording and context personalization in the solving of mathematical word problems. *Journal of Educational Psychology 83,* 61–68.

Davison, A. & Green, G., eds. (1987). *Linguistic complexity and text comprehension: a re-examination of readability with alternative views.* Hillsdale, NJ: Erlbaum.

DiGisi, L.L. & Willett, J.B. (1995). What high school biology teachers say about their textbook use: a descriptive study. *Journal of Research in Science Teaching 32* (2), 123–42.

Dorner, J. & Hartley, J. (1993). Writers and machines: the role of computers in writing journalistic and academic text. Paper to the 6th U.K. Conference on Computers and Writing, University of Wales, Aberystwyth, April 1993.

Dwyer, F.M. (1978). *Strategies for improving visual learning.* State College, PA: Learning Services.

Ehrenberg, A.S.C. (1977). Rudiments of numeracy. *Journal of the Royal Statistical Society,* A, 140, 227–97.

Entwistle, N.J. (1992). Student learning and study strategies. *In* B.R. Clark & G. Neave, eds. *The Encyclopedia of Higher Education,* Vol. 3, 1730–40. Oxford, U.K.: Pergamon.

Evans, H. (1972). *Editing and design,* Vol. 1. London: Heinemann.

Fisher, D. (1976). Spatial factors in reading and research: the case for space. *In* R.A. Monty & J.W. Senders, eds. *Eye*-

movements and psychological processes, 417–28. Hillsdale, NJ: Erlbaum.

Foos, P.W., Mora, J.J. & Tkacz, S. (1994). Student study techniques and the generation effect. *Journal of Educational Psychology 86* (4), 567–76.

Foster, J.J. (1979). The use of visual cues in text. *In* P.A. Kolers, M.E. Wrolstad & Bouman, H., eds. *Processing of visible language,* Vol. 1., 189–203.

Freeman, D.J. & Porter, A.C. (1989). Do textbooks dictate the content of mathematics instruction in elementary schools? *American Educational Research Journal 26* (3), 403–21.

Gagné, E.D. (1984). *The cognitive psychology of school learning.* Boston, MA: Little, Brown.

Garner, R. & Alexander, P.A., eds. (1994). *Beliefs about text and instruction with text.* Hillsdale, NJ: Erlbaum.

Glover, J.A. & Krug, D. (1988). Detecting false statements in text: the role of outlines and inserted headings. *British Journal of Educational Psychology 58,* 301–06.

Glynn, S.M., Britton, B.K. & Muth, D. (1985). Text-comprehension strategies based on outlines: immediate and long-term effects. *Journal of Experimental Education 53,* 129–35.

Guri-Rosenblit, S. (1989). Effects of a tree diagram on students' comprehension of main ideas in an expository text with multiple themes. *Reading Research Quarterly 14* (2), 226–47.

Hall, R., Dansereau, D.F. & Skaggs, L.P. (1992). Knowledge maps and the presentation of related information domains. *Journal of Experimental Education 61* (1), 5–18.

Hamaker, C. (1986). The effects of adjunct questions on prose learning. *Review of Educational Research 56* (2), 212–42.

Hamilton, R.J. (1985). A framework for the evaluation of the effectiveness of adjunct questions and objectives. *Review of Educational Research 55* (1), 47–85.

Hartley, J. (1984). The role of colleagues and text editing programs in improving text. *IEEE Transactions on Professional Communication 27* (1), 42–44.

— (1985). Developing skills of learning. *In* A. Branthwaite & D. Rogers, eds. *Children growing up,* 112–21. Milton Keynes, U.K.: Open University Press.

— (1986). Learning skills and their improvement. *In* A. Gellatly, ed. *The skillful mind,* 143–55. Milton Keynes, U.K.: Open University Press.

— (1987). Typography and executive control processes in reading. *In* B.K. Britton & S.M. Glynn, eds. *Executive control processes in reading,* 57–79. Hillsdale, N.J.: Erlbaum.

— (1989). Text design and the setting of Braille (with a footnote on Moon). *Information Design Journal 5* (3), 183–90.

— (1991). Thomas Jefferson, page design and desktop publishing. *Educational Technology XXXI,* 1, 54–57.

— (1992). *Technology & writing.* London: Kingsley.

— (1993a). The layout of computer-based text. *In* R. Sassoon, ed. *Computers and typography,* 16–31. Oxford, U.K.: Intellect.

— (1993b). Recalling structured text: does what goes in determine what comes out? *British Journal of Educational Technology 24* (3), 85–91.

— (1994a). *Designing instructional text,* 3d ed. East Brunswick, NJ: Nichols.

— (1994b). Designing instructional text for older readers: A literature review. *British Journal of Educational Technology 253,* 172-88.

— (1994c). Three ways to improve the clarity of journal abstracts. *British Journal of Educational Psychology 64* (2), 331–43.

—, Burnhill, P. & Davies, L. (1978). The effects of line-length and paragraph denotation on the retrieval of information from prose text. *Visible Language 12* (2), 183–94.

— & Trueman, M. (1982). The effects of summaries on the recall of information from prose text. *Human Learning 1,* 63–82.

— & — (1985). A research strategy for text designers: the role of headings. *Instructional Science 14* (2), 99–155.

—, — & Burnhill, P. (1980). Some observations on producing and measuring readable writing. *Programmed Learning and Educational Technology 17* (3), 164–74.

—, — & Rodgers, A. (1984). The effects of verbal and numerical quantifiers on questionnaire responses. *Applied Ergonomics 11,* 149–55.

Hershberger, W.A. & Terry, D.F. (1965). Typographic cueing in conventional and programmed texts. *Journal of Applied Psychology 49* (1), 55–60.

Hinchman, K. (1987). The textbook and those content-area teachers. *Reading Research and Instruction 26,* 247–63.

James, S., Lewis, A. & Allison, F. (1987). *The comprehensibility of taxation: a study of taxation and communications.* Aldershot, U.K.: Avebury.

Jandreau, S. & Bever, T.G. (1992). Phrase-spaced formats improve comprehension in average readers. *Journal of Applied Psychology 77,* 143–46.

Jonassen, D.H. (1982). Introduction to section III: electronic text. *In* D.H. Jonassen, ed. *The technology of text: principles for structuring, designing and displaying text,* 379–81. Englewood Cliffs, NJ: Educational Technology.

—, Hartley, J. & Trueman M. (1986). The effects of learner-generated versus text-provided headings on immediate and delayed recall and comprehension. *Human Learning 5* (3), 139–50.

Jones, B.F. (1988). Text learning strategy instruction: guidelines from theory and practice. *In* C.E. Weinstein, E. Goetz & P.A. Alexander, eds. *Learning and study strategies,* 233–60. San Diego, CA: Academic.

Kahn, A., ed. (1991). *How to write and speak better.* London: Readers Digest Association.

Kinross, R. (1994). Unjustified text and the zero hour. *Information Design Journal 7* (3), 243–52.

Kirby, J.R. & Pedwell, D. (1991). Students' approaches to summarization. *Educational Psychology 11,* 297–307.

Kohut, G.F. & Gorman, K.J. (1995). The effectiveness of leading grammar/style software packages in analyzing business students' writing. *Journal of Business and Technical Communication 9* (3), 341–61.

Lambiotte, J.G. & Dansereau, D.F. (1992). Effects of knowledge maps and prior knowledge on recall of science lecture content. *Journal of Experimental Education 60* (3), 189–204.

Lapp, D., Flood, J. & Ranck-Buhr, W. (1995). Using multiple text formats to explore scientific phenomena in middle school classrooms. *Reading and Writing Quarterly: Overcoming Learning Difficulties 11,* 173–86.

Lewis, C. & Walker, P. (1989). Typographic influences on reading. *British Journal of Psychology 80* (2), 241–58.

Lipman, P.D. & Caplan, L.J. (1992). Adult age differences in memory for routes: the effects of instruction and spatial diagram. *Psychology and Aging 7* (3), 435–42.

Lockwood, F. (1992). *Activities in self-instructional texts.* East Brunswick, NJ: Nichols.

Lorch, R.F. & Chen, A.H. (1986). Effects of number signals on reading and recall. *Journal of Educational Psychology 78* (4), 263–70.

—, Lorch, E.P. & Inman, W.I. (1993). Effects of signalling topic structure on text recall. *Journal of Educational Psychology 85* (2), 281–90.

—, — & Klusewitz, M. (1993). College students' conditional knowledge about reading. *Journal of Educational Psychology 85* (2), 239–52.

Loxterman, J.A., Beck, I.L. & McKeown, M.G. (1994). The effects of thinking aloud during reading on students' comprehension of more or less coherent text. *Reading Research Quarterly 29* (4), 353–68.

Macdonald-Ross, M. & Scott, B. (1995). Results of the survey of OU students' reading skills. Text and Readers Programme Technical Report #3. Institute of Educational Technology, The Open University, Milton Keynes, MK7 6AA, U.K.

Marland, P., Patching, W. & Putt, I. (1992). *Learning from text: glimpses inside the minds of distance learners.* Townsville, Australia: James Cook University of North Queensland.

—, —, — & Putt, R. (1990). Distance learners' interactions with text while studying. *Distance Education 11* (1), 71–91.

—, —, — & Store, R. (1984). Learning from distance-teaching materials: a study of students' mediating responses. *Distance Education 5* (2), 215–36.

Marton, F. & Saljo, R. (1984). Approaches to learning. *In* F. Marton, D. Hounsell & N. Entwistle, eds. *The experience of learning,* 36–55. Edinburgh: Scottish Academic Press.

Meyer, B.J.F., Young, C.J. & Bartlett, B.J. (1989). *Memory improved: reading and memory enhancement across the life-span through strategic text structures.* Hillsdale, NJ: Erlbaum.

Michael, D. (1988). User differences and graphic design. Unpublished Ph.D. Thesis, University of Keele, Staffordshire, ST5 5BG, U.K.

Miles, J. (1987). *Design for desktop publishing.* San Francisco, CA: Chronicle.

Misanchuk, E.R. (1992). *Preparing instructional text: document design using desktop publishing.* Englewood Cliffs, NJ: Educational Technology.

Morrell, R.W. & Park, D.C. (1993). The effects of age, illustrations and task variables on the performance of procedural assembly tasks. *Psychology and Aging 8* (3), 389–99.

—, — & Poon, L.W. (1990). Effects of labelling techniques on memory and comprehension of prescription information in young and old adults. *Journal of Gerontology 45* (5), 166–72.

Moxey, L.M. & Sanford, A.J. (1993). *Communicating quantities: a psychological perspective.* London: Erlbaum.

Muncer, S.J., Gorman, B.S., Gorman, S. & Bibel, D. (1986). Right is wrong: an examination of the effect of right justification on reading. *British Journal of Educational Technology 17* (1), 5–10.

Newton, D.P. (1994). Textbooks in science teaching. *School Science Review 66,* 235, 388–91.

Paterson, D.G. & Tinker, M. (1929). Studies of typographical factors influencing speed of reading. II. Size of type. *Journal of Applied Psychology 13,* 120–30.

Posner, G.J. & Strike, K.A. (1976). A categorization scheme for principles of sequencing content. *Review of Educational Research 46,* 685–90.

Raban, B. (1982). Text display effects on the fluency of young readers. *Journal of Research in Reading 5* (1), 7–28.

Reder, L.M. & Anderson, J.R. (1980). A comparison of texts and their summaries: memorial consequences. *Journal of Verbal Learning and Verbal Behavior 19,* 121–34.

Renninger, K.A., Hidi, S. & Krapp, A. (1992). *The role of interest in learning and development.* Hillsdale, NJ: Erlbaum.

Rice, G.E., Meyer, B.J.F. & Miller, D.C. (1989). Using text structure to improve older adults' recall of important medical information. *Educational Gerontology 15,* 527–42.

Rook, K. (1987). Effects of case-history versus abstract information on health attitudes and behaviors. *Journal of Applied Social Psychology 17* (6), 533–53.

Roth, K. & Anderson, C. (1988). Promoting conceptual change learning from science textbooks. *In* Ramsden, P., ed. *Improving learning: new perspectives,* 109–41. London: Kogan Page.

Rowntree, D. (1992). *Exploring open and distance learning.* London: Kogan Page.

Schallert, D.L., Alexander, P.A. & Goetz, E. (1988). Implicit instruction of strategies for learning from text. *In* C.E. Weinstein, E. Goetz & P.A. Alexander, eds. *Learning and Study Strategies,* 193–214. San Diego, CA: Academic.

Schlosser, B. (1994, Aug.). Books have already entered the stage of obsolescence. *A.P.A. Monitor 25* (8).

Schumacher, G.M. (1985). Reaction to "Americans develop plans for government." *Journal of Curriculum Studies 17* (3), 263–67.

Shaw, A. (1969). *Print for partial sight.* London: Library Association.

Sherrard, C. (1988). What is a summary? *Educational Technology 28* (9), 47–50.

Small, J.P. (1997). *Wax tablets of the mind: cognitive studies of classical antiquity.* In press.

Smith, S.L. & Aucella, A.F. (1983). Numbering formats for hierarchic lists. *Human Factors 25* (3), 343–48.

Spencer, H. (1969). *The visible word.* London: Lund Humphries.

Spiegel, G. & Barufaldi, J.P. (1994). The effects of a combination of text structure awareness and graphic postorganizers on recall and retention of scientific knowledge. *Journal of Research in Science Teaching 31* (9), 913–32.

Spyridakis, I.H. & Standal T.C. (1987). Signals in expository prose: effects on reading. *Reading Research Quarterly 12* (3), 285–98.

Swann, A. (1989). *How to design grids.* London: Phaedon.

Tannenbaum, P., Jacobson, H. & Norris, E. (1964). An experimental investigation of typeface connotations. *Journalism Quarterly 41* (1), 65–73.

Thomas, J.M. (1984). Four introductions to psychology. *Contemporary Psychology 29* (8), 629–32.

Tinker, M.A. (1963). *Legibility of print.* Ames, IA: State University Press.

— (1965). *Bases for effective reading.* Ames, IA: State University Press.

— & Paterson, D.G. (1928). Influence of type form on speed of reading. *Journal of Applied Psychology 12* (4), 359–68.

Townsend, M.A.R., Moore, D.W., Tuck, B.F. & Wilton, K.M. (1990). Headings within multiple-choice tests as facilitators of test performance. *British Journal of Educational Psychology 60,* 153–60.

Turner, T.N. (1989). Using textbook questions intelligently. *Social Education 53,* 58–60.

U.S. Department of Justice. (1988). Access to printed information by visually impaired persons, Technical Assistance Guide: Civil Rights Division, Washington, DC.

Van Patten, B., Chao, C. & Reigeluth, C.M. (1986). A review of strategies for sequencing and synthesizing information. *Review of Educational Research 56,* 437–72.

Walczyk, J.J. & Hall, V.C. (1989). Effects of examples and embedded questions on the accuracy of comprehension self-assessments. *Journal of Educational Psychology 81* (3), 435–37.

Walker, E., Tobin, M. & McKennell, A. (1992). *Blind and partially sighted children in Britain: the RNIB Survey,* Vol. 2. London: HMSO.

Waller, R. (1979). Typographic access structures for educational texts. *In* P.A. Kolers, M.E. Wrolstad & H. Bouma, eds. *Processing of visible language,* Vol. 1., 175–88. New York: Plenum.

Waller, R. (1980). Notes on transforming No. 4: numbering systems in text. *In* J. Hartley, ed. *The psychology of written communication,* 145–53. London: Kogan Page.

Watts, L. & Nisbet, J. (1974). *Legibility in children's books.* London: National Foundation for Educational Research.

Weiten, W., Guadagno, R.E. & Beck, C.A. (1996). Students' perceptions of textbook pedagogical aids. *Teaching of Psychology 23* (2), 105–06.

— & Wight, R.D. (1992). Portraits of a discipline: an examination of introductory textbooks in America. *In* A.E. Puente, J.R. Matthews & C.L. Brewer, eds. *Teaching psychology in America: a history.* Washington, DC: American Psychological Association.

Welsh, T., Murphy, K., Duffy, T.M. & Goodrum, D.A. (1993). Accessing elaborations on core information in a hypermedia environment. *Educational Technology Research and Development 41* (2), 19–34.

Wilhite, S.C. (1989). Headings as memory facilitators: the importance of prior knowledge. *Journal of Educational Psychology 81,* 115–17.

Zahorik, J.A. (1991). Teaching styles and textbooks: *Teaching and Teacher Education 7* (2), 185–96.

28. AUDITORY PRESENTATIONS AND LANGUAGE LABORATORIES

Steven D. Tripp
UNIVERSITY OF AIZU, JAPAN

Warren B. Roby
WASHINGTON STATE UNIVERSITY

28.1 INTRODUCTION AND HISTORICAL OVERVIEW

The use of mediated audio for instructional purposes is nearly a century old, and there is a deep history of studies of audio media in education, but in recent years the subject has been relatively dormant. Perhaps this is because technological advances in video and computing have led researchers in the direction of visual and textual presentations. Whatever the reason, much of the literature on this topic is not new. This chapter tends to emphasize work that cannot be called up-to-date.

This chapter is presented in two parts. The first part reviews research and makes recommendations about the design of auditory instructional materials. The second part of the chapter reviews research and makes recommendations about the most common application of auditory instruction, language laboratories.

28.1.1 Scope of the Auditory Instruction Review

This review of the literature on audio instruction is limited in its scope. It covers the use of audio, whether live or through conventional media such as tape, radio, or telephone. It does not address the use of audio for music instruction, nor does it include the applications of audio for various special education situations where students are suffering from handicaps that limit the effectiveness of other conventional media. Additionally, no attempt is made to include the use of nonverbal audio such as sound effects.

28.2 MEMORY FOR AUDITORY PRESENTATIONS

28.2.1 Memory Theory

A short description of current thinking may be helpful in order to put auditory memory in perspective (see also 3.2,

3.3). Potter (1990) distinguishes between three kinds of short-term memory: iconic, very short-term conceptual, and short-term verbal memory. Potter notes that these three types of memory are subject to differing types of interference and differing rates of forgetting. Iconic memory serves as a short-term visual buffer. It recognizes objects in 200 to 300 milliseconds and then holds that information for about 200 milliseconds. Very short-term conceptual memory receives scenes from iconic memory and stores them temporarily in conceptual form. These memories are not interfered with by iconic memory, but may be by other conceptual tasks. Very short-term conceptual memory decays in about 1 second. If these concepts are not embedded into a train of thought, they are lost. Finally, we have short-term verbal memory. This memory consists of an auditory buffer, which is severely limited in its capacity but may be maintained by continuous rehearsal. Its capacity is about 1.3 to 1.7 seconds, and its decay rate is nearly the same, allowing us to "replay" words or sounds heard a short time before. Meaningful background noise can interfere with verbal memory, and because this buffer is used for understanding written text, interference between the two channels may be experienced. This relates to the multichannel theories of learning that will be discussed later.

Potter (1990) stated that long-term memory may have three forms corresponding to the three forms of short-term memory. The dominant form of long-term encoding is conceptual, but visual and auditory long-term memories are also available. One implication of this conception of memory is that the extremely limited capacity of short-term memory implies that we should limit the number of chunks to be associated at any one time to three or four and that these *not* be redundant, because the short-term conceptual and verbal buffers are so vulnerable to interference. There is no reason to believe that information stored in any of one of the three short-term memories is more likely to be remembered because it was in that memory.

28.2.2 Early Comparison Studies

There have been many attempts to compare the relative instructional effectiveness of material presented through an audio or through a textual or visual medium. Erickson and King (1917) performed one of the earliest studies of the effectiveness of the auditory medium. Four groups of students from third to ninth grade were chosen, and each group was divided in half. One-half received the lesson from silent reading, whereas the other half was given similar material orally by the teacher. The following day, the order was reversed as to which half would read or listen. This procedure was followed two more times, for a total of four lessons. At the third- and fourth-grade level, the median score of the oral group was much higher than the medians of the group that read. At the fifth- and sixth-grade levels, the results were inconclusive. At seventh-, eighth-, and ninth-grade levels, the medians of the oral groups were much higher than in the groups that read the lesson. Needless to say, in these early studies experimental design was not what might be desired. Specific variables such as teachers' skill and interest were not taken into account, nor was the subject matter. Also, the only datum that was examined was the median score of the group.

Worchester (1925) tested 13 students to see whether oral or reading presentation of connected material was remembered better after 1 day, 2 days, and 7 days. In spite of methodological shortcomings, the author concluded that neither medium has a marked degree of superiority in the rate of learning of meaningful connected material.

The relative effectiveness of visual and auditory presentations of advertising material was studied by DeWick (1935). A group of 73 college students was divided into two groups. Three presentations of audio and visual advertisements were based on real advertising found in current magazines and on radio. One group heard the advertisement; the other looked at it in the booklet form. The auditory and visual advertisements were different. Time was held constant. After the experiment, the students were asked to write the names of products in order of presentation and then to describe the content. Next, the groups were switched and the same procedure followed. Five months later, all students were given the opportunity to recall the advertisements presented in both media. DeWick reported that: (a) The auditory presentation was superior in the recall of trade names after a delay of from 5 days to 5 months; (b) in immediate recall, both were similar; (c) recall was progressively weaker with visual presentations; (d) recall of ideas expressed in the advertisements was greater with the auditory method than with the visual.

Stanton (1934) conducted a follow-up study of DeWick, whose work was unpublished at the time. The auditory presentation was given without embellishments, such as music, and the visual material was presented without illustrations or other attention-getting devices. The same procedure was followed as in DeWick's study. Recall and recognition tests were given at three time intervals: 1 day, 7 days, and 21 days. The auditory method of presentation was superior. Recall was highest for auditory presentations at 7 days, and recognition was highest at 21 days.

The above studies addressed memory, but they did not investigate comprehension. Young (1936) tested comprehension with 2,000 intermediate students from Iowa and Texas. Four modes were used to present the material: (a) The teacher read aloud to students; (b) teacher read aloud and students read the selection silently; (c) students read selection once; and (d) students read for the time allotted the teacher to read orally. At the end of each presentation, a comprehension test was given; a delayed test was given 1 month later. Young reported that the students got very little information from an oral presentation and remembered even less after a month. However, the oral presentation was more effective than either of the silent readings, both immediately and after a month. He also found that the children who do poorly in comprehending through reading also do poorly in comprehending through hearing.

Larsen and Feder (1940) asked whether psychological abilities differentiate between the processes involved in reading and listening comprehension. After hearing and reading selected materials that varied in difficulty, 151 students were given both reading and listening comprehension tests. On these tests, there was a superiority of performance on reading comprehension over listening comprehension. However, this superiority depended on the aptitude of the student. Students with lower aptitudes tended to show equal results in listening and reading. The higher-ability groups showed a superiority in the reading comprehension tests. The authors concluded that comprehension is a central function operating independently of the mode of presentation. This study foreshadows modern results that emphasize the relative effectiveness of auditory presentations for students, who, for age or other reasons, do not read well.

In general, these studies, whatever their shortcomings, indicate that auditory presentations can be at least as effective as live or print presentations and are practical alternatives to conventional instruction. Under certain circumstances, especially when the materials are well prepared, auditory presentations may be superior.

28.3 AUDIO TECHNOLOGY

Early educational technology such as the radio, the telephone, the tape recorder, and the loudspeaker attracted the attention of researchers. Loder (1937) compared the retention of factual materials presented over a loudspeaker system and directly by a speaker. Two groups totaling 449 students were rotated in the experiment. A pretest, a test immediately after the lesson, a test 1 day later, and one 20 days later were given. One group saw the speaker, and the other group heard him from another room. The direct group performed better, but later tests showed that the means were not significantly different.

Cook and Nemzek (1939) compared the effectiveness of radio instruction and conventional teaching. Two intermediate school groups were match-paired by age, sex, and intelligence for this experiment. Pretests and posttests were given. Their results showed a superiority for the radio-taught classes.

Rulon (1943a), using phonographic recordings, conducted an experiment to compare the amount of information gained by students who listened and those who studied the same material in printed form. Time was equalized. A total of 418 students listened to the recordings; 426 students studied the printed material. All students involved took a pretest, a posttest, and a test 1 week after the experiment was completed. Separate *t* tests were used to compare means of the pretest and posttest and also the delayed test. According to Rulon, the study of the printed material was superior to the method employing the recordings. However, a comparison in tests taken after a week showed little difference in methods employed. From this result, he concluded illogically that recordings make more of a lasting impression than printed materials.

Rulon (1943b) later conducted a similar experiment to compare the amount of information gained by students using phonographic recordings with the amount gained by students who studied a unit incorporating the same material presented in a textbook. This experiment probably is closer to an actual classroom situation, although, in this case, the textbook was prepared using the recordings as a primary source. Instructional methods using the textbook were not controlled. Testing procedures were similar to those above. The results, also using the *t* test, showed that phonographic recordings failed to show any superior effectiveness in teaching the "informational" aspects of the lesson.

In a third study on the effects of phonographic recordings, Rulon (1943c) investigated the motivational values of recordings. Using the same recordings and textbooks prepared for the earlier experiment, two groups of students were given access to supplementary reading materials after one group had heard the recordings and the other had read the material. Motivation was measured by which group used more supplementary reading materials. A total of 193 students used the recording, and 187 used the textbook presentation. Rulon's study showed no difference between the groups in terms of motivation to use supplementary reading material.

Kramer and Lewis (1951) investigated whether there was a difference in memory and comprehension between two groups of students in which one group sees and hears the speaker and another group only hears him. In the visual group were 128 students, and 120 were in the audio group. Both groups were in the same lecture room separated by a large, heavy curtain. Loudspeakers were used, and the lecture was given simultaneously to both groups. After the lecture, both groups took the same test. Both groups had been told that grades would not be counted. Kramer and Lewis reported that the mean of the visual group was higher than that of the audio group and that the visual group had a wider range. They concluded that the speaker's visible action somehow contributed to the ability to understand and remember the ideas in the lecture.

Leshan (1942) used a phonograph record to determine if a habit could be broken by suggestion while the subjects were asleep. At a summer camp, three small groups of young boys, all fingernail biters, were chosen for the study. The experimental group heard the suggestion to stop biting nails played 300 times a night over a period of a month and a half. The control groups received no auditory messages. Leshan reports that, at the end of the experiment, 40% of the experimental group had stopped nail biting, whereas none in the control groups had.

Similarly, a series of research studies with tape recorders attempted to determine whether or not students could be taught while they were sleeping. Fox and Roblin (1952) selected 30 people who had no knowledge of Chinese. Pretests and posttests were given. A tape recorder with a pillow microphone and an automatic timer switch was used for one-half hour during the night. Matched Chinese words with English words were given. Three groups were chosen: group 1 heard Chinese words and true English equivalents, group 2 heard Chinese words with false English equivalents, and group 3 heard music only. There were several weaknesses in the design, including the fact that the students were not observed at night. Fox and Roblin reported that the following morning the group that had the true translations learned the same list much more quickly than the other two groups, with the false translation group taking the longest. The authors conclude that learning can occur during sleep.

Gallacher and Stevens (1954) found that the use of tape recorders to teach spelling improved performance from 50 to 100%. The published description of this study was incomplete. However, as a result of this report, other studies were conducted on the effectiveness of tape recording used with spelling.

Gibson (1958, 1959, 1960) reported a 3-year experimental comparison of a tape teaching program with conventional instruction at an Omaha, Nebraska, junior high school. Two areas were chosen to study the effectiveness of tape recording: spelling and conversational Spanish. Oral and written tests were used. Results of findings included the assertion that tape instruction was superior to conventional instruction when the criterion was in the number of words correctly spelled. Both methods were similar with respect to the recognition of words misspelled. Spanish classes taught by a non-Spanish teacher using Spanish tapes, and classes taught by a Spanish teacher were similar in achievement scores. The following conclusions were made: (a) Tape recording is an effective method for teaching conversational Spanish to seventh-graders; (b) regular classroom teachers can effectively teach conversational Spanish by means of tape prepared by Spanish specialists; (c) students can learn to spell as effectively with a tape as with conventional classroom procedures; (d) with proper orientation, large groups can be taught spelling effectively; and (e) teaching with tapes produced no adverse effect on attitudes toward the subject.

Popham (1962) studied the effectiveness of tape-recorded lectures in teaching a college-level education class. Thirty-six students were divided into 18 matched pairs. Chi-square analysis revealed no significant difference between assorted variables. One group was a conventional lecture discussion; the other group was taught by tape-recorded lectures with student-led discussions. This experiment continued over one semester. Pretests in achievement and a test to measure student opinion were given. Both tests were repeated at the completion of the course. Popham reports that both groups had increased performance on the achievement tests; there was no significant difference between them. There was no significant difference on reactions to the courses. However, the opinions of the tape-lecture sections were generally favorable towards the technique.

In a similar study, Menne, Klingenschmidt, and Nord (1969) provided taped lectures, tape recorders, and printed notes to 209 college students. Another 408 students attended regular lectures. Overall, there was no significant difference, but students in the lowest quartile showed an advantage in the tape condition. Also the dropout rate was lower with the students using tape.

As a result of the interest in taped instruction, the National Center for Audio Tapes (NCAT) was established in 1955 and was known popularly as the National Tape Repository (DeKieffer, 1973). The repository originated at Kent State University and by 1960 housed approximately 2,000 titles. The NCAT was moved to the University of Colorado in 1960 because of the facilities for high-speed duplication that had been established. A survey of tape duplication facilities by NCAT in 1965 determined that of 350 institutions responding, 223 had tape-duplication libraries. The majority were in institutions of higher learning. In 1973 the NCAT had over 14,000 titles and duplicated more than 17,000 tapes.

In addition to the tape recorder, there was interest in the telephone as an instructional medium. Cutler, McKeachie, and McNeil (1958) conducted a study concerning the relative effectiveness of teaching via the telephone. Two matched groups of 10 were selected. One group was taught elementary psychology in the traditional manner, the other by telephone alone. No text was used, but a list of suggested readings was furnished. The telephone group was connected to a system in which all participants could speak to each other. Gains in knowledge were found in both groups, and there was no significant difference in the gain between the two classes. Although there was evidence of a novelty effect, the method appeared practical. Rao (1977) summarized the limited research on telephone teaching and concluded, ". . . the research done on the effectiveness of teleteaching indicates that teleteaching is an economical and effective tool" (p. 483).

In conclusion, audiotechnology such as the tape recorder, has been generally shown to be as instructionally effective in conventional teaching. In addition, such technologies lend themselves to special situations. The telephone obviously allows distance education where students are unable to attend classes. In addition, it appears that the tape recorder allows learning while asleep. Although it is difficult to assess the validity of these sleep-learning studies,

they point out that auditory media may have applications under conditions when conventional media are not feasible.

28.4 AUDIO-TUTORIALS

There are few cases of the large-scale, systematic application of audio technology to instruction. One interesting and extensive implementation of audio for instructional purposes is Postlethwaite's "audio-tutorial instruction" (ATI). This approach, which has been widely reported (Postlethwaite, 1970, 1972, 1978, 1980; Svoboda, 1978; Button, 1991), is more a complete instructional system than just an application of audio, but its long history and wide application make it an important source of information. Because of its well-elaborated structure, I will describe it in depth.

ATI began almost by accident in 1961 at Purdue University (Postlethwaite, Novak & Murray, 1972), when Postlethwaite was attempting to provide supplementary materials for weaker students in freshman botany. Simple lecture material was made available on a self-study basis through the audiovisual department. During the semester, these tapes evolved into programmed experiences that directed the students' attention to sections of the textbook, pictures, and diagrams, as well as live plants. Eventually experiments were added, and the entire week's study could be covered without attending any formal sessions. Student reaction was favorable, so in 1961–62, an experimental section of 36 students was taught entirely by audio-tutorial. Results on the conventional exam showed that the experimental group performed as well as the regular students. Interviews with the students led to the creation of a completely restructured course.

In designing the new course, Postlethwaite studiously avoided using words like lecture, recitation, and laboratory, which he felt connoted formality and passivity. The new course consisted of "independent study sessions," "general assembly sessions," "small assembly sessions," which included "integrated quiz sessions," and other small assembly sessions. Other additional activities were sometimes included.

The independent study session is the heart of Postlethwaite's system. Students would check into a special learning center with 36 booths equipped with tape recorders, movie projectors, and other materials. Armed with a list of behavioral objectives and the tape, the student would proceed through a series of activities. The tape was not a lecture. Rather it was a kind of programmed guide that would direct the student's attention to certain parts of the book or other materials. The tape acted as a kind of tutor, suggesting activities and pointing out important information. The student would perform experiments, read short segments of text, fill in diagrams or charts, view films, or examine specimens. The program could be interrupted at any time, and students could talk with other students or instructors if they were confused. Students could also omit activities if they felt they understood the content.

The general assembly sessions were held at the end of the week and were intended to support activities that could not be performed at the individual session, such as exams, guest lecturers, and long films.

The integrated quiz sessions had an especially interesting structure. About eight students would be seated around a table covered with items drawn from that week's objectives. On the assumption that the best way to learn about something is to teach it, the students would be asked to discuss an item chosen at random. The student would first name the object, relate it to the behavioral objective, and then explain or demonstrate the object to the class. Once all students had completed this graded, oral quiz, a 20-point written quiz was given.

Another interesting feature was that although a small project involving the collection and analysis of data was compulsory for all students, any students desiring a grade of "A" were required to complete a second, original project.

It appears that Postlethwaite was acutely aware that an audiotape-mediated course might take on the appearance of impersonality. To avoid this, several measures were taken. The tapes were made with an informal, conversational quality. The instructors in the learning center were apparently told to maintain a pleasant personal manner. The senior instructor spent 3 hours per week in the small quiz sessions, meeting with about 48 students. Another 3 hours were spent informally visiting the learning center. He also held a weekly coffee hour to which all students were invited. Finally, he held an open house (for 600 students!) at his home once a semester. Postlethwaite considered this emphasis on personal contact and a well-structured sequence of learning events to be the essential ingredients of ATI.

As a result of his experience, Postlethwaite and his colleagues (Postlethwaite, Novak & Murray, 1972) were able to provide guidelines for the production of audio-tutorial lessons: First, they emphasized the importance of behavioral objectives. All course objectives should be listed first and test questions should be written concurrently, if possible. Second, you should list on cards all activities needed to reach the objectives. This should include the medium of presentation of the activity. Third, you assign the activities to the different kinds of sessions, as appropriate. Finally, you arrange the activities in a proper sequence, taking into account prerequisite knowledge. Once this is completed, the program tapes can be produced. Postlethwaite also provided guidelines for this step: First, assemble the required materials for an activity and make a demo tape. It is helpful to have an average student present as you do this, because the student's questions will trigger necessary elaborations and will give the tape a true tutorial feeling. Next, transcribe the tape and edit it critically. This eliminates redundancy and imprecision. Finally, make the final tape from the edited script, which may have emphasis or other helpful markings added.

In the production of the actual tape, Postlethwaite gave the following guidelines: First, with regard to voice, use a conversational tone, speaking clearly and cheerfully. Vary your tone frequently. Speak rapidly. Avoid "uh's" and other annoying speech habits. Second, concerning the content,

aim for critical thinking. Do not lecture. Do not read the directions. Involve the students by directing their attention to actual things. Keep things simple but don't repeat, because the students can play back the tape if necessary. Proceed from the known to the unknown. Keep the lesson as short as possible, but be sure to clarify critical points. A variety of voices and sounds can increase realism. Finally, with regard to the mechanics, adjust the volume and tone to an appropriate level. Keep a constant distance from the microphone. To make corrections, find a natural pause in the conversation and begin there. Signal the student to stop the tape while performing an activity. A sound effect is better here than a spoken instruction that will have to be repeated many times.

Since a good part of design is avoiding errors, Postlethwaite and his colleagues listed some pitfalls associated with ATI. Since these pitfalls may be encountered with any mediated course, they are worth repeating. First, they list problems associated with the structure of ATI. One problem may be the lack of specific objectives. The sequencing of instructional events requires the clear specification of objectives. Also, ATI cannot be a lecture-on-tape. This is certain to be more boring than the original. Visuals that are too complex, lengthy, or irrelevant can detract from learning. Study materials that are unnecessary to the objectives are wasteful of time and money. Auxiliary experiences outside the learning center can be very valuable, but discussion and evaluative feedback are essential. Synchronization of mediated lessons with actual activities is difficult to predict and requires trial-and-error adjustment.

There are also psychological issues associated with ATI. First, the structure of the course is crucial to learning. Postlethwaite recommended Ausubel's subsuming structures, but augmented this where appropriate. Equally important, substructures of the course should also be paced and subsumed appropriately. This is very difficult to predict in advance, and almost always requires adjustment as a result of student feedback. Because older students have extensive vocabularies, direct experience is not always necessary, but when new concepts are being introduced, direct experience supports meaningful learning. Student feedback is essential to determining whether instruction is effective. On the other hand, feedback on small objectives may not be useful because it does not reflect the larger structure of the course, which is intended to clarify difficult concepts by repeated experiences. Finally, affective factors are easy to over- or underestimate. However, they cannot be ignored. Individualized audio-tutorial instruction capitalizes on the students' desire to be in control of learning, but it does not satisfy their social drives. For this reason, group work needs to be included.

In summary, in spite of the age of the Postlethwaite book (1972), it can still be recommended as a guide for the individualization of courses, especially where they are to be audiomediated.

Despite the widespread use of ATI, evaluation studies are not numerous. The common results reported (e.g.,

Postlethwaite, Novak & Murray, 1972) indicate that it is as good as conventional instruction with positive attitudinal ratings. However, there are a few reports of an advantage for ATI. For example, in Huppert and Lazarowitz (1990), 15 students used an ATI unit to learn cell biology. Standard classroom lab techniques were used with 65 others. Although the control group had significantly higher pretest scores, posttest scores were equal, indicating greater gains by the ATI group Also, higher-ability students tended to score higher with ATI. In another study, Carter and Cooney (1983) reported that undergraduates exposed to modified ATI in a statistics class showed a significant increase in performance, even under low-motivational conditions. Low motivation was indicated by the fact that students generally expressed the belief that the course was irrelevant to their career. Despite some methodological shortcomings, Carter and Cooney's effect size was 1.8 standard deviations, an astonishing gain under the circumstances. However, this gain was against a control group that received no instruction. Thus, these numbers reflect the effectiveness of ATI, not its superiority to conventional instruction.

The most comprehensive review of ATI is Kulik, Kulik, and Cohen (1979). This meta-analysis of 48 reports of ATI found a small but significant achievement effect for ATI over conventional instruction. However, ATI had little effect on course evaluations or withdrawal rates. Also, aptitude and achievement correlated highly, indicating that ATI does not have a leveling effect as might have been expected with such a self-directed, self-paced approach. Thus, the best available evidence seems to indicate that ATI does have a small positive effect on achievement, but given the fact that it does not seem to have other advantages over conventional instruction, it appears that its use can only be justified when special circumstances apply.

One kind of special circumstance is when well-trained content teachers are not available. An excellent example of this is elementary science education. Joseph Novak (of the previous Postlethwaite group) developed elementary science lessons using ATI. In an extensive longitudinal investigation of the effects of ATI, Novak and Musunda (1991) reported a 12-year study of science concept learning. Twenty-eight of their best science concept ATI lessons were provided to 191 first- and second-grade children. Each lesson required 15 to 25 minutes to complete. As with the Postlethwaite materials, students were directed by the tape to interact with materials and pictures. The lesson were sequenced according to Ausubel's ideas about subsumption. Lessons were replaced after all students in the class had a chance to interact at least once. With few exceptions, all students were capable of proceeding through the lessons. Grade-1 students completed lessons 1 to 16, and grade-2 students completed lessons 16 to 28. Lesson 16 was repeated. All lessons covered basic science concepts and principles. These children were compared by means of interviews to 48 uninstructed students in grades 2, 7, 10, and 12. Early on, the interviews included the use of tests with pictures or diagrams. However, these were later aban-

doned because they were judged to be confusing or misleading. Data collection evolved into Piagetian clinical interviews that were then translated into concept maps. Concept maps were then graded for valid and invalid notions. Instructed subjects showed significantly more valid concept understandings and fewer misconceptions. A significant interaction showed that instructed subjects, over the 12 years, had a greater tendency to increase their number of correct concepts and decrease the number of incorrect concepts. This exceptional study strongly supports the validity of ATI even under conditions where the instructors are not well trained. Valid concepts were learned from ATI and evidently "scaffolded" more learning throughout the children's 12 years of schooling.

In summary, audio-tutorial instruction is the most complete and most well-documented method of auditory presentation. It has a general record of success, and, although it is not noticibly superior to conventional approaches, it has many valuable ideas, even for other nonaudio forms of mediated instruction.

28.5 COMPRESSED SPEECH

Because people were found to learn as effectively from tape recordings as from live speech, a variation on research on auditory comprehension emerged. This research was based on a simple observation: People can comprehend speech faster than narrators can speak. If a technology for speeding up the delivery rate of a tape recording could be developed, an apparent gain in instructional efficiency might be realized. This simple idea has generated a large body of research.

28.5.1 Processing Capacity

One way of measuring cognitive processing capacity is the comprehension of words per minute (wpm). Conversation typically takes place at a rate of 12 to 150 wpm (Benz, 1971; Nichols & Stevens, 1957). Since in conversation, one is simultaneously listening and composing speech, it was assumed that perhaps another 125 to 150 wpm of unused capacity might be available in simple listening. Because the rate for speed reading (Taylor, 1965) is 250 to 300 wpm, it was assumed that that much capacity might be available for listening. In fact Fairbanks, Guttman, and Miron (1957) found that rates of up to 300 wpm were possible with compressed speech.

28.5.2 Compression Technology

In early studies, compressed speech was produced by playing back a recording at a speed faster than that used to make the original recording. While this method is simple to produce, the vocal pitch and intelligibility were affected. The limitations of the "speed changing" technique generally rendered research findings questionable.

Miller and Lichlinder (1950) first demonstrated the tape-sampling method accomplished by deleting segments of the speech signal. A switching device was used that turned off the signal periodically. Garvey (1953) performed further experimentation in compressed speech by editing out segments of the audiotape and splicing the ends of the retained tape together. While Garvey's technique was successful, it was deemed too tedious except for research purposes. Fairbanks, Everitt, and Jaeger (1954) produced the first electromechanical apparatus that allowed both the expansion and compression of recorded tape.

Technological developments in the 1960s improved the Fairbanks technique. Scott (1965) utilized a computer to dispose of empty time intervals between words and to sample the time interval occupied by words differentially. While the computer proved to be the best means of producing compressed speech, the cost of computer time negated the application of this approach for other than experimental purposes. Electronic developments of the last 2 decades have now allowed the mass marketing of completely electronic compressor/expander tape recorders.

28.5.3 Comprehension

Numerous researchers have varied the rate of compression and measured the resulting effect on comprehension. Fairbanks, Guttman, and Miron (1957) found little difference in comprehension of selections compressed to 141, 201, and 282 wpm. Diehl, White, and Burke (1959) determined that listening comprehension was unaffected by changes between 126 and 272 wpm. Foulke (1962) used both literary and technical presentations and found that listening comprehension was slightly higher in the 175- to 272-wpm range than the 272- to 375-wpm range, at which point an accelerated loss in listening comprehension occurred. Foulke and Sticht (1967) measured a 6% loss in comprehension between 225 and 325 wpm, and a loss of 14% between 325 and 425 wpm. These and other subsequent studies (Boyle, 1969; Carver, 1973; Foulke, 1968; Foulke & Stich, 1969; Rossiter, 1970; Sticht, 1968; Wasserman & Tedford, 1973; Williams, Moore & Sewell, 1983–84) indicated that as word rate is increased beyond about 250 to 300 wpm, there is a decline in comprehension. Recall that Potter's verbal short-term memory buffer has a capacity of about 1.5 seconds. At 300 wpm that is about 7.5 words. Since these words must be processed as concepts to be understood, and our conceptual short-term memory has a capacity of only five to seven items, a limit of about 300 wpm seems reasonable. Indeed, Carver (1982) found that the optimal rate (which sacrifices some comprehension) for both reading and listening is about 300 wpm, indicating that there is an innate bottleneck in human information processing beyond which improved technology cannot take us.

However, numerous intervening variables must be considered before a determination of the optimum degree of compression can be made (Duker, 1974). Researchers believe that the ability of subjects to comprehend compressed speech may be dependent on the difficulty of the material. Readability has sometimes been found to influence normal audio comprehension (May & Lumsdaine, 1958; Chall & Dial, 1948), but others (e.g., Molstad, 1955) were unable to replicate this finding. Foulke (1962) determined that the comprehension of a scientific selection was less than the comprehension of a literary work at normal speed. However, at various levels of compression, the comprehension scores of the scientific selection declined less than those for the literary selection. This phenomenon may be because the comprehension scores for the scientific selection were lower at the normal rate; therefore the range in which they could vary was relatively small (Duker, 1974). Fairbanks, Guttman, and Miron (1957) investigated the effect of time compression on messages of various difficulty levels. The study seemed to indicate that, within the range explored, listening comprehension did not depend on the difficulty of the listening material. Goldhaber (1967) and Reid (1968) found that comprehension decreased as wpm increased, and that simplified material was better comprehended than more difficult material. Carver (1982) presented data that relate reading difficulty with efficiency. His data showed that for college students, listening to compressed materials written at the eighth-grade level produced the greatest efficiency. Raising the difficulty level of the materials caused comprehension to drop off abruptly.

Comprehension may also be measured in terms of delayed recall. George (1970) studied various rates of compression and two levels of material difficulty. He determined that more was forgotten at the lowest levels of compression in a delayed measurement, 1 day and 1 week following treatment. George indicated that although simplified materials were accompanied by some initial forgetting, the amount of forgetting with the passage of time was less than with more difficult materials. Friedman, Freedle, Norris, and Orr (1966) conducted retention studies among college freshmen and sophomores at speeds ranging from 175 to 475 wpm. After a 30-day delay, the posttest was administered again. The retention for the two highest rates, 425 and 475 wpm, were 117% and 90%, respectively, of their first-session scores. These authors reported that information presented in compressed format is retained as well as information that has not been compressed. Foulke (1966) pointed out that forgetting is not limited to the recall of information presented at accelerated word rates. In other words, there is no indication that compression, within broad limits, has a unique effect on the retention of information.

Length of presentation may also be a factor in comprehension and memory. Adelson (1975) examined comprehension by a group of college students listening to a 1-hour lecture at 175 wpm, as compared to the same group of college students listening to an equated 1-hour lecture compressed at 275 wpm for 40 minutes. Compressed materials produced less comprehension than did the normal rate materials. The author concluded that with compressed materials, the length of presentation appeared to be a critical factor, perhaps because of attentional fatigue or other factors.

Narrators of both sexes differ in vocal pitch, average word rate, variation in word rate, pitch, and loudness (Foulke & Sticht, 1969). Foulke (1968) examined the extent to which these factors interacted with word rate in determining listening comprehension. Three versions of a selection were presented to college students at normal and compressed rates by narrators of both sexes. Significant differences in scores on a listening comprehension test were associated with the word rate variable, but narrator's style did not interact with rate. Rossiter (1972) had college undergraduates listen to short informative messages by both male and female presenters. Students were tested on the content of the messages. Data analysis showed an interaction of the sex of the speaker with the sex of the listener, but the author dismissed its importance, concluding that the sex of the speaker was not of much consequence in determining listening scores of subjects participating in the study.

Learner characteristics may influence the comprehension of compressed speech. Some of these variables include the subjects' sex, age, intelligence, and reading ability. Duker (1974) determined that the comprehension scores of male and female subjects revealed no sex-related differences for word rates varying from 174 to 475 wpm. This conclusion is supported by other research studies conducted by Foulke and Sticht (1967), Orr and Friedman (1964), Ross (1964), Bell (1969), Ludrick (1974), and Klavon (1975).

Fergen (1954) and Wood (1966) found that ability to comprehend compressed speech increases with age and grade level of school children. However, beyond age 12, little difference is noted until age 60 or so. Goldhaber (1970) found significantly better comprehension for junior high school students over college freshmen and sophomores. Goldhaber attributed the difference to the interest level and the level of motivation for each population. Duker (1974) agreed that the effects of age and education on the comprehension of compressed speech cannot be generalized. Lysaght (1969) tested elderly, middle-aged, and young adult subjects. He determined that elderly subjects performed lower on a posttest measuring comprehension. Duker (1974) noted that the decline in the ability to comprehend compressed speech may result from ". . . changes in the central nervous system" as opposed to the variable of age, per se (p. 494).

Aptitude or intelligence may also interact with comprehension. Eckhardt (1970) used a 1-hour multimedia presentation at various rates of compression with Air Force recruits of varying aptitudes. Eckhardt concluded that test differences between the groups were due to aptitude and an aptitude-rate interaction. There was a comprehension loss for lower aptitude subjects at the higher compression levels. Sticht and Glasnap (1972) determined that low-aptitude men learned easier material better than more difficult material as a function of decreased wpm. High-aptitude men tended to learn material best at 175 wpm, independent of difficulty level. However, other researchers (Sticht, 1968; Watts, 1971; Williams, Moore & Sewell, 1983–84) found that subjects with lower aptitudes or lower reading ability performed as well at higher rates of compression as at normal rates. Fergen (1954) found no relationship between the IQ of grade school children and their ability to comprehend compressed speech selections. On the other hand, Goldstein (1940) and Nelson (1948) found a positive relationship between intelligence and comprehension of compressed speech. Cicardo (1974) examined the retention of a compressed speech message presented to junior high school students of various intelligence levels. Cicardo determined that IQ level affects factual retention of material presented, but there appeared to be no interaction with rate. Foulke and Sticht (1969) pointed out that the relationship between lower intelligence and the decline in comprehension may be attributed to the lower scores of less intelligent subjects, which have a lower variance. For this reason, Foulke and Sticht (1969) and Duker (1974) argued that the difference in comprehension cannot be attributed directly to intelligence level.

Reading ability may influence comprehension of compressed speech. Breed (1977) tested adult vocational technical school students to determine the differences in listening comprehension when subjects were categorized according to reading ability. The subjects in Breed's study listened to tapes that were time expanded and time compressed, varying in rate from 60 to 240 wpm. Breed indicated that listening comprehension and reading ability appear to be related to verbal skills. The poorest readers exhibited the poorest listening comprehension, and better readers were better listeners as measured by scores on tests of listening comprehension. Goldstein (1940) and Orr, Friedman, and Williams (1965) found a positive correlation between reading rate and ability to comprehend compressed speech. Conversely, both studies further determined that practice in listening to compressed speech resulted in an improved reading rate. Robertson (1977) determined that the comprehension of subjects is not affected when they are presented recorded materials within two reading levels below or three reading levels above their particular grade level. In general, it appears that a relationship between better reading ability and the comprehension of compressed speech can be established, although this may reflect an underlying verbal ability.

28.5.4 Training

It has often been speculated that practice might influence comprehension of compressed speech. This research has attempted to provide appropriate training prior to treatment in order to improve comprehension. Voor and Miller (1965) exposed subjects to five listening sessions at 380 wpm. Test scores indicated that comprehension increased as a function of exposure up to 7 minutes, and remained constant thereafter. Orr, Friedman, and Williams (1965) exposed blind subjects to listening material presented initially at 325 wpm and increased in 25 wpm intervals to a rate of 475 wpm. Subjects were tested for comprehension at 475 wpm and compared to equivalent pretraining test scores. An improvement of 29.3%

was noted. Friedman, Orr, Freedle, and Norris (1966) compared the comprehension scores of subjects given 35 hours of massed practice with test scores of subjects given 14 to 21 hours of distributed practice in listening to compressed speech. The authors concluded that the comprehension of the distributed-practice group was as good or better than the comprehension demonstrated by the mass-practiced group. Duker (1974) suggested that gradually increasing the wpm rate might have some benefit on comprehension of compressed speech. Klavon (1975) tested this idea, without effect, in at attempt to provide a controlled transition period. In general, studies (Foulke, Amster, Bixler & Nolan, 1962; Friedman, Orr & Norris, 1966) have found that although no particular method of training or practice appears to be any more effective than another, even small exposure to compressed speech can improve comprehension.

28.5.5 Affective Factors

There are some interesting affective factors to consider when using compressed speech (see also 34.7). Listener attitudes toward the speaker are improved significantly (Maclachlan, 1982). Maclachlan notes that people associate fast, fluent speech with confidence, knowledge, and enthusiasm. Because attitude learning is influenced strongly by feelings toward the speaker, compressed speech may have an unexpected application in such situations. Additionally, college students prefer listening to compressed speech over normal tapes (Short, 1977), apparently because of the time savings. Also, for students under about 14 years old, there is a preference for listening over reading, presumably because of their slow reading rates (Boyle, 1969).

28.5.6 Efficiency

Recall that the original impetus for speech compression was potential efficiency. The instructional implications of using compressed speech for efficiency are limited. When the time saved in compression was used (Fairbanks, Guttman & Miron, 1957) to elaborate certain parts of the text, comprehension for that part of the text increased. But as Sticht (1971) pointed out, the time saved in compression was lost in elaboration, and overall comprehension was not improved. Similarly, hearing the same text twice at double speed resulted in no more learning than hearing the same text once at normal speed (Schramm, 1972). Thus it appears that the instructional use of compression cannot be based on efficiency arguments.

28.5.7 Summary

In conclusion, a great body of research has been done on speech compression. It has confirmed the hypothesis that listeners can process speech at a much higher rate than normal conversational speech, with some loss of comprehension.

Usually, any short exposure to compressed speech will result in improved comprehension. In general, no differences were detected for sex, or age between about 12 and 60. However, some differences in the ability to comprehend compressed speech may be due to aptitude or verbal ability. Compressed speech may be preferred to normal speech and may cause positive attributions to the speaker. However, the early hopes that it could lead to more efficient instruction appear to have been unjustified.

28.6 DISTANCE AUDIO EDUCATION

28.6.1 Radio

Although the history of the use of radio in education (see 13.4.2.8) is long, there is not a plethora of empirical data concerning its effectiveness (see also 13.4). Saettler (1990) gives an institutional history of early educational radio in the U.S., but does not mention more than a few empirical studies. After World War II, interest in instructional radio declined, so the situation has not improved.

Educational radio began at the University of Iowa in 1911 (Wolcott, 1993). The University of Wisconsin followed in 1919, and the Ohio School of the Air was established in 1929. Other "schools of the air" were established at many institutions, but the Wisconsin effort appears to have been the most successful, surviving until this day. Various attempts were made to evaluate the effectiveness of these broadcasts, and Saettler (1990) reports on two important ones. The first, the Ohio Evaluation of School Broadcasts Project, enumerated objectives that might be met by radio. Armed with these materials, the CBS American School of the Air was evaluated in 1940–41. It was determined that teachers who used the broadcasts found the broadcast extremely valuable. In spite of this, various defects were identified. First, purposes were not always well defined. Second, there was a need for printed aids. Third, there were errors of content selection which reflected a lack of understanding of the backgrounds of the pupils. Fourth, although the broadcasts were enjoyable, they were not as interesting as they might have been.

The second evaluation study, the Wisconsin Research Project, among other efforts, compared radio instruction with conventional instruction in six subject areas from 1937 to 1939. The differences were not significant, and only with music was the small difference in the direction of radio. Although there are not many other studies, those that exist (e.g., Constantine, 1964; NHK, 1956; Cook, 1964) typically showed that radio students performed at least equally as well as live audiences.

Bates (1983) reported that the British Open University's experience with radio instruction showed that the broadcasts tended to help the weaker students more than the successful ones. It must be remembered that Open University courses were taught primarily through correspondence texts and that the radio broadcasts were intended to supplement the texts. It is not surprising that students who found the texts difficult would welcome the added help afforded by the radio.

Radio is no longer widely used in education in the wealthier countries, but Wolcott (1993) reports that interactive radio is still used where long distances are involved, as in Alaska and Australia. In the poorer nations, radio is used widely because it is cost effective compared to other more sophisticated technologies. Radio is not expensive to produce or receive and can cover long distances using the AM band. The Agency for International Development (no date) reports that from 1974 to 1990 radio instruction programs existed in Nicaragua, Thailand, Kenya, Nepal, Dominican Republic, Papua New Guinea, Honduras, Bolivia, Lesotho, Costa Rica, Ecuador, Belize, Swaziland, and Guatemala. Reported results are encouraging. For example, in Bolivia effect sizes as large as .91 were reported for radio math as compared to traditional math. By dividing effect size by cost per pupil, a measure of cost effectiveness was obtained. According to data from the Agency for International Development, interactive radio was generally much more cost effective than textbooks or teacher training. In a related case study of radio-assisted community basic education (Eshgh, Hoxeng, Provenzano & Casals, 1988) in the Dominican Republic, gains in both math and reading as a result of radio instruction are reported.

In summary, as with other media, radio instruction has been found to be at least as effective as conventional instruction, although the literature is limited. Under certain circumstances, such as when conventional instruction is inadequate, the radio can be a cause of improved learning. Given the cost and reach of radio, it appears to be a viable medium in places where other media are too expensive or unavailable.

28.6.2 Other Media

In distance education, other recent audio-based technologies, besides radio, are now entering the field. Audioconferencing, both audio only and audioconferencing with images or data, is now possible through existing public telephone lines. Audiographic technologies such as the fax machine, the electronic blackboard, and both still and motion video images are becoming common. Use of high-speed data compression techniques will make these media more and more convenient and cost effective. Although these technologies are audio based, in the sense that they use telephone lines, they are not strictly speaking auditory and so will not be discussed here. A very complete study of these technologies and their limitations, along with suggestions to overcome those limitations, has recently been published (Wolcott, 1993), and the reader is referred to that source for further details (see also 13.4).

28.7 AUDITORY LEARNING VS. PRINT PRESENTATIONS

Since the general topic of multichannel presentations is covered in another chapter (see 29.3), it will not be discussed here. However there is some value to examining the specific question of the effects of learning the same material by listening or by reading. Olsen and Bruner (1974) stated that, "Each form of experience, including the various symbol systems tied to the media, produces a unique pattern of skill for dealing with or thinking about the world" (p. 149). Similarly, Salomon (1979) stated that, "Media's ways of structuring and presenting information—that is, their symbols systems—are media's most important attributes when learning and cognition are considered and should serve as the focus of our inquiry" (p. 216). These seem to imply that there should be some cognitive difference between listening to or reading a text.

This notion seems to contradict Clark's well-known hypothesis that media do not influence achievement. After an extensive review of the literature, Clark (1983) concluded that, "The best current evidence is that media are mere vehicles that deliver instruction but do not influence student achievement any more than the truck that delivers our groceries causes changes in our nutrition" (p. 445). He has defended his position by arguing that even where apparent differences are detected, they are rendered dubious by various forms of confounding. Some of the forms of confounding that Clark cited are the novelty effect, the "John Henry Effect," unequal instructional strategies, unequal opportunity to learn, and unequal quality of instructional design.

A comparison of learning from print or audio seems to provide a convenient test of Clark's hypothesis, because it is relatively easy to control both content and instructional strategy. Since both audio and print are used to convey verbal information, the essential difference between a print or audio presentation (if otherwise equal in quality) is precisely the medium of delivery.

28.7.1 Audio and Print

Reading and listening seem to demand the same underlying linguistic competence (Mosenthal, 1976–77). In general, comparisons of learning from audio and print have shown no difference, as Clark would predict. Nugent (1982) and Rohwer and Harris (1975) found no differences for children, while Nasser and McEwen (1976) found no difference for college students. Needless to say, this assumes that the printed text is within the reading ability of the student.

Other research on reading and listening sometimes suggests an advantage for dual-channel presentation. Some studies showed that recall was higher when the very same material was read and heard than when it was presented in one channel alone (Hartman, 1961; Nasser & McEwen, 1976). However, Nugent (1982) found no advantage with children for print plus audio over either print or audio alone.

Recent research in England may shed light on this question. The research has largely been done by a pair of scholars, Furnham and Gunter, and their colleagues while studying the effects of mass communication on the recall of factual information. These researchers are apparently unaware of Clark's hypothesis and thus have not addressed it.

Although Furnham and Gunter have found a variety of results under differing conditions, they have consistently found that subjects remember material presented in the print medium better than identical material presented in the audio medium or the audiovisual medium. Gunter (1987) concluded that this was due to the inherent capacities of these different media to convey knowledge. These differences were found for samples drawn from populations of schoolchildren, university students, military personnel, and nonstudents. Across these categories, the most consistent result was that subjects remember better from print materials than audio or audiovisual materials. Table 28-1 (adapted from Furnham, Gunter & Green, 1988) illustrates their findings.

Furnham and Gunter's research methodology may be best exemplified by their 1986 article (Gunter, Furnham & Leese, 1986). An approximately 5-minute television broadcast was delivered to university students in three groups. Group 1 received the TV broadcast in its normal form. (We are not concerned with this treatment here, but it is included for completeness.) Group 2 received the broadcast with audio only. Group 3 received a transcribed script of the broadcast. Time was held constant in all treatments. Memory was tested with free recall, cued recall, and multiple-choice questions, in that order. Results, as reported above, indicated that retention was always superior with print materials. Note that the content was designed for TV and that the print condition was the least "natural." These methods and results are typical. It is important to note that because these methods appear to be more rigorous than many of the earlier studies, and because the results have been replicated many times, they should be given greater weight.

Although Furnham and Gunter repeatedly found significant differences in achievement with print and audio, their work may have confounding factors. It is important to examine it in terms of Clark's list of possible confounds. First, it seems that the "John Henry" effect, the unequal

instructional strategies, and the unequal quality of design arguments can be dismissed as irrelevant. No teacher was involved, so the "John Henry" effect cannot have occurred. Second, the content delivered was identical in terms of text and time; therefore no differing strategy or quality could be involved. Again, remember that in many cases the print version was derived from an audioscript, so, if anything, the print version should have been "inferior" in quality.

Different media may not be equally "novel" or familiar. But in this case, it is unlikely that either print or audio would be perceived as novel, so this objection seems weak.

Possibly, reading may be superior to listening because of greater opportunity to learn. Although Furnham and Gunter held total time constant, it is normal that people can read faster than an announcer speaks. Thus the subjects in the print condition may have been able to read the text more than once. Clark mentions this "reviewability" problem in his original article, but this objection seems to be unwarranted. If print is inherently "reviewable," then it is precisely this quality of the medium itself which influences student achievement. Thus media do influence achievement.

In a recent study, Tripp (1994) tested the differences between audio and print in a direct comparison that attempted to hold other factors constant, including reviewability and novelty, by presenting the same text by computer through either the audio or video (printed text) medium while holding speed and reviewability. As with Furnham and Gunter, the students who read the text remembered significantly more correct semantic units than the students who heard the passage. Clark (personal communication) has suggested that affective factors such as those mentioned by Salomon (1984) may account for the differences, but my students expressed the belief that learning from "tapes" was more difficult than learning from "books." Contrary to Salomon, they also expressed the belief that they would

---

TABLE 28-1. AUDIO AND PRINT (Adapted from Furnham, Gunter & Green, 1988)

Content	Source	Ss	Results*
News	Gunter, Furnham & Gietson, 1984a	128 school children	P > A = AV
	Furnham & Gunter, 1985	68 students	P > A > AV
	Gunter & Furnham, 1986	117 military students	P > A = AV
	Furnham & Gunter, 1987	101 adults	P > A > AV
Political broadcast	Gunter, Furnham & Leese, 1986	65 students	P > AV > A
Ad	Furnham, Benson & Gunter, 1987	69 students	P > AV > A
Magazine program	Furnham, Proctor & Gunter, 1988	63 students	P > AV > A
Science program	Furnham, Gunter & Green, 1988	60 students	P > AV > A (free recall) P > AV = A (cued recall)
Insect biology text (easy and hard)	Furnham, Gunter & Green, 1988	60 students	P > AV = A (free recall, hard text) P > A > AV (cued recall, hard text) P > AV > A (free recall, easy text) P = AV > A (cued recall, easy text)

*P = paper; A = audio; AV = audiovisual.

also expend more effort with books. Thus, if these attributions transfer to audio and text presented by computer, students may have tried harder with text, but there was no external indication of this. In any case, whether achievement differences are attributable to intrinsic qualities of the medium or student attributions of intrinsic qualities, or an interaction between the two, in this highly controlled case student achievement did vary as a function of the medium of delivery to the detriment of the audio presentation.

Given the robust results demonstrated by Furnham and Gunter and replicated by Tripp with differing content and audiences, it seems that it must be concluded that print is superior to audio as a presentational medium, when the content to be delivered is to be held constant.

28.7.2 Conclusions about Auditory Instruction

There is a considerable body of evidence that audio presentations, through a variety of technologies, can be at least as effective as other forms of instruction, and audio-based media may be usable when other media or live presentations are impossible or impractical. However, the Furnham and Gunter studies indicate that when audio and print are identical and time is held constant, people learn more from print. Under normal instructional circumstances, however, this is not the case. Typically, audio presentations are adapted to suit the instructional situation. Under these modified conditions, there is no reason to doubt the effectiveness of audio. The best example of this is Postlethwaite's audio-tutorial method which uses audiotapes as a kind of programmed guide in a larger instructional system. This system has been widely implemented and may serve as a model for other forms of individualized instruction. Finally, although there has been a great deal of interest in compressed speech for instructional purposes and it has been demonstrated to be effective, its practical applications are limited.

28.8 LANGUAGE LABORATORIES

28.8.1 History

Because of the nature of their task, foreign-language educators have been heavily involved in the use of audio equipment. They welcomed the first audio device, the phonograph, and have immediately adopted other advances in audio technology such as magnetic tape and digital media. Unfortunately, the history of the use of audio technology to teach languages has not been duly noted by historians of educational technology. Paul Saettler, in his definitive *The Evolution of American Educational Technology,* only makes passing references to foreign-language teaching, and language laboratories are granted merely one paragraph (p. 187). It will be demonstrated that this disregard is startling in view of the extensive use of, and massive investment in, audio equipment by foreign-language educators. Moreover, it will be shown that the research that

accompanied these commitments has not been appreciated by the larger educational technology community.

28.8.1.1. History of the Use of Audio Resources in Foreign-Language Education: 1877 to 1945.   Leon (1962) and Peterson (1974) have documented the early use of audio recordings by foreign-language educators since the invention of the phonograph by Thomas Edison in 1877. By 1893 there were commercial record sets available for Spanish and English as a foreign language. The phonograph was used in regular classes and for self-study at home, but to what extent is difficult to ascertain. In their 340-page annotated bibliography of "modern" language methodology (the references commence in 1880s), Buchanan and MacPhee (1928) include only nine entries concerning the phonograph. Three of these are listings of recorded courses; none of the six articles is a controlled study of the merit of the phonograph. The 491-page Bagley et al. volume (1930) contains no mention of the phonograph. This paucity of references is surprising when one considers that in the 1880s the field of phonetics was born out of the effort to teach proper foreign-language pronunciation. The literature of the period is full of articles on phonetics, and many pronunciation textbooks and teaching materials were published. One would have expected greater enthusiasm in the language-teaching community for the equipment that could provide native speaker models.

According to a contemporary (Keating, 1936), initial use of the phonograph and other devices such as the stereopticon (an early slide projector) was haphazard, and interest waned because there was no real absorption of modern inventions into the teaching program (p. 678). The Depression may have prohibited a wider use of the phonograph in the 1930s. A definite discouragement to its use was the Carnegie-funded Coleman report of 1929, which stated that the reading skill should be emphasized (Parker, 1961). Nevertheless, it should be noted that the decade saw much interest in the use of radio for foreign-language instruction. From October 1935 (volume 20) through December 1946 (volume 30), the *Modern Language Journal* had a radio "department."

It is not until 1908 that there is any evidence of a laboratory arrangement of phonographic equipment (Léon, 1962). By this is meant a dedicated facility for foreign-language study. This lab was at the University of Grenoble in France. An American, Frank C. Chalfant, who studied there in the summer of 1909, appears to have been the one who brought the idea back to this country. He installed a "phonetics laboratory" at Washington State College in Pullman during the 1911–1912 academic year. Pictures of this installation in use show students listening via networked earphones. This lab also had a phonograph recording machine so that students could compare their pronunciation with the native-speaker models.

Near the time that Chalfant established his phonetics laboratory, the U.S. Military and Naval Academy set aside rooms for listening to foreign-language records (Clarke, 1918). Another early facility was set up at the University of Utah in 1919 by Ralph Waltz (1930). He moved to Ohio

State and built another lab about which he published several articles (Waltz, 1930, 1931, 1932). Waltz is usually credited with coining the term *language laboratory* in 1930 (Hocking, 1964). In fact, Chalfant had used it as early as 1916 in the Washington State College yearbook, the *Chinook,* and probably in the regional foreign-language education circles of which he was a leader. In any event, the preferred term until after WWII was "phonetics lab." During the 1930s many institutions established labs (Gullette, 1932), but, as in the case of the phonograph, discussions of their use did not loom large in the methodological literature. For example, the *Modern Language Journal*'s annual annotated bibliography of monographs and articles only had four entries prior to 1945 besides the three articles by Waltz. The bibliography of the language laboratory for the years 1938–1958 compiled by Sanchez (1959) only added four items to the total for the prewar period. Eddy (1944) and Whitehouse (1945) describe the equipment and use of two labs at the end of the period under consideration.

28.8.1.2. History of the Use of Audio Resources in Foreign-Language Education: 1946 to 1958.

The year 1946 is considered to mark the beginning of the modern language laboratory movement (Hocking, 1964; Koekkoek, 1959). The labs at Louisiana State University (Hocking, 1964) and the University of Laval in Quebec City, Canada (Kelly, 1969), were built that year. Whether these postwar labs owed anything to the previous phonetics labs is unclear, but probable. Claudel's (1968) use of "predecessor" (p. 221) expresses linkage. However, according to Koekkoek, "the beginning of the language laboratory movement was a new start, albeit with similar means and ends, rather than a direct expansion of the limited phonetics laboratory tradition" (1959, p. 4). Sanchez (1959) is ambiguous on the question. The earliest entry in his annotated bibliography of the "modern" language laboratory is a reference to a phonetics laboratory (Peebles, 1938), but he included the note "not related to the modern language lab, as such" (p. 231). The record at the universities of Iowa (Funke, 1949) and Tennessee (Stiefel, 1952) indicate continuity with phonetics labs. It thus appears that Koekkoek's statement must be tempered. Most institutions that built language labs after the war did so for the first time, whereas a few others updated their prewar phonetics labs.

A point of difference between phonetics labs and language labs were individual booths or carrels. Although the lab at Ohio State had long tables divided into "compartments" (Waltz, 1930, p. 28) by 18-inch-tall boards, these did not provide sufficient acoustic isolation (Schenk, 1930). Levin (1931) suggested that the facility he described would be improved by the installation of soundproof booths. These became standard equipment in the postwar labs. Labs of the period were principally audio installations, but movie, slide, and filmstrip projectors were sometimes present as well (Newmark, 1948; Hirsch, 1954).

Also at issue is the impulse for the modern lab movement. It is certain that the military's success in language training during the war caught the attention of the foreign-language teaching profession at large. In 1945, the *Modern Language Journal*'s annual bibliography began a separate category for the "Army" (Army Specialized Training Program, ASTP) method. It contained far more entries than any of the other 21 categories. Regarding labs specifically, Gaudin (1946) demonstrated enthusiasm for the Army experience in her design of a facility. Koekkoek maintained that "the language laboratory and its spread is a postwar development, fostered by a climate of experimentation which was stimulated by the Army language teaching program during the war" (1959, p. 4). Pictures of labs in the 1950s certainly have a military air to them. Students sitting in rows with eyes straight ahead suggests columns of soldiers at attention. The individual student in a booth wearing a headset evokes an image of a navigator or radar technician at his post on a ship or airplane.

Hocking (1964), however, adamantly denied that the ASTP method drove the establishing of labs. He is echoed by Barrutia:

> . . . we have Elton Hocking to thank for almost single-handedly trying to keep the record straight about the fiction of the supposed extended use of recording equipment and aural-oral techniques in the A.S.T.P. . . . the Army Specialized Training Program did not, as is so widely believed, pioneer language laboratories . . . (1967, p. 890).

To what then did Hocking and Barrutia attribute the postwar interest in labs? They cite the availability of magnetic tape and tape-recording machines from 1946. Hitherto, labs were outfitted with phonographs or wire recorders. These had several problems: Their sound fidelity was low, they were fragile, and they were difficult to edit. Plastic disc player/recorders such as the SoundScriber (first advertised in the *Modern Language Journal* in October 1946) were an improvement, but according to Hocking "the superiority of the tape recorder-reproducer was immediately apparent" (1964, p. 18), and the verdict of history confirmed this first impression.

This major technological improvement does not fully account for the language laboratory movement. Roughly concurrent with the invention of magnetic tape was the development of the audiolingual method. It is here that the ASTP can be given some deserved credit. It stressed the listening and speaking skills more than reading and writing—the priorities of prewar methods. The Army method relied much on small-group practice to develop the learners' aural and oral abilities. Another important feature of the ASTP was the preponderate use of native-speaker instructors. Stack connects these developments in equipment and methodology:

> The language laboratory owes its existence to the recognition that the spoken form of language is central to effective communication, and that it should have as large a share in instruction as do written forms. In order to implement this new orientation of language teaching, the textbook (which is essentially graphic) was supplemented by sound recordings of native speakers. The coincidental advent of the tape recorder created a fortuitous juncture of technology and pedagogy (1971, p. 3).

By 1958, in the United States there were 64 labs in secondary schools and 240 in colleges and universities (Johnston & Seerley, 1960). The passage of the National Defense Education Act that year ushered in a new phase in language laboratory history.

28.8.1.3. History of the Use of Audio Resources in Foreign-Language Education: 1959 to Present.

Responding to the challenge to Yankee know-how and American ingenuity by the Soviet's launching of Sputnik on October 4, 1957, Congress passed the National Defense Education Act, which President Eisenhower signed on September 2, 1958. The act sought to strengthen the teaching of mathematics, science, and foreign languages in America's schools. The intent of the foreign-language provisions of this important legislation has been described by Derthick (1959). The history of the language laboratory in the first years following the NDEA has been written by Parker (1961), Hocking (1964), and Diekhoff (1965). There was an explosion in the number of facilities, thanks to generous federal support: $76 million in matching funds by 1963 (Diekhoff, 1965). By 1962 there were approximately 5,000 installations in secondary schools (Hocking, 1964). Another 1,000 secondary schools had labs by 1964 (Diekhoff, 1965). This represents a thousandfold increase in the number of labs at the secondary level from 1958! Most of these were in medium-to-large school districts (Godfrey, 1967). Although colleges and universities were not eligible for equipment funds under the NDEA, they were caught up in the national enthusiasm for language study, and thus committed their own monies to labs. By 1962 there were 900 labs in higher education (Hocking, 1964). More postsecondary labs were built from 1965 when matching funds became available under Title VI-A of the Higher Education Act (Ek, 1974).

Unquestionably, the 1960s were the golden years of the language laboratory. Those involved in these facilities felt an urgent need to gather and compare experiences. William Riley Parker wrote this about the motivation for the first of the Indiana and Purdue universities–sponsored language laboratory conferences in 1960 (the others were in 1961, 1962, and 1965):

> . . . foreign language teachers feel themselves suddenly involved in a technological revolution, suddenly chin-deep in a tide of new demands upon their competencies, and they seek, some almost frantically, enlightenment and practical help (1960, p. v).

B. F. Skinner spoke at the first of these meetings (January 22, 1960) on the use of teaching machines for foreign-language instruction. One of the respondents to Skinner's paper was Robert Glaser. Neither of these men were foreign-language educators by training, but both were already well known in the educational technology community. Their presence at this conference is testimony both to the interest the larger educational community of the day had in foreign-language instruction and to the willingness of foreign-language professionals to accept insights from other disciplines, notably psychology. In addition to the Indiana conferences, there were many lab-related presentations at

meetings of the various professional associations to which language educators belonged: the Modern Language Association (MLA), the American Association of Teachers of French (AATF), the American Association of Teachers of German (AATG), and the American Association of Teachers of Spanish and Portuguese (AATSP).

A spate of books, articles, and dissertations also accompanied the flow of money and the many installations. Most of the entries in Davison's (1973) 780-item bibliography of the language laboratory from 1950 through 1972 are from the 1960s, and thus post-NDEA. The first edition of Edward Stack's textbook, *The Language Laboratory and Modern Language Teaching,* appeared in 1960. It should be consulted by those interested in the literature of the period, because it explains the terminology of installations and operations current at the time. Also appearing in the early 1960s were Hutchinson's monograph concerning labs in high schools (1961), and the technical guide to facilities by Hayes (1963). Léon's book *Laboratoire des Langues et Correction Phonétique* (1962), although written in French and published in France, circulated widely in this country, as evidenced by the numerous citations of it. The Scherer and Wertheimer (1964) book-length report of an experiment involving language labs will be discussed in the section on research. As for articles, hundreds appeared in all ranges of periodicals from school district newsletters to long-established refereed journals such as *The Modern Language Journal, Language Learning, Hispania, The French Review,* and *The German Quarterly.* A publication that focused on language laboratories, *The Audio-Visual Language Journal,* was founded in Great Britain in 1962. Both *The International Review of Applied Linguistics* and *Foreign Language Annals* carried articles about the language laboratory from their inceptions in 1963 and 1967, respectively. The major research articles of the period will be noted in a later section.

During the first half of the decade, language laboratory professionals held caucuses at the conventions of the Modern Language Association and the Department of Audiovisual Instruction, but they soon felt the need for their own organization. The National Association of Language Laboratory Directors (NALLD) was founded in 1965. The NALLD began publishing a newsletter the following year. The inaugural issue reported that at the first NALLD meeting in Chicago in December 1965, there had been much discussion of the lab director's job description and the problem schools face in recruiting qualified applicants. Job openings were featured regularly from the start of this publication.

The major technical development of note during the decade was the audiocassette (Dodge, 1968). The advantages of this were the lower price and smaller, lighter machines that could play it. However, it did have the drawbacks of lower fidelity and greater difficulty of editing by cutting and splicing. The quality of sound was eventually ameliorated, and the editing problem was not sufficient to prevent the cassette from replacing reel tape in language labs in the 1970s. Another technical advance was the speech compressor-expander (see 28.5). This device allowed a recording to be sped up (compressed) or slowed down (expanded). Articles on this technology were numerous in the general educational literature from the start of the decade. Paradoxically, it was not until 1978 that anything on it appeared in the NALLD Journal (Harvey, 1978). One would have expected a greater enthusiasm among the foreign-language community. The ability to slow down a tape would seem to be a boon to students struggling with a difficult passage. Moreover, variable-speed technology was not unknown in foreign-language teaching, for Hirsch (1954) had commended the use of the *sound stretcher* (p. 22) in the early 1950s.

Machines with a repeat or skip-back function came on the scene at this time as well. This feature permitted students to replay easily a tape segment, and thus was well suited to dictations and audiolingual listen-and-repeat drills. The cassette Canon Repeat-Corder L was first advertised in the *NALLD Journal* in the October 1970 issue. Aikens and Ross (1977) wrote an article in the same journal describing a reel-to-reel machine they fabricated. By the end of the decade, the major manufacturers, such as Sony and Tandberg, were producing machines with skip-back capability.

Language laboratories ended the 1960s on a mixed note. On the one hand, federal funding was diminished:

> . . . the amount of equipment funding in Title III-A of the National Defense Education Act (NDEA) and Title VI-A of the Higher Education Act (HEA), two large sources for equipment funds, dropped from an allotment in fiscal year 1968–69 of $91.24 million to nothing in fiscal year 1969–70. The portent of this budgetary reduction is not as black as it might seem: any program for which the federal government is still offering subsidy, e.g., bilingualism, poverty, etc., still has access to equipment funds, but the inflated years of the mid-sixties have come to a close (Dodge, 1968, p. 331).

On the other hand, Smith (1970) did not lament this decline in federal support as entirely negative, because he candidly acknowledged that "the recent years have seen much professional neglect and misuse of the language laboratory (p. 191). He sensed a positive development in the unanimous agreement that the laboratories should be used to "individualize instruction," in the university community and provide the corresponding "increase in expenditures for equipment and materials for tutorial and individualized instruction" (p. 192). Heinich (1968) also commented on the problems associated with labs and the insights that were gained by both language educators and instructional technologists:

> The *language laboratory* movement threw content and media specialists together in an intimate working relationship that produced very strange and startling experiences. For the first time, language teachers discovered that the mode and materials of instruction interact with instructional behavioral objectives and methods. Many language teachers did not understand that a language laboratory requires a different method of instruction: that print stimulus methods are not audio stimulus methods. On the other hand, the audiovisual specialist was shaken out of a comfortable

bookkeeping-procurement function and introduced, often for the first time, to the rigors of developing curriculum materials to meet specific curricular objectives. The novelty of the roles played by both has caused so many difficulties that the language laboratory has not yet reached its potential value. One of the lessons learned by audiovisual directors in this encounter is the incredible quantity of materials required by technology when media are used for direct instruction. The classroom teacher, at the same time, was experiencing another instance of shared responsibility with media (pp. 50–51).

The 1970s and early 1980s were a period of malaise for the language laboratory. Coinciding with the drying up of funds was a sharp dropoff in the number of articles published. An index of this change can be seen in the ACTFL yearbooks. The first two volumes contained the articles by Dodge (1968) and Smith (1970), with 84 and 95 citations, respectively. The 1971 volume had one paragraph about labs and two references! From then on until 1983, many volumes contained no mention of labs, and those that did accorded a page at most. Labs had their vocal defenders to be sure (Jarlett, 1971), but frank avowals of their problems (Altamura, 1970; Racle, 1976) and their need for revitalization (Strei, 1977) were prominent.

A turnaround in the decline of the language lab could be seen from the early 1980s. A 3-day colloquium with the theme "A Renaissance for the Language Lab" was held at Concordia University in July of 1981 (Kenner, 1981). McCoy and Weible maintained that the recent "revival of interest in language laboratories" was "directly attributable to the 'domestication' of the tape recorder, made possible through the invention of the audiocassette" (1983, p. 110). What this indicates is that it took nearly 2 decades for the audiocassette to fully work its way into the instructional mores of teachers.

The lab of the 80s was not to be limited to audio technology. The year 1983 saw the founding of the Computer Assisted Learning and Instruction Consortium (CALICO), a group that was (and still is) dominated by language educators. It should not be thought that the invention of the personal computer in the late 70s was solely responsible for the interest in computer-assisted language instruction (known as CALL). Mainframes had already been much used for this purpose, most notably in the PLATO system at the University of Illinois. Computers were welcomed for their potential, but cautions were issued about the need to avoid the unrealistic expectations associated with early language labs and the need to learn other lessons from language lab history (Marty, 1981; McCoy & Weibel, 1983; Lemon, 1986; Pederson, 1987; Otto, 1989).

Ely's *Bring the Lab Back to Life* was published in 1984. In 1985 the president of the International Association of Learning Laboratories (IALL, the new name for the NALLD as of November 1982), Glyn Holmes, could affirm that the professional group was showing new signs of *vitality* (Holmes, 1985, p. 5). This rebirth was also indicated by volumes 18 and 19 of the ACTFL Foreign Language Education Series, which were devoted entirely to technology (Smith, 1987, 1989). With new life came a new look. By 1989, Otto could write that "language laboratories have been redefined as multimedia learning centers that deliver computer and video services to faculty and students in addition to familiar audio resources" (1989, p. 38). Since 1988 the reinvigorated IALL has published several monographs dealing with learning-center design and pedagogical use (e.g., Stone, 1988) and has produced several "video tours" of facilities around the country.

A further sign of the broadening of focus of language laboratories is the greater attention placed on reading and writing. A prime example of the former is the popular series of software produced by the Transparent Language Company. The Systeme-D writing assistant program of Heinle & Heinle Publishers is an indication of the latter. Major research has accompanied its usage (Bland et al., 1990).

The use of video is firmly established in foreign-language teaching. A prominent instance is the innovative first- and second-year French course that appeared in 1987, French in Action. Interestingly, an early leader in the post-NDEA labs, Pierre Capretz, was the driving force behind it. French in Action and its subsequent Spanish equivalent, Destinos, received major funding from the Annenberg Foundation and are broadcast on many Public Broadcasting System stations.

28.8.1.4. Conclusion.   Surely language laboratories represent the single largest investment and installment of audio resources in education. It is no accident that the foreign-language teaching community has been heavily involved in using audio. Audio has face validity in foreign-language instruction simply because much of language use is oral/aural. Granted, there has been concern that the reading and writing skills might be neglected in methodologies that make much use of recordings such as audiolingualism. Nevertheless, for foreign-language educators it has never been an issue of whether to use audio; it has been a question of how.

28.8.2 Research

The preceding historical account detailed the growth and extent of a particular application of audio technology. What has not yet been assessed is the effectiveness of this massive expenditure of effort and money. This is the task of research. This section will give the main currents of research for each period in the language laboratory's history. Details of each study will not be mentioned except insofar as they are crucial to interpreting the chief findings. The bibliography will permit the interested reader to locate and directly consult the reports cited for further information about the design and conditions of each study.

28.8.2.1. Research on the Use of Audio Resources in Foreign-Language Instruction: 1877 to 1946.   There appears to have been very little attempt to provide an empirical justification for the use of the phonograph and phonetics laboratories before World War II. This is not entirely surprising, given that before the 1960s very few foreign-language scholars had training in quantitative experimental techniques: They were humanists schooled in literary and philological research methods. There are, however, accounts of problems with the use of phonographs and phonetics labs which can perhaps be classified as observational research. These observations will be noted, for they raise issues that were to be examined more rigorously later. Moreover, these records demonstrate that there was some notion of accountability among those who used early audio resources. That is, the phonograph and phonetics labs were not accepted and used uncritically.

Based on his *long experimentation,* C. C. Clarke (1918, p. 120) provided the first guidelines to appear in the scholarly literature on the proper use of the phonograph in teaching foreign languages. He granted that some teachers found the *mechanism* (p. 122) troublesome, time-consuming, and distracting. To this he countered that it afforded learners the opportunity to hear consistent native-speaker models that never suffered fatigue. He concluded that "the true success of the speech record is in teaching pronunciation and that nothing else should be expected of it" (p. 120). The emphasis on pronunciation training certainly became the hallmark of the phonetics laboratories. Waltz, the founder of the lab at Ohio State University, also cited the benefit of having tireless native-speaker models to imitate. By having the "constant control sounding in his ears" (p. 29), the student could exclude the imperfect approximations of his peers and gain confidence in his own speaking ability. However, a colleague of Waltz, Emma Schenk, complained that the earphones did not adequately keep out others' voices (1930). In addition, she complained of the poor audio quality and the lack of supervision in the Ohio State lab. She worried that students would "cultivate errors" (p. 30). She also noted much cheating on time slips and many students who were not on task while in the lab. Levin (1931) was sympathetic to labs and sought to offer constructive criticism of their use. He stressed the need for immediate feedback so as to avoid the problem Schenk had feared, namely, the development of bad speech habits. Gullette (1932) showed that this fear was justified. He noted with consternation that many students working alone in the lab reverted back to the poor pronunciation practices that earlier had been eradicated in class drill sessions. He stressed that imitation was not sufficient; what was needed was ear training such as was done in music classes. This would allow for self-diagnosis and correction.

Waltz's report (1932) of two studies he consulted on, but did not conduct himself, is the first record of an attempt to establish empirically the phonetic/language laboratory's effectiveness. It is ironic, in view of the identification of the language laboratory with foreign languages, that neither investigation involved their teaching! The first experiment had to do with the teaching of the Irish accent; the second was concerned with correct English diction. Both studies can be faulted for the low number of subjects (20 and 24), the apparent nonrandom assignment of subjects to treatments, and the lack of statistical analysis beyond a comparison of group means. Nevertheless, Waltz did note that the groups were equivalent by using scores on standardized tests of intelligence, hearing, and pitch discrimination. In the first study, the lab group's mean was 10.1 (out of a possible 20 points). The control group's mean was 8.04. In the second study, both the lab and nonlab groups showed similar gains. Waltz argued that the comparable improvement was actually evidence in favor of the efficiency of the lab: Class and instructor time was saved by having students work independently in the lab.

For the sake of comprehensiveness, Peebles' master's thesis (1938) must be mentioned. It was included in the annotated bibliography compiled by Sanchez (1959). Students who volunteered to use the Phonetics Laboratory at the University of Colorado and who received one or two French pronunciation tutorial sessions were compared with students who did not avail themselves of these opportunities. Amazingly, she did not specify how much the volunteers used the lab. Neither were the total number of subjects, nor the number of subjects per group, specified. These omissions bespeak a blatant lack of control that invalidates any conclusions that might be drawn from her data, which in fact consisted only of mean numbers of pronunciation mistakes on a posttest.

28.8.2.1.1. Summary. Obviously, no firm conclusions can be drawn about the effectiveness of the phonograph and the prewar phonetics laboratory from these few observations and two cursory investigations. There appears to have been a consensus among practitioners that the best use of this equipment was for pronunciation training. All saw a potential benefit in untiring, consistent, native speaker models for students to imitate. However, complaints were raised about the sound quality of recordings, and it was observed that many learners lacked the self-monitoring ability to profit fully from them. Just as the next period of language laboratory history saw an increase in the number and sophistication of facilities, so there was similar growth in the inquiries concerning their value.

28.8.2.2. Research on the Use of Audio Resources in Foreign-Language Instruction: 1946 to 1958. Language laboratory research of the postwar and pre-NDEA period may be described as nascent. Certain features of empirical research are seen; some are only partially present, and others are completely absent. For example, one sees the first use of standardized tests as criterion measures, and this use is universal. On the other hand, only one study (Allen, 1960) randomly assigned subjects to treatments; intact classes were used otherwise. Only two-group designs and *t* tests were used. The number of subjects, when reported, was uniformly low. There certainly was not an agreed-upon research agenda. In fact, researchers of the day were either unaware of what their peers were doing (there is little citation of others' work) or they simply ignored it. With these limitations in view, the following discussion will list five studies of the period in chronological order and present

their conclusions. According to Kelly (1969), more experiments were conducted than this number would suggest, "but we only know of those whose authors had the time and energy to write articles about them" (p. 245). This is corroborated by Johnson and Seerley (1960), who refer to studies done at a high school and two universities (all unnamed) and of research that was planned at the University of Massachusetts.

Stiefel's description (1952) of the language laboratory at the University of Tennessee and its usage is barely beyond the anecdotal level. Yet its mention of the University of Chicago language investigation tests and the cooperative tests (created by the forerunner of Educational Testing Services) does represent the first, inchoate desire of those involved in language labs to have an objective benchmark with which to compare groups of learners who used the lab with those who did not. In this case, Stiefel compared the scores of lab classes on these measures and on an in-house test with classes from previous years. Thus, this is an ex post facto study. He noted higher scores for lab groups on the in-house tests, but he was hesitant to draw any strong conclusions from these. He found that both groups were comparable on the standardized tests. This he took as heartening evidence that the reading ability (as measured by the cooperative test) of the lab groups did not suffer because of their emphasis on the listening and speaking skills. This last point was of great concern to the scholarly community of the day, as further evidenced by the following study.

Supported by a grant from the Carnegie Foundation for the Advancement of Teaching, Brushwood and Polmantier (1953) at the University of Missouri sought to determine whether dialogue repetition and memorization in the language lab increased learners' aural skills. Although for administrative reasons they were unable to randomly assign subjects to treatments, these researchers did take the trouble to administer the Iowa Foreign Language Aptitude Test to the intact classes that constituted the treatment groups. Moreover, the researchers obtained access to the scores on two English proficiency tests that all the subjects had taken previously. All these tests revealed that the control and experimental groups were matched on these measures, as they were in age.

Four groups were formed: two groups of 19 subjects each who were enrolled in elementary Spanish, and two groups of 23 who were enrolled in elementary French. The control groups simply attended the standard 5-hour per week (1 hour daily) course as taught at the University of Missouri. The experimental groups covered the same material (grammar, reading, and composition) as the control groups, but did so in 4 hours instead of 5. The experimental groups also attended two 1-hour laboratory sessions during the first 4 days of the week. In these sessions, they worked with a dialogue written for the experiment that incorporated the grammar and vocabulary that was studied that week. The work consisted of listening to the dialogue via earphones and chorally repeating it until it was memorized. A graduate student or upperclassman lab attendant controlled the tape player and thus directed the sessions. His or her only other task was to correct gross pronunciation errors. The experimental group then had a fifth class session in which the regular instructor had the students review and act out the dialogues. The dialogue was then manipulated by changing number, person, tense, object, etc., as a transition to free conversation. This fifth hour was deemed "the crucial point in the achievement of the oral-aural objective" (p. 8).

At the end of the semester the groups were given the cooperative tests on reading, vocabulary, and grammar, and an aural comprehension test created for the experiment. For whatever reason, both *t* tests and *F* tests were calculated for the two Spanish and two French groups, but no tests were run on a combination of control and experimental groups across languages. The results showed that there were no significant differences on the cooperative measures. There were significant *t*s, but not *F*s, in favor of the experimental groups on the aural comprehension test.

This study can be faulted on several grounds, but perhaps the most serious flaw may be the lack of control for amount of instruction. Although the authors claimed that the 2 hours of lab practice for the experimental groups were in lieu of homework required of the students in the control groups, it must be noted that the lab sessions were scheduled and monitored. Whether students in the control sections did their work or not is unknown. Moreover, the significant difference between the groups on aural comprehension was measured by a nonstandardized test, the validity and reliability of which is open to question. All of these criticisms aside, Brushwood and Polmentier's study was certainly more rigorous than previous investigations of the use of audio resources in foreign-language teaching.

Next in chronological order are two ex post facto studies that are included here for the sake of completeness. The first is the description by Fotos (1955) of the use of the language laboratory at Purdue University. In direct opposition to the Brushwood and Polmentier study, the lab at Purdue was used for "*predrilling* [emphasis added] the student on the French text of the basic grammar or reading lesson" (p. 142). Fotos reported that students in first-year French scored 60.1 on the cooperative tests; second-year students scored 71.3. The national averages were 56.7 and 68.8, respectively. Whether this was a significant difference cannot be ascertained.

Mueller and Borglum (1956) looked at correlations between lab attendance and course grade, final exam score, and cooperative test score at Wayne University. They noted that students who voluntarily attended the lab more than the minimum requirement of 30 minutes per week generally did better on these measures. They drew special attention to the heavy lab users' 10% increase on the cooperative reading test: "an unprecedented jump in 8 years of recorded scores" (p. 325). Moreover, they observed that even students who only attended the lab 30 minutes per week scored better than students from previous years who had no lab experience. They also noted a lower drop rate for heavy lab users. One can surmise that greater time-on-task natu-

rally produced greater learning. In their discussion, Mueller and Borglum also acknowledged a significant teacher effect: The lab's director "succeeded in getting the students of his sections to attend the laboratory 2 or 3 times more frequently than other instructors" (p. 322).

Allen (1960) conducted a study during the 1957–58 academic year which represents the last investigation of language laboratories in the 1946–58 period. The 54 subjects were 15- and 16-year-old students in a high school operated by Ohio State University. Allen created eight groups based on level (elementary or intermediate), language (French or Spanish), and use of the lab (55 minutes per week or none). These divisions made for groups as small as five. He administered three standardized tests in order to have a basis for pairing subjects. Once the pairs were established, he used a random-choice technique to assign students to the lab or nonlab treatments.

The lab groups spent one classroom hour listening to instructor-made tapes of "humorous or suspenseful tales" (p. 355) and answering questions about them in the target language. They recorded their answers and then spent the rest of the period listening to commercially prepared recordings. There was absolutely no written material presented during the lab hour. The nonlab group read the same stories and answered the questions in writing. If any time remained, they did free reading from a collection of books at their level.

At the end of the school year, all groups were given three standardized tests (including the cooperative) that measured reading, vocabulary, grammar, speaking, and listening. Allen only reports means and standard deviations. In all cases except one, the laboratory groups scored identical to or higher than the nonlab groups. The exception was the Intermediate Spanish lab group ($n = 5$), which scored lower on the speaking test. In several cases, the differences between the means were large, but Allen did not compute any test of significance. In his brief conclusion, however, he claimed that the laboratory groups "achieved significantly higher scores in reading, vocabulary, and grammar" (p. 357), but that there were no differences in speaking or listening. This author calculated a *t* test on the cooperative French test means for the largest groups, those in Elementary French ($n = 10$ each). The lab group had a mean of 57 (s.d. = 23); the nonlab group mean was 39.4 (s.d. = 20). This turned out to be significant at the 0.001 level.

It is fitting that the last of the studies of the 1946–58 period should be the one with the highest methodological standards. Yet the number of subjects was quite low for the design chosen, and it is baffling that Allen claimed to have found a significant difference in favor of the lab groups, but did not bother to report any data beyond means and standard deviations. Moreover, it is ironic that reading, grammar, and vocabulary scores were enhanced by listening in the language laboratory, whereas listening scores proper did not reveal any difference between the lab and nonlab groups. Thus, Allen's study gives weak but curious evidence of the language laboratory's contribution to foreign-language learning.

28.8.2.3. Summary. Writing in the early 1960s, Carroll (1963) stated that virtually all previous foreign-language research "has only rarely been adequate with respect to research methodology" (p. 1094). For him, language laboratory research was not an exception to this rule. He briefly reviewed three studies concerning labs; these were not included in this section because they did not contain important results, were not widely circulated at the time (two were institutional reports), and were not cited by subsequent researchers. Therefore, what one can conclude from Carroll's review and this summary is that while the research during the 1946–1958 period did not firmly establish the positive value of language laboratories, it did provide circumstantial, and in one case (Allen, 1960) empirical, evidence in favor of this conclusion.

Writing at the close of the period under consideration, Koekkoek (1959) stated that labs were so "firmly established" in language teaching that "no teacher can remain today unaffected and disengaged" (p. 5). He went on to describe the ambivalence about them within the profession and closed his article with the hope that subsequent experience would resolve "basic questions to be expected from the use of laboratory machines and the best methods of obtaining the results" (p. 5). If the nascent body of research could only offer a cautious "thumbs-up" assessment, it also showed that those promoting labs were willing to be held responsible for their use. This was fortunate, for during the next phase of the lab's existence, a period of great growth because of major expenditures, the public would eventually demand an accounting.

28.8.2.4. Research on the Use of Audio Resources in Foreign-Language Instruction: 1959 to the Present. The massive increase in the number of language laboratories, thanks to the NDEA, prompted a comparable increase in the amount of research concerning their effectiveness. In fact, some of the studies were funded by the NDEA under its Title VI provisions. The extent of this research is such that this section cannot detail every investigation that was undertaken. The several dissertations listed by Davison (1973) will not be treated. This discussion will focus on four large-scale studies of labs: three in high schools and one in a university. These all received much attention at the time. Moreover, those studies that have been thoroughly reviewed elsewhere will be only briefly described.

During the 1961–62 school year, Keating (1963) conducted a study of the use of the language laboratory in French classes in New York City high schools. He cited Allen's study (1960) as the "only exception" (he was evidently unaware of the Brushwood & Polmantier study) to the rule that "the literature abounds with articles that describe the benefits of using language laboratories" but "contains virtually no reports upon the empirical validation" (p. 8) of them. He called Allen's results "quite interesting" but noted a possible Hawthorne effect, which he felt "severely compromised" (p. 8) them. Keating knew of the research being simultaneously conducted in New York City by Lorge (to be described later).

Keating's was a large-scale study involving approximately 5,000 subjects in 21 school districts. Schools were divided between laboratory and nonlaboratory users based on a questionnaire filled out by each district's foreign-language coordinator. Besides this factor, groups were formed according to year of study (first through fourth years) and IQ scores (five levels). The dependent measures were reading comprehension, listening comprehension, and speech production. The cooperative test was used to test the first two skills; however, first-year students were not given the listening portion because it was designed for intermediate and advanced students. The French speech production test was used to evaluate speaking. This instrument was constructed specifically for the study. Of note is that it was not administered to all subjects: only 519 students from 12 of the participating school districts were given it. The results showed a sole significant finding in favor of the lab groups, on speaking among first-year students. Otherwise, there were several cases of the nonlab groups scoring significantly higher.

Keating's findings were promptly and vehemently disputed. The April 1964 issue of the *Modern Language Journal* included four rebuttals (Anderson, Grittner, Porter & Porter, Stack). The criticisms showed much overlap. Keating was taken to task for numerous methodological flaws: failure to define what was meant by language laboratory and the activities that went on there, failure to control for amount of time spent in the lab, failure to control for the socioeconomic level of the schools and the quality of their lab installations, use of *t* tests when ANOVAs were called for, and sloppy reporting of results (the number of subjects per group was not consistent). Keating was also criticized for using several different IQ tests, rather than one, to group subjects. The validity of his speaking test was challenged for being in fact only a pronunciation measure. Keating was shown no mercy: Despite the disclaimers he gave about the generalizibility of his results, he was accused of spreading anti-lab propaganda by Grittner.

Because the literature of the period contains no defense of Keating's study, it can be concluded that it was dismissed by the scholarly community of the day. Unfortunately, the public was of another mind. It seized on the notion that if language laboratories are not useful, then the massive investment of tax dollars in facilities was a waste. An example of this attitude was a newspaper editorial about the Keating study entitled "Backwards Via 'Aid'" that was reprinted in the *Modern Language Journal* issue containing the four rebuttals. Such a response gives credence to the propaganda charge made by Grittner. He and Stack and Anderson pointed out, with great dismay, that the Institute of Administrative Research of Columbia Teacher's College, which had sponsored Keating's study, mailed out a five-page preliminary report to school administrators across the country. They viewed such an action as unprofessional; it was clearly inflammatory in its impact.

Lorge (1964) conducted two experiments in New York City high schools. The first took place during the 1961–62 school year, and the second was done the following year. Thus, the first study coincided with Keating's investigation. Whether there was any overlap of subjects between the two studies is unknown, but could hardly be problematic given that only two schools were involved in Lorge's first inquiry; Keating's entailed 21 districts. Lorge described the purpose of her study thus:

> The object of the study was not to compare what a student learns from a teacher alone as opposed to what he learns from laboratory work alone. The question was whether the teacher improves the teaching-learning situation by using the laboratory as a teaching aid. The research was intended not to give the laboratory a passing or failing mark—if it passes, use it; if it fails, rip it out—but rather to determine in which areas it had proved to be successful, and how its use could be made more effective (p. 409).

The first study compared first-, second-, and third-year French classes. Unfortunately, the number of classes and subjects is not specified in the article, and the full report of the study is not available for consultation; by 1965 it was already out of print (Lorge, 1965). All that is known is that the classes were determined to be comparable based on the Stanford reading test and the Gallup-Thorndike vocabulary test. Half of the classes had 60 minutes a week of supervised lab practice in lieu of a fifth class period. The other half had five class meetings. The course content was the same for both groups. At the end of the school year, all classes were given the cooperative French test to gauge reading, vocabulary, and grammar skills. A speaking test and a listening test, both written by the experimenters, were also administered. All the tests contained subtests for which separate statistics were calculated. There were no differences between the groups on the cooperative test. The first- and second-year laboratory groups tested significantly higher than the control groups on the fluency component of the speaking test. The second-year laboratory group also scored significantly higher on the intonation component. The third-year laboratory group was significantly superior in listening.

The second experiment compared two types of laboratory equipment: audio-active and recording-playback. The first was a headset with earphones and a microphone; the second was an identical headset plus a tape recorder for each student. The other factor was time. Daily usage of 20 minutes was compared to a once-a-week 60-minute session. Five groups of second-year French students were formed. It should be stressed that none of the subjects had previous laboratory experience. Moreover, during the study, the control group did not use any equipment. The other four groups were formed by crossing equipment type and usage time. The dependent measures were the same as in the first study, with the addition of a mimicry test.

The *t* test results from the 14 components are difficult to interpret. Some differences are reported at a .01 level of significance, others at a .05 level, but it is impossible to determine whether one group was significantly higher than all the other groups or only some of them. The rankings that

were also reported are more helpful, for they allow trends to be detected. On measures of enunciation, the order was thus: (1) daily record-playback, (2) daily audio-active, (3) weekly record-playback, (4) weekly audio-active, and (5) control. Thus greater time, frequency, and more elaborate equipment favor one aspect of the speaking skill. However, as regards lexical and syntactic features of speech, the control group was ranked first, with the daily record-playback group coming in second. This finding should be considered along with the result from the composite score on the cooperative test. Here, the daily record-playback group ranked first and the control group was second. The difference between the two groups was not significant, but both groups were significantly higher than the other three groups. What emerges is this: The daily record-playback group and the control group scored similarly, and significantly better than the other groups, on both oral and written measures of vocabulary and grammar.

From the above findings, one is tempted to draw an "all or nothing" conclusion: Either use a fully equipped lab daily or dispense with it altogether. It seems that certain outcomes will be the same in either case. The corollary is that infrequent usage of a modest lab actually appears to be detrimental to the lexical and syntactic aspects of language learning! However, Lorge does not make such a counterintuitive deduction. She noted that in the first study, there were no differences between the lab and nonlab groups on the vocabulary and grammar tests. In the second study, she maintained that any measure showing statistically significant differences showed at least one laboratory group that equalled or exceeded the gains made by the control group. This appears to indicate that time spent in the laboratory contributes to conventional learnings as well as to listening and speaking skills (p. 419).

The last sentence is crucial. Taken together, these studies indicated an overall advantage for the language lab. Lorge also noted that a higher percentage of students in lab sections continued studying French beyond the 3 years required for high school graduation and college admission.

Lorge's study appears to have been well received by the scholarly community. Stack (1964) praised Lorge's work in his critique of the Keating study. Only Green (1965) ventured criticisms. Some of his complaints had to do with the manner in which the results were reported. He was more concerned with the apparent addition of another group after the study was underway. Lorge (1965) answered these objections easily in her rebuttal, which was included in the same issue of the *Modern Language Journal* as Green's piece.

In 1966, Philip D. Smith began an investigation of beginning high school French and German teaching and learning, which lasted through 1969. It was sponsored by the Federal Office of Education under Titles VI and VII of the NDEA and is commonly referred to in the literature as the Pennsylvania project because all the participating schools were in that state. Smith summarized his findings in 1969 articles in *Foreign Language Annals* (Smith, 1969a) and the *French Review* (Smith, 1969b), which are more accessible than the technical reports he submitted as part of the grant's requirements. The October 1969 issue (volume 53, number 6) of the *Modern Language Journal* contained six articles critiquing the Pennsylvania studies. The December 1969 issue (volume 3, number 2) of *Foreign Language Annals* contained the summary article by Smith and two review articles. Contemporary synopses of the project and its reviews by D. L. Lange (1968) and W. F. Smith (1970) will be relied on for this discussion.

In the first year of the study, 2,171 students participated. Three teaching strategies and three language laboratory systems were compared. The strategies were: traditional, functional skills, and functional skills with grammar. By *traditional* was meant that an emphasis was placed on vocabulary acquisition, reading and writing skills, translation, and grammatical analysis. *Functional skills* was a synonym for the audiolingual method; the command of a core vocabulary and key syntactic patterns was emphasized, as were the speaking and listening skills. *Functional skills with grammar* was, as the name indicates, the addition of grammatical explanations to the audiolingual method. The three language laboratory systems were: audio-active, audio-active record, and tape recorder in the classroom. The first consisted of two, 25-minute practice sessions each week in which a 10-minute drill tape was played twice. The second arrangement differed from the first in that the students recorded their first practice with the tape and then listened to their own responses. Both of the audio-active groups also practiced in the classroom with a tape recorder each day under the supervision of the instructor for one-fifth of the period. The tape recorder in the classroom group did no lab practice. What they did was at least 10 minutes of guided practice with the tape each day in class.

The results from the first year indicated no significant differences between the teaching strategies, except for reading, where the traditional group outperformed the two audio-active groups. There were no significant differences detected between laboratory systems. During the second year of the project, 639 first-year students participated in a replication study, and 1,090 of the original 2,171 subjects were observed in their second year of language study. The results from this second year of the investigation were in line with those of the first. In the third, year the number of subjects (third-year students) dropped to 277, and by the fourth year it was down to 144 fourth-year students. The findings from these last 2 years showed the traditional students faring significantly better than the audio-active students in both reading and listening. In none of the 4 years of the study was a significant difference in outcomes found according to the laboratory system.

Although the Pennsylvania project generally received higher marks for its methodology than did the Keating report with which it was often compared, there were nevertheless several critiques leveled and questions raised. Some of these involved control issues, such as the degree of teacher adherence to experimental guidelines, the consistency of laboratory installations and maintenance between schools, and the

lack of data as to the amount of time the labs where actually used. Carroll (1969b) detected stowaway variables and practice effects. Perhaps the most serious criticism was the claim (Valette, 1969) that the cooperative test was an inappropriate measure of listening achievement. It was maintained that the vocabulary in this test was closer to what was in the textbook used by traditional groups than the one used by the lab groups. Moreover, evidence from other sources was cited which indicated that the cooperative test was simply too difficult for students in their first 3 years of foreign-language study. This second criticism had broad implications: It cast doubt on the instrument that had been used in all previous language laboratory studies and in many other studies of foreign-language teaching.

Carroll (1969b) and Smith (1970) assessed the implications of the Pennsylvania project. For them, the supposed findings in favor of the traditional groups did not warrant a return to former means of teaching. Rather, they viewed the report, despite its faults, as a credible demonstration that the enthusiastic adoption of new approaches and accompanying materiel does not guarantee success. "The Pennsylvania studies have removed us from our tower of false security" (Smith, 1970, p. 208). For Carroll, the specific lessons to be learned were that audiolingual textbooks needed more linguistic content and that less emphasis should be placed on drills and other "habit formation" activities (1969; p. 235). Smith ended his review on an upbeat note: "It is time to meet the challenge of a new decade" (1970, p. 208). But such a positive attitude did not prevail. As was noted in the historical section above, language laboratories were in the doldrums in the 1970s and early 1980s. Davies (1982) singled out the Pennsylvania project for making complete the growing disillusionment of the period with labs. Moreover, it appears that the study discouraged other research, for it was the last of the large-scale inquiries into the language laboratory's effectiveness.

The only major inquiry of the language laboratory involving postsecondary students will now be discussed. Scherer and West (1964) described in a 246-page book the 2-year NDEA-sponsored investigation they conducted from September 1960. Their goal was to compare the audiolingual approach to the traditional grammar-reading method. Thus, this was not an examination of the language laboratory per se; rather, it was an inquiry similar to the Pennsylvania project (not yet conducted), which was interested in the language lab because of its intimate connection to the audiolingual method. The subjects were beginning German students at the University of Colorado. Intact classes were used, and these were determined to be similar on measures of general academic ability, language learning aptitude, and motivation, as well as sex, age, and year in school.

All of the teaching staff received a week of training in the respective methods prior to the start of the experiment. In addition, there were weekly meetings and frequent observations by the principal investigators and outside consultants to ensure that the instructors adhered to the experiment's guidelines. The traditional approach is only scantily described, but the audiolingual procedures are elaborately detailed in Scherer and Wertheimer's book. The essence of the latter was dialogue memorization and related drill and practice in class. The frequency and duration of the lab sessions were unfortunately not specified; they were for "overlearning" (p. 83) the material presented in class. It is stated that the lab sessions were unmonitored and were of the "library-type" (p. 83), which presumably means the students attended at their convenience. Of note is the postponement of reading for the audiolingual group until the 12th week of the semester. To be specific, the audiolingual group saw absolutely no written German until that point. When reading began, it consisted of the dialogues that had been previously memorized and recombinations of the vocabulary contained in them.

The investigators claimed that they conducted a "persistent and continuous search" (p. 108) for standardized tests to use to measure the outcomes of the two teaching approaches. They were not satisfied with what they found, because "nothing that the major test distributors had to offer seemed to meet the requirements of our situation" (p. 108). They therefore constructed tests of the four language skills and two for translation: German-to-English and vice versa. The *t* test statistic was used for comparisons. At the end of the first year, the audiolingual students were significantly superior to the traditional students in speaking and listening. The superiority in speaking was maintained in the second year, but the advantage for listening was not. On the other hand, the traditional students significantly outperformed the audiolingual students on reading and writing during the first year, and maintained their edge on the latter skill during the second year. The traditional students also were higher in German-to-English translation during both years, and better in English-to-German translation in the first year.

In addition to these measures of linguistic proficiency, Scherer and Wertheimer also used standardized scales and questionnaires they constructed to evaluate the subjects' motivation to study German and their attitude to it and its speakers. They were also concerned with "habituated direct association." By this was meant the ability of the students to think in German, their inclination to translate or not, and their sensitivity to semantic nuances between the two languages. Numerous intercorrelations between these and measures of affective constructs such as anomie, social inhibition, and desire for further German study were calculated. The researchers summarized their work thus:

> The experiment has demonstrated that the two methods, while yielding occasionally strong and persisting differences in various aspects of proficiency in German, result in comparable overall proficiency. But the audiolingual method, whether its results are measured objectively or estimated by the students themselves, appears to produce more desirable attitudes and better habituated direct association (p. 245).

John B. Carroll (1969a) characterized the Scherer and Wertheimer study as "ambitious" (p. 869) and more rigor-

ously designed than any previous examination of the audiolingual approach. He accepted the investigators' conclusions as valid, but offered the following:

> The conclusion that emerges from this experiment is that the differences between the audiolingual and traditional methods are primarily differences of objectives; not surprisingly, students learn whatever skills are emphasized in the instruction (pp. 869–870).

Besides the large-scale and well-publicized studies of Keating, Lorge, Smith, and Scherer and Wertheimer, there have been many smaller investigations since 1959. Eight studies that appeared in major journals have been selected for inclusion here according to chronological order. Only their main findings will be given, since these studies in general did not generate the interest of the larger studies that were described above.

Bauer (1964) found that university students who used the language laboratory in a supervised group-practice condition performed significantly better on oral and dictation measures, but not on a writing measure, than students who studied individually and were not supervised. Two drawbacks to the study were the low number of subjects ($N = 24$) and the use of nonstandardized tests. Moreover, a close examination of the data reveals that the supervised subjects as a group used the lab 125 minutes more over a 3.5-week period than the unsupervised subjects, so the observed differences could possibly be attributed to greater time-on-task.

Young and Choquette's NDEA-sponsored study (1965) was a series of seven experiments that sought to determine whether any of four language laboratory equipment configurations made a difference in the subjects' abilities to self-monitor their pronunciation. The systems were characterized by the feedback options they presented: (1) passive, (2) active, (3) long-delayed comparison, and (4) short-delayed comparison. The first three systems were standard options for language laboratory installations at the time. An apparatus for the fourth condition was specially fashioned for the study by the investigators. In the passive arrangement, the subjects repeated after taped prompts, but they could not clearly hear their responses because the headsets muffled their voices. In the active arrangement, subjects could hear their responses amplified through their headsets as they spoke. In third option, subjects could record their answers for later comparison. In the fourth setup, the students could hear their recorded response within $1\frac{1}{2}$ seconds of making them. Subjects in the active feedback configuration were found to have slightly superior pronunciation than subjects in the other arrangements. However, the authors qualified this finding on several grounds. Of note was the lower sound quality of the fabricated equipment used in the short-delay condition. The authors admitted that this hampered a true comparison with the other three conditions.

Buka, Freeman, and Locke (1962) and Freeman and Buka (1965) conducted experiments that sought to establish psychoacoustic parameters for language laboratory equipment.

The first study determined that a high-frequency cutoff of less than 7,300 cps hindered subjects (high school students) from perceiving certain phonemic contrasts in German and French. The second study found that a low-frequency cutoff of 500 cps caused subjects (again high school students) to make significantly more errors in German phoneme discrimination than a 50-cps cutoff. However, no significant differences were found between these two levels for French phoneme discrimination. It was also found that consonant distinctions were more affected than vowel distinctions by the degradation of sound quality brought on by filtering.

Benathy and Jordan (1969) reported on a post hoc comparison of achievement scores in Bulgarian courses at the Defense Language Institute. The scores of 13 classes (87 students) that completed the course between August 1959 and September 1963 were compared to the scores of 15 classes (103 students) that finished between November 1963 and July 1967. The difference between these classes was the introduction in the fall of 1963 of the Classroom Laboratory Instructional System (CLIS): CLIS is a designed interaction of live instruction and a set of different kinds of learning experiences that make use of preprepared and recorded instructional materials, delivered through the electronic media (p. 473).

The authors stressed that the CLIS system kept the learners on task much more than in a typical classroom. This was because the earphones both isolated each learner from the erroneous responses and pronunciations of others and provided quality native-speaker models. Moreover, the learner did not wait to be called on as in a regular class; it was always his or her "turn." The equipment used appeared to be that of a typical audio-active language laboratory, although the authors do not use the term in their article. Curiously, they do not cite any language laboratory literature in their discussion, yet their description and justification for CLIS are identical to those commonly found in language laboratory writings.

The two groups were found to be very similar in ages and scores of the Army Language Aptitude Test. Class sizes were nearly identical, and the same textbooks and proficiency test were used throughout the 8-year period. It was found that the CLIS classes scored significantly higher than the pre-CLIS classes on the two skills measured by the test, namely, reading and listening. The differences were especially pronounced in the case of the latter skill.

Despite the many experimental controls and the marked differences between the groups, there are three questions that may be raised about this study. First of all, as no mention of instructors is made, one wonders whether teacher effects were held constant. Secondly, the generalizability of the results to high school and university students is doubtful, given that the subjects were all adults studying for specific career purposes at the Defense Language Institute. A third consideration is a question: Why did Benathy and Jordan not more fully report on the synchronous study that preceded the longitudinal one? They claimed similar significant results from it in favor of the CLIS. More information

(i.e., number of subjects, a figure showing t values) about it would give greater credibility to their overall conclusion.

The Chomei and Houlihan (1970) study compared three language laboratory systems: instant playback, long-delay playback, and audio-active. The instant playback option allowed the subjects to have their recorded response to the program stimulus echoed back within half a second. The long-delay group had to rewind the tape to hear their recordings. The audio-active group did not record their responses. It can thus be seen that this study closely resembled what had been done by Young and Choquette (1965), but, surprisingly, this earlier work was not cited. The subjects in the Chomei and Houlihan investigation were 140 Japanese 10th-graders, who were all taught by the same instructor. It was found that the instant-playback group performed significantly better than the other groups on one out of five translation tests and on four out of five speaking tests that had been specially created for the experiment.

Sisson (1970) did a study that was sponsored by the U.S. Office of Education. Its aim was to settle the controversy among language educators as to the benefit (or lack thereof) of delayed comparison on students' ability to perceive and produce the phonemes of another language. Thus, this study shared the same goal as the work of Young and Choquette (1965) and Chomei and Houlihan (1970). That Sisson did not cite the latter is understandable, since it was contemporary to his own. What is surprising is that he ignored the former, yet did cite 39 other articles. In this oversight he followed Chomei and Houlihan, as pointed out before. Why a major study published in a leading journal was so ignored is an unanswered question in the record.

Sisson claimed that "the variables of learning environment were controlled as closely as possible with respect to identity of instructors, scheduling of laboratory lessons, and use of classroom and laboratory materials" (p. 82). The special equipment used in the study, the Plurilingua language laboratory, was thoroughly described. The subjects were 24 students of English as a second language at the University of Michigan. They were in three intact classes of eight students each. The classes were matched on the basis of a modified version of the test of Aural Perception for Latin American Students. This instrument had a phoneme discrimination section and two phoneme production portions.

Two conditions were compared. Half of the students (four from each of the three classes) listened to a taped stimulus and recorded their answer. On completion of an exercise, these subjects rewound the tape and repeated the exercise in the same manner. These subjects formed the "active group." The other group of subjects recorded their responses, as did the active group. However, at the completion of the exercise, these subjects rewound their tape and listened to their first responses rather than record them a second time. This was the "delayed-comparison group." Both groups spent 1 hour per week in the language laboratory during the 8-week term. The modified version of the test of Aural Perception for Latin American Students, which had been used as the pretest was also used as the posttest. Sisson found no significant difference between the two groups on either discrimination or production.

Smith (1980) conducted a study to determine whether the slowing down of recorded material had a beneficial effect on listening comprehension. The reader will recall from the section on history that, during the 1960s, equipment became available which was capable of slowing down (expanding) or speeding up (compressing) recordings without distortion. Smith claimed that his search of the literature turned up no reference to studies addressing the specific application of this technology to foreign-language instruction. This claim was proved incorrect in Driscoll's article (1981), which listed several such studies. However, it should be pointed out that Driscoll was also guilty of oversight; he omitted Smith's study even though it was in the same outlet, the *NALLD Journal,* as his article.

Smith's subjects were second-semester students of French at West Chester State College in Pennsylvania. The control group had 11 members, and the experimental, 12. The cooperative test was administered as a pretest, and the control group was found to be significantly better in reading ability than the experimental group, but both groups were equal in listening comprehension, the skill at issue in the investigation. The study stretched over the fall 1978 semester. The control group covered 12 audio lessons that were recorded at normal speed. The experimental group listened to four lessons that were slowed by 20%, four that were slowed by 10%, and four that were at normal speed. At the end of semester, the students were again given the cooperative tests. Contrary to expectations, the ANCOVA and Finney *t* test procedures showed that the control group scored significantly higher on listening comprehension than the experimental group who listened to expanded material.

Despite such a clearcut albeit counterintuitive finding, Smith cautioned that the study needed to be replicated with a larger number of subjects and for other languages before it could be reasonably concluded that expanded speech was not beneficial, or perhaps even harmful, for the acquiring of listening proficiency in a foreign language. Unfortunately, there is no record of replications by Smith or others. Whether the magnitude of Smith's findings squelched any other initiatives can only be conjectured. It should be pointed out that manufacturers continued to include expansion and compression capabilities in the "deluxe" models of their equipment. It can only be concluded that many practitioners appreciated these features and purchased them, although they had no independent, empirical confirmation of their effectiveness.

28.8.2.4.1. Summary. Twelve studies conducted since the passage of the NDEA in 1958 were discussed in this section. They differed considerably in scale, populations, and methodology. Although all concerned language laboratories in some way, they did not all seek to answer the same questions other than the general one of effectiveness. For these reasons, it is difficult to draw a conclusion. This body of research does not offer clearcut confirmation of the utility of language laboratories, yet neither does it suggest that they

are detrimental to language learning. Perhaps the inconclusiveness of the record is because the investigations that were conducted were not following an agreed-upon agenda. The larger educational technology community began the period with such an agenda (Allen, 1959; Meierhenry, 1962). This lack of focus was costly: Pederson (1987) claimed that it was the lack of solid research concerning courseware that led to the decline of language laboratories.

It would be hasty, however, to dismiss all language laboratory research. It can readily be determined that the use of audio resources within the foreign-language community has differed significantly from that of the larger educational technology community. Not surprisingly, this different use fostered different research. What was unique to the utilization and study of audio resources within foreign-language circles? One can first note the interest in psychophysics and the acoustic parameters of equipment. Besides Buka, Freeman, and Locke (1962) and Freeman and Buka (1965), who were discussed above, Hayes (1963) should be mentioned. He culled a wide range of human factors literature in order to offer standards to be used in laboratory purchase specifications. At this time, the broader educational technology community was more concerned with visual rather than auditory perception. A clear example of this pictorial bias is the fifth issue of volume 10 of the *Audio-Visual Communication Review* (1962), which was entitled "Perception Theory and AV Education." It contained no mention of the aural sense. Such a slanting of interest belies the "audio" component in the name of the flagship journal of the educational technology field at the time. Saettler's *The Evolution of American Educational Technology* shows that this inclination persists; visual media are accorded much more attention than are audio media.

Related to acoustic and perceptual matters are equipment features. Some of the studies reviewed in this section of the chapter (e.g., Young & Choquette, 1965; Chomei & Houlihan, 1970) were concerned with this issue. This is also unique to the body of language laboratory research. Only the studies of compressed and expanded speech showed an interest in machine capabilities.

The reader must be aware that in foreign-language teaching, audio materials are not used merely to present declarative information in an alternative medium; rather audio is the medium. What is meant is that language as normally used in everyday life is predominantly oral and aural rather than visual. Knowledge of a language is more properly considered to be procedural; such knowledge must be inculcated and learned by doing. This perhaps explains why the foreign-language community showed little, if any, interest in the channel effectiveness literature and audio-tutorial instruction (ATI). That the latter was not pursued is somewhat surprising when one considers that Smith (1970), in his essay in the prominent ACTFL yearbook, had proposed that ATI held promise for better foreign-language courseware.

The record shows that periodically foreign-language practitioners have been diligently involved in the use of audio technology. The record also shows that this enthusiasm has waned, and the blame was put on the lack of adequate research. In order to avoid a repeat of this mistake, it would appear that research is required. Audio technology is still in use: less and less alone, but more and more in computer-based multimedia systems. These systems permit the easy collecting of usage data. One can hope that audio technology research will enter a new phase with this new equipment.

28.8.3 Conclusions about Language Labs

According to Last (1989), "language teachers as a body have been more ready than most to accept and explore the pedagogical potential of new technologies as they have emerged" (p. 15). Yet Richards and Nunan (1992) judge that "technology at present is underexploited in language learning and teaching" (p. 1203). It is not the purpose of this chapter to resolve this contradiction. Suffice it to say that there is evidence for both positions, and one has reason to be optimistic about the future. In 1990 the U.S. Department of Education funded the first National Foreign Language Resource Center. Two centers, the University of Hawaii and San Diego State University, have been offering workshops on the use of technology. The FLAME (Foreign Language Applications in Multimedia Environment) project at the University of Michigan is another reason for hope.

At the outset of this portion of the chapter, it was stated that the larger educational technology community has not fully appreciated the history of language laboratories. The scant attention paid to them in Saettler's *The Evolution of American Educational Technology* was cited to support this point. Nor has the history of the research that accompanied language laboratories been acknowledged heretofore. The proof of this contention can be seen in Allen's (1971) review of past research. This essay in the AVCR by its long-time editor contained no mention of what were then recent studies, some of which had attracted much attention in the popular press. It is hoped that this summary will contribute to setting the record straight.

REFERENCES

Adelson, L. (1975). Comprehension by college students of time compressed lectures. *Journal of Experimental Education 44,* 53–59.

Agency for International Development (n.d.). *Interactive radio instruction.* Newton, MA: Education Development Center.

Aikens, H.F. & Ross, A.J. (1977). Immediate, repetitive playback/record—a practical solution. *NAALD Journal 11* (2), 40–46.

Allen, E.D. (1960). The effects of the language laboratory on the development of skill in a foreign language. *Modern Language Journal 44,* 355–58.

Allen, W.H. (1959). Research on new educational media: summary and problems. *Audio-Visual Communication Review 7,* 83–96.

— (1971). Instructional Media research: past, present, and future. *Audio-Visual Communication Review 19,* 5–18.

Altamura, N.C. (1970). Laboratory a liability. *French Review 43,* 819–20.

Anderson, E.W. (1964). Review and criticism. *Modern Language Journal 48,* 197–206.

Bagster-Collins, E.W., et al. (1930). *Studies in modern language teaching.* New York: Macmillan.

Barrutia, R. (1967). The past, present, and future of language laboratories. *Hispania 50,* 888–99.

Bates, A.W. (1983). Adult learning from educational television: the open university experience. *In* M.J.A. Howe, ed. *Learning from television: psychological and educational research,* 213–27. Washington, DC: American Psychological Association.

Bauer, E.W. (1964). A study of the effectiveness of two language laboratory conditions in the teaching of second year German. *International Review of Applied Linguistics 2,* 99–112.

Bell, R. (1969). An analysis of certain elements of an audio-take approach to instruction. Unpublished doctoral dissertation, University of Washington.

Benathy, B.H. & Jordan, B. (1969). A classroom laboratory instructional system (CLIS). *Foreign Language Annals 2,* 466–73.

Benz, C.R. (1971). Effects of time compressed speech upon the comprehension of a visual oriented television lecture. Unpublished doctoral dissertation, Wayne State University.

Boyle, V.A. (1969). Visual stimulation and comprehension of compressed speech. (Doctoral dissertation, George Peabody College for Teachers, 1969). Dissertation Abstracts International, 30, 5221B.

Breed, P.A. (1977). The relative effect of the controlled reader and the speech compressor on reading rate and comprehension. Unpublished Doctoral Dissertation, Northern Illinois University.

Brushwood, J. & Polmantier, P. (1953). *The effectiveness of the audio-laboratory in elementary modern language courses.* Columbia, MO: The University of Missouri.

Buchanan, M.A. & MacPhee, E.D. (1928). *An annotated bibliography of modern language methodology.* Toronto, Canada: University of Toronto Press.

Buka, M., Freeman, M.K. & Locke, W.N. (1962). Language learning and frequency response. *International Journal of American Linguistics 28,* 62–79.

Button, G.E. (1991). Audio-tutorial biology, andragogy, and self-esteem: relationships among independent and dependent variables. Dissertation Abstracts International, 53/02, 457. (University Microfilms No. AAC 9211068.)

Carroll, J.B. (1963). Research on teaching foreign languages. *In* N.L. Gage, ed. *Handbook of research on teaching,* 1060–1100. Chicago, IL: Rand McNally.

— (1969a). Modern languages. *In* R.L. Ebel, ed. *Encyclopaedia of educational research, 4th ed.,* 866–78. New York: Macmillan.

— (1969b). What does the Pennsylvania foreign language research project tell us? *Foreign Language Annals 3,* 214–36.

Carter, K.R. & Cooney, J.B. (1983). The audio-tutorial applied in psychology classes to minimize individual differences and save class time. *Teaching of Psychology 10,* 201–04.

Carver, R.P. (1973). Understanding, information processing, and learning from prose materials. *Journal of Educational Psychology 64,* 76–84.

— (1982). Optimal rate of reading prose. *Reading Research Quarterly 18* (1), 56–88.

— (1973). Effect of increasing the rate of speech presentation upon comprehension. *Journal of Educational Psychology 65,* 118–26.

Chomei, T. & Houlihan, R. (1970). Comparative effectiveness of three language lab methods using a new equipment system. *AV Communication Review 18,* 160–68.

Chall, J.S. & Dial, H.E. (1948). Predicting listener understanding and interest in newscasts. *Educational Research Bulletin 27,* 141–53.

Cicardo, A.R. (1974). An analysis of retention of a compressed speech message among various intelligence levels, rates of compression, and retention levels. Unpublished doctoral dissertation, Northwestern State University of Louisiana.

Clark, R.E. (1983). Reconsidering research on learning from media. *Review of Educational Research 53,* 445–59.

Clarke, C.C. (1918). The phonograph in modern language teaching. *Modern Language Journal 3,* 116–22.

Claudel, C.A. (1968). The language laboratory. *In* J.S. Roucek, ed. *The study of foreign languages,* 219–36. New York: Philosophical Library.

Constantine, M. (1964). Radio in the elementary school. *Science Education 48,* 121–32.

Cook, D.C. & Nemzek, C. (1939). Effectiveness of teaching by radio. *The Journal of Educational Research 33* (2), 105–09.

Cook, H.R. (1964). The effects of learning of structural drills in Spanish broadcast via high frequency AM radio (NDEA Title VII Project No. 1018). Bloomington, IN: Indiana University.

Cutler, R.L., McKeachie, W.J. & McNeil, E.B. (1958). Teaching psychology by telephone. *The American Psychologist 13* (9), 551–52.

Davies, N.F. (1982). Foreign/second language education and technology in the future. *NAALD Journal 16* (3/4), 5–14.

Davison, W.F. (1973). *The language laboratory: a bibliography, 1950-1972.* Pittsburgh, PA: University Center for International Studies and The English Language Institute, University of Pittsburgh.

Derthick, L.G. (1959). The purpose and legislative history of the foreign language titles in the National Defense Education Act, 1958. *Publications of the Modern Language Association 74,* 48–51.

Diekhoff, J.S. (1965). *NDEA and modern foreign languages.* New York: Modern Language Association.

DeKieffer, R.E. (1973). The national center for audio tapes. *In* J.W. Brown, ed. *Educational Media Yearbook,* 56–59. New York: Bowker.

DeWick, H.N. (1935, Jun.). The relative recall effectiveness of visual and auditory presentation of advertising material. *The Journal of Applied Psychology 19,* 245–64.

Diehl, C.F., White, R.D. & Burke, K. (1959). Rate and comprehension. *Speech Monographs 26,* 229–32.

Dodge, J.W. (1968). Language laboratories. *In* E.M. Birkmaier, ed. *Britannica review of foreign language education, Vol. 1,* 331–35. Chicago, IL: Encyclopaedia Britannica.

Driscoll, J. (1981). Research trends in rate-controlled speech for language learning. *NALLD Journal 15* (2), 45–51.

Duker, S. (1974). *Time compressed speech.* Metuchen, NJ: Scarecrow.

Eckhardt, W.W. (1970). Learning in multi-media programmed instruction as a function of aptitude and instruction rate controlled by compressed speech. Unpublished doctoral dissertation, University of Southern California.

Eddy, F.D. (1944). The language studio. *Modern Language Journal 28,* 338–41.

Ek, J.D. (1974). Grant fever. *NALLD Journal 9* (1), 17–23.

Ely, P. (1984). *Bring the lab back to life.* Oxford, England: Pergamon.

Erickson, C.I. & King, I. (1917). A comparison of visual and oral presentations of lessons in the case of pupils from third to ninth grade, *School and Society 6* (136), 146–48.

Eshgh, R., Hoxeng, J., Provenzano, J. & Casals, B., eds. (1988). Radio-assisted community basic education (RADE-CO). Pittsburgh, PA: Duquesne University Press.

Fairbanks, G., Everitt, W.L. & Jaeger, R.P. (1954). Method for time or frequency compression-expansion of speech. *Transactions of the Institute of Radio Engineers, Professional Groups on Audio, AU 2,* 7–12.

—, Guttman, N. & Miron, M.S. (1957). Auditory comprehension of repeated high speech messages. *Journal of Speech and Hearing Disorders 22,* 23–32.

Fergen, G.K. (1954). Listening comprehension at controlled rates for children in grades iv, v, and vi. Unpublished doctoral dissertation, University of Missouri.

Fotos, J.T. (1955). The Purdue laboratory method in teaching beginning French classes. *Modern Language Journal 39,* 141–43.

Foulke, E. (1968). Listening comprehension as a function of word rate. *Journal of Communication 18,* 198–206.

—, ed. (1966). *Proceedings of the Louisville conference on time-compressed speech.* Louisville, KY: Center for Rate Controlled Recordings.

—, Amster, C.H., Bixler, R.H. & Nolan, C.Y. (1962). The comprehension of rapid speech by the blind. *Exceptional Children 11,* 134–41.

Foulke, E.A. & Sticht, T.G. (1967). *The intelligibility and comprehension of accelerated speech.* Proceedings of the Louisville Conference on Time Compressed Speech, Louisville, KY, 21–28.

— (1969). *Proceedings of the second Louisville conference on rate and/or frequency controlled speech.* Louisville, KY: University of Louisville. (ERIC Document Reproduction Service No. Ed 61 682.)

— (1962, Mar.). *A comparison of two methods of compressing speech.* Symposium at the Southeastern Psychological Association, Louisville, KY.

— & Sticht, T.G. (1969). A review of research on the intelligibility and comprehension of accelerated speech. *Psychological Bulletin 72,* 50–62.

Fox, B. & Roblin, J.S. (1952). Retention and sleep. *Journal of Experimental Psychology 43* (1), 75–79.

Freeman, M.Z. & Buka, M. (1965). Effect of frequency response on language learning. *AV Communication Review 13,* 289–95.

Friedman, H.L., Freedle, R.O., Norris, C.M. & Orr, D.B. (1966). *Further research on speeded speech as an educational medium.* (Report No. AIR-E-50-7-66-TR-3.) Silver Spring, MD: American Institute for Research in the Behavioral Sciences (ED 044 903).

—, Orr, D. & Norris, C. (1966). *Further research on speeded speech as an educational medium—the use of listening aids.* (Report No. 3.) Silver Spring, MD: American Institutes for Research in Behavioral Sciences (ED 044 903).

Funke, E. (1949). Rebuilding a practical phonetics laboratory.

German Quarterly 21, 120–25.

Furnham, A. & Gunter, B. (1985). Sex, presentation mode and memory for violent and non-violent news. *Journal of Educational Television 11,* 99–105.

— & Gunter, B. (1987). Effects of time of day and medium of presentation on recall of violent and non-violent news. *Applied Cognitive Psychology 1,* 255–62.

—, Benson, I. & Gunter, B. (1987). Memory for television commercials as a function of the channel of communication. *Social Behaviour 2,* 105–12.

—, Gunter, B. & Green, A. (1988). Remembering science: the recall of factual information as a function of presentation mode. *Applied Cognitive Psychology 4,* 203–12.

—, Proctor, T. & Gunter, B. (1988). Memory for material presented in the media: the superiority of written communication. *Psychological Reports 63,* 935–38.

Gallacher, T. & Stevens, R. (1954). Teaching with a tape recorder. *California Journal of Secondary Education 29,* 312–14.

Garvey, W.D. (1953). The intelligibility of speeded speech. *Journal of Experimental Psychology 45,* 102–08.

George, R.G. (1970). Retention of prose material as a function of rate of presentation and difficulty of material. *Audio Visual Communication Review 18,* 291–99.

Gibson, R. (1958). Tape recordings are used to teach seventh-grade students in Westside Junior-Senior High School, Omaha, NE. *Bulletin of the National Association of Secondary Principals 42,* 81–93.

— (1959). The tape recordings experiment is expanded in Westside Junior-Senior High School, Omaha, NE. *Bulletin of the National Association of Secondary Principals 43,* 49–72.

— (1960). Final report on the Westside High School Teaching-by-Tape Project. *Bulletin of the National Association of Secondary Principals 44,* 56–62.

Godfrey, E.P. (1967). *The state of audiovisual technology: 1961–1966.* Washington DC: Department of Audiovisual Instruction, National Education Association.

Goldhaber, G. (1967). Listener comprehension of compressed speech when the difficulty level of the content and the sex of the listener varied. Unpublished master's thesis, University of Maryland.

— (1970). Listener comprehension of compressed speech as a function of the academic grade level of the subjects. *The Journal of Communications 20,* 167–73.

Goldstein, H. (1940). Reading and listening comprehension at various controlled rates. *Teacher's College Contributions to Education,* No. 821.

Green, J.R. (1965). Language laboratory research: a critique. *Modern Language Journal 49,* 367–69.

Grittner, F. (1964). The shortcomings of language laboratory findings in the IAR-Research Bulletin. *Modern Language Journal 48,* 207–10.

Gullette, C.C. (1932). Ear training in the teaching of pronunciation. *Modern Language Journal 16,* 334–36.

Gunter, B. (1987). *Poor reception: misunderstanding and forgetting broadcast news.* Hillsdale, NJ: Erlbaum.

— & Furnham, A. (1986). Sex and personality differences in recall of violent and non-violent news from three presentational modalities. *Personality and Individual Differences 7,* 829–37.

—, — & Gietson, G. (1984). Memory for the news as function of the channel of communication. *Human Learning 3,* 265–71.

—, — & Leese, J. (1986). Memory for information from a party political broadcast as a function of channel of communication. *Social Behaviour 1,* 135–42.

Hartman, F.R. (1961). Single and multiple communication: a review of research and proposed model. *Audio Visual Communication Review 9,* 235–62.

Harvey, T.E. (1978). The matter with listening comprehension isn't the ear: hardware & software. *NALLD Journal 13* (1), 8–16.

Hayes, A.S. (1963). *Language laboratory facilities: technical guide for the selection, purchase, use, and maintenance.* Washington, DC: U.S. Department of Health, Education, and Welfare.

Heinich, R. (1968). The teacher in an instructional system. *In* F.G. Knirk & J.W. Childs, eds. *Instructional technology: a book of readings,* 45–60. New York: Holt.

Hirsch, R. (1954). *Audio-visual aids in language teaching.* Washington, DC: Georgetown University Press.

Hocking, E. (1964). *Language laboratory and language learning.* Washington, DC: Division of Audiovisual Instruction, National Education Association.

Holmes, G. (1985). From the president. *NALLD Journal 19* (2), 5–7.

Huppert, J. & Lazarowitz, R. (1990). Pupils abilities and academic achievement in an individualized biology curriculum. *Research in Science and Technological Education 8,* 117–31.

Hutchison, J.C. (1961). *Modern foreign languages in high school: the language laboratory.* Washington DC: U.S. Department of Health, Education, and Welfare.

Jarlett, F.G. (1971). The falsely accused language laboratory: 25 years of misuse. *NALLD Journal 5* (4), 27–34.

Johnston, M.C. & Seerley, C.C. (1960). *Foreign language laboratories in schools and colleges.* Washington, DC: U.S. Department of Health, Education, and Welfare.

Klavon, A.J. (1975). Time-compressed lecture: an alternative for increased teacher learner interaction. Unpublished doctoral dissertation, University of Maryland.

Keating, L.C. (1936). Modern inventions in the language program. *School and Society 44,* 677–79.

Keating, R.F. (1963). *A study of the effectiveness of language laboratories.* New York: Teachers College, Columbia University.

Kelly, L.G. (1969). *25 centuries of language teaching.* Rowley, MA: Newbury.

Kenner, R. (1981). Report on the Concordia Colloquium on language laboratories. *NALLD Journal 16* (2), 15–18.

Koekkoek, B.J. (1959). The advent of the language laboratory. *Modern Language Journal 43,* 4–5.

Kramer, E.J. & Lewis, T.R. (1951). Comparison of visual and non-visual listening. *Journal of Communication 1* (2), 16–20.

Kulik, J.A., Kulik, C.-L.C. & Cohen, P.A. (1979). Research on audio-tutorial instruction: a meta-analysis of comparative studies. *Review of Educational Research 11,* 321–41.

Lange, D.L. (1968). Methods. *In* E.M. Birkmaier, ed. *Britannica Review of Foreign Language Education, Vol. 1,* 281–310. Chicago, IL: Encyclopaedia Britannica.

Larsen, R.P. & Feder, D.D. (1940). Common and differential factors in reading and hearing comprehension. *The Journal of Educational Psychology 31,* 241–51.

Leshan, L. (1942). The breaking of a habit by suggestion during sleep. *The Journal of Abnormal and Social Psychology 37,* 406–08.

Last, R.W. (1989). *Artificial intelligence techniques in lan-*

guage learning. Chichester, England: Horwood.

LeMon, R.E. (1986). Computer labs and language labs: lessons to be learned. *Educational Technology 26,* 46–47.

Leon, P.R. (1962). *Laboratoire de langues et correction phonétique.* Paris: Didier.

Levin, L.M. (1931). More anent the phonetic laboratory method. *Modern Language Journal 15,* 427–31.

Lorge, S.W. (1964). Language laboratory research studies in New York City high schools: a discussion of the program and the findings. *Modern Language Journal 48,* 409–19.

— (1965). Comments on "language laboratory research: a critique." *Modern Language Journal 49,* 369–70.

Loder, J.E. (1937). A study of aural learning with and without the speaker present. *Journal of Experimental Education 6,* 46–60.

Ludrick, J.A. (1974). A study of the effects of controlled delivery instruction upon the achievement of college students using compressed speech audio and television pictorials. Unpublished doctoral dissertation, the University of Oklahoma.

Lysaght, C.E. (1969). Geriatrics: effect of speech rate and pacing procedures upon the responses to verbal stimuli by three age groups. Unpublished doctoral dissertation, Boston University.

Maclachlan, J. (1982). Listener perception of time-compressed spokespersons for radio commercials. *Journal of Advertising 22,* 47–51.

May, M.A. & Lumsdaine, A.A. (1958). *Learning from films.* New Haven, CT: Yale.

McCoy, I.H. & Weible, D.M. (1983). Foreign languages and the new media: the videodisc and the microcomputer. *In* C.J. James, ed. *Practical applications of research in foreign language teaching,* 105–52. Lincolnwood, IL: National Textbook.

Meierhenry, W.C. (1962). Needed research in the introduction and use of audiovisual materials: a special report. *Audio-Visual Communication Review 10,* 307–16.

Miller, G.A. & Lichlinder, J.C. (1950). The intelligibility of interrupted speech. *Journal of the Acoustical Society of America 22,* 167–73.

Molstad, J. (1955). Readability formulas and film grade-placement. *Audio-Visual Communication Review 3,* 99–108.

Mosenthal, P. (1976–77). Psycholinguistic properties of aural and visual comprehension as determined by children's abilities to comprehend syllogisms. *Reading Research Quarterly 12,* 55–92.

Mueller, T. & Borglum, G. (1956). Language laboratory and target language. *French Review 29,* 322–31.

Menne, J.W., Klingenschmidt, J.E. & Nord, D.L. (1969, Mar.). *The feasibility of using taped lectures to replace class attendance.* Paper presented at the annual meeting of American Educational Research Association, Los Angeles.

Nasser, D.L. & McEwen, W.J. (1976). The impact of alternate media channels: recall and involvement with messages. *AV Communication Review 24,* 263–72.

Nelson, H.E. (1948). The effect of variations of rates on the recall by radio listeners of straight newscast. *Speech Monographs 1,* 173–80.

Newmark, M. (1948). Teaching materials: textbooks, audiovisual aids, the language laboratory. *In* M. Newmark, ed. *Twentieth century modern language teaching,* 456–62. New York: Philosophical Library.

Nichols, R.G. & Stevens, L.A. (1957). *Are you listening?* New York: McGraw-Hill.

Novak, J.D. & Musunda, D. (1991). A twelve-year longitudinal study of science concept learning. *American Educational Research Journal 28,* 117–53.

Nugent, G.C. (1982). Pictures, audio, and print: symbolic representation and effect on learning. *Educational Communication and Technology Journal 30,* 163–74.

NHK Radio-Television Cultural Research Institute (1956). *The listening effect of radio English classroom.* Tokyo: NHK.

Otto, S. (1989). The language laboratory in the computer age. *In* W.F. Smith, ed. *Modern technology in foreign language education: applications and projects,* 13–41. Chicago, IL: National Textbook.

Parker, W.R. (1960). Foreword. *In* F.J. Oinas, ed. *Language teaching today,* pp. v–viii. Bloomington, IN: Indiana University Research Center in Anthropology, Folklore, and Linguistics.

— (1961). *The national interest and foreign languages,* 3d ed. Washington, DC: U.S. Department of State.

Pederson, K.M. (1987). Research on CALL. *In* W.F. Smith, ed. *Modern media in foreign language education: theory and implementation,* 99–131. Chicago, IL: National Textbook.

Peebles, S. (1938). *The phonetics laboratory and its usefulness.* Unpublished MA thesis. Boulder, CO: University of Colorado.

Peterson, P. (1974). Origins of the language laboratory. *NALLD Journal 8* (4), 5–17.

Olsen, D.R. & Bruner, J.S. (1974). Learning through experience and learning through media. *In* D.R. Olsen, ed. *Media and symbols,* 125–50. Chicago, IL: University of Chicago Press.

Orr, D.B. & Friedman, H.L. (1964). *Research on speeded speech as an educational medium.* (Progress Report, Grant No. 7-48-7670-203.) U.S. Department of Health, Education, and Welfare, Office of Education, Washington, DC.

—, — & Williams, J.C. (1965). Trainability of listening comprehension of speeded discourse. *Journal of Educational Psychology 56,* 148–56.

Popham, W.J. (1962). Tape recorded lectures in the college classroom II. *AV Communication Review 10,* 94–101.

Porter, J.J. & Porter, S.F. (1964). A critique of the Keating report. *Modern Language Journal 48,* 195–97.

Racle, G.L. (1976). Laboratoire de langues: problèmes et orientations. *Canadian Modern Language Review 32,* 384–88.

Postlethwaite, S.N. (1970). The audio-tutorial system. *American Biology Teacher 32,* 31–33.

— (1972). The audio-tutorial system: incorporating minicourse and mastery. *Educational Technology 12* (9), 35–37.

— (1975). Students are a lot like people! *American Biology Teacher 37,* 205.

— (1978). Principles behind the audio-tutorial system. *NSPI Journal 17,* 3–4,18.

— (1980). Improvement of science teaching. *BioScience 30,* 601–04.

—, Novak, J. & Murray, H.T., Jr. (1972). *The audio-tutorial approach to learning,* 3d ed. Minneapolis, MN: Burgess.

Potter, M.C. (1990). Remembering. *In* D.N. Osherson & E.E. Smith, eds. *Thinking: an invitation to cognitive science,* 3–32. Cambridge, MA: MIT Press.

Rao, P.V. (1977). Telephone and instructional communication. *In* I.D.S. Pool, ed. *The social impact of the telephone,* 473–86. Cambridge, MA: MIT Press.

Reid, R.H. (1968). Comprehension of compressed speech as a function of difficulty of material. Unpublished doctoral dissertation, Florida State University.

Richards, J. C. & Nunan, D. (1992). Second language teaching and learning. *In* M.C. Aikin, ed. *Encyclopaedia of educational research*, 6th ed., 1200–08. New York: Macmillan.

Robertson, E.M. (1977). The effects of different rates of recorded speech on the listening comprehension of adult remedial readers. Unpublished doctoral dissertation, University of Georgia.

Rohwer, W.D. & Harris, W.J. (1975). Media effect on prose learning in two populations of children. *Journal of Educational Psychology 67,* 651–57.

Ross, R.A. (1964). Look at listeners. *Elementary School Journal 64* (7), 369–72.

Rossiter, C.M., Jr. (1972). Sex of the speaker, sex of the listener, and listening comprehension. *The Journal of Communication 22,* 64–69.

— (1970). The effects of rate of presentation on listening test scores for recall of facts, recall of ideas, and generation of inferences. Unpublished doctoral dissertation, Ohio University.

Rulon, P.V. (1943a) A comparison of phonographic recordings with printed material in terms of knowledge, *The Harvard Educational Review 8,* 63–76.

— (1943b). A comparison of phonographic recordings with printed material in terms of knowledge gained through their use in a teaching unit, *The Harvard Educational Review 8,* 163–75.

— (1943c). A comparison of phonographic recordings with printed motivation to further study. *The Harvard Educational Review 8,* 246–55.

Saettler, P. (1990). *The evolution of American educational technology.* Englewood, CO: Libraries Unlimited.

Salomon, G. (1979). *Interaction of media, cognition, and learning.* San Francisco, CA: Jossey-Bass.

— (1984). Television is "easy" and print is "tough": the differential investment of mental effort in learning as a function of perceptions and attributions. *Journal of Educational Psychology 76,* 647–58.

Sanchez, J. (1959). Twenty years of modern language laboratory (an annotated bibliography). *Modern Language Journal 43,* 228–32.

Schenk, E.H. (1930). Practical difficulties in the use of the phonetics laboratory. *Modern Language Journal 15,* 30–32.

Scherer, G.A.C. & Wertheimer, M. (1964). *A psycholinguistic experiment in foreign-language teaching.* New York: McGraw-Hill.

Schramm, W. (1972). What the research says. *In* W. Schramm, ed. *Quality instructional television,* 44–79. Honolulu: HI: University Press of Hawaii.

Scott, R.J. (1965). Temporal effects in speech analysis and synthesis. Unpublished doctoral dissertation, University of Michigan.

Short, H.S. (1977). A comparison of variable time-compressed speech and normal rate speech based on time spent and performance in a course taught by self-instructional methods. *British Journal of Educational Technology 8,* 146–57.

Sisson, C.R. (1970). The effect of delayed comparison in the language laboratory on phoneme discrimination and pronunciation accuracy. *Language Learning 20,* 69–88.

Smith, P.D. (1969a). The Pennsylvania foreign language research project: teacher proficiency and class achievement in two modern languages. *Foreign Language Annals 3,* 194–207.

— (1969b). An assessment of three foreign language teaching strategies and three language laboratory systems. *The French Review 43,* 289–304.

— (1980). A study of the effect of "slowed speech" on listening comprehension of French. *NALLD Journal 14* (3/4), 9–13.

Smith, W.F. (1970). Language learning laboratory. *In* D.L. Lange, ed. *Britannica review of foreign language education, Vol. 2,* 191–237. Chicago, IL: Encyclopaedia Britannica, Inc.

— (1987). *Modern media in foreign language education: theory and implementation.* Chicago, IL: National Textbook.

— (1989). *Modern technology in foreign language education: applications and projects.* Chicago, IL: National Textbook.

Stack, E.M. (1964). The Keating report: a symposium. *Modern Language Journal 48,* 189–210.

— (1971). *The language laboratory and modern language teaching.* New York: Oxford University Press.

Stanton, F.N. (1934). Memory for advertising copy presented visually and orally, The *Journal of Applied Psychology 18,* 45–64.

Stich, T.G. (1968). Some relationships of mental aptitude, reading ability, and listening ability using normal and time-compressed speech. *Journal of Communication 18,* 243–58.

— & Glasnap, D.R. (1972). Effects of speech rate, selection difficulty, association strength, and mental aptitude on learning by listening. *The Journal of Communication 22,* 174–88.

— (1971). Failure to increase learning using the time saved by the time compression of speech. *Journal of Educational Psychology 62,* 55–59.

Stiefel, W.A. (1952). Bricks with straw—the language laboratory. *Modern Language Journal 36,* 68–73.

Strei, G. (1977). Reviving the language lab. *TESOL Newsletter 11,* 10.

Svoboda, R.G. (1978). Audio-tutorial courses for college algebra and trigonometry: a progress report. Fort Wayne, IN: Indiana University. (ED 167125.)

Taylor, S.E. (1965). Eye movements in reading: facts and fallacies. *American Educational Research Journal 2,* 187–202.

Tripp, S.D. (1994, Aug. 5). Do media affect memory? Paper presented at the 3d Practical Aspects of Memory Conference, College Park, MD.

Valette, R.M. (1969). The Pennsylvania project, its conclusions and its implications. *Modern Language Journal 53,* 396–404.

Voor, J.B. & Miller, J.M. (1965). The effect of practice on the comprehension of time compressed speech. *Speech Monographs 32,* 452–54.

Waltz, R.H. (1930). The laboratory as an aid to modern language teaching. *Modern Language Journal 15,* 27–29.

— (1931). Language laboratory administration. *Modern Language Journal 16,* 217–27.

— (1932). Some results of laboratory training. *Modern Language Journal 16,* 299–305.

Wasserman, H.M. & Tedford, W.H. (1973). Recall of temporally compressed auditory and visual information. *Psychological Reports 32,* 499–502.

Watts, M.W. Jr. (1971). Differences in educational level and subject matter difficulty in the use of compressed speech with adult military students. *Adult Educational Journal 21,* 27–36.

Whitehouse, R.S. (1945). The workshop: a language laboratory. *Hispania 28,* 88–90.

Williams, D.L., Moore, D. M., & Sewell, E.H., Jr. (1983–84). Effects of compressed speech on comprehension of community college students. *Journal of Educational Technology Systems 12,* 273–84.

Wolcott, L.L. (1993). Audio tools for distance education. *In* B. Willis, ed. *Distance education: strategies and tools,* 135–64, Washington, DC: American Psychological Association.

Wood, C.D. (1966). Comprehension of compressed speech by elementary school children. Indiana University, Bloomington, Indiana (ED 003 216.)

Worchester, D.A. (Jan., 1925). Memory by visual and auditory presentation. *The Journal of Educational Psychology 16* (1), 18–27.

Young, W.E. (1936). The relation of reading comprehension and retention to hearing comprehension and retention. *Journal of Experimental Education 5* (1), 30–39.

Young, C.W. & Choquette, C.A. (1965). An experimental study of the effectiveness of four systems of equipment for self-monitoring in teaching French pronunciation. *International Review of Applied Linguistics 3,* 13–49.

29. MULTIPLE-CHANNEL COMMUNICATION: THE THEORETICAL AND RESEARCH FOUNDATIONS OF MULTIMEDIA

David M. (Mike) Moore
VIRGINIA POLYTECHNIC INSTITUTE
AND STATE UNIVERSITY

John K. Burton
VIRGINIA POLYTECHNIC INSTITUTE
AND STATE UNIVERSITY

Robert J. Myers
WHEELING
JESUIT COLLEGE

29.1 INTRODUCTION*

The ability of technology to make information available quickly and provide an individualized learning opportunity has long been discussed and dreamed of. These desires go back to Pressey's teaching machines of the 1920s and Bush's theoretical "Memex" information retrieval system of the 1940s. Since the beginning of the microcomputer computer revolution in the late 1970s, however, the dream has become a reality. Proponents have extolled the virtues of instruction supported, assisted, or conducted by the computer (e.g., Papert, 1977; Suppes, 1980). Others have exercised less enthusiasm about the effects of any media per se. Clark (1983), for example, said that mediated environments are merely sufficient, not necessary, for the learning process. Teachers, as practitioners, will ultimately decide whether incorporation of new technologies into the classroom is worth the time and effort (Moore, Myers & Burton, 1994).

This chapter focuses on the theories and effects related to multiple-channel communication, which undergirds notions of multimedia instruction. Because cognitive notions of learning currently have widespread acceptance, we will use them as the perspective for the review. Specifically, we will use the information-processing view of the cognitive system because it, like current views of multimedia itself, relies so heavily on the computer. The information-processing approach focuses on how the human memory system acquires, encodes, retrieves, and uses information. This approach applies information theory and computer analogies to human learning. Within the information-processing model, topics and research reviewed include multiple-channel communication, including modalities of instruction, cue

summation and stimulus generalization, channel interference, and capacity. We, however, resisted the temptation to include and thus report on cueing strategies and other remotely related theories. Related research literature in areas of multi-image and subliminal perception are also investigated and summarized.

The term *multimedia* has been used for a long time by educators as well as those in the technology industry, yet there is little consensus as to what, exactly, the concept includes (Strommen & Ravelle, 1990). Until recently, the term has meant the use of several media devices in a coordinated fashion (e.g., synchronized slides with audiotape). Advances in technology, however, have combined these media so that information previously delivered by several devices is now integrated into one device (Kozma, 1987, 1991). Obviously the computer plays a central organizing role in this environment, and just as obviously the computer allows interactivity and, constrained only by the size of the lesson, unlimited branching. Because of this history, many authors (see, for example, Matchett & Elliot, 1991) argue that multimedia should encompass interactive systems. This allows the notion of multimedia not only to accommodate interactive video, for example, but also to absorb the historically older concept of hypermedia (Moore, Myers & Burton, 1994). In part because we don't agree (we tend to see multimedia as a special case of hypermedia with one, linear path specified), and in part because of the more practical reason that such things as interactive video, etc., are covered elsewhere in this handbook, we will limit our definition, and hence our coverage, to systems that include two or more of the following: motion, voice, data, text, graphics, and still images.

Multimedia research is evaluated with the intent of answering the question: Does multimedia really work? Speculation on multimedia message design based on past and current research concludes this chapter.

*The authors appreciate the research assistance of James A. DeChenne, Helen B. Miller, John F. Moore, and Joanne B. Whitley.

29.2 INFORMATION -PROCESSING APPROACH TO HUMAN COGNITION

29.2.1 Historical Perspectives

Notions such as seeing with our "mind's eye" or "listening" to our inner "voices" portray an ancient metaphor of a mind with sense organs much like the body. The mind feels pain (e.g., "it hurts me when I think about . . ."), has a sense of taste (e.g., "I want this so bad I can taste it"), and smell (e.g., "the more I think about this the more it smells"), etc. Moreover, our language reflects specific, organ-based memories, as in "I'll never forget the look on his face or the sound of his voice," or "I can still feel (or smell) it after all these years." Yet, the nature of sensory image processing, storage, interpretation, and generation is not nearly as clear (nor as noncontroversial) as our conversational descriptions would imply.

Images are mentioned in Greek scrolls that date as early as 500 BC. A few hundred years later, a building collapsed during an earthquake. Simonodes, a survivor, related his use of mental images to recreate the seating arrangement at the feast he had been attending in the building. The power of the mind to "see" is exemplified, for example, by authors such as St. Augustine (who refers to *inner sight* or *insight*) and Descartes (who believed that during dream states the mind could both see and hear during its "travels").

To understand the current views of these historical concepts, however, it is necessary to take a position on how the human memory system works. For simplicity sake, and to make discussions about modality easier, we have selected the model that began the current rise of cognitive psychology: information processing.

29.2.2 Cognitive Overview

The information-processing approach to human cognition (see 1.4.4, 5.2.4, 28.1.2.1, 30.2) relies on the computer as a metaphor. Gardner (1985) states that cognitive science was "officially" recognized at the Symposium on Information Theory held at MIT in 1956. While Broadbent (1958) published the first model, it was Neisser, in his 1967 book *Cognitive Psychology,* who synthesized earlier attempts to apply information theory and computer analogies to human learning (see, e.g., Bartlett, 1958; Broadbent, 1958; Miller, 1953; Posner, 1964).

The information-processing approach focuses on how the human memory system acquires, transforms, compacts, elaborates, encodes, retrieves, and uses information. The memory system is divided into three main storage structures: sensory registers, short-term memory (STM), and long-term memory (LTM). Each structure is synonymous with a type of processing.

The first stage of processing is registering stimuli in the memory system. The sensory registers (one for each sense) briefly hold information until the stimulus is recognized or lost. Pattern recognition is the matching of stimulus information with previously acquired knowledge. Klatzky (1980)

referred to this complex recognition process as assigning meaning to a stimulus. Unlike the sensory registers, STM does not hold information in its raw sensory form, (e.g., visual—"icon," auditory—"echo") but in its recognized form. For example, the letter *A* is recognized as a letter rather than as just a group of lines. STM can maintain information longer than the sensory registers through a holding process known as *maintenance rehearsal,* which recycles material over and over as the system works on it. Without rehearsal, the information would decay and be lost from STM.

Another characteristic of STM is its limited capacity for information. Miller (1956) determined that STM has room for about seven items (chunks) of information. Moreover, STM has a "limited pool of effort" or cognition capacity (see, e.g., Britton, Meyer, Simpson, Holdredge & Curry, 1979; Kahneman, 1973; and Kerr, 1973). This limited pool is assumed to affect everything from decision making to the sizes of visual images that can be processed (e.g., Kosslyn, 1975). Klatzky (1980) defined STM as a "work space" in which information may be rehearsed, elaborated, used for decision making, lost, or stored in the third memory structure: long-term memory.

LTM is a complex and permanent storehouse for individuals' knowledge about the world and their experiences in it. LTM processes information to the two other memory structures and in turn receives information from the sensory registers and STM. First, the stimulus is recognized in the sensory registers through comparison with information in LTM. Second, information manipulated in STM can be permanently stored in LTM.

Perception is an interpretive process involving a great deal of unconscious inference (Helmholtz, 1866, as cited in Malone, 1990). An important characteristic of STM for our purposes is that despite the fact that it can apparently manipulate visual information (e.g., Cooper & Shepard, 1973), phonemic coding is the preferred modality (Baddeley, 1966; Conrad, 1964; Sperling, 1960). Related to this phenomena is that STM apparently treats printed text and spoken words the same: acoustically (e.g., Pellegrino, Siegel & Dhawan, 1974, 1976a, b). Basic research studies not only tend to confirm this treatment but also suggest that while people can remember information as being presented by picture or spoken word, printed text is identified as printed (versus spoken) at about a chance level (Burton, 1982; Burton & Bruning, 1982).

To understand how an individual is able to interpret information, the researcher must first focus on decisions made at each memory storage structure. Within the information-processing model, attention and pattern recognition determine the environmental factors that are processed. A large amount of information impinges on the sensory registers, but it is quickly lost if not attended to. Attention, therefore, plays an important role in selecting sensory information.

Early information-processing models viewed attention as a filler or bottleneck (e.g., Broadbent, 1958). For example, an individual could follow an auditory message across many "ears" (headphones) but could attend to only one message; the rest were filtered out. Work by Cherry (1953, 1957), Moray (1959), and Treisman (1960) indicated, however, that information in an unattended channel (same modality) can penetrate this proposed bottleneck. Current models (e.g., Shiffrin & Geisler, 1973) view attention as attenuation with unlimited capacity for recognition of stimuli coming from different channels at the same time. Recognizing a stimulus in one channel does not disturb the process of recognizing a second stimulus in another channel (Bourne, Dominowski, Loftus & Healy, 1986). Attention is conceived of as being a very limited mental resource (Anderson, 1985). It is difficult to perform two demanding tasks at the same time. While all information is registered by the sensory registers, only information attended to and processed to a more permanent form is retained. Bruner, Goodnow, and Auston (1967) stated that a person tends to focus attention on cues that have seemed useful in the past. Pattern recognition enables the individual to organize perceptual features (cues) so that relevant knowledge from LTM is activated. In other words, recognition is attention (Norman, 1969). Pattern recognition integrates information from a complex interaction that uses both bottom-up and top-down processing (Anderson, 1985). Bottom-up processing is the use of sensory information in pattern recognition. Top-down processing is the use of pattern context and general knowledge. In fact, attention is assumed to use both processes; that is, it is interactive (Neisser, 1967). Once relevant information is activated from LTM, the individual focuses attention on the relevant stimulus and brings it into the working memory (STM).

Long-term memory contains large quantities of information that have to be organized efficiently so they can be effectively encoded, stored, and retrieved. These three processes are interdependent. For example, the method of presentation determines how information is stored and retrieved (Klatzky, 1980). Encoding is related to the amount of elaboration and rehearsal conducted in STM. Elaboration uses information received from LTM after the stimulus is recognized. As new information is compared to the old and manipulated information, it is either added or subsumed into the existing schema, then encoded in LTM (Anderson, Greeno, Kline & Neves, 1981). These schema or "set of past experiences" are the cognitive structures that, when related to new information, cause meaning (Mayer, 1983, p. 68). As information is restructured and added, new structures are formed that result in new conceptualizations (Magliaro, 1988). These knowledge structures combine information in an organized manner. Evidence for memory storage indicates that representations can be both meaning based and perception based. Retrieval of information is also an active process. Information is accessed by a search of the memory structures. The speed and accuracy of retrieval is directly dependent on how the information was encoded and the attention being given to the stimulus. To be recalled from LTM, information must be activated. The level of activation seems to depend on the associative strength of the path. The strength of the activation increases with practice and with the associative properties (Anderson, 1985).

29.2.3 Dual Coding

Imagery theorists obviously make a distinction between the codes used for images versus verbal information. Paivio (1971, 1986) developed the dual-code model (see 16.2.1), which stated that the two types of information (verbal and imaginal) are encoded by separate subsystems, one specialized for sensory images and the other specialized for verbal language. The two systems are assumed to be structurally and functionally distinct. Paivio (1986) defined structure as the difference in the nature of representational units and the way in which these units are organized into higher-order systems. Structure, therefore, refers to LTM operations that correlate to perceptually identifiable verbal or visual objects and activities.

It is important to note that Paivio defines his two systems very broadly. An image can be a picture or a sound or even perhaps a taste, while the verbal store, on the other hand, is construed broadly to mean a language store (Burton & Bruning, 1982). In Paivio's (1971) words, image refers to:

> concrete imagery, that is, *nonverbal* memory representations of concrete objects and events, or nonverbal modes of thought (e.g., imagination) in which such representations are actively generated and manipulated by the individual. This will usually be taken to mean *visual* imagery, although it is clear that other modalities (e.g., auditory) could be involved, and when they are, this must be specified. Imagery, so defined, will be distinguished from verbal symbolic processes, which will be assumed to involve implicit activity in an auditory-motor speech system (p. 12).

Functionally, Paivio's two hypothesized subsystems are independent, meaning that either can operate without the other, or both can work parallel to each other. Even though independent of one another, these two subsystems are interconnected so that a concept represented as an image can also be converted to a verbal label in the other system, or vice versa (Klatzky, 1980). Paivio is very explicit, however, about the power of images: While words that can be imaged *may* be, images (and presumably all concrete sensory input) that can be translated *will* be, automatically. Paivio argues that this is why pictures are often remembered better than verbal information (Pressley & Miller, 1987).

Dual-code theorists accept that mental images are not exact copies of pictures but instead contain information that was encoded from a sensory event after perceptual analysis and pattern recognition (Klatzky, 1980). It is thought that the images are organized into subunits at the time of perception (Anderson, 1978). Paivio (1986) further explained that mental representations have their developmental beginnings in perceptual, motor, and affective experience and are able to retain these characteristics when being encoded so that the structures and the processes are modality specific. For example, a concrete object such as the ocean would be recognized by more than one modality—by its appearance, sound, smell, and taste. Therefore, a continuity between perception and memory as well as behavioral skills and cognitive skills is implied (Paivio).

There are, however, the same limits on imaginal processing that we see throughout the information-processing model. The concept of limited space was demonstrated by Kosslyn (1975), who asked students to visualize two named objects and then to answer questions about one of the objects. Students were slower to find parts that were next to an elephant than to find those next to a fly. STM for visuals appeared to have a processing limitation. Large objects like elephants (or even *very large* flies) "fill up" the system and slow it down. Retrieval of visually coded material also differs from other forms of internal representation. As previously stated, information is available simultaneously rather than by a sequential search and can be located by template or by an unlimited-capacity parallel search (Anderson, 1978).

Dual-coding theory can account for our personal impression of having images. The theory is often supported by research studies that conclude that individuals have a continuous and analog ability to judge space from images, in at least some cases (Kosslyn, 1975), and finally for studies that indicate strong visual-memory abilities. Paivio's theory is also able to effectively support the recurrent finding that memory for pictures is better than memory for words (Shepard, 1967), otherwise known as the *pictorial superiority effect* (Levie, 1987). Imagery theories have been used by researchers to construct and test hypotheses on learning from graphics (Winn, 1987) and seem a fruitful heuristic source for multimodality research in the future.

29.2.4 Detail and Experience

In terms of simple recognition, text modality detail does not seem to be important. Nelson, Metzler, and Reed (1974), for example, varied visual representations of the same scene from nondetailed drawings to photographs and compared recognition for the visuals versus text descriptions. As we would expect, pictures were superior in recognition tests, but there were no differences among the detail levels used. For recall, however, detail is important in at least two ways. Mandler and Parker (1976) showed that the location of detail elements are best recalled if they are organized in a meaningful way. Thus, for example, graphic elements of classroom items that are placed in their "usual" locations are superior to the same elements when they are not organized in a meaningful manner. Obviously, "meaningful" reflects prior knowledge, including culture. In a related way, specific expertise impacts memory for visuals. Egan and Schwartz (1979) demonstrated that skilled electronics technicians showed superior recall for circuit diagrams compared to novices, *as long as* the diagrams made "sense," that is, were organized in a meaningful manner.

Images can also be used to organize incoming information. The classic demonstration of this use of visuals to "make sense" of subsequent textual information is Bransford and Johnson's (1972) *Balloons* passage. In their study, people found text without the visuals (or the visual following the text) to be difficult to comprehend and remember

relative to the same text following an organizing visual. A related effect, "priming" (see, e.g., Neely, 1977; Posner & Snyder, 1975), has been demonstrated with text. Basically, a categorical prime, such as a bird, facilitated access to a specific bird, such as a robin. Conversely, an incorrect categorical prime inhibits access. A representative of the category in whatever modality should produce a similar effect (Miller & Burton, 1994).

Theory, basic research, and applied research predict and support the efficacy of images (and instructions to image) in learning and memory. Yet, images are prone to the same processes (and problems) that affect all aspects of the human system: distortions from "reality." We assume that human sensation is about the same for all of us. When confronted with a visual stimulus, we assume that our rods, cones, optic nerves, and so forth react about the same. Perceptually, however, we do not *see* the same things. We extract (and create) meaning from visual stimuli just as we do from text. Therefore, our prior experience, inferences, expectations, beliefs, physical state, and other factors determine what we see as surely as the stimulus before us. A similar process operates when we recall an image from memory: We reconstruct from our constructed images. Naturally, like memory for text, we forget details (Miller & Burton, 1994).

Finally, where there are gaps, we unconsciously fill them. As you will see in later chapters, images are effective for connecting items to be remembered and, if the level of detail is correct, for learning new facts and relationships. However, these tasks are rather low level and rote. In general, unless images are entrained to the point of pattern recognition, we can assume that the human memory system deals with images as it deals with text: generally or prototypically. The system is great at "gist" or meaning and poor at specifics. Thus, images may work "better" than text in many applications, but they probably do not work differently (Miller & Burton, 1994).

29.3 MULTIPLE-CHANNEL COMMUNICATION

Of major interest to communication theorists and instructional designers is whether humans can accommodate simultaneous audio and visual stimuli and, if so, the amount and types of information that could be so processed. Multiple-channel communication involves simultaneous presentations of stimuli ". . . through different sensory channels (i.e., sight, sound, touch, etc.) which will provide additional stimuli reinforcement" (Dwyer, 1978, p. 22).

Broadbent (1958) and later Feigenbaum and Simon (1963) espoused the single-channel theory, in which, if information arrives simultaneously in separate channels, information jamming will occur. Broadbent (1958, 1965) suggests that one reason for reduced learning in multiple-channel presentations is a result of the filtering process (bottleneck) occurring in an individual's information-processing system which reduces superfluous elements and permits only essential or basis information to be received; the nervous system acts as a single channel. Similarly, research conducted by Hernandez-Peon (1961) has led to a hypothesis known as the *Hernandez-Peon effect* that contends that when information is being processed via one sense, this act may cause an impediment to the processing of a stimuli through other senses. Likewise, Jocobson (1950, 1951) contended that the brain is able to process only small proportions of the large amounts of stimuli received. Thus, regardless of the amount of information presented in any sensory modality, learners are able to accept only limited amounts in the information-processing center (Attneave, 1954; Brown, 1959; Dwyer, 1972; Livingstone, 1962). Broadbent (1958) asserts that information-processing of human beings can receive information from only one source at a time; the additional information is temporarily stored (in the sensory register). However, Hartman (1961b) also points out that Broadbent's thesis regarding the filtering of information in the central nervous system is based on data obtained from presenting unrelated information to learners through two or more modalities simultaneously. If after this momentary storage the information is not used, it is not retained. Thus, people viewing multiple-channel presentations are presented with the problem of switching from one channel to another (Broadbent, 1956, 1965). Other researchers, including Shannon and Weaver (1949), Spaulding (1956), and Cherry (1953) support this theory. Corballis and Reaburn (1970), Clark (1969), Herman (1965), and Welford (1968) have documented the reduction (impairment) of the processing of information in multiple-channels communication situations. Travers (1968) concurs in his review of multiple-channel communication. He suggests that there is no convincing evidence that *multiple-channel communications* were any more effective in producing learning than single-channel inputs. There appears to be major concerns, however, involved in determining the amount of information a human being can process at any one time. Travers (1968) indicates unequivocally that the human processing system is one of limited capacity (see also Miller, 1956). To recognize information simultaneously, the various receptors (eyes, ears) would have to analyze a great variety of different cues. At this initial stage, the system *does* function as a multiple-channel system. But once recognition has occurred and, hence, attention (see also Norman, 1969), the remainder of operations on the incoming information is undertaken by a system with a limited capacity, the STM. The system from this point on operates as a single-channel system, Travers (1968) states, ". . . unless the rate at which the incoming information being received is less than the capacity of the system for handling information. Only under the latter condition can two separate and distinct sequences of messages be received at the same time" (p. 10). Human beings are able to deal with the vast complexities of various types of data from the environment. These data are then simplified to be handled by the perceptual system. Much of the simplification of this huge amount and complex data involves the discarding of redundant information. This process is referred to as "information compression" (Travers, 1968, p. 11).

It is also related to the information-processing system's strength: gist. Travers's perceptual model thus includes a high-capacity information system up to the point of recognition and a very limited system beyond. Lack of retention and understanding of many multiple-channel presentations are examples of this model in action. Travers's (1964a, 1964b, 1966) studies support this contention that human beings cannot receive more information if exposed to two or more sources simultaneously than if exposed to just one source, or if the information is transmitted by two different modalities. Van Mondfrans (1963), in a study using nonsense syllables and words, showed no advantage for an audiovisual presentation over presentations via audio and visual modalities alone. Cherry (1953) concluded that the utilization of information by the brain can be represented by a single-channel input. Travers (1968) continues and states that since the perceptual channel is very limited, we must assume that the receiver (learner) cannot process multiple-channel inputs as efficiently as "designers of audiovisual materials have commonly assumed" (p. 10).

Other researchers have supported the efficacy of single-channel presentations. These include Fleming (1970) who reviewed research studies dealing with single- and multiple-channel presentations and noted the possibility that many instructional programs are already "perceptually overloaded." He suggests that additional "jamming" of the perceivers' senses through multiple-media (channel) may have negative results. Fleming suggests that the only possible instructional situation where "stepped-up sensory environments" are useful is when the desire is to "overwhelm, impress, or to exhilarate." Hartman (1961a) concludes that multiple-channel presentations do not produce increases in learning (however defined) over single-channel communication, unless the situation in which the learning takes place also contains the necessary additional cues. Hartman (1961b) has also expressed concern about the act of increasing the number of cues and/or the number of channels used with the expectation that more learning will occur. He states:

> A common practice among multiple-channel communicators has been to fill the channels, especially the pictorial, with as much information as possible. The obvious expectation is for additional communication to result from the additional information. However, the probability of interference resulting from the additional cues is very high. The hoped-for enhanced communication resulting from a summation of cues occurs only under special conditions. Most of the added cues in the mass media possess a large number of extraneous cognitive associations. The possibility that these associations will interfere with one another is probably greater than that they will facilitate learning (p. 255).

Hsia (1971) drew several conclusions from an extensive review of literature comparing multiple- and single-channel presentations. These include: (1) Human information-processing functions as a multiple-channel system until the capacity of the system is overloaded; (2) when input becomes greater than the system's capacity, the system reverts to a single-channel system; and (3) an increase in the amount of information presented does not necessarily increase the rate of information transmission. Hsia (1971) asserts that, since all incoming information needs to be coded prior to being processed by the human processing system, it would seem reasonable that all extraneous, irrelevant, and superfluous information be eliminated or reduced at that time. Hsia (1971) contends that by reducing this "extra" information, the learner is spared from having to discriminate the relevant from the irrelevant. In addition to filtering information, a large part of redundancy and noise are eliminated. Hsia (1971) and Carpenter (1953) feel that the processing capability of an individual is limited by the physiological aspects of the individual. A person can receive far more stimuli than he or she can effectively process. Clark (1969), Corballis and Reaburn (1970), Herman (1965), and Welford (1968) indicate that there are a substantial number of research results that support the position that single-channel communication can be as effective as multiple-channel orientations. Dwyer (1978) cites approximately 50 studies in which the contention that additional cues—"provided by the use of two or more information channels simultaneously—or excessive realistic cues within a single-channel may be distracting or even evoke responses in opposition to the desired types of learning" (pp. 29, 30).

There is also much criticism of the research which supports the single-channel view. For example, Norberg (1966) takes Travers to task for basing his assumption concerning single-channel communication on experiments using verbal material in both auditory and visual channels (i.e., no pictures presented). Norberg (1966) explains that Travers's studies:

> . . . deal exclusively with verbal symbols, whereas most two-channel presentations actually used in instructional situations typically combine nonverbal signs in the visual channel with verbal auditory stimuli. . . . But it is still necessary to distinguish carefully between the actual experimental findings and theoretical statements regarding nonverbal "realistic " stimuli which have not entered into the experimental work cited. . . . It is one thing to say that the "density" of information in stimulus materials presented to the leaner may become a factor impeding efficient transmission; i.e., some presentations may be too realistic (p. 307).

Other criticisms of single-channel research are that much of the data collected were from studies where unrelated and/or contradictory stimuli was presented to the learners simultaneously. It would seem reasonable under these circumstances that a person would attend to one stimulus (message) and not the other. The following section looks at multiple-channel communication and the influences of the cue summation theories.

29.4 CUE SUMMATION AND MULTIPLE-CHANNEL COMMUNICATION

It is relatively easy to find current literature extolling the virtues of multimedia or hypermedia environments. Among the commonly mentioned advantages are:

- The ability to place learners in a context-rich environment
- An increase in learning due to the combination of text, graphics, full-motion video, and signs
- The ability to navigate complex nonlinear "hyperspace"
- An increase in motivation due to intrinsic aspects of the media

Desktop hardware and software have become more powerful, flexible, and sophisticated in the types of presentations that they can author and deliver. Moreover, such systems are within the budgets of many, if not most, K-12 classrooms. There has been a proliferation of authoring packages and CD-ROM–based programs that can deliver high-fidelity sound, realistic color images in stills, graphics, and full-motion video. The central issue in this chapter, however, is whether multiple-channel presentations provided by multimedia environments contribute to an increase in the amount of learning.

The terms *multiple-channel communication* and *cue summation* are routinely used interchangeably in the literature. Is there a difference? The cue summation principle of learning theory predicts that learning is increased as the number of available cues or stimuli is increased (Severin, 1967a). Does this mean the addition of cues within a single-channel, such as adding color to a picture? Or does it mean adding cues across channels such as adding audio to a visual presentation? For the purposes of this review, cue summation will include both the addition of cues within and across channels. Therefore the multiple-channel communication research in this review may be subsumed under the cue summation theories. Supporting this approach is Miller's (1957) view concerning cue summation, which is frequently cited:

> When cues from different modalities (or different cues within the same modality) are used simultaneously, they may either facilitate or interfere with each other. When cues elicit the same responses simultaneously, or different responses in the proper succession, they should summate to yield increased effectiveness. When the cues elicit incompatible responses, they should produce conflict and interference (p. 78).

Hoban (1949), in a summary of the instructional value of increasing the number of cues and/or realistic detail (which some call *single-channel realism theory*) in a visual presentation, concluded that the power of a medium of communication is determined by "the richness of the symbols employed" (p. 9) within that medium. These cues lead to greater understanding of the message by the audience.

Miller (1957) cites his views on the need to increase the number of cues in a presentation. He states that if one stimulus complex is to be identified versus another, the individual may use any number (even one) of available cues to make this discrimination. Increasing the number of available cues will increase the likelihood of an individual's making the correct discrimination over time and increasing the likelihood of a number of individuals making the correct discrimination simultaneously.

Dwyer (1978) suggests that the above views can be classified under the theoretical orientation collectively referred to as *realism theories*. The assumption is that:

> Learning will be more complete as the number of cues in the learning situation increases. They suggest that an increase in realism in the existing cues in a learning situation increases the probability learning will be facilitated (p. 6).

(It should be noted that by making a learning situation more complex does not necessarily make it more realistic.)

Allen and Cooney (1963) suggest that age and maturity have effects on recall of information from multiple- or single-channel presentations. The mode of presentation has less effect on learning than does maturity. Hsia (1969) studied the relationships between modalities and learner intelligence; he concluded that less-intelligent learners would be assisted positively if input, noise, and redundancy were controlled. Audiovisual (multiple-channel) presentations rather than single-channel presentations were suggested to optimize the information-processing rate of less-intelligent subjects. Further, Hsia recommended keeping cross-channel redundancy high in audiovisual (multiple-channel) presentations. Hsia (1968) similarly states that:

> . . . in dual or multi-channel information-processing, dimensionality of information generally increases, and one channel provides cues and clues for the other, provided that the amount of information to be presented has not reached the capacity limit, thereby eliminating probable interference or information jamming. Increase in dimensionality usually results in the increase of information-processing (p. 326).

Severin (1967b) suggests that "multiple-channel communications appear to be superior to single-channel communications when relevant cues are summated across channels; neither is superior when redundant between channels, and are inferior when irrelevant cues are combined (presumably because irrelevant cues cause interference between them)" (p. 397).

Severin's theory of cue summation differs slightly from others in that he stresses the addition of "relevant" cues. This is somewhat of a caveat to the general theory of cue summation, which states that an increase in cues will summate in more learning. Severin (1967c) also places emphasis on the use of pictorial presentations as the vehicle to add cues.

Van Mondfrans and Travers (1964) found that redundant information presented over two sense modalities (auditory plus visual) resulted in no better learning than from either sense modality used alone. Severin (1967a) points out that the work of Van Mondfrans and Travers did not deal with nonredundant information presented over two channels. Their work looked at verbal material in both channels—omitting the use of pictorial information.

Baggett and Ehrenfeucht (1983) reported that when college age subjects are watching a film presentation and related information is presented simultaneously across two mediums—visual and auditory—there is no competition for resources. When encoding visual and auditory information

sequentially, the extraction of information is not increased. They concluded that synchronous visual/auditory input is an efficient way to present information. Baggett (1984) reported superiority of a simultaneous presentation of narrative and visuals over a presentation of the narration prior to corresponding visual sequence, but speech given slightly after a visual sequence resulted in recall just as good as a simultaneous presentation. Nugent (1982) studied content redundancy of content across three channels and found that when the content was the same, subjects learned equally as well from all modes, and by combining modes generally maximized learning.

It is not surprising that much of the multiple-channel (audiovisual) research has been conducted in the television venue, particularly with studies dealing with questions of redundancy (see 11.2.3). Findahl (1971), Reese (1983), and Drew and Grimes (1987) reported the superiority of redundant audio and video presentations in the recall and retention of verbal information and understanding of content. Likewise, Pezdek and Stevens (1984) found that with kindergarten students audio and video channels with "'matched' information was better for memory than when channels were 'mismatched.'" They concluded that a high degree of redundancy helps learning in the audio channel and hinders the visual channel. With nonredundant material, the students relied primarily on the video for meaning however. Calvert, Hudson, Watkins, and Wright (1982) reported that children learned more when verbal content was supported by understandable video than when abstract audio was accompanied by recognizable video.

Rolandelli (1989) reports that in television presentations, the visual mode is more important than the auditory mode when visual component competes with incongruent audio tract, but when visual superiority is confounded with complexity and comprehensibility, comprehensibility appears to be a more critical factor in viewer behavior. Audio can enhance comprehensibility by signaling what is worthy of attention and conveys information that can be understood independently of the visual mode (being present). In studies exploring irrelevant visual distractions (Festinger & Maccoby, 1964; Ostehouse & Brock, 1970; Bither, 1972), it was found that irrelevant visual distractions have an adverse effect on audio recall.

Lumsdaine and Gladstone (1958), Kale, Grosslight, and McIntyre (1955), and Kopstein and Roshal (1954) found the use of pictorial information or picture-word combinations more effective than words alone. Setting out to develop a hypothesis for these findings, Severin (1967a) suggested that the principles of cue summation and stimulus generalization accounted for improvement in learning. Stimulus generalization implies that "learning" improves as testing situations become more similar to the presentation situation.

Additional studies have shown the superiority of the multiple-channel presentations of information. Severin (1967b, 1967c) reported that subjects receiving information with audio and related pictures received the highest scores of four treatments (sound only, picture only, sound and pictures, sound and unrelated pictures). He also reported finding that individual intelligence scores were less important in predicting learning than types of treatments. Hartman (1961a), in summarizing his study on multiple-channel effectiveness, indicated that "redundant information simultaneously presented by the audio and print channels is more effective in producing learning than the same information in either channel alone" (p. 42). Likewise, reviews of literature by Day and Beach (1950) that focused on the comparisons of audio and print channels, and the Hoban and Van Ormer studies (1950a) that concentrated on pictorial comparisons, concluded similar findings. However, Hartman (1961a) distinguished four relationships between multiple-channel messages and those on studies: redundant, related, unrelated, and contradictory. If multiple-channel messages are unrelated or contradictory, they compete with each other, and information interference is the result. That is why multiple-channel presentations were less effective in some studies. But if audio and visual messages were identical or closely related, they complement the other to form one thought and improve learning (Hanson, 1989; Ketcham & Heath, 1962). In educational practices, we seldom deliver unrelated or contradictory messages through multiple channels. Therefore, an improvement of learning is expected by adopting the multiple-channel approach (Yang, 1993).

The implications of this work for development of multimedia products is considerable. It suggests that the addition of "bells and whistles" may contribute unrelated cues. As Severin (1967b) says: "If interference is accidentally introduced between channels, then much effort, time, and money is wasted, for one channel could then communicate more effectively" (p. 399). This work could provide advice for those engaged in the development of multimedia products for "at-risk" audiences. For these groups, less emphasis on print material, combined with the summation of cues using relevant material in the other channels, may be more appropriate.

Smith and Smith (1966) critiqued earlier multiple-channel research (sometimes called *audiovisual research*). The Smiths stated:

> Implicit in many of the older research designs which tried to make direct comparisons between different techniques was the assumptions that different types of instruction promoted the same type of learning—presumably the learning of verbal knowledge. These experimental comparisons usually were based on verbal criterion tests, for it was not realized that specialized audiovisual procedures might teach specialized nonverbal knowledge (p. 142).

Dwyer (1978) identified 19 factors that complicate interpretation and cause contradictory results of the single- and multiple-channel communication research studies. Some criticisms include weakness in experimental design, studies lacking hypotheses, research conducted in nonrealistic situations, and lack of relationship content used in one channel versus another.

Hartman (1961b), commenting on a review of 30 studies of channel comparisons, suggested that for presenting related information either through one or two channels, there is a strong indication of an advantage of combining channels. Severin (1967a) points out, however, that most of these studies were completed prior to 1940, and many contained poor research designs, lacked controls, and had test channel bias. Interference between channels, due to unrelated or opposing information, were not recognized in many of the studies. Severin (1967a) continues that a common practice among many communication researchers was to fill all channels in a multiple-channel situation with as much information (cues) as possible, with the expectation that this additional information would increase communication. The probability is quite high, however, that the additional information will only "evoke irreverent cues" (p. 234). Also see a strikingly similar statement by Hartman (1961b, p. 255).

Severin (1967a) attempts to explain the contradictory research findings of those who have studied multiple-channel and single-channel communication. Severin asks why some studies show an increase in learning in cross- (multiple) channel redundancy and others do not? Severin (1967a) suggests that educators sometimes use multiple channels without understanding the possibilities of interference between them, and information may be presented via two channels and testing mode presented with only one channel. If, as Broadbent (1957) suggests, the central nervous system is a single system, separate presentations across two channels may not exceed its capacity, but together could overload and jam. Gulo and Baron (1965) and Williams and Ogilvie (1957) suggest that presentations do not always use the second channel to convey information and thus add nothing, not even redundancy, and might cause interference.

Hsia (1968) also questions the inconsistent findings. He feels that a major cause is the failure to take into account the capacity limit theorem and redundancy. First, redundancy causes information processing to fluctuate. Second, equivocation (loss of information) is caused by overloading the capacity limit. Hsia suggests that decreasing input information in accordance with the information-processing capacity will eliminate or reduce equivocation. Error, he submits, will be eliminated by adjusting redundancy to an optimum level so that maximum transfer may take place.

Conway (1968), however, suggests that "the distinction between redundant and related information must now be regarded as an artifact of faulty conceptualization" (p. 409). He opines that equivalence in referential function is the criterion for redundancy. That is, "two items are redundant in that, as sign vehicles, they are interpreted to make reference in an equivalent fashion" (Conway, 1968, p. 409). Two important issues are implied in this discussion. First, Conway questions Severin's hypotheses concerning cue summation and stimulus generalization and the criteria upon which they are made. Second, Conway goes to some length in discussing whether relationships involving two signs or two modalities are redundant or related. If, as Conway proposes, most of the above relationships are redundant, as opposed to related, then there is no advantage in combining signs or sensory modalities. In refuting the hypothesis that presentations combining two sensory modalities are more efficient than either one of the modalities used alone, Conway cites findings from Van Mondfrans and Travers (1964), and from Severin (1967a, c). Severin's (1967a) position states there is no advantage in using "redundant" information over two modalities versus either one used alone. An example would be a presentation of the spoken word *moose* and the written word *moose*. Severin (1967a) hypothesizes that "related or relevant" presentations using two signs offer the greatest gain in communications. An example of the latter would be a picture of a moose and the written word *moose,* or a picture of a *moose* along with the spoken word *moose.*

Conway (1968), in an attempt to analyze the cue summation and stimulus generalization theories, tested word-plus-picture presentations against other conditions. He found that the present-picture/test-picture condition to be superior to those of present-word/test-word plus picture or those of present-word/test-word. He failed to find significance in the present-word/test-picture and present-picture/test-word conditions. Conway suggests that the dual-coding theory (Paivio, 1971) may account for the failure to support the stimulus generalization theory. For example:

> . . . simple pictorial (line drawing) sign vehicles, although presented as single units, are, it is suggested, most likely to be coded and stored in two internal forms and therefore more likely than either word or word-plus-picture presentations to be readily assessed by the sign-vehicle presentations used to test memory (p. 412).

Using somewhat analogous reasoning to explain Van Mondfrans and Travers's (1964) failure to support an advantage to combined spoken- and printed-word presentations, Conway suggests that these messages are functionally equivalent and are already stored in word form. Therefore, using either spoken or printed-word presentations would be equal in learning to a combined presentation. It would follow that recall would also be equal under either stimulus, because the material is stored as a verbal string under both modes of presentation.

Much kinder to cue summation theory and Severin's (1967a, 1967b) views is Hsia (1968, 1971). He submits that ". . . tangible evidence suggests the possibility that when the amount of information to be processed is optimal, the audiovisual channels may be a more effective means of communication than either single channel" (p. 246). Hsia (1971) makes a very thorough literature review of the discrete ranges of audio, visual, and audiovisual information-processing rates and capacities. One of his conclusions is that combined audiovisual presentations produce more dimensionality than audio or visual alone. This dimensionality, he says, brings about an increase in information transfer within the information-processing capacity.

Hsia (1968) cautions, however, that multimodal information-processing seems to reach the overloading point faster than using single channels alone, especially when the between-channel redundancy is low. In essence, Hsia (1968) is proposing that designers remain cognizant of the principle that audiovisual communications will provide dimensionality and address individual-learner differences when used within the capacity of the nervous system. He also addresses individual-learner traits. For example, he cites research that supports use of the audio channel for young children, poor readers, and those of limited ability. In dealing with literate subjects, however, he provides evidence for using visual presentations. We could easily deduce that this information supports a need for multiple-channel presentations, especially when resources do not permit developing presentations for specific-learner types. Severin (1967a) makes the following predictions based on research when comparing single-channel communication and multiple-channel communication. Multiple-channel presentations that combine words and relevant visuals across channels will be the most effective and superior to single channels alone. This is due to cue summation across the channels. Multiple-channel communication with unrelated cues across both channels will cause interference, and thus single-channel presentations will be superior. Single-channel communication will be as effective as multiple-channel presentations when words (aurally and visually) are combined across channels.

Whether one subscribes to Severin's (1967) theory of using related multiple-channel communications, or the more generally held notion of using redundant information (Hsia, 1968), there is a considerable body of research supporting combined presentations (Levie & Lentz, 1982). From a review of over 155 experiments, Levie and Lentz (1982) suggest that: using attention-getting pictorials increase the possibility that material will be looked at; using text-redundant illustrations will facilitate learning the textual material; illustrations will help learners understand and remember readings; learners often need prompting to pay attention to critical information found in illustrations; learners' enjoyment and affective reactions may be evoked from illustrations; poor readers may benefit from illustrations; and learner-generated imaginal pictures are generally less useful than supplied illustrations.

Supporting both cue summation and stimulus generalization were two studies by Beck (1987). His findings indicated that labeled pictures used during instruction provided more effective encoding cues than arrowed or noncued pictures. During evaluation, the repetition of identical cues appeared to assist learners in retrieving critical information.

Rigney and Lutz (1976) found that the use of images significantly improved learning of complex concepts. Students also found the graphics versions to be more enjoyable. The enjoyment, it appears, increases involvement, so that students may acquire concepts from verbal instructional materials. Their research also supports Levie and Lentz's (1982) findings that supplied illustrations are better than user-generated imaginal pictures.

Mayer (1989) found evidence that the use of labeled illustrations helped students with limited prior knowledge of mechanical systems recall more explanative information and perform better on problem-solving transfer. He suggested that a meaningful learning model using illustrations helps focus attention on explanative textual information and to assimilate the information into useful mental models.

Mayer and Gallini (1990) tested two major features of illustrations that would assist learners in building mental models: system topology and component behavior. The former portrays each major system component; the latter portrays state changes in major components and the relationships of the components as the system functions. An example would be the major component of a braking system and the changes each component undergoes in relationship to the others as the system is employed. Findings supported their hypothesis that these illustrations would assist explanative recall and improve creative problem solving for low prior-knowledge learners.

Mayer and Anderson (1991) extended previous research (Mayer, 1989; Mayer & Gallini, 1990) by using voice narration and animation. While inconclusive, the results supported the theory that coordinated presentation of narrative and visuals (animations) (see 16.2.1) results in better performance on tests of creative problem solving than the word-before-pictures group. This research on integrated dual coding was adapted from Paivio's (1971) dual-code hypothesis. This extended theory posits that learners can build both visual and verbal representations as well as connections between them. Significant for designers was the finding that animation without narration had about the same effect as no instruction. Further, they found presenting unconnected words and pictures is not as useful as coordinated verbal narration simultaneous with animation.

Reynolds and Baker (1987) were interested in the notion of selective attention and its influence on using text and graphical representations. They found that texts with graphs, and texts without graphs, did not differ in degree of learning effect. Presenting materials on a computer, however, did increase attention and learning. Further, they found that interactive, graphical representation increased attention. The amount learned, although not significant, did show an increase. Their research suggested that when attention was increased, so was the amount of learning.

As noted earlier, questions over the superiority of individual channels have intrigued researchers for years. Conflicting results can be found which favor either channel. Katz and Deutsch (1963) and Travers (1964), for examples, reported results that supported the visual channel over the auditory channel. However, Carterette and Jones (1967), Hartman (1961a, b), Henneman (1952), and Mowbray (1952) determined that auditory presentations were superior for young children and had more resistance to interference. Other researchers (Beagles-Roos & Gat, 1983; Meringoff, 1980) found that recall by children is comparable for visual and auditory modalities. However, Hayes, Kelly, and Mandel (1986) disagree and feel that verbal information recalled was incidental to the central plot of a televised program. Mudd and McCormick (1960) reported that, provided the information is related, auditory cues of various dimensions appreciably decrease the time involved in a visual-search task. Warshaw (1978) reported on a series of experiments in which

subjects were shown commercials with various juxtapositioning of different levels of audio and video information. He reported that when auditory information was presented without background video (a blank screen), more content was recalled than when audio appeared simultaneously with relevant video, regardless of the level of information content in the second channel. Warshaw continued and stated that multiple-channel presentations do attract more attention than either channel alone, but perceptual interferences across multiple channels will hamper assimilation of the content.

Other studies supporting the single-channel, nervous system theory (Broadbent, 1958)) found no difference between modalities (Baker & Alluisi, 1962; Hill & Hecher, 1966). Lorch, Bellock, and Augsback (1987) also noted that in televised presentations, children's recall of "central" content was comparable to audio only, visual only, or simultaneous across both modes. Grimes (1991) continues: In studies conducted with television where two channels—audio and visual—are highly redundant, people view the two channels as components of a single message. In a medium-redundancy situation, attention was shifted away from the visual channel and more attention was applied to the auditory channel. He reported contradictory results in a nonredundant presentation in one study in which the group attended to the video and in another study in which they did not. However, in the two experiments with nonredundant presentations, viewers' memory dropped for auditory messages and suggested low visual attention but high visual memory.

29.5 MULTI-IMAGE PRESENTATIONS

The concept of multi-image is closely akin to properties of cue summation research, which suggests increased learning from more cues within a single channel or using more cues across (multiple) channels. Multi-image research was very popular in the 1960s and 1970s. The multi-image format (see 16.4.2.4) in these earlier studies generally referred to the use of more than one image, with or without audio synchronization on single- or multiple-projection screens. Millard (1964) stated that simultaneous images can be used advantageously in instructional situations that require comparisons, the development of interrelated concepts, and illustrations of relationships, or in the presentation of dimensional and spatial characteristics of objects. Perrin's (1969) theory of using multi-images is based on the simultaneous presentation of images in which images interact; this may be of significance in making comparisons and establishing relationships. Film, slides, television, etc. (not current interactive multimedia formats), presented content and images in a sequential, linear format. The meaning was based on the context (content that preceded) of the image. However, multi-image allows, as Perrin states:

> . . . the viewer to process larger amounts of information in a very short time. Thus information density is effectively increased, and certain kinds of information are more efficiently learned (p. 369).

However, questions raised earlier by Hartman (1961), Hsia (1971), and others concerning the efficacy of simultaneously presenting information across (and within) channels also apply to the concept of multi-image presentations.

Burke and Leps (1989) indicated that there may have been a "failure" by multiple-image enthusiasts to prove its effectiveness. Multi-image, like other specific technologies, has always had to use traditional media comparison studies with their inherent problems (see 4.2.4). Fradkin (1974, 1976) noted that although there was wide use of multi-image in education, there was little empirical evidence in support of increased learning. Moreover, Burke and Leps (1989) note that little research on multi-image presentations has investigated the validity of aspects of Perrin's theory, and that many studies of multiple-image presentations have been limited to self-serving individuals involved in the hardware and production processes.

All of these instructional situations require association, which, according to Gagné (1965), is one of the basic mechanisms of learning. According to Perrin (1969), the number of instances available to the viewer to make associations by visual comparison are greater with simultaneously presented images than with sequentially presented images. Low (1968) pointed out that in single-image presentations one image follows another, thus determining the interrelationships between images. In multiple-image presentations, several images appear simultaneously and "interact upon each other *at the same time,* and this is of significant value in making comparisons and relationships" (Perrin, 1969, p. 90).

Perrin (1969) stressed that images are especially rich in information and in the range of associations they stimulate. Without careful control by the communicator, there is the possibility that some associations can conflict with the intended message, causing interference. Relevance, realism, and simplicity have been found to be important in learning from book illustrations (Spaulding, 1956) and in learning from films (May & Lumsdaine, 1958). These factors are equally important in presentations utilizing multiple imagery (Perrin, 1969). A viewer's ability to determine relationships between images has an effect on memory and recall (Berger, 1973; Low, 1968). Low stated that no single image can establish certain memory combinations, but a group of images perceived simultaneously often recalls long-forgotten memories. Berger (1973) found that multi-image techniques are effective in expediting the recall of events and thought-feeling associations in analytic psychology. The recall of memories and of events attributed to simultaneous images may be a function of the viewers' freedom to select their own sequence (Bruner, 1967; Gagné & Briggs, 1974). Therefore, as Perrin (1969) pointed out, presenting images simultaneously and allowing viewers to select their own sequential order may have an effect on the learning taking place. Roshka (1960), Malandin (cited in Perrin, 1969), and Allen and Cooney (1963) found simultaneous presentation of images effective in instruction with younger children. Roshka (1960) found that simultaneous images had less effect with older

children, and Allen and Cooney (1963) stated that simultaneous images had a significant effect on learning of sixth-graders, but not eighth-graders. Malandin (cited in Perrin, 1969) found that primary classes had difficulty with recall from sequential images, but that grouping the images permitted an increase in the number of recollections and organization of the recollections. These studies support Perrin's (1969) view that image simultaneity is a significant factor in some learning situations. Beck (1983), in a study that supported Perrin's views, found that subjects exposed to simultaneous picture formats achieved significantly higher scores than subjects exposed to successive (linear) formats. Goldstein (1975) stated that the simultaneous presentation of multiple images is in many respects "like the environment; it contains meaningful material, it surrounds us, and it is constantly changing" (p. 63).

A caution that emerges from the literature concerning the simultaneity of multiple images is that the theory of cue summation may not be valid in some contexts. Recall that cue summation, as noted earlier, is the general theory that posits that the more cues that are given through various communications channels, the more learning occurs (Whitley, 1977). Perrin (1969) notes that the use of simultaneous multiple images places a burden on the visual channel and that in the multiplication of visual stimuli, irrelevant as well as relevant detail is increased. Therefore, care must be taken to ensure that the visual stimuli are clear and simple and that detail included is relevant. Otherwise, the result is not cue summation but confusion. A study by Fradkin and Meyrowitz (1975) supports this hypothesis that cue summation and the avoidance of conflicting cues is important in the design of multiple-image presentations produced for cognitive learning situations.

29.5.1 Screen Size

The use of a large screen coupled with the simultaneous projection of two or more images has been cited as one of the major, inherent advantages of multiple imagery. A large screen provides better approximations of "real" environments by supplying the physical and psychological factors (see 16.11.1, 36.3.10) necessary for realism and involvement (Perrin, 1969).

Blackwell (1968) indicated that tasks requiring high visual acuity, such as detecting differences in texture or patterns, might benefit from the use of large-screen presentations. Two factors affecting usefulness of large screens were identified by Schlanger (1966): visual impact and visual task. Visual impact is the amount and forcefulness of information available to the sense of sight. The visual impact is proportional to the amount of the viewer's field of view that the screen occupies. According to Blackwell (1968), visual impact on the viewer is greater in large-screen presentations because more of the viewer's field of vision is occupied by the projected image—therefore limiting the chance of distraction from the surrounding environment. Schlanger

(1966) stated that large screens can produce information rich in detail for the visual channel and simulate real environments, but Blackwell (1968) warned that any channel of communication loaded with information details may be distracting if the details are irrelevant to the learning situation. Travers (1966), while attempting to deal with excess details, hypothesized that line drawings would be advantageous because they eliminated superfluous detail. His experiments with oversimplified drawings, however, indicate poor transfer of learning to real situations. Blackwell (1968) stated that the advantage of a large screen to reduce the visual task factor is conditional. Presented images, for example, must contain enough irrelevant detail to convey the proper message (which may not have been the situation in Travers's experiments), but not so much detail as to distract learners. Barr (1963) stated that a large screen opens up the frame and gives a greater sense of continuous space. The more open the frame, the greater the impression of depth; the image is more vivid. This suggests that simultaneous images produce an increase in information density during presentations.

29.5.2 Information Density

A greater density of information is possible with multiple than with linear imagery. There are several dimensions to information density in multiple-image presentations (Whitley, 1977). Perrin (1969) believes that it is important to distinguish between the method of presentation and the mechanism of perception. He states that the theory of multiple images suggests that for making contrasts and comparisons, and for learning relationships, "simultaneous images reduce the task of memory (a dimension of visual task) and enable the viewer to make immediate comparisons" (p. 376).

Langer (1957) utilizes the terms *linear* and *nonlinear* to distinguish between verbal and iconic signs. She stresses the sequential ordering, the "strung-out" arrangement of linear (verbal) signs in time and contrasts this to the "all-at-once" (parallel) character inherent in pictorial signs (p. 83). Her position is that even single pictures shown in sequential order are essentially nonlinear (Whitley, 1977).

Nonlinearity and simultaneity go hand in hand. The use of visual images, inherently nonlinear, allows the presentation of a great deal of information simultaneously rather than sequentially, as with words arranged in sentences and thus bound to grammatical ordering and syntax. Perrin (1969) expands this line of analysis and hypothesizes that when visual images are combined in multi-image presentations, the result is an increase in the amount of information presented simultaneously, or in the information density of the presentation.

Information density can be further increased if the information is organized properly (Whitley, 1977). McFee (1969) believes that visual organization is more important than the actual amount of information present. Much of our responding occurs so quickly that we are unaware of our own processing. Selecting and organizing visuals in advance makes the information for the user easier to assimilate (p. 85).

Investigative confirmation of the importance of organization is illustrated by the introduction of a carefully organized and automated televised instructional system called TeleMation at the University of Wisconsin. Hubbard found (1961) that information density could be significantly increased through proper organization without loss of material or loss of learning by students. A similar finding resulted when the Army Ordinance Guided Missile School conducted a series of evaluative studies in 1958 (U.S. Army, 1959). Instruction time was reduced 19.5% to 41% for a similar level of achievement, and an increase in learning was reported for the experimental groups 9 weeks later. Allen and Cooney (1963), however, suggested that time saved in instruction was as much a function of care in preparation as it was a function of the multi-imaged delivery of the subject matter.

Commercial producers claim that information density created through multiple imagery results in motivation and arousal. A serious question is whether or not this arousal is beneficial (Whitley, 1977). Research on motivation indicates that an increase in motivation improves performance (Smith, 1966) but that there is an optimum level. Eysenck (1963) found that for complex tasks, optimum performance is achieved when drive is relatively low; only for simple tasks is the optimum achieved with relatively high drive. Kleinsmith and Kaplan (1963, 1964) and Kleinsmith, Kaplan, and Tarte (1963) found that there is some confusion between learning and performance, with a person sometimes performing very poorly in highly arousing situations, yet tending to remember most vividly those incidents in his life that were most traumatic or arousing. These researchers measured skin conductivity, and their findings indicated that high-arousal associates showed stronger permanent memory and weaker immediate memory than low-arousal associates. Low arousal was accompanied by the normal forgetting curve. High-arousal responses showed poor immediate recall. This may explain some inconsistencies in research with regard to long-term retention. For example, Vander-Meer (1951) found that color films did not increase immediate learning but produced greater long-term retention. The findings of Kleinsmith suggest that the cause may have been the arousal produced by the color films.

Fleisher (1969) stated that the mind and eye have proved to be capable of tremendous speed and versatility in accepting multiple impressions, and that during a multi-image presentation the viewer's eyes explore the entire screen and keep the viewer very conscious of what is happening. In contrast, Goldstein (1975) indicated that multi-image presentation may cause information overload by presenting more information than the viewer can process and thus create arousal through frustration. This arousal may cause multi-image presentations to be highly motivating but not very informative (Kreszock, 1981). Goldstein (1975) stated that when presenting specific concepts or highly technical information, multi-image presentations should be used with restraint. Perrin (1969) concluded that it is clear that great densities of information can be perceived during a multi-image presentation, but he went on to question whether great amounts of information were learned from these perceptions.

Several studies have compared different aspects of single-image and multi-image presentations. Lombard (1969) used both a single-image and multi-image format to teach synthesis skills in history to 11th-grade students. He found no significant differences in males between the single-image and multi-image presentations at any achievement level, and the only female group to demonstrate any significant difference were the low achievers. These low-achieving females who received the multi-image presentations surpassed both the males and females in the average- and high-achiever groups who received the single-image format. Some of the procedures used in Lombard's study, however, make his findings dubious.

Conducting a study to explore the affective impact of multi-image presentations, Bollman (1970) experimented to see if there was any difference in the amount of shift in evaluative meaning of audiences viewing multi-image presentations and audiences viewing single-image presentations, and to ascertain if the persons' relationship to the screen had any effect on shifts in evaluative meaning. In his conclusions, Bollman (1970) stated that this experiment did not produce significant statistical evidence or conclusive answers.

Atherton (1971) conducted a study to determine if a multi-image slide presentation would result in greater affective and cognitive learning than similar content presented by a 16-mm film. No significant differences were found between groups in the amount of attitudinal change elicited as a result of the presentation, or between treatment of groups relative to the cognitive learning resulting from viewing the presentations. These analyses indicated that one treatment was not significantly more effective (or even affective) than the other in producing positive increases in affective or cognitive learning (Atherton, 1971). Didcoct (1958) conducted a study of the cognitive and affective responses of college students to single-image and multi-image presentations. He found no significant difference in attitude or cognitive retention between a group viewing a single-image presentation and a group viewing a multi-image presentation.

Westwater (1972), in conducting a descriptive study to gather information about the field use of a multi-image presentation, found that about 80% of the teachers who participated in the study would like to use such presentations to a greater degree. Westwater, however, pointed out two major limitations to the development of multi-image presentations. These are that few teachers were familiar with the characteristics and capabilities of large multi-image presentations, and they lack knowledge concerning their utility.

Jonassen (1979) states that it is generally believed that research on multi-image presentation revolves around linear vs. simultaneous presentation factors. Using Perrin's theory, most researchers predict that learning will increase (however it is measured) when "the viewer makes his own montage of different image elements, increasing the probability of learning comparative information" (Perrin, 1969,

p. 369). Jonassen (1979) indicates that the mere presentation of simultaneous images does not necessarily lead to simultaneous mental processing. The view still must provide a cognitive strategy for processing and make sense of the presentation order. Just as linear-sequenced material must be processed based on content and syntactic associations, multi-image presentations must also. Jonassen (1979) found that the literature on multi-image (simultaneous) presentations has yielded contradictory results. He feels that incomplete questions in the research hypothesis were asked instead of just questions about linearity vs. simultaneity. Researchers should consider "how simultaneous images can best be structured to facilitate specific types of learning behavior" (p. 292). Jonassen (1979) continues by indicating that proponents have assumed that multi-image presentations are a unique form of communication. Multi-imagery is "not a medium," it is a presentation mode that can manipulate visual perception. Therefore, study on multi-image presentations should be based on established principles of concept learning. To date, little research in this area has been conducted with concept teaching in mind. An exception would be the study conducted by Whitley and Moore (1979) which found significant interactions between a student perceptual type (visual vs. haptics) and presentation mode (linear vs. simultaneous). Haptics scored higher with multi-image presentations. Another exception was completed by Ausburn (1975), which found that both haptics and visuals benefited from multi-image presentations.

Burke and Leps (1989), gleaning information from the limited (and possibly flawed) research on multi-image presentations (see 16.4.2.4), feel that multi-image as a concept offers little to learners to improve cognitive potential or "affective impact." This is due to conceptually weak studies. The limited number of reviews concerning multiple-image research (Allen & Cooney, 1964; Burke, 1987; Burke & Leps, 1989) have revealed few usable results. There is, of course, the seemingly ever-present problem of research design and implications. These basic problems included retention studies comparing single-image and multiple-image presentations that were flawed by the presence of unnecessary recall data in both sound tracks. In addition, "the comparisons were usually of single- and multiple-screen versions of the same material, thereby canceling out Perrin's theoretical call for multi-image to enhance a basic message" (Burke & Leps, 1989, p. 185). Burke and Leps, however, feel that multi-image presentations were given little opportunity to prove themselves due to cost and technical execution of the presentations.

29.6 SUBLIMINAL PERCEPTION AND INSTRUCTION

Subliminal perception refers to visual and auditory information presented at a speed and or intensity that is below the conscious threshold of perception through one or more channels and thus not readily apparent to the subject

(Moore, 1982). Subliminal perception, like multi-image presentations, is also closely related to the theoretical bases of cue summation and multiple-channel research. All are interested in providing the learner with the maximum amount of usable cues, with the idea that these cues will support and reinforce each other. This is similar to multiple-channel theory, which suggests that additional simultaneous cues within and across sensory channels provides greater reinforcement in organizing and structuring information.

Experiments using subliminal exposure to visual and audio stimuli have been reported in psychological journals since 1863 (*Application of Subliminal Perception in Advertising,* 1958). Reviews of experimentation in subliminal perception have contributed summaries of various points of view. Three excellent sources on the subject were published by Miller (1942), Adams (1957), and McConnell, Cutler, and McNeil (1958). All three sources indicate that research results have differed widely (DeChenne, 1975).

In reviewing three summaries of research on subliminal perception (Bevan, 1964; Dixon, 1971; McConnell, Cutler & NcNeil, 1958), several generalizations become apparent. Susceptibility to subliminal stimulation varies among people and is dependent on factors such as anxiety, attentiveness, and need state. Sensitivity to subliminal effects tends to be cumulative, since repeated viewing of subliminal materials tend to make a person more aware of the technique. Differences in awareness thresholds also determine whether subliminal messages are perceived. Perception thresholds can be lowered if the duration of the subliminal exposure increases or is of different brightness than the surrounding visual field. In other words, the closer to being consciously visible the material is, the more likely it is to be perceived (Moore, 1982).

Early experiments were designed to provide evidence that the psychological phenomenon of subliminal perception was a reality. One of the earliest of these experiments was reported by Hollingworth (1919). Others included experiments by Maker (1937), Coyne, King, Zubin, and Landis (1943), McGinnus (1949), Lazarus and McClearey (1951), and Wilcot (1953). All except Wilcot reported results that there had been definite unconscious recognition or influence by stimuli below the conscious threshold. These studies gained attention for the concept of subliminal perception but brought about additional research that was often inconclusive and contradictory (Moore, 1982). More recent experiments have focused on determining relationships between subliminal perception and behavior. Studies of this type included those of Klein, Spence, Holt, and Gourevtich (1958), and Smith, Spence, and Klein (1959), all of which reported tendencies of a positive nature concerning the effectiveness of subliminal perception.

Several studies have been conducted to determine whether subliminal shapes or words could be detected when superimposed on a still or moving picture. One method of operationalizing subliminal stimulation is to superimpose a message at a very low relative brightness for a long period of time. This method was used by DeFleur and Petranoff (1959) in one of the first studies of subliminal perception using television as a carrier medium. The subliminal material in this experiment was superimposed as an extremely faint image, relative to the main program. Analysis of the results indicated that significantly more correct guesses had occurred than would have been expected by chance. It was not reported if the participants were asked whether they had consciously seen any of the shapes during the film. Nevertheless, the results seemed to indicate that TV images of extremely low brightness influenced their responses.

Moore (1982) commented on the procedures used in DeFleur and Petranoff's (1959) study. The low-intensity, constant-image technique that was used by DeFleur and Petranoff could result in the "subliminal" image being consciously visible. Because the visual field of the motion picture was dynamic (the images moved and changed), the faint subliminal words or shapes that were on the screen may have become partially unmasked at times as the foreground images changed. For example, if the constantly superimposed, subliminal images were white and the foreground images (the motion picture) in the same area of the screen were momentarily dark, then the resulting contrast differences may have been sufficient to unmask and reveal the subliminal word or shape or an identifiable segment of it. If the superimposed words or shapes were quickly flashed rather than constantly exposed, then the visual threshold of viewers would remain higher and the images would more likely remain subliminal (Moore, 1982).

Similar experiments have been reported by several other researchers. In these experiments, the subliminal shapes or words were nonmoving images on a neutral background, as compared to the moving foreground images used by DeFleur and Petranoff (1959). Schiff (1961) and King, Landis, and Zubin (1944) reported positive results, while Champion and Turner (1959) and Calvin and Dollenmayer (1959) concluded that there was no definitive evidence that behavior was altered by subliminal presentations. The relationship between subliminal stimulation and cognitive functions has been studied in a number of experiments. Kolars (1957) (two studies) and Gerard (1960) used a problem-solving task in which rows of geometric figures were simultaneously presented by a tachistoscope. Kolars concluded that the presentations of subliminal stimuli did influence the frequency of correct answers in both studies. Gerard tested participants' ability to reconstruct mentally a composite, geometric figure into alternative assemblies. One group saw the correct solution, another group saw an incorrect solution, and the control group saw no subliminal solution.

The results indicated that the control group did better than either of the subliminal treatment groups. However, the group shown the correct answer did better than the group shown the incorrect answers, as hypothesized. Gerard's results partially confirmed Kolers' findings, however, that subliminal presentations could affect performance on problem-solving tests (DeChenne, 1975; Moore, 1982; Moore & Moore, 1984).

The research described above (Calvin & Dollenmayer, 1959; DeFleur & Petranoff, 1959; Gerald, 1960; Kolers,

1957) indicates that subliminal perception can occur among certain people in laboratory settings. Research dealing with educational uses has been conducted by Murch (1965) and Sharp (1959) who demonstrated that the test-taking behavior of students can be subliminally influenced. DeChenne (1975), Skinner (1969), and Taris (1970) studied either teaching subject matter or teaching a skill entirely by subliminal means (DeChenne, 1975, Moore, 1982).

In contrast to Murch (1965) and Sharp (1959), who demonstrated that choice behavior could be altered in a test-taking situation, the experiments of DeChenne (1975), Skinner (1969), and Taris (1970) failed to demonstrate that direct teaching by subliminal perception can occur. Although various laboratory experiments have produced evidence that subliminal perception can occur, field experiments conducted to test direct teaching by subliminal perception have not yielded collaborative results.

Moore (1982) contends that when teaching by a subliminal means under conditions when the subject matter to be taught is transmitted with films that are unrelated and/or irrelevant to the subject matter, the possibility for content interference is great and the lack of conductive and focused learning setting would seem to hinder learning further. "Expecting subliminally produced learning to occur now seems less realistic than expecting a classroom teacher to teach while students are watching an Abbott and Costello comedy" (pp. 19, 20).

A number of studies investigated the possibilities that motivation might be influenced by subliminal perception. Among these were studies by Byrne (1959) and Goldstein and Davis (1961), whose results indicated no influence on the subjects. Goldstein and Barthal (1968) and Zuckerman (1960) conducted studies to determine whether subliminal stimulation could influence elaborative thinking. In both studies, positive and negative words were subliminally flashed with pictures from the Thematic-Apperception Test. Both studies reported contradictory results when participants were asked to create and elaborate on stories and the amount written as directed in the subliminal constructions. Shevrin and Luborsky (1958) and Johnson and Erikson (1961) reported similar results to support their theory that there was a tendency for tachiscopically presented material to appear in daydreams and dreams.

In addition to content reinforcement, Moore (1982) asks what effect individual cognitive style differences may have on learning from subliminal media treatments. Most early subliminal perception research limited consideration of individual participant differences to sex, race, and IQ. Other (undetected) differences in sample populations might explain why many replication attempts have failed to confirm original findings, and why many findings are contradictory. In a review of subliminal research, McConnell et al. (1958) stated that individual differences "must be taken into account by anyone who wishes to deal with individuals. It is quite likely that many differences in the perception of subliminal stimuli do exist between individuals of differing classes, ages, and sexes" (p. 236). Allison (1963), Murch (1965), and Sackeim,

Packer, and Gur (1977) have shown that individual differences such as thought strategies, cognitive set, and hemisphericity were related to susceptibility to subliminal stimulation. DeChenne (1975) and Skinner (1969) did not collect data on individual differences in learning styles or abilities within their samples. By not doing so, detecting the effect of the treatment would have been more difficult if aptitude-treatment interaction effects were occurring, as the slight increase in treatment effectiveness in these two studies may have indicated. The term *individual differences* is also associated with the concept of cognitive styles.

Past studies questioned whether subliminal perception could be a useful tool for producers of educational television and explored the feasibility of teaching one topic while students were watching a program unrelated in content (DeChenne, 1975; Skinner, 1969; Taris, 1970). The results indicated that subliminal messages were generally not powerful enough to cause learning when students were concentrating on an unrelated topic. In other words, it is unrealistic for educational producers to expect that students could be taught two topics simultaneously, one through normal channels and the other through subliminal perception (Moore, 1982; Moore & Moore, 1984). However, there was some evidence (DeChenne, 1975) that some students seeing subliminal cues performed better on a criterion task. This suggested that individual differences such as intelligence or perceptual abilities may be related to the ability to profit from subliminal messages implanted in a television program. This is generally consistent with Calvin and Dollenmayer (1959), Gerard (1960), Murch (1965), and Sharp (1959).

The properties of visual subliminal messages include being faintly and quickly embedded within a surrounding visual field. A student's ability to profit from subliminal messages could be related to the ability to dissembed the message from the surrounding television picture. Therefore, it was thought that the cognitive style of field dependence may have some relationship to the potential usefulness of subliminal perception. Since people have different ways of perceiving their environment, these differences may have been associated with the differences in subliminal learning seen in various studies (Calvin & Dollenmayer, 1959; DeChenne, 1975; Gerard, 1960; Kolers, 1957). Based on the literature, it also could be expected that field-independent individuals, because they have highly developed skills at dissembedding one object or image from a surrounding array of objects or images, should likewise be able to distinguish the embedded subliminal messages in a television picture (Greco & McClung, 1979; Hessler, 1972). The real benefit in learning, however, could occur for those students who are field dependent, since they typically benefit from more salient content organization cues (Witkin, Moore, Goodenough & Cox, 1977). Thus, the use of subliminal reinforcement cues (captions) could be of most value to field-dependent students, because the captions would supplant students' reduced ability to distinguish between relevant and nonrelevant cues and would make the relevant cues more salient.

In Moore's (1982) experiment, these differences in cognitive style were studied as a possible intervening factor for consideration in the production and utilization of subliminal materials. In the analysis of data, it was found that students having prior experience with the subject matter, such as in a previous course, averaged highest on the recall test, as one would expect. These students were eliminated from subsequent analysis, since their recall may have reflected prior knowledge or outside influence.

The available experiments and observations on subliminal perception seem to indicate that in certain instances human subjects are capable of responding to audio and visual stimuli that are so weak in duration, intensity, or clarity that they are not consciously aware of them. Researchers have varying opinions as to the effectiveness of subliminal stimulation, and there is no conclusive evidence as to its ineffectiveness or effectiveness. However, the body of evidence does indicate that, effective or not, there is perception below the threshold of awareness (DeChenne, 1975). There appears to be major concerns, however, involved in determining the amount of information a human can process at any one time. To recognize information simultaneously, the various receptors (eyes, ears) would have to analyze a great variety of different cues. All the findings noted in preceding sections, e.g., multiple-channel, multi-image, and subliminal perception, have import to the design of multimedia presentations. Basic decisions have to be made to determine how the presentation is to be developed, the number of cues to be available, and the number of channels to be used.

29.7 MULTIMEDIA RESEARCH

Technology does not stand still. While the debate as to the efficacy of technology's impact on learning continues, microcomputers become more powerful and flexible. As opposed to the first microcomputers, today's classroom machines can easily have thousands of times the amount of internal memory available before. Audio and visual capabilities will soon exceed those of today's television, and auxiliary storage will soon be practically unlimited (Moore, Myers & Burton, 1994). Because of these (and related technological advances in software), everyday users, and most particularly educators, have access to systems called *multimedia* and *hypermedia* (see 24.6.3). Yet the development of the interactive technologies that we now call *multimedia* has not been without controversy or unfulfilled promises (Gleason, 1991).

Although the concept of multimedia has been present for a long time, educators and the technology industry cannot decide exactly what the concept of multimedia (see 21.1, 24.6.1) includes (Strommen & Revelle, 1990). Until recently, the term has meant the use of several media devices, sometimes in a coordinated fashion (e.g., synchronized slides with audiotape). Advances in technology, however, have combined these media so that information previously delivered by several devices is now integrated into one device (Kozma, 1991, p. 199). The computer now plays a central organizing role in this environment. Questions remain: Does multimedia include, for example, interactive video, CDI, and DVI, as well as traditional slide shows supplemented by sound and many other media formats?

The most commonly accepted definition of multimedia appears to support the concept of computer-driven interactivity with the learner's ability to determine and control the sequence and content selection. Matchett and Elliott (1991) argue that these "interactive multimedia" should include motion, voice plus data, text, graphic, and still images. This definition permits multimedia to "absorb" the historically older and somewhat broader notion of hypermedia, which will be discussed in more detail later. As such, interactive video is a "high-bandwidth" source in the sense that a great deal of information, in many modes, or channels, are available at once (i.e., parallel fashion). DeBloois (1982) indicates that "it is important to realize that interactive video (multimedia) is not merely a merging of video and computer mediums; it is an entirely new media with characteristics quite unlike each of the composites" (p. 33). The attraction of interactive multimedia is that it includes two of the more powerful educational technologies: the computer and video. Unlike some of the earlier linear technologies that allowed the user to remain passive, the new interactive programs not only allow viewers to become involved but also demand it (Gleason, 1991). By doing so, these technologies have closed the gap between some of the earlier theories of learner control and learning styles. Interactive multimedia allows the user to see, hear, and do. Through this mix of presentation techniques, interactive multimedia can appeal to learners who prefer to receive information by reading, those who learn best through hearing, and those who prefer hands-on environments (Moore, Myers & Burton, 1994).

29.7.1 Multimedia

Research concerning the learning impact of this medium is still sketchy. Its potential is important because it can combine all the symbol systems discussed above. An important distinction in this medium, however, is that the computer controls the use of the various system states. Distinct potential advantages accrue when using this media-rich environment. The learner can develop pattern recognition skills from the video and access information (in all modes) in a random manner. The latter capability takes the learner out of the traditional sequential environment and into one in which he or she can explore the domain from multiple perspectives (Cognition and Technology Group, 1990; see 26.4.2.2). Using interactive videodisc, the learner can be placed into contexts that simulate the "real world." This type of learning has been referred to as "situated cognition" (Brown, Collins & Duguid, 1989) because the information learned is tied to retrieval cues in the environments in which it will be needed.

An excellent example of situated cognition is the use of the "anchored instruction" work (see 23.4.1.) done by the Cognition and Technology Group at Vanderbilt (1990).

They believe that young students learn better in meaningful, socially organized contexts. Their research indicates that problem-oriented approaches are more effective than fact-oriented approaches in overcoming inert knowledge (knowledge people know but often fail to use during problem-solving situations). The methodology is designed to help students develop rich mental models as the basis for future learning, create environments that permit sustained exploration by students and teachers, help students explore the domain from multiple perspectives, and develop integrated knowledge structures that help students transfer knowledge to more complex tasks. (It should be noted that the above comments are speculative and are not confirmed by direct research.)

29.7.2 Hypermedia

This technology parallels mental models by forming associations or links between various ideas, then constructing meaning among these relationships (Kozma, 1991). Research suggests that a number of concepts can be explored by using hypermedia's cognitive flexibility (see 12.2.3.5.4, 21.1). For example, users might be interested in pursuing information about land navigation. Searching on this area might turn up information about magnetic principles, topography, uses of the compass, terrain orientation, the coordinate system, and celestial navigation. The learner could follow one or all of these links—all of which would provide further links. There might also be an opportunity to watch a video of participants engaged in the sport of orienteering, or simulations using triangulation to determine location. While research on hypermedia is in its infancy, the learner will have access to a multitude of information. This information will allow the formation (and tracking) of mental models or schemata on unlimited types of domains.

Kozma (1991) suggests that "various aspects of the learning process are influenced by the cognitively relevant characteristics of media: their technologies, symbol systems, and processing capabilities" (p. 205). He also submits that learning is influenced by taking ". . . advantage of the medium's cognitively relevant capabilities to complement the learner's cognitive abilities and prior knowledge and cognitive skills" (p. 205). The discussion has considered basic cognitive learning theory and the dual-code theory that links learning to the symbol systems inherent in multimedia. Also important is the strategy used by the instructional designer or teacher to take advantage of cognitive psychology in employing media. The discussion now turns to two approaches in which multimedia applications demonstrate the use of cognitive theory.

29.7.3 Using Evidence to Evaluate Multimedia Programs

Does multimedia really work? To answer this question, it is necessary to note some of the earlier-mentioned learning theories (see 24.6.3) and also to note earlier media-related

research. It may also be useful to differentiate between evaluation studies and research. Evaluation is practical and is concerned with how to improve a product or whether to buy/use a product. Studies that compare one program/media against another (or a control for that matter) are primarily evaluations. Evaluation seeks to find programs that "work" more cheaply, efficiently, quickly, effectively, etc. Research, on the other hand, tends to be more concerned with testing theoretical concepts and constructs or attempting to isolate variables to observe their contributions to a process or outcome. Having said this, we should point out that the terms *evaluation* and *research* are often used interchangeably in the fields of education and media (Moore, Myers & Burton, 1994).

Multimedia is a combination of many technologies, most notably the computer, which allows for true interaction. Strommen and Revelle (1990) stress the importance of existing research literature on computer usage for understanding the pragmatic requirements of developing interactive tasks in the multimedia programs that were developed at the Children's Television Workshop. This literature helped "take children's special needs into account and . . . (delineate) what the content of our interactive tasks should be and how those tasks should be structured" (pp. 77, 78). Smith (1987) indicated that there are three major sectors in our society that use and conduct research on the effects of interactive multimedia: the military, industry, and education. Educational use of multimedia programs is still limited and in most cases still experimental. Two multimedia formats (videodisc and videotape) are predominate in education. As you would expect, multimedia researchers are still debating their relative values and virtues (Smith, 1987). However, the marketplace may decide the winner, and DVI technologies such as CD-ROM and Quicktime™ may well settle the debate in a practical sense. Despite the short duration of multimedia's availability, Smith (1987) reports evidence for both the effectiveness and efficiency of the interactive media on learning. Other researchers argue that there is little to support the contentions of the effectiveness of interactive media. They contend that little progress has been made since Clark (1983) argued that media in general have little substantial impact on learning (Hannafin, 1985; Slee, 1989). Hannafin (1985) asserts that while the interactive technology, as noted earlier, offers interesting potential, interactive video differs little from the allied technology from either "learning or cognitive perspectives."

Ragan, Boyce, Redwine, Savenye, and McMichael (1993) summarized the findings of seven major reviews of research on multimedia. The 139 reviews were from a variety of settings, but the majority concerned adults. Among (which are obviously not independent) their findings were:

1. Multimedia is at least as effective as conventional forms and has substantial cost benefits and efficiency.
2. Frequently, multimedia instruction is more effective than conventional instruction.
3. Multimedia is more efficient in terms of learning time than is conventional instruction (30% savings).

Ragan et al. (1993) stated that they were unable to determine why multimedia was appreciably more effective than conventional instruction, and cautioned that it would be inappropriate to say that multimedia is always the most effective delivery system. They suggested that certain instructional design features appear to enhance the quality of multimedia instruction. Among them are higher levels of interactivity, program or advised learner control, integration of multimedia with other delivery forms, and structured rather than totally exploratory learning.

Smith, Hsu, Azzarello, and McMichael (1993) reviewed 28 group-based multimedia studies. They indicate that group-based multimedia can be as effective as individualized multimedia, and it can be as effective or more so than traditional forms of instruction. They also found that learners prefer group-based multimedia to individualized multimedia and traditional instruction. Again, Smith et al. (1993) stated that they were unable to predict which situations are appropriate for group-based multimedia, and that it would be erroneous to state that group-based multimedia is always superior to traditional instruction or individualized multimedia.

Though hypermedia is relatively new, there are hundreds of reports and studies about its implementation. However, most of them deal with the excitement of adopting this new technology or envision its potentials in education (Yang, 1993). Only a few of these reports are experimental studies. In these limited studies, some positive results of using hypermedia have been reported. Abrams and Streit (1986), as well as Jones and Smith (1989), reported significant gains in learning achievement. Janda (1992) found a positive attitude toward the use of hypermedia systems. Higgins and Boone (1992) reported a decreased demand on teaching time. Hardiman and Williams (1990) noted that the completion rate of courses was increased with the use of hypermedia. Liu (1992) found that hypermedia was very effective in the teaching of English as a second language. In a review, Smith (1987) summarized the findings: "The effective evidence seems to indicate that the medium is both effective and efficient . . ." (p. 2). Thompson, Simonson, and Hargrave (1992) also suggested that hypermedia was promising in a learning context (Yang, 1993).

What does the research say about multimedia and its interactive technologies? Unfortunately, not much. The terms *multimedia* and *interactivity* are defined universally by neither the developers nor the researchers. Many of the current guidelines for the development of multimedia programs can be traced to just a few sources. One source is the behaviorist learning theory tradition of Thorndike and Skinner; the second is existing research investigating computer-assisted instruction. The most prevalent sources, however, are assumption, intuition, and (apparently) common sense. After reflection on an extensive review of the literature, there appears to be little useful research on multimedia (Moore, Myers & Burton, 1994). Quite frankly, with few exceptions there is *not* a body of research on the design, use, and value of multimedia systems. The few exceptions include the meta-analysis of some 60 studies of McNeil and Nelson (1991),

the work at the Children's Television Workshop (Strommen & Revelle, 1990), and the reviews of Ragan et al. (1993). The lack of research concentrating on the interactive features that maximize learning effectiveness has been noted by both practitioners and researchers alike. Specific programs of research have been suggested to fill these gaps, e.g., Hannafin (1985) and Kozma (1991). Until these calls are taken seriously, multimedia development will have a less-than-adequate research base (Moore, Myers & Burton, 1994).

29.8 DISCUSSION AND SUMMARY

Design decisions are not made based solely on a given foundation, but upon presumed processing requirements, the strategies and methods deemed reasonable in supporting those processes, and the manner in which technology options support or hinder combinations of learning strategies and cognitive processes (Park & Hannafin, 1993, p. 67).

Among important variables are teacher-student interactions, methods, learner traits, and motivation. Based on our review of the literature, finding a multiple-channel research article that addressed more than one of these variables was an exception. At the beginning of this chapter, we highlighted the information-processing model, its impact on research, and the implications research results have on instructional design.

To briefly recap, the information-processing model hypothesizes several information storage areas governed by processes that convert stimuli to information. The goal for instructional designers is to take advantage of suggestions from multiple-channel research in order to facilitate cognitive processes particularly in the development of multimedia presentations.

Our review has focused on the effectiveness that multiple-channel communications, cue summation, and related areas such as multi-image and subliminal perception research may play in learning situations. Unfortunately, most literature addressing these issues is conflicting and/or dated. Not once did we encounter research that thoroughly investigated these theories in the context of hypermedia or multimedia. In addition, much of the research reported is based on the well-documented limitations of media comparison studies. We also feel that the literature dealing with multiple-channel communications and cue summation should provide a portion of the foundation from which to design learning environments in the multimedia arena. Based on the review of pertinent research that are the antecedents of the concept of multimedia—e.g., multiple-channel, cue summation, multi-image, and subliminal perception—what did we find? We feel that instructional designers, looking for simple rationale methods or guidelines for effective multimedia (multiple-channel) presentations will be disappointed in the relevant research. While much of the evidence from the research studies appears to support multiple-channel design, the overall evidence on the effectiveness of single-channel versus multiple-channel presentations is confusing at best. The human information-processing system appears to function as a multiple-channel system until the system capacity overloads. When the system capacity is reached, the processing system seems to revert to a single-channel system. In other words, a fixed cognitive capacity limits the absolute amount of information that the individual can "handle." Adding information channels does not enlarge the system, rather it distributes the capacity across the two input channels. Conflicting research results are also present concerning the use of redundant information presented across two or more channels. People apparently view highly redundant information presented over two or more channels as components of a single message. Research on the cue summation and stimulus generalization theories have produced opposing results (no surprise). However, there appears to be some evidence to suggest that multiple-channel presentations are superior to single-channel presentations when cues are summed across channels, but when neither channel is superior or when content is redundant or irrelevant across channels. Redundancy may cause information processing to fluctuate and become less efficient. There also may be failure to take into account the theory about processing capacity in human beings. It is suggested that designers sometime do not understand the possibility that in multiple-channel communication irrelevant cues in either channel can cause interference. Research on multi-image presentations suggest that the mere presentation of simultaneous images does not necessarily lead to simultaneous mental processing. Like the other research in this area, multi-image research has revealed few usable results. The familiar problem of how much information an individual processes at any one time is also raised by multi-image presentations and with studies on subliminal perception. Inconclusive results leaves us with no definite evidence as to subliminal perception's effectiveness or ineffectiveness. However, there appears to be evidence that there is human perception below the threshold of awareness. Where does this leave us in relationship to multimedia? For one thing, educators appear unable to determine a universal definition for the concept of multimedia. Secondly, there is little research concerning the design and value of multimedia systems. Certainly, the use of the research and theoretical antecedents of multimedia reviewed in this paper (e.g., multiple-channel communication and cue summation theory) have not for the most part made it into the research literature on multimedia. Most of the literature appears to deal with their adoption and implementation or the visions of their potential use. Some of the evaluative studies available, however, tend to support the use of such presentations.

There is a rather obvious lesson to be learned in reviewing the literature in this area and, we suspect, many of the areas that this handbook is meant to deal with. Theory-based research, such as that grounded in dual-coding theory, cue summation theory, etc., "add up" over time. Research comparing media against media (see 4.3.4.2), which we have characterized as evaluations, does not. As Clark (1983) readily acknowledges, such studies were criticized long before he put forth his delivery truck metaphor. This metaphor does not seem counterintuitive or, for that matter, controversial. We invite you to look up the term *media* in any dictionary. It will say *vehicle,* as in television or radio, or words to that effect. The concept, though blindingly simple, is still misunderstood. Evaluating media against media in terms of learning outcomes (as in film versus television,) has not helped us. Testing media attributes (e.g., text and audio) against another doesn't help us either (see 4.4.4.6). What the argument doesn't have is a theory that explains what happens from a human learning/memory point of view. Clark and others suggest that there are "deeper processes" at work in learning and that the various media attributes employed are surrogates for those processes that can be cued or accessed in many ways. Simply put, that learning may be unaffected by a particular media and that learning of any type can be achieved through a variety of paths (media) if the methods of providing information are well designed, have a theoretical base and are well executed. If research in multimedia does not move quickly from evaluation to theory-based research, we will not only repeat the mistakes of the past, we also, as a discipline, will be made redundant by those working in human computer interface (HCI) and industrial systems engineering (ISE), who are grounding their work in theory.

REFERENCES

Adams, J.K. (1957). Laboratory studies of behavior without awareness. *Psychological Bulletin 54,* 383–405.

Abrams, A. & Streit, L. (1986). Effectiveness of interactive video in teaching basic photography. *T.H.E. Journal 14* (2), 92–96.

Allen, W.H. & Cooney, S.M. (1963). A study of the non-linearity variable in filmic presentation. Los Angeles, CA: University of Southern California. NDEA Title VII, Project No. 422.

— & — (1964). Non-linearity in filmic presentation. *AV Communication Review 12* (2), 164–76.

Allison, J. (1963). Cognitive structure and receptivity to low-intensity stimulation. *Journal of Abnormal and Social Psychology 67,* 132–38.

Anderson, J.R. (1985a). *Cognitive psychology and its implications.* New York: Freeman.

— (1985b). *Theories of learning,* 5th ed. Englewood Cliffs, NJ: Prentice Hall.

— (1978). Arguments concerning representations for mental imagery. *Psychological Review 85,* 249–77.

Anderson, R.C., Greeno, J.G., Kline, P.J. & Neves, D.M. (1981). Acquisition of problem solving skill. *In* J.R. Anderson, ed. *Cognitive skills and their acquisition.* Hillsdale, NJ: Erlbaum.

Advertising Research Foundation (1958). *Application of subliminal perception in advertising.* New York: ARF.

Atherton, L.L.(1971). A comparison of movie and multi-image presentation techniques on affective and cognitive learning. Doctoral dissertation, Michigan State University. *Dissertation Abstracts International 32* (6-A), 5924. (University Microfilms, No. 71-31,154.)

Attneave, F. (1954). Some informational aspects of visual perception. *Psychological Review 61,* 183–93.

Ausburn, F.B. (1975). *Multiple versus linear imagery in the presentation of a comparative visual location task to visual and haptic college students.* Unpublished doctoral dissertation, University of Oklahoma.

Baddeley, A.D. (1966). Short-term memory for word sequences as a function of acoustic, semantic, and formal similarity. *Quarterly Journal of Experimental Psychology 18,* 362–65.

Baggett, P. (1984). Role of temporal overlap of visual and auditory material in forming dual media associations. *Journal of Educational Psychology 76,* 408–17.

— & Ehrenfecucht, A. (1983). Encoding and retaining information in the visuals and verbals of an educational movie. *Educational Communication and Technology 31* (1), 23–32.

Baker, E.J. & Alluisi, E.A. (1962). Information handling aspect of visual and auditory form perception. *Journal of Engineering Psychology 1,* 159–79.

Bartlett, F.C. (1958). *Thinking.* New York: Basic Books.

Beagles-Roos, J. & Gat, I. (1983). Specific impact of radio and television on children's story comprehension. *Journal of Educational Psychology 75,* 128–37.

Beck, C.R. (1983). Successive and simultaneous picture and passage formats: visual, tactual, and topical effects. *Educational Communications and Technology 31* (3), 145–52.

— (1987). Pictorial cueing strategies for encoding and retrieving information. *International Journal of Instructional Media 14* (4), 332–46.

Berger, M.M. (1973). A preliminary report on the multi-image immediate impact on video self-confrontation. *American Journal of Psychiatry 130,* 304–06.

Bevan, W. (1964). Subliminal stimulation: a pervasive problem for psychology. *Psychological Bulletin 61,* 81–99.

Bither, S.W. (1972). Effects of distraction and commitment on the persuasiveness of television advertising. *Journal of Marketing Research 9,* 1–5.

Blackwell, H.R. (1968). Lighting in the learning module. *American Annals of the Deaf 113* (5), 1063–74.

Bollman, C.G. (1970). The effect of large screen multi-image display of evaluative meaning. Doctoral dissertation, Michigan State University. *Dissertation Abstracts International 31* (11-A), 5924. (University Microfilms, No. 71-11,789.)

Bourne, C.E., Dominowski, R.L., Loftus, E.F. & Healy, A.F. (1986). *Cognitive processes,* 2d ed. Englewood Cliffs, NJ: Prentice Hall.

Bransford, J.D. & Johnson, M.K. (1972). Contextual prerequisites for understanding: some investigations of comprehension and recall. *Journal of Verbal Learning and Verbal Behavior 11,* 717–26.

Bransford, J.D., Sherwood, R., Vye, N.J. & Rieser, J. (1986). Teaching thinking and problem solving: research foundations. *American Psychologist 41* (10), 1078–79.

Britton, B.K., Meyer, B.J.F., Simpson, R., Holdredge, T. & Curry, C. (1979). Effects of organization of text on memory: test of two implications of selective attention. *Journal of Experimental Psychology: Human Learning and Memory 5,* 496–506.

Broadbent, D.E. (1956). Successive responses to simultaneous stimuli. *Quarterly Journal of Experimental Psychology 8,* 145–52.

— (1957). Immediate memory and simultaneous stimuli. *Quarterly Journal of Experimental Psychology 9,* 1–11.

— (1958). *Perception and communication.* New York: Pergamon.

— (1965). Information-processing in the nervous system. *Science 150,* 457–62.

Brown, J. (1959). Information, redundancy, and decay of the memory trace. In *Mechanization of the thought, Vol. 2.* National Physical Laboratory, Symposium No. 10. London: Her Majesty's Stationery Office.

Brown, J.S., Collins, A. & Duguid, P. (1989). Situated cognition and the culture of learning. *Educational Researcher 18* (1), 32–41.

Bruner, J.S. (1967). *Towards a theory of instruction.* Cambridge, MA: Harvard University Press.

—, Goodnow, J.J. & Auston, G.A. (1967). *A study of thinking.* New York: Wiley.

Burke, K.(1987). AMI research bibliography. AMI Archives and Clearinghouse No. CAb1.

— & Leps, A.A. (1989). Multi-image research: a thirty-year retrospective. *International Journal of Instructional Media 16* (3), 181–95.

Burton, J.K. & Bruning, R.H. (1982). Interference effects on the recall of pictures, printed words, spoken words. *Contemporary Educational Psychology 7,* 61–69.

— (1982). Dual coding of pictorial stimuli by children. *Journal of Mental Imagery 6* (1), 159–68.

Byrne, D. (1959). The effect of a subliminal food stimulus on verbal responses. *Journal of Applied Psychology 43,* 249–52.

Calvert, S.L., Huston, A.C., Watkins, B.A. & Wright, J.C. (1982). The relation between selective attention to television forms and children's comprehension of content. *Child Development 53,* 601–10.

Calvin, A.D. & Dollenmayer, K.S. (1959). Subliminal perception: some negative findings. *Journal of Applied Psychology 43,* 187–88.

Carpenter, C.R. (1953). A theoretical orientation for instructional film research. *AV Communication Review 1,* 38–52.

Carterette, E.C. & Jones, M.H. (1965). Visual and auditory information-processing in children and adults. *Science 156,* 986–88.

Champion, J.M. & Turner, W.W. (1959). An experimental investigation of subliminal perception. *Journal of Applied Psychology 43,* 382–84.

Cherry, C.E. (1953). Some experiments on the recognition of speech with one and two ears. *Journal of the Acoustical Society of America 25,* 975–74.

— (1957). *On human communication: a review, a survey, and a criticism.* New York: Wiley.

Clark, R.E. (1983). Reconsidering research on learning from media. *Review of Educational Research 53,* 445–59.

Clark, S.E. (1969). Retrieval of color information from preperceptual memory. *Journal of Experimental Psychology 82,* 263–66.

Cognition and Technology Group at Vanderbilt (1990). Anchored instruction and its relationship to situated cognition. *Educational Researcher 19* (5), 2–10.

Conrad, R. (1964). Acoustic confusions in immediate memory. *British Journal of Psychology 55,* 75–84.

Conway, J.K. (1967). Multiple-sensory modality communication and the problem of sign types. *AV Communication Review 15* (4), 371–83.

— (1968). Information presentation, information-processing, and the sing vehicle. *AV Communication Review 16* (4), 403–14.

Cooper, L.A. & Shepard, R.N. (1973). Chronometric studies of the rotation of mental images. *In* W.G. Chase, ed. *Visual information-processing.* New York: Academic.

Corballis, M.C. & Raeburn, B.J. (1970). Recall strategies in three-channel immediate memory. *Canadian Journal of Psychology 24*, 109–16.

Coyne, J.W., King, H.E., Zubin, J. & Landis, C. (1943). Accuracy of recognition of subliminal auditory stimuli. *Journal of Experimental Psychology 33*, 508–13.

Day, W.F. & Beach, B.R. (1950). A survey of the research literature comparing the visual and auditory presentation of information. Charlottesville, VA: University of Virginia (Contract No. W33-039-ac-21269, E.O. No. 694-37).

DeBloois, M.L. (1982). *Videodisc/microcomputer courseware design*. Englewood Cliffs, NJ: Educational Technology.

DeChenne, J.A. (1975). An experimental study to determine if a task involving psychomotor and problem-solving skills can be taught subliminally. Doctoral dissertation, Virginia Polytechnic Institute and State University. *Dissertation Abstracts International 37*, 1947a. (University Microfilms NO. 76-23213.)

DeFleur, M.L. & Petranoff, R.M. (1959). A televised test of subliminal persuasion. *Public Opinion Quarterly 23*, 168–80.

Didcoct, D.H. (1958). *Comparison of the cognitive and affective responses of college students to single-image and multi-image audio-visual presentations*. Unpublished doctoral dissertation, Cornell University.

Dixon, N.F. (1971). *Subliminal perception: the nature of a controversy*. New York: McGraw-Hill.

Drew, D.G. & Grimes, T. (1987). Audio-visual redundancy and TV news recall. *Communication Research 14*, 452–61.

Dwyer, F.M. (1972). *A guide for improving visualized instruction*. State College, PA: Learning Services.

— (1978). *Strategies for improving visual learning*. State College, PA: Learning Services.

Egan, D.E. & Schwartz, B.J. (1979). Chunking in recall of symbolic drawings. *Memory & Cognition 7*, 149–58.

Eggen, P. D. & Kauchak, D. (1992). *Educational psychology: classroom connections*. New York: Merrill.

Emmer, E.T. (1981). *Effective management in junior high mathematics classrooms*. Austin, TX: University of Texas (R&D Report No. 6111).

Evertson, C.M., Anderson, L.M. & Brophy, J.E. (1978). *Process-outcome relationships in the Texas junior high school study: compendium*. Washington, DC: National Institute of Education (ERIC #ED 166 192).

Eysenck, N.J. (1963). The measurement of motivation. Reprinted from *Scientific American*. (May). New York: Freeman (Print No. 477).

Feigenbaum, E.A. & Simon, H.A. (1963). Brief notes on the EPAM theory of verbal learning. *In* C.N. Confer & B.S. Musgrave, eds. *Verbal behavior and learning*. New York: McGraw-Hill.

Festinger, L. & Maccoby, N. (1964). On resistance to persuasive communications. *Journal of Abnormal and Social Psychology 68*, 359–66.

Findahl, O. (1981). *The effect of visual illustrations upon perception and retention of news programmes*. (ERIC Document Reproduction Service No. ED 054 631.)

Fleisher, R. (1969). Multiple-image technique for "The Boston Strangler." *American Cinematographer*, 202–205 *et passim*.

Fleming, M.L. (1970). Perceptual principles for the design of instructional material. *Viewpoints*. Bloomington, IN: Indiana University, Bulletin of the School of Education, 69-200.

Fortune, J.C. (1967). *A study of the generality of presenting behavior in teaching*. Memphis, TN: Memphis State University (ERIC # ED 016 285).

Fradkin, B.M. (1974). Effectiveness of multi-image presentations. *Journal of Educational Technology Systems 2*, 231–326.

— (1976). A review of multiple image presentation research. (Contract No. WIE -C-74-0027.) Washington, DC. National Institute of Education (ERIC No. 130 680).

— & Meyowitz, J. (1975). Design of multi-image instructional presentations. Paper presented at the national convention of the Association for Educational Communications and Technology, Dallas, TX.

Gardner, H. (1985). *The mind's new science: a history of the cognitive revolution*. New York: Basic Books.

Gerard, E.O. (1960). Subliminal stimulation in problem solving. *American Journal of Psychology 73*, 121–26.

Gersten, R.M., Carine, D.W. & Williams, P.B. (1982). Measuring implementation of a structural educational model in a urban school district: an observational approach. *Educational Evaluation and Policy Analysis 4*, 67–79.

Gleason, J. (1991). *Development of an interactive multimedia presentation for use in a public delivery setting*. Unpublished doctoral dissertation, Virginia Tech University.

Goldstein, B. (1975). The perception of multiple images. *AV Communication Review 23* (1), 34–68.

Goldstein, M.J. & Barthol, R.P. (1960). Fantasy responses to subliminal stimuli. *Journal of Abnormal and Social Psychology 60*, 22–26.

— & Davis, D. (1961). The impact of stimuli registering outside of awareness. *Journal of Personality 29*, 247–57.

Greco, A. & McClung, C. (1979). Interaction between attention directing and cognitive style. *Educational Communications and Technology Journal 27*, 97–102.

Grimes, T. (1991). Mild auditory-visual dissonance in television news may exceed viewer attentional capacity. *Human Communication Research 18*, (2), 268–98.

Gulo, E. & Baron, A. (1965). Classroom learning of meaningful prose by college students as a function of sensory mode of stimulus presentation. *Perceptual and Motor Skills 21*, 183–86.

Hannafin, M.J. (1985). Empirical issues in the study of computer assisted interactive video. *ECTJ 33* (4), 235–47.

Hanson, L. (1989). Multichannel learning research applied to principles of television production: a review and synthesis of the literature. *Educational Technology 29* (10), 15–19.

Hardiman, B. & Williams, R. (1990). Teaching developmental mathematics: the interactive video approach. *T.H.E. Journal 17*, 63–65.

Hartman, F.R. (1961a). Investigation of recognition learning under multiple-channel presentation and testing conditions. *AV Communication Review 9*, 24–43.

— (1961b). Single and multi-channel communication: a review of research and a proposed model. *AV Communication Review 9*, 235–62.

Hayes, D.S., Kelly, S.B. & Mandel, M. (1986). Media differences in children's story synopses: radio and television contrasted. *Journal of Educational Psychology 78*, 341–46.

Henneman, R.H. (1952). Vision and audition as sensory channels for communication. *Journal of Speech 38*, 161–66.

Herman, L.M. (1965). Study of the single channel hypothesis and input regulation within a continuous, simultaneous task situation. *Quarterly Journal of Experimental Psychology 17*, 37–46.

Hernandez-Peon, R. (1961). Reticular mechanisms of sensory control. *In* W.A. Rosenblith, ed. *Sensory communication,* 497–517. New York: Wiley.

Hessler, D.W. (1972). Interaction of 'visual compression' and field-dependence in relation to self-instruction and transfer. Doctoral dissertation, Michigan State University, 1972. *Dissertation Abstracts International 33,* 6235a. (University of Microfilms No. 73-12735.)

Higgins, K. & Boone, R. (1992). Hypermedia computer study guides: adapting a Canadian history text. *Social Education 56* (3), 154–59.

Hill, S.D. & Hecker, E.E. (1966). Auditory and visual learning of paired associate tasks by second grade children. *Perceptual & Motor Skills 23,* 814.

Hoban, C.F. & VanOrmer, E.B. (1950). *Instructional film research.* University Park, PA: Pennsylvania State University (SDC 269-7-19).

— (1949). Some aspects of learning from films. Incidental Report No. 2. State College, PA: Pennsylvania State College, Instructional Film Research Program.

Hollingworth, H.L. (1919). *Advertising and selling.* New York: Appleton.

Hooper, S. & Hannafin, M.J. (1991). Psychological perspectives on emerging instructional technologies: a critical analysis. *Educational Psychologist 26* (1), 69–95.

Hsia, H.J. (1968). On channel effectiveness. *AV Communication Review 16,* 245–67.

— (1969). Intelligence in auditory, visual, and audiovisual information-processing. *AV Communication Review 17,* 272–82.

— (1971). The information-processing capacity of modality and channel performance. *AV Communication Review 19* (1), 51–75.

Hubbard, R.D. (1961). Telemation: AV automatically controlled. *Audio-visual Instruction 6,* 437–39.

Janda, K. (1992). Multimedia in political science: sobering lessons from a teaching experiment. *Journal of Educational Multimedia and Hypermedia 1,* 341–54.

Jacobson, H. (1950). The informational capacity of the human ear. *Science 112,* 143–44.

— (1951). The informational capacity of the human eye. *Science 113,* 292–93.

Johnson, H. & Eriksen, C.W. (1961). Preconscious perception: a re-examination of the Poetzl phenomenon. *Journal of Abnormal and Social Psychology 62,* 497–503.

Jonassen, D. (1979). Implications of multi-image for concept acquisition. *Educational Technology Communication Journal 27* (4), 291–302.

Jones, L.L. & Smith, S.G. (1989). Lights, camera, reactions! The interactive videodisc: a tool for teaching chemistry. *T.H.E. Journal 16,* 78–85.

Kahneman, D. (1973). *Attention and effort.* Englewood Cliffs, NJ: Prentice Hall.

Kale, S.U., Grosslight, J.H. & McIntyre, D.J. (1955). *Exploratory studies in the use of pictures and sound for teaching foreign language vocabulary.* Technical Report SDC 269-7-53. Port Washington, New York: Special Devices Center.

Katz, P.A. & Deutsch, M. (1963). Visual and auditory efficiency and its relationship to reading in children. Final Report, Project 1009, Washington, DC: Office of Education.

Kerr, B. (1973). Processing demands during mental operations. *Memory and Cognitions 1,* 401–412.

Ketcham, C.H. & Heath, R.W. (1962). Teaching effectiveness of sound with pictures that do not embody the material being taught. *AV Communication Review 10,* 89–93.

King, H.E., Landis, C. & Zubin, J. (1944). Visual subliminal perception where a figure is obscured by the influences upon conscious thought. *Journal of Experimental Psychology 34,* 60–69.

Klatzky, R.L. (1980). *Human memory: structures and processes.* New York: Freeman.

Klein, G.S., Spence, D.P., Holt, R.R. & Gourevitch, S. (1958). Cognition without awareness: subliminal influences upon conscious thought. *Journal of Abnormal and Social Psychology 57,* 255–66.

Kleinsmith, L.J. & Kaplan, S. (1963). Paired-associate learning as a function of arousal and interpolated interval. *Journal of Experimental Psychology 65,* 190–93.

— & — (1964). Interaction of arousal and recall interval in nonsense syllable paired-associate learning. *Journal of Experimental Psychology 67,* 124–26.

—, — & Tarte, R.D. (1963). The relationship of arousal to short- and long-term verbal recall. *Canadian Journal of Psychology 17,* 393–97.

Kolers, P.A. (1957). Subliminal stimulation in problem solving. *American Journal of Psychology 70,* 437–41.

Kopstein, F.F. & Roshal, S.M. (1954). Learning foreign vocabulary from pictures versus words. *The American Psychologist 9,* 407–08.

Kosslyn, S.M. (1975). Information representation in visual images. *Cognitive Psychology 7,* 341–70.

Kozma, R.B. (1987). The implications of cognitive psychology for computer-based learning tools. *Educational Technology,* Nov., 20–25.

— (1991). Learning with media. *Review of Educational Research 61* (2), 179–211.

Kreszock, C.M. (1981). An experimental study to compare the affective and cognitive responses of female and male college students to single-image, multi-image, and time compressed single-image presentations. Unpublished doctoral dissertation, Virginia Tech University.

Langer, S.D. (1957). *Philosophy in a new key: a study of the symbolism of reason, rite, and art.* Cambridge, MA: Harvard University Press.

Lazarus, R.S. & McCleary, R.A. (1951). Automatic discrimination without awareness: a study of subception. *Psychological Review 58,* 113–22.

Levie, W.H. & Lentz, R. (1982). Effects of text illustrations: a review of research. *Educational Communications and Technology Journal 30* (4), 195–232.

Levie, W.L. (1987). Research on pictures: a guide to the literature. *In* D.M. Willows & H.A. Houghton, eds. *The psychology of illustration.* New York: Springer.

Lorch, E.P., Bellack, D.R. & Augsbach, L.H. (1987). Young children's memory for televised stories: effects of importance. *Child Development 58,* 453–62.

Lillie, D.L., Hannum, W.H. & Stuck, G.B. (1989). *Computers and effective instruction.* White Plains, NY: Longman.

Liu, M. (1992). The application of research-based instructional design principles in developing a hypermedia assisted instruction courseware for second language learning. Paper presented at the 34th ADCIS meeting.

Livingstone, R.B. (1962). An adventure shared psychology and neurophysiology. *In* S. Koch, ed. *Psychology: a study of science*. New York: McGraw-Hill.

Lombard, E.S. (1969). Multi-channel, multi-image teaching of synthesis skills in 11th-grade U.S. history. Unpublished doctoral dissertation, University of Southern California.

Low, C. (1968). Multi-screen and Expo 67. *Journal of the Society of Motion Picture and Television Engineers 77*, 185–86.

Lumsdaine, A.A. & Gladstone, A. (1958). Overt practice and audio-visual embellishments. *Learning from films* (edited by M.A. May & A.A. Lumsdaine). New Haven, CT: Yale University Press.

Magliaro, S. (1988). Expertise in problem identification: a descriptive analysis of the cue selection and hypothesis generation of reading diagnosticians. Unpublished doctoral dissertation, Virginia Polytechnic Institute and State University.

Malandin, C. (n.d.). Research on the understanding of film-strips. Ministere de l'Education Nationale, Ecole Normale Superieur de Saint-Cloud, France (Mimeo) (b).

Mandler, J.M. & Parker, R.E. (1976). Memory for descriptive and spatial information of complex pictures. *Journal of Experimental Psychology: Human and Learning Memory*, 38–48.

Matchett, J.R. & Elliott, S.A. (1991). Multimedia: the potential is startling, but . . . *Inform 6* (4), 48–50.

May, M.A. & Lumsdaine, A.A., eds. (1958). *Learning from films*. New Haven, CT: Yale University Press.

Mayer, R.E. (1983). *Thinking, problem solving, cognition*. New York: Freeman.

— (1984). Aids to text comprehension. *Educational Psychologist 19*, 30–42.

— & Anderson, R.B. (1991). Animations need narrations: an experimental test of a dual-coding hypothesis. *Journal of Educational Psychology 83* (4), 484–90.

— (1989). Systematic thinking fostered by illustrations in scientific text. *Journal of Educational Psychology 81* (2), 240–46.

— & Gallini, J.K. (1990). When is an illustration worth ten thousand words? *Journal of Educational Psychology 82* (4), 715–26.

McConnell, J.W., Cutler, R.L. & McNeil, E.B. (1958). Subliminal stimulation: an overview. *American Psychologist 13*, 229–42.

McFee, J.K. (1969). Visual communication. *In* R.V. Wiman & M.C. Meierhenry, eds. *Educational media: theory into practice*. Columbus, OH: Merrill.

McGinnus, E. (1949). Emotionality and perceptual defense. *Psychological Review 56*, 244–51.

McNeil, B.J. & Nelson, K.R. (1991). Meta-analysis of interactive video instruction: a 10-year review of achievement effects. *Journal of Computer-Based Instruction 18* (1), 1–6.

Meringoff, L.K. (1980). Influence of the medium on children's story apprehension. *Journal of Educational Psychology 72*, 24–49.

Nugent, G.C. (1982). Pictures, audio, and print: Symbolic representation and effect on learning. *Educational Communication and Technology 30* (3),163–74.

Millard, W.L. (1964). Visual teaching aids: production and use. *The encyclopedia of photography*. New York: Greystone.

Miller, G.A. (1953). What is information measurement? *American Psychologist 17*, 748–62.

— (1956). The magical number seven, plus or minus two: some limits on our capacity for processing information. *Psychological Review 63*, 81–97.

Miller, H.B. & Burton, J.K. (1994). Images and imagery theory. *In* D.M. Moore & F.M. Dwyer, eds. *Visual literacy: a spectrum of visual learning*, 65–85. Englewood Cliffs, NJ: Educational Technology.

Miller, J.G. (1942). *Unconsciousness*. New York: Wiley.

Miller, N.E., ed. (1957). Graphic communication and the crisis in education. *In* collaboration with W.A. Allen et al. *AV Communication Review 5*, 1–120.

Moore, D.M., Myers, R.J. & Burton, J.K.(1994). What multimedia might do and . . . what we know about what it does. *In* A. Ward, ed. *Multimedia and learning: a school's leaders guide*. Alexandria, VA: National School Boards Association.

Moore, J.F. & Moore, D.M. (1984). Subliminal perception and cognitive style in a concept learning task taught via television. *British Journal of Educational Technology 3* (15), 22–31.

— (1982). An exploratory study of subliminal perception and field dependence in a concept learning task taught by television. Unpublished doctoral dissertation, Virginia Polytechnic Institute and State University.

Moray, N. (1959). Attention in dichotic listening: affective cues and the influence of instructions. *Quarterly Journal of Experimental Psychology 11*, 59–60.

Mowbray, G.H. (1952). Simultaneous vision and audition: the detection of elements from over-learned sequences. *Journal of Experimental Psychology 44*, 292–300.

Mudd, S.A. & McCormick, E.J. (1960). The use of auditory cues in a visual search task. *Journal of Applied Psychology 44*, 184–88.

Murch, G.M. (1965). A set of conditions for a consistent recovery of subliminal stimulus. *Journal of Applied Psychology 49*, 257–60.

Myers, R. (1993). *Problem-based learning: a case study in integrating teachers, students, methods, and hypermedia databases*. Unpublished doctoral dissertation, Virginia Polytechnic Institute and State University, Blacksburg, VA.

Neely, J.H. (1977). Semantic priming and retrieval from lexical memory: roles of inhibitionless spreading activation and limited-capacity attention. *Journal of Experimental Psychology: General 106*, 226–54.

Neisser, U. (1967). *Cognitive psychology*. New York: Appleton-Century-Crofts.

Nelson, T.O., Metzler, J. & Reed, D.A. (1974). Role of details in the long-term recognition of pictures and verbal descriptions. *Journal of Experimental Psychology 102*, 184–86.

Norberg, K. (1966). Visual perception theory and instructional communication. *AV Communication Review 14*, 301–16.

Norman, D.A. (1969). *Memory and attention*. New York: Wiley.

Nuthall, G. & Alton-Lee, A. (1990). Research on teaching and learning: thirty years of change. *The Elementary School Journal 90* (5), 547–70.

Osterhouse, R.A. & Brock, T.C. (1970). Distraction increases yielding to propaganda by inhibiting counterarguing. *Journal of Personality and Social Psychology 15*, 344–58.

Paivio, A. (1971). *Imagery and verbal processes*. New York: Holt, Rinehart & Winston.

— (1986). *Mental representations: a dual coding approach*. New York: Oxford University Press.

Papert, S. (1977). A learning environment of children. *In* R.J. Seidel & M. Rubin, eds. *Computers and communications: implications for education*, 271–78. New York: Academic.

Park, I. & Hannifin, M.J. (1993). Empirically-based guidelines for the design of interactive multimedia. *Educational Technology Research and Development 41* (3), 63–85.

Pellegrino, J.W., Siegel, A.W. & Dhawan, M. (1974). Short-term retention of pictures and words: evidence for dual coding systems. *Journal of Experimental Psychology: Human Learning and Memory 1*, 95–102.

—, — & — (1976a). Short-term retention of pictures and words as a function of type of distraction and length of delay interval. *Memory & Cognition 4*, 11–15.

—, — & — (1976b). Differential distraction effects in short-term and long-term retention of pictures and words. *Journal of Experimental Psychology: Human Learning and Memory 2*, 541–47.

Perrin, D.G. (1969). A theory of multiple-image communication. *AV Communication Review 17* (4), 368–82.

Pezdek, K. & Stevens, E. (1984). Children's memory for auditory and visual information on television. *Developmental Psychology 210*, 212–18.

Posner, M.I. & Snyder, C.R.R. (1975). Facilitation and inhibition in the processing of signals. *In*. P.M.A. Rabbitt & S. Dornic, eds. *Attention and performance,* Vol. 5. New York: Academic.

— (1964). Information reduction in the analysis of sequential tasks. *Psychology Review 71*, 491–504.

Pressley, M. & Miller, G. (1987). Effects of illustrations on children's listening comprehension and oral prose memory. *In* D.M. Willows & H.A. Houghton, eds. *The psychology of illustration.* New York: Springer.

Ragan, T., Boyce, M., Redwine, D., Savenye, W.C. & McMichael J. (1993). *Is multimedia worth it?: a review of the effectiveness of individualized multimedia instruction.* A paper presented at the Association for Educational Communications and Technology Convention, New Orleans, LA.

Reese, S.D. (1983). *Improving audience learning from television news through between-channel redundancy.* (ERIC Document Reproduction Service No. Ed 229 777.)

Reed, S.K. (1985). Effect of computer graphics on improving estimates to algebra word problems. *Journal of Educational Psychology 77* (3), 285–98.

Reynolds, R.E. & Baker, D.R. (1987). The utility of graphical representations in text: some theoretical and empirical issues. *Journal of Research in Science Teaching 24* (2), 161–73.

Rigney, J.W. & Lutz, K.A. (1976). Effect of graphic analogies of concepts in chemistry on learning and attitude. *Journal of Educational Psychology 68*, 305–11.

Rolandelli, D.R. (1989). Children and television: the visual superiority effect reconsidered. *Journal of Broadcasting & Electronic Media 33* (1), 69–81.

Roshka, A.U. (1960). Conditions facilitating abstraction and generalization. *Voprosy Psikhologii, 1958, 4* (6) 89–96. (Reported by I.D. London, *Psychological Abstracts 34*, 85.)

Sackeim, H.A., Packer, I.K. & Gur, R.C. (1977). Hemisphericity, cognitive set, and susceptibility to subliminal perception. *Journal of Abnormal Psychology 86*, 624–30.

Samuels, S.J. (1970). Effects of pictures on learning to read, comprehension and attitudes. *Review of Educational Research 40* (3), 397–407.

Schiff, W. (1961). The effect of subliminal stimuli on guessing accuracy. *American Journal of Psychology 74*, 54–60.

Severin, W.J. (1967a). Cue summation in multiple-channel communication. Unpublished doctoral dissertation, University of Wisconsin.

— (1967b). Another look at cue summation. *AV Communication Review 15* (4), 233–45.

— (1967c). The effectiveness of relevant pictures in multiple-channel communication. *AV Communication Review 15* (4), 386–401.

Shannon, C.E. & Weaver, W. (1949). *The mathematical theory of communication.* Urbana, IL: University of Illinois Press.

Sharp, H.C. (1959). Effect of subliminal cues on test results. *Journal of Applied Psychology 43*, 369–71.

Sheehan, J. (1992). Multimedia down under. *Multimedia and Videodisc Monitor 10* (6), 20.

Shepard, R.N. (1967). Recognition memory for words, sentences, and pictures. *Journal of Verbal Learning and Verbal Behavior 6*, 156–63.

Shevrin, H. & Luborsky, L. (1958). The measurement of preconscious perception in dreams and images: an investigation of the Poetzl phenomenon. *Journal of Abnormal and Social Psychology 56*, 285–94.

Shiffrin, R.M. & Geisler, W.S. (1973). Visual recognition in a theory of information-processing. *In* R.L. Solso, ed. *Contemporary issues in cognitive psychology: the Loyola symposium.* Washington, DC: Winston.

Skinner, W.S. (1969). The effect of subliminal and supraliminal words presented via video-taped motion pictures on vocabulary development of ninth-grade students. Doctoral dissertation, Arizona State University, Tempe, AZ: University Microfilms, No. 69-20802.

Slee, E.J. (1989). *A review of the research on interactive video.* A paper presented at the Educational Communications and Technology Annual meeting, Dallas, TX.

Smith, E.E. (1987). Interactive video: an examination of use and effectiveness. *Journal of Instructional Development 10* (2), 2–10.

Smith, R.L. (1966). *Monotony and motivation: a theory of vigilance.* Santa Monica, CA: Dunlap.

Smith, G.J.W., Spence, D.P. & Klein, G.S. (1959). Subliminal effects of verbal stimuli. *Journal of Abnormal and Social Psychology 59*, 167–76.

Smith, K.U. & Smith, M.F. (1966). *Cybernetic principles of learning and educational design.* New York: Holt, Rinehart & Winston.

Smith, P.L., Hsu, S, Azzarello, J. & McMichael, J. (1993). *Group-based multimedia: research conclusions and future question.* A paper presented at the Association for Educational Communications and Technology Convention, New Orleans, LA.

Smith, S.M., Glenbert, A. & Bjork, R.A. (1978). Environmental context and human memory. *Memory and Cognition 6*, 342–53.

Spaulding, S. (1956). Communication potential of pictorial illustration. *AV Communication Review 4*, 31–46.

Sperling, G. (1960). The information available in brief visual presentations. *Psychological Monographs 74*, 1–29.

Strommen, E.F. & Revelle, G.L. (1990). Research in interactive technologies at the Children's Television Workshop. *Educational Technology Research and Development 38* (4), 65–80.

Suppes, P. (1980). The teacher and computer-assisted instruction. *In* R.P. Taylor, ed. *The computer in the school: tutor, tool, tutee,* 231–35. New York: Teachers College Press.

Taris, L.J. (1970). Subliminal perception: an experimental study to determine whether a science concept can be taught subliminally to fourth grade pupils. Doctoral dissertation,

Boston University, Boston, MA: University Microfilms, No. 70-22527.

Thompson, A.D., Simonson, M.R. & Hargrave, C.P. (1992). *Educational technology: a review of the research.* Association for Educational communications and Technology.

Travers, R.M.W. (1964a). The transmission of information to human receivers. *AV Communication Review 12,* 373–85.

—, ed. (1964b). *Research and theory related to audiovisual information transmission.* Salt Lake City, UT: Bureau of Educational Research, University of Utah.

— et al. (1966). *Studies related to the design of audiovisual teaching materials.* Final Report Contract No. 3-20-003, U.S. Department of Education.

— (1967). Research and theory related to audiovisual information transmission. Rev. ed. Contract No. 3-20-003, U.S. Department of Health, Education and Welfare.

— (1968). *Theory of perception and the design of audiovisual materials.* Paper presented at the faculty on educational media, Apr. 22, 1968, Bucknell University.

Treisman, A.M. (1960). Contextual cues in selective listening. *Quarterly Journal of Experimental Psychology 12,* 242–48.

United States Army (1959). Training by television and television prompting equipment. New York: Redstone Arsenal, Ordnance Guided Missile School.

VanderMeer, A.W. (1951). Relative effectiveness of color and black and white in instructional films. Port Washington, NY: Office of Naval Research, Human Engineering Division, Special Devices Center. Technical Report No. SDC-269-7-28.

VanMondfrans, A.P. (1963). An investigation of the interaction between the level of meaningfulness and redundancy in the content of the stimulus material, and the mode of presentation of the stimulus material. Unpublished masters thesis, University of Utah.

— & Travers, R.M.W. (1964). Learning of redundant materials presented through two sensory modalities. *Perceptual and Motor Skills 19,* 743–51.

Warshaw, P.R. (1978). Application of selective attention theory to television advertising displays. *Journal of Applied Psychology 63* (3), 366–72.

Webb, N.M. (1982). Group composition, group interaction and achievement in cooperative small groups. *Journal of Educational Psychology 74,* 475–84.

Westwater, J.N. (1973). A wide-screen multi-image presentation used as a multidimensional resource for experimental education: a study of teacher-user perceptions. Doctoral dissertation, Ohio state University. *Dissertation Abstracts International 33* (8-a), 3976 (University Microfilms No. 73-02, 159).

Whitley, J.B. (1977). The effects of perceptual type and presentation mode in a visual location task. Unpublished doctoral dissertation, Virginia Polytechnic Institute and State University.

— & Moore, D.M. (1979). The effects of perceptual type and presentation mode in a visual location task. *Educational Communication and Technology Journal 27* (4), 281–90.

Wilcot, R.C. (1953). A search for subthreshold conditioning at four different auditory frequencies. *Journal of Experimental Psychology 46,* 271–77.

Williams, D. & Ogilvie, J. (1957). Mass media, learning, and retention. *Canadian Journal of Psychology 11,* 157–63.

Winn, B. (1987). Charts, graphs, and diagrams in educational materials. *In* D.M. Willows & H.A. Houghton, eds. *The psychology of illustration.* New York: Springer.

Witkin, H.A., Moore, C.A., Goodenough, D.R. & Cox, P.W. (1977). Field-dependent and field-independent cognitive styles and their educational implications. *Review of Educational Research 47,* 1–64.

Welford, A.T. (1968). *Fundamentals of skills.* London: Methuen.

Yang, C.S. (1993). Theoretical foundations of hypermedia. Unpublished paper. Virginia Polytechnic Institute and State University, Blacksburg, VA.

Zuckerman, M. (1960). The effects of subliminal and supraliminal suggestion on verbal productivity. *Journal of Abnormal and Social Psychology 60,* 404–11.

V

INSTRUCTIONAL STRATEGIES RESEARCH

Marcy P. Driscoll, Florida State University

Associate Editor

30. CONTROL OF MATHEMAGENIC ACTIVITIES

Ernst Z. Rothkopf
COLUMBIA UNIVERSITY TEACHERS COLLEGE

The purpose of this chapter is to discuss the concept of mathemagenic activities. I intend to review its theoretical and empirical origins and to contrast mathemagenic activities with several other conceptions of the dynamics of information gathering such as motivation and learning strategies. In addition, I will describe the critical role of mathemagenic activities in a macrotheoretical model of teaching and explore their role in the management of instruction. Finally, I would like to point to some unsolved scientific and practical problems and to offer a brief discussion of appropriate supports for effective mathemagenic activities with the newer instructional technologies.

30.1 ORIGINS

Mathemagenic activities are the activities that give birth to learning (Rothkopf, 1963, 1965, 1968). The coined word *mathemagenic* comes from the Greek *mathemain,* that which is learned, and *gineisthos,* to give birth. *Study activities, metacognition, inspection behaviors, epistemic activities,* and even *motivation,* are other terms in the psychological literature that overlap to some degree in meaning with this coined word.

The term *mathemagenic activities* was chosen to emphasize that learning is an active process. The information that we acquire about the world is not the passive consequence of bombardment by informative environmental particles.[1] Rather, learning is the result of intense activity in which learners expose themselves to information and select from it. Learners structure, organize, and elaborate the acquired information and integrate it into memory. *Mathemagenic activities are both observable and covert activities that are relevant to achieving particular learning goals when a specific information base is available.* It should be pointed out, however, that in purposive learning, not all mathemagenic activities are consistent with achieving a particular goal. Some mathemagenic activities can produce stillbirths, useless information monsters, or nothing much at all. The key term in the definition of mathemagenic activities is *relevant.* Mathemagenic activities are relevant to attaining a particular goal. Some mathemagenic activities help, while others may hinder. For the purposes of this discussion, mathemagenic activities are those activities that provide or structure information, regardless of whether purposive learning is involved. Some learning may result from any information procurement activities, but we have no feasible way of checking definitively whether some learning has resulted from an information-procurement act. As a consequence, we consider that all of the following are examples of mathemagenic activities: (a) looking up a number in the telephone book, (b) reading directions for using epoxy to repair a boat, (c) finding out how to use large fonts in printing a computer document, (d) figuring out what a botched word in a fax means from the remainder of the transmission, and (e) studying a textbook to pass a history examination.

The success of any *instructive event* depends critically on what the learner does when the event occurs. *An instructive event is a physical change in the environment.* The description of an instructive event is simply a description of a stimulus object, the nominal stimulus. Whether this nominal stimulus produces learning depends strongly on acts by the students: whether they attend to it, process it to a sufficient degree, and form an adequate internal representation. Students must transform the nominal stimulus into a sufficiently effective stimulus for the desired learning to occur. The importance of this simple idea is obvious when learning from written material is considered. The successful utilization of written instructive events depends on highly

---

[1] In apology for adding another strange word to psychology's already murky vocabulary, it should be kept in mind that I coined the term around 1960. At that time, much instructional research emphasized the calculus of practice, i.e., effective organization and sequencing of instructional elements. Relatively little attention was paid to the learner's role in translating instructive information into internal representations. This was due to the mindset of instructional researchers rather than the behaviorist Zeitgeist. Contrary to the current cognitivist party line, learners' activities were frequently considered in behavioral literature (e.g., Hull, 1943; Postman, 1964; Underwood, 1963).

skilled acts by the students, namely, reading. Reading to learn is a complex set of activities, most of which cannot be directly observed. These activities vary widely in different circumstances. They are all essentially under the control of the readers whether consciously or not. No learning takes place without them. Students' processing activities are even harder to observe in the case of nonwritten instructive events such as lectures, films, etc. But the importance of these processing activities under those circumstances is also clear.

Mathemagenic activities involve a variety of observable and unobservable student actions that range from postural adjustments and eye movements to hypothetical mental acts. Mathemagenic activities may include those required to decode written language into some kind of internal representation, to pay attention, to form mnemonic devices, as well as inference and other forms of intellectual elaborations of the representations of stimulus objects. They may also include other important activities of which the learner is unaware and about which we can only speculate.

Discourse about mathemagenic activities is not a single coherent scientific theory. These activities do not represent a unitary class of natural phenomena that form a simple focus for research. Rather, the concept of mathemagenic activities refers to a class of related scientific and practical questions about the role of students and information users in learning and in the use of informative documents and other information sources. The concept is intended to distinguish concern with the role of the information user from concern with the design and use of cultural artifacts to transmit knowledge. Concern with such cultural artifacts and their use has dominated applied psychological and educational research, as well as discussions of national policy.

30.2 COGNITIVE MODELS OF LEARNING PROCESSES

How does the notion of mathemagenic activity differ from *cognitive* models that have emerged from information-processing research during the past decades? Many of these cognitive approaches share psychological perceptions of man as an active, resource-limited transformer of information. Cognitive models of study processes differ on several important points of emphasis from the conceptions that have grown around mathemagenic activities.

Numerous cognitivist conceptions deal with learning and learning-related activities.[2] These include a cluster of

similar or related notions such as metacognition, learning strategies, study strategies, networking, concept learning, mnemonic techniques, and constructivist conceptions (see 7.3). All portray the learner as an active agent who plays a critical role in acquiring information. Clearly, in this respect these views resemble mathemagenic conceptions. The difference is that the notion of mathemagenic activity includes *dispositional* elements as well-skilled acts acquired through experience. Disposition refers to the likelihood that learners will carry out acts that they are capable of carrying out. It refers to optional, and perhaps volitional, aspects of acts. Cognitive formulations tend to concentrate on *know-how*. The mathemagenic concept stresses the *likelihood of execution* as well. This is an important difference. If there is such a thing as a mathemagenic hypothesis,[3] it is that mastering of learning activities is a necessary but not a sufficient condition for their execution.

One additional important difference between Rothkopf's (1970, 1976) approaches to mathemagenic activities and cognitive formulations such as that of Kintsch and van Dijk (1978), Frederiksen (1972), and Meyer (1975) concern the specifiability of the content of instruction.[4] For example, it is assumed by the cognitivists that text passages have innumerable content. All measures of the successful use of the text, e.g., understanding or recall, are derived from characterizations of content. The major theoretical focus is the explication of understanding and recall. This position is fraught with logical complexities when it is applied to instructional expository text and, in fact, any other fixed instructional message.

The mathemagenic conception rejects the proposition that text or any other tangible instructional product has *true* specifiable content for which the reader signals receipts by demonstrating comprehension. The logic of this position is as follows. Assume that an operational definition of *text content* is the set of questions that a prudent and intelligent observer can generate about a passage. Generally, many questions can be produced for each *text element*. Additional unique questions can be generated from pairs of text elements and other multiples. As the text grows longer— the number of questions that can be asked—with it our conceptions of content increase geometrically. As a result, content becomes much more difficult to specify as text length approaches the size usually found in school assignments. A basic assumption in our work is that the successful use of expository, instructional text or any other instructional product must be evaluated with reference to a criterion outside a text. The most likely of these outside criteria is derived from the purposes of instruction, i.e., a specifica-

---

[2]Introspection provides everyone with a front-row seat on mental processes, and this has led some cognitivist researchers to propose protocols of inspection as data for the analysis of learning processes. Thanks to the articulate advocacy by Simon and his coworkers (e.g., Ericsson & Simon, 1980), protocol analysis is currently a widely practiced form of inquiry into strategic learning processes. The shortcomings of this method are legion. Perhaps the most serious of these is that the analysis of protocols is highly selective informants. For these reasons, this technique can be of only limited heuristic value in the analysis of learning-related processes.

---

[3]The term *mathemagenic* hypothesis is not mine; it has appeared frequently in the literature.

[4]It is difficult to characterize the currently popular constructivist's position (van Glaserfeld, 1987) on the enumerability of content, but it must, at least in practical domains, devolve to the pragmatics of constructed representations. In this respect, the constructivist's view on content may be closer to the mathemagenics position.

tion of what we want students to know when they are finished reading. This approach makes it possible, for example, to compare the value of several texts, a task that is awkward with text-centered, cognitivist approaches.

Cognitivist approaches have tended to be content centered. Accounts of mathemagenic activities, on the other hand, look to the pragmatics of teaching—to what we hope readers or learners will achieve—for criteria of successful use of text or any other instructional message. Mathemagenic activity is always considered with respect to a specific purpose. The characterization of instructional material that is of greatest importance, according to this view, is not the content but the relationship between material and instructional goals. The cognitivist-structuralist asks whether the instructional material is understood and how this is accomplished. We ask whether a particular purpose can be achieved with a text and what can be done to help learners achieve their goals.

Another difference is that cognitive models have tended to focus on relatively *fixed* components of learning processes that are used by expert learners and that can be taught like any other procedural skill. Research on mathemagenic activities, on the other hand, has concentrated on *changeable* processes that not only have flexible skill components but also include important dispositional elements. There has been an inclination in much information-processing research (see 5.4.1) to regard reading processes as the same or very similar in all readers, or that, at most, they may vary in the time constants associated with each processing stage. Work on mathemagenic activities has emphasized process differences among learners, and within learners from time to time.

The matter of fixed versus changeable, and of uniform versus diverse, learning processes is of course not only a matter of emphasis but also involves questions about empirical facts. These empirical issues have often received cavalier treatment by information-processing researchers. The preferred form of their theoretical models is the decomposition of information flow into component stages or the postulation of algorithmic processes that have functional properties similar to stage models. In work on reading models, for example, tachistoscopic experiments on letter or word recognition and on the speed of making categorical semantic judgments, are used to infer basic stages of the reading process—a process that is optimistically alleged to be the same for all. The discovery of processing stages is, in itself, not sufficient proof that these operative functions cannot be changed by suitable environmental pressures such as task demands or learning. The uniformity hypothesis is rarely questioned.

Whether these hypotheses are adequately tested or not, information-processing research has aimed at discovering fixed psychological functions that are common to all readers. By contrast, work on mathemagenic activities has focused on how environmental pressures can alter the transformation of information that takes place during study. In part, this emphasis rests on the belief that any complex human activity is flexible, adaptive, and determined by the diverse experiential histories of individuals. In part, it is motivated by the desire to account for failure, for lack of persistence, and to deal with changeable purpose. Furthermore, practical theories about the instructional uses of any media such as text should deal not only with models of possible reading processes but also with instructional intervention that can modify these processes.

It must also be recalled, particularly with respect to text, that its structure is *not* an unchangeable characteristic of language and human thought. Text structure is determined by the psychology of writers, by changeable custom, by aesthetics, and by current methods for the manufacture of text. For this reason, text structure and organization may prove to be a fickle subject for studies. To be sure, text structured in customary ways has a lasting place among the artifacts of our civilization and thus is a proper subject for study. But current written instructional forms may change, as may any other technical or cultural artifact. Written communication is now entering a new, electronic era, and new forms are likely to evolve at an increasing pace. Structural features will change in order to capitalize on new electronic means. Writing forms are to an important degree determined by current means of production. Those whose research focuses on into traditional text structure may find that text forms in practical services have been greatly altered by electronic presentation media.

Another difference between the two approaches to the study of learning processes is that the cognitivists are usually too optimistic about their ability to analyze covert mental processes. Information-processing models have usually been fairly sanguine about how much detail about studying can be revealed by current experimental methods (see 55.4.1). Mathemagenic research, on the other hand, has followed a somewhat more conservative line. The resulting conceptual models try to anchor functions on the level of observation and seek to live within their empirical income, even if this limits the internal complexity of models.

30.3 SOME HISTORY

Research on mathemagenic activities has become confused with the flimsy issue of whether adjunct questions are a useful instructional method. The confusion was probably caused by misreading of early research and an insidious preoccupation with method in the educational research community. Early work on the modification of mathemagenic activities relied on the experimental use of questions. However, the matter of the educational value of questions is on the periphery of research on mathemagenic activities and does not generate many interesting practical questions. No report from our laboratory has ever concluded that questions are necessarily an effective instructional maneuver.

The use of adjunct questions in early research on mathemagenic activities grew out of the analysis of active responding in programmed instruction (Rothkopf, 1963). It was proposed by some, at that time, that corrective feedback (i.e., knowledge of results) for student responses reinforced substantive knowledge gained from self-instructional material (e.g., McDonald, 1965, pp. 90–91). The analytic metaphor was taken from studies of instrumental learning in birds and small mammals. Contingencies between key pecking by pigeons and food reinforcement was known to increase the likelihood of the future occurrence of key pecking. By analogy, it was thought that contingencies between responses to a program frame and evaluative feedback strengthened the subject-matter competence underlying that response (McDonald, 1965). The equation of the effect of knowledge of results on substantive learning with reinforcement of substantive knowledge seemed faulty. In instrumental conditioning in animals, withdrawal of reinforcement leads to a weakening of the learned response. Similar effects in human substantive learning have not been observed, i.e., elicitation of subject-matter knowledge without feedback did not result in the deterioration of this knowledge. This suggested that one important effect of active student responses during the use of programmed material was on reading and studying activities rather than on substantive knowledge. Active responses and corrective feedback might shape and maintain study activities. This concept broadly equated the use of specially programmed materials calling for student responses with any reading activity that was accompanied by intermittent questions.

Two reports in the literature of reading supported our working hypothesis. Hoffman (1946), studying visual fatigue, observed college students during a 4-hour reading period. He recorded their eye movements using electro-oculographic methods for 5 minutes every half hour. Hoffman reported sharp deterioration of reading activities (e.g., fewer fixations, fewer lines read, increases in regressions and in blinking) after only 30 minutes of reading, and this deterioration progressed throughout the entire 4-hour period. By contrast, Carmichael and Dearborn (1947) observed readers during a 6-hour period, using similar procedures and subjects. As can be seen in Figure 30-1, the change in eye movements due to prolonged reading was much less marked for Carmichael and Dearborn's subjects than for Hoffman's. The Carmichael and Dearborn experiment differed in one important respect from the Hoffman study: Carmichael and Dearborn administered a comprehension test every 25 pages. This test included about one question for each page in the preceding 25-page reading section. The implications were fairly clear. Systematic use of questions, asked by an authoritative source, maintained effective reading patterns that would otherwise deteriorate. These results supported the conjecture that periodic questions *could* exert some influence on reading activities. The Hoffman (1946) and the Carmichael and Dearborn (1947) reports are the result of very substantial

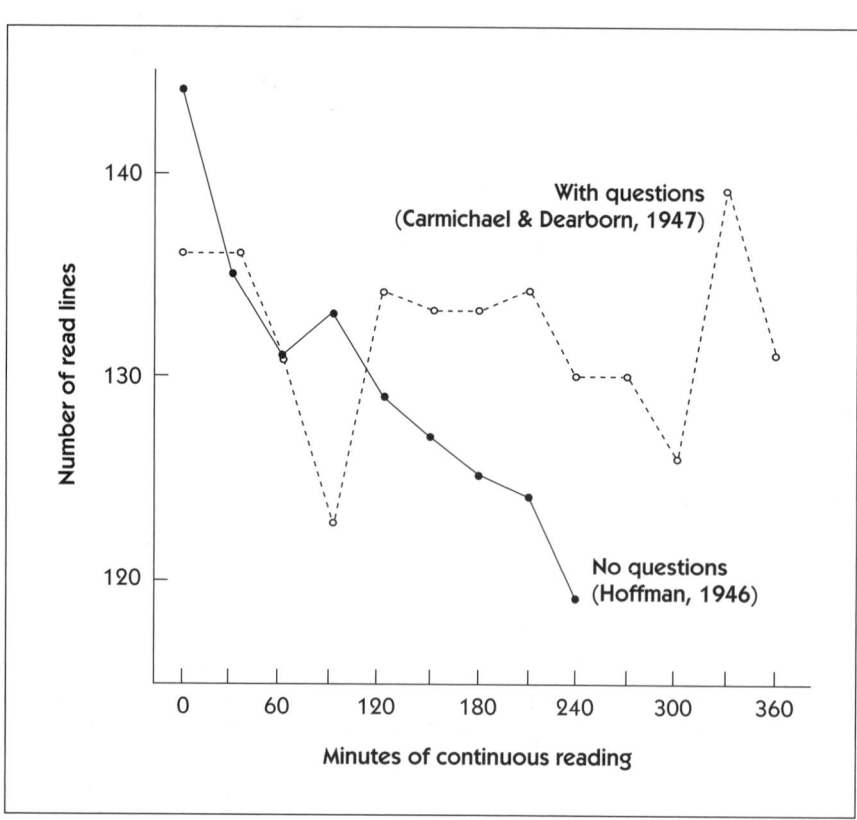

Figure 30-1. Persistence of close inspection during extended reading as function of the use of intermittent questions. The plot shows the number of lines read during 5-minute samples. (After Rothkopf, 1982.)

experimentation, but their work has not received the attention that it deserves. They clearly stimulated our early work.

30.4 CHARACTERISTICS OF MATHEMAGENIC ACTIVITY

General mathemagenic activities may be viewed as falling into two classes. The first of these involves gross activities that bring learners within physical reach of the instructive information. They are readily observable. The second class consists of covert mental processes, i.e., hypothetical internal processes such as the representation, collation, elaboration, and integration of information.

Overt mathemagenic activities include the gross body movements and postural adjustments that we usually associate with attendance, compliance with assignments, the procurement and inspection of information-bearing objects such as books, videocassettes, examining specimens, turning pages, keyboarding, and other gross information-gathering and exploratory activities. Also linked to overt mathemagenic activities are eye movements, changes in skin resistance, and other physiological responses, although these are mainly used to infer covert mathemagenic activities (e.g., Rothkopf, 1978; Rothkopf & Billington, 1979).

Covert mathemagenic activities are hypothetical mental processes that are characterized by their function such as, for example, selection, segmentation, rehearsal, etc. (e.g., Rothkopf, 1965). These processes control the flow and transformation of information during learning and comprehension. Their functions may include selection, analysis, or interpretation. The invisibility and importance of covert processes makes them ripe for speculation, but this temptation should be resisted. In doing a reading assignment for homework, for example, the gross mathemagenic activities might include taking notes about the assignment, picking up the necessary books, finding a quiet location, and looking at the assigned pages. The covert mathemagenic activities might include reading, interpreting what is read, and, perhaps, extrapolating from it. Of course, it is hardly possible to do this without engaging in gross activities, but the converse is easy. It is not uncommon to hold a book, even to turn the pages and move one's eyes across the lines of type, and still extract hardly any information from what is written.

Gross, overt mathemagenic activity for an accountant who does not know how to use a particular feature of a spreadsheet might be to find the relevant section of the manual. The covert activity might be to extract the required information from the text and apply it to the task at hand.

In the laboratory, we make inferences about covert mathemagenic activities both through the manipulations by which we induce them and by the observable consequences that are produced. For research purposes, antecedent manipulations, such as questions, are designed not to be instructive by themselves. They simply accompany a standardized instructional delivery. Therefore, if the antecedent experimental manipulation is found to influence learned performance, it can be inferred that the manipulation has altered the manner in which the instructional message was processed, i.e., that it has altered mathemagenic activities.

A distinction must be made between (a) the methods that are used to induce mathemagenic activities in the laboratory and to infer their effects, and (b) the methods that are used to manipulate them and to apply the concept in practical situations. In the laboratory, great pains have to be taken to ensure that the inducing operations are not informative or instructive with respect to criterion measurements. In practical situations, this is not necessary. It is wasted motion. Opportunities should be fully exploited that would combine interventions to enhance useful mathemagenic activities with operations that communicate substantive information, strengthen memory for information, or facilitate subsequent retrieval. Practical applications will be discussed in somewhat greater detail later in this chapter.

General characteristics of mathemagenic activities include lability, topography, and persistence. These will be briefly sketched below. A more detailed discussion follows later.

30.4.1 Lability

From a practical point of view, the most important characteristic of mathemagenic activities, whether overt or covert, is their lability. They can be changed by many situational factors including environmental conditions and task demands. They are adaptive in the sense that they are responsive to environmental pressures. Because they are labile they offer opportunities for instructional intervention.

30.4.2 Topography

Operationally this simply means that the effective processing induced by demand characteristics for certain materials or content is not necessarily transferred to other materials and topics. Demand characteristics shape mathemagenic activities. Association linkages occur if certain situations reliably produce the same demand characteristics. Subsequently these situations will tend to elicit particular topographies. This means that topographies may have specific linkages to content and instructional forms. Selection, elaboration, and rehearsal, indexed with respect to instructive sources, are examples of topography.

Our ability to infer the topography of covert mathemagenic activities is very limited. But a functional analysis of these covert activities is feasible, i.e., it is possible to infer to a certain degree what transformations the learner has performed on instructional information. The postulation of hypothetical mathemagenic functions and inferences about functional topography is useful in planning practical interventions. It is of particular value in devising adjunct techniques to induce effective mathemagenic activities and in avoiding procedures that will interfere with purposive learning.

Not all mathemagenic processes should be categorized as executive functions, i.e., as strategies that are purposefully focused on learning. It is not unlikely that the most effective mathemagenic activities involve the invocation of processes that *incidentally* produce the desired learning outcomes. The highest art in teaching is the skillful management of such processes.

30.4.3 Persistence

Mathemagenic processes can be maintained by incentives, and they can be eroded by difficulties and through effortfulness. It is very likely the case that some mathemagenic activities behave like operants in the sense that they require appropriate reinforcement schedules to maintain them. Such mathemagenic activities will deteriorate if reinforcement contingencies are haphazardly managed or are removed from instructional situations. There are also good reasons to expect that the law of least effort modifies mathemagenic activities and that effort itself can erode them. For this reason, it is not enough to teach learners how to handle information. Schools have to create environments that will sustain mathemagenic activities at vigorous levels by managing reinforcement contingencies and reducing obstacles. It must not be assumed that study skills or metacognitive strategies will be practiced once they are mastered.

The factors that shape and sustain mathemagenic activities are partially in instructional environments because such environments can model appropriate activities, create task demands, and provide contingencies between activities and consequences. Other shaping and sustaining factors can be found in intrinsic consequences of learning activities. Finding interesting information in books, lessons, or other instructive sources makes it more likely that these sources will continue to be consulted.

30.5 INDUCTION, MODIFICATION, AND MAINTENANCE

Mathemagenic activities can be induced, shaped, and maintained by a variety of methods. A rather questionable trend in the literature is to treat individual control techniques such as adjunct questions, directions, learning goals, etc., as if they were pharmaceuticals that had to be evaluated for curative effectiveness. The empirical assessment of *methods* poses many well-known logical and practical problems, and this approach will not be used here. Instead, the nature of possible controls will be considered with respect to their influence on the functional topography of mathemagenic activities.

Mathemagenic activities are always analyzed with respect to some specific educational goals or some achievement reference. Effective functional topographies are likely to differ among various instructional media such as texts, film materials, computers, lectures, and so on. We know most about topographies that are effective with text because most of the relevant research was done with text.

Several useful distinctions need to be pointed out before discussing the management of mathemagenic activities.

The first is between (a) *general* instructional material that is *used* for a particular purpose, and (b) *specific* instructional material that has been *prepared* for a particular purpose. These two types of material differ sharply in how selective the learner has to be.

Another useful distinction is between (a) materials in which the learner has relatively *weak control* over inspection, such as a film or videotape; and (b) material in which learners have *strong control* over sequence and timing, such as text or certain computer courseware. Weak control materials offer poorer opportunities for reinspection. This raises capacity limitation problems that may limit mathemagenic activities.

The third distinction that needs to be made is between operations (a) that directly elicit mathemagenic activities, and (b) those that shape and dispose towards such activities in future efforts. This distinction is similar to the contrast between the *direct* and *indirect* effects of adjunct questions (Rothkopf, 1966). One operation directly induces actions that will produce learning and strengthen memory or the ability to retrieve it, e.g., rehearsal. The indirect operation makes it more likely that instructional material will be processed in some particular way in the future (e.g., Sagerman & Mayer, 1987).

30.6 INTERVENTIONS

The major kinds of interventions to elicit, shape, and maintain mathemagenic activities are task demands, modeling, and incentive manipulations. Task demands include adjunct questions and exercises, directions, and process-inducing tasks.

30.6.1 Adjunct Questions

The role of adjunct questions in the control of mathemagenic activities has frequently been misunderstood. The problem has been the obsessive concern of many educators with *method* and their unsound belief in a pharmacological model for the empirical evaluation of methods of instruction. As a result of these mistaken beliefs, much effort was wasted in a flurry of experiments that were carried out to determine whether adjunct questions were instructionally effective.

It is historical fact that adjunct questions were used in the experiments that first demonstrated mathemagenic activities and provided existential proof for them. These adjunct questions were carefully designed to provide *no* information that could be directly useful in responding to a text-based criterion test, and this design feature was empirically checked before experimentation. Such questions, nevertheless, were found to improve criterion test performance. They shaped mathemagenic activities that yielded information needed to answer criterion test questions. The point of these early experiments (e.g., Rothkopf, 1966; Rothkopf & Bisbicos, 1967) was to show that mathemagenic activities were labile and adapted to environmental pressures. The adjunct questions shaped and maintained effective mathemagenic activities. Unhappily, this caused the *methods* addicts to pay attention. To make the misunderstanding worse, recall of the material actually covered by the adjunct questions was greatly improved, in part, because the questions also provided direct rehearsal of the relevant information.

Not enough people paid attention to the governing principles proposed by Rothkopf (e.g., 1982). First, adjunct questions have to be consistent with instructional goals to be effective. Mathemagenic activities are labile, and it is possible to write adjunct questions that will result in mathemagenic behaviors that will *depress* test performance. This was clearly demonstrated by Rothkopf and Coke (1963, 1966) using overprompting techniques.

The second principle is that beneficial mathemagenic effects will be produced by adjunct questions, chiefly when the mathemagenic activities of the learner are inadequate. Good learners hardly need a boost. This was demonstrated (Rothkopf, 1972) by having learners read a very long (96-page) passage on geology. Adjunct questions were never used before page 12. We kept track of whether (a) people accelerated their reading rate during the first 12 pages or not, and (b) if they remembered more than average about the first 12 pages. It is safe to assume that mathemagenic activities were not adequate to the task in the group members who did not learn much from the first 12 pages but who increased their reading rate. Our experiment showed that it was exactly this group that showed the greatest gain due to adjunct questions. Other subsequent reports that adjunct question are more likely to be useful to ineffective learners (e.g., Serethy & Dean, 1986) have similarly attracted very little attention.

The size of the "mathemagenic" effect produced by adjunct "post" questions also depends on how representative the adjunct question set is of the criterion test and on the malleability of appropriate mathemagenic activity. In order to estimate the effect on the population mean, the experimental effect must then be multiplied by the proportion of the student population who bring inadequate mathemagenic activities to the learning situation. The gross effect of the intervention, however, is substantially larger when the criterion test is only a small sample of the total knowledge domain that was covered by instruction. This is commonly the case. As a crude estimate, if the experimental gain in incidental learning is only 4%, and the criterion test was derived from 50 out of a 1,000 sentences, then the expected gross gain from the intervention averages 40 sentences per person. It will average a lot more per inefficient learner if such learners represented only a small proportion of the total student population.

Adjunct questions or exercises have several consequences. First of all, they are acts of rehearsal that strengthen memory, prepare for future interrogation or use (Landauer & Bjork, 1978; Landauer & Ainslie, 1975; Glover, 1989), and provide context for future recall and use (e.g., Ross, 1984). Whether knowledge of results is made available or not, adjunct questions provide feedback that will strengthen or weaken

learning processes that have been applied in the recent past, depending on the results that they have produced.

Adjunct questions also influence selection mechanisms (e.g. Rothkopf & Bisbicos, 1967; Reynolds & Anderson, 1982; Reynolds, Standiprot & Anderson, 1979). Learners are sensitive to the tenor of the questions and any biases in the nature of the information that is asked for. Such bias shapes selective attention. It works on the instructive events that follow adjunct questions (see Rothkopf, 1966; Sagerman & Mayer, 1987). The selection mechanism is important when teachers are trying to adapt general instructional materials to their special instructional purposes. They are especially useful in the unhappy case when teachers are unable to state their purpose clearly but have a good intuitive sense of those goals. The questions the teachers then ask can provide an inductive basis for tuning the selective attention of the student to the teacher's intuitive aims.

The notion of selection implies that particular instructive elements (e.g., text elements) are favored with a different level or kind of mathemagenic activities than other instructive components. We may not be able to specify in detail what these activities are, but they seem to result in increased demands on cognitive resources. This has been shown through inspection time measurements (e.g., Reynolds et al., 1979) and by demonstration of threshold increases through ingenious secondary task monitoring techniques (e.g., Britton, Piha, Davis & Wethausen, 1978; Burton, Niles, Lalik & Reed, 1986).

Finally, another beneficial usage of questions is to communicate to the student that someone cares about what they derive from instruction. There is some evidence that suggests that social questioning is more effective than questions from inanimate sources. Questions directly relevant to the reading task that were personally asked by a teacherlike figure were found to result in more effective learning activities than automatically presented questions or than nonsubstantive questions (e.g., Is the chair at a comfortable height?) asked by a teacherlike person during a periodic visit to the workstation (Rothkopf & Bloom, 1970). Such contingent reinforcement procedures may be especially helpful in maintaining gross overt mathemagenic actions.

Questions that can be answered through information obtained through trivial processes will depress effective mathemagenic activities. Examples of such trivially based queries are adjunct questions made up preeminently from picture captions (which I have actually observed in the teachers' version of a prominent social science textbook) or questions that can be answered from short-term memory.

30.6.2 Goal-Descriptive Directions

When general instructional materials are used and the teacher can specify what students should accomplish with these materials, then the students should be informed as precisely as possible about these goals. That is the purpose of directions that describe goals. This fairly obvious point is worth reiterating. Adjunct questions can be used as inductive guides to goals that teachers consider important but cannot describe specifically. When teachers can describe goals in explicit language, then questions are still useful because they act as rehearsal. But when goals can be described, explicit direction can guide the student in selecting from the instructional material. This is especially useful if teachers wish to adapt general materials for specific purposes of their own. Directions have been found instructionally effective with text (e.g., Rothkopf & Kaplan, 1972; Ellis, Konoske, Wulfeck & Montague, 1982). Eye movement studies (Rothkopf, 1978; Rothkopf & Billington, 1978) have shown that goal-descriptive directions can effectively control selective attention in reading. There are indications that there is a fall-off in efficiency as the number of directions increases (Rothkopf & Kaplan, 1974). For text, this is most likely due to failures in the search set rather than from capacity stresses during reading, because the observed fall-off in efficiency was due to the number of directions rather than to the density of direction-relevant sentences in the text. It is highly likely that the density of direction-relevant material might play a role if exposure to the instructional material were externally paced.

Much of the work on directions seems to have been carried out with text. But Mager and McCann's (1961) elegantly simple use of goal directions with engineering trainees at Varian Industries demonstrates the broad usefulness of goal descriptions. Recently graduated, newly hired engineers were given short orientation assignments in various departments of the Varian plant. Their subsequent professional development was greatly aided if they were given descriptions of what they were to find out during each departmental assignment.

Goal-descriptive directions operate on mathemagenic selection. The major technical challenge is to understand the discriminations that must be made by the learners when they detect instructional elements (such as text components) that match the goals that have been identified through the directions. It seems clear that goals can be described too broadly or vaguely, so that the processing focus is scarcely narrowed or is described so badly that the focus is misdirected. Empirical techniques can be devised for determining whether directions highlight the appropriate instructional elements (e.g., Rothkopf & Kaplan, 1972). Asking a representative sample of students to identify instructional elements that are relevant to a particular goal provides much useful information about the effectiveness of the directions.

Several additional points should be made about goal-descriptive directions. First, some skill is required to identify the instructional components that are relevant to a goal. For example, trivial misidentifications occur when a sentence in a text shares a word or two with the goal description. A particularly difficult situation arises when the goal-descriptive directions require concatenation of two or more elements that are widely dispersed in the text (e.g., Gagné & Rothkopf, 1975; Rothkopf & Billington, 1975; Rothkopf

& Koether, 1978). Second, identifying goal-relevant instructional elements is not a sufficient condition for learning. Although cognitivists tend to overvalue the importance of intention, the incidental learning literature is replete with demonstrations that intention is nice, but not sufficient, and not needed (e.g., Mechanic, 1962; for a discussion, see Postman, 1964).

Finally, the clever experiments of Frase and Keitzberg (1975) have shown that the positive identification of goal-relevant elements, as well as other kinds of categorization, can be an effective mathemagenic act. Their experiments show that the processes required to identify a sentence as containing relevant elements may be sufficient for learning.

30.6.3 Other Task Demands

Students can be asked to carry out tasks that involve elements of the instructional information. Such demands can result in mathemagenic processes that will lead to the acquisition of targeted information. The search for goal-relevant information, alluded to above—i.e., the examination of instructional elements to see whether they contained goal-relevant material—may internalize the information sufficiently to cause it to be understood and remembered. Sorting instructional information according to certain attributes can result in sufficient processing for important learning. Frase and Kammann (1974), for example, showed that sorting animal names according to a dual criterion resulted in better recall than sorting them according to a single feature. A number of tasks (other than the directions to learn) can be devised that will result in processes sufficient for learning.

Inventing tasks that will induce appropriate and sufficient mathemagenic processes to accomplish instructional goals, without necessarily revealing to learners that they are working to achieve these goals, is an exciting challenge. It is a challenge because of an intriguing mystery, which some ingenious researcher may help us understand some day, namely, that many people perceive efforts to learn as painful. Such pain prevents many learners from accomplishing what they are asked to do. Yet these very same people will willingly perform other tasks with the instructional materials—tasks such as searching for content elements, classification or sorting, rewriting text, or explaining the instructional content to others—and thus process the material sufficiently to induce the desired learning outcomes. This is the reason why well-conceived task demands often result in effective mathemagenic activities, while hortatory directions to learn will only produce modest results.

30.6.4 Control by Revealing Consequences

Since mathemagenic activities are labile, they tend to be responsive to environmental pressures. The incorporation of indicators of progress into the instructional stream therefore makes it more likely that these activities will be shaped into effective topographies. Two kinds of consequences of mathemagenic activities appear useful. One is essentially informative. It lets learners know if they are moving in the right directions and warns them of difficulties. The second involves consequences with hedonistic tone, for example the recognition or praise of study activities or of accomplishments. There are some suggestions in the literature (e.g., Dweck, 1986) that some learners may perceive information about their accomplishments as particularly pleasant and encouraging. Others flourish when their learning activities gain the attention of teachers or other persons. As pointed out earlier, we have observed that the effectiveness of adjunct questions can be enhanced by having them delivered (live) by a teacherlike person (Rothkopf & Bloom, 1970).

It is hardly worthwhile experimentally to evaluate the advisability of providing consequences, i.e., making the instructive environment transparent to results. Even if consequencing did not work all the time, gauges and mileage markers are usually installed without much cost, and they are unlikely to do much harm. Instructional materials that have been developed for very specific purposes ought to be transparent enough to provide learners with an accurate sense of progress. Interactive instructional systems offer many opportunities for providing consequences with which learners might evaluate their efforts.

30.7 DISPOSITIONAL SOCIAL INFLUENCES

30.7.1 Intrinsic Factors

It is something of a truism that the control of mathemagenic activities does not depend entirely on external interventions but may result from well-internalized dispositions such as interests and immediate or long-range goals. One has the impression that such controls function better if there are immediate concrete linkages between instruction and the disposition. For example, the instructional materials work better if they are interesting rather than if they were just logically related to the learner's career goals. It is a common observation that some students can be very articulate about the importance for their career of certain skills (such as programming or calculus) but consistently fail to pursue the appropriate studies in a serious vein. Afterward, they often express keen regret. Intrinsic controls can often be established by certain experiences that are calculated to create interest and establish the value of outcomes.

30.7.2 Modeling

Social modeling is probably the most powerful of several possible learning-inducing mechanisms (Bandura, 1977). It is likely to have a direct influence on overt gross mathema-

genic activities and is likely to shape covert mental activity indirectly through the modeling of values. Models have been shown to affect persistence (Zimmerman, 1979). Models of information gathering and intellectual preparation and models of positive attitudes towards such activities are also likely to induce these in others. If the models for information gathering and problem solving that are provided by family and neighborhood are sparse, public media such as television and films are likely to play an important role in shaping behaviors and attitudes towards the use of information. Television (and other powerful media) cultivates attitudes and influences behavior when other influences are weak. This has been demonstrated by a number of studies. For example, the perception of danger from crime and attitudes towards aging have been shown to be influenced by television watching (e.g., Gerber, Gross, Jackson-Beek & Signorelli, 1978; Gerber, Gross, Signorelli & Morgan, 1980). American students average over 1,200 hours per year before television sets—more time than they spend in school. Yet television fare is exceedingly short of models of behavior in which information is diligently gathered to master some skill or to solve a problem. Portrayals of success gained through hard study, the acquisition of useful knowledge, training, and problem solving have poor dramatic value and are therefore very rarely portrayed. The exceptions are sweaty preparations for sports, which appear both in news programs and in drama (e.g., *Rocky*), and the grunty travails of becoming a Kung Fu master. But mad and brilliant scientists and engineers in the movies seem to have arrived at work without preparatory schooling or labor, just as tycoons succeed by greed and cunning and rarely by the knowledge they have acquired. Cowboys learn to ride, shoot, and sing without much visible effort, and police drive their cars masterfully in hair-raising chases without any hint of schooling or frustrating practice. The studying and gathering of information for problem solving does not offer good dramatic possibilities. Preparation like the passage of time is often portrayed as the wind riffing through the calendar. It is therefore not too difficult to extract the message from the media that accomplishments are due mainly to special talent—a popular contemporary form of magic—rather than hard work and the diligent, judicious acquisition of information. For this reason, it is not surprising that Americans blame lack of talent for failures in mathematics, while Asians, both here and abroad, attribute such failures to lack of hard effort (Stigler & Barnes, 1988). The convergent theme is that success is achieved through magic and talent and not by marshaling information resources and molding them into a lever that will serve a prechosen purpose.

30.7.3 Mathemagenic Activities and Motivation

Insufficient motivation is often blamed when instruction fails, and success is often attributed to good motivation.

These attributions are probably incorrect in many cases. Of course, motivation is a fairly broad, portmanteau kind of concept. But it may frequently be the case that what is attributed to motivation should be attributed to the shaping and maintenance of mathemagenic activities. The purpose of this section is to contrast briefly mathemagenic activities with motivational concepts.

Psychology has evolved three kinds of explanatory engines to account for why people act. They are motivation, incentive, and the learned-skill dispositions, which behaviorists like Hull (1943) called *habits*. None of these concepts is very crisply defined when taken away from its original experimental contexts, and the boundaries between concepts are a bit fuzzy. Both motivation and incentive are frequently invoked to explain *why* students study. Habitlike concepts (e.g., study strategies, concept mapping) are used almost exclusively to describe *how* they study. When failures to study occur (e.g., compliance), regardless of how effective the available study skills are, the failure is usually attributed to lack of motivation or lack of suitable incentives. Yet the results from research on mathemagenic activities suggests that habitlike concepts should be assigned a more important role in descriptions of *why* students do or do not study.

Undoubtedly all three—motivation, incentive, and habitlike dispositions—influence study performance. Of course, most motivation relevant to human study activities is not directly derived from basic tissue needs such as hunger and thirst but rather stems from complex experiential factors that have largely social origins. It is safe to say that motivation in instructional situations is less under immediate environmental control than either incentives or habit.

We infer motivation both from what we know about people (a test, an attitude questionnaire) and what we tell them (that others will "hold their manhoods cheap" because they did not stand and fight on St. Crispin's day or that "the eyes of Texas are upon you"). Incentives, on the other hand, refer to objects or states of affairs that are associated with satisfaction of drivelike motivational states (a high grade, money, a smile from Texas, or even some wanted information obtained from study). Incentives can be thought of as exercising both direct and indirect control on study performance. It is direct control when the incentive is present in the study situation and is reached for. Indirect control is exerted when the attainment of incentive objects in similar situations is remembered and serves as an internalized incentive.

The most complete theoretical statement about the relationships between motivation, incentive, and habit was offered by the latter-day behaviorist Clark Leonard Hull (1943). Habits as learned, skill-like entities are conceptualized as taking place when certain external or internal demands are made. Motivation and incentive are rather closely related. An object or event acts as an incentive only for particular motivational states. In practice, many motivational conditions are named for the incentives that are operative when a given motivational state is in effect.

Furthermore, when the term *incentive* is used to include internalized representations of the goal object, the distinction between motivation and incentive almost disappears.

Habit, on the other hand (and with it mathemagenic activity), is quite distinct from the other two concepts. The growth and decline of habit depends either (a) on contingencies between the student's actions and events in the instructional environment, or (b) on modeling or mimicry. For this reason, growth and decline of habits occur only in the performance situation, whereas motivation can be thought to arise in many contexts. Motivation may increase gradually and with weak references to any particular external event. We say that Laura and Joanna study hard because they want college scholarships, or like to be praised, love mathematics, or because their mother has promised them a space shuttle if they get all A's.

Study habits refers to whether students study at the same time each day, whether they shut off radio, TV, or CD while reading, and whether they paraphrase and write down what they have read. Covert mathemagenic activities (as well as overt) also fall into the habit category that can be caused to change and to wax and wane as a consequence of instructional contingencies or through modeling.

30.8 LEARNING IN SCHOOLS AND OTHER INSTRUCTIVE SETTINGS

30.8.1 Study Skills Training

Training in study skills has long been on the educational scene (e.g., Deese, 1957; Robinson, 1970), usually on an individual basis. The study skills targeted in these courses involve actions that might be termed *mathemagenic* under many circumstances. The following section offers a critical perspective on study skills training and contrasts study skills training with shaping and support of mathemagenic activities.

Failure to meet academic standards is sometimes due to inadequate teaching or inadequate teaching materials. Another very important contributor to low achievement is insufficient or ineffective learning or study activities. Many students don't do enough homework or remember little of what they have studied. Students pay poor attention in class or gain little from instructional episodes from which other students have profited. Some of these failures have been ascribed to low abilities. But hardly anyone doubts that the exercise of appropriate learning activities can improve academic results. For this reason, many educators feel that training in study or learning skills will solve the achievement problems. They reason that part of the difficulty is that students do not know how to study and need to be taught. In the past, institutional efforts were usually fairly perfunctory. In recent years, however, stimulated by concern about low academic achievements, many schools have adopted systematic instruction in study skills. These training courses tended to be guided by the rationalistic conception of learning processes that are endemic among cognitivists.

Strong claims have been made for the educational efficacy of these courses, although evaluation studies provide mixed results (see Nicholson, 1988).

We see the inadequate study activities problem, instead, as a matter of the instructional management of mathemagenic activities. There are three major differences between this view and the study skills approach to bolstering academic achievement. The first centers on the relative importance of *the knowledge about how to study* versus *the disposition to use this knowledge.* Mathemagenic research has emphasized the second concern. The second difference has to do with the general applicability of learning strategies to instructional situations. Much mathemagenic research points to content and form-specific improvements in the effectiveness of learning processes (including Rothkopf & Bisbicos, 1967; Duchastel, 1979; Glover, Plake & Roberts, 1981; Mayer, 1980; Reynolds & Anderson, 1982; Reynolds, Standiford & Anderson, 1979; Sagerman & Mayer, 1987). The third substantial difference between these two points of view is the degree of faith they place on intention during learning.

30.8.2 Knowledge versus Disposition

What is the nature of the skills that have been proposed for inclusion in formal learning-skill training programs? They are not like typing or serving a tennis ball, so automatic that highly proficient performers can barely describe what they do? Nor are they like folding a parachute or describing Wellington's maneuvers at the Battle of Waterloo. Neither are they like algebra or calculus, ready to be used whenever the situation demands it except for the erosions of forgetting.

No, they are more like the many skills for which the critical characteristic is not only knowing but also in translating knowledge into action. They are much more like good manners. Many of the folks in the subway who are staring at the elderly pregnant woman with the broken leg know they should offer her their seat. Yet sometimes such women stand all the way to the hospital.

Study skills are like dietary information that diabetics can describe in fastidious detail but neglect at the dinner table. They are like knowing how to protect the roses in your garden from aphids but failing to do so. They are like knowing about calories while wishing to be thin and continuing to eat too well.

Study skills training is like information about birth control. General educational programs produce results, but a substantial number of unwanted conceptions persist that are not due to deficiencies of method, or lack of knowledge or skill, but simply from failure to act in an appropriate way. Driving safety, industrial accident prevention, village sanitation—all of these involve skills from the same category as those trained in study and learning skills programs.

The concern of teachers with learning activities in practical settings is not only whether students know how to study effectively but also whether they are willing or

disposed to do so. The relative importance of these two components is an interesting question for debate, analysis, and experiment. But it is fair to conclude that the disposition to translate learning skill into action is very important. This clearly has been one of the focuses of research on mathemagenic actions.

30.8.3 Learning Strategies and Educational Styles

Gross learning strategies that are taught tend to have three general components: (1) selection, (2) mnemonic mooring, and (3) integration (Cook & Mayer, 1983; Dansereau et al., 1979; Jones et al., 1984; Weinstein, 1978). Mayer (1987) has made similar distinctions, calling them selection, internal and external connection. Mayer's and other careful studies have shown that learning maneuvers, executed in any one of a number of variations, can produce gains in academic achievement and in retention. There is little evidence, however, that these learning strategies are universal, portable tools that can help students in any learning task whatsoever.

Learning strategies are neither content independent nor context-free. As most are taught today, their value to the learner depends on subject matter and educational goals. They depend on the structure and form of instructional information. Perhaps most important, their value depends on the intellectual outlook and style favored by academics and educationists who manage the schools. The latter is, of course, important if the aim of learning strategy training is to foster academic success. But such training will not necessarily be useful in preparation for life and for the world of work. Clearly, a successful experimental demonstration in a particular setting is not a sufficient reason for a school to adopt a training program for a particular set of learning skills. The most important question is whether the targeted learning skills are really useful to the student.

The argument can be made that what certain learning (and some reasoning) strategies accomplish is to reduce information into forms that are currently in vogue in the academic/educational community. Such strategies are of immediate advantage to the learner because academic success depends on approval by members of this community. But it is uncertain whether these learning strategies will be useful in the long term, in the world of work or in more open, less-structured learning settings. To put it in blunter language, such learning strategy training teaches students to extract what their teachers want to hear and to put it into an approved form. And what teachers want to hear and the forms that are approved may change from time to time or from circumstance to circumstance. It depends on educational fashions. The notion of the *main idea of a passage,* for example, smacks of educationists' cant. It also carries with it the tacit assumption that the main aim of reading is reproduction of information in a testlike setting. There may be more to education than this. The developer of learning skill training must make sure that what is taught is sufficiently flexible to avoid fashionable educational traps. Learning strategies training should be determined by the information needs of the learner in the contemporary world and not necessarily by current pedagogic fashion!

One important difference between study strategy training and the conception of mathemagenic behavior is that the first tends to be oriented to general goals—towards receipt theories of understanding—while the latter is pragmatic and always oriented to a very specific educational purpose. Interest in practical exploration in learning strategies was at least partially stimulated by experimental work in learning laboratories, and by attendant theoretical conceptions. But the condition that makes learning skill training viable as an academic tool is uniformity of expectations about academic outcomes, the routine application of certain teaching methods, and the nature of currently used instructional media.

30.8.4 Selecting Learning Strategies and the Strategy of Selection

As indicated before, selection is an important component of learning skill. Selection includes two distinct but related components: (a) the choice of strategies appropriate for particular conditions and tasks, and (b) the choice from the instructional content of appropriate elements to which particular learning strategies may be applied. Selection is a critical component of learning activities because learning maneuvers and mnemonic devices, no matter how skillfully executed, are ineffective if they are inappropriately applied or if applied to inappropriate content elements. Inappropriate applications may result from mismatches between learning goals and the nominal purposes of a study maneuver. The nominal aim of the study maneuver may not be the most efficient method for achieving the actual learning goal, even when the nominal aim of the study maneuver appears to match the actual goal.

Selecting learning strategies according to nominal descriptions of their purposes is not necessarily efficient because incidental consequences of processes are sometimes more powerful than intentional, systematic approaches. Everyone wants the learner to acquire intelligent flexibility in the choice of learning maneuvers. Almost every learning-skill–training program teaches that different learning goals require different learning activities. But broad identification of learning goals may not be sufficient for adapting the most efficient strategies. For example, if the actual study goal is to remember the exact sequence of events in a descriptive passage, it may be more efficient to try to remember the exact wording of the event description. These phenomena were very neatly demonstrated by the classical (and now apparently largely forgotten) study of Postman and Senders (1946). They asked subjects to read a Chekov short story under one of six goal-setting directions, e.g., general comprehension, or to remember the sequence of events, the details of wording, etc. Recall was tested using items appropriate to each goal. While some directions

facilitated performance on relevant items, others produced reliable improvements in unrelated items, improvements that were in some cases substantially larger than those produced by directions relevant to the test questions. The Postman and Senders' experiment (1946) proved quite neatly that the nominal character of learning goals is not necessarily a good predictor of what the learner will achieve with the study activities that are induced by these descriptions of learning goals.

The second important selection activity does not involve choice of strategy but rather choice of appropriate content elements. Skill in content choices is probably the most difficult of all learning strategies to train, because it is so closely tied to the semantics of teaching materials and the pragmatics of the instructional tasks. Much learning material, and in particular text, is intended for many uses. Consequently, ordering of content elements with respect to centrality or importance does not depend on the material alone but also on instructional purpose or demand. An encyclopedia article, for example, is not like a blueplate special that can simply be analyzed into meat, accompanying vegetable, and decorative garnishes. In practical settings, cut-and-dried selection formulas will very likely flounder on the rocky complexities of human knowledge. It is interesting to speculate that much of the progressive gain in incidental learning that results from adjunct postquestions is probably due to the focusing of selection by inductive processes.

Two conclusions may be drawn about selection. The first is that the relationship between actual learning goals and the nominal intent of the learning maneuvers we teach can be surprisingly devious. Postman and Senders' (1946) work suggests that effective intentional control of learning activities can benefit from a little sophistication about the incidental consequences of learning activities. The second point is that when teachers have very specific instructional purposes but use general, multiuse materials, the materials themselves cannot be sufficient guides about what is important information.

30.9 MACROTHEORY OF INSTRUCTION

How does the concept of mathemagenic activities fit into a broad theoretical framework that deals with the impact of instruction on a large aggregate of learners? Rothkopf (1981) has proposed such a theory, centered around the notion of an *instructive event* as the basic counting unit of instructive experience. *An instructive event is an informative presentation, event, or happening that is sufficient to induce a targeted competence in at least some learners in at least some situations at least some of the time.* Many possible experiences may serve as instructive events for a given targeted competence. The competence to erase an entire line with a simple maneuver in a word-processing program may be produced by a paragraph of text in a manual, a personal demonstration, a labeled diagram, or clips from videotapes of a working writer or secretary. All of these instructive events support competence. All or some of these may be part of a training program. As may be seen in Figure 30-2, the likelihood of encountering an instructive event is the first major factor of the macrotheory for forecasting the number of individuals who will have the competence to erase an entire line with a simple maneuver. The likelihood of *encountering* an instructive event is determined by two variables: (1) the number of relevant instructive events—their density or redundancy in the instructional stream, and (2) compliance with directions and assignments (e.g., do students read what they are supposed to read?). Compliance is clearly an important variable in determining the number of instructive events that will be encountered. Compliance represents a class of overt mathemagenic activities and is affected both by consequencing and by modeled behaviors and modeled values.

Encountering an instructive event is not sufficient for the acquisition of competence. For that, the instructive event must be successfully processed. Three variables determine the likelihood of successfully processing an instructive event once it has been encountered. As may be seen in Figure 30-2, the three variables are: (1) the disparity between the representation of the instructional information and some canonical representation of the target competence, (2) persistence and topography of elicited mathemagenic activity, and (3) the instruction-relevant experience and knowledge of the learner. Disparity can be thought of as the

logical distance between the instructional representation of the required knowledge and a simple hypothetical mental representation. It is a conceptualization of the obstacles that the mathemagenic processes must overcome in order to produce the required knowledge. In text for example, the information about erasing a line may be simply and directly stated, or it may be said in an involuted indirect manner that requires much analysis and inference. Mathemagenic activity of a given topography and vigor may be sufficient for simple instructive representation but may fail when encountering a complex instructive event. Hence, there is a trade-off between disparity and mathemagenic activities. The last variable, instruction-relevant experience, also trades off with disparity and mathemagenic activities. Instruction-relevant experience refers to familiarity with elements of the instructive representation such as word knowledge or particular pictorial techniques. The simple metaphor of a successful leap across a ditch describes the interaction of the three variables. Disparity represents the width of the ditch. The persistence of mathemagenic activities describes the energy of the leap. Mathemagenic topography describes its direction. Finally, instruction-relevant experience refers to how little weight you are carrying when the leap is made: the more experience, the less weight.

The remaining aspects of the model deal with successful retrieval, and we do not need to concern ourselves with them here.

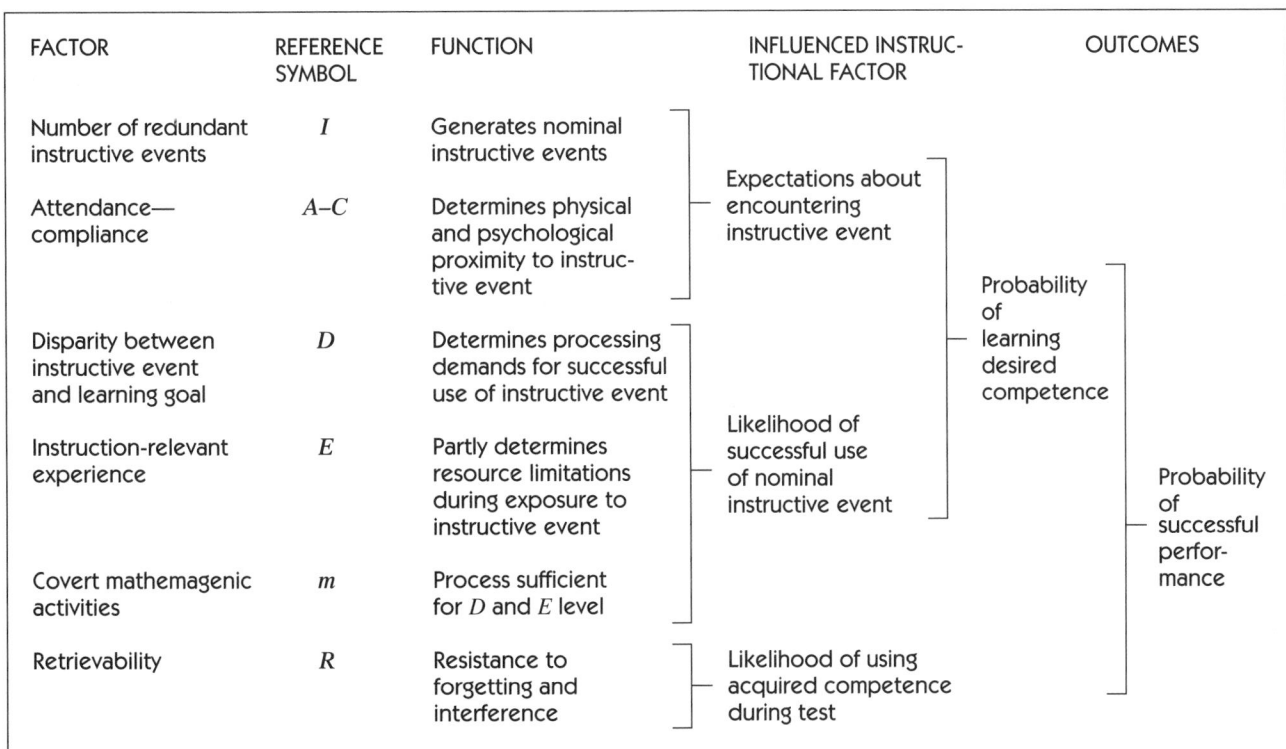

Figure 30-2. Factors in Rothkopf's macrotheoretic model that determine the success of instruction. The likelihood of acquiring the targeted competence depends on the likelihood of encountering a suitable instructive event and the likelihood of successfully processing an encountered instructive event. (After Rothkopf, 1981.)

To sum up, mathemagenic activities are involved in two aspects of acquisition within the macrotheoretic model. Overt *compliance* influences the likelihood of encountering an instructive event. *Covert mathemagenic activities* determine the successful processing of instructive events once they are encountered.

The intervention and control variables for acquisition in the macromodel can range widely in molarity. For a given system, indicators of instructional-event density may range from actual counts of instructive events judged relevant for a particular competence in a particular body of materials to computer-based statistical approximations obtained from key word counts, to the salaries paid to teachers in systems where teachers are the main instructive-event generators. Disparity indicators may include judged disparity and quantitative measures of sentence length and complexity. Schools can be evaluated with respect to measures that are taken to foster compliance, although socioeconomic and cultural characteristics of the student population are bound to play an important role. Vigorous management of compliance enhances achievements. The control of covert mathemagenic activities requires micromanagement for which technological aids to teachers are very useful. A computer-aided homework help system via telephone is an example of such technological aid.

30.10 RESEARCH ISSUES AND THE ROLE OF MATHEMAGENIC ACTIVITIES IN NEW INSTRUCTIONAL TECHNOLOGIES

Like any scientific conception, our notion of mathemagenic activities may change as new data become available and as theory becomes further elaborated and tested. There clearly are several open questions that are at present too broadly cast for systematic scientific solutions. An example of such is the relative contribution of instrumental and cognitive processes in shaping and maintaining mathemagenic activities. The following section deals with selected theoretical and empirical issues for which further research is required and for which, at least in principle, workable research resolutions can be foreseen. These include questions about the relationship between prior subject-matter knowledge and the disposition to process new information, about a wave theory of attention, and the support of effective mathemagenic topographies with newer instructional technologies.

30.10.1 *e* and *m*: Unsolved Riddle

In the macrotheory described earlier, the likelihood of successfully processing an encountered instructive event depends on three factors. It is inversely related to the disparity (*d*) between the representation of the relevant information in the instructional stream and the simple canonical representation of this information, i.e., it is inversely related to the complexity of the transformation

that the learner has to perform. Successful processing is positively related to instruction-relevant experience (*e*) and appropriate mathemagenic activity (*m*). For example, the likelihood of acquiring targeted knowledge from a group of written sentences depends both on degree of familiarity with the words in the sentences (*e*) and the topography and persistence of mathemagenic processes (*m*). Rothkopf and Billington (1979), in accounting for the effects of goal directions, have proposed the expression $e + (1 - e)m$ to describe the interaction between instruction-relevant experience such as previously acquired knowledge (*e*) and process (*m*). In other words, with respect to particular purpose, the contribution of mathemagenic process to performance is greatest when *e* is small.

Theoretical problems arise because, for simplicity, the assumption has been made that *e* and *m* are independent. But there are circumstances when the independence of *e* from *m* is suspect. For example, strong interest in a particular topic may increase not only instruction-relevant knowledge but also the likelihood that information-bearing elements of topical interest will be attended. People are more likely to focus on information that is of interest to them and are more likely to try to understand it. One possible solution to this theoretical quandary is to collapse instruction-relevant experience and mathemagenic activity into a single variable. This would work in many cases, since both *e* and *m* have positive effects on the likelihood of successful process. This solution is not appealing, however, because there are many situations where the determinants of *e* and *m* are clearly independent. Low *e* is an obstacle here against which *m* is played. The problem clearly needs a resolution. In general, issues relating the external control of mathemagenic activities to intrinsic control factors such as interest await careful analysis and formalization.

30.10.2 No Broad Wave Effects for *m*

It has been possible to develop indirect measuring techniques to study fluctuations in attention and engagement during purposive reading of text (Rothkopf & Billington, 1975). The measurement techniques are based on the assumption that, if engagement has systematic wavelike fluctuations in time, then the recall of contiguous items from text should be correlated. If engagement is strong, both of two adjacent items should be remembered. If engagement is weak, items from adjacent text segments should be failed together. The rationale behind this approach can be understood by imagining text going by the learner on an ever-moving tape. The learner sometimes closes his or her eyes (low *m* engagement), and sometimes the eyes are open (full *m* engagement). One way of deciding when the eyes were open and when they were shut is to look for clusters of test items (from adjacent sections of the text) that tended to be passed or that tended to be failed.

Using the correlational methods referred to above, it has been found that mathemagenic engagement with text materials fluctuates fairly capriciously in time but is effectively entrained by task demands or by endogenous content factors (Rothkopf & Billington, 1975). Mathemagenic selection appears to become finely tuned quickly. In a study on the effects of goal-descriptive directions, inspection time and eye movement measures have shown sharp rises in inspection activities around goal-relevant instructional elements with little or no spread of this effect to other material within the same close text neighborhood (Rothkopf & Billington, 1979).

The sharp tuning may be due to the profound mathemagenic effects of the act of discovering that an instructional element is relevant to a learning goal. Frase and Kreitzberg (1975), in an important study, asked subjects to learn about aspects of Nathaniel Bowditch's life and career. They gave them directions that referenced certain kinds of sentences (e.g., sentences that contain information about Bowditch's childhood, or that included certain words). They then told some subjects that: (a) their learning goal was the information in the referenced sentences, and directed others that (b) their learning goal was the information in the sentences that did *not* include referenced elements. The number of referenced and not-referenced sentences were the same in the passage. But subjects remembered more information from sentences that were both referenced and had goals than from the compliment sentences that were goals but were not referenced. This simple, elegant experiment suggests that the processes required to decide that a sentence contains referenced elements has more profound mathemagenic consequences than detecting the absence of such elements.

The following general principles are worth testing and may be testable. First, that the most dramatic and accessible aspect of mathemagenic activities is selectivity, i.e., high-process densities for some elements of the instructional materials rather than others. Second, the selection processes involve comparisons between learners' conceptions of their goals and elements of the instructional materials. These comparisons invoke mental activities that transform instructional materials in important ways and that must be considered effective mathemagenic acts. The Frase and Kreitzberg (1975) results as well as those of Rothkopf and Billington (1979) provide a certain degree of support for these conjectures.

The mathemagenic character of comparison processes does not depend on the intention to learn. Directions to search or to categorize the instructional information, without any intention to learn, may be useful teaching maneuvers. The comparisons involved in search (e.g., Do these materials contain any information about Nathaniel Bowditch's grammar school education?) or in categorization (Find any mention of food! Find any mention of fruit!) (Frase & Kammann, 1974) are also effective producers of learning. Clever search directions or requests to categorize are mathemagenic control maneuvers that are worth exploring further, particularly since very powerful, new storage media such as CD-ROM will open vast challenging horizons for application of search and categorization techniques.

30.11 MATHEMAGENIC ACTIVITIES AND DEVELOPMENTS IN INSTRUCTIONAL TECHNOLOGY

30.11.1 Superbooks, Hypertext, CD ROM Databases

The development and instructional use of densely indexed information media allow students to embark on highly individualized explorations of subject matter. Automated cross-indexing of a quite sophisticated character permits extended searches that often lead to the emergence and pursuit of new search goals. This promises many new educational opportunities but casts the student in the often unaccustomed role of solitary explorer/adventurer.

Explorations in a hypertext or in a rich CD-ROM database is a class of mathemagenic activities that has not received much attention in the research literature. The first reaction of many educators will be to rely on intrinsic interest and curiosity, but this may not be enough to sustain and guide appropriate activities. Not only do ways have to be found to maintain the intelligent collection of information but, for practical reasons, some topical focus has to be fostered. Another problem that may be anticipated stems from technological means that are becoming readily available for recording the found information either on disk or by printing it out. This activity may supplant covert interpretive process. The student, rather than trying to understand and learn, collects information fragments and stores it in machine memory as a kind of digital amulet against ignorance. The phenomenon is already observable in the educational research community where the collections of reprints and photocopies sometimes serve as a surrogate for reading.

The basic problem with superbooks or hypertext is that following your nose into interesting crannies is nice and may lead to serendipitous discoveries. But using such text to accomplish a particular purpose requires judgment and discipline about selection, as well as persistence. Mathemagenic activities will have to be shaped and supported, perhaps with greater care and energy than is required for ordinary reading assignments. It would be a serious mistake to think that all students will be irresistibly charmed by an information wonderland. One possibility that might be worth exploring is the kind of task demand that requires productive reportage about specified and open subject matter. This is likely to engage the selection mechanism. Classification and restructuring may induce sufficient process. Information shopping lists similar to those used by Mager and McCann (1961) in the Varian Associates experiments described before may also be a useful control mechanism for mathemagenic activities with super- or hypertext.

Finally it should be noted here that the theoretical modeling of structural and sequential text features (e.g., Kintsch & van Dijk, 1978) that has captured the attention of many researchers during the past decade will require very substantial revision before it can be applied to text that can be traversed in a very large number of ways.

30.11.2 Adaptive, Computer-Based Instruction

Sustained, "intelligent" interactions between learners and a shrewdly configured computer program are excellent opportunities for maintaining gross and covert mathemagenic activities at a high level. If the interactive program is conversationally dense, i.e., if frequent response demands are made, short-term memory support tends to reduce topographic shaping. Some processing fetch is required in order for feedback to have much selective effect on process. It seems advisable to require substantial elaboration and synthesis in the learner's responses to avoid too much recent memory support. Answers fresh out of the echo box usually do not shape useful mathemagenic activities. It would pay to reach, from time to time, well back into the instructional scenario for elements that the learner must use to solve problems. There is some evidence that lengthening the acquisition-recall/exercise interval improves subsequent retention (Landauer & Bjork, 1978; Landauer & Ainslie, 1975).

The external management of instruction through the creation of an effort-sustaining environment is probably at least as important as the internal courseware structure for the effective use of sophisticated computer-based instructional systems.

30.12 SUMMING UP

The aims of this paper were to (a) review characteristics of mathemagenic activities, (b) disentangle the concept of mathemagenic activities from rather short-sighted concerns with the efficacy of adjunct aids to learning, (c) contrast the mathemagenic concept with cognitivist notions such as metacognition and with over-rationalized ideas about learning processes such as study skill training, (d) discuss the place of mathemagenic acts in a broad macrotheory of instruction, (e) consider some issues that invite research, and (f) explore the role of mathemagenic activities in the use of advanced instructional technologies.

Mathemagenic activities are labile. They can be shaped and trained. They are adaptive and are modified by learners according to information structures, task demands, and the transparency of results. Not all adaptive responses support the goals of instruction. Certain instructional circumstances can create undesirable mathemagenic activities.

The concept of mathemagenic activities stresses not only topography ("know how") but also maintenance. The latter is generally not the focus of concern for cognitivist and other skill approaches. The instructional situation must contain support elements to ensure the persistence of learning-related activities.

In a macrotheoretical instructional model, mathemagenic activities play two roles. First, degree of gross compliance with instructional transactions, such as assignments, influences the number of encountered instructional events. Second, mathemagenic activities operate in a reciprocal trade-off with the number and "difficulty" of instructive events, to determine the likelihood of successfully processing an encountered instructive event.

New technological instrumentalities afford learners many diverse paths through instructional information. Goal-consistent guidance and maintenance of excursions through informationally rich paths pose new challenges for the control of mathemagenic activities.

REFERENCES

Bandura, A. (1977). *Social learning theory*. Englewood Cliffs, NJ: Prentice Hall.

Britton, B.K., Piha, A., Davis, J. & Wehausen, E. (1978). Reading and cognitive capacity usage: adjunct question effects. *Memory & Cognition 6*, 266–73.

Burton, J.K., Niles, J.A., Lalik, R.M. & Reed, W.M. (1986). Cognitive capacity engagement during and following interspersed mathemagenic questions. *Journal of Educational Psychology 78*, 147–52.

Carmichael, L. & Dearborn, W.F. (1947). *Reading and visual fatigue*. Boston, MA: Houghton Mifflin.

Cook, L.K. & Mayer, R.E. (1983). Reading strategies training for meaningful learning from prose. *In* M. Pressley & J.R. Levin, eds. *Cognitive strategy research: educational applications*. New York: Springer.

Dansereau, D.F., Collins, K.W., McDonald, B.A., Holley, C.D., Garland, J., Dickhoff, G. & Evans, S.H. (1979). Development and evaluation of a learning strategy training program. *Journal of Educational Psychology 71*, 64–73.

Deese, V. (1957). *How to study*. New York: McGraw-Hill.

Duchastel, P. (1979) Learning objectives and the organization of prose. *Journal of Educational Psychology 71*, 100–06.

Dweck, C. (1986). Motivational processes affecting learning. *American Psychologist 41*, 1041–48.

Ellis, J.A., Konoske, P.V., Wulfeck, W.H. II & Montague, W.E. (1982) Comparative effects of adjunct postquestions and instructions on learning from text. *Journal of Educational Psychology 74*, 860–67.

Ericsson, K.A. & Simon, H.A. (1980). Verbal reports as data. *Psychological Review 87*, 215–51.

Frase, L.T. & Kammann, R. (1974). Effects of search criterion upon unanticipated free recall of categorically related words. *Memory and Cognition 2*, 181–84.

— & Keitzberg, V.S. (1975). Effect of topical and indirect learning directions on prose recall. *Journal of Educational Psychology 67*, 320–24.

Frederiksen, C.H. (1972). Effects of task-induced cognitive operations on comprehension and memory processes. *In* R.O. Freedle & J.B. Carroll, eds. *Language comprehension and the acquisition of knowledge*, 211–46. New York: Wiley.

Gagné, E.D. & Rothkopf, E.Z. (1975). Text organization and learning goals. *Journal of Educational Psychology 67*, 445–50.

Gerber, G., Gross, L, Jackson-Beek, M. & Signorelli, N. (1978) Cultural indicators: violence profile No. 9. *Journal of Communications 28*, 176–207.

—, —, Signorelli, N. & Morgan, M. (1980) Aging with television: images on television drama and conceptions of social reality. *Journal of Communication 30*, 37–47.

Glover, J.A. (1989). The "testing" phenomenon: not gone

but nearly forgotten. *Journal of Educational Psychology 81,* 392–99.

—, Plake, B.S. & Roberts, B. (1981) Distinctiveness of encoding: the effects of paraphrasing and drawing inferences on memory for prose. *Journal of Educational Psychology 73,* 736–44.

Halpain, D.R., Glover, J.A. & Harvey, A.L. (1985). Differential effects of higher and lower order questions: attention hypothesis. *Journal of Educational Psychology 77,* 703–15.

Hoffman, A.C. (1946). Eye-movements during prolonged reading. *Journal of Experimental Psychology 36,* 95–118.

Hull, C.L. (1943). *Principles of behavior.* New York: Appleton-Century-Crofts.

Jones, B.F., Friedman, L.B., Tinzmann, M. & Cox, B.E. (1984). Content-driven comprehension instruction: a model for army training literature, Technical Report, Army Research Institute, Alexandrea, VA.

Kaplan, R. & Rothkopf, E.Z. (1974). Instructional objectives as direction to learners: effect of passage length and amount of objective-relevant content. *Journal of Educational Psychology 66,* 448–56.

Kintsch, W. & van Dijk, T.A. (1978). Towards a model of text comprehension and production. *Psychological Review 85,* 363–94.

Koether, M.E. & Rothkopf, E.Z. (1978). Instructional effects of discrepancies in content and organization between study goals and information sources. *Journal of Educational Psychology 70,* 67–71.

Landauer, T.K. & Ainslie, K.I. (1975). Exams and use as preservatives of course-aspired knowledge. *Journal of Educational Research,* 69–104.

— & Bjork, R.A. (1978). Optional rehearsal patterns and name learning. *In* M.M. Gruneberg, P.M. Morris & R.N. Sykes, eds. *Practical aspects of memory,* 52–60. London: Academic.

Mager, R.F. & McCann. (1961). *Learner-controlled instruction.* Belmont, CA: Varian.

McDonald, F.J. (1965). *Educational psychology.* Belmont, CA: Wadsworth.

Mayer, R.E. (1980). Elaboration techniques that increase the meaningfulness of technical text: an experimental test of the learning strategy hypothesis. *Journal of Educational Psychology 72,* 720–84.

Mechanic, A. (1962). Effects of orienting task, practice, and incentive on simultaneous incidental and intentional learning. *Journal of Experimental Psychology 64,* 393–99.

Meyer, B.J.F. (1975). *The organization of prose and its effect on memory.* Amsterdam: North-Holland.

Nickerson, R.S. (1988). On improving thinking through instruction. *In* E.Z. Rothkopf, ed. *Review of research in education,* Vol. 15, 3–57. Washington, DC: American Educational Research Association.

Postman, L. (1964). Short-term memory and incidental learning. *In* A.W. Melton, ed. *Categories of Human Learning,* 146–201. New York: Academic.

— & Senders, V.L. (1946). Incidental learning and generality of set. *Journal of Experimental Psychology 36,* 153–65.

Reynolds, R.E. & Anderson, R.C. (1982). Influence of questions on the allocation of attention during reading. *Journal of Educational Psychology 74,* 623–32.

—, Standiford, S.N. & Anderson, R.C. (1979). Distribution of reading time when questions are asked about a restricted category of text information. *Journal of Educational Psychology 71,* 183–90.

Robinson, F. (1970). *Effective study,* 4th ed. New York: Harper & Row.

Ross, B.H. (1984). Remindings and their effects in learning a cognitive skill. *Cognitive Psychology 16,* 371–416.

Rothkopf, E.Z. (1963). Some conjectures about inspection behavior in learning from written sentences and the response mode problem in programmed self-instruction. *Journal of Programmed Instruction 2,* 31–46.

— (1965). Some theoretical and experimental approaches to problems in written instruction. *In* J.D. Krumboltz, ed. *Learning and the educational process,* 193–221. Chicago, IL: Rand McNally.

— (1966). Learning from written instructive material: an exploration of the control of inspection behavior by test-like events. *American Educational Research Journal 3,* 241–49.

— (1968). Two scientific approaches to the management of instruction. *In* R. Gagné & W.J. Gephart, eds. *Learning research and school subject learning,* 107–32. Itasca, IL: Peacock.

— (1970). The concept of mathemagenic activities. *Review of Educational Research 40,* 325–36.

— (1971). Experiments on mathemagenic behavior and the technology of written instruction. *In* E.Z. Rothkopf & P.E. Johnson, eds. *Verbal learning research and the technology of written instruction,* 284–303. New York: Columbia University Teachers College Press.

— (1972). Variable adjunct question schedules, interpersonal interaction and incidental learning from written material. *Journal of Educational Psychology 63,* 87–92.

— (1976). Writing to teach and reading to learn: a perspective on the psychology of written instruction. *In* N.L. Gagné, ed. *The psychology of teaching methods. The 75th yearbook of the National Society for the Study of Education,* 91–129.

— (1978). Analyzing eye movements to infer processing styles during learning from text. *In* J.W. Senders, D.F. Fisher & R.A. Monty, eds. *Eye movement and the higher psychological functions,* 209–23. Hillsdale, NJ: Erlbaum.

— (1981). A macroscopic model of instruction and purposive learning: an overview. *Instructional Science 10,* 105–22.

— & Billington, M.J. (1975). A two-factor model of the effect of goal-descriptive directions on learning from text. *Journal of Educational Psychology 67,* 692–704.

— & — (1979). Goal-guided learning from text: inferring a descriptive processing model from inspection times & eye movements. *Journal of Educational Psychology 71,* 310–27.

— & Bisbicos, E.E. (1967). Selective facilitative effects of interspersed questions on learning from written material. *Journal of Education Psychology 58,* 55–61.

— & Bloom, R.D. (1970). Effects of interpersonal interaction on the instructional value of adjunct questions in learning from written material. *Journal of Educational Psychology 61,* 416–22.

— & Coke, E.U. (1963). Retention interval and rehearsal method in learning equivalences from written sentences. *Journal of Verbal Learning and Verbal Behavior 2,* 406–16.

— & — (1966). Variations in phrasing, repetition interval, and the recall of sentence materials. *Journal of Verbal Learning and Verbal Behavior 5,* 86–91.

— & Kaplan, R. (1972). An exploration of the effect of density and specificity on instructional objectives on learning from text. *Journal of Educational Psychology 63,* 295–302.

Sagerman, N. & Mayer, R.E. (1987) Forward transfer of different reading strategies evoked by adduct questions in science text. *Journal of Educational Psychology 79,* 189–91.

Seretny, M.L. & Dean, R.S. (1986) Interspersed postpassage questions and reading comprehension achievement. *Journal of Educational Psychology 76,* 228–29.

Stigler, V.W. & Barnes, R. (1988). Culture and mathematical thinking. *In* E.Z. Rothkopf, ed. *Review of research in education,* Vol. 15, 253–306. Washington, DC: American Educational Research Association.

Underwood, B.V. (1963) Stimulus selection in verbal learning. *In* C.N. Cofer & B.S. Musgrave, eds. *Verbal behavior and learning,* 33–47. New York: McGraw-Hill.

Von Glaserfeld, E. (1987). Learning as a constructive activity. *In* C. Janvier, ed. *Problems of representation in the teaching and learning of mathematics,* 3–18. Hillsdale, NJ: Erlbaum.

Weinstein, C.E. (1978). Elaboration skills as a learning strategy. *In* H.F. O'Neill, ed. *Learning strategies.* New York: Academic.

Zimmerman, B.V. (1979). Effects of model persistence and success on children's problem solving. *Journal of Educational Psychology 71,* 508–13.

31. GENERATIVE LEARNING: PAST, PRESENT, AND FUTURE

Barbara L. Grabowski
PENNSYLVANIA STATE UNIVERSITY

31.1 INTRODUCTION*

Over the past 20 years, attention has gradually shifted from investigating the effects of the external, physical form of *instruction* to examining what internal processes of *learning* are stimulated or induced by external stimuli. As a result, models and prescriptions for learning are founded on theoretical and empirical evidence about cognitive functioning, processes, and structure of memory (see 5.4). Using this foundation, designers develop a conception of what occurs within the learner, and use this conception to guide designs of learning rather than instructional environments. While instructional and learning environments both contain facts or data points (information with which learners interact), the key difference is who does what with that information. In a learning environment, the learner and his or her learning processes, styles, and activities take on prime importance. A learning environment is not devoid of instruction or an instructor, but rather the external stimuli simply take on a secondary role. In an instructional environment, the role of learner and instruction are reversed.

Generative learning theory and its companion model of generative teaching is one such significant area of investigation whose theoretical foundation lies in neural research, research regarding the structure of knowledge and cognitive development, and whose focus is on the learner. This chapter defines generative learning and its foundation, reviews relevant research that tested the theory, describes the generative model of teaching and implications for instructional design, and concludes with a discussion of future directions for research.

*Recognition and appreciation are extended to Eileen Schroeder for her insightful comments on this manuscript, and to Christopher P. Rynd for his editorial assistance.

31.1.1 Generative Learning Defined

Wittrock (1974a, 1974b) initially conceived of the model of generative learning that integrated several areas of cognitive psychology (see Chapter 5), including cognitive development, human learning, human abilities, information processing, and aptitude treatment interactions (see 22.3.3). His work stems from an attempt to explain and prescribe teaching strategies to maximize reading comprehension. While most of the original research deals specifically with reading comprehension, in theory there is much transferability to learning for understanding in general, regardless of the medium or form of the external stimuli. This article embraces the broader interpretation of this theory and model of learning.

From his initial conception to now, Wittrock emphasized one very significant and basic assumption: The learner is not a passive recipient of information; rather she or he is an active participant in the learning process, working to construct meaningful understanding of information found in the environment. The importance of asking the learner to generate his or her own meaning is clearly summarized by Wittrock's statement that "although a student may not understand sentences spoken to him by his teacher, it is highly likely that a student understands sentences that he generates himself" (Wittrock, 1974b, p. 182). It is as Harlen and Osborne (1985) call it, "learning through the person" (p. 137).

While there are and have been four parts to his model, I find it interesting that in his current writing, Wittrock (1990, 1991, 1992, 1993) explains more thoroughly his second essential attribute, which he feels distinguishes his from other theories and models of learning. He elaborates on the importance of and difference between two types of learner-generated *relationships*: first, among the different parts of the information that are being perceived and, second, between that information and the learner's prior knowledge and other memory components. Comprehension occurs by formulating connections, rather than solely by the function of "placing" information or "transforming" information in memory. The subtle difference lies in the *creation of new* understanding of the information by the learner, rather than *changing* the presented information. (An analogy characterizing these important and subtle differences is presented in the next section in which generative learning is compared with other theories.)

These two combined attributes comprise only one of the four parts of his generative-learning theory, namely, the processes of generation. The three other component processes that explain learning are motivational processes, learning processes, and knowledge creation processes. Metacognitive processes also play a key role in his model, although in most cases he folds this idea into the learning processes component.

The concept maps portrayed in Figures 31-1 and 31-2 are illustrative of generative learning in action. These figures represent my comprehension of the ideas presented in Wittrock's (1974a, 1974b, 1985, 1990, 1991, 1992) writings regarding the progression of generative learning from neural brain processes research to models of thinking and teaching. The lines depict personally generated relationships between different concepts and ideas presented in his writings.

As shown in Figure 31-1, Wittrock conceptualized this model of generative learning based on a neural model of brain functioning and cognitive research on the process of knowing. From this foundation, the four components of the model are presented in shaded, rounded-corner rectangles with examples of each process presented as ovals under each. For example, "Attribution" is one example of motivational processes, and "Preconceptions" is one example of the knowledge creation processes. The process of generation is divided into the two types of possible relationship creations—between different parts of the information in the text and between the information in the text and prior learning and experience. This figure also implies a flow between the four processes of the model, with motivational processes activating learning processes, which in turn affects whether the process of generation will occur. The knowledge creation processes also affect the process of generation, but in a different way: Beliefs, preconception, prior concepts, and metacognition influence the quality and type of links that are created. Depending on the type of relationships generated, the four components converge for the purpose of learner-constructed reorganization, elaboration, or reconceptualization of the information to result ultimately in comprehension, as shown by the hexagons. Each of these processes will be discussed in detail later.

Figure 31-2 denotes the research by Luria (1973), as described by Wittrock (1992), on which generative learning was founded. As depicted here, Luria identified three functional units of the brain that are activated through the ascending and descending reticular activating systems and the frontal lobes of the cortex. In each of these units,

responsibility for cognitive functioning originates, which then activates or manages one of the processes of knowing, which then influences one of the four components of Wittrock's generative-learning model—again depicted by the shaded, rounded rectangles.

The first unit, arousal and intention, influences an individual's learning processes and motivation. External stimuli arouse attention through the ascending reticular activating system. Without active, dynamic, and selective attending of environmental stimuli, it follows that meaning generation cannot occur regarding that environmental stimuli. The influence of arousal on attention flows from the environment outside of the learner, but interacts internally. Intention is activated by the descending reticular activating system, which stimulates attribution and interest. Attribution and interest influence the motivation of the learner. Attribution of effort, or the process of giving credit for success or failure to one's own effort, can influence whether or not the learner will exert the effort to be "attentive to the underlying structure of the information to be learned" (Wittrock, 1985, p. 123) and thereby become actively involved in generating understanding. If the learners attribute success to themselves, it follows that motivation to exert effort will be greater than if they attribute success to external forces (Weiner, 1979). The influence of intention on motivation for meaning generation flows from within the learner.

The second functional unit is the unit for receiving, analyzing, and storing information. The coding of information is managed by the frontal lobes of the cortex. The functions of the brain in this unit are influenced by the knowledge creation processes. Wittrock identifies many parts to the knowledge creation processes in several of his writings. Primarily, he includes beliefs, concepts, preconceptions, metacognitions, and experiences (see Fig. 31-1.). In other words, these are the components of memory. It is between these existing beliefs, concepts, preconceptions, etc., and environmental stimuli that relationships are formed and, thereby, understanding and comprehension are generated. According to Wittrock (1974a), "cognitive theory implies that learning can be predicted and understood in terms of what the learners bring to the learning situation, how they relate the stimuli to their memories, and what they generate from their previous experiences" (p. 93).

The third functional unit is the unit for planning, organizing, and regulating cognition and behavior. This unit operates through the frontal lobes of the cortex to coordinate learning and integrate information. These are the processes of metacognitive monitoring and generative processes—the heart and soul of generative-learning theory. By generating relationships between parts of what the learners see and hear, and by integrating that information with what exists in memory, learners reorganize, elaborate, and/or reconceptualize information, not simply "stuff in more information." It is a process for which meaningful understanding and comprehension are predicted outcomes. (see Fig. 31-1.)

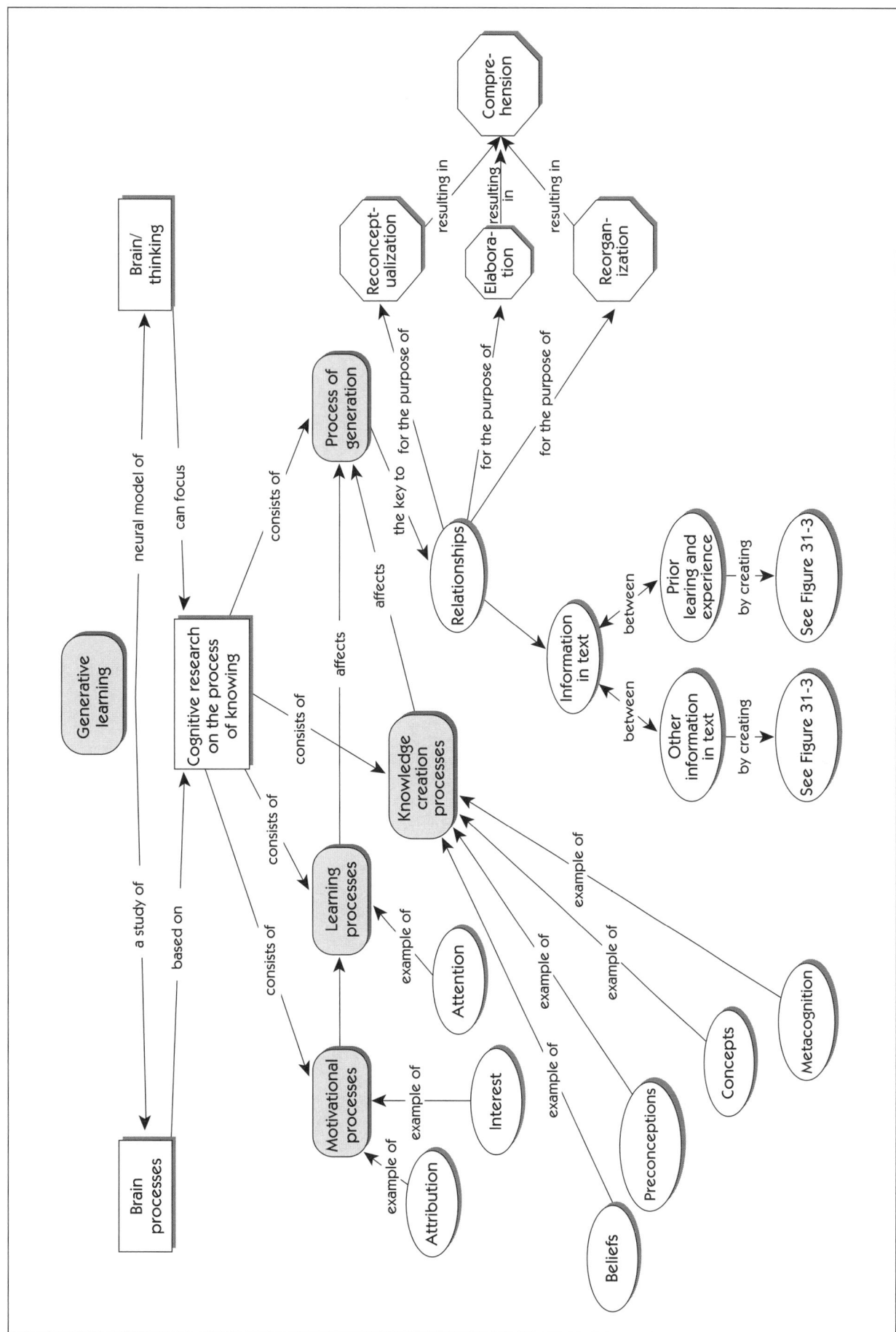

Figure 31-1. Generative-learning concept map.

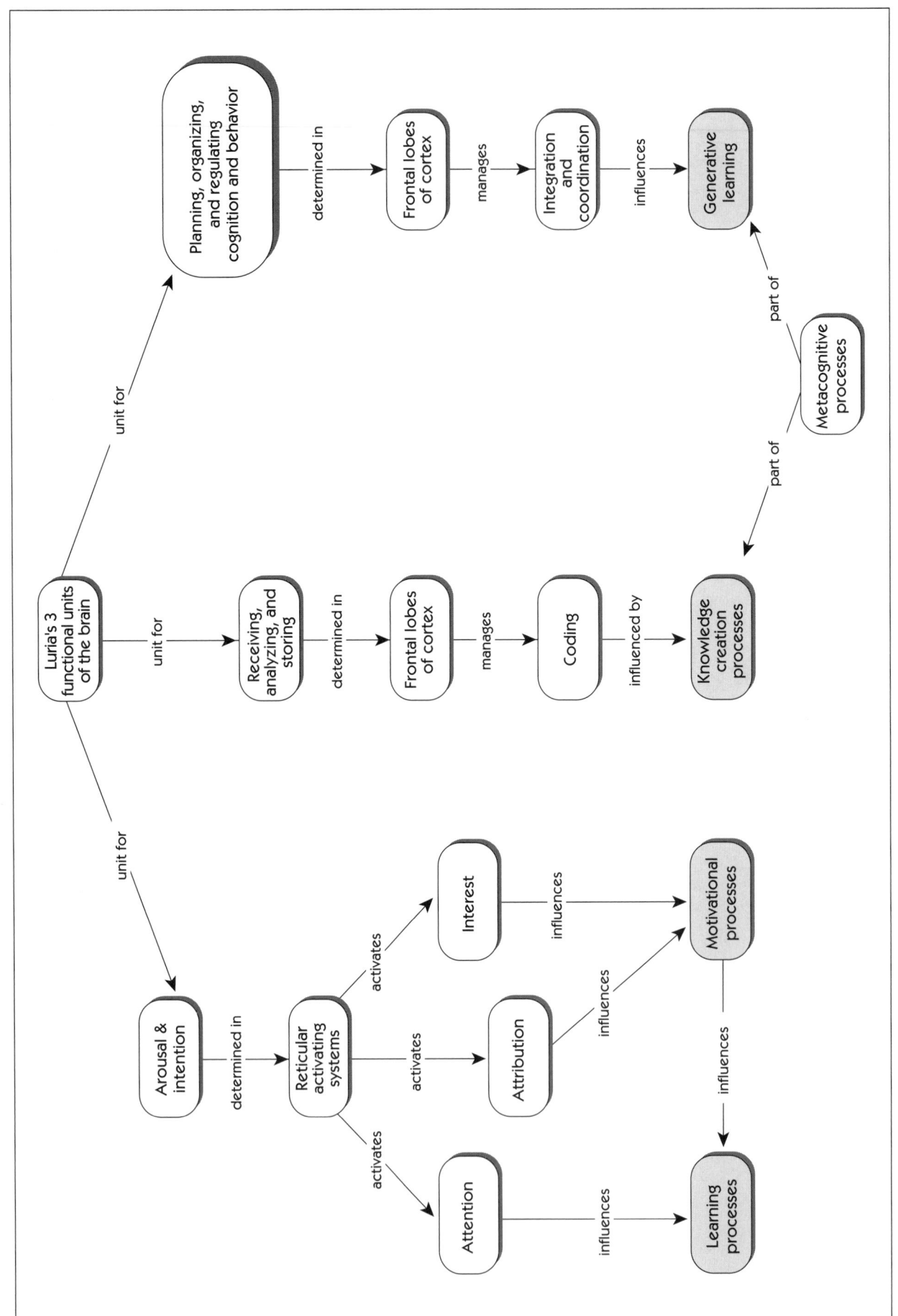

Figure 31-2. Neural functions concept map.

Wittrock (1990) claimed that there are two types of activities that can be judged as generative. Activities that generate organizational relationships between different components of the environment include "titles, headings, questions, objectives, summaries, graphs, tables, and main ideas," while those that generate integrated relationships between the external stimuli and the memory components include "demonstrations, metaphors, analogies, examples, pictures, applications, interpretations, paraphrases, and inferences" (p. 354). In Figure 31-3, those examples are shown in the ovals connected to one of the two types of relationships. From other activities proposed by DiVesta (1989), Goetz (1983), and Jonassen (1986), concept maps, diagrams, outlines, and identifying scripts within narratives seem appropriate to be added to the organizational relationship list. Mnemonics, clarifying, and predicting seem appropriate for his second, the integrated relationship list, linking external stimuli to internal components of memory. Notetaking, diagrams, and concept maps could be appropriate for both lists, depending on which cognitive processes were used to create which type of link—organizational or integrative. That is, if learners were only relating different ideas extracted directly from a text passage, together it would be classified as organizational, whereas if they related the information to prior knowledge, it would qualify as integrative. Figures 31-1 to 31-3 represent organizational maps. Table 31-1, shown in the next section, portrays generation as integration by reconceptualization and elaboration.

Only those activities that involve the actual *creation* of relationships and meaning would be classified as examples of generative-learning strategies. Restructuring or manipulation of environmental information presented to the learner by definition requires him or her to generate either organizational or integrated relationships and constructed personal meaning, thereby qualifying as a generative activity. If this activity were simply tracing with no generation of relationships or meaning apparent, rather than involve new positioning, the activity would *not* qualify as a generative activity. Other controversial activities such as highlighting or underlining can be argued as *not* being generative, since the activity involves examining only single components, even though the learner may be selecting author-written main ideas. Even if the learner is integrating the sentences with prior knowledge, there is no covert evidence of that integration, as the focus of the activity is a selection task in which he or she is simply selecting from among many parts. An activity must involve *meaning making* in order to qualify as generative. An activity in which the learner simply selects sentences that someone else has already composed cannot be considered a generative activity. The generated main idea *relates* all or some of the ideas presented in the passage together. If learners are relating the textual information to their own prior experience, knowledge, or preconception, however, it could be argued that highlighting or underlining would be generative. As will be seen in the applied research section, Rickards (1979) would support this notion.

31.1.2 Relationship of Generative Learning to Other Schools of Thought

Wittrock (1991, 1992) often compares his own theory with other theories. These comparisons are quite useful for understanding the nuances of his teaching recommendations. In Table 31-1, by depicting an integrative restructured elaboration, generative-learning theory is compared with other contemporary schools of thought: behaviorism, connectionism, schema theory, information processing, and constructivism.

These schools of thought differ in many ways, the most significant being what unit of analysis is examined and explained, and how thinking and learning are defined and exemplified. These basic differences are often subtle, yet they contribute directly to the type of model that has been constructed and the implications that are drawn for instruction. The purpose of this section is not to describe each of these theories in detail (see other chapters for further description); rather, it is to discuss overall salient differences between the various models and generative-learning theory and what these differences imply for instruction. The last two rows of Table 31-1 depict those differences, one directly, and the other in an analogical reconceptualization.

Of all the theories, behaviorism (see 2.2; Skinner, 1990) presents the most extreme difference from generative learning. That difference lies in how the role of the learner is perceived and what this perception implies for learning. For generative learning, the learner is the key—the controller of whether information is learned or not. Understanding all of the neural processes that affect learning, from intention to components in memory to attribution, will aid the designer in selecting or creating appropriate activities that take these factors into account when encouraging the learner to code or integrate information. The learner must also be actively and consciously relating ideas. For behaviorism, the learner plays no role, except as a passive recipient of information. The behavioral design of instruction must center on creating a stimulating message that reinforces by positive or negative feedback. Higher-level coding or integration is irrelevant in the prescription.

Connectionism (Wittrock, 1992) is similar to behaviorism, in that its intent is in strengthening associations. However, the network of individual memory is important, as in generative-learning theory. Connectionists, however, establish networks by strengthening associations by externally driven, repeated practice rather than creating personally drawn relationships between and among ideas. Understanding is internally created in generative-learning theory, making repetitions unnecessary.

Schema theory (Rummelhart, 1981; Rummelhart & Ortony, 1977) is similar to connectionism in that it deals with patterns of data points or schema. Basically, these data points form the knowledge units that are manipulated in generative-learning theory. Because of the way knowledge is stored, instructional and learning activities must connect new to existing knowledge so that it is easily retrievable.

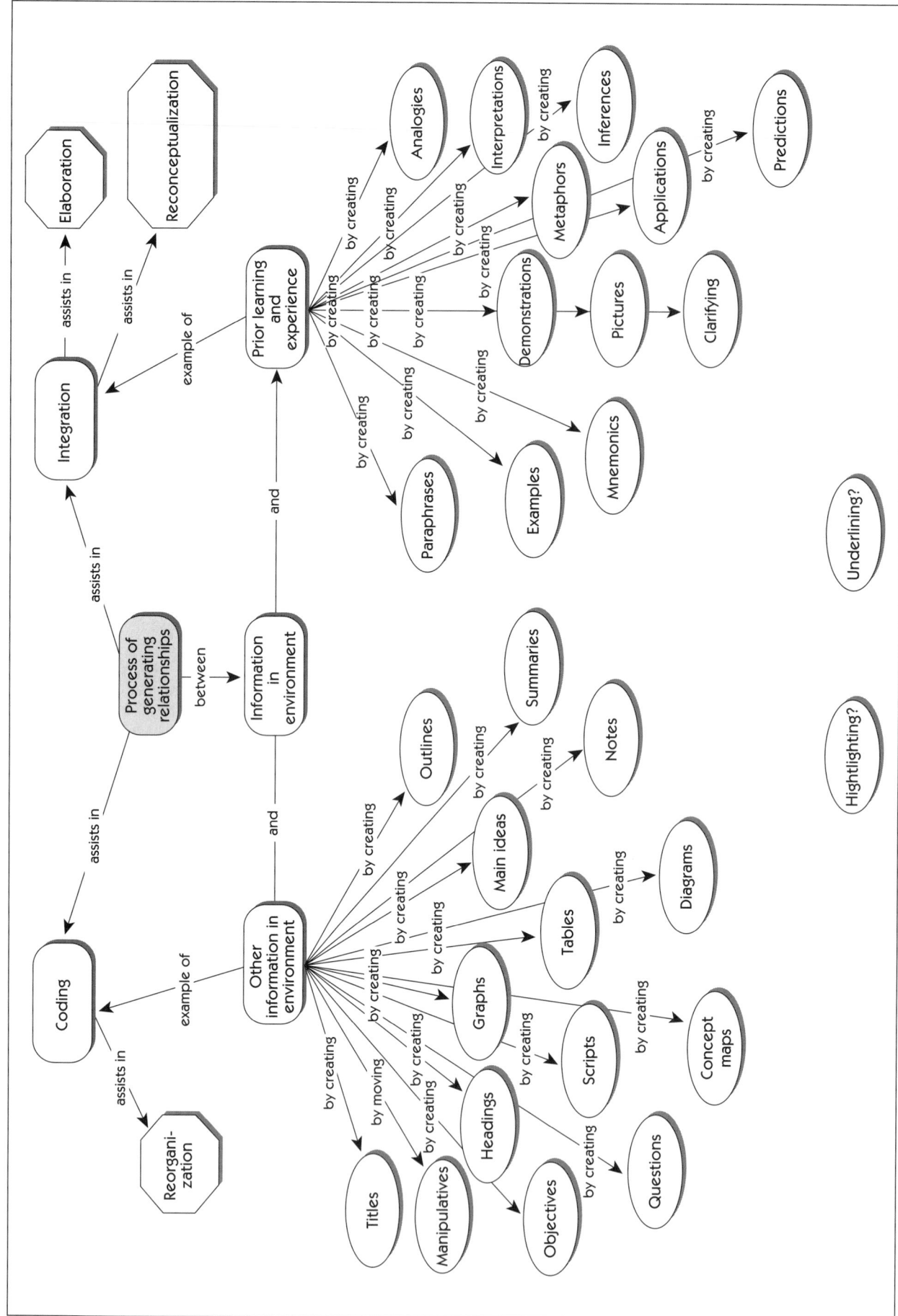

Figure 31-3. Generative activities concept map.

TABLE 31-1. COMPARISON OF RELATED SCHOOLS OF THOUGHT

Comparison	Generative Learning Theory (Wittrock, 1992)	Behaviorism (Skinner, 1990)	Connectionism (Wittrock, 1992)	Schema Theory (Rumelhart, 1981)	Information Processing (Bell-Gredler, 1986)	Constructivism (Jonassen, 1990)
A study of:	brain as controller	neural connections	memory associations	knowledge representation in memory	stages and levels of processing	philosophy of constructed meaning
Learning defined by:	learner-generated relationships	behavioral change	associations	creation of, addition to, restructuring of, or fine-tuning of schema	process of encoding information for retrieval	individually constructed understanding
Type of thinking:	brain as model builder by controlling the 4 processes	automatic paired response in S-R chain	neurally induced	schemata construction and reconstruction	transference of external stimuli to memory so it may be retrieved	building understanding from experiences
Levels of thinking:	comprehension/ understanding— coding, elaboration, reorganization, reconceptualization	unnecessary unit of analysis	conceptual	comprehension	rehearsal, coding, organization, conceptualization, integration, and translation	unspecified
Type of model:	neurally controlled learning	stimulus-response chains	subconceptual network model of memory	structural (networked) knowledge representation of memory	representation of the sequence of mental operation and form of stored knowledge	n/a
Components of the theory:	4 processes: motivation, learning, knowledge creation, and generation	operant conditioning, response formation, shaping, reinforcement schedules	networks of patterns and weights of nodes and connections	schema, schemata, scripts, and plans	stages: sensory receptors, short-term store, working memory, long-term memory; levels: deep and surface processing	source of reality, learner as builder
Implications for instruction:	activities that guide (induce) mental processes relating information	careful construction of the physical form of messages with repeated, rewarded practice	activities that strengthen connections through repetition	activities that relate new to existing knowledge so it is easily retrievable	activities that activate attention, facilitate processing in working memory, and facilitate transfer into long-term memory	creation of a contextualized learning environment

TABLE 31-1. Continued

Comparison	Generative Learning Theory (Wittrock, 1992)	Behaviorism (Skinner, 1990)	Connectionism (Wittrock, 1992)	Schema Theory (Rumelhart, 1981)	Information Processing (Bell-Gredler, 1986)	Constructivism (Jonassen, 1990)
Comparison with generative-learning theory:	n/a	claims a very different role for the learner, as passive recipient rather than active generator	explains learning as external neural induction instead of being neurally controlled internally; externally imposed not necessarily personally relevant	explains the basic knowledge unit used in generative learning theory	explains learning as a transformation of information rather than generation	Provides a philosophical basis rather than a neuro-logical explanation of learning
Comparative analogy—task: purchasing clothing for an outing	*approach:* active and conscious selection of items	*approach:* passive and reinforced by salesperson	*approach:* passive, externally driven	*approach:* not specified, but rather the units of clothing that can be chosen are more representative here	*approach:* active but not necessarily inter-nally controlled— represents the process one goes through from attending to those items in the store, to trying various combinations, and then taking them home to store in the closet using a variety of grouping strategies	*approach:* active— represents a philosophy that what is fashionable is constructed by individual tastes rather than predefined combi-nations proffered in society
	item purchased: the intent is creating a *new* fashion statement	*item purchased:* outfit selected and laid out by another	*item purchased:* selection of combi-nation of items for outfit determined by those most commonly seen on peers or in magazines	*item purchased:* some-thing to add to an existing outfit, tailor-ing of an old item, or creating of a new combination of items	*item purchased:* some-thing to add to an existing outfit, tailor-ing of an old item, or creating of a new combination of items	*item purchased:* that which has been created by the individual rather than the salesperson

This connection is made by adding information to schema, restructuring, or tuning it. While connections are made by links, those linkages are not defined or labeled, as in creating a pattern note without labeling the lines. Generative-learning theory, on the other hand, is similar in concept to creating a pattern note with all the links labeled. Activities designed by schema theorists would include those that reminded learners of prior knowledge and related the information to what the learner already knows. It is less relevant who selects those connection points over the fact that they *are* made.

Information-processing theory (Bell-Gredler, 1986) explains the process of thinking and memory storage (see 5.4.1)—in other words, the stages and levels of processing. What we get out of information-processing theory is an emphasis on how we think, rather than on what we think, or that we think. Its focus is on that process of transforming external stimuli into some recallable form to be stored in memory. The emphasis of generative-learning theory is on the generation of *new* conceptual understandings, not just on transforming information.

Finally, constructivism (Jonassen, 1990) is a philosophy that underlies learning (see 7.3). It parallels generative theory in considering the learner to be an active processor of information; however, it is extreme in its position about the nonexistence of an objective reality. Wittrock has not addressed this notion in any of his writings.

To explain some of these subtle differences, a comparative analogy of an individual tasked with purchasing clothing for an outing was generated showing how the approach to the task (the purchase process) and the ultimate outcome (what item would ultimately be purchased) differ between schools of thought. The approach in generative buying would be exemplified as a buyer-controlled activity, with intention, motivation, and prior conceptions and beliefs about the outing and the people invited driving what types and styles of clothing are perceived as needed. The generative buyer would purchase cloth and create a *new* style based on those internally stimulated factors. The salesperson will query the buyer on how each article fits with those other influences, and how the articles would go with other items the buyer had at home. This buyer seeks a totally new fashion statement, rather than one already prepared.

A behavioristic example is simple: In a salesperson-driven environment, the approach is very passive with an outfit having been preselected, and the salesperson giving much praise and lauding for purchasing the item. In a connectionism scenario, the approach is also passive. Choices are driven by society-defined fashion that have been repeatedly seen (connected) in fashion magazines, television, and on peers. A buyer would purchase an outfit based on the frequency of seeing the outfit in fashion magazines. Intention or personal conception would already have been programmed.

Following schema theory, the buyer and seller play equal roles. Though the approach is not specified by this theory, the articles of available clothing in the store and at home will play the key role. How these articles are combined is the important aspect of this theory. Accessories could be added, items rearranged, the outfit tailored to reach different desired effects. The coordination factors, however, would remain undefined. Intention, personal conceptions, or the generation of some new fashion item are irrelevant.

For information processing, both the buyer and sales environment are essential players, meaning that the approach by the buyer is active, but not necessarily internally controlled. The information-processing buyer would attend to featured items that catch his or her attention, select a few, try on various combinations, and purchase a standard outfit, embellish it with accessories, or ask for it to be tailored. The key difference here is that what is purchased is transformed from a rack in a store into an appropriate outfit following established rules of fashion, rather than generating totally new fashion statements or a totally new garment from different pieces of cloth.

A constructivistic buyer would hold a philosophy that what is fashionable is constructed by individual tastes and needs rather than predefined combinations proffered by society. The approach would be very active, independent, and individually driven. The ultimate item or combination of items would make an individual statement.

In each case, the notable difference is in the role of the buyer (learner) as he or she is related to the salesperson (instructor) or store items (instruction). This is exemplified through the approach (learning process) taken to the task, and the final selection of the item (learning).

31.2 APPLIED RESEARCH

Studies investigating the viability of the generative model of learning have tested the effects of simple coding strategies such as underlining, notetaking, and adjunct or inserted questions; more complex coding/organizational strategies such as creating hierarchies, headings, summaries, and concept maps, or the manipulation of objects; elaborative integration strategies such as imaging, and creating examples, interpretations, or analogies; and, finally, metacognitive generative-learning training. Table 31-2 organizes and summarizes some of the most significant work testing Wittrock's theory. The table divides the types of research into those that represent a coding generative activity and those that represent an integrative generative activity. Those that exemplify coding interrelate concepts from the instruction together to create one level of understanding through various levels and types of organizational activities. Those exemplifying integration interrelate the concepts from the instruction with prior knowledge to create a higher level of understanding by reconceptualization and elaboration. A discussion and summary of the results from each of these areas is provided. This discussion begins with the most controversial—underlining—so that it neither gets lost among the other significant, noncontroversial

TABLE 31-2. SUMMARY OF SELECTED APPLIED GENERATIVE RESEARCH STUDIES

Generative Activity	Author/Year	Dependent Variable	Content	Age Level	Results
Coding—Underlining?					
underlining	Rickards & August, 1975	reading comprehension	educational psychology	college students	Increased achievement on posttest when learner underlined most relevant information.
Coding—Notetaking					
notetaking	Peper & Mayer, 1986	recall, problem solving	auto engines	high school & college students	Notetaking increased achievement for far-transfer problem solving but not near-transfer fact retention.
notetaking	Shrager & Mayer, 1989	recall, problem solving	how to use a camera	college students	Confirmed above findings, also significant differences for students with low prior knowledge.
notetaking	Barnett, DiVesta & Rogozenski, 1981	immediate and delayed recall	history	college students	Notetaking produced better results than no note-taking, but no significant difference between elaborated review and simple review of notes. Review of instructor-prepared notes resulted in greater learning than review of learner-generated notes. Delayed retention scores higher for questions from learner notes.
Coding—Adjunct Questions					
adjunct questions: frequency, nature of, need for feedback, overt/covert responses	Anderson & Biddle, 1975	facts, motivation, and higher-order thinking	across content areas	across age levels	Better learning with more frequent questions. No difference if feedback is given. Overt response needed depending on if questions were embedded.
adjunct postquestions with no overt responses	Sutliff, 1986	facts, inference	electrical engineering	low- and upper-ability college students	No significant differences between groups.
adjunct questions super/subordinate postquestions	Burton, Niles Lalik & Reed, 1986	recall of main ideas and details	description of a mythical country	undergraduates	More main ideas were recalled. General questions were more engaging than detailed ones.
adjunct postquestions	Woods & Bernard, 1987	recall of intentional and incidental ideas	weather forecasting	adults—aged 60 or older	Adjunct questions aided recall of intentional ideas only.
adjunct pictures	Brody & Legenza, 1980	reading comprehension	history	undergraduates	Postpictures were more beneficial than prepictures.

TABLE 31-2. Continued

Generative Activity	Author/Year	Dependent Variable	Content	Age Level	Results
Coding—Organizational Strategies					
organization hierarchies	Wittrock & Carter, 1975	free recall	mineral tables	undergraduates	Learner-generated hierarchies for disorganized lists significantly better than simply reproducing them. Reproducing organized hierarchies significantly better than learner-generated ones.
organization headings, sentence meaning	Doctorow, Wittrock & Marks, 1978	reading comprehension	SRA literature	elementary school students	Learner-generated sentences combined with experimenter-provided headings produced increased comprehension followed by generative only.
organization -concept vs. semantic maps	Beissner, Jonassen & Grabowski, 1993	drawing, identification, terminology, comprehension, and problem solving	heart content	undergraduates	Learner-generated concept maps better strategy for holists. Learner-generated semantic maps better for serialists for problem solving learning only.
organization concept maps— learner generated vs. system provided	Smith & Dwyer, 1995	drawing, identification, terminology, and comprehension	heart content	undergraduates	Learners using instructor-provided concept maps performed better on identification tests only. No other differences found.
Coding—Manipulation of Objects					
physical manipulation of objects	Sayeki, Ueno & Nagasaka, 1991	calculating an area	math	elementary school children	Posttest showed physical manipulation facilitated problem solving.
mouse-manipulated graphics	Haag & Grabowski, 1994	terminology, identification, comprehension, and problem solving	heart content	undergraduates	Learner-manipulated graphics increased problem solving over static or computer-manipulated graphics.
Integration—Imaging					
imaging	Anderson & Kulhavey, 1972	prose learning	fictitious description of a tribe of people	high school seniors	Significant differences in favor of those who actually used an imaging strategy.
imaging— experimenter provided/ learner generated	Bull & Wittrock, 1973	recall of verbal definitions	definitions of nouns	elementary school children	Recall was significantly higher for imaging than verbal/copying strategy.
verbal and image elaborations: sequence	Kourilsky & Wittrock, 1987	economic understanding	economics	high school students	Verbal-to-image elaborations significantly better than image to verbal or either used singularly.
verbal only; image only; and combined elaborations	Laney, 1990	reasoning in decision making	economics	third-grade children	Verbal-only and verbal-to-image integrated strategies facilitated reasoning better than imagery only.

TABLE 31-2. Continued

Generative Activity	Author/Year	Dependent Variable	Content	Age Level	Results
Integration—Elaborations					
elaborations elaborated sentences	Stein & Bransford, 1979	retention	language arts	undergraduates	Performance facilitated only when elaborations clarified precise objectives—prompting encouraged subjects to ask more relevant questions.
elaboration examples	DiVesta & Peverley, 1984	concept attainment—near and far transfer	fictitious concepts	undergraduates	Students who generated their own examples did significantly better on far-transfer tasks than those given instructor-provided examples.
elaboration interpretation	Johnsey, Morrison & Ross, 1992	recall, recognition, application, type of elaborations	professional development	adults	Results favored the use of embedded *vs.* detached elaboration strategies. Elaborations better than no elaborations. No difference between leaner generated *vs.* experimenter provided.
Combination of Coding and Integration Strategies					
images, verbalization of the image and summaries, structural adjunct questions	Carnine & Kinder, 1985	reading comprehension	social studies and science	low-performing elementary school children	Comprehension increased significantly but not more than when inserted questions on passage structure were used.
summaries and analogies	Wittrock & Alesandrini, 1990	text	marine life	undergraduates	Summaries facilitated reading comprehension better than analogies, and both did better than reading alone.
summaries and analogies: alone and in pairs	Hooper, Sales & Rysavy, 1994	achievement, efficiency, and generations	marine life	undergraduates	Those who generated summaries performed better than those who generated analogies. Students working alone did better than those working in pairs.
combination of generative strategies—images, summary sentences, and analogies/ metaphors	Linden & Wittrock, 1981	factual retention and comprehension	reading	elementary school children	All generations increased and correlated with comprehension. More generations were produced when images were produced before verbal elaborations. No difference by generation sequence. Results were mixed for factual recall.
Metacognitive Processes					
generative learning processes training	Kourilsky & Wittrock, 1992	comprehension, confidence, misunderstanding	economics	high school seniors	Generative learning procedures significantly increased confidence and decreased level of misunderstanding.
generative teaching training	Kourilsky, 1993	comprehension, misunderstanding	economics	professional teachers	Pre- to posttest gains on both exams were significant when misconceptions were clarified and learning recovered.

studies nor is given the same importance of many of the other studies reported here.

31.2.1 Simple Coding

31.2.1.1. Underlining. As previously discussed, an argument can be made for the activation of generation processes in the learner by having her or him consciously and interactively relate information in the passage with prior beliefs and conceptions. This is, in essence, what Rickards and August (1975) did in their study. They investigated subject-generated versus experimenter-provided underlining strategies under six treatment conditions. Their results indicated that when college students had an opportunity to underline text that they considered most relevant, they performed much better on the posttests on both objective-specific and incidental learning (total recall). In fact, a very interesting result was that in the learner-generated condition, in which the subjects were asked to underline the least important items, they did poorest of all. Rickards (1979) explained that since learners were asked to underline those sentences that were more relevant *to them,* a mental interaction between sentences and between what they read and their own preconceptions had to occur, thereby establishing plausible evidence that learner-constructed generative learning occurred.

31.2.1.2. Notetaking. Notetaking is considered an organizational, coding strategy, which has some controversy connected with it as well. No generation of understanding occurs when a learner simply copies sentences from a page. As with the Rickards' argument, however, a learner that rewords sentences to combine ideas from the passage or relate them to prior knowledge is engaging in generative activity. This is an important distinction for teachers as they teach learners how to take notes and give them feedback in the process. To illustrate, three studies have been selected that include both high school and college students in both vocational and liberal arts areas.

Peper and Mayer (1986) found from two experiments, one with high school and one with college-level students, that notetakers performed better than non-notetakers on far-transfer tasks of problem solving but were worse on near-transfer tasks of fact retention and verbatim recognition (p. 34). Shrager and Mayer's (1989) study of college students instructed to take notes or not to take notes from a videotaped lesson confirmed these findings and found the effect on recall and transfer highest for learners with low prior knowledge. Peper and Mayer also tested the effects of other generative strategies, such as taking summary notes and answering conceptual questions during breaks in lectures, which produced similar results. This study points out the importance of examining the effects of generative strategies on the quality vs. quantity of learning.

Notetaking in two studies by Barnett, DiVesta, and Rogozenski (1981) was hypothesized to aid college students in the processing of information. Notetaking produced better results in learning from text than no notetaking, but

elaboration of the notes during a review period, a generative activity, produced similar results in terms of amount of learning as those who simply reviewed their notes. An interesting dimension to this study was the inclusion of instructor-prepared notes vs. learner-generated notes. For immediate recall tests during which learners had an opportunity to review or elaborate on instructor-prepared notes, they performed better than the learner-generated notes group. A second study tested whether the effects were the same for different types of questions: those common to the group, those from their own notes, those from others' notes, and those from others' elaborations. Scores for the delayed test using questions from their own notes were dramatically higher than the other groups. This provides a strong case for notetaking causing generative effects. In other words, these results showed that learners remembered what they originally perceived and encoded versus what others had intended them to remember.

To summarize, at least with these studies, notetaking has shown positive effects, but there were mixed findings when compared with type of learning. Notetaking may be a highly generative activity; however, quality of notes, type of elaborations, and opportunity for review can affect what, how much, and for how long information is learned.

31.2.1.3. Adjunct or Inserted Questions. Adjunct questions have been classified by Wittrock (1990) as a generative activity. They function as a coding and organizational guide. While questions can be generated by the learner, Wittrock also believes that they serve a teaching function to induce generative thinking by causing the learner to organize the information presented by relating ideas from a passage together, thereby creating personally meaningful understanding.

Over the past 25 years, the effects of inserted or adjunct questions have been studied extensively across content areas and age levels. Two important reviews of this research have summarized those findings. Anderson and Biddle (1975) and Rickards (1979) have concluded that inserted postquestions have been shown to increase recall of incidental learning (where criterion questions are unrelated to the inserted questions) as well as increasing recall on intentional learning (i.e., where criterion questions are the same as the inserted questions). Prequestions have been shown to increase intentional learning only.

According to Anderson and Biddle (1975), adjunct questions have also been examined in terms of frequency, the need for feedback, the nature of the question, the need for overt responding, and motivation. They summarized that: The more frequent the questions the better; feedback increased learning, but so did inserted questions without feedback; while most of the research focused on fact-level questions, there was also a positive effect from higher-level questions; free recall was generally better than multiple choice; a need for overt responding was dependent on how the questions were embedded; and the questions did motivate learners in some cases. They also found that these effects held across age level, content, length of text, and medium used.

Sutliff (1986) investigated the effect of inserted questions on reducing passivity in a self-instructional slide-tape presentation as evidenced by increased learning of facts (direct learning) and inference (indirect learning). His findings were opposite those of Anderson and Biddle in that there were no significant differences between groups. He interpreted the nonsignificance to be a result of not requiring overt responses to the questions, again contrary to previous research. Because of this "veto power over learning," described by Rothkopf (1976, p. 94), results such as this need to be examined further to determine just where overt manifestations may be necessary to ensure that processing occurs.

Burton, Niles, Lalik, and Reed (1986) investigated the effect of superordinate and subordinate questions on the amount of mental effort (level of cognitive capacity engagement) by using a secondary task probe technique and a passage about a mythical country. They found that superordinate questions have a greater learning effect, and that the effect carries over into subsequent text. The overall result also indicated that more main ideas were recalled than details. The explanation of the effect offered was that superordinate information is pulled into short-term memory more frequently, so it gets more practice. In other words, they found that general questions are more mentally engaging than detailed ones.

Woods and Bernard (1987) also found effects contrary to those of the reviews of Anderson and Biddle and Rickards. They investigated the effects of adjunct conceptual postquestions for encouraging greater depth of processing of verbal information of adults 60 and older. From results on intentional and incidental free-recall tests, they found that adjunct questions helped older learners process only intentional text at a greater depth.

In an interesting twist of the research question, Brody and Legenza (1980) studied the effect on learning of inserted pictures as opposed to inserted questions and hypothesized that the effect would be the same as the results on adjunct questions. Their findings supported their hypothesis that postpictures were more beneficial to reading comprehension than prepictures.

To summarize the numerous studies: Postquestions and postpictures have been shown to be most effective for increasing both intentional and incidental learning; superordinate questions have been more effective than subordinate detail questions; and overt responses have been more effective than allowing covert responses.

31.2.2 Complex Coding

31.2.2.1. Organizational Strategies. This topic deals with a variety of coding/organizational activities including creating hierarchies, headings, and sentence meanings, and mapping techniques across all age levels from elementary school children to professionals in a variety of topics from science to language arts. These organizational tasks require learners to relate ideas from a passage together by using a variety of symbolic representations. Each addresses at least one of three key questions regarding the generative model of learning: the effect of learner-generated learning vs. the effect of learner-reproductive learning; learner-generated vs. instructor-provided constructions of meaning—including organization as a variable; or the general effects of generated elaborations.

Wittrock and Carter (1975) studied free-recall responses of undergraduates in generative vs. reproductive treatments using hierarchies with varying degrees of order. The generative group was directed to organize the hierarchies, while the reproductive group was directed to simply copy them. The results showed better performance for the generative treatment groups than for the reproductive groups for the disorganized and randomly organized hierarchies. However, the organized reproductive group performed better than the unrelated generative group. This means that organization in the stimuli can compensate somewhat for a lack of learner-generated strategies, but providing organization in the instruction *and* opportunities for generative activity will be the best.

In two experiments with elementary school children, Doctorow, Wittrock, and Marks (1978) studied the effect of learner-generated vs. experimenter-provided paragraph headings and sentence meanings on comprehension. Again, the combination of text organized through the use of headings plus learner-generated sentences about the paragraphs produced dramatic gains in comprehension and recall. Generative instructions without experimenter-provided headings followed as the next most effective, and paragraph headings alone were more effective than the control group. This strategy also increased comprehension more for high-ability students than for low-ability students, perhaps because high-ability students have better organizational cognitive abilities to make sense out of disorganized information.

Beissner, Jonassen, and Grabowski (1993) tested the effects of two organizational strategies against learner differences at four levels of learning. Their findings showed an interaction between learner-generated concept vs. semantic maps and serialist learners on the problem-solving questions only, with serialists performing better with semantic maps, and holists performing better with concept maps. While this study did not compare their results with instructor-provided maps, it does contribute evidence to considering the importance of learner cognitive strengths and patterns of thinking when selecting organizational learning activities.

Also studying the effects of concept maps, Smith and Dwyer (1995) found a significant difference only on lower-level terminology tasks in favor of instructor-provided maps. This result is consistent with that of Wittrock and Carter (1975). For lower-level tasks, organization helps, especially when a learner is tested with questions that show similarity to the organization that an instructor may have possessed when creating the test.

To summarize the findings of these studies: The results show that learner-generated activities are more effective in improving achievement than instruction-provided organizational schemes. Performance is increased even more when the text is organized. The selection of activities should be tempered by cognitive ability.

31.2.2.2. Manipulation of Objects. The next organizational activity deals with manipulating objects. While this activity extends beyond the printed page as designated by Wittrock's work, it qualifies as a generative activity because a relationship is being drawn and extended between parts of the environment.

Sayeki, Ueno, and Nagasaka (1991), in a very interesting study, investigated the effects of transforming mediational objects in the learning of mathematical principles. Their results supported the hypothesis that manipulatives would increase comprehension. While they do not specifically call this a generative activity, the act of creating understanding by generating both mental and physical relationships from different shapes of a manipulable rectangle manifests the same required attributes defined by Wittrock. Their results from mathematics should be tested for conceptual learning and problem solving in other content areas.

Haag and Grabowski (1994) extended this work to computer-manipulated graphics. Most applications of moving or manipulated graphics are done through generated animation. In this study, they found that learners who manipulated the graphics on the screen using a preorganized organizational framework increased problem solving over those using no organizational framework or having the computer create the graphic statically. These results are consistent with those of other organizational strategies reported in the previous section.

Both studies lend support to the use of manipulatives for generating understanding for both children and undergraduates in math and science.

31.2.3 Integration Strategies

The next series of studies examine the effects of activities that require a student to relate information to prior knowledge. In these activities, learners are integrating that information through imaging, elaborations, and analogies.

31.2.3.1. Imaging. The effects of imaging have also been investigated extensively with four of those studies summarized here. They include fictitious descriptions, language arts, and economics topics studied by elementary or high school students.

Anderson and Kulhavey (1972) studied high school seniors to determine the effect of imaging on prose learning. In this study, half of the subjects were told to image, while the other half were not. Results indicated no difference in prose learning between the groups. On further probing, the researchers discovered that not all of the students in the imaging group actually created images (only 50% did), and

many in the control group did create images (about one-third)! Comparing those subjects from both groups who actually used imaging with those who did not showed significant differences in favor of the imaging strategy. This illustrates the fact that mental activity cannot be strictly controlled by instruction and, again, raises the issue that requiring an overt response may be more effective in encouraging the desired result than just simply providing direction to image, as Sutliff (1986) found with adjunct questions.

Bull and Wittrock (1973) compared the effect of experimenter-provided vs. learner-generated imagery with elementary school children. Groups were directed to either draw, trace, or copy verbal information on definitions they were to learn. As predicted, results showed that the group that generated images performed significantly better than those who copied definitions; however, there was no significant difference between the imagery provided (tracing) and the copied definitions groups.

Kourilsky and Wittrock (1987) investigated what effect the sequence of the use of verbal or imaging generative activities would have on economic understanding by high school students. They found that using verbal elaborations first, followed by imaging, significantly increased economic understanding. They also found significantly greater gains by using both generative activities (verbal and imaginal) over just verbal elaboration only.

Laney (1990) found a slightly different result. Examining economic reasoning in the decision making of third-graders, he found that the verbal-only and integrated strategies were more effective than the imaging-only strategy. While using both symbol systems increased learning in both studies, the verbal-only elaboration was more effective than both the imagery-only and the use of dual-symbol systems. He felt his results were consistent with Wittrock's notion that the effective use of imagery is developmental. Laney's third-grade subjects had not yet developed this ability and were more familiar with verbal instruction. These are important results given the confusion that could result from the use of a generative imagery strategy too early in a learner's developmental cycle.

These studies have shown that overt imaging is more effective than covert; learner-generated imaging is more effective than instruction-provided imaging; and visual images may be more effective than verbal ones, only in cases in which students have progressed developmentally to the point where they can understand them.

31.2.3.2. Elaborations. Stein and Bransford (1979) conducted two studies to determine the effects of learner generated or experimenter provided by type of sentence elaborations. They hypothesized that congruence of the elaboration with the topic would be the determining variable and, in fact, did find differences in two experiments with undergraduates. In those cases where elaborations were incongruent, students did worse than those in the treatments with no elaborations at all. Two important findings indicated that "elaborations facilitated performance only when they clarify the precise significance of target concepts . . . and that prompting subjects to ask relevant questions facilitated both the precision of elaboration and subsequent retention" (p. 769).

DiVesta and Peverley (1984), in a very complex study, tested learner-organized vs. preorganized examples on near and far transfer in a concept attainment lesson. Additional variables included variability of examples, and sequence. Their results on the active vs. passive element of their study indicated that students who generated their own examples did significantly better on both transfer tests than the preorganized group.

Johnsey, Morrison, and Ross (1992) investigated the effects of embedded vs. detached and learner-generated vs. experimenter-provided elaboration on recall, recognition, and application learning. The type of elaborations tested in this study in the area of adult professional development included two types of statements relating the content of the lesson to their job, and stating implications of the information presented to their job environment. When these elaborations were embedded in the CAI training, significant gains were found; however, there were no differences between the learner-generated or experimenter-provided elaborations. Teaching students how to generate elaborations at the time they will need them appears to be consistent with "just-in-time" training, especially when the technique may be new or more mentally difficult to implement.

31.2.4 Combination and Comparison of Coding and Integration Strategies

Carnine and Kinder (1985) expanded on the Anderson and Kulhavey study on imaging. In their investigation, elementary school subjects were asked to form an image, then verbalize it, and were then given corrective feedback. They were also asked to create a summary at the end. This strategy was compared to a "schema-based strategy" in which learners were asked structurally related questions about the passage composition. They found significant gains in reading comprehension from pre- to posttests for both narrative and expository text for both treatments. One cannot be sure whether the positive results were due to the additional instructional effects of the feedback. Nevertheless, the question of the need for feedback on learner-generated activities is an important one since significant differences favoring adjunct questioning over the imaging strategy were observed for learning of expository materials.

Linden and Wittrock (1981) conducted a study with elementary children that found that students who were asked to generate text-related summaries, analogies, metaphors, and pictures had better comprehension than those who were not. When instructed to generate images before verbal explanations, students produced more generations.

Wittrock and Alesandrini (1990) also investigated the effects of learner-generated summaries and analogies by analytic and holist undergraduates. The results followed the predicted rank ordering, with the most positive effects found for generating summaries, followed by generating analogies, both of which were significantly better than the control group, which contained no generative activities. They also found that individual differences of analytic and holist ability correlated with learning differently in the three treatments: analytic ability with learning in the generate analogies group, the holist ability with the text-only control group, and both analytic and holist abilities in the generate summaries treatment.

Finally, Hooper, Sales, and Rysavy (1994) tested undergraduates on achievement efficiency and generations when given summaries and analogies while working alone and in pairs. They found that those who generated summaries performed better than those who generated analogies. Contrary to expected predictions, students working alone did better than those working in pairs.

When using a combination of strategies, the difficulty of the task must be taken into consideration, and, where possible, the effects of cognitive strengths must be factored in. Imaging is a more difficult task than adjunct questions, and analogies more difficult than summaries. If learners are not developmentally ready for such a task, it may cause more frustration than positive effects.

31.2.5 Metacognitive Processes

Kourilsky and Wittrock (1992), in a very powerful study, investigated the effect of teaching the overall generative model of teaching, including its four processes and activities, to senior high school students. The seniors were taught economics in cooperative learning groups. Those students who were taught this way of thinking were found to be more confident, had significantly fewer misconceptions, and had greater comprehension than those without this training. A fascinating result consistent with the Hooper, Sales, and Rysavy (1994) study was that just using cooperative learning groups alone did not produce as great an effect.

Kourilsky (1993) taught professional teachers generative teaching strategies and economic misconceptions. She found that pre- to posttest gain on exams of comprehension and misunderstanding were significant when misconceptions were clarified.

31.2.6 Summary

As can be seen, a variety of studies reporting on results of generative strategies have been summarized here. This section is not intended to be exhaustive; rather the studies have been selected as representative of the kind of research that has been conducted across content areas, learning types, and age levels. However, all articles that could be found that specify generative learning as the theory being tested are included. In general, results have shown increased gains in learning when the learner is an active vs. a passive participant in the learning process and when instruction includes activities that relate new information together and new information to prior knowledge. These studies on generative learning have shown that in most cases, active learner involvement produced increased learning—i.e., learner-generated activities have resulted in significant gains in learning, although issues of organization of lesson content and quality of response may affect the degree of the effect.

31.3 FOR THE PRESENT: THE GENERATIVE MODEL OF TEACHING AND IMPLICATIONS FOR THE DESIGN OF INSTRUCTION

The goal of instructional message design which follows generative learning theory is to create effective instruction that is organized and causes some level of mental activity on the part of the learner. "Effective instruction [in the generative model of learning] causes the learner to generate a relationship between new information and previous experience" (Wittrock, 1974a, p. 182). As a generative model of teaching, generative learning theory offers many practical guidelines and suggestions that extend beyond simply suggesting those learning activities that induce relationship building. From the description of the components of generative-learning theory presented earlier in this chapter, one must recall that generative-learning theory has four processes that work in tandem to create learning: motivation, learning, knowledge creation, and generation. Ignoring any one of these processes could result in the learner's taking a "passive," mentally disengaged approach to learning.

The generative model of teaching (Wittrock, 1991) takes into consideration these four components. Creating a teaching model to provide practical prescriptions for teachers was his original intent in pursing this area of research. As such, he provides some important teaching recommendations that affect the four processes of his model.

31.3.1 Motivation Processes

Wittrock (1991) specifies interest and attribution as the two essential and linked components of motivation processes (see Figs. 31-1 and 31-2) that are activated by arousal and intention through the descending reticular activation system. Research from other areas suggests that attribution of effort, or the process of giving credit for success or failure to one's own effort, can influence whether or not the learner will exert the effort to learn actively. If the learners attribute success to themselves, it follows that motivation to exert effort will be greater than if they attribute success to external forces (Weiner, 1979). The influence of intention on motivation for meaning generation flows from within the learner. Wittrock (1990, 1991) suggests that addressing this component means providing opportunities for the learner to "take control and responsibility for being active in learning" (p. 175). Teaching and design strategies that deal with

attribution should result in enduring interest, persistence, and motivation. He suggests those activities or teaching strategies that:

- Attribute learning to their own effort
- Improve self-concept
- Create satisfaction from the process of learning
- Modify their perception of themselves as learners
- Create control and increase responsibility and accountability for learning
- Use rewards and praise that can be directly attributable to their effort

31.3.2 Learning Processes

Arousal and intention in the brain also influence an individual's learning processes. External stimuli arouse attention through the ascending reticular activating system. Without active, dynamic, and selective attending of environmental stimuli, it follows that meaning generation cannot occur regarding that environmental stimuli. The influence of arousal on attention flows from the environment outside of the learner, but interacts internally. The learning process that is key to this model is attention. Without attention, learning cannot occur. Teaching and design activities that can assist in gaining and maintaining attention include those that:

- Provide attention training by self-control, planning, and organizing
- Provide behavioral objectives and adjunct questions
- Provide interpretation of the importance of topic selected
- Use problems, mysteries, inconsistencies, suspense, and enigmas
- Direct students' voluntary attention to meaning

31.3.3 Knowledge Creation Processes

Knowledge creation processes are those components of memory—including preconceptions, beliefs, concepts, metacognitions, and experiences—activated through the frontal lobes of the cortex, which manage the receipt, coding, and storage of information. It is between these existing beliefs, concepts, preconceptions, etc., and environmental stimuli that relationships are formed, and, thereby, understanding and comprehension are generated (Wittrock, 1990, 1991). Much of his writing and research with colleagues addresses the notion of preconceptions as they influence learning misconceptions (Kourilsky & Wittrock, 1987). Some would assert that creating dissonance in the learner is one way to "unteach" misconceptions. Wittrock (1990) would argue that those dissonant situations must be carefully selected experiences that are real to the learners so that the situation cannot be easily dismissed by the learner as untrue. He also suggests teaching scientific conceptions early—before preconceptions are formed.

Preconceptions about learning and the learning process also function as a primary influence on learning. It may be necessary to change one's beliefs about learning and the learner's role in order to understand the value of participating in generative activities.

Other strategy recommendations offered by Wittrock (1990, 1991) include:

- Relating instruction to background knowledge and interest
- Teaching metacognitive processes to monitor learning actively
- Demonstrating tangible results from active learning

31.3.4 Generation Processes

"The art of generative teaching is knowing how and when to facilitate the learner's construction of relations among the parts of the text and their knowledge" (Wittrock, 1990, p. 353). Stimulated by the frontal lobes of the cortex, learners generate relationships between parts of what they see and hear. By integrating that information with what exists in memory, learners reorganize, elaborate, and/or reconceptualize information.

There are two types of activities that can be judged as generative. Those that generate organizational relationships between different components of the environment include "titles, headings, questions, objectives, summaries, graphs, tables, and main ideas." Those that generate integrated relationships between the external stimuli and the memory components include "demonstrations, metaphors, analogies, examples, pictures, applications, interpretations, paraphrases, inferences" (Wittrock, p. 354).

Both of these types of activities can be used in an instructor-provided or learner-generated format. In other words, the teacher can create titles and headings as organizers, or ask the learner to create a title or heading. When the instructor provides the actual relationship, it should be done in a manner that would direct attention. One way to do that is to relate those connections to ideas that are highly relevant to the learner. They should capture attention *and* motivate learners to think actively about the information. Wittrock advises that even though the instructor makes connections for the learners, learners must make those connections actively themselves in order for them to be learned. Passive observation will not suffice.

Given that there are many types of relationship-building activities that can be selected, a guide for selecting from among those activities is appropriate. Although Wittrock claims that levels of thinking are not represented in his theory and only designates two types of relationship building, it is evident that, by examining the level of mental effort required for each of these activities, the two categories can be broken down even further. Those activities that relate parts of the information in the environment together include coding, organization, and conceptualization levels of thinking, while those that relate parts of the information to prior knowledge include integration and translation tasks. Those

activities that relate to the various levels are shown in Table 31-3 (Grabowski, 1995).

31.3.5 Summary

The recommendations that follow from Wittrock's writings provide straightforward ideas to be implemented by teachers and designers for any instructional medium, and should not be ignored. Whether we are designing for the computer, print, television, or instructor-led training, these principles hold. Engaging the learner in active processing of the information should be our primary goal.

The computer can be exploited as a powerful means to engage learners by tapping its capability as a mental construction tool, rather than in the traditional page-turner sense. Following Wittrock's principles, one should put the control of learning in the hands of the learner by creating an advisory environment in which learners manipulate information by moving text, graphics, and media segments around mentally or physically, testing their own ideas. This does not mean placing the learner in a total learner-controlled *information* environment, but rather in one in which success can be guided, rewarded, and reinforced.

Creating a transactive environment (between the learner and the materials) is more of a challenge when designing for more static media, but it can be done cleverly by giving conscious attention to the design of the message to induce thinking—such as "stop and think activities" (Arnone & Grabowski, 1992), incomplete messages, and rhetorical adjunct questions to direct and engage thought.

The second important message from Wittrock is that more time and effort be spent on identifying important

---

TABLE 31-3. MATCH OF GENERATIVE ACTIVITY WITH LEVEL OF PROCESSING

Level of Cognitive Processing	Recommended Generative Activities
Coding	creating titles and headings
Organization	outlining summarizing diagramming
Conceptualization	paraphrasing explaining/clarifying creating concept maps identifying important information
Integration	creating relevant examples relating to prior knowledge creating analogies creating metaphors synthesizing
Translation	evaluating questioning analyzing predicting inferring

factors about the learner than is traditionally spent in the instructional design process. Identifying the learner has always been an important step in the instructional design process; however, how to do this, or the kind of key information to gather, is rarely specified. Wittrock's writings show some clear elements: Gather conceptual preconceptions, preconceptions about their learning the topic, preconceptions about their role as learners, prior knowledge relating to the topic, general prior knowledge, and metacognitive abilities. This knowledge, combined with a good understanding of appropriate activities that draw relationships, should result in very effective instruction.

31.4 THE FUTURE

31.4.1 Implications for Research

The potential for continuing and extending research on the effects of generative activities is considerable. What is currently evident from past research is the validity of Wittrock's basic premise of active learner engagement. Further research is necessary to help in selecting the type and mode of activity. In other words, we need to ask when various generative activities are more appropriate than others, and whether they should be used in an instructor-provided format or learner-generated one. Given past research results and these capabilities, these two broad agendas can be specified.

31.4.1.1. Selection of the Type of Generative Activity. In the previous section, a table of activities was proposed which matches generative activities to desired levels of cognitive processing. This matching must be empirically tested. Questions such as the following take this into account:

1. What are the effects of each generative activity on higher-level learning? Much of the previous research has emphasized fact and concept-level learning and has not dealt with higher-level learning such as application, synthesis, or problem solving.
2. Are there clusters of generative activities that are best used for specific learning tasks or levels of learning? Are, for example, analogies appropriate for fact-level learning?

31.4.1.2. Use of Generative Activities. Previous research has also indicated mixed results from activities requiring overt/covert responses. Because of a "veto power over learning," described by Rothkopf (1976, p. 94), further research should explore the conditions that may require overt manifestations to ensure that processing occurs.

3. Is there a differential effect from requiring or not requiring overt manifestations of generative activity? What are the best strategies (instructional and mechanical) for controlling that information is manipulated in the mind?

31.4.1.3. Motivation, Learner, and Knowledge Creation Processes. Another very significant area of research is identifying strategies that will enhance the perception of learner responsibility. This indicates a need to merge the learner control research with that of generative learning. From Wittrock's writing, it seems apparent that learner control with advisement would be recommended, but it needs to be empirically tested with questions such as:

4. What are the best methods for providing advisory feedback on learner-generated conceptions of the instruction content, and what are their effects?
5. What is the effect on learning of directive, embedded, or inductive control when motivation level varies? Several strategies have been proposed by various researchers. Directive control, as defined by Rothkopf (1976), takes the form of directions that are given to a learner to perform a particular task. Embedded strategies are similar to Rothkopf's inductive control in that they may not be obvious to the learner. Inductive control does not force a response, however, while an embedded strategy expects the learner to perform the behavior before going on (Rigney, 1980).

31.4.1.4. Instructor Provided or Learner Generated? Some of the research results reported earlier indicate that both developmental and cognitive strengths may play a part in selecting appropriate and successful activities. Besides learner-generated activities in which the learner actively makes connections, Bovy (1981) suggests that instructor-provided activities supplant cognitive connections that are provided for the learner by the instruction itself (instructor generated, not learner generated, but personally relevant). There is also another category of instruction in which no control is provided: offering no suggestions, no forced responses, and no supplanted cognitive strategies. The following table proposes a matching of cognitive strengths with levels of thinking and recommended generative activities. If the activity is one that matches the cognitive strengths of individuals, then perhaps it should be presented in a learner-generated format. If it is an activity that would frustrate the learner—i.e., it is not a cognitive strength—then it should be presented in an instructor-provided format, so that the mental effort can be concentrated on the meaning of the message, rather than on a frustrated attempt at using a technique that does not match one's cognitive style. Providing no guidance may well be saved for learners with well-developed metacognitive abilities (see Table 31-4).

Research designs should then test the effect of these three presentational strategies (learner generated, supplanted, or no control) for each generative-learning strategy matched by cognitive style or other individual difference factors against desired levels of learning or the cognitive processing requirements of the specific task. Cognitive developmental issues should also be considered. The following research questions should yield very important prescriptions:

6. Is there an appropriate use for supplanted vs. generated learning? Does this vary by task or learner?
7. Which activities match with developmental levels of learners?

TABLE 31-4. THEORETICAL MATCH OF GENERATIVE ACTIVITY WITH COGNITIVE STRENGTHS

Cognitive Style Type	Cognitive Strength	Learner-Generated Activity	Instructor-Provided Activity
Breadth of Categorization—Organizational Thinking			
	broad	create summaries create main ideas	provide outlines
	narrow	outline	provide summaries provide main ideas
Organizational Patterns—Organizational Thinking			
	global	create summaries create diagrams	provide outline
	analytic	create outline	provide summaries provide diagrams
Variation in Memory—Organizational Thinking			
	leveling	create summaries	provide outlines
	sharpening	create outlines	provide summaries
Conceptual Styles—Conceptualization			
	relational	create concept maps	explain/clarify identify important information provide paraphrases
	analytic/ descriptive	explain/clarify identify important information	provide concept maps provide paraphrases
	categorical/ inferential	paraphrase	provide concept maps explain/clarify identify important information
Cognitive Dimension—Integration			
	complexity (abstract)	create analogies create metaphors	provide relevant examples relate to prior knowledge
	simplicity (concrete)	create relevant examples relate to prior knowledge	provide analogies provide metaphors
Thinking Patterns—Organization, Conceptualization, Integration, Translation			
	Convergent		
Organizational		creating outlines creating diagrams	provide summaries
Conceptualization		explaining/clarifying identifying important information	provide concept maps paraphrase
Integration		relate to prior knowledge create relevant examples	provide analogies provide metaphor
Translation		evaluation analysis inference	question provide predictions
	Divergent		
Organizational		create summaries	provide outlines provide diagrams
Conceptualization		create concept maps paraphrase	explain/clarify identify important information
Integration		create analogies create metaphors	relate to prior knowledge provide relevant examples
Translation		question make predictions	evaluation analysis inference

31.5 CONCLUSION

The principles behind generative learning offer the instructional designer much guidance for developing effective instruction that emphasizes the learner as an active partner in the instructional process. There is much research that has been done to support this position, and there is much research to do to figure out how to help the designer to create a learning environment that promotes this active mental processing at all stages and levels of learning. All of the evidence indicates, in my view, that it is an area of very fruitful work that should continue.

REFERENCES

Anderson, R.C. & Biddle, W.B. (1975). On asking people questions about what they are reading. *In* G. Bower, ed. *Psychology of learning and motivation,* Vol. 9. New York: Academic.

— & Kulhavey, R.W. (1972). Imagery and prose learning. *Journal of Educational Psychology 63*(3), 242–43.

Arnone, M. & Grabowski, B.L. (1992). Effects of variation in learner control over an interactive video lesson children's achievement and curiosity. *Educational Technology: Research and Development 40*(1), 15–27.

Barnett, J.E., DiVesta, F.J. & Rogozenski, J.T. (1981). What is learned in notetaking? *Journal of Educational Psychology 73* (2), 181–92.

Barry, R.J. (1974). The concept of mathemagenic behaviors: an analysis of its heuristic value. *Perceptual and Motor Skills 38,* 311–21.

Beissner, K., Jonassen, D. & Grabowski, B.L. (1993). Using and selecting graphic techniques to convey structural knowledge. *In* M.R. Simonson, ed. *Proceedings of selected research paper presentations,* 79–114. Ames, IA: Iowa State University.

Bell-Gredler, M.E. (1986). Learning and instruction: theory into practice. New York: Macmillan.

Blanchard, J., Chang, F., Logan, I. & Smith, K. (1985). An investigation of computer based mathemagenic activities. *Texas Tech Journal of Education 12*(3), 159–74.

Bovy, R.C. (1981). Successful instructional methods: a cognitive information processing approach. *Educational Communications and Technology Journal 29*(4), 203–17.

Brody, P. & Legenza, A. (1980). Can pictorial attributes serve mathemagenic functions? *Educational Communications and Technology Journal 28*(1), 25–29.

Bull, B.L. & Wittrock, M.C. (1973). Imagery in the learning of verbal definitions. *British Journal of Educational Psychology 43*(3), 289–93.

Burton, J.K., Niles, J.A., Lalik, R.M. & Reed, M.W. (1986). Cognitive capacity engagement during and following interspersed mathemagenic questions. *Journal of Educational Psychology 78*(2), 147–52.

Carnine, D. & Kinder, C. (1985). Teaching low-performing students to apply generative and schema strategies to narrative and expository materials. *Remedial and Special Education 6*(1), 20–30.

DiVesta, F.J. (1989). Applications of cognitive psychology to education. *In* M.C. Wittrock & F. Farley, eds. *The future of educational psychology.* Hillsdale, NJ: Erlbaum.

— & Peverley, S. (1984). The effects of encoding variability, processing activity, and rule-examples sequence on the transfer of conceptual rules. *Journal of Educational Psychology 76*(1), 108–19.

Doctorow, M., Wittrock, M.C. & Marks, C.B. (1978). Generative processes in reading comprehension. *Journal of Educational Psychology 70*(2), 109–18.

Goetz, E. (1983). Elaborative strategies: promises and dilemmas for instruction in large classes. ERIC Document: Reproduction Services, ED 24307.

Grabowski, B.L. (1995). Mathemagenic and generative learning: a comparison and implications for designers. *In* A.J. Romiszowski & C. Dills, eds. *Instructional developments: state of the art, Vol 3: the paradigms.* Englewood Cliffs, NJ: Educational Technology.

Harlen, W. & Osborne, R. (1985). A model for learning and teaching applied to primary science. *Journal of Curriculum Studies 17*(2), 133–46.

Haag, B.B. & Grabowski, B.L. (1994). The effects of varied visual organizational strategies within computer-based instruction on factual, conceptual and problem solving learning. *In* M.R. Simonson, N. Maushak & K. Abu-Omar, eds. *16th annual proceedings of selected research and development presentations,* 235–246B. Ames, IA: Iowa State University.

Hooper, S., Sales, G. & Rysavy, S. (1994). Generating summaries and analogies in Paris. *Contemporary Educational Psychology 19,* 53–62.

Johnsey, A., Morrison, G.R. & Ross, S.M. (1992). Using elaboration strategies training in computer-based instruction to promote generative learning. *Contemporary Educational Psychology 17,* 125–35.

Jonassen, D.H. (1986). *Technology of text, Vol. 2.* Englewood Cliffs: Educational Technology.

— (1990). Objectivism versus constructivism: do we need a new philosophical paradigm? *Educational Technology: Research and Development 39*(3), 15–26.

Kourilsky, M. (1993). Economic education and a generative model of mislearning and recovery. *Journal of Economic Education 25* (Winter), 23–33.

— & Wittrock, M.C. (1987). Verbal and graphical strategies in teaching economics. *Teaching and Teacher Education 3*(1), 1–12.

— & — (1992). Generative teaching: an enhancement strategy for the learning of economics in cooperative groups. *American Educational Research Journal 29*(4), 861–76.

Laney, J.D. (1990). Generative teaching and learning of cost-benefit analysis: an empirical investigation. *Journal of Research and Development in Education 23*(3), 136–44.

Linden, M. & Wittrock, M.C. (1981). The teaching of reading comprehension according to the model of generative learning. *Reading Research Quarterly 17*(1), 44–57.

Luria, A. (1973). *The working brain: an introduction to neuropsychology* (B. Haigh, trans.). New York: Basic Books.

Peper, R.J. & Mayer, R.E. (1986). Generative effects of notetaking during science lectures. *Journal of Educational Psychology 78*(1), 34–38.

Rickards, J.P. (1979). Adjunct post-questions in text: a critical review of methods and processes. *Review of Educational Research 49*(2), 181–96.

— & August, G.J. (1975). Generative underlining strategies

in prose recall. *Journal of Educational Psychology 67* (6), 860–65.

Rigney, J.W. (1980). Cognitive learning strategies and dualities in information processing. *In* R.E. Snow, P. Frederico & W.E. Montague, eds. *Aptitude, learning and instruction, Vol. 1.* Hillsdale, NJ: Erlbaum.

Rothkopf, E.Z. (1976). Writing to teach and reading to learn: a perspective on the psychology of written instruction. *In* N.L. Gagné, ed. *The psychology of teaching methods.* Chicago, IL: University of Chicago Press.

Rummelhart, D.E. (1981). Understanding understanding. Technical Report: National Science Foundation, Washington DC (ED 198–497).

— & Ortony, A. (1977). The representation of knowledge in memory. *In* R.C. Anderson, R.J. Spiro & W.E. Montague, eds. *Schooling and the acquisition of knowledge.* Hillsdale, NJ: Erlbaum.

Sayeki, Y., Ueno, N. & Nagasaka, T. (1991). Mediation as a generative model for obtaining an area. *Learning and Instruction 1,* 229–42.

Shrager, L. & Mayer, R.E. (1989). Note-taking fosters generative learning strategies in novices. *Journal of Educational Psychology 81*(2), 263–64.

Skinner, B.F. (1990). Can psychology be a science of mind? *American Psychologist 45*(11), 1206–10.

Smith, K. & Dwyer, F.M. (1995). The effect of concept mapping strategies in facilitating student achievement. *International Journal of Instructional Media 22*(1), 25–31.

Stein, B.S. & Bransford, J.P. (1979). Constraints on effective elaboration: effects of precision and subject generation. *Journal of Verbal Learning and Verbal Behavior 18* (6), 769–77.

Sutliff, R. (1986). Effect of adjunct postquestions on achievement. *Journal of Industrial Teacher Education 23*(3), 45–54.

Weiner, B. (1979). A theory of motivation for some classroom experiences. *Journal of Educational Psychology 71*(1), 3–25.

Wittrock, M.C. (1974a). Learning as a generative process. *Educational Psychologist 11*(2), 87–95.

— (1974b). A generative model of mathematics education. *Journal for Research in Mathematics Education 5* (4), 181–96.

— (1985). Teaching learners generative strategies for enhancing reading comprehension. *Theory into Practice 24*(2), 123–26.

— (1990). Generative processes of comprehension. *Educational Psychologist 24,* 345–76.

— (1991). Generative teaching of comprehension. *Elementary School Journal 92,* 167–82.

— (1992). Generative learning processes of the brain. *Educational Psychologist 27*(4), 531–41.

— & Alesandrini, K. (1990). Generation of summaries and analogies and analytic and holistic abilities. *American Educational Research Journal 27,* 489–502.

— & Carter, J. (1975). Generative processing of hierarchically organized words. *American Journal of Psychology 88* (3), 489–501.

Woods, J.H. & Bernard, R.M. (1987). Improving older adults retention of text: a test of an instructional activity. *Educational Gerontology 13*(2), 107–20.

32. FEEDBACK RESEARCH

Edna Holland Mory
UNIVERSITY OF NORTH CAROLINA AT WILMINGTON

32.1 INTRODUCTION

In this chapter, the use of feedback in the facilitation of learning will be examined according to various historical and paradigmatic views in the research literature. Most of the research in the area of feedback has been completed with specific assumptions as to what purpose feedback serves. Feedback may have various functions according to the particular learning environment in which it is examined and the particular learning paradigm under which it is viewed. In fact, feedback is incorporated in both behavioral (see 2.2) and cognitive (see Chapter 5) learning paradigms and is an essential element of theories of learning and instruction (Bangert-Drowns, Kulik, Kulik & Morgan, 1991). The use of feedback will be discussed according to the way in which it is to function and to what purpose it is to serve.

32.2 DEFINITION OF FEEDBACK

Feedback is defined in *Webster's New World Dictionary* (1984) as "a process in which the factors that produce a result are themselves modified, corrected, strengthened, etc., by that result" (p. 513). While this definition could fit a host of situations or systems, most educational researchers consider the term *feedback* in the context of instruction. Feedback has been widely perceived as an important component of general systems operations and may be viewed under a variety of settings (Kowitz & Smith, 1985, 1987). In the purely instructional sense, feedback can be said to describe any communication or procedure given to inform a learner of the accuracy of a response, usually to an instructional question (Carter, 1984; Cohen, 1985; Kulhavy, 1977; Sales, 1993). This type of feedback acts as one of the events of instruction described by Gagné (1985) (see 18.3) and usually follows some type of practice task. More broadly, feedback allows the comparison of actual performance with some set standard of performance (Johnson & Johnson, 1993). In technology-assisted instruction, it is information presented to the learner after any input with the purpose of

shaping the perceptions of the learner (Sales, 1993). Information presented via feedback in instruction might include not only answer correctness but also other information such as precision, timeliness, learning guidance, motivational messages, lesson sequence advisement, critical comparisons, and learning focus (Hoska, 1993; Sales, 1993). In fact, Wager and Wager (1985) refer to feedback in computer-based instruction as being *any* message or display that the computer presents to the learner after a response.

Most studies that have examined feedback use contrived experimental learning situations where feedback is given from an external source after a learner responds to a question during instruction. The main purpose of this feedback is to confirm or change a student's knowledge as represented by answers to practice or test questions. However, some researchers (Butler & Winne, 1995) have suggested that viewing feedback in such a unilateral context fails to take into account variances in behavior that might be the result of self-regulation and student engagement. Further, feedback can also be viewed in even less traditional settings, such as its role in program evaluation. When used in situations that are not necessarily instructional, the best definition of feedback is information presented that allows comparison between an actual outcome and a desired outcome. Tucker (1993) points out that feedback is particularly important when evaluating dynamic instructional programs because its presence or absence can "dramatically affect the accuracy required of human judgment and decision making" (p. 303).

In order to illustrate some of the various purposes of feedback, the next section presents the evolution of feedback research in instruction from its early beginnings through the present. The principle feedback variables that have interested researchers are then discussed.

32.3 EVOLUTION OF FEEDBACK RESEARCH

Many of us may assume that the most recent studies of feedback are the result of several current trends and accepted paradigms—for example, the information-processing model and newer theories of motivation. However, three definitions of feedback dating back to the early 1900s are surprisingly similar to the ones we use today. Kulhavy and Wager (1993) refer to these as the "feedback triad" (p. 5) and point out that these definitions still prevail in our views of feedback we currently hold. The first view was that feedback served as a motivator or incentive for increasing response rate and/or accuracy. Secondly, feedback acted to provide a reinforcing message that would automatically connect responses to prior stimuli—the focus being on correct responses. Lastly, feedback provided information that learners could use to validate or change a previous response—the focus falling on error responses.

32.3.1 Law of Effect

The earliest studies of feedback date back to E. L. Thorndike's Law of Effect that postulated that feedback would act as a "connector" between responses and preceding stimuli (see 2.2.1.3; Kulhavy & Wager, 1993). Researchers such as Thorndike were examining the use of postresponse information as early as 1911 (cited in Kulhavy & Wager, 1993). Thorndike's work showed that a response followed by a "satisfying state of affairs" is likely to be repeated and increases the likelihood of learning. The view of feedback as information emphasized the role that the learner had in learning, with the ability to adapt his or her response according to information in the feedback and thus correct his or her errors. The first researcher to emphasize error correction was Sidney Pressey (1926). However, a later study using his "teaching machine" (see 2.3) emphasized both the error-correcting function of feedback as well as its acting as a punishment for errors—a Thorndike viewpoint that supports the notion of feedback as a reinforcer (Pressey, 1927). Thus we see that the confusion in the feedback research began quite early and that, given the early "feedback triad," the research has not evolved as much as one might expect.

32.3.2 Programmed Instruction

Thorndike's pioneering work paved the way for the next avenue of research on feedback, B. F. Skinner's study of programmed instruction (Skinner, 1958; see 2.3). Using principles from the Law of Effect and the application of reinforcement on learners, Skinner proposed that a solution to instructional problems lay in the use of strategically designed classroom materials that would take learners through information in a step-by-step fashion, shaping behavior and strengthening desired responses. By the year 1960, the programmed instruction movement was well under way, purporting that feedback in programmed instruction served as both a reinforcer and a motivator and perpetuating a confusion between learning and incentive.

During this period, instructional errors were either ignored or considered as "aversive consequences" to be avoided (Skinner, 1968). The fact that errors were deemed as aversive implies an emotional element from which the early motivational view of feedback was derived. The viewpoint that incorrect responses cause distress and influence self-concept is used even today (Fischer & Mandl, 1988). Kulhavy and Wager (1993) suggest that such motivational variables should be separated from the feedback message, keeping them extrinsic to the lesson content itself. Certainly this would help remove the confusion between the instructional content of feedback and other factors that might affect performance.

32.3.3 Feedback as Reinforcement

Programmed instruction (see 2.3.4, 22.4.1) emphasized an operant approach to learning (see 2.2.1.3.2), one that had the concept of reinforcement at its heart. Programs were designed to shape a student's responses, using a small lock-step approach with a high level of redundancy. Operant psychologists of the time argued that learning tasks should be analyzed and broken down into small enough steps such that the probability of a successful response was ensured (Cohen, 1985). By telling a student that an answer is correct, the student is "reinforced" to answer correctly again on a later test (Kulhavy, 1977).

Around 1970, most researchers began to doubt the feedback-as-reinforcement view. In fact, 10 years of research under this paradigm showed no systematic effects for feedback (see Kulhavy & Wager, 1993). Studies provided little evidence that feedback following positive responses acts in a reinforcing manner (Anderson, Kulhavy & Andre, 1972; Bardwell, 1981; Barringer & Gholson, 1979; Kulhavy, 1977; Roper, 1977). Researchers then had to look at the basic functions of feedback to discover what was actually occurring. A series of studies by R. C. Anderson and his colleagues found that students will not use feedback as the researcher intends unless this use is controlled (Anderson et al., 1971, 1972). For instance, students will simply copy answers from feedback if allowed to do so, with little or no processing or learning of information. Kulhavy (1977) coined the term *presearch availability* to describe the ease in which learners can find a correct answer without reading the lesson material. If presearch availability is high, then students will usually copy the answer itself, bypassing the instruction and yielding little learning (Anderson & Faust, 1967). In programmed material, feedback significantly facilitates learning only if students must respond *before* seeing the feedback.

32.3.4 Feedback as Information

The data collected by Anderson and his colleagues (Anderson et al., 1971, 1972) not only provided insight into the importance of the learner's processing of the lesson material before his or her response to a question but also, perhaps more importantly, provided indication that feedback functions primarily to correct errors, not merely to "reinforce" correct answers. Numerous studies during this time supported feedback's ability to correct inaccurate information (Anderson et al., 1971, 1972; Bardwell, 1981; Barringer & Gholson, 1979; Kulhavy, 1977; Kulhavy & Anderson, 1972; Roper, 1977; Tait, Hartley & Anderson, 1973). Concurrently, cognitive psychology was coming into vogue (see 5.2), and many educational psychologists were shifting from a behavioral to a cognitive view of feedback. Such researchers became more interested in how feedback influenced primary cognitive and metacognitive processes within a learner (Briggs & Hamilton, 1964; Kulhavy, 1977). Consequently, feedback was said to serve primarily as information and not as reinforcement.

Examining feedback from an information-processing perspective (see 5.4), the learner participates in the system to correct his or her errors. Kulhavy and Stock (1989) use the concept of servocontrol theory, contrasting the two feedback systems (feedback-as-reinforcement vs. feedback-as-information) as either open loop or closed loop. Feedback acting as reinforcement would be an example of an open-loop system, in which errors are ignored because the system is not affected by input information. The operant approach does not provide error-correcting mechanisms. In contrast, the feedback-as-information position acts as a closed-loop system. Since this type of system has ways of correcting errors, errors are of primary importance. In light of this view, studies indeed emerged which made the correction and analysis of errors a major goal (Anderson et al., 1971; Birenbaum & Tatsuoka, 1987; Elley, 1966; Gilman, 1969; Kulhavy & Parsons, 1972).

It is from the information-processing perspective that most research of the past 20 years has been conducted. In a later portion of this chapter, the prevailing concerns of researchers during this period to the present will be discussed in detail. But first, it is helpful to present two current models of feedback as a framework for what follows.

32.4 TRADITIONAL MODELS OF FEEDBACK

32.4.1 A Certitude Model of Feedback

Kulhavy and Stock (1989) have proposed a model of feedback in written instruction that attempts to clarify and explain previous findings in the literature. Their model also goes beyond these basic explanations to make testable predictions undergirded by theoretical rationales. The model has been scrutinized (Bangert-Drowns et al., 1991; Dempsey, Driscoll & Swindell, 1993; Mory, 1991, 1992, 1994) and tested by current researchers (Kulhavy & Stock, 1989; Kulhavy, Stock, Hancock, Swindell & Hammrich, 1990; Kulhavy, Stock, Thornton, Winston & Behrens,

1990; Mory, 1991, 1994; Swindell, 1991, 1992; Swindell, Peterson & Greenway, 1992). It is cited as the most comprehensive treatment of feedback in facilitating learning from written instruction (Dempsey, Driscoll & Swindell, 1993), since it integrates the factors of learner confidence, feedback complexity, and error correction, and has been investigated under different modes of presentation and timing. (Note that each of these components will be discussed individually and in depth later.)

Kulhavy and Stock (1989) assert that much of the prior research on feedback is conceptually flawed. For one thing, researchers always treated responses as being absolutely right or wrong, a dichotomy that virtually ignored the complexity of learning behavior. Consider that a correct answer may be just a lucky guess, or that a wrong answer may be anything from a careless mistake to a total miscomprehension of the material. Even more puzzling were studies that resulted in initial correct answers being *changed* to *wrong* responses on a posttest, and instances in which initial errors were never corrected, in spite of what was included in the feedback (Lhyle & Kulhavy, 1987; Peeck, van den Bosch & Kreupeling 1985).

The model proposes that the feedback process is made of three cycles that constitute each instructional episode. In cycle I, the learner is presented with a task to which he or she needs to respond. In cycle II, feedback is presented based on the input from the learner in cycle I. In cycle III, the original task is presented again as a test item to which the learner again responds. Within each cycle, a common series of steps ensues. Put succinctly, each cycle involves an input from the task at hand to the learner, a comparison of the input to some sort of reference standard that then results in an output. The degree of mismatch between the perceived stimulus and reference standard results in a measure of error. The discrepancy between these two entities causes the system to exert effort to reduce the discrepancy. Dempsey and his colleagues (Dempsey, Driscoll & Swindell, 1993) have graphically represented the Kulhavy and Stock model, as seen in Figure 32-1.

During each cycle, the learner engages in mental activity aimed at processing the input and preparing an appropriate response. The model emphasizes the learner's level of certainty (termed *response certitude*) between the demands of the instructional task in cycle I and his or her prior knowledge and current understanding of that task. If this perceived match is good, the learner will select a response with a high level of certainty or confidence. The worse the match, the lower the learner's confidence level will be. In cycle II, when the learner receives feedback on his or her response, the feedback acts as verification to allow the learner to compare the response to the information contained in the feedback. When this verification is combined with the learner's initial response confidence level, a discrepancy value results. If learners receive verification of a correct answer when they are certain they were correct, there is no discrepancy. Conversely, learners who are informed that their answer was wrong when they were confident that their answer was correct will produce a high level of discrepancy.

Kulhavy has represented this discrepancy value in the equation

$$f_v \times c = d$$

where f_v is the verification component, c is the initial certitude level, and d is discrepancy. The verification component f_v is set to equal $(-1)^m$, where $m = 0$ for initial error responses and $m = 1$ for initial corrects. This is explained as having the effect of assigning an algebraic sign to d, where $[(-1)^0 = +1]$ for errors and $[(-1)^1 = -1]$ for correct responses. The response certitude variable, c, usually employing a 5-point Likert-type scale, results in a discrepancy, d, from (-5) to $(+5)$ (Kulhavy & Stock, 1989; Kulhavy, Stock, Hancock et al., 1990).

In this model, it is predicted that the level of discrepancy is a major factor influencing how much time and effort a student will naturally expend in error correction. In the case of a high-certitude correct answer (low discrepancy), the student has little need for extensive or elaborated feedback. But when students think an answer is correct but was in reality an incorrect response (high discrepancy), they will exert much effort to find out what was remiss in their thinking. In the case of low-certitude responses, regardless of whether the student's answer is correct or wrong, the student likely does not understand the information and would likely benefit from feedback that acts as new instruction. Even in Kulhavy's (1977) prior research, we see that high-confidence correct answers yield the shortest feedback study times, high-confidence errors yield the longest time, and low-confidence responses fall somewhere in between (Kulhavy, White, Topp, Chan & Adams, 1985; Kulhavy, Yekovich & Dyer, 1976, 1979). Obviously, discrepancy must mediate effects of different types of feedback in terms of their complexity or elaboration. Further, according to the model, prescriptions can be made as to how much and what type of information to include in feedback for the varying levels of discrepancy.

Kulhavy and Stock's (1989) predictions have been shown to prevail in a number of conditions, thus suggesting its robustness. In testing the model, they performed three studies relating to discrepancy and feedback times and the durability of correct answers under low discrepancy (Kulhavy & Stock, 1989). As predicted by the model, learners who thought they answered correctly when in fact they were in error (high discrepancy) spent more time studying feedback. To further test this finding, students in a second study (Kulhavy & Stock, 1989) were told that an answer was wrong when it was in fact correct, and vice versa. Because the students *thought* their answer was wrong when they had assumed they were correct (even though in actuality the answer *was* correct), they indeed spent more time studying the feedback. Again, these results support the model. And in their third study (Kulhavy & Stock, 1989), they demonstrated that the probability of a correct posttest response increased with the initial response certainty level, particularly when practice responses were also correct. In this way, feedback served to increase the durability of initially correct responses.

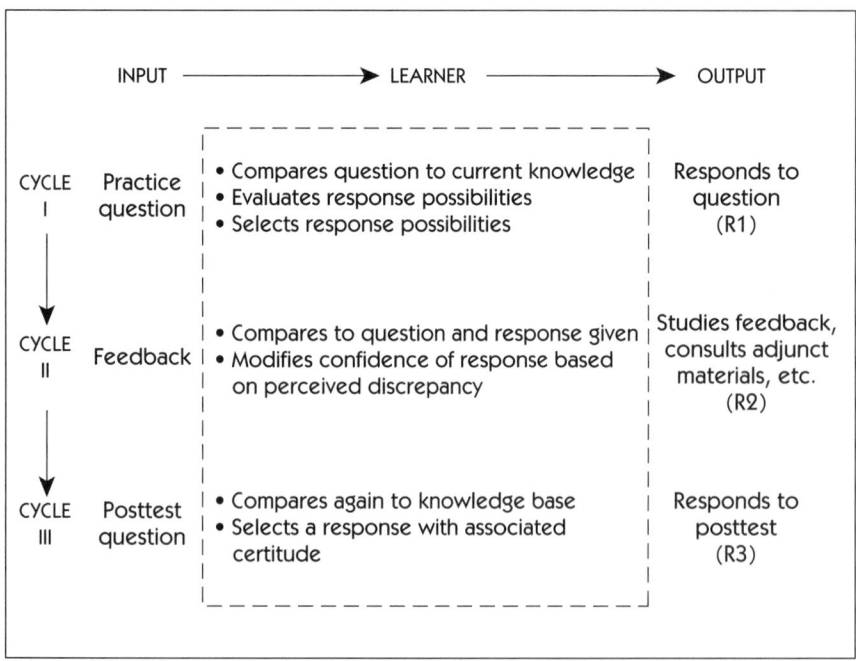

Figure 32-1.   Representation of Kulhavy and Stock's (1989) certitude model of text-based feedback. (From *Interactive Instruction and Feedback*, p. 42, by J. V. Dempsey & G. C. Sales, eds., 1993, Englewood Cliffs, NJ, Educational Technology.) Copyright 1993 by Educational Technology Publications. Reprinted with permission.

Several other studies have also supported the model. Kulhavy and his associates (Kulhavy, Stock, Hancock et al., 1990) found that in the absence of feedback, response confidence and the probability of a correct posttest response are positively related. The model suggests that feedback elaboration should be useful in correcting particularly high-certitude errors, a prediction that a study by Swindell (1991) supports. One problem in the Swindell study, however, is that feedback elaboration consisted of presenting the stem and all of the alternatives listed with the correct alternative designated by an asterisk. As will be discussed later, feedback elaborations usually provide more information than was operationalized in the Swindell (1991) study, usually informing the learner of why an answer is incorrect or re-presenting a portion of the original instruction.

The prediction that there is a direct relationship between increases in discrepancy and increased study effort is supported by another study by Swindell (1992). In this study, she also constrained the time that students were allowed to study feedback, expecting that as feedback reading time became increasingly constrained, the probability of a correct posttest response would decrease. This was generally true, but for groups receiving feedback at both slow and average presentations speeds, high certitudes resulted in lower probabilities of correct responses, and lower certitude resulted in higher probabilities. She explains this through interference theory, suggesting that in the case of errors, certitude may reflect response competition that results in an inaccurate perception of comprehension. Her study was not able to support a durability hypothesis that high-certitude response alternatives would be better remembered and carry over to a posttest, and that low-certitude judgments are more likely to be forgotten over time and are less likely to be chosen again on a posttest. No systematic relationship could be determined from her study.

Swindell and her colleagues (Swindell, Peterson et al., 1992) also have attempted to extend the model to younger learners, since the original model was developed from a research base of adult learners. Certainly the developmental stage a child is at will likely determine whether or not the child is able to assess accurately his or her own learning confidence. The results of the study suggest that fifth-graders demonstrated the pattern that high-confidence errors (maximum discrepancy) were more likely to be corrected on a posttest than were low-confidence errors. However, third-graders in the study demonstrated an opposite pattern: high-confidence errors were less likely to be corrected than those of low confidence. Further, fifth-graders were more likely to correct high-confidence errors than were the third-graders.

Dempsey and his associates (Dempsey, Driscoll & Swindell, 1993) point out that the Kulhavy and Stock (1989) model also provides a useful framework for past research results. The durability hypothesis explaining why initially correct responses are better remembered than errors, assuming that learners are more likely to make higher-confidence judgments for correct responses than for

incorrect responses, is supported by Peeck & Tillema (1979) and Peeck et al. (1985). Measures of response certitude and durability should be positively related because high confidence should represent better comprehension and will therefore be better remembered. Further, the model supports the finding that learners were not only more likely to recall initially correct responses, they were also more likely to correct initial errors if they could recall their initial response. And a recent study (Swindell, Kulhavy & Stock, 1992) found similar response patterns for durability as well.

Although the Kulhavy and Stock (1989) model of feedback is the most comprehensive to date, it does have some problematic aspects. For one thing, response certitude is a self-report measure. While response certitude judgments do provide some useful information about the cognitive status of the learner (Kulhavy et al., 1976; Metcalfe, 1986; Nelson, Leonesio, Landwehr & Narens, 1986), the nature of determining certitude has some underlying problems. The idea behind response certainty lies in the learner's metacognitive process of predicting his or her criterion performance on a task. This process can be related to "feeling of knowing" research (Butterfield, Nelson & Peck, 1988; Metcalfe, 1986; Nelson, 1988; Nelson et al., 1986). Feeling of knowing has been shown to be accurately predicted for memory recognition tasks and has been found to exist over all age groups, and the reliability of feeling of knowing has been found to be generally excellent. However, the stability of an individual's feeling-of-knowing accuracy has been found to fluctuate significantly (Nelson, 1988). In Nelson's (1988) findings, when a subject gives a higher feeling-of-knowing rating to one item over another, there is perfect retest reliability in that the same outcome occurs if the person subsequently makes feeling-of-knowing responses on those same items (Nelson et al., 1986). Conversely, individuals having a relatively high level of feeling-of-knowing accuracy at one time do not also have a relatively high level of feeling-of-knowing accuracy at another time (see Nelson, 1988). Since individual differences of feeling-of-knowing accuracy may be inconsistent, it raises the question of whether or not a response certitude estimate is valid for prescribing feedback, if certitude statements may not be a stable measure of an individual's true knowledge. Perhaps if a variable or variables could be identified that influence these changes, researchers would have more insight into the process. For example, learners' general level of self-esteem or motivation might be influencing the learners' perceptions of certainty.

Further inconsistency predominates when comparing the levels of tasks involved in feeling-of-knowing research. Learners were able to predict accurately their feeling-of-knowing in memory tasks, but overestimated their likelihood of success on problem-solving tasks or problems requiring insight (Metcalfe, 1986). Other researchers (Driscoll, 1990) have found a contrary finding, that students learning concepts tended to underestimate their feelings of answer correctness. These cases of over- and underestimation show that students generally possess an inaccurate perception of their own knowledge. Of further concern, most feedback studies using response certitude have employed verbal information tasks only; in fact, the model itself was built on a vast well of studies that involved rote memorization of verbal information. As researchers are discovering (Dempsey & Driscoll, 1994; Mory, 1991, 1994), tasks of learning intellectual skills may produce different results, especially in light of the prior findings, suggesting that subjects tend to wrongly estimate their feeling of knowing during studies using higher-level tasks. Indeed, this was the case in a recent study (Mory, 1994) that used response certitude estimates as part of the feedback cycle for both verbal information and concept-learning tasks. Students tended to have a high level of certitude for concept questions, regardless of actual answer correctness. Thus, low-certitude feedback designed to give the most information was not encountered when it was truly needed. Learners simply were not able to give accurate assessments of their own abilities to classify a particular concept.

Another issue that regards the application of response certitude estimates within an instructional situation is that of efficiency. Corrective efficiency results from taking the total number of correct answers on a posttest and dividing it by the amount of time spent during an instructional task. Kulhavy and his associates (1985) examined efficiency using two separate measures. One measure isolated the amount of time spent reading the instruction, thus accounting for the efficiency of only the instruction or "text" portion of the lesson. When this measure was tested across varying feedback groups, there were no significant differences found. A second measure used was the amount of time spent just in studying the feedback, since less complex forms of feedback are usually more time efficient in terms of what Kulhavy and his colleagues (1985) call "posttest yield per unit of study time invested" (p. 289). The amount of time a learner spends on feedback is affected by two things: (1) the amount of information included in the feedback message (load) and (2) response certitude levels. Results from the study confirmed that the less-complex forms of feedback were more time efficient, and also that efficiency rose as a function of increases in confidence values. Considering that high-confidence responses should reflect an understanding of subject matter and content, the learner would be more likely to make efficient use of the feedback presented (Kulhavy et al., 1985).

One should note that the Kulhavy study (Kulhavy et al., 1985) examined efficiency in terms of the feedback portion of a lesson only. But the process of giving a response confidence rating for each question could possibly add considerable time and interference to the overall lesson for the student. Mory (1991, 1994) investigated adaptive feedback that was based on levels of discrepancy and prescriptions of the model. The study supports that feedback efficiency can be increased by varying the amount of feedback information according to levels of discrepancy; however, the added time for response certitude evaluations resulted in lower overall lesson efficiency. Further, when a typical nonadaptive feedback sequence was compared with

an adaptive one that employed response certitude as part of the cycle, adaptive feedback was significantly less efficient than traditional feedback in terms of overall lesson efficiency (Mory, 1994).

And lastly, one might question the generality of a model that was built around experimental testing environments and usually limited to the use of multiple-choice questions (see Kulik & Kulik, 1988). Many of the studies present brief paragraphs of text information, followed by multiple-choice questions based on the preceding paragraph (Chanond, 1988; Kulhavy et al., 1976, 1979; Lhyle & Kulhavy, 1987). Many of these studies used generic topics with limited relevance to current topics being studied by learners within the experimental groups. And to further confound matters, in several studies students were not given instruction at all, but questions and feedback alone served as "instruction" (Anderson et al., 1971, 1972; Kulhavy & Anderson, 1972; Kulhavy & Stock, 1989; Swindell, 1991). In fact, recent findings (Clariana, Ross & Morrison, 1991) support the notion that feedback effects tend to be stronger in conditions where materials involve no text but use questions and feedback only, than in conditions in which text was used before questions and feedback. This leads to the question of whether or not the model will be supported in "real-world" instructional environments. Researchers (Chanond, 1988; Dempsey, Driscoll & Litchfield, 1993; Mory, 1991, 1992, 1994; Peterson & Swindell, 1991) are beginning to recommend that the model be examined under more typical classroom learning situations.

Researchers interested in exploring the Kulhavy and Stock (1989) model further should consider some of the aforementioned issues, both supportive and problematic. Dempsey, Driscoll, and Swindell (1993) point out that the model has made more precise predictions for high-confidences responses than for low-confidence responses, and that midrange levels of confidence have no such predictions. This means that the entire range of metacognitive judgments should be examined. Further, if response confidence could be linked to a variable other than self-report, the adaptation of feedback might more readily fit the needs of the learner. For example, Dempsey and others (Dempsey, 1988; Dempsey, Driscoll & Litchfield, 1993) used levels of fine and gross discrimination error during a concept-learning task to adapt feedback to the needs of learners.

32.4.2 A Five-Stage Model of Mindfulness

Bangert-Drowns and his associates (1991) organize the findings of previous researchers' investigations of text-based feedback into a five-stage model, describing the state of the learner as he or she is going through a feedback cycle. The model emphasizes the construct of mindfulness (Salomon & Globerson, 1987), described as "a reflective process in which the learner explores situational cues and underlying meanings relevant to the task involved" (Dempsey, Driscoll & Swindell, 1993, p. 38). They describe both behavioral and cognitive operations that occur in learning. To direct behavior, a learner needs to be able to monitor physical changes brought about by the behavior. Learners change cognitive operations and, consequently, activity by adapting it to new information and matching it with his or her own expectations about performance (Bangert-Drowns et al., 1991). These researchers emphasize that:

> . . . any theory that depicts learning as a process of mutual influence between learners and their environments must involve feedback implicitly or explicitly because, without feedback, mutual influence is by definition impossible. Hence, the feedback construct appears often as an essential element of theories of learning and instruction (p. 214).

The five stages include (1) the learner's initial state, (2) what search and retrieval strategies are activated, (3) the learner's response, (4) the learner's evaluation of the response, and (5) adjustments the learner makes. A graphic representation of the model by Dempsey and colleagues may be viewed in Figure 32-2.

This model emphasizes the construct of mindfulness, in which activities are exactly the opposite of automatic, over-learned responses. Feedback can promote learning if it is received mindfully. However, it also can inhibit learning if it encourages mindlessness, as when the feedback message is made available before learners begin their memory search or if the instruction is too easy or redundant. The inhibition of learning effect relates to research conducted on processes that "kill" learning (Clark, Aster & Hession, 1987) and presearch availability (Anderson et al., 1971, 1972; Kulhavy, 1977).

These researchers (Bangert-Drowns et al., 1991) examined 40 studies using meta-analytic procedures looking at such variables as type of feedback, timing of feedback, error rates, among others, in terms of their various effect sizes. They report generally weak effects of feedback on achievement. Also, feedback indicating only whether an answer was correct or wrong resulted in lower effect sizes than feedback containing the correct answer. Further, using a pretest within a study significantly lowered effect sizes, as did uncontrolled presearch availability of answers.

Dempsey and his colleagues (Dempsey, Driscoll & Swindell, 1993) point out that the emphasis on mindfulness is an important framework for future research involving text-based feedback. While the studies examined by the Bangert-Drowns et al. (1991) meta-analysis "may be too simple or specific" (Bangert-Drowns et al., 1991, p. 234), it leads us to believe that future studies should examine feedback in more complex environments that involve higher learning outcomes.

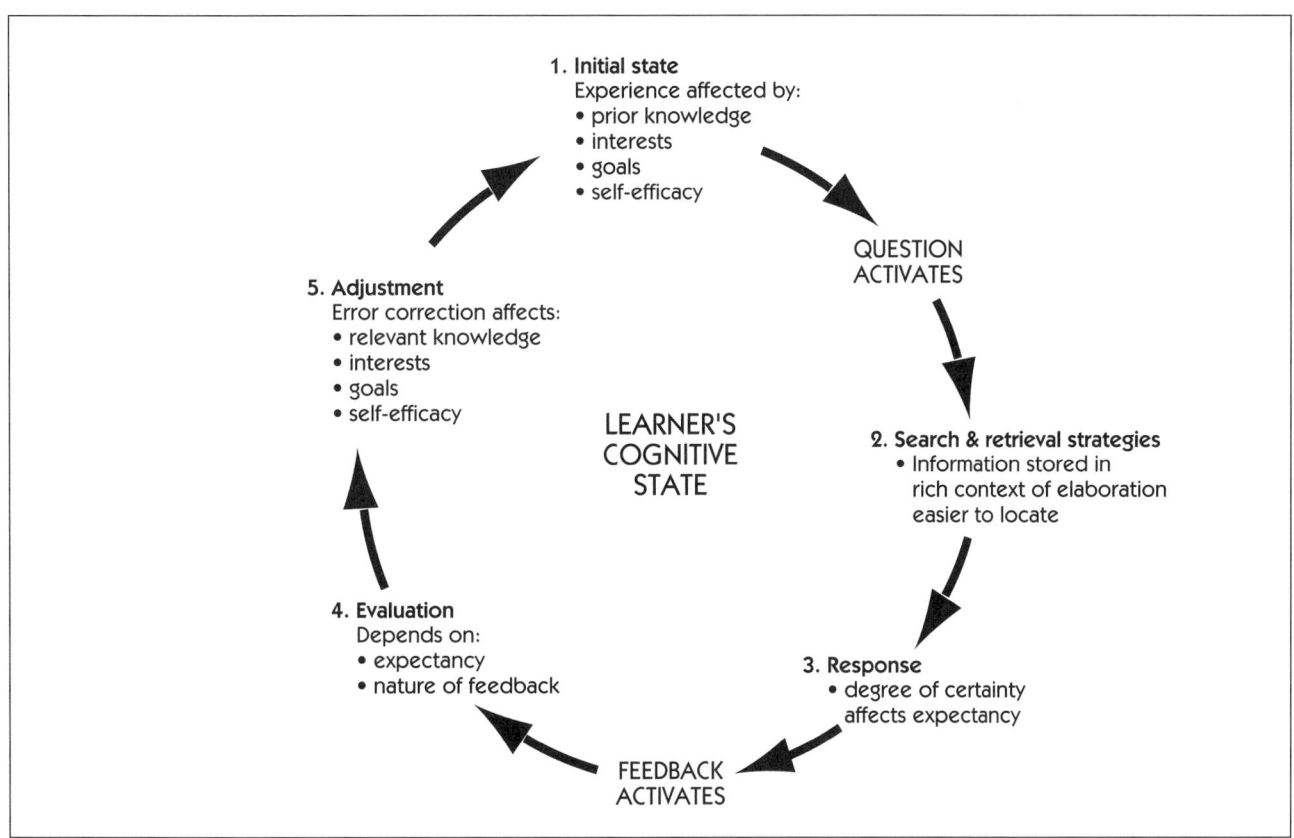

Figure 32-2. The state of the learner receiving feedback, based on Bangert-Drowns et al., 1991. (From Dempsey, Driscoll & Swindell, 1993.) (From *Interactive Instruction and Feedback*, p. 40, by J. V. Dempsey & G. C. Sales, eds., 1993, Englewood Cliffs, NJ: Educational Technology.) Copyright 1993 by Educational Technology Publications. Reprinted with permission.

32.5 FEEDBACK RESEARCH VARIABLES OF INTEREST

32.5.1 Information Content and Load

32.5.1.1. Complexity. Feedback complexity refers to how much and what information should be included in the feedback messages. There is an abundance of literature concerning feedback complexity. Dempsey, Driscoll, and Swindell (1993) have organized the major variables of interest in most corrective feedback studies as follows:

1. *No feedback* means the learner is presented a question and is required to respond, but no indication is provided as to the correctness of the learner's response.
2. *Simple verification feedback or knowledge of results (KR)* informs the learner of a correct or incorrect response.
3. *Correct response feedback or knowledge or correct response (KCR)* informs the learner what the correct response should be.
4. *Elaborated feedback* provides an explanation for why the learner's response is correct or incorrect or allows the learner to review part of the instruction.
5. *Try-again feedback* informs the learner of an incorrect response and allows the learner one or more additional attempts to try again (from Dempsey, Driscoll & Swindell, 1993, p. 25).

If feedback is to serve a corrective function, even the simplest feedback should verify whether or not the student's answer is right or wrong. This verification is usually combined with an elaboration component in order to provide more information to the learner. Studies that have examined the type and amount of information in feedback have not yielded very consistent results (Kulhavy, 1977; Schimmel, 1988).

What types of elaborative information have been used along with the verification component in the feedback message? In a review of the feedback literature, Kulhavy and Stock (1989) suggest that there are basically three possible elaboration types to employ during feedback. They categorize them as: (1) *task-specific*, which is drawn from the initial task demand or initial question (e.g., restatement of the correct answer); (2) *instruction-based*, which contains information derived from the specific lesson material, but not directly from the actual question completed before the feedback (e.g., explanation of why an answer is correct, based on the original instruction, or a display of the original instructional text that contains the correct answer); and (3) *extra-instructional*, which is the addition of information from outside the immediate lesson environment (e.g., new information to clarify meaning). The majority of elaboration studies fall within the task-specific and instruction-based types.

First, consider task-specific types of feedback, where the feedback is a restatement of the correct answer. Usually studies that contain this type of feedback have examined

changes in the amount of information, sometimes referred to as *load*. A study by Phye (1979) examined three types of feedback for multiple-choice questions. One contained the question stem and only the correct alternative; another contained the stem and designated correct answer with incorrect alternatives from the question; and a third contained the stem with designated correct answer with the two incorrect alternatives from the question plus two previously unseen incorrect alternatives. No differential effect was produced by type of feedback on the posttest. However, in a second experiment in the study, immediate feedback in the form of only the correct answer plus an answer sheet from the practice was superior to other forms of feedback. Thus, the type of feedback thought to provide the least information produced the greatest improvement on the posttest. Phye suggests a threshold hypothesis to account for this unexpected finding, positing that when more than sufficient information needed to correct or confirm an answer is provided to the student, it does not have a facilitative effect on his ability to use the feedback.

Some studies that have added increases of task information to feedback have actually produced lower scores on a posttest. Phye and his associates (Phye, Gugliamella & Sola, 1976) used feedback very similar to that used in the Phye (1979) study, adding either the correct answer only, the initial item plus all original distracters, or the correct alternative and three extra-list distracters. Feedback in the form of correct answer only was superior to the other types that contained more information. This would imply that the feedback with more load contained considerable distracting information in the form of incorrect alternatives.

Another similar finding was provided by Sassenrath and Yonge (1969) in providing two types of feedback cues: with or without the stem of the question, and with or without correct plus wrong alternative answers. Students who received information feedback without the stem of the question performed better than those who received information feedback with the question stem. This refutes the results of a previous study they completed (Sassenrath & Yonge, 1968), in which students receiving the stem of the question and the alternatives performed better on a retention test than those only receiving the alternatives. The researchers explain this discrepancy by the fact that the earlier (1968) study gave feedback after the students had responded to the entire list of questions, so that the question stem conveyed valuable information in addition to the alternatives. But in the second study (1969), feedback was presented after each item response, and it is suggested that the stem was distracting when used in feedback given within such a short time lapse after a response.

Wentling (1973) compared the effects of (1) partial feedback that contained knowledge of results, to (2) total feedback that contained knowledge of correct answer and required a re-response, or (3) no feedback at all. The partial feedback treatment exceeded the other two treatments on immediate achievement scores, and, surprisingly, the total feedback treatment was least effective in terms of immediate achievement.

Another study (Hanna, 1976) comparing partial feedback, total feedback, and no feedback found that partial feedback produced highest scores for high-ability students, and total feedback produced the highest scores for lower-ability students. There were no differential effects between partial and total feedback for middle-ability students, but both of these types of feedback were superior to no feedback.

Three studies do show positive results for task-specific item elaborations. Roper (1977) provided students with either no feedback, yes-no verification, or an opportunity to restudy the correct answer. Scores on the posttest increased as more information was added to the feedback. There was also evidence that the correction of errors and not just reinforcement of responses was the major effect of feedback. Also, Winston and Kulhavy (cited in Kulhavy & Stock, 1989) found that using feedback consisting of a multiple-choice item stem plus the correct response and all of the original distracter alternatives was more effective at correcting errors than when using feedback containing the stem plus only the correct alternative. And finally, an early study (Travers, van Wagenen, Haygood & McCormick, 1964) gave an interesting variation of task-specific feedback for corrects and wrongs. One group received verification for both corrects and wrongs; a second group received verification only for wrongs and nothing for corrects; a third group received verification only for corrects and verification plus the correct answer for wrongs; and a fourth group received nothing for corrects and verification plus the correct answer for wrongs. A relationship between information content of the feedback condition and extent of learning was found to exist. Highest criterion test performance occurred under the last two feedback conditions—the ones that were the most information laden. The second feedback condition of merely saying "That's wrong" was significantly inferior to all other conditions studied.

An even more inconsistent pattern of results is found in studies that have used instruction-based elaborations, in which information in the feedback is taken from the instruction itself. The information used in this type of feedback has been quite diverse, including explanations of the correct answer (Gilman, 1969), supplying solution rules (Birenbaum & Tatsuoka, 1987; Lee, 1985; J. Merrill, 1987) and re-presenting original instruction (Peeck, 1979).

Gilman (1969) employed "additive" feedback, comparing (1) no feedback, to (2) feedback of "correct" or "wrong," (3) feedback of correct response choice, (4) feedback appropriate to the student's response, or (5) a combination of (2), (3), and (4). The means of the groups that had guidance toward the correct answer [groups (3), (4), and (5)] performed better than the groups who had to search for the correct answer. Gilman points out that providing learners with a statement of which response was correct or with a statement of why the correct response is correct may be of more value than merely telling the learner "correct" or

"wrong." In terms of error correction, knowledge-of-results feedback resulted in the least number of corrected errors. In terms of retention rates, Gilman suggests that extensive information in feedback messages show advantages in retention rates.

Merrill employed both corrective feedback and attribute isolation feedback in his 1987 study of feedback to aid concept acquisition. Corrective feedback informed the learners of the correctness or incorrectness of their answers and also provided the full text of the correct answer when a student's answer was wrong. The full text consisted of a single word, phrase, or short paragraph. Attribution isolation feedback also informed the learners of the correctness of their responses, but then included the attributes of the concepts being studied. Attribution isolation is used to help focus attention on the variable attributes of a concept (M. Merrill & R. Tennyson, 1977). No main effects for feedback form were found, possibly due to the attribute isolation feedback being presented after two incorrect responses and, consequently, not being encountered enough times in the lesson to make a difference.

Another study (Lee, 1985) that provided solution rules in its feedback used either (1) "right/wrong" feedback only, (2) "right/wrong" plus the correct answer after an error, or (3) "right/wrong" plus the rule restated and the correct answer after an error. No significant main effects were found in the feedback treatments.

One unique approach using feedback solution rules was devised by Tatsuoka and her colleagues (cited in Kulhavy & Stock, 1989). The seriousness of instructional errors were analyzed from a pretest in order to assess the effect of additive feedback elaborations on a later criterion measure. Students received feedback as either (1) "OK/No" verification, (2) the correct answer to the problem, or (3) a statement of correct and incorrect rules for solving the problem. They found that for nonserious errors, more feedback elaborations result in a greater probability of these errors being corrected. But for serious errors, correction was relatively unaffected by the amount of elaboration. This finding suggests that more complex errors or misunderstandings are not as likely to be corrected by typical feedback treatments.

Schloss and his colleagues (P. J. Schloss, Sindelar, Cartwright & C. N. Schloss, 1987) presented either instructions to try again or a re-presentation of the instruction after student errors in computer-assisted instructional modules to test if error correction procedures would interact with question type, such that higher-cognitive questions with feedback loops and factual questions with re-presentation of questions would yield maximum results. They concluded that when factual questions are used in CAI modules, allowing a student to attempt a second answer after an error results in more learning than re-presenting the part of the instruction in which the answer appears.

Sassenrath and Garverick (1965) compared more traditional classroom types of feedback: looking up wrong answers in the textbook to having answers discussed by the instructor or checking over answers from correct ones written on the board. These three feedback groups did perform significantly better on a retention test than a no-feedback control group. The discussion group also performed better than the groups that looked up answers in the textbook.

Students in a different study (Peeck, 1979) were either given feedback sheets identical to immediate test sheets, with the correct alternatives circled or were given both the original text and the feedback sheets with correct alternatives circled. Also, to test if the effectiveness of different forms of feedback was influenced by the kind of test question presented, both fact and inference multiple-choice questions were used. There was little difference in scores between the two feedback conditions. More inference questions were answered correctly when subjects could refer to the original text during the feedback. But for fact questions, subjects were more successful on a delayed test when the text was absent during the feedback.

Similarly, two types of questions (factual and application) and two types of feedback (correct-answer feedback, self-correction feedback, and no feedback control) were employed in a study by Andre and Thieman (1988). Both types of feedback facilitated performance on the same concept questions but did not facilitate the application to new examples. This suggests that such feedback may be helpful in tasks where the students memorize an answer but be ineffective for tasks that require application to new cases.

Even large-scale additions to the feedback have failed to influence posttest performance, as was the case for Kulhavy and his colleagues (Kulhavy et al., 1985). Four types of feedback were developed additively. Four components could be used in the feedback: (1) test item stem and the correct alternative; (2) incorrect response alternatives; (3) four sentences, each explaining why one of the error choices was incorrect; and (4) the relevant section of the passage in which the correct answer was identified. One group received only component number (1); a second group received components (1) and (2); a third group components (1), (2), and (3); and a fourth group all four components. The principle was that increases in the feedback complexity are closely tied to corresponding increases in the amount of information available to the learner. Results showed that more complex versions of feedback had a small effect on error correction, with the least complex feedback correcting a significantly greater portion of errors than the more complex third feedback group.

In a CAI drill-and-practice program using a concept-learning task, it was indicated that immediate extended feedback following both correct and incorrect responses is superior to minimal feedback (Waldrop, Justen & Adams, 1986). In the first of three treatment conditions, subjects received only minimal feedback of "correct" or "incorrect." In a second treatment condition, subjects received minimal feedback ("that's correct") if a response was correct, but received minimal feedback ("that's incorrect") for three trials if a response was wrong. After the third trial, if a response was still incorrect, students were provided extend-

ed feedback relating the example given to the definition of the type of consequence involved in that example. The third treatment condition provided a detailed explanation of the correct answer following both correct and incorrect responses. The results of this study agrees with a suggestion made by Gilman (1969), that providing the student with a statement of which response was correct after errors and providing reasons for correctness of a correct response are essential.

Noonan (1984) examined the presence or position of knowledge of results (KR), knowledge of correct response (KCR), and elaborated and try-again feedback. In this study, knowledge of results with an explanation and a second attempt was no less effective than giving KCR and moving on or giving KCR and another second attempt. In support of error analysis, Noonan suggests that explanations should depend more on the type of error made by the learner and not merely on the correct answer.

Varying types and amounts of information in feedback given after specific combinations of answer correctness and response certitude in a CAI lesson was used by Chanond (1988). If a subject's answer was correct, and he or she was confident of the answer, the subject received knowledge of result feedback. If a subject's answer was correct, but he was not confident of his answer, he received knowledge of result and a statement of why the response was correct. If a subject's answer was incorrect, but she was confident of her answer, she received knowledge of result, a statement of why the response was incorrect, knowledge of correct response, and a statement of why the correct answer was correct. If a subject's answer was incorrect, and he was not confident of his answer, he received knowledge of result, knowledge of correct response, and a statement of why the correct answer was correct.

Subjects were given both an immediate and delayed posttest at the end of the lesson. Results indicated that for immediate retention of verbal information in terms of overall correct responses, the feedback had a significant effect. No significant effect was found for delayed retention, however. Further analyses indicated that, regardless of the level of confidence for the response, feedback following incorrect responses had a significant effect on both immediate and delayed retention.

The use of extra-instructional feedback types has been studied very little (Kulhavy & Stock, 1989). However, adaptive feedback that additively used all three types—task-specific, instruction-based, and extra-instructional feedback—was implemented by Mory (1991) and involved two levels of learning tasks: verbal information and concepts. Varying combinations of task-specific, instruction-based, and extra-instructional feedback were prescribed according to a combined assessment of answer correctness and response certitude level for an adaptive feedback group. When compared to nonadaptive feedback that utilized task-specific and instruction-based elaborations only, there were no significant differences in posttest performance for either verbal information or concept tasks.

To summarize the feedback elaboration literature, only half the studies utilizing task-specific feedback produced any significant improvements in learning. An even greater inconsistency is found in studies using information-based feedback, perhaps partially due to the diverse types of information manipulations tried. Such variance has made it difficult to prescribe any set rule for the use of either type of elaborations (Kulhavy & Stock, 1989). Extra-instructional feedback types have not been researched enough to draw conclusions as to their effectiveness on learning.

32.5.2 Timing of Feedback

Recall from the early reports of feedback research that the idea of feedback as reinforcement—a Skinnerian view—would suggest that feedback should follow a response as closely in time as possible in order to be most effective (see 2.2.1.3.2). Skinner himself is quoted as saying, ". . . the lapse of only a few seconds between response and reinforcement destroys most of the effect" (cited in Kulhavy & Wager, 1993, p. 13). But when researchers began comparing the effects of immediate versus delayed feedback, discrepancies from such an operant approach were soon discovered. Kulhavy (1977) reports that studies showed repeatedly that delaying the presentation of feedback for a day or more results in significant increases in student retention on posttest scores (Sassenrath & Yonge, 1968, 1969; Sturges, 1969, 1972). This phenomenon was termed the Delay-Retention Effect (DRE) (Brackbill, Bravos & Starr, 1962; Brackbill & Kappy, 1962) and was found to occur predominantly in studies concerned with multiple-choice testing. The explanation for the DRE is thought to lie in the proactive interference from initial error responses upon the acquisition of correct answers given via immediate feedback. That is, when a learner is presented immediate feedback showing the correct response after an error, his or her error response interferes with the correction of the response due to the immediacy of the feedback. Thus delayed feedback eliminates this type of interference, and the learner is better able to remember the correct response. Several studies support this hypothesis: interference-perseveration hypothesis, explaining the DRE through the assumption that initial errors tend to be forgotten over time (Bardwell, 1981; Kulhavy & Anderson, 1972; Kulik & Kulik, 1988; Sassenrath, 1975; Surber & Anderson, 1975). But others have found that either the delay did not make a difference (Peeck et al., 1985; Phye et al., 1976), that initial responses were not forgotten (Peeck & Tillema, 1979), or that the DRE was not present when subjects were required to re-respond (Phye & Andre, 1989).

In a 1988 meta-analysis conducted by Kulik and Kulik, the issue of immediate versus delayed feedback was examined more thoroughly. In analyzing the available research on the timing of feedback, they found that studies using actual classroom quizzes and materials usually found that immediate feedback was more effective than delayed feed-

back. Apparently the studies that supported the effects of delayed feedback over immediate feedback for improving retention of material were conducted using contrived, experimental learning situations, such as list learning. These findings challenge both the use of delayed feedback in more practical learning environments and the explanations afforded by the interference-perseveration hypothesis in "real-world" learning situations. Dempsey, Driscoll, and Swindell (1993) suggest that delaying feedback in many instructional contexts "is tantamount to withholding information from the learner that the learner can use" (p. 24). And a pragmatic suggestion postulated by Tosti (1978) and Keller (1983) is to present feedback containing pertinent information from the learner's prior performance right before the next learning trial, when the learner would be able to use the information to improve his or her subsequent learning. As Dempsey and his associates (Dempsey, Driscoll & Swindell, 1993) point out, this amounts to providing feedback at what is commonly referred to as "the teachable moment" (p. 24). An interesting variation involving a delay of feedback was designed by Richards (1989) using a declarative knowledge task involving labels and facts. In this case, feedback was more effective when delayed temporarily and when the learner was required to respond covertly a second time to the question—that is, a covert second try, *prior* to feedback.

In a 1989 study conducted to examine the timing of feedback with respect to the acquisition of motor skills, shorter feedback times improved acquisition and performance while feedback was present, but delayed feedback resulted in improved subsequent performance once feedback had been withdrawn (Schmidt, Young, Swinnen & Shapiro, 1989). They explain these findings as what is termed the *guidance hypothesis,* which suggests that during the initial stages of skill acquisition, immediate feedback guides the learner and results in superior initial performance. But this guidance can lead to dependence on the feedback and obscure the need to learn the secondary skills (such as detection and self-correction) necessary to perform the task without feedback (Schmidt et al., 1989).

The guidance hypothesis is supported by a previous study that examined the effects of immediate versus delayed feedback within the context of an adventure game on subsequent performance (Lewis & Anderson, 1985). Subjects that received immediate feedback were more likely to select appropriate operators, but those that received delayed feedback were better able to detect errors. But a differing trend was found by Anderson, Conrad, and Corbett (1989) when assessing the effects of immediate and delayed feedback within the context of the GRAPES LISP Tutor. Subjects receiving immediate feedback moved through the material more quickly than did those subjects receiving delayed feedback, but there was no significant difference in test performance. A more recent study by Schooler and Anderson (1990) found that when students were acquiring LISP skills, subjects receiving immediate feedback went through the training material in 40% less time than those receiving delayed feedback, yet with no detrimental effects on learning. In a second experiment during the same study, subjects were using an improved LISP editor and less supportive testing conditions. During this trial, subjects in the immediate feedback group completed the problems 18% faster than those in the delayed feedback group, but they were slower on the test problems and made twice as many errors. A final experiment, a partial replication of the first two experiments, indicated that delayed feedback was an advantage in terms of errors, time on task, and the percentage of errors that subjects self-corrected. They suggest that immediate feedback competes for working-memory resources, forcing out necessary information for operator compilation—a finding that would support the interference-perseveration hypothesis mentioned above. In contrast, delay feedback in the study fostered the development of secondary skills such as error detection and self-correction (Schooler & Anderson, 1990).

In terms of what to recommend in terms of immediate versus delayed feedback, as several researchers concur (Dempsey, Driscoll & Swindell, 1993; Kulhavy, 1977; Kulik & Kulik, 1988), in most learning situations delayed feedback appears to function to hinder the acquisition of needed information. Only under very special experimental situations has the use of delayed feedback helped learning. As Kulik and Kulik (1988) point out,

> The experimental paradigms that show superiority of delayed feedback are very similar to paradigms used for testing effects of massed versus distributed practice. When experiments deviate from this paradigm, they show results similar to those in applied studies. In such experiments, immediate feedback produces a better effect than delayed feedback does (p. 94).

One only has to look at the myriad of definitions that past researchers have used in each of the areas of immediate and delayed feedback to understand why this area of study has been muddied throughout the research. Dempsey and Wager (1988) have summarized the types of immediate and delayed feedback as shown in Figure 32-3.

Some researchers suggest that as newer technologies offer more instructional delivery options and a wider variety of modalities through which to deliver feedback, these issues will become even more complex (Dempsey, Driscoll & Swindell, 1993). Perhaps as delivery options increase, researchers will be better able to determine when delayed feedback might aid learners.

32.5.3 Error Analyses

In the early 1930s, Thorndike demonstrated that errors made in rote learning tasks tend to persist. By the year 1958, Skinner argued that errors made within programmed instruction will tend to persist as well. Elley (1966) tested the hypothesis that errors play different roles in rote and meaningful learning tasks. Results supported the hypothesis, showing that fewer errors were associated with better reten-

---

Immediate feedback is informative corrective feedback given to a learner or examinee as quickly as the computer's hardware and software will allow during instruction or testing.

Types of immediate feedback are:
1. item-by-item
2. learner-controlled
3. logical content break
4. end-of-module (end of session)
5. break by learner
6. time-controlled (end of session)

Delayed feedback is informative, corrective feedback given to a learner or examinee after a specified programming delay interval during instruction or testing.

Types of delayed feedback are:
1. item-by-item
2. logical content break
3. less than 1 hour (end of session)
4. 1–24 hours (end of session)
5. 1–7 days (end of session)
6. extended delay (end of session)
7. before next session

Figure 32-3. Immediate and delayed feedback with CBI: definitions and categories. (From Dempsey & Wager, 1988.)

---

tion in rote tasks but not in meaningful types of learning. Both experiments supported the hypothesis that errors are undesirable in rote learning and tend to be repeated even with immediate feedback. However, when learners were given meaningful problems, incidence of errors was unrelated to ultimate performance.

The current view considers an error to be a valuable opportunity to clarify misunderstanding in the learner. Thus, errors play an important role in feedback studies today. The belief that feedback's main function lies in correcting errors makes error analyses more critical for gaining insight into the corrective process.

Kulhavy and Parsons (1972) examined errors that are never corrected, or that "perseverate" to a posttest. They suggest that error perseveration is a function of at least three factors: (1) the rated meaningfulness of the items used, (2) the amount of incorrect material available during learning, and (3) the response mode required of the learner. In their study, students were forced to respond incorrectly to see if these errors would be repeated on a posttest. But their analyses revealed that forcing a student to make an error does not automatically result in the transference of that error to the posttest.

Patterns of pretest-posttest responses were introduced in a limited way by Phye and his colleagues (Phye et al., 1976). This work was later extended to include three error types (Peeck & Tillema, 1979; Phye, 1979). An error analysis model was developed independently by Peeck and Tillema (1979) and Phye (1979), and this model has been used by several researchers (Peeck, 1979; Phye & Andre, 1989; Phye & Bender, 1989). Their research has served to help further understand how feedback is being used by learners in most experimental settings.

Whenever informative feedback is used in a pretest-feedback-posttest design, five possible outcomes for pretest-posttest response sequences exist. First, when feedback has a *confirmatory* function, the feedback serves to confirm a correct answer at pretest (a combination sequence of Correct → Correct). Secondly, when feedback has a *corrective* function, it serves to correct an error made on the pretest (a sequence combination of Wrong → Correct). And finally, feedback can have *no* function, as in cases when errors result on the posttest (Phye & Bender, 1989).

The three error types where feedback is considered nonfunctional are described as follows. One type is a *same* error and is perseverative in nature. A same error occurs when an initial incorrect response reoccurs on the posttest, regardless of any correct answer feedback that was provided. A second type of error is a *different* error, in which an item is missed on both the pretest and posttest, but was not the same error across trials. That is, the posttest error was a different error than the pretest error. Perhaps insufficient information was encoded during feedback, so that on the posttest the learner remembers that his or her initial response was wrong, but he or she does not remember information well enough to respond correctly. The final type of error is a *new* error, in which an item was initially correct on the pretest or practice but for some reason was changed to a wrong answer, or new error, on the posttest. Perhaps in this instance, the initial response was a lucky guess, feedback was basically ignored, and a new error resulted on the test.

Thus, the five possible combinations of pretest → posttest responses are: (1) Correct → Correct, (2) Wrong → Correct, (3) Wrong → Same wrong, (4) Wrong → Different wrong, and (5) Correct → New wrong (see Fig. 32-4).

When put into a response pattern profile in terms of percentage of occurrence, a more exhaustive account of test performance is facilitated (Peeck et al., 1985). Response pattern profiles have been used for multiple-choice formats (Peeck, 1979; Phye, 1979). Some researchers (Peeck et al., 1985) argue that in order to interpret the cognitive processes involved in such sequences, it is important to determine to what extent learners remember their initial responses after the pretest. Peeck et al. (1985) included "guess questions" that could not be answered from the text and "factual questions" that could be answered from the text. The most important finding was that learners remembered their initial responses in the wrong-changed-to-correct category. This indicates that retention of initial responses did not prevent subjects from learning the correct answer from feedback, casting serious doubt, incidentally, on the assumption that subjects tend to forget their responses on the initial task after a delay and that error tendencies interfere with learning the correct answers from feedback—an assumption that was a major component of the interference-perseveration

interpretation of the delayed-retention effect studies (Kulhavy & R. C. Anderson, 1972). Data also indicated that when subjects changed their initial response after feedback (correct to a new wrong, wrong to correct, and wrong to a different wrong), the highest identification scores were obtained in the category of corrected errors (wrong to correct).

The construct validity of error analysis was addressed by Phye and Bender (1989) and demonstrated when Peeck et al. (1985) examined pooled data from four previous experiments (cited in Peeck et al., 1985). Proportional frequencies for the three error types when averaged across the four studies were .10 for same errors, .06 for different errors, and .05 for new errors. These averages were quite similar when compared to results of Phye and Bender (1989) in which same errors equaled .08, different errors equaled .05, and new errors equaled .04. These data contribute to the construct validity of the error analysis model and suggest its value when combined with correct response and conditional probability data to assess feedback effectiveness.

Further research from an information-processing perspective should address feedback effectiveness and efficiency by considering not only correct responses but also an analysis of processing errors (Phye & Bender,

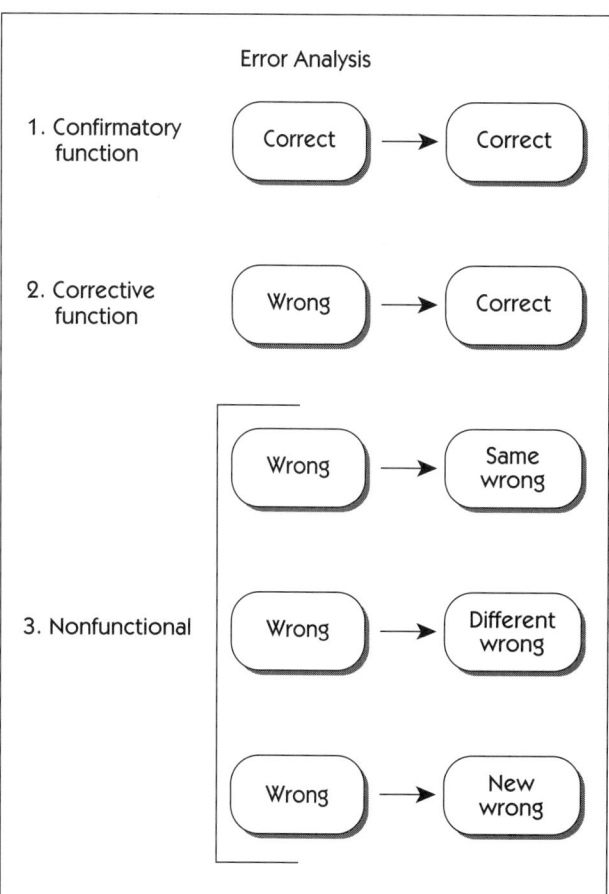

Figure 32-4. Five response pattern combinations, based on Phye and Bender response pattern analysis (1989).

1989). Error data, when used with correct response data and conditional probability data, "provides a multivariate account of feedback utilization by the learner in a learning situation involving practice" (p. 109).

Another way of analyzing errors is to classify them in some way that is related to the specific learning outcome involved. In rule-using tasks, an example would be the classification of errors as "serious" or "nonserious," as was done in an analysis developed by Tatsuoka (see Birenbaum & Tatsuoka, 1987). The measure of seriousness of error types indicated to what extent a wrong rule deviates from the right rule. Using an "error vector" system to analyze signed-number problems, error codes were developed based on the absolute number operation and the sign operation involved in solving problems. Students' response patterns to test items were then classified into three categories: serious errors, nonserious errors, and correct answers.

In concept learning, errors are categorized according to three kinds of concept classification errors: overgeneralization, undergeneralization, and misconception (cited in R. D. Tennyson & Cocchiarella, 1986). When students are learning to classify a member of a concept class, they must make discriminations between examples and nonexamples of the concept. Certain nonexamples may be quite difficult to discriminate from a given concept example (termed a *close-in* nonexample), and others may be easy to discriminate from an example (termed a *far-out* nonexample) (Dempsey, 1988). When a learner is consistently making a particular overgeneralization error of accepting nonexamples, it is likely that he is having a problem with fine discrimination of the concept. Fine discrimination errors occur when close-in nonexamples are classified by the learner as an example of a concept. But if the student is regularly classifying a far-out nonexample as a true example, he may be undergeneralizing by rejecting the examples, resulting in an error of gross discrimination. In general, fine discrimination errors result from classification problems on close-in nonexamples, whereas gross discrimination errors result from a student's having classification problems on far-out nonexamples. Since close-in nonexamples are more difficult to discriminate from examples than are far-out nonexamples, more close-in errors (or fine discrimination errors) should be expected to occur. This indeed was the case in a study by Dempsey (1988). In the same study, it was found that learners who made fewer fine discrimination errors during instruction scored significantly higher on a retention test. In fact, 4 out of 10 errors made during the instruction were those that were predetermined as fine discrimination errors. These findings encourage the analysis of close-in and far-out nonexamples associated with fine and gross discrimination errors when employing concepts-learning tasks.

Finally, Meyer (1986) identifies four errors reflected in a review of research on teachers' correction of students that include (1) lack-of-information errors, (2) motor errors, (3) confusions, and (4) rule application errors. Lack-of-information errors result when student's mistakes are caused by

missing knowledge. Motor errors result when a student knows the information but cannot express it. Confusions occur when students fail to discriminate correctly between concepts or ideas. And rule application errors result when students apply rules incorrectly in problem-solving situations. Meyer asserts that feedback should be designed to fit each type of misunderstanding.

Since the correction of errors appears to be where feedback has its most promising effects, researchers should continue to examine ways in which to manipulate feedback to maximize this outcome. As Noonan (1984) points out, more sophisticated procedures that involve analysis of common errors or error patterns might be more useful than traditional correct-answer feedback. Adaptive-feedback information can easily be facilitated within a computer-based instruction environment, where the computer can record and analyze the types of errors being made and give appropriate feedback based on error types.

32.5.4 Learning Outcomes

A detailed overview of suggested feedback for various learning outcomes has been offered by Smith and Ragan (1993). These researchers discuss their views of what information to include for each type of learning outcome according to Gagné's taxonomy (see 18.3). Instructional design theorists have proposed that different types of learning tasks require different strategies and instructional methods (Gagné, 1985; Merrill, 1983; Reigeluth & Stein, 1983) (see 18.3, 18.4). Very few researchers have attempted to investigate the differences in feedback needs for differing types of learning. Schimmel (1983) found differences in informative feedback given for declarative knowledge versus procedural knowledge. The studies that have been conducted are summarized below. In terms of testing current views of feedback, recall that results from the Mory (1991) study indicated that predictions from the Kulhavy and Stock (1989) model held for verbal information learning, but not for concept acquisition. Swindell (1991) also reported a study attempting to examine the same model (Kulhavy & Stock, 1989) under the conditions of higher-level learning. Although results of the study claim to suggest the generalizability of the model to higher learning, questions required recall of verbal information only, with no guarantee that intellectual skill learning had occurred.

The vast majority of feedback studies have dealt with verbal information tasks (Schimmel, 1988). Consequently, it is not known if certain patterns or inconsistencies that have emerged from these studies would necessarily result when involving other types of learning. This question has been acknowledged by a few researchers, an example of which is clear in Andre and Thieman's (1988) statement: "Whether feedback on questions facilitates concept learning as well as factual learning is not known from available research" (p. 297). Indeed, Schimmel discovered differences in the value of informative feedback for declarative knowledge versus procedural learning in the results of a 1983 meta-analysis.

Smith and Ragan (1993) estimate feedback requirements for different learning outcomes based on the theoretical cognitive processing requirements of each outcome. Thus their suggestions are predominantly theory based, and the reader should note that each area is a source of much-needed research to test these conjectures. The following sections address the feedback requirements suggested by either research or theory, or both.

32.5.4.1. Learning Outcome Comparisons. In an effort to bridge the gap between learning outcome differences, some researchers have compared declarative information tasks with higher cognitive tasks. Lee (1985) compared verbal information with rule using, hypothesizing that feedback for rule-using tasks should be more complex than feedback for learning verbal information. Three levels of feedback were compared. Correct-answer feedback was the same for all three levels (i.e., "right"). Differences in feedback only occurred if the student missed the question. For an error, students in the first level of feedback simply received the statement "Wrong." Students in the second level were told "Wrong. The answer is. . . . " for errors made. Errors for the students in the third level of feedback were presented with "Wrong. The rule is. . . . The correct answer is. . . ." There were no significant differences between feedback levels, suggesting that more-complex feedback did not prove more effective in either task. An additional finding was that there were no differences between feedback that was given immediately or feedback that was delayed.

Another study comparing verbal information with rule using was completed by Char (1978). Char refers to his intellectual skill task as "higher-order learning," which he describes as both identifying concepts and applying rules. The purpose was to examine the effects of both informative feedback versus no feedback, and delayed versus immediate feedback on retention of verbal information and higher-order learning. As one might predict, informative feedback did significantly enhance retention of both verbal information and higher-order learning. There were no differences between immediate and delayed feedback. It is regrettable that he did not categorize each higher-order question separately as being either a concept or rule application, so as to more clearly delineate between the specific kinds of learning being applied.

S. U. Wager (1983) also compared verbal information learning with a type of intellectual skill—specifically, defined concepts. She examined the effects of timing and type of feedback on retention of an instructional task involving verbal information and defined concepts learning. Both immediate- and delayed-feedback timing were used, and feedback was either simple or elaborated. Simple feedback presented a knowledge of results only, and elaborated feedback presented a combination of knowledge of results, knowledge of correct response, and response contingent feedback, which explained why a particular response choice was correct or not. Results indicated that neither timing of feedback nor type of feedback made any significant differences between groups. These results were partially attributed to the fact that the feedback may have assumed a lesser role when students were given tutorial instruction.

Gaynor (1981) also compared across verbal tasks and higher-level tasks. Rather than using Gagné's categorizations of "verbal information" and "intellectual skill," Gaynor classified her materials according to Bloom's taxonomy. She compared test items that fell into three levels of intellectual ability: knowledge, comprehension, and application. She concluded that when degree of original learning is equated, immediate feedback, end-of-session feedback, or even no feedback have little effect on short- or long-term retention of materials at Bloom's first three taxonomy levels.

Mory (1991, 1994) attempted to test the Kulhavy and Stock (1989) model of response certitude using two different types of learning outcomes for her subjects to try to determine if the model would generalize to a concept-learning task. The model was derived from studies that used predominantly verbal information and rote memorization of facts. In the Mory (1991, 1994) study, feedback was adaptive based on a combined assessment of answer correctness and level of certitude. The rationale was that by varying the type and amount of information contained in the feedback to fit the prescriptive state of learners under high- and low-certitude conditions and correct and error responses, learners would be given only the most "economic" form of feedback. Further, this type of adaptive feedback treatment was compared with a traditional form of non-adaptive feedback that essentially contained a verification component combined with knowledge of correct response. While there were no significant differences in posttest performance between the adaptive and nonadaptive groups, there was a significant increase in feedback efficiency for the adaptive group. Mory postulates that one reason that adaptive feedback did not seem to improve scores in the higher-level learning task of concept learning was that students did not accurately predict their answer correctness and thus were not able to receive the appropriate feedback for that condition. Data in the study revealed that certitude levels tended to be high throughout the adaptive program, regardless of actual answer correctness. This means that students did not receive low-certitude feedback when needed most. Learners simply could not give accurate assessments of their own abilities to classify a particular concept. As stated earlier, these findings are supported by previous studies involving "feeling of knowing" judgments (which are similar to response-certitude estimates) that propose that when learning involved higher-level tasks, judgments tended to be overestimated by learners (Metcalfe, 1986). In contrast to this, some researchers have found that students learning concepts tended to underestimate their belief about their answer correctness (M. P. Driscoll, personal communication, Aug. 30, 1990). Despite the opposing nature of these two separate results, it would appear that learners do not accurately predict their knowledge in higher-cognitive tasks.

32.5.4.2. Declarative Knowledge. This type of knowledge is what is referred to as *verbal information* in Gagné's (1985) taxonomy (see 18.3) and specifically by Smith and Ragan (1993) as including labels, facts, lists, and organized discourse. For labels and facts, feedback should give some evaluation of whether the learner's response is complete and whether the learner's associations are complete. Lists will possibly involve the elements of both completeness and sequence to be evaluated. They suggest that feedback might point out errors in incorrect combinations of associations and that simple correct/incorrect feedback may be sufficient. In Schimmel's work (1983), confirmation feedback was found to be more potent than correct-answer feedback in verbal information tasks. Simpler feedback was more effective than complex feedback in a study by Siegel and Misselt (1984). Further, Kulhavy and his colleagues (1985) found that knowledge of correct response was more beneficial than more complex feedback.

In terms of organized discourse, they (Smith & Ragan, 1993) assert that feedback must act as an intelligent evaluator or provide model responses. This "intelligent" evaluation may be provided by a knowledgeable human being or by computerized intelligent tutors. In terms of a model response, feedback should be constructed with attention to modeling organization, links of information, and elaborations that would be considered essential for an appropriate answer.

32.5.4.3. Concept Learning. Four feedback studies were found which dealt specifically with concept-learning tasks. Although already described under the feedback elaboration research, they will be discussed in this section for their importance as involving concepts. But before discussing these studies, an overview of concepts is presented from the major tenets of concepts-learning research.

Concepts are types of classifying rules (Gagné & Driscoll, 1988; Gagné, Briggs & Wager, 1992) that are used to facilitate the classification of instances through acquiring definitions, attributes, and examples (Tessmer, Wilson & Driscoll, 1990). The two categories of concepts are concrete concepts and defined concepts (Gagné & Driscoll, 1988). Concrete concepts represent categories determined on the basis of perceptual features, whereas defined concepts represent semantic categories that may or may not have a perceptual basis (Tessmer et al., 1990). Defined concepts must be identified through the use of a definition, rather than by actual sight.

Concepts have both declarative and procedural components that require instruction designed to convey both of these learning outcomes. Declarative strategies help make information about the concept meaningful to the learner, and procedural strategies produce accuracy and ease in performance of concept classification skills (Tessmer et al., 1990). Conceptual knowledge is more than just the storage of declarative (or verbal information) knowledge, embodying also an understanding of a concept's operational structure

within itself and between associated concepts (Park & R. D. Tennyson, 1986; R. D. Tennyson & Cocchiarella, 1986). Since conceptual knowledge is the storage and integration of information, and procedural knowledge is the retrieval of knowledge in the service of solving problems, instruction could typically include portions that focus on verbal information outcomes (the declarative component) and intellectual skill (concept) outcomes (the procedural component). Although testing how well a student has stored information in the form of verbal information outcomes is not a guarantee that the student also understands and can integrate the information, it still is an indicator of how much he or she can remember in order to apply it.

The primary method of teaching concepts usually involves presenting a definition or classification rule, followed by sets of examples and nonexamples. Examples and nonexamples are in the form of both (1) statement presentations to the student (expository instances) and (2) question presentations to the student (interrogatory instances) (R. D. Tennyson & Cocchiarella, 1986). Additionally, critical attributes of a concept may be presented. Critical attributes are what define a concept and must be present in any given case to be an example of the concept. The presence of these critical attributes constitutes both "necessary and sufficient conditions for judging the presence of the concept" (Wilson, 1986, p. 16). The test of whether a concept has been learned is to present the student with new instances of the concept that he has not previously encountered to see if he can classify the instance correctly.

Further, a concept is a set of specific objects, symbols, or events that share common characteristics (critical attributes) and can be categorized by a particular name or symbol (R. D. Tennyson & Park, 1980). Most concepts do not exist in isolation but as part of a set of related concepts. The placement of a given concept in relation to other concepts having similar attributes implies that certain concepts would be subordinate while others would be superordinate. Those concepts that are placed in the same general location in the content structure and are neither subordinate or superordinate may be defined as coordinate concepts (M. Merrill & R. Tennyson, 1977; R. D. Tennyson & Park, 1980). Coordinate concepts fall at the same level of specificity, and the members of any coordinate class are not members of any other coordinate class (Klausmeier, 1976). For coordinate concept learning, the nonexamples of one concept are examples of other coordinate concepts. Usually a set of concepts are presented simultaneously, making it easy for the learner to confuse specific attributes of one concept with another one and resulting in an error of misclassification. But simultaneous presentation is helpful in enabling learners to compare and contrast similarities and differences between concepts and thus aid in clarification of individual concepts (Litchfield, 1987).

The first study to involve both feedback and concepts is by Waldrop and his colleagues (Waldrop et al., 1986). They approach feedback with an emphasis on feedback only being effective under certain conditions, relating the importance of this when using feedback in CAI. They compared three types of feedback during a drill-and-practice CAI program. The program presented a series of 20 examples of 4 types of consequences for behavior (positive reinforcement, negative reinforcement, punishment, and extinction). Although the classification of concepts was used in the practice, they did not test the learning of the concepts by giving them new instances on the posttest. Instead, the criterion measure consisted of the same 20 items used in the CAI modules, only presented in a random order and within a test booklet. At least in terms of retention of the original examples, immediate extended feedback following both correct and incorrect responses was superior to minimal feedback. It would have been of value if the researchers had tested the concepts in the manner typically in line with what theorists would say constitutes successful learning of the concept—that is, being able to classify previously unencountered examples—and not merely by a repetition of the same examples.

A second feedback study to employ the use of concepts was by J. Merrill (1987). High- and low-level questions were used in combination with corrective feedback and attribute isolation feedback to form four versions of a computer-based science lesson that taught Xenograde terminology concepts. J. Merrill chose attribute isolation feedback based on M. Merrill and R. Tennyson's (1977) proposition that the correct classification of newly encountered examples of a concept is more likely if attribution isolation is presented both in the instructional presentation of examples and in the feedback given after practice examples. The primary hypothesis of the study was that students who received high-level questions and attribute isolation feedback would perform better than the other groups. Although there was a question-level main effect of students in the high-level question treatments performing significantly better than those in low-level question treatments, there was an absence of a feedback form main effect. J. Merrill suggests that this absence may be due to the fact that potential benefits of either feedback form were not fully available to the students. The attribute isolation feedback was only presented after two wrong responses and consequently was not encountered very often. This is unfortunate, considering that results from previous studies (cited in J. Merrill, 1987) yielded significant posttest results from the addition of attribute isolation to the concept-learning task.

Andre and Thieman (1988) approached the concept issue by directly addressing the problem that feedback research has used tests that measure only factual learning and thus has stood "mute on the issue of concept/principle acquisition" (p. 297). Unlike the Waldrop et al. (1986) study, these researchers measured both retention of the presented examples as well as performance on new instances of the concept. They broke student scores into performance on four types of questions: (1) repeated factual, (2) repeated application, (3) new factual, and (4) new application. Performance on the new application questions was cited as the main variable of interest, since the major purpose of the

study was to determine the effects of type of question and type of feedback on concept learning. Subjects were given either factual, application, or both types of adjunct questions immediately after reading an instructional passage. A day later, subjects were given either (1) no feedback, (2) correct-answer feedback, or (3) self-correction feedback in which the students received a list of incorrect items without the correct answer, the instructional passage, and instructions to find the correct answers to the incorrect items.

One major finding of the study was that adjunct application questions significantly improved student performance on later use of concepts, and that this improvement occurred without any loss of incidental factual learning. This beneficial effect was obtained only when application questions were used in isolation. When both factual and application adjunct questions were used in the practice, poor performance occurred on new application items. This suggests some sort of interference when the two different types of questions are presented together.

A second major finding was that feedback did not influence concept learning (i.e., performance on new instances) but did influence performance on repeated examples of concepts. Thus, feedback did not facilitate the acquisition of a concept that could be applied to new examples. They suggest that more than one trial of feedback may have been insufficient to induce concept acquisition, and cited Park and R. D. Tennyson's (1980) finding that students required approximately four examples to learn a particular concept.

Dempsey and his associates (Dempsey, 1988; Dempsey, Driscoll & Litchfield, 1993) examined concepts in terms of achievement on a retention test, feedback study time, and type and numbers of discrimination errors. These studies examined the effects of four methods of immediate corrective feedback on retention, discrimination error, and feedback study time in computer-based instruction. Also, the studies explored the relationship between types of corrective feedback and the types of errors made by learners. The four feedback conditions included: (1) feedback that gave knowledge of correct response only, (2) feedback that informed students of the correct response and then required that they make that response, (3) feedback that gave knowledge of the correct response and also presented anticipated wrong-answer feedback, and (4) feedback that gave knowledge of correct response and allowed a second try to answer the question. No significant differences in retention rates resulted for any feedback group, but the group receiving knowledge of correct response only used significantly less feedback study time and was more efficient than the other conditions. Type of feedback made no difference in the number of errors during instruction. Students making fewer fine discrimination errors during the instruction performed better on a retention test. More fine than gross discrimination errors were made on the retention test. Regarding feedback study times and discrimination error, almost twice as much feedback study time was consumed for fine discrimination errors. This last finding may suggest a link between fine discrimination errors and high-certitude errors from Kulhavy's work, since in both cases, the longest feedback study times result.

32.5.4.4. Rule Learning.

According to Smith and Ragan (1993), rules may be one of two types: relational rules and procedural rules. Relational rules involve relationships between two or more concepts, often being described in terms of "if-then" or "cause-effect" (p. 84). Relational rules have also been referred to as propositions, principles, laws, axioms, theorems, and postulates. These researchers (Smith & Ragan, 1993) describe suggested feedback for rule learning in terms of various practice stages for using the rule. When practicing verbalizing or visualizing the rule, feedback should provide information concerning the key concepts of the rule and their relationships. Note that this would basically qualify as verbal information and not rule utilization itself.

When practice involves the recognition of situations in which the rule is applicable, feedback should identify (1) whether the rule is applicable, and (2) what features of the situation make the rule applicable or not. They (Smith & Ragan, 1993) suggest that the explanatory portion of the feedback be placed under learner control, as explanatory feedback has been shown to confuse some learners (Phye, 1979).

When learners begin actually applying the rule, feedback should provide the outcome of the application of the rule. Explanatory feedback might include a step-by-step solution of the problem, highlighting critical features that influence the application of the rule or illustrating in graphic form how a solution can be drawn. Such explanatory feedback was found to be significantly superior than simple correct/incorrect feedback on college students' ability to apply rules in computer programming (Lee, Smith & Savenye, 1991).

When learners determine whether a rule has been correctly applied, feedback should include simple correct-answer feedback. For situations in which the rule has been applied incorrectly, feedback should point out the specific error in application and give the correct way that rule should have been applied. Feedback might also serve to provide hints for modification of the learner's use of a rule or be adapted to correct specific misconceptions or error patterns that a learner is making (Smith & Ragan, 1993).

The second type of rule, procedural rules, involves learning a series of steps to reach a specific goal. Procedural rules may be simple, with only one set of steps to complete linearly; or they may be complex, with many decision points leading to different paths or branches. The first step in learning procedural rules involves determining if the procedure is required. Smith and Ragan (1993) recommend feedback that is confirmatory, informing the learner whether he or she has appropriately identified the situations that require the application of the procedure. Learners should also be given feedback about the accuracy of their completion of each step in the procedure. During initial practice stages, feedback should be detailed and given during the practice of each step of the procedure. Then, as the learner is able to perform the entire procedure, feedback

would both determine whether each step was correctly completed and provide qualitative information concerning selection, criterion, and precision and efficiency. These researchers (Smith & Ragan, 1993) also recommend that feedback be given about the remembrance of steps in the procedure and their correct sequence of completion. And finally, feedback should be provided about the appropriateness of a completed procedure in the form of correct-answer feedback.

Departing from the usual fare of verbal-learning studies in the feedback elaboration research, only a few experimenters have chosen to look at rule using alone. Birenbaum and Tatsuoka's (1987) study examined the seriousness of errors committed by eighth-graders using rules to add signed numbers in a CAI task. For serious errors, it did not matter how much elaboration was in the feedback; correction was relatively unaffected by feedback. Feedback elaborations for nonserious errors did have an increasing probability of being corrected as more information was added to the feedback.

A second group of researchers (Tait et al., 1973) examined rule using in a CAI environment designed to help children multiply two- and three-digit numbers by one-digit numbers. Treatment conditions included (1) no feedback, (2) passive feedback, and (3) active feedback. The active feedback procedure required an overt response to be given for each step in the procedure for computing the answer. The passive procedure merely printed a message to the student and required no overt response. The active feedback was designed to alleviate the problem of children not attending to feedback messages that explained the procedure. Children seemed to be copying the answer presented at the end of the feedback and ignoring other information in the feedback. Active feedback required the student's active engagement with the feedback at each step within solving the problem. Additionally, active feedback contained more information than did passive feedback.

Even when using both active and passive feedback, there was still little improvement from pretest to posttest. The researchers concluded then that with the active feedback, children were still able to copy answers without understanding the procedure behind them. Consequently, a second experiment was designed which required the pupils to repeat the question until it had been answered correctly. The correct answer was required in both passive and active feedback groups before the child was allowed to continue on to a new problem. Even under these conditions, active feedback was no more beneficial than passive feedback. However, pupils who had scored low on the pretest did perform much better on the posttest when given active feedback than similar pupils in the passive feedback group.

32.5.4.5. Problem Solving.

In the domain of problem solving, a learner must select and combine multiple rules in order to reach a solution. This may require that learners use declarative knowledge and cognitive strategies within a content domain, and combine previously learned relational and procedural rules to solve a previously unencountered problem (Gagné, 1985). According to Smith and Ragan (1993, p. 92), the following stages often occur during a problem-solving task, and not necessarily in the same sequence:

1. Clarify the given state, including any obstacles or constraints.
2. Clarify the goal state, including criteria for knowing when the goal is reached.
3. Search for relevant prior knowledge of declarative, rule, or cognitive strategies that will aid in solution.
4. Decompose problems into subproblems with subgoals.
5. Determine a sequence for attacking subproblems.
6. Consider possible solution paths to each subproblem using related prior knowledge.
7. Select solution path and apply production knowledge (rules) in appropriate order.
8. Evaluate to determine if goal is achieved. If not, revise by returning to (1) above.

Since this type of learning involves the use of several other types of learning, feedback during a problem-solving task must work to help the learner see where his or her strategies or information gaps are occurring. According to Smith and Ragan's (1993) suggestions, initial feedback may be in the form of hints or guiding questions. It may include information as to which information has been used or misused, the appropriateness of selected solutions, whether individual phases of the solution have been correctly performed, and the efficiency of the solution process. As learners progress from novice to expert, their approaches to a problem should become more automatic. At this expert level, learners will need feedback on the efficiency or speed of their problem solving. The extent of this type of feedback will depend on the extent that genuine expertise is an expected part of the learning goal.

In simulations, feedback is often provided in terms of presenting learners with the consequences of their decisions. Open-ended response questions may be followed by feedback presenting a model of the solution process. And during the initial stages of practice, immediate feedback will be most helpful for intermediate stages, when responses can keep the learner from an eventual successful solution (cited in Smith & Ragan, 1993).

It should be noted that more recent views of problem solving are found in the literature on constructivism, to be presented later in this chapter. In particular, recent research in the areas of anchored instruction, situated cognition, situated learning, and generative learning have examined what might be thought to be "problem solving," but with very different philosophical assumptions about the way that learning takes place (Cognition & Technology Group at Vanderbilt [CTGV], 1990, 1991a, 1991b, 1992a, 1992b, Young, 1993). It is from this broadened perspective that researchers will find the most need for research on types of feedback that can aid learners as they construct solutions to authentic problems.

32.5.4.6. Cognitive Strategies. Cognitive strategies are techniques that learners use to help them attend to, organize, elaborate, manipulate, and retrieve knowledge, thus controlling their own cognitive processes (see Gagné, 1985). Smith and Ragan (1993) relate the use of cognitive strategies with problem solving, since the selection, application, and evaluation of a cognitive strategy is similar to problem-solving techniques. Given that similarity, feedback will have some of the same functions as stated for problem solving—that of modeling appropriate decisions and stating explicitly whether the decisions and performance of the learner were adequate or not. Feedback should also contain explanations as to why the model is appropriate. Characteristics such as the learners' capabilities, requirements of the task, learner efficacy, and applications of various strategies should be considered as well. They (Smith & Ragan, 1993) suggest that for open-ended trials toward a solution, feedback should involve reviewing appropriateness of a particular strategy and the critical details of the strategy for a given problem/solution.

In a study by Ahmad (1988), college-age learners participating in a guided discovery lesson were taught strategies that were either compatible or incongruent with their prior cognitive strategies. When feedback on the effective or ineffective use of a particular strategy was provided, better performance resulted when the strategy was compatible with previously employed strategies. But when the strategy used by the learner was incompatible with her or his prior strategy use, feedback containing only whether or not a solution was correct or incorrect proved more effective.

Since cognitive strategies can be very subject domain oriented, it would probably be fruitful to explore the uses of various cognitive strategies within specified subject areas and contexts. Also, as stated above, researchers should consider examining cognitive strategies in terms of their applications to a learner's construction of solutions of more authentic learning tasks. In fact, one of the goals underlying the development of the Jasper series (CTGV, 1990, 1991a, 1992a, 1992b) is the importance of helping students learn to become independent thinkers, learning to identify and define issues and problems on their own (CTGV, 1992a). The whole notion of cognitive strategies should begin to be viewed as learners themselves generate the relevant subproblems and data necessary to satisfy subgoals that they themselves have generated on their own, referred to as "generative learning" (CTGV, 1990, 1992a).

32.5.4.7. Psychomotor Skills. Psychomotor learning involves skills that are physical in nature, often with coordinated muscular movements. Psychomotor skills require a cognitive component, particularly in the early stages of learning the skill. As the skill becomes more automatic, the cognitive awareness becomes an unconscious part of performing the skill. Two components of psychomotor skill are (1) executive subroutines to control decisions and supply subordinate hierarchical skills and (2) temporal patterning of skills to integrate the sequence of performance over time, involving pacing and anticipation (cited in Smith & Ragan, 1993). Further, psychomotor skills are sometimes classified on a continuum from "closed" to "open." Closed skills are predictable and do not require much adaptation to the environment, thus referred to as "internally paced" (Singer, as cited in Smith & Ragan, 1993). Open skills, on the other hand, must be adapted to unpredictable aspects of a changing environment.

The function of feedback in the learning of psychomotor skills is to provide a surrogate for the learner of self-evaluation, at least until the learner reaches a skill level where he or she can provide this role for themselves. However, as Smith and Ragan (1993) point out, this transfer is more pronounced than in other types of learning tasks. Learners are able, through their own seeing and hearing, to determine when a skill has been performed correctly, thus providing themselves a type of internal feedback.

Feedback may be given about (1) the product (the quality of the response outcome) or (2) the process (what causes the response outcome). During the beginning practice stages of motor skill, feedback serves the critical function of providing information about the process of executing the motor skill. Then, as a learner advances in his or her ability to execute the skill, feedback can focus on the response outcome (product) itself. Ho and Shea (cited in Smith & Ragan, 1993) found that learners appeared to learn simple motor skills better when feedback was withdrawn or at least not given after every single response. Also, quantitative feedback (using a measurable criterion) appears to be superior to qualitative feedback (e.g., "too fast," "too low") (Smoll, as cited in Smith & Ragan, 1993). However, there is an optimal precision point to include in feedback, past which point can result in detrimental learning (Rogers, as cited in Smith & Ragan, 1993).

Graphic representations can be very beneficial to learners when included in feedback about the quality of a psychomotor response. Sometimes referred to as "kinematic" feedback, it can increase both efficiency and effectiveness of the learner during the acquisition of a psychomotor skill. Further, feedback that is interspersed throughout the learning of a motor task is more effective than massed feedback at the end of practice (cited in Smith & Ragan, 1993).

32.5.4.8. Attitude Learning. The final type of learning capability that will be discussed in this section is that of attitude learning (see 34.2). The desired outcome of attitude learning is that a learner will choose to behave in a particular way. A person's attitude about something is reflected in the decisions or choices he or she makes. The goal of instruction for attitude learning would be to influence what a learner chooses to do after the instruction is completed (Gagné, 1985; Gagné et al., 1992). Obviously before a person can "choose" to do something, there are cognitive and behavioral components that have to be learned beforehand. The person has to cognitively "know how" to practice the attitude. Also, a person has to see the need to apply the attitude, behaviorally responding to opportunities to make decisions and make the particular choice. This can be accomplished through his or her own experience or vicariously through others' experiences. The affective side of attitude learning merely involves "knowing why."

Feedback for the cognitive and behavioral components can simply include information concerning whether they have successfully employed the knowledge or skill that the attitude will require. Feedback can also include information about the congruency of their responses with the desired attitude. In terms of mediating attitudes through feedback, learners can be presented with information concerning the anticipated consequences of their choices, incorporating the affective component of why the behavior that reflects the attitude is important (Smith & Ragan, 1993).

32.5.5 Motivation

When one begins to speak of motivation in feedback, it is easy to bring to mind the reinforcement view of feedback, and indeed, theories of motivation have tended to focus on behavioral reinforcement and performance rather than on increasing motivation through instructional means (Jacobs & Dempsey, 1993). In order to understand ways in which feedback can be used to help the motivational level of students, whether from a behavioral or a cognitive view, it will be useful to examine briefly some of the basic theories of motivation that psychologists have constructed to explain motivation in the learning process.

32.5.5.1. Goals and Goal Discrepancy Feedback. Past research in the area of motivation (cited in Covington & Omelich, 1984) has shown that for a learner to remain motivated and involved depends on a close match between a learner's aspirations or goals and his or her expectations that these goals can be met. If these aspirations are set so high that they are unattainable, the learner will likely experience failure and discouragement. Conversely, when goals are set so low that their attainment is certain, success loses its potency in promoting further effort (Birney, Burdick & Teevan, 1969). Covington and Omelich (1984) have suggested that setting performance goals beyond present capabilities, particularly in the case of low self-perception of success, can become a main source of gratification. Apparently the statement of a worthy goal is enough to boost self-regard irrespective of goal attainment. One might say that feedback is a means to allow a learner to study and "retest" information, actions that, according to some researchers, would encourage greater performance aspirations coupled with increased confidence to achieve these elevated goals. Findings suggest that motivation is a key mediating factor in the performance of learners (Covington & Omelich, 1984).

Feedback can be a powerful motivator when it is given in response to goal-driven efforts. Some researchers suggest that the learner's goal orientation should be considered when designing instruction, particularly when feedback can encourage or discourage a learner's effort, thus regulating sustained effort and future goal orientations (Dempsey, Driscoll & Swindell, 1993). Other researchers claim that feedback enters into the actual goal-setting process, as a basis for evaluating assigned goals and in guiding the formation of a learner's personal goals (Erez & Zidon,

1984; Locke, Shaw, Saari & Latham, 1981). Malone (1981) asserts that there are certain attributes that a goal must have in order to challenge the learner to attain them. First, they should be personally meaningful and easily generated by the learner. This is supported by Locke and others who contend that goals may enhance performance only when the learner conscientiously accepts them (Locke et al., 1981). Indeed, Erez and Zidon (1984) found a linear decrease in performance after assigned goals were rejected.

Malone (1981) also suggests that learners need some type of performance feedback as to whether or not they are achieving their goals. This notion was explored in a study by Vance and Coella (1990) in which goal discrepancy feedback (GDF) and past-performance discrepancy feedback (PDF) were used to examine acceptance of assigned goals and personal goal levels of learners. GDF conveyed to what level learners were performing above or below the assigned goals. PDF indicated the learner's performance level from one trial to the next. Interestingly, assigned goals were designed to become increasingly difficult over given trials. This meant that, concurrently, the GDF became increasingly negative and, consequently, the learner's acceptance of the goals because less likely. Learners were found to switch over to PDF for evaluating assigned goals and for selecting new goals, what one would expect given the uncomfortable nature of the GDF over time.

Hoska (1993) refers to goals in terms of whether they help in acquiring something desirable or in avoiding something undesirable. These *acquisition* and *avoidance goals* can be external (in which the learner's focus is performing for others) or internal (in which the learner's focus is on learning for oneself). Several researchers (Dweck, 1986; Dweck & Legget, 1988; Nolen-Hoeksema, Seligman & Girgus, 1986) have found that an individual's general goal orientation falls on a continuum between an ego-involved performing-goal orientation to a task-involved learning-goal orientation. She further explains that learners who have performing goals want to demonstrate high ability and to avoid poor performance. They tend to view their success as a display of their abilities, which they measure in terms of the perceived abilities of others. To an ego-involved learner, ability is his key to success, and effort is merely a means to achieve such external goals. In contrast, individuals who have learning goals pursue learning and extend effort to gain skills. They view their competence as improved mastery, attained through effort. To a task-involved learner, effort is perceived as being beneficial since it helps the learner attain mastery.

When learners are successful, individual goal orientation is not a critical issue since success breeds the desire to extend effort, regardless of the goal. But when looking at instances of performance failure, the two goal orientations can produce very different results. If an individual with a learning-goal orientation perceives an impending failure, it results in his or her exerting more effort to the task. To this task-focused individual, obstacles are a challenge to be overcome through effort. Task-involved learners believe

that effort, not ability, is the key to success and, consequently, they will look for ways to overcome any difficulties that arise. Their satisfaction lies in effort, which has been shown to result in higher mastery scores and produces 50% more work than with other learners (Dweck, 1986).

In contrast, learners with a performance goal orientation will react quite differently to an impending failure. Obstacles become a threat to success and, therefore, a threat to their self-worth. Even high-ability learners in this group will set up defenses to protect themselves against the emotional threat. These self-defense reactions include such tactics as discounting (Kelley, 1973); avoiding the task, feigning boredom, or engaging in task-irrelevant actions to bolster their self-image (Dweck & Legget, 1988); and using inefficient strategies, resulting in learned helplessness (Seligman, Maier & Geer, 1968).

According to Hoska (1993), if learners begin a task without a predisposition toward one of these two goal orientations, they will probably approach the task with both the goals of learning and performing. If learners do not receive cues favoring one type of goal over another, they will act according to their predisposition. But if a learning situation is structured to foster a particular type of goal, learners will respond. Thus a learner's goal orientations can be temporarily and, over time, permanently altered by intervention. This is where feedback can have a great effect on this aspect of motivation.

Providing lesson feedback can be used to influence a learner's goal orientation by increasing her or his incentives to learn and minimize a learner's incentives to perform. Hoska (1993) classifies these modifications into three approaches: (1) changing the learner's view of intelligence, (2) modifying the goal structure of the learning task, and (3) controlling the delivery of learning rewards. In terms of modifying a learner's view of intelligence, feedback can help learners view intelligence in a way that helps them see that ability and skill can be developed through practice, that effort is critical to increasing this skill, and that mistakes are part of the skill-developing process.

In terms of altering a learner's goal structure, one should consider the type of learning environment within which the lesson is taking place. Often goal structures are set within competitive, cooperative, and individualistic learning environments. Competitive goal structures emphasize performance success and failure and cause learners to become ego involved. Cooperative goal structures teach a learner that the task is important, thus helping to foster learning goals (Johnson & Johnson, 1993). In individualized goal structures, although noncompetitive, a learner will not necessarily be task focused, but the learner's orientation will be determined by the reward system of the learning experience.

Lastly, the control of the delivery of learning awards usually involves providing external awards, offering praise and blame feedback, and offering unrequested help that can increase the learner's chance for success, and the comparison of the learner's performance to that of others.

Unfortunately, providing external rewards to learners can easily undermine any personal learning goals that a learner has. Researchers have found that learners will often select less-difficult tasks to increase their probability of success (Deci, 1972; McCullers, Fabes & Moran, 1987), and this effect increases under competitive conditions (Covington & Omelich, 1979). Further, learners often think that only difficult or boring tasks require reward (McCullers et al., 1987). Hoska (1993) offers the suggestion that feedback on the development of skills at various stages of a learning task can help redirect the learner to a focus on internal rewards.

Praise and blame feedback, once thought to provide positive and negative reinforcement, has been shown to be interpreted by learners as estimates of their ability (Deci, 1972). While most learners associate praise and blame in terms of how much effort they expended, ego-involved learners and learners in competitive tasks often interpret praise-and-blame feedback as indicators of both ability and success levels, sometimes even producing learned helplessness (Koestner, Zuckerman & Koestner, 1987). Hoska (1993) summarizes the effects of praise-and-blame feedback in terms of whether or not the learner felt the comments were warranted, the difficulty of the task involved, and the goal structure of the learning environment. She points out that praise has the most potential for being misinterpreted by learners. When high praise occurs after successful completion of an easy task, it is interpreted to mean that the evaluator thinks the learner must have low ability. When minimal praise occurs after the successful completion of a difficult task, learners may believe that the evaluator believes they have high ability, with success occurring due to this high ability rather than effort. And when praise or no feedback occurs after a failure, learners will tend to believe that this indicates low ability.

Blame feedback for incorrect responses can have more positive effects than praise feedback does for successes. Learners will tend to perceive blame as a result of their withheld effort. Hoska (1993) cautions that blame feedback must be used carefully since it also can be harmful in instances when a learner has invested a high degree of effort and has achieved at least some level of success. In such cases, the feedback can teach learners that small, sustained improvements do not help them reach mastery—an undesirable outcome. In general, praise-and-blame feedback should focus on individual learner responses rather than on overall success levels so as to associate the feedback with effort and not with ability.

It should be noted that having the option of being retested, in which a learner is given feedback and allowed to improve, also increases the number of failures experienced by a learner (Covington & Omelich, 1982). These failures have been shown to lead to decreases in self-estimates of ability, which in turn trigger hopelessness, shame, and anxiety (Covington, 1983; Covington & Omelich, 1981). But under a mastery format, positive perceptions of ability have been shown to be maintained even in the event of failure as long as learners eventually reached their grade goals or

showed improvement (Covington & Omelich, 1984). In the same study (Covington & Omelich, 1984), while isolated failures were temporarily demoralizing, they were shown to play little part in determining overall motivational reactions. When students do not have opportunity to make good their failures, the result is greater student demoralization even though students experience fewer failures. The study makes the point that task-oriented learning may be especially beneficial for slow learners who may require several tries before mastering the subject matter.

Although the mastery learning approach is not new, nor is the idea of mastery being a desirable approach for slow learners, it is important to note here that the motivational element at work in such approaches should not be ignored. This line of motivation research suggests that students who are given the chance to improve through practice and feedback of some sort will have a positive perception of ability and will retain a high level of motivation overall. Thus the "retesting" effects of feedback have implications for improving and sustaining motivation, irrespective of the numbers of errors made.

32.5.5.2. Self-Efficacy and Expectancy. Self-efficacy and task expectancy have been said to be equally as important in determining how a learner will respond to a learning task (Hoska, 1993). Self-efficacy is the learner's perception of how well he or she can perform the learning tasks to achieve his or her goals. It helps the learner select attainable goals and determine the amount of effort that will be involved for reaching success. Self-efficacy affects learning because it influences how much effort a learner will invest in a task. For example, low self-efficacy can cause learners to dwell on their deficiencies, resulting in inaccurate personal assessments of task difficulty and excessive attention devoted to the possibility of failure, resulting in a learning detriment (Bandura, cited in Hoska, 1993). On the other hand, high self-efficacy does not always result in maximum effort, because the amount of effort extended by learners is said to depend on not only self-efficacy but also on goal incentives and the perceived demand or load of a task. Hoska (1993) points out that when learners are aware that a task is demanding, high self-efficacy will usually result in the effort needed for optimal performance. But when learners perceive tasks as being easy, high self-efficacy may cause them to feel that minimal effort is needed.

Bandura (1977) cites three information sources from which learners derive their general sense of self-efficacy. One is through vicarious experiences, in which self-efficacy is increased through viewing others' successes, or decreased when viewing others' failures. Self-efficacy is also developed through the learner's own personal performance. The impact of a success or failure affects self-efficacy by how the learner interprets the outcome. Any success that is achieved through a minimal amount of effort is viewed to indicate high ability and can result in increased self-efficacy. Some learners view success that requires high effort to mean low ability, thus reducing self-efficacy of those learners. The third area that learners build their self-efficacy from is verbal persuasion. Verbal persuasion comes in the form of opinions from parents, teachers, and peers concerning the learner's ability to perform various tasks and tend to affect learners' own perceptions about their abilities. Even learners with an initially high level of self-efficacy are said to have their own opinions of their ability affected by continual exposure to negative criticism (Hoska, 1993). Self-efficacy levels can also be temporarily affected by the learner's physiological state (Bandura, 1977), role assignment, familiarity with a task, or presence of a highly confident person (Bandura, 1982).

Expectancy is determined by the amount of effort a learner deems as appropriate for a task, based on the learner's goal incentives. Hoska (1993, p. 119) lists several elements of expectancy as follows:

- Belief that an outcome, or goal, is possible given the current situation. (Learners must feel that they have some control over goal attainment; this goal may or may not be task completion.)
- Belief that an outcome, which can be achieving either an acquisition or an avoidance goal, will have desired consequences. (The consequences of goal achievement must have some value to the learner.)
- Determination of the amount of effort appropriate for goal attainment. (The greater the goal incentive, the more effort the learner is willing to invest to achieve the goal.)
- Determination of whether or not the selected amount of effort will lead to goal attainment.

Keller and Suzuki (1986) assert that learners tend to evaluate outcomes against their own expectations. Recall that Kulhavy's research in the area of response certitude gives support for the importance of learner's expectancy level. Dempsey and his colleagues (Dempsey, Driscoll & Swindell, 1993) note that Kulhavy's work supports the hypothesis that "corrective feedback should be personally relevant to the learner and tailored to the learner's expectancy for success" (p. 28) and that this link has major implications for both motivational and instructional designs.

Hoska (1993) asserts that self-efficacy and expectancy levels can be modified. Figure 32-5 depicts the relationship between a learner's goals and self-efficacy with level of effort and task expectancy.

As can be seen in Figure 32-5, a learner's self-efficacy and strength of task goals influence the level of effort that the learner will decide to invest in the task. This selected level of effort will then affect the learner's task expectancy, which will in turn influence further effort decisions. A learner's level of effort can be increased by providing him with experiences that are positive and internally satisfying, such as experiencing continually increasing levels of competence. Another method of increasing self-efficacy is by modifying the learner's attributes of success and failures (see the following section on attribution theory).

32.5.5.3. Attribution Theory. One classic approach to motivation emphasizes the importance of causal attributions in explaining the consequences of academic failure and success (Weiner, 1972, 1979, 1980). According to

attribution theory, a learner's striving for achievement, affective reactions, and expectations concerning future outcomes are determined in part by the learner's attributional conclusions. Following performance on a learning task, students will react in a generally positive or negative manner, formulate causes to explain their performance (causal attributions), and then experience affect and expectancy changes dependent on the nature of these attributions. Note how closely this last description matches what Kulhavy and his associates (Kulhavy, 1977; Kulhavy & Stock, 1989) described for a learner's processing of feedback and the comparison of his or her response to the feedback information. Recall that Kulhavy explained how a learner's level of response confidence combined with the actual correctness of response determined how feedback was used.

Forsyth and McMillan (1981) describe Weiner's proposed model of educational attributions and attempt to assess the relationship between the attributions, affect, and expectations of college students following a course exam. They cite previous research that suggests that when students attribute their success to factors such as ability or the nature of the task, their expectations for success increased, whereas students who attribute their success to luck or effort report less positive expectancies. Further, according to self-worth theory, "failure is more likely to lead to

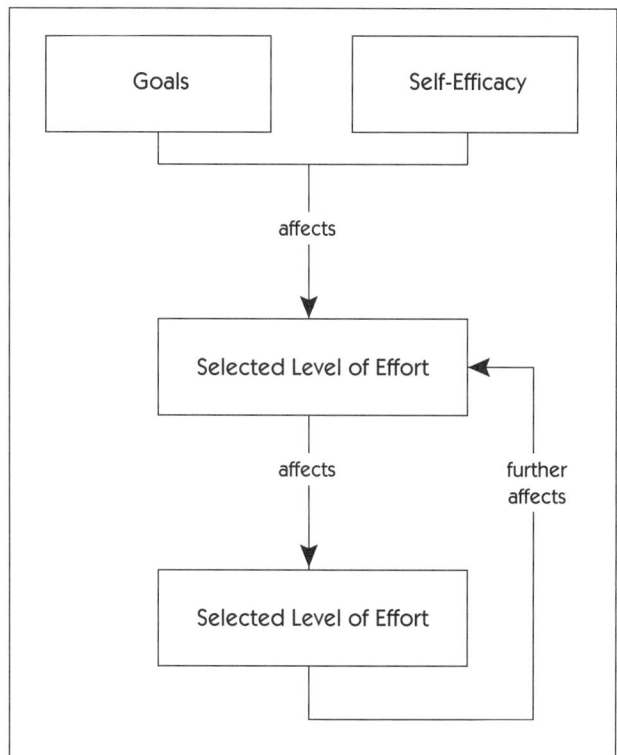

Figure 32-5. Relationship between goals, self-efficacy, learner's selected level of effort, and task expectancy (Hoska, 1993, p. 121). (From *Interactive Instruction and Feedback*, p. 121, by J. V. Dempsey & G. C. Sales, eds., 1993, Englewood Cliffs, NJ: Educational Technology.) Copyright 1993 by Educational Technology Publications. Reprinted with permission.

shame, depressed expectations, and lowered self-worth when it is ability linked rather than effort linked" (p. 394). Effort is something that is within the learner's control and has been found to have a strong relationship to affect. In the Forsyth and McMillan (1981) study, the affective reactions of students who felt that their performance was caused by factors they could control were more positive than the reactions of students who believed they did not control the cause of their outcome. This supports studies of learned helplessness in that even students who did well on the test yet believed they could not control their outcomes reported less-positive affect.

Learned helplessness has been described by Seligman as "the giving-up reaction, the quitting response that follows from the belief that whatever you do doesn't matter" (1990, p. 15). In his 25 years of research in this area, Seligman has isolated what he believes to be "the great modulator of learned helplessness," that of *explanatory style.* Whenever events happen to a person, whether good or bad, each individual has a habitual manner in which he or she explains those events. These explanatory styles can either prevent helplessness or spread helplessness, depending on the person's explanations about the event. He further divides these explanations into the areas of *permanence, pervasiveness,* and *personalization.* He has found that if you can alter the way in which a pessimistic person explains a success or failure—that is, alter the levels of permanence, pervasiveness, and personalization they surround their self-talk with—you can change that person's outlook to one of optimism. Optimism, in turn, prevents the person from remaining in a state of helplessness so that he or she can be a more productive individual.

Since students' "perceived that noncontingency" (Forsyth & McMillan, 1981, p. 400) is associated with loss of achievement motivation, it seems reasonable to suggest that feedback could help students directly see a link between their level of effort and success, and provide information concerning various factors that the learner has under control. This will be elaborated on further in the next section, in which strategies for modifying learner's motivational perspectives are examined.

32.5.5.4. Modifying Learner's Perspectives Through Feedback.
Hoska (1993) cites several steps that learners go through when they select and perform tasks, based on Weiner (1979). The steps are as follows. A learner:

1. Selects a goal.
2. Evaluates task difficulty.
3. Evaluates his or her abilities and develops a level of self-efficacy.
4. Selects an effort level and decides if that level will yield task success.
5. Invests effort to complete the task and evaluates progress toward task completion.
6. Determines and dimensions the cause of the success or failure.
7. Modifies his or her learner perspective.

As learners go through these steps, Hoska suggests feedback according to its motivational function. This is summarized in Table 32-1.

32.5.5.5. ARCS Model of Motivation.
Some researchers (Keller, 1983, 1987a, 1987b, 1987c; Keller & Kopp, 1987; Keller & Suzuki, 1987) have developed a model for increasing student motivation through instructional design, emphasizing instructional components that serve to motivate learners. The model grew from a macrotheory of motivation and instruction developed by Keller (1983). It is grounded in expectancy value theory that assumes that "people engage in an activity if it is perceived to be linked to the satisfaction of personal needs (the value aspect), and if there is a positive expectancy for success (the expectancy aspect)" (Keller, 1987a, pp. 2, 3). The model came about by dividing the value components into the categories of *interest* and *relevance. Interest* refers to attentional factors in the environment, and *relevance* refers more to goal-directed activities (p. 3). The expectancy component remained as a category, and a fourth category was added that was originally called *outcomes. Expectancy* refers to one's own expectation for being successful, and *outcomes* refers to the reinforcing value of instruction. Outcomes include both reinforcement as described in operant-conditioning theory, but they also include any environmental outcomes that help maintain intrinsic motivation (see Deci, 1972).

The ARCS model was created by generating a large list of motivational strategy statements, derived from research findings and from practices that have resulted in motivated learners. The four original categories of *interest, relevance, expectancy,* and *outcomes* were renamed to strengthen the central feature of each component and to generate a useful acronym (Keller, 1987a). The model now focuses on the four categories: attention, relevance, confidence, and satisfaction, and is hence referred to as the ARCS model in reference to these areas. By using each of these four categories as a framework, instructional designers are able to incorporate strategies that relate to each.

When Keller (1987a) refers to *attention,* he is referring to the interest level of the learner—whether or not the learner's curiosity is aroused and is sustained over an appropriate period of time. Whether the learner perceives the instruction to satisfy personal needs or to help achieve personal goals is referred to by the *relevance* component of the model. *Confidence* refers to the learner's perceived likelihood of success (expectancy) and whether the learner perceives success as being under his or her control. Intrinsic and extrinsic motivation are referred to under the *satisfaction* component and focuses on the learner's intrinsic motivation and response to extrinsic awards.

Keller (1987c) notes that one of the challenges of motivation is that it is just as detrimental to learning and performance for learners to be overmotivated as it is for them to be undermotivated. Undermotivation results in low productivity levels, while overmotivation results in high error rates and poor efficiency due to stress and overconfi-

TABLE 32-1. MOTIVATING LEARNERS THROUGH FEEDBACK (modified from Hoska, 1993, pp. 126–129)

Type of Feedback	Function of the Feedback	Technique	Cautions
Feedback to strengthen the incentive of learning goals	Help learner view his or her abilities as improvable.	In intro. to lesson or as feedback when learner has difficulty: • Suggest that abilities are skills that can be developed. • Identify the skills that the lesson is aimed at developing. • Indicate that effort is the main tool for increasing skills. • Treat mistakes as an important part of skill development.	Help learner view his or her abilities as improvable. If learner are working in pairs or small groups, set up a cooperative environment.
	Present a task-focused, noncompetitive learning environment.	When presenting feedback for both correct and incorrect responses: • Keep comments task focused. • Have the learner set goals related to completion of small-task stages. • Do not tie goals to accuracy rate or the time required for mastery. • Avoid comparisons. Do not rate the learner's progress against the progress of previous lesson users. • Do not offer rewards such as bonus points.	
Feedback to minimize the effect of difficulty level	In the case of CBI feedback, counteract learner's tendency to view the computer as solely an entertainment source.	As an introduction to the lesson and intermittently within feedback, reinforce the idea that the lesson is designed to help the learner develop skills. During feedback, occasionally stress the importance of paying close attention to presented information.	Do not suggest that the learner needs to work hard before he or she is presented with a learning task. This may cause him or her to overestimate task difficulty.
	Convince learner that difficulties and challenges are positive and do not reflect ability level.	Introduce the idea that the learner may easily complete some parts of the lesson, while having difficulty with others. Present the need for increasing levels of difficulty as a necessary part of skill development.	
Feedback to increase a learner's self-efficacy	Steadily increase the self-efficacy of learners.	To develop a sense of self-efficacy, use the following strategy throughout the lesson: 1. Use feedback that provides support during the early stages of learning a task. Either give the learner some type of advised control over help sequences or attempt to put some aspect of forced support under learner control. 2. As the learner progresses, slowly reduce the amount of available help, letting the learner know that he or she is starting to do well on his or her own. 3. As the learner gains skill, begin to give him or her increasing control over the lesson. Let learners know that they have earned the ability to direct their study. If trackable factors are present, such as the speed at which the learner selects answers to questions, indicate that poor performance may be due to guessing; suggest to the learner that guessing is a waste of time, and lesson mastery is possible if he or she takes time and concentrates.	Do not offer high verbal praise for successes; a learner can easily misinterpret praise as a sign of low ability. Simple verification of a success is usually enough. Do not admonish learners every time they do poorly. If a learner with low self-efficacy is trying, blame may cause him or her to give up. Do not always force help on a learner. Provide help only when the learner really needs it.
Learner gains a sense of control over his or her learning	Help learner to attribute his or her success and failures to effort.	Provides feedback related to effort levels for both successes and failures. Track the learner's performance and: • If a learner responds incorrectly to several problems in a row, suggest that the difficulty does not mean failure. Encourage effort and suggest that if the learner tries hard, he or she will achieve success. Follow this advice with a slightly less-difficult problem. • If a learner has had difficulty and is now improving, point out the success and suggest that the cause is effort. Encourage continued effort. Follow this advice with a problem the learner has a fairly good chance of answering correctly. • If the learner is having difficulty, guide the learner to select a different, more-effective strategy. Relate the search for and use of strategies to effort.	Make certain that the learning environment is task focused and noncompetitive. Present the effort feedback after the learner responds to a problem. Offer effort-directed feedback only when the learner is working on problems of medium difficulty.

dence (pp. 2, 3). The typical graphical representation of this is the inverted-U curve illustrating this result (see Fig. 32-6).

Keller (1987c) uses this inverted-U depiction when he completes audience analyses, plotting the levels of attention, relevance, confidence, and satisfaction on the curve. The rise and fall in performance in relationship to levels of motivation has implications for instruction. It appears that enhancing motivation for learning is an area that should be of concern to researchers, and, as we shall see momentarily, an area that feedback potentially may influence.

In Keller's (1983) original description of the motivational design of instruction, he lists several strategies to enhance motivation, many that are recommendations for the use of feedback to the learner. For our purposes of considering areas for future feedback research, these deserve closer inspection. They are as follows.

To enhance expectancy, what is now included in the model as *confidence,* "increase expectancy for success by using *attributional feedback* and other devices that help students *connect success* to personal effort and ability" (p. 420).

Attributional feedback is important when a student does not perceive a connection between his or her effort and its consequences. This is what has been referred to earlier as *learned helplessness.* A person who has developed learned helplessness towards a task does not perceive any causal link between behavior (effort) and its consequences. This type of learner cannot see the connection between ability and persistence as the key to success. When working with this type of learner, a sequence of problems or assignments should be developed that are initially easy but become challenging. After each success, feedback would be given as encouragement to keep trying, and after success at the more difficult problems, attributional feedback would be presented. Basically attributional feedback tells the learner that his or her success occurred because he or she kept trying. Keller (1983) refers to this feedback as being given verbally by a teacher in a classroom situation, but it is easily conceivable that adaptive feedback in other forms that contain the same type of messages would be appropriate.

To enhance the learner's perception of outcomes is now referred to as *satisfaction* and involves both intrinsic and extrinsic motivation. Keller (1983, pp. 426, 427) recommends to teachers to:

1. Maintain intrinsic satisfaction with instruction; use *verbal praise* and *informative feedback* rather than threats, surveillance, or external performance evaluation.
2. Maintain quantity of performance; use *motivating feedback* following the response.
3. Improve the quality of performance; provide *formative* (corrective) feedback when it will be immediately useful, usually just *before* the next opportunity to practice.

This first strategy is concerned with the types of consequences that will enhance or suppress intrinsic motivation. Keller (1983) points out that intrinsic motivation tends to flourish more in a context of positive but noncontrolling

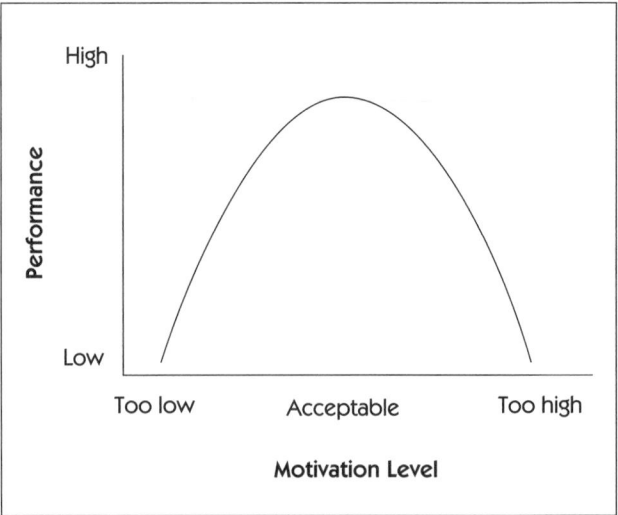

Figure 32-6.   Inverted-U curve depiction of the relationship between motivation and performance. (Based on Keller, 1987c.)

consequences than when excessive evaluation and aversive forms of control are used (p. 426). In terms of motivating feedback in the second strategy, the behavioral view of operant conditioning using positive reinforcement again surfaces. As Keller emphasizes, we are more likely to repeat behaviors that have pleasurable consequences than those that do not. When a learner receives positive reinforcement following a desired response, it affects the quantity of performance. One might contest this view of feedback in light of the evolution of feedback research from this type of behavioral view to that of cognition only. But it does make sense in terms of increasing and maintaining motivation or morale.

The last strategy refers to formative feedback, used to affect the quality of performance. It signals a gap between the given performance of the student versus the desired performance, and it indicates the actions to take to close the gap. Again, it is easy to see that this is feedback with the purpose to correct errors, as seen in the latest feedback studies that view feedback from a cognitive standpoint with a predominantly corrective function.

32.5.6 Feedback from a Constructivist View

32.5.6.1. Paradigm Shifts. The majority of feedback studies in the literature have examined feedback under the traditional learning theory paradigms of behaviorism and information processing. Both of these theories can be classified as viewing learning from an *objectivist* perspective. The philosophy of objectivism basically holds that "reliable knowledge about the world" exists (Jonassen, 1991b, p. 8) and that instruction serves to present this real-world knowledge to the student who will in turn be tested and "give back" this knowledge in order to demonstrate effective learning. Feedback would then serve to correct misinformation about this external, objective reality. This is, indeed, how most feedback studies are conceived.

The latest philosophy of learning, however, postulates that there is no external knowledge the student merely "takes in"; rather the student must *construct* his or her own reality or knowledge, and this construction will be based on the learner's prior experiences, mental structures, and beliefs (Brown, Collins & Duguid, 1988; Cooper, 1993; Duffy & Jonassen, 1991; Jonassen, 1991b). Put succinctly, "Knowledge is constructed in the mind of the learner" (Bodner, 1986, p. 873). This espouses the philosophy called *constructivism,* in which each learner constructs his or her own reality through interpretation of experiences of the external world (see 7.1). And given this new view of learning, feedback will likely function differently than from an objectivist view of learning (Mory, 1995).

Recall how early studies of feedback evolved from a behavioral view of feedback as reinforcement to more recent research that advocates an information-processing perspective with an emphasis on error correction. Feedback's main function is that of providing corrective information. Recall also the recently developed models of feedback (Bangert-Drowns et al., 1991; Kozma & Bangert-Drowns, 1987; Kulhavy, 1977; Kulhavy & Stock, 1989) that attempt to explain what happens within the feedback process. These models also contribute to an organization of the many variables that have been examined or even overlooked by past research. All of these studies were conceived under a philosophy of learning that embraces certain assumptions about learning from an objectivist viewpoint. These assumptions and the resulting use of feedback may be seen in Figure 32-7.

Although there has been progress in determining ways in which feedback can best be used under certain conditions, there are still many areas in which the feedback literature is not consistent, and yet other areas that have been left unexplored. One must critically examine feedback in light of the philosophical assumptions underlying these studies in order to highlight how feedback functions within such contrived experimental settings. The basic assumptions of the objectivist philosophy are presented in order to contrast these assumptions with those of a constructivist view (Fig. 32-7). Suggestions for the use and function of feedback within the constructivist philosophy are presented in light of these basic assumptions in an effort to identify areas in need of further research (see Fig. 32-8).

Given such an array of inconsistencies in the feedback literature, it is essential to question whether or not researchers are focusing on feedback variables that have real value for the world of the classroom. Many feedback studies are computer-based training (CBT) studies and are not intended to be generalized to a large group setting such as a "typical classroom." In most instructional settings, feedback is presented within some sort of interactional environment, one that is not necessarily one of computer-based or programmed instruction. Perhaps some of the most potent feedback is received within a setting in which the student interacts with some problem he or she is trying to solve, with feedback resulting as a natural phenomenon of the context of instruction. For example, students who are trying to learn to play a musical instrument receive constant feedback from their mistakes just by hearing the sounds that are being produced, regardless of whether or not there is any other external mechanism in place to correct these sounds. Feedback occurs as a natural result of interactions between the learner and his or her own constructions of knowledge. Further, the relevance of topics typically being presented within traditional feedback studies are usually a far cry from being anything the learner would be motivated to learn, this being purposefully the case in order to maximize feedback differences. The context in which learning takes place in most of these studies is often artificial and distanced from what a typical learner's interactions with a problem would be. Certainly the inconsistencies in the feedback literature warrant some fresh ideas and perspectives. This researcher proposes that feedback be critically examined within a paradigm that embraces the philosophy of constructivism, in which the learner must construct his or her own knowledge based on interactions within authentic learning environments (see 7.3, 12.3).

32.5.6.2. Applications of Feedback in Constructivism.
The philosophy of constructivism opens a new avenue for

OBJECTIVISM	
ASSUMPTIONS	FEEDBACK
• Reality is external to knower.	• Feedback is based on response match to external reality.
• Mind acts as processor of symbols.	• Feedback contains symbols for learner to process.
• Thought is independent of human experience; reflects external reality.	• Feedback not related to human experience; reflects external reality.
• Meaning corresponds to categories in the world.	• Meaning within feedback information corresponds to categories in the world.
• Symbols represent external reality.	• Feedback contains symbols that represent external reality.

Figure 32-7.   Assumptions of objectivism (from Jonassen, 1991b) and suggested use of feedback.

CONSTRUCTIVISM

ASSUMPTIONS	FEEDBACK
• Reality is determined by knower.	• Feedback is to guide learner toward internal reality; facilitates knowledge construction.
• Mind acts as builder of symbols.	• Feedback aids learner in building symbols.
• Thought grows out of human experience.	• Feedback in context of human experience.
• Meaning does not rely on correspondence to world; determined by understander.	• Meaning within feedback information determined by internal understanding.
• Symbols are tools for constructing an internal reality.	• Feedback provides generative, mental construction "tool kits."

Figure 32-8.   Assumptions of constructivism (from Jonassen, 1991b) and suggested use of feedback.

feedback research. Feedback in a constructivist context would provide intellectual tools and serve as an aid to help the learner construct his or her internal reality. Because learners would be solving complex problems through social negotiation between equal peers and within contextual settings, feedback might also occur in the form of discussion among learners and through comparisons of internally structured knowledge.

Perhaps to understand better what feedback would represent in a constructivist paradigm, consider the earlier transition of research foci from a behavioral view (reinforcement) to a cognitive view (information). As Cooper (1993, p. 16) suggests:

> The move from behaviorism through cognitivism to constructivism represents shifts in emphasis away from an external view to an internal view. To the behaviorist, the internal processing is of no interest; to the cognitivist, the internal processing is only of importance to the extent to which it explains how external reality is understood. In contrast, the constructivist views the mind as a builder of symbols—the tools used to represent the knower's reality. External phenomena are meaningless except as the mind perceives them.

One constructivist principle is that instruction should occur in relevant contexts (Brown et al., 1989; Jonassen, 1991a). Referred to as *situated cognition,* the notion is that learning occurs most effectively in context, and that the context becomes part of the actual knowledge base for that learning (Jonassen, 1991b). One approach to this is called *cognitive apprenticeship* (Brown et al., 1989; Collins, Brown & Newman, 1987; see 7.4, 20.3), in which learners engage in activity and make deliberate use of both social and physical context, just as an apprentice would do. Feedback in this view would occur in the form of the interactions between the learner and the activity of solving real-world problems. Rather than providing predetermined instructional sequences, feedback could be used as a coaching mechanism that analyzes strategies used to solve these problems (Jonassen, 1991b).

Another constructivist strategy has been termed *cognitive flexibility theory* and involves the presentation of multiple perspectives to learners (Jonassen, 1991b; Spiro, Feltovich, Jacobson & Coulson, 1991a, 1991b) (see 7.3, 23.4). By stressing conceptual interrelatedness, providing multiple representations of content, and emphasizing "case-based instruction" that includes inherent multiple themes (Jonassen, 1991b), feedback can help learners acquire advanced knowledge in ill-structured domains. Spiro and associates (Spiro et al., 1991a, 1991b) propose the use of multidimensional and nonlinear hypertext (see 21.3) systems to convey ill-structured aspects of knowledge domains and thus promote cognitive flexibility. When a learner approaches a problem from a certain perspective, feedback can serve to guide the learner to revisit the same material in a rearranged context, for a different purpose, from a different conceptual perspective (Spiro et al., 1991a), and any combination of these. Although implementing cognitive flexibility theory is not just a matter of, as Spiro et al. (1991a) state, using a computer to "connect everything with everything else" (p. 30), feedback can be designed into a hypertext system to lead the learner to approach concepts from new perspectives and to provide locator information when a learner feels lost in a "labyrinth of incidental or ad hoc connnections" (p. 30). Feedback traditionally has been used to allow the learner to evaluate preset goals through reinforcement of matching responses or through control of instruction. But in the constructivist view, evaluation provided by feedback would become more of a tool for self-analysis (Jonassen, 1991a).

Another constructivist invention is that of the *microworld*—"a small but complete subset of reality in which one can go to learn about a specific domain through personal discovery and exploration" (cited in Rieber, 1992, p. 94) (see 12.3). Instructional applications of microworlds conform to Vygotsky's idea of the "zone of proximal development" (see 7.4), in which learners who are on the threshold of learning are often unable to attain understanding without some external intervention or assistance (Rieber, 1992).

Rieber contends that learning environments like microworlds should be designed with a "self-oriented feedback loop" (p. 100) that provides a rich and continual stream of information to help students establish and maintain goal setting and goal monitoring. Further, because many complex problems contain so many individual variables that can inundate a novice to the point of frustration, microworlds offer a way to structure the learning environment to a finite set of variables, something Piaget termed *variable stepping* (Rieber, 1992). Feedback received can be judged against a learner's individually defined goals. Rieber (1992) also suggests using a variety of feedback features to complement one another, such as presenting verbal feedback at the same time as visual feedback.

A report by Edwards (1991) focused on how children used feedback from a computer microworld for transformational geometry to discover and correct instances of overgeneralizations that emerged as they solved problems with the microworld. Although there was a tendency towards symbolic overgeneralization in some activities, the children were able to use visual feedback from the microworld and discussions with their partners to correct their own errors.

A summary of the functions of feedback under a constructivist philosophy are presented in Figure 32-9. Researchers are encouraged to pursue the study of feedback under this paradigm.

32.5.7 Bridging the Gap: A Synthesis Model of Feedback with Self-Regulated Learning

The most recent synthesis of contemporary feedback models views feedback in the context of self-regulated learning (Butler & Winne, 1995). Butler and Winne (1995) propose a more elaborated examination of feedback that takes into account how feedback affects cognitive engagement with tasks and how engagement relates to achievement. Self-regulated students are aware of aspects of their own knowledge, beliefs, motivations, and cognitive processing,

and the most effective learners are self-regulating. The model couples elements from traditional feedback research with processes involved in self-regulation. My view is that the Butler and Winne (1995) model quite possibly may supply the "missing link" between the findings presented in recent reviews (Bangert-Drowns et al., 1991; Kulhavy & Stock, 1989; Mory, 1992) and elements of motivation theory and constructivistic philosophies. They (Butler & Winne, 1995) point out that many studies of self-regulated learning (SRL) have looked at global or aggregate results of multiple SRL activities, rather than at individual instances of self-regulation. They suggest a more "fine-grained analysis of feedback's roles in dynamic cognitive activities that unfold during SRL" (p. 247).

While most studies of feedback have focused on externally provided information, these researchers (1995) postulate that internal feedback is also inherent as self-regulated learners monitor their own engagement in tasks. The most effective learners develop their own distinct cognitive routines for creating this internal feedback, which in turn affects how the learner will use information presented within feedback externally. Thus, the feedback serves a multidimensional role in aiding knowledge construction that fits into a model of self-regulation.

While not usually found in feedback or self-regulated learning (SRL) research, Butler and Winne (1995) cite several different areas of research and integrate these areas to aid in understanding the process of self-regulation as it relates to feedback. These include (1) how affect relates to persistence during self-regulation, (2) what the role of learner-generated feedback plays in decision making, (3) how students' beliefs affect learning, and (4) what beliefs learners have in the process of conceptual change or restructuring when faced with misconceptions.

Self-regulation is the recursive process of interpreting information based on beliefs and knowledge, goal setting, and strategy applications to generate both mental and behavioral products (see Fig. 32-10). Mental products can include both cognitive and affective domains. Learners monitor their own process of engagement and updated products through internal feedback. They then reinterpret the task and their own engagement, which then affects subsequent engagement. Modifications can include altering goals or setting new ones, reviewing and adapting their strategies of learning, and developing new skills. At this point, if external feedback is provided, additional information can be added to help the learner in this process (see Fig. 32-10).

32.5.7.1. Self-Regulated Engagement. Four lines of research are featured in Butler and Winne's (1995) review of self-regulation. One is a model of self-regulation in terms of engagement and affect. Several researchers (Bandura, 1993; Carver & Scheier, 1990; Kuhl & Goschke, 1994; Mithaug, 1993; Zimmerman, 1989) have found that "students' goals couple with motivational beliefs and affective reactions to shape self-regulation" (Butler & Winne,

---

- Aids learner in constructing an internal reality by providing intellectual tools

- Helps learner solve complex problems within contextual, relevant settings

- Occurs as social negotiation between equal peers

- Provides guidance for multiple modes of representation

- Guides learner through ill-structured domains, reminding learner of goals

- Challenges learner toward potential development

Figure 32-9. Suggested constructivist functions of feedback (Mory, 1995).

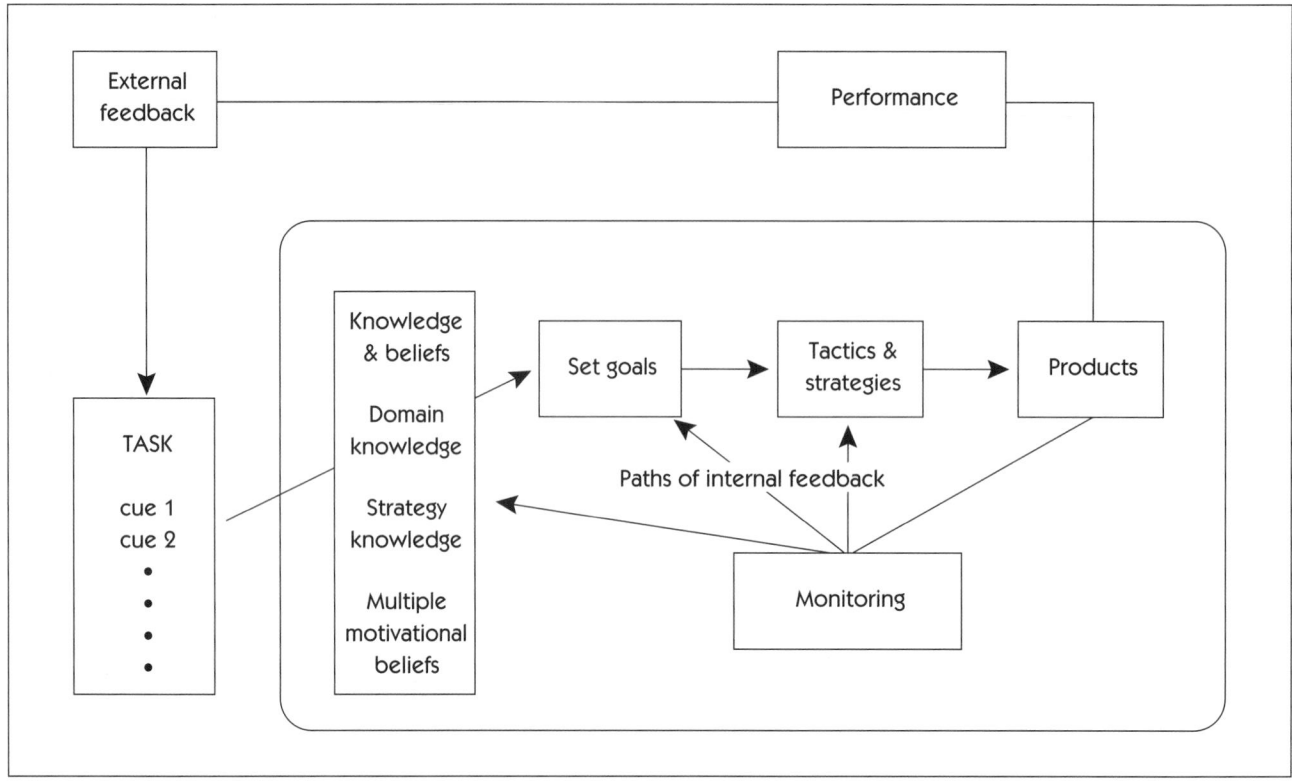

Figure 32-10. A model of self-regulated learning (from Butler & Winne, 1995). (From "Feedback and Self-regulated Learning," by D. L. Butler & P. H. Winne, 1995, *Review of Educational Research 65*, p. 248.) Copyright 1995 by the American Educational Research Association. Reprinted with permission.

1995, p. 249). Positive affect results when progress is achieved faster than predicted, and negative affect results when the learner's rate of progress is slower than predicted. According to this model of SRL (Carver & Scheier, 1990), it is predicted that when learners make progress exactly as planned, the affect level that results is neutral rather than positive, and that under some conditions, achievement actually results in a negative affect. These affect levels influence future engagement on the task through the shaping of confidence judgments during the learner's internal monitoring process (Carver & Scheier, 1990; Eisenberger, 1992; Kuhl & Goschke, 1994).

32.5.7.2. A Lens Model. A second line of SRL research is from the viewpoint of what is termed a "lens model," in which both task characteristics and students' progress on tasks are used to predict final performance. Traditional feedback studies focus on *outcome feedback,* many times referred to as *knowledge-of-results.* While several studies do focus on adding elaborations to outcome information, most have ignored the role of giving learners guidance that can aid in their own self-regulation. Butler and Winne (1995) propose that data on students' perceptions of cues and their value, along with expectations for success and perceptions of actual achievement, can help researchers in knowing what to provide in elaborated feedback to support self-regulated engagement and to enhance self-calibration. Such feedback has been termed *cognitive*

feedback (Balzer, Doherty & O'Connor, 1989) and can provide learners information that links cues and achievement. Cognitive feedback includes (1) task validity feedback, (2) cognitive validity feedback, and (3) functional validity feedback. *Task validity feedback* includes information provided from an external source that describes that source's perceived relationship between a task's cues and achievement (Butler & Winne, 1995; Elawar & Corno, 1985; Winne, 1989, 1992; Zellermayer, Salomon, Globerson & Givon, 1991). *Cognitive validity feedback* includes information describing the learner's own perceptions about the cue and achievement relationship (Butler & Winne, 1995). And *functional validity feedback* describes the relationship between the learner's own achievement estimation and actual end performance. In a review by Balzer and associates (1989), feedback that provided various forms of validity-related information was found to be more effective than outcome feedback, and task validity feedback was somewhat more effective in supporting learning and problem solving than cognitive validity feedback information alone.

Several implications of examining feedback from a lens model viewpoint become evident. When providing outcome feedback, researchers should realize that the effectiveness of the feedback depends on several learner characteristics and behaviors. Students must be attentive to many cues, have accurate memories of cue features when receiving outcome feedback, and be strategic enough to generate effective internal feedback to themselves. Outcome feedback provides little guidance to the learner on how to self-regulate. However, when applying cognitive feedback, researchers should use information that helps students identify cues and monitor their own task engagement. This monitoring is an essential part of self-regulation.

32.5.7.3. Learners' Beliefs. A third line of SRL research examines the relationships between what the learner believes about learning, his or her use of strategies, and resulting performance (Schommer, 1990, 1993; Schommer, Crouse & Rhodes, 1992). Beliefs about learning can affect a student's persistent effort on a given task and goal orientation (Boekaerts, 1994; Carver & Scheier, 1990). These beliefs thus influence subsequent engagement on a task.

32.5.7.4. Misperceptions in Content. A learner's prior misconceptions about content area can hinder his or her subsequent revisions of that incorrect knowledge (Chinn & Brewer, 1993; Perkins & Simmons, 1988). While students can be receptive and correct misunderstandings through feedback, Chinn and Brewer (1993) identify six negative responses to feedback under such conditions. Students can (1) ignore the feedback, (2) reject feedback, (3) judge feedback to be irrelevant, (4) consider the feedback to be unrelated to the belief, (5) reinterpret the feedback to fit the misconceived belief, or (6) make superficial as opposed to fundamental changes in the erroneous belief. In this way, feedback is "filtered" through a learner's existing beliefs about the content.

Butler and Winne (1995) conclude that SRL is inherent in students' construction of knowledge. They assert that differentiating functions of feedback using a broadly framed model of self-regulation synthesizes the diversity of students on feedback and instruction. They identify the potential roles of feedback in remedying both strategy implementation failure and ineffective monitoring.

Students' knowledge and beliefs are linked with their self-regulated engagement in tasks. In addition to their epistemological beliefs, research on self-regulation also points to four other types of knowledge that learners bring to a task. These include domain knowledge, task knowledge, strategy knowledge, and motivational beliefs. In terms of domain knowledge, students' strong incorrect knowledge structures within a domain result in erratic application of productive learning strategies (Burbules & Linn, 1988). As domain knowledge increases, students tend to acquire, use, and transfer cognitive strategies that support SRL (Salomon & Perkins, 1989). Task knowledge influences self-regulation as well, and learners' beliefs or interpretations of tasks can influence the goals they establish, as well as the cues attended to and acted on as they work on a task (Schommer, 1990).

Strategy knowledge results as students complete tasks. Winne and Butler (1994) identify three types of strategy knowledge. The first, declarative knowledge, involves stating what the strategy is. The second, procedural knowledge, involves how to use a particular strategy. And the third, conditional knowledge, addresses the utility of a strategy, such as when and where to use a strategy and how much effort will be required.

Finally, motivational knowledge involves learners' "beliefs about their capabilities to exercise control over their own level of functioning and over events that affect their lives" (Bandura, 1993, p. 118), referred to as *self-efficacy*. Self-efficacy affects the goals a learner will set, his or her commitment to those goals, decision making while striving to reach those goals, and persistence (Bandura, 1993).

As mentioned in the research on motivation, students can adopt two types of task-related goals: learning goals versus performance goals. Butler and Winne (1995) hypothesize that cognitive feedback containing information about task cues will be most effective when given to students that adopt learning goals. Further, the effects of feedback depend on both the students' overall goal as well as the item-to-item change in their total knowledge as they review their wrong answers. The goals that students adopt may be different from the goals intended by the instructor, designer, or researcher. When that is the case, feedback would probably have less stable or predictable effects. Since goals are central in the process of self-regulated learning, feedback must address the types of goals students adopt and support their processes for prioritization, selection, and maintenance of these goals (cited in Butler & Winne, 1995).

In terms of students selecting and generating strategies to reach their goals, Winne (1982) notes four particular problems that students encounter. A learner may fail to recognize the conditions under which to employ the strategy. Secondly, learners may not understand the task or perceive the task goals and mismatch strategies to goals. Another problem occurs when students select good strategies but do not know how to apply them. And lastly, students may lack the motivation to expend effort in applying a strategy.

Monitoring is another important aspect of self-regulated learning. Monitoring generates internal feedback in the learner that links his or her past performance to the next successive task. The points of linkage are the prime times that feedback should be given to be most useful (Butler & Winne, 1995).

The ideas put forth by Butler and Winne (1995) may well be the key to linking the two areas of motivation and constructivist philosophy as presented earlier in this chapter. Through the blending of self-regulated learning research with research on feedback, both the motivational elements involved in learning and the philosophy of constructivism can be addressed. Their model (Butler & Winne, 1995) suggests that feedback is contextualized according to the learner's prior knowledge and beliefs and, consequently, provides insufficient information to affect knowledge construction. They further suggest that for learning in authentic complex tasks, feedback should provide information about cognitive activities that promote learning and the relationships between cues and successive states of achievement.

Note also that the Kulhavy and Stock (1989) model emphasizing response certitude judgments adds credence to the notion that learners both set goals and monitor themselves. But Butler and Winne (1995) fine-tunes the issue by hypothesizing that students actually monitor their own *calibration.* Calibration is the extent to which monitoring creates accurate certitude judgments. They (Butler & Winne, 1995) suggest that high-confidence errors result in longer and more intense study of feedback because it is at this point that calibration is at its worst.

Traditional feedback research has been directed narrowly to the effects of feedback on achievement. The Butler and Winne (1995) model is a bridge allowing us to combine diverse studies on feedback, self-regulation, and instruction in such a way that future researchers have a schema for integrating instruction, self-regulation, feedback, and knowledge construction.

32.5.8 Advances in Technology

Perhaps one of the most important contributions to the use of adaptive feedback for facilitating learning lies in the advent of the microcomputer and its use for instruction. Unlike many of its technological predecessors, the computer has opened a door to interactivity, the precise recording of student response information, and the ability to adapt feedback and instruction to the changing needs of the learner within the interactive environment almost instantaneously. Further, recent developments in the use of multimedia and hypermedia open a vast set of questions for researchers to consider. For example, how does feedback function when presented via different modes of sensory input? Multimedia PCs common today involve the use of both auditory and visual stimuli to aid learning. What was once only possible through the integration of specialized media such as the interactive laserdisc now becomes more commonplace as newer technologies such as CD-ROM become increasingly commonplace and available. Hypertext and hypermedia designs await the learner using today's interactive CD software, with icons and "hotwords" linking vast amounts of information in the form of text, pictures, animations, and sounds.

A common problem with such open hypermedia environments is that learners often get lost along their exploratory way, unaware of how they were taken to the point at which they now rest. Navigation is just one of many variables to consider when examining such complex environments. Search (1994) suggests that if the communication potential of hypermedia is to reach its peak, designers must develop interfaces with orientation cues that help users navigate through large, multimedia databases. As she phrases it, "hypermedia computing is a temporal medium in which spatial relationships change dynamically, leaving the user with few references for orientation" (p. 369).

To understand adequately how the nature of computer-based learning has transformed, it is helpful to consider its evolution from its emergence in the 1960s as the pro-grammed instruction movement to now. Jonassen (1993) notes that even early computer-assisted instruction was merely programmed instruction delivered on a computer. The evolutionary path unfolded from programmed instruction, computer-based drills and tutorials, adaptive tutorials, and simulations. An important conceptual framework for hypertext and hypermedia environments is presented by Jonassen (1993). The growth of hypertext, hypermedia, and multimedia since the 1980s has provided designers with the capabilities necessary to develop complex, content-oriented learning environments. In order to make such large quantities of information more accessible, a variety of conceptual models are being "mapped" onto these environments. As Jonassen (1993, p. 332) describes it:

> Recent advances in learning theory have fueled a more rapid and extensive revolution in computer-supported learning systems. Rather than using the computer as a delivery vehicle for displaying and purveying information, generative learning systems and knowledge construction environments are designed to form partnerships with learners/users, to distribute the cognitive load and responsibility to the part of the learning systems that performs the best. Learners are engaged by these environments because their intellectual involvement in the learning process is essential. They are no longer passive recipients of information . . . they are actively involved in knowledge construction and meaning making. The computer's computational functionality is being used to support those processes rather than to present information.

The open architecture of hypermedia and multimedia have made them the platform of choice for implementing such knowledge construction environments (see 24.6). The computers of the future will function as "intellectual toolkits for enhancing the intellectual and perceptual capacities of humans" (p. 333).

A useful framework for designing feedback by incorporating the powers of emerging instructional technologies to present, manipulate, control, and manage educational activities has been proposed by Hannafin, Hannafin, and Dalton (1993). They point out that emerging technologies provide the potential for a dramatic range of varied feedback not possible or practical to present before.

Feedback design helps in the ability to present information and support encoding. The range of presentation dimensions include visual, verbal, sensory, or multiple modalities. In order to optimize both individual processing capabilities and technological potential requires an expansion of our notion of both feedback and technology.

According to Hannafin et al. (1993), emerging technologies have provided six major areas of improvement for instruction: adaptability, realism, hypermedia, open-endedness, manipulability, and flexibility. To design feedback effectively requires the psychological, technological, and pedagogical foundations of lesson design (Hannafin, 1989). Psychological foundations emphasize the role of the learner in processing inputs, organizing and restructuring knowledge, and generating responses. Particularly relevant are processing requirements, the role of prior knowledge, the role of active processing, and strength encoding (Hannafin et al., 1993, p. 272).

Technological foundations concern the capabilities of the actual hardware and devices for providing output, receiving input, and processing data. Emphasis is on input-output capability, symbol manipulation, and management. In many instances, technological capabilities far exceed human processing capacity. Therefore, what is most important is not what the outer limits of technology are, but rather how to utilize those technological capacities (Hannafin et al., 1993).

Pedagogical foundations of design are rooted in beliefs about how to organize lesson knowledge, how to sequence activities in the lesson, and how to support the learner as he or she acquires knowledge. Many times, pedagogical factors are identified during a needs assessment or front-end analysis and include the resources and constraints of learner, task, and setting characteristics (Hannafin et al., 1993).

As one might expect, even with emerging, high-profile technologies, distinctions of "good instruction, bad instruction" hold true (Hannafin et al., 1993). This includes the design of "good and bad" feedback within instruction as well.

32.6 RECOMMENDATIONS FOR FUTURE RESEARCH

To summarize areas in feedback research that need further attention, this author offers the following suggestions:

1. Examine how feedback functions within a wider variety of learning domains. Higher-order learning such as concept acquisition, rule use, problem solving, and the use of cognitive strategies offer a rich source for researchers to explore.
2. Analyze individual learner motivations and attitudes and prescribe feedback based on factors such as tenacity, self-efficacy, attributions, expectancy, and goal structure.
3. Identify measurable variables that can reflect internal cognitive and affective processes of learners that might potentially affect how feedback is perceived and utilized.
4. Examine how feedback functions within constructivist learning environments and test new feedback strategies within these environments.
5. Examine the role of monitoring and how both external and internal feedback generation effects the learning from a viewpoint of self-regulation.
6. As technologies continue to advance, design feedback that utilizes the improved capabilities for instruction.
7. Continue to identify and test interactive patterns between the learner, environment, individual internal knowledge construction, and varying types of feedback.

One could venture to say that no learning would occur unless some type of feedback mechanism was at work. What we do know is that feedback serves a critical function

in knowledge acquisition, regardless of the particular learning paradigm we are choosing to examine it through.

REFERENCES

Ahmad, M. (1988). The effect of computer-based feedback on using cognitive strategies of problem solving. *Proceedings of selected research papers, Association for Educational Communications and Technology, Research and Theory Division* (pp. 1–22). New Orleans, LA.

Anderson, J.R., Conrad, C.G. & Corbett, A.T. (1989). Skill acquisition and the LISP Tutor. *Cognitive Science 13,* 467–505.

Anderson, R.C. & Faust, G.W. (1967). The effects of strong formal prompts in programmed instruction. *American Educational Research Journal 4,* 345–52.

—, Kulhavy, R.W. & Andre, T. (1971). Feedback procedures in programmed instruction. *Journal of Educational Psychology 62,* 148–56.

—, Kulhavy, R.W. & Andre, T. (1972). Conditions under which feedback facilitates learning from programmed lessons. *Journal of Educational Psychology 63,* 186–88.

Andre, T. & Thieman, A. (1988). Level of adjunct question, type of feedback, and learning concepts by reading. *Contemporary Educational Psychology 13,* 296–307.

Balzer, W.K., Doherty, M.E. & O'Connor, R. (1989). Effects of cognitive feedback on performance. *Psychological Bulletin 106,* 410–33.

Bandura, A. (1977). Self-efficacy: toward a unifying theory of behavior change. *Psychological Review 84* (2), 191–215.

— (1982). Self-efficacy mechanism in human aging. *American Psychologist 37* (2), 122–47.

— (1993). Perceived self-efficacy in cognitive development and functioning. *Educational Psychologist 28,* 117–48.

Bangert-Drowns, R.L., Kulik, C.C., Kulik, J.A. & Morgan, M.T. (1991). The instructional effect of feedback in test-like events. *Review of Educational Research 61* (2), 218–38.

Bardwell, R. (1981). Feedback: how does it function? *Journal of Experimental Education 50,* 4–9.

Barringer, C. & Gholson, B. (1979). Effects of type and combination of feedback upon conceptual learning by children: implications for research in academic learning. *Review of Educational Research 49* (3), 459–78.

Birenbaum, M. & Tatsuoka, K.K. (1987). Effects of "on-line" test feedback on the seriousness of subsequent errors. *Journal of Educational Measurement 24* (2), 145–55.

Birney, R.C., Burdick, H. & Teevan, R.C. (1969). *Fear of failure.* New York: Van Nostrand.

Bodner, G.M. (1986). Constructivism: a theory of knowledge. *Journal of Chemical Education,* 63.

Boekaerts, M. (1994). Action control: how relevant is it for classroom learning? *In* J. Kuhl & J. Beckmann, eds. *Volition and personality: action versus state orientation,* 427–35. Seattle, WA: Hogrefe & Huber.

Brackbill, Y., Bravos, A. & Starr, R.H. (1962). Delay improved retention of a difficult task. *Journal of Comparative Psychology 55,* 947–52.

— & Kappy, M.S. (1962). Delay of reinforcement and retention. *Journal of Comparative and Physiological Psychology 55,* 14–18.

Briggs, L.J. & Hamilton, N.R. (1964). Meaningful learning

and retention: practice and feedback variables. *Review of Educational Research 34,* 545–58.

Brown, J.S., Collins, A. & Duguid, P. (1989). Situated cognition and the culture of learning. *Educational Researcher 18* (1), 32–42.

Burbules, N.C. & Linn, M.C. (1988). Response to contradiction: scientific reasoning during adolescence. *Journal of Educational Psychology 80,* 67–75.

Butler, D.L. & Winne, P.H. (1995). Feedback and self-regulated learning: a theoretical synthesis. *Review of Educational Research 65* (3), 245–81.

Butterfield, E.C., Nelson, T.O. & Peck, V. (1988). Developmental aspects of the feeling of knowing. *Developmental Psychology 24* (5), 654–63.

Carter, J. (1984). Instructional learner feedback: a literature review with implications for software development. *The Computing Teacher 12* (2), 53–55.

Carver, C.S. & Scheier, M.F. (1990). Origins and functions of positive and negative affect: a control-process view. *Psychological Review 97,* 19–35.

Chanond, K. (1988). The effects of feedback, correctness of response and response confidence on learners' retention in computer-assisted instruction. (Doctoral dissertation, University of Texas at Austin, 1988). *Dissertation Abstracts International 49,* 1358A.

Char, R.O. (1978). The effect of delay of informative feedback on the retention of verbal information and higher-order learning, for college students. (Doctoral dissertation, Florida State University, 1978). *Dissertation Abstracts International 40,* 748A.

Chinn, C.A. & Brewer, W.F. (1993). The role of anomalous data in knowledge acquisition: a theoretical framework and implications for science instruction. *Review of Educational Research 63,* 1–49.

Clariana, R.B., Ross, S.M. & Morrison, G.R. (1991). The effects of different feedback strategies using computer-administered multiple-choice questions as instruction. *Educational Technology Research & Development 39* (2), 5–17.

Clark, R.E., Aster, D. & Hession, M.A. (1987, Apr.). *When teaching kills learning: types of mathemathantic effects.* Paper presented at the annual meeting of the American Educational Research Association, Washington, DC.

Cognition and Technology Group at Vanderbilt (1990). Anchored instruction and its relationship to situated cognition. *Educational Researcher 19* (6), 2–10.

— (1991a). Technology and the design of generative learning environments. *Educational Technology 31* (5), 34–40.

— (1991b). Some thoughts about constructivism and instructional design. *Educational Technology 31* (9), 16–18.

— (1992a). The Jasper experiment: an exploration of issues in learning and instructional design. *Educational Technology Research & Development 40* (1), 65–80.

— (1992b). The Jasper series as an example of anchored instruction: theory, program description, and assessment data. *Educational Psychologist 27* (3), 291–315.

Cohen, V.B. (1985). A reexamination of feedback in computer-based instruction: implications for instructional design. *Educational Technology 25* (1), 33–37.

Collins, A., Brown, J.S. & Newman, S.E. (1987). Cognitive apprenticeship: teaching the craft of reading, writing, and mathematics. *In* L. Resnick, ed. *Learning, knowing, and instruction: essays in honor of Robert Glaser,* 453–94. Hillsdale, NJ: Erlbaum.

Cooper, P.A. (1993). Paradigm shifts in designed instruction: from behaviorism to cognitivism to constructivism. *Educational Technology,* May 1993, 12–19.

Covington, M.V. (1983). Motivated cognitions. *In* S.G. Paris, G.M. Olson & H.W. Stevenson, eds. *Learning and motivation in the classroom.* Hillsdale, NJ: Erlbaum.

— & Omelich, C.L. (1979). Are causal attributions causal? A path analysis of the cognitive model of achievement motivation. *Journal of Personality and Social Psychology 37,* 1487–1504.

— & Omelich, C.L. (1981). As failures mount: affective and cognitive consequences of ability demotion in the classroom. *Journal of Educational Psychology 73,* 796–808.

— & — (1982). Achievement anxiety, performance and behavioral instruction: a cost/benefits analysis. *In* R. Schwarzer, H. van der Ploeg & C. Speilberger, eds. *Test anxiety research,* Vol. 1. Amsterdam: Swets & Zeitlinger.

— & — (1984). Task-oriented versus competitive learning structures: motivational and performance consequences. *Journal of Educational Psychology 76* (6), 1038–50.

Deci, E.L. (1972). Intrinsic motivation, extrinsic reinforcement, and inequity. *Journal of Personality and Social Psychology 22* (1), 113–20.

Dempsey, J.V. (1988). The effects of four methods of immediate corrective feedback on retention, discrimination error, and feedback study time in computer-based instruction. (Doctoral dissertation, Florida State University, 1988.) *Dissertation Abstracts International 49,* 1434A.

— & Driscoll, M.P. (1994). *Conceptual error and feedback: the relationship between content analysis and confidence of response.* Manuscript submitted for publication.

— & Wager, S.U. (1988). A taxonomy for the timing of feedback in computer-based instruction. *Educational Technology 28* (10), 20–25.

—, Driscoll, M.P. & Litchfield, B.C. (1993). Feedback, retention, discrimination error, and feedback study time. *Journal of Research on Computing in Education 25* (3), 303–26.

— Driscoll, M.P. & Swindell, L.K. (1993). Text-based feedback. *In* J.V. Dempsey & G.C. Sales, eds. *Interactive instruction and feedback,* 21–54. Englewood Cliffs, NJ: Educational Technology.

Driscoll, M.P. (1990, Aug. 30). Personal communication.

Duffy, T.M. & Jonassen, D. (1991). Constructivism: new implications for instructional technology? *Educational Technology,* May 1991, 7–12.

Dweck, C.S. (1986). Motivational processes affecting learning. *American Psychologist 41* (10), 1040–48.

Dweck, C.S. & Legget, E.L. (1988). A social-cognitive approach to motivation and personality. *Psychology Review 95* (2), 256–73.

Edwards, L.D. (1991). Children's learning in a computer microworld for transformation geometry. *Journal for Research in Mathematics Education 22* (2), 122–37.

Eisenberger, R. (1992). Learned industriousness. *Psychological Review 99,* 248–67.

Elawar, M.C. & Corno, L. (1985). A factorial experiment in teachers' written feedback on student homework: changing teacher behavior a little rather than a lot. *Journal of Educational Psychology 77,* 162–73.

Elley, W.B. (1966). The role of errors in learning with feedback.

British Journal of Educational Psychology 35–36, 296–300.

Erez, M. & Zidon, I. (1984). Effect of goal acceptance on the relationship of goal difficulty to performance. *Journal of Applied Psychology 69,* 69–78.

Fischer, P.M. & Mandl, H. (1988). Knowledge acquisition by computerized audio-visual feedback. *European Journal of Psychology of Education 111,* 217–33.

Forsyth, D.R. & McMillan, J.H. (1981). Attributions, affect, and expectations: a test of Weiner's three-dimensional model. *Journal of Educational Psychology 73*(3), 393–403.

Gagné, R.M. (1985). *The conditions of learning,* 4th ed. New York: CBS College.

—, Briggs, L.J. & Wager, W.W. (1992). *Principles of instructional design,* 4th ed. New York: Holt, Rinehart & Winston.

— & Driscoll, M.P. (1988). *Essentials of learning for instruction,* 2d ed. Englewood Cliffs, NJ: Prentice Hall.

Gaynor, P. (1981). The effect of feedback delay on retention of computer-based mathematical material. *Journal of Computer-Based Instruction 8* (2), 28–34.

Gilman, D.A. (1969). Comparison of several feedback methods for correcting errors by computer-assisted instruction. *Journal of Educational Psychology 60* (6), 503–08.

Hanna, G.S. (1976). Effects of total and partial feedback in multiple-choice testing upon learning. *Journal of Educational Research 69,* 202–05.

Hannafin, M.J. (1989). Interactive strategies and emerging instructional technologies: psychological perspectives. *Canadian Journal of Educational Communication 18* (3), 167–80.

Hannafin, M.F., Hannafin, K.M. & Dalton, D.W. (1993). Feedback and emerging instructional technologies. *In* J.V. Dempsey & G.C. Sales, eds. *Interactive Instruction and Feedback,* 263–86. Englewood Cliffs, NJ: Educational Technology.

Hoska, D.M. (1993). Motivating learners through CBI feedback: developing a positive learner perspective. *In* J.V. Dempsey & G.C. Sales, eds. *Interactive Instruction and Feedback,* 105–32. Englewood Cliffs, NJ: Educational Technology.

Jacobs, J.W. & Dempsey, J.V. (1993). Simulation and gaming: fidelity, feedback, and motivation. *In* J.V. Dempsey & G.C. Sales, eds. *Interactive instruction and feedback,* 197–227. Englewood Cliffs, NJ: Educational Technology.

Johnson, D.W. & Johnson, R.T. (1993). Cooperative learning and feedback in technology-based instruction. *In* J.V. Dempsey & G.C. Sales, eds. *Interactive instruction and feedback,* 133–57. Englewood Cliffs, NJ: Educational Technology.

Jonassen, D.H. (1991a). Context is everything. *Educational Technology 31* (6), 33–34.

— (1991b). Objectivism versus constructivism: do we need a new philosophical paradigm? *Educational Technology Research and Development 39* (3), 5–14.

— (1993). Conceptual frontiers in hypermedia environments for learning. *Journal of Educational Multimedia and Hypermedia 2* (4), 331–35.

Keller, J.M. (1983). Motivational design of instruction. *In* C.M. Reigeluth, ed. *Instructional-design theories and models: an overview of their current status,* 383–434. Hillsdale, NJ: Erlbaum.

— (1987a). Development and use of the ARCS model of instructional design. *Journal of Instructional Development 10* (3), 2–10.

— (1987b). Strategies for stimulating the motivation to learn. *Performance & Instruction 26* (8), 1–7.

— (1987c). The systematic process of motivational design. *Performance and Instruction 26* (9), 1–8.

— & Kopp, T. (1987). An application of the ARCS model of motivational design. *In* C.M. Reigeluth, ed. *Instructional theories in action: lessons illustrating selected theories and models,* 289–320. Hillsdale, NJ: Erlbaum.

— & Suzuki, K. (1987). Use of ARCS motivation model in courseware design. *In* D.H. Jonassen, ed. *Instructional designs for microcomputer courseware,* 409–34. Hillsdale, NJ: Erlbaum.

Kelley, H.H. (1973). The processes of causal attribution. *American Psychologist 28,* 107–28.

Klausmeier, H.J. (1976). Instructional design and the teaching of concepts. *In* J.R. Levin & V.L. Allen, eds. *Cognitive learning in children,* 191–217. New York: Academic.

Koestner, R., Zuckerman, M. & Koestner, J. (1987). Praise involvement and intrinsic motivation. *Journal of Personality and Social Psychology 53* (2), 383–90.

Kowitz, G.T. & Smith, J.C. (1985). The dynamics of successful feedback. *Performance & Instruction Journal,* Oct., 4–6.

— & — (1987). The four faces of feedback. *Performance & Instruction,* Oct., 33–36.

Kozma, R. & Bangert-Drowns, R.L. (1987). Design in context: a conceptual framework for the study of computer software in higher education. Ann Arbor, MI: University of Michigan, National Center for Research to Improve Postsecondary Teaching and Learning. ERIC Document Reproduction Service No. 287 436.

Kuhl, J. & Goschke, T. (1994). A theory of action control: mental subsystems, modes of control, and volitional conflict-resolution strategies. *In* J. Kuhl & Beckmann, eds. *Volition and personality: action versus state orientation,* 93–124. Seattle, WA: Hogrefe & Huber.

Kulhavy, R.W. (1977). Feedback in written instruction. *Review of Educational Research 47* (1), 211–32.

— & Anderson, R.C. (1972). Delay-retention effect with multiple-choice tests. *Journal of Educational Psychology 63* (5), 505–12.

— & Parsons, J.A. (1972). Learning-criterion error perseveration in text materials. *Journal of Educational Psychology 63* (1), 81–86.

— & Stock, W.A. (1989). Feedback in written instruction: the place of response certitude. *Educational Psychology Review 1* (4), 279–308.

—, Stock, W.A., Hancock, T.E., Swindell, L.K. & Hammrich, P. (1990). Written feedback: response certitude and durability. *Contemporary Educational Psychology 15,* 319–32.

—, —, Thornton, N.E., Winston, K.S. & Behrens, J.T. (1990). Response feedback, certitude and learning from text. *British Journal of Educational Psychology 60,* 161–70.

— & Wager, W. (1993). Feedback in programmed instruction: historical context and implications for practice. *In* J.V. Dempsey & G.C. Sales, eds. *Interactive instruction and feedback,* 3–20. Englewood Cliffs, NJ: Educational Technology.

—, White, M.T., Topp, B.W., Chan, A.L. & Adams, J. (1985). Feedback complexity and corrective efficiency. *Contemporary Educational Psychology 10,* 285–91.

—, Yekovich, F.R. & Dyer, J.W. (1976). Feedback and

response confidence. *Journal of Educational Psychology 68* (5), 522–28.

—, — & — (1979). Feedback and content review in programmed instruction. *Contemporary Educational Psychology 4,* 91–98.

Kulik, J.A. & Kulik, C.-L.C. (1988). Timing of feedback and verbal learning. *Review of Educational Research 58* (1), 79–97.

Lee, O.M. (1985). The effect of type of feedback on rule learning in computer-based instruction. (Doctoral dissertation, Florida State University, 1985). *Dissertation Abstracts International 46,* 955A.

Lee, D., Smith, P.L. & Savenye, W. (1991). The effects of feedback and second try in computer-assisted instruction for rule-learning task. *Proceedings of selected research papers, Association for Educational Communications and Technology, Research and Theory Division,* 441–32. Orlando, FL.

Lewis, M.W. & Anderson, J.R. (1985). Discrimination of operator schemata in problem solving: learning from examples. *Cognitive Psychology 17,* 26–65.

Lhyle, K.G. & Kulhavy, R.W. (1987). Feedback processing and error correction. *Journal of Educational Psychology 79* (3), 320–22.

Litchfield, B.C. (1987). The effect of presentation sequence and generalization formulae on retention of coordinate and successive concepts and rules in computer-based instruction. (Doctoral dissertation, Florida State University, 1987). *Dissertation Abstracts International 49,* 486A.

Locke, E.A., Shaw, K.N., Saari, L.M. & Latham, G.P. (1981). Goal setting and task performance: 1969-1980. *Psychological Bulletin 90,* 125–52.

Malone, T.W. (1981). Toward a theory of intrinsically motivating instruction. *Cognitive Science 4,* 333–69.

McCullers, J.C., Fabes, R.A. & Moran, J.D., III (1987). Does intrinsic motivation theory explain the adverse effects of rewards on immediate task performance? *Journal of Personality and Social Psychology 52* (5), 1027–33.

Merrill, J. (1987). Levels of questioning and forms of feedback: instructional factors in courseware design. *Journal of Computer-Based Instruction 14* (1), 18–22.

Merrill, M.D. (1983). Component display theory. *In* C.M. Reigeluth, ed. *Instructional design theories and models,* 279–333. Hillsdale, NJ: Erlbaum.

Merrill, M. & Tennyson, R. (1977). *Teaching concepts: an instructional design guide.* Englewood Cliffs, NJ: Educational Technology.

Metcalfe, J. (1986). Feeling of knowing in memory and problem solving. *Journal of Experimental Psychology: Learning, Memory, and Cognition 12* (2), 288–94.

Meyer, L. (1986). Strategies for correcting students' wrong responses. *Elementary School Journal 87,* 227–41.

Mithaug, D.E. (1993). *Self-regulation theory: how optimal adjustment maximizes growth.* Westport, CT: Praeger.

Mory, E.H. (1991). *The effects of adaptive feedback on student performance, feedback study time, and lesson efficiency within computer-based instruction.* Unpublished doctoral dissertation. Florida State University, Tallahassee.

— (1992). The use of informational feedback in instruction: implications for future research. *Educational Technology Research and Development 40* (3), 5–20.

—(1994). The use of response certitude in adaptive feedback: effects on student performance, feedback study time, and efficiency. *Journal of Educational Computing Research 11* (3).

— (1995, Feb.). *A new perspective on instructional feedback: from objectivism to constructivism.* Paper presented at the annual meeting of the Association for Educational Communications and Technology, Anaheim, CA.

Nelson, T.O. (1988). Predictive accuracy of the feeling of knowing across different criterion tasks and across different subject populations and individuals. *In* M.M. Gruneberg, P.E. Morris & R.N. Sykes, eds. *Practical Aspects of Memory,* Vol. 1, 190–96. New York: Wiley.

—, Leonesio, R.J., Landwehr, R.S. & Narens, L. (1986). A comparison of three predictors of an individual's memory performance: the individual's feeling of knowing versus the normative feeling of knowing versus base-rate item difficulty. *Journal of Experimental Psychology: Learning, Memory, and Cognition 12* (2), 279–87.

Nolen-Hoeksema, S., Seligman, M.E. & Girgus, J.S. (1986). Learned helplessness in children: a longitudinal study of depression, achievement, and explanatory style. *Journal of Personality and Social Psychology 51* (2), 435–42.

Noonan, J.V. (1984). *Feedback procedures in computer-assisted instruction: knowledge-of-results, knowledge-of-correct-response, process explanations, and second attempts after errors.* Unpublished doctoral dissertation. University of Illinois, Urbana-Champaign.

Park, O.C. & Tennyson, R.D. (1986). Computer-based response-sensitive design strategies for selecting presentation form and sequence of examples in learning of coordinate concepts. *Journal of Educational Psychology 78* (2), 153–58.

Peeck, J. (1979). Effects of differential feedback on the answering of two types of questions by fifth- and sixth-graders. *British Journal of Educational Psychology 49,* 87–92.

— & Tillema, H.H. (1979). Delay of feedback and retention of correct and incorrect responses. *Journal of Experimental Education 47,* 171–78.

—, van den Bosch, A.B. & Kreupeling, W.J. (1985). Effects of informative feedback in relation to retention of initial responses. *Contemporary Educational Psychology 10,* 303–13.

Perkins, D.N. & Simmons, R. (1988). Patterns of misunderstanding: an integrative model for science, math, and programming. *Review of Educational Research 58,* 303–26.

Peterson, S.K. & Swindell, L.K. (1991, Apr.). *The role of feedback in written instruction: recent theoretical advance.* Paper presented at the annual meeting of the American Educational Research Association, Chicago, IL.

Phye, G.D. (1979). The processing of informative feedback about multiple-choice test performance. *Contemporary Educational Psychology 4,* 381–94.

— & Andre, T. (1989). Delayed retention effect: attention, perseveration, or both? *Contemporary Educational Psychology 14,* 173–85.

— & Bender, T. (1989). Feedback complexity and practice: response pattern analysis in retention and transfer. *Contemporary Educational Psychology 14,* 97–110.

— Gugliamella, J. & Sola, J. (1976). Effects of delayed retention on multiple-choice test performance. *Contemporary Educational Psychology 1,* 26–36.

Pressey, S.L. (1926). A simple device which gives tests and

scores—and teaches. *School and Society 23,* 373–76.

— (1927). A machine for the automatic teaching of drill material. *School and Society 25,* 549–52.

Reigeluth, C.M. & Stein, F.S. (1983). The elaboration theory of instruction. *In* C.M. Reigeluth, ed. *Instructional design theories and models,* 335–81. Hillsdale, NJ: Erlbaum.

Richards, D.R. (1989). A comparison of three computer-generated feedback strategies. *Proceedings of selected research papers, Association for Educational Communications and Technology, Research and Theory Division,* 357–68, Dallas, TX.

Rieber, L.P. (1992). Computer-based microworlds: a bridge between constructivism and direct instruction. *Educational Technology Research & Development 41* (1), 93–106.

Roper, W.J. (1977). Feedback in computer-assisted instruction. *Programmed Learning and Educational Technology 14,* 43–49.

Sales, G.C. (1993). Adapted and adaptive feedback in technology-based instruction. *In* J.V. Dempsey & G.C. Sales, eds. *Interactive instruction and feedback,* 159–75. Englewood Cliffs, NJ: Educational Technology.

Salomon, G. & Globerson, T. (1987). Skill may not be enough: the role of mindfulness in learning and transfer. *International Journal of Educational Research 11,* 623–37.

— & Perkins, D.N. (1989). Rocky roads to transfer: rethinking mechanisms of a neglected phenomenon. *Educational Psychologist 24,* 113–42.

Sassenrath, J.M. (1975). Theory and results on feedback and retention. *Journal of Educational Psychology 67* (6), 894–99.

— & Garverick, C.M. (1965). Effects of differential feedback from examinations on retention and transfer. *Journal of Educational Psychology 56* (5), 259–63.

— & Yonge, G.D. (1968). Delayed information feedback, feedback cues, retention set, and delayed retention. *Journal of Educational Psychology 59* (2), 69–73.

— & — (1969). Effects of delayed information feedback and feedback cues in learning on delayed retention. *Journal of Educational Psychology 60* (3), 174–77.

Schommer, M. (1990). Effects of beliefs about the nature of knowledge on comprehension. *Journal of Educational Psychology 82,* 498–504.

— (1993). Epistemological development and academic performance among secondary students. *Journal of Educational Psychology 85,* 406–11.

—, Crouse, A. & Rhodes, N. (1992). Epistemological beliefs and mathematical text comprehension: believing it is simple does not make it so. *Journal of Educational Psychology 84,* 435–43.

Schmidt, R.A., Young, D.E. Sinnen, S. & Shapiro, D.C. (1989). Summary knowledge of results for skill acquisition: support for the guidance hypothesis. *Journal of Experimental Psychology: Learning, Memory, and Cognition 15* (2), 352–59.

Schooler, L.J. & Anderson, J.R. (1990). The disruptive potential of immediate feedback. *Proceedings of the Twelfth Annual Conference of the Cognitive Science Society,* 702–08, Cambridge, MA.

Schimmel, B.J. (1983, Apr.). A meta-analysis of feedback to learners in computerized and programmed instruction. Paper presented at the annual meeting of the American Educational Research Association, Montreal. ERIC Document Reproduction Service No. ED 233 708.

— (1988). Providing meaningful feedback in courseware. *In* D.H. Jonassen, ed. *Instructional designs for microcomputer courseware,* 183–95. Hillsdale, NJ: Erlbaum.

Schloss, P.J., Sindelar, P.T., Cartwright, P.G. & Schloss, C.N. (1987-88). The influence of error correction procedures and question type on student achievement in computer-assisted instruction. *Journal of Educational Technology Systems 16* (1), 17–27.

Search, P. (1993). HyperGlyphs: using design and language to define hypermedia navigation. *Journal of Educational Multimedia and Hypermedia 2* (4), 369–80.

Seligman, M.E. (1990). *Learned optimism.* New York: Knopf.

— Maier, S.F. & Geer, J.H. (1968). Alleviation of learned helplessness in the dog. *Journal of Abnormal Psychology 73,* 256–62.

Siegel, M.A. & Misselt, A.L. (1984). Adaptive feedback and review paradigm for computer-based drills. *Journal of Educational Psychology 76,* 310–17.

Skinner, B.F. (1958). Teaching machines. *Science 128,* 969–77.

— (1968). *The technology of teaching.* New York: Appleton-Century-Crofts.

Smith, P.L. & Ragan, T.J. (1993). Designing instructional feedback for different learning outcomes. *In* J.V. Dempsey & G.C. Sales, eds. *Interactive instruction and feedback,* 75–103. Englewood Cliffs, NJ: Educational Technology.

Spiro, R.J., Feltovich, P.J., Jacobson, M.J. & Coulson, R.L. (1991a). Cognitive flexibility, constructivism, and hypertext: random access instruction for advanced knowledge acquisition in ill-structured domains. *Educational Technology,* May 1991, 24–33.

—, —, — & — (1991b). Knowledge representation, content specification, and the development of skill in situation-specific knowledge assembly: Some constructivist issues as they relate to cognitive flexibility theory and hypertext. *Educational Technology,* Sep. 1991, 22–25.

Sturges, P.T. (1969). Verbal retention as a function of the informativeness and delay of information feedback. *Journal of Educational Psychology 60,* 11–14.

— (1972). Information delay and retention: effect of information in feedback and tests. *Journal of Educational Psychology 63,* 32–43.

Surber, J.R. & Anderson, R.C. (1975). Delay-retention effect in natural classroom settings. *Journal of Educational Psychology 67* (2), 170–73.

Swindell, L. (1991, Apr.). *Testing a model of feedback in written instruction.* Paper presented at the annual meeting of the American Educational Research Association, Chicago, IL.

Swindell, L.K. (1992). Certitude and the constrained processing of feedback. *Contemporary Educational Psychology 17,* 30–37.

—, Kulhavy, R.W. & Stock, W.A. (1992). *The role of response confidence in comprehension and memory for written instruction.* Manuscript submitted for publication.

—, Peterson, S.E. & Greenway, R. (1992). Children's use of response confidence in the processing of instructional feedback. *Contemporary Educational Psychology 17,* 379–85.

Tait, K., Hartley, J.R. & Anderson, R.C. (1973). Feedback procedures in computer-assisted arithmetic instruction. *British Journal of Educational Psychology 43,* 161–71.

Tennyson, R.D. & Cocchiarella, M.J. (1986). An empirically

based instructional design theory for teaching concepts. *Review of Educational Research 56* (1), 40–71.

— & Park, O.C. (1980). The teaching of concepts: a review of instructional design research literature. *Review of Educational Research 50* (1), 55–70.

Tessmer, M., Wilson, B. & Driscoll, M. (1990). A new model of concept teaching and learning. *Educational Technology Research and Development 38* (1), 45–53.

Tosti, D.T. (1978). Formative feedback. *NSPI Journal 13,* 19–21.

Travers, R.M., van Wagenen, R.K., Haygood, D.H. & McCormick, M. (1964). Learning as a consequence of the learner's task involvement under different conditions of feedback. *Journal of Educational Psychology 55* (3), 167–73.

Tucker, S.A. (1993). Evaluation as feedback in instructional technology: the role of feedback in program evaluation. *In* J.V. Dempsey & G.C. Sales, eds. *Interactive instruction and feedback,* 301–42. Englewood Cliffs, NJ: Educational Technology.

Vance, R.J. & Coella, A. (1990). Effects of two types of feedback on goal acceptance and personal goals. *Journal of Applied Psychology 75* (1), 68–76.

Wager, S.U. (1983). The effect of immediacy and type of informative feedback on retention in a computer-assisted task. (Doctoral dissertation, Florida State University, 1983.) *Dissertation Abstracts International 44,* 2100A.

Wager, W. & Wager, S. (1985). Presenting questions, processing responses, and providing feedback in CAI. *Journal of Instructional Development 8* (4), 2–8.

Waldrop, P.B., Justen, J.E. & Adams, T.M. (1986). A comparison of three types of feedback in a computer-assisted instruction task. *Educational Technology 26,* 43–45.

Webster's New World Dictionary of the American Language, 2d ed. (1984). New York: Simon & Schuster.

Weiner, B. (1972). *Theories of motivation: from mechanism to cognition.* Chicago, IL: Rand McNally.

— (1979). A theory of motivation for some classroom experiences. *Journal of Educational Psychology 71,* 3–25.

— (1980). *Human motivation.* New York: Holt, Rinehart & Winston.

Wentling, T.L. (1973). Mastery versus nonmastery instruction with varying test item feedback treatments. *Journal of Educational Psychology 65* (1), 50–58.

Wilson, B. (1986). What is a concept? Cognitive teaching and cognitive psychology. *Performance and Instruction 25* (10), 16–18.

Winne, P.H. (1989). Theories of instruction and intelligence for designing artificially intelligent tutoring systems. *Educational Psychologist 24,* 229–59.

— (1992). State-of-the-art instructional computing systems that afford instruction and bootstrap research. *In* M. Jones & P.H. Winne, eds. *Foundations and frontiers of adaptive learning environments,* 349–80. Berlin: Springer.

Young, M.F. (1993). Instructional design for situated learning. *Educational Technology Research & Development 41* (1), 43–58.

Zellermayer, M., Salomon, G., Globerson, T. & Givon, H. (1991). Enhancing writing-related metacognitions through a computerized writing partner. *American Educational Research Journal 28,* 373–39.

Zimmerman, B.J. (1989). A social-cognitive view of self-regulated learning. *Journal of Educational Psychology 81,* 329–39.

—, ed. (1990). Self-regulated learning and academic achievement [special issue]. *Educational Psychologist 25* (1).

— & Martinez-Pons, M. (1992). Perceptions of efficacy and strategy use in the self-regulation of learning. *In* D.H. Schunk & J.L. Meece, eds. *Student perceptions in the classroom,* 185–207. Hillsdale, NJ: Erlbaum.

33. LEARNER-CONTROL AND INSTRUCTIONAL TECHNOLOGIES

Michael D. Williams
NANYANG TECHNOLOGICAL UNIVERSITY (SINGAPORE)

This chapter has several purposes: (a) to update the literature base of learner-control studies provided in previous reviews; (b) to review the paradigms employed in CBI research on learner control in instructional technologies; (c) to focus and expand on the suggestions made or implied in these reviews that a number of individual learner differences (and by implication the mental processes they reflect) can greatly contribute to both the choices students make and to the effectiveness of those choices; (d) to explore the impact on learner-control effectiveness of both rational-cognitive processes and emotional-motivational states of the learner; (e) to propose some instructional prescriptions for the use of learner-controlled activities; and (f) to suggest avenues for future research.*

33.1 LEARNER CONTROL AND COMPUTERS

The thrust of discussion here involves learner control over instructional activities that are based on or delivered by a computer (including interactive videodisc, CD-ROM, and related technologies). The exploration of learner control within more traditional delivery systems—for example, the *Audio-Tutorial Approach* (see 22.2.2) of Postlethwait, Novak, and Murray (1972) and the *Personalized System of Instruction* (*PSI* or *Keller Plan*) of F. S. Keller (1974)—is comprehensively addressed in Reiser's (1987) chapter on the history of educational technology. (See also 22.2.)

*I thank the University of Minnesota, San Diego State University, the Educational Communications and Technology Foundation, and Wilson Learning Corporation for supporting much of the preliminary work that culminated in this chapter.

33.2 LEARNER CONTROL IN INSTRUCTION

In general, "learner-controlled instruction," regardless of the instructional delivery system employed, refers to those instructional designs where learners make their own decisions regarding some aspect of the "path," "flow," or "events" of instruction. Such an instructional process is not in any way new or novel; in fact, when examined closely, most instructional designs are seen to consist of a mixture of learner-controlled and instructor-prescribed events.

Designers may wish to base their decisions about the provision of learner control around any of several instructional models or theories commonly used to guide the selection of instructional methods. These models or theories (e.g., Gagné, Briggs & Wager, 1988; Merrill, 1983) usually consist of very small elements or component activities (see 18.4) (e.g., motivating activities, informing students of the objective, presenting information, providing feedback to learners on their performance) to be drawn upon or assembled into an instructional design. These models, too, coincidentally function very handily as practical menus of instructional components about which the designer may decide whether, when, and how to place under the learner's control.

Possibilities for learner control of these types of learner-controlled activities would apply to any format of instructional delivery system. However, because the literature base focusing specifically on learner control in computer-based instructional environments is a fairly well-defined subset of studies within the larger domain of general learner control (including, e.g., correspondence courses and independent study), the remainder of this paper will focus specifically on those issues of learner control that are related to technology-based instructional delivery systems.

(For additional discussions of issues related to learner control, see also 7.4.5, 12.2.3, 13.3.1, 14.6.2, 22.3.9, 22.5.5., 23.7.2, and 25.9.4.)

33.3 LEARNER CONTROL IN COMPUTER-BASED INSTRUCTIONAL DELIVERY SYSTEMS

A supposed advantage of computer-based instruction (CBI) over more traditional forms of instruction is its capability to deliver to students "individualized" lessons. That is, the computer can assemble and present to different students tailored lessons with wide variations in sequence of information, amounts of examples and practice questions, or kinds of feedback and review, to name just a few possibilities. In such situations, the computer program assumes the role of manager or guide of instructional activities. In such situations, students "receive" the instruction and have little or no explicit choice over what is given.

Alternatively, the instructional computer program may abrogate such decisions and allow learners to select the instruction they are to receive. Here, the learner operates to control the "flow" or "path" of instructional materials. Although it is certainly possible that learner choices might be afforded at a "macro" level of instruction, i.e., at the level of curricula, units, or lessons (see Romiszowski, 1986, for a discussion of instructional levels), typically the types of instructional choices provided in computer-delivered instruction operate at the "micro" scale, that is, at the level of small instructional elements, activities, or components.

There are many common instances of instructionally related activities that fall within the general framework of technology-based "learner control." For example:

- Standard computer-based and multimedia (e.g., videodisc, CD-ROM) instruction for direct instruction (e.g., drill and practice, and tutorial). This type of software follows an overall instructional design strategy but permits students to make their own decisions about, for example, what topics to see and when, how many exercises to take, or when to quit the lesson.
- Computer-based simulations (see 17.4, 17.5). These programs operate almost entirely under the learner's control (Reigeluth & Schwartz, 1989) in that the continual and often complex manipulations of the simulation's parameters are nearly totally left to the discretion of the learner.
- Tools for indirect learning such as word processing, programming, telecommunications, and databases. Billings (1982) argues that these tools are of a different class from typical computer-assisted instructional lessons. She argues that in these applications, learner control is inherent in the software and offers the potential for more complex learning by the students than more traditional instruction. These are called *tools for indirect learning* in that students should not learn the

tools for their own sake, but rather that these softwares be utilized in the pursuit of other learning outcomes (e.g., writing skills, mathematical reasoning, critical thinking).
- Instructional and informational applications developed around hypertext or hypermedia technologies (e.g., Bowers & Tsai, 1990). Such innovations offer to learners previously unconceived freedom of movement and choice of media displays. So-called "electronic encyclopedias," especially those designed for K-12 school use, are examples of this type of technology. The structures of these databases have important implications for information accessibility and the ease of navigation around the database, i.e., what learner control features are offered (Duchastel, 1986a; Wilson & Jonassen, 1989).
- On-line computer documentation, which allows the user the options of either following a detailed walk-through of major procedures and functions, or jumping around according to the needs of the moment (so-called "just-in-time" helps). These features most commonly serve as simply performance job aids, but they are frequently used as aids for learning, as well (Rossett & Gautier-Downes, 1991).

33.4 RATIONALE FOR LEARNER CONTROL IN CBI

There seems to be several philosophical, practical, and theoretical reasons for allowing learners some control over events occurring during CBI lessons. In fact, the use of traditional, rather rigidly controlled computer-assisted instruction may actually run counter to the educational philosophies promoted by many teachers in the arts and humanities, and which encourage student exploration and expression. D. W. Hansen (1982/1983) argues that allowing students more user control will increase the chance these teachers would want to include computer-based activities in their classes.

Additionally, to many educators and instructional designers, the expression "learner-controlled instruction" suggests a class of instructional events or tactics intended to increase learner involvement, mental investment ("mindfulness," as Salomon, 1983, phrased it), and achievement. The approach is to emphasize the learner's freedom to choose those learning activities that suit his or her own individual preferences and needs.

On a more pragmatic level, Steinberg (1984) says that, if learning is found to be equivalent in both learner- and computer-controlled settings, design costs should shrink, time spent learning should be reduced, and attitudes and motivation should become more positive if a learner-controlled framework for instruction is adopted.

Instructional design theorists, too, have found ample reasons for including provisions for learner control in computer-based designs. In his design theory, Merrill (1983) prescribes learner control of content (encompassing curriculum, lesson, and module selection) and of strategy (spanning various forms of presentation). Bunderson (1974), Faust (1974), and Fine (1972) each present an assortment of learner-controlled activities derived from Merrill's early design theory (Merrill, 1973; Reigeluth, 1979). The *TICCIT* (*T*ime-Shared *I*nteractive, *C*omputer *C*ontrolled *I*nformation *T*elevision) system, derived from Merrill's early theory, provides the learner with many types of options, some of which are dependent on the current course (such as reviews, menus, quizzes, faster/slower type of feedback, level of question difficulty, and topic surveys), while others are constant across any course delivered by the system (such as backward or forward movement, access to a calculator, access to a glossary, and opportunity to leave an on-line comment; there is even a feature that gives the student the option to "CUSS" at the computer when things go wrong!).

Reigeluth and Stein (1983) in their instructional design theory also hypothesize that ". . . instruction generally increases in effectiveness, efficiency, and appeal to the extent that it permits informed learner control by motivated learners" (p. 362). Federico (1980), too, suggests that learner control might be a useful alternative to the classic aptitude-by-treatment interaction approach (see 22.3.3), in that "learners can become system independent by enabling them to manipulate and accommodate treatments to their own momentary cognitive requirements" (p. 17).

A rationale from a different perspective comes from a survey of adult learning preferences. Penland (1979) found that the top four reasons why adults prefer learning on their own were expressed as desires to "set my own learning pace," "use my own style of learning," "keep the learning strategy flexible," and "put my own structure on the learning project." Discussing the differences between adults and children, Hannafin (1984) argues that under CBI conditions, older students should realize the benefits from learner control more than younger students because they have acquired more (and presumably better) learning strategies.

Some of the research from the psychology of basic learning processes also implies possible advantages of learner control. For example, one might expect a learner-controlled instructional treatment to induce more elaborate mental processing by students as a result of their having to ponder the choices they face. Salomon (1983, 1985) refers to the degree of such mental activity as "invested mental effort." The more such effort expended, he implies, the more mental elaborations the student performs, resulting in deeper, more meaningful learning. In contrast, one might not expect as much cognitive elaboration from students proceeding through a more "passive" instructional treatment. In plain language, learners given control over their instruction might be more likely to think about what they are doing as a result of having to make choices along the way.

Hartley (1985), too, argues for the need for more attention to basic psychological processes when studying the impact of computers on learning, and he supports the use of learner control of instruction as a means for students to develop their own cognitive structures. That is, consistent with a constructivist view of knowledge development (see 7.3), he proposes that the learning of complex knowledge structures is facilitated when the learner himself or herself can participate in the construction of those mental structures. This constructivist approach is also promoted by Salomon and Gardner (1986) who suggest that ". . . individuals mold their own experiences by the traits and goals they bring to the encounter, the way they apprehend the technology and the situation, and the *particular volitional choices they make.* In so doing, learners, particularly when given interactive opportunities with computers, are likely to affect the way these opportunities are going to affect them" (p. 16, emphasis added).

Indeed, the emerging constructivist paradigm of learning as an inventive learning process rather than an acquisitive one almost requires some type of attention to the degree and types of control the learners will exert during the learning process. Lebow (1993), for example, suggests that, to constructivists, the strategic availability of learner control options can provide structural support for the values of personal autonomy, personal relevance, active engagement, and reflectivity, all important characteristics undergirding the constructivist philosophy of education. (See 7.4.5 for further discussion of constructivisim and learner control.)

33.5 THE EFFECTIVENESS OF LEARNER CONTROL IN CBI

Unfortunately, the empirical research on learner control in instructional contexts does not support its unconditional use (Carrier, 1984; Hannafin, 1984; Milheim & Martin, 1991; Steinberg, 1977, 1989). Many authors of texts on CBI design caution against cavalierly offering a variety of options to learners (e.g., Alessi & Trollip, 1985; Jonassen & Hannum, 1987; Steinberg, 1984) because such a strategy does not seem to improve overall learning. O'Shea and Self (1983, Chapter 3) summarize much of the unpublished research on the effectiveness of the early TICCIT system and conclude that it is difficult to support its widespread use. Merrill (1983), too, concludes that college-level students generally do not make good use of learner control options, a position also taken by Carrier (1984). Snow (1980), commenting on the use of learner control in adaptive instruction, argues that far from eliminating the effects of individual differences on learning, providing learner control may actually exacerbate these differences.

Research on learner control in CBI has typically compared learner-controlled and program-controlled treatments in a fashion reminiscent of, and analogous to, media comparison studies conducted in the 1960s and 70s (and with analogous methodological problems; see Reeves, 1993, for a thorough critique). The following is an updated summary of research findings comparing learner-controlled computer-based instruction with either partial learner-controlled versions or complete computer-controlled versions for the three most common types of dependent variables measured in such studies, namely, learning, time-on-task, and attitudes and affect.

Generally speaking, these studies compare treatments that present a mixture of the specific instructional events actually subject to learner control. Also, contrary to Hannafin's (1984) claim, both adults and children seem to have been well represented in these studies. Many of these studies were also reviewed by Carrier, (1984), Hannafin, (1984), Milheim and Martin (1991), and Steinberg (1977, 1989), but are discussed in this chapter with more stress given to attempting to understand the underlying processes governing students' choices. Additionally, many studies are examined here which have not been included in previous review papers.

33.5.1 Learning

On the whole, results have been mixed, but instructional treatments under the learner's control have been shown most often to be as effective or less effective than treatments under more computer control. Also contrary to a suggestion by Hannafin (1984), findings from the literature reviewed here indicate that children do not seem to be less able to handle learner-controlled situations than adults.

A few studies have supported the use of learner control of at least some instructional events (Avner, Moore & Smith, 1980; Campanizzi, 1978; Ellermann & Free, 1990; Kinzie, Sullivan & Berdel, 1988; Mayer, 1976; Newkirk, 1973; Shyu & Brown, 1992). Most of these support Hannafin's (1984) suggestion that learner control promotes a deeper or more long-lasting effect on memory. Newkirk (1973), for example, found a long-term learning benefit for learner control, but not for program control. Mayer (1976) found that more complex outcomes were learned better when learners were able to control the order of presentation, while simple outcomes were learned better under experimenter-controlled conditions. In one of the few long-term studies of the effects of learner control in CBI, Avner et al. (1980) found that students using highly "interactive" learner control showed a greater degree of high-level skills than did the students within a more "passive" type of CBI. There were no differences between these groups on low-level skills, however. In a paired-associate task investigated by Ellermann and Free (1990), students who could select the order of presentation seemed to have a stronger memory trace, implying more engagement of cognitive structures.

In contrast, studies by R. C. Atkinson (1972), Belland, Taylor, Canelos, Dwyer, and Baker (1985), Johansen and Tennyson (1983), Lee and Wong (1989), MacGregor (1988), Morrison, Ross, and Baldwin (1992), Olivier (1971), Pollock and Sullivan (1990), Reinking and Schreiner (1985), Rivers (1972), C. L. Tennyson, Tennyson, and Rothen (1980), Tennyson and Buttrey (1980), Tennyson, Park, and Christensen (1985), Tennyson, Welsh, Christensen, and Hajovy (1985), all found various types or degrees of program control superior to learner control of the same instructional elements for posttest achievement. Many of these authors speak of learners not having or not knowing how to utilize appropriate strategies when they are left to themselves to manage their learning environment.

Interestingly, most studies in which the computer controlled the rate of pacing, that is, the length of time in which screenfuls of information were presented to the student (Belland et al., 1985; Dalton, 1990; Tennyson, Park & Christensen, 1985; Tennyson, Welsh, Christensen & Hajovy, 1985), found learning under those conditions better than self-paced conditions (in which the learner controls the speed at which material is presented), the usual fixture in most CBI programs. One study by Milheim (1990), however, did find learning better under a learner-controlled pacing condition.

Additionally, in a meta-analysis of 10 years of interactive video instruction, McNeil and Nelson (1991) conclude generally that program-controlled conditions are superior to learner-controlled condition. They suggest however, that partial (i.e., "guided") learner control over review and practice activities might be better for learning than program control over these activities, although they caution that too few studies included such conditions to make the conclusion unequivocal.

Most studies, however, found no differences overall between learner-controlled and program-controlled treatments (Arnone & Grabowski, 1992; Balson, Manning, Ebner & Brooks, 1984/1985; Beard, Lorton, Searle & Atkinson, 1973; Carrier, Davidson, Higson & Williams, 1984; Carrier, Davidson & Williams, 1985; Carrier, Davidson, Williams & Kalweit, 1986; Fredericks, 1976; Goetzfried & Hannafin, 1985; Gray, 1987; Hannafin & Colamaio, 1987; Holmes, Robson & Steward, 1985; Hurlock, Lahey & McCann, 1974; Judd, Bunderson & Bessent, 1970; Judd, O'Neil & Spelt, 1974a; Kinzie & Sullivan, 1989; Klein & Keller, 1990; Lahey, 1978; Lahey & Coady, 1978; Lahey, Crawford & Hurlock, 1976; Lahey, Hurlock & McCann, 1973; Lee & Lee, 1991; López & Harper, 1989; McCann, Lahey & Hurlock, 1973; Murphy & Davidson, 1991; Pridemore & Klein, 1991; Relan, 1991; Ross, Morrison & O'Dell, 1988, 1989; Schloss, Sindelar, Cartwright & Smith, 1988; Schloss, Wisniewski & Cartwright, 1988; Strickland & Wilcox, 1978; Wilcox, Richards, Merrill, Christensen & Rosenvall, 1978). The various conclusions drawn from this "no-difference" finding are interesting and tend to reflect a good deal of rationalization. Some of the researchers use this finding to support the use of learner control, saying that programming the computer to handle the myriad complex types of branching that could potentially occur in a lesson is far too difficult. So therefore, since their research indicates it would at least do no harm, it is better to let students handle their own lesson branching. Other researchers use the "no-difference" result to justify program control of instruction, saying that other benefits, such as time savings (discussed next), are realized by not letting learners control their own instructional paths. Still other researchers look more closely at their data to discern any interaction effects that may be operating; that is, learner control or program control might be better for some people or under some conditions, but not on the whole. These types of studies are discussed in more detail later in this chapter.

33.5.2 Time-on-Task

Several studies also included as a dependent variable the length of time students took to complete a lesson. A few studies found students in learner-controlled CBI groups taking more time to finish the lesson than program-controlled groups. In a study by MacGregor (1988), elementary students worked in pairs, and those in the learner-controlled group were given the opportunity to participate in an on-line instructional game; students in the program-controlled group were not. The author attributed the time-on-task differences to the fact that the game aroused quite a bit of interest, thus generating a lot of talking and other social activity within the pairs, thus naturally consuming more time in the process. Dalton (1990) also found that students in a condition in which the computer controlled the pacing of materials spent more time than those in learner-controlled pacing. He, too, suggests that the amount of socializing observed among the paired members of the learner-controlled condition accounted for the longer time spent. Shyu and Brown (1992) explain that longer times in their study for students under learner control can be explained by those students needing more time to figure out how to operate the learner control features of the computer program. Another study (Avner et al., 1980) found that while students in learner control conditions spent more time during on-line tasks, they spent less time during related off-line tasks, in this case laboratory activities. Interestingly, none of these authors of studies attributed the additional time spent by students in learner-controlled conditions to a greater or deeper degree of cognitive engagement, even though there is theoretical justification for such a conclusion.

A few studies found no differences in time spent (Hurlock et al., 1974; Kinzie & Sullivan, 1989; Lahey et al., 1973). The bulk of studies, however, found that learner-controlled groups spent considerably less time than program-controlled groups (Fredericks, 1976; Johansen & Tennyson, 1983; Lahey et al., 1976; Murphy & Davidson, 1991; Rivers, 1972; Ross et al., 1988; Schloss, Sindelar, Cartwright & Smith, 1988; C. L. Tennyson et al., 1980; Tennyson, 1980; Tennyson & Buttrey, 1980).

Researchers investigating "efficiency" of time spent during a lesson have found mixed results. Dalton (1990) found no differences on achievement-per-time-spent between self-paced and lesson-paced interactive video formats, although Relan (1991) did find such differences in a CBI study favoring the least amount of learner control. Another study (Goetzfried & Hannafin, 1985) did find differences between groups on an efficiency variable they define as the number of concepts a student sees per minute. In their study, however, learner control was the least efficient; that is, it promoted a slower progression through the lesson.

In some of these studies (Goetzfried & Hannafin, 1985; Johansen & Tennyson, 1983; C. L. Tennyson et al., 1980; Tennyson, 1980; Tennyson & Buttrey, 1980), shorter time was also linked to poorer performance. One possible explanation for these findings lies in the confounding of instructional control, time-on-task, and amount of instructional material seen. That is, learners navigating their way through a lesson might spend less time because they opted to skip over large amounts of instructional material. If this omitted material were crucial for overall lesson performance, these students might naturally be expected to perform more poorly than would students progressing through a program-controlled, but more "complete," lesson package. This notion is also offered by Lepper (1985), who suggests that students under learner control might see differing amounts or kinds of instructional material than students under program-controlled treatments. (In fact, for some situations it is entirely likely that each student under learner control selected his or her way through a completely different instructional treatment!) Therefore, in these studies we do not know whether the culprit for the supposed failure of learner control is the fact that students were granted control, per se, or simply saw suboptimal amounts of instruction as a result of "poor" choices. Indeed, several of these studies do report that students in learner control spent less time because they saw fewer instructional screens (e.g., fewer examples).

Commenting on the problem of learners choosing low amounts of instruction, Higginbotham-Wheat (1988) and Ross and Morrison (1989) draw the conclusion that learner-controlled instruction should allow naive or otherwise unprepared students to select context, sequence, and presentation style variables only, and should not allow students to choose instructional events that could alter the amount of content support, unless they have the prerequisite skills or training. It seems safe to say that the confounding of learner control, time-on-task, and amount of instructional material is a matter that can prevent clear conclusions about the relative merits of offering control to learners. This issue surfaces again later in this chapter.

As with the findings of no difference in learning between learner- and program-controlled groups mentioned earlier, the authors of the studies who found shorter times for learner control also are quite creative in the implications they draw from that finding. Some authors claim that if learning is equivalent, but time spent is shorter, learner control is desired because of the time "savings" or "economies." Others say that the shorter times from the learner control groups mean less time-on-task and time for cognitive processing, inherently undesirable outcomes, and thus should be avoided.

33.5.3 Attitudes and Affect

Most of the studies that measured the students' attitudes toward computer-assisted instruction or toward learner control over instruction found either no differences or a favorable attitude from students who experienced a learner-controlled treatment compared with program-controlled groups. The author of the one study that did find relatively negative attitudes in the learner control group (Gray, 1987) explained the findings as due to resentment and frustration at the complexity of the instructional decisions the students under the learner-controlled condition were required to make.

A few studies (Arnone & Grabowski, 1992; Beard et al., 1973; Judd et al., 1970; Kinzie et al., 1988; Lahey, 1978; Pridemore & Klein, 1991; Shyu & Brown, 1992) found no differences between learner-control and program-control groups in student attitude toward CBI. Additionally, one review (Judd, 1972) also concluded that, generally, learner control does not contribute to improved attitudes. However, it is quite possible that the early computer studies included in Judd's paper do not represent the highly interactive approaches used for instruction on modern microcomputers.

Six studies did find positive attitude effects for students in learner-control groups (Hintze, Mohr & Wenzel, 1988; Hurlock et al., 1974; Judd et al., 1974a; Milheim, 1989; Morrison et al., 1992; Newkirk, 1973). For example, the study by Milheim (1989) exploring interactive videodisc instruction found better attitudes toward the instructional activity for students under learner-control pacing compared with students who experienced program control of lesson pacing. In most of the studies examining attitudes, students were exposed only to one type of program (i.e., they only saw a learner-controlled version or a program-controlled version). One of the most interesting of all the studies examining attitudes is presented by Hintze et al. (1988), who compared attitudes in dental students in Denmark, each of whom actually had a chance to experience several versions: completely learner-controlled, partially learner-controlled, and computer-controlled instructional situations. They found the overwhelming majority of students preferred at least some learner control. Interestingly, males by far preferred complete learner control, while female preferences were split between partial and total learner control. They suggest possible explanations for this finding, including that it might be due to the fact that males typically have spent more time with computers, and thus are more likely to want to explore with them when given the chance. Dalton (1990) also found some interesting interactions between gender and learner- or program-controlled treatments on attitudes. Specifically, he found that females

under lesson-controlled pacing ended up with better attitudes toward instruction and toward the content of the lesson than females under learner-controlled pacing. Males, however, under program-controlled pacing had significantly worse attitudes toward content than males under learner-paced lessons. However, convincing explanations for these gender effects and interactions were not provided by the authors of these studies and remain to be drawn, particularly as they relate to the underlying social, motivational, or cognitive processes involved. For example, it is possible that males have a greater comfort level (less anxiety) when they sit at the computers, and thus feel more confident to "take charge" of them.

Some researchers investigated the effects of learner-controlled instruction on one particular type of attitude measure called *continuing motivation* (Maehr, 1976; Seymour, Sullivan, Story & Mosley, 1987), which indicates how likely is a student's ongoing willingness to return to a learning activity at a later time without external pressure, essentially a variable measuring the student's desire to learn voluntarily. Kinzie and Sullivan (1989) found positive effects on the students' desires to pursue science activities following computer-assisted instruction, generally, and following learner-controlled CAI, specifically. However, this effect was not replicated by López and Harper (1989), who found no advantage for learner control over program control on continuing motivation in science. López and Harper (1989) do not offer any specific explanation to reconcile this discrepancy, but they imply that there might be characteristics of the population studied (high-risk Hispanic students), which had a unique bearing on the findings in their study.

Lastly, a few early studies investigated the effects of learner-controlled computer-based instruction on student state (i.e., temporary) anxiety, with mixed results. Judd (1972) recaps one study that shows a reduction in anxiety as a result of learner-controlled CBI. J. B. Hansen (1974) also found a lowering of initial state anxiety as a result of learner control over computer-delivered feedback. However, neither Judd, O'Neil, and Spelt (1974b), nor Judd, Daubek, and O'Neil (1975), were able to lower state anxiety as a result of their particular types of learner control (control over access to mnemonic devices in the first case, and control over access to pictures in the second case).

33.5.4 Summary of the Effectiveness of Learner Control of CBI

After reviewing all of these findings for the various types of dependent variables, we are presented with an apparent dilemma: Given the rationale for learner control provided earlier, there are good reasons to believe that learner control is a desirable instructional approach. However, the bulk of studies conducted to assess that notion found that students left on their own do not uniformly make good use of such strategies. Duchastel (1986b) sums up the frustrating ambiguity of learner control research:

. . . the research leads one to be cautious about the general learner control hypothesis, namely, that the student is the best judge of the instructional strategy to be adopted. Some results in instructional research indicate that not all students are capable of making appropriate educational decisions. Other results, however, indicate the tremendous benefits of learner control in particular situations. The sophistication of the learner and the type of objectives pursued, as well as the particular context of the system, will probably impact on the nature and effectiveness of learner control in given situations (p. 391).

But there are problems with the research itself, which also limits the conclusions we might draw from this body of literature. Reeves (1993) presents a very thorough critique of the bulk of learner control research, suggesting that the lack of unambiguous findings is in fact due to bad research. He lists a variety of shortcomings with the literature spanning four crucial areas. First, he presents some problems in many studies with the definition of learner control used. That is, many authors fail to provide adequate operational definitions of their learner control treatments, and so end up with, at best, muddy and ambiguous experimental designs. Secondly, he discusses the lack of adequate theoretical foundations undergirding the experiments. Studies often proceed, he says, without even a tenuous connection with the literature of basic learning or instructional theories. (Whether this type of uninformed research activity is necessary for the "theory-building" phase required of any school of systematic scientific investigation, or instead bluntly demonstrates intellectual expedience or laziness on the part of researchers, is a matter of separate debate.) The last two problem areas he finds in the learner-control literature are methodological and analytical, with researchers too seldom using adequate designs (often including poor instrumentation, control of procedures and sampling; see 39.2.1) and procedures for analyzing the data (e.g., improperly employing quantitative paradigms when qualitative approaches would make more sense; see 39.4.1.2).

As an example, a typical problem in learner-control research is the confounding of learner-control or program-control treatments with the amount of instruction students see during the lesson, a problem mentioned earlier in this chapter. That is, as Lepper (1985) points out, the often-repeated failure to demonstrate the effectiveness of learner control might simply be a function of the fact that less instructional material is selected by those students; hence they received an "incomplete" lesson compared with their program-controlled counterparts. In other words, learner-control ineffectiveness would be an artifact of the particular set of instructional events they experienced (or, more likely, did not experience).

Indeed, Ross and Rakow (1981), C. L. Tennyson et al. (1980), Tennyson (1980), and Tennyson and Buttrey (1980), all showed that students in the learner-controlled treatments saw many fewer instructional examples than did students under program control. However, in these studies, lower amounts of instructional material were inextricably confounded with the learner-control treatments. Carrier and Williams (1988) experimentally controlled the amount of material seen, and found a positive effect for amount of material separate from learner-control or program-control effects. In a study by Morrison et al. (1992), amount of instructional material was controlled for by having two program-controlled versions: one with "minimum" instructional support, one with "maximum." They found that the students under learner control actually performed poorer than those with the "minimum" program-control treatment. The type of studies that attempt to control for amount of instruction separately from learner control have been fairly rare, but they do allow for a clearer examination of the effects of learner choices independent from amount of instruction.

These criticisms also prevent researchers from conducting statistical meta-analyses on the literature as a way to provide a little more concrete basis for making statements about the effectiveness of learner control. Because the studies about learner control are so incredibly varied (each study seems to offer unique operationalizations, instrumentations, designs, and analyses), it would be practically impossible to arrange the studies into sets of reasonably equivalent dependent and independent variables, and to conduct a meta-analysis so as to avoid the concerns Slavin (1986) has voiced about improper use of the meta-analysis technique.

Similarly, a "best-evidence" approach (Slavin, 1986) to synthesizing the learner-control literature would also be difficult to defend, because the criteria for inclusion of studies in such a synthesis (e.g., relevance, minimal bias, external validity) are frequently not met, as Reeves (1993) has forcefully presented. If a best-evidence synthesis were attempted, it is likely that after gleaning from the literature the studies worthy of examination, there might not be that many "clean" articles left that could provide any useful information for inclusion in the synthesis.

If, as seems amply demonstrated by Reeves (1993), there are problems that prevent us from drawing confident conclusions from the domain of learner-control research in CBI, the next logical question would be, "Is there anything we *can* say from looking at these studies?" Depending on the research perspective taken, reviewers might reject the body of research to date (because of the flaws); or they might conduct a type of salvage operation, examining the studies post mortem for clues and commonalities across the papers that might help both explain the diverse findings previously cited, and to provide new researchable questions. Kinzie (1990), for example, provides a very helpful mapping of some research findings in the learner-control literature, with various theoretical perspectives in motivation, individual differences, social psychology, and self-regulated learning. However, as with all post hoc types of examinations of literature (including this chapter), it is important to stress that conclusions drawn should be considered in large part to be conjectures, inferred from the studies, and which remain to be a priori tested in their own right.

33.6 THE ROLE OF
LEARNER CHARACTERISTICS

Educators know that individual learner characteristics play a huge role in how fast and how well overall learning occurs. Generally speaking, since its inception CBI has continually been held up as a promising vehicle able to somehow tailor instruction to meet the individual needs of each learner (Suppes, 1966; U.S. Congress, Office of Technology Assessment, 1988). Just how these instructional adaptations are best concocted, however, is a matter of debate.

Some models for adaptive CBI are largely program controlled and attempt to present to each student appropriately matched instructional events according to some relevant individual difference variable. Examples of such approaches include regression models that assign optimized instructional conditions based on either stable trait variables (McCombs & McDaniel, 1981; see also 22.3) or on-task state variables (Rivers, 1972; Ross & Morrison, 1988; see also 22.5) and schemes to branch instruction according to some optimizing mathematical model (R. C. Atkinson, 1972; Holland, 1977; Smallwood, 1962; Tennyson, Christensen & Park, 1984; see also 22.4). Few of these approaches have made it into commercially produced CBI, however.

On the other hand, for reasons of feasibility, attractiveness, and understandability, most of the CBI found in school software libraries has at least some learner-controlled features that their manufacturers tout as helping to accommodate the learning needs of each individual student. The idea, as Merrill (1973, 1975) and Federico (1980) have propounded, is that students will make their own decisions throughout a lesson so as to best match their own learning styles, personality, or other relevant traits.

As we have seen, however, learner control does not seem to be a superior overall instructional strategy. A closer examination does seem to indicate differential student effectiveness of instructional choices, although perhaps not in the way the software producers had intended. That is, some students are able to use learner control to their advantage; others, however, use it actually to their detriment.

33.6.1 Paradigms

It is useful at this point to review the major paradigms employed in research that focuses on the relationship between learner characteristics and learner-controlled CBI. There are several methods available to researchers wishing to study such interactions. One common approach adopts an "aptitude-by-treatment interaction" or ATI perspective (see 22.5; Carrier & Jonassen, 1988; Cronbach & Snow, 1977). That is, students' stable cognitive and personality "trait" variables are viewed as possibly interacting with predetermined instructional features to produce differentially effective learning, particularly within a learner-controlled context (Snow, 1980). One example (Judd et al., 1974a) found that the personality variable of "achievement via independence" predicts certain behaviors under learner control (see 22.3.4.6). Snow (1979) also takes an ATI

approach and presents some data using various statistical profiling techniques that appear to be fairly successful at sorting college students enrolled in a BASIC programming course into good and poor options selectors according to their scores on a variety of aptitude measures.

The usual aim of ATI studies is to find instructional treatments that would somehow benefit students possessing different learner characteristics or profiles. However, in spite of Federico's (1980) suggestion that learner control might allow students to select effectively instances based on their own cognitive requirements, there is ample evidence that learner control serves to magnify student differences rather than eliminate them. Wilcox (1979), for instance, presents a review of non-computer–based ATI studies and concludes that learner control tends to exacerbate problems arising from individual differences instead of minimizing them. Snow (1980), too, argues that a learning environment that allows learners to control instruction might possibly produce stronger relationships between individual differences and learning to the degree that these individual differences are free to operate than would "fixed" instruction. In a variation on ATI approaches, which Tobias (1976) calls "achievement-by-treatment interactions" (see 22.3.7), differential results have also been found for effectiveness of options selection for students with differing amounts of prior knowledge (Ross & Rakow, 1981; Tobias, 1987a).

Merrill (1975) discusses several frequently invalidated assumptions regarding "aptitudes" and "treatments" in a typical ATI model. He points out that quite often the most germane learner characteristics are actually unstable, varying from moment to moment during instruction. Likewise, treatment effects may similarly not always hold under the variety of conditions present in typical educational settings. Lastly, he argues that instead of instruction being adapted to the individual, we should allow students to adapt the instruction for themselves. This forms one of the bases for the inclusion and importance of learner control in his theory of instruction.

While standard ATI approaches seek to understand the differential effectiveness of learner control with individual differences measured *prior* to instructional intervention ("trait" variables), other approaches choose to explore learner variables measured *during* the instructional task, so-called "within-task" variables (Federico, 1980) or situational "state" variables. These presumably reflect momentary variations in certain learner characteristics that also could interact with the specific instructional situation. Tennyson and Park (1984) discuss the need to investigate the phenomena of moment-by-moment interactions of instruction and individual differences, in particular within learner-controlled environments.

Studies by Seidel, Wagner, Rosenblatt, Hillelsohn, and Stelzer (1975) examining students' ongoing expectancies of success, by Fisher, Blackwell, Garcia, and Greene (1975) on momentary changes in attributions for success and failure, and by Goetzfried and Hannafin (1985), Johansen and Tennyson (1983), Tennyson (1981), and Tennyson and Buttrey (1980) investigating on-task mastery self-assessment by students, illustrate the utility of variables that occur during the course of learner-controlled CBI.

However, still another possibility not discussed by either Carrier and Jonassen (1988) or Merrill (1975) is to not necessarily adapt instruction to fit the student, but rather to attempt to change the student to optimally use the instruction. That is, if we can identify modifiable characteristics of the students which typically produce dysfunctional interactions with instructional treatments, we might attempt to alter those characteristics so that the student and instruction are better matched. Suggested approaches using this paradigm are presented later in this chapter.

Thus, both person and instruction variables can be considered either stable or unstable, perhaps reciprocally changing throughout the course of instruction. This paradigm also allows for the occurrence of aptitude-by-treatment "corrections" (Gehlbach, 1979), that is, selecting treatments to eliminate the effects of individual differences rather than to accommodate them.

This expanded "adaptive instruction" paradigm presents a revised set of larger questions to the researcher: When might instruction respond to variations (both stable and unstable) in individual learners, and how might learners react and respond to changes (macro and micro) in the instruction? Within this framework, there seems to be sufficient theoretical, empirical, and practical justification for investigating the mutual relationship between learner differences and instruction under some degree of learner control.

33.7 INSTRUCTIONAL CHOICE

A fundamental question that should guide investigators of learner control is: Why do students make the choices they do? Learner-controlled instruction is, by definition, instruction in which students are required to make decisions at various points. In order to guide the design and use of learner control, it is necessary to understand the composition of such decisions: that is, can we specify the precursors and effects of the decisions students will make? However, as has been argued by Reeves (1993), very few learner control studies have been grounded on such learning-theoretical questions. Rather, in the simple pursuit of the winner in the contest between learner control and program control, too much learner-control research has proceeded in the absence or ignorance of relevant basic psychological research that might clarify the actual phenomenon being studied, namely, the act of learner choice.

We seek at this point to identify the different kinds of person variables that, it is conjectured, in combination with the actual choices made (i.e., the instructional materials encountered), help to account for the unevenness of learning found under learner-controlled instruction.

As was pointed out earlier, Reigeluth and Stein (1983) advocate the use of "*informed* learner control by *motivated* learners" [emphases added]. This statement suggests two qualitatively different sets of individual difference variables that could influence the effectiveness of learner-controlled instruction.

We should first be interested in a student's capacity to make rational choices (i.e., an "informed" student). "Rational" means how adequately they can appraise both the demands of the task and their own learning needs in relation to that task in order to select appropriate instructional support. Tennyson and Park (1984) seem to call this the student's "perception of learning need," and also point out the need for its further study in order to be of use in effective learner-controlled instruction. These perceptions of learner need, too, will vary across learners.

Secondly, because both motivation and learner-controlled instruction are, at least in part, defined by choice activities, individual differences in motivational variables might also contribute to our understanding of the differential effects of learner-controlled instruction on learning. In contrast to attempting to specify some rationally based determinants of choice, here we need to ask if there are certain emotion-related characteristics of the student that would allow us to predict how inclined (i.e., motivated) a person is to make a particular choice. We are particularly concerned here with identifying "gut-level" predispositions, tendencies, and preferences of the students that operate to direct a choice toward one alternative or another.

The remainder of this review examines the relationships between students' rational understanding of their learning needs, their motivations to choose on an emotional level, their on-task performances, and learning when offered instruction to some degree under their control. First, the rationally-cognitively oriented variables are presented. Following that is a discussion of emotional-motivational variables that influence choice and learning.

33.8 RATIONAL-COGNITIVE ASPECTS OF CHOICE AND LEARNING

Several reviews of learner control in instruction (Hannafin, 1984; Milheim & Martin, 1991; Steinberg, 1989) have identified two kinds of cognitive traits, prior knowledge and ability, which may explain some of the negative results of providing learners with choices during instruction. The relationships of learner control with achievement and with ability are presented in turn, together with some hypothetical instructional prescriptions that could take advantage of these relationships.

33.8.1 Prior Knowledge

The review presented earlier in this chapter amply demonstrates that learners given control over their instruction too often make suboptimal choices. One possible explanation for these findings is that individuals do make appropriate decisions, but within their own perceptions of the problem at hand, not according to some optimal outside decision rules. This view suggests that an increase in an individual's accuracy of perception of his or her learning state in relation to the learning task should result in the individual's making more appropriate choices. Students are therefore expected to make instructional choices that are rational only to the degree they have accurate information about their current learning state. This suggests an approach based on learner prior knowledge or achievement.

There is substantial evidence that, left on their own, both children and adults very often overestimate how much they know about a given topic, and, indeed, those with more knowledge are often better able to judge their knowledge level than people fairly ignorant in that area (Flavell, 1979; Lichtenstein & Fischhoff, 1977; Nelson, Leonesio, Shimamura, Landwehr & Narens, 1982).

This finding that students are generally poor at estimating their current state of knowledge has been found also in computer-based contexts. Lee and Wong (1989) found students unable to predict their own learning of both general and specific types of knowledge. Additionally, Garhart and Hannafin (1986) and Relan (1991) found little correlation between self-rating of knowledge and performance on several tests. Garhart and Hannafin (1986) use this finding to explain plausibly why many students under learner-controlled conditions tend to terminate instruction prematurely.

It could very well be, then, that people often really don't know what they don't know, and that those who know very little know even less about what they don't know. (Apologies for the last sentence.) If this is the case, one might predict that students with higher levels of knowledge would make better (more judicious) instructional decisions than those with lower knowledge levels. Evidence for this phenomenon is provided by Seidel et al. (1975) and Fredericks (1976). In these learner-control CBI studies, high performers were much more able than low performers to estimate their performance capabilities prior to their taking quizzes on the lesson material.

The notion that poor performers are incapable of judging how much they know has implications for the idea of instructional support, as well. That is, if students are unable to estimate their current state of knowledge, they may also be unable to assess whether they need additional instruction when given the chance to choose more. This would imply that a pretest given prior to instruction could predict the success of students given learner-controlled instruction, an extension of the achievement-treatment interaction paradigm of Tobias (1976, 1981), but here the instructional support is controlled by the learners. Such an interaction has indeed been found in studies by Gay (1986), Ross and Rakow (1981), and Ross, Rakow, and Bush (1980), although neither of these last two studies occurred in a computer-based environment. In all cases, college students scoring higher on a pretest performed as well under learner control as similar students under program control. This was not the case for low-prior-knowledge students who performed much worse under learner control. It is plausible that low-prior-knowledge students were not as able to judge the instructional support they needed as were higher-prior-knowledge students.

Additional evidence within a CBI context is provided by Tobias (1987a), who found that knowledgeable students (as measured by a pretest) opted to see more review material

than did less knowledgeable students. He states, " . . . the presence of instructional support is no guarantee that less-knowledgeable students will use it frequently or effectively to improve learning" (p. 160). This is echoed by Judd et al. (1970), who found a similar result in their early study, namely, that students who needed additional instructional support tended to avoid seeking it.

In another paper, Lee and Lee (1991) found that, consistent with the prior-knowledge hypothesis, students with the lowest levels of prior achievement related to their lesson topic performed poorest on a posttest when given learner control during the beginning phase of the lesson, the phase designed for learners to acquire their initial knowledge of the content area. However, another group of learners, also with low pretest scores, who were given learner control during a review phase of the lesson, performed the best of all the students in the study, even better than both program-control groups (both in the initial knowledge acquisition and in the knowledge review phases). They clarify the distinctive findings for the two lesson phases:

> In other words, the LC strategy cannot function effectively when learners have to learn new materials. It makes intuitive sense that when LC subjects have to learn new materials [initial knowledge acquisition], they would work through CAL sessions under the pervasive influence of their previous knowledge base. Learners' management of learning activities is less influenced by previous knowledge differences when they have some grasp of the target knowledge [knowledge review] (p. 496).

In sum, prior achievement has been found to be a major factor affecting the effectiveness of learner-controlled instruction. Additionally, unlike many learner-control studies on other factors, this area of research is well grounded in relevant theory. Generally, it seems that students with some knowledge about the topic being taught seem better able to sense at any given choice point what they need from instruction and to choose additional instructional support accordingly. Here the key instructional variable seems to be amount of instructional support. Students with low amounts of topic knowledge have inaccurate perceptions of what they know, and consequently make poor use of needed instructional support.

Three possibilities are suggested for improving the effectiveness of learner control in relation to learner prior knowledge: (a) informing learners directly of their progress (i.e., supplanting the self-monitoring function); (b) instructing students to try to gauge their current knowledge (i.e., activating the self-monitoring function); and (c) training the students to better monitor their learning.

The students' continual estimation of their level of knowledge (a metacognitive strategy, according to Flavell, 1979) affects the effectiveness of their choices. Without feedback data from the instruction about their knowledge level, students with more prior learning seem better able to assess what they do and do not know, and therefore how much more or what kinds of instruction (i.e., optional material) they need to see. Hannafin (1984), Milheim and

Martin (1991), and Steinberg (1989) each suggests that learner control that regularly informs learners of the state of their learning might provide an aid, perhaps in the form of coaching or advisement to the students, in deciding whether they need more instruction. Additionally, Steinberg (1989) suggests that instruction should gradually wean the student from such crutches in order to promote more internalization of the metacognitive processes. Such information supports to the learner fall under the category of "decision aids," which have been shown to be quite useful in helping people make judgments and select appropriate courses of action (Pitz & Sachs, 1984).

Studies by Arnone and Grabowski (1992), Holmes et al. (1985), Schloss et al. (1988), Tennyson (1980, 1981), and Tennyson and Buttrey (1980) support the contention that providing students with updated information as to their moment-by-moment mastery level would improve the effectiveness of learner control over providing no such information. Here the researchers provide students under learner control with such information and show beneficial effects in comparison to students not given such information. A related study by Steinberg, Baskin, and Hofer (1986) showed that providing informative feedback to students during the course of a CBI lesson increased the chances that learner-controlled memory tools would be used. That is, students were able to use the feedback information to help them decide when and how to use the memory tools.

Results are not unequivocal, however. Ross et al. (1988) did not find an interaction between student selection of density of text displayed on the computer screen (high and low densities) and student pretest scores. Additionally, Goetzfried and Hannafin (1985) did not replicate in a CBI setting the achievement-by-treatment interaction that was demonstrated by Ross and Rakow (1981) in a non-CBI setting.

An additional wrinkle is suggested in results reported by Pridemore and Klein (1991), who compared selection of feedback by students (see 32.5.5.4) under two learner-controlled conditions differing in the elaborateness of feedback information provided. They found generally that students in the less-elaborate condition selected less feedback than those in the more-elaborate condition. The authors suggest that the amount of information contained in the feedback message helps students decide whether choosing to see such feedback is worthwhile. This might imply that students select their instructional support only to the degree they perceive it will help them. It's possible, then, that students choose to experience more instruction, not just on their perceived learning need but also on the perceived usefulness of the material to be offered. Instruction then, designed for learner control, should have as its goal the expansion and clarification of the student's own perception of the task as well as their progress toward it, particularly for those who are deficient in the accuracy of their self-monitoring. This notion builds on the prior-knowledge hypothesis, in that because students with low knowledge of an area tend to bypass additional optional instructional support, an improvement in the accuracy of perception of students as to their own knowledge level or to the task requirements would be expected to result in better decision making during learner-controlled instruction.

However, it is not known at this point whether students even need to be aware that self-monitoring of knowledge is important in learner-controlled instruction as a type of learning strategy (Garner & Alexander, 1989). It might be that simple directions to the student to think about what or how much they know might be enough to dislodge them from more habitual "mindless" activity. If we could somehow activate the learner's own untapped self-monitoring skills, it is speculated, then, that it may be unnecessary to inform them directly of their mastery using some decision superstructure (e.g., Bayesian probabilities; see 22.4.2.3; Tennyson & Rothen, 1979). This approach, however, has not been explored in learner-controlled CBI contexts.

In addition to supplanting a student's monitoring activities, or activating existing monitoring strategies, instruction might attempt to actually improve the student's conscious use of metacognitive strategies. This would involve some type of strategy training (see Garner & Alexander, 1989, for a review of some of these training approaches). Tobias (1987a) supports metacognitive strategy training, indicating that many students might need to be taught when and why to use various instructional supports. Kinzie (1990), too, advocates an approach to help the learners become better managers of their learning with the suggestion that perhaps,

> . . . students should be given the training to become self-managers as well as instructional assistance in self-management, and that those without a strong knowledge base should be assisted in making the links that will help establish the structure for new knowledge.

However, at this point, metacognitive strategy training has not been much investigated in a learner-control CBI context.

33.8.2 Learning Strategies and Ability

In addition to the prior-knowledge hypothesis and related issues just discussed, there is another explanation for the general ineffectiveness of providing instructional options. This notion begins with the suggestion that individuals have developed either good or poor strategies for dealing with learning problems. The metacognitive self-monitoring processes mentioned in the previous section on prior knowledge in fact represent a subset of a larger collection of cognitive processing strategies most often called *learning strategies*. Jonassen (1985) reviews some of the research on learning strategies, and describes four classes of strategies, all of which have clear implications for learner-controlled instruction:

- Metacognitive strategies are those processes by which students tell themselves how much they know. It is often described as "self-monitoring," and reflects a sense of both knowledge and ignorance.

- Information-processing strategies make up the largest group of learning strategies. These strategies include developing readiness, reading/viewing for meaning, recalling material, integrating it with prior knowledge, expanding or elaborating on the material, and finally reviewing what has been learned. These strategies seem to correspond to what Merrill (1984) calls "conscious cognition" processes.
- Study strategies (occasionally called *study skills*) are explicit techniques to help learners actively process information. These consist of such activities as note taking, outlining, underlining, and the identification and noting of patterns in the new material.
- Support strategies relate to the mental climate or attitude at the time of learning, such as the degree students can internally motivate themselves and stay on-task during the instruction. Jonassen (1985) says these last strategies are a sine qua non for learning, and are required in order for the other strategies to be effective.

When many people using both good and poor strategies are averaged in a study, a less-than-ideal picture is painted of the effectiveness of decision making as a whole. Some researchers suggest that the use of such learning strategies as Jonassen (1985) presents is linked closely with the concept of general intelligence (Snow & Yalow, 1982). It is not unreasonable to imagine that higher-ability students might have a greater repertoire of strategies to draw on when faced with a learning problem. In fact, as Snow and Yalow (1982) point out, very often the concept of ability is equated with the capacity to learn.

If indeed we can infer that (a) higher-ability students consciously or unconsciously bring to bear the mental resources appropriate to the learning task and avoid using inefficient ones, (b) lower-ability students somehow either lack or don't know how or when to activate their learning strategies, and (c) the success of learner control depends to a large degree on students judiciously applying their mental resources to the learning problem, then we can begin to explain the mixed results of learner control of instruction as being to a degree a function of learner ability, with higher-ability students capitalizing on learner control and lower-ability students left floundering.

An opposing viewpoint that higher ability will predict use of better learning strategies comes from Clark (1982). From a review of aptitude-treatment interaction studies, he first hypothesizes that high-ability students would profit most from activating or cueing methods, that is, techniques that prompt the student to adopt appropriate mental strategies from their repertoire of strategies for a given problem. Second, he suggests that low-ability students would do best under the supplanting or modeling methods, which are techniques that do not rely on the student to use his or her own mental resources, but rather explicitly guide the student through the optimal learning strategies. But regardless of what high-ability students would need, he suggests that they would prefer to choose supplantation or modeling,

while low-ability students would *prefer* activating or cueing methods. Each group does so because that is the method perceived to be the lowest "mental workload" for the student. In this case, he proposes, neither group would select an appropriate strategy.

There is the additional question, however, of what the patterns of "optimal" choices would look like in a learner-controlled lesson. Would the best students generally choose more options, regardless of the specific type of instructional event put under their control? In this case, "more" of anything would be perceived by students as being "better." Or would their effective strategy use lead them to select only those specific types of options they feel would produce the greatest benefit? In this case, we would be able to see only some kinds of options being chosen by higher-ability students, while by others, perhaps not at all. Lower-ability students would perhaps manifest converse types of options-selection patterns, or maybe even random patterns.

It is possible to examine the notion of ability being related to overall amount of options selection only in those studies that offer a variety of options to the student. Otherwise, for studies that offer only one type of selectable instructional event, it is difficult to conclude anything about selective strategy choice and ability level. Of studies that do offer several types of options to students, Carrier et al. (1985) did find a strong positive relationship between a measure of general ability and general amount of options selected, regardless of the type of instructional event. This was not replicated in a follow-up study, however (Carrier et al., 1986), which included some additional motivational feedback in one of the treatments. Perhaps the presence of encouraging feedback (which did increase overall options selection in the study) was a more salient factor affecting decisions by the students to choose or to skip over material, so much so that ability affects were minimized. Other studies, too, found little or no relationship between overall level or frequency of options selection and ability measures. Snow (1979), for example, found near-zero correlations between standard ability and achievement measures and frequency of choice of instructional options. Reinking and Schreiner (1985), too, found no differences between low- and high-reading ability groups in any type of options selected. Another study by Morrison et al. (1992), although more indirect in its implication about ability level relationships, reports no association between amount of instructional support selections made by students under learner-controlled conditions and their posttest performance (posttest performance also being assumed to be generally related to student ability level). From these findings, it is difficult to conclude that higher-ability students make indiscriminately more frequent use of any and all instructional options that they might be offered.

Connections between ability and selective use of specific types of options seem a little more evident in the literature. In a study that looked for a possible curvilinear connection between options use and ability, Carrier and Williams (1988) found that students with the highest ability levels chose medium frequency levels of instructional options. The suggestion they made was that high-ability students do not act compulsively, indiscriminately selecting all options presented to them, but rather act more reflectively, choosing some as needed, but skipping over others deemed not useful. Another study by Sasscer and Moore (1984) found that when students in a TICCIT lesson were given the option of terminating the lesson, the dropout rate was related to the types of options chosen. The students who left the lesson early typically chose the "easier" kinds of options in the lesson. Snow (1979) found that aptitude measures of fluid-analytic ability and perceptual speed predicted the choice activities of successful college students in a BASIC programming task. The best choice activities he described as indicating a reflective and thoughtful style, and were more frequently selected by high-ability students. (Some caution is urged in reading this study, however, as the data analysis presented is sketchy and contains too few subjects to trust unequivocally the stability of the multivariate analysis employed.)

A couple of other studies are worth mentioning, although they offer somewhat qualified tests of associations between ability and type of options selected. For example, a study by Kinzie et al. (1988) found that students higher in reading ability selected a high proportion of options to review material than did lower-ability students. This was the only type option offered to subjects in the study, but because it was highly germane for the particular lesson, higher-ability students seemed perhaps better able to gauge the benefits of frequently selecting it. Additionally, if we use posttest performance as a type of surrogate ability measure, we find in a reanalysis of data presented in Seidel et al. (1975, p. 29, Table 6) that while low-posttest performers selected overall more options, high performers selected proportionally more of certain types of options—namely, options to take quizzes—than did low performers. This was not the case for options to recap or review material presented in the lesson. This finding seems not to have occurred for Holmes et al. (1985), however, who found no relationship between pretest scores (here taken as a surrogate ability measure) and particular strategy use—in their case, either opting to take unit tests before proceeding through the lesson, or going through instruction first before taking the tests.

There is also evidence that ability plays an important role on the attrition of students in large instructional units. An early example, the TICCIT system (Merrill, 1973) offered college students a great deal of choice in selection of both content and strategy. Results showed a high dropout rate, but positive effects on achievement for those who persisted. Those who stayed were generally higher-ability students to begin with (O'Shea & Self, 1983, p. 92).

The mixed results from these studies, while indicating the potential for ability and learning strategies to explain overall performance in learner-controlled CBI, also demonstrate that more research needs to be done. The hypothesis of Clark (1982) that higher-ability students will probably seek more instructional support (even though they do not need it) appears supported in some studies, but not in others. There is also some evidence that high-ability learners have some capacity to choose their instructional support with some circumspection and discrimination, rather than wholesale. It might be that the specific type of tasks presented to the students need to be more precisely matched to the specific learning strategies with which they most correspond. Overall, though, ability measures do not seem to have the power to differentiate the more relevant learning strategies adopted by a given student at a given time.

Some types of instructional interventions do appear to work to compensate for the poor use of mental resources in low-ability learners. Jonassen (1985) presents within the four learning strategy categories listed earlier several suggestions for improving the use of strategies in computer-based instruction. Most of these approaches have yet to be tried in learner-control CBI studies, however.

Ability appears to predict, in addition to the individual's perception of need for instructional support (a metacognitive strategy), other types of mental learning strategies in which the student might engage. Although the relationship between ability and choice seems more tenuous than that of prior achievement and choice, there still seems cause to believe that appropriate choice strategies can be made salient to the learners when these learners lack the inclination to spontaneously make their own decisions, perhaps via simple instructions or suggestions, and perhaps by changing the attractiveness of the various choices to be made. Additionally, the types of options selected appear more related to ability than quantity of options chosen.

Only two instances were found of learner-controlled CBI studies that attempted to improve students' strategy use. Elementary school students in Jacobson and Thompson's (1975) study were given prompts at various points to help them make appropriate instructional decisions. Although the instructional treatments used in the study were quite large and in many ways not comparable, the authors still conclude that such strategic prompting can help students to make appropriate decisions. In another study by Relan (1991), three types of strategy-training groups (comprehensive, partial, or no training) were experimentally crossed with two levels of learner control over review of material (complete or limited). She found that, for the immediate posttest at least, both strategy-training groups did improve performance, but only for the limited learner-control treatment group. She hypothesizes that the complete learner-control group with strategy training added on top was simply overloaded. The implication is that strategy training might be most effective when close attention is paid to matching appropriately that training to the context of the lesson.

Reigeluth (1979) proposed that learner-controlled instruction offer students an "advisor" option, a sort of prescriptive "help" feature, which would suggest to the student various so-called "optimal" strategies for how to process information or what to do next in the lesson. The potential flaw in this proposal is that students might not know how or when to access the optional advisor. Another intervention system is proposed by Allen and Merrill (1985), which provides to the learners varying amounts of learning-strategy suggestions depending on their aptitudes for accomplishing the learning tasks. For students of low abilities, for example, the computer would provide explicit processing representations for the students to follow; for medium-ability students, the system would "guide" the learner to use certain previously learned strategies; high-ability students would be left with the most freedom to select and apply their previously acquired processing strategies without external suggestions or interference from the computer system. This type of system has not yet been tested.

The idea behind all these approaches is to promote the conscientious and mindful use of instructional options according to individual needs for instructional support. The following section shifts the examination from the rational predictors of learner choices to the emotional or affective predictors.

33.9 EMOTIONAL-MOTIVATIONAL ASPECTS OF CHOICE AND LEARNING

"Motivation" is a very slippery concept. J. M. Keller (1983) defines motivation as the "magnitude and direction of behavior. In other words, it refers to the choices people make as to what experiences they will approach or avoid, and the degree of effort they will exert in that respect" (p. 389). Both intuition and research (Tobias, 1987b) inform us that poorly motivated students are also very often poor performers in educational settings, too. However, the derivation of instructional prescriptions to help students improve their motivation to learn requires a much more detailed exploration of both the determinants of motivated behavior and the effects of motivation on choice and learning. That is, we need to uncover the reasons (motives) behind particular choices a student may make, to clarify which variables determine, or at least predict, both general patterns and levels of choice and situation-specific choices students will make. Additionally, we need to investigate the relationship between motivation and learning. In path-analytic terms, both direct and indirect (via the actual instructional choices made) relationships of motivation and learning require clarification.

A terminology issue needs to be raised at this point. Many researchers would argue that a "motivated" behavior might be based on rational, logical decision-making processes, and thus is not best described in terms of "emotional-motivational" processes. This is true to a large extent (although some could argue it is moot). However, for clarity's sake in this chapter, learner "motivation" refers primarily to the emotional states and reactions (and their consequent overt behaviors) experienced before, during, and after instruction which have an impact on learning and choice. So-called "rationally" motivated behaviors were discussed earlier in this paper.

A large body of research and several psychological theories exist that attempt to describe and explain the relationships among emotional-motivational variables, choice, and learning, and will only be touched on here. Instead, the implications of these findings about motivation and learning for the design of learner-controlled instruction will be explored. (For further discussion of motivation issues in educational technology, see also 32.5.5.)

33.9.1 Achievement Motivation and Learner-Controlled Instruction

The history of motivation research contains a sizable body of literature concerning what is called *achievement motivation*—in simple terms, a person's desire to perform and achieve. J. W. Atkinson (1974b) presents a theory, sprung from a behaviorist tradition, which connects so-called "motivated behavior" with performance based on what he calls "resultant achievement motivation." This construct has been defined and operationalized in many ways, but according to Heckhausen, Schmalt, and Schneider (1985), the measures of achievement motivation which tend to yield the most fruitful research are those indicators that are most overt, such as an individual's tendencies to persist (J. W. Atkinson, 1974a) or otherwise exert effort (Revelle & Michaels, 1976; Thomas, 1983) at some task or tasks. Because "achievement motivation" is largely defined by overt behaviors such as persistence and perseverance, there would seem to be at least on the surface clear reasons to attempt to extend experimental findings from the theory into the domain of learner-controlled instruction, so to try to provide more grounded explanations of student behaviors in such situations.

In J. W. Atkinson's theory (1974b), a person's level of achievement motivation at any given time is described as being the function of several variables. The first set of these variables includes motive to succeed and motive to avoid failure. The second type of variable influencing achievement motivation is the perceived probability of task success (also called *expectancy*). Last, extrinsic motivational factors (such as rewards or social approval) also play a role in the level of resultant achievement motivation. Various combinations of these variables produce both *approach* tendencies (i.e., a person's inclination to engage in some type of performance situation) and *avoidance* tendencies (i.e., a person's likelihood of shunning a particular performance situation). It is these two tendencies that taken together indicate a person's level of achievement motivation.

Expanding on the achievement-motivation tradition, Lepper (1985) suggests a link between motivation and achievement which is related to covert states in the learner. It is possible that a person's level of motivation during the performance of a learning task affects key components of information processing related to learning, a position also taken by Salomon (1983). Emotional-motivational variables may influence the direction and intensity of attention processes, arousal, depth of processing, and problem representation. Even though Lepper (1985) points out that many of these information-processing ideas are at present hypothetical, there does seem to be an emerging unification of the underlying mechanisms linking motivation and achievement (Humphreys & Revelle, 1984).

Some researchers suggest that the relationship between persistence or effort and achievement is generally linear (Revelle & Michaels, 1976; Salomon, 1983). That is, they say that highly achievement-motivated individuals will usually outperform those with lower motivation levels. However, theorists following J. W. Atkinson's original model (1974b) treat motivation as having a curvilinear (inverted-U shape) relationship with learning performance (Brophy, 1983; Humphreys & Revelle, 1984; J. M Keller, 1983). That is, both excessively low and high motivational levels can have dysfunctional effects on learning. This effect is moderated depending on either task difficulty or task complexity (J. W. Atkinson, 1974b; Humphreys & Revelle, 1984).

Given this relationship, it would be interesting to look for interactions of level of motivation and learner- or program-controlled instructional treatments. Such an ATI has been found by Carrier and Williams (1988). Using task persistence as the overt motivational index, they found that under two program-controlled treatments (with low and high amounts of instruction) students performing best were those in the middle levels of persistence; under learner control, however, the best performers had the highest levels of persistence. In other words, the curvilinear relation between motivation and learning was found under program control, but a mostly linear relationship was found under learner control. (Similar data were collected in a study by Morrison et al., 1992. However, they only reported on a posited linear relationship—none found—between task persistence and achievement. It would be interesting to reanalyze their data to see if such a curvilinear relationship emerges.)

A possible explanation for these differential treatment effects can be inferred from a paper by Humphreys and Revelle (1984). Following their theory describing the underlying relationships between effort and performance, it is speculated that the students in the Carrier and Williams (1988) study behaved as though learner control were an easier or less complex condition; i.e., it placed fewer demands on their learning resources. In addition, it's possible the learner-controlled treatment produced less overall anxiety that could have interfered with learning. This interpretation is also consistent with Salomon's (1983) general notion of "perceived demand characteristics" of instructional treatments.

Although still hypothetical, three instructional factors are proposed here which might be expected to interact with a person's average general level of achievement motivation: learner or program control, task complexity, and extrinsic motivation variables.

Learner- and program-controlled treatments might be perceived by different students to be easier or more difficult to manage. It is possible that general motivational level could have an influence on performance by interacting with these treatments in a linear or curvilinear fashion, depending on the perceived "ease" of learning under the treatment.

Second, fairly simple tasks given under both learner- and program-controlled treatments might find no differences for highly motivated students. However, for difficult tasks, or those tasks requiring careful and deliberate thinking, one might expect learner control to surpass program control, at least for highly motivated (persistent) students. It is not clear yet what to expect for students of low or middle levels of motivation under tasks of varying difficulty or complexity.

Last, the object of using extrinsic motivators would be to try to increase the learner's persistence or effort expenditure through instructional manipulations, particularly for those students with low motivation levels. J. W. Atkinson (1974a) lists as examples of extrinsic motivators authority, competition, social approval, and external rewards. Several studies from the learner control literature support the use of these extrinsic motivators. Tennyson and Buttrey (1980) and Tennyson (1981) found that providing students under learner control with computer-delivered *advisements*—that is, instructional recommendations about whether they should select more material (based on a mastery diagnosis)—did result in higher amounts of material chosen and in learning equivalent to the program-controlled version. In this case, the computer can be viewed as an extrinsic motivator because of the presumed authority its recommendations carry to the learner. Peters (1988), too, found that students receiving advisements requested more practice and answered more practice questions correctly on the first attempt than did students with no advisements, although there were no differences on posttest performance. Similarly, Carrier et al. (1986) found that simple encouragements within a learner-controlled treatment did increase the amount of material chosen by the students over a learner-controlled treatment without encouragements. Hicken, Sullivan, and Klein (1992) employed another external incentive approach by varying the type of task orientation in a lesson (i.e., students were told either that simply completing the lesson was sufficient to receive credit, or that a performance criterion level of 70% was required). The result was that students in the performance criterion condition, even without selecting any additional options or by spending more time-on-task, outperformed the group with the less-stringent conditions. The authors suggest that this extrinsic type of instructional manipulation functions to improve students' effort or concentration levels. There is evidence, then, that the type of task orientation given or simple instructional guidance in learner-controlled settings can alter performance, or at least the overall level of task persistence and other on-task behaviors.

33.9.2 Emotional-Motivational Patterns and Learner-Controlled CBI

The remainder of this section attempts to peer beneath the overt motivational variables (e.g., persistence) to see how learner emotional states might have direct or indirect impacts on learner-control effectiveness. Dweck (1986) and Dweck and Leggett (1988) offer a useful integrative approach to understanding student behaviors in terms of the student's own internal beliefs about the nature of their performances and their striving to confirm those beliefs. In their model, students are continually forming implicit theories about themselves which orient them to seek particular goals related to confirming these theories. Dweck (1986) describes so-called *adaptive* (or "mastery-oriented") and *maladaptive* ("helpless") motivational patterns. The maladaptive pattern is characterized by an avoidance of challenge and a deterioration of performance in the face of obstacles. Students who exhibit an adaptive pattern, in contrast, tend to seek challenging tasks and the maintenance of effective perserverance under failure circumstances.

What follows is an example of one avenue of promising theory, to date fairly unresearched within CBI contexts, which holds promise for explaining the heretofore mixed effects of learner-controlled CBI and suggesting means of improving instructional designs that adopt learner control. The investigation of other related theoretical frameworks is encouraged, however, as well. Kinzie (1990), for example, folds into her discussion of self-regulation and learner control another promising avenue of motivation theory, namely, self-efficacy (Bandura, 1986), and suggests ways of pursuing the topic in future research. But regardless of the stance on motivation research an investigator might adopt, the idea is to try to understand the nature of emotional states the learner experiences which produce healthy (*adaptive*) or dysfunctional (*maladaptive*) expression in terms of choices, persistence, and perseverance during learner-controlled instruction.

33.9.2.1. Attribution Theory and Learner Control.
A major portion of Dweck and Leggett's (1988) model is based on research in the area of student *attributions* of their success and failures. Here the conception of motivation becomes that of a somewhat unstable factor affected on a moment-by-moment basis by the person's perception of events happening during instruction and their own inferred role in those events. Generally, an "attribution" refers to an individual's perceived causes of his or her own success or failures. Early conceptualizations by Kukla (1978) and Weiner (1974) explain that the degree to which students ascribe the causes of their own success or failures to ability, effort, task difficulty, or luck will differentially predict whether or what kinds of subsequent performance opportunities the student is likely to select voluntarily. These four variables can be grouped along two primary dimensions: internal versus external (analogous to, but not the same as, the familiar "locus of control" dimension of Rotter, 1966); and stable versus unstable.

Other researchers have recently extended, refined, and reconceptualized attribution theory. For example, Covington and Omelich (1984a, 1984b, 1985) attempt to frame student attributions in terms of emotional states they imply, such as pride, shame, guilt, and humiliation. Additionally, Dweck and Leggett (1988) present a model that seeks to explain

the precursors of an individual's attributions along the "controllability" dimension. That is, they attempt to explain why some individuals feel more in control of their performances outcomes and others feel more "helpless." These developments in attribution theory have potentially important consequences for the design of motivational interventions during instruction.

Very few studies have explicitly examined attribution-like variables in connection with learner-controlled CBI. Treating perception of internality/externality of reinforcement (or "locus of control"; Rotter, 1966) as a predictor variable has yielded generally unimpressive results in differentially predicting learning under several instructional conditions (Tobias, 1987b) and in predicting overall choice levels or learning in learner-controlled instruction (Carrier et al., 1985, 1986; Gray, 1989; Klein & Keller, 1990; López & Harper, 1989; Santiago & Okey, 1992). In fact, López and Harper (1989) conclude that there is little to be gained by further research investigating Rotter's locus-of-control construct in connection with learner-controlled instruction. Nevertheless, these negative findings could be masking potentially valid discriminations within groups broadly labeled *externals* or *internals*. For example, the differences between the two internal attribution styles, ability and effort, might be expected to affect options selection in either adaptive or maladaptive ways.

One early study (Fisher et al., 1975) treated various attributional variables as dependent variables under conditions of learner- and program-controlled problem selection. The authors found that subjects in the choice group made significantly more internal and stable attributions during or following instruction than did students in the program-controlled group. They also found no treatment differences for an attribution variable they called *control–no control,* but they do not provide an operational definition of this variable to aid interpretation. Additionally, even though these researchers did not take baseline measures of attribution, nor plot the changes in attributions occurring over time, their study still supports the short-term modifiability of attributions as a possible result of treatment variables.

Within J. M. Keller's ARCS model of motivational design (1983, 1987a, 1987b), both attribution theory and learner control would potentially play useful roles when attempting to improve student confidence. In some strategies, Keller suggests, students might receive attributional feedback to enhance the feeling of that "they can do it." Additionally, they could be given some degree of control over their learning situation to enhance feelings of their own self-efficacy. The attributional feedback would seem to apply mostly to situations under learner control where students are asked to choose performance-related options. These options could include the selection of such specific instructional events as optional practice items, feedback, test situations, and, possibly, remediation or review following test conditions.

However, J. M. Keller's model is fairly nonspecific about the types of attributional feedback that should be offered to students and under which circumstances it would function optimally. Milheim and Martin (1991), too, suggest the utility of attribution theory for explaining the mixed effects found in the learner-control literature, but they, too, offer few specific suggestions for possible instructional design strategies that incorporate the theory.

Manipulations directed toward attaining these treatment goals would seem to fall into three classes of instructional strategies: (1) those affecting an entire lesson condition; (2) those preceding specific choice situations, taking the form of guidance, advice, or recommendations; and (3) those immediately following performance situations, taking the form of interpretations and attributions of success or failure generated by instruction.

The first strategy class includes attempts to adapt instruction to whatever overall attributional style a person seems to possess. Here, diagnosis of attribution levels would take place once, prior to the start of the lesson. All instruction might be subsequently modified accordingly in the manner of an ATI.

Additionally in this class, instruction could at the outset inform learners that they have control over what they see, and that their performance will be determined by how much they try. Given this, it would be necessary that the instruction monitor performance throughout the lesson and adjust task difficulty so as to minimize the discouraging effects of frequent failure.

Also in this class are manipulations related to task or ego involvement. Norm-referencing (ego-involving) suggestions to the student by the instructional system could be presented to students with high success rates. Examples of such presentations might be general statements that a student's performance will be compared to others, or perhaps comments to the students that they did better than most people on a particular task. Low-performing students might be best placed under task-involved conditions that encourage value placed on task improvement.

The second class also subscribes to a typical adaptive instruction paradigm, although here we are dealing with microinstructional adaptations of task-specific attributions. In particular, strategies in this class are forward looking, and include encouragement and advisement techniques such as those mentioned in the earlier section on achievement motivation. Some specific techniques might include recommending to the student that they choose a task of hard-difficulty (medium, easy) level depending on what the student's current performance level and attributional tendencies are at the moment. They might also include such motivating statements as "try harder on this one . . .," or "the next task is an easy one. . . ." Another possibility might be to describe a subsequent task in terms compatible with the student's attributional style, but again on a very local level.

In the last class of instructional manipulations, the instruction could make evaluative and interpretive comments on a student's performance immediately following the success or failure of the task. The goal of these reflective or backward-looking instructional strategies is to alter attributions intentionally. Comments to the student might attribute failure to his not trying hard enough or, when appropriate, to a task being difficult. Successful performance would always be attributed by the instruction to an internal factor. A study by Carrier et al. (1986) gave students a variety of backward-looking encouraging feedback (though not attributionally related) and found positive effects for task persistence. It is expected that feedback engineered more specifically to counteract maladaptive attributional patterns in the students would be even more fruitful.

A doctoral dissertation conducted by this author (Williams, 1992) examined the impact of attributionally related feedback on learners of differing attributional tendencies (or styles) within learner- and program-controlled conditions. The type of feedback employed in the study was specifically intended to affect students' temporary perceptions of the causes of their learning successes and failures, that is, their *attributions* of their performance outcomes, so to minimize the dysfunctional behaviors of learners with maladaptive attributional styles. Providing specific attributionally related feedback to learners in an attempt to alter attributions temporarily has a well-established research base (Andrews & Debus, 1978; Barker & Graham, 1987; Borkowski, Weyhing & Carr, 1988; Dweck, 1975; Fowler & Peterson, 1981; Graham & Barker, 1990; Medway & Venino, 1982; Meyer & Dyck, 1986; Schunk, 1982, 1983, 1990a; Schunk & Cox, 1986) which hitherto had not been investigated in a computer-based context.

Findings from the study generally support the notion that, overall, certain types of attributional styles are maladaptive. (Examples of types of these maladaptive attributional styles include tendencies to attribute personal success to external causes, or to attribute personal failure to lack of ability.) That is, students who exhibit such motivational patterns tend not to exert as much effort or mental investment in their learning activities, and thus are prone to perform poorly.

The study by Williams (1992) also showed that the granting of a relatively small degree of learner control within the CBI lesson succeeded in improving the performance of students who otherwise showed certain types of maladaptive motivational patterns, namely, those who attribute their successes to either effort or to external causes. Also, students who attributed their successes to external causes, a generally maladaptive attributional style, showed markedly improved performance when given appropriate attributionally related feedback following their on-task performances. Such feedback was designed in accordance with recommendations from researchers on attribution theory, and consisted of reflective interpretations given by the computer to the student that a particular successful performance on the first try was due to ability (e.g., "You seem to know this material well!"), and on a second try was due to effort (e.g., "Terrific! It pays to try a little harder the second time."). Similarly, a failed performance on the first try was ascribed by the computer to lack of effort (e.g., "Perhaps you weren't concentrating enough on the question."), and on a second try to external causes (e.g., "You made a good try. That question was particularly hard."). In other words, giving these types of attributional feedback moderated the maladaptive tendencies of these students.

The Williams (1992) study supports the utility of the adaptive instruction paradigm of Gehlbach (1979). In this framework, unlike the classic ATI approach of Cronbach and Snow (1977), students who are deficient in some relevant aptitude are administered an instructional treatment intended to "correct" the difficulty, not operate around it or on top of it. In the current case, students who exhibited suboptimal motivational patterns were provided with appropriate feedback in an attempt to encourage more healthy emotional self-perceptions and hence more functional behaviors.

To summarize, the previous section posits that the general ineffectiveness of learner-controlled CBI can be explained, at least in part, by the fact that some learners have acquired maladaptive motivational tendencies and as a result exhibit dysfunctional or suboptimal choices (e.g., showing low persistence or perseverance, or terminating a lesson early). There is some evidence, although scant, that one particular motivational theory, namely, attribution theory, can be exploited to improve the on-task motivational behaviors for learners within learner-controlled situations. Other related theoretical approaches, e.g., learned helplessness and self-efficacy, also need explicating as to their potential relationships with learner-control effectiveness. The goal is to increase both motivation to achieve, where such motivation is low and motivational patterns are maladaptive, and to help students optimize their selection of instructional support.

33.10 SUMMARY

This paper has reviewed many studies comparing various forms of learner-controlled, computer-based instruction with program-controlled CBI. These studies had been theoretically predicted to show learner control superior to program control. However, empirical findings related to these predictions have been disappointing.

A closer examination of these studies showed that a number of mediating factors were likely responsible for the poor performance under learner control. It was found that many students simply were not capable of making good use of the control they were given. Two large categories of individual difference variables were suggested to be important in identifying these students: rational-cognitive variables and emotional-motivational variables.

In particular, both student prior knowledge and ability were found to predict student success under learner control. Prior knowledge was found to be related to the capacity of the students to estimate the amount of instructional support they would need. Students with little knowledge were not able effectively to monitor their comprehension, and thus were not able to gauge the degree of instructional support they would need. Additionally, student ability was viewed

as related to the learning strategies individual students bring to bear when faced with a learning problem. Lower-ability students typically do not have the repertoire of learning strategies available to them that higher-ability students do. Some suggestions were offered for accommodating these differences within learner-controlled instruction.

The student's level of motivation was also found to be a potentially important variable in explaining the overall effects of learner control. In particular, attributional theory was offered as an example of a well-grounded framework for understanding motivated student behaviors and effort, and for adapting instruction to meet the needs of students with maladaptive attributional patterns.

33.11 AN INSTRUCTIONAL THEORY OF LEARNER CONTROL?

Can a comprehensive, integrative, deductive, prescriptive, and testable theory of learner control be developed? I suspect not, not if we demand of such a theory (any more than any other educational theory) that it be falsifiable in the Popper (1968) sense. An alternative question, however, is whether we can still develop instructional prescriptions for the use of learner control which are at least pragmatic and are grounded in some reasonable psychological and educational principles. I suspect we probably can. In fact, work to develop such prescriptions can be found in many of the existing learner-control reviews.

Steinberg (1984), for example, lists a range of these events that might be offered within a learner-controlled lesson, together with some conditions that might mitigate their success: which topics to study and in what order, number of exercises to practice and their level of difficulty, presentation of review or supplementary materials, or the option not to answer questions. Other activities, too, could be made optional: amount or kind of feedback to see following practice questions, whether to exit the instruction, mode of presentation (e.g., verbal or graphic), and even the option of whether to allow further learner control at all.

Laurillard (1987) presents another assortment of computer-based learning strategies of which learners might judiciously be given control. One category of these strategies, *control of content sequence,* includes provisions for the student to skip forward or backward a chosen amount or to retrace a route through the material, and options to control when to view such features as content indexes or content maps. [A rather remarkable early example of learner control of content sequence in computer-based instruction comes from Grubb (1968). He describes a system whereby the student, with the aid of a light pen and a content map on the screen, is able to point and jump to any subtopic in the lesson. This approach presages the current "hypertext" environments in which students proceed through instruction in a nonlinear "browsing" fashion.]

Another category presented by Laurillard (1987) is called *control of learning activities,* and includes options for the student to see examples, do exercises, receive information, consult a glossary, ask for more explanation, and take a quiz. Most of her list of learner-controlled activities is included in Steinberg's (1984) list, but Laurillard's seems more complete and grounded in educational-psychological theory.

Milheim and Martin (1991) discuss when and how to prescribe three types of variables for which students might be granted control: *control of pacing,* that is, the speed of presentation of instructional materials; and *control of content,* permitting students to skip over certain instructional units. They suggest that these categories, in addition to *control of sequence* (similar to Laurillard's *control of content sequence*), represent the most germane sets of instructional variables affecting the success or failure of learner-controlled CBI.

Recently others, most notably Chung and Reigeluth (1992), have worked to synthesize an empirically based and pragmatic listing of instructional prescriptions that link a variety of learner-control strategies (over content, sequence, pace, display/strategy, internal processing, and use of advisor systems) to instructional conditions (learner characteristics, learning objectives or domains, and instructional systems) and broad outcomes (learning achievement, transfer, and retention, time efficiency, cost efficiency, and attitudes toward learning and instruction). These authors recognize the multidimensional nature of learner control, and provide a helpful set of do's and don'ts for deciding when to employ which learner-controlled instructional events. Their recommendations are many, and only a few are presented here as illustrations of their approach.

For example, they recommend that students should be offered control of content when they have significant previous knowledge in the content area, because presentation of already known material could be irrelevant and interesting. If students are already prepared with some content knowledge, they can more effectively manage their own content. Additionally, content control might be given when the learning objectives are of a higher-order type, as opposed to factual information.

Similarly, they list conditions that allow for learner control of sequence, such as when the instructional program is quite lengthy (sequence control can help maintain learner motivation and interest), or when they are familiar with a topic. Likewise, students should not be given control over sequence when learning objectives have a clear prerequisite order, or when it would be impractical to break up and resequence existing materials.

In a similar vein, they provide many conditions for using learner control of specific instructional elements such as pacing, displaying information or using instructional strategies, internal processing (including some metacognition strategies), and use of advisory systems. To justify many of these prescriptions, Chung and Reigeluth (1992) cite empirical studies from the learner-control literature; many others, however, are derived from current instructional theories (e.g., Gagné, 1985; Merrill, 1983) and need empirical validation in their own right. Given the overall structure

they give to their instructional prescriptions, essentially a series of "if-then" conditions, it would be interesting to see developed a type of computer-based decision tree or expert system based on the "mix and match" combinations of instructional strategies, outcomes, and conditions presented in their paper. Such a prescriptive system of learner control might then be validated with research across a variety of instructional systems and contexts, and would provide some tests of the generalizability of their recommendations.

All of the categorization schemes providing advice on if, how, and when to use learner control in CBI overlap to a large degree and differ primarily in perspective or orientation. And all provide useful information for designers attempting to decide whether and how to include learner-controlled events in their instructional designs. None, however, is comprehensive or definitive.

33.12 RECOMMENDATIONS FOR FUTURE RESEARCH

Several researchers recently have apparently stopped asking this research question: "Which is better: learner- or program-controlled CBI?" It seems that enough research has been produced to date to justify conclusions of "it depends" or "take your pick." Rather, these researchers fundamentally alter the question to read, "How can I make learner-controlled CBI effective?" Within their experimental studies, these investigators do not include a program-control treatment at all, deciding instead to focus on the question of how to improve the design of instruction, given learner control. For example, a study by Santiago and Okey (1992), investigating various forms of advisement conditions all under learner control, provides a good example of how research might be conducted with the aim of improving learner-controlled instruction. Another good example of this framework is shown in a study by Pridemore and Klein (1991), who looked at variations in feedback elaborations, each operating within the same learner-controlled feedback structure. Another study by Hicken et al. (1992) investigated whether within a completely learner-controlled lesson, options to skip material in a "full" lesson might be more beneficial than learner options to see more material in a "lean" lesson. The likelihood is that the number of this type of study will continue to grow.

Additionally, many other specific issues that might be pursued include the following:

1. What specific instructional events are most or least amenable to providing or withdrawing learner control? That is, of the many instructional strategies, methods, activities, and events from which designers may draw upon to build lesson designs, which ones are most promising? Theoretical work by Laurillard (1987), Milheim and Martin (1991), and Steinberg (1989) go a long way toward providing prescriptive guidelines for designers; however, more specific recommendations need to be explored. I also strongly concur with the suggestion of Milheim and Martin

(1991) to conduct more empirical and theoretical work on the nature and role of learner motivations in learner-controlled CBI settings.

2. What exactly is the nature of a learner's mental processes as he or she proceeds through learner-controlled instruction? If we can better understand both the rational-cognitive thought processes and the emotional-motivational states of the learner, we might be able to devise means to encourage optimal processes and perhaps attempt to alter or at least compensate for dysfunctional processes. This type of investigation has been suggested before (Clark, 1984; Robson, Steward & Whitfield, 1988) but has not yet been adequately pursued, perhaps because of the inherently qualitative nature of the data and the lack of comfort with such methodologies by many learner-control investigators. Reeves (1993) goes so far as to suggest that, "Perhaps a moratorium should be called on the types of quantitative studies described in this [Reeves's] paper, replacing them with extensive, in-depth efforts to observe human behavior in our field and relate the observations to meaningful learning theory that may later be susceptible to quantitative inquiry" (p. 44). (See also 40.1.)

3. Related to the previous suggestion, it is time investigators more closely examined the social nature of learner-controlled activities. Anyone who has observed classroom situations where students navigate through instruction has informally noticed that there can be a great deal of discussion among students, both those sitting at separate computers and those working at the same computer. Rather than attempt to eliminate such interactions in order to investigate the "pure" effects of learner or program control, researchers may wish to adopt methodologies closer to field studies or naturalistic inquiry to study how learners can feed off each other's comments and actions during instruction. Although some experimental studies have been conducted to try to sort out the relative effects of learner control or program control for cooperative groups or for individual students (Hooper, Temiyakarn & Williams, 1993; Temiyakarn & McDonald, 1993), more work remains to be done before general conclusions, if any, can be drawn. (See also 35.9.4.)

4. A perhaps erroneous assumption undergirding most learner-control research is the implicit value placed on an individualistic and internally referenced system of control over instruction. That is, we tend to say that it is a good thing for learners to develop a capacity for intelligent control over their instructional experiences. This assumption might, however, be culture dependent. There is the additional question of whether the psychological bases discussed earlier (cognitive-rational and emotional-motivational) will operate similarly for students of differing cultural backgrounds. Wong (1988), for example, found that for students in a study conducted in Singapore, those who were under learner-controlled conditions selected more instructional options than students received under program control, a finding contrary to most learner-control research. Cross-

cultural studies of learner control are sparse, but are needed to shed light on the question of whether learner control can be viewed with the same assumptions for children of different cultural backgrounds and values.

5. Learner control should be much more closely investigated under other common or developing types of computer-based environments, such as simulations, hypertext/hypermedia (including browsing through internet systems such as the World Wide Web), on-line databases (such as electronic encyclopedias), on-line help and other support tools, and distance education. All of these contexts (possibly excepting distance education), by definition, intrinsically allow learner control to a greater or lesser degree. And it is likely that these types of computer-based experiences will soon be more frequent experiences for students than standard tutorials or "drills & practice." However, research to sort out the peculiar learner-control factors, each of which needs attention or support in these instructional systems, is still in its infancy (Trumbull, Gay & Mazur, 1992; McGrath, 1992; Saba & Shearer, 1993). Nevertheless, Chung and Reigeluth (1992) have given a jolt to this area of investigation by providing some useful instructional prescriptions for the use of learner control in hypermedia learning systems which they induced from the standard learner-control literature.

6. There needs to be a greater link made between learner-controlled CBI research and a growing body of literature on the topic of *self-regulated learning*. Briefly, this area of investigation, contributed to notably by McCombs and associates (McCombs, 1982, 1984; McCombs & Marzano, 1990) and by Zimmerman and associates (Zimmerman, 1990; Zimmerman & Martinez-Pons, 1986, 1988, 1990) conceptualizes students as "metacognitively, motivationally, and behaviorally active participants in their own learning processes" (Zimmerman & Martinez-Pons, 1988, p. 284). Although the research so far has primarily focused on understanding on a rather macro level the mental strategies occurring during successful self-regulated learning, this literature has clear implications for the inclusion of motivational variables in the design of learner-controlled instructional systems. In fact, some investigators have recently begun to explicitly address motivational variables operating in self-regulated learners (e.g., Schunk, 1990b; Zimmerman & Martinez-Pons, 1990). Additionally, there is beginning to emerge an interest in the application of self-regulated learning models to other formats of CBI, such as computer programming (Armstrong, 1989; Fischer & Mandl, 1988). Finally, a recent integrative paper by Kinzie (1990) provides a much-needed conceptual framework for discussion of the related areas of self-regulation, continuing motivation, and learner control.

7. The constructivist paradigm for learning would seem to have great implications for both the explanation of findings from the existing literature on learner control as well as to offer suggestions for new types of research questions based on the perspective it brings. Lebow (1993), in fact,

suggests that constructivism provides a much-needed framework for interpreting the often confusing results from learner-control research. These reinterpretations of the learner-control literature from this point of view remain to be done, however. Additionally, he points out, as do others (e.g., Jonassen, Wilson, Wang & Grabinger, 1993; see also 7.4.5), that constructivist instructional perspectives are associated with a high degree of learner control and imply many new types of research questions. Indeed, Jonassen et al. (1993) discuss how constructivist approaches and learner control are inextricably linked, "The more learner-controlled the instructional systems are, the more generative they are; that is, they require learners to generate or construct their own knowledge" (p. 87). Certainly future investigators who adopt this type of philosophy would ask questions that are far removed from "Which is better: learner or program control?"

33.13 CONCLUSION

Lepper and Chabay (1985) succinctly summarize the problem of differentially providing learners with control over their own instruction: "It is unlikely that any choice of level of control will be optimal for all students, or even that the same level of control will be optimal for a single student for all activities or in all situations" (p. 226). Of the many approaches for accommodating differences among learners, one is to allow them to adapt the instruction themselves to meet their own needs as they see fit. Instruction would not be linear and lockstep; that is, all students could receive different instructional events. This strategy is not as highly prescriptive or determined or complicated as branching or other adaptive schemes sometimes found in computer-based approaches. Rather, learner control is a way of allowing individual differences to exert a positive influence without trainer control or intervention based on these individual differences. However, great care needs to be exercised by designers in constructing their learner-controlled lessons to optimize effectiveness for all types of learners.

In sum, after all that has been written about the virtues of giving trainees control over their own learning, such activities alone offer no guarantee of successful learning. This might have been forecast by Dewey, that strong proponent of experiential education, who voiced concerns about unconditional learner self-management: "The ideal aim of education is creation of the power of self-control. But the mere removal of external control is no guarantee for the production of self-control" (1938, p. 64).

REFERENCES

Alessi, S.M. & Trollip, S.R. (1985). *Computer-based instruction.* Englewood Cliffs, NJ: Prentice Hall.

Allen, B.S. & Merrill, M.D. (1985). System assigned strategies and CBI. *Journal of Educational Computing Research 1* (1), 3–21.

Andrews, G.R. & Debus, R.L. (1978). Persistence and the causal perception of failure: modifying cognitive attributions. *Journal of Educational Psychology 70*(2), 154–66.

Armstrong, A.-M. (1989). The development of self-regulation skills through the modeling and structuring of computer programming. *Educational Technology Research and Development 37*(2), 69–76.

Arnone, M.P. & Grabowski, B.L. (1992). Effects on children's achievement and curiosity of variations in learner control over an interactive video lesson. *Educational Technology Research and Development 40*(1), 15–27.

Atkinson, J.W. (1974a). The mainsprings of achievement-oriented activity. *In* J.W. Atkinson & J.O. Raynor, eds. *Motivation and achievement,* 13–41. Washington, DC: Winston.

— (1974b). Strength of motivation and efficiency of performance. *In* J.W. Atkinson & J.O. Raynor, eds. *Motivation and achievement,* 193–218. Washington, DC: Winston.

— (1972). Optimizing the learning of a second-language vocabulary. *Journal of Experimental Psychology 96* (1), 124–29.

Avner, A., Moore, C. & Smith, S. (1980). Active external control: a basis for superiority of CBI. *Journal of Computer-Based Instruction 6*(4), 115–18.

Balson, P.M., Manning, D.T., Ebner, D.G. & Brooks, F.R. (1984/1985). Instructor-controlled versus student-controlled training in a videodisc-based paramedical program. *Journal of Educational Technology Systems 13*(2), 123–30.

Bandura, A. (1986). The explanatory and predictive scope of self-efficacy theory. *Journal of Social and Clinical Psychology 4,* 359–73.

Barker, G.P. & Graham, S. (1987). Developmental study of praise and blame as attributional cues. *Journal of Educational Psychology 79*(1), 62–66.

Borkowski, J.G., Weyhing, R.S. & Carr, M. (1988). Effects of attributional retraining on strategy-based reading comprehension in learning-disabled students. *Journal of Educational Psychology 80*(1), 46–53.

Beard, M.H., Lorton, P.V., Searle, B.W. & Atkinson, R.C. (1973). *Comparison of student performance and attitude under three lesson-selection strategies in computer-assisted instruction.* Stanford University: California Institute of Mathematical Studies in the Social Sciences. (ERIC Document Reproduction Service No. ED 088 466.)

Belland, J.C., Taylor, W.D., Canelos, J., Dwyer, F. & Baker, P. (1985). Is the self-paced instructional program, via microcomputer-based instruction, the most effective method of addressing individual differences? *Educational Communications and Technology Journal 33*(3), 185–98.

Billings, K. (1982). Computer-assisted learning: a learner-driven model. In *The computer: extension of the human mind.* Proceedings of the 3rd annual summer conference, University of Oregon. (ERIC Document Reproduction Service No. ED 219 863.)

Bowers, D. & Tsai, C. (1990). HyperCard in educational research: an introduction and case study. *Educational Technology 30*(2), 19–24.

Brophy, J. (1983). Conceptualizing student motivation. *Educational Psychologist 18*(3), 200–15.

Bunderson, C.V. (1974). The design and production of learner-controlled courseware for the TICCIT system: a progress report. *International Journal of Man-Machine Studies 6* (4), 479–91.

Campanizzi, J.A. (1978). Effects of locus of control and provision of overviews in a computer-assisted instruction sequence. *Association for Educational Data Systems (AEDS) Journal 12*(1), 21–30.

Carrier, C.A. (1984). Do learners make good choices? A review of research on learner control in instruction. *Instructional Innovator 29*(2), 15–17.

Carrier, C.A., Davidson, G., Higson, V. & Williams, M. (1984). Selection of options by field independent and dependent children in a computer-based concept lesson. *Journal of Computer-Based Instruction 11*(2), 49–54.

Carrier, C.A., Davidson, G. & Williams, M. (1985). Selection of instructional options in a computer-based coordinate concept lesson. *Educational Communications and Technology Journal 33*(3), 199–212.

Carrier, C.A., Davidson, G.V., Williams, M.D. & Kalweit, C.M. (1986). Instructional options and encouragement effects in a microcomputer-delivered concept lesson. *Journal of Educational Research 79*(4), 222–29.

Carrier, C.A. & Jonassen, D.H. (1988). Adapting courseware to accommodate individual differences. *In* D.H. Jonassen, ed. *Instructional designs for microcomputer courseware,* 203–26. Hillsdale, NJ: Erlbaum.

Carrier, C.A. & Williams, M.D. (1988). A test of one learner control strategy with students of differing levels of task persistence. *American Educational Research Journal 25*(2), 285–306.

Chung, J. & Reigeluth, C.M. (1992). Instructional prescriptions for learner control. *Educational Technology 32*(10), 14–20.

Clark, R.E. (1982). Antagonism between achievement and enjoyment in ATI studies. *Educational Psychologist 17* (2), 92–101.

— (1984). Research on student thought processes during computer-based instruction. *Journal of Instructional Development 7*(3), 2–5.

Covington, M.V. & Omelich, C.L. (1984a). An empirical examination of Weiner's critique of attribution research. *Journal of Educational Psychology 76*(6), 1214–25.

— & — (1984b). Controversies or consistencies? A reply to Brown and Weiner. *Journal of Educational Psychology 76*(1), 159–68.

— (1985). Ability and effort valuation among failure-avoiding and failure-accepting students. *Journal of Educational Psychology 77*(4), 446–59.

Cronbach, L.J. & Snow, R.E. (1977). *Aptitudes and instructional methods: a handbook for research on interactions.* New York: Irvington.

Dalton, D.W. (1990). The effects of cooperative learning strategies on achievement and attitudes during interactive video. *Journal of Computer-Based Instruction 17*(1), 8–16.

Dewey, J. (1938). *Experience and education.* New York: Collier.

Duchastel, P. (1986a). Computer text access. *Computer Education 10* (4), 403–09.

Duchastel, P. (1986b). Intelligent computer assisted instruction systems: the nature of learner control. *Journal of Educational Computing Research 2*(3), 379–93.

Dweck, C.S. (1975). The role of expectations and attributions in the alleviation of learned helplessness. *Journal of Personality and Social Psychology 31*(4), 674–85.

— (1986). Motivational processes affecting learning. *American Psychologist 41*(10), 1040–48.

— & Leggett, E.L. (1988). A social-cognitive approach to motivation and personality. *Psychological Review 95* (2), 256–73.

Ellermann, H.H. & Free, E.L. (1990). A subject-controlled environment for paired associate learning. *Journal of Computer-Based Instruction 17*(3), 97–102.

Faust, G.W. (1974). Design strategy and the TICCIT system. *Viewpoints 50*(4), 91–101.

Federico, P.-A. (1980). Adaptive instruction: trends and issues. *In* R.E. Snow, P-A. Federico & W.E. Montague, eds. *Aptitude, learning, and instruction: Vol. 1. cognitive process analyses of aptitude,* 1–26. Hillsdale, NJ: Erlbaum.

Fine, S.R. (1972). *Learner control commands for computer-assisted instruction systems* (Tech. Rep. No. 15). Washington, DC, National Science Foundation. (ERIC Document Reproduction Service No. ED 072 633.)

Fischer, P.M. & Mandl, H. (1988). Knowledge acquisition by computerized audiovisual feedback. *European Journal of Psychology of Education 3*(2), 217–33.

Fisher, M.D., Blackwell, L.R., Garcia, A.B. & Greene, J.C. (1975). Effects of student control and choice on engagement in a CAI arithmetic task in a low-income school. *Journal of Educational Psychology 67*(6), 776–83.

Flavell, J.H. (1979). Metacognition and cognitive monitoring. *American Psychologist 34*(10), 906–11.

Fowler, J.W. & Peterson, P.L. (1981). Increasing reading persistence and altering attribution style of learned helpless children. *Journal of Educational Psychology 73*(2), 251–60.

Fredericks, P.S. (1976, Apr.). *The effects of locus of control on CAI performance.* Paper presented at the annual meetings of the American Educational Research Association, San Francisco, CA. (ERIC Document Reproduction Service No. ED 125 545.)

Gagné, R.M. (1985). *The conditions of learning and theory of instruction,* 4th ed. New York: Holt, Rinehart & Winston.

—, Briggs, L.J. & Wager, W.W. (1988). *Principles of instructional design,* 3rd ed. New York: Holt, Rinehart & Winston.

Garhart, C. & Hannafin, M. (1986). The accuracy of cognitive monitoring during computer-based instruction. *Journal of Computer-Based Instruction 13*(3), 88–93.

Garner, R. & Alexander, P.A. (1989). Metacognition: answered and unanswered questions. *Educational Psychologist 24* (2), 143–58.

Gay, G. (1986). Interaction of learner control and prior understanding in computer-assisted video instruction. *Journal of Educational Psychology 78*(3), 225–27.

Gehlbach, R.D. (1979). Individual differences: implications for instructional theory, research, and innovation. *Educational Researcher 8*(4), 8–14.

Goetzfried, L. & Hannafin, M.J. (1985). The effect of locus of CAI control strategies on the learning of mathematics rules. *American Educational Research Journal 22*(2), 273–78.

Graham, S. & Barker, G.P. (1990). The down side of help: an attributional-developmental analysis of helping behavior as a low-ability cue. *Journal of Educational Psychology 82*(1), 7–14.

Gray, S.H. (1987). The effect of sequence control on computer assisted learning. *Journal of Computer-Based Instruction 14*(2), 54–56.

— (1989). The effect of locus of control and sequence control on computerized information retrieval and retention. *Journal of Educational Computing Research 5*(4), 459–71.

Grubb, R.E. (1968). Learner-controlled statistics. *Programmed Learning and Educational Technology 5*(1), 38–42.

Hannafin, M.J. (1984). Guidelines for using locus of instructional control in the design of computer-assisted instruction. *Journal of Instructional Development 7*(3), 6–10.

— & Colamaio, M.E. (1987). The effects of variations in lesson control and practice on learning from interactive video. *Educational Communications and Technology Journal 35*(4), 203–12.

Hansen, D.W. (1982/1983). User-controlled technology in the humanities. *Journal of Educational Technology Systems 11*(2), 131–42.

Hansen, J.B. (1974). Effects of feedback, learner control, and cognitive abilities on state anxiety and performance in a computer-assisted instruction task. *Journal of Educational Psychology 66*(2), 247–54.

Hartley, J.R. (1985). Some psychological aspects of computer-assisted learning and teaching. *Programmed Learning and Educational Technology 22*(2), 140–49.

Heckhausen, H., Schmalt, H.-D. & Schneider, K. (1985). *Achievement motivation in perspective* (M. Woodruff & R. Wicklund, trans.). Orlando, FL: Academic. (Original work published in 1979.)

Hicken, S., Sullivan, H. & Klein, J. (1992). Learner control modes and incentive variations in computer-delivered instruction. *Educational Technology Research and Development 40*(4), 15–26.

Higginbotham-Wheat, N. (1988, Nov.). *Perspectives on implementation of learner control in CBI.* Paper presented at the annual meetings of the Mid-South Educational Research Association, Lexington, KY. (ERIC Document Reproduction Service No. ED 305 898.)

Hintze, H., Mohr, H. & Wenzel, A. (1988). Students' attitudes towards control methods in computer-assisted instruction. *Journal of Computer Assisted Learning 4*(1), 3–10.

Holland, J.G. (1977). Variables in adaptive decisions in individualized instruction. *Educational Psychologist 12*(2), 146–61.

Holmes, N., Robson, E.H. & Steward, A.P. (1985). Learner control in computer-assisted learning. *Journal of Computer Assisted Learning 1*(2), 99–107.

Hooper, S., Temiyakarn, C. & Williams, M.D. (1993). The effects of cooperative learning and learner control on high- and average-ability students. *Educational Technology Research and Development 41*(2), 5–18.

Humphreys, M.S. & Revelle, W. (1984). Personality, motivation, and performance: a theory of the relationship between individual differences and information processing. *Psychological Review 91*(2), 153–84.

Hurlock, R.E., Lahey, G.F. & McCann, P.H. (1974). *Student-controlled versus program-controlled* CAI. San Diego, CA: Naval Personnel Research and Development Center. (ERIC Document Reproduction Service No. ED 089 681.)

Jacobson, E. & Thompson, M. (1975). *Self-managed learning using CAI.* Washington, DC: National Institute of Education and National Science Foundation. (ERIC Document Reproduction Service No. ED 104 362.)

Johansen, K.J. & Tennyson, R.D. (1983). Effect of adaptive advisement on perception in learner-controlled, computer-based instruction using a rule-learning task. *Educational Communications and Technology Journal 31*(4), 226–36.

Jonassen, D.H. (1985). Learning strategies: a new educational technology. *Programmed Learning and Educational Technology 22* (1), 26–34.

— & Hannum, W.H. (1987). Research-based principles for designing computer software. *Educational Technology 27* (12), 7–14.

—, Wilson, B.G., Wang, S. & Grabinger, R.S. (1993). Constructivist uses of expert systems to support learning. *Journal of Computer-Based Instruction 20*(3), 86–94.

Judd, W.A. (1972). *Learner-controlled computer-based instruction.* Paper presented at the International School on Computers in Education, Pugniochiuso, Italy. (ERIC Document Reproduction Service No. ED 072 635.)

—, Bunderson, C.V. & Bessent, E.W. (1970). *An investigation of the effects of learner control in computer-assisted instruction prerequisite mathematics (MATHS).* Austin, TX: University of Texas. (ERIC Document Reproduction Service No. ED 053 532.)

—, Daubek, K. & O'Neil, H.F., Jr. (1975). *Individual differences in learner-controlled CAI.* Paper presented at the annual meetings of the American Educational Research Association, Washington, DC. (ERIC Document Reproduction Service No. ED 107 215.)

—, O'Neil, H.F., Jr. & Spelt, P.F. (1974a). *Individual differences and learner control II: investigation of control over pictorial mediators in computer-assisted instruction.* Lowry AFB, CO: Air Force Human Resources Lab. (ERIC Document Reproduction Service No. ED 094 733.)

—, — & — (1974b). *Individual differences and learner control I: program development and investigation of control over mnemonics in computer-assisted instruction.* Lowry AFB, CO: Air Force Human Resources Lab. (ERIC Document Reproduction Service No. ED 094 732.)

Keller, F.S. (1974). Ten years of personalized instruction. *Teaching of Psychology 1*(1), 4–9.

Keller, J.M. (1983). Motivational design of instruction. *In* C.M. Reigeluth, ed. *Instructional-design theories and models,* 386–434. Hillsdale, NJ: Erlbaum.

— (1987a). Strategies for stimulating the motivation to learn. *Performance & Instruction 26*(8), 1–7.

— (1987b). The systematic process of motivational design. *Performance & Instruction,* 26(9–10), 1–8.

Kinzie, M.B. (1990). Requirements and benefits of effective interactive instruction: learner control, self-regulation, and continuing motivation. *Educational Technology Research and Development 38*(1), 1–21.

— & Sullivan, H.J. (1989). Continuing motivation, learner control, and CAI. *Educational Technology Research and Development 37*(2), 5–14.

—, Sullivan, H.J. & Berdel, R.L. (1988). Learner control and achievement in science computer-assisted instruction. *Journal of Educational Psychology 80*(3), 299–303.

Klein, J.D. & Keller, J.M. (1990). Influence of student ability, locus of control, and type of instructional control on performance and confidence. *Journal of Educational Research 83*(3), 140–46.

Kukla, A. (1978). An attributional theory of choice. *In* L. Berkowitz, ed. *Advances in experimental social psychology: Vol. 11,* 113–44. New York: Academic.

Lahey, G.F. (1978). *Learner control of computer-assisted instruction: a comparison to guided instruction.* Paper presented at the annual meetings of the Association for the

Development of Computer-Based Instructional Systems, Dallas, TX. (ERIC Document Reproduction Service No. ED 165 716.)

— & Coady, J.D. (1978). *Learner control of instructional sequence in computer-based instruction: a comparison to programmed control.* San Diego, CA: Naval Personnel Research and Development Center. (ERIC Document Reproduction Service No. ED 211 049.)

—, Crawford, A.M. & Hurlock, R.E. (1976). *Learner control of lesson strategy: a model for PLATO IV system lessons.* San Diego, CA: Naval Personnel Research and Development Center. (ERIC Document Reproduction Service No. ED 125 543.)

—, Hurlock, R.E. & McCann, P.H. (1973). *Post lesson remediation and student control of branching in computer-based training.* San Diego, CA: Naval Personnel Research and Development Center. (ERIC Document Reproduction Service No. ED 083 797.)

Laurillard, D.M. (1987). Computers and the emancipation of students: giving control to the learner. *Instructional Science* 16(1), 3–18.

Lebow, D. (1993). Constructivist values for instructional systems design: five principles toward a new mindset. *Educational Technology Research and Development* 41(3), 4–16.

Lee, S.-S. & Wong, S.C.-H. (1989). Adaptive program vs. learner control strategy on computer-aided learning of gravimetric stoichiometry problems. *Journal of Research on Computing in Education* 21(4), 367–79.

— & Lee, Y.H.K. (1991). Effects of learner-control versus program-control strategies on computer-aided learning of chemistry problems: for acquisition or review? *Journal of Educational Psychology* 83(4), 491–98.

Lepper, M.R. (1985). Microcomputers in education: motivational and social issues. *American Psychologist* 40(1), 1–18.

— & Chabay, R.W. (1985). Intrinsic motivation and instruction: conflicting views on the role of motivational processes in computer-based education. *Educational Psychologist* 20(4), 217–30.

Lichtenstein, S. & Fischhoff, B. (1977). Do those who know more also know more about how much they know? *Organizational Behavior and Human Performance* 20(2), 159–83.

López, C.L. & Harper, M. (1989). The relationship between learner control of CAI and locus of control among Hispanic students. *Educational Technology Research and Development* 37(4), 19–28.

MacGregor, S.K. (1988). Instructional design for computer-mediated text systems: effects of motivation, learner control, and collaboration on reading performance. *Journal of Experimental Education* 56(3), 142–47.

Maehr, M.L. (1976). Continuing motivation: an analysis of a seldom considered educational outcome. *Review of Educational Research* 46(3), 443–62.

Mayer, R.E. (1976). Some conditions of meaningful learning for computer programming: advance organizers and subject control of frame order. *Journal of Educational Psychology* 68(2), 143–50.

McCann, P.H., Lahey, G.F. & Hurlock, R.E. (1973). *A comparison of student options versus program controlled CAI training.* San Diego, CA: Naval Personnel Research and Development Center. (ERIC Document Reproduction Service No. ED 081 233.)

McCombs, B.L. (1982). Learner satisfaction, motivation, and performance: capitalizing on strategies for positive self-control. *National Society for Performance and Instruction Journal* 21(4), 3–6.

— (1984). Processes and skills underlying continuing intrinsic motivation to learn: toward a definition of motivational skills training interventions. *Educational Psychologist* 19(4), 199–218.

— & Marzano, R.J. (1990). Putting the self in self-regulated learning: the self as agent in integrating will and skill. *Educational Psychologist* 25(1), 51–70.

— & McDaniel, M.A. (1981). On the design of adaptive treatments for individualized instructional systems. *Educational Psychologist* 16(1), 11–22.

McGrath, D. (1992). Hypertext, CAI, paper, or program control: do learners benefit from choices? *Journal of Research on Computing in Education* 24(4), 513–32.

McNeil, B.J. & Nelson, K.R. (1991). Meta-analysis of interactive video instruction: a 10-year review of achievement effects. *Journal of Computer-Based Instruction* 18(1), 1–6.

Medway, F.J. & Venino, G.R. (1982). The effects of effort feedback and performance patterns on children's attributions and task persistence. *Contemporary Educational Psychology* 7(1), 26–34.

Merrill, M.D. (1973). *Premises, propositions and research underlying the design of a learner-controlled computer assisted instruction system: a summary of the TICCIT system.* Working paper No. 44. Provo, UT: Division of Instructional Sciences, Brigham Young University.

— (1975). Learner control: beyond aptitude-treatment interactions. *AV Communication Review* 23(2), 217–26.

— (1983). Component display theory. *In* C.M. Reigeluth, ed. *Instructional-design theories and models,* 279–334. Hillsdale, NJ: Erlbaum.

Merrill, M.D. (1984). *What is learner control?* (ERIC Document Reproduction Service No. ED 298 905.)

Meyer, N.E. & Dyck, D.G. (1986). Effects of reward-schedule parameters and attribution retraining on children's attributions and reading persistence. *Bulletin of the Psychonomic Society* 24(1), 65–68.

Milheim, W.D. (1989, Feb.). *Perceived attitudinal effects of various types of learner control in an interactive video lesson.* Paper presented at the annual meetings of the Association for Educational Communications and Technology, Dallas, TX. (ERIC Document Reproduction Service No. ED 308 828.)

— (1990). The effects of pacing and sequence control in an interactive video lesson. *Educational & Training Technology International* 27(1), 7–19.

— & Martin, B.L. (1991). Theoretical bases for the use of learner control: three different perspectives. *Journal of Computer-Based Instruction* 18(3), 99–105.

Morrison, G.R., Ross, S.M. & Baldwin, W. (1992). Learner control of context and instructional support in learning elementary school mathematics. *Educational Technology Research and Development* 40(1), 5–13.

Murphy, M.A. & Davidson, G.V. (1991). Computer-based adaptive instruction: effects of learner control on concept learning. *Journal of Computer-Based Instruction* 18(2), 51–56.

Nelson, T.O., Leonesio, R.J., Shimamura, A.P., Landwehr, R.F. & Narens, L. (1982). Overlearning and the feeling of knowing. *Journal of Experimental Psychology: Learning,*

Memory, and Cognition 8(4), 279–88.

Newkirk, R.L. (1973). A comparison of learner control and machine control strategies for computer-assisted instruction. *Programmed Learning and Educational Technology* 10(2), 82–91.

Olivier, W.P. (1971, Feb.). *Learner and program-controlled sequences of computer-assisted instruction.* Paper presented at the annual meetings of the American Educational Research Association, New York. (ERIC Document Reproduction Service No. ED 046 246.)

O'Shea, T., & Self, J. (1983). *Learning and teaching with computers.* Englewood Cliffs, NJ: Prentice Hall.

Penland, P. (1979). Self-initiated learning. *Adult Education* 29(3), 170–79.

Peters, C.L. (1988). The effects of advisement, content mapping, and interactive video on learner control and achievement in computer-based instruction. *Dissertation Abstracts International* 50(2), 348A.

Pitz, G.F. & Sachs, N.J. (1984). Judgment and decision: theory and application. *Annual Review of Psychology* 35, 139–63.

Pollock, J.C. & Sullivan, H.J. (1990). Practice mode and learner control in computer-based instruction. *Contemporary Educational Psychology* 15(3), 251–60.

Popper, K.W. (1968). *Conjectures and refutations in the growth of scientific knowledge.* New York: Harper Torchbooks.

Postlethwait, S.N., Novak, J. & Murray, H.T., Jr. (1972). *The audio-tutorial approach to learning,* 3d ed. Minneapolis, MN: Burgess.

Pridemore, D.R. & Klein, J.D. (1991). Control of feedback in computer-assisted instruction. *Educational Technology Research and Development* 39(4), 27–32.

Reeves, T.C. (1993). Pseudoscience in computer-based instruction: the case of learner control research. *Journal of Computer-Based Instruction* 20(2), 39–46.

Reigeluth, C.M. (1979). TICCIT to the future: advances in instructional theory for CAI. *Journal of Computer-Based Instruction* 6(2), 40–46.

— & Schwartz, E. (1989). An instructional theory for the design of computer-based simulations. *Journal of Computer-Based Instruction* 16(1), 1–10.

— & Stein, F.S. (1983). The elaboration theory of instruction. *In* C.M. Reigeluth, ed. *Instructional-design theories and models,* 335–82. Hillsdale, NJ: Erlbaum.

Reinking, D. & Schreiner, R. (1985). The effects of computer-mediated text on measures of reading comprehension and reading behavior. *Reading Research Quarterly* 22 (5), 536–52.

Reiser, R.A. (1987). Instructional technology: a history. *In* R.M. Gagné, ed. *Instructional technology: foundations,* 11–48. Hillsdale, NJ: Erlbaum.

Relan, A. (1991). Effects of two levels of strategy training and learner control on performance and choice behavior in a computer-based concept-classification task. *Dissertation Abstracts International* 52(11), 3895-A.

Revelle, W. & Michaels, E.J. (1976). The theory of achievement motivation revisited: the implications of inertial tendencies. *Psychological Review* 83(5), 394–404.

Rivers, L.C. (1972). *Development and assessment of an adaptive strategy utilizing regression analysis for the presentation of instruction via computer* (Tech. Rep. No. 27). Florida State University, Computer-Assisted Instruction Center. (ERIC Document Reproduction Service No. ED 077 228.)

Robson, E.H., Steward, A.P. & Whitfield, G.E. (1988). Pupils' choices in learning with computers. *Journal of Computer Assisted Learning* 4(2), 93–102.

Romiszowski, A.J. (1986). *Developing auto-instructional materials.* New York: Nichols.

Ross, S.M & Morrison, G.R. (1988). Adapting instruction to learner performance and background variables. *In* D.H. Jonassen, ed. *Instructional designs for microcomputer courseware,* 227–46. Hillsdale, NJ: Erlbaum.

— & — (1989). In search of a happy medium in instructional technology research: issues concerning external validity, media replications, and learner control. *Educational Technology Research and Development* 37(1), 19–33.

—, — & O'Dell, J.K. (1988). Obtaining more out of less text in CBI: effects of varied text density as a function of learner characteristics and control strategy. *Educational Communications and Technology Journal* 36(3), 131–142.

—, — & — (1989). Uses and effects of learner control of context and instructional support in computer-based instruction. *Educational Communications and Technology Journal* 37(4), 29–39.

— & Rakow, E.A. (1981). Learner control versus program control as adaptive strategies for selection of instructional support on math rules. *Journal of Educational Psychology* 73(5), 745–53.

—, — & Bush, A.J. (1980). Instructional adaptation for self-managed learning systems. *Journal of Educational Psychology* 72(3), 312–20.

Rossett, A. & Gautier-Downes, J. (1991). *A handbook of job-aids.* San Diego, CA: Pfeiffer.

Rotter, J.B. (1966). Generalized expectancies for internal versus external control of reinforcement. *Psychological Monographs,* 1 (whole no. 609).

Saba, F. & Shearer, R.L. (1993, Jan.). *Instructional transactions in distance education.* Paper presented at the annual meeting of the Association for Educational Communications and Technology, New Orleans, LA.

Salomon, G. (1983). The differential investment of mental effort in learning from different sources. *Educational Psychologist* 18(1), 42–50.

— (1985). Information technologies: what you see is not (always) what you get. *Educational Psychologist* 20 (4), 207–16.

— & Gardner, H. (1986). The computer as educator: lessons from television research. *Educational Researcher* 15 (1), 13–19.

Santiago, R.S. & Okey, J.R. (1992). The effects of advisement and locus of control on achievement in learner-controlled instruction. *Journal of Computer-Based Instruction* 19 (2), 47–53.

Sasscer, M.F. & Moore, D.M. (1984). A study of the relationship between learner control patterns and course completion in computer-assisted instruction. *Programmed Learning and Educational Technology* 21(1), 28–33.

Schloss, P.J., Sindelar, P.T., Cartwright, G.P. & Smith, M.A. (1988). Learner control over feedback as a variable in computer assisted instruction. *Journal of Research on Computing in Education* 20 (4), 310–20.

—, Wisniewski, L.A. & Cartwright, G.P. (1988). The differential effect of learner control and feedback in college students' performance on CAI modules. *Journal of Educational Computing Research* 4(2), 141–50.

Schunk, D.H. (1982). Effects of effort attributional feedback on children's perceived self-efficacy and achievement. *Journal of Educational Psychology 74*(4), 548–56.

— (1983). Ability versus effort attributional feedback: differential effects on self-efficacy and achievement. *Journal of Educational Psychology 75*(6), 848–56.

— (1990a, Apr.). *Socialization and the development of self-regulated learning: the role of attributions.* Paper presented at the annual meeting of the American Educational Research Association, Boston, MA. (ERIC Document Reproduction Service No. ED 317 581.)

— (1990b). Goal setting and self-efficacy during self-regulated learning. *Educational Psychologist 25*(1), 71–86.

— & Cox, P.D. (1986). Strategy training and attributional feedback with learning disabled students. *Journal of Educational Psychology 78*(3), 201–09.

Seidel, R.J., Wagner, H., Rosenblatt, R.D., Hillelsohn, M.J. & Stelzer, J. (1975). *Learner control of instructional sequencing within an adaptive tutorial CAI environment* (Report No. HumRRO-TR-75-7). Alexandria, VA: Human Resources Research Organization. (ERIC Document Reproduction Service No. ED 111 338.)

Seymour, S.L., Sullivan, H.J., Story, N.O. & Mosley, M.L. (1987). Microcomputers and continuing motivation. *Educational Communications and Technology Journal 35*(1), 18–23.

Shyu, H.-Y. & Brown, S.W. (1992). Learner control versus program control in interactive videodisc instruction: what are the effects in procedural learning? *International Journal of Instructional Media 19*(2), 85–96.

Slavin, R.E. (1986). Best-evidence synthesis: an alternative to meta-analytic and traditional reviews. *Educational Researcher 15*(9), 5–11.

Smallwood, R.D. (1962). *A decision structure for teaching machines.* Cambridge, MA: MIT Press.

Snow, R.E. (1979, Apr.). *Aptitude, learner control, and adaptive instruction.* Paper presented at the annual meeting of the American Educational Research Association, San Francisco, CA. (ERIC Document Reproduction Service No. ED 180 447.)

— (1980). Aptitude, learner control, and adaptive instruction. *Educational Psychologist 15*(3), 151–58.

— & Yalow, E. (1982). Education and intelligence. *In* R.J. Sternberg, ed. *Handbook of human intelligence,* 493–585. Cambridge, England: Cambridge University Press.

Steinberg, E.R. (1977). Review of student control in computer-assisted instruction. *Journal of Computer-Based Instruction 3*(3), 84–90.

— (1984). *Teaching computers to teach.* Hillsdale, NJ: Erlbaum.

— (1989). Cognition and learner control: a literature review, 1977–88. *Journal of Computer-Based Instruction 16*(4), 117–24.

—, Baskin, A.B. & Hofer, E. (1986). Organizational/memory tools: a technique for improving problem solving skills. *Journal of Educational Computing Research 2*(2), 169–87.

Strickland, S. & Wilcox, W.C. (1978). *Regression study of learner control data.* Washington, DC, National Science Foundation. (ERIC Document Reproduction Service No. ED 208 012.)

Suppes, P. (1966). The uses of computers in education. *Scientific American 215*(3), 206–20.

Temiyakarn McDonald, C.S. (1993). Learner-controlled lesson in cooperative learning group during computer-based instruction. *Dissertation Abstracts International 54* (12), 4414–A.

Tennyson, C.L., Tennyson, R.D. & Rothen, W. (1980). Content structure and instructional control strategies as design variables in concept acquisition. *Journal of Educational Psychology 72*(4), 499–505.

Tennyson, R.D. (1980). Instructional control strategies and content structure as design variables in concept acquisition using computer-based instruction. *Journal of Educational Psychology 72*(4), 525–32.

— (1981). Use of adaptive information for advisement in learning concepts and rules using computer-assisted instruction. *American Educational Research Journal 18* (4), 425–38.

— & Buttrey, T. (1980). Advisement and management strategies as design variables in computer-assisted instruction. *Educational Communications and Technology Journal 28*(3), 169–76.

—, Christensen, D.L. & Park, O.-C. (1984). The Minnesota Adaptive Instructional System: a review of its theory and research. *Journal of Computer-Based Instruction 11* (1), 2–13.

— & Park, O.-C. (1984). Computer-based adaptive instructional systems: a review of empirically based models. *Machine-Mediated Learning 1*(2), 129–53.

—, — & Christensen, D.L. (1985). Adaptive control of learning time and content sequence in concept learning using computer-based instruction. *Journal of Educational Psychology 77*(4), 481–91.

— & Rothen, W. (1979). Management of computer-based instruction: design of an adaptive control strategy. *Journal of Computer-Based Instruction 5*(3), 63–71.

—, Welsh, J.C., Christensen, D.L. & Hajovy, H. (1985). Interactive effect of information structure, sequence of information, and process learning time on rule learning using computer-based instruction. *Educational Communications and Technology Journal 33*(3), 213–33.

Thomas, E.A.C. (1983). Notes on effort and achievement-oriented behavior. *Psychological Review 90*(1), 1–20.

Tobias, S. (1976). Achievement-treatment interactions. *Review of Educational Research 46*(1), 61–74.

— (1981). Adapting instruction to individual differences among students. *Educational Psychologist 16*(2), 111–20.

— (1987a). Mandatory text review and interaction with student characteristics. *Journal of Educational Psychology 79*(2), 154–61.

— (1987b). Learner characteristics. *In* R.M. Gagné, ed. *Instructional technology: foundations,* 207–31. Hillsdale, NJ: Erlbaum.

Trumbull, D., Gay, G. & Mazur, J. (1992). Students' actual and perceived use of navigational and guidance tools in a hypermedia program. *Journal of Research on Computing in Education 24*(3), 315–28.

U.S. Congress, Office of Technology Assessment (1988). *Power on! New tools for teaching and learning* (OTA-SET-379). Washington, DC: U.S. Government Printing Office.

Weiner, B. (1974). An attributional interpretation of expectancy-value theory. *In* B. Weiser, ed. *Cognitive views of human motivation,* 51–69. New York: Academic.

Williams, M.D. (1992). The differential effectiveness of attributional feedback and learner control in a computer-based economics lesson. *Dissertation Abstracts International 53*(1), 129–A.

Wilson, B.G. & Jonassen, D.H. (1989). Hypertext and instructional design: some preliminary guidelines. *Performance Improvement Quarterly 2*(3), 34–49.

Wilcox, W.C. (1979, Apr.). *Interaction of learner control and student aptitudes.* Paper presented at the annual meetings of the American Educational Research Association, San Francisco, CA. (ERIC Document Reproduction Service No. ED 208 011.)

—, Richards, B.F., Merrill, M.D., Christensen, D. & Rosenvall, J. (1978). *Learner control of number of instances in a rule-using task.* Washington, DC: National Science Foundation. (ERIC Document Reproduction Service No. ED 201 531.)

Wong, S.K.P. (1988). The effects of different visual strategies, selected individual differences, and learner control on student word-problem solving performance. *Dissertation Abstracts International 49*(6), 1366-A.

Zimmerman, B.J. (1990). Self-regulated learning and academic achievement: an overview. *Educational Psychologist 25* (1), 3–18.

— & Martinez-Pons, M. (1986). Development of a structured interview for assessing student use of self-regulated learning strategies. *American Educational Research Journal 23*(4), 614–28.

— & — (1988). Construct validation of a strategy model of student self-regulated learning. *Journal of Educational Psychology 80*(3), 284–90.

— & — (1990). Student differences in self-regulated learning: relating grade, sex, and giftedness to self-efficacy and strategy use. *Journal of Educational Psychology 82*(1), 51–59.

34. INSTRUCTIONAL TECHNOLOGY AND ATTITUDE CHANGE

Michael Simonson   Nancy Maushak

IOWA STATE UNIVERSITY

"A companion's words of persuasion are effective." —*The Iliad,* Homer, c. 700 BC

Attitudes are learned "predispositions to respond." Attitudes serve to provide direction to subsequent actions. Because attitudes are acquired they can be changed fairly predictably (Zimbardo & Leippe, 1991). Increasingly, instructional media have been used to deliver attitude change messages. This chapter will discuss the use of media to present instructional messages that persuade instead of inform. Unfortunately, when media are used for attitude change, the relationship between the medium of delivery and the message of persuasion is unclear.

Chaiken and Egly (1976) reported on the results of what now is considered a classic study of attitude change using media. It demonstrated the difficulty of drawing conclusions about mediated instruction and attitude change. In their experiment, subjects were exposed to either an easy- or difficult-to-comprehend message that was presented in written, audiotaped, or videotaped form. The easy version of the message, which dealt with a dispute between a company and its union, used short sentences with simple vocabulary. The difficult version used complex sentences and sophisticated vocabulary. The results showed that in the difficult message treatment, both attitude change and learning were greater when the message was presented in written form. For the easy-to-comprehend message, a different pattern emerged. Comprehension was high no matter what delivery medium was used, but the amount of attitude change was greatest when the message was videotaped, slightly less when it was audiotaped, and least when the message was written (Table 34-1).

Apparently, the amount of attitude change was related to the difficulty of the message content and to the delivery medium. Chaiken and Egly discussed why this differential effect occurred, but they did not explain the apparent media effect. Results such as this one demonstrate the difficulty of developing conclusions or offering guidelines about the

persuasive impact of messages delivered using media. Actually, any careful study of the literature leads the serious, if conservative, reviewer to conclude that there is little if any "medium effect," and to agree with Clark (1994, 1983) that media are "mere vehicles" that do not directly influence attitudes any more than they do achievement. However, instructional media are often used to deliver persuasive messages. There is a wealth of interesting and useful research examining attitudes and media that can be applied by the educator. This literature will be reviewed, criticized, and summarized in this chapter.

34.1 INTRODUCTION

Attitude change and instructional technology will be discussed as follows. First, the nature of attitudes will be explained. Attitudes will be defined and the characteristics of attitude constructs will be presented. Also included will be a rationale for why attitude change is an important concern of those interested in instructional technology. Second, there will be a review of the theories of attitude change. Understanding some of the various theories of attitude change is fundamental to any discussion of the relationship between persuasion and instructional technology. Third, a review of the long-continuing debate about the relationship between attitudes and behaviors will be included. Historically, many have felt that attitudes are not related to actions, but others have taken a more moderate approach. This debate will be summarized.

Next, an overview of the techniques for measuring attitudes will be provided. It is obvious from any review of the literature that attitude measurement is done poorly. Researchers often do not use even the most basic procedures for effective measurement when they investigate attitude variables. Generally accepted procedures for measuring

TABLE 34-1.   ATTITUDE CHANGE AND RETENTION OF MESSAGE CONTENT AS A FUNCTION OF MEDIUM AND MESSAGE DIFFICULTY (Chaiken & Egly, 1976)

	Easy Message			Difficult Message		
	Written	Audio	Video	Written	Audio	Video
Attitude change	2.94	3.75	4.78	4.73	2.32	3.02
Number of messages recalled	2.45	2.21	2.17	2.29	1.74	1.67
Number of short answer items correct	4.57	3.93	4.45	4.21	3.71	3.36
Perceived message difficulty	4.76	4.21	4.83	5.31	7.50	7.43

Note: Higher numbers indicated greater attitude change, message comprehension, and perceived message difficulty.

attitudes will be presented. Fifth, there will be a review of previous attempts to organize the attitude change and instructional technology literature. At least two schemes (Simonson, 1979; Bednar & Levie, 1993) for explaining the use of instructional technology for attitude change have been proposed and will be discussed.

Finally, a set of six guidelines for designing persuasive instructional messages will be offered. These guidelines will be linked using a "Model of Cumulative Effect" that proposes a method for improving the likelihood of attitude change. The model is an attempt to provide the practitioner with techniques for building a persuasive message that is to be delivered with media.

It is also important to explain what is *not covered* in this discussion of attitude change and instructional technology. First, the very important and rich literature about motivation is not reviewed. Motivation is obviously related to attitude change, especially to most of the current theories used to predict behaviors, such as the theory of reasoned action and the theory of planned action. However, motivation is a broad topic that requires its own discussion. (see 32.5.5).

Second, attitude toward media or technology is presented only peripherally. This is because the main concern of this review is to discuss persuasive instructional messages presented with media. In other words, attitude change toward the content of messages is the focus of this chapter, not attitude toward the medium itself. Finally, this review should not be considered a comprehensive examination of the extremely broad body of literature related to attitudes and attitude change. Rather, it is a handbook-type summary of the literature that relates, at least tangentially, to the chapter's theme: how to design messages using media when attitude changes are desired. For a more complete review of attitude literature, one of the recently published books on this topic should be consulted (e.g. Eagly & Chaiken, 1993; O'Keefe, 1990).

34.2 THE NATURE OF ATTITUDES

Research on attitudes has been popular in many disciplines. However, the construct is considered more central to social psychology than to any other academic area. Allport (1935) claimed 60 years ago that "the concept of attitude is probably the most distinctive and indispensable concept in contem-

porary American social psychology." This assessment is as appropriate today as it was then. Most information on attitudes is reported in the literature of social psychology (see 6.6, 32.5.4.8).

34.2.1 Attitudes Defined

Attitudes and attitude change have been discussed at least since the beginning of this century (Thomas & Znaniecki, 1918). The study of attitudes has been an important area of interest to psychologists, who often were also interested in related concepts such as propaganda. Educators have been interested in attitudes because of their possible impact on learning, and while attitudes have not been convincingly linked to achievement, they have been long considered an important component of the most important outcome of education: learning.

Attitude has been a difficult concept to define adequately, primarily because it has been defined by so many, but also because of the word's differing lay uses and connotations. One of the earliest definitions of attitude was proposed by Thomas and Znaniecki (1918). They defined attitude as:

A mental and neural state of readiness, organized through experience, exerting a directive or dynamic influence upon the individual's response to all objects and situations with which it is related.

More recently, Zimbardo and Leippe (1991) defined attitude as:

An evaluative disposition toward some object based upon cognitions, affective reactions, behavioral intentions, and past behaviors . . . that can influence cognitions, affective responses, and future intentions and behaviors.

Attitudes are latent and not directly observable in themselves, but they act to organize or provide direction to actions and behaviors that are observable. Many refer to attitudes as "predispositions to respond" (Zimbardo & Leippe, 1991). Attitudes are related to how people perceive the situations in which they find themselves. Also, attitudes vary in direction (either positive or negative), in degree (the amount of positiveness or negativeness), and in intensity (the amount of commitment with which a position is held; Smith, 1982).

34.2.2 Attitude Systems

Attitude positions are the summary aggregation of four components: (a) *affective responses,* (b) *cognitions,* (c) *behaviors,* and (d) *behavioral intentions* (Zimbardo & Leippe, 1991). The *affective* component of attitude is said to consist of a person's evaluation of, liking of, or emotional response to some situation, object, or person. Affective responses reflect one's attitude with sensations of pleasure, sadness, or other levels of physical arousal. For example, for the attitude construct of *computer anxiety,* a topic of current interest, the affective component would be a person's liking of the computer and his feeling of excitement, or dread, when she or he used one.

The *cognitive* component of an attitude is conceptualized as a person's factual knowledge of the situation, object, or person, including oneself. In other words, the cognitive component refers to how much a person knows about a topic, such as computers. The cognitive component of computer anxiety would be based on how much a person knows about computers and her level of understanding of computer operation.

The *behavioral* component of an attitude involves the person's overt behavior directed toward a situation, object, or person. For example, the behavioral component of computer anxiety would be related to how often a person had used a computer, and what kind of experience he had. Persons who routinely use computers, especially if they choose to use them freely, would be more likely to have positive attitudes toward computers, and be less anxious, than would others who have fewer experiences with computers.

Finally, the *behavioral intention* component involves the person's plans to perform in a certain way, even if sometimes these plans are never acted upon. An example, once again, is the construct of computer anxiety. Computer anxiety is defined by Maurer and Simonson (1993, 1994, p. 206) as "the fear or apprehension felt by an individual when considering the implications of utilizing computer technology, or when actually using computer technology." The behavioral intention component of this attitude construct would be the "apprehension felt by an individual when considering the implications of utilizing computer technology." In other words, if people knew that they were going to have to use computers in an upcoming class, this would partially shape their level of computer anxiety. If the class were to be a difficult one, say in statistics, then computer anxiety would be likely to be increased.

These four components of attitude form an attitude system. The components are not isolated but are interrelated and produce an organizing framework or mental representation of the attitude construct. Cognitive schemata provide structure to interrelated attitudes and guide the information processes of attending, interpreting, and reconstructing (Smith, 1982). Behavioral research supports the idea that actions lead to the formation of cognitive schemata, which lead to the creation of attitudes. It would seem that the opposite is also true. Attitudes help form cognitive relationships, which in turn predispose behaviors.

34.2.3 Attitude Formation

Situational stimuli or events in the environment directly influence behavior and the formation of attitudes. Strict behaviorists would argue that internal events that form attitudes are the result of observable actions. A change in attitude or beliefs occurs as a result of actions that have been influenced by reinforcers. Social-learning theory expands this principle. According to social-learning theorists, it is not essential to learn behaviors directly through action and reinforcement, as traditional behavioral psychologists would propose. Indirect learning through observing a model and receiving verbal instruction has a powerful impact on behavior and attitude formation (Zimbardo & Leippe, 1991).

Situations that include a change in the behavioral component of attitude lead to changes in attitudes. But there is also a reciprocal action. Since the components of attitude systems are interrelated, a change in liking (affect) may result in a change in behaviors (Smith, 1982). For example, the currently popular concept of the cognitive apprenticeship is based on the idea of learners participating as apprentices in real-world activities with those who are more knowledgeable than they. If designed correctly, these situations are perceived by learners as important and realistic, and learners come to value them. The overt activities of cognitive apprenticeships produce in students favorable dispositions (i.e., affects), which in turn promote a sense of value and often a desire to learn more.

34.2.4 An Example

Some professions use computers more than others. For example, stockbrokers use computers routinely, and their use of computers, especially computer networks, is directly related to positive consequences, such as increased profits. Students who work as apprentices with stockbrokers will most likely see the importance of computers and gain an appreciation of them (an affective reaction). They also learn a great deal about using computers (a cognitive reaction) as they navigate through various options included in the stockbroker's network of computer databases and on-line sources of information (a behavioral reaction), and certainly this real-world use of the computer is perceived as important. Finally, future uses (behavioral intentions) are important because the apprentice stockbroker learns quickly from the mentor that financial success may be directly related to continued use of computers and computer systems. In this case, cognitive apprenticeships are effective attitude change strategies because they often place learners in situations where an entire attitude system is influenced.

Maurer (1983) has reported that computer anxiety is lower for those who see an observable benefit to computer use, such as stockbrokers who can use computer skills to increase productivity. Stockbrokers usually have relatively low levels of computer anxiety because their computer attitude systems are continuously and positively modified during their work.

Maurer (1983) also reported, as have others, that all groups, even computer-intensive professionals such as stockbrokers, have individuals that are more or less computer anxious than their peers. These computer-using professionals just tend to be less anxious than some other groups of people. A characteristic of attitudes is that they are variable, not discrete. Attitudes are analog, not digital. Attitudes vary among individuals.

34.2.5 Importance of Attitudes

Traditionally when instruction is designed, there are two categories of outcomes in mind: those directed toward cognitive goals, and those related to the attitudes of the learner. There is little necessity to argue the importance of the acquisition of knowledge by a student as a result of instruction. Achievement is the paramount objective of most instructional activities. However, it may also be important to recognize the need for establishing attitudinal goals and for planning activities designed to facilitate affective outcomes in learners as a consequence of an instructional situation. As a matter of fact, it has become increasingly apparent to those involved in educational technology research that one of the major, and possibly unique, consequences of instructional situations involving media is the likelihood of the development of positive attitudinal positions in students (Simonson, 1985).

The most powerful rationale for the need to promote attitude positions in learners would be to demonstrate a direct relationship between attitudes and achievement, or liking and learning. Numerous researchers have identified such a relationship (Fenneman, 1973; Greenwald, 1965, 1966; Lamb, 1987; Levy, 1973; Perry & Kopperman, 1973; Simonson, 1977; Simonson, 1978; Simonson & Bullard, 1978). However, most educational and psychological researchers are reluctant to claim that there is any cause-and-effect linkage between these two learner variables (Zimbardo & Leippe, 1991). There are too many intervening forces likely to influence the relationship between how a person feels and how he or she behaves. Attitudes are thought to "predispose" persons to act. Positive attitudes toward a topic are felt to orient the person in a positive manner toward that idea, but not to predict actions directly.

The impact of attitude on learning is only one reason for interest in attitudes. There are other arguments that explain why attitudes of learners are important. First, most educators would agree that there are times when it is legitimate, and important, for learners to accept the truth of certain ideas—in other words, to accept an attitudinal position. The importance of voting is an attitude position that most would agree is important. Civics teachers routinely "teach" this attitude.

Second, while the strength of the relationship between attitudes and achievement is unclear, it seems logical that students are more likely to remember information, seek new ideas, and continue studying when they react favorably to an instructional situation or like a certain content area. Students who like chemistry will tend to stay after class to work on experiments, read about chemistry outside of class, and be more likely to elect to take a chemistry course than will those who do not like chemistry. Learners tend to do what they like, not what they do not like. They gravitate toward their interests.

Third, there are some instances when influencing student's attitudes is not desirable, so educators should be aware of which techniques affect attitudes. In this way, possible bias can be recognized and eliminated. The gender biases found in textbooks are considered partially responsible for gender biases in people. For example, the use of the generic *he* was long considered appropriate by textbook authors and publishers. Now it is obvious that the use of this term helped form an inappropriate attitude position in both boys and girls that males were more important.

Last, student attitudes toward a situation can tell the teacher a great deal about the impact of that situation on the learning process. Obviously, attitudes need to be measured in order to know if they have been influenced. As a result of quantitatively and qualitatively assessing the opinions of students toward the learning activities in which they are participating, it may be possible to improve the quality of procedures. One of the most important techniques of evaluation is to ascertain attitudes toward some event, object, or person. End-of-course evaluations of attitude toward courses and course content are a standard activity in schools and training centers.

In summary, attitudes, as shall be discussed later, are complex phenomena. They have been studied for decades by social scientists and educators and are beginning to be understood as organizers related to learning processes and outcomes. Attitudes are learned "predispositions to respond" held by individuals that make them likely to act in certain ways. Attitudes are not observable, but they do serve to help produce observable actions in people.

Social psychologists, and others, have proposed a number of theories of attitude change. Many of the theories are related, so there has been considerable effort to categorize them. Because of the comprehensiveness of the attitude change literature, it is considered important to review the theories of attitude change as a foundation for proposing guidelines for persuasion.

34.3 THEORIES OF ATTITUDE CHANGE

Several attitude change categorization schemes have been proposed in the literature (Eagly & Chaiken, 1993; O'Keefe, 1990), and most are similar. For this discussion, attitude theories have been organized into four categories (see 11.6):

- Consistency theories
- Learning theories
- Social judgment theories
- Functional theories

The study of attitudes has been approached with varying emphases and methods during most of this century. Prior to

World War II, the emphasis was on definition issues and attitude measurement. Most studies were of a survey nature and provided important correlational findings, but little insight into causality. Experimental techniques such as control groups or comparison groups were notably absent (Himmelfarb & Eagly, 1974).

This changed dramatically during World War II. Attitude change was an important topic of Army-sponsored research (see 1.10). Because of the influence of experimental psychologists such as Carl Hovland, true experimental techniques were used to study the persuasive effects of propaganda. The work of Hovland and his associates in the area of attitude change research was continued after the war at Yale University. Theories developed by this group served as an organizational framework for the study of attitude change (Hovland, Janis & Kelley, 1953; Himmelfarb & Eagly, 1974; Insko, 1967; O'Keefe, 1990). Most of Hovland's attitude change research can be considered classical. Most of this research and theory building approached the concept of attitude from the behaviorist perspective, and most research activities dealt with trying to relate attitudes to observable outcomes in learners.

An example of research of the classical type that demonstrated a consistency theory approach was Simonson's (1977) study of dissonance theory principles. In this study, cognitive dissonance theory (Festinger, 1957) assumptions, one of the most influential consistency theories, were used in a formal program of attitude change in order to improve student attitude toward an instructional activity. Student achievement in this instructional activity was then measured to determine if achievement was influenced by a change in student attitude toward instruction.

Randomly assigned to one of three treatment groups were 218 students. Students in the experimental treatments were asked to make a videotape about their attitudes toward an instructional activity. An "Instructional Improvement Needs Assessment" was the title given to the fictitious activity that in reality was the research study. First, students were given a camouflaged attitude pretest. Then, students were met individually by a researcher who told them that:

> I am a member of a committee in the college called the Instructional Improvement Needs Assessment Committee. We are attempting to obtain as much information as possible about student's opinions of college courses. This is difficult, so we are asking for several different types of information.

Then, depending on the random treatment group assignment, the students were told:

1. Control group: "I would like you to complete this Needs Assessment opinionnaire. You can fill it out in the next room. Answer on the score sheet and when you finish place the opinionnaire and answer sheet in the box."
2. Nonrelevant treatment group: "The entire committee would like to study your opinions, so I will give you several minutes to think of everything positive you

can about (a course irrelevant to the study and to the attitude tests). Then I will take you to the next room where we will ask you to state your positive comments while you are being videotaped. We need to videotape you so that the entire committee can get together and observe all the videotapes. I'll give you 5 minutes to collect your thoughts."
3. Relevant experimental group: The experimenter read the same comments to students assigned to this group, with one exception; they were given the name of the course that the study was attempting to change attitudes about.

Students in the "irrelevant" and "relevant" groups were given time to jot down ideas and then were escorted into the video-recording room where their comments were recorded. When they were finished, they were told that "faculty and students will be viewing this tape." Next, they signed a release and were given a questionnaire that contained the attitude test embedded among other items.

Subjects in the "relevant experimental treatment" who initially had low attitudes toward the course in question were expected to experience dissonance when they stated positive comments about this course. The dissonance-producing experience was heightened by leading the students to believe that a group of peers and faculty would view the videotapes. The videotaping session and the signing of the release were included to make the treatment procedures as forceful and irreversible as possible. The two other treatments were included to control for the impact of videotaping and for change due to extraneous events.

Results of this classical dissonance theory study demonstrated that attitude changes could be produced. Students in the relevant videotaping group changed their attitudes toward the course they were asked to talk about more than one standard deviation ($p < .0001$). Simonson (1977) also tested the persistence of the attitude changes and reported that while there was a regression to the mean, student's attitudes remained positive 6 weeks later. There was only a minor and statistically insignificant relationship between attitude change and achievement.

This study showed in an experimental situation with real-world implications, that it was possible, even simple, to modify student attitudes toward an instructional event, in this case a college course. Simonson used video recording as a technique to "cement" and make irreversible a student's attitude positions. No one would argue that the video recording itself changed attitudes. The forces that changed attitudes were the arguments created by the student that were recorded on the video. In this situation, the video recording was a methodological tool of the researcher. This chapter will tend to show that in media and attitude research the role of media is as a tool. Media do not influence attitudes; messages and methods do.

Simonson's (1977) study is an example of the type of attitude change research often reported in the literature between the 1950s and today. Certainly, human subject regulations would force modification in Simonson's approach if it were replicated today. However, the behavioral and experimental approach taken is typical of the research used to identify and support the consistency theories of attitude change summarized next. Early attitude change literature is firmly anchored in traditional experimental psychology and draws heavily on behaviorism (see 2.2; Eagly & Chaiken, 1993).

34.3.1 Consistency Theories

The basic assumption of these theories is the need of the individual for consistency. There must be consistency between attitudes, between behaviors, and among attitudes and behaviors. A lack of consistency causes discomfort so that an individual attempts to ease the tension by adjusting attitudes or behaviors in order to once again achieve balance or consistency. One of the earliest consistency theories was balance theory (Himmelfarb & Eagly, 1974; Kiesler, Collins & Miller, 1969; O'Keefe, 1990).

Relationships among the perceiver, another person, and an object are the main focus of balance theory (Heider, 1958). Relationships are either positive or negative, based on the cognitive perceptions of the perceiver. In this theory, there are eight possible configurations; four balanced and four unbalanced. Unbalanced states are recognized as being unstable. Under these conditions, perceivers attempt to restore balance by changing their attitudes toward objects or other persons.

Two extensions of Heider's balance theory include the work of Newcomb (1961) and that of Abelson (Abelson & Rosenberg, 1958). Newcomb studied interpersonal situations as well as cognitive balancing and transferred these ideas to research on the pressures for uniformity in groups. Abelson proposed four additional modes of restoring balance: (a) denial, (b) bolstering, (c) differentiation, and (d) transcendence (Himmelfarb & Eagly, 1974; Kiesler, Collins & Miller, 1969; Insko, 1967; O'Keefe, 1990). Establishing balance was critical to individuals. Attitude changes occurred when the individual attempted to reestablish balance by modifying their attitudes.

Affective-cognitive consistency theory examines the relationship between attitudes and beliefs (Rosenberg, 1956). An unstable state occurs when an individual's attitudes toward an object and knowledge about an object are inconsistent. Persuasive communications (see 4.4) attempt to change the affective component of an attitude system by changing the cognitive component of attitude. In other words, providing an individual with new information that changes the cognitive component of attitude will tend to cause that individual to change overall attitudes toward an object.

An alternative to Rosenberg's theory is Festinger's theory of cognitive dissonance (Festinger, 1957). While Rosenberg's theory deals with affect and cognition, Festinger's theory examines consistency among cognitive elements or beliefs

about oneself, behavior, or environment. Dissonance occurs when elements are logically inconsistent or psychologically inconsistent because of cultural mores, specific opinions deviating from more encompassing opinions, or information or experiences that are contrary to previous information or experiences. Dissonance motivates the individual to reduce the dissonance and return to consonance. When faced with dissonance, the individual seeks to avoid situations or information that may increase dissonance.

To test dissonance theory, Festinger and Carlsmith (1959) reported on an experiment that is considered one of the most controversial ever conducted in the area of attitude change. It was also one of the most influential. This study lead to numerous modified replications, including Simonson's (1977) study reported here earlier.

Male undergraduates spent an hour performing two tasks that had been designed to be very boring: putting spools onto a tray and turning pegs on a board. Afterwards, the experimenter told them that the study concerned the effect that a prior expectation had on task performance and explained that participants in another experiment were being given a favorable expectation about the task. According to the researcher, this expectation was usually conveyed by an assistant who told a waiting subject of the study that the experience had been enjoyable and intriguing. The experimenter then claimed (a white lie, one of several told by researchers) that the assistant who was supposed to perform the chore had not shown up. The researcher then asked the student who had just finished the boring task to fill in for the absent assistant by conveying this story to the study's next participant. The researcher promised the student money for this service and for being on call in the future if help were needed again. The college male was told that the decision to help was up to him.

Festinger and Carlsmith (1959) introduced the critical dissonance theory incentive at the point when money was mentioned. Half the study's subjects were offered $1, and half were offered $20, for engaging in the counterattitudinal behavior. Because the inducement to comply with the researcher's request was much greater with the larger amount of money, the counterattitudinal behavior should have been considered by the students as justified, and little dissonance and attitude change produced. The $1 payment was designed to provide just enough pressure to induce compliance but insufficient reason for subjects to believe their actions were warranted by money alone. This was predicted to produce maximum dissonance and maximum attitude change.

In both the $1 and the $20 conditions, the students engaged in a brief role playing by praising the experiment to a confederate of the researcher who pretended to be waiting to participate in the study. This person appeared to be convinced by the student's story. Next, the students were referred to an interviewer who was supposedly conducting a survey unrelated to the experiment. This interviewer asked, among other things, how interesting and enjoyable the experimental tasks involving the spools and pegs had been. The results showed that the subjects who had been offered $1 for praising the experiment evaluated the tasks significantly more favorably than did the subjects who had been offered $20. The attitudes of students who received $20 did not differ from the control subjects, who participated in the dull tasks, but not the part of the experiment that involved making insincere statements to the confederate.

The results of the experiment confirmed Festinger's prediction that increased justification for role playing (i.e., more money) would reduce attitude change. In other words, the students who received $1 for their actions experienced dissonance. Their actions advocating the enjoyability of the peg and spool activity, and the reality of the boring activity, were dissonant from one another. In order to reduce the dissonance, it was easier to change their attitudes toward the activity to be more positive than it was to change their praising of the activity. Thus, attitude change occurred to reduce the student's level of dissonance. The $20 subjects did not experience dissonance. They were able to say in their minds: "I did it for the money; it really was boring." This study was the first of many that demonstrated clearly the need for consistency between attitude positions and behaviors. Consistency theories, notably cognitive dissonance theory, provide relatively straightforward, if incomplete, information about attitude change.

Studies on counter-attitudinal advocacy are based on dissonance theory. Individuals who are asked to write an essay or present a speech promoting a position contrary to their beliefs become committed to certain aspects of the contrary position. This causes dissonance, which the individuals attempt to reduce by changing their original position or attitude. The stronger the magnitude of the dissonance, the stronger the need to change the original attitude.

The simple act of decision making creates dissonance, too. The magnitude of the dissonance is related to the importance of the decision and the attractiveness of both the chosen and the unchosen alternatives (O'Keefe, 1990). For example, hypermedia-based instructional systems (see 21.1, 23.3.), with their many learner choices, provide a great deal of decision making that may influence learner's attitudes in either a positive or negative direction, depending on the success and attractiveness of the decisions.

One of the major criticisms of consistency theories is that there are too many of them. Since they all work from the similar theme of an individual's trying to maintain consistency, it has been suggested that the area would be stronger if the various subtheories were consolidated. Today, interest in dissonance theory specifically, and consistency theories generally, has waned considerably in social psychology (Eagly & Chaiken, 1993). This loss of interest is, in part, due to the growth of understanding about the conditions and processes responsible for the phenomena dissonance theorists investigated. Researchers have a better understanding of the interactions between attitudes and opinions and actions and behaviors, so consistency theories that are not directly related to processes are of little interest

to today's cognitive scientists who tend to be more process oriented than behaviorists who studied consistency theories.

34.3.2 Early Learning Theories

This section might more accurately be called *behavioral theories of attitude change*. These theories were also developed during the 1950s and 1960s. During this time, learning theories reflected behavioral psychology (see 2.2). A major commonality of these theories was their emphasis on the stimulus characteristics of the communication situation.

Staat's (Insko, 1967) work reflected the ideas of classical conditioning, and focused almost entirely on the formation of attitudes. Events in the environment create an emotional response in an individual. As new stimuli are consistently paired with old stimuli (events), the new stimuli develop the power to create an emotional response in the individual (O'Keefe, 1990).

Learning theories of attitude change received major emphasis by Hovland and his associates in the Yale Communication Research Program (Hovland, Janis & Kelley, 1953). They proposed that opinions tended to persist unless the individual underwent some new learning experience. Persuasive communications that both present a question and suggest an answer serve as learning experiences. Acceptance of the suggested answer is dependent on the opportunity for mental rehearsal or practice of the attitude response, and on the number of incentives included in the communication. Hovland and his colleagues assumed that as people processed persuasive message content, they rehearsed the message's recommended attitudinal response, as well as their initial attitude. For attitude change to occur, more than rehearsal and practice had to take place. The Yale researchers emphasized the role of incentives and the drive-reducing aspects of persuasive messages as mechanisms for reinforcement, thereby creating acceptance of new beliefs and attitudes.

In the Yale model of attitude change emphasis is placed on attention, comprehension, and acceptance. An individual must attend to and comprehend the communication before acceptance can occur. It is during the attending and comprehending phases that the individual has the opportunity to practice the recommended new opinion. Practice alone does not lead to acceptance, but when combined with incentives and recommendations imbedded in the communication, attitude change is likely. Incentives are broadly defined by Hovland et al. (1953). They could be direct financial or physical benefits (e.g., money, improved health), or they could take on more abstract forms such as the knowledge gain from persuasive arguments, social acceptance by others who are respected, or self-approval from the feeling that one is correct.

Hovland and his associates identified three classes of variables that influenced the effectiveness of the message: (a) source characteristics, (b) setting characteristics, and (c) communication content elements. Research using the

Yale model focuses on variables in one or more of these three classes. Examples include research in communicator credibility (trustworthiness and degree of expertness), fear-arousing appeals, and the placement of persuasive arguments within the communication (Himmelfarb & Eagly, 1974; Kiesler et al., 1969; Insko, 1967).

A Skinnerian approach (see 2.5) to the study of attitude change was employed by Bem (1967), whose major assumptions reflected the viewpoint that attitudes were learned as a result of previous experience with the environment. Bem proposed that since the person trying to change attitudes usually lacked direct knowledge of the internal stimuli available to the learner, it was necessary to rely on external cues in order to reward and punish the individual. It was the combination of external cues and observable behaviors that produced changes in attitude (Himmelfarb & Eagly, 1974; Kiesler et al., 1969; Insko, 1967).

Today, few attitude change theorists feel that the early research by Hovland and others has direct impact on current procedures (Eagly & Chaiken, 1993). Newer research and theory building is directed toward approaches that emphasize multiple modes of processing information. However, these early researchers investigated basic issues, such as reinforcement, incentives, and drive-reduction constructs, that are related to how motivational states influence information processing and persuasion. Early-learning theorists' efforts provided a foundation for more modern process models of attitude change.

34.3.3 Social Judgment Theory

Social judgment theory focuses on how people's prior attitudes distort their perceptions of the positions advocated in persuasive messages, and how such perceptions mediate persuasion. In general terms, the theory assumes that a person's own attitudes serve as a judgmental standard and anchor that influences where along a continuum a persuader's advocated position is perceived to lie (Sherif & Hovland, 1961). Social judgment theory is an attempt to apply the principles of judgment to the study of attitude change.

According to Sherif, Sherif, and Nebergall (1965), an individual's initial attitude serves as an anchor for the judgment of related attitude communications. Opinions are evaluated against this point of reference and are placed on an attitudinal continuum. Opinions that most characterized the individual's own opinion are in the latitude of acceptance. Those opinions found most objectionable are placed in the latitude of rejection. The latitude of noncommitment consists of those opinions that are neither accepted nor rejected.

Communication that falls within the latitude of acceptance is assimilated, and if judged to be fair and unbiased will result in a change in attitude. Within the limits of the latitude of acceptance, the greater the difference between the initial opinion and the communicated opinion, the greater the attitude change. Though some change is possible when opinions fall within the latitude of rejection, the greater the

discrepancy the less the change in attitude (Himmelfarb & Eagly, 1974; Kiesler et al., 1969; Insko, 1967).

Social judgment theory's core propositions can be summarized as follows (Eagly & Chaiken, 1993):

1. A person's current attitude serves as a judgmental anchor for new attitude positions.
2. Latitude widths determine whether a message's position will be assimilated or contrasted (e.g., accepted or rejected). Positions falling within the latitude of acceptance will be assimilated toward a person's current attitude. Positions falling within the latitude of rejection will be contrasted away from the person's own attitude.
3. Ego involvement of a person broadens the latitude of rejection and narrows the latitude of noncommitment.
4. Both assimilation and contrast effects increase as a positive function of a message's position and the recipient's attitude.
5. Ego involvement increases the anchoring property of initial attitudes.
6. Greater assimilation produces more positive evaluation of message content, which produces greater amounts of attitude change. Conversely, greater contrast produces more negative evaluations of message content, which produces lesser amounts of attitude change.
7. Ambiguity enhances the likelihood of judgmental distortions. Therefore, other effects are greater when recipients are exposed to persuasive messages whose content positions are ambiguous.

In summary, social judgment theory predictions for attitude change are largely borne out by the research literature and by practice. Recently however, researchers have questioned the basic principles of social judgment theory and how the theory's principles relate to one another. Social judgment theory is important because it demonstrates the importance of people's prior attitudes. Most other approaches only deal marginally with previous attitudes. Newer theories incorporate social judgment principles as covariates and control variables in experimental designs (Wood, 1982).

34.3.4 Functional Theories

A fundamental question about attitudes concerns their purpose: That is, what functions do attitudes serve? Understanding the purposes of attitudes is the identifying characteristic of functional theories. Attitudes serve different functions for different individuals or for the same individual in different settings. The reasons for attitude changes are individualized and related to personal functions of attitudes.

Functional theories of attitude entered the literature in the 1950s when researchers developed the idea that attitudes served varying psychological needs and thus had variable motivational bases. A common and central theme of these early efforts was the listing of the specific person- ality functions that attitudes served for individuals. Unlike other theoretical approaches developed during this golden decade of attitude research, functional theories are still relevant and important today (Eagly & Chaiken, 1993).

Functional theories hold that successful persuasion entails implementing change procedures that match the functional basis of the attitude one is trying to change. Katz (1960) proposed that any attitude held by an individual served one or more of the four distinct personality func- tions. The more of these functions that contributed to an attitude system, the stronger and less likely it was that the attitude could be changed.

Katz (1960) identified four personality functions of atti- tudes as follows: (a) utilitarian function, (b) knowledge function, (c) ego-defensive function, and (d) value-expressive function. In order for attitude change to occur, there must be a discrepancy between the need being met by the attitude and the attitude itself. Attitude change is accomplished by recognizing the function of the attitude for the individual, and designing strategies to produce a disparity between the attitude and one or more of the attitude functions.

The *utilitarian function* acknowledges the behaviorist principle that people are motivated to gain rewards and avoid punishments from their environment. Utilitarian attitudes are instrumental in securing positive outcomes or preventing negative ones. For example, parents' opposition to busing might be based on the utilitarian belief that it would be harmful to their child. Often, utilitarian beliefs are associations to stimuli. For example, children often acquire a positive feeling about the month of December because they associate it with holidays, presents, and vacations (Eagly & Chaiken, 1993).

The *knowledge function* of attitudes presumes a basic human need to gain a meaningful, stable, and organized view of the world. Attitudes supply a standard for organizing and simplifying perceptions of a complex and ambiguous environment. Attitudes provide a way of sizing up objects and events so they can be reacted to in a meaningful way. If people's attitudes toward school are positive, then when they are asked about schools they will be likely to say positive things without needing to "think about it too much."

Katz's *ego-defensive function* emphasizes the psychoan- alytic principle that people use defense mechanisms such as denial, repression, and projection to protect their self-con- cepts against internal and external threats. People protect their feelings by developing convenient, if sometimes biased, attitudes that do not require active involvement in threatening or unfamiliar situations. For example, a high school student may think: "Chemistry is for nerds, and I do not want to be a nerd; that is why I do not like chemistry." Or a student might think: "Only really smart people study chemistry, and I study chemistry, so I must be really smart; that is why I like chemistry."

Finally, Katz's *value-expressive function* acknowledges the importance of self-expression and self-actualization.

Attitudes are a means for expressing personal values and other aspects of self-concept. A person who draws self- esteem from being a liberal and an environmentalist is motivated to hold attitudes that reflect these ideologies (Eagly & Chaiken, 1993).

The central theme of functional theories is that changing an attitude requires understanding its motivational basis, or its function for the individual. Knowing what function an attitude performs for a person helps guide the designer of the persuasive message who wants to change the attitude. Whatever function attitudes perform they provide a frame of reference for comprehending and categorizing objects, persons, and events, and only by understanding an atti- tude's function can attitude change efforts be successful.

An alternative and related theory looks at social relation- ships that occur in social influence situations (see 6.2). Kelman (1958) looked at three processes of opinion change: (a) compliance, (b) identification, and (c) internal- ization. Compliance results in only a surface level change. Attitudes are changed only to receive a favorable reaction from another person or group. This attitude is only expressed when the other person is present.

The attitude change resulting from identification occurs both publicly and privately but does not become part of the person's value system. The change is dependent on the rela- tionship with the source but not with the source's presence. Attitudes that are internalized become part of an individual's value system.

McGuire's (1964) inoculation theory is concerned with resistance to change (see 37.4). Research in this area inves- tigates the treatments individuals could receive which would allow them to resist successfully attacks on their belief systems. An analogy is drawn from the biological process of inoculation. Once people are inoculated, they are immune when exposed to the disease. Attitudes are often established in a relatively "germ-free" environment, free from attack. Thus, the individual has little chance to devel- op resistance to future attacks. McGuire's research strategy was to expose the individual to mild attacks in a control setting in order to motivate the individual to defend his or her beliefs (Himmelfarb & Eagly, 1974; Kiesler et al., 1969; Insko, 1967).

Functional theories are in the mainstream of attitude research. Their theoretical approaches remain conceptually intriguing to investigators because of their breadth and unique focus on the functional bases for attitudes. Func- tional theories provide a link between the behavioral theories proposed during the 1950s (consistency theories, early-learning theories, social judgment theories) and the processing and cognitive themes of more recent theorizing.

Attitude and persuasion research is a major area of interest to those in social psychology. Theory building has been characteristic of this research. Only a fraction of this literature has been reviewed in this section of this chapter; however, the information presented provides a basis for information presented later. These theories, especially the functional theories discussed last, provide guidance to the development of recommendations for the design of persuasive messages delivered by media.

34.4 ATTITUDES AND BEHAVIOR

In 1969, Wicker reported on a review of 42 experimental studies that assessed attitudes and then included an observation of related behaviors. Wicker found few studies where the correlation between attitudes and behavior were as high as .30 ($r = .30$). The average correlation was about .15 ($r = .15$). Wicker concluded that "taken as a whole, these studies suggest that it is considerably more likely that attitudes will be unrelated or only slightly related to overt behaviors than that attitudes will be closely related to actions" (p. 65).

The impact of Wicker's review was immediate. By the early 1970s most social psychologists had readily accepted the negative verdict about the attitude-behavior link. Most felt that attitudes had little importance and direct relation to actions. Also during this time frame, many studies were conducted and reported that examined the impact of behaviors on attitudes, rather than the other way around. Festinger's (1957) dissonance theory was very popular, and its emphasis on the influence of behaviors on attitudes seemed to make it difficult for researchers to believe that the opposite link could be strong or even stronger.

Simonson's (1977) study discussed earlier showed that attitudes could be changed predictably by following dissonance theory guidelines, but that the impact of attitudes on achievement was not easily identified. Simonson's results demonstrated a one standard deviation improvement in attitude scores, but no significant improvement in related achievement scores. This study was one of many reported during this period which supported the position taken by many that attitude and behavior had little relationship to each other. Most research of the 1970s dealing with attitudes did not attempt to demonstrate a direct link between attitudes and behavior (Eagly & Chaiken, 1993).

Since then, however, there has been a serious reexamination of the attitude-behavior link, and a resurgence of interest in this area has occurred. As a matter of fact, the generalization that attitudes do not predict behavior is now considered inaccurate (Eagly & Chaiken, 1993). Parenthetically, as one reads the debate about attitudes and behaviors that raged in the social psychology literature during the 1970s and 1980s, it is interesting to compare it to the ongoing debate in instructional technology between those who say "media will never influence achievement" (Clark, 1983, 1994) and those who take a more moderate approach to the relationship between mediated instruction and achievement. The similarities are interesting. In the attitude-behavior debate, subsequent research has shown that neither extreme position was correct, and the following section of this chapter will present what currently is known about the attitude-behavior link.

This section will include a brief explanation of the approaches taken recently by attitude researchers and will concentrate on theories of social psychology. The section will conclude with a discussion of attitudes and instructional behaviors.

First, while Wicker's (1969) premise about the weak link between attitudes and behavior gained widespread acceptance, many took issue with his study's methods. Wicker reviewed only a narrow sample of studies that were heavily weighted toward laboratory research. Many outstanding studies were not examined by Wicker, and several writers who reviewed survey research reported that this literature showed a moderately strong relationship between attitudes and behaviors (Kelman, 1974; Schuman & Johnson, 1976). This critique of Wicker led to a series of new proposals about, and new examinations of, the relationship between attitudes and behavior.

First, researchers began to examine attitudes as being related to an aggregate of behaviors. It was found that relatively high attitude-behavior correlations were obtained by comparing a general attitude (e.g., attitude toward chemistry or attitude toward homework) to a measure with an aggregate of attitude-relevant behaviors (e.g., taking chemistry courses, talking about chemistry in the study hall with friends, using chemistry examples in other classes).

Fishbein and Ajzen (1975) reported that attitudes typically predicted multiple-act criteria better than single-act criteria. They generalized that attitudes and behaviors must be compatible to ensure a strong relationship. In other words, general attitudes are good predictors of general behaviors (e.g., attitudes toward affirmative action are predictors of actions related to affirmative action), and specific attitudes, especially attitudes toward behaviors, are good predictors of specific actions (attitudes toward studying chemistry predict nicely the act of studying). Unfortunately, many researchers had examined, and still are examining, quite general attitudes (e.g., attitudes toward chemistry), and quite specific behaviors (e.g., achievement on a chemistry test).

Fishbein and Ajzen maintained that a consistent terminology was needed. In other words, specific attitude constructs should be identified if specific actions are to be correlated to them. An attitude toward studying chemistry every evening could be measured by an attitude test, and subsequent studying of chemistry could be determined by asking students' parents to keep a journal of their child's study habits. Fishbein and Ajzen predicted that the correlation between this kind of specific attitude and specific behavior would be quite high.

Fishbein's efforts in this area produced a model that he and Ajzen called the *theory of reasoned action*. It is now considered an excellent model of the psychological processes that explain observed links between attitudes and behaviors. The theory of reasoned action suggests that the cause of behavior is a person's intention to engage in the behavior. Attitudes influence behavior by their influence on intentions, which are decisions to act in a particular way. The issue of how an attitude was transformed into action was resolved by adding another psychological event, the formation of an intention. Intention was explained to be the person's motivation to exert effort to carry out a behavior.

This theory was popular since it had an inherent reasonableness about it. People were assumed to behave as they intended to behave. They were theorized to act in ways that allowed them to obtain favorable outcomes and to meet the expectations of others. The theory of reasoned action can be summarized as follows:

a. Behavior is determined by the intention to engage in the behavior.
b. Intention is determined by attitude toward the behavior and the subjective norm to which the attitude is related.
c. Attitude is determined by behavioral beliefs and evaluation of the likely outcomes of a behavior.
d. Subjective norms are determined by the normative beliefs of the person and the motivation to comply with the relevant actions.

Many believe that this theory provides a complete theory of voluntary behavior. Critics have indicated that they do not consider the theory of reasoned action to be a general theory of behavior. Rather, it is considered by them to be a theory of the immediate causes of voluntary action.

In part because of criticisms, Ajzen proposed an alternative *theory of planned behavior* that attempted to enlarge the Fishbein-Ajzen model (Ajzen, 1991). Ajzen stated that for nonhabitual behaviors that are easily executed by almost everyone without special circumstances, the theory of reasoned action was adequate. When behaviors are more difficult to execute, and when a person needs to take control over needed resources in order to act, the theory of planned behavior is a better predictor of behavior than the theory of reasoned action. In the theory of planned behavior, control is taken into account as a variable labeled "perceived behavioral control," which is defined as a person's perception of how easy or difficult it would be to perform the action.

Perceived control affects behavior in two ways: First, it influences the intention to perform the behavior. Second, it may have a direct impact on the behavior itself. Ajzen proposed that people tend to engage in behaviors to the extent that they believe that they have control over the behaviors, in other words, to the extent that they have confidence in their ability to perform the behavior.

In a series of studies that examined the prediction of behavior, it was found that when perceived behavioral control was taken into account, along with attitude toward a behavior, the average R for predicting intentions was .71 (Ajzen, 1991). Research suggests that the addition of perceived control to the model of reasoned action results in a more comprehensive model that applies to behaviors that require skills, resources, and other inputs that are not available merely because people decide to act.

From the low point of the late 1960s, when many social scientists believed that attitudes were not closely related to behaviors, new information has been made available to the point where most now believe there is considerable interaction between attitudes, behaviors, and other variables. High correlations between attitudes and overt behaviors can be produced by aggregating several behaviors to create a measure that corresponds to the attitude measure. The theory of reasoned action and the theory of planned action provide direction to the study of the prediction of behavior, especially where attitudes are concerned.

Eagly and Chaiken (1993) also proposed a composite attitude-behavior model that is especially attractive because of its comprehensiveness (Fig. 34-1). This model demonstrates that behavior is likely to be partially determined by attitudes, but that the relation between attitudes and behavior is best understood by placing attitudes in the context of other factors that also help to determine behavior, such as habits, intentions, and perceived utilitarian outcomes.

Ultimately we must return to the purposes of this chapter: the design of persuasive messages that are delivered by media, and the relationship between media and attitudes. It is apparent from the literature of social psychology that a direct relationship between attitude formation and the production of educational behaviors such as achievement is not straightforward. Rather, the development of attitude positions that are desirable and planned is only one step in the process of promoting educational relevant actions. Attitudes contribute to learning outcomes, but are only one of several important variables. Arguments listed previously in this chapter provide support for the need to understand the use of mediated messages designed to persuade. Later in this chapter, a series of guidelines for producing attitude changes will be proposed.

It would be inappropriate to assume that the development of new attitude positions will directly and predictably influence educational behaviors. Rather, attitudes are one component of a system that predicts behaviors. For those interested in predicting behavior from attitudes, the literature provides guidelines. First, single general attitudes are not likely to predict general actions. At the very least, very specific attitudes and very specific behaviors should be identified for correlation. Second, general attitudes are probably related to a collection, an aggregate, of behaviors. Finally, other variables such as motivation, intention, and personality traits are intervening forces that should be considered in the attitude-behavior formula. Interestingly, even the critics of attitude-behavior research are consistent in their opinion that it is possible, even easy, to modify attitudes predictably, and that attitudes play *some* role in determining actions.

34.5 MEASURING ATTITUDES

When reviewing the literature that deals with attitude change and instructional technology, it is very apparent that attitude measurement is often done very poorly. Simonson (1979a) commented on the sad state of attitude measurement in the educational technology literature, and more recent reviews have not revealed any improvements in testing methodology (Simonson & Maushak, 1995). The move to more qualitative-based research (see 40.2) and measurement has not changed this situation, and may be contributing to a decline in the quality of attitude testing (see 6.1).

Before beginning this discussion of attitude measurement, it is important once again to establish a frame of reference for this review. Attitude research is largely conducted by those called *empiricists, objectivists,* and *reductionists.* They tend to take the approach of the scientific empiricist who believes that there are laws of nature that the scientist must discover. The vast body of attitude and attitude-change literature is authored by those attempting to "discover the answer" and to determine "truth." These researchers usually apply quantitative approaches in their research designs (see 39.4).

Those advocating naturalistic inquiry (see 40.2) may be uncomfortable with the approach taken by this chapter. A general question often asked by qualitative researchers, "What is going on here?", does not readily translate to results of the kind summarized in this chapter and the type of measurement techniques recommended next. Certainly, it would be unwise to discount qualitative techniques for examining the critical issues of the field. Just as certainly, the vast body of literature about attitudes and attitude measurement were generated by scientists who applied quantitative approaches to measurement.

Problems with attitude measurement are of three types. First, researchers are not clearly defining their attitude variables. In other words, they are not operationalizing the constructs that they are setting out to measure. This prob-

lem is heightened by the failure of many to include attitude hypotheses or research questions in their research designs. Rather, attitude constructs are often included as post-hoc components of research studies. Qualitative researchers also tend to show little interest in attitude constructs.

Second, attitudes are not measured well. Certainly, quantitative measurement of attitudes has evolved into a fairly exact process (Henerson, Morris & Fitz-Gibbon, 1987). However, reports about the methods used to develop measures of attitudes are reported in only a minority of the research studies found in the literature. Simonson (1979a) reported that only 50% of the studies reviewed reported on the validation of attitude measures, and only 20% reported descriptive information about their attitude tests. Most measures then, and today, tended to be locally prepared and used only once—in the specific study reported. Researchers who were otherwise extremely careful to standardize their achievement measures did not do the same for their tests of attitudes.

One alarming trend was the use of single items to measure attitudes. Researchers reported using a single item to determine a person's attitude (e.g., Do you like chemistry?), and then used the responses to this question in powerful statistical analyses. Apparently, reliability and validity concerns were not worrisome to these researchers.

Finally, attitude measurement has tended to be of only peripheral importance to researchers. Often, as stated above, attitudes are relegated to post-hoc examinations, often conducted without controls or design considerations being taken into account. As a matter of fact, it is obvious that attitude

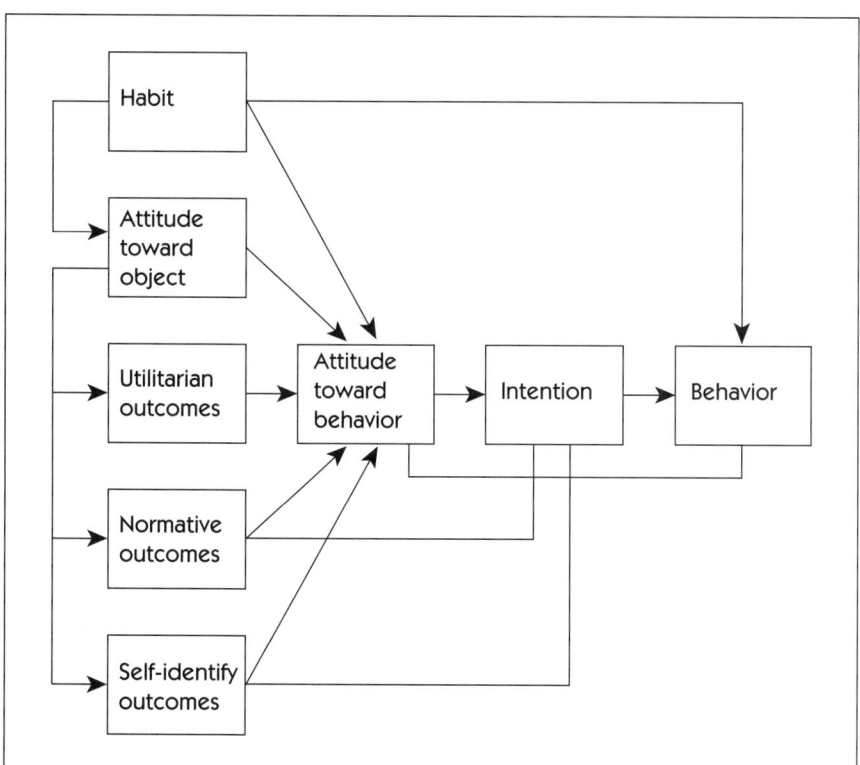

Figure 34-1. A composite model of the attitude-behavior relationship (Eagly & Chaiken, 1993).

study is not an area of interest or importance in mainstream instructional technology research. Of the hundreds of studies published in the literature of educational communications and technology since Simonson's review (1979a) of attitude research, less than 5% examined attitude variables as a major area of interest. This lack of interest was discouraging, especially when contrasted with the wealth of attitude research in the literature of social psychology.

One reason attitudes may be studied so rarely is the difficulty many have in clearly identifying how attitudes should be measured. The characteristics of attitude contribute to this perception of difficulty, as does the recent move away from quantitative research procedures. In a recent review of the indexes of five textbooks dealing with methods of qualitative analysis, the term *attitude* was not found in any, even in the recently published *Handbook of Qualitative Research* (Denzin & Lincoln, 1994).

Since attitudes are defined as latent, and not observable in themselves, the educator must identify some action that would seem to be representative of the attitude in question so that this behavior might be measured as an index of the attitude. This characteristic of attitude measurement is justifiably one of the most criticized of this area of educational evaluation. However, there are several generally recognized procedures used to determine quantitatively an individual's, or group's, attitude toward some object or person. It is those procedures that are described below. Two excellent sources for information on attitude measurement should be reviewed by those interested in quantitatively testing for attitudes. First is Himmelfarb's (Eagly & Chaiken, 1993) comprehensive review of the basic concepts and ideas behind attitude measurement. It also contains an explanation of the various techniques for quantifying attitude positions. Himmelfarb's discussion is a scholarly explanation of attitude measurement.

For those interested in more specific procedures for attitude measurement, Henerson, Morris, and Fitz-Gibbon's (1987) manual is excellent. It would be unfair to call the manual a *cookbook* because it is more than that. It does contain step-by-step, cookbook-like, procedures for validly and reliably developing measures of attitudes. It is a *must* reference for those interested in quantifying attitudes as part of a research study, but who do not wish to become attitude measurement experts. Henerson, Morris, and Fitz-Gibbon even include a section labeled "alternative approaches to collecting attitude information" designed to appeal to the qualitative researcher.

34.5.1 Characteristics of Quantitative Attitude Measurement

Before procedures for measuring attitudes are discussed, there are several general characteristics of measurement that should be considered in order to determine if an evaluation technique is an effective one. Good tests have these characteristics. Basically, a quantitative approach to attitude measurement requires that measures be:

- Valid. The instrument must be appropriate for what needs to be measured. In other words, a valid test measures the construct for which it is designed. A test of "attitude toward chemistry" will have items that deal directly with the concept of chemistry.
- Reliable. The measure should yield consistent results. In other words, if people were to take a reliable test a second time, they should obtain the same, or nearly the same, score as they got the first time they took the test, assuming no changes occurred between the two testings.
- Fairly simple to administer, explain, and understand. Generally, the measures that yield a single score of an attitude position epitomize the intent of this characteristic, although the single score may be deficient in meeting the intent of other characteristics of good measurement. Most tests of single attitudes have about 10 to 30 items, are valid, and have reliability estimates above .80.
- Replicable. Someone else should be able to use the measure with a different group, or in a different situation, to measure the same attitude. Replicable tests of attitude should be usable in a variety of situations. In other words, a test of computer anxiety should measure the existence of that construct in college students, parents, elementary schools students, and even stockbrokers.

34.5.2 Categories of Attitude Measurement Techniques

There are four widely used and accepted categories, or approaches, for collecting attitude information. These approaches are:

- Self-reports, where the members of a group report directly about their own attitudes. Self-reports include all procedures by which a person is asked to report on his or her own attitudes. This information can be provided orally through the use of interviews, surveys, or polls, or in written form through questionnaires, rating scales, logs, journals, or diaries. Self-reports represent the most direct type of attitude assessment and should be employed, unless the people who are being investigated are unable or unwilling to provide the necessary information. Questions like "How do you feel about X?" where X is the attitude construct under investigation are often asked in self-reports.
- Reports of others, where others report about the attitudes of a person or group. When the people whose attitudes are being investigated are unable or unlikely to provide accurate information, others can be questioned using interviews, questionnaires, logs, journals, reports, or observation techniques. Parents of children can be asked how their children feel about X, where X is the attitude construct under investigation.
- Sociometric procedures, where members of a group report about their attitudes toward one another. Sociometrics are used when the researcher desires a picture of the

patterns within a group. Members of groups can be asked questions like "Who in your group fits the description of *X*?" where *X* is the attitude position being studied.

• Records, which are systematic accounts of regular occurrences, such as attendance reports, sign-in sheets, library checkout records, and inventories. Records are very helpful when they contain information relevant to the attitude area in question. For example, when a researcher is trying to determine if a schoolwide program to develop a higher level of school pride is working, the school's maintenance records might give an index of the program's effectiveness. If school pride is improving, then vandalism should decline, and maintenance costs should be lower. The amount of trash picked up from the school's floors might yield relevant information, too. Students who have school pride are less likely to throw trash on the floor.

Within each of these categories, there are strategies for measuring attitude-related behaviors. Most commonly, attitude measurement is accomplished by one of the following techniques:

• Questionnaires and rating scales. Questionnaires and rating scales are instruments that present information to a respondent in writing and then require a written response, such as a check, a circle, a word, a sentence, or several sentences. Attitude rating scales are special kinds of questionnaires. They are developed according to strict procedures that ensure that responses can be summed to yield a single score representing one attitude. Questionnaires and rating scales are often used because they permit anonymity, permit the responder time to answer, can be given to many people simultaneously, provide uniformity across measurement situations, permit relatively easy data interpretation, and can be mailed or administered directly. Their main disadvantage is they do not permit as much flexibility as do some other techniques.

• Interviews. Interviews are face-to-face meetings between two or more people in which the respondent answers questions. A survey is a highly structured interview. Often surveys are conducted over the telephone, an approximation of face-to-face interviewing. A poll is a headcount. Respondents are given a limited number of options and asked to select one. For example, word-of-mouth procedures, such as interviews, surveys, and polls, are useful because they can be read to people who cannot read or who may not understand written questions. They guarantee a relatively high response rate, they are best for some kinds of information especially when people might change their answers if responses were written, and they are very flexible. There are two major problems with interviews. First, they are very time consuming. Second, it is possible that the interviewer may influence the respondent.

• Written reports, such as logs, journals, and diaries. Logs, journals, and diaries are descriptions of activities, experiences, and feelings written during the course of the program. Generally they are running accounts consisting of many entries prepared on an event, on a daily or weekly basis. The main advantage of this approach is that reports provide a wealth of information about a person's experi-

ences and feelings. The main problem is in extracting, categorizing, and interpreting the information. Written reports require a great deal of time by both the respondent and the researcher.

• Observations. These procedures require that a person dedicate his or her attention to the behaviors of an individual or group in a natural setting for a certain period of time. The main advantage of this approach is its increased credibility when pretrained, disinterested, unbiased observers are used. Formal observations often bring to attention actions and attitudes that might otherwise be overlooked. Observations are extremely time consuming, and sometimes observers produce discomfort in those they are observing. The presence of an observer almost always alters what is taking place in a situation.

A specific strategy for attitude measurement should be chosen which is appropriate for the type of attitude construct of interest, the type of learner, and the situation being examined (Henerson, Morris & Fitz-Gibbon, 1987). The procedures summarized above are those most often used. Others strategies are available, but attitude researchers are cautioned to select a technique appropriate to their research questions and a technique they are competent to carry out.

34.5.3 A Recommended Process for Attitude Measurement

Attempts at measurement, including the evaluation of attitude, require that a systematic process be followed. Using structured procedures increases the likelihood of an effective measurement taking place. Guidelines for attitude measurement usually recommend that at least six steps be followed (Henerson, Morris & Fitz-Gibbon, 1987):

1. *Identify the construct to be measured.* A construct is simply defined as the attitude area of interest. It is usually best to identify specific attitude constructs. Narrow attitude constructs such as "desire to take a course in chemistry" are probably better than "liking of chemistry," and "importance of knowing about the chemical elements" might be an even better attitude to measure. A learner can conceivably have an attitude position toward any object, situation, or person. When mediated instruction is designed, those attitudes that are important to the learning activity should be clearly identified and defined. An example of an attitude that an instructional developer might be interested in would be "attitude toward learning about titrations by video."

2. *Find an existing measure of the construct.* Once a certain attitude construct has been identified, an attempt should be made to locate an instrument that will measure it. Published tests are the first choice for measuring attitudes because they have usually been tried out in other instructional situations and include some statement of test validity and reliability. Additionally, instructions for administration of published tests often are available. The use of standardized measures simplifies the job of attitude evaluation.

The most obvious disadvantage to using a predesigned test is that it may not be evaluating the specific attitude being studied. Even if this is the case, it may sometimes be possible to extract valuable information from an instrument designed to test an attitude position similar to the one of specific instructional interest.

Possibly the best source of published tests is the research literature. Researchers who have conducted attitude research will often have developed or identified measures of their dependent variables that can be used in new experimental situations. If the research literature does not yield an appropriate measure of an attitude construct, then published indexes of tests can be reviewed. *Mental Measurements Yearbooks,* and *Tests in Print* are general sources for tests of all kinds. Often, standardized tests, such as those listed in general indexes, can be used to provide direction to the development of more specific attitude tests.

3. *Construct an attitude measure.* If no existing test of the relevant attitude is available, and a quantitative measure is needed, then it is necessary to construct a new test. Of the many types of attitude measurement possible, one widely used technique that seems to possess most of the characteristics of a good measure is the Agreement, or Likert-type, Scale. This technique involves the use of statements about the attitude that are either clearly favorable or unfavorable. Each student responds to each test item according to his or her perceived attitude "intensity" toward the statement. Often, students are asked to answer test items using a five-point scale that has responses varying in the amount of agreement to the statement from "strongly disagree" to "strongly agree." Advantages of this technique are ease of scoring and ease of summarizing the information obtained.

When a test is constructed, it is critical that validity and reliability information be collected for the measure. Of these two concepts, validity (i.e., appropriateness of instrument) is the most difficult to determine.

Validity for a test depends on a number of factors, such as the type of test and its intended use. Basically, there are four categories of validity:

• *Construct validity.* This concept refers to the extent to which the measure accurately represents the attitude construct whose name appears in its title. This can be determined by:

a. *Opinions of experts.* Experts are asked to review the test, and their reactions to it are used to modify the test, or if they do not have negative reactions, then the test is considered valid.

b. *Correlations to other measures of the same construct.* In some situations there may be other, often more complex, measures of the same variable that are available. Validity can be determined by asking a sample of learners to complete both the complex and the simpler versions and then correlating their scores. This procedure was used by Maurer (1983) when he validated his Computer Anxiety Index by correlating student's scores on it to Spielberger's (1970) much more complex and expensive State Anxiety Index.

c. *Measures of criterion group subjects (those who have been proved to possess the construct).* Maurer (1983) vali-

dated his computer anxiety index also using this technique. He observed learners and identified those who possessed the obvious characteristics of the computer anxious person. He then examined their Computer Anxiety Index scores and determined that their Index scores were also high, indicating that it was validly measuring computer anxiety.

d. *Appeals to logic.* Many times, particularly when the attitude can be easily defined, audiences will accept an instrument as logically related to the attitude, as long as they know it will be administered fairly.

• *Content validity.* This refers to the representativeness of the sample of questions included in the instrument. Content validity is usually determined by careful analysis of the items in the test. There is no simple process to determine content validity other than a close, thoughtful examination of each item separately, and all items collectively.

• *Concurrent validity.* This refers to the agreement of a test with another test on the same topic that was administered at approximately the same time. Concurrent validity is determined by correlating the results of the two parallel measures of the same attitude. This correlation coefficient is reported as an index of concurrent validity. For example, if an attitude test measuring "willingness to study chemistry" was administered and scores were obtained, it could be correlated to the instructor's assessments of the "completion rate of chemistry homework assignments" in order to determine an index of concurrent validity.

• *Predictive validity.* This refers to how well a measure will predict a future behavior, determined by comparing the results of an attitude test to a measure of behavior given in the future. This type of validity is usually expressed by a correlation coefficient found by comparing the results of two measures. For example, the results of an attitude test that measured "willingness to take additional chemistry courses" could be compared to actual course enrollment figures to determine the predictive validity of the attitude test.

Determining validity is not simple, however. Every educator who constructs a test of any type should be acutely aware of the need to develop valid instruments. Because there is no single, established method for determining validity, the test originator should exercise great care when constructing, administering, and interpreting tests.

Reliability is the ability of a measure to produce consistent results. It is usually less difficult to determine than validity. Reliability also refers to the extent to which measurement results are free of unpredictable kinds of error.

There are several methods of determining reliability that can be easily used by the attitude test developer. The "Test-Retest" method involves a second administration of the instrument to the target group and correlation of the results. The "Split-Half" method uses a random division of the instrument into two halves. Results from each half are correlated and reported as a reliability coefficient. "Alternate-Form" reliability involves the correlation of the results of two parallel forms of tests of the same attitude construct. In this method, each subject takes each form, and the resulting correlation is reported as a reliability estimate. Internal consistency reliability is a determination of how well the items of an attitude test correlate with one another. Measures of internal consistency, such as the Cronbach-alpha, are often used by attitude test developers (Ferguson, 1971).

Both the Test-Retest and Alternate Form techniques will yield a score between -1.00 and +1.00. The higher the number, the more reliable the test. Reliability coefficients above .70 are considered respectable. Scores above .90 are not uncommon for standardized attitude tests. As with validity, the results of reliability estimation should be reported to the test's consumer (Anastasi, 1968; Cronbach, 1970; Talmage, 1978; Henerson et al., 1987).

4. *Conduct a pilot study.* While it is possible to obtain validity and reliability data during the actual testing portion of the instructional activity, it is preferable to administer attitude instruments to a pilot audience before any formal use is undertaken. This is done to obtain appropriate data, and to uncover minor and potentially troublesome administrative problems such as misspellings, poor wording, or confusing directions. A group of learners similar to those who are the target group for the attitude test should be given the measure. Results should be used to revise the test and to determine validity and reliability information.

5. *Revise tests for use.* Results of pilot testing are used to revise, and refine, attitude instruments. Once problems are eliminated, the measure is ready to be used with its intended target audience.

6. *Summarize, analyze, and display results.* After testing is completed, the resulting data should be interpreted. Attitude test results are handled similarly to any other quantitative test information. Attitude responses should be summarized, analyzed, and displayed in such a manner that results are easily and quickly understood by others.

Descriptive statistics should be reported about the attitude test results. Most often, means, standard deviations, and the range of scores should be reported. In experimental situations, tests of inference are often performed using the results of attitude tests. Most attitude test results can be analyzed using standard parametric tests, such as t tests and analysis-of-variance tests. However, attitude data about instructional method or content area are often useful even if they are only averaged and compared to other averages. In other words, did the class average change for "Attitude Toward the Happiness of People in India" after viewing the video, or did the class react favorably to "The Importance of Wearing Seat-Belts" after participating in a hypermedia computer lesson?

Displaying data is another effective method of analysis. Charts, graphs, and bar diagrams are examples of data display techniques that are useful in assisting the reader in developing an understanding of what test results indicate. Whatever the process, the developer of an attitude test should make every effort to decipher the results of the measure and to explain apparent conclusions and implications derived from the test.

Attitude measurement is certainly not an exciting topic, and may be of less interest than other issues discussed in this chapter. However, attitude testing specifically, and identifying attitudes generally, are apparently not understood and probably not valued by many educational technology researchers. Certainly, the trend toward more qualitative approaches to investigation may convince some that attitude measurement, and even attitude identification, are irrelevant to the important issues of the field. However, those who are still approaching research questions from an objectivist perspective will want to be sure that they are correctly following the accepted principles of measurement.

34.6 ATTITUDES AND INSTRUCTIONAL MEDIA—THE LITERATURE

In the last 15 years, two attempts have been made to organize the literature related to attitude change and instructional technology. In the late 1970s and early 1980s, Simonson reported on a series of reviews of the literature that culminated in a set of guidelines for designing mediated messages for obtaining attitudinal outcomes. Several studies were reported during the following years that attempted to validate Simonson's (1979) guidelines.

In 1993, Bednar and Levie proposed a series of attitude change principles. These principles facilitated the design of instruction to change attitudes and for the processes used for structuring lessons that targeted affective goals.

Simonson's research will be summarized first, then Bednar and Levie's principles will be reviewed. Finally, there will be a discussion of other research literature that relates to the use of media for persuasion.

34.6.1 Designing Instruction for Attitudinal Outcomes—The Iowa State Studies

In 1977, the first of a number of reviews and research studies dealing with media-attitude research was published by Simonson. A three-part approach was followed. First, literature about media and attitudes was located, reviewed, and synthesized (Simonson & Burch, 1977; Simonson, Thies & Burch, 1979a; Simonson, 1979; Simonson, 1980). Next, Simonson proposed a series of guidelines for designing instruction for attitudinal outcomes (Simonson, 1979, 1983, 1984). Finally, a series of research studies were conducted that evaluated various aspects of Simonson's guidelines (Simonson, 1985; Simonson, Aegerter, Berry, Kloock & Stone, 1987; Treimer & Simonson, 1988; Dimond & Simonson, 1988). This research agenda will be reviewed.

Several publications by Simonson reviewing the media and attitude literature were published during the 3-year period between 1977 and 1980. The purpose of these reviews was to summarize the status of the research in this area and to attempt to synthesize conclusions about the results of this research. Simonson identified 211 research studies that experimentally examined some aspect of the relationship between attitudes, attitude change, and instructional media. Published or abstracted in *AV Communications Review* were 138 articles, and 73 articles were found that were published elsewhere (Simonson, Thies & Burch, 1979; Simonson, 1979a).

Simonson (1979a) arrived at several general conclusions after reviewing this literature. Five observations, with each having impact on those preceding it, were offered.

Observation #1: Mediated instruction *does* contribute to desired attitudinal outcomes in learners, especially when the instruction is designed specifically to produce certain attitudes or attitude changes.

Observation #2: The state of the art of media-attitude research is such that no specific guidelines for producing attitudinal outcomes can be generated. This is no theory of "media-produced attitude change."

Observation #3: Procedures *most likely* to produce desired attitudinal outcomes toward content as a result of instruction delivered by media include:

- Use of follow-up activities (e.g., discussions) and open-ended questions after the mediated instruction
- Maximum use of realistic types of media with as many nondistracting/noncontradictory visual cues (e.g., color, motion) as possible (e.g., the story film)
- Creation of an aroused state in the learner through direct participation, intermittent distractions to reorient the learner from previously held attitudinal positions, or dramatic presentations that involve the viewer emotionally and intellectually in the content shown

Observation #4: Procedures *least likely* to produce desired attitudinal outcomes toward content as a result of instruction delivered by media include:

- Varying only the channel through which the instruction is delivered (e.g., a videotaped replay of a live lecture probably would not produce more favorable viewer attitudes toward the lecture topic, and might even produce more negative attitudes than would the live lecture)
- Including distractions in the form of extraneous information or cues in the mediated instruction (e.g., a videotaped presentation on the need for better study habits probably would not change viewers' attitudes toward the use of the public library as a source of information even though this was included as part of the videotape script; too much irrelevant information inhibits attitude change)
- Presenting unrealistic, highly symbolic information using visual media (e.g., a slide set which included many frames containing written information probably would not produce positive attitudes toward the topic presented)
- Presenting problem/conflict situations but providing no mechanism for conflict alleviation or problem solving, either as part of the mediated messages or in follow-up discussions (e.g., a film on the problem of soil erosion probably would not change farmer's attitudes unless the film showed solutions to the problem of soil erosion)

Observation #5: Media-attitude experimentation is not currently a high priority for researchers in media or related areas.

Simonson (1979a) stated that these five observations were opinions, but that any careful review of the 221 studies summarized would produce the same or similar conclusions. Simonson (1980) stated that if mediated instruction was broadly defined to include the entire learning process of which television, film, or still pictures were a part, then mediated instruction did seem to contribute to attitude formation and change. When only the media were evaluated, then conclusions were much less conclusive. Simonson stated that only one, broad, general conclusion about the relationship between media and attitudes was apparent and that this conclusion was an obvious one. Instructional media are primarily carriers of information and play their greatest role in the attitude change process as delivery vehicles. Characteristics of media such as flexibility of use, accessibility of information, and ability to encode ideas were more important than any inherent communication-related characteristics of a medium, which probably were of secondary importance to any development of attitudes or attitude changes (Simonson, 1980).

Simonson, Thies, and Burch (1979) also identified four trends in media-attitude research. These trends were listed as phases that characterized the research about media and attitudes.

Phase #1. Liking. A number of early research studies evaluated the media-attitude link in the simplest form by attempting to determine if the learner liked the lesson delivered by media or the medium itself. Usually, researchers reported on the results of an evaluation of learners. They were asked questions like, "Did you like this lesson?" or "Do you like learning from film?"

Phase #2. Change in liking. The logical second level of attitude evaluation conducted by media researchers was the study of *change in liking* as a result of media exposure. Usually pre- or postsurveys of learner attitude were conducted in order to determine if there was a positive or negative change.

Phase #3. Attitude comparison. A slightly more sophisticated design was the use of two treatments to determine the impact of attitude change procedures. Often, one treatment was a mediated one and the other was traditional, teacher-centered instruction. These comparison studies suffered from the same problems as media comparison studies of achievement: Results from many studies produced contradictory findings.

Phase #4. Media-attitude interaction. In the late 1970s, researchers began to design experimental studies using an aptitude-treatment-interaction approach (Allen, 1975). This approach made it possible to determine with greater specificity the relationship between attitudes and media. While relatively few studies were found that used this approach, the ones that were found did provide considerable information for the development of guidelines for designing persuasive mediated instruction (Simonson, 1979).

Next, a number of methodological problems common to the media-attitude literature were summarized by Simonson. These concerns related directly to the problems encountered by those who subsequently attempted to synthesize this area of research.

First, attitudes were poorly defined. Often researchers did not operationally define the attitude constructs they were investigating. Rather, statements such as "attitudes were measured and students liked learning about chemistry from films" were reported. Measurement of attitudes was also considered inadequate. Most measures were locally prepared, and most researchers did not report validity or reliability information about their attitude tests.

Most studies reviewed by Simonson were considered to be quasi-experimental or experimental (Campbell & Stanley, 1963). Often, however, attitude testing was only of peripheral importance to the main purposes of the research study. Many times, attitudes were evaluated after the fact, as follow-ups to an experiment. Clearly stated attitude hypotheses or research questions were rarely reported.

Finally, it was rare that follow-ups of the results of attitude change treatments were reported. Many critics of attitude research considered then, as they do now, that attitudes are transitory and attitude changes short-lived. Social psychology literature tends to refute this criticism. Few media-attitude researchers reported studying the long-term consequences of their persuasive efforts.

Simonson (1979a) concluded that the research on media and attitudes was not significantly different from media research in general. However, Simonson did feel that there were important implications to the research that made possible the proposal of general guidelines pertaining to the design of mediated instruction for attitudinal outcomes. Simonson offered a series of six guidelines (1979, 1983, 1984), which are included next.

34.6.2 Guidelines for Designing Instruction for Attitudinal Outcomes

Several versions of six guidelines for designing mediated instruction for attitudinal outcomes were proposed by Simonson (1979, 1983, 1984). In all cases, they were supported by research literature and were offered with two purposes in mind. First, the guidelines were generated for instructional developers to apply during the instructional design process (1979). They were also offered to researchers so they could test the effectiveness of the guidelines.

Simonson's six guidelines for designing instruction of attitudinal outcomes are:

Guideline #1: Learners react favorably to mediated instruction that is realistic, relevant to them, and technically stimulating.

Guideline #2: Learners are persuaded, and react favorably, when mediated instruction includes the presentation of new information about the topic.

Guideline #3: Learners are positively affected when persuasive messages are presented in as credible a manner as possible.

Guideline #4: Learners who are involved in the planning, production, or delivery of mediated instruction are likely to react favorably to the instructional activity and to the message delivered.

Guideline #5: Learners who participate in postinstruction discussions and critiques are likely to develop favorable attitudes toward delivery method and content.

Guideline #6: Learners who experience a purposeful emotional involvement or arousal during instruction are likely to change their attitudes in the direction advocated in a mediated message.

Simonson (1979) concluded his discussion of these six guidelines by repeating the position, taken several times previously, that media are primarily carriers of information. There was no "best medium" found for producing attitude outcomes. However, there apparently was a best approach for the maximizing of the likelihood of desirable attitudes being fostered in learners in a specific situation. The guidelines were thought to be useful for developing specific attitude change messages.

Apparently, the six guidelines received a lukewarm reception from the profession. While no rebuttals were published, neither were there many research studies published that cited the guidelines as the basis for either a research plan or an instructional design process. One exception to this were the studies conducted at Iowa State University during the 1980s that attempted to investigate one or more of the guidelines. Six of these studies will be discussed next.

34.6.3 Media and Attitude Change: Six Studies

Simonson's (1979) guidelines were derived from previous research dealing with media and attitudes. In order to evaluate them, a number of research studies were completed and reported. The first four were published as a group (Simonson, Aegerter, Berry, Kloock & Stone, 1987). One was published in the journal *Teaching and Learning Technologies* (Simonson, 1985) and replicated and presented at a convention of the Association for Educational Communications and Technology (Dimond & Simonson, 1988), and the last study was published in the *Journal of Social Psychology* (Treimer & Simonson, 1988).

The first four studies were part of a research program that investigated whether instructional media could be used to deliver persuasive messages effectively. The studies attempted to provide evidence about the following questions:

1. Is there a hierarchy of media types related to effectiveness in delivering persuasive messages? In other words, are media that deliver messages realistically,

as defined by Dale (1946), more effective than media that depict messages less realistically?

2. Does learner aptitude interact with media type when attitude change is the goal of the message? Specifically, do the learner characteristics of field dependence/field independence and hemisphericity interact with media type when persuasive messages are delivered?

Study #1. This study attempted to determine if a motion picture was more effective than a nearly identical slide with audiotape presentation at changing attitudes of viewers toward the need for greater soil conservation efforts. This study used a posttest only, control group design (Campbell & Stanley, 1963). There were three randomly assigned groups of subjects, two experimental and one control. The two experimental treatments were based on a 23-minute film entitled *We Are of the Soil.* This motion picture was designed to introduce soil conservation practices, such as conservation tillage, and to convince viewers that these practices were important. It was selected by a panel of experts as a film that was technically excellent (Cook, 1979), and as one that seemed to have been produced more to change attitudes than to provide information.

Subjects in the first treatment viewed the motion picture. Students in the second treatment watched a 2 × 2 slide presentation and listened to an accompanying audiotape. To produce this slide presentation, each scene in the film was analyzed, and the most important still picture from each scene was made into a slide. The film's narration was duplicated on an audiotape. The slides were projected using a dissolve unit and two carousel slide projectors, a treatment that was reported by Cook (1979) to be comparable in technical quality to the motion picture from which it was derived. The motion picture was considered to be the medium that would deliver the message the most realistically (Dale, 1946).

Subjects. Students enrolled in an undergraduate teacher education course were assigned randomly to one of the three treatment groups. Before treatments were administered, all subjects were given the Group Embedded Figures Test (GEFT) (Witkin, Oltman & Raskin, 1971). The GEFT was used to determine whether students tended to be either field-dependent (FD) or field-independent (FI) learners. This learner characteristic was examined because it was felt that the impact of the mediated treatments might be different for subjects who were either FD or FI.

FD and FI are considered to be pervasive, stable cognitive styles that influence a person's perception of messages (McLeod, McCormack, Carpenter & Skvarcius, 1978). FD learners are influenced more by their surroundings than are FI learners, who are influenced more by internal factors. FD individuals seem to be more socially oriented and are more affected by praise and criticism from their peers. FD persons tend to take a passive, spectator role in learning. FI learners, on the other hand, seem more adept at taking a message apart and at understanding its component parts, and tend to be more active learners who often have a strong self-concept. People are not totally field dependent

or field independent, rather they have tendencies one way or the other.

Subjects were given the GEFT, then were categorized as being either FD or FI, depending on their score on the GEFT. Students who had scores within one raw score of the average of all scores were not included in treatments. They were excused from the experiments because the GEFT did not satisfactorily identify them as tending to be either FD or FI.

Design. This study employed a 2 × 3 factorial design. There were three treatment groups. One group watched the motion picture, one group watched the slide presentation, and the third was a control group. Within each group there were two levels of each treatment: those students considered to be FD and those considered to be FI.

After treatments were viewed, subjects were given the Soil Conservation Attitude Test (SCAT). The SCAT was developed by Cook (1979) and revised by Kloock (1981). It contained 24 statements to which subjects reacted using a five-response Likert-type scale. The SCAT was reported to have a reliability estimate of .85 (Kloock, 1981).

Results of Study #1. Descriptive statistics are reported in Table 34-2. There was a statistically significant difference in attitude reported that was attributable to the experimental treatments. The average scores of students in all four experimental treatment cells indicated a more positive attitude toward the importance of soil conservation than did the scores of control subjects. Because one of the main goals of this study was to determine if any of the experimental groups of subjects reacted to treatments significantly differently from the others, a Duncan's test (Ferguson, 1971) was used to identify where significant differences occurred among cells. It was found that the subjects in the motion picture treatment who were identified as being field independent had more positive attitudes than did subjects in any of the other five treatment groupings.

Study #2. This study was a modified replication of study 1, with the same general purpose. However, three changes were made. First, the topic of the experimental

TABLE 34-2. ATTITUDES TOWARD SOIL CONVERSATION: STUDY #1

		Treatments			
		Film	**Slides**	**Control**	**Total**
Field-dependent subjects	$\overline{x}=$	64.69	65.33	61.14	63.62
	$N=$	13.00	12.00	14.00	39.00
	$sd=$	6.76	7.39	8.47	7.64
Field-independent subjects	$\overline{x}=$	69.86	65.31	63.69	66.19
	$N=$	14.00	13.00	16.00	43.00
	$sd=$	4.85	7.69	7.95	7.42
Totals	$\overline{x}=$	67.37	65.32	62.50	64.96
	$N=$	27.00	25.00	30.00	82.00
	$sd=$	6.31	7.53	8.16	7.59

Higher scores indicate a more positive attitude toward soil conservation. Possible range of scores was 24 to 120.

treatments was changed. A film entitled *The Right Approach* was selected by a jury of media specialists as an excellent persuasive film. Its topic was the employment of the handicapped. A slide presentation, with accompanying audiotape, was produced from the most relevant scenes of the film in a manner similar to the slide treatment produced for study 1. The two treatments (motion picture and slide with audiotape) were judged by experts to be generally of comparable technical quality.

Since the topic of the treatments changed, the test of the dependent variable also had to be changed. A standardized text of attitude toward disabled persons was found in the *Mental Measurements Yearbook* (Buros, 1978). The Attitudes Toward Disabled Persons (ATDP) was reported to have a reliability estimate of .76 (Yucker, Block & Young, 1970).

The second change for study 2 was to use fifth- and sixth-grade students as subjects. They ranged in age from 10 to 13. Last, a follow-up test was given to a small subsample of subjects 3 weeks after treatment to determine if attitude changes produced by the treatments persisted.

The posttest-only design for this study had two independent variables, field dependence/field independence and treatment. The 2×3 factorial design had three treatments (motion picture, slide with audiotape, and control), and two levels of the cognitive style, field dependence/independence.

Results of Study #2. Results of descriptive tests are reported in Table 34-3. There was a statistically significant difference in attitude attributable to treatments and to the learner cognitive style field dependence/independence. After treatments, the subjects who had viewed the motion picture generally had more positive attitudes toward disabled persons than did subjects who watched the slide/audiotape presentation. Average attitude scores of subjects in both of the experimental treatments were significantly more positive than were the average scores of control subjects.

Average scores of several treatment cells deserve note. Three of the experimental treatment cells, Film/FD, Film/FI, and Slide/FI, had approximately equal attitude scores, while the fourth treatment group, Slide/FD, had significantly less positive attitudes toward the disabled than did students in any of the other three experimental cells.

This study added a follow-up testing session. Three weeks after treatments were administered, a smaller number of the subjects were randomly selected for retesting. There were no significant differences found, even though the trends of scores were similar to those obtained from the original administration of the attitude test. There seemed to be a regression effect. It was also apparent that field-independent subjects generally remained more positive toward disabled persons than did field-dependent subjects. However, because such a small number of subjects were included in this retesting, it is not possible to draw generalizable conclusions from the data.

Study #3. This experiment could also be considered a modified replication of study 1. For this experiment, there were two major changes made to the design of study 1. First, junior and senior high school students were used as subjects. These students attended school in a small town in an agricultural state in the Midwest and ranged in age from 13 to 18. The second change in this study was the examination of the independent variable hemisphericity instead of field dependence/independence.

Researchers have reported that in spite of a great deal of overlap of function, the two hemispheres of the brain organize and encode information in two different ways. Generally, the left hemisphere is more logical, convergent, and analytical. It is responsible for language and processes information sequentially. The right hemisphere is more holistic, intuitive, spatial, and divergent (Ornstein, 1977).

It also has been determined that individuals tend to have a dominant hemisphere. That is, one hemisphere tends to take priority when information is processed. It has been proposed that this hemispheric dominance is related to effective learning. In other words, how a person's brain perceived data determines in part how much is learned.

In order to assign subjects to treatments, the Conjugate Lateral Eye Movement (CLEM) Test was used to identify a person's dominant hemisphere (Day, 1964). The CLEM is an individually administered test that requires observation of a subject's eye movement after reflective questions are asked of them. The CLEM Test has a reliability of .78 ($r = .78$).

Subjects were tested using the CLEM and were assigned to treatment groups. Individuals who did not have a clearly dominant hemisphere, as indicated by the CLEM, were excused from the experiment. Specifically, subjects who did not move their eyes in a predictable pattern when they were asked reflective questions were not included in data analyses.

The first treatment group viewed the persuasive film *We Are of the Soil*. The second group watched the slides with accompanying audiotape prepared from this motion picture. The third group was a control. After treatments were completed, the SCAT was administered. This study used a 2×3, posttest only, control group design.

Results of Study #3. Descriptive statistics are reported in Table 34-4. There were no statistically significant differences found, although the trends of the mean scores

TABLE 34-3. ATTITUDES TOWARD DISABLED PERSONS: STUDY #2

		Film	Slides	Control	Total
Field-dependent subjects	$\overline{x} =$	86.08	75.25	67.83	76.64
	$N =$	25.00	24.00	23.00	72.00
	$sd =$	14.61	18.96	21.29	19.65
Field-independent subjects	$\overline{x} =$	85.17	87.24	78.35	83.50
	$N =$	24.00	21.00	23.00	68.00
	$sd =$	4.85	7.69	7.95	7.42
Totals	$\overline{x} =$	85.63	80.84	73.09	79.97
	$N =$	49.00	45.00	46.00	140.00
	$sd =$	15.67	17.91	19.52	18.35

Higher scores indicate a more positive attitude toward disabled persons. Possible range of scores was 24 to 120.

**TABLE 34-4. ATTITUDES TOWARD SOIL
CONSERVATION: STUDY #3**

		Film	Slides	Control	Total
		Treatments			
Right-brain–	$\overline{x} =$	57.26	57.47	55.56	56.81
dominant	$N =$	19.00	17.00	16.00	52.00
subjects	$sd =$	8.26	11.35	9.80	9.65
Left-brain–	$\overline{x} =$	59.78	60.64	57.29	59.02
dominant	$N =$	18.00	14.00	21.00	53.00
subjects	$sd =$	4.85	7.69	7.95	7.42
Totals	$\overline{x} =$	58.49	58.90	56.54	57.92
	$N =$	37.00	31.00	37.00	105.00
	$sd =$	9.84	9.81	8.54	9.36

Higher scores indicate a more positive attitude toward soil conservation.
Possible range of scores was 24 to 120.

were interesting. Left-brain–dominant subjects generally were more positive than were right-brain subjects in all treatment categories.

In order to examine the data more completely, a post-hoc analysis of SCAT scores for subjects in grades 9 through 12 was conducted. While results were not significant, it was found that subjects in the senior high school grades who were in experimental treatments had more positive attitudes when compared to control subjects in the same grade. In other words, the difference between control group subjects' and experimental group subjects' attitude scores were greater in the higher grades than they were in the lower grades.

Study #4. This experiment took a slightly different approach than studies 1, 2, or 3. At its foundation was the principle reported by Simonson (1984) and Rogers (1973) that the use of fear may be an effective technique for attitude change, especially if cures to the problem or probabilities of exposure to a fear-provoking event are included in the message. In other words, a persuasive message that showed the dire consequences of not following some course of action—such as stopping smoking, or wearing seat belts—could be made more effective if cures for the problem or techniques for how to change behavior were included in the message.

Study #4 used a 2 × 3, posttest only, control group design. As before, field dependence/independence was the second factor in the design. This learner characteristic was hypothesized as possibly being related to the impact of a fear-provoking message, especially when information to reduce the tension produced in viewers as a consequence of the fear was included in one treatment and not in the other. The college students who participated in the experiment were tested using the GEFT and assigned to one of the three treatment groups, just as they were in study 1.

Experimental treatments were based on a film entitled *The Feminine Mistake,* a 23-minute, antismoking motion picture sponsored by the American Cancer Society. This film was selected by a group of media specialists because

of its high technical quality. Permission was obtained from the copyright holder to produce two 15-minute videotape versions of the film. The first version showed only the fear-provoking scenes included in the film. Narrated by Bonnie Franklin, star of the television program *One Day at a Time,* this version showed scenes designed to scare viewers so they would stop smoking. These scenes included an interview with a young woman undergoing chemotherapy for lung cancer, sequences showing how smoke deteriorated the tissues of the skin, and a presentation by a doctor of the results of medical tests that demonstrated the effects of cigarette smoke on the unborn.

The second 15-minute videotape version included the most dramatic, fear-provoking scenes used in the first version, but also included about the 5 minutes of information on how to stop smoking. These scenes gave information on smokers' support groups and how the body recovered once a smoker quit.

The two video versions of the motion picture were evaluated several times during production. They were also evaluated by subjects during the experiment and in all cases were judged to be generally of high and comparable technical quality.

After treatments were administered, subjects completed the Smoking Attitude Scale (SAS; Baer, 1966). The SAS is a 21-item measure using a five-response, Likert-type scale. It is reported to have a reliability estimate of .84.

Results of Study #4. Results are reported in Table 34-5. It was found that both experimental treatments were successful at significantly influencing subjects' attitudes toward smoking. Subjects assigned to one of the two versions of the videotaped adaptations of *The Feminine Mistake* had more negative attitudes toward smoking after viewing treatments than did control subjects. There was no statistical difference found between subjects categorized as being either field dependent or field independent, nor was there a significant interaction between field dependence and treatment.

34.6.3.1. Discussion of the Four Studies. Earlier, two specific questions were posed that served as guides for the design of the four studies included in this research program.

**TABLE 34-5. ATTITUDES TOWARD
SMOKING: STUDY #4**

Treatments

		Fear with Alleviation	Fear Alone	Control
Field-dependent	$\overline{x} =$	41.23	38.93	47.50
subjects	$N =$	22.00	15.00	14.00
	$sd =$	11.67	7.78	6.76
Field-independent	$\overline{x} =$	40.21	39.85	48.32
subjects	$N =$	24.00	20.00	22.00
	$sd =$	8.95	10.87	13.16

Higher scores indicate a more positive attitude toward smoking. Possible range of scores was 21 to 105.

Question 1. Is there a hierarchy of media types related to effectiveness in delivering persuasive messages? It seems obvious that media can be used to effectively deliver persuasive messages. Studies 1, 2, and 4 all reported attitude positions that were significantly different for subjects who viewed experimental treatments when compared to control subjects. There also seemed to be some evidence that motion pictures generally were more effective at persuading than were slide presentations. This conclusion was supported by the results of studies 1 and 2.

The impact of realistic persuasive messages on attitude change has been studied by social psychologists for over 4 decades. Reinforcement theory is based on the assumption that realistic messages have more cues for the viewer, and thus are more effective at persuading. Specifically, since motion pictures have more visual information, theoretically this should make motion pictures more effective than still pictures at persuading. The results from these studies seem to support the assumptions of this theory. While no hierarchy of media types could be developed based on this series of experiments, it does seem that this question should be investigated further.

Question 2. Does learner aptitude interact with media type when attitude change is the goal of a message? Based on the results of studies 1 and 2, there may be a relationship between field independence and filmed persuasive messages for the topics of soil conservation and hiring the disabled. Field-independent subjects seem more likely to be influenced favorably. It also seemed that films were, in general, better than slide presentations at delivering messages that changed attitudes.

34.6.3.2. Conclusions from the Four Studies. A fundamental assumption of the research presented above was that attitude change is an important concern of the educator, and that if attitudes are important, information on how attitudes might be formed or changed with media is needed. These four studies were conducted to examine the use of media to deliver persuasive messages. The results of the four studies tended to support the following conclusions: First, attitudes toward educationally relevant topics, such as conservation, smoking, and disabled persons, can be modified by using persuasive messages delivered by media. Next, it appeared that some types of media may be more effective than others at delivering information designed to change attitudes. Motion pictures seem to be more effective than slides. There also seems to be sufficient evidence to warrant further investigation into the relationship between the content of persuasive messages, the media used to deliver those messages, and the characteristics of the students who view the message.

Realistic media, such as films and video, were reported most often to be vehicles for delivering attitude change messages. The next step in Simonson's research agenda was to query filmmakers about the techniques they used when they designed persuasive motion pictures.

Study #5. Persuasive Films: Techniques Used to Change Attitudes (Simonson, 1985; Dimond & Simonson, 1988)

Purpose of the study. The four studies reported above indicated that persuasive films can change attitudes. The next study attempted to determine how films were planned and produced, and what makes it possible for a film to persuade a viewer to accept an attitudinal position.

Alfred Hitchcock is supposed to have once remarked to an executive producer that he never looked at motion pictures, to which the producer replied, "But where do you get all your ideas then?" (Rose, 1963). "How they did it" in a film starts a description heard in many film production conferences. The techniques used by one filmmaker in a successful film are often used as models for similar films. Filmmakers often produced films by formula. Many times they do not even realize what formula they are following (Rose, 1963). Most often, filmmakers decide on, or are hired, to present a position in a film. The filmmaker then works backwards, planning the presentation to include, through emphasis and selection, the ideas and techniques that would be most likely to elicit the desired reaction in the viewer. In other words, the desired attitude is identified, then filmmakers decide how to persuade the audience to accept this attitude as a consequence of viewing their film (Rose, 1963).

The identification of the specific techniques used by the filmmaker to accomplish these persuasive goals was the purpose of this study. Simonson's (1979) guidelines were used in the development of the questions asked.

Procedures. In order to obtain information from filmmakers about persuasive films, a *Film-Makers Survey* (FMS) was developed. A pilot version of the FMS was sent to a small sample of filmmakers and a revised version based on their comments and suggestions was developed. This revised FMS had two parts. Part 1 dealt with the filmmaker's background and experience. Part 2 asked the filmmaker to rate, discuss, or evaluate techniques used in persuasive filmmaking. Each item in part 2 of the FMS was directly related to one of the six design guidelines identified by Simonson (1979).

The catalog of the Council on International Non-Theatrical Events (CINE) listed 150 filmmakers who were sent a copy of the FMS with a cover letter explaining the purpose of this study. These filmmakers were sampled because their films were listed in the CINE catalog as Golden Eagle Award winners and because the accompanying descriptions of their films seemed to indicate that their motion pictures were persuasive. A random selection of cinematographers was not considered appropriate because the purpose of this study was to have individuals with experience in persuasive filmmaking evaluate techniques used to produce this type of film. Experience in persuasive filmmaking was necessary in order for a person to be able to satisfactorily complete the FMS. Included with the questionnaire and cover letter was a stamped, addressed, return envelope. No follow-ups to filmmakers who failed to return the questionnaire were attempted, because the cover letter stated that if addressees had not produced persuasive films, they should disregard the FMS. Because subjects were selected based on a two- or three-sentence description of one of their films in the CINE catalog, it was very likely that many of them were not actually persuasive filmmakers and, consequently, discarded the FMS.

Results. Of the questionnaires, 51 were returned, for a response rate of 34%. This fairly small percentage of returns was expected because of the technique used to select subjects and because no follow-ups were attempted. A careful analysis of the completed questionnaires did not reveal any discernible, confounding pattern. An analysis of the known characteristics of those filmmakers who completed the survey as compared to those who did not return it failed to reveal any significant relationships that might have indicated that a biased subset of filmmakers answered the FMS as compared to those who did not.

Background information on the responding filmmakers. All 51 of the filmmakers who responded indicated that producing motion pictures was their primary method of employment. The average length of time respondents had been employed as filmmakers was slightly more than 18 years. The range of years of employment was 1 to 40. Of the respondents, 91% were males. Their average age was 46. Ages ranged from 25 to 68 years.

The average number of films of all types produced by each filmmaker was 142. The average number of persuasive films produced was 29 (range = 1 to 200). For persuasive films, the average film length was 18.3 minutes. The shortest persuasive film was reported to be 2 minutes. The longest was 30 minutes. There were a large number of 28-minute films reported, probably because this was a popular length for films that were to be broadcast. Filmmakers reported working in production companies with an average of 11 employees. The smallest company was a one-person freelance operation. The largest company employed 35.

Of the filmmakers, 37% reported that they had no formal school training in filmmaking, only on-the-job training; 16% had some college experience. Those who had masters degrees or more were 21%; 5% reported that they had attended a trade school. Only 9% reported having any formal training in producing persuasive films.

The definition of persuasive film used for this study was considered appropriate by 78% of the filmmakers who answered the FMS. Almost without exception, those who did not like the definition thought that it was too narrow and should be expanded to include broadcast, noneducational uses of films. The definition used for this study was: "A persuasive film is a training or educational film that has influencing, persuading, or changing of attitudes as its primary purpose.

Most respondents thought that the market for persuasive films would increase in the future (73%), and that about 40% of the educational film market was for films that primarily persuade rather than inform. The average cost of a 10-minute persuasive film was estimated at $29,000, or $2,900 per minute (range = $13,000 to $65,000). This price was estimated as being only slightly higher than the cost of an informative film of the same length.

Persuasive-film production techniques. One of the major goals of this study was to determine how filmmakers would go about producing a film when persuasion was their goal. Filmmakers responding to the FMS considered persuasive films to be planned and produced a little differently than other educational films ($X = 3.79$; $5 =$ very differently; $1 =$ exactly the same). One major difference was the importance of a prescript writing target audience assessment that most filmmakers considered critical to the success of their persuasive films ($X = 4.27$; $5 =$ critical; $1 =$ not necessary). Technical quality of persuasive films was considered important, but only slightly more so than for any film ($X = 3.59$; $5 =$ critical; $1 =$ less important than for other films). The "outs," the percentage of film not used, for persuasive motion pictures was estimated at being only slightly greater than for informative films ($X = 3.59$; $5 =$ much greater; $3 =$ about the same; $1 =$ much less).

To determine the production techniques considered most effective for persuasive films, several somewhat overlapping groups of procedures were presented in the FMS for the filmmakers to rate. An analysis of this rating process follows.

I. WHEN COMPARING PERSUASIVE FILMS TO OTHER EDUCATIONAL FILMS, HOW IMPORTANT IS IT TO:

Rank

Most important	1.	Use motion rather than static actors, objects, or graphics?
	2.	Use believable, realistic scenes, events, and actors?
	3.	Present new information on the topic?
	4.	Use an arousing or dramatic musical score?
	5.	Use many rather than few scenes?
	6.	Produce a shorter rather than longer film?
Least important	7.	Use color rather than black and white?

II. HOW WOULD YOU RATE THE FOLLOWING TECHNIQUES IN TERMS OF THEIR LIKELIHOOD OF INFLUENCING YOUR AUDIENCE?

Rank

Most effective	1.	Conduct a target audience pre-assessment.
	2.	Hire professional actors rather than amateurs.
	3.	Present new information on the topic.
	4.	Have people in the film that are as similar to the target audience as possible.
	5.	Include a teacher's guide with the film to use during follow-up discussions.
	6.	Use testimonials from the "man on the street."
	7.	Hire a big-name star to promote your position.
	8.	Present inspirational messages.
	9.	Use title scenes to present verbal information visually.
Least effective	10.	Use graphs and charts for presenting facts.

III. RATE THE FOLLOWING CHARACTERISTICS OF FILMS IN TERMS OF THEIR IMPORTANCE FOR USE IN A PERSUASIVE FILM.

Rank

Effective techniques	1.	Attempt to "arouse" the audience intellectually, sexually, or emotionally.
	2.	Be as realistic in presenting the story as possible.
	3.	Make the film "fun" to watch.
	4.	Present facts.
	5.	Be as nonverbal as possible.
	6.	Use physically attractive actors and actresses.
	7.	Present both sides of an argument.
	8.	Use animation.
	9.	Use talking faces.
Not effective techniques	10.	Scare the audience by presenting the dire consequences of not following the recommendations presented in the film.
	11.	Use many written scenes.

When asked to rank three general statements concerning how important each was to persuasive filmmaking, the filmmakers considered the need to arouse the viewer emotionally or to promote some reaction in the viewer relative to the content of the persuasive film as the most important of the three presented ($X = 1.23$; 1 = most important; 3 = least important). The technical quality of the film ($X = 2.37$) and the need to present considerable information in the film about the topic ($X = 2.31$) were not considered as important as involving the viewer in the message of the motion picture.

Because the production of persuasive films is considered controversial by some, several questions were included in the FMS to determine what filmmakers thought about the propriety of producing films that were meant to persuade rather than to inform. Most considered persuasive films to be much more exciting to produce than other types of motion pictures ($X = 4.25$; 5 = much more exciting; 1 = not much fun). Only 10% reported having problems with the morality of producing attitude change films. However, most indicated that they would refuse to produce a film that was intended to promote a position they did not believe in.

Based on the FMS results reported above, it would seem that there were several ingredients agreed on by the filmmakers as being likely to promote attitude changes when they were included in the planning or production of persuasive films. Techniques considered important for successful persuasive films were that they should:

- Be planned and based on the results of a target audience assessment
- Arouse and promote in the viewer some action, either intellectual or behavioral
- Present new information to the viewer on the topic
- Be realistic and believable to the viewer
- Include motion and action in scenes rather than static visuals

- Be enjoyable, or fun, to watch
- Be as nonverbal as possible
- Be used with follow-up discussions as outlined in a teacher's guide that should accompany the film

This hypothetical persuasive film should be no longer than necessary and have a budget of about $3,000 per minute. Technical quality would be important for this motion picture, but only slightly more so than for any film. The "outs" ratio would probably be slightly greater for this film than for a regular informative motion picture of the same length.

Techniques not considered important or effective for persuasive films were the use of considerations of:

- Color rather than black and white
- Film length
- Graphs, charts, and other written scenes
- "Scare" tactics that would attempt to show the dire consequences of not adhering to the message of the persuasive film
- Talking faces
- Animation
- Inspirational messages

Generally, it was thought that an effective persuasive film was one that was believable and realistic, presented new information, was fun to watch, promoted involvement or action in the viewer, was more visual than verbal, and was used correctly by the teacher. These results were the amalgamation of those found in two studies (Simonson, 1985; Dimond & Simonson, 1988).

Study #6. Subliminal Messages, Persuasion, and Behavior Change (Treimer & Simonson, 1988). In 1988, Treimer and Simonson published the results of a slightly different type of study that attempted to investigate the impact of subliminal messages on the level of emotional involvement felt by the viewer of videotapes. It was felt that subliminal messages, if effective, might provide an alternative method of intellectually or emotionally involving the viewer of a videotape in the persuasive message, as proposed by guideline #6 (Simonson, 1979).

Subliminal perception was defined as any word, image, or sound that is not perceived within the normal range of consciousness but that makes an impression on the mind. This phenomenon involves words or pictures that are flashed so quickly that the eye cannot transmit them to the conscious brain, or words spoken at such a volume that they evoke no conscious memory.

The purpose of the Treimer and Simonson (1988) study was to determine whether viewing a commercial videotape containing written and aural subliminal messages was more effective at producing weight loss and attitude change toward weight loss than a videotape containing the same visible message but with no subliminals. *Weight Loss Video Programming,* by Hypnovision, Inc., was the videotape selected for this study. It endorsed no specific weight loss or exercise plan and required nothing of viewers other than their willingness to change diet and exercise habits and to watch the videotape that contained subliminal messages daily for 30 days.

Participants were measured to see if changes occurred in the following areas:

1. Food and Exercise Attitude (FEAT; $r = .72$). This test of attitudes was administered at the beginning and end of the treatment period.
2. Food Intake Recall (FIR). FIR was measured by using a 1-day recall of food intake at the end of the testing period.
3. Weight and Skinfold Test (WST). WST was measured at the beginning and end of the treatment period.

It was hypothesized that participants who viewed the videotapes with subliminals would change their attitudes toward dieting, would have a healthier food intake, and would lose weight. A pretest/posttest control group design was used. Participants were volunteers who were randomly assigned to one of two treatment groups: video with subliminals or video with no subliminals. Both groups watched the 22-minute video at least 25 times in a 35-day period. Two versions of the video were prepared, one with the subliminals and one without.

Results of Study #6. The results of the study showed that FEAT scores improved for the group watching the video with the subliminals (11.8 vs. 7.37), but that the difference was not statistically significant. Results of the FIR and WST testing showed little numerical difference in the scores of participants in either group. It was concluded that subliminal messages did not appear to have an impact on either attitude or behavior.

This study is included in this review because it represents a slightly different approach than the five studies summarized previously. The results of this study effectively closed the door on research on subliminals. As a matter of fact, several months later Hypnovision, Inc., stopped marketing subliminal videos.

34.6.4 Attitudes and Instructional Media (Bednar & Levie, 1993)

Fleming and Levie proposed a series of attitude change principles in 1978 that were based on their comprehensive review of the media and attitude research. Their discussion had three categories of information. The first was based on the classic SMCR model of communication (see 4.3). (The *Source* presents a *Message* through a *Channel* to a *Receiver*). They also developed principles related to modeling of appropriate behaviors, and they concluded with principles related to creating and managing dissonance. In 1993, Fleming and Levie included an updated and revised series of attitude change principles (Bednar & Levie, 1993) that are included next.

SMCR Principles—the Source. The first series of guidelines proposed by Bednar and Levie were concerned with the source of the persuasive message and were based

on the position that "the likelihood that a receiver will accept the conclusion advocated in a given lesson is in part a function of the receiver's perception of the source's or model's credibility" (p. 286).

Principle 1.1. High-credibility sources exert more persuasive influence than low credibility sources.

Principle 1.2. Sources perceived by the receiver as attractive are more influential.

Principle 1.3. The quality and structure of the arguments in a persuasive message are more critical for credible sources than for attractive sources.

Message Principles. Next, Bednar and Levie identified principles that were concerned with the content of the persuasive message. Message principles were considered to be closely related to source-based principles.

Principle 1.4. Be sure the receiver is informed of the expertise of a high-credibility communicator.

Principle 1.5. To enhance communicator attractiveness, establish belief congruence with the receiver by arguing in favor of positions the receiver is known to hold.

Principle 1.6. Arguments are more effective if they are relevant to the receiver's needs.

Principle 1.7. Generally, two-sided arguments are slightly more effective than one-sided messages.

Principle 1.8. It is almost always advisable to state the conclusion explicitly rather than to allow receivers to draw their own conclusions.

Principle 1.9. Repetition helps, but only one or two repetitions are likely to have any additional effect.

Channel Principle. A principle related to the channel of communication was presented next by Bednar and Levie. Channels were explained to refer to both media and to senses.

Principle 1.10. No one media type has been explicitly shown to have greater persuasive effectiveness than any other media type. Face-to-face communication, however, is more effective in promoting acceptance than mediated communication, particularly in difficult cases.

Receiver Principle. Finally, Bednar and Levie proposed one principle related to the receiver of a persuasive message. They stated that is very important for the designer of the attitude change lesson to know as much as possible about the student who will receive the lesson.

Principle 1.11. It is very difficult to change the attitudes of receivers who are highly committed to their positions on an issue.

Modeling Principles. Next, Bednar and Levie proposed five principles that dealt with the use of modeling as an instructional strategy and with the credibility of the model.

Principle 2.1.   High-credibility models exert more persuasive influence than low-credibility models.

Principle 2.2.   In order for modeling to be effective, the learners must comprehend the presentation as a demonstration of specific behaviors.

Principle 2.3.   In addition to observing the model demonstrating the behavior, learners should observe the model being reinforced for that behavior.

Principle 2.4.   Role playing can have a powerful persuasive impact.

Principle 2.5.   Active participation produces more attitude change than passive reception of information.

Dissonance Principles. Last, Bednar and Levie offered six principles for creating and managing dissonance in order to produce attitude changes. Their principles were based on Festinger's (1957) cognitive dissonance theory.

Principle 3.1.   If a person can be induced to perform an important act that is counter to the person's own private attitude, attitude change may result.

Principle 3.2.   When a person is induced to perform an attitudinally discrepant act because of promise of reward or punishment, attitude change will occur only to the extent that the person feels that the magnitude of the reward or punishment was insufficient to justify the attitudinally discrepant behavior.

Principle 3.3.   A message should demonstrate the social acceptability of the desired attitude and the reward available socially for behavior consistent with the attitude.

Principle 3.4.   The message should alternate between presenting information discrepant with existing beliefs and inducing behaviors discrepant with existing attitudes to maximize dissonance.

Principle 3.5.   Attitude change lessons should be structured so that attention is paid to the cognitive (information), affective (feeling), and behavioral (acting) elements of the attitude.

Principle 3.6.   Messages should use approximations to move attitudes gradually between a current status and a desired state.

Bednar and Levie (1993) included with each principle a discussion of the literature that supported it. The Bednar and Levie principles are practical and effective, and provide considerable guidance to the designer of persuasive messages. They stated in their conclusion that "common to all of these (principles) are opportunities for free choice and control by students, opportunities for success, and lessons which present and confront alternative perspectives" (p. 302).

34.6.5 Summary

Simonson's six studies, Bednar and Levie's 22 principles, and other research reported during the 1980s and 1990s have provided considerable information about attitude change and instructional technology. The next section of this chapter will propose a set of guidelines for designing mediated messages that persuade. These guidelines are based on the research reviewed above and on the other studies that were found in the literature. It is important to note that revisiting this research area produced no startling changes from the reviews reported a decade and a half ago. Attitude change is quite predictable if mediated instruction is correctly designed. Media, at best, play a minor role in persuasion when compared to the message delivered by the medium or the methodology of instruction.

34.7 CONCLUSION: DESIGNING MEDIATED MESSAGES FOR ATTITUDE CHANGE AND THE MODEL OF CUMULATIVE EFFECT

Based on the literature reviewed above, a series of guidelines have been developed for designing mediated messages that change attitudes. These guidelines are based on Simonson's (1979) previous work in this area and have been modified in three ways. First, the recent attitude literature of social psychology was incorporated where appropriate. Second, the Iowa State University research agenda reviewed above provided guidance about techniques that seemed effective. Finally, Bednar and Levie's (1993) 22 principles for attitude change validated the proposed guidelines. Bednar and Levie's principles can be subsumed within one or more of the following guidelines.

The guidelines are organized into two groupings. The first three guidelines refer to *message design,* and the second three relate to *learner involvement.* A "model of cumulative effect" is also proposed (Fig. 34-2). This model states that for attitude change, at least one guideline should be selected from each category, and the more of the guidelines that are appropriately included in a persuasive communication, the more likely will be the development of attitude changes.

34.7.1 Message Design Guidelines

Guideline #1: *Learners are persuaded, and react favorably, when mediated situations include the discovery of useful new information about a topic.*

Most students like to learn. They react positively when relevant new information is presented to them. Inert knowledge, knowledge that can be recalled but is not spon-

Message Design Guidelines:

1. New information

2. Realistic, relevant, and technically stimulating

3. Presented in a credible manner

PLUS

Learner Involvement Guidelines:

4. Involved in planning, production, and/or delivery

5. Purposeful emotional involvement or arousal

6. Participation in postinstruction discussions or critiques

Figure 34-2.   Model of cumulative effect.

taneously used in problem solving (Whitehead, 1929), is often not perceived positively by learners. Sherwood, Kinzer, Hasselbring, and Bransford's (1987) interesting work on logarithms demonstrates this point. Most youngsters do not see the importance of learning logarithms, even though almost everyone remembers studying them. To many students, logarithms are inert knowledge. On the other hand, mathematicians, statisticians, and computer programmers do not feel this way. They use logarithms and realize their power as tools to solve problems. While no attitude study investigating attitudes toward logarithms was found in the literature, it is safe to say that those who use these powerful tools have a much more positive attitude about them than those that do not use them. To the users of logarithms, they are important tools, not inert knowledge. This is because mathematicians use logarithms to solve real-world problems.

Levonian's (1960, 1962, 1963) landmark studies support this guideline. As a critical part of Levonian's study, the audience for a film was surveyed about India. The developer of the film used this information to ascertain previous knowledge about India so that new information could be presented. This new information was included in the film to support the attitude position desired by Levonian. In other words, Levonian produced a film that presented useful and relevant information. The content of the film was selected so that it would not be knowledge for the sake of knowledge but that it would be cognitively relevant to the previous knowledge and needs of the audience.

Jouko (1972) reported related results. It was found that the less preinstruction knowledge students had about a topic, the more attitude change that was produced after an informational and persuasive lesson. There was a negative relationship between preinstruction familiarity about a topic and attitude change as a result of participating in a relevant persuasive situation.

A similar conclusion was proposed in a study by Knowlton and Hawes (1962). In this study, it was determined that knowledge about a topic was often a necessary prerequisite

for a positive attitude position toward the idea. Stated another way, new knowledge may need to be discovered by learners when attitude changes are desired (e.g., Jouko, 1972), or knowledge may need to be present for learners to have a favorable attitudinal position toward the situation in which they are involved (Knowlton & Hawes, 1962). The results of two additional studies using video reported similar findings (Thirion, 1992; Harkins & Petty, 1981).

> Guideline #2: *Attitude change is likely because of, and learners react favorably to, mediated situations involving the use of instructional technologies that are authentic, relevant to them, and technically stimulating.*

One practical technique for instruction using technology is based on the concept of anchored instruction. Anchored instruction, as described by the Vanderbilt Cognition and Technology Group (1990), uses technology to provide a realistic situation for learning. Media are used to present real-world events that become the anchor for learning. While the Vanderbilt Group's studies concentrated on the cognitive consequences of anchored instruction, there is ample anecdotal evidence that anchored instruction also influences attitudes.

Simonson et al. (1987) reported on a series study that attempted to determine if a situation where media were used to deliver messages authentically was more effective in creating attitude change than media that presented a situation less authentically. It was found that authentic mediated situations could be designed to promote desired attitudinal change.

Dimond and Simonson (1988) studied filmmakers who produced persuasive films. These filmmakers indicated that presenting authentic situations in their films was critical to the success of their persuasive messages, much more so than for informational films and videos. In other words, filmmakers indicated that the presentation of authentic, real-world situations was a critical ingredient of successful persuasive films. Filmmakers also indicated that when they produced persuasive films, they almost always "believed" in the attitudinal positions advocated in their films. Dimond and Simonson hypothesized that the act of filmmaking was an authentic situation that acted to influence the filmmaker's attitudes.

Similar results have been reported in the literature for decades. Levonian's (1960, 1962, 1963) landmark study that incorporated the use of a preproduction survey of the target audience to determine their attitudinal positions towards India was summarized above. The results of this survey were used as input for the production of a persuasive film on India. This approach made the resulting motion picture about India more authentic and realistic to the audience, and this contributed to desired attitude changes.

Authenticity and realism were examined further by Croft, Stimpson, Ross, Bray, and Breglio (1969) and Donaldson (1976). Both studies reported that authentically presented situations were most effective in producing attitude changes toward intercollegiate athletics and the disabled. Booth and Miller (1974) and Winn and Everett

(1978) investigated the authenticity provided by pictures produced in color versus those produced in black and white. They reported a relationship between the use of color, authenticity, and attitude formation.

Authentic instruction, typically instruction anchored in technically stimulating media such as the Vanderbilt Group's Jasper series (Vanderbilt, 1990), has a positive attitudinal impact on learners. The assumption is that positive predispositions, developed during participation in authentic situations, orient students to actively pursue additional learning.

Guideline #3: *Learners are positively affected when persuasive messages are encountered in mediated situations that are as authentic and credible as possible.*

Modern strategies such as situated learning are based, in part, on the concepts of the credibility and authenticity of instruction. A direct relationship exists between attitude about a situation and the individual's perception of the authenticity and relevance of the situation. For example, source credibility has been recognized as an important criteria for attitude change since the early 1950s. When mediated situations are planned, they will often be valued positively, and attitudinal positions advocated in the materials will be influential, if persuasive messages are delivered by a credible source or discovered in a credible situation. Kishler's (1950) classic study found that when the actor in a persuasive film was cast as a member of a highly credible occupational group, it was likely that the attitude changes advocated by the actor would be produced. Viewers considered the message to be authentic, so it influenced them.

A study by Carter (1990) supports this relationship between source credibility and attitude change. Results indicated that when subjects were told that the message was prepared by an expert, attitude changes tended to be more positive.

Physical attractiveness and celebrity status also contribute to source credibility. Maddux and Rogers (1980) used photographs of people with varying levels of physical attractiveness to identify the relationship between physical attractiveness and source credibility. The attractive source was evaluated as being more sociable, warm, outgoing, poised, and more credible. In a study by Mehta (1990), celebrities were rated significantly higher on source variables of trustworthiness, believability, and physical attractiveness and were found to be effective persuasive sources. This was especially true for field-dependent subjects.

Two studies reported that the use of social modeling was an effective means of promoting attitude change. Slide/tape and print materials using positive role models had a significant effect on student attitudes toward nontraditional careers (Savenye, 1990). Evans, Rozelle, Maxwell, Raines, Dill, Guthrie, Henderson, and Hill (1981) used students as real-world models in films created to deter smoking. Groups viewing the films considered their messages to be credible and authentic and exhibited less smoking behavior and indicated less intention to smoke.

These studies have looked at human sources of information delivered by media. However, one study in the literature examined the effects of credible and noncredible computer sources of information. Gahm (1986) found that persuasion increased as the authenticity of the computer message increased.

The content of media-based instructional situations is a critical variable in determining attitude formation and change. If information is presented authentically and intelligently (i.e., credibly), it is likely that it will be favorably received and will be persuasive.

34.7.2 Learner Involvement Guidelines

Guideline #4: *Learners who are involved in a situation requiring their participation in the planning, production, or delivery of media-based instruction are likely to react favorably to the situation and to the message delivered by the media.*

Involving learners in the planning, production, and delivery of mediated lessons can be considered a form of cognitive apprenticeship (see 20.4). If learners participate in a situation they feel is realistic and not fabricated, they will generally react by indicating they have a positive attitude about it. Simsek (1993) investigated the issue of audience involvement by studying the effects of learner control in computer-based cooperative learning. A comparison was made between students exercising control over pacing and sequencing and students using software that controlled the pacing and sequencing. The students with control over the lesson had a more positive attitude toward the delivery system and the subject matter. Learner control as opposed to program control was found to promote better attitudes (see 33.5).

Video is traditionally a very passive instructional medium. When merged with computer technology, video allows the learner to become involved in the instruction. In other words, it becomes more real. Dalton and Hannafin (1986) found that interactive video instruction produced significant improvements in learner attitudes when compared with computer-based instruction and video alone.

Active involvement (see 12.3.1.1) in the learning situation has been examined as a component of many research studies. For example, Erickson (1956) found that students who actually produced a film on science concepts reacted more favorably toward instruction and toward science than did students who only watched science films. Coldevin (1975) involved students in message delivery through the use of various review and summarization techniques that were a part of the instructional sequence. It was found that a short review after the TV lesson subunits produced the most favorable attitude reports from students.

Simonson (1977) conducted an experiment in which students were convinced to make counter attitudinal videotapes without realizing that attitude change was the primary purpose of the activity. The process of involving subjects in making these videotapes was found to be successful in producing significant attitude changes in subjects. In these studies, learners were solving real-world problems. They were learning by doing, and were often apprentices to more knowledgeable mentors.

It would seem that in the affective domain, the active learner perceives instruction and information more favorably than does the passive learner. Student involvement is an important technique for promoting desirable attitudinal outcomes.

Guideline #5: *Learners who experience purposeful emotional involvement or arousal during media-rich instructional situations are likely to change their attitudes in the direction advocated in the situation.*

Participating in an authentic event requires intellectual involvement that can elicit emotions in the learner. For this reason, the research seems to indicate that this guideline is extremely powerful. For example, the use of subliminal messages to arouse emotion and therefore affect attitude change was examined in two studies. In a pretest-posttest control group study on weight loss, videotapes were used that differed only in the inclusion of visual and aural subliminals. While the subliminal messages had no identifiable impact on weight loss, subjects who viewed the videotape with subliminal messages showed an improved attitude toward food and exercise (Treimer & Simonson, 1988).

Edwards (1990) used a series of 10 supraliminal and 10 subliminal slides in a study of affect-based and cognition-based attitude change. Subjects were aware of the cognitive manipulation, but not the affective manipulation (subliminal slides). Results indicated that emotion-arousing subliminal slides were effective in inducing affect-based attitude changes, and supraliminal knowledge, or information slides, were effective in inducing cognition-based attitude changes.

Janis and Feshbach (1953) presented a slide/audiotape program on the effects of poor dental hygiene to high school students. The intensity of a fear-arousing appeal in three versions of the presentation were varied to determine the most influential delivery technique. All three methods were successful in producing aroused, affective reactions in the students. However, it was found that a minimal fear-arousing appeal was most successful in modifying attitudes because the stronger versions left students in a state of tension that was not alleviated by the remedies offered during the slide show.

Janis and Feshbach concluded that strong, fear-producing appeals were not as effective in changing attitudes as were more moderate appeals, because the audience became motivated to ignore the importance of the threat to reduce the tension they felt. The more-frightening message was not as authentic, and therefore was not as effective. It was found that only those fear-provoking messages that were considered to be authentic influenced attitudes. The more dramatic and fearsome presentations were not considered to be realistic or authentic, and were less effective.

Rogers (1973) reported on a study that supported this position. Public-health films dealing with cigarette smoking, safe driving, and venereal disease were tested in three different studies. It was found that the more noxious a film was, the more fear was aroused in viewers. However, it was

also reported that these fear-arousing films were most effective in changing attitudes when preventatives or statements of probability of exposure to the malady discussed in the film were included as part of the motion picture.

Another study addressing the relationship between fear-arousing videos and attitude change was conducted by Berry and Simonson (1983). Subjects viewed either a fear-provoking persuasive video or a fear-provoking video with remedies. The message was about smoking. Experimental treatments significantly influenced subjects' attitudes as compared to subjects in the control group, and the more authentic situations presented by the videos were considered to be the most effective at changing attitudes.

The studies supporting guideline #5 indicate also that viewers' participation in the learning process is important when attitudinal outcomes are desired. In these cases, involvement was emotional rather than behavioral. It would seem that learner involvement in a situation is a powerful technique if attitudinal outcomes are to be important consequences of instruction.

Guideline #6: *Learners who participate in situations where technology-based instructional situations are openly critiqued in an attitudinally appropriate way are likely to develop favorable attitudes toward the situations and toward the message.*

The learner who is actively involved in what is perceived as a real event is more likely to react in an attitudinally positive way to the situation and to instruction. Johnson (1989) found that the use of discussion questions following a mediated situation resulted in significant attitude changes toward careers with regard to learners' confidence in their ability to be successful.

Follow-up discussions, a powerful technique for promoting positive attitudes, were evaluated by several researchers (Howard, 1990). Follow-ups usually involved learners in an analysis or critique of the instructional situation and message presented. Allison (1966) found that significant attitude changes occurred only when postviewing discussions were held. Fay (1974) reported similar findings in a study that used follow-ups to a film on the problems of the handicapped and the need for barrier-free buildings. Attitudes toward continuing education were significantly altered after classroom teachers saw a film and participated in a discussion on the subject (Burrichter, 1968). These studies demonstrated the importance of learner involvement in authentic situations which, in these cases, were discussion activities. The researchers carefully constructed the learning situations to make sure the students felt that their opinions were important.

Lamb (1987) found that including social interaction in the form of postinstruction discussion was an effective instructional technique to promote changes in attitudes toward wearing seat belts. This study examined the effects of three learner involvement strategies incorporated into a persuasive, computer-based instruction lesson. The situations that included postinstruction discussions were found to be the most effective in promoting attitude change.

The study also found that the absence of emotional involvement by the learner toward the message was shown to be detrimental to attitude change. Students stated that they considered the discussion to be real (i.e., authentic), and that this was important to them.

These six guidelines can be used singly or in combination to design mediated instructional situations that are likely to change attitudes. However, it is hypothesized that there is likely to be a cumulative effect that will take place if more than one technique from each category is used. Certainly, one media design guideline and one learner involvement guideline should be considered as part of any persuasive instructional strategy (Fig. 34-2).

34.7.3 Summary

The "model of cumulative effect" is based on the principle that a persuasive message must be designed effectively. First, *new information* should be presented (guideline #1). Next, the message should be *realistic, relevant, and stimulating* (guideline #2). Finally, a persuasive message should be delivered in as *credible* a manner as possible (guideline #3).

The effectiveness of persuasive messages is improved if the target of the message, the learner, is involved actively, cognitively, and emotionally. First, learners who are involved in the *planning, production, or delivery* of persuasive messages are more likely to be influenced (guideline #4). *Purposefully emotional involvement* of the learner is an extremely powerful attitude change activity. The aroused learner is the involved learner (guideline #5). Finally, the use of *postinstruction activities* that relate to the intent of the persuasive message is extremely powerful and may produce attitude changes even if other guidelines are improperly or inadequately followed (guideline #6).

Certainly, these guidelines and the model of cumulative effect must now be offered to the researchers of the discipline for further validation. However, based on current evidence, it is safe to assume that attitudes of learners can be changed if mediated instructional events incorporate as many of the activities referred to in the guidelines as possible.

Attitudes are predispositions to respond, and media are primarily carriers of information. There is no best medium for attitude change. However, there probably are best situations involving media that will maximize the likelihood of developing desirable attitudes in learners. Critically applying the general guidelines listed above will promote the discovery of attitudinal positions by students that are likely to contribute to healthy, positive learning situations.

Companion none is like
Unto the mind alone;
For many have been harmed by speech,
Through thinking, few or none.

Of a Contented Mind, 1557
Sir Thomas Vaux

REFERENCES

Abelson, R. & Rosenberg, M. (1958). Symbolic psychologic: a model of attitudinal cognition. *Behavioral Science 3*, 1–13.

Ajzen, I. (1991). The theory of planned behavior. *Organizational Behavior and Human Decision Processes 50*, 179–211.

Allen, W. (1975). Intellectual abilities and instructional media design. *AV Communication Review 23*, 139–70.

Allison, R.W. (1966). The effect of three methods of treating motivational films upon attitudes of fourth, fifth, and sixth grade students toward science, scientists, and scientific careers (doctoral dissertation, Pennsylvania State University, 1966). *Dissertation Abstracts 28*, 994.

Allport, G. (1935). Attitudes. *In* C. Murchison, ed. *Handbook of social psychology*, 798–844. Worcester, MA: Clark University Press.

Anastasi, A. (1968). *Psychological testing*. New York: Macmillan.

Baer, D. (1966). Smoking, attitude, behavior, and beliefs of college males. *The Journal of Social Psychology 11*, 65–78.

Bednar, A. & Levie, H. (1993). Attitude-change principles. *In* M. Fleming & H. Levie, eds. *Instructional message design*, 283–304. Englewood Cliffs, NJ: Educational Technology.

Bem, D. (1967). Self-perception: an alternative interpretation of cognitive dissonance phenomena. *Psychological Review 74*, 183–200.

Berry, T. & Simonson, M.R. (1983, Jan.). *Use of fear in persuasive messages.* Paper presented at the 1983 Annual Convention of the Association for Educational Communication and Technology, New Orleans, LA.

Booth, G.D. & Miller, H.R. (1974). Effectiveness of monochrome and color presentations in facilitating affective learning. *AV Communication Review 22*, 409–22.

Buros, O. (1978). *The eighth mental measurement yearbook.* Highland Park, NJ: Gryphon.

Burrichter, A.W. (1968). *A study of elementary public school personnel attitudes toward continuing education in selected communities in Wyoming: an experiment in changing adult attitudes and concepts.* Unpublished doctoral dissertation, University of Wyoming.

Campbell, D. & Stanley, J. (1963). Experimental and quasi-experimental designs for research on teaching. *In* N. Gage, ed. *Handbook of research on teaching*. Chicago, IL: Rand McNally.

Carter, R.W. (1990). Effects of expertise and issue involvement on rehabilitation counselors in the selection of computer technology for their clients. *Dissertation Abstracts International 51*, 1545B.

Chaiken, S. & Egly, A. (1976). Communication modality as a determinant of message persuasiveness and message comprehensibility. *Journal of Personality and Social Psychology 34*, 605–14.

Clark, R. (1983). Reconsidering research on learning from media. *Review of Educational Research 53*(4), 445–59.

— (1994). Media will never influence learning. *Educational Technology Research and Development 42*(2), 21–29.

Coldevin, G.O. (1975). Spaced, massed, and summary as review strategies for ITV production. *AV Communication Review 23*, 289–303.

Cook, S. (1979). *Persuasive messages with varying amounts of stimuli and their influence on the attitude changes of learners.* Unpublished masters thesis, Iowa State University, Ames, IA.

Croft, R.G., Stimpson, D.V., Ross, W.L., Bray, R.M.

& Breglio, V.J. (1969). Comparison of attitude changes elicited by live and videotape classroom presentation. *AV Communication Review 17,* 315–21.

Cronbach, L. (1970). Test validation. *In* R. Thorndike, ed. *Educational measurement.* Washington, DC: American Council on Education.

Dale, E. (1946). *Audiovisual methods in teaching.* New York: Dryden.

Dalton, D. & Hannafin, M.J. (1986). The effects of video-only, CAI only, and interactive video instructional systems on learner performance and attitude: an exploratory study. *In* M.R. Simonson, ed. *Proceedings of the Annual Convention of the Association for Educational Communication and Technology,* 154–62.

Day, M. (1964). An eye movement phenomenon relating to attention, thought, and anxiety. *Perceptual and Motor Skills 19,* 443–46.

Denzin, N. & Lincoln, Y., eds. (1994). *Handbook of qualitative research.* Thousand Oaks, CA: Sage.

Dimond, P. & Simonson, M.R. (1988). Film-makers and persuasive films: a study to determine how persuasive films are produced. *In* M.R. Simonson, ed. *Proceedings of the Annual Convention of the Association for Educational Communication and Technology,* 200–12.

Donaldson, J. (1976). Channel variations and effects on attitudes toward physically disabled individuals. *AV Communication Review 24,* 135–44.

Eagly, A. & Chaiken, S. (1993). *The psychology of attitudes.* Fort Worth, TX: Harcourt, Brace.

Edwards, K. (1990). The interplay of affect and cognition in attitude formation and change. *Journal of Personality and Social Psychology 59* (2), 202–16.

Erickson, C.W.H. (1956). Teaching general science through film production. *AV Communication Review 4,* 268–78.

Evans, R.I., Rozelle, R.M., Maxwell, S.E., Raines, B.E., Dill, C.A., Guthrie, T.J., Henderson, A.H. & Hill, P.C. (1981). Social modeling films to deter smoking in adolescents: results of a three-year field investigation. *Journal of Applied Psychology 66*(4), 399–414.

Fay, F.A. (1974). Effects of a film, a discussion group, and a role playing experience on architecture student's attitudes, behavioral intentions, and actual behavior toward barrier free design (doctoral dissertation, University of Illinois, 1974). *Dissertation Abstracts International, 34,* 6445A.

Fenneman, G.C. (1973). *The validity of previous experience, attitude, and attitude toward mathematics as predictors of achievement in freshman mathematics at Wartburg College.* Unpublished doctoral dissertation, University of Northern Colorado.

Ferguson, D. (1971). *Statistical analysis in psychology and education.* New York: McGraw-Hill.

Festinger, L. (1957). *A theory of cognitive dissonance.* Stanford, CA: Stanford University Press.

— & Carlsmith, J. (1959). Cognitive consequences of forced compliance. *Journal of Abnormal and Social Psychology 58,* 203–10.

Fishbein, M. & Ajzen, I. (1975). *Belief, attitude, intention, and behavior: an introduction to theory and research.* Reading, MA: Addison-Wesley.

Fleming, M. & Levie, W. (1978). *Instructional message design.* Englewood Cliffs, NJ: Educational Technology.

— & — (1993). *Instructional message design,* 2d ed. Engle-wood Cliffs, NJ: Educational Technology.

Gahm, G.A. (1986). The effects of computers, source salience and credibility on persuasion. *Dissertation Abstracts International 46,* 4063B.

Greenwald, A.G. (1965). Behavior change following a persuasive communication. *Journal of Personality 33,* 370–91.

— (1966). Effects of prior commitment on behavior change after a persuasive communication. *Public Opinion Quarterly 29,* 595–601.

Harkins, S.G. & Petty, R.E. (1981). Effects of source magnification of cognitive effort on attitudes: an information-processing view. *Journal of Personality and Social Psychology 40*(3), 401–13.

Heider, F. (1958). *The psychology of interpersonal relations.* New York: Wiley.

Henerson, M., Morris, L. & Fitz-Gibbon, C. (1987). *How to measure attitudes.* Beverly Hills, CA: Sage.

Himmelfarb, S. & Eagly, A.H. (1974). *Readings in attitude change.* New York: Wiley.

Hovland, C., Janis, I. & Kelley, H. (1953). *Communication and persuasion.* New Haven, CT: Yale University Press.

Howard, D.J. (1990). Rhetorical question effects on message processing and persuasion: the role of information availability and the elicitation of judgment. *Journal of Experimental Social Psychology 26,* 217–39.

Insko, C.A. (1967). *Theories of attitude change.* New York: Appleton-Century-Crofts.

Janis, I.L. & Feshbach, S. (1953). Effects of fear-arousing communications. *Journal of Abnormal and Social Psychology 48,* 78–92.

Johnson, J. (1989). Effects of successful female role models on young women's attitudes toward traditionally male careers. *In* M.R. Simonson, ed. *Proceedings of the Annual Convention of the Association for Educational Communication and Technology.*

Jouko, C. (1972). *The effect of directive teaching materials on the affective learning of pupils.* Jyvaskyla. Finland: Institute for Educational Research, Report 139.

Katz, D. (1960). The functional approach to the study of attitudes. *Public Opinion Quarterly 24,* 163–204.

Kelman, H. (1958). Compliance, identification, and internalization: the process of attitude change. *Journal of Conflict Resolution 2,* 51–60.

Kiesler, C.A., Collins, B.E. & Miller, N. (1969). *Attitude change.* New York: Wiley.

Kishler, J.P. (1950).*The effects of prestige and identification factors on attitude restructuring and learning from sound films.* University Park, PA: The Pennsylvania State University. (ERIC Document Reproduction Service No. ED 053 568.)

Kloock, T. (1981). *Relationship of persuasively mediated instruction and learner characteristics.* Unpublished masters thesis, Iowa State University, Ames, IA.

Knowlton, J. & Hawes, E. (1962). Attitude: helpful predictor of audiovisual usage? *AV Communication Review 10,* 147–57.

Lamb, A.S. (1987). Persuasion and computer-based instruction: the impact of various involvement strategies in a computer-based instruction lesson on the attitude change of college students toward the use of seat belts. *Dissertation Abstracts International 49,* 238A.

Levonian, E. (1960). Development of an audience-tailored film. *AV Communication Review 8*(1), 62–68.

— (1962). The use of film in opinion measurement. *AV Communication Review 10*(4), 250–54.

— (1963). Opinion change as mediated by an audience-tailored film. *AV Communication Review 11*(4), 104–13.

Levy, J. (1973). *Factors related to attitudes and student achievement under a high school foreign language contingency contract.* Unpublished doctoral dissertation, University of Southern California.

Maddux, J.E. & Rogers, R.W. (1980). Effects of source expertness, physical attractiveness, and supporting arguments on persuasion: a case of brains over beauty. *Journal of Personality and Social Psychology 39*(2), 235–44.

Maurer, M. (1983). *Development and validation of a measure of computer anxiety.* Unpublished masters thesis, Iowa State University, Ames, IA.

— & Simonson, M. (1993-1994). The reduction of computer anxiety: its relation to relaxation training, previous computer coursework, achievement, and need for cognition. *Journal of Research on Computers in Education 26,* 205–19.

McGuire, W. (1964). Inducing resistance to persuasion. *In* L. Berkowitz, ed. *Advances in experimental social psychology,* Vol. 1. New York: Academic.

McLeod, D., McCormack, R., Carpenter, T. & Skvarcius, R. (1978). Cognitive style and mathematics learning. *Journal of Research in Mathematics Teaching 9,* 163–74.

Mehta, A. (1990). Celebrity advertising: a cognitive response approach. *Dissertation Abstracts International 51,* 1311A.

Newcomb, T. (1961). *The acquaintance process.* New York: Holt.

O'Keefe, D. (1990). *Persuasion.* Newbury Park, CA: Sage.

Ornstein, R. (1977). *The psychology of consciousness,* 2d ed. New York: Harcourt, Brace.

Perry, G.A. & Kopperman, N. (1973). *A better chance-evaluation of student attitudes and academic performance, 1964–1972.* Boston, MA: A Better Chance.

Rogers, R.W. (1973). *An analysis of fear appeals and attitude change.* Final report, University of South Carolina, Grant No. 1 RO3 MH2215701 MSM, National Institute of Mental Health.

Rose, E. (1963). Motion picture research and the art of the film-maker. *Journal of the University Film Association 15*(2), 8–11.

Rosenberg, M. (1956). Cognitive structure and attitudinal affect. *Journal of Abnormal and Social Psychology 53,* 367–72.

Savenye, W.C. (1990). Role models and student attitudes toward nontraditional careers. *Educational Technology, Research and Development 38*(3), 5–13.

Schuman, H. & Johnson, M. (1976). Attitudes and behavior. *Annual Review of Sociology 2,* 161–207.

Sherif, M. & Hovland, C. (1961). *Social judgment: assimilation and contrast effects in communication and attitude change.* New Haven, CT: Yale University Press.

Sherif, C., Sherif, M. & Nebergall, R. (1965). *Attitude and attitude change.* Philadelphia, PA: Saunders.

Sherwood, R., Kinzer, C., Hasselbring, T. & Bransford, J. (1987). Macro-contexts for learning: initial findings and issues. *Journal of Applied Cognition 1,* 93–108.

Simonson, M. (1977). Attitude change and achievement: dissonance theory in education. *Journal of Educational Research 70*(3), 163–69.

— (1978). Liking and learning go hand-in-hand. *Audiovisual Instruction 23*(3), 18–20.

— (1979). Designing instruction for attitudinal outcomes.

Journal of Instructional Development 2(3), 15–19.

— (1979a). Media and attitudes: an annotated bibliography of selected research, Part II. *Educational Communication and Technology Journal 28*(1), 47–61.

— (1980). Instructional media, attitude formation and change: a critical review of the literature, *In* M. Simonson, ed. *Proceedings of Selected Research Papers, Denver, CO,* 1980, 473–526.

— (1983). Designing instructional media for attitudinal outcomes. *In* J. Wilson, ed. *Materials for teaching adults: selection, development, and use.* San Francisco, CA: Jossey-Bass.

— (1984). Media and persuasive messages. *Instructional Innovator 29*(2), 23–24, 48.

— (1985). Persuasive films: a study of techniques used to change attitudes. *Journal of Teaching and Learning Technologies 1*(2), 39–48.

—, Aegerter, R., Berry, T., Kloock, T. & Stone, R. (1987). Four studies dealing with mediated persuasive messages, attitude, and learning styles. *Educational Communications and Technology Journal 35*(1), 31–41.

— & Bullard, J. (1978). Influence of student expectations and student sex on predicting academic success. Paper presented at the meeting of the Midwest Educational Research Association, Chicago, IL. *Resources in Education,* ERIC Document Reproduction Service No. 114049.

— & Burch G. (1977). Media influence on affective learning: a review of the literature. Paper presented at the annual convention of the Association for Educational Communications and Technology, Miami Beach, FL.

— & Maushak, N. (1994, 1995). Situated learning, instructional technology, and attitude change. *In* H. McLellan, ed. *Perspectives on situated learning.* Englewood Cliffs, NJ: Educational Technology.

—, Thies, P. & Burch, G. (1979). Media and attitudes: a bibliography, Part I: articles published in *AV Communication Review. Educational Communications and Technology Journal 27*(3), 217–36.

Simsek, A. (1993). The effects of learner control and group composition in computer-based cooperative learning. *In* M.R. Simonson, ed. *Proceedings of the Annual Convention of the Association for Educational Communication and Technology,* 953–90.

Smith, M.J. (1982). *Persuasion and human action.* Belmont, CA: Wadsworth.

Spielberger, C. (1970). *In* R. Gorsuch & R. Lushene, eds. *STAI manual.* Palo Alto, CA: Consulting Psychologists.

Talmage, H. (1978). Statistics as a tool for educational practitioners. Berkeley, CA: McCutchan.

Thirion, E.M. (1992). Attitude and behavior change of a group of young masculine road-users. *Masters Abstracts 31,* 440.

Thomas, W.I. & Znaniecki, F. (1918). *The Polish peasant in Europe and America.* Boston, MA: Badger.

Treimer, M. & Simonson, M. (1988). Subliminal messages, persuasion, and behavior change. *Journal of Social Psychology 128*(4), 563–65.

Vanderbilt Cognition and Technology Group. (1990, Aug.–Sep.). Anchored instruction and its relationship to situated learning. *Educational Researcher,* 2–10.

Whitehead, A.N. (1929). The aims of education. New York: Macmillan.

Wicker, A. (1969). Attitude versus actions: the relationship of verbal and overt behavioral responses to attitude objects. *Journal of Social Issues 25*(4), 41–78.

Winn, W. & Everett, R. (1978). *Differences in the affective meaning of color and black and white pictures.* Paper presented at the Annual Convention of the Association for Educational Communication and Technology.

Witkin, H., Oltman, P. & Raskin, E. (1971). *The embedded figures test manual.* Palo Alto, CA: Consulting Psychologists.

Wood, W. (1982). Retrieval of attitude-relevant information from memory: effects on susceptibility to persuasion and on intrinsic motivation. *Journal of Personality and Social Psychology 42*, 246–59.

Yucker, H., Block, J. & Young, J. (1970). *The measurement of attitudes towards disabled persons (ATDP).* Albertson, NY: Human Resources Center.

Zimbardo, P. & Leippe, M. (1991). *The psychology of attitude change and social influence.* Philadelphia, PA: Temple University Press.

35. COOPERATION AND THE USE OF TECHNOLOGY

David W. Johnson   Roger T. Johnson

UNIVERSITY OF MINNESOTA

35.1 TECHNOLOGY IN THE CLASSROOM

We live in an age that needs people who can work collaboratively designing, using, and maintaining the tools of technology. These tools pervade every aspect of our lives, from automatic teller machines, to bar codes on the things we buy, to copy machines, computers, and fax machines. Our society has moved from manufacturing-based work on which individuals generally competed or were independent from each other to information and technological-rich work on which individuals generally work in teams. Technology and teamwork will continuously play a larger role in our lives. Children, adolescents, and young adults have no choice but to develop and increase their technological and teamwork literacy. There is no better place for them to start than in school. Learning in cooperative groups while utilizing the tools of technology should occur in all grade levels and subject areas.

Because the nature of technology used by a society influences what the society is and becomes, individuals who do not become technologically literate will be left behind. Influences of a technology include the nature of the medium, the way the medium extends human senses, and the type of cognitive processing required by the medium. Harold Adam Innis (1964, 1972) proposed that media biased towards lasting a long time, such as stone hieroglyphics, lead to small, stable societies because stone was difficult to edit and rewrite and was too heavy to distribute over great distances. In contrast, media biased toward traveling easily across distances, such as papyrus, enabled the Romans to build and run a large empire. Marshall McLuhan (1964) believed that the way the media technology balances the senses creates its own form of thinking and communicating and eventually alters the balance of human senses. He believed that oral communication makes hearing dominant and thought simultaneous and circular. Written communication makes sight dominant, and thought may be linear (one thing follows another), rational (cause and effect), and abstract. Electronic technology tends to recreate the village on a global scale through instantaneous and simultaneous communication in which physical distance between people becomes irrelevant. On a more negative note, Neil Postman (1985) expressed fears that our ability to reason with rigor and self-discipline is being eroded as fewer people read systematically and more people watch and listen to electronic media. Their thinking may become more reactive and impressionistic.

Given the pervasive and powerful effects media technologies can have on the nature of society and the thinking and communicating of its members, there can be little doubt that technology will increasingly be utilized in instructional situations. In the past, however, teachers and schools have been very slow in adopting new technologies and very quick in discontinuing its use (Cuban, 1986). Cuban documents a cyclic pattern in which: (a) the potential of a technology leads to fervent claims and promises by advocates, (b) its utility is demonstrated by academic research in a small set of classrooms rich with human and technical support, (c) teachers who have little or no resources adopt the technology and are frustrated by their failure to make it work, and (d) the use of the new technology gradually declines.

The failure of schools to adopt available instructional technologies and to maintain (let alone continuously improve) their use may be at least in part due to two barriers: (a) the individual assumption underlying most hardware and software development and (b) the failure to utilize cooperation learning as an inherent part of using instructional technologies. The purpose of this chapter is to clarify the interdependence between instructional technologies and cooperation among students in using the technologies as an inherent part of classroom life. In order to understand how cooperative learning may be used with instructional technologies, the nature of cooperative learning needs to be defined, the theoretical foundations on which it is based need to be clarified, the research validating its use needs to be reviewed, distinctions between cooperative learning and other types of instructional groups needs to be made, and

1017

the basic elements that make cooperation work must be defined. At that point, the interrelationships between cooperative learning and technology-assisted instruction can be noted and their complementary strengths delineated. The future of technology-assisted cooperative learning can then be discussed.

35.2 THE INDIVIDUAL ASSUMPTION

Many hardware and software designers (as well as teachers) automatically assume that all technology-assisted instruction should be structured individualistically. One student to a computer has been the usual assumption, and computer programs have been written accordingly. A strength of the computer and interactive technologies has been perceived to be their apparent ability to deliver individualized instruction. Tailoring instruction to each student's personal learning needs has strong intuitive appeal, as students differ in aptitude, learning style, personality characteristics, and motivation. The ability of designers to adapt instruction sequences to the cognitive and affective needs of each learner, however, is limited by three factors:

1. Substantial variation exists in types of learning styles and personality traits and, although many of them are sometimes correlated with achievement, few have been shown to predict achievement consistently.
2. Little agreement exists on how to translate differences in learning styles and personal traits into instructional prescriptions. The only design rule widely accepted is that students should control the flow of information.
3. Creating algorithms to adapt instruction to individual needs and designing and producing multiple versions of lessons are both time consuming and expensive.

Thus, the potential for individualized instruction may be limited due to the difficulties associated with identifying individual differences and translating them into instructional prescriptions. In addition, individualized instruction has several shortcomings:

1. Individual work isolates students, and working alone for long periods may lower personal motivation by increasing boredom, frustration, anxiety, and the perception that learning is impersonal.
2. Individual instruction limits the resources and the technology available for individual effort. The support and encouragement of peers and the cognitive benefits associated with explaining to peers and developing shared mental models is lost.
3. Individualized instruction greatly increases development and hardware costs. A workstation is required for each learner, which entails considerable hardware expense. Substantial development and software expenses are required when lessons have to be designed to personalize instruction and to adapt the instructional sequence to individual processing requirements.

The difficulties associated with identifying and accommodating individual needs severely limit designers' ability to individualize instruction. The shortcomings of individualized instruction call into question the wisdom of designing individualized programs. Despite these problems, however, virtually all instructional software is designed, developed, and marketed for individual use.

In his description of the implementation of the Apple Classrooms of Tomorrow, Dwyer (1994) notes that the cooperative, task-related interaction among students was spontaneous and more extensive than in traditional classrooms, with students interacting with one another while working at computers, spontaneously helping each other, showing curiosity about each other's activities, wanting to share what they had just learned to do, working together to build multimedia presentations about diverse topics, and combining their group's work into whole-class, interdisciplinary projects. The spontaneous cooperation often reported around technology both casts doubt on the individual assumption made by hardware and software designers and points toward the use of cooperative learning in technology-assisted instruction. To use cooperative learning, however, educators must understand its nature.

35.3 THE NATURE OF COOPERATIVE LEARNING

The best way to conduct technology-assisted instruction is to embed it in cooperative learning. To understand technology-assisted cooperative learning, you must understand the nature of cooperative learning, the theoretical foundations on which it is based, the research validating its use, the distinctions between cooperative learning and other types of instructional groups, and the basic elements that make cooperation work.

Cooperation is working together to accomplish shared goals (Johnson & Johnson, 1989). Within cooperative activities, individuals seek outcomes that are beneficial to themselves and beneficial to all other group members. *Cooperative learning* is the instructional use of small groups so that students work together to maximize their own and each other's learning. In cooperative-learning situations, there is a positive interdependence among students' goal attainments; students perceive that they can reach their learning goals if and only if the other students in the learning group also reach their goals (Deutsch, 1962; Johnson & Johnson, 1989). There are four types of cooperative learning that may be used in combination with instructional technology: formal cooperative learning, informal cooperative learning, cooperative base groups, and academic controversy.

Formal cooperative learning is students working together, for one class period to several weeks, to achieve shared learning goals and complete jointly specific tasks and assignments—such as decision making or problem solving, completing a curriculum unit, writing a report, conducting a survey or experiment, or reading a chapter or reference book, learning vocabulary, or answering questions at the end of the chapter (Johnson, Johnson & Holubec, 1992, 1993). Any course requirement or assignment may be reformulated to be cooperative. In formal cooperative learning groups, teachers:

1. *Specify the objectives for the lesson.* In every lesson there should be an academic objective specifying the concepts and strategies to be learned and a social skills objective specifying the interpersonal or small-group skill to be used and mastered during the lesson.

2. *Make a number of preinstructional decisions.* A teacher has to decide on the size of groups, the method of assigning students to groups, the roles students will be assigned, the materials needed to conduct the lesson, and the way the room will be arranged.

3. *Explain the task and the positive interdependence.* A teacher clearly defines the assignment, teaches the required concepts and strategies, specifies the positive interdependence and individual accountability, gives the criteria for success, and explains the expected social skills to be engaged in.

4. *Monitor students' learning and intervene within the groups to provide task assistance or to increase students' interpersonal and group skills.* A teacher systematically observes and collects data on each group as it works. When assistance is needed, the teacher intervenes to assist students in completing the task accurately and in working together effectively.

5. *Evaluate students' learning and help students process how well their groups functioned.* Students' learning is carefully assessed and student performances are evaluated. Members of the learning groups then process how effectively they have been working together.

Informal cooperative learning consists of having students work together to achieve a joint learning goal in temporary, ad-hoc groups that last from a few minutes to one class period (Johnson, Johnson & Holubec, 1992; Johnson, Johnson & Smith, 1991). During a lecture, demonstration, or film, ad-hoc groups can be used to focus student attention on the material to be learned, set a mood conducive to learning, help set expectations as to what will be covered in a class session, ensure that students cognitively process the material being taught, and provide closure to an instructional session. During direct teaching, the instructional challenge for the teacher is to ensure that students do the intellectual work of organizing material, explaining it, summarizing it, and integrating it into existing conceptual structures. Informal cooperative learning groups are often organized so that students engage in 3- to 5-minute *focused discussions* before and after a lecture, and 2- to 3-minute *turn-to-your-partner* discussions interspersed throughout a lecture.

Cooperative base groups are long-term, heterogeneous cooperative learning groups with stable membership

(Johnson, Johnson & Holubec, 1992; Johnson, Johnson & Smith, 1991). *The purposes of the base group are to give the support, help, encouragement, and assistance each member needs to make academic progress (attend class, complete all assignments, learn) and develop cognitively and socially in healthy ways.* Base groups meet daily in elementary school and twice a week in secondary school (or whenever the class meets). They are permanent (lasting from one to several years) and provide the long-term caring peer relationships necessary to influence members consistently to work hard in school. They formally meet to discuss the academic progress of each member, provide help and assistance to each other, and verify that each member is completing assignments and progressing satisfactorily through the academic program. Base groups may also be responsible for letting absent group members know what went on in class when they miss a session. Informally, members interact every day within and between classes, discussing assignments and helping each other with homework. The use of base groups tends to improve attendance, personalizes the work required and the school experience, and improve the quality and quantity of learning. The larger the class or school and the more complex and difficult the subject matter, the more important it is to have base groups. Base groups are also helpful in structuring homerooms and when a teacher meets with a number of advisors.

When students work together in cooperative groups, they will often disagree and argue with each other. Using intellectual conflicts for instructional purposes is one of the most dynamic and involving, yet least-used, teaching strategies. The fourth type of cooperative learning is *academic controversy,* which exists when one student's ideas, information, conclusions, theories, and opinions are incompatible with those of another, and the two seek to reach an agreement (Johnson & Johnson, 1992). Teachers structure academic controversies by choosing an important intellectual issue, assigning students to groups of four, dividing the group into two pairs, and assigning one pair the "pro" position and the other pair a "con" position. Students then follow the five-step controversy procedure of (a) preparing the best case possible for their assigned position, (b) persuasively presenting the best case possible for their position to the opposing pair, (c) having an open discussion in which the two sides argue forcefully and persuasively for their position while subjecting the opposing position to critical analysis, (d) reversing perspectives, and (e) dropping all advocacy coming to a consensus as to their best reasoned judgment about the issue.

In all four types of cooperative learning, repetitive lessons can be scripted so they become classroom routines. *Cooperative learning scripts* are standard cooperative procedures for conducting generic, repetitive lessons and managing classroom routines (Johnson, Johnson & Holubec, 1993). They are used to organize course routines and generic lessons that occur repeatedly. These repetitive cooperative lessons provide a base on which the cooperative classroom may be built. Some examples are checking homework, preparing for and reviewing a test, drill-review of facts and events, reading of textbooks and reference materials, writing reports and essays, giving presentations, learning vocabulary, learning concepts, doing projects such as surveys, and problem solving. Each of these instructional activities may be done cooperatively and, once planned and conducted several times, will become automatic activities in the classroom. They may also be used in combination to form an overall lesson.

Cooperative learning is being used throughout preschools, elementary and secondary schools, colleges, and adult education programs because of its blend of theory, research, and practice. It is not a strictly American educational phenomenon; it is touted from Finland to New Zealand, from Israel to Japan. What underlies cooperative learning's popularity is that it is based on well-formulated theories that have been validated by numerous research studies.

35.4 THEORETICAL FOUNDATIONS OF COOPERATIVE LEARNING

There are at least three general theoretical perspectives that have guided research on cooperative learning: cognitive-developmental, behavioral, and social interdependence. The *cognitive-developmental perspective* is largely based on the theories of Piaget and Vygotsky. The work of Piaget and related theorists is based on the premise that when individuals cooperate on the environment, sociocognitive conflict occurs that creates cognitive disequilibrium, which in turn stimulates perspective-taking ability and cognitive development. The work of Vygotsky and related theorists is based on the premise that knowledge is social, constructed from cooperative efforts to learn, understand, and solve problems. The *behavioral learning theory perspective* focuses on the impact of group reinforcers and rewards on learning. Skinner focused on group contingencies; Bandura focused on imitation; and Homans, as well as Thibaut and Kelley, focused on the balance of rewards and costs in social exchange among interdependent individuals. While the cognitive-developmental and behavioral theoretical orientations have their followings, by far the theory dealing with cooperation that has generated the most research is *social interdependence theory*.

Social interdependence exists when individuals share common goals (see 6.4), and each person's success is affected by the actions of the others (Deutsch, 1962; Johnson & Johnson, 1989). It may be differentiated from *social dependence* (i.e., the outcomes of one person are affected by the actions of a second person, but not vice versa) and *social independence* (i.e., individuals' outcomes are unaffected by each other's actions). There are two types of social interdependence: cooperative and competitive. The absence of social interdependence and dependence results in individualistic efforts. Social interdependence is one of the most fundamental and ubiquitous aspects of being a human being and it affects all aspects of our lives (Deutsch, 1949, 1962).

Theorizing on *social interdependence* began in the early 1900s, when one of the founders of the Gestalt School of Psychology (see 5.2.2), Kurt Koffka, proposed that groups were dynamic wholes in which the interdependence among members could vary. One of his colleagues, Kurt Lewin, refined Koffka's notions in the 1920s and 1930s while stating that: (a) The essence of a group is the interdependence among members (created by common goals), which results in the group's being a "dynamic whole," so that a change in the state of any member or subgroup changes the state of any other member or subgroup; and (b) an intrinsic state of tension within group members motivates movement toward the accomplishment of the desired common goals. For interdependence to exist, there must be more than one person or entity involved, and the persons or entities must have impact on each other in that a change in the state of one causes a change in the state of the others. From the work of Lewin's students and colleagues, such as Ovisankian, Lissner, Mahler, and Lewis, it may be concluded that it is the drive for goal accomplishment that motivates cooperative and competitive behavior.

In the late 1940s, one of Lewin's graduate students, Morton Deutsch, extended Lewin's reasoning about social interdependence and formulated a theory of cooperation and competition (Deutsch, 1949, 1962). Deutsch conceptualized three types of social interdependence: positive, negative, and none. Deutsch's basic premise was that the type of interdependence structured in a situation determines how individuals interact with each other, which, in turn, largely determines outcomes. Positive interdependence tends to result in promotive interaction; negative interdependence tends to result in oppositional or contrient interaction; and no interdependence results in an absence of interaction. Depending on whether individuals promote or obstruct each other's goal accomplishments, there is substitutability, cathexis, and inducibility. The relationships between the type of social interdependence and the interaction pattern it elicits is assumed to be bidirectional. Each may cause the other. Deutsch's theory has served as a major conceptual structure for this area of inquiry for the past 45 years.

35.5 RESEARCH ON SOCIAL INTERDEPENDENCE

The research on social interdependence is notable for the sheer amount of work done, the long history of the work, the wide variety of dependent variables examined, the generalizability and external validity of the work, and the sophistication of the research reviews.

A great deal of research on social interdependence has been conducted over 10 decades. Between 1898 and 1989, over 550 experimental and 100 correlational studies were conducted on social interdependence (see Johnson & Johnson, 1989, for a complete listing of these studies). Hundreds of other studies have used social interdependence as the dependent rather than the independent variable. In our own research program at the Cooperative Learning

Center at the University of Minnesota over the past 25 years, we have conducted over 85 studies to refine our understanding of how cooperation works. In terms of sheer quantity of research, social interdependence theory is one of the most examined aspects of human nature.

A wide variety of dependent variables has been examined in the research on social interdependence. Social interdependence is a generic human phenomenon that affects many different outcomes simultaneously. Over the past 95 years, researchers have focused on such diverse dependent variables as individual achievement and retention, group and organizational productivity, higher-level reasoning, moral reasoning, achievement motivation, intrinsic motivation, transfer of training and learning, job satisfaction, interpersonal attraction, social support, interpersonal affection and love, attitudes toward diversity, prejudice, self-esteem, personal causation and locus of control, attributions concerning success and failure, psychological health, social competencies, and many others. These numerous outcomes may be subsumed within three broad categories (Johnson & Johnson, 1989): effort to achieve, positive interpersonal relationships, and psychological health.

The research on social interdependence has an external validity and a generalizability rarely found in the social sciences. The more variations in places, people, and procedures the research can withstand and still yield the same findings, the more externally valid the conclusions. The research has been conducted in 10 different historical decades. Research subjects have varied as to age, sex, economic class, nationality, and cultural background. A wide variety of research tasks, ways of structuring the types of social interdependence, and measures of the dependent variables have been used. The research has been conducted by many different researchers with markedly different theoretical and practical orientations working in different settings and even in different countries. The diversity of subjects, settings, age levels, and operationalizations of social interdependence and the dependent variables give this work wide generalizability and considerable external validity.

If research is to have impact on theory and practice, it must be summarized and communicated in a complete, objective, impartial, and unbiased way. In an age of information explosion, there is considerable danger that theories will be formulated on small and nonrepresentative samples of available knowledge, thereby resulting in fallacious conclusions that in turn lead to mistaken practices. A quantitative reviewing procedure allows for more definitive and robust conclusions. To establish the current state of knowledge about social interdependence, therefore, the meta-analysis process was applied. *Meta-analysis* is a method of statistically combining the results of a set of independent studies that test the same hypothesis and using inferential statistics to draw conclusions about the overall result of the studies. The essential purpose of meta-analysis is to summarize a set of related research studies so that the size of the effect of the independent variable on the dependent variable is known.

The basic premise of social interdependence theory is that the way interdependence among goals is structured determines how individuals interact, which in turn largely determines outcomes. Research, therefore, has focused on both the interaction patterns found among interdependent individuals and the outcomes resulting from their efforts.

35.5.1 Interaction Patterns

Two heads are better than one.—Heywood

Positive interdependence (see Fig. 35-1) creates *promotive interaction*, which occurs as individuals encourage and facilitate each other's efforts to reach the group's goals (such as maximizing each member's learning). Group members promote each other's success (Johnson & Johnson, 1989) by:

1. Giving and receiving help and assistance. In cooperative groups, members both give and receive work-related and personal help and support. Hooper (1991) found a positive and significant correlation between achievement and helping behaviors.

2. Exchanging resources and information. Group members seek information and other resources from each other, comprehend information accurately and without bias, and make optimal use of the information provided (e.g., Cosen & English, 1987; Hawkins et al., 1982; Webb, Ender & Lewis, 1986). There are a number of beneficial results from (a) orally explaining, elaborating, and summarizing information and (b) teaching one's knowledge to others. Yueh and Alessi (1988) found that a combination of group and individual rewards resulted in increased peer teaching. Explaining and teaching increase the degree to which group members cognitively process and organize information, engage in higher-level reasoning, attain insights, and become personally committed to achieving. Listening critically to the explanations of groupmates provides the opportunity to utilize other's resources.

3. Giving and receiving feedback (see 32.2) on taskwork and teamwork behaviors. In cooperative groups, members monitor each other's efforts, give immediate feedback on performance, and, when needed, give each other help and assistance. Carrier and Sales (1987) found that students working in pairs chose elaborative feedback more frequently than did those working alone.

4. Challenging each other's reasoning. Intellectual controversy promotes curiosity, motivation to learn, reconceptualization of what one knows, higher-quality decision making, greater insight into the problem being considered, higher-level reasoning, and cognitive development (Johnson & Johnson, 1992). Logo environments (see 12.3.2.1, 24.5.1.3) may especially engender conflicts among ideas and subsequent negotiation and resolution of that

conflict (Clements & Nastasi, 1985, 1988; Lehrer & Smith, 1986).

5. Advocating increased efforts to achieve. Encouraging others to achieve increases one's own commitment to do so.

6. Mutually influencing each other's reasoning and behavior. Group members actively seek to influence and be influenced by each other. If a member has a better way to complete the task, groupmates usually adopt it quickly.

7. Engaging in the interpersonal and small-group skills needed for effective teamwork.

8. Processing how effectively group members are working together and how the group's effectiveness can be continuously improved.

Negative interdependence typically results in *oppositional interaction,* which occurs as individuals discourage and obstruct each other's efforts to achieve. Individuals focus both on increasing their own success and on preventing anyone else from being more successful than they are. *No interaction* exists when individuals work independently without any interaction or interchange with each other. Individuals focus only on increasing their own success and ignore as irrelevant the efforts of others.

Each of these interaction patterns affects outcomes differently. The outcomes of social interdependence may be organized into three major areas.

35.5.2 Effort to Achieve

In *Look Homeward Angel,* Thomas Wolfe records how in grammar school Eugene learned to write from a classmate, learning from a peer what "*all instruction failed*" to teach him. Is Eugene an isolated case? No. Between 1898 and 1989, researchers conducted over 375 experimental studies on social interdependence and achievement (Johnson & Johnson, 1989). A meta-analysis of all studies indicates that cooperative learning results in significantly higher achievement and retention than does competitive and individualistic learning (see Table 35-1). The more conceptual and complex the task, the more problem solving required; and the more creative the answers need to be, the greater the superiority of cooperative over competitive and individualistic learning. When we examined only the methodological high-quality studies, the superiority of cooperative over competitive or individualistic efforts was still pronounced.

Some cooperative procedures contained a mixture of cooperative, competitive, and individualistic efforts, while others contained pure cooperation. The original jigsaw procedure (Aronson, 1978), for example, is a combination of resource interdependence and an individualistic reward structure. Teams-games-tournaments (see 17.3; DeVries & Edwards, 1974) and student-teams-achievement-divisions (Slavin, 1986) are mixtures of cooperation and intergroup competition. Team-assisted instruction (Slavin, Leavey & Madden, 1982) is a mixture of individualistic and coopera-

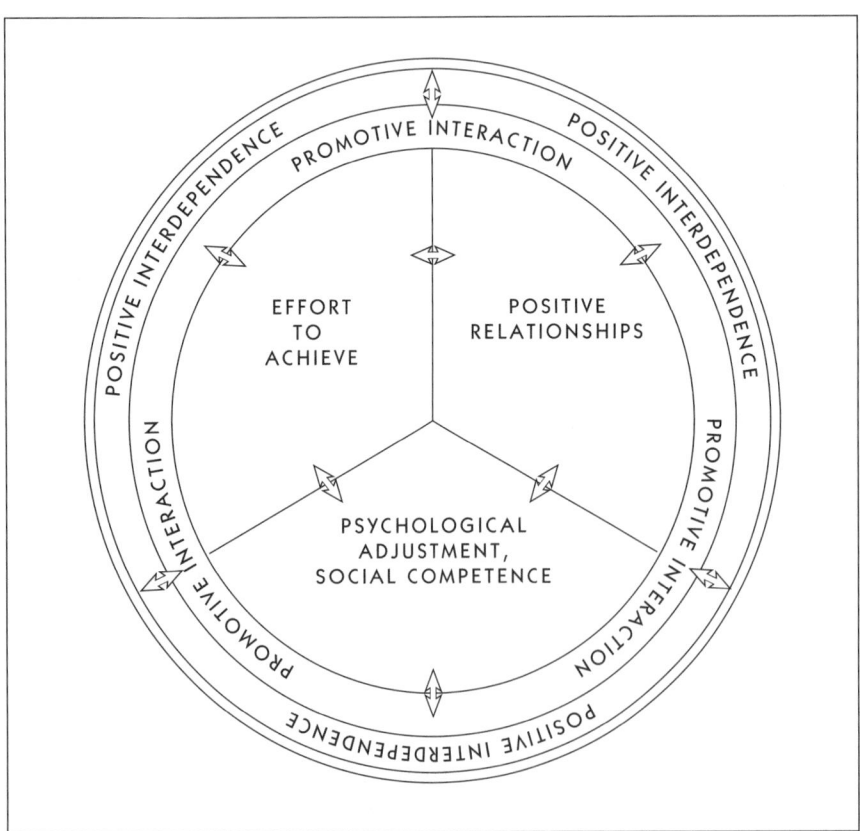

Figure 35-1. Outcomes of cooperation. Reprinted by permission from Johnson, D. W., Johnson, R. & Holubec, E. (1993). *Circles of Learning,* 4th ed. Edina, MN: Interaction Book Company.

TABLE 35-1. MEAN WEIGHTED EFFECT SIZES OF SOCIAL INTERDEPENDENCE ON DEPENDENT VARIABLES

	Mean	s.d.	*n*
Achievement			
Cooperative vs. competitive	0.67	0.93	129
Cooperative vs. individualistic	0.64	0.79	184
Competitive vs. individualistic	0.30	0.77	38
Interpersonal attraction			
Cooperative vs. competitive	0.67	0.49	93
Cooperative vs. individualistic	0.60	0.58	60
Competitive vs. individualistic	0.08	0.70	15
Social support			
Cooperative vs. competitive	0.62	0.44	84
Cooperative vs. individualistic	0.70	0.45	72
Competitive vs. individualistic	-0.13	0.36	19
Self-esteem			
Cooperative vs. competitive	0.58	0.56	56
Cooperative vs. individualistic	0.44	0.40	38
Competitive vs. individualistic	-0.23	0.42	19

Reprinted by permission from: Johnson, D. W., Johnson, R. & Holubec, E. (1993). *Circles of Learning*, 4th ed. Edina, MN: Interaction Book Company.

tive learning. When the results of "pure" and "mixed" operationalizations of cooperative learning were compared, the pure operationalizations produced higher achievement.

Besides higher achievement and greater retention, cooperation, compared with competitive or individualistic efforts, tends to result (Johnson & Johnson, 1989) in more:

1. Willingness to take on difficult tasks and persist, despite difficulties, in working toward goal accomplishment.
2. Long-term retention of what is learned.
3. Higher-level reasoning (critical thinking) and metacognitive thought. Cooperative efforts promote a greater use of higher-level reasoning strategies and critical thinking than do competitive or individualistic efforts (effect sizes = 0.93 and 0.97, respectively). Even on writing assignments, students working cooperatively show more higher-level thought.
4. Creative thinking (process gain). In cooperative groups, members more frequently generate new ideas, strategies, and solutions that they would think of on their own.
5. Transfer of learning from one situation to another (group to individual transfer). What individuals learn in a group today, they are able to do alone tomorrow.
6. Positive attitudes toward the tasks being completed (job satisfaction). Cooperative efforts result in more positive attitudes toward the tasks being completed and greater continuing motivation to complete them. The positive attitudes extend to the work experience and the organization as a whole.

7. Time on task. Cooperators spend more time on task than do competitors (effect size = 0.76) or students working individualistically (effect size = 1.17).

Kurt Lewin often stated, *"I always found myself unable to think as a single person."* Most efforts to achieve are a personal but social process that require individuals to cooperate and to construct shared understandings and knowledge. Both competitive and individualistic structures, by isolating individuals from each other, tend to depress achievement.

35.5.3 Positive Interpersonal Relationships

Heartpower is the strength of your corporation.— Vince Lombardi, famous coach of the Green Bay Packers

Since 1940, over 180 studies have compared the impact of cooperative, competitive, and individualistic efforts on interpersonal attraction (Johnson & Johnson, 1989). Cooperative efforts, compared with competitive and individualistic experiences, promoted considerably more liking among individuals (see Table 35-1). The effects sizes were higher for (a) high-quality studies and (b) the studies using pure operationalizations of cooperative learning than for studies using mixed operationalizations. These positive feelings were found to extend to superiors in the organizational structure. Thus, *individuals tend to care more about each other and to be more committed to each other's success and well-being when they work together cooperatively than when they compete to see who is best or work independently from each other.*

A major extension of social interdependence theory is social judgment theory that focuses on relationships among diverse individuals (Johnson & Johnson, 1989). Cooperators tend to like each other, not only when they are homogeneous but also when they differ in intellectual ability, handicapping conditions, ethnic membership, social class, culture, and gender (see 6.4). Individuals working cooperatively tend to value heterogeneity and diversity more than do individuals working competitively or individualistically. The positive impact of heterogeneity results from a process of acceptance that includes frequent and accurate communication, accurate perspective taking, mutual inducibility (openness to influence), multidimensional views of each other, feelings of psychological acceptance and self-esteem, psychological success, and expectations of rewarding and productive future interaction.

Closely related to the research on the impact of social interdependence on interpersonal relationships is the study of group cohesion (Johnson & F. Johnson, 1994). Generally, the more positive the relationships among group members, the lower the absenteeism, the fewer the members who drop out of the group, and the more likely students will commit effort to achieve educational goals, feel personal responsibility for learning, take on difficult tasks, be motivated to learn, persist in working toward goal achievement, have high morale, be willing to endure pain and frustration on behalf of learning, listen to and be influenced by classmates and teachers, commit to each other's learning and success, and achieve and produce.

In addition, positive peer relationships influence the social and cognitive development of students and such attitudes and behaviors as educational aspirations and staying in school (Johnson & Johnson, 1989). Relationships with peers influence what attitudes and values students adopt, whether students become prosocial or antisocial oriented, whether students learn to see situations from a variety of perspectives, the development of autonomy, aspirations for postsecondary education, and whether students learn how to cope with adversity and stress. Mevarech et al. (1987), for example, found that altruism increased among students learning in cooperative pairs.

Besides liking each other, cooperators give and receive considerable social support, both personally and academically (Johnson & Johnson, 1989). Since the 1940s, over 106 studies comparing the relative impact of cooperative, competitive, and individualistic efforts on social support have been conducted. Social support may be aimed at enhancing another person's success (task-related social support) or at providing support on a more personal level (personal social support). Cooperative experience promoted greater task-oriented and personal social support than did competitive (effect size = 0.62) or individualistic (effect size = 0.70) experiences. Social support tends to promote achievement and productivity, physical health, psychological health, and successful coping with stress and adversity.

Interpersonal relationships are at the heart of communities of practice. Learning communities are based as much on relationships as they are on intellectual discourse. The more positive the relationships among students and the more committed students are to each other's success, the harder students will work and the more productive they will be.

35.5.4 Psychological Health

Ashley Montagu was fond of saying, *"With few exceptions, the solitary animal is, in any species, an abnormal creature."* Karen Horney said, *"The neurotic individual is someone who is inappropriately competitive and, therefore, unable to cooperate with others."* Montagu and Horney recognized that the essence of psychological health is the ability to develop and maintain cooperative relationships. *Psychological health* may be defined, therefore, as the ability to develop, maintain, and appropriately modify interdependent relationships with others to succeed in achieving goals. To manage social interdependence, individuals must correctly perceive whether interdependence exists and whether it is positive or negative, be motivated accordingly, and act in ways consistent with normative expectations for appropriate behavior within the situation. The major variables related to psychological health studied by researchers interested in social interdependence are psychological adjustment, self-esteem, perspective-taking ability, social skills, and a variety of related attitudes and values.

A number of studies have been conducted on the relationship between social interdependence and psychological health (Johnson & Johnson, 1989). Working cooperatively with peers and valuing cooperation results in greater psychological health than does competing with peers or working independently. *Cooperativeness* is positively related to a number of indices of psychological health, such as emotional maturity, well-adjusted social relations, strong personal identity, ability to cope with adversity, social competencies, and basic trust in and optimism about people. Personal ego strength, self-confidence, independence, and autonomy are all promoted when cooperative efforts are involved. *Individualistic attitudes* tend to be related to a number of indices of psychological pathology such as emotional immaturity, social maladjustment, delinquency, self-alienation, and self-rejection. *Competitiveness* is related to a mixture of healthy and unhealthy characteristics. Cooperative experiences are not a luxury; they are an absolute necessity for healthy psychological development.

The relationship between social interdependence and self-esteem has been examined by interested researchers. A process of self-acceptance is posited to be based on (a) internalizing perceptions that one is known, accepted, and liked as one is, (b) internalizing mutual success, and (c) evaluating oneself favorably in comparison with peers. A process of self-rejection may occur from (a) not wanting to be known, (b) low performance, (c) overgeneralization of self-evaluations, and (d) the disapproval of others. Since the 1950s there have been over 80 studies comparing the relative impact of cooperative, competitive, and individualistic experiences on self-esteem (Johnson & Johnson, 1989). Cooperative experiences promoted higher self-esteem than did competitive (effect size = 0.58) or individualistic (effect size = 0.44) experiences. Our research demonstrated that cooperative experiences tend to be related to these beliefs: One is intrinsically worthwhile; others see one in positive ways; one's attributes compare favorably with those of one's peers; and one is a capable, competent, and successful person. In cooperative efforts, students (a) realize that they are accurately known, accepted, and liked by one's peers, (b) know that they have contributed to their own, others, and group success, and (c) perceive themselves and others in a differentiated and realistic way that allows for multidimensional comparisons based on complementary of their own and others' abilities. Competitive experiences tend to be related to conditional self-esteem based on whether one wins or loses. Individualistic experiences tend to be related to basic self-rejection.

A number of studies have related cooperative, competitive, and individualistic experiences to perspective-taking ability (the ability to understand how a situation appears to other people) (Johnson & Johnson, 1989). Cooperative experiences tend to increase perspective-taking ability, while competitive and individualistic experiences tend to promote egocentrism (being unaware of other perspectives other than your own) (effect sizes of 0.61 and 0.44, respectively). Individuals, furthermore, who are part of a cooperative effort learn more social skills and become more socially competent than do persons competing or working individualistically. Finally, it is through cooperative efforts that many of the attitudes and values essential to psychological health (such as self-efficacy) are learned and adopted.

35.5.5 Everything Affects Everything Else

Deutsch's (1985) crude law of social relations states that the characteristic processes and effects elicited by a given type of social interdependence also tend to elicit that type of social interdependence. Thus, positive interdependence elicits promotive interaction, and promotive interaction tends to elicit positive interdependence. Deutsch's law may also be applied to the three types of outcomes resulting from cooperative experiences.

Each of the outcomes of cooperative efforts (effort to achieve, quality of relationships, and psychological health) influences the others, and, therefore, they are likely to be found together (Johnson & Johnson, 1989). *First,* caring and committed friendships come from a sense of mutual accomplishment, mutual pride in joint work, and the bonding that results from joint efforts. The more individuals care about each other, on the other hand, the harder they will work to achieve mutual goals. *Second,* joint efforts to achieve mutual goals promote higher self-esteem, self-efficacy, personal control, and confidence in one's competencies. The healthier psychologically individuals are, on the other hand, the better able to they are to work with others to achieve mutual goals. *Third,* psychological health is built on the internalization of the caring and respect received from loved ones. Friendships are developmental advantages that promote self-esteem, self-efficacy, and general psychological adjustment. The healthier people are psychologically (i.e., free of psychological pathology such as depression, paranoia, anxiety, fear of failure, repressed anger, hopelessness, and meaninglessness), on the other hand, the more caring and committed their relationships. Since each outcome can induce the others, you are likely to find them together. They are a package, with each outcome a door into all three. Together they induce positive interdependence and promotive interaction.

35.6 WHAT IS AND IS NOT A COOPERATIVE GROUP

It is the potential for such outcomes that make cooperative groups the key to successful education. *The truly committed cooperative learning group is probably the most productive instructional tool educators have.* Creating and maintaining truly committed cooperative learning groups, however, require an understanding of the differences between cooperative learning groups and other forms of classroom grouping, the forces hindering group performance, and the basic elements that make cooperative work.

35.6.1 Making Potential Group Performance a Reality

Not all groups are cooperative groups. Placing people in the same room and calling them a cooperative group does not make them one. Having a number of people work together does not make them a cooperative group. Study groups, project groups, lab groups, committees, task forces, departments, and councils are groups, but they are not necessarily cooperative. Groups do not become cooperative groups simply because that is what someone labels them.

The authors have studied cooperative learning groups for 30 years. We have interviewed thousands of students and teachers in a wide variety of school districts in a number of different countries over three different decades to discover how groups are used in the classroom and where and how cooperative groups work best. On the basis of our findings and the findings of other researchers such as Katzenbach and Smith (1993), a learning group performance curve has been developed to clarify the difference between various types of learning groups (Fig. 35-2).

The *learning group performance curve* illustrates that how well any small group performs depends on how it is structured. On the performance curve, four types of learning groups are described. It begins with the individual members of the group and illustrates the relative performance of these students to pseudo groups, traditional classroom groups, cooperative learning groups, and high-performance cooperative learning groups.

A *pseudo-learning group* is a group whose members have been assigned to work together, but they have no interest in doing so. They meet but do not want to work together or help each other succeed. Members often block or interfere with each other's learning, communicate and coordinate poorly, mislead and confuse each other, loaf, and seek a "free ride." The interaction among group members detracts from individual learning without delivering any benefit. The result is that the sum of the whole is less than the potential of the individual members. The group does not mature, because members have no interest in or commitment to each other or the group's future.

A *traditional classroom learning group* is a group whose members have accepted that they are to work together but see little benefit from doing so. Interdependence is low. The assignments are structured so that very little if any joint work is required. Members do not take responsibility for anyone's learning other than their own. Members interact primarily to share information and clarify how the assignments are to be done. Then they each do the work on their own. And their achievements are individually recognized and rewarded. Students are accountable as separate individuals, not as members of a team. Students do not receive training in social skills, and a group leader is appointed who is in charge of directing members' participation. There is no processing of the quality of the group's efforts.

A *cooperative learning group* is more than a sum of its parts. It is a group whose members are committed to the common purpose of maximizing each other's learning. A *high-performance cooperative learning group* is a group that meets all the criteria for being a cooperative learning group and outperforms all reasonable expectations, given its membership. What differentiates the high-performance group from the cooperative learning group is the level of commitment members have to each other and the group's success. Jennifer Futernick, who is part of a high-performing, rapid-response team at McKinsey & Company, calls the emotion binding her teammates together a form of love (Katzenbach & Smith, 1993). Ken Hoepner of the Burlington Northern Intermodal Team (also described by Katzenbach & Smith, 1993) stated: *"Not only did we trust each other, not only did we respect each other, but we gave*

a damn about the rest of the people on this team. If we saw somebody vulnerable, we were there to help." Members' mutual concern for each other's personal growth enables high-performance cooperative groups to perform far above expectations, and also to have lots of fun. The bad news about high-performance cooperative groups is that they are rare. Most groups never achieve this level of development.

35.6.2 Forces Hindering Group Performance

Performance and small groups go hand in hand. Although cooperative groups outperform individuals working alone, there is nothing magical about groups. There are conditions

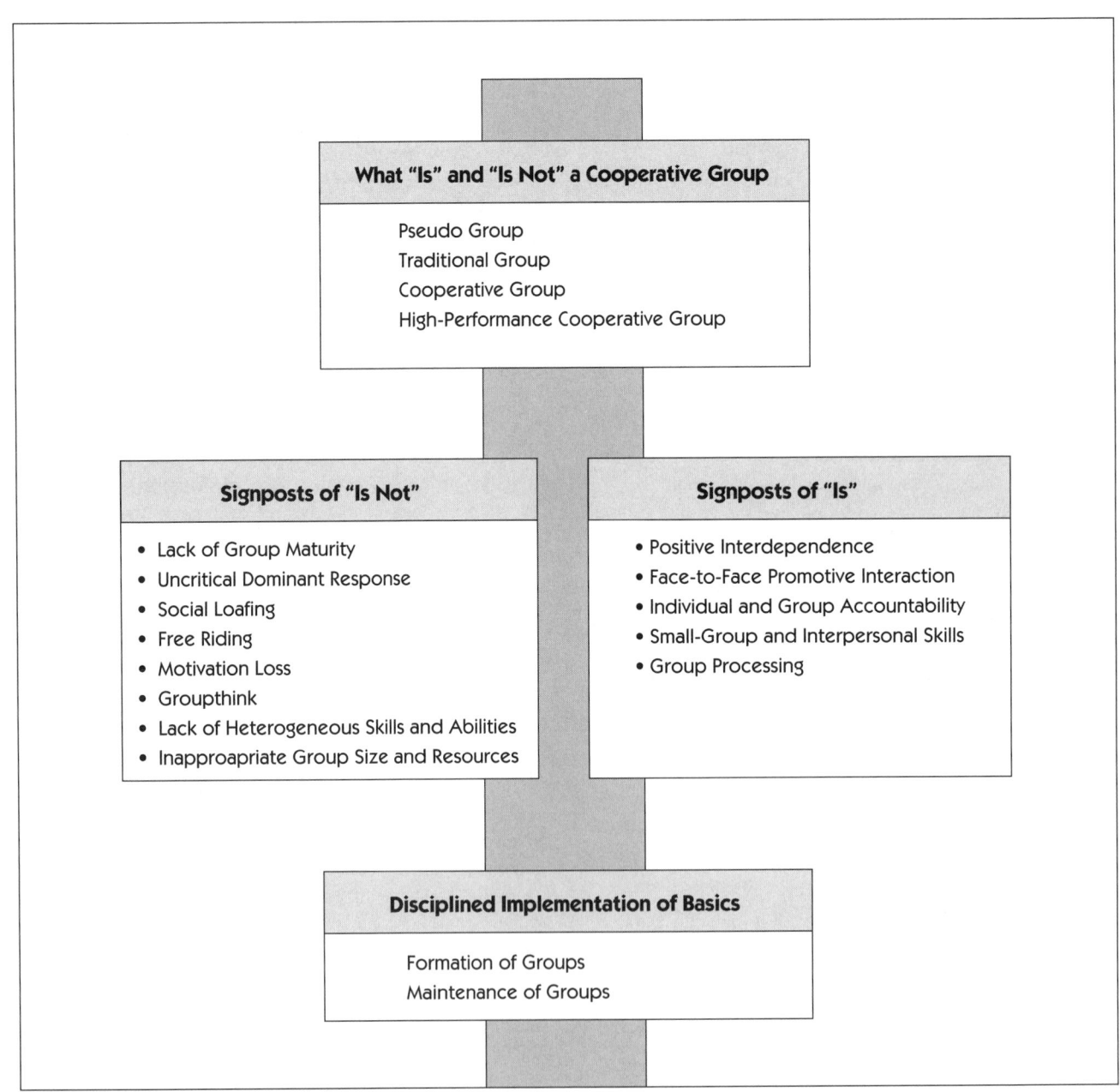

Figure 35-2. Making cooperative groups work. Reprinted by permission from Johnson, D. W., Johnson, R. & Holubec, E. (1993). *Circles of Learning,* 4th ed. Edina, MN: Interaction Book Company.

under which groups function effectively, and conditions under which groups function ineffectively. *Potential barriers to group effectiveness* (Johnson & F. Johnson, 1994) are:

1. *Lack of group maturity.* Group members need time and experience working together to develop into an effective group. Temporary, ad-hoc groups usually do not develop enough maturity to function with full effectiveness.

2. *Uncritically giving one's dominant response.* A central barrier to higher-level reasoning and deeper-level understanding is the uncritical giving of members' dominant response to academic problems and assignments. Instead, members should generate a number of potential answers and choose the best one.

3. *Social loafing—hiding in the crowd.* When a group is working on an additive task (group product is determined by summing together individual group members' efforts), and individual members can reduce their effort without other members realizing that they are doing so, many people tend to work less hard. Such social loafing has been demonstrated on a variety of additive tasks such as rope pulling, shouting, and clapping.

4. *Free riding—getting something for nothing.* On disjunctive tasks (if one member does it, all members receive the benefit), there is the possibility of a free ride. When group members realize that their efforts are dispensable (group success or failure depends very little on whether or not they exert effort), and when their efforts are costly, group members are less likely to exert themselves on the group's behalf.

5. *Motivation losses due to perceived inequity—not being a sucker.* When other group members are free riding, there is a tendency for the members who are working to reduce their efforts to avoid being a "sucker."

6. *Groupthink.* Groups can be overconfident in their ability and resist any challenge or threat to their sense of invulnerability by avoiding any disagreements and seeking concurrence among members.

7. *Lack of sufficient heterogeneity.* The more homogeneous the group members, the less each member adds to the group's resources. Groups must develop the right mix of taskwork and teamwork skills necessary to do their work. Heterogeneity ensures that a wide variety of resources are available for the group's work.

8. *Lack of teamwork skills.* Groups with members who lack the small-group and interpersonal skills required to work effectively with others often underperform their most academically able members.

9. *Inappropriate group size.* The larger the group, the fewer the members who can participate, the less essential each member views his or her personal contribution, the more teamwork skills required, and the more complex the group structure.

Not every group is effective. Most everyone has been part of a group that wasted time, was inefficient, and generally produced poor work. But there are groups that accomplish wondrous things. Educators must be able to spot the above characteristics of ineffective groups and take action to eliminate them. The hindering factors are eliminated by the basics of cooperation.

35.7 APPLYING THE BASICS OF COOPERATION

Educators fool themselves if they think well-meaning directives to "work together," "cooperate," and "be a team" will be enough to create cooperative efforts among students. *There is a discipline to creating cooperation.* The "basics" of structuring cooperation are not a series of elements that characterize good groups. They are a regimen that, if followed rigorously, will produce the conditions for effective cooperation. Cooperative learning groups are rare because educators (and students) seek shortcuts to quality groupwork and assume that "traditional classroom groups will do." Like persons who wish to lose weight without dieting, they seek easy alternatives to the disciplined application of the basics of effective groups, which are positive interdependence, face-to-face promotive interaction, individual and group accountability, appropriate use of social skills, and group processing.

35.7.1 Positive Interdependence: We Instead of Me

All for one and one for all.—Alexandre Dumas

In a football game, the quarterback who throws the pass and the receiver who catches the pass are positively interdependent. The success of one depends on the success of the other. It takes two to complete a pass. One player cannot succeed without the other. Both have to perform competently if their mutual success is to be assured. If one fails, they both fail.

The discipline of using cooperative groups begins with structuring positive interdependence (see Johnson & Johnson, 1989, 1992b, 1992c). The heart of cooperation is positive interdependence. Group members must believe that they sink or swim together and know that they cannot succeed unless all other members of their group succeed. It is positive interdependence that requires group members to work together to accomplish something beyond individual success. Positive interdependence creates the realization that members have two responsibilities: to learn the assigned material and to ensure that all members of their group learn the assigned material. When positive interdependence exists in a group, all group members realize they (a) *share a common fate* where they all gain or lose on the basis of the overall performance of group members, (b) *are striving for mutual benefit* so that all members of the group will gain, (c) *have a long-term time perspective* so that long-term joint productivity is perceived to be of greater value than short-term personal advantage, and (d) *have a shared identity based on group membership* (besides being a separate individual, one is a member of a team). When positive interdependence is clearly understood, it highlights that (a) each group member's efforts are required and indispensable for group success (i.e., there can be no "free riders"), and (b) each group member has a unique contribution to make to the joint effort because of his or her resources and/or role and task responsibilities (i.e., there can be no social loafing).

To structure positive interdependence, the teacher *first* assigns the group a clear, measurable task (members have to know what they are supposed to do) and, *second,* explains the positive goal interdependence (mutual goals) so that members believe that they can attain their goals if and only if their groupmates attain their goals. Positive goal interdependence ensures that the group is united around a common goal, a concrete reason for being, such as *"learn the assigned material and make sure that all members of your group learn the assigned material." Third,* the teacher supplements positive goal interdependence with other types of positive interdependence, such as joint rewards, divided resources, complementary roles, and a team identity. The more types of interdependence used in a group, the greater the impact on outcomes.

The authors have conducted a series of studies investigating the nature of positive interdependence and the relative power of the different types of positive interdependence (Frank, 1984; Hwong, Caswell, Johnson & Johnson, 1993; Johnson, Johnson, Stanne & Garibaldi, 1990; Johnson, Johnson, Ortiz & Stanne, 1991; Lew, Mesch, Johnson & Johnson, 1986a, 1986b; Mesch, Johnson & Johnson, 1988; Mesch, Lew, Johnson & Johnson, 1986). Our research indicates that positive interdependence provides the context within which promotive interaction takes place, group membership and interpersonal interaction among students do not produce higher achievement unless positive interdependence is clearly structured, the combination of goal and reward interdependence increases achievement over goal interdependence alone, and resource interdependence does not increase achievement unless goal interdependence is present also.

35.7.2 Individual Accountability/ Personal Responsibility

> *What children can do together today, they can do alone tomorrow.*—Vygotsky

Among the early settlers of Massachusetts, there was a saying: *"If you do not work, you do not eat."* Everyone had to do his or her fair share of the work. *The discipline of using cooperative groups includes structuring group and individual accountability. Group accountability* exists when the overall performance of the group is assessed, and the results are given back to all group members to compare against a standard of performance. *Individual accountability* exists when the performance of each individual member is assessed, the results given back to the individual and

the group to compare against a standard of performance, and the member is held responsible by groupmates for contributing his or her fair share to the group's success. On the basis of the feedback received, (a) efforts to learn and contribute to groupmates' learning can be recognized and celebrated, (b) immediate remediation can take place by providing any needed assistance or encouragement, and (c) groups can reassign responsibilities to avoid any redundant efforts by members.

The purpose of cooperative groups is to make each member a stronger individual in his or her own right. Individual accountability is the key to ensuring that all group members are in fact strengthened by learning cooperatively. After participating in a cooperative lesson, group members should be better prepared to complete similar tasks by themselves. There is a pattern to classroom learning. *First,* students learn knowledge, skills, strategies, or procedures in a cooperative group. *Second,* students apply the knowledge or perform the skill, strategy, or procedure alone to demonstrate their personal mastery of the material. Students learn it together and then perform it alone. Hooper, Ward, Hannafin, and Clark (1989) found that cooperative technology-assisted instruction resulted in higher achievement when individual accountability was structured than when it was not.

35.7.3 Positive Interdependence and Accountability

In cooperative situations, group members share responsibility for the joint outcome. Each group member takes personal responsibility for (a) contributing his or her efforts to accomplish the group's goals and (b) helping other group members do likewise. The greater the positive interdependence structured within a cooperative learning group, the more students will feel *personally responsible* for contributing their efforts to accomplish the group's goals. The shared responsibility adds the concept of "ought" to members' motivation: One *ought* to do one's share, contribute, and pull one's weight. The shared responsibility also makes each group member personally accountable to the other group members. Students will realize that if they fail to do their fair share of the work, other members will be disappointed, hurt, and upset.

35.7.4 Face-to-Face Promotive Interaction

> *In an industrial organization, it's the group effort that counts. There's really no room for stars in an industrial organization. You need talented people, but they can't do it alone. They have to have help.*—John F. Donnelly, President, Donnelly Mirrors

The discipline of using cooperative groups includes ensuring that group members meet face to face to work together to complete assignments and promote each other's success. Group members need to do real work together. *Promotive interaction* exists when individuals encourage and facilitate each other's efforts to complete tasks in order to reach the group's goals. Through promoting each other's success, group members build both an academic and a personal support system for each member. Promotive interaction is characterized by individuals providing each other with efficient and effective help and assistance, exchanging needed resources such as information and materials and processing information more efficiently and effectively, providing each other with feedback in order to improve subsequent performance, challenging each other's conclusions and reasoning in order to promote higher-quality decision making and greater insight into the problems being considered, advocating the exertion of effort to achieve mutual goals, influencing each other's efforts to achieve the group's goals, acting in trusting and trustworthy ways, being motivated to strive for mutual benefit, and a moderate level of arousal characterized by low anxiety and stress. Promoting each other's success results in group members' getting to know each other on a personal as well as a professional level.

While electronic communication has many positive features, face-to-face communication has a richness that electronic communication may never match. There is evidence that up to 93% of people's intent was conveyed by facial expression and tone of voice, with the most important channel being facial expression (Druckman, Rozelle & Baxter, 1982; Meherabian, 1971). Harold Geneen, the former head of ITT, believed that his response to requests was different face to face than through teletype: *"In New York, I might read a request and say No. But in Europe, I could see that an answer to the same question might be Yes. . . . It became our policy to deal with problems on the spot, face to face"* (cited in Trevino, Lengel & Draft, 1987). For this and other reasons (such as lack of effective groupware), instructional programs may be most effective when they use face-to-face rather than electronic teams. Learning teams, however, may be electronically linked with other training teams in other sites.

35.7.5 Interpersonal and Small-Group Skills

I will pay more for the ability to deal with people than for any other ability under the sun.—John D. Rockefeller

The fourth arena in the disciplined use of cooperative groups is teaching group members the small-group and interpersonal skills they need to work effectively with each other. In cooperative learning groups, students are required to learn academic subject matter (*taskwork*) and also to learn the interpersonal and small-group skills required to function as part of a group (*teamwork*). If the teamwork skills are not learned, then the taskwork cannot be completed. If group members are inept at teamwork, their taskwork will tend to be substandard. On the other hand, the greater the members' teamwork skills, the higher will be the quality and quantity of their learning. Cooperative learning is inherently more complex than competitive or individualistic learning because students have to engage simultaneously in

taskwork and teamwork. In order to coordinate efforts to achieve mutual goals, students must (a) get to know and trust each other, (b) communicate accurately and unambiguously, (c) accept and support each other, and (c) resolve conflicts constructively (Johnson, 1991, 1993; Johnson & F. Johnson, 1994).

The more socially skillful students are, and the more attention teachers pay to teaching and rewarding the use of social skills, the higher the achievement that can be expected within cooperative learning groups. In their studies on the long-term implementation of cooperative learning, Marvin Lew and Debra Mesch (Lew, Mesch, Johnson & Johnson, 1986a, 1986b; Mesch, Johnson & Johnson, 1988; Mesch, Lew, Johnson & Johnson, 1986) investigated the impact of a reward contingency for using social skills as well as positive interdependence and a contingency for academic achievement on performance within cooperative learning groups. In the cooperative skills conditions, students were trained weekly in four social skills, and each member of a cooperative group was given two bonus points toward the quiz grade if all group members were observed by the teacher to demonstrate three out of four cooperative skills. The results indicated that the combination of positive interdependence, an academic contingency for high performance by all group members, and a social skills contingency promoted the highest achievement.

35.7.6 Group Processing

Take care of each other. Share your energies with the group. No one must feel alone, cut off, for that is when you do not make it.—Willi Unsoeld, Renowned Mountain Climber

The final phase of the discipline of using cooperative groups is structuring group processing. Effective group work is influenced by whether or not groups reflect on (process) how well they are functioning. A process is an identifiable sequence of events taking place over time, and process goals refer to the sequence of events instrumental in achieving outcome goals (Johnson & F. Johnson, 1994). *Group processing* occurs when members discuss how well they are achieving their goals and maintaining effective working relationships among members. Cooperative groups need to describe what member actions are helpful and unhelpful and make decisions about what behaviors to continue or change. The *purposes* of group processing are to clarify and improve the effectiveness of members in contributing to the collaborative efforts to achieve the group's goals by (a) enabling groups to improve continuously the quality of member's work, (b) facilitating the learning of teamwork skills, (c) ensuring that members receive feedback on their participation, and (d) enabling groups to focus on group maintenance (Johnson, Johnson & Holubec, 1993). Groups that process how effectively members are working together tend to higher achievements than do groups that do not process or than individuals working alone. The combination of teacher and student processing resulted in greater problem-solving success than did the other cooperative conditions. And the combination of group and individual feedback resulted in higher achievement (Archer-Kath, Johnson & Johnson, 1994; Johnson, Johnson, Stanne & Garibaldi, 1990; Yager, Johnson & Johnson, 1985).

Group processing and self-monitoring are interrelated. Discussing the observations of members' actions results in (a) a heightened self-awareness of the effective and ineffective actions taken during the group meetings, (b) public commitment to increase the frequency of effective actions and decrease the frequency of ineffective actions, and (c) an increased sense of having the ability to be more effective if appropriate effort is exerted (i.e., self-efficacy). Participating in group processing inherently increases the self-monitoring by group members. There is evidence, however, that high- and low-ability students may differ in their self-monitoring capacity. Ames and Lau (1982) found that ability and effort, among other things, played a significant role in determining students' help-seeking and self-monitoring behaviors. Zimmerman (1986) found that high school students' effective use of self-monitoring skills was related to their achievement level. Thus, because low-ability students are often lacking in self-monitoring skills, it seems reasonable to expect that they would benefit by working with students who typically exhibit more effective monitoring during the learning process.

Group processing leads not only to self-monitoring, it also leads to *self-efficacy,* which is the expectation of successfully obtaining valued outcomes through personal effort. The opposite of self-efficacy is helplessness. Sarason and Potter (1983) examined the impact of individual self-monitoring of thoughts on self-efficacy and successful performance and found that having individuals focus their attention on self-efficacious thoughts is related to greater task persistence and less cognitive interference. They concluded that the more that people are aware of what they are experiencing, the more aware they will be of their own role in determining their success. The greater the sense of self- and joint-efficacy promoted by group processing, the more productive and effective group members and the group as a whole become.

Effective processing focuses group members on positive rather than negative behaviors. Monitoring one's own and one's collaborators' actions begins with deciding which behaviors to direct one's attention toward. Individuals can focus either on positive and effective behaviors, or on negative and ineffective behaviors. Sarason and Potter (1983) found that when individuals monitored their stressful experiences, they were more likely to perceive a program as having been more stressful than did those who did not. But when individuals monitored their positive experiences, they were more likely to perceive the group experience as involving less psychological demands, were more attracted to the group and had greater motivation to remain members, and felt less strained during the experience and more prepared for future group experiences. When individuals are anxious about being successful, and are then told they have failed, their performance tends to decrease significant-

ly, but when individuals anxious about being successful are told they have succeeded, their performance tends to increase significantly (Turk & Sarason, 1983).

35.8 THE COOPERATIVE SCHOOL

The new electronic tools are radically changing the way people access and use information and, therefore, have profound implications for the educational process. Education, on the other hand, is stuck with organizational patterns and professional traditions that negate many of the advantages of the new technologies. For technology to be fully utilized in schools, the organizational structure of the school has to change as well as the organizational structure of the classroom. To utilize the new technologies most effectively, schools need to change from a mass-manufacturing organizational structure to a team-based, high-performance organizational structure. This new organizational structure is created when cooperative learning is used the majority of the time in the classroom, and cooperation is used to structure faculty and staff work in (a) colleagial teaching teams, (b) school-based decision making, and (c) faculty meetings (Johnson & Johnson, 1994a).

Just as the heart of the classroom is cooperative learning, the heart of the school is *colleagial teaching teams*: small cooperative groups in which members work to improve continuously each other's (a) instructional expertise and success in general and (b) expertise in using cooperative learning in particular. Administrators may also be organized into colleagial support groups to increase their administrative expertise and success.

School-based decision making may be structured through the use of two types of cooperative teams. A *task force* considers a school problem and proposes a solution to the faculty as a whole. The faculty is then divided into *ad-hoc decision-making groups* and considers whether to accept or modify the proposal. The decisions made by the ad-hoc groups are summarized, and the entire faculty then decides on the action to be taken to solve the problem.

Faculty meetings represent a microcosm of what administrators think the school should be. The clearest modeling of cooperative procedures in the school may be in faculty meetings and other meetings structured by the school administration. All four types of cooperative learning (formal, informal, base groups, and controversy) may be used at faculty meetings to increase their productivity, build faculty cohesion, and improve the faculty's social competence.

Technological innovation lags in schools. A key obstacle to the use of technology in schools is the limited support teachers have for integrating unfamiliar technologies into instruction. Just as students group together to learn cooperatively how to use new software or hardware, teachers need to group together to learn how to use the new technologies and then how to integrate them into the instruction. As long as each teacher works in isolation from his or her peers, the implementation of technology represents a personal decision on the part of each teacher, rather than an organizational change at the school and district levels. Many teachers are unfamiliar with the new technologies and feel unable to master them. In order to implement technology fully, the organizational structure of the school has to change from the old mass-manufacturing organizational structure to a team-based, high-performance organizational structure where teams of teachers can explore the new technologies, learn how to use them, and implement them together.

35.9 COOPERATIVE LEARNING AND TECHNOLOGY-BASED INSTRUCTION

In order to enhance learning, technology must promote cooperation among students and create a shared experience. *Technology-assisted cooperative learning* exists when the instructional use of technology is combined with the use of cooperative learning groups. Students, for example, may be assigned to cooperative groups of two or three members and given a cooperative assignment to complete a task for which a technology is to be utilized. Positive interdependence is typically established at the terminal so that students are aware of their dependence on other group members in accomplishing their learning goals.

Adding technology to a lesson inherently increases the lesson's complexity. When students participate in technology-assisted instruction, they have the dual tasks of (a) learning how to use the technology (i.e., the hardware and software required by the lesson) and (b) mastering the information, skills, procedures, and processes being presented within the technology. When cooperative learning groups are used, students have the additional task of learning teamwork procedures and skills. The complexity may be worth it. Technology-assisted cooperative learning tends to be a cost-effective way of teaching students how to use technology, increasing academic achievement, giving learners control over their learning, creating positive attitudes toward technology-based instruction and cooperative learning, promoting cognitive development, and increasing social skills. Computers themselves promote cooperative interaction among learners. The composition of the group and the gender of the learners are factors that have been hypothesized to affect the success of technology-assisted cooperative learning. Through technology, individuals in different settings can be networked into electronic cooperative learning groups.

35.9.1 Cost Effectiveness

The use of cooperative learning increases the cost effectiveness of technology. Although the range of technology that could be used in schools is increasing yearly (Hancock & Betts, 1994), the cost of adopting new technologies is an inhibiting factor to its use. Ensuring that every student is provided with the latest technology is beyond the financial resources of most school districts. Giving each cooperative learning group access to the latest technology is much more cost effective. An historical example is the adoption of computers by schools. By having groups work at computers (instead of individuals), schools were able to reduce significantly the cost of obtaining and maintaining computers (Johnson & Johnson, 1985; Wizer, 1987).

35.9.2 Learning How to Use Technology

Cooperative learning may reduce hardware and software problems that decrease achievement when students work alone (Hativa, 1988). Students naturally form groups when learning how to use a new technology or software program (Becker, 1984). When technology-assisted lessons require complex procedures (such as learner-controlled lessons), cooperative learning promotes greater mastery of the procedures than does individualistic learning. Trowbridge and Durnin (1984) found that students working in groups of two or three seemed more likely to interpret program questions as the authors of the materials intended. Discussions of multiple interpretations tended to converge on the correct interpretation. Hooper (1992) reported that students were frustrated and could not master the computer-assisted lesson when they worked alone with a learner-controlled lesson. Dyer (1993) compared structured cooperative pairs, unstructured cooperative pairs, and individuals completing a computer-assisted series of math problem-solving lessons. Structured cooperative pairs communicated more frequently and used the computer more efficiently and skillfully than did the unstructured cooperative pairs or students in the individualistic condition. McDonald (1993) found that students in the learner-controlled/cooperative learning condition selected more options during the lesson and spent more time interacting with the tutorial than did the learner-controlled/individual learning condition. When teachers wish to introduce new technology and new software programs of some complexity, they will be well advised to use cooperative learning. Hooper, Temiyakarn, and Williams (1995) found that cooperative learning established a mutually supportive learning environment among group members in which both cognitive difficulties and navigational disorientation were overcome in using the computer to complete a symbolic-reasoning task. Students studying alone had greater difficulty reading and understanding lesson directions, used the help option more often, and required more attempts to master embedded quizzes than did students in cooperative learning groups. Generally, this evidence indicates that students will learn how to use hardware and software more quickly and effectively when they learn in cooperative groups rather than alone.

In learning how to use computers, Webb (1984a) and Webb, Ender, and Lewis (1986) found that, in cooperative groups, explaining how to do computer programming was not related to skill in doing so (see also 24.5.3), and receiving explanations only influenced the learning of basic commands (not the interpretation of programs or the ability to generate programs). Fletcher (1985), on the other hand, investigating cognitive facilitation, found on a computer task calling for solving equations in an Earth spaceship game that individuals who were told to verbalize their decisions did as well in problem-solving performance on the game as groups told to come to consensus (both of which had superior results to individuals working silently). King (1989) asked groups of fourth-graders to reproduce a stimulus design using LOGO computer graphics (see 24.5.1.3) after they had watched a videotape modeling of "think-aloud problem solving." The groups were instructed to think aloud as they performed their task. More successful groups asked more task-related questions, spent more time on strategy, and reached higher levels of strategy elaboration than did groups who were less successful on the task.

35.9.3 Academic Achievement

We conducted several studies examining the use of cooperative, competitive, and individualistic learning activities at the computer (D. Johnson, Johnson, Stanne & Garibaldi, 1989, 1990; R. Johnson, Johnson & Stanne, 1985, 1986; R. Johnson, Johnson, Stanne, Smizak & Avon, 1987; Richards, Johnson & Johnson, 1986). The studies included students from the eighth grade through college freshmen and lasted from 3 to 30 instructional hours. The tasks were a computerized navigational and map-reading problem-solving task and word-processing assignments. Computer-assisted cooperative learning, compared with competitive and individualistic efforts at the computer, promoted (a) higher quantity of daily achievement, (b) higher quality of daily achievement, (c) greater mastery of factual information, (d) greater ability to apply one's factual knowledge in test questions requiring application of facts, (e) greater ability to use factual information to answer problem-solving questions, and (f) greater success in problem solving. Cooperation at the computer promoted greater motivation to persist on problem-solving tasks. Students in the cooperative condition were more successful in operating computer programs. In terms of oral participation, students in the cooperative condition, compared with students in the competitive and individualistic conditions, made fewer statements to the teacher and more to each other, made more task-oriented statements and fewer social statements, and generally engaged in more positive, task-oriented interaction with each other (especially when the social skill responsibilities were specified and group processing was conducted). Finally, the studies provided evidence that females were perceived to be of higher status in the cooperative than in the competitive or individualistic conditions.

In addition to our work, there are a number of studies that have found that students using a combination of cooperative learning and computer-based instruction learn better than do students using computer-based instruction while working individually (Cox & Berger, 1985; Dalton, 1990; Dalton, Hannafin & Hooper, 1987; Hooper, 1992; Hooper, Temiyakarn & Williams, 1995; Hythecker, Rocklin, Dansereau, Lambiotte, Larson & O'Donnell, 1985; Love, 1969; Mevarech, Stern & Levita, 1987; Okey & Majer, 1976; Repman, 1993; Rocklin, O'Donnell, Dansereau, Lambiotte, Hythecker & Larson, 1985; Shlecter, 1990; Stephenson, 1992; Webb, 1984; Yueh & Alessi, 1988). There are also a number of studies that found no statistically significant differences in achievement between subjects who worked in groups and subjects who worked alone (Carrier & Sales, 1987; Cosden & English, 1987; Hooper & Hannafin, 1988; Trowbridge & Durnin, 1984). No study has reported significantly greater learning when students work alone.

Simon Hooper and his colleagues have conducted a series of studies on technology-assisted cooperative learning involving fifth- to eighth-graders and college students (Dyer, 1993; Hooper, 1991; Hooper & Hannafin, 1988a, 1988b, 1991; Hooper, Ward, Hannafin & Clark, 1989; Huang, 1993; McDonald, 1993). They found that: (a) Cooperative group members achieved significantly higher than did students working under individualistic conditions; (b) cooperative learning groups in which individual accountability was carefully structured achieved higher than did cooperative learning groups in which no individual accountability was structured; (c) the achievement of low-ability students in heterogeneous cooperative groups was consistently higher than the achievement of low-ability students in homogeneous groups; (d) a positive and significant correlation was found between achievement and helping behaviors, and increases in achievement and cooperation to be significantly related within heterogeneous groups; and (e) cooperative (compared with individualistic) learning resulted in greater willingness to learn the material, options selection, time on task, perceived interdependence, and supportiveness for partners. Carlson and Falk (1989) and Noell and Carnine (1989) found that students in cooperative groups perform higher than students working alone on learning tasks involving interactive videodiscs. Adams, Carson, and Hamm (1990) suggest that cooperative learning can influence attention, motivation, and achievement when students use the medium of television.

35.9.4 Learner Control

Combining cooperative learning and technology-assisted instruction results in students having more control over their learning (see 33.1 to 33.3). Simon Hooper and his associates (Hooper, 1992; Hooper, Temiyakarn & Williams, 1993) note that three forms of lesson control are used in the design of technology-based instruction: learner, program, and adaptive control. *Learner control* involves delegating instructional decisions to learners so that they can determine what help they need (see 33.2), what difficulty level or content density of material they wish to study, in what sequence they wish to learn material, and how much they want to learn. *Program or linear control* prescribes an identical instructional sequence for all students regardless of interest or need. *Adaptive control* modifies lesson features according to student aptitude (see 22.1; Snow, 1980), prior performance (see 22.3.4.4; Tobias, 1987), or ongoing lesson needs (e.g., Tennyson, Christensen & Park, 1984).

Of the three, learner control may be the most important, as Hooper (1992) notes that the field of technology-assisted instruction seems to be moving toward learner-controlled environments, such as simulations, hypermedia (see Chapter 21), and on-line databases. He suggests that as learner control increases so does instructional effectiveness and efficiency (Reigeluth & Stein, 1983) and learner independence, efficiency, mental effort, and motivation (Federico, 1980; Salomon, 1983, 1985; Steinberg, 1984). On the other hand, linear or program control may impose an inappropriate lesson sequence on learners and thereby lower their motivation, and adaptive instruction may foster learner dependence (Hannafin & Rieber, 1989).

Technology-assisted cooperative learning tends to increase the effectiveness of learner control. When students work alone, in isolation from their peers, they tend not to control the learning situation productively, making ineffective instructional decisions and leaving instruction prematurely (Carrier, 1984; Hannafin, 1984; Milheim & Martin, 1991; Steinberg, 1977, 1989). Students working cooperatively tend to motivate each other to seek elaborative feedback to their responses to practice items during learning control and to seek a greater variety of feedback types more frequently than did those working alone (Carrier & Sales, 1987). Additionally, the cooperative pairs spent longer times inspecting information on the computer screen as they discussed which level of feedback they needed and what the answers were to practice items. McDonald (1993) found that students in the learner-controlled/cooperative learning condition selected more options during the lesson, and spent more time interacting with the tutorial, than did students in the learner-controlled/individual learning condition. Hooper, Temiyakarn, and Williams (1995) found that students in the program-control conditions attempted more than 4 times as many examples and nearly twice as many practice questions as did the students in the learner-control conditions. The LOGO computer environment (see 12.3.2.1, 24.5.1.3) tends to promote more actual learner control over the task structure and the making of rules to govern it than does the CAI computer environment (Battista & Clements, 1986; Clements & Nastasi, 1985, 1988; Nastasi, Clements & Battista, 1990). Learner control seems to be most effective when prior knowledge is high or when students possess well-developed metacognitive abilities (Garhart & Hannafin, 1986). What these studies imply is that cooperative learning is an important variable in improving the effectiveness of learner-controlled environments.

35.9.5 Attitudes Toward Technology-Based Instruction

Cooperative learning tends to promote positive attitudes toward technology-based instruction. A key aspect of technology-assisted instruction is the student attitudes generated by the experience. Students are more likely to learn from and to use technology-based instruction in the future when their self-efficacy toward technology and attitudes about

technology-based instruction are positive (Sutton, 1991). Hooper, Temiyakarn, and Williams (1995) found that students developed more positive attitudes toward the computer-based instructional lesson when they worked in cooperative learning groups than when they worked individually. McDonald (1993) found that students developed more positive attitudes toward learning with a computer in the cooperative conditions than in the individualistic conditions. Huang (1993) found that students working cooperatively had more positive attitudes toward the computer-based lesson than did students working individually. Students appear to enjoy using the computer to engage in cooperative activities (Bonk, Southerly, Brantmayer & Smith, 1991).

35.9.6 Attitudes Toward Cooperative Learning

Closely related to the attitudes toward technology (see 34.6) are students' attitudes toward cooperative learning. Students with negative attitudes about cooperative learning may be less likely to invest effort in the group process and to engage in actions that mediate achievement. Mevarech et al. (1985) found that students who learned in pairs were more positive in their attitudes toward cooperative learning than were students who worked individually with the computer. Evaluations obtained by Rocklin et al. (1985) from students involved in computer-based cooperative learning were more positive towards cooperative learning and how it affected them personally than were subjects who worked individually. Hooper, Temiyakarn, and Williams (1995) found that students working in cooperative pairs developed more positive attitudes toward cooperative learning than did students working alone. Hooper et al. (1993) found that students rated cooperative learning in a computer-assisted lesson almost a point higher on a five-point scale than did students who worked alone. Dyer (1993) found that students in the structured cooperative learning conditions developed more positive attitudes toward working cooperatively than did students in the unstructured cooperative learning or the individualistic learning condition. McDonald (1993) and Huang (1993) both found that students in the cooperative conditions developed more positive attitudes toward working cooperatively than students working alone. Thus, when technology-assisted instruction is used, students' attitudes toward the instructional experience will be more positive when cooperative learning is an inherent part of the lesson.

35.9.7 Cognitive Development: Cooperation and Controversy

Social-cognitive theory posits that cognitive development is facilitated by individuals (Bearison, 1982; Johnson & Johnson, 1979, 1992; Perret-Clermont, 1980): (a) working cooperatively with peers on tasks that require coordination of actions or thoughts, (b) collaborators contradicting and challenging each other's intuitively derived concepts and points of view (i.e., engaging in *academic controversy*), thereby creating cognitive conflict within and among group members, and (c) the successful and equitable (members contributing approximately equally) resolution of those conflicts (learners have to go beyond mere disagreement to benefit from cognitive conflict [Bearison, Magzament & Filardi, 1986; Damon & Killen, 1982]). In order to create the conditions under which cognitive development takes place, students must work cooperatively, challenge each other's points of view, and resolve the resulting cognitive conflicts. Douglas Clements and Bonnie Nastasi have conducted a series of studies on the occurrence of cooperation and controversy in technology-assisted instruction (Battista & Clements, 1986; Clements & Nastasi, 1985, 1988; Nastasi & Clements, 1992; Nastasi, Clements & Battista, 1990). They have found that both LOGO (see 12.3.2.1, 24.5.1.3) and CAI/CBI-W computer environments promoted considerable cooperative work and conflict (both social and cognitive). The LOGO environment (compared to CAI/CBI-W computer and traditional classroom tasks environments) promoted (a) more peer interaction focused on learning and problem solving, (b) self-directed problem solving (i.e., learners solve problems they themselves have posed) in which there is mutual "ownership" of the problem, (c) more frequent occurrence and resolution of cognitive conflicts, (d) greater development of executive level problem-solving skills (planning, monitoring, decision making), higher-level reasoning, and cognitive development. The development of higher-level cognitive processes seemed to be facilitated by the resolution of cognitive conflict that arises out of cooperating. They also found that the LOGO (compared with the CAI) computer environment resulted in more learner satisfaction and expressions of pleasure at the discovery of new information and their work, variables reflective of intrinsic and competence motivation. Clements and Nastasi conclude that the LOGO environment generally promotes the development of motivated, self-directed learners who seek to validate their ideas not only through their own reasoning but also through meaningful communication with others.

35.9.8 Increasing Social Competencies

If students are to work effectively in cooperative groups, they must have the teamwork skills to do so. In order to examine the importance of social skills training on the productiveness of cooperative groups, it is possible to compare studies that have included cooperative skills training and those that have not. A number of studies have found that when teamwork procedures and skills are present, cooperative learning results in higher achievement in technology-assisted instructional lessons than individualistic learning (Hooper & Hannafin, 1991; Hooper & Hannafin, 1988a; Hooper, 1991; Johnson R., Johnson & Stanne, 1985, 1986). In studies where teamwork procedures and skills were not emphasized, reliable differences in achievement in

cooperative and individualistic technology-assisted instruction were not found (Meuarech, Stern & Leuita, 1987; Underwood & McCaffrey, 1990; Hooper, Ward, Hannafin & Clark, 1989).

Software designers may be able to facilitate the development use of the interpersonal and small-group skills required for teamwork in several ways:

1. Before students engage in the actual instruction, they might first be required to complete a tutorial activity designed to introduce or refresh their understanding of cooperative skills. This could include a discussion of each member's role and its value in determining the overall group success.
2. Teachers' guides can suggest roles to assign to each group member to perform in the group (keyboarder, recorder, checker for understanding, encourager of participation).
3. Allow time for group processing to analyze and discuss how effectively they are working together and how they may work more effectively together in the future. Software could be designed to include pauses during which group members are directed to focus on their progress, discuss the records they are keeping, or reflect on improvements or changes they might make to increase performance.
4. The software could periodically remind students to monitor their own performance and to assist in optimizing group performance.
5. Yueh and Alessi (1988) suggest that group reward is crucial to provide a group goal motivating everyone to work well together, and individual accountability is needed to create a feeling of fairness among group members. Tangible prizes are recognition for individual successes, and group achievement offers motivation to succeed on both levels. One computer-generated reward would be a printout of collective characters, coupons, or certificates that are assigned points or a relative value, or are valued based on the number accumulated. These items could be displayed by students where they would be acknowledged by the teacher and other classmates.

35.9.9 Preference for Using Technology Cooperatively

There is a natural partnership between technology and cooperation. There is evidence that individuals prefer to work cooperatively at the computer (Hawkins, Sheingold, Gearhart & Berger, 1982; Levin & Kareev, 1980; Muller & Perlmutter, 1985). The introduction of computers into classrooms increases cooperative behavior and task-oriented verbal interaction (Chernick & White, 1981, 1983; Hawkins, Sheingold, Gearhart & Berger, 1982; Levin & Kareev, 1980; Rubin, 1983; Webb, 1984). Working at a computer collaboratively with classmates seems to be more fun and enjoyable, as well as more effective, to most students. Students are more likely to seek each other out at the computer than they normally would for other school work. Even when students play electronic games, they prefer to have partners and associates. The computer may not only be a good place to cooperate but may also be a good place to introduce cooperative learning groups in schools.

35.9.10 Group Composition

A factor hypothesized to effect the success of technology-assisted cooperative learning is whether cooperative learning groups are composed homogeneously or heterogeneously. There is considerable disagreement. Advocates of heterogeneous grouping point out that students are more likely to gain sophistication and preparation for life in a heterogeneous society by working cooperatively with classmates from diverse cultures, attitudes, and perspectives rather than by learning in homogeneous groups or studying alone. Proponents of heterogeneous ability grouping point out that (a) high-achieving students benefit by the cognitive restructuring that occurs when providing in-depth explanations to peers, and (b) less academically successful students benefit from the extra attention, alternative knowledge representations, and modeling that more academically successful students provide (Johnson & Johnson, 1989; Webb, 1989). Students in heterogeneous-ability groups learned more than did students in homogeneous-ability groups (Yager, Johnson & Johnson, 1985; Yager, Johnson, Johnson & Snider, 1986). Beane and Lemke (1971) found that high-ability students benefited more from heterogeneous than homogeneous grouping. The academic discussion and peer interaction in heterogeneous groups promotes the discovery of more effective reasoning strategies than would occur in homogeneous groups (Johnson & Johnson, 1979; Berndt, Perry & Miller, 1988).

Proponents of homogeneous-ability grouping, however, state that heterogeneous-ability grouping may fail to challenge high-ability students (Willis, 1990) and that less academically successful students benefit at the expense of their more successful partners (Mills & Durden, 1992; Robinson, 1990). Many of the most carefully conducted studies aimed at resolving this controversy have been focused on ability grouping in technologically-assisted instruction. Webb (1982) and Swing and Peterson (1982) reported that heterogeneous grouping hinders the performance of average-performing students when groups include a wide range of student performance levels.

In a week-long study on the learning of LOGO, Webb (1984) investigated whether the higher-ability students in cooperative groups of three would try to monopolize the computer. She found that (a) student ability did not relate to contact time with the computer, and (b) student success in programming was predicted by different profiles of abilities and by group process variables such as verbal interaction. Yueh and Alessi (1988) used group ability composition as

one of their treatments for students utilizing the computer to learn three topics in algebra. They formed groups of medium-ability students and groups of mixed-ability students, and found that group composition had no significant effect on achievement.

In a study with 40 eighth-grade students, Hooper and Hannafin (1988a) had students work in cooperative groups of three or four which were classified as homogeneous low, homogeneous high, or heterogeneous. Students worked on a computer task. Low-ability students working with high-ability partners achieved higher than did low-ability students studying in homogeneous groups or alone, and the achievement of high-ability students was basically the same whether they worked with a low-achieving partner, a high-achieving partner, or studied alone.

Hooper and Hannafin (1991) conducted a study involving 125 sixth- and seventh-grade students. Subjects were randomly assigned to homogeneous or heterogeneous pairs, and the pairs were randomly assigned to cooperative or individualistic conditions. The high-ability students interacted equally across treatments, but low-ability students interacted 30% more when placed in heterogeneous pairs. Increases in achievement and cooperation were significantly related within heterogeneous groups.

Simsek and Hooper (1992) compared the effects of cooperative and individual learning on student performance and attitudes during interactive videodisc instruction. Thirty fifth- and sixth-grade students were classified as high or low ability and randomly assigned to cooperative or individual treatments. Students completed a level II interactive videodisc science lesson. The achievement, attitudes, and time-on-task of high- and low-ability students working alone or in cooperative groups were compared. Results indicated that both high- and low-ability students performed better on the posttest when they learned in cooperative groups than did their counterparts who learned alone. Students who worked individually spent less time-on-task. Members of cooperative groups developed more positive attitudes toward instruction, teamwork, and peers than did students studying alone.

Simsek and Tsai (1992) compared the effects of homogeneous- versus heterogeneous-ability grouping on performance and attitudes of students working cooperatively during interactive videodisc instruction. After two cooperative training sessions, 80 fourth- through sixth-grade students, classified as high and low ability, were randomly assigned to treatments. Students completed a level II interactive videodisc science lesson. The amount of instructional time for each group was also recorded. Homogeneous low-ability groups scored significantly lower than the other three groups, while the difference between achievement of high-ability students in homogeneous and heterogeneous groups was not statistically significant. Homogeneous low-ability groups consistently used the least amount of time. Low-ability students in heterogeneous groups had significantly more positive attitudes than did their high-ability groupmates.

Hooper (1992) compared individual and cooperative learning in an investigation of the effects of ability grouping on achievement, instructional efficacy, and discourse during computer-based mathematics instruction. A total of 115 fifth- and sixth-grade students were classified as having high or average ability and were randomly assigned to group or individual treatments. Students in the cooperative condition were assigned to either heterogeneous or homogeneous dyads, according to ability. Results indicated that students completed the instruction more effectively in groups than alone. In groups, achievement and efficiency were highest for high-ability homogeneously grouped students and lowest for average-ability homogeneously grouped students. Generating and receiving help were significant predictors of achievement, and average-ability students generated and received significantly more help in heterogeneous groups than in homogeneous ones.

Hooper, Temiyakarn, and Williams (1995) compared cooperative and individualistic learning on academically high- and average/low–performing students. They classified 175 fourth-grade students as high or average/low performing academically and randomly assigned them to paired or individual conditions strategies by performance level. Performance level was determined by scores on the mathematics subscale of the California Achievement Test. High-performing students scored at or above the median, and average/low–ability students scored below the median score of all fourth-grade students in the school. All cooperative pairs consisted of one high and one average/low–performing student. They found that the students in the cooperative conditions performed higher on a computer-assisted symbolic reasoning task than did the students in the individualistic conditions. The greatest benefactors from the group learning experience appeared to be the highest-performing students. Overall achievement increased by almost 20% for high-academic-ability students, but only 4% for average-ability students. High-ability students may have benefited from generating explanations for their less-able partners. Less-able partners might have adopted more passive roles. Mulryan (1992) found that the highest-achieving students adopted the more active roles in cooperative learning groups and the least-able students demonstrated high levels of passive behavior, a pattern that according to Webb (1989) further decreases the achievement of the passive students.

Siann and Macleod (1986) found that mixed-gender pairs working on a LOGO programming exercise were dominated by the males (females were less motivated and successful). Underwood and McCaffrey (1990) studied pairs of students (10 and 11 years of age) on a computer task filling in missing letters from words. They were not told how to work together. Single-sex pairs were more productive than mixed-sex pairs, who did not improve in performance over the individual performance of group members. Single-sex pairs worked by discussion and agreement, with each member of the pair contributing and both sharing keyboard control. In contrast, the mixed-gender

pairs tended simply to divide the labor, with one taking over the keyboard and the other instructing the typist, with little discussion of or negotiation about alternative solutions.

The results of these studies indicate that cooperative learning may be used effectively with both homogeneous and heterogeneous groups, but that the greatest educational benefits may be derived when heterogeneous groups work with technology-assisted instruction. In heterogeneous cooperative learning groups, low-ability students increased their achievement considerably, and high-ability students generally either increased their achievement or achieved at the same levels as did their counterparts in homogeneously high groups.

35.9.11 Gender

The gender of group members has been hypothesized to be an important factor in determining the success of technology-assisted cooperative learning. Johnson, Johnson, Richards, and Buckman (1986) found that computer-assisted cooperative learning, compared with competitive and individualistic computer-assisted learning, increased the positiveness of female students' attitudes toward computers, equalized the status and respect among group members regardless of gender, and resulted in a more equal participation pattern between male and female members. While females in cooperative groups liked working with the computer more than males did, there was no significant difference in oral interactions between males and females. Dalton et al. (1987) examined interactions between instructional method and gender and found that cooperative learning was rated more favorably by low-ability females than by low-ability males. Other studies noted no significant differences in performance between males and females in computer-based instruction cooperative learning settings (Mevarech, Stern & Levita, 1987; Webb, 1984). Carrier and Sales (1987) compared female pairs, male pairs, and mixed pairs among college juniors and noted that female pairs verbalized the most while male pairs verbalized the least, and that male-female pairs demonstrated the most off-task behavior. Lee (1993) found that males tended to become more verbally active and females tended to become less verbally active in equal-ratio, mixed-gender groups.

A study that looked at mixed-gender groups versus single-gender groups was done by Underwood and McCaffrey (1990) in England. Two classes of students between the ages of 10.5 years and 11.4 years from a single school were the subjects in this study. Forty girls and 40 boys were randomly assigned to three types of pairs: male/male, female/female, and male/female. The study was divided into three sessions. The first session had the subjects working individually. In the second session, subjects worked in pairs. The third session also involved pairs, but subjects who were in mixed pairs were shifted to single-gender pairs, and single-gender pairs were assigned to mixed pairs. The subjects worked with a computer program in language tasks that required them to place missing letters into text. The results showed that single-gender pairs completed more stories and had more correct responses than did mixed-gender pairs. When subjects were shifted from single-gender pairs to mixed-gender pairs, their level of activity decreased, but there was no change in their overall performance. The study found no overall differences for gender on any of the measures. No cooperative training of subjects was undertaken for this study, and it was found that mixed pairs rarely discussed their answers. Rather, one subject operated the keyboard and the other gave directions.

Overall, there is mixed evidence concerning the impact of technology-assisted instruction on males and females. A conservative interpretation of the existing research is that there will be no performance differences between males and females on technology-assisted cooperative learning, but females will have more positive attitudes toward using technology when they learn in cooperative groups.

35.9.12 Networking into Teams

Technology such as electronic mail, bulletin boards, and conferences can be used to create teams made up of individuals who are widely separated geographically. In an electronically networked team, interaction no longer has to be face to face; team members can be anywhere in the world. In electronically networked teams, members may depend on one another differently than they do in face-to-face teams. Meetings only require that members be at their terminals. Communication between meetings can be asynchronous and extremely fast in comparison with telephone conversations and interoffice mail. Participation may be more equalized and less affected by prestige and status (McGuire, Kiesler & Siegel, 1987; Siegel, Dubrovsky, Kiesler & McGuire, 1986). Electronic communication, however, relies almost entirely on plain text for conveying messages, text that is often ephemeral, appearing on and disappearing from a screen without any necessary tangible artifacts. It becomes easy for a sender to be out of touch with his or her audience. And it is easy for the sender to be less constrained by conventional norms and rules for behavior in composing messages. Communicators can feel a greater sense of anonymity, detect less individuality in others, feel less empathy, feel less guilt, be less concerned over how they compare with others, and be less influenced by social conventions (Kiesler, Siegel & McGuire, 1984; Short, Williams & Christie, 1976). Such influences can lead both to more honesty and more "flaming" (name calling and epithets).

35.9.13 The Need for Groupware

For cooperation to take place, students must have a joint workspace. One of the promises of the computer is to allow students all over the world to create powerful shared spaces: super blackboards and super models. Instead of sharing a blackboard or a worktable, people from a wide variety of locations can share a computer screen. The future of technology-assisted cooperative learning will be greatly enhanced by developing both appropriate software and hardware to create workspaces that may be shared by all members of a group, all groups within the same classroom (or school), and all groups in a network that stretches throughout the world. Increasingly, work is being done in self-managing teams, networked electronically with other teams throughout the company and the world. The ability of the hardware to allow or even require people to work cooperatively is an important design issue. Developers of hardware need to think seriously about how technology can increase human cooperation within education and within the workplace. In addition, a challenge facing software programmers is to write *groupware* to support group rather than individual work. The availability of groupware will increase the productivity of joint efforts. In order to write such software, programmers need to understand the nature of cooperation and the five basic elements that mediate its effectiveness.

35.10 QUESTIONS ABOUT TECHNOLOGY-ASSISTED COOPERATIVE LEARNING

Given the powerful effects of cooperation on achievement, relationships, and psychological adjustment, and given the numerous advantages of using technology-assisted cooperative learning, there are a number of questions about the use of technology that may tentatively be answered. The first question is: *Does technology effect achievement or is it merely a means of delivering instruction?* In a review of research, Clark (1983) concluded that technology is merely a means of delivering instruction. Our results support his conclusion. There are cognitive consequences of discussing what one is learning with classmates that technology cannot duplicate. Social interaction is essential for effective learning, the transformation of the mind, and the development of expertise.

The second question is: *Is a "dialogue" with a computer as effective in promoting achievement, higher-level reasoning, and ability to apply learning as a "dialogue" with a peer?* It takes more than the presentation of information to have a dialogue. There needs to be an exchange of knowledge that leads to epistemic conflict and intellectual challenge and curiosity. Such an exchange is personal as well as informational. It involves respect for and belief in each other's abilities and commitment to each other's learning. Our results and the results of other researchers indicate that a dialogue with a peer is far more powerful than one with a computer. The third question is: *Can a computer pass as a person?* Our research leads to the tentative conclusion that a person interacts quite differently with a computer than he or she does with another person. Machines and people are not equally interesting or persuasive. With another person, there is a commitment to his or her learning and well-being. It is rare to feel the same emotions toward a machine. Fourth: *Is the effectiveness of a message separate from the medium?* Generally, the research on cognitive development indicates that the same information, presented in other formats (especially nonsocial formats), is only marginally effective in promoting genuine cognitive development (Murray, 1983; Johnson & Johnson, 1989).

Fifth: *Is technology an amplifier or a transformer of the mind?* An *amplifier* serves tool function like note taking or measuring. A *transformer* leads to the discovery and invention of principles. If technological learning devices are transformers, the habitual technology users eventually will be in a new stage of mental functioning. Neil Postman (1985) believes that the introduction into a culture of a technique such as writing or a clock is not merely an extension of the power of human beings to record information or bind time but a transformation of their way of thinking and the content of human culture. Generally, therefore, it may be concluded that technology such as the computer is a tool to amplify the minds of students. As a tool, the computer (as well as the calculator) can free students from the rote memorization of methods of mathematical formulation and formula-driven science, allowing more time for underlying concepts to be integrated with physical examples. A danger of the computer is that a student will know what button to push to get the right answer without understanding the underlying process or developing the ability to solve the problem on his or her own without the computer. There is far more to expertise than knowing how to run hardware and software.

Finally, the sixth question is: *Can technology such as computers prepare a student for the "real world"?* Technological expertise is helpful in finding and holding a job. Working in a modern organization, however, requires team skills such as leadership and conflict management and the ability to engage in interpersonal problem solving. While it is clear that cooperative learning is an analog to modern organizational life, experience in using technology in and of itself may only marginally improve employability and job success. A person has to have interpersonal competence as well as technical competence.

35.11 THE FUTURE OF TECHNOLOGY-ASSISTED COOPERATIVE LEARNING

Technology-assisted cooperative learning has yet to realize its great promise. It currently rests on the strengths of cooperative learning. Cooperative learning has a well-formulated theory validated by hundreds of research studies, translated into a set of practical procedures that teachers and administrators may use, and actually implemented in tens-of-thousands of classrooms throughout the world. Despite the success of cooperative learning, there are three great shortcomings of technology-assisted cooperative learning.

First, there is a lack of theorizing. Conceptual models of how technology and teamwork may be productively integrated are practically nonexistent. The variables unique to the combination of technology and cooperation have not been identified and defined. *Second*, relatively little research has been done. Overall, the quality of the existing research is quite high. Only a few of the potential outcomes, however, have been studied. The unique strengths of technology-assisted cooperative learning have not been assessed and documented. Rather, investigators have examined more general variables such as the composition of cooperative groups and the gender of members. *Third*, the lack of conceptual models and the scarcity of research has created a corresponding lack of guidelines for practice. Teachers can be trained to implement cooperative learning, but training is underdeveloped in the specific procedures for implementing technology-assisted cooperative learning. Operational procedures are needed for designing and implementing instructional procedures that optimize the impact of technology-assisted cooperative learning on student achievement and other important outcomes. Equivalent procedures need to be designed for work environments where technology and teamwork are used together.

What is needed is theory to stimulate research, which, in turn, will validate and modify the theory. The results need to be used to design specific procedures for operationalizing technology-assisted cooperative learning in every grade level and subject area. Without systematic research, proponents of technology-assisted cooperative learning cannot present a persuasive case for the adoption of an effective training program for teachers. On the positive side, there has been so little research on technology-assisted cooperative learning that the future is wide open to interested social scientists.

There are, however, several areas for researchers to focus on. *First*, there is a need to look at outcomes other than achievement. The impact of technology-assisted cooperative learning on relationships among students and aspects of psychological health need to be examined. *Second*, there is a need for long-term studies that track the use of technology across at least one school year and ideally for several years. Short-term studies of initial use are not enough. The real question is whether the use of the technology will be maintained over several years. *Third*, the implementation process by which technology-assisted cooperative learning is institutionalized within schools needs to be documented and studied. While advocates of technology see a revolution coming in instruction, historians point to the virtual absence of lasting or profound changes in classroom practice over the past 100 years. Despite brief periods of popularity, new instructional technologies such as education television, language labs, and programmed learning were tried and dropped. Life in classrooms remains largely unchanged. Lepper and Gurtner (1989) argue that the last "technology" to have had a major impact on the way schools are run is the blackboard. Most often new technologies are used in ways that do not disrupt regular classroom practices, which means that they can be dropped with no disruption to ongoing classroom life. Similarly, software selection is often conducted with the intention of supporting existing classroom practices rather than transforming them. Considerably more research is needed on the implementation process by which the combination of cooperative learning and learning technologies become integrated and institutionalized in classroom and schools.

Fourth, studies need to focus on the role of teachers and administrators in the implementation process. No matter how good technology is, unless teachers decide to use it and gain some expertise in how to implement it, the technology will not be adopted by schools. *Fifth,* there need to be studies examining the support services required for technology to be used in the classroom. Who repairs the technology and how often are repairs needed are important questions. Teachers, for example, cannot be expected to be computer technicians.

Sixth, cognitive growth and the development of problem-solving skills depend on epistemic conflict, that is, the collision of adverse opinion (Bearison, 1982; Johnson & Johnson, 1992; Piaget, 1950). Students need the opportunity to experience and resolve academic controversies. Computers and multimedia presentations rarely engage students in intellectual conflict the same way other students can. The role of technology in promoting and facilitating intellectual conflicts among students has not been investigated.

Seventh, there is a question whether technology-assisted instruction will increase inequality in educational outcomes (Becker & Sterling, 1987). Students who have access to the new technologies in their homes will be more skilled and sophisticated in their uses than will students who have no access. Equality in the classroom may require heterogeneous grouping where students who are skilled in the use of instructional technologies work with students who are not. Cooperative learning is an essential aspect of such equalization. New studies need to be conducted on group composition focusing on the ability of students to use instructional technologies.

Schools eventually may have to make greater use of appropriate technologies and cooperative learning. Multiple ongoing revolutions in technology and classroom organization require schools to prepare students to make wise choices in situations where there is an overabundance of information and they are part of a team. It may be technology-assisted cooperative learning that best prepares students to live in the modern world.

35.12 SUMMARY

Media technologies can have pervasive and powerful effects on the nature of society and the thinking and communicating of its members. There can be little doubt that technology will increasingly be utilized in instructional situations. In the past, however, teachers and schools have been very slow in adopting new technologies and very quick in discontinuing its use. The failure of schools to adopt available instructional technologies and to maintain (let alone continuously improve) their use may be at least in part due to two barriers: (a) the individual assumption underlying most hardware and software development and (b) the failure to utilize cooperation learning as an inherent part of using instructional technologies.

A recurrent problem is that most technologies traditionally have carried an individualistic bias. Individualized instruction is difficult, as meaningful individual differences are hard to identify, let alone translate into instructional practice. As long as hardware and software designers are fixated on individuals, the potential for technology in education is limited.

The alternative to individual use of technologies is their use by cooperative learning groups. *Cooperative learning* is the instructional use of small groups so that students work together to maximize their own and each other's learning. There are four basic types of cooperative learning: formal cooperative learning, informal cooperative learning, base groups, and academic controversies. *Technology-assisted cooperative learning* exists when the instructional use of technology is combined with the use of cooperative learning groups. What underlies cooperative learning's popularity is that it is based on a well-formulated theory that has been validated by numerous research studies and translated into practical procedures that can be used at any level of education. The three theoretical perspectives that have contributed to cooperative learning are cognitive-developmental theory, behavioral learning theory, and social interdependence theory. It is the latter perspective that has had the most profound influences on the development of cooperative learning. Between 1898 and 1989, over 550 experimental and 100 correlational studies were conducted comparing the relative effectiveness of cooperative, competitive, and individualistic efforts. Their findings verify that positive interdependence results in promotive interaction among students; negative interdependence results in oppositional interaction; and no interdependence results in the absence of interaction. The multiple outcomes resulting from promotive interaction (compared with oppositional and no interaction) may be classified into three categories: effort to achieve, positive interpersonal relationships, and psychological health. Generally, cooperative efforts result in higher achievement, more positive relationships, and greater psychological health than do competitive or individualistic efforts.

Not all groups, however, are cooperative groups. Teachers may assign students to pseudo-learning groups, traditional-learning groups, or cooperative-learning groups. Pseudo- and traditional-learning groups are characterized by lack of group maturity, uncritically giving one's dominant response, social loafing, free riding, motivational losses, and group think. To be a cooperative learning group, five basic elements must be structured within the learning situation: positive interdependence, face-to-face promotive interaction, individual accountability, social skills, and group processing. It is these five elements that give cooperation its power. In order for schools to adopt technology and maintain its use over time, the school organizational structure must change from a mass-manufacturing structure to a team-based, high-performance structure (known as the *cooperative school*).

From the research on technology-assisted cooperative learning, a number of conclusions may be made:

1. Cooperative learning is more cost effective in using technology-assisted instruction than is competitive or individualistic learning.
2. When students are taught to use technology, cooperative-learning groups produce higher achievement than do competitive or individualistic learning.
3. There is a great deal of evidence that when technology-assisted learning is to be used, cooperative learning (compared with competitive and individualistic learning) will result in higher achievement, higher-level reasoning, and long-term retention. There can be little doubt that when technology is involved, individuals should work in teams rather than individualistically or competitively.
4. Cooperative-learning groups provide more productive use of learner control during technology-assisted instruction than do competitive or individualistic learning.
5. Learners will have more positive attitudes toward technology-based instruction and cooperative learning when they participate in cooperative rather than competitive or individualistic learning.
6. Cooperative-learning experiences promote greater cognitive development during technology-assisted instruction than do competitive or individualistic learning.
7. Cooperative-learning experiences promote higher achievement on technology-assisted learning tasks when social skills are taught and emphasized.
8. Learners tend to prefer to work cooperatively at the computer.
9. While technology-assisted cooperative learning may be used with either homogeneous or heterogeneous groups, learners will often achieve more in heterogeneous groups.
10. Females will achieve equally to males and have more positive attitudes toward technology and technology-assisted instruction when they learn in cooperative groups than when they learn competitively or individualistically.
11. Technology creates the possibility of cooperative groups in which members from widely different locations are electronically networked to achieve common goals.

What this research illuminates is that cooperative learning and technology-assisted instruction have complementary strengths. The more technology is used to teach, the more necessary cooperative learning is. The computer, for example, can control the flow of work, monitor accuracy, give electronic feedback, and do calculations. Cooperative learning provides a sense of belonging, the opportunity to explain and summarize what is being learned, social models, respect and approval for efforts to achieve, encouragement of divergent thinking, and interpersonal feedback on academic learning and the use of the technology.

There are a number of questions that must be asked about technology-assisted instruction. Does technology affect achievement or is it only a means for delivering instruction? Current evidence indicates that computers deliver instruction, but they do not affect achievement in and of themselves. Is a dialogue with the computer as effective as a dialogue with another person in promoting achievement and higher-level reasoning? The answer seems to be No. Can the computer pass as a person? The answer seems to be No. Cooperators are people, not machines. Is the effectiveness of a message separate from the medium? The answer seems to be Yes; messages from other people are more powerful and influential than are messages from machines. Is technology an amplifier or a transformer of the mind? The answer seems to be an amplifier. Technology amplifies communication, but it takes other people to transform each other's minds.

The dearth of research on technology-assisted instruction and the absence of theoretically relevant, well-controlled studies on technology-assisted cooperative learning are major barriers for implementation. The interdependence between the use of technology-assisted instruction and cooperative learning is relatively unexplored. Technologies can either facilitate or obstruct cooperation. The future of technology-assisted cooperative learning depends on the development of software written for cooperative groups and the development of hardware that both requires and facilitates cooperative efforts within the group, among groups in the classroom, and among groups throughout the world.

REFERENCES

Archer-Kath, J., Johnson, D.W. & Johnson, R. (1994). Individual versus group feedback in cooperative groups. *Journal of Social Psychology.*

Adams, D., Carson, H. & Hamm, M. (1990). *Cooperative learning and educational media.* Englewood Cliffs, NJ: Educational Technology.

Ames, R. & Lau, S. (1982). An attributional analysis of student help-seeking in academic settings. *Journal of Educational Psychology 74,* 414–23.

Aronson, E. (1978). *The jigsaw classroom.* Beverly Hills, CA: Sage.

Bandura, A. (1977). *Social learning theory.* Englewood Cliffs, NJ: Prentice Hall.

Battista, M. & Clements, D. (1986). The effects of Logo and CAI problem-solving environments on problem-solving abilities and mathematics achievement. *Computers in Human Behavior 2,* 183–93.

Beane, W. & Lemke, E. (1971). Group variables influencing the transfer of conceptual behavior. *Journal of Educational Psychology 62* (3), 215–18.

Bearison, D. (1982). New directions in studies of social interaction and cognitive growth. *In* F. Serafica, ed. *Social-cognitive development in context,* 199–221. New York: Guildford.

Bearison, D., Magzamen, S. & Filardo, E. (1986). Socio-cognitive conflict and cognitive growth in young children. *Merrill-Palmer Quarterly 32,* 51–72.

Becker, H. (1984). *School uses of microcomputers: reports from a national survey* (Issue No. 6). Baltimore, MD: Johns Hopkins University, Center for Social Organization of Schools.

— (1985). *The second national U.S. school users of microcomputers survey.* Paper presented at the Second World Conference on Computers in Education, Norfolk, VA.

— & Sterling, C. (1987). Equity in schools computer use: national data and neglected considerations. *Journal of Educational Computing Research 3,* 289–311.

Berndt, T., Perry, T. & Miller, K. (1988). Friends' and classmates' interactions on academic tasks. *Journal of Educational Psychology 80,* 506–13.

Bonk, C., Medury, P. & Reynolds, T. (1995). Cooperative hypermedia: the marriage of collaborative writing and mediated environments. *Computers in the Schools.*

Carlson, H. & Falk, D. (1989). Effective use of interactive videodisc instruction in understanding and implementing cooperative group learning with elementary pupils in social studies. *Theory and Research in Social Education 17* (3), 241–58.

Carrier, C. (1984). Do learners make good choices? A review of research on learner control in instruction. *Instructional Innovator 29* (2), 15–17.

— & Sales, G. (1987). Pair versus individual work on the acquisition concepts in a computer-based instructional lesson. *Journal of Computer-Based Instruction 14* (1), 11–17.

Chernick, R. & White, M. (1981). *Pupils' interaction with microcomputers vs. interaction in classroom settings.* New York: Teachers College, Columbia University, Electronic Learning Laboratory.

— & White, M. (1983, May). *Pupil cooperation in computer learning vs. learning with classroom materials.* Paper presented at the New York State Psychological Association, Liberty, NY.

Clark, R. (1983). Reconsidering research on learning from media. *Review of Educational Research 53,* 445–59.

Clements, D. (1986). Research on Logo and social development. *Logo Exchange 5* (3), 22–24.

— & Nastasi, B. (1985). Effects of computer environments on social-emotional development: Logo and computer-assisted instruction. *Computers in the Schools 2* (2/3), 11–31.

— & Nastasi, B. (1988). Social and cognitive interaction in educational computer environments. *American Educational Research Journal 25,* 87–106.

Cohen, E. (1986). *Designing groupwork: strategies for heterogeneous classrooms.* New York: Teachers College Press.

Cosden, M. & English, J. (1987). The effects of grouping, self-esteem, and locus of control on microcomputer performance and help seeking by mildly handicapped students. *Journal of Educational Computing Research 3,* 443–60.

Cox, D. & Berger, C. (1985). The importance of group size in the use of problem-solving skills on a microcomputer. *Journal of Educational Computing Research 1,* 459–68.

Cuban, L. (1986). *Teachers and machines: the classroom use of technology since 1920.* New York: Teachers College Press.

Dalton, D. (1990a). The effects of cooperative learning strategies on achievement and attitudes during interactive video. *Journal of Computer-Based Instruction 17,* 8–16.

— (1990b, Apr.). *The effects of prior learning on learner interaction and achievement during cooperative computer-based instruction.* Paper presented at the annual meeting of the American Educational Research Association, Boston, MA.

—, Hannafin, M. & Hooper, S. (1989). Effects of individual and cooperative computer-assisted instruction on student performance and attitudes. *Educational Technology Research and Development 37* (2), 15–24.

Damon, W. & Killen, M. (1982). Peer interaction and the process of change in children's moral reasoning. *Merrill-Palmer Quarterly 28,* 347–67.

Deutsch, M. (1949). A theory of cooperation and competition. *Human Relations 2,* 129–52.

— (1962). Cooperation and trust: some theoretical notes. *In* M.R. Jones, ed. *Nebraska symposium on motivation,* 275–319. Lincoln, NE: University of Nebraska Press.

DeVries, D. & Edwards, K. (1974). Student teams and learning games: their effects on cross-race and cross-sex interaction. *Journal of Educational Psychology 66* (5), 741–49.

Dickson, W. & Vereen M. (1985). Two students at one microcomputer. *Theory into Practice 22* (4), 296–300.

Druckman, D., Rozelle, R. & Baxter, J. (1982). *Nonverbal communication: survey, theory, and research.* Beverly Hills, CA: Sage.

Dwyer, D. (1994). Apple classrooms of tomorrow: what we've learned. *Educational Leadership 51* (7), 4–10.

Dyer, L. (1993). *An investigation of the effects of cooperative learning on computer monitored problem solving.* University of Minnesota, Ph.D. dissertation.

Federico, P. (1980). Adaptive instruction: trends and issues. *In* R. Snow, P. Federico & W. Montague, eds. *Aptitude, learning, and instruction: Vol. 1. Cognitive process analysis of aptitude,* 1–26. Hillsdale, NJ: Erlbaum.

Fletcher, B. (1985). Group and individual learning of junior high school children on a micro-computer-based task. *Educational Review 37,* 252–61.

Frank, M. (1984). A comparison between an individual and group goal structure contingency that differed in the behavioral contingency and performance-outcome components (doctoral dissertation, University of Minnesota). *Dissertation Abstracts International 45*/05, 1341-A.

Garhart, C. Hannafin, M. (1986). The accuracy of cognitive monitoring during computer-based instruction. *Journal of Computer-Based Instruction 13,* 88–93.

Hancock, V. & Betts, F. (1994). From the lagging to the leading edge. *Educational Leadership 51* (7), 24–29.

Hannafin, M. (1984). Guidelines for using locus of instructional control in the design of computer-assisted instruction. *Journal of Instructional Development 7* (3), 6–10.

Hannafin, M. & Rieber, L. (1989). Psychological foundations of instructional design for emerging computer-based interactive technologies: Part II. *Educational Technology Research and Development 37* (2), 102–14.

Hawkins, S., Sheingold, K., Gearhart, M. & Berger, C. (1982).

Microcomputers in schools: impact on the social life of elementary classrooms. *Journal of Applied Developmental Psychology 3,* 361–73.

Hill, G. (1982). Group versus individual performance: are N+1 heads better than one? *Psychological Bulletin 91,* 517–39.

Hooper, S. (1992). Effects of peer interaction during computer-based mathematics instruction. *Journal of Educational Research 85* (3), 180-189.

— (1992). Cooperation learning and computer-based instruction. *Educational Technology Research and Development 40* (3), 21–38.

— & Hannafin, M. (1988). Cooperative CBI: the effects of heterogeneous versus homogeneous groups on the learning of progressively complex concepts. *Journal of Educational Computing Research 4* (4), 413–24.

— & — (1991). The effects of group composition on achievement, interaction, and learning efficiency during computer-based cooperative instruction. *Educational Technology Research and Development 39* (3), 27–40.

—, Temiyakarn, C. & Williams, M. (1993). The effects of cooperative learning and learner control on high- and average-ability students. *Educational Technology Research and Development 41* (2).

—, Ward, T., Hannafin, M. & Clark, H. (1989). The effects of aptitude composition on achievement during small group learning. *Journal of Computer-Based Instruction 16,* 102–09.

Hwong, N., Caswell, A., Johnson, D.W. & Johnson, R. (1993). Effects of cooperative and individualistic learning on prospective elementary teachers' music achievement and attitudes. *Journal of Social Psychology 133* (1), 53–64.

Huang, C. (1993). The effects of feedback on performance and attitude in cooperative and individualized computer-based instruction. Minneapolis, MN: University of Minnesota, doctoral dissertation.

Hythecker, V., Rocklin, T., Dansereau, D. Lambiotte, J., Larson, C. & O'Donnell, A. (1985). A computer-based learning strategy training module: development and evaluation. *Journal of Educational Computer Research 1* (3), 275–83.

Innis, H. (1964). *The bias of communication.* Toronto, Canada: University of Toronto Press.

— (1972). *Empire and communication.* Toronto, Canada: University of Toronto Press.

Johnson, D.W. & Johnson, F. (1994). *Joining together: group theory and group skills,* 5th ed. Englewood Cliffs, NJ: Prentice Hall.

— & Johnson, R. (1979). Conflict in the classroom: controversy and learning. *Review of Educational Research 49,* 51–70.

— & — (1986). Computer-assisted cooperative learning. *Educational Technology 26* (1), 12–18.

— & — (1989). *Cooperation and competition: theory and research.* Edina, MN: Interaction.

— & — (1992a). *Creative controversy: intellectual challenge in the classroom.* Edina, MN: Interaction.

— & — (1992b). Positive interdependence: key to effective cooperation. *In* R. Hertz-Lazarowitz & N. Miller, eds. *Interaction in cooperative groups: the theoretical anatomy of group learning,* 174–99. Cambridge, England: Cambridge University Press.

— & — (1992c). Positive interdependence: the heart of cooperative learning. Edina, MN: Interaction.

— & — (1994). *Leading the cooperative school,* 2d ed. Edina, MN: Interaction.

—, — & Holubec, E. (1992). *Advanced cooperative learning.*
Edina, MN: Interaction.

—, — & Holubec, E. (1993). *Cooperation in the classroom.* Edina, MN: Interaction.

—, — & Smith, K. (1991). *Active learning: cooperation in the college classroom.* Edina, MN: Interaction.

—, — & Stanne, M. (1989). Impact of goal and resource interdependence on problem-solving success. *Journal of Social Psychology 129* (5), 621–29.

—, —, Stanne, M. & Garibaldi, A. (1990). The impact of group processing on achievement in cooperative groups. *Journal of Social Psychology 130,* 507–16.

—, —, Richards, S. & Buckman, L. (1986). The effect of prolonged implementation of cooperative learning on social support within the classroom. *Journal of Psychology 119,* 405–11.

Johnson, R. & Johnson, D.W. (1979). Type of task and student achievement and attitudes in interpersonal cooperation, competition, and individualization. *Journal of Social Psychology 116,* 211–19.

—, — & Stanne, M. (1985). Effects of cooperative, competitive, and individualistic goal structures on computer-assisted instruction. *Journal of Educational Psychology 77,* 668–77.

—, — & — (1986). A comparison of computer-assisted cooperative, competitive, and individualistic learning. *American Educational Research Journal 23,* 382–92.

—, —, —, Smizak & Avon (1987). *Effect of composition pairs at the word processor on quality of writing and ability to use the word processor.* Minneapolis, MN: Cooperative Learning Center, University of Minnesota.

Kiesler, S., Siegel, J. & McGuire, T. (1984, Oct.). Social psychological aspects of computer-mediated communication. *American Psychologist 39* (10), 1123–34.

King, A. (1989). Verbal interaction and problem solving within computer-assisted cooperative learning groups. *Journal of Educational Computing Research 5* (1), 1–15.

Lee, M. (1993). Gender, group composition, and peer interaction in computer-based cooperative learning. *Journal of Educational Computing Research 9* (4), 549–77.

Lehrer, R. & Smith, P. (1986, Apr.). *Logo learning: are two heads better than one?* Paper presented at the annual meeting of the American Educational Research Association, San Francisco, CA.

Lepper, M. & Gurtner J. (1989). Children and computers: approaching the twenty-first century. *American Psychologist 44* (2), 170–78.

Levin, J. & Kareev, Y. (1980). Problem-solving in everyday situations. *The Quarterly Newsletter of the Laboratory of Comparative Human Cognition 2,* 47–51.

Lew, M., Mesch, D., Johnson, D.W. & Johnson, R. (1986a). Positive interdependence, academic and collaborative-skills group contingencies and isolated students. *American Educational Research Journal 23,* 476–88.

—, —, — & — (1986b). Components of cooperative learning: effects of collaborative skills and academic group contingencies on achievement and mainstreaming. *Contemporary Educational Psychology 11,* 229–39.

Love, W. (1969). *Individual versus paired learning of an abstract algebra presented by computer assisted instruction.* The Florida State University. (ERIC Document Reproduction Service No. ED 034 403.)

McLuhan, M. (1964). *Understanding media: the extensions of man.* New York: New American Library.

McDonald, C. (1993). *Learner-controlled lesson in coopera-*

tive learning groups during computer-based instruction. University of Minnesota, Ph.D. dissertation.

Mehrabian, A. (1971). *Silent messages.* Belmont, CA: Wadsworth.

Mesch, D., Lew, M., Johnson, D.W. & Johnson, R. (1986). Isolated teenagers, cooperative learning and the training of social skills. *Journal of Psychology 120,* 323–34.

—, Johnson, D.W. & Johnson, R. (1988). Impact of positive interdependence and academic group contingencies on achievement. *Journal of Social Psychology 128,* 345–52.

Mevarech, Z., Stern, D. & Levita, I. (1987). To cooperate or not to cooperate in CAI: that is the question. *Journal of Educational Research 80* (3), 164–67.

Mevarech, Z., Silber, O. & Fine, D. (1991). Learning with computers in small groups: cognitive and affective outcomes. *Journal of Educational Computing Research 7* (2), 233–43.

Milheim, W. & Martin, B. (1991). Theoretical bases for the use of learner control: three different perspectives. *Journal of Computer-Based Instruction 18* (3), 99–105.

Mills, C. & Durden, W. (1992). Cooperative learning and ability groups: an issue of choice. *Gifted Child Quarterly 36* (1), 11–16.

Muller, A. & Perlmutter, M. (1985). Preschool children's problem-solving interactions at computers and jigsaw puzzles. *Journal of Applied Developmental Psychology 6,* 173–86.

Mulryan, C. (1992). Student passivity during cooperative small groups in mathematics. *Journal of Educational Research 85,* 261–73.

Murray, F. (1983). *Cognitive benefits of teaching on the teacher.* Paper presented at American Educational Research Association Annual Meeting, Montreal, Quebec.

Nastasi, B. & Clements, D. (1992). Social-cognitive behaviors and higher-order thinking in educational computer environments. *Learning and Instruction 2,* 215–38.

—, — & Battista, M. (1990). Social-cognitive interactions, motivation, and cognitive growth in logo programming and CAI problem-solving environments. *Journal of Educational Psychology 82,* 150–58.

Noell, J. & Carnine, D. (1989). Group and individual computer-based video instruction. *Educational Technology 29* (1), 36–37.

Okey, J. & Majer, K. (1976). Individual and small-group learning with computer-assisted instruction. *AV Communication Review 24* (1), 79–86.

Perret-Clermont, A. (1980). *Social interaction and cognitive development in children.* New York: Academic.

Piaget, J. (1950). *The psychology of intelligence.* New York: Harcourt, Brace.

Postman, N. (1985). *Ourselves to death: public discourse in the age of show business.* New York: Viking Penguin.

Reigeluth, C. & Stein, F. (1983). The elaborative theory of instruction. *In* C. Reigeluth, ed. *Instructional design theories and models,* 335–82. Hillsdale, NJ: Erlbaum.

Repman, J. (1993). Collaborative, computer-based learning: cognitive and affective outcomes. *Journal of Educational Computing Research 9* (2), 149–63.

Riel, M. (1990). Cooperative learning across classrooms in electronic learning circles. *Instructional Science 19,* 445–66.

Robinson, A. (1990) Cooperation or exploitation? The argument against cooperative learning for talented students. *Journal of Education of the Gifted 14* (3), 9–27.

Rocklin, T., O'Donnell, A., Dansereau, D., Lambiotte, J.,

Hythecker, V. & Larson, C. (1985). Training learning strategies with computer-aided cooperative learning. *Computers in Education 9* (1), 67–71.

Rubin, A. (1983). The computer confronts language arts: cans and shoulds for education. *In* A. Wilkinson, ed. *Classroom computers and cognitive science,* 201–18. San Diego, CA: Academic.

Rysavy, D. & Sales, G. (1991). Cooperative learning in computer-based instruction. *Educational Technology Research and Development 39* (2), 70–79.

Salomon, G. (1983). The differential investment of mental effort in learning from different sources. *Educational Psychologist 18* (1), 42–50.

— (1985). Information technologies: what you see is not (always) what you get. *Educational Psychologist 20* (4), 207–16.

Sarason, I. & Potter, E. (1983). *Self-monitoring: cognitive processes, and performance.* Seattle, WA: University of Washington.

Shlechter, T. (1990). The relative instructional efficiency of small group computer-based training. *Journal of Educational Computing Research 6,* 329–41.

Short, J., Williams, E. & Christie, B. (1976). *The social psychology of telecommunications.* London, England: Wiley.

Showers, C. & Cantor, N. (1985). Social cognition: a look at motivated strategies. *In* M. Rosenzweig & L. Porter, eds. *Annual review of psychology, Vol. 36,* 275–306. Palo Alto, CA: Annual Reviews.

Siann, G. & MacLeod, G. (1986). Computers and children of primary school age: issues and questions. *British Journal of Educational Technology 17,* 133–44.

Siegel, J., Dubrovsky, V., Kiesler, S. & McGuire, T. (1986). Group processes in computer-mediated communication. *Organizational Behavior and Human Decision Processes 37,* 157–87.

Simpson, J. (1986). Computers and collaborative work among students. *Educational Technology 26* (10), 37–44.

Simsek, A. & Hooper, S. (1992). The effects of cooperative versus individual videodisc learning on student performance and attitudes. *International Journal of Instructional Media 19* (3), 209–18.

Simsek, A. & Tsai, B. (1992). The impact of cooperative group composition on student performance and attitudes during interactive videodisc instruction. *Journal of Computer-Based Instruction 19* (3), 86–91.

Slavin, R. (1986). *Using student team learning.* Baltimore, MD: Center for Social Organization of Schools, Johns Hopkins University.

—, Leavey, M. & Madden, N. (1982). *Team-assisted individualization: Mathematics teacher's manual.* Baltimore, MD: Center for Social Organization of Schools, Johns Hopkins University.

Snow, R. (1980). Aptitude, learner control, and adaptive instruction. *Educational Psychologist 15,* 151–58.

Steinberg, E. (1977). Review of student control in computer-assisted instruction. *Journal of Computer-Based Instruction 3* (3), 84–90.

— (1984). *Teaching computers to teach.* Hillsdale, NJ: Erlbaum.

— (1989). Cognition and learner control: a literature review, 1977–88. *Journal of Computer-Based Instruction 16* (4), 117–24.

Stephenson, S. (1992). Effects of student-instructor interaction and paired/individual study on achievement in computer-based training (CBT). *Journal of Computer-Based Instruction 19* (1), 22–26.

Swing, S. & Peterson, P. (1982). The relationship of student ability and small group interaction to student achievement. *American Educational Research Journal 19,* 259–74.

Tennyson, R., Christensen, D. & Park, O. (1984). The Minnesota Adaptive Instructional System: a review of its theory and research. *Journal of Computer-Based Instruction 11* (1), 2–13.

Trevino. L., Lengel, R. & Daft, R. (1987). Media symbolism, media richness, and media choice in organizations: a symbolic interactionist perspective. *Communication Research 14,* 553–74.

Tobias, S. (1987). Mandatory text review and interaction with student characteristics. *Journal of Educational Psychology 79,* 154–61.

Trowbridge, D. & Durnin, R. (1984). *Results from an investigation of groups working at the computer.* Washington, DC: National Science Foundation.

Turk, S. & Sarason, I. (1983). *Test anxiety and causal attributions.* Seattle, WA: University of Washington, Department of Psychology.

Underwood, G. & McCaffrey, M. (1990). Gender differences in a cooperative computer-based language task. *Educational Research 32,* 44–49.

Webb, N. (1982). Group composition, group interaction, and achievement in cooperative small groups. *Journal of Educational Psychology 74* (4), 475–84.

— (1984). Microcomputer learning in small groups: cognitive requirements and group processes. *Journal of Educational Psychology 76,* 1076–88.

— (1987). Peer interaction and learning with computers in small groups. *Computers in Human Behavior 3,* 193–209.

— (1989). Peer interaction and learning in small groups. *International Journal of Educational Research 13,* 21–39.

—, Ender, P. & Lewis, S. (1986). Problem solving strategies and group processes in small group learning computer programming. *American Educational Research Journal 23* (2), 243–61.

Willis, S. (1990). Cooperative learning fallout. *ASCD Update 32* (8), 6, 8.

Yager, S., Johnson, D.W. & Johnson, R. (1985). Oral discussion, group-to-individual transfer, and achievement in cooperative learning groups. *Journal of Educational Psychology 77* (1), 60–66.

Yueh, J. & Alessi, S. (1988). The effects of reward structure and group ability composition on cooperative computer-assisted instruction. *Journal of Computer-Based Instruction 15,* 18–22.

Zimmerman, B. (1986). Becoming a self-regulated learner: which are the key subprocesses? *Contemporary Educational Psychology 11,* 303–13.

36. ERGONOMICS AND THE LEARNING ENVIRONMENT

G. F. McVey

BOSTON UNIVERSITY

36.1 BACKGROUND OF TOPIC

36.1.1 Introduction

In seeking a universally acceptable definition of the *learning environment,* I have borrowed from Tessmer and Harris's useful publication *Analyzing the Instructional Setting* (1992, p. 15): "The learning environment is the physical space allotted for learning. This environment may be a classroom, training center, computer lab, study room at home, office desk, car, or some combination of any of these." In citing the work of Spivak (1975) and David (1975), Tessmer and Harris note (p. 18): "The environment exerts a powerful influence on learning and behavior, even though we may not be aware of it or may choose to disregard it." These authors go on to state that ". . . environment-based (facility) design is still more art than science." While I recognize that this represents the popular conception, I believe that it was more true in the past than it is today. And it is my hope that this chapter will serve to change such perceptions.

Recently there have been significant gains made in our understanding and awareness of ergonomics as applied to the design and utilization of various kinds of environments where people perform tasks not dissimilar to those performed in schools and training centers. I believe that much of that information is readily transferable to the educational sector. In addition, there have been other studies conducted by myself, my students, and by other academicians and their students specifically assessing the merits of design features in educational facilities, which I believe if used collectively with the previously mentioned information are sufficient to make possible educational-facilities design decisions based on hard science. That is one of the primary goals of this chapter, a goal that also embraces my own singular professional objective for more than 25 years.

36.1.2 The Components and Function of the Learning Environment

The learning environment consists of all those physical-sensory elements such as lighting, color, sound, space, furniture, and so on that characterize the place in which a student is expected to learn. This surround should be designed so that learning may proceed with minimum stress and maximum effectiveness. Thus, it should promote sensory comfort and high auditory and visual acuity; and its dimensions and physical layout should accommodate scheduled activities, allow for people's sense of personal space, and promote desirable patterns of social interaction and communication.

In addition to supporting human functioning, the learning environment must accommodate the equipment, tools, and materials that are used in education and training. The introduction of these media, be it chalkboard, computer terminal, video, or film display, inevitably alters the nature of the environment. When a medium is prudently integrated into the learning environment, it may be effectively employed in ways that are coordinated with basic human sensory processes. However, when media technology adds glare, noise, or excessive heat to the learning situation, it vitiates the design of that environment and interferes with those same processes

Consequently, guidelines are required that will enable the facility designer to create learning environments that recognize both how human beings function and how instructional tools operate. The science that investigates such matters is called either *human factors engineering* or *ergonomics,* and knowledge from this science is, I believe, essential for those who design educational facilities. And similarly, I believe that an understanding of ergonomics will help the educator better manage both the equipment and the physical surround to promote effectively his or her educational objectives. Thus, the facility designer, through prudent design in accordance with established ergonomic principles, and the educator, through effective teaching and media utilization, create the learning environment (McVey, 1985).

36.1.3 Defining Ergonomics Relative to the Learning Environment

Ergonomics simply stated is the study of the relationship between people, the work that they perform, and the environment in which such mental and physical activities take place. The term is derived from the Greek words *ergos,* meaning *work,* and *nomos,* meaning *laws.* Consequently ergonomic research methodologies are generally applied toward the multiple goals of determining how work (tasks) can be best designed to maximize an individual's performance, and how the work environment, including tools and equipment, can be best designed to promote the safety, comfort, and the effectiveness and efficiency of the worker in the performance of those tasks.

As noted above, another term considered today to be synonymous with ergonomics is *human factors engineering.* Alphonse Chapanis (1959), one of the long-time academic leaders in the field, describes human factors engineering as "the name applied to that branch of modern technology which deals with ways of designing machines, operations, and work environments so that they match human capacities and limitations." And more recently, the educational technologist Frederick Knirk (1992) identified the objective of ergonomics as ". . . to systematically define, design, and develop effective, safe, comfortable and efficient working, learning, and living environments." Up until around 1980, there seemed to be some minor distinctions between the two terms, with *ergonomics* being a term generally employed in Europe and characterized by a greater physiological focus, while *human factors engineering* was the term primarily used in the United States and characterized by a greater psychological emphasis. Today, such distinctions seem to have evaporated, and the term *ergonomics* has gained the wider usage on both sides of the Atlantic, as well as in the many other countries around the world boasting such organizations and programs.

36.1.4 Ergonomics in Education: A Short History

During the first half of this century, the focus of ergonomic study was on industrial and military tasks and settings. Beginning around the late 1940s and early 1950s, a good amount of this attention was turned toward transportation, the commercial sector, and office work. A smaller and less significant portion was directed toward education. Notable exceptions to this included a series of publications by the National Council on Schoolhouse Construction (today known as the Council of Educational Facility Planners International) aimed at applying research findings toward school facilities design, actually with some efforts made as early as 1921, but becoming more comprehensive during the early 1950s and continuing up to the present time. The initial and continuing purpose of this organization was "to promote the establishment of reasonable standards for school buildings and equipment with regard for economy of expenditure, dignity of design, utility of space, healthful conditions and safety of human life" (Gardner, 1971). As previously noted in recent years, this organization's publications have become increasingly more comprehensive, with such efforts including higher-education facilities and stressing guiding principles and planning goals rather than standards. Its bimonthly publication, *The Educational*

Facility Planner, continues to offer summaries of research having a practical utilitarian bent for the facilities manager, planner, and designer.

36.1.4.1. The Pioneers, Bennett and Harmon. Another notable exception in educational ergonomics began during the early 20s as a doctoral study investigating the posture of elementary and secondary students and their classroom furniture. This study, involving about 4,000 students, was conducted in the schools of Des Moines, Cleveland, Philadelphia, and Winnetka by Henry Eastman Bennett, and culminated in the publication of his findings in the book *School Posture and Seating: A Manual for Teachers, Physical Directors and School Officials* (Bennett, 1928). From the time of that publication and for about a decade, little activity took place in school ergonomics until around 1940, when a series of highly significant studies were initiated by Darrell Boyd Harmon and completed in the early 50s. These involved a series of pioneering epidemiological studies of the physical effects of the school environment on elementary-level students and culminated in a series of comprehensive and highly informative monographs, chief among them *The Co-ordinated Classroom* (Harmon, 1951). Interestingly, this monograph and another by Harmon, *Controlling the Thermal Environment of the Co-ordinated Classroom* (Harmon, 1953), were published by a school furniture company and a heating control systems company, likely indications of the lack of interest shared in "classroom ergonomics" during that time period by the principal publishers in the field of education. In reviewing Harmon's *The Co-ordinated Classroom* and its implications for more ergonomically correct learning environments at the school and college level, Barrett Caldwell (1994) has succinctly stated:

> Harmon's approach conceived of the classroom environment as "an occupational environment—a working surround in which (students), through participating in organized experiences, can grow and develop in an optimum manner, and channel their unfolding capacities into constructive and satisfying living." He advocated a systematic approach to "occupational hygiene" to evaluate and improve the classroom, focusing on enhancing student's learning performance. Harmon's ideas integrate several major elements of the human factors perspective: organization of information and resources devoted to improving performance and satisfaction of persons in a complex environment. Nonetheless, his work, and that of his few intellectual successors, is largely ignored in modern classroom design.

Two of the main strengths and distinctions of the Harmon studies were its epidemiological approach and the reliability and validity of its findings, borne by the large population of its subjects (more than 160,000 school children) and supported by the controls only possible when conducted under the mantle of a governmental agency. A number of Harmon's findings were summarized and reported by the author in his own dissertation (McVey, 1969) and later in a monograph, *Sensory Factors in the Classroom Learning Environment* (McVey, 1971), funded by the National Education Association for its *What*

Research Says to the Teacher series, and then used in the development of the educational specifications that were used in the design of a new, ergonomically correct educational facility for the University of Wisconsin's School of Education. Figure 36-1 includes photographs of the then new (1972) instructional spaces designed in accordance with the environmental design principles, human factors guidelines, and design development details that I provided to the architect, and which, because of my full-time involvement in all phases of the project, ensured inclusion in the project. These photographs display a number of ergonomic features that will be discussed throughout this chapter.

36.1.4.2. Progress in the 60s. In the 1960s, the activity in school facility research, including but not specifically naming ergonomic issues, increased significantly, funded mostly by the government; in the U.K. through its Building Performance Research Unit, and, in this country, through various state departments of education and such private organizations like the Educational Facilities Laboratories. One of EFL's most influential school facility research projects culminated in the publications *SER 1, 2, and 3* produced by the *School Environment Research Project,* an activity of the Architectural Research Laboratory at the University of Michigan in Ann Arbor and directed by C. T. Larson.

SER 1: Environmental Abstracts is basically a collection of annotated abstracts of research that the project's investigators believed would advance the readers knowledge of the various relationships that link environment with human behavior, particularly as it applies to educational settings. *SER 2: Environmental Evaluations* presents "a series of technical papers, prepared by individual project staff members, which summarize and analyze what is now (was) generally known about the environment and its interactions with the individual and the effects of space, the thermal environment, the luminous environment, the sonic environment, and the social environment (Larson, 1965)." The third publication, *SER 3: Environmental Analysis,* presented proposed methods for investigation and processing of information needed in environmental design.

36.1.4.3. Today's Organizational Efforts and Research Dissemination. In the 1970s, 80s, and 90s, we have seen numerous publications on human factors engineering, ergonomics, environmental design, architectural research, and applied ergonomics flood our libraries from printing presses literally spanning the globe. During this period, we have also seen professional organizations such as the Human Factors Society (now the Human Factors and Ergonomics Society) and the Environmental Design Research Association gain in membership and prominence. Unfortunately, such progress has not brought with it a commensurate increase in ergonomic research specifically applied to educational settings. And, in fact, some educational facility planners even today have reported difficulty in finding relevant ergonomic research that they can use in their planning efforts. In a recent issue of the *Educational Facility Planner,* Lane and Richardson (1993) stated: "The litera-

ture dealing with human factors engineering and education is almost nonexistent. A literature search yielded few resources and little usable information." These authors went on to list only six citations they were able to find that they felt had some relationship to human factors engineering and educational-facilities design!

36.1.4.4. An Overview of the Research. The topic areas, and research designs considered appropriate for use in ergonomic research are no different from those traditionally conducted in the other behavioral sciences. An overview of such research is offered by Aikman (1994), who states:

Research designs share a common element, namely, a systematic view of a given phenomenon by determining relationships among variables with the purpose of explaining and predicting the phenomenon. Once a research problem linking an aspect of environment and human behavior has been formulated clearly enough to designate the explanatory variables, the researcher must develop a research plan or design. Specific research variables are selected from the several possible explanatory variables. They are the variables among which the researcher wishes to find and to measure some specific relationships. They include both the "dependent" and "independent" variables, that is, the "predictand" and the "predictor" variables.

Although there is no such thing as a single "correct" design, a design should include procedures not only related to the variables which are the objects of study, but also procedures for the control of as many as possible of other explanatory variables not included as objects of study. If the relationships among variables, the characteristics of which are ready-made, such as human characteristics, a given classroom environmental characteristic, an architectural feature of an educational facility, etc., the type of design of study is descriptive. Causality is not established. In contrast, in an experimental design, an independent variable is manipulated by the research to determine what effect or relationship it has, with a dependent variable as well as determining its relationship with other explanatory variables, either manipulated or controlled.

Descriptive and experimental studies are sometimes defined by the setting in which a study is conducted, for example, field studies, field experiments, or laboratory experiments. Some of the other descriptive terms employed to designate studies in the behavioral sciences are "qualitative" versus "quantitative" and differentiated primarily by the precision of measurement; cross-sectional versus longitudinal, which reflect some variation in time orientation; single factor versus multiple factor, indicating the number of explanatory factors involved in the study. The two major statistical procedures employed in both descriptive and experimental studies in determining relationships among the research variables are various forms of regression analysis or analysis of variance.

The majority of ergonomic studies to date have been of an experimental nature carried out in laboratory settings specifically set up for this purpose. As such, these studies when properly conducted have included the four important features that Chapanis (1965) states must be present in human factors research : (a) controlled observations in (b)

306-Seat Multimedia Lecture Hall

132-Seat Multimedia Lecture Room

20–90-Seat Flexible Classroom

20-Seat Media Conference Room

Figure 36-1. University of Wisconsin instructional complex displaying ergonomic features specified by author.

an artificial situation with (c) the deliberate manipulation of some variable(s) in order to answer (d) specific hypotheses.

36.1.4.5. Studies to Be Included and Limitations. Later, I will review in detail a cross section of specific ergonomic/educational environment studies. Only representative studies with which I have been directly involved and that deal with ergonomic topics that relate specifically to educational facilities design have been selected. Others that relate to comparative instructional methodologies, instructional design, instructional coding and mapping, and so forth, and which given another interpretation or context could very well claim educational-ergonomic relevance, cannot be presented here. Ergonomic studies related to the design and utilization of environments other than educational will not be treated (cf. Burton, 1980).

36.1.4.6. Influences. Several educators and specialists from other fields played important roles in promoting the ergonomic or scientific approach toward educational facilities design during the past 3 decades. These individuals subsequently had a great influence on the research and on my own facility design efforts and countless others. Such direct and personal influences included the guidance and example of James MacConnell and his planning team from San Francisco in the preparation of the University of Wisconsin School of Education *educational specifications*—the critical building block for all good facilities design; the knowledge and environmental assessment examples of Drs. Darrell Boyd Harmon and Philip Lewis of the University of Wisconsin; Gene Ferris and John Moldstad of Indiana University for their pioneering 1961 survey, *Improving the Learning Environment,* which influenced the future direction of my own academic pursuits; Gaylen B. Kelley of Boston University's School of Education, for his practical insight into what constituted good media presentation facilities; Alan Green, formerly of the Educational Facilities Laboratory, and Don Ely of Syracuse University, for their tireless efforts at collecting and disseminating relevant information. Key influences outside the field of education included William Lam (lighting design), Robert Newman and Lyle Yerges (acoustical design), Jerry Dommer, O'Neil Ford, and Byron Bloomfield (architectural design), and Ray Wadsworth (audiovisual systems design); and from the field of human factors engineering, for their knowledge, critical analysis, and creative applications, Drs. Alphonse Chapanis, Harry Snyder, and H. Mac Parsons. The valued legacy of all of the above individuals can still be seen in numerous educational facilities across the country and overseas.

36.2 REVIEW OF SELECTED ERGONOMIC/ LEARNING ENVIRONMENT STUDIES

36.2.1 Introduction

The aim of this review is to summarize what constitutes ergonomic research as applied to educational facilities, and thus is intended to be representative and not comprehensive. In making my selection of ergonomically representative studies, I have chosen (1) two user preference survey studies

that related student responses on a rating scale–type questionnaire to the physical measurements of environmental and display features; (2) an experimental study of social interaction patterns with different classroom seating arrangements employing television as an observational tool; (3) an experimental study investigating the effect of photometric brightness contrast on student preference, attention, visual comfort, and fatigue; and (4) an experimental study on display legibility that explored qualitative differences between front- and rear-screen projection. The first study reported is one of my own, and the other four were doctoral dissertations that I supervised at Boston University between 1976–91. By providing such a sampler, it is hoped that the reader will acquire some insight into representational methodologies in educational ergonomic research, as well as an awareness of the substance of their findings, which I believe hold considerable significance today relative to learning environment design and utilization.

36.2.2 Environmental and Ergonomic Features in Educational Facilities: Two User Preference Studies (McVey, 1979; Bethune, 1991)

36.2.2.1. Rationale for the Studies. Every year, millions of dollars are spent on the construction and renovation of educational facilities that are often inadequate for both students and instructors. Students and faculty alike frequently complain that classrooms are too hot or too cold, that they have uncomfortable seating, or that the seating location does not permit clear and accurate viewing of the room's display systems. Additional complaints relate to the difficulty in hearing lectures because of excessive internal noise or because of excessive sound reverberation within the room. Other problems are more subtle and frequently result in complaints like "My eyes seem to hurt after a lecture," or "I just can't seem to concentrate for very long in that room," or "I'm just not comfortable in there. I don't like the room."

These classroom conditions and complaints point out the need to determine why such facilities fail to meet the objectives of facility planners and architects. One reason proposed for this failure is the source material for the guidelines used in the planning and design of educational facilities. Discussions with numerous architects indicate that most rely almost exclusively on architectural standards such as those found today in Ramsey and Sleeper's *Architectural Graphic Standards* (1988), or those published by BOCA (Building Officials and Code Administration International, 1990), and rarely adopt or refer to long-standing and widely available ergonomic standards and references such as contained in the publications of Woodson (1981), Woodson and Conover (1973), Bennett (1977), Van Cott and Kinkade (1972), and Grandjean (1969, 1987).

To determine the relative efficacy of these two different sources of planning and design information, in either their earlier or current editions, the assessments of two college student populations, one from a large midwestern university, and the other from a large eastern university, were recorded approximately 20 years apart using two slightly different versions of the same questionnaire. In spite of the passage of time and changes in the student population and the schools' curricula and the increased sophistication of available educational technology, and although the statistical tools employed and the analysis procedures differed, the results of both studies were strikingly similar. Given the similarity of the research methodology employed in these two studies and their results, they will be presented here as a two-part case study.

36.2.2.2. Method (1973 Study). The first study conducted at a large midwestern university in 1973, and reported in 1979 (McVey, 1979), was basically a posttest- only comparison of the assessments of a static group of college freshmen, sophomores, and juniors ($N = 214$) who, during semester I, were assigned to three popular lecture halls that had been constructed in accordance with guidelines found in standard architectural handbooks, with a comparable static group ($N = 289$) assigned to a lecture hall constructed in accordance with guidelines found in ergonomic handbooks and other guidelines developed from the author's own human factors literature search (McVey, 1969) and verified by in-house laboratory experiments. The user assessment instrument consisted of a Likert-type scale (questionnaire) made up of 59 measurement items related to specific interior environmental factors, 10 items that tested face validity, and 10 subject identification items. The 59 measurement items were divided into 10 categories: seating, desks, acoustics, audio systems, visual display systems, lighting, color and reflectance, and two "other" considerations.

36.2.2.3. Rationale for Employing a User Assessment Methodology. My reasons follow for employing a combination of questionnaire (with a rating scale) to solicit student assessments of their classroom environments, with an analysis of those findings in light of actual physical measurements taken in the environments being assessed:

One approach gaining popularity is the utilization of the users themselves as evaluators. Armed with instruments ranging from simple attitudinal scales and various modifications of the semantic differential originally developed by Osgood, Suci, and Tannenbaum (1957) to the more complex Guttman scales (Markus, 1974) and the various adaptations of the multitrait-multimethod model originally proposed by Campbell and Fiske (1959), researchers have evaluated such wide-ranging environmental settings as "school study areas" (Sommer, 1968), "landscaped offices" (Boyce, 1974), and "low and high use housing" (Francescato et al., 1975). Through these and other studies, strong justification for employing users as evaluators of their environments has emerged (Canter, 1975; Lee, 1973; Preiser, 1970; Wools, 1970), as has support for using the questionnaire to record this evaluation.

Canter (1970) notes:

Using a questionnaire is one stage towards getting the user to set up hypotheses about the effect of the physical environment and to explain his interaction with it. . . . The investigator does not pressure to understand or to hypothe-

size the nature of the mechanisms by which the subject deals with the physical environment, but rather to get the subject to show how satisfied he is with the functioning of the environment in which he is (p. 14).

Discussing the legitimacy of this measurement approach as opposed to the more traditional, physiological response recording methods, Sommer and Becker (1971) state:

A psychologist can take the position that a check mark on a scale indicating dissatisfaction, particularly when the respondent has no incentive to falsify or distort his reply, is just as legitimate a basis for remedial action as a physiological measure. . . . Our results make clear that psychologists must deal with organisms or environments separately (p. 416).

Other researchers believe that while the questionnaire can reveal important information about the efficacy of an environment, much can be gained by using a design that also allows the researcher to relate the user's subjective assessment to specific causes, i.e., the physical variables inherent in that environment. For example, asking students to rate a desk's design in terms of "How well does it support accurate and comfortable note taking" will reflect on such physical variables as the size, height, and inclination of the desk being evaluated.

An approach along this line was used with success by the Building Performance Research Unit of the United Kingdom to assess school buildings, one major basis for comparison being a building performance profile called a *psarchigraph* (Patterson & Passini, 1974). A similar multimethod approach also has been used to evaluate acoustic experience in concert auditoria (Hawkes & Douglas, 1970). It is theorized that such an approach should make it possible for the researcher to relate subjective effects to physical causes, thus improving the predictability of subjective experiences from physical data. Such information, on the face of it, would seem to be of considerable value to architects and facility planners as they make decisions regarding the design of new construction or remodeling projects.

36.2.2.4. Validity, Reliability, and Analytical Measures (1973 Study). The following statistical data were obtained for each variable in each class: arithmetic mean, standard error of the mean, standard deviation, unbiased variance, coefficient of skewness, coefficient of kurtosis, and .05 confidence interval for the mean. One-way analysis of the variance also was conducted for each group across the two semesters and the results of that analysis expressed as analysis of variance tables. Other data included statistics relating to the validity (UWMACC Factor 2 Program) and stability of the questionnaire (Hoyt Reliability Index), individual student seat location, and anthropometric data regarding the student population taking part in the study.

36.2.2.5. Results and Discussion (1973 Study). In the 1973 study, the completion of the questionnaire took an average of 25 minutes, with some students taking as long as 35 minutes and others only 15 minutes. Examinations of the distributions indicated that the 5-point rating scale (5 = exceptionally good, 1 = unacceptable) yielded considerable variance, since every point on the scale was used. Results found that students gave statistically significantly higher ratings ($p < .05$) to Room 204, the lecture hall that had been designed and constructed in accordance with ergonomic recommendations, than they did for the three designed and constructed in accordance with published architectural standards. Overall mean student ratings for each of the major categories are shown in Table 36-1.

When reporting the findings of this study in 1979, comparisons were made between the overall mean scores per category received by the ergonomically derived lecture hall and the overall mean scores received by the three architecturally derived lecture halls. These data supported the study's hypothesis. However, because of space limitations in that publication, it was only possible to report on the overall student responses to the main environmental and display system design features in the rooms. In order to determine the student's individual responses to specific room characteristics, it was left to the reader to look at each of those responses while cross-checking those ratings with the room photographs and the 60-item physical descriptor developed for each room.

Given the importance of specificity in design, that study has now been revisited by its author in order to compile a set of empirically defensible lecture hall design guidelines. These generalizations follow.

36.2.2.5.1. Viewing Location and Visual Display

- Given free choice in seat location and given the design features of an ergonomically derived room layout where viewers are located at distances between 2 and 6 times a projected image width and at lateral locations not greater than 60° off screen axis, students will rate all seat locations equally high.
- Maximum acceptable viewing distances are determined not so much by the apparent size of the screen but by the legibility of the materials (words, captions) displayed. Acceptable boundaries of the horizontal viewing sector are determined more by the ability of the display system (projector, lens, and screen) to deliver an adequately bright image than by the amount of trapezoidal distortion caused by oblique viewing.
- Sight lines with inclination angles greater than +25° (to the top of the display) and depression angles

greater than -10° (to the bottom of the display) will be criticized by college students. Rear projection can be more effective than front projection when projection screen type, size, and location are carefully selected and coordinated with the room's viewing sector.

36.2.2.5.2. Lighting and Color and Reflectance

- Illumination levels of 30 foot-candles from either incandescent or warm-white fluorescent will satisfy a student's note-taking requirement. Cool-white fluorescent illumination will require 50 foot-candles in order to achieve as satisfactory a rating as the above-mentioned lighting relative to the same student activity.
- Matte-finished, warm-colored walls (off-white, parchment, buckskin) and light-colored furniture (brown, tan, cream) will produce a more visually comfortable environment than specular finished dark-colored walls, even when the illumination level of the latter is double that of the former.
- While incandescent downlighting is well received by most students, some of those who wear glasses will report distraction and discomfort. The degree of this response will be affected by ceiling height, fixture design and spacing, and the overall brightness in the room.

36.2.2.5.3. Acoustics and Audio Systems

- College students are extremely sensitive to noise intrusion, either from outside student traffic or from inside mechanical, electrical, or heating and air-conditioning systems.
- An ambient noise level of NC10 will be perceived as being too low in terms of masking unwanted sounds, while ambient noise levels of NC30 and above will interfere with students' ability to hear clearly the unamplified speech of a lecturer.
- Amplified audio response systems will be well received by students in large lecture halls (4,000 SF +) but will not be as important in the smaller halls (1,200–2,000 SF) as will be room acoustics.

36.2.2.5.4. Space, Desks, and Seating

- In terms of physical comfort, ease of access and egress, a sense of personal space, and for book and coat storage, students will prefer separate swivel seats and fixed desks (counter) in a seating layout providing them with 7.5–8.0 SF over fixed nonswivel chairs with tablet arms in a layout providing 6.3 SF or less per station.
- In rating the following design features of chairs, students will give the highest ratings to the features shown in bold print: floor-seat pan height (**17"**, 15", 16"), seat inclination (**3°**, 0°, 10°, 17°), back inclination (**10°**, 20°, 22°), lateral spacing (**25-31"**, 20", 21"), frontal spacing (**48"**, 32", 28", 34").
- A linear span of 28"–31" of 18"–deep and inclined (15°) continuous counter writing surface will promote

TABLE 36-1. STUDENT (MEAN) RATINGS (1–5) OF LECTURE HALLS (P < .05)

Room	204	147	2650	112
Thermal	3.7	3.2	2.8	2.7
Viewing location	4.3	3.3	3.7	3.3
Visual display system	4.4	4.0	3.7	3.5
Lighting	4.0	3.1	3.4	3.4
Color and reflectance	4.1	3.1	3.5	3.0
Seating	3.9	2.6	2.5	2.4
Desks or tablet arms	3.8	3.4	3.0	2.8
Acoustics	3.8	3.4	2.6	3.2
Audio system	3.9	3.4	2.9	2.9

more accurate and comfortable note taking during lectures and visual presentations than will flat or moderately inclined (2°–7°) movable tablet arms offering between 81 and 116 SF of writing surface.

36.2.2.5.5. Thermal

- When attending classes having the following thermal factors, students will prefer the combination of temperature, relative humidity, and air velocity as noted in bold print: Room A: (82°F, 15% RH, front: 0–75 fpm, rear: 0–280 fpm,), Room B: (82°F, 29% RH, 0–75 fpm), **Room C: (69.5°F, 47% RH, 0–25 fpm),** and Room D: (77°F, 29% RH, w/o AC: 0–10 fpm, w/ AC: 0–75).
- Students will complain of drafts when air velocities exceed 75 fpm.

36.2.2.6. Method (1991 Study). A second user assessment study—a doctoral dissertation by James Bethune employing a modified version of the questionnaire—used in the 1973 study was conducted in 1991 at a large eastern university to determine whether today's college students would also prefer educational facilities constructed on the basis of ergonomic design guidelines over those constructed in accordance with standard architectural references. Freshmen, sophomore, junior, and senior students ($N = 145$) evaluated the four lecture halls in which they regularly attended classes. Using a 5-point Likert-type rating scale questionnaire consisting of 152 items, organized into 46 major interior environmental factors, the students rated each item as it existed in each of the rooms. The results of this activity were then analyzed in an effort to determine the validity of current architectural standards and recommendations as applied to the design of lecture halls.

A comparison was then made in the 1991 study between what the students found acceptable and the current architectural standards in the design and construction of lecture halls. A similar comparison was then made between the student's ratings and the recommendations found in published ergonomic sources. A *t* test, developed by Kruskal-Wallis and Dunn (Dunn, 1964), and simultaneous confidence intervals were used to analyze statistically the student's responses and to validate their significance.

36.2.2.7. Results and Discussion (1991 Study). The 1991 study built on the work of the 1973 investigation and extended the user assessment techniques used in that study in order to evaluate the efficacy of applying ergonomic recommendations to the design of lecture halls. The four lecture halls used in the 1991 study were all built or remodeled within the last 10 years and therefore reflected current architectural practices.

A comprehensive set of measurements was taken of each architectural feature in each of the four rooms, and each item was categorized as being either in agreement with architectural standards or ergonomic guidelines. Modifications were made to the original questionnaire by eliminating a number of audiovisual display system items

not present in the current rooms and by setting up four cross-comparisons between rooms. This resulted in 38 individual test items and a total of 152 evaluation factors. The questionnaire was distributed to each of the 145 students taking part in the study. The statistical analysis first tried to determine what a student's response should be to a hall that was acceptable both in terms of architectural standards and ergonomic recommendations.

This resulted in a mean score of 3.554, with a standard deviation of 0.411 ($p < .01$). A Kruskal-Wallis test and Dunn's method were used to show that the results from the four different lecture halls were statistically related, and "simultaneous confidence" intervals were used to compare the responses within a specific question. The evaluation concluded that the results both between the individual halls and the individual questions were reliable at the 95% confidence level.

Table 36-2 shows the mean responses to the individual items in the questionnaire. It was concluded that any response of less than 3.000 indicated student dissatisfaction, as 3.000 is greater than one standard deviation from the 3.554 expected satisfactory mean response. The same mean satisfaction level of 3.000 can be applied to the data in Table 36-1 from the 1973 study, showing a statistical similarity in student's assessments of their classroom environments despite the 20 years between the studies.

The results of the evaluation showed that of the 152 measured factors, students agreed with ergonomic recommendations 82% of the time. For 103 of the factors, the agreement was positive; that is, the factor was in agreement with ergonomic recommendations, and the student's mean assessment was within the satisfaction level. For 22 of the factors, students found specific room features to be unacceptable, a position consistent with ergonomic sources but not with architectural standards. There were 16 cases where students found specific factors acceptable which were not supported by the ergonomic sources. These factors were primarily related to seat spacing. Interestingly, students accepted frontal seating closer (34") than recommended by ergonomic sources (40") for seating comfort during notetaking, but rejected that same spacing when evaluating it for ease of access and egress. Similarly, 11 items related to lateral seat spacing that were within ergonomic recommendations (24") were found to be too close and therefore unsatisfactory.

The results of the 1991 study confirmed the conclusions of the 1973 study and serve to point out that when it comes to the design of lecture halls, there is still a discrepancy between architectural standards and ergonomic recommendations, differences that are noticeable to college students and who for the most part find greater agreement with the ergonomic guidelines than with the architectural standards. Students were invited to make written comments throughout the questionnaire. These qualitative responses in general supported the quantitative results presented above, as well as most of the findings of the 1973 study.

36.2.2.7.1. Student Comments. Some of the interesting

TABLE 36-2. MEAN RESPONSE SCORES: INDIVIDUAL QUESTIONARE ITEMS

	B33	SED130	Nick II	RM150
Lighting	1. 4.08	3.62	<u>2.66</u>	4.27
	2. 3.29	3.52	*	4.36
	3. 3.43	3.37	*	3.30
	4. 3.68	3.82	<u>2.54</u>	3.95
Color & reflectance	1. 3.56	3.82	3.17	3.93
	2. 3.84	4.12	3.67	4.20
	3. 3.57	3.74	3.34	4.06
	4. 3.79	4.03	<u>2.82</u>	3.88
	5. 3.76	4.18	*	3.88
	6. 3.88	3.85	*	3.50
Seating	1. 3.42	<u>2.53</u>	3.52	3.39
	2. <u>2.19</u>	<u>1.41</u>	<u>2.18</u>	<u>2.80</u>
	3. 3.42	<u>2.59</u>	4.07	3.18
	4. <u>2.96</u>	<u>1.71</u>	3.79	3.43
	5. <u>2.81</u>	<u>2.03</u>	3.80	3.44
Desks	1. 3.20	<u>2.91</u>	*	3.32
	2. 3.75	3.35	*	3.61
	3. 3.47	<u>2.68</u>	*	3.50
	4. 3.42	<u>2.88</u>	*	3.54
Acoustics	1. 3.68	4.32	3.57	4.07
	2. 3.08	3.59	3.61	3.39
	3. <u>2.96</u>	3.18	3.05	3.32
	4. 4.00	3.91	3.93	3.18
Thermal	1. <u>2.69</u>	3.68	3.86	4.05
	2. <u>2.46</u>	3.32	3.75	3.69
	3. <u>2.35</u>	3.41	3.59	3.70
	4. <u>2.54</u>	3.44	3.27	3.82
	5. <u>2.62</u>	3.70	3.80	3.62
Viewing location	1. 4.20	4.20	4.14	3.97
	2. 3.76	3.79	4.15	3.18
	3. 3.84	3.82	3.84	3.78
	4. 3.84	4.03	3.34	3.79
	5. 3.04	3.35	3.84	3.23
Other considerations	1. 350	3.47	3.15	3.42
	2. <u>264</u>	<u>1.68</u>	3.45	3.11
	3. 3.00	3.50	<u>2.80</u>	3.21
	4. 3.44	3.03	3.30	3.59
	5. <u>1.64</u>	<u>1.47</u>	<u>2.80</u>	<u>2.14</u>
	6. <u>2.24</u>	<u>1.94</u>	<u>2.03</u>	3.03

* = Question is not applicable to room. For example, there are no desks in NICK II.

student responses included the following:

- Only the small students or those of average height registered complaints with the seating. But the lack of response from the very tall or large students was apparently due not to their satisfaction but simply to the resignation they had developed over the years with the unsatisfactory seating to which they were continuously subjected.
- The combination of tight lateral and frontal seat spacing resulted in very low scores for the tablet armchairs relative to book and coat storage. Frequently, this situation combined with poor tablet arm design led to books and notes spilling onto the floor when students tried to enter or leave their seats.

- While Nick II was rated acceptable as a movie theater, its use as a lecture hall was very poorly received by the students. This result speaks to the frequent failure of multiuse designs for lecture halls, as well as the unwise assignment of such spaces as large-group classrooms by college administrators.
- Provisions for left-hand tablet arms were absent in all of the rooms used in this study. This omission was duly noted in the students' evaluations.

36.2.2.8. Conclusion. Both of these studies, although performed approximately 20 years apart, indicate the firm and continuing existence of a strong student preference for lecture halls designed in accordance with existing ergonomic guidelines than for those designed in accordance with standard architectural references and building codes. Consequently, it is recommended that now and in the future, facility planners and architects make every effort to utilize existing ergonomic guidelines and standards in their educational facility design, construction, and remodeling efforts. Many of these important guidelines and standards will be found in section 36.3. Others can be found in existing ergonomic handbooks and in the growing number of journals that are directing their focus toward ergonomic applications.

While the two studies just presented raise a number of interesting questions about the current state of educational facilities design, their results also generate some concerns relative to the current preparation of architects, inasmuch as valuable ergonomic information continues to be ignored in their work product. One of the questions that surfaces is: In the face of such evidence, why haven't architectural programs adopted the ergonomic guidelines that have been available for more than 20 years? A second question is: Why have architects ignored past research findings that clearly have demonstrated the benefits of designing educational facilities in accordance with ergonomic guidelines?

These questions go beyond the scope of this study, but they are clearly implied by the study's results. A third question raised by the study is: In light of the fact that both studies clearly showed that college students are reliable and objective evaluators of their learning environments, why are they not consulted more often in educational facilities planning and evaluation? While these questions merit considerable discussion, one can conclude from the findings of both the 1973 and 1991 studies the following recommendations:

- Educational facility planning and architectural design references and standards should adopt time-tested and proven ergonomic guidelines.
- Architects should seek out the observations and comments of college students in determining the successful and unsuccessful elements of their educational facilities before making final determinations as to the specific design features to be contained in new and proposed facilities.
- Architectural educational programs should include the study of ergonomic principles and guidelines.

36.2.3 An Observational Study of Classroom Seating Arrangements on Student Attention, Participation, Fatigue, and Preferences (Fulrath, 1976)

36.2.3.1. Background and Rationale for Study.
In the mid-60s, the work of E. T. Hall and specifically his book *The Hidden Dimension* (Hall, 1966) advanced the science of "proxemics" and the concepts of "socieopital" and "sociefugal" spaces, i.e., those spaces that promoted human interaction and those that promoted noninteraction. This work followed the acceptance of earlier works on social interaction by Bass and Klubeck (1952), Steinzor

(1950), and Leavitt (1951). It was also during this period that the sociologist Robert Sommer published research findings (1959, 1965, 1967, 1969, 1970, 1974) that strongly supported and justified specific seating arrangements to promote desired patterns of social interaction. It was in this context that the following study was rationalized and conducted.

Fulrath (1976, p. 23) states:

Increasingly, educational and business facilities are being designed with spaces for small-group work. Schools, libraries, offices, and hotels have conference areas designated for, or classrooms that accommodate, both small-group work and media use. Typically, the furniture arrangement of the classroom is still that of the straight row, though rectangle arrangements prevail in offices. However, these arrangements may not be best for the individual, especially in view of increased media use, if they contribute to a negative response condition by the individual, either behaviorally or attitudinally. Other arrangements, such as the circle/hexagon, may better help to facilitate a positive response set, particularly where media tasks are concerned. The design implications of this issue concern future use of furniture arrangements that facilitate the optimal response of the user. In studying user responses to these varied arrangements, the question of whether to design predominately for comfort or for interaction may be partially answered.

Similarly, use of the small group as a problem-solving mechanism is common in both education and business, as is the attendant use of media for information transfer. In the examination of the relationship of time to these factors, the results of this study may provide some specific answers about appropriate limits to task duration and involvement for the individual. That information would, in turn, augment existing knowledge about the appropriate utilization of media and small-group work.

36.2.3.2. The Research Question and Method.
This study focused on two environmental variables and their effects on selected behavioral and attitudinal responses of the learner. The specific purpose was to determine the effects of seating arrangement and task duration on fatigue, attention, participation, and preference of individuals engaged in small-group media tasks. Circle, rectangle, and straight-row patterns constituted the three levels of the independent variable seating arrangement. Similarly, three levels of the independent variable task duration were 1 hour, 2 hours, and 3 hours. There were three hypotheses in the study:

1. There would be significant differences in fatigue and participation as task duration increased from 1 to 3 hours.
2. There would be significant increases in fatigue, attention, and participation between people in the circle seating arrangement and those in the rectangle or straight-row patterns.
3. There would be significant increases in preference for a seating arrangement between people in the circle pattern and those in the other arrangements.

The sample consisted of 54 adult students from various schools in the university who were nonmedia majors. Subjects were randomly assigned to six small groups of nine members each, and two groups each were then assigned to one of three seating arrangements.

The task used in the study was a 3-hour, visual-verbal media task in which groups rated 35-mm slide images according to criteria of visual design. The measurement instruments for fatigue included the *Pearson Fatigue Checklist* (Pearson, 1956), and a *Visual Discomfort Evaluator* developed by the researcher based on the work of Hultgren, Knave, and Werner (1974). Videotape recordings were used to assess attention and participation; and preference was measured by *Mehrabian's Approach-Avoidance Test* (Mehrabian & Russell, 1974). Testing occurred at four time intervals of the study, including the start of task, first hour, second hour, and third hour. The resulting data were scored analyzed by multifactor analysis of variance procedures.

Figure 36-2. below shows the layout of the experimental setting used in this study.

36.2.3.3. Results and Analysis of Findings. Results confirmed the first hypothesis and revealed significant increases in fatigue between the start of task and the first, second, and third hours ($p < .001$). Similar results were recorded for three symptoms of visual discomfort as the incidence of tired eyes, sore eyes, and headache increased significantly between start of task and the third hour ($p < .05$). However, no significant differences in discomfort were found for five other symptoms (itchy eyes, watery eyes, sandy eyes, blurred vision, and double vision). Attention increased significantly between the third hour of the task and each of the other task times ($p < .001$), but here were no significant differences in participation.

These results held in all groups regardless of seating arrangement, and, with one exception, no significant differences were found between groups for either the second or

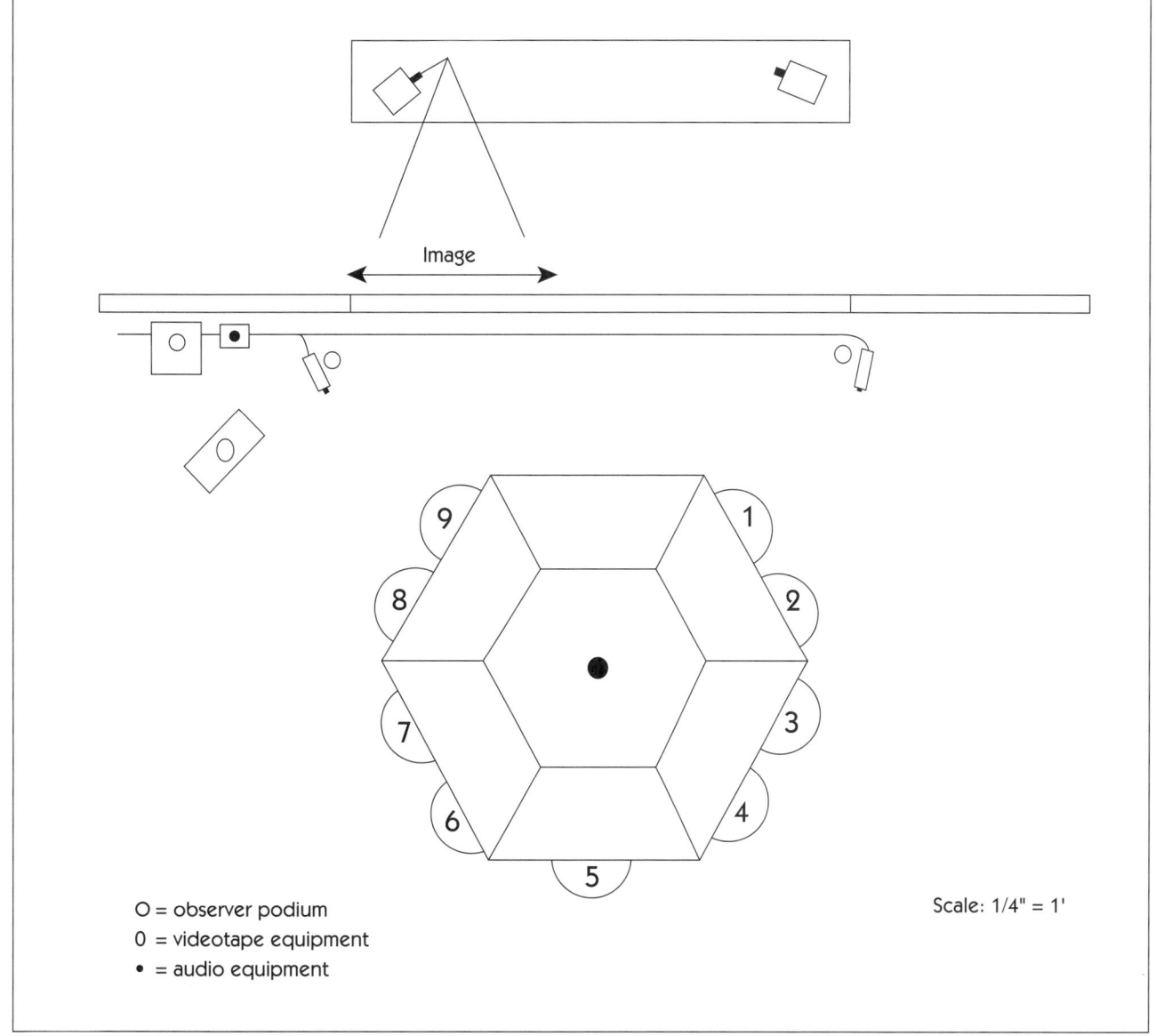

Figure 36-2. Layout of experimental room used in Fulrath study.

third hypotheses. The single exception was that attention in the straight-row arrangement was significantly greater than that recorded in the other two patterns ($p < .01$). Additionally, the use of blink rate as an index of fatigue and the relationship between fatigue and performance were examined and found to confirm the reservations that some behavioral researchers have found with this device as a reliable index of fatigue.

Several specific conclusions based on the general acceptance of the first hypothesis were formulated from the results of the study. The conclusions also reflect the clinical observations video recorded during testing. Those conclusions led to several recommendations, including two primary ones. It was recommended that, when using media tasks with groups of adults, optimal task duration should not exceed 1 hour without a break, or 2 hours if rest breaks are used. Study results also suggested that a single 15-minute break after 1.25 hours might foster changes in arousal levels and would be more conducive to continued task performance. Given media use, the straight-row arrangement may be preferred if attention to the screen were most important, but the rectangle may be preferred if attention to the group, or group interaction, were most important. Though equal to the other two patterns, the circle/hexagon arrangement could neither be recommended or rejected as being superior based on the results of the study.

Secondly, the *Pearson Fatigue Checklist* (Pearson, 1956) was found to be a valid, sensitive instrument, and its use was recommended for fatigue studies that would investigate other task types, task durations, learning situations, and age groups. It was further recommended that such studies also investigate the nature and pattern of the fatigue response as well as the psychophysical law to which it conforms. Finally, the study confirmed the value of television recording as a valued tool in the analysis of student behavior.

36.2.4 The Effect of Image/Surround Brightness Contrast Ratios on Student Preference, Attention, Visual Comfort, and Visual Fatigue (DesRosiers, 1976)

36.2.4.1. Background and Rationale for the Study. In the 1950s and early 1960s, Domina Spencer (1954) and her associate at M.I.T., Parry Moon (1961), created a stir in academic and engineering circles with their studies regarding luminance contrasts that attempted to quantify the patterns of photometric brightness that promoted comfortable and accurate viewing through enhancing figure/ground separation and three dimensionality of objects in interior environments. At the same time, Darrell Boyd Harmon's monograph *The Coordinated Classroom* (1951) related this work and that of others in the illuminating engineering profession to the classroom settings of elementary school children.

Two decades later, the lighting designer William Lam (1977) took major steps toward quantifying the perceptual aspects of lighting in school and office environments. Around the same time, LaGuisa and Perney of the Illumi-

nating Engineering Society's Research Institute conducted their research of supplementary illumination on visual displays (1973, 1974) and discovered that attention was sustained longer and distractions reduced when classroom charts were illuminated in excess of the surround. Thus it was only natural that educational researchers in the field of media and technology would look toward establishing, through their own research, operational guidelines for establishing appropriate contrast ratios in media-related rooms. If such luminance contrast ratios could be verified, they could then be adopted with confidence in future educational facility design practices.

Such was the background of the DesRosier's study. Surprisingly, this study remains one of the only experimental studies to deal specifically with photometric brightness contrast ratios and remains uncited in the literature, even though influential organizations such as the Illuminating Engineering Society of North America and the Human Factors and Ergonomic Society regularly include similar luminance ratios in their published *Standards and Recommendations*. One would expect that those organizations could find their recommendations strengthened by referencing the DesRosiers' study (Fig. 36-3).

36.2.4.2. Method. One aspect of the visual environment, the photometric brightness contrast ratio (BCR) between a projected image and its surround, was investigated in two experiments. The nature of these two experiments was established by DesRosiers to include the four important features called for by Chapanis (1965): (a) controlled observations in (b) an artificial situation with (c) the deliberate manipulation of some variables in order to answer (d) specific hypotheses. In describing the experimental setting DesRosiers states:

> The experimental setting was essentially the same for both experiments 1 and 2. The room dimensions were 17'× 17' × 11'. The main feature of the room was a vinyl rear projection screen 10' × 15' which served as a translucent wall dividing the room into two smaller rooms, one for projection, one for viewing. Portions of the rear projection screen were designated for specific tasks:
>
> *Visual task,* the centrally located portion 26" × 17" on which the test slide presentation image was projected. *Distractor,* that portion 8" × 12" on which the distractor slides were projected. The position of this screen was 45° left of the center of the test screen. This distance was chosen based on earlier research findings. *Surround,* the remaining portion of the rear projection screen was transilluminated by supplementary lighting. The rear projection screen used had a gain of 120% at 0°. *Projection area,* the inner portion of the laboratory, 11.5' × 17', served as the projection area. Test *presentation system,* two carousel slide projectors, an audiocassette tape recorder with sync pulse capacity, a dissolve unit, a buffer relay system, a dimmer to control image brightness, and a rectangular image frame, a device to ensure that all illumination from the projectors (and only illumination from them) reached the portion of the screen where the visual task (image) was projected. The slide presentation system was controlled by a custom power supply and relay system to ensure that all luminances were as specified.

The videotape observation recording system consisted of a low-light sensitive video camera, a camera adapter, and a TV monitor. Forty one-half-inch 30-minute videotapes were used. *The audio-grid* is an instrument devised by DesRosiers to ensure consistent reading of the videotapes after the test period. This system required an audiocassette player and an audiocassette with oral cues to announce the change of slides. When played in sync with the videotape, the investigator could know what slide was being projected at any moment of the videotape. The *student station* consisted of a chair-desk combination positioned two screen widths from the screen. A dimmer for controlling the brightness of the image was positioned on the student's desk. The luminous environment of the viewing area was defined by identifying the range of the illumination on the subject and on the desk. A photo research illuminance meter and 2° luminance meter were used in the measurements.

36.2.4.3. Problem Statement and Methodology of Experiment 1.
The first experiment attempted to answer these questions: What are the image/surround brightness contrast ratios preferred by students? How do these correspond to the task/surround brightness contrast ratios recommended by the literature? The currently recommended task/surround BCRs for conventional tasks suggest the hypothesis that, given a specific surround brightness, students will select an image brightness no less than that of the surround (1:1), and no greater than 10 times that of the surround (10:1). In a controlled laboratory environment, 14 high school students, given the surround brightness levels of 2, 6, and 20 footlamberts (FL), were asked to select their preferred image brightnesses. The mean brightness levels preferred were established, and the resultant BCRs were calculated.

36.2.4.3.1. Results of Experiment 1. AT 20 FL, the students selected a BCR of approximately 1:1 ratio; at 6 FL, a 3:1 ratio, and at 2 FL, an 8:1 ratio. Since the BCRs chosen were within the 1:1 to 10:1 range, there was strong

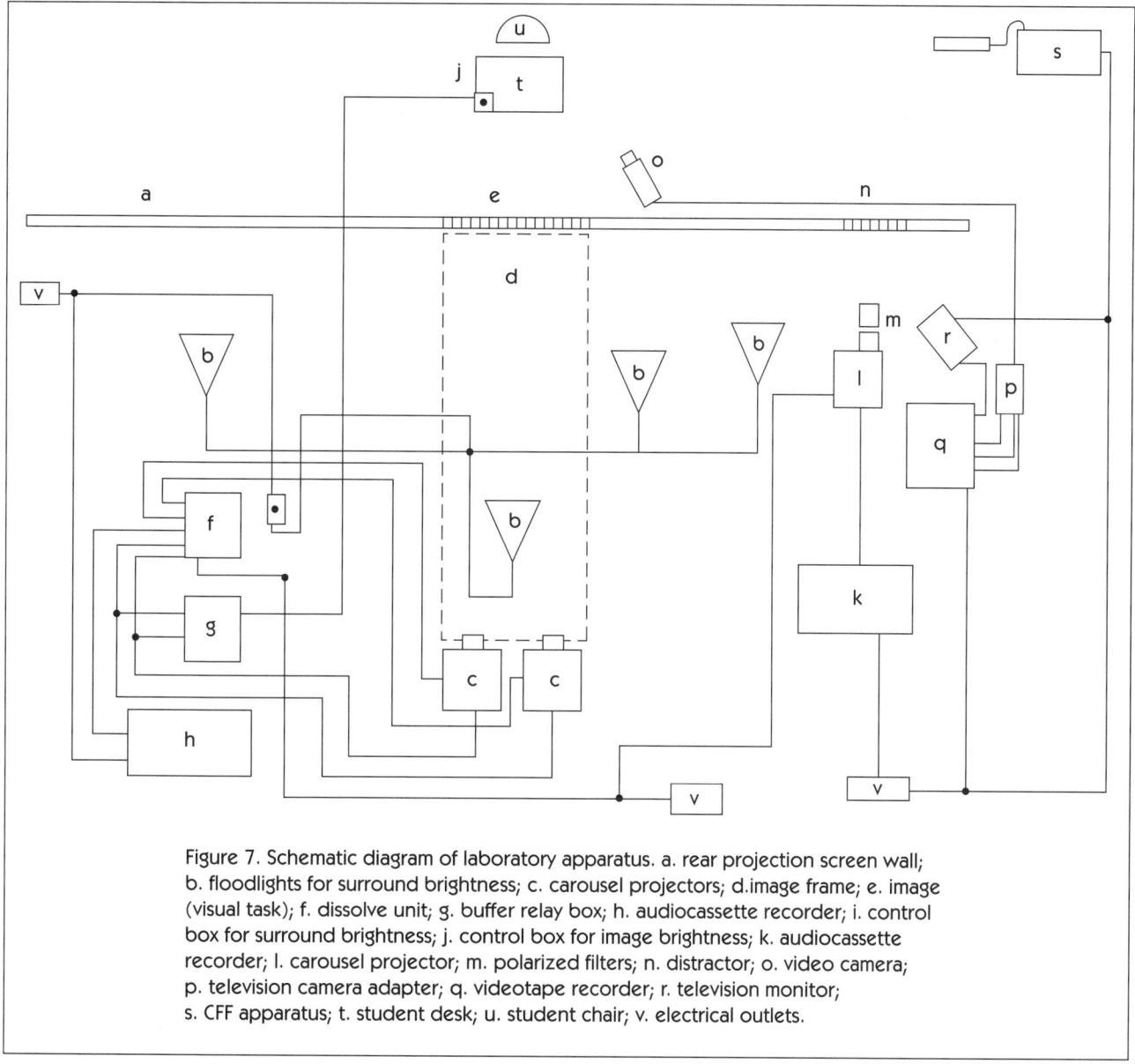

Figure 7. Schematic diagram of laboratory apparatus. a. rear projection screen wall; b. floodlights for surround brightness; c. carousel projectors; d. image frame; e. image (visual task); f. dissolve unit; g. buffer relay box; h. audiocassette recorder; i. control box for surround brightness; j. control box for image brightness; k. audiocassette recorder; l. carousel projector; m. polarized filters; n. distractor; o. video camera; p. television camera adapter; q. videotape recorder; r. television monitor; s. CFF apparatus; t. student desk; u. student chair; v. electrical outlets.

Figure 36-3. A sample of one of the measurement systems developed by DesRosiers for her study.

indication given that the general recommendations for task/surround BCRs are equally applicable to the projected image/surround BCRs. Furthermore, students chose a similar image brightness (17 FL) regardless of the surround brightness. As a result of this stable choice, a recommendation of 15 ± 2 FL was established as a "brightness task requirement for projected images." It should be noted that this recommendation is approximately the same as that recommended by the Society of Motion Picture Engineers (Kloepfel, 1969) for motion pictures for more than 3 decades.

36.2.4.4. Problem Statement and Methodology of Experiment 2. Current literature has suggested that the root of problems like inattention, visual discomfort, and visual fatigue encountered in media environments seems to lie in the characteristics of the visual display system and how it interfaces with its viewers, that is, the viewing angles, the luminance contrast between the display and its surround, etc. Experiment 2 dealt with this problem and investigated the effect of image/surround brightness contrast ratios on attention, visual comfort, and visual fatigue. DesRosiers states:

> Thirty-seven students between ages 14 to 19, assigned randomly to one of four experimental groups, viewed a slide presentation individually at an image/surround BCR of 40:1, 10:1, 3:1, or 1:1. The footlambert levels for these were 20:0.5, 20:2, 20:6.7, and 20:20, respectively. The Kruskal-Wallis One-Way Analysis of Variance by Ranks was applied to see if any relationship existed within the four BCRs. Each student was tested for attention by videotaped observation, for visual comfort by subjective evaluation using a checklist, and for visual fatigue by the two objective measures of critical flicker fusion (CFF) and threshold and eye blink rate recorded by videotape.

36.2.4.4.1. Results of Experiment 2. The hypothesis tested was: When the brightness contrast between image and surround is high, attention is greater, visual comfort is lower, and visual fatigue is greater. The Mann-Whitney U test for k independent samples was applied to the combined attention scores at 40:1 and 10:1 and to the combined scores at 3:1 and 1:1, yielding results that permitted acceptance of the first part of the hypothesis (that when BCR is high, attention is greater).

Results of the subjective evaluation of visual comfort gave some evidence that the second part of the hypothesis is true, that comfort is lower when BCR is high. Because of problems with the experimental process and the instrumentation used to measure visual fatigue (CFF and eye blink), there was no way of concluding whether or not visual fatigue was greater at high BCRs. It may be concluded that when the image/surround BCR is high, attention is greater and visual comfort is lower. It was also found that a "contamination effect" may occur when CFF tests and eye blink counts are employed in close succession.

In discussing her rationale for using the Mann-Whitney U test, DesRosiers stated:

> This test is used in order to determine whether the two independent groups have been drawn from the same popu-

lation. One of the most powerful of the nonparametric tests, it is most useful as an alternative to the parametric t test when the researcher wishes to avoid the t test's assumptions (Siegel, 1956). The U test does not require that data be normally distributed or that sample variances be equal. It calls for a nominal independent variable and an ordinal dependent variable (Tuckman, 1972).

36.2.4.5. Implications of Study. In her study, DesRosiers concluded that:

> This study pointed out that often visual discomfort is the cost paid for a media environment conducive to high attention. Research is needed to determine a brightness contrast ratio which is the best compromise between these competing elements. The findings in this study have direct application to designers and users of media facilities, especially in preparing for the projection of slides, filmstrips, and motion pictures with rear-screen projection for high school students. They apply less directly for front-screen projection and for a broader range of audience than the target population in the current study. They have possible implications to designers and users of facilities for any visual presentation, including nonaudio visual setting, since the structural patterns of brightness used by architects are basically the same for all designs and environmental settings.

At the time of DesRosiers' study (1976), VDT use was in its infancy relative to educational environments, and so it is understandable that DesRosiers did not relate her findings to lighting and viewing conditions in VDT workstations. If provided that opportunity today, there is no doubt that given the validity and reliability of her findings, she could and would apply them to such educational environments with a high degree of confidence.

36.2.5 The Accuracy Recognition of Positive and Negative Symbols on Front- and Rear-Projection Screens Under Self-Selected Illumination (Hamilton, 1983)

36.2.5.1. Rationale for the Study. This study represents a response to two basic questions most educational media specialists were asking themselves during the early 1980s: How can I be sure that I am producing legible instructional materials? Should I use front- or rear-screen projection to display those materials? Adding confusion to the issue was the fact that most educational media guidelines available to the media specialist specified print size by dimensions such as $1/8''$, $1/4''$, etc., without any consideration of the distance at which those materials would be viewed. And second, there was considerable disagreement among information display specialists as to which was the preferred medium for information display, rear- or front-screen projection. In an effort to provide other media specialists with some "hard science" for guidance relative to making such choices, Mark Hamilton (1983) decided to investigate both sides of this issue and include as a modifying factor the self-selection of illumination level. By doing this, Hamilton anticipated discovering luminance-illuminance interrelationships that would affect performance and possibly serve as a guide for establishing ambient illuminance levels for future media presentation spaces. In noting his motivation, Hamilton stated:

> This investigation originated from recent visibility-orientated research and concern for possible misconceptions regarding the use of front and rear screens for projecting positive and negative symbols. . . . The study of projected visual images in teaching is one area in which there has been a move toward more systematic research. The increased use of projected images has amplified the potential benefits to be gained from good message design and optimum projection practice and has magnified the negative effects of inadequate materials and poor projection. An examination of published standards and research findings, as well as current classroom practices, show widespread confusion and disagreement on what should be the proper level of various factors of the projection environment.

36.2.5.2. Problem Statement. This study was designed to determine the effects of projection screens, symbol polarity, and symbol size on accuracy recognition of projected symbols. The dependent variable was accuracy recognition. Three independent variables were: film-based projection systems, consisting of front and rear screens; symbol contrast, consisting of positive (white symbols on black) and negative (black symbols on white); and subtended visual angle, consisting of 7, 5, and 3 minutes of arc.

36.2.5.3. Procedure. Hamilton describes his procedure as follows:

> One hundred sixty college students with tested visual acuities ranging from 20/40 to 20/10 and including those with normal or corrected-to-normal vision were individually presented 81 randomly ordered letters for a total of nine slides displayed in a laboratory specifically set up for this purpose during evening sessions at a small private New England college. Subjects were randomly assigned to one of four treatments, i.e., front screen with positive symbols; front screen with negative symbols; rear screen with positive symbols; and rear screen with negative symbols, each having symbol sizes of 7, 5, and 3 minutes of arc. Subjects attempted to correctly identify the self-paced stimulus materials. Additionally, subject's preference for a general illumination level and responses were recorded. Data from the $2 \times 2 \times 3$ factorial design were subjected to a three-way analysis of variance. Where significance at the .05 level was evident, individual differences between means were examined with the Newman-Keuls test.

36.2.5.4. Apparatus, Description, and Specification of Stimulus Materials, Display System, Lighting System. An excerpt of Hamilton's lengthy and precise description of his experimental setting and controls follows (Fig. 36-4):

> The photographic equipment used throughout was a 35-mm, single-lens reflex camera (Canon AE1), with a 50-mm macro lens (f3.5). The exposure used was f/11 for 1 second for the positive materials and f/8 for 4 seconds for the negative materials. The letters were originally derived from a Kroy lettering machine using the Helvetica Regular

(24 point) disk. Letters were graphically laid out on grid paper to provide uniform spacing. The single sheet of letters and sample Es were then photographically reduced on a stat to a uniform height of 10 mm. When this appropriate size was attained, the letters were reduced by 30, 50, and 70% to produce symbol sizes of 7, 5, and 3 millimeters. . . . To eliminate slide "popping" due to heat, Gepe glass slide mounts were used. Each test slide, in the horizontal format, was projected on a front or a rear screen at an appropriate distance (12 feet) to provide the specified subtended visual

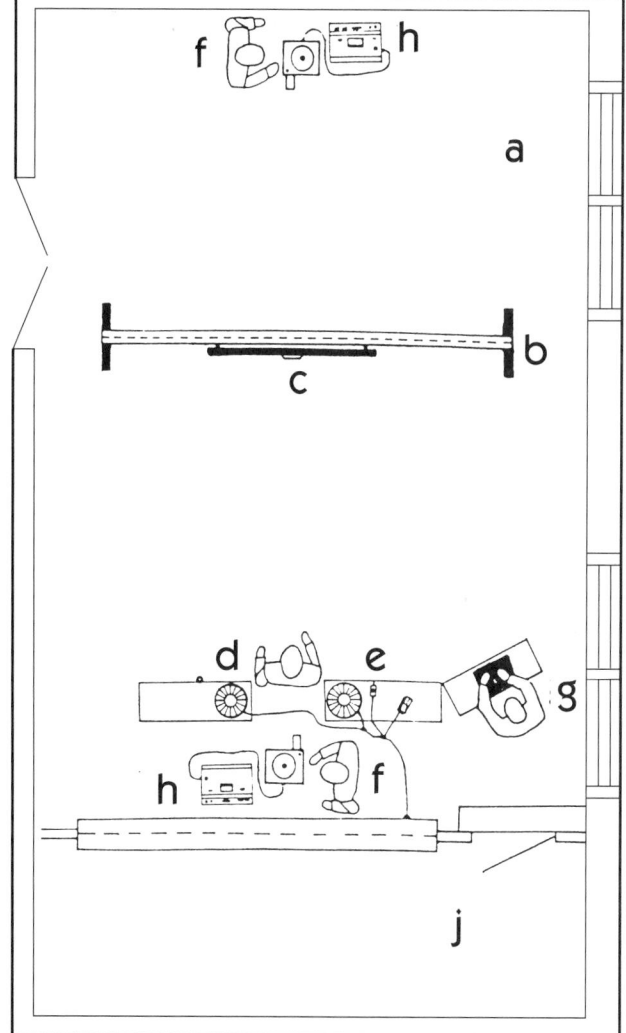

a. Rear projections area for treatments 3 & 4. **b.** Wooden partition (divides the room for rear projection, supports the 9×12-foot rear screen, and supports the 6×6-foot front screen to be pulled down for front-screen treatments). **c.** Front screen. **d.** Subject. **e.** Rheostate dimmer control for self-selection of illumination. **f.** Experimenter. **g.** Assistant. **h.** Slide projector and cassette player. **i.** Table lamps. **j.** Front projection booth (was not utilized).

Figure 36-4. Graphic representation of Hamilton's experimental setting.

angle of 7, 5, and 3 minutes of arc for the symbol. Projected image brightness for each of the test slides was 18 footlamberts. Two multiple slide sets were produced to control potential bleaching of the slides due to exposure of the projector lamp.

A single Kodak Ektagraphic AF-2 slide projector with a Kodak 100–150-mm f/3.5 flat field lens with a 300-watt ELH lamp was used in the tests. Screen luminance was determined by projecting stimulus slides on the projection screen and measuring it with a photometer calibrated in footlamberts. Test instructions and procedures were pre-taped and synchronized on a cassette tape recorder to provide uniform presentation of test procedures. The range of illumination intensities available at the work plane was approximately 0 to 50 footcandles. General illumination was derived from two table top lamps, each fitted with one 150-watt bulb, positioned behind and to either side of the subject. One commercial, 100-volt (600 watts maximum) rheostat dimmer, wired to the 115-volt, 60-cycle electrical source, was utilized to provide a range of 0 to 50 footcandles at the work plane. The dimmer was contained in an enclosure and located to the right of the subject to allow easy selection of room light for each of the four treatments. The rheostat dimmer was preset to 0 before each subject entered the testing room.

In the remaining portion of his lengthy description of the experimental setting and controls, Hamilton provides specifications of the measuring instruments and display system characteristics, and describes his measurement procedures.

36.2.5.5. Research Design and Data Analysis. The dependent variable for the study was the number of judgments made on the criterion task, which consisted of one self-paced recognition accuracy task of symbols projected via 35-mm, 2×2 slides. Subject responses were judged either correct or incorrect, and therefore ratio data were obtained from the tests. The number of correct recognitions made by the subjects were computed and analyzed. There were three independent variables manipulated in this investigation. The first independent-variable, film-based projection system had two levels: (1) front-projection screen and (2) rear-projection screen. The second independent variable, direction of symbol contrast, also had two levels: (1) positive (W/B) projected symbols and (2) negative (B/W) projected symbols. The third independent variable manipulated in the study was subtended visual angle. This variable had three levels: (1) 7 minutes of arc, (2) 5 minutes of arc, and (3) 3 minutes of arc.

The basic design for the study was a true experimental design, Design 6, the Posttest-Only Control Group Design (Campbell & Stanley, 1963). This design was utilized because it can be delivered to students or groups as a single natural package and eliminates the awkwardness of a pretest. This design was also used because it permits an evaluation of treatment effects upon the criterion task while minimizing the effects of confounding variables (Issac & Michael, 1981).

The Posttest-Only Control Group Design consisted of a 2 (film-based projection system) $\times$ 2 (direction of symbol contrast) $\times$ 3 (subtended visual angle) factorial design with repeated measures on the third factor. The use of this design enables the investigator to assess interaction between the three independent variables (Ary, Jacobs & Razavieh, 1979). A three-way analysis of variance of the criterion task scores was applied to ascertain the presence of differences between treatments (Ary, Jacobs & Razavieh, 1979; Campbell & Stanley, 1963). Results with a statistical significance at the .05 level were considered demonstrative of reportable treatment effects. Kerlinger (1973) suggests the .05 level as adequate, being ". . . neither too high nor too low for most social scientific research" (p. 170). The Newman-Keuls multiple comparison test was used to compare means on the criterion task scores after analysis of variance had been performed if the results indicated its appropriateness. The Newman-Keuls test is an a posteriori comparison test and is employed when the investigator intends to make all possible simple pairwise comparisons among means if a significant overall F ratio is obtained in the analysis of variance (Howell, 1982).

The range of brightness patterns created in the testing environment for the present investigation was caused by the reflectance of the walls, ceiling, and floor surfaces, as well as the reflectance of screen areas adjacent to the projected image. Figure 18 illustrates the visual field of the present investigation, as seen by the subject during projection of stimulus materials. Specific target areas were preselected by the investigator, and footlambert readings were taken at each to determine a specific brightness pattern selected by the subject. All testing was conducted during the evening to eliminate external light sources from the testing environment. The 10 preselected target points are numbered.

36.2.5.6. Results and Discussion. Hamilton offers the following in his Results and Discussion section:

1. Given the relatively ideal viewing conditions and display systems used in this study, film-based projection systems, i.e., front and rear screens, of similar performance did not significantly affect the accuracy recognition of either positive (W/B) or negative (B/W) projected symbols of either 7, 5, or 3 subtended arc minutes. In fact, for all the single and multiple interactions with the other independent variables, there were no significant effects revealed in the accuracy recognition scores ($F = 0.44$).

2. For 7 minutes of arc little difference was found between the accuracy recognition of positive (W/B) symbols (94.6%) and negative (B/W) symbols (98.7%). For 5 and 3 minutes of arc, negative symbols (B/W) were more accurately recognized than the positive (W/B) symbols (p < .01).

It should be noted here that when determining the symbol sizes to be used in this study, it was assumed that any size symbol less than 10 arc minutes would result in accuracy recognition reductions, and that these losses would be directly proportional to the amount of reduction. This study proved this to be true, with 100% accuracy scores recorded in the field test conducted prior to the start of the study employing a symbol size of 10 arc minutes, and the following results recorded during the Hamilton study with the three smaller symbol sizes (see Table 36-3).

3. In the self-selection of ambient illuminance when displaying white symbols on the front screen, 31% preferred a light level between 0–1 FC, while the remainder of the test population were evenly distributed (about 15% each) in their selections of the following levels: 1–5 FC; 5–15 FC; 15–30 FC; over 30 FC. In the self-selection of ambient illuminance when displaying black symbols on the front screen, there were no majority preferences for any of the 5 footcandle ranges and were found to be fairly equal (20–25%) at the various footcandle ranges. Only at the 1–5 FC range did subject preferences drop to 9%. One interpretation of these findings is that when subjects view white symbols on a black background, projected on front screen, they prefer low illumination. On the other hand, when subjects view black symbols on a white background, projected on a front screen, they prefer a wide range of illumination.

4. In the self-selection of ambient illuminance when displaying white symbols on the rear screen, subject's selections for ambient light conditions were fairly evenly distributed for each of the 5 footcandle ranges, but with a slight reduction in preference for the 5–15 FC range. In the self-selection of ambient illuminance when displaying black symbols on the rear screen, a majority of the subject's selections (60.8%) fell on or with the 0–5 FC range, with the remainder equally spread over the range of 5 to over 30 ranges.

In explaining these results, it should be remembered that black symbols projected on a white background produce a bright image and hence a brighter room than do white symbols projected on a black surround. As a result of conditioning or believing that the existing light in the room was sufficient, subject preferences did not group around the higher footcandle ranges. In fact, in treatment 4, 24% of the subjects selected no additional illumination at their workplace. It should also be noted that this finding might have been different had the subjects been required to take notes during their period of participation.

TABLE 36-3. HAMILTON'S RESULT: MEANS AND STANDARD DEVIATIONS* ON PERCENTAGE ACCURATE BY FILM-BASED PROJECTION SYSTEM, DIRECTION OF SYMBOL CONTRAST, AND SUBTENDED VISUAL ANGLE

Minutes of Arc	Front Screen		Rear Screen	
	Positive	Negative	Positive	Negative
7	97.0 (5.2)	99.5 (1.9)	92.7 (10.6)	98.0 (11.6)
5	(84.6) (20.3)	97.6 (4.5)	72.3 (28.7)	94.9 (16.8)
3	(20.4) (20.6)	(50.8) (32.8)	17.5 (23.3)	51.7 (34.5)

*SD in parentheses.

5. The range of luminance contrasts for the target area and its near and far surrounds as expected were higher when projecting black symbols on a white background than when projecting white symbols on a black background. This was true for both front- and rear-screen display, with front-screen projection having more variance and slightly higher luminance levels recorded than rear screen. However, in all cases there were no luminance ratios that exceeded 3:1

36.2.6 Future Research Needs

There is a need for educators, architects, and ergonomists to continue the kind of research sampled in this section. User assessments have yielded important findings that have proved valid and reliable. Current research has applied a modified version of the instrument used in the McVey (1979) and Bethune (1991 studies in the evaluation of music education multimedia workstations. Preliminary results from this study appear to support the findings of the two earlier studies (Badolato, 1995).

But more importantly, there is a critical need to conduct the kind of epidemiological research that was conducted by Harmon and Bennett decades ago and unfortunately not repeated since. We need to find out how our young students are being affected by the learning environments in which they are expected to dedicate increasingly more time in VDT workstations and carrels. Are their maladaptations to the current nonergonomic facilities simply creating surmountable stress and fatigue? Or are they being exposed to conditions that threaten their normal growth and development, due to the fact that their physiological and sensory systems are yet fully developed? It is my own personal belief that we educators are sitting on a time bomb in this regard. And while substantive and well-sponsored research in the field of office design has produced corrective designs to mitigate if not eliminate repetitive motion disorders, no such mandate has yet been directed toward the learning environment. Hopefully, some concerned and well-positioned educational leaders will discover this author's quiet alarm signal and respond accordingly.

36.3 ERGONOMIC RESEARCH FINDINGS AND DESIGN GUIDELINES FOR THE LEARNING ENVIRONMENT

36.3.1 Foreword

Two of the primary purposes of research are to either effect change in an undesirable condition or to verify the efficacy of an existing condition. Consequently, when seeking guidance in developing learning environments, the educational facilities planner looks to the research and to planning handbooks for guidance. This is also true of educators when seeking ways in which a given learning environment may be utilized in order to have the most positive effect on a student's physical well-being and learning. Unfortunately, the topic of effecting learning gains through environmental design or manipulation of its features is beyond the scope and allotted length of this paper. Where I am aware of documentation of specific cause and effect relationships between some physical or sensory aspect of educational facilities and learning, I will report them, but the focus of this part of the chapter will be on those guidelines that are believed to contribute to the health, safety, and physical well-being of the student, as well as those that contribute to his or her orientation toward tasks and localization of information transmissions either from a teacher, other classroom discussants, or from some form of educational technology. For those readers interested in more substantive sources specifically regarding the environment and its effect on human learning, as an initial step toward acquiring such information the author recommends consulting Bruner (1961) and Tessmer and Harris (1992).

36.3.2 Introduction

In 36.1.4.3, I referenced Lane and Richardson (1993) who stated: "The literature dealing with human factors engineering and education is almost nonexistent. . . . A literature search yielded few resources and little usable information." Taking such statements at face value, we must then look to ergonomic research conducted in other physical settings and other relevant academic and professional disciplines like architecture and engineering in order to find guidance regarding the design and utilization of the learning environment. This approach is justified when one considers the similarity of tasks that take place in business and high-tech offices, conference rooms, auditoria, etc., and those that take place in educational facilities. In this way, I believe it becomes possible to establish supportable guidelines for educational facilities design.

In *Analyzing the Instructional Setting,* Tessmer and Harris (1992) offer six general questions that those involved in planning educational facilities need to ask of themselves and their project associates:

1. Will the learning space suit the attendance and strategies of the instruction?
2. Does seating facilitate the intended learning activities in the environment?
3. Are the instruction and resource environments accessible to learners?
4. Will the environment's temperature conditions be comfortable during the instructional activities?
5. Does lighting allow for sustained concentration and attention?
6. Will acoustics inhibit the aural messages of the instruction?

Should the answers to the first five questions be No, or to the last question, Yes, and should the facility's construction not yet be underway or, at worst, not yet completed, then some rethinking of the facility's design is warranted. If the facility is already constructed, then some form of inter-

vention on the part of its instructors will be needed until the problems are corrected.

36.3.3 Objective

In this section, it is my intention to present guidelines and supporting documentation that should help the reader address these and related questions. And in addressing such questions and reviewing relevant materials, my focus will be on establishing guidelines to promote the efficacy of the learning environment and, as such, improving the comfort, safety, and task performance of the student or trainee. Developing a relationship between task performance and cognitive, affective, and psychomotor learning is beyond the scope of this chapter.

Furthermore, the primary audience sought for this chapter are those who have some say in the shaping of educational environments. This audience would include educational administrators, educational facility planners, media specialists, teachers who are members of a building development team, and the architects who serve them all. However, where deemed appropriate, suggestions are offered to help the teacher, trainer, the conference leader, and so forth to utilize better a given learning/training/presentation environment. These are presented in the form of classroom *interventions.* The number of such entries is intentionally limited and in no way should be viewed as comprehensive. For those interested specifically in finding more information on the environment's effect on learning or how a teacher can manipulate environmental factors for a desired effect, the following sources are recommended: Bugelski (1971); DeCecco (1968); Gagné (1965); Levy-Leboyer (1982); Proshansky, Ittleson, and Revlin (1970); Bruner (1961); and Tessmer and Harris (1992).

36.3.4 Getting Started

Traditionally, facility planning handbooks have proven to be a useful starting point toward the creation of an effective learning environment (Castaldi, 1977; DeChiara & Callender, 1980). However, even they need to be verified, modified, or simply supplemented and updated by information from the fields of environmental design and ergonomics in order to maintain their relevance. The relevance of the contributions of ergonomics to facilities design is supported by Hunt and Bernotat (1977), who stated:

> . . . the ergonomist is concerned both with improving the health and well-being of the individual human being and with improving the efficiency of the system of which the individual is a part. The improvement of man-environment combinations involves altering the machine and the environment; this part of the ergonomist's work has been called "fitting the job to the man."

The importance of continually updating educational facility planning guidelines has been given additional reinforcement by past and recent ergonomic studies (McVey,

1979, 1990; Bethune, 1991; Caldwell et al., 1993), three of a number of studies that specifically addressed educational facilities. In the McVey and Bethune studies, students rated specific environmental, display system, and ergonomic features in their classrooms and showed an overwhelming preference for rooms designed in accordance with well-established ergonomic standards. In the Caldwell et al. study, a student productivity loss of 26.2% was recorded and attributed to inappropriate environmental and ergonomic features in a lecture hall.

In addition and of equal importance are a number of the findings from ergonomic research conducted in libraries and nonconventional educational settings such as offices, word-processing rooms, and other work settings where computer terminals and visual-display units (collectively referred to as VDTs or VDUs) are employed and where tasks are similar to those found in today's schools, training centers, and conference facilities.

What follows is an updated look at those guidelines that have been shown to contribute to the establishment of efficacious learning environments. The focus of this discussion (lighting, acoustics, thermal factors, display systems, etc.) relate generally to all learning environments, including training and conference facilities. However specifics relative to space allocations and furniture dimensions, because of their anthropometric nature, relate specifically to post-ninth-grade students and adults. Those seeking information regarding elementary school and pre-tenth-grade settings are advised to seek it out in other available sources (Packard, 1988; CEFP, 1969; Castaldi, 1977).

36.3.5 The Physical Space

36.3.5.1. Room Size and Seating Considerations.
The size of the teaching-learning space should be such that it comfortably accommodates the required number of students, space for the instructor's teaching station and apparatus, and the activities planned for that space. If these intended activities include media use, then additional space should be provided for the setup and use of equipment and for whatever empty floor space is needed to keep viewers from being seated too close to the display surfaces, i.e., chalk and marker boards, projection screens, television monitors, and so forth (McVey, 1985).

The importance of appropriate space allocations in classroom design is not only appreciated by teachers but also by their students. In a recent article, "The Learning-Friendly Classroom," Caldwell recounts the results of a survey he and Kathy Hoyt conducted involving eight classrooms at the University of California-Davis. In that study, an "uncrowded facility" was cited by 43 faculty members and 890 students as being one of the most important criteria determining the acceptably of a classroom's design (Caldwell, 1994).

The use of the word *seating* in this paper follows the description employed in the work of Tessmer and Harris (1992), who state (p. 31):

Seating refers to both the kind and placement of seats within the learning environment. The seats may be chairs, desks, chair-and-table combinations, or computer workstations. They may be in a classroom, office, home or laboratory. . . . The arrangement of seats refers to the positioning of the students' and instructor's seats in relation to each other. The "type" of seating refers to the style, weight and features of the seat (back support, table-top, etc.).

36.3.5.2. Seating Arrangements and Social Interactions.
Seating arrangements play an important role in determining social interactions in the classrooms. Students have been shown to experience greater feelings of equality and uniformity when seated around a rectangular table than when seated at a V- or Y-shaped one (Bass & Klubeck, 1952). In a rectangular arrangement, students tend to speak primarily to those opposite and closest to them. However, as soon as a person is seated at the head of the rectangular table, this interaction pattern changes dramatically; now those seated diagonally across from each other tend to engage in conversation about 6 times as often as those directly opposite each other, and about twice as often as those seated side by side (Hall, 1966).

Interaction in circular seating arrangements is affected by placement and distance as well as by postures and other physical impressions individuals make on each other (Steinzor, 1950). Students in small circular arrangements tend to speak to those opposite them, while those in larger circular arrangements (I have found to be a diameter of more than 18 feet) tend to have more interaction with those seated next to them. When there is an authority figure in the center of a circular seating arrangement, students tend to show more progress and produce a greater number of ideas. Nevertheless, students generally prefer the circular arrangement without the central authority figure (Leavitt, 1951). Figure 36-5 shows some seating arrangements and anticipated interaction patterns.

As implied in the work of Fulrath (1976), reported in 36.2.3.1, the theater style and conventional-row seating arrangement is generally recommended for lecturing, orientation, and media presentations (Fulrath, 1976). My own experience with designing training facilities finds the *U*-shaped seating arrangement, a minor variation of the circle, to be the most popular with high-tech and management training sessions, and with interaction patterns similar to those found with the circular arrangement. It has been noted above that a rectangular conference seating arrangement promotes interaction, with the locus of authority generally vested with those seated at each end of the table, and that the circular and "case method" seating patterns promote more uniform social interaction among the group (McVey, 1971). *Classroom Intervention:* As the manager of such environmental factors, the instructor needs to be made aware of the attributes of different seating arrangements and then employ them for their desired effect in the classroom.

Figure 36-6 is a photograph of a 40-student classroom designed by the author in collaboration with DRA Architects of Newton, Massachusetts, which employs a circular seating pattern, with each successive row of seats on risers for improved viewing of the rear-screen display, vertical operable marker board (behind wainscot), and flip-chart displays.

36.3.5.3. Seating Capacity, Configuration, and Room Size. Seating capacity and configuration are major factors in determining room size. As noted by Menell (1976): "Generally speaking, a 20- × 32-foot room will seat about 49 people theater style, 24 people classroom style, 18 people at a U-shaped table, and 15 people at a conference table." My own studies involving a room 25 feet wide by 32 feet long confirm Menell's assertions. Figure 36-7 shows four examples of the same-sized class/conference room with different seating arrangements, table requirements, and the occupancy levels possible.

The following are some guidelines relative to space allocations for different types of teaching spaces that have been substantiated through my own research and found to be useful in facility planning. Additional considerations can be found in the literature (Leed & Leed, 1987; Terlaga, 1990). My own recommendations follow:

1. Lecture halls and auditoria with tablet arm chairs (12 SF/student), with 18" × 30" countertop writing surfaces (15 SF/student). Arranging seating in the "case method" design will require between 50 and 75% more SF/student space allocation, depending whether fixed or castered seats are used.

2. Classrooms with conventional row-seating arrangement and movable tablet armchairs, spaced on 28-inch centers with 42-inch rows (15-18 SF/student); with 18" × 28" fixed table area and 48" rows (20–22 SF/student), and with 24" × 36" fixed table area and 60" rows (28–33 SF/student). These last dimensions are also acceptable for supporting a VDT if the tables or desks are equipped with a supplementary keyboard drawer. If not, then the VDT work surface should have a minimum dimension with a depth of 30" and width of at least 30" and preferably 36".

3. Classrooms or conference rooms with U-shaped arrangement and 24" × 30" table area (35–42 SF/participant); with 24" × 36" table area (45–50 SF/participant). Employing a circular seating arrangement will require approximately 10% more space per participant than the U-shaped arrangement.

Figure 36-8 shows a room I designed to employ the teacher-student, student-student interaction features of the

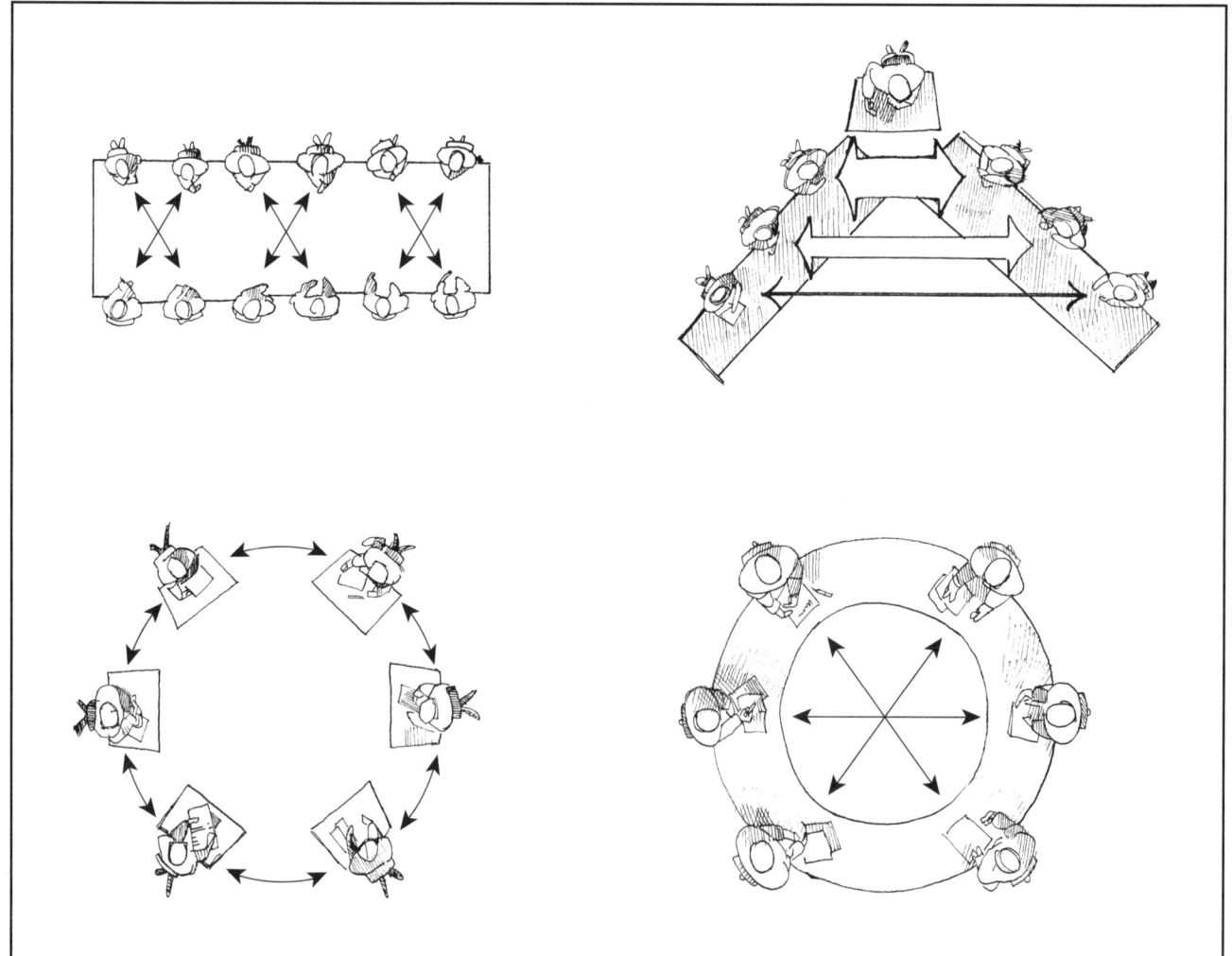

Figure 36-5. Seating patterns and social interaction.

Figure 36-6. Circular seating pattern in media presentation room.

case method plan modified for improved viewing of projected media and demonstrations. This design also employs movable ergonomic chairs on casters and as such requires about 10% more space than the conventional case method plan using fixed seating.

36.3.5.3.1. Determining Classroom Size. In light of the variety of potential interactions available to the classroom teacher through employing different seating patterns in the classroom, Tessmer and Harris (1992) recommend that facility planners provide enough space to accommodate the

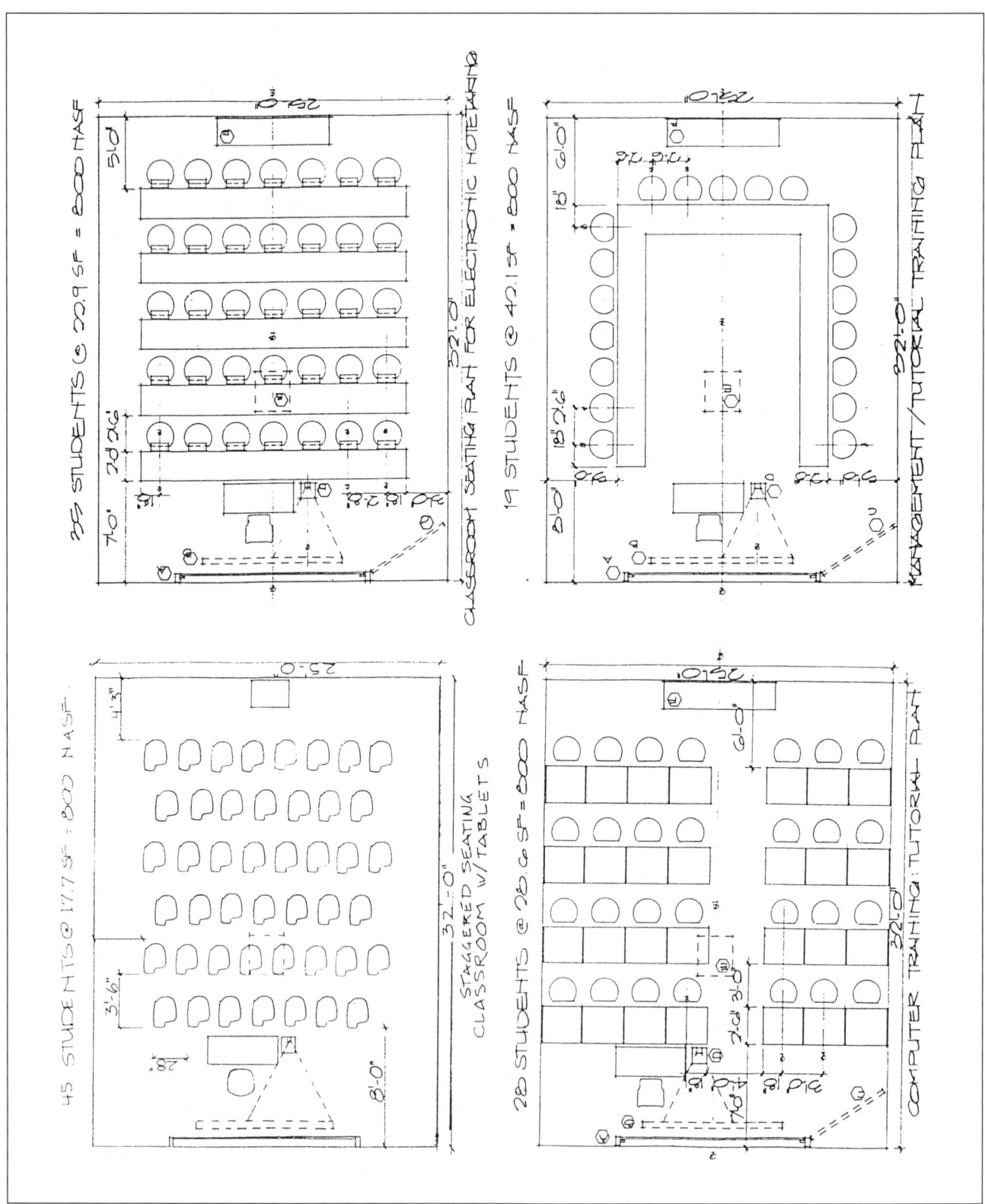

Figure 36-7. Room capacity relative to seating arrangement and table requirements.

Figure 36-8. Modification of case method room design for improved viewing of presentation media.

conventional seating pattern that requires the most space, i.e, the U-shaped arrangement. When provided with the space needed to accommodate such space demands, then all of the other less space-demanding seating patterns will be possible.

However, the application of the above space allocation recommendations will not be met without some resistance. In the college, government, and business sectors, the primary reason will be budget, since additional space equates to additional cost. But relevant ergonomic data have been successfully employed in overcoming this argument. The greater challenge lies with the public school sector. The reason for this is that many states require strict adherence to their own less-generous program standards, standards that in most cases were developed before the computer arrived on the scene and before teachers were motivated to employ a variety of classroom seating arrangements in their teaching methodology. The inappropriateness of the space standards currently being enforced in most states was recently addressed by Ross and Stewart (1993):

> Documented space requirement standards for a technology classroom are still in development. The space requirements are larger than traditional classrooms requiring more area than student desks and involving many factors including the type of equipment involved, the instructional methodology anticipated, student age and size, and furniture and storage requirements.

Consequently, the school facility planner is currently faced with a dilemma. Ergonomic studies may provide more appropriate space guidelines, but legislation will dictate that current Department of Education (DOE) standards be applied. Operating under this constraint will require some ingenuity on the part of the educational facility planner. One approach would be to see that classrooms employing computers and other space-demanding technologies be programmed as "lecture/laboratory" spaces. This category traditionally applied to science-teaching rooms usually receives a more generous space allocation in the DOE program standards. And no doubt, there are other approaches that could and should be considered in the worthwhile pursuit for classrooms sized appropriately for the next decade.

36.3.5.4. Ceiling Height. One of the structural features of a room which often reduces the potential effectiveness of projected media is ceiling height (McVey, 1985). A room's ceiling height should accommodate a projection screen large enough to display images of adequate size and positioned high enough from the floor so that sight lines are unobstructed. In the conventional classroom, one can determine the required ceiling height by dividing the room's length by 6 to determine the vertical length of the required screen, and adding to this dimension a minimum of 4 feet (where the bottom of the screen will be positioned) and 6 inches for trim at the top of the screen. Additional ceiling height above the top of the projection screen is required in an auditorium to accommodate an acoustical canopy or "cloud" that can also serve as an enclosure for the room's program playback speakers.

However, it is also important that where generous ceiling heights have been provided, this vertical span is not used to raise the projection screen to a height that will cause viewer discomfort. According to Ramsey and Sleeper's Architectural Graphic Standards (Packard, 1988), the vertical viewing angle of the first row occupant to the top of the screen should generally not exceed $+30°$, and never $35°$. However, this popular handbook provides no empirical evidence to support this guideline. And a major research study (McVey, 1979) clearly showed college students finding a $+24°$ to the top of the projection screen to be more acceptable ($p < .05$) than ones of $+32°$ and $+47°$. And subsequent field experiments in instructional spaces by the author indicate that sight lines with inclinations greater than $+25°$ (to the top of the display) and depression angles greater than $-24°$ (to the bottom of the display) brought about negative responses from viewers.

Sometimes having added ceiling height makes it possible to conduct functions that would otherwise be difficult if not impossible. And example of this is the divisible auditorium I designed in collaboration with the architects at Shepley, Bullfinch, Abbott, and Richardson for the Tufts New England College (see Fig. 36-9). Given the instructors' need to project video to one or both halves of the room while simultaneously video recording a conference setup at the front of the room, a high ceiling was the answer. Employing rear-screen projection above the video-recording stage permitted the beams from the video-recording light to be directed away from the screens, where it would have "washed out" the display, and focused on the people who were being recorded. Note that this screen does not begin at the second-floor level (an undesirable but popular procedure in the past) but is cantilevered forward and downward so that the bottom of it is only 7'3" above the finished floor (AFF). Note also that the screen is tilted forward in order to minimize geometric distortion and maximize uniform image brightness for the greatest number of viewers. It should also be noted that such an arrangement does increase the angle of the front-row vertical sight line to $35°$, which, though not ideal, is still in keeping with Ramsey and Sleeper's recommendations cited above, and, admittedly, given the special needs of this project, appear to be an acceptable compromise.

36.3.5.5. Room Shape, Seat Location, and Spacing. A room's shape is a major factor contributing to a space's aesthetic character, its overall sense of perceptual appropriateness, and the kind of social interaction pattern that its planners desire to promote. In rooms planned for extensive media use, the configuration of a room and its viewing area can be one of the most significant factors contributing to the effectiveness of the display system, the viewer's comfort, and the strength and clarity of the instructor's voice.

36.3.5.5.1. Room Dimensions and Viewing Distances. The basic dimensions for lecture halls, auditoria, and large media presentation rooms should be 2:3 (width to length), with seating contained in a fan-shaped area beginning at a distance 2 times the height of the projected image [1.5 times

Figure 36-9. Divisible auditorium used for videoconferencing and distance learning by Tufts New England College.

the width (1.5W) for rooms employed for dual-image display systems, and 1W for triple-image display] and extending to a distance of 6 times the projected image height (3W for multi-image rooms) for media employing standard symbol sizes (minimum of 10 arc-min).

When displaying computer screens, this maximum viewing distance will vary considerably and be governed primarily by the character size employed in the display. For example, when displaying, say, a Powerpoint screen consisting of large alphanumerics (40 characters per line, C/L), the maximum viewing distance can be 12H. If the display consists of 60 C/L (as produced by 12 pt on a 9-inch Macintosh screen), this maximum distance needs to be reduced to 8H, and for 80 C/L = 6H. For "windows" where a 9-inch screen sometimes consists of 100–120 C/L, the maximum should be 4.5H. These minimum and maximum viewing distances differ from the widely used earlier recommendations (Wadsworth, 1983) in that they attempt to go beyond accommodating film-based media and consider the viewing legibility of computer screens at terminals or via video projection (McVey, 1991).

36.3.5.5.2. Off-Axis Viewing and the Shape of the Viewing Sector. As a viewer moves away from the axis perpendicular to a displayed image, an increasing amount of distortion will be experienced because a flat surface is being seen from a more and more oblique angle. The effect of this geometric distortion on symbol legibility can be compensated for by moving off-axis viewers closer to the display, thus increasing the observed symbol size. *Classroom Intervention:* Set up seating so that the seats off-axis at a point 45° from the display are 80% of the maximum viewing distance, and those located at a point 60° from the display axis are only 60% of the maximum viewing distance.

The viewing-seating area itself is fan shaped to improve horizontal sight lines. The boundary for the acceptable viewing area proposed by Ramsey and Sleeper (Packard, 1988) is an area within two lines extended out 45° from the far sides of the screen or other display surface, i.e., chalkboard, dry marker, etc. However, experimental research (McVey, 1979) has broadened that area to extend to two lines extending out approximately 30° (actually 27° in the study) from the far sides of the display. Such a wide viewing sector assumes the use of a well-designed display system. See Figure 36-10 for some of these relationships.

36.3.5.5.3. Recommended Room Configurations. The length-to-width ratios for standard-size classrooms are meant to accommodate different seating arrangements and room acoustics. These follow:

- Classroom style: a room 1.15 to 1.5 times longer than it is wide.
- U-shaped seating pattern: a room 1.0 to 1.3 times longer than it is wide.
- Circular seating pattern: a room 1.0 to 1.25 times longer than it is wide.
- Lecture hall or auditorium with standard seating patterns: a room 1.25 to 1.5 times longer than it is wide.

With a "case method" seating arrangement: a room 0.8 to 1.2 times longer than it is wide.

Note that in classrooms, conference rooms, and auditoria where there is a requirement for simultaneous side-by-side projection and extensive marker board use, the length-to-width ratio approaches 1:1 and thus requires extra attention for acoustical treatment. Because of their relatively large size, auditoria also require special acoustical considerations. Figure 36-11 is a photograph of a computer classroom I recently designed to feature side-by-side simultaneous projection and marker board display. Note that both halves of the front wall are angled out at each end about 15° so that each display is perpendicular to the center of the viewing area.

36.3.5.5.4. Seat Spacing and Access and Egress. Research has shown that access and egress to seating areas in lecture halls is dramatically improved when seats are spaced a minimum 26 inches on center, and 38 inches front to back. When these chairs are equipped with tablet arms, the preferred spacing is 28 inches on centers and 42 inches frontal. For fixed 18-inch tables with pedestal chairs, the minimum frontal spacing should be 48 inches, including the table (McVey 1979).

Movable chairs with five-star pedestal and casters provide stability and ease of access and egress, and because of this are often employed in carrels, conference settings, and "case method" arrangements. This type of seating requires a minimum space of 32 inches, and preferably 36 inches between tables if the occupants are to have unrestricted access and egress, and 42 inches if an instructor expects personally to monitor a student's activities at a particular workstation.

Accessibility for all is an important design principle. An accommodation for the special needs of the physically challenged is the law of the land, and also provides access and egress as well as many other benefits to all occupants of a facility. It also contributes to one's sense of acceptance or rejection. As Burch (1993) stated: "Height, size, openness, and accoutrements are all part of the package that is this piece of instructional equipment." The need for accessibility is not limited to seats in the learning environment. Safe, easy, and convenient access to learning resources is also important (Tessmer & Harris, 1992).

36.3.6 The Chair, the Desk, and the Computer Workstation

36.3.6.1. Seating Design. Proper seating is an important factor in determining a student's relative comfort and effectiveness as a perceiver, recorder, and processor of information. Furthermore, there is a long history of evidence that improper seating may result in improper skeletal development in children between the ages of 11 and 16 (CCSE, 1938). Since chairs need to accommodate the body dimensions of those who use them, most schools need a variety of chair sizes to serve their student population. In fixed workstations, such as audiovisual/television carrels, video-display terminal stations, and operational control rooms, where a chair has to accommodate a varied user population, pneumatically adjustable chairs are recommended.

36.3.6.1.1. The Seat Pan. A chair's seat pan should have a modest concave contour so that an individual's weight is distributed evenly in the ischia area of the buttocks. The seat pan should have a "waterfall" shape at its front and should be lightly padded (about 1 inch) and covered with a porous textured "breathable" nonvinyl fabric. Overpadding the seat pan should be avoided, since the research indicates that leg discomfort increases with low, soft seat pans, suggesting that postural constraint is more important than thigh

compression as a risk factor for leg discomfort (Sauter & Schlifer, 1991).

36.3.6.1.2. Materials and Components. The seat and frame parts that come in contact with its occupant should be made of wood or some other thermally nonconductive material. It should be equipped with a padded backrest that provides support both in the lower back (lumbar) and midback regions. Chairs that swivel are recommended for large-group lecture halls and other settings where tasks involve rotation of the torso (Tichauer, 1978). Adding a pneumatic seat height adjustment is desirable for conference rooms, and this along with numerous other adjusting mechanisms are required for chairs used in VDT workstations.

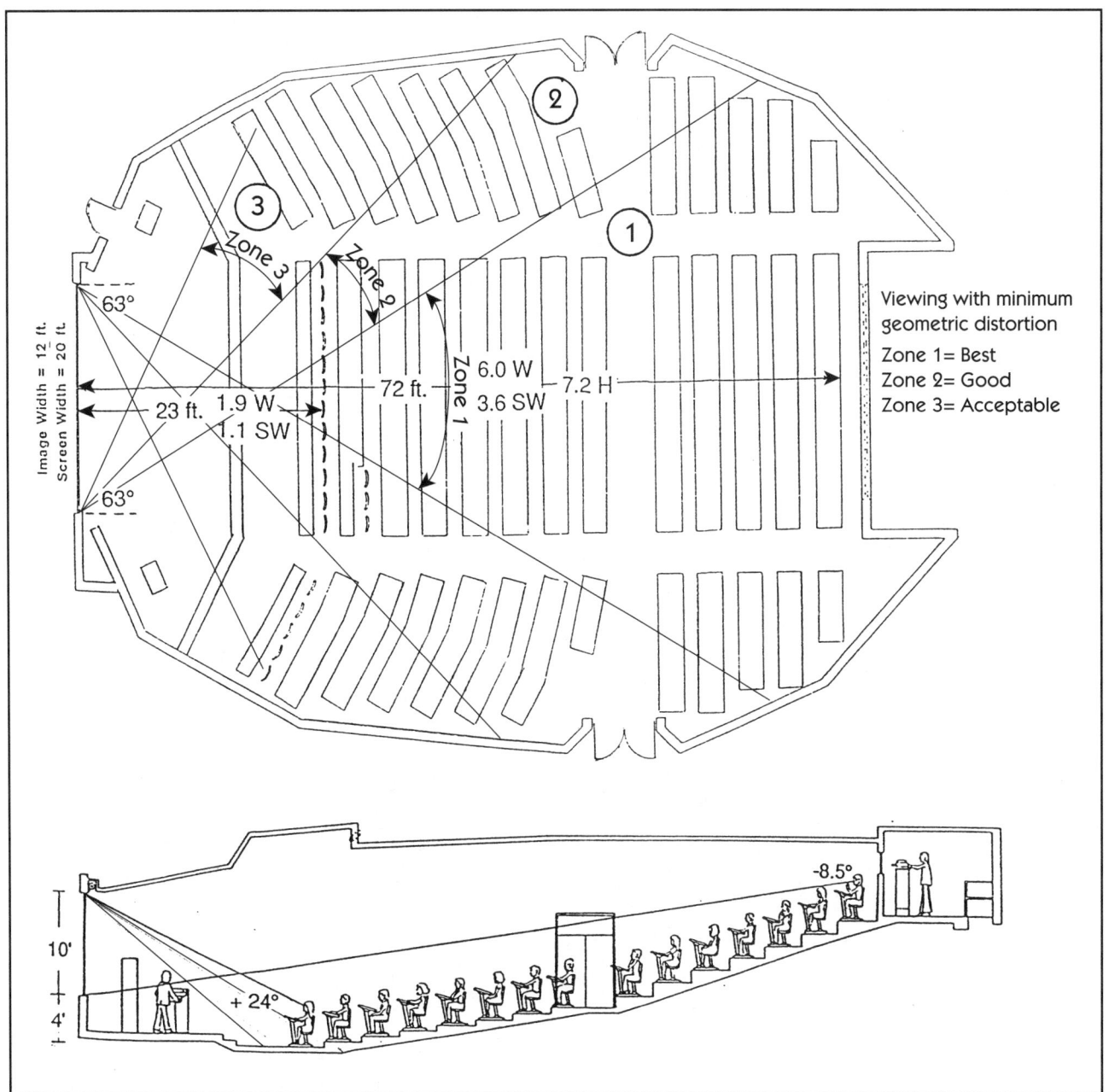

Figure 36-10. University of Wisconsin auditorium viewing parameters.

Figure 36-11. Computer classroom with simultaneous rear-screen and marker board display and individual VDT workstations.

36.3.6.1.3. Range of Adjustments. Since people, desks, and chairs all vary in height, units with adjustable height and tilt allow the greatest flexibility in avoiding problems (Davis, 1988). According to the Canadian National Standard (Carnovale et al., 1989), a workstation chair should have a minimum adjustable range between 15 inches to 20.5 inches, and ideally a desk's height should be adjustable between 24.8 inches to 30.0 inches. But if it has to be nonadjustable, then it should have a height between 27.9 inches to 28.3 inches. The use of a footrest is recommended, and a chair's backrest should be adjustable 104° to 120°, and the seat pan inclined backward 4° to 6° (Grandjean, 1988). Being able to change a chair's height, angle, and pitch will promote postural shifting, which is an important determinant for both physical comfort and work effectiveness. Such postural shifts are recommended for educational settings by Knirk (1992), "particularly for high cognitively loaded tasks such as those for computer-based training."

Classroom Intervention: Unfortunately, all too often the classroom teacher "inherits" chairs and desks that have little if any ergonomic merit. In such situations, Tessmer and Harris (1992) recommend adopting the following classroom management procedures in order to reduce the effects on learning of seating discomfort and inappropriate arrangement:

- Break instruction into shorter modules, thus encouraging students to take breaks from uncomfortable seating.
- Direct or advise learners to break sessions after no longer than 20 minutes via a message built into the materials they use.
- Provide seating graphics and user directions within instructor or student guides.

While the above procedures were intended for elementary and secondary classrooms, they are also appropriate for college and adult learning situations, with the exception of perhaps an adjustment of a seating interval being extended to 45 minutes.

36.3.6.2. The Desk, Computer Workstation, and Working Postures. The design of the notetaking, reading, and working surfaces also contributes to an individual's operational comfort and effectiveness. Horizontal writing and reading surfaces force students to bend forward excessively, setting up stresses in their skeletal and visual systems which can cause digestive, respiratory, visual, and postural problems (Harmon, 1951). And as early as 1938, one can find orthopedic reports showing that improper seating support can result in kyphosis (curved or bent back) and scoliosis (twisted spine) in children between the ages of 11 and 16 (CCSE, 1938). Another but more benign problem created by flat desks is noted by Tessmer (1994), who believes that excessive bending forward can affect a student's attention to learning tasks.

36.3.6.2.1. Inclined Reading/Writing Surfaces. Proper reading and writing posture is promoted by a desk or writing surface that is tilted somewhere between 10 to 20° from the horizontal (Freudenthal et al., 1991; Diffrient et al., 1974; deWall et al., 1991). In a major study at a large university, a writing/reading surface tilted 15° from the horizontal received significantly higher ratings from college students than did writing surfaces that were inclined 0°, 2°, and 7° (McVey, 1979). Figure 36-12 is a photograph of the desk designed by the author and constructed by the Haywood Wakefield Company for the University of Wisconsin's two lecture halls in the then-new (1972) School of Education facility. Note the 15° inclination of the surface and also its light color and matte texture. Also note the flatness of the paper/book restraining device. This was done to minimize pressure on the student's forearms and wrists when writing.

Having inclined writing surfaces is not only recommended for college age students but also has been shown to be particularly favorable for children (Bendix & Hagberg, 1984). Inclining the desk top 30° to 45° places reading and viewing materials at even more comfortable inclinations but will not allow items to remain unattended without falling off. This is why less-acute inclinations have thus far been favored. And it stands to reason that horizontal work surfaces have been found best for three-dimensional manipulative tasks.

About 40 years ago, the physiologist Darrell Boyd Harmon, in an effort to meet this challenge, designed for the American Seating Company a solid wood-metal seat-desk combination that was adjustable for students of different sizes and had swivel seats and an adjustable top that could accommodate the various work surface angles that were recommended for the full range of activities found in the standard classroom of the day (Harmon, 1951).

Classroom Intervention: Since most worktables and desks available to the student will probably be horizontal, the teacher should demonstrate for the students and encourage them to prop up their reading material with a thick book (3 inches), or by writing on a clipboard propped up by a 2-inch book. By placing these two tasks at these angles, the teacher will be promoting better posture, visual comfort, and speed and accuracy in reading and writing.

36.3.6.2.2. Accommodating the Computer (VDT). Today, the term VDT (visual-display terminal) is used primarily to mean computer monitor and keyboard, but its application is also extended to cover any display device employed at a workstation and its research findings applicable to all variations on this theme, i.e., video-display terminals, CRTs (cathode ray tubes), VDUs (visual-display unit, i.e., microfiche readers), etc.

Working at VDT workstations can be fatiguing and create physiological stress if seating-display relationships are not ergonomically correct. Working with VDTs, Sauter and Schlifer (1991) have found the erect seating posture to be associated with less-frequent discomfort than either stooped or reclining postures. This association is consistent with the classic view regarding healthy seating postures

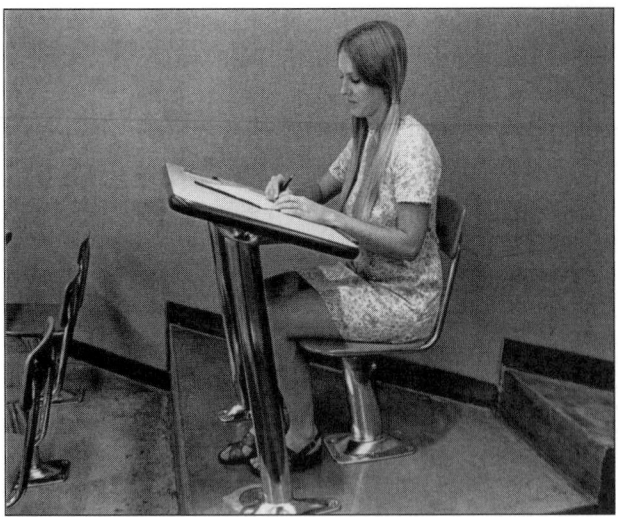

Figure 36-12a. Ergonomic reading and writing unit at the University of Wisconsin (circa 1972).

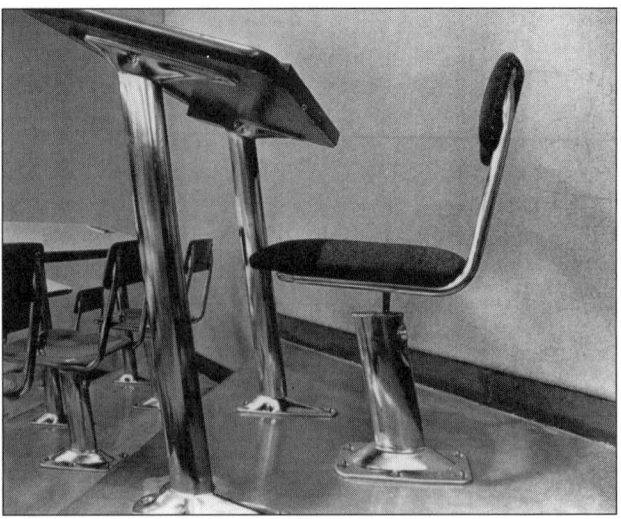

Figure 36-12b. Chair modified with addition of fabric-covered padding.

(Akerblom, 1954), but contrasts with at least one study that showed preference for reclining posture in VDT work (Grandjean et al., 1983).

36.3.6.2.3. Recommended Postures. Horowitz (1992) indicates that the right kind of furniture can help VDT users avoid crippling injuries by promoting what we have come to know as good posture. She recommends that furniture should be installed which promotes student posture with the following characteristics. It should be noted that these recommendations also apply to conventional reading and writing activities.

- The head should be directly over the shoulders, without straining forward or backward, about an arm's length from and at the same height as the screen.
- The neck should be elongated and relaxed.
- Shoulders should be kept down, with chest open and wide.
- The back should be upright or inclined slightly forward from the hips.
- Elbows should be relaxed and in a neutral position without flexing up or down.
- Knees should be slightly lower than the hips.
- Feet should be firmly planted on the floor.

One of the obvious objectives of Horowitz's recommendations is to establish a posture where the neck, back, upper arms, hips, and ankles are aligned at an angle approximately 90° to the floor, and with the forearms parallel to it. This is consistent with established ergonomic guidelines for VDT workstations (HFS, 1988). This arrangement will avoid positioning the head forward over the spine, with the shoulders and upper back following to produce an undesirable slump.

Given that the head represents a considerable weight (about 10% of the total body), maintaining such an unbalanced load sets up stresses in the musculoskeletal system. Sustaining such a posture while operating a keyboard for an extended period of time will result in excessive compression of the nerves and blood vessels in the neck, over the upper ribs, and down the arm. This cumulative trauma is referred to as a thoracic outlet syndrome. In addition to upsetting nerve control and circulation to the arms, the syndrome can also contribute to other CTD problems further down the arm (Hebert, 1989)

36.3.6.3. VDT Keyboard Height and Configuration.
The coordination of seating, viewing, and work positions is important to those whose learning activities involve computer terminals, using microfiche readers, video monitors in carrels, or VDT workstations. Research indicates that "many existing desks are not deep enough to accommodate a VDT and leave room for a generous wrist/forearm support for the use of a keyboard" (Porter et al., 1992). Whatever the support mechanism, it is important that the VDT keyboard height be on a plane with, or slightly below, elbow level. Sauter and Schlifer (1991) found that arm discomfort increased with increases in keyboard height above elbow level, and their findings are in agreement with Bendix and Jensen's (1986) electromyographic data that showed reduced trapezius loads with lower keyboard placement.

The angle of the keyboard should be such that the user can assume a position where the hands can be held in a neutral position, without excessive "extension" (palm down and wrist bent upward), "flexion" (palm down and wrist bent downward), "ulnar deviation" (rotating or tipping the hand toward the little finger). Experiments with a "split" keyboard design and with solid keyboards where the two keyboard halves have an opening angle of 25° and shaped with a lateral support of 10° were found to lessen the extent of inward rotation of the forearms and wrists and reduce physiological strain (Zipp, 1983). Other recommendations relative to keyboard design include detachability (HFS, 1988) or movability on a desk, with a support for forearms and wrists, the keyboard having a minimum depth of approximately 6 inches (Grandjean, 1988).

Figure 36-13, taken from one of my student's current studies (Badolato, 1995), summarizes the principle characteristics and dimensions recommended by different respected sources regarding computer workstation design. In his study, Badolato has applied these to the analysis of his own experimental settings, a series of music training classrooms at the Berklee School of Music in Boston. Readers should find this summary useful in their own future design and furniture selection activities.

36.3.6.4. The VDT and Viewing Distances. Because of the time-intensive nature of most VDT work, this subject has received considerable attention by leading ergonomists. Their work concerning viewing distance and viewing angle is summarized in the form of recommendations, as follows:

36.3.6.4.1. Viewing Distance from the VDT Screen. The absolute minimum distance according to a British standard (BS7179, 1990) is 15.7 inches. But according to the research of Jaschinski-Kruza (1988), the minimum distance should be 19.6 inches. And according to a widely respected source (Grandjean et al., 1984), that minimum distance should be 24 inches. The recommended maximum viewing distance also varies depending on the above sources, with the Jaschinski-Kruza study recommending 32 inches as the preferred maximum viewing distance and the Grandjean study, 36.6 inches. The author's own studies indicate student preferences for VDT viewing distances between 20 to 28 inches.

36.3.6.4.2. Viewing Angle to the VDT Screen. Some sources recommend that the top of the VDT screen be on a plane with a person's eyes (Eggleton, 1983). Other sources recommend a more acute downward angle (Ankrum & Nemeth, 1995). Hill and Kroemer (1988) recommend that the line of vision center on a downward angle between -29° to -38°, with the viewing distance decreasing at greater downward viewing angles. Support for this change in recommended viewing distance with increased declination angles is offered by Ripple (1952), who describes the "near" visual field as being "a curved surface concave toward the eye and curving deeper in and down and flatter up and out."

The author's own experiments have shown a preference for a viewer-monitor arrangement where the top of the display does not extend above the viewer's -5° horizontal line of sight, and the bottom not below the viewer's -40° horizontal line of sight. Where lighting conditions permit, the display screen should be inclined backward somewhere between 20° to 45° from the perpendicular. It should be noted that while inclining the monitor in this manner minimizes perceived geometric distortion and makes use of the increased visual accommodation experienced at downward viewing angles, it will require special care in the room's lighting design in order to control for excessive reflected glare. Figure 36-14 shows a computer training classroom I designed employing student workstations where the computer monitor is located inside the desk and below its glass work surface. This concept has been shown to have merits as well as some limitations, particularly in educational programs in which students often work in pairs. Complaints

with it relative to glare of its glass surface, as well as off the monitor, were generally eliminated with the use of the glare hood provided by the manufacturer and by fitting each monitor with an antiglare polarizing screen.

36.3.6.5. Repetitive Motion Problems. With the increased use of VDTs primarily in offices has come increased incidents referred to as *repetitive motion disorders* (RMD) or *cumulative trauma disorders* (CTD) affecting different parts of the body (arms, shoulders, neck, legs) and a variety of sensory functions. A 5-year prevalence rate for RMDs of nearly 35% has been reported in some Australian organizations (Hocking, 1987), and Japan experienced a similar phenomenon during the 1970s (Nakaseko et al., 1982).

In the U.S., the most prevalent RMDs are carpal tunnel disorder (CTD) problems, which are primarily caused by the excessive compression of the median nerve in the wrist and which account to up to 3% of all VDT users. According to the National Institute of Occupational Safety and Health (NIOSH, 1991), CDTs are primarily caused by inadequate physical and psychological workplace design or ergonomic factors (NSWI, 1992).

While great strides have been made in improving the ergonomics of the office work environment, little attention to date has been given to classrooms, libraries, and resource centers where extensive VDT use is a regular occurrence. It is anticipated that significant levels of RMDs including CDTs will soon be noted in the education sector. Today's educational facility planners should look to office design research results for guidance in preventing the onset of such problems.

36.3.7 The Acoustical Environment

36.3.7.1. Room Shape and Acoustical Treatment. There are a number of sources that can help the facility planner and designer create the proper acoustics for a space (Yerges, 1969; Doelle, 1972). The following generalizations apply: A room's shape affects its acoustics. The orientation of a room's walls, ceiling, and floor should be such that sound is reflected from the front of the room toward the back. To accomplish this, side walls should be nonparallel (splayed). In large-group media rooms and auditoria, floors should be stepped or inclined.

The ceiling section over the instructor should also be inclined toward the audience so that the speaker's voice is projected forward, although part of this sound should also be reflected at a slight downward angle so that instructors will have no difficulty hearing their own voice. A room's shape should propagate sound throughout, but in a diffused fashion. Consequently, concave curved walls are usually not recommended, since they tend to refocus reflected sound waves.

The character of each room surface should be consistent with the general acoustical treatment of the space. The ceiling above the lecture stage should be sonically reflective. If reflecting panels (acoustical clouds) are used, they should be no smaller than 8 feet wide, or else they will not

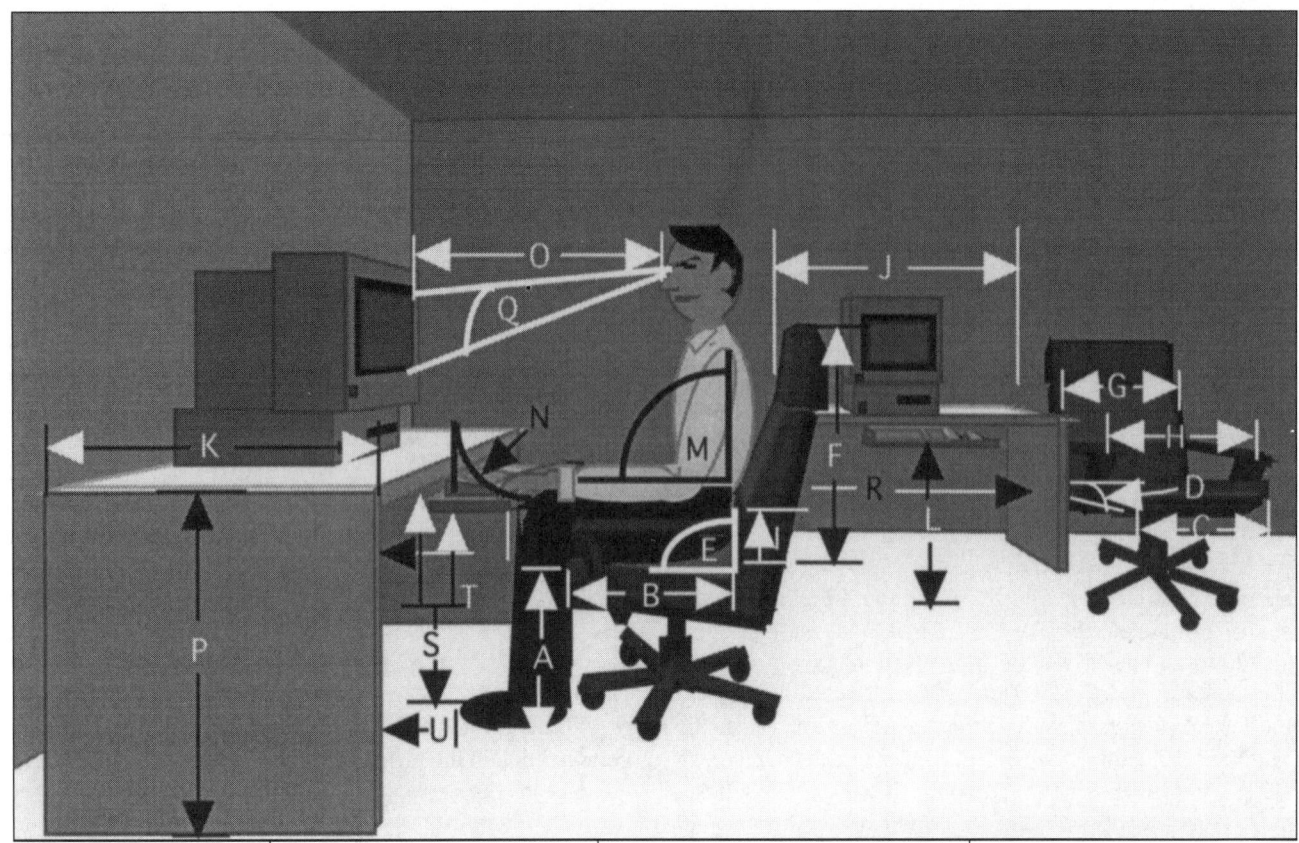

Dimension	ANSI/HFS (1988)	Grandjean (Salvendy 1987)	Woodson (1992)
Seating			
A–Height	16.0–20.5 in. (40.6–42.0 cm)	13.0–22.0 in. (32.0–55.0 cm)	15.0–18.0 in. (38.0–46.0 cm)
B–Depth	15.0–17.0 in. (38.0–43.0 cm)		16.0 in. (43.2 cm)
C–Width	18.2 in. (45 cm) minimum		19.0 in. (48.0 cm)
D–Pan angle	0–10°		5°
E–Angle btw back and pan	90–105°	90–120°	105° (10° free pivot)
F–Backrest height	no specific recommendation		15.0–18.0 in. (38.0–46.0 cm)
G–Backrest width	12 in. (30.5 cm) minimum		
H–Distance btw armrests	18.2 in. (45 cm) minimum		
I–Lumber support	6–10 in. (15.2–24.4 cm) abv seat	4.0–8.0 in. (10–20) abv seat	
Worksurface			
J–Width	sufficient for equipment and task		32.0 in. (81.0 cm)
K–Depth	sufficient for equipment and task		24.0 in. (61.0 cm)
Keyboard			
L–Support surface height	23.0–28.0 in. (58.4–71.1 cm)	27.5–33.4 (70.0–85.0 cm)	
M–Upper arm/forearm angle	70–135°	90° observed avg posture	
N–Slope	0–25°		
Video Display			
O–Viewing Distance	12.0 in. (30.5 cm) minimum	19.6–29.5 in. (50.0–75.0 cm)	
P–Support surface height	position within viewing angle Q	35.4–45.2 in. (90.0–115.0 cm)	
Q–Viewing angle	0–60° below horiz. line of sight	+2 to -26° observed	
Clearance Envelopes			
R–Leg clearance width	20.0 in. (50.8 cm) minimum		
S–Leg clearance height	26.2 in (66.5 cm) minimum	23.6 in. (60.0 cm) minimum	23.0–28.0 in. (58.4–71.0 cm)
T–Depth at knee level	15.0 in. (38 cm)		
U–Depth at toe level	23.5 in. (59.0 cm)		

Figure 36-13. Principle characteristics and dimensions of VDT workstation design. (After Badolato, 1995.)

Figure 36-14. Below-surface VDT student workstation.

should be no smaller than 8 feet wide, or else they will not reflect the lower sound frequencies. While it is generally recommended that the front half of the space be acoustically reflective, it is also recommended that the rear half of the room be acoustically absorptive so that sound waves will not be reflected back toward the front of the room. This condition can usually be accomplished by putting acoustical tiles on the rear one-third of the ceiling and acoustical carpet or other sound-absorptive material on the rear and side rear walls.

Installing carpeting on the floor area usually completes the acoustical treatment of a room while adding a welcomed bit of texture and color to the space. In a large auditorium that is used for a variety of activities involving groups of varying numbers, the addition of upholstered chairs may be required to keep the room's reverberation time near a desired constant.

The reader should note, however, that getting an educational institution to provide upholstered chairs for its lecture halls is not an easy task. Back in 1970 when I had selected the seating for the University of Wisconsin's ergonomically designed auditorium/lecture hall, I was successful in getting the university to agree to adding padding and fabric to the seat pan and backrests of the Haywood Wakefield swivel chairs selected and installed at the site. And, interestingly, the only justification they would accept for such an expenditure was for improved acoustics. Student comfort was not enough. However, before the modifications could be made, the university's swimming pool sprung a leak, and the money allocated for the chair modification was diverted to that emergency. And since I left that institution at the start of the next fiscal year, there was no one to "champion" spending the additional money to make the desired modifications, and so that particular ergonomic improvement was never made.

36.3.7.2. Noise and Performance. Noise, i.e., unwanted sound, is generally not desired in learning environments. However, broadband "white" or "pink" noise, sounding somewhat like an open TV channel or an air-conditioning unit, is used at moderate amplitudes as a noise-masking agent to create speech privacy in open offices and open classrooms. Some of the general affects unwanted sound has on people include annoyance, distraction, or interference with communications, leading to altered performance of some tasks (Eggleton, 1983). The effects of noise have been investigated by a number of people (Broadbent, 1957; Cohen, 1969; Kryter, 1970; Miller, 1971; Taylor, 1988; Kjellberg & Skoldstrom, 1991).

36.3.7.2.1. Noise Measurement. Ambient noise is usually measured either in decibels on the "A" scale (the scale most closely approximating the human hearing curve) or by plotting decibel levels at each of the nine major center octave bands. The set of curves that results from this activity are either called *noise criterion* or *NC curves* or *preferred noise criterion* or *PNC curves*. The PNC curves were developed by the originators of the NC curves, about 14

years later, as an improved version of ambient spectra that could be recommended for specific activities. The two sets of curves are nearly identical, except with the PNC being less permissive in the very low and very high frequencies by 4 to 5 dB. Basically, one determines a room's NC or PNC curve by plotting the sound pressure levels of the principle octave band frequencies on either set of curves, i.e., contours, and notes the highest rank contour tangent to or touched by any one of these readings. That upper-curve designation is used to identify the room's NC or PNC number. And, since the research cites both versions, as well as the benefits of decibel levels on the A scale as predictors for acceptability, all three versions will be used as they were originally cited in the literature.

36.3.7.2.2. Noise Limits. While total quiet is never recommended, it is important that the learning environment provide spaces of relative quiet to serve as retreats from the din of school and nonschool activities. Noise levels exceeding 70 dBA will not only interfere with communication and mental performance but also produce a disorienting, chaotic learning environment. Noise levels of 85 dBA and above are generally considered psychologically and physiologically excessive. It is well known that prolonged exposure to excessive noise levels causes both temporary and permanent hearing loss. Such loss is usually thought of as an adult problem, but this is a misconception. Even our youngest citizens are not immune. One study of 3,000 students at three grade levels revealed that 5% of the sixth-graders, 14% of the ninth-graders, and 20% of the twelfth-graders showed some measurable hearing loss induced by the general noise level of their environment (Lexan, 1969). Temporary hearing loss may become permanent unless the victim is given a sufficient hearing recovery period away from the noise. Other disabilities that can be caused by excessive noise include cardiovascular disorders, nausea, weight loss, fatigue, irritability, insomnia, and impaired tactile functioning (CEQ, 1968). Again, relief can be found only by eliminating the noise or by moving away from it to a quieter environment.

Classroom Intervention: Efforts to reduce noise are based on isolation, absorption, and containment. *Isolation* means eliminating the medium a sound needs in order to travel. For example, placing a rubber or neoprene pad under a noisy projector or printer can do much to keep its noise from being transmitted via the table and floors. Likewise, placing audiospeakers away from the front wall of a classroom will keep their sound from being transmitted as vibration through the structure and disturbing the adjacent room.

36.3.7.2.3. The Character of Noise and Its Consequences. Excessive decibel levels are not the only problem. Someone else's music or conversation can be perceived as noise by others. Grandjean (1987) has shown that conversation is one of the most disturbing types of noise that can intrude on mental concentration, specifically because of the informational content it contains. It has also been shown that excessive conversational noise, in the range of 60 decibels on the "A" weighted scale (60 dBA), can negatively affect reading comprehension, particularly of students most susceptible to such distractions (Veitch, 1990). And while noise adversely affected performance on a proofreading task, this affect was only significant when this task was machine paced as opposed to when it was self-paced (Kjellberg & Skoldstrom, 1991). Weinstein (1979) found that noise levels between 68 to 70 decibels decreased student performance even on short-term tasks. Glass (1985) found that loud, distracting noises interfered with the performance of complex mental tasks and led to fatigue. Noise features that are likely to degrade performance include:

- Variability in level or content
- High-level repeated noises
- Intermittency
- Frequencies above approximately 2,000 Hz
- Any combination of the above

Ross and Stewart (1993) cite the work of Bobker (1991) in making their case that technological equipment by itself tends to make annoying and disconcerting sounds. They report that some computer users have complained of ringing in their ears (tintinnabulation), and that many multimedia programs, employed in schools, have built-in sound effects for student motivation. They state: "The continual din of these can be disconcerting to classroom instruction." It is important that designers of computers be encouraged in their continued efforts at quieting their machines, and it is critical that the problems associated with the audio components of multimedia workstations be thoroughly researched so that these new technologies be made to coexist with other important learning activities, otherwise their continual adoption by educators may be resisted because of their "noise" intrusiveness.

36.3.7.2.4. The Too-Quiet Room. It is also known that an environment that is too quiet can also lead to distractions and annoyance. Given the tasks that a student is likely to perform when using a VDT, one can predict greater awareness to noise distractions if the ambient noise level is lower than 35 dBA or NC30. Generally, one can usually expect the lighting and the heating, ventilation, and air-conditioning (HVAC) systems, and the fans in the computer itself, to generate at least this level of ambient sound. However, when an environment is too quiet for its programmed activities, the addition of artificially generated broad spectrum sound is recommended. It is in this regard that Harmon (1966) noted that the addition of 30 dBA of "white" noise, a soft "whooshing" sound, produced the optimum body tonus necessary for alignment of attention to a performance task.

Classroom Intervention: When students need to concentrate on a demanding task, a small amount of "white noise" (meaningless sound made up of tones of all audible frequencies) may be used as a sound-masking device to keep them from being disturbed by extraneous classroom sounds like talking or traffic. Personal "white noise" generators are currently available for around $100, but the class-

room teacher can produce an acceptable substitute by simply making a tape recording of the sound generated by a TV set when it is turned to an unoccupied channel. The teacher can then play this recording, at a low level, which will sound very much like white noise in the classroom whenever he or she wishes to mask extraneous and distracting noises. The currently available environmental recordings of the sea, wind, etc., can also be used as noise-masking devices.

While people have different reactions to noise-masking systems, most seem to accept broadband steady-state sounds as a constant element in their environment as long as the levels do not exceed 47 dBA or NC43 (Yerges, 1978; ASTM, 1976). Given that spaces with many VDTs require more cooling than the standard classroom environment, extra care needs to be taken with HVAC design to ensure that the general background noise level correlates with the levels recommended for its programmed activities and in no instance exceeds 47 dBA.

36.3.7.2.5. The Role of Background Music. Music, in general, tends to speed up the fundamental physiological processes and to raise the level of body tonus (the muscular and nerve readiness to perform). Because it also tends to increase muscle endurance, music can reduce or delay the fatigue associated with a physical worktask. In recent years there have been many attempts to use music as background sound for various school tasks. The success or failure of such attempts has depended on the nature of the music and the nature of the task. While nonfamiliar music, especially if it has few major frequency and volume shifts, can help many students concentrate on their work, familiar music can be an informational distraction. The rhythm of the music is most important. If it does not match the rhythm of the worktask (typing, handwriting, or whatever), it can cause a decrement in the student's performance.

36.3.7.3. Noise and Communication. Figure 36-15 shows the preferred noise criteria (PNC) curves and the excessive ambient noise conditions I recorded in six elementary classrooms. These readings show the extent of the problems that can be created by window ventilators and room air–handling systems.

Most of the experts are in agreement with Kryter (1970) that in classrooms where unamplified speech is used in teaching, the background-noise level should be not less than NC 25 (30 dBA) and no more than NC 35 (35 dBA). These same classroom background-noise levels are also recommended for classrooms serving students with hearing disabilities (Ross, 1972; John, 1960). The recommended ambient noise level for auditoria is NC 25, and for recording facilities, NC 15-20 (Doelle, 1972). See Table 36-4 for the preferred noise criteria ranges recommended for various indoor-activity areas deemed relevant to the reader.

Increasingly, a variety of media are being employed in educational and training environments at all grade levels from elementary schools through postdoctoral and corporate educational programs. Today it is not uncommon to find anywhere from 10 to 30 VDT workstations in a classroom setting where background-noise levels have to be low in order for accurate verbal communications, an essential element in the teaching-learning process. Here again, the NC 35 level has been shown to provide an acceptable noise level for such activities.

36.3.7.3.1. Signal-to-Noise Ratios. The contribution to communications efficacy made by relatively low ambient noise levels is seen in the signal-to-noise (S/N) ratios found in classrooms. The relationship of the sound pressure level (SPL) of a person's voice to a room's background or ambient sonic-energy levels is termed the *signal-to-noise ratio* (S/N). Woodson and Conover (1973) note that at S/N ratios of +15, +10, +5, and 0, one can expect word intelligibilities of 82%, 78%, 70%, and 58%, respectively. And Van Cott and Kinkade (1972) indicate that 75% word intelligibility is required for reliable conversation to take place.

Furthermore, this same source notes that reliable conversation will barely exist for people as close as 12 feet using normal voice levels (reported by Van Cott & Kinkade to be 49 dB at 12 feet) when the room noise level is 43 dB (S/N +6). They also report that when this background noise level is raised to 49 dB, accurate conversation is barely possible even at 12 feet when using a raised-voice level of 53 dBA (S/N +4). It should be noted that ambient noise levels of 49 dB and even 43 dB, while considered excessive, are not uncommon in today's classrooms where window air circulators or overhead air diffusers are improperly set up or balanced, or where the noise from computer peripherals such as printers is not attenuated through either acoustic absorption or isolation.

Figure 36-16 offers a good visual representation of how reductions in S/N ratios, caused by window ventilators,

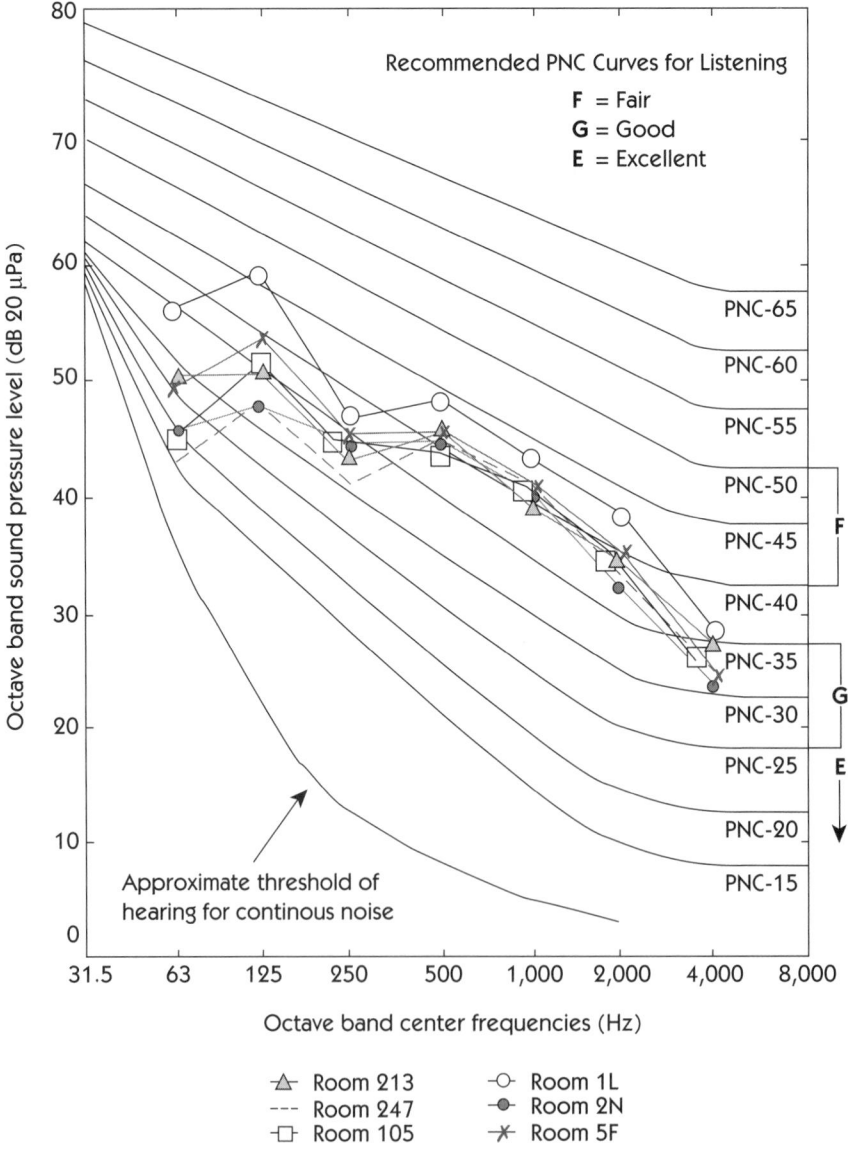

Figure 36-15. Preferred noise criteria (PNC) curves with noise spectra plotted for six elementary classrooms.

TABLE 36-4. NOISE CRITERIA RANGE FOR VDT-RELATED ENVIRONMENTS
(Adapted from AFSC-DH 1-3, 1980, Kryfer, 1970, Doelle, 1972)

Type of Space (and Approximate Acoustical Requirements)	PNC Curve	LA, dBA
Broadcast and recording studios (distant microphone pickup), concert and recital halls (for listening to faint musical sounds)	10–20	21–27
Large auditoria, large drama theaters (for excellent to good listening conditions)	Not to exceed 20–25	Not to exceed 25–30
Broadcast television and recording studios (close microphone pickup only), video conferencing room, small auditoria	Not to exceed 25	Not to exceed 30
General 25–30 seat classroom	25–35	Not to exceed 35
Libraries, private or semiprivate offices, small conference rooms, etc. (for good listening conditions)	30–40	38–47
Large meeting and conference rooms (for good listening), or executive offices and conference rooms for 50 people (no amplificaiton)	Not to exceed 35	Not to exceed 42
Large offices, reception areas (for moderately good listening conditions)	35–45	42–52
Laboratory work spaces, drafting and engineering rooms, general secretarial areas (for fair listening conditions)	40–50	47–56
Light maintenance shops, offices, and computer equipment rooms (for moderately fair listening conditions)	45–55	52–61
Shops, garages, power-plant control rooms, etc. (for just-acceptable speech and telephone communications). Levels above PNC-60 are not recommended for any office or communication situation.	50–60	56–66
For work spaces where speech or telephone communications is not required, but where there must be no risk of hearing damage	60–70	66–80

affected speech intelligibility by masking consonant sounds as heard in six different elementary classrooms tested by the author.

Classroom Intervention: The classroom teacher can promote a desirable signal-to-noise ratio by preventing extraneous sounds from entering the classroom through open doors or windows. The S/N ratio for a student sitting by a door leading into a noisy corridor often approaches zero. Whenever climatically feasible, classroom doors and windows should remain closed during those hours that require mental and verbal activity. Students as well as teachers have a right to quiet, and they should express that right whenever noise intrusion hinders their learning activities. The sense of freedom in the classroom should be such that a student who is being disturbed by outside sounds will not hesitate to leave his or her seat and close a door or window.

A common occurrence is where instructors leave a slide or overhead projector on long after they have finished showing their visual materials. This unwanted noise reduces the intelligibility of the instructor's voice at a time when continued use of these devices serves no useful purpose. It is one thing to suffer unwanted background noise while the

media are in use, but it is simply inconsiderate and poor classroom management to continue to generate such noise and negatively affect S/N ratios after such equipment operations are no longer required.

36.3.7.4. Reverberation Time. A room's reverberation time (RT) refers to its liveness and deadness and is expressed as the number of seconds that it takes for a sound level to decay 60 decibels. Traditionally, recommendations for RTs have been associated with the size and function of a given space, and according to Kryter (1978), "Normally, smaller rooms should have shorter times than larger rooms; and music spaces usually require longer times than spaces used principally for speech." Today's study areas, resource centers, and open-plan classrooms and offices, however, while large in overall size, consist of numerous small and independent workstations where speech privacy and accurate personal and, in many cases, telephone communications are to take place. Consequently, it is recommended that such spaces have RTs at the lower end of the scale, i.e., 0.6 to 0.8 seconds. Classroom RTs between 0.7 and 0.9 seconds are considered optimum for normal-hearing individuals (Ross, 1972), with a RT of 1.0 second as a limit for the conventional-size classroom (Niemoeller, 1968).

36.3.7.4.1. Reverberation Time and the Hearing Impaired. Given that mainstreaming hearing-impaired students into general educational programs is the norm, we should look at their special needs regarding reverberation time. Studies from the field of clinical audiology and sensory disabilities have shown that such individuals experience noticeable difficulty when RTs exceed 0.7 seconds (Niemoeller, 1968; John, 1960), leading John (1960) to recommend that RTs for rooms in which hearing-impaired students are to be placed not exceed 0.5 seconds. The only practical way such low RTs can be achieved in today's classrooms is through adding significant amounts of sound-absorbing materials to a room's surfaces. The positive effect of such acoustical treatment on speech discrimination in general classrooms has recently been supported by the research of Pekkarinen and Viluanen (1990).

Classroom Intervention: The different reverberation times in different rooms should always be considered by teachers making tape recordings, for these will affect the intelligibility of the tapes when they are played back. When an audiotape made in a recording studio or a classroom having a short reverberation time is played back in an auditorium or classroom having a long reverberation time, words seem to run into each other, pauses are lost, and speech becomes unintelligible. A teacher can compensate for this problem somewhat by making a concerted effort to slow down his or her speech when recording in a studio or any other room with a short reverberation time.

36.3.7.5. Acoustical Design and Corrective Work. Guidance for acoustical procedures, including isolation, containment, and surface treatments, can be found in numerous sources (Doelle, 1972; Harris, 1957; Close,

1966; Yerges, 1978; Propst, 1968; Packard, 1981). The need for innovative acoustical design is expected to increase in importance with the development of new educational technologies. Parsons (1986) claims that the demands of new electronic technology are not getting the attention of individuals who traditionally are responsible for designing learning environments. According to Allen and Charles (1986), "as more voice-operated machines are introduced, effective sound separation will become even more crucial, so that machines will be able to identify and respond to their masters." Thus, the acoustical needs of the tomorrow's learning environments will increase rather than lessen.

36.3.7.6. Sound Systems

36.3.7.6.1. Sound System Quality and Directionality. Sound enhances visual perception by giving it contrast and adding information. Sounds can be used to direct attention to related visual elements (Broadbent, 1958). People tend to position their bodies in a direct line with the apparent source of a sound. Therefore, in setting up audiovisual aids, teachers should coordinate the placement of a projector's loudspeaker with the projected image and, of course, the classroom seating. The better-designed movie theaters provide the ideal arrangement: The loudspeaker used to play back dialog and critical localizing sounds is located directly behind the projection screen at a height approximately two-thirds the vertical span of the screen. Such theaters use a fixed perforated projection screen that allows sound to pass undisturbed right through it, thus creating the illusion that the sound is coming from the elements appearing on the screen.

Classroom Intervention: For most classroom audiovisual presentations with portable equipment, placing the loud-

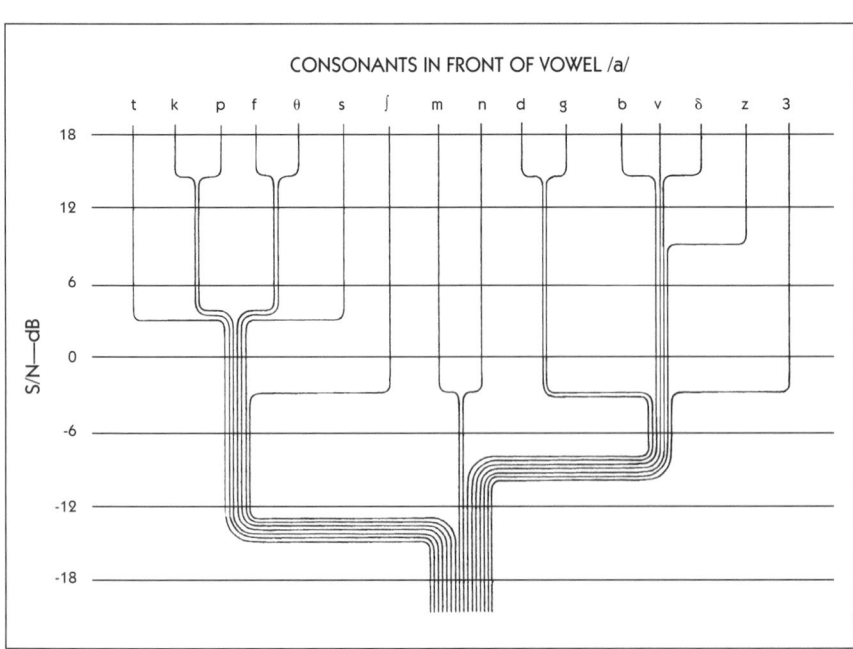

Figure 36-16. How reduced S/N ratios affect speech intelligibility. (After Kryter, 1970.)

speaker on a bench or chair directly in front of and below the extended projection screen will be acceptable.

36.3.7.6.2. Sound System Selection. It is a well-known fact that audio amplification and distribution systems can contribute to the effectiveness of audiovisual materials. A good playback sound system should reproduce both monophonic and stereo signals and have sufficient power, good sensitivity, low distortion, and smooth frequency response. Ideally, as noted above, reinforced sound should appear to emanate from the informational display area (e.g., the projection screen). In an auditorium, this effect can be achieved by mounting a central monophonic speaker cluster or stereo speakers in the acoustical cloud above the projection screen or in smaller rooms at each side of the projection screen about 7 1/2 feet from the floor, preferably recessed into the wall.

While it is possible to use the program playback speakers for voice amplification, usually in lecture halls and auditoria, it is recommended that a separate distributed speaker system be installed in the ceiling. Standard-size classrooms and conference rooms generally require only program playback speakers, not voice amplification systems.

A ceiling-distributed speaker system is a practical solution that works well for rooms with low ceilings or poor acoustics. This is because people have difficulty sensing the displacement of a sound's source when it is in the vertical plane, unless it is displaced from the vertical by more than 45° (Wysotsky, 1971). Consequently, in a properly spaced ceiling-speaker system, the illusion that the sound is coming from the lecturer or the display is maintained even though the speakers are located overhead. In such a system, speakers are spaced at distances from each other equal to the ceiling height minus 4 feet, multiplied by a factor of choice between 1.25 to 1.34. For example, given a finished ceiling height of 10 feet, speakers should be spaced no farther apart than on 8-foot centers, i.e., 1.34 (10 − 4) = between 7.5 and 8.0 feet; while with a 16-foot-high ceiling, they would be spaced on centers between 15 to 16 feet. Understandably in an auditorium with a stepped or sloped floor, the ceiling-speaker distances from each other should vary with the changing ceiling height.

36.3.7.6.3. Assistive Listening Devices. In auditoriums and other educational spaces where the public is likely to gather for special events, provisions for assistive listening devices need to be provided for the hearing challenged. Since there are a variety of different types, with each type having unique features, it is recommended that a detailed study of the particular needs of a facility and its likely occupants be conducted before any specific system is purchased.

36.3.8 The Luminous Environment

36.3.8.1. Lighting Systems

36.3.8.1.1. General Lighting. A learning environment requires lighting that produces a pattern of brightness from room surfaces which is aesthetically pleasing and which promotes good depth perception. Illumination or, using the currently more correct terminology, *illuminance,* on major and supplementary task areas, such as chalk or dry-mark boards, tackboards, desks, and other work surfaces, should allow participants to complete visual tasks in comfort and with a high degree of efficiency. Because of their long life and energy efficiency, fluorescent luminaires are preferred over incandescents, except in special situations where directionality and modeling are critical or where room aesthetics are a major factor (Bennett, 1985).

36.3.8.1.2. Supplementary Lighting. The use of supplementary lighting on flip charts, maps, models, etc., capitalizes on the natural attraction that people have toward bright areas within their visual field. Research shows that people are less distracted by a room's surroundings and give more attention to displays with supplementary illumination than those without (LaGuisa & Perney, 1973, 1974). The message here for both the facility designer and the classroom teacher is a fairly simple one: Provide and utilize supplementary lighting on all principal display surfaces.

36.3.8.1.3. Indirect Lighting. Wide-angle dispersion indirect lighting has proved particularly desirable in rooms where VDTs are used, since it minimizes distracting reflections from luminaires seen on the VDT screen (Hedge et al., 1989). But a direct-lighting component is a practical requirement during media projection where notetaking is required and control of light away from the display areas is necessary. Consequently, the ideal lighting system for today's classrooms is one that combines a wide-dispersion indirect-lighting unit for general learning activities and computer work, and a second component with narrow-dispersion direct low-level illuminance on notetaking task areas, separately controlled, to be used during audiovisual presentations.

36.3.8.1.4. Lighting Control and Windowless Rooms. Illuminance control is imperative, particularly in rooms where visual-display media are used. Ideally, there should be no windows in rooms used primarily for computer training and for media presentations. They introduce unwanted light, heat, and noise. However, if windows are required, then the room should be equipped with sunscreens, audiovisual blinds, and/or opaque drapes so that sunlight does not "wash out" projected images or create glare on marker boards and VDT screens. The controversy surrounding the absence or presence of windows in educational spaces has yet to be settled. Knirk (1992) covered the topic about as thoroughly as anyone when he stated:

> Research does not support those claiming that windowless learning spaces will allow increased concentration and thus higher achievement. . . . On the other hand, data do not support those educators fearing that the absence of windows will have harmful psychological or physical effects on the students and staff. Windowless learning spaces provide more control over the learner's environment. . . the level of visual and auditory distractions are lower . . . with computers, windowless environments reduce glare and light levels. Temperature can be regulated and chances of vandalism are lessened in windowless environments.

My own experience has indicated that having both windowed and windowless rooms in a learning environment are desirable. The windowed spaces should be allocated to standard classrooms and office spaces, while the windowless areas relegated to those spaces that are to be used to house computers and training/conference rooms having extensive media-display components. And while the preference at the elementary and secondary school level is clearly for windowed rooms, college students seem to accept equally both kinds of spaces, if the wall color treatment and the lighting of the windowless rooms is to their liking. And in high-tech and business training and meeting environments, particularly those having extensive display facilities, there seems to be a preference for windowless rooms, particularly where the room lighting has been appropriately designed. Figure 36-17 shows photographs of one of six windowless rooms I designed for the New England Telephone Learning Center in Marlboro, Massachusetts. These rooms all featured an indirect-lighting ceiling cove that served to draw the attention of the occupants inward and away from the room's perimeter. They also included scene switched fluorescent lights, incandescent downlights on dimmer, and wall washers. These room's proved to be more popular to the attendees and their session leaders than the 12 other rooms having windows. One of the reasons cited for this preference by the session leaders was the additional tackable walls for displaying their flip-chart materials and product display artwork. The attendees on the other hand seemed to feel that the windowless rooms were less distracting and visually more comfortable over long sessions than the windowed rooms. It should be noted that in this environment and in the training program, there were many opportunities and places for the attendees to have extended views of the outdoors.

36.3.8.2. Illumination (Illuminance) Levels. The preferred term for illumination today is *illuminance,* measured in either foot-candles (FC) or Lux (1 FC = approximately 10.7 Lux). Since most of the research cited herein has used "foot-candles," this term will be used throughout. However, with the unit equivalent just provided, readers may easily make their own conversions to Lux. And where research and luminance standards specifically refer to Lux, such units will be cited.

36.3.8.2.1. General Tasks. Illuminance levels of 30 to 50 foot-candles (FC) are recommended for general educational activities, with the lower end of that range being appropriate for exclusively VDT work (Zmirak, 1993), and the upper end for reading books and writing (McVey, 1971). According to Zmirak (1993), providing an illuminance level of 30 FC in computer labs where students only work off the screen will result in improved student efficiency and reduced energy costs. Christinaz and Knirk (1987), while accepting a 30 to 75 FC range for general activities, note that when designing for VDT use, illuminance levels should be based on the readability of associated materials and the surrounding area. They warn that strict adherence to raw foot-candle standards will not in themselves ensure sufficient or efficient task illumination. Support for this more qualitative approach can be found in Grandjean (1982a), who states (p. 271) that:

> Specifications for lighting levels can be no more than general guidelines, and other circumstances must be taken into account in any particular situation, for example: (a) the reflectivity (color and material) of the working materials and of the surroundings, (b) the extent of difference from natural lighting, (c) whether it is necessary to use artificial lighting during the daytime, and (d) the age of the people concerned.

36.3.8.2.2. Visually Demanding Tasks. Levels of 100 to 150 FC are recommended for critical visual tasks (artwork, etc.). A variable illumination range of 0 to 30 FC is recommended for AV/TV use (the lower levels used for video, LCD panel display, and motion picture projection; the upper levels for slide projection, and even higher levels for standard overhead transparency projection). Classrooms and conference rooms used for participants 50 years old and older need more illumination for notetaking than rooms used exclusively by their younger counterparts (NRC,1987).

36.3.8.3. Reflectances. *Gloss* refers to the specular (mirrorlike) nature of some finishes. The combination of excessive gloss and direct illuminance can create distracting glare. Consequently, low levels of gloss, i.e., matte or satin finishes, are recommended for all furnishings that students are to read from. And the ANSI/HFS (1988) standards specifies this limit to be 45% or less when measured with a 60° gloss meter or equivalent device.

The term *reflectance* refers to the percentage of light that a finish is capable of reflecting. Too little reflectance in a finish can create a "gloomy" environment, while reflectances that are too high can contribute to a "glaring" environment. To keep reflections at comfortable levels, the following surface reflectances are recommended (Kaufman, 1981):

- Desktops: matte finish, 30–50%
- Floors: natural woods or light-colored tile or carpet, 30–50%
- Chalkboards: green, not to exceed 20%; gray or black, under 10%
- Walls: matte finish, 40–60%
- Ceiling: 70–90%

36.3.8.4. Brightness (Luminance) Contrast Ratios. The term *brightness* refers to a perceptual value and has been incorrectly used for many years; researchers meant *photometric* or *measurable* brightness. The preferred term for photometric brightness today is *luminance;* it is measured in either footlamberts (FL) or candela per square meter (cd/m^2), sometimes called a *nit.* One nit is equal to approximately 0.3 footlamberts. Since most of the research cited herein has used *footlamberts,* this term will be used throughout. However, with the unit equivalent just provided, readers may make their own conversions to cd/m^2. And where research and luminance standards specifically refer to cd/m^2, such units will be cited.

Figure 36-17a. Windowless training conference rooms showing special lighting and display features. (Note vertically operable marker board in "use" position in front of rear screen.)

Figure 36-17b. Same room but set up in U-shaped seating arrangement. (Note extensive use of acoustic/tack panels, chart trays, magnetic strips, flip charts, and perimeter lighting.)

As noted in 36.2, for about 50 years the Illumination Engineering Society of North America has promoted guidelines that state that the LCR of large adjoining areas should fall somewhere between 1:1 and 3:1, with the task area brighter than its surroundings. For areas adjacent to the visual task, the acceptable LCR should fall somewhere between 3:1 and 10:1 (Kaufman, 1981; Woodson, 1987).

It is believed that observance of the recommended luminance ratio limits will lessen or eliminate visual problems, such as transient adaptation and disability glare at the VDT workstation. The rationale used to support this is based on the fact that when the eye fixates on a task, an adaptation level is established. This adaptation level is initiated by a combination of task luminance and field luminance. As the eye redirects its focus from an area having one luminance level to another area having a different luminance, the eye readapts to the new luminance level. If that luminance difference is significant, the adaptation process will require time. And if that luminance difference is excessive, the reaction will be discomfort, attended by a transient pupillary response. To avoid this, luminance levels of large adjoining areas need to be kept within appropriate limits.

There is, however, recent evidence to indicate that the recommended luminance contrast range between task and surround, i.e, between a VDT screen and its adjacent source document, given certain conditions may be extended to a ratio as high as 1:20 without affecting visual performance (Haubner & Kokoschka, 1983).

This extended range of luminances seems particularly appropriate when the central visual task involves a VDT with a negative polarity screen (light characters on a dark field). It is thought that this is due to the lower average luminance levels created by the dark screen. Support for this can be found in studies by Grandjean (1987), where he noted a marked preference for lower illuminances (and thus luminances) in workstations supporting negative polarity screens than in those supporting positive polarity screens. One reason for this is that negative polarity screens are more adversely affected by excessive ambient illuminance than are positive polarity displays.

This extended luminance range may also be appropriate for users of multimedia software or computer-aided-design workstations. Here, users may require lower surround luminances in order to enhance the readability of text and discrimination of the fine detail that is usually present in these types of displays.

Figure 36-18, taken from Badolato's (1995) current study, provides an example of the kind of luminances he found at his music workstations. This figure should help readers conceptualize the concept of plotting luminance patterns and lead them toward taking the same approach in evaluating their own learning environments.

36.3.8.5. Glare. When recommended luminance contrast ratios are exceeded by a significant amount, such as when there is an unduly bright source of light in the visual field or when specular (mirrorlike) reflectances fall on a display surface, they create glare. Glare is a luminous condition that brings about discomfort and/or a reduction in visual acuity (Kaufman, 1981). Most glare in the learning environment equipped with VDTs can be eliminated or reduced by the following methods:

- Place the display perpendicular to the light source to reduce reflected glare.
- Shield the eyes from light sources.
- Use filters or a coating of the VDT screen; a flat or even slightly concave filter will reduce the area reflected by a curved VDT screen.
- For lighting, use indirect sources or use several low-intensity lights rather than one light of high intensity.

As people age beyond 50 years, they become increasingly more sensitive to glare (NRC, 1987). The careful control of all glare sources is especially important for the comfort and visual efficiency of older members of the workforce and training programs.

36.3.8.5.1. Controlling Luminaire Glare. In order to keep glare from light fixtures (luminaires) at acceptable levels at the VDT screen, the Illuminating Engineering Society of North America produced a standard for VDT workspaces (IES, RP-24). Under this standard, indirect lighting systems are strongly recommended and luminance emission limits for direct lighting luminaires given maximum limits relative to specific viewing angles. The maximum allowable luminance at a viewing angle 85° from the vertical is 175 cd/m²; at 75°, 350 cd/m²; and at 65°, 850 cd/m². This standard is currently being complied with or even exceeded by today's luminaire manufacturers. While compliance with this standard will reduce excessive glare at the VDT screen, it will also result in perimeter walls being excessively dark, unless illuminated by supplemental wall washer lighting or unless the spacing currently used between luminaires is reduced significantly. Consequently, there are those who find this IES standard problematic (Rea, 1991).

36.3.8.5.2. Display/Surround Luminance Ratios. There is a perceptual conflict when a display is surrounded by areas of greater brightness than its own, such as when a TV monitor or computer screen is set up next to an unshaded window. If this difference is modest, then at best this conflict will result in only a distraction from the visual task. If this difference is great, then viewers are faced with the dilemma of attempting to attend to the visual task while their autonomic defensive mechanism is unconsciously directing them to look away from the area in order to maintain visual comfort.

Classroom Intervention: Set up visual displays where there are no excessively bright areas to surround it. If the display is not the self-illuminated kind, i.e., TV, computer screen, then provide supplementary illumination on the display.

36.3.8.5.3. Luminance Contrasts within the Visual Display. The above luminance contrast limits between adjoining visual areas relates to relatively large areas, i.e., the overall VDT screen brightness relative to the area surrounding it. However, these contrast limits should not be confused with those recommended for visual elements within the task itself—for example, print in a book, chalk or marker on a board, alphanumerics on a slide or vugraph foil, a motion picture scene, etc., all of which need to be greater than those recommended for large adjoining areas. Lack of sufficient contrast between the design elements within the visual itself will seriously affect its legibility and readability. Contrast ratios of 10:1 between the dark and light elements of video or vugraph display are generally accepted, while ratios of 25:1 for slides with dark elements on a light background and 5:1 for light elements on a dark background are recommended. Recommended contrast ratios between dark and light elements in a motion picture film can be as high as 100:1 (Caravaty & Winslow, 1964).

Classroom Intervention: Chalkboards and marker boards should be kept clean of old chalk and marker dust so that there is sufficient contrast between what is written on the board and the board itself. All projected visual media should be shown in rooms dark enough so that image details and colors are accurately rendered, but no darker.

36.3.8.6. Other Properties of Light. In addition to providing radiant energy with which to see objects, there are spectral aspects of lighting that can effect how accurately colors can be seen, the appearance of the lamps themselves, and contribute to a number of psychological and physiological conditions affecting people.

36.3.8.6.1. Light Quality and Control for Media Use. Since all types of artificial illumination reproduce colors differently, the selection of lamps should be based not only on the amount of light they produce but also on their color appearance (how they will look in the room) and color-rendering qualities (how objects will appear under their illumination). Also, since there is a need to control illuminance levels during media presentations, this factor should enter into the decision in lamp selection as well. To accommodate such special needs, it is recommended that one use incandescent downlights on dimmers (or low-wattage compact fluorescent in parabolic fixtures) for low light levels in front-screen presentation rooms, and quartz lights or asymmetric fluorescent fixtures with lamp color temperatures between 3,000° and 3,500° Kelvin and color indices of 80 or higher for rooms where video conferencing and video recording are planned.

Classroom Intervention: The teacher needs to realize that objects will take on a different color appearance when illuminated by different lamps. Efforts should be made to acquire lamps with high color rendition accuracy for art rooms and to display artworks under the same kind of illumination under which they were created. Replacing the three or four lamps in a fixture above a critical display is a relatively simple and inexpensive matter, and the lamps have a life expectancy of about 20,000 hours. When trying to match colors, and where high color rendition fluorescent lighting is not available, do your matching under daylight, which has a color rendition of 100.

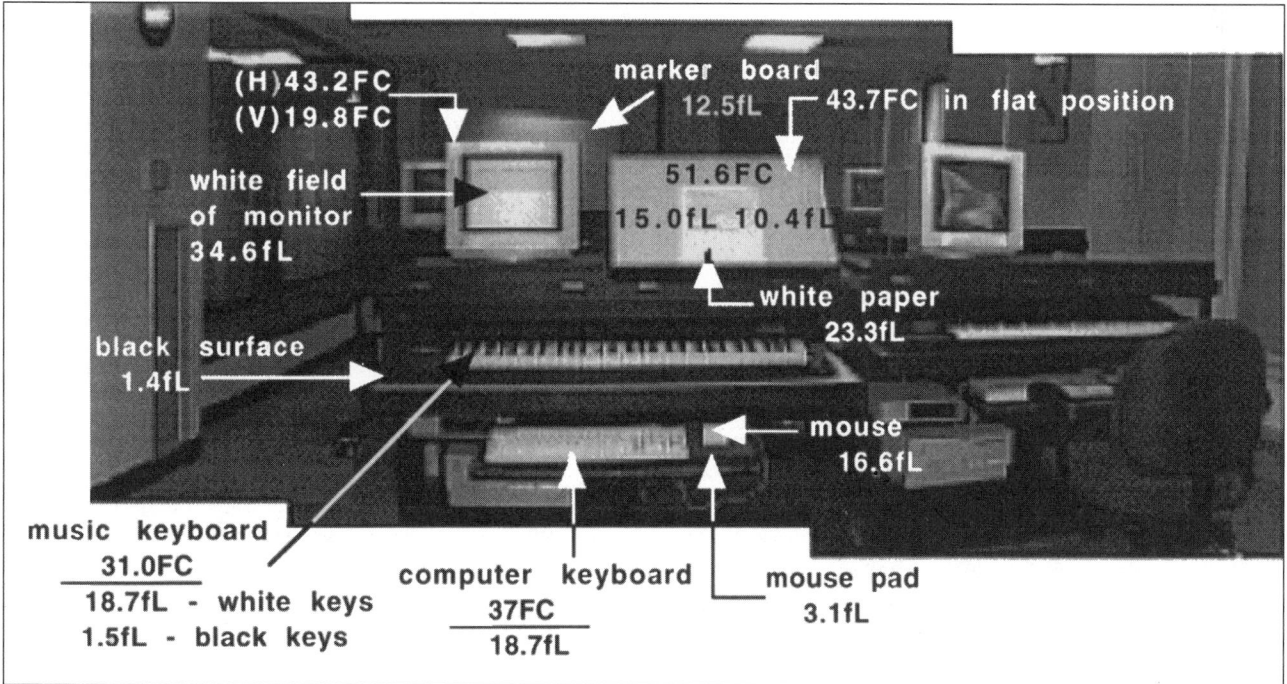

Figure 36-18. Illuminance levels and resultant luminance patterns in a music education workstation. (After Badolato, 1995.)

36.3.8.6.2. Light Quality, Moods, and Physiological Benefits. Research by Hathaway (1988) has shown that the color of light and its quality are important to the learning atmosphere, and he recommends UV-enhanced full-spectrum lighting, particularly for geographic areas where seasonal affective disorders (SAD) are noted. According to Hathaway (1994), under such lighting, elementary students developed fewer dental cavities (an accepted stress index) and had better attendance, achievement, and growth and development than students under other lights. This study went on to report that students under high-pressure sodium vapor lamps had the slowest rates of growth and development, as well as the poorest attendance and achievement. While the full-spectrum UV-enhanced lamps appeared to offer some physical benefits over cool-white fluorescent, there were no differences found in achievement. It is unfortunate that this study did not include the 32w T8 tri-phosphor lamps that currently are being selected for many schools and offices because of their high color rendition, pleasant color appearance, and energy benefits. It would be useful to know how such lamps stack up to the full-spectrum UV-enhanced lamps promoted in Hathaway's study. A review of the literature finds the research to be equivocal on the benefits of full-spectrum lighting (Boray et al., 1989).

36.3.8.6.3. Light Quantity and Physiological Benefits. Similarly, there are strong advocates for using inordinately high light levels (300 FC+) to "optimize human health, performance, and well-being, and recommend such levels for treating depression, sleep disorders, and dysfunctions of the circadian system related to jet travel and shift work" (Brainard, 1994). However, more research will be required before facility planners will be able to justify the added energy costs required to produce such levels, and to mount effective arguments for exceeding state energy codes. In the meantime, the popularity of tri-phosphor T8 lamps for general classroom/training rooms has grown over the past decade and seems to be here to stay for some time, given their high color rendition and color appearance qualities and their reduced energy consumption.

36.3.9 Color

36.3.9.1. The Power of Color. Color is a vital part of our lives. It can change moods and judgments of size, weight, and distance, induce body tonus, and in general enhance the quality of life. Many of our psychophysical responses to light have been attributed to the phenomenon known as *chromatic aberration*, where the lens of the eye has to physically change its shape in order to bring different colors into focus. Depending on the direction of this adjustment, a color will appear to be perceived as "approaching" or "receding." At least one researcher (Harmon, 1951) believes that chromatic aberration is the likely physiological basis for the psychological effects of colors, i.e., for our perception of colors as "warm" and "stimulating" or "cool" and "relaxing."

When used properly and combined with the right kind of illumination, color can be an effective tool for the facility designer and the classroom teacher. In spite of some ambiguity in the literature as to the uniformity of human responses to different colors (Cohen & Trostle, 1990; Mikellides, 1990), it is generally accepted that color has relatively predictable behavioral concomitants both as a surface treatment and as a light source. Different colors evoke different physiological awareness levels and emotional/attitudinal responses (Gerard, 1958; Ali, 1972; Birren, 1969) as well as producing different psychospatial effects.

36.3.9.2. Responses to Color. Burch (1993) recently referred to cognitive and emotional responses as being byproducts of the lighting and color used in the learning environment when he stated:

> Architects have known . . . that light and color created moods within spaces. Now we know that the neo-cortex of the brain, the conscious rational side, responds to subtle, sophisticated colors, while the limbic, or emotional set of the brain, responds to vivid hues.

Other researchers have noted the effect of colors on blood pressure, respiration, task confusion, and reaction time (Kwallek & Lewis, 1990; Sanders & McCormick, 1987). Knirk (1987) believes that room colors are powerful instructional tools that can be used to "assist the student into a mental state conducive to the behaviors required by the objectives." In making his case, he goes on to report the work of Zental (1986), who found that test scores increased by 12 points on an IQ test in a room that was light blue; whereas in a white or brown room, the scores decreased by 14 points. Knirk concludes from this and other studies that ". . . in classrooms and labs, where there is close visual and mental work, tints of blue-green, gray, or beige are desirable colors."

My own research supports these statements leading to the following generalizations:

- Room colors, particularly areas within the visual field, should be relatively neutral and in desaturated tones, such as off-white with umbra added, light gray, sandalwood, light buckskin, etc. If bold colors are desired in the classroom, they should be confined to surfaces outside the line of sight of the students, such as the back and side walls, and the floor.
- Fully saturated bold colors, particularly blues and reds, are stressful, and should be avoided on walls, especially on surfaces that may be used as backgrounds for visual displays. Such colors should be confined to artwork, wall murals, display exhibits, and the like, where exaggerated feelings of depth or visual excitement are specifically desired.
- Light chalk green, gray with a touch of umbra, off-white, and beige are visually neutral and should be used for end walls that are planned as backgrounds for visual displays or projection screen locations (McVey, 1988).

Classroom Intervention: Many elementary school teachers make use of the effects of chromatic aberration by wearing bright and colorful clothes on days when they plan to introduce new and difficult lessons. Their experience has been that the students seem to sense that something new and interesting is going to happen. Visual displays such as slides, bulletin boards, and dioramas can also make good use of the psychospatial effects of colors by highlighting the most important elements with red and orange and adding depth to the backgrounds with shades of blue.

36.10 Thermal and Air Quality Factors

Thermal comfort is a product of many interactions. Auliciems (1989) cites the interaction of such personal and atmospheric factors as a person's metabolic rate, which relates to the physical demands of the task, clothing insulation, air temperature, radiant temperature of surroundings, rate of air movement, and atmospheric humidity as the contributory factors. To this, Heijs and Stringer (1988) add the personal factors of one's knowledge and experience, gender, age, and place of residence, as well as such architectural elements as lighting and furnishings. Figure 36-19, adapted from Woodson (1992), illustrates the effects of season, clothing, relative humidity, or temperature requirements. It is because of such interactions that ASHRAE developed its concept of the "effective temperature" scale as a better predictor of comfort than the standard temperature scale.

36.3.10.1. General Effects of Heat and Humidity.
The nature of the exchange of heat and humidity between people and their surroundings is a major factor affecting mental alertness, level of comfort, and the effectiveness with which they complete their tasks. The amount of environmental heat necessary for comfort will vary with a person's age, level of physical activity, clothing, and adaptation to local climate. Girls, in general, seem to prefer a warmer environment than boys, and young children prefer a cooler one than all but the oldest adults.

One study indicates that a student's achievement level may affect his or her sensitivity to heat (Lane, 1966).

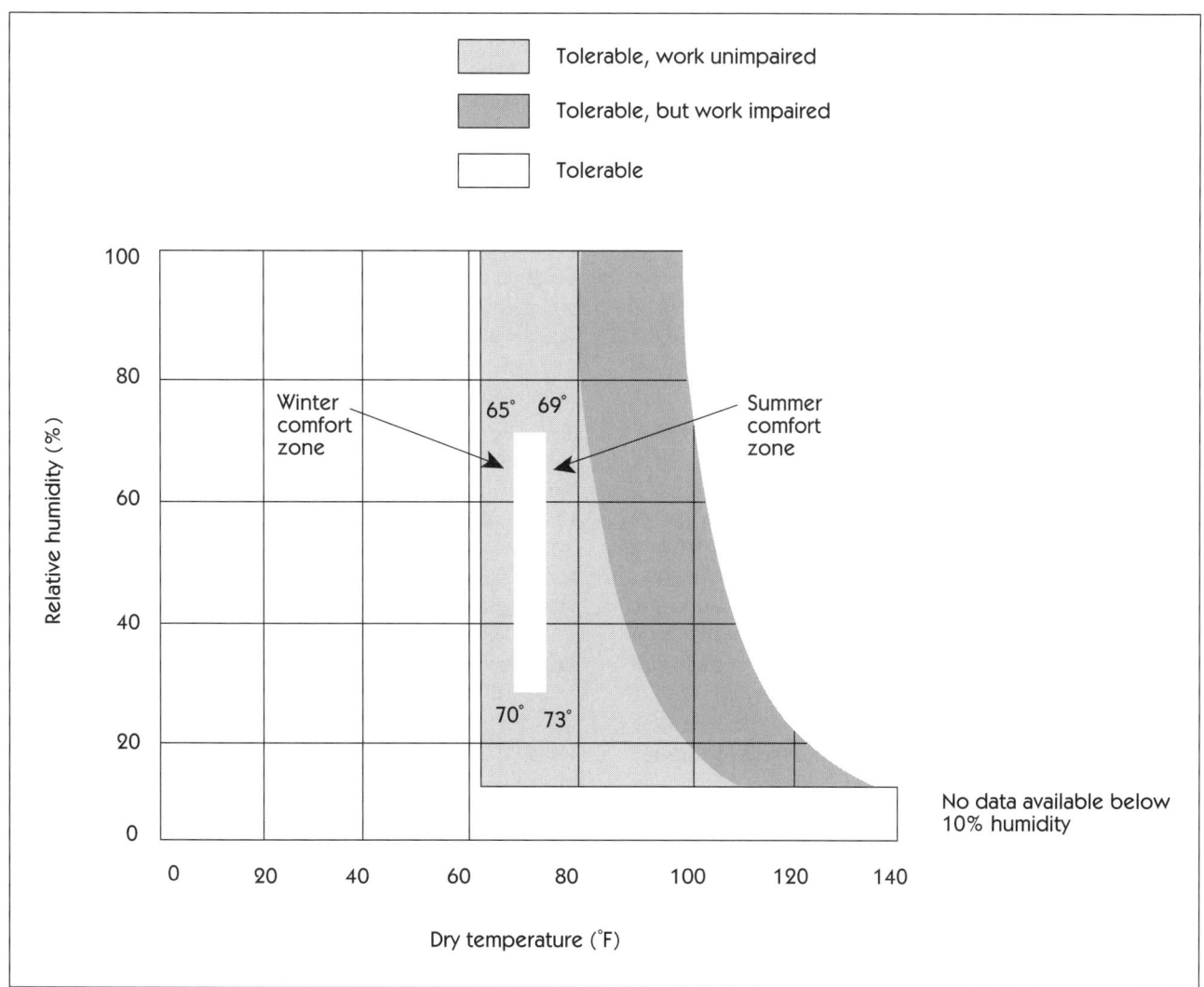

Figure 36-19. Effect of season, clothing, and relative humidity on temperature requirements.

Another study has found that certain temperatures evoke high levels of arousal, while others evoke dull attention (Wyon, 1970). An improper thermal environment can alter growth, development, and learning (Harmon, 1953). Children tend to become restless in a cold room and listless in a hot one. According to one researcher, there is reason to believe that students may experience a 2% reduction in learning ability for every degree that the room temperature rises above the optimum (Gilliland, 1969). Room temperatures between 68°F and 76°F generally promote normal functioning, given standard recommended levels of relative humidity and air velocity.

36.3.10.2. Effects of Heat on Performance. There is support in the literature for one to accept that thermal and air quality factors are perhaps *the* most important environmental elements in the work environment (Rohles, 1989). High temperatures can influence performance of various tasks. With young adults, Eckenrode and Abbot (1959) found 80°F to be the maximum temperature for the normal performance of the following tasks, with 87°F being the temperature where demonstrable impairment was noted:

Typewriter code (scrambled letters), locations (spatial relations code), mental multiplications (problems), number checking (error detection), pursuit (visual maze), and lathe operations (hand coordination).

Additional tasks and their normal performance/demonstrable impairment (N/I) temperatures follow:

Morse code reception 87.5/92, block coding (problem solving) 83/87.5, visual attention (erratic clock test) 79/87.5, Pursuitmeter 87.5/92, reaction time (simple response) 93/. . . , motor coordination 64.5/91.

There are not many studies available concerning the optimum classroom temperature for the very young student. One such study from Canada by Partridge and MacLean (1935) indicates that the optimum temperature in summer for young children is 70.5°F, with a relative humidity of 50% or a dry bulb temperature of 75.5°. In winter, this optimum temperature was said to change to 66.5°F, with a relative humidity of 35% or a dry bulb reading of 71°. This, however, cannot be accepted as a rigid recommendation, for thermal needs are quite individualistic, and, furthermore, these readings are not totally consistent with the most recent ASHRAE recommendations, which will be discussed later.

Classroom Intervention: There are those who cite the higher rate of metabolism that children have as being the reason why they seem to operate more effectively at lower temperatures than adults, and this has led to the suggestion that an effective rule of thumb for a teacher to follow is to wear a sweater or jacket in class and set the temperature for his or her comfort. The children, because of their higher rate of metabolism, should now be comfortable in their shirt sleeves. Tessmer (1994) suggests that moving the seat locations of students further apart from each other can increase airflow between seats, thus reducing the sense of a classroom feeling too hot as well as too crowded. This is particularly true when students have returned from a gym session or recess.

36.3.10.3. Solar Heat Gain. Radiation from the sun may also aid or play havoc with student comfort. Solar energy radiated in the form of visible light passes through classroom windows and is absorbed by objects lying directly in its path, which then convert the light into heat. This heat, in turn, is radiated to the rest of the room. The average classroom is like a greenhouse, a one-way trap for infrared radiation. While the glass windows allow sunlight in, they do not allow much of the resultant radiant heat to escape. This heat can affect the overall room temperature and cause wide temperature swings during a day. Most affected are students seated next to the windows, who may actually be receiving excessive heat exposure even though the average room temperature is not above normal. This "greenhouse effect" can be minimized by (a) better site planning with regard to the sun's transit, (b) large roof overhang, (c) tinted windows, (d) fewer or no windows, and (e) reflected shades or blinds.

Classroom Intervention: The classroom teacher should monitor the seats closest to the windows for excessive solar heat gain, adjust the shades accordingly, and provide additional ventilation when needed by opening windows at student work height. The students should also feel free to make adjustments on their own, as long as doing so does not negatively affect others nearby, or simply move to another seat if bothered by excessive solar heat exposure.

36.3.10.4. Air Movement. Some researchers feel that providing enough heat for the students is not the problem; the problem is providing proper ventilation, air circulation, and cooling. In one study, it was found that any time the outdoor temperature reached 50°F, the classroom temperature rose above the desirable level, unless cooling was introduced (Lane, 1966). No wonder, since physiologists tell us that each child of elementary school age radiates heat equivalent to that radiated by a 100-watt incandescent lamp. It is not unusual for a classroom to show a 4° to 5° rise in temperature shortly after the students return from an active recess. In educational facilities, air conditioning should not be considered a luxury, but rather an integral and critical environmental component.

Air movement's role in the thermal environment is to promote convection and evaporation, two natural methods of heat dispersion that help the body rid itself of excessive heat buildup during the performance of work and study tasks. If this work-related body heat is not lost, performance and physical comfort will be affected. In fact, some specialists have gone so far as to claim that most of the headaches, fatigue, dizziness, and nausea experienced in crowded, poorly ventilated rooms are caused not by high temperature, high humidity, or even high concentration of carbon dioxide, but rather by inadequate body heat loss due to lack of air movement (Lane, 1966). Although air movement is vital for the elimination of superfluous body heat, excessive air movement results in too much body heat loss and makes it necessary to increase the overall room temperature in order to maintain comfort. Needless to say, drafty rooms should be avoided as places of study.

36.3.10.5. Effect of Humidity on Performance. Knirk (1992) notes that when a room's relative humidity (RH) rises above 70%, it impairs human performance. He goes on to cite the work of other researchers who found that low relative humidities also reduced the quality of the learning experience and that "students attending schools with relative humidities between 22% and 26% experienced nearly 13% greater illness and absenteeism than students in schools with 27% and 33% RH."

Excessive humidity in the thermal environment can also affect the reliability of equipment. Excessive humidity has been known to cause serious damage to computer equipment. General recommendations adapted from the 1992 ASHRAE handbook, which will serve both people and sensitive electronic equipment, follow:

1. Air temperature should be kept constant within a range of 68 to 74°F during the winter and 73 to 79°F during the summer (with lighter clothing).
2. Relative humidity should be kept within a range of 30 to 60% in most classrooms and 50% constant in computer training rooms.
3. Air velocity should be kept with 15 to 25 feet per minute for low-activity rooms. and 25 to 50 fpm for rooms programmed for greater physical activity.
4. Outside air in quantities of 10 to 25 cubic feet per minute should be provided for each occupant.
5. The room's ambient temperature should be uniform (+/− 2°F) at working height throughout the room, within 1 foot from exterior walls.
6. The room should be serviced by automatic control systems, integrated thermostats, and automatic timing devices for day-night operations.
7. Fully operational heating, ventilation, and air-conditioning systems should be available whenever possible, particularly for those schools and training and conference centers that operate year round.
8. Rooms that employ extensive audiovisual equipment and computer-related equipment should have additional cooling in direct proportion to the heat produced by these media.

36.3.10.5.1. Thermal Limits for Media and Technology. While adhering to the thermal conditions cited in 36.3.10.5 will accommodate both people and audiovisual equipment, in 1970 the Educational Facilities Laboratories issued guidelines in terms of thermal limits for various media. Perhaps the reader will find their inclusion here of some practical value (EFL, 1970):

1. Computer facilities: Constant temperature of 75°F with 50% RH. Operational limits: Dry-bulb temperature of 60–90°F, relative humidity of 20–80%, maximum dry-bulb temperature of 78°F. Recommend 1/4-ton cooling per computer-assisted instruction (CAI) sta-

tion. (*Author's note:* This last recommendation was based on what constituted a CAI station in 1970; a more accurate assessment can be made today by adding up the total wattage of each component in a VDT workstation, i.e., monitor, CPU, printers, server, etc., and multiply this number by 3.42 to determine the number of BTUs per hour that can be expected from this equipment during operations.)
2. Film projectors (slide, motion picture, etc.): 65–70°F and 25–40% RH.
3. Film storage: Below 80°F and 25–60% RH.
4. Audiotape storage: 60–90°F and 20–80% RH.

36.3.10.6. Air Distribution. The standard air distribution system for most rooms is centralized, with air being supplied from specific locations in the ceiling. This works well for standard workspaces and classrooms but is problematic in open-plan offices and learning resource centers because of the presence of work and study stations with self-standing partitions. Because of these partitions, the room's central air supply is often short circuited across the ceiling, and "still air" pockets are created. In response to such problems, newly designed heat distribution and ventilation systems that operate in a decentralized manner are now available.

One version is a "task-under-floor" ventilation system (TUFV). A study employing this system and involving six facility managers and 151 office workers found that the facility managers recorded fewer complaints about thermal discomfort and ventilation problems than in their previous buildings where a standard system had been employed. And the majority of the 151 office workers said that TUFV improved thermal comfort and perceived air quality, as well as providing good temperature and ventilation conditions, better supporting work productivity, and worker alertness (Hedge et al., 1990).

36.3.10.7. Air Quality

36.3.10.7.1. The Sick Building Syndrome. In considering air quality, it is noted that a growing number of schools and daycare centers and libraries are included in the category of "sick buildings" (Norbock et al., 1990; Yeung et al., 1991). Causes for this are symptoms such as itching skin, eye irritation, headache, nausea, respiratory problems, fatigue, and complaints of odor and disagreeable taste. These complaints center on the concentration of volatile organic hydrocarbons and the presence of wall-to-wall carpet (Noback & Widstrom, 1989). There is growing consensus that these symptoms are related to physical factors such as air temperature, pollutants, and biological factors like pollen and mold, as well as psychological factors (Potter, 1988). Excessive levels of static electricity are also cited as contributory causes of eye and skin irritations (Wedberg, 1987).

The causes of the recent increase in the level of pollutants found in our newly constructed offices and learning environments are attributed to new construction techniques and materials. According to Chant (1986) "new office buildings [and presumably schools] aimed at creating a uniform and perfect environment have been designed largely on the basis of building shape and engineering economics, with cheaper materials and construction shortcuts that have in many cases resulted in dangerous working environments." Commenting on this situation, Parsons (1992) stated that: "new building materials often give off fumes, particularly fumes containing formaldehyde. New office partitions and furniture, especially those made from particle board and other manufactured wood products, contain high concentrations of formaldehyde." Parsons goes on to indicate that formaldehyde can also be released from rugs, drapes, and other textiles. He also adds paints, solvents, wood preservatives, asbestos, glass fibers, cleaning agents, correction fluid, and pesticides to his list of building pollutants.

36.3.10.7.2. Air Quality and Emissions. Classroom and conference room air quality should meet and, where possible, exceed the requirements for office environments as specified in ANSI/ASHRAE 62-1992 standard. This standard stipulates that the maximum emission rate for total volatile organic compounds released in a room should not exceed 0.25 mg/hr/m^3, and carbon dioxide should be kept below 800 ppm.

Other emissions of concern include the electromagnetic emissions that are created by VDTs, building wiring, low-voltage lamps, and other electrical devices (Pool, 1990). Such emissions fall into the primary divisions: ELF, 5 Hz–2 kHz, VLF, 2 kHz–400 kHz, RF, and microwave. At the present time a causal relationship between EMFs and physical discomfort and illness has not been clearly established.

On the other hand, there is considerable scientific evidence that raises concern and promotes continued research on the subject (Burgess, 1992). And, compounding this problem is the cumulative effect likely to be found in the computer laboratory where 20 or more monitors operate simultaneously (Ross & Stewart, 1993; Frost, 1992). Facility planners, architects, and school administrators need to monitor this potential problem and give consideration to relevant research findings.

36.3.11 Display Systems

36.3.11.1. Basic Requirements. One of the most important components of the learning environment, and particularly of spaces used for media presentations, is the display system. Display systems range in sophistication from a basic setup that typically includes a television monitor, a slide projector, and a matte white screen, to highly complex front- and rear-projection multimedia systems. They can be as simple to operate and maintain as an overhead transparency projector or as complex as light-valve television projectors or plasma displays hooked up to an interactive computer program. In all cases they require the same basic considerations if they are to serve the function for which they were designed. It has been long established

that display systems in order to be effective should have the following characteristics (Meister et al., 1969):

1. High legibility of individual characters and meaningful groups of symbols and words easily recognizable
2. Easy detectability of weak signals at all display ranges and at long and short viewing distances
3. Comfortable and accurate viewing at any required viewing angle
4. Minimum fall-off in image brightness at all viewing angles
5. Appropriate brightness-contrast, good resolution, and minimal image distortion
6. Qualities that elicit high observer accuracy and response time in performing visual functions
7. No apparent flicker for any of the viewers
8. Effective viewing within entire operating range of ambient illumination
9. Response with minimal equipment delay to user's request for display, as in information retrieval systems
10. Display parameters (brightness and contrast) adjustable by user
11. Audio signals of sufficient strength and fidelity to provide accurate and comfortable hearing for all listeners
12. Sound and image that appear to emanate from same location
13. Properly coded display controls for ease and accuracy of operation
14. Equipment and components that can be maintained by in-house technical staff
15. Adaptability for the inclusion of new presentation devices

36.3.11.2. Front- and Rear-Screen Projection. The two display systems commonly employed in classrooms, auditoria, and technical presentation facilities are front- and rear-screen projection. Each system has its merits and limitations. Consequently, it is not unusual and frequently advisable for a facility to be provided with both systems.

36.3.11.2.1. Front-Screen Projection. In a front-projection system, an image is produced by reflection off an opaque screen. Screen types include matte, ultramatte, beaded, lenticular, and aluminum foil. The standard matte screen is recommended for general applications and wide-angle viewing; the ultramatte should be used for higher image luminance, while still providing wide-angle viewing. Beaded screens are often recommended for rooms with narrow viewing sectors and where higher image luminance is required from standard projection equipment. Fixed, perforated lenticular screens are standard equipment for motion picture theaters, and the aluminum foil screen is used for special situations involving high ambient illumination and low-luminance television projection.

36.3.11.2.2. Rear-Screen Projection. In a rear-projection system, an image is produced by transmission through a translucent vinyl, acrylic, or glass screen. Rear-projection screens have found high acceptance in conference and training centers, where media presentations generally occur in rooms with high ambient illumination (McVey & Powell, 1985). These screens are widely available in a variety of colors and "gain" features.

36.3.11.2.3. Screen Gain. The "gain" of a screen refers to its light distribution characteristics. The most popular are the low-gain (1.2 to 1.8) screens for wide viewing sectors, and the moderately high-gain screens (2.0 to 3.0) for the more narrow viewing sectors or where greater image luminance is required under higher ambient illumination levels. Standard microdiffusion rear-projection screens with higher gains are usually unsatisfactory for general applications since they project noticeable hot spots. But recently a number of manufacturers have developed acrylic screens that employ fresnel lens technology and lenticulation to produce wide-angle viewing and higher gain (principally in the horizontal sector). These screens appear ideally suited for video display but are limited in size (about 12.5 feet diagonal) and cost significantly more than conventional RP screens.

While it has been generally accepted that front projection provides better image quality than rear projection, at least one study found that in terms of rendering print legible, both forms of projection (matte white vs. RP with 2.0 gain) yielded equivalent scores from graduate students, even when using alphanumerics measuring only 10, 8, and 6 subtended arc-minutes (Hamilton, 1983).

36.3.11.2.4. Rear or Front. A survey of the 10 leading conference centers in the United States relative to their existing and desired facilities found that the greatest number of requests by the managers was for fixed rear-projection facilities (McVey & Powell, 1985). Similar responses are now coming from business and higher-education organizations. Information relative to projection systems is continually updated and readily found in the literature (Utz, 1992).

Figure 36-20 shows a marketing/presentation room I recently designed for a computer company, in collaboration with Carl Franceschi of DRA Architects, showing both front- and rear-screen capabilities. This recognizes the fact that each medium has its own special attributes, and that having both provides the users with the capability of modifying their presentation approaches in the future when new technologies may make one of these two display approaches more desirable than the other.

36.3.11.2.5. Coordinating Lighting with Projection. As noted above, rear projection can be more effective in displaying media in conditions where there is more illumination than most front-projection systems can accommodate. Actually, both rear- and front-screen display can be made more effective by controlling the amount of illumination that falls off the display surface from room lighting during projection. The limits of this nonimage illuminance will vary with the light output of the display system and the reflectivity of the screen surface. For decades, the standard in the motion picture industry for nonimage illuminance in theaters has been 0.3 foot-candles (Kloepfel, 1969). My own experiments with conventional media indicate the

following relative to currently typical media use in today's educational/training environments. These recommendations for permissible light levels may be modified upward where new developments increase the light output of tomorrow's standard projection equipment:

> Permissible ambient light levels on front projection screens are 0.3 FC with movie and video projection, 1.0 FC with slides and LCD display, and 2.5 FC with overhead projection of high-contrast transparencies. These ambient light levels may be increased significantly with rear-projection display, in direct proportion to the reflectivity of the screen surface. For rear screens having 10% reflectivity, the above levels may be tripled, but for rear screens having a 30% reflectivity, such levels can only be doubled.

36.3.12 Controls

In the learning environment, instructors, presenters, and students are faced on a daily basis with the need to operate various kinds of controls. Some of the controls that the instructor or presenter have to deal with are environmental, and include lighting, window drapery, or shades, and, in some cases, room thermostats. Other controls they operate involve the room's presentation systems, such as projectors, audio- and videotape recorders and players, sound system levels and balance, etc. And others include those that involve the room's security and electrical power systems. The students also are expected to operate many controls. Most of these involve the operation of equipment in their computer workstation, i.e., mouse, joy stick, optical scanner, etc., or portable audiovisual equipment employed in their project activities.

For many years now, one of the byproducts of human factors engineering efforts in the military and space programs was the development of practical and effective guidelines for the control of equipment and building systems by the operator. For example, even at the most general level, ergonomists such as Woodson (1981) offered such guidelines relative to control selection, design, and use (p. 570).

1. Type of control: The control should be chosen as though it were an extension of the operator's limb, i.e., it would be operable in terms of the natural motions of the arm, wrist, finger, leg, ankle, or foot, and it should not require awkward and unnatural positioning, extension, or motion on the part of the operator.
2. Feedback: The control interface and basic controller system should provide feedback so that the operator knows at all times what his or her input is accomplishing.
3. Resistance: There should be sufficient resistance to operator inputs to dampen spurious inputs, but not so much that the operator has to put great force into the control, so that his or her muscles are not quickly fatigued or that the operator has difficulty maintaining the nominal operating position.

Figure 36-20. Marketing/presentation room with both front- and rear-screen projection.

4. Position of the control: Controls should be placed where they do not require the operator to assume awkward body positions or make frequent long-reaching movements. The position should reflect consideration of the excursion requirements of the control system so that there is no chance that the operator will be unable to reach a critical point in the control movement path.

5. Size and shape: The size and shape of control interfaces (handles, knobs, buttons, etc.) should be compatible with the size of the operator's hands, fingers, or feet. The shape of a control should also be compatible with the kind of grip or motion required to operate the control interface.

6. Interface surface: The surface of a control handle should depend on the type of operation required, i.e., it may need serrations or knurling in order to apply a firm grip for maximum force.

7. One-hand versus two-hand operations: Two hands often provide more precision or force.

Today's equipment designers seem, however, to be ignoring the above and other guidelines that have proved so effective in controlling the complex systems found in military and space programs for past 4 decades. Instead they seem to be driven by a misplaced concept of uniformity and symmetry. Andre and Segal (1994) recently studied what happens when designers attempt to design control panels with total symmetry: "Typically these types of layouts do not allow the user to easily differentiate between controls that serve different functions." They go on to cite that they found amplifiers with as many as 28 similar buttons laid out in a symmetrical pattern. They note: ". . . such similarity in form between controls further hinders differentiation and requires the user to adapt to the product." According to these authors, the operators are expected to rely on memory and verbal labels to differentiate among variables that are in essence quite different. And this is where the conflict lies: "Switches on computer monitors, buttons on phones, calculators, etc., all are deliberately made less visible (or are omitted) so as not to detract from the so-called aesthetic quality of the product." The direct consequence of designing for reduced visibility is reduced feedback.

The psychologist Donald A. Norman (1988, p. 3) addressed this problem of reduced feedback through efforts toward design aesthetics via simplicity when he described how he had tried to operate a particular slide projector: "With only one button to control the slide advance, how could one switch from forward to reverse?" When he asked a technician how he could initiate both functions from one button, he was told that a brief push of the button would send the slide forward; a long push and it would reverse itself. However, even after having an explanation of the system's "logic" without the necessary feedback, he was still unable to operate the projector successfully. This motivated Norman to note that there are psychological principles that should be followed in order to make controls understandable: visibility, appropriate clues, and feedback of one's actions, constituting a psychology of how people interact with things and thus how they should be designed.

In designing or selecting a control system for purchase, one needs to be reminded of the "locus of control" theory, which states that a control, system as well as other human-technology interfaces, should permit the user to feel in control of the system, and not vice versa (Robson & Crelin, 1989). If an ergonomist, is to successfully prescribe the learning environment, he or she must direct attention toward the design of all elements in the learning environment, and that includes the systems that control audiovisual presentation systems as well as room features. Figures 36-21a, b, and c show examples of the product for which I was asked to design control systems for room lighting and audiovisual equipment.

The methods employed on the lectern controls systems (Fig. 36-21a) included clustering related controls, color coding, shape coding, and employing knobs for quantitative elements, such as sound levels from both the voice reinforcement and program playback systems, and illuminated feedback switches. The lighting controls (Fig. 36-21b) are set up so that an instructor or presenter simply picks a "scene," i.e., general, vugraph, slides, or video, and in each case the correct light fixtures are left on, with the appropriate number of lamps, for the media to be effectively used and to maximize the available light for the students.

The touch AV control panel (Fig. 36-21c) represents a hybrid of modern LCD selection screens, along with discrete buttons to the side of the touch panel which duplicate some of the most frequently used functions. The reason for this is that many people do not need or want to go sequentially through selecting a menu to control such things as volume level, lights, draper, or a projection screen's descent. Readers should be aware that ample information is available to guide their efforts at developing efficacious control systems. These sources include but are not limited to: Woodson and Conover (1973), Van Cott and Kinkade (1972), and Sanders and McCormick (1987).

36.4 Conclusion

This chapter considered some of the environmental, ergonomic, and display system factors that contribute to the effectiveness of learning environments in general, with particular emphasis on classroom and conference room settings, and workstations where educational media, including VDTs, are used extensively. When such factors are prudently integrated into a learning environment's design, they have gained acceptance and appreciation from both students and faculty (McVey, 1979). Trainers and trainees working in similarly designed environments also recognize and appreciate their features.

Figure 36-22 is a photograph of an auditorium I recently designed in collaboration with Mark Sweeney of OmniArchitecture Inc., Charlotte, North Carolina. The photograph shows many of the ergonomic features discussed in the preceding pages of this chapter. Such features include the following:

• NASF of 2,928 SF, serving a total of 219 occupants, 28 in movable castered seats behind tables, 189 in fixed seats, plus 3 handicap locations (13.4 SF/occupant) plus a 11' × 42' rear-projection room, a 7' × 20' front-projection room, and a 230 SF enclosure for a chairlift.

- 189 fixed seats, 12 with regular 21" seat pan widths, and 177 large modules of 22.75–23.50", with side-to-side spacing of 26.5–27.0", true staggered arrangement, on risers spaced 42" apart and with a tablet arm and two arm rests per person. Left-hand tablet arms clustered at desired viewing locations, with a "L" label on the chair back to simplify locating the left-handed seats.

- Ambient noise level equal to PNC 26, with a reverberation time of approximately 1.2". Acoustical gain of voice amplification system 20+ dBA. The physical acoustics of the room make possible two-way communications between presenter and audience without microphones.

- Fluorescent levels for general activities variable by scene selection up to 70 FC, downlighting on dimmer for AV activities = 0–25 FC. Videoconferencing illuminance levels variable by dimmer up to 139 FC.

- Rear-screen image luminances ranged from 28 FL, as seen from audience center, to 5 FL at most angular viewing locations.

- All vertical viewing angles between 25° to top of display and -10° to bottom of display. All horizontal viewing angles within acceptable standards.

Planning and designing ergonomically correct learning environments require a concerted effort to make the proposed facility's educational specifications reflect what we have learned from ergonomic research. It is hoped that readers, whether facility planners, architects, media specialists, or teachers, will adopt the principles and guidelines presented in this paper and make every effort, consistent with their role on a school systems' building committee or on a college or university's planning committee, to see that these principles and guidelines are employed in the planning of their own future facilities.

In addition, it is hoped that classroom teachers, college instructors, and high-tech trainers or presenters will, after reading this chapter, have a better understanding of how the physical factors inherent in the design of their spaces affect the comfort, well-being, and task performance of their charges, and aggressively seek ways of employing or modifying elements to achieve their instructional goals in an

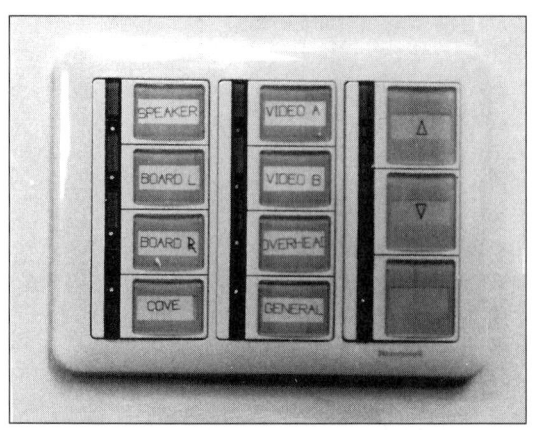

a. Scene selection and dimming lighting control.

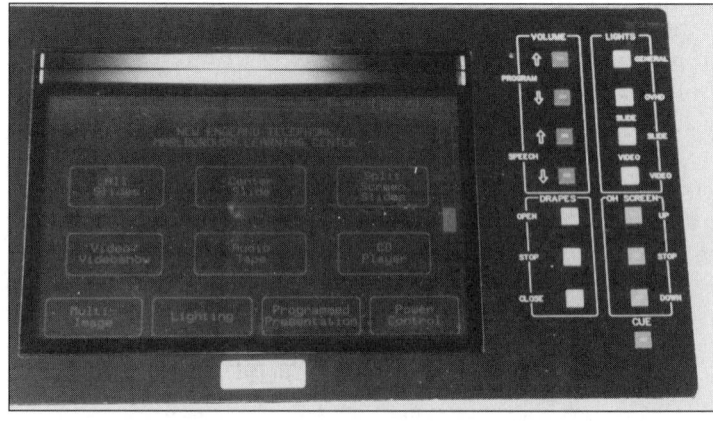

b. LCD AV touch control panel with supplementary hard-wired controls.

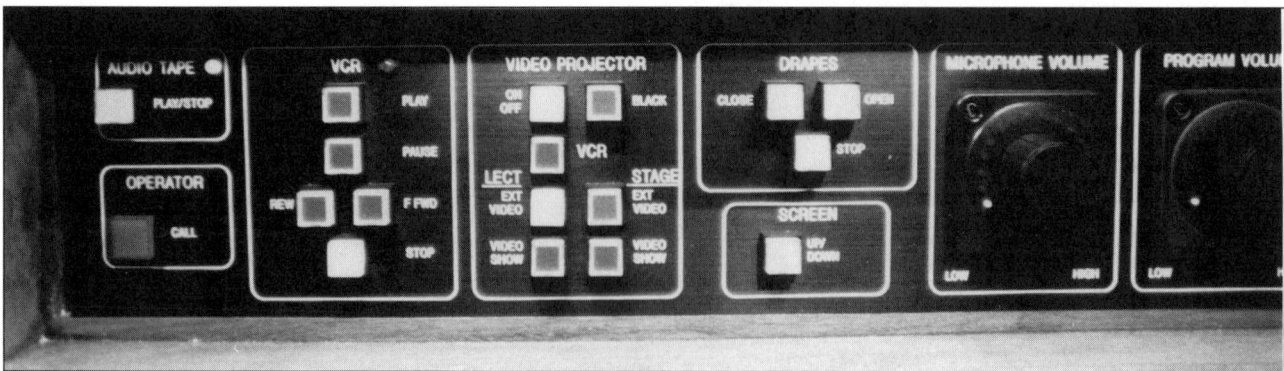

c. Hard-wired AV control panel for lectern.

Figure 36-21a, b, c. Lighting and audiovisual controls designed or specified by author.

Figure 36-22. Photo of Hoechst/Celanese auditorium showing ergonomic features.

ergonomically appropriate manner—and where doing so may not be possible, then guide their charges in adapting teaching activities and materials accordingly.

For educational researchers, it is hoped that this chapter has provided the kind of introduction with appropriate examples that will spur them on to conduct their own ergonomic research. It is hoped that the approximately 200 citations presented in this chapter's reference section can assist in such efforts. It is imperative that we add to our ergonomic knowledge base if our future learning environments are to be developed on the basis of "hard science" with justifiable expectations and not left to the whims of trends and design affectations. Figure 36-23 is a visual summary of many of the design details that affect the comfort, attention, and notetaking effectiveness of students in lecturing environments.

36.4.1 Summarizing Questions

In concluding this chapter, I would like to suggest a series of questions and concerns that I feel need to be addressed each time those involved in planning the learning environment get together to assess the ergonomic needs of the facility's occupants in the process of developing the critical document known as the *educational specifications.* Of course such discussions should not be limited to these questions but also include the many others that relate to the school or training center's mission, demographics, staffing, and so forth. However, since it is usually the ergonomic concerns that seem to get short shrift, and since that is the topic of this chapter, I will focus my coverage on the major ergonomic issues. However, I will also include a couple of related issues that I feel need to be mentioned. These same questions need to be asked at the conclusion of the facility's construction and occupancy in order to help the facility's administration to determine if all of the important considerations have been made or whether physical corrections are already in order. Asking oneself these questions will also alert the teacher or trainer to the need for classroom interventions.

Area. This is the net assignable area allocated to the various spaces in a facility. Will the various space allocations make it possible for a teacher/trainer to set up seating in the patterns they desire, with appropriate viewing distances and viewing angles? Will the space allocations accommodate the easy access and storage of instructional materials and equipment? Is there a need to use a chalk and/or marker board simultaneously with media projection, and if so is the room sufficiently wide enough to permit this side-by-side display arrangement?

HVAC. Has there been an accurate estimate made regarding the anticipated heat that will be produced in the areas by people, activities, technology, lighting, etc.? Have the electrical and HVAC systems been appropriately "sized" to accommodate such estimated full-load amperes (FLA) and British thermal units per hour (BTUH)? Will the thermal environment provide the appropriate amount of air exchange in the spaces, with an appropriate number of fresh-air changes per hour? Will the resultant air velocities at each student location be sufficient to dissipate heat buildup but not cause drafts? Will the spaces' relative humidity be kept within acceptable limits throughout all months of the year for both occupants and sensitive educational technology? Will there be any "off gassing" problems expected from the building materials used in the facilty's construction?

Acoustical factors. Will the spaces have the ambient noise spectra (preferred noise criteria curve) appropriate for the programmed activities. Will the room's walls sufficiently attenuate (sound transmission class) sound in one room from interfering with the activities of an adjacent room? Will the air-handling units create too much background noise for effective speech communication to occur? Will the spaces have reverberation times appropriate for the programmed activities and the needs of special students? Are there any hard parallel walls that should have acoustical treatment in order to avoid excessive reverberation, echoes, flutter, etc.? Will the ballasts used in the lighting systems be appropriately quiet for the spaces intended activities?

Lighting. Will there be sufficient horizontal illuminance for the proposed visual tasks? Will there be sufficient and uniform vertical illuminance to illuminate the chalk and/or marker board areas appropriately? Will the resultant display surfaces have a luminance at least equal to, and preferably a bit greater than, the adjacent wall areas? Can the ambient illuminance in the projection screen area be effectively and easily controlled during projection so that images are not "washed out"? Have all possible sources of glare been considered and eliminated through either design or product selection? Will the luminaires have color temperatures and color rendition indices appropriate for the spaces intended activities? Has daylighting been employed effectively and its control such that solar-heat gain and glare will not be problematic for occupants, and that it will not compromise media projection when in use? Will the pattern of luminances created by lighting and surface finishes be such that they promote visual efficiency, visual comfort, and aesthetic value?

Reflectances. Will the reflectances chosen for the wall and desk finishes be such that they will produce backgrounds for near and distant visual tasks that will promote orientation to the task and in general contribute to a glare-free environment when illuminated by the lighting systems chosen for the spaces? Are the chalkboards and/or marker boards of a reflectance appropriate to display chalk or liquid markers with sufficient contrast for legibility, but not so great as to create contrast ratios that are visually uncomfortable?

Utility factors. Are there sufficient electrical circuits and outlets to support the technology needs of the spaces? Are there sufficient data/voice lines and connections in the spaces for the programmed activities? Will there need to be electrical filtration or transient "spike" suppressions systems? Is water (hot and cold) or compressed air required in any of the spaces?

Seating. Are the chairs ergonomically appropriate for the programmed activities and the physical sizes of the intended user population? Do the chairs have all of the required

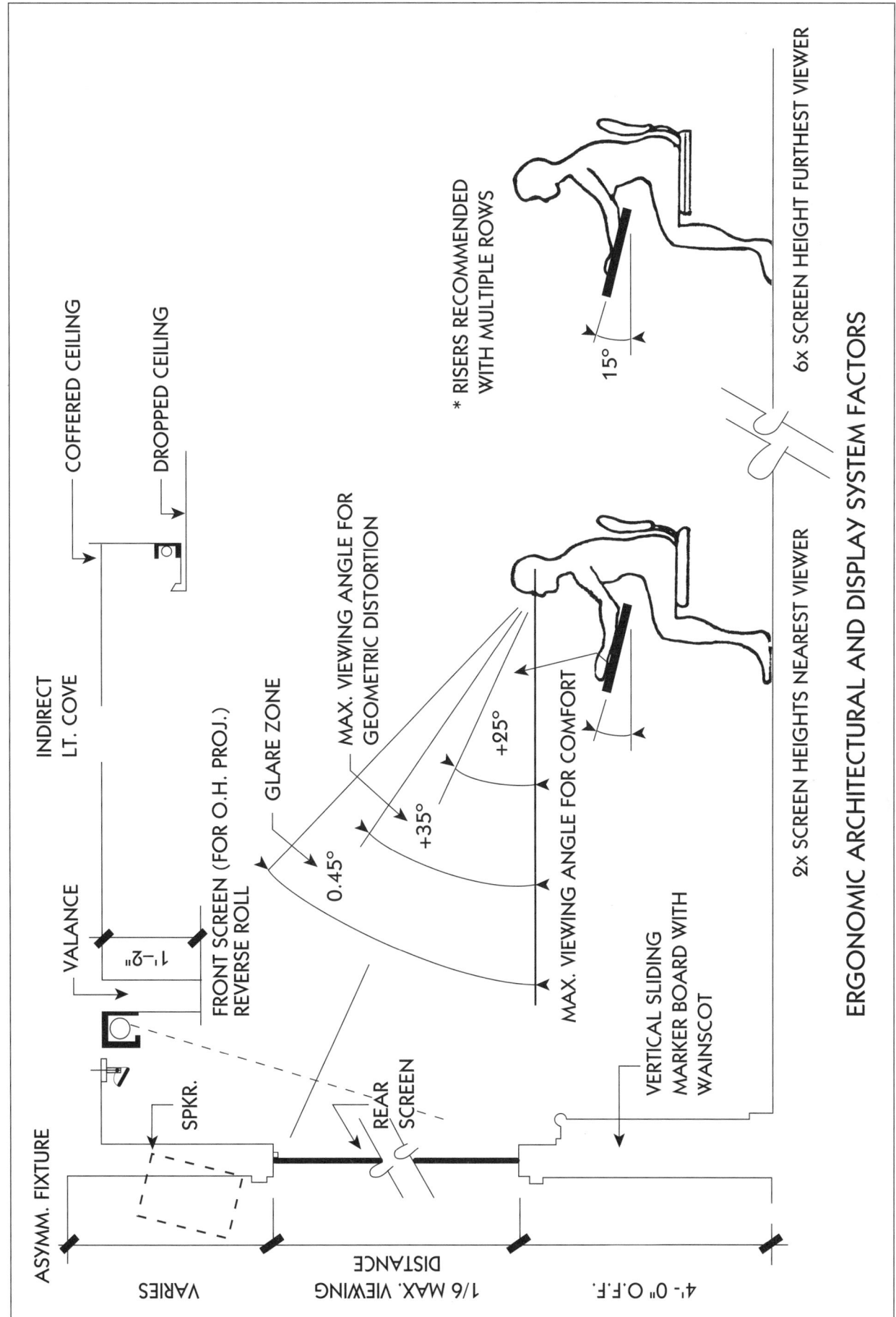

Figure 36-23. Ergonomic design details for lecture environments with media.

1099

adjustment features needed, and, if so, will they be able to be operated easily by an inexperienced occupant? Will the desks be of an appropriate height and provide sufficient surface area for the programmed activities? Will the reading and writing surface have an inclination sufficient to promote the comfortable and effective completion of near visually centered tasks such as taking notes, writing, and reading? Will there be desks or tables available with flat work surfaces for three-dimensional tasks, i.e., assembly work, models, etc.?

Display system factors. Has the most appropriate display system (rear screen or front screen) been selected for each of the spaces where display systems are required? Do the screens have light distribution patterns (gain) appropriate for the intended media and the width of the spaces? Is it possible for simultaneous use of marker board and media display where required? Are horizontal and vertical sight lines to all parts of the screen physically comfortable as well as unobstructed by occupants seated in front of each other? Have the display systems been coordinated with the lighting fixtures (luminaires), dimmers and/or switches, and scene selection "controls" to permit appropriate image/non-image "brightness" ratios?

Audio system factors. Has the most appropriate type(s) of audio system(s) been selected for each of the presentation spaces? Will these systems be capable of producing sound levels to promote orientation and adequate signal-to-noise ratios for effective communications? Is "sound masking" needed in any of the "open" multipurpose spaces?

Safety and security factors. Have all possible egress scenarios been considered and provided for? Have the appropriate fire suppression systems been provided for people and equipment? Are there any electrical or hazardous substance conditions that need to be accommodated? Have medical and first-aid services been considered and provided where a need is anticipated? Have security measures been provided to ensure personal safety and hazard and intrusion avoidance? Are there pockets of invisibility where potential hazards for people are likely to be hidden from view? Is the parking area safe? Are all locks clearly visible so that using one's keys is not problematic at any time of the day or night the facility is in use?

Handicapped/elderly. Have the physical, auditory, and visual needs of the handicapped and elderly learners been accommodated?

Anthropometric factors. Have corridors, door openings, etc., been designed to make passage safe and nonclaustrophobic. Will they accommodate prosthetic devices including wheelchairs? Are all critical controls for environmental and equipment elements within easy reach for all of the intended population? Are all physical clearances into spaces of sufficient height and width to accommodate all of the intended population? Have furnishings been selected on the basis of anthropometric appropriateness and not solely on the owners's aesthetic values or organizational image?

Orientation factors. Is the floor plan logic such that people new to a space will have no difficulty getting to where they want to go? Has sufficient attention been given to space differentiation, and to color and graphic usage, to promote efficient "way finding"? Is the logic such that there is not excessive transition time from entrances to information sources, i.e., reception desks, the message center, or message monitors?

Proxemics. Have the spaces been designed to provide a sense of personal space where desired and the number of socieopital and sociofugal spaces needed to compliment the facility's program? Does the facility convey a sense of openness and/or territoriality where desired?

Aesthetics and interaction. Will the facilty convey a sense of familiarity, cultural identity, and naturalness? Are there sufficient window views and areas that capitalize on natural light? Will the facility provide sensory variation for its occupants that is stimulating but not so distracting that it will interfere with their task performance?

Housekeeping. Have the problems associated with beverages, food use, and smoking been accommodated, through both facility design and the establishment of rules and regulations?

Control systems. Are there control systems for room lighting, drapery, and HVAC? Are these accessible to the appropriate people? Are the media control systems designed in a logical manner so that their operation is self-evident, i.e., one does not need to read a manual in order to use them? Are all operations labels visible and legible given the lighting conditions under which they are expected to be used? Can a student turn on and operate all elements in his or her workstation without needing to involve someone else? Are important operating instructions clearly visible and understandable by all of the intended users? Do all controls provide the operator with feedback, i.e, tactile, kinesthetic, visual, auditory, etc., so that the operator knows immediately the consequence of his or her action?

REFERENCES

Aikman, L. (1994). Personal communication, Newton, MA.

Akerblom, B. (1954). Chairs and sitting. *In* W.F. Floyd & A.T. Welford, eds. *Symposium on Human Factors Design. Proceedings of the Ergonomics Research Society*, Vol. II, 29–35, Loughborough, U.K., Ergonomics Society.

Ali, M.R. (1972). Pattern of EEG recovery under photic stimulation by light of different colors, *Electroencephalography and Clinical Neurophysiology 33*, 332–35.

Allen, W. & Charles, J.G. (1986). The aural environment. *In* R. Lueder, ed. *The ergonomic payoff: designing the electronic office.* New York: Nichols.

Andre, A. & Segal, L. (1994, Oct.). Design functions. *Ergonomics in Design.*

Ankrum, D.R. & Nemeth, K.J. (1995). Posture, comfort, and monitor placement. *Ergonomics in Design*, April, 7–9.

ASHRAE (1992). Thermal environmental conditions for human occupancy. *ANSI/ASHRAE,* 55-1992, Atlanta, GA.

Ary, D., Jacobs, L.C. & Razavieh, A. (1979). *Introduction to research in education.* New York: Holt, Rinehart & Winston.

ASTM (1976). *Acoustical environment in the open-plan office.* Report of ASTM Task Group E33.04C.

Au Yeung, Y.N., et al. (1991). Sick building syndrome—a case study. *Building and Environment 26,* 319–30.

Auliciems, A. (1989). Thermal comfort. *In* N.M. Ruck, ed. *Building design and human performance.* New York: Van Nostrand.

Badolato, M. (1995). An ergonomic analysis and assessment of selected music education classrooms, Doctoral dissertationin progress, Boston University.

Bass, B.H., & Klubeck, S. Effects of seating arrangements on leaderless group discussions. *Journal of Abnormal Social Psychology 47,* 724-27.

Bendix, T. & Hagberg, M. (1984). Trunk posture and load on the trapezius muscle whilst sitting at sloping tables. *Ergonomics 27,* 873–82.

— & Jensen, F. (1986). Wrist support during typing: a controlled electromyographic-graphic study. *Applied Ergonomics 17,* 162–68.

Bennett, C. (1977). *Spaces for people.* Englewood Cliffs, NJ: Prentice Hall.

— (1985). Three comparisons of incandescent and fluorescent: color or luminaire. *Proceedings of the Human Factors Society,* 29th annual meeting.

Bennett, H.E. (1928). *School posture and seating: a manual for teachers, physical directors, and school officials.* Boston, MA: Ginn.

Bethune, J. (1991). A user assessment of selected lecture halls to determine the relative merits of architectural standards and ergonomic guidelines. Doctoral dissertation, Boston University. Ann Arbor, MI: University Microfilms.

BS7179 (1990). *Ergonomics of design and use of visual display terminals (VDTs) in Offices, Parts 1-6.* Milton Keynes, England: British Standards Institute.

Beranek, L., Blazier, W. & Figwer, J. (1971). Preferred noise criterion (PNC) curves and their application to rooms. *Journal of the Acoustical Society of America 50* (5.1), 1223–28.

Birren, F. (1969). *Light, color and environment.* New York: Van Nostrand.

Bobker, S. (1991). Work smart, work safe. *MacUser 7,* (12), 221–23.

BOCA (1990). *The BOCA National Building Code/1990,* 11th ed. International Country Club Hills, IL: Building Officials and Code Administration.

Boray, P.F., et al. (1989). Effects of warm-white, cool-white, or full-spectrum fluorescent lighting on simple cognitive performance, mood, and ratings of others, *Journal of Environmental Psychology 9,* 297–308.

Boubekrl, M., et al. (1991, Jul.). Impact of window size and sunlight penetration on office workers' mood and satisfaction. *Environment and Behavior 23,* (4), 474–93.

Boyce, P.R. (1974, Sep.). User's assessment of a landscaped office. *Journal of Architectural Research 3,* 44–62.

Brainard, G.C. (1994, Oct.). *Special report: impact of light on human health, performance and well-being.* Unpublished Report. Boston, MA: Tradeline Symposium.

Broadbent, D.E. (1957). Effects of noise on behavior. *In* Harris, ed. *Handbook of noise control,* Chap. 10. New York: McGraw-Hill.

Bruner, J. (1961). The cognitive consequences of early sensory deprivation. *In* P. Solomon, ed. *Sensory deprivation.* Cambridge, MA: Harvard University Press.

Bugelski, B.R. (1971). *The psychology of learning applied to teaching.* New York: Bobbs-Merrill.

Burch, L. (1993). Architects and educators: the total is greater than the parts. *The Educational Facility Planner.* CEFPI, 32, No. 3, 5–6.

Burgess, C.G. (1992, Dec.). Electromagnetic fields (EMF) and health hazards. *CSTG Bulletin,* Human Factors and Ergonomics Society.

Burton, Daniel, J. (1980). *Human needs assessment, performance-based programming, construction and user evaluation of a facility for the elderly and the handicapped, utilizing man-environment data.* Doctoral dissertation, School of Education, Boston University. Ann Arbor, MI: University Microfilms.

Cakir, A., et al. (1980). *Visual display terminals.* Chichester, U.K.: Wiley.

Caldwell, B. (1994, Jan.). The learning-friendly classroom. *Ergonomics in Design,* 30–35.

Caldwell, B., et al. (1995, Jan.). Classroom environment analysis and improvement strategies, Proceedings 37th Annual Meeting of the Human Factors and Ergonomics Society.

Campbell, D.T. & Fiske, D.W. (1959). Convergent and discrimination validation by the multitrait-multimethod matrix. *Psychological Bulletin 56,* 81–105.

— & Stanley, J.C. (1963, 1966). Experimental and quasi-experimental designs for research. Chicago, IL: Rand McNally.

Canter, D., ed. (1970). Architectural psychology. Proceedings of the conference held at Dalandhui, University of Strathclyde, Glasgow, Scotland, 28 Feb.–2 Mar., 1969. London: Royal Institute of British Architects.

— (1975). Psychology for architects. New York: Halsted Press, Wiley.

Carnovale, R., et al. (1989). *A guideline on office ergonomics.* CSA Standard CAN/CSA-Z412-M89. Rexdale, Ontario: Canadian Standards Association.

Castaldi, B. (1977). *Educational facilities.* Boston, MA: Allyn & Bacon.

CCSE (1938). *Report of the Consultative Committee on Secondary Education.* London: CCSE, HMSO.

CEFP (1969). *Guide for planning educational facilities.* Columbus, OH: CEFP.

CEQ (1968). *Noise: sound without value.* PB 180299, Committee on Environmental Quality, Federal Council for Science and Technology. Washington, DC: Government Printing Office.

Chant, R. (1986). Air quality. *In* R. Lueder, ed. *The ergonomic payoff: designing the electronic office.* New York: Nichols.

Chapanis, A. (1965). *Research techniques in human engineering.* Baltimore, MD: John Hopkins.

Close. P.D. (1957). *Sound control and thermal insulation of buildings.* New York: Reinhold.

Cohen, A. (1969, Feb.). Effects of noise on psychological state. In *Noise as a public health hazard.* ASHRAE Reports 4, 74–88, Proceedings of the American Speech and Hearing Association, Washington, DC.

Christinaz, D. & Knirk, F. (1987). Environmental requirements for computer-assisted instruction, Proceedings of the Human Factors Society, 31st Annual Meeting, 228–32. Santa Monica, CA.

Davis, G. (1991, May). The electronic office. In *Building Operating Management.* GTE Sylvania.

DeCecco, J.P. (1968). *The psychology of learning and instruction: educational psychology.* Englewood, NJ: Prentice Hall.

DeChiara J. & Callender, J. (1980). *Time saver standards for building types,* 2d ed., New York: McGraw-Hill.

DesRosiers, E. (1976).The effect of image/surround brightness contrast ratios on student preference, attention, visual comfort, and visual fatigue. Doctoral dissertation, Boston University. Ann Arbor, MI: University Microfilms.

Diffrient, N., et al. (1974). *The human scale.* Cambridge, MA: MIT Press.

Doelle, Leslie, L. (1972). *Environmental acoustics.* New York: McGraw-Hill.

Dunn, O. (1964). Multiple comparisons using rank sums. *Technometrics 6,* 241–52.

Eckenrode, A. & Abbot, L. (1959). *In* C.T. Larson, ed. *SER 2,* 1965. Ann Arbor, MI: University of Michigan.

EFL (1970): *Instructional hardware: a guide to architectural requirements,* 66–98. New York: Educational Facilities Laboratories.

Eggleton. E., ed. (1983). *Ergonomic design for people at work, Vol. 1.* Belmont, CA: Lifetime Learning.

Ferris, G. & Moldstad, J. (1961). *Improving the learning environment.* Bloomington, IN: Indiana University.

Francescato, A., et al. (1975). Evaluating residents' satisfaction in housing for low- and moderate-income families: a multimethod approach. *In* C. Lozar, ed. EDRA 5: Sec. 5, methods and measures: 1974. Milwaukee, WI: University of Wisconsin.

Freudenthal, A., et al. (1991, Oct.). The effect on sitting posture of a desk with a ten-degree inclination, using an adjustable chair and table. *Applied Ergonomics,* 329–36.

Frost, M. (1992). Mac LC and IIsi color display systems. *MacUser 8* (2), 157–70.

Fulrath, D. (1976). Some effects of seating arrangement and task duration on fatigue, attention, participation, and preference of individuals engaged in small group media tasks. Doctoral dissertation, Boston University. Ann Arbor, MI: University Microfilms.

Gagné, R. (1965). *Conditions of learning.* New York: Holt, Rinehart & Winston.

Gardner, D.E. (1971). *Guide for planning educational facilities.* Columbus, OH: Council of Educational Facility Planners.

Gerard, R.M (1958). Differential effects of colored lights on psychophysiological functions. Doctoral dissertation, University of California, Ann Arbor, MI: University Microfilms.

Grandjean, E. (1969). *Fitting the task to the man.* New York: Taylor & Francis.

— (1984). VDT workstation settings, body posture and physical impairments. *Applied Ergonomics 15,* 99–104.

— (1987). *Ergonomics in computerized offices.* London: Taylor & Francis.

—(1987a). Design of VDT workstations. *In* G. Salvendy, ed. *Handbook of human factors,* Chap. 11. New York: Taylor & Francis.

— (1988). *Fitting the task to the man,* 4th ed. New York: Taylor & Francis.

— et al. (1983). VDT workstation design: preferred setting and their effects. *Human Factors 25,* 161–76.

Green, A., ed. (1966). *Educational facilities with new media.* Washington, DC: AECT.

Hall, E.T. (1966). *The hidden dimension.* New York: Doubleday.

Hamilton, M. (1983). The accuracy recognition of positive and negative symbols of seven, five, and three minutes of arc on front and rear projection screens under self-selected illumination. Doctoral dissertation, Boston University. Ann Arbor, MI: University Microfilms.

Harmon, D.B. (1951). *The coordinated classroom.* File No. 35-B, Washington, DC: A.I.A.

— (1953). *Controlling the thermal environment of the coordinated classroom.* ERIC ED 033531, Minneapolis, MN: Honeywell.

— (1966). Class lecture notes: environmental design program. Madison, WI: University of Wisconsin.

Harris, C.M. (1957). *Handbook of noise control.* New York: McGraw-Hill.

Hathaway, W. (1988). Educational facilities: designing to enhance learning and human performance. *Education Canada 28,* (4), 28–35.

Haubner, P. & Kokoschka, S. (1983). *Characteristics of performance.* International Commission on Illumination (CIE), 20th Session in Amsterdam, 52 Bd. Malesherbes 75008 Paris, France.

Hawkes, R.J. & Douglas, H. (1970, Nov.). Subjective acoustic experience in concert auditoria. *Architectural Research and Teaching* (2), 34–35.

Hebert, L.A. (1989). *The neck-arm-hand book.* Bangor, ME: IMPACC.

Hedge, A., et al. (1989). Lighting the computerized office: a comparative study of parabolic and lensed indirect office lighting systems. *Proceedings of the Human Factors Society, 33d annual meeting.*

— (1990). Improving thermal comfort of offices: the impact of underfloor task ventilation. *Proceedings of the Human Factors Society, 34th annual meeting.*

Heijs, W. & Stringer, P. (1988). Research on residential thermal comfort: some contributions from environmental psychology. *Journal of Environmental Psychology 8,* 235–47.

HFS (1988). *American National Standards for Human Factors Engineering of Visual Display Terminal Workstations.* ANSI/HFS Standard No. 100-1988. Santa Monica, CA: Human Factors Society.

Hill, S. & Kroemer, E. (1986). Preferred declination of the line of sight. *Human Factors 28* (2) 127–34.

Hocking, W. (1987) Epidemiological aspects of repetition strain injury. *Medical Journal of Australia 147,* 218–22.

Horowitz, J. (1992, Oct.). Crippled by computers. *Time 12,* 70–72.

Howell, D.C. (1982). *Statistical methods for psychology.* Boston, MA: Duxbury.

Hultgren, G., Knave, B. & Werner, M. (1974). Discomfort thru microfilm in different enlargers. *Applied Ergonomics,* 194–210.

Hunt, D.P. & Bernotat, R. (1977). *University curricula in ergonomics.* Forschungsinstitut fur Anthropotecnic, Meckenhim.

IES (1989). IES-RP-24: *VDT lighting.* Washington, DC: Illuminating Engineering Society of North America.

Issac, S. & Michael, W.B. (1981). *Handbook in research and evaluation.* San Diego, CA: Edits Publications.

ISO (1988) Visual display terminals (VDTs) used for one tasks-ergonomic requirements. *International Standard* ISO/DIS 9241-1.

Ittleson, W., Rivlin, L. & Proshansky, H. (1970). The use of behavioral maps. *In* H. Proshansky, W. Ittleson & L. Rivlin, eds. *Environmental psychology.* New York: Holt, Rinehart & Winston.

Jaschinski-Kruza, W. (1988). *Visual strain during VDU work:*

the effect of viewing distance and dark focus. Ergonomics *32* (10), 1449–65.

John, J.E.J. (1960). The efficiency of hearing aids as a function of architectural acoustics. *In* AW. Ewing, ed. *The modern educational treatment of deafness.* Manchester, U.K.: Manchester University Press.

Kaufman, J.E., ed. (1981). 1981 *lighting handbook,* Vols. 1, 2. New York: Illuminating Engineering Society of North America.

Kerlinger, F.N. (1973). *Foundations of behavioral research.* New York: Holt, Reinhart & Winston.

Kjellberg, A. & Skoldstrom, B. (1991). Noise annoyance during the performance of different non-auditory tasks. *Perceptual and Motor Skills 73,* 39–49.

Kloepfel, D.V. (1969). *Motion picture projection and theater presentation manual.* New York: S.M.P.T.E.

Kwallek, N. & Lewis, C.M. (1990). Effects of environmental colour on males and females. *Applied Ergonomics 21* (12), 275–78.

Knirk, F.G. (1992, Sep.). Facility requirements for integrated learning systems. *Educational Technology 33* (9), 26–32.

Kryter, Karl, D. (1970). *The effects of noise on man.* New York: Academic.

LaGuisa, F. & Perney, L. (1973, May). Effects of brightness variation on attention span in a learning environment. *Lighting Design and Application* (3) 6, 28–29.

— (1974) Further studies on effects of brightness variations on attention spans. *Journal of the Illuminating Engineering Society 3,* 249–52.

Lam, W. (1977). *Perception and lighting as formgivers for architecture.* New York: McGraw-Hill.

Lane, K.E. & Richardson, M.D (1993). Human factors engineering and school furniture: a circular odyssey. *The Educational Facility Planner,* CEFPI 31, No. 3, 22–23.

Larson, C.T. (1965). SER 1, 2, 3, school environment project. Ann Arbor, MI: University of Michigan.

Leavitt, H.J. (1951, Jan.). Some effects of certain communication patterns on group performance. *Journal of Abnormal Social Psychology 46,* 38–50.

Lee, S.A. (1973). Environmental perception, preferences and the designer. *In* R. Kuller, ed. *Architectural Psychology, Proceedings of the Lund Conference.* Stroudsburg, PA: Dowden, Hutchinson & Ross.

Leed, S. & Leed, J. (1987). *Building for adult learning.* Cincinnati, OH: LDA.

Levy-Leboyer, C. (1982). *Psychology and environment.* Beverly Hills, CA: Sage.

Lexan, H. (1969, May). The noise is killing us. *St. Anthony Messenger 76,* 12–17.

Markus, T. (1974, May). The why and how of research into 'real building.' *Journal of Architectural Research* (2), 19–23.

McVey, G.F. (1969). An analysis, synthesis, and application of selected research findings to visual design and presentation by the visual specialist. Doctoral dissertation, University of Wisconsin-Madison. Ann Arbor, MI: University Microfilms.

— (1971). *Sensory factors in the classroom learning environment.* Washington, DC: NEA.

— (1979, Summer) User assessment of media presentation rooms. *Educational Communication and Technology Journal, 27* (2), 121–47.

— (1985). The learning environment. In *The international encyclopedia of education.* New York: Pergamon.

— (1991, Jul.). Twelve ergonomic guidelines for integrating AV into conference room design. *Facility Planning News.*

— (1992). In search of equitable learning environments: the acoustics of classrooms used in mainstreaming hearing-disadvantaged students. *Proceedings of EDRA/23.* Environmental Design Research Association, Apr. 9–12, Boulder, CO.

— & Bethune, J. (1992). User assessment of selected lecture halls and the relative merits of architectural standards and ergonomic guidelines. *Proceedings of the Human Factors Society,* Oct. 12–16.

— & Powell, J. (1985, Aug.). *An audiovisual facility and production status study of selected national conference centers.* Cambridge, MA: B & M Technologies.

Mehrabian, A. & Russell, J. (1974). *An approach to environmental psychology.* Cambridge, MA: MIT Press.

Meister, D., et al. (1969, Aug. 30). *Guide to human engineering design for visual displays.* Canoga Park, CA: Bunker-Ramo.

Menell, J. (1976). Training facilities and equipment. *In* American Society for Training and Development. *Training and development handbook: a guide to human resource development,* 2d ed. New York: McGraw-Hill.

Mikellides, B. (1990, Spring). Color and physiological arousal. *Journal of Architectural and Planning Research 7* (1), 13–19.

Miller, J.D. (1971). Noise and performance. In *Effects of noise on people,* 118–21. NTID 300 7. Washington, DC: Environmental Protection Agency.

Moon, P. (1961). *The scientific basis of illuminating engineering.* New York: Dover.

Nakaseko, P. (1982). History of occupational cervicobrachial disorders in Japan. *Journal of Human Ergology 11,* 7–16.

Niemoeller, A.F. (1968). Acoustical design of classrooms for the deaf. *American Annals of the Deaf 113,* 1040–45.

NIOSH, (1991). *The occupational safety and health office of communication workers of America: a survey.* Washington, DC: NIOSH.

Norback, D., et al. (1990). Volatile organic compounds, respirable dust, and personal factors related to prevalence and incidence of sick-building syndrome in primary schools. *British Journal of Industrial Medicine 47,* 733–41.

Norman, Donald A. (1988). *The design of everyday things.* New York: Doubleday.

NRC (1987). *Work, aging, and vision: report of a conference.* Washington, DC: National Academy Press.

NSWI (1992, Jun. 15). *The healthy office report.* Chicago, IL: National Safe Workplace Institute.

Packard, R., ed. (1988). *Ramsey and Sleeper architectural graphic standards,* 8th ed., New York: Wiley.

Parsons, H.M. (1992). Human factors/ergonomics in office design and automation. *Proceedings: 1982 Meeting of the American Psychological Association.*

Partridge, R.C. & MacLean, D.L. (1935). Determination of the comfort zone for school children. *Journal Industrial Hygiene 17,* 66–71.

Patterson, A.H. & Passini, R. (1974). The evaluation of physical setting: to measure attitudes, behavior, or both? EDRA 5: Proceedings. Milwaukee, WI: University of Wisconsin.

Pearson, R. (1956). The development and evaluation of a

checklist for measuring subjective fatigue, USAF No. 56-115. Randolf AFB, TX.

Pekkarinen, E. & Viluanen, V. (1990). Effect of sound-absorbing treatment in speech discrimination in rooms. *Audiology 29,* 219–27.

Pool, R. (1990, Sep. 21). Electromagnetic fields: the biological evidence. *Science 249,* 1378–81.

Porter, J.M., et al. (1992). An evaluation of a tilting computer desk. *In* E.J. Lovesey, ed. *Contemporary ergonomics.* London, U.K.: Taylor & Francis.

Potter, I.N. (1988). The sick building syndrome: symptoms, risk factors and practical design. BSRIA Technical Note 4/88.

Preiser, W. (1970). Behavioral design criteria in student housing. *In* H. Sanoff & S. Cohn, eds. *EDRA 1: Proceedings.* Raleigh, NC: North Carolina State University.

Proshansky, E., Ittleson, W. & Rivlin, L., eds. (1970). *Environmental psychology.: man and his physical setting.* New York: Holt, Rinehart & Winston.

Propst R. (1968). *The office: a facility based on change.* Zeeland, MI: Herman Miller.

Rea, M.S. (1991). Technics: solving the problem of VDT reflections. *Progressive Architecture 10.*

Ripple, P.H. (1952). Variation of accommodation in vertical directions of gaze. *American Journal of Ophthalmology 35,* 1630–34.;

Rosenthal, N.E. (1984). Seasonal affective disorder: a description of the syndrome and preliminary findings with light therapy. *Archives of General Psychiatry 42,* 72–80.

Ross, M. (1972). Classroom acoustics and speech intelligibility. *In* J. Katz, ed. *Handbook of clinical audiology,* 756–71. Baltimore, MD: Williams & Wilkins.

Ross, T.W. & Steward, G.K. (1993). Facility planning for technology implementation. *The Educational Facility Planner,* CEFPI, 31, No. 3, 9–12.

Sanders, M.S. & McCormick, E.J. (1987). *Human factors in engineering and design,* 6th ed., New York: McGraw-Hill.

Sauter, S. & Schlufir, L. (1991). Work posture, workstation design, and musculoskeletal discomfort in a VDT data entry task. *Human Factors 33* (2) 151–67.

Sommer, R. (1959). Studies in personal space. *Sociometry 22,* 247–60.

— (1965). Further studies of small group ecology. *Sociometry 28,* 337–48.

— (1967). Small group ecology. *Psychological Bulletin 67,* (2) 145–50.

— (1968). *The ecology of study areas.* University of California Cooperative Research Project No. 6-1121., U.S. Office of Education, Washington, DC.

— (1969). *Personal space: the behavioral basis of design.* Englewood Cliffs, NJ: Prentice Hall.

— (1974). *Tight spaces: hard architecture and how to humanize it.* Englewood Cliffs, NJ: Prentice Hall.

— (1970). Studies of small group ecology. *In* R.S. Cathcart & L.A. Samovar, eds. *Small group communication.* Dubuque, IA: Wm. C. Brown.

— & Becker, F.D. (1971, Dec. 2). Room density and user satisfaction. *Environment and Behavior* (4), 412–17.

Spencer, D.E. (1954). Comparative analysis of comfort and glare. *Illuminating Engineering 49,* 39–49.

Steinzor, B. (1950, Jul.). The spatial factor in face to face discussion groups. *Journal of Abnormal Social Psychology 45,* 552–55.

Tannenbaum, P.H. (1957). *In* C.E. Osgood, G.J. Sochi & P.H. Tannenbaum. *The measurement of meaning.* Urbana, IL: University of Illinois Press.

Terlaga, K.L. (1990) *Training room solutions.* Howe Furniture.

Tessmer, M. (1994). Personal communication.

— & Harris, D. (1992). *Analyzing the instructional setting.* London, U.K.: Kogan Page.

Tichauer, E.R. (1978). *The biomechanical basis of ergonomics: anatomy applied to the design of workstations.* New York: Wiley.

Tuckerman, B.W. (1972). *Conducting educational research.* New York: Harcourt, Brace.

Utz, P. (1992, Oct.). Video projector ergonomics: the basics of screen and audience placement. *AV Video,* 70–88.

Van Cott, D. & Kinkade, R. (1972). *Human engineering guide to equipment design.* New York: McGraw-Hill.

Veitch, J.A. (1990). Office noise and illumination effects on reading comprehension. *Journal of Environmental Psychology 10,* 209–17.

deWall, M., et al. (1991). The effect on sitting posture of a desk with a 10° inclination for reading and writing. *Ergonomics 34* (5), 575–85.

Wadsworth, R. (1983). *Basics of audio visual systems design.* Indianapolis, IN: Sams.

Wedberg, W. (1987). Facial particle exposure in the VDU environment: the role of static electricity. *In* B. Knave & P.G. Wideback, eds. *Work with display units.* New York: Elsevier.

Weinstein, C. (1979). The physical environment of the school. *Review of Educational Research 49* (4), 577–610.

Woodson, W.E. (1987). *Human factors design handbook.* New York: McGraw-Hill.

— (1992). *Human factors design handbook: information and guidelines for the design of systems, facilities, equipment, and products for human use,* 2d ed. New York: McGraw-Hill.

— & D. Conover, (1973). *Human engineering guide for equipment designers.* Berkeley, CA: University of California Press.

Wools, R. (1970). The assessment of room friendliness. *Architectural Psychology: Proceedings of the Conference at Dalandhui.* University of Strathclyde, Glasgow, Scotland, 28 Feb.-2 Mar. 1969. London: Royal Institute of British Architects.

Wysotsky, M.Z. (1971). Wide-Screen Cinema and Stereophonic Sound. New York: Communication Arts Books.

Yerges, L. (1978). *Sound, noise and vibration control.* New York: Van Nostrand.

Zental, S.S. Color stimulation on performance and activity of hyperactive and non-hyperactive children. *Journal of Educational Psychology 78* (2), 159–65.

Zipp, P., et al. (1983). Keyboard design through physiological strain measurements. *Applied Ergonomics 14,* 117–22.

Zmirak, J.P. (1993). Workplace utopia. *Success 40* (2), 35–40.

VI

ISSUES OF ORGANIZATION AND CHANGE IN EDUCATIONAL COMMUNICATIONS AND TECHNOLOGY

Donald P. Ely, Syracuse University

Associate Editor

37. DIFFUSION AND ADOPTION OF EDUCATIONAL TECHNOLOGY: A CRITIQUE OF RESEARCH DESIGN

Robert E. Holloway
NORTHERN ARIZONA UNIVERSITY

Studies of diffusion and adoption help to explain the what, where, and why of technology acceptance or rejection in education. The types of studies done and their sponsors significantly shape professional, public, and political perceptions of educational technology. A primary thesis of this review is that the results of the majority of these studies create an "equipment centered" view of the field. The focus in this review is on the impact of research design on the results of the studies. Numbers from surveys, for instance, capture the attention of decision makers and the public. Discussions are presented in technical terms and potential. The context of educational technology—especially the economics of marketing technology to schools, demonstrated learning outcomes, and microlevel realities of classroom use—are much less known and less acknowledged in policy and decision. Until we focus on macro-forces such as marketing of technology and micro-events such as barriers to teachers using technology, we will be unable to explain diffusion or affect adoption.

The body of research reviewed here is divided into three logical categories: (1) descriptive surveys of equipment diffusion, (2) correlational studies of technology and demographic variables, and (3) constructivist and action research on adapting technology. It is assumed that the diffusion process is similar to a market model based on a knowledge cycle (Rich, 1981). This cycle, somewhat simplified, moves through invention, commercial production, and eventual sale to secondary markets. Technology is developed for other markets first. Education is a secondary or tertiary market where technology is adapted. *Technology,* used in this context, is a combination of equipment and its use. Learning, except for activities such as in-service training, is not a dependent variable in these studies. Neither is

the research driven by theory. Taking one area, the literature on microcomputer adoption, Gillman (1988, p. 192) concluded that:

It is notable that few of the studies in the 8 years of research under review were theoretically based or utilized a methodology based on multivariate analysis. The breakdown of the types of research pursued in the 70 studies reviewed was as follows:

Case studies, 11
Exploratory field studies, 21
Surveys, 21
Ex post facto (quasi-experimental), 12
Experimental (controlled), 2
Reviews, 3

The intervening years do not appear to have brought substantive changes. Data are descriptive. Statistical procedures are correlational. Survey and case study are the primary techniques used. This is not a criticism of the instructional technology field in particular. Journals have a similar distribution across education, with the exception of journals that are design specific, such as *Experimental Psychology.*

An unevenly distributed but full range of research methods exists among studies of diffusion and adoption. Survey studies are over represented, likely because they are inexpensive and simple compared to experimental studies. Most federal longitudinal studies of all kinds are of short duration because of political and economic factors. Those commercial studies that are available must be compared with caution because there are significant differences in methods used for sampling techniques, instrumentation, and analysis. Kinnaman (1993) suggested using multiple studies for decision making, since reported research represents a wide range of competence, care, and sources. From this and other sources, an overview list of issues can be constructed.

- Research methods in studies of diffusion and adoption reflect the same strengths and weakness as other research foci in educational technology.
- Multimethod studies, needed to provide holistic understanding of diffusion and, especially, adoption, are gradually evolving.
- Results of diffusion and adoption studies are more likely to be used in marketing and journalism in the popular press than results from research on learning.
- Baseline data and tracking of simple indicators of diffusion are sporadic, focused on success, and often do not meet the cannons of research.

The most important distinction among the three categories used in this review is the intent of the research. Survey or diffusion studies are to find what is happening: Who is buying how much of which kind of technology? The most common reporting statistic is descriptive. Demographic and trend generalizability are important outcomes. The correlational studies in this section are designed to find relationships, usually using survey data. The differences are in the additional data collected, such as personality differences among adopters, shifting to measures of beliefs and attitudes, and in generating more testable hypotheses. The last category, action research, has the potential to help us understand why diffusion and adoption occur as they do.

Some of the earliest studies of innovation in education included such variables as school wealth (see Mort, 1938). More sophisticated than this simple description, correlational studies share the goal of generalization about factors associated with purchase and use. The last, action research, centers on the user's perception of the world and is usually less concerned with generalizations. The three categories form a progression. The survey literature tells us what is and perhaps what has quantitatively changed; the correlational studies tell us about the factors associated with change; and the constructivist and action research seeks to understand and bring about change at qualitative and quantitative levels. Of the three areas, the correlational studies are currently the richest in grounded speculation about why technology is in schools and how it is used. Factors affecting adoption, such as district wealth, help explain the presence of technology. Such factors do not address use or adaptation. In contrast, models, such as Morehouse & Stockdill's (1991) five-stage process—(1) front-end analysis, (2) prototype development, (3) small-scale implementation, (4) organizational adoption, and (5) institutionalization—or Stages of Concern (Hall, George & Rutherford, 1977) are common ways of describing innovation and planning for intentional change in educational technology. The stages are still descriptive and do not directly deal with attitudes and beliefs effectively. It is likely, as Cuban suggests, that

education has a value system that is positive toward personal contact and views technology as impersonal. Dealing with such subjective beliefs is difficult for survey and correlational designs.

37.1 CATEGORY OVERVIEW

37.1.1 Survey Research

Research on diffusion of educational technology has been dominated by descriptive survey research (see 41.2.1). The federal government is the primary source of longitudinal studies (Atkenson & Jackson, 1992). The main sources of longitudinal data are four agencies that serve as conduits for educational research and development information to Congress. They are the Congressional Research Service (CRS), the General Accounting Office (GAO), the Congressional Budget Office (CBO), and the former congressional Office of Technology Assessment (OTA). Data collection in education is more politics than policy according to Hill (1985): "Only a few lines of research have been sustained for the time needed to bring them to fruition" (Atkenson & Jackson, 1992, p. 3). The most significant descriptive studies are government studies such as the National Center for Educational Statistics report, "Schools and Staffing in the United States: A Statistical Profile" (1992b); Becker's Office of Technology Assessment report (Becker, 1994a); or a government grant-sponsored report such as "Telecommunications and K-12 Educators: Findings from a National Survey" (Honey & Henriquez, 1993). Doctoral dissertations make up the larger volume of research, but these are usually limited in scope. This body of work, both the national and dissertation surveys, is largely atheoretical. A recent National Center for Education Statistics report has no narration and is entirely made up of tables of equipment inventories and connectivity (see Heaviside, Farris, Malitz & Carpenter, 1995). Learning and use are not reported. Although survey studies remain more descriptive of equipment than of its use, this is changing. For example, time or frequency of use and kind of use are now more commonly reported as indicators.

37.1.2 Correlational Studies

The second category, correlational studies, is slightly more sophisticated. The research on innovation and change is distinguished by correlational techniques, especially pairing attitudes and demographic variables with adoption of equipment. The title of a sample study illustrates this category: "Socioeconomic Status and the Early Diffusion of Personal Computing in the United States" (Dutton, Sweet & Rogers, 1989). This line of inquiry moves the focus from descriptions of "what is" and "how many" to relationships between decision makers and technology choices. Correlational studies lead to tentative hypotheses about why and what kind of technology exists in an educational setting. Student learning and teacher change are not common variables. There are, however, some models proposed to explain diffusion events. For instance, in a body of studies by the Minnesota Extension Service, "A Technology Adoption Model" (Morehouse & Stockdill, 1991), one finds a five-stage adoption process grounded in four case studies. The models have the empirical base of an S-shaped curve of adoption that makes similarities obvious in different lines of research from medical sociology to marketing. The similarity of findings across disciplines leads to comparisons and proposals for a common model. (See Mahajan & Peterson's "Models for Innovation Diffusion," 1985.)

37.1.3 Action Research

Action research is designed to bring about change. Constructivist and qualitative work help us understand why adopters do what they do. (It is acknowledged that this category is somewhat contrived.) Bogdan and Bilken (1992), while specifying it is the systematic collection of information, limit action research to social change. Kemmis (1988) defines the term as reflection on praxis. A formal requirement is that truth is determined by the way it relates to practice (p. 43). As used in this review, *action research* is a synonym for *applied research* (see 42.2). The social-order concerns remain, but utility moves into a more central position. The perception of the participants remains as a guide to interpretation. Early studies in this category simply reported the effects of training or impact of the technology in the workplace. They were often one-shot case study, workshoplike efforts to introduce change. Earlier work on describing change in a variety of fields led to several models focused on stages of change. The first models of prescriptive change (see, for example, Havelock, 1973) used a process approach and were based on low-level generalizations from research. There was little model-specific empirical evidence. Current work on the process of change has been parsed out in prescriptive stages in a series of studies that has established its own research tradition. Most of these studies are based on Hall and Hord's (1987) concerns-based approach to change. Some of these are specific to technology, such as Hall and Win's 1981 study of implementation of computers in classrooms. More studies are being done with the intent to modify practice through an iterative intervention focus on in-service training using variations of Hall's "Concerns-Based Adoption Model" (C-BAM) as a guide. (See, for example, Winner's 1982 dissertation "Introducing the Microcomputer into the Elementary Classroom: An Inservice Program for Teachers.")

Policy, gender, and equity studies are also included in this category. (See, for example, Turkle & Papert's "Epistemological Pluralism and the Revaluation of the Concrete," 1992.) An illuminating subcategory, placed here because few studies are available, is qualitative research focused on perceptions of adopters. For example, Mehan's 1989 study uses qualitative data to speculate on the weight of social practice in the use of microcomputers in classrooms. A more basic study is Nordenbo's (1990) description of how computer novices perceive information technology. Often these studies emphasize a constructivist perspective and grounded research in a context that is naturalistic.

37.2 MARKET MODEL

Educators do not usually discuss technology acquisition and implementation as a market activity. The reasons educators do not describe acquisition as a market activity may be due to ignorance of markets, feelings that learning should be preeminent, belief that financial profit is not appropriate in education, or a combination of factors. Still, studies of diffusion and implementation in all disciplines strongly resemble market research. To the degree that this claim can be supported, a credible case for education as a market, or acting as a market, and needing to be understood as a market, is justified. There is at least one clear indicator that the education market is significant. It is that the most current and comprehensive studies, including those used by the federal government, are done by private commercial marketing research corporations. The marketing model is clearly the basis for most of these studies.

If market models explain in large part the spread of technology in education, they can perform a valuable function in improving our understanding of why events unfold the way they do. Marketing research about consumer behavior is clearly focused on the same variables of characteristics of innovations and adopters as education. These variables have been shown to be common across many settings, especially in the diffusion of technology in the private sector. The difference between industry and education is the emphasis on monetary rewards that provide the motivation for the commercial sector to make technology available to schools; that is, the profit for schools in acquiring technology is not monetary. It is more likely that increased status and reputation, sometimes feeling modern, and the facilitation of work are profits. This is still a market model, but value is set by the subjective perception of the actors. These perceptions are based on interpersonal utility comparisons, not on the economic value of technology. Social-exchange theory (Cook, 1987) attempts to explain patterns of social relations in structural terms. The model is not developed to the point Simon's decision making is in economics. However, Simon's bounded rationality in reaching "satisficing" decisions is closely related to social-exchange theory. The exchange of some currency, be it status or public relations, takes place when educators adopt technology. As social-exchange theory matures and deals with variations in social structure in schools, the kinds of exchanges will become more evident. One possibility, for instance, is that an administrator acquires technology for the school, advances the acquisition as an innovative improvement in learning, and trades the increase in status for professional advancement.

37.3 CONTEXT

The majority of instructional technology studies, especially in diffusion and adoption, are about artifacts such as videodisc players or software and, to a lesser degree, about knowledge, such as on-line search strategies or teaching techniques. The intent of this research is straightforward: to tell us what equipment and practices are used in instruction, where they are used, what trends to anticipate, and, less often, why technology is applied in a particular way. The majority of studies do this by describing current events, such as the number of television sets per school or funding sources for technology. In the last decade, more of these studies have described context and use, such as school size or programs using drill versus problem-solving instruction. This descriptive survey strand is used to forecast trends, such as how much and which kind of technology will be purchased by schools. Many of these studies are done by commercial marketing groups such as Market Data Retrieval or Quality Education Data. A few studies trace histories, such as the spread of instructional television. (See, for example, Marovitz, 1994.) The relationship between commercial antecedents and use of the technology in education is evident. It is this relationship that supports the claim for a market model as the best causal description of educational technology's spread.

The descriptive and explanatory robustness of these descriptive strands is mitigated by weaknesses in research on managing change and prescribing implementation practice. Studies of the implementation and adaptation processes are important (see Fullan & Pomfret, 1977; Fullan with Stiegelbauer, 1991), but few use the diffusion of technologies as independent variables with learning outcomes as dependent variables. For the most part, the focus is on installing technology in instructional settings rather than on the effects of technology in instructional settings. This distinction sets the genre aside from most research in educational technology where learning is the explicit, if not demonstrated, concern.

Most of the research on the spread of technology in education follows the transfer of equipment from the commercial sector to schools. Since equipment is an easily measured and visible record of one dimension of educational technology, it is most often used as the major indicator in diffusion research. Campbell (1971) identified this kind of study as the result of a "corrupting" effect of quantitative measures. The effect is to emphasize diffusion over use and things over process. This is evidence of expediency in research. Instructional development and design, learning, motivation, cost, and even diffusion of materials are less visible and thus less easily measured aspects of educational technology. The market model is demonstrably robust since it is known that "courseware can sell regardless of effec-

tiveness" (Roblyer, 1988, p. 11). Most research on learning comes after equipment is marketed.

The academic research community in educational technology has de-emphasized machines. It has emphasized learning-centered technology. For instance, in one authoritative review of research in educational technology, five types of educational media are covered. They include computer-based learning and hypermedia with references to behaviorism, cognitive theory, communications theory, and systems theory (Thompson, Simonson & Hargrave, 1992). The relationship of learning technology to equipment is intentionally distant. Another illustration: In a national study of educational technology research concerns as identified by 89 recognized leaders in the field, 12 areas were identified as priorities: (1) learner control, (2) instructional strategies, (3) cognitive psychology and educational technology, (4) interactivity, (5) cost/benefit–cost effectiveness, (6) higher-order and creative mental processes, (7) theoretical bases for new technologies, (8) learning styles and media, (9) adoption and diffusion, (10) theory building and instructional development, (11) effective factors in instructional design, and (12) societal effects of technologies (Zoski, 1989). This priority agenda is clearly focused on learning. It is in contrast with the popular focus on technology as equipment. Clearly, research on learning is important and can identify and demonstrate best practice. As a reflective and refining process, research on learning is productive in postdiffusion applications. The true rationale for educational technology is found in learning, cost efficiency, and access. Specifically, cost efficiency and access are demonstrated effects. For cost, the rationale for use is logistical. Access is the rationale for distribution of educational resources through technology for rural and other disenfranchised groups. Learning is assumed rather than demonstrated.

Regrettably, learning research lacks explanatory power for diffusion and implementation of technology. Cuban (1993) holds that three impulses converged in reforming schools through electronic technologies. First came a drive to bring schools technologically in step with the workplace because of the fear that students would be unprepared to compete in the job market and to adjust to the changing marketplace. A second impulse has come from a diverse coalition of academics, educators, and foundation officials with "neoprogressive" values, including that of self-directed learning for children. Finally, there is the impulse for productivity or teaching more in less time for less cost. The lack of success in implementing technology, Cuban explains, lies in the conflicting cultural beliefs of the teacher. It is a belief system, not an economic or empirical warrant, that determines acceptance and success.

Diffusion and implementation research are productive in understanding why the field is in a given condition at a particular time. Decision researchers have long known that rational models do not explain decisions. The alternatives are explanations that are administrative, sociological, or economic. In the best of all worlds, learning and diffusion strands of research come closer together. One purpose of this chapter, then, is to argue that both strands are needed and are complementary. One way to make this case is to show that improved student learning is not related to diffusion of technology. And, conversely, that diffusion of technology does not show improved learning even though there may be powerful potential to make such a change.

Using these assumptions, educational technology will be defined in two different ways in this section. The first definition, used in the review of survey research on diffusion, is what Clark (1992) names *technocentric* research. It is focused on machines, what Ely (1983) classes as the *physics of technology*. The second focus, used in the latter half of this review on implementation, is on proactive change. This shifts the focus to why various educational technologies are accepted or rejected and how implementation can be facilitated. This approach is part of research traditions in sociology that were synthesized in the 1970s in early works of Miles (1964), Rogers and Shoemaker (1971), and Havelock (1973). About the same time, Hall, Wallace, and Dossett (1973) provided a transition to proactive studies in education.

The presence of Ely's "physics" of technology in education stems from commercial sector marketing of equipment and materials. The physical technology in education is near the end of what Rich (1981) described as the knowledge cycle: invention, demonstration, production, primary market, and secondary market. A similar development path by Herbig (1994) has eight steps: fundamental science, discovery or development of a new theory, observation of a possible practical application, feasibility, development, decision to implement, innovation (commercial production), and diffusion. Herbig describes the process of technology implementation in the context of culture at both company and country level. Education, as a part of this process, can be understood better using culture as the mediating factor than using learning.

The cycle can be clearly illustrated with the history of television. The concept was invented early in the century, demonstrated in the late 1930s, produced just after World War II, and sold to the primary market. Interestingly, the first adoption both in the United States and in developing countries was the commercial setting of taverns and bars. Now, at the end of the century, schools (but not classrooms) approach the television equipment saturation of homes. This is true of almost all technologies except the overhead projector. The telephone, among the most common technologies, is in less than 15% of classrooms across the United States, and only 3% have access to electronic networks. Education is clearly a secondary or tertiary market.

If the spread or diffusion of educational technology is tied to the invention, production, and commercial sales of equipment and materials, then the process is easy to trace. In addition, some common elements of the process emerge across sectors. Early studies of technologies used in schools demonstrated a phenomenon that has held true over time: Products are widely disseminated to other sectors before they are adopted by education. Record players, for instance, were in over half the homes in the United States before they were adopted for school use. Thomas Edison predicted that motion pictures would be essential to schools, but it was the commercial entertainment sector that developed the technology and supplied the first materials to schools. From paper and chalkboards, developed for record keeping, to computers and television, the only technology developed for instruction appears to be the overhead projector, and that was for instruction in the military where there were ambient light problems in field training.

Education is a secondary market because it is not an economic power compared to the commercial sector. Sales of computers to the workplace were 20 million units compared to 2 million in education in 1988, a ratio of 10 to 1 (U.S. Department of Commerce, 1992). Electronic networks growing at the rate of 100% a year (Harris, 1995) and company growth of 75% revenue increase in one quarter (Netscape Communications Corporation news release, Oct. 24, 1995) stand as powerful indicators of the driving forces in connectivity. With this economic leverage, it is not surprising that manufacturers moved toward meeting workplace needs rather than instructional needs. If technology is not designed for and does not originate in education, there are two obvious questions: "How does technology get from its initial applications to education?" and "How is technology adapted for use in education?"

The answer to the first question must draw heavily on economics, since diffusion is in large part driven by profits from selling equipment and materials. This is described as sales push. However, what was market push has become in good part market pull, at least in policy if not in funding. The National Education Association, as an example of market pull, recommends that every teacher have a computer for administrative use. Apple creating loyalty by grants is another. Equipment, such as a videotape player or a computer, is developed for uses outside education. It is not significantly modified for transfer to education, since such a change increases the production cost. This explains why there is a lack of studies about machines developed for education. With the exception of early Skinnerian programmed instruction, the history of machine development is outside education. The assumption here is that a model of consumer (schools) behavior and profit (vendors) have more descriptive and predictive power for the diffusion of technology than increases in learning.

The answer to the second question, "How is technology adapted for use in education?", is in implementation research. This somewhat contrived category includes in-service and preservice training, professional organization interests, the consulting industry, and the use of materials developed within and for education. Training, ingenuity, and materials form a bridge for adapting the physics of technology to learning. It is in this area that professionals face the greatest challenges in encouraging use. Increased use of technology may maintain poor teaching methods or support of a deleterious status quo for class or gender (Pea, 1988). Adaptation of practice during implementation rather than simple adoption of machines is where professionals have the greatest potential for bringing about significant changes.

An important part of the argument for the importance of the adaptation process is that the characteristics of a technology are antecedents. The motivation for equipment or software development is done in noninstructional sectors and precedes plans or efforts to use the technology for learning. Further, the selection of machine-based technology is usually done by personnel other than the users. If there is a mismatch between needs of the users, teachers for instance, and what the technology is perceived to be able to do, such as calculate spread sheets, implementation will be nominal. If, instead, implementation is seen as an adaptation process, educators can make optimum use of the technology. These context forces and assumptions are powerful determinates of adoption and use.

37.4 SURVEYS AS DIFFUSION

As noted earlier, research on diffusion of educational technology has been dominated by survey methods (see 42.2.1). This section will focus more on the survey method as implemented than a review of findings from the surveys. The surveys are largely atheoretical and focused on the acquisition of equipment that, for better or worse, defines and shapes the field. Examples are easy to find. In his seminal history of the field, Saettler (1990) traces the growth of educational technology. In this account, he cites a 1922 survey of visual instruction in teacher education, a 1923 study of administrative practices, and a 1940 U.S. Office of Education survey of courses. The growth of the field is in fact tracked by such surveys. The central point in this section is that survey research is overrepresented and obscures how technology is used. The quantitative survey shapes public perception and policy and distorts the current construct of educational technology as defined in professional literature. The kinds of survey research used, especially data collection by mailing forms with convergent closed-end questions, has conceptual limits. However, the method will probably continue to dominate descriptions of the status of technology because equipment surveys are quick, easy to quantify, have high face validity, and are economical. Given the continuing popularity of this method, professionals must examine and provide perspective on survey methods.

Equipment acquisition surveys are the most common. They parallel economic activity and report or even lead to some of the growth. An early example is cited by Saettler (1990). He reports a U.S. Office of Education survey of 21,000 superintendents in 1935. There were 9,000 respondents, a substantial response, and results were simple tabulations such as the number of lantern slide projectors, an impressive 17,040. From this study, Saettler traces a resulting 1936 conference of motion picture projector manufacturers who, working out market needs and having the survey results, saw an opportunity and offered schools

price breaks on projectors. In this case, the relationship between education and the commercial sector is close, even symbiotic. The method, a survey, generated a particular type of data that described one likely market need in education. The equipment manufacturers developed a strategy for sales that built on this and then created a greater demand for equipment and eventually materials.

One of the most valuable results of surveys is that there is a rough index of change and diffusion. With reflection, the findings also point out where future inquiry might be fruitful. However, studies of downward trends are missing from the literature. Still, diffusion studies do provide us with the equivalent of an irrefutable grounded theory: Something is going on.

37.4.1 Methods

The ideal way to subdivide this section is by type of study. However, differences among study methods are not as important as the intent of a sponsoring agency. To recognize those differences, a sampling of survey studies is reported by sponsoring agency or association. This approach helps set out different standards, largely a function of different purposes, by which the studies are done. Since the majority of the work is traditional survey research, conventional standards for the method are used to discuss the studies.

The conventional technical canons for quantitative survey research are widely accepted, especially compared to those of qualitative methods. The National Center for Education Statistics Statistical Standards (1992b, p. 3) specify design parameters:

1. Response rates for universe surveys of at least 95% if the data are not going to be weighted, and 90% if the data are to be weighted.
2. A response rate of at least 90% for longitudinal sample surveys.
3. Within any stratum of a sample, the response rate must be at least 85%.
4. The desired target item response rate for each critical variable must be at least 90%.

While uncomfortably rigorous for most studies, the federal standards are clear and set the mark. Few studies in the field meet these standards for sample size, stratification, and selection, even at the outset. Returns are even more problematic, and many studies fall critically short on this criterion. This shortcoming is usually acknowledged in the reports, but users tend to look at the total number of returns and less at the implications of the nonrespondents in the sample. Serious though this error is, the more insidious shortcoming is the nonsampling error. Nonsampling errors include different interpretation of questions by respondents and researcher or, less often, errors in collection or processing. These errors are difficult to identify, and even federal guidelines are vague on qualitative checks of nonsampling errors. However, the NCES standards are clear on the need for pilot testing and documentation. It is in this process of development, or lack of it, where nonsampling errors occur most often. Much reported research falls short in documentation. Limited documentation is understandable, since journals are restricted in space and the information is essentially uninteresting. Since limited background reporting is unlikely to change, caution in interpretation is a more reasonable course than exhortations for additional public documentation. The use of a table of specifications for instrument development is rarely reported. Phrasing, grammar, and the response options in many questionnaires raise doubts about pilot test rigor.

Construct validity is also a difficult standard to determine. Here the field has a serious source of errors that must be engaged. For example, items on questionnaires are bound to be limiting because the framing of the inquiry must be focused to avoid ambiguous or vague items. At the end, responses are aggregated for ease of responding, analysis, and reporting. For instance, in response to the survey item "Is your state involved in the use of telecommunications to provide education either for academic course credit or academic enrichment at the elementary and/or secondary levels?" 90% checked "yes" (England, 1991). A respondent would answer "yes" if any of four conditions existed to some degree: academic credit at the elementary level, academic credit at the secondary level, enrichment at the elementary level, or enrichment at the secondary level. Such a question gives very basic quantitative information that cannot be disaggregated. Operationalizing or reporting the constructs of educational technology in such parsimonious ways truncates the range and richness of the results. Easily quantifiable research reduces the study of educational technology to simple indicators. Yet because surveys are so visible, the findings define the field to the public. This does particular violence to the construct of educational technology in what Clark (1992) describes as equipment-focused or technocentric research.

37.4.1.1. Federal Studies. Publications by the Office of Technological Assessment and most of the survey studies already mentioned are easily accessible. The most current analysis of survey results is Becker's Office of Technology Assessment report (Becker, 1994a). Becker analyzes and compares several seminal surveys, tracks trends, and critiques the technical limits of this research. Likely growth and use of particular technologies, such as the modem, are grounded in survey data cited in the report. A number of Becker's cautions in interpreting the data are insightful lessons in limits of interpretability imposed by compromised methods.

The federal government's annual *Digest of Educational Statistics* is an excellent example of scientific description with continuity (National Center for Education Statistics, 1992a). Federal studies have advantages of access, high return rates, and large samples. The primary charge to NCES, to describe the progress of more than 40 million students, displaces longitudinal or fine-grained studies of facilities, methods, and equipment. However, federally sponsored studies, as opposed to those done directly by NCES, are commissioned through contract and grant mechanisms and offer unique contributions. It is necessary to make a distinction between federal studies and contracted or grant studies reported in federal documents. The databases and methods often differ.

The standards, if not the exemplars, for the survey method are studies done by the National Center for Educational Statistics (1992b). The best of these draw on the Common Core of Data (CCD) for all states and areas. Even with this database, there are problems of slow return or inaccurate reporting, but it is at the top end for the size of population, including over 85,000 public schools, and has procedures to follow up and correct errors. The CCD is intended to be a census, not a sample, of basic statistics on education. Obviously the degree of inference needed is lower for the census studies. The advantage of the CCD base is that it gives a baseline to compare smaller studies using sampling. It is a description of one universe to which we want to generalize.

The methods used to survey technology are not in the same league as the CCD collection methods. Technology and media studies are collected periodically and instruments are frequently revised. The most recently reported federal study of school libraries, for instance, was done in 1985 with a sample of 4,500 public schools and, in 1986, with a sample of 1,700 private schools. These were contracted surveys with satisfactory return rates: 92% for public schools and 85% for private schools. NCES is careful to point out problems in interpretation and fully discloses shortcomings. The obvious concern is that the study was done in 1984–85, and there have been some changes since then in the number of computers, media centers, and software. The next study of this type was conducted in 1995.

Trend analysis using several databases collected by different or private agencies is subject to large error, perhaps as much as 30%, and only the most general changes can be inferred. The sources of data are mixed in NCES reports. Close attention to headings and footnotes is needed to estimate the generalizability of the results. Some, such as student use of computer by level of instruction or household income, is based on unpublished Bureau of the Census data (NCES, 1992c, p. 434). This is sample data, not a census, and based on 1989 data. In the same set of tables, a report on the number of public schools with microcomputers is based on data collected by a commercial marketing research firm, Market Data Retrieval, rather than federal data collection. In some cases, reports are done on contract with supervision by NCES. In other instances, NCES fills in using available sources. The *Digest* is an excellent tool to determine sources, but each source needs to be evaluated on its own merits because methods vary. Obtaining information on methods used by Market Data Retrieval, a subsidiary of Dun & Bradstreet, requires buying the $500 report. This does not mean the methods are suspect, just that they are not easily accessible, and judgments must be reserved.

37.4.1.2. Professional Associations. Association studies are usually important since they originate from a direct need for information. Associations are charged with representing members at the national level, usually in funding and legislation, and maintaining a mailing list. Associations do not usually seek research opportunities. When they do research, it is typically to influence policy and funding decisions. A current study is a National Education Association (NEA) phone survey of teachers. Clearly, NEA is interested in representing the need for federal support for teachers to gain access to technology. Oddly, associations in technology, such as the Association for Educational Communications and Technology (AECT) or the International Society for Technology in Education (ISTE), made up of technology professionals, do not currently research changes in technology at this level. There are surveys of academic programs at the master's and doctoral level which reflect employment in the field (see Ely & Minor, 1993). The development of the profession and training, especially related to certification, is part of the sociology of the field (see 6.3). These and similar reports, such as Roberts's (1985) Corporation for Public Broadcasting survey of Training of Teachers in the Instructional Use of Technology, make significant but loosely connected and isolated contributions to describing the status of educational technology. The Corporation for Public Broadcasting has an active agenda of fund raising through donations and grants. To the degree need can be demonstrated, surveys are used to move funding for PBS up on government and corporate agendas. A research agenda is incidental in these studies.

In higher education, the American Association of Higher Education (AAHE) and institutional computing's EDUCOM are the major organizations at the national level. The focus of AAHE is on teaching and learning and, to some degree, faculty productivity. EDUCOM started as a consortium of campus computer administrators and now focuses on high-level decision makers. Both associations sponsor or endorse surveys. Community college associations are among the most active in professional development and worth contacting for reports. The methods in both associations are mailed surveys. EDUCOM's most recent survey is of computing equipment used at the institutional level and networks. Lukesh's 1987 survey of microcomputers in higher education is one of the most recent full reports. Since this survey includes instructional as well as administrative uses, the results were of value for institutional planning, the administrative population that makes up most of the EDUCOM membership. EDUCOM's method is a census of the 600 member institutions. The reports, though distributed to members, are difficult to find in public collections. A more recent study is Green's (1993) Survey of Desktop Computing, sponsored by EDUCOM and the James Irvine Foundation Center for Scholarly Technology. This series of studies of academic computing continues under the sponsorship of AAHE from 1994 on.

An example of an association survey of technology use in elementary and secondary schools is a National Educa-

tion Association study (National Education Association, 1993). Telephone surveys are unusual in education, so the methods are worth examining. This was a survey of 1,206 teachers. The survey was conducted by Princeton Survey Research Associates on contract. Most surveys deal with newsworthy topics such as computers and video. While these topics are covered, the NEA survey reflects teacher concerns more than those of a market researcher or a journalist. This atypical focus included asking about copying machines, clerical assistance, paper supplies, use of a telephone to call parents, condition of buildings, and other basic resources. The intent is clear. Data showing low levels of available technology can be used to influence policy and funding to increase technology for classroom instruction.

37.4.1.3. Commercial Studies. There are two kinds of surveys in the private sector. The most visible surveys are done by marketing companies. The results are sold to vendors and producers as information for market planning or, most often, as mailing lists that are generated on criteria spelled out by the equipment or materials vendor. In this way, a mailing on a new high-cost item can be targeted to those schools or training groups reporting large recent purchases. This market research is significant in portraying technology to decision makers and the public, and so will be discussed in more detail in the methods section.

Private-sector studies done as for-profit works are important, especially for decision making by equipment manufacturers and material producers. Market Data Retrieval's 1992 report is based on reports from 85% of all public, private, and Catholic schools in the United States. Such studies are detailed in reporting specific brands and options. But even commercial surveys now collect data on training and in-service. The high cost for published results, usually several hundred dollars, limits access to businesses or large agencies with discretionary budgets. For example, the 1993 discounted price for QED's School Trend Series is $1,495 (Quality Education Data Catalog, 1993).

The second kind of commercial survey is done by trade organizations. Trade association studies are usually not available beyond the membership of the association. The databases and findings are used by lobbyists and members of the association, but the influence of both methods and findings must be acknowledged as significant in shaping the field. For example, the Software Publishers Association (SPA) figures represent reported sales by vendors. As with most such studies, the quantitative information on sales are by company and regarded as proprietary, so they are only reported in aggregated total for the approximately 1,000 members of the association. To disseminate the findings, the Software Publishers Association uses press releases rather than published studies. SPA (1993) findings are noteworthy because they provide unique information. For instance, the sales volume of home education software in North America for the first half of 1993 was over $73 million. We can determine that something is being disseminated. Beyond that, the methods are not verifiable. Members of the association furnish their sales figures to an accounting firm, Arthur Anderson, to maintain confidentiality. While there is no indication which companies reported, one could assume the information reported is likely valid. The cautions in using such data are obvious. The number of respondents, mortality of poorly performing vendors, and the representativeness of the association membership are not available. Generalizability is severely limited when the responding population is either undefined or small. However, the cautions observed by the research community are not necessarily applied in generating or using these data. The results of the Software Association survey, disseminated as a press release, will be used in lobbying funding agencies, and may influence policy in ways the formal research community seldom achieves. As a research activity, the reported work of marketing companies approaches minimum standards. The trade association data are significant in forming public perceptions and must be acknowledged, but the data can only be used for forming testable hypotheses in diffusion research.

37.4.1.4. State and Local Studies. State and local studies, including doctoral dissertations, make up the larger volume of research. These are usually limited in scope, not replicated, and poorly disseminated. Most are best left to a local audience, since knowledge of the population and collection procedures are needed to interpret results. For instance, a survey of who uses TV, computers, and film/video by Computer Using Educators (CUE) had 125 responses (Marshall, 1993). The number, instrumentation, the sampling technique, and the demographics of the respondents were not reported. This does not mean the survey was faulty or that these were not known, but that any use of the four-page analysis is more an illustrative case than quantitative research, even though numbers are used. Most valuable in the study may be the more qualitative comments such as responding nonusers of TV reporting scheduling difficulties and access problems. These face valid findings point the way for studies of barriers to use.

37.4.1.5. Dissertations Studies. The details of a dissertation study are more public than other studies, and some of the best work is done at this level. Few established professionals work as hard as students do in constructing a literature review. The result is that a dissertation on a topic of interest is an excellent place to start a new search. However, as a group, there are limits. Dissertations usually lack longitudinal data, and the economic constraints of graduate students often mean the study is limited in scope. Fortunately, since the procedures used are detailed in a dissertation, each study can be taken on its own merits.

A number of states are gradually accumulating trend data on the installed base of technologies. How often equipment is used, who uses it, and for what purposes are now categories commonly included in studies. Most start with simple measurements: "How many television receivers do you have in your district?" The next level of sophistication is determining the ratio of machines to teachers or students and the kind of programs used. It is also typical that more detail on use and the demographics of respondents are

collected. This is often part of policy development and, with the establishment of telecommunications groups in state departments, provides justification for funding. This accumulation will no doubt continue. Unlike student or facility counts, the technology database in states is not commonly maintained by law or mandate. This leaves the form and focus of data collection open to reinvention with changes in technologies and agendas. Rapid changes in technology make the reinvention desirable, but the lack of consistent data over time makes prediction less trustworthy, since trend data are lost.

37.4.2 Case Analysis

An example is often more informative than a definition. A study by Honey and Henriquez (1993), "Telecommunications and K-12 Educators: Findings from a National Survey," provides important information and illustrates typical problems in using a single study beyond the respondent population. The study was funded by a grant from the Office of Educational Research and Improvement, U.S. Department of Education. This study of accomplished users joins an embryonic body of studies on the characteristics of those teachers who are deeply involved in technology (e.g., Becker, 1994b).

This study has clear antecedents and intent. Honey and Henriquez grounded the study in three strands of literature: educational reform, collegial collaboration, and student learning. The grounding provides a face valid rationale and significance for the study. The intent of the survey was to provide a profile of telecommunications activities used by current K-12 educators. The sample was limited to educators who were current users. This type of study is found in other areas, most notably the "wellness" studies in the health field. How educators become users of technology is at the heart of diffusion research.

The criteria for analysis and judgment of this work (logical validity, sampling, instrumentation, nonrespondent bias, conclusions) are adapted from Smith and Glass (1987). The categories are traditional validity and reliability concerns of survey research. They are used here to facilitate the analysis, which is not exhaustive, but rather illustrative of the strengths and limits of this type of study.

1. *Logical validity.* This criterion compares the congruity of the study purpose with the questions, population, and conclusions. The purpose of Honey and Henriquez's study was to determine the types of telecommunications activities being conducted by teachers for either professional development or student learning. Telecommunications is defined as computer-based information systems utilizing modems hooked up to computers that allow communication over telephone lines. This is limited but clear. Sensational wording, such as "cyberspace interactivity," is avoided.

To the casual reader, the use of "national survey" in the title may imply a random sample of teachers and create a mindset for generalization to the national level. However, the authors are careful to describe the population so that any conclusions can be interpreted with clear limits. There had been no systematic analysis of the range and type of telecommunications activities of teachers who are heavy users of new technologies. Additionally, by using respondents' comments, the study documents the benefits and obstacles in using telecommunications from a user's perspective. Technology is being largely defined by equipment and databases used.

2. *Population and sampling.* The population of interest was K-12 educators using telecommunications. A study to describe a population must have a sample from that population, preferably stratified in the same proportions. Since the study was to find out what telecommunication-using teachers do, sampling the larger population of teachers was not within the purpose. The researchers announced the study and requested participation through electronic networks. This makes it likely that the respondents were in fact telecommunications users, but not all or even representative of the universe of teachers or users. The respondents in this study can be described as a convenience, volunteer, or purposive sample. The researchers compared demographics from the Federal Common Core of Data to survey respondents. They noted a number of differences that suggest the responding population differed from the K-12 universe. The comparison provides an excellent perspective for interpreting the findings. For instance, 29% of the respondents were from rural schools, and 39% from suburban schools. The CCD figures are 55% for rural schools and 18% for suburban. The bias toward suburban schools is clear. The quality of the study is determined more by the clarity of this comparison by the researchers than the representativeness. Readers may easily be misled in studies where population comparisons are not as explicit as they were in this study. However, the title of the study can still lead the casual reader to believe that the "national survey" included all teachers.

This approach begs the question of how representative the sample is of the universe of telecommunications-using teachers. The size of the population, the differences among the population, and thus the differences in response are not determined. The respondents are not a random sample of telecommunications-using teachers; to generalize to such a population would amount to pure speculation.

3. *Instrumentation.* The standards for development at the federal level require piloting and revision. The final survey form in this study was a 30-page questionnaire. The report included a section on the development of the instrument. Five focus groups were used to develop specifications for the instrument. Developing a questionnaire from a table of specifications or map is a recommended step. Piloting of the draft was not described. This is a step frequently omitted because it takes considerable time. While piloting may have been done, this is a point where nonsampling errors are made.

One detailed example illustrates the level of analysis needed to judge a study. Typically, there are item validity questions. It is the degree to which an item is vague or ambiguous that must be determined. Different referents for a word or idea are difficult to identify, especially for authors. For instance, item 36a is to be rated on an agreement scale from 1 to 6. The item "Telecommunications helps students to gain familiarity with basic computer applications and helps them become computer literate adults" could be difficult to answer, since there are two parts. "Basic computer applications" may fall short of a teacher's definition of what it means to be "computer literate." This does not seem a serious flaw, but the two-part question has more than two answers. Measured reliability, validity (reactivity), and other technical concerns are not reported. Generally we are asked to assume these have been checked.

4. *Mortality.* Those who do not respond in survey research are more likely to be forgetful or busy than dead. To determine reasons for nonresponse, phone calls and sampling of nonrespondents can be done to measure differences, if any, between respondents and nonrespondents. This step is often ignored because of the additional time required. In this study there were 1,100 responses to the e-mail solicitation for participants, with a final response rate of 50% (550). This is far below the 95% standard set by the National Center for Educational Statistics. This clearly limits generalizability. However, the purpose of the study was not to generalize but to describe a unique population. The responsible reporting of the response rate redeems any error in fulfilling the purpose of the study. That is, if the data are used to generate testable hypotheses, the purpose has been served.

5. *Conclusions.* Sometimes claims, generalizations, go far beyond the data. There are several levels of conclusions in most reports. Those justified by the data are easy to identify by the empirical evidence. The next level, claims made on the basis of inference, are usually plausible. Implications are generally understood to be predictions. The focus of this part of the analysis is on the extent of the generalizations and the degree to which they are justified by the data.

Within the report, findings are presented in concise low-inference statements. The authors reported that 78% of the teachers were in telecommunications because they were "personally intrigued by the technology," and that 88% were self-taught, mostly by attending conferences on topics of interest. At the next level of inference, they report the findings that strongly suggest that school support of telecommunication at school or district level is virtually nonexistent. They carefully limit the conclusions by reiterating the findings to "suggest that these educators represent a very specialized group" (p. 34). At the next level, the implications or predictions based on the findings are framed as recommendations. Here again, the interpretation is conservative. They also appeal to face validity and are similar to findings in other studies. For instance, the conclusion that "phone lines need to become much more widely available in schools" if telecommunications are to be used can be logically concluded from the evidence and is supported by the finding of the NEA study that only 12% of teachers have phone lines in their classrooms.

In summary, the study contributes to an important new area of inquiry. It is not rigorous in the traditional sense of high internal validity. Yet more valid implications can be drawn from the data collected than were reported. The study is readable, cautious, and useful. It succeeds in the authors' intent to be sensitive to the respondents and "reflect their stories." They clearly report most of the soft areas of survey research. The use of focus groups was appropriate as a technique and a service to mention as a process. Pilot testing of the form was, as usual, not reported, though it was done. The soft areas are typical—low returns, convergent items, no longitudinal plans, no triangulation for validity—resulting, finally, in limited generalizability. Overall, the study is an excellent exploratory contribution and stakes out very promising areas for further research and development.

The purpose of this section was to illustrate some of the concerns addressed in an analysis and critique of a research study. While the study itself is well done, the method and stage of inquiry limit generalization or application. The next section uses this same analytical framework as implicit criteria to summarize survey findings in general.

37.4.3 Findings

What do the findings tell us about the diffusion of educational technology? Reported findings show continued and increasing diffusion of the artifacts of technology in all sectors. Not reported are sales or use of less-popular technologies or those of low market value. What is reported tells us of public and private interest. What is not reported could provide us with the contrasts we need to determine the success or failure of diffusion of a technology. The findings do not address learning or teaching. The implications for learning and teaching are, however, potentially profound. The findings do support claims of growing technology availability in education.

It is reasonable to expect this type of research study to continue because the advantages of mailed surveys to a sample population are several. The most compelling is low cost. The need to produce data and identify trends can easily be satisfied with the results. Perhaps the most dangerous flaw among these studies is the lack of information on sampling and response rate. No one expects a single study to be without error. Sampling procedures and respondent mortality are weak points in all such research. It is the degree of possible error that we need to judge. When data are arrayed as though the entire population of schools is sampled, then it is important to have evidence that the assertion is supported. Returns from nontechnology schools and small schools are always in smaller proportion than suburban technology-using schools. The respondents must

be stratified on several criteria to determine how the data apply to a given population of interest. These cautions represent a significant area of concern because such errors are not usually part of the publicized results. The advantages of surveys are obvious, but the weaknesses are hidden.

Surveys are at their best in tracing trends. In a national survey of higher education, Green (1993) reports that campus networks are the top priority for institutions in all sectors (scale score of 6.3, up from 6.2 in 1992 and 6.1 in 1991). Networking issues rank highest in research universities, although the gap has narrowed across institutional segments in the past 2 years. Indeed, nearly three-fourths (73%) of the respondents indicate that networking issues are "more important this year than last," up from 69% in 1992. The finding that may be most important in such studies may be that there is what economists term *market pull.* Education is not a passive market for technology. At this point, there is little need for a market push of technology by manufacturers and vendors. Education wants and is planning for technological growth. Where the demand has been passive, there are incentives to move schools to planning. Texas, the best example, implemented a policy giving each district a starting technology allotment of $30 per student, an allotment scheduled to increase through the year 2000, and requires in turn that 75% be spent on classroom-based technology. Allotments go only to districts that submit a 5-year technology plan and report (Kinnaman, 1992). Policies that create funding create market demand. The survey interest, however, is in what the schools acquire, not in what students will learn. The focus on equipment is most clear in marketing studies.

A market research study by Quality Education Data (QED) (1992) reported that 98% of all schools have microcomputers in 1992 compared to 37% for 1982. The dollar figures from sales surveys increase each quarter, and market shares held by competing manufacturers change. These findings are reported as news. For instance, the Software Publishers Association reports Windows applications accounted for 56% of all word-processing program sales in the second quarter of 1993, compared to 11% for Macintosh. This seems closer to a business report than an educational technology study. The difference may be only in the emphasis on sales and dollar figures. The same news release from the Software Publishers Association (1993) showed that home education was the fastest-growing software category. Here are data that can form the basis for testable and significant hypotheses. We can empirically determine that the cost threshold for home buyers of MS-DOS machines has been reached and that equipment sales are increasing in the home market. Home education software sales are increasing because the machines are below the price breakpoint for home consumers. This fact may be an incidental finding for the association but one with major implications for education and training. Because education is a small market compared to other sectors, there are no data reported. The challenge in much of these data is teasing out the implications on a speculative tightrope supported by the quality of the research design. The balance is made difficult, since emotions about such things as platforms, Macintosh versus MS-DOS, make survey results news, while research design is often seen as an uninteresting minor technical issue.

The methodological concern of aggregated data without a context of use is an understandable insufficiency in commercial studies. The industry is interested in sales rather than use. The attention paid to these studies means that professionals who see themselves as change agents must know the limits and findings. For instance, Market Data Retrieval (MDR) reports that modem "penetration" in schools is about 65% in a study sampling of 3,927 districts with 31,172 schools (Market Data Retrieval, 1993). Limits of the finding are easy to list: Modems may be used for attendance reports, school lunch programs, and administrative e-mail, as well as for instructional uses. Since administrative uses are usually implemented before instructional uses, a small portion of modem use is attributable to teachers or students. District staff are survey respondents, not school administrators or classroom teachers. The respondent mortality may be high and selective. Stripped of context then, the data are of only rudimentary use. The cost of a more fine-grained analysis is so high that the nature of most market research is unlikely to change dramatically.

There are frustrating differences between databases. QED reported that 33% of districts and 22% of schools have modems (QED, 1992). MDR reported that the percentage of schools with modems for 1993 at 64.8% (Market Data Retrieval, 1993). While one expects results to differ, a contrast of this magnitude means significant reporting or sample differences. The difference is great enough so that conclusions, except that there is growth, must be tentative. These results could be an artifact of the modem, something small enough that it can be overlooked as easily as overestimated. Another comparison can make the case. Integrated learning systems (ILS) are major investments and major changes for schools. The MDR results show 20% of the schools have ILS. QED found 45.6% (QED, 1992, p. 94). QED reports discuss sample size and return rate, and include a copy of the instrument. The responding sample was 217 districts for the study. MDR based figures on 3,927 districts.

In the 2-year comparison, Market Data Retrieval reported that four technologies increased by 100%: CD-ROM drives, videodisc players, local area networks, and distance learning. Additionally, integrated learning systems and downlinks were almost at the 100% increase level. The spread among districts was small compared to the growth in schools that were in high-use districts in the 1991 study. These data can be valuable if used within the limits of the sample. The findings do suggest that there is something to look at in districts with high use, and that high use builds on itself. The increase within those districts is dramatic, and budgets were found to support the growth—significant factors well worth studying. The caution is that data are

from a subset of the total population, and generalization is limited. The vendors of the data, asking $495 for this report, do not emphasize the limited generalizability of the data. The results are often presented in speeches and testimony in which the context and limits are omitted. The effect of overgeneralization may not be dramatic since most decision makers are suspicious of all data. It may, however, create an expectation in the public's perception of what is going on in schools. Where no other data are available, questionable data fill in.

Skewing of data is not limited to special-interest sectors. Public and private research suffers from a bias toward positive results. We know that a number of technologies have dropped by the wayside and are not much examined. Language laboratories, for instance, at least in premultimedia configurations, are gradually disappearing. There are reasons for this shift that could provide fruitful inquiry and guidance for other technologies, but few want to report failures in detail.

37.4.4 Summary

Equipment surveys have and do inform policy. For the most part, the picture is accurate in identifying trends, but there is a lack of continuity. The problem is that in one year television is the focus of surveys; another year, computers, with no overlap and no follow-up after political and commercial interests wane. This has left some gaps, especially in less-newsworthy technologies. Regrettably, other kinds of studies, those describing use, have not balanced out the larger picture of technology in education. Cohen cited a study from the turn of the century that found that the flexibility of the textbook let the innovation be adapted to existing practice rather than opening new ways of teaching. "The very attribute that innovators thought would revolutionize education made it easy for schools to adapt this innovation to existing organization and purposes" (Cohen, 1988, p. 235).

The federal government has provided the most consistent survey program about education issues in the *Digest of Educational Statistics* (see National Center for Education Statistics, 1992a). Reports of Department of Education expenditures for television and other instructional equipment start in 1968. From a 1975 high of $19 million, expenditures went to a low of $2 million in 1980. Such trend statistics imply rapid change in priorities. Rapid changes such as a $17 million reduction whipsaws the commercial sector and drastically affects planning by educators.

Does this research capture what is going on in educational technology? Along one dimension, yes. Small research budgets, large numbers of schools, and widely geographic distribution have lead to the use of mailed surveys in diffusion studies. The time and cost of more detailed information, such as site visits, or even frequent or extensive mailings, are beyond education research and development budgets. If the kind of information needed is simple description, and that alone, survey methods are appropriate. Surveying equipment in schools is an important strand of research, but the absence of surveys of use, especially those using good qualitative techniques, leave us with a one-dimensional picture. The major concern with this method is construct validity. Survey research captures one kind of activity in educational technology. Survey results are powerful in policy and commercial applications but inadequate in providing for understanding of motivation, processes, and successful or unsuccessful teaching or learning interventions.

37.4.5 Recommendations

The databases on diffusion are in their infancy. The discussion of combining databases, such as Hilton's (1992) work on unifying national databases in educational research, are at a large aggregate level where educational technology and information literacy do not have enough presence to merit a footnote. The quality and quantity of data collected in such work as the Research Triangle Institute National Science Survey or the Metropolitan Achievement Tests set standards that we do not, and likely never will, meet. Nor perhaps do we need to. These set the high end of the scale. It is in quality and consistency that diffusion studies can be most fruitfully improved. Long-term trends reliably and validly collected do have value.

Existing data have considerable untapped potential for secondary and tertiary analyses. Becker (1991), Cuban (1986), and Cohen (1988) have made good use of existing data to develop arguments and support one policy or another. The corpus of Becker's work represents the best use of quantitative data, and Cohen's the widest societal scope. Many of the databases are available in machine-readable form, and all have latent insights to be drawn out. The School District Data Book electronic database combines the NCES information on 17,000 school districts with the 1990 census, providing the best available data in easy access form. All one needs are good questions.

Secondary analysis of valid, reliable data is more valuable than a primary study with serious sampling flaws. The conceptual challenge in secondary analysis is more than the simple numerical reporting of responses: It offers an analysis of data with resulting insights of comparison and objectivity inherently unavailable to the primary researcher. This is advanced as the single most consequential recommendation for existing diffusion research. It is also an area for significant and efficient dissertation work that is often overlooked in the belief that "original" data must be collected. The value of another underfinanced survey by a graduate student trying to complete a study by May pales compared to the potential of analyses and comparison of the best available data collected at great expense by some of the best survey researchers in education. With increasing size and availability of databases, secondary analysis is becoming more accepted.

Commercial market research can improve the quality of data collection with changes in sampling and context of use questions. The changes in sampling need not include a larger initial sampling, since the total already exceeds the size used by most national polls. The sampling does need focused follow-through to obtain returns from a proportionally stratified sample.

The use of context questions is a delicate balance between the length of the survey, the patience of the respondent, and detailed information. The degree to which more detailed information can be collected can be determined empirically, but matrix sampling, using different questions within a set total survey form, is a first step. Academic researchers with less of a stake in reporting sales may advocate for different designs. These designs are not precluded by market research in the private sector and may, in fact, be welcomed.

Descriptive research at the national level, especially in the Department of Education, has been the mainstay of diffusion studies. Data on use and context are becoming more common, and sophistication is growing. The continuity of this database is the best available, but it too is subject to the vagaries of popular interest that appear and disappear as a function of budget and political agendas. It is unlikely that nationally funded surveys will show brands of computers by districts as the market researchers do, but they can focus on conditions of use and adaptation in detail. Dissertation descriptive research suffers from unreplicated one-shot studies, and surveys by states are directly connected to political or policy opportunities. Taken as a whole, a great deal can be gleaned from such studies, but there is generally no unifying review of this work. The closest is Becker's (1994a) summary for the Office of Technological Assessment.

Survey research will continue for policy and marketing decisions and budget leverage, and as grist for dissertations. Following trends over time has value if the field takes time to reflect on the meaning of such trends. Writers such as Cuban (1986), Pea (1988), and Cohen (1988) lift the discussion from counting equipment to paradigmatic propositions. Their models can lead to higher-level generalizations for practice. Their work is less quantitative and more conceptually complex; the field, if not the public, must turn to such thinkers or be forever mired in numbers rather than knowledge.

37.5 CORRELATIONAL STUDIES OF VARIABLES

The second category, correlational studies, is similar to survey research. It is still basic description but provides more support for inferences. Many of the speculations drawn from surveys are logical but without empirical support. The correlational studies give support for relationships, though causality is still a matter of speculation. Correlational studies move beyond counting to relationships among demographics and variables such as personality or training. A key difference between correlational studies and diffusion surveys is that personality, stage of implementation, and other differentiating characteristics at the individual or site level take on greater significance.

37.5.1 Dominant Paradigm of Change

The majority of the correlational studies stem from innovation diffusion literature. This literature has been more focused on developing generalizations and tentative hypotheses about change. At the empirical level, theory is not used as a guide. However, practitioners frequently use the data to support a theory borrowed from another area, especially psychology, such as Bandura's theory of self-efficacy or Lewin's change theory, to categorize data. For instance, Jorde-Bloom (1988) investigated the relationship between self-efficacy expectations (after Bandura) and computer use by early childhood administrators. The assumption was that the adoption of technological innovations is to some degree a function of an individual's feelings of self-efficacy. This self-efficacy in large part regulates the degree of commitment and ego involvement that individuals are willing to invest in implementation of the innovation. To determine this, a 12-page questionnaire was mailed to measure both the independent and dependent variables. The method, then, is similar to that used in equipment surveys. Visits to sites, interactive data from qualitative interviews, and triangulation from other data sources were not part of the study. However, the intent of the study is clearly different. The relationship between personality and use of technology is focused on human variations across sites. Early studies of diffusion and adoption behavior found significant correlations between some traits and innovation. In a summary, Rogers and Shoemaker (1971) reported that "earlier adopters are less dogmatic than later adopters. Dogmatism is a variable representing a relatively closed belief system . . . " (p. 187). The higher a score on a dogmatism scale, the less likely a subject was to innovate.

The data in this category are not experimental, and the use of theory is often post hoc. Gillman (1988) identified 14 out of 70 research reports that used some form of experimental design in studying microcomputer implementation. The 20% that were attempts at more causal statements generally suffer from small populations and idiosyncratic treatments. There are, after a decade, few experimental studies to draw on. Studies that focus on isolated instances of learning may guide development of instruction but have little to do with the factors that affect diffusion or implementation.

Development of models to explain diffusion events is more common than theory among researchers in this tradition. For instance, in a body of practical studies by the Minnesota Extension Service, "A Technology Adoption

Model" (Morehouse & Stockdill, 1991), a five-stage adoption process is proposed from four case studies. This is not as slim a base as it seems, since there is a large body of research to give face validity to such generalizations.

The popularity of prescriptive and causal models stem from the empirical base of an S-shaped curve of adoption that makes isomorphism or similarities obvious in different lines of research. The similarity of findings across disciplines leads to comparisons and proposals for a common model:

> In particular, diffusion models [using the sigmoid curve] have been developed to represent the level or spread of an innovation among a given set of prospective adopters in a social system in terms of a simple mathematical function of the time that has elapsed from the introduction of the innovation (Mahajan & Peterson, 1985 p. 10).

This diffusion pattern is also true of education in general. Since any study, quantitative or qualitative, is time and resource intensive, a slim base of studies of diffusion of educational technology is advanced by drawing heavily on a research tradition of studies across disciplines.

Work by Rogers (1983) in weaving together almost two dozen research traditions in innovation shows the value of this approach. The weakness is that differences in settings and culture are less apparent. Cuban (1993) holds that schools as institutions are substantially different from businesses, industries, and other organizations. Further, technology is resisted because of "certain cultural beliefs about what teaching is, how learning occurs, what knowledge is proper in schools, and the teacher-student relationship" (p. 86). Still, the diffusion curve remains the same in education, even if the reasons for decisions by educators are different from other sectors.

Berman and McLaughlin (1975, 1977) reported on federal programs and change in education. These studies were important methodological and substantive contributions. The series, done with federal grant monies through the Rand Corporation from 1973 to 1978, is widely cited in education, especially the change literature, and generalized far beyond the initial data. The generalizations from the series have been updated by occasional articles. The original recommendations for effective strategies in implementation, such as teacher participation in project decisions, or that adoption and implementation or continuation are different processes, have become doctrine in change literature. Subsequent commentary expands the original themes (McLaughlin, 1990). The original study was post hoc. The factors identified as associated with change were identified from what McLaughlin (1990) describes as top-down study . . . reflecting "macro-level concerns, not micro-level realities" (p. 14). Part of the transition is recognition that local variability is the rule and that uniformity is the exception. McLaughlin observes that "variability has been an anathema to policymakers and cast as the plague of efforts to reform schools because it signaled uneven local responses to policy objectives" (p. 13). In this, she comes close to

House (1991) in focusing on specific settings and specific solutions rather than generalizing. This "local" theme anticipates the next section on action research. Much of the same tradition in education is represented in Fullan's (1992) work on educational change.

37.5.2 Factors in Change

To identify a teacher as a technology user, as Honey and Henriquez (1993) did, does not address the process of how to implement change. However, they identify likely reasons these teachers are technology users, what factors in their experience lead them to develop skills and motivate them to use technology in teaching, and further, what these users perceive as barriers to use. If we know that professional communication and materials preparation are the most important reported uses of technology by teachers, then those activities are more likely to be appealing in training sessions than techniques for a large number of students to use a small number of computers. More efficient diffusion and effective adaptation can be developed using the findings.

The addition of different variables as well as the limitations of the data are clear. Cohen and Forde (1992) surveyed 59 dental schools to determine factors supportive of development of instructional technology. This is in the mainstream of survey method, but it does include measures that lead the authors to conclude that faculty felt unrewarded for innovation. So, while expected variables and findings are reported (testing and record keeping were the most common computer applications; individualized instruction and paper-and-pencil simulation are used in most schools; support services influence technology use), qualities such as "unenthusiastic" or "unrewarded" pave the way for prescriptive generalizations. The "perception" variables—those beyond a physical count of equipment, hours of use, and training—set these studies apart from the descriptive survey genre.

A study of 400 Kentucky elementary teachers and factors supportive of instructional technology has similar conclusions. The general findings indicated that the frequency with which instructional technology was used in the classroom was related to: (1) the availability of technological hardware in the classroom, building, and district media center, in that order; (2) the amount of teacher input into the purchase of hardware and software; (3) the level of administrative encouragement; and (4) the amount of training teachers had in the use of each medium (Henry, 1987). This kind of study is still basic survey and description. However, variables such as administrative encouragement reflect a search for ways to change existing practice.

The next evolution of complexity is captured in a survey of 231 teachers by Wiley (1992). Wiley used measures of "Attitudes Toward Computer Usage Scale" (ATCUS), a form of the "ENLIST Micros" knowledge instrument, the "Stages of Concern Questionnaire" (SoCQ), and the "Computer Needs of Teacher and Students." The measure of perceptions or attitudes is a large part of this study, and it is these variables that distinguish this category. The use of a discriminant analysis to compare groups of teachers who were participants and nonparticipants in computer-related staff development again reflects the prescriptive change intent. It also shows a more sophisticated statistical analysis than used in most survey research. The discriminant analysis is a good selection for exploration, since the contributions of different variables can be measured. A lack of statistical significance found by Wiley suggests a common problem in the social sciences. The concepts are difficult to operationalize or measure, and there is considerable measurement error as well as confounding of variables in a field setting.

Separate from the statistical analysis, Wiley found that teachers may view educational computing as an "add-on" to the existing curriculum. Wiley projects that teachers' concerns may be redirected to the "impact" phase through staff development programs that are aligned with concerns. The perspective of the adopter, in this case the teacher, is an important marker in this study. The factor is measured in terms of attitude toward technology and as a function of the personal history of implementation. This presages a constructivist model that turns to the adopter's point of view as the significant reality. Proposing ways to change, in this case by training, is typical of both technology studies and studies of innovation in general.

That teachers may view educational computing as an add-on (Wiley, 1992) is common in education. Anderson and others (1979) selected teachers in a study because they are different from clerical workers or computer-related professionals for whom computer use is required. For educators, there is a choice. Nowhere is choice more an article of faith than in higher education. Todd (1992) reported on faculty concerns in integrating computer technologies into teacher education at the university level. The variables are typical of this type of study. Faculty concerns were assessed with a "Stages of Concern About an Innovation" questionnaire. Todd used existing course objectives, a guide for computer-based technology practice (Sheingold & Hadley, 1990), a computer guideline from a professional association (International Society for Technology in Education), and a technology evaluation item as dependent variables. Different concerns by faculty related to different uses they made of the technology. This differentiation is a rich guide to addressing adopter concerns.

Moving across national boundaries shows dissemination effects of culture and economics. Pelgrum's (1993) analysis of attitudes of school principals and teachers towards computers in 14 countries found significant variations among countries and between those who use and those who do not use computers. The Pelgrum analyses used data from the International Association for the Evaluation of Educational Achievement, the sponsor of the 1987 International Computers in Education Study (see also Pelgrum & Plomp, 1993). The causal relationship of variance in attitude on use of technology is supported by these studies.

To push this line of research one step further, a study rejecting the traditional rationale for adoption serves as a pointer to a different focus in research on implementation. Anderson, Hansen, Johnson, and Klassen (1979) surveyed 3,576 secondary school teachers of mathematics, science, and business education—half of whom had adopted instructional computing—to determine factors related to acceptance and rejection. This NSF-supported study was reported in the journal *Sociology of Work and Occupations,* far outside the mainstream of educational research but in the center of the research tradition in innovation. The authors state that the study provides a test for technological versus cultural theories of social change. They further cite Schramm, a major figure in educational technology, and class him as a technological determinist who holds that adoption is a function of cost, efficiency, and similar factors. They grant that the technological determinism perspective has value but does not account for adoption behavior. Anderson and others (1979) hold that sociocultural factors of attitudes and setting must be taken into account for a complete explanation of the variance in adoption behavior. Mitchell's (1990) findings that "innovations in information technology . . . appear to be diffused most successfully in components of the educational system not directly related to instruction" (p. 89) suggest differences among populations in education.

Anderson and others (1979) use multiple regression analysis to demonstrate the necessity of sociological analysis of acceptance and rejection of computer innovations. They conclude that individual, occupational, school, and community factors are all predictive of adoption of computer technology. At the macro-level, Herbig (1994) concludes that:

> the barriers to innovation are almost never technological but rather social, political, financial, or economic. The primary barriers to such innovation in any society are (1) the structure of the society itself and the state of business, political, and educational institutions; (2) the society's "reward system" or lack of it; (3) attitudes and concepts among the labor force and philosophy of the people involved; (4) the political forces; and (5) any standards which are based on product rather than performance expectations (p. 140).

37.5.3 Case Analysis

The study selected for analysis, "Socioeconomic Status and the Early Diffusion of Personal Computing in the United States," is by Dutton, Sweet, and Rogers (1989). This example captures a feel for the diffusion research tradition through the influence of the third author, Everett Rogers, originally a rural sociologist, who summarized and popularized innovation research. The variables, socioeconomics and diffusion, move us beyond counting equipment and toward examining context variables.

This study is not about schools. It is the kind of study that precedes educational technology. It deals with the factors that develop the capacity to use educational technology. Use of computers in the home is most likely, on the face of it, to be work related. A secondary market factor is entertainment. With this installed base, the $73-million-dollar sale of educational software in the first half of 1993 reported by Software Publishers Association makes logical sense. It is a very large market. A market this large will have an effect on what is available in smaller markets, including education. The authors clearly ground the analysis in the larger corpus of diffusion literature and anticipate that a number of studies must be done to develop strong generalizations. Still, most readers of the study will be interested in the content, not the research tradition, and read the findings without reflecting on the design. The analysis is to show the limits of the findings.

The criteria for judging the survey (logical validity, sampling, instrumentation, nonrespondent bias, conclusions) are after Smith and Glass (1987). The categories are traditional validity and reliability concerns of survey research. They are used here to facilitate the analysis. The analysis is not exhaustive but illustrative of the strengths and limits of this type of study.

1. *Logical validity.* This category is to compare the congruity of the study purpose with the questions, population, and conclusions. The purpose of the study was to determine socioeconomic factors related to adoption of home computing. The dependent variable was having a computer in the home. Dutton and others (1989) concluded that socioeconomic factors were significantly related to having a computer at home.

The logical connection is easy to follow. A member of each identified household with a computer was asked about socioeconomic status. A mulivariate analysis was used to reduce findings. Similar studies were identified and summarized to support the significance of the socioeconomic factors selected. The study clearly achieved this standard.

2. *Population and sampling.* A study to describe a population must have a sample of that population, preferably stratified in the same proportions. This was a secondary analysis. The population was a database available to academic researchers. The sample size was 1,561 households. A commercial firm (Harris & Associates) collected the data in 1983 as a national probability sample.

Secondary analysis is generally laudable, since much of the cost of research is in the data collection. Few databases are exhaustively analyzed. This sample size is large enough to meet the assumptions of multivariate analysis. The selection process is not reported, and the commercial firm generally does not make reports public since they are contract work, in this case for a telephone company. The population, the selection, and their characteristics are not reported or easily determined. The source cited in the article, a conference paper, does not appear in the ERIC database. However, in this case what appears to be a report of the original study on privacy is in ERIC under Westin (1979). This report is 4 years earlier than the date of the paper cited in the article. If the 1983 citation was in fact based on the 1979 study, we know that the stage of evolution of home computing in 1979—2 years at most after the personal computer was marketed—is different from home computing in 1989, 10 years later. The authors express concern about the findings being "transient" and point out several factors, especially cost, that have changed since the original data were collected.

The total proportion of computer households in the sample is small. For a total population in a total of 1,409 respondents, 1,248 did not have computers and 152 responses had missing data. This leaves 161 computer households distributed over six categories. One cell has three respondents. In other tables, cells under 30 are common. While the statistical technique is robust, the assumption of homoscedasticity is not achieved.

3. *Instrumentation.* The standards for development at the federal level require piloting and revision. Harris & Associates is a professional opinion poll firm with a national presence. However, the techniques used are not reported. At this point, research can become a matter of faith and authority. The primary difficulty with this is that the particular kinds of questions asked, however well selected and refined, may have a slightly different meaning that is obvious only in reviewing the questions themselves. Since this study was for a telephone company and focused on privacy, the context of the original data collect differs from the use made in this study. This does not mean it is wrong, of course, just that interpretation must be cautious since we have the answers and not the questions.

4. *Mortality.* In survey studies, mortality deals with nonrespondent bias. The researchers chose the database because it had less selection bias than similar databases. Other databases focused on owners of personal computers, while this one defined having a computer in the household as the selection criterion. The "owner" criterion in those studies eliminated computer-using households where the computer was owned by an employer. The refusal of households to participate in the study is not reported. The number of cases with missing data was reported for each variable examined.

5. *Conclusions.* Did the method of analysis support the conclusions? Such variables as tricotomized income were correlated with computer and noncomputer households. The conclusions were that income played a more pivotal role in the early diffusion of personal computing than previously thought. Education and occupation have indirect effects, while income has a significant direct effect. The analysis, based on correlations to examine how findings fit with theoretical assumptions, showed a large number of significant relationships at or above the .001 level. However, as the authors note, socioeconomic status accounts for only a small proportion of the total variance in adoption of this technology. They also note that "more intensive, participant-observer research is needed" (p. 268). In this vein Giacquinta, Bauer, and Levin (1993) found in their 3-year qualitative study that children use computers in the home mostly for games. This kind of finding requires a participant-observer, or at least an on-site observer, for data collection. This leaves us with well-framed questions and suggestions for research. It would have been incorrect to go further with the data. At the same time, the understanding of diffusion remains at an abstract level for practitioners. The most likely problem in this study is that the data are over a decade old. The recent publication date obscures the outdated database.

37.5.4 Findings

The diffusion research tradition is as demonstrable a paradigm in education as in other sectors. Adoption curves from diffusion data are similar to other sectors. This makes it tempting to generalize reasons for adoption from diffusion findings. It is here that the findings of studies on diffusion of technology in education provide little guidance. Studies based on adoption data generate the familiar sigmoid adoption curve, true. But it is not clear what factors account for this distribution. Significant factors in other sectors, such as improved output, standardization, or better control, are not easily generalized to teaching and learning settings, nor do the studies use teaching and learning as dependent variables.

There are differences in adopters' perceptions over time in the adoption process (Gilberson-Anderson, 1992). This study also found differences among educators. Innovators, for instance, believe that education can benefit as much from technology as society has benefited. (Early innovators have been described as different from other adopters, especially in risk taking, throughout innovation research.) A key shift in the focus of research is reflected by the word *believe* as a way of describing a variable. Gilberson-Anderson concluded that the informants in the study held educational beliefs that were compatible with the meaning given to the computer. It is even more dramatic that the source of definition is ascribed to the adopter rather than assumed to be an objective fact.

Similar to McLaughlin's (1990) expansion of the original findings of the Rand studies to "recognize instances in which belief follows practice" (p. 13), Mitchell (1990) found that change results from the adoption of an idea of object. The complexity of the process is captured by Morehouse and Stockdill's (1991) description of implementation:

> Each stage involves a number of developmental and information-gathering tasks. Movement to the next step is based on findings on the efficacy of the technology, and on a series of increasingly complex decisions by stakeholders and organizational decision makers. Full-scale organizational implementation is more directly affected by interrelated political and communication forces within the organization than by rational information about the technology itself. In addition, adoption by the organization does not guarantee individual adoption or institutionalization (p. 3).

In general, as Wiley (1992) found, teachers view educational computing as an "add-on" to the existing curriculum. Decker Walker (1992) concluded that results of a statewide study indicated that computer use, not adoption, was uneven. The conclusion is that technology is subjectively defined.

37.5.5 Recommendations

Earlier studies of motion pictures, programmed instruction, language laboratories, and television came in waves closely associated with early introduction of equipment and commercial availability. While it is clear that different learning tasks can be accomplished with different technologies, it is much less clear that learning tasks have a demonstrated role in the diffusion and implementation of technology. The focus on equipment also obscures the thread of learning research and implementation findings across time. It is important to make the distinction between equipment and learning in research on educational technology. It is also important to acknowledge that the equipment has a powerful effect on the research agenda. It is a face valid claim that surveys of computers have a higher probability of publication than radio or language lab equipment.

There is a pull of opposite forces, one to generalize about the change process and the other to look at specific personal history, setting, and beliefs. These can comfortably coexist, but the purpose of any given study needs to address directly the intent. Generalizations about the change process will develop as the body of studies grows large enough to support meta-analyses. More use of secondary analysis can benefit the field. The laudable goal to generalize practice should be encouraged but carefully qualified when derived from correlational data. Generalizations must yield to specific contexts that ultimately motivate adoption and use.

37.6 ACTION RESEARCH AND ADAPTATION OF TECHNOLOGY

This section is a three-part review (technical change, social change, and policy) from the perspective of action research. Action research in this section is loosely defined to include studies that focus on social concerns, values, and perspectives of participants and their context rather than the innovation itself. Applied research and aspects of qualitative data are also bundled in this category. The thread of intentional change as part of the research process connects several kinds of studies that are in other ways dissimilar. Among these are themes of equity, policy studies, some qualitative methods, and constructivist research. In these studies the canons of experimental methods are less important or expressed in different ways. The approaches generally sacrifice classical validity concerns of control for results. Validity in qualitative research is a complex issue well described by Maxwell (1992) who concludes that "validity categories" are of much less direct use in qualitative research than they are (or are assumed to be) in quantitative and experimental research (p. 296). Wolcott (1990) is even more circumspect, and Bogdan and Biklen (1992) do not index the word *validity* in their basic text on qualitative

research. Maxwell and others are not devaluing accuracy, systematic inquiry, or objectivity. They do reflect a concern that the goal of generalizability obscures much of what is important in specific studies.

Doubt about the traditional approach to validity does not represent a cavalier attitude toward accuracy or truth, but it does set the direction toward a different kind of realism. These approaches question the utility of validity as it serves generalizability. The site or setting differences in the social sciences make attempts at generalizability weak imitations of physical sciences where conditions are controlled. Knowledge, Garrison says, is not based on similarities across settings but is contextual (1994). The attempt to generalize and establish grand theory has been cited as a marginal activity by a number of researchers in the social sciences. This doubt has a kinship with the "scientific realism" reorientation proposed by House (1991). In this aspect, action research is compatible with qualitative and most constructivist orientations. A full discussion of the relevance of validity in these several approaches is beyond the scope of this review. The important aspect of validity in action research as used here is the emphasis on authenticity, usually at the microlevel.

It is easy to draw distinctions among these several ways of conceptualizing and doing research, but they share the belief that the subjective interpretation of the world determines action. One of those actions is making decisions based on effort and returns. This kind of decision is described by the model developed by Herbert Simon's Nobel Prize–winning economic theory called *satisficing*. Simon (1982) concluded that decisions are not made on a rational basis. The "good enough" motto seems to be an accurate description of decision making in education. The maximizing of returns, such as learning, held up as an ideal, has no explanatory power.

The proactive aspect of all these approaches implies that knowing the subjective view of the population of interest can lead to understanding motivations and the reasons for adopting and adapting, among other things, technology. Generally, the belief is that "major alterations in the school's behavioral and programmatic regularities—in short, educational innovations, require changes in the culture of the school" (Schmuck & Runkel, 1985, p. 5). So far, technology does not attract this type of research as much as organization research. For instance, Gillman (1988), in a study of K-12 computing, derived 375 propositions from 70 studies and classifies them using organizational theory. The change process is advanced as an objective organizational alteration rather than a cultural shift at the individual level. However, the few studies that have been done provide critical insights about the use of technology in education. Harasim (1990) concludes that on-line education's success must be viewed in "the web of social expectations and consequences that inseparably accompany and indeed make possible the operation of the technology" (p. 7).

The focus of studies may vary, but the purpose, bringing about change, remains a distinction. The management of change, regardless of the research used or the techniques advocated, deals with how to bring about change, not why change should be brought about. This "technical" process is well represented in change studies. Social change as a function of technology, or the effects of technology, such as access or gender studies, is driven by a valuing of a particular kind of change rather than the change process. Policy studies, often closely related to the social change approach, cover a wide range of concerns about change. A key understanding must be that policy can direct innovation with or without research. Last, economics, both money and resources in general, have more explanatory power in diffusion and adoption than research on educational technology or learning. The purpose in all these approaches is to change current practice.

37.6.1 Technical Aspects of Change

The earlier uses of "action research" described formative, problem-solving activity with a social or organizational change focus. The action, especially in sociology in the 1960s, was direct involvement in advocating social change. Education has been more conservative. More of the research on change in education has been to facilitate implementation of organization-determined change. There is an assumption in this research that change is needed and desirable. However, most change models in education implicitly value change of an evolutionary rather than revolutionary nature. The most dominant model is managed change using variations on Hall's C-BAM description of the steps in the change process (Hall, George & Rutherford, 1977).

Hall's model, and action research in general in education, is now closely associated with in-service training. The intent is to modify practice through iterative intervention. Frame (1991) studied the effect two institutes would have on participants' concerns and level of instructional computer use. In this case, participants completed a questionnaire that included 35 Concerns-Based Adoption Model (C-BAM) qualifying statements. In addition there were on-site visits, observation, and interviews. Frame found that the workshops decreased concerns and increased computer use at the mechanical level. Similarly, Mitchell (1990) used the C-BAM model to identify examples of strategies and levels of success of various approaches used to provide sufficient hardware, software, training, technical assistance, and time needed to get educators using the technology. The method combined a survey of 41 computer-using educators and 6 in-depth interviews to test proactive change processes. The data are partly qualitative and recognize the orientation of the user as important. For instance, Glaude (1991) studied a staff development model using the Stages of Concern questionnaire. In addition to questionnaires, the study included recordings of discussion issues. This adds another color to a full picture of technology in schools. As might be expected in looking at a process over time, the study supported a plan that accommodated concerns that varied greatly during the implementation year. Longer periods of data collection give more detail on the antecedents and consequences

of educational technology. The primary focus was a staff development plan. The C-BAM change process has a top-down orientation. Teachers are being managed after the goal has been set. The data collection method has shifted to personal perspective, but the locus of control has not. The data are "subjective," but the goal setting is organizational. Much less emphasis was on the staff planning for development.

Some studies are transitions. In a 10-year period, a qualitative study by Gilberson-Anderson (1992) captured a description of the diffusion of the computer as an innovation in one rural school district. Similar to the stages of concern model, three phases of the change process were parsed out: adoption, implementation, and continuation. The researcher analyzed patterns of meaning given to the change effort by the innovators and early adopters in the district. This study included interviews, documentation of board meetings and committee meetings, and videotapes of classroom instruction and meetings. The more intensive field-based collection of data is part of the shift in focus for implementation of educational technology. This falls short of being action research, but it does represent data collection closer to the user's experience.

The importance of knowing users' subjective points of view is recognized in the larger body of school improvement literature. The rationale for a study of knowledge utilization by Cousins and Leithwood (1993) is that individuals "must actively reconstruct the meaning they attribute to their work before lasting change will occur" (p. 305). They cite extensive references to support the need for meaning as developed in a social context. The study was guided by a review of findings from 65 empirical studies on the use of evaluation. They examined the influence of a large array of factors, derived from knowledge utilization framework, on educators' use of several types of information for improvement purposes. A total of 233 elementary school principals and 155 central board office staff members completed a survey instrument inquiring about most useful sources of information for improving curriculum. The results on the characteristics of the source of information, setting, and interactive processes are a mix of top-down and bottom-up strategies.

The research method used by Cousins and Leithwood, a written survey, is removed from the vivid, thick description for qualitative approaches suggested by Bogden and Biklen (1992). The results, the effect of the status of the information source for credibility, are reminiscent of marketing and propaganda studies. So, while the value of subjective socially constructed interpretation is recognized, the research activity itself is removed from the population studied and resembles managed change studies. Their careful integrating of previous research with the findings of the study is capped by a strong case for empowerment strategies. The study meets high standards for research, is reflective, and is part of a strong research tradition. That empowerment is suggested as a strategy to bring about change rather than as a moral value highlights a dividing point in research orientation.

The use of educational technology has advocates, viz., those who see the technology and the commercial sector as a source of better techniques. Others see the advent of technology as a given to be accommodated and developed. Canning's (1988) most notable finding in a qualitative study of six teachers was that the informants did not make a conscious decision to proceed or not to proceed: They believed that adoption was inevitable. These can be classed as advocacy or accepting perspectives toward technology.

More articulate but less popular are those who see commercialization and technology as social-political problems. This concern is expressed in philosophical terms, particularly about an increasing logical-determinist approach to education (e.g., Bors, 1987). The theme is that innovators are technocrats who belong to a subculture that values order and rational process (Wolcott, 1977). Earlier, Weizenbaum (1976) identified computers as having potential for significant misuse in this regard and wrote critical essays on the social effects of technology. The critics start from specific values and outline a progression that may dehumanize society. Oskamp and Spacapan (1990) studied people's reactions to technology in factories, offices, and aerospace. The thesis was that the:

> . . . introduction of any new technology has predictable consequences in shaping the structure and activities of organizations and individuals. Other more pessimistic determinists have emphasized the negative results of factory technology (p. 20).

The authors countered that open systems can optimize both the technical and social subsystems in two important functions involved in group activity: (1) task or production functions and (2) social-emotional or group maintenance functions. The danger, some maintain, is the dehumanization of schools and workplace by technology. It is more likely that the computer systems *mirror* the existing work environment rather than alter it (Oskamp & Spacapan, 1990). So, the existing research on technology in education seems mixed in findings.

The objective discussion of the change process is fragmented into many, often opposing, suggestions. Lehming and Kane (1981) wrote that fundamental elements of successfully initiating and managing such programs have been overlooked and "the various conceptual approaches we encountered were difficult to integrate, the methods employed frequently open to criticism, and the findings apparently contradictory and of uneven coverage" (p. 9). Washington-Bunkley (1988), in a survey study of teachers and administrators, found complicated factors that influence the fate of computer innovations in schools, particularly in the areas of orientation, communications, and support of project decision. However, the temptation to reduce and simplify this complexity by overgeneralizing is a strong one.

Studies of technology-using teachers have produced broad descriptions that help one to understand in general ways what needs to be available to foster greater technology use. Becker (1994b) has listed implications from survey studies for what is needed for such teachers. Technology-using teachers appear to be in schools:

1. Where there is a strong social network of many computer-using teachers
2. With a full-time technology coordinator on staff
3. In a district that provides teachers with formal staff development for (a) using tool-based software and (b) using technology . . . in curriculum
4. That have made a long-term commitment to students using word processing . . . in subject-matter classrooms
5. That have policies ensuring equity of access between boys and girls
6. Where pattern of use extends beyond basic math, language arts, and computer literacy to social studies, the fine arts
7. That allocate time at school for teachers to use school computers . . . for their own professional tasks
8. That are faced with additional maintenance . . .
9. That need, perhaps most costly of all, smaller class sizes for computer-using teachers

The process of getting to this stage is described in other works. Some of the conditions are organizational (see Ely, 1990) while others are demographic. The demographic puzzle has many pieces. One demographic piece reported by Whiteside and James (1986) was that older teachers were more concerned about collaboration and younger ones about management. They also report that males have higher collaboration concerns. Furst-Bowe (1992) found that first-year technology education teachers used microcomputers, models, overhead transparencies, and videotapes most frequently. Mitchell (1990) used multimethods in a case study of microcomputer-using teachers. The finding that a single-person model (a lone teacher) was most common led to the recommendation that change agents need to develop better methods to determine strategies that will move individual teachers to higher levels of use. Similarly, Washington-Bunkley's (1988) study of attitudes of teachers and administrators was designed to provide data to guide future decisions on adoption, diffusion, and evaluation of computer technology in schools. Similarly, Allum (1991) studied social processes of organizational change using participant observation, interviews, questionnaires, and secondary data analysis to identify normative "sacred" and "profane" cultural elements influencing teacher behavior in integrating technology in instruction. Nordenbo (1990) interviewed 39 adult computer novices to "reveal the self-view and global understanding of the individual learner." Concepts, such as Allum's "sacred and profane cultural elements," are clearly different factors from those identified in equipment surveys.

The methods in this kind of research are focused on the individual's world view. For instance, Canning (1988) used interviews and observation to determine what teacher perceptions were associated with successful adoption. The conditions identified by the informants included compatibility of computing to existing values, self-images, practices, and environment; a strong sense of self-efficacy; and a psychological state of self-actualization. The effort to bring about adoption is clear in the recommendation: "Empowering competent teachers can be an effective tool for change in the school setting."

House (1991) used a metaphor of a pool game to distinguish two different concerns of research. The dominant and traditional concern is what happens when one ball strikes another. This technical point of view is represented by correlation studies of the factors and methods associated with adoption. House has a second question: "Who struck the cue ball?" In other words, it may be possible to determine similarities across situations and manage change, but the initial motivation to change, the why question, is outside technical studies using C-BAM and managed change.

37.6.2 Social Change

Social change as a function of technology is made up of many issues. It includes, among other things, perceived control, moral or belief positions, and economics. One argument on ways of thinking holds that there are inherent shaping features of the machines, such as the way computer programming logic affects content. These features shape the way technology is used and what it is used for. Effects are subtle, similar to the problem with left-handed scissors. The cutting edge of scissors have an opposed design that works only for the right hand. Left-handed use is awkward and ineffective because of the design, not because of the dexterity of the user. So scissors are not used with the left hand. What is not seen in technologies, from the scissors to computers, is less likely to be researched even though it has an effect on how we do tasks, including thinking. Such studies use logical argument and history more than quantitative data. Another view, from a study in four elementary school classrooms, concludes that how people use a microcomputer, and not the machine's inherent features, determines how a microcomputer will be used in education (Mehan, 1989). It is likely that both the machine's inherent features and how it is used are important determinants. Since little can be done by adopters and adapters about the machine's inherent features, it is reasonable to focus on how it is used. In this, the machine and its technology come closer to the academic definition of educational technology as a process of developing instruction. Such a process has adaptation as part of the purpose.

The adaptation process is a negotiation between preadoption factors in the design of the technology and setting factors. This is a process Rogers (1983) names *reinvention*. (See Buttolph, 1992, for a general discussion of adaptation.) Much of the success of this process depends on understanding the belief systems in schools. Bowers suggests that:

. . . educational computing [educational technology] is more properly and fully understood within the conceptual frameworks of . . . the sociological knowledge of Alfred Schutz . . . Martin Heidegger, Frederick Nietzsche, and

Gregory Bateson . . . than the traditions of thought that go back to René Descartes, Frederick Taylor, and B. F. Skinner (1988, p. x).

Bowers also cautions against using the technical language of machines to describe adaptation, since the user perspective becomes secondary.

Cuban (1993), in "Computers Meet Classroom: Classroom Wins," maintains that schools are substantially different from businesses, industries, and other organizations. In one way, schooling is less vulnerable to electronic technologies than these other institutions because "certain cultural beliefs about what teaching is, how learning occurs, what knowledge is proper in schools, and the teacher-student relationship" focus on human rather than machine interaction (p. 86). Cuban argues that schools are not culturally compatible with technology but that there are external counter pressures to adopt it. He maintains that schools are caught up in the press for using technology because of (1) the economics of the workplace—the fear that students will be unprepared both to compete in the job market and to adjust to the changing marketplace, (2) a neoprogressive coalition advocating new ways of learning, and (3) teacher productivity (Cuban, 1993). There are empirical grounds for school culture being the determining factor. Mehan (1985), in a study of four classroom teachers, found that there was no significant change in the way in which teachers arranged space and used time in their classrooms as a result of having microcomputers available for instruction on a full-time basis. The microcomputers were incorporated into previously established practices for organizing instruction, regardless of the teacher's previous knowledge of computers. This supports the position that there are social and organizational forces that have effects on how technology is perceived and used.

The perceived control of technology has an effect on how the technology is used. McInerney (1989) used data drawn from written analyses prepared by 7 teachers and 17 administrators in 10 school districts. The framework for analysis was Leavitt's sociotechnical systems model made up of four components: task, people, technology, and structure. The social effects were determined to be related to control. "Control" in this qualitative study is illustrated by the data. Two informants reported: "No one asked the administration or the actual users of the program what they felt their needs were; the software was just dropped on them like a lead weight. There was no training" (p. 500). The two ends of the spectrum are clearly different. McInerney concludes:

Where control is internal to the individual, it is manifested in the development of computer champions. Where control is external and formal, it is manifested in the development of technicians, defined as people using computers to do programmed work directed primarily toward organizational goals (p. 491).

Concern for control is also reflected in Apple and Jungck's worry about "curriculum on a cart" (1991, p. 29). The control issue is closely related to House's "Who struck the cue ball" question and must be addressed before attention is turned to what happens after events are set in motion.

The title of a study by Apple and Jungck (1991) conveys the concern with control: "You Don't Have to Be a Teacher to Teach in This Unit: Teaching, Technology and Control in the Classroom." In their study of two teachers who developed a computer literacy unit using audiotapes and worksheets to reduce lab time, they traced an effort by the teachers to accommodate an instructional need (computer literacy) with very limited resources (no computers). The result was that the response of teachers and students to the paper-and-pencil computer literacy unit was mildly negative. The irrelevance likely accounts for this outcome. Apple and Jungck conclude that training is sensitive to context:

> School systems are often caught between two competing goals—accumulation and legitimation. They must both support an economy, especially when it is in crisis, and at the same time maintain their legitimacy with a wide range of different groups. . . . Given this, many goals will simply be symbolic" (pp. 36–37).

Their findings suggest control issues, mostly control held by the institution, but does not point to a solution as clearly. Control and participation remain powerful issues, even determining issues, in adoption and adaptation of technology in education.

Control concerns are found outside education. Counting keystrokes and errors in clerical staff is one potentially egregious use of control. Kaufman, Parcel, Wallace, and Form (1988) examined technological change in an ultra-high-technology firm. They propose a contingency theory on how occupations condition responses to technological and organizational changes. Their stratified random sample represented the main occupations in the company. Occupation best explained supervisory and technological work control. Specialty professionals, computer operators, and secretaries reported being the most controlled by the work process, while computer specialists reported being the least. Computer operators, computer professionals, and product specialists were the most apprehensive about future technological changes, while managers were the least. Technology and how it is used were strongly linked to perceptions of control and empowerment. Apple and Jungck's (1991) concern with control by teachers or Cuban's (1993) description of economic forces affecting schools suggests that the issues are shared in education.

Equity and access studies are often surveys of how many people of what gender, socioeconomic level, or ethnicity are using technology. Data are used to support moral positions. Bors (1987) holds the position that the introduction of computers into the classroom is not merely a technical matter but one involving values implications that will affect various groups in society differently. The argument is advanced within the framework of sociology. (See also Mehan, 1992, on social interaction, and Doty, 1992, on social aspects of machines in education.) The moral posi-

tion is that to avoid increasing inequalities that already exist in society, the promises of classroom computerization must be critically addressed (Bors, 1987). The underlying belief is represented by the organizing questions in a study by Mehan (1985). As schools acquire and use computers for educational purposes, two major questions arise: (1) whether students from different strata of society will obtain equal access to computers, and (2) whether students from different strata of society will be taught similar or different uses of the computer (Mehan, 1985). The distinction between an empirical argument and a moral argument is that a moral argument does not need empirical support. What is being demonstrated in equity and access studies is the degree to which equity and change exist in the use of technology.

Ekker (1986) conducted a survey and experiment to determine whether unequal access to microcomputer technology will increase inequalities in educational and occupational aspirations. The sample consisted of 160 students from two high schools. Students were divided into low- and high-access groups, and the low-access group was randomly assigned to either the control or the treatment group. The treatment was a tutorial designed to introduce the participants to the use of "spreadsheet" software as an application of microcomputer technology. While the data suggest that expected educational attainment is not attributable to the independent variable, the level of access to microcomputer technology, it is likely that Ekker's experimental treatment was not of sufficient duration or strength to draw robust conclusions. However, the survey part of the study did show that the (control group) participants with a high level of access to microcomputer technology expect, on the average, to achieve a higher occupational status based on Duncan SEI scores. Thus, unsurprisingly, covariance exists but the cause is not identified.

Turkle and Papert (1992) argue that computers are a medium through which different styles of scientific thought can be observed in women whose learning styles differ from the way programming and problem solving in computer-related exercises are taught. The implication is that a different kind of instruction is appropriate. A grounding line of inquiry is found in Anderson (1987), who has pursued differences in gender and access over 2 decades. A related concern of Bowers is that the

> . . . people writing the educational software have tended to ignore the tacit dimension of . . . computer technology based on the Cartesian view of knowledge; the problem of representing the tacit, contextual, and metaphorical dimension of cultural experience . . ., developing a conceptual framework for making explicit how the culture is mediated through the process of educational computing, as well as the specific cultural orientations that are reinforced by this technology . . . (1988, p. 36).

Mehan's (1985) observations of computer use in 21 classrooms found a very strong relationship between the type of students and the type of instruction. There were gender differences in access, and ethnic and class differences in the kind of instruction. White middle-class students' instruction encouraged initiative (programming and problem solving), while lower-class and ethnic minority students were controlled through computer-aided drill and practice.

It appears that there are differences by gender and socioeconomic status, but the source or solution may not be technology. For instance, in a study of computers, using observations and interviews in 32 rural schools in Canada, small impact was found. This kind of study describes what is happening with technology. Why it is happening this way in rural settings heavily populated by Native Americans is speculation. Archer surmised it may be because there is a difference between the officially recognized functions of schooling and those actually performed. In particular, if the most important actual function of schooling is to allocate individuals to social strata, rather than to educate them, then this severely limits the extent to which the potential of the computer can be realized in the public school system (Archer, 1988). Technology is not the cause of the kinds of problems Archer cites, though it can be used to perpetuate them. A full understanding of the diffusion and adoption of educational technology must include the effects of social and organizational forces.

37.6.3 Policy

The policies of technology are better described as the politics of technology. The milieu includes the entire group of laws, regulations, programs, decisions, and other governmental interventions that influence the extent and direction of technological change (Dalpe, 1989). An example of problems with policy was reported in a study of a 1984 decision to purchase microcomputers for local schools by the Quebec Ministry of Education. The Quebecan government wanted a computer specialized to meet the needs of education, but attractive to French-speaking markets. To meet this standard, the computer had to operate entirely in French, its parts had to be at least 50% Quebecan, and at least 10% of the cost of the order had to be applied to research. The government subsidized programs: one for production and one for purchases by the education system. Although the primary goal of the Quebecan computers was to satisfy the needs of education (instruction), the government imposed a second—that of accelerating industrial development. The educational niche that the Quebecan educational computer occupied was too limited to support development of competitive businesses, and the project failed.

Policy affects the diffusion and adoption of technology, often with unintended outcomes. Studies of policy, especially at the international level, identify inhibiting aspects of policy. Studies of national educational technology policy suggest that funding has an effect on diffusion. Policies are not usually based on research (Atkenson & Jackson, 1992) but on political positions. (For example, see Doyle, 1994, adapting Goals 2000, a political statement, to information literacy, an education-based construct.)

37.7 SUMMARY OF DIFFUSION AND ADOPTION RESEARCH

From simple surveys to learning experiments, Atkenson and Jackson found "that the effects of research on educational practice are for the most part indirect and slow" (p. 52). There is no long-term program for collecting or using research at the federal level. There are excellent studies, but they are limited by short time spans. Since this is the state of educational research in general, it is a magnitude greater for educational technology. However rough the indicators, it is clear there have been waves of equipment technology diffused in education. The amplitude of those waves is increasing. The diffusion of the use of technology has been marginalized. There has been little change in classroom practice (Cuban, 1993; Mehan, 1985).

There are consistent findings in research on how change can be brought about. Training, resources, and involvement appear to be consistent determining factors. These findings are almost self-evident but difficult to implement. For instance, Stuhlmann (1994) found that telecommunications were more likely to be incorporated into teaching if teachers received support from other users and had access to computer equipment at home. Support and computer access at home are effective but not easy to provide. Fullan (1993) suggests that change at the microlevel is most productive and that teachers must be the change agents. The Rand studies (McLaughlin, 1990) made clear that local context and human factors are powerful determents of change in education, as have studies by Mitchell (1990) and Cousins and Leithwood (1993). Changes take time, often measured in years (Honey & Henriquez, 1993). Rejection of technology appears to be a combination of poor implementation and the culture of schools.

Generally research does not have impact on policy or practice. If, for instance, there is strong evidence that computer technologies produce more student learning than do conventional approaches, then the technophile and optimist scenarios become worthy of support, regardless of one's values, one could argue. "Sadly enough, the research evidence . . . is ambiguous and unhelpful in determining policy" (Cuban, 1993, p. 205). Educational technology has a symbolic value, a place to play out equity, learning, and curriculum issues. Educational technology is not the cause of gender differences or inequity, but it can perpetuate patterns. Policies and practice in technology are not the solutions to equity problems, but they do reflect the larger realities of society.

37.7.1 Generalizability

For those working in more controlled environments, especially learning research, the entire corpus of research in diffusion and adaptation of educational technology seems less rigorous in technique and design and weak in causal findings. If the traditional standards of the hard sciences are applied, the judgments are correct. Two positions counter or at least mitigate this conclusion. One, a traditional counter, is that causal relationships are difficult to demonstrate in the social sciences. Clearly, the large number of variables, their interactions, and low internal validity mean that the generalizability of diffusion and adaptation research is very limited. The critique can be easily argued, since few studies consistently identify the same sets of variables, treatments are idiosyncratic, and follow-up is negligible. The history of studies of in-service training must also be generalized with great caution. A traditional position on these problems is that the descriptive research must accumulate so that meta-analyses can eventually point the way. Then, it follows, controlled studies may be worth the investment.

A second counterargument, advanced by House (1991), is that seeking a high level of generalizability is a waste of time in education since no two days, settings, or events represent uniform interactions among common sets of variables. Solving problems in a specific site, House reasons, is the correct approach, and spending resources on grand generalizations is a disciplinary self-indulgence of small benefit. This is a credible argument to practitioners but not widely accepted by those vested in research aimed at generalizability. The approach certainly deserves consideration, since education has a long tradition of limited risk monies for research and a short tradition of experimental science that is largely derivative.

Part of the charge to those working in diffusion and adaptation research is to recognize how large the sets of variables are and how interactions are so complex they seem idiosyncratic. Pea (1988) holds that knowledge transfer . . . has "as much to do with recognizing the impacts of the sociocultural organizations of activities in which learning takes place as they do with psychological findings from research on learning" (p. 169). The recognition of the power of social forces has been increasingly recognized in determining change and innovation (House, 1979). Yeaman (1990) encourages an anthropological paradigm as a way to bridge the schism between researchers and practitioners in educational technology. Herbig (1994), writing on technology in business and industry at the national level, concluded that the barriers to innovation are almost never technological but rather social, political, financial, or economic. These are cautions that interpretation should be a soft and cautious process. Given this state of the art, a holistic view, one that attends to descriptions but does not advocate for a single factor solution such as more computers or different software, seems right. The change process is too often approached as an objective organizational alteration, a visit to the parts shop, rather than a cultural shift at the individual level and the context in which the innovation occurs. If we are to understand how technology is diffused and what kind of adaptation is needed, we must understand the context of technology and education in the larger culture. The perceptions of the teachers, students, and other stakeholders in the process, their real reasons for use and nonuse, require research that is reflective, grounded, and open. Studies that focus on the social context of technology for decision makers, teachers, publics, and students are the most productive new perspectives for diffusion and adoption research.

REFERENCES:

Allum, K.F. (1991). Technological innovation in a high school mathematics department: a structural and cultural analysis. *Dissertation Abstracts International*, 52/04, 1283A.

Anderson, R.E. (1987). Females surpass males in computer problem solving: findings from the Minnesota Computer Literacy Assessment. *Journal of Educational Computing Research 3* (1), 39–51.

— (1987). The unresolved need for research on computers and education. *Education and Computing 3* (1–2), 15–20.

—, Hansen, T., Johnson, D.C. & Klassen, D.L. (1979). Instructional computing: acceptance and rejection by secondary school teachers. *Sociology of Work and Occupations 6* (2), 227–50.

Apple, M.W. & Jungck, S. (1991). You don't have to be a teacher to teach in this unit: teaching, technology and control in the classroom. *In* A. Hargreaves & M. Fullan, eds. *Understanding teacher development,* 20–42. London: Cassell.

Archer, E.G. (1988). The use of computers in rural education. *Dissertation Abstracts International,* 49/05, 1122A.

Atkinson, R.R. & Jackson, G.B., eds. (1992). *Research & education reform.* Washington, DC: National Academy.

Becker, H.J. (1991). How computers are used in United States schools: basic data from the 1989 I.E.A. Computers in Education Survey. *Journal of Educational Computing Research 7,* 385–406.

— (1994a). Analysis and trends of school use of new information technologies. Office of Technology Assessment. Washington, DC: U.S. Government Printing Office (1996).

— (1994). How our best computer-using teachers differ from other teachers: implications for realizing the potential of computers in schools. *Journal of Research on Computing in Education 26* (1996).

Berman, P. & McLaughlin, M. (1975). Federal programs supporting educational change, Vols. 1–5. Santa Monica, CA: Rand.

— & — (1977). Federal programs supporting educational change, Vols. 6–8. Santa Monica, CA: Rand.

Bogdan, R. & Biklen, S.A. (1992). Qualitative research or education. Needham Heights, MA: Allyn & Bacon.

Bors, D.A. (1987). Introducing microcomputers into schools: a social-political issue. *Education and Society 5* (1–2), 55–63.

Bowers, C.A. (1988). The cultural dimensions of educational computing: understanding the non-neutrality of technology. New York: Teachers College Press.

Buttolph, D. (1992). A new look at adaptation. *Knowledge: Creation, Diffusion, Utilization 13,* 460–70.

Campbell, D.L. (1971). Administrative experiments, institutional records, and non-reactive measure. *In* W. Evans, ed. *Organizational experimentation.* New York: Harper & Row.

Canning, C.L. (1988). Adoption of computing: the experience of six teachers. *Dissertation Abstracts International,* 49/05, 1119A.

Clark, R.E. (1992). Six definitions of media in search of a theory. *In* D.P. Ely & B.B. Minor, eds. *Educational media and technology yearbook,* 65–76. Englewood, CO: Libraries Unlimited.

Cohen, D.K. (1988). Educational technology and school organization. *In* R.S. Nickerson & P.P. Zodhaiates, eds. *Technology in education: looking toward 2020,* 231–64. Hillsdale, NJ: Erlbaum.

Cohen, P.A. & Forde, E.B. (1992). A survey of instructional technology in dental education. *Journal of Dental Education 56* (2), 123–27.

Cook, Karen S., ed. (1987). *Social exchange theory.* Beverly Hills, CA: Sage.

Cousins, J.B. & Leithwood, K.A. (1993). Enhancing knowledge utilization as a strategy for school improvement. *Knowledge: Creation, Diffusion, Utilization 14,* 305–33.

Cuban, L. (1986). *Teachers and machines: the classroom use of technology since 1920.* New York: Teachers College Press.

— (1993). Computers meet classroom: classroom wins. *Teachers College Record 95* (2), 185–210.

Dalpe, R. (1989). Political dimensions of public interventions in technology. *Recherches-Sociographiques 30* (3), 447–63. (Dept. Science Politique, University of Montreal, Quebec.)

Doty, L.H. (1992). Machine technology: the social aspects of teaching machines and computers in education. *In* D.P. Ely & B.B. Minor, eds. E*ducational media and technology yearbook,* 117–26. Englewood, CO: Libraries Unlimited.

Doyle, C.S. (1994) Information literacy in an information society: a concept for the information age. Syracuse, NY: ERIC Clearinghouse on Information & Technology, Syracuse University (ERIC Monograph).

Dutton, W.H., Sweet, P.L. & Rogers, E.M. (1989). Socioeconomic status and the early diffusion of personal computing in the United States. *Social Science Computer Review 7* (3), 259–71.

Ekker, K. (1986). Technological innovation and the implications for social differentiation: the case of microcomputer technology. *Dissertation Abstracts International,* 47/06, 2323A.

Ely, D.P. (1990). Conditions that facilitate the implementation of educational technology innovations. *Journal of Research on Computing in Education 23* (2) 298–305.

— (1983). The definition of educational technology: an emerging stability. *Educational Considerations 10* (2), 2–4.

— & Minor, B.B. (1993). *Educational media and technology yearbook.* Englewood, CO: Libraries Unlimited.

England, R. (1991). A survey of state-level involvement in distance education at the elementary and secondary levels. ACSDE Research Monograph, No. 3. University Park, PA: The American Center for the Study of Distance Education.

Frame, J.A. (1991). Moving toward a staff development model for computer learning. *Dissertation Abstracts International,* 52/03, 756A.

Fullan, M.G. (1993). Why teachers must become change agents. *Educational Leadership 50* (6), 12–17.

— (1992). *Teacher development and educational change.* Washington, DC: Falmer.

— (1992). *Successful school improvement: the implementation perspective and beyond.* Philadelphia, PA: Open University Press.

— & Pomfret, A. (1977). Research on curriculum and instruction implementation. *Review of Educational Research 47,* 335–97.

Furst-Bowe, J. (1992). The utilization of instructional technology by beginning technology education teachers. *International Journal of Instructional Media 19,* 229–34.

Garrison, J. (1994). Realism, Deweyan pragmatism, and educational research. *Educational Researcher 23* (1), 5–14.

Geiss, G.R. (1987). Information technology: human impacts and national policies. *Education and Computing 3,* 49–62.

Giacquinta, J.B., Bauer, J.A. & Levin, J.E. (1993). *Beyond technology's promise.* New York: Cambridge University Press.

Gilberson-Anderson, M.S. (1992). The diffusion of computers as an innovation in rural school district. *Dissertation Abstracts International,* 53/12, 4287A.

Gillman, T.V. (1988). Adoption, implementation, and integration of instructional microcomputing (K-12): a synthesis of findings. *Dissertation Abstracts International,* 49/12, 3567A.

Glaude, C.A. (1991). A description of the concerns of selected Maine educators involved in the implementation of a computer innovation called NovaNet. *Dissertation Abstracts International,* 52/08, 2896A.

Green, K. (1993). Campus computing 1992: the EDUCOM-USC survey of desktop computing in higher education. Los Angeles, CA: The James Irvine Foundation Center for Scholarly Technology, University of Southern California.

Hall, G.E. & Hord, S.M. (1987). *Change in schools: facilitating the process.* Albany, NY: SUNY.

— & Loucks, S.F. (1977). Developmental model for determining whether the treatment is actually implemented. *American Educational Research Journal 14* (3), 263–76.

—, George, A.A. & Rutherford, W.L. (1977). Measuring stages of concern about the innovation: a manual for the use of the SoC Questionnaire. Austin, TX: Research and Development Center for Teacher Education, University of Texas.

— Wallace, R.C. & Dossett, W.F. (1973). A developmental conceptualization of the adoption process within educational institutions. Austin, TX: Research and Development Center for Teacher Education, University of Texas.

Harasim, L.P., ed. (1990). *Online education.* New York: Praeger.

Harris, J. (1995) Knowledge-making in the information age: beyond information access. *Learning & Leading with Technology 23* (2), 57–60.

Havelock, R.G. (1973). *The change agent's guide to innovation in education.* Englewood Cliffs, NJ: Educational Technology.

Henry, S.A. (1987). A study of the relationships among selected factors affecting Kentucky teachers' instructional technology use in the elementary classroom. *Dissertation Abstracts International,* 48/12, 3094A.

Herbig, P.A. (1994). *The innovation matrix: culture and structure prerequisites to innovation.* Westport, CT: Quorum.

Heaviside, S., Farris, E., Malitz, G. & Carpenter, J. (1995). Advanced telecommunications in U.S. public schools, K-12. National Center for Educational Statistics 95-73. Washington, DC: U.S. Government Printing Office.

Hill, P.T. (1985). The politics of educational data collection. Washington, DC: National Center for Education Statistics.

Hilton, T.L. (1992). *Using national data bases in educational research.* Hillsdale, NJ: Erlbaum.

Honey, M. & Henriquez, A. (1993). *Telecommunications and K-12 educators: findings from a national survey.* New York: Bank Street College of Education, Center for Technology in Education.

House, E.R. (1991). Realism in research. *Educational Researcher 20* (6), 2–9.

House, E.R. (1979). Technology versus craft: a ten-year perspective on innovation. *Journal of Curriculum Studies 11* (1) 1–15.

Jorde-Bloom, P. (1988). Self-efficacy expectations as a predictor of computer use: a look at early childhood administrators. *Computers in the Schools 5* (1/2), 45–63.

Kaufman, R.L., Parcel, T.L., Wallace, M. & Form, W. (1988). Looking forward: responses to organizational and technological change in an ultra-high-technology firm. *Research in the Sociology of Work 4,* 31–67.

Kemmis, S. (1988) Action research. *In* J.P. Keeves, ed. *Educational research, methodology, and measurement: an international handbook,* 42–49. Oxford, England: Pergamon.

Kinnaman, D.E. (1992). Newsline. *Technology & Learning 13* (2), 38, 40.

— (1993). Research in education: approach with caution. (The leadership role) (column) *Technology & Learning 14* (2), 78.

Lehming, R. & Kane, M., eds. (1981). *Improving schools: using what we know.* Beverly Hills: Sage.

Leonard-Barton, D. (1984). Diffusing innovations when the users are not the choosers: the case of dentists. *Knowledge: Creation, Diffusion, Utilization 6,* 89–111.

Lukesh, S.S. (1987). *Microcomputer use in higher education.* New York: Peat Marwick.

Mahajan, V. & Peterson, R.A. (1985). Models for innovation diffusion. Sage University Paper series on quantitative applications in the social sciences. Beverly Hills, CA: Sage.

Market Data Retrieval (1993). *Education and technology.* Shelton, CA: Author (flyer).

— (1992). *The survey of microcomputers in schools.* Shelton, CT: Author.

Marovitz, M. (1994). The diffusion and implementation of instructional television at the U.S. Military Academy. (Syracuse University) *Dissertation Abstracts International,* 1996.

Marshall, G. (1993). Who uses TV, computers, and film/video? *CUE Newsletter 15* (5), 15–18. Alameda, CA: Computer Using Educators.

Maxwell, J.A. (1992). Understanding and validity in qualitative research. *Harvard Educational Review 62* (3), 279–300.

McInerney, W.D. (1989). Social and organizational effects of educational computing. *Journal of Educational Computing Research 5* (4), 487–506.

McLaughlin, M.W. (1990). The Rand change agent study revisited: macro perspectives and micro realities. *Educational Researcher 19* (9), 11–16.

Mehan, H. (1989). Microcomputers in classrooms: educational technology or social practice? *Anthropology and Education Quarterly 20* (1), 4–22.

— (1985a). Microcomputers and classroom organization: the more things change the more they change each other. *Interactive Technology Laboratory Report 10* (ED311874).

— (1985). Computer literacy and social stratification. *Interactive Technology Laboratory Report 9* (ED311873).

Miles, M.B., ed. (1964). *Innovation in education.* New York: Teachers College.

Mitchell, J.C. (1990). A comprehensive study of implementation strategies for microcomputer use in public elementary schools. *Dissertation Abstracts International,* 51/11, 3712A.

Morehouse, D.L. & Stockdill, S.H. (1991). A technology adop-

tion model. (TDC Research Report No. 16.) St. Paul, MN: University of Minnesota Extension Service.

Mort, P.R. (1938). *Adaptability of public school systems.* New York: Teachers College, Columbia University.

National Center for Education Statistics (1992a). Digest of education statistics. Washington, DC: U.S. Government Printing Office, 1976, Annual.

— (1992b). NCES Statistical Standards. Washington DC: U.S. Department of Education, Office of Research and Improvement.

— (1992c). Schools and staffing in the United States: A statistical profile, 1987-88. Washington DC: U.S. Department of Education, Office of Research and Improvement.

National Education Association (1993). *Technology in the classroom: a teacher perspective.* Washington DC: Author.

Nordenbo, S. (1990). How do computer novices perceive information technology? A qualitative study based on a new methodology. *Scandinavian Journal of Educational Research 34* (1), 43–76.

Oskamp, S. & Spacapan, S., eds. (1990). People's reactions to technology. Beverly Hills, CA: Sage.

Pea, R.D. (1988). Putting knowledge to use. *In* R.S. Nickerson & P.P. Zodhaiates, eds. *Technology in education: looking toward 2020,* 239–52. Hillsdale, NJ: Erlbaum.

Pelgrum, W.J. (1993). Attitudes of school principals and teachers towards computers: does it matter what they think? *Studies in Educational Evaluation 19,* 199–212.

Pelgrum, W.J. & Plomp, T. (1991). The use of computers in education Worldwide: results from a comparative survey in 18 countries. (ED 337 157.)

Quality Education Data (1993). Education mailing lists and marketing services. 1993–94. Denver, CO: Author (brochure).

— (1992). Technology in public schools 1992–93. Denver, CO: Author.

Rich, R.F. (1981). *The knowledge cycle.* Beverly Hills, CA: Sage.

Roberts, L.G. (1985). Training of teachers in the instructional use of technology. Corporation for Public Broadcasting, Washington, DC: National Center for Educational Statistics (ED 297 694).

Roblyer, M.D. (1988). Fundamental problems and principles of designing effective courseware. *In* D. Jonassen, ed. *Instructional designs for microcomputer courseware,* 7–33. Hillsdale, NJ: Erlbaum.

Rogers, E.M. (1993). *Diffusion of innovations,* 3d ed. New York: Free Press.

— & Shoemaker, F.F. (1971). *Communication of innovations: a cross-cultural approach.* New York: Free Press.

Saettler, L.P. (1990). *The evolution of American educational technology.* Englewood, CO: Libraries Unlimited.

Shaw, S.G. (1992). An examination of the arguments against the naturalistic paradigm of research in educational technology and their implications for current research practices. *Dissertation Abstracts International,* 53/01, p. 97.

Schmuck, R. & Runkel, P. (1985). *The handbook of organizational development in schools,* 3d ed. Palo Alto, CA: Mayfield.

Sheingold, K. & Hadley, M. (1990). *Accomplished teachers: integrating computers into classroom practice.* New York: Bank Street College of Education, Center for Technology in Education.

SIMBA Information (1992). *Electronic media for the school*

market: review, trends & forecast. Wilton, CT: SIMBA Information.

Simon, H.A. (1982). Models of bounded rationality. Cambridge, MA: MIT Press.

— (1987). Satisficing. *In* J. Eatwell, M. Milgate & P. Newman, eds. *The new Palgrave: a dictionary of economics,* 243–44 New York: Macmillan.

Smith, M.L. & Glass, G.V. (1987). *Research and evaluation in education and the social sciences.* Englewood Cliffs, NJ: Prentice Hall.

Software Publishers Association. (1993). Market Study Report press release. Washington DC: Author.

Stelnikov, E. (1991). Marketing instructional technology: the science of seduction. *Contemporary Education 63,* 54–57.

Stuhlmann, J.M. Circumstances and experience that lead to incorporating telecommunications into teaching practices. AERA. New Orleans, LA, Apr. 4–8, 1994, University of Virginia.

Thompson, A.D., Simonson, M.R. & Hargrave, C.P. (1992). *Educational technology: a review of the research.* Washington, DC: AECT.

Todd, N.I. (1992). A model for integrating computer-based technologies in teacher education. *Dissertation Abstracts International,* 53/06, 1878A.

Turkle, S. & Papert, S. (1992). Epistemological pluralism and the revaluation of the concrete. *Journal of Mathematical Behavior 11* (1), 3–33.

U.S. Department of Commerce (1992). Statistical abstract of the United States. Washington, DC: U.S. Government Printing Office.

Walker, D. (1992). Computers in California high schools: implications for teacher education. *Journal of Computing in Teacher Education 8* (4), 6–18.

Washington-Bunkley, W.C. (1988). Computer technology in Ohio schools: an investigation of its adoption, implementation, and outcomes. *Dissertation Abstract International,* 49/07, 1776A.

Weizenbaum, J. (1976). On the impact of the computer on society. *In* J.M. Adams & D.H. Haden, eds. *Social effects of computer use and misuse,* 276–86. New York: Wiley.

Westin, A.F., et al. (1979). The dimensions of privacy: a national opinion research survey of attitudes toward privacy. (ED177634.)

Whiteside, C. & James, R.K. (1986). Utilizing teachers' concerns to improve microcomputer implementation. *Computers in the Schools 2* (4), 29–41.

Wiley, L.G. (1992). Relationships between teachers' attitudes, knowledge and concerns about computers in education and a concerns-based approach to staff development. *Dissertation Abstracts International,* 54/01, 151A.

Williams, F., Rice, R.E. & Rogers, E.M. (1988). *Research methods and the new media.* New York: Free Press.

Winner, A. (1982). Introducing the microcomputer into the elementary classroom: an inservice program for teachers. *Dissertation Abstracts International,* 43/10, 3212A.

Wolcott, H.F. (1977). Teachers vs. technocrats. Center for Educational Policy and Management, University of Oregon.

— (1990). On seeking—and rejecting—validity in qualitative research. *In* E.W. Eisner & A. Peshkin, eds. *Qualitative inquiry in education,* 121–52. New York: Teachers College Press.

Yeaman, A.R.J. (1990). An anthropological view of educational communications and technology: beliefs and behaviors in research and theory. *Canadian Journal of Educational Communication 19* (3), 237–46.

Zoski, K.W. (1989). Research needs in educational technology for 1990's: a Delphi study. *Dissertation Abstracts International,* 50/05, 1284A.

VII

RESEARCH METHODOLOGIES IN EDUCATIONAL COMMUNICATIONS AND TECHNOLOGY

Rhonda Robinson, Northern Illinois University

Associate Editor

38. PHILOSOPHY, RESEARCH, AND EDUCATION

J. Randall Koetting
UNIVERSITY OF NEVADA, RENO

The concern of teacher educators must remain normative, critical, and even political. Neither the teachers colleges nor the schools can change the social order. Neither colleges nor schools can legislate democracy. But something can be done to empower teachers to reflect upon their own life situations, to speak out in their own ways about the lacks that must be repaired, the possibilities to be acted upon in the name of what they deem decent, humane, and just (Greene, 1978, p. 71).

38.1 INTRODUCTION: PHILOSOPHY AND PERSONAL STRUGGLE

It has been a struggle writing this chapter. Eisner (1991) helps me to understand part of the nature of my struggle. He states that for some researchers within the social sciences, philosophy is often viewed as an "academic distraction." It is a distraction because:

> Philosophy is nagging. It conjoles students into asking questions about basic assumptions, it generates doubts and uncertainties, and, it is said, it keeps people from getting their work done. Many appear to believe that it is better to leave the unanswerable questions and unsolvable problems alone and get down to brass tacks. I regard such attitudes as short-sighted. Core concepts in the social sciences are philosophical in nature: Objectivity, Validity, Truth, Fact, Theory, Structure. Why neglect to examine them, even if their examination will never yield a single unassailable meaning? (pp. 4–5).

Trying to deal with the "big picture" in education gets complicated. There is a greater sense of urgency felt today to come up with answers to educational problems. Philosophy takes too much time. There is the sense of "Let's get down to brass tacks." Like Eisner, I experience philosophy as a study that does nag at my thinking because, at its best, it has me question and doubt. Because I question and doubt, sometimes it keeps me from getting my work done. Also, I agree with Eisner that core concepts in the social sciences are philosophical in nature. And this is my struggle.

My perspective is that of teacher-student, one who has found much value in the study of philosophy that has helped

me to better understand issues in education. My main struggle has been in determining how to convey to the reader my strong sense of the importance of philosophy for research and philosophical inquiry. How should I discuss and analyze, in a philosophic way, philosophy, education, and research? In this chapter, I want to argue for the critical importance of using a philosophical perspective in studying education. I will do this by situating my discussion of philosophy, inquiry, and education within a general discussion of educational research. I will then examine education as a moral undertaking, and therefore the need for not only continued inquiry into the process of schooling but also the need for foundational (theoretical), diverse, and critical questioning. I will argue that the study of philosophy/philosophy of education will provide a framework needed for inquiry into schooling that is foundational (theoretical), diverse, and critical. I will briefly look at the notion of theory and the importance of having or taking a theoretical (foundational) perspective. Modes of philosophical inquiry will be discussed throughout the chapter.

38.1.1 Education and Research

I would like to begin this chapter with a brief definition and discussion of what I would consider a mainstream position of what constitutes educational research (Anderson, 1990). I do this in order to situate my discussion of philosophy, research, and education:

> Research in education is a disciplined attempt to address questions or solve problems through the collection and analysis of primary data for the purpose of description, explanation, generalization, and prediction (Anderson, 1990, p. 4).

Anderson's (1990) discussion in his first chapter entitled "The Nature of Educational Research" expands this definition. He views educational research as primarily problem solving as opposed to testing of hypothesis. This research is based on "systematic and objective observation, recording and analysis"; it seeks to find "general principles and theories which can lead to the prediction of behaviors and events in the future"; its goals are "understanding, prediction, and ultimately control"; controlled, accurate observation and recording information allows for prediction to be "accurately measured and assessed"; the researcher should be "unbiased" and strive for "objectivity" (p. 5). Furthermore, "research is a scientific process which assumes that events in the world are lawful and orderly" and that the laws are "discoverable." This lawfulness provides the meaning of determinism and the

> researcher acts in the belief that the laws of nature can be understood and ultimately controlled to at least some degree. In a nutshell, educational research is the systematic process of discovering how and why people in educational settings behave as they do (pp. 4–5).

As I stated, I believe this is a mainstream position on educational research.

Anderson also identifies "four different levels at which educational research takes place: descriptive, explanatory, generalization, and basic or theoretical" (1990, p. 7). It is within the basic/theoretical level that Anderson places philosophy as an associated discipline:

> While philosophy does not typically incorporate primary source data, empirical evidence, or observation, it is included as an associated discipline since it relies on similar approaches to other forms of theoretical research (p. 7).

At the same time, in a previous passage, philosophy is not considered research within the definition quoted earlier:

> There is another domain of investigation which some scholars consider research. It includes philosophical analysis, especially conceptual analysis, the situation of educational issues within a philosophical tradition, the examination of epistemological and axiological assumptions, criticism, and so forth. I view such activities as scholarship, but not as research in the sense in which it is used in this text. The principal difference is the lack of primary data in those approaches which rely entirely on critical thinking and analysis of existing literature and theory (Anderson, 1990, p. 5).

The above discussion places philosophy outside legitimate educational research and identifies it as "scholarship." The opening quote by Maxine Greene identifies what is implicit in the writing of this chapter, namely, the belief that the study of philosophy and philosophy of education is most critical for educators and educational researchers. The study of philosophy/philosophy of education can provide the possibility for the empowering practices that Maxine Greene identifies: reflection on one's own life situation, one's own voice with which to speak, and the possibility for action based on decency, humaneness, and justice.

38.1.2   Education as a Moral Undertaking

The study of philosophy/philosophy of education can provide greater insight and understanding into the complexities of schooling. By complexities of schooling I mean that educational practice does not "just happen," does not take

place as an isolated activity. Wingo (1974) identifies the complexities of the school setting:

> Behind every approach to teaching method, behind every plan for administrative organization of the schools, behind the structure of every school curriculum stands a body of accepted doctrine—assumptions, concepts, generalizations, and values. In short, every practical approach to the art of teaching is shored up by some constellation of accepted ideas. Very often, however, the very presence of this body of ideas goes unnoticed. Its acceptance is largely unconscious and based on tradition (p. 6).

Let me be more explicit about this.

As educators, we are concerned with philosophical issues and perspectives in our daily work within classrooms. As we debate curricular issues, as we decide educational policy, as we work with students and their "behavior," as we "test" students' "knowledge," etc., we are concerned with philosophy. However, as Wingo stated in the above quote, the underlying ideas behind our practice may go unnoticed, may be unconscious, may be unquestioned. The importance of philosophical inquiry in education is exactly at this point: It can illuminate, inform, or call into question the taken-for-granted notions that we have. Philosophical inquiry and analysis can help conceptual clarification, as well as inform our praxis, and vice versa.

The Western tradition in philosophy has wrestled with the following questions: What is real (metaphysics/ontology)? How do we know (epistemology)? What is of value (axiology)? Understanding and identifying the nature of reality, what counts for knowledge, and making judgments as to what is of value are all philosophical positions. I will use the term *philosophical inquiry* to mean a form of questioning into (to inquire into) the nature of reality, knowledge, and value. This notion of inquiry is the beginning of doing philosophy, of inquiring into the nature of things (Greene, 1974).

The three questions/positions regarding the nature of reality, knowledge, and value also identify the nature of the concerns of schooling as well as form the basis for philosophical inquiry. If this is so, the lives of educators/researchers are rooted in philosophical and moral struggles and questions, and consequently they cannot view their work as a neutral enterprise. Their lives are rooted in philosophical, moral, and nonneutral (political) realities because educators, schools, communities, interest groups, legislators, religious organizations, and private and corporate enterprise presuppose some conception of reality that they wish to transmit, or pass on to the young. As Childs (1950) stated:

> . . . deliberate education is never morally neutral. A definite expression of preference for certain human ends, or values, is inherent in all efforts to guide the experience of the young. No human group would ever bother to found and maintain a system of schools were it not concerned to make of its children something other than they would become if left to themselves and their surroundings (p. 19).

School practice reflects the interests of divergent groups. The metaphysical/ontological, epistemological, and axiological questions of philosophy are educational questions as well. Research in education reflects this. The differing groups mentioned have interests, and those interests identify the political nature of education (see 1.4).

School curricula reflect multiple world views. Curricula reflect the possibilities of humankind. Curricula can raise critical questions about the nature of the social world and how we know that world, or it can dogmatically repress such exploration. To chose a specific curriculum is to chose from among many possibilities. Curricular decision making is hence a political decision. To say that "... education is a moral undertaking involves choices that make a difference in the individual and social lives of human beings" (Morris & Pai, 1976, p. 18).

The concept of *moral* as used here is from Child's work (1950) *Education and Morals*. He uses the term quite specifically regarding educators' intervention in the lives of their students. Moral refers to:

> ... the more elemental fact that choices among genuine life-alternatives are inescapably involved in the construction and the actual conduct of each and every educational program. These choices necessarily have consequences in the lives of the young, and through them in the life of the society. Viewed from this perspective, education undoubtedly ranks as one of the outstanding moral undertakings of the human race (p. 20).

Furthermore, education is rooted in philosophical and political realities. The philosophical and political roots come in when we are required to make choices from among many possible world-views.[1] [*]

If education is a moral undertaking, as Childs rightly suggests, it is encumbent upon educators to "inquire into their work," to question their theory and practice. Philosophical inquiry provides various ways of doing that.

38.2 PHILOSOPHY AND INQUIRY

Although I was critical of Anderson's (1990) discussion of philosophy and research, I do think he accurately represented the processes of philosophical inquiry: conceptual analysis, situating educational issues within a philosophical tradition, and the examination of epistemological and axiological assumptions, criticism, etc. He also emphasized critical thinking and analysis of existing literature and theory as part of philosophical inquiry. These processes are modes of philosophical inquiry, ways of doing philosophy.

My criticism of Anderson's position centered on his viewing philosophy as an "associated discipline" for research, whereas I believe it to be a foundation (theory) for educational research. To begin to address philosophy as foundation, I will return to the three questions that have concerned philosophers within the Western traditions from the beginning.

What is the nature of reality? What is the nature of knowledge? What is of value (metaphysics, epistemology, axiology, respectively)? These questions provide a *conceptual framework* that gives coherence to the study of philosophy. These questions also identify the major concerns of education and provide the possibility for a coherence in educational practice. By coherence I mean they provide educators with a possible framework for posing questions from multiple perspectives that allow us to reflect on our work. For example, they allow us to pose multiple questions regarding the nature of curricula. They allow us to examine whose knowledge we are promoting, and, even prior to that, what knowledge is of most worth. Questions of value ask us why we choose this particular knowledge and leave all of the rest out, etc. Engaging in this questioning is philosophical inquiry, is "doing" philosophy.

Another framework I can use in looking at the relationship among philosophy, research, and education would be an examination of the differing approaches to the study of philosophy. Wingo (1974) states that we can approach the study of philosophy in three different ways (these ways may also be looked at as the main functions of philosophy): the descriptive, the normative, and the analytic (pp. 15–16).

To engage in descriptive philosophical inquiry, a student would be involved in the study of the history of philosophy. She or he would be studying

> ... what is (and has been) the field of philosophy. Working comprehensively, he is trying to picture the general development of philosophical thought (p. 15).

This is more than studying "intellectual history." As Wingo points out, it is possible to study about what philosophers have said, and at the same time be doing philosophy in that students are "analyzing and clarifying concepts and the language in which ideas are expressed" (p. 15). This is the area that Anderson (1990) identified as situating educational issues within a philosophical tradition—for example, educational issues looked at from the viewpoint of different philosophies, and what writers within those philosophical traditions said about the issues, how they would go about making sense of those issues, establish a world view (metaphysics/ontology), a way of knowing (epistemology), and a way to make decisions regarding action (axiology). Philosophy of education textbooks would be good examples of the descriptive perspective.[2]

To engage in normative philosophical inquiry a student would be involved with values (axiology). Interests could focus on

> ... ethics or aesthetics. He will be involved with advocating some ends or objectives (values) that he believes to be desirable and with explaining the reasons for their desirability. He may also be involved in suggesting means for advocating these values. His main concern is not what is, but what ought to be (p. 15).

Normative philosophical inquiry explores and critiques philosophical positions, as well as makes decisions as the

---

"rightness and wrongness" of those positions (see Webb et al., 1992). The normative perspective reflects Anderson's (1990) earlier position regarding examination of epistemological and axiological assumptions, as well as critical thinking and analysis of existing literature and theory as part of inquiry.[3]

To engage in analytic philosophical inquiry is to engage in the "analysis of language, concepts, theories, and so on" (Wingo, 1974, p. 15). This is the practice that analytic philosophers consider "doing philosophy." According to Webb et al. (1992), analytic philosophy has as its goal

> . . . to improve our understanding of education by clarifying our educational concepts, beliefs, arguments, assumptions. For example, an analytic philosophy of education would attempt to understand such questions as: What is experience? What is understanding? What is readiness? (pp. 174–75).

Anderson referred to the analytic perspective as conceptual analysis.[4]

The framework of the "functions" of philosophy suggests the foundations position mentioned earlier. Each of these three functions can provide multiple possibilities for educational research and, more specifically, philosophical inquiry. The descriptive, normative, and analytic forms of philosophical inquiry suggest in-depth study of the philosophy of education. Looking at different philosophical traditions with regard to metaphysics/ontology, epistemology, and axiology requires study in philosophy. Movements in education, e.g., reconstructionism, perrenialism, Marxism and education, and more recent movements rooted in critical theory, postmodern analyses, and renewed emphasis on democratic schooling and forms of emancipatory praxis represent major areas of study for researchers (see Chapters 9, 10). These areas of study have their own world views and concerns. Writers within these positions offer differing conceptual frameworks, differing questions posed, and hence challenges to status quo practice. And they all engage the student in philosophical inquiry.

I believe that the study of the philosophy of education from the normative, descriptive, and analytic perspectives offers critical means of inquiry into educational realities for researchers. Writing within these frameworks is doing philosophy. Doing philosophy is doing research. The descriptive perspective works out of systems of philosophical thought, schools of thought, and offering foundational positions from which to work; the normative perspective offers a "process of inquiry into ideas and basic beliefs that will enable us to form reasoned attitudes about the important issues of our time" (Wingo, 1974, p. 22). The analytic perspective allows us to inquire into the use of language, the meaning and clarification of language used to talk about education. This is philosophical inquiry. This is doing philosophy.

Education, being a very complex social undertaking, has many important dimensions that can be examined from psychological (see Chapters 2, 5), sociological, and political perspectives, yet there is one question that is uniquely philosophical (see Chapter 6): "the question of determining

the ends of education" (Wingo, 1974, p. 22). The means and ends of education are inseparably united. Wingo (1974) quotes Max Black:

> All serious discussion of educational problems, no matter how specific, soon leads to consideration of educational aims, and becomes a conversation about the good life, the nature of man, the varieties of experience. But these are the perennial themes of philosophical investigation. It might be a hard thing to expect educators to be philosophical, but can they be anything else? (p. 22).

Conceptualizations about "the good life," the nature of humankind, etc., are problematic in the sense that there are no final, all-inclusive positions on these concepts. Inquiry into these issues can take place through the descriptive, normative, and analytic perspectives. Each of these perspectives, again, will demand that different questions be posed. This process is doing philosophy, doing philosophical inquiry.

To understand how the three perspectives can be used in the study of education, Wingo (1974) suggests that there are three assumptions that underlie the nature of philosophical inquiry in education. These three assumptions are critical to an understanding of the importance, scope, and possibility the study of philosophy has for the study of education. As obvious as it may seem, the first assumption is: "The primary subject matter of philosophy of education is education itself" (p. 24). Thus the phenomena of education, in all its myriad forms, are the "subject matter" for study. From a research point of view this can mean looking at curricula, the outcomes of learning, testing, organizational matters, place of schools within the social setting, the means-ends of education, etc., etc.

The second, and perhaps the most insightful and critical assumption, states that "Education always takes place within a certain constellation of cultural conditions and therefore it cannot be studied as a set of universal and independent phenomena" (p. 24). This assumption means that there is no "one best system" to model schools after and no single answer to complex educational situations. This assumption suggests that we need to view education relationally, in context (cf. Apple, 1979; Beyer, 1986; Purpel, 1993), and clearly identifies the complex nature of understanding education. At the same time, this assumption suggests the myriad possibilities for inquiry into the process of schooling. By this I mean that the nature of the inquiry is dependent on the researcher. It is not standardized; it is not given (cf. Eisner, 1991).

The third assumption states that the "basic purpose of philosophy of education applies to the ends and means of education and their interrelationships" (Wingo, 1974, p. 24). The assumption suggests the complexity of educational experience and the many variables/factors that influence the process. These assumptions clearly call for the descriptive, normative, and analytic perspectives of viewing educational realities, but also point toward the need for expanding our decision to accommodate other perspectives such as interpretive and critical forms of inquiry, as well as the empirical.

A way to expand my discussion to accommodate other perspectives that can be used in looking at the relationship between philosophy, inquiry, and education can be found in examining research paradigms. This framework (research paradigms) extends the more-traditional descriptive, normative, and analytic perspectives by looking at methodological/epistemological viewpoints. This framework allows the researcher to identify human interests within modes of inquiry.[5]

Bredo and Feinberg (1982) discuss differing paradigms according to the research methodologies utilized. These methodologies have inherent interests in the kind of research findings sought and generated. The paradigms identified are the positivistic, the interpretive, and the critical approaches to social and educational research. These paradigms have fundamental differences that separate the positivistic from the interpretive and critical approaches. These differences are of a philosophical nature concerning metaphysics, subject-object dualism, generalization, causality, and axiology (Koetting, 1985).

If I pose the question "Why do we do research?", my response will allow me to explore the framework (research paradigms) as follows:

We do research in order to gain a clear/clearer perception of reality and our relationship to that reality. This clearer perception can be of benefit to us and others depending on our interests: What are we searching for? (Truth? Knowledge? Information? Understanding? Explanation? Emancipation?) This notion of interest also bears on why we ask certain research questions, as well as what the nature of the research question/problem/situation under investigation might be. Positivist science has an interest in technical control; interpretive science has an interest in understanding; and critical science has an interest in emancipation. For example, I may try to better control reality in order to make predictions, develop lawlike theories and explanations, establish causal relationships, etc. This would correspond to the positivist, empirical approach to research. I may want to better understand reality, and hence understand myself and others within a particular context. I may want to understand the meanings attached to social customs, the diversity of meaning in multiple interpretations of singular events, etc. This would correspond to the interpretive approach to research. I may want to better understand reality, and hence understand myself and others within a particular context in order to act within that context, to effect change. This corresponds to the critical approach to social and educational research.

There are fundamental differences that separate forms of inquiry, and the differences are of a philosophical nature. The differences are concerned with the three questions of philosophy stated earlier: metaphysics/ontology, epistemology, and axiology (also cf. Koetting, 1985, 1993). These concerns keep us rooted in doing philosophy.

Although I have used the term *foundations* frequently in this section, I am not talking about the establishment of a "metanarrative" (Lyotard, 1989; Hlynka & Yeaman, 1992).

I am not talking about "doing philosophy in the grand manner" of building systems of thought (Wingo, 1974). I do not believe that there is only one complete explanation or understanding of our social world and that given the time and effort we will be able to "figure things out." What I am saying about foundations is the way in which philosophy is carried out—within philosophical inquiry, the problem posing, the questioning, the search for clarification, the quest for seeing things relationally—provides multiple ways of inquiring into the world of social and educational realities (see Chapters 9, 10).

Martusewicz and Reynolds (1994) state a similar position regarding foundations. They see the "job" of foundations

> . . . to raise questions and offer points of view that ask us to see what we do as teachers or as students in new or at least unfamiliar ways, from another side, perhaps from the inside, of perhaps from both inside and outside. It is an invitation to look at education both socially and historically as well as practically, that is, from the inside (the complex processes, methods, and relations that affect individuals in schools, for example) within the context of the outside (the larger social, economic, and political forces that have affected those processes over time) (p. 2).

This notion of inside/outside (school/world) suggests the "flux of boundaries," and allows the researcher/participant to see the relationships of seemingly separate realities, as well as questions the idea of foundations as a "stable set of knowledges, concepts, or principles to be discovered, defined, and then presented in a unilinear way" (Martusewicz & Reynolds, 1994, p. 3; also see Greene, 1974). Again, there is no one best way to explain what happens in the world or in education. Possibilities for understanding, however, can take place when we pay "particular attention to perspectives that maintain a critical stance, a willingness to put existing assumptions and interpretations into question" (Mantusewicz & Reynolds, 1994, p. 3).

As I become engaged in this form of critical inquiry, I become involved in theory (foundations). There are multiple theoretical perspectives on the world, knowledge, value.[6] However, there is no metanarrative. There is no grand philosophy (Greene, 1974, 1994; Martusewicz & Reynolds, 1994). Returning to an assumption made earlier in this chapter from Wingo (1974),

> Education always takes place within a certain constellation of cultural conditions and therefore it cannot be studied as a set of universal and independent phenomena. Some set of relations among education, politics, and social institutions is inevitable and cannot be ignored in any useful analysis (p. 24).

There are multiple explanations/understandings of schooling, of the "world," and multiple ways of knowing. In the next section of this chapter, I will turn to a discussion of theory. Understanding the notion of theory can provide insight into the multiple interpretations of the world and experience. Theorizing is a mode of philosophical inquiry that suggests the complexities and possibilities for creating/constructing knowledge.

38.3 THEORY AND PHILOSOPHICAL INQUIRY

Theorizing is a mode of philosophical inquiry. It is an important mode of inquiry in that, as educators/researchers, we take a theoretical stance with regard to our work (Koetting, 1993). Stated another way, as educators/researchers, we work out of a theoretical framework that is very closely related to our orientation to the world. This happens whether we are conscious of it or not. Furthermore, it is important that we reflect on that stance, that we try to understand how that stance affects our practice, and, vice versa, that we understand how the practice influences our theoretical stance. This is directly related to my earlier discussion of the moral nature of our work (we intervene in the lives of people).

How do I define/talk about theory that helps shape my practice, and about how practice helps to shape theory? Stated simply, theory is a "worldview, a way of looking at and explaining a set of phenomena" (Martusewicz & Reynolds, 1994, p. 5). In relation to philosophy and education, Gutek (1988) refers to theory as a "grouping or clustering of general ideas or propositions that explain the operations of an institution, such as school, or a situation, such as teaching or learning," and that these ideas are "sufficiently abstract or general that they can be transferred and applied to situations other than those in which they are directly developed" (p. 250). Theory can also refer to an "opinion that originates from trying to establish generalizable patterns from facts, information, or practices" (Gutek, 1988, p. 251).

Where do educational theories come from? How do educators arrive at theoretical positions? Gutek (1988) discusses three sources of educational theory. Educational theory can be derived from philosophies or ideologies; educational theory can be constructed from reactions to certain "social, political, and economic situations"; and theories can be constructed from educational practice. I will discuss each of these sources.

First, theories are derived from philosophies and ideologies. This is the study of philosophy of education. Education is examined within the broader context of individual philosophical systems. Although these systems may not have dealt specifically with education, educators, writers, and scholars derive educational positions from these philosophies and apply principles from their study to schooling. For example, progressivism, as a theory of education, is derived from elements of pragmatism and naturalism. Similarly, I can derive a theory of education from ideological positions. For example, a view of the American democratic ideology can be found in public school settings. Theories of education can be derived from a Marxist ideology. And finally, educational theories can be derived from blending philosophy and ideology, as in social reconstructionism, a blending of philosophical elements found in pragmatism, and ideological elements found in utopianism (cf. Gutek, 1988, pp. 250–55). This theorizing is philosophical inquiry.

A second way to develop educational theory is from reactions to certain "social, political, and economic situations." Gutek (1988) suggests studying the history of American education to understand the reactive nature of educational theories. For example, in the late 19th and early 20th centuries, educational critics said that:

> Schools had become too formal, devitalized, and geared to rote learning. In some of the big cities, school systems were mired in political patronage and corruption. Progressivism as an educational movement and the various experimental schools that it simulated, including John Dewey's at the University of Chicago, were reactions designed to bring about the reform of American society and education (p. 252).

This examination and critique of existing literature (cf. Anderson, 1990) is philosophical inquiry, is doing philosophy.

Finally, educational theories can be constructed from educational practice. The effective schools movement provides an example of theory derived from practice (Gutek, 1988). Schools, teachers, and administrators are singled out for their effectiveness in bringing about higher levels of student achievement. Research is conducted, findings are analyzed, generalizations and principles are offered. A research report is published by the Department of Education entitled *What Works: Research about Teaching and Learning* (1986, quoted in Gutek). The report

> . . . is based on a research investigation and analysis of school practices. Information about these practices is organized as findings. These findings have sufficient generality about them that they can be applied in various school settings. In other words, they represent an emerging theory of education (pp. 253–54).

Examples of theoretical generalizations and principles from the report are:

> Parents are their children's first and most influential teachers. What parents do to help their children learn is more important to academic success than how well-off the family is.
> Children learn science best when they are able to do experiments, so they can witness "science in action."
> Belief in the value of hard work, the importance of personal responsibility, and the importance of education itself contribute to greater success in school (all quoted in Gutek, 1988, pp. 253–54).

These three sources allow us to engage in philosophical inquiry, theorizing possible understandings of realities/schooling. This theorizing is a mode of doing research, a way of doing philosophy. As stated at the beginning of this section, inquiry happens whether we are aware of it or not, and suggests the importance of "thinking about what we are doing" (Greene, 1974, quoting Arendt, p. 6). This theorizing, this doing philosophy, is what Greene (1974) refers to as "wide-awakeness," thinking about commitment and action wherever we "work and make" our lives. "In other words, we shall attempt to do philosophy with respect to teaching, learning, the aims and policies of education, the choices to be made in classrooms, the goods to be pursued" (p. 6).

Another way of talking about theory, to identify the nature of differing theoretical positions, is to view theory in relation to method and interest (Koetting & Januszewski, 1991). From this viewpoint, knowledge of the world is constructed through a dialectical relationship with that world; i.e., we are shaped by our world, and we help to shape that world. Thus:

> . . . theorizing about that world is part of a social process, and therefore, theory itself can be considered a social construction. Theorizing, as a social construction/social process, arises out of humankind's desire to explain and/or understand and/or to change the world (Koetting & Januszewski, 1991, p. 97).

This analysis is based on the work of Habermas (1971) and thus has a philosophical position within critical theory. Habermas's theory of knowledge and interests has three forms/processes of inquiry: empirical-analytic, historical-hermeneutic, and critical. Drawing upon a previous work (Koetting & Januszewski, 1991), I will briefly present these processes.[7]

Theory can serve to explain both the conscious and unconscious. Theory can be seen as a "hypothetical position which can be proven/disproven through empirical testing." It suggests causal relationships:

> This notion of explaining things is the basis for rational thought. Nomological knowledge is the result of such endeavours. Nomological suggests law-like propositions based on the results of the testing of hypotheses. This form of theory (empirical/ analytic theory) has an interest in prediction and control (Koetting & Januszewski, 1991, p. 97).

Theory can serve to help us better understand/make sense of the world, as well ourselves and others within that world. When we are engaged in this form of investigation, our interest is not explanation but understanding. Thus we are involved in an

> . . . interpretive mode of understanding/theorizing and this theoretical stance to the world sees reality as a social construction. This form of theory (historical/hermeneutic theory) has an interest in better understanding social construction through consensual agreement (Koetting & Januszewski, 1991, pp. 97–98).

The third use of theory can help us gain insight into seemingly "given" realities. Through a process of reflective critique we can:

> . . . examine the social construction of reality and seek ways to analyze the contradictions found in reality (the "is" and the "ought"). Through a shared vision we can begin to set about the enormous difficulty of changing (our) individual and group context (p. 98).

To effect change within that context a different understanding of reality is needed. This form of theorizing (critical theory) has an interest in emancipation. In this context emancipation means:

> . . . the possibility of individuals freeing themselves from "law-like rules" and patterns of action in "nature" and his-

tory so that they can reflect and act on the dialectical process of creating and recreating themselves and their institutions' (Apple, 1975, p. 126). In this sense, emancipation is a continual process of "critique of everyday life" (Koetting & Januszewski, 1991, p. 98).

This discussion of theory/theorizing returns us to the main focus of this chapter: philosophy, inquiry, and education. There are fundamental differences within the empirical, hermeneutical, and critical modes of knowing and theorizing, and these differences are of a philosophical nature. Each form of inquiry has its own understanding of the nature of reality, the nature of knowledge, and the nature of value (metaphysics, epistemology, axiology) (see 9.3). Hence theory and theorizing raise questions of a philosophical nature. To become engaged in raising these questions is philosophical inquiry, is doing philosophy. This is the sense in which Eisner (1991) referred to philosophy as being nagging, "conjoling us" into asking more questions about the nature of things, generating "doubt and uncertainties," and, perhaps, hindering us in getting our work done.

Theory and theorizing does lead us to ask questions of a philosophic nature. Giarelli and Chambliss (1984) state that it is the philosopher's "task to ask the unasked questions" (p. 36). They state that "without a formulated question, there can be no inquiry" (p. 36). They identify the special task of philosophy as

> . . . the formulation of questions for reflective thought. The philosopher, as a qualitative thinker, tries to cultivate a sensitivity to the situation as a whole and to the qualities that regulate it. . . . For the philosopher, the issue always is, "What is the problem?" which in turn depends on a prior question, "What is this all about?" (p. 37).

The philosopher as "qualitative thinker" does not seek certain knowledge or truth, but rather is concerned with meaning. In this sense,

> Philosophy does not aim at making the world, for its concern is not action, but qualities. Rather, philosophy serves an educational role. It mediates between immediate experience and experiment and promotes the intelligent development of value (Giarelli & Chambliss, 1984, p. 38).

The educational role of philosophy can be seen within public philosophy of education. Public philosophers of education "see the context of educational problems to be social and cultural life" (p. 40). The social and historical processes of education include the interactions of differing institutions and participants whose intent is to conserve, create, and criticize culture. Public philosophy focuses on creating a context for understanding the process of education as a whole.

> Their methods are synthetic rather that analytic and aim to integrate and give synoptic meaning to knowledge from all perspectives (e.g., history, sociology, economics, anthropology, psychology, etc.), about all educative institutions (e.g., family, school, workplace, church, community, media, etc.), in order to construct a context or a vision of education in its widest cultural sense. Without such a con-

text, efforts to resolve educational problems will be short-sighted and short-lived (p. 40).

This position of the public philosophers of education relates to Wingo's (1974) second assumption that underlies the nature of inquiry in the study of philosophy and education, namely, that "Education always takes place within a certain constellation of cultural conditions and therefore it cannot be studied as a set of universal and independent phenomena" (p. 24). Giarelli and Chambliss (1984) build on Wingo's assumption and show the broader context of the discussion.[8] They discuss the nature of questioning:

> All questions arise from within a perceptual field, a whole, a context, or a situation. Inquiry is the exploration of questions (or queries) that arise and take particular shape in a situation. The same may be said for "research," which word comes from the Latin *re-circere,* "to go around again." Research is going around, exploring, looking within a situation, context, or field. Inquiry, then, is not simply questioning or searching. It is questioning and searching with an intent, with some limits, or with an object in mind (p. 36).

This questioning is a mode of philosophical inquiry and will help to identify the fundamental problems in education, which depend on an aesthetic judgment (axiology) of "where the difficulty is and on qualitative thinking to bring these difficulties into the form of questions and problems that can be researched" (Giarelli & Chambliss, 1984, p. 45). In other words, these "questions and problems that can be researched" are not arbitrary; they do not just "appear." They are contextual, purposive, limited in scope, necessitating further questioning, and have a particular "object" in mind which changes as we question, search, re-question, re-search.

My discussion in this section has gone from theory and theorizing as philosophical inquiry to the nature of questioning within the context of a public philosophy of education. The nature of questioning, our engagement in the process of questioning, is philosophical inquiry, is doing philosophy.

The present status of "doing philosophy," particularly philosophy of education, has broadened into multiple discourses. Ozmon and Craver (1995) suggest that the "current mood" in philosophy of education is moving away from "overriding systems of thought" and is concerned with problems and issues in particular contexts, becoming the new arena for philosophy of education. At the same time, the philosophical task remains one of "constant probing and inquiry" (p. xxv). This suggests to me the notion of public philosophy of education mentioned above in the work of Giarelli and Chambliss (1984). This "new arena of philosophy" is what was meant by the construction of a "context or vision of education in its widest cultural sense" (p. 40).

38.4 CONCLUDING DISCUSSION: DOING PHILOSOPHY

I want to revisit some concepts/terms used during the course of this chapter. This will be done matter-of-factly, cryptically, to the point.

- Education is a moral undertaking, and therefore our practice within education must be open to reflective inquiry.
- To engage in philosophical inquiry is to theorize, to analyze, to critique, to raise questions about, and/or to pose as problematic.
- Theory can be derived from other systems of thought—from social, political, and/or economic situations—and can be constructed from practice.
- Philosophical inquiry is concerned with (i.e., "inquires into") the nature of reality, knowledge, and value.
- Philosophical inquiry is descriptive, normative, and analytic. It is interpretive and critical.
- Modes of philosophical inquiry have interests: interpretive inquiry has an interest in understanding; critical inquiry has an interest in emancipation.
- Critical inquiry is a mode of philosophical inquiry that questions the nature of things, questions reality, looks for contradictions, and is change oriented.
- The major task of philosophy is the posing of questions. It is the basis for research; it is the foundation. Without good questions, there is no inquiry.
- Philosophical inquiry is doing philosophy.
- Philosophical inquiry is philosophical research.

Quantitative research also relies on philosophical inquiry. Sherman, Webb, and Andrews (1984) argue that even a study (e.g., a dissertation) that has a "quantitative formulation" has a

> . . . qualitative context out of which it grows and to which its conclusions must be put. The "statement of the problem" in such a study, to be made clearly, calls on philosophy, and the chapter in which conclusions are suggested to be important (for further research or for practice) is philosophical in its axiological import. And one may see a "review of the literature" in any study as an historical account of what has been tried in reference to the problem at hand (p. 33).

This position captures the sense in which I believe philosophy and its modes of inquiry are the foundation for educational research.

As I have stressed during this chapter, philosophical inquiry is doing philosophy. Maxine Greene (1974) has captured, in a very insightful and existential way, what it means to do philosophy. I have used her work in the course of this chapter, and I would like to present a few more of her thoughts on what it means to do philosophy.

Greene (1974) regards philosophy as a way to approach (a way to look at, or to take a stance with respect to) knowledge gained through study of the sciences and the arts, as well as the personal understandings and insights that each of us acquires through daily life. Philosophy allows us a way to ask questions that have to do with:

> . . . what is presupposed, perceived, intuited, believed, and known. It is a way of contemplating, examining, or thinking about what is taken to be significant, valuable, beautiful, worthy of commitment. It is a way of becoming self-aware, of constituting meanings in one's life-world.

Critical thinking is demanded, as are deliberate attempts to make things clear (p. 7).

There is the exploration of "background consciousness" and boundaries; there is the creation of "unifying perspectives"; there is normative thinking; there is the "probing of what might be, what should be," and the "forging of ideals." Doing philosophy is becoming conscious of the world as it presents itself to our consciousness. "To do philosophy, as Jean-Paul Sartre says, is to develop a fundamental project, to go beyond the situations one confronts and refuse reality as given in the name of a reality to be produced" (p. 7).

To do educational philosophy, we must become critically aware of the complexities of the teaching and learning context. We must clarify the meanings of education and the language of schooling. We must become clear about preferences for the "good" and the "right" which motivate pressure groups as they place demands on schools (Greene, 1974, p. 7). This calls for critical, analytic, and normative philosophical inquiry.

We do philosophy (theorize) when, for whatever reason, we are:

. . . aroused to wonder about how events and experiences are interpreted and should be interpreted. We philosophize when we can no longer tolerate the splits and fragmentations in our pictures of the world, when we desire some kind of wholeness and integration, some coherence which is our own (Greene, 1974, pp. 10–11).

This requires that we be "wide-awake" within our world, with others, within our communities. To be closed off because of

. . . snobbery, ignorance, or fear is to be deprived of the content that makes concepts meaningful. It is, as well, to be deprived of the very ground of questioning. For this reason, the teacher who dares to do philosophy must be open to such a multiplicity of realities. He cannot do so if he cannot perceive himself, in both his freedom and his limitations, as someone who must constitute his own meanings with the aid of what his culture provides. Nor can he do so if he is incapable of "bracketing," or setting aside, on occasion the presuppositions that fix his vision of the world (Greene, 1974, p. 11).

I sense that this feeling of a fractured, fragmented world is part of the human condition, our sense of not "being at home" in the world. To remain open to multiple perspectives of the world, to create our own meanings and yet have to bracket them to understand another, etc., leaves one with a sense of unquietness (cf., Koetting, 1994). And yet not to be able to do this, leaves us (teachers), like our students, to live in a world that is primarily prefabricated by others for what they consider to be "the public." Thus:

On occasion, he must be critically attentive; he must consciously choose what to appropriate and what to discard. Reliance on the natural attitude—a commonsense taking for granted of the everyday—will not suffice. In some fashion, the everyday must be rendered problematic so that questions may be posed (Greene, 1974, p. 11).

Greene is speaking of the difficult task of maintaining a philosophical attitude, a person/teacher who sees philosophically, and can communicate that attitude to students, that sense of empowerment to transform their situations. Thus students:

. . . need to be enabled—through habituation and stimulation—to initiate inquiries. To be equipped for inquiry is to be equipped to engage in a process through which objects and events can be seen in connection with other objects and events in the experienced world (Greene, 1974, p. 158).

This is working with students to do philosophy, to develop the philosophical attitude/orientation; this is seeing realities relationally and not in isolation. We need to show, as well as believe, that students are capable of doing philosophy.

Maxine Greene identifies what it means to do philosophy, to engage in philosophical inquiry. I have presented many of the theoretical positions that she demonstrates. I have referred to this as the philosophical attitude/orientation. There are many texts that will convey this attitude which would be helpful for initiating or continuing study in educational research.

There are texts on inquiry that are of a philosophical nature, that present in great depth the theoretical positions, the modes of inquiry, and examples of critical research.[9] There are texts within the field of educational technology that convey the theoretical positions for engaging in multiple forms of research.[10] And there are texts of critical essays that are examples of the forms of philosophical inquiry discussed in this chapter. They are examples of doing philosophy.[11]

In conclusion, I refer you to the following work: Schubert, William H. (1991). Philosophical inquiry: the speculative essay. *In* Edmund C. Short, ed. (1991). *Forms of curriculum inquiry*. Albany: SUNY Press. Engage yourself in doing philosophy.

ENDNOTES

1. Recent educational critics suggest that we have lost this sense of education as a moral undertaking. Representative essays of a philosophical nature would be Beyer, 1988; Purpel, 1993; Giroux, 1988; Aronowitz & Giroux, 1985.
2. Examples of descriptive philosophical inquiry can be found in the following philosophy of education texts: Wingo, 1974; Gutek, 1988; Ozmon & Craver, 1995.
3. See Kaufmann, 1974, and Dewey, 1904 (1964), for examples of normative philosophical inquiry.
4. Examples of analytic inquiry would be Tom, 1984; Wilson, 1963.
5. The foundational (theoretical) text that influenced my study was Jurgen Habermas, 1971. Also, as secondary texts, Bernstein (1976) offers an historical perspective and overview of mainstream social science and moves through theoretical positions of language, analysis, phenomenology, and critical theory (also Schroyer, 1973).
6. Note the chapters in this volume on "Postmodern and Poststructuralist Theory" (Yeaman et al., Chapter 10)

and on "Critical Theory and Educational Technology" (Nichols & Allen-Brown, Chapter 9).

7. This discussion of theorizing relates to my earlier discussion of research paradigms and interest.

8. Giarelli & Chambliss (1984) identify Dewey's *Democracy and Education* (1944) as a "classic example" of public philosophy of education. Also, cf. Aronowitz & Giroux, 1985.

9. Bredo & Feinberg, 1982; Carr & Kemmis, 1986; Eisner, 1991, 1994; Kincheloe, 1991; Popkewitz, 1984; Cherryholmes, 1988.

10. Hlynka & Belland, 1991; Muffoletto & Knupfer, 1993; *Educational Technology,* Vol. 34, No. 2, Yeaman, guest ed., 1994; Robinson, 1990.

11. Short, 1991; Beyer & Apple, 1988; Martusewicz & Reynolds, 1994; Greene, 1978; Pinar, 1988; McLaren & Leonard, 1993; Dobson, Dobson & Koetting, 1985.

REFERENCES

Anderson, G. (1990). *Fundamentals of educational research.* New York: Falmer.

Apple, M.W. (1979). *Ideology and curriculum.* London: Routledge.

— (1975). Scientific interests and the nature of educational institutions. *In* W. Pinar. *Curriculum theorizing: the reconceptualists.* Berkeley, CA: McCutchan.

Aronowitz, S. & Giroux, H.A. (1991). *Postmodern education: politics, culture, and social criticism.* Minneapolis, MN: University of Minnesota Press.

— & — (1985). Education and the crisis of public philosophy. *In* S. Aronowitz & H.A. Giroux, *Education under siege: the conservative, liberal and radical debate over schooling.* Boston, MA: Bergin & Garvey.

Bernstein, R.J. (1978). *The restructuring of social and political theory.* Philadelphia, PA: University of Pennsylvania Press.

Beyer, L.E. (1988). Schooling for the culture of democracy. *In* L.E. Beyer & M.W. Apple, *The curriculum: problems, politics, & possibilities.* Albany, NY: SUNY Press.

— (1986, Mar., Apr.). Beyond elitism and technicism: teacher education as practical philosophy. *Journal of Teacher Education 37* (2).

Bredo, E. & Feinberg, W. (1982). *Knowledge and values in social and educational research.* Philadelphia, PA: Temple University Press.

Carr, W. & Kemmis, S. (1986). *Becoming critical: education, knowledge, and action research.* Philadelphia, PA: Falmer.

Cherryholmes, C. (1988). *Power and criticism: poststructural investigations in education.* New York: Teachers College Press.

Childs, J.L. (1950). *Education and morals.* New York: Wiley.

Dewey, J. (1944). *Democracy and education: an introduction to the philosophy of education.* New York: Free Press.

— (1904/1964). *The relation of theory to practice in education.* New York: Modern Library.

Dobson, R.L., Dobson, J.E. & Koetting, J.R. (1985). Looking at, talking about, and living with children: reflections on the process of schooling. New York: University Press of America.

Eisner, E.W. (1994). *The educational imagination: on the design and evaluation of school programs,* 3d ed. New York: Macmillan.

— (1991). *The enlightened eye: qualitative inquiry and the enhancement of educational practice.* New York: Macmillan.

Giarelli, J.M. & Chambliss, J.J. (1984). Philosophy of education as qualitative inquiry. *Journal of Thought 19* (2).

Giroux, H.A. (1988). *Teachers as intellectuals: toward a critical pedagogy of learning.* Boston, MA: Bergin & Garvey.

Greene, M. (1994). Epistemology and educational research: the influence of recent approaches to knowledge. *In,* L. Darling-Hammond, ed. *Review of research in education,* Vol. 20. Washington, DC: AERA.

— (1978). *Landscapes of meaning.* New York: Teachers College Press.

— (1974). *Teacher as stranger: educational philosophy for the modern age.* Belmont, CA: Wadsworth.

Gutek, G.L. (1988). *Philosophical and ideological perspectives on education.* Englewood Cliffs, NJ: Prentice Hall.

Habermas, J. (1971). *Knowledge and human interests.* Boston, MA: Beacon.

Hlynka, D. & Belland, J.C., eds. (1991). *Paradigms regained: the uses of illuminative, semiotic, and post-modern criticism as modes of inquiry in educational technology.* Englewood Cliffs, NJ: Educational Technology.

— & Yeaman, A.R.J. (1992). Postmodern educational technology. *ERIC Digest.* EDO-IR-92-5.

Kaufmann, W. (1966). Educational development from the point of view of a normative philosophy. *In* G. Barnett, ed. *Philosophy and educational development.* Boston, MA: Houghton Mifflin.

Kincheloe, J.L. ((1991). *Teachers as researchers: qualitative inquiry as a path to empowerment.* New York: Falmer.

Koetting, J.R. (1994). Postmodern thinking in a modernist cultural climate: the need for an unquiet pedagogy. *Educational Technology 34* (2).

— (1993). Educational technology, curriculum theory, and social foundations: toward a new language of possibility. *In* R. Muffoletto & N.N. Knupfer, eds. *Computers in education: social, political, and historical perspectives.* Cresskill, NJ: Hampton.

— & Januszewski, A. (1991). The notion of theory and educational technology: foundation for understanding. *Educational and Training Technology International 28* (2).

— (1985). Foundations of naturalistic inquiry: developing a theory base for understanding individual interpretations of reality. *Media and Adult Learning 6* (2).

— (1983). Philosophical foundations of instructional technology. *Proceedings.* RTD-AECT, Dallas, TX, 1983.

— (1979). *Towards a synthesis of a theory of knowledge and human interests, educational technology and emancipatory education: a preliminary theoretical investigation and critique.* Unpublished doctoral dissertation. University of Wisconsin-Madison.

Lyotard, J-F. (1984). *The postmodern condition: a report on knowledge.* Minneapolis, MN: University of Minnesota Press.

Martusewicz, R.A. & Reynolds, W.M., eds. (1994). *Inside/out: contemporary critical perspectives in education.* New York: St. Martin's.

McLaren, P. & Leonard, P., eds. (1993). *Paulo Freire: a critical encounter.* New York: Routledge.

Morris, V.C. & Young, Pai (1976). *Philosophy and the American school: an introduction to the philosophy of education,* 2d ed. Boston, MA: Houghton Mifflin.

Muffoletto, R. & Knupfer, N.N., eds. (1993). *Computers in education: social, political, and historical perspectives.* Cresskill, NJ: Hampton.

Nichols, R. & Allen-Brown, V. (1996). Critical theory and educational technology. *Handbook of research on educational communications and technology.* This volume.

Ozmon, H. & Craver, S. (1995). *Philosophical foundations of education,* 5th ed. Westerville, OH: Merrill.

Pinar, W.F., ed. (1988). *Contemporary curriculum discourses.* Scotsdale, AR: Gorsuch Scarisbrick.

Popkewitz, T.S. (1984). *Paradigm and ideology in educational research: the social functions of the intellectual.* New York: Falmer.

Purpel, D.E. (1993). Educational discourse and global crisis: what's a teacher to do? *In* H. Shapiro & D.E. Purpel, eds. *Critical social issues in American education: toward the 21st century.* New York: Longman.

Robinson, R.S., ed. (1990). *Journal of Thought 25* (1 & 2).

Schroyer, T. (1973). *The critique of domination.* Boston, MA: Beacon.

Schubert, W.H. (1991). Philosophical inquiry: the speculative essay. *In* E.C. Short, ed. *Forms of curriculum inquiry.* Albany, NY: SUNY Press.

Sherman, R.R., Webb, R.B. & Andrews, S.D., eds. (1984). Qualitative inquiry: an introduction. *Journal of Thought 19* (2).

Short, E.C. ed. (1991). *Forms of curriculum inquiry.* Albany, NY: SUNY Press.

Simon, R.I. (1992). *Teaching against the grain: texts for a pedagogy of possibility.* Boston, MA: Bergin & Garvey.

Webb, L.D., Metha, A. & Jordan, K.F. (1992). *Foundations of American education.* Westerville, OH: Merrill.

Wilson, J. (1969). *Thinking with concepts.* Cambridge, MA: Cambridge University Press.

Winch, P. (1958). *The idea of a social science and its relation to philosophy.* London: Routledge.

Wingo, M. (1974). *Philosophies of education: an introduction.* Lexington, MA: Heath.

Yeaman, A.R.J. & Hylinka, D. (1996). Postmodern and poststructuralist theory. This volume.

— , Koetting, J.R. & Nichols, R.G. (1994). Critical theory, cultural analysis, and the ethics of educational technology as social responsibility. *Educational technology 34* (2).

39. EXPERIMENTAL RESEARCH METHODS

Steven M. Ross   Gary R. Morrison

UNIVERSITY OF MEMPHIS

39.1 EVOLUTION OF EXPERIMENTAL RESEARCH METHODS

Experimental research has had a long tradition in psychology and education. When psychology emerged as an infant science during the 1900s, it modeled its research methods on the established paradigms of the physical sciences, which for centuries relied on experimentation to derive principals and laws. Subsequent reliance on experimental approaches was strengthened by behavioral approaches to psychology and education that predominated during the first half of this century. Thus, usage of experimentation in educational technology over the past 40 years has been influenced by developments in theory and research practices within its parent disciplines.

In this chapter, we shall examine practices, issues, and trends related to the application of experimental research methods in educational technology. The purpose is to provide readers with sufficient background to understand and evaluate experimental designs encountered in the literature and to identify designs that will effectively address questions of interest in their own research. In an introductory section, we shall define experimental research, differentiate it from alternative approaches, and identify important concepts in its use (e.g., internal vs. external validity). We shall also suggest procedures for conducting experimental studies and publishing them in educational technology research journals. Next, we shall analyze uses of experimental methods by instructional researchers, extending the analyses of 2 decades ago by Clark and Snow (1975). In the concluding section, we shall turn to issues in using experimental research in educational technology, to include balancing internal and external validity, using multiple outcome measures to assess learning processes and products, using item responses vs. aggregate scores as dependent variables, and media replications vs. media comparisons.

39.2 WHAT IS EXPERIMENTAL RESEARCH?

The experimental method formally surfaced in educational psychology around the turn of the century, with the classic studies by Thorndike and Woodworth on transfer (Cronbach, 1957). The experimenter's interest in the effect of environmental change, referred to as "treatments," demanded designs using standardized procedures to hold all conditions constant except the independent (experimental) variable. This standardization ensured high *internal validity* in comparing the experimental group to the control group on the dependent or "outcome" variable. That is, when internal validity was high, differences between groups could be confidently attributed to the treatment, thus ruling out rival hypotheses attributing effects to extraneous factors. Traditionally, experimenters have given less emphasis to external validity, which concerns the generalizability of findings to other settings, particularly realistic ones. One theme of this chapter is that current orientations in instructional theory and research practices necessitate achieving a better balance between internal and external validity levels.

During the past century, the experimental method has remained immune to paradigm shifts in the psychology of learning, including behaviorism to cognitivism, objectivism to cognitivism (see 5.5), and instructivism to constructivism (see Jonassen, 1991; Jonassen, Campbell & Davidson, 1994; see 7.2, 24.3). Clearly, the logical positivism of behavioristic theory created a fertile, inviting framework for attempts to establish causal relationships between variables, using experimental methods (see 2.2). The emergence of cognitive learning theory in the 1970s and 1980s initially did little to change this view, as researchers changed the locus of inquiry from behavior to mental processing, but maintained the experimental method as the basic way they searched for scientific truths (see 5.2). Today, the increasing influences of constructivist theories are making the fit between traditional scientific methods and current perspectives on learning more difficult (see 7.3). As Jonassen et al. (1994) state, it is now viewed as much more difficult ". . . to isolate which components of the learning system, the medium, the attributes, the learner, or the environment affect learning and in what ways" (p. 6). Accordingly, without knowing the ultimate impact or longevity of the constructivist view, we acknowledge its contribution in conveying instruction and learning as less orderly than preceding paradigms had depicted, and the learner rather than the "treatment" as deserving more importance in the study of learning processes. Our perspective in this chapter, therefore, is to present experimental methods as continuing to provide valuable "tools" for research, but ones whose uses need to be altered or expanded relative to their traditional functions to accommodate the changing complexion of theory and scientific inquiry in instructional technology.

39.2.1 Types of Experimental Designs

Complete descriptions of alternative experimental designs are provided in Campbell and Stanley (1963) and conventional research textbooks (e.g., Borg, Gall & Gall, 1993; Kerlinger, 1986; McMillan & Schumacher, 1989; Wiersma, 1991). For purposes of providing common background for the present chapter, we have selected four major design approaches to review. These particular designs appeared to be the ones instructional technology researchers would be most likely to use for experimental studies or find in the literature. They are also "core" designs in the sense of including basic components of the more complex or related designs not covered.

39.2.1.1. True Experiments. The "ideal" design for maximizing internal validity is the true experiment, as diagrammed below. The *R* means that subjects were randomly assigned; *X* represents the treatment (in this case, alternative treatments 1 and 2); and *O* means observation (or outcome), for example, a dependent measure of learning or attitude. What distinguishes the true experiment from less powerful designs is the random assignment of subjects to treatments, thereby eliminating any systematic error that might be associated with using intact groups. The two (or more) groups are then subjected to identical environmental conditions, while being exposed to different treatments. In educational technology research, such treatments frequently consist of different instructional methods (see X_1 and X_2 below).

$$R \quad X_1 \quad\quad O$$
$$R \quad X_2 \quad\quad O$$

Example. An example of a true experiment involving an educational technology application is the study by Park and Gittelman (1992) on animation and feedback. College students were randomly assigned to six treatments, 15 subjects per group, comprised of two conditions of visual display (static graphics and animation) crossed with three conditions of feedback (explanatory, knowledge of results, and natural). All subjects were treated identically, with the exception of the manipulation of the assigned visual-feedback treatment combination in the CAI program administered. The major outcome variable (observation) was an achievement posttest on the lesson material. Findings favored the groups that received animation, while showing no effects for the feedback variations. Given the true experimental design employed, the authors could infer that the learning advantages obtained were due to properties of the animation rather than to extraneous factors relating to the

lesson, environment, or instructional delivery. In research parlance, "causal" inferences can be made regarding the effects of the independent (manipulated) variable (in this case, type of display) on the dependent (outcome) variable (in this case, degree of learning).

39.2.1.2. Repeated Measures. A variation of the above experimental design is the situation where all treatments (X_1, X_2, etc.) are administered to all subjects. Thus, each individual (S_1, S_2, etc.), in essence, serves as his or her own control and is tested or "observed" (O), as diagrammed below for an experiment using *n* subjects and *k* treatments. Note that the diagram shows each subject receiving the same sequence of treatments; a stronger design, where feasible, would involve randomly ordering the treatments to eliminate a sequence effect.

$$S_1 \quad X_1 0 - X_2 0 \ldots X_k O$$
$$S_2 \quad X_1 0 - X_2 0 \ldots X_k O$$
$$\cdot$$
$$\cdot$$
$$\cdot$$
$$S_n \quad X_1 0 - X_2 0 \ldots X_k O$$

Suppose that an experimenter is interested in whether learners are more likely to remember words that are italicized or words that are underlined in a computer text presentation. Twenty subjects read a paragraph containing five words in each form. They are then asked to list as many italicized words and as many underlined words as they can remember. (To reduce bias, the forms in which the 10 words are represented are randomly varied for different subjects.) Note that this design has the advantage of using only one group, thereby effectively doubling the number of subjects per treatment relative to a two-group (italics only vs. underline only) design. It also ensures that the ability level of subjects receiving the two treatments will be the same. But there is a possible disadvantage that may distort results. The observations are not independent. Recalling an italicized word may help or hinder the recall of an underlined word, or vice versa.

Example. An example of a repeated-measures design is the recent study by Winn and Solomon (1993). Pairs of nonsense words were presented in one of three diagrammatic positions (horizontal boxes, vertical boxes, and "included" boxes) and described by one of three types of sentences ("*X* has *Y*," "*X* is *Y*," and "*X* causes *Y*," where *X* and *Y* were the nonsense words). By reversing the position of the words in each sentence (e.g., "*Y* has *X*"), there were six possible interpretations (three sentence types × two orders) of each diagram. Subjects viewed all possible combinations of interpretations for each of the three diagrams (45 in all); thus each subject experienced each "treatment." Findings showed that interpretations followed the syntactic rules of English, such that, for example, if *X* were the included (inner) box in a diagram, the sentence "*Y* has *X*" was favored over other choices. In a replication experiment using English words (experiment 2), syntactic conventions ("junk food causes indigestion") created biases in interpretations that sometimes conflicted with a diagram's spatial arrangement.

Again, by using the repeated-measures design, Winn and Solomon (1993) were able to reduce the number of subjects needed while controlling for individual differences across treatments. But the disadvantage was the possible "diffusion" of treatment effects caused by earlier experiences with other treatments (i.e., types of diagrams). We'll return to diffusion effects, along with other internal validity threats, in a later section.

39.2.1.3.   Quasi-Experimental Designs. Oftentimes in educational studies, it is neither practical nor feasible to randomly assign subjects to treatments. Such is especially likely to occur in school-based research, where classes are formed at the start of the year. These circumstances preclude true-experimental designs, while allowing the quasi-experiment as an option. A common application in educational technology would be to expose two similar classes of students to alternative instructional strategies and compare them on designated dependent measures (e.g., learning, attitude, classroom behavior) during the year.

An important component of the quasi-experimental study is the use of pretesting or analysis of prior achievement to establish group equivalence. While in the true experiment, randomization makes it improbable that one group will be significantly superior in ability to another, in the quasi-experiment, systematic bias can easily (but often unnoticeably) be introduced. For example, although the first- and third-period algebra classes may have the same teacher and identical lessons, it may be the case that honors English is offered third period only, thus restricting those honors students to taking first-period algebra. The quasi-experiment is represented diagrammatically as follows. Note its similarity to the true experiment, with the omission of the randomization component. That is, the Xs and Os show treatments and outcomes, respectively, but there are no Rs to indicate random assignment.

$$X_1 \quad O$$
$$X_2 \quad O$$

Example. Use of a quasi-experimental design is reflected in a recent study by the present authors on the long-term effects of computer experiences by elementary students (Ross, Smith & Morrison, 1991). During their fifth- and sixth-grade years, one class of students at an inner-city school received classroom and home computers as part of a computer-intensive learning program sponsored by Apple Classrooms of Tomorrow (ACOT). A class of similar students, who were exposed to the same curriculum but without computer support, was designated to serve as the control group. To ensure comparability of groups, scores on all subtests of the California Achievement Test (CAT), administered before the ACOT program was initiated, were analyzed as pretests; no class differences were indicated. The Ross et al. (1990) study was designed to find members of the two cohorts and evaluate their adjustment and progress in the seventh-grade year, when, as junior-high students, they were no longer participating in ACOT.

Although many more similarities than differences were found, the ACOT group was significantly superior to the control group on CAT mathematics. Can this advantage be attributed to their ACOT experiences? Perhaps, but in view of the quasi-experimental design employed, this interpretation would need to be made cautiously. Not only was "differential selection" of subjects a validity threat, so was the "history effect" of having each class taught in a separate room by a different teacher during each program year. Quasi-experimental designs have the advantage of convenience and practicality but the disadvantage of reduced internal validity.

39.2.1.4.   Time Series Design. Another type of quasi-experimental approach are time series designs. This family of designs involves repeated measurement of a group, with the experimental treatment induced between two of the measures. Why is this a quasi-experiment as opposed to a true experiment? The absence of randomly composed, separate experimental and control groups makes it impossible to attribute changes in the dependent measure directly to the effects of the experimental treatment. That is, the individual group participating in the time series design may improve its performances from pretesting to posttesting, but is it the treatment or some other event that produced the change? There are a variety of time series designs, some of which provide higher internal validity than others.

A single group time series design can be diagrammed as shown below. As depicted, one group (G) is observed (O) several times prior to receiving the treatment (X) and following the treatment.

$$G \quad O_1 \quad O_2 \quad O_3 \quad X \quad O_4 \quad O_5$$

To illustrate, suppose that we assess on three successive days the percentage of students in a class who successfully complete individualized computer-based instructional units. Prior to the fourth day, teams are formed and students are given additional team rewards for completing the units. Performance is then monitored on days 4 and 5. If performance increases relative to the pretreatment phase (days 1 to 3), we may "infer" that the CBI units contributed to that effect. Lacking a true-experimental design, we make that interpretation with some element of caution.

A variation of the time series design is the single-subject study in which one individual is examined before and after the introduction of the experimental treatment. The simplest form is the A-B design, where A is the baseline (no-treatment) period and B is the treatment. A potentially stronger variation is the A-B-A design that adds a withdrawal phase following the treatment. Each new phase (A or B) added to the design provides further data to strengthen conclusions about the treatment's impact. On the other hand, each phase may inherit cumulative contaminating effects from prior phases. That is, once B is experienced, subsequent reactions to A and B may be directly altered as a consequence.

Example. An example of a time series design is the study by Alper, Thoresen, and Wright (1972), as described by Clark and Snow (1975). The focus was the effects of a videotape on increasing a teacher's positive attention to appropriate student behavior and decreasing negative responses to inappropriate behavior. Baseline data were collected from a teacher at two times: (1) prior to the presentation of the video and feedback on ignoring inappropriate behavior, and (2) prior to the video and feedback on attending to positive behavior. Teacher attention was then assessed at different points following the video modeling and feedback. Interestingly, the analysis revealed that, although the teacher's behavior changed in the predicted directions following the video-feedback interventions, undesirable behavior tended to reappear over time. The time series design, therefore, was especially apt for detecting the unstable behavior pattern.

39.2.1.5. Deceptive Appearances: The Ex Post Facto Design. Suppose that in reviewing a manuscript for a journal, you come across the following study that the author describes as quasi-experimental (or experimental). The basic design involves giving a class of 100 college educational psychology students the option of using a word processor or paper and pencil to take notes during three full-period lectures on the topic of cognitive theory. Of those who opt for the two media (say, 55 for the word processor and 45 for paper and pencil), 40 from each group are randomly selected for the study. Over the 3 days, their notes are collected, and daily quizzes on the material are evaluated. Results show that the word processor group writes a greater quantity of notes and scores higher on the quizzes.

Despite the appearances of a treatment comparison and random assignment, this research is not an experiment but rather an ex post facto study. No variables are manipulated. Existing groups that are essentially self-selected are being compared: those who chose the word processor vs. those who chose paper and pencil. The random selection merely reduced the number of possible participants to more manageable numbers; it did not assign students to particular treatments. Given these properties, the ex post facto study may look sometimes like an experiment but is closer in design to a correlational study. In our example, the results imply that using a word processor is *related* to better performance. But a causal interpretation cannot be made, because other factors could have just as easily accounted for the outcomes (e.g., brighter or more motivated students may have been more likely to select the word-processing option).

39.2.2 Validity Threats

As has been described, internal validity is the degree to which the design of an experiment controls extraneous variables (Borg et al., 1993). For example, suppose that a researcher compares the achievement scores of students who are asked to write elaborations on a CBI lesson vs. those who do not write elaborations on the same lesson. If findings indicate that the elaborations group scored significantly higher on a mastery test than the control group, the implication would be that the elaborations strategy was effective. But what if students in the elaborations group were given more information about how to study the material than were control students? This

extraneous variable (i.e., additional information) would weaken internal validity and the ability to infer causality.

When conducting experiments, instructional technology researchers need to be aware of potential internal validity threats. In 1963, Campbell and Stanley identified different classes of such threats. We'll briefly describe each below, using an illustration relevant to educational technology interests.

39.2.2.1. History. This validity threat is present when events, other than the treatments, occurring during the experimental period can influence results.

Example. A researcher investigates the effect of using cooperative learning (treatment) vs. individual learning (control) in CBI. Students from a given class are randomly assigned to different laboratory rooms where they learn either cooperatively or individually. During the period of the study, however, the regular teacher begins to use cooperative learning with all students (see 35.9). Consequently, the control group feels frustrated that, during the CBI activity, they have to work alone. *Due to their "history," with cooperative learning, the control group's perceptions were altered.*

39.2.2.2. Maturation. During the experimental period, physical or psychological changes take place within the subjects.

Example. First-grade students receive two types of instruction in learning to use a mouse in operating a computer. One group is given active practice, and the other group observes a skilled model followed by limited practice. At the beginning of the year, neither group performs well. At the end of year, however, both substantially improve to a comparable level. *The researcher (ignoring the fact that students became more dexterous, as well as benefiting from the training) concluded that both treatments were equally effective.*

39.2.2.3. Testing. Exposure to a pretest or intervening assessment influences performance on a posttest.

Example. A researcher who is interested in determining the effects of using animation (see 12.2.3.2.2) versus static graphics in a CBI lesson pretests two randomly composed groups of high school students on the content of the lesson. Both groups average close to 55% correct. One of the groups then receives animation and the other the static graphics on their respective lessons. At the conclusion of the lesson, all students complete a posttest that is nearly identical to the pretest. No treatment differences, however, are found, with both groups averaging close to 90% correct. *Students report that the pretest gave them valuable cues about what to study.*

39.2.2.4. Instrumentation. Inconsistent use is made of testing instruments or testing conditions; or the pretest and posttest are uneven in difficulty, suggesting a gain or decline in performance that is not real.

Example. An experiment is designed to test two different procedures for teaching students to write nonlinear stories (i.e., stories with branches) using hypermedia (see 24.6). Randomly composed groups of eighth-graders learn from a modeling method or a direct instruction method, and are then judged by raters on the basis of the complexity and quality of a writing sample they produce. The "modeling" group completes the criterion task in their regular writing laboratory, whereas the "direct instruction" group completes it on similar computers, at the same day and time, but in the *journalism room* at the local university. Results show significantly superior ratings for the modeling group. *In fact, both groups were fairly comparable in skills, but the modeling group had the advantage of performing the criterion task in familiar surroundings.*

39.2.2.5.   Statistical Regression.   Subjects who score very high or very low on a dependent measure naturally tend to score closer (i.e., regress) to the mean during retesting.

Example.   A researcher is interested in the effects of learning programming on the problem-solving skills of high-ability children. A group of 400 sixth-graders are pretested on a problem-solving test. The 50 highest scorers are selected and randomly assigned to two groups of 25 each. One group learns programming during the semester, while the other learns a spreadsheet application. At the end of the year, the students are posttested on the same problem-solving measure. There are no differences between them; in fact, the means for both groups are actually slightly lower than they were on the pretest. *These very high scorers on the pretest had regressed to the mean (due, perhaps, to not having as "good of a day" on the second testing).*

39.2.2.6.   Selection.   There is a systematic difference in subjects' abilities or characteristics between the treatment groups being compared.

Example.   Students in the fourth-period American history class use an electronic encyclopedia during the year as a reference for historical events, while those in the sixth-period class use a conventional encyclopedia. The two classes have nearly identical grade point averages and are taught by the same teacher using the exact same materials and curriculum. Comparisons are made between the classes on the frequency with which they use their respective encyclopedias and the quality of the information they select for their reports. The control group is determined to be superior on both of these variables. Further examination of student demographics, however, shows that a much greater percentage of the control students are in advanced placement (AP) courses in English, mathematics, and science. In fact, the reason many were scheduled to take history sixth period was to avoid conflicts with AP offerings. *Differential selection therefore resulted in higher-achieving students being members of the control group.*

39.2.2.7.   Experimental Mortality.   The loss of subjects from one or more treatments during the period of the study may bias the results.

Example.   An instructional designer is interested in evaluating a college-level CBI algebra course that uses two learning orientations. One orientation allows the learner to select menu and instructional support options (learner-control treatment); the other prescribes particular options based on what is considered best for "typical" learners (program-control treatment). At the beginning of the semester, 40 students are assigned to each treatment and begin work with

the corresponding CBI programs. At the end of the semester, only 50 students remain in the course, 35 in the learner-control group and 15 in the program-control group. Achievement results favor the program-control group. *The greater "mortality" in the program-control group probably left a higher proportion of more motivated or more capable learners than in the learner-control group.*

39.2.2.8.   Diffusion of Treatments.   The implementation of a particular treatment influences subjects in the comparison treatment.

Example.   A researcher is interested in examining the influences on attitudes and achievement of fifth-graders' writing to pen pals via electronic mail. Half the students are assigned pen pals; the other half complete the identical assignments on the same electronic mail system but send the letters to "fictitious" friends. The students in the latter group, however, become aware that the other group has real pen pals and feel resentful. On the attitude measure, their reactions toward the writing activities are very negative as a consequence. *By learning about the experimental group's "treatment," the perceptions and attitudes of the control group were negatively influenced.*

39.2.3   Dealing with Validity Threats

In many instances, validity threats cannot be avoided. The presence of a validity threat should not be taken to mean that experimental findings are inaccurate or misleading. By validity "threat," we mean only that a factor has the *potential* to bias results. Knowing about validity threats gives the experimenter a framework for evaluating the particular situation and making a judgment about its severity. Such knowledge may also permit actions to be taken to limit the influences of the validity threat in question. Examples are as follows:

- Concern that a pretest may bias posttest results leads to the decision not to use a pretest.
- Concern that two intact groups to be used for treatment comparisons (quasi-experimental design) may not be equal in ability leads to the decision to pretest subjects on ability and employ a statistical adjustment (analysis of covariance) if the groups significantly differ.
- Concern that subjects may mature or drop out during the period of the experiment leads to the decision to shorten the length of the treatment period, use different types of subjects, and/or introduce noncontaminating conditions (e.g., incentives) to reduce attrition.
- Concern that the posttest may differ in difficulty from the pretest in an experiment design to assess learning gain leads to the decision to use each test form as the pretest for half the students and the posttest for the other half.
- Concern about the artificiality of using of *X*'s and *O*'s as the stimulus material for assessing computer screen designs leads to the addition of "realistic" nonsense words and actual words as additional treatments.

• Concern that subjects might not be motivated to perform on an experimental task leads to the development of an actual unit of instruction that became an alternative form of instruction for the students.

Even after all reasonable actions have been taken to eliminate the operation of one or more validity threats, the experimenter must still make a judgment about the internal validity of the experiment overall. In certain cases, the combined effects of multiple validity threats may be considered inconsequential, while in others, the effects of a single threat (e.g., differential sample selection) may be severe enough to preclude meaningful results. When the latter occurs, the experiment needs to be redone. In cases less severe, experimenters have the obligation to note the validity threats and qualify their interpretations of results accordingly.

39.3 THE PRACTICE OF EXPERIMENTATION IN EDUCATIONAL TECHNOLOGY

39.3.1 How to Conduct Experimental Studies: A Brief Course

For the novice researcher, it is often difficult to get started in designing and conducting experimental studies. Seemingly, a common problem is putting the cart before the horse, which in typical cases translates into selecting methodology or a research design before deciding what questions to investigate. Research questions, along with practical constraints (time and resources), should normally dictate what type of study to do, rather than the reverse. To help readers avoid such problems, we have devised the following seven-step model that presents a sequence of logical steps for planning and conducting research (Ross & Morrison, 1992, 1993b). The model begins at a level where the individual is interested in conducting research (such as for a dissertation or scholarly activity) but has not even identified a topic. More advanced researchers would naturally start at the level appropriate to their needs. To illustrate the various steps, we'll discuss our recent experiences in designing a research study on applications of an interactive computer-based chemistry unit.

39.3.1.1. Step 1. Select a Topic. This step is self-explanatory and usually not a problem, except for those who are "required" to do research (e.g., as part of an academic degree program) as opposed to initiating it on their own. The step simply involves identifying a general area that is of personal interest (e.g., learner control, picture perception, mathematics learning) and then narrowing the focus to a researchable problem (step 2).

Chemistry CBI Example. In our situation, Gary Morrison received a grant from FIPSE to develop and evaluate interactive chemistry units. We thus had the interest as well as the formal responsibility of investigating how the completed units operated.

39.3.1.2. Step 2. Identify the Research Problem. Given the general topic area, what specific problems are of

interest? In many cases, the researcher already knows the problems. In others, a trip to the library to read background literature and examine previous studies is probably needed. A key concern is the importance of the problem to the field. Conducting research requires too much time and effort to be examining trivial questions that do not expand existing knowledge. Experienced researchers will usually be attuned to important topics, based on their knowledge of the literature and current research activities. Novices, however, need to be more careful about establishing support for their idea from recent research and issues-oriented publications (see step 3). For experts and novices alike, it is always a good practice to use other researchers as a sounding board for a research focus before getting too far into the study design (steps 4 and 5).

Chemistry CBI Example. The topic and the research problem were presented to us through the objectives of the FIPSE grant and our interest in assessing the "effectiveness" of the completed CBI chemistry units. The research topic was "CBI usage in teaching college chemistry courses"; the research problem was "how effectively interactive CBI units on different chemistry concepts would teach those concepts." Later, this "problem" was narrowed to an examination of the influences on student learning and attitudes of selected features of a specific CBI unit, Gas Laws.

39.3.1.3. Step 3. Conduct a Literature Search. With the research topic and problem identified, it is now time to conduct a more intensive literature search. Of importance is determining what relevant studies have been performed; the designs, instruments, and procedures employed in those studies; and, most critically, the findings. Based on the review, direction will be provided for (a) how to extend or compliment the existing literature base, (b) possible research orientations to use, and (c) specific research questions to address. Helpful information about how to conduct effective literature reviews is provided in other sources (e.g., Borg et al., 1993; Ross & Morrison, 1992; Wiersma, 1991).

Chemistry CBI Example. For the chemistry study, the literature proved important in two ways. First, it provided general background information on related studies in the content area (chemistry) and in CBI applications in general. Second, in considering the many specific features of the chemistry unit that interested us (e.g., usage of color, animation, prediction, elaboration, self-pacing, learner control, active problem solving), the literature review helped to narrow our focus to a restricted, more manageable number of variables and gave us ideas for how the selected set might be simultaneously examined in a study.

39.3.1.4. Step 4. State the Research Questions (or Hypotheses). This step is probably the most critical part of the planning process. Once stated, the research questions or hypotheses provide the basis for planning all other parts of the study: design, materials, and data analysis. In particular, this step will guide the researcher's decision as to whether an experimental design or some other orientation is the best choice.

For example, in investigating uses of learner control in a math lesson, the researcher must ask what questions does he or she really want to answer. Consider a question such as: How well do learners like using learner control with math lessons? To answer it, an experiment is hardly needed or even appropriate. A much better choice would be a descriptive study in which learners are interviewed, surveyed, and/or observed relative to the activities of concern (see 40.1, 41.2). In general, if a research question involves determining the "effects" or "influences" of one variable (independent) on another (dependent), use of an experimental design is implied.

Chemistry CBI Example. The questions of greatest interest to us concerned the effects on learning of (a) animated vs. static graphics, (b) learners predicting outcomes of experiments vs. not making predictions, and (c) learner control vs. program control. The variables concerned were expected to operate in certain ways based on theoretical assumptions and prior empirical support. Accordingly, hypotheses such as the following were suggested: "Students who receive animated graphics will perform better on problem-solving tasks than do students who receive static graphics." "Low achievers will learn less effectively under learner control than program control." Where we felt less confident about predictions or where the interest was descriptive findings, research questions were implied: "Would students receiving animated graphics react more positively to the unit than those receiving static graphics?" "To what extent would learner-control students make use of opportunities for experimenting in the 'lab'?"

39.3.1.5. Step 5. Determine the Research Design. The next consideration is whether an experimental design is feasible. If not, the researcher will need to consider alternative approaches, recognizing that the original research question may not be answerable as a result. For example, suppose the research question is to determine the effects of students watching Channel 1 on their knowledge of current events. In planning the experiment, the researcher becomes aware that no control group will be available, since all classrooms to which she has access receive Channel 1. While an experimental study is implied by the original "cause-effect" question, a descriptive study examining current events scores (perhaps from pretest to posttest) will probably be the most reasonable option (see 41.1). This design may provide some interesting food for thought on the "possible effects" of Channel 1 on current events learning, but it cannot validly answer the original question.

Chemistry CBI Example. Our hypotheses and research questions implied both experimental and descriptive designs. Specifically, hypotheses concerning the effects of animated vs. static graphics and between prediction vs. no prediction implied controlled experimental comparisons between appropriate treatment conditions. Decisions were needed to be made about which treatments to manipulate and how to combine them (e.g., a factorial or balanced design vs. selected treatments). We decided on selected treatments representing targeted conditions of interest. For example, we did not use static graphics with no prediction, since that treatment would have appeared awkward given

the way the CBI program was designed, and we had little interest in it for applied evaluation purposes. Because subjects could be randomly assigned to treatments, we decided to use a true-experimental design.

Other research questions, however, implied additional designs. Specifically, comparisons between high and low achievers (in usage of CBI options and relative success in different treatments) required an ex post facto design, because members of these groups would be identified on the basis of existing characteristics. Research questions regarding usage of learner control options would further be examined via a descriptive approach.

39.3.1.6. Step 6. Determine Methods. Methods of the study include (a) subjects, (b) materials and data collection instruments, and (c) procedures. In determining these components, the researcher must continually use the research questions and/or hypotheses as reference points. A good place to start is with subjects. What kind and how many participants does the research design require? (See, e.g., Glass & Hopkins, 1984, p. 213, for a discussion of sample size and power.) Next consider materials and instrumentation. When the needed resources are not obvious, a good strategy is to construct a listing of data collection instruments needed to answer each question (e.g., attitude survey, achievement test, observation form, etc.).

An experiment does not require having access to instruments that are already developed. Particularly in research with new technologies, the creation of novel measures of affect or performance may be implied. From an efficiency standpoint, however, the researcher's first step should be to conduct a thorough search of existing instruments to determine if any can be used in their original form or adapted to present needs. If none is found, it would usually be far more advisable to construct a new instrument rather than "force fit" an existing one. New instruments will need to be pilot tested and validated. Standard test and measurement texts provide useful guidance for this requirement (e.g., Gronlund & Linn, 1990; Popham, 1990). The experimental procedure, then, will be dictated by the research questions and the available resources. Piloting the methodology is essential to ensure that materials and methods work as planned.

Chemistry CBI Example. Our instructional material consisted of the CBI unit itself. Hypotheses and research questions implied developing alternative forms of instruction (e.g., animation-prediction, animation–no prediction, static-prediction) to compare, as well as original (new) data collection instruments because the instructional content was unit-specific. These instruments included an achievement test, attitude survey, and on-line assessments or recording of lesson option usage (e.g., number of lab experiments selected), learning time, and predictions.

39.3.1.7. Step 7. Determining Data Analysis Techniques. While statistical analysis procedures vary widely in complexity, the appropriate options for a particular experiment will be defined by two factors: the research questions and the type of data. For example, a t test for independent samples would be implied for comparing one experimental group (e.g., CBI with animation) to one control group (CBI with static graphics) on an *interval*-dependent measure (e.g., performance on a problem-solving test). Add a third treatment group (CBI without graphics), and a one-way ANOVA will be implied for the same interval data, but now comparing more than two means. If an additional outcome measure were a categorical response on, say, an attitude survey ("liked the lesson" or "didn't like it") a chi-square analysis would be implied for determining the relationship between treatment and response on the resultant *nominal* data obtained.

Educational technology experimenters do not have to be statisticians. Nor do they have to set analytical procedures in stone prior to completing the research. Clearly formulated research questions and design specifications will provide a solid foundation for working with a statistician (if needed) to select and run appropriate analyses. To provide a convenient guide for considering alternative analysis, Table 39-1 lists common statistical analysis procedures and the main conditions under which they are used. Note that in assessing causal relationships, experiments depend on analysis approaches that compare outcomes associated with treatments (nominal or categorical variables) such as *t* tests, analysis of variance, analysis of covariance, and chi square, rather than correlational-type approaches such as Pearson *r*, multiple regression, and discriminant analysis.

39.3.2 Reporting and Publishing Experimental Studies

Obviously, for experimental studies to have impact on theory and practice in educational technology, their findings need to be disseminated to the field. Thus, part of the experimenter's role is publishing research in professional journals and presenting it at professional meetings. Discussing these activities in any detail is beyond the scope of the present chapter; also, articles devoted to these subjects can be found elsewhere (e.g., Levin, 1993; Ross & Morrison, 1991; Ross & Morrison, 1993b; Sternberg, 1988). However, given the special features and style conventions of experimental reports compared to other types of educational technology literature, we consider it relevant to review the former, with a specific concentration on journal publications. It is through referred journals—such as *Computers and Human Behavior*, *Performance Improvement Quarterly*, and *Educational Technology Research and Development*—that experimental studies are most likely to be disseminated to members of the educational technology field. The following is a brief description of each major section of the paper.

39.3.2.1. Introduction. The introduction to reports of experimental studies accomplishes several functions: (a) identifying the general area of the problem (e.g., CBI or cooperative learning), (b) creating a rationale to learn more about the problem (otherwise, why do more research in this area?), (c) reviewing relevant literature, and (d) stating the

specific purposes of the study. Hypotheses and/or research questions should directly follow from the preceding discussion and generally be stated explicitly, even though they may be obvious from the literature review. In basic research experiments, usage of hypotheses is usually expected, since a theory or principle is typically being tested. In applied research experiments, hypotheses would be used where there is a logical or empirical basis for expecting a certain result (e.g., "The feedback group will perform better than the no-feedback group"); otherwise, research questions might be preferable (e.g., "Are worked examples more effective than incomplete examples on the CBI math unit developed?").

39.3.2.2. Method. The *method* section of an experiment describes the participants or subjects, materials, and procedures. The usual convention is to start with *subjects* by clearly describing the population concerned (e.g., age or grade level, background) and the sampling procedure. In reading about an experiment, it is extremely important to know if subjects were randomly assigned to treatments or if intact groups were employed. It is also important to know if participation was voluntary or required, and whether level of performance on the experimental task was consequential to the subjects.

Learner motivation and task investment are critical in educational technology research, because such variables are likely to impact directly on subjects' usage of media attributes and instructional strategies (see Hicken, Sullivan & Klein, 1992; Morrison, Ross, Gopalakrishnan & Casey, 1995). For example, when learning from a CBI lesson received as part of an experiment rather than actual course, a volunteer subject may be primarily concerned with completing the material as quickly as possible and, therefore, not select any optional instructional support features. In contrast, subjects who were completing the lesson for a grade would probably be motivated to take advantage of those options. A given treatment variable (e.g., learner control or elaborated feedback) could therefore take very different forms and have different effects in the two experiments.

Once subjects are described, the type of design employed (e.g., quasi-experiment, true experiment) should be indicated. Both the independent and dependent variables also need to be identified.

Materials and *instrumentation* are covered next. A frequent limitation of descriptions of educational technology experiments is lack of information on the learning task and the context in which it was delivered. Since media attributes can impact learning and performance in unique ways (see Clark, 1983, 1994; Kozma, 1991, 1994; Ullmer, 1994; see also 23.6), their full description is particularly important to the educational technologist. Knowing only that a "CBI" presentation was compared to a "textbook" presentation suggests the type of senseless media comparison experiment criticized by Clark (1983; see also 4.4) and others (Hagler & Knowlton, 1987; Knowlton, 1964; Ross & Morrison, 1989) In contrast, knowing the specific attributes of the CBI (e.g., animation, immediate feedback, prompting) and textbook presentations permits the more

TABLE 39.1. COMMON STATISTICAL ANALYSIS PROCEDURES USED IN EDUCATIONAL TECHNOLOGY RESEARCH

Analysis	Type of Data	Features	Example	Test of Causal Effects?
t test (independent samples)	Independent variable = nominal Dependent = one interval-ratio measure	Testing the difference between 2 treatment group means	Does the cooperative-treatment group surpass the individual-treatment group?	Yes
t test (dependent samples)	Independent variable = nominal (repeated measure) Dependent = one interval-ratio measure	Testing the difference between 2 treatment means for a *given group*	Will subjects change their attitudes toward drugs, from pretest to posttest, following a film on drug effects?	Yes
Analysis of variance (ANOVA)	Independent variable = nominal Dependent = one interval-ratio measure	Testing the difference between 2 or more treatment means. If ANOVA is significant, follow-up comparisons of means are performed.	Will there be differences in learning between three groups that receive advance organizers, objectives, or neither?	Yes
Multivariate analysis of variance (MANOVA)	Independent variable = nominal Dependent = two or more interval-ratio measures	Testing the difference between 2 or more treatment group means on 2 or more learning measures. Controls type I error rate across the measure. If MANOVA is significant, an ANOVA on each individual measure is performed.	Will there be differences between 3 feedback strategies on problem solving and knowledge learning?	Yes
Analysis of covariance (ANCOVA) or multivariate analysis of covariance (MANCOVA)	Independent variable = nominal Dependent = one or more interval-ratio measures Covariate = one or more interval-ratio measures	Replicates ANOVA or MANOVA but employs an additional variable to control for treatment group differences in aptitude and/or to reduce error variance in the dependent variable(s).	Will there be differences in concept learning between learner-control, program-control, and advisement strategies, with differences in prior knowledge controlled?	Yes
Pearson r	Two interval-ratio measures	Tests relationship between the two variables	Is anxiety related to test performance?	No
Multiple linear regression	Independent variable = two or more interval-ratio measures Dependent = one interval-ratio measure	Tests relationship between set of predictors (independent) variables and an outcome variable. Shows the relative contribution of each predictor in accounting for variability in the outcome variable.	How well do experience, age, gender, and grade-point average predict time spent in completing a task?	No
Discriminant analysis	Nominal variable (groups) and 2 or more interval-ratio variables	Tests relationship between a set of predictor variables and subjects' membership in particular groups.	Do students who favor learning from print materials *vs.* computers *vs.* television differ with regard to ability, age, and motivation?	No
chi-square test of independence	Two nominal variables	Tests relationship between two nominal variables.	Is there a relationship between gender (males vs. females) and attitudes toward the instruction (liked, no opinion, disliked)?	No

meaningful interpretation of results relative the influences of these attributes on the learning process.

Aside from describing the instructional task, the overall method section should also detail the instruments used for data collection. For illustrative purposes, consider the following excerpts from a highly thorough description of the instructional materials used by Reiser, Williamson, and Suzuki (1988):

> The instructional materials used in this study were three videotapes of specially edited versions of "Sesame Street." . . . Each tape ran for approximately 35 minutes and began with the opening song and ended with the closing credits regularly used on the television program. Each tape included 18 "instructional" segments, 3 segments for each of the following 6 concepts: the letters *P*, *Q*, *V*, and *W* and the numbers 6 and 9. . . . In each segment, one of the letters or numbers listed above was shown and named (p. 17).

The next main methodology section is the *procedure*. It provides a reasonably detailed description of the steps employed in carrying out the study (e.g., implementing different treatments, distributing materials, observing behaviors, testing, etc.). Here, the rule of thumb is to provide sufficient information on what was done to perform the experiment so that another researcher could replicate the study.

39.3.2.3. Results. This major section describes the analyses and the findings. Typically, it should be organized such that the most important dependent measures are reported first. Tables and/or figures should be used judiciously to supplement (not repeat) the text.

39.3.2.4. Discussion. To conclude the report, the *discussion* section explains and interprets the findings relative to the hypotheses or research questions, previous studies, and relevant theory and practice. Where appropriate, weaknesses in procedures that may have impacted results should be identified. Other conventional features of a discussion may include suggestions for further research and conclusions regarding the research hypotheses/questions. For educational technology experiments, drawing implications for practice in the area concerned is highly desirable.

39.3.3 Why Experimental Studies Are Rejected for Publication

After considering the above discussion, readers may question what makes an experimental study publishable or perishable in professional research journals. Given that we have not done a formal investigation of this topic, we will make only a brief subjective analysis based on our experiences with *ETR&D*. We strongly believe, however, that all of the following factors would apply to every educational technology research journal, although the relative importance they are assigned may vary. Our "top 10" listing is as follows:

1. Low internal validity of conditions: Treatment and comparison groups are not uniformly implemented. One or more groups have an advantage on a particular condition (time, materials, encouragement) other than the independent (treatment) variable. Example: The treatment group that receives

illustrations and text takes 1 hour to study the electricity unit, whereas the text-only group takes only one-half hour.

2. Low internal validity of subject selection/assignment: Groups assigned to treatment and comparison conditions are not comparable (e.g., a more experienced group receives the treatment strategy). Example: In comparing learner control versus program control, the researcher allows students to select the orientation they want. The higher-aptitude students tend to select program control, which, not surprisingly, yields the better results!

3. Invalid testing: Outcomes are not measured in a controlled and scientific way (e.g., observations are done by the author without validation of the system or reliability checks of the data). Example: In a qualitative study of teachers' adaptations to technology, only one researcher (the author) observes each of the 10 teachers in a school in which she works part time as an aide.

4. Low external validity: Application/importance of topic/findings is weak. Example: The findings show that nonsense syllables take more time to be identified if embedded in a border than if they are isolated.

5. Poor writing: Writing style is unclear, weak in quality (syntax, construction), and/or does not use appropriate (APA) style. Example: The *method* section contains no subheadings and intermixes descriptions of participants and materials, then discusses the procedures, and ends with introducing the design of the study. Note that the design would be much more useful as an organizer if presented first.

6. Trivial/inappropriate outcome measures: Outcomes are assessed using irrelevant, trivial, or insubstantial measures. Example: A 10-item multiple-choice test is the only achievement outcome in a study of cooperative learning effects.

7. Inadequate description of methodology: Instruments, materials, and/or procedures are not described sufficiently to evaluate the quality of the study (see 24.11). Example: The author describes dependent measures using only the following: "A 10-item posttest was used to assess learning of the unit. It was followed by a 20-item attitude scale regarding reactions to the unit. Other materials used. . . ."

8. Inappropriate analyses: Quantitative and/or qualitative analyses needed to address research objectives are not properly used or sufficiently described (see 40.4). Example: In a qualitative study, the author presents the "analysis" of 30 classroom observations exclusively as "holistic impressions," without reference to any application of systematic methods of documenting, transcribing, synthesizing, and verifying what was observed.

9. Inappropriate discussion of results: Results are not interpreted accurately or meaningfully to convey appropriate implications of the study. Example: After finding that motivation and performance correlated significantly but very weakly at $r = .15$, the author discusses for several paragraphs the importance of motivation to learning, "as supported by this study." (Note that although "reliable" in this study, the .15 correlation indicates that motivation accounted for only about 2.25% of the variable in performance: $.15 \times .15 = .225$).

10. Insufficient theoretical base or rationale: The basis for the study is conveyed as manipulating some combination of variables essentially "to see what happens." Example: After reviewing the literature on the use of highlighting text, the author establishes the rationale for his study by stating, "No one, however, has examined these effects using color vs. no-color with males vs. females." No theoretical rationales or hypotheses relating to the color or gender variable are subsequently provided.

39.4 THE STATUS OF EXPERIMENTATION IN EDUCATIONAL TECHNOLOGY

39.4.1 Uses and Abuses of Experiments

The behavioral roots of educational technology and its parent disciplines have fostered usage of experimentation as the predominant mode of research (see 2.3). As we will show in a later section, experiments comprise the overwhelming proportion of studies published in the research section of *Educational Technology Research and Development (ETR&D)*. The representation of alternative paradigms, while gradually increasing, remains quite small.

39.4.1.1. The Historical Predominance of Experimentation. Why is the experimental paradigm so dominant? According to Hannafin (1986), aside from the impetus provided from behavioral psychology, there are three reasons. One is that experimentation has been traditionally viewed as the definition of "acceptable" research in the field. Researchers have developed the mentality that a study is of higher quality if it is experimental in design. Positivistic views have reinforced beliefs about the importance of scientific rigor, control, statistical verification, and hypothesis testing as the "correct" approaches to research in the field. Qualitative researchers have challenged this way of thinking, but until recently, acceptance of alternative paradigms has been reluctant and of minimal consequence (see Guba, 1981).

Second, Hannafin (1986) proposes that promotion and tenure criteria at colleges and universities have been strongly biased toward experimental studies. If this bias occurs, it is probably attributable mainly to the more respected journals having been more likely to publish experimental designs (see next paragraph). In any case, such practices are perpetuated by creating standards that are naturally favored by faculty and passed down to their graduate students.

Third, the research journals have published proportionately more experimental studies than alternative types. This factor also creates a self-perpetuating situation in which increased exposure to experimental studies increases the likelihood that beginning researchers will also favor the experimental method in their research.

As will be discussed in later sections, however, practices are changing in the direction of greater acceptance of alternative methodologies, such as qualitative methods. The pendulum may swing far enough to make the highly controlled experiment with low external validity less valued than eclectic orientations that use a variety of strategies to balance internal and external validity.

39.4.1.2. When to Experiment. The purpose of this chapter is neither to promote nor criticize the experimental method, but rather to provide direction for its effective usage in educational technology research. On the one hand, it is fair to say that, probably for the reasons just described, experimentation has been overused by educational technology researchers. The result has frequently been "force fitting" the experiment in situations where research questions could have been much more meaningfully answered using an alternative design or a combination of several designs.

For example, we recall a study on learner control that was submitted about a year ago to *ETR&D* for review. The major research question concerned the benefits of allowing learners to select practice items and review questions as they proceeded through a self-paced lesson. The results showed no effects for the learner control strategy compared to conventional instruction on either an achievement test or attitude survey. Despite the study's being well designed, competently conducted, and well described, the decision was *not* to accept the manuscript for publication. In the manner of pure scientists, the authors had carefully measured outcomes but totally omitted any observation or recording of how the subjects used learner control. Nor did they bother to question the learners on their usage and reactions toward the learner control options. The experiment thus showed that learner control did not "work," but failed to provide any insights into why (see 24.11).

On the other hand, we disagree with the sentiments expressed by some writers that experimental research conflicts with the goal of improving instruction (Guba, 1969; Heinich, 1984). The fact that carpentry tools, if used improperly, can potentially damage a bookcase does not detract from the value of such tools to skilled carpenters who know how to use them appropriately to build bookcases. Unfortunately, the experimental method has frequently been applied in a very strict, formal way that has blinded the experimenter from looking past the testing of the null hypothesis to inquire why a particular outcome occurs. In this chapter, we take the view that the experiment is simply another valuable way, no more or less sacrosanct than any other, of increasing understanding about methods and applications of educational technology.

39.4.1.3. Experiments in Evaluation Research. In applied instructional design contexts, experiments could potentially offer practitioners much useful information about their products, but will typically be impractical to perform. Consider, for example, an instructional designer who develops an innovative way of using an interactive medium to teach principles of chemistry. Systematic evaluation of this instructional method (and of the unit in particular) would comprise an important component of the design process (Dick & Carey, 1985; Kemp, Morrison & Ross, 1994; Ross & Morrison, 1993a; Tennyson, 1978; see also 42.1, 42.2). Of major interest in the evaluation would certainly be how effectively the new method supports instructional objectives as compared to conventional teaching procedures. Under normal conditions, it would be difficult logistically to address this question via a true experiment. But if conditions permitted random assignment of students to "treatments" without compromising the integrity (external validity) of the instruction, a true experimental design would likely provide the most meaningful test. If random assignment were not viable, but two comparable groups of learners were available to experience the instructional alternatives, a quasi-experimental design might well be the next best choice. The results of either category of experiment would provide useful information for the evaluator, particularly when combined with outcomes from other measures, for either judging the method's effectiveness (summative evaluation) or making recommendations to improve it (formative evaluation). Only a very narrow, short-sighted approach would use the experimental results as isolated evidence for "proving" or "disproving" program effects.

In the concluding sections of this chapter, we will further examine applications and potentialities of "applied research" experiments as sources of information for understanding and improving instruction. First, to provide a better sense of historical practices in the field, we'll turn to an analysis of how often and in what ways experiments have been employed in educational technology research.

39.4.2 Experimental Methods in Educational Technology Research

To determine practices and trends in experimental research on educational technology, we decided to examine comprehensively the studies published in a single journal. The journal, which is now called *Educational Technology Research and Development (ETR&D)*, is published quarterly by the Association for Educational Communications and Technology (AECT). *ETR&D* is AECT's only research journal, is distributed internationally, and is generally considered a leading research publication in educational technology. The journal started in 1953 as *AV Communication Review* and was renamed *Educational Communication and Technology Journal (ECTJ)* in 1978. *ETR&D* was established in 1989 to combine *ECTJ* (AECT's research journal) with the *Journal of Instructional Development* (AECT's design/development journal) by including a research section and a development section. The research section, which is of present interest, solicits manuscripts dealing with "research in educational technology and related topics." Nearly all published articles are blind refereed, with the exception of infrequent solicited manuscripts as part of special issues.

39.4.2.1. Analysis Procedure. The present analysis began with the Volume 1 issue of *AVCR* (1953) and ended with Volume 40 (1992) of *ETR&D*. All research studies in these issues were examined and classified in terms of the following categories:

Experimental Studies

True-experiment
Quasi-experiment
Time series (single subject, repeated measures)

Nonexperimental (Descriptive) Studies

Correlational
Ex post facto
Survey
Observational/ethnographic

A total of 303 articles were classified into one of these seven categories. Experimental studies were then classified according to two additional criteria:

Stimulus Materials

Actual content. Stimulus materials classified in this category were based on actual content taught in a course from which the subjects were drawn. For example, Tennyson, Welsh, Christensen, and Hajovy (1985) worked with a high school English teacher to develop stimulus materials that were based on content covered in the English class.

Realistic content. Studies classified in this category used stimulus materials that were factually correct and potentially usable in an actual teaching situation. For example, Beck (1984) used a unit on carnivorous plants with fourth-graders that was not part of the curriculum.

Contrived content. This stimulus material category included both nonsense words (Morrison, 1986) and fictional material. For example, Feliciano, Powers, and Kearl (1963) constructed fictitious agricultural data to test different formats for presenting statistical data. Studies in this category generally used stimulus materials with little if any relevance to subjects' knowledge base or interests.

Experimental Setting

Actual setting. Studies in this category were conducted in either the regular classroom, computer lab, or other room used by the subjects for real-life instruction.

Realistic setting. This category consisted of new environments designed to simulate a realistic situation. For example, if elementary students from a university lab school were tested in one of the university's computer labs, the study was classified in this category.

Contrived setting. Studies requiring special equipment or environments were classified in this study. For example, Niekamp's (1981) eye movement study required special equipment that was in-lab designed especially for the data collection.

The final analysis yielded 266 articles classified as experimental (88%) and 37 classified as descriptive (12%). In instances where more than one approach was used, a decision was made by the authors as to which individual approach was predominant. The study was then classified into the latter category. The authors were able to classify all studies into individual design categories. Articles that appeared as reports and lacked the rigor of other articles in the volume were not included in the list of 303 studies. The results of the analysis are described below.

39.4.2.2. Utilization of Varied Experimental Designs. Of the 266 articles classified as experimental, 182 (60%) were classified as true-experiments using random assignment of subjects; 74 (24%) of the studies were classified as using quasi-experimental designs; and 10 (3%) were classi-

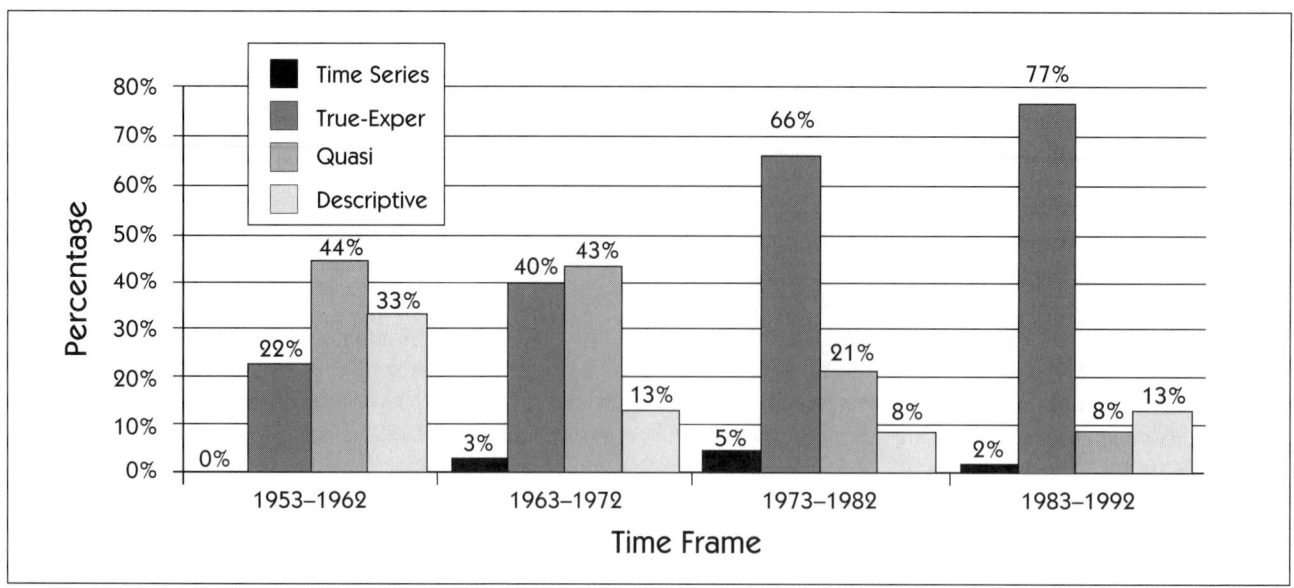

Figure 39-1.   Experimental design trends.

fied as employing time-series designs. Thus, following the traditions of the physical sciences and behavioral psychology, usage of true-experimental designs has predominated educational technology research.

An analysis of the publications by decade (e.g., 1953–1962, 1963–1972, etc.) revealed the increased use of true-experimental designs and decreased use of quasi-experimental designs since 1953 (see Fig. 39-1). In the first 10 years of the journal (1953–1962), there was a total of only six experimental studies and three descriptive studies. The experimental studies included two true-experiments and four quasi-experimental designs. During the next 30 years, there was an increase in the number of true-experimental articles. Table 39-2 presents the number of articles published with each design in each of the 4 decades. It's interesting to note that quasi-experimental designs reached a peak during the 1963–1972 period with 43 articles and then decreased to only 7 articles in the 1983–1992 time period.

39.4.2.3. Utilization of Stimulus Materials. An additional focus of our analysis was the types of stimulus materials used in the studies. For example, did researchers use actual materials that were either part of the curriculum or derived from the curriculum? Such materials would have high external validity and provide additional incentive for the subjects to engage in learning process. Figure 39-2 illustrates the three classifications of materials used by the various studies published during the past 40 years. In the

1963 to 1972 period, actual materials were clearly used more often than realistic or contrived. Then, starting in 1972, the use of actual materials began a rapid decline while use of realistic materials tended to increase. There are two possible explanations for this shift from actual to realistic materials. First is the increasing availability of technology and improved media production techniques. During the 1963–1972 time frame, the primary subject of study was film instruction (actual materials). The increased utilization of realistic materials during the 1973–1982 period may have been the result of the availability of other media, increased media production capabilities, and a growing interest in instructional design as opposed to message design. Similarly, in the 1983–1992 time frame, the high utilization of realistic materials may have been due to the increase in experimenter-designed CBI materials using topics appropriate for the subjects, but not necessarily based on curriculum objectives.

39.4.2.4. Utilization of Settings. The third question concerns the settings used to conduct the studies. As shown in Figure 39-3, actual classrooms have remained the most preferred locations for researchers, although the classroom site has decreased in popularity during the last 10 years, while usage of realistic labs has increased. One possible explanation for the increased use of the realistic lab during the 1983–1992 period may be the increased number of CBI studies conducted in university computer labs not normally

TABLE 39-2. DESIGNS × TIME FRAME				
Design	1953–1962	1963–1972	1973–1982	1983–1992
Time Series	0	3	5	2
True-Experiment	2	40	70	70
Quasi-Experimental	4	43	22	7
Descriptive	3	13	9	12

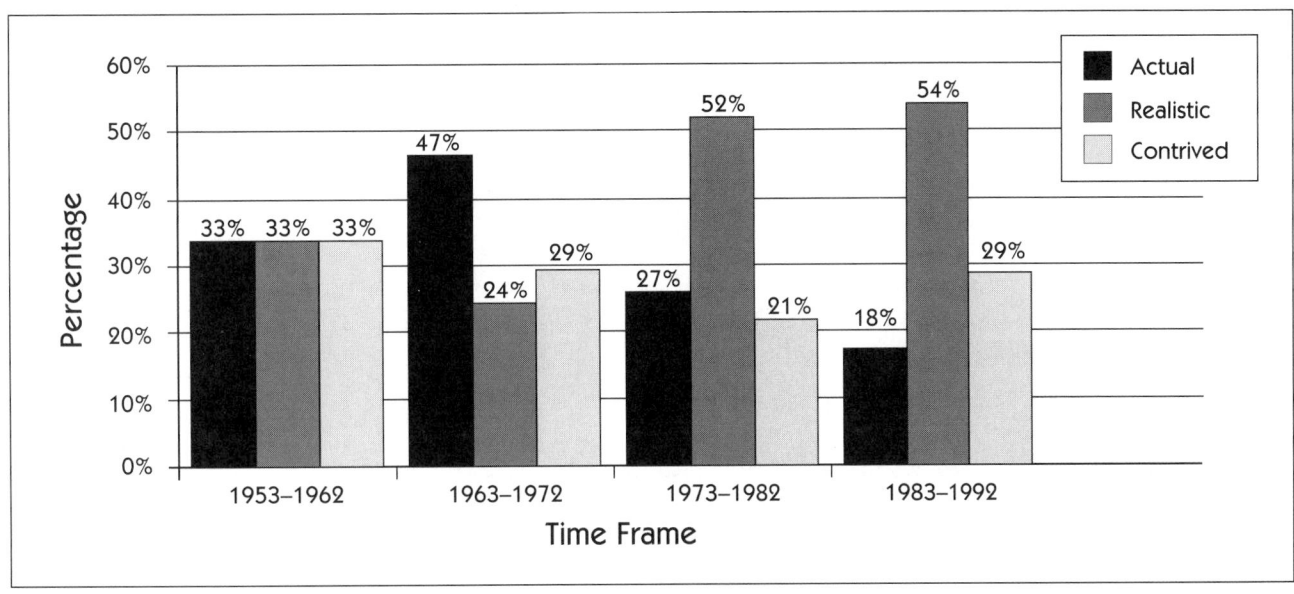

Figure 39-2. Trends in stimulus materials.

accessible to the subjects (hence, the classification as a realistic lab). Utilization of contrived settings, as was the case for contrived materials (see Fig. 39-2), has remained fairly constant over time.

39.4.2.5. Interaction Between Usage Variables. Extending the preceding analyses is the question of which types of stimulus materials are more or less likely to be used in different designs. As shown in Figure 39-4, realistic materials were more likely to be used in true-experimental designs (48%), while actual materials were used most frequently in quasi-experimental designs. Further, as shown in Figure 39-5, classroom settings were more likely to be chosen for studies using a quasi-experimental (82%) than for true-experimental designs (44%). These relationships are

predictable, since naturalistic contexts would generally favor quasi-experimental designs over true-experimental designs given the difficulty of making the random assignments needed for the latter.

The nature of educational technology research seems to create preferences for realistic as opposed to contrived applications. Yet, the trend over time has been to emphasize true-experimental designs and fewer classroom applications. Internal validity thus appears to have acquired relatively greater value than external validity in the design of many studies. Changes in publishing conventions and standards in favor of high experimental control have certainly been influential. Affecting future patterns will be the growing usage and acceptance of qualitative methods in educa-

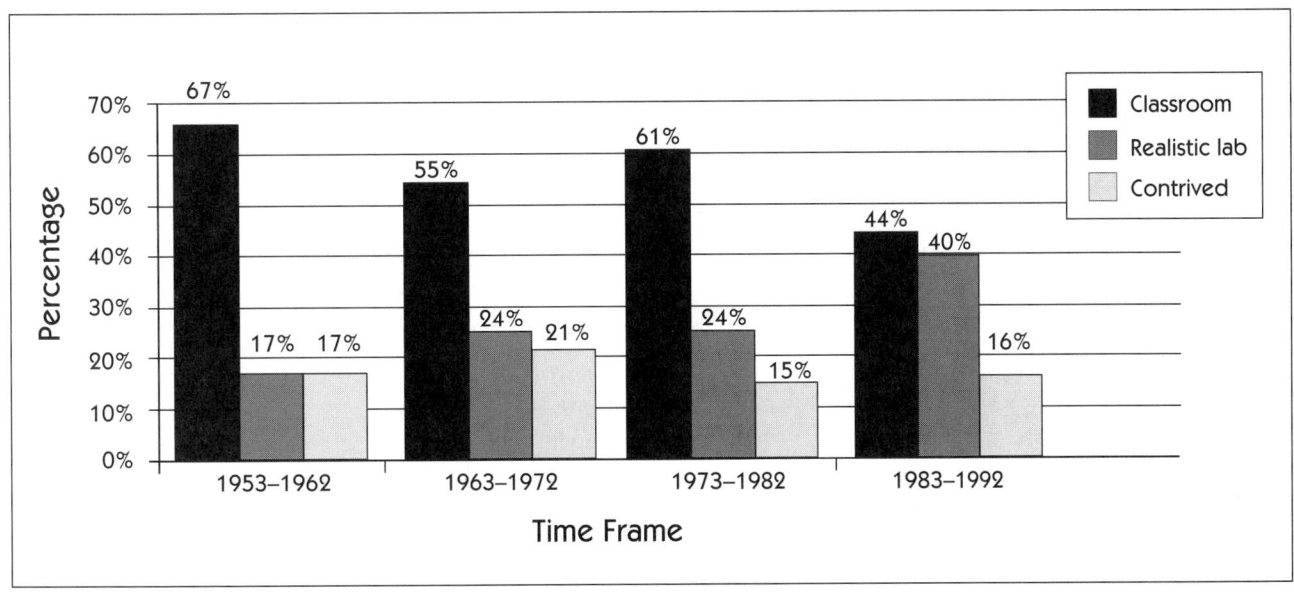

Figure 39-3. Trends in settings.

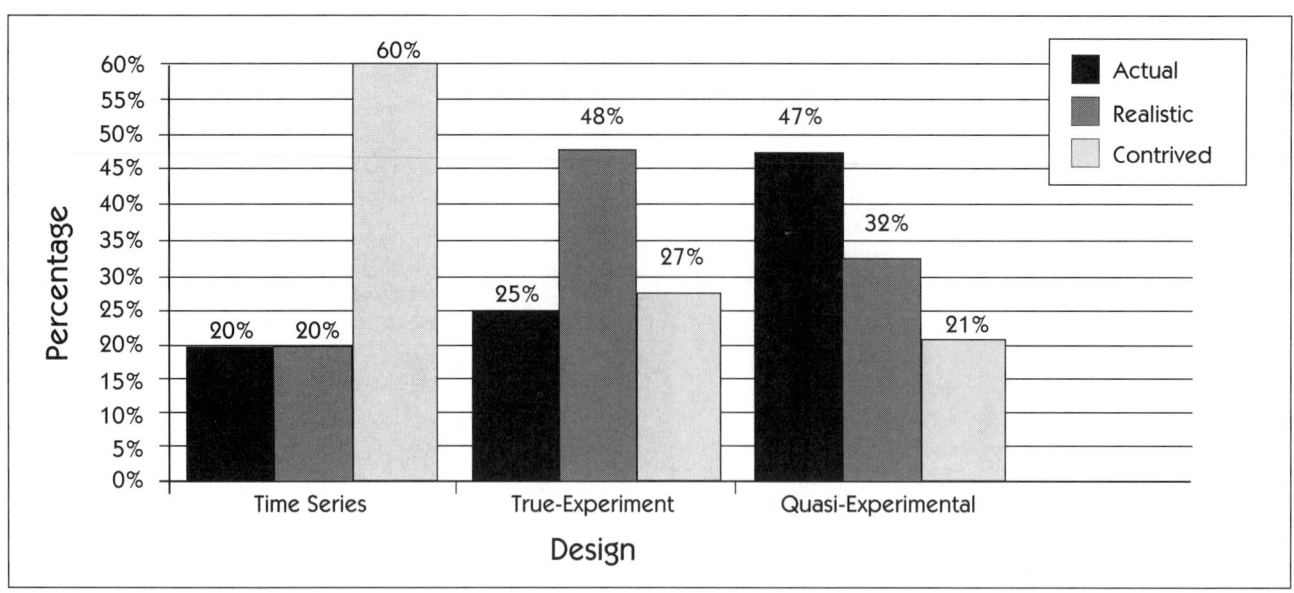

Figure 39-4. Experimental settings × materials.

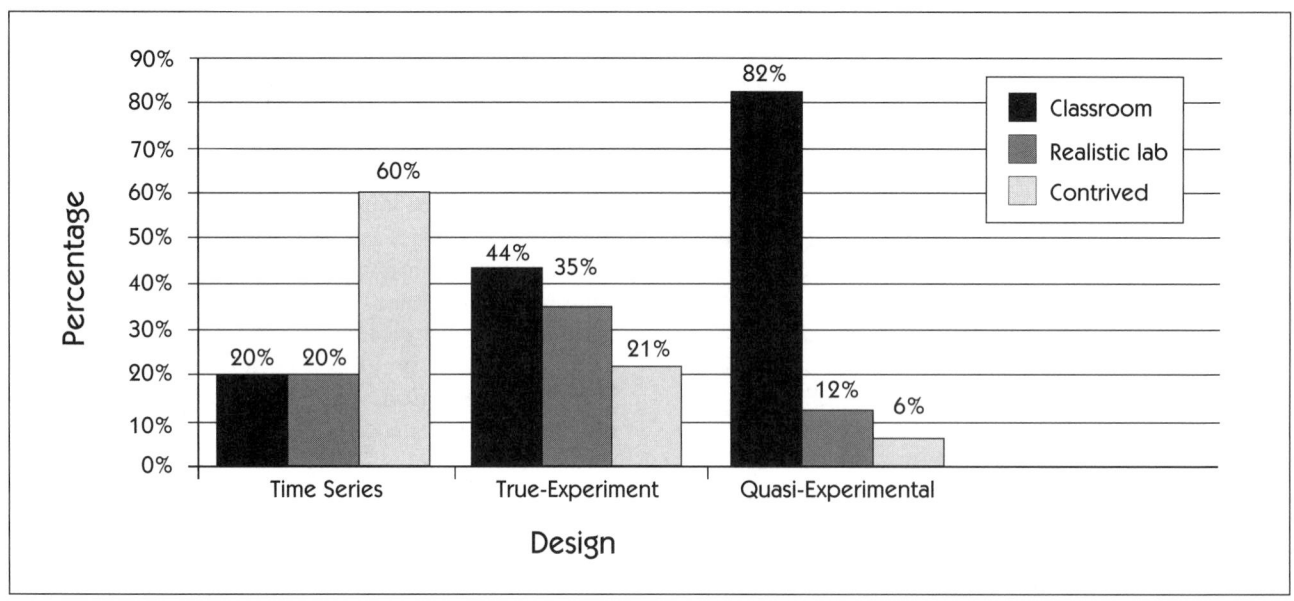

Figure 39-5. Experimental design × setting.

tional technology research. Although qualitative methods are currently popular, that pattern was not noticeable in the studies reviewed in the present analyses, all of which were published by 1992.

39.5 CONTEMPORARY ISSUES IN EDUCATIONAL TECHNOLOGY EXPERIMENTATION

39.5.1 Balancing Internal and External Validity

Frequently in this chapter, we have discussed the traditional importance to experimenters of establishing high internal validity by eliminating sources of extraneous variance in

testing treatment effects. Consequently, any differences favoring one treatment over another can be attributed confidently to the intrinsic properties of those treatments rather than to confounding variables, such as one group having a better teacher or more comfortable conditions for learning (see e.g., reviews by Ross & Morrison, 1989; Slavin, 1993).

The quest for high internal validity orients researchers to design experiments in which treatment manipulations can be tightly controlled. In the process, using naturalistic conditions (e.g., real classrooms) is discouraged, given the many extraneous sources of variance that are likely to operate in those contexts. For example, the extensive research conducted on "verbal learning" in the 1960s and 1970s largely involved associative learning tasks using simple words and nonsense syllables (e.g., see Underwood, 1966). With simplicity and artificiality come greater opportunity for control.

This orientation directly supports the objectives of the basic learning or educational psychology researcher whose interests lie in testing the generalized theory associated with treatment strategies, independent of the specific methods used in their administration. Educational technology researchers, however, are directly interested in the interaction of medium and method (Kozma, 1991, 1994; Ullmer, 1994). To learn about this interaction, realistic media applications rather than artificial ones need to be established. In other words, external validity becomes as important a concern as internal validity.

Discussing these issues brings to mind a manuscript that one of us was asked to review about 5 years ago for publication in an educational research journal. The author's intent was to compare, using an experimental design, the effects on learning of programmed instruction and computer-based instruction. To avoid Clark's (1983) criticism of performing a media comparison, i.e., confounding media with instructional strategies (see 23.6), the author decided to make the two "treatments" as similar as possible in all characteristics except delivery mode. This essentially involved replicating the exact programmed instruction design in the CBI condition. Not surprisingly, the findings showed no difference between treatments, a direct justification of Clark's (1983) position. But, unfortunately, this result (or one showing an actual treatment effect as well) would be meaningless for advancing theory or practice in educational technology (see 3.4). By stripping away the special attributes of a normal CBI lesson (e.g., interaction, sound, adaptive feedback, animation, etc.), all that remained were alternative forms of programmed instruction and the unexciting finding, to use Clark's (1983) metaphor, that groceries delivered in different, but fundamentally similar, ways still have the same nutritional value. Needless to say, this study, with its high internal validity but very low external validity, was evaluated as unsuitable for publication. Two more appropriate orientations for educational technology experiments are proposed in the following sections.

39.5.1.1. Randomized Field Experiments.

Given the importance of balancing external validity (application) and internal validity (control) in educational technology research, an especially appropriate design is the randomized field experiment (Slavin, 1993) in which instructional programs are evaluated over relatively long periods of time under realistic conditions. In contrast to descriptive or quasi-experimental designs, the randomized field experiment requires random assignment of subjects to treatment groups, thus eliminating differential selection as a validity threat.

For example, Reiser, Driscoll, and Vergara (1987) randomly assigned undergraduate students in a mastery-oriented educational psychology course to one of three treatment groups differing in mastery criteria (ascending difficulty on unit quizzes, descending difficulty, and fixed criterion). At the end of 15 weeks, students completed a comprehensive final examination. Results indicated that those in the fixed criterion group proceeded through the course at the steadiest pace and performed better than the other students.

The obvious advantage of the randomized-field experiment is high external validity. Had Reiser et al. (1987) assigned volunteer subjects to the same treatments for a 1- or 2-hour "experimental" lesson, the actual conditions of learning would have been substantially altered and likely to have yielded different results. On the other hand, the randomized-field experiment concomitantly sacrifices internal validity, since its length and complexity permit interactions to occur with confounding variables. Reiser et al.'s (1987) results, for example, might have been influenced by subjects discussing the study and its different conditions with one another after class (e.g., diffusion of treatments). The experimental results from such studies, therefore, reflect "what really happens" from combined effects of treatment and environmental variables rather than the pure effects of an isolated instructional strategy.

39.5.1.2. Basic-Applied Design Replications.

Basic research designs demand a high degree of control to provide valid tests of principles of instruction and learning. Once a principle has been thoroughly tested with consistent results, the natural progression is to evaluate its use in a real-world application. For educational technologists interested in how learners are affected by new technologies, the question of which route to take, basic versus applied, may pose a real dilemma. Typically, existing theory and prior research on related interventions will be sufficient to raise the possibility that further basic research may not be necessary. Making the leap to a real-life application, however, runs the risk of clouding the underlying causes of obtained treatment effects due to their confounding with extraneous variables.

To avoid the limitations of addressing one perspective only, a potentially advantageous approach is to look at both using a replication design. "Experiment 1," the basic research part, would examine the variables of interest by establishing a relatively high degree of control and high internal validity. "Experiment 2," the applied component, would then reexamine the same learning variables by establishing more realistic conditions and high external validity. Consistency of findings across experiments would provide strong convergent evidence supporting the obtained effects and underlying theoretical principles. Inconsistency of findings, however, would suggest influences of intervening variables that alter the effects of the variables of interest when converted from their "pure" form to realistic applications. Such contamination may often represent "media effects," as might occur, for example, when feedback strategies used with print material are naturally made more adaptive (i.e., powerful and effectual) via interactive CBI (see Kozma, 1991). (For example, a learner who confuses discovery learning with inquiry learning in response to an inserted lesson question may be branched immediately to a remedial CBI frame that differentiates between the two approaches, whereas his or her counterpart in a parallel print lesson might experience the same type of feedback by having to reference the response selected on an answer page and manually locate the appropriate response-sensitive feedback in another section of the lesson.) The next implied step of a replication design would be further experimentation on the nature and locus of the altered effects in the applied situation. Several examples from the literature of the basic-applied replication orientation follow.

Example 1. In a repeated-measures experiment conducted by our research group, adult subjects were asked to indicate their preferences for screen designs representing differing degrees of text density (Ross, Morrison, Schultz & O' Dell, 1989). In one experiment, high internal validity was established by having learners judge only the *initial* screen of a given text presentation, thus keeping the number of displays across higher- and lower-density variations constant. In realistic lessons, however, using lower-density displays requires the use of additional screens (or more scrolling) to view the content fully. Accordingly, a parallel experiment, having higher external validity but lower internal validity, was conducted in which the number of screens was allowed to vary naturally in accord with the selected density level.

Both experiments produced similar results, supporting higher- over lower-density displays, regardless of the quantity of screens that conveyed a particular density condition. Consequently, we were able to make a stronger case both for the theoretical assumption that higher density would provide greater contextual support for comprehending expository text and for the practical recommendation that such density levels be considered for the design of actual CBI lessons.

Example 2. In the previously described replication design by Winn and Solomon (1993), nonsense syllables were used as verbal stimuli in experiment 1. Findings indicated that the interpretation of diagrams containing verbal labels (e.g., "Yutcur" in box A and "Nipden" in box B) was mainly determined by syntactic rules of English. For example, if box B were embedded in box A, subjects were more likely to select, as an interpretation, "Yutcur are Nipden" then the converse description. However, when English words were substituted for the nonsense syllables (e.g., "sugar" in box A and "spice" in box B) in experiment 2, this effect was overridden by common semantic meanings. For example, "Sugar is spice" would be a more probable response than the converse, regardless of the diagram arrangement. Taken together, the two experiments supported theoretical assumptions about the influences of diagram arrangement on the interpreted meaning of concepts, while suggesting for designers that appropriate diagram arrangements become increasing critical as the meaningfulness of the material decreases.

Example 3. Although using a descriptive rather than experimental design, Grabinger (1993) asked subjects to judge the readability of "model" screens that presented symbolic notation as opposed to real content in different formats (e.g., using or not using illustrations, status bars, headings, etc.) Using multidimensional scaling analysis, he found that evaluations were made along two dimensions: organization and structure. In a second study, he replicated the procedure using real content screens. Results yielded only one evaluative dimension that emphasized organization and visual interest. In this case, somewhat conflicting results from the basic and applied designs required the researcher to evaluate the implications of each relative to the research objectives. The basic conclusion reached was that while the results of study 1 were free from content bias, the results of study 2 more meaningfully reflected the types of decisions that learners make in viewing CBI information screens.

Example 4. Recently, Morrison et al. (1995) examined uses of different feedback strategies in learning from CBI. Built into the experimental design was a factor representing the conditions under which college student subjects participated in the experiment: simulated or realistic. Specifically, in the simulated condition, the students from selected education courses completed the CBI lesson to earn extra credit toward their course grade. The advantage of using this sample was increased internal validity, given that students were not expected to be familiar with the lesson content (writing instructional objectives) or to be studying it during the period of their participation. In the realistic condition, subjects were students in an instructional media course for which performance on the CBI unit (posttest score) would be computed in their final average.

Interestingly, the results showed similar relative effects of the different feedback conditions; for example, knowledge of correct response (KCR) and delayed feedback tended to surpass no-feedback and answer-until-correct (AUC) feedback. Examination of learning *process* variables, however, further revealed that students in the realistic conditions performed better, while making greater and more appropriate use of instructional support options provided in association with the feedback. While the simulated condition was valuable as a more basic and purer test of theoretical assumptions, the realistic condition provided more valid insights into how the different forms of feedback would likely be used in combination with other learning resources on an actual learning task.

39.5.2 ASSESSING MULTIPLE OUTCOMES IN EDUCATIONAL TECHNOLOGY EXPERIMENTS

The classic conception of an experiment might be to imagine two groups of white rats, one trained in a Skinner Box under a continuous schedule of reinforcement and the other under an intermittent schedule. After a designated period of training, reinforcement (food) is discontinued, and the two groups of rats are compared on the number of trials to extinction. That is, how long will they continue to press the bar even though food is withheld?

In this type of experiment, it is probable that the single dependent measure of "trials" would be sufficient to answer the research question of interest. In educational technology research, however, research questions are not likely to be resolved in so straightforward a manner (see 24.11). Merely knowing that one instructional strategy produced better achievement than another provides little insight into how those effects occurred or about other possible effects of the strategies. Earlier educational technology experiments, influenced by behavioristic approaches to learning (see 2.2), were often subject to this limitation.

For example, Shettel, Faison, Roshal, and Lumsdaine (1956) compared live lectures and identical film lectures on subjects (Air Force technicians) learning fuel and rudder systems. The dependent measure was immediate and delayed multiple-choice tests on three content areas. Two outcomes were significant, both favoring the live-lecture condition on the immediate test. Although the authors concluded that the films taught the material less well than the "live" lectures, they were unable to provide any interpretation as to why. Observation of students might have revealed greater attentiveness to the live lecture; student interviews might have indicated that the film audio was hard to hear; or a problem-solving test might have shown that application skills were low (or high) under both presentations.

Released from the rigidity of behavioristic approaches, contemporary educational technology experimenters are likely to employ more and richer outcome measures than did their predecessors. Two factors have been influential in promoting this development. One has been the predominance of cognitive learning perspectives in the past 2 decades (Tennyson, 1992; Tennyson & Rasch, 1988; Snow & Lohman, 1989; see also 5.2); the other has been the growing influence of qualitative research methods (see 40.1).

39.5.2.1. Cognitive Applications.

In their comprehensive review paper, Snow and Lohman (1989) discuss influences of cognitive theory to contemporary educational measurement practices. One key contribution has been the expansion of conventional assessment instruments so as to describe more fully the "cognitive character" of the target. Among the newer, cognitively derived measurement applications that are receiving greater usage in research are tests of declarative and procedural knowledge, componential analysis, computer simulations, faceted tests, and coaching methods, to name only a few.

Whereas behavioral theory stressed learning products, such as accuracy and rate, cognitive approaches also emphasize learning processes (Brownell, 1992). The underlying assumption is that learners may appear to reach similar destinations in terms of observable outcomes but take qualitatively different routes to arrive at those points. Importantly, the routes or "processes" used determine the durability and transferability of what is learned (Mayer, 1989). Process measures may include such variables as the problem-solving approach employed, level of task interest, resources selected, learning strategies used, and responses made on task. At the same time, the cognitive approach expands the measurement of products to include varied, multiple learning outcomes such as declarative knowledge, procedural knowledge, long-term retention, and transfer (Tennyson & Rasch, 1988).

This expanded approach to assessment is exemplified in a recent experiment by Hicken, Sullivan, and Klein (1992). The focus of the study was comparing two types of learner control ("FullMinus" vs. "LeanPlus" under two conditions of incentives (performance contingent vs. task contingent). In the FullMinus condition, learners could selectively bypass elements of a full instructional program, whereas in the LeanPlus condition, they could opt to add elements to a core program. Degree of learning, assessed via a posttest on the unit studied, reflected advantages for FullMinus learner control and performance-contingent incentives. This information alone, however, would have provided little insight into why those strategies were effective. Accordingly, Hicken et al. also examined learner-control option use (i.e., optional examples, practice examples, and review screens), which showed that FullMinus subjects used 80% of the options, whereas LeanPlus subjects used only 37%. Apparently, learners, given individual control over instruction, are inclined to choose the "default" option, which in the case of FullMinus produces exposure to higher levels of instructional support and, in turn, better learning. Further analyses showed typical patterns of option use by learners in the four conditions, time spent on the overall program and on option usage, and student attitudes. Using these multiple outcome measures, the researchers acquired a comprehensive perspective on how processes induced by the different strategies culminated in the learning products obtained.

Use of special assessments that directly relate to the treatment is illustrated in a study by Shin, Schallert, and Savenye (1994). Both quantitative and qualitative data were collected to determine the effectiveness of leaner control with elementary students who varied in prior knowledge. An advisement condition that provided the subject with specific directions as to what action to take next was also employed. Quantitative data collected consisted of both immediate and delayed posttest scores, preferences for the method, self-ratings of difficulty, and lesson completion time. The qualitative data include an analysis of the path each learner took through the materials. This analysis revealed that nonadvisement students became lost in the hypertext "maze" and often went back and forth between two sections of the lessons as though searching for a way to complete the lesson. In contrast, students who received advisement used the information to make the proper decisions regarding navigation more than 70% of the time. Based on the qualitative analysis, they concluded that advisement (e.g., orientation information, what to do next) was necessary when learners can freely access (e.g., learner control) different parts of the instruction at will. They also concluded that advisement was not necessary when the program controlled access to the instruction.

Another example of multiple and treatment-oriented assessments is found in Neuman's (1994) study on the applicability of databases for instruction. Neuman used observations of the students using the database, informal interviews, and document analysis (e.g., review of assignment, search plans, and search results). This triangulation of data provided information on the design and interface of the database. If the data collection were limited to only the number of citations found or used in the students' assignment, the results might have shown that the database was quite effective. Using a variety of sources allowed the researcher to make specific recommendations for improving the database rather than simply concluding that it was beneficial or not.

39.5.2.2. Qualitative Research. In recent years, educational researchers have shown increasing interest in qualitative research approaches (see 40.2). Such research involves naturalistic inquiries using techniques such as in-depth interviews, direct observation, and document analysis (Patton, 1990). Unfortunately, in recalling our personal experiences at recent AECT meetings, the reaction by some researchers has been to view quantitative and qualitative paradigms as competing or even mutually exclusive (see Bruner, 1990). Our position, in congruence with what is likely the majority opinion (albeit a silent one at times), is that quantitative and qualitative research are each more useful when used together than when used alone (Warwick, 1990, as cited by Peshkin, 1993). Both provide unique perspectives, which, when combined, are likely to yield a richer and more valid understanding.

Presently, in educational technology research, experimentalists have been slow to incorporate qualitative measures as part of their overall research methodology. To illustrate how such an integration could be useful, we recall conducting an editorial review of a manuscript submitted for publication in *ETR&D* by Klein and Pridemore (1992). The focus of their study was the effects of cooperative learning and need for affiliation on performance and satisfaction in learning from instructional television. Findings showed benefits for cooperative learning over individual learning, particularly when students were high in affiliation needs. While we and the reviewers evaluated the manuscript positively, a shared criticism was the lack of data reflecting the nature of the cooperative interactions. It was felt that such qualitative information would have increased understanding of why the treatment effects obtained occurred. Seemingly, the same recommendation could be made for nearly any applied experiment on educational technology uses. The following excerpt from the *published* version of Klien and Pridemore (1992) illustrates the potential value of this approach:

> . . . observations of subjects who worked cooperatively suggested that they did, in fact, implement these directions [to work together, discuss feedback, etc.]. After each segment of the tape was stopped, one member of the dyad usually read the practice question aloud. If the question was unclear to either member, the other would spend time explaining it . . . [in contrast to individuals who worked alone] read each question quietly and would either immediately write their answer in the workbook or would check the feedback for the correct answer. These informal observations tend to suggest that subjects who worked cooperatively were more engaged than those who worked alone (p. 45).

Qualitative and quantitative measures can thus be used collectively in experiments to provide complementary perspectives on research outcomes.

39.5.3 Item Responses vs. Aggregate Scores as Dependent Variables

Consistent with the "expanded assessment" trend, educational technology experiments are likely to include dependent variables consisting of one or more achievement (learning) measures, attitude measures, or a combination of both types. In the typical case, the achievement or attitude measure will be a test comprised of multiple items. By summing item scores across items, a total or "aggregate" score is derived. To support the validity of this score, the experimenter may report the test's internal-consistency reliability (computed using Cronbach's alpha or the KR-20 formula) or some other reliability index. Internal consistency represents "equivalence reliability"—the extent to which parts of a test are equivalent (Wiersma & Jurs, 1985). Depending on the situation, these procedures could prove limiting or even misleading with regard to answering the experimental research questions.

A fundamental question to consider is whether the test is designed to measure a unitary construct (e.g., ability to reduce fractions or level of test anxiety) or multiple constructs (e.g., how much students liked the lesson and how much they liked using a computer). In the latter cases, internal consistency reliability might well be low, because students vary in how they perform or how they feel across the separate measures. Specifically, there may be no logical reason why good performances on, say, the "math facts" portion of the test should be highly correlated with those on the problem-solving portion (or why reactions to the lesson should strongly correlate with reactions to the computer). It may even be the case that the treatments being investigated are geared to affect one type of performance or attitude more than another. Accordingly, one caution is that, where multiple constructs are being assessed by *design*, internal-consistency reliability may be a poor indicator of construct validity. More appropriate indices would assess the degree to which: (a) items within the separate subscales intercorrelate (subscale internal consistency), (b) the makeup of the instruments conforms with measurement objectives (content validity), (c) students answer particular questions in the same way on repeated administrations (test-retest reliability), and (d) subscale scores correlate with measures of similar constructs or identified criteria (construct or predictive validity).

Separate from the test validation issue is the concern that aggregate scores may mask revealing patterns that occur across different subscales and items. We will explore this issue further by examining some negative and positive examples from actual studies.

39.5.3.1. Aggregating Achievement Results. Recently, we evaluated a manuscript for publication which described an experimental study on graphic aids. The main hypothesis was that such aids would primarily promote better understanding of the science concepts being taught. The dependent measure was an achievement test consisting of factual (fill-in the-blank), application (multiple-choice and short-answer), and problem-solving questions. The analysis, however, examined total score only in comparing treatments. Because the authors had not recorded subtest scores and were unable to rerun the analysis to provide such breakdowns (and, thereby, directly address the main research question), the manuscript was rejected.

39.5.3.2. Aggregating Attitude Results. More commonly, educational technology experimenters commit comparable oversights in analyzing attitude data. When attitude questions concern different properties of the learning experience or instructional context, it may make little sense to compute a total score, unless there is an interest in an overall attitude score. For example, in a study using elaborative feedback as a treatment strategy, students may respond that they liked the learning material but did not use the feedback. The overall attitude score would mask the latter, important finding.

For a brief illustration, we recall a manuscript recently submitted to *ETR&D* in which the author reported only aggregate results on an postlesson attitude survey. When the need for individual item information was requested, the author replied, "the KR-20 reliability of the scale was .84; therefore, all items are measuring the same thing." While high internal consistency reliability implies that the items are "pulling in the same direction," it does not also mean necessarily that all yielded equally positive responses. For example, as a group, learners might have rated the lesson material very high, but the instructional delivery very low. Such specific information might have been useful in furthering understanding of why certain achievement results occurred.

Effective reporting of item results was done by Welsh, Murphy, Duffy, and Goodrum (1993) in investigating the effects of different link displays for accessing information in a hypermedia system. The three displays were (a) an arrow indicating that some type of elaboration was available; (b) six unique icons, each designating a different elaboration type; and (c) a submenu structure. In addition to an assessment of the number and type of elaborations students accessed, one of the dependent measures was an attitude measure of "ease of reading." The analysis of *total* attitude scores showed, as the only trend, a predictable preference for the submenu (since the display was less cluttered). Individual item results further revealed that participants in general tended to agree with the statements, "The arrows that I clicked on in the text were distracting," and "A computer text screen without arrows would have been easier to read." The authors concluded on this basis that, regardless of the link strategy used, novice users of hypermedia are initially distracted by unfamiliar symbols embedded in the text (p. 31). More insight into user experiences was thus obtained relative to examining the aggregate score only. It is important to keep in mind, however, that the multiple statistical tests resulting from individual item analyses can drastically inflate the chances of making a type I error (falsely con-

cluding that treatment effects exists). Usage of appropriate statistical controls, such as MANOVA (see Table 39-1) or a reduced alpha (significance) level, is required.

39.5.4 Media Studies vs. Media Comparisons

As confirmed by our analysis of trends in educational technology experimentation, a popular focus of the past was comparing different types of media-based instruction to one another or to teacher-based instruction to determine which approach was "best." The fallacy or, at least, unreasonableness of this orientation, now known as "media comparison studies," was forcibly explicated by Clark (1983) in his now classic article (see also Hagler & Knowlton, 1987; Petkovich & Tennyson, 1984; Ross & Morrison, 1989; Salomon & Clark, 1977). As previously discussed, in that paper, Clark argued that media were analogous to grocery trucks that carry food but do not in themselves provide nourishment (i.e., instruction). It, therefore, makes little sense to compare delivery methods when instructional strategies are the variables that impact learning.

For present purposes, these considerations present a strong case against experimentation that simply compares media. Specifically, two types of experimental designs seem particularly unproductive in this regard. One of these represents treatments as amorphous or "generic" media applications, such as CBI, interactive video, Personalized System of Instruction, lecture, and the like. The focus of the experiment then becomes which medium "produces" the highest achievement. The obvious problem with such research is the confounding of results with numerous media attributes. For example, because CBI may offer immediate feedback, animation, and sound, while a print lesson may not, differences in outcomes from the two types of presentations would be expected to the extent the differentiating attributes impact criterion performance.

A second type of inappropriate media comparison experiment is to create artificially comparable alternative media presentations, such that both variations contain identical attributes but use different modes of delivery. In an earlier section, we described a study in which CBI and a print manual were used to deliver the identical programmed instruction lesson. The results, which predictably showed no treatment differences, revealed little about CBI's capabilities as a medium compared to those of print lessons. Similarly, to learn about television's "effects" as a medium, it seems to make more sense to use a program like *Sesame Street* as an exemplar (see, e.g., Reiser et al., 1988) than a "talking head" from a taped, unedited lecture. (This does not mean, however, that comparing the talking head to a live head would be inappropriate in an *evaluation* study of a particular instructional program that uses taped lectures.)

So where does this leave us with regard to experimentation on media differences? We propose that researchers consider two related orientations for "media studies." Both orientations involve conveying media applications realistically, whether "conventional" or "ideal" (cutting edge) in form. Both also directly compare educational outcomes from the alternative media presentations. However, as will be explained below, one orientation is deductive in nature and the other is inductive.

39.5.4.1. Deductive Approach: Testing Hypotheses about Media Differences. In this first approach, the purpose of the experiment is to test a priori hypotheses of differences between the two media presentations based directly on analyses of their different attributes (see Kozma, 1991, 1994). For example, it might be hypothesized that for teaching an instructional unit on a cardiac surgery procedure, a conventional lecture presentation might be superior to an interactive video presentation for facilitating retention of factual information, whereas the converse would be true for facilitating meaningful understanding of the procedure. The rationale for these hypotheses would be directly based on analyses of the special capabilities (embedded attributes or instructional strategies) of each medium in relation to the type of material taught. Findings would be used to support or refute these assumptions.

An example of this a priori search for media differences is the recent study by Aust, Kelley, and Roby (1993) on "hyperreference" (on line) and conventional paper dictionary use in foreign-language learning. Because hyperreferences offer immediate access to supportive information, it was hypothesized and confirmed that learners would consult such dictionaries more frequently and with greater efficiency than they would conventional dictionaries.

39.5.4.2. Inductive Approach: Replicating Findings Across Media. The second type of study, which we have called *media replications* (Ross & Morrison, 1989), examines the consistency of effects of given instructional strategies delivered by alternative media. Consistent findings, if obtained, are treated as corroborative evidence to strengthen theoretical understanding of the instructional variables in question as well as claims concerning the associated strategy's effectiveness for learning. If inconsistent outcomes are obtained, methods and theoretical assumptions are reexamined and the target strategy subjected to further empirical tests using diverse learners and conditions. Key interests are why results were better or worse with a particular medium and how the strategy might be more powerfully represented by the alternative media. Subsequent developmental research might then explore ways of incorporating the suggested refinements in actual systems and evaluating those applications. In this manner, media replication experiments use an inductive, post hoc procedure to identify media attributes that differentially impact learning. At the same time, they provide valuable generalizability tests of the effects of particular instructional strategies.

The continuing debate on media effects (Clark, 1983, 1994; Kozma, 1994) is important for sharpening conceptualization of the role of media in enhancing instruction. However, Clark's focal argument that media do not affect learning should not be used as a basis for discouraging experimentation that compares educational outcomes *using*

different media. In the first orientation reviewed above, the focus of the experiment is hypothesized effects on learning of instructional strategies embedded in media. In the second orientation, the focus is the identified effects of media in altering how those strategies are conveyed. In neither case is the medium itself conceptualized as the direct cause of learning. In both cases, the common goal is increasing theoretical and practical understanding of how *to use* media more effectively to deliver instruction.

39.6 SUMMARY

In this chapter, we have examined the historical roots and current practices of experimentation in educational technology. Initial usage of experimental methods received impetus from behavioral psychology and the physical sciences. The basic interest was to employ standardized procedures to investigate the effects of treatments. Such standardization ensured high internal validity or the ability to attribute findings to treatment variations as opposed to extraneous factors.

Common forms of experimentation consist of true experiments, repeated-measures designs, quasi-experiments, and time series designs. Internal validity is generally highest with true experiments due to the random assignment of subjects to different treatments. Typical threats to internal validity consist of history, maturation, testing, instrumentation, statistical regression, selection, experimental mortality, and diffusion of treatments.

Conducting experiments is facilitated by following a systematic planning and application process. A seven-step model suggested consists of (1) selecting a topic, (2) identifying the research problem, (3) conducting a literature search, (4) stating research questions or hypotheses, (5) identifying the research design, (6) determining methods, and (7) identifying data analysis approaches.

For experimental studies to have an impact on theory and practice in educational technology, their findings need to be disseminated to other researchers and practitioners. Getting a research article published in a good journal requires careful attention to writing quality and style conventions. Typical write-ups of experiments include as major sections an introduction (problem area, literature review, rationale, and hypotheses), method (subjects, design, materials, instruments, and procedure), results (analyses and findings), and discussion.

Given their long tradition and prevalence in educational research, experiments are sometimes criticized as being overemphasized and conflicting with the improvement of instruction. However, experiments are not intrinsically problematic as a research approach, but have sometimes been used in very strict, formal ways that have blinded educational researchers from looking past results to gain understanding about learning *processes*. To increase their utility to the field, experiments should be used in conjunction with other research approaches and with nontraditional, supplementary ways of collecting and analyzing results.

Analysis of trends in using experiments in educational technology, as reflected by publications in *ETR&D* (and its predecessors) over the last 4 decades, show consistent trends as well as some changing ones. True experiments have been much more frequently conducted over the years relative to quasi-experiments, time series designs, and descriptive studies. However, greater balancing of internal and external validity has been evidenced over time by increasing usage in experiments of realistic but simulated materials and contexts as opposed to either contrived or completely naturalistic materials and contexts.

Several issues seem important to current uses of experimentation as a research methodology in educational technology. One is balancing internal validity and external validity, so that experiments are adequately controlled while yielding meaningful and applicable findings. Two orientations suggested for achieving such balance is the randomized field experiment and the "basic-applied" design replication. Influenced and aided by advancements in cognitive learning approaches and qualitative research methodologies, today's experimenters are also more likely than their predecessors to use multiple data sources to obtain corroborative and supplementary evidence regarding the learning processes and products associated with the strategies evaluated. Looking at individual item results as opposed to only aggregate scores from cognitive and attitude measures is consistent with the orientation.

Finally, the continuing debate regarding "media effects" notwithstanding, media comparison experiments remain interesting and viable in our field. The goal is not to compare media generically to determine which are "best," but rather to further understanding of (a) how media differ in their capabilities for conveying instructional strategies, and (b) how the influences of instructional strategies are maintained or altered via different media presentations.

REFERENCES

Alper, T., Thoresen, C.E. & Wright, J. (1972). *The use of film-mediated modeling and feedback to change a classroom teacher's classroom responses.* Palo Alto, CA: Stanford University, School of Education, R&D Memorandum 91.

Aust, R., Kelley, M.J. & Roby, W. (1993). The use of hyperference and conventional dictionaries. *Educational Technology Research & Development 41,* 63–71.

Beck, C.R. (1984). Visual cueing strategies: pictorial, textual, and combinational effects. *Educational Communication and Technology Journal 32,* 207–16.

Borg, W.R., Gall, J.P. & Gall, M.D. (1993). *Applying educational research,* 3d ed. New York: Longman.

Brownell, W.A. (1992). Reprint of criteria of learning in educational research. *Journal of Educational Psychology 84,* 400–04.

Bruner, E. (1990). The scientists vs. the humanists. *Anthropology Newsletter 31,* 28.

Campbell, D.T. & Stanley, J.C. (1963). Experimental and quasi-experimental designs for research on teaching. *In* N.L. Gage, ed. *Handbook of research on teaching,* 171–246.

Chicago, IL: Rand McNally.

Clark, R.E. (1983). Reconsidering research on learning from media. *Review of Educational Research 53,* 445–59.

— (1994). Media will never influence learning. *Educational Technology Research and Development 42,* 21–29.

— & Snow, R.E. (1975). Alternative designs for instructional technology research. *AV Communication Review 23,* 373–94.

Cronbach, L.J. (1957). The two disciplines of scientific psychology. *American Psychologist 12,* 671–84.

Dick, W. & Carey, L. (1985). *The systematic design of instruction,* 2d ed. Glenview, IL: Scott, Foresman.

Feliciano, G.D., Powers, R.D. & Kearl, B.E. (1963). The presentation of statistical information. *AV Communication Review 11,* 32–39.

Glass, G.V. & Hopkins, K.D. (1984). *Statistical methods in education and psychology.* Englewood Cliffs, NJ: Prentice Hall.

Grabinger, R.S. (1993). Computer screen designs: viewer judgments. *Educational Technology Research & Development 41,* 35–73.

Gronlund, N.E. & Linn, R.L. (1990). *Measurement and evaluation in teaching,* 6th ed. New York: Macmillan.

Guba, E.G. (1969). The failure of educational evaluation. *Educational Technology 9,* 29–38.

Guba, E.G. (1981). Criteria for assessing the trustworthiness of naturalistic inquiries. *Educational Communication and Technology Journal 29,* 75–92.

Hagler, P. & Knowlton, J. (1987). Invalid implicit assumption in CBI comparison research. *Journal of Computer-Based Instruction 14,* 84–88.

Hannafin, M.J. (1986). The status and future of research in instructional design and technology. *Journal of Instructional Development 8,* 24–30.

Heinich, R. (1984). The proper study of educational technology. *Educational Communication and Technology Journal 32,* 67–87.

Hicken, S., Sullivan, H. & Klein, J. (1992). Learner control modes and incentive variations in computer-delivered instruction. *Educational Technology Research & Development 40,* 15–26.

Jonassen, D.H. (1991). Chaos in instructional design. *Educational Technology 30,* 32–34.

—, Campbell, J.P. & Davidson, M.E. (1994). Learning with media: restructuring the debate. *Educational Technology Research & Development 42,* 31–39.

Kemp, J.E., Morrison, G.R. & Ross, S.M. (1994). *Designing effective instruction: applications of instructional design.* Columbus, OH: Merrill.

Kerlinger, F.N. (1986). *Foundations of behavioral research: educational and psychological inquiry,* 3d ed. New York: Holt, Rinehart & Winston.

Klein, J.D. & Pridemore, D.R. (1992). Effects of cooperative learning and the need for affiliation on performance, time on task, and satisfaction. *Educational Technology Research & Development 40,* 39–48.

Knowlton, J.Q. (1964). A conceptual scheme for the audiovisual field. *Bulletin of the School of Education: Indiana University 40* (3), 1–44.

Kozma, R.B. (1991). Learning with media. *Review of Educational Research 61,* 179–212.

— (1994). Will media influence learning? Reframing the debate. *Educational Technology Research and Development 42,* 7–19.

Levin, J.R. (1993). Editorial: publishing in the *Journal of Educational Psychology*: reflections at midstream. *Journal of Educational Psychology 85,* 3–6.

Mayer, R.E. (1989). Models for understanding. *Review of Educational Research 59,* 43–64.

McMillan, J.H. & Schumacher, S. (1989). *Research in education,* 2d ed. Glenview, IL: Scott, Foresman.

Morrison, G.R. (1984). Communicability of the emotional connotation of type. *Educational Communication and Technology Journal 43,* 235–44.

—, Ross, S.M. & Baldwin, W. (1992). Learner control of context and instructional support in learning elementary school mathematics. *Educational Technology Research & Development 40,* 5–14.

—, Ross, S.M., Gopalakrishnan, M. & Casey, J. (1995). The effects of incentives and feedback on achievement in computer-based instruction. *Contemporary Educational Psychology 20,* 32–50.

—, Ross, S.M., Schultz, C.W. & O'Dell, J.K. (1989). Learner preferences for varying screen densities using realistic stimulus materials with single and multiple designs. *Educational Technology Research & Development 37,* 53–62.

Neuman, D. (1994). Designing databases as tools for higher-level learning: insights from instructional systems design. *Educational Technology Research & Development 41,* 25–46.

Niekamp, W. (1981). An exploratory investigation into factors affecting visual balance. *Educational Communication and Technology Journal 29,* 37–48.

Park, O. & Gittelman, S.S. (1992). Effects of cooperative learning and need for affiliation on performance. *Educational Technology Research & Development 40,* 27–38.

Patton, M.G. (1990). *Qualitative evaluation and research methods,* 2d ed. Newbury Park, CA: Sage.

Peshkin, A. (1993). The goodness of qualitative research. *Educational Researcher 22,* 23–29.

Petkovich, M.D. & Tennyson, R.D. (1984). Clark's "Learning from media": a critique. *Educational Communication and Technology Journal 32,* 233–41.

Popham, J.W. (1990). *Modern educational measurement: a practitioner's perspective,* 2d ed. Englewood Cliffs, NJ: Prentice Hall.

Reiser, R.A., Driscoll, M.P. & Vergara, A. (1987). The effects of ascending, descending, and fixed criteria on student performance and attitude in a mastery-oriented course. *Educational Communication and Technology Journal 35,* 195–202.

—, Williamson, N. & Suzuki, K. (1988). Using "Sesame Street" to facilitate children's recognition of letters and numbers. *Educational Communication and Technology Journal 36,* 15–23.

Ross, S.M. & Morrison, G.R. (1989). In search of a happy medium in instructional technology research: issues concerning external validity, media replications, and learner control. *Educational Technology Research and Development 37,* 19–34.

— & — (1991). Delivering your convention presentations at AECT. *Tech Trends 36,* 66–68.

— & — (1992). Getting started as a researcher: designing and conducting research studies in instructional technology. *Tech Trends 37,* 19–22.

— & — (1993a, July). *Evaluation as a tool for research and development: issues and trends in its application in educational technology.* NATO Institute, Grimstad, Norway.

— & — (1993b). How to get research articles published in professional journals. *Tech Trends 38,* 29–33.

—, Smith, L.S. & Morrison, G.R. (1991). The longitudinal influences of computer-intensive learning experiences on at-risk elementary students. *Educational Technology Research & Development 39,* 33–46.

Salomon, G. & Clark, R.W. (1977). Reexamining the methodology of research on media and technology in education. *Review of Educational Research 47,* 99–120.

Shettel, H.H., Faison, E.J., Roshal, S.M. & Lumsdaine, A.A. (1956). An experimental comparison of "live" and filmed lectures employing mobile training devices. *AV Communication Review 4,* 216–22.

Shin, E.C., Schallert, D.L. & Savenye, W. (1994). Effects of learner control, advisement, and prior knowledge on students' learning in a hypertext environment. *Educational Technology Research and Development 42,* 33–46.

Slavin, R.E. (1993). *Educational psychology.* Englewood Cliffs, NJ: Prentice Hall.

Snow, R.E. & Lohman, D.F. (1989). Implications of cognitive psychology for educational measurement. *In* R.L. Linn, ed. *Educational measurement,* 3d ed., 263–331. New York: Macmillan.

Sternberg, R.J. (1988). *The psychologist's companion: a guide to scientific writing for students and researchers.* Cambridge, MA: Cambridge University Press.

Tennyson, R.D. (1978). Evaluation methodology in instructional development. *Journal of Instructional Development 2,* 19–26.

— (1992). An educational learning theory for instructional design. *Educational Technology 32,* 36–41.

— & Rasch, M. (1988). Linking cognitive learning theory to instructional prescriptions. *Instructional Science 17,* 369–85.

—, Welsh, J.C., Christensen, D.L. & Hajovy, H. (1985). Interactive effect of information structure sequence of information and process learning time on rule learning using computer-based instruction. *Educational Communication and Technology Journal 33,* 212–23.

Ullmer, E.J. (1994). Media and learning: are there two kinds of truth? *Educational Technology Research & Development 42,* 21–32.

Underwood, B.J. (1966). *Experimental psychology.* New York: Appleton-Century-Crofts.

Warwick, D.P. (1973). Survey research and participant observation: a benefit-cost analysis. *In* D.P. Warwick & S. Osherson, eds. *Comparative research methods,* 189–203. Englewood Cliffs, NJ: Prentice Hall.

Welsh, T.M., Murphy, K.P., Duffy, T.M. & Goodrum, D.A. (1993). Assessing elaborations on core information in a hypermedia environment. *Educational Technology Research & Development 41,* 19–34.

Wiersma, W. (1991). *Research methods in education,* 5th ed. Needham Heights, MA: Allyn & Bacon.

Wiersma, W. & Jurs, S.G. (1985). *Educational measurement and testing.* Newton, MA: Allyn & Bacon

Winn, W. & Solomon, C. (1993). The effect of spatial arrangement of simple diagrams on the interpretation of English and nonsense sentences. *Educational Technology Research & Development 41,* 29–41.

40. QUALITATIVE RESEARCH ISSUES AND METHODS: AN INTRODUCTION FOR EDUCATIONAL TECHNOLOGISTS

Wilhelmina C. Savenye
ARIZONA STATE UNIVERSITY

Rhonda S. Robinson
NORTHERN ILLINOIS UNIVERSITY

INTRODUCTION*

Educational technology research is changing. Assumptions, questions, methods, and paradigms that formerly dominated research in the field are changing. Research questions and methods that might once have been deemed unacceptable are gaining acceptability; studies published using alternate paradigms may now be published. Are these "new methods" really so new? Are they based on the same perceptions of quality as the well-established quantitative methods? Are we losing the big picture in research? Are researchers really calling for the end of quantitative research, the positivistic research paradigm, all that has gone before?

It is the goal of this chapter to introduce educational technology researchers, both new and experienced, to the conceptual basis and methods of qualitative research. The goal is a modest one, due to the need for brevity in a small chapter in a large handbook. Controversy will not be sidestepped, but will not specifically be entered in to. Readers will be introduced, for example, to the "paradigm debate" currently swirling in the field and to the assumptions of various researchers who adhere to one view or another. Just as one cannot learn to conduct research by reading one book, a researcher who determines to conduct research to be labeled *qualitative* will need to study sources beyond this chapter to determine his or her own assumptions on which to base the work. The researcher must thus enter the debate, and will be responsible for describing the foundational ideas of the study. He or she will want to conduct the study with the utmost attention to quality, therefore will want to turn to more-detailed texts to learn more deeply how to apply qualitative methods. This chapter will point the researcher to such references and resources; however, we do not intend the chapter to be a definitive self-study text in conducting quali-

tative research. We intend to make the chapter a small and useful tool, a simple guide to assist educational technologists in learning and making decisions about qualitative research. It is thus intended as a beginning point, a brief tour of qualitative methods that may serve an educational technology researcher well in preparing to answer chosen questions, and serve the field in allowing new questions to be explored.

Objectives

The objectives of this chapter are listed below. It is hoped that after reading this chapter, educational technology researchers will be able to:

1. Define the term *qualitative research* and compare it with other terms, including naturalistic inquiry and ethnography.
2. Describe some of the assumptions underlying qualitative research and compare these assumptions with those underlying quantitative research.
3. Describe and select from various qualitative research methods.
4. Begin to be able to use qualitative research methods at a basic level in research studies.
5. Describe common problems in conducting—and evaluate the quality of—qualitative research studies.
6. Describe a few of the ethical issues involved in conducting qualitative research.
7. Describe issues related to analyzing and reporting qualitative findings.

40.1 INTRODUCTION TO QUALITATIVE RESEARCH

40.1.1 What Is Qualitative Research?

Qualitative research is a term with varying meanings in educational research. Borg and Gall (1989), for example,

---

*The authors would like to thank Marcy Driscoll, David Jonassen, and Susan Tucker for their support and comments.

suggest that the term is often used interchangeably with terms such as *naturalistic, ethnographic, subjective,* or *postpositivistic.* Goetz and LeCompte (1984) choose to use the term *ethnographic* as an overall rubric for research using qualitative methods and for ethnographies.

In this chapter, *qualitative research* will be defined as research devoted to developing an understanding of human systems, be they small, such as a technology-using teacher and his or her students and classroom, or large, such as a cultural system. Qualitative research studies typically include ethnographies, case studies, and generally descriptive studies (see 41.2). They often are called *ethnographies,* but these are somewhat more specific. Goetz and LeCompte, for instance, based on the work of Spradley and McCurdy (1972), define ethnographies as "analytic descriptions or reconstructions of intact cultural scenes and groups" (1984, p. 2). A case study may indeed be viewed as an ethnography; however, the investigator may have set out to answer a particular question rather than to describe a group or scene as a whole.

Qualitative research methods typically include interviews and observations, but may also include case studies, surveys, and historical and document analysis. Case study and survey research are also often considered methods on their own. Survey research (see 37.1, 37.4, 41.2.1) and historical and document analysis (see, for instance, 41.2.4) are covered in other chapters in this book; therefore they will not be extensively discussed in this chapter.

Qualitative research has several hallmarks. It is conducted in a natural setting, without intentionally manipulating the environment. It typically involves highly detailed rich descriptions of human behaviors and opinions. The perspective is that humans construct their own reality, and an understanding of what they do may be based on why they believe they do it. There is allowance for the "multiple realities" individuals thus might construct in an environment. The research questions often evolve as the study does, because the researcher wants to know "what is happening," and may not want to bias the study by focusing the investigation too narrowly. The researcher becomes a part of the study by interacting closely with the subjects of the study. The researcher attempts to be open to the subjects' perceptions of "what is"; that is, researchers are bound by the values and world views of the subjects. (For a discussion of self-reflexivity, see 10.4.4.) In qualitative research, it is not necessarily assumed that the findings of one study may be generalized easily to other settings. There is a concern for the uniqueness of a particular setting and participants.

In the following section, we will present some of the many points of debate about the definition and use of qualitative methods.

40.1.2 Comparisons Between Qualitative and Quantitative Methods

Some authors have chosen to posit qualitative and quantitative research as diametrically opposed constructs. This may confuse a beginning researcher in that it simplistically implies that qualitative research might never use numbers, while quantitative research might never use subjects' perceptions. [Discussion of quantifying qualitative data will follow later in this chapter, but for an example the reader need only look at the title of Johnson's (1978) introduction to qualitative research design, *Quantification in Cultural Anthropology.*]

More useful, perhaps, is the comparison of Borg and Gall (1989) who name the two approaches *positivistic* and *naturalistic* and compare them on the dimensions of the vision of the nature of reality, relationship of the researcher to the research subject, issues of generalizability, discussion of causality, and role of values.

Lincoln and Guba (1985) and Denzin and Lincoln (1994) define the term *paradigm* as a systematic set of beliefs, and their accompanying methods, which provide a view of the nature of reality. They contend that the history of human inquiry can be divided into eras based on people's view of the world and how to study it. They argue that scientific inquiry is defined by the positivist paradigm, which has prevailed until recently. They call the earliest era the *prepositivist era,* which included human scientific endeavors from about the time of Aristotle to the middle of the 1700s. This was the precursor to a more modern perspective. Lincoln and Guba say that research during this era consisted of passive observation and description. They consider the modern scientific method to have emerged in the positivist era, from about the middle 1700s to the present. Positivism, they note, can be identified by scientific research that involves posing hypotheses, manipulation, active observation of occurrences, and, thus, testing of hypotheses. These authors argue that the positivist paradigm is limited and is challenged currently by the emerging postpositivist paradigm, which they also call the *naturalistic paradigm.* [Readers unfamiliar with the evolution of paradigms in research may refer to Kuhn's (1970) seminal work, *The Structure of Scientific Revolutions,* although Lincoln and Guba (1985) appear to consider Kuhn's views part of the positivist paradigm.]

This conception of the naturalistic paradigm is echoed by Erlandson, Harris, Skipper, and Allen (1993) who note in their book, *Doing Naturalistic Inquiry,* that naturalistic inquiry is a new paradigm as opposed to the older prevailing positivist one. They say that while naturalistic research may use qualitative research methods, it cannot be equated with these methods. They mention the "paradigm wars" raging in research in general. They note that constructivism and naturalistic inquiry have evolved together. [Readers may wish to refer to Guba's (1990) book, *The Paradigm Dialog,* in the first few chapters of which these points of view are explored further, as well as Chapters 7 to 10 in this handbook for newer views of educational technology research.]

The paradigm debate as it has evolved in educational technology is more recent. The introduction of critical theory issues (see 9.7), the presentation of qualitative workshops at AECT national conferences, and the discussion of alternative research techniques are all indicators of change (see Yeaman, 1994; Robinson & Driscoll, 1993; Driscoll, 1995; Robinson, 1995). One aspect of the paradigm debate is the issue of how one's perspective directs the type of research questions studied and how methods are chosen. Some believe that researchers must declare a paradigm from which they work, and that the paradigm naturally dictates methods and questions. This is a different approach from that taken in this chapter, namely, that methods may be chosen based on questions to be studied.

Other authors, such as Goetz and LeCompte (1984), contend that it is perhaps not useful to build simplistic dichotomies of research models. They argue that dichotomies such as generative verificative, inductive-deductive, subjective-objective, and constructive-enumerative to describe research models must be examined carefully and that "all factors must be balanced in composing a research design" (p. 48).

While many of the authors above use the term *naturalistic inquiry,* it is perhaps more useful for that term to be applied to the paradigm as Lincoln and Guba (1985) and Erlandson et al. (1993) apply it. Goetz and LeCompte use the term *ethnographic* for research using qualitative methods, but ethnography is just one form that qualitative research may take. In this chapter, we will use the term *qualitative* research. This seems to be a less value-laden term and one that has come to the fore recently. (As evidence, one major publisher of textbooks for social science research, Sage Publications, California, publishes an extensive series of references for all aspects of conducting this type of research under the title "qualitative methods.") It remains to be seen whether this is the term that in decades hence will continue to be used.

In sum, we in this chapter agree that forcing a choice between using qualitative or quantitative methods limits and inhibits the quality of research. Our argument is that the questions a researcher strives to answer should drive the choice of methods. Our assumption is that there is no reason data-gathering methods cannot be combined in a study, that a researcher cannot investigate carefully and creatively any questions he or she chooses (see 11.2.4.2, 39.5.2.2). Rather than limiting our endeavors in this time of tremendous strides in technology development, this approach should enable researchers to take chances, to make leaps, to enhance development in the field by yielding both "answers" and "understanding." As will be seen in the next section, this approach has a solid tradition in educational communications and technology.

That said, given the tremendous ferment in educational research today, it behooves any researcher using qualitative methods to be aware of the "paradigm war" discussions. A researcher may choose to build a study using qualitative methods to answer certain questions, in a study that blends these methods with experimental or quasi-experimental methods. The researcher may design an entirely qualitative study to come to a deep understanding about what is happening in a setting, or how the participants perceive of their world. This study may stand on its own, or be used as a sort of pilot study to generate questions and hypotheses prior to conducting an experimental study. In any case, the researcher should be specific about how he or she defines the assumptions of the study and why what was done was done—in short, to be able to enter into the current and upcoming discussions as a thoughtful, critical, and creative researcher.

40.1.3 How Has Qualitative Research Historically Been Defined in Educational Technology?

In educational communications and technology research, and in educational research in general, there is similar debate about the definition and purpose of qualitative methods. This can be viewed as a natural consequence of discussion in education about the utility of constructivist as opposed to positivist views of education. This discussion can be enjoyed at national and regional conferences in the field, and in the journals. It can be said that the larger debate regarding naturalistic versus positivistic research is creating a more open arena in which studies can be presented and published. Indeed, the editors of the leading journals in the field have indicated they welcome the submission of well-crafted qualitative studies. While not many such reports have been published, it is hoped that this chapter may positively influence the future. We will therefore, in this chapter, avoid the larger debate and focus on qualitative methods as tools.

It may come as a surprise to some that use of qualitative data collection methods has a long tradition in educational technology research. Early research efforts often used qualitative methods to evaluate and describe the use of media in the classroom. Experimental researchers have often used qualitative methods to collect attitude data, for instance, to yield possible explanations of students' behavior. These data are typically collected using surveys, but may be collected using interviews. It is not unusual for an experimental researcher to further inform the study by conducting observations of the subjects. Researchers often conduct a case study to unobtrusively learn more about students, teachers, and trainers who use a new technology. Case studies present detailed data that may be used to derive questions later to be investigated in an experiment. Evaluation researchers have long used qualitative methods, in particular surveys, interviews, observations, and historical and document analysis (see also 34.3, 34.6, Chapter 42).

While not researchers, per se, instructional systems designers have always used the qualitative methods of surveys, interviews, and observations during the front-end analysis and evaluation phases of development. Markle (1989), for example, contends that even in the early, more "behaviorist" days of instructional design, developers listened to their learners, watched them carefully, and humbly incorporated what learners taught them into their drafts of instructional materials. Similarly, what recent authors, especially computer scientists, are calling testing in "software engineering" (Chen & Shen, 1989), "prototype evaluation" (Smith & Wedman, 1988), "prototype testing," "quality assurance" (McLean, 1989), or "quality control" (Darabi & Dempsey, 1989–90) is clearly formative evaluation, usually incorporating some qualitative methods.

Beyond these basic uses of qualitative methods, however, there have been calls in the field to use these methods to address new research questions.

With the increasing use of computer-based interactive technologies in education and industry, opportunities, and at times the responsibility, to explore new questions about the processes of learning and instruction are evolving. Educational technologists have issued the call for the use of more qualitative research methods to explore training and school processes (Bosco, 1986; Clark, 1983; see also 6.5). Driscoll (1995) suggests that educational technologists select research paradigms based on what they perceive as the most critical questions. Noting the debate regarding paradigms, she adds that educational technology is a relatively young field in which "numerous paradigms may vie for acceptability and dominance" (p. 322). Robinson (1995) and Reigeluth (1989) concur, noting the considerable debate within the field regarding suitable research questions and methods. Winn (1989) also calls for more descriptive studies yielding information about learning and instruction. Clark agrees with Winn, calling for reconsideration of how media are studied (1983), and stating that researchers should conduct planned series of studies, selecting methods based on extensive literature reviews (1989). He recommends that prescriptive studies be conducted to determine why instructional development methods work. Qualitative methods can serve these purposes admirably.

The approach taken in this chapter, that choosing qualitative or quantitative methods need not be an either/or proposition, is similar to the approach of Hannafin and his associates (Hannafin & Rieber, 1989; Hooper & Hannafin, 1988) in their development of the ROPES guidelines for designing instruction. Their guidelines blend behaviorist with cognitive principles in what they call *applied cognitivism* (see 12.4.4).

In our field, new educational technologies are continually being developed. Recent developments have been interactive multimedia, new distance learning systems, information technologies such as hypertext databases and the Internet, interactive learning environments, microworlds, and virtual-reality systems. Many teachers, trainers, administrators, managers, community members, and institutional leaders contend that the evolution of new technologies will continue to change the nature of teaching, training, instruction, and learning (Ambron & Hooper, 1990, 1988; Lambert & Sallis, 1987; Schwartz, 1987; Schwier, 1987; U.S. Congress, OTA, 1988).

It is not only new technologies that require new research methods. The more recent developments in critical theory (see Chapter 9), postmodernism (see Chapter 10), and philosophical thought presented in this handbook and elsewhere (see Yeaman et al., 1994) also suggest distinctive changes and additions to our research endeavors and to the questions and problems in education with which technology is involved.

A recent study that used new technologies and combined qualitative and quantitative methods is that of Wiegmann (1996). In her dissertation, she combined techniques to examine preservice teachers' attitudes and perceptions of efficacy regarding instructional technologies. Her quasi-experimental study used a nonequivalent control-group design to investigate the effects of presentation techniques used in a science methods class. Her data were collected using pre- and postsurveys. She also collected student artifacts in the form of student lesson plans, daily technology-use surveys, and reflective journals focusing on topics pertinent to science education and the use of technology in the classroom. Quantitative data analyses in the form of chi-square and factor analysis were combined with qualitative, more-narrative data about the student journals and lesson plans. Questions included, "Does the method used affect teachers' attitudes toward technology?" and "Does the method used to present preservice teachers with ways to use technology in instruction affect the instructional strategies they incorporate into their lesson plans?"

New technologies also enable researchers to study learners and learning processes in new ways. Computers allow sophisticated tracking of the paths that learners take through a lesson. We can view each decision a learner makes and analyze the relationship among the patterns of those decisions and their performance and attitudes (Dwyer & Leader, 1995).

New technologies may also require that we ask new questions in new ways. We may need to expand our views of what we should investigate and how. For instance, a qualitative view of how teachers and their students use a new technology may yield a view of "what is really happening" when the technology is used. Developers are well aware that instruction is not always delivered as designed, and this holds true for technology-based instruction. The history of educational technology includes records of the failures of a technological approach, often for reasons stemming from poorly planned implementation. We need to know what is really occurring when technologies or new approaches are used. Newman (1989) holds that learning environments can affect instructional technologies. He writes, "How a new piece of educational technology gets used in a particular environment cannot always be anticipated ahead of time. It can be argued that what the environment does with the technology provides critical information to guide design process" (p. 1). He adds, "It is seldom the case that the technology can be inserted into a classroom without changing other aspects of the environment" (p. 3).

A lucid discussion of the issues related to using qualitative techniques in investigating aspects of the technology of computer-based instruction is presented by Neuman (1989). She presents, for example, her findings on teacher perceptions and behaviors for integrating this type of interactive technological innovation into their classrooms. In another qualitative study of an instructional innovation, Jost (1994) investigated aspects of effective use of calculators in teaching calculus (see 12.3, 12.4.4, 14.7, 15.6, 17.7, 19.6, 20.5, 23.5, 23.6, 24.11, 26.7, and 29.7 for discussions of the impact of new technologies and research in educational technology).

40.1.4 Assumptions of This Chapter

Well-designed research is never easy to conduct. Qualitative research studies typically require considerably more time to design, collect, and analyze data and to report the results than do quantitative studies. Yet professors in the field often hear students stating that they plan to do a qualitative study because it will be easier or quicker. Unfortunately, all too often poorly conceived and conducted studies are called *qualitative* in an effort to avoid defining and describing methods used to collect data, to avoid assumptions of the study, and even to clearly describe results. At conferences, one often hears editors of the leading journals exhorted to publish more qualitative research. Editors reply that they will publish such studies, provided reviewers and editors can determine that the studies are sound and relevant. [See, for example, Smith's (1987) paper signifying that the journal *AERJ* welcomes the submission of qualitative reports.]

It should be noted that there is still some concern regarding the acceptance of qualitative research by journals. Not every editor or reviewer is an expert in identifying well-developed research reports of qualitative studies. Questions of sample size and validity may be inappropriately raised about qualitative studies, indicating that reviewers may need more experience with qualitative methods, or that reviewers with more experience with qualitative methods could be selected.

The concerns with regard to quality of research are not confined to educational technology. Lincoln and Guba (1985) note that "The naturalistic inquirer soon becomes accustomed to hearing charges that naturalistic studies are undisciplined; that he or she is guilty of 'sloppy' research, engaging in 'merely subjective' observations, responding indiscriminately to the 'loudest bangs or brightest lights' " (p. 289).

Methods for evaluating the soundness of a qualitative study, and for conducting a study ethically, will be presented in a later section. However, before discussing the methods qualitative researchers use, it is critical to illustrate the characteristics of good qualitative research. Not all will be present in any one study, as each study is designed differently to investigate different issues. However, it is worth considering what makes a study "qualitative."

In addition to the characteristics described in the earlier definition of qualitative research, in this chapter many of Lincoln and Guba's (1985) characteristics of naturalistic research will be assumed to apply to qualitative research. Qualitative research is done in a natural setting. The main data-gathering instrument is the human researcher. The researcher uses tacit, that is, intuitive or felt, knowledge, as well as propositional knowledge. Qualitative methods are used generally, but not to the exclusion of quantitative methods. Sampling is often purposive or theoretical rather than random or representative. Data analysis is typically inductive rather than deductive, but again, not exclusively. In naturalistic studies, theory is grounded in the data rather than determined a priori, although in qualitative studies theories often do drive the processes used in the investigation.

In contrast to experimental studies, in qualitative studies the design often emerges as the study progresses, with the researcher continually refining the methods and questions. Similarly, the focus of the study determines what data are collected, and the boundaries of what is studied may change during the study as new issues and questions emerge. In qualitative research, the "reality" or the meaning of a situation and setting are negotiated among the researcher and those studied, with the understanding that multiple realities are always present. Many qualitative studies use a case study approach in the report, rather than a scientific report; some, in fact, describe the results by building a narrative or sort of story. A qualitative researcher tends to interpret results of a study or draw conclusions based on the particulars of that study, rather than in terms of generalizability to other situations and settings. Similarly, such a researcher is likely to be hesitant about advocating broad application of the findings of one study to other settings (Lincoln & Guba, 1985).

A final assumption of this chapter is that qualitative studies can be evaluated for quality, and rigor is not tossed out because a study is not quantitative in nature. While some of the criteria may be different from those used in quantitative research, many criteria for evaluating what Lincoln and Guba call the "trustworthiness" of a qualitative study will be discussed, many related to the particular methods used in qualitative research.

In summary, we concur with the call of Salomon (1991) that it is time to transcend the debate about qualitative versus quantitative research. In a stronger message, Robinson (1995) suggests that, "The paradigm debate should be declared a draw. . . . [We should] accept the dual perspectives of our paradigm debate, if we are to meet the challenges of the future and be at all helpful in shaping the educational success of the next century" (pp. 332–333). Robinson continues, "All ways of knowing and all social constructs should be equally accepted and represented in our literature . . . individuals should be encouraged to question and consider how they approach the world, how they understand learning, and how they believe knowledge is achieved" (p. 332).

The range of methods we may use to conduct qualitative research will be explored in the next section. Examples of educational technology studies that use these methods will be woven into the discussion. As this chapter is an introduction, issues of analysis and reporting will be briefly introduced, but not in great detail.

40.2 QUALITATIVE RESEARCH METHODS

Designing qualitative studies is quite different from designing experimental studies. In fact, designs and methods are continually refined while the researcher conducts a qualitative study. As suggested by Jacobs (1987), the researcher initially chooses methods based on the questions to be addressed; however, the questions, issues, and topics of the study themselves may change as the researcher's conception of the reality of the "world" being studied changes. This may be uncomfortable for those experienced with more quantitative, experimental, or quasi-experimental research. However, most qualitative researchers recommend this process of continual refinement. Goetz and LeCompte (1984), for example, note that methods are "adjusted, expanded, modified, or restricted on the basis of information acquired during the mapping phase of fieldwork. . . . Only after final withdrawal from the field can researchers specify the strategies they actually used for a particular study" (p. 108).

Lincoln and Guba (1985) address the contradictory idea of "designing" a naturalistic study completely prior to beginning the study, calling this a "paradox" in that most funding agencies require specificity regarding methods, while methods in a good qualitative study may be expected to change as the study progresses. Erlandson et al. (1993) take the middle road. They say that the answer to whether a naturalistic study should be designed in advance is "Yes—to some extent" (p. 66). They recommend beginning the study by specifying a research problem, selecting a research site, developing working hypotheses, and using interactive processes to refine the research questions. They further suggest that the researcher plan for the stages of conducting the study. These may include negotiating entry to the site, planning for purposive (rather than random) sampling and for data collection, planning for data analysis, determining how quality will be ensured in the study, deciding how the findings of the study will be disseminated, and developing a logistical plan. [For further information regarding the logistical operations of field research, the reader may refer to Fiedler's book (1978), *Field Research: A Manual for Logistics and Management of Scientific Studies in Natural Settings.*] Erlandson et al. (1993) also recommend reviewing the design of the study regularly.

In determining what the research problem is, Bernard (1988, p. 11) suggests that the researcher ask himself or herself five questions:

1. Does this topic (village—i.e., setting, school, organization, institution—and data collection method) really interest me?
2. Is this a problem that is amenable to scientific inquiry?
3. Are adequate resources available to investigate this topic? (To study this population? To use this particular method?)
4. Will my research question, or the methods I want to use, lead to unresolvable ethical problems? (Ethical issues will be addressed later in this chapter.)
5. Is the topic (community, method) of theoretical interest?

Once a question or issue has been selected, the choice of qualitative methods falls roughly into the categories of observations, interviews, and document and artifact analysis. Qualitative methods, however, form continua on various dimensions, and researchers espouse many views of how methods may be categorized and conceptualized.

Pelto and Pelto (1978) in their frequently cited text on anthropological research methods remind us that the human investigator is the primary research instrument. These authors categorize methods as either verbal or nonverbal techniques. Verbal techniques include participant observation, questionnaires, and various forms of structured and unstructured interviews. Nonverbal techniques include observations and measures of interactions; proxemics, kinesics, and research involving videotaped observations; use of various types of technical equipment for collecting data; content analysis; and analysis of artifacts and records. Pelto and Pelto (1978) add that methods may be described as having an "emic" or insider's view, as in participant observation, versus an "etic" or outsider's view, as in nonparticipant stream-of-behavior analyses.

Other researchers use variations of these taxonomies. Goetz and LeCompte (1984) divide methods into interactive (participant observation and several types of interviews) versus noninteractive methods (forms of nonparticipant observation, as well as artifact collection and analysis). Lincoln and Guba (1985) classify methods as those that collect data from human sources (observations and interviews) as opposed to those that collect data from nonhuman sources (documents and records).

Other authors, however, note that methods can rarely be classified as simple dichotomies, such as interactive or not, in large part because the researcher is a human being and thus involved, and plays a role even in nonparticipant observation (see Atkinson & Hammersley, 1994). Bogdan and Biklen (1992) provide the example of the "participant/observer continuum" (p. 88), describing the ways observers who refrain from being overt participants may still interact to varying degrees with those subjects. Researchers who work using an ethnographic perspective consider all methods "doing fieldwork" (cf. Bogdan & Biklen, 1992). Similarly, Bernard (1982) calls participant observation the "foundation of anthropological research" (p. 148); some would say this deep, involved method of interacting with subjects defines qualitative research.

It is assumed that educational technologists will use methods ethically and with a view to doing quality research, but may not always be bound by anthropological tradition. We are in another field with other questions to answer than those in which anthropologists or sociologists may be interested. For instance, it is now possible to design instruction using a multitude of techniques, using many delivery systems. As noted by McNeil and Nelson (1991) and Reeves (1986), many design factors contribute to the success of instruction using new technologies, such as distance education, interactive multimedia, and Internet-based delivery systems. Educational technologists may successfully use and adapt qualitative methods to investigate new and challenging questions.

In this chapter, we will discuss specific methods that may be called *observations, interviews,* and *document and artifact analysis.* As in all qualitative research, it is also assumed that educational technology researchers will use and refine methods with the view that these methods vary in their degree of interactiveness with subjects. Each of these methods, in their various forms, along with several research perspectives, will be examined in detail below (see 23.6 and 41.2 in this handbook for discussion of other aspects of qualitative methods).

40.2.1 Grounded Theory

Grounded theory is considered a type of qualitative methodology. Strauss and Corbin (1994), however, in their overview of grounded theory note that it is "a *general methodology* for developing theory that is grounded in data systematically gathered and analyzed" (p. 273), adding that it is sometimes called the *constant comparative method* and that it is applicable as well to quantitative research. In grounded theory, the data may come from observations, interviews, and videotape or document analysis, and, as in other qualitative research, these data may be considered strictly qualitative or may be quantitative. The purpose of the methodology is to develop theory, through an iterative process of data analysis and theoretical analysis, with verification of hypotheses ongoing throughout the study. A grounded theory perspective leads the researcher to begin a study without completely preconceived notions about what the research questions should be, assuming that the theory on which the study is based will be tested and refined as the research is conducted.

The researcher collects extensive data with an open mind. As the study progresses, he or she continually examines the data for patterns, and the patterns lead the researcher to build the theory. Further data collection leads to further refinement of the questions. The researcher continues collecting and examining data until the patterns continue to repeat and few relatively, or no clearly, new patterns emerge. The researcher builds the theory from the phenomena, from the data, and the theory is thus built on, or "grounded" in, the phenomena. As Borg and Gall (1989) note, even quantitative researchers see the value of grounded theory and might use qualitative techniques in a pilot study without completely a priori notions of theory to develop a more-grounded theory on which to base later experiments.

A recent example of a grounded-theory approach in an educational technology study is that of Oliver's (1992). This research investigated and described the activities used in a university televised distance education system, analyzing the use of camera techniques as they related to interaction in class. Oliver videotaped hours of two-way video instruction and analyzed the amount and kind of classroom interactions that occurred. She also examined and described the various television shots and transitions used. Outside observers also coded the videotapes. Using grounded-theory techniques, Oliver used the data she transcribed and the emerging categories of data to create a theory of televised instruction. The theory involved the use of close-up camera techniques and the "clean-cut" transition to enhance interaction.

40.2.2 Participant Observation

Participant observation is a qualitative method frequently used in social science research. It is based on a long tradition of ethnographic study in anthropology. In participant observation, the observer becomes "part" of the environment, or the cultural context. The method usually involves the researcher's spending considerable time "in the field," as anthropologists do. Anthropologists typically spend a year or more in a cultural setting in order to really understand the culture in depth, even when they begin the study with a broad overall research question. The hallmark of participant observation is interaction among the researcher and the participants. The main subjects take part in the study to varying degrees, but the researcher interacts with them continually. For instance, the study may involve periodic interviews interspersed with observations so that the researcher can question the subjects and verify perceptions and patterns. These interviews may themselves take many forms, as noted in an upcoming section. For example, a researcher may begin by conducting open-ended unstructured interviews with several teachers to begin to formulate the research questions. This may be followed by a set of structured interviews with a few other teachers, based on results of the first series, forming a sort of oral questionnaire. Results of these interviews may then determine what will initially be recorded during observations. Later, after patterns begin to appear in the observational data, the researcher may conduct interviews asking the teachers about these patterns and why they think they are occurring, or if indeed those are categories of information. Similarly, a researcher might conduct videotaped observations of a set of teachers, analyze the tapes to begin to make taxonomies of behaviors, and then conduct interviews with the teachers, perhaps while they view the tapes together, to determine how the teachers themselves categorize these behaviors. Thus, the researcher becomes a long-term participant in the research setting.

Educational researchers have come under some criticism, at times legitimately so, for observing in educational settings for very brief periods of time, such as once for a few hours, and then making sweeping generalizations about teachers, schools, and students from these brief "slices of time." Yet, educational researchers typically do not have the resources to "live" in the observed settings for such extended periods of time as anthropologists do. There are several exceptions, including, but not limited to, Harry Wolcott's studies of a Kwakiutl village and school (1967) and of one year in the life of a school principal (1973); John Ogbu's (1974) ethnography of urban education; and Hugh Mehan's (1979) collaborative study of social interactions in a classroom, done with Courtney Cazden and her cooperating teacher, LaDonna Coles.

It is reasonable that fine educational technology research can be conducted using participant observation techniques, with somewhat limited research questions. Not every phenomenon can possibly be recorded. Most qualitative observational studies rely on the researcher's writing down what occurs in the form of extensive field notes. The researcher then analyzes these notes soon after observations are carried out, noting patterns of behaviors and events and phenomena to investigate in further observations. Still, the researcher is the instrument in most participant observations and, being human, cannot observe and record everything. Therefore, in most educational research studies, the investigator determines ahead of time what will be observed and recorded, guided but not limited by the research questions.

In an example of a limited participant observation case study, Robinson (1994) observed classes using "Channel One" in a midwestern middle school. While Robinson was not there for more than one semester, she did observe and participate in the class discussions for many hours of classroom instruction, as well as interview about 10% of the students. She did not focus on all school activities, or on all the categories of interaction within the classrooms, but focused her observations and field notes on the use of the televised news show and the reaction to it from students, teachers, administrators, and parents.

It should be noted that novice observers initially think they can avoid the observational limitations by simply videotaping everything that goes on in the setting, such as the classroom. The use of videotape and audiotape in data collection is useful, particularly in nonparticipant observational studies of particular behaviors and phenomena. However, it can be readily seen that videotaping everything is usually not a way to avoid defining or focusing research questions. For instance, without an exceptionally wide-angle lens, no video camera can record all that goes on in one classroom. If such a lens is used, then the wide view will preclude being able to see enough detail to understand much of what is going on. For example, computer screens will not be clearly visible, nor will specific nonverbal behaviors. In addition, if conversations are of interest in order to understand the types of behaviors students are engaged in, no one camera at the back of the room will be able to record all the conversations. Finally, those who have conducted microanalysis of videotaped classroom observations find it is not unusual to require 10 hours to analyze the behaviors and language recorded in 1 hour of videotape. It can easily be seen that the decision to videotape dozens of hours of classroom behaviors with one camera in the room might result in little useful data being collected, even after hundreds of hours of analysis. Videotape can successfully be used in data collection when the researcher knows what he or she wants to analyze. The preceding note of caution is just a reminder to the qualitative researcher that "shotgun" data collection is no substitute for determining ahead of time what the study is all about.

What can happen with videotape can also happen with written field notes. Trying to glean meaning by sifting through notebook after notebook of descriptions of classroom happenings, especially long after observations were made, is nearly impossible. What is needed is for observations to be at least loosely guided by purposes and questions. Even in studies using a grounded theory approach, observers generally analyze for patterns in observations throughout the entire data collection phase.

Spradley's (1980) book details how to conduct participant observations. He discusses the variety of roles the observer might take, noting that the observer becomes to varying degrees an "insider," in line with what Pelto and Pelto (1978) call the *emic* view. Spradley suggests that the research site and setting, of course, be selected to best answer the research questions, but with an eye toward simplicity, accessibility, possibility of remaining relatively unobtrusive, permissibleness, assurance that the activities of interest will occur frequently, and degree to which the researcher can truly become a participant.

Spradley (1980) provides specific techniques for conducting observations, for conducting iterative interviews with subjects, and for analyzing behaviors, especially language used by informants in interviews. In particular, he notes that cultural domains, or categories of cultural meaning, can be derived from interviews and observations with participants. Finally, he provides advice regarding how to analyze data and write the ethnography.

The stages of participant observation, from an anthropological perspective, have been delineated by Bernard (1988). He describes the excitement, and sometimes fear, of the initial contact period; the next stage, which is often a type of shock as one gets to know the culture in more detail; a period of intense data collection he identifies with discovering the obvious, followed by the need for a real break; a stage in which the study becomes more focused; followed by exhaustion, a break and frantic activity; and finally, carefully taking leave of the field setting.

Spradley (1980) advises that ethical issues be addressed throughout the study. These issues are common to most types of qualitative research methods. For instance, Spradley advises that the researcher consider the welfare and interests of the informants, that is, the collaborating subjects first. He says informants' rights, interests, and sensibilities must be safeguarded; informants should not be exploited. Subjects should be made aware of the purposes of the research study. Their privacy should be protected. Many of these issues are common to all types of research. However, Spradley adds that reports should be made available to informants, so that they too are participants in the study. In some of the interview techniques described later, in fact, verifying analyses and preliminary reports with subjects is one way to ensure the authenticity of the results and to delve deeper into the research questions. Ethical issues in qualitative research, as well as criteria for evaluating the rigor and quality of such research, will be discussed in further detail later in this chapter.

Borg and Gall (1979) discuss the types of questions one might address using participant observation techniques. These include such questions as who the participants are; what are their typical and atypical patterns of behavior; and where, when, how, and why the phenomena occur. In short, participant observation is often successfully used to describe what is happening in a context and why it happens. These are questions that cannot be answered in the standard experiment.

Another example of participant observation is described by Reilly (1994). His use of videotaping and video production instruction as a project in a California high school involved defining a new type of literacy, combining print, video, and computer technologies. Students produced videotapes that were then transferred to disc and made available for others' use. The research involved many hours of in-school data collection and analysis, and was very action oriented, with a product from the students as well as a written report from the researcher.

The work of Higgins and Rice (1991) is another excellent example of a qualitative study with an educational technology focus. These researchers investigated teachers' perceptions of testing. They used triangulation, by using a variety of methods to collect data; however, a key feature of the study was participant observation. Researchers observed six teachers for a sample of 10 hours each. Trained observers recorded instances of classroom behaviors that could be classified as assessment.

Another exemplary study that used multiple methods to triangulate data but that relied primarily on participant observation is that of Moallem (1994). This researcher investigated an experienced teacher's model of teaching and thinking by conducting a series of observations and interviews over a 7-month period. Using a constant comparative style, she analyzed the data, which allowed categories of the teacher's frames of reference, knowledge and beliefs, planning and teaching techniques, and reflective thinking to emerge. She then built a model of the teacher's conceptions. This study may also be called a form of case study.

The study and the triangulation of data and refinement of patterns using progressively more-structured interviews and multidimensional scaling will be described in more detail later in this chapter.

40.2.3 Nonparticipant Observation

Nonparticipant observation is one of several methods for collecting data considered to be relatively unobtrusive. Many recent authors cite the early work of Webb, Campbell, Schwartz, and Sechrest (1966) as laying the groundwork for use of all types of unobtrusive measures.

Several types of nonparticipant observation have been identified by Goetz and LeCompte (1984). These include stream-of-behavior chronicles, recorded in written narratives or using videotape or audiotape; proxemics and kinesics, that is, the study of uses of social space and movement; and interaction analysis protocols, typically in the form of observations of particular types of behaviors, categorized and coded for analysis of patterns. Bernard (1988) describes two types of nonparticipant observation, which he calls *disguised field observation* and *naturalistic field experiments*. He cautions in the first case for care to be taken that subjects are not harmfully deceived. Reflecting recent postmodern and constructivist (as well as deconstructionist) trends, Adler and Adler (1994) extend paradigms of observational research to include dramaturgical constructions of reality, and auto-observation, as well as more typical ethnomethodology.

In nonparticipant observation, the observer does not interact to a great degree with those he or she is observing [as opposed to what Bernard (1988) calls direct, reactive observation]. The researcher primarily observes and records, and has no specific role as a participant. Usually, of course, the observer is "in" the scene, and thus affects it in some way; this must be taken into account. For instance, observers often work with teachers or instructors to have them explain to students briefly why the observer is there. Care should be taken once more not to bias the study. It is often desirable to explain the observations in general terms rather than to describe the exact behaviors being observed, so that participants do not naturally increase those behaviors. Some increase may occur; if the researcher suspects this, it would be appropriate to note it in the analyses and report.

As with participant observation, nonparticipant observers may or may not use structured observation forms, but are often more likely to. In this type of study, often several trained observers make brief sampled observations over periods of time, and observation forms help to ensure consistency of the data being recorded.

Nonparticipant observation is often used to study focused aspects of a setting, in order to answer specific questions within a study. This method can yield extensive detailed data, over many subjects and settings, if desired, in order to search for patterns, or to test hypotheses developed as a result of using other methods, such as interviews. It can thus be a powerful tool in triangulation. Observational data may be coded into categories, frequencies tabulated, and relationships analyzed, yielding quantitative reports of results.

Guidelines for conducting nonparticipant observation are provided by Goetz and LeCompte (1984), among others. They recommend that researchers strive to be as unobtrusive and unbiased as possible. They suggest verification of data by using multiple observers. The units of analysis, thus data to be recorded, should be specified before beginning; recording methods should be developed; strategies for selection and sampling of units should be determined; and finally all processes should be tested and refined, before the study is begun in earnest. (See 35.5 and 35.6 for a discussion of research on social interaction in cooperative learning settings.)

Examples of studies in which observations were conducted that could be considered relatively nonparticipant observation were Savenye and Strand's (1989) in the initial pilot test, and Savenye (1989) in the subsequent larger field test of a science videodisc and computer-based curriculum. Of most concern during implementation was how teachers used the curriculum. Among other questions researchers were interested in are: how much teachers followed the teachers' guide, the types of questions they asked students when the system paused for class discussion, and what teachers added to or didn't use from the curriculum. In the field test (Savenye, 1989), a careful sample of classroom lessons was videotaped and the data coded. For example, teacher questions were coded according to a taxonomy based on Bloom's (1984), and results indicated that teachers typically used the system pauses to ask recall-level rather than higher-level questions.

Analysis of the coded behaviors for what teachers added indicated that most of the teachers in the sample added examples to the lessons which would provide relevance for their own learners, and that almost all of the teachers added reviews of the previous lessons to the beginning of the new lesson. Some teachers seemed to feel they needed to continue to lecture their classes; therefore they duplicated the content presented in the interactive lessons.

Developers used the results of the studies to make changes in the curriculum and in the teacher training that accompanied it. Of interest in this study was a comparison of these varied teacher behaviors with the student achievement results. Borich (1989) found that learning achievement among students who used the interactive videodisc curriculum was significantly higher than among control students. Therefore, teachers had a great degree of freedom in using the curriculum, and the students still learned well.

If how students use interactive lessons is the major concern, researchers might videotape samples of students using an interactive lesson in cooperative groups, and code student statements and behaviors, as did Schmidt (1992). In a study conducted in a museum setting, Hirumi, Allen, and Savenye (1994) used qualitative methods to measure what visitors learned from an interactive videodisc-based natural history exhibit.

Nonparticipant observations may be used in studies that are primarily quantitative experimental studies in order to answer focused research questions about what learners do while participating in studies. For instance, a researcher may be interested in what types of choices learners make while they proceed through a lesson. This use of observations to answer a few research questions within experimental studies is exemplified in a series of studies of cooperative learning and learner control in television or computer-delivered instruction by Klein, Sullivan, Savenye, and their colleagues.

Jones, Crooks, and Klein (1995) describe the development of the observational instrument used in several of these studies. Klein and Pridemore (1994), in a study of cooperative learning in a television lesson, observed four sets of behaviors. These were coded as helping behaviors, on-task group behaviors, on-task individual behaviors, and off-task behaviors. In a subsequent experimental study using a computer-based lesson, Crooks, Klein, Jones, and Dwyer (1995) observed students in cooperative dyads, and recorded, coded, and analyzed helping, discussion, or off-task behaviors.

In another study of cooperative use of computer-based instruction (Wolf, 1994), only one behavior was determined to be most related to increased performance, and that was giving elaborated explanations, as defined by Webb (1991, 1983). Instances of this behavior, then, were recorded and analyzed.

An example of using technology to assist in recording and analyzing behaviors is shown in Dalton, Hannafin, and Hooper's (1989) study on the achievement effects of individual and cooperative use of computer-based instruction.

These researchers audiotaped the conversations of each set of students as they proceeded through the instruction.

A variation on nonparticipant observations represents a blend with trace-behavior, artifact, or document analysis. This technique, called *read–think-aloud protocols,* takes the form of asking learners to describe what they do and why they do it, that is, their thoughts about their processes, as they proceed through an activity, such as a lesson. Smith and Wedman (1988) describe using this technique to analyze learner tracking and choices. Researchers may observe and listen as subjects participate, or researches can use audiotape or videotape to analyze observations later. In either case, the resulting verbal data must be coded and summarized to address the research questions. Techniques for coding are described by Spradley (1980). However, protocol analysis (cf. Ericsson & Simon, 1984) techniques could be used on the resulting verbal data. These techniques also relate to analysis of documentary data, such as journals, discourse, recalled learning measures, and even forms of stories, such as life or career histories (see 23.6.3).

Many qualitative studies using observational techniques are case studies, and many in educational technology have involved the use of computers in schools. One such study was conducted by Dana (1994), who investigated how the pedagogical beliefs of one first-grade teacher related to her classroom curriculum and teaching practices. The teacher was an experienced and creative computer user who modeled the use of computers for her peers. Many hours of interviews and observations of the classes were made. Classroom videotapes were coded by outside reviewers who were trained to identify examples of the teacher's beliefs, exemplified in classroom practice. Her study provided insights into the methodology and teaching and learning in a computer-rich environment. She suggested changes that schools could make to encourage teachers to become better able to incorporate technology into their classrooms.

Another qualitative case study was conducted by Pitts (1993). He investigated students' organization and activities when they were involved in locating, organizing, and using information in the context of a research project in a biology class. Pitts relied on cognitive theory and information models in developing her theoretical construct. She described how students conducted their research leading to their preparation and use of video to present the results of their research.

40.2.3.1. Scope. A study using observational techniques may investigate a broad set of research questions, such as how a reorganization has affected an entire institution, or it may be much more narrowly focused. The outcome of the study may take the form of a type of "rich story" that describes an institution or a classroom or another type of cultural setting. A more narrowly focused participant observation study, however, may investigate particular aspects of a setting, such as the use of an educational innovation or its effects on particular classroom behaviors.

While some qualitative researchers might believe that only studies rich in "thick description," as described by

Lincoln and Guba (1985) (cf. Geertz, 1973), are legitimate, other researchers might choose to use qualitative techniques to yield quantitative data. This blend of qualitative and quantitative data collection is also being used in anthropological studies. An example of a more narrowly focused relatively nonparticipant observation study is the Savenye and Strand (1989) study described earlier, in which the researchers chose to focus primarily on what types of interactive exchanges occurred between students and teachers while they used an electronic curriculum.

40.2.3.2. Biases. Educational researchers who choose to do observational studies would do well to remember that although they do not spend years observing the particular instructional community, they may quickly become participants in that community. Their presence may influence results. Similarly, their prior experiences or upbringing may bias them initially toward observing or recording certain phenomena, and later in how they "see" the patterns in the data. In subsequent reports, therefore, this subjectivity should be honestly acknowledged, as is recommended in ethnographic research.

40.2.3.3. The Observer's Role. In participant observation studies, the researcher is a legitimate member in some way in the community. For instance, in the videodisc-science curriculum study mentioned above, Strand was the senior instructional designer of the materials, Savenye had been an instructional design consultant on the project, and both researchers were known to the teachers through their roles in periodic teacher-training sessions. Observers have limited roles to play in the setting, but they must be careful not to influence the results of the study, that is, to make things happen that they want to happen. This may not seem so difficult, but it may be—for example, if the researcher finds himself or herself drawn to tutoring individuals in a classroom, which may bias the results of the study. Schmidt (1992) describes an example in which she had difficulty not responding to a student in class who turned to her for help in solving a problem; in fact, in that instance, she did assist. More difficult would be a researcher observing illegal behaviors by students who trust the researcher and have asked him or her to keep their activities secret. Potential bias may be handled by simply describing the researcher's role in the research report, but the investigator will want to examine periodically what his or her role is, and what type of influence may result from it.

40.2.3.4. What Should Be Recorded. What data are recorded should be based on the research questions. For example, in a study of classroom behaviors, every behavior that instructors and students engage in could potentially be recorded and analyzed, but this can be costly in money and time and is often not possible. A researcher using a completely "grounded-theory" approach would spend considerable time in the field recording as much as possible. However, another researcher might legitimately choose to investigate more narrowly defined research questions and primarily collect data related to those questions. Again, what is excluded may be as important as what is included.

Therefore, even in a more-focused study, the researcher should be observant about other phenomena occurring and be willing to refine data collection procedures to collect emerging important information, or to change the research questions as the data dictate, even if this necessitates added time collecting data.

40.2.3.5. Sampling. In observational research, sampling becomes not random but purposive (Borg & Gall, 1989). For the study to be valid, the reader should be able to believe that a representative sample of involved individuals were observed. The "multiple realities" of any cultural context should be represented. The researcher, for instance, who is studying the impact of an educational innovation would never be satisfied with only observing the principals in the schools. Teachers and students using the innovation would obviously need to be observed. What is not so obvious is that it is important in this example to observe novice teachers, more experienced teachers, those who are comfortable with the innovation and those who are not, along with those who are downright hostile to the innovation. Parents might also be observed working with their youngsters or interacting with the teachers. How these various individuals use the innovation becomes the "reality of what is," rather than how only the most enthusiastic teachers or experienced technologists use it.

40.2.3.6. Multiple Observers. If several observers are used to collect the data, and their data are compared or aggregated, problems with reliability of data may occur. Remember that human beings are the recording instruments, and they tend to see and subsequently interpret the same phenomena in many different ways. It becomes necessary to train the observers and to ensure that observers are recording the same phenomena in the same ways. This is not as easy as it may sound, although it can be accomplished with some effort. A brief description of these efforts should be described in the final research report, as this description will illustrate why the data may be considered consistent.

One successful example of a method to train observers has been used by Klein and his colleagues in several of the studies described earlier (cf. Klein & Pridemore, 1994; Klein, Erchul & Pridemore, 1994). In the study investigating effects of cooperative learning versus individual learning structures, Crooks et al. (1995) determined to observe instances of cooperative behaviors while students worked together in a computer-based lesson. Several observers were trained using a videotape made of a typical cooperative-learning group, with a good-quality audio track and with close views of the computer screens. Observers were told what types of cooperative behaviors to record, such as instances of asking for help, giving help, and providing explanations. These behaviors were then defined in the context of a computer-based lesson and the observation record form reviewed. Then observers all watched the same videotape and recorded instances of the various cooperative behaviors in the appropriate categories. The trainer and observers next discussed their records, and observers were given feedback regarding any errors. The following segment of videotape was viewed, and the observers again recorded the behaviors. The training was repeated until observers were recording at a reliability of about 95%. Similarly, Wolf (1994) in her study trained observers to record instances of just one behavior, providing elaborated explanations.

It should be noted that in studies in which multiple observers are used and behaviors counted or categorized and tallied, it is desirable to calculate and report interrater reliability. This can easily be done by having a number of observers record data in several of the same classroom sessions or in the same segments of tape, and then computing the degree of their agreement in the data.

Other references are also available for more information about conducting observational studies in education, for example, Croll's (1986) book on systematic classroom observation (see 41.2.4).

40.2.4 Interviews

In contrast with the relatively noninteractive, nonparticipant observation methods described earlier, interviews represent a classic qualitative research method that is directly interactive (see 41.2.2). Interview techniques, too, vary in how they may be classified, and again, most vary in certain dimensions along continua, rather than being clearly dichotomous. For instance, Bernard (1988) describes interview techniques as being structured or unstructured to various degrees. He describes the most informal type of interviewing, followed by unstructured interviewing that has some focus. Next, Bernard mentions semistructured interviewing and finally structured interviews, typically involving what he calls an *interview schedule,* which others call *interview protocols,* that is, sets of questions, or scripts. Fontana and Frey (1994) expand this classification scheme by noting that interviews may be conducted individually or in groups. Again, exemplifying modern trends in qualitative research, these authors add that unstructured interviews now may include oral histories, and creative and postmodern interviewing, the latter of which may include use of visual media and polyphonic interviewing, that is, almost verbatim reporting of respondents' words, as well as gendered interviewing in response to feminist concerns.

Goetz and LeCompte (1984) note that other classification schemes may include scheduled versus nonscheduled or standardized versus nonstandardized. However, their division of interview techniques into key-informant interviews, career histories, and surveys represents a useful introduction to the range of interviewing techniques.

An interview is a form of conversation in which the purpose is for the researcher to gather data that address the study's goals and questions. A researcher, particularly one who will be in the setting for a considerable period of time or one doing participant observations, may choose to conduct a series of relatively unstructured interviews that seem more like conversations with the respondents. Topics will be discussed and explored in a somewhat loose but probing

manner. The researcher may return periodically to continue to interview the respondents in more depth, for instance to focus on questions further or to triangulate with other data.

In contrast, structured interviews may be conducted in which the researcher follows a sort of script of questions, asking the same questions, and in the same order, of all respondents. Goetz and LeCompte (1984) consider these to be surveys, while other authors do not make this distinction, and some consider surveys and questionnaires to be instruments respondents complete on their own without an interview.

Interviews or a series of interviews may focus on aspects of a respondent's life and represent a standard technique in anthropology for understanding aspects of culture from an insider's view. Fontana and Frey (1994) call these *oral histories.* Goetz and LeCompte (1984) note that for educators such interviews, which focus on career histories, may be useful for exploring how and why subjects respond to events, situations, or, of interest to educational technologists, particular innovations.

Guidelines for conducting interviews are relatively straightforward if one considers that both the researcher, as data-gathering instrument, and the respondents are human beings with their various strengths and foibles at communicating. The cornerstone is to be sure that one truly listens to respondents and records what they say, rather than to the researcher's perceptions or interpretations. This is a good rule of thumb in qualitative research in general. It is best to maintain the integrity of raw data, using respondents' words, including quotes liberally. Most researchers, as a study progresses, also maintain field notes that contain interpretations of patterns, to be refined and investigated on an ongoing basis. Bogdan and Biklen (1992) summarize these ideas:

> Good interviews are those in which the subjects are at ease and talk freely about their points of view. . . . Good interviews produce rich data filled with words that reveal the respondents' perspectives (p. 97).

Bernard (1988) suggests letting the informant lead the conversation in unstructured interviews, and asking probing questions that serve to focus the interview at natural points in the conversation. While some advocate only taking notes during interviews, Bernard stresses that memory should not be relied on, and tape recorders should be used to record exact words. This may be crucial later in identifying subjects' points of view and later in writing reports.

Ensuring the quality of a study by maintaining detailed field journals is also emphasized by Lincoln and Guba (1985). They suggest keeping a daily log of activities, a personal log, and a methodological log. They add that safeguards should be implemented to avoid distortions that result from the researcher's presence, and bias that arises from the researcher, respondents, or data-gathering techniques. They add that participants should be debriefed after the study.

Stages in conducting an interview are described by Lincoln and Guba (1985). They describe how to decide whom to interview, how to prepare for the interview, what to say to the respondent as one begins the interview [Bogdan & Biklen mention that most interviews begin with small talk (1992)], how to pace the interview and keep it productive, and, finally, how to terminate the interview and gain closure.

One example of the use of interviews is described by Pitlik (1995). As an instructional designer, she used a case study approach to describe the "real world" of instructional design and development. Her primary data source was a series of interviews with individuals involved in instructional design. She conducted group interviews with members of the International Board of Standards for Performance and Instruction, and conducted individual interviews with about 15 others. From the data she collected, she approached questions about the profession, professional practices, and the meaning of the term *instructional designer.* Her data included interview transcripts and literature on the profession. She coded her data and found that themes that emerged described four distinct types of practitioners. Her results led to recommendations for programs that train instructional designers, as well as for practitioners.

Many old, adapted, new, and exciting techniques for structured interviewing are evolving. For example, Goetz and LeCompte (1984) describe confirmation instruments, participant-construct instruments, and projective devices. Confirmation instruments verify the applicability of data gathered from key-informant interviews or observations across segments of the population being studied. (It may be added that this type of structured interview could be adapted as a questionnaire or survey for administering to larger subject groups; see 41.2.1). Participant-construct instruments may be used to measure degrees of feelings that individuals have about phenomena, or to use in having them classify events, situations, techniques, or concepts from their perspective. Goetz and LeCompte say that this technique is particularly useful in gathering information about lists of things, which respondents can then be asked to classify.

One example of such a use of interviews is in the Higgins and Rice (1991) study mentioned earlier. At several points during the study teachers were asked to name all the ways they test their students. In informal interviews, they were asked about types of assessment observers recorded in their classrooms. The researchers later composed lists of the types of tests teachers mentioned and asked them to sort the assessment types into those most alike. Subsequently, multidimensional scaling was used to analyze these data, yielding a picture of how these teachers' viewed testing.

A third type of structured interview mentioned by Goetz and LeCompte is the interview using projective techniques. Photographs, drawings, other visuals or objects may be used to elicit individuals' opinions or feelings. These things may also be used to help the researcher clarify what is going on in the situation. Pelto and Pelto (1978) describe traditional projective techniques in psychology, such as the Rorschack ink-blot test and the Thematic Apperception Test. Spindler (1974), for example, used drawings to elicit parents', teachers', and students' conceptions of the school's role in a German village. McIssac, Ozkalp, and Harper-Marinick (1992) effectively used projective techniques with subjects viewing photographs.

Types of questions to be asked in interviews are also categorized in a multitude of ways. Goetz and LeCompte (1984) describe these as "experience, opinion, feeling questions, hypothetical questions, and propositional questions" (p. 141). Spradley (1980) provides one of the more extensive discussions of questions, indicating that they may be descriptive, structural, or contrast questions. He further explains ways to conduct analyses of data collected through interviews and observations. In an earlier work (1972), he explicates how cultural knowledge is formed through symbols and rules, and describes how language can be analyzed to begin to form conceptions of such knowledge.

Of particular use to educational technologists may be the forms of structured interviews that Bernard (1988) says are used in the field of cognitive anthropology. Educational technologists and psychological researchers are interested in how learners learn, and how they conceive of the world, including technological innovations. Some of the techniques that Bernard suggests trying out include having respondents do *free listing* of taxonomies, as was done in the Higgins and Rice (1991) study of teachers' conceptions of testing. These items listed can later be ranked or sorted by respondents in various ways. Another technique is the *frame technique* or *true/false test.* After lists of topics, phenomena, or things are developed through free listing, subjects can be asked probing questions, such as, "Is this ___ an example of ___?" *Triad tests* are used to ask subjects to sort and categorize things that go together or do not. Similarly, respondents can be asked to do *pile sorting,* to generate categories of terms and how they relate to each other, forming a type of concept map. Bernard adds that other types of rankings and ratings can also be done.

To learn further techniques and the skills needed to use them, the reader may refer to Weller and Romney's book, *Systematic Data Collection* (1988). Also for a more in-depth perspective on analyzing verbal protocols and interview data for insight into cognitive processes, one may look to several chapters in the Spradley (1972) work mentioned earlier. For instance, Bruner (1972) discusses categories and cognition, and Frake (1972) presents uses of ethnographic methods to study cognitive systems. More recent works include work in semiotics (see 16.4.2.1; cf. Manning & Cullum-Swam, 1994).

The earlier-mentioned study by Moallem (1994) relied heavily on use of interviews along with participant observation to build the model of an experienced teacher's teaching and thinking. Another good study in educational technology which used interview techniques as one of several methods to gather data is that of Reiser and Mory (1991). These researchers investigated the systematic planning techniques of two experienced teachers. The teachers were administered a survey at the beginning of the year and were interviewed early in the year about how they planned and designed lessons. They were subsequently observed once a week while they taught the first science unit of the year.

Before and after each observation, the teachers were interviewed in depth. In addition, copies of their written plans were collected (a form of document analysis, to be discussed later in this chapter). Thus a deep case study approach was used to determine the ways experienced teachers plan their instruction. In this study, the teacher who had received instructional design training appeared to use more systematic planning techniques, while the other planned instructional activities focused on objectives.

As with observations, interviews may be conducted as part of an experimental, quantitative study in educational technology. For instance, Nielsen (1990) conducted an experimental study to determine the effects of informational feedback and second attempt at practice on learning in a computer-assisted instructional program. He incorporated interviews with a sample of the learners in order to further explain his findings. He found that some of his learners who received no feedback realized their performance depended more on their own hard work, so they took longer to study the material than did those who determined that they would receive detailed informational feedback, including the answers.

Other detailed examples of how interview techniques may be used are illustrated in Erickson and Shultz's work, *The Counselor as Gatekeeper* (1982).

40.2.5 Document and Artifact Analysis

Beyond nonparticipant observation, many unobtrusive methods exist for collecting information about human behaviors. These fall roughly into the categories of document and artifact analyses, but overlap with other methods. For instance, the verbal or nonverbal behavior streams produced during videotaped observations may be subjected to intense microanalysis to answer an almost unlimited number of research questions. Content analysis, as one example, may be done on these narratives. In Moallem (1993), Higgins, and Rice (1991) and Reiser and Mory (1991) studies of teacher's planning, thinking, behaviors, and conceptions of testing, documents developed by the teachers, such as instructional plans and actual tests, were collected and analyzed.

This section will present an overview of unobtrusive measures. [Reader's interested in more detailed discussion of analysis issues may refer to DeWalt and Pelto's (1985) work, *Micro and Macro Levels of Analysis in Anthropology*, as well as other resources cited in this chapter.]

Goetz and LeCompte (1984) define artifacts of interest to researchers as things that people make and do. The artifacts of interest to educational technologists are often written, but computer trails of behavior are becoming the objects of analysis as well. Examples of artifacts that may help to illuminate research questions include textbooks and other instructional materials, such as media materials; memos, letters, and, now, e-mail records, as well as logs of meetings and activities; demographic information, such as enrollment, attendance, and detailed information about sub-

jects; and personal logs kept by subjects. Webb et al. (1966) add that archival data may be running records, such as those in legal records or the media, or they may be episodic and private, such as records of sales and other business activities and written documents.

Physical traces of behaviors may be recorded and analyzed. Webb et al. (1966) describe these as including types of wear and tear that may appear on objects or in settings naturally, as in police tracing of fingerprints or blood remains.

In recent studies in educational technology, researchers are beginning to analyze the patterns of learner pathways and decisions they make as they proceed through computer-based lessons. Based on the earlier work of Hicken, Sullivan, and Klein (1992), Dwyer and Leader (1995) describe the development of a HyperCard-based researcher's tool for collecting data from counts of keypresses to analyze categories of choices made within computer-based instruction, such as the mean numbers of practice or example screens chosen. In a recently conducted study, Savenye, Leader, Dwyer, Jones, and Schnackenberg (1996) used this tool to collect information about the types of choices learners made in a fully student-controlled, computer-based learning environment. In a similar use of computers to record data, Shin, Schallert, and Savenye (1994) analyzed the paths that young learners took when using a computer-based lesson to determine the effects of advisement in a free-access, learner-controlled condition.

As noted earlier, the records made using videotape or audiotape to collect information in nonparticipant observation may be considered documentary data and may be subjected to microanalysis.

Guidelines for artifact collection are provided by Goetz and LeCompte (1984). They identify four activities involved in this type of method: "locating artifacts, identifying the material, analyzing it, and evaluating it" (p. 155). They recommend that the more informed the researcher is about the subjects and setting, the more useful artifacts may be identified and the more easily access may be gained to those artifacts.

Hodder (1984) suggests that from artifacts, a theory of material culture may be built. He describes types of objects and working with respondents to determine how they might be used. (Anyone who has accompanied older friends to an antique store, especially one that includes household tools or farm implements from bygone eras, may have experienced a type of interactive description and analysis of systems and culture of the past based on physical artifacts.) Hodder continues with discussion of the ways that material items in a cultural setting change over time and reflect changes in a culture.

Anthropologists have often based investigations about the past on artifacts such as art pieces, analyzing these alone, or using them in concert with informant and projective interviews. As noted in some of the current debate in anthropology or regarding museum installations that interpret artifacts, the meaning of artifacts is often intensely personal and subjective, so that verification of findings through triangulation is recommended. [The reader intrigued with these ideas may wish to refer to some of the classic anthropological references here cited, or to current issues of anthropology and museum journals. Two interesting examples appear in the January 1995 issue of *Smithsonian* magazine. Secretary I. Michael Heyman discusses the many points of view represented in the public's perceptions of the initial form of the installation of the Enola Gay exhibit. In a different vein, Haida Indian artist Robert Davidson describes how he used art and dance and song to help elders in his tribe remember the old ways and old tales (Kowinski, 1995).]

Content analysis of prose in any form may also be considered to fall into this artifact-and-document category of qualitative methodology. Pelto and Pelto (1978) refer to analysis of such cultural materials as folktales, myths, and other literature, although educational technologists would more likely analyze, for example, content presented in learning materials. For more information about content analysis see, for instance, Manning and Cullum-Swan (1994).

This concludes our introduction to general methods in conducting qualitative research. We can look forward to other methods being continually added to the repertoire.

40.3 ANALYZING QUALITATIVE DATA

Qualitative data are considered to be the "rough materials researchers collect from the world they are studying; they are the particulars that form the basis of analysis" (Bogdan & Biklen, 1992, p. 106). As described earlier, qualitative data can take many forms, such as photos, objects, patterns of choices in computer materials, videotapes of behaviors, etc. However, words often are the raw materials that qualitative researchers analyze, and much advice from researchers discusses analyzing these words.

The need for brevity in this chapter precludes an extensive discussion of analyzing qualitative data. However, we will introduce the researcher to the issues underlying decisions to be made and provide several views of how to analyze data. As noted by Miles and Huberman (1994) in their in-depth sourcebook, beginning researchers may quake in the face of the "deep, dark question" regarding how to have confidence that their approach to analysis is the right one (p. 2). Yet we concur with the thoughtful and yet practical approach of these authors, that one must just begin and that more energy is often spent discussing analysis, and research for that matter, than "doing it." Miles and Huberman note, in a decidedly unnaive approach, that ". . . any method that works, that will produce clear, verifiable, credible meanings from a set of qualitative data," is "grist" for their mill. They add, ". . . the creation, testing, and revision of simple, practical, and effective analysis methods remain the highest priority of qualitative researchers," adding that, "We remain convinced that concrete, shareable methods do indeed belong to 'all of us'" (p. 3). It is in this spirit that we present approaches to analyzing qualitative data.

One of the major hallmarks of conducting qualitative research is that data are analyzed continually, throughout

the study, from conceptualization through the entire data collection phase, into the interpretation and writing phases. In fact, Goetz and LeCompte (1984) describe the processes of analyzing and writing together in what they call *analysis and interpretation*. How these activities may be done will be explored below.

40.3.1 Overall Approaches to Analyzing Qualitative Data

Qualitative researchers choose their analysis methods not only by the research questions and types of data collected but also based on the philosophical approach underlying the study. For example, Miles and Huberman (1994) outline three overall approaches to analyzing qualitative data. An "interpretive" approach would be phenomological in nature or based on social interactionism. Researchers using this approach would seek to present a holistic view of data rather than a condensed view. They might seek to describe a picture of "what is." They would generally not choose to categorize data to reduce it. Miles and Huberman note that the interpretive approach might be used by qualitative researchers in semiotics, deconstructivism, aesthetic criticism, ethnomethodology, and hermeneutics.

A second approach described by these researchers is "collaborative social research," often used by action researchers in partnerships composed of members of many, and sometimes opposing, organizations.

The final approach to analyzing data described by Miles and Huberman is that of "social anthropology," which relies primarily on ethnography. Researchers using this approach seek to provide detailed, or rich, descriptions across multiple data sources. They seek regular patterns of human behavior in data, usually sifting, coding, and sorting data as they are collected, and following up analyses with ongoing observations and interviews to explore and refine these patterns, in what Goetz and LeCompte call a *recursive approach* (1994). Researchers using a social anthropology approach also tend to be concerned with developing and testing theory. Researchers who develop life histories, work in grounded theory and ecological psychology, and develop narrative studies, applied studies, and case studies often base their analyses on this social anthropology approach. Many of the methods for, and views about, analyzing qualitative data can be seen to be based on this social anthropology approach.

40.3.2 Methods for Analyzing Qualitative Data

Depending on the basic philosophical approach of the qualitative researcher, many methods exist for analyzing data. Miles and Huberman state that qualitative data analysis consists of "three concurrent flows of activity: data reduction, data display, and conclusion drawing/verification" (1994, p. 10). Most researchers advocate that reducing and condensing data, and thereby beginning to seek meaning, should begin as the study begins and continue throughout data collection.

40.3.2.1. Data Reduction. Goetz and LeCompte (1994) describe the conceptual basis for reducing and condensing data in this ongoing style as the study progresses. The researcher theorizes as the study begins and builds and tests theories based on observed patterns in data continually. Researchers compare, aggregate, contrast, sort, and order data. These authors note that while large amounts of raw data are collected, the researcher may examine in detail selected cases or negative cases to test theory. They describe analytic procedures researchers use to determine what the data mean. These procedures involve looking for patterns, links, and relationships. In contrast to experimental research, the qualitative researcher engages in speculation while looking for meaning in data; this speculation will lead the researcher to make new observations, conduct new interviews, and look more deeply for new patterns in this "recursive" process.

Researchers may derive patterns in many ways. They may, for example, engage in what Goetz and LeCompte call "analytic induction" (p. 179), reviewing data for categories of phenomena, defining sets of relationships, developing hypotheses, collecting more data, and refining hypotheses accordingly. As noted earlier, interpretivists would be unlikely to use this method. They would not tend to categorize, but would scan for patterns in order to build a picture or tell a story to describe what is occurring.

Another method, constant comparison, would be relied on by those using a grounded-theory approach. This method involves categorizing, or coding, data as they are collected, and continually examining data for examples of similar cases and patterns. Data collection can cease when few or no new categories of data are being encountered. Goetz and LeCompte contend that researchers using constant-comparison code data look for patterns as do those using analytic induction, but the categories are thus processed differently.

Bogdan and Biklen (1992) describe in detail practical approaches to writing up field notes, one of the main forms the "words" that make up qualitative data take. They recommend writing field notes with large margins in which to write later notes as data are later analyzed, as well as in which to write codes for these data. They also advise that text be written in blocks with room left for headings, notes, and codes.

It should be noted that virtually all researchers who use an ethnographic approach advocate writing up field notes immediately after leaving the research site each day. Observations not recorded will quickly be forgotten. Researchers may not realize the importance of some small phenomenon early on, so these details should be recorded each day. Most authors further recommend that researchers scan these data daily, analyzing thoughtfully for patterns and relationships, and perhaps adding to or modifying data collection procedures accordingly.

Field notes consist of observations and the researcher's interpretations. Bogdan and Biklen (1984) call these two types of field notes contents the *descriptive part* (p. 108) and the *reflective part* (p.121). They state that the descriptive part consists of detailed descriptions of the subjects and settings, the actual dialogue of participants, descriptions of events and activities, as well as descriptions of the observer's behavior, to enable determining how this may have influenced participants' behaviors. The reflective part of field notes, they add, consists of the observer/researcher's analysis. The researcher records speculations about patterns and how data can be analyzed, thoughts about methods and ethical concerns, and even ideas about his or her own state of mind at the time. These authors provide many pages of actual field notes from studies done in elementary and secondary education classrooms, which the beginning researcher will find helpful.

If researchers collect data using audiotape or videotape, written transcripts of language recorded are often prepared. Later analysis can be done, but notes should still be recorded immediately after being in the field. Such notes, for instance, will include observations about participants' nonverbal behaviors, what was occurring in the immediate surroundings, or what activities participants were engaging in. Even in the case of interviews, notes might include these descriptions, as well as what participants were doing just prior to interviews. As noted in the discussion of data collection methods, audiotapes and videotapes may be subjected to detailed microanalysis. Usually data are coded and counted, but, due to the labor-intensive nature of this type of analysis, segments of these "streams of behavior" are often systematically selected for analysis.

It is advisable to collect data in its raw, detailed form and then record patterns. This enables the researcher later to analyze the original data in different ways, perhaps to answer deeper questions than originally conceived. The researcher many weeks into data collection may realize, for example, that some phenomena previously considered unimportant hold the keys to explaining participants' views and actions. In addition, preserving the raw data allows other researchers to explore and verify the data and the interpretations.

If researchers have collected documents from subjects, such as logs, journals, diaries, memos, and letters, these can also be analyzed as raw data. Similarly, official documents of an organization can be subjected to analysis.

Collecting data in the form of photographs, films, and videotapes, either those produced by participants or by the researcher, has a long tradition in anthropology and education. These data, too, can be analyzed for meaning. (See, for instance, Bellman & Jules-Rosette, 1977, *A Paradigm for Looking*; Bogdan & Biklen, 1992; Bogaart & Ketelaar, 1983, *Methodology in Anthropological Filmmaking*; Collier, 1967, and Collier & Collier, 1986, *Visual Anthropology as a Research Method*; Heider, 1976, *Ethnographic Film*; and Hockings, 1975, *Principles of Visual Anthropology.*)

40.3.2.2. Coding Data. Early in the study, the researcher will begin to scan recorded data and to develop categories of phenomena. These categories are usually called *codes*. They enable the researcher to manage data by labeling, storing, and retrieving it according to the codes. Of course, the codes created depend on the study, setting, participants, and research questions, because the codes are the researchers' way of beginning to get at the meaning of the data. There are therefore as many coding schemes as researchers. Still, examples of coding schemes will here be provided in an attempt to guide the reader.

Miles and Huberman (1994) suggest that data can be coded descriptively or interpretively. Unlike some authors, they suggest creating an initial "start list" (p. 58) of codes and refining these in the field. Researchers using a strictly inductive approach might choose not to create any codes until some observations and informal interviews were conducted from which codes could be induced.

Bogdan and Biklen (1992) recommend reading data over at least several times in order to begin to develop a coding scheme. They describe coding data according to categories and details of settings; types of situation observed; perspectives and views of subjects of all manner of phenomena and objects; processes, activities, events, strategies, and methods observed; and social relationships. Goetz and LeCompte (1984) describe coding to form a taxonomic analysis, a sort of outline of what is related to what, and in what ways.

In one of many examples he provides, Spradley (1979) describes in extensive detail how to code and analyze interview data, which are semantic data as are most qualitative data. He describes how to construct domain, structural, taxonomic, and componential analyses. We will discuss, as one example, domain analysis. Domains are names of things. Spradley proposes "universal semantic relationships" that include such categories as "strict inclusion," that is, "*X* is a kind of *Y*"; "spatial," "*X* is a place in *Y*, *X* is a part of *Y*"; and "cause-effect," "rationale," "location of action," "function," "means-end," "sequence," and "attribution" (p. 111). Spradley provides an example from his own research. In a study on tramps, he found from interviews that the cover term *flop,* as a place to sleep, included such things as box cars, laundromats, hotel lobbies, and alleys.

An example of the types of codes that might be developed to investigate patterns of teacher use of an educational technology innovation is presented in the Savenye and Strand observational study described earlier (1989). The researchers videotaped teachers and students using the multimedia science course in 13 physical science classrooms in four states. Samples of videotapes from three teachers were selected for approximate equivalence; in the samples, the teachers were teaching approximately the same content using the same types of lesson components. The researchers were interested not in all the behaviors occurring in the classrooms but in the types of language expressed as teachers taught the lessons.

After reviewing the videotaped data several times, the researchers developed codes for categorizing teacher language. Most of these codes were created specifically for this study. For example, the most frequent types of teacher language observed were instances of "teacher statements," which included data coded as "increasing clarity or coherence of information presented." Examples of codes in this category included PR, for providing preview or organizers of lessons; RP, reminding students to remember prior knowledge; EL, elaborating by providing new information about a scientific concept in the lesson; and R, providing a review of lesson content. Another example of a code created for teacher statements was REL, for instances of when a teacher relates content to student's own experience with everyday examples.

Savenye and Strand were also interested in the types of questions teachers added to the curriculum to encourage their students to participate actively during the whole-class presentations of content. Along with a few created codes, the researchers developed codes based on Bloom's taxonomy of cognitive objectives (1984). Such codes included REC, for questions that asked students to recall information just presented by the multimedia system; APP, for questions that required students to apply or extend lesson content to new content or situations; and ANAL/SYN, for questions that require a student to analyze a situation to come up with solutions or to synthesize a solution. In a result similar to those of many studies of teacher-questioning strategies, but which may disappoint multimedia developers, the majority of the teachers' questions simply asked students to recall information just presented, rather than to apply or analyze or synthesize knowledge learned.

In this study, as in most qualitative studies, coding schemes were continually added to, collapsed, and refined as the study progressed. However, in some studies, only preassigned codes are used to collect and/or analyze data. As in the use of Bloom's categories by Savenye and Strand (1989), usually these codes have been derived from studies and theories of other researchers, or from pilot studies conducted by the researchers themselves. These studies may use observational coding forms or protocols on which data are recorded in the coding categories.

Another example of using preassigned codes is a study conducted to investigate how visitors to a botanical garden use interactive signs (Savenye, Socolofsky, Greenhouse & Cutler, 1995). Among other types of data collected in this study, these researchers trained observers to record behaviors visitors engaged in while they used signs. Observers recorded whether visitors stopped to read a sign at all; if so, for how long, and the level of interactivity visitors exhibited. Based on the work of Bitgood (1990), interactivity was coded as stopping briefly and glancing only; obviously reading the sign and looking at the plant exhibit near it; and, finally, engaging in highly active behaviors, such as reading the sign aloud, pointing to the plants displayed, discussing information being learned, and pulling friends and family over to the sign to read it. In a blend of coding methods typical in many studies, observers also wrote ethnographic-style notes to describe what if any content on the signs was being discussed, what misconceptions appeared, what excited visitors most, etc. In this study, visitor surveys and interviews were also used.

In any qualitative study, codes can be used to count frequencies or, as Goetz and LeCompte call it, conduct *enumer-*

ation (1984) to develop quantitative data, as was done in the studies described above. Similarly, quantitative data, such as attendance or production figures, from other sources, may be analyzed. Most researchers suggest caution when counting that the "big picture" is not lost, and also note that quantitative data from other sources can also be biased. Even what is collected in a school district, for instance, may be determined by financial, administrative, and political concerns.

For more examples of coding schemes and strategies, see Strauss (1987). (See also 41.2.4 for some discussion of coding observational data.)

40.3.2.3. Data Management

40.3.2.3.1. Physically Organizing Data. Analysis of data requires examining, sorting, and reexamining data continually. Qualitative researchers use many means to organize, retrieve, and analyze their data. Many researchers simply use notebooks and boxes of paper. Bogdan and Biklen (1992) describe what they call two *mechanical means* to organize and begin to review data. One way they describe is to write initial codes in margins of field notes, photocopy the notes and store the originals, then cut up and sort the text segments into piles according to codes. These coded data can be stored in boxes and resorted and analyzed on an ongoing basis. A second method they describe is to record field notes on pages on which each line is numbered, code the field notes, and then write the page number, line numbers, and a brief description of each piece of data on a small index card. These cards can then be sorted and analyzed. The authors note that this second method is better suited for small sets of data, as it often requires returning to the original field notes to analyze the actual data.

30.2.3.2. Organizing Data Using Computers. Computers are increasingly the tool of choice for managing and analyzing qualitative data. It is interesting to note that computers have long been used in anthropological analysis. (See, for instance, Hymes, 1965, *The Use of Computers in Anthropology.*) Computers may be used simply for word processing in developing field notes. However, there is now considerable software specifically developed for qualitative research, and it can be expected that many new programs will be developed in the upcoming decade. Some software uses text entered with a word processor to retrieve words and phrases or to manage text in databases. Software is also available to code and retrieve data, and some programs also allow for building theories and conceptual networks. Programs are available for IBM (e.g., QUALPRO, The Ethnograph) or for Macintosh microcomputers (e.g., HyperQual, SemNet) or multiple systems (QSR NUD-IST) (Miles & Weitzman, 1994). For much more on using computers for analysis, the reader may refer to the following books: Tesch (1990), *Qualitative Research: Analysis Types and Software Tools,* or Wietzman and Miles (1995), *A Software Sourcebook: Computer Programs for Qualitative Data Analysis.*

40.3.2.3.3. Data Display. Seeking the meaning in data is made easier by displaying data visually. Research data are displayed using charts, graphs, diagrams, tables, matrices, and any other devices, such as drawings, that researchers devise. Frequency tables are typically developed for categories of coded behaviors. In the Reiser and Mory (1991) study, for example, teachers' planning behaviors were coded and tables of behaviors presented.

Miles and Huberman (1994) hold that data display is a critical and often underutilized means of analysis. They describe many forms of data display, illustrated with examples of actual data. They recommend that researchers initially create categories of data, code data, and revise codes, as do other authors. They note that increasingly qualitative research involves analyzing what they call *within-case* data, for instance, from one classroom or one school, as well as "cross-case" data, from many participants and many sites. Whereas in one case study, it may not be necessary to present visual displays—narrative descriptions might suffice—studies involving data from many cases can greatly benefit from visual displays. Miles and Huberman present many options. For example, for within-case data they show context charts or checklist matrices, but they also discuss using a transcript as a poem. They also illustrate time-ordered displays, role-ordered displays, and conceptually ordered displays. For cross-case studies, these researchers mention some of the earlier displays for reviewing and presenting data, along with case-ordered displays. They illustrate other displays for examining cross-case data and provide extensive advice for creating matrix displays.

An example of the use of matrix displays is the Higgins and Rice participant observation study described earlier (1991). The researchers analyzed teachers' conceptions of all the activities that represent "assessment." These data were derived from a series of structured interviews with the teachers, conducted in conjunction with observations of the teachers and their students. The researchers analyzed these data using multidimensional scaling and displayed the data using a matrix to show the relationships among types of assessments teachers used and how different teachers conceived of them differently.

That data analysis is woven into interpreting results and writing up the study is indicated by the fact that Miles and Huberman describe the third type of data analysis activity as drawing and verifying conclusions. Similarly, Goetz and LeCompte (1984) include writing up the study in their chapter on analysis and interpretation of data, describing the writing phase as developing an ethnographic analysis, and integrating and interpreting the study. While recognizing that analysis continues as the research report is written, and that writing should begin during analysis, in this chapter, we will present ideas and issues for writing up a study.

40.4 WRITING QUALITATIVE RESEARCH REPORTS

The report of a qualitative study may take many forms, both those common to more quantitative research and also forms likely to be unfamiliar to those who conduct only experimental research. The best advice for the beginning researcher is to recognize that it is not unusual for even experienced researchers to feel overwhelmed by the amount of data to be analyzed and described, as well as to feel a lack of confidence that the interpretations and conclusions the researcher has drawn represent "the truth." Most authors simply advise writers to "do it," or to "begin" to write and refine, and write and refine again. A later section will discuss ethical issues and criteria for evaluating the quality of a study. As with analysis, there exist many books of guidelines and advice for writing qualitative research reports. In this section we will briefly discuss a few of the issues.

In writing up a qualitative study, researchers have many choices of presentation styles. Bogdan and Biklen (1984) consider qualitative researchers fortunate in that there is not one accepted convention for writing qualitative reports. For example, the qualitative report may take the form of a case study, as in the Reiser and Mory (1991) study. If a case study, the report may include considerable quantification and tables of enumerated data, or it may take a strictly narrative form. Recent studies have been reported in more nontraditional forms, such as stories, plays, and poems showing what is happening for these participants in that setting.

A few examples of less-traditional approaches to reporting results are the presentations by Barone and Lather at the 1995 conference of the American Educational Research Association (AERA). Barone presented an arts-based phenomological inquiry in a narrative format (1995). Lather, in an AERA Qualitative Research SIG interactive symposium on reframing the narrative voice, discussed her study, in which she divided pages in her report into three sections in which she presented her interpretation, the participants' interpretation, and then her response to the participants (Tierney, Polkinghorn, Lincoln, Denzin, Kincheloe, Lather & Pinar, 1995).

Richardson (1995) describes other components and styles of less-traditional writing, including ways to reference historical contexts, using metaphors, documentary styles, and various experimental representations, including "narrative of the self," "ethnographic fictional representations," "poetic representations," "ethnographic dramas," and "mixed genres" (pp. 521, 522). Richardson additionally provides advice to the researcher who wishes to explore these experimental formats.

Fetterman (1989) explicates the nature of qualitative writing. As do many others, he stresses the use of "thick description" and liberal use of verbatim quotations, that is, the participants' own words to illustrate the reality of the setting and subjects. (This serves as another reminder to the researcher to record and preserve raw data in the participants' language with quotes.) Fetterman adds that ethnographies are usually written in what he calls the "ethnographic present" (p. 116), as if the reality is still ongoing. However, in educational technology research in which innovations are often described, the researcher may or may not choose to use this approach. Qualitative reports typically will be woven around a theme or central message, and will include an introduction, core material, and conclusion (Bogdan & Biklen,

1984). However, what constitutes the core of the report, of course, will vary depending on the style of the writing.

A cogent and enjoyable manual for writing up qualitative research is Wolcott's (1990). [For additional information about writing reports of qualitative studies, see Meloy (1994) and Van Maanen (1988).]

40.5 ETHICAL ISSUES IN CONDUCTING QUALITATIVE RESEARCH

In addition to the ethical issues raised by authors cited earlier in discussions of specific methodologies, there continues to be great concern that qualitative researchers conduct and report their studies in an ethical manner. Punch, in his recent work (1994), however, suggests that qualitative researchers not be daunted or deterred by ethical issues. In fact, under the heading "Just do it!" he advises that "Fieldwork is fun; it is easy; anyone can do it; it is salutary for young academics to flee the nest; and they should be able to take any moral or political dilemmas encountered in their stride" (p. 83). He describes the ethical issues that are in common with most scientific research, such as biomedical research in this country at this time. For instance, all researchers must be concerned with preventing subjects from being harmed, protecting their anonymity and privacy, not deceiving them, and securing their informed consent. In discussing recent debate about qualitative methods, however, Punch adds other issues that arise. Questions may include: Does the pursuit of scientific knowledge justify the means? What is public and what is private? When can research be said to be "harming" people? Does the researcher enjoy any immunity from the law when he or she refuses to disclose information? (p. 89). He discusses the concepts of codes, consent, privacy, confidentiality, and trust and betrayal in detail. He further describes three developments that have stirred up the debate. These include the women's movement and its attendant concern that women have been studied as subjects/objects, the trend toward conducting action research in which participants are partners or stakeholders to be empowered and therefore not to be duped, and, finally, the concern of funding agencies for ethics that has led to requirements for the inclusion of statements of ethics in proposals and reports. Croll (1986) addresses similar issues and recommends that researchers conduct their studies in good faith, and that the research should be not only not harmful to subjects but also worthwhile.

Erlandson et al. (1993), in their discussion of ethical issues, echo the previously mentioned concerns with regard to privacy, confidentiality, harm, deception, and informed consent. They add that in contracted research, situations may arise that could compromise the research by restricting freedom or encouraging suppression of negative results. From a more "action research" type of perspective, these authors add to Croll's idea that studies should be of value to subjects, that they should educate subjects (see 9.7.5). Educational technology researchers must determine for themselves their answers to ethical questions, realizing that their work may or may not fall into the category of action research.

For a broader and more in-depth discussion about ethical issues, the reader may wish to refer to *Ethics and Anthropology: Dilemmas in Fieldwork,* by Rynkiewich and Spradley (1976); the Beauchamp, Faden, Wallace, and Walters (1982) book, *Ethical Issues in Social Science Research*; or the Bower and Gasparis (1978) book, *Ethics in Social Research: Protecting the Interest of Human Subjects.*

Many authors blend concerns for ethics with criteria for evaluating the quality of qualitative studies, in that an unethically conducted study would not be of high quality. The criteria to use in determining whether a qualitative study is sound and strong will be illustrated in the following section.

40.6 CRITERIA FOR EVALUATING QUALITATIVE STUDIES

Criteria for evaluating the quality and rigor of qualitative studies vary somewhat, based on methods used. Most concerns, however, apply to most studies. Adler and Adler (1994) say that one of the primary criticisms of observational studies, whether participant or nonparticipant methods are used, is the question of their validity due to the subjectivity and biases of the researcher. These authors contend that this concern is one of the reasons studies based solely on observations are rarely published. They suggest that validity can be increased in three ways. Multiple observers in teams can cross-check data and patterns continually. The researcher can refine and test propositions and hypotheses throughout the study, in a grounded theory approach. Finally, the researcher can write using "verisimilitude" or "varisemblance" (p. 383), or writing that makes the world of the subjects real to the reader; the reader recognizes the authenticity of the results. Adler and Adler also address the issue of reliability in observational studies. They suggest systematically conducting observations repeatedly under varying conditions, particularly varying time and place. Reliability would be verified by emergence of similar results.

Borg and Gall (1989) listed several criteria for evaluating the quality of participant observation studies, including that:

1. Using involved participant observers is less likely to result in erroneous reported data from individuals or organizations.
2. The researcher should have relatively free access to a broad range of activities.
3. The observations should be intense, that is, conducted over a long period of time.
4. In more recent studies, both qualitative and quantitative data are collected.
5. Using a "triangulation of methodology" (p. 393), researchers can be assured that the picture they present of the reality of a setting or situation is clear and true. Multiple methods may be used to address

research questions, but also, in line with Adler and Adler's (1994) recommendations for enhancing reliability, the same data may be collected from other samples at other times and in other places.
6. Researchers should strive to gain an overall view of the issues and context, and then sample purposely in order to collect data that represent the range of realities of participants in those settings. Borg and Gall, as do others, caution that researchers be sensitive to both what is excluded as well as what is included.
7. Finally, in all observational studies they recommend that researchers should be ready to observe, record, and analyze, not just verbal exchanges but also subtle cues by using unobtrusive measures.

Ethical issues also relate to the quality of a study. Issues specific to conducting interviews are delineated by Fontana and Frey (1994). They add to the general concerns already mentioned the issues of informed consent and the right to privacy and protection. They mention that there is some debate regarding whether covert methods for gathering data are ethical although they may reflect real life. They describe the dilemma a researcher may face in deciding how involved to become with respondents and suggest some degree of situational ethics, cautioning that a researcher's participation may enable or inhibit certain behaviors or responses. Finally, they raise the issue that interviewing itself is manipulative, still treating human beings as objects.

Hammersley (1990) provides additional criteria for assessing ethnographic research, many of which will apply to most qualitative studies. He puts forward two main criteria for judging ethnographic studies, namely, validity and relevance. He discusses the validity of a study as meaning the "truth" of the study. He suggests three steps for assessing the validity of ethnographic finds or conclusions. He recommends asking first if the findings or claims are reasonable; secondly "whether it seems likely that the ethnographer's judgment of matters relating to the claim would be accurate given the nature of the phenomena concerned, the circumstances of the research, the characteristics of the researcher, etc." (p. 61); finally, in cases in which the claim does not appear to be plausible or credible, evidence of validity is required to be examined. Clearly in reports of qualitative research studies, the reader must be provided enough information about the perspective, sampling and choice of subjects, and data collected in order to determine with some confidence the validity or "truth" represented in a study.

With regard to the second criterion, relevance, Hammersley advises that studies have broadly conceived public relevance or value. On a practical level, Nathan (1979, pp. 113–115), in Abt's book on the costs and benefits of applied social research, provides what he calls rules for relevant research. A selection includes:

1. Be as evenhanded as you can.
2. Focus on the most policy-relevant effects.

3. When faced with a choice between the direct and the more elaborate expression of statistics and concepts, choose the former.
4. Get your hands dirty.
5. Be interdisciplinary.
6. Sort out carefully description, analysis, and your opinions.

Lincoln and Guba (1985) describe criteria that are frequently cited for evaluating qualitative studies. They address the criticisms leveled at naturalistic research and determine that quality rests in trustworthiness of the study and its findings. They agree with others that conventional criteria are inappropriate for qualitative studies and that there do exist alternative criteria. These criteria are: (1) credibility, (2) transferability, (3) dependability, and (4) confirmability. These authors go on to recommend activities the researcher may undertake to ensure that these criteria will be inherent in the study. In particular, in order to make credible findings more likely, they recommend that prolonged engagement, persistent observation, and triangulation be done. Further, they recommend peer debriefing about the study and its methods, opening the researcher and the methods up for review. They also recommend analyzing negative cases in order to revise hypotheses; testing for referential adequacy by building in the critical examination of findings and their accompanying raw data; and conducting checks of data, categories used in analysis, and interpretations and findings with members of the subject audience.

Lincoln and Guba (1985) provide a similar level of helpful suggestions in the area of ensuring confirmability. They recommend triangulation with multimethods and various sources of data, keeping a reflexive journal and, most powerfully, conducting a confirmability audit. In their book, they include detailed descriptions of the steps in conducting an audit and recommend the following categories of data that can be used in the audit, including raw data, products of data analysis, products of the synthesis of data such as findings and conclusions, process notes, personal notes about intentions, and information about how instruments were developed.

In the tradition of Lincoln and Guba, Erlandson et al. (1993) describe these techniques for ensuring the quality of a study:

- Prolonged engagement
- Persistent observation
- Triangulation
- Referential adequacy
- Peer debriefing
- Member checking
- Reflexive journal
- Thick description
- Purposive sampling
- Audit trail

The Association for Educational Communications and Technology (AECT) has shown strong support for qualitative research in the field. For several years, the ECT Foundation and the Research and Theory Division supported the Special Research Award. The ECT Foundation has recently decided to support the creation of a Qualitative Research Award. Ann De Vaney (1995), currently the chair of this award committee, provided the following criteria, developed by numerous AECT members, which will be used to evaluate the quality of papers submitted for this award:

1. Is the problem clearly stated? Does it have theoretical value and currency? Does it have practical value?
2. Is the problem or topic situated in a theoretical framework? Is the framework clear and accessible? Does the document contain competing epistemologies or other basic assumptions that might invalidate claims?
3. Is the literature review a critique or simply a recapitulation? Is it relevant? Does it appear accurate and sufficiently comprehensive?
4. Are the theses stated in a clear and coherent fashion? Are they sufficiently demonstrated in an accessible manner? Are there credible warrants to claims made about the theses?
5. Does the method fit the problem, and is it an appropriate one given the theoretical framework?
6. Do the data collected adequately address the problem? Do they make explicit the researcher's role and perspective? Do the data collection techniques have a "good fit" with the method and theory?
7. Are the data aggregates and analysis clearly reported? Do they make explicit the interpretive and reasoning process of the researcher?
8. Does the discussion provide meaningful and warranted interpretations and conclusions?

Lest it appear that there is universal agreement about the quality criteria, it may be noted that the postmodern trend toward questioning and deconstruction have led to continued debate in this area. Wolcott, in his book about transforming qualitative data (1994, pp. 348–356), argues for rejecting validity in qualitative research, and then describes activities he undertakes to address the challenge of validity. These include "talk a little, listen a lot . . . begin writing early . . . let readers 'see' for themselves . . . report fully . . . be candid . . . seek feedback . . . try to achieve balance . . . write accurately."

40.7 LEARNING MORE ABOUT DOING QUALITATIVE RESEARCH

The preceeding discussion of evaluating qualitative research, rather than being a conclusion, is a fitting beginning point for you, the researcher, to go onward and conduct your studies. It is hoped that this chapter has served as an introduction, pointing you toward more useful resources and references.

Below is a subjective list of the authors' "top" books, listed in alphabetical, not ranked, order, for learning about qualitative research in education (full citations appear, right after, in the reference list):

Bogdan & Biklen (1992). *Qualitative research for education,* 2d ed.

Denzin & Lincoln, eds. (1994). *Handbook of qualitative research.*

Eisner (1991). *The enlightened eye: qualitative inquiry and the enhancement of educational practice.*

Erlandson, Harris, Skipper & Allen (1993). *Doing naturalistic inquiry: a guide to methods.*

Fetterman (1989). *Ethnography: step by step.*

Goetz & LeCompte (1984). *Ethnography and qualitative design in educational research.*

Lincoln & Guba (1985). *Naturalistic inquiry.*

Marshall & Rossman (1984). *Designing qualitative research.*

Meloy (1994). *Writing the qualitative dissertation: understanding by doing.*

Miles & Huberman (1994). *Qualitative data analysis: an expanded sourcebook,* 2d ed.

Spradley (1980). *Participant observation.*

Strauss (1987). *Qualitative analysis for social scientists.*

Van Maanen (1988). *Tales of the field: on writing ethnography.*

Wolcott (1990). *Writing up qualitative research.*

Wolcott (1994). *Transforming qualitative data: description, analysis, and interpretation.*

Yin (1989). *Case study research.*

Additional references appear in Robinson and Driscoll's (1993) handout for their AECT workshop on qualitative methods.

The researcher is also wise to keep up with new publications in methodology, including new editions of these books and others. Several journals specialize in publishing qualitative research, including the *International Journal of Qualitative Studies in Education, Journal of Contemporary Ethnography, Journal of Visual Literacy,* and the research section of *Educational Technology.* In addition, researchers may wish to join the qualitative research bulletin board, which can be reached via Judith Preissle at the University of Georgia.

We wish you well in your explorations!

REFERENCES

Adler, P.A. & Adler, P. (1994). Observational techniques. *In* N.K. Denzin & Y.S. Lincoln, eds. *Handbook of qualitative research,* 377–92. Thousand Oaks, CA: Sage.

Altheide, D.L. & Johnson, J.M. (1994). Criteria for assessing interpretive validity in qualitative research. *In* N.K. Denzin & Y.S. Lincoln, eds. *Handbook of qualitative research,* 485–99. Thousand Oaks, CA: Sage.

Ambron, S. & Hooper, K., eds. (1988). *Interactive multimedia: visions of multimedia for developers, educators & information providers.* Redmond, WA: Microsoft.

— & —, eds. (1990). *Learning with interactive multimedia: developing and using multimedia tools in education.* Redmond, WA: Microsoft.

Atkinson, P. & Hammersley, M. (1994). Ethnography and participant observation. *In* N.K. Denzin & Y.S. Lincoln, eds. *Handbook of qualitative research,* 248–61. Thousand Oaks, CA: Sage.

Barone, T. (1995, Apr.). *An example of an arts-based phenomenological inquiry.* Paper presented at the annual conference of the American Educational Research Association, San Francisco, CA.

Beauchamp, T.L., Faden, R.R., Wallace, R.J., Jr. & Walters, L. (1982). *Ethical issues in social science research.* Baltimore, MD: Johns Hopkins University Press.

Bellman, B.L. & Jules-Rosette, B. (1977). *A paradigm for looking: cross-cultural research with visual media.* Norwood, NJ: Ablex.

Bernard, H.R. (1988). Research methods in cultural anthropology. Newbury Park, CA: Sage.

Bitgood, S. (1990, Nov.). *The role of simulated immersion in exhibition.* Jacksonville, AL: Center of Social Design.

Bloom, B.S. (1984). *Taxonomy of educational objectives, handbook 1: cognitive domain.* New York: Longman.

Bogaart, N.C.R. & Ketelaar, H.W.E.R., eds. (1983). *Methodology in anthropological filmmaking: papers of the IUAES—Intercongress, Amsterdam, 1981.* Gottingen, Germany: Edition Herodot.

Bogdan, R.C. & Biklen, S.K. (1992). *Qualitative research for education: an introduction to theory and methods,* 2d ed. Boston, MA: Allyn & Bacon.

Borg, W.R. & Gall, M.D. (1989). *Educational research: an introduction,* 5th ed. New York: Longman.

Borich, G.D. (1989). Outcome evaluation report of the TLTG Physical Science Curriculum, 1988–89. Austin, TX: Texas Learning Technology Group of the Texas Association of School Boards.

Bosco, J. (1986). An analysis of evaluations of interactive video. *Educational Technology 16* (5), 7–17.

Bower, R.T. & de Gasparis, P. (1978). *Ethics in social research: protecting the interests of human subjects.* New York: Praeger.

Bruner, J.S., Goodnow, J.J. & Austin, G.A. (1972). Categories and cognition. *In* J.P. Spradley, ed. *Culture and cognition: rules, maps, and plans,* 168–90. San Francisco, CA: Chandler.

Chen, J.W. & Shen, C.W. (1989, Sep.). Software engineering: a new component for instructional software development. *Educational Technology 9,* 9–15.

Clark, R.E. (1983). Reconsidering research on learning from media. *Review of Educational Research 53* (4), 445–59.

— (1989). Current progress and future directions for research in instructional technology. *Educational Technology Research and Development 37* (1), 57–66.

Collier, J. (1967). *Visual anthropology: photography as a research method.* New York: Holt, Rinehart & Winston.

— & Collier, M. (1986). *Visual anthropology: photography as a research method.* Albuquerque, NM: University of New Mexico Press.

Croll, P. (1986). *Systematic classroom observation.* London: Falmer.

Crooks, S.M., Klein, J.D., Jones, E.K. & Dwyer, H. (1995, Feb.). *Effects of cooperative learning and learner control modes in computer-based instruction.* Paper presented at the annual meeting of the Association for Communications and Technology, Anaheim, CA.

Darabi, G.A. & Dempsey, J.V. (1989–90). A quality control system for curriculum-based CBI projects. *Journal of Educational Technology Systems 18* (1), 15–31.

Dalton, D.W., Hannafin, M.J. & Hooper, S. (1989). Effects of individual and cooperative computer-assisted instruction on student performance and attitude. *Educational Technology Research and Development 37* (2), 15–24.

Denzin, N.K. & Lincoln, Y.S., eds. (1994). *Handbook of quali-*

tative research. Thousand Oaks, CA: Sage.

DeWalt, B.R. & Pelto, P.J., eds. (1985). *Micro and macro levels of analysis in anthropology.* Boulder, CO: Westview.

Driscoll, M.P. (1995). Paradigms for research in instructional systems. *In* Anglin, ed. *Instructional technology: past, present and future,* 2d ed., 322–29. Englewood, CO: Libraries Unlimited.

Dwyer, H. & Leader, L. (1995, Feb.). *The Researcher's HyperCard Toolkit II.* Paper presented at the annual meeting of the Association for Educational Communications and Technology, Anaheim, CA.

ECT Foundation (1995). *Suggested criteria for qualitative research.* Association for Educational Communications and Technology.

Eisner, E. (1991). *The enlightened eye: qualitative inquiry and the enhancement of educational practice.* New York: Macmillan.

Erickson, F. & Shultz, J. (1982). *The counselor as gatekeeper: social interaction in interviews.* New York: Academic.

Ericsson, K.A. & Simon, H.A. (1984). *Protocol analysis—verbal reports as data.* Cambridge, MA: MIT Press.

Erlandson, D.A., Harris, E.L., Skipper, B.L. & Allen, S.D. (1993). *Doing naturalistic inquiry: a guide to methods.* Newbury Park, CA: Sage.

Fetterman, D.M. (1989). *Ethnography: step by step.* Applied Social Research Methods Series, Vol. 17. Newbury Park, CA: Sage.

Fiedler, J. (1978). *Field research: a manual for logistics and management of scientific studies in natural settings.* San Francisco, CA: Jossey-Bass.

Fontana, A. & Frey, J.H. (1994) Interviewing: the art of science. *In* N.K. Denzin, & Y.S. Lincoln, eds. *Handbook of qualitative research,* 361–77. Thousand Oaks, CA: Sage.

Frake, C.O. (1978). The ethnographic study of cognitive systems. *In* J.P. Spradley, ed. *Culture and cognition: rules, maps, and plans,* 191–205. San Francisco, CA: Chandler.

Geertz, C. (1973). Thick description. *In* C. Geertz, ed. *The interpretation of cultures,* 3–30. New York: Basic Books.

Goetz, J.P. & LeCompte, M.D. (1984). *Ethnography and qualitative design in educational research.* Orlando, FL: Academic.

Guba, E.G., ed. (1990). *The paradigm dialog.* Newbury Park, CA: Sage.

Hammersley, M. (1990). *Reading ethnographic research: a critical guide.* London: Longman.

— & Atkinson, P. (1983). *Ethnography: principles in practice.* London: Tavistock.

Hannafin, M.J. & Rieber, L.P. (1989). Psychological foundations of instructional design for emerging computer-based instructional technologies: Part 1. *Educational Technology Research and Development 37* (2), 91–101.

Heider, K.G. (1976). *Ethnographic film.* Austin, TX: University of Texas Press.

Heyman, I.M. (1995, Jan.). Smithsonian perspectives. *Smithsonian,* 8.

Hicken, S., Sullivan, H. & Klein, J. (1992). Learner control modes and incentive variations in computer delivered instruction. *Educational Technology Research and Development 40* (4), 15–26.

Higgins, N. & Rice, E. (1991). Teachers' perspectives on competency-based testing. *Educational Technology Research and Development 39* (3), 59–69.

Hirumi, A., Savenye, W. & Allen, B. (1994). Designing interactive videodisc-based museum exhibits: a case study. *Educational Technology Research and Development 42* (1),

47–55.

Hockings, P., ed. (1975). *Principles of visual anthropology.* The Hague, Netherlands: Mouton.

Hodder, I. (1994) The interpretation of documents and material culture. *In* N.K. Denzin & Y.S. Lincoln, ed. *Handbook of qualitative research,* 393–402. Thousand Oaks, CA: Sage.

Hooper, S. & Hannafin, M.J. (1988). Learning the ROPES of instructional design: guidelines for emerging interactive technologies. *Educational Technology 28,* 14–18.

Hymes, D., ed. (1965). *The use of computers in anthropology.* London: Mouton.

Jacob, E. (1987). Qualitative research traditions: a review. *Review of Educational Research 57* (1), 1–50.

Johnson, A.W. (1978). *Quantification in cultural anthropology.* Stanford, CA: Stanford University Press.

Jones, E.K., Crooks, S. & Klein, J. (1995, Feb.). *Development of a cooperative learning observational instrument.* Paper presented at the annual meeting of the Association for Communications and Technology, Anaheim, CA.

Jost, K.L. (1994, Feb.). *Educational change: the implementation of technology and curriculum change.* Paper presented at the annual meeting of the Association for Communications and Technology, Nashville, TN.

Kowinski, W.S. (1995, Jan.). Giving new life to Haida art and the culture it expresses. *Smithsonian,* 38–46.

Klein, J. D., Erchul, J.A. & Pridemore, D.R. (1994). Effects of individual versus cooperative learning and type of reward on performance and continuing motivation. *Contemporary Educational Psychology 19,* 24–32.

— & Pridemore, D.R. (1994). Effects of orienting activities and practice on achievement, continuing motivation, and student behaviors in a cooperative learning environment. *Educational Technology Research and Development 41* (4), 41–54.

Kuhn, T.S. (1970). *The structure of scientific revolutions,* 2d ed. Chicago, IL: University of Chicago Press.

Lambert, S. & Sallis, J., eds. (1987). *CD–I and interactive videodisc technology.* Indianapolis, IN: Sams.

Lather, P. (1995, Apr.) *At play in the field of theory: from social scientism to paradigm proliferation.* Paper presented at the annual conference of the American Educational Research Association, San Francisco, CA.

Lincoln, Y.S. & Guba, E.G. (1985). *Naturalistic inquiry.* Beverly Hills, CA: Sage.

Manning, P.K. & Cullum-Swan. (1994). Narrative, content, and semiotic analysis. *In* N.K. Denzin & Y.S. Lincoln, eds. *Handbook of qualitative research,* 463–77. Thousand Oaks, CA: Sage.

Markle, S.M. (1989, Aug.). The ancient history of formative evaluation. *Performance & Instruction,* 27–29.

Marshall, C. & Rossman, G. (1989). *Designing qualitative research.* Newbury Park, CA: Sage.

McIsaac, M.S., Ozkalp, E. & Harper-Marinick, M. (1992). Cross-generational perspectives on gender differences and perceptions of professional competence in photographs. *International Journal of Instructional Media 19* (4), 349–65.

McLean, R.S. (1989). Megatrends in computing and educational software development. *Education & Computing 5,* 55–60.

McNeil, B.J. & Nelson, K.R. (1991). Meta-analysis of interactive video instruction: a 10-year review of achievement effects. *Journal of Computer-Based Instruction 18* (1), 1–6.

Mehan, H. (1979). *Learning lessons: social organization in the classroom.* Cambridge, MA: Harvard University Press.

Meloy, J.M. (1994). *Writing the qualitative dissertation: understanding by doing.* Hillsdale, NJ: Erlbaum.

Miles, M.B. & Huberman, A.M. (1994). *Qualitative data analysis: an expanded sourcebook,* 2d ed. Thousand Oaks, CA: Sage.

— & Weitzman, E.A. (1994). Appendix: choosing computer programs for qualitative data analysis. *In* M.B. Miles & A.M. Huberman. *Qualitative data analysis: an expanded sourcebook,* 2d ed., 311–17. Thousand Oaks, CA: Sage.

Moallem, M. (1994, Feb.). *An experienced teacher's model of thinking and teaching: an ethnographic study on teacher cognition.* Paper presented at the annual meeting of the Association for Communications and Technology, Nashville, TN.

Nathan, R. (1979). Ten rigorous rules for relevant research. *In* C.C. Abt. *Perspectives on the costs and benefits of applied social research.* Cambridge, MA: Abt.

Neuman, D. (1989). Naturalistic inquiry and computer-based instruction: rationale, procedures, and potential. *Educational Technology Research and Development 37* (3), 39–51.

Newman, D. (1989, Mar.). *Formative experiments on technologies that change the organization of instruction.* Paper presented at the annual conference of the American Educational Research Association, San Francisco, CA.

Nielsen, M.C. (1989). *The effects of varying levels of informational feedback on concept learning in CAI programs.* Unpublished doctoral dissertation, The University of Texas at Austin.

Ogbu, J.U. (1974). *The next generation: an ethnography of education in an urban neighborhood.* New York: Academic.

Oliver, E.L. (1992). *Interaction at a distance: mediated communication in televised courses.* Unpublished doctoral dissertation, Northern Illinois University, DeKalb, IL.

Pelto, P.J. & Pelto, G.H. (1978). *Anthropological research: the structure of inquiry,* 2d ed. Cambridge, MA: Cambridge University Press.

Pitlik, D. (1995). *A description of the real profession of instructional design.* Unpublished doctoral dissertation, Northern Illinois University, DeKalb, IL.

Pitts, J.M. (1993). *Personal understandings and mental models of information: a qualitative study of factors associated with the information seeking and use of adolescents.* Unpublished doctoral dissertation, Florida State University, Tallahassee, FL.

Punch, M. (1994). Politics and ethics in qualitative research. *In* N.K. Denzin & Y.S. Lincoln, eds. *Handbook of qualitative research,* 83–97. Thousand Oaks, CA: Sage.

Reeves, T.C. (1986). Research and evaluation models for the study of interactive video. *Journal of Computer-Based Instruction 13* (4), 102–06.

Reigeluth, C.M. (1989). Educational technology at the crossroads: new mindsets and new directions. *Educational Technology Research and Development 37* (1), 67–80.

Reilly, B. (1994). Composing with images: a study of high school video producers. *Proceedings of ED-MEDIA 94, Educational multimedia and hypermedia.* Charlottesville, VA: Association for the Advancement of Computing in Education.

Reiser, R.A. & Mory, E.H. (1991). An examination of the systematic planning techniques of two experienced teachers. *Educational Technology Research and Development 39* (3), 71–82.

Richardson, L. (1994) Writing: a method of inquiry. *In* N.K. Denzin, & Y.S. Lincoln, eds. *Handbook of qualitative*

research, 516–29. Thousand Oaks, CA: Sage.

Robinson, R.S. (1995). Qualitative research—a case for case studies. *In* Anglin, ed. *Instructional technology: past, present and future,* 2d ed., 330–39. Englewood, CO: Libraries Unlimited.

— (1994). Investigating channel one: a case study report. *In* De Vaney, ed. *Watching channel one.* Albany, NY: SUNY Press.

— & Driscoll, M. (1993). Qualitative research methods: an introduction. *In* M.R. Simonson & K. Abu-Omar, eds. *15th annual proceedings of selected research and development presentations at the 1993 national convention of the Association for Educational Communications and Technology, New Orleans, LA,* 833–44. Ames, IO: Iowa State University.

Rynkiewich, M.A. & Spradley, J.P., eds. (1976). *Ethics and anthropology: dilemmas in fieldwork.* New York: Wiley.

Salomon, G. (1991). Transcending the qualitative-quantitative debate: the analytic and systemic approaches to educational research. *Educational Researcher 20* (6), 10–18.

Savenye, W., Socolofsky, K., Greenhouse, R. & Cutler, N. (1995, Feb.). *Evaluation under Sonoran sun: formative evaluation of a desert education exhibit.* Paper presented at the annual conference of the Association for Educational Communications and Technology, Anaheim, CA.

— (1989). *Field test year evaluation of the TLTG interactive videodisc science curriculum: effects on student and teacher attitude and classroom implementation.* Austin, TX: Texas Learning Technology Group of the Texas Association of School Boards.

—, Leader, L., Dwyer, H., Jones, E., Schnackenberg, H. & Jiang, B. (1996, Feb.). *Relationship among patterns of choices, achievement, incentive, and attitude in a learner-controlled computer-based lesson for college students.* Paper presented at the annual conference of the Association for Educational Communications and Technology, Indianapolis, IN.

— & Strand, E. (1989, Feb.). Teaching science using interactive videodisc: results of the pilot year evaluation of the Texas Learning Technology Group Project. *In* M.R. Simonson & D. Frey, eds. *11th annual proceedings of selected research paper presentations at the 1989 annual convention of the Association for Educational Communications and Technology in Dallas, TX.* Ames, IA: Iowa State University.

Schmidt, K.J. (1992). *At-risk eighth-grade student feelings, perceptions, and insights of computer-assisted interactive video.* Unpublished doctoral dissertation, The University of Texas at Austin.

Shin, E.J., Schallert, D. & Savenye, W.C. (1994). Effects of learner control, advisement, and prior knowledge on young students' learning in a hypertext environment. *Educational Technology Research and Development 42* (1), 33–46.

Smith, M.L. (1987). Publishing qualitative research. *American Educational Research Journal 24* (2), 173–83.

Smith, P.L. & Wedman, J.F. (1988). Read-think-aloud protocols: a new data-source for formative evaluation. *Performance Improvement Quarterly 1* (2), 13–22.

Spindler, G.D. (1974). Schooling in Schonhausen: a study in cultural transmission and instrumental adaptation in an urbanizing German village. *In* G.D. Spindler, ed. *Education an cultural process: toward an anthropology of education.* New York: Holt, Rinehart & Winston.

Spradley, J.P. (1972). *Culture and cognition: rules, maps, and plans.* San Francisco, CA: Chandler.

— (1979). *The ethnographic interview.* New York: Holt, Rinehart & Winston.

— (1980). *Participant observation.* New York: Holt, Rinehart & Winston.

Straus, A.L. (1987). *Qualitative analysis for social scientists.* Cambridge, MA: Cambridge University Press.

Strauss, A.L. & Corbin, J.M. (1994) Grounded theory methodology: an overview. *In* N.K. Denzin & Y.S. Lincoln, eds. *Handbook of qualitative research,* 273–85. Thousand Oaks, CA: Sage.

Tesch, R. (1990). *Qualitative research: analysis types and software tools.* New York: Falmer.

Tierney, W., Polkinghorne, D.E., Lincoln, Y.S., Denzin, N.K., Kincheloe, J., Lather, P. & Pinar, W. (1995, Apr.). *Representation and text: reframing the narrative voice.* Interactive symposium presented at the annual conference of the American Educational Research Association, San Francisco, CA.

U.S. Congress, Office of Technology Assessment (1988, Sep.). *Power on! New tools for teaching and learning* (OTA-SET-379). Washington, DC: U.S. Government Printing Office.

Van Maanen J. (1988). *Tales of the field: on writing ethnography.* Chicago, IL: University of Chicago Press.

Webb, E.J., Campbell, D.T., Schwartz, R.D. & Sechrest, L. (1966). *Unobtrusive measures: nonreactive research in the social sciences.* Chicago, IL: Rand McNally.

Webb, N.M. (1983). Predicting learning from student interaction: defining the interaction variable. *Educational Psychologist 18* (1), 33–41.

— (1991). Task-related verbal interaction and mathematics learning in small groups. *Journal of Research in Mathematics Education 22* (5), 366–89.

Weitzman, E.A. & Miles, M.B. (1995). *A software sourcebook: computer programs for qualitative data analysis.* Thousand Oaks, CA: Sage.

Weller, S.C. & Romney, A.K. (1988). *Systematic data collection.* Newbury Park, CA: Sage.

Wiegmann, B.A. (1996). *Utilizing technology: the effects of methods instruction on preservice teacher planning.* Unpublished doctoral dissertation, Northern Illinois University, DeKalb, IL.

Winn, W. (1989). Toward a rationale and theoretical basis for educational technology. *Educational Technology Research and Development 37* (1), 35–46.

Wolcott, H.F. (1994). *Transforming qualitative data.* Thousand Oaks, CA: Sage.

— (1990). *Writing up qualitative research.* Newbury Park, CA: Sage.

— (1973). *The man in the principal's office.* New York: Holt, Rinehart & Winston.

Wolf, B.A. (1994). *Effects of cooperative learning and learner control in computer-based instruction.* Unpublished doctoral dissertation, Arizona State University, Tempe, AZ.

Yeaman, A., Koetting, J. & Nichols, R. (1994). Special issue: the ethical position of educational technology in society. *Educational Technology 34* (2), 5–72.

Yin, R.K. (1989). *Case study research,* 2d ed. Beverly Hills, CA: Sage.

41. DESCRIPTIVE RESEARCH METHODOLOGIES

Nancy Nelson Knupfer
KANSAS STATE UNIVERSITY

Hilary McLellan
MCLELLAN WYATT DIGITAL

Descriptive statistics play an important role in educational research, and thus it is essential to understand the nature and function of such research. As researchers consider possible study designs, statistical analysis, and final reports about any particular topic, it is critical that they maintain focus on the questions to be answered by the research. Those questions will determine the appropriate approach to the investigation and its resulting methodology. The research questions will position the analysis into one of two areas: that which describes data according to a particular organization, and that which draws inferences about cause and effect.

The former, descriptive research, holds a valuable place within education, because in contrast to laboratory experiments, the human nature of educational research is critical to the result. Educational environments and experiences inherently contain many extraneous variables that cannot be controlled in a realistic situation, often call for careful observation of specific life situations, and can require the collection of data from a large number of people spread throughout a wide geographic region.

While writing this chapter, we discussed the topic of descriptive research with several people and discovered that some people were confused about the definition and purpose of descriptive research. As we discussed the possibilities of descriptive research and compared it to other types of research methodologies, we had to conclude that all research contains some degree of description, and thus the term itself could be confusing to the reader. The research discussions that one typically encounters are "quantitative" versus "qualitative" methodology, designs labeled "experimental," "quasi-experimental," "case study," and so on. It is rare to find a research methods class or even a chapter that focuses strictly on descriptive research. Indeed, the term is often given a paragraph or two of importance or ignored altogether. Yet a review of the leading journals related to the field of educational technology shows that descriptive research holds an important place in the study of human interaction and learning (see 39.1, 39.5.2.2, 40.1, 40.1.1, 42.1). Indeed, the descriptive component is critical to educational research,

because educational events cannot be reduced to a controlled laboratory environment. The types of questions generated in educational research, particularly with respect to the constructivist paradigm and social implications, require descriptions that help to explain the data and direct emergent prescriptions for educational events.

41.1 WHAT IS DESCRIPTIVE RESEARCH?

Descriptive research does not fit neatly into the definition of either quantitative or qualitative research methodologies, but instead it can utilize elements of both, often within the same study. The term *descriptive research* refers to the type of research question, design, and data analysis that will be applied to a given topic. Descriptive statistics tell what is, while inferential statistics try to determine cause and effect.

The type of question asked by the researcher will ultimately determine the type of approach necessary to complete an accurate assessment of the topic at hand. Descriptive studies, primarily concerned with finding out "what is," might be applied to investigate the following questions: Do teachers hold favorable attitudes toward using computers in schools? What kinds of activities that involve technology occur in sixth-grade classrooms and how frequently do they occur? What have been the reactions of school administrators to technological innovations in teaching the social sciences? How have high school computing courses changed over the last 10 years? How do the new multimediated textbooks compare to the print-based textbooks? How are decisions being made about using Channel One in schools, and for those schools that choose to use it, how is Channel One being implemented? What is the best way to provide access to computer equipment in schools? How should instructional designers improve software design to make the software more appealing to students? To what degree are special-education teachers well versed concerning assistive technology? Is there a relationship between experience with multimedia computers and problem-solving skills? How successful is a certain satellite-delivered Spanish course in terms of motivational value and academic achievement? Do teachers actually implement technology in the way they perceive? How many people use the AECT gopher server, and what do they use if for?

Descriptive research can be either quantitative or qualitative. It can involve collections of quantitative information that can be tabulated along a continuum in numerical form, such as scores on a test or the number of times a person chooses to use a certain feature of a multimedia program, or it can describe categories of information such as gender or patterns of interaction when using technology in a group situation. Descriptive research involves gathering data that describe events and then organizes, tabulates, depicts, and describes the data collection (Glass & Hopkins, 1984). It often uses visual aids such as graphs and charts to aid the reader in understanding the data distribution. Because the human mind cannot extract the full import of a large mass of raw data, descriptive statistics are very important in reducing the data to manageable form. When in-depth, narrative descriptions of small numbers of cases are involved, the research uses description as a tool to organize data into patterns that emerge during analysis. Those patterns aid the mind in comprehending a qualitative study and its implications.

Most quantitative research falls into two areas: studies that describe events and studies aimed at discovering inferences or causal relationships. Descriptive studies are aimed at finding out "what is," so observational and survey methods are frequently used to collect descriptive data (Borg & Gall, 1989). Studies of this type might describe the current state of multimedia usage in schools or patterns of activity resulting from group work at the computer. An example of this is Cochenour, Hakes, and Neal's (1994) study of trends in compressed video applications with education and the private sector.

Descriptive studies report summary data such as measures of central tendency including the mean, median, mode, deviance from the mean, variation, percentage, and correlation between variables. Survey research commonly includes that type of measurement, but often goes beyond the descriptive statistics in order to draw inferences. See, for example, Signer's (1991) survey of computer-assisted instruction and at-risk students, or Nolan, McKinnon, and Soler's (1992) research on achieving equitable access to school computers. Thick, rich descriptions of phenomena can also emerge from qualitative studies, case studies, observational studies, interviews, and portfolio assessments. Robinson's (1994) case study of a televised news program in classrooms and Lee's (1994) case study about identifying values concerning school restructuring are excellent examples of case studies.

Descriptive research is unique in the number of variables employed. Like other types of research, descriptive research can include multiple variables for analysis, yet unlike other methods, it requires only one variable (Borg & Gall, 1989). For example, a descriptive study might employ methods of analyzing correlations between multiple variables by using tests such as Pearson's Product Moment correlation, regression, or multiple regression analysis. Good examples of this are the Knupfer and Hayes (1994) study about the effects of the Channel One broadcast on knowledge of current events, Manaev's (1991) study about mass media effectiveness, McKenna's (1993) study of the relationship between attributes of a radio program and it's appeal to listeners, Orey and Nelson's (1994) examination of learner interactions with hypermedia environments, and Shapiro's (1991) study of memory and decision processes.

On the other hand, descriptive research might simply report the percentage summary on a single variable. Examples of this are the tally of reference citations in selected instructional design and technology journals by Anglin and Towers (1992); Barry's (1994) investigation of the controversy surrounding advertising and Channel One; Lu, Morlan, Lerchlorlarn, Lee, and Dike's (1993) investigation of the international utilization of media in education (1993); and Pettersson, Metallinos, Muffoletto, Shaw, and Takakuwa's (1993) analysis of the use of verbo-visual information in teaching geography in various countries.

Descriptive statistics utilize data collection and analysis techniques that yield reports concerning the measures of central tendency, variation, and correlation. The combination of its characteristic summary and correlational statistics, along with its focus on specific types of research questions, methods, and outcomes is what distinguishes descriptive research from other research types.

Three main purposes of research are to describe, explain, and validate findings. Description emerges following creative exploration, and serves to organize the findings in order to fit them with explanations, and then test or validate those explanations (Krathwohl, 1993). Many research studies call for the description of natural or man-made phenomena such as their form, structure, activity, change over time, relation to other phenomena, and so on. The description often illuminates knowledge that we might not otherwise notice or even encounter. Several important scientific discoveries as well as anthropological information about events outside of our common experiences have resulted from making such descriptions. For example, astronomers use their telescopes to develop descriptions of different parts of the universe, anthropologists describe life events of socially atypical situations or cultures uniquely different from our own, and educational researchers describe activities within classrooms concerning the implementation of technology. This process sometimes results in the discovery of stars and stellar events, new knowledge about value systems or practices of other cultures, or even the reality of classroom life as new technologies are implemented within schools.

Educational researchers might use observational, survey, and interview techniques to collect data about group dynamics during computer-based activities. These data could then be used to recommend specific strategies for implementing computers or improving teaching strategies. Two excellent studies concerning the role of collaborative groups were conducted by Webb (1982), and Rysavy and

Sales (1991). Noreen Webb's landmark study used descriptive research techniques to investigate collaborative groups as they worked within classrooms. Rysavy and Sales also apply a descriptive approach to study the role of group collaboration for working at computers. The Rysavy and Sales approach did not observe students in classrooms, but reported certain common findings that emerged through a literature search.

Descriptive studies have an important role in educational research. They have greatly increased our knowledge about what happens in schools. Some of the important books in education have reported studies of this type: *Life in Classrooms,* by Philip Jackson; *The Good High School,* by Sara Lawrence Lightfoot; *Teachers and Machines: The Classroom Use of Technology Since 1920,* by Larry Cuban; *A Place Called School,* by John Goodlad; *Visual Literacy: A Spectrum of Learning,* by D. M. Moore and Dwyer; *Computers in Education: Social, Political, and Historical Perspectives,* by Muffoletto and Knupfer; and *Contemporary Issues in American Distance Education,* by M. G. Moore.

Henry J. Becker's (1986) series of survey reports concerning the implementation of computers into schools across the United States as well as Nancy Nelson Knupfer's (1988) reports about teacher's opinions and patterns of computer usage also fit partially within the realm of descriptive research. Both studies describe categories of data and use statistical analysis to examine correlations between specific variables. Both also go beyond the bounds of descriptive research and conduct further statistical procedures appropriate to their research questions, thus enabling them to make further recommendations about implementing computing technology in ways to support grassroots change and equitable practices within the schools. Finally, Knupfer's study extended the analysis and conclusions in order to yield suggestions for instructional designers involved with educational computing.

41.1.1 The Nature of Descriptive Research

The descriptive function of research is heavily dependent on instrumentation for measurement and observation (Borg & Gall, 1989). Researchers may work for many years to perfect such instrumentation so that the resulting measurement will be accurate, reliable, and generalizable. Instruments such as the electron microscope, standardized tests for various purposes, the United States census, Michael Simonson's questionnaires about computer usage, and scores of thoroughly validated questionnaires are examples of some instruments that yield valuable descriptive data. Once the instruments are developed, they can be used to describe phenomena of interest to the researchers.

The intent of some descriptive research is to produce statistical information about aspects of education that interests policymakers and educators. The National Center for Education Statistics specializes in this kind of research. Many of its findings are published in an annual volume called *Digest of Educational Statistics.* The center also administers the National Assessment of Educational Progress (NAEP), which collects descriptive information about how well the nation's youth are doing in various subject areas. A typical NAEP publication is *The Reading Report Card,* which provides descriptive information about the reading achievement of junior high and high school students during the past 2 decades.

On a larger scale, the International Association for the Evaluation of Education Achievement (IEA) has done major descriptive studies comparing the academic achievement levels of students in many different nations, including the United States (Borg & Gall, 1989). Within the United States, huge amounts of information are being gathered continuously by the Office of Technology Assessment, which influences policy concerning technology in education. As a way of offering guidance about the potential of technologies for distance education, that office has published a book called *Linking for Learning: A New Course for Education,* which offers descriptions of distance education and its potential.

There has been an ongoing debate among researchers about the value of quantitative (see 40.1.2) versus qualitative research, and certain remarks have targeted descriptive research as being less pure than traditional experimental, quantitative designs. Rumors abound that young researchers must conduct quantitative research in order to get published in *Educational Technology Research and Development* and other prestigious journals in the field. One camp argues the benefits of a scientific approach to educational research, thus preferring the experimental, quantitative approach, while the other camp posits the need to recognize the unique human side of educational research questions and thus prefers to use qualitative research methodology. Because descriptive research spans both quantitative and qualitative methodologies, it brings the ability to describe events in greater or less depth as needed, to focus on various elements of different research techniques, and to engage quantitative statistics to organize information in meaningful ways. The citations within this chapter provide ample evidence that descriptive research can indeed be published in prestigious journals.

Descriptive studies can yield rich data that lead to important recommendations. For example, Galloway (1992) bases recommendations for teaching with computer analogies on descriptive data, and Wehrs (1992) draws reasonable conclusions about using expert systems to support academic advising. On the other hand, descriptive research can be misused by those who do not understand its purpose and limitations. For example, one cannot try to draw conclusions that show cause and effect, because that is beyond the bounds of the statistics employed.

Borg and Gall (1989) classify the outcomes of educational research into the four categories of description, prediction, improvement, and explanation. They say that descriptive research describes natural or man-made educational phenomena that is of interest to policymakers and educators. Predictions of educational phenomenon seek to determine whether certain students are at risk and if teachers should use different techniques to instruct them. Research about improvement asks whether a certain technique does something to help students learn better and whether certain interventions can improve student learning by applying causal-comparative, correlational, and experimental methods. The final category of explanation posits that research is able to explain a set of phenomena that leads to our ability to describe, predict, and control the phenomena with a high level of certainty and accuracy. This usually takes the form of theories.

The methods of collecting data for descriptive research can be employed singly or in various combinations, depending on the research questions at hand. Descriptive research often calls upon quasi-experimental research design (Campbell & Stanley, 1963). Some of the common data collection methods applied to questions within the realm of descriptive research include surveys, interviews, observations, and portfolios.

41.2 DESCRIPTIVE RESEARCH METHODOLOGY

41.2.1 Survey Methods

Although survey research can yield data that are compared and analyzed at a more complicated level, the simplest use to which survey data can be put is a description of how the total sample has distributed itself on the response alternatives for a single questionnaire item (see 6.6.1, 37.4). These are sometimes called *marginal tabulations.* For example, news media often report the result of public-opinion polls in terms of marginal tabulations: 50% of the sample were in favor of a particular governmental policy, 30% disagreed with it, and 20% were unsure or had no opinion. Survey research in education often yields this type of normative description.

As an illustration, we may consider a study by N. N. Knupfer (1994) that was designed to investigate the interest of junior high and high school students in viewing the Channel One news program. A Likert-type scale of 34 items plus open-ended questions, each describing an element of the televised news program, was administered to a sample of approximately 2,000 students randomly drawn from an eligible population of approximately 16,000 high school students in a Southwest school district. Students were asked to describe their level of agreement with the statements about the value of the Channel One program based on a five-point scale. In the data analysis, the mean score of the entire sample on each opinion item was determined. This form of data analysis provides an interesting description of students' interest in this form of educational programming and their opinion about its quality. We find, for instance, that the junior high students liked the program more than the high school students, even though Channel One was originally designed for the high school audience. This, of course, has implications for the future design of the program.

Descriptions of this type often provide important leads in identifying needed tactics and changes within the instructional design of such material. Also, we should note that since proper sampling procedures were employed, Knupfer was able to generalize these descriptive findings from the sample to the population from which they were drawn.

In addition to summary statistics, survey data may be used to explore relationships between two or more variables. Researchers who are aware of the possibilities of investigating relationships in the survey data will make a more substantial research contribution than researchers who limit their data analysis to single variable descriptions. Questionnaires may refer to past, present, or future phenomena, so they have a great deal of flexibility.

Because of the various data analysis techniques that can be applied to survey research, surveys cannot automatically be assumed to be strictly descriptive. Consider a study by Davidson and Ritchie (1994) as an example. Their survey collected information from students, teachers, and parents within a school, analyzed the data with descriptive methods, conducted *t* tests to look for significant differences between groups, and was labeled as a "case study" within the title of their publication.

Two critical components of survey research are sound methodology and well-designed data collection instruments. It is important that data collection instruments used for surveys ensure the ability to collect standardized information and do so in a way that will yield quantifiable results. The same instruments should be distributed to all subjects so that data can be summarized and compared. Although there are a variety of potential methods and instruments, questionnaires and individual interviews are the most common collection techniques used in survey research (Borg & Gall, 1989).

One also can conduct telephone interviews or examine records as part of the main data collection or as follow-up with nonrespondents to assess any differences between the respondent and nonrespondent groups. A common mistake that researchers make is to ignore the nonrespondents. Nonrespondents can indicate bias in the study results and need some follow-up analysis.

It is also important to determine if the variables are related to each other in terms of time-bound or time-ordered association. Time-bound association refers to the same point in time for all questions worded a certain way. Time-ordered association means that the items can be temporarily ordered relative to each other. For example, now ask respondents to tell how they feel about *X* and to recall how they felt about *Y.*

Surveys can use cross-sectional, longitudinal, or Delphi techniques (Borg & Gall, 1989). Cross-sectional surveys use simple random, stratified, or cluster sampling techniques. Longitudinal surveys are administered at different points of time in order to study changes or explore time-ordered associations. The Delphi technique employs questionnaires but is quite different from the typical questionnaire survey.

Common types of longitudinal studies include trend studies, cohort studies, and panel studies. Trend studies sample a given general population at each data collection point, and although the same individuals are not surveyed, the sample is drawn from the same population. Because the population is general, the specific individuals in it are constantly changing.

Cohort studies follow a specific population over a period of time. Like trend studies, different individuals are drawn from the same population at each data collection point. The difference is that the cohort group does not shift in the makeup of the population, so the sample is always drawn from the same pool of people. To illustrate this concept, envision the population as being fixed, such as the group of people who received the doctor of philosophy degree in educational technology in a specific year. The sample will always be drawn from that group of people.

Finally, panel studies involve the repeated surveying of the same individual subjects at the outset of the study and then again at each subsequent data-collection point. Since the study follows the same individuals, the researcher can note data about individual changes over time and explore possible reasons why the individuals have changed. Loss of participants in this type of study would be a serious problem (Borg & Gall, 1989).

The Delphi technique was developed by the RAND Corporation as a method of predicting future defense needs, but it can be modified to various situations wherever consensus is needed. It can be used to identify problems, define needs, establish priorities, and identify and evaluate solutions (Borg & Gall, 1989). Basically, the Delphi technique asks a set of questions, then revises that set of questions repeatedly, based on the responses to each step before it. Constant refining eventually whittles the information down to a key set of refined data.

Surveys can take several forms and data can be collected in many ways. Surveys can be in the form of written questionnaires, personal interviews, or telephone interviews. They can be distributed by mail (paper or electronic), in person, or electronically. Commercial sources often use electronic devices to help collect the data, but educational surveys tend to be the low-budget variety that lean toward inexpensive data collection techniques.

No matter what method is eventually used, there are certain major issues involved in choosing a data collection strategy. Some of these issues include sampling, type of population, question form, question content, response rates, costs, available facilities, length of data collection, and computer-assisted techniques for data collection. The type of data collection mode can vary with each situation, and the selection of a particular method is a complex process involving consideration of many aspects of the survey research process (Fowler, 1993).

Subjects are more likely to answer a survey if they can relate to it as being purposeful, if it is not time consuming, if it appears aesthetically pleasing and legible, and if it presents itself as an ethical piece of research. But even the most well-designed study and survey instrument will do no good unless the researcher has determined a way to obtain the best possi-

ble return rate. Although specific respondents should not be matched with their answers, the researcher will need a way to keep track of respondents and nonrespondents. Mailed surveys always require a second or third mailing to obtain a higher return rate. Keeping track of the respondents will save the trouble, expense, and waste associated with resending the survey to the entire sample group, not to mention the irritation it will cause and the possibility of tainted data if people were to send in two responses. The goal is to collect one response from each subject, not multiple responses from some of the subjects. Color coding survey instruments by groups can greatly aid organization and follow-up data collection, as can a good recording system for tracking survey returns.

41.2.2 Interviews

Face-to-face interviews and telephone interviews provide an opportunity to follow a line of questioning to obtain more in-depth information. Telephone interviews can be more time efficient, but face-to-face interviews would be appropriate for studies that need the feeling of personal contact, because they allow the researcher to establish rapport with the respondent. In general, interviews produce a better return rate than mailed questionnaires (Fowler, 1993).

To increase the reliability of data collected by interviews, it is important to follow certain guidelines and to train all interviewers to use the same techniques. The most effective interviews require that the researcher develop a guide to use during the interview process. The guide will help organize the information and is usually followed in order.

Personal-interview procedures can be advantageous because they promote the highest response rate and allow the researcher to respond to questions from the respondent, probe for adequate answers, follow complex instructions that might otherwise confuse the respondent, and provide longer interviews than those conducted by telephone. In addition, personal interviews offer the opportunity to use multiple methods of data collection such as observations and visual cues (Fowler, 1993). Disadvantages of personal interviews are that they require more staff time and travel, leading to more expense than telephone interviews and mailed questionnaires. In addition, certain populations are more difficult to reach due to physical factors.

Telephone interviews are potentially advantageous because they are less time consuming and less expensive. They can also employ random dialing to access a truly randomized sample. Disadvantages of telephone interviews include sampling limitations due to restrictions imposed by access to telephones, lack of ability to provide visual information, and lack of ability for the researcher to observe the participant.

41.2.3 Mailed Questionnaires

The major advantages of mailed questionnaires are that one can reach large numbers of people from wide geographic areas, the respondents have time to reflect on their answers or even check information prior to responding, and the relatively low cost of administration that results from the distribution method, as well as the need for only a small staff of people and minimal facilities (Fowler, 1993). The major disadvantages include the lower response rate and the need to take special care with designing questions that will be self-administered.

Although all surveys should contain some open-ended questions to allow for participant ideas to emerge, a significant number of respondents will not take the time to answer those questions with in-depth answers, and some respondents will not understand the instructions for completing the open-ended questions. Therefore, simple formats that allow users simply to check responses on the questionnaire work the best (Belson, 1981; J. Converse, 1987; Fowler, 1993). Brevity will be helpful there.

A letter of transmittal on letterhead stationery will be critical for mailed questionnaires. The content of the letter as well as its presentation will have an influence on the response rate. To provide a good visual presentation, make the letter look professional by its style and print quality. Be sure to include a postage-paid return envelope.

Within the body of the letter, it is important to state the purpose of the research, the importance of study, the importance of respondents, a reasonable but specific time limit, an assurance of confidentiality, and an offer to share results, as well as to thank the respondent. Concise wording should make it possible to keep this letter to one page. Special delivery options increase the look of importance but also can be detrimental in terms of attitude. Some people get annoyed with the packaging, so you need to make decisions about how it would likely be perceived by the respondents.

41.2.3.1. Designing Good Questions. Good surveys use questions that are interesting because of their relationship to what they are supposed to be measuring. Good questionnaires provide a script for the entire process that the researchers are to follow, word questions so that they mean the same thing to everyone, and inform participants about the kinds of answers that are appropriate. Questionnaires should provide definitions for any terminology that might be confusing; use complete sentences, and offer a limited set of answers. The expression "I don't know" should be used very carefully because it can encourage participants to mark it rather than think more deeply about the question (Fowler, 1993).

41.2.4 Observational Research Methods

Observational research has a long tradition across a large number of disciplines. Observational methods are concerned with naturally occurring behaviors observed in natural contexts or in contexts that are contrived to be realistic. Suen and Ary (1989) delineate two approaches to the direct observation of behavior: a quantitative approach that employs structured observation methods, and a qualitative approach that features unstructured observation. Unstructured observational methods are often used for pilot studies; the data collected yield categories shaped into instruments that are then employed for structured observation on a larger scale.

Observational research requires the systematic, direct observation of behavior. Many analysts consider it superior to other methods of data collection because the data are gathered directly without intermediary instruments such as tests or questionnaires. Since observation provides a direct approach, it requires very little conceptual inference to connect the data to the phenomenon under scrutiny (Suen & Ary, 1989). Further, if used properly, the observational method can overcome the limitations of the self-report method, for example, biased or selective reporting (Borg & Gall, 1989).

The systematic observation of behavior in educational and psychological research can yield a wealth of valuable information, but it is a complicated and labor-intensive process. The process of defining and developing coding schemes, then training observers to acceptable levels of agreement, can be time consuming (Bakeman & Gottman, 1986; Borg & Gall, 1989). The complexity of both the behavior and observation methods can lead to technical errors, such as miscoding, as well as problems in achieving and maintaining satisfactory interrater agreement (Borg & Gall, 1989). But structured observation offers a degree of certainty and replicability that unstructured narrative reports cannot achieve (Bakeman & Gottman, 1986). Both structured and unstructured observational methods can yield thick, rich descriptions that achieve the depth that other research methodologies lack.

This section deals primarily with structured observation research. However, unstructured observation, naturalistic contrived situations, situational testing, and portfolios will also be considered as topics in this section on observational research.

41.2.4.1. Purposes of Observational Research in Educational Technology. Observation methods can be employed productively to support many purposes in the area of educational communication and technology. Observation may be used to understand how people interact with technology in various stages of design and implementation. Observational data can help to improve the materials design as well as their utilization within particular settings. For example, observation can be used in both formative evaluation and summative evaluation of educational software. Questions answered might be: How do learners respond to and interact with a specific program? How do learners interact with a new hardware system? Observational research can help to determine if one has a technology that works. Observation makes it possible both to explore the implementation of a particular technological innovation and assess the instructional outcomes.

Flagg (1990) reports that observation is especially useful with children, because they frequently produce verbal and nonverbal behaviors from which one infers their comprehension of media program segments. Many analysts (Amarel, 1982; Chen, 1985; Dickson, 1985; Fraser & Burkhardt, 1984; McLellan, 1991; McLellan, 1994; Sheingold, Kane & Endreweit, 1983; Webb, 1982; Webb, Ender & Lewis, 1986) have suggested that the social interactions that emerge in a computer-learning environment are a fundamental aspect of the computer-mediated experience for students and teachers. Thus an understanding of the characteristics of social interaction is vital to understanding the educational significance of any implementation of computers in the schools.

41.2.4.2. Types of Observational Research

41.2.4.2.1. Structured Observations. Structured observation can be defined as a particular approach to quantifying behavior. Two fundamental components of observational research include the use of predefined, behavior-code catalogs and reliable observers. Because human observers are so important to the instrumentation, reliability issues loom especially large in observational research (Bakeman & Gottman, 1986).

In contrast to informal observations, structured observations are systematic and controlled. Many parameters must be rigidly prescribed and followed, including what, when, where, and how to observe, as well as the methods for recording and analyzing the data. Investigators must articulate beforehand what they hope to find out, what seems important conceptually, and specify accurate, reliable ways to measure those concepts (Suen & Ary, 1989). A hypothesis that tentatively describes the relationships among the variables is also established before the actual observation is carried out. The process of observation is rigidly controlled, and the nature of the data gathered is well defined so that data quality can be assessed by interobserver comparisons, and quantitative data analysis can be employed. The analysis of structured, observational data may examine frequency, duration, and interrelationships between events in an attempt to identify meaningful patterns that are reported with descriptive statistics.

Thus, complex phenomenon, such as human interaction with technology, is first conceptually reduced to a number of measurable and observable behavioral variables. These variables are fine tuned and defined, often through unstructured observation and review of videotaped recordings. A system for measuring these variables is determined before the actual observation is implemented. Structured observation codes define specifically, before observation begins, the behaviors and situations thought to be relevant to the focus and purpose of the study (Flagg, 1990). Other behaviors are inferential, requiring some conclusions on the part of the observer. For example, from verbal or nonverbal behavior the observer infers why someone initiates the use of a technology system.

The structured observation record usually includes frequency counts of how often specific behaviors occur and the duration or interval involved (Flagg, 1990). The data can provide a quantitative description or explanation of the phenomenon (Suen & Ary, 1989; Flagg, 1990). It may be possible to gather observational data "live," during ongoing events as they unfold, or it may be possible to videotape events for later observation and analysis. In some instances,

observations are made through a one-way mirror so that the subjects of the study are not aware of the observation. Statistical analyses are performed on these quantitative observational data to determine whether evidence of the hypothesized relationships indeed exist.

Observational research is susceptible to several common mistakes that the researcher must take into consideration and work to avoid. These mistakes include insufficient training of observers, use of a complex observation form that requires too much from the observer or requires observers to make excessively precise discriminations among behaviors, failure to take adequate precautions to avoid having observers disturb or change the situation they are to observe, failure to use at least two observers in order to determine interrater reliability, failure to ensure that observers work independently of each other, contamination of data collection, failure to use random sampling techniques when appropriate, and lack of tight controls that help prevent observer drift and reliability decay (Bakeman & Gottman, 1986).

41.2.4.2.2. Unstructured Observations. The purpose of unstructured observation is to furnish an unselective, detailed, continuous description of behavior (Flagg, 1990). In unstructured observation, the evaluator records all of the user's activities, and if the user is interacting with a media program, the program status is continually recorded. Thus, the observation is continuous and unselective while it is ongoing. This technique may be valuable in a preliminary study to determine observational categories for subsequent structured observation. Or it may be useful for the formative evaluation of media programs, studying the actual interaction between the user and the program content and the machine (interfaces, screen, etc.).

Flagg (1990) emphasizes that unintended effects of a media system are best detected through unstructured observation. Related to this, Norman (1991) claims the best kind of task analysis is in the field. You have to learn how to watch people. It can help to bring in a trained observer, an anthropologist, psychologist, or sociologist who knows about the people who are under study, can make videotapes of typical interactions of people with technology, and show you how computers are used in the environment for which your design is destined. Studying people as they perform familiar, well-understood tasks can provide valuable insights about possible ways to represent tasks on the computer, providing a valuable resource for the design of future media as well as formative evaluation of new designs that are in development (Mountfort, 1991).

Unstructured observation offers several advantages in evaluating user friendliness issues. For example, the frequency of use of functions and the length of time the system is used can be calculated from an unstructured observation record, just as from structured observation. Furthermore, the unstructured record adds a richness to the evaluation that is missing from the structured approach. Unstructured observation can be continuous, or it can be structured around time sampling for example, recording observations once every 5 minutes for 1 minute, or by sampling only when certain events occur, for example, whenever the help mode in a program is accessed (Flagg, 1990).

Flagg (1990) reports that eventually, for analysis and interpretation, the unstructured observation record is coded in categories and tallied in a manner similar to the structured observation. At the same time, the rich qualitative observations are still available to whatever happens, including unexpected interactions or sources of confusion that are extremely valuable to document. Consequently, the categories resulting from this method might be different from those defined a priori in the structured observation schedule. It is possible to go back into an unstructured narrative to study questions that might not have occurred to the evaluators earlier.

According to Flagg (1990), the main disadvantage of unstructured observation for formative evaluation is the time and labor required to collect and analyze sets of extensive observations. And training is needed so that observers are recording similar data in an unbiased manner. Since it is time intensive, unstructured observations on a small sample are sometimes used to define the behaviors for a larger-scale, structured-observation study.

41.2.4.3. Considerations within Observation

41.2.4.3.1. Types of Observational Variables. Three types of observational variables may be distinguished: descriptive, inferential, and evaluative. Borg and Gall (1989) report that descriptive variables have the advantage that they require little inference on the part of the observer, so that they generally yield reliable data. Descriptive variables are considered to be "low inference" variables.

Other observational variables call upon the observer to make an inference before a variable can be scored. As Borg and Gall (1989) explain:

Observers may be asked to record the self-confidence with which a teacher explains a mathematical concept. Some teachers may speak with a good deal of confidence, whereas others may appear uncertain, confused, or anxious because their understanding of the topic is weak. Confidence, uncertainty, confusion, and anxiety are not behaviors but rather are inferences made from behavior. These are often referred to as "high inference variables." It is much more difficult to collect reliable data when observers are asked to make inferences from behavior (p. 493).

Finally, with the third type of observational variable, the observer must make an evaluative judgment. The researcher may be interested in evaluating the quality of the teacher's explanation of a mathematical concept. Quality ratings are not behavior but rather are inferences made from behavior. Because it is difficult to make reliable observations of evaluative variables, we need to collect examples of behavior that define points along the continuum of excellent-to-poor explanations and use these in training the observers (Borg & Gall, 1989).

In the progression from low inference to high inference to evaluative variables, the observers' task becomes more complex (Borg & Gall, 1989). Any changes in the observa-

tional task that make it more complex tends to lower observer reliability or agreement (Reid, 1987). Reid has devised some methods for estimating the complexity of the variables to be observed.

To ensure accurate recording, require observers to score only one behavior at a given point in time. For example, most observers would find it quite difficult to record certain aspects of the teacher's talk and at the same time record the percentage of children who appear to be paying attention to the teacher. Concomitantly, the reliability of both sets of observations would probably be low, although in order to understand complex interactions, including the duration of events that start and stop in overlap, it may be desirable to monitor more than one event simultaneously. Thus mediated observations such as video records or a computer-based coding system such as PLEXYN, which automates the observations as much as possible through a carefully designed coding system, may be extremely valuable.

41.2.4.3.2. The Observation Form. Once the observational variables to be used in the research study are identified, you need to develop a form on which they can be recorded. A paper-and-pencil observational form is one option that can accommodate a variety of scoring procedures. This form of scoring can be designed so as to require a minimum of effort on the part of the observer and can usually be developed so as to require the observer to make a few inferences. However, it is also possible to develop media-based observation forms where data are entered with a hand-held device or a computer keyboard.

With some more complex observation forms, the observer must record not only the behavior as it occurs but also evaluate the behavior on a rating scale. This scoring procedure requires a higher level of inference on the part of the observer (Borg & Gall, 1989). The observer must not only record the behavior but must also evaluate it, and this is much more difficult to do objectively. If you use a rating scale as part of your scoring procedure, you should avoid the common mistake of attempting to obtain excessively precise discrimination from the observer. Most human behavior studied in educational research cannot be reliably rated on more than five levels. The 3-point rating scale, breaking the behavior observed into such categories as "above-average," "average," and "below-average," is often as fine a discrimination as can be made with satisfactory reliability. Five-point rating scales, however, are often used in educational research and can be employed effectively in observing well-defined behavior. It is almost never advisable to attempt to obtain ratings for finer than the 5-point scale. Furthermore, the more inference the observer must use in making the rating, the fewer ratings levels should be employed (Borg & Gall, 1989).

41.2.4.3.3. Mediated Observation Techniques. Traditionally, paper and pencil have been used to record observational data. However, newer mediated observation techniques are available to support data recording and analysis. Behaviors can be recorded on audio and videotape so that observations can be made from these records rather than, or in addition to, the "live" event. Computers and related hand-held devices can be used as tools to facilitate and improve data gathering by human observers either during the "live" event or during a review of an audio- or videotape recording (Borg & Gall, 1989; Stephenson, 1979, 1983; Fraser & Burkhart, 1984; McLellan, 1991; McLellan, 1994). Observational codes can be entered directly via keyboard or other input, making later analysis easier and more efficient.

Computers offer the advantage of on-line monitoring. On-line monitoring is the process of capturing characteristics of the human-computer interaction automatically, in real time, from an operating system (Borgman, 1986). *Keystroke records, audit trails,* and *logging data* are other terms used to describe on-line monitoring. Computers can directly record and store information about a user's interactions with a program, including both transactional (keystroke, screen viewed, etc.) and temporal (duration) features of the interactions (Neal & Simons, 1984; Chen, Liberman & Paisley, 1985; Hawkins, Bosworth, Chewning, Day & Gustafson, 1985; Hasselbring, 1992).

With virtual-reality technology, position-tracking devices make it possible to record human performance precisely and in great detail. These data can be used to provide performance replays as well as performance reports and data graphing. For example, a baseball pitch or a golf swing can be recorded electronically with position-monitoring devices linked to a computer (McLellan, 1994). Sophisticated simulators can electronically "replay" a learner's performance based on the learner's precise movements and interactions with simulator controls.

Video- or audiotaping the target behavior has several advantages. These technologies are relatively unobtrusive, and their use can decrease the number of observers necessary, thereby increasing observational reliability (Flagg, 1990). Furthermore, when recorders are used, observers no longer need to make ratings at the time particular events are occurring. These events may be recorded on audiotape or videotape so that they can be replayed several times for careful study or for several observers to rate at their convenience.

Another advantage of recording observations is that the recordings permit you to obtain data on behavior that you did not anticipate you would need at the outset of your study (Borg & Gall, 1989; Flagg, 1990). Recording devices can provide a permanent record for alternate analyses. And recording devices can be used to collect samples of behavior to facilitate the development of an observation form and to provide the basis for training observers. The recordings can be replayed repeatedly, thus making it easier to develop observational categories and to test the reliability with which observers can use these categories in rating behavior (Borg & Gall, 1989). In formative evaluation studies, the recordings can play an additional role by showing user reactions directly to the production staff that must revise the product (Flagg, 1990).

The cost and availability of audio, video, and computer recording equipment is a vital consideration. Each type of media is limited in terms of what it captures. The audiotape

records only verbal comments, with no contextual information. The videotape has a restricted field of view. And on-line monitoring by the computer results in a record of user activities only as they impact on the machine itself. To increase the completeness of the observational data, these methods can be used together or in conjunction with a human observer (Flagg, 1990). In certain situations, technical problems or complexities may pose serious problems. For example, it may be necessary to have several microphones and to adjust the camera frequently so that a reasonably complete record of classroom behavior can be obtained (Borg & Gall, 1989). Technical competence may be required in order to obtain satisfactory audio and video recording.

In some situations it is humanly impractical to collect all of the desired observational data at the same time, so that supplemental data gathering via technology may be all the more helpful in meeting research goals. For example, if several of the behaviors to be rated occur at the same time or closely together, or if more than one person's behavior is monitored, media records may help to capture the data more fully. Media-based recordings offer another advantage in assessing the interrater reliability of observational data; observers can rate the same sample of behavior recorded on videotape (Borg & Gall, 1989).

For interactive media, keystroke records furnish an objective way to observe the learning process. One can pinpoint comprehension difficulties by analyzing what segments of the program were accessed in what sequence, by reviewing right and wrong answers in task and test situations, and by examining error messages and help requests. Keystroke records identify what pathways to revise or eliminate and what new branches to add (Flagg, 1990).

In addition to collecting and examining data recorded directly by the computer, computer tools have been devised to alleviate some of the technical problems of research observation. Borg and Gall (1989) and other analysts report that microcomputers, handheld recording devices, and even handheld calculators have all been used as tools in observational data collection. Possible-event recorders appropriate for behavioral observation have been identified by, among others, Celhoffer, Boukydis, Minde, and Muir (1977); Crossman, Williams, and Chambers (1978); Fernald and Heinecke (1974); Gass (1977); Repp et al. (1985); Sackett, Stephenson, and Ruppenthal (1973); Sanson-Fisher, Poole, Small, and Fleming (1979); Stephenson and Roberts (1977); Stephenson (1979); and Torgerson (1977). With real-time observations of more complicated designs (e.g., multiple subject or multiple behavior), some type of electronic aid such as an electronic real-time event recorder may have to be used.

These tools make it possible to increase both the amount and the complexity of data that a human observer can collect. One example is PLEXYN (Stephenson, 1979, 1983), an event-recording system that encodes the incidence, duration, coincidence, and sequence of human observation entries in real time for subsequent high-speed transcription by computer. The PLEXYN system includes statistical analysis programs for analyzing the data once the observations have been recorded and reviewed for errors. And it includes programs that make it possible to edit and correct the data transcript and combine files (for example, where video recordings make it possible to record data for the same event more than once). PLEXYN has been applied to a wide array of research problems, including the interactions of student partners in a computer lab (McLellan, 1991; McLellan, 1994).

Berger, Shermis, and Stemmer (1992) list several ways that microcomputers can be used to support observational research. These include recording and timing the events being observed, transcribing the data onto coding sheets, transferring the data from the coding sheets into computer storage ready for data analysis, cleaning up the data by locating coding errors, aggregating and analyzing the data, and interpreting the results of data analysis. Microcomputers have the capacity to produce a variety of graphic data representations, which can greatly help the researcher in understanding his results. Often the cost of doing this activity on a large computer is prohibitive.

41.2.4.3.4. Coding Schemes. A critical component of structured observational research is the catalog of behavior codes identifying the behaviors that will be the basis for data gathering. In fact, Bakeman and Gottman (1986) suggest that the coding scheme is the most important component of observational research. The coding catalog is the measuring instrument of observational research, specifying which behavior is to be selected from the passing stream of activity and recorded for subsequent study.

Developing a coding scheme can be time consuming, involving extensive preparation and fine tuning. Many analysts (Bakeman & Gottman, 1986; Flagg, 1990; Suen & Ary, 1989) recommend that a good starting point for developing a coding scheme is to conduct extensive preparatory unstructured observation, either "live" or using videotapes that can be reviewed many times. As successively refined versions of the coding scheme are developed, they should be extensively reviewed, critiqued, and finally validated by other appropriate experts.

In addition to selecting a coding scheme, the researcher must select a recording procedure. Most recording procedures can be classified into four major categories, including frequency-count recording, duration recording, interval recording, and continuous recording (Bakeman & Gottman, 1986). Before selecting a particular recording strategy, the researcher must determine the units and types of measures that should be used.

Frequency count refers to the number of times a behavioral event occurs. Here, observers wait for an event of interest to occur, and when such an event occurs, it is recorded. *Duration events* can be conceptualized as "behavioral states" or the specific length of time during which a behavioral state continues to take place. The onset and offset times for the event are recorded, as well as the type of event under observation. Interval recording is similar to this, but instead of recording specific time duration, codes are assigned for successive time intervals during which behavioral events transpire. Continuous recording can refer to the use of some type of automated event recorder or to human recorders who are continuously alert, paying attention, ready to record whenever a behavioral state changes, or whenever a specific time interval elapses (Bakeman & Gottman, 1986, p. 50).

Is it better to code events, intervals, or durations? That depends on several factors, including the kind and complexity of the coding scheme, the desired accuracy, and the kind of recording equipment available (Bakeman & Gottman, 1986). Sometimes investigators are concerned only with how often certain events occur, or in what order they occur, and are not much concerned with how long they last. At other times, there is a fundamental concern with duration or the mean amount of time a particular kind of event lasts or the proportion of time devoted to a particular kind of event. A common procedure used in observations of group interaction is to record the frequency of a certain behavior (e.g., helping) in a group without tying this information to specific group members.

Information at the group level has limited utility, however, for predicting and understanding the impact of the group experience on the achievement of individual members. For example, a high frequency of helping in a group may not be beneficial for the achievement of all group members if explanations are not directed to those who need it most. Furthermore, even a high correlation between the frequency of helping behavior in a group and achievement sheds no light on the effects of giving help separate from those of receiving help (Suen & Ary, 1989).

41.2.4.3.5. Observational Schedules. Many standard observational schedules that have been developed by researchers in education and other fields are available. Instead of developing a new observational schedule for a research project, it may be possible that one of these existing schedules will fit the project at hand (Bakeman & Gottman, 1986; Borg & Gall, 1989; Suen & Ary, 1989).

The standard observational schedules that have been developed vary in complexity, the type of behavior they record, and the setting in which they can be used. They offer several advantages. First, as is true of standardized personality and aptitude tests, standard observational schedules have usually reached a stage of development where they are valid and reliable measuring instruments. Second, use of a standard schedule saves the considerable amount of time that it takes to develop and validate a new schedule. Third, because most of these standard schedules have been used in a number of research studies, you can compare your findings with those obtained by other researchers using the same instrument.

But the standard schedules may not include all the variables that you are interested in measuring. In this case, it is possible to use only the part of the schedule that is needed, keeping in mind that previously reported reliability and validity data will not apply if only part of the instrument is used.

The book *Mirrors for Behavior and Evaluating Classroom Instruction* by Simon and Boyer (1974) provides an extensive inventory of older classroom observation forms.

The references are now 20 years old, but many of the instruments described are still in use. The Educational Testing Service (ETS) offers a test collection bibliography entitled *Systematic Observation Techniques*. This is a valuable resource for locating observation schedules, since it is updated frequently. Many of the observation forms listed in the ETS bibliography are experimental forms developed for use in a specific research project; however, many of the instruments listed have been carefully developed and are comparable to standard observational schedules (Borg & Gall, 1989).

41.2.4.3.6. Selecting and Training Observers. Selecting and training observers is critically important since careless or unmotivated observers can destroy the most carefully planned study. The observers who produce the most reliable data tend to be persons of above-average intelligence and verbal fluency who are highly motivated to do a good job (Borg & Gall, 1989; Hartman, 1982).

Observer training should begin with a thorough understanding of what is to be observed and how it is to be recorded, including the observation categories and their definitions, as well as the form that data gathering will take (paper and pencil, recording device, etc.). The observer trainees should become very familiar with the observation coding form and behavior definitions before moving to the next level of training. After the initial training, observers can practice data recording with videotape recordings of situations similar to those to be observed in the study. Practice observations on site, in which all observer trainees participate, are also highly recommended (Borg & Gall, 1989).

During the practice sessions, watch the trainees to determine if there are still deficiencies in the observation form or the instructions for implementing the observations, in case further fine tuning is warranted. Borg and Gall (1989) report that common problems at this stage include: (1) requiring the observer to record too many behaviors, (2) including behaviors on the form that cannot be reliably identified by the observers, even after extensive training, and (3) poor format that slows down recording or causes observer errors or omissions. Sometimes the observation form will include two behaviors that are quite similar. Thus, when borderline cases occur, the observers have difficulty deciding which behavior to record. This problem can be resolved in several ways. The two behaviors can be combined into one redefined behavior, or, if it is essential to get data separately on the two behaviors, a rule can be established to resolve borderline cases. Such cases can be placed in a "can't decide" category, or can be assigned to the two categories alternately, or can be assigned to the two categories randomly by flipping a coin (Borg & Gall, 1989, p. 488).

Different videotape segments should be used for practice observations until the observer trainees reach the desired level of agreement. Borg and Gall (1989, p. 489) recommend that:

For tallying highly specific descriptive behavior, such as counting the number of times the teacher smiles, the percentage of agreement between observers should be above 90%. When the observer must make inferences or evaluations about the behavior being observed, however, 70 to 90% agreement is usually considered satisfactory.

If observational data gathering is to extend for more than 1 week, observers should be checked frequently, and a weekly refresher training session should be held for the observers to maintain the reliability of the observations (Borg & Gall, 1989; Taplin & Reid, 1973). Otherwise, observers will gradually lose the common frame of reference they developed during training. This "observer drift" can be a major source of error in observational studies. Research has determined that observers sometimes lose their objectivity, the proper frame of reference, in their use of observational schedules. This must be guarded against since the resulting research data will reflect the biases and characteristics of the observer rather than the observational variables that the research seeks to measure (Borg & Gall, 1989).

41.2.4.3.7. Reliability and Validity. In earlier years, observational researchers assumed that direct observation of behavior was by definition bias-free and valid (Cone, 1978). At that time, conventional psychometric issues such as reliability and validity were regarded as irrelevant. However, it is now understood that reliability and validity are as significant for observational recording as for any other data-gathering measure (Suen & Ary, 1989). *Reliability* refers to the dependability, consistency, predictability, and stability of the data. *Validity* refers to the ability of the data to reflect the underlying attribute of interest. The fact that the observer is more often a human being rather than a mechanical device highlights the importance of recording reliability (Flagg, 1990).

Suen and Ary (1989) report that in literature concerning psychometrics of behavioral observation, much time and space has been devoted to the issue of reliability, whereas validity has not received much attention. Part of this neglect can be attributed to the widespread belief that observational data are inherently valid because of the minimal amount of inferences required on the part of the observers. This belief is justified for some behaviors but not for others, depending on the degree of complexity (Suen & Ary, 1989).

41.2.4.3.8. Validation of the Coding Scheme. The use of predefined catalogs of behavior is a central feature of structured observational research. Coding systems reduce the task of an observer either to assigning the behavioral occurrences to categories or to assigning a numerical value to each behavioral occurrence (Suen & Ary, 1989). The behavioral category codes are measuring instruments that must be validated to ensure that these categories do indeed represent the phenomenon of interest.

Validity can be improved by fine tuning behavioral categories based on unstructured (and increasingly structured) observation within the study setting and by review of videotaped recordings of sample behavior streams. Validity is further enhanced if this process of identifying and fine tuning behavioral categories is carried out by more than one researcher trained in observational methods.

As the categories are fine tuned and ultimately selected, they should be reviewed and approved by outside experts.

Each category should be defined briefly and precisely so that there is no possible confusion. The ultimate approach to validating an observational catalog is repeated testing. Standard observational schedules have usually reached a stage of development where they have been extensively validated.

In educational communication and technology, as well as in other fields, observational methods may be applied to unique or innovative settings and purposes that offer less opportunity for extensive validation. For example, classroom research focusing on student interactions with computers is less than 15 years old; few catalogs of behavior have as yet been devised specifically for this area (Amarel, 1982; Chen, 1985; Dickson, 1985; Fraser & Burkhardt, 1984; McLellan, 1991; Sheingold, Kane & Endreweit, 1983; Webb, 1982; Webb, Ender & Lewis, 1986).

Another specialized application is the formative evaluation of a specific media program. A catalog of behaviors must be developed and validated specifically for that purpose, where users are observed interacting with the media program or a prototype. In sum, adequate validation can be obtained with careful fine tuning and repeated review of categories by qualified experts. The ideal would be to validate thoroughly a catalog of behaviors through rigorous testing, but this is extremely time consuming, often prohibitively so. Suen and Ary (1989) advise that validity can never be proved, and it cannot be described quantitatively; it is only possible to accumulate evidence in support of the validity of data obtained through a specific observation system.

Traditionally, observation codes were fairly simple and were based on readily observable and identifiable behaviors so that validation was fairly easy. But in recent years, the goals of observational research have often become much more complex, in tandem with sophisticated recording devices that make it possible to gather more observational data. A trend has emerged that threatens effective validation of observation codes. Increasingly, more than one behavior is observed in a study within a sophisticated scheme. In other situations, certain behaviors are observed to reflect an abstract variable or construct. For example, the occurrences and nonoccurrences of eye contact, appropriate speech, and so on may be observed to assess a subject's social skills. The earlier direct connection between the observed behavior and the object of inquiry no longer exists.

This trend toward greater complexity suggests that research should be directed toward improving observational techniques to meet emerging research needs. Research methods will need to be adapted to meet the growing awareness of the complexity of human behavior and interactions. Already there has been a shift in focus from observing individuals to observing groups. For example, instead of observing only teacher behavior, researchers attempt to observe both teacher and student behavior in coordination (Amarel, 1982; Peterson & Janicki, 1979; Peterson, Wilkinson & Hallinan, 1984; Peterson, Wilkinson, Spinelli & Swing, 1984; Webb, 1982; Webb, 1983; Webb, Ender & Lewis, 1986). Mediated observation techniques can help in this effort.

41.2.4.3.9. Interobserver and Intraobserver Agreement and Reliability. Human observers require a much greater concern for recording reliability than do mechanical recording devices. Human observers may have biasing expectations, and their recording methods may change over time due to fatigue or practice. Observer training is critically important; it may be necessary for ongoing training to maintain consistency over time on the part of individual observers.

Observational research calls for an assessment of both interobserver and intraobserver reliability. *Interobserver reliability* refers to data gathered by two or more observers, while *intraobserver reliability* refers to data gathered by the same observer on different occasions. The simplistic definition of reliability is the classical theory, as data consistency is inherently incapable of accommodating the idea that there can be more than one reliability estimate. The classical theory is incapable of accommodating the idea that for a given set of data there can be more than one reliability coefficient, since it assumes that a score contains only a true score component and a random error component and that reliability is the proportion of true variance relative to the sum of true and random error variances . Since two types of reliability are of concern in observational research, the generalizability approach to reliability is utilized in place of classical theory (Suen & Ary, 1989).

The generalizability approach, introduced by Cronbach, Gleser, Nanda, and Rajartnam (1972), is designed to accommodate the coexistence of more than one reliability estimate, making it possible to come to terms with the multifaceted nature of reliability. The generalizability theory has been praised as a powerful new psychometric tool by many analysts (Berk, 1979; Brennan, 1983; Brennan, 1984; Bakeman & Gottman, 1986; Hartmann, 1982; Mitchell, 1979; Suen & Ary, 1989). One advantage of this approach is that it makes it possible to identify sources of error so that an investigator can take steps to improve data (Hartmann, 1982).

The generalizability theory departs from conventions in two respects: (1) Statistically, it approaches the task of estimating reliabilities through an alternative technique known as the *intraclass correlation*; and (2) conceptually, it systematically defines for each reliability assessment situation its unique frame of reference. It is unique in its fundamental idea of reliability and error. Within the generalizability framework, reliability is not an absolute concept. Rather, depending on the question asked, it is relative to a certain context with a specific set of dimensions (e.g., time, observer, environment, instrumentation, etc.). When a set of observational data is said to be reliable, it implies that the results can be expected to be consistent over a variety of conditions (Suen & Ary, 1989).

In the classical theory, the context for reliability is undefined. But by contrast, within the generalizability theory, reliability is not an absolute concept without a context. Thus, whether or not a set of scores are reliable depends on what question is being asked.

A third group of techniques has been suggested as a superior approach to reliability (Suen & Ary, 1989). This set of techniques is known alternatively as *observer accuracy, criterion-referenced agreement,* and *transduction accuracy.* At this time, however, there is no clear consensus as to exactly what is being determined by these techniques.

41.2.4.3.10. Reducing Observer Effect. Another problem involved in conducting observational research is the degree to which the presence of the observer changes the situation being observed. In some cases, it may be possible to disguise the observer's role in order to direct less attention to the presence of a researcher. Any changes in the observational situation that will make the observation less obtrusive so that it appears to be more a part of the regular classroom situation will reduce reactivity (Borg & Gall, 1989). Observer effects can include the following:

1. Effect of observer on the observed: Person(s) observed change their behavior because they are aware of the observation.
2. Effect of the observer on the setting: Presence of the observer may lead to anxieties or expectations that change the climate of the observed situation.
3. Observer personal bias: Systematic errors are traceable to characteristics of the observer or the observational situation.
4. Error of leniency: When using a rating scale, observer tends to make most ratings at the favorable end of the scale.
5. Error of central tendency: When using a rating scale, observer tends to make most ratings around the midpoint.
6. Halo effect: Observer's initial impression distorts later evaluations or judgments of the subject.
7. Observer omissions: Because the observation system includes variables that occur very rapidly or simultaneously, the observer overlooks some behavior that should be recorded.
8. Observer drift: The tendency for observers to redefine gradually the observational variables, so that the data collected do not reflect the original categories.
9. Reliability decay: Toward the end of training, observer reliability is high, but in the field, as monitoring and motivation decrease, observers become less reliable.
10. Contamination: The observer's knowledge of one aspect of a study influences his or her perception of events observed in another part of the study. Observer expectations are a common form of contamination (Everton & Green, 1986; Borg & Gall, 1989).

Some analysts recommend that the following precautions should be taken as appropriate to minimize these observer effects and errors (Borg & Gall, 1989; Kazdin, 1977; Rosenthal, 1978; Suen & Ary, 1989):

1. Structure the observational situation so that the observer is as unobtrusive as possible.
2. Explain the common rating errors to the observers, and structure the observation schedule to minimize these errors.

3. Be sure the observation schedule does not require the observer to record more data or record at a higher rate than can be done accurately.
4. Make the observational task as objective as possible. Avoid requiring the observer to make evaluations, interpretations, or high-level inferences.
5. Give the observer as little information as possible about your hypotheses, research design, and expectations.
6. Do not reveal to the observer information about the characteristics of your subjects—such as social class, IQ, or composition of experimental and control groups—that the observer need not know.
7. Train observers to a high level of reliability and objectivity, and retrain as necessary to avoid observer drift.
8. Monitor observers on a random basis to minimize reliability decay.
9. Construct your observation form to minimize recording errors.
10. Check for bias when training observers, and eliminate those who submit biased observations.

41.2.4.4. Naturalistic Contrived Situations. In the naturalistic contrived approach, the researcher intervenes in a natural situation in a manner that cannot be detected by the subject; thus, the naturalness of the situation is preserved (Flagg, 1990). Manipulating the situation helps to ensure that the events of interest will occur. For example, by using pupil confederates, contrived situations can be set up to collect the necessary data in a reasonably short time. Naturalistic observations can require many hours of observation to record a short, 2-minute event. For example, suppose you want to observe teachers' responses to deviant student behavior such as cheating, fighting, or abusing computer equipment. Since these behaviors occur at a very low frequency in most classrooms, a great deal of observer time would be needed to gather data on a reasonable sample of such behavior.

There is another advantage of establishing contrived situations to be observed: The level of intensity of the situation can be manipulated. Thus, behavior can be observed at several specific and clearly defined levels of intensity. These variations in intensity are fairly easy to achieve in contrived situations, but in many cases they are virtually impossible to observe in natural situations (Flagg, 1990).

Borg and Gall (1989, p. 507) report that there are two serious limitations to observing in contrived situations:

> First, in many cases believable situations cannot be contrived without arousing the suspicion of the subjects. Second, difficult ethical problems may arise because of the deception involved. When one or both of these problems rule out the use of naturalistic contrived observation, a similar technique, situational testing, can be employed.

41.2.4.5. Situational Testing. Situational testing is another form of contrived observation. In this case, the subjects are aware that they are playing a role (Flagg, 1990). The researcher "devises a situation and assigns appropriate roles to the subjects, who are asked to play the roles to the best of their ability." Typically, all participants except the person being tested have been trained to play their roles. The roles create a situation toward which the person being tested must respond. For example, the person might make a decision or try to resolve a conflict. The situations are aimed at teasing out the specific types of behavior that the researcher is interested in observing (Flagg, 1990).

Like other forms of contrived observation, situational testing has advantages over the observation of behavior in natural settings (Flagg, 1990). By setting up the situation, you can control the behavior that is likely to occur to a greater degree than is usually possible in the naturalistic, contrived situation. This permits you to focus the observation on behavior that appears to be critical in the area being studied. In order to observe such critical behavior in a natural situation, the observer may need to be present for weeks or even months (Flagg, 1990).

41.2.4.6. Portfolios. Portfolios provide a descriptive measure of student work based on actual performance. Portfolios consist of learner-created products that reflect the processes of learning and development over time. Many analysts have recommended portfolios as a mechanism for integrating learning and assessment (Belland & Best, 1991; Collins, 1990; Paulson, Paulson & Meyer, 1991; Pearlman, 1990; Schon, 1987; Wolf, 1989). There is currently a trend toward using portfolios of student work as a basis for assessing learner performance and mastery. For example, in Vermont, 135 schools are piloting the use of student portfolios to measure student abilities in math and writing (Pearlman, 1990).

41.2.4.6.1. Types of Portfolios. The portfolios can take many forms. For example, portfolios can record the student's best compositions, game performances, multimedia projects, artwork, or problem solutions. Portfolios serve as relatively complete process records of a student's learning, providing a cognitive map of his involvement in projects and his exploration of a particular domain or craft. One advantage of portfolios is that they enlarge the view of what is learned. Portfolios provide a developmental point of view so they can provide a mechanism for assessing progress. Furthermore, portfolios offer students an opportunity to learn about their own learning while they require active student responsibility and self-assessment (Paulson, Paulson & Meyer, 1991).

41.2.4.6.2. Constructing Portfolios. There is a strong tradition of using portfolios in the creative arts, and this is now being extended to other fields of study, including various subjects within education. Portfolios may center around such mediated projects produced by students as print-based materials produced with desktop publishing, videotaped recordings of student presentations, audiotaped recordings of student performances, student-produced videos, as well as computer-based and multimedia projects. The process of assessing portfolios is of central concern, and calls for systematic and refined analysis.

In the context of the Key School, a private school in Indianapolis that is piloting innovative educational prac-

tices based on his model of seven intelligences, Howard Gardner (1993) recommends that student portfolios be assessed in terms of five separate dimensions, including individual profile, quality of work, communication, reflection, and mastery of facts, skills, and concepts. The individual profile includes consideration of the specific cognitive strengths, weaknesses, and proclivities of the student. The profile includes the student's disposition toward work, such as taking risks and persevering, as well as the student's particular intellectual propensities, such as linguistic, logical, spatial, and interpersonal skills.

Usually a bargain is struck between the student and teacher. The teacher can ask the student to draw on school knowledge and understanding in creating a project, and the student has the opportunity to select from a range of school-work those facts, skills, and concepts desirable for the project. Quality of work is assessed in terms of the criteria of a particular genre; this may include innovation and imagination, aesthetic judgment and technique, or the execution of a performance such as a puppet show. In terms of communication, the projects go beyond the classroom situation and offer an opportunity for students to communicate with a wider audience, including with peers, teachers, and other adults. Finally, reflection involves monitoring one's goals, assessing what progress has been made, evaluating how the course can be corrected, and how to make use of knowledge that has been attained. One example of a system that has been developed for assessing student work in language arts is the 6-point scale for written reports that comes from the state of Vermont, as shown in Figure 41-1.

In the Vermont system, several judges score each student essay based on this 6-point scoring system. This is far more time intensive than scoring a multiple-choice test, but it gives a deeper understanding of student learning and achievement. Gardner (1993) states that assessing the portfolio is no easy matter, but that it should be possible to trace various forms of growth in production, perception, and reflection through a judicious examination of the portfolio.

Noting the need to support educators in the use of portfolios, The Northwest Evaluation Association, based in Lake Oswego, Oregon, publishes a *Portfolio Assessment Newsletter* that is available on a regular basis. Portfolios represent an area of descriptive technique that is at an early stage, but it promises to expand in importance over the coming years as more people find ways for meaningful implementation and interpretation.

Good descriptive studies use data collection instruments that are reliable and valid. *Reliability* refers to the ability to provide consistent answers in comparable situations, and *validity* refers to the ability to provide answers that correspond to what they are intended to measure. One way of maintaining reliability is to make sure that the same research instrument is used for all participants within a particular study and that the research staff is well trained for using the same procedure for collecting the data (Borg & Gall, 1989; J. Converse, 1987; Fowler, 1993). It is also important to attend to the clarity of materials used within

SCORE DESCRIPTION OF ACHIEVEMENT

[6] **Exceptional achievement.** The student produces convincingly argued evaluation; identifies a subject, describes it appropriately, and asserts a judgment of it; gives reasons and specific evidence to support the argument; engages the reader immediately, moves along logically and coherently and provides closure; reflects awareness of reader's questions or alternative evaluations.

[5] **Commendable achievement.** The student produces well-argued evaluation; identifies, describes, and judges its subject; gives reasons and evidence to support the argument; is engaging, logical, and attentive to the reader's concerns; is more conventional or predictable than the writer of a [6].

[4] **Adequate achievement.** The student produces adequately argued evaluation; identifies and judges its subject; gives at least one moderately developed reason to support the argument; lacks the authority and polish of the writer of a [5] or [6]; produces writing that, although focused and coherent, may be uneven; usually describes the subject more than necessary and argues a judgment less than necessary.

[3] **Some evidence of achievement.** The student states a judgment and gives one or more reasons to support it; either lists reasons without providing evidence or fails to argue even one reason logically or coherently.

[2] **Limited evidence of achievement.** The student states a judgment but may describe the subject without evaluating it or may list irrelevant reasons or develop a reason in a rambling, illogical way.

[1] **Minimal evidence of achievement.** The student usually states a judgment but may describe the subject without stating a judgment; either gives no reasons or lists only one or two reasons without providing evidence; usually relies on weak and general personal evaluation.

Figure 41-1. State of Vermont's 6-point scale for written reports.

the study so that the respondents are able to understand precisely what is meant by any question.

41.3 IMPACT AND FUTURE ROLE OF DESCRIPTIVE RESEARCH

Although descriptive studies are important, most educational studies involve questions about causes (Borg & Gall, 1989), such as "What causes underachievement?" or "Will multimedia cause students to be more motivated or lead to higher achievement levels?" It is not always possible to isolate the variables that will explain those causes, so descriptive research can play an important role in providing information from another perspective. By gathering descriptions of "what is" and comparing them to "what we would like," educators can see the area that needs to be addressed. Further, descriptive statistics can provide information that can help to isolate

the variables that will eventually be used to measure cause and effect, and at the least can help provide surrounding information that will aid logical interpretations of research questions within the context of a specific situation.

Descriptive research has gained acceptance as a valid form of research in education, and in recent years the number of descriptive studies published in research journals and conference proceedings has increased. This is probably due to a couple of reasons. First, educational researchers have realized that trying to mimic scientific research does not work for educational settings. The purely scientific approach reduces educational research to trivial questions that do not address the important, overarching issues within education. Instead, researchers need to address the questions at hand and be willing to use a variety of methodologies in order to ensure the most appropriate and accurate investigation. Second, the rapidly changing technologies available to educators have everyone scrambling for information. Educators are likely to be observing students using media in new ways and for new purposes. It is extremely difficult to set up control groups that adequately control all of the variables that might affect the outcome of the research while providing the same type of learning experience for all of the students. The new classroom activities lend themselves nicely to descriptive research.

In addition, educators want to know how others are implementing the new multimediated technologies, the national information infrastructure, and so on, and are very happy to hear reports that describe what others are doing, as well as what happens as a result of the process. Analysis of descriptive research patterns leads to prescriptions that instructional designers and educators can heed as they consider future direction. Within the realm of cognitive skill building and the constructivist paradigm, these patterns and prescriptions become part of the whole process of education rather than isolated components. If current patterns continue, we are likely to see more acceptance of properly conducted descriptive research in the future.

REFERENCES

Amarel, M. (1982). Classrooms and computers as instructional settings. *Theory into Practice 22* (4), 260–66.

Anglin & Towers (1992). Reference citations in selected instructional design and technology journals, 1985–1990. *Educational Technology Research and Development 40* (1), 40–43.

Bakeman, R. & Gottman, J.M. (1986). *Observing interaction: an introduction to sequential analysis.* Cambridge, England: Cambridge University Press.

Bales, R.F. (1950). *Interaction process analysis: A method for the study of small groups.* Chicago, IL: University of Chicago Press.

Barry, A.M. (1994). Advertising and Channel One: controversial partnership of business and education. *In* A. DeVaney, ed. *Channel One: the convergence of students, technology and private business,* 102–36. Albany, NY: State University of New York Press.

Becker, H.J. (1986). Instructional uses of school computers. *Reports from the 1985 national survey.* Issues No. 1, 2 & 3. Center for Social Organization of Schools, The Johns Hopkins University.

Belson, W.A. (1981). *The design and understanding of survey questions.* Aldershot, England: Gower.

Boehm, A.E. & Weinberg, R.A. (1977). *The classroom observer—a guide for developing observation skills.* New York: Teachers College Press.

Borg, W.R. & Gall, M.D. (1989). *Educational research: an introduction,* 5th ed. White Plains, NY: Longman.

Borich, G.D. & Madden, S.K. (1977). *Evaluating classroom instruction: a source book of instruments.* Reading, MA: Addison-Wesley.

Brown, R. (1989, Apr.). Testing and thoughtfulness. *Educational Leadership,* 31–33.

Campbell, D.T. & Stanley, J.C. (1963). *Experimental and quasi-experimental designs for research.* Boston, MA: Houghton Mifflin.

Celhoffer, L., Boukydis, C., Minde, C. & Muir, E. (1977). The DCR-II event recorder: a portable high-speed digital cassette system with direct computer access. *Behavior Research Methods and Instrumentation 10,* 563–66.

Cochenour, J., Hakes, B. & Neal, P. (1994). 1993 Survey compressed video applications: higher education, K-12, and the private sector. *Proceedings of the annual international conference of the Association of Educational Communications and Technology* (AECT), 123–35.

Collins, A. (1990). Reformulating testing to measure learning and thinking. *In* N. Frederiksen, R. Glaser, A. Lesgold & M.G. Shafto, eds. *Diagnostic monitoring of skill and knowledge acquisition,* 75–87. Hillsdale, NJ: Erlbaum.

Converse, J. (1987). *Survey research in the United States.* Berkeley, CA: University of California Press.

Croll, P. (1986). *Systematic classroom observation.* Philadelphia, PA: Falmer.

Cronbach, L.J., Gleser, G.C., Nanda, H. & Rajaratnam, N. (1972). *The dependability of behavioral measurements: theory of generalizability for scores and profiles.* New York: Wiley.

Crossman, E.K., Williams, J.C. & Chambers, J.H. (1978). Using the PET microcomputer for collecting and analyzing observational data in the classroom. *Behavior Research Methods and Instrumentation 10, 563–66.*

Davidson, G.V. & Ritchie, S.D. (1994). How do attitudes of parents, teachers, and students affect the integration of technology into schools?: a case study. *Proceedings of the annual international conference of the Association of Educational Communications and Technology* (AECT), 161–72.

Evertson, C.M. & Green, J.L. (1986). Observation as inquiry and method. *In* Merlin C. Wittrock, ed. *Handbook of research on teaching.* New York: Macmillan.

Fernald, R.D. & Heinecke, P. (1974). A computer-compatible multi-purpose event recorder. *Behavior 49,* 268–75.

Flagg, B.N. (1990). *Formative evaluation for educational technologies.* Hillsdale, NJ: Erlbaum.

Fowler, F.J., Jr. (1993). *Survey research methods,* 2d ed. Newbury Park, CA: Sage.

Fraser, R. & Burkhardt, H. (1984). Technology, triangles, and teaching. Paper presented at the American Educational Research Association. New Orleans, LA.

Galloway, J.P (1992). Teaching educational computing with analogies: a strategy to enhance concept development. *Journal of Research on Computing in Education 24* (4), 499–512.

Gardner, H. (1993). *Multiple intelligences. the theory in practice.* New York: Basic Books.

Gass, C.L. (1977). A digital encoder for field recording of behavioral, temporal, and spatial information in directly computer-accessible form. *Behavior Research Methods and Instrumentation 9,* 5–11.

Glass, G.V., & Hopkins, K.D. (1984). *Statistical methods in education and psychology.* Englewood Cliffs, NJ: Prentice Hall.

Goodlad, J. (1983). *A place called school.* New York: McGraw-Hill.

Hartmann, D.P., ed. (1982). *Using observers to study behavior.* San Francisco, CA: Jossey-Bass.

Hayes-Roth, B. & Hayes-Roth, F. (1979). A cognitive model of planning. *Cognitive Science 3,* 275–310.

Herbert, J. & Altridge, C. (1975). A guide for developers and users of observation systems and manuals. *American Educational Research Journal 12,* 1–20.

Jackson, P.W. (1968). *Life in classrooms.* New York: Holt.

Knupfer, N.N. (1994). Channel One: reactions of students, teachers, and parents. *In* A. DeVaney, ed. *Channel One: the convergence of students, technology and private business,* 61–86. Albany, NY: State University of New York Press.

— (1988). Teachers' beliefs about instructional computing: implications for instructional designers. *Journal of Instructional Development (JID) 11* (4), 29–38.

— & Hayes, P. (1994). The effects of the Channel One broadcast on students' knowledge of current events. *In* A. DeVaney, ed. *Channel One: the convergence of students, technology and private business,* 42–60. Albany, NY: State University of New York Press.

Krathwohl, D.R. (1993). Methods of educational and social research: an integrated approach. New York: Longman.

Lamb, M.E., Suomi, S.J. & Stephenson, G.R. (1979). *Social interaction analysis: methodological issues.* Madison, WI: University of Wisconsin Press.

Lee, I.S. (1994). Identifying values: the front-end of systemic school restructuring. *Proceedings of the annual international conference of the Association of Educational Communications and Technology* (AECT), 389–422.

Lightfoot, S.L. (1983). *The good high school.* New York: Basic Books.

Lu, M.Y., Morlan, J.E., Lerchlorlarn, C., Lee, B. & Dike, H. (1993). Media utilization by teachers in the United States, Taiwan, Thailand, and Nigeria. *Educational Technology Research and Development (ETR&D) 41* (1), 107–11.

Manaev, O. (1991). The disagreeing audience: change in criteria for evaluating mass media effectiveness with the democratization of Soviet society. *Communication Research 18* (1), 25–52.

McKenna, L.M. (1993). The relationship between attributes of a children's radio program and its appeal to listeners. *Educational Technology Research and Development (ETR&D) 41* (1), 17–28.

McLellan, H. (1991). Teachers and classroom management in a computer learning environment. *International Journal of Instructional Media 18* (1), 19–27.

— (1993, Mar.). Evaluation in a situated learning environment. *Educational Technology 33* (3), 39–45.

— (1994, Spring). Virtual reality and multiple intelligences: potentials for higher education. *Journal of Computing in Higher Education 5* (2), 31–64.

— (1994). Interactions of student partners in a high school astronomy computer lab. *Computers in the Schools.*

Moore, M.G., ed. (1990). *Contemporary issues in American distance education.* Elmsford, NY: Pergamon.

Moore, D.M. & Dwyer, F.M., eds. (1994). *Visual literacy: a spectrum of learning.* Englewood Cliffs, NJ: Educational Technology.

Muffoletto, R. & Knupfer, N.N., eds. (1993). *Computers in education: social, political, and historical perspectives.* Cresskill, NJ: Hampton.

Nolan, P.C.J., McKinnon, D.H. & Soler, J. (1992). Computers in education: achieving equitable access and use. *Journal of Research on Computing in Education 24* (2), 189–203.

Office of Technology Assessment (1991). *Linking for learning: a new course for education.*

Orey, M.A. & Nelson, W.A. (1994). Visualization techniques for examining learner interactions with hypermedia instruction. *Proceedings of the annual international conference of the Association of Educational Communications and Technology (AECT),* 629–40.

Paulson, F.L., Paulson, P.R. & Meyer, C.A. (1991, Feb.). What makes a portfolio a portfolio? *Educational Leadership 48* (5), 60–63.

Pearlman, R. (1991, Jan.). Restructuring with technology: a tour of schools where it's happening. *Technology and Learning,* 30–37.

Peterson, P.L. & Janicki, T. (1979). Individual characteristics and children's learning in large-group and small-group approaches. *Journal of Educational Psychology 71,* 677–87.

—, Wilkinson, L.C. & Hallinan, M. (1984). *The social context of instruction: group organization and group processes.* New York: Academic.

—, —, Spinelli, F. & Swing, S.R. (1984). Merging the process-product and the sociolinguistic paradigms: research on small group processes. *In* P.L. Peterson, L.C. Wilkinson & M. Hallinan (1984). *The social context of instruction: group organization and group processes.* New York: Academic.

Pettersson, R., Metallinos, N., Muffoletto, R., Shaw, J. & Takakuwa, Y. (1993). The use of verbo-visual information in teaching geography: views from teachers. *Educational Technology Research and Development (ETR&D) 41* (1), 101–07.

Repp, A.C., Harman, M.L., Felce, D., Van Acker, R. & Karsh, K.L. (1985, Sep.). *A real-time, parallel entry, portable computer system for observational research.* Paper presented at the annual meeting of the Midwestern Educational Research Association, Chicago, IL.

Robinson, R.S. (1994). Investigating Channel One: a case study report. *In* A. DeVaney, ed. *Channel One : the convergence of students, technology and private business,* 21–41. Albany, NY: State University of New York Press.

Rysavy, S.D.M. & Sales, G. (1991). Cooperative learning in computer-based instruction. *Educational Technology Research and Development 39* (2), 70–79.

Sackett, G.P., Stephenson, E. & Ruppenthal, G.C. (1973). Digital data acquisition systems for observing behavior in laboratory and field settings. *Behavior Research Methodology and Instrumentation 5,* 344–48.

Sanson-Fisher, R.W., Poole, A.D., Small, G.A. & Fleming, I.R. (1979). Data acquisition in real time—an improved system for naturalistic observations. *Behavior Therapy 10,* 543–44.

Schatzman, L. & Strauss, A.L. (1973). *Field research.* Englewood Cliffs, NJ: Prentice Hall.

Shapiro, M. (1991). Memory and decision processes in the construction of social reality. *Communication Research 18* (1), 3–25.

Signer, B.R. (1991). CAI and at-risk minority urban high school students. *Journal of Research on Computing in Education 24* (2), 189–203.

Simon, A. & Boyer, E.G. (1974). *Mirrors for behavior III: an anthology of observation instruments.* Wyncote, PA: Communications Materials Center.

Stephenson, G.R. (1979). PLEXYN: a computer-compatible grammar for coding complex social interactions. *In* M.E. Lamb, S.J. Suomi & G.R. Stephenson. (1979). *Social interaction analysis: methodological issues,* 157–84. Madison, WI: University of Wisconsin Press.

— (1983). *Technical manual for PLEXYN users.* Madison, WI: SSR Associates.

— & Roberts, T.W. (1977). The SSR system 7: a general encoding system with computerized transcription. *Behavior Research Methods and Instrumentation 9,* 434–41.

Suen, H.K. & Ary, D. (1989). *Analyzing quantitative behavioral observation data.* Hillsdale, NJ: Erlbaum.

Torgerson, L. (1977). Datamyte 900. *Behavior research methods and instrumentation 9,* 405–06.

Webb, N.M. (1982, Fall). Student interaction and learning in small groups. *Review of Educational Research 52* (3), 421–45.

— (1983). Predicting learning from student interaction: defining the interaction variables. *Educational Psychologist 18* (1), 33–41.

—, Ender, P. & Lewis, S. (1986, Summer). Problem-solving strategies and group processes in small groups learning computer programming. *American Educational Research Journal 23* (2), 243–61.

Wehrs, W.E. (1992). Using expert systems to support academic advising. *Journal of Research on Computing in Education 24* (4), 545–62.

Wolf, D.P. (1989, Apr.). Portfolio assessment: sampling student work. *Educational Leadership 46* (6), 35–39.

42. DEVELOPMENTAL RESEARCH

Rita C. Richey
WAYNE STATE UNIVERSITY

Wayne A. Nelson
SOUTHERN ILLINOIS UNIVERSITY AT EDWARDSVILLE

The field of instructional technology has traditionally involved a unique blend of theory and practice. This blend is most obvious in developmental research, which involves the production of knowledge with the ultimate aim of improving the processes of instructional design, development, and evaluation. It is based on either situation-specific problem solving or generalized inquiry procedures. Developmental *research,* as opposed to simple instructional development, has been defined as "the systematic study of designing, developing and evaluating instructional programs, processes, and products that must meet the criteria of internal consistency and effectiveness" (Seels & Richey, 1994, p. 127). In its simplest form, developmental research could be either:

- A situation in which someone is *performing* instructional design, development, or evaluation activities and *studying* the process at the same time
- The study of the impact of someone else's instructional design and development efforts
- The study of the instructional design, development, and evaluation process as a whole, or of particular process components

In each case, the distinction is made between performing a process and studying that process. Reports of developmental research may take the form of a case study with retrospective analysis, an evaluation report, or even that of a typical experimental research report.

The purposes of this chapter[1] are to:

- Explore the nature and background of developmental research
- Describe the major types of developmental research by examining a range of representative projects

- Analyze the methodological approaches used in the various types of developmental research
- Describe the issues, findings, and trends in recent developmental research
- Discuss the future of this type of research in our field

42.1 THE NATURE OF DEVELOPMENTAL RESEARCH

Today, even amid the calls for increased use of alternative research methodologies, the notion of developmental research is often unclear, not only to the broader community of educational researchers but to many instructional technology researchers as well. An understanding of this topic is rooted in the nature of development and research in general, as well as a more specific understanding of the purpose, focus, and techniques of developmental research itself.

42.1.1 The Character of Development

Development, in its most generic sense, implies gradual growth, evolution, and change. This concept has been applied to diverse areas of study and practice. For example, developmental psychology is concerned with human growth. It may concentrate on particular age groups, such as in the areas of adolescent development or life span development. Organizational development is a strategy for changing "the beliefs, attitudes, values, and structure of organizations so that they can better adapt to new . . . challenges" (Bennis, 1969, p. 2). Educators are familiar with the notion of professional or staff development. Lieberman and Miller (1992) define this as "the knowledge, skills, abilities, and the necessary conditions for teacher learning on the job" (p. 1045). This same concept is often applied to other professional areas. In the corporate arena, the term *executive development* also refers to learning processes, and in this setting learning, as a developmental activity, often integrates both classroom instruction and work experience (Smith, 1993).

---

[1]The authors would like to thank Phil Doughty (Syracuse University) for the extensive contributions he made to this chapter. In addition, we would like to thank reviewers Walter Dick (Florida State University), Barbara Seels (University of Pittsburgh), Nick Smith (Syracuse University), and Martin Tessmer (University of South Alabama) for their helpful suggestions and guidance.

In the field of instructional technology, development has a particular, somewhat unique, connotation. The most current definition views development as "the process of translating the design specifications into physical form" (Seels & Richey, 1994, p. 35). In other words, it refers to the process of *producing* instructional materials. Development is viewed as one of the five major domains of theory and practice in the field.[2] Even though this varies from many other uses of the term *development,* it is consistent with the fundamental attribute of being a process of growth, and in our field *development* is a very creative process.

Historically *development* has been an ambiguous term to many instructional technologists and has generated considerable discussion regarding its proper interpretation. This debate has focused typically on the distinctions between instructional *design* and instructional *development.* Heinich, Molenda, and Russell (1993) define instructional development as "the process of analyzing needs, determining what content must be mastered, establishing educational goals, designing materials to reach the objectives, and trying out and revising the program in terms of learner achievement" (p. 445). To many, this is a definition of the instructional systems design (ISD) process.

The confusion is further exacerbated. In 1977, Briggs defined "instructional design" as "the entire process of analysis of learning needs and goals and the development of a delivery system to meet the needs; includes development of instructional materials and activities; and tryout and revision of all instruction and learner assessment activities" (p. xx). In this interpretation, *design* is the more generic term, encompassing *both* planning and production. The 1994 definition of the field attempts to clarify these issues by viewing design as the planning phase in which specifications are constructed, and development as the production phase in which the design specifications are actualized (Seels & Richey, 1994). This is not a new distinction (Cronbach & Suppes, 1969; National Center for Educational Research and Development, 1970), even though the past use of the term *instructional developer* (see Baker, 1973) typically referred to a person who was doing what today we would call both design and development. All would agree, however, that design and development are *related* processes, and Connop-Scollard (1991) has graphically demonstrated these relationships in a complex chart that identified hundreds of interrelated concepts.

Instructional development traditionally does not include a *comprehensive* notion of evaluation. For example, the Heinich, Molenda, and Russell definition directly speaks to both formative evaluation of products and programs and needs assessment, but by implication it would also encompass test item construction. Likewise, the majority of instructional design models also address only these aspects

of evaluation (Andrews & Goodson, 1980). Notable exceptions are the design models of Dick and Carey (1996) and Seels and Glasgow (1990), both of which include a summative evaluation phase.

However, the word *development* has a broader definition when it is used within the research context than it has when used within the context of creating instructional products. The focus is no longer only on production, or even on both planning and production. It also includes comprehensive evaluation. As such, developmental research may well address not only formative but summative evaluation as well. It may address not only needs assessment but also broad issues of front-end analysis, such as contextual analysis issues, as conceived by Tessmer and Harris's (1992) environmental analysis, or systemic design issues as described by Richey (1992). When evaluation is approached in a comprehensive manner, the scope of the research effort is often correspondingly expanded to encompass product utilization and management, as well as product creation. Table 42-1 displays the scope of development as discussed in this chapter.

The next step beyond "Utilization & Maintenance" in the schemata of Table 42-1 would be "Impact," the follow-up analysis of the effects of an instructional product or program on the organization or the learner. This type of research typically falls within the scope of traditional evaluation research.

42.1.2 The Character of Research

While research methodologies vary, there are key attributes that transcend the various research orientations and goals. An understanding of these characteristics can shed light on the process of developmental research.

42.1.2.1. The Dimensions of Research. Gay (1987) defines research as "the formal, systematic application of the scientific method to the study of problems" (p. 4). One result of such an effort is the creation of knowledge. Even though research is typically rooted in societal problems, all knowledge produced by research is not necessarily in a form conducive to quick resolution of society's problems. Some knowledge (which is usually generated by *basic* research) must be specifically transformed to enable its application to a given problem. Other knowledge (which is usually generated by *applied* research) lends itself to the immediate solution of practical problems. Developmental research clearly falls in the latter category. In this respect, it is similar to other methodologies such as action research.

While the objective of research is to produce knowledge, these products may take a variety of forms. Diesing (1991, p. 325) has noted that:

> . . . the philosophers suggest that social science produces at least three kinds of knowledge: (1) systems of laws, which describe interconnected regularities in society; (2) descriptions, from the inside, of a way of life, community, person, belief system, or scientific community's beliefs; (3) structural models, mathematical or verbal, of dynamic processes exemplified in particular cases.

---

[2] In addition to development, the domains also include design, management, utilization, and evaluation. Brief histories of each of these domains can be found in Chapter 2 of Seels and Richey (1994).

**TABLE 42-1. THE SCOPE OF DEVELOPMENT
IN A RESEARCH CONTEXT**

Design	Development	Utilization & Maintenance
Analysis and planning for development, evaluation, utilization & maintenance	Production & formative evaluation	Usage, management & summative evaluation

Research orientations tend to conform to the pursuit of a particular type of knowledge. Experimental research (see 39.1) tends to contribute to the construction of a system of laws. Characteristic of this method is a series of routine checks to ensure self-correction throughout the research, and in the logical positivist tradition, such checks are considered to be rooted in objectivity (Kerlinger, 1964). Qualitative research (see 40.1) primarily contributes to the development of "mirrors for man" so that we can see ourselves better (Kluckhohn, as noted in Diesing, 1991). In the various forms of qualitative research, context and contextual influences become a integral part of the investigation (Driscoll, 1991; Mishler, 1979).

Diesing's third type of knowledge is process knowledge presented in model form. This is usually of great interest to instructional designers and developers, given our history of working with many kinds of process models, such as the graphic models of systematic design procedures and the models of media selection. When inquiry procedures result in this type of knowledge, these endeavors can legitimately be placed in the research realm.

Another traditional characterization of research is as a facilitator of understanding and prediction. In this regard "understanding results from a knowledge of the process or dynamics of a theory. Prediction results from investigation of the outcomes of a theory" (Schwen, 1977, p. 8). These goals can be achieved by either: (1) providing a logical explanation of reality, (2) anticipating the values of one variable based on those of other variables, or (3) determining the states of a model (Dubin, as cited by Schwen, 1977). While these ends, especially the first two, can be achieved through traditional research methodologies, the third is uniquely matched to the goals of developmental research. This was emphasized by Schwen (1977, p. 9):

> Inquiry in educational technology may be associated with the planning, implementing, and/or evaluation of the management-of-learning process, where that process employs systematic technological analysis and synthesis . . . current definitions of technological process may be found in development models . . . (having) the common attributes of (1) disciplined analysis of problem, context, constraints, learners, and task, and (2) disciplined synthesis involving the design of replicable forms of instruction and formative and summative evaluation.

42.1.2.2. The Relationships Between Research and Development. The more typical view of research is the discovery of new knowledge and development as the translation of that knowledge into useful form (Pelz, 1967). This conceptual framework has not only been commonly subscribed to but it was also subsequently extended into the research, development, and diffusion model (Brickell & Clark, and Guba, as cited in Havelock, 1971). Early research methods texts addressed development as the "research and development" process (Borg & Gall, 1971). The processes were separate, though related, dependent, and sequential. In some situations, this orientation still prevails. This view emphasizes development's function of linking practice to research and theory, and recognizes the likelihood that instructional development can highlight researchable problems, and thus serve as a vehicle for stimulating new research (Baker, 1973).

Stowe (1973) has shown the parallels between scientific research and the general methodology of instructional systems design. He notes that both:

- Are objective, empirical problem-solving approaches
- Employ procedural models "couched in the language of mathematics" (p. 167)
- Have a predictive power dependent on the degree to which they represent the most critical aspects of reality
- Can generate new problems and hypotheses

Nonetheless, Stowe rejected the proposition that systematic design procedures can be viewed as research to a great extent because of the inability of ISD to discover generalizable principles and its intent to produce context-specific solutions. In addition, Stowe cited the distinctions between ISD's orientation toward explanations of "how?" as opposed to research's orientation toward explanations of "why?".

In the contemporary orientation toward research, Stowe's arguments can be interpreted as an overly rigid expression of positivist philosophy. The contextual richness of the typical design and development task increases the likelihood that research on such topics be especially ripe for a qualitative orientation. The ability to provide process explanations exemplifies a type of knowledge production using the Diesing framework, and an avenue to understanding and prediction using Schwen's paradigm. Stowe's arguments drafted over 20 years ago could lead to diametrically opposite conclusions today, provided one accepts the premise that research can have a broader function than the creation of generalizable statements of law. We are taking the position that research can also result in context-specific knowledge and can serve a problem-solving function. This is true of developmental research, as it has commonly thought to be true of evaluation research.

While instructional development typically *builds* on previous research, developmental research attempts to produce the models and principles that guide the design, development, and evaluation processes. As such, *doing* development and *studying* development are two different enterprises.

42.1.3 The Background of Developmental Research[3]

The field of instructional technology as it exists today emerged primarily from a convergence of the fields of audiovisual education and instructional psychology (see 1.5, 2.3, 5.2). In audiovisual education the emphasis was on the role of media as an enhancement of the teaching/learning process and an aid in the communication process, and there was much interest in materials production. On the other hand, in instructional psychology the nature of the learner and the learning process took precedence over the nature of the delivery methodology, and there was much interest in instructional design. Complementing the instructional psychology roots was the application of systems theory to instruction (see 3.2) that resulted in the instructional systems design movement (Seels & Richey, 1994). This conceptual and professional merger came to fruition in the 1960s and 1970s. During this period, instructional design and development came to assume the role of the "linking science" that John Dewey had called for at the turn of the century (Reigeluth, 1983).

Not surprisingly, it was during this same period that the term *developmental research* emerged. This new orientation was exemplified by the shift in topics between the *First and Second Handbooks of Research on Teaching* (Gage, 1963; Travers, 1973). In the 1963 handbook, media was addressed as an area of research with a major emphasis on media comparison research, and all research methodologies considered were quantitative. In the 1973 handbook, media continued to be included as a research area, but the research methodologies were varied, including Eva Baker's chapter on "The Technology of Instructional Development." This chapter describes in detail the process of systematic product design, development, and evaluation. Of significance is the fact that the entire methodology section was titled "Methods and Techniques of Research *and Development.*"

This was a period in which federal support of educational research mushroomed. Regional research and development laboratories were established, and the ERIC system was devised for dissemination. Clifford (1973) estimated that appropriations for educational "research and development for 1966 through 1968 alone equaled three-fourths of all funds ever made available" (p. 1). Research-based prod-

uct and program development had become firmly established as part of the scientific movement in education. At this time, Wittrock (1967) hailed the use of empirical measurement and experimentation to explain product effectiveness. Such activities "could change the development of products into research, with empirical results and theory generalizable to new problems" (p. 148).

Hilgard (1964) characterized research as a continuum from basic research on topics not directly relevant to learning through the advocacy and adoption stages of technological development. Saettler (1990) maintained that the last three of Hilgard's research categories were directly within the domain of instructional technology. These included laboratory, classroom, and special teacher research; tryout in "normal" classrooms; and advocacy and adoption. Note that these are portrayed as types of research, rather than applications of research, and they are all encompassed within the framework of developmental research.

While instructional technology is not the only field concerned with learning in applied settings, few would dispute the critical role played by these three types of research in our field. Moreover, our uniqueness among educational fields is not only our concern with technology, but rather our emphasis on the design, development, and use of processes and resources for learning (Seels & Richey, 1994). Given this definition of the field, developmental research is critically important to the evolution of our theory base.

42.1.4 The Character of Developmental Research

The distinctions between "doing" and "studying" design and development provide further clarification of developmental research activities. These distinctions can be described in terms of examining the focus, techniques, and tools of developmental research.

42.1.4.1. The Focus of Developmental Research. The general purposes of research have been described as knowledge production, understanding, and prediction. Within this framework, developmental research has particular emphases that vary in terms of the extent to which the conclusions are generalizable or contextually specific. Table 42-2 portrays the relationships between the two general types of developmental research.

The most straightforward developmental research projects fall into the first category of Table 42-2. This category typically involves situations in which the product development process used in a particular situation is described and analyzed, and the final product is evaluated, such as Buch's (1988/1989) documentation of the development of an industrial microcomputer training program. Driscoll (1991) called this research paradigm *systems-based evaluation.* Some Type 1 developmental studies reflect traditional evaluation orientations in which the development process is not addressed, and only the product or program evaluation is described. An example of this type of study is O'Quin, Kin-

---

[3]A history of instructional development can be found in Baker (1973), which primarily summarizes the work in research-based product development from the turn of the century to 1970. Baker, however, does not address developmental research as it is presented in this chapter.

TABLE 42-2. A SUMMARY OF THE TWO TYPES OF DEVELOPMENTAL RESEARCH

<table>
<tr><td colspan="3" align="center">Developmental Research</td></tr>
<tr><td></td><td align="center">Type 1</td><td align="center">Type 2</td></tr>
<tr><td>Emphasis</td><td>Study of specific product or program design, development &/or evaluation projects</td><td>Study of design, development, or evaluation processes, tools, or models</td></tr>
<tr><td>Product</td><td>Lessons learned from developing specific products and analyzing the conditions that facilitate their use</td><td>New design, development, and evaluation procedures &/or models, and conditions that facilitate their use</td></tr>
<tr><td></td><td align="center">Context-specific conclusions $\Rightarrow \Rightarrow \Rightarrow \Rightarrow$</td><td>Generalized conclusions</td></tr>
</table>

sey, and Beery's (1987) report of the evaluation of a microcomputer training workshop for college personnel. Regardless of the nature of the Type 1 study, the results are typically context and product specific, even though the implications for similar situations may be discussed.

The second type of developmental study is oriented toward a general analysis of either design, development, or evaluation processes as a whole or any particular component. They are similar to those studies Driscoll (1991) calls *model development* and *technique development research.* While there are fewer studies that focus on the more global orientation, Taylor and Ellis's (1991) study did so by evaluating the use of instructional systems design in the Navy, and Kress (1989/1990) did so by comparing the impact of systematically designed training with a nonsystematic approach. Other studies in this category focus on only one phase of the design/development/evaluation process, such as Jonassen's (1988) case study of using needs assessment data in the development of a university program. Type 2 research may draw its population from either one target project such as King and Dille's (1993) study of the application of quality concepts in the systematic design of instruction at the Motorola Training and Education Center, or from a variety of design and development environments. Examples of the latter approach include Riplinger's (1985/1987) survey of current task analysis procedures, and Cambre's (1978/1979) historical study of formative evaluation in instructional film and television. Typically, conclusions from Type 2 developmental research are generalized, even though there are instances of context specific conclusions in the literature.

42.1.4.2. Nondevelopmental Research in the Field. A critical aspect of any concept definition is the identification of nonexamples as well as examples. This is especially important with respect to developmental research, since it often seems to overlap with other key methodologies used in the field. Even so, developmental research does *not* encompass studies such as the following:

- Instructional psychology studies
- Media or delivery system comparison or impact studies
- Message design and communication studies

- Policy analysis or formation studies
- Research on the profession

While results from research in these areas impact the development process, the study of variables embedded in such topics does not constitute developmental research. For example, design and development is dependent on what we know about the learning process. We have learned from the research literature that transfer of training is impacted by motivation, organizational climate, and previous educational experiences. Therefore, one may expand a front-end analysis to address such issues, or even construct design models that reflect this information, but the foundational research would not be considered developmental. If the new models were tested, or programs evaluated that were designed using such models, this research would qualify as developmental.

A fundamental distinction should be made between reports that analyze actual development projects, and *descriptions* of recommended design and development procedural models. While these models may represent a synthesis of the research, they do not constitute research in themselves. A good example of this latter situation is Park and Hannafin's (1993) guidelines for designing interactive multimedia. These guidelines are generalized principles that speak to the development process, and they are based on a large body of research. Nonetheless, the identification and explanation of the guidelines is not in itself an example of developmental research. The instructional technology literature includes many examples of such work. They often provide the stimulus for a line of new research, even though these articles are not considered to be research reports themselves. There are many examples today of such work, including explorations of topics such as cognitive task analysis (Ryder & Redding, 1993), or the nature of design and designer decision making (Rowland, 1993).

42.1.4.3. The Techniques and Tools of Developmental Research. Developmental researchers employ a variety of research methodologies, applying any tool that meets their requirements. Summative evaluation studies often employ classical experimental designs. Needs assessments may incorporate qualitative approaches. Process studies may adopt descriptive survey methods. Even historical research methods may be used in developmental projects.

Traditional research tools and traditional design tools facilitate the developmental endeavor. Expertise is often required in statistical analysis, measurement theory, and methods of establishing internal and external validity. Likewise, the developmental researcher (even one studying previously designed instruction) requires a command of design techniques and theory. Additional design proficiency is frequently required when using electronic design systems and aids, conducting environmental analyses, and defining ways to decrease design cycle time.

A developmental research project may include several distinct stages, each of which involves reporting and analyzing a data set. Merely conducting a comprehensive design and development project does not constitute conducting a developmental research project, even using its most narrow Type 1 definition. One must also include the analysis and reporting stage to warrant being classified as developmental research.

Developmental research projects may include a number of component parts. Substudies may be conducted to analyze and define the instructional problem, to specify the content, or to determine instrument reliability and validity. Substudies may be conducted to provide a formative evaluation, a summative evaluation, or a follow-up of postinstruction performance. Consequently, reports of developmental research are frequently quite long, often prohibiting publication of the full study.

Reports of developmental projects can often be found in:

- Professional journals
- Doctoral dissertations
- Educational Resource Information Center (ERIC) collections of unpublished project reports
- Conference proceedings

The nature of the reports varies depending on the dissemination vehicle. Sometimes, full developmental projects are split into more easily publishable units (or even summarized) to facilitate publication in the traditional research journals. Developmental research reports are also published in practitioner-oriented journals and magazines, and the methodology and theoretical base of the studies is omitted to conform to the traditions of those periodicals. The next section will further define the nature of developmental research by summarizing studies that are representative of the wide range of research in this category.

42.2 AN OVERVIEW OF REPRESENTATIVE DEVELOPMENTAL RESEARCH

We have identified representative developmental research studies in the literature so that we might:

- Further describe the character of this type of research
- Identify the range of settings and foci of developmental research
- Summarize developmental tools and techniques commonly used

- Identify the range of research methodologies used
- Describe the nature of the conclusions in such research

The literature will be described in terms of the two types of developmental research. This review covers research from the past 15 years, with a concentration on the most recent work.

42.2.1 Type 1 Developmental Research

Type 1 research is the most context-specific inquiry. These studies are essentially all forms of case studies, and emanate from a wide range of educational needs. Table 42-3 presents an analysis of 40 studies representative of this category of research. These studies are described in terms of their focus, methodology, and the nature of their conclusions. Focus is examined in terms of the:

- Type of program or product developed
- Particular design, development, evaluation or utilization process emphasized in the study
- Particular tools and techniques emphasized
- Organizational context for which the product is intended

The most common characteristics among the studies are found in relation to their process foci, the research methodologies employed, and the nature of their conclusions. The product and technique focus and the user context seem to reflect individual researcher interests or subject availability more than they reflect the inherent nature of this type of research.

42.2.1.1. Process Foci of Type 1 Developmental Research. Type 1 research studies all originate with the design and development of an instructional product or program. This is the crux of Type 1 research. The process orientation in Type 1 developmental research is marked, and for many a key purpose of reporting such research is to encourage replication and further experimentation with the target process or media. Typically the entire design, development, and evaluation process is documented. Consistent with predominant practice in the field, the procedures employed usually follow the tenets of instructional systems design (ISD), encompassing a form of front-end analysis through the summative evaluation and the ongoing maintenance of the system. Nearly half the studies cited in Table 42-3 describe in detail the entire design, development, and evaluation process as it occurred in a particular environment (studies classified in terms of an "A" process focus). Petry and Edwards's (1984) description of the systematic design, development, and evaluation of a university applied phonetics course describes the application of a particular ISD model, as well as the use of elaboration theory in content sequencing. The study also addresses the production of course materials, as well as the results of an evaluation of student performance and attitudes in the revised course. This is a classic Type 1 study with a course focus.

Those studies that did not document the entire design, development, and evaluation process tended to concentrate instead on the production aspect (See Table 42-3 for studies

TABLE 42-3. AN ANALYSIS OF REPRESENTATIVE TYPE 1 DEVELOPMENTAL RESEARCH LITERATURE

Reference	Product or Program Focus	Process Focus	Use Context	Tools and Techniques Emphasized	Research Methods Used	Nature of Conclusions
Albero-Andes, M. (1982/1983)	C, F, I	A, E, F	A	B	A	B
Alessi, S.M. (1988)	J	A, H	B	H, K	A	C
Aukerman, M.E. (1986/1987)	J	G, J	D	H	D, G, I	A
Bednar, A.K. (1988)	B	B	B	A, B	A	B
Blackstone, B.B. (1989/1990)	H	E, F, I, J	F		A, E, D, J	A
Bowers, D. & Tsai, C. (1990)	J	E, G	G	K	A, E	D
Buch, E.E. (1988/1989)	C	A, J	C	B, F	A, D, E	B
Cantor, J.A. (1988)	D, E, F, G	E	E	K	A, D	B
Capell, P. & Dannenberg, R.B. (1993)	J	C, D	A, B	F, G, L	A, D	B
Coscarelli, W.C. & White, G.P. (1982)	A	A, G, H	B	E	A, D	B
Coyle, K. (1985/1986)	B, J	G, J	B		A, G	B
Coyle, L. (1992)	B	E, G	B		D	A
Crane, G. & Mylonas, E. (1988)	J	E	B	K	A	A
Cregger, R. & Metzler, M. (1992)	A	A, G, H	B	G	A, D, J	B

Product/ Program Focus	Process Focus	Use Context	Tools and Techniques	Research Methods	Nature of Conclusions
A. Full Course	A. Gen. Des/Devel./ Evaluation Proc.	A. K-12 Schools	A. Problem Analysis	A. Case Study	A. Context/Product Specific
B. Full Program	B. Needs Assessm't.	B. Post-Secondary	B. Needs Assessm't	B. Descriptive	B. Context/Product Specific with some Generalz'tn
C. Workshop	C. Content Selection	C. Business and Industry	C. Environm'tal Anal.	C. Ethnography	C. Generalizations with some context/product specific
D. Gen. Print Mat.	D. Design	D. Health Care	D. Job Analysis	D. Evaluation	D. Generalizations
E. Instruct. Module	E. Production	E. Military and Govt.	E. Task Analysis	E. Experimental	
F. Study Guide	F. Form. Evaluation	F. Continuing and Community Educ.	F. Learning Hierarchy	F. Historical	
G. Job Aid	G. Utilization/Delivery	G. Employee Trng. — Other	G. Sequencing	G. Observational	
H. Games/Simulation	H. Management	H. International	H. Cost Analysis	H. Philosophical	
I. Instruc. Television	I. Summative Evaluation	I. Context-Free	I. Dissemination	I. Qualitative	
J. Computer-Based	J. Learner Outcomes		J. Learner Verification	J. Survey	
K. Any Project	K. No Dev. Involved		K. Specific Technology		

TABLE 42-3. /

Reference	Product or Program Focus	Process Focus	Use Context	Tools and Techniques Emphasized	Research Methods Used	Nature of Conclusions
Dick, W. (1991)	B	B, D	C, H	B, F	A	A
Gay, G. & Mazur, J. (1993)	J	E, H	G	K	A, F	C
George, T. (1979/1981)	E	A, J	A		A, C	A
Gustafson, K.L. & Reeves, T.C. (1990)	K	A	G	B, C, D, E, H	D	C
Harris, M. & Cady, M. (1988)	J	E	A	K	A	A
Jonassen (1988)	B	B, D	B	B	J	A
Jones, R.H. (1985/1986)	C	J	B		A, C, E, J	A
Kanyarusoke, C.M.S. (1983/1985)	A, F,	A, B, C, J	B		A, B, J	A
Kearsley, G. (1985)	G	G	I	K	D	B
Lewis, E.L. Stern, J.L. & Linn, M.C. (1993)	H, J	E	A		A, B	A
Li, Z. & Merrill, M.D. (1991)	C, D	C, D	I		A, D	C
Link, N. & Cherow-O'Leary	B, F	B, F	A, F, G		B, G, J	B
Medsker, K.L. (1992)	A, H, J	A, H, J	B, C, G	A	A. B	D

Product/ Program Focus	Process Focus	Use Context	Tools and Techniques	Research Methods	Nature of Conclusions
A. Full Course	A. Gen. Des/Devel./ Evaluation Proc.	A. K-12 Schools	A. Problem Analysis	A. Case Study	A. Context/Product Specific
B. Full Program	B. Needs Assessm't.	B. Post-Secondary	B. Needs Assessm't	B. Descriptive	B. Context/Product Specific with some Generalz'tn
C. Workshop	C. Content Selection	C. Business and Industry	C. Environm'tal Anal.	C. Ethnography	C. Generalizations with some context/product specific
D. Gen. Print Mat.	D. Design	D. Health Care	D. Job Analysis	D. Evaluation	D. Generalizations
E. Instruct. Module	E. Production	E. Military and Govt.	E. Task Analysis	E. Experimental	
F. Study Guide	F. Form. Evaluation	F. Continuing and Community Educ.	F. Learning Hierarchy	F. Historical	
G. Job Aid	G. Utilization/Delivery	G. Employee Trng. — Other	G. Sequencing	G. Observational	
H. Games/Simulation	H. Management	H. International	H. Cost Analysis	H. Philosophical	
I. Instruc. Television	I. Summative Evaluation	I. Context-Free	I. Dissemination	I. Qualitative	
J. Computer-Based	J. Learner Outcomes		J. Learner Verification	J. Survey	
K. Any Project	K. No Dev. Involved		K. Specific Technology		

TABLE 42-3. *Continued*

Reference	Product or Program Focus	Process Focus	Use Context	Tools and Techniques Emphasized	Research Methods Used	Nature of Conclusions
Mielke, K.W. (1990)	I	A	A, F		A	A
Munro, A. & Towne, D.M. (1992)	J	D, E	A, B, E, G	K	A, D	B
Noel, K. (1991)	B	A, B	A, H	C	A	C
O'Quin, K.; Kinsey, T.G. & Beery, D. (1987)	C, J	I, J	B, G / G		D, E	A
Parer, M. (1977/1978)	E, I	A, J	B	B	A, D, E	B
Petry, B. A. & Edwards, M.L. (1984)	A	A	I	G	A	A
Pirolli, P. (1991)	J	C, D	C		A, D,	B
Pizzuto, A.E. (1982/1983)	C, H,	A, C, E, F, I, J	C	F, G, K	A, D, G, J	A
Plummer, K.H.; Gillis, P.D.; Legree, P.J. & Sanders, M.G. (1992)	G	E, I	B		A, E, J	A
Russell, C.M. (1988/1990)	J	A, E, F, G, J	I	D, E	D, E	B
Russell, D.M. (1988)	J	C, D	A	F, G, K	A, D	B
Sullivan, H.J. (1984)	B	D, F, G	I		A,	C
Watson, J.E. & Belland, J.C. (1985)	E	B	B, D	K	A	B

Product/ Program Focus	Process Focus	Use Context	Tools and Techniques	Research Methods	Nature of Conclusions
A. Full Course	A. Gen. Des/Devel./ Evaluation Proc.	A. K-12 Schools	A. Problem Analysis	A. Case Study	A. Context/Product Specific
B. Full Program	B. Needs Assessm't.	B. Post-Secondary	B. Needs Assessm't	B. Descriptive	B. Context/Product Specific with some Generalz'tn
C. Workshop	C. Content Selection	C. Business and Industry	C. Environm'tal Anal.	C. Ethnography	C. Generalizations with some context/product specific
D. Gen. Print Mat.	D. Design	D. Health Care	D. Job Analysis	D. Evaluation	D. Generalizations
E. Instruct. Module	E. Production	E. Military and Govt.	E. Task Analysis	E. Experimental	
F. Study Guide	F. Form. Evaluation	F. Continuing and Community Educ.	F. Learning Hierarchy	F. Historical	
G. Job Aid	G. Utilization/Delivery	G. Employee Trng. — Other	G. Sequencing	G. Observational	
H. Games/Simulation	H. Management	H. International	H. Cost Analysis	H. Philosophical	
I. Instruc. Television	I. Summative Evaluation	I. Context-Free	I. Dissemination	I. Qualitative	
J. Computer-Based	J. Learner Outcomes		J. Learner Verification	J. Survey	
K. Any Project	K. No Dev. Involved		K. Specific Technology		

classified in terms of an "E" process focus.) Often these studies concerned the development of technology-based instruction, such as Bowers and Tsai's (1990), Crane and Mylonas's (1988), and Harris and Cady's (1988) research on the use of hypertext as a vehicle for creating computer-based instructional materials. The reports describe authoring procedures so specifically that one could replicate the innovative development processes. These same tactics were employed with respect to developing instructional television by Albero-Andes (1982/1983) and Parer (1977/1978), and they were used in interactive videodisc projects by Alessi (1988) and C. M. Russell (1988/1990). Similar studies can be found in the research of our field as each new technological advancement emerges.[4]

At times, Type 1 developmental research reports emphasize a particular phase of the design and development process, even though all phases were completed. For example, Link and Cherow-O'Leary (1990) document the needs assessment procedures followed by the Children's Television Workshop (CTW) to determine the needs and interests of elementary school teachers. Such data are then used to guide the development of a magazine published by the CTW. Furthermore, they describe formative evaluation techniques for testing the effectiveness of children's and parent's magazines. Other studies emphasize different components of the overall design-development process which are particularly pertinent to their topics. Sullivan (1984) documented the design, field testing, and installation of a large-scale grade K-12 energy education program; however, this particular report does not emphasize the needs assessment or evaluation stages.

Type 1 developmental studies demonstrate the range of design and development procedures currently available to practitioners. In addition, these studies commonly encompass an evaluation of the products and programs that were created, including an examination of the changes in learners who had interacted with the newly developed products.

42.2.1.2. Research Methodologies Employed in Type 1 Developmental Research. A basic premise of this chapter is that the design-development-evaluation process itself can be viewed as a form of inquiry. This is accomplished in a developmental research project by embedding traditional research methodologies[5] into the development projects. The type of research method used in a particular project tends to vary with the type of developmental research, and Type 1 studies are most likely to employ case study techniques. (See Table 42-3 for studies classified in terms of a "A" methodology use.)

The manner in which case study techniques are used varies widely in developmental research. Most commonly, the case study is seen as a way in which one can explore or describe complex situations that consist of a myriad of critical contextual variables as well as process complexities. For example, Coscarelli and White (1982) described the steps they followed in working together as subject-matter expert and designer to revise a university course in production-operations management so that student decision-making skills could be developed through the course of the semester. The study includes a description of the goals, the process used (including how unexpected problems were resolved), general evaluation data, and reflections on the experiences with implications for future development efforts. Likewise, Dick (1991) described a corporate design project in Singapore aimed at training instructional designers. The report of his Type 1 study focuses on the needs assessment and actual design phases rather than on the entire design-development-evaluation process. Both of these projects are approached from a research point of view in a qualitative manner.

Less often do studies heed the admonition of Yin (1992), who indicates that case studies are more appropriate when one is attempting to establish causal relationships rather than simply providing detailed descriptions. This approach requires a more quantitative orientation to the development case study as one seeks to explain (as well as describe) the nature of the development process. More often quantitative aspects of a Type 1 developmental research project concern efforts to determine the effectiveness or impact of the resulting instruction. In these cases, the studies have experimental designs, with or without the case study component. (See Table 42-3 for studies classified in terms of a "E" methodology use.) An example of this methodological approach is Plummer, Gillis, Legree, and Sanders (1992) whose study used two research methodologies—case study and experimental—in conjunction with the design and development task. This project involved the development of a job aid used by the military when operating a complicated piece of communications equipment. The experimental phase of the evaluation of the job aid was a study to evaluate the effectiveness of the job aid. Three instructional situations were compared: using the job aid alone, using it in combination with a demonstration, and using the technical manual in combination with a demonstration. Consequently, not only was impact information secured but

---

[4] Although this is not the emphasis of this chapter, one could construct a type of history of the field of instructional technology by tracing the Type 1 developmental research. The audiovisual emphasis could be documented through a series of studies such as Greenhill's (1955) description of producing low-cost motion pictures with sound for instructional purposes. Procedural changes could be traced through studies such as Rouch (1969) and Gordon (1969) who describe early applications of the systems approach to designing education and training programs. Programmatic trends could be seen in studies of the design and development of competency-based teacher education programs, such as Cook and Richey (1975). Today, the development of new technologies is documented in a variety of studies, many of which are discussed here.

[5] More specific information on other methodologies used in research in our field can be found in Chapters 38 to 41.

information relating to the superior conditions for using the newly developed product was also obtained.

Evaluation components of Type 1 developmental research often use a variety of methodological approaches, including systematic learner observations (see "G" classifications on Table 42-3) and diverse types of qualitative techniques (see "C" and "I" classifications). However, one of the most commonly used developmental research tools are surveys and their matching research methodologies. Surveys are used (see Table 42-3 for studies classified in terms of a "J" methodology use) as they were in Pizzuto's (1982/1983) study of the development of a simulation game used in a corporate environment to make change agents aware of diffusion communication strategies for bringing about changes in on-the-job behavior. He used surveys to determine the attitudes of trainees who had used the new game. This is a typical application of survey methodology in Type 1 developmental research.

42.2.1.3. The Nature of Conclusions from Type 1 Developmental Research.

Type 1 studies are characterized by their reliance on contextually specific projects and contextually specific conclusions that emerge from such research. This is consistent with the more qualitative orientation of the research, with the applied nature of the research and with the field's history of using practitioner experience as a source of knowledge.

Over three-quarters of the Type 1 representative developmental studies identified in Table 42-3 have conclusions that are either exclusively directed toward the target product and situation in which the project occurred, or have predominantly context-specific conclusions, even though they did generalize to some extent to other situations. (See Table 42-3 for studies classified in terms of "A" and "B" types of conclusions.) These context-specific conclusions address issues such as the following:

- *Suggested improvements in the instructional product or program* (Albero-Andres, 1982/1983; Coyle, 1985/1986; Crane & Mylonas, 1988; Cregger & Metzler, 1992; Kanyarusoke, 1983/1985; Link & Cherow-O'Leary, 1990; Munro & Towne, 1992; C.M.Russell, 1988/1990)
- *The conditions that promote successful use of the product or program* (Munro & Towne, 1992; Pizzuto, 1982/1983)
- *The impact of the particular product or program* (Aukerman, 1986/1987; Blackstone, 1989/1990; Cantor, 1988; Jones, 1985/1986; Kearsley, 1985; Pirolli, 1991; Petry & Edwards, 1984; Plummer et al., 1992; D.M. Russell, 1988)
- *The conditions that are conducive to efficient design, development, and/or evaluation of the instructional product or program* (Albero-Andres, 1982/1983; Bednar, 1988; Blackstone, 1989/1990; Buch, 1988/1989; Capell & Dannenberg, 1993; Coyle, 1992; Dick, 1991; George, 1979/1981; Harris & Cady, 1988; Jonassen, 1988; Jones, 1985/1986; Kearsley, 1985; Link &

Cherow-O'Leary, 1990; Mielke, 1990; Munro & Towne, 1992; Parer, 1977/1978; Petry & Edwards, 1984; Pirolli, 1991; C.M. Russell, 1988/1990; D.M. Russell, 1988; Watson & Bellend, 1985)

Even though these conclusions are directed toward a particular product or program, it is clear that the foundational design and development procedures are as important as the product. However, it is possible for these conclusions, even though they are context specific, to provide direction to others who are confronting similar design and development projects.

Some Type 1 studies did present conclusions that were directed toward applications of a more general nature, and two studies even emphasized such recommendations. It should be noted that *all* of these studies (see "C" and "D" classifications) were published in journals with a national audience. This may have influenced the manner in which the report was written, or it may have been recommended by a reviewer, or may even have been a condition of publication. In any case, many journal articles tend to be less focused upon context-specific conclusions than dissertation research reports. The conclusions of these studies, especially those with a less formal quantitative design or with a more descriptive qualitative design, tend to be presented as "lessons learned" rather than as hypothesized relationships or predictions. These generalized lessons are often supported by, and discussed in the context of, current related literature as well as the design, development, and evaluation project that prompted them. The content of the conclusions in the six studies identified in Table 42-3 with more generalized conclusions all relate to the conditions that are conducive to efficient design, development, and/or evaluation of instructional products or programs (Alessi, 1988; Bowers & Tsai, 1990; Gay & Mazur, 1993; Medsker, 1992; Noel, 1991; Sullivan, 1984).

42.2.1.4. Typical Type 1 Developmental Studies.

This section has described the nature of Type 1 developmental research in terms of their focus, specifically examining the design, development, and evaluation processes addressed, the research methodologies employed, and the nature of their conclusions. While recent studies have been used to exemplify the range of Type 1 research, thus far particular studies have not been described in detail. Here, we will summarize the research of C. M. Russell (1988/1990)[6] and Noel (1991) as studies that are representative of the group. These studies reflect the two key Type 1 research formats; Russell's work was a doctoral dissertation and Noel's was a large-scale project published in a research journal. The topics, a computer-based instructional product and an international secondary education program, are representative of the contemporary issues addressed through developmental research.

---

[6] Christina Russell's research was completed at the University of Pittsburgh under the direction of Barbara Seels and won the 1989 outstanding dissertation award of AECT's Division of Instructional Development.

The C. M. Russell (1988/1990) study addressed the development and evaluation of an interactive videodisc system to train radiation therapy technology students in the process of treating malignancies using a linear accelerator. As with any traditional research project, it is guided by predetermined questions and hypotheses and is embedded into the theoretical framework supported by current literature, including instructional design theory and generally related research on programmed instruction and computer-assisted instruction, as well as more specifically related research on interactive video and simulations.

The development procedures were described and documented in detail. These procedures included the ways in which the following tasks were performed:

- Project management and advisory committee operations
- Needs assessment
- Identification of goals and objectives
- Task analysis and development of learning hierarchies
- Scriptwriting and storyboarding
- Production of audio and video components
- Computer programming
- Formative evaluation of the prototype

The products of each phase were provided. Finally, the effectiveness of the prototype product was determined through the used of a nonequivalent control group design.

The conclusions of this research supported the proposition that the interactive videodisc approach to training was not only effective in increasing cognitive achievement but was also more efficient instruction than the traditional lecture approach. When comparing the two delivery methodologies, no differences were apparent in terms of posttraining clinical performance or student attitudes. However, conclusions were also drawn with respect to managing other videodisc development projects and to specific techniques of designing and developing such mediated instruction. Attention was drawn to the importance of the skills of the project manager, the front-end analysis, the choice of dominant information presentation mode, the format of reviews and test items, the extent of realism used, and the use of visual cues for highlighting major points. The amount of structure provided for the student was an issue. Christina Russell concluded that "when accuracy is critical in skills performance, or the lack thereof results in death to a patient, the mainline content should be highly structured. However, once mainline content is given, an unstructured approach would work well with practice segments" (p. 120).

C. M. Russell's work (1988/1990) is a detailed report of an extensive study that includes both context-specific and generalized conclusions, although the clear focus of the study is the particular product that will be used by university-level radiation therapy students. Since it is a study completed as part of the requirements of a doctoral degree, length is not an issue, and the format was undoubtedly dictated by the degree requirements. Noel's (1991), on the other hand, is not only reported in a different medium—a

professional journal—but it addresses a project with a much larger scope. Consequently, this study and its published report take on a different form, even though it too is representative of Type 1 developmental research.

Noel's research concerned the design of a junior secondary education program for the country of Botswana. This is essentially the design of a nationwide junior high school curriculum. The project, guided by an instructional systems design model, encompassed not only the program design but also the development and production of instructional materials and the development and implementation of a support system that included teacher training and school management systems.

Noel (1991) stresses the initial stages of project implementation, especially the needs assessment phase. Noel places the project into a cultural and historical framework when he describes the role of education and schooling in Botswana. The study is also viewed as a testing ground for the use of ISD principles. Special needs assessment procedures were used: sector assessment and contextual review. Sector assessment is a method of tailoring general development strategies to a unique situation, and the contextual review process ensures project implementation according to the original plans. Both can be viewed as part of an ongoing needs assessment activity. The use of these two design and development processes in Botswana are described in Noel (1991).

While the ISD process served as an excellent model for curriculum development in Botswana, particular techniques were identified which proved most useful. Noel (1991) notes, however, that the most productive aspects of the model were those "that directly addressed the perceived needs of various curriculum developers" (p. 103), and identifies techniques used to infuse ISD concepts into Botswanian practice. One way of ensuring successful use of ISD is through the use of contextual review procedures that provide a way of updating the project plan, build project teams, promote clear communication, and provide opportunities for dissemination and diffusion of project products.

Noel (1991) describes these strategies and makes recommendations for their more general use based on the experiences of the large-scale Botswana research and development effort. Thus, even though the conclusions and recommendations are written in a more general tone, they are lessons learned from a specific practical situation.

Each of these studies exemplify Type 1 developmental research. They are case studies that:

- Describe and document a particular design, development, and evaluation project
- Utilize a range of traditional research methodologies, in addition to standard design and development procedures
- Draw conclusions from their research which are highly context specific
- Tend to serve as dissemination vehicles for exemplary design, development, and/or evaluation strategies

42.2.2 Type 2 Developmental Research

Type 2 developmental research is the most generalized of the various orientations, and typically addresses the design, development, and evaluation processes themselves rather than a demonstration of such processes. The ultimate objective of this research is the production of knowledge in the form of a new (or an enhanced) design or development model. This research tends to emphasize:

- The use of a particular design technique or process, such as formative evaluation
- The use of a comprehensive design, development, or evaluation model
- A general examination of design and development as it is commonly practiced in the workplace

Thirty-eight examples of Type 2 research have been analyzed using the same framework previously employed in the analysis of Type 1, and the results are presented in Table 42-4.

42.2.2.1. Process Foci of Type 2 Developmental Research. We have previously distinguished between *doing* development and *studying* development. In Type 1 research there is a pattern of combining the doing and the studying in the process of discovering superior procedures. However, unlike Type 1, Type 2 research often does *not* begin with the actual development of an instructional product or program, concentrating instead on previously developed instruction. These studies are more likely to focus on the more generic use of development processes, offering implications for *any* design or development project.

Whether the research is product focused or process focused, Type 2 studies are more likely to concentrate on a particular process rather than on the more comprehensive view of development. (See those studies in Table 42-4, Process Focus column, which are labeled "B" through "J" as opposed to those labeled "A.") For example, Abdelraheem (1989/1990) and Cambre (1978/1979) both studied formative evaluation processes, one with respect to instructional module design and the other in reference to the design and development of instructional television. But while Abdelraheem was involved in a specific design and development project, Cambre was not. She was studying the manner in which this task had been conducted in many situations over a 50-year period. The key difference between Type 1 and Type 2, studies that focus on a particular aspect of the total process, is that goals of Type 2 studies tend to be more generalized, striving to enhance the ultimate models employed in these procedures. Type 1 research, on the other hand, is more confined to the analysis of a given project.

Developmental research projects span the entire range of design and development process components. Those studies included in Table 42-4 tend to emphasize needs assessment and formative and summative evaluation. In addition, there are studies that address design processes in a more generic fashion. Sample studies of this nature include Nelson (1988/1990), Rowland (1992), and Wedman and Tessmer (1993). This research is part of the growing body of literature contributing to an understanding of the nature of designer decision making. It provides another topical orientation in addition to those studies that examine the various components of traditional instructional systems design models.

It is less common to see Type 2 developmental research that addresses materials production procedures. While Spector, Muraida, and Marlino (1992) do this to some extent with respect to authoring computer-based instruction, it is far more common for production processes to be analyzed within the context of a demonstration of such procedures. These situations are more likely to form the basis of a Type 1 developmental study as discussed earlier.

While the majority of the studies cited in Table 42-4 do not tackle the entire design and development process in a comprehensive fashion, some do. For example, Spector, Muraida, and Marlino (1992) proposed an enhanced ISD model for use in courseware authoring grounded in cognitive theory. This use of this model was then described and evaluated in a military training environment. This is a good example of a Type 2 study. Likewise, Richey (1992) proposed a modified ISD procedural model that was based on an empirical examination of those factors that influence employee training effectiveness. This is another example of a comprehensive Type 2 study.

42.2.2.2. Research Methodologies Employed in Type 2 Developmental Research. While the case study served as the dominant methodological orientation of Type 1 developmental research, it is far less prominent in Type 2 studies. This is not surprising given the fact that Type 2 research typically does not involve a specific design and development project. There is a much greater diversity of research methods employed in the representative Type 2 studies identified in Table 42-4. Not only are experimental and quasi-experimental studies common, but this table even shows studies using philosophical and historical techniques, as well as a variety of qualitative methodologies. (See Table 42-4, "Research Methods Used" column.)

Even though case studies are not the overwhelming norm in Type 2 research, they are nonetheless found. (See Table 42-4 for studies classified in terms of "A"-type research methodology.) As with other developmental studies, case study techniques are sometimes employed in Type 2 research that includes a description of the actual design and development process followed in the creation of a particular product, or in the demonstration of a particular process. Wreathall and Connelly (1992) document the development of a method of using performance indicators as a technique for determining training effectiveness. In true Type 1 fashion, they describe the technique and the manner in which they applied it in a given context. This facet utilizes case study methods. However, they extend their study to verify the relevance of their technique through the use of a structured survey interview of other professionals in the field. (This latter phase of the research warrants its classification as a Type 2 study.) The Wreathall and Connelly study is typical of the Type 2 research that uses case study methods, in that the methods are used in combination with other research techniques as well.

TABLE 42-4. AN ANALYSIS OF REPRESENTATIVE TYPE 2 DEVELOPMENTAL RESEARCH LITERATURE

Reference	Product or Program Focus	Process Focus	Use Context	Tools and Techniques Emphasized	Research Methods Used	Nature of Conclusions
Abedelraheem, A.Y. (1989/1990)	E	F, J	A, H	J, K	E	C
Baghdadi, A.A. (1980/1981)	E	F, J	B	J, K	E	D
Beauchamp, M. (1990/1991)	K	A	A	B	J	D
Burkholder, B.L. (1981/82)	E, A	F	B	K	E	D
Cambre, M. (1978/1979)	I	F	I		F	D
Capell, P. (1989/1990)	J	A	B		B, I	D
Carl, D. (1977/1978)	I	A, B	B	A, B	A, G, J	B
Cummings, O.W. (1985)	K	B	C		J	D
Driscoll, M.P. & Tessmer, M. (1985)	E, K,	D, J	A	G, J	E	D
Ford, J.M. & Wood, L.E. (1992)	K	D	I	E, F, G	D	C
Fuchs, L.S. & Fuchs, D. (1986)	A, K	F	A	J	K	D
Gauger, E.P. (1985/1987)	B	I	B, D		D	C
Goel, V. & Pirolli, P. (1988)	K	A, K	C		G, I	D

Product/ Program Focus	Process Focus	Use Context	Tools and Techniques	Research Methods	Nature of Conclusions
A. Full Course	A. Gen. Des/Devel./ Evaluation Proc.	A. K-12 Schools	A. Problem Analysis	A. Case Study	A. Context/Product Specific
B. Full Program	B. Needs Assess'mt.	B. Post-Secondary	B. Needs Assessm't	B. Descriptive	B. Context/Product Specific with some Generalz'tn
C. Workshop	C. Content Selection	C. Business and Industry	C. Environmental Anal.	C. Ethnography	C. Generalizations with some context/product specific
D. Gen. Print Mat.	D. Design	D. Health Care	D. Job Analysis	D. Evaluation	D. Generalizations
E. Instruct. Module	E. Production	E. Military and Govt.	E. Task Analysis	E. Experimental	
F. Study Guide	F. Form. Evaluation	F. Continuing and Community Educ.	F. Learning Hierarchy	F. Historical	
G. Job Aid	G. Utilization/Delivery	G. Employee Trng. — Other	G. Sequencing	G. Observational	
H. Games/Simulation	H. Management	H. International	H. Cost Analysis	H. Philosophical	
I. Instruc. Television	I. Summative Evaluation	I. Context-Free	I. Dissemination	I. Qualitative	
J. Computer-Based	J. Learner Outcomes		J. Learner Verification	J. Survey	
K. Any Project	K. No Dev. Involved		K. Specific Tech.		

TABLE 42-4. Continued

Reference	Product or Program Focus	Process Focus	Use Context	Tools and Techniques Emphasized	Research Methods Used	Nature of Conclusions
Harrison, P.J., et al. (1991)	B	A, G, H	B		I, J	C
Higgins, N. & Reiser, R. (1985)	K	D	C		E	D
Keller, J.M. (1987)	A, K	D	A, I	J	E, J, K	C
Kerr, S.T. (1983)	A, E	A	A, B		J	C
Kim, S.O. (1983/1984)	K	A	H			C
King, D. & Dille, A. (1993)	K	A	C	H	A	B
Kress, C. (1989/1990)	A	A	C		E, J	D
Luiz, T. (1982/1983)	K	A	I		H	D
McAleese, R. (1988)	K	D	I	E, F, G	D	C
Milazzo, C. (1981)	H	F	B, D			
Nelson, W.A. (1988/1990)	K	A, K	G	A, D, E	G, I	D
Nicolson, R. (1988)	K	D, E	B	E, F, G	D	C

Product/ Program Focus	Process Focus	Use Context	Tools and Techniques	Research Methods	Nature of Conclusions
A. Full Course	A. Gen. Des/Devel./ Evaluation Proc.	A. K-12 Schools	A. Problem Analysis	A. Case Study	A. Context/Product Specific
B. Full Program	B. Needs Assessm't.	B. Post-Secondary	B. Needs Assessm't	B. Descriptive	B. Context/Product Specific with some Generalz'tn
C. Workshop	C. Content Selection	C. Business and Industry	C. Environmental Anal.	C. Ethnography	C. Generalizations with some context/product specific
D. Gen. Print Mat.	D. Design	D. Health Care	D. Job Analysis	D. Evaluation	D. Generalizations
E. Instruct. Module	E. Production	E. Military and Govt.	E. Task Analysis	E. Experimental	
F. Study Guide	F. Form. Evaluation	F. Continuing and Community Educ.	F. Learn'g Hierarchy	F. Historical	
G. Job Aid	G. Utilization/Delivery	G. Employee Trng. —	G. Sequencing	G. Observational	
H. Games/Simulation	H. Management	Other	H. Cost Analysis	H. Philosophical	
I. Instruc. Television	I. Summative Evaluation	H. International	I. Dissemination	I. Qualitative	
J. Computer-Based	J. Learner Outcomes	I. Context-Free	J. Learner Verification	J. Survey	
K. Any Project	K. No Dev. Involved		K. Specific Tech.	K. Other	

TABLE 42-4. Continued

Reference	Product or Program Focus	Process Focus	Use Context	Tools and Techniques Emphasized	Research Methods Used	Nature of Conclusions
Piper, A.J. (1990/1991)	K	H	C	J	A	D
Pirolli, P. (1991)	K	D, E	I	E, F, G	D	D
Richey, R.C. (1992)	C, K	A, J	C	B, C	I, J	D
Riplinger, J.A. (1985/1987)	K	B, C	J	E	B, J	D
Rojas, A.M. (1988)	C	I	C		D	D
Rowland, G. (1992)	K	A, K	B, C, E		G, I	D
Spector, J.M., Muraida, D.J. & Marlino, M.R. (1992)	J	A, E	E	K	G	B
Taylor, R.L.M. (1986/1987)	J					
Taylor, B. & Ellix, J. (1991)	A	A	E		D	B
Wagner, N. (1984)	A, K	I	B	J, K	E	D
Wedman, J. & Tessmer, M. (1993)	K	A, K	C		J	D
Wreathall, J. & Connelly, E (1992)	K	I, J	E	J, K	A, J	C
Zemke, R. (1985)	K	A, K	C		J	B

Product/ Program Focus	Process Focus	Use Context	Tools and Techniques	Research Methods	Nature of Conclusions
A. Full Course	A. Gen. Des/Devel./ Evaluation Proc.	A. K-12 Schools	A. Problem Analysis	A. Case Study	A. Context/Product Specific
B. Full Program	B. Needs Assessm't.	B. Post-Secondary	B. Needs Assessm't	B. Descriptive	B. Context/Product Specific with some Generalz'tn
C. Workshop	C. Content Selection	C. Business and Industry	C. Environmental Anal.	C. Ethnography	C. Generalizations with some context/product specific
D. Gen. Print Mat.	D. Design	D. Health Care	D. Job Analysis	D. Evaluation	D. Generalizations
E. Instruct. Module	E. Production	E. Military and Govt.	E. Task Analysis	E. Experimental	
F. Study Guide	F. Form. Evaluation	F. Continuing and Community Educ.	F. Learn'g Hierarchy	F. Historical	
G. Job Aid	G. Utilization/Delivery	G. Employee Trng. — Other	G. Sequencing	G. Observational	
H. Games/Simulation	H. Management	H. International	H. Cost Analysis	H. Philosophical	
I. Instruc. Television	I. Summative Evaluation	I. Context-Free	I. Dissemination	I. Qualitative	
J. Computer-Based	J. Learner Outcomes		J. Learner Verification	J. Survey	
K. Any Project	K. No Dev. Involved		K. Specific Tech.		

Experimental and quasi-experimental techniques (see 39.2.1) can serve a variety of functions in Type 2 developmental research. (See Table 42-4 for studies classified in terms of a "E"-type research methodology.) They are often used as a way of verifying the procedure in terms of learner outcomes. Driscoll and Tessmer (1985) confirmed the utility of the rational set generator as a way of creating examples and nonexamples in instruction by using an experimental design to compare its impact on student performance. Keller (1987) used quasi-experimental methods to test the impact of the ARCS Model of Motivation Design as it was applied to the development of teacher in-service training workshops. In both cases, the experimentation is critical to the verification and evaluation of a particular design and development technique. This is not unlike the use of experimental and quasi-experimental techniques in other types of developmental research.

Surveys (see 41.2.1) are frequently used in Type 2 developmental studies. In Type 1 studies, surveys were typically another means of determining product impact or effectiveness with learners and/or instructors in a given education or training situation. This technique is also used in Type 2 research as in the studies of Keller (1987) and Richey (1992). However, in Type 2 studies the survey is frequently used as a means of gathering data from designers in a variety of settings. Beauchamp (1990/1991), Cummings (1985), Riplinger (1985/1987), Rowland (1992), and Wedman and Tessmer (1993) all conducted surveys across a range of typical design environments—Beauchamp to validate the use a wide range of affective variables in the instructional design process, Cummings to gather widespread data on the effectiveness of three needs assessment techniques, Riplinger to determine the type of task analyses used in the field, and Rowland and Wedman and Tessmer to analyze the nature of designer decisions.

Most of the surveys conducted in Type 2 research are either mail surveys or on-site, on-demand surveys. In both cases they are completed by the subject. However, survey methodologies can also be employed in other forms to obtain data of a more qualitative nature. For example, Richey (1992) conducted structured personal interviews with trainees to verify and/or expand the more quantitative data collected in her study. Similarly, Rowland (1992) used a systematic posttask interview in addition to other data collection techniques designed to document one's decision-making processes. Survey methodologies can also be used to gather existing data on organizations or learners, for example, in a systematic fashion.

While Type 1 developmental research studies tend to be more quantitative in nature, it is not uncommon for Type 2 studies to have a qualitative facet to their design. Not only is interview data often utilized, but other examples are seen as well. Harrison et al. (1991) used qualitative data analysis techniques in the development of a distance education assessment instrument. Nelson's (1988/1990) and Rowland's (1992) use of "think-aloud protocols" not only reflects a cognitive orientation but a qualitative one as well.

42.2.3. The Nature of Conclusions from Type 2 Developmental Research.

Type 2 studies are unique among developmental research in that they are ultimately directed toward general principles that are applicable in a wide range of design and development projects. Those studies described in Table 42-4 are typical. Almost all of these studies present generalized conclusions (see the studies in Table 42-4 that are classified in terms of "C" and "D" types of conclusions), and the vast majority of these studies have *all* generalized conclusions. Again, this is consistent with the methodologies typically used in such research and the greater tendency toward quantitative techniques.

The nature of the conclusions in Type 2 research also varies somewhat from those of Type 1. The most noticeable difference is that the Type 2 conclusions pertain to a technique or model, as opposed to a product or program. The issues that are addressed in these conclusions can be summarized in the following manner:

- *Evidence of the validity and/or effectiveness of a particular technique or model* (Baghdadi, 1980/1981; Beauchamp, 1990/1991; Burkholder, 1981/82; Driscoll & Tessmer, 1985; Fuchs & Fuchs, 1986; Gauger, 1985/1987; Harrison et al., 1991; Keller, 1987; Kim, 1983/1984; Kress, 1989/1990; Richey, 1992; Wagner, 1984; Wreathall & Connelly, 1992)
- *Conditions and procedures that facilitate the successful use of a particular technique or model* (Abdelraheem, 1989/1990; Baghdadi, 1980/1981; Beauchamp, 1990/1991; Burkholder, 1981/1982; Carl, 1977/1978; Cummings, 1985; Ford & Wood, 1992; Fuchs & Fuchs, 1986; Gauger, 1985/1987; Goel & Pirolli, 1988; Keller, 1987; Kim, 1983/1984; King & Dille, 1993; Kress, 1989/1990; Nelson, 1988/1990; Nicholson, 1988; Piper, 1990/1991; Rowland, 1992; Spector, Muraida & Marlino, 1992)
- *Explanations of the successes or failures encountered in using a particular technique or model* (Cambre, 1978/1979; Carl, 1977/1978; Higgins & Reiser, 1985; Kerr, 1983; King & Dille, 1993; Kress, 1989/1990; McAleese, 1988; Nicolson, 1988; Pirolli, 1991; Taylor & Ellis, 1991; Wedman & Tessmer, 1993; Zemke, 1985)
- *A synthesis of events and/or opinions related to the use of a particular technique or model* (Cambre, 1978/1979; Luiz, 1982/1983; Pirolli, 1991; Riplinger, 1985/1987; Rojas, 1988)
- *A new or enhanced design, development, and/or evaluation model* (Beauchamp, 1990/1991; King & Dille, 1993; McAleese, 1988; Richey, 1992; Spector, Muraida & Marlino, 1992; Wedman & Tessmer, 1993).

It is not uncommon for a given Type 2 study to generate more than one type of conclusion. This was less likely to be the case with respect to the other type of developmental research.

42.2.2.4. Typical Type 2 Developmental Studies.

We will describe in more detail two typical studies, one that looks at a particular component of the design and development process, and another that involves the construction and validation of a model for integrating learner affect into the design process (a more global study). First, Higgins and Reiser (1985) studied media selection by comparing the decisions made by novice developers making intuitive decisions with those using a media selection model. The "correct" answers were determined by experienced instructional designers. They found that those inexperienced designers who used a selection model were more likely to match the decisions of experienced professionals than those simply using intuition. Moreover, those who had received instruction on media selection were more likely to consider a greater number of selection factors than those simply using common sense. They also learned that merely having or reviewing a media selection model does not ensure proper use of the model. They can be sufficiently complex, so that instruction appears necessary to ensure that one can use the model to make correct decisions. This research employed experimental techniques and methods.

The Higgins and Reiser (1989) research is an example of a fairly straightforward study of the use of a particular aspect of an ISD model. Other Type 2 studies are broader in scope. Beauchamp (1990/1991), for instance, was interested in the extent to which designers consider affective variables during their work. His task was twofold. First, Beauchamp devised an integrative model of learner affect and instructional systems design. This model was a synthesis of an extensive review of the literature on affect and affective instructional design practices. The format of the model was a taxonomic matrix. Learner affect variables were classified as either internal/emotional (including items such as motivation and self-esteem), cognitive (including items such as beliefs and moral judgments), or behavioral (including items such as creativity and interpersonal skills). The instructional systems design categories were traditional design phases: needs assessment, goals and objectives, delivery, and evaluation. Affective variables were related to the design stage in which they would be addressed. Thus, the needs assessment would consider attributes of affect such as interests (internal/emotional), values (cognitive), and attendance (behavioral). Similarly, affective-related content variables were related to goals and objectives, affective delivery considerations were identified, and evaluation techniques cited.

The second purpose of Beauchamp's (1990/1991) research was to validate this model by determining the extent to which it reflects affective learner components and current practice in alternative education settings. In addition, the extent to which the characteristics of the teachers, the schools, and the community impacted the use of the various parts of the model was determined. The cognitive components of the model proved to be of significantly less importance than the internal/emotional or behavioral components. However, there did not appear to be any differences in the design and delivery of affective instruction related to internal/emotional factors as opposed to behavioral factors. Moreover, as the instructional design process progresses from needs assessment to evaluation, the importance of addressing affective variables seems to dimin-

ish. In general, older, more experienced educators were more likely to use the elements of the affective design model. The model also tended to be used more in communities with higher income levels, and less in schools with larger proportions of minority students. Rural and urban communities seemed to use the affective model less than the small-town and suburban communities. Implications and recommendations for developing affective instruction were identified in the context of general principals of curriculum innovation.

Beauchamp's study did not involve any product or program development, but did address the nature of design and development. It primarily used survey research techniques.

Each of these studies represent Type 2 developmental research. Even though they do not describe or relate to an actual development project, they are typical of Type 2 studies because of the following characteristics:

- An orientation towards studying the design and development process, rather than demonstrating particular strategies
- A tendency toward use of quantitative research methodologies
- A tendency to develop generalized principles and conclusions with respect to the design and development process, or a part of the process
- An effort to identify, describe, explain, or validate those conditions that facilitate successful design and development

42.3 THE METHODOLOGY OF DEVELOPMENTAL RESEARCH

The aim of this section is to provide some methodological direction to those entertaining a developmental research project. Since many topics can be addressed in a number of different ways, this section may also help one recognize the potential of a given problem to be addressed as a developmental topic by describing the developmental orientation to the traditional stages of planning and reporting research projects.

42.3.1 Defining the Research Problem

Putting the developmental "twist" on a research project begins in the problem definition stage. This is done by focusing the research problem on a particular aspect of the design, development, or evaluation *process*, as opposed to focusing on a particular variable that impacts learning, or perhaps the impact of a type of media (to name two alternative approaches). A developmental focus typically involves one of the following dimensions:

- A given *type* of developmental research
- A given design, development, or evaluation *model* or *process*
- A given instructional *product, program, process or tool*
- An interest in identifying either general development *principles* or *situation-specific recommendations*

The problem definition stage must also establish the research parameters and identify the scope of the study. At the minimum, this involves determining whether the:

- *Development* (or part of the development) of the instruction will be considered as part of the study, or if the research will be directed toward a *previously* developed program or set of materials
- *Evaluation* of the instruction or the development process will be considered as part of the study, and if so whether the evaluation in point will be formative, and/or summative, and/or confirmative
- *Revision and retesting* of the prototype instruction will be encompassed in the study

Seels (1994) describes typical processes one uses to explain the goals of a developmental research project. For example, *research questions,* rather than hypotheses, may guide the study. This tactic may be selected due to the lack of a firm base in the literature which one can use as a basis for formulating a hypothesis. However, one can use *objectives* as a substitute for both research questions and hypotheses. Project objectives are typically used to describe the design, development, evaluation, and/or revision processes or models that will be followed in the early parts of the study.

Because developmental research is often context specific, one must be particularly concerned with the limitations or unique conditions that may be operating in a particular study. Such limitations will affect the extent to which one may generalize the conclusions of the study. The results may be applicable only in the situation studied, or to others with similar characteristics, rather than being generalizable to a wider range of instructional environments.

42.3.2 The Review of Related Literature

Typically, literature reviews concentrate on the specific variables being studied, usually the independent and dependent variables. The literature review in developmental studies may also address other topics, such as:

- Procedural models that might be appropriate for the task at hand
- Characteristics of effective instructional products, programs, or delivery systems
- Factors that have impacted the use of the target development processes in other situations
- Factors that have impacted the implementation and management of the target instructional product, program, or delivery system in other situations
- The methodology of developmental research

In developmental studies directed toward innovative instructional environments or innovative design and development processes, it would not be unusual to find little research in the literature that is *directly* relevant. In such cases the researcher must still identify literature that is rele-

vant to the foundational theory of the project, even though the link may be indirect. For example, there *is* literature on factors that affect the use of computers and other media in instruction, but there may be little on factors related to the specific use of virtual reality as a delivery system. In developmental research, the conceptual framework for the study may be found in literature from actual practice environments (such as an evaluation report) as well as from traditional research literature that is directed toward theory construction.

42.3.3 The Research Procedures

Many developmental studies take more time to complete than other types of research. Moreover, it is likely that there will be more changes made in one's research plans and procedures as a result of unanticipated events than is typical in other types of research. Consequently, detailed research procedures and timelines are most important.

42.3.3.1. Population and Sample. There may be several populations and/or samples in a developmental research project. While the nature of the population varies with the type of developmental research being conducted, typical populations include:

- Designers, developers, and evaluators
- Instructors and/or program facilitators
- Learners

In many developmental studies, the project itself is considered to be the object of study. In such situations, each dimension of the project would need to be carefully profiled, including factors such as resources available, time constraints, and designer expertise. The project then would be the unit of analysis, rather than the designers, for example. Some of these studies may also have a component in which individual learners are the units of analysis as well.

42.3.3.2. Research Design. The procedures should address both the development facet of the study and the traditional research facet. First, the critical design and development processes should be explicated (i.e., how and when will the development take place, how and when will the instruction be implemented, how and when will the evaluation take place). Then those procedures of the component research methodologies should be described. For example, will the research encompass an experimental study? If so, what is the design? Will the research encompass survey research? If so, describe the steps. Will the research encompass a case study? If so, how will it be conducted?

Table 42-5 presents a summary of those research methods that are most frequently used in the various types of developmental research. This table is built upon analyses of the representative developmental studies presented in Tables 42-3 and 42-4. It highlights those points made earlier regarding the methodological trends that appear when comparing the two types of developmental research.

Even though these data are incomplete, there seem to be methodological patterns for the two types of developmental research. While the selection of a given methodology is certainly not *mandated* by the type of research, Table 42-5 may provide some selection guidelines for those new to developmental research.

42.3.3.3. Data Collection and Analysis Procedures.
Data collection in a developmental study takes a variety of forms depending on the focus of the research. Typical types of data collection in developmental research relate to factors such as:

- Documentation of the design, development, and evaluation tasks
- Documentation of the conditions under which the development and implementation took place
- Conducting the needs assessment, the formative and summative evaluations
- Profiling the target populations
- Profiling the design and/or implementation contexts
- Measuring the impact of the instruction and the conditions that are associated with this impact

Data analysis and synthesis are not unlike those of other research projects. There are likely to be descriptive data presentations, qualitative data analyses using data from documentation and observations, and correlational and comparative analyses.

42.3.4 Results and Conclusions

The results of a developmental study are likely to be extensive, given the wide range of data typically collected. The format for presenting these results varies depending on the nature of the reporting medium. Dissertations or reports to funding agencies provide more opportunity for full data presentation. Articles in the professional journals must be kept succinct. In all formats, however, data synthesis becomes critical. However, longer reports may allow one to include raw data in an appendix. For example, full results of a needs assessment may be included in this situation.

We have previously discussed the nature of conclusions derived from both types of developmental research. Seldom do we find a single project that confines itself to one type of conclusion, and most often *all* projects attempt to make additions to the field's knowledge of instructional design, development, and evaluation. This may be done by constructing new procedural models, or formulating generalized principles, or by describing the "lessons learned" in a particular project.

42.4 RECENT INNOVATIVE DEVELOPMENTAL RESEARCH

Recently, there have been innovative lines of developmental research occurring in the discipline. This research has extended the boundaries of the more traditional orientation to developmental research previously discussed in this chapter. By and large, this work concerns the development of instruction using the newer models and procedures of instructional design (see 5.5, 7.5, 12.4, 18.5, 20.1). These new models reflect the influence of cognitive science, especially with respect to higher-level cognitive skills (van Merrienboer, Jelsma & Paas, 1992). Moreover, constructivist influences are evident in a new emphasis on the role of context in design (Richey & Tessmer, 1995) and in the development of anchored instruction (Bransford, Sherwood, Hasselbring, Kinzer & Williams, 1990). This research is progressing even as new methods and techniques of designing technology-based instruction are being developed. The more recent research to be considered here addresses areas such as designer decision making (see 2.5), knowledge acquisition tools (see 19.2), and the use of automated development tools (see 18.4).

By its very nature, the research on designer decision making is Type 2 research aimed at understanding and improving the design process. The other research tends to focus on improving the design process through the development of new tools and techniques. Sometimes this is Type 1 research involving a particular product or context, but more frequently it is Type 2 research oriented toward the development of generic tools. The following section summarizes important findings and issues emerging from these newer lines of developmental research activity.

42.4.1 Trends in Research on Design and Designer Decision Making

Depending on the situation, design (in the general sense) has been described as decision making, simulation, a creative activity, a scientific process, or "a very complicated act of faith" (Freeman, 1983, p. 3). Recently, engineers,

TABLE 42-5. AN OVERVIEW OF COMMONLY USED RESEARCH METHODS IN DEVELOPMENTAL RESEARCH STUDIES

Type of Developmental Research	Documentation of Development Process	Primary Research Methods Used
Type 1	Yes	Case study, evaluation
Type 2	Sometimes	Survey, experimental, evaluation, qualitative

architects, commercial designers, computer scientists, and instructional designers have become interested in the question of how humans design or, by way of definition, how they select certain elements from a large number of possibilities and combine these elements to develop a functional and aesthetically pleasing solution to a problem (Zaff, 1987). As of yet, there is no definitive answer to the question of how people design. What is suspected, however, is that design combines both rational and intuitive thought processes that are derived from the knowledge and creativity of the designer (Nadin & Novak, 1987).

Part of the problem in understanding the design process is distinguishing design activities from other forms of thinking (see 5.4). The theoretical basis for most studies of design comes from the literature on human problem solving. Simon (1981) suggests an all-encompassing view of design that incorporates nearly any kind of planning activity. In fact, he considers design as a fundamental characteristic of human thought: Everyone designs who devises courses of action aimed at changing existing situations into preferred ones. Simon's conception of design as problem solving leads to the characterization of design as a process of optimization among various solution alternatives.

In contrast, Schon (1983, 1987) believes that design is a process of reflection-in-action. In this sense, design problems are constructed by the designer through a process of "dialogue" with the situation in which the designer engages in metaphorical processes that relate the current design state to the repertoire of objects/solutions known by the designer. In part, this involves "seeing" the current situation in a new way (Rowland, 1993). As a designer moves through the design process, the situation "talks back" to the designer, causing the designer to reframe the problem, often relating the current situation to previous experiences. Obstacles or difficulties in the design situation often provide opportunities for new insights into the problem. In some sense, a designer is engaged in learning as well as design, because the designer's personal knowledge structures are altered by the information present in the design environment (McAleese, 1988).

42.4.1.1. The Design Task Environment. What makes design a special form of problem solving, in part, is the nature of design problems. Reitman (1964) has suggested a classification of problem types that includes a category he calls "ill-defined" problems, where starting states, goal states, and allowable transformations of the problem are not specified. Simon (1973) generally agrees with this classification, but notes that problems fall along a continuum between well defined and ill defined. The point at which a problem becomes ill defined is largely a function of the problem solver, in that the goals, attitudes, and knowledge of the problem solver determine the degree to which a problem may be ill defined. Goel and Pirolli (1988) take issue with Simon's broad characterization of design described above, noting that unlike cognitive science theorists, designers generally describe their activities as the specification of an artifact that includes considerations of performance and realizability. They claim that the design task environment includes several features that distinguish design from other forms of problem solving, including many degrees of freedom in the problem statement, limited or delayed feedback from the world during problem solving, an artifact that must function independently from the designer, and "no right or wrong answers, only better and worse ones" (Goel & Pirolli, 1988, p. 7). Chandrasekaran (1987) also characterizes design problems in a more limiting classification scheme than Simon. At one extreme are those rare design problems that require innovative behavior where neither the knowledge sources nor the problem-solving strategies are known in advance. Such activity might be more properly termed *creating* or *inventing,* and results in a completely new product. Other design problems are closer to routine, but may require some innovation because of the introduction of new requirements for a product that has already been designed. The most common type of design routinely proceeds "by selecting among previously known sets of alternatives" (Chandrasekaran, 1987, p. 122). The designer knows at each stage what options are available and in which order to select them.

42.4.1.2. The Instructional Design Task Environment. Certainly, how a designer proceeds in the design process is related to what is being designed, that is, the design task environment. Initially, design goals are often poorly specified, and can involve the performance goals for the object or system, constraints on the development process (such as cost), or constraints on the design process (such as time required for completion). Part of the designer's task is to formulate more specific goals based on the constraints of the problem. The designer then identifies criteria for selecting and eliminating various elements, and finally makes decisions based on these criteria (Kerr, 1983). Pirolli and Greeno (1988) have described the instructional design task environment in similar terms. Their analysis, based on the notion that instructional design is a problem-solving task, recognizes that the task environment, or problem space, consists of "the alternatives that a problem solver has available and the various states that can be produced during problem solving by the decisions that the problem solver makes in choosing among alternatives" (p. 182). They suggest that instructional design has three levels of generality—global, intermediate, and local—and at each level designers are concerned with three types of issues: goals and constraints, technological resources, and theoretical resources. Global-level design decisions are mainly concerned with the content and goals of instruction. At the intermediate level, lessons and activities are identified and sequenced. At the local level, instructional designers make decisions about how information is to be presented to learners, and how specific learning tasks are to be organized.

This description of the instructional design task environment is similar in many respects to the "variables" of instruction identified by Reigeluth (1983a). But Pirolli and Greeno (1988) also note an interesting gap in instructional design research: Nearly all of the descriptive and prescriptive theories of instructional design focus on instructional products, while there is little research dedicated to describing the instructional design process (see 2.5).

42.4.1.3. The Cognitive Processes of Instructional Design.

Studies of the cognitive processes of designers in domains other than instructional design indicate that the design process is iterative and cyclical, rather than linear. For example, studies of architectural designers have reported two distinct categories of designer behavior: problem structuring and problem solving (Akin, Chen, Dave & Pithavadian, 1986). Problem structuring transforms the information obtained through functional analysis into scenarios that partition the design space into a hierarchical organization of design units along with the parameters of the units and relationships between units. The design units are then arranged in various ways until a solution is found that meets the requirements and constraints established earlier. Furthermore, the structure of the problem can affect the designer's performance. When the information of a design problem is provided in a more hierarchical structure, solutions tend to be faster, more clustered, stable, and more successful in satisfying design requirements (Carroll, Thomas, Miller & Friedman, 1980). While problem structuring establishes the problem space, problem solving completes the design task by producing solutions that satisfy the requirements and constraints for each design unit. Solution proceeds under a control structure that is established through problem structuring, and consists of successive generate/test actions that progress toward the final solution. Problem solving in design also contains a feedback component that communicates results of the solution to higher levels, where restructuring of the problem space can be undertaken if the partial solution demands such an action (Akin, Chen, Dave & Pithavadian, 1986).

In their studies of the design process, Goel and Pirolli (1988) have noted a number of additional characteristics of design problem solving. Observations of three experienced designers (an architect, a mechanical engineer, and an instructional designer) using think-aloud protocols revealed that during the design task these designers engaged in extensive problem structuring (decomposing the problem into modules) and performance modeling of the artifact at various stages of its design. Each designer also employed evaluation functions and "stopping rules" that controlled the decomposition of the problem. Designers tended to evaluate their decisions at several levels continuously through the process: immediately upon making a decision, and on local terms that ignored the context of the complete design; in terms of the current context (the design as it existed so far); and in a later, more complete context while reconsidering previous decisions.

Another interesting feature of the design process that emerged in the study was the cognitive strategy used to control problem decomposition into "leaky modules" (Goel & Pirolli, 1988, p. 20). While extensive restructuring of the design problem into several modules was observed, the designers did not encapsulate each module, but rather they monitored the design process to ensure that decisions made

in one module did not adversely affect other modules. The designers handled "leaks" between modules by "plugging" the leaks, that is, ignoring the effects of low-level decisions in one module after making high-level assumptions about the other modules. For example, after decomposing the problem into lessons, the instructional designer worked on the first lesson without regard to any of the details of the third lesson. A second method for dealing with "leaks" was termed *opportunistic* (Hayes-Roth & Hayes-Roth, 1979). The designers actually stopped work on the current module in order to attend to the interrelated modules immediately.

The studies described above provide valuable insights into the design process. But do instructional designers exhibit similar characteristics when they design? The small number of studies completed to date seems to suggest that the instructional design process, when viewed as a type of problem solving, is similar to design in other domains. Kerr (1983) studied the thought processes of 26 novice instructional designers using interviews and planning documents produced by the designers during a graduate course in instructional design. He found that the processes employed by the designers were not systematic, that their solutions were generated largely based on their personal experiences in various instructional settings, and that problem constraints greatly influenced their solutions. Kerr concluded that the speed at which the designers settled on solutions for their problems (some as quickly as 1 or 2 days, even though they had 6 weeks to work out the design) points out the need to find methods to help novice designers "maintain an open set of options for longer into the initial phases of design work" (p. 56). Designers in this study also found it difficult to describe how they represented the problem, generated solution alternatives, and made decisions. Kerr suggests that new methods should be found to represent instructional design problems in symbol systems other than the typical flow diagrams used by many instructional designers.

Using a think-aloud task and protocol analysis, Nelson (1988/1990) studied the initial phase of problem structuring in four experienced instructional designers. While the experimental task only approximated a "first pass" at the problem, several interesting findings were described. The designers tended to focus on information related to available resources, the learners, and the skills to be trained. Specific information regarding content and learning tasks was not examined in detail. It was also apparent that specific pieces of information, in this case a small budget for the hypothetical training program, constrained the possible solutions that the designers considered. In other words, a "stopping rule" was evoked that led the designers to a particular solution without considering additional alternatives (Goel & Pirolli, 1988). Finally, the process employed to organize the information of the problem seemed to be controlled by an internalized cognitive structure, as had been shown in other types of design (Akin, Chen, Dave & Pithavadian, 1986; Eastman, 1972).

A more comprehensive study of instructional designers was reported by Rowland (1992), where four expert and four novice designers were given a task to design instruction for an industrial setting involving training employees to operate two hypothetical machines. Verbal reports of the designers' thoughts while completing the task were coded and analyzed, and the results of this study suggest that the design process alternates between two phases that Rowland terms *problem understanding* and *solution generation* (p. 71). Experts tended to take much more time in the problem understanding phase, constructing a rich representation of the problem that was guided by a template, or mental model, of the process (Rowland, 1992). After problem understanding, the expert designers specified solution elements that were linked in varying strengths to the different elements of the problem, without making further reference to the problem materials. In some cases, the tentative solution elements acted as alternative solutions to be considered later. The novice designers in the study employed design processes that differed significantly from the experts. Novices did not develop a rich representation of the problem, relying on the materials given rather than making inferences about the constraints of the problem or the structure of the content. They also quickly began to generate possible solutions after briefly examining the problem materials, and frequently returned to the problem materials as the process unfolded. Consequently, their problem representation grew as they progressed through the solution generation phase.

Observations of designer behavior using a case study methodology (Spector, Muraida & Marlino, 1992) have revealed that many variables affect the ability of designers to author effectively computer-based instruction, especially prior experience (both as a designer and with computer-based authoring systems). But since this study was conducted without a firm theoretical framework, few conclusions can be drawn. Other studies of instructional design practice have employed self-report methods using surveys to elicit designers' opinions about how they actually practice instructional design. Zemke's (1985) survey indicated that instructional designers in business and industry are selective in terms of the design activities in which they engage, often ignoring needs assessment, task analysis, and follow-up evaluations. Wedman and Tessmer (1993) extended this work by examining the factors that might contribute to the selective use of instructional design activities. Surveys of more than 70 instructional design professionals indicated that activities such as writing learning objectives, developing test items, and selecting media and instructional strategies are nearly always completed. On the other hand, these designers reported that needs assessment, task analysis, assessing entry level skills, and pilot testing instruction are performed selectively, if ever. Reasons for not performing some activities included lack of time or that the decisions had already been made by others. Interestingly, lack of money or expertise in performing the activity were rarely cited as reasons the activities were not performed.

42.4.1.4. The Role of Knowledge in the Design Process. The success of the designer's problem-solving processes is directly related to the designer's experience and knowledge in the problem domain (see 5.3). Akin (1979) has observed that environmental cues can evoke a precompiled solution from the designer's memory very early in the process, indicating the influence that various declarative and procedural knowledge structures have on the design process. Jeffries, Turner, Polson, and Atwood (1981) contend that a general cognitive structure for design, containing both the elements of a designed product and the processes necessary for generating the design, exists for individual computer software designers. This cognitive structure controls the process of problem decomposition, as well as evoking other subordinate structures for each subproblem. After the subproblems are solved, another high-level cognitive structure is retrieved to tie together the various solutions in order to form the final design. Their study reported significant similarities between the cognitive structures of experienced designers, although individual differences were found because of variations in prior experience with software design.

Goel and Pirolli (1988) also discuss the role of knowledge in the design process, noting that the personal knowledge of the designers in their study was organized in rich and intricate structures that contained both general knowledge (extracted from the totality of an individual's life experiences) consisting of concepts, procedures, and patterns (pictorial, linguistic, musical, etc.), as well as domain-specific knowledge derived from their professional training, which was similarly organized and integrated with their general knowledge. This knowledge was used in many cases as a template for understanding the characteristics of the design task, as well as for generating solutions.

So it seems that a well-organized knowledge base for instructional design is crucial to the process (see 5.3, 7.2). The knowledge available to instructional designers, either individual knowledge stored in memory or other forms of knowledge embodied in the models and tools used for design, will influence the kinds of instruction they create (Nelson & Orey, 1991). An instructional designer's knowledge base should include not only conceptual and procedural structures for controlling the design process but also cases or scenarios of exemplary instructional products and solutions that can be recalled and applied to particular situations (Nelson, Magliaro & Sherman, 1988; Rowland, 1993). It is also necessary for an instructional designer to be familiar with concepts and procedures derived from general systems theory, psychological theory, instructional theory, and message design (Richey, 1993). In fact, it has been argued that successful implementation of instructional design procedures ultimately depends on whether designers have "adequate understanding and training in higher-order problem-solving principles and skills such that the necessary expertise can be applied in the process" (McCombs, 1986, p. 78).

42.4.1.5. Overview of Designer Decision-Making Studies as Developmental Research. Designer decision-making research is typically Type 2 research and has the ultimate goal of understanding the design process, and at times to produce design models that more closely match actual design activity. The populations of the studies are naturally designers—not learners—and frequently designers are classified as either novice or expert. The effort to identify the impact of various design environments is a common secondary objective. Consequently, the project itself is often a second unit of analysis, and data are collected on the nature of the content, work resources, and constraints. Methodologically, the studies tend to be more qualitative in nature, although survey methods are not uncommon.

42.4.2 Trends in Research on Techniques for Knowledge Acquisition

One of the major tasks to be completed by the instructional designer is to identify and structure the content of instruction. Both instructional designers and instructional developers consult with subject-matter experts to determine the knowledge that must be acquired by the learners, and the form in which this knowledge might best be communicated to the learners. In this respect, instructional design activities are similar to the knowledge engineering process that is utilized in the development of expert systems and intelligent tutoring systems (McGraw, 1989; Nelson, 1989; Rushby, 1986).

42.4.2.1. Tools of Content Determination.
Knowledge engineers typically work with subject-matter experts to identify and organize the knowledge that is necessary for solving problems in a domain. While the ultimate goals of knowledge acquisition for instructional design and knowledge engineering differ, the processes and tools used by instructional designers and knowledge engineers are complimentary. In fact, many of the techniques and tools used in knowledge engineering are becoming common in instructional design (see 18.4, 19.3, 22.6, 25.8).

These new tools and techniques reflect the assumptions about the role of knowledge in learning and problem solving that forms the basis of research in cognitive science. Various theories of knowledge representation have been proposed in the psychology literature (e.g., Anderson, 1983; Gentner & Stevens, 1983; Greeno, 1989), and an even greater number of knowledge representation schemes for artificial intelligence applications have been implemented (see Wenger, 1987). The knowledge representation employed in any system, including instructional systems, needs to be tailored to the nature of the problem domain, just as the knowledge acquisition techniques used to identify and structure the knowledge need to be appropriate for the domain. As described below, this becomes especially important as systems are developed to automate the knowledge acquisition process, allowing the subject-matter expert to interact directly with a computer system instead of with a knowledge engineer or instructional designer. Until recently, the procedures utilized for knowledge acquisition in instructional design and development largely relied on task analysis (e.g., Merrill, 1973) and information-processing analysis (Gagne, Briggs & Wager, 1988). A large number of task analysis procedures have been employed for

instructional design and development, as summarized by Jonassen, Hannum, and Tessmer (1989). In general, these analysis techniques are used by designers to describe the nature of the learning tasks, and to identify and sequence the content of the instruction (see 2.3). Information-processing analysis further delineates the decision-making processes that may underlay a task, allowing the designer to identify any concepts or rules that may be necessary to complete the task.

As research in cognitive science has advanced in recent years, theories describing the nature and structure of knowledge, and how it is used by experts to solve problems, have been elaborated (Glaser, 1990). Many of the techniques used by researchers have been adapted by knowledge engineers and instructional designers, becoming important components of several computer-based design tools and systems described below. The process of knowledge acquisition generally follows several stages, including: (1) a descriptive phase, where basic domain concepts and relations are identified; (2) a structural phase, where the declarative knowledge is organized into integrated structures; (3) a procedural phase, where the reasoning and problem-solving strategies are identified; and (4) a refinement phase, where the knowledge structures, procedures, and strategies are tested with a wider range of problems, and modified as needed (Ford & Wood, 1992; McGraw, 1989).

Using structured interviews and a variety of documentation activities, concepts and relations can be identified during the descriptive phase of knowledge acquisition. McGraw (1989) recommends the use of concept dictionaries or cognitive maps to represent graphically the major domain concepts. Ford and Wood (1992) discuss a tool for constructing such initial conceptual representations where the expert interacts with a computer system to define the concepts and relations in the domain. Many of the automated tools for instructional design discussed below feature some kind of graphical representation tool to help define domain concepts and relations (e.g., McAleese, 1988; Nicolson, 1988; Pirolli, 1991).

During the structural phase, the concepts and relations identified earlier are organized into larger units. This phase has been described as "a precondition to effective instructional design" (Jones, Li & Merrill, 1990, p. 7) and is critical to the specification of domain knowledge. While the methods for organizing the declarative knowledge into these larger units vary depending on the type of knowledge representation being used, interviewing is generally the most widely employed technique. However, at this stage it is important to begin prompting the expert to clarify distinctions between concepts in order to structure the knowledge (Ford & Wood, 1992). Besides interviews, various statistical procedures such as multidimensional scaling (e.g., Cooke & McDonald, 1986), path analysis (Schvaneveldt, 1990), ordered trees (Naveh-Benjamin, McKeachie, Lin & Tucker, 1986), and repertory grid techniques (Kelly, 1955; Boose, 1986) can be used to help structure the knowledge. Johnson (1988) has also described a method for eliciting the mental models used by experts during troubleshooting activities.

Knowledge does not consist solely of concepts and relations. Experts also possess highly proceduralized knowledge in the form of rules and heuristics that help them solve problems (see 5.3). The third phase of knowledge acquisition focuses on the elicitation of the reasoning strategies and solution procedures employed by the expert. A variety of methods can be used to identify and describe these procedures. Task analysis methods yield a description of the tasks that constitute performance, along with the skills necessary to perform each task (Jonassen, Hannum & Tessmer, 1989). Additional methods that provide useful descriptions of domain expertise include time-line analysis for sequencing tasks, information-processing analysis for describing decision making, and process tracing to determine the thinking strategies used by the expert during task performance (McGraw, 1989). Protocol analysis (Ericsson & Simon, 1984) is a particularly effective process-tracing technique, although it is time consuming because of the extensive data analysis that is required. Observations, constrained tasks (Hoffman, 1987), and simulations can also be useful at this stage of knowledge acquisition, especially when two or more experts collaborate to solve or "debug" a problem (Tenney & Kurland, 1988). It is also advisable to perform similar analyses of novices in order to identify specific difficulties that learners are likely to encounter (Means & Gott, 1988; Orey & Nelson, 1993).

Cognitive task analysis may be an effective alternative to behavioral task analysis or process-tracing methods that can produce a rich description of the precursors, explanations, and alternatives for actions that are considered by experts as they solve problems. Several procedures for conducting cognitive task analysis have been proposed (e.g., Redding, 1992), but despite variations in procedures, the advantages of this method lie in the resulting description of expert performance. Instead of decomposed tasks and isolated knowledge components, cognitive task analysis produces an integrated description of expert performance, including a highly structured knowledge base, that can be used to design instruction. While little research validating the method has been reported, Ryder and Redding (1993) have presented a model for integrating cognitive task analysis into instructional design activities, and as research focusing on the effectiveness of cognitive task analysis is completed, the benefits of using the methodology for designing instruction will become clear.

42.4.2.2. Overview of Studies of Knowledge Acquisition Techniques as Developmental Research. These studies are also Type 2 research, although they are focusing on only one phase of the design process: producing content identification and analysis. This research is primarily directed toward producing new content analysis tools and procedures, and then determining the conditions under which they can be best used. There are often multiple units of analysis in these studies, including designers, subject-matter experts, and the design tasks themselves. Much of this research is based on "artificial" design tasks, projects that have been devised solely for the purposes of the research. Again, it is common for researchers to use qualitative techniques in these studies.

42.4.3 Trends in Research on Automated Instructional Design Tools

The systematic instructional design and development procedures common to our field have been developed as a means to organize and control what is essentially a very complicated engineering process. Even with systematic methods, however, the instructional design process can become very time consuming and costly (O'Neil, Faust & O'Neil, 1979). As computer technology has proliferated in society, and as more training has become computer based, it is not surprising that efforts in the instructional design field have concentrated on the development of computer-based tools intended to streamline the design and development of instruction, both for novice designers as well as expert designers.

42.4.3.1. Knowledge-Based Design Systems. Knowledge-based design systems are becoming common in many design professions as researchers strive to acquire and represent in computer systems the kinds of knowledge and reasoning necessary to interpret design problems, control design actions, and produce design specifications (Coyne, Rosenman, Radford, Balachandran & Gero, 1990). Some computer-based design environments have been developed as extensions of the tools used by designers, such as the computer-aided design (CAD) systems used in professions where sketches or blueprints are used as a part of the design specifications (architecture, electronics, automobiles, etc.). The designer uses the computer system as a "drafting table" that can significantly increase the designer's capabilities to render drawings and thereby consider alternative solutions. Other systems, such as those used in computer-aided software engineering (CASE), have been developed around "libraries" or "templates" of primitive design elements, so that the designer may construct a solution to a particular problem by combining design elements from the database of possible solution components. Other systems have been developed to include critiquing facilities that monitor the designer's activities and suggest alternatives when an action that may be inappropriate is taken (Fischer, 1991). These types of knowledge-based design systems require an extensive database of rules that functions in the background as the designer works with the system.

While a wide variety of approaches to knowledge-based instructional design have been attempted, all are characterized by the need to formalize the knowledge and decision-making processes necessary for effective instructional design so that the knowledge can be stored in the memory of a computer. Research and development efforts in this area have employed knowledge engineering techniques similar to those described earlier in order to develop systems and tools to support the instructional design process. These efforts began with attempts to provide "job aids" for novice instructional designers, especially those in military settings (Schulz & Wagner, 1981). Early efforts using computers to automate various instructional development tasks focused on the production of print-based materials for programmed instruction (Braby & Kincaid, 1981; Brecke & Blaiwes, 1981) and adaptive testing systems (Weiss, 1979), and, more recently, paper-based training materials (Cantor, 1988). A more ambitious project was undertaken in conjunction with the PLATO system. Beginning with libraries of code to produce various types of test items, Schulz (1979) completed extensive research to produce and test a number of on-line authoring aids designed to be integrated with the military's IPISD model. Various activities specified by the model were identified and the associated tasks analyzed. Flowcharts of the design activities were then converted to interactive instructional segments that could be accessed by users as on-line aids during authoring activities. Findings indicated that the aids were accepted by the authors and that development time was significantly decreased.

More recently, a number of additional projects have begun to develop knowledge-based instructional design systems and tools. This research has wide-ranging implications for instruction, as evidenced by the fact that individuals in fields as diverse as cognitive science, instructional design, artificial intelligence, and computer-based instruction are engaged in the development of these systems. While many of these efforts have been reviewed elsewhere and described in more detail than is appropriate here (Pirolli, 1991; Wilson & Jonassen, 1990/91), a brief summary of the advances being made in knowledge-based instructional design systems can serve to characterize the work in light of what is known about the instructional design process. In general, the research represents three approaches to the problem of designing tools for the instructional design process: individual tools for various self-contained instructional design tasks, integrated systems that provide decision support and structure for the process, and integrated systems that act as "drafting boards" for the design process.

42.4.3.2. Design Productivity Tools.
Numerous tools based on expert system technology have been developed to aid instructional designers in making decisions about various aspects of instructional design. These tools function as intelligent "job aids" where the designer enters information about the present situation in response to system queries, and the system then provides a solution based on domain-specific rules and reasoning strategies. Such tools do not provide a complete working environment for the design task, but rather can serve as an expert consultant when the designer is not sure how to proceed in a particular situation (Jonassen & Wilson, 1990). A number of expert system tools for instructional design have been developed by Kearsley (1985) to provide guidance for classification of learning objectives, needs assessment, cost-benefit analysis, and decisions about the appropriateness of computers for delivery of instruction. Other expert system tools have been developed to aid in media selection (Gayeski, 1987;

Harmon & King, 1985) and job/task analysis (Hermanns, 1990), while researchers in artificial intelligence are developing tools to analyze a curriculum for an intelligent tutoring system based on prerequisites and lesson objectives (Capell & Dannenberg, 1993).

Expert system technology has also been employed in the development of integrated instructional design systems that provide guidance and support for the complete design process. Merrill (1987) was an early advocate for the development of authoring systems for computer-based instruction that provide guidance for the user throughout the design process. His work has focused on the development of a comprehensive instructional design environment that queries the user about the nature of the problem, guides in the specification and structuring of content, and recommends strategies and instructional transactions (Li & Merrill, 1991; Merrill & Li, 1989). The strength of this system is that it is explicitly based on component display theory (Merrill, 1983) and elaboration theory (Reigeluth & Stein, 1983), and thereby provides more specific support for making design decisions than is available in other systems. A similar system, the Instructional Design and Development Advisor (IDD Advisor), has been described by Jonassen and Wilson (1990). IDD Advisor represents an ambitious attempt to develop expert system consultation modules for all phases of the design process. At the time of this writing, four of the modules had been developed as prototypes, and extensive analysis and specification of rules had been completed for the system. Nicolson (1988) has described a similar system named SCALD (Scriptal CAL Designer) that was developed to produce automatically computer code for computer-assisted instruction systems. Using a script representation, SCALD users enter descriptions of the instructional components of the system by filling out forms to specify the script for each component. The system then creates an appropriately organized and sequenced "shell" from the scripts, and content (specific questions, information, graphics, etc.) can then be added to the shell by the developer.

Alternative approaches to rule-based expert system technologies for knowledge-based instructional design have been examined by other researchers. Some of these systems serve as working environments for the instructional designer, but without the system-controlled advisory sessions common to expert system approaches. Instead, these systems provide structured environments and tools to facilitate the instructional design process, sometimes in very specific domains such as the tools described by Munro and Towne (1992) for the design and development of computer-based simulations, sometimes comprehensive systems to support all aspects of the instructional design process, including tutorials and support for novice designers (Gayeski, 1987; Seyfer & Russell, 1986). IDioM (Gustafson & Reeves, 1990) is an instructional design environment used by Apple Computer employees to aid in their training design activities. Consisting of several modules related to analysis, design, development, evaluation, implementation, and management activities, IDioM helps to impose structure on the design process while maintaining flexibility for the designer to engage in various design and development activities. The Instructional Design Environment (IDE), developed at Xerox, is a similar system that allows designers to enter and manipulate the information necessary for analysis and specification activities (Pirolli, 1991). The environment is completely open, allowing the designer to represent the problem in a way that is comfortable and appropriate for the situation. Tools are provided to assist the designer in activities related to task and content analysis, sequencing, delivery, and evaluation. Another set of tools, the IDE-Interpreter, has been developed to generate automatically instructional plans based on the specifications previously stored in the IDE knowledge base by the designer (D. M. Russell, 1988). Other researchers are investigating the possibilities of intelligent tutoring system architectures for automated instructional design (Spector, Muraida & Marlino, 1992), and in Europe a system that includes knowledge-based instructional design components is being developed to author and deliver instruction on computer networks (Muhlhauser, 1992).

42.4.3.3. The Practicality of Automated Instructional Design.
The question that remains unanswered with respect to research in the area of knowledge-based instructional design systems is whether such systems will be used by practicing instructional designers. Gayeski (1988, 1990) has pointed out several problems with automating instructional design processes, especially the difficulty of representing instructional design expertise as decision algorithms that can be executed by a computer. She also speculates that using an automated instructional design system may stifle creativity, and that systems may need to be customized and tailored to the design procedures and practices of a particular organization (see 6.2).

There is also some question whether the expert system approach to knowledge-based instructional design is an appropriate solution that can adequately support the kinds of cognitive processes in which designers engage during the design task, and whether novice designers will successfully learn proper design procedures by using such systems. Expert system architectures for knowledge-based instructional design systems may prove useful for novice designers, helping them to make correct decisions regarding content structure and instructional strategies, but experts may find such systems tedious and intrusive. If the intent is to help novices acquire instructional design expertise through interaction with an expert system, it is important to remember that expert systems have been difficult to operationalize as tutoring systems. History has shown that converting an expert system into a tutoring system is difficult, if not impossible, because of problems involving knowledge representation and explanation of decisions (Clancey, 1986). Although the most recent version of ID Expert allows more user control than many expert systems, it remains to be seen whether efforts to incorporate an explanation facility into ID Expert will be successful (Li, O'Neil & Baker, 1991), and whether novice users of the system

will learn appropriate instructional design practices through their interactions with the system.

The open-ended workbench approach to knowledge-based instructional design also poses problems for some users, even though it may be a more appropriate architecture given the nature of the instructional design task (Duchastel, 1990). Because of the high degree of user control, an instructional design workbench can be useful for experienced instructional designers, helping them to streamline their work and providing assistance in documenting and managing the design process. But a system such as IDioM or IDE is not designed to provide guidance to novice instructional designers, and therefore may not be useful in many situations where trained instructional designers are in short supply.

The most appropriate architecture for knowledge-based instructional design systems may be a hybrid system that incorporates open-ended tools for experts along with an advisory system and solution library for novices. Fischer (1991) has developed such a system for architectural design that includes several modules: a construction kit, simulation generator, hypertext database of design principles, and a design catalog. As the designer works, an on-line design critic monitors activities, interrupting the user when a design principle has been violated. At such times, the design critic module presents an argument for modification of the design, supporting the argument with a design principle retrieved from a hypertext database along with examples of correct designs in the design catalog. The user can then browse both modules to obtain more information about the principle that was violated and other related principles and examples. The user can also access the simulation generator to test the current design using "what-if" scenarios that simulate usage in various situations. Duchastel's design for a knowledge-based instructional design system for the McDonnell Douglas Corporation includes many similar features (Duchastel, 1990).

Even if we never use a knowledge-based instructional design system on a daily basis, research in this area has not been futile. In part, the interest in developing automated instructional design systems has precipitated research into the nature of the instructional design process (Pirolli, personal communication). Work in this area may also help to identify those instructional design tasks that can be successfully automated, leaving the tasks that require creativity and "fuzzy" reasoning to human designers. And finally, attempts to acquire and represent instructional design expertise will result in a better understanding of the nature of that expertise, suggesting alternative approaches to the teaching of instructional design (Rowland, 1992).

42.4.3.4. Overview of Studies of Automated Instructional Design Tools as Developmental Research.
These studies are Type 2 developmental research directed toward the production and testing of tools which would change design procedures. However, they do not preclude developmental Type 1 studies that would describe and analyze design projects using these new automated tools and evalu-

ate the impact on learners of the materials produced using these tools. The focus of analysis in the Type 2 studies of automated design tools tends to be the tools themselves, and in some instances the designers who use such tools are also studied. The studies are typically descriptive and observational in nature, and typically seek to identify those conditions that facilitate successful use.

42.5 CONCLUSIONS

The history of developmental research, in spite of frequent misunderstanding of the concept, nonetheless parallels the past growth of instructional technology, and it is likely that this trend will continue in the future. Findings from past research provide a record of the technological development of the field, as well as a record of the development of the instructional design movement. The impetus for further developmental research undoubtedly will originate from the current concerns of the field at any point in time. For example, presently the field is grappling with ways of reducing design and development cycle time while maintaining quality standards; issues such as these give rise to new research.

The obstacles to disciplinary growth are not typically those of problem identification and definition. Rather, the obstacles are more likely to be created by the daily pressures within education and training environments which prevent us from the systematic construction and testing of solutions to our problems. Developmental research methodologies facilitate the *study* of new models, tools, and procedures so that we can reliably anticipate their effectiveness and efficiency. In this way, we can determine the relevance of context-specific findings for other teaching and learning environments, as well as identify new general principles of design, development, and evaluation.

The recognition and encouragement of developmental research techniques not only expands the empirical methodologies of the field but also expands the *substance* of instructional technology research. In this respect, developmental research differs from other research methodologies that are totally process oriented and devoid of content in and of themselves. Consequently, the proliferation of developmental research projects, as well as the subsequent publication and dissemination of their findings (in the same manner as we disseminate other research findings), can be important vehicles in our field's efforts to promote effective design and, in turn, effective learning.

REFERENCES

Abdelraheem, A.Y. (1990). Formative evaluation in instructional development: a multiple comparison study. (Doctoral dissertation, Indiana University, 1989.) *Dissertation Abstracts International-A 50* (10), 3381.

Akin, O. (1979). Exploration of the design process. *Design Methods and Theories 13* (3/4), 115–19.

Akin, O., Chen, C.C., Dave, B. & Pithavadian, S. (1986). A schematic representation of the designer's logic. *Proceedings of the Joint International Conference on CAD and Robotics in Architecture and Construction,* 31–40. London: Kogan Page.

Albero-Andres, M. (1983). The use of the Agency for Instructional Television instructional development model in the design, production, and evaluation of the series of Give and Take. (Doctoral dissertation, Indiana University, 1982.) *Dissertation Abstracts International-A 43* (11), 3489.

Alessi, S.M. (1988). Learning interactive videodisc development: a case study. *Journal of Instructional Development 11* (2), 2–7.

Anderson, J.R. (1983). *The architecture of cognition.* Cambridge, MA: Harvard University Press.

—, Boyle, C.F., Corbett, A.T. & Lewis, M.W. (1990). Cognitive modeling and intelligent tutoring. *Artificial Intelligence 42* (1), 7–49.

Andrews, D.H. & Goodson, L.A. (1980). A comparative analysis of models of instructional design. *Journal of Instructional Development 3* (4), 2–16.

Aukerman, M.E. (1987). Effectiveness of an interactive video approach for CPR recertification of registered nurses. (Doctoral dissertation, University of Pittsburgh, 1986.) *Dissertation Abstracts International-A 47* (06), 1979.

Baghdadi, A.A. (1981). A comparison between two formative evaluation methods. (Doctoral dissertation, Indiana University, 1980.) *Dissertation Abstracts International 41* (08), 3387.

Baker, E.L. (1973). The technology of instructional development. *In* R.M.W. Travers, ed. *Second handbook of research on teaching,* 245–85. Chicago, IL: Rand McNally.

Beauchamp, M. (1991). The validation of an integrative model of student affect variables and instructional systems design. (Doctoral dissertation, Wayne State University, 1990.) *Dissertation Abstracts International-A 51* (6), 1885.

Bednar, A.K. (1988). Needs assessment as a change strategy: a case study. *Performance Improvement Quarterly 1* (2), 3–39.

Bennis, W.G. (1969). *Organizational development: its nature, origins, and prospects.* Reading, MA: Addison-Wesley.

Blackstone, B.B. (1990). The development and evaluation of a simulation game about being a believer in the Soviet Union. (Doctoral dissertation, University of Pittsburgh, 1989.) *Dissertation Abstracts International-A 50* (7), 2024.

Boose, J.H. (1986). *Expertise transfer for expert system design.* New York: Elsevier.

Borg, W.R. & Gall, M.D. (1971). *Educational research: an introduction,* 2d ed. New York: McKay.

Bowers, D. & Tsai, C. (1990). Hypercard in educational research: an introduction and case study. *Educational Technology 30* (2), 19–24.

Braby, R. & Kincaid, J.P. (1981). Computer aided authoring and editing. *Journal of Educational Technology Systems 10* (2), 109–24.

Bransford, J.D., Sherwood, R.D., Hasselbring, T.S., Kinzer, C.K. & Williams, S.M. (1990). Anchored instruction: why we need it and how technology can help. *In* D. Nix & R. Spiro, eds. *Cognition, education, and multimedia,* 115–42. Hillsdale, NJ: Erlbaum.

Brecke, F. & Blaiwes, A. (1981). CASDAT: an innovative approach to more efficient ISD. *Journal of Educational Technology Systems 10* (3), 271–83.

Briggs, L.J., ed. (1977). *Instructional design: principles and applications.* Englewood Cliffs, NJ: Educational Technology.

Buch, E.E. (1989). A systematically developed training program for microcomputer users in an industrial setting. (Doctoral dissertation, University of Pittsburgh, 1988.) *Dissertation Abstracts International-A 49* (4), 750.

Burkholder, B.L. (1981–82). The effectiveness of using the instructional strategy diagnostic profile to prescribe improvements in self-instructional materials. *Journal of Instructional Development 5* (2), 2–9.

Cambre, M.A. (1979). The development of formative evaluation procedures for instructional film and television: the first fifty years. (Doctoral dissertation, Indiana University, 1978.) *Dissertation Abstracts International-A 39* (7), 3995.

Cantor, J.A. (1988). An automated curriculum development process for navy technical training. *Journal of Instructional Development 11* (4), 3–12.

Capell, P. (1990). A content analysis approach used in the study of the characteristics of instructional design in three intelligent tutoring systems: The LISP tutor, Bridge, and Piano Tutor. (Doctoral dissertation, University of Pittsburgh, 1989.) *Dissertation Abstracts International-A 50* (7), 2024.

— & Dannenberg, R.B. (1993). Instructional design and intelligent tutoring: theory and the precision of design. *Journal of Artificial Intelligence in Education 4* (1), 95–121.

Carl, D. (1978). A front-end analysis of instructional development in instructional television. (Doctoral dissertation, Indiana University, 1977.) *Dissertation Abstracts International-A 38* (9), 5198.

Carroll, J.M., Thomas, J.C., Miller, L.A. & Friedman, H.P. (1980). Aspects of solution structure in design problem solving. *American Journal of Psychology 95* (2), 269–84.

Chandrasekaran, B. (1987). Design as knowledge-based problem solving activity. *In* B. Zaff, ed. *Proceedings of a symposium on the cognitive condition of design,* 117–47. Columbus, OH: The Ohio State University.

Clancey, W.J. (1986). From GUIDON to NEOMYCIN and HERACLES in twenty short lessons: ONR final report 1979–1985. *AI Magazine 7* (3), 40–60.

Clifford, G.J. (1973). A history of the impact of research on teaching. *In* R.M.W. Travers, ed. *Second handbook of research on teaching,* 1–46. Chicago, IL: Rand McNally.

Connop-Scollard, C. (1991). The ID/D chart: a representation of instructional design and development. *Educational Technology 31* (12), 47–50.

Cook, F.S. & Richey, R.C. (1975). A competency-based program for preparing vocational teachers. *Journal for Industrial Teacher Education 12* (4), 29–38.

Cooke, N.M & McDonald, J.E. (1986). A formal methodology for acquiring and representing expert knowledge. *Proceedings of the IEEE 74* (1), 1422–30.

Coscarelli, W.C. & White, G.P. (1982). Applying the ID process to the guided design teaching strategy: a case study. *Journal of Instructional Development 5* (4), 2–6.

Coyle, K. (1986). The development and evaluation of an experimental computer simulation for animal science students. (Doctoral dissertation, Iowa State University, 1985.) *Dissertation Abstracts International-A 46* (12), 3581.

Coyle, L. (1992). Distance education project: extending extension programming via telecommunications technology. *Educational Technology 32* (8), 57–58.

Coyne, R.D., Rosenman, M.A., Radford, A.D., Balachandran, M. & Gero, J.S. (1990). *Knowledge-based design systems.* Reading, MA: Addison-Wesley.

Crane, G. & Mylonas, E. (1988). The Perseus project: an interactive curriculum on classical Greek civilization. *Educational Technology 28* (11), 25–32.

Cregger, R. & Metzler, M. (1992). PSI for a college physical education basic instructional program. *Educational Technology 32* (8), 51–56.

Cronbach, L.J. & Suppes, P., eds. (1969). *Research for tomorrow's schools—disciplined inquiry for education.* Report of the Committee on Educational Research of the National Academy of Education. London: Macmillan, Callien Macmillan.

Cummings, O.W. (1985). Comparison of three algorithms for analyzing questionnaire-type needs assessment data to establish need priorities. *Journal of Instructional Development 8* (2), 11–16.

Dick, W. (1991). The Singapore project: a case study in instructional design. *Performance Improvement Quarterly 4* (1), 14–22.

Dick, W. & Carey, L. (1996) *The systematic design of instruction,* 4th ed. HarperCollins.

Diesing, P. (1991). *How does social science work? Reflections on practice.* Pittsburgh, PA: University of Pittsburgh Press.

Driscoll, M.P. (1991). Paradigms for research in instructional systems. *In* G. Anglin, ed. *Instructional technology: past, present, and future,* 310–17. Englewood, CO: Libraries Unlimited.

— & Tessmer, M.. (1985). The rational set generator: a method for creating concept examples for teaching and testing. *Educational Technology 25* (2), 29–32.

Duchastel, P.C. (1990). Cognitive design for instructional design. *Instructional Science 19,* 437–44.

Eastman, C.M. (1972). On the analysis of intuitive design processes. *In* G.T. Moore, ed. *Emerging methods in environmental design and planning,* 21–37. Cambridge, MA: MIT Press.

Ericsson, K.A. & Simon, H.A. (1984). *Protocol analysis.* Cambridge, MA: MIT Press.

Fischer, G. (1991). Supporting learning on demand with design environments. *In* L. Birnbaum, ed. *The International Conference on the Learning Sciences: Proceedings of the 1991 Conference.* Charlottesville, VA: Association for the Advancement of Computing in Education.

Ford, J.M. & Wood, L.E. (1992). Structuring and documenting interactions with subject-matter experts. *Performance Improvement Quarterly 5* (1), 2–24.

Freeman, P. (1983). Fundamentals of design. *In* P. Freeman, ed. *Software design tutorial,* 2–22. New York: IEEE Computer Society Press.

Fuchs, L.S. & Fuchs, D. (1986). Effects of systematic formative evaluation: a meta-analysis. *Exceptional Children 53* (3). 199–208.

Gage, N.L., ed. (1963). *Handbook of research on teaching.* Chicago, IL: Rand McNally.

Gagné, R.M. (1985). *The conditions of learning and theory of instruction,* 4th ed. New York: Holt, Rinehart & Winston.

Gagné, R.M., Briggs, L.J. & Wager, W.W. (1988). *Principles of instructional design,* 3d ed. New York: Holt, Rinehart & Winston.

Gauger, E.P. (1987). The design, development, and field test of a prototype program evaluation approach for medical residency rotations. (Doctoral dissertation, Michigan State

University, 1985.) *Dissertation Abstracts International-A 47* (1), 69.

Gay, G. & Mazur, J. (1993). The utility of computer tracking tools for user-centered design. *Educational Technology 33* (4), 45–59.

Gay, L.R. (1987). *Educational research: competencies for analysis and application,* 3d ed. Columbus, OH: Merrill.

Gayeski, D.M. (1987). *Interactive toolkit.* Ithaca, NY: OmniCom.

— (1988). Can (and should) instructional design be automated? *Performance and Instruction 27* (10), 1–5.

— (1990). Are you ready for automated design? *Training and Development Journal,* 61–62.

Gentner, D. & Stevens, A.L. (1983). *Mental models.* Hillsdale, NJ: Erlbaum.

George, T. (1981). The development and evaluation of an instructional package systematically designed to teach fifth-grade children nonaggressive alternatives to verbal aggression. (Doctoral dissertation, University of Pittsburgh, 1979.) *Dissertation Abstracts International-A 41* (1), 164.

Glaser, R. (1990). The reemergence of learning theory within instructional research. *American Psychologist 45* (1), 29–39.

Goel, V. & Pirolli, P. (1988). *Motivating the notion of generic design within information processing theory: the design problem space.* (Report No. DPS-1.) Washington, DC: Office of Naval Research. (ERIC Document Reproduction Service No. ED 315 041.)

Gordon, J.J. (1969). A system model for civil defense training and education. *Educational Technology 9* (6), 39–45.

Greenhill, L.P. (1955). *A study of the feasibility of local production of minimum cost sound motion pictures* (Pennsylvania State University Instructional Film Research Program). Port Washington, NY: U.S. Naval Training Device Center, Office of Naval Research, Technical Report No. SDC 269-7-48.

Greeno, J.G. (1989). Situations, mental models, and generative knowledge. *In* D. Klahr & K. Kotovsky, eds. *Complex information processing,* 285–318. Hillsdale, NJ: Erlbaum.

Gustafson, K.L. & Reeves, T.C. (1990). IDioM: a platform for a course development expert system. *Educational Technology 30* (3), 19–25.

— & — (1991). Introduction. *In* L.J. Briggs, K.L. Gustafson & M.H. Tillman, eds. *Instructional design: principles and applications,* 2d ed., 3–16. Englewood Cliffs, NJ: Educational Technology.

Harmon, P. & King, D. (1985). *Expert systems: artificial intelligence in business.* New York: Wiley.

Harris, M. & Cady, M. (1988). The dynamic process of creating hypertext literature. *Educational Technology 28* (11), 33–40.

Harrison, P.J, Seeman, B.J., Behm, R., Saba, F., Molise, G. & Williams, M.D. (1991). Development of a distance education assessment instrument. *Educational Technology Research and Development 39* (4), 65–77.

Havelock, R.G. (1971). The utilisation of educational research and development. *British Journal of Educational Technology 2* (2), 84–98.

Hayes-Roth, B. & Hayes-Roth, F. (1979). A cognitive model of planning. *Cognitive Science 3,* 275–310.

Heinich, R., Molenda, M. & Russell, J.D. (1993). *Instructional media and the new technologies of instruction,* 4th ed. New York: Macmillan.

Hermanns, J. (1990). Computer-aided instructional systems development. *Educational Technology 30* (3), 42–45.

Higgins, N. & Reiser, R. (1985). Selecting media for instruction: an exploratory study. *Journal of Instructional Development 8* (2), 6–10.

Hilgard, E.R., ed. (1964). *Theories of learning and instruction.* 63rd National Society for the Study of Education Yearbook. Chicago, IL: University of Chicago Press.

Hoffman, R.R. (1987). The problem of extracting the knowledge of experts from the perspective of experimental psychology. *AI Magazine 8* (2), 53–67.

Jeffries, R., Turner, A.A., Polson, P.G. & Atwood, M.E. (1981). The processes involved in designing software. *In* J.R. Anderson, ed. *Cognitive skills and their acquisition,* 255–83. Hillsdale, NJ: Erlbaum.

Johnson, S.D. (1988). Cognitive analysis of expert and novice troubleshooting performance. *Performance Improvement Quarterly 1* (3), 38–54.

Jonassen, D.H. (1988). Using needs assessment data to design a graduate instructional development program. *Journal of Instructional Development 11* (2), 14–23.

—, Grabinger, R.S. & Harris, N.D.C. (1991). Analyzing and selecting instructional strategies and tactics. *Performance Improvement Quarterly 4* (2), 77–97.

—, Hannum, W.H. & Tessmer, M. (1989). *Handbook of task analysis procedures.* New York: Praeger.

Jonassen, D.H. & Wilson, B.G. (1990). Analyzing automated instructional design systems: metaphors from related design professions. Paper presented at the annual meeting of the Association for Educational Communications and Technology, Anaheim, CA. (ERIC Document Reproduction Service No. 323 935.)

Jones, M.K., Li, Z. & Merrill, M.D. (1990). Domain knowledge representation for instructional analysis. *Educational Technology 30* (10), 7–32.

Jones, R.H. (1986). The development and analysis of an interactive video program for paralegal students in a university setting. (Doctoral dissertation, University of Pittsburgh, 1985.) *Dissertation Abstracts International-A 46* (6), 1604.

Kanyarusoke, C.M.S. (1985). The development and evaluation of an external studies form of the introductory course in educational communications and technology. (Doctoral dissertation, University of Pittsburgh, 1983.) *Dissertation Abstracts International-A 45* (2), 387.

Kearsley, G. (1985). An expert system program for making decisions about CBT. *Performance and Instruction 24* (5), 15–17.

— (1986). Automated instructional development using personal computers: research issues. *Journal of Instructional Development 9* (1), 9–15.

Kelly, G.A. (1955). *The psychology of personal constructs.* New York: Norton.

Kerlinger, F.N. (1964). *Foundations of behavioral research: educational and psychological inquiry.* New York: Holt, Rinehart & Winston.

Kerr, S.T. (1983). Inside the black box: making design decisions for instruction. *British Journal of Educational Technology 14* (1), 45–58.

Kim, S.O. (1984). Design of an instructional systems development process for Korean education in harmony with Korean culture. (Doctoral dissertation, The Ohio State University, 1983.) *Dissertation Abstract International-A 44* (4), 974.

King, D. & Dille, A. (1993). An early endeavor to apply quality concepts to the systematic design of instruction: successes and lessons learned. *Performance Improvement Quarterly 6* (3), 48–63.

Kress, C. (1990). The effects of instructional systems design techniques on varying levels of adult achievement in technical training. (Doctoral dissertation, Wayne State University, 1989.) *Dissertation Abstracts International-A 50* (11), 3447.

Lewis, E.L., Stern, J.L. & Linn, M.C. (1993). The effect of computer simulations on introductory thermodynamics understanding. *Educational Technology 33* (1), 45–58.

Li, Z. & Merrill, M.D. (1991). ID Expert 2.0: design theory and process. *Educational Technology Research and Development 39* (2), 53–69.

—, O'Neil, H.F. & Baker, E.L. (1991). Developing a research reference interface for knowledge-based instructional design tools. *Educational Technology 31* (8), 7–16.

Lieberman, A. & Miller, L. (1992). Professional development of teachers. *In* M.C. Alkin, ed. *Encyclopedia of educational research,* 6th ed., 1045–51. New York: Macmillan.

Link, N. & Cherow-O'Leary, R. (1990). Research and development of print materials at the Children's Television Workshop. *Educational Technology Research & Development 38* (4), 34–44.

Luiz, T. (1983). A comparative study of humanism and pragmatism as they relate to decision making in instructional development processes. (Doctoral dissertation, Michigan State University, 1982.) *Dissertation Abstracts International-A 43* (12), 3839.

McAleese, R. (1988). Design and authoring: a model of cognitive processes. *In* H. Mathias, N. Rushby & R. Budgett, eds. *Designing new systems for learning,* 118–26. New York: Nichols.

McCombs, B.L. (1986). The instructional systems development model: a review of those factors critical to its implementation. *Educational Communications and Technology Journal 34* (2), 67–81.

McGraw, K.L. (1989). Knowledge acquisition for intelligent instructional systems. *Journal of Artificial Intelligence in Education 1* (1), 11–26.

Means, B. & Gott, S. (1988). Cognitive task analysis as a basis for tutor development: articulating abstract knowledge representations. *In* J. Psotka, L.D. Massey & S.A. Mutter, eds. *Intelligent tutoring systems: lessons learned,* 35–57. Hillsdale, NJ: Erlbaum.

Medsker, K.L. (1992). NETwork for excellent teaching: a case study in university instructional development. *Performance Improvement Quarterly 5* (1), 35–48.

Merrill, M.D. (1973). Cognitive and instructional analysis for cognitive transfer tasks. *Audio Visual Communications Review 21* (1), 109–25.

— (1983). Component display theory. *In* C.M. Reigeluth, ed. *Instructional design theories and models,* 279–338. Hillsdale, NJ: Erlbaum

— (1987). Prescriptions for an authoring system. *Journal of Computer-Based Instruction 14* (1), 1–10.

— & Li, Z. (1989). An instructional design expert system. *Journal of Computer-Based Instruction 16* (3), 95–101.

— & Jones, M.K. (1990a). Limitations of first generation instructional design. *Educational Technology 30* (1), 7–11.

— (1990b). Second generation instructional design. *Educational Technology 30* (2), 7–14.

— (1991). Instructional transaction theory: an introduction. *Educational Technology 31* (6), 7–12.

Mielke, K.W. (1990). Research and development at the Children's Television Workshop. *Educational Technology Research & Development 38* (4), 7–16.

Milazzo, C. (1981). Formative evaluation process in the development of a simulation game for the socialization of senior nursing students. (Doctoral dissertation, Columbia University Teachers College.) *Dissertation Abstracts International-A 42* (5), 1935.

Mishler, E.G. (1979). Meaning in context: is there any other kind? *Harvard Educational Review 49* (1), 1–19.

Mulhauser, M. (1992). Hypermedia and navigation as a basis for authoring/learning environments. *Journal of Educational Multimedia and Hypermedia 1* (1), 51–64.

Munro, A. & Towne, D.M. (1992). Productivity tools for simulation-centered training development. *Educational Technology Research and Development 40* (4), 65–80.

Nadin, M. & Novak, M. (1987). MIND: a design machine. *In* P.J.W. ten Hagen & T. Tomiyama, eds. *Intelligent CAD systems I,* 146–71. New York: Springer.

National Center for Educational Research and Development (1970). *Educational research and development in the United States.* Washington, DC: United States Government Printing Office.

Naveh-Benjamin, J., McKeachie, W.J., Lin, Y. & Tucker, D.G. (1986). Inferring students' cognitive structures and their development using the "ordered tree technique." *Journal of Educational Psychology 78,* 130–40.

Nelson, W.A. (1990). Selection and utilization of problem information by instructional designers. (Doctoral dissertation, Virginia Polytechnic Institute and State University, 1988.) *Dissertation Abstract International-A 50* (4), 866.

— (1989). Artificial intelligence knowledge acquisition techniques for instructional development. *Educational Technology Research and Development 37* (3), 81–94.

—, Magliaro, S.G. & Sherman, T.M. (1988). The intellectual content of instructional design. *Journal of Instructional Development 11* (1), 29–35.

— & Orey, M.A. (1991). Reconceptualizing the instructional design process: lessons learned from cognitive science. Paper presented at the annual meeting of the American Educational Research Association, Chicago, IL. (ERIC Document Reproduction Service No. ED 334 268.)

Nicolson, R. (1988). SCALD—towards an intelligent authoring system. *In* J. Self, ed. *Artificial intelligence and human learning,* 236–54. London: Chapman & Hall.

Noel, K. (1991). Instructional systems development in a large-scale education project. *Educational Technology Research & Development 39* (4), 91–108.

O'Neil, H.L., Faust, G.W. & O'Neil, A.F. (1979). An author training course. *In* H.L. O'Neil, ed. *Procedures for instructional systems development,* 1–38. New York: Academic.

O'Quin, K., Kinsey, T.G. & Beery, D. (1987). Effectiveness of a microcomputer-training workshop for college professionals. *Computers in Human Behavior 3* (2), 85–94.

Orey, M.A. & Nelson, W.A. (1993). Development principles for intelligent tutoring systems: integrating cognitive theory into the development of computer-based instruction. *Educational Technology Research and Development 41* (1), 59–72.

Parer, M. (1978). A case study in the use of an instructional development model to produce and evaluate an instructional television program. (Doctoral dissertation, Indiana University, 1977.) *Dissertation Abstracts International-A 38* (6), 3229.

Park, I. & Hannafin, M.J. (1993). Empirically based guidelines for the design of interactive multimedia. *Educational Technology Research and Development 41* (3), 63–85.

Pelz, D.C. (1967, Jul.). Creative tensions in the research and development climate. *Science,* 160–65.

Petry, B.A. & Edwards, M.L. (1984). Systematic development of an applied phonetics course. *Journal of Instructional Development 7* (4), 6–11.

Piper, A.J. (1991). An analysis and comparison of selected project management techniques and their implications for the instructional development process. (Doctoral dissertation, Michigan State University, 1990.) *Dissertation Abstracts International-A 51* (12), 4010.

Pirolli, P. (1991). Computer-aided instructional design systems. *In* H. Burns, J.W. Parlett & C.L. Redfield, eds. *Intelligent tutoring systems: evolutions in design,* 105–25. Hillsdale, NJ: Erlbaum.

Pirolli, P.L. & Greeno, J.G. (1988). The problem space of instructional design. *In* J. Psotka, L.D. Massey & S.A. Mutter, eds. *Intelligent tutoring systems: lessons learned,* 181–201. Hillsdale, NJ: Erlbaum.

Pizzuto, A.E. (1983). The development and evaluation of a simulation game demonstrating diffusion communications in a corporate organization. (Doctoral dissertation, University of Pittsburgh, 1982.) *Dissertation Abstracts International-A 43* (4), 1273.

Plummer, K.H., Gillis, P.D., Legree, P.J. & Sanders, M.G. (1992). The development and evaluation of a job aid to support mobile subscriber radio-telephone terminal (MSRT). *Performance Improvement Quarterly 5* (1), 90–105.

Redding, R.E. (1992). A standard procedure for conducting cognitive task analysis. (ERIC Document Reproduction Service No. ED 340-847).

Reigeluth, C.M. (1983). Instructional design: what is it and why is it? *In* C.M. Reigeluth, ed. *Instructional design theories and models: an overview of their current status,* 3–36. Hillsdale, NJ: Erlbaum.

— & Curtis, R.V. (1987). Learning situations and instructional models. *In* R.M. Gagné, ed. *Instructional technology: foundations,* 175–206. Hillsdale, NJ: Erlbaum.

— & Stein, F.S. (1983). The elaboration theory of instruction. *In* C.M. Reigeluth, ed. *Instructional design theories and models: an overview of their current status.* Hillsdale, NJ: Erlbaum.

Reitman, W. (1964). *Cognition and thought.* New York: Wiley.

Richey, R.C. (1992). *Designing instruction for the adult learner: systemic training theory and practice.* London/Bristol, PA: Kogan Page/Taylor & Francis.

— (1993). The knowledge base of instructional design. a paper presented at the 1993 annual meeting of the Association for Educational Communications and Technology, New Orleans, LA.

— & Tessmer, M. (1995). Enhancing instructional systems design through contextual analysis. *In* B. Seels, ed. *Instructional design fundamentals: a reconsideration,* 189–99. Englewood Cliffs, NJ: Educational Technology.

Riplinger, J.A. (1987). A survey of task analysis activities used by instructional designers. (Doctoral dissertation, University of Iowa, 1985.) *Dissertation Abstracts International-A 47* (3), 778.

Rojas, A.M. (1988). Evaluation of sales training impact: a case study using the organizational elements model. *Performance Improvement Quarterly 1* (2), 71–84.

Rouch, M.A. (1969). A system model for continuing education for the ministry. *Educational Technology 9* (6), 32–38.

Rowland, G. (1992). What do instructional designers actually do? An initial investigation of expert practice. *Performance Improvement Quarterly 5* (2), 65–86.

— (1993). Designing and instructional design. *Educational Technology Research and Development 41* (1), 79–91.

Rushby, N. (1986). A knowledge-engineering approach to instructional design. *The Computer Journal 29* (5), 385–89.

Russell, C.M. (1990). The development and evaluation of an interactive videodisc system to train radiation therapy technology students on the use of the linear accelerator. (Doctoral dissertation, University of Pittsburgh, 1988.) *Dissertation Abstracts International-B 50* (3), 919.

Russell, D.M. (1988). IDE: the interpreter. *In* J. Psotka, L.D. Massey & S.A. Mutter, eds. *Intelligent tutoring systems: lessons learned,* 323–49. Hillsdale, NJ: Erlbaum.

Ryder, J.M. & Redding, R.E. (1993). Integrating cognitive task analysis into instructional systems development. *Educational Technology Research and Development 41* (2), 75–96.

Saettler, P. (1990). *The evolution of American educational technology.* Englewood, CO: Libraries Unlimited.

Schon, D.A. (1983). *The reflective practitioner: how professionals think and act.* New York: Basic Books.

— (1987). *Educating the reflective practitioner: toward a new design for teaching and learning in the professions.* San Francisco, CA: Jossey-Bass.

Schulz, R.E. (1979). Computer aids for developing tests and instruction. *In* H. L. O'Neil, ed. *Procedures for instructional systems development,* 39–66. New York: Academic.

— & Wagner, H. (1981). *Development of job aids for instructional systems development (ARI Technical Report No. ARI-TR-527).* Alexandria, VA: U.S. Army Research Institute. (ERIC Document Reproduction Service No. 205 202.)

Schvaneveldt, R.W. (1990). *Pathfinder associative networks: studies in knowledge organization.* Norwood, NJ: Ablex.

Schwen, T.M. (1977). Professional scholarship in educational technology: criteria for judging inquiry. *Audio Visual Communication Review 25* (1), 5–24.

Seels, B. (1994). An advisor's view: lessons learned from developmental research dissertations. A paper presented at the 1994 annual meeting of the Association for Educational Communications and Technology, Nashville, TN.

Seels, B. & Glasgow, Z. (1990). *Exercises in instructional design.* Columbus, OH: Merrill.

Seels, B.B. & Richey, R.C. (1994). *Instructional technology: the definition and domains of the field.* Washington, DC: Association for Educational Communications and Technology.

Seyfer, C. & Russell, J.D. (1986). Success story: computer managed instruction development. *Performance and Instruction 25* (9), 5–8.

Simon, H.A. (1973). The structure of ill-structured problems. *Artificial Intelligence 4,* 181–201.

— (1981). *The sciences of the artificial,* 2d ed. Cambridge, MA: MIT Press.

Smith, M. (1993). Evaluation of executive development: a case study. *Performance Improvement Quarterly 6* (1), 26–42.

Spector, J.M., Muraida, D.J. & Marlino, M.R. (1992). Cognitively based models of courseware development. *Educa-*

tional Technology Research and Development 40 (2), 45–54.

Stowe, R.A. (1973). Research and the systems approach as methodologies for education. *Audio-Visual Communications Review 21* (2), 165–75.

Sullivan, H.J. (1984). Instructional development through a national industry-education partnership. *Journal of Instructional Development 7* (4), 17–22.

Taylor, B. & Ellis, J. (1991). An evaluation of instructional systems development in the navy. *Educational Technology Research and Development 39* (1), 93–103.

Taylor, R.L.M. (1987). An analysis of development and design models for microcomputer-based instruction. (Doctoral dissertation, Syracuse University, 1986.) *Dissertation Abstracts International-A 47* (8), 3011.

Tenney, Y.J. & Kurland, L.J. (1988). The development of troubleshooting expertise in radar mechanics. *In* J. Psotka, L.D. Massey & S.A. Mutter, eds. *Intelligent tutoring systems: lessons learned,* 59–83. Hillsdale, NJ: Erlbaum.

Tessmer, M. & Harris, D. (1992). *Analyzing the instructional setting: environmental analysis.* London/Bristol, PA: Kogan Page/Taylor & Francis.

Travers, R.M.W., ed. (1973). *Second handbook of research on teaching.* Chicago, IL: Rand McNally.

van Merrienboer, J.J.G.V., Jelsma, O. & Paas, R.G.W.C. (1992). Training for reflective expertise: a four-component instructional design model for complex cognitive skills. *Educational Technology Research and Development 40* (2), 23–43.

Wagner, N. (1984). Instructional product evaluation using the staged innovation design. *Journal of Instructional Development 7* (2), 24–27.

Watson, J.E. & Belland, J.C. (1985). Use of learner data in selecting instructional content for continuing education. *Journal of Instructional Development 8* (4), 29–33.

Wedman, J. & Tessmer, M. (1993). Instructional designers' decisions and priorities: a survey of design practice. *Performance Improvement Quarterly 6* (2), 43–57.

Weiss, D.J. (1979). Computerized adaptive achievement testing. *In* H.L. O'Neil, ed. *Procedures for instructional systems development,* 129–64. New York: Academic.

Wenger, E. (1987). *Artificial intelligence and tutoring systems.* Los Altos, CA: Morgan Kaufmann.

Wilson, B.G. & Jonassen, D.H. (1990/91). Automated instructional systems design: a review of prototype systems. *Journal of Artificial Intelligence in Education 2* (2), 17–30.

Wittrock, M.C. (1967). Product-oriented research. *The Educational Forum 31* (1), 145–50.

Wreathall, J. & Connelly, E. (1992). Using performance indicators to evaluate training effectiveness: lessons learned. *Performance Improvement Quarterly 5* (3), 35–43.

Yin, R.K. (1992). Case study design. *In* M.C. Alkin, ed. *Encyclopedia of educational research,* 134–37. New York: Macmillan.

Zaff, B.S., ed. (1987). The cognitive condition of design. *Proceedings of a Symposium on the Cognitive Condition of Design.* Columbus, OH: The Ohio State University.

Zemke, R. (1985, Oct.). The systems approach: a nice theory but . . . *Training,* 103–08.

INDEX